U.S. INDUSTRY & TRADE OUTLOOK® 2000

U.S. INDUSTRY & TRADE OUTLOOK® 2000

The McGraw-Hill Companies

U.S. Department of Commerce/International Trade Administration

McGraw-Hill

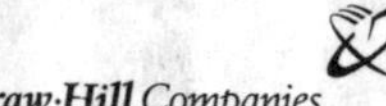

A Division of The ***McGraw-Hill*** *Companies*

1 2 3 4 5 6 7 8 9 0 QPD/QPD 0 9 8 7 6 5 4 3 2 1 0

ISBN 0-07-135245-7

The sponsoring editor for this book was Griffin Hansbury and the editing and production manager was Fred Bernardi. The book was set in Times Roman with Univers by North Market Street Graphics.

At the back of the book is a list of associations, organizations, and companies that have given permission to use data and other information for this publication.

Printed and bound by Quebecor/Dubuque.

ACKNOWLEDGMENTS

The ***U.S. Industry & Trade Outlook® 2000*** is the product of a partnership between the U.S. Department of Commerce and The McGraw-Hill Companies. The Office of Trade and Economic Analysis within the U.S. Department of Commerce provided concept development, authorship, interagency coordination within the government, U.S. government data, and editorial support. Those with major responsibilities for this 38th edition include the following: **Jonathan C. Menes,** Project Director; **Richard A. Eberhart,** Project Manager; **John J. Bistay,** Managing Editor; **Howard L. Schreier,** Computer Support Coordinator; **Rebecca Krafft, Francine Krasowska,** Technical Editors; **Jeffrey W. Lins,** Senior Economist/Economic Reviewer; **Kemble Stokes,** Senior Economist; **Michael Goodwin, Joanne Hepburn, Marjorie Pavliscak, Allen Unsworth,** Economic/Statistical Reviewers; **Bruce Miller, Jean Janicke,** Policy Reviewers; **John Jelacic,** Consulting Economist; **David Barton, Indumati Jasani,** Statistical Support; and **Miralette Herbert,** Administrative Support.

Contributing McGraw-Hill Companies are Standard & Poor's DRI for industry analysis and the Professional Book Group for production and distribution. Within Professional Book, special thanks go to **Philip Ruppel,** Publisher; **Susan Barry,** Editorial Director; **Roger Kasunic,** Production Director; **Griffin Hansbury,** Associate Editor; and **Fred Bernardi,** Editing Manager. **Cynthia H. Braddon** is Vice President, Washington Affairs, for The McGraw-Hill Companies, and **Tracey Thomson** is Manager, Government Marketing & Communications.

The National Technical Information Service, of which **Walter Finch** is Associate Director for Business Development, is McGraw-Hill's distribution partner.

The Bureau of the Census provided most of the data on which the analyses are based. Many other federal agencies also contributed data, but special recognition goes to the Bureau of Economic Analysis, the Bureau of Labor Statistics, the Council of Economic Advisers, the Board of Governors of the Federal Reserve System, the Department of Transportation, the Department of the Interior, the Department of Health and Human Services, the Securities and Exchange Commission, and the Commodity Futures Trading Commission.

Special appreciation also goes to the Department of Energy for its coverage of crude petroleum and natural gas and petroleum refining; the U.S. Geological Survey of the Department of the Interior for the chapter on metals and industrial minerals mining; the Maritime Administration and Federal Railroad Administration of the Department of Transportation for the chapters on shipbuilding and repair, water transportation, and railroads; and the Federal Deposit Insurance Corporation for the chapter on financial institutions.

A message from the Secretary of Commerce

The United States is an economic powerhouse! We have just set an endurance record for all economic expansions by topping the previous record held by the 1961-69 expansion, which lasted 106 months. Fueled by a revolution in information technology (IT), we are experiencing the lowest unemployment rate in 30 years, with more than 20 million new jobs created. Help wanted ads are seen everywhere extolling the need for professional, technical and support staff to fill the thousands of IT job vacancies in established and start-up companies across the United States. Inflation has been held in check and is now at its lowest rate since 1965. The stock market capped its fifth straight year of phenomenal returns at the end of 1999.

As we enter the new millennium, the global economy is again showing signs of recovery and world trade will resume its rapid growth creating major opportunities for U.S. industries. In order for U.S. businesses to capitalize on new opportunities, they will need to meet the many challenges created by growth in the Internet and electronic commerce around the globe. It is often said that with great challenge comes great opportunity. If U.S. businesses continue to meet the challenges of the new digital economy, they are virtually certain to reap huge rewards in the future.

To compete in and win world markets, businesses must identify promising markets, produce high quality goods and services, and seize opportunities. As American companies rise to meet the challenges of this global marketplace, the *U.S. Industry & Trade Outlook®* can be a valuable tool.

The 2000 *Outlook*, a joint effort of the Department of Commerce and The McGraw-Hill Companies, chronicles the performance of industry in our economy and provides insight into how key segments are likely to fare in the year ahead. To accentuate the role of these new technologies on our economy, this year's *Outlook* spotlights the growing impact of the IT revolution on individual U.S. industries and includes a special feature on how it will affect commerce and business in the 21st century.

To the extent that the *Outlook* stimulates profitable business ideas, contributes to increased competitiveness, and provides information that allows American business managers to make better decisions, its purpose has been fulfilled.

William M. Daley

The **McGraw·Hill** Companies

For over three decades the *U.S. Industrial Outlook®* proved to be a critical reference tool for government, businesses, and nonprofit entities both in the United States and abroad. Under the title *U.S. Industry & Trade Outlook®*, the 2000 edition marks the third year of The McGraw-Hill Companies' collaboration with the U.S. Department of Commerce in producing this important publication. We are proud to be a part of the process and to assist in providing the public with this vital economic and trade information.

Founded in 1888, The McGraw-Hill Companies is a leading information services provider meeting worldwide needs in education, business, finance, the professions, and government. Because of our expertise in financial information and publishing, we are in a unique position to assist in creating an updated objective outlook on U.S. industry and trade.

The McGraw-Hill Companies is pleased that both Standard & Poor's DRI and our Professional Publishing group are able to make a valuable contribution to the revival of this important resource volume. *Outlook 2000* encompasses deeper, richer content, is more customer friendly, provides a more global perspective, and promotes wide distribution of valuable information.

In addition, *Outlook 2000* preserves underlying government information principles, strongly supported by The McGraw-Hill Companies, which assure that such information remains available to the public. The McGraw-Hill Companies provides the government with free copies for distribution to depository libraries and the Library of Congress as well as for internal government use. We strongly support products such as the *Outlook* entering into the National Depository Library program.

The *U.S. Industry & Trade Outlook®* partnership is a prime example of how the government and the private sector can successfully work together and provide valuable information that the public wants and needs.

HAROLD McGRAW III

Contents

FEATURES

INDUSTRY REVIEWS AND FORECASTS

NATURAL RESOURCES AND ENERGY

CONSTRUCTION AND RELATED INDUSTRIES

INDUSTRIAL MATERIALS AND COMPONENTS

PRODUCTION AND MANUFACTURING EQUIPMENT

INFORMATION AND COMMUNICATIONS

THE CONSUMER ECONOMY

HEALTH CARE

FINANCIAL, BUSINESS, AND EDUCATION SERVICES

TRANSPORTATION

A

Getting the Most Out of *Outlook 2000*

Welcome to the third edition of *U.S. Industry & Trade Outlook®*, a joint publication of the U.S. Department of Commerce and The McGraw-Hill Companies. This series replaces *U.S. Industrial Outlook,* which the Department of Commerce had published annually until 1994. Like its predecessor, *U.S. Industry & Trade Outlook®* is a single reference source that business professionals, investors, researchers, and students can use to get information on U.S. industries, how those industries affect the U.S. economy, and where they are going in an increasingly global marketplace. Most of the chapters have been written by government analysts; also participating were McGraw-Hill authors (principally from Standard & Poor's Equity Investor Services and Standard & Poor's DRI) and independent analysts and industry experts. To ensure that the articles and forecasts are objective and unbiased, government economists have reviewed all chapters.

ANALYTICAL APPROACH: SIC CODES

Data in the *2000 Outlook* are based on the *Standard Industrial Classification Manual–1987,* which classifies industries by SIC codes. These codes have been used as the basis for collecting most of the data on domestic industries. This classification system includes all sectors, from manufacturing and service industries to construction, agriculture, and natural resources. The SIC system begins with nine major categories: (1) agriculture, forestry, and fishing, (2) mining, (3) construction, (4) manufacturing, (5) transportation, communications, and public utilities, (6) wholesale trade, (7) retail trade, (8) finance, insurance, and real estate, and (9) services. These basic categories, in turn, are divided into groups with two-digit, three-digit, and four-digit industry codes; each additional digit indicates a greater degree of specificity.

A NEW APPROACH: THE NAICS SYSTEM

In an effort to standardize their data collection systems, the United States, Canada, and Mexico collaborated in developing a new economic classification system, the North American Industry Classification System (NAICS). This also served to address the criticism that the SIC system focused too heavily on manufacturing, giving too little recognition to the growing services sector. NAICS is based on a production concept, defining industries by grouping together establishments that use similar processes and inputs to produce a good or a service. Inputs include types of labor and skills, capital equipment, and intermediate materials. In many cases, intangible inputs may be important, especially in service industries. The final listing of NAICS industries appeared in the *Federal Register* of April 9, 1997, and is available on the Internet at www.census.gov/epcd/www/naics.html#fedreg. The United States adopted and began presenting data based on NAICS with the release of the 1997 Economic Census reports. Eventually, all U.S. industrial statistics will be tabulated according to NAICS rather than SIC definitions. Industry data based on NAICS were released too late to have been included in *Outlook 2000.*

DATA FEATURED IN EACH CHAPTER

Economic and Trade Trends Graphs

Each chapter begins with four overview graphs depicting information on the particular industry segment. A common format is used for all manufacturing industries. For nonmanufacturing industries, graphs were chosen that are pertinent to the specific industry. The four graphics used consistently for manufacturing industries are U.S. international trade, world export market shares, U.S. export dependence and import penetration, and U.S. output and output per worker.

U.S. International Trade. This graph depicts worldwide U.S. exports and imports and the resulting trade balance.

World Export Market Share. The world export market share data have been developed from international trade information collected by the United Nations. These data are classified by Standard International Trade Classifications (SITC), Revision 3, which does not correspond to the 1987 SIC system used for U.S. domestic industries. An attempt was made to develop comparable statistics by identifying the SITCs that accounted for a preponderance of trade at the chapter level. In some cases, an appropriate match could not be made. Where the worldwide international trade data do not accurately reflect the SIC industries included in the chapter, no data are presented.

Export Dependence and Import Penetration. The export dependence ratio is derived by dividing exports by comparable domestic shipments; the import penetration ratio is derived by dividing imports by the sum of comparable shipments and imports minus exports (apparent consumption). The ratios do not necessarily use the shipments data included in the trends and forecasts tables (discussed below); shipment data were modified to reflect all traded commodities of a particular sector.

Output and Output per Worker. The industry output and productivity series were constructed by using published and unpublished indexes from the Bureau of Labor Statistics (BLS). Indexes comparable to the SICs covered in each chapter were rebased to 1992 (i.e., 1992 = 100). Then a weighted index was constructed, using the 1996 value of industry shipments as weights. At the national level, output is for private nonfarm business, adjusted for inflation. Private nonfarm business output is gross domestic product (GDP) minus the sum of agricultural output and the output of the government sector. BLS provided data on total employment.

Trends and Forecasts Tables

The trends and forecasts table is a standard feature in manufacturing chapters. This table defines the industry by SIC codes and contains up to 9 years of statistics. This edition contains industry and product data from 1992 through 2000. Shipments data through 1996 are actual; data for 1997, 1998, and 1999 are estimates, and data for 2000 are forecasts. The chapters in *Outlook 2000* were being prepared while 1997 Census data were being released. Applicable 1997 Census statistics, when available, were taken into consideration by the authors, but their inclusion was at the author's discretion, based on his or her evaluation of the impact that the conversion to the NAICS basis would have on the relevant industry statistics. Trade data through 1998 are actual. The value of shipments in the trends and forecasts tables generally is shown in both "current" and "constant" dollars. The constant dollars in the trends and forecasts tables are identified as "value of shipments (1992$)." This means that output is valued using 1992 prices. (See the accompanying glossary for further explanation.) Historical data also are provided for capital investment and earnings (both in current dollars) and employment.

The difference between industry and product shipments is important for interpreting the statistics in this book. Shipments data are collected separately for individual factories or establishments rather than for entire companies. Although most factories or establishments make or sell a variety of products, for statistical purposes, individual concerns are classified under the industry of their most prominent product. For instance, if 80 percent of a plant's total output consists of tires and 20 percent consists of hose and belting, that plant is classified as a tire industry plant. The total output of all such plants makes up the shipments for the industry. Other measures of activity under the "industry" heading, such as employment and hourly earnings, are reported for the establishments classified as being in that industry.

The value of all tires shipped by all establishments is added to derive "product shipments." In other words, "industry shipments" refers to the total value of all activities conducted by the establishments classified in an industry. "Product shipments" can be thought of as the total value of specific products classified within an industry shipped by all establishments regardless of how those establishments are classified.

When a plant's products change substantially, the industry under which the plant is classified may change as well. Despite such changes, historical data are not revised, and this can result in significant discontinuities. The reader therefore should use care in relating industry statistics (such as employment) to product statistics because an industry's product mix may change.

Trade Patterns Tables

These tables include data on exports and imports for the six major areas of the world and data on the United States' top purchasers and suppliers of merchandise. The six major regions are NAFTA (North American Free Trade Agreement countries of Canada and Mexico), Latin America (all other countries in the western hemisphere except Canada and Mexico), Western Europe (all countries in that region, whether a European Union member or not), Japan/Chinese Economic Area (Japan, China, Hong Kong, and Taiwan), Other Asia (all countries on the Asian continent except the Japan/Chinese Economic Area and the Middle East), and the Rest of World (eastern Europe and the former Soviet states, the Middle East, Africa, Australia, New Zealand, and other Pacific countries and territories).

Data Sources and Methods

Industry and Product Data. For manufacturing industries, the most reliable and consistent federal source of historical data on items such as value of shipments, employment and wages, and capital investments is the *Census of Manufactures,* revised and updated by the *Annual Survey of Manufactures.* Mining industry data are published in the *Census of Minerals;* data for subsequent years are available from the U.S. Department of Interior, Bureau of Mines. Data for many service industries are included in the Census of Service Industries and the Census Bureau's Service Annual Surveys, which are current through 1996. New Censuses of Manufactures and Minerals are taken every five years. Recent editions of the *Outlook* have been based on the *1992 Census of Manufactures* and the *1992 Census of Minerals.* (For the latest available data from the Economic Census, see www.census.gov/epcd/www/econ97.html.)

Trade Data. Trade data are collected using the Harmonized System (HS), a procedure the United States adopted in 1989. Most major industrial countries and many less developed countries use the HS, making it easier to assess and compare recent (but not pre-1989) international trade by commodity for various countries. Census trade data (exports and imports) are tabulated by following the Bureau of the Census's trade concordance, as adjusted by the various analysts to approximate their four-digit SIC industry groupings. Census data on U.S. merchandise trade are current through 1997. In preparation for the adoption of the NAICS as the new U.S. domestic industry classification, the U.S. Bureau of the Census modified the SIC-based trade concordance. It also took this opportunity to correct SIC assignments of HS codes. The trade statistics presented in *Outlook 2000* have been revised to reflect those changes.

Analysis of trade data over a longer period is more difficult. Since trade data used to be collected and tabulated differently, one cannot determine whether apparent changes in the value of trade by category before and after 1989 are due to actual trade developments or to changes in reporting and classifying practices.

WHERE TO FIND MORE INFORMATION

Two federal government resources of general interest to U.S. businesses are *A Basic Guide to Exporting,* which discusses exporting strategies and related issues, and the U.S. Trade Information Center (1-800-USA-TRADE), the definitive source for information on U.S. government export programs and activities.

Free catalogs listing government publications can be ordered from the superintendent of documents at the U.S. Government Printing Office (GPO) by calling (202) 512-1800 or faxing an order to (202) 512-2250. (The GPO's Internet address is www.access.gpo.gov.) Call the National Technical Information Service at (703) 487-4650 for information and to order catalogs on thousands of government publications or visit the Web site at www.ntis.gov. In addition, the U.S. Bureau of the Census has made statistical information available on its Web site at www.census.gov.

The government documents mentioned here can be found in the reference section of many libraries and on the Web sites of university and state libraries that participate in the Federal Depository Library program. Useful nongovernment sources of business information include *Thomas' Register, Standard & Poor's Register, Ward's Business Directory, Dun's Industrial Guide,* and reports by Dun & Bradstreet and Standard & Poor's, among others. Directories of trade associations that can be found in reference sections of libraries include the *Encyclopedia of Associations, National Trade & Professional Associations of the U.S.,* and the *Yearbook of International Organizations.*

GLOSSARY OF KEY TERMS AND ABBREVIATIONS

APEC: The Asia-Pacific Economic Cooperation group was established in 1989 and has become the primary regional vehicle for promoting open trade and economic cooperation within that region. Currently, its members are (in order of joining) Australia, Brunei Darussalam, Canada, Indonesia, Japan, South Korea, Malaysia, New Zealand, the Philippines, Singapore, Thailand, the United States, China, China–Hong Kong, Taiwan, Mexico, Papua New Guinea, Chile, Peru, Russia, and Vietnam.

Antidumping duty: A duty imposed by the United States to offset any profits a foreign firm attempts to make by dumping merchandise on the U.S. market. (See *Dumping.*)

ASEAN: Association of Southeast Asian Nations, consisting of Brunei Darussalam, Cambodia, Indonesia, Laos, Malaysia, Myanmar, the Philippines, Singapore, Thailand, and Vietnam.

CAGR: Compound annual growth rate.

Caribbean Basin Initiative (CBI): An inter-American program, led by the United States, of increased economic assistance and trade preferences to Caribbean and Central American countries. CBI provides duty-free access to the U.S. market for most products from the region and promotes private sector development in the region.

c.i.f.: Cost, insurance, and freight. A pricing term indicating that the cost of the goods, insurance, and freight is included in the quoted price.

Constant dollars ("real" dollars): Output-valued base-year prices, calculated by dividing current (or actual) dollars by a deflator. The use of constant dollars eliminates the effects of price changes between the year of measurement and the base year and allows the calculation of real changes in output.

Consumer Price Index (CPI): Presents a weighted average cost of a representative basket of goods and services purchased by consumers relative to the cost of the same basket in the base year.

Countervailing duty: A retaliatory charge that a country places on imported goods to counter direct or indirect subsidies or bounties granted to the exporters of the goods by their home governments.

Current dollars: The actual dollar amount paid in sales transactions.

Dumping: A term used in international trade to refer to the sale of a product in export markets below the selling price for that product in the exporter's domestic market or lower than the cost of manufacturing and marketing such goods in the domestic market.

Durable goods (durables): Items with a normal life expectancy of 3 years or more, such as automobiles, furniture, and major household appliances. Sales of durable goods generally are postponable and therefore are the most volatile component of consumer expenditures.

Euro: The basic unit of the new common European currency, which was put into use on January 1, 1999. Initially, only 11 of the 15 European Union member countries participate. Denmark, Greece, Sweden, and the United Kingdom will continue to maintain their national currencies. Euro notes and coin are scheduled to be put into circulation on January 1, 2002, and all bank accounts must be converted to Euros by that date.

Eurodollars: Deposits held in denominations of U.S. dollars in commercial banks outside the United States.

European Union (EU): A regional economic/political organization forming the largest trading bloc in the world. Its 15 members are Austria, Belgium, Denmark, Finland, France, Germany, Greece, Ireland, Italy, Luxembourg, the Netherlands, Portugal, Spain, Sweden, and the United Kingdom.

Export-Import Bank (Eximbank): An autonomous agency of the U.S. government created in 1934 to facilitate the export trade of the United States.

f.a.s. (free alongside ship): The transaction price of an export product, including freight, insurance, and other charges incurred in placing the merchandise alongside the carrier in the U.S. port.

f.o.b. (free on board): Without charge for delivery of export merchandise to, and placing on board, a carrier at a specified point.

Foreign trade zones (FTZs): Designated areas in the United States, usually near ports of entry, considered to be outside the customs territory of the United States. Also known as free trade zones.

G-7 (Group of Seven): Seven industrial countries: the United States, Japan, Germany, France, the United Kingdom, Italy, and Canada. G-7 heads of state and/or government have met at annual economic summits since 1975. G-7 finance ministers meet periodically to discuss economic issues of common concern.

General Agreement on Tariffs and Trade (GATT): An international organization and code of tariffs and trade rules that evolved out of the multilateral trade treaty signed in 1947. It was replaced by the World Trade Organization (WTO) on January 1, 1995.

Generalized Agreement on Trade in Services (GATS): Expands the rules on trade in goods that were negotiated under GATT auspices to include trade in services.

Generalized System of Preferences (GSP): A system approved by GATT in 1971 that authorizes developed countries to give preferential tariff treatment to developing countries.

Gross domestic product (GDP): The value of all goods and services produced in a country during a specified time period. (See *Value Added.*)

Harmonized System (HS): An international convention that was implemented by the United States in 1989 for classifying imports and exports so that data from different countries are comparable.

Industry shipments: The total value of products shipped by establishments classified as being in an industry, plus miscellaneous receipts.

Intellectual property: Includes trademarks, copyrights, patents, and trade secrets.

Intellectual property rights (IPR): In general, the right to possess or control the use of intellectual property.

International Monetary Fund (IMF): Established in 1945, the IMF serves as a permanent forum for its member countries to discuss and coordinate economic and financial policies. Its capital is derived from subscriptions from member countries. Its resources are used to provide assistance to members facing relatively short-term economic difficulties.

ISO 9000: A series of five standards (9000–9004) of the International Standards Organization (ISO), an international agency that promotes quality standards in products and systems. The ISO 9000 family of standards applies to quality assurance in design, development, production, installation, and servicing (ISO 9001); production, installation, and servicing (ISO 9002); and final inspection and testing (ISO 9003). ISO 9004 contains guidelines.

Maquila (maquiladora): A Mexican assembly plant generally, but not necessarily, near the U.S.–Mexican border; most of its production is exported to the United States.

Most-favored-nation (MFN) trade status: An arrangement in which GATT countries must extend to all other members the most favorable treatment granted to any trading partner, thus assuring that any tariff reductions or other trade concessions are extended automatically to all GATT parties. Under WTO, this status is known as "normal trading relations."

n.e.c.: Not elsewhere classified.

NIC/NIE: A newly industrialized (or industrializing) country/economy that has experienced rapid growth in GDP, industrial production, and exports in recent years.

Nondurable goods (nondurables): Items that last less than 3 years, such as food, beverages, and clothing. Generally, purchases of these items cannot be postponed significantly.

North American Free Trade Agreement (NAFTA): Agreement creating a free trade area among the United States, Canada, and Mexico. The agreement became effective January 1, 1994.

North American Industry Classification System (NAICS): A new economic classification system adopted by the United States, Canada, and Mexico for defining industries and classifying establishments by industry. It replaces the SIC in the United States.

OEM: Original equipment manufacturer.

Organization for Economic Cooperation and Development (OECD): A group of 29 industrialized, market economy countries that aims to promote its members' economic and social welfare and stimulate economic development efforts in developing countries. The OECD was established in 1961 and is headquartered in Paris. Member countries are Australia, Austria, Belgium, Canada, the Czech Republic, Denmark, Finland, France, Germany, Greece, Hungary, Iceland, Ireland, Italy, Japan, Luxembourg, Mexico, the Netherlands, New Zealand, Norway, Poland, Portugal, South Korea, Spain, Sweden, Switzerland, Turkey, the United Kingdom, and the United States.

Organization of Petroleum Exporting Countries (OPEC): An association of important oil-exporting countries that are highly dependent on oil revenues, formed in 1960. Its major objective is to coordinate and unify petroleum policies among its 11 member nations: Algeria, Indonesia, Iran, Iraq, Kuwait, Libya, Nigeria, Qatar, Saudi Arabia, the United Arab Emirates, and Venezuela.

Pacific Rim: A term that technically means all countries bordering the Pacific Ocean, although it often refers only to east Asian countries.

Product shipments: The total value of specific products shipped by all establishments irrespective of these establishments' industry classification.

Standard industrial classification (SIC): The former U.S. government–established standard for defining industries and classifying establishments by industry.

Uruguay Round: The eighth and final round of multilateral trade negotiations held under GATT auspices. Named for the country where initial discussions began in September 1986 and concluded in December 1993; most of the negotiations have taken place in Geneva, Switzerland.

Value added: The difference between the value of goods produced and the cost of the materials and services purchased to produce those goods. It includes wages, interest, rent, and profits. The sum of value added of all sectors of the economy equals GDP.

Voluntary restraint agreement (VRA): An import relief device to limit foreign trade in a particular commodity to protect domestic industry from injury by foreign competition. Sometimes referred to as a "voluntary export restraint" or an "orderly marketing agreement."

World Bank: This term refers to the International Bank for Reconstruction and Development (IBRD) and the International Development Association (IDA). The World Bank is the largest provider of development assistance to developing countries and countries in transition, committing about $20 billion in new loans each year. Its main focus is to help people in developing countries raise their standard of living through financing for agriculture, schools, health programs, transportation, and other essential needs.

World Trade Organization (WTO): Created by the Uruguay Round to succeed GATT on January 1, 1995. It expands GATT's rules to apply to trade in services and intellectual property rights. A tribunal to adjudicate trade disputes also was established.

B

Economic Assumptions of *Outlook 2000*

U.S. Industry and Trade Outlook 2000 provides estimates of near-term growth for major industries of the economy. These estimates reflect the knowledge of analysts from the U.S. Department of Commerce and Data Resources, Inc., regarding the specific circumstances that influence the industries they follow. The estimates also reflect the broad economic projections that were made in about midyear 1999. The midyear assumptions were more conservative than those presented in this chapter, which incorporate the effects of the comprehensive revisions to the national income and product accounts published in October 1999 and also reflect current views on the economic outlook.

In early 2000, private sector analysts anticipated that the U.S. economy would grow at a strong pace in 2000 and 2001, but less than the 4.1 percent average gain registered over the prior 4 years. Expectations also included moderate inflation and a low unemployment rate. Table B-1 shows the private sector forecasts published by *Blue Chip* Consensus in January 2000.

TABLE B-1: Economic Forecasts for 2000 and 2001

	Actual		Forecast	
	1998	1999	2000[1]	2001[1]
Real GDP (% change)	4.3	4.0	3.1–4.0	2.3–3.7
Consumer price index (% change)	1.6	2.2	2.0–2.9	1.9–3.0
Unemployment rate (percent)	4.5	4.2	3.9–4.4	3.9–4.7

[1] Private sector forecasts published by the *Blue Chip* Consensus, January 2000. Range reflects the average of the top 10 and bottom 10 forecasts.

To emphasize the uncertainty of the gross domestic product (GDP) and related forecasts, ranges that indicate likely trends rather than point estimates are shown in the table.

The administration's forecasts for the years 2000 and 2001 fall within the indicated range of private sector forecasts.

The Economy in 1999

A brief review of economic developments in 1999 provides an introduction to the projections for 2000 and 2001. The U.S. economy ended the year on a very strong note and grew 4.0 percent in the year as a whole (year-over-year growth rates are shown in Figure B-1).

The current economic expansion set an endurance record in February 2000 and will complete its ninth year in March 2000. The previous record was held by the 1961–1969 expansion, which lasted 106 months and coincided with the Vietnam War.

Growth in 1999 again surpassed expectations. At the start of each of the past 4 years, private sector and administration forecasts anticipated an increase of about 2¼% in the coming year. In those years, actual growth outdid expectations by a large 1.8 percentage points on average.

In 1999, domestic spending continued to be the major force driving the U.S. economy. Exports were limited by less vigorous growth in foreign economies and contributed modestly to overall U.S. growth.

Household spending—consumer spending plus residential construction—accounted for much of the strength in domestic spending in 1999. That vigorous spending reflected a combination of large gains in real disposable income and payroll

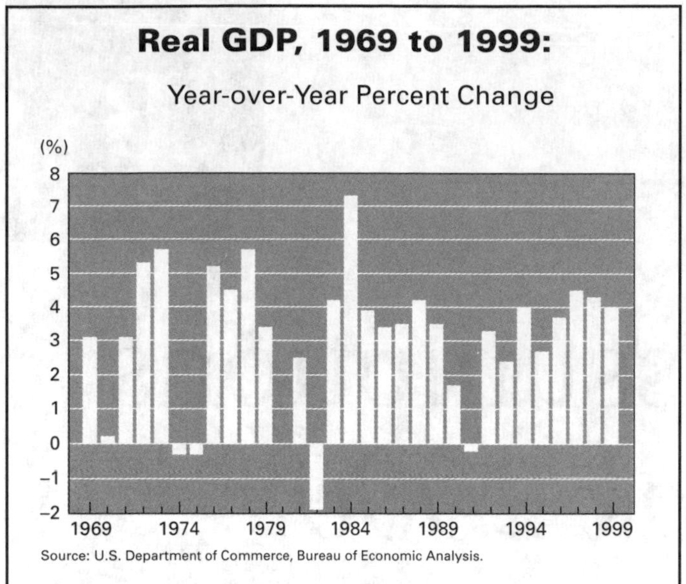

FIGURE B-1

employment, low interest rates for home mortgages, and a surge in household wealth caused by higher equity prices and increases in the value of existing homes. The strength in spending caused the personal saving rate to fall further. The personal saving rate trended downward from the recent high of 8.7 percent in 1992 to 2.4 percent in 1999, the lowest annual level since the series began in 1959.

Business spending for equipment and software continued to account for a significant and stable share of the growth in domestic spending. Purchases of computers and other information-processing equipment accounted for most of the growth in business spending as companies incorporated new technologies and innovations into their production processes.

Y2K concerns had a small impact on U.S. business activity in 1999. Available data suggest that firms and public agencies spent about $30 billion in that year to hunt down and correct error-prone technologies. Total Y2K-related spending in the second half of the 1990s reached an estimated $100 billion. The changeover from 1999 to 2000 caused no major disruptions.

Consumer prices rose a modest 2.2 percent in 1999. That pace represented a pickup from the 1.7 percent advance in 1998. However, the sharp rebound in energy prices more than accounted for the acceleration. The rate of inflation in core prices remained subdued. Figure B-2 shows that this rate of inflation, measured by consumer prices excluding those for food and energy, has trended downward throughout the current expansion.

Resource utilization in the product and labor markets continued to diverge in 1999. Throughout 1999, capacity utilization in manufacturing remained below its long-term (1967–1998) average of 81.1 percent. As a result, inflationary pressures in core consumer prices remained limited. The rate of inflation in core consumer prices tends to ease when manufacturing capacity utilization is below its long-term average but tends to increase when utilization is above that average.

In contrast, the unemployment rate averaged 4.2 percent for the year, the lowest yearly rate since 1969. This tightness in the labor markets did not lead to significant upward pressures on labor costs. Hourly compensation in the nonfarm business sector rose 4.8 percent in 1999, a smaller increase than the 1998 advance of 5.2 percent. In addition, businesses achieved solid gains in labor productivity. As a result, the rate of increase in labor costs per unit of output, a major component of total costs, rose only 1.8 percent in 1999, down from the 2.4 percent increase in 1998.

Strong domestic demand contributed to rapid growth in U.S. imports of goods and services, while the subdued performance of foreign economies led to little growth in U.S. exports. Available data suggest that the U.S. economy grew roughly 1 percentage point faster than a weighted average of key foreign economies in 1999. As a result, the U.S. trade deficit in goods and services rose to a record $267 billion on an annual basis in the first 11 months of 1999 from $164 billion in 1998. Relative to GDP, the deficit jumped to 2.9 percent in the period from January to November from 1.9 percent in 1998. The record ratio for a complete year remains 3.2 percent in 1987.

Oil prices also affected U.S. trade. The price of imported oil fell from $21.86 per barrel in January 1997 to $9.19 in January 1999 and then rebounded to $22.67 per barrel in December 1999 (the latest available data). The volume of monthly crude oil imports fluctuated around a flat trend between mid-1997 and late 1999, and the large price movements caused the petroleum trade deficit to fall in 1998 and rise sharply in 1999.

The economy's vigorous expansion in 1999 contributed to another increase in the federal government surplus. The budget surplus rose to $122.7 billion in fiscal year (FY) 1999. Relative to GDP, the budget shifted from a 4.7 percent deficit in FY 1993 to a surplus of 1.3 percent in FY 1999.

FIGURE B-2

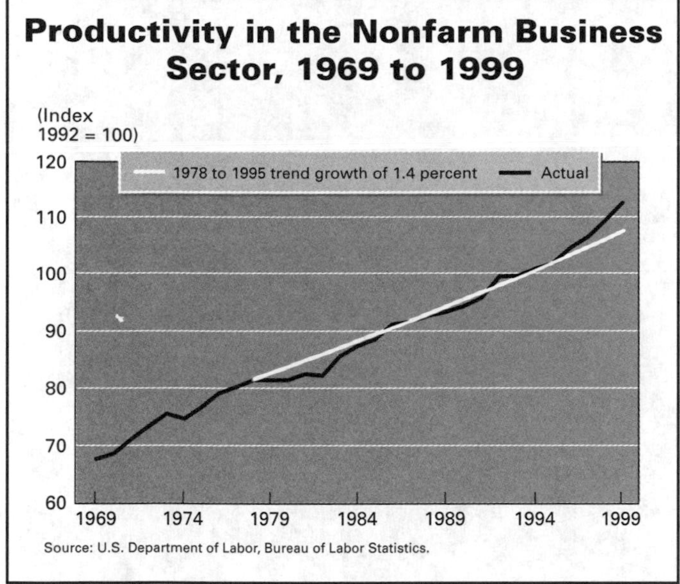

FIGURE B-3

The Federal Reserve tightened monetary policy in 1999. Actions in July, August, and November raised the federal funds and discount rates by three-quarters of a percentage point. Those actions reversed the policy moves made in the second half of 1998 in response to unsettled conditions in the financial markets. Shifts in monetary policy usually take 6 to 9 months to affect GDP growth. Thus, the 1998 actions supported GDP growth in 1999 while the 1999 actions will tend to restrain growth in the year 2000.

The Economy in 2000 and 2001

Most analysts expect the U.S. economy to grow strongly in the next 2 years. This expectation of strong growth represents a substantial upward shift in outlook compared with expectations of moderate growth at the start of each of the past 4 years. As was noted earlier, forecasters (including the administration) anticipated 2¼ percent growth in each of the past 4 years. The forecast for 2000 represents roughly a 1¼ percentage point upward shift in expectations.

The outlook for the year 2000 reflects in part the marked acceleration in the rate of productivity growth in the second half of the 1990s from the trend rate between 1978 and 1995. Productivity in the nonfarm business sector trended upward at a rate of 1.4 percent per year between 1978 and 1995 (see Figure B-3). Since 1995, productivity has grown at a pace of 2.6 percent per year, 1.2 percentage points faster than the 1978–1995 trend rate. Further rapid gains in productivity would limit potential inflationary pressures from a tight labor market.

A recession is not anticipated over the forecast horizon. Economic expansions do not die from old age. Rather, they die when serious imbalances develop that bring inflationary pressures and rising interest rates.

The deficit in international trade remains a concern. The outlook for 2000 and 2001 is for a modest pickup in foreign economic growth from the 1999 performance, but the U.S. trade deficit is likely to widen further in the near term before it begins to improve.

Upward pressures in prices for crude oil and for commodities at the early stages of production developed in 1999. Those pressures partly reflected the stabilization or upturn of some Asian economies as well as strong growth in the North American economies. The decline in import prices for nonpetroleum goods apparently has ended.

Stock prices remain an uncertain factor in the outlook. Slower growth in consumer spending, reflecting a leveling off in stock prices as well as the tightening by the Federal Reserve, could contribute to more sustainable overall economic growth in 2000 and 2001 and probably slow the decline in the personal saving rate. Slower overall growth would reduce the labor market pressures that have been a concern of the Federal Reserve.

Lee Price, Chief Economist, U.S. Department of Commerce, February 2000.

C

World Economic Outlook

At the outset of the new year, the outlook for the world economy is positive. For the first time since 1997, the prospect is for the world's economy to grow at a nearly normal rate of growth of around 3.5 percent, the average rate for the decade 1985–1995. In most areas, economic conditions continue to improve after the financial crises in 1997 and 1998.

The improved outlook has emerged in the last few months as economic data from Asia have shown that most of the countries that were most severely affected by that region's 1997 financial crisis are improving. In Latin America, positive growth should return after a smaller than anticipated downturn in 1999 after the Russian financial crisis in August 1998. Emerging markets in areas other than Asia and Latin America also are facing better prospects as the prices of petroleum and a few other raw materials, important exports of those countries, continue to strengthen.

During the economic slowdown in 1998–1999, positive economic growth continued in almost all the world's developed industrial economies (Japan being a major exception) while the brunt of the crisis was felt in the emerging markets, particularly in Asia, South America, and the transitional economies of the former Soviet Union (see Table C-1). Among the industrial developed economies, Japan suffered a major contraction in 1998 and most of the larger economies in Europe saw their economies slow somewhat at the end of that year. The best economic performances were turned in by the North America economies, Australia, and the smaller economies in the European Union. Strong economic growth in the United States in particular is credited with preventing the financial crisis from degenerating into a world recession.

In the year 2000, stronger growth in the world economy is expected to be based on more balanced growth throughout the world's economies. Indeed, some of the growing imbalances in the world economy in the last 2 years, particularly the growth of the U.S. current account deficit, are seen by many analysts as potential risk factors amid the generally good outlook for the coming months. As a group, the developed industrial economies are predicted to grow at about the same rate as they did in thc last 2 years, but the source of that growth will shift as the U.S. economy slows while the economies of Europe and Japan grow a little faster.

Across the board, the emerging markets are expected to record faster growth in the year 2000 compared with 1998–1999. One exception may be the emerging markets of Asia. That region probably will grow at about the same rate in 2000 as it did in 1999 as faster growth in the crisis economies of Asia will be offset to some extent by slower growth in China, the world's second largest economy. In 2000, all five of the crisis economies (South Korea, Malaysia, Thailand, Indonesia, and the Philippines) should show positive growth. The rise in world oil prices has been of particular benefit to Indonesia and will offset some of the economic and political turmoil associated with the crisis in East Timor and the political transition to a new government.

After Asia, Latin America accounts for the second largest share of emerging market output. The downturn in that region began after the Asian crisis pushed down commodity prices and accelerated after the Russian crisis in August 1998. The Russian crisis precipitated a rush of capital from the region and was a key factor in the easing of monetary policy in the United States,

TABLE C-1: World, Regional, and Country Growth, 1985–2000

	Average 1985–1995	1996	1997	1998	1999 Estimate	2000 Forecast
World	3.5	4.4	4.2	2.5	3.2	3.7
Industrial economies	2.7	3.1	3.2	2.6	2.8	2.8
United States	2.8	3.7	4.5	4.3	4.1	3.3
Canada	2.3	1.7	4.0	3.1	3.6	3.0
Japan	3.0	5.1	1.4	–2.8	1.0	1.2
European Union	2.4	1.8	2.5	2.7	2.1	2.8
United Kingdom	2.4	2.6	3.5	2.2	1.5	2.7
Euro-11	2.5	1.6	2.3	2.8	2.2	2.8
Germany[1]	2.7	0.8	1.5	2.3	1.4	2.6
France	2.1	1.6	2.0	3.4	2.5	2.9
Italy	2.1	0.9	1.5	1.3	1.2	2.4
Australia	3.3	4.0	3.9	5.1	4.0	3.3
Emerging economies	4.6	6.0	5.4	2.4	3.7	4.7
Africa	2.2	5.6	2.2	3.2	2.8	4.3
Asia	8.1	8.0	6.4	3.0	5.7	5.7
China	9.9	9.6	8.8	7.8	7.2	6.6
India	5.8	7.4	5.0	6.0	6.0	5.8
NICs[2]	8.8	6.1	3.5	–3.7	5.6	5.2
South Korea	8.7	6.8	5.0	–5.8	7.5	5.5
ASEAN[3]	7.3	7.2	3.9	–8.6	2.2	4.0
Indonesia	7.4	8.0	4.9	–13.2	0.3	3.0
Middle East	3.4	4.9	4.4	2.4	1.7	3.6
Central and South America	2.8	3.7	5.4	2.1	0.0	3.3
Brazil	2.5	2.8	3.7	0.2	–0.2	3.1
Mexico	1.6	5.2	7.0	4.8	3.5	3.7
Eastern, Central, and Southern Europe, CIS, and Central Asia	n.a.	–0.9	1.4	–1.4	0.8	2.6
Russia	n.a.	–3.4	0.9	–4.6	0.5	2.0
Poland	1.6	6.1	6.8	4.8	3.5	4.8
Big Emerging Markets[4]	6.4	7.3	6.4	2.9	4.5	5.2

[1] Data before 1990 refer to West Germany only.
[2] Newly industrialized countries (Hong Kong, Singapore, South Korea, Taiwan).
[3] Association of Southeast Asian Nations (Indonesia, Malaysia, Phillipines, Thailand, Singapore, Brunei Darrussalam, and Vietnam).
[4] Argentina, Brazil, Mexico, Chinese Economic Area, ASEAN, India, South Korea, Poland, South Africa, and Turkey.
Source: OECD, International Monetary Fund, U.S. Department of Commerce. Forecasts by U.S. Department of Commerce.
NOTE: Country groupings weighted on the basis of GDP as measured by purchasing power parities (PPP).

Europe, and the United Kingdom in the fall of 1998. The easing of world credit is cited as an important reason why this region has not suffered as sharp a decline as was anticipated after the Brazilian devaluation early in 1999. Relatively strong financial institutions, firmer commodity prices, and the strong U.S. export market also are given credit for halting the region's economic slide at midyear. The prospect is that the region's growth rate will climb to around 3.5 percent in 2000.

The fall of oil prices to $10 per barrel at the beginning of 1999 and their subsequent rise to over $30 after production cuts instituted by the Organization of Petroleum Exporting Countries (OPEC) in March of that year tell much about the economic fortunes of the countries in the Middle East. In 1997, OPEC had expanded output and Iraq began selling more oil under United Nations authority, when the Asian crisis hit and demand for oil and other commodities fell sharply. The price of oil began falling, and that trend was not reversed until the OPEC cuts in March. The movement in oil prices has paralleled economic growth in the region. The region's economies expanded over 4 percent in 1997 but grew only around 1 percent in 1999. With the recovery in oil prices, growth should top 3 percent in the year 2000.

Among the countries that constitute the leading export markets for U.S. manufactured goods, growth slowed quite sharply in 1998 but began recovering in 1999 (see Table C-2). Trade-weighted growth for the top 20 U.S. export markets fell to an estimated 2.1 percent in 1998, one-half the level recorded in 1997. That slowdown in growth affected most of the top 20 markets, with Germany, France, and Australia being notable exceptions. The sharp fall in the rate of growth in those markets, combined with the continued rapid growth of the U.S. economy, explains most of the explosion in the U.S. trade deficit in the last 2 years.

As sharp as the downturn in growth was in the country's principal export markets, Table C-2 shows that on a gross domestic product (GDP)-weighted basis, 1998 growth among U.S. partners, at 2.6 percent, was significantly better than total world growth outside the United States, which was only 2.0 percent. Undoubtedly, U.S. trading partners did better than others in part because the strong U.S. economy acted as an engine of growth and pulled those economies along with it.

TABLE C-2: Economic Growth in the Top 20 Purchasers of U.S. Manufactured Goods
(ranked according to 1998 U.S. trade data; annual percent change in real GDP)

	1991	1992	1993	1994	1995	1996	1997	1998	1999 Estimate	2000 Forecast
1. Canada	−1.9	0.9	2.3	4.7	2.8	1.7	4.0	3.1	3.6	3.0
2. Mexico	4.2	3.6	2.0	4.4	−6.2	5.2	7.0	4.8	3.5	3.7
3. Japan	3.8	1.0	0.3	0.6	1.5	5.1	1.4	−2.8	1.0	1.2
4. United Kingdom	−1.5	0.1	2.3	4.4	2.8	2.6	3.5	2.2	1.5	2.7
5. Germany	5.0	2.2	−1.1	2.4	1.8	0.8	1.5	2.3	1.4	2.6
6. France	0.8	1.2	−1.3	2.8	2.1	1.6	2.0	3.4	2.5	2.9
7. Netherlands	2.3	2.0	0.8	3.2	2.3	3.1	3.8	3.7	2.9	2.7
8. Taiwan	7.6	6.8	6.3	6.5	6.0	5.7	6.8	4.8	5.4	6.0
9. Singapore	7.1	6.6	12.8	11.4	8.2	7.5	7.8	1.5	4.9	6.0
10. Brazil	1.0	−0.5	4.9	5.9	4.2	2.8	3.7	0.2	−0.2	3.1
11. South Korea	9.2	5.4	5.5	8.3	8.9	6.8	5.0	−5.8	7.5	5.5
12. China	9.2	14.2	13.5	12.6	10.5	9.6	8.8	7.8	7.2	6.6
13. Belgium and Luxembourg	1.6	1.5	−1.5	2.6	2.3	1.3	3.2	3.0	1.8	2.6
14. Australia	−1.0	2.6	3.8	5.0	4.4	4.0	3.9	5.1	4.0	3.3
15. Hong Kong	5.1	6.3	6.1	5.4	3.9	4.5	5.3	−5.1	0.5	2.6
16. Saudi Arabia	8.4	2.8	−0.6	0.5	0.5	1.4	2.7	−2.0	5.0	1.3
17. Malaysia	8.6	7.8	8.4	9.3	9.4	8.6	7.7	−7.5	3.3	6.0
18. Italy	1.4	0.8	−0.9	2.2	2.9	0.9	1.5	1.3	1.2	2.4
19. Switzerland	−0.8	−0.1	−0.5	0.5	0.5	0.3	1.7	2.1	1.3	1.9
20. Israel	5.7	6.8	3.4	6.9	6.8	4.7	2.7	2.0	1.7	3.0
Top 20, trade-weighted growth	2.2	2.5	2.7	4.6	2.6	3.5	4.2	2.1	3.0	3.2
Top 20, PPP GDP-weighted growth	3.7	3.9	3.6	5.2	4.1	4.6	4.4	2.6	3.4	3.7
U.S. growth	−0.2	3.3	2.4	4.0	2.7	3.7	4.5	4.3	4.1	3.3
World growth	2.2	2.8	2.8	4.2	3.9	4.4	4.2	2.5	3.2	3.7
World less U.S., growth	2.9	2.7	2.9	4.3	4.2	4.6	4.1	2.0	3.0	3.8

Source: OECD, International Monetary Fund, U.S. Department of Commerce. Forecasts by U.S. Department of Commerce.

In 1999, the disparity in growth between the United States and the rest of the world, including its major partners, continued, but the contrast in growth rates was not as stark as it had been in 1998. In 2000, the forecast is for the U.S. economy to grow at a slower rate while growth in the rest of the world will accelerate to levels higher than U.S. growth. These projected trends in relative growth rates should result in a slowdown in the rate of increase in the U.S. trade deficit during that year. Whether the trade deficit will begin to shrink by the year's end will depend on other factors, including the dollar's value and world trade prices.

NAFTA ECONOMIES: NORTH AMERICA

In 1999, economic growth in North America continued at a very strong pace for the fourth consecutive year. The average PPP-weighted growth rate for the region was an estimated 4.0 percent compared with 4.3 percent in 1998. Economic growth in both the United States and Canada is expected to slow slightly in the year 2000, while a moderate acceleration of growth is expected in Mexico (see Figure C-1).

Both Canada and Mexico have benefited greatly from the consumer-led boom in the United States. Canada relies on the U.S. market to absorb more than 85 percent of its exports, and those exports equal around 30 percent of Canada's GDP. Strong export growth to the United States was important in maintaining overall growth in the last 2 years because of a one-third drop in exports to Asia. Automobiles are becoming an increasingly important component in Canada's shipments to the United States, and Canada has seen its share of North American auto production increase as a result. Canada's economy also was helped in 1999 by an increase in consumer spending and a strengthening of commodity prices.

The potential for continued strong Canadian growth looks very good. Growth has become more balanced in recent months with the increase in consumer spending and an increase in

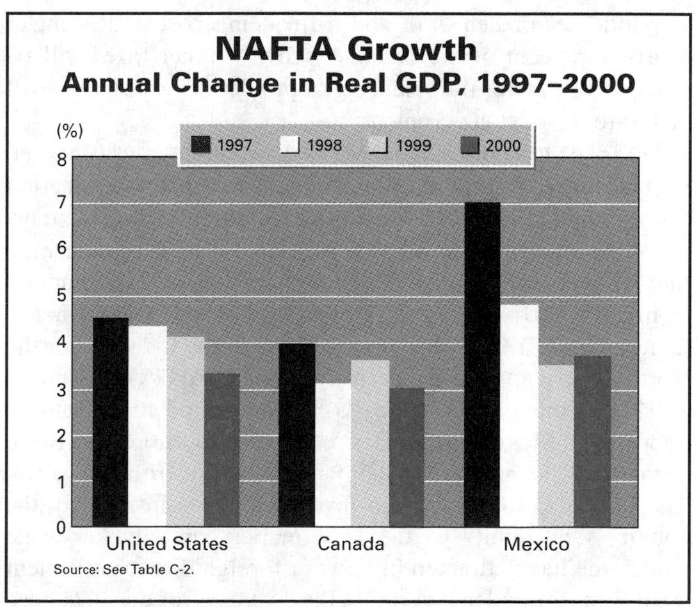

FIGURE C-1

investment. Unemployment has dropped to its lowest level in nearly a decade. Government fiscal policy was tightened several years ago, and the growing economy has put the budget into surplus. Price inflation remains low, and a growing trade surplus has allowed the Bank of Canada to maintain interest rates below U.S. rates.

A troubling trend in Canada's otherwise good economic picture is the country's inability to match the productivity growth of the United States. Studies indicate that productivity in Canada may be only 70 percent of the U.S. level. The low value of the Canadian dollar allows exports to be competitive, but long-term prospects for increases in living standards are not good unless productivity growth can be increased.

With low inflation, low interest rates, and growing consumer confidence, the short-term outlook for Canada's economy is excellent, with the only possible threat being a significant slowdown in the U.S. growth rate.

The growth rate in Mexico slowed to around 3.5 percent in 1999, somewhat lower than the rate in the last 2 years. Mexico's economy suffered virtually no ill effects from the currency crisis in Brazil. Only around 1 percent of Mexico's trade is with Brazil, and Mexico's fiscal, monetary, and exchange rate policies are such that there was no capital flight from that country when Brazil devalued. However, Mexico's economy did suffer from the sharp decline in oil prices in 1998. Around 10 percent of Mexico's export earnings come from oil, and oil income provides the government with around one-third of its revenues. Before oil prices began climbing in March, the government was forced to make cuts in its spending plans to keep the deficit within around 3 percent of GDP. The subsequent increase in oil prices has relieved some of that pressure.

One ongoing fiscal policy issue that has not been relieved by higher oil prices is the cost associated with financing the huge ($65 billion or more) debt assumed by the government from the country's bank deposit insurance fund. The debt resulted from bank failures after the 1995 crisis. The conversion of bad loans to public sector debt will add a financing cost equivalent to nearly 1 percent of the country's GDP. Higher taxes will be required to pay for the financing, a problem that probably will be left to the next government.

As in the case of Canada, Mexico's economy has benefited from strong U.S. growth. The United States is the destination for around 80 percent of Mexico's exports. In 1999, U.S. merchandise imports from Mexico increased nearly 16 percent, a rate of increase one-third higher than that of U.S. imports from the world. Most of this import growth has been in manufactured goods. Over the 5 years between the inception of the North American Free Trade Agreement (NAFTA) in January 1994 and the end of 1998, U.S. imports of manufactured goods from Mexico grew 20 percent per year, more than twice as fast as U.S. imports of manufactured goods from the world. The liberalization of foreign investment laws in Mexico, the country's proximity to the U.S. market, and its low-wage workforce have attracted billions in foreign direct investment from firms around the world. In the 3 years after the 1994 peso crisis, an estimated $12 billion in foreign investment created 600,000 new jobs in the export manufacturing sector.[1] Despite those job gains, real incomes of typical Mexican workers are an estimated one-third below the levels that existed before the peso crisis.

For 2000, the outlook is for the Mexican economy to grow almost 4 percent. Inflation has been coming down, falling to around 13 percent in 1999 and perhaps a little lower in 2000. In the near term, Mexico's economy faces two potential risks: that the U.S. economy may have a sharp downturn and that risk and uncertainty are associated with the July 2000 presidential elections. Under President Zedillo, Mexico has introduced political as well as economic reforms, and the midyear elections are expected to be the most fairly contested in the nation's history. If the ruling Institutional Revolutionary Party (PRI) fails to win the election, ending 70 years of rule, the change could introduce a great amount of uncertainty into the way the economy is managed.

INDUSTRIAL ECONOMIES: WESTERN EUROPE

Economic growth slowed in western Europe in the second half of 1998, in part because of the loss of exports to Asia. In 1999, economic prospects picked up significantly as a result of a number of factors. First, the beginning of an Asian recovery helped boost exports. Second, easier monetary policy lowered interest rates. Third, the region's new currency, the Euro, lost about 8 percent of its value, and this increase in the region's competitiveness gave a real boost to exports. Business and consumer confidence has picked up in most countries, and significant job creation has occurred in many countries around Europe's periphery, although not to any great extent in the large core countries. Among the major economies at its center, the economy of France is expected to turn in the best performance in 2000, but many of the smaller countries—Spain, Ireland, and Finland, for example—are expected to grow much faster. Overall, economic growth for the European Union is expected to reach about 2.8 percent in the year 2000, nearly a full percentage point higher than the level in 1999.

Inflation throughout the region is very low at just over 1 percent. Within the 11-country region of the Euro, inflation is even lower. Finally, most countries in the region have seen significant improvements in their fiscal budgets. The better performance of fiscal budgets resulted partially from faster growth and partially from low interest rates, which significantly reduced finance costs for many of Europe's economies where government debt is large, exceeding 100 percent of GDP in a few cases. This respite from large government deficits promises to be brief, however, unless those countries reign in their public pension systems. For many European countries, the problem of future public pension funding is much more serious than that which confronts the U.S. Social Security system.

[1] Joel Millman, "The Outlook: Is the Mexican Model Worth the Pain?" *Wall Street Journal,* March 8, 1999, p. A1.

Despite the very low rate of inflation, moderate growth in the major economies, and significant slack in labor markets, the European Central Bank (ECB) raised interest rates by 0.5 percent in early November, reversing a cut that had been made in April. On the same day, the Bank of England raised rates 0.25 percent. Many analysts questioned those moves in view of the underlying economic conditions.

When the Euro was born on January 1, 1999, many analysts expected that it would gain value against the U.S. dollar. Instead, it lost ground steadily through the first 6 months of that year. As was noted above, that fall helped the competitiveness of the Euro-area countries, and by some calculations the real effective exchange rate of the countries in the Euro zone is as low as it has been since the early 1980s. Also, the drop in the Euro's value has had only a minimal impact on inflation within the area, since imports account for only about an eighth of total Euro output.

Another impact that the new currency has had is in capital markets. Although the European Union has been in effect a single market for some time, the introduction of the Euro has spurred a sharp increase in mergers and acquisitions throughout the Euro area. Also, there has been a large increase in the issuance of bonds denominated in the new currency.

Europe has undergone tremendous changes in the last decade. From the opening of the Berlin Wall and the end of communism in central Europe, to the signing of the Maastricht treaty in 1992 and the subsequent taming of large budget deficits and inflation, to the recent introduction of the Euro, the economies in this region have had to adapt to a very different economic environment.

Germany, the region's giant with over 20 percent of the European Union's (EU) total output, is where many of the decade's changes began and the country whose central bank served in many respects as a model for the new European Central Bank with its clear focus on controlling price inflation. While Germany's growth exceeded total EU growth in the late 1980s and early 1990s, since 1993 that growth rate has been below the EU growth rate. Part of that sluggish growth can be attributed to the tight monetary policy that was pursued in reaction to the liberal fiscal spending associated with reunification. Of late, much blame for slow growth has been placed on the country's high labor costs and rigid labor laws. Also, the eastern part of the country has been much more slow to recover than was originally expected. The unemployment rate in the region remains more than twice the level in the western section. The recovery in Asia and the drop in the Euro's value provided the impetus for much of Germany's recent growth. The outlook for the year 2000 is for growth to pick up to around 2.6 percent (see Figure C-2), but recent data have not been very robust and consumer sentiment is subdued, unlike the situation in most of the rest of Europe.

French economic growth led the big four European economies in the last 3 years. In part the good growth in France was a result of very positive consumer sentiment, and in part it was the result of expansionary fiscal policy; also, strong domestic demand offset the weak demand for France's exports from Asia as well as from its two major markets, Germany and Italy. Public spending in France is among the continent's highest, and the country's social benefits and restrictive labor laws are blamed for unemployment rates that are nearly 2 percent above the EU's average rate. In recent quarters, France's rate of growth has been slowing, but better prospects for exports are expected to lead to slightly faster growth (around 2.9 percent) in the year 2000.

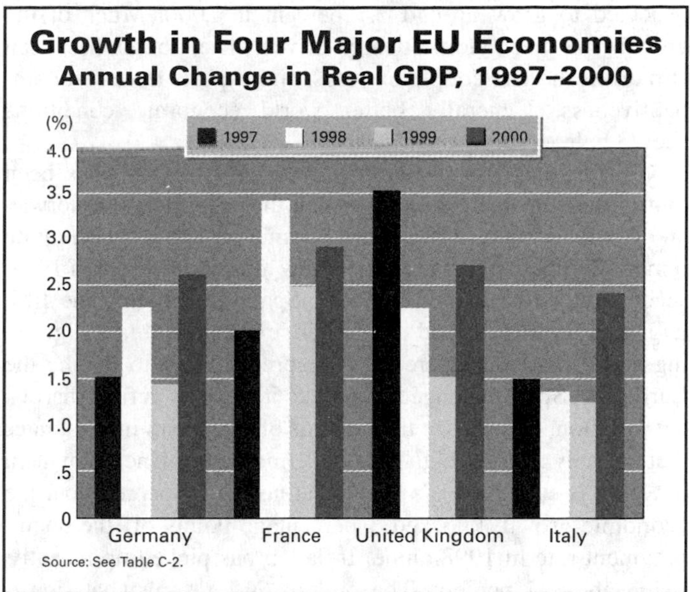

FIGURE C-2

Italy turned in the weakest performance of all the Euro-area economies in 1999, growing only a little over 1 percent. In fact, in all of the EU, only Norway, with its oil price problems, and Denmark grew more slowly. Italy's sluggish growth was partially the result of the tight fiscal policies (mainly higher taxes) that were imposed to meet the Maastricht criteria for inclusion in the Euro currency zone. Italy's economy also was constrained by its adoption of the Euro and the loss of export competitiveness. In late 1999, the economy began to grow more rapidly than expected, in part because of exports to Asia, and growth in 2000 is predicted to be twice as great as that in 1999. The outlook will not improve significantly in the longer term, however, until the country fixes its public pension system. Payments from that system now total around 14 percent of GDP, twice the EU average, and revenue shortfalls in the program equal around 4 percent of GDP.

The last of the big four European economies and the only one outside the Euro zone is the United Kingdom (UK). In a period of scarcely a year, the UK economy took a roller coaster ride that saw it nearly slip into a recession in late 1998 after the financial fallout from Russia, only to quickly recover and approach a state of near overheating by late summer 1999. Interest rate cuts that were made by the Bank of England in the fall of 1998 to offset a feared downturn were reversed in the waning months of 1999, largely because of rapidly rising real estate prices and growing wage pressures. The UK economy is expected to grow around 2.7 percent in 2000. Much of the growth has been domestically driven. The pound has been strong for the last couple of years, and exports have lost competitiveness. Generally better world economic conditions should help exports somewhat.

Outside the large economies, economic growth has been quite robust in western Europe with the exceptions of Norway and Denmark. In a few cases, economic growth has been quite remarkable. Spain, for example, grew almost 4 percent in 1998, second only to Ireland. In 1999, Spain's economy, the fifth largest in the EU, turned in another strong performance, growing an estimated 3.7 percent. As a precondition to joining the Euro area, Spain managed to reduce its budget deficit sharply, cut inflation, and realize the benefits of long-term interest rates that are only slightly higher than German rates. Unemployment in Spain is still the EU's highest at nearly 16 percent, but the economic growth knocked 3 percentage points off the unemployment rate in 1998 alone. Inflation has picked up recently, rising above 2 percent. The outlook is for somewhat slower growth of around 3.5 percent in 2000.

Another economy that has turned in superb economic performances for several years is that of Ireland. The Irish economy has averaged nearly 9 percent per year growth in the last 4 years. Sharp increases in productivity and an expanding labor force have allowed this rapid growth. Drawn by the healthy economy, many Irish people have returned home in recent years. These added workers, together with a growing female labor market participation rate that is approaching the EU average, have provided the added workers needed to keep the surging economy growing. Recently, however, there have been signs that the economy may have reached its capacity. Aside from shortages of skilled workers in many areas, the country's infrastructure is becoming overburdened, housing prices are escalating, and inflation is a notch above the EU average. Rapid growth has allowed the government to balance its budget, and the unemployment rate is 50 percent below the EU average. In the year 2000, the Irish economy is expected to grow slightly more than 7 percent, around a percentage point lower than the rate in 1999.

In Scandinavia, two economies—Sweden's and Finland's—realized better than average growth in 1999 (3.5 percent and 3.4 percent, respectively), while the other two—Norway's and Denmark's—managed growth estimated at only 0.5 percent and 1.4 percent, respectively. In Scandanavia, only Finland is a member of the Euro zone, and membership by the other three countries lacks strong popular support. Except for slightly slower growth in Sweden, the other countries in this group are expected to grow more rapidly in 2000. Sweden, the largest country in this group and the country with the strongest welfare system in Europe, has transformed itself remarkably in recent years. High-tech industries have grown vigorously, and when other countries slowed in 1998 because of diminished export sales, Sweden's economy had continued strong growth. Unemployment is a couple of percentage points below the EU average, and the fiscal budget is in surplus. Sweden has relinquished none of its social programs, but the government has reduced its involvement in the economy.

Economic deregulation, privatization, and more vigorous competition are evident in many of Europe's economies, and these trends are one factor in the more vigorous growth that has appeared in recent years. In many European countries, labor market restrictions have been relaxed, and part-time employment is a much more important ingredient in labor markets today than it was just a few years ago.

INDUSTRIAL ECONOMIES IN THE EAST: JAPAN, AUSTRALIA, AND NEW ZEALAND

The three countries in this group include the only two developed industrial economies that experienced a recession in 1998 and one country that is among the economic stars of the Organization for Economic Cooperation and Development (OECD) group. Australia, the star, was among the two or three fastest-growing developed industrial economies in both 1997 and 1998. In contrast, both Japan and New Zealand experienced recessions in 1998 (see Figure C-3) and are now in the early stages of slow recoveries that are predicted to continue through the year 2000.

Japan's turnaround began with a surprisingly strong burst of growth. The economy grew 2 percent in the first quarter of 1999 before slowing to a much more moderate pace in the second quarter and recording slightly negative growth in the third quarter. The source of Japan's initial rapid growth was no mystery as a \$228 billion fiscal spending program provided much of the impetus behind the spurt. Investment also was strong in the first quarter, in part because of the establishment of a government-guaranteed credit plan. The fiscal spending package was the eighth such government package since 1992. The total announced value of those packages topped \$1 trillion. They all

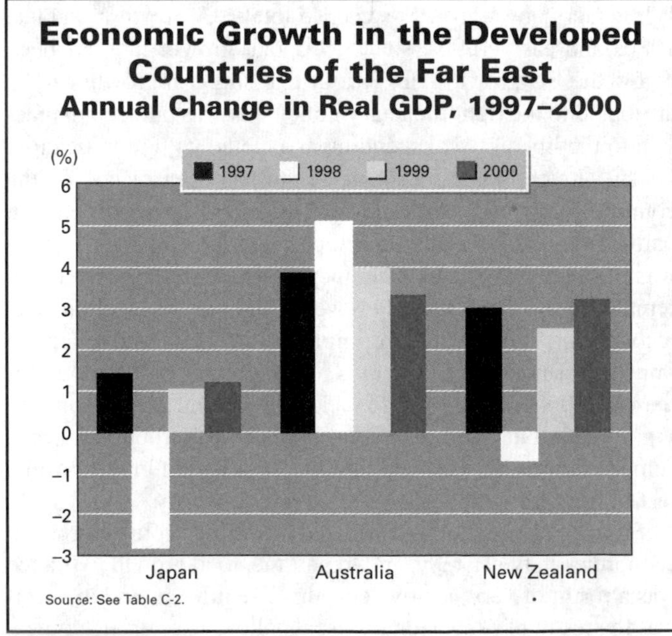

FIGURE C-3

succeeded in temporarily boosting growth, but they have not provided the impetus for the long-term recovery they promised. In early November 1999, a ninth major package was announced. This package, along with the earlier packages and ongoing government deficit spending, has ballooned Japanese government debt to nearly 120 percent of GDP, around twice the relative size of the U.S. federal debt. Whether this new spending plan will succeed in sparking a recovery remains to be seen. What is certain, however, is that the economy has been in a decadelong slump.

Since Japan's bubble economy burst at the end of the 1980s, there has been little growth. The collapse of equity and land prices destroyed immense amounts of wealth and left the banking system burdened with bad loans of at least 77 trillion yen (around $700 billion). This huge overhang of bad loans has prevented banks from making new loans and extending the credit necessary to fuel an economic revival. Even if the problem of the banks' bad loans were removed (there is a plan in place for dealing with the problem), it is unlikely that there would be a rush for new credit since the economy is faced with much unused capacity and business investment plans have been scaled back. Consumers, with nearly two-thirds of Japan's spending power, are another potential source of growth, but incomes are falling, unemployment is at record levels, and the rapidly aging population is worried about the public pension program. The recovery in Asia, the market for two-thirds of Japan's exports, promised some boost to Japan's economy early in 1999, but the jump in the value of the yen has stifled growth from that source.

Forecasters of Japan's growth in 2000 predict slightly higher growth than in 1999, perhaps around 1.2 percent. Given the problems facing Japan's economy, this projection is one of the less certain ones in the overall world economic outlook.

With a majority of their exports going to Asia, consisting largely of raw materials and agricultural products, the economies of Australia and New Zealand were expected to take severe hits when the Asian financial crisis began in mid-1997. New Zealand did suffer a mild contraction in 1998, but many analysts now attribute that downturn to poor policy decisions rather than to the Asian flu. Australia, by contrast, defying most predictions, shrugged off the Asian downturn, boomed along, and in the process recorded the third highest growth rate for the decade among developed economies.

Australia's successful navigation of the Asian financial crisis can be attributed in part to interest rate cuts that were made before the Asian downturn. Those cuts helped boost domestic spending and offset export losses. Also, the Australian dollar was allowed to fall, reaching record lows, as the current account deficit grew. The lower dollar and a diversion of exports from Asia and to the United States and Europe helped prop up export earnings. Australia also has been a favorite destination for foreign direct investment in recent years, in part because of a series of economic reforms that have been implemented over the years, including liberalizing labor markets and cutting tariffs. One payoff is that job creation has been robust, with a growth rate comparable to that of the U.S. job engine.

Healthy job creation is only one of several areas in which the Australian economy resembles that of the United States. Equity markets have boomed, creating a strong wealth effect, and household saving is at a low level. Productivity has grown rapidly, inflation is low at about 1.5 percent, and the fiscal balance is in surplus. The outlook is that the economy will slow a bit in the year 2000 to around 3.3 percent. The central bank did raise interest rates a quarter of a percent in early November 1999 as a precaution against any overheating as the country readies itself to host the summer Olympics, an event expected to give the economy a further boost.

The risks that Australia's economy faces are similar in many respects to U.S. risks. The large current account deficit (6 percent of GDP) leaves the country's currency open to a possible speculative attack. There is also the danger of a decline in asset prices and a reversal of wealth effect spending. Probably most worrisome, however, is the fear of a sharp U.S. slowdown and the resulting loss of export sales to the U.S. market.

Unlike Australia, New Zealand boosted interest rates when its currency fell at the onset of the Asian crisis. The policy move was based on the strategy that a decline in a country's real exchange rate has a an impact on aggregate spending similar to that of a cut in interest rates. Interest rates were boosted to offset an anticipated increase in export demand. However, exports fell instead, and the higher interest rates pushed the economy into recession in early 1998. The economy began a recovery in late 1998 and recorded growth of 2.5 percent in 1999. Slightly faster growth is projected for the year 2000. Most of the growth has come from domestic demand, however, and the current account deficit has grown to 7 percent of GDP. As a result, the New Zealand dollar has fallen to record low levels. Despite the recent improvements, there is general dissatisfaction with the economy, and a new government is expected to roll back some of the economic reforms of the last 15 years. Promises of new high-tech industries have not been fulfilled, and the economy still is heavily dependent on agriculturally based industries whose prices continue to decline in world markets.

EMERGING MARKETS: LATIN AMERICA

After several years of rapid economic growth after a slow recovery from the financial crisis of the early 1980s, Latin America once again found itself in a regionwide recession at the beginning of 1999 (see Figure C-4). Regional growth began slowing in late 1997 as a result of the impact of the Asian financial crisis on South American exports and raw materials prices, but the Russian financial crisis in mid-1998 was the impetus for a domino effect that saw first a foreign exchange rate crisis in Brazil and then a general retreat of private sector capital from countries in the region. With its relatively low savings rates, the region is very dependent on outside financing for its capital needs, and capital flight sharply pushed up interest rates. Except for Mexico (see the NAFTA section) and Peru, none of the larger countries in the region managed positive economic growth in 1999.

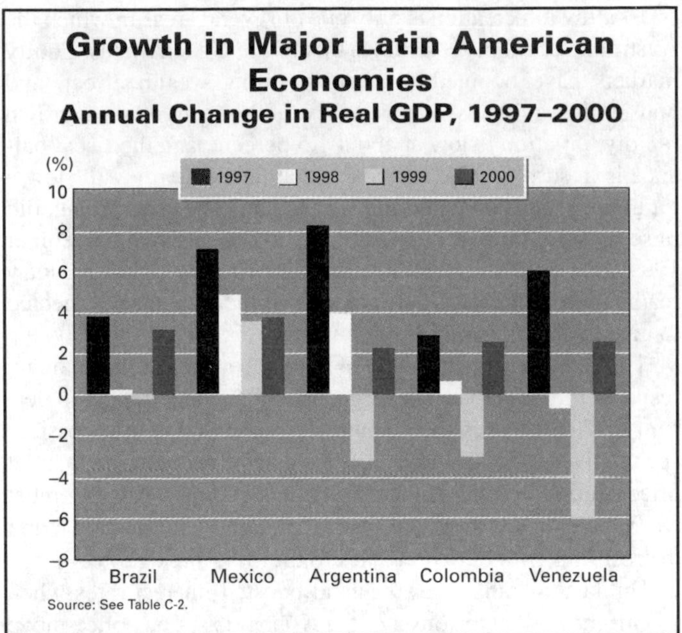

FIGURE C-4

The beginning of a recovery in Asia and the firming of mineral resource prices have helped many of the countries in this region with their current account balances and fiscal balances, and prospects for the region for the year 2000 are a lot brighter than they were just a few months ago. In the case of fiscal budgets, the improvement in resource prices helps both directly, since several countries depend on that source for revenue, and indirectly as economic conditions improve, increasing tax revenues and reducing social spending.

The region remains at risk, however, for a variety of reasons. To close fiscal deficits, many of these countries have been forced into painful contractions in government spending programs. With increasing unemployment and falling real wages in many countries, cuts in government spending have fueled unrest and popular opposition. In recent elections in Venezuela and Argentina, center-left candidates were elected as a result of the growing backlash. In Brazil, the government is facing difficulties in reforming the country's pension system, an important drain on government revenues. In addition, because of its reliance on foreign funding and high levels of government debt, any increase in world interest rates would place an additional strain on the economies in this region.

Most of the countries in the region are in the difficult position of having to balance their external financial accounts against the growing internal needs of their populations. After the "lost decade" of the 1980s, when incomes throughout the region fell, the growth spurt of the 1990s was just beginning to increase the regional standard of living when the latest blows struck. Efforts to "streamline," privatize, and reduce public budget deficits have resulted in the loss of thousands of better-paying jobs, growing unemployment, and greater income inequality in a region that leads the world in that regard.

Brazil is the largest economy in Latin America by far. Its output equals more than a third of the region's total (44 percent if Mexico is excluded). When a financial crisis forced Brazil to allow its currency to float in January 1999, that event prompted capital flight and a sharp jump in interest rates in many countries in the region. As the crisis unfolded, initial forecasts were that Brazil's economy would contract around 4 percent in 1999. That outlook proved unduly pessimistic. The country's economy actually began recovering during the second quarter of 1999, and growth for the year was essentially flat. Inflation also remained fairly constrained. One fear was that a devaluation would push the country back toward hyperinflation, a chronic problem before the currency reform was adopted. However, although price inflation increased to around 7 percent, the increase was far less than expected.

Allowing the currency to float had an immediate positive impact on Brazil's equity markets, as most analysts had come to the conclusion that the currency, the real, was overvalued at the time of the crisis. However, the devaluation of the real has not helped the balance of payments as much as had been hoped and has strained relations with the country's trade partners, especially Argentina, in the MERCOSUR trade pact. Since Argentina's currency is fixed to the dollar, the real's devaluation has put Argentina at a distinct competitive disadvantage in the region. Brazil continues to attract a substantial amount of foreign direct investment, and the long-term prognosis for the economy is positive. In the short term, however, the country faces the difficult hurdle of reforming its pension and tax systems. Until those goals are met, interest rates will remain high because of the government's need to finance its deficits and growth will be retarded.

The third largest country in Latin America, Argentina, experienced a sharp economic downturn in 1999 as output fell more than 3 percent and unemployment rose above 15 percent. Low commodity prices; the country's fixed exchange rate system, which ties the peso to the U.S. dollar through a currency board system; capital flight; and high interest rates combined to push the economy into recession. Besides the general capital flight from the region that was prompted by the Russian debacle, foreign investors tended to shy away from Argentina because of the uncertainty associated with the October 1999 elections. The new president, Fernando de la Rua, has pledged to cut the government's fiscal deficit and work toward streamlining the country's labor laws. Prospects for the economy are brightening with increasing resource prices and the negative trend in the value of the U.S. dollar. Assuming that progress is made on the fiscal deficit, interest rates should continue to decline, and the economy is expected to rebound with positive growth of over 2 percent in 2000.

Colombia is South America's third largest economy and has enjoyed largely uninterrupted growth for several decades, but recently that country has been beset by instability and is in its worse recession since the 1930s. Beginning in 1996, Colombia has had problems with a growing fiscal deficit. Economic growth in 1996 was only 2 percent, well below the region's average. Growth rebounded to 3.2 percent in 1997, but spillover effects from the Asian financial crisis (primarily low coffee and oil prices), adverse El Nino impacts, and an economic slowdown in Venezuela, Colombia's second most important trading partner, hit the country hard. Currently, unemployment is running at around 20 percent. The country's banking system is burdened with high levels of bad debt, and losses of foreign exchange reserves have forced two devaluations in the last year. Finally, in September 1999, the country followed Chile and other countries in the region that have abandoned currency bands and allowed their currencies to float. An earthquake, continuing problems with leftist guerrillas and rightist paramilitary groups, and the country's large illegal cocaine and heroin trade are added sources of uncertainty. Repair of the nation's banking system and tightening of the fiscal deficit are sorely needed before Colombia can hope to return to a semblance of normal economic growth. Nevertheless, the competitive effect of the currency devaluation, together with firming export prices, should increase economic growth to over 2 percent in 2000.

No country in the region has benefited more from the recent increase in oil prices than has Venezuela. The rebound in oil prices will help stabilize a deteriorating current account and ease growing fiscal deficits. Perhaps a larger problem in the short term, however, is the great amount of uncertainty about the policies of the populist president, Hugo Chavez. Chavez was elected in February 1999, and he pushed through a new constitution that gives the presidency added power. Chavez has pledged to honor all the country's foreign debts, but doubts abound, and the value of Venezuela's outstanding debt is trading at prices little above those of countries that are in default. The oil price hike, together with efforts to spur domestic demand, may result in minimal positive economic growth in 2000 after an economic decline of around 6 percent in 1999.

Low prices for copper, the source of over one-third of Chile's export earnings, and interest rates that were boosted to 14 percent in 1998 in an effort to protect the value of the currency are blamed for the 1999 recession. The boost in interest rates proved futile as Chile eventually relaxed its currency bands, in effect allowing the peso to float. A severe drought also played a role in the economy's troubles in 1999. Not only did the drought cause damage to agriculture, it also caused reductions in hydroelectric power, leading to several brownouts and reductions in industrial output. Interest rates have been reduced, inflation is very low, and a sharp reduction in imports has kept the current account deficit low. A sharp rebound in economic output is expected in the year 2000, with economic growth expected to approach 5 percent.

Peru's economy slumped badly in 1998, but minimal positive growth was accomplished despite the triple whammies of El Nino, falling commodity prices, and the Asian financial crisis. Output in 1999 was up almost 3 percent, in contrast to most Latin economies. A much better marine harvest, the source of 20 percent of the country's export earnings, was a big reason. Peru is hoping for a return of healthy levels of foreign investment to boost economic growth above 5 percent in the year 2000.

The eighth largest country in Latin America, Ecuador, also is ailing. Faced with the highest debt burden of any country in the region and hammered by the dual blows of El Nino floods and falling oil prices, the country became the first ever to default on its holdings of Brady bond liabilities when it failed to make a $96 million interest payment on that debt in September 1999. (Brady bonds consist of defaulted commercial bank debt from the Latin American financial crisis of the 1980s. The debt was repackaged and backed by U.S. Treasury bonds named after then Treasury secretary Nicholas Brady. Ecuador's Brady bond debt is rather small compared with the $43.4 billion of such debt owed by Brazil.) The International Monetary Fund (IMF) allowed the default when it failed to extend emergency credit to Ecuador after that country's congress refused to pass a series of tax and fiscal spending reforms that the IMF required as a condition for the emergency credit. (Financial markets see the IMF's lack of action as a step toward shifting some of the cost of country defaults from public institutional creditors such as the IMF to private sector creditors. Many believe that removing public sector guarantees of such debt will reduce or eliminate the "moral hazard" problem that has led some in the private sector to make ill-considered and risky loans to emerging markets. The consequence may be that interest costs to emerging markets will increase.) After the default, Ecuador's economy continued to spiral out of control as 1999 came to a close. In early January 2000, Mahuad took the unpresidented step of announcing that Ecuador would "dollarize" its economy, replacing the rapidly depreciating currency, the sucre, with U.S. dollars. The outlook is very uncertain.

EMERGING MARKETS: THE MIDDLE EAST AND EUROPE

Before the successful implementation of OPEC oil production cutbacks in March 1999, this region's prospects, along with the price of crude oil, were headed downward. As the price of oil neared $10 a barrel (in real terms a record low price by some calculations), governments throughout the region were preparing austerity budgets to limit the growth of fiscal deficits that were in some cases nearing 20 percent of GDP. Regional efforts to diversify economically have not been successful, and countries in the area, particularly Arabian Gulf coast countries, remain heavily dependent on oil revenues for up to 75 percent of their annual income. Largely as a result of the rebound in oil prices, growth in the region should recover to over 3 percent in 2000, slightly lower than the region's average growth in the last decade (see Table C-1 and Figure C-5).

At the time of the OPEC meeting in March 1999, some OPEC observers doubted that the organization could maintain the discipline needed to reverse the fall in oil prices. Now that prices have reached $30 per barrel, some of those voices anticipate that as in the past, some members may begin cheating on the production quotas. Indeed, some within the organization have voiced the opinion that prices have perhaps been driven too high so that non-OPEC members may increase production and undercut the organization, as happened in the past. In light of the fact that there has been virtually no new investment in

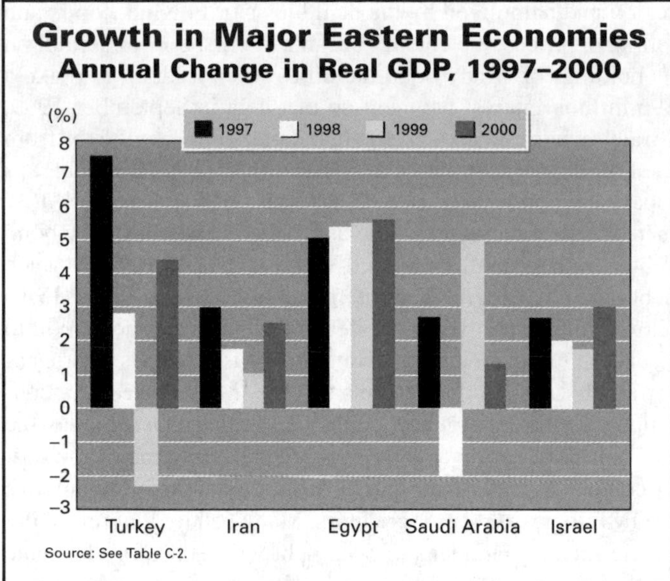

FIGURE C-5

exploration in recent years, this argument apparently carried little weight within OPEC, which has elected to maintain current quotas at least until March 2000.

The Middle East region, with a few notable exceptions, has made the least progress toward economic reform in recent years. By and large, oil revenues are used to subsidize inefficient economic operations. Rapidly growing populations and surging unemployment rates are making these policies increasingly untenable and there is a growing realization that reforms are needed, but little progress has been made. The rapid rebound in oil prices after the March 1999 OPEC accord is therefore somewhat of a mixed blessing in that the extra revenue may again allow those countries to set aside reform.

Four economies in this region—Egypt, Iran, Turkey, and Saudi Arabia—account for about three-quarters of the region's total output, with Israel accounting for another 5 percent. Of the four large economies, Egypt has made the most progress in implementing stabilization and structural reforms. Egypt's reform measures have been very successful and have resulted in several years of solid growth. Inflation rates have declined, and government budget deficits have been virtually eliminated. Economic growth was at nearly 6 percent in 1999 and is expected to be about the same in the year 2000.

Egypt pegs its currency to the dollar, and the dollar's high value has led some to suggest that Egypt should devalue. Its foreign exchange reserves have slipped around 10 percent, partly because revenues from tourism have yet to return to the levels reached before the murder of dozens of foreign tourists at the Luxor archaeological site in November 1997. The increase in oil prices has helped balance the country's foreign accounts, and the current account deficit is now well under 2 percent of GDP. Economic reform efforts are continuing, but the most attractive public assets have been sold, and the country has been slowed in its continuing efforts to privatize the assets that remain under government control. The financial crises that have wracked the emerging markets in the last 2 years have not helped in these privatization efforts.

Turkey is the largest country in the region and, unlike the other large economies there, is an oil importer, and so the boost in oil prices is not advantageous. However, the fact that several of its major trading partners, including Russia, have benefited from higher oil prices indirectly helps the Turkish economy. The country had several years of rapid growth in the mid-1990s but fell into a recession in late 1998. The economy apparently had turned the corner when the devastating earthquake struck in mid-August 1999. Just before the quake, the newly elected government had passed a series of new laws to pave the way for economic reform. The IMF had been pressuring the country to bring its budget deficits under control. Those deficits have been the major reason for Turkey's chronically high rates of inflation. In the wake of the tragedy, the government pledged to continue the reform process. Indications are that except for severe damage to one of its refineries, the country's manufacturing physical plant escaped major damage. The outlook is for an rebound in 2000 with growth of over 4 percent.

The remaining major economies in the region—Saudi Arabia and Iran—and most of the smaller economies all depend on petroleum for import and state revenues. The rebound in oil prices will result in better growth in 2000 than was the case in 1999. In Saudi Arabia, as in most of these economies, the oil industry is state-owned and -controlled, and there has been little progress on economic reform other than some restructuring in the electrical power sector and the private contracting of transportation services. Iran also has made little progress in economic reform. Conservative clerics are in charge of many of the state industries that dominate the economy, and there is strong resistance to fundamental changes in the way the economy operates. As in other Gulf states, oil earnings account for about 75 percent of state revenues, which are used to support inefficient state industries. Parliamentary elections at the end of February 2000 resulted in a victory by Iranian moderates, which may portend a change in economic policy.

EMERGING MARKETS: AFRICA

As in most emerging markets, the adverse impact of falling resource prices after the Asian financial crisis was felt powerfully in Africa, and growth in 1999 was off compared with that in 1998. The continent is very dependent on commodity exports, and most countries will find their export earnings limited in the year 2000. With the recovery of oil prices, some countries, particularly those in west and north Africa, will see a rebound in 2000. On the whole, while growth is expected to be stronger in 2000 because of stronger world trade growth, the region will not grow rapidly enough to ensure sustainable development in the coming years (see Table C-1 and Figure C-6).

Unlike emerging economies in most of the world's regions, countries in Africa did not suffer from the panic of capital flight when the Asian and Russian crises occurred, but only because

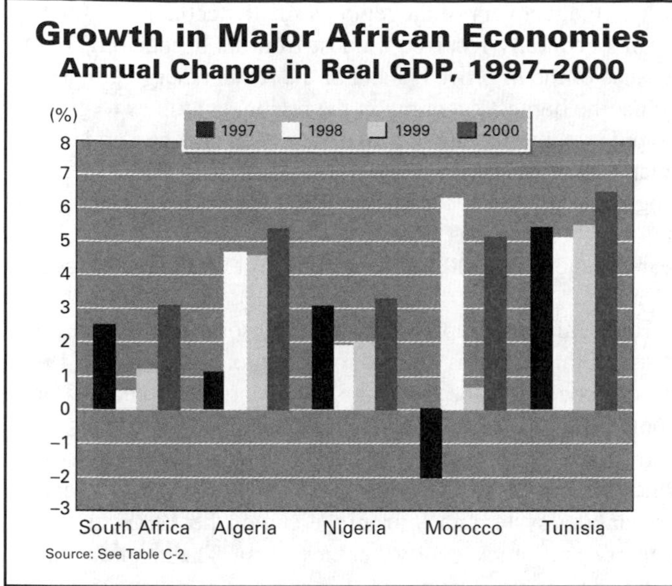

FIGURE C-6

the continent receives very little foreign capital investment to begin with. Sub-Saharan Africa attracts barely 5 percent of the total of foreign direct investment in emerging markets, down from more than 20 percent in 1980. Foreign direct investment grew somewhat during the 1990s, but most of it went to Nigeria and South Africa. At the same time, official assistance has been on the decline as industrial countries have cut back on foreign aid. High levels of indebtedness also impede efforts to increase investment in many African countries. By most measures, the debt burdens of sub-Saharan countries continue to worsen, and 28 of the 33 low-income countries with severe debt problems are in Africa.

Aside from the geographic, infrastructure, and political problems that make investment in the region unattractive, Africa contains many small countries with markets that are too small to benefit from economies of scale. To rectify this problem, efforts are under way to create free-trade zones within the region. Two prominent groupings in the region—the 14-member South African Development Community (SADA) and the 21-member Common Market for Eastern and Southern Africa (COMESA)—are undertaking efforts to establish free-trade zones and common external tariffs, but progress has been slow, in part because of the dominant role of South Africa's economy in the region. South Africa has a surplus with most countries on the continent, and other countries fear competition with South Africa's relatively efficient industries, particularly in textiles.

South Africa's economy is the largest on the continent, accounting for around 14 percent of total output. That country successfully concluded its second all-race democratic elections in June 1999, and the African National Congress party (ANC) led by Thabo Mbeki won. Mbeki was elected state president, replacing Nelson Mandela, on June 16, 1999. The new government has promised to continue economic reforms. The fiscal budget and other macroeconomic measures indicate that the economy is in reasonably good condition. Foreign investment continues to lag, however, and economic growth is expected to increase only 3 percent in 2000.

Nigeria, with the continent's third biggest economy, also got a new government in 1999. After 15 years of military dictatorship, a democratically elected government headed by President Olusegun Obasanjo entered office in May. Obasanjo inherited a country with enormous economic problems. Fortunately, the rise in the price of oil has returned the state budget to the black. As in the case of many other oil exporters, Nigeria's government depends on oil revenues for a majority of its funding (around 70 percent). Oil revenues also dominate the country's foreign exchange earnings. Obasanjo's most serious challenge will be to reform corrupt political and economic institutions. Meanwhile, on the strength of higher oil prices, the economy is expected to grow over 3 percent in the year 2000.

Three of the five largest economies in Africa are in north Africa. Algeria, Morocco, and Tunisia are predicted to grow 5 percent or more in 2000. As in the Sub-Saharan region, there were positive political developments during 1999 to unite the region in a common market and increase stability. After years of strife, north African governments met in 1999 to try and revive the United Maghreb Arab Union, which was founded in 1989 with the goal of creating a common market. Positive movement on many political fronts has been the key to the revival of the talks. In Algeria, an agreement between the government and the Islamic Freedom Front ended years of violence. In Libya, the government handed over accused terrorists to stand trial in the Lockerbie aircraft bombing case; United Nations sanctions were lifted in return. Morocco and Algeria are working toward an agreement over their dispute on the status of the Western Sahara.

EMERGING MARKETS: ASIA

The rapid recovery in this region is the key to the much more optimistic world outlook today compared with the outlook a few short months ago. While signs of an Asian recovery began to appear in late 1998, growth sharply accelerated in the first half of 1999, and it is now believed that with the possible exception of Indonesia and Hong Kong, all major economies in the region recorded positive growth in 1999, with prospects for even faster growth in 2000 (see Table C-1 and Figure C-7).

The recovery in the region has been spurred by numerous stimuli. The sharp currency devaluations after the 1997 financial crisis, coupled with continued strong demand from North America, helped spur export growth. As recovery in the region has progressed, intraregional trade has picked up. The abrupt turnaround in current account balances has been phenomenal. The IMF reports that the five crisis economies in the region—South Korea, Indonesia, Malaysia, Thailand, and the Philippines—saw their collective current account balances reversed from a total deficit of $53 billion in 1996 to a total surplus of $68.8 billion in 1998. Capital flight from the region in the wake

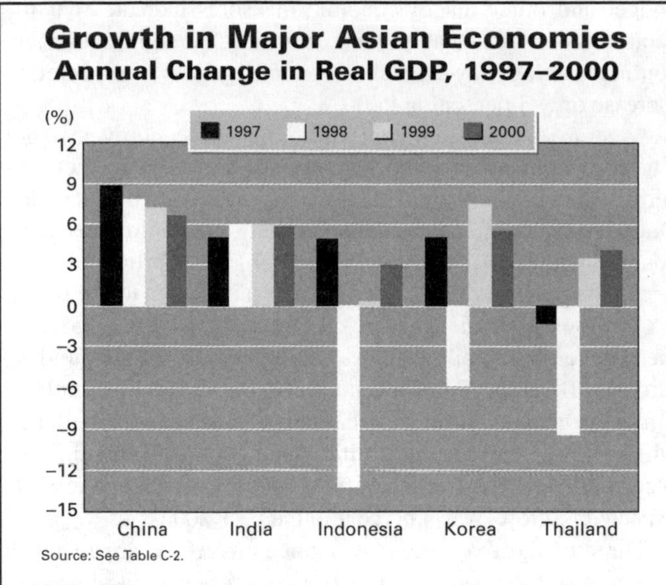

FIGURE C-7

of the mid-1997 financial crisis forced the abrupt rebalancing. Most of the adjustment was accomplished through large declines in imports. Now that the region has stabilized and financial markets have recovered, private capital inflows have resumed to some extent, and imports are recovering.

Aside from the stimulus from sharply higher net exports, the countries in the region benefited from expansionary fiscal and monetary policies. Interest rates have come down across the region. Firming commodity prices have added to the export earnings of some of these countries. The recovery of oil prices helped Indonesia in particular. Several countries, notably India, Indonesia, and the Philippines, have had gains in agricultural output. Finally, with recoveries well under way, consumers have begun to spend again.

The speed of the recovery has led more than a few analysts of the region to express the worry that an overly rapid recovery may result in the postponement or avoidance of recommended structural reforms. The lack of transparency in business institutions, inefficient capital allocation because of "crony capitalism," and state ownership of enterprises are among the problems that led to the bursting of Asia's economic boom. Without a full rectification of these problems, some fear that too rapid a recovery may result in another collapse down the road. The pace of structural reforms has been uneven. In general, there has been good progress in developing a framework for repairing the region's financial institutions in most of the crisis countries. However, progress in restructuring the region's industries has been less rapid. The incomplete nature of this work leaves a source of potential future instability and is one of the major risk factors in regard to continued growth in the region.

The other risk factors relate to the economies of the two regional giants, China and Japan. Together, those two countries account for roughly half of Asia's output, and they contributed little to the recovery of the region's smaller economies. Indeed, Japan's economy received a boost from its decadelong slump because of the improved health of the Asian emerging markets. China, the biggest economy in the region, continues to grow at a rapid rate, but its rate of growth has been slowing, and of late much of its growth has come from government fiscal spending programs. Domestic consumption in China has been sluggish, and the economy has been experiencing price deflation for 2 years. In the year 2000, China's growth is expected to be around 6.6 percent.

Both China and Japan are plagued by some of the same sorts of structural problems that led to the regional collapse in 1997. In both countries, the banking systems are burdened by large amounts of bad debts. In China, much the bad debt stems from loans made to inefficient state-owned enterprises, a majority of which are believed to be unprofitable. Japan's debt overhead in the banking system dates from the end of the 1980s, when its property and stock equity bubbles burst. The manufacturing sectors in the two countries also share at least one common characteristic: overcapacity. Japan's manufacturing sector is for the most part among the most efficient in the world, but overinvestment in the late 1980s, together with a policy of lifetime employment, has reduced profitability. In China, the industrial sector is inefficient. China's possible entry into the World Trade Organization (WTO) may lead to a needed restructuring of its industrial sector if it opens its markets to foreign competition. Any industrial restructuring, however, will lead to even more unemployment in the short run, and one of the biggest problems is the huge number of unemployed and underemployed workers in the Chinese economy.

The bottom line is that both of these economic giants have significant structural problems to overcome, and the risk of either of them stumbling on the way to reform will threaten the economic health of the entire region despite any progress the smaller economies make in their efforts to rebuild their economies.

EMERGING MARKETS: CENTRAL EUROPE AND THE CIS

Ten years after the fall of the Berlin wall and the beginning of the end of central planning, the economies of the former Soviet Union and its eastern bloc partners have undergone a dramatic transformation. Although no two economies in this group have followed the same path from where they began in 1989 to where they find themselves today, one can generalize to some extent about the relative success or failure they have realized in their transformations. No country has had an easy transformation, and almost all suffered sharp declines in output in the years immediately after the demise of central planning.

In the last 5 or 6 years, several economies in this group have begun to recover; they have realized several years of continuous growth, and a few of them have reached or surpassed the levels of output attained before the transformation process began. By and large, the more successful economies are in central Europe.

Those countries have made great strides in their transformation to market economies. They have established or reformed commercial and legal institutions to support a market economy. To a large extent, the operation and ownership of those countries' economic assets have been transferred to private ownership, including foreign ownership, a development that has been welcomed and encouraged.

For the countries that are members of the Commonwealth of Independent States (CIS), the former republics of the Soviet Union (except the Baltic states of Latvia, Lithuania, and Estonia), the results have not been nearly as positive. Only two in this group of economies currently produce as much as two-thirds of the output they produced at the beginning of the transition decade. More troubling, more than half these economies have seen their output fall to one-half or less of their 1989 levels. Included in this group of countries are Russia and Ukraine, the two giants within the CIS.

There is much debate about the reason or reasons for these divergent outcomes between most of the central European countries and the CIS countries. Certainly the CIS countries failed to implement the institutional and economic policy reforms required to realize a successful transition. Instead, the limited reforms that were initiated were not pursued as vigorously as was required. The result has been the evolution of a system that is highly corrupt and inefficient, a system somewhere between a market economy and the old command structure. In fact, in much of the CIS, including Russia, privatization involved the transfer of the ownership of state enterprises to the former managers of those enterprises under highly questionable, if not patently illegal, means. These "nomenklatura capitalists" proceeded to systematically expropriate as many resources as possible from the populace by using various monopolistic practices. The inability of the government to collect taxes on those transactions because of corruption and a weak legal structure was a major factor in the financial crisis caused by the Russian default in August 1998, which caused a second round of destabilizing capital flight throughout much of the world's financial system.

Central Europe

The aftershocks of the Russian default have affected most of the countries in the region, but since the economies of central Europe have been cutting their economic ties with Russia and the east and have become much more closely integrated with the economies of the west, the macroeconomic impact of the crisis was not as severe as had been predicted initially. Overall, economic growth in central Europe and the Baltic states was roughly halved between 1997 and 1999. Besides the adverse consequences of the Russian default, some of the economic slowdown was the result of slower economic growth in the EU. The outlook for the year 2000 is that overall growth in central Europe should return to the 1997 level of around 3.5 percent. Within this group of countries there are sharp differences. Poland has had the most successful economic transformation, and the European Bank for Reconstruction and Development (EBRD) estimates that that country's output is now around 17 percent larger than it was in 1989. Growth slowed to around 3.5 percent in 1999, and the fiscal and external deficits increased somewhat. Foreign investment has been adequate to close most of the current account deficit. In 2000, growth is projected to reach almost 5 percent (see Figure C-8). Perhaps Poland's major current concern is the growing disparity in income and wealth both geographically and between different occupational groups. In early 1999, the country witnessed its largest public demonstrations since 1989 as various groups of public servants, including teachers and doctors, along with farmers demonstrated for higher wages. The problem of rural poverty and the 25 percent of the workforce in agriculture is an issue that must be faced before Poland can attain full membership in the EU.

Like Poland, Hungary is a success story in the region. Its growth also slowed in 1999 for some of the same reasons that Poland's slowed but also because of serious flooding during the summer. Strong domestic demand and a better export outlook will result in faster growth in 2000. Hungary may be the fastest-growing country in the region. The economy's output is just returning to the levels reached before the economic transformation. Hungary moved slowly and carefully on the way to economic transformation, and its economy may be the first to be accepted for membership in the EU.

In contrast to Hungary, the Czech Republic moved to transform its economy much more quickly after the fall of communism. Unfortunately, its plan has proved to be defective in that the country's banks ended up with major ownership stakes in Czech industries. Since the government owned the banks, the relationship produced a system in which generous loans continued to subsidize inefficient industries. The country is in the process of correcting that problem. Banks are being privatized and industry is being restructured, but the process has cost the country. Growth for the last 3 years has been flat. A moderate

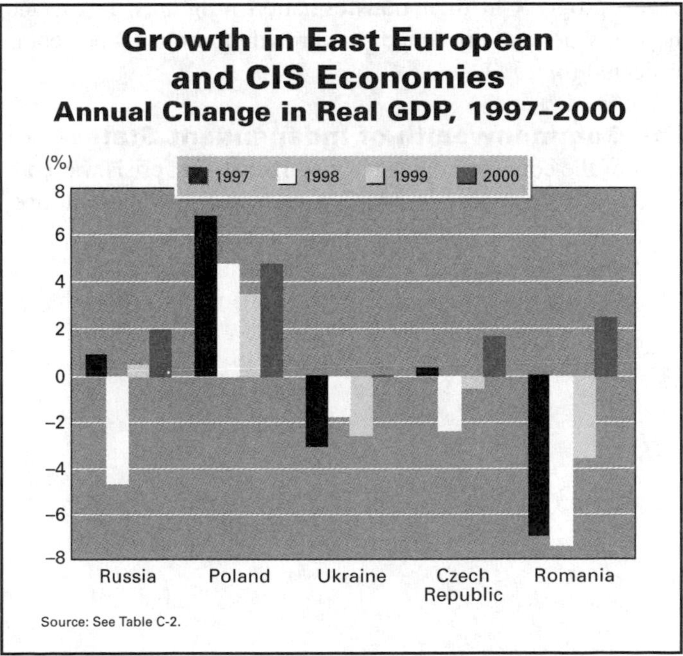

FIGURE C-8

upturn with growth approaching 2 percent is expected in the year 2000. Slovakia had rapid growth between 1995 and 1998, but the fiscal and current accounts became unbalanced and growth was reigned in to around 2 percent in 1999. Growth is expected to be the same in 2000 as the country confronts economic restructuring issues.

In the Balkans, the Kosovo war and the political and economic isolation of Yugoslavia have adversely affected this region's economies. In 1999, Yugoslavia's eastern neighbors, the economies of Romania and Bulgaria, were both adversely affected by the war. Downed bridges are blocking traffic on the Danube River, and those blockages have caused transportation problems in the area. Beyond this common problem, the economies of the two countries are heading in opposite directions. Bulgaria has moved ahead with economic reforms and has used a currency board to halt inflation. The economy grew 3.5 percent in 1998 but was flat in 1999, in large part because of the war. Growth of around 4 percent is expected in 2000. In contrast to Bulgaria's successes, Romania has made scant progress in restructuring its economy. In addition to its internal problems, Russia is a major trading partner, and exports to that country have slowed. As the trade turns around and after 3 consecutive years of sharp declines, moderate growth is expected in 2000. In 1999, Albania's economy grew despite the Kosovo conflict, while the economies of Croatia and Macedonia suffered setbacks. The economies in all three countries are expected to improve in 2000. Slovenia has made the most progress toward restructuring its economy among the former Yugoslav republics. That country was relatively unscathed by the Kosovo conflict, had solid growth in 1997–1999, and is projected to grow around 4 percent in 2000. It may be one of the early entrants into the EU.

The Russian crisis caused some economic damage to Estonia, Latvia, and Lithuania. Those three Baltic states have made steady progress in their transformation programs. Fiscal and monetary policies are sound, and growth of around 4 percent is projected for 2000.

The Commonwealth of Independent States

Most of the collateral damage from the Russian crisis was confined to Russia's closest trading partners in east-central Europe. Belarus, Moldova, and Ukraine all experienced economic declines or slowdowns in 1998–1999. Of course, separating the negative impacts from Russia from the general mismanagement of those economies is a difficult task. As was discussed above, the countries of the CIS have made the least progress in transforming their economies.

In Russia, the economy registered a slight increase in 1997, the first since the fall of communism, but the 1998 financial crisis caused a sharp contraction in the aftermath of default and the devaluation of the ruble. That devaluation, however, has increased the competitiveness of Russia's producers, and domestic manufactures have replaced imports in Russian stores. The increase in oil prices has helped the country's energy exporters. The increase in manufacturing and the boost in oil exports helped stabilize the economy in 1999. Inflation has cooled, and government finances arc in better shape. There is cautious optimism that the economy may record moderate growth in 2000. However, to stem capital flight from the country; reenergize foreign investment, which has declined sharply since the crisis; and put the economy on a positive long-term growth trajectory, Russia must make the structural reforms necessary to assure investors, domestic and foreign, that their investments are secure and protected by a strong legal system.

In the CIS economies of the Transcaucasus and central Asia, several countries, including Armenia, Azerbaijan, and Uzbekistan, have registered several years of solid growth. Kazakhstan, the largest economy in the region, has not fared as well. In that country, the recovery in oil prices will help.

John Jelacic, U.S. Department of Commerce, Office of Trade and Economic Analysis, (202) 482-2403, February 2000.

■ GLOSSARY

Purchasing Power Parity (PPP) Exchange Rates: Exchange rates that have been adjusted for relative prices between countries for the same or similar products so that the PPP exchange rate would equalize the purchasing power between countries if a given amount of money in one country's currency was to be converted to the other country's currency.

D

The Electronic Commerce Landscape: Technology and Business Converging

The early 1990s saw the convergence of key communications and information technologies. Computers got dramatically faster and cheaper. Deregulation in the U.S. telecommunications industry spurred innovation by communications companies, and a little-known computer network called the Internet became widely accessible to the general public as a result of the development of the World Wide Web and a graphics-based, point-and-click Web browser called Mosaic. Those innovations have brought about changes that are touching every part of the economy and society.

Digital economy technologies[1] are having a profound effect on commerce and business. For manufacturers and suppliers, they are creating new opportunities to extend market reach around the globe and generating new business opportunities. For purchasers, E-commerce can mean increased convenience and choice as well as more competition and reduced prices. Both groups may be able to streamline purchases, reduce costs, and take advantage of new market efficiencies.

As businesses integrate new, rapidly changing technologies into their processes, a new and different marketplace centered on the Internet is forming. More people and companies are going on-line. More of the people and businesses that are on-line are using the Internet as a marketplace, that is, exploring what is out there for sale, checking and comparing prices, and asking questions about the characteristics of the goods and services that are for sale. Finally, more people and businesses are buying and selling on-line.

These opportunities, however, have not come without challenges. In the process of taking up E-commerce, businesses are being forced to reevaluate the competition and their own operations. The competitive environment appears to be changing. Web-based start-ups such as E-Loan and E*Trade are challenging established firms. Producers and manufacturers such as Dell and Cisco are forgoing traditional wholesale and retail outlets and selling directly to the final consumers on-line. Intermediaries such as FedEx are expanding their services and becoming more deeply involved in the supply and distribution chains of other firms. Cyberintermediaries such as eBay are creating new markets.

As business models change, new business are invented, and consumers embrace or reject those changes, there is a continuous effort to assess what is taking place. With that in mind, this overview touches on various facets of E-commerce and

[1] There are no strict definitions of many of the terms used to describe the digital economy. This can lead to confusion, particularly when terms are used inconsistently or interchangeably. In this chapter, "digital economy technologies" is used as a catchall term that encompasses everything from new TCP/IP protocols to games. "E-commerce" refers to transactions made over computer networks, such as the Internet, and "E-business" refers to changes in business and business processes brought about by digital economy technologies. Much of the innovation related to E-commerce has been made possible by the World Wide Web, an application the runs on the Internet; however, the term "Internet" is used broadly here to refer to both the Internet and the World Wide Web.

E-business. The following sections outline the potential benefits of E-commerce and E-business, provide an overview of the E-commerce environment, and discuss some of the challenges that businesses face as they enter this marketplace.

POTENTIAL BENEFITS OF ELECTRONIC COMMERCE AND ELECTRONIC BUSINESS

Digital economy technologies are new and are changing rapidly. This makes it difficult to assess their impact on businesses and business processes. Evidence of the potential of these technologies to broaden and/or create markets, streamline supply chains and other business processes, and reduce costs tends to be anecdotal rather than systematic. Part of the difficulty stems from the scale of the changes taking place, which is so great that government statistical agencies have to reassess and revamp the statistics they collect. Another source of difficulty is the pace of change. Ideas sweep through the on-line marketplace. An Internet auction site is a success, and then all the major sites introduce auctions. One company gives away free E-mail accounts, and then every major site gives away E-mail accounts. Changes within firms may occur more slowly and are much less evident to observers.

Despite these difficulties in evaluating the on-line marketplace, a number of trends are emerging. The Internet and Internet-like networks enable firms to lower costs. One means is to shift sales and information dissemination to lower-cost channels. Solomon Smith Barney, for example, estimates that the airlines are saving $20 to $40 per ticket on tickets sold on-line compared with those sold off-line. That firm estimates that savings may increase another $15 per ticket. Use of the Internet for customer service—order tracking, software downloads, technical support information, and so on—is also saving firms money and improving customer satisfaction. Cisco Systems, for example, reported that by putting customer service and technical support on-line, it increased customer service productivity 200 to 300 percent, resulting in savings of $125 million in customer service costs.

Firms also are saving money by shortening production cycles by reducing the time it takes to transmit, receive, and process routine business communications such as purchase orders, invoices, and shipping notifications. By reducing product cycle time, a firm potentially reduces the fixed costs associated with production, including depreciation of equipment and building costs as well as managerial and supervisory time.

Another E-business means of lowering costs is to lower procurement prices by broadening procurement markets and increasing procurement competition. By using an on-line procurement system, GE Lighting reduced processing time for outgoing bid packages from 7 days to 2 hours, increased the number of suppliers receiving requests for quotes, and decreased error rates. This enabled GE Lighting to decrease the division's labor costs 30 percent and redeploy 60 percent of the procurement staff.

The Internet and Internet-like networks such as Extranets also enable sellers to reach broader markets. Almost every country in the world has some Internet connectivity, although the level of access varies substantially, ranging from E-mail only to full Internet access. A company that opens an on-line business potentially has a worldwide market, although there are certain limiting factors. International shipping costs are an important factor for tangible goods. For intangible goods, limited bandwidth in other countries may be a constraint. In both cases, there may be legal and regulatory differences. In addition, as with more traditional technologies, linguistic and cultural differences can create significant barriers to trade.

Digital economy technologies have provided firms with unprecedented tools that can be used to track and analyze their customers' interests and purchasing habits. For example, by tracking a customer's purchases, on-line companies can tailor on-line advertising to that customer's revealed interests. Companies also are tailoring their products and services to customers' preferences and developing one-to-one marketing. (The use of these capabilities has raised concern about invasion of privacy; this is discussed below.)

The processing power and connectivity of digital economy technologies are allowing the creation of markets, such as on-line auctions and spot markets, that previously would have been impossible. Examples are distributed across the Internet. eBay, one of the most prominent on-line trading communities, has 5.6 million registered users, lists 2.4 million items for sale, and is open 24 hours a day, 7 days a week. There are also business-to-business (B2B) sites such as Fastparts.com, which hosts a site at which original equipment manufacturers, contract assemblers, part makers, and distributors can trade electronic components and equipment.

The Internet gives purchasers a wider selection of products. It also provides them with powerful tools for comparison shopping. The Web also holds out the promise of lower prices for purchasers. Sites such as Price Watch and CNET Shopper let buyers search the Web for the best price. Furthermore, recent research suggests that on-line prices of standardized products such as books and compact discs appear to be lower than those at conventional outlets.

It is critical not to underestimate the ability of consumers and purchasers who use the Internet to comparison shop and research products and services. Jupiter Communications estimates that 47 percent of the on-line population uses the Internet to research products even though those shoppers may not buy a product on-line. Consumers increasingly are likely to be better informed about the characteristics and prices of the products they are purchasing. Factors such as these appear to be shifting market power to the customer.

THE ON-LINE MARKETPLACE

An increasing number of individuals are on-line. On the low end, IntelliQuest estimates that 82 million people are on-line in the United States. On the high end, Nielsen Netratings estimates that there are as many as 108 million. Early users of the Internet were likely to be young, well educated, affluent, white, and male. As the Internet has become more of a mass medium, it has begun to reach a broader, more diverse group of people and firms. IntelliQuest's research suggests that in 1999 Internet users still tended to be younger, have higher incomes, and have higher education levels than the U.S. population as a whole. However, the demographics of new Internet users in that year were more reflective of the overall population.

Only a fraction of Web users are making purchases on-line, but estimates indicate that that number is growing and that on-line spending is increasing. Estimates of 1999 on-line retail sales in the United States range from $11.9 billion (Jupiter Communications) to $36 billion (Boston Consulting Group/Shop.Org). Even the most optimistic estimates indicate that current on-line sales still account for less than 1 percent of total retail sales. However, forecasts such as Forrester Research's projection that on-line sales will grow to as much as $184 billion in 2004 point to rapid growth. If these projections prove correct, the Internet is likely to become an important sales channel in the near future.

On-line sales showed dramatic increases during the 1998 holiday shopping season, which appears to have been a turning point for mainstream acceptance of buying on-line. More people made purchases on-line, and those purchasers spent more. Sales estimates vary dramatically, ranging from $1.1 billion (eMarketer) to as high as $8.2 billion (Marketing Corp of America). Regardless of the dollar value of the estimates, the consensus is that the forecasts were outstripped by on-line sales. Estimates for the 1999 holiday shopping season reveal further increases. American Express estimated that the number of Internet shoppers nearly tripled during the holiday shopping season in 1999—16 percent of U.S. consumers bought gifts on-line in 1999 compared to 6 percent in 1998.

Just as retail sales are moving on-line, more businesses are using the Internet to purchase products and services. A 1999 study at Georgetown University's McDonough School of Business found that 72 percent of *Fortune* magazine's Global 250 had Web sites that were interactive enough to allow Web users to communicate with the company. Furthermore, a study by Zona Research suggests that corporate purchasing on the Internet is increasing. Like business-to-customer (B2C) E-commerce, B2B E-commerce is forecast to grow dramatically over the next few years. Forrester Research estimates that U.S. on-line B2B E-commerce will total $109 billion in 1999 and $1 trillion in 2003.

ELECTRONIC COMMERCE DEVELOPMENTS

Businesses that have entered the on-line marketplace have discovered that putting up a Web page is not enough to create a successful on-line business. The costs of going on the Web, of course, vary with a firm's level of commitment to the Internet marketplace. A business's use of the Internet can range from simply posting information about a company (known as brochureware) to integrating a firm's Internet strategy with its overall business strategy (becoming an E-business). After the physical cost of going on-line (Internet service provider, Web page design, Web page hosting), substantial off-line investments such as advertising and marketing are needed to attract consumers to the Web site.

The Internet is an active rather than a passive medium; that is, a Web user must choose to visit a site. The Online Computer Library Center estimates that there are 2.2 million publicly assessable sites on the Web, and so an important part of any on-line strategy is to bring users to a company's Web site. Businesses currently use numerous strategies to draw users to their sites, including linking to or advertising on sites with heavy traffic and listing themselves with Internet search engines. Many Web-based start-up companies have spent heavily on advertising and marketing. Advertising by Internet companies on television networks alone could surpass $500 million during 2000.

Building trust is also critical in both B2C and B2B E-commerce. The same characteristics that offer opportunities—the ability to sell to remote customers with a minimum of person-to-person interaction—create the potential for fraud. It is important for businesses to provide an environment where Web users feel confident that the information is accurate and that if they buy something on-line, it will be delivered. Providing on-line customers with features that are routine in the brick and mortar world, such as clear policies on returning goods and customer service contact information, helps develop this trust.

While potential fraud is a problem for consumers trying to distinguish the real on-line businesses from the phony ones, it is also a problem for businesses that face fraudulent payments. The authors of the *Nilson Report,* a credit card industry newsletter cited in the *New York Times,* estimated that in late 1999, 2 percent of on-line transactions were fraudulent. That figure was down from 15 percent in the early 1990s, but all but the largest on-line retailers still pay at least a 1 percent premium in transactions fees to credit card companies because of the risks associated with on-line transactions. Credit card issuers reportedly lose about 8 cents for every $100 in on-line sales from fraudulent credit card use. New technologies such as customer profiling, special credit cards, and credit card readers designed for use with personal computers may reduce the costs associated with fraud.

Firms that have established brand names and trust in the off-line world may have an advantage over start-ups. In a study of on-line retailing for Shop.org, Boston Consulting Group found that over half the 1998 on-line revenues were from retailers that had businesses that predated the Web. However, there are other factors that matter in the on-line environment, and start-ups can quickly become dominant players in the on-line marketplace. For example, during the fourth quarter of 1998, the Web-based eToys moved aggressively into the top slot in on-line toy selling. Although eToys' fourth quarter 1998 revenues of $22.9 million represented only a tiny share of the $23 billion U.S. toy market, the company's success in competing against the Web stores of established toy sellers such as Toys "R" Us and Wal-Mart has made brick and mortar firms scramble to revamp their Web sites.

On-line consumers are demanding. They expect extensive product information, real-time order confirmations and status information, and around-the-clock customer service. In addition to providing evidence of a general acceptance of the Internet for shopping, the 1998 holiday shopping season provided vivid examples of how firms selling to consumers over the Internet needed to improve to meet consumers' expectations. Some companies, such as Toys "R" Us and Barnes and Noble, were unprepared for the heavy traffic on their sites and had to shut them down temporarily. Others were unprepared to fulfill the volume of orders that accompanied the surge in on-line demand. Postholiday news reports revealed on-line shoppers expressing annoyance with orders that were misdelivered or delivered late, slow notification that items were out of stock, and their inability to reach customer service staff.

Established firms also have to deal with potential conflicts between on-line sales channels and existing distribution channels. Since the onset of Internet E-commerce, brick and mortar businesses have been concerned that opening a Web-based store would shift sales from existing channels instead of generating new sales. This is a legitimate concern. Even companies that have gone to considerable lengths to make sure the products they are selling over the Internet do not compete with those provided by resellers have had difficulties. Compaq Computer Corp., for example, began selling computers on-line in 1998. That company created a new line of business-oriented computers and targeted its on-line efforts at a market segment that was not a focus of its resellers. Despite Compaq's strategy, brick and mortar dealers retaliated by refusing to stock Compaq personal computers. This loss of sales in off-line channels was one of the reasons the company cited for lower than expected profits in the first quarter of 1999. However, if on-line commerce grows as it is projected to, sales in the on-line channel may come largely at the expense of sales at brick and mortar outlets. Jupiter Communications estimates that only 6 percent of on-line sales in 1999 were sales that would not have occurred otherwise. Companies that ignore the on-line sales channel thus may cede market share to competitors and start-ups.

Getting It There

The Internet makes finding, researching, and ordering goods easier and more efficient for both businesses and consumers. It enables disparate businesses to find each other and buy and sell the products they produce, but this is only one part of a transaction. If the goods are physical—books, clothing, cars, refrigerators, engines, wheels, bearings—they must be physically moved from the producer to the final consumer. This makes shipping and logistics increasingly important in the digital economy and a vital consideration for E-businesses. Web-based businesses that deliver physical goods often have large brick and mortar facilities. For example, Amazon.com has seven distribution facilities and the Web-based grocer Webvan Group recently announced that it will spend $1 billion on a nationwide network of automated warehouses.

Shipping firms also are taking on a direct role in E-commerce by becoming more closely involved in the inner workings of their partner companies. FedEx, for example, orchestrates the assembly and shipping of laptop computers for Fujitsu; this has enabled Fujitsu to decrease the time customers have to wait for an order from 10 days to 3 or 4 days. By turning over much of its computerized distribution system to FedEx, Fujitsu has been able to remove the warehousing and inventory costs from its supply chain. The company reportedly has saved millions of dollars, increasing profits 25 percent and cutting inventory 90 percent.

If the goods are digital—software and digitized images and sounds—rather than physical, there are challenges in delivering them to the end user. Some challenges are associated with the capacity, or bandwidth, of telecommunications channels. Bandwidth determines how fast digitized information can be moved over a wireline or wireless connection. This is a major factor in determining which digital products realistically can be offered on-line. Most large businesses already have access to broadband communications. The availability of broadband for residences and small business is increasing, but it is still limited. Consumers often will not wait for large files to transfer or for graphics-laden Web pages to load. A study by Zona Research suggests that E-commerce vendors that do not take into account the download times associated with their Web pages face lost sales as a result of customer frustration.

THE BUSINESS ENVIRONMENT AND ELECTRONIC COMMERCE

Digital economy technologies have enabled businesses and individuals to engage in unprecedented commercial activities. The examples given above demonstrate some of the many challenges associated with integrating E-commerce into business processes. Just as individual businesses are working to incorporate digital economy technologies into their business models, the communities that jointly create the business environment—business groups, governments, and international organizations—are working to resolve issues arising from the use of those technologies.

The Legal Environment

Many businesses and consumers are wary of conducting extensive business over the Internet because of the lack of a predictable legal environment governing transactions. This is particularly true for international commercial activity, where E-commerce accentuates existing issues related to cross-border activities, such as the enforcement of contracts and legal dispute jurisdiction. For example, a European company may operate servers in the United States that allow transactions to take place between the European headquarters and customers in Latin America. If a contract is developed using these computer-mediated communications channels, the legal jurisdiction for any subsequent disputes may be unclear.

Taxation

Numerous questions surround taxation and E-commerce. Sales taxes represent a substantial revenue source for U.S. state and local governments. The U.S. Supreme Court held in *Quill v. North Dakota* that states cannot require out-of-state sellers that do not have a physical presence in, or "nexus" to, the taxing state to collect that state's sales or use tax. Thus, although in most cases a mail order purchaser is required to pay tax in his or her home state on goods purchased remotely (e.g., via mail order catalog), states do not have effective collection and enforcement mechanisms. State governments have expressed concern that analogous treatment of E-commerce transactions could result in tremendous revenue losses.

In 1998, Congress created a process to resolve E-commerce taxation issues. The Internet Tax Freedom Act, which was signed into law on October 21, 1998, imposed a 3-year moratorium on state and local taxation of Internet access and on discriminatory, multiple-state, or local taxation of E-commerce. It also created a congressional advisory commission to consider the tax and trade issues associated with E-commerce and comparable sales activities. A report by that commission is due in April 2000.

Privacy

The proliferation of technologies that enable customer tracking and profiling raises questions about the use and sale of data collected over the Internet. Electronically collected information can now be compiled, matched, and "mined" to reveal the characteristics and habits of individuals and groups. Furthermore, applications, such as "cookies," text files automatically stored on a Web user's hard drive by a Web site, allow the tracking of Web users' on-line activities. These tools help businesses manage their inventories and customize the products they offer, but they also raise concern about an individual's right to keep information private.

Different countries have differing views on individuals' rights to privacy and on how to enforce the privacy rights of their citizens. The United States has taken a self-regulatory approach; that is, the government has strongly encouraged industry to provide the information and tools to empower Web users to protect their privacy, control the content they see, and protect themselves against inappropriate commercial behavior. This has involved promoting the use of privacy policies and encouraging the development of responsible privacy practices through industry associations. In contrast, other countries and regional organizations, such as the European Union, have taken a more regulatory approach.

Authentication and Security

The ease with which information can be duplicated and transmitted raises issues related to the effective control of intellectual property. Related to most of these issues are questions of security and authentication. Both of these issues tend to have technological solutions; that is, the questions relate to how to achieve these goals in light of current technologies, notably encryption technologies. Authentication means assuring that a file or document has not been altered since its creation and that it came from the person or organization indicated as the sender. These issues are particularly important for legal records such as contracts and in situations where control of duplication can be the key to profits, such as limiting the distribution of digitized copyrighted materials. Encryption technologies are a key component in authentication schemes, since the point of encryption is to make it impossible or at least very difficult for anyone other than the intended recipients to decrypt a message.

Related to authentication are issues of security. When data are transferred across a computer network, interception is always a possibility. Even if the data are not tampered with (i.e., the original message is still authentic), unauthorized access to the data can be damaging. For example, a common concern of individuals purchasing over the Internet is the security of their credit card information while it is in transit. Again, encryption is a key technology for ensuring the security of electronic communications.

Security and authentication issues can be controversial because various communities have differing opinions about the development and use of encryption technologies. The law enforcement community argues that the availability of encryption reduces law enforcement capabilities and represents a threat to national security. Others argue for encryption on the grounds that sensitive electronic information—government, commercial, and private personal information—requires protection against unauthorized and unlawful access.

The issues surrounding the development and proliferation of MP3 technology demonstrate the importance of authentication and security issues on the Internet. MP3 is an audiocompression file format that is used to store recorded music. MP3 technology offers a potentially important new distribution channel for companies in the music industry. However, content stored in MP3 file formats is not secure and cannot be authenticated, since it can be duplicated easily and a duplicate is indistinguishable from the original. Music companies have opposed dissemination of this technology because of concerns over piracy. Despite their resistance, the use of MP3 technology for music files has spread rapidly across the Internet. Some Web sites offer illegally copied copyrighted material, and others legally distribute non-copyrighted songs. A number of companies have developed portable MP3 players that enable users to play downloaded MP3 files away from their computers. Again, encryption holds a potential solution. Instead of resisting the new technologies, some companies, such as Liquid Audio Inc and AT&T's A2B unit, are developing software to compress, encrypt, and track music delivered over the Internet, potentially creating files for which it is possible to check the authenticity.

CONCLUSION

The digital economy is still in the early stages of development. The technologies that are driving the business and the market changes described in this overview are still in their infancy. The Internet as a type of "mass media" network is less than a decade old. The evidence, even though it is less systematic and comprehensive than one would wish, suggests that these new technologies have created opportunities for greater efficiency, new markets, larger markets, and a better understanding of customers. Along with these new opportunities have come new challenges and risks.

Sabrina L. Montes, U.S. Department of Commerce, Economics and Statistics Administration, (202) 482-6495, February 2000.

■ REFERENCES

American Express, "American Express Retail Index Finds Consumers Spent an Average of $1,557 on Holiday Gifts, Entertaining, Travel and Decorations," American Express Press Release, January 17, 1999. http://home3.americanexpress.com/corp/latestnews/post_holiday99.asp.

Armstrong, Larry, "This Toy War Is No Game," *Business Week,* August 9, 1999.

Beckett, Jamie, "Personal Technology/E-Shopping's Big Test/Holiday Buyers Like Ease, Not Delivery, Supply Glitches," *San Francisco Chronicle,* January 7, 1999.

Boston Consulting Group/Shop.Org., "Online Retailing to Reach $36 Billion in 1999: Shop.org Releases New Market Figures in Study by the Boston Consulting Group," Shop.Org press release, July 19, 1999. http://www.bcg.com/features/shop/main_shop.html.

Brull, Steven V., "Net Nightmare for the Music Biz," *Business Week,* March 2, 1998.

Brynjolfsson, Erik, and Michael D. Smith, "Frictionless Commerce? A Comparison of Internet and Conventional Retailers," paper presented at "Understanding the Digital Economy Conference," May 1999 (August 1999 version available at http://ecommerce.mit.edu/papers/friction).

Cyber Source. "Visa® U.S.A. and CyberSource® Join Forces to Reduce Internet Fraud: Partnership of Industry Leaders Enhances Fraud Screening Solution," CyberSource press release, September 1, 1999. http://www.cybersource.com/press/releases/1999/99090101.html.

Czinkota, Michael R., "Global Giants Slow to Join Net Revolution," *Journal of Commerce,* November 5, 1999.

eBay, "Carclub.com Teams Up with eBay to Provide Automotive Service for eBay Users," eBay press release, August 3, 1999. http://www.ebay.com/community/aboutebay/releasesindex.html.

eMarketer. "eMarketer Forecasts Online Holiday Spending to Reach $1.1 Billion," eMarketer press release, November 9, 1998. http://www.emarketer.com/estats/110998_holiday.html.

Flint, Joe, "Advertising Spending to Get Big Boost From Internet Companies Next Year," *Wall Street Journal,* December 7, 1999.

Forrester Research. Forrester Findings Web page, September 22, 1999. http://www.forrester.com/ER/Press/ForrFind/0,1768,0,FF.html.

Forrester Research. "Forrester Forum to Explore the Future of Internet Retail," Forrester Research press release, September 20, 1999. http://www.forrester.com/ER/Press/Release/0,1769,163,FF.html.

Gleckman, Howard, "On Congress' Hit List: Crucial Business Data," *Business Week,* September 13, 1999, p. 40.

Goldberg, Laura, "A Click and a Prayer: Airlines' Net Offerings Have Opened Up the Skies to Everyday Traveler," *Houston Chronicle,* September 19, 1999, Business section, p. 1.

Harris Interactive, "Online Holiday '99: Executive Summary," *Harris Interactive,* August 27, 1999, p. 4. http://www.ecommercePulse.com.

IntelliQuest, "IntelliQuest Internet Tracking Service Total Market Coverage of U.S. Users and Non-Users: Summary and Trends Report: Second Quarter 1999," 1999.

Jupiter Communications, "Jupiter Communications: Digital Commerce Growth Will Be an Expense of Off-line Dollars," Jupiter Communications press release, August 4, 1999. http://www.jup.com/jupiter/press/releases/1999/0804.html.

Jupiter Communications, "Jupiter: 14 Percent Fewer Online Shoppers Satisfied after Holiday Season: Loyalty to Ill-Prepared Sites Threatened by Poor Performance," Jupiter Communications press release, January 18, 1999. http://www.jup.com/jupiter/press/releases/1999/0118a.html.

Jupiter Communications, "Preparing for the Holiday Crush: Web Ventures Must Begin Testing Immediately," Jupiter Communications sample analyst note, August 9, 1999. http://www.jup.com/research/sos/samples/notes/036/.

McWilliams, Gary, "E-Commerce (A Special Report)—A New Model—Dealer Loses? Retailers Are Finding It Tough to Balance Traditional Outlets with Selling on the Web. Just Ask Compaq," *Wall Street Journal,* July 12, 1999.

Nielsen NetRatings. "Weekly Internet Ratings From Nielsen: NetRatings: Data for Monday August 23 through Sunday, August 29, 1999," September 2, 1999. http://www.nielsennetratings.com/press_releases/pr_090299.htm.

Online Computer Library Center, Inc., "OCLC Research Project Measures Scope of the Web," OCLC press release, September 8, 1999. http://www.oclc.org/oclc/press/19990908a.htm.

"Online Holiday Shopping Is Pegged at $8.2 Billion," *Wall Street Journal,* January 14, 1999.

Petersen, Andrea, "E-Commerce (A Special Report)—A New Model—Getting Noticed: You Can Have the Greatest E-Commerce Site on the Web: The Trick Is to Get People to Come to It," *Wall Street Journal,* July 12, 1999.

Saccomano, Ann, "So You've Got a Web Page. Now What Do You Do?" *Traffic World,* vol. 259, no. 4, July 26, 1999.

Smart, Tim, "Delivering Packages, Partnerships: FedEx's Ties with Fujitsu Show How Firm Is Meeting Demands of E-Commerce," *Washington Post,* May 2, 1999.

Tedeschi, Bob, "E-Commerce Report: A New Piece of Hardware Could Help Internet Merchants Cut Fraud-Associated Costs, If It Catches On," *New York Times,* September 20, 1999, Section C, p. 5.

U.S. Department of Commerce, "Elements of Effective Self Regulation for the Protection of Privacy and Questions Related to Online Privacy," Federal Register Notice. Docket No. 980422102-8102-01, June 1998. http://www.ntia.doc.gov/ntiahome/privacy/6_5_98fedreg.htm.

U.S. Department of Commerce, "The Emerging Digital Economy," Washington D.C., April 1998, p. 19. http://www.ecommerce.gov.

White House Office of the Press Secretary, "Statement by the Press Secretary: Administration Announces New Approach to Encryption," White House press release, September 16, 1999. http://www.bxa.doc.gov/Encryption/whpr99.htm.

Zona Research, "Estimated $4.35 Billion in Ecommerce Sales at Risk Each Year: Zona Research Report Reveals Consequences of Unacceptable Download Times," Zona Research press release, June 1999. http://www.zonaresearch.com/info/press/99-jun30.htm.

Zona Research, "Online Purchasing Activities Picking Up Steam," results from Zona Enterprise usage study, "Electronic Economy—Q2 1999," cited in *Zona Quiniela QStat,* September 7, 1999.

Zona Research, "Online Shopping: Is Web-Based Buying Reaching Critical Mass?" January 1999, p. 10.

E

Highlights of *Outlook 2000*

In 1999 the economy outperformed expectations at the beginning of the year. Initially, forecasters had thought the economy would slow toward a long-term growth rate of about 2.5 percent, in fact, however, the economy showed continued strength. For 2000, most forecasters anticipate some slowing, but growth will still be above what had historically been considered the trend rate of growth.

Information technology industries are expected to continue to be strong, with demand also holding up well in consumer goods. Traditional capital goods industries will show little growth, and the export sector is expected to continue to be weak in the face of weak foreign demand.

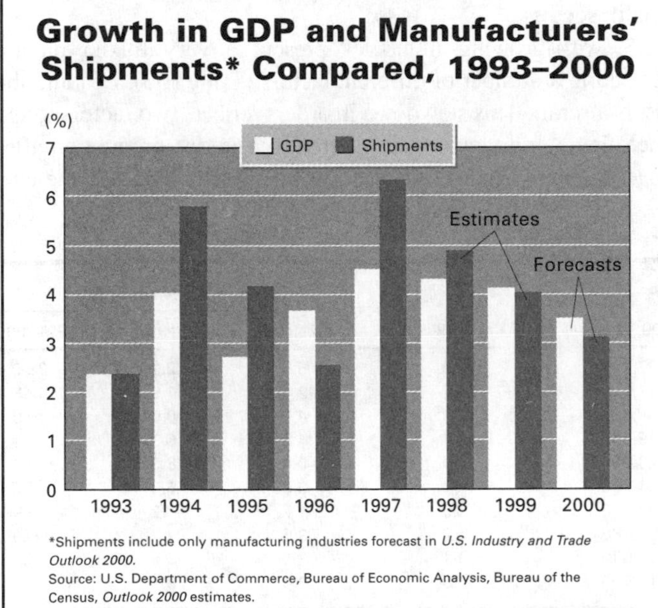

*Shipments include only manufacturing industries forecast in *U.S. Industry and Trade Outlook 2000.*

Source: U.S. Department of Commerce, Bureau of Economic Analysis, Bureau of the Census, *Outlook 2000* estimates.

FIGURE E-1

In aggregate the trends in industry shipments generally reflect the trend in GDP growth (see Figure E-1). Because they are constructed quite differently and have significant compositional differences the two can diverge significantly from time to time.

TRADE

Trade continues to be a key weakness for the economy. In 1999 exports increased only 2.6 percent. This is an improvement over 1998 when exports fell by 0.4 percent, but still well below earlier rates of growth. While exports as a percent of GDP are just below 11 percent, exports of goods represents more than 20 percent of

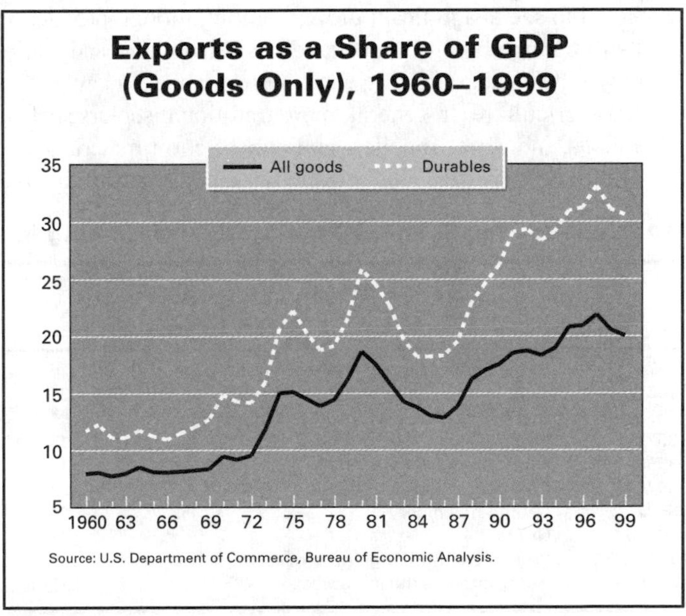

Source: U.S. Department of Commerce, Bureau of Economic Analysis.

FIGURE E-2

TABLE E-1: Trends in Major Manufacturing Sectors
(millions of 1992 dollars except where noted)

Sector	Value of Industry Shipments, 2000	Annual Growth Rates, %		
		92–99	98–99	99–2000
Aerospace	131,367	–0.97	6.30	–11.95
Chemicals, plastics, and rubber	177,575	1.66	2.33	1.73
Construction materials	104,904	3.49	2.36	1.97
Consumer durables (selected)	69,825	3.36	3.02	1.46
Food and kindred products	406,963	1.71	2.40	1.76
Industrial supplies	225,013	2.00	0.13	1.98
Information technology	210,681	13.76	10.98	12.41
Health—Drugs, medical, and dental equipment	107,327	4.30	2.64	4.60
Machinery and equipment	79,093	4.24	–5.62	–0.53
Motor vehicles and parts	262,150	6.68	5.65	1.67
Printing and publishing	166,153	1.79	3.50	2.24
Textiles, apparel, and leather	151,421	0.29	–1.63	0.05
Instruments	56,849	3.96	0.49	2.60

Source: U.S. Department of Commerce, Bureau of the Census, and *U.S. Industry and Trade Outlook 2000.*

GDP goods output. For durable goods, exports represent more than 30 percent of output (see Figure E-2). Hence, the weakness in foreign markets can have a very heavy impact on goods, especially manufacturing. Traditional capital goods such as machinery, equipment, and aircraft are especially dependent upon exports.

MANUFACTURING SECTORS

The outlook for domestic industrial growth is mixed despite the overall strength of the domestic economy. The information technology (IT) sector—computers, telecommunications, and semiconductors—will continue to lead the economy. Output of the IT sector will maintain a double-digit growth in 2000. This mirrors the strong investment in information sectors as well as strong consumer demand for information products and services. At the other end of the spectrum, the aerospace industry is expected to see a significant drop in output, though production will still be high by historical standards. Machinery and equipment will be weak, reflecting weak performances in key sectors such as agriculture. In general, more traditional sectors such as chemicals, industrial supplies, and construction materials will all see modest growth. This reflects the modest growth in construction and slowing growth in the motor vehicles sector. Despite the expected strong growth in consumer spending in 2000, output of the consumer durables sectors will grow only modestly. This reflects in part the composition of the sectors forecast as well as the fact that much of the growth will be met by imports, especially consumer electronics (Table E-1).

The ten fastest-growing manufacturing sectors are predominantly high tech and related to information technologies (Table E-2). Semiconductors lead and are the basic components of 5 of the fastest-growing industries. The second and third fastest-growing sectors, both telecommunications-related, reflect the growth in the Internet as well as mobile telephony. Oil and gas field equipment shows signs of recovery from its fall-off in 1999 as a result of low energy prices. This recovery is being driven by higher energy prices, but output levels are still well below 1998 levels. Mining equipment, after a fall-off in 1999, is returning to earlier strong growth trends. The growth in drugs reflects the growing reliance on technology and drugs in the health sector.

Slowest-growing industries present a very mixed picture reflecting a number of different factors (Table E-3). Leading the list is aircraft. This slowdown in orders reflects two factors. First, there is natural slowdown in output of aircraft production after meeting the surge of orders in the mid-1990s. Second, the cur-

TABLE E-2: Ten Fastest-Growing Manufacturing Industries

SIC	Industry	Chapter	2000 Value	Rank 92–99	Annual Growth Rates, %		
					92–99	98–99	99–2000
3674	Semiconductors and related devices	16	187,701	9	8.1	22.2	23.0
3661	Telephone and telegraph apparatus	31	51,591	2	12.4	11.9	12.3
3663	Radio and TV communications equipment	31	48,634	24	4.5	10.0	10.0
3672	Printed circuit boards	16	15,645	1	24.9	6.9	9.2
3533	Oil and gas field machinery	18	3,806	110	–0.4	–38.0	9.1
357*	Computers and peripherals	27	131,900	17	5.6	5.0	8.0
3532	Mining machinery	18	2,756	120	–1.7	–3.2	6.9
283	Drugs	11	91,488	42	3.6	1.7	5.6
2015	Poultry slaughtering and processing	35	31,270	51	3.1	5.0	5.1
371P	Automotive parts and accessories	37	210,900	98	0.4	8.1	5.1

*Current dollars.
Source: U.S. Department of Commerce, Bureau of the Census, and *U.S. Industry and Trade Outlook 2000.*

TABLE E-3: Ten Slowest-Growing Manufacturing Industries

SIC	Industry	Chapter	2000 Value	Rank 92–99	Annual Growth Rates, % 92–99	98–99	99–2000
3721	Aircraft	21	50,433	104	0.1	8.0	–20.4
3171	Women's handbags and purses	34	136	136	–14.3	–13.3	–13.4
3172	Personal leather goods, nec	34	193	133	–9.3	–9.2	–10.6
3151	Leather gloves and mittens	34	73	132	–7.7	–25.2	–8.8
3724	Aircraft engines and engine parts	21	23,524	69	1.9	2.4	–8.0
3728	Aircraft parts and equipment, nec	21	21,314	62	2.5	1.5	–7.8
279	Printing trade services	25	4,024	123	–2.4	–5.5	–6.0
3161	Luggage	34	848	117	–1.1	–10.9	–5.1
3523	Farm machinery and equipment	18	9,937	41	3.6	–30.0	–5.0
3812	Search and navigation equipment	31	24,353	127	–4.5	–3.7	–3.9

Source: U.S. Department of Commerce, Bureau of the Census, and *U.S. Industry and Trade Outlook 2000.*

TABLE E-4: Trends in Nonmanufacturing Industries

Sector	SIC Code	Chapter	Unit of Measure	Annual Growth Rates, % 2000[1]	99–00	96–00[2]
Nonservices						
Coal mining	12	2	Production, million short tons	1,168.0	1.2	2.1
Electricity production and sales	4911	5	Revenue, $ billions	215.1	–1.4	—
Electricity production and sales		5	Total sales, billions of kilowatt-hours	3,258	1.7	—
Construction	na	6	Value of new-construction-put-in-place, billions of $ 1992	568	0.5	2.9
Lead metal production		14	Thousands of metric tons	1,460	1.8	1.6
Refined copper production		14	Thousands of metric tons	1,820	–16.5	–6.2
Tintanium ingot production		14	Metric tons	35,000	–10.3	–9.2
Shipments of aluminum		14	Thousands of metric tons	11,325	1.0	4.2
Zinc metal production		14	Thousands of metric tons	380	2.7	0.9
Services						
U.S. Environmental Industry	na	20	Revenues, $ millions	203,500	2.9	3.0
Professional computer services	7371,7373,73 77,7378,7379	26	Receipts, $ millions	214,795	20.0	22.9
Data processing and network services	7374,7376	26	Receipts, $ millions	65,696	12.0	10.6
Information retrieval services	7375	26	Receipts, $ millions	19,943	30.0	30.3
U.S. CAD/CAM/CAE software Market	na	28	$ millions	3,613	11.6	—
Telecommunications services	4812,4813 4822	30	Operating revenues, $ millions	282,094	7.0	7.4
Motion picture theaters	783	32	Box office receipts, $ billions	7.8	5.4	7.2
Home video	7841	32	Revenues, $ billions	18.7	3.9	3.7
Recorded music	3652	32	Revenues, $ billions	15.4	5.5	5.4
Wholesale distribution	50, 51	41	Wholesale sales, $ millions	2,668,000	1.8	2.9
Retailing	52–59	42	Retail sales, $ millions	3,044,422	4.5	5.0
National health expenditures	na	43	$ millions	1,316,200	7.1	6.0
Commercial banking		45	Commercial and industrial loans, $ billions	1,046	5.8	7.7
Commercial banking		45	Consumer debt, excluding mortgages, $ billions	1,472	6.5	5.6
Life insurance		46	Premium receipts, $ millions	469,190	—	5.5
Nonlife insurance		46	Premium receipts, $ millions	309,712	—	3.6
New York Stock Exchange firms	6221,6231	47	Total income, $ millions	211,300	10.1	15.1
Commodity trading industry	628	47	Futures contracts, $ millions	616.7	11.0	11.8
Accounting, auditing, and bookkeeping services	8721	48	Revenues, $ millions	82,056	12.0	10.8
Management, consulting, and public relations services	874	48	Revenues, $ millions	170,771	12.0	13.0
Legal services	81	48	Revenues, $ millions	158,605	5.5	6.2
Advertising services	731	48	Revenues, $ millions	40,050	5.5	6.9
Education and training	na	49	Cost of public and private education, $ 1997/98 billions	600.8	1.5	2.0
Travel and tourism		50	Total travel and tourism spending, $ billions	570	5.6	—
Air transportation		51	Revenue passenger miles, $ billions	657	3.0	3.6
Water transportation	44	52	Real GDP, billions of $ 1992		—	—
Railroads	4011	53	Ton-miles, $ billions	1,405	1.1	0.9

[1] Forecast.
[2] Compound annual growth rate.
Source: *U.S. Industry and Trade Outlook 2000.*

tailment of existing orders as a result of the Asian financial crisis has also led to cutbacks in output. Both leather goods of various kinds and footwear, which face strong import competition, are also weak. The decline in farm machinery reflects the weak U.S. farm sector hit by low prices and weak foreign demand.

SERVICES

In the services sector, information technology-related services continue to dominate as far as growth is concerned (Table E-4). The two fastest growth sectors are information retrieval services and professional computer services. Also in the top ten are data processing and network services, CAD/CAM software, and telecommunications services. Business services, in particular management consulting and accounting, continue strong performance. Not surprisingly, given the strong stock market, brokers are also expected to do well. The growth rate for expenditures on health services is up in 2000 after several years of more moderate growth, which many had attributed to the rise of HMOs.

TABLE E-5: Forecast Growth Rates for 135 Manufacturing Industries and Groups
(millions of 1992 dollars except as noted)

SIC	Industry	Chapter	Value of Industry Shipments, 2000	2000 Rank	Rank based on 92–99 Growth	Annual Growth Rates, %		
						92–99	98–99	99–2000
2015	Poultry slaughtering and processing	35	31,270	9	51	3.1	5.0	5.1
201A	Red meat	35	74,650	105	89	0.9	1.0	0.0
2068	Salted and roasted nuts and seeds	35	3,640	11	57	2.9	8.4	4.9
2082	Malt beverages	35	18,335	72	93	0.6	1.5	1.1
2084	Wines, brandy, and brandy spirits	35	5,855	38	28	4.1	2.0	2.5
2085	Distilled and blended liquors	35	3,445	66	105	0.0	0.0	1.3
2096	Potato chips and similar snacks	35	9,860	12	39	3.7	6.2	4.9
221	Cotton broadwoven fabric mills	9	6,454	55	84	1.2	−2.0	1.8
222	Manmade broadwoven fabric mills	9	9,738	69	82	1.3	0.0	1.2
223	Wool broadwoven fabric mills	9	1,694	74	94	0.6	−1.4	1.0
225A	Weft, lace, and warp knit fabric mills	9	7,619	85	95	0.5	0.5	0.9
227	Carpets and rugs	9	12,360	35	56	2.9	2.9	2.7
2281	Yarn spinning mills	9	8,969	88	68	2.2	0.2	0.7
2311	Men's and boys' suits and coats	33	1,754	107	128	−4.5	−1.5	−0.1
2321	Men's and boys' shirts	33	5,040	95	122	−2.3	1.6	0.3
2322	Men's & boys' underwear and nightwear	33	592	90	129	−4.6	1.6	0.5
2323	Men's and boys' neckwear	33	603	100	109	−0.4	−0.7	0.2
2325	Men's and boys' trousers and slacks	33	6,794	111	92	0.7	−0.8	−0.5
2326	Men's and boys' work clothing	33	1,746	115	64	2.3	0.1	−1.2
2331	Women's and misses' blouses and shirts	33	3,556	93	119	−1.6	0.0	0.3
2335	Women's, junior's, and misses' dresses	33	6,983	52	43	3.5	1.1	2.0
2337	Women's and misses' suits and coats	33	3,830	53	121	−2.2	0.2	1.9
2341	Women's and children's underwear	33	2,214	97	116	−1.0	−0.3	0.3
2342	Bras, girdles, and allied garments	33	1,720	103	83	1.3	−1.2	0.1
2361	Girls' and children's dresses, blouses	33	1,566	106	111	−0.5	−0.1	−0.1
2369	Girls' and children's outerwear, nec	33	2,295	71	15	5.8	1.7	1.1
2386	Leather and sheep-lined clothing	34	256	51	60	2.7	5.5	2.0
239A	Textile house furnishings	33	6,866	101	107	−0.1	0.1	0.1
239B	Miscellaneous textile products	33	13,659	108	75	1.6	1.4	−0.4
2421	Sawmills and planing mills, general	7	24,225	65	71	1.8	1.5	1.4
2435	Hardwood veneer and plywood	7	2,365	33	99	0.4	1.1	2.9
2436	Softwood veneer and plywood	7	5,385	83	106	0.0	0.7	0.9
2451	Mobile homes	8	7,800	92	8	8.2	−3.0	0.4
2452	Prefabricated wood buildings	8	2,558	68	65	2.3	2.9	1.3
2493	Reconstituted wood products	7	4,860	45	61	2.6	2.1	2.2
251	Household furniture	38	27,017	59	37	3.8	5.7	1.7
2611	Pulp mills	10	5,042	44	118	−1.5	2.0	2.2
2653	Corrugated and solid fiber boxes	10	23,852	31	66	2.2	2.9	3.0
2657	Folding paperboard boxes	10	8,635	67	88	1.0	1.3	1.3
26A	Paper and paperboard mills	10	54,828	64	79	1.4	1.2	1.5

[1] Shipments in current dollars.
Source: U.S. Department of Commerce, Bureau of the Census, and *U.S. Industry and Trade Outlook 2000*.

TABLE E-5: Forecast Growth Rates for 135 Manufacturing Industries and Groups *(Continued)*
(millions of 1992 dollars except as noted)

SIC	Industry	Chapter	Value of Industry Shipments, 2000	2000 Rank	Rank based on 92–99 Growth	Annual Growth Rates, % 92–99	98–99	99–2000
2711	Newspapers	25	32,002	76	115	–0.9	0.5	1.0
2721	Periodicals	25	24,963	49	78	1.5	4.1	2.0
2731	Book publishing	25	19,982	36	67	2.2	3.9	2.7
2732	Book printing	25	5,129	89	85	1.2	1.5	0.7
2741	Miscellaneous publishing	25	11,161	99	100	0.3	5.0	0.2
275	Commercial printing	25	74,923	22	40	3.6	5.4	3.8
2761	Manifold business forms	25	5,185	63	131	–5.2	0.9	1.5
2771	Greeting cards	25	4,266	86	102	0.1	0.5	0.8
2782	Blankbooks and looseleaf binders	25	4,778	41	52	3.1	4.5	2.5
2789	Bookbinding and related work	25	1,662	61	45	3.4	3.3	1.6
279	Printing trade services	25	4,024	130	123	–2.4	–5.5	–6.0
281	Industrial inorganic chemicals	11	26,200	62	114	–0.8	1.2	1.6
2821	Plastics materials and resins	11	43,517	30	26	4.2	7.0	3.0
2822	Synthetic rubber	12	5,143	96	59	2.8	0.0	0.3
282A	Man-made fibers	9	15,950	70	55	3.0	0.1	1.2
283	Drugs	11	91,488	8	42	3.6	1.7	5.6
286	Industrial organic chemicals	11	67,750	57	96	0.5	1.6	1.8
2873	Nitrogenous fertilizers	11	3,030	77	113	–0.8	1.7	1.0
2874	Phosphatic fertilizers	11	4,400	84	103	0.1	1.4	0.9
2879	Agricultural chemicals, nec	11	10,070	56	87	1.1	1.7	1.8
289	Miscellaneous chemical products	11	23,270	94	72	1.8	0.2	0.3
308P	Plumbing parts	8	8,770	42	12	6.5	3.9	2.5
3111	Leather tanning and finishing	34	3,065	102	90	0.8	5.1	0.1
3142	House slippers	34	121	125	134	–11.1	–13.2	–3.2
3143	Men's footwear, except athletic	34	1,682	73	125	–4.0	–13.5	1.0
3144	Women's footwear, except athletic	34	434	123	135	–12.0	–13.2	–2.9
3149	Footwear, except rubber, nec	34	230	17	130	–4.7	–17.5	4.1
3151	Leather gloves and mittens	34	73	133	132	–7.7	–25.2	–8.8
3161	Luggage	34	848	129	117	–1.1	–10.9	–5.1
3171	Women's handbags and purses	34	136	135	136	–14.3	–13.3	–13.4
3172	Personal leather goods, nec	34	193	134	133	–9.3	–9.2	–10.6
3211	Flat glass	8	2,787	87	27	4.2	1.2	0.8
3241	Cement, hydraulic	8	5,152	37	53	3.1	2.2	2.5
331A	Steel mill products	13	69,600	26	63	2.4	–1.4	3.1
3441	Fabricated structural metal	8	13,900	32	14	6.1	3.8	3.0
3448	Prefabricated metal buildings	8	3,500	58	54	3.0	1.2	1.7
3451	Screw machine products	15	6,383	25	11	7.0	1.0	3.5
3452	Bolts, nuts, rivets, and washers	15	6,785	28	44	3.4	0.0	3.0
349A	Valves and pipe fittings	15	9,073	75	77	1.5	–6.0	1.0
3511	Turbines and turbine generator sets	19	6,294	124	86	1.2	5.9	–2.9
3523	Farm machinery and equipment	18	9,937	128	41	3.6	–30.0	–5.0
3524	Lawn and garden equipment	38	6,501	118	7	8.6	–3.5	–1.8
3531	Construction machinery	18	22,623	126	10	7.6	–3.1	–3.2
3532	Mining machinery	18	2,756	7	120	–1.7	–3.2	6.9
3533	Oil and gas field machinery	18	3,806	5	110	–0.4	–38.0	9.1
3545	Machine tool accessories	17	5,299	43	49	3.2	3.7	2.4
3546	Power-driven handtools	17	3,760	15	13	6.3	5.4	4.7
3548	Welding apparatus	17	4,403	14	81	1.4	5.0	4.7
354A	Machine tools	17	4,858	120	25	4.3	–12.0	–2.0
3554	Paper industries machinery	18	2,709	122	34	3.8	–5.8	–2.3
3555	Printing trades machinery	18	3,466	80	97	0.5	0.8	1.0
3556	Food products machinery	18	2,595	18	58	2.8	1.6	4.0
3562	Ball and roller bearings	15	5,266	79	22	4.7	–3.0	1.0

[1] Shipments in current dollars.
Source: U.S. Department of Commerce, Bureau of the Census, and *U.S. Industry and Trade Outlook 2000.*

TABLE E-5: Forecast Growth Rates for 135 Manufacturing Industries and Groups *(Continued)*
(millions of 1992 dollars except as noted)

SIC	Industry	Chapter	Value of Industry Shipments, 2000	2000 Rank	Rank based on 92–99 Growth	Annual Growth Rates, % 92–99	98–99	99–2000
3565	Packaging machinery	18	4,438	48	4	10.2	2.0	2.0
357A	Computers and peripherals[1]	27	131,900	6	17	5.6	5.0	8.0
3585	Refrigeration and heating equipment	18	28,833	110	29	4.1	3.2	–0.5
3612	Transformers, except electronic	19	5,349	121	70	1.8	–0.9	–2.0
3613	Switchgear and switchboard apparatus	19	6,415	113	32	3.9	–2.4	–0.6
3621	Motors and generators	19	10,546	114	48	3.3	–1.1	–0.9
3625	Relays and industrial controls	19	9,662	109	30	4.0	–2.8	–0.4
3631	Household cooking equipment	38	4,033	19	35	3.8	6.0	4.0
3632	Household refrigerators and freezers	38	5,655	29	33	3.9	6.0	3.0
3633	Household laundry equipment	38	4,510	21	36	3.8	6.5	4.0
3634	Electric housewares and fans	38	3,790	81	23	4.7	2.0	1.0
3635	Household vacuum cleaners	38	2,735	20	108	–0.1	7.0	4.0
3639	Household appliances, nec	38	3,391	27	3	12.2	4.0	3.0
3661	Telephone and telegraph apparatus	31	51,591	2	2	12.4	11.9	12.3
3663	Radio and TV communications equipment	31	48,634	3	24	4.5	10.0	10.0
3671	Electron tubes	16	4,396	40	5	10.1	4.4	2.5
3672	Printed circuit boards	16	15,645	4	1	24.9	6.9	9.2
3674	Semiconductors and related devices	16	187,701	1	9	8.1	22.2	23.0
367A	Passive components	16	55,391	23	31	3.9	6.2	3.7
371A	Motor vehicles and bodies	36	201,250	117	6	9.6	3.3	–1.7
371P	Automotive parts and accessories	37	210,900	10	98	0.4	8.1	5.1
3721	Aircraft	21	50,433	136	104	0.1	8.0	-20.4
3724	Aircraft engines and engine parts	21	23,524	132	69	1.9	2.4	–8.0
3728	Aircraft parts and equipment, nec	21	21,314	131	62	2.5	1.5	–7.8
3732	Boat building and repairing	39	5,711	116	50	3.2	0.6	–1.2
3761	Guided missiles and space vehicles	21	21,752	98	76	1.6	10.6	0.2
3764	Space propulsion units and parts	21	3,790	54	126	–4.5	9.7	1.9
3769	Space vehicle equipment, nec	21	1,889	91	112	–0.6	12.6	0.5
3812	Search and navigation equipment	31	24,353	127	127	–4.5	–3.7	–3.9
3825	Instruments to measure electricity	23	13,370	34	16	5.7	3.4	2.8
3841	Surgical and medical instruments	44	20,168	13	19	5.3	5.7	4.8
3842	Surgical appliances and supplies	44	15,765	60	74	1.7	2.8	1.7
3843	Dental equipment and supplies	44	2,780	16	21	4.8	7.3	4.5
3844	X-ray apparatus and tubes	44	3,556	104	80	1.4	0.0	0.0
3845	Electromedical equipment	44	10,336	50	20	5.0	5.0	2.0
3861	Photographic equipment and supplies	24	25,400	47	73	1.7	–4.6	2.0
38A	Laboratory instruments	23	14,611	24	18	5.3	3.9	3.5
38B	Measuring and controlling instruments	23	21,244	39	38	3.7	3.0	2.5
3911	Jewelry, precious metal	40	5,358	78	46	3.4	1.0	1.0
3931	Musical instruments	40	1,045	82	91	0.8	1.0	1.0
3949	Sporting and athletic goods, nec	39	9,710	46	47	3.3	1.5	2.1
394A	Dolls, toys, and games	39	4,574	112	101	0.2	–0.6	–0.5
3961	Costume jewelry	40	1,084	119	124	–3.7	–2.0	–2.0
	Total		2,414,360	137	137	4.3	4.0	3.1

[1] Shipments in current dollars.
Source: U.S. Department of Commerce, Bureau of the Census, and *U.S. Industry and Trade Outlook 2000.*

METALS AND INDUSTRIAL MINERALS MINING
Economic and Trade Trends

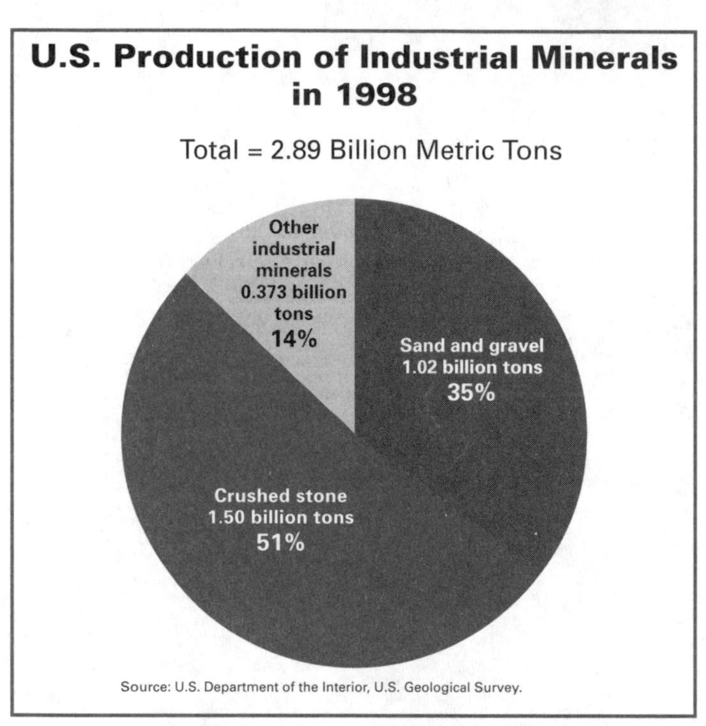

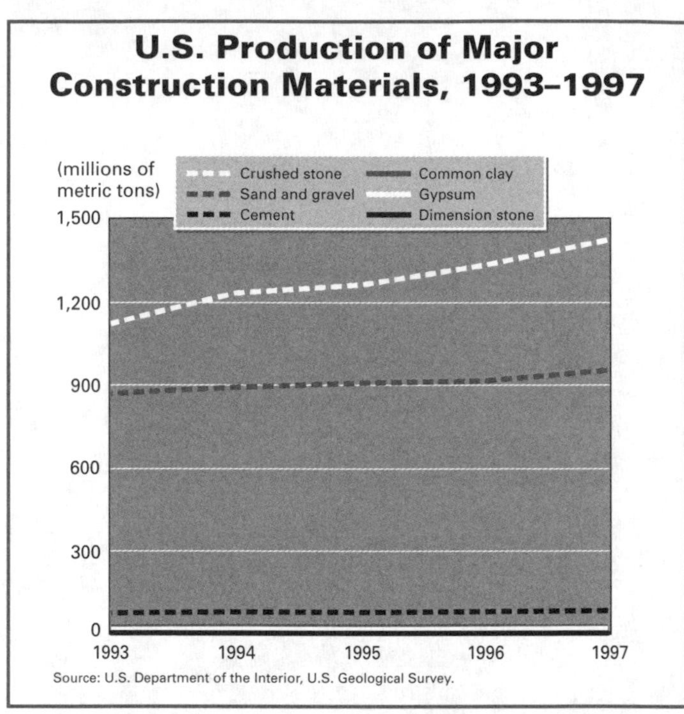

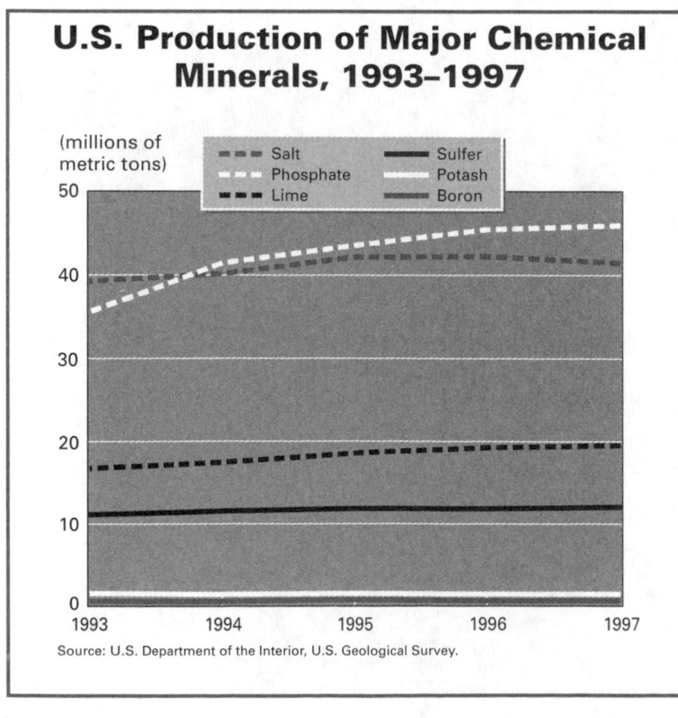

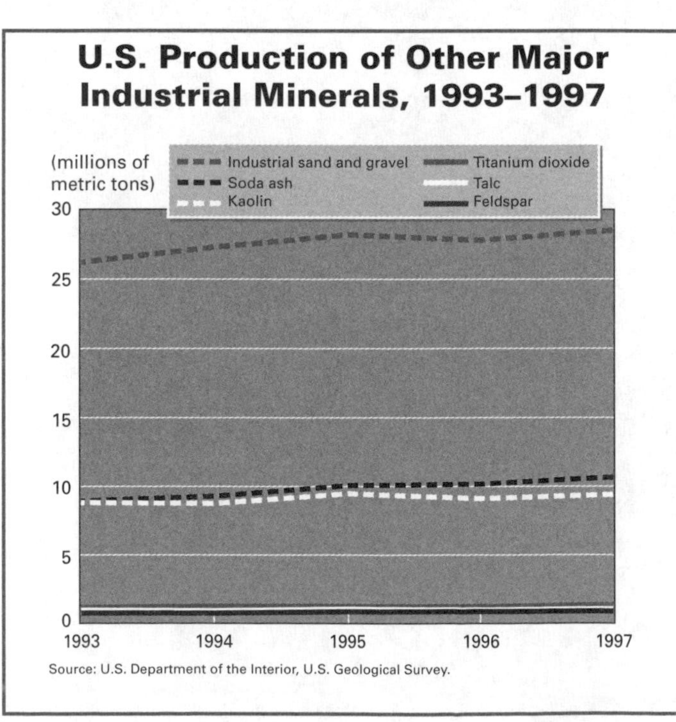

See "Getting the Most Out of *Outlook 2000*" for definitions of terms.

1

Metals and Industrial Minerals Mining

INDUSTRY DEFINITION The mining industry, as it is described in this chapter, includes the mining of ores containing metals (SIC 10) such as copper, gold, iron, lead, lithium, molybdenum, silver, and zinc. It also includes the extraction of industrial minerals (SIC 14) such as boron, clays, phosphate rock, potash, salt, sand and gravel, soda ash, and stone.

RECENT TRENDS

In 1999, the U.S. economy continued its longest peacetime expansion after growing 3.9 percent in 1998. However, the performance of U.S. metals and industrial minerals mining was mixed. Increases in construction activity helped push the production of industrial minerals higher in 1998 than it had been in 1997, while an excess supply of metals worldwide held down production in U.S. metal mines.

Adding to the problem of an oversupply of metals was the continuing decline in economic growth in Asia, Latin America, and parts of Europe. Poor economic performances in those regions along with high inventories of metals caused metal prices to fall in 1998 and early 1999, forcing the closing of some U.S. mines. The United States increased its imports of metal ores during that period, while exports dropped dramatically, partly as a result of the high value of the U.S. dollar and economic problems in other parts of the world. As a result, early data show that the total value of metal ores mined in the United States fell 19 percent in 1998 from that in 1997 even though physical production as measured by the Federal Reserve Board remained about the same as it was in 1997. The total value of mine production of industrial minerals grew 7.7 percent in constant dollars between 1997 and 1998, while the Federal Reserve Board's production index for stone and earth minerals climbed 3.3 percent. The 1998 values of mine production for metallic and industrial mineral ores (see Table 1-1) are preliminary and probably will be revised when more data become available.

The number of metal mining operations in the United States has been dropping since the early 1980s, while industrial mineral operations have been increasing. For metal ores and concentrates, the value of imports exceeded the value of exports for most of the 1990s, while the United States for the most part exported more raw industrial minerals than it imported.

Issues and Regulation

The United States has large reserves of important metals such as copper, iron ore, and zinc, but it depends on other nations to provide metals that it lacks or cannot readily mine. In 1998, for instance, the United States produced 6 percent of the world's iron ore but relied on other countries to supply roughly 17 percent of the iron ore it consumed. Other metals that the United States counts on foreign producers to supply include bauxite and alumina, chromium, cobalt, manganese, nickel, platinum-group metals, tin, tungsten, and zinc.

The long-term outlook of U.S. mining industries is affected by factors such as access to public lands, the regulatory environment, advances in mining technology, and the location, quality, and potential profitability of ore deposits. For metal mining, one of the most important issues in recent years has been access to public lands for the exploration and development of mineral deposits.

In the United States, access to federal lands for mining is determined by the 1872 Mining Law. That law allows anyone to enter open public lands to explore for hardrock minerals and file claims to extract minerals discovered on them. There are more than 330,000 active claims on federal lands operating under this law.

TABLE 1-1: Metals and Industrial Minerals Mining (SIC 10, 14) Trends
(millions of dollars unless otherwise noted)

	1992	1993	1994	1995	1996	1997	1998	Percent Change 96–97	Percent Change 97–98	Compound Annual Growth Rate, % 92–98
Industry Data										
Value of mine production										
SIC 10	11,547	10,800	12,100	14,000	13,000	13,100	10,600	0.8	−19.1	−1.4
SIC 14	20,574	21,200	23,100	24,600	25,800	27,400	29,500	6.2	7.7	6.2
Value of mine production (1992$)										
SIC 10	11,547	10,879	11,310	11,679	11,517	11,564	10,029	0.4	−13.3	−2.3
SIC 14	20,574	20,714	21,816	22,365	23,092	24,121	25,542	4.5	5.9	3.7
Total employment (thousands)										
SIC 10	53	50	49	51	54	54	50	0.0	−7.4	−1.0
SIC 14	102	102	104	105	106	108	109	1.9	0.9	1.1
Production workers (thousands)										
SIC 10	42	40	39	41	42	41	38	−2.4	−7.3	−1.7
SIC 14	76	76	78	80	81	82	83	1.2	1.2	1.5
Average hourly earnings ($)										
SIC 10	15.26	15.29	16.08	16.77	17.35	17.82	18.24	2.7	2.4	3.0
SIC 14	12.25	12.68	13.10	13.38	13.74	14.17	14.69	3.1	3.7	3.1
Trade Data										
Value of exports										
SIC 10	1,084	799	1,018	1,562	1,091	1,251	981	14.7	−21.6	−1.7
SIC 14	1,148	1,107	1,199	1,296	1,302	1,375	1,377	5.6	0.1	3.1
Value of imports										
SIC 10	1,167	1,108	1,283	1,413	1,407	1,407	1,509	0.0	7.2	4.4
SIC 14	734	767	839	894	1,035	1,619	1,506	56.4	−7.0	12.7

Source: U.S. Geological Survey (USGS), Bureau of Labor Statistics (BLS), and Bureau of the Census. Value of mine production in 1992 dollars was estimated by the USGS with commodity-based producer price indexes (BLS codes 101, 102, and 13). The values of mine production for 1998 are preliminary.

In the last few years, both the administration and Congress have made efforts to reform the mining law and restrict access to public lands, primarily because hardrock mining companies do not pay royalties to the federal government for mining minerals on public lands and because mining companies with approved claims can "patent," or buy, land for $2.50 or $5.00 per acre, depending on the type of claim. More efforts to reform the mining law probably will be made in the future, with guidelines for mine claim maintenance and reclamation of abandoned mines also subject to reform.

In 1999, Congress considered other legislation that would affect the availability of public and private lands for mining. The American Land Sovereignty Protection Act, for example, would require congressional approval of any lands recommended by the administration for United Nations–sponsored World Heritage Sites or biosphere reserves. Congress also has considered legislation concerning the acquisition of private lands by the federal government to prevent economic development and legislation to revise the requirements for designating critical habitats for endangered species.

Like many other industries in the United States, metals and industrial minerals mining must comply with environmental regulations at the federal, state, and local government levels. At the federal level, environmental impacts are regulated primarily by the Resource Conservation and Recovery Act (RCRA), which covers the treatment and disposal of hazardous and nonhazardous solid wastes; the Clean Water Act, which regulates discharges into surface waters; the Clean Air Act, which is designed to prevent and control air pollution; and the Comprehensive Environmental Response, Compensation, and Liability Act (CERCLA), also known as Superfund, which established a mechanism for cleaning up closed and abandoned hazardous waste sites. There are about 70 mining-related sites among the 1,200 sites that are on the Superfund Priority List. In 1999, the metal mining sector also began reporting to the U.S. Environmental Protection Agency to comply with its Toxics Release Inventory (TRI) program. The TRI was enacted as part of the Emergency Planning and Community Right-to-Know Act of 1986. The TRI tracks certain chemicals that can be released to water, air, and land during mining operations.

Outlook

Early data from the Federal Reserve Board show that production in the nation's metal mines continued to fall through the middle of 1999 because of mine closures and production cutbacks. Mine closings and cuts in production, which also have occurred in other parts of the world, have caused the growth of metals inventories to begin to slow and in some cases to decline, causing prices for some metals, such as copper and zinc, to move higher in 1999.

U.S. manufacturing activity, which had slowed in 1998, began picking up in the first half of 1999, as did overall economic growth in southeast Asia and western Europe. Moreover, several international cyclical indicators, such as the Organization for Economic Cooperation and Development (OECD) Total Leading Index, are pointing to increases in future industrial production for many of the world's major economies, and that should help increase demand for metals. The total value of mine production for U.S. metal mining was expected to register a decline in 1999, but it is likely to rebound during the year 2000 as economic growth in other countries increases. Slower growth in U.S. construction, which began in the first half of 1999, and rising interest rates could mean a slower rate of growth in the value of mine production for industrial minerals in 1999 and 2000.

METALS MINING

The value of U.S. mine production of metals (SIC 10) declined significantly in 1998 in current and constant (1992) dollars, dropping 19.1 percent and 13.3 percent, respectively (see Table 1-1), owing to falling metal prices. Over the period 1992–1998, metal mine production value in real terms declined 2.3 percent annually on average, with the value of production peaking at $11.7 billion in 1995. Growth in constant dollars also trended downward slightly over that period and trended upward slightly in current dollars. The growth in the value of total output in constant dollars for iron and other ferrous ores, copper ore, and miscellaneous nonferrous ores rose slightly over the 3-year period 1996–1998 and is projected by Standard & Poor's DRI to be about 2 percent per year between 1998 and 2004. The recent slow growth in metal mine production value does not reflect the relatively high demand for most metal commodities over that period. Oversupply has kept prices down for many metals even as high demand in the United States has kept production rates relatively high in recent years, except for 1998.

Some important metals in which the United States is nearly self-sufficient or produces the majority of its supply are, in order of increasing self-sufficiency, zinc, lead, iron ore, and copper. The United States is a net exporter of molybdenum and gold. The relative positions of these commodities with respect to net import reliance were nearly unchanged in 1998 compared with 1997, except that iron ore and copper exchanged places. Although completely dependent on imports of bauxite and alumina, the United States is the world's largest exporter of aluminum metal.

Total employment in metal mining was about 50,000 in 1998, down more than 7 percent from 1997. Over the longer term (1992–1998), employment declined at a rate of 1 percent per year on average. With the value of mine production in real terms generally declining at a slightly higher rate than did total employment, value of output per employee also declined slightly over that period.

With respect to the value of mine production in 1998, gold was highest among metals at $4.0 billion, followed by copper at $3.3 billion, iron ore at $1.9 billion, zinc at $840 million, molybdenum at $454 million, and lead at $440 million. The value of iron and steel and ferrous foundry industry production was $73 billion, and the value of primary aluminum produced at U.S. smelters was $5.3 billion. Economic conditions in 1998 and 1999 were generally good, particularly in transportation, housing, and construction, resulting in a relatively high demand for metals. Favorable economic indicators point to a moderation of this trend through 2004 in several indexes that are important to metals consumption. For example, as projected by the U.S. Department of Commerce, Bureau of the Census, total housing starts will decline slightly between 1999 and 2003. Total multiunit structures are expected to remain about the same, but total single-unit structures are projected to decrease approximately 10 percent. Light vehicle construction is expected to fall slightly from 15.7 million units in 1999 to 15.3 million units in 2000 but rise to 15.7 million units by 2003.

Recycling remained a strong component of metals supply in the United States in 1998 and 1999. The commodities with the highest recycling rates (defined as metal recovered from old and new scrap as a percentage of apparent supply) were lead (66 percent), steel (59 percent), titanium (50 percent), aluminum (39 percent), copper (37 percent), nickel (29 percent), tungsten (28 percent), cobalt (23 percent), chromium (21 percent), and tin (21 percent). In steel, scrap-based electric arc furnaces have captured a major portion of steelmaking capacity: 45 percent in 1998. The impact of the Asian financial crisis on U.S. metals markets could be felt most in iron and steel scrap. U.S. exports to that region declined significantly in 1998. Consequently, prices for carbon steel scrap also experienced a substantial drop. Stainless steel scrap prices experienced a similar price decline. With signs of recovery in Asia in 1999, the scrap markets are expected to rebound in 2000 with a sustained high level of economic activity in the United States.

Ferrous Metals

In addition to iron, the ferrous metals include chromium, cobalt, columbium (niobium), manganese, molybdenum, nickel, rhenium, silicon, tantalum, tungsten, and vanadium. With the exception of cobalt, rhenium, and tantalum, all these metals are commonly alloyed with iron. They often tend to follow trends in steel production and also are referred to as ferroalloy elements, or ferroalloys. Cobalt, rhenium, and tantalum generally are not used in steelmaking because of their high cost and limited supply but can be added as alloying agents in the more expensive superalloys used to fabricate parts for the hot sections of jet aircraft engines. Each of these metals has other important applications not related to steel.

The United States is a major producer of iron ore for the steel industry. About 40 percent of the iron units for U.S. steel production are supplied by the U.S. iron ore industry. From 1994 to 1997, the production of usable iron ore (gross weight) trended upward from 60.6 million metric tons (Mt) to an estimated 63.0 Mt, an average annual growth rate of 0.7 percent (see Figure 1-1). The production of iron ore was expected to decrease approximately 2 percent in 1999 compared with 1998; con-

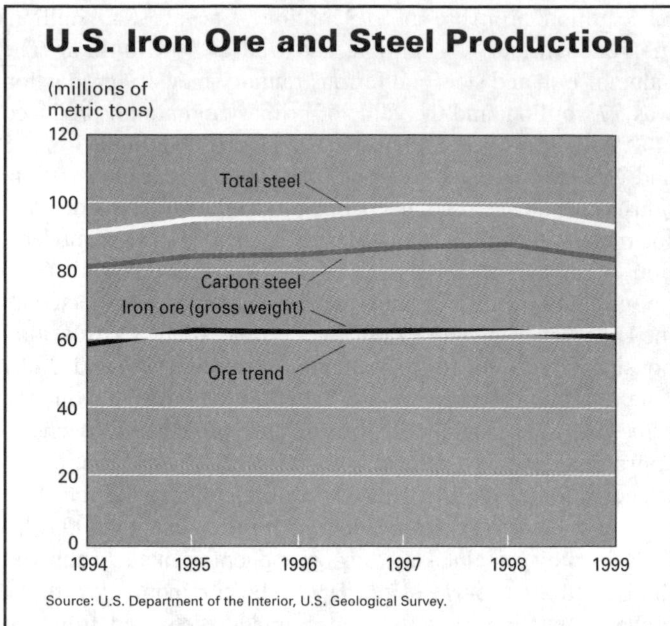

FIGURE 1-1

sumption was expected to decrease about 1 percent, and trade (net imports) to decline less than 1 percent. Domestic production of iron ore generally represents about 75 percent of domestic consumption. In any given year, some of this production may be exported and some may go into stocks. Thus, the United States relies on imports for a portion of its supply. From 1993 to 1997, the United States depended on imports to satisfy on average about 15 percent of its demand for iron ore. Between 1997 and 1998, iron ore prices rose about 2.8 percent.

Steel production was expected to decline slightly more than iron ore production in 1999 compared with 1998, a decline approaching 2.5 percent. The iron and steel industry and ferrous metal foundries produced goods valued at about $73 billion in 1998. Imports of steel increased 22 percent in 1998 because the weak Asian economies, which were in a deep recession, exported relatively cheap steel. Steel imports were a record high 25 percent of apparent supply. However, imports were expected to decline significantly in 1999 as the situation in Asia appeared to be stabilizing. Average annual growth of output in constant 1992 dollars for iron and other ferrous metal ores has been projected by Standard & Poor's DRI to grow from $2.4 billion to $4.7 billion over the period 1997–2004, an average annual growth rate of 2.4 percent.

U.S. metals markets were noticeably affected in 1998 by the deep recession in Asia that was part of the Asian financial crisis, particularly in iron and steel scrap, which is exported in significant quantities to that region. For example, between 1997 and 1998, total U.S. exports of iron and steel scrap dropped almost 45 percent. A substantial portion was destined for Asia. At the same time, U.S. iron and steel scrap prices declined nearly 20 percent.

Because of environmental concerns about the effects of emissions from coke ovens and concern about the availability of low-residue scrap for electric arc furnaces, companies have increasingly invested in alternative ironmaking technologies, especially direct reduced iron. The ratio of steel production from basic oxygen furnaces, which use mostly primary ore products, to that from electric arc furnaces, which use mostly scrap or direct reduced iron, was nearly unchanged over the period 1994–1999, holding at about 60:40. Domestic demand for steel remained high in 1998 and 1999 and was increasing along with domestic steelmaking capacity, but pessimism about market conditions grew as steel spot prices and exports declined while imports increased.

There has been an upward trend in the consumption of most ferroalloys, but there have been significant fluctuations in demand since 1993, notably in chromium. Carbon steel production had slow but steady growth from 1994 through 1998, and, while experiencing a downturn in 1999, consumption in 2000 is expected to remain strong. The specialty steel industry, including stainless steel, is a major consumer of chromium and nickel, among other commodities (see Figure 1-2). Stainless steel production continued to account for only about 2 percent of raw steel production in 1998, the last year for which data are available. Stainless steel is subject to market conditions that may be different from those which apply to carbon steel. A robust economy is expected to extend into the year 2000, with the construction and transportation sectors, two important users of stainless steel, performing well. This probably will result in rising demand for chromium and nickel.

Figure 1-3 shows the weight fraction of total ferrous metal consumption accounted for by the major metal types. The markets for the bulk ferroalloys manganese and silicon are tied to the fortunes of the carbon steel industry and show similar pat-

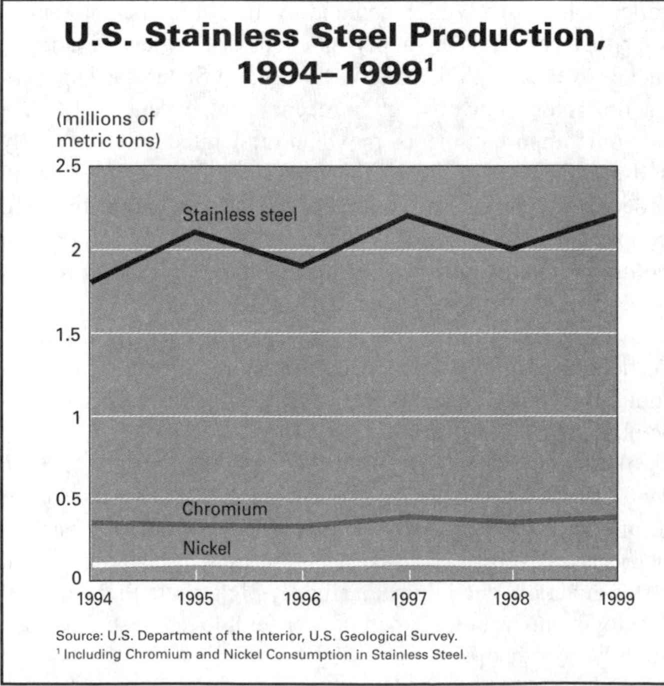

FIGURE 1-2

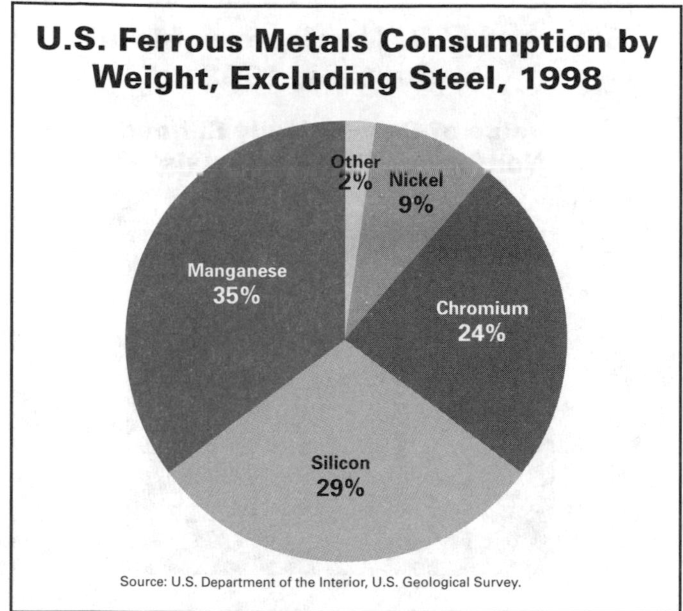

FIGURE 1-3

terns of use. The fraction of the value of U.S. consumption held by each ferrous metal is shown in Figure 1-4. There is a much more even distribution of the ferrous commodities when they are compared by value rather than by weight.

Net import reliance of ferrous metals is high, except for molybdenum and iron and steel scrap, for which the United States is a net exporter (see Figure 1-5). The United States had a 100 percent reliance on imports of manganese and columbium in 1998 and was partially dependent on imports of tantalum at 80 percent, chromium at 79 percent, tungsten at 77 percent, cobalt at 73 percent, nickel at 64 percent, vanadium at an estimated 60 percent, silicon at 32 percent, iron and steel at 25 percent, and iron ore at 12 percent. Most of the balance of the alloy metal supply comes from scrap material, except for iron ore, silicon, and iron and steel, which are domestically produced. Commodities with high import reliance and their most significant countries of origin (4-year average, 1994–1997) were chromium (South Africa, 39 percent), cobalt (Norway, 22 percent), columbium (Brazil, 70 percent), iron and steel (European Union, 27 percent), iron ore (Canada, 54 percent), manganese (South Africa, 27 percent), nickel (Canada, 37 percent), silicon (Norway, 25 percent), tantalum (Australia, 31 percent), tungsten (China, 33 percent), and vanadium (Canada, ferrovanadium, 40 percent; South Africa, vanadium pentoxide, 89 percent).

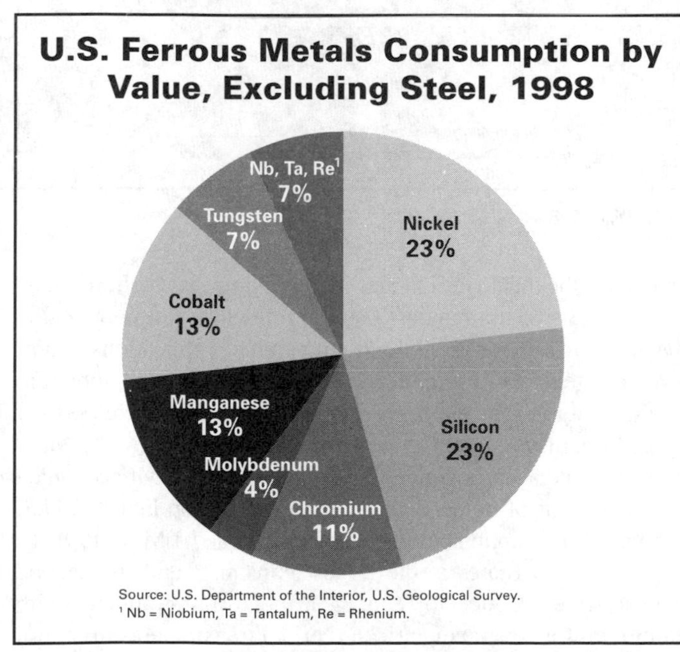

FIGURE 1-4

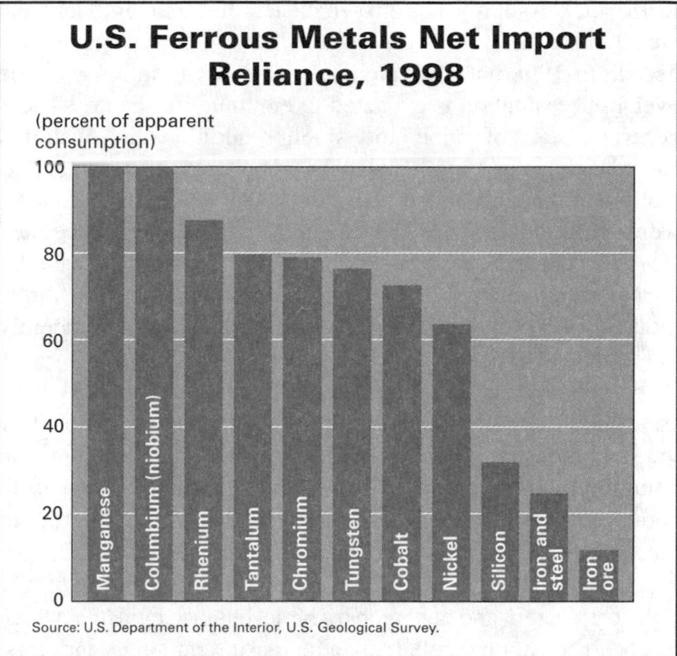

FIGURE 1-5

Steel consumption remained strong throughout 1998 and into 1999, but a large proportion of that consumption was satisfied by steel imports, which were cheaper for U.S. consumers, partly because of the strength of the U.S. dollar. Steel prices and capacity utilization worldwide were gradually recovering in 1999. Along with a slight decline in steel production, prices generally declined across the board, especially after mid-1998, for the bulk ferroalloys manganese and silicon and for chromium and nickel. For manganese, while prices for high- and medium-carbon ferromanganese declined in the first half of 1999, ore prices fell slightly in 1998–1999, as did those of silicomanganese. The silicon metal market also weakened in terms of price in the first half of 1999. The domestic ferrous metals industries were influenced in some cases by the Asian financial crisis, which forced down Asian-produced stainless steel prices. This resulted in pressure to lower the price of stainless steel produced in North America and Europe, which affected chromium and nickel prices. U.S. production of nickel-bearing stainless steel was down about 6 percent in 1998 from the near-record 1.36 Mt in 1997. Imports of stainless steel grew. The world nickel supply has grown faster than demand, and the nickel price in current dollars reached its lowest point in a decade in 1998 but recovered substantially by mid-1999. The oversupply situation is expected to continue for the next 4 to 5 years because of mine and smelter additions in Australia, Canada, Indonesia, and Venezuela. Tougher environmental regulations, especially those restricting coke oven gas emissions, were expected to force the closure of some older integrated steel facilities. Five direct reduced iron projects were under consideration that, if completed, would increase U.S. direct reduced iron production capacity from 0.5 Mt to considerably more than 4 Mt per year.

For the ferrous alloying metals, specialized markets have controlled prices, but nearly all are to some degree affected by the steel industry, particularly for molybdenum, vanadium, and columbium. For cobalt, in the near to medium term—up to about 5 years—various industry sectors are expected to increase their consumption. In particular, increases from the superalloy industry, which consumes the most cobalt of any industry sector, and the rechargeable battery industry, which has been consuming cobalt at an increasing rate in recent years, are anticipated to contribute to an overall growth in cobalt demand in the range of 3 to 6 percent per year. World consumption of tungsten has remained higher than world mine production, with the shortfall being met by releases of stockpiled tungsten materials from Russia, Kazakhstan, and eastern Europe. Demand is expected to continue strong into the year 2000. Very little tantalum is used in the steel industry. Tantalum consumption increased 5 percent in 1998 and was expected to remain strong or increase into 2000 because of strong demand for tantalum capacitors in products such as portable telecommunication devices, personal computers, and automotive electronics.

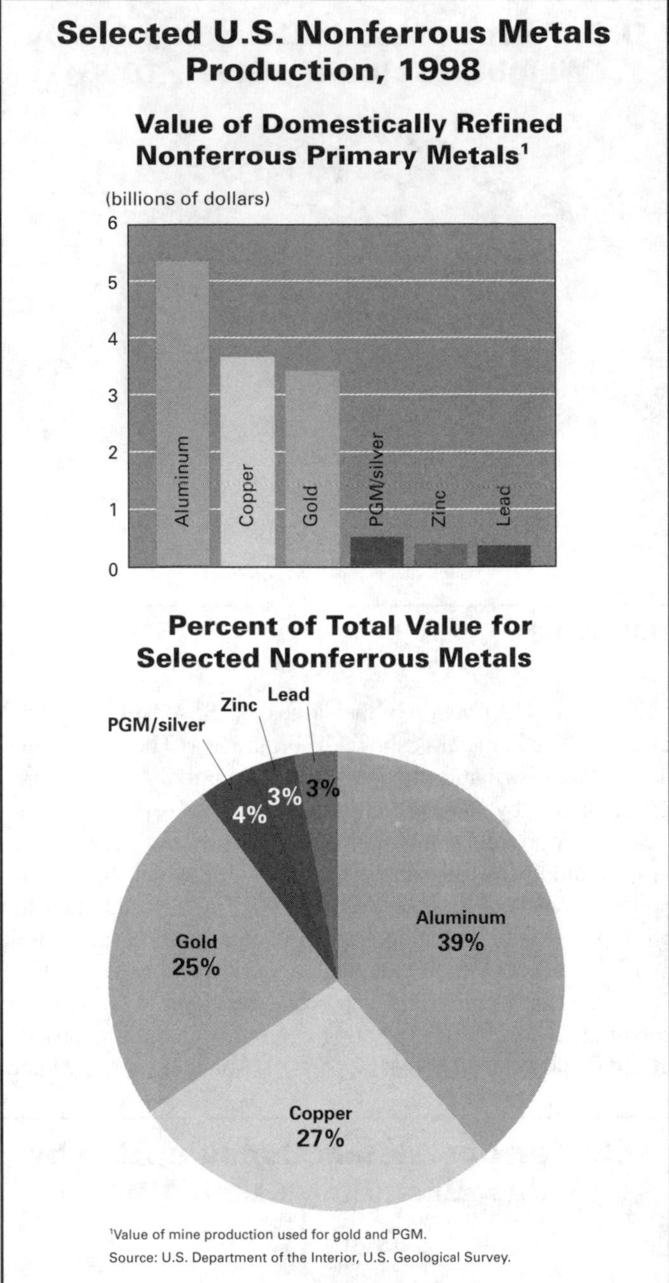

FIGURE 1-6

Nonferrous Metals

The nonferrous metals include more than four dozen metals that are mined in quantities that range from a few kilograms per year to several million tons per year and that have diverse uses. The more economically important of these metals are the base metals (aluminum, copper, lead, tin, and zinc) and the precious metals (gold, silver, and the six platinum-group metals). The base metals are important because they are produced and used in large quantities, and the precious metals because they have high unit values. The United States produces large amounts of most of these economically important nonferrous metals and uses large quantities of all of them. In terms of the dollar value of production or consumption, all these important metals rank among the top two dozen of the 90 or so mineral commodities used in the domestic economy (see Figure 1-6 for domestically refined values of some of these metals). Standard & Poor's DRI projects real annual growth of 3.2 percent between 1998 and 2004.

The United States is the world's largest producer and user of aluminum. It imports substantial quantities of aluminum metal and is completely dependent on foreign sources for the aluminum ore—bauxite—it needs. It also imports large quantities of the intermediate product alumina, of which more than 90 percent is smelted to the metal; the balance of this alumina and some domestically produced alumina are used in refractories (a nonmetallic material suitable for use in high-temperature applications), abrasives, and several other applications. Domestic primary aluminum production grew from 3.3 Mt in 1994, at the peak of imports of metal from the countries of the former Soviet Union, to 3.7 Mt in 1998. Secondary production from old scrap at 1.5 Mt accounted for 21 percent of domestic aluminum production in 1998. U.S. apparent consumption of aluminum was about 7.1 Mt in 1998.

The United States is the largest consumer and the second largest mine producer of copper, a metal that competes with aluminum for several electrical, thermal transfer, and structural applications. Domestic mine production grew slowly in recent years from 1.85 Mt in 1994 to 1.94 Mt in 1997 before dipping back to an estimated 1.86 Mt in 1998. At the same time, consumption rose steadily from 2.69 Mt in 1994 to more than 3.0 Mt in 1998. As more environmentally compliant smelter capacity came on-stream and concentrate production declined, the United States became a net importer of copper concentrates after 15 years as a net exporter.

As with copper, the United States is the largest consumer and the third largest producer of lead. Lead is the preeminent metal in batteries for automotive starting, lighting, and ignition systems and industrial backup power systems. Domestic lead mine production grew fairly rapidly in recent years, from 370 thousand tons (kt) in 1994 to 481 kt in 1998. Lead consumption grew almost as fast, increasing from 1.49 Mt in 1994 to 1.72 Mt in 1998. Lead is recycled extensively in the United States; secondary metal accounts for more than two-thirds of the lead consumed. Nearly all of the scrap is postconsumer (old) scrap, more specifically, battery scrap. Battery scrap alone provided about 1 Mt of metal, or 62 percent of the lead consumed.

The United States is the sixth largest mine producer of zinc and by far the largest consumer. Because of limited refinery capacity, it imports nearly two-thirds of the refined metal it requires. At the same time, it exports large quantities of zinc in concentrate to foreign smelters. Mine production grew substantially, increasing from 570 kt of recoverable zinc in 1994 to 722 kt in 1998. Consumption grew more slowly, increasing from 1.40 Mt in 1994 to about 1.58 Mt in 1998. Although zinc is an important constituent of brass, bronze, and die casting alloys and has a variety of other uses, about 55 percent of the metal consumed domestically is used as the protective coating on galvanized steel.

Since 1992, the United States has been the second leading mine producer of gold after South Africa. Annual domestic mine production increased dramatically in the 1970s and 1980s and by 1993 had reached 331 tons. It remained at about that level until 1997, when it rose to 362 tons. In 1998, despite falling bullion prices, production was about 366 tons. The United States is the fourth largest fabricator of gold after India, Italy, and China. As is the case elsewhere in the world, the largest end use by far is jewelry.

Annual domestic mine production of silver grew slowly from 1.49 kt in 1994 to 1.57 kt in 1996 and then rose abruptly to 2.15 kt in 1997; it has been estimated to be about the same (2.06 kt) in 1998. Domestic silver consumption, more than half of which goes for photographic uses, is estimated to have been about 5 kt in 1997 and 1998. Silver, like lead, is recycled extensively, with secondary silver satisfying about one-third of total demand. The sole domestic platinum-group metals (PGM) mine, which yields palladium and platinum in a 3.3:1 ratio along with minor quantities of rhodium, has increased production of PGM substantially in the last 5 years, from 8.4 tons in 1994 to 13.8 tons in 1998. The six metals in the group have many technological uses, of which their use as catalysts, especially as automotive emissions control catalysts, is the most important quantitatively. The use of PGM in jewelry is almost negligible in the United States.

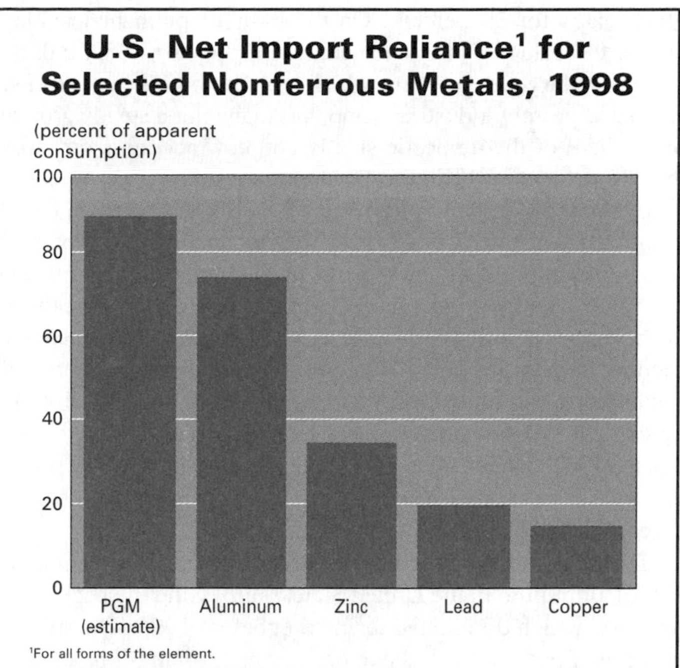

FIGURE 1-7

U.S. net import reliance (NIR), expressed as a percentage of consumption, ranges widely among the nonferrous metals. About 75 percent of aluminum is imported, principally as bauxite and alumina and a lesser amount as aluminum metal and its alloys. Other NIR figures are copper, 15 percent; lead, 20 percent; zinc, 35 percent; and PGM, 90 percent (see Figure 1-7). The United States is a net exporter of gold and refined silver.

The prices of most nonferrous metals declined in 1998. The annual average price per pound in the United States of aluminum ingot fell 15 percent to 65.5 cents. The price of copper cathode plunged 26 percent to 78.9 cents, and the price of zinc fell 10 percent to 48.7 cents. The price of lead, however, declined less than 3 percent to 45.3 cents. The average price per troy ounce of gold also fell, by 11 percent, to $295, and the price of platinum declined nearly 6 percent to $375. However, the price per troy ounce of silver rose 13 percent to $5.54, and the price of palladium, buoyed by strong demand for use in automotive emissions control catalysts, climbed 57 percent to $290.

METAL INDUSTRY SUBSECTORS

Aluminum

Domestic Production and Use. The domestic supply of aluminum includes three major components: primary ingot production, secondary (scrap) recovery, and trade. In 1998, 3.7 Mt of primary aluminum metal was produced by 13 companies operating 23 primary aluminum smelters. Montana, Oregon, and Washington accounted for 39 percent of the production; Maryland, New York, Ohio, and West Virginia for 22 percent; and other states for 39 percent. On the basis of published market prices, the value of primary metal production was $5.4 billion. The secondary metal sector, which includes both postconsumer scrap and prompt industrial scrap, has maintained steady growth in its share of the domestic supply and now accounts for more than 38 percent of the domestic aluminum supply.

Imports for consumption increased significantly in 1998 compared with 1997. Canada is the dominant trading partner for aluminum imports and exports, accounting for about 60 percent of U.S. imports of ingot and approximately 55 percent of both imported mill products and scrap. Russia remained the second largest supplier of aluminum materials. Imports of crude metal and alloys from Russia increased dramatically (43 percent) in 1998, returning to a level that had not been seen since 1994. Canada received about 45 percent of U.S. ingot exports in 1998, and Mexico accounted for an additional 30 percent of the U.S. primary ingot shipments.

The transportation sector continued to be the dominant market for aluminum in the United States, surpassing the packaging industry, which dominated the market before 1995. Transportation uses for aluminum accounted for more than 35 percent of domestic consumption, with packaging accounting for about another 25 percent. Building and construction, electrical, consumer durables, machinery and equipment, and other uses accounted for the remainder.

Recent Events, Trends, and Issues. The Defense Logistics Agency completed the sale of aluminum metal from the National Defense Stockpile (NDS) in 1998. On April 24, the sale of 323 metric tons exhausted the inventory of aluminum metal held by the NDS and completed the 2-year sales program of 57,000 tons of aluminum metal.

Domestic primary aluminum production increased 3 percent in 1998 compared with 1997. Domestic smelters continued to operate at about 88 percent of engineered or rated capacity. Although there were significant changes in the ownership or operating status of several domestic smelters, overall domestic production capacity remained essentially unchanged. World production also increased 3 percent in 1998. Aluminum demand continued to be strong in the United States, and demand in Europe, although tempered by the Asian economic crisis, remained relatively strong. The Asian aluminum markets, however, reflected the economic and financial crises in that area.

Indications that the economic crisis in Asia may be easing a bit suggest that world aluminum demand will improve. Aluminum demand in the United States is expected to remain relatively strong, and demand in western Europe, though weaker, is expected to continue to be positive. World production is expected to continue to increase as smelter capacities increase. The two greenfield smelter projects under construction in Canada and Mozambique should come on-stream in the next couple of years. Additional projects are being considered, and so in the near term, metal supply should be sufficient to meet overall world demand. Demand is expected to continue to grow, with the major growth area continuing to be the domestic and foreign transportation industries.

Copper

Domestic Production and Use. In 1998, copper mine production reversed a 15-year upward trend, declining about 80,000 tons (4 percent) as capacity utilization fell to 90 percent, the lowest level since 1995. The five principal mining states in descending order—Arizona, Utah, New Mexico, Nevada, and Montana—accounted for 98 percent of domestic production; copper also was recovered at mines in five other states. Although copper was recovered at about 38 U.S. mines, 15 mines accounted for about 97 percent of the output. Mine production was processed at seven primary and three secondary smelters, seven electrolytic and four fire refineries, and 15 electrowinning operations. U.S. production of refined copper was essentially unchanged in 1998. Approximately 35 brass mills, 15 wire-rod mills, and 600 foundries, chemical plants, and miscellaneous plants consumed refined copper and/or copper base scrap. In 1998, consumption of refined copper rose about 3 percent to a record high 2.88 Mt. The principal markets for copper and copper alloy products were building construction (42 percent), electric and electronic products (25 percent), industrial machinery and equipment (11 percent), transportation equipment, (13 percent), and consumer and general products (9 percent). U.S. net imports of refined copper, principally from Canada, Chile, and Mexico, amounted to about 600,000 tons, or, adjusting for stock increases, 15 percent of the demand for refined copper.

Recent Events, Trends, and Issues. World mine production of copper rose significantly for the fourth consecutive year, increasing by about 600,000 tons (5 percent) in 1998 to 12.2 Mt. Most of the increase in production came from Chile and Indonesia, where production rose 300,000 tons and 260,000 tons, respectively. World refined copper production rose about 500,000 tons (4 percent) to 13.4 Mt and continued to outstrip world demand for refined copper. Reported world inventories rose about 340,000 tons, accumulating mostly in London Metal Exchange (LME) warehouses in the United States. Domestic inventories rose to 500,000 tons, the highest level since 1985, amid industry concerns about warehouse incentives that resulted in the eventual intervention of the LME to limit further accumulations. In response to the growing oversupply, copper prices declined sharply from the already low year-end 1997 level.

The United States maintained its position as the second largest mine producer of copper and the world's largest smelter, refiner, and consumer. While U.S. mine capacity remained essentially unchanged at 2.1 Mt, production declined owing to closures and cutbacks attributed to low copper prices. Significant cutbacks included the curtailment of sulfide production at BHP Copper Corp.'s Pinto Valley Mine and a reduction in mill throughput at several other mines that closed high-cost mill segments. Primary smelter production rose about 5 percent owing to improved capacity utilization at Kennecott's Utah copper smelter, and the United States went from being a net exporter of copper concentrates in 1997 to a net importer in 1998. Secondary smelter production declined sharply, reflecting the impact of low copper prices on scrap availability and processing margins, and by year end only two secondary smelters remained in operation. Refined copper production was essentially unchanged in 1998 as an increase in primary production was balanced by lower secondary production. Despite increased imports of concentrate, cutbacks in mine and secondary production led to an anode feed shortage, and by year end, ASARCO Incorporated had announced an 80,000-ton refinery cutback. The increased consumption of refined copper was driven by strong demand for wire mill products and increased substitution of refined copper for scrap at domestic brass mills. In June, a new wire-rod mill began production in Texas.

With most analysts projecting a continued oversupply and depressed copper prices, further production curtailments were announced in 1999 as companies attempted to reduce unit operating costs. Asarco announced that it would close its El Paso smelter at the beginning of the year for a minimum of 3 years and make further reductions at its 450,000-ton refinery that would reduce capacity utilization to 67 percent. BHP closed its San Manuel Smelter for renovation in May and on June 25, after months of industry speculation about sale or closure, announced that it would cease operations at its North American properties by the end of August. BHP operates the San Manuel Mine in Arizona and the Robinson Mine in Nevada, with a combined capacity of about 150,000 tons of copper per year, as well as a smelter, refinery, and wire-rod mill, all at San Manuel. On June 30, Phelps Dodge Corp. announced a cost reduction program that included a shutdown of its Hidalgo, NM, smelter and the smaller of its two concentrators at Morenci, AZ, during the third quarter of 1999. The company anticipated an annual reduction in copper output of 68,000 tons at the mines and a 5 percent reduction (195,000 tons) at its El Paso refinery.

On July 15, Cyprus Amax Minerals Co. and ASARCO Incorporated announced an agreement for the combination of the two companies in a "merger-of-equals" transaction. The new company, Asarco Cyprus Incorporated, would be the largest publicly traded copper producer in the world, with mine production of about 900,000 tons of copper per year. The merger was expected to realize an annual cost saving of $150 million from corporate overhead, administrative, and other cost savings. In August, Phelps Dodge Corp. sought to halt the merger by offering to purchase the two companies separately or in total.

On the basis of announced cutbacks, irrespective of the impact of the pending mergers, U.S. copper mine production is expected to decline by about 180,000 tons in 1999 and a further 200,000 tons in 2000, while refinery production is expected to decline by as much as 280,000 tons and 350,000 tons, respectively. The United States is expected to relinquish to Chile its position as the largest world producer of refined copper. Consumption of refined copper in 1999 and 2000 is expected to grow a modest 2 percent per year, and domestic import dependence for refined copper is expected to grow significantly.

Gold

Domestic Production and Use. In 1998, the United States was the second largest producer of gold, after South Africa, with about 366 tons of production. Gold is produced at about 70 major lode mines; a dozen or more large placer mines, nearly all in Alaska; and numerous smaller placer mines, mostly in Alaska and the western states. The top 8 mines produced two-thirds of the domestic gold and the top 25 mines about 90 percent in 1998. Mines in Nevada and California continued to dominate domestic gold production. The value of U.S. gold production stood at about $3.5 billion in 1998. The leading use of gold in the United States is jewelry. Canada supplies the overwhelming majority of American gold imports. Generally, palladium, platinum, and silver are the leading substitutes for gold.

Recent Events, Trends, and Issues. As in many commodity fields, U.S. gold-mining operations sought opportunities abroad. Much of the foreign investment took place in Latin American countries, with their promising geologic terranes and liberalized regulations on foreign direct investment. Additional gold-related foreign direct investment took place in Australia as well as parts of Africa, Canada, and Pacific and southeastern Asia.

There was a decline in price beginning toward the end of 1996 and continuing into mid-1999, with the price dipping to the lowest level in 20 years in July 1999. Central bank gold sales contributed to the negative sentiment in the gold market. However, a wake-up call that has very serious implications was issued to the gold industry in the form of world gold exploration expenditures. After 5 consecutive years of significant increases, almost 40 percent less was spent on gold exploration in 1998 than in the peak year, 1997. Lower gold exploration expenditures are expected to continue in the year 2000 with predicted low prices for gold. As less and less gold is discovered and old mines are closed, a gap will be created between the world's future gold supply and its demand.

Iron Ore

Domestic Production and Use. It is estimated that the value of usable ores shipped from Minnesota, Michigan, and six other states in 2000 will be $1.7 billion. Iron ore was produced by 12 mines that had 10 concentration plants and 10 pelletizing plants. Those mines included 11 open pit mines and one underground operation. Virtually all the ore was concentrated before shipment. Nine mines managed by five companies accounted for 98.9 percent of production. It is estimated that production of iron ore in 2000 will be 60 Mt; consumption will be approximately 78 Mt.

Recent Events, Trends, and Issues. Virtually all iron ore is consumed by the steel industry. The domestic iron ore industry provides about 70 percent of the ore used in the United States. Almost all domestic iron ore reserves are low-grade and require extensive processing. The U.S. iron ore industry is able to compete with foreign producers largely because the iron ore mines and most of the integrated steel industry it supplies are close to the Great Lakes, which offer low-cost transportation. Most, if not all, East Coast and Gulf coast integrated steelmakers are supplied by foreign producers. Virtually all U.S. exports consisted of pellets shipped via the Great Lakes to Canadian steel companies that are partners in U.S. taconite mines in Michigan and Minnesota.

The U.S. steel industry is undergoing a structural change that has the potential to affect the domestic iron ore industry. The U.S. steel industry can be viewed as having two primary parts: the integrated steelmakers, which use iron ore as feedstock, and the minimills, which use iron and steel scrap and direct reduced iron as feed. Iron ore is used as feedstock to produce direct reduced iron. The minimills' share of the steel market has increased steadily, rising from 15 percent in 1970 to about 50 percent in 2000. This trend is expected to continue and will affect the domestic iron ore industry negatively (feedstock for direct reduced iron produced domestically is imported) unless one or more domestic iron ore producers begins producing direct reduced iron.

Lead

Domestic Production and Use. Mine production, based on the net quantity of lead recovered in the smelting of concentrate, increased about 7 percent in 1998 to 481 kt. Lead was produced at 17 mines in Alaska, Colorado, Idaho, Missouri, Montana, New York, and Tennessee; 9 mines in Alaska and Missouri accounted for about 91 percent of the production. The value of the recovered lead was about $480 million, calculated on the basis of an average North American producer price of $0.4527 per pound. Lead concentrate was processed at two smelter-refineries in Missouri and a smelter in Montana. Primary refinery production decreased 1.8 percent in 1998.

Lead was consumed principally in the transportation industries, where about 72 percent was used in automotive-type starting-lighting-ignition (SLI) storage batteries, fuel tanks, solder, seals, casting metals, and bearings. The use of lead in electrical, electronic, and communications applications, including industrial-type lead-acid storage batteries, and its use in ammunition, television glass, construction, radiation shielding, and protective coatings accounted for approximately 24 percent of consumption. The balance was used in ballast and weights, ceramics and crystal glass, tubes, containers, foil, and wire. The demand for lead in all forms of lead-acid storage batteries, SLI-type and industrial-type, represented about 88 percent of consumption in 1998.

Recent Events, Trends, and Issues. Two lead-producing mines were expanded in 1998, one in Alaska and one in Idaho, and acquisition of additional mining rights was made by another Alaskan producer through a land exchange agreement with the U.S. government. In 1998 and 1999, exploration was begun at several undeveloped properties in Alaska, and efforts continued to reopen five mines: two in Utah and one each in Idaho, Nevada, and Washington.

Mine production in the United States should increase about 2 to 3 percent per year through 2000 as a result of continued higher production at some of the larger facilities and the resumption of mining at some of the currently closed operations. Total refined lead production in the United States from primary and secondary refineries is expected to increase at an annual rate of about 2 percent through 2000.

Consumption of lead in the industrialized nations was expected to grow only marginally in 1999 but will begin to accelerate in 2000, leading to the resumption of a 2 to 3 percent yearly growth rate between 2001 and 2003. Lead-acid battery demand, dominated by automotive-type replacement batteries, will continue to drive consumption higher as it continues to increase its share of total consumption.

Worldwide production of primary and secondary lead is expected to increase modestly through 1999 and 2000 despite the continuation of low lead prices. With respect to secondary production, the pool of potential lead scrap feed for secondary smelters worldwide will continue to expand in that period, probably easing some of the operating difficulties experienced by smelters in 1998 that were associated with low lead prices and the high cost and shortage of available lead scrap.

Molybdenum

Domestic Production and Use. In 1998, 11 U.S. mines produced molybdenum with a value of approximately $200 million. Major end-use applications include machinery, 35 percent; electrical products, 15 percent; transportation, 15 percent; chemicals, 10 percent; and the oil and gas industry, 10 percent. The U.S. ratio of exports to imports has remained about the same in recent years at 3:1. Potential substitutes for molybdenum include chromium, vanadium, columbium, and boron in alloy steels; tungsten in tool steels; and graphite, tungsten, and tantalum for refractory materials in high-temperature electric furnaces.

Recent Events, Trends, and Issues. In 1998, molybdenum mine production decreased 12 percent and reported consumption increased 21 percent compared with 1997. That change contrasts with changes in production and consumption from 1996 to 1997, when mine production of molybdenum increased about 11 percent while reported consumption decreased about 1 percent. In 1998, exports increased slightly but imports decreased slightly. The United States produces about 39 percent of the world's mined molybdenum.

Zinc

Domestic Production and Use. In 1998, production of zinc in concentrate was about 755 kt, of which nearly 95 percent came from four states: Alaska, Missouri, New York, and Tennessee. More than 67 percent of zinc in concentrate originated in Alaska. Production of zinc metal was 368 kt, valued at about $417 million. Zinc metal was produced by three primary smelters and eight secondary smelters. Apparent consumption of zinc metal reached 1.28 Mt in 1998. About 75 percent of the output was used in Illinois, Indiana, Michigan, New York, Ohio, and Pennsylvania. Of the total zinc consumed, about 55 percent was used in galvanizing, 20 percent in zinc-based alloys, 11 percent in brass and bronze, and 14 percent in other applications. Zinc compound and zinc dust were used mainly by the agriculture, chemical, paint, and rubber industries. Major coproducts of zinc mining and smelting, in decreasing order, were lead, sulfur, cadmium, silver, gold, and germanium. Major competitors for zinc include aluminum, cadmium, magnesium, plastics, and steel.

Recent Events, Trends, and Issues. The large increase in ore production was due mainly to the completion of a production rate increase project by Cominco Ltd. at the Red Dog Mine in Alaska. Production of zinc concentrate at the Red Dog Mine was about 799 kt in 1998 and was expected to reach more than 900 kt in 1999. Most of this increased production will be exported because all three primary smelters are producing at or near capacity. The planned tripling of capacity of the Clarksville, TN, smelter was shelved after Savage Resources Ltd. was bought by Pasminco Mining Ltd. of Australia. Korea Zinc Co. Ltd. is planning to gradually expand production at its Sauget, IL, smelter from the current 105,000 to 120,000 tons per year. Inadequate domestic metal production will continue to be compensated for by imports and increased secondary production. Because of geographic proximity and lower tariffs, most imports are from Canada and Mexico. Spurred by strict environmental protection laws, an ever-increasing share of zinc is being recycled. Currently, about one-third of consumption is met by secondary production.

INDUSTRIAL MINERALS

The production and use of industrial minerals showed strong growth in the 1990s, generally following the trend of the domestic economy. In 1997 and 1998, in both current and constant dollars, the value of industrial minerals production grew at a slightly higher rate than did the economy as a whole. Owing to the low unit value of most industrial minerals, production comes for the most part from domestic resources. Most industrial minerals are produced for their physical or chemical properties and require limited processing other than crushing and sizing or separation from other minerals before their end use. Several are produced from brines, which are concentrated by solar evaporation or chemically processed into end-use products. Many are building blocks for end-use manufactured products.

In terms of value of mine production in 1998, crushed stone was the largest commodity at $8.8 billion, followed by construction sand and gravel at $4.7 billion. Those two commodities were also the largest in terms of quantity at 1.5 and 1.02 billion tons, respectively (see Economic and Trade Trends at the beginning of the chapter). Cement at $6.5 billion (ex plant) was used to make portland cement concrete that had a value of about $30 billion. Titanium dioxide pigment was valued at about $3 billion. Chemical minerals with important value to the economy were lime ($1.2 billion), phosphate rock ($1.1 billion), salt, ($0.96 billion), soda ash ($0.84 billion), boron ($0.45 billion), and sulfur ($0.45 billion) (see Economic and Trade Trends at the beginning of this chapter). By-product production of industrial minerals from nonmining sources is significant for sulfur and sodium sulfate and has significant potential for flue-gas desulfurization gypsum. Very few industrial minerals are recycled; refractory brick, construction and demolition concrete, and road asphalt are exceptions.

The value of trade in industrial minerals showed considerable growth in the 1990s. The value of exports increased about $0.5 billion to a total of $2.8 billion from 1990 to 1997, and the value of imports increased about $220 million to a total of nearly $9.8 billion in that period. (Note: These foreign trade values include some materials of mineral origin produced in SICs 28 and 32.) U.S. import reliance, expressed as a percentage of domestic consumption, varies widely for industrial minerals. The United States is totally dependent on foreign sources for fluorspar, graphite, sheet mica, and strontium minerals and more than 50 percent dependent for barite, dimension stone, gemstones, iodine, peat, and potash. Although the United States is among the top three world producers, it has some import dependence for cement, gypsum, lime, perlite, salt, and sulfur. The United States is an important exporter of soda ash, talc, and titanium dioxide. Industrial minerals contributed to U.S. exports; many chemicals, compounds, and finished products are based solely or partly on domestically produced materials.

INDUSTRIAL MINERALS INDUSTRY SUBSECTORS

Aggregates

Domestic Production and Use. Preliminary estimates indicate that 2.52 billion tons of aggregates was produced in 1998 in the United States. Of this total, nearly 1.5 billion tons consisted of crushed stone produced by 1,411 companies at 3,362 quarries and 1.02 billion tons consisted of construction sand and gravel produced by 3,838 companies at 5,288 operations. U.S. production of aggregates has increased steadily since 1991, in response to continued high-level activity in the commercial, public, and private sectors of the construction industry. The production for consumption of both mineral commodities in 1998 represents the highest U.S. production levels ever recorded.

Fifty-two percent of the crushed stone produced in 1998 came from the following 10 states, listed in order of tonnage: Pennsylvania, Texas, Florida, Ohio, Virginia, Georgia, Missouri, Illinois, North Carolina, and Tennessee. For sand and gravel, the leading states, in order of tonnage, were California, Texas, Michigan, Ohio, Arizona, Washington, Colorado, Utah, Illinois, and Minnesota, which together accounted for about 53 percent of total U.S. output.

Aggregates are used mainly for construction purposes in portland cement concretes and asphalt concretes and as road base materials. A small but important percentage of crushed stone is used for chemical and metallurgical processes, including cement and lime manufacture; for agricultural uses; and in environmental applications such as soil erosion control, water purification, and reduction of sulfur dioxide emissions generated mostly by fossil-fueled electric power plants. The widespread distribution of domestic deposits of aggregates and the high cost of transportation combine to limit foreign trade to mostly local transactions across international borders. U.S. imports and exports of aggregates are small, representing less than 1 percent of domestic consumption.

Outlook. The demand for aggregates is expected to continue to grow on the basis of the volume of work on the infrastructure that will be financed by the new Surface Transportation Efficiency Act for the Twenty-First Century (PL 105-178) and the growth of the U.S. economy in general. The projected increases will be influenced by construction activity in the public as well as private construction sectors. The demand for crushed stone in 1999 was expected to be about 1.6 billion tons, a 6.6 percent increase over 1998. The demand for construction sand and gravel in 1999 was expected to be 1.07 billion tons, a 4.9 percent increase over 1998. Gradual increases in demand for aggregates were anticipated after 1999 as well. The free on board (FOB) mine prices for aggregates are not expected to increase significantly in the near future. Delivered prices, however, are expected to increase, especially in and near metropolitan areas, mainly because more aggregates will be transported from distant sources.

Gypsum and By-Product Gypsum

Domestic Production and Use. In 1998, U.S. output of mined gypsum reached a record high of 19 Mt valued at $132 million. The leading producer states were Oklahoma, Iowa, Texas, Michigan, California, Nevada, and Indiana, which together accounted for about 72 percent of total output. Overall, 32 companies produced gypsum at 61 mines in 19 states and 10 companies calcined gypsum at 65 plants in 28 states. More than two-thirds of domestic consumption, which was about 31 Mt, was accounted for by manufacturers of wallboard and plaster products. About 5 Mt for cement production, 3 Mt for agricultural applications, and small amounts of high-purity gypsum for a wide range of industrial processes, such as smelting and glassmaking, accounted for the remaining consumption. About one-third of the consumption was supplied by imports, almost all from Canada and Mexico.

In addition to mined gypsum, by-product gypsum is generated by various industrial processes and by flue-gas desulfurization (FGD) operations at coal-burning power plants. Some of this by-product gypsum is used for wallboard manufacturing, agriculture, roadbase, and fill material. Industrial plants in at least 11 states sold an estimated 500,000 tons of by-product gypsum in 1998, principally for agricultural uses. Also, approximately 60 domestic coal-fired power plants generated at least 25 Mt of FGD product in 1998. Although less than 10 percent of this material is used as a substitute for mined gypsum, primarily for wallboard manufacturing (1.6 Mt in 1998), consumption has been increasing in recent years.

Recent Events, Trends, and Issues. Forecasts indicate that gypsum demand in North American markets will remain high for the next few years. This demand will be driven by and depend on the continued strength of the construction industry, particularly in the United States, where more than 90 percent of the gypsum consumed is used for wallboard products (which reached a record high in 1998), building plasters, and the manufacture of portland cement. Several large wallboard plants under construction and designed to use only by-product gypsum will accelerate substitution significantly as they become operational in a few years. Federal funding authorized in 1998 for road building and repair through 2003 will help increase gypsum consumption in the cement industry.

Phosphate Rock

In 1998, phosphate rock ore was mined by 11 companies in four states and upgraded into 44.2 Mt of marketable product, 4 percent less than 1997 output. Twelve mines in Florida and one in North Carolina accounted for 88 percent of domestic production; four mines in Idaho and one in Utah produced the remainder. World production of phosphate rock was estimated at 145 Mt, with the United States the largest producer, followed by Morocco and China. The manufacture of wet-process phosphoric acid and superphosphoric acid, which were used as intermediates in the manufacture of granulated and liquid fertilizers and animal feed, accounted for 93 percent of domestic phosphate rock consumption. The remaining 7 percent was used to produce elemental phosphorus and phosphorus compounds for use in industrial applications. Production of wet-process phosphoric acid was slightly higher than it was in 1997. The United States accounted for 43 percent of estimated world concentrated phosphate production. More than 50 percent of the wet-process phosphoric acid produced in the United States was exported in the form of fertilizer materials or as merchant-grade phosphoric acid. Overall, the United States accounted for 41 percent of world concentrated phosphate trade in 1998. U.S. exports of phosphate rock increased slightly in 1998 as one producer became a major supplier to an elemental phosphorus plant in the Netherlands. However, other producers have reduced exports and switched their emphasis to exporting higher-value phosphoric acid and fertilizer materials. Imports of marketable phosphate rock were estimated at 1.8 Mt, nearly all from Morocco.

In September, Nu-Gulf Industries, Inc., reopened the Wingate Creek mine in Manatee County, FL, which had been closed since 1992. Wingate Creek will supply the Mulberry Phosphates, Inc., phosphoric acid plant and the Piney Point Phosphates, Inc., plant that was scheduled to reopen in mid-1999. All three companies are subsidiaries of Mulberry Corp.

IMC-Agrico Co. began a restructuring program in the fourth quarter to consolidate its potash and phosphate business into a single unit. The phosphate operation will be known as IMC-Phosphates. As part of its reorganization, one mine was slated to be closed because of depleted reserves and two other mines were to be closed temporarily in 1999 to conserve resources and reduce stockpiles. IMC-Agrico Co. also purchased 5,000 hectares of phosphate rock reserves in Hardee County, FL, from Mississippi Chemical Co. for $57 million. The company continued the process of obtaining permits for two new mines that will be located south of the current active mining area in central Florida. The new mines will be necessary when reserves at existing mines are depleted in the next 5 to 10 years.

Domestic phosphate rock production was expected to decrease slightly over the next 5 years as mine output will be influenced by a reduction in exports of fertilizer materials and the prolonging of the life of several mines in Florida. Exports of phosphate fertilizers, primarily diammonium phosphate (DAP), to Asia have been a major factor in the domestic consumption of phosphate rock. In 1998, 78 percent of U.S. DAP exports went to that region. Several mine expansions and new DAP plants in Australia, China, India, and Pakistan are scheduled in the next 2 years, and those sources will displace fertilizers supplied by U.S. producers. The projects in Australia and the Indian subcontinent will have the strongest impact on U.S. producers, since the planned increase in annual production capacity will equal U.S. import tonnage to the region in the last year. Domestic consumption has remained steady over the last several years, with some minor fluctuations, and probably will follow the same trend in the near future.

Soda Ash

Soda ash, also known as sodium carbonate, is an alkali chemical that is refined from the mineral trona or naturally occurring sodium carbonate–bearing brines (both referred to as natural soda ash) or manufactured from one of several chemical processes (referred to as synthetic soda ash). It is an essential raw material in glass, chemicals, detergents, and other important industrial products. In 1998, soda ash was the eleventh largest inorganic chemical in terms of production of all domestic inorganic and organic chemicals, excluding petrochemical feedstocks. Although soda ash represented 2 percent of the total estimated $40 billion U.S. nonfuel mineral industry, its use in many diversified products consequently contributes substantially to the gross domestic product of the United States. Because soda ash is used to make flat glass and fiberglass, both of which are used by the domestic automotive and construction industries, monthly soda ash production statistics canvassed by the U.S. Geological Survey are used to develop monthly economic indicators for industrial production that measure the conditions of the U.S. economy.

Production. Total U.S. soda ash production in 1998 decreased 6 percent to 10.1 Mt because of reduced export sales. The domestic soda ash industry consisted of six companies: five in Wyoming and one in California. The names and annual nameplate capacities of the Wyoming producers are FMC Wyoming Corp., 3.22 Mt; General Chemical Corp., 2.40 Mt; OCI Chemical Corp., 2.81 Mt; Solvay Minerals Inc., 2.09 Mt; and Tg Soda Ash Inc., 1.18 Mt. IMC Chemical's (formerly North American Chemical Co.) plant in California has an annual capacity of 1.31 Mt. In 1998, the industry operated at 78 percent of total nameplate capacity, which was 13.02 Mt. Each of the U.S. companies is wholly owned or partially owned by foreign soda ash–producing companies or foreign soda ash consumers. Those countries include Australia, Belgium, France, Japan, and the Republic of South Korea. U.S. ownership represented 54 percent of total production capacity.

World soda ash production in 1998 was estimated at 31.7 Mt. Of the 29 countries that produce natural and synthetic soda ash, the United States is the world's largest producer, accounting for 32 percent of total world output. Only the United States, Botswana, China, and Kenya produce soda ash from natural sources; other countries manufacture soda ash through various chemical processes, primarily the Solvay process. Total world natural soda ash production represented about 33 percent of combined world soda ash production. The five leading nations that produce soda ash are the United States, China, Russia, India, and Germany. Those five countries accounted for 69 percent of total world production in 1998.

Consumption. Soda ash is a mature commodity that tends to parallel growth in population and gross domestic product. U.S. reported consumption in 1998 was 6.55 Mt, a slight increase from 1997. The distribution of soda ash by end use was glass, 49 percent (containers, 50 percent; flat, 34 percent; fiber and specialty, 8 percent each); chemicals (mainly sodium phosphates, sodium silicates, sodium bicarbonate, and sodium chromate), 27 percent; soaps and detergents, 11 percent; distributors, 5 percent; FGD, 3 percent; pulp and paper and water treatment, 2 percent each; and miscellaneous uses, 1 percent. Domestic soda ash consumption has been relatively flat for several years, with domestic markets growing only about 1 percent annually. The glass container sector, which is the single largest consuming market, has been declining since about 1980 because of competition from polyethylene terephthalate (PET) plastic beverage containers, which are lighter and unbreakable. Glass container recycling has adversely affected soda ash consumption in glass container manufacture. In 1998, the domestic recycling rate for glass containers was about 35 percent. In certain uses, particularly in the pulp and paper, water treatment, and some chemical sectors, sodium hydroxide (also known as caustic soda) can be substituted for soda ash. The price and availability of both commodities usually determine which chemical is preferred by those sectors. Normally, about 300,000 tons of displacement can occur between both chemicals when the cycle shifts from one to the other. Caustic soda can be produced from soda ash and can substitute for the traditional electrolytic form of sodium hydroxide.

U.S. Trade. The export market is the major growth sector for U.S. soda ash. In 1998, exports were 3.66 Mt and represented 36 percent of total U.S. soda ash production. By comparison, exports accounted for only 5 percent of U.S. production in 1970. The downturn in the Asian economies in late 1997 that continued throughout 1998 caused the U.S. export market to decline 14 percent in 1998 compared with 1997. With world soda ash demand estimated to grow at about 2.5 to 3 percent annually, however, the United States will continue to be the main supplier to many foreign markets for the foreseeable future.

The percentage distribution of U.S. soda ash exports on a regional basis in 1998 were Asia, 39 percent; South America, 22 percent; North America, 20 percent; Europe, 10 percent; the Middle East and Africa, 3 percent each; and Central America and Oceania, 1 percent each. The 10 leading nations for U.S. soda ash exports in 1998 were Mexico (14 percent); Japan (8 percent); the Republic of Korea and Taiwan (7 percent each); Canada, Indonesia, and Venezuela (6 percent each); Brazil (5 percent); and Chile and Thailand (4 percent each). Those countries accounted for 67 percent of total U.S. exports.

The majority of U.S. soda ash imports come from Canada, where General Chemical Corp. operates a synthetic soda ash facility at Amherstburg, Ontario. That plant produces dense and light soda ash, a large quantity of which is shipped to the United States for special markets that require soda ash with a lighter bulk density, such as detergents.

Outlook. Despite the economic problems in several Asian countries, soda ash consumption has remained constant as several Asian consumers have imported lower-priced soda ash from major U.S. competitors such as China. In the last 2 years, Chinese soda ash production has exceeded internal consumption, causing an excess supply of material to become available for export at favorable prices. The proposed formation of an export association by the major soda ash producers in China may adversely affect U.S. export sales in the future.

World soda ash consumption has been forecast to remain favorable for 1999 and into the twenty-first century because of growing demand for soda ash in developing nations, especially in the Far East and South America. Exports will continue to be the most important category for increased U.S. soda ash sales. Consolidation in the U.S. soda ash industry will reduce the number of suppliers but should strengthen sales and prices. Domestic soda ash consumption will remain about the same in the short term; however, overall consumption could increase if more soda ash companies conduct market research to find innovative uses for additional soda ash. FMC Corp., for example, assisted in developing technology to convert spent solutions reacted with soda ash into useful products for sale, increasing soda ash consumption.

Sulfur

The United States has been the world's leading sulfur producer since it surpassed Italy in about 1915, shortly after the Frasch method for mining sulfur was perfected in Louisiana. In this unusual mining process, native sulfur is melted underground with superheated water and brought to the surface by compressed air. More recent years have seen significant changes in the sulfur industry, although the United States has maintained its dominance and is expected to do so in the foreseeable future.

In 1982, the most important change in sulfur production was the shift from Frasch sulfur to recovered sulfur as the most important source. Recovered sulfur is produced primarily to comply with environmental regulations that are applicable directly to emissions from the processing facility or indirectly by restricting the sulfur content of the fuels sold or used by a facility. Recovered sulfur is produced at oil refineries, natural gas processing plants, and coking plants in the United States. Another important source of domestic sulfur is by-product sulfuric acid from nonferrous metal smelters.

In the United States, more elemental sulfur is recovered from petroleum refining than from natural gas processing and Frasch mining combined. Natural gas processing is the most important source of sulfur in the world market. Pyrite, because of its high sulfur content, is also an important source of sulfur in a few countries, although its importance is diminishing everywhere.

The general trend in sulfur production is that intentional production (in which elemental sulfur, sulfur ores, and pyrites are produced for the sole purpose of providing sulfur raw materials) is declining, and there is little likelihood of reversing that trend. Sulfur that is produced as a result of environmental regulation is expanding globally, and as economies improve in developing countries, this expansion is likely to accelerate.

Sulfur consumption trends are relatively stable. The production of phosphate fertilizers is by far the largest consumer of sulfur and sulfuric acid. Consumption in phosphate production and other agricultural areas varies from year to year for an assortment of reasons, including weather conditions in various regions throughout the world, economic circumstances in different locations, and government programs that increase or decrease agricultural support programs over time. Although difficult to predict over the short term, sulfur consumption in the phosphate industry is expected to rise moderately as new projects are completed around the world. Little growth is expected in the United States.

One agricultural use that has potential for a global increase is that of plant nutrient sulfur. Sulfur has been recognized as a requirement for the growth of healthy crops. Sulfur deficits in soil have been identified around the world and could stimulate a large market for additional sulfur, but the application of sulfur as a fertilizer is not expanding quickly.

Other uses for sulfur are significantly smaller than those in agriculture, and growth in use is harder to predict. In general, growth in other areas will be moderate at best. In all end uses, growth in sulfur consumption is expected to lag behind increased production. Unless additional requirements for sulfur are developed, supply will continue to surpass demand.

Titanium

Commercial forms of titanium concentrates include ilmenite, leucoxene, rutile, synthetic rutile, and titaniferous slag. In 1998, mineral concentrate producers were in the process of substantially increasing the supply of high-grade mineral concentrates suitable for use by chloride-route titanium pigment producers. As a result of the these upgrades, new chloride-grade slag production capacity exists in Canada, Norway, and South Africa. Previously, South Africa was the exclusive source of chloride-grade slag. U.S. production of natural and synthetic mineral concentrates was 601,000 tons in 1998.

Approximately 95 percent of titanium is used to produce titanium dioxide (TiO_2), a white pigment used in paints, paper, and plastics. The leading producer countries of titanium pigments include France, Germany, Japan, the United Kingdom, and the United States. Domestic production of TiO_2 pigment was 1.33 Mt in 1998, a slight decrease from 1997.

The world's producers of titanium sponge, the primary form of titanium metal, are located in China, Japan, Kazakhstan, Russia, and the United States. In 1998, an estimated 65 percent of titanium metal was used in aerospace applications. The remaining 35 percent was used in chemical process, power generation, marine, ordnance, medical, and other nonaerospace applications. In 1998, domestic sponge production data were withheld to avoid revealing company proprietary data. U.S. production of titanium ingot and mill products decreased 7 percent compared with 1997. Decreased consumption of titanium metal was attributed to cancellations of orders by the commercial aircraft industry.

Over the next few years, the development of new programs in Australia and South Africa will substantially increase the availability of titanium concentrates. Further expansions in supply are expected through ongoing exploration and development activities in Australia, Canada, Kenya, Madagascar, Russia, South Africa, Sri Lanka, and the United States. Consumption of TiO_2 pigment is linked to the growth of the overall economy and is expected to increase at an annual rate of 2 to 3 percent. Global demand for titanium metal products is driven primarily by demand from the commercial and military aerospace industries. The recent fall in demand was expected to continue in 1999; however, this trend is not expected to continue beyond the year 2000.

Minerals Information Team, U.S. Department of the Interior, U.S. Geological Survey, (703) 648-4919, September 1999.

REFERENCES

American Geological Institute, Government Affairs Program, http://www.agiweb.org.

American Metal Market, Cahners, Inc., 350 Hudson Street, New York, NY 10014-4504. (212) 519-7550.

Census of Mineral Industries, 1992, U.S. Department of Commerce, Bureau of the Census, Washington, DC 20233.

Early Economic Outlook, Foundation for International Business and Economic Research, Inc., 60 East 42 Street, Suite 3219, New York, NY 10165. (212) 983-2222.

International California Mining Journal, California Mining Journal, Inc., 9011 Soquel Drive, Aptos, CA 95001-2260. (831) 662-2899.

National Mining Association, Issues, http://www.nma.org.

Statistical Abstract of the United States 1997, U.S. Department of Commerce, Bureau of the Census, Washington, DC 20233.

The Wall Street Journal.

RELATED CHAPTERS

2: Coal Mining
6: Construction
8: Building Products and Materials
13: Steel Mill Products
14: Nonferrous Metals
36: Motor Vehicles
37: Automotive Parts

COAL MINING
Economic and Trade Trends

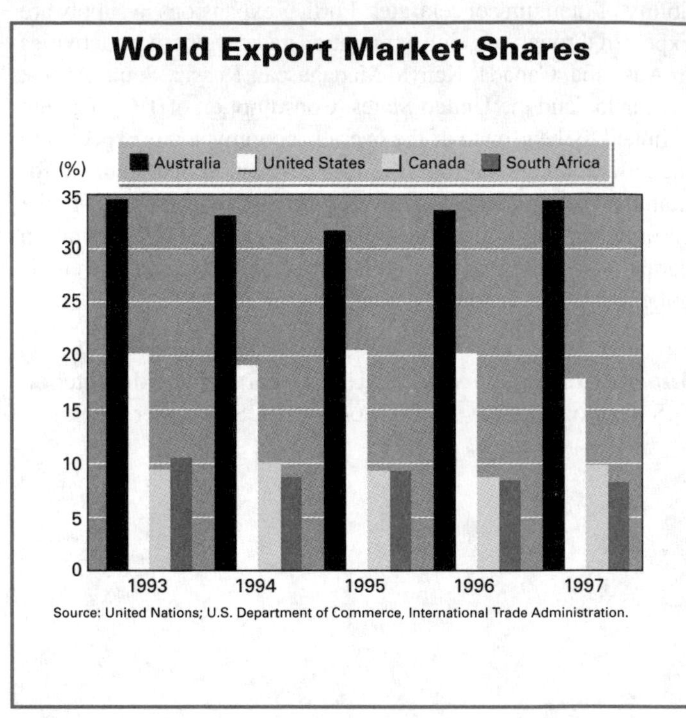

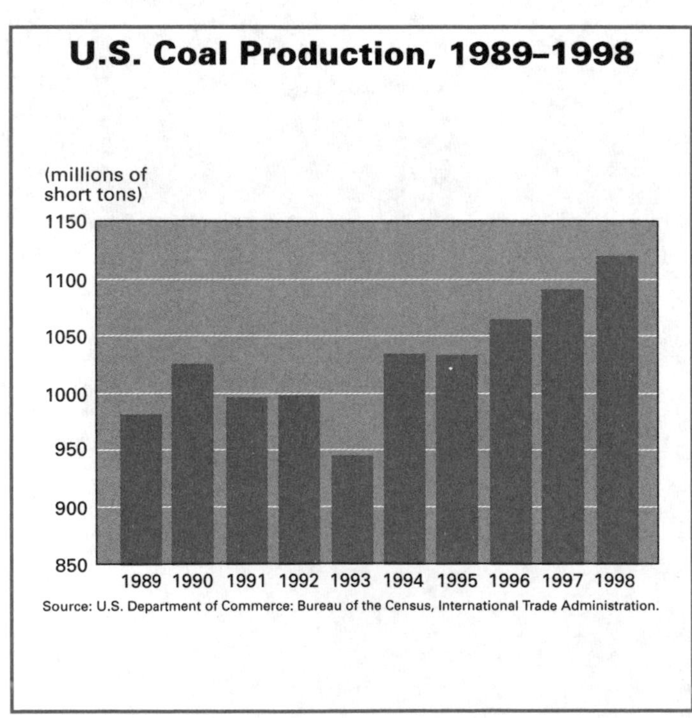

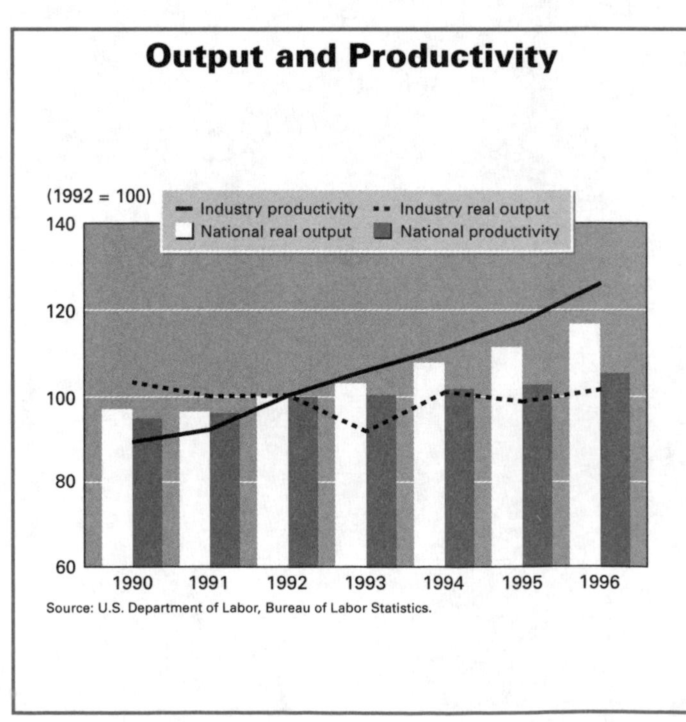

See "Getting the Most Out of *Outlook 2000*" for definitions of terms.

2

Coal Mining

INDUSTRY DEFINITION The U.S. coal industry is composed of establishments engaged primarily in producing and developing bituminous coal or lignite at surface mines (SIC 1221), bituminous coal or lignite at underground mines (SIC 1222), and anthracite (SIC 1231). The industry includes underground mining, auger mining, strip mining, culm bank mining, and other surface mining as well as coal preparation plants engaged in cleaning, crushing, screening, or sizing coal. It also includes establishments that perform primarily coal mining services for others on a contract or fee basis (SIC 1241).

GLOBAL INDUSTRY TRENDS

The U.S. coal industry and the international coal sector appear to have a common outlook, at least in the short run. The use of coal as a fuel for generating electricity will continue to remain strong, if not dominant, for at least the next 5 years. Both in the United States and internationally, the status of coal may become more problematic after that period, largely because of environmental concerns and competition from so-called cleaner fuels such as natural gas.

At present, the use of coal is affected by various clean air regulations in many countries, and looming on the horizon is the potential for even more regulation of the release of carbon dioxide from the burning of coal. The United Nations Framework Convention on Climate Change is being considered by many countries, although the momentum behind the Kyoto Protocol, which was created under United Nations auspices in December 1997, may be waning in the United States. That protocol set limits on greenhouse gas emissions in the major industrialized countries. The United States has not ratified the protocol and is unlikely to in the near future, with the Senate having voted 96 to 0 to postpone ratification until the treaty addresses emissions from major developing countries such as China and India.

The counterbalance to concern over emissions from coal-fired power plants lies in the realm of technology, where a number of options are available currently or close to maturity in terms of being adopted for commercial use in electricity generation. As recently as the fall of 1999, the top executive of one of the largest U.S. electric power companies noted the beneficial aspects of adopting clean coal technologies and the contribution those technologies could make toward extending the time frame for the significant use of coal in power generation. Thus, the inherently low cost of coal as a fuel provides an opportunity for power generators to invest in technology for using coal in such a way that the total cost of fuel plus the adoption of newer technologies still allows the cost-effective use of coal-fired electric plants.

No matter how the long-term situation evolves regarding the interplay of an inherently low-cost fuel, a concern for the environment, and the economics of fuel technology, the short-run outlook for coal is stable. Both international and U.S. forecasts show that for the next 3 years at least, the use of coal will grow, although at modest annual rates.

For example, global demand for coal is expected to grow at an annual rate of 2.2 percent between 1995 and 2020, with the highest rates of growth occurring in China and other Asian countries. However, in the most active international coal-trading markets, which involve the most industrialized countries, the rate of growth is lower than the overall international rate, with primary coal demand growing at an annual rate of only 1.2 percent per year in the Organization for Economic Cooperation and Development (OECD) countries. Within the OECD, coal demand is expected to grow at a rate of 2.1 percent in North America and 0.5 percent in the Asia-Pacific region and to decline about 0.5 percent per year in Europe.

In the United States, total demand for coal for all uses, which reached 1.04 billion tons in 1998, is expected to grow to 1.06

billion tons in 1999 and 1.09 billion tons in the year 2000. In the electric power sector in the United States, coal-fired power plants account for well over half of all power generation, with a market share of just over 52 percent in 1998. That share is expected to dip slightly in 1999 and then increase a bit in 2000. The slight decline in 1999 resulted from a warmer winter that was not completely offset during the summer peak air-conditioning period. Also in 1999, U.S. coal exports were expected to decline as lower-cost coal from Poland and South Africa, coupled with lower demand in Asia, dampened coal exporters' enthusiasm for participating in the export trade. U.S. coal exports traditionally amount to less than 7 percent of total demand for U.S.-produced coal.

U.S. COAL INDUSTRY OVERVIEW

The coal industry in the United States is characterized by three major factors:

1. Coal is relatively abundant.
2. Coal is inexpensive compared with other fuels.
3. Improving productivity in the mining and production of coal ensures that coal will remain cost-competitive with other fuels.

However, the U.S. coal industry still faces a challenging business environment. Air pollution regulations now on the books that address the discharge of emissions from coal-fired power plants will have a great impact on how much coal is consumed and, importantly, where the coal that is consumed is produced. For example, western U.S. coal, which generates a lower level of emissions when burned in power plants, will continue to replace the higher-sulfur coal produced in the eastern and midwestern United States. In addition, the coal industry must comply with an array of worker safety and health regulations as well as regulations governing the physical impact of mining such as strip mine operation, subsidence, and water pollution.

Environmental concerns do not stop with the regulations that are already in place. Continuing concern about carbon dioxide emissions from coal burning and their relation to global warming have created negative public perceptions about the use of coal that eventually may be translated into public policy. Those concerns have created a climate of uncertainty about the advisability of using coal to generate electricity and thus may work to coal's disadvantage as electricity producers decide which fuels to use when building new power plants.

However, over the next 5 years, it is unlikely that the dominant role of coal as a fuel for electric power generation will change significantly (see Figure 2-1). In the longer term, technological changes associated with power generation may head off challenges to the coal industry's dominant position, but in any case it appears that any meaningful challenge to the strong position of coal as a fuel is at least a decade away.

The dominant position of coal as a fuel for power generation is reflected in current measurements of the industry's performance.

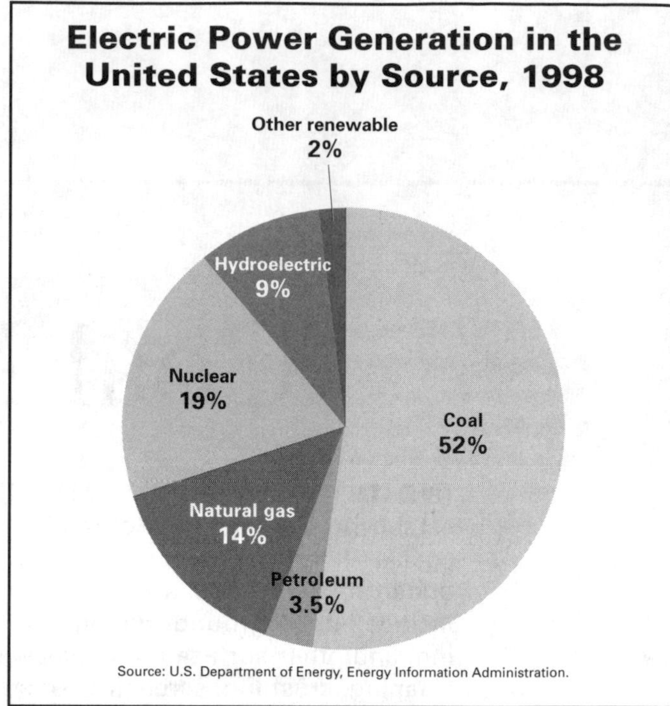

FIGURE 2-1

Production, Consumption, and Prices of U.S. Coal

Coal production in the United States reached 1.12 billion tons in 1998, the highest level on record, reflecting an 8.2 percent gain over the production rate of 1.03 billion tons in 1994. However, not all coal-producing regions made similar gains in that 5-year period. For example, coal production in the Appalachian region amounted to 460.4 million tons in 1998, a gain of only 3.3 percent from the 1994 level of 445.4 million tons. In the interior region, consisting largely of western Kentucky, Illinois, and Indiana, coal output in 1998 amounted to 168.4 million tons, a decline from 179.9 million tons in 1994. Finally, in the western U.S. region, coal production amounted to 489 million tons in 1998 versus 408.3 million tons in 1994, a 19.6 percent gain, with Wyoming accounting for 314.4 million tons in 1998 versus 237.1 million tons in 1994. Wyoming coal has become attractive because its low sulfur content results in lower levels of emissions when it is burned.

Using the same time frame of 5 years, the consumption of coal for electric power generation in the United States amounted to 941.6 million tons in 1998 versus 839 million tons in 1994 (see Figure 2-2). In 1998, coal accounted for 52.3 percent of the fuel used for electricity generation in the United States, versus 14.3 percent for natural gas, 3.5 percent for oil, 18.7 percent for nuclear power, 8.9 percent for hydropower, and 1.6 percent for other sources. On the negative side, as the U.S. steel industry has declined somewhat in recent years, the use of coal to produce blast furnace coke used in steelmaking has declined. Coal used for coke amounted to 27.8 million tons in 1998, a 13 percent decline from 32 million tons in 1994.

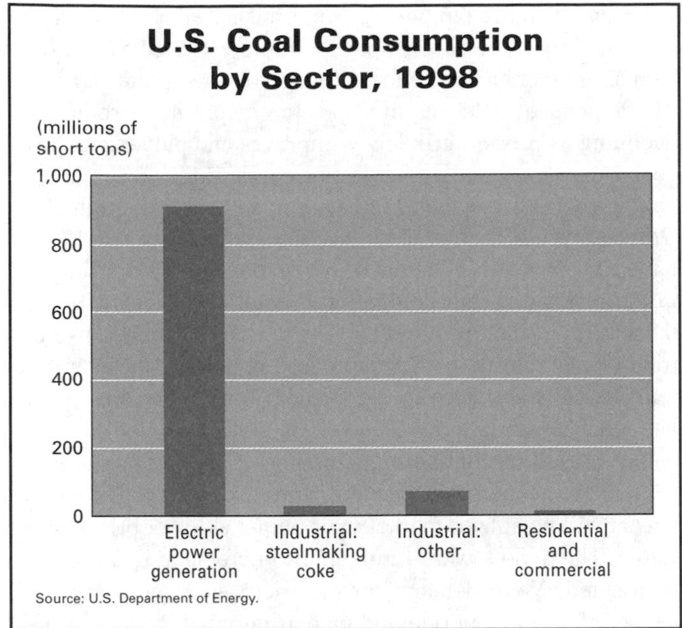

FIGURE 2-2

The United States is a major exporter of coal, although exports overall amount to only a small fraction of domestic coal production. U.S. coal exports tend to fluctuate because of the role of the United States as a "swing" supplier, filling coal orders on the basis of the occurrence of excess supplies in the United States or shortfalls in supplies from other exporting countries. In 1998, the United States exported 30.1 million tons of coal for electric power generating (known as steam or thermal coal) and 47.1 million tons of coal used for blast furnace coke production (known as coking coal). Total U.S. coal exports are likely to decline in the near term, falling from 77.2 million tons in 1998 (see Figure 2-3) to 63 million tons in 1999 and 62.7 million tons in the year 2000. Competition from lower-cost suppliers and lingering weak demand in Asia account for the short-term decline in coal exports. However, a recent forecast by the U.S. Department of Energy still has U.S. coal exports growing over the next decade.

Compared with other fossil energy sources, coal is by far the least expensive fuel. In 1998, the national average cost of using coal for power generation in the United States amounted to 125.1 cents per million British thermal units (Btu) of power generation, compared with oil at 213.5 cents per million Btu and natural gas at 238.4 cents per million Btu. It is highly likely that coal can continue to remain a low-cost fuel solely because of productivity gains. In the last reported annual tally, the U.S. coal industry produced 6.04 short tons of coal per miner per hour in 1997, whereas the rate was only 4.70 short tons per miner per hour in 1993 (see Figure 2-4). The rate was 3.55 short tons per miner per hour in 1988.

U.S. COAL INDUSTRY OUTLOOK

The staying power of coal is reflected in the expectation that U.S. domestic coal demand will increase from 1.03 billion tons in 1997 to 1.28 billion tons in 2020, a gain of 245 million tons. This steady increase in demand stems largely from growth in the use of coal for electricity generation. The demand for coal in other U.S. domestic markets will increase only 3 million tons during that period, based on the expectation that U.S. coking coal consumption will decline while demand for coal for industrial cogeneration will increase (cogenertion is the dual production of power and heat used for industrial purposes from the combustion of coal). Coal use for power generation (excluding industrial cogeneration) should increase to 1.17 billion tons in 2020 from 924 million tons in 1997, largely as a result of increased utilization of existing generation capacity and, in later years, additions of new electric power capacity.

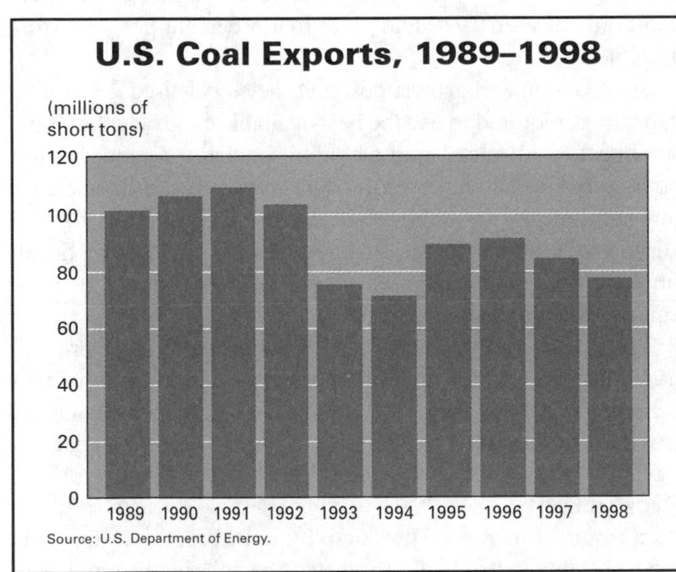

FIGURE 2-3

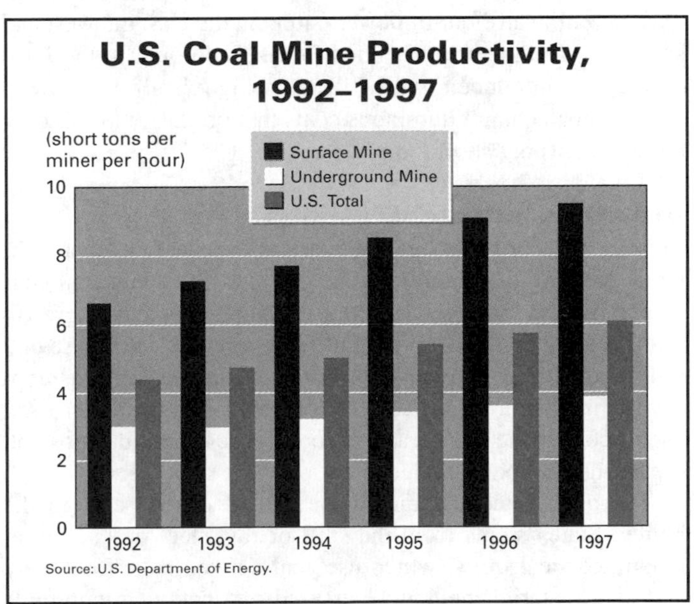

FIGURE 2-4

The issue of power generation capacity is interesting, since natural gas appears to be favored for new power plants. As power generators add "peaking" units, or relatively smaller generating units designed to be used during periods of peak demand, such as for heavy air-conditioning use, the fuel of choice has been natural gas for such units.

However, the "baseload" stock of power plants used for normal electricity generation in the United States is in general not fully utilized. Given the high price tag of upward of $400 million to construct a new power plant, the use of smaller peaking units and the "tweaking" of existing coal-fired plants to render them more efficient constitute an inviting strategy for power generators in meeting increased power demands.

It is expected in one major forecast that the average utilization rate for coal-fired power plants will increase from 67 percent to 79 percent between 1997 and 2020. Thus, any challenge to coal from natural gas in baseload generation will have to await the full utilization of existing coal-fired plants, according to the coal industry's view. In a recent industry analysis, the economic advantage of boosting efficiency in coal-fired plants also involved an environmental advantage. This analysis noted that every 1 percent increase in generating efficiency with coal yields a 3 to 4 percent decrease in carbon dioxide output per unit of power produced. The efficiency gains available through upgrades of existing electric generation plants may offer power at 6 to 12 percent less carbon dioxide, the analysis noted.

In terms of capital, operating, and fuel costs, it appears that natural gas–fired electricity generation is the most cost-effective option for the construction of new power plants through 2010. However, between 2010 and 2020, rising natural gas costs and nuclear power plant retirements are projected to cause increasing demand for coal-fired baseload capacity.

Coal consumption per kilowatt-hour of generation is higher for softer subbituminous and lignite coals than it is for harder bituminous coal. As a result, the shift to desirable "cleaner" low-sulfur subbituminous western coal will increase the tonnage per kilowatt-hour of power output in the U.S. midwest and southeast. In the eastern United States, according to the forecast, power producers will shift from higher-sulfur to lower-sulfur Appalachian bituminous coals that produce more energy (Btu content) per short ton.

Growth in Industrial Markets

In other coal consumption markets, it is expected that there will be an increase of 12 million tons in industrial steam coal consumption between 1997 and 2020 (a 0.7 percent annual growth rate), but that gain will be partially countered by a decrease of 9 million tons in coking coal consumption. Increasing consumption of industrial steam coal results primarily from increased use of coal in the chemical and food processing industries and greater use of coal for cogeneration.

The anticipated decline in the use of coking coal in the United States stems from the shift of raw steel production in integrated steel mills (which use coal-derived coke for energy and as a material input) to increased production in minimills (which use electric arc furnaces that require no coal-derived coke) and increased imports of semifinished steel. There is also a small amount of coke imported into the United States from China, another factor in the slippage of U.S.-produced coke. The amount of coke required per ton of pig iron produced is declining as process efficiency improves and pulverized steam coal is used increasingly in blast furnaces. U.S. consumption of coking coal is projected to fall 1.7 percent a year through 2020. Domestic production of coking coal is stabilized in part by sustained levels of export demand. While total energy consumption in the residential and commercial sectors probably will grow 0.8 percent a year, most of that growth will be captured by electricity and natural gas. Coal consumption in these sectors remains constant, accounting for less than 1 percent of total U.S. coal demand.

As a result of continuing gains in coal mining productivity, which have averaged 6.2 percent per year since 1977, coal producers will be able to market their output at lower prices in the future. The trend toward future gains in productivity appears to be assured. More demand for electricity will cause a greater demand for coal, but demand increasingly will be conditioned by environmental regulations that require a fixed sulfur emissions cap dictated by the Clean Air Act of 1990. The use of western coal can result in up to 85 percent lower sulfur emissions compared with the use of many types of higher-sulfur eastern coal. This bodes well for producers of low-sulfur western coal, which is less costly to produce than much of the coal in the east, and will result in a major expansion of western coal production, according to a U.S. Department of Energy (DOE) forecast.

The inherent advantage of low-sulfur western coal produced largely in the Powder River Basin region of Wyoming and in Montana will result in coal production from that region increasing at a much higher rate than will be the case for coal produced elsewhere. It is anticipated that coal production west of the Mississippi will reach 772 million tons in 2020 versus 534 million tons in 1998 (see Table 2-1). However, the annual growth rate for western coal is likely to decline from the 9.4 percent achieved between 1970 and 1997 to 1.8 percent per year from 1997 to 2020.

As coal demand grows, however, new coal-fired generating capacity is required to use the best available control technology: scrubbers or advanced coal technologies that can reduce sulfur emissions 90 percent or more. Thus, even as the demand for low-sulfur coal grows, there will still be an opportunity to market low-cost higher-sulfur coal. (A scrubber or flue-gas desulfurization unit is an apparatus designed to capture the sulfur emissions from coal combustion.)

From 1997 to 2020, high- and medium-sulfur coal production will grow from 654 million tons to 662 million tons (0.1 percent a year) and low-sulfur coal production should increase from 445 million tons to 696 million tons (2 percent a year).

Productivity

As a result of increased productivity in the coal industry, with reduced labor costs in the east and the inherently more economical surface mining in the west, mine mouth coal prices

TABLE 2-1: Coal Trends and Forecasts
(millions of short tons per year unless otherwise noted)

	1996	1997	1998	1999	2000	2001	2005	2010	2015	2020	Percent Change[1] 1997–2020
Production[2]											
Appalachia	461	477	481	491	483	488	482	482	479	466	−0.1
Interior	173	171	170	168	169	157	129	127	146	164	−0.2
West	439	451	474	495	516	542	589	627	670	728	2.1
East of the Mississippi	573	589	591	599	593	587	561	563	580	586	0.0
West of the Mississippi	500	511	534	554	575	600	640	672	714	772	1.8
Total	1073	1099	1125	1154	1168	1187	1200	1236	1294	1358	0.9
Imports	7	7	7	7	7	7	8	8	8	8	0.2
Exports	90	84	82	83	84	85	87	90	91	93	0.5
Net imports	−83	−76	−75	−75	−76	−77	−80	−82	−84	−86	0.5
Total supply[3]	989	1023	1050	1078	1092	1109	1121	1154	1211	1272	1.0
Consumption by sector											
Residential and commercial	6	6	6	6	6	6	6	7	7	7	0.4
Industrial[4]	71	70	71	72	72	73	74	77	79	82	0.7
Coke plants	32	29	29	29	29	28	26	24	22	20	−1.7
Electric generators[5]	897	924	934	967	985	1002	1014	1050	1103	1166	1.0
Total	1006	1030	1040	1075	1092	1109	1120	1156	1211	1275	0.9
Delivery Price (1997$/short ton)[6]											
Industrial	32.90	32.41	30.46	30.14	29.86	29.55	28.53	27.40	26.15	24.96	−1.1
Coke plants	48.24	47.36	46.41	45.89	45.37	45.01	43.61	41.98	40.16	38.74	−0.9
Electric generators											
1997 dollars/short ton	26.96	26.16	25.25	24.88	24.47	24.20	23.21	21.66	20.03	18.77	−1.4
1997 dollars/million Btu[7]	1.31	1.27	1.23	1.21	1.19	1.18	1.14	1.06	0.99	0.93	−1.3
Average	28.05	27.20	26.20	25.82	25.39	25.08	24.04	22.46	20.80	19.49	−1.4
Exports[8]	41.54	40.55	39.38	38.83	38.32	37.90	36.58	35.15	33.38	31.90	−1.0

[1] Compound annual rate.
[2] Includes anthracite, bituminous coal, lignite, and waste coal.
[3] Production plus net imports and net storage withdrawals.
[4] Includes consumption by cogenerators.
[5] Includes all electric power generators except cogenerators.
[6] Sectoral prices weighted by consumption tonnage; weighted average excludes residential/commercial prices and export (f.a.s.) prices.
[7] Btu = British thermal unit.
[8] F.a.s. = price at U.S. port of exit.
Note: Totals may not equal sum of components due to independent rounding.
Source: U.S. Department of Energy, Energy Information Administration, *Annual Energy Outlook 1999.*

should continue to decline. The mine mouth coal price is the price of coal either at the actual production source or at a nearby preparation plant where some of the impurities are removed. The mine mouth price usually is compared with the delivered price, which is the price at origin plus the cost of transportation to the delivery point, such as an electric power generation plant. Mine mouth coal production costs were reduced $4.97 per ton in 1997 dollars between 1970 and 1997 and are projected to decline 1.5 percent a year, or $5.40 per ton, between 1997 and 2020. The price of coal delivered to electricity generators, which was essentially unchanged between 1970 and 1997, is likely to decline to $18.77 per ton in 2020, a 1.4 percent annual rate of decline.

Gains in coal mine labor productivity result from technological improvements, economies of scale, and better mine design. At the national level, however, average labor productivity also will be influenced by changing regional production shares. Competition from very low sulfur, low-cost western and imported coals is projected to limit the growth of eastern low-sulfur coal mining. Western low-sulfur coal has been used successfully in most regions except New England and the mid-Atlantic states, and its penetration of eastern markets is projected to increase, according to a DOE forecast.

In the eastern or Appalachian region, extensive reserves of higher-sulfur coal are situated in moderately thick seams (or geologic layers) that are well suited to longwall mining, a highly mechanized means of slicing through coal seams, versus more labor-intensive methods. Maturing technologies for extracting and hauling high coal volumes in both surface and underground mining indicate that further reductions in mining costs are likely. The use of air pollution credits within the framework of the Clean Air Act could extend the competitive position of some high-sulfur coal mines, according to an analysis by Merrill Lynch. (Credits accrue to power generators that reduce power plant pollution more than is required. Those credits can be applied to other power facilities within a utility's system or can be sold or traded to other utilities.) Improvements in labor productivity in coal mining have been and are expected to remain the key to lower extraction costs. As labor productivity improved between 1970 and 1997, the number of miners fell 2.1 percent a year. With improvements continuing through 2020, a further decline in the number of miners of 1.3 percent a year is projected. The share of wages in mine mouth coal prices, which fell from 31 percent to 17 percent between 1970 and 1997, is projected to decline to 15 percent by 2020, according to a DOE analysis.

Using projections of significant increases in productivity of 2.3 percent per year and assuming that wage rates are held constant in 1997 dollars, the national mine mouth coal price should decline 1.5 percent a year to reach $12.74 per ton in 2020. Assuming a potentially even lower-cost case in which productivity increases 3.8 percent a year and real wages decline 0.5 percent a year, the mine mouth price will decline to $10.42 per ton in 2020, according to a DOE forecast. However, if productivity gains are much more modest, on the order of only 1.2 percent a year, and are accompanied by an increase in real wages of 0.5 percent per year, the average mine mouth price of coal will still decline 0.8 percent a year to $14.94 per ton in 2020.

Thus, one of the "high cards" held by coal in the energy game appears to be an extremely competitive cost structure with enduring reductions in costs and gains in productivity.

Average U.S. labor productivity follows the trend for eastern mines most closely, because eastern mining is more labor-intensive than is western mining. The mines of the northern Great Plains, with thick seams and low overburden ratios, have had higher labor productivity than other coal fields, and that advantage is anticipated to continue for the next two decades.

Transportation

No matter how productive the U.S. coal industry becomes in extracting coal from the mine and no matter how attractive mine mouth prices may be, coal customers must incur the transportation costs of moving coal from mines to power stations or industrial facilities. The competition between coal and other fuels and among mining regions is influenced by coal transportation costs. However, as with coal itself, railroad operations should become less costly in the future and the cost of service to railroad customers is likely to be reflected in rates that will keep the total costs of obtaining coal competitive with those of other fuels.

It is expected that average coal transportation rates will decline 1.1 percent a year between 1997 and 2020. There appears to be a symbiotic relationship between the most efficient coal mines and railroad service. The DOE contends that railroads are likely to invest in routes that serve the most efficient coal mines, since the low mine mouth cost of coal probably will yield high demand for that coal and generate high volumes of rail traffic. Railroad investment in those lines yields the most cost-effective service and higher rates of transport productivity, and thus, the assumption goes, attractive rail rates for customers. This in turn contributes to an attractive "delivered" price for coal. Therefore, the coal fields that are most successful in improving productivity and lowering mine mouth prices are likely to obtain the lowest transportation rates and consequently the largest markets at competitive delivered prices.

Expansion of the national market for Powder River Basin coal slowed in 1996 and 1997 as a result of rail service problems after the Union Pacific–Southern Pacific railroad merger. Many Gulf Coast and midwest consumers had problems maintaining coal stocks as the frequency and predictability of unit train coal deliveries deteriorated. Improvements in 1998 indicate that service efficiency returned to premerger levels and even improved. Activities resulting from other mergers, such as the current integration of Conrail within Norfolk Southern and CSX, may cause similar short-term problems, but one forecast projects that rail rates for coal will continue their historic decline in real terms.

Role of Exports

U.S. coal exports are expected to grow, although at quite modest rates, from 84 million tons in 1997 to 93 million tons in 2020, primarily as a result of higher demand for steam coal imports in Asia. Exports of metallurgical coal in 2020 probably will be lower than the 1997 level. Worldwide trade in metallurgical coal is expected to decline slightly as a result of generally slow growth in steel production and improved steelmaking efficiency, but the U.S. market share should remain unchanged. U.S. steam coal exports to Europe are likely to increase from 13 million tons in 1997 to 20 million tons in 2020, a 1.9 percent annual growth rate. Europe's steam coal imports could increase from 119 million tons in 1997 to 135 million tons in 2020, an increase of 0.5 percent a year, reflecting reduced subsidies for domestic coal production as well as some new generating capacity. The DOE forecast for European imports is lower than some that have been provided by the governments of the importing nations, where environmental considerations, including emerging carbon emissions issues, limit fuel choices. The International Energy Agency (IEA) expects a slight decline in European coal imports over the next 20 years. While the United States may gain market share in Europe as a result of sharp declines in the indigenous production of coal in European countries, simply holding on to market share in Europe will be considered a significant achievement for U.S. coal exporters. Trade patterns in 1998 for the coal industry are shown in Table 2-2.

U.S. coal exports to Asia are likely to increase 1.6 percent a year, rising from 14 million tons in 1997 to 20 million tons in 2020 as metallurgical exports fall 1.5 percent and steam coal exports rise 3.8 percent annually. Asian imports of coal from all sources should increase 1.6 percent a year, rising from 274 million tons in 1997 to 394 million tons in 2020 as Pacific Rim nations without indigenous fossil fuel resources base electricity generation on imported coal, according to the DOE forecast, which adds that most of the growth in Asian imports is projected to be supplied by Australia, South Africa, China, and Indonesia.

Consolidation of the U.S. Coal Industry

In the future, the U.S. coal industry is likely to continue the recent trend toward consolidation of major producers. In 1997, there were approximately 1,828 coal mines in the United States, but 68 mines produced 571.7 million tons of coal, just over half of total U.S. production. The top 13 producing mines had out-

TABLE 2-2: U.S. Trade Patterns in Coal Mining[1] in 1998
(millions of dollars; percent)

Exports			Imports		
Region[2]	Value[3]	Share, %	Region[2]	Value[3]	Share, %
NAFTA	662	22	NAFTA	43	15
Latin America	306	10	Latin America	185	66
Western Europe	1,371	45	Western Europe	2	1
Japan/Chinese Economic Area	354	12	Japan/Chinese Economic Area	0	0
Other Asia	110	4	Other Asia	45	16
Rest of world	232	8	Rest of world	6	2
World	3,036	100	World	281	100
Top Five Countries	Value	Share, %	Top Five Countries	Value	Share, %
Canada	602	20	Colombia	109	39
Japan	298	10	Venezuela	76	27
Brazil	278	9	Indonesia	45	16
Italy	247	8	Canada	43	15
United Kingdom	232	8	Australia	3	1

[1] SIC 12.
[2] For definitions of regional groupings, see "Getting the Most Out of *Outlook 2000.*"
[3] Values may not sum to total due to rounding.
Source: U.S. Department of Commerce, Bureau of the Census.

put rates ranging from 10 million tons to 37 million tons. The largest U.S. coal mine in terms of output was the Black Thunder mine in Wyoming's Powder River Basin with 37.7 million tons of production in 1997, the latest year with available full year compilations.

Not only will there be continued movement to fewer but larger coal mining complexes in the United States, it is expected that there will be a continuation of the trend toward fewer but larger producers. Again, using data based on 1997 compilations, 57 companies accounted for 83.5 percent of the coal produced in the United States. By midyear 1999, the second largest U.S. coal producer, Cyprus Amax, was no longer producing coal in the United States, having sold its coal units in two segments to two separate owners. Each of the new owners already had affiliations within the coal industry, and one of them, RAG International Gmbh of Germany, which took over Cyprus Amax's large western properties, has coal industry interests in Germany and Australia.

The involvement of Germany's RAG is notable because it marks the second major international venture into the U.S. coal industry in recent years. Kennecott Energy, a major existing coal producer, added to its portfolio in 1997 and 1998 by acquiring other large western U.S. coal mines. Kennecott Energy is a unit of the London-based Rio Tinto Ltd., which has mineral holdings worldwide and is involved in coal production in Australia and Colombia. Another major U.S. coal producer, CONSOL Energy Inc., has been affiliated with an international coal industry player since 1991, when Germany's RWE A.G., through its direct and indirect subsidiaries Rheinbraun A.G. and Rheinbraun U.S.A. Gmbh, became part owners of CONSOL Energy, currently holding more than 60 percent of the U.S. coal producer.

Also in 1999, the oil giant Chevron announced its intention to sell its Pittsburg & Midway coal operation. Negotiations with a possible buyer that already owned another major U.S. coal entity were pending in the third quarter of 1999. Ashland Inc., an oil and chemical company that saw its Ashland Coal unit merge with the independent coal producer Arch Mineral in 1997 to form Arch Coal, announced in 1999 that it was considering the sale of its remaining share of Arch Coal obtained through the merger process. The major U.S. engineering and construction company Fluor Inc. has indicated its willingness to divest its A.T. Massey coal operation.

The Role of Utilities

The shape and character of the U.S. coal production industry are likely to be influenced significantly by the fate of its major customer—in this case the U.S. electric power industry—which is being "deregulated" in a move to instill more competition in the electric power market. Coal is the primary fuel for generating electricity in the United States and will remain so in the future, especially in the new era of deregulated electric utilities, a top executive of one the major U.S. coal producers contends. No other fuel can realistically replace coal over the next several decades as electricity use continues to grow, he noted.

Electric utilities are undergoing great change with federal and state government deregulation of their operations, and that deregulation will do more than transform formerly regulated monopolies into unregulated entrepreneurs, that executive observed. As a result of deregulation, there will be fewer but larger players in electricity, and those players are likely to be more diversified. Many will be global, and they will do business with their customers and vendors in ways that reflect the less regulated nature of business.

"For companies in the coal industry with operational and financial strength, there will be opportunities to form strategic alliances with [electric] generators in which we will be asked to share in the risk in return for a share of the rewards. But there is one thing that won't change. They will still need coal. And they will need more of it every year. Even if they don't build a single new plant in the next ten years, they will use more coal," the executive said.

One reason for this assertion is that existing U.S. coal-fired power plants will be better utilized. In 1998, the average electric power plant capacity utilization factor was 67 percent. However, coal plants can achieve 85 percent on a sustained basis, and existing coal-fired capacity therefore has great value, the coal industry executive noted. Companies that have acquired electric power plants are betting that existing facilities will be among the first to be run, and these new owners will want to maximize output because of the premium paid for those facilities.

"We believe that coal demand could increase about 150 million tons in the next ten years as a result of this increased utilization of existing capacity. In addition to increasing plant utilization, I am convinced that generators will invest in modern pollution control technology for these plants," the coal executive said.

It is likely that coal mining companies also will continue consolidating, he noted. "Fewer but larger and better capitalized companies will produce most of the coal in the United States and will have the ability to invest in technology to drive production and productivity," the executive stated. One major impact of consolidation could be more discipline among producers to adjust the rate of coal production to the natural demand of the marketplace and thus avoid oversupply and uneconomical prices for coal producers. In 1999, there was a spate of coal mine closures as well as temporary shutdowns (or idling) of mines in the midwest and the east. While painful for laid-off workers, these moves are necessary to balance supply with demand, producers contend, underscoring a determination by coal producers to be more disciplined in coal production.

OUTLOOK

In conclusion, despite concerns about the impact of coal on the environment, it appears that the U.S. coal sector will remain a major factor in the energy industry in the near term and possibly in the long run as well. The challenge for individual coal producers will be to serve the market well while making an acceptable profit. As a result of the soft market in the United States in the winter of 1998 and the spring of 1999, even the largest and most efficient U.S. producers struggled to make a profit in 1999. Industry consolidation and continued productivity appear to be the major routes for the surviving producers to profitably exploit the opportunity to be significant and enduring players in the U.S. energy market.

John K. Higgins, Coal Week, (202) 383-2190, October 1999.

REFERENCES

Coal Industry, Caution—Contents under Pressure, April 1999, Shane C. Larson and Daniel A. Rolling, Merrill Lynch & Co., New York. (212) 449-1793.

Coal Week, McGraw-Hill Companies, 1200 G. Street, NW, Suite 1100, Washington, DC 20005. (202) 383-2190.

CONSOL Energy Inc., 1800 Washington Road, Pittsburgh PA 15241-1421. (412) 831-4000. Address by J. Brett Harvey, chairman and chief executive officer, at the Longwall Mining USA conference in September 1999.

National Mining Associaition, 1130 17 Street, Washington, DC 20036. (202) 463-9780. Address by Richard Lawson, president, at the Canadian Conference on Coal, September 1999.

U.S. Department of Energy, Energy Information Administration, various references, including *Annual Energy Outlook, 1999; Coal Industry Annual, 1997; Short Term Energy Outlook September 1999.* National Energy Information Center, Washington, DC 20585. (202) 586-5880.

World Energy Outlook, 1998 edition, International Energy Agency, Paris, IEA/OECD, Publications Service, 2, rue Andre-Pascal, 75775 PARIS CEDEX 16, France.

RELATED CHAPTERS

3: Crude Petroleum and Natural Gas
4: Petroleum Refining
5: Electricity Production and Sales
13: Steel Mill Products
18: Production Machinery
20: Environmental Technologies and Services
53: Water Transportation
54: Railroads

GLOSSARY

Bituminous coal: The most common coal, with moisture content less than 20 percent and a calorific value of 10,500 to 14,000 Btu per pound; typically found in the midwestern United States.

Coke: A hard, dry carbon substance produced by heating coal to a very high temperature in the absence of air; used in the manufacture of iron and steel.

Continuous mining: Underground mining method using a machine that rips or cuts coal from the solid seam and loads it onto conveyors or into shuttle cars for removal from the mine.

Conventional mining: A deep mining method that includes inserting explosives in a coal seam, blasting the seam, and removing the coal onto a conveyor or shuttle car.

Demonstrated reserve base: The portion of the identified resource base that is measured and indicated and published by the Department of Energy.

Identified resources: Measured, indicated, and inferred resources that are published by the Department of Energy and the U.S. Geological Survey.

Lignite coal: A brownish-black coal that contains a high moisture content and volatile matter and has a low heat content, ranging from 6,300 to 8,300 Btu per pound.

Longwall mining: An underground mining method that uses equipment that cuts coal from large faces of coal deposits. Conveyors then remove the coal, and movable hydraulic roof supports collapse the roof evenly once mining from an area is complete. More of the coal can be removed than with more traditional methods that leave pillars to support the ceilings.

Metallurgical coal: Various grades of coal suitable for carbonization to make coke for steel manufacturing.

Mine-mouth price: The price of coal that is sold from the mine and therefore does not include transportation and other consumer costs.

Pulverized coal processes: Processes that use pulverized, powderlike coal and are predominantly found in utilities that burn coal, and are increasingly used in blast furnaces.

Recoverable reserve base: The portion of the demonstrated reserve that is likely to be recovered using standard technologies, taking economics into account, as published by the Department of Energy.

Steam coal: Coal used by electric power plants and industrial steam boilers to produce electricity.

Subbituminous coal: A coal that is ranked between bituminous and lignite.

Total resources: Estimates of both identified resources and undiscovered resources, as published by the Department of Energy and the U.S. Geological Survey.

CRUDE PETROLEUM AND NATURAL GAS
Economic and Trade Trends

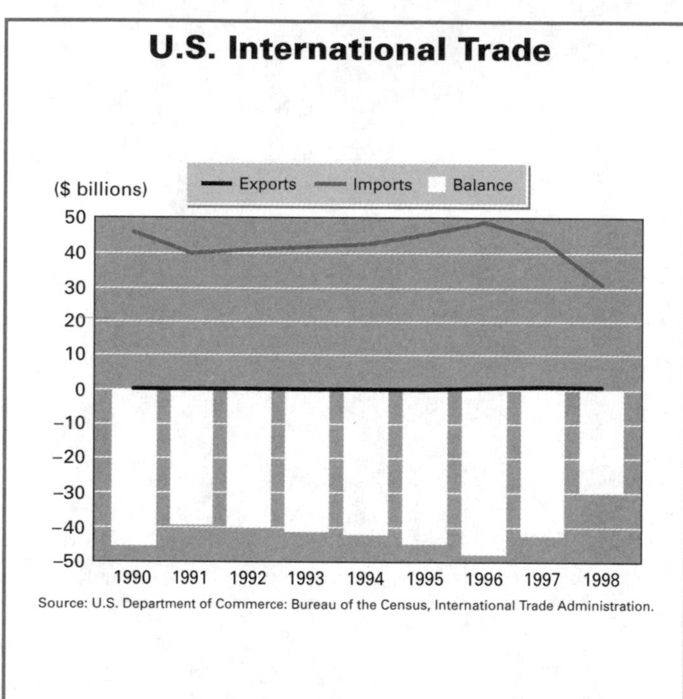

Source: U.S. Department of Commerce: Bureau of the Census, International Trade Administration.

Source: United Nations; U.S. Department of Commerce, International Trade Administration.

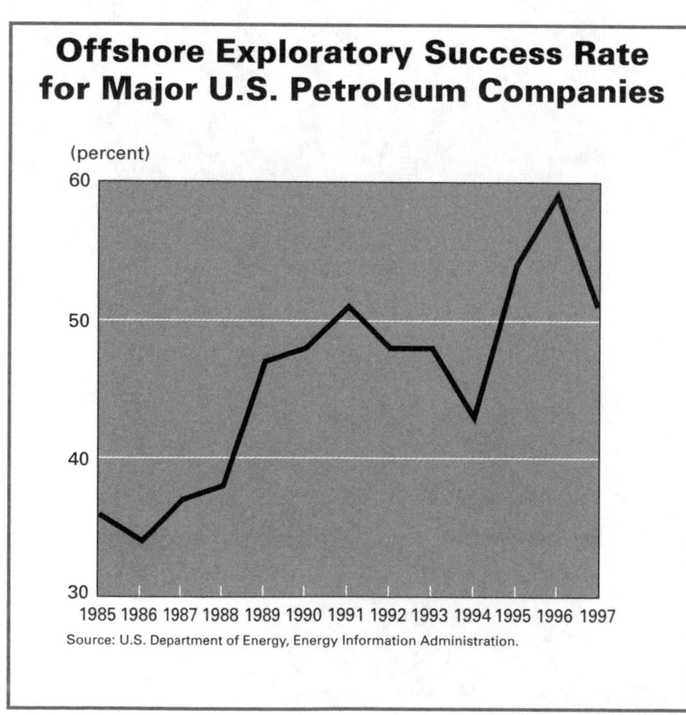

Source: U.S. Department of Energy, Energy Information Administration.

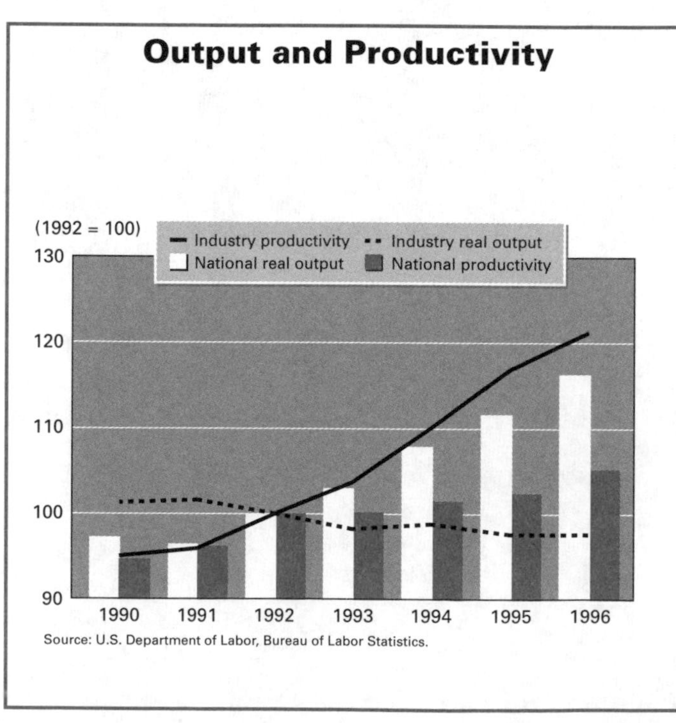

Source: U.S. Department of Labor, Bureau of Labor Statistics.

See "Getting the Most Out of *Outlook 2000*" for definitions of terms.

3

Crude Petroleum and Natural Gas

INDUSTRY DEFINITION The crude oil and natural gas extraction industry (SIC 1311) consists of establishments engaged in operating oil and gas fields. The industry's activities include exploration for crude oil and natural gas; drilling, completing, and equipping wells; operating separators, emulsion breakers, and desilting equipment; and all other activities involved in making crude oil and natural gas marketable up to the point of shipment from the producing property. This industry also includes the mining and extraction of oil from oil shale and oil sands and the production of gas and hydrocarbon liquids through gasification, liquefaction, and pyrolysis of coal at the mine site.

DOMESTIC OPERATIONS

The production of oil in the United States has been declining since 1986, after higher-cost projccts were abandoned in the wake of that year's price collapse. In 1998, the average annual imported crude oil price in real terms was for the first time below that in 1973, the year of the Organization of Petroleum Exporting Countries (OPEC) oil embargo. This low price is one of the major reasons why crude oil production in the United States in 1998 was at its lowest level since the early 1950s. Sustained low crude oil prices led many domestic independent producers to shut in or idle their wells in 1998.

The effects of lower oil prices have been offset in part by the increased productivity of U.S. exploration, development, and production activities, which is reflected in a decline in the cost of producing oil and gas (lifting costs) and, except in the last few years, a decline in the cost of adding reserves (finding costs). Declines in exploration, development, and production costs appear to be due largely to technological advances in the industry. Lifting costs in the United States for the major domestic petroleum companies generally have been declining moderately since 1986. Adjusted for inflation, domestic lifting costs for those companies in 1997 were 38 percent lower than their level in 1986. In the same period, finding costs fell even more: 54 percent. However, between 1995 and 1997, domestic finding costs for the major U.S. petroleum companies increased, especially offshore. It is too early to tell whether this apparent reversal in trend will continue or whether technological advances will lower finding costs over the long run.

Nonmajor Companies Challenge Majors in U.S. Oil and Gas Production

The structure of the petroleum production industry in the United States has been changing. Smaller companies have continued to play a larger role in the development of U.S. oil and gas resources. The share of production from nonmajors (including independent oil and gas producers, pipeline companies, foreign-based companies, and a variety of other companies) generally has been increasing since at least 1986. [For the purpose this analysis, major petroleum companies are defined as the companies reporting to the Energy Information Administration's (EIA) Financial Reporting System, which included 24 large petroleum companies in 1997. Nonmajors are defined as all the other petroleum companies.] Oil production by nonmajors from the lower 48 onshore part of the United States has exceeded that by majors since the early 1990s. These smaller companies tend to drill smaller fields and have faster depletion rates compared with the majors. However, with access to advanced technologies, the smaller companies have been able to reduce their finding costs to levels comparable to those of the majors.

The share of oil and gas produced by nonmajor companies (on a barrel of oil equivalent basis) rose from 44 percent in 1993 to 47 percent in 1997 (based on net ownership, which includes all of a company's fractional ownership shares in oil and gas properties but excludes royalty interests) (see Figure 3-1). Production of oil (crude oil and natural gas liquids) by the major integrated U.S. energy companies generally has declined since 1987. While the major companies' domestic production of gas (dry natural gas) has increased, it has not grown any faster over the past decade than has gas production by the nonmajor companies.

In 1997, the nonmajor companies produced an estimated 44 percent of U.S. oil, up from 39 percent in 1993. Nonmajor companies produced 49 percent of U.S. gas in 1997, the same share they produced in 1993 (see Figures 3-2 and 3-3). Nonmajor companies also have increased their amount and share of U.S. oil and gas reserves in recent years. Nonmajor companies' U.S. oil reserves increased 22 percent between 1994 and 1997. The major companies' U.S. oil reserves fell 6 percent over that period; their domestic oil reserves have fallen every year since 1988. The amount of nonmajor company gas reserves increased 10 percent from 1995 to 1997; the major companies' gas reserves decreased 6 percent over that period. At the end of 1997, the share of U.S. gas reserves held by nonmajor companies was almost as high as their share of gas production; their share of oil reserves, at 38 percent, was less than their share of oil production.

U.S. Oil Production Shares for Majors and Nonmajors by Region

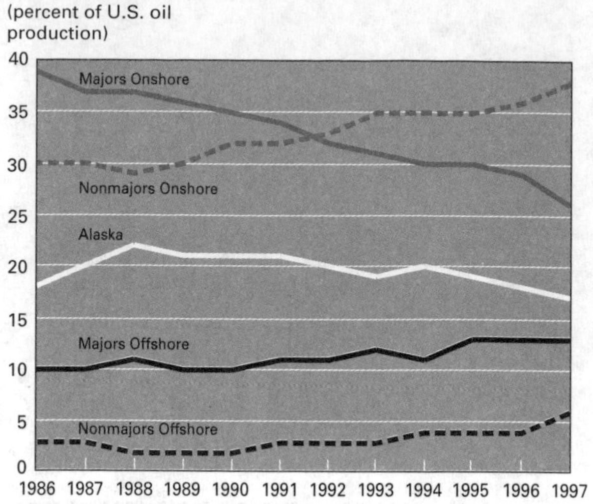

(percent of U.S. oil production)
40
35
30
25
20
15
10
5
0
Majors Onshore
Nonmajors Onshore
Alaska
Majors Offshore
Nonmajors Offshore
1986 1987 1988 1989 1990 1991 1992 1993 1994 1995 1996 1997

Sources: Majors: Financial Analysis Team, Office of Energy Markets and End Use, Energy Information Administration (Financial Reporting System); total United States: Energy Information Administration, *U.S. Crude Oil, Natural Gas, and Natural Gas Liquids Reserves 1997 Annual Report,* DOE/EIA-0216(97), Washington, DC, September 1998, and preceding issues.

FIGURE 3-2

Shares of U.S. Oil and Gas Production on a Net Ownership Basis

(percent)
70
60
50
40
30
Majors
Nonmajors
1986 1987 1988 1989 1990 1991 1992 1993 1994 1995 1996 1997

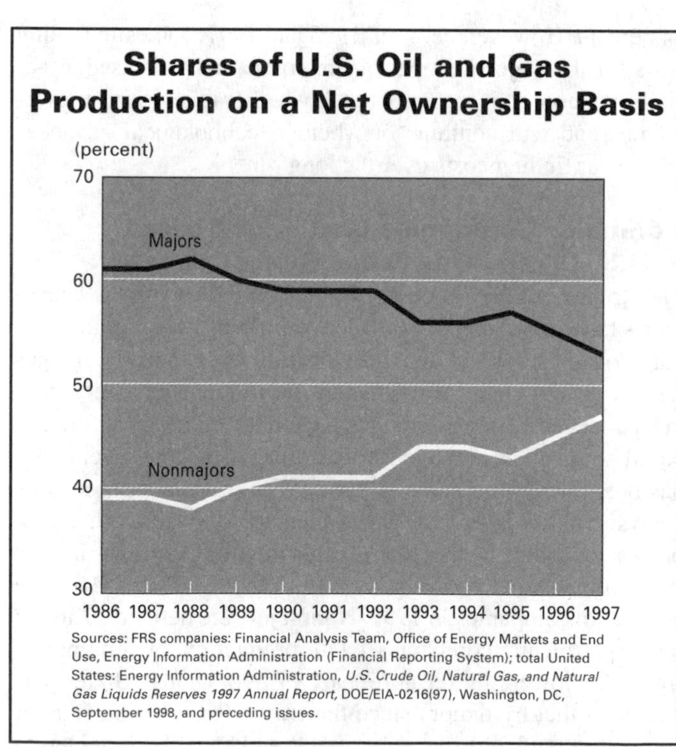

Sources: FRS companies: Financial Analysis Team, Office of Energy Markets and End Use, Energy Information Administration (Financial Reporting System); total United States: Energy Information Administration, *U.S. Crude Oil, Natural Gas, and Natural Gas Liquids Reserves 1997 Annual Report,* DOE/EIA-0216(97), Washington, DC, September 1998, and preceding issues.

FIGURE 3-1

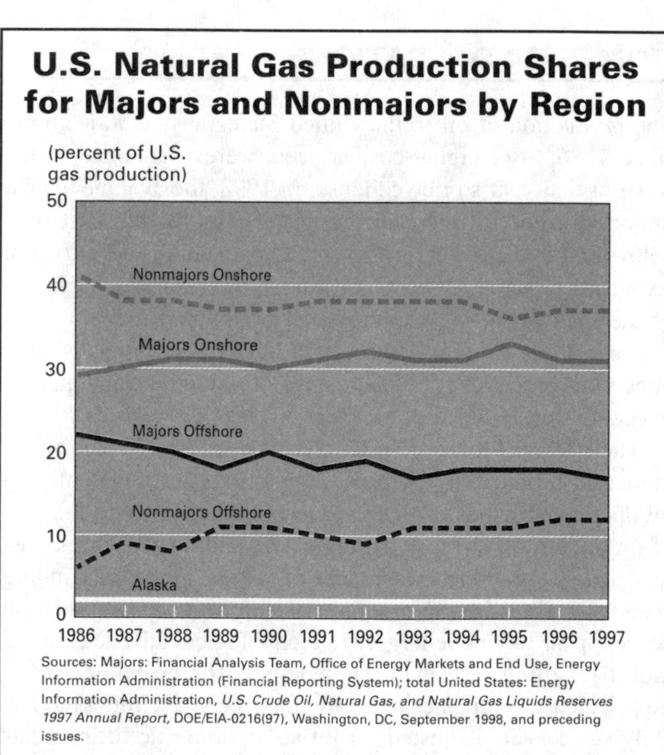

U.S. Natural Gas Production Shares for Majors and Nonmajors by Region

(percent of U.S. gas production)
50
40
30
20
10
0
Nonmajors Onshore
Majors Onshore
Majors Offshore
Nonmajors Offshore
Alaska
1986 1987 1988 1989 1990 1991 1992 1993 1994 1995 1996 1997

Sources: Majors: Financial Analysis Team, Office of Energy Markets and End Use, Energy Information Administration (Financial Reporting System); total United States: Energy Information Administration, *U.S. Crude Oil, Natural Gas, and Natural Gas Liquids Reserves 1997 Annual Report,* DOE/EIA-0216(97), Washington, DC, September 1998, and preceding issues.

FIGURE 3-3

From 1993 through 1997, the nonmajor companies improved their exploration and development results substantially. This was true for oil and gas, both onshore and offshore. Purchases of the major companies' castoff properties are no longer necessary as a strategy to maintain reserve levels (see Figure 3-4). This is not to say that nonmajor companies have ceased all reserve purchases from major companies. Overall, such purchases have continued, especially for additions to oil reserves in the lower 48 states (see Table 3-1).

Domestic Oil Production

Domestic crude oil production peaked in 1970 and generally has been falling since 1986. In 1998, it was at its lowest level since 1950. Historically, low returns on investment in oil and gas production operations account for much of the long-term decline in U.S. exploration and development activity. Despite higher rates of return in the last couple of years, domestic crude oil production has not revived. (In 1996, the rate of return on domestic investment in oil and gas production for the major U.S. petroleum companies exceeded that on foreign investment in production for the first time since 1977, the first year in which these data were collected. Although the gap narrowed in 1997, domestic rates of return again exceeded foreign rates and were the highest rate of return for any line of business for the U.S. majors.) Production (see Table 3-2) still may decline in the near term, in part because of relatively high finding costs and lifting costs in the United States.

The Gulf of Mexico and California are two areas in the United States where crude oil production may increase notably in the next several years. Most of the crude oil reserve additions from new fields and new reservoirs in 1997 occurred in the federal offshore areas of the Gulf of Mexico. In the deepwater part of the gulf, major U.S. operators continue to evaluate and develop large prospects, using the newest deepwater technology. In California, the largest part of the reserve increase in 1997 came from revisions and adjustments in the heavy oil fields of the San Joaquin basin. The application of the continuous-injection steam flood process is expected to increase production and lower per-barrel production costs over the next 3 years in the basin's Kern River Field.

Changes in U.S. Oil and Gas Reserves for Nonmajors, 1993–1997

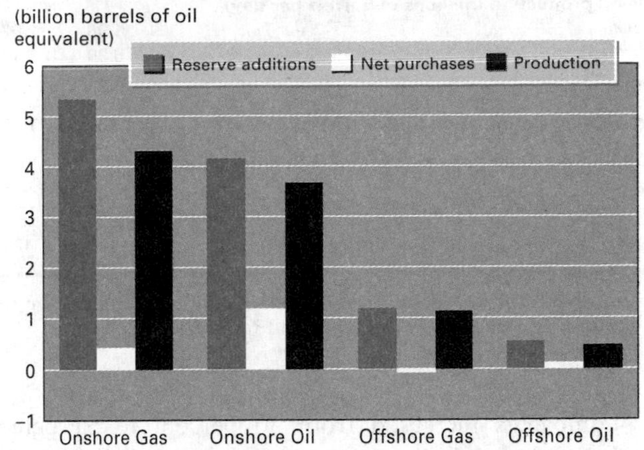

Sources: FRS companies: Financial Analysis Team, Office of Energy Markets and End Use, Energy Information Administration (Financial Reporting System); total United States: Energy Information Administration, *U.S. Crude Oil, Natural Gas, and Natural Gas Liquids Reserves 1997 Annual Report*, DOE/EIA-0216(97), Washington, DC, September 1998, and preceding issues.

FIGURE 3-4

The Role of Seismic Advances in the Gulf of Mexico

The possibility of increased oil production in the Gulf of Mexico is in large part based on advances in seismic technology that have led to a drilling renaissance of vast proportions there. (Other important factors are the high productivity rates of the wells in the deepwater part, recently enacted royalty relief legislation for deepwater production, and advances in production technologies such as the introduction of tension-leg platforms.) As a result of these advances, the percentage of wells drilled in the Gulf where three-dimensional (3-D) technology has been employed increased from 5 percent in 1989 to 80 percent in 1996. Another indicator of the usefulness of 3-D seismology and other improvements in exploration technology is the dramatic increase in the success rate of exploratory wells drilled offshore. Over the period 1985–1997, the offshore exploratory success rate of the major

TABLE 3-1: Petroleum Reserves and Production for Nonmajors, 1994–1997
(million barrels of oil equivalent)

	Onshore		Offshore	
	Liquids	Gas	Liquids	Gas
Beginning of 1994 reserves	7,734	9,900	444	880
Plus reserve additions, 1994–1997	4,157	5,337	535	1,192
Plus net purchases from majors, 1994–1997	1,195	427	118	–9
Minus production, 1994–1997	3,670	4,317	450	1,140
End of 1997 reserves	9,416	11,347	647	924

Note: Components may not sum to total due to rounding.
Sources: Majors: Financial Analysis Team, Office of Energy Markets and End Use, Energy Information Administration (Financial Reporting System); total United States: Energy Information Administration, *U.S. Crude Oil, Natural Gas, and Natural Gas Liquids Reserves 1994*, DOE/EIA-0216(94), Washington, DC, November 1995; Energy Information Administration, *U.S. Crude Oil, Natural Gas, and Natural Gas Liquids Reserves 1995*, DOE/EIA-0216(95), Washington, DC, November 1996; Energy Information Administration, *U.S. Crude Oil, Natural Gas, and Natural Gas Liquids Reserves 1996*, DOE/EIA-0216(96), Washington, DC, November 1997; and *U.S. Crude Oil, Natural Gas, and Natural Gas Liquids Reserves 1997*, DOE/EIA-0216, Washington, DC, December 1998.

TABLE 3-2: U.S. Crude Oil and Natural Gas Production, 1987–1997

	1987	1988	1989	1990	1991	1992	1993	1994	1995	1996	1997
Crude oil production (millions of barrels per day)											
Alaska	1.96	2.02	1.87	1.77	1.80	1.71	1.58	1.56	1.48	1.39	1.30
Lower 48	6.39	6.12	5.74	5.58	5.62	5.46	5.26	5.10	5.08	5.07	5.16
Total	8.35	8.14	7.61	7.36	7.42	7.17	6.85	6.66	6.56	6.46	6.45
Dry natural gas production (trillions of cubic feet)	16.62	17.10	17.31	17.81	17.70	17.84	18.10	18.82	18.60	18.79	18.91
Crude oil production (percent of total U.S. production)											
Alaska	23.5	24.8	24.6	24.0	24.3	23.8	23.1	23.4	22.6	21.6	20.1
Lower 48	76.5	75.2	75.4	76.0	75.7	76.2	76.9	76.6	77.4	78.4	79.9
Total	100	100	100	100	100	100	100	100	100	100	100

Sources: 1986–1996: Energy Information Administration, *Annual Energy Review 1997,* July 1998, Table 5.2 and Table 6.2; 1997: Energy Information Administration, *Monthly Energy Review,* Table 3-2a and Table 4-1.

U.S. companies increased from 36 percent to 51 percent despite the fact that the price of oil, which historically has tended to have a positive influence on the success rate, declined 50 percent in real terms (see Economic and Trade Trends earlier in this chapter).

Through the use of 3-D seismic technology, a geologist can construct a 3-D image of the earth beneath the surface before drilling and thus significantly increase the probability that the drilling will yield sufficient reserves and production rates to warrant development. In addition to the deepwater region, this technology has been indispensable in the exploration of the subsalt play of the gulf. This region spans a vast area south of Louisiana totaling approximately 36,000 square miles that is characterized by tabular salt bodies or salt sheets.

Geologists began to experiment with 3-D seismic technology in the 1970s. However, commercialization of that technology was inhibited by its huge data-processing requirements. Before 1990, the computations associated with processing 3-D seismic data could tie up the largest processors for weeks. New processing algorithms, more powerful workstations, and advances in satellite positioning have dramatically reduced the amount of time required to collect and process the data.

Domestic Natural Gas

Natural gas production in the United States occurs chiefly onshore, but offshore production generally has been increasing its share of the total. The two areas that produce the most natural gas are the Gulf of Mexico and Texas. As was noted previously, drilling in the deepwater parts of the gulf has increased greatly in the last few years; however, in 1997, Texas had the most reserve additions by means of extensions at already discovered reservoirs.

Increases in U.S. natural gas production have lagged behind increases in demand in recent years, leading to increased imports (see Table 3-3). Canada is the source of virtually all U.S. natural gas imports because natural gas is generally cheaper to transport via pipeline, and Canada has an extensive and growing gas pipeline system that is integrated with the U.S. system. Between 1986 and 1996, Canada more than doubled its dry natural gas production, while U.S. production experienced only modest growth. Canada is expected to continue increasing exports of natural gas to the United States in the future. An additional expansion of the trans-Canada pipeline near the end of 1999 and the new Alliance pipeline to the U.S. midwest, which will be completed in the year 2000, are expected to allow for increased imports beginning in that year.

TABLE 3-3: U.S. Net[1] Imports of Energy by Source, 1987–1997

Year	Crude Oil, millions of barrels per day	Petroleum Products, millions of barrels per day	Natural Gas,[2] trillions of cubic feet
1987	4.52	1.39	0.94
1988	4.95	1.63	1.22
1989	5.70	1.50	1.27
1990	5.79	1.38	1.45
1991	5.67	0.96	1.64
1992	5.99	0.94	1.92
1993	6.69	0.93	2.21
1994	6.96	1.09	2.46
1995	7.14	0.75	2.69
1996	7.40	1.10	2.78
1997	8.12	1.04	2.84

[1] Gross imports minus gross exports.
[2] Dry natural gas.
Sources: 1986–1996: Energy Information Administration, *Annual Energy Review 1997,* July 1998, Table 5.1 and Table 6.3; 1997: Energy Information Administration, *Monthly Energy Review,* Table 3-1b and Table 4-3.

Natural gas consumption in the United States is expected to grow over the next few years. Most new electricity generation capacity planned for the next 5 years is expected to be natural gas–fired. There are several reasons that may account for this. New technologies are expected to allow natural gas–fired electricity generation to be as cheap as if not cheaper than coal-fired generation, formerly the lowest-cost fuel for generation. Natural gas has an environmental advantage over coal and crude oil. In addition, gas-fired generation has much lower capital costs, giving it a financial advantage in the uncertain environment surrounding electricity deregulation.

U.S. PETROLEUM COMPANIES' INVESTMENTS ABROAD

In 1997, 4 of the world's 20 largest crude oil producing companies were U.S.-based investor-owned companies, 2 were European-based investor-owned companies (both of which had affiliates among the major U.S. oil companies), and 14 were state-owned. If the planned merger between Exxon and Mobil is completed (no date has been proposed), there will be only 3 U.S.-based companies and 15 state-owned companies in the worldwide top 20.

Nonetheless, opportunities for U.S. multinational petroleum companies to explore, develop, and produce crude oil and natural gas in many areas of the world continue to increase. Since the oil price crash of 1986, the major U.S. petroleum companies have more than doubled their foreign exploration and development spending in nominal terms. Domestic exploration and development expenditures by those companies have not evidenced a similar pattern, but they did increase extraordinarily in 1997, exceeding foreign expenditures again after falling behind in 1995 and 1996 (see Table 3-4). (Some U.S. independent oil and gas companies have overseas oil and gas production operations, but their collective value constitutes a small fraction of the overseas operations of the U.S. majors.) For every year since 1977 except two, Organization for Economic Cooperation and Development (OECD) Europe (primarily the North Sea) has been the leading area for the U.S. majors' foreign exploration and development expenditures, followed by Canada, Asia and the Pacific Rim, and Africa. (The year 1977 is as far back as consistent data are available; the North Sea began producing notable amounts of petroleum after the oil price spike of 1974.)

North Sea. OECD Europe (principally the North Sea) continues to be the largest target of the major U.S. petroleum companies' overseas oil and gas exploration and development spending, accounting for about 39 percent of those expenditures in 1997. While spending by these companies on their upstream North Sea operations should continue to be substantial in the years ahead, that area has exhibited the highest lifting costs and among the highest finding costs of any region in the last few years. These high costs may constrain future exploration and development in the region.

Asia and the Pacific Rim. As is shown in Table 3-4, the "Other Eastern Hemisphere" region (essentially Asia and the Pacific Rim) is one of the two next most important targets of the major U.S. petroleum companies' exploration and development spending, accounting for about 17 percent of total foreign expenditures in 1997. Since 1990, that region has been in second place for foreign expenditures. However, in 1997, foreign expenditures in the region fell by 28 percent, in part because one transaction, Mobil's acquisition of Ampolex Ltd. (Australia), added $1.4 billion to expenditures in 1996. Expenditures in 1997

TABLE 3-4: Domestic and Foreign Petroleum Exploration and Development Expenditures of Major U.S. Energy Companies by Region, 1986–1997, Selected Years
(millions of dollars)

	1986	1989	1994	1995	1996	1997
U.S. exploration and development expenditures						
Onshore	12,496	8,973	7,815	7,695	7,913	13,201
Offshore	4,906	6,016	4,773	4,739	6,719	8,827
Total	17,402	14,989	12,588	12,434	14,632	22,028
Foreign exploration and development expenditures						
Canada	1,125	6,266	1,835	1,899	1,565	1,998
OECD Europe	3,168	3,539	4,439	5,204	5,567	7,052
Former Soviet Union and eastern Europe			297	359	461	628
Africa	1,064	1,024	1,392	2,043	2,793	2,978
Middle East	340	406	445	361	463	643
Other Eastern Hemisphere	1,186	2,284	2,758	2,430	4,132	2,984
Other Western Hemisphere	642	609	743	875	1,637	1,648
Total	7,526	14,128	11,909	13,171	16,618	17,931

Sources: 1986: Energy Information Administration, *Performance Profiles of Major Energy Producers 1986,* DOE/EIA-0206(86), Washington, DC, January 1988, Table B28; 1989: Energy Information Administration, *Performance Profiles of Major Energy Producers 1989,* DOE/EIA-0206(89), Washington, DC, January 1988, Table 55; 1994–1997: Energy Information Administration, *Performance Profiles of Major Energy Producers 1997,* DOE/EIA-0206(97), Washington, DC, January 1999, Table B16.

also may have been reduced in part as a response to the Asian economic crisis, especially for liquefied natural gas projects.

Africa. The U.S. majors' spending for exploration and development in Africa was about the same as that in Asia and the Pacific Rim in 1997. In the earlier part of the 1990s, expenditures by the majors in this region rose from forth to third place. U.S. majors' African exploration and development spending more than doubled between 1994 and 1996 while increasing just 7 percent in 1997. At least two countries in Africa have recently opened their upstream petroleum assets to foreign investment: Algeria and Angola. Part of the motivation for both countries is to encourage new investments that involve advanced technologies.

Latin America. Exploration and development expenditures by the U.S. majors in 1997 in the "Other Western Hemisphere" region shown in Table 3-4 (principally Latin America) maintained their 1996 level, an increase of 87 percent from 1995. Petroleum assets in Latin America have been privatized as part of recent free market economic reforms. The extent of those reforms has varied among countries. For example, Argentina has privatized its formerly state-owned petroleum company completely, while Mexico (Latin America's second largest crude oil producer) has given more latitude to foreign investors in the petrochemical industry but has largely maintained its state-owned monopoly in petroleum. For a discussion of reforms in the largest crude oil producing country in Latin America, Venezuela, see "Venezuela Offers Full Market Value to Encourage Foreign Investment in Oil," http://www.eia.doe.gov/emeu/finance/usi&to/ upstream/ venezuela.html.

Canada. In 1997, Canada was a leader in the worldwide upswing in developmental drilling. One of the factors contributing to this increase was the ongoing rise in the exportation of natural gas from Canada to the United States. Several major U.S. petroleum companies have played a role in this increase. Enron is actively developing gas fields in Alberta, Manitoba, and Saskatchewan. At the end of 1997, Mobil made its first shipment of oil from the vast Hibernia field in eastern Canada, off the coast of Newfoundland. Hibernia could prove to be the largest North American project since the development of the Prudhoe Bay, Alaska, deposits. Mobil also reported continued progress in the development of the enormous gas fields in the Sable Island area, 125 miles off the coast of Nova Scotia. Unocal has received government approval to expand its natural gas storage facilities at Aitken Creek in British Columbia, and Exxon has heavy oil projects in Cold Lake, Alberta.

Former Soviet Union and Eastern Europe. The breakup of the Soviet Union opened up this area to substantial investment by U.S. companies. However, unlike other parts of the world, that investment started virtually from ground zero less than a decade ago, and it has taken time for U.S. companies to learn how to do business in this region. For example, an official for Texaco said in 1998 that Texaco is "hopeful to get off the ground [sic] in Azerbaijan." Not surprisingly, investment by the U.S. majors in the former Soviet Union and eastern Europe represented less than 4 percent of total foreign petroleum exploration and development expenditures by the U.S. majors in 1997 (see Table 3-4). Other problems plague this region. An undeveloped infrastructure hinders the transportation of produced oil and gas to consumers. Although the Russian government has taken steps in recent years toward privatizing the oil industry and attracting foreign investment to it, federal and regional governments within Russia have continued to impose high taxes on petroleum revenues, have not approved production-sharing agreements that would insulate companies from changes in tax regimes, and have failed to pass laws protecting foreign investments in oil and gas. In addition,

TABLE 3-5: U.S. Trade Patterns in Crude Petroleum and Natural Gas[1] in 1998
(millions of dollars; percent)

Exports			Imports		
Regions[2]	Value[3]	Share, %	Regions[2]	Value[3]	Share, %
NAFTA	518	57	NAFTA	14,570	47
Latin America	1	0	Latin America	4,940	16
Western Europe	1	0	Western Europe	1,144	4
Japan/Chinese Economic Area	279	31	Japan/Chinese Economic Area	60	0
Other Asia	115	13	Other Asia	278	1
Rest of world	0	0	Rest of world	9,820	32
World	913	100	World	30,812	100
Top Five Countries	Value	Share, %	Top Five Countries	Value	Share, %
Canada	487	53	Canada	10,745	35
Japan	167	18	Mexico	3,825	12
South Korea	115	13	Saudi Arabia	3,180	10
China	78	9	Venezuela	3,174	10
Taiwan	34	4	Nigeria	2,288	7

[1] SIC 1311.
[2] For definitions of regional groupings, see "Getting the Most Out of *Outlook 2000.*"
[3] Values may not sum to total due to rounding.
Source: U.S. Department of Commerce, Bureau of the Census.

FORECASTS FOR THE U.S. PETROLEUM AND NATURAL GAS INDUSTRY

Forecasts for energy production, consumption, and supply change frequently in response to current conditions. The Energy Information Administration, an independent statistical and analytical agency of the U.S. Department of Energy, updates its short-term forecasts monthly and its longer-term forecasts in its publications *Annual Energy Outlook* and *International Energy Outlook.* For the latest forecasts of world oil price projections, world oil consumption and production, world natural gas consumption and production, U.S. energy consumption, and U.S. oil and gas production, consumption, and imports, go to http://www.eia.doe.gov and select "forecasts."

recent trouble in the Russian economy has slowed foreign investment there.

U.S. trade patterns in crude petroleum and natural gas in 1998 as determined by the U.S. Department of Commerce, Bureau of the Census, are shown in Table 3-5.

Larry Spancake, U.S. Department of Energy, Energy Information Administration, (202) 586-8597, larry.spancake@eia.doe.gov, June 1999.

■ REFERENCES

Beck, Robert J., and Laura Bell, "OGJ200 Companies Posted Strong Financial Year in 1997," *Oil and Gas Journal,* vol. 96, no. 36, September 7, 1998, p. 56.

Beck, Robert J., and Marilyn Radler, "Government Oil Companies Dominate OGJ100 List of Production Leaders Outside U.S.," *Oil and Gas Journal,* vol. 96, no. 36, September 7, 1998, p. 78.

Bohi, Douglas R., "Changing Productivity in U.S. Petroleum Exploration and Development," *Resources for the Future,* Discussion Paper 98-38, June 1998.

Collett-White, Mike, "Texaco to Ride Oil, Economic Woes in CIS," *Financial Express,* March 4, 1999.

Energy Information Administration, *International Energy Annual 1996,* DOE/EIA-0219(96), Washington, DC, February 1998.

Energy Information Administration, *Oil and Gas Developments in the Early 1990's: An Expanded Role for Independent Producers,* DOE/EIA-0600, Washington, DC, October 1995.

Energy Information Administration, *Performance Profiles of Major Energy Producers 1997,* DOE/EIA-02069(97), Washington, DC, January 1999.

Energy Information Administration, *Privatization and the Globalization of Energy Markets,* DOE/EIA-0609, Washington, DC, October 1996.

Energy Information Administration, *U.S. Crude Oil, Natural Gas, and Natural Gas Liquids Reserves 1996,* DOE/EIA-0216(96), Washington, DC, November 1997.

Energy Information Administration, *U.S. Crude Oil, Natural Gas, and Natural Gas Liquids Reserves 1997,* DOE/EIA-0216, Washington, DC, December 1998.

Energy Information Administration, "The U.S. Petroleum Refining and Gasoline Marketing Industry," June 28, 1999, http://www.eia.doe.gov/emeu/finance/usi&to/downstream/index.html.

Forbes, Kevin, and Ernest Zampelli, "Technology and the Offshore Success Rate," United States Association for Energy Economics, 19th Annual North American Conference, October 1998.

"Trade Groups Pursue Strategies to Provide Hope for Beleaguered Independent Producers," *The Oil Daily,* December 9, 1998, pp. 3–4.

Unocal Corp., "Unocal Canada to Expand Capacity of Aitken Creek Gas Storage Facility," news release, November 5, 1998.

"U.S. E&P Surge Hinges on Technology, Not Oil Prices," *Oil and Gas Journal,* vol. 95, no. 2, January 13, 1997, p. 42.

■ RELATED CHAPTERS

2: Coal Mining

4: Petroleum Refining

5: Electricity Production and Sales

PETROLEUM REFINING
Economic and Trade Trends

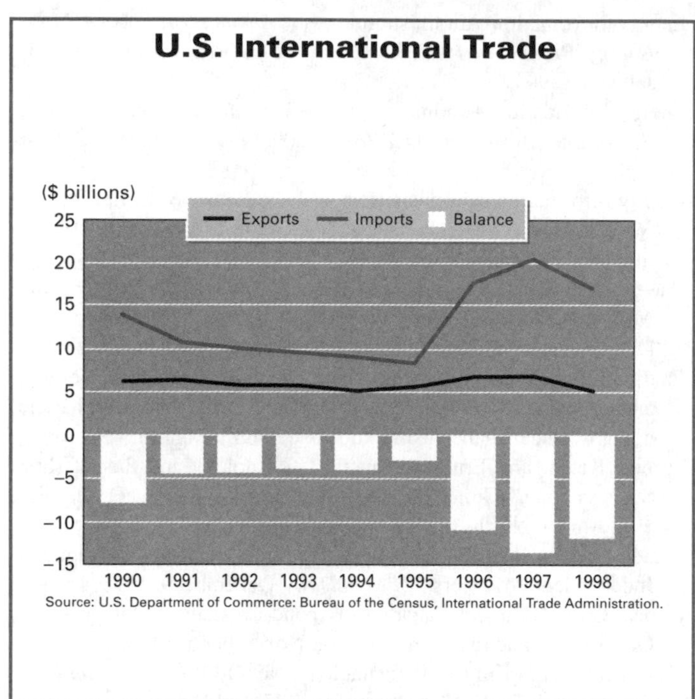

Source: U.S. Department of Commerce: Bureau of the Census, International Trade Administration.

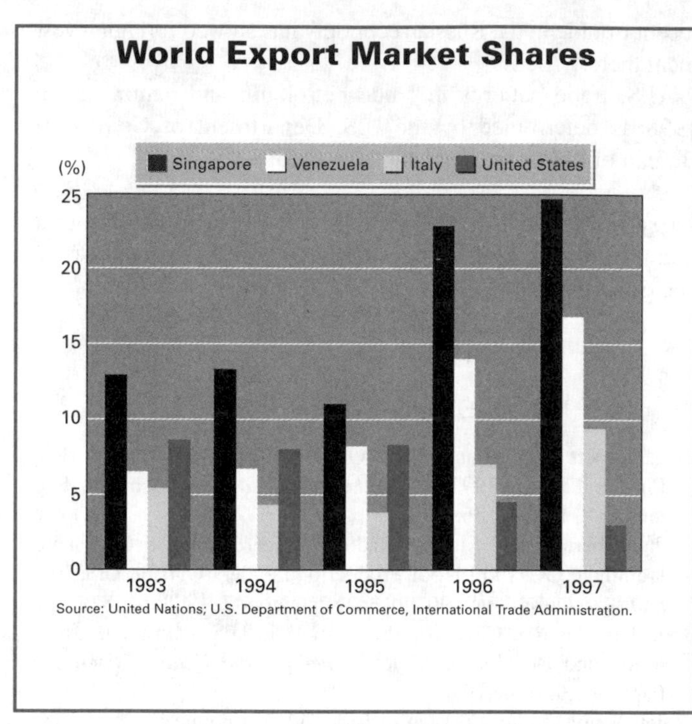

Source: United Nations; U.S. Department of Commerce, International Trade Administration.

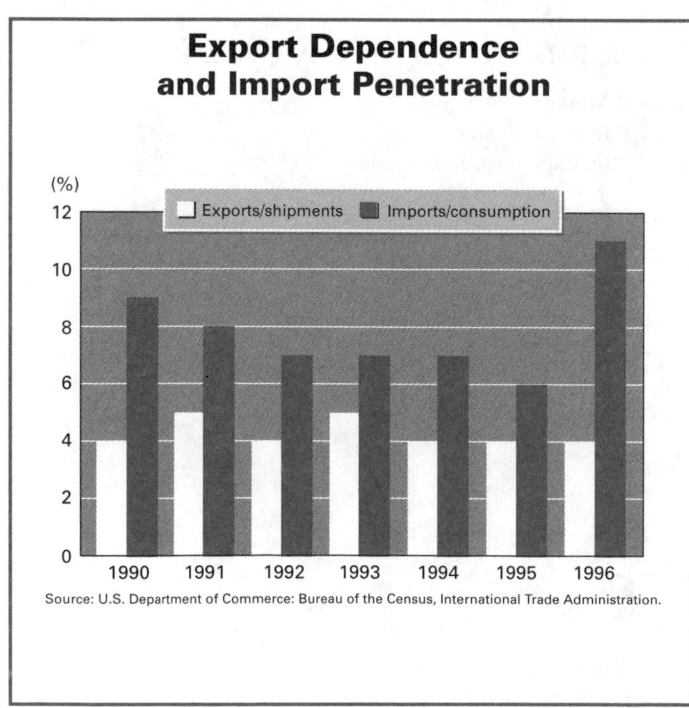

Source: U.S. Department of Commerce: Bureau of the Census, International Trade Administration.

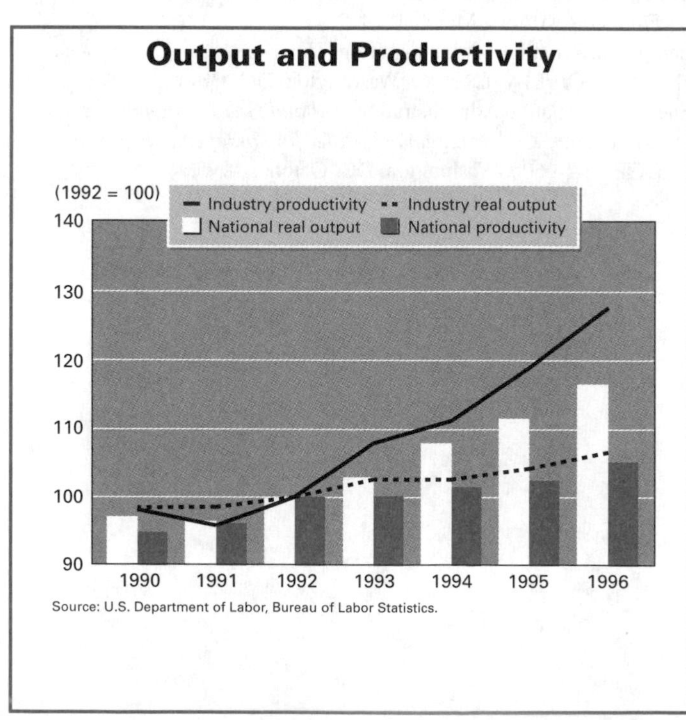

Source: U.S. Department of Labor, Bureau of Labor Statistics.

See "Getting the Most Out of *Outlook 2000*" for definitions of terms.

4

Petroleum Refining

INDUSTRY DEFINITION The petroleum refining industry (SIC 2911) consists of establishments engaged primarily in producing gasoline, kerosene, distillate fuel oils, residual fuel oils, and lubricants through straight distillation of crude oil, redistillation of unfinished petroleum derivatives, cracking, and other processes. Establishments in this industry also produce aliphatic and aromatic chemicals as by-products.

The U.S. petroleum refining and marketing industry was characterized by unusually low product margins, low profitability, selective retrenchment, and substantial restructuring throughout the 1990s. The costs involved in complying with environmental laws grew substantially during that period and affected the profitability of the domestic industry. Profitability (measured by the rate of return on investment) from the refining operations of domestic petroleum companies varied widely even before the 1990s (see Figure 4-1). Consequently, refiners' ability to recoup their investment has been impaired.

However, the profitability of U.S. refining and marketing in 1997 was the highest since 1989, when the return on investment from those operations last exceeded 10 percent (see Figure 4-1). Refiners were able to achieve that high level of profitability in 1997 partly because of events such as lower energy costs and partly because of efforts and developments over the last several years (such as lower marketing costs). Cost cutting through downstream mergers, alliances, and joint ventures also has contributed to the current profitability of downstream operations.

The experience of the majors illustrates financial developments in U.S. petroleum refining and marketing. The average price received by U.S. majors for refined petroleum products fell 4 percent between 1996 and 1997. Motor gasoline prices registered a 1 percent decline, with most of the overall price decline in refined products attributable to other products. This pattern of price change reflected the relatively greater growth in demand for transport fuels resulting from generally strong economic growth and a drop in demand for heating fuels caused by mild winter weather in 1997.

In total, the U.S. majors more than survived these price reductions and the resulting reduction in their revenues because their costs for purchased materials and products (mainly crude oil costs) fell more than did refined product prices overall. Consequently, gross margins (refined product revenues minus raw material and product purchases divided by refined product sales volume) were substantially higher in 1997 than in 1996 and were the highest since 1992 after adjusting for inflation.

Although gross margins were at their highest level since 1992, the primary reason why net refined product margins (petroleum product revenues minus all out-of-pocket refining

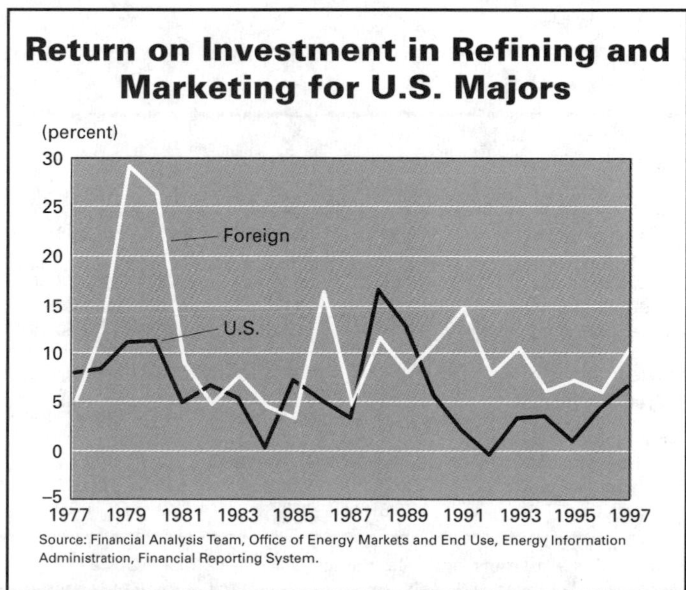

Source: Financial Analysis Team, Office of Energy Markets and End Use, Energy Information Administration, Financial Reporting System.

FIGURE 4-1

and marketing expenses divided by refined product sales volume) were so high in 1997 was that majors reduced their operating costs 6 percent between 1996 and 1997. This reduction was part of a longer-term trend.

All categories of operating costs, such as marketing, energy, and other costs to operate refineries, have been reduced since 1990 (see Table 4-1). Marketing costs were reduced 28 percent between 1990 and 1997 and 5 percent between 1996 and 1997. That reduction in marketing costs was due partially to the fact that many U.S. majors divested themselves of their credit card operations and undertook other cost reduction efforts in the 1990s. (This trend continued through 1997, when Texaco reported that it received $13 million for the sale of its credit card operation.) Additionally, the U.S. majors reduced their number of branded outlets by 34 percent over that period, becoming more regional in their approach to marketing, a move that led to reduced expenses.

The U.S. majors reduced energy costs 24 percent between 1990 and 1997 and almost 6 percent between 1996 and 1997. Many of them began to utilize cogeneration to provide at least some of their electricity needs. (For example, in 1997, both Exxon and Phillips mentioned in their annual reports that cogeneration plants had been completed at refineries or were under construction.) Thus, although the gross refined product margin fell 21 percent between 1990 and 1997, the net refined product margin increased almost 1 percent over that period because of the substantial reduction in costs.

Between 1996 and 1997, the average net refined product margin increased almost 70 percent. Although the refined product margin increased for all groups of U.S. majors (ranked by the size of total energy assets), the largest U.S. majors led with an increase of 108 percent. The group of smallest companies closely followed the group of largest companies with an increase of 76 percent. Trailing was the group of midsize companies, which had an increase of 33 percent.

UPGRADING CAPACITY: SOPHISTICATED REFINERS MAY BUY LOW AND SELL HIGH

Since the late 1970s, the U.S. majors have invested heavily in their refineries in order to utilize heavier, more sulfurous crude oils as inputs. Over that period, the U.S. majors have invested in upgrading their refineries to produce greater proportions of lighter, higher-valued products, particularly motor gasoline. The actual returns on these investments not only depend on the levels of input and product prices but also can be strongly affected by the differences in prices of light versus heavy petroleum products and high- versus low-quality crude oils.

A refinery with a large capital investment directed toward processing lower-quality crude oils will do better financially than will less versatile refineries when the difference in price between high-quality crude oils and low-quality crude oils is large. In recent years, the U.S. majors have made numerous upgrades that have enabled them to process relatively lower-quality crude oil. In 1996 and 1997, the spread between high-quality and low-quality crude oil increased, reversing a 5-year trend (see Figure 4-2). The majors' upgraded refinery capacity contributed significantly to their 1997 profitability.

Those upgrades also resulted in proportionately more valuable light products as well as greater quantities through the addition of downstream processing units such as catalytic cracking and catalytic reforming units. A refinery that has been upgraded to produce a larger yield of light products will do better than a less sophisticated refinery when the difference between lighter products (e.g., motor gasoline) and heavier products (e.g., residual fuel oil) is large.

In recent years, the difference between the selling price for light products and that for heavier products has increased after narrowing in the early 1990s (see Figure 4-3). Higher-quality products include motor gasoline, jet fuel, and aviation gasoline;

TABLE 4-1: Petroleum Product Refining and Marketing Margins and Production Costs, 1988–1997
(1997 dollars per barrel)

	1988	1989	1990	1991	1992	1993	1994	1995	1996	1997	Percent Change 1996–1997
Gross refining margin	**8.91**	**8.29**	**8.60**	**8.18**	**7.73**	**7.42**	**6.38**	**5.77**	**6.62**	**6.78**	**2.4**
Minus:											
Marketing costs	2.05	2.28	2.45	2.78	3.03	2.38	1.92	1.82	1.86	1.76	–5.2
Energy costs	1.39	1.33	1.36	1.35	1.26	1.28	1.02	0.86	1.09	1.03	–5.5
Other operating costs	3.16	2.83	3.39	3.20	3.01	2.97	2.68	2.57	2.78	2.52	–9.5
Equals:											
Net refining margin	**2.32**	**1.85**	**1.41**	**0.85**	**0.42**	**0.78**	**0.76**	**0.51**	**0.89**	**1.47**	**65.2**
Refined product sales (thousands of barrels per day)	14,868	12,088	14,114	13,015	13,089	13,178	13,455	13,641	14,024	13,294	–5.2
GDP deflator	76.6	79.8	83.3	86.6	89.0	91.3	93.5	95.9	98.0	100.0	

Sources: Costs, margins, and sales: Financial Analysis Team, Office of Energy Markets and End Use, Energy Information Administration, Financial Reporting System; GDP deflator: U.S. Department of Commerce, Bureau of Economic Analysis.

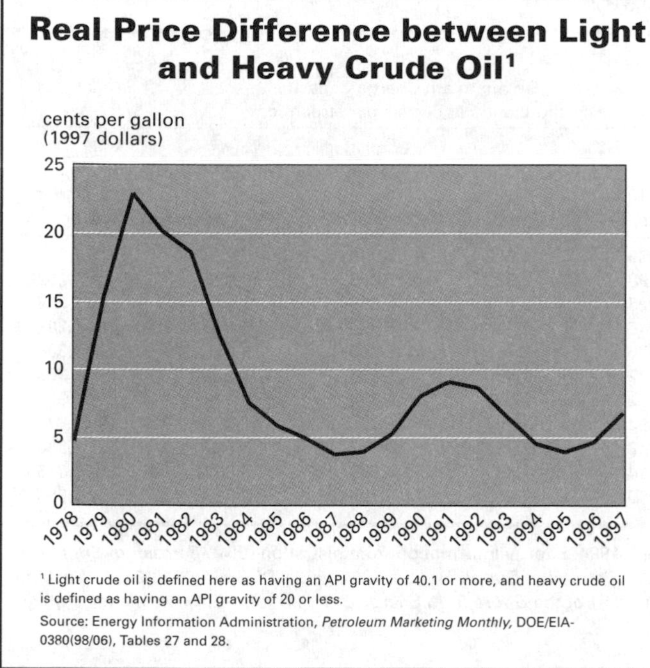

[1] Light crude oil is defined here as having an API gravity of 40.1 or more, and heavy crude oil is defined as having an API gravity of 20 or less.

Source: Energy Information Administration, *Petroleum Marketing Monthly*, DOE/EIA-0380(98/06), Tables 27 and 28.

FIGURE 4-2

lower-quality products are those such as residual fuel oil. The quality cost spread is the difference between the prices of higher-quality (i.e., lighter and sweeter) crude oil and lower-quality (i.e., heavier and more sour) crude oil. The increase in quality price spreads from 1995 to 1997 favored upgraded refineries and contributed to the recent upswing in the profitability of the U.S. majors' U.S. refining and marketing operations.

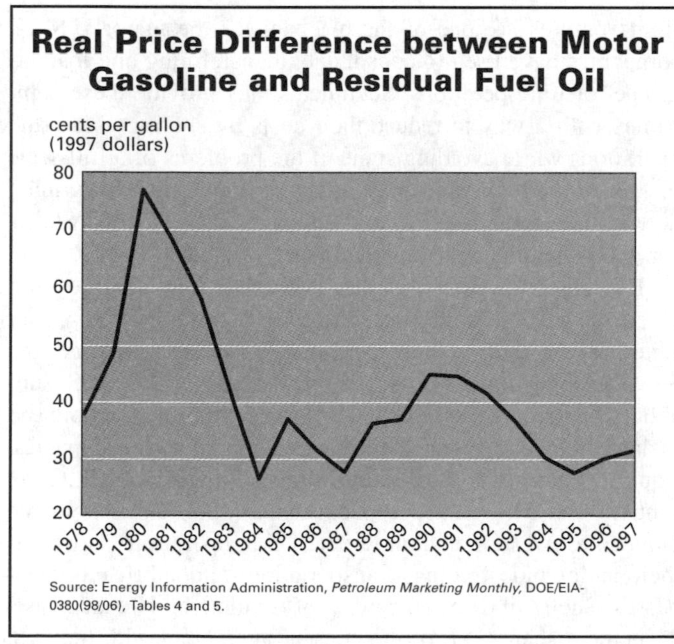

Source: Energy Information Administration, *Petroleum Marketing Monthly*, DOE/EIA-0380(98/06), Tables 4 and 5.

FIGURE 4-3

Further impetus to upgrade the refineries of the U.S. majors has been provided by the creation of joint ventures with several non-U.S. producers of crude oil. Venezuela's Petroleos de Venezuela, S.A. (PdVSA), Mexico's PEMEX, and, more recently, Norway's Statoil have allied themselves with U.S. refiners. For example, Coastal Corporation and PdVSA formed a joint venture to operate Coastal's Corpus Christi refinery. The refinery will process heavy crude produced in Venezuela by the joint venture. Similarly, Phillips Petroleum plans to construct a 58,000-barrel-per-day (b/d) coker unit and related facilities in Venezuela to allow heavy, sour Venezuelan crude to be upgraded (transformed into lighter crude oil). In addition to making a long-term agreement to provide crude oil to their refineries, in some cases crude oil producers have provided a portion of the funding for the refinery upgrades needed to enhance a refiner's ability to manufacture light petroleum products such as motor gasoline, jet fuel, and diesel fuel.

Domestic refinery capacity also has expanded through conventional projects (e.g., adding a catalytic cracking unit) and debottlenecking investments, which are marginal investments in upgrades that increase throughput and thus create additional refining capacity from the same physical structure without making any direct changes to it. Such relatively inexpensive investments in a refinery may result in substantial increases in the capacity of that refinery. The additional capacity gained through debottlenecking is termed "capacity creep." Total U.S. crude oil distillation capacity has increased substantially since 1990 (more than 340,000 b/d) as a result of both conventional investments and debottlenecking investments, even though 41 refineries with more than 1.1 million b/d of crude distillation capacity have been closed (see Table 4-2). As a result, capacity per operating refinery increased 28 percent to 97,060 b/d over the 1990–1998 period.

ENVIRONMENTAL ISSUES AND COSTS

In recent years, refining investment has been driven largely by the environmental requirements of the Clean Air Act Amendments of 1990 (CAAA90). The CAAA90 required a phased reduction in vehicle emissions of regulated pollutants primarily through the use of reformulated gasoline. Phase 1 of CAAA90 required refiners to produce oxygenated gasoline by November 1992. Low-sulfur diesel fuel was required by October 1993. By January 1, 1995, reformulated gasoline (RFG) had to be available. Thus, consistently through the first half of the 1990s, domestic refiners were faced with deadlines for new products that required new capital investment.

Since reaching a 1992 peak of $5.2 billion, domestic refining capital expenditures by the major U.S. oil companies have fallen an average of 15 percent per year, reaching the decade's low point in 1996 at $2.1 billion. Correspondingly, investment related to pollution abatement also peaked in 1992 and then declined, according to information from the American Petroleum Institute.

TABLE 4-2: U.S. Refineries and Refining Capacities, 1987–1997

Year	Operable Refineries, number		Crude Distillation Capacity, thousands of barrels per calendar day		Downstream Charge Capacity, thousands of barrels per stream day					
	Total	Operating	Total	Operating	Total	Vacuum Distillation	Thermal Cracking	Catalytic Cracking (Fresh and Recycled)	Catalytic Reforming	Catalytic Hydrocracking
1987	219	195	15,566	14,940	28,656	6,935	1,928	5,716	3,805	1,189
1988	213	195	15,915	15,018	29,347	7,198	2,080	5,806	3,891	1,202
1989	204	193	15,655	15,012	29,537	7,225	2,073	5,650	3,911	1,238
1990	205	194	15,572	15,063	29,823	7,245	2,108	5,755	3,896	1,282
1991	202	184	15,676	14,959	30,206	7,276	2,158	5,862	3,926	1,308
1992	199	183	15,696	14,966	30,074	7,172	2,100	5,888	3,907	1,363
1993	187	175	15,121	14,777	29,560	6,892	2,082	5,784	3,728	1,397
1994	179	171	15,034	14,704	30,642	6,892	2,107	5,777	3,875	1,376
1995	175	165	15,434	15,081	31,292	7,248	2,123	5,752	3,867	1,386
1996	170	162	15,333	n.a.	31,353	7,314	2,153	5,599	3,852	1,385
1997	164	159	15,452	15,168	31,150	7,349	2,050	5,595	3,727	1,388

Sources: 1987–1993: U.S. Department of Commerce, *1994 U.S. Industrial Outlook,* p. 4–2; 1994: Energy Information Administration (EIA), *Petroleum Supply Annual 1993,* vol. 1, DOE/EIA-0340(93)/1, Washington, DC, June 1994, Table 36; 1995: EIA, *Petroleum Supply Annual 1994,* vol. 1, DOE/EIA-0340(95)/1, Washington, DC, May 1995, Table 41; 1996: EIA, Short-Term Integrated Forecasting System in support of the *Short-Term Energy Outlook;* 1997: EIA, *Petroleum Supply Annual 1996,* vol. 1, DOE/EIA-0340(96)/1, Washington, DC, June 1997.

Nonetheless, compliance with environmental regulations most likely will continue to affect domestic refiners. One recent environmental restriction affecting the U.S. downstream petroleum industry was the December 22, 1998, deadline set for upgrading or replacing underground storage tanks installed at marketing outlets before December 22, 1988. Although the U.S. Environmental Protection Agency (EPA) issued the regulation in 1989, an estimated 20,000 outlets (about 11 percent of total U.S. outlets according to the latest *National Petroleum News* survey) had not completed the necessary work by the deadline. A grace period announced by the EPA just before the deadline led to criticism by some trade associations and created uncertainty concerning the end of the grace period as well as the penalties, if any, that will be assessed for noncompliance.

Two other significant environmental considerations facing U.S. refiners are Phase 2 CAAA90 reformulated motor gasoline requirements and the growing public opposition to the use of methyl tertiary butyl ether (MTBE). To meet Phase 2 RFG requirements, U.S. refiners will incur numerous expenses and will have to make substantial investments.

MTBE is an additive that increases the oxygen content of motor gasoline, causing more complete combustion of the fuel and less pollution. A relatively inexpensive way for petroleum refiners to meet Phase 1 CAAA90 RFG requirements was to blend MTBE into the motor gasoline. In March 1999, California's governor called for a 3-year phase-in of a ban on the use of MTBE and congressional representatives and senators from California and New Jersey have proposed similar federal legislation. If MTBE is banned in California and other states, the effects may be widespread and highly variable. For example, California motor gasoline prices could increase substantially as more costly alternatives to MTBE are utilized, which at least initially will be imported from other regions of the United States, exposing California to production and price variability from those regions.

Another interesting development related to the environment is the announcement of two partnerships between major U.S. oil companies and U.S. auto manufacturers to "develop cleaner and more efficient fuels." The partnerships will focus on producing improved conventional fuels in addition to alternative fuels such as fuel cells and natural gas.

STRUCTURAL CHANGES IN U.S. REFINING

Joint ventures are one of the mechanisms the major U.S. oil companies have used to consolidate their refining and marketing petroleum operations. Such deals may provide these companies with a way to reduce their costs by sharing assets and operations while avoiding some of the problems of a full-scale merger of the two companies involved. (In addition to forming downstream joint ventures and alliances in the United States, some U.S. majors are forming alliances abroad.)

The largest recently completed domestic joint venture combined the U.S. refining and marketing assets of Texaco; Star Enterprise, a joint venture between Texaco and Aramco, the Saudi Arabian state oil company; and Shell Oil, the U.S. subsidiary of Royal Dutch/Shell. The joint venture was announced in late 1996 and resulted in the creation of two companies, Equilon Enterprises L.L.C. and Motiva Enterprises L.L.C., in January and May 1998, respectively. Equilon consists of the companies' western and midwestern U.S. operations as well as their nationwide trading, transportation, and lubricants businesses. Shell Oil owns 56 percent of Equilon, and Texaco has a 44 percent share. Part of the consent agreement with the U.S. Federal Trade Commission reduced Equilon's assets. In particular, Texaco agreed to sell 60 retail outlets in southern California and Hawaii and Shell Oil agreed to sell its Anacortes, WA, refinery (108,200 b/d capacity). Motiva consists of the companies' eastern and Gulf Coast U.S. operations, with the exception of Shell's Deer Park, TX, refinery, which is operated as a joint venture between Shell Oil and the state oil company of Mexico, Petroleos Mexicanos.

The resulting venture has combined assets with a book value of approximately $10 billion. Equilon has seven refineries with a total crude oil distillation capacity of approximately 846,000 b/d and slightly more than 9,000 retail outlets in 32 states. Motiva has four refineries with a total crude oil distillation capacity of 819,000 b/d and almost 14,000 retail outlets in 27 states. Overall, the Texaco-Star-Shell alliance is expected to reduce the aggregate operating costs of those companies by $800 million annually.

On January 1, 1998, USX-Marathon Group, a subsidiary of the USX Corporation, and Ashland Oil, an affiliate of Ashland Inc., merged their downstream assets into a joint venture called Marathon Ashland Petroleum L.L.C. USX-Marathon Group is operating the joint venture and is the majority partner with a controlling interest of 62 percent. The venture has a combined refining capacity of 924,300 b/d and more than 3,000 retail outlets. The joint venture is expected to result in savings of $200 million annually in operating costs.

Other joint ventures are more limited in scope, involving a single refinery with each partner having a 50 percent share of the venture. As with the larger ventures, they are aimed at reducing costs through reducing or eliminating redundancies, reducing logistical costs, or reducing unused capacity.

Amerada Hess and PdVSA, the state oil company of Venezuela, formed a refinery joint venture in 1998. Hess provided its St. Croix, Virgin Islands, 495,000 b/d refinery, receiving $62.5 million in cash and a 10-year note for $562.5 million. A delayed coking unit will be constructed at the refinery. The resulting joint venture company, Hovensa L.L.C., signed a long-term supply contract with PdVSA under which it will receive 155,000 b/d of Venezuelan crude and another 115,000 b/d of heavy Venezuelan crude after the delayed coking unit is completed.

Mobil and Citgo, the wholly owned U.S. affiliate of PdVSA, formed a joint venture in 1997 to operate Mobil's Chalmette, LA, refinery beginning in 1998. Mobil contributed the 159,000 b/d refinery, and PdVSA will contribute at least part of the crude oil processed at the refinery.

Along the same lines, in late 1998, Phillips Petroleum and PdVSA finalized a refinery joint venture involving Phillips's 200,000 b/d Sweeny, TX, refinery. Phillips and PdVSA will each own 50 percent of a $450 million, 58,000 b/d coking unit scheduled to be operational by the end of the year 2000. The unit upgrades the refinery's ability to process heavy crude oil. Additionally, PdVSA will supply as much as 165,000 b/d of heavy Venezuelan crude oil for processing at the refinery.

With the announcement of two megamergers, 1998 was one of the more eventful years in U.S. petroleum history. The first megamerger was the acquisition of the U.S.-based Amoco Corporation by the United Kingdom–based British Petroleum (BP), resulting in the creation of BP Amoco p.l.c., at the time the second-largest oil company in the world behind Royal Dutch/Shell. However, if the second merger, Exxon's acquisition of the Mobil Corporation (both U.S.-based companies), is approved by regulatory authorities, it will result in the creation of world's largest oil company.

The merger of BP and Amoco was approved on December 30, 1998, by the U.S. Federal Trade Commission, subject to a consent agreement. The consent agreement required the sale of nine terminals and 134 retail outlets, mostly in the southeastern United States, and gave 1,600 independent branded outlets the opportunity to change brands if they wish. BP stockholders received ownership of 60 percent of the resulting company, BP Amoco p.l.c. The two companies produced a total of 1.89 million barrels of crude oil and natural gas liquids (3 percent of world production) and 5.66 billion cubic feet of natural gas (7 percent of world production) per day in 1997. Also during that year the merging companies sold 4.5 million barrels per day of petroleum products through 27,200 outlets worldwide, 15,960 of which were in the United States and constituted 9 percent of all domestic motor gasoline retail outlets. The companies reported combined revenues of $108 billion and net income of $7.3 billion from assets valued at $53 billion.

On December 1, 1998, Exxon announced that it had signed a merger agreement with Mobil that would create the world's largest oil company, with $80 billion of assets. The two companies had joint revenues of $203.1 billion in 1997, resulting in net income of $11.8 billion. The companies had worldwide crude oil and natural gas liquids production of 2.5 million barrels (3 percent of world production) and 10.9 billion cubic feet of natural gas production per day (14 percent of world production). Also during 1997, the two companies sold 8.7 million barrels per day of petroleum products through 48,500 motor gasoline retail outlets, 15,900 of which were in the United States and amounted to 9 percent of all domestic motor gasoline retail outlets.

In addition, during 1997 and 1998 substantial mergers occurred between independent refiners and marketers in the United States, and the resulting companies appear to be interested in pursuing joint ventures. For example, in October 1998, the independent refiner and marketer Ultramar Diamond Shamrock (UDS), which acquired Total Petroleum North America in 1997 (including three refineries and more than 2,100 marketing outlets), announced a joint venture with Phillips Petroleum. However, the venture was abandoned in March 1999 when the firms could not reach agreement on the final terms. This effort represented Phillips's second unsuccessful attempt to form a downstream joint venture. In 1996, Phillips's attempt to form a downstream joint venture with DuPont/Conoco was thwarted when the companies were unable to agree on the value of the assets each would contribute to the venture.

Thus, as the 1990s drew to a close, distinctions in downstream petroleum operations between the majors and the independents were substantially less than they had been at the outset of the decade.

CONSOLIDATION OF MARKETING OPERATIONS

Gasoline marketing in the United States has undergone dramatic changes over the last 15 years. The major U.S. oil companies have refocused their marketing operations, narrowing their focus to the regions in which they have had the most success, that is, the greatest profitability or the greatest market share.

The number of states in which the major oil companies operate declined 28 percent from 32 states in 1984 to 23 in 1997. However, that decline is only part of the consolidation story, as the majors now also have substantially fewer branded outlets. Majors' branded outlets fell from 92,344 in 1984 to 33,753 in 1997, a 63 percent decline. The 5 percent average annual decline in the number of majors' branded outlets between 1991 and 1997 was much greater than the 2 percent average annual decline in the total number of U.S. gasoline stations (regardless of ownership) in that period. In other words, as a result of consolidating and refocusing their gasoline marketing efforts, the majors closed gasoline stations at a rate more than twice as fast as the national average.

In contrast to the majors, foreign-owned and independent refining and marketing companies have expanded their scope of operations by acquiring refineries, outlets, or both. For example, Citgo, a wholly owned subsidiary of PdVSA, expanded its operations from 31 states in 1984, just before its 1986 acquisition by PdVSA, to 48 states in 1997, an increase of 55 percent. Similarly, the Connecticut-based Tosco went from retail operations in no states in 1990 (it had only wholesale operations) to 37 states in 1997.

U.S. DOWNSTREAM INDEPENDENTS ACQUIRE NATIONAL PROMINENCE

After a long period of low profitability in the refining and marketing line of business, in the 1990s the U.S. majors began a process of selective refining and marketing divestiture. In 1990, the U.S. majors, including their joint ventures, held 72 percent of U.S. refining capacity. The independent refiner/marketers that pursued acquisition growth strategies in the 1990s (the "fast-growing independent refiners") then held only 8 percent of domestic capacity, with 20 percent being held by all other refiners. By October 1998, the U.S. majors' share of domestic crude distillation capacity had fallen to 54 percent (60 percent including their joint ventures), and the seven fast-growing independent refiners had earned their name by increasing their share to 23 percent, an almost threefold increase. The remaining capacity (18 percent) is still held by all other refiners (see Figure 4-4).

The majors' divestitures of downstream assets created opportunities for smaller, independent U.S. refiner/marketers to acquire domestic refineries and petroleum marketing outlets and move into market areas formerly dominated by the U.S. majors. (For the purposes of this discussion, an independent refiner/marketer is one that has no significant crude oil production.)

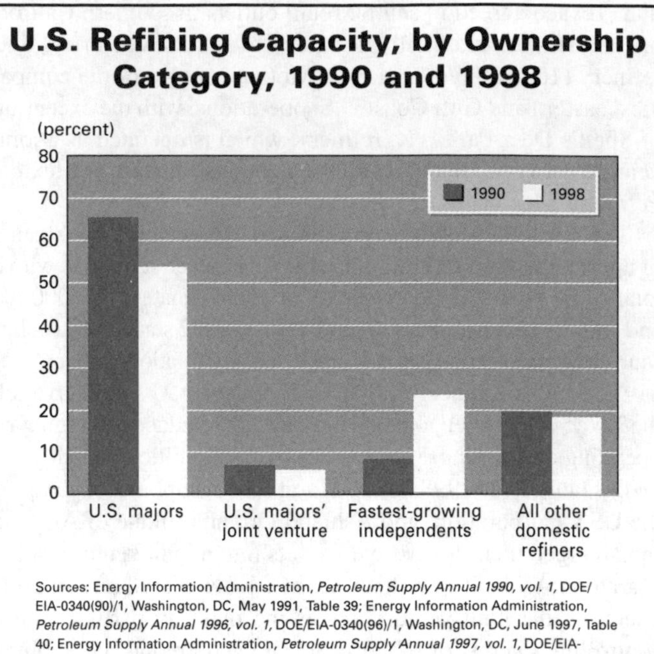

Sources: Energy Information Administration, *Petroleum Supply Annual 1990, vol. 1,* DOE/EIA-0340(90)/1, Washington, DC, May 1991, Table 39; Energy Information Administration, *Petroleum Supply Annual 1996, vol. 1,* DOE/EIA-0340(96)/1, Washington, DC, June 1997, Table 40; Energy Information Administration, *Petroleum Supply Annual 1997, vol. 1,* DOE/EIA-0340(90)/1, Washington, DC, June 1998, Tables 37 and 38; various news sources.

FIGURE 4-4

The first independent to acquire a refinery from a U.S. major was Tosco Corporation, which acquired Exxon's 200,000 b/d Bayway, NJ, refinery in April 1993. Several other independents subsequently pursued a similar strategy of acquisition and growth. As a result, a large amount of the U.S. majors' refining and marketing assets changed hands in the 1990s.

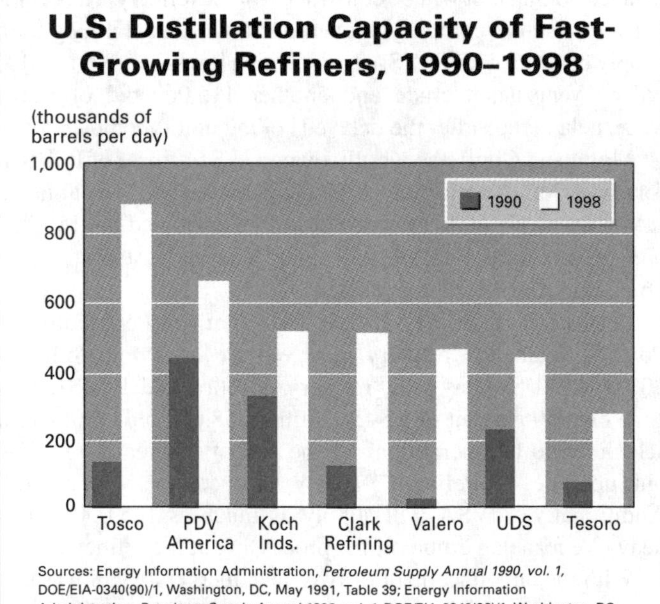

Sources: Energy Information Administration, *Petroleum Supply Annual 1990, vol. 1,* DOE/EIA-0340(90)/1, Washington, DC, May 1991, Table 39; Energy Information Administration, *Petroleum Supply Annual 1996, vol. 1,* DOE/EIA-0340(96)/1, Washington, DC, June 1997, Table 40; Energy Information Administration, *Petroleum Supply Annual 1997, vol. 1,* DOE/EIA-0340(90)1, Washington, DC, June 1998, Tables 37 and 38; various news sources.

FIGURE 4-5

TABLE 4-3: Fast-Growing Independents' Refining Capacity and Acquisitions, 1990 and October 1998
(thousands of barrels per day)

Company	1990 Crude Oil Distillation Capacity	Capacity Additions: Acquisition of U.S. Majors' Refineries	Capacity Additions: Acquisition of Other Refineries	Capacity Additions: Refinery Expansion	October 1998 Crude Oil Distillation Capacity
Tosco	131.9	699.3	0	50.3	881.5
PDV America	435.0	181.7	0	43.0	659.7
Koch Industries	325.0	104.0	0	85.0	514.0
Clark Refining	121.6	346.5	0	41.4	509.5
Valero Energy	25.0	152.0	279.6	4.9	461.5
Ultramar Diamond Shamrock	227.0	0	147.0	64.0	438.0
Tesoro Petroleum	72.0	108.2	95.0	−1.5	273.7
Total	1,337.5	1,591.7	521.6	287.1	3,737.9

Sources: Energy Information Administration, *Petroleum Supply Annual 1990,* vol. 1, DOE/EIA-0340(90)/1, Washington, DC, May 1991, Table 39; Energy Information Administration, *Petroleum Supply Annual 1996,* vol. 1, DOE/EIA-0340(96)/1, Washington, DC, June 1997, Table 40; Energy Information Administration, *Petroleum Supply Annual 1997,* vol. 1, DOE/EIA-0340(97)/1, Washington, DC, June 1998, Tables 37 and 38; various news sources.

The U.S. majors have added some capacity to the refineries that they retained, and other capacity gains have been made by the same independent refiner/marketers that undertook a growth strategy in the 1990s (see Figure 4-5). The seven fastest-growing independents increased their distillation capacity significantly. In 1990, they owned 12 refineries with a combined refining capacity of slightly more than 1.3 million barrels per day. By October 1998, those companies owned a total of 29 refineries with a combined refining capacity of approximately 3.7 million barrels per day.

This near tripling of this group's refining capacity was accomplished largely through acquisition of refining capacity (88 percent), 66 percent of which was acquired from the U.S. majors (see Table 4-3). The rate of refining capacity acquisition in the United States was especially high during 1998; 33 percent of the capacity acquired between 1991 and 1998 was acquired during 1998 alone.

GASOLINE MARKETING OPERATIONS REDISTRIBUTED

Not only has the crude distillation capacity of the fast-growing independent refiners grown markedly since 1990, so has their presence in gasoline retailing, as measured by the number of motor gasoline retail outlets. In contrast to the U.S. majors, the fast-growing independent refiners have expanded their scope of operations, through both acquiring and building new outlets. The number of branded outlets of the fast-growing independent refiners nearly doubled from 1990 to 1997, reaching 25,000 (see Table 4-4). Rather than consolidating the geographic scope of their gasoline marketing networks (the concentration strategy pursued by the majors), the fast-growing independent refiners expanded their scope. For those independent refiners owning gasoline outlets in 1997, the average number of states in which they retailed gasoline increased from 14 states in 1990 to 24 in 1997.

Recent gasoline marketing acquisitions by independents include Tosco, which has added approximately 2,000 outlets (632 from BP and 1,317 from Unocal) since April 1993. Additionally, in 1996, Tosco acquired the Circle K convenience store chain and its 1,900 gasoline outlets. Before that acquisition, Tosco had owned relatively few convenience store operations. Ultramar Diamond Shamrock (UDS) was created in 1996 when Ultramar (with 420 retail outlets in California) merged with Diamond Shamrock (with 1,324 retail outlets in eight midwestern states). Since then, UDS acquired Total Petroleum (with a total of 560 outlets) but failed in attempts to create joint ventures with Petro-Canada in 1998 and Phillips Petroleum in

TABLE 4-4: Branded Retail Outlets of U.S. Majors and Fast-Growing Independent Refiners, 1990 and 1997

Group	Average Number of States with Branded Outlets: 1990	Average Number of States with Branded Outlets: 1997	Number of Branded Outlets: 1990	Number of Branded Outlets: 1997
U.S. majors	28	25	51,085	33,753
Fast-growing independent refiners	14	24	13,117	25,248

Sources: *National Petroleum News* (mid-June 1991), pp. 44–51; *National Petroleum News* (mid-July 1998), pp. 44–52. Used by permission of Adams Business Media.

TABLE 4-5: U.S. Trade Patterns in Petroleum Refining[1] in 1998
(millions of dollars; percent)

Exports			Imports		
Region[2]	Value[3]	Share, %	Region[2]	Value[3]	Share, %
NAFTA	2,251	43	NAFTA	2,635	15
Latin America	1,229	24	Latin America	5,443	32
Western Europe	527	10	Western Europe	2,763	16
Japan/Chinese Economic Area	404	8	Japan/Chinese Economic Area	213	1
Other Asia	323	6	Other Asia	497	3
Rest of world	452	9	Rest of world	5,509	32
World	5,187	100	World	17,060	100
Top Five Countries	Value	Share, %	Top Five Countries	Value	Share, %
Mexico	1,433	28	Venezuela	3,323	19
Canada	818	16	Saudi Arabia	2,039	12
Japan	247	5	Canada	1,830	11
Panama	156	3	Nigeria	1,452	9
Australia	134	3	Mexico	805	5

[1] SIC 2911.
[2] For definitions of regional groupings, see "Getting the Most Out of *Outlook 2000.*"
[3] Values may not sum to total due to rounding.
Source: U.S. Department of Commerce, Bureau of the Census.

1999. Despite those recent setbacks, the significance of UDS and, more generally, the group of fast-growing independent refiner/marketers in the U.S. downstream petroleum industry became greater during the 1990s.

Trade patterns in refined petroleum products in 1998, as determined by the U.S. Department of Commerce, Bureau of the Census, are shown in Table 4-5.

FORECASTS FOR U.S. PETROLEUM REFINING AND GASOLINE MARKETING

Forecasts for petroleum refining and gasoline marketing change frequently in response to current conditions. The Energy Information Administration, an independent statistical and analytic agency of the U.S. Department of Energy, updates its short-term forecasts monthly and its longer-term forecasts on a regular basis. For new data and analysis of this sector, go to http://www.eia.doc.gov and select "forecasts."

Neal C. Davis, U.S. Department of Energy, Energy Information Administration, (202) 586-6581, neal.davis@eia.doe.gov, August 1999.

REFERENCES

American Petroleum Institute, *Petroleum Industry Environmental Performance,* 6th Annual Report, Washington, DC.

British Petroleum, *BP 1997: BP Statistical Review of World Energy,* June 1998.

Coastal Corporation, "Refining, Marketing, and Chemicals," October 25, 1998.

Energy Information Administration, *Annual Energy Review 1997,* DOE/EIA-0384(97), Washington, DC, July 1998.

Energy Information Administration, "Financial Performance: Low Profitability in U.S. Refining and Marketing," November 3, 1997.

Energy Information Administration, "The Impact of Environmental Compliance Costs on U.S. Refining Profitability," November 3, 1997.

Energy Information Administration, *International Energy Annual 1997,* DOE/EIA-0219(97), Washington, DC, April 1999.

Energy Information Administration, *Performance Profiles of Major Energy Producers 1997,* DOE/EIA-0206(97), Washington, DC, January 1999.

Energy Information Administration, *Petroleum Supply Annual 1996,* vol. 1, DOE/EIA-0384(96/1), Washington, DC, June 1997.

Energy Information Administration, *Petroleum Supply Annual 1997,* vol. 1, DOE/EIA-0384(97/1), Washington, DC, June 1998.

Energy Information Administration, *Privatization and Globalization of Energy Markets,* DOE/EIA-0609, Washington, DC, October 1996.

Energy Information Administration, *Short-Term Energy Outlook* (pdf format), April 8, 1999.

Energy Information Administration, "The U.S. Petroleum and Natural Gas Industry," June 28, 1999.

Energy Information Administration, "Why Do Motor Gasoline Prices Vary Regionally? California Case Study," June 9, 1998.

Exxon Corporation, *Annual Report 1997,* Refining and Marketing, October 25, 1998.

Hart's Oxy-Fuel News, Hart's Publishing, Potomac, MD.

Mobil Corporation, *1997 Annual Report.*

National Petroleum News, Adams Business Media, Arlington Heights, IL.

Oil and Gas Journal, Penn Well Publishing Co., Tulsa, OK.

The Oil Daily, Energy Intelligence Group, Washington, DC.

Petroleum Intelligence Weekly, Energy Intelligence Group, New York, NY.

Phillips Petroleum, *1997 Annual Report.*

Shell Oil, *1997 Annual Report.*

Texaco, *1997 Annual Report.*

RELATED CHAPTERS

2: Coal Mining
3: Crude Petroleum and Natural Gas
11: Chemicals and Allied Products

GLOSSARY

Catalytic cracking: uses a catalytic agent to break down the larger, heavier, and more complex hydrocarbon molecules into simpler and lighter molecules; it is a highly effective process for increasing the yield of gasoline from crude oil.

Catalytic reforming: uses controlled heat and pressure with catalysts to rearrange certain hydrocarbon molecules, converting paraffinic and naphthenic hydrocarbons (e.g., low-octane gasoline boiling range fractions) into petrochemical feedstocks and higher-octane stocks that are suitable for blending into finished gasoline.

Downstream: Refers to petroleum refining, marketing, and transportation (e.g., interstate pipelines and tankers).

Gross margin: Refined product revenues minus raw material and product purchases divided by refined product sales volume.

Net margin: The difference between petroleum product revenues and all out-of-pocket refining and marketing expenses per barrel of refined products sold.

Residual fuel oil: The heavier oils that remain after the distillate fuel oils and lighter hydrocarbons are distilled away in refinery operations. Used in commercial and industrial heating and electricity generation and to power ships.

Upstream: Refers to oil and gas exploration, development, and production.

U.S. majors: Major public companies with audited financial statements that have at least 1 percent of U.S. oil, natural gas, or coal reserves or production or refinery crude oil distillation capacity. The companies are selected by the administrator of the Energy Information Administration to submit Form EIA-28 (Financial Reporting System). In 1997, the companies were Amerada Hess Corporation; Amoco Corporation; Anadarko Petroleum, Inc.; Ashland Inc.; Atlantic Richfield Co. (ARCO); BP America, Inc.; Burlington Resources Inc.; Chevron Corporation; Coastal Corporation; DuPont (Conoco); Enron Corporation; Exxon Corporation; Fina, Inc.; Kerr-McGee Corporation; Mobil Corporation; Occidental Petroleum Corporation; Oryx Energy Company; Phillips Petroleum Company; Shell Oil Company; Sonat Inc.; Texaco; Union Pacific Resources; Unocal Corporation; and USX Corporation. A historical list of the respondent companies and the years in which they were respondents can be found at http://www.eia.doe.gov/emeu/perfpro/tab a1.gif.

ELECTRICITY PRODUCTION AND SALES
Economic and Trade Trends

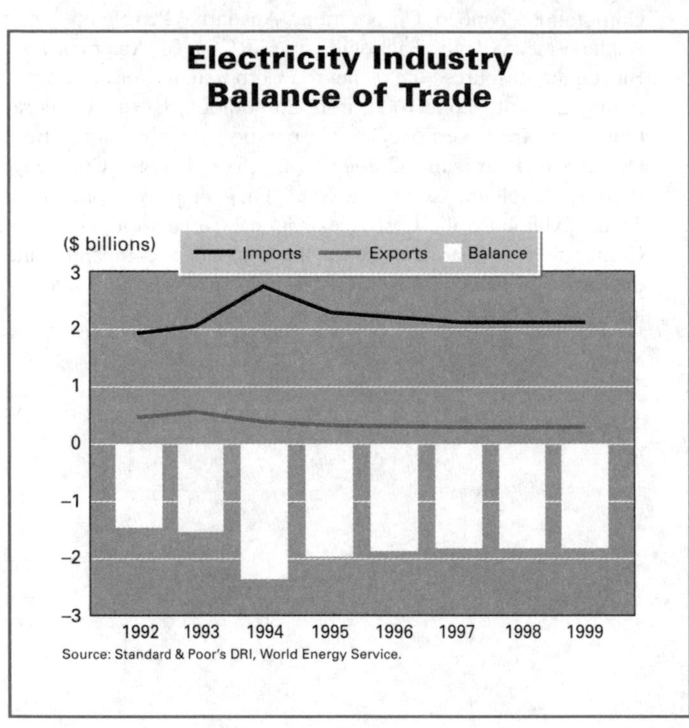

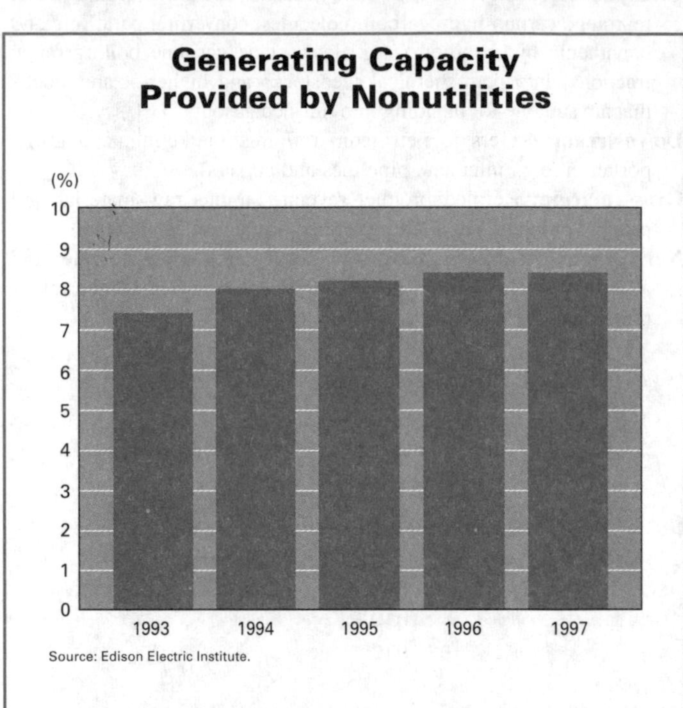

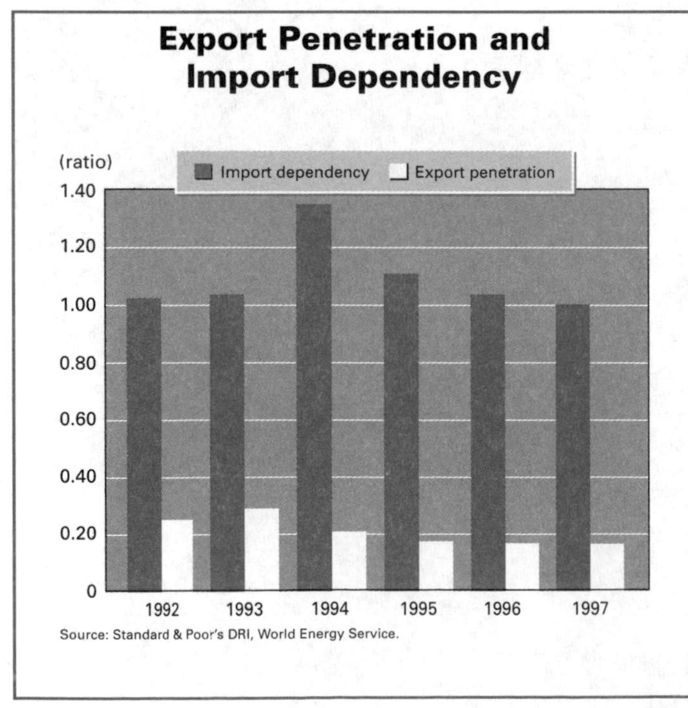

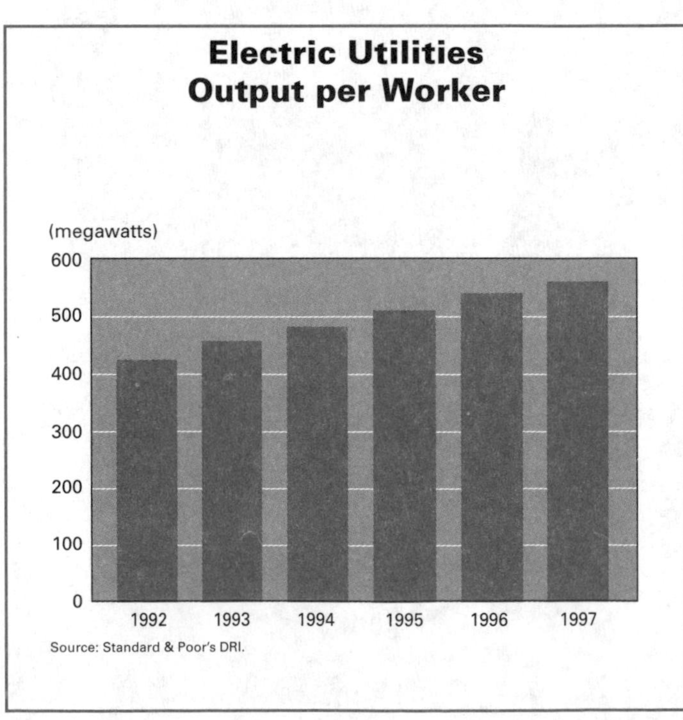

See "Getting the Most Out of *Outlook 2000*" for definitions of terms.

5

Electricity Production and Sales

INDUSTRY DEFINITION The electricity supply industry in the United States is the largest in the world, with approximately one-fourth of global generation capacity and 120 million retail customers. The present industry is still dominated by large vertically integrated utilities and smaller distribution-only utilities, with nonutility power generators and power marketers that act as intermediaries between sellers and buyers of energy playing a lesser role. However, this traditional pattern is changing in some regions as a result of restructuring, which is creating new corporate structures characterized by varying mixtures of unbundled generation, distribution, and marketing units as well as groups specializing in only one or two functions.

Supplying electricity involves numerous commercial and industrial activities, including purchasing fuel, constructing power stations, generating electricity, building and operating transmission and distribution networks, trading bulk electricity, marketing to retail customers, metering retail sites, and operating customers' billing and accounting systems.

Regulated electricity suppliers fall into two categories: investor-owned utilities and publicly owned utilities. Public power, which serves about 24 percent of all retail users in the United States, is subdivided into municipally owned utilities and rural cooperatives. There are also federally owned power generation utilities and systems that supply the wholesale market and some large retail users.

Nonutility power producers fall into several categories, including industrial groups that own on-site generation and cogeneration facilities, small independent power producers and cogenerators that have special "qualifying facility" status, and large-scale independent power producers (IPPs). Companies in the IPP group both develop new power projects and buy existing plants as utilities are forced to divest as a result of restructuring; they are often nonregulated affiliates of large utilities.

Other market participants include power marketers that buy and sell energy, energy brokers that facilitate trades without owning energy, and energy service companies (ESCOs) that sell utility-related services such as conservation upgrades and energy purchasing. Transmission capacity tends to be owned by large utilities that sell in an increasingly active market for third-party wheeling. However, in some regions, management of the grid has been transferred to an independent system operator to ensure open access for all grid users.

GLOBAL INDUSTRY TRENDS

In most countries, formerly dominant models of large, vertically integrated utilities and extensive state ownership of the electricity industry are disappearing as a result of independent power producer (IPP) development, privatization, and deregulation. However, the pace has been different in each region.

Most foreign countries, facing rising power demand, have invited western energy companies to build new generation capacity and sell power to the existing national or regional utilities. This can be done on a build-own-operate basis in which the developer permanently owns the project or on a build-own-transfer basis in which the developer runs the plant for a fixed period to recoup the initial investment and then transfers it to the host government. Developers also may acquire long-term concessions to operate facilities without buying them.

Privatization of state-owned electricity assets in countries such as the United Kingdom has been motivated by the need to break up the national monopoly and shift to private ownership. However, in many cases, local governments are selling assets to raise cash to balance their budgets or attract foreign capital to pay for modernization and expansion of their aging electric systems.

The European Union (EU) as a whole began deregulation in 1999. Currently, about half the EU members—including the United Kingdom, Germany, and the Scandinavian countries—have opened their markets completely, while the others are phasing in deregulation over several years and starting with large industrial users. Most western European countries have privatized their utilities and broken them up into competitive units. Only France appears likely to remain with a monolitic, state-owned power company. However, the pressures of deregulation and price reductions are forcing consolidation of utilities in some European countries, especially Germany and Austria. In others, such as Holland, foreign groups are buying up utilities that are too small to compete in continent-wide markets.

In eastern Europe, the demise of the communist system brought a broad restructuring of national power industries, including the creation of separate generation and distribution groups. IPP development and privatization have moved ahead slowly, with Hungary and Poland ahead of other countries. However, the need to make energy policy reforms in preparation for EU membership has accelerated the shift toward private deregulated market systems and forced the retirement of aging nuclear plants.

In South America, Argentina adopted a United Kingdom (UK)-style pooling system in 1992, setting off a local investment boom. In the later 1990s, Chile and Brazil moved steadily to invite in new power projects, reform market structures, and privatize state-owned generation and distribution companies, setting a pattern for the entire continent. In general, European and U.S. investor interest in the South American energy market has remained strong despite currency fluctuations and other problems because privatization has been widespread, giving the outside groups a chance to build up integrated operations across the region. Some countries, such as Mexico, have resisted privatization while encouraging IPP development, and there has been a local backlash against privatization in Brazil.

In Asia, an IPP development boom in the early and middle 1990s was stifled by the financial crisis of the late 1990s, and many generation projects were canceled or delayed. Also, Asian governments have been less willing to privatize existing generation and distribution operations and move to competitive market systems, making IPP developers more dependent on deals with government-owned utilities.

In the United States, the national wholesale market was opened up by the landmark 1992 Energy Policy Act, which gave buyers and sellers open access to the national transmission system. The push for full retail competition has gained in intensity since that time. Most actions to establish retail choice have occurred at the state level so far, with Congress still debating a national restructuring law that would set a target date and policy framework for action by all the states.

Privatization of the remaining federally owned generation assets in the United States is being debated in the context of deregulation of the generation market, but public power groups, which have priority access to the power generated by federal facilities, oppose any such change.

INDUSTRY RESTRUCTURING ISSUES IN THE UNITED STATES

Restructuring has advanced rapidly at the state level in the last 3 years. A limited number of states with high power costs, led by California, Massachusetts, Rhode Island, Maine, New York, Connecticut, New Jersey, Pennsylvania, and Illinois, have already approved deregulation for the period 1998–2000. Several other states are debating the issue, and some, such as Ohio, Texas, Montana, and Arkansas, already have adopted laws that will initiate retail choice in the 2001–2002 period. States close to a decision on restructuring plans include Maryland, Michigan, and West Virginia, while many states in the southeast and the west have not begun a serious debate of the issue, and some may chose not to restructure at all. In general, state actions on deregulation have been determined by local price conditions and political considerations and are not keyed to federal action, although once a federal law is passed, it could affect states that have not acted already.

In March 1998, the Clinton administration went on record with a plan that would create a "flexible mandate" for states to deregulate by 2003 but would give them the option to decide against retail choice if their state regulators determined that it would not be in the public interest. In 1999, Congress made some progress on deregulation legislation, with the House Commerce Energy Subcommittee marking up a comprehensive plan. However, it remains unlikely that the full Congress will act on the issue in the year 2000.

Regardless of the outcome at the federal level, the trends among state plans are clear. Electricity distribution and transmission are being functionally separated from electricity generation, which is being deregulated, resulting in a new competitive market for energy, which is slowly evolving at the retail level.

TABLE 5-1: Installed Generation Capacity in the United States by Type of Producer
(as of December 31 in each year; megawatts, nameplate)

	1993	1994	1995	1996	1997
Total electric utility	774,689	745,954	750,541	756,481	759,875
Investor-owned	575,163	574,834	578,668	582,214	582,508
Government and public	169,526	171,120	171,874	174,267	177,367
Total nonutility	58,134	65,101	66,416	69,328	70,301
Total	802,823	810,964	816,958	825,809	830,176

Source: Edison Electric Institute.

States are maintaining traditional regulations over electricity distribution and transmission and are using either full divestiture or strict codes of conduct to prevent anticompetitive actions in local retail markets by energy sellers affiliated with distribution companies.

In general, northern states with strong traditions of public utility regulation have ordered utilities to divest generation to eliminate unfair advantage in competitive markets and help establish stranded cost levels. Southern states have tended to let utilities keep generation assets and instead plan to use administrative sanctions to control their market power.

On the basis of Federal Energy Regulatory Commission (FERC) guidelines, states and regions are using nonprofit independent system operators (ISOs) to supervise transmission grids and ensure nondiscriminatory access to those grids by all energy sellers. ISOs have no allegiance or business connection to any market group. FERC also may allow regional grid companies such as one proposed by the energy marketer Entergy, in which the grid owners would operate the system through an independent for-profit subsidiary.

States generally have upheld the principle of stranded cost recovery, in which customers pay for above-market costs of unneeded generation, although some, such as New Hampshire and Pennsylvania, have approved less than full recovery. So far states have worked out the issue through voluntary agreements with utilities, and the legality of charging stranded costs to users has not been tested. Establishing the value of stranded costs also has been a major issue, but asset divestitures have helped defuse this problem by automatically setting values on the basis of the sales prices of the plants. The Clinton administration generally supports the recovery of "prudent" and "verifiable" stranded costs and would give FERC the power to step in if states did not approve such recovery.

As several states have implemented deregulation since 1998, several practical impacts have come into play. In California, stranded cost charges were pegged high and users got little initial saving from deregulation. In reaction to negligible initial rate cuts, many states have ordered utilities to guarantee specific rate cuts of 10 percent and more to users at the time of deregulation and also have required utilities to provide low-cost "standard offer" rate packages for all customers who have not sought competitive supplies.

The second major impact of deregulation was large-scale asset divestitures that totaled 66,000 megawatts (MW) by the end of 1999. In many cases, asset buyers paid well above book value for plants in order to get market access. This helped reduce stranded cost charges for several utilities. Also, the deregulated markets led to a boom in the construction of economical new gas-fired generation capacity that could compete effectively against existing plants and get a market edge.

Industry Participants

There are more than 3,100 electric utilities in the United States, including 243 investor-owned utilities (IOUs), 2,000 publicly owned (mainly municipal) utilities, and about 930 cooperative utilities (see Tables 5-1, 5-2, and 5-3). Municipal utilities are owned by local towns, while co-ops are owned by their customers. All states regulate IOUs, but only some regulate publicly owned utilities and co-ops. IOUs provide distribution service to about 76 percent of all retail customers, with municipals and co-ops accounting for the remaining 24 percent.

TABLE 5-2: Electricity Generation in the United States by Type of Producer
(million kilowatt-hours)

	1993	1994	1995	1996	1997
Total electric utility	2,882,525	2,910,712	2,994,529	3,073,149	3,119,098
Investor-owned	2,271,185	2,308,684	2,340,482	2,372,985	2,385,484
Government and public	611,340	602,028	654,047	700,164	733,623
Total nonutility	327,398	372,015	400,506	400,220	416,648
Total	3,209,922	3,382,727	3,395,034	3,473,369	3,535,746

Source: Edison Electric Institute.

TABLE 5-3: Regulated U.S. Electric Utility Industry, 1997

	IOU	Public[1]	Federal	Co-op	Total
Number of utilities	243	2,010	10	932	3,195
Customers (millions)	91.5	17.5	1	13.2	122.2

[1] Includes municipals, public power districts, state authorities, irrigation districts, and other state organizations.
Source: Edison Electric Institute.

There are also 10 federally owned generation utilities that provide power to wholesale users on a not-for-profit basis. These include the Tennessee Valley Authority, four regional Power Marketing Administrations, and several agencies, such as the U.S. Army Corps of Engineers, that own large hydroelectric projects.

Until the late 1990s, IOUs, public utilities, and co-ops owned more than 90 percent of the installed nameplate generation capacity in the United States, but this is beginning to change as individual states order utilities to divest their generation assets and utilities close uneconomical units because of increased competition but do not build new capacity. Asset divestitures since 1998 have shifted close to 70,000 MW of generation capacity, or about 10 percent of the nation's installed capacity, from regulated utilities and to nonregulated companies. Also, the United States is adding about 15,000 MW a year of new capacity, most of which is nonregulated.

Until the mid-1990s, most nonutility generation capacity was owned by cogeneration and small power producers that had built projects under the guidelines of the 1978 Public Utilities Regulatory Policy Act (PURPA). Such "qualifying facilities" were given special rights to sell power to utilities under protected contracts. However, as competitive wholesale markets developed in the United States in the wake of the 1992 Energy Policy Act, IPPs began to build new "merchant" power plants designed to sell in wholesale markets without long-term contracts or special legal protection. Nonregulated affiliates of utilities also were permitted to participate more freely in this market by a provision in the 1992 act allowing "exempt wholesale generator" (EWG) status for their plants.

As utility asset sales have begun, the existing plants that are being auctioned off have entered the same merchant category, frequently with energy sell-back deals with the utilities that formerly owned those assets (see Table 5-4). These developments have created a new class of large independent generation owners, including both nonregulated affiliates of existing utilities and traditional IPP groups. Such groups also frequently have large-scale energy marketing operations that started up in the mid-1990s for wholesale markets and are expanding to emerging retail markets.

IPP generation and marketing operations are becoming more closely intertwined, frequently coming under the same management in large energy groups. Also, some large generators use tolling arrangements under which outside marketers supply fuel and sell all output from IPP plants, freeing the generator to focus on plant operation.

Utility Mergers and Other Company Combinations

The number of mergers between IOUs increased dramatically in the late 1990s (see Table 5-5) as utilities attempted to form larger groups to enhance their efficiency and prepare for competitive markets. While state and federal authorities have begun to take a harder line against mergers that appear to be anticompetitive, so far most of these deals have been approved (see Table 5-6). A mid-1997 plan to merge American Electric Power with Central and South West broke new ground as the first to join utilities in two separate regions, Texas and Ohio, that have no physical connection. While that plan was still awaiting final approval in late 1999, similar transregional megamergers have been proposed in Pennsylvania and Illinois (PECO and Unicom) and in Colorado and Minnesota (New Centuries Energy and Northern States Power). Also under study is a plan to merge Consolidated Edison in New York with Northeast Utilities in New England to form a dominant utility in the northeast.

Another major trend has been for IOUs to merge with or acquire gas companies (see Table 5-7). This "combined energy" strategy is aimed at deregulated retail markets in which a single market entity can offer users one-stop shopping for a range of fuels and sell British thermal units (Btu) in the most economical package rather than selling specific energy resources. Such mergers have tended to require less antitrust review because of the different market segments of the players, and major 1997 deals between Duke Power and PanEnergy Corp. and between Reliant Energy and Noram were closed rapidly. There are several variations on this approach, such as the deal between Southern Company and Vastar to merge their electricity and gas marketing businesses but not the parent companies. There also has been increased movement by traditional electric utilities to acquire new gas distribution units and provide retail users with both gas and power options.

A new trend in 1999 was the invasion of the U.S. utility market by foreign energy groups, with the UK-based National Grid buying several New England utilities and Scottish Power buying PacifiCorp. Also in 1999, independent power groups in the United States began buying regulated utilities, led by AES, which purchased the Illinois-based CilCorp. to help develop its business in the midwest.

Another key trend that picked up steam in the mid-1990s involved electric utilities diversifying into other service businesses, including energy purchasing and management, energy conservation, telecommunications, and home security. In these cases, utilities are looking for new, nonregulated revenue streams to provide growth once electricity deregulation flattens

TABLE 5-4: Utility Asset Sales in the United States, Nonnuclear and Nuclear, 1997–1999

Nonnuclear utility	Buyer	Capacity, MW	Price, $millions	Status
New England Electric	PG&E Gen	4,000	1,600	Closed 9/98
Cental Maine Power	FPL Group	1,185	846	Closed 4/99
Boston Edison	Sithe Energies	2,000	536	Closed 5/98
EUA	Southern Energy	280	75	Closed 1/99
ComElec	Southern Energy	984	462	Closed 1/99
EUA	NRG Energy	160	55	Closed 1/99
Maine Public Service	Wisconsin PS	92	37	Closed 6/99
PG&E	Duke Energy	2,645	501	Closed 6/98
SoCal Edison	AES	3,556	781	Closed 6/98
SoCal Edison	Dynergy-NRG	1,020	87	Closed 4/98
SoCal Edison	Thermo Ecotek	280	9	Closed 5/98
San Diego G&E	Dynergy NRG	951	356	Closed 12/98
Montana Power	PP&L Global	1,315	745	Closed 12/99
PG&E	Southern Energy	3,065	801	Closed 4/99
GPU, NYSE&G	Edison Mission	1,884	1,800	Closed 3/99
GPU	Sithe Energies	4,117	1,680	Closed 12/99
NYSE&G	AES	1,424	950	Closed 5/99
Bangor Hydro	PP&L Global	89	89	Closed 5/99
United Illuminating	Wisconsin Energy	1,056	272	Closed 4/99
Western Mass.	Con Ed	290	47	Closed 7/99
Conn. P&L	NRG Energy	2,235	460	Closed 12/99
Conn. P&L	NU Gen	1,329	865	Pending
Con Ed	NRG Energy	1,456	505	Closed 6/99
Con Ed	KeySpan	2,168	597	Closed 8/99
Puget Sound	PP&L Global	735	549	Pending
Portland General	PP&L Global	323	163	Pending
Orange & Rockland	Southern Energy	762	345	Closed 7/99
Con Ed	Southern Energy	814	135	Closed 7/99
Niagara Mohawk	NRG Energy	1,360	355	Closed 9/99
Niagara Mohawk	Orion	661	425	Closed 8/99
San Diego G&E	San Diego Port	693	110	Closed 12/98
SoCal Ed	Dynergy/NRG	530	30	Closed 4/98
Orlando	Reliant	619	205	Closed 10/99
Con Ed	Orion	1,855	550	Closed 8/99
Niagara Mohawk/Rochester G&E	NRG	1,700	91	Closed 9/99
PP&L	Wisconsin PS	431	106	Closed 6/99
Duquense Light	Orion	2,614	1,705	Pending
Niagara Mohawk	PSEG Power	400	48	Pending

Nuclear utility (1998–1999)	Buyer	Plant	Capacity, MW	Price, $millions	Status
GPU	AmerGen	TMI-1	916	23	Pending
Boston Ed	Entergy	Pilgrim	690	80	Closed 7/99
Illinova	AmeGen	Clinton	950	20	Pending
Niagara Mohawk	AmerGen	NMP-1	618	72	Pending
Niagara Mohawk/ NYSE&G	AmerGen	NMP-2 (59%)	1,136	91	Pending
GPU	AmerGen	Oyster Creek	619	10	Pending
13 NE utilities	Amergen	Vermont Yankee	504	23	Pending

Source: *Electric Utility Week.*

revenue growth from their core electricity business. A key aim of utilities is to leverage existing retail customer bases, brand names, and distribution networks by providing new products. In some cases, the dynamic is reversed, as in a 1997 bid by the gas and electricity marketer Enron to acquire Portland General Electric to provide a base for developing retail products and pursuing west coast and national energy marketing activities. However, this trend toward diversification showed signs of slowing in mid-1998 as Entergy announced that it would sell several noncore businesses and several companies reined in their power marketing operations.

This expansion of electric utilities into new businesses is occurring at the same time that restructuring at the state level is breaking down the traditional model in which electric utilities are vertically integrated (the same company generates, transmits, and sells power to retail users and charges a bundled rate covering all costs). While some states are forcing total divestiture of electricity generation to create "distribution-only" utilities, others are expected to require only "functional" unbundling, in which utilities will be able to retain all their original upstream and downstream businesses but will have to operate them separately.

The end result has been a general division between nonregulated energy production and marketing functions on one side and regulated energy distribution and services functions on the other side. Utilities are being forced to make key business deci-

TABLE 5-5: Mergers of U.S. Investor owned Electric Utilities, 1994–1999

Company 1	Company 2	New Company	Status
Consolidated Edison	Northeast Utilities		Pending
MCM	Detroit Edison	DTE Energy	Pending
PECO	Unicom		Pending
Carolina P&L	Florida Progress		Pending
Energy East	Central Maine Power		Pending
Green River	Henderson Union	Kenergy	Pending
New Century Energies	Northern States Power	Xcel Energy	Pending
UtiliCorp	St. Joseph L&P		Pending
New England Electric	EUA		Pending
BEC Energy	ComElec	NSTAR	Closed 8/99
Orange & Rockland	Consolidated Edison		Pending
Nevada Power	Sierra Pacific		Pending
Wisconsin Public Service	Upper Peninsula Power		Pending
American Electric Power	Central and South West		Pending
LG&E Energy	KU Energy		Pending
Wisconsin Energy	Edison Sault Electric		Closed 6/98
Ohio Edison	Centerior Energy	First Energy	Pending
Kansas City P&L	Western Resources	Westar Energy	Pending
WPL Holdings	IES Industries	Alliant Energy	Closed 4/98
Allegheny Power	DQE		Canceled 10/98
Atlantic Energy	Delmarva	Connectiv	Closed 3/98
Union Electric	Central Illinois Power	Ameren	Closed 1/98
Baltimore G&E	Potomac Electric Power	Constellation	Canceled 12/97
Public Service Colorado	Southwestern PS	New Century Energies	Closed 8/97
Northern States Power	Wisconsin Energy	Primergy	Rejected 5/97
Washington Water Power	Sierra Pacific Resources	Altus	Canceled 6/96
Midwest Resources	Iowa-Illinois G&E	MidAmerican Energy	Closed 7/95
Cincinnati G&E	PSI Resources	CINergy	Closed 10/94

Source: *Electric Utility Week.*

sions about whether to keep only their regulated business side or remain active in both areas.

Prices and Demand

Restructuring is bringing more competition to the electricity supply industry, and this should lower prices through the action of normal market forces. This downward price trend will be hastened by the introduction of new baseload gas combined-cycle generation technology, which provides extremely low-cost power to replace high-cost output from older fossil fuel and nuclear plants.

After it became clear that the California deregulation plan, which went into effect in March 1998, would provide only minimal up-front rate cuts because of high charges for stranded cost recovery, some states proposed plans that would directly mandate rate cuts of 10 percent or more after stranded cost charges were accounted for to ensure up-front savings for consumers. In Massachusetts, rate cuts of 10 to 20 percent have been assured by allowing utilities to provide a low-cost "standard offer" service for a few years that is based on purchases from groups that have bought their generation assets.

However, in Massachusetts the energy component of the standard offer was set too low at 3.7 cents per kilowatt-hour (kwh) and provided no margin for competitive suppliers. Therefore, a true retail market has not developed in that state and virtually all customers use standard offer supplies. Other states, such as Connecticut, Maine, New Jersey, and Pennsylvania, have reacted to this and set higher energy rates or "shopping credits" in the range of 4 to 6 cents/kwh to attract competitive suppliers to their markets.

Major cost reductions for retail users will tend to take place in states that have retail prices well above the national average of 6.5 cents/kwh and have pushed the hardest for deregulation. Therefore, the first major result of restructuring will be to bring energy prices in those states more in line with those in the rest of the country. A reduction in average rates nationwide should follow, but some states that now have below-average rates are concerned that national restructuring will raise their costs as their cheap supplies flow elsewhere.

With generally lower electricity prices nationwide, consumption will continue to rise steadily, but it is unlikely that there will be a price-related surge in the demand for power, in part because of the major drive over the last 15 years to encourage the use of more energy-efficient appliances, lighting, indus-

TABLE 5-6: Takeovers of U.S. Investor-Owned Utilities by Independent Power Groups and Foreign Utilities

IPP Group	IOU	Status
Dynegy	Illinova	Pending
AES	CILCORP	Closed 9/99
Cal Energy	MidAmerican Energy	Closed 3/99
National Grid (UK)	NEES/EUA	Pending
Scottishpower (UK)	Pacificorp	Closed 12/99

Source: *Electric Utility Week.*

TABLE 5-7: Recent Electricity-Gas Mergers and Acquisitions in the United States

Electric Company	Gas Company	Status	Name
Dominion Resources	Consolidated Natural Gas	Pending	
Keyspan	Eastern Enterprises	Pending	
Energy East	CTG Resources	Pending	
Energy East	Connecticut Energy	Pending	
Energy East	Berkshire Resources	Pending	
El Paso Energy	Sonat Energy	Pending	
Northeast Utilities	Yankee Energy	Pending	
Southern Indiana G&E	Indiana Gas	Pending	Vectren
Carolina P&L	North Carolina NG	Closed 7/99	
Sempra Energy	KN Energy	Canceled 6/99	
NiSource Inc.	Bay State Gas	Closed 2/99	
Enova Corp.	Pacific Enterprises	Closed 7/98	Sempa Energy
Portland General	Enron	Closed 4/98	
Long Island Lighting	Brooklyn Union Gas	Closed 5/98	
Midwest Energy	KN Energy	Closed 4/98	
Western Resources	ONEOK	Closed 12/97	
Houston Industries	NorAm Energy	Closed 8/97	Reliant Energy
PG&E Co.	Valero Energy	Closed 7/97	
Duke Power	Pan Energy Corp.	Closed 7/97	Duke Energy
Puget Sound P&L	Washington Energy	Closed 7/97	Puget Sound
TECO Energy	Lykes Energy Inc.	Closed 6/97	
PacifiCorp	TCP Corp.	Closed 3/97	

Source: *Electric Utility Week.*

trial machinery, and building construction materials. This produced a real demand reduction of about 2 percent, or 30,000 MW, nationwide in 1996.

Since that time, ratepayer-supported energy conservation efforts have been reduced or ended in many states in favor of market-based programs. However, a conservation infrastructure probably will remain in place, and customers will be able to get conservation services from private suppliers or from marketers as part of energy sales packages.

Other factors that are expected to limit demand growth include aging of the population, which implies a declining number of persons per household, and the increasing importance in the economy of services and trade jobs relative to traditional manufacturing jobs. Even though commercial demand for power will grow, these industries are not as energy-intensive as manufacturing is.

GLOBAL INDUSTRY TRENDS OF U.S. COMPANIES

Large U.S.-based IPPs and some nonregulated utility affiliates entered overseas energy markets in the early 1990s after opportunities to initiate new independent projects diminished in the domestic market. Their activities included acquiring privatized assets and developing greenfield projects, often through competitive bidding against other energy groups. That trend intensified in the mid-1990s for several reasons. The international marketplace has expanded exponentially as governments have sold existing generation and distribution companies and have begun to depend totally on foreign developers for the large new projects needed to keep up with rapid growth in domestic demand. At the same time, U.S. utilities stepped up overseas expansion as another way to create a new nonregulated revenue stream and leverage their world-class expertise in the electricity business.

In the mid-1990s, several large American utilities acquired British regional electric utilities and made major acquisitions in South America and Australia. Southern Company led the pack by being the first into the British market in 1995 and then taking over the Hong Kong–based Consolidated Electric Power of Asia in 1997. Other utility-related developers with extensive overseas activities include Edison Mission Energy, CMS Generation, Duke Energy, and NRG Energy.

Among American IPP players, the most successful overseas operator by far is AES, which has amassed a worldwide portfolio of over 20,000 MW of capacity and has been active in up to 50 countries. Other key U.S. IPP players in international markets include Enron and International Generating.

U.S. regulators so far have taken a lenient attitude toward U.S. utility investment in foreign electricity markets despite some concerns that domestic customers could be affected negatively by bad overseas investments. There have been some financial setbacks, such as a 1997 decision by the new British government to impose a windfall profits tax on regional electric companies, which resulted in over $1 billion in write-offs by the U.S. parent companies. Also, the 1998 recession in several Asian countries crimped development plans, and some U.S. groups, including Entergy and Dominion Resources, have sold off large foreign electric distribution assets. Southern is backing out of some South American countries, and AES has taken large losses on Brazilian operations as a result of that country's 1998 devaluation. Overall, however, foreign investments have been successful and continue to grow.

However, in 1998 and 1999, as the impact of deregulation in the United States grew, the balance shifted and U.S. energy

TABLE 5-8: Electric Utilities Industry (SIC 4911) Trends and Forecasts

Year	1997	1998	1999	2000[1]	2001[1]	2005[1]	2010[1]	2015[1]	2020[1]	Percent Change 98–10	Percent Change 10–20
Average retail rate (cents/kwh)	6.9	6.7	6.6	6.6	6.1	6.1	5.7	5.5	5.3	−1.4	−0.6
Revenues ($billions)	215.6	216.3	218.1	215.1	212.9	212.9	213.8	222.4	229.0	−0.1	+0.7
Imports ($millions)	2,123	2,139	2,148								
Exports ($millions)	311	311	311								

[1] Forecast.
Source: DRI McGraw-Hill.

groups began to focus more of their resources on building up domestic operations through new plant construction and asset purchases. AES began a campaign to secure new U.S. assets, in part to balance its portfolio and calm shareholders' jitters about too much foreign exposure. Entergy sold off over $4 billion in foreign assets and began a round of new power plant construction in the United States. Overall new plant construction in the United States mushroomed from about 1,000 MW/year in the mid-1990s to 15,000 MW/year by 1999. At the same time, overseas power plant development peaked at about 35,000 MW/year and settled back to about 25,000 MW/year.

Also, several large European-based energy groups have invested in the U.S. IPP markets. They include Tractebel of Belgium, which bought the Texas-based CRSS; the French-owned Sithe Energies, which bought Boston Edison's generation assets; and Britain's National Power, which now owns American National Power.

Actual imports and exports of electricity are a minor issue for the U.S. electricity industry. Exports are minimal, and imports have tended to remain in the range of $2 billion per year, or about 1 percent of all sales (see Table 5-8). The main source of imports has been Canadian shipments to the northeast and the upper midwest, where there is a logistic and economic advantage. In New England, an emerging issue is the competition between low-cost hydroelectric power from new Canadian projects and power from efficient new plants in the region that are fueled by imported Canadian gas.

U.S. INDUSTRY GROWTH PROJECTIONS FOR THE NEXT 1 AND 5 YEARS

Electricity Prices

Retail competition, a proliferation of suppliers, low coal prices, efficient new generation technology, low interest rates, and lower supplier reserve margins have all contributed to the continuation of a fall in electricity prices. While the ability of utilities to win stranded cost payments from retail customers through "transition" charges will prevent a price plunge once restructuring is complete, the collection of such charges will be limited to 5 to 10 years, after which the full impact of competitive pricing will be felt.

By 2005, the average nationwide price of electricity should be 11.5 percent lower than the price in 1997, which will mean an average annual decline of roughly 1.4 percent (see Table 5-8). Regional price differentials should narrow as a result of restructuring from a maximum of 150 percent in the mid-1990s to 130 percent by the mid-2000s, measured by average prices in each region relative to the average U.S. price.

Generating Capacity

Through the early 1980s virtually all new power plants were built by electric utilities in the context of traditional regulation, which guaranteed a specific rate of return on new rate-based additions and secured franchised distribution territories. This began to change in the mid-1980s as federal law required utilities to buy supplies from qualifying facilities under PURPA and state regulators adopted least-cost planning rules that forced utilities to seek competitive bids for new supplies and build capacity themselves only when that was economically justified.

From the mid-1980s to the late-1990s, about half the approximately 100,000 MW of new generation capacity in the United States was built by utilities and half was built by nonutility generators. For the utilities, this has included several large nuclear plants that had been under construction since the 1970s as well as a large number of small oil- and gas-fired units to meet peaking needs without adding to baseload capacity, which has remained sufficient to meet normal nonpeak demand.

U.S. nuclear capacity nearly doubled from 55,000 NW in 1980 to 103,000 MW in 1990. However, since that time, nuclear plant additions have stopped, with the last one coming in 1995 with the Tennessee Valley Authority's 1,250-MW Watts Bar 1 plant. No new nuclear plants have been ordered in the United States since 1978, and several projects have been canceled. Also, because of competition and increasingly tough safety regulations, the number of nuclear plants that have closed before their 40-year licenses expired has increased.

Also starting in 1999, a lively market developed for existing nuclear capacity as specialized nuclear generation companies began buying plants that were put on the market because of divestiture rules or because the utility owners did not want to deal with nuclear regulations. The buyers, including AmerGen and Entergy, believe that the plants can be operated competitively because of the low fuel cost. They estimate that most nuclear capacity will gravitate to specialized owners over the next 5 years.

By 1997, nonutility generators owned 70,301 MW, or 8.4 percent of generation capacity, in the United States and produced 416.6 billion kwh of energy, 11.5 percent of U.S. output (see Tables 5-1 and 5-2). Cogenerators, which also sell steam to industrial hosts, supplied about 9.2 percent of total energy, selling about half their output to utilities. Small power producers, mainly small hydroelecric units, contributed 1.5 percent of supply, and IPP plants now provide less than 1 percent of total energy.

However, this situation is changing rapidly for several reasons, including deregulation, weather trends, and a perceived capacity shortage. The total amount of capacity is beginning to rise rapidly, and the percentage of capacity that is non-utility-owned also is increasing.

The capacity shortage became apparent in 1998 and 1999 but was due to several longer-term trends. Utilities' additions to capacity virtually stopped in the mid-1990s because of the trend toward lower reserve margins and the advent of restructuring, which made recovery of plant investment costs uncertain. Many states have set a cutoff date for restructuring plans, after which utilities cannot claim stranded cost recovery for new investments. Most utilities simply stopped adding capacity, and by 1997 Southern Company was considered unconventional because of its proposal to build 2,000 MW of new gas-fired capacity in Mississippi and Alabama under normal rate regulation. It won state approval only after pledging not to seek stranded cost recovery for those projects.

At the same time, growth in the cogeneration and small power sector has stalled as the rates providers are offered by utilities for such power have dropped with the overall trend toward lower prices. This has made it almost impossible for new cogeneration plants to get contracts under PURPA rules. This situation may change somewhat, as some states have passed rules requiring competitive energy sellers in deregulated markets to use a fixed percentage of power from renewable and cogeneration sources.

By 1998, however, as deregulation took hold in several areas, the highly favorable economic structure of new gas-fired combined cycle generation led to a surge in proposals for new projects in several regions, including California, Texas, the northeast, and the midwest. This building boom was expedited by unusually hot summer weather in 1998 and 1999 in the eastern half of the country and the Mississippi Valley, which led to some power shortages and price spikes in spot markets. This resulted in a new wave of project proposals, especially in the southeast and the midwest.

Assets sales totaling close to 70,000 MW doubled the amount of nonregulated generation in the United States by 1999, and analysts predict that between asset sales and new capacity additions, the IPP share of U.S. electricity capacity will increase to close to 200,000 MW, or about 25 percent of the national total, by 2002, with about 15 large energy groups holding over half the assets. Groups with integrated marketing arms should be able to offer energy in the range of 2 to 3 cents/kwh, forcing down prices in the entire market.

In the mid-1990s, coal with about 56 percent and nuclear with about 22 percent were by far the main fuel sources for U.S. power plants. However, this has begun to change. Gas use should rise steadily from a base of about 10 percent as new capacity under construction comes on line, and nuclear use is expected to drop gradually as no new plants are added and retirements continue. Coal also may be affected by tougher emission standards and the gradual retirement of older plants but should remain the dominant fuel for the next decade. Hydro should remain steady at about 10 percent, and oil, now under 2 percent, should continue to fade.

Electricity Consumption

Electricity consumption rose steadily in the mid-1990s at a rate somewhat below 1 percent annually, and electricity use generally has grown faster than has the use of other energy sources. Demand for electricity is expected to grow 1.3 percent per year between 1996 and 2010, driven especially by increases in commercial and industrial demand. Residential growth will remain flat at 1 percent per year. Total demand should top 3.5 trillion kwh by the year 2005 (see Table 5-9).

The value of electricity sales in the United States in 1999 was estimated at $218.1 billion. Sales in constant dollars have risen just over 2 percent per year since the early 1990s. This growth will flatten out through the next decade as rate decreases offset growth in demand (see Table 5-9).

Commercial

Electricity consumption in the commercial sector traditionally has been lower than that in the industrial and residential sectors, accounting for 32.1 percent of total demand in 1999. However,

TABLE 5-9: U.S. Electricity Sales
(billions of kilowatt-hours)

	1997	1998	1999	2000[1]	2001[1]	2005[1]	2010[1]	2015[1]	2020[1]	Percent Change 98–10	Percent Change 10–20
Commercial	996	1,028	1,038	1,060	1,074	1,146	1,246	1,339	1,400	1.6	1.2
Industrial	1,032	1,058	1,052	1,066	1,082	1,177	1,300	1,409	1,505	1.7	1.5
Residential	1,071	1,126	1,103	1,124	1,136	1,175	1,223	1,296	1,375	0.7	1.2
Other	9	7	9	8	7	8	9	9	9		
Total	3,108	3,219	3,202	3,258	3,299	3,506	3,778	4,053	4,289	1.3	1.3

[1] Forecast.
Source: DRI McGraw-Hill.

this sector showed strong growth in the early 1990s and is predicted to increase its use of electricity 1.6 percent per year through 2010, surpassing residential use in that year (see Table 5-9). This strong growth has been pushed by the explosion in personal computing over the last 15 years, along with increased use of photocopiers, printers, fax machines, and communications devices. Indoor shopping centers, amusement complexes, and mass transit systems have increased the demand for electricity in this sector.

Over time, the amount of electricity used per square foot has increased. If that trend continues, it should raise the electricity intensity of the commercial sector to 46 percent by 2002 from 44.5 percent in 1995. In addition to gas absorption chillers and some gas heat pumps in specialized locations, electricity has captured the commercial sectors' growth markets. A 1.5 percent annual growth rate in commercial square footage combined with a rise of 0.25 percent per year in electricity used per square foot will lead to an expected 1.6 percent annual growth increase through 2010.

Commercial users have been less vocal in pushing for retail competition but are expected to make major use of competitive energy sellers and special purchasing and load aggregation techniques once that choice becomes available. Large institutional users such as school districts, hospitals, and state governments also have made aggressive efforts to tap the competitive market.

Industrial

The industrial sector, with total usage of 1.2 trillion kwh per year, is the largest consumer of electricity in the United States, including both purchases from outside sources and self-generation. This sector purchased just over 1 trillion kwh from utilities and other generators in 1999, and demand growth is expected to continue in the range of 1.7 percent per year through 2010 and then drop off slightly (see Table 5-9).

While industrial users have greatly improved their efficiency in the use of power in the last 10 years, this has been closely matched by growth in new applications for electricity in automated production lines, robotics, computers, and heating systems. In this period, industrial use of other fossil fuels has declined fairly steadily, driven by high prices, environmental pressures, and the shift of the industrial mix away from so-called smokestack industries. From just 15 percent of final industrial energy consumption in 1980 (excluding raw material uses), electricity now accounts for almost 25 percent of total industrial energy usage.

Industrial users have been able to win major price concessions from utilities in recent years, especially in high-cost states, where they have made a legitimate case that they will be forced to move their operations out of state unless they get energy at lower prices. They also have played a key political role in pushing state governments to consider retail competition. However, because of this early success, they generally will tend to get smaller new price gains than other classes will once competition starts.

Residential

Residential use at 1.1 trillion kwh in 1999 accounts for 34.2 percent of U.S. electricity consumption. While residential use rose in the early 1990s, it is expected to stabilize at a steady average annual growth rate of about 1 percent over the next 10 to 20 years. (see Table 5-9). This slow growth will be caused by the modest overall growth in the population and in household formation. Also, gas is expected to share in the growth in residential energy use, along with electricity, over the survey period. Gas provides competition in traditional areas of cooking, water heating, and clothes drying and increasingly in space heating and cooling as gas heat pumps gain market share.

Home energy savings resulting from more energy-efficient appliances and promotions that encourage the use of such appliances and lighting will be offset by the increased use of appliances and a modest gain in electricity-heated homes, keeping energy use per person constant during this period. With the faster growth of demand for electricity in the commercial and industrial sectors, residential use gradually will fall below one-third of total U.S. demand after 2005.

Electricity Trading

Since the passage of the 1992 Energy Policy Act, which encouraged a greater use of regional transmission grids for energy trading, energy sales on the wholesale market have risen dramatically. These sales are carried out by a large group of energy marketers and brokers that are licensed by FERC to deal at market rates.

In 1998, energy marketers handled 2.3 trillion kwh of wholesale energy sales, twice the 1997 level and a 10-fold increase over the 1996 level. In 1999, marketers were expected to exceed 2.5 trillion kwh in sales. The volumes handled by markets do not include about 1.5 trillion kwh in wholesale sales made by utility affiliates directly to their own operating companies or to other utilities. Leading national energy marketers by sales volume in 1998 included Enron, Southern Energy Marketing, PG&E Energy, and Aquila Power. Overall, about 150 separate marketers were registered with FERC and reported some trading activity in 1998.

In 1998, futures trading in electricity began to emerge, with large commodity exchanges in New York and Chicago setting up trading hubs.

Because of the spring price fluctuations in 1998 and 1999 in wholesale markets, as a result of especially weather-related demand spikes, markets have deemphasized speculative trading that is based on market supplies and focused on asset-based trading in which they deal in energy volumes backed by physical generation assets that usually are owned by the same corporation or are under firm contract.

Also in 1998 and 1999, specialized retail marketers began to emerge, focused on state markets where deregulation had occurred. However, the slow start-up of retail competition in key states has hampered development. Retail marketers are divided into groups that cater to large business users and groups that carry out mass marketing to residential and small business users.

CONCLUSIONS

The movement toward restructuring of the U.S. electricity industry appeared to gain irreversible momentum in the late 1990s, and the only questions now are how many states will voluntarily change to a deregulated system and whether federal legislation will force the others to follow suit or allow the system to evolve with both regulated and deregulated states.

For the electricity supply industry, the introduction of choice will shift the focus of regulation but not eliminate it. Unbundled generation and energy marketing activities will be free from traditional rate regulation but still come under scrutiny from FERC and state commissions, especially in regard to market power and environmental issues. Most states will have a simple procedure for registering marketers but also will impose a code of conduct to ensure fair competition and protect retail customers from shady sales practices.

Existing utilities generally will retain their transmission assets, but transmission rates and access issues will be supervised by the new ISO groups, usually at the regional level. ISOs also will control system expansion and other reliability-related issues and manage regional pools for energy, capacity, reserves, and ancillary services.

The distribution operations of current utilities generally will remain intact. These utilities will serve the same franchise areas under regulated distribution rates with an obligation to serve, provide default service, and collect stranded cost charges.

A key question remains how quickly true competitive retail markets will develop in states that have deregulated.

Paul Kemezis, *Electric Utility Week,* (931) 695-5485, December 1999.

■ REFERENCES

Capacity and Generation of Non Utility Sources of Energy (annual), Edison Electric Institute.

Electric Power Annual (annual), Energy Information Administration, Department of Energy.

Electric Utility Week, McGraw-Hill, New York.

Electrical World (monthly), McGraw-Hill, New York.

Electricity Supply & Demand, Summary of Electric Utility Supply and Demand Projections (annual), North American Electric Reliability Council.

Global Power Report (biweekly), McGraw-Hill, New York.

International Private Power Quarterly, McGraw-Hill, New York.

Power Generation Markets Quarterly, McGraw-Hill, New York.

Statistical Yearbook of the Electric Utility Industry (annual), Edison Electric Institute.

■ RELATED CHAPTERS

2: Coal Mining
4: Petroleum Refining

■ GLOSSARY

British thermal unit (Btu): The standard unit for measuring quantities of heat energy, such as the heat content of fuel. A Btu is the amount of heat energy required to raise the temperature of 1 pound of water 1 degree Fahrenheit.

Cogeneration: Electricity generation in which both electrical energy and excess heat are produced. The heat, usually in the form of steam, is sold as a separate commodity to a host industrial user. Power output from the plant may be sold directly to the host industry, the local electric utility, or both. Cogeneration plants can be owned by the industrial host or an independent developer.

Combined cycle unit: A type of generation unit, usually gas- or oil-fired, that uses waste heat from an initial combustion turbine cycle to assist a second topping combustion cycle, creating extra efficiencies in fuel use. Gas-fired combined cycle units in the range of 400 to 600 MW currently represent the leading-edge technology for new baseload plants in the United States.

Electricity intensity: Energy used per dollar of gross domestic product (GDP) measured in real dollars is referred to as *energy intensity;* electricity used per dollar of GDP in real dollars is referred to as *electricity intensity.*

Electricity used per square foot: The average number of kilowatt-hours used per square foot of a building or building sector, such as commercial buildings.

End-use sectors: Residential, commercial, industrial, and transportation markets in which energy is sold at retail.

Final demand: The demand for electricity, natural gas, coal, and oil, excluding the demand for those fuels when they are used to generate electricity.

Independent power producers (IPPs): Private companies that develop, own, or operate electric power plants and sell power on the wholesale market mostly to utilities and do not have a responsibility to serve a retail load. IPPs also are defined as a class of large nonutility generators that produce electricity only and are not cogeneration plants or small power producers.

Investor-owned utilities (IOUs): Utilities that are financed by the sales of securities and whose business operations are overseen by a board representing their shareholders.

Nameplate capacity: The guaranteed continuous output in megawatts of an electricity generation plant when it operates under optimal conditions.

Nonutility generators (NUGs): A broad class of privately owned power generators that sell power in wholesale markets. Unlike traditional vertically integrated utilities, they do not sell directly to retail users in franchise territories, although this is changing with the advent of restructuring. NUGs include cogenerators, small power producers, and IPPs.

Qualifying facilities (QFs): Nonutility generation plants that have a special status under the 1978 Public Utilities Regulatory Policy Act and have the right to sell their power to utilities if they can meet a utility's avoided cost. QFs include cogeneration plants and small power units fueled by renewable energy sources.

Restructuring: Action by a state government or the federal government that requires utilities to unbundle their operations into separate generation, transmission, and distribution companies' wires and allows retail customers to access the competitive market directly.

Self-generation: Production of electricity on site by a retail customer for the customer's use as an alternative to buying from the local utility.

Small power producers (SPPs): Private nonutility power producers whose generating facilities use renewable resources and produce power below a set capacity.

Standard offer: A set rate for electricity offered by a restructured distribution utility to its retail customers as an alternative to buying from outside suppliers. Standard offers usually are set for transition periods of up to 4 years and set an energy market ceiling that competitive suppliers must beat to gain customers.

Stranded costs: The value of generation assets owned by utilities that become too costly to operate once restructuring takes place and retail users can access competitive supplies at lower market-based costs. Most state and federal restructuring proposals allow utilities to recover some or all of their stranded costs, usually through a universal "transition" charge on all retail users over a fixed period.

Unbundling: The process of separating the generation, transmission, and distribution assets of vertically integrated utilities into distinct operating units that can be individual subsidiaries of a parent corporation or can be divested into independent unaffiliated companies. Also refers to the practice of breaking down utility rates into separate energy, transmission, and generation components as a preliminary step toward restructuring.

CONSTRUCTION
Economic and Trade Trends

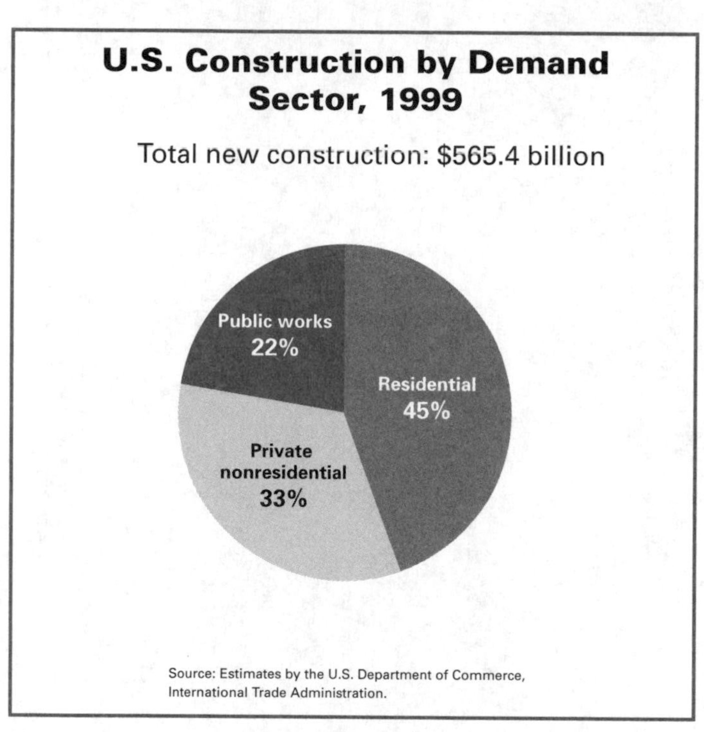

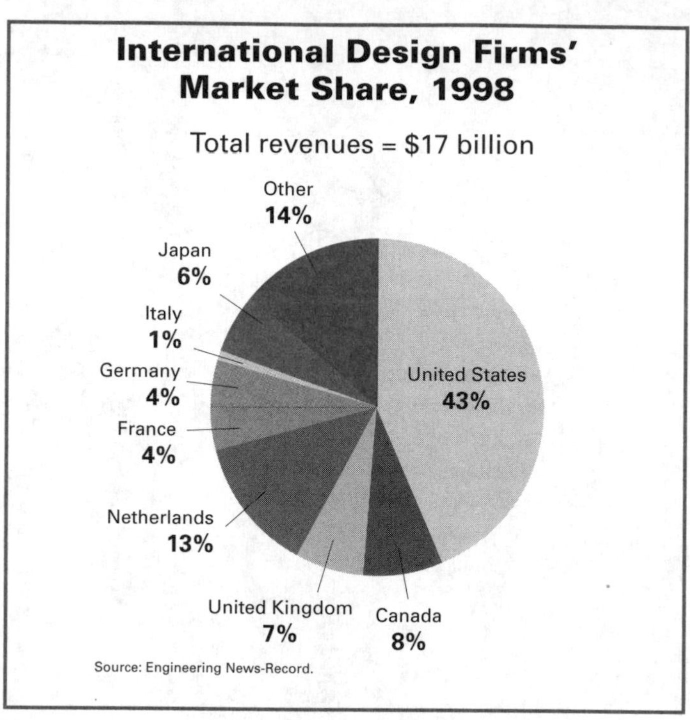

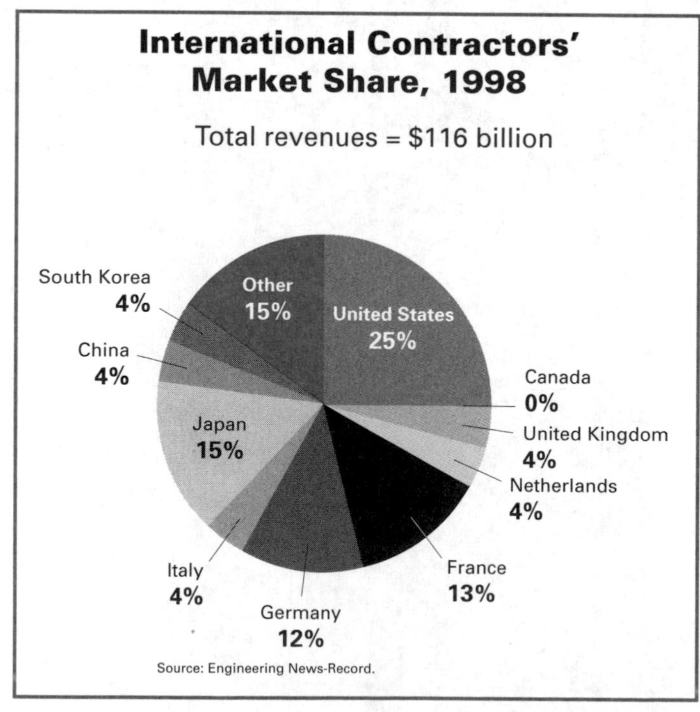

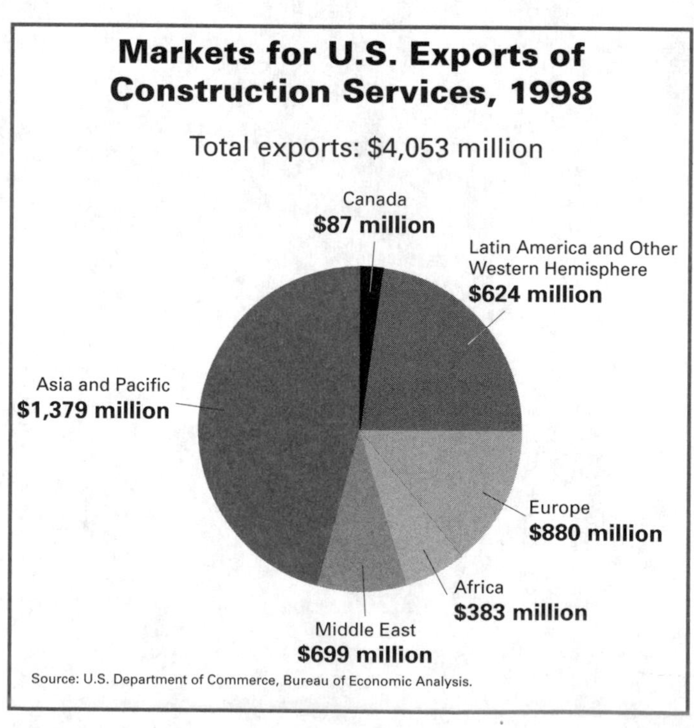

See "Getting the Most Out of *Outlook 2000*" for definitions of terms.

6

Construction

INDUSTRY DEFINITION This chapter covers construction contracting (SIC 15, 16, 17). Architectural, engineering, and surveying services (SIC 8710) are not included in the domestic analyses, but their international activities are covered in the analysis of the international contracting subsector. This chapter does not cover real estate (SIC 65), manufactured housing (SIC 245), construction equipment (SIC 3462), and construction equipment leasing (SIC 735).

OVERVIEW

In the year 2000, the constant dollar value of new construction put in place is expected to increase 1 percent from its record level in 1999. The home building sector will dip slightly because of higher interest rates (see Table 6-1). Nonresidential construction will gain 2 percent from the 1999 level. Public works construction will increase 3 percent over the 1999 level as a result of increasing federal and state government investment in infrastructure. U.S. exports of construction services will decline about 5 percent because of lackluster foreign construction markets and tight capacity in the domestic market.

GLOBAL CONSTRUCTION TRENDS

The United States is one of the leading construction markets in the world, employing 7.9 million workers and accounting for nearly 8 percent of U.S. gross domestic product (GDP). Nevertheless, about 80 percent of the world's construction activity occurs outside the United States. Enterprising American construction and engineering firms have been successful competitors in the international contracting business, although most of their overseas construction is done by foreign affiliates that use local labor rather than involving cross-border exports of U.S. services.

TABLE 6-1: Construction Trends and Projections

	1995	1996	1997	1998	1999[1]	2000[2]
Value of new construction put in place ($ billions)[3]	537.4	583.4	618.2	665.4	700.0	
Value of new construction put in place (1992 $billions)[3]	477.4	506.5	520.1	544.6	565	568
Number of private housing starts (thousands of units)	1,354	1,477	1,475	1,630	1,660	1,550
Shipments of mobile homes (thousands of units)[4]	340	363	353	373	375	360
International construction contracts, U.S. companies ($millions)[5]	18,900	22,800	24,600	28,246	29,000	
Exports of construction services ($millions)[6]	2,550	3,560	4,084	4,300	4,100	
Imports of construction services ($millions)[6]	345	489	346	450	480	
Employees (thousands)[7]	5,158	5,400	5,600	6,300	6,300	
Self-employed workers (thousands)	1,455	1,475	1,500	1,550	1,600	
Average hourly earnings of construction workers ($)	15.09	15.46	16.00	16.60	17.22	
Construction cost index (1992 = 100)	112.5	115.0	118.7	122.0	127.0	
Producer price index for construction materials (1982 = 100)	138.8	139.6	146.5	146.8	150.0	

[1] Estimated.
[2] Forecast.
[3] The data on new construction put in place do not include maintenance and repair work.
[4] Manufactured Housing Institute and U.S. Bureau of the Census.
[5] Proprietors and working partners, not counted as employees.
[6] U.S. Department of Commerce, Bureau of Economic Analysis.
[7] Based on establishments surveyed by the Bureau of Labor Statistics. Excludes self-employed workers.
Source: U.S. Department of Commerce: Bureau of Census, International Trade Administration; U.S. Department of Labor, Bureau of Labor Statistics.

U.S. exports of construction services measured on a cross-border transactions basis totaled over $4 billion in 1998. The actual value of contracts won by American-owned companies was much larger at over $28 billion. The difference can be explained chiefly by the fact that cross-border transactions exclude most construction done by foreign affiliates, subcontractors, and labor forces. Legal U.S. imports of construction services were about $0.6 billion, giving the United States a large surplus in the balance of trade in construction services. Most U.S. exports of construction services involve management services, engineering know-how, and specialized technology.

U.S. CONSTRUCTION INDUSTRY

In 1999, the inflation-adjusted value of new construction put in place increased 4 percent to set an all-time record. (The 1999 current dollar value of about $700 billion is also an all-time record.) This performance was partly the result of a small increase in the number of housing starts to 1.66 million units. Public works construction increased 5 percent, led by increases in school and road construction. Private nonresidential construction increased modestly to set a new record, with commercial buildings and utilities accounting for most of the gain (see Table 6-2).

Residential remodeling and repair work increased in 1999, reflecting the growing stock of housing and a heavy turnover of used homes. Although the data for maintenance and repair construction are not as complete as those for new construction, the available information indicates that 1999 was a record year for maintenance and repair work. Nonresidential building improvements (commercial remodeling and renovation) also appeared to be at record levels.

The value of new construction put in place as a percentage of GDP (about 7.8 percent in 1999) has risen slightly in recent years but is well below the post–World War II peak of 11.9 percent attained in 1966. This measure tends to understate the importance of construction in the economy because several types of construction activity that are not included in new con-

TABLE 6-2: Value of Construction Put in Place
(billions of 1992 dollars; percent)

						Percent Change[3]		
Type of Construction	1997[1]	1998[2]	1999[2]	2000[2]	2004[2]	98–99	99–00	99–04
Total new construction	520.1	544.6	565.4	567.7	597.5	4	1	1
Residential	221.8	239.2	252.7	246.5	251.8	6	–2	–0
Single-family	137.2	153.9	163.6	155.4	155.6	6	–5	–1
Multifamily	19.1	19.9	21.1	21.7	21.1	6	3	0
Home improvement	65.5	65.4	68.0	69.4	75.1	4	2	2
Private nonresidential	177.0	185.1	186.2	190.0	194.8	1	2	1
Manufacturing facilities	26.4	26.3	22.1	21.7	25.6	–16	–2	3
Office	28.9	33.8	37.2	39.8	37.2	10	5	0
Hotels and motels	10.9	12.1	13.0	13.3	13.0	7	2	0
Other commercial	43.6	43.7	44.1	44.1	39.9	1	0	–2
Religious	4.9	5.5	6.2	6.3	6.8	12	2	2
Educational	7.3	7.8	7.0	7.2	8.5	–10	2	4
Hospital and institutional	11.4	11.1	10.3	10.5	12.0	–7	2	3
Miscellaneous buildings	7.8	7.6	8.4	8.5	9.2	10	2	2
Telecommunications	10.0	10.6	11.0	11.5	12.8	4	4	3
Railroads	4.2	4.5	4.6	4.7	4.9	3	2	1
Electric utilities	9.8	9.8	9.8	10.0	11.4	0	2	3
Gas utilities	5.8	5.7	5.8	5.8	6.4	2	0	2
Petroleum pipelines	0.8	1.1	1.1	1.1	1.0	0	3	–2
Farm structures	3.2	3.2	3.2	3.2	3.6	1	–2	2
Miscellaneous structures	2.0	2.3	2.3	2.4	2.6	2	2	2
Public works	121.3	120.3	126.4	131.2	151.0	5	3	4
Housing and redevelopment	3.2	3.3	3.1	3.1	3.4	–7	2	2
Federal industrial	0.8	0.8	0.7	0.8	1.0	–10	7	6
Educational	24.3	24.3	25.8	26.8	29.9	6	4	3
Hospital	4.2	3.3	3.1	3.2	3.5	–5	1	2
Other public buildings	20.9	22.1	22.1	22.3	25.6	0	1	3
Highways	37.8	37.5	40.5	43.7	54.2	8	8	6
Military facilities	2.2	2.1	1.8	1.7	1.5	–15	–7	–4
Conservation and development	4.8	4.7	5.0	5.0	5.3	7	0	1
Sewer systems	7.8	7.4	8.1	8.1	8.6	10	0	1
Water supply	4.8	4.9	5.5	5.5	6.4	12	1	3
Miscellaneous public structures	10.5	9.9	10.7	10.9	11.8	8	2	2

[1] Estimate.
[2] Forecast.
[3] Average annual rate of growth.
Percent changes calculated on unrounded data. Values may not sum to totals due to independent rounding.
Source: U.S. Department of Commerce: Bureau of Census, International Trade Administration.

struction data have grown rapidly in the last decade, including maintenance and repair, some commercial and industrial renovation, factory-built structures, and environmental restoration.

Construction costs increased about 4 percent in 1999, as measured by the U.S. Bureau of the Census's fixed-weight construction cost deflator. This was faster than the average annual rate of increase during the previous 5 years and faster than the rate of increase in the consumer price index. Prices for building materials rose an average of about 2 percent in 1999, although there were serious materials shortages during the peak construction season. Land prices appear to be escalating, and double-digit increases are common in some of the stronger markets. (Land prices are not included in the construction cost index.) Insurance and bonding costs have continued to increase, although the overall availability of insurance is better. Labor costs have increased because of tight labor markets, with average hourly earnings of construction workers increasing about 4 percent in 1999 (see Table 6-1).

There were an estimated 6.3 million employees in the construction industry in 1999, about the same as the 1998 level, which was an all-time record. In addition, about 1.6 million people are self-employed in construction as proprietors and working partners, and so the total number of persons employed in the industry is about 7.9 million. Construction is one of the higher-paying industries in the United States as measured by average hourly and weekly earnings (see Table 6-1).

OUTLOOK FOR 2000

The constant dollar value of new construction in the year 2000 is expected to increase slightly from the 1999 level to set another record. Home building will lag behind nonresidential construction (see Tables 6-1 and 6-2). The most promising markets are commercial buildings, educational buildings, highways, and electric utilities. The weaker construction markets will be factories, military facilities, and single-family homes. (Detailed prospects for various types of construction are discussed in the subsector sections of this chapter.)

Housing starts are expected to be about 1.55 million units in the year 2000, about 5 percent lower than the figure in 1999. This drop is entirely attributable to single-family housing starts, which are projected to decrease 6 percent to 1.05 million units. Private nonresidential construction will be about 2 percent higher than in 1999, with declines in factory construction offset by gains in other categories. Public works construction are expected to increase in 2000 as a result of increases in federal, state, and local construction expenditures.

OUTLOOK TO 2004

Between 2000 and 2004, new construction is expected to increase modestly from current levels. The overall growth rate for construction will be about 1 percent annually, compared with 2 percent for GDP. Public works construction is expected to increase faster than is private nonresidential construction. Remodeling and repair construction is expected to increase at about the same rate as GDP.

A key factor supporting construction during the next 5 years will be stable or even declining interest rates after the year 2000. This forecast assumes a very small federal deficit and modest inflation rates, which should lead to lower interest rates and a fairly good macroeconomic climate for construction.

Despite the record levels of commercial building construction, supply and demand are not wildly out of line as they were in the mid-1980s. Store construction will be affected by the adjustments under way in the retailing industry, which could last several years. The demand for new housing construction will be affected by the public's enormous wealth held in equities as well as by demographic trends. Federal government spending for public works, especially highways, will increase, and state and local governments also will increase their investment in infrastructure.

The large trade deficit will result in weak levels of demand for industrial construction in 2000 and for several years thereafter. Electric utility construction and repair also will be a large growth market (see Table 6-3). Hospital construction will recover despite strenuous cost-cutting efforts and regulatory uncertainties. Educational construction will be a large and growing market because of favorable demographics and public support for school improvements. Remodeling and repair work, both residential and nonresidential, will continue to increase as the U.S. stock of structures becomes older and more extensive.

In addition to market factors, the U.S. construction industry will face a number of supply-side challenges during the next 5 years, including foreign competition, the supply of workers, and the cost of insurance. Most of the foreign construction contractors that compete in the U.S. market are well financed and have world-class construction expertise. The strong U.S. market has made foreign penetration easier than it was 5 years ago. The supply of young workers, who make up most of the construction labor force, is fairly tight because of economic and demographic trends. In 1999, there were labor shortages, especially of skilled workers, in local markets. Some of those shortages were eased by labor migration, but as the economic boom continues, shortages of labor and skills are becoming more general. The cost of liability insurance has stabilized, but the cost of health insurance and worker's compensation insurance has continued to increase rapidly.

PRIVATE RESIDENTIAL CONSTRUCTION

In 1999, the home building industry put up an estimated 1.66 million homes (excluding mobile homes) and the value of housing construction set an all-time record at $320 billion. The current recovery has lasted 8 years, and 1999 was the sixth consecutive year in which housing starts exceeded 1.35 million. In the year 2000, home building expenditures are expected to decline about 2 percent in real terms.

Demand for new housing was very strong in 1999 despite the higher interest rate environment. The strength in multifamily

TABLE 6-3: Construction Expenditures by Type of Structure
(billions of 1992 dollars; percent)

	1997[1]	1998[2]	1999[2]	2000[2]	2004[2]	Percent Change[3] 98–99	99–00	99–04
Total Construction	520.1	544.6	565.4	567.7	597.5	4	1	1
New building construction	350.9	375.5	387.8	384.7	392.2	3	−1	0
New housing units	156.3	173.8	184.7	177.1	176.7	6	−4	−1
Private nonresidential	141.2	147.9	148.4	151.3	152.2	2	2	1
Publicly owned	53.4	53.8	54.8	56.2	63.3	2	3	3
Other new structures	103.7	103.7	109.6	113.7	130.2	6	4	4
Private nonresidential	35.8	37.2	38.0	38.7	42.6	2	2	2
Publicly owned	67.9	66.5	71.6	75.0	87.7	8	5	4
Home improvements[4]	65.5	65.4	68.0	69.4	75.1	4	2	2
Home repairs[5]	31.7	32.0	33.0	34.0	38.3	3	3	3

[1] Estimate.
[2] Forecast.
[3] Average annual rate of growth.
[4] Home improvements are included in total new construction, but nonresidential building improvements are not included.
[5] Excludes industrial and agricultural buildings as well as buildings owned by the federal government or private utilities. Also excludes buildings of 1,000 square feet or less.
Source: U.S. Department of Commerce: Bureau of Census, International Trade Administration.

housing comes in spite of the record rate of home ownership in America and is due chiefly to strong demographic trends and low vacancy rates. Although housing starts data do not include mobile homes (see Chapter 7), they do include panelized and modular units that are built to local or statewide codes for factory-built buildings.

Expenditures for residential upkeep and improvements totaled $120.7 billion in 1998. About $81 billion was for improvements and additions to existing structures, while $39 billion was for maintenance and repair of structures. Expenditures for these purposes are expected to increase by about 2 percent annually in 1999 and 2000. Improvements over the last few years have averaged about 67 percent of all such expenditures, leaving maintenance and repair with the remainder.

Outlook for 2000

New housing starts are expected to total 1.55 million units in the year 2000, a slight decline from 1.65 million units in 1999. Single-family units are expected to decrease slightly to 1.2 million, while the multiunit segment is forecast to increase about 6 percent to 0.35 million units (see Table 6-4). Home improvement expenditures are expected to rise about 2 percent (see Table 6-3).

Interest rates should be slightly higher in the year 2000, with a modest impact on the single-family sector. Other factors affecting this sector are the continued moderate growth expected in GDP and consumer income, the lure of other investment options, the heavy debt load of consumers, the price and availability of building materials, and the ready availability of construction loans to contractors and mortgage funds to home buyers.

Multifamily construction activity has been spurred by the demographic surge of increasing numbers of 18- to 25-year-old young adults. Because of the post-1976 recovery from the "baby bust" and as a result of immigration, this population cohort is increasing again. With the strong job market these consumers are much more able to rent new apartments than they were in the previous decade.

Spending for residential upkeep and improvements is expected to increase about 3 percent in the year 2000. Home repair expenditures probably will match the 3 percent increase expected for improvements. This gain will result largely from solid sales of new and existing homes over the last few years. (More than half of all improvements occur within 18 months after a new owner moves in or within 12 months before a home is sold.) In addition, the moderately strong economy will allow more home owners to better maintain and improve their homes.

Outlook to 2004

Annual housing starts for the period 1999–2004 probably will average about 1.45 million units. This will be lower than the level in 1999, but the average size of housing units will increase in line with long-term trends at about 2 percent annually. Home improvement and repair work will continue to increase at about the same rate as GDP.

Demographic factors will restrain the demand for new single-family housing in the first few years of the new century. Because of the baby bust that occurred in the United States between 1965 and 1976, there will be declining numbers of Americans in the 25- to 45-year-old age group, the prime home-buying age. Demographic support for apartment construction is currently strong and will improve steadily over the next 5 years because the 18- to 25-year-old age cohort will be increasing, as will the over-65 population.

Financial factors affecting the demand for housing are less certain and often offsetting. Interest rates may have reached their lows for this business cycle, but rising real incomes should improve the affordability of home ownership. Low inflation

TABLE 6-4: Private Housing Starts by Type of House
(thousands of units)

		Single-Unit Structures			Multiunit Structures			
Period	Total Housing Starts	Total One-Unit	Detached Houses	Town Houses[1]	Total Multiunit	Two- to Four-Unit Structures	Town House–Style Apartments	Apartment Units[2]
1980	1,292	852	774	78	440	110	45	285
1981	1,084	705	628	77	379	91	39	249
1982	1,063	663	577	86	400	80	27	293
1983	1,703	1,068	897	171	635	113	44	478
1984	1,750	1,085	875	210	665	121	40	504
1985	1,745	1,075	905	170	670	93	53	524
1986	1,807	1,179	1,013	166	628	84	52	492
1987	1,623	1,146	1,004	142	477	65	35	377
1988	1,488	1,081	968	113	407	59	30	318
1989	1,376	1,003	916	87	373	55	31	287
1990	1,193	895	832	63	298	38	20	240
1991	1,014	840	789	51	174	36	12	126
1992	1,200	1,030	958	72	170	31	14	125
1993	1,288	1,126	1,031	95	162	29	12	120
1994	1,457	1,198	1,091	107	259	35	19	204
1995	1,354	1,076	972	104	278	34	13	231
1996	1,477	1,161	1,054	107	316	45	15	256
1997	1,475	1,134	1,030	104	341	44	17	280
1998	1,630	1,271	1,154	117	346	43	11	292
1999[3]	1,660	1,330			330			
2000[4]	1,550	1,200			350			
2004[4]	1,460	1,100			360			

[1] A single-unit town house is one that is separated from adjoining units by a ground-to-roof wall and has separate utilities. Town house-style apartments, though attached, are not separated by a ground-to-roof wall and may share infrastructural facilities.
[2] Apartment buildings are conventional multifamily buildings in which dwelling units may share a common basement, heating plant, stairs, entrance halls, water supply, or sewage disposal system.
[3] Estimate.
[4] Forecast.
Source: U.S. Department of Commerce; Bureau of the Census.

rates are likely to restrain a buildup in home owners' equity, which will limit owners' ability to trade up to newer and larger houses. The recent pickup in housing prices is likely to increase the investment appeal of home ownership, especially for more expensive homes. Also, the record capital gains being made by stock market investors may lead them to purchase more luxurious housing. The net effect of these mixed trends will be a small reduction in the number of housing starts through the beginning years of the twenty-first century.

Home improvement and repair construction will continue to grow faster than will new home construction. Much of this demand will result from home owners adding rooms and amenities. In addition, the stock of housing is steadily growing larger and older, providing a growing base demand for home improvement and repair construction.

Single-Family Home Building

Many factors influenced the single-family housing market in the 1990s, including affordable interest rates, solid economic growth, surging personal wealth, and changing demographic patterns. The investment appeal of home ownership has been improved by tax law changes that have enhanced the tax benefits of owner-occupied housing.

Whereas first-time buyers and trade-up buyers account for most of the demand for new homes, the role of retirement and other specialized housing is also significant. Retirement housing is becoming a much greater factor in this market, with the units usually being smaller and having special design features for seniors. Many of these units are being built outside metropolitan areas.

New housing competes with housing resales and sales of manufactured homes in the single-family market. Family income, consumer confidence, and affordability remain the key considerations that affect decisions to buy or rent. Among the key factors affecting affordability are mortgage interest rates, the availability of funds, and the variety of mortgage options.

About 90 percent of new single-family houses are detached. According to the U.S. Bureau of the Census, the median sales price of new single-family units has continued to rise, with the 1999 level at about $158,000. The size of new single-family homes has been increasing steadily and now averages over 2,100 square feet. New one-family units are also characterized by the inclusion of more amenities, which include units with central air-conditioning, two and a half or more bathrooms, fireplaces, two-car garages, full basements, and three or more bedrooms.

Multiunit Home Building

Multifamily housing starts exceeded 330,000 units in 1999, in response to low vacancy rates and strong demographic trends for the next decade. This was one of the best years of the 1990s. Increasing interest rates are expected to restrain this market in the year 2000, although an increase is still likely. The 350,000 units expected in 2000 contrast with annual totals in the mid-1980s that were nearly twice as large.

Multiunit houses are characterized as having two or more dwelling units. They are usually either town house structures or apartment units. Rentals make up about 80 percent of multiunit housing, and most of those units are in structures with five or more dwelling units. In 1999, multiunit housing accounted for 21 percent of all housing starts, compared with about 38 percent in 1985 (see Table 6-4).

Among the major factors that influence the levels of new multiunit housing construction are tax laws, demographics, economic conditions, the financial strength or weakness of the real estate and lending institution sectors, and various regulatory requirements, such as accessibility for handicapped persons. Another factor supporting greater multiunit construction is the aging of the population. Credit problems and mobility among workers also tend to discourage home buying and favor rentals.

Alterations, Repairs, and Additions

This category encompasses spending for upkeep and repairs as well as improvements to existing residential structures. Maintenance and repairs continue to account for the bulk of spending for rental properties, while improvements account for the greater share of spending on owner-occupied units.

Included in this work are projects such as painting, appliance replacement parts and repair, and roof repairs. The improvements category involves additions to structures and major replacements of structures and other property. Examples of improvements include major exterior and interior structural changes, fences, and the replacement of furnaces and water heaters. For do-it-yourself work, the cost of materials and parts is included but the labor cost element is not.

Expenditures for home improvement and repair increased fairly steadily in the 1990s. Spending for this type of work tends to be less volatile than that for new construction, and the growth has been somewhat greater over the long term. This trend is expected to continue into the twenty-first century. The stock of housing will grow larger and older, and sales of existing homes will continue to increase.

PRIVATE NONRESIDENTIAL CONSTRUCTION

The value of new private nonresidential construction put in place during 1999 was estimated at $188 billion, of which $144 billion was for buildings and $44 billion was for other structures. In constant 1992 dollars, the total was about 2 percent higher than that in 1998 and set an all-time record (see Table 6-2). The largest increases were for hotels, offices, and telecommunications.

Private nonresidential construction includes all the buildings and other structures owned by American businesses and nonprofit organizations except for housing and mining. This includes manufacturing plants, office buildings, stores, hotels, hospitals, nursing homes, farm buildings, electric power plants, gas pipelines, telephone and electric lines, churches, railroads, and private schools (see Table 6-2).

Although demand for each of these categories of construction is influenced by macroeconomic variables such as interest rates and GDP growth, each category also has a unique set of factors that influence demand. For example, store construction is influenced heavily by the trend toward "big box" stores and "demalled" shopping centers rather than traditional malls. Hospital construction is affected by corporate cost cutting and health care legislation. Manufacturing plant demand is influenced by capacity utilization rates as well as international competitiveness factors.

Outlook for 2000

New private nonresidential construction is expected to remain at the current high levels as the economic expansion continues for the ninth year. The largest construction increases in the year 2000 are expected to be in offices, telecommunications, and petroleum pipelines. The outlook is weaker for hotels and other commercial construction.

Construction of the world's tallest skyscraper is expected to begin in 2000. The building would be erected in Chicago and would carry a mix of apartments, offices, retail spaces, and parking. In the 1990s, several new skyscrapers were temporarily able to claim to be the world's tallest building, and advancing technology will allow even taller buildings.

In the year 2000, business investment in plant and equipment is expected to increase. Although construction of manufacturing facilities and utility plants is expected to share in that increase, most of the investment will be in capital equipment rather than in buildings and other structures. Investments in equipment tend to be cost-saving measures and are less risky than are those in new industrial plants.

In the late 1990s real estate investment trusts (REITs) became important funding sources for nonresidential construction. These companies are dependent on developments in the stock market, and their ability to channel large amounts of equity into commercial real estate will depend heavily on their share prices.

Nonresidential repair and renovation markets probably will continue to grow in 2000 and for the next 5 years. Electric utilities in particular are likely to increase their maintenance and repair expenditures substantially. Investment in nonresidential building improvements will remain at high levels as the owners of commercial buildings attempt to keep their buildings attractive in the competitive rental markets. A side effect of the turmoil in the retailing industry will be massive remodeling of existing stores.

Outlook to 2004

Total private nonresidential construction is likely to increase moderately over the next 5 years, rising a little more slowly than the average growth in GDP of about 2 percent. Prospects look best for industrial, educational, utility, and hospital construction. The repair and renovation market will grow about as fast as will the new construction market during the next 5 years but will be less cyclical.

Despite the currently modest oversupply situation in commercial real estate, investor interest in commercial construction is expected to be strong enough to maintain the building boom through the first years of the twenty-first century. Strong investor demand will help support commercial construction even if interest rates rise. The recovery in this office building cycle has been slower but more sustainable than were several earlier recoveries. It is unlikely that a 1980s-style boom, characterized by surging construction in spite of rising vacancy rates, will result except in local situations because of tax law changes, tighter regulatory scrutiny, and greater wariness in the investment community.

Technological trends in the twenty-first century will affect the demand for commercial buildings by favoring telecommuting, Internet shopping, home offices, teleconferencing, and globalization of information services. Business management trends toward downsizing, temporary workforces, and inventory reduction also will have an effect. Although the boom in the construction of big box stores will abate, a potential growth area could be automobile "megadealers" selling used cars and multiple brands of new cars.

By 2004, private nonresidential construction will be 5 or 10 percent above current levels. However, spending on factories, utilities, and hospitals will account for a larger share of the total and commercial construction will account for a substantially lower proportion.

Manufacturing Facilities

Industrial construction has been a declining market category since 1997, chiefly because of intense international competition. With increasing imports and declining exports, most manufacturers are concentrating their investments on improving productivity rather than increasing efficiency. Thus, over 80 percent of manufacturers' capital expenditures go for equipment rather than structures. Nevertheless, enough manufacturers have been investing in industrial construction (to increase capacity, replace old buildings, and adjust to changing conditions) that construction of manufacturing facilities was expected to total an estimated $27 billion in 1999. The inflation-adjusted value of industrial construction put in place probably will decline again in the year 2000, but a recovery is expected before 2004. The long-term rate of increase may be slower than it was in most previous recoveries because of concern over global competition, but the upswing will last longer.

The need to modernize the capital stock of U.S. manufacturers will provide strong underlying demand for new construction as well as for repair and renovations. Even though the bulk of plant and equipment expenditures go for equipment rather than structures, the construction potential is huge.

Although the long-term outlook is uncertain, industrial construction is likely to be one of the stronger construction markets during the next 5 years. Because the U.S. economy and U.S. exports are expected to grow during this period, the economic climate should be moderately favorable for industrial construction. Strong common stock prices and fairly low interest rates will make it easier to finance industrial expansion. Negative factors include continued uncertainty about the economy, international competitiveness, regulatory burdens, and the heavy debt loads of many companies.

Office Buildings

In 1999, the value of office construction was about 10 percent higher than it was in 1998 but was still below its 1985 record. Further gains are expected beyond 1999 for both new construction and office renovation.

There is increasing investor interest in office construction despite the recent increase in long-term interest rates. In addition, lending institutions have gradually eased restrictions on commercial real estate loans, and the value of new real estate loans has surged.

The long-term office supply and demand situation includes fairly high vacancy rates, forecasts of slower growth in white-collar employment, and technology trends that favor the substitution of home offices for office buildings. Nevertheless, absorption of space has been good, and prices have been rising for investment-grade buildings.

In the year 2000, white-collar employment will increase very slowly because of tight labor markets, modest economic growth, and corporate cost cutting. During the 2000–2004 period, growth in office-type employment will be about 1 percent annually, according to U.S. Department of Labor forecasts. In addition, the trend toward telecommuting will increase as the falling cost and increasing availability of technology make it more feasible to work at home.

The office renovation business has fared better than has new office construction in recent years. In some markets, expenditures for office renovation are probably greater than those for new office construction put in place. Much of the growth in this market segment is caused by competition for tenants, which has compelled owners to upgrade and modernize older buildings. Although expenditures for office remodeling are likely to remain at high levels, the era of rapid growth is largely over because of market maturation.

Hotels and Other Commercial Buildings

Although hotel construction is usually a small category of construction, it has been booming since the mid-1990s. The 1999 value of hotel construction was more than double the 1994 value. Many gambling casinos are classified as hotels in construction statistics, and much of the current boom is attributable to that factor. In addition to casinos, travelers' demand for lodging has increased, although since 1998 the level of construction has been running ahead of the underlying demand for hotel lodging.

The construction category of "other commercial buildings" consists of all commercial buildings except office buildings and hotels and includes warehouses, grain elevators, shopping centers, parking garages, banks, fast-food restaurants, and gasoline stations. In recent years, shopping centers have accounted for about half the value of construction work in this category, and warehouses for about one-fourth.

The value of store construction put in place has remained high despite the financial woes of many established retail chains and weak gains in retail spending. Much of the current strength in store construction is in big box stores and centers, which are nonmall discount stores or large stores that carry a narrow category of products (such as electronics, building supplies, or pet supplies) at discount prices. The boom in big box store construction has waned, but this type of construction will be a major component of commercial construction for the next 5 years. Softness in consumer spending is affecting even the most successful discounters, and some of them are suffering from growing pains as well.

Another important segment consists of "neighborhood" shopping centers close to new housing subdivisions. The fairly high level of housing starts between 1996 and 2000 has created numerous opportunities for new neighborhood shopping centers over the next few years.

Construction of service stations and automobile repair garages is expected to remain at high levels in the year 2000. The auto service business has benefited from the increasing complexity of automobiles and the increasing proportion of older cars. Although the number of gasoline stations has declined sharply over the last three decades, most of the remaining stations are investing large amounts in construction to become high-volume sales outlets, convenience shops, fast-food outlets, or specialized service stations. According to economic and demographic forecasts for the next 5 years, there will be further increases in the number of vehicle-miles driven and the demand for auto service and repair.

Private Electric Utilities

This category of construction includes new power plants, transmission lines, pollution control facilities, the conversion of existing power plants from oil and gas to coal, and the modernization of existing power plants and other buildings. It does not include government-owned facilities and power plants owned by manufacturers.

The electric utility industry is experiencing a moderate construction boom as demand for electricity approaches capacity in many regions. This trend should continue in the year 2000 and through 2004. The rate of gain over the long term will be strongly affected by interest rates and demand for electricity, with new construction gaining at about the same rate as GDP and repair construction growing at a faster rate.

Although the industry has experienced good growth in the demand for electricity, competition has increased because of the National Energy Policy Act of 1992 and actions by certain state utility commissions. This has resulted in less construction by the regulated utility companies but more construction for cogeneration projects, nonregulated power generators, and municipal supplies. There probably will be a quickening in the pace of new construction starts, but utilities are unlikely to order large numbers of new power plants. Instead, the emphasis will be on energy conservation, the expansion of existing facilities, and heavier use of existing capacity.

Expenditures for the maintenance and repair of electric utility systems have grown rapidly and are almost as large as new utility construction spending. Maintenance and repair expenditures will continue to grow rapidly in the twenty-first century as the average age of operating power plants increases and operations become more complex.

Hospital and Institutional Building

This category includes hospitals, outpatient clinics, nursing homes, convalescent homes, orphanages, and similar institutions for prolonged care. (Buildings that are used primarily as doctors' offices are classified as office buildings.) About 70 percent of the value of this construction goes for hospitals and clinics; the remainder goes for nursing homes and similar facilities. Seventy percent of hospital and institutional construction expenditures are for additions and modernization at existing facilities, and only 30 percent are for new facilities. About 75 percent of this construction is for privately owned facilities, and 25 percent for publicly owned facilities.

Construction of health care facilities declined in 1999, in part reflecting uncertainty about health care financing. Recent legislation regulating health maintenance organizations (HMOs) has increased uncertainty and may affect construction plans. In addition, the health care sector has been affected by many of the downsizing and cost-cutting trends that have affected the rest of the U.S. economy.

The decline in hospital construction caused by these financial factors is likely to be brief and mild, as was the case in the mid-1980s, during a different round of cost containment. After about 2001, hospital construction probably will resume its long-term upward trend and be one of the faster-growing markets.

Aside from health care financing, the most important factor in the longer-term outlook for hospital and institutional construction is the rapid increase in the number of elderly Americans. People over age 65 average about six times as much hospitalization per capita as do persons under that age.

Nursing home construction is likely to increase even faster than overall health care construction because it is focused on the most rapidly growing segment of the population. Nearly 90 percent of the 1.8 million Americans in nursing homes are age 65 or older. Within this group, people over 85 years old are by far the most likely to be in nursing homes, and they are the fastest-growing age group in the United States.

Additional factors that will support health care construction are the increasing use of new and sophisticated medical treatments, the possibility of major increases in federally mandated health insurance coverage, and the need to modernize to attract paying patients and scarce health care personnel. Negative factors in an otherwise bullish outlook include the poor fiscal condition of hospitals with large proportions of charity patients, the increasing number of Americans without health insurance, and aggressive cost reduction by major insurance payers. Publicly owned hospitals are less able to cope with these negative factors, and so their construction is expected to lag behind that of privately owned hospitals.

PUBLICLY OWNED CONSTRUCTION

In 1999, the total value of publicly owned construction in current dollars was about $158 billion, of which $50 billion was for highways and bridges and $34 billion was for educational buildings. The constant dollar value of publicly owned construction put in place was $126 billion, about 5 percent greater than that in 1998. Most categories of public construction increased, with the exception of federal construction, military facilities, and public housing (see Table 6-2).

Public works construction is expected to set an all-time record in the year 2000, although in per capita terms it is expected to be below the level reached in 1968. This category of construction will remain at high levels to prevent the deterioration of U.S. infrastructure and accommodate population growth and movements and economic development. The condition of infrastructure not only is a quality-of-life issue, it also is an important factor in U.S. productivity and international competitiveness. In particular, the vast U.S. highway network increases industrial productivity by allowing faster and cheaper transportation of products. Other types of infrastructure, such as airports, schools, waterworks, and mass transit, also contribute to the productivity of the U.S. economy.

The Transportation Efficiency Act for the 21st Century (TEA-21), which was passed in June 1998, will be one of the most important determinants of public works construction over the next 5 years. TEA-21 not only set high budget levels for the federal-aid highways program but contained policy directives on how the funds should be spent. The budget levels set by TEA-21 exceed the previous 6-year authorization, known as the Intermodal Surface Transportation Efficiency Act of 1991 (ISTEA), and allow even more flexibility in terms of highway versus mass transit construction and new construction versus repair construction.

The federal budget is the source of financing for about 40 percent of all public works construction. Federal construction spending programs will increase about 6 percent in the year 2000 (see Table 6-5) because of the high level of obligations incurred during fiscal years 1998 and 1999. (Because of lags in approvals and construction, most obligations do not result in construction put in place for a year or more.)

State and local governments will increase their total construction spending in 2000 as a result of larger federal grants, the booming economy, and the need to curtail the backlog of deferred projects. State and local government spending is especially important for education, highways, water and sewer projects, and public safety.

Outlook for 2000

The overall value of publicly owned construction is expected to increase modestly from the 1999 level. On a level-of-government basis, federal spending for public works construction will increase 3 percent faster than will inflation, while state and local government spending will increase 4 percent faster in the aggregate. The largest increases are expected in federal industrial facilities, prisons, highways, and water supply systems. Few categories of public works construction other than military facilities are expected to decline.

The President's budget in January 1999 projected a 6 percent increase in federal construction spending in 2000, and there probably will be a significant increase in spending because of additional authorizations by Congress. The budget anticipates large reductions for military construction, defense family housing, energy programs, and federal office buildings, while spending for highways, mass transportation, pollution abatement, and the U.S. Postal Service is expected to increase (see Table 6-5).

TABLE 6-5: Federal Construction Outlays by Fiscal Year
(millions of dollars; percent)

	1996[1]	1997[1]	1998[1]	1999[2]	2000[3]	Percent Change 99–00
Military construction	3,398	3,161	3,515	3,170	2,955	−7
Defense family housing	1,078	1,012	883	966	803	−17
Atomic energy defense activities	933	537	689	640	703	10
Highways and bridges	19,653	20,502	20,063	23,150	25,517	10
Mass transportation	3,698	4,041	3,892	3,789	3,960	5
Railroad transportation	282	372	465	107	16	−85
Air transportation	1,675	1,514	1,541	1,684	1,766	5
Water transportation	125	111				
Community development block grants	4,545	4,517	4,621	4,965	4,856	−2
Other community and regional development	1,530	1,507	1,479	1,438	1,414	−2
Pollution control and abatement	3,668	3,646	3,521	3,616	4,104	13
Water resources	2,318	2,078	2,350	3,297	3,295	−0
Federal prison system	486	307	33	459	414	
Housing assistance	6,757	6,849	6,406	6,501	7,264	12
General science, space, and technology	611	615	517	479	551	15
Energy	1,918	1,128	778	961	843	−12
Veterans hospitals and other health	1,404	1,538	1,565	1,633	1,652	1
Postal service	1,138	1,261	1,528	1,032	1,225	19
Federal buildings funds	1,478	1,362	1,375	1,069	1,016	−5
International affairs	279	315	150	318	392	23
Other construction programs	917	1,373	1,420	1,420	1,420	0
Total federal construction outlays	57,891	57,746	58,394	61,002	64,717	6

[1] Actual.
[2] Estimated.
[3] Budgeted.
Source: Budget of the U.S. government, fiscal years 1998 through 2000.

Outlook to 2004

Public works construction will increase about 4 percent annually during the next 5 years, assuming moderate economic growth and interest rates. Federal construction spending will pick up substantially because of the balanced budget situation and TEA-21 funding. The increases in new construction obligations in 1998 and 1999 will be felt mostly after 2000. Over the past two decades, construction programs have borne a disproportionate share of the budget cuts needed to control the deficit, and the expected budget surpluses will reduce this severe pressure on infrastructure investment. Since the $64.7 billion in federal construction spending accounts for only 2 percent of the total federal budget, substantial increases in public works would have relatively modest effects on overall spending. Furthermore, if the economy performs as predicted, growing tax revenues will allow state and local funding for public works to remain at high levels.

Government maintenance and repair spending probably will increase at least as fast as will spending for new construction because the public works infrastructure is becoming steadily older and larger. While increased maintenance and repair expenditures will provide work for certain types of contractors, this often will consume funds that could have been spent on new construction.

Highway construction will be the largest and most reliable public works market for the next 5 years. Water and sewer construction will remain at high levels but will not increase much. Construction of schools and other public buildings also may increase. Military construction and federal industrial construction probably will decline as measured by new construction put in place, but environmental restoration funded by those programs will remain at high levels.

Transportation Infrastructure

New road and bridge construction, which was at a record level in 1999, is expected to set another record in the year 2000. Expenditures for highway maintenance and repair have increased and will continue to set records as well.

About 25 percent of the value of highway construction put in place consists of bridges, overpasses, and tunnels; flatwork (primarily roads) accounts for the remaining 75 percent. Bridge work is expected to grow faster than flatwork during the next several years because of the need to replace obsolete or unsafe bridges with new bridges for the twenty-first century. According to the Federal Highway Administration's latest estimate, 23 percent of the highway bridges in the United States are structurally deficient and an additional 21 percent are functionally or structurally obsolete.

Highway maintenance and repair expenditures have grown during the last two decades as the road network has become larger and older. In 1999, the current dollar cost of highway maintenance and repair was about $31 billion, compared with $50 billion in new highway construction put in place. While some of this work consists of routine maintenance such as mowing grass, much of it is typical construction activity such as repaving roads and painting bridges. Highway maintenance and repair expenditures probably will grow more rapidly than will new construction over the next decade.

Mass transit construction was expected to decline slightly in 1999 despite the increase in new federal budget authority because of lags in the spending process. However, after 2000, mass transit construction is expected to increase sharply because of increasing federal financial support. The outlook for mass transit construction is heavily dependent on the TEA-21 funding discussed above. Of the $235 billion in TEA-21 funds authorized from 1998 through 2004, $35 billion was earmarked for mass transit projects. In addition, a large share of the remaining funds can be diverted from highways to mass transit because of concern about air pollution and local development policies.

Airport construction will gain dramatically in the next 5 years in response to the record levels of traffic in both passengers and cargo. Federal government spending for airport construction is not budgeted to change much in the year 2000, but local investments in airports are booming. Legislation is pending in Congress (AIR-21) that could boost airport construction even more than is currently expected (see Chapter 51).

Water and Sewer Systems

Water supply and sewerage construction increased 12 percent and 10 percent, respectively, in 1999 in response to new building construction and the need to upgrade existing infrastructure. Both of these construction categories did well in the mid-1990s, reflecting high levels of building construction as well as work on long-deferred projects. The strong construction market expected in the year 2000 will help both categories remain at high levels.

In the longer term, waterworks probably will be one of the more rapidly growing categories of public construction. The aqueduct systems of most older cities are so old that extensive replacement work must be done each year. The current level of construction in the United States is much lower than that needed to replace waterworks every 50 years, which is the recommended practice. Most water utilities are in a good position to raise the needed capital, and so a steady increase in replacement construction is likely. The Safe Drinking Water Act requires numerous upgrades and replacements of water supply facilities, which will continue well into the twenty-first century.

After the year 2000, sewerage construction probably will continue to grow, although at a slower rate than will the overall economy. Federal spending may not keep up with inflation, but the state and local share will increase steadily. A growing market factor is the need to repair, modernize, and replace sewage treatment plants that were built during the boom in the 1970s. The sustained recovery in building construction also will support sewerage construction.

Solid waste disposal facilities, including those for resource recovery, constitute a small but rapidly growing construction market. Resource recovery facilities are increasingly common because of improved efficiency, rising land prices, and environmental objections to landfills.

Educational Buildings

New construction expenditures for schools, libraries, and museums were at near-record levels in 1999, and another solid increase is expected in 2000. About 70 percent of the spending was for primary and secondary schools, and colleges and other higher education facilities accounted for an additional 25 percent. More than 80 percent of educational construction expenditures were for publicly owned buildings; the rest went for privately owned buildings.

The school construction boom, which began in the late 1980s, is being affected by the budget problems of state and local governments. The underlying demand for school construction is very strong because of the record number of school-age Americans, the need to replace dilapidated schools, and population expansion into underbuilt areas. The net result of these conflicting pressures will be for school construction to remain at high levels with slower growth rates.

Patrick MacAuley, U.S. Department of Commerce, Office of Metals, Materials, and Chemicals, (202) 482-0132, October 1999.

INTERNATIONAL CONSTRUCTION MARKET

The international construction market was hurt as much as any industry by the financial disruptions in southeast Asia in late 1997 and 1998 and Brazil's financial troubles in 1998 and early 1999. The dramatic tumble in currencies in the Young Tiger economies of Thailand, Indonesia, and Malaysia, along with financial disruptions in South Korea and the Philippines, caused the delay or cancellation of major state-funded infrastructure projects and resulted in a huge outflow of development capital from the region. Also, the rush of investment into Brazil stalled. While there remains a hangover in the international construction market, U.S. engineers, architects, and contractors working abroad are experiencing a gradual recovery.

According to *Engineering News-Record* magazine (*ENR*), the 500 largest construction engineering, architectural, and environmental design firms in the United States generated $7.7 billion in design revenue from projects outside the United States in 1998, up 4.9 percent from the 1997 level. As a measure of the impact of the Asian financial crisis on the U.S. design export market, revenue for the *ENR* Top 500 Design Firms fell 8.5 percent in Asia in 1998 to $2.25 billion while advancing in nearly every other region.

Significantly, 1998 revenue from Latin American projects for this group rose 30 percent to $888 million, mostly as a result of increasingly stable regional economies and a greater emphasis on privatization. Brazil's economic woes are not reflected in these numbers. The largest overall regional jump in numbers for the Top 500 in 1998 was the 61.2 percent increase in the Caribbean to $199 million. Africa showed a healthy 16.9 percent gain to $370.4 million in 1998. Europe, the largest international design market for the top 500, increased to $2.9 billion in revenue, up 9.8 percent over 1997. The Middle East rose 8.9 percent in 1998 to $741.4 million for the Top 500.

On *ENR*'s list of the Top 400 International Design Firms, reflecting export design revenue for architects and engineers around the world, U.S. design firms dominated. There were 80 U.S. firms among the top 200 of that list, generating $7.36 billion in revenue, a 43.4 percent share of the total of $16.97 billion by the group.

Among *ENR*'s Top 400 general contractors, U.S. contractors reported $28.44 billion in international revenue in 1998. This was a very healthy 11.8 percent increase over the figures for 1997. One warning sign for contractors in the international market was the fact that new contract awards for work abroad reported by the *ENR* Top 400 dropped 24.6 percent in 1998, moving down to $27.9 billion.

On a regional basis, contractors tend to be more on the trailing edge of trends than are their counterparts among design firms. Thus, U.S. contractors working abroad did not begin to experience the troubles in Asia until 1998. The Top 400 contractors reported $7.6 billion in revenue in Asia in 1998, up only 0.4 percent. Surprisingly, Latin America also was flat for the Top 400, with a drop-off in metals prices that depressed the mining market offsetting an upswing in manufacturing and infrastructure in that year. Overall, revenue in Latin America fell 0.9 percent in 1998 to $3.56 billion for *ENR*'s Top 400 contractors.

Other regional markets were more vigorous. U.S. contractors generated $4.86 billion in revenue in the Middle East in 1998, up 42.1 percent over the level in 1997. Europe provided $7.04 billion in revenue for U.S. contractors, up 11 percent. Africa showed more promise than in the past, rising 28.5 percent to $1.95 billion, and the Canadian market improved 23.2 percent to reach $2.39 billion.

Among *ENR*'s top 225 international contractors, U.S. firms led those from all other nations, although not to the extent that U.S. design firms dominate the market. There were 64 U.S. contractors in the top 225, generating $28.25 billion in revenue from projects abroad. This constituted 24.3 percent of the total of $116.39 billion for the top 225 as a whole.

As a measure of the international construction market as a whole, *ENR* measured the world construction market at $3.22 trillion in 1998. The U.S. represented the single largest market at $651 billion in total construction spending, followed closely by Japan at $626.5 billion. Other major national construction markets included: Germany, $315.0 billion; China, $185.9 billion; the United Kingdom, $104.9 billion; Brazil, $102.1 billion; France, $98.0 billion; Italy, $95.3 billion; South Korea, $73.6 billion; and Canada, $72.0 billion. On a regional basis, *ENR* estimates total construction spending as follows: Asia, $1.12 trillion; Europe, $995.6 billion; Latin America, $238.6 billion; the Middle East, $76.7 billion; and Africa, $59.4 billion.

Financing

While construction is a multi-trillion-dollar market worldwide, private financing remains a major driver for U.S. construction firms' export opportunities. However, the southeast Asian financial crisis caused a significant reduction in the overall willingness of private investors to commit funds to developing economies. For example, gross private financings to emerging market economies took a nosedive in 1998, falling nearly 50 percent to $148.5 billion from $286.1 billion in 1997, according to the International Monetary Fund, citing a study by Capital Data Loanware and Bondware.

Much of this drop-off came as a direct result of the Asian economic crisis. Gross private financings to Asia collapsed in 1998, falling from $127.5 billion in 1997 to $34.1 billion in 1998. The Middle East and Africa also saw a major drop in private financings, falling from $30.8 billion in 1997 to $13.7 billion in 1998, while financings in the Americas fell from $90.3 billion to $64.6 billion. Only the developing nations in Europe held the line, dropping only from $37.5 billion to $36.1 billion.

It is a measure of the recovery of many of the economies in Asia that gross private financings were on the rise in that region in 1999. Through August 1999, financings from private sources stood at $38.2 billion, exceeding in the first 8 months of the year the region's total for 1998. By contrast, private financings in developing countries in the Americas continued to lag in 1999, off nearly 20 percent from their 1998 level.

It is a measure of the importance of private financing in generating infrastructure, development, and construction opportunities that multinational development organizations are stepping up their efforts to involve private investors in projects. An example is the increasing emphasis the Asian Development Bank (ADB) is placing on its Private Sector Group (PSG).

Through the PSG, the ADB will provide up to 25 percent of the financing to a maximum of $50 million for projects in any of its developing member countries. The PSG places particular emphasis on infrastructure projects, including build-operate-transfer and build-own-operate arrangements, in areas such as power, water supply, transportation, and telecommunications. It also will help facilitate projects in agribusiness and industrial development on a limited basis. It already has approved power projects in China [1,000 megawatts (MW)], India (500 MW), and the Philippines (1,200 MW) as well as industrial projects in Bangladesh, Nepal, Pakistan, and Vietnam. Other countries with approved projects are Indonesia, South Korea, Malaysia, Sri Lanka, and Thailand.

U.S.-based agencies also are working to provide incentives for international construction opportunities for U.S. construction firms. The U.S. Trade and Development Agency will provide seed money for proposed projects with export potential. It maintains a proposed project database of about 1,000 projects with construction potential, including about 600 power projects.

However, U.S. firms must keep in mind that large-scale financial commitments to developing nations have an element of risk. Even experienced firms employing sophisticated currency hedges lost money during the Asian currency crisis. There are indications that the vast expansion of power capacity in some Asian countries may result in customers who signed supply contracts being unable to meet them. Thus, construction firms must have a thorough understanding of the economic circumstances of the areas in which they hope to operate.

Markets

Privatization is one of the keys to the developing international construction market. The scale of some of these privatization projects is huge. One of the largest is a proposal by the Taiwan Environmental Protection Administration to privatize its solid waste disposal responsibilities. That long-term nationwide program, which would include the building of 39 solid waste incinerators under individual contracts, would cost an estimated $27 billion.

Taiwan's plan provides just one demonstration that water and wastewater projects have large export potential for U.S. construction firms. Another proposed large-scale water and wastewater project is China's Chengdu province's $2 billion plan to upgrade its drinking water and wastewater treatment program. SABESP, the water company for the state of São Paulo, Brazil, is planning a wide-scale upgrade of that state's water and sewage treatment plant system, a series of projects worth an estimated $1.6 billion. Other large-scale water and waste projects on the boards include those in the province of Tucaman, Argentina; Ankara, Turkey; the state of Victoria, Australia; and in the areas around Mexico City.

Transportation projects provide another source of export potential for U.S. construction companies. Among the major proposed privatized projects, one of the largest is a proposal by the governor of the Brazilian state of Minas Gerais to privatize about 2,500 kilometers of roads. The proposal would parcel out the project into seven parts with a cumulative value of $1.5 billion. Other large-scale road projects in the planning stage are the Bregana–Zagreb–Dubrovnik highway in Croatia, the Kuwait–Subbiya causeway, the rebuilding of the Florianpolis–Osorio highway in Brazil, a highway development plan in Portugal, and, potentially the largest, a 163-kilometer mountain highway in Yunnan as part of an $8.2 billion regional development plan.

Rail systems, particularly light rail, are an extremely promising sector for U.S. construction firms. Taiwan has possibly the most aggressive rail program in the world, with light rail projects on the boards for Taipei, Taoyuan, Kaoshing, and Tainan as well as a high-speed rail system to connect Taipei and Kaoshing. Other cities planning new or upgraded light rail lines are Bogota, Colombia; Hong Kong; Singapore; Delhi, India; and several connector lines in Korea.

The airport market is experiencing a worldwide boom. Among the large international projects under consideration are a new Inchon International Airport in Korea, which is ticketed at $4 billion, and the Berlin International Airport project, which would replace Tegel and Templehof airports, an estimated $2 billion project presenting substantial export opportunities for U.S. firms. China is planning two new international airports, one at Pudong, Shanghai, and the other at Baiyun, Guangzhou, both estimated to cost $2 billion each.

The largest potential new airport projects are the $7.0 billion proposed Chubu New International Airport near Nagoya, Japan, and Kitakyushu Airport in Kitakyushu, Japan, estimated at $5 billion. Argentina has a large airport privatization program with work worth an estimated $2.1 billion at 55 airports in that country.

Regional Markets

A trend toward stabilization and openness has improved the outlook for the Middle East in the year 2000. The orderly transition of power from Jordan's King Hussein to his son, King Abdullah, is a symbol of the new order. Jordan had suffered because its economy was tied to Iraq and it had few natural resources aside from the mineral-rich Dead Sea. An $80 million plant, now under construction, that will extract magnesium fluoride from Dead Sea brine and convert it to high-grade magnesium oxide is part of a strategy to exploit that resource. Two boom years in the petrochemical sector are winding down in the Middle East and north Africa. Many of the current ethylene projects under construction will come on-line in 2001. One new project is a 500,000-ton-per-year ethylene cracker in Mesaieed, Qatar.

Led by Hong Kong, the Asian construction market is beginning to recover. There are still underlying economic problems in countries such as Japan, South Korea, and Thailand, and Japan still presents barriers to international competition. The Philippines is a bright spot for some firms, which cite projects in the planning stages such as a $1.5 billion rail line from Manila to Clark air base.

Africa's poverty and virtually constant political unrest have put a damper on development for years, but there are indications that conditions are becoming more favorable for tapping its oil and gas reserves even in countries such as war-torn Angola. One pending petroleum project may produce Africa's single largest construction job: a $3.5 billion, 1,070-kilometer pipeline from southern Chad to the coast of Cameroon. The World Bank may lend the two governments $90 million to finance their equity shares, and if it does that, construction will start in the year 2000. Another major area of development is the "Maputo Corridor" in Mozambique, where one of the projects is a $1.3 billion aluminum smelter now under construction.

Fortunately for the Latin American region, the Brazilian financial crisis of early 1999 was nipped in the bud and never spread to the closely interdependent neighboring countries. The region is experiencing a burst of privatization in water and wastewater treatment plants. With more than 500 municipalities that have more than 100,000 people, the field presents a major opportunity for international investors. In the power sector, many projects are on hold, but demand is not decreasing, and capacity additions over the next 10 years could reach 44,000 MW.

The pace of construction in Europe could creep up a notch in the year 2000 after several years of slow going. Development is getting a boost from the establishment of a single currency and a single central bank for the European Union, which has put interest rates at a historically low level. The effort to stimulate a single market, however, has not had much success. There has been little effect on cross-border exchange. The Irish construction market, although worth only about $13 billion, is the most active in western Europe, growing at four times Europe's average growth rate of 2.5 percent. In eastern Europe, although the combined volume of work in Poland, Hungary, the Czech Republic, and Slovakia is small, the growth rate is predicted to be 6.5 percent in the year 2000.

The U.S. construction market marked its eighth consecutive year of expansion in 1999, making it a magnet for international firms. These firms are coming not only to do projects but also to buy U.S. firms. Notably, the Essen, Germany–based Hochtief AG bought all outstanding shares of the New York City–based Turner Corp. for $370 million. The major challenge facing firms in the U.S. market is finding qualified personnel. Recruiting and retaining staff is a major management focus.

Canada has finally felt the surge of work spilling over from the United States. Construction activity was expected to grow 3 to 5 percent in 1999 and approach $70 billion. Every province experienced growth except British Columbia, which traditionally is influenced more by Asian markets than by North American affairs. Growth is being spurred by high-tech industries in Calgary and Ottawa, auto manufacturing in Ontario, and airport work. Lester B. Pearson International Airport has a development program worth $2.5 billion over 10 years, for example.

Long-Term Outlook

The outlook for international construction has brightened considerably. Southeast Asia's economic struggles seem to be coming to an end in most countries, although Malaysia and Indonesia continue to experience some economic and political problems. While Thailand, the Philippines, Indonesia, and Malaysia saw their combined GDPs fall 9.8 percent in 1998, the International Monetary Fund estimated that these Association of Southeast Asian Nations (ASEAN-4) countries would rebound in 1999 with an overall increase in economic output of 1.4 percent and rise again in 2000 by 3.6 percent. This turnaround, coupled with the slow recovery of Brazil's economy, should provide the impetus for a new round of investment and growth in major construction markets in developing countries.

In Asia, Japan continues to be far and away the largest construction market. However it has experienced negative growth in the past 2 years, and was projected to show slow growth in 1999, with little indication of a major recovery in 2000. This, coupled with the difficulty of penetrating the Japanese construction market, should leave little room for growth there.

China has been struggling to balance its growth against inflationary pressure. However, it remains a strong market, and the Chinese government has indicated a greater willingness to use foreign construction firms, especially if they can provide economic assistance to boost project viability.

India also continues to show strong growth in the construction market. However, political considerations in light of U.S. economic sanctions in 1998 after India tested its first nuclear device, coupled with growing nationalism, make it a difficult market for U.S. construction firms.

In terms of overall growth, Asia's total economic output should grow 4.5 to 5.0 percent in 1999 and another 5 percent in 2000. Despite some difficulties in Japan and India, the increased willingness of the private sector to return to investing in Asia should allow U.S. construction firms to experience growth in revenue in Asia of at least that level and perhaps in the range of 6 to 7 percent in 1999 and 2000.

In Latin America, strong corporate investment in Brazil and Argentina and an increase in industrial investment in Venezuela and major infrastructure expansions throughout the region were expected to mitigate the overall downturn in Brazil's economy during 1999. Thus, the overall Latin American construction market was expected to remain flat in 1999, and U.S. construction firms should experience significant growth of 3 to 5 percent in 2000. That figure could increase if metals prices rebound, allowing countries, such as Chile, with economies heavily influenced by mining to come back.

The economies of many Middle Eastern countries are so closely tied to the price of oil that much of that region's construction market is dependent on oil price movements. The International Monetary Fund (IMF) anticipates an average increase in the price of oil of about 7.5 percent in the year 2000, which should help regional construction patterns expand. However, if recent patterns in oil pricing hold, IMF's projections may be on the high side. Overall, the construction market in the Middle East should increase, but only in the range of 2 to 3 percent, in 1999 and 2000.

The African market, while relatively small and often difficult for U.S. construction firms, has shown steady growth over the last 3 years and should continue to grow in 1999 and 2000. However, political problems in Nigeria and economic stagnation in South Africa, the two largest construction markets in sub-Saharan Africa, have blunted the promise of the region. In addition, the AIDS crisis, which has affected up to 20 percent of the adult population of several countries in the region, has forced many countries to devote their limited resources to health care and social services rather than much-needed infrastructure improvements. Therefore, the construction outlook in Africa, while positive, remains less than its potential otherwise indicates. The market should increase 2 to 3 percent in 1999 and 5 percent in 2000.

Europe is still one of the world's largest construction markets, but it remains sluggish as it adjusts to a united economy. Overall growth rates for the continent have ranged from 2 to 3 percent. Large privatization projects in the United Kingdom and major industrial developments there and in Ireland have spurred major construction opportunities. However, overall, there is little to indicate that the European construction market will grow more than 3 percent a year in the foreseeable future.

Taken as a whole, the international construction market is recovering from the shocks to its system in 1997–1998 in Asia and in 1999 in Brazil. The overall international construction market should grow at least 2 percent in 1999 and 4 to 5 percent in 2000. As long as the U.S. economy remains strong and the dollar remains stable, there is every reason to believe that a steady growth rate of 4 percent in the international market is sustainable through 2003.

Jan Tuchman and Gary Tulacz, *Engineering News-Record,* The McGraw-Hill Companies, 212-904-3251, November 1999.

■ REFERENCES

Call the Bureau of the Census at (301) 457-1242 for information about ordering Census documents.

America's Infrastructure: Effects of Construction Spending, Associated General Contractors, 1957 E St. NW, Washington, DC 20006. (202) 393-2040.

Automated Builder (monthly), P.O. Box 120, Carpinteria, CA 93014. (805) 684-7659.

Cahners Building & Construction Market Forecast (monthly), Cahners Publishing Co., 275 Washington Street, Newton, MA 02158-1630. (617) 630-2105.

Census of Construction, 1997, Bureau of the Census, U.S. Department of Commerce, Washington, DC 20233. (301) 457-1242.

Construction Review (quarterly), International Trade Administration, Room H4045, U.S. Department of Commerce, Washington, DC 20230. (202) 482-0132.

Dodge/Sweet's Construction Outlook, McGraw-Hill Information Systems Company, 1221 Avenue of the Americas, New York, NY 10020.

Engineering News-Record (weekly), McGraw-Hill Publishing Co., 1221 Avenue of the Americas, New York, NY 10020. (212) 512-4634.

Expenditures for Nonresidential Improvements and Upkeep, 1997, Bureau of the Census, U.S. Department of Commerce, Washington, D.C. 20233. (301) 457-1605.

Housing Starts (Construction Reports, Series C-20), Bureau of the Census, U.S. Department of Commerce, Washington, DC 20233. (301) 457-4666.

Infrastructure: Investing in Our Future, Portland Cement Association, 54 Old Orchard Road, Skokie, IL 60077. (708) 966-6200.

International Construction Review On-Line, International Trade Administration, U.S. Department of Commerce. ita.doc.gov/forestprod/construction.

Manufacturing Report (monthly), Manufactured Housing Institute, 2101 Wilson Boulevard, Arlington, VA 22201-3062. (703) 558-0400.

1998 Year-End Report (annual), National Association of Home Builders, Building Systems Councils, 1201 15th Street, NW, Washington, DC 20005. (202) 822-0576.

Quick Facts (annual), Manufactured Housing Institute, 2101 Wilson Boulevard, Arlington, VA 22201-3062. (703) 558-0400.

Value of New Construction Put in Place (Construction Reports, Series C-30), Bureau of the Census, U.S. Department of Commerce, Washington, DC 20233. (301) 457-1605.

■ RELATED CHAPTERS

5: Electricity Production and Sales
7: Wood Products
8: Building Products and Materials
43: Health and Medical Services

WOOD PRODUCTS
Economic and Trade Trends

Source: U.S. Department of Commerce: Bureau of the Census, International Trade Administration.

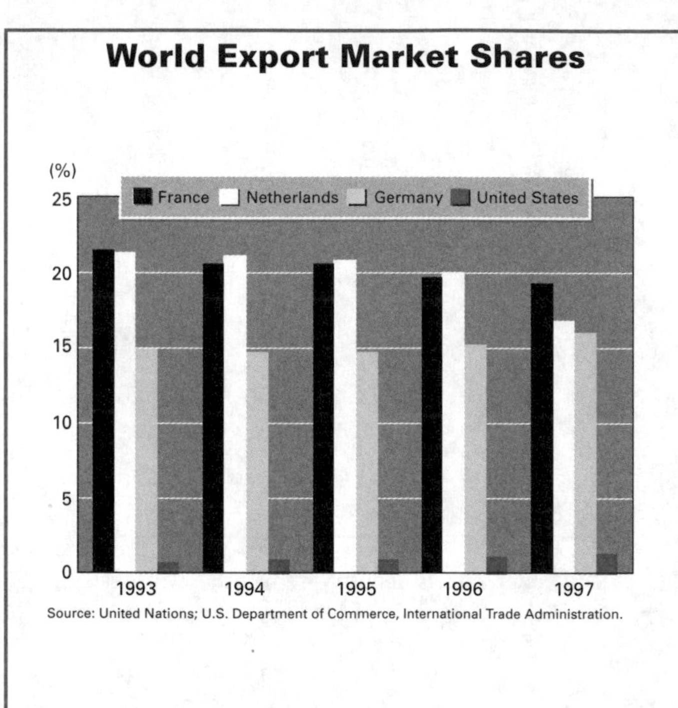

Source: United Nations; U.S. Department of Commerce, International Trade Administration.

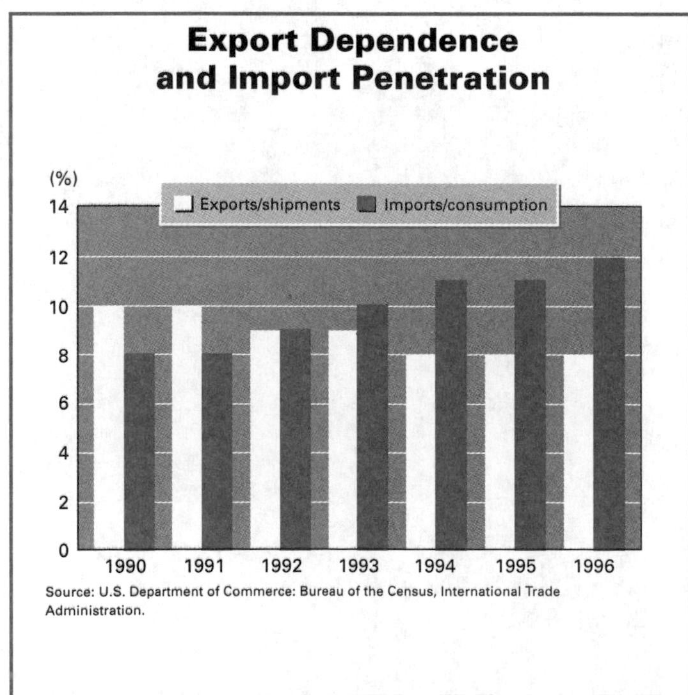

Source: U.S. Department of Commerce: Bureau of the Census, International Trade Administration.

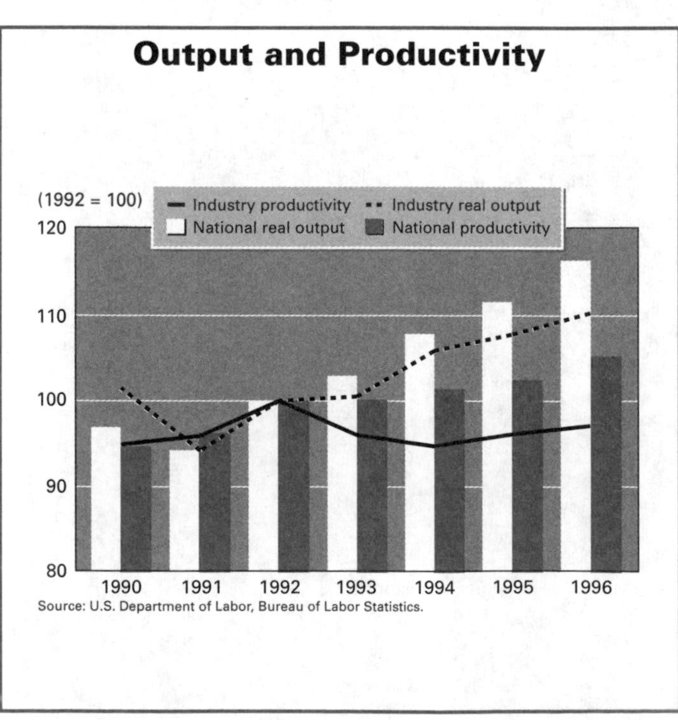

Source: U.S. Department of Labor, Bureau of Labor Statistics.

See "Getting the Most Out of *Outlook 2000*" for definitions of terms.

7

Wood Products

INDUSTRY DEFINITION The U.S. wood products industry consists of 14 manufacturing sectors that process timber and pulpwood into products such as lumber, panel products, and other basic wood materials. This chapter covers the following wood products sectors: general sawmills and planing mills (SIC 2421), hardwood veneer and plywood (SIC 2435), softwood veneer and plywood (SIC 2436), and reconstituted wood products (SIC 2493). Manufactured housing and prefabricated wood buildings are not covered in this chapter.

GLOBAL INDUSTRY TRENDS

The U.S. wood products industry remains a world leader in the production of and trade in a multitude of products used for residential and light commercial construction as well as consumer-oriented products. Residential and light commercial construction end uses dominate the market for its products, with more than 81 percent of softwood lumber and 65 percent of structural panels used in those activities. Highly skilled labor, access to raw materials, efficient transportation, and strong capital investments in machinery and information technologies make the United States the world's premier producer of wood products.

International trade is an important component of the wood products industry. The net value of imports and exports increased

TABLE 7-1: Lumber and Wood Products (SIC 24) Trends and Forecasts
(millions of dollars except as noted)

										Percent Change			
	1992	1993	1994	1995	1996	1997[1]	1998[1]	1999[2]	2000[3]	97–98	98–99	99–00	96–00[4]
Industry data													
Value of shipments[5]	81,565	94,272	103,501	104,944	106,518	112,500	116,325	120,150	121,766	3.4	3.3	1.3	3.4
Value of shipments (1992$)	81,565	81,696	86,175	87,769	90,035	93,636	95,509	97,515	99,270	2.0	2.1	1.8	2.5
Total employment (thousands)	656	685	718	740	739	739	738	738	737	−0.1	0.0	−0.1	−0.1
Production workers (thousands)	540	569	595	614	613	613	613	612	612	0.0	−0.2	0.0	−0.0
Average hourly earnings ($)	9.37	9.51	9.62	9.83	10.17	10.42	10.63	10.92	11.10	2.0	2.7	1.6	2.2
Capital expenditures	1,760	1,949	2,657	3,060	3,305	3,330	3,395	3,450	3,600	2.0	1.6	4.3	2.2
Product data													
Value of shipments[5]	78,061	90,329	98,798	99,853	101,319	104,359	107,594	111,037	113,568	3.1	3.2	2.3	2.9
Value of shipments (1992$)	78,061	78,291	82,258	83,506	85,611	86,895	88,546	90,494	91,625	1.9	2.2	1.2	1.7
Trade data													
Value of imports	6,736	8,888	10,513	10,394	12,176	13,506	14,002	14,744	15,100	3.7	5.3	2.4	5.5
Value of exports	6,821	7,361	7,252	7,424	7,401	7,312	5,960	6,115	6,206	−18.5	2.6	1.5	−4.3

[1] Estimate except imports and exports.
[2] Estimate.
[3] Forecast.
[4] Compound annual rate.
[5] For a definition of industry versus product values, see "Getting the Most Out of *Outlook 2000*."
Source: U.S. Department of Commerce: Bureau of the Census; International Trade Administration.

consistently from $13.6 billion in 1992 to almost $20 billion in 1998. However, 1998 was a weak year for exports, with their value falling 18.5 percent, mostly as a result of languishing Asian economies, especially Japan. Imports, by contrast, increased 3.7 percent, reflecting strong demand in the United States (see Table 7-1). Although trade is an important factor in the industry, the domestic market is by far the main contributor to the financial health of the U.S. wood products industry. Demand for wood products is primarily a function of the housing market, and with the sustained strength of that sector, demand has been increasing.

IMPORTANT FACTORS AFFECTING FUTURE U.S. INDUSTRY GROWTH

The strength of the domestic housing market, including new construction and remodeling, is the key to growth in the U.S. wood products industry. Certain sectors, such as the wood products utilized in furniture and commercial displays, are not as reliant on the robustness of the housing industry but still depend on the strength of the overall economy.

In 1998, the value of new residential construction put in place for private residential buildings rose 9.5 percent over its level in 1997. In fact, the value of one-unit housing starts grew a dramatic 14 percent in 1998 to $294 billion, while growth in single-family housing market was flat but remained at a relatively lofty historical level. While the single-family sector has remained strong, growth in private nonresidential construction increased a healthy 8.5 percent in 1998 as developers scrambled to build office parks and hotels and motels.

Continued financial difficulties in Asia, especially in Japan, have caused increased concern in the industry in light of the robust domestic market, because high levels of domestic activity cannot be maintained for a long period and producers will have to expand their markets and recapture markets lost as a result of the financial crisis in Asia. The industry has not experienced the pricing setbacks it faced in 1997 and early 1998. However, it appears that general prices became much more volatile later in 1998 and throughout 1999, indicating efficiencies in the pricing mechanisms as manufacturers took into account the reduced Asian demand for wood. Suggestions in 1997 and 1998 that some producers were increasing production to meet financial obligations such as employee payrolls vanished in 1999—a sign of the maturity of the wood products market.

A further sign of maturity in the wood products market is that the former reliance on stumpage (standing timber) from federal lands has been mostly replaced by the use of stumpage from private lands. In the early 1990s, it was not uncommon to hear that segments of the U.S. wood products industry could not survive without access to federal stumpage. Despite the reduction in federal-origin timber being offered for sale, U.S. wood products production experienced healthy gains in 1999. However, storm clouds may be gathering for the industry, including the forecast slowdown in the domestic housing market and mounting pressure from factions intent on eliminating the harvesting of stumpage.

Although the domestic market is relatively secure, uncertainty clouds the international markets for wood products. Japan, traditionally the largest market for U.S. wood products, has been slow in recovering from its economic malaise.

U.S. INDUSTRY GROWTH PROJECTIONS FOR THE NEXT 1 AND 5 YEARS

The U.S. gross domestic product (GDP) is forecast to continue to grow. However, one of the main engines of its growth, the level of single-family housing starts, is expected to decline 9.1 percent annually to 1.5 million units in the next 5 years. Although this decline in housing starts will affect the wood products industry, the forecast 4 percent annual increase in the repair and remodeling sector should counteract it. As a result, shipments of wood products were expected to increase slightly (2.2 percent) in 1999.

Improved access to foreign markets will be a key determinant of growth in the wood products industry over the next 5 years. In light of the uncertainty of attaining such improved market access for wood products, the outlook for improvement in the U.S. export performance remains bleak, with some signs that it may improve in the medium term.

GLOBAL MARKET PROSPECTS

Growth of U.S. exports of wood products is dependent on how the Asian economies, especially Japan, recover from their economic difficulties. Exports to Japan, the leading market for U.S. wood products, declined slightly in 1999 to $1.62 billion, and it is expected that exports to that country in 2000 should stabilize around 1999 levels. Continuing difficult economic conditions in Japan are stunting consumer demand for wood products, especially in housing applications. According to Japanese government sources, the Japanese economy continues to show prolonged weakness and stagnation. Data for 1998 showed negative GDP growth, and most economists in Japan predicted another year of anemic growth in 1999. The consumption tax increase in April 1, 1997, from 3 percent to 5 percent often is cited as the catalyst for the downturn, yet consumer confidence and business confidence continued to sag into 1999. Japan's overall economic ills, punctuated by the increase in the consumption tax, negatively affected U.S. wood exports to that country and served to create supply-demand distortions in the Japanese wood products market. However, the worst of the severe wood fiber inventory adjustments, which took place in 1997 and 1998, have subsided.

The housing market, which accounts for the majority of demand for wood products, declined even further in 1998. Total Japanese housing starts during 1998 reached 1.198 million units, down over 13 percent from the 1997 level. Wood housing accounted for 44 percent of all housing starts. If all construction starts are counted, including commercial nondwellings, wood structures still accounted for over 35 percent of the floor space of new starts, according to the Ministry of Construction.

The Japanese economy was projected to show little growth in fiscal year 1999 despite low interest rates and government spending that has totaled more than $800 billion over the last 8 years. In an economic package announced in 1998, the government introduced nearly $200 billion worth of tax cuts, loans, public spending, and other economic stimulants. The government even resorted to issuing shopping vouchers in the spring of 1999, hoping to reverse the slide in consumer spending. Although these were widely viewed as stopgap measures, the implementation of these steps was expected to temper excessive pessimism over Japan's financial status.

The outlook for U.S. wood product exports to Japan continues to be lackluster. Housing starts, which are the engine for wood demand, were expected to be flat, with 1999 levels predicted to be at or near 1998 levels. The Japanese government forecast just under 1.3 million units, while house builders and economists predicted that starts would be under 1.2 million. Certain factors could have paved the way for a recovery in the housing sector in 1999. They included historically low interest rates adding to the incentive for consumers to make purchases, since rates may rise in the future; stabilization of the decline in land prices; the implementation of a temporary mortgage interest rate deduction system; and perceptions among certain sectors that the worst of the financial crisis had passed. The distortion in supply and severe adjustments in inventory over the previous 2 years stabilized in late 1998, indicating the return of a more rational balance between supply and demand.

The changes in the Japanese economy, as well as the overall economic malaise throughout Asia, have also had a major impact on the distribution channels for U.S. wood products going to Japan. The U.S. industry recognizes that many of these changes have affected and will continue to affect the sale of U.S. wood products in Japan. Only by understanding the changes in the distribution channels will the U.S. industry be able to compete. The U.S. wood products industry has seen a rise in competition in Japan over the last 2 years from New Zealand, Europe, and other Asian countries

The wood products industry remains a key sector in the various multilateral market-opening forums, such as the Asia-Pacific Economic Cooperation (APEC), the Transatlantic Economic Partnership, and the Free Trade Area of the Americas. All these forums address key issues, including the removal of tariffs and harmonization of product standards and the adoption of performance-based building codes, all key impediments to increased growth in U.S. wood product exports, among their objectives.

Elimination of the remaining global tariffs on wood products is being sought in the World Trade Organization (WTO) through an initiative called Advanced Tariff Liberalization (ATL). ATL was born in the APEC forum, where the heads of state from the various APEC economies endorsed a package of tariff liberalization measures in nine sectors, including a forest products sector that covered wood products. At the APEC leaders' meeting held in Kuala Lumpur in 1998, the leaders agreed to move tariff elimination initiatives to the WTO in order to achieve a critical mass of support, including non-APEC economies.

The implementation of the North American Free Trade Agreement (NAFTA) on January 1, 1994, should continue to benefit U.S. exporters by phasing out tariffs and nontariff barriers in Canada and Mexico. U.S. exports to Mexico continued to rebound from the difficulties they experienced when the Mexican economy contracted at the end of 1994. Wood product exports to Mexico increased 26 percent to $373 million in 1998 (see Table 7-2), while exports to Canada contracted slightly to just below $1.6 billion.

Electronic Commerce

The wood products industry is paying more attention to the utility of E-commerce. In light of the structure of the industry as a whole, the widespread use of E-commerce applications will be limited to manufacturers of specialty-type items. For example, the increasing use of E-commerce and the Internet is becoming more important to hardwood lumber producers that have a distinctive product to sell and enough variation in product grades that consumers traditionally have searched out producers of unique hardwood lumber items.

However, hardwood lumber producers are not necessarily making full use of the internet and E-commerce applications to sell directly to the consumer but instead are using them to market their products to consolidators that ultimately ship to brick and mortar outlets. A factor limiting the utility of E-commerce in the hardwood lumber industry is the shipping costs and limitations imposed by conventional consumer-oriented shippers such as United Parcel Service and FedEx on size and weight. Hardwood lumber commonly is sold in 8-foot lengths; this exceeds the limits set by the main shipping companies.

Because of the bulk of the majority of wood products, manufacturers are somewhat constrained from making full use of the powers of E-commerce. Most E-commerce applications for wood products are business-to-business transactions. Some products, such as hardwood veneer, could be poised to take advantage of E-commerce because they are relatively easy to ship and Web designers could showcase the variety of figures and species consumers look for. While there are established grades for hardwood veneer, it is bought primarily on the basis of appearance.

An event to watch is how the "big box" home improvement retailers position themselves in the exploding world of E-commerce. Some industry watchers contend that once these well-known retail stores go on-line, wood product shipments will increase. However, since big-box retailers account for only about 15 percent of wood product sales, their presence in the E-commerce economy will have only a negligible impact on the structure of wood product sales.

Another potential beneficiary of E-commerce is the millwork sector. Homebuilders and remodelers can use the Internet to get specifications for windows and doors and employ that information to generate computer images of a planned home or home improvement. The consumer could choose from a wide

TABLE 7-2: U.S. Trade Patterns in Wood Products[1] in 1998
(millions of dollars; percent)

Exports			Imports		
Region[2]	Value[3]	Share,%	Region[2]	Value[3]	Share,%
NAFTA	1,932	32	NAFTA	10,357	74
Latin America	427	7	Latin America	889	6
Western Europe	1,319	22	Western Europe	765	5
Japan/Chinese Economic Area	1,864	31	Japan/Chinese Economic Area	796	6
Other Asia	212	4	Other Asia	932	7
Rest of world	207	3	Rest of world	262	2
World	5,960	100	World	14,002	100
Top Five Countries	Value	Share,%	Top Five Countries	Value	Share,%
Japan	1,640	28	Canada	9,956	71
Canada	1,559	26	China	630	4
Mexico	373	6	Indonesia	467	3
Germany	286	5	Brazil	403	3
United Kingdom	247	4	Mexico	401	3

[1] SIC 24.
[2] For definitions of regional groupings, see "Getting the Most Out of *Outlook 2000.*"
[3] Values may not sum to total due to rounding.
Source: U.S. Department of Commerce, Bureau of the Census.

variety of window and door manufacturers to achieve the desired appearance and performance within his or her budget.

SAWMILLS AND PLANING MILLS

Industry Performance in 1999

Sawmills and planing mills are the largest sector in the solid wood products industry. Product shipments in constant dollars in 1999 were valued at almost $24.2 billion. The continuation of strong domestic demand for softwood and hardwood lumber was the major reason why product shipments increased by a very healthy 4.1 percent in real terms in 1999 (see Table 7-3), and are expected to remain strong for the next couple of years. The factors driving this increase in demand are the relatively high level of single-family housing starts, the largest consumer of lumber products, and the vigorous residential repair, remodeling, and home improvement sectors.

Prices for softwood lumber, which were relatively stable throughout 1998, became more volatile in 1999 but not as volatile as they were in late 1996 and early 1997. The strength of the U.S. housing sector is the key reason for the strength in softwood lumber prices. However, attendant to the strong housing sector, builders and producers have kept inventories tighter, increasing the volatility of prices. One key technical reason for increased volatility in the softwood lumber markets is that producers did not take any considerable downtime in production as a way to even out the volatility of prices. As a result of the surge in demand, producers ramped up production in anticipation of increasing revenues; however, since the majority of end users do not stock inventories of lumber, the producers were caught with excess inventories when prices fell from their highs.

Softwood lumber producers experienced healthy gains in production in 1998 and were expected to exceed industry expectations in 1999. As supplies from federally owned lands were expected to be curtailed for various environmental and political reasons, mills, especially in the western United States, were forced to derive supplies from private landowners if they did not own any land themselves. The decrease in softwood log exports has benefited the softwood lumber industry by increasing the available supply, keeping raw material input costs low, and ultimately leading to an increase in demand-driven production. Softwood log exports declined after 1992 from 13.8 million cubic meters to 9.7 million cubic meters in 1998. Continued weakness in Japanese demand accounted for most of the decline in softwood log exports; those exports are expected to remain weak because of the state of the Japanese economy and the use of more value-added materials from the United States and other suppliers.

Single-family residential construction remains the main consumer of softwood lumber, and according to industry data, the average unit uses 14,000 board-feet of framing lumber. Multiplied by the number of single-family housing starts, this figure shows the importance of construction activity for the softwood lumber industry. Although single-family residential construction is the most important consumer of softwood lumber, the residential repair and remodeling market is a close second and is viewed as a growth segment as more homeowners refurbish their existing houses. However, the market demand from the remodeling sector fell slightly in 1998. According to industry data, the remodeling sector consumed 28.1 percent of softwood lumber production in 1998, down from almost 30.0 percent in 1997. Buoyed by financial gains from the U.S. stock market and high consumer confidence, homeowners are spending an increasing amount of money for new housing instead of remodeling their existing houses; since new construction uses more lumber, demand from the remodeling sector is relatively lower. Expenditures on home improvements increased 2.4 percent in 1998 to a

TABLE 7-3: Sawmills and Planing Mills, General (SIC 2421) Trends and Forecasts
(millions of dollars except as noted)

	1992	1993	1994	1995	1996	1997[1]	1998[1]	1999[2]	2000[3]	Percent Change 97–98	98–99	99–00	96–00[4]
Industry data													
Value of shipments[5]	21,061	24,460	26,964	25,776	26,740	28,125	29,100	29,900	30,585	3.5	2.7	2.3	3.4
Value of shipments (1992$)	21,061	19,662	21,181	21,716	22,700	23,100	23,550	23,900	24,225	1.9	1.5	1.4	1.6
Total employment (thousands)	138	142	142	143	138	137	137	135	134	0.0	−1.5	−0.7	−0.7
Production workers (thousands)	118	122	122	122	118	118	117	117	116	−0.8	0.0	−0.9	−0.4
Average hourly earnings ($)	9.65	9.83	9.97	10.24	10.51	10.70	10.93	11.15	11.90	2.1	2.0	6.7	3.2
Capital expenditures	459	548	694	852	1,000	1,050	1,085	1,105	1,210	3.3	1.8	9.5	4.9
Product data													
Value of shipments[5]	20,347	23,641	26,001	24,945	25,849	26,577	27,861	29,366	30,147	4.8	5.4	2.7	3.9
Value of shipments (1992$)	20,347	19,004	20,425	21,015	21,943	22,382	23,277	24,231	25,020	4.0	4.1	3.3	3.3
Trade data													
Value of imports	3,626	5,187	6,187	5,686	6,986	7,566	6,920	7,588	7,855	−8.5	9.7	3.5	3.0
Value of exports	2,823	2,903	2,917	2,999	2,989	3,025	2,431	2,064	2,219	−19.6	−15.1	7.5	−7.2

[1] Estimate except imports and exports.
[2] Estimate.
[3] Forecast.
[4] Compound annual rate.
[5] For a definition of industry versus product values, see "Getting the Most Out of *Outlook 2000.*"
Source: U.S. Department of Commerce: Bureau of the Census; International Trade Administration.

total of $80.4 billion, and this upward trend is expected to continue, boding well for the softwood lumber industry.

In 1998, imports accounted for nearly 35.7 percent of apparent consumption of products from this sector, and import dependency was expected to increase slightly in 1999. Imports of softwood lumber from Canada are by far the single largest component of this sector and the entire solid wood products industry.

International Competitiveness

The U.S. sawmills and planing mills industry faces formidable competition in international markets, especially in softwood lumber commodities. Despite this competition, U.S. exports of softwood lumber were estimated to increase 8.7 percent in 1999 from 1998 levels in value and 9.5 percent in volume. Japan remains the largest U.S. export market for softwood lumber, with a 26 percent share in 1998, down considerably from 1996, when 54 percent of U.S. softwood lumber exports went to that country, reflecting the sluggish Japanese economy, especially in terms of demand for new residential housing. Canada and Spain are the second and third largest markets, respectively, for U.S. softwood lumber.

Financial difficulties in Asia are having a profound impact on the international competitiveness of the U.S. sawmills and planing mills industry. Since lumber products are priced internationally in U.S. dollars, the depreciation of Asian currencies has had a depressing effect on lumber exports. Furthermore, Asian demand for imported hardwood and softwood logs, which also are priced in U.S. dollars, has fallen dramatically, allowing domestic sawmillers to process these high-quality logs for domestic consumption. Even with the very strong U.S. housing market, U.S. producers have not been able to pass along price increases because of the weak Asian markets. In fact, the U.S. market is so strong and lumber prices are so relatively weak (largely because of the Asian difficulties) that consumers are reaping large benefits.

Industry and Trade Projections for the Next 1 and 5 Years

In constant dollars, shipments of products from sawmills and planing mills grew about 4.0 percent in 1998 and about 4.1 percent in 1999. According to industry data, while the volume of production is expected to increase around 2 to 4 percent, prices will remain stable despite the very strong domestic markets.

With a domestic economy expected to grow 2.4 percent in 2000, U.S. housing markets are expected to retain most of their vitality but slowly retract from their lofty levels of 1997 and 1998. Since the average size of homes built in the United States are predicted to increase slightly, more lumber products are expected to be consumed domestically in 2000–04. Increasing activity in the repair and remodeling end-use segments was expected to further bolster lumber consumption. Homeowners, flush with receipts from a historically high equities market, have been funneling some of those gains into additions, decks, and furniture, causing the production of lumber products to increase.

Producers have been caught between strong domestic demand and tepid international demand, especially in Japan and other Asian countries, and have not been able to increase prices readily. However, the hardwood lumber segment has been able to pass along price increases more readily than have its softwood cousins, since international demand for hardwood has not been affected as much as it has been in the softwood lumber commodity sector. Hardwood lumber, with its vast range of varieties, is differentiated from the softwood sector because softwood lumber products are used primarily in construction and moulding and millwork applications, where species differentiation is not critical. Lighter-colored hardwood lumber such as hard maple has seen a tremendous rise in price, and that price is expected to remain high for the next 2 or 3 years. Production of light-colored hardwoods has been increasing slowly but cannot fully satisfy demand because of increasing logging restrictions on federal lands in the hardwood-producing regions of the country. The Allegheny National Forest in Pennsylvania, a prime location for hard maple and other highly sought after Appalachian hardwoods, has seen a moratorium on logging as a result of various environmental measures. This has occurred despite the fact that this area is not experiencing the same degree of restrictions on federal lands that the Pacific Northwest is facing. Privately owned land in the eastern United States has been used to increase production to meet the demand, but this has not been totally successful because ownership of the hardwood forest resource is so highly fragmented.

Internationally, U.S. exports were expected to experience significant setbacks, mainly as a result of continued lackluster demand in Asia. However, 1999 saw a rebound in exports as the Asians returned to the marketplace and as European economies increased their growth. A major wild card in the future growth of exports in this sector is China's housing reform, launched in 1998, and that country's acceptance of the use of wood products such as softwood lumber and hardwood lumber in domestic residential construction. China has not been affected as strongly by the Asian financial difficulties as some of its regional neighbors have, but its economy has slowed somewhat and the Chinese government has focused on the residential housing market as a key to increasing growth to its set targets. However, China's housing reform efforts have been progressing more slowly than expected because of the complexity of the domestic housing industry. In the past, the Chinese government allocated housing at minimal or no cost. China's housing market is expected to increase rapidly in 2000–04 and will increase demand for certain sawmill products like millwork and mouldings.

The recovering European markets will have a positive influence on the growth of this industry, mostly in the hardwood lumber market but also in softwood lumber commodities. However, the United States faces formidable competition in the European market from Canada and the Scandinavians, especially the Swedes. Sweden's European Union membership and proximity to the European market is likely to make it the primary beneficiary of increased European activity.

Growth in the sawmills and planing mills sector is expected to be moderate over the 1999–2004 period. While the Asian economies sort out their difficulties, especially Japan, U.S. mills will benefit from an increasing supply of logs that once were destined for Asian markets that will be available for transformation into lumber products. The healthy U.S. economy will allow this sector to grow and absorb some of the lumber that was manufactured from previously destined log exports. However, plentiful supply will have a dampening effect on lumber prices, leading to only moderate growth for this sector.

Chris Twarok, Office of Metals, Materials, and Chemicals, (202) 482-0377, October 1999.

HARDWOOD VENEER AND PLYWOOD

Industry Performance in 1999

Strong demand from the furniture, cabinetry, and fixtures sector was the main factor fueling a 2.4 percent increase in constant dollar product shipments of hardwood veneer and plywood in 1999. Also contributing to the growth in product shipments were the strong European and Canadian markets, leading to a 16 percent increase in U.S. exports to $431 million in 1997 (see Table 7-4).

According to data from the U.S. Bureau of the Census, hardwood plywood is the dominant product in this group, accounting for over 65 percent of product shipments in 1997. Commodities manufactured by this sector are used in applications that range from furniture and case goods to residential repair and remodeling and manufactured housing units.

Hardwood plywood producers can make panels in nearly any dimension that an application demands. A customer can make special orders for sizes that go beyond the standard sizes that are normally available. However, most hardwood plywood panels are produced in stock sizes, generally 4 feet wide by 8 to 10 feet long. Industry data show that production of hardwood plywood increased 3 percent, the thirteenth consecutive year of growth, to 89.5 million square meters. Continued growth is expected as a result of increased consumption by the furniture industry and other case good manufacturers.

Stock hardwood production accounts for slightly more than half of all the hardwood plywood produced. Of this amount, eastern producers, with their proximity to the hardwood forest resource, produce 53 percent of hardwood plywood while western producers account for 46 percent of production, with the Great Lakes states making up the remainder. In the not too distant past, western producers were besieged by escalating fiber costs resulting from harvesting restrictions and the impact on producer prices of the exportation of unprocessed logs primarily to Asia.

Hardwood plywood producers use a wide range of species for the face veneers of their products. Red oak remains the most popular species at 38 percent of the market, followed by birch (29 percent) and maple (17 percent). Maple continues to increase in popularity as consumers specify lighter-colored woods, especially for kitchen cabinetry and other furniture items. The popularity of maple should plateau at around 17 or 18 percent of the market because maple is a very difficult species to stain, whereas oak and birch are more readily adaptable to changing consumer preferences in the colors of wood. A trouble spot for maple's popularity is price. As maple becomes more expensive because of difficult sourcing conditions, consumers will look at cherry more closely. In the past, cherry was much more expensive than maple, but the gap is closing.

The cores used in the hardwood plywood industry vary from veneer plies at 63 percent of the market to medium-density fiberboard (MDF) cores at 16 percent. The use of MDF and particleboard cores has increased steadily since 1991, as those materials allow a panel to be flatter and more dimensionally stable. Furthermore, these cores are cheaper to manufacture than are veneer or lumber cores.

TABLE 7-4: Hardwood Veneer and Plywood (SIC 2435) Trends and Forecasts
(millions of dollars except as noted)

	1992	1993	1994	1995	1996	1997[1]	1998[1]	1999[2]	2000[3]	Percent Change 97–98	98–99	99–00	96–00[4]
Industry data													
Value of shipments[5]	2,238	2,537	2,609	2,642	2,623	2,652	2,725	2,805	2,915	2.8	2.9	3.9	2.7
Value of shipments (1992$)	2,238	2,371	2,292	2,277	2,236	2,250	2,272	2,298	2,365	1.0	1.1	2.9	1.4
Total employment (thousands)	19.9	19.8	21.9	22.0	21.3	22.0	22.1	22.1	22.0	0.5	0.0	–0.5	0.8
Production workers (thousands)	16.9	16.8	18.8	18.8	18.3	19.2	19.3	19.3	19.0	0.5	0.0	–1.6	0.9
Average hourly earnings ($)	8.12	8.55	8.21	8.75	8.95	9.80	10.10	10.40	10.80	3.1	3.0	3.8	4.8
Capital expenditures	45.1	46.6	52.5	32.2	37.7	38.1	35.0	36.2	39.0	–8.1	3.4	7.7	0.9
Product data													
Value of shipments[5]	2,023	2,305	2,444	2,520	2,556	2,633	2,701	2,771	2,862	2.6	2.6	3.3	2.9
Value of shipments (1992$)	2,023	2,154	2,148	2,173	2,179	2,234	2,284	2,339	2,405	2.2	2.4	2.8	2.5
Trade data													
Value of imports	729	857	890	924	997	994	965	1,250	1,370	–2.9	29.5	9.6	8.3
Value of exports	278	297	348	376	371	431	399	462	475	–7.4	15.8	2.8	6.4

[1] Estimate except imports and exports.
[2] Estimate.
[3] Forecast.
[4] Compound annual rate.
[5] For a definition of industry versus product values, see "Getting the Most Out of *Outlook 2000.*"
Source: U.S. Department of Commerce: Bureau of the Census; International Trade Administration.

International Competitiveness

U.S. hardwood veneer and plywood exports increased over 16 percent in 1999 as demand from the European and Canadian markets increased. Canada, Germany, Spain, and the United Kingdom are the top four markets, representing nearly 60 percent of U.S. exports of these products. U.S. exports are expected to increase slightly in 2000 as exports to Europe pick up. The United States will continue to face strong competition from southeast Asian, South American, and eastern European producers but is insulated somewhat because plywood produced from species indigenous to the United States is still highly sought after in foreign markets.

U.S. imports of these products increased dramatically in 1999, totaling nearly $1250 million. U.S. importers of these products have numerous choices that are not available from domestic sources. Aided by a strong domestic economy, U.S. imports are expected to remain robust. Indonesia is expected to remain the largest supplier.

Industry and Trade Projections for the Next 1 and 5 Years

While there was not much change in the hardwood veneer and plywood industry in 1999, a couple of developments could profoundly affect the industry's domestic and international performance in the next 5 years.

Continued growth in furniture and mobile home construction and a healthy domestic construction market were expected to result in higher product shipments in 1998 and 1999. Constant dollar product shipments were expected to increase 2.4 percent in 1999 and 2.8 percent in 2000 as domestic demand was sustained and demand from Europe and Canada strengthened. All categories of products in this sector should share in the growth, even the recently declining prefinished hardwood paneling plywood used in prefabricated and modular housing units.

Exports of hardwood veneer and plywood products were expected to increase about 2.6 percent in 1999 (see Table 7-4), continuing the strong export growth of these products. Europe, Canada, and South America are expected to be the main markets in 2000–04. Imports are expected to continue to increase, especially hardwood plywood from Indonesia (luaun) as the rupiah was pummeled in foreign exchange markets, making luaun very price competitive in the United States.

Over the 1999–2004 period, the hardwood veneer and plywood industry is expected to increase shipments 2 percent annually as the markets for those products grow. Domestic producers are expected to face an increasing amount of competition from Asian countries for the lower end-use markets, especially inexpensive furniture items that once used hardwood plywood and now are increasingly using vinyl overlaid particleboard and other composite products, thus tempering the growth potential of this sector.

Chris Twarok, Office of Metals, Materials, and Chemicals, (202) 482-0377, October 1999.

SOFTWOOD VENEER AND PLYWOOD

Industry Performance in 1999

The softwood veneer and plywood industry continued to experience difficult times as product shipments rose less than 1 percent. Despite the strong construction, renovation, and housing markets, production could not capitalize on those trends as the other sectors of the wood economy did. The softwood plywood and veneer sector has shown its resilience by shifting production from the Pacific northwest to the south to meet changing fiber conditions. Even though shipments were up slightly, the real news in this sector has been the explosion of imports and the slowdown in exports. Softwood plywood and veneer exports are facing stiff competition from Canada, Indonesia, and Brazil, especially in the European and Japanese markets.

Production of softwood plywood has been enhanced by technological and economic breakthroughs in the use of adhesives. The use of phenol-formaldehyde adhesives, which are thermoreactive and set to an infusible solid, allow the use of veneer sheets with a higher moisture content than that of veneer sheets glued with protein-based adhesives such as casein. This allows a lower production cost because the manufacturer does not need to reduce the moisture content of the veneer sheets below the equilibrium moisture content to ensure a good bond. Furthermore, the plywood panel is less likely to warp or shrink because the moisture content of the veneers is near equilibrium with the ambient environment.

One of the greatest challenges to the softwood plywood and veneer industry is the formidable competition from oriented strand board (OSB). OSB is a structural panel with alternating layers of compressed wood strands that are glued with exterior-grade adhesives. Since 1992, when OSB was certified to perform as well as softwood plywood as defined by Performance Standard PS-2, OSB has been rapidly eroding the market share of softwood plywood. This certification allows OSB to compete directly for the same markets while offering the consumer a lower cost because OSB is much cheaper to produce than plywood (see the section on reconstituted wood products, below). However, certain applications are still dominated by the use of softwood plywood, such as underlayment for floors.

In the United States, there are 92 plywood-producing mills and nearly 50 OSB-producing mills. Nearly 75 percent of all grades of softwood plywood are produced in the south. The west, the traditional producer of softwood plywood, especially Douglas fir plywood, is slowly being reduced to serving niche markets because of the changing patterns of raw material procurement that have favored landowners in the south over the publicly derived stumpage that a large percentage of western mills have relied on.

International Competitiveness

Exports of softwood plywood and veneer dropped precipitously in 1998 to $222 million, the lowest level in 8 years (see Table 7-5). This was a remarkable reversal, since 1997 saw the highest level of exports in 8 years. Exports to the traditionally strong European markets languished in 1998 and 1999 because demand from the United Kingdom, Germany, and the Netherlands weakened as construction activity in those countries slowed.

Softwood plywood remains the largest export sector in this category accounting for nearly 88 percent of exports. However, that percentage has been declining over the last couple of years as international acceptance of OSB and increasing competition from Canada, Brazil, and Indonesia have slowly eroded softwood plywood's dominance of exports.

U.S. imports of softwood plywood and veneer increased over 37 percent to $150 million in 1998, with over 75 percent originating in Canada. This increase was due mainly to the strong U.S. housing market and repair and remodeling sectors.

Industry and Trade Projections for the Next 1 and 5 Years

Sales of softwood plywood and veneer barely continued their modest increase in 1998 and should match those very small

TABLE 7-5: Softwood Veneer and Plywood (SIC 2436) Trends and Forecasts
(millions of dollars except as noted)

	1992	1993	1994	1995	1996	1997[1]	1998[1]	1999[2]	2000[3]	Percent Change 97–98	98–99	99–00	96–00[4]
Industry data													
Value of shipments[5]	5,350	6,035	6,544	6,828	6,033	6,095	6,185	6,200	6,255	1.5	0.2	0.9	0.9
Value of shipments (1992$)	5,350	5,172	5,417	5,376	5,264	5,270	5,296	5,335	5,385	0.5	0.7	0.9	0.6
Total employment (thousands)	30.9	30.7	30.3	32.4	31.9	28.8	28.5	28.5	28.3	–1.0	0.0	–0.7	–2.9
Production workers (thousands)	27.7	27.7	27.2	29.1	28.6	26.1	25.7	25.2	25.0	–1.5	–1.9	–0.8	–3.3
Average hourly earnings ($)	11.08	11.42	11.83	12.14	12.36	13.10	13.40	13.80	14.10	2.3	3.0	2.2	3.3
Capital expenditures	94.5	118	150	184	208	168	172	180	185	2.4	4.7	2.8	–2.9
Product data													
Value of shipments[5]	4,778	5,321	5,700	5,953	5,225	5,088	5,152	5,255	5,360	1.3	2.0	2.0	0.6
Value of shipments (1992$)	4,778	4,560	4,719	4,688	4,559	4,593	4,639	4,674	4,702	1.0	0.8	0.6	0.8
Trade data													
Value of imports	59.0	76.9	96.4	99.4	88.4	109	150	265	302	37.6	76.7	14.0	36.0
Value of exports	336	369	323	334	314	379	222	211	205	–41.4	–5.0	–2.8	–10.1

[1] Estimate except imports and exports.
[2] Estimate.
[3] Forecast.
[4] Compound annual rate.
[5] For a definition of industry versus product values, see "Getting the Most Out of *Outlook 2000.*"
Source: U.S. Department of Commerce: Bureau of the Census; International Trade Administration.

gains in 1999 and 2000. The 5-year outlook for this sector indicates that softwood plywood is increasingly being relegated to niche markets as competition from OSB continues. The market perception is that softwood plywood is now seen as a "luxury" wood product, and high-end homebuilders and customers are specifying the use of softwood plywood instead of OSB because of its perceived superiority even though softwood plywood and OSB are structurally equivalent.

A key factor in reviving growth in this sector is the export market, especially in Europe. Even with a slight revival in European construction markets, there is cause for concern in Asia, especially in Japan. As that region's financial difficulties slowly abate, competition from Indonesia threatens any further increases in softwood plywood exports to that region.

While the traditional European and Asian markets should remain the main markets, nontraditional markets such as South America and eastern Europe need to be exploited. Softwood plywood has some advantages over OSB in developing these markets because OSB currently is not seen as a performance-based product equivalent to plywood. Also, developments in China and that country's massive restructuring of its housing market could be a boon to plywood producers, especially for concrete forming applications.

The south is expected to increase its dominance in production over the west and by 2004 should account for 80 percent of all plywood production. While the timber constraints that western producers have been facing for the last 10 years are starting to abate, the south is a much lower-cost producer. However, the west will still have the niche markets for high-end construction applications. Douglas fir and fir plywood products will still be demanded by consumers drawn to the appearance of those products.

Chris Twarok, Office of Metals, Materials, and Chemicals, (202) 482-0377, October 1999.

RECONSTITUTED WOOD PRODUCTS

Industry Performance in 1999

Product shipments of reconstituted wood products increased 4.6 percent in constant dollars 1998, reaching an estimated nominal value of $4.9 billion. The strong domestic housing market and the increased activity in residential repairs and remodeling projects contributed significantly to this growth. The strong furniture market and other similar end-use markets also contributed to this growth.

The reconstituted wood products sector produces items such as OSB, hardboard, particleboard, MDF, and insulation board. U.S. Bureau of the Census data indicate that OSB and particleboard constitute the largest portion of this industry, accounting for 24 percent of total product shipments, followed by hardboard (18 percent) and MDF (9 percent). According to industry data, production of OSB, the main structural item in this group, increased significantly over the last couple of years, growing from slightly over 7.0 million square feet in 1994 to nearly 10.5 million square feet in 1998. OSB uses compressed strands of wood laid in alternating layers with a phenol-formaldehyde adhesive and is structurally equivalent to plywood. OSB has a distinct advantage over plywood in that OSB utilizes tree species that once were considered very undesirable, especially aspen. OSB started production in the Great Lakes states, where aspen is very abundant; it grows in pure stands because it is a pioneer species and is very prolific in propagation from cuttings. Scientists utilized this wood and tweaked the production processes to yield OSB. Since peeler logs are not needed, as they are in the production of plywood products, producers have lower costs for raw materials. Furthermore, producers can use smaller-diameter logs and are not as reliant on raw material derived from publicly owned lands.

Pricing volatility in OSB markets exhibited behavior similar to that of softwood lumber. As competition increases for OSB markets from domestic and international sources, volatility is expected to remain a problem for brokers and the homebuilding industry. However, the price spread between OSB and softwood plywood is narrowing, reflecting strength in the OSB market and simultaneous weakness in the plywood market.

The other products in this category are used mainly in decorative and furniture and case good applications. These products are very fiber-efficient and average around 93 percent recovery of a log during the production process. Also, as in OSB production, producers can use smaller-diameter logs, which are less expensive and more available than are the peeler logs used in other types of panel production. Many producers also buy waste products such as sawdust from lumber mills and turn it into particleboard, MDF, and hardboard products. Because of its uniformity, flatness, and dimensional stability, particleboard is used primarily for floor underlayment (a panel product to be used under the finish flooring or countertop), kitchen counter underlayment, furniture components, and cabinet components. According to industry data, in 1998 particleboard shipments totaled 5.8 billion square feet on a ¾-inch basis, a 5.1 percent increase over 1997.

Hardboard is used primarily in the construction industry for exterior siding in new residential construction. Unlike particleboard, which uses a relatively high amount of binders, hardboard is produced mainly by compressing wood fibers under extreme heat and pressure to form a panel. Hardboard also is used in industrial applications such as furniture and case goods as well as in the repair and remodeling sector.

MDF is used primarily in furniture and cabinetry applications because of its smoothness, dimensional stability, and paintability and the sharp lines that are left after a decorative cut is made on the panel. MDF uses wood fibers and binders and then is heated and pressed to yield a panel. Consumption of MDF is increasing in the moulding and millwork industries. An increasing amount of newly constructed housing may use MDF wainscoting and other decorative applications. MDF shipments continue to increase, and in 1998 shipments grew to 1.4 billion square feet on a ¾-inch basis. Competition for MDF sales is increasing as capacity rises in both established and new mills.

TABLE 7-6: Reconstituted Wood Products (SIC 2493) Trends and Forecasts
(millions of dollars except as noted)

	1992	1993	1994	1995	1996	1997[1]	1998[1]	1999[2]	2000[3]	Percent Change 97–98	98–99	99–00	96–00[4]
Industry data													
Value of shipments[5]	3,986	4,669	5,344	5,202	5,141	5,300	5,434	5,560	5,695	2.5	2.3	2.4	2.6
Value of shipments (1992$)	3,986	4,180	4,388	4,264	4,470	4,565	4,658	4,755	4,860	2.0	2.1	2.2	2.1
Total employment (thousands)	22.8	23.5	24.3	25.0	26.1	25.3	25.2	25.1	25.1	–0.4	–0.4	0.0	–1.0
Production workers (thousands)	18.6	19.2	19.7	20.4	21.1	20.6	20.6	20.6	20.5	0.0	0.0	–0.5	–0.7
Average hourly earnings ($)	11.49	11.72	11.85	11.92	12.73	13.20	13.40	13.70	14.10	1.5	2.2	2.9	2.6
Capital expenditures	143	171	333	438	573	330	401	445	500	21.5	11.0	12.4	–3.3
Product data													
Value of shipments[5]	3,987	4,658	5,338	5,160	5,111	5,168	5,338	5,664	5,965	3.3	6.1	5.3	3.9
Value of shipments (1992$)	3,987	4,170	4,382	4,229	4,444	4,688	4,904	5,140	5,386	4.6	4.8	4.8	4.9
Trade data													
Value of imports	402	581	834	963	1,067	1,146	1,652	2,100	2,565	44.2	27.1	22.1	24.5
Value of exports	244	256	292	307	308	355	308	316	328	–13.2	2.6	3.8	1.6

[1] Estimate except imports and exports.
[2] Estimate.
[3] Forecast.
[4] Compound annual rate.
[5] For a definition of industry versus product values, see "Getting the Most Out of *Outlook 2000.*"
Source: U.S. Department of Commerce: Bureau of the Census; International Trade Administration.

International Competitiveness

The real international story for this sector is the strength of U.S. imports. In 1998, imports grew 44.2 percent (see Table 7-6), and this strong trend is expected to be sustained in 1999 and 2000. As with other wood product sectors, housing and related items such as furniture and cabinetry are driving this increase. Exports, by contrast, had a lackluster year in 1998, dropping 13.2 percent to $308 million, and it is expected that 1999 and 2000 will see slight improvements in the level of exports.

Canada, Mexico, and the United Kingdom are the largest markets for these products, while Japan, the third largest market in 1998, fell to fourth place. Exports should improve in 1999 and 2000 as a result of the increasing global acceptance of OSB for use in construction applications. In 1998, imports from Canada increased 54.3 percent to $1.4 billion, accounting for 83.8 percent of U.S. imports, and are expected to increase at a rate higher than that of export growth because of the intense competition from Canada and the additional capacity Canada has added in the last couple of years.

Industry and Trade Projections for the Next 1 and 5 Years

Reconstituted wood products are forecast to increase shipments 4.8 percent in constant dollars from 1999 to 2000 as strong demand from the furniture market will prove to be especially beneficial to particleboard, MDF, and hardboard producers. Furthermore, the increased use of OSB in residential construction and the increase in the number of producing mills should allow this sector to increase shipments.

However, as in other sectors in the wood products industry, growth in this sector will be restrained by the economic conditions in Japan and throughout Asia. OSB has been making significant inroads into the Japanese residential construction market as Japan and the United States have worked successfully to address the building code and product standards issues affecting the use of OSB. However, its use is threatened by Japan's recession. As an increasing amount of OSB production is coming online in North America, increased export opportunities are paramount for this sector's longer-term health. Over the 1999–2004 period, export growth is expected to increase 2.2 percent per year as the furniture markets remain healthy, along with residential construction.

Chris Twarok, Office of Metals, Materials, and Chemicals, (202) 482-0377, October 1999.

■ REFERENCES

Crow's Weekly Letter, C.C. Crow Publications, Inc., P.O. Box 25749, Portland, OR 97225. (503) 646-8075.

Market Barometer, Composite Panel Association, 1828 Premier Court, Gaithersburg, MD 20879. (301) 670-0604.

1998 Statistical Yearbook of the Western Lumber Industry, Western Wood Products Association, Yeon Building, 522 SW Fifth Avenue, Portland, OR 97204. (503) 224-3930.

Panels: Products, Applications and Production Trends, 2d Edition, Miller-Freeman, Inc., 600 Harrison Street, San Francisco, CA 94107.

Random Lengths, Random Lengths Publications, Inc., P.O. Box 867, Eugene, OR 97440. (503) 686-9925.

Solid Wood Products Statistical Roundup, American Forest and Paper Association, 1111 19 Street, NW, Suite 800, Washington, DC 20036. (202) 463-2700.

Structural Panels, C.C. Crow Publications, Inc., P.O. Box 25749, Portland, OR 97225. (503) 646-8075.

Structural Panels and Engineered Wood Products, APA—The Engineered Wood Association, P.O. Box 11700, Tacoma, WA 98411. (206) 565-6600.

Weekly Hardwood Review, P.O. Box 471307, Charlotte, NC 28247. (704) 543-4408.

Woodshop News, Soundings Publications L.L.C., 35 Pratt Street, Essex, CT 06426.

RELATED CHAPTERS

6: Construction
8: Building Products and Materials
38: Household Consumer Durables

BUILDING PRODUCTS AND MATERIALS
Economic and Trade Trends

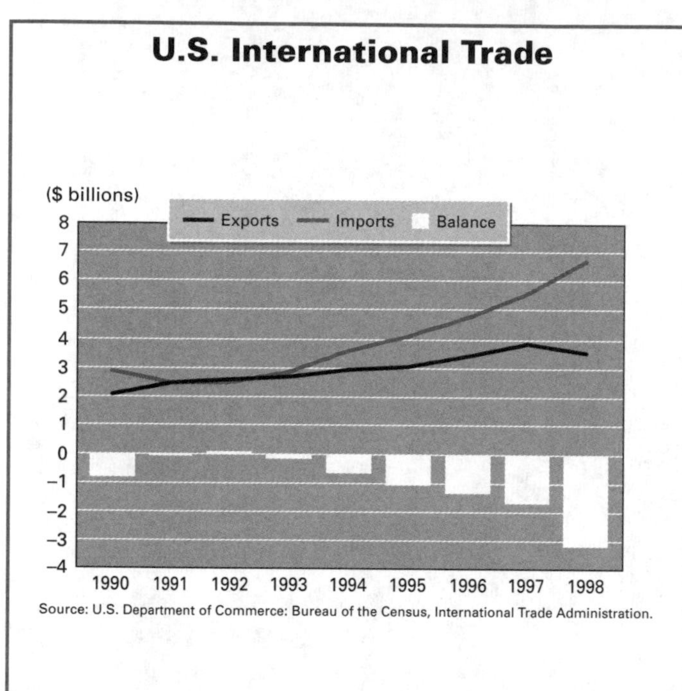

Source: U.S. Department of Commerce: Bureau of the Census, International Trade Administration.

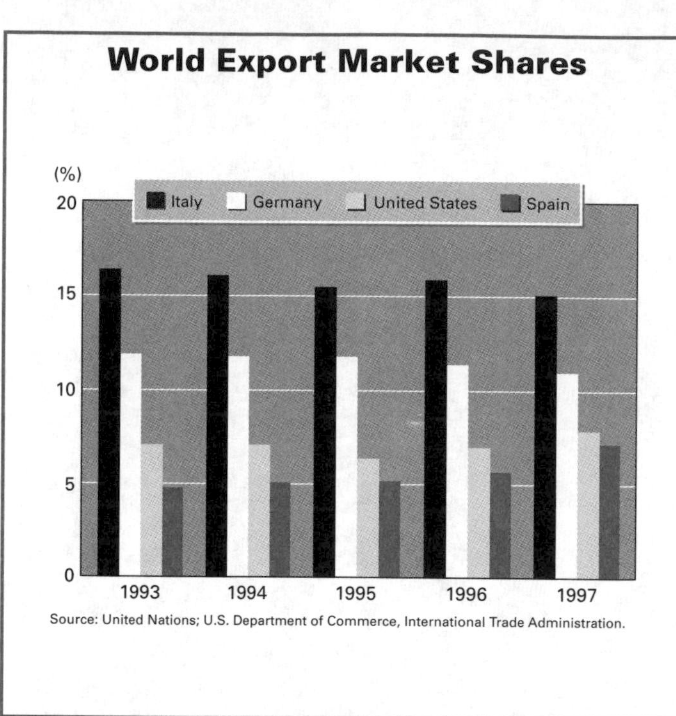

Source: United Nations; U.S. Department of Commerce, International Trade Administration.

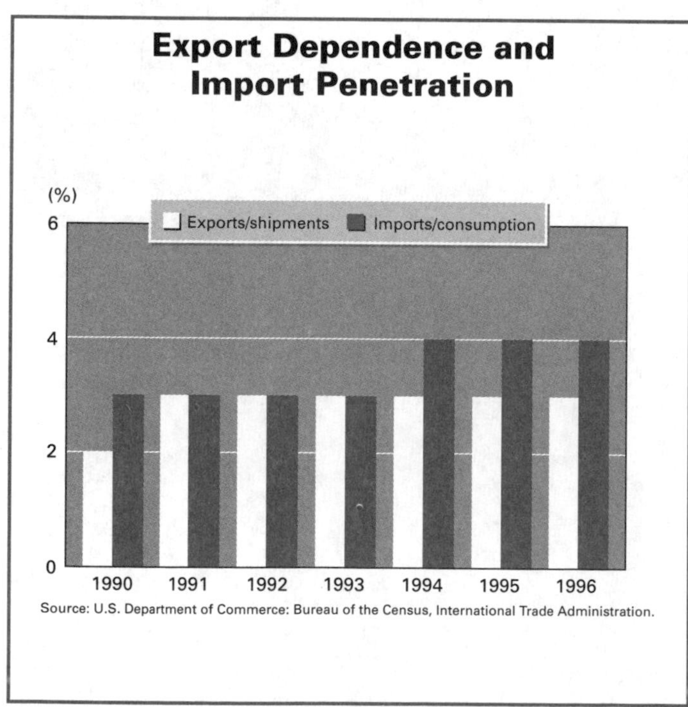

Source: U.S. Department of Commerce: Bureau of the Census, International Trade Administration.

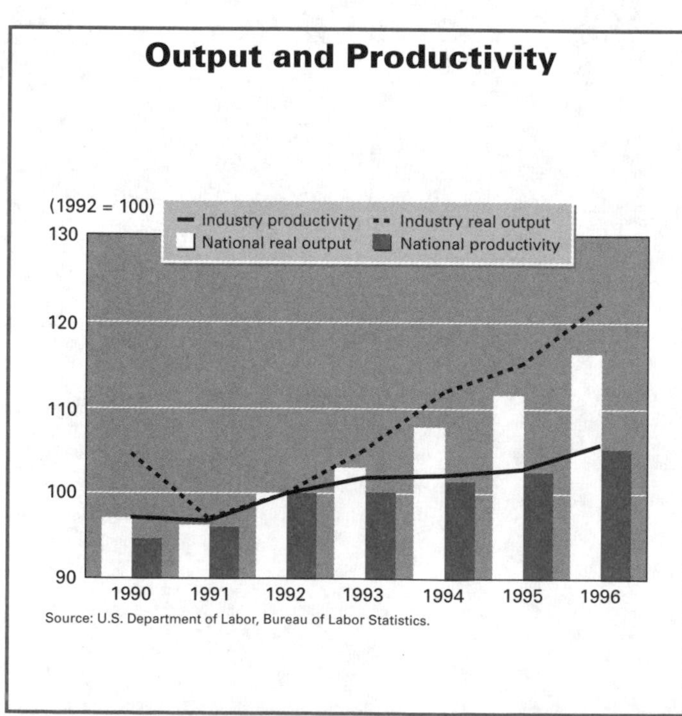

Source: U.S. Department of Labor, Bureau of Labor Statistics.

See "Getting the Most Out of *Outlook 2000*" for definitions of terms.

8

Building Products and Materials

INDUSTRY DEFINITION The industries described in this chapter produce a variety of products that range from cement, to roofing shingles, to nearly complete buildings. The defining common characteristic of these industries is that the bulk of their output is sold to the construction sector. This chapter excludes lumber and millwork, which are covered in Chapter 7. More than 30 building product industries are covered in this chapter, and 10 of those industries are discussed in detail: fabricated structural metal (SIC 3441), cement (SIC 3241), flat glass (SIC 3211), mobile homes (SIC 2451), prefabricated wooden buildings (SIC 2451), prefabricated metal buildings (SIC 3448), and various plumbing products (SIC 30881, 3261, 3431, 3432).

GLOBAL INDUSTRY TRENDS

U.S. manufacturers of building products prospered in 1999 as the domestic construction market set an all-time record. As a result of trends in most of the world, however, U.S. exports of building products declined while imports surged.

Although construction products tend to be bulky, this industry has become more global. U.S. exports totaled just below $4.8 billion in 1998, which accounted for about 3 percent of the almost $168 billion in total shipments. Imports of just under $8.1 billion accounted for about 7 percent of U.S. consumption (see Table 8-1).

Of the 32 building product industries shown in Table 8-1, 22 showed a trade deficit in 1998, and that number increased in 1999. (This is similar to the overall pattern for the U.S. manufacturing sector.) The international competitiveness of specific products varies widely; for example, the trade deficit in ceramic tile was equal to 41 percent of consumption, while the trade surplus in flat glass was equal to 8 percent of production.

The United States had a trade surplus in building products as recently as 1992. The trade balance has been in deficit since that time because of the strong domestic construction market, the strong U.S. dollar, and the increasing sophistication of foreign suppliers. By 1998, the surplus had become a $3.3 billion trade deficit, and that trend intensified in 1999.

Canada and Mexico traditionally have been the largest customers for U.S. exports of building products, and they are also among the major suppliers of imports (see Table 8-2). The North American Free Trade Agreement (NAFTA) has reinforced these relationships. Other large customers include western Europe (notably Great Britain and Germany) and the Pacific Rim countries of Asia. Imports from countries in the Pacific Rim have surged since 1997, because their local construction markets have been in recession. China and Japan both have large amounts of excess capacity, and cheap ocean freight rates have made it profitable to ship cement, gypsum board, structural steel, and builders' hardware to U.S. Pacific Coast markets.

Although U.S. construction materials companies of all sizes are active exporters, most of the smaller companies do not export because they are regional businesses that have not yet reached most of the domestic market. For regional companies seeking growth, it usually is easier to enter other regional markets than it is to go international.

Most of the larger firms export and/or produce overseas. Increasingly, the larger firms are multinational companies that ship between facilities across national boundaries. Many U.S. building product industries have high levels of foreign owner-

TABLE 8-1: Value of Shipments and International Trade for U.S. Building Product Industries in 1998
(millions of current dollars)

	SIC Code	Product Shipments[1]	International Trade		
			Exports	Imports	Balance of Trade
Total building products		167,850	4,794	8,055	-3,261
Mobile homes	2451	10,276	27	6	21
Prefabricated wooden buildings	2452	2,943	53	56	-3
Asphalt paving mixtures	2951	6,135	21	50	-29
Asphalt roofing	2952	5,753	74	46	28
Hard-surfaced floor coverings	3996	2,257	112	228	-116
Rubber floor coverings	30694	831	54	55	-1
Plastic pipe	3084	5,019	222	99	123
Plastic plumbing fixtures	3088	2,191	41	89	-48
Miscellaneous plastic construction products	3089[2]	8,427	462	541	-79
Flat glass	3211	2,779	738	510	228
Cement	3241	6,741	58	963	-905
Clay brick and structural tile	3251	1,681	16	6	10
Ceramic wall and ceiling tile	3253	1,091	27	860	-833
Structural clay products nec	3259	222	10	13	-3
Vitreous plumbing fixtures	3261	983	75	233	-158
Concrete block and brick	3271	3,375	11	24	-13
Concrete products nec	3272	10,319	105	426	-321
Ready-mixed concrete	3273	19,241	0	1	-1
Gypsum products	3275	4,826	66	155	-89
Cut stone and stone products	3281	1,699	37	883	-846
Mineral wool	3296	2,422	350	158	192
Cast iron pipe and fittings	33211	287	134	35	99
Builders' hardware	34294	5,988	586	676	-90
Metal plumbing fixtures	3431	1,179	71	154	-83
Plumbing fittings (metal)	3432	5,148	67	399	-332
Fabricated structural metal	3441	15,300	472	537	-65
Metal doors, windows, and trim	3442	10,175	188	261	-73
Sheet metal work	3444	17,963	66	22	44
Architectural metal work	3446	4,538	41	81	-40
Prefabricated metal buildings	3448	3,997	201	58	143
Fences and screens	3496[3]	406	71	169	-98
Building heating equipment	3433	3,658	338	261	77

[1] Estimate.
[2] Only plastic construction products are included.
[3] Component of SIC 3496, miscellaneous fabricated wire products.
Source: U.S. Department of Commerce: Bureau of the Census, International Trade Administration; U.S. Customs Service.

ship. Among the industries in which foreign-based multinationals own much of U.S. production capacity are cement, clay brick, and flat glass. U.S.-based multinationals with high levels of foreign investment are in the flat glass, fiberglass, flooring, and gypsum board industries.

DOMESTIC TRENDS

The boom in the U.S. construction market continued in 1999, with the value of new construction easily exceeding the record set in 1998. Shipments of building products also increased to record levels, although surging imports absorbed some of the increased demand.

The value of U.S. building product shipments by the 32 industries shown in Table 8-1 was about $168 billion in 1998 and $176 billion in 1999. The largest industries measured by the value of shipments were concrete products, sheet metal work, fabricated structural metal, doors and windows, and mobile homes. The output of those 32 industries accounted for 25 percent of the $665 billion value of U.S. construction in 1998.

Shipments of building products measured in constant 1992 dollars grew about 3 percent in 1999. This was about the same rate of growth that was seen in the value of construction put in place. The fastest-growing industries in 1999 measured by shipments in constant 1992 dollars were asphalt paving mixtures and fabricated structural metal. This was due largely to the boom in highway construction funded by the Transportation Efficiency Act for the 21st Century (TEA-21) (see Chapter 6). Shipments of plumbing fixtures also were very strong because of the boom in large new homes and improvements to existing homes.

Capacity shortages have limited shipments of some building products, especially cement, gypsum board, bricks, and fiberglass insulation. Shortages of these products have been com-

TABLE 8-2: U.S. Trade Patterns in Building Products and Materials[1] in 1998
(millions of dollars; percent)

Exports			Imports		
Region[2]	Value[3]	Share, %	Region[2]	Value[3]	Share, %
NAFTA	1,562	44	NAFTA	2,916	44
Latin America	435	12	Latin America	332	5
Western Europe	488	14	Western Europe	2,124	32
Japan/Chinese Economic Area	529	15	Japan/Chinese Economic Area	1,015	15
Other Asia	205	6	Other Asia	226	3
Rest of world	320	9	Rest of world	83	1
World	3,539	100	World	6,695	100
Top Five Countries	Value	Share, %	Top Five Countries	Value	Share, %
Canada	1,216	34	Canada	2,016	30
Mexico	346	10	Italy	904	14
Japan	292	8	Mexico	900	13
China	90	3	China	608	9
Germany	89	3	Spain	361	5

[1] SIC 2451, 2452, 2951, 2952, 3084, 3088, 3211, 3241, 3251, 3253, 3259, 3261, 3271, 3272, 3273, 3275, 3281, 3296, 3431, 3432, 3433, 3441, 3442, 3444, 3446, 3448, 3996.
[2] For definitions of regional groupings, see "Getting the Most Out of *Outlook 2000*."
[3] Values may not sum to total due to rounding.
Source: U.S. Department of Commerce, Bureau of the Census.

pensated for by increased imports, product substitution, construction delays, and reduced construction output.

Price increases were fairly moderate in 1999. The producer price index for construction materials increased about 1 percent from 1998 to 1999. However, price increases for individual products increased widely, with prices for asphalt paving mixtures gaining 9 percent while the price index for water heaters declined 12 percent. A notable feature of the 1999 peak construction season was the tight supply of key materials such as gypsum board and fiberglass insulation. Those shortages varied geographically and were worst between June and September.

Electronic Commerce in Building Products

Because sales of building products tend to involve large orders of physical goods, E-commerce opportunities are different than they are in consumer product industries and information industries. The principal uses of the Internet for building products are to enable purchasers to announce their requirements and to allow suppliers to broadcast product brochures widely and cheaply. Although this significantly increases efficiency, negotiations usually need to be concluded in the traditional manner.

A noteworthy Internet innovation is the on-line *Thomas Register of American Manufacturers* (www.thomasregister.com), which is becoming an important vehicle for exporting U.S. building products. Although the register is intended primarily for American customers, it automatically provides foreign buyers with the same service. This has dramatically reduced the difficulties faced by foreign buyers by making product brochures and lists of U.S. suppliers available instantly and for free. Since access to the Web site is on a 24-hour basis, most of the communications problem caused by time zones is eliminated.

OUTLOOK FOR THE YEAR 2000 AND BEYOND

Shipments of building products will increase moderately in the year 2000, because the domestic construction market is expected to remain strong and several important export markets are expected to recover. The biggest increases will be in products used in highway and commercial building construction, such as asphalt, cement, and fabricated structural metal. Since housing starts are expected to decline slightly, shipments of products used chiefly in homebuilding, such as asphalt roofing, water heaters, and plastic pipe, will not experience much change (see Table 8-3).

The trade deficit in construction products probably will narrow in 2000, but the situation will vary among products. Although the international economic conditions that caused the trade deficit in building products will ease, foreign suppliers probably will have to struggle to keep their market shares in the United States. In the export markets, U.S. producers will have to struggle to regain market share. Excess production capacity in China will cause a major competitive challenge for years.

Over the period 2000–2004, the U.S. construction sector is expected to grow slowly from its current record levels, and building products shipments should increase approximately in line with increases in construction. The best market in the long term is likely to be highway construction, which will require cement, asphalt, concrete products, and structural steel. The number of housing starts will not increase much, but the long-term trend toward larger and more luxurious homes will continue. This will benefit most building products companies, especially those selling gypsum board, plumbing fixtures, doors and windows, and sheet metal work. Home improvement

TABLE 8-3: Value of Product Shipments of U.S. Building Product Industries, 1998–2000
(millions of 1992 dollars except as noted)

		Current Dollars	Constant 1992 Dollars			Annual Percent Change	
	SIC Code	1998[1]	1998[1]	1999[1]	2000[2]	98–99	99–00
Total building products		167,850	140,340	144,730	146,835	3.1	1.4
Mobile homes	2451	10,276	7,929	8,200	8,237	−3	1
Prefabricated wooden buildings	2452	2,943	2,317	2,387	2,418	3	1
Asphalt paving mixtures	2951	6,135	5,402	5,726	6,012	6	5
Asphalt roofing	2952	5,753	7,100	7,313	7,386	3	1
Hard-surfaced floor coverings	3996	2,257	2,362	2,433	2,433	3	0
Rubber floor coverings	30694	831	804	820	811	2	−1
Plastic pipe	3084	5,019	4,244	4,414	4,414	4	0
Plastic plumbing fixtures	3088	2,191	1,895	1,971	1,971	4	0
Miscellaneous plastic construction products	3089[3]	8,427	7,747	8,135	8,297	5	2
Flat glass	3211	2,779	2,609	2,640	2,670	1	1
Cement	3241	6,741	4,771	4,878	5,002	2	3
Clay brick and structural tile	3251	1,681	1,405	1,461	1,475	4	1
Ceramic wall and ceiling tile	3253	1,091	1,301	1,340	1,340	3	0
Structural clay products nec	3259	222	228	237	239	4	1
Vitreous plumbing fixtures	3261	983	774	769	777	0	1
Concrete block and brick	3271	3,375	2,968	3,058	3,088	3	1
Concrete products nec	3272	10,319	7,679	7,909	7,988	3	1
Ready-mixed concrete	3273	19,241	15,406	15,868	16,027	3	1
Gypsum products	3275	4,826	2,887	2,974	3,033	3	2
Cut stone and stone products	3281	1,699	1,539	1,570	1,601	2	2
Mineral wool	3296	2,422	2,014	2,075	2,116	3	2
Cast iron pipe and fittings	33211	287	251	261	258	4	−1
Builders' hardware	34294	5,988	5,078	5,231	5,335	3	2
Metal plumbing fixtures	3431	1,179	928	934	946	1	1
Plumbing fittings (metal)	3432	5,148	4,338	4,511	4,511	4	0
Fabricated structural metal	3441	15,300	11,944	12,588	12,997	6	4
Metal doors, windows, and trim	3442	10,175	8,966	9,325	9,418	4	1
Sheet metal work	3444	17,963	15,364	15,825	15,983	3	1
Architectural metal work	3446	4,538	3,660	3,806	3,844	4	1
Prefabricated metal buildings	3448	3,997	3,147	3,189	3,253	2	2
Fences and screens	3496[4]	406	364	379	382	4	1
Building heating equipment	3433	3,658	2,919	3,007	3,067	3	2

[1] Estimate.
[2] Forecast.
[3] Only plastic construction products are included.
[4] Component of SIC 3476, miscellaneous fabricated wire products.
Source: Forecasts and estimates by International Trade Administration.

will increase faster than will new housing construction, with a disproportionate benefit going to vendors of plumbing fixtures, asphalt roofing, and sheet metal work. Past trends toward more prefabrication and the use of more plastic building products will continue, benefiting those industries.

Patrick MacAuley, U.S. Department of Commerce, Forest Products and Building Materials Division, (202) 482-0132, September 1999.

PREFABRICATED BUILDINGS

This section covers three industries that produce prefabricated buildings in permanent plants. The prefabricated metal buildings industry (SIC 3448) is composed of firms that fabricate the components of complete low-rise nonresidential building systems such as office buildings, retail stores, fast-food restaurants, warehouses, recreational facilities, manufacturing facilities, schools, churches, storage buildings, and agricultural buildings. The mobile home industry (SIC 2451) produces units, now also called manufactured homes, that are made to the U.S. Department of Housing and Urban Development National Manufactured Housing Standard. The prefabricated wood building industry (SIC 2452) includes firms that make panelized and modular units for residential use. Prefabricated wood units are built to either local building codes or statewide codes for factory-built housing.

A major advantage of prefabrication in all types of buildings is that these units are built faster and are available to the buyer much sooner. Factory quality and cost controls are also key factors in the success of these industries. In 1999, 7 percent of all new residential structures built in the United States consisted of prefabricated wooden buildings and mobile/manufactured homes. Prefabricated metal buildings had a 65 percent market share of nonresidential structures, particularly for commercial properties.

Prefabricated Metal Buildings

Prefabricated metal buildings (SIC 3448) are particularly popular as nonresidential structures of less than 150,000 square feet, especially for commercial properties. These buildings have a 65 percent share of this nonresidential market compared with about 50 percent in 1990 and 35 percent in the early 1970s. These structures often are sold through manufacturer representatives that act as builder-dealers. Most of those dealers are independent and provide the staff for engineering and erecting the buildings.

Among the reasons for the popularity of these structures are affordability, faster completion and occupation times, and high quality. Faster construction results in a quicker return on investment for the owner. Factory fabrication of components for these structures usually offers easier quality control and reduces the weather and seasonality factor.

Because of the popularity of this kind of building, consumption of prefabricated metal structures grew about 2 percent in 1999. Average annual consumption through the year 2000 is also expected to increase approximately 2 percent. The value of product shipments for prefabricated metal structures increased about 1 percent in constant dollars in 1999 (see Table 8-4), with 1 to 2 percent annual average growth forecast for the year 2000. Despite the forecast for no growth in the commercial building sector, shipments of prefabricated metal buildings will increase because prefabricated buildings capture slightly more market share in the commercial structure and manufacturing facility construction sectors than they did in the past.

Exports of these structures dropped to $190 million in 1999, down from $201 million in 1998. However, exports were up from $143 million in 1992 and are forecast to remain steady through 2000. Although the value of exports is substantial, they represent only about 5 percent of domestic output. The U.S. industry is considered a leader in the design and production of these units and enjoys a reputation for quality and service. Among the major foreign markets are Canada, Syria, Egypt, Mexico, and China (see Table 8-5). The devastating earthquake in Turkey in 1999 may generate export opportunities for these nonresidential structures.

The overall import trend suggests slow import growth from Canadian, European, and Taiwan companies with products that can compete with those of U.S. firms in developing country markets and even the United States.

Mobile/Manufactured Homes

These units, now called manufactured homes (SIC 2451), are produced as single-section or multisection dwelling units. Before 1996, the industry produced more single-section units than multisection units. In 1999, 65 percent of all units shipped were double-wide or triple-wide units (see Table 8-6). A small percentage of these units are used for schoolrooms, bank branches, construction site offices, and other commercial applications.

Unit shipments of manufactured homes rose 5.6 percent in 1998 to 373,000 homes and declined 6 percent in 1999 (see Table 8-6). The forecast for unit shipments in the year 2000 is a 1.3 percent decline. However, the value of shipments will increase slightly, reflecting the trend toward larger and more expensive units.

The challenges facing this industry include dispelling the "trailer park" or "mobile home" image. Although these units have improved, safety and quality concerns still exist. The

TABLE 8-4: Prefabricated Metal Buildings (SIC 3448) Trends and Forecasts
(millions of dollars except as noted)

										Percent Change			
	1992	1993	1994	1995	1996	1997	1998[1]	1999[2]	2000[3]	97–98	98–99	99–00	96–00[4]
Industry data													
Value of shipments[5]	2,789	3,314	3,857	4,352	4,512	4,206	4,332	4,520		3.0	4.3		
Value of shipments (1992$)	2,789	3,190	3,532	3,775	3,853	3,400	3,400	3,440	3,500	0.0	1.2	1.7	−2.4
Total employment (thousands)	20.3	23.2	25.3	27.4	28.7	25.9	26.0	26.5		0.4	1.9		
Production workers (thousands)	13.1	15.6	17.1	19.3	20.0	17.8	18.0	18.3		1.1	1.7		
Average hourly earnings ($)	10.03	10.69	10.51	10.82	10.77	12.30							
Capital expenditures	28.9	34.3	50.5	67.4	73.0	57.1	60.0	63.0		5.1	5.0		
Product data													
Value of shipments[5]	2,579	3,048	3,581	3,982	3,998	3,872	3,997	4,177		3.2	4.5		
Value of shipments (1992$)	2,579	2,934	3,279	3,454	3,414	3,115	3,147	3,189	3,253	1.0	1.3	2.0	−1.2
Trade data													
Value of imports	7.7	12.7	20.4	33.9	40.2	62.3	58.0	65.0	70.0	−6.9	12.1	7.7	14.9
Value of exports	143	198	197	201	233	230	201	190	210	−12.6	−5.5	10.5	−2.6

[1] Estimate except imports and exports.
[2] Estimate.
[3] Forecast.
[4] Compound annual rate.
[5] For a definition of industry versus product values, see "Getting the Most Out of *Outlook 2000*."
Source: U.S. Department of Commerce: Bureau of the Census; International Trade Administration.

TABLE 8-5: U.S. Trade Patterns in Prefabricated Metal Buildings[1] in 1998
(millions of dollars; percent)

Exports			Imports		
Region[2]	Value[3]	Share, %	Region[2]	Value[3]	Share, %
NAFTA	71	36	NAFTA	51	87
Latin America	37	18	Latin America	0	0
Western Europe	19	9	Western Europe	5	9
Japan/Chinese Economic Area	16	8	Japan/Chinese Economic Area	1	2
Other Asia	7	4	Other Asia	0	1
Rest of world	51	25	Rest of world	1	1
World	201	100	World	58	100
Top Five Countries	Value	Share, %	Top Five Countries	Value	Share, %
Canada	62	31	Canada	50	87
Syria	12	6	United Kingdom	2	4
Egypt	10	5	Taiwan	1	2
Mexico	10	5	Germany	1	1
China	8	4	Belgium	1	1

[1] SIC 3448.
[2] For definitions of regional groupings, see "Getting the Most Out of *Outlook 2000*."
[3] Values may not sum to total due to rounding.
Source: U.S. Department of Commerce, Bureau of the Census.

industry continues to encounter zoning restrictions, which in many areas virtually "zone out" the use of mobile/manufactured homes unless they are placed in a manufactured housing park (community).

The industry's efforts to reinvent itself are showing results, and demand has grown. Financing options for buyers of manufactured homes are now closer to those for buyers of conventional housing. Owners who place these units on private property can finance the land with the unit for up to 30 years. Prices per square foot for manufactured housing are about half those for site-built units. When put on private lots, manufactured homes often appreciate at a rate similar to that of conventional units. There is also a sizable market for preowned manufactured homes. Product shipments are projected to grow less than 1 percent in the year 2000, compared with a 6 percent annual decline forecast for new housing starts (see Table 8-7).

Because these units are shipped in a three-dimensional mode, relatively few are exported. Their weight and volume result in very high transportation costs. Most exports are sent across the border to Canadian customers. U.S. imports are insignificant.

Prefabricated Wood Buildings

In 1999, industry shipments of prefabricated wood building units (SIC 2452) increased over 3 percent in real terms over 1998 levels (see Table 8-8). The forecast for 2000 is that shipments will

TABLE 8-6: Manufactured Housing Units
(thousands of units; percent)

Year	Single-Wide Shipments	Multiwide Shipments	Total Shipments	Annual Percent Change in Total Shipments	Single-Family Housing Starts	Annual Percent Change	Single-Family Total Housing Additions[1]	Manufactured Housing, Percent of Total Additions
1987	139.1	93.5	232.6		1,146.4		1,379.0	16.9
1988	122.4	96.0	218.4	–6.1	1,081.3	–5.7	1,299.7	16.8
1989	103.3	94.9	198.3	–9.2	1,003.3	–7.2	1,201.6	16.5
1990	98.6	89.6	188.2	–5.1	894.8	–10.8	1,083.0	17.4
1991	91.1	79.7	170.7	–9.3	840.4	–6.1	1,011.1	16.9
1992	112.1	98.7	210.8	23.5	1,029.9	22.5	1,240.7	17.0
1993	134.4	119.8	254.3	20.6	1,125.7	9.3	1,380.0	18.4
1994	156.2	147.8	303.9	19.5	1,198.4	6.5	1,502.3	20.2
1995	173.8	165.8	339.6	11.7	1,076.2	–10.2	1,415.8	24.0
1996	173.7	189.7	363.4	7.0	1,160.9	7.9	1,524.3	23.8
1997	148.8	204.6	353.4	–2.8	1,133.1	–2.4	1,486.5	23.8
1998	144.3	228.5	372.8	5.5	1,271.4	12.2	1,644.2	22.7
1999	122.0	228.0	350.0	–6.0	1,330.0	4.6	1,680.0	20.8

[1] Manufactured housing shipments are not included in housing starts. This column is the total of the shipments and housing starts.
Source: Manufactured Housing Institute, U.S. Department of Commerce, Bureau of the Census.

TABLE 8-7: Mobile Homes (SIC 2451) Trends and Forecasts
(millions of dollars except as noted)

	1992	1993	1994	1995	1996	1997	1998[1]	1999[2]	2000[3]	Percent Change 97–98	98–99	99–00	96–00[4]
Industry data													
Value of shipments[5]	4,484	5,786	6,890	8,115	9,019	9,290	10,404	10,250		12.0	–1.5		
Value of shipments (1992$)	4,484	5,537	6,135	6,791	7,338	7,484	8,010	7,770	7,800	7.0	–3.0	0.4	3.1
Total employment (thousands)	36.8	42.4	48.4	54.5	60.4	68.3	71.7	71.5		5.0	–0.3		
Production workers (thousands)	30.6	35.7	40.5	45.8	51.4	57.3	60.5			5.6			
Average hourly earnings ($)	9.52	10.07	10.19	10.43	10.96	11.75							
Capital expenditures	50.4	78.4	124	89.3	140	137	140	150		2.2	7.1		
Product data													
Value of shipments[5]	4,446	5,755	6,844	7,964	8,876	9,141	10,276	10,140		12.4	–1.5		
Value of shipments (1992$)	4,446	5,507	6,095	6,664	7,222	7,347	7,931	7,770	7,740	7.9	–3.0	0.5	3.3
Trade data													
Value of imports	1.1	0.6	1.1	1.2	1.2	2.0	5.9	7.0	8.0	195.0	18.6	14.3	60.7
Value of exports	17.4	13.8	13.1	17.7	17.3	21.7	26.8	25.0	26.0	23.5	–6.7	4.0	10.7

[1] Estimate except imports and exports.
[2] Estimate.
[3] Forecast.
[4] Compound annual rate.
[5] For a definition of industry versus product values, see "Getting the Most Out of *Outlook 2000.*"
Source: U.S. Department of Commerce: Bureau of the Census; International Trade Administration.

increase less than 1 percent. Product shipments for prefabricated wood buildings also rose 3 percent in 1999. The forecast for 2000 is that product shipments will grow another 1 percent or so, compared with a 6 percent annual decline forecast for new housing starts. The market for prefabricated wood buildings normally follows the trend in new single-family housing. This steady pattern of slow growth reflects the growing popularity of factory-built housing. Prefabricated wood buildings accounted for just under 7 percent of all homes built in 1999, up from 6 percent in 1992.

Because prefabricated wood buildings are built to local building codes or statewide factory-built codes, they do not encounter serious zoning problems. Also, the difference in appearance between these units and conventional housing has become less apparent. However, a prefabricated unit often is less expensive, and quality control generally is better in a plant than it is at a building site. These units normally can be put in place faster than can site-built units. Although most of the output of this industry is used for residential purposes, some units,

TABLE 8-8: Prefabricated Wood Buildings (SIC 2452) Trends and Forecasts
(millions of dollars except as noted)

	1992	1993	1994	1995	1996	1997	1998[1]	1999[2]	2000[3]	Percent Change 97–98	98–99	99–00	96–00[4]
Industry data													
Value of shipments[5]	2,161	2,327	2,688	2,745	2,871	3,054	3,112	3,280		1.9	5.4		
Value of shipments (1992$)	2,161	2,155	2,337	2,284	2,343	2,460	2,455	2,526	2,558	–0.2	2.9	1.3	2.2
Total employment (thousands)	19.2	19.5	20.7	21.5	21.4	23.3	24.0	24.5		3.0	2.1		
Production workers (thousands)	13.7	14.1	15.4	16.1	16.1	17.1	18.0	18.5		5.3	2.8		
Average hourly earnings ($)	9.60	9.32	9.84	9.61	10.07	10.52							
Capital expenditures	25.2	39.9	44.3	49.5	41.6	56.8	60.0	62.0		5.6	3.3		
Product data													
Value of shipments[5]	2,164	2,325	2,749	2,644	2,715	2,888	2,943	3,103		1.9	5.4		
Value of shipments (1992$)	2,164	2,153	2,391	2,199	2,216	2,323	2,318	2,387	2,418	–0.2	3.0	1.3	2.2
Trade data													
Value of imports	8.5	9.4	21.4	22.5	41.2	41.7	56.0	62.0	65.0	34.3	10.7	4.8	12.1
Value of exports	59.8	45.8	74.3	73.1	93.0	97.0	53.2	50.0	70.0	–45.2	–6.0	40.0	–6.9

[1] Estimate except imports and exports.
[2] Estimate.
[3] Forecast.
[4] Compound annual rate.
[5] For a definition of industry versus product values, see "Getting the Most Out of *Outlook 2000.*"
Source: U.S. Department of Commerce: Bureau of the Census; International Trade Administration.

TABLE 8-9: U.S. Trade Patterns in Prefabricated Wood Buildings[1] in 1998
(millions of dollars; percent)

Exports			Imports		
Region[2]	Value[3]	Share, %	Region[2]	Value[3]	Share, %
NAFTA	2	5	NAFTA	51	91
Latin America	3	6	Latin America	0	1
Western Europe	2	4	Western Europe	4	7
Japan/Chinese Economic Area	42	78	Japan/Chinese Economic Area	0	1
Other Asia	2	3	Other Asia	0	0
Rest of world	2	4	Rest of world	0	0
World	53	100	World	56	100
Top Five Countries	Value	Share, %	Top Five Countries	Value	Share, %
Japan	41	77	Canada	51	91
Guatemala	2	4	United Kingdom	3	4
Mexico	2	3	Finland	1	1
South Korea	1	2	China	0	1
Germany	1	2	Costa Rica	0	1

[1] SIC 2452.
[2] For definitions of regional groupings, see "Getting the Most Out of *Outlook 2000.*"
[3] Values may not sum to total due to rounding.
Source: U.S. Department of Commerce, Bureau of the Census.

particularly modular ones, are used for schoolrooms, offices, and other commercial applications.

The 1999 "State of the Industry Shapiro Report" published by *Automated Builder* showed that in 1998 there were approximately 3,500 panelizer firms (including dome, log, conventional, foam-core, steel frame, plastic block, and retail or mass merchandiser lumberyards). Those figures indicate that there were 7,000 major production builders, 200 residential modular producers, and 90 U.S. Department of Housing and Urban Development (HUD)-code home manufacturers operating over 300 factories. Not included were about 2,200 firms that produce components for homes (roof trusses, wall and floor units, etc.) and a large group (about 7,000) of "production builders" that make their own components in a factory (permanent or temporary) or buy them from component producers.

Exports of prefabricated wooden buildings account for only a small proportion of production. In 1998, exports totaled about $53 million. The single largest consumer of U.S. prefabricated wooden buildings was Japan at $41 million (see Table 8-9). Other countries buying U.S. prefabricated wooden buildings included Guatemala and Mexico. The recent earthquake in Turkey has generated a market opportunity for this product. Exports were expected to fall in 1999 and are forecast to rebound in the year 2000 as east Asian markets recover from their economic crises.

Imports of these units grew in 1998 and 1999, reflecting the healthy domestic construction market. In 1998, import value ($56 million) exceeded export value, generating the first trade deficit for the prefabricated wood building industry. In part, that deficit was caused by domestic demand outpacing supply, along with material and labor shortages. In 1998, most U.S. imports originated from Canada, valued at $51 million. Imports are forecast to rise through 2000. However, U.S. exports are forecast to outpace imports in that year.

Kathryn Hollander, U.S. Department of Commerce, Forest Products and Building Materials Division, (202) 482-0132, September 1999.

PLUMBING EQUIPMENT

The plumbing equipment sector includes industries that produce fixtures made of various materials: plastic (SIC 3088), vitreous (SIC 3261), and metal (SIC 3431). Also covered in this section is the plumbing fixture fittings and trip industry (SIC 3432), which makes faucets, drains, and showerheads. Most larger plumbing equipment producers make products in several, if not all, of these industries. There are, however, hundreds of small companies specializing in products classified under just one or two of these industries.

Product shipments in these four industries rose about 6 percent in 1998 (see Table 8-10). The 3 to 4 percent gain in constant dollars in 1999 reflected the housing market slowdown in the latter part of that year. A 2.4 percent rise is forecast for 2000.

Growth and continuing strength in the new building construction and renovation markets have resulted in favorable trends in the overall plumbing equipment markets. The market for plumbing fixtures is dependent mainly on housing demand, but commercial and institutional buildings are also important. There are also significant plumbing equipment replacement and addition markets. Adding and renovating bathrooms and modernizing kitchens have become a very big business for contractors, distributors, and producers. The market situation for fixture fittings, however, is different from that for fixtures. Fittings have much stronger repair and replacement market because they are easier and often less costly to replace than are fixtures and tend to wear out faster.

TABLE 8-10: Plumbing Parts (SIC 3088, 3261, 3431, 3432) Trends and Forecasts
(millions of dollars except as noted)

	1992	1993	1994	1995	1996	1997	1998[1]	1999[2]	2000[3]	Percent Change 97–98	98–99	99–00	96–00[4]
Industry data													
Value of shipments[5]	5,507	6,007	6,539	6,899	7,753	9,132	9,862	10,450		8.0	6.0		
Value of shipments (1992$)	5,507	5,886	6,277	6,395	6,979	7,771	8,237	8,560	8,770	6.0	3.9	2.4	4.6
Total employment (thousands)	43.1	45.7	47.5	49.0	50.0	52.5							
Production workers (thousands)	33.5	35.0	36.3	37.5	38.7	41.0							
Average hourly earnings ($)	11.08	11.03	10.78	11.24	10.85								
Capital expenditures	137	137	167	180	169	170							
Product data													
Value of shipments[5]	5,224	5,705	6,294	6,647	7,427	8,747	9,501	10,100		8.6	6.0		
Value of shipments (1992$)	5,224	5,586	6,037	6,156	6,679	7,444	7,935	8,185	8,380	6.6	3.2	2.4	4.9
Trade data													
Value of imports	385	431	533	582	666	724	883			22.0			
Value of exports	261	267	266	273	258	288	262			–9.0			

[1] Estimate except imports and exports.
[2] Estimate.
[3] Forecast.
[4] Compound annual rate.
[5] For a definition of industry versus product values, see "Getting the Most Out of *Outlook 2000.*"
Source: U.S. Department of Commerce: Bureau of the Census; International Trade Administration.

Material trends in plumbing fixtures show that plastic fixtures and fittings experienced higher growth over the years than did metal and vitreous ones. Plastics have gained in the residential bathtub, shower stall, lavatory sink, and whirlpool markets at the expense of vitreous and metal materials. Vitreous fixtures are used primarily in bathrooms (sinks and toilets), while metal fixtures are employed most often in kitchen sinks (stainless and enameled) and are still used in bathtubs. Vitreous still has much of the toilet market but has lost market share to plastics in the toilet water tank and lavatory sink markets. The plastics category includes fiberglass-reinforced plastic (FRP) and other plastics, including cultured marble. FRP products are gel-coated or acrylic. The U.S. Bureau of the Census's *Current Industrial Report: Plumbing Fixtures* shows that overall shipments of plastic fixtures (fiberglass and plastics) reached $1.7 billion in 1998, accounting for about 50 percent of total plumbing fixture shipments. Vitreous china accounted for $884 million, or 26 percent of the total. Metal fixtures reached $700 million, a 21 percent share. Other materials accounted for the remaining 3 percent.

Another favorable factor for the plumbing equipment markets is the long-term trend toward including more bathrooms in new homes. The U.S. Bureau of the Census's *Characteristics of New Housing: 1994–1998* shows that the number of new homes with three or more bathrooms rose to 8 percent of the total of new homes. The proportion with two and a half baths was 34 percent, with those with two baths at 41 percent and those with one and a half baths or less at just 8 percent.

Water conservation is a major issue in this industry. Water supply devices and toilet flush designs and devices are the key factors. The Energy Policy Act of 1992 set the maximum number of gallons per flush at less than 1.6, less than half the amount per flush previously used in most toilets. Some of the first new devices and designs did not provide satisfactory flushing. There also have been problems with some supply devices, such as showerheads, which decrease water pressure and volume to the point of not cleaning properly. Manufacturers have spent much time and money developing products that work satisfactorily for the consumer but still meet government standards.

Foreign trade in plumbing equipment is significant, but the low growth in exports has been overshadowed by the rapid increase in imports. In 1998, imports were more than triple the value of exports, with most imports coming from Canada, Mexico, and Taiwan. Export value dropped 9 percent in 1998 from 1997 levels, with most exports going to Canada, Japan, and Hong Kong. The deficit increased again in 1999 because of the strong U.S. domestic market and a strong dollar. The deficit is forecast to decline slightly in the year 2000 as U.S. housing starts decline and the Asian economies recover.

Kathryn Hollander, U.S. Department of Commerce, Forest Products and Building Materials Division, (202) 482-0132, September 1999.

CEMENT

Cement (SIC 3241) is a fundamental building material for the construction sector. It is used in virtually all types of construction activity, but its major market is nonresidential construction. The ready-mix concrete industry is the major customer for cement, accounting for about 72 percent of shipments. Concrete product producers (pipe, block, brick, precast, prestressed, and dry mix) purchase another 11 percent. Direct

TABLE 8-11: Hydraulic Cement (SIC 3241) Trends and Forecasts
(millions of dollars except as noted)

	1992	1993	1994	1995	1996	1997	1998[1]	1999[2]	2000[3]	Percent Change 97–98	98–99	99–00	96–00[4]
Industry data													
Value of shipments[5]	4,051	4,187	4,808	5,342	5,818	6,254	6,942	7,282	7,726	11.0	4.9	6.1	7.3
Value of shipments (1992$)	4,051	3,987	4,278	4,437	4,618	4,546	4,914	5,024	5,152	8.1	2.2	2.5	2.8
Total employment (thousands)	17.0	16.6	16.6	16.8	16.9								
Production workers (thousands)	12.8	12.5	12.4	12.6	12.5								
Average hourly earnings ($)	15.15	15.48	15.80	16.40	16.75								
Capital expenditures	226	227	280	282	495								
Product data													
Value of shipments[5]	3,929	4,051	4,699	5,172	5,650	6,075	6,741	7,073	7,503	11.0	4.9	6.1	7.3
Value of shipments (1992$)	3,929	3,858	4,180	4,296	4,484	4,414	4,771	4,878	5,002	8.1	2.2	2.5	2.8
Trade data													
Value of imports	251	284	444	542	596	753	963	1,100	1,050	27.9	14.2	−4.5	15.2
Value of exports	50	49	47	56	59	60	58	60	60	−3.2	2.9	0.0	0.4

[1] Estimate except imports and exports.
[2] Estimate.
[3] Forecast.
[4] Compound annual rate.
[5] For a definition of industry versus product values, see "Getting the Most Out of *Outlook 2000*."
Source: U.S. Department of Commerce: Bureau of the Census; International Trade Administration.

sales to construction contractors account for about 7 percent of demand, and sales to building materials dealers, hardware stores, lumberyards, and home centers account for another 3 percent. The rest is purchased directly by the government, oil well drillers, and miscellaneous users.

In 1998, cement consumption followed the trend illustrated by that year's record high level of new construction (see Chapter 6). Total construction activity increased nearly 5 percent in that year and was expected to grow 4 percent in 1999. Demand for cement closely follows the market for nonresidential construction and public works projects, which in 1998 accounted for 56 percent of total new construction. The consumption of cement surpassed the construction growth rate in 1998, perhaps indicating new material use or a modest price hike in response to heavy demand (see Table 8-11). Domestic demand began to increase steadily in 1994 after spending allocated by the first federal highway bill (ISTEA) in 1992 led to a greater concentration of construction in the transportation and public works sector. As a result, the ratio of cement shipments to construction activity has risen steadily. The passage of TEA-21 in 1998 to fund federal highway construction promises to support demand for cement and aggregates through 2004. Even if overall construction activity flattens during the next several years, annual cement shipments are likely to continue to remain strong (2 to 4 percent) because of the funding slated for federal highways.

The internationalization of the U.S. and world cement industries continues. In the 1980s, large international firms began to purchase plants around the world. As a result, production capacity in the United States is now more than two-thirds foreign-owned. This trend continued to characterize the industry in 1998. With recent acquisitions in the industry, foreign-owned production capacity could be as high as 71 percent. The owners of U.S. production facilities also purchase the bulk of U.S. imports.

The United States has long been a net importer of cement. The gap between U.S. cement imports and exports widened further in 1998 as imports increased 28 percent and exports declined 3 percent. As domestic cement production has been stretched to full or nearly full capacity, imports have become an important part of the U.S. supply. The bulk of U.S. cement imports come from Canada, China, Spain, Greece, Venezuela, Colombia, and Mexico. In 1998, China became the United States' second largest cement source, supplying 14 percent of all imports, a 432 percent increase from 1997. Thailand is another producer country supplying cement to the United States. After the financial crisis in that country began, domestic production reoriented itself to supply export markets. In 1998, U.S. imports of cement satisfied 23 percent of U.S. consumption as measured by volume, up from 18 percent the previous year, and in 1999 imports accounted for 27 percent of consumption. This compares to similar peaks in 1987 and 1988, when U.S. demand was strong and imports were abundant, and contrasts with the 8 to 9 percent levels in 1992 and 1993, when the U.S. construction sector was recovering from a recession. Imports are likely to continue to increase through 2004, although at diminishing levels. The United States has little cement available for export. Exports account for about 1 percent of U.S. production, and most are sent to Canada.

The capacity for cement production is expanding worldwide, including in the United States. Despite the enormous cost associated with building a new plant (capital outlay and energy costs), strong domestic demand justifies the expansion. New plants can cost as much as $300 million, and major modernization and expansion can cost more than $50 million. Most capital expenditures in the late 1980s and early 1990s were for replacement equipment (kilns, crushers, mixers, etc.), to meet environmental requirements, and for energy conservation projects. No new plants were built in that period, largely because of the high capital financial status of the producers. Starting in the second half of the 1990s, however, the number of major modernizations increased, and a few new plants are being built or are in the planning process.

In addition to the cost issue, cement manufacturers must minimize energy consumption to reduce the release of harmful air emissions. After the energy crisis of the 1970s, government programs required the industry to convert from natural gas and oil to coal. To save energy, the industry accelerated the conversion of kilns from a wet process to a dry process and introduced "tightening-up" measures to save energy. The most recent annual review by the USGS stated that 72 percent of clinker production occurred in entirely dry process plants and 26 percent was in wet process plants. In the 1990s, there was pressure to switch back to natural gas because of the environmental climatic change and ozone layer issues involved with coal use. Coal burning and the chemical process in which limestone and other materials are transformed into cement clinker and are subsequently mixed with gypsum and finely ground into finished cement cause the emission of carbon dioxide, nitrogen oxide, and sulfur dioxide, which have been named as contributors to climatic change, the thinning of the ozone layer, and urban smog. An inordinate amount of energy is required to sustain a manufacturing process that involves a high-temperature, 7-days-a-week, around-the-clock operation. As a result, energy accounts for 30 to 40 percent of total cement manufacturing costs. Legislation that requires plants to further restrict their emissions could negatively affect the U.S. industry by limiting capacity expansion and encouraging imports. This will be determined over the next few years as U.S. and international regulations related to changes in climate are approved and enforced.

Many cement plants in the United States also burn various waste materials and have worked with some hazardous waste materials in accordance with U.S. Environmental Protection Agency (EPA) and state regulations. Manufacturers that use waste fuel benefit from a less expensive fuel source. Environmental legislation may restrict the ability of manufacturers to use waste, which is an inexpensive fuel source. Another cost-saving tactic is the greater use of blended cements, which require less cement in concrete mixes and allow for a greater use of waste material substitutes such as coal ash and slag.

Susan H. Lusi, U.S. Department of Commerce, Forest Products and Building Materials Program, (202) 482-0133, susan_lusi@ita.doc.gov, September 1999.

FLAT GLASS

The U.S. flat glass industry (SIC 3211) consists of manufacturers of flat or float glass and those which fabricate flat glass products. The North American Industry Classification System (NAIC) eventually will replace this SIC code with NAIC 327211. The two systems define the industry in terms of the same types of establishments. The NAIC code considers establishments primarily engaged in manufacturing flat glass by melting silica sand or cullet or manufacturing both flat glass and laminated glass by melting silica sand or cullet as part of the sector.

In 1998, flat glass prices declined 4 percent from 1997 levels. As a result, the nominal value of shipments increased almost 4 percent while the constant dollar value increased 8

TABLE 8-12: Flat Glass (SIC 3211) Trends and Forecasts
(millions of dollars except as noted)

	1992	1993	1994	1995	1996	1997	1998[1]	1999[2]	2000[3]	Percent Change 97–98	98–99	99–00	96–00[4]
Industry data													
Value of shipments[5]	2,073	2,283	2,600	2,598	2,671	2,788	2,910	2,822	2,963	4.4	–3.0	5.0	2.6
Value of shipments (1992$)	2,073	2,234	2,346	2,213	2,417	2,523	2,732	2,766	2,787	8.3	1.2	0.8	3.6
Total employment (thousands)	11.8	11.3	11.2	11.2	11.5	11.5							
Production workers (thousands)	9.7	9.2	9.2	9.1	9.3	9.4							
Average hourly earnings ($)	17.45	18.03	19.01	19.73	19.39								
Capital expenditures	148	159	137	170	248	177							
Product data													
Value of shipments[5]	1,994	2,151	2,474	2,474	2,555	2,785	2,888	2,781	2,930	3.7	–3.7	5.3	2.7
Value of shipments (1992$)	1,994	2,105	2,233	2,107	2,312	2,415	2,609	2,640	2,670	8.0	1.2	1.1	3.7
Trade data													
Value of imports	278	341	416	399	463	492	510	520	520	3.7	2	0.0	2.9
Value of exports	499	583	620	687	793	810	738	700	725	–8.9	–5	3.5	–2.2

[1] Estimate except imports and exports.
[2] Estimate.
[3] Forecast.
[4] Compound annual rate.
[5] For a definition of industry versus product values, see "Getting the Most Out of *Outlook 2000.*"
Source: U.S. Department of Commerce: Bureau of the Census; International Trade Administration.

percent. As the industry has globalized production, there has been considerable expansion of overseas capacity, leading to increased imports and declining exports, as was the case in 1998 (see Table 8-12). The forecast for the year 2000 calls for shipments to increase by over 1 percent. The longer-term outlook is for about a 2 percent average annual increase through the year 2004. This forecast is based on expectations of modest growth in the construction and automotive sectors.

Like the manufacture of cement, the production of float glass is energy- and capital-intensive and therefore costly. The manufacturing process takes place around the clock, requiring considerable energy consumption. Capital expenditures for a new plant are likely to run between $100 million and $120 million. In the United States, flat glass manufacturers use natural gas or fuel oil in their production processes, and energy costs account for approximately 8 percent of total production costs.

Demand for flat glass has been particularly strong in recent years as the construction and motor vehicle sectors have rebounded from the recession of the early 1990s. The production capacity utilization rate for float glass production grew from about 80 to 85 percent in 1989 and 1990 to almost 100 percent currently. Construction applications account for 50 to 55 percent of total flat glass use, and motor vehicles account for another 25 percent. Other products, such as furniture, appliances, machines, and other transportation equipment (primarily naval, aircraft, and aerospace equipment), account for the rest. The glass replacements market is also a significant factor in the construction and automotive sectors.

The trend toward rising flat glass exports throughout the 1990s reversed itself in 1998, when exports declined 9 percent from $810 million in 1997 to $738 million, significantly lower than in 1996, when exports reached $793 million. U.S. exports to Japan declined 29 percent, probably because of displacement by imports from regional sources in response to the Asian economic crisis that began in 1997. Similarly, U.S. exports to most markets in Asia declined (China, 28 percent; Korea, 13 percent; Hong Kong, 33 percent). Exports to Europe and Canada tended to increase (France, 62 percent; Belgium, 133 percent; Canada, 10 percent), while exports to the third largest U.S. export market, Mexico, fell 3 percent to $76 million. U.S. imports totaled $510 million in 1998, up from $492 million in 1997 and about $278 million in 1992. Canada, Mexico, and Germany were the source of most U.S. imports in 1998.

Susan H. Lusi, U.S. Department of Commerce, Forest Products and Building Materials Program, (202) 482-0133, susan_lusi@ita.doc.gov, September 1999.

FABRICATED STRUCTURAL METAL

The output of the fabricated structural metal industry (SIC 3441) is consumed mostly in the construction of nonresidential buildings and infrastructure facilities. In recent years, structural metal applications for home construction have increased, and this has been reflected in consumption patterns. Industrial and commercial buildings account for 65 percent of the type of construction work that consumes structural metals. A variety of buildings fall under this category: hospitals, sports arenas, churches, government buildings, utility facilities, and infrastructure such as bridges and tunnels. The NAIC code 332312 is a nearly perfect match to the products covered under SIC 3441 and eventually will replace the SIC code.

TABLE 8-13: Fabricated Structural Metal (SIC 3441) Trends and Forecasts
(millions of dollars except as noted)

										Percent Change			
	1992	1993	1994	1995	1996	1997	1998[1]	1999[2]	2000[3]	97–98	98–99	99–00	96–00[4]
Industry data													
Value of shipments[5]	8,919	9,245	9,857	10,918	11,744	15,260	16,700	17,700		9.4	6.0		
Value of shipments (1992$)	8,919	9,144	9,450	10,166	10,551	12,500	13,000	13,500	13,900	4.0	3.8	3.0	7.1
Total employment (thousands)	72.0	70.7	71.4	74.3	75.5	92.5							
Production workers (thousands)	50.8	50.8	51.6	54.3	55.7	66.9							
Average hourly earnings ($)	10.97	11.16	11.24	11.45	11.69								
Capital expenditures	133	130	149	166	172	294							
Product data													
Value of shipments[5]	8,073	8,455	8,915	9,897	10,751	13,997	15,300	16,200		9.3	5.9		
Value of shipments (1992$)	8,073	8,363	8,548	9,215	9,659	11,449	11,900	12,400	12,800	3.9	4.2	3.2	7.3
Trade data													
Value of imports	115	160	196	265	329	398	537	700	750	34.9	30.4	7.1	22.9
Value of exports	302	317	371	387	451	570	472	450	475	−17.2	−4.7	5.6	1.3

[1] Estimate except imports and exports.
[2] Estimate.
[3] Forecast.
[4] Compound annual rate.
[5] For a definition of industry versus product values, see "Getting the Most Out of *Outlook 2000.*"
Source: U.S. Department of Commerce: Bureau of the Census; International Trade Administration.

U.S. shipments of fabricated structural steel have increased in real terms over the last few years as a result of rising levels of all types of construction. Increases in the range of 4 to 5 percent occurred in 1997 and 1998 and were expected to continue at that level through 1999 until construction activity leveled off (see Table 8-13). Federal funding of highways over the next several years will support the use of structural steel, particularly in bridges and tunnel reconstruction and road work. Expectations through the year 2004 are for average annual increases of 1 to 2 percent, although as the residential market is penetrated further by the industry, shipments could grow at a higher rate.

In 1998, product shipments were estimated at over $15 billion, a 9.3 percent increase over nearly $14 billion in 1997. The surge in steel imports that provide the raw material for prefabricated structural steel probably supported the increase, but imports of prefabricated structural metal itself also increased 62 percent in 1998. By volume, Canada imported the largest amount in 1998 at $181 million; Mexico was sent $24 million, and Japan received $10 million. Respectively, these importing countries expanded 57 percent, 28 percent, and over 1,000 percent from their 1997 levels, when total imports of structural metal grew from $151 to $246 million.

The trend in shipments was supported by a decline in U.S. exports of structural metal of 17 percent in 1998, a reversal of the 1996–1997 increase of 23 percent. The largest customers for U.S. exports were Canada, Mexico, and Venezuela, which each consumed more U.S. structural metal than it did the previous year. The overall decline reflects a loss in production capacity resulting from plant closings or reductions in line operations and the imbalance created by the 62 percent increase in imports.

To remain competitive, U.S. steelmakers are interested in creating new markets for steel products. The residential housing market has been a focus of interest for fabricated structural steel companies. Metal framing systems have been developed and are being used in single-family and multifamily houses, replacing traditional lumber products. Homebuilding organizations have been encouraging the use of this technology as they have encountered higher prices for lumber and wood products and fear future shortages. Research and development continue to strengthen fabricated structural steel sales and encourage the use of steel products in the residential construction field.

Prefabricated steel competes mainly with reinforced concrete construction and factory-produced precast/prestressed concrete and prefabricated metal building systems. Brick also competes with steel, but it increasingly is used only as facing rather than structurally. American Institute of Steel Construction data indicate that steel has about a 50 percent share of the industrial building market and a slightly higher share of the market for commercial and office buildings. Masonry (clay brick and concrete) construction accounts for the balance of the nonresidential building market.

Susan Lusi, U.S. Department of Commerce, Forest Products and Building Materials Program, (202) 482-0133, susan_lusi@ita.doc.gov, September 1999.

■ REFERENCES

Call the Bureau of the Census at (301) 457-1242 for information about ordering Census documents.

American Institute of Steel Construction, Inc., One East Wacker Drive, Suite 3100, Chicago, IL 60601-2001. (312) 670-2400.

Automated Builder, "AB Exclusive State of the Industry Report," January 1999, 1445 Donlon Street, Suite 16, Ventura, CA 93003. (805) 642-9735.

Brick Institute of America, 11490 Commerce Park Drive, Reston, VA 22091. (703) 620-0010.

Building Systems Councils, National Association of Home Builders, 1201 15 Street, NW, Washington, DC 20005. (202) 822-0576.

Construction Review (quarterly), International Trade Administration, Room H4309, U.S. Department of Commerce, Washington, DC 20230. (202) 482-0134.

Current Construction Reports: Characteristics of New Housing: 1998 (annual), C25/98, U.S. Bureau of the Census.

Current Industrial Reports: Clay Construction Products (quarterly), MQ32D, U.S. Bureau of the Census.

Current Industrial Reports: Plumbing Fixtures (quarterly), MQ34E, U.S. Bureau of the Census.

Glass Digest (monthly), Ashlee Publishing Co., 110 East 42 Street, New York, NY 10017. (212) 682-7681.

Gypsum Association, 810 First Street, NE, Washington, DC 2002. (202) 289-5440.

International Construction Review (on-line), International Trade Administration, Room H4309, U.S. Department of Commerce, Washington, DC 20230. www.ita.doc.gov/forestprod/construction/.

Manufactured Housing Institute, 2101 Wilson Boulevard, Arlington, VA 22201-3062. (703) 558-0400.

Metal Building Manufacturers Association, 1300 Summer Avenue, Cleveland, OH 44115-2851. (216) 241-7333.

Mineral Industry Surveys: Cement (monthly), Industrial Minerals Section, U.S. Geological Survey, 983 National Center, Reston, VA 20192.

Mineral Industry Surveys: Gypsum (monthly), Industrial Minerals Section, U.S. Geological Survey, 983 National Center, Reston, VA 20192.

National Glass Association, 8200 Greensboro Drive, McLean, VA 22102. (703) 442-4890.

New Steel (monthly), the Chilton Company, Chilton Way, Radnor, PA 19089. (610) 964-4000.

Plumbing Manufacturers Institute, 1340 Remington Road, Suite A, Schaumburg, IL 60173. (847) 884-9775.

Portland Cement Association, 5420 Old Orchard Road, Skokie, IL 60077-1083. (847) 966-6200.

Systems Builders Association, 28 Lowry Drive, West Milton, OH 45383. (515) 698-4127.

Tile Council of America, P.O. Box 1787, Clemson, SC 29633. (803) 646-4021.

Thomas Register of American Manufacturing Companies. www.thomasregister.com.

■ RELATED CHAPTERS

6: Construction
7: Wood Products
13: Steel Mill Products
15: General Components
18: Production Machinery

TEXTILES
Economic and Trade Trends

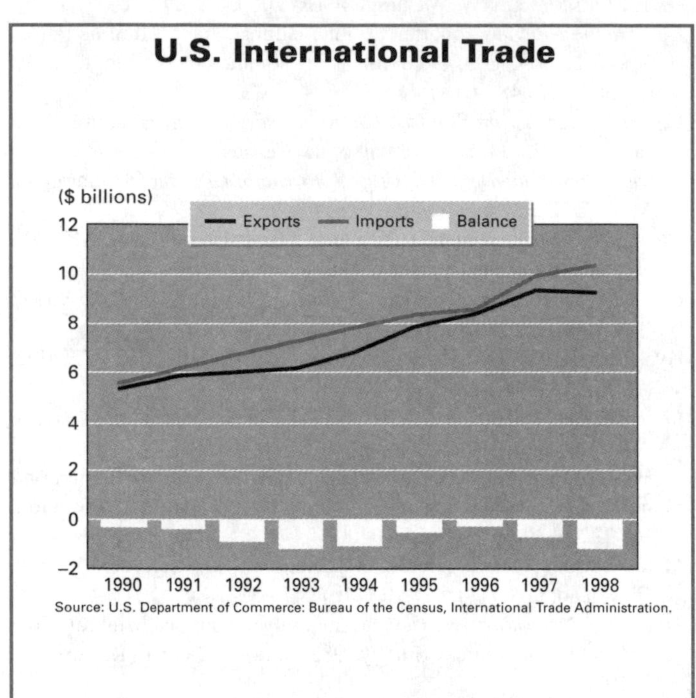

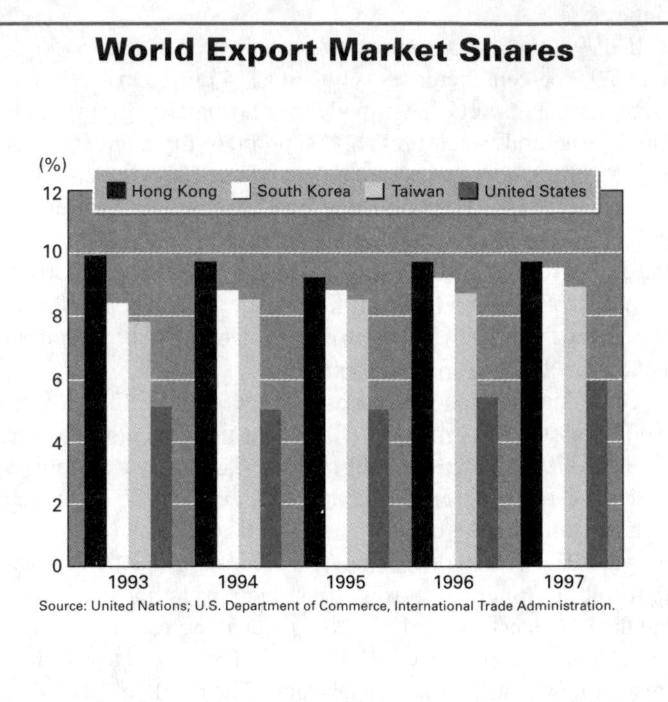

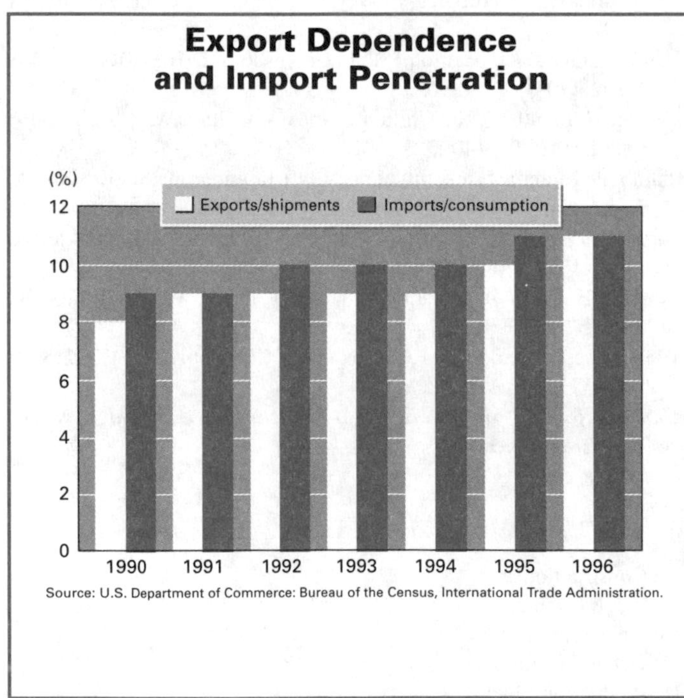

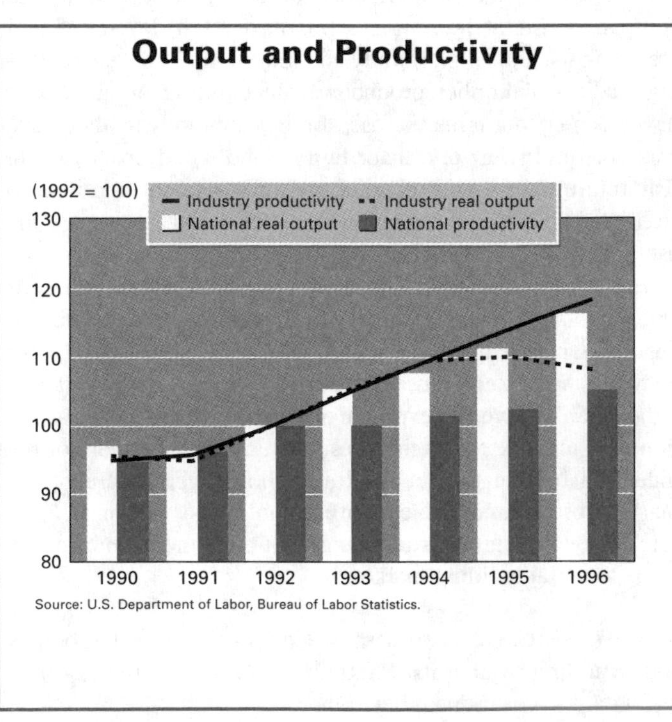

See "Getting the Most Out of *Outlook 2000*" for definitions of terms.

9

Textiles

INDUSTRY DEFINITION In this chapter portions of the textile mill products sector (SIC 22) are covered: broadwoven fabric mills (SIC 221, 222, 223); weft, lace, and warp knit fabric mills (SIC 2257, 2258); carpets and rugs (SIC 227); and yarn spinning mills (SIC 2281). The chapter also covers the man-made fiber industry (SIC 2823, 2824), which provides primary raw material inputs for textile products. Also included in SIC 22 but not covered in this chapter are narrow fabric and other smallwares mills, cotton, wool, silk, and man-made fiber (SIC 224); women's full-length and knee-length hosiery except socks (SIC 2251); hosiery not elsewhere classified (SIC 2252); knit outerwear mills (SIC 2253); knit underwear and nightwear mills (SIC 2254); knitting mills not elsewhere classified (SIC 2259); dyeing and finishing textiles except wool fabrics and knit goods (SIC 226); yarn texturizing, throwing, twisting, and winding mills (SIC 2282); thread mills (SIC 2284); and miscellaneous textile goods (SIC 229).

FACTORS AFFECTING FUTURE INDUSTRY GROWTH

Global Industry Trends

Global market trends in the textile industry increasingly are being determined by the transition to a quota-free textile trade environment. The quota system that has been in place since the early 1960s will end on December 31, 2004. However, quota growth rates have been increasing and will continue to increase until the end of 2004. This situation is driving a realignment of markets and a restructuring of the industry that are well under way.

The Asian economic crisis has provided a further spur to global market restructuring. The Asian exporting countries remain subject to quotas, but currency devaluations combined with an urgent need to export at nearly any price to garner foreign exchange impelled many of those countries to export textiles and apparel to the United States and other markets at rock-bottom prices. While recovery of Asian domestic markets and strengthening of certain currencies may mitigate the stress on world markets in the near term, intense competitive pressure is likely to characterize the global textile market in the future.

The response of textile manufacturers to intensifying global competition has been threefold. First, industry product mixes are shifting among countries. There is ongoing rationalization of production to emphasize products in which the manufacturer has the greatest competitive advantages and deemphasize products that are more vulnerable to foreign competition. In the United States and other developed countries, this implies a deemphasis on textile products consumed in the apparel industry and a greater emphasis on other products, such as home furnishings and industrial textiles. Second, companies continue to invest in new, more productive plant and equipment. Textile production is no longer a low-technology, labor-intensive industry enterprise. Textile firms around the world are under constant pressure to become more efficient through technology upgrades. Third and perhaps most important, manufacturing is expanding into countries close to home markets. This is being undertaken primarily to support production sharing arrangements for apparel, sometimes in partnership with customers, suppliers, or other textile manufacturers.

For U.S. textile producers, the most important regional expansion and partnering are taking place with Mexico. According to a report by Kurt Salmon Associates, broad market forces, including Asian pricing pressures, have accelerated the flow of textile capital into Mexico. The Asian crisis has accelerated the trend toward vertical integration and has prompted stronger vendor-supplier alliances. These trends, in addition to the benefits of lower manufacturing costs, are driving textile manufacturers that serve the apparel market to move closer to their customer base. By locating a mill in the same region as apparel manufacturers, textile companies reduce delivery times and help forge stronger ties to their apparel manufacturing customers.

Other partnerships are taking place between U.S. textile manufacturers and apparel producers in the Caribbean Basis Initiative (CBI) beneficiary countries and European textile and apparel producers in eastern Europe and north Africa. In the man-made fiber industry, cross-border joint ventures and partnerships have advanced to an especially high degree on both a regional and an extraregional basis.

Domestic Trends

To sharpen their competitive edge, many U.S. textile companies are (1) restructuring their operations through mergers, acquisitions, and divestitures, (2) concentrating on more profitable niche markets and product diversification, (3) improving productivity through new capital investment, (4) building strategic partnerships with retail and apparel companies, and (5) using quick response and other communication-oriented techniques to enhance their overall flexibility and competitiveness.

U.S. textile companies have been acting to improve their competitive positions through reorganization, restructuring, and downsizing. By merging, textile companies gain market share and access to capital. Through acquisitions and vertical integration, textile companies have been able to achieve economies of scale and expand the range of their services.

Another trend is for U.S. mills and converters to move slowly away from staple fabrics for the apparel industry and toward niche products and diversification into multiple sewn products markets. Technical fibers for sportswear and activewear have experienced tremendous growth. Other profitable growth opportunities in nonapparel fabric markets include automotive, medical, fire safety, and telecommunications (fiberoptics).

The U.S. textile industry is a technologically advanced industry, achieving such advancement through restructuring and investment in modern machinery. Spinning, weaving, and knitting processes are highly modernized in many companies, and this has allowed them to reduce the share of labor in production costs and increase quality and speed.

There has been a substantial job loss in the U.S. textile industry, a trend that has been ongoing for almost 30 years. This job loss can be attributed partly to imports, but like many other industries in the United States, the textile industry has been able to increase its production through new technologies while decreasing the number of employees. Overall textile production has increased more than 20 percent since the beginning of the decade even though industry employment has dropped over 13 percent. The textile industry continues to invest in machinery and technology, spending upward of $2 billion a year to maintain modern manufacturing facilities. Continued investment in modern technology, including information technology, is very important. Textile production is very capital intensive, and up-to-date technology is essential to meet the increasingly rigorous demand for high-quality products.

Some fabric manufacturers are finding success in integrating forward into apparel production either through ownership of the sewing or by finding contractors for their apparel customers. This has simplified apparel sourcing for retailers and significantly reduced the time needed to go from an idea to a retail store. The benefit to the textile mill is increased revenue and a stronger relationship with the customer.

Quick response (QR) is a system that shortens the interval between the placement of retail orders and the delivery of textile goods to stores. The benefits of QR include reduced lead time, lower inventories, increased order accuracy, reduced paper processing costs, improved customer service, improved quality, and improved operating margins.

Electronic commerce—business conducted over the Internet and the World Wide Web—is becoming a major engine of economic growth. For the U.S. textile industry, electronic commerce is facilitating links between all stages of the manufacturing and distribution process. To support electronic commerce, the American Textile Manufacturers Institute has developed a set of Fabric and Suppliers Linkage Council (FASLINC) voluntary standards for bar coding, labeling, and electronic data interchange (EDI). FASLINC voluntary standards facilitate electronic business between the textile industry and its suppliers, including suppliers of dyes, chemicals, natural and synthetic fibers, natural and synthetic yarns, and indirect materials and distributors of those products and supplies. Bar coding and EDI are the first steps in implementing QR. By providing standard bar coding and EDI formats, FASLINC is an integral part of a QR business strategy.

The American Textile Partnership (AMTEX), a collaborative research and development program involving representatives from the textile industry, the U.S. Department of Energy and its laboratories, other federal agencies, and universities, is developing the Textile Industry Data-Sharing Network (TEXNET) and the Supply Chain Integration Program (SCIP) to facilitate electronic commerce for the U.S. textile industry. TEXNET is a communications infrastructure that is part of an overall decision support system that will bridge the fiber, textile, apparel, and retail businesses. It is the only known software system with four security features that uses the Internet to share data among companies. SCIP is a computer-based tool for supply and demand analysis that uses supply-chain information exchanged among strategic business partners in a customer-supplier relationship. SCIP will enable business partnerships to analyze consumer demand, material availability, and resource capacity to reduce the product time in the supply-chain pipeline and meet inventory and safety stock targets. TEXNET and SCIP are tools of Demand Activated Manufacturing Architecture (DAMA), AMTEX's main project to link the fiber-textile-apparel-retail complex in an electronic marketplace where companies will identify, compare, buy, and sell resources, products, and services in support of innovative business partnerships.

PROJECTIONS OF INDUSTRY AND TRADE GROWTH FOR THE NEXT 1 AND 5 YEARS

While the U.S. economy showed strong growth in 1998 and consumers continued to spend, trends in the U.S. textile industry painted a mixed economic picture. Textile mill industry shipments were down 3 percent from 1997 to 1998. Meanwhile, textile inventories remained under control during 1998 and ended the year 3 percent above the December 1997 level. The Federal Reserve Bank's industrial production index for textile mill products was essentially flat in 1998 compared with the 1997 level, and the capacity utilization rate declined from 85.3 percent to 83.2 percent. According to the Fiber Economics Bureau, in 1998, U.S. mill fiber consumption declined from the previous year's all-time record by 1 percent, falling to 16.6 billion pounds, including a 0.5 percent increase for man-made fibers and a 3.5 percent decline for cotton fibers.

After-tax profits for U.S. textile operations fell 54 percent in the last quarter of 1998 from the previous quarter even though operating costs and nonoperating expenses were down for that quarter. However, profits for the year were $2.1 billion, up 11 percent from 1997 and the highest profit level since 1992.

The Asian economic crisis had a negative impact on the U.S. textile industry, the effects of which became apparent in the latter part of 1998. Financial problems in Asian countries led to a significant decline in textile prices in that region. Lower prices made Asian textiles more attractive on the global market. As a result, low-cost textiles imported from Asia, especially man-made fibers, put substantial pressure on the sales and margins of U.S. textile firms. Moreover, the influx of lower-priced imports from Asia led to a decline in U.S. textile sales. Weakened Asian economies also decreased consumer spending in Asia, leading to lower U.S. exports to that region.

While the U.S. economy was off to a good start in 1999, with business and consumer confidence both very high, the performance of the textile industry lagged behind that of the overall economy. Several factors should make for textile industry recovery over the long term: (1) a strong U.S. economy, (2) growing signs that the Asian financial crisis is abating, (3) expected stable or lower fiber costs, and (4) continued rationalization of U.S. mill capacity. Textile industry employment will continue to decline, but there will be gains in productivity. With the Asian financial crisis and intense competition, operational efficiencies will become critical for success. Companies must focus on high-margin, value-added products along with productivity and cost improvements. Nominal growth in the value of textile industry shipments should be approximately 1 percent between 1999 and 2000. The value of exports will continue to increase, although at a slower pace in 1999, by about 6 percent between 1999 and the year 2000. Imports are expected to grow about 10 percent over that period (see Table 9-1).

Several observers anticipate that pricing will remain problematic for the industry in the short term. In fact, in the first half of 1999, the producer price index for textile mill products was running about 2 percent below the same period a year earlier. However, one long-term forecast indicates that textile prices will improve. A forecast by the WEFA Group puts average annual textile mill product price increases in the range of 1 to 1.5 percent over the 2000–2008 period. Low fiber costs should provide a cushion for textile producers. Industry analysts predict that fiber prices will continue to fall or remain low and stable.

TABLE 9-1: Textile Mill Products (SIC 22) Trends and Forecasts
(millions of dollars except as noted)

										Percent Change			
	1992	1993	1994	1995	1996	1997[1]	1998[1]	1999[2]	2000[3]	97–98	98–99	99–00	96–00[4]
Industry data													
Value of shipments[5]	70,753	73,955	78,027	79,874	80,242	83,700	81,600	79,968	80,768	−2.5	−2.0	1.0	0.2
Value of shipments (1992$)	70,753	74,285	78,213	77,715	77,227	79,789	77,055	74,809	74,858	−3.4	−2.9	0.1	−0.8
Total employment (thousands)	617	610	624	610	577								
Production workers (thousands)	528	524	534	520	489								
Average hourly earnings ($)	8.62	8.92	9.29	9.38	9.62								
Product data													
Value of shipments[5]	70,008	73,216	77,249	79,200	79,334	82,863	80,791	79,176	79,967	−2.5	−2.0	1.0	0.2
Value of shipments (1992$)	70,008	73,539	77,448	77,035	76,336	78,991	76,291	74,068	74,117	−3.4	−2.9	0.1	−0.7
Trade data													
Value of imports	5,849	6,162	6,535	6,974	7,176	8,385	8,793	9,900	10,850	4.9	12.6	9.6	10.9
Value of exports	4,506	4,707	5,172	5,721	6,195	7,102	7,193	7,450	7,900	1.3	3.6	6.0	6.3

[1] Estimate except imports and exports.
[2] Estimate.
[3] Forecast.
[4] Compound annual rate.
[5] For a definition of industry versus product values, see "Getting the Most Out of *Outlook 2000.*"
Source: U.S. Department of Commerce: Bureau of the Census; International Trade Administration.

Exports will continue to play a major role in the future growth of the U.S. textile industry. Many U.S. textile companies have the potential to export successfully to selected markets, particularly speciality fabrics that are not produced in other countries. In addition to exporting, U.S. textile companies will continue to invest in plants and joint ventures overseas in order to compete in international markets.

GLOBAL MARKET PROSPECTS

Increased trade in this hemisphere through the North American Free Trade Agreement (NAFTA) and CBI has made U.S. textile companies more competitive with Asian producers. These arrangements have benefited the U.S. textile industry because the vast majority of apparel imported from Mexico and the Caribbean contains U.S. yarn and fabric, whereas apparel imported from Asian countries has virtually no U.S. content. Because NAFTA and the CBI encourage production sharing in the textile and apparel sector, Mexican and Caribbean plants purchase large quantities of U.S. components, allowing U.S. companies to increase exports, enhance efficiencies, and keep jobs in the United States.

In 1998, U.S. exports of textile mill products to Canada and Mexico accounted for 51 percent of total U.S. exports, up from 40 percent in 1993, reflecting a combined export increase of almost 100 percent to NAFTA countries during that period. U.S. exports of textiles to Canada and Mexico in 1998 were 10 times greater than U.S. exports to China, Taiwan, Hong Kong, and South Korea combined and three times as large as exports to Japan and the European Union countries combined. Exports to beneficiary countries of the CBI increased 10 percent between 1997 and 1998 and accounted for 12 percent of total U.S. textile exports in 1998 (see Table 9-2).

Aside from strong exports to NAFTA and CBI countries, 1998 was a difficult year for textile exports. The Asian economic crisis took a particularly heavy toll on U.S. exports. Exports to Japan dropped 27 percent from 1997 levels, while exports to Hong Kong and South Korea dropped 19 percent and 37 percent, respectively. With financial turmoil spreading into South America, that market was also weak for U.S. textile exporters. Exports to South America as a whole fell 10 percent, while exports to Brazil, which experienced a substantial currency devaluation in 1998, fell 14 percent. A generally weak economy in the European Union countries in 1998 also hampered exporters as textile exports fell 7 percent. With encouraging signs of economic recovery in some Asian countries and strengthening in Europe, there is cause for optimism that declines in textile exports to non-NAFTA and CBI markets will be reversed in the years ahead.

The trend toward regional export growth shows no sign of abating, as regional tariff preferences, combined with the possible expansion of such arrangements in various parts of the world, encourage U.S. textile companies to focus their efforts largely on regional markets. Various proposals for Caribbean Basin trade enhancement have been introduced by the administration and Congress in recent years. The proposals differ in specifics, but in general they would provide CBI beneficiary countries with access to the U.S. market for textiles and apparel, including tariff treatment, similar to that accorded to Mexico under NAFTA. Additionally, negotiations are under way to create a Western Hemisphere Free Trade Area of the Americas by 2005. These pending agreements will increase trade and cooperation within the Western Hemisphere, and eventually those countries could represent more attractive investment opportunities for U.S. textile companies.

In many emerging markets, U.S. textile exporters face high tariffs and a variety of nontariff barriers. A new multilateral

TABLE 9-2: U.S. Trade Patterns in Textiles[1] in 1998
(millions of dollars; percent)

Exports			Imports		
Region[2]	Value[3]	Share, %	Region[2]	Value[3]	Share, %
NAFTA	3,696	51	NAFTA	1,929	22
Latin America	1,227	17	Latin America	447	5
Western Europe	1,086	15	Western Europe	2,093	24
Japan/Chinese Economic Area	481	7	Japan/Chinese Economic Area	1,720	20
Other Asia	234	3	Other Asia	2,169	25
Rest of world	469	7	Rest of world	434	5
World	7,193	100	World	8,793	100
Top Five Countries	Value	Share, %	Top Five Countries	Value	Share, %
Canada	2,024	28	Canada	1,210	14
Mexico	1,672	23	Mexico	720	8
United Kingdom	315	4	South Korea	650	7
Dominican Republic	215	3	Italy	621	7
Hong Kong	209	3	China	577	7

[1] SIC 22.
[2] For definitions of regional groupings, see "Getting the Most Out of *Outlook 2000.*"
[3] Values may not sum to total due to rounding.
Source: U.S. Department of Commerce, Bureau of the Census.

round of trade negotiations could result in greater opportunities for U.S. textile producers to access those markets.

INDUSTRY SUBSECTORS

Broadwoven Fabric Mills

The broadwoven fabric mills subsector consists of cotton broadwoven fabric mills (SIC 221), man-made fiber broadwoven fabric mills (SIC 222), and wool broadwoven fabric mills (SIC 223).

According to data published by the U.S. Bureau of the Census, the quantity of broadwoven fabric production declined by almost 4 percent between 1997 and 1998, falling from 17.0 to 16.4 billion square yards. Particularly hard hit were wool broadwoven fabrics, which declined 24 percent over that period, partly as a result of a relatively warm winter and low-priced fabrics coming into the U.S. market from Asia. Between 1997 and

TABLE 9-3: Broadwoven Fabric Mills (SIC 221, 222, 223) Trends and Forecasts
(millions of dollars except as noted)

										Percent Change			
	1992	1993	1994	1995	1996	1997[1]	1998[1]	1999[2]	2000[3]	97–98	98–99	99–00	96–00[4]
Industry data													
Value of shipments[5]	16,190	16,816	17,638	18,389	18,204	18,800	18,276	17,643	17,898	−2.8	−3.5	1.4	−0.4
221 Cotton fabric mills	5,811	5,990	6,172	6,751	6,699	6,967	6,725	6,422	6,487	−3.5	−4.5	1.0	−0.8
222 Man-made fabric mills	8,767	9,145	9,605	9,810	9,750	10,042	9,841	9,546	9,737	−2.0	−3.0	2.0	0.0
223 Wool fabric mills	1,612	1,681	1,861	1,829	1,756	1,791	1,710	1,675	1,675	−4.5	−2.0	0.0	−1.2
Value of shipments (1992$)	16,190	16,927	17,916	18,164	17,769	18,263	17,788	17,633	17,886	−2.6	−0.9	1.4	0.2
221 Cotton fabric mills	5,811	5,930	6,068	6,375	6,325	6,629	6,466	6,337	6,454	−2.4	−2.0	1.9	0.5
222 Man-made fabric mills	8,767	9,303	9,964	9,949	9,682	9,845	9,620	9,620	9,738	−2.3	0.0	1.2	0.1
223 Wool fabric mills	1,612	1,693	1,884	1,840	1,761	1,789	1,701	1,677	1,694	−4.9	−1.5	1.0	−1.0
Total employment (thousands)	157	155	151	151	139								
221 Cotton fabric mills	55.9	55.0	55.0	55.8	51.9								
222 Man-made fabric mills	87.2	85.8	81.5	80.8	73.9								
223 Wool fabric mills	13.7	13.8	14.6	13.9	13.4								
Production workers (thousands)	139	137	134	132	121								
221 Cotton fabric mills	50.1	49.9	50.0	50.4	46.7								
222 Man-made fabric mills	76.7	75.0	71.4	69.7	63.0								
223 Wool fabric mills	11.8	11.9	12.6	12.1	11.7								
Average hourly earnings ($)	9.04	9.38	9.86	10.08	10.35								
221 Cotton fabric mills	8.92	9.38	9.82	9.96	10.32								
222 Man-made fabric mills	9.21	9.46	9.91	10.20	10.48								
223 Wool fabric mills	8.46	8.87	9.70	9.92	9.78								
Product data													
Value of shipments[5]	15,597	16,218	17,045	17,819	17,558	18,136	17,634	17,019	17,269	−2.8	−3.5	1.5	−0.4
221 Cotton fabric mills	5,708	5,863	6,084	6,640	6,582	6,845	6,605	6,308	6,371	−3.5	−4.5	1.0	−0.8
222 Man-made fabric mills	8,500	8,853	9,442	9,716	9,549	9,835	9,638	9,349	9,536	−2.0	−3.0	2.0	0.0
223 Wool fabric mills	1,388	1,502	1,518	1,463	1,427	1,456	1,390	1,362	1,362	−4.5	−2.0	0.0	−1.2
Value of shipments (1992$)	15,597	16,324	17,314	17,595	17,129	17,609	17,156	17,009	17,254	−2.6	−0.9	1.4	0.2
221 Cotton fabric mills	5,708	5,805	5,982	6,270	6,215	6,513	6,351	6,224	6,340	−2.5	−2.0	1.9	0.5
222 Man-made fabric mills	8,500	9,006	9,795	9,854	9,483	9,642	9,422	9,422	9,537	−2.3	0.0	1.2	0.1
223 Wool fabric mills	1,388	1,513	1,537	1,472	1,431	1,454	1,383	1,363	1,377	−4.9	−1.4	1.0	−0.9
Trade data													
Value of imports	3,182	3,294	3,309	3,414	3,370	3,755	3,752	3,997	4,221	−0.1	6.5	5.6	5.8
221 Cotton fabric mills	1,475	1,525	1,482	1,614	1,507	1,689	1,694	1,800	1,890	0.3	6.3	5.0	5.8
222 Man-made fabric mills	1,468	1,540	1,585	1,548	1,596	1,774	1,757	1,880	2,000	−1.0	7.0	6.4	5.8
223 Wool fabric mills	240	230	242	252	267	292	301	317	331	3.1	5.3	4.4	5.5
Value of exports	1,569	1,680	1,840	2,026	2,205	2,376	2,410	2,533	2,761	1.4	5.1	9.0	5.8
221 Cotton fabric mills	579	621	704	813	881	938	983	1,050	1,150	4.8	6.8	9.5	6.9
222 Man-made fabric mills	891	974	1,049	1,099	1,209	1,303	1,277	1,328	1,450	−2.0	4.0	9.2	4.6
223 Wool fabric mills	99.3	84.6	87.2	114	116	134	150	155	161	11.9	3.3	3.9	8.5

[1] Estimate except imports and exports.
[2] Estimate.
[3] Forecast.
[4] Compound annual rate.
[5] For a definition of industry versus product values, see "Getting the Most Out of *Outlook 2000.*"
Source: U.S. Department of Commerce: Bureau of the Census; International Trade Administration.

1998, imports of wool broadwoven fabrics from Asia (excluding Japan) increased at a faster rate than did imports from the rest of the world: 29 percent versus 2 percent, respectively.

Industry shipments of broadwoven fabrics fell 0.9 percent in real terms between 1998 and 1999. U.S. exports of broadwoven fabrics to the NAFTA countries increased from 37 percent of total broadwoven fabric exports in 1993 to 50 percent in 1998. U.S. imports of broadwoven fabrics increased over 6 percent from 1998 to 1999, rising to an estimated $4 billion (see Tables 9-3 and 9-4).

Measures being taken by the broadwoven fabrics industry to enhance its competitive position include investing in modern technology and innovative manufacturing techniques; product diversification; market and product research and development to meet the demands of each market (apparel, home furnishing, industrial) in regard to the fabric's suitability of purpose, design, coloration, styling, quality, delivery, and price; marketing to a global customer base; and better customer service.

Technology will play a major role in shaping the future of the weaving industry. Weaving mills are investing in newer, faster, and more flexible equipment. This has resulted in greater productivity, with the amount of square yards of fabric produced per loom hour almost doubling since 1990. The biggest change in weaving equipment over the last two decades has been the steady decline in the number of shuttle looms. According to U.S. Bureau of the Census statistics, there were 4,813 shuttle looms in place at year end 1998, down from 29,102 at year end 1992. Other technological developments that have enhanced weaving productivity and flexibility include quick-style-change systems, off-loom take-ups, and new monitoring systems. Computer-integrated manufacturing (CIM) has been used by the weaving industry for several years, allowing pattern data and machine settings to be downloaded directly to the loom from workstations.

Weft, Lace, and Warp Knit Fabric Mills

The weft, lace, and warp knit fabric mill sector had real growth of 0.6 percent in the value of industry shipments between 1998 and 1999. In contrast to other textile industry segments, imports are relatively low, although they are growing. Between 1992 and 1999, the share of imports in the domestic market grew from 3 percent to an estimated 11 percent. U.S. exports of weft, lace, and warp knit fabrics rose 2.5 percent from 1998 to 1999, reaching an estimated $685 million (see Table 9-5). This increase primarily reflects larger shipments to the NAFTA countries, which increased from 39 percent of U.S. knit fabric exports in 1993 to 50 percent in 1998 (see Table 9-6).

Weft knits are the principal knit fabric made in the United States, representing more than 80 percent of total knit fabric production. Because most weft knits are in tubular form, they are commonly known as circular knits. Circular knit fabric includes single knits, double knits, and fleece. Most weft knit fabrics are high-volume commodity fabrics used for the production of T-shirts, underwear, and fleece apparel.

Carpets and Rugs

A solid economy, a surge in new homes, and a trend toward frequent home redecoration have created a retail environment ripe for growth and profit for the carpet and rug industry. Reflecting a robust housing market, industry shipments of carpets and rugs achieved real growth of approximately 3 percent between 1998 and 1999. Carpet and rug shipments were expected to reach 1.9 billion square yards in 1999, almost 30 percent higher than the amount produced in 1992. Exports were particularly hard hit by the Asian financial crisis and a generally weak European economy, as exports declined over 3 percent between 1998 and 1999. Imports increased by almost 5 percent over that period (see Table 9-7).

TABLE 9-4: U.S. Trade Patterns in Broadwoven Fabric Mills[1] in 1998
(millions of dollars; percent)

Exports			Imports		
Region[2]	Value[3]	Share, %	Region[2]	Value[3]	Share, %
NAFTA	1,204	50	NAFTA	621	17
Latin America	383	16	Latin America	41	1
Western Europe	441	18	Western Europe	948	25
Japan/Chinese Economic Area	125	5	Japan/Chinese Economic Area	820	22
Other Asia	73	3	Other Asia	1,188	32
Rest of world	184	8	Rest of world	135	4
World	2,410	100	World	3,752	100
Top Five Countries	Value	Share, %	Top Five Countries	Value	Share, %
Canada	608	25	Italy	401	11
Mexico	596	25	Canada	371	10
Belgium	102	4	South Korea	341	9
United Kingdom	97	4	China	296	8
Honduras	94	4	Mexico	249	7

[1] SIC 221, 222, 223.
[2] For definitions of regional groupings, see "Getting the Most Out of *Outlook 2000*."
[3] Values may not sum to total due to rounding.
Source: U.S. Department of Commerce, Bureau of the Census.

TABLE 9-5: Weft, Lace, and Warp Knit Fabric Mills (SIC 2257, 2258) Trends and Forecasts
(millions of dollars except as noted)

	1992	1993	1994	1995	1996	1997[1]	1998[1]	1999[2]	2000[3]	Percent Change 97–98	98–99	99–00	96–00[4]
Industry data													
Value of shipments[5]	7,270	7,526	8,110	7,858	7,537	7,600	7,494	7,569	7,720	–1.4	1.0	2.0	0.6
Value of shipments (1992$)	7,270	7,544	8,182	7,752	7,414	7,469	7,506	7,551	7,619	0.5	0.6	0.9	0.7
Total employment (thousands)	63.9	60.6	61.2	57.7	54.8								
Production workers (thousands)	53.9	50.6	51.5	48.5	46.3								
Average hourly earnings ($)	8.54	8.90	9.43	9.47	9.58								
Product data													
Value of shipments[5]	7,436	7,478	8,102	7,841	7,580	7,650	7,543	7,618	7,771	–1.4	1.0	2.0	0.6
Value of shipments (1992$)	7,436	7,492	8,172	7,736	7,459	7,494	7,555	7,600	7,669	0.5	0.6	0.9	0.7
Trade data													
Value of imports	233	302	354	354	540	804	810	845	900	0.7	4.3	6.5	13.6
Value of exports	377	375	400	495	547	675	668	685	715	–1.0	2.5	4.4	6.9

[1] Estimate except imports and exports.
[2] Estimate.
[3] Forecast.
[4] Compound annual rate.
[5] For a definition of industry versus product values, see "Getting the Most Out of *Outlook 2000.*"
Source: U.S. Department of Commerce: Bureau of the Census; International Trade Administration.

TABLE 9-6: U.S. Trade Patterns in Weft, Lace, and Warp Knit Fabric Mills[1] in 1998
(millions of dollars; percent)

Exports: Region[2]	Value[3]	Share, %	Imports: Region[2]	Value[3]	Share, %
NAFTA	336	50	NAFTA	258	32
Latin America	151	23	Latin America	6	1
Western Europe	53	8	Western Europe	92	11
Japan/Chinese Economic Area	66	10	Japan/Chinese Economic Area	225	28
Other Asia	32	5	Other Asia	211	26
Rest of world	30	4	Rest of world	17	2
World	668	100	World	810	100
Top Five Countries	**Value**	**Share, %**	**Top Five Countries**	**Value**	**Share, %**
Canada	214	32	Canada	205	25
Mexico	122	18	South Korea	184	23
Dominican Republic	52	8	Taiwan	179	22
Hong Kong	31	5	Mexico	53	7
Honduras	27	4	Italy	40	5

[1] SIC 2257, 2258.
[2] For definitions of regional groupings, see "Getting the Most Out of *Outlook 2000.*"
[3] Values may not sum to total due to rounding.
Source: U.S. Department of Commerce, Bureau of the Census.

Significant consolidation has taken place in the carpet and rug industry, with four firms—Shaw, Mohawk, Beaulieu, and Interface—accounting for the majority of production of carpets and rugs in the United States. Those large firms also have formed new alliances with fiber suppliers, yarn producers, and retailers to increase the share of carpets in the floor covering industry. Most carpet manufacturers extrude their own fiber. In fact, U.S. volume of in-house extrusion of carpet fiber is almost 2 billion pounds annually, almost half of total fibers consumed in carpet production. Nylon has been the predominant fiber in the production of carpets, accounting for more than 60 percent of fiber use. Polypropylene has been gaining in market share, representing over 20 percent of carpet fiber usage, up from 11 percent in 1992. Polypropylene is the fiber of choice for molded and/or felted automotive carpets and trunk liners and primary and secondary carpet backing.

Yarn Spinning Mills

The yarn spinning subsector of the textile industry had real growth of 0.2 percent between 1998 and 1999. U.S. exports of

TABLE 9-7: Carpets and Rugs (SIC 227) Trends and Forecasts

(millions of dollars except as noted)

	1992	1993	1994	1995	1996	1997[1]	1998[1]	1999[2]	2000[3]	Percent Change 97–98	98–99	99–00	96–00[4]
Industry data													
Value of shipments[5]	9,828	10,234	10,600	10,762	11,184	11,800	12,500	13,000	13,500	5.9	4.0	3.8	4.8
Value of shipments (1992$)	9,828	10,286	10,537	10,551	10,722	11,164	11,697	12,033	12,360	4.8	2.9	2.7	3.6
Total employment (thousands)	49.4	50.6	55.1	55.5	55.0								
Production workers (thousands)	38.9	39.6	42.9	43.5	43.8								
Average hourly earnings ($)	8.83	9.17	9.54	9.58	9.55								
Product data													
Value of shipments[5]	9,518	9,953	10,141	10,405	10,806	11,400	12,075	12,560	13,040	5.9	4.0	3.8	4.8
Value of shipments (1992$)	9,518	10,003	10,081	10,201	10,360	10,785	11,300	11,630	11,940	4.8	2.9	2.7	3.6
Trade data													
Value of imports	709	671	748	858	845	961	1,109	1,163	1,200	15.4	4.9	3.2	9.2
Value of exports	725	730	713	686	757	858	826	800	780	–3.7	–3.1	–2.5	0.8

[1] Estimate except imports and exports.
[2] Estimate.
[3] Forecast.
[4] Compound annual rate.
[5] For a definition of industry versus product values, see "Getting the Most Out of *Outlook 2000*."
Source: U.S. Department of Commerce: Bureau of the Census; International Trade Administration.

spun yarn increased steadily to an estimated $352 million in 1999, primarily as a result of NAFTA. In 1998, U.S. exports of spun yarn to the NAFTA countries were more than three times the 1993 level and represented 65 percent of total spun yarn exports. U.S. imports of spun yarn increased almost 4 percent between 1998 and 1999 (see Table 9-8).

Like most sectors of the U.S. textile industry, the yarn spinning industry has undergone major restructuring marked by mill closures, mergers and acquisitions, and divestitures. The surviving producers have been able to sharpen their competitive edge by installing more efficient machinery, increasing automation, and providing value-added products to customers.

Man-Made Fibers

The global man-made fiber industry hit another record high in 1998. According to the Fiber Economics Bureau, 1998 world production of man-made fibers was 29.8 million metric tons. However, whereas production increased 9 percent between 1996 and 1997, output was only 2 percent higher in volume terms in 1998. Given the impact of the Asian financial crisis and

TABLE 9-8: Yarn Spinning Mills (SIC 2281) Trends and Forecasts

(millions of dollars except as noted)

	1992	1993	1994	1995	1996	1997[1]	1998[1]	1999[2]	2000[3]	Percent Change 97–98	98–99	99–00	96–00[4]
Industry data													
Value of shipments[5]	7,669	7,618	7,999	8,465	8,543	8,725	8,800	8,840	8,925	0.9	0.5	1.0	1.1
Value of shipments (1992$)	7,669	7,960	8,289	8,324	8,526	8,831	8,886	8,905	8,969	0.6	0.2	0.7	1.3
Total employment (thousands)	68.7	65.6	66.1	64.5	60.6								
Production workers (thousands)	62.6	59.7	60.2	58.8	55.1								
Average hourly earnings ($)	8.48	8.62	8.95	9.13	9.47								
Product data													
Value of shipments[5]	7,756	7,696	8,196	8,619	8,771	8,790	8,865	8,910	9,000	0.9	0.5	1.0	0.6
Value of shipments (1992$)	7,756	8,041	8,493	8,475	8,753	8,897	8,950	8,970	9,030	0.6	0.2	0.7	0.8
Trade data													
Value of imports	321	337	388	400	420	529	584	607	630	10.4	3.9	3.8	10.7
Value of exports	169	146	209	299	327	355	344	352	365	–3.1	2.3	3.7	2.8

[1] Estimate except imports and exports.
[2] Estimate.
[3] Forecast.
[4] Compound annual rate.
[5] For a definition of industry versus product values, see "Getting the Most Out of *Outlook 2000*."
Source: U.S. Department of Commerce: Bureau of the Census; International Trade Administration.

the resulting slowdown in the global textile sector, 1998 was a year of adjustment, although the slowdown in growth in the man-made fiber industry was more severe than had been anticipated by most industry analysts. By the end of the year 2000, man-made fiber capacity is expected to reach 39.3 million metric tons, 3 percent above the March 1999 level. The main producer of man-made fibers is Asia with 51 percent of world production, followed by the NAFTA partners (19 percent) and western Europe (16 percent).

Man-made fiber production capacity will continue to shift incrementally to the developing countries as textile mills and finishing industries improve the ability of those countries to process a wider variety of fibers. Future growth in Asia probably will remain slower than it has been in recent years as a result of the Asian financial crisis. However, several capacity expansion projects are under way, and the region will continue to increase its share of world man-made fiber output.

The U.S. man-made fiber industry experienced no growth in the value of industry shipments between 1998 and 1999. Exports grew almost 5 percent during that period, and imports grew about 4 percent (see Table 9-9). Major trading partners include the NAFTA countries and European Union countries, which account

TABLE 9-9: Man-Made Fibers (SIC 2823, 2824) Trends and Forecasts
(millions of dollars except as noted)

										Percent Change			
	1992	1993	1994	1995	1996	1997[1]	1998[1]	1999[2]	2000[3]	97–98	98–99	99–00	96–00[4]
Industry data													
Value of shipments[5]	12,861	13,293	13,366	14,035	14,179	14,700	14,500	14,650	14,875	−1.4	1.0	1.5	1.2
Value of shipments (1992$)	12,861	13,289	13,217	13,421	13,425	15,740	15,742	15,765	15,950	0.0	0.1	1.2	4.4
Total employment (thousands)	55.4	51.6	46.9	44.7	44.5								
Production workers (thousands)	41.7	39.8	36.6	35.0	35.1								
Average hourly earnings ($)	14.22	14.63	14.23	14.87	15.28								
Product data													
Value of shipments[5]	10,924	11,092	11,779	12,529	12,383	12,500	12,325	12,450	12,640	−1.4	1.0	1.5	0.5
Value of shipments (1992$)	10,924	11,092	11,709	12,023	11,768	13,383	13,388	13,400	13,560	0.0	0.1	1.2	3.6
Trade data													
Value of imports	899	1,126	1,299	1,381	1,398	1,552	1,573	1,630	1,712	1.4	3.6	5.0	5.2
Value of exports	1,433	1,385	1,571	2,052	2,093	2,146	1,961	2,050	2,125	−8.6	4.5	3.7	0.4

[1] Estimate except imports and exports.
[2] Estimate.
[3] Forecast.
[4] Compound annual rate.
[5] For a definition of industry versus product values, see "Getting the Most Out of *Outlook 2000.*"
Source: U.S. Department of Commerce: Bureau of the Census; International Trade Administration.

TABLE 9-10: U.S. Trade Patterns in Man-Made Fibers[1] in 1998
(millions of dollars; percent)

Exports			Imports		
Regions[2]	Value[3]	Share, %	Region[2]	Value[3]	Share, %
NAFTA	674	34	NAFTA	586	37
Latin America	197	10	Latin America	12	1
Western Europe	512	26	Western Europe	394	25
Japan/Chinese Economic Area	303	15	Japan/Chinese Economic Area	238	15
Other Asia	181	9	Other Asia	276	18
Rest of world	93	5	Rest of world	66	4
World	1,961	100	World	1,573	100
Top Five Countries	Value	Share, %	Top Five Countries	Value	Share, %
Canada	455	23	Canada	416	26
Mexico	219	11	South Korea	207	13
Belgium	127	6	Mexico	170	11
Hong Kong	110	6	Japan	133	8
Germany	105	5	Germany	130	8

[1] SIC 2823, 2824.
[2] For definitions of regional groupings, see "Getting the Most Out of *Outlook 2000.*"
[3] Values may not sum to total due to rounding.
Source: U.S. Department of Commerce, Bureau of the Census.

for more than 60 percent of U.S. exports and imports (see Table 9-10). There are fewer major international textile fiber producers operating in the United States today. A number of operations have been sold or merged with smaller fiber producers. For many man-made fiber producers, profit margins have evaporated as these fibers have increasingly become commodity products.

Maria A. D'Andrea, U.S. Department of Commerce, Office of Textiles and Apparel, (202) 482-4058, August 1999.

■ REFERENCES

America's Textiles International (ATI), 2100 Powers Ferry Road, Atlanta, GA 30339. (770) 955-5656, http://www.billian.com.

American Textile Manufacturers Institute, Inc., 1130 Connecticut Avenue, NW, Suite 1200, Washington, DC 20036-3954. (202) 862-0500, http://www.atmi.org.

American Textile Partnership (AMTEX), Industry Program Office, P.O. Box 4670, Wilmington, DE 19807. (302) 633-9259, http://amtex.sandia.gov.

Consumption on the Cotton System and Stocks, Current Industrial Report M22P, U.S. Department of Commerce, Bureau of the Census, Washington, DC 20233. (301) 457-4810, http://www.census.gov/cir/www/m22p.html.

Consumption on the Woolen System and Worsted Combing, Current Industrial Report MQ22D, U.S. Department of Commerce, Bureau of the Census, Washington, DC 20233. (301) 457-4698, http://www.census.gov/cir/www/mq22d.html.

Daily News Record. Fairchild Publications, Inc., 7 West 34 Street, New York, NY 10001-8191. (212) 630-4000.

Federal Reserve Statistical Release G.17, *Industrial Production and Capacity Utilization,* Board of Governors of the Federal Reserve System, Washington, DC 20551. (202) 452-3245, http://www.federalreserve.gov/releases/G17.

Monthly Investment Review, Standard & Poor's, 25 Broadway, New York, NY 10004. (800) 221-5277, http://www.stockinfo.standardpoor.com.

Producer Price Index, Bureau of Labor Statistics, Postal Square Building, 2 Massachusetts Avenue, NE, Washington, DC 20212. (202) 606-7717, ext. 220, http://stats.bls.gov/ppihome.htm.

Quarterly Financial Report for Manufacturing, Mining, and Trade Corporations, U.S. Department of Commerce, Bureau of the Census, Washington, DC 20233. (301) 457-3343/3379, http://www.census.gov/prod/www/abs/msqfr-mm.html.

Textile HiLights, American Textile Manufacturers Institute, Inc., 1130 Connecticut Avenue, NW, Suite 1200, Washington, DC 20036. (202) 862-0544.

Textile Outlook International, Textiles Intelligence Limited, Derwent House, 31 Alma Lane, Wilmslow, Cheshire SK9 5EY, United Kingdom. (44) (0) 1625 539067, E-mail: textintell@aol.com.

Textile Transactions & Trends: Perspectives on Mergers and Acquisitions in the Textile Industry, Summer 1999. Kurt Salmon Associates, Inc., 1355 Peachtree Street, NE, Suite 900, Atlanta, GA 30309-0090. (404) 892-0321, http://www.kurtsalmon.com/KSA_home/homeindex.html.

Textile World. Intertec Publishing Corporation, 9800 Metcalf Avenue, Overland Park, KS 66212-2215, (913) 341-1300.

Broadwoven Fabrics

Broadwoven Fabrics (Gray), Current Industrial Report MQ22T. U.S. Department of Commerce, Bureau of the Census, Washington, DC 20233. (301) 457-4620. http://www.census.gov/cir/www/mq22t.html.

Discount Store News, September 21, 1998. Discount Store News, 425 Park Avenue, New York, NY 10022. http://www.discountstorenews.com.

Weft, Lace, and Warp Knit Fabric Mills

Knit Fabric Production, Current Industrial Report MA22K, U.S. Department of Commerce, Bureau of the Census. (301) 457-4620, http://www.census.gov/cir/www/ma22k.html.

Knitted Textile Association, 386 Park Avenue South, Suite 901, New York, NY 10016. (212) 689-3807, http://www.kta-usa.org.

Carpets and Rugs

Carpet and Rug Institute, 310 Holiday Street, Dalton, GA 30720. (706) 278-3176, http://www.carpet-rug.com.

Carpets and Rugs, Current Industrial Report MA22Q, U.S. Department of Commerce, Bureau of the Census, Washington, DC 20233. (301) 457-4810, http://www.census.gov/cir/www/ma22q.html.

Yarn Spinning Mills

American Yarn Spinners Association, PO Box 99, Gastonia, NC 28053. (704) 824-3522, http://www.aysa.org.

Yarn Production, Current Industrial Report MA22F, U.S. Department of Commerce, Bureau of the Census, Washington, DC 20233. (301) 357-4810, http://www.census.gov/cir/www/ma22f.html.

Man-Made Fibers

Fiber Organon, Fiber Economics Bureau, Inc., 1150 17 Street, NW, Suite 306, Washington, DC 20036. (202) 467-0916, http://www.fibersource.com.

International Fiber Journal, 7401 Carmel Executive Park Drive, Suite 202, Charlotte, NC 28226. (704) 544-1969, http://www.ifj.com.

■ RELATED CHAPTERS

18: Production Machinery
33: Apparel and Fabricated Textile Products
42: Retailing

■ GLOSSARY

Off-loom take-up: An automated process for winding up fabric as it is woven.

Quick-style-change system: Refers to production techniques designed to minimize the time required to change styles.

Shuttle loom: A loom that uses an oblong device (shuttle) to carry filling yarns through the warp yarns in the weaving process. Newer shuttleless looms (e.g., air-jet, water-jet) have much higher weaving speeds.

PAPER AND ALLIED PRODUCTS
Economic and Trade Trends

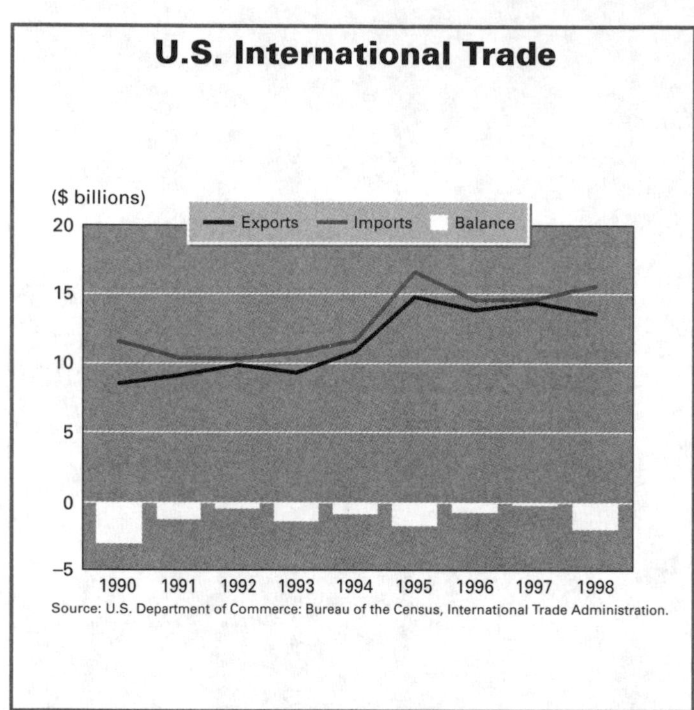

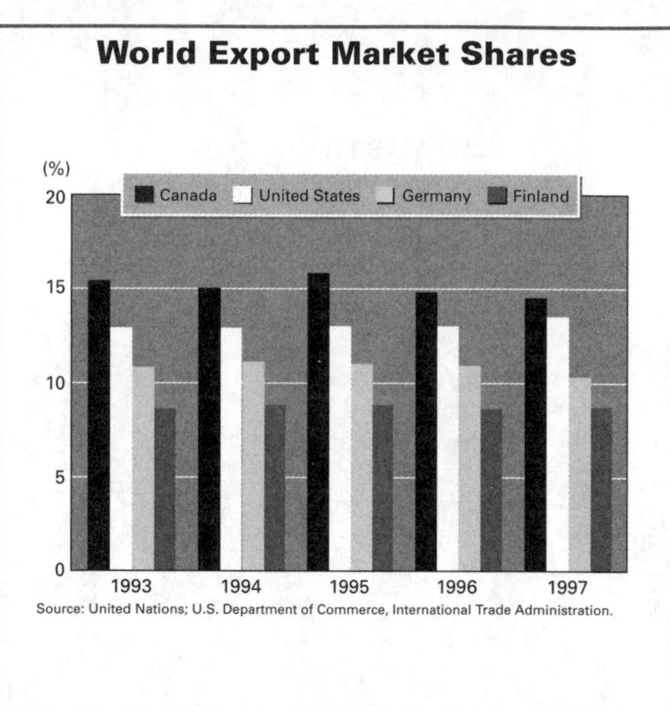

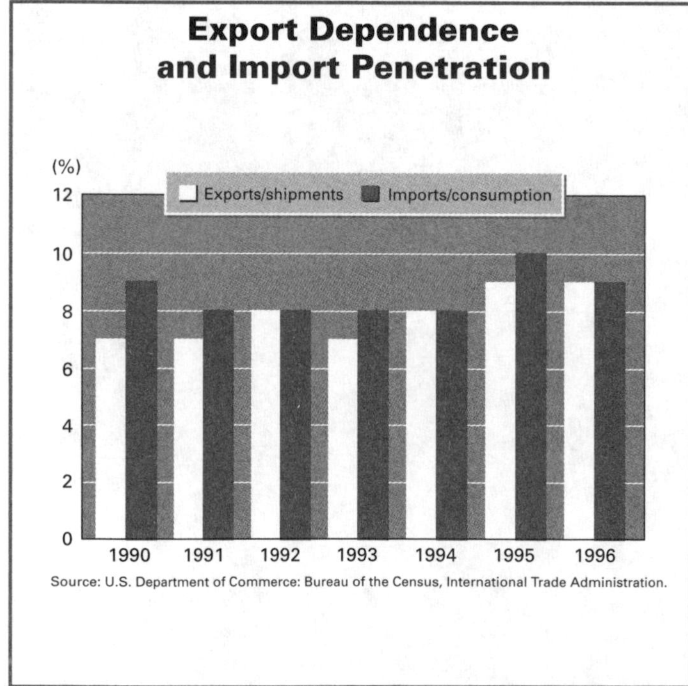

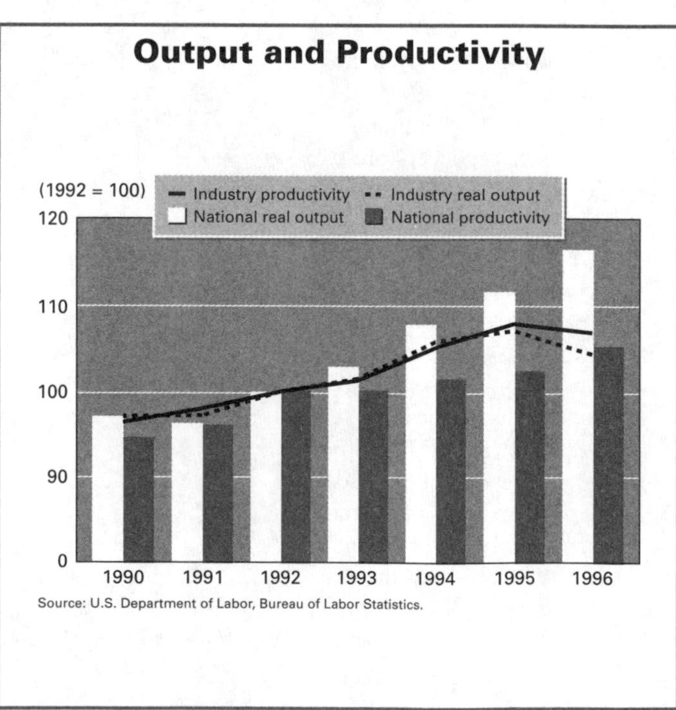

See "Getting the Most Out of *Outlook 2000*" for definitions of terms.

10

Paper and Allied Products

INDUSTRY DEFINITION The U.S. paper and allied products sector consists of 17 separate manufacturing industries that process wood, recovered paper and paperboard, other cellulose fiber sources, and certain plastic and metal films into thousands of end-use products. This sector is divided into three major commodity groupings: (1) SIC 261, 262, and 263, which produce primary products, covering the production of pulp, paper, and paperboard; (2) SIC 265, which consists of five paperboard containers and box producers; and (3) SIC 267, which contains nine nonpackaging converted paper and paperboard products, including pressure-sensitive tapes, labels, and packaging films; plastic and paper bags; envelopes, stationery, and paper office supplies; pressed and molded pulp goods; certain wall coverings; and gift-wrap paper.

GLOBAL INDUSTRY TRENDS

The global paper and allied products industry is one of the most important contributors to the overall health of the world economy. Although recognized in many circles as a mature sector, it is also one of the world's most dynamic industries in terms of product development, technological improvements, distribution and handling, processing and converting, and environmental protection. This industry is continuing to go through a globalization process in which producers are expanding their raw material holdings; improving product manufacturing, converting, and distribution networks; and streamlining order procedures to foreign markets previously seen strictly as competitors. Leading world producers, especially in the developed industrialized nations, can no longer be contented simply to focus on the domestic market for sales growth. It is essential to expand their customer base to the world marketplace as globalization in the paper and allied products industry continues into the new millennium. Competition is increasing rapidly from producers in many developing countries that have a number of advantages over their industrialized counterparts in terms of cost and raw materials. A number of less developed competitor countries, such as Indonesia and Malaysia, have achieved the same level of technological advancement in production but do not have the inherent costs of environmental compliance that affect U.S. producers. The growing influence of this globalization process will continue into the twenty-first century as global free trade becomes more of a reality and market access barriers are removed to create a more even-surfaced, open, fair trading marketplace.

The U.S. paper and allied products industry is the world's leading producer and exporter of a variety of consumer-directed commodities, trading many of the industry's commodities with more than 125 countries worldwide. Its large modern manufacturing base, combined with an adequate transportation and distribution network and a highly skilled labor force, has made the U.S. industry the most competitive and highest-volume supplier in the world. Although the domestic market consumes more than 90 percent of the U.S. industry's output, the industry has become a major player in the world paper and allied products market, especially in the commodity grades of pulp, paper, and paperboard. After 1993, exports as a percentage of total U.S. paper and allied products shipments increased from 7.3 percent to 8 percent in 1999 as exports on a value basis grew from $10 billion to nearly $13.5 billion (see Table 10-1). As much as 65 percent of the industry's growth in shipments over the past decade is directly attributable to increases in foreign shipments of paper and allied products.

As domestic sales have stagnated (up 1.5 to 2 percent) over the last 5 years, the industry has refocused on export sales, placed greater emphasis on increased exports by directing more resources toward world markets, and gained a global market share. The globalization of world paper and allied products manufacturers has been an ongoing development for more than a decade. Many U.S. paper and allied products companies are

TABLE 10-1: Paper and Allied Products (SIC 26) Trends and Forecasts
(millions of dollars except as noted)

	1992	1993	1994	1995	1996	1997[1]	1998[1]	1999[2]	2000[3]	Percent Change 97–98	98–99	99–00	96–00[4]
Industry data													
Value of shipments[5]	133,201	133,262	143,649	173,716	160,661	163,213	165,659	167,876	175,522	1.5	1.3	4.6	2.2
Value of shipments (1992$)	133,201	135,059	141,192	141,915	140,102	139,498	138,743	140,130	142,933	–0.5	1.0	2.0	0.5
Total employment (thousands)	627	626	622	629	631	633	628	612	615	–0.8	–2.5	0.5	–0.6
Production workers (thousands)	479	479	480	487	488	489	487	484	486	–0.4	–0.6	0.4	–0.1
Average hourly earnings ($)	13.81	14.09	14.52	14.73	15.02	15.31	15.78	16.25	16.77	3.1	3.0	3.2	2.8
Capital expenditures	7,963	7,370	7,731	8,369	9,302	9,276	9,417	9,532	9,646	1.5	1.2	1.2	0.9
Product data													
Value of shipments[5]	128,941	128,695	138,560	168,137	155,319	162,286	166,444	169,506	177,226	2.6	1.8	4.6	3.4
Value of shipments (1992$)	128,941	130,523	136,231	137,048	135,455	138,706	139,400	141,491	144,321	0.5	1.5	2.0	1.6
Trade data													
Value of imports	10,361	10,793	11,676	16,624	14,608	14,667	15,621	15,692	16,084	6.5	0.5	2.5	2.4
Value of exports	9,919	9,363	10,892	14,837	13,896	14,417	13,632	13,416	13,785	–5.4	–1.6	2.8	–0.2

[1] Estimate except imports and exports.
[2] Estimate.
[3] Forecast.
[4] Compound annual rate.
[5] For a definition of industry versus product values, see "Getting the Most Out of *Outlook 2000.*"
Source: U.S. Department of Commerce: Bureau of the Census; International Trade Administration.

active exporters, but they also are engaged in foreign production, converting, and packaging operations as well as joint ventures and direct foreign capital investment in partnerships and ownerships.

From 1992 through 1998, U.S. paper and allied products exports increased at a 4.2 percent compound annual growth rate. Most of the increase came from expanded shipments to Canada, Mexico, southeast Asia, and certain Latin American and European countries. The commodities exported by the industry are divided into market wood pulp, recovered paper (although this is not included in SIC data), paper and paperboard, and converted paper and paperboard products. In 1999, exports of paper and paperboard on a volume basis represented 38 percent of the industry's exports, followed by recovered paper (31 percent), market wood pulp (22 percent), and converted paper and paperboard products (9 percent). On a value basis, paper and paperboard exports represented 45 percent of the industry's exports, followed by converted paper and paperboard products (27 percent) and wood pulp (21 percent), with the balance coming from exports of recovered paper and paperboard.

FACTORS AFFECTING FUTURE GROWTH OF THE U.S. INDUSTRY

The U.S. paper and allied products sector is recognized worldwide as a high-quality and high-volume low-cost producer that benefits from a number of key operating advantages, including a large domestic consumer market; the world's highest per capita consumption; a modern manufacturing infrastructure; adequate raw material, water, and energy resources; a highly skilled labor force; and an efficient transportation and distribution network. The U.S. industry is among the most modern in the world because of continued large capital expenditures. This spending, which is driven mainly by production improvements (existing machine upgrades, retrofits, and new installed equipment), environmental concerns, and the goal of increased recycling, totaled an estimated $9.5 billion in 1999.

The industry ranks among the top 10 among U.S. manufacturing industries and is in the top 5 for sales of nondurables. Although the sector is the third leading energy consumer (behind chemicals and metals), it has the second highest rate of self-generated energy (behind chemicals), totaling 56 percent in 1998–1999. Because nearly all of the industry's products are consumer-oriented, product shipments are affected mostly by the overall health of the U.S. economy, but the growth of the world economy is playing a more important role in the industry's outlook than ever before. Gross domestic product (GDP) growth and sector shipment growth typically are tied together closely. In the future, growth in demand in a number of key foreign paper and paperboard markets will play an increasingly important role in the health and expansion of U.S. paper and allied products industries.

After a poor performance in 1996, the U.S. paper and allied products industries experienced 3 consecutive years of increased domestic sales, slowly improving prices, higher capacity utilization rates, and moderating inventories. As a result, total shipments of paper and allied products increased 1.5 percent in real terms and 1.8 percent in current dollar terms in 1999. A modest movement upward in prices for a number of primary commodity grades of paper and paperboard and certain converted paper products and packaging materials resulted in an increase in the current value of shipments. Real GDP increased about 3 percent in 1999, leading to noticeable increases in real disposable income, total U.S. industrial production, and purchases of nondurable goods, which combined to increase domestic paper and paperboard demand and cause an expansion of the industry's shipments.

New paper and paperboard tonnage capacity in 1999 was estimated at 1.3 percent above that of the previous year. This helped producers draw down their inventories and set up better industry fundamentals going into the year 2000. Much of this tonnage is due to come on line when price and demand levels begin to rise again. By controlling operating rates and allowing inventories to draw down and stabilize for most of 1998–1999, domestic pulp and paper producers were in a better economic and operative position throughout most of 1999. This should bode well for the industry in 2000. Industry capital expenditures increased 1.5 percent in 1998 to $9.41 billion and increased an additional 1.2 percent in 1999 to $9.53 billion. Since 1992, there has been a leveling off of industry spending after the record high levels of the late 1980s. Over the 1998–2000 period, expenditures for environmental and energy (non-output-related) projects are forecast to account for nearly 23.5 percent of total capital outlays over that 3-year period.

Electronic Commerce

As the new millennium arrives, the U.S. paper and allied products industry is well under way in its effort to become "Net-friendly" in a global environment where more and more advertising, sales, product introduction, and information are being generated and utilized every day by global papermakers. Companies that do not embrace the new electronic marketplace will be left on the sidelines as smart, progressive, innovative, and aggressive companies make maximum use of the communication and information technologies that are readily available for global paper makers, buyers, and consumers.

Producers at all levels within the U.S. paper and allied products have already been implementing electronic commerce (E-commerce) procedures and communication networks that have greatly increased efficiency and reduced costs. Information technologies are playing an increasingly important role in the supply chain and are boosting productivity by allowing better data exchange by both end users and suppliers. The use of E-commerce creates an avenue for the on-line trading of paper, paperboard, and many other products through the Internet. Despite arguments that the advent of the Internet and E-commerce will result in reduced paper consumption and ultimately the "paperless office," evidence clearly indicates that the use of electronic media will lead to increased consumption of paper and paperboard products. Although certain segments of the paper industry (newsprint, magazines, catalogs, directories) will experience some erosion, overall the industry stands to benefit through increased consumption of office-type papers, packaging materials, and containers and boxes. A recent study indicates that by 2003, the consumption of cut-size office paper (principally used in home and office computer printers) will double from the 1996 level as it benefits from increased installation of home computers and expansion of home offices.

According to recent industry surveys, most U.S. paper and allied products manufacturers are already on-line with the Internet and E-commerce systems. One survey indicates that approximately 85 to 90 percent of all U.S. mill managers have on-line access. However, the proportion of middle managers drops to around 80 percent. This is an area that clearly needs improvement. Through the use of electronic information technologies, many U.S. paper companies have already implemented computer-based systems that feature multisite inventory and shipment tracking, order and reorder forms and systems, up-to-the-minute shipment tracking systems (complete with links to various shippers and handlers), on-line training programs, detailed product specifications and production capabilities, information on mill suppliers (chemicals, coatings, dyes), and on-line requests for samples and brochures. As the electronic screen replaces certain types of the printed page, leaders and managers in the industry are preparing to meet the challenge head-on and develop new management strategies and marketing techniques to increase overall consumption of paper and paperboard products.

Profits and Earnings

Earnings for domestic paper and paperboard companies are estimated to have improved slowly in 1999 as a result of increasing demand, slightly higher prices, increased operating rates, and the end of a major inventory drawdown cycle. Virtually every major U.S. pulp and paper company saw overall sales, net profits, and average earnings per share improve slightly in 1999 from a year earlier. Costs for labor, chemicals, and wood raw materials generally were kept in check, but energy prices increased slightly in 1999.

Environmental Issues U.S. paper and allied products manufacturers traditionally have been at the forefront of a number of environmental issues. They have a history of successfully addressing many key environmental issues, particularly those relating to air and water quality, forestation and reforestation, recycling, recovery of pre- and postconsumer paper and paperboard, and energy. Protection of the environment not only has become a major capital expenditure but also is one of the industry's most challenging and hard-to-solve public relations matters. Although the industry's expenditures for the environment increased substantially in the last decade, the public still generally perceives the industry as damaging, not improving, the environment. Significant improvements have been made in environmental protection over the last several years, and producers have worked closely with the U.S. government on a number of key domestic and international environmental policy issues. As the industry looks to the future, it will see the need to continue to improve its environmental performance and increase its collection and utilization of recovered paper and paperboard. Corporate decisions will be made not only on how to increase production and improve sales but also on how to improve the corporate image, increase recycling, and adapt to increasingly stringent environmental regulations.

The United States is the global leader in the generation, recovery, consumption, and export of recovered paper and paperboard. What was once a fiber supplement has become a critical source of raw materials for papermaking. In 1999, the U.S. paper and paperboard industries consumed 33.4 million metric tons of paper and paperboard, less than a 1 percent increase over the record level in 1998. U.S. paper and allied products companies not only are the world's leading collectors and consumers of recovered paper, they also are the global leader in exporting. Based on 6-month 1998 data, the United States exported nearly 8 million metric tons to about 80 world markets. These tremendous improvements in pre- and postconsumer paper recovery operations will have to continue if the primary paper and paperboard industry is to meet its self-imposed 50 percent recycling goal by the year 2000.

U.S. INDUSTRY GROWTH PROJECTIONS FOR THE NEXT 1 AND 5 YEARS

With U.S. GDP forecast to continue to expand in 2000, product shipments by the U.S. paper and allied products industries should follow suit with a 2 percent increase. Over the 2000–2004 forecast period, product shipments in real terms should increase 2.1 percent annually. The attempt by the industry to improve its fundamentals over the last couple of years should allow it to reap benefits, especially if demand remains high and the industry is able to control its capacity additions. The U.S. paper and allied products industry should experience improved sales, prices, and earnings over the forecast period, driven by increases in domestic and foreign shipments. As foreign market access barriers are reduced through both the North American Free Trade Agreement (NAFTA) and World Trade Organization (WTO), the industry should be in an excellent position to increase exports. This forecast is dependent on the economic performance of key world paper consuming markets. U.S. exports should increase 2.8 percent in 2000 and 3 percent annually over the next 5 years. However, imports also should increase as the U.S. economy expands, leading to increased paper and paperboard demand. U.S. imports are forecast to increase 2.5 percent in 2000 and 3 percent annually over the 2000–2004 forecast period. The large U.S. paper-consuming market will continue to be the principal target for many foreign paper producers.

GLOBAL MARKET PROSPECTS

Growth of U.S. exports of paper and allied products will be dependent on the improved economies of many key foreign markets. Over the last 5 years, the industry has been successful in penetrating a number of emerging markets, including Mexico, China, South Korea, and Brazil. In addition, there has been substantial growth in a number of nontraditional developing markets in Latin America, southeast Asia, and portions of eastern Europe. However, it is still too early to determine the long-term impact of the Asian financial crisis that nearly paralyzed the economies of important paper-consuming markets, including Thailand, Malaysia, the Philippines, Korea, and Indonesia. The full extent of the impact on Asian financial markets probably will not be felt until late in the forecast period. It is certain that a number of the pulp, paper, and paperboard capacity announcements made by several key Asian producers will be delayed or perhaps canceled as a result of that region's financial problems. However, some of the projects that initially were delayed have been slated for restart during the forecast period.

The successful implementation of key bilateral and multilateral trade pacts will greatly increase the U.S. paper and allied products industry's ability to compete. The Mexican economy has been experiencing a number of difficulties over the last several years as that country makes the transition to a more business-oriented economy. As a result, the benefits of NAFTA to the U.S. paper industries have not been fully realized. In the first couple of years of implementation, U.S. paper products manufacturers had significantly higher exports to Mexico, reaching \$1.9 billion in 1995. However, the devaluation of the peso had a negative impact on the ability to compete in the Mexican market in 1996, as U.S. exports to that country dropped to less than \$1.8 billion. In 1997, the Mexican economy stabilized and the peso strengthened, giving U.S. exporters of paper and allied products an opportunity to increase their exports to Mexico. In 1997, U.S. exports increased 13 percent in value to \$2.03 billion. This trend continued in 1998 as exports to Mexico expanded an additional 11 percent to \$2.27 billion and in 1999 as exports expanded an additional 2.5 percent to \$2.33 billion. This has allowed Mexico to become a solid number two export market, surpassing Japan and trailing only Canada as the leading foreign destination for U.S. paper and allied products (see Table 10-2). Over the next 5 years, NAFTA should bring further benefits to the U.S. paper industry as the Mexican economy strengthens and market access barriers, both tariff and nontariff, are reduced. Beginning January 1, 1994, NAFTA phases out trade barriers on the majority of primary pulp, paper, and paperboard products over a 5-year period. Tariff and nontariff barriers to corrugated boxes will be eliminated over 7 years, while tariffs on most converted products will be eliminated after a 10-year phaseout.

The ongoing implementation of the Uruguay Round Agreements should have a positive impact on future trade opportunities for the U.S. paper and allied products industries. As a result of the Uruguay Round tariff agreement for paper and allied products, tariff barriers in key European and Asian markets will be eliminated by 2005. In the implementing congressional legislation of both the Uruguay Round and NAFTA accords, there is specific language that permits the U.S. government to enter into follow-up negotiations that could lead to a shortening of the tariff reduction period. In addition, efforts are under way that were initiated by the Asia-Pacific Economic Cooperation (APEC) members and then transferred to the WTO in the Accelerated Tariff Liberalization (ATL) initiative to liberalize trade significantly within several product groupings, as agreed at the November 1997 and November 1998 APEC ministerial meetings. Included in these initiatives is the paper and allied products sector. Domestic producers have been very active in supporting the U.S. government's efforts to this end.

PULP MILLS

According to the current Standard Industrial Classification, manufacturers in SIC 2611 produce a variety of chemical and mechanical paper-grade pulps, special alpha and dissolving

TABLE 10-2: U.S. Trade Patterns in Paper and Allied Products[1] in 1998
(millions of dollars; percent)

Exports			Imports		
Region[2]	Value[3]	Share, %	Region[2]	Value[3]	Share, %
NAFTA	5,460	40	NAFTA	11,191	72
Latin America	1,580	12	Latin America	485	3
Western Europe	2,812	21	Western Europe	2,394	15
Japan/Chinese Economic Area	2,212	16	Japan/Chinese Economic Area	995	6
Other Asia	789	6	Other Asia	431	3
Rest of world	778	6	Rest of world	125	1
World	13,632	100	World	15,621	100
Top Five Countries	Value	Share, %	Top Five Countries	Value	Share, %
Canada	3,201	23	Canada	10,889	70
Mexico	2,260	17	Finland	703	5
Japan	1,105	8	Germany	499	3
Germany	503	4	Japan	447	3
United Kingdom	486	4	China	403	3

[1] SIC 26.
[2] For definitions of regional groupings, see "Getting the Most Out of *Outlook 2000*."
[3] Values may not sum to total due to rounding.
Source: U.S. Department of Commerce, Bureau of the Census.

pulps, and pulp by-products that include turpentine, tall oil, and other cooking liquor–based by-products. The various grades of pulp are made from softwoods, hardwoods, and other fibrous raw material sources, including recovered fiber, rags, flax, and other agricultural fibers (cotton linters, straw, bagasse, and kenaf). Product shipments by this sector, both for export and domestic, represent 13 to 16 percent of annual U.S. pulp production and do not include pulp utilized in captive paper and paperboard operations and domestic transfer shipments to affiliated and/or nonaffiliated paper and paperboard mills.

Industry Performance in 1999

The U.S. market pulp industry followed a disappointing sales performance in 1998 with increased shipments in 1999. Based on 6-month industry data, U.S. market pulp product shipments in real terms increased 2 percent in constant dollars in 1999 (see Table 10-3). Although the industry continued to find foreign demand sluggish and increased its utilization of secondary fiber and recovered paper, it benefited from a stronger than expected domestic pulp market. The industry continues to deal with fluctuating prices and an almost perpetual

TABLE 10-3: Pulp Mills (SIC 2611) Trends and Forecasts
(millions of dollars except as noted)

										Percent Change			
	1992	1993	1994	1995	1996	1997[1]	1998[1]	1999[2]	2000[3]	97–98	98–99	99–00	96–00[4]
Industry data													
Value of shipments[5]	5,466	4,282	4,827	7,513	5,508	5,783	5,242	5,239	5,622	–9.4	–0.1	7.3	0.5
Value of shipments (1992$)	5,466	4,758	4,992	4,920	4,931	5,091	4,836	4,933	5,042	–5.0	2.0	2.2	0.6
Total employment (thousands)	15.9	14.2	13.3	14.6	15.0	14.8	14.7	14.4	14.6	–0.7	–2.0	1.4	–0.7
Production workers (thousands)	12.1	10.8	10.2	11.3	11.1	11.0	10.9	10.7	10.8	–0.9	–1.8	0.9	–0.7
Average hourly earnings ($)	19.15	19.49	20.08	20.40	20.16	20.76	21.46	21.89	22.61	3.4	2.0	3.3	2.9
Capital expenditures	772	426	315	564	698	663	605	613	646	–8.7	1.3	5.4	–1.9
Product data													
Value of shipments[5]	6,104	4,995	5,952	8,911	6,329	6,640	6,024	6,020	6,663	–9.3	–0.1	10.7	1.3
Value of shipments (1992$)	6,104	5,550	6,156	5,836	5,666	5,850	5,558	5,669	5,794	–5.0	2.0	2.2	0.6
Trade data													
Value of imports	2,104	1,868	2,285	3,745	2,601	2,572	2,392	2,129	2,193	–7.0	–11.0	3.0	–4.2
Value of exports	3,236	2,482	2,954	4,698	3,358	3,253	2,774	2,524	2,650	–14.7	–9.0	5.0	–5.7

[1] Estimate except imports and exports.
[2] Estimate.
[3] Forecast.
[4] Compound annual rate.
[5] For a definition of industry versus product values, see "Getting the Most Out of *Outlook 2000*."
Source: U.S. Department of Commerce: Bureau of the Census; International Trade Administration.

global oversupply situation, but overall, the industry experienced a better sales performance in 1999. Exports represented about 59.5 of the volume of all U.S. market pulp shipments in 1999, which was below the 1998 share of 63 percent and represents the lowest market share for exports in a decade. Despite improved demand in portions of Europe and Latin America, there were still indications that the Asian financial crisis significantly affected the global pulp sector.

The U.S. Commerce Department's Bureau of the Census divides the sector's shipments into four major commodity groupings: (1) special alpha and dissolving pulps, representing 16 percent of the product shipment in current dollar value, (2) sulfate (or kraft) paper-grade pulp, accounting for 73 percent, (3) sulfite paper-grade pulp, accounting for 2 percent, and (4) nonwood pulp and pulp by-products, accounting for 9 percent. On a volume basis, sales by the domestic market pulp sector are dominated by chemical paper-grade pulp produced by either the kraft or the sulfite cooking process. In 1999, shipments of those commodities accounted for nearly 85 percent of the total quantity of U.S. market pulp shipments. The majority of shipments in this category in 1999 consisted of bleached and semibleached kraft pulp, amounting to nearly 97 percent of chemical paper-grade market pulp shipments. The remaining paper grade chemical pulp sales in 1999 came from product shipments of sulfite pulps and unbleached kraft pulp. Domestic market pulp capacity currently is dominated by the kraft process rather than mechanical pulping or other chemical processes. Bleached and unbleached kraft pulps have distinct advantages over mechanical and other chemical process–based pulps, including high physical strength and appearance properties, valuable and economically retrievable pulp by-products (including tall oil and turpentine), improved yields, and lower costs for environmental pollution control. In addition, the kraft pulping process is better adapted to the indigenous hardwood and softwood tree species grown in the United States.

Shipments of special alpha and dissolving pulps accounted for 14 percent (on a volume basis) of the sector total in 1999. These higher-valued pulps are specialty grades of chemical pulps produced from alpha cellulose, wood, or cotton linters and are tailored for use in the manufacture of man-made fibers (rayon and acetate), certain cellulose-based plastics, textiles, cellophane film, photographic paper, chemicals, and other value-added specialty papers. The alpha and dissolving pulp market has been going through a difficult transition period over the last couple of years. For instance, the rayon market, which is one of the bigger end-use markets for alpha and dissolving pulps, is slowly being transferred from industrialized nations to less developed countries. This is further slowing domestic sales of alpha pulp. Global capacity has experienced significant changes over the last 5 years as several mills in the United States, Canada, Europe, and Scandinavia have closed or retrofitted their equipment to make paper-grade chemical pulp, while new mills have been added in Asia and Latin America. According to the Food and Agriculture Organization (FAO) of the United Nations in its Pulp and Paper Capacities survey, world special alpha and dissolving pulp capacity decreased from 4.6 million metric tons in 1992 to 3.6 million metric tons in 1998. Approximately 70 percent of this capacity is in the form of market pulp. The FAO estimates that world capacity of this pulp grade will decrease 0.4 percent annually over the 1997–2002 period to less than 3.5 million metric tons. In the United States, annual production capacity declined to less than 1.3 million metric tons in 1999 with the permanent closure of several large mills.

A Global Commodity

Chemical paper-grade market pulp, which is used primarily in the manufacture of coated and uncoated free sheet printing and writing paper grades, is recognized as a global commodity and a bellwether for the general health of the world paper and paperboard sector. Unfortunately, it was not a very profitable sector in the 1990s. With the exception of the early 1994–early 1996 period, many global pulp producers have not made a profit. Chronic oversupply, cyclical demand, rapidly fluctuating operating rates, sharp inventory swings, and uneven world demand have plagued the global pulp market for more than a decade. Nevertheless, this commodity is still produced in about 27 countries worldwide, with 1999 global capacity amounting to nearly 38.4 million metric tons. About 62 percent, or 23.7 million metric tons, of world output came from the Norscan countries (United States, Canada, Sweden, Finland, and Norway) in 1999. The combined capacity of Canada (the global leader) and the United States is just under 47 percent (17.9 million metric tons) of the world chemical paper-grade market pulp total. For more than a decade, the Norscan market share for pulp shipments has declined as a result of significant new capacity coming on-stream from a number of suppliers in Latin America, Asia, and Africa. After 1992, the Norscan market share gradually declined from 68 to 65 percent in 1996 to the 1998 level of just below 62 percent. Most of the new output is coming from modern, state-of-the-art, technically advanced pulping facilities in Brazil, Chile, and Indonesia. Those countries have a number of operating advantages over their Norscan counterparts, including low-cost, rapid-growing hardwood and softwood tree species and lower costs for labor, energy, and environmental protection. Countries with lower delivered costs are able to undersell Norscan producers in a global market where price is the principal driving force.

Prices, Inventories, and Operating Rates

Despite the recent pressure from a variety of nontraditional producers, Norscan producers, with their well-established global presence, large domestic processing facilities, and major share of global market pulp output, are the most critical producers to watch in terms of production levels, prices, and inventories. Generally, Norscan producers need to carry no more than 1.5 million metric tons (the equivalent of a 25- to 26-day supply) of inventory for the market to be considered firm. At the end of 1998, Norscan inventory levels decreased 65,000 metric tons to 1.6 million tons, which represented 27 days of supply compared to the 32-day supply level that existed at the end of 1997. However, the ramifications of the Asian financial crisis were felt at the same time that inventories declined. The financial upheaval resulted in lower pulp and paper demand throughout the region, lower market pulp prices, and a slump in market pulp shipments to Asia, which has been the fastest-growing pulp-consuming market for the last decade. As a result, at the beginning of 1999, list prices for Northern Bleached Softwood Kraft (NBSK) remained soft. However, as global producers reduced operating rates and allowed inventory levels to remain low (1.4 million metric tons in mid-1999), there were several opportunities to raise pulp prices during 1999. The industry was successful in instituting small price increases in March, June, and September that brought the price of NBSK from $490 per metric ton to $580 per metric ton in September 1999. If global producers remain successful in keeping intact the often delicate supply-demand-inventory balance, further price increases for market pulp in the final quarter of 1999 and early 2000 are possible if demand remains at the same level. Operating rates, which were at the 85 percent level at the end of 1998, increased to nearly 90 percent at the end of 1999. U.S. capacity utilization was by far the worst among Norscan producers. Sweden led the way among Norscan producers in 1999 with a 98 percent operating rate, followed by Finland with 96 percent and Canada and Norway with 95 percent. U.S. market pulp producers typically prefer to run at operating rates of 93 to 96 percent, but this has not happened since 1995.

The practical maximum chemical paper-grade market wood pulp capacity for U.S. mills in 1999 was essentially unchanged from the 1998 level of 8.6 million metric tons. According to industry estimates, capacity increased less than 1 percent, primarily as a result of a definition-related shift in capacity from captive pulp to market pulp by a domestic manufacturer. Through the year 2001, capacity is forecast to increase less than 1 percent annually and will remain in the range of 8.6 to 8.8 million metric tons during that 3-year time frame.

Recovered paper and paperboard consumption by the domestic paper industry continues to increase, partly as a result of the industry's goal of a 50 percent recycling rate (consumption and export) of paper stock by the year 2000. Increased consumption of secondary fiber has come at the expense of virgin papermaking fibers. In 1999, U.S. paper and paperboard mills consumed an all-time high of 33.4 million metric tons of paper and paperboard, less than a 1 percent increase over the record attained in 1998. In 1999, domestic paper mills consumed an estimated 90.5 million metric tons of total papermaking fiber. Of that total, the share of virgin fiber was 63 percent and that of secondary fiber was 37 percent. Since 1994, the secondary fiber share of total papermaking fiber consumption has increased steadily from 30 percent to the record 37 percent in 1999. Over the next 3 years, paper and paperboard consumption is forecast to increase at an average annual rate of 2 percent, about double the growth rate of virgin wood pulp consumption. By the year 2000, paper consumption will reach nearly 38 percent of the domestic paper industry's total papermaking fiber consumption.

International Competitiveness

The pulp market has a global nature in which large quantities of virgin papermaking fiber are traded principally duty-free internationally from countries with a net surplus of fiber to papermaking countries that by nature are fiber-deficient. Norscan countries are the leading suppliers because of their adequate forest resources, large domestic pulping infrastructures, adequate transportation and distribution facilities, and low-cost pulp-processing facilities. Canada and the United States are the world's leading producers and exporters of market pulp. For most of the 1980s and the early 1990s, the United States was the global leader in market pulp production, but in 1996, Canada surpassed the United States. Currently, the United States is the world's largest captive pulp supplier and the second leading market pulp supplier. Canada's total practical maximum market pulp capacity is 10.4 million metric tons compared with the market pulp capacity of 8.66 million metric tons of the United States.

The United States is a large exporter and importer of market pulp and has had a trade surplus in that sector since 1987. The majority of international trade in this commodity grouping for the United States consists of bleached and semibleached kraft pulp. In 1998, more than 76 percent of U.S. exports and 80 percent of U.S. imports were composed of this particular grade. U.S. exports of market pulp fell for the fourth consecutive year in 1999, decreasing 10 percent in quantity to 4.92 million metric tons and 9 percent in value to $2.52 billion, driven by substantially lower demand in Asia caused by the financial crisis that affected many leading pulp-purchasing countries and contributed to a global oversupply of pulp. In 1999, there were year-over-year declines in U.S. pulp exports to each of its top five export markets: Japan (down 10 percent), Italy (down 22 percent), Germany (down 19 percent), Mexico (down 9 percent), and France (down 36 percent). In 1999, U.S. market pulp imports decreased about 7 percent to 5.05 million metric tons, the lowest level since 1993. Because of falling pulp prices, the value of those exports declined 11 percent to $2.12 billion. As was the case with exports, there were declines in imports from each of the three principal U.S. suppliers of pulp: Canada (down 11 percent), Brazil (down 9.5 percent), and South Africa (down 12.5 percent).

Prospects for the Year 2000

A turnaround in the important Asian pulp-consuming economies combined with an increase in production by domestic paper producers should result in increased demand for U.S. market pulp in the year 2000. As a result, market pulp shipments should increase 2.2 percent. Higher demand by U.S. and Asian producers for printing and writing paper is expected to contribute to the expansion. The industry should experience higher shipments, prices, and operating rates in 2000, resulting in a return to profitability for the sector.

The volume of U.S. exports of pulp should grow about 4 percent and increase the U.S. product share of total pulp shipments to more than 60 percent. For U.S. pulp exporters to improve their sales in 2000, significant improvements will have to be made in the Asian economies that have been adversely affected by the recent financial crisis. The sector's ability to export to Korea, Thailand, Malaysia, and the Philippines is critical if exports are to increase. The rebound of Japan's and China's economies, as well as key European markets, are also important to the sector's export prospects for 2000. The strengthening of the U.S. dollar throughout the east Asian region has reduced the price competitiveness of U.S. market pulp in that region. A strengthening of the local currencies in the east Asian region will aid U.S. exporters' ability to export to those large paper-producing, fiber-deficient markets.

As the world's leading paper and paperboard manufacturer, the United States will continue to be the target of many countries' pulp output. As a result, U.S. imports of pulp are forecast to increase 2.5 percent on a volume basis and 3 percent on a value basis. U.S. suppliers that ship to the U.S. market probably will face increased competition from low-cost, high-volume producers in Indonesia, Brazil, South Africa, and Chile. U.S. producers of pulp will need to monitor their own capacity utilization rates as well as consumer and producer inventory levels around the world and their relationship with the current level of global paper and paperboard production to prevent further significant increases in surplus pulp on the market.

Long-Term Prospects

Over the 2000–2004 forecast period, U.S. market pulp suppliers should experience increased global demand and a corresponding increase in domestic sales as product shipments increase about 1.75 percent annually over those 5 years. Much of the growth in sales will be linked to foreign demand as exports continue to be the major end use for U.S. market pulp shipments. The U.S. dollar must stabilize, especially in the east Asian region, if the United States is to remain competitive in world pulp markets. Exports as a proportion of total market pulp shipments are likely to increase back to the 70 percent level over the 5-year period as U.S. paper and paperboard producers continue to consume even larger quantities of recovered paper and paperboard and pulp imports (especially bleached hardwood kraft) find new markets in the U.S. paper and paperboard sector, which is by far the world's leading market. Other economic and performance characteristics that are important to this sector include domestic and foreign paper and paperboard demand (especially printing and writing paper), capacity utilization rates, various pulp inventory levels, and market pulp prices. For this industry to remain productive and profitable, utilization rates in the range of 92 to 96 percent should be maintained and producer inventory levels should stay near the 25-day supply level.

U.S. suppliers will continue to experience increased competition from Asian, African, and Latin American suppliers not only in the global pulp market but also in the U.S. market, which is by far the world's largest pulp-consuming market. Despite these factors, virgin market pulp will continue to be papermakers' fiber of choice because of its high strength and appearance properties, uniformity of quality, cleanliness, and ease of processing. In the U.S. market, virgin pulp will maintain about a 62 to 64 percent share of the fiber consumed in domestic paper and paperboard mills. According to a recent report, total world demand and supply for chemical paper-grade market pulp are forecast to increase by about 3 million metric tons (an average of 1.7 percent per year) from 1997 to 2002. The additional supply during that period will come mostly from Latin American suppliers, which are forecast to add nearly 2.1 million metric tons of pulp over that 5-year period. This amounts to a 7.2 percent annual average increase in pulp capacity for the region. During that period, additional pulp production will be coming on-stream from Asian, African, Nordic, and U.S. suppliers; that could adversely affect the supply and demand balance and cause prices to come under intense pressure during the forecast period.

Gary Stanley, U.S. Department of Commerce, Office of Metals, Materials, and Chemicals, (202) 482-0376, September 1999.

PAPER AND PAPERBOARD MILLS

According to the current SIC, paper and paperboard mills (SIC 262, 263) are engaged primarily in manufacturing a variety of commodity grades of coated and uncoated paper and paperboard from wood pulp and other fiber pulp. They also may manufacture converted and packaging paper and paperboard products. Among the commodities manufactured by this sector are newsprint, coated and uncoated printing and writing papers, tissue, packaging and converting paper, boxboard, bristols, milk carton board, containerboard, pressboard, special food board, wet machiner board, and construction paper and paperboard.

Industry Performance in 1999

The U.S. paper and paperboard industry experienced a disappointing sales performance in 1998 as product shipments declined 0.5 percent in real terms. This was the first year-over-year drop in shipments since 1985. However, in 1999, the industry experienced a turnaround in its sales performance as product shipments by the U.S. paper and paperboard mills sector increased about 1.2 percent in real terms (see Table 10-4). This improvement was driven primarily by an increase in domestic consumption of paper and paperboard, which was fueled by an expanding U.S. economy (a 2.7 percent increase in real GDP).

After experiencing numerous frustrations (weak foreign demand, high inventories, soft prices, low profitability) in 1998, the industry saw a number of improvements in operating conditions in 1999, including an easing of overcapacity, which had plagued the industry for a couple of years, and the end of a long inventory drawdown cycle. There were year-over-year increases in product shipments for most paperboard commodity sectors and in certain paper commodity sectors, including coated and uncoated free sheet printing and writing paper grades, tissue, and several converting and packaging paper grades. The commodity sectors that showed negative results in 1999 were newsprint and coated and uncoated groundwood papers.

The current value of product shipments by U.S. paper and paperboard mills in 1999 decreased 0.6 percent as prices for paper commodities continued to come under intense pressure from stagnant foreign demand and excess supply on the world market. The weak price structure that had been in place since mid-1995 was slowly coming to an end in mid-1999, but prices

TABLE 10-4: Paper and Paperboard Mills (SIC 262, 263) Trends and Forecasts
(millions of dollars except as noted)

	1992	1993	1994	1995	1996	1997[1]	1998[1]	1999[2]	2000[3]	Percent Change 97–98	98–99	99–00	96–00[4]
Industry data													
Value of shipments[5]	48,926	48,267	53,381	69,638	59,837	59,028	59,782	59,420	61,956	1.3	–0.6	4.3	0.9
Value of shipments (1992$)	48,926	48,625	52,187	53,571	51,107	53,662	53,377	54,018	54,828	–0.5	1.2	1.5	1.8
Total employment (thousands)	182	180	177	175	171	170	169	170	171	–0.6	0.6	0.6	0.0
Production workers (thousands)	140	138	136	135	132	131	134	134	134	2.3	0.0	0.0	0.4
Average hourly earnings ($)	17.97	18.22	19.17	19.76	20.34	20.55	21.31	21.84	22.32	3.7	2.5	2.2	2.3
Capital expenditures	4,952	4,507	4,960	4,859	5,502	5,384	5,454	5,508	5,663	1.3	1.0	2.8	0.7
Product data													
Value of shipments[5]	47,232	46,513	51,110	67,052	57,971	57,189	57,920	57,569	60,026	1.3	–0.6	4.3	0.9
Value of shipments (1992$)	47,232	46,866	49,945	51,571	49,514	51,990	51,714	52,335	53,120	–0.5	1.2	1.5	1.8
Trade data													
Value of imports	6,708	7,190	7,338	10,198	9,117	9,007	9,827	10,338	10,596	9.1	5.2	2.5	3.8
Value of exports	4,263	4,189	4,813	6,437	6,339	6,545	6,240	5,955	6,163	–4.7	–4.6	3.5	–0.7

[1] Estimate except imports and exports.
[2] Estimate.
[3] Forecast.
[4] Compound annual rate.
[5] For a definition of industry versus product values, see "Getting the Most Out of *Outlook 2000*."
Source: U.S. Department of Commerce: Bureau of the Census; International Trade Administration.

had not shown any significant improvement, primarily on the paper side of the industry. The paperboard sector was in a better position throughout most of 1999 because demand remained fairly strong, consumer inventories dropped, additional capacity additions were minimal, and production rates stabilized. Operating rates for the industry, which had shown a steady decline in 1995–1996, improved in 1997 but declined further in 1998.

However, in 1999, there was slight improvement for the paper and paperboard sectors. For the U.S. paperboard sector, domestic mill operating rates declined from the 1994 high of nearly 97 percent, to just under 95 percent in 1995, to less than 93 percent in 1996. As the inventory drawdown process continued and demand remained high in 1997, domestic paperboard sector operating rates improved to 95 percent. However, in 1998, operating conditions declined to 92 percent as foreign demand, especially in the area affected by the Asian financial crisis, remained soft. Operating rates for the paperboard segment increased to almost 95 percent in 1999, driven by stronger demand in the U.S. market fueled by the improvement in the domestic economic performance. Results for the paper segment of the industry were similar. Operating rates declined from the 1994 level of nearly 95 percent to only 90 percent in 1996. Although operating rates jumped back to 94 percent in 1997, they fell to 92 percent in 1998. However, operating rates improved to nearly 94 percent in 1999. As a result, domestic producers were able to reduce their inventories and pass along legitimate price increases on several important paperboard and printing and writing paper grades for the first time in several years.

A particularly troublesome area for the industry in 1999 was the decrease in the quantity of paper and paperboard exports. The globalization of the world paper and paperboard sector has been ongoing for more than a decade. The United States produces about 28.5 percent of the world's paper and paperboard output. As a result, the domestic industry is well suited to take advantage of growing world paper and board demand. However, for the last 2 years, U.S. paper and paperboard exports have declined, primarily as a result of the Asian financial crisis and a European economic slowdown. In 1999, because of lower foreign demand and excess global paper and paperboard supply, U.S. exports of paper and paperboard decreased more than 8 percent to 8.3 million metric tons after a 9 percent decline in 1998. The Asian financial crisis, which affected a number of that region's key paper-purchasing markets (e.g., Korea, Thailand, the Philippines, Malaysia) in 1998–1999, led to a surplus of paper and paperboard not only from North American and European papermakers but also from Latin American and Asian producers looking for markets in which to sell their excess output.

Despite the problems of the last 2 years, international trade continues to be the sector's major source of growth. After 1985, U.S. exports of paper and paperboard jumped from 3.7 million metric tons to 10.9 million metric tons, an 8 percent compound annual growth rate (tonnage basis) over that period. Through an aggressive trade policy and trade promotion activities, the U.S. paper and paperboard sector has been able to expand foreign sales greatly over the past 15 years. This has moved the domestic industry from primarily looking to the domestic market, to marketing its products, to aggressively seeking new customers abroad.

In 1999, U.S. production of paper and paperboard reached a new record as output totaled 86.8 million metric tons. Paperboard commodities accounted for 53.2 percent (46.2 million metric tons) of the sector's output, while paper commodities were responsible for 46.8 percent (40.6 million metric tons). On a current dollar basis, however, paper commodities have a higher per unit value; therefore, shipments of paper accounted for 62 percent of the paper and paperboard mills total, while paperboard shipments accounted for the remainder.

Paper Mills

Slowly improving operating rates, increases in domestic demand, and moderately improved prices for certain grades of printing and writing paper characterized the U.S. paper mills sector in 1999. Overall production was up 0.5 percent in the paper segment of the industry. Although the drawdown of inventories that started in mid-1995 was slower than expected, it contributed to an overall better performance by U.S. producers in 1999, especially manufacturers of coated and uncoated free sheet printing and writing paper. The process of inventory downsizing resulted from producers' efforts to keep operating rates in check, minimize capacity additions, and take advantage of stronger demand. The strength in the U.S. economy, with real GDP increasing 2.7 percent, was the principal cause of the increase in domestic demand. Although exports of paper and paperboard have increased strongly over the last decade, 90 percent of the output from U.S. paper mills is destined for the domestic market. According to a leading industry survey, from 1999 through 2001, domestic papermaking capacity is forecast to increase at a rate of less than 1 percent annually. This should allow supply and demand to continue to be brought more into balance as the industry moves into the year 2000.

In 1999, production from U.S. paper mills was divided into four principal commodity segments: (1) printing and writing paper, (2) newsprint, (3) tissue, and (4) packaging and converting paper. Printing and writing paper is the single largest commodity group in paper-related production. In 1999, domestic output of this high-value paper products segment was 23.8 million metric tons, or 59 percent of all paper-related production. Within this commodity grouping, moderate increases in shipments came from the coated and uncoated free sheet sector. The lower-valued coated and uncoated groundwood papers segment experienced small declines in production in 1999 as a result of overcapacity and low-cost imports from European, Canadian, and Asian paper producers. Uncoated free sheet, which is used extensively in a variety of printing, communication, and publishing applications, was the single largest printing and writing paper commodity in 1999, amounting to 12.4 million metric tons, or 52 percent of all U.S. printing and writing paper production. Production in the uncoated free sheet segment was up 2.7 percent in 1999, a significant turnaround from the 1 percent decline in 1998. The second leading commodity grouping in the paper sector in 1999 was newsprint. Production of this newspaper, periodical, and journal raw material in 1999 was just under 6.4 million metric tons, down about 2.5 percent from the 1998 level. Newsprint production represented 16 percent of all paper-related output in 1999.

Paperboard Mills

In 1999, U.S. production of paperboard commodities increased just over 1 percent because of a slight increase in domestic sales. Paperboard for export declined significantly in 1999 as exports of U.S. containerboard mills and boxboard mills experienced significant declines. U.S. producers of containerboard (linerboard and corrugating medium) had noticeably higher sales in only one major end-user segment: the domestic corrugated and solid fiber box sector. Despite the decline in exports in 1999, U.S. paperboard mills, especially those in the containerboard sector, have over the last several years enjoyed record sales opportunities for many of their products in corrugated box, shipping container, and carton plants in southeast Asia, Europe, and Latin America, leading to a noticeable increase in the sector's exports. However, the Asian financial crisis, which led to a downturn in the economies of major paperboard-consuming economies (Japan, South Korea, Thailand, Malaysia, the Philippines, Hong Kong, Taiwan), suppressed U.S. paperboard exports in 1999 (see Table 10-4).

U.S. production of paperboard falls into two product lines: containerboard and boxboard. Containerboard sales amounted to 31.8 million metric tons (63 percent) of all domestic paperboard production in 1999, a 1 percent decline increase from the 1998 level. Domestic boxboard production amounted to 14 million metric tons in 1999 (28 percent) of total paperboard production, a 2.5 percent increase over the 1998 level. Stronger than expected demand by some folding carton and sanitary food and beverage container end users contributed to a significant increase in boxboard production in 1999. Although domestic boxboard sales to folding carton plants were strong in 1999, the export market was very weak as foreign shipments by U.S. boxboard producers decreased nearly 15 percent to 1.4 million metric tons.

The production of linerboard, which is used by the corrugated box and container sector and is the largest domestic paperboard commodity, accounted for 61 percent (19.4 million metric tons) of domestic containerboard production in 1999. This was a 1.6 percent increase over the 1998 level and reflects a new record for domestic producers, providing an indication of strong demand by U.S. corrugators. Domestic production of corrugating medium, the other component of a corrugated box, increased 2 percent in 1999 to 8.7 million metric tons. As a result of the positive situation for containerboard sector fundamentals in 1999, there were several significant price increases for linerboard and corrugating medium. In September 1999, several leading linerboard producers announced an increase of $40 per ton for standard number 42 kraft linerboard, which brought the price up to $430 per ton. This was a 15 percent increase from the same period in 1998. At the same time, corrugating medium producers announced an increase of $50 per ton, which brought the price of standard number 26 semichemical corrugating medium up to $405 per ton. This reflected a 29 percent increase over the same period in 1998. Additional price increases in late 1999 and early 2000 are possible because of the fundamentals in place in the fourth quarter of 1999 if the export market opens up for U.S. suppliers.

According to a recent industry capacity survey, domestic paperboard mills will add more than 1.4 million metric tons of capacity over the 1999–2001 period. This reflects an average annual growth rate of 1 percent over that 3-year period. This is a noticeable drop from the 3 percent average annual increase in capacity over the 1988–1998 period. Approximately one-half of the new capacity will be added in the containerboard sector.

International Competitiveness

Weak foreign demand and a global oversupply situation in 1999 led to a significant decline in both quantity (down 8 percent to 8.3 million metric tons) and value (down 4.6 percent to just under $6 billion). Foreign demand was weakest in certain Asian markets but also was lower in many European, Latin American, and African markets. Paper exports represented 33.5 percent (on a volume basis) of the total and paperboard represented 66.5 percent of the total in 1999. On the paper side, the only sectors that had higher exports in 1999 were coated and uncoated free sheet printing and writing papers at 12 and 6 percent, respectively. Exports of the other paper sector commodities declined, including tissue (down 10 percent), packaging and converting paper (16 percent), uncoated groundwood printing and writing paper (27 percent), and newsprint (7 percent). On the paperboard side, there were decreases in exports of all major paperboard grades, including bleached and unbleached linerboard (down 19 percent), recycled paperboard (6 percent), semichemical corrugating medium (28 percent), and unbleached kraft paperboard (19 percent).

In 1999, the strong U.S. economic performance led to significant increases in paper and paperboard consumption. Other paper-producing countries, including Canada, Sweden, Finland, Brazil, Indonesia, and several other Asian nations, seized the opportunity to increase their exports to the United States to take advantage of the increase in demand. As a result, there was a 5 percent increase in the volume of U.S. imports of paper and paperboard and a 5.2 percent increase in the value of U.S. paper and paperboard imports in 1999. The U.S. market is not protected by significant tariff and nontariff market access barriers. This makes the U.S. market, which is by far the global leader in terms of apparent paper consumption, vulnerable to low-cost or surplus paper and paperboard output from a number of foreign competitors.

As a result of the dependence of the U.S. newspaper publishing market on newsprint imports, primarily from Canada, the U.S. paper and paperboard sector traditionally has run a trade deficit. In 1999, U.S. imports of newsprint amounted to 6.1 million metric tons, nearly a 2 percent increase over the 1998 level. In addition, U.S. imports of nearly every other commodity grade of paper and paperboard surged in 1999. This included significant increases in imports of printing and writing paper (6 percent), unbleached kraft packaging and converting paper (6 percent), semichemical corrugating medium (38 percent), kraft paperboard (39 percent), and paperboard (17 percent).

Forecast for the Year 2000

Shipments from domestic paper and paperboard mills are forecast to increase at least 1.5 percent in the year 2000 as the U.S. economy continues to expand, resulting in higher domestic demand for a variety of paper and paperboard commodity grades. This forecast is contingent not only on an improving domestic economy but also on better economic conditions in key Asian, Latin American, and European markets and reduced market access barriers in key foreign markets. A stabilized U.S. dollar vis-à-vis foreign currencies, especially in Asia and Latin America, will help U.S. exporters increase their exports in 2000. Although domestic producers traditionally have directed much of their output to domestic converters and packagers, significant future growth will be centered in vital international markets, especially in Asia and Latin America. Exports to Europe, although still important, will not grow as fast because of competition from Canadian and Scandinavian producers, which already have a strong presence in the European market. Exports of paper and paperboard will increase 2.5 percent on a volume basis and 3.5 percent on a value basis in 2000. However, the combination of the large and open U.S. market, insignificant market access barriers, and an expanding U.S. economy will result in additional U.S. imports of paper and paperboard. Canadian, west European, Latin American, and Asian paper-producing economies will again find the U.S. market the best outlet for their output in 2000. As a result, U.S. imports of commodity paper and paperboard should increase 2 percent in volume and 2.5 percent in value. If the U.S. economy expands at a level beyond 2.5 percent, the rate of increase of imports could easily double. Prices for principal paper and paperboard grades, which have struggled to increase over the past 2 years, should go up in the year 2000 if operating rates and inventories are kept in check and the balance of supply and demand is maintained.

The outlook for the global paper and paperboard sector is uncertain. Although world demand is forecast to increase about 1.4 percent over the 1998–2001 period, that rate of expansion is not close to the 2.3 to 2.5 percent levels of the late 1980s and early 1990s or equal to the 2 percent annual increase from 1997 through 2000. The long-term impact of the Asian financial crisis will continue to unfold in 2000. The countries hardest hit by the crisis (Thailand, Indonesia, Malaysia, the Philippines, South Korea) are just beginning to recover. Those five countries will attempt to move rapidly to protect and stabilize key manufacturing sectors, including the paper and paperboard sector. Asia represents the fastest-growing paper-consuming and paper-producing region. Many projects that were mothballed or delayed because of the financial crisis may be back on track now that the region's economic and investment climate seems to be stabilizing. According to the latest United Nations FAO Pulp and Paper Capacities survey, Asian papermakers will add more than 2 million tons of capacity over the 1998–2001 period. China and Indonesia have indicated that additional projects, including several paper machine installations and mill constructions, are possible in the Asian region. The survey also indicates that significant capacity additions will be coming on-stream from both western European and Latin American papermakers, with the fastest growth coming from European producers in Finland, Sweden, Italy, and Germany.

After successfully passing along numerous price increases in 1994 through mid-1995, global paper and paperboard producers saw steep price declines from mid-1995 through most of 1996. The cycle of peak-to-valley pricing has been something that global paper and board producers have been unable to avoid over the past half century despite their concerted efforts. In 2000, relationships between producers, stockholders, and consumers will experience more friction as producers seek to make up for their disappointing results over the last 24 months. U.S. paper and paperboard producers will have to monitor closely domestic and foreign demand, supply, and inventory levels to prevent further dramatic price swings in the year 2000. U.S. paper and paperboard mill fundamentals and operating conditions appear to be relatively solid for 2000. As a result, operating rates should increase and prices should improve.

Over the next 2 years, the domestic paper and paperboard mills sector is expected to add 2.9 million metric tons of capacity, with new output being added to the paper and paperboard sectors (although paperboard increases will constitute 55 percent of the added capacity). If the global economy improves over the next 24 months, the additional output from U.S. mills will be easily absorbed by the global paper and paperboard market. If it does not, operating rates in domestic production plants will probably remain in the upper eighties or low nineties to prevent mill and consumer stocks from increasing significantly and causing downward pressure on prices.

Long-Term Prospects

Over the 2000–2004 period, the U.S. paper and paperboard mills sector should see shipments increase about 1.8 percent annually. The large, price-competitive, high-quality, and low-cost U.S. paper and paperboard sector is well prepared to move into the new millennium and should find new domestic and international end users, spurring overall growth among domestic producers. As major Asian paper-consuming markets recover and other global economies grow, resulting in increased consumption of paper and paperboard, the U.S. industry should be in the best position to supply much of the increased demand. As U.S. capacity is added, the industry will expand its overseas activities in Mexico, southeast Asia, Latin American countries, and eastern Europe. The United States has the world's largest paper and paperboard industry, producing nearly 30 percent of world paper and paperboard output. As market access barriers are reduced over the next 5 years through the implementation of the NAFTA and WTO agreements, demand for U.S. paper and paperboard products will increase. As a result, U.S. exports (on a volume basis) will increase at least 2.3 percent annually through 2004. As the world's leading paper-consuming market, the United States will continue to be the target for many countries' surplus paper and paperboard output. Low-cost imports from Indonesia, Brazil, Canada, and certain European countries will increase during the forecast period. There are practically no market access barriers that will impede other countries from exporting to the U.S. market. As a result, imports will increase 3 percent annually during the 2000–2004 period.

Competition on a global scale is expected to increase over the forecast period as world producers attempt to maintain current market share and broaden their customer base. According to the FAO, global paper and paperboard capacity is forecast to grow from 333.6 million metric tons in 1998 to 348.1 million metric tons by 2001, an increase of 14.5 million metric tons over those 3 years. Although the United States will remain the global leader in output, its share of total world production probably will decline over the forecast period when competition from Asian, Latin American, Canadian, and western European producers increases. The greatest amount of growth is expected from Asia as producers in China, South Korea, Japan, and Indonesia seek to satisfy more domestic demand and move into the export arena. By 2004, the U.S. sector's share of global paper and board production will have dropped from the current level of just over 29 percent to 27 percent. However, there will be further technological, product, and distribution innovations by U.S. suppliers, and that will enable domestic producers to remain a powerful player in the still-expanding global paper and paperboard market.

Gary Stanley, U.S. Department of Commerce, Office of Metals, Materials, and Chemicals, (202) 482-0376, September 1999.

CORRUGATED AND SOLID FIBER BOXES

According to the current SIC, the corrugated and solid fiber box industry (SIC 2653) consists of establishments that are engaged primarily in the manufacture of corrugated and solid fiber boxes and containers and related products from purchased paperboard (produced in SIC 263). The industry's principal commodities are corrugated and solid fiberboard boxes, pads, partitions, display items, pallets, single face products, and corrugated sheets. According to the *Annual Survey of Manufactures (ASM),* product shipments for the industry represent more than 60 percent of total U.S. paperboard container and box shipments (SIC 265).

Industry Performance in 1999

The U.S. corrugated and solid fiber boxes industry experienced a fourth consecutive year of significant growth in 1999 as product shipments increased 2.9 percent (see Table 10-5). The 1999 increase is in line with trend growth for corrugated product shipments for the past 10 years, even considering the 1.5 percent decline in 1995. Domestic corrugators experienced record domestic and foreign demand in 1999, which saw the industry ship a record 405.4 billion square feet of finished corrugated boxes, cartons, and shipping containers. Shipments of corrugated products represented just over 99 percent (403.3 billion square feet) of the 1999 industry total, and shipments of solid fiber boxes made up the remainder.

Strong growth in the U.S. economy in 1999 resulted in increased U.S. manufacturing output (the principal driving force behind corrugated box demand) and higher shipments of industrial and consumer nondurable goods. Internationally, this growth was tempered by the Asian economic crisis, continued global overcapacity, and a strong U.S. dollar. Although the industry struggled in the first half of 1999, it was able to recover in the latter half, buoyed by the continued growth in the U.S. economy (real GDP increased nearly 2.7 percent) and increased domestic consumption.

In 1999, the U.S. corrugated and solid fiber boxes industry continued to find excellent export opportunities. U.S. exports of a wide variety of corrugated boxes, shipping containers,

TABLE 10-5: Corrugated and Solid Fiber Boxes (SIC 2653) Trends and Forecasts
(millions of dollars except as noted)

	1992	1993	1994	1995	1996	1997	1998[1]	1999[2]	2000[3]	Percent Change 97–98	98–99	99–00	96–00[4]
Industry data													
Value of shipments[5]	19,834	20,623	22,681	27,965	25,914	25,644	26,541	27,310	28,130	3.5	2.9	3.0	2.1
Value of shipments (1992$)	19,834	20,895	21,297	20,472	21,051	22,190	22,505	23,158	23,852	1.4	2.9	3.0	3.2
Total employment (thousands)	112	114	120	125	127	125	124	126	127	–0.8	1.6	0.8	0.0
Production workers (thousands)	81.4	82.6	89.3	93.5	94.7	91.8	90.9	91.7	92.1	–1.0	0.9	0.4	–0.7
Average hourly earnings ($)	11.37	11.85	11.92	11.77	12.12	13.46	13.70	14.30	14.80	1.8	4.4	3.5	5.1
Capital expenditures	465	530	531	788	862	962	980	950	900	1.9	–3.1	–5.3	1.1
Product data													
Value of shipments[5]	19,139	19,876	21,703	26,724	24,816	24,145	24,868	25,589	26,357	3.0	2.9	3.0	1.5
Value of shipments (1992$)	19,139	20,138	20,379	19,564	20,159	20,677	20,888	21,493	22,138	1.0	2.9	3.0	2.4
Trade data													
Value of imports	62.8	74.7	102	131	139	141	151	157	159	7.1	4.0	1.3	3.4
Value of exports	392	421	533	698	789	818	879	923	972	7.5	5.0	5.3	5.4

[1] Estimate except imports and exports.
[2] Estimate.
[3] Forecast.
[4] Compound annual rate.
[5] For a definition of industry versus product values, see "Getting the Most Out of *Outlook 2000.*"
Source: U.S. Department of Commerce: Bureau of the Census; International Trade Administration.

and related packaging materials have increased each year since 1989. This growth has been remarkable in that the total quantity of exports has increased as well as the actual number of markets. In 1999, the industry experienced another year of record demand despite the Asian financial crisis and the slow growth of many European and Latin American economies. Exports as a proportion of total shipments have grown noticeably over the last 8 years, increasing from less than 1 percent in 1989 to nearly 4 percent in 1999. Although the overall percentage remains relatively low, exports have become one of the fastest growing end-use segments for domestic corrugators. The ability of the domestic industry to develop new, innovative packaging and shipping commodities to meet the increasingly stringent criteria of foreign customers has enabled U.S. corrugators to become the world's leading exporters of finished corrugated products. The superior quality, price competitiveness, and high strength of U.S.-produced corrugated materials continue to open new export opportunities for U.S. suppliers.

Prices and Inventories

To smooth earnings volatility, the need of corporations to integrate within the industry has intensified. The corrugated boxes industry is more than 80 percent integrated, and this percentage is rising weekly as a result of the acquisition strategies of several leading producers of corrugated boxes. Since the output of the corrugated box industry is a commodity product, consolidation is seen as a necessity to balance supply with demand and support pricing that will encourage the growth of the industry. After the disappointing current dollar sales value of 1996, the corrugated box industry experienced back-to-back years of higher current dollar sales, primarily as a result of the recovery of prices for domestic corrugators. The Producer Price Index (using 1980 as the base year) for SIC 2653 shows a slow, moderate increase since the final quarter of 1996, which equates to higher current dollar value sales for the sector over the last couple of years. The combination of growing domestic and foreign demand and closely monitored inventories gave U.S. corrugating converters an opportunity to implement several small price increases in 1998 and 1999. Box prices were able to catch up to the price hikes made for linerboard and corrugating medium in the final quarter of 1998. A recent price increase of 11 to 12 percent came from four of the major U.S. corrugated container manufacturers, the second round of price increases in 1999.

The domestic corrugating industry was able to draw down its containerboard (i.e., linerboard and corrugating medium) inventories to manageable levels (about 2,530 million tons, which is equivalent to a 4-week supply) and moderate operating levels for most of 1998 and the early months of 1999.

International Competitiveness

Spurred by an increase in foreign demand for high-quality, high-strength, competitively priced U.S. corrugated shipping containers and boxes, domestic exports of corrugated paperboard products experienced their ninth consecutive year of growth in quantity and value in 1999 with a 5 percent increase in value and a 3 percent increase in volume. U.S. corrugators exported a record 820,000 metric tons of finished corrugated boxes and containers in 1999.

Despite the Asian financial crisis, U.S. corrugators increased their sales noticeably to Indonesia, China, and Thailand. U.S. exports of corrugated containers and finished packaging commodities were shipped mainly to Mexico (60 percent) and Canada (20 percent) in 1999. However, there were large increases in exports to Guatemala, Chile, and several other Latin American markets in 1999.

Although imports of corrugated containers and other finished corrugated products totaled only $157 million in 1999, they increased for the eighth straight year. Growth in the U.S. economy was the principal driver behind the increase in imports in 1999. The only significant suppliers of corrugated containers and related materials to the U.S. market in 1999 were Canada (72 percent) and Mexico (6 percent).

Prospects for 2000

The U.S. corrugated and solid fiber boxes sector should experience higher domestic and foreign demand in 2000, resulting in a 3 percent increase in product shipments. The U.S. economy is expected to continue to grow in 2000, resulting in increased industrial activity and larger shipments of nondurable goods. If domestic corrugators are to experience an increase in the current dollar value of shipments, they will have to do a better job of monitoring finished product inventories and adjusting operating rates to reflect current domestic and foreign demand patterns.

The availability of raw materials may become a problem for the industry in the year 2000. The combination of additional linerboard and corrugating medium output coming on line and the recovery of important containerboard export markets in Asia may lead to difficulty for domestic corrugators in securing adequate box-making materials at reasonable prices. Significant recent mergers in the containerboard sector could affect the availability, flow, and price of linerboard and corrugating medium. As a result, domestic corrugators, especially independent corrugators, will need to monitor their raw material inventories closely to ensure that high production levels are maintained.

Foreign sales will grow in the year 2000, with exports increasing on a value basis by 5 percent to $920 million, which will become a new record high for U.S. corrugators. Despite a slow recovery in important Asian markets, U.S. corrugated box, carton, and related product converters should find expanded sales opportunities in traditional markets and also develop new markets. Growth in the U.S. economy (with real GDP growth averaging 2.4 percent) will result in increased imports of corrugated packaging materials. For 2000, imports are forecast to increase 2 percent to a new record high of $159 million because of the growing U.S. economy, which provides new sales opportunities for foreign box and carton manufacturers.

In 1999, shipments of nondurable goods accounted for 76 percent of the total volume of corrugated boxes and related materials shipments, reflecting a slight decrease from the share in 1998. This share will decrease slightly in the year 2000 to 75.5 percent as durable goods capture a slightly larger proportion of the sector's shipments. Growth in demand by the food and kindred products (39 percent of corrugated shipments) and paper and allied products sectors (22 percent) contributed to the increase in the share of nondurable goods in 1999 and will continue to expand in 2000. Durable goods accounted for just over 24.5 percent of total corrugated products shipments in 1999 and will increase their percentage of shipments further in 2000. The leading durables end-use segments in 2000 will be miscellaneous manufacturing, which includes toys, amusements, sporting and athletic goods (6 percent of corrugated shipments), electrical machinery, equipment and supplies (4 percent of corrugated shipments), and stone, clay, and glass products (4 percent of corrugated shipments).

Long-Term Prospects

Product shipments by the U.S. corrugated and solid fiber boxes sector are expected to grow nearly 3 percent per year over the next 5 years. This places that sector first in projected average annual growth among all domestic paperboard packaging sectors (SIC 265). The food and kindred products and paper and allied products industries will continue to be the leading end-use markets throughout the forecast period. However, durable goods sectors, as they have done over the last several years, will continue to consume larger quantities of corrugated containers, cartons, and boxes. Competition for domestic and international market share for shipping mediums probably will intensify from flexible plastic films, metal and plastic laminates, and related materials as well as within the paperboard packaging sectors. For instance, in 1999, some customers in the food industry, notably the meat and fresh fruit and vegetable sectors, began to replace traditional brown corrugated boxes with returnable, reusable plastic containers. This trend has been under way for some time in portions of Europe. However, there has been a backlash against plastics in the United States because of environmental concerns.

Despite increased competition, corrugated packaging materials should be able to maintain their dominant role as a shipping medium through more innovative, eye-appealing, environmentally friendly, recyclable, cost-effective products that increasingly will be directed to the retail marketplace in the form of consumer-oriented point-of-purchase displays. The continued growth of large "warehouse-style" grocery outlets offering bulk and jumbo-size items will provide new marketing and sales opportunities for domestic corrugators. Although traditional shipping containers (the so-called brown box) will continue to dominate sales into the twenty-first century, specialty corrugated products, which are largely consumer-directed, will show the fastest rate of growth. The development of new mini-flutes (known as E-, F-, and K-flutes) have opened up many end-use segments previously unavailable to domestic corrugators. These new products are very popular as point-of-purchase consumer-oriented displays in both grocery stores and other retail stores and outlets.

U.S. exports of corrugated boxes, containers, and related products are projected to continue to climb through the forecast period, although at slightly lower growth rates than has been the case recently, spurred by increasing sales to Latin American countries, the recovery of Asian market economies, and the development of new markets in Europe. Canada and Mexico will remain the dominant foreign markets for U.S. corrugated products not only because of their proximity but also because of a projected acceleration of demand. The removal of market access barriers through the U.S.–Canada Free Trade Agreement and the ongoing reduction of barriers through NAFTA have created a more level playing field for U.S. corrugated products exporters, which have seen their export opportunities improve. Further implementation of NAFTA should help U.S. producers continue to increase exports.

During the next 5 years, the domestic corrugating sector will see expanded product development; increased recycled content of its corrugated board through improved technologies, paper stock handling, and collection procedures; new uses for preprinted linerboard; increased use of mini- and microfluted combination board in point-of-purchase displays; increased use of computerization throughout each aspect of corrugated box design, assembly, and distribution; expanded use of flexographic color printing; and improvements in graphic design. As the world's lowest-cost, highest-volume, most technologically advanced, and highest-quality producer of containerboard and corrugated products, the United States is expected to remain highly competitive in the ever-expanding global marketplace for corrugated shipping containers and similar products over the forecast period.

Sarah Smiley, U.S. Department of Commerce, Office of Metals, Materials, and Chemicals, (202) 482-0577, September 1999.

FOLDING PAPERBOARD BOXES

According to the current SIC, the folding paperboard box (also known as the folding carton) industry (SIC 2657) is made up of establishments that are engaged primarily in the manufacture of folding paperboard boxes from purchased paperboard (manufactured in SIC 263), including folding sanitary food boxes and cartons, except milk cartons. Milk and milk-type paperboard containers and cartons are classified under SIC 2656, sanitary food containers. The principal products manufactured include a variety of folding paperboard boxes, packaging containers, and food packaging components for a number of food and produce (i.e., dry foods, beverages, frozen foods, fast-food restaurant items) and nonfood items (i.e., soaps, detergents, cosmetics, medicinal products, personal health and hygiene products, paper products). The industry is second only to the corrugated and solid fiber box industry in terms of domestic paperboard container and box industry sales. The *Annual Survey of Manufactures (ASM)* shows that product shipments for this industry represent nearly 30 percent of total U.S. paperboard container and box shipments (SIC 265).

Industry Performance in 1999

The strength of the domestic economy, which led to increased domestic sales, enabled the folding paperboard box industry to enjoy record sales in nearly all of its end-use markets. This was the second consecutive year of marked growth for this sector after a disappointing sales performance in 1997. The growth of the industry was tempered in 1999 by the resin-based alternatives that are becoming prominent in the market. Based on annualized 9-month 1999 industry data, product shipments in real terms increased 1.14 percent in 1999 after a 0.53 percent increase in 1998 (see Table 10-6). On a value basis, prices for folding cartons and related products increased modestly in 1999, resulting in a 1 percent increase in the current dollar value of shipments.

A combination of factors led to the increase in the volume of folding carton product shipments by domestic box makers in 1999. Those factors included (1) real GDP growth of 2.7 percent in the U.S. economy, (2) significant improvements in real disposable income (up 2.7 percent), (3) strong growth in total U.S. industrial production (up 1.7 percent), (4) growth in purchases of nondurable goods (up 1.6 percent), and (5) record

TABLE 10-6: Folding Paperboard Boxes (SIC 2657) Trends and Forecasts
(millions of dollars except as noted)

	1992	1993	1994	1995	1996	1997	1998[1]	1999[2]	2000[3]	Percent Change 97–98	98–99	99–00	96–00[4]
Industry data													
Value of shipments[5]	7,929	8,009	8,284	8,782	9,026	8,942	9,031	9,122	9,386	1.0	1.0	2.9	1.0
Value of shipments (1992$)	7,929	7,993	8,267	8,253	8,396	8,355	8,415	8,523	8,635	0.7	1.3	1.3	0.7
Total employment (thousands)	52.6	52.5	53.1	53.0	53.2	50.2	49.9	50.0	50.1	–0.6	0.2	0.2	–1.5
Production workers (thousands)	41.7	41.5	42.7	42.5	42.8	40.0	39.0	39.2	39.5	–2.5	0.5	0.8	–2.0
Average hourly earnings ($)	12.14	12.63	12.43	12.66	13.00	13.79	14.00	14.23	14.40	1.5	1.6	1.2	2.6
Capital expenditures	296	333	282	240	350	419	400	410	407	–4.5	2.5	–0.7	3.8
Product data													
Value of shipments[5]	7,731	7,754	7,986	8,545	8,814	8,606	8,700	8,788	8,875	1.1	1.0	1.0	0.2
Value of shipments (1992$)	7,731	7,738	7,970	8,031	8,199	8,067	8,110	8,203	8,308	0.5	1.1	1.3	0.3
Trade data													
Value of imports	144	147	197	275	294	315	350	371	382	11.1	6.0	3.0	6.8
Value of exports	130	179	192	212	242	278	262	263	264	–5.8	0.4	0.4	2.2

[1] Estimate except imports and exports.
[2] Estimate.
[3] Forecast.
[4] Compound annual rate.
[5] For a definition of industry versus product values, see "Getting the Most Out of *Outlook 2000.*"
Source: U.S. Department of Commerce: Bureau of the Census; International Trade Administration.

U.S. exports of folding cartons and related paperboard boxes materials (up 0.5 percent on a volume basis).

Sales in the folding carton industry traditionally have been very seasonal. The industry typically begins the year on a strong note after a slowdown in sales during December. Sales for the industry typically slow moderately from April to July and then experience a turnaround from August through November before slowing again in December. In 1999, this traditional pattern held true for most of the year.

Prices and Inventories

Fortunately for the domestic folding carton industry, the cost of its raw materials (predominantly bleached board, recycled board, and kraft paperboard) has changed very little over the last couple of years, allowing the industry to control a portion of input costs. According to published price statistics for the 1997–1999 period, prices for each of the pertinent raw material grades of folding boxboard changed less than 5 percent during that period.

According to industry data, the sector's inventory of finished goods was kept at fairly even levels throughout most of 1999, with the exception of April through June, which is traditionally the season of inventory buildup for the fall sales push. In a year-over-year comparison, finished folding carton inventories increased about 3.5 percent from 1998 to 1999. The industry's operating rates remained high for most of the year, contributing to the slight increase in the sector's finished goods inventory. However, domestic producers were able to adjust output and operating levels to prevent a large inventory buildup, which would have contributed to lower prices.

Environmental Profile

The U.S. folding paperboard box industry has an excellent environmental performance record, surpassing that of other domestic paper and paperboard segments as well as that of other packaging materials, including plastics, metals, and glass. The industry has a long-established reputation as a leading consumer of paper and paperboard, with many of its products containing more than 75 percent secondary fiber. In many of its applications, there is as much as 100 percent secondary fiber content. Unfortunately, the industry's environmental performance is overlooked by many consumers. As a result, a mechanism has been created to promote the environmental efforts and benefits of the folding paperboard box industry. In conjunction with the National Paperbox Association (NPA) and the American Forest and Paper Association (AFPA), the Paperboard Packaging Council has created the American Paperboard Packaging Environmental Council (APPEC), which was established to promote the recyclability, renewability, functionality, and durability of paperboard containers. To date, APPEC has established support and recognition for recovery programs in at least 10 major U.S. cities and has provided product and process informational kits to manufacturers, legislators, and the general public.

Product and Process Innovations

The U.S. folding paperboard box industry has been very aggressive over the last decade in improving its overall productivity and expanding its range of products. This industry has the reputation of providing excellent technical and sales service, innovative packaging ideas, and flexibility in response to customers' requests. As a result, the industry has become increasingly competitive in an increasingly competitive packaging materials market. The industry has enhanced its printing, pressing, folding, and die-cutting technologies in recent years, establishing itself as a quality supplier of environmentally preferable packaging. Although competition from other packaging alternatives (plastics and corrugated products) has increased in recent years, the industry has experienced slow but steady growth in sales over the last decade.

Domestic folding carton producers have expanded their customer bases to include some nontraditional end-use markets. Those markets include cartons and boxes for software and computer-related products; alcoholic beverages, including wines and champagnes; photographic equipment and supplies; and new restaurant and fast-food businesses. Domestic and foreign customers have responded strongly to new lighter-weight, more attractively styled (including multicolored graphics and designs), and more tamper-resistant features. Utilizing this type of protective, visually appealing packaging, folding carton producers have aggressively pursued increased sales opportunities in the high-value pharmaceutical, soap, cosmetics, and toiletries end-use segments as well as the traditional food, bakery, and related products segments. In addition, U.S. folding carton producers have improved their overall operating efficiencies to keep operating costs down and remain competitive in the large U.S. packaging sector. As the industry's more mature markets have begun to experience either fluctuating or stagnating sales, the industry has moved to offer a wider range of modernized, upscaled products to spur consumption. Efforts to increase sales to a larger proportion of the generic and private label marketers in hopes of making inroads into the national brands' market share have led to higher demand for folding cartons in a number of markets.

Industry Structure

According to the 1992 Census of Manufactures report, the domestic folding carton industry consists of 445 companies operating 599 establishments. This reflects a slight decline from the similar 1987 report. These estimates vary noticeably from industry sources. In 1998, a leading publication reported new figures of approximately 300 companies operating 495 folding carton plants in the United States, essentially unchanged from the 1997 level. Although the industry had announced several new folding carton installations, an equal number of facilities were closed, acquired, merged, or sold. The survey indicates that the reason for the discrepancy between the government and industry reports is that many of the facilities in the government data are considered very small or captive operations that produce only minimal output for specific packaging applications. These facilities are not included in the overall industry statistics.

Shipments by the U.S. folding carton industry are broken down into four principal geographic regions: eastern, southern, north central, and western. The north central region continues to be the leading geographic region for folding carton shipments, accounting for over 44 percent of the industry total. The southern and eastern regions follow at about 28 percent and 20 percent, respectively, while the western region remains at slightly over 7 percent. The southern region continues to be the fastest-growing carton-producing region, while the share of the western region continues to slip.

Folding Carton End-Use Market Profile

The fastest-growing end user, the beverage carrier industry, continues to be one of the most competitive and innovative sectors for domestic folding carton producers. As soft drink consumption has increased in recent years, the industry has developed a number of different display units, a variety of carton designs, and creative advertising and packaging products for holding 12 to 24 cans. With many soft drink companies expanding their product lines to include different varieties (regular versus diet, caffeine versus decaffeinated), the folding carton sector has been able to provide the necessary products and services for different customers' requirements. The beer industry has been responsive to the "cube" and "twin stack" carton adaptations typically utilized by the soft drink industry. Colorful graphics and eye-catching displays have proved to be effective advertising schemes for domestic beer producers. Competition in the dry foods area, especially for snack-related foods and breakfast cereals, has increased tremendously in recent years. The snack food and breakfast cereal industries have been very aggressive in their promotional efforts in recent years, and folding carton manufacturers have been able to use new and innovative advertising campaigns and gimmicks to attract many new customers in these dry food segments. U.S. folding carton producers have created many new products for this competitive sector, including some for pretzels, popcorn, chips, and cookies and for a number of different breakfast cereals. The prospects for this area look equally positive as these sectors continue to show flexibility in developing new and different dry food varieties.

International Competitiveness

International trade for the U.S. folding carton industry falls essentially under two separate commodity groupings. The first is under Harmonized System (HS) code 4819.20.0020, which includes sanitary food and beverage containers of noncorrugated paper and paperboard. The second is under HS code 4819.20.0040, which includes folding cartons, boxes, and cases of noncorrugated paper and paperboard.

U.S. exports of all folding carton sector–related commodities in 1999 totaled 135,700 metric tons and were valued at $240 million. This represents increases of 1 percent and 5 percent, respectively, over the 1998 levels. In 1999, folding cartons represented about two-thirds of the total quantity shipped and sanitary food and beverage containers made up one-third.

Exports of sanitary food and beverage containers totaled 30,800 metric tons in 1999, a 13 percent decline in the quantity shipped from the 1998 level. This was the second decline in U.S. exports of noncorrugated sanitary food and beverage containers over the last 7 years. Fortunately, U.S. suppliers were able to make up for the significant drop in the quantity shipped by increasing prices in certain markets, resulting in an overall increase in the value of U.S. exports. On a quantity basis, the leading U.S. sanitary food and beverage container export markets in 1999 were Mexico (25 percent), Canada (35 percent), and Panama (10 percent).

In 1999, U.S. exports of finished folding cartons totaled 104,900 metric tons, a 3.4 percent increase in the volume of exports. The increase in foreign demand, combined with local folding carton shortages in certain Asian and Latin American markets, enabled the industry to pass along several price increases in 1999, boosting the value of those shipments. As a result of the recovery of certain Asian economies in 1999, U.S. suppliers of folding cartons were able to increase their exports to some east Asian markets, including Hong Kong (up 28 percent). The leading U.S. export markets (on a quantity basis) for finished folding cartons in 1999 were Canada (43 percent), Mexico (38 percent), and China (5 percent).

The continued expansion of the U.S. economy in 1999 resulted in an increase in demand for a variety of shipping containers, cartons, boxes, and related packaging materials, including folding carton–related products. In 1999, sanitary food and beverage containers represented 30 percent of the total quantity imported and finished folding cartons represented 70 percent. In recent years, the import share of sanitary food and beverage containers has risen substantially because of moderate growth in U.S. demand by the domestic soda and beer end-use markets.

In 1999, U.S. imports of sanitary food and beverage containers totaled 43,000 metric tons. This reflects a 2 percent increase in the quantity shipped. Canada is by far the leading supplier to the U.S. market with a 91 percent market share. The only other noteworthy suppliers in 1999 were Denmark (4 percent) and Venezuela (2 percent).

In 1999, U.S. imports of finished folding cartons totaled 117,110 metric tons. The level of imports in 1999 increased 2 percent. As is the case with most paper and paperboard products, Canada is by far the largest supplier of folding cartons to the U.S. market. In 1999, Canada supplied 87 percent of the finished folding cartons imported into the United States. Other suppliers included China (5 percent), Taiwan (2 percent), and the Netherlands (1 percent).

Prospects for the Year 2000

Product shipments by the U.S. folding paperboard box industry should increase 1.2 percent in real terms in the year 2000, buoyed by the continued expansion of the U.S. economy, and this should translate into higher consumer spending, increased real disposable income, and increased consumer purchases of nondurable food products (fast-food items and dry foods). Economic growth in important export markets, combined with a comparatively high-valued U.S. dollar, will translate into higher overseas demand and a 2 percent increase (on a quantity basis) in U.S. exports of sanitary food and beverage containers and finished folding cartons. However, U.S. imports of these products should again reach an all-time record in 2000 as a stronger U.S.

economy leads to increased demand for folding cartons and a 3 percent increase (on a volume basis) in U.S. imports.

If historical paperboard packaging trends continue, the industry should see higher shipments not only because of the stronger U.S. economy but also as a result of the growth of domestic box consumer inventories. Most of the industry's end-use markets should grow in the year 2000 as a result of the improved U.S. economy. The strength of the folding paperboard box industry has always been in its ability to adapt to an ever-changing domestic packaging sector and develop new products to maintain its end-user market share. The industry's new technologies and equipment have allowed the development of lighter-weight, more colorful graphics, producing more visually appealing boxes without sacrificing the folding carton's dimensional stability and structural integrity. The industry is expected to continue its gradual increase in the use of flexography printing at the expense of the more traditional rotogravure process. This should reduce the industry's printing costs and improve production turnaround time. About 25 to 30 percent of the industry uses flexography.

Long-Term Prospects

Product shipments of folding paperboard containers and boxes should increase about 1.6 percent annually over the next 5 years as the domestic economy grows around 2.2 percent per year. Exports and imports of folding carton products should increase about 6 and 7 percent, respectively, on a quantity basis annually throughout the 5-year period. Mexico and Canada will remain the principal export markets, but the industry will develop a number of new, nontraditional markets over the next year, primarily in Latin America, east Asia, and eastern Europe.

The north central region of the United States will remain the industry's largest consumer market, but the south will continue to be the fastest-growing production and sales region for domestic folding carton producers. The eastern region, with improving economies in portions of New York, New Jersey, and Pennsylvania, also should see sales increase, but the growth will fluctuate more than it does in the southern region. The western region has experienced a slow decline over the last decade because of natural disaster damage in California and the decline in the Mexican economy and the devaluation of the Mexican peso. Nevertheless, sales in this region should stabilize in the range of 7 to 7.5 percent of total shipments as California's economy improves and gains in Washington and Oregon also take place.

Competition in the U.S. packaging sector is expected to escalate in the future as makers of plastic packaging and other paperboard packaging products (corrugated and solid fiber boxes) attempt to develop new end-use markets at the expense of the folding paperboard box market's share. However, with continuing improvements in process technologies, product development, and operating efficiencies, the folding carton industry is well positioned not only to secure traditional end users but to expand into new product sectors. The functional durability of the folding carton will find increased uses for products such as soaps, pharmaceutical and medicinal products, alcoholic and soft drink beverages, and fast and frozen foods. The industry's environmental performance should capture sales from companies and organizations seeking to utilize products that are environmentally preferable or have a minimal environmental impact. The industry's continuing attempts to promote its environmental efforts will continue to reap benefits.

Sarah Smiley, U.S. Department of Commerce, Office of Metals, Materials, and Chemicals, (202) 482-0577, September 1999.

REFERENCES

Boxboard Containers, Maclean Hunter Publishing Co., 29 North Wacker Drive, Chicago, IL 60606. (312) 726-2802.

Fibre Box Association, 2850 Golf Road, Rolling Meadows, IL 60008. (847) 364-9600.

Monthly Statistical Summary, American Forest and Paper Association, 1111 19th Street, NW, Suite 800, Washington, DC 20036. (202) 463-2700.

1994–1998 Paper, Paperboard, and Pulp Capacity and Fiber Consumption, American Forest and Paper Association, 1111 19th Street, NW, Suite 800, Washington, DC 20036. (202) 463-2700.

1995–1998 Statistics of Paper, Paperboard, and Wood Pulp, American Forest and Paper Association, 1111 19th Street, NW, Suite 800, Washington, DC 20036. (202) 463-2700.

North American Factbook, Miller Freeman Publications, 600 Harrison Street, San Francisco, CA 94107. (415) 905-2200.

Paper Age, Global Publications, Inc., 51 Mill Street, Hanover, MA 02339. (617) 829-4581.

Paperboard Packaging Council, 888 17 Street, Suite 900, Washington, DC 20006. (202) 289-4100.

Papermaker Magazine, 57 Executive Park, Suite 310, Atlanta, GA 30329. (404) 325-9153.

Pulp and Paper, Miller Freeman Publications, 600 Harrison Street, San Francisco, CA 94107. (415) 905-2200.

Pulp and Paper International, Miller Freeman Publications, 600 Harrison Street, San Francisco, CA 94107. (415) 905-2200.

TAPPI Journal, Technology Park/Atlanta, P.O. Box 105113, Atlanta, GA 30348. (404) 446-1400.

Walden's Fiber and Board Report, Walden-Mott Publications, 225 North Franklin Turnpike, Ramsey, NJ 07446. (201) 818-8630.

RELATED CHAPTERS

7: Wood Products

18: Production Machinery

25: Printing and Publishing

CHEMICALS AND ALLIED PRODUCTS
Economic and Trade Trends

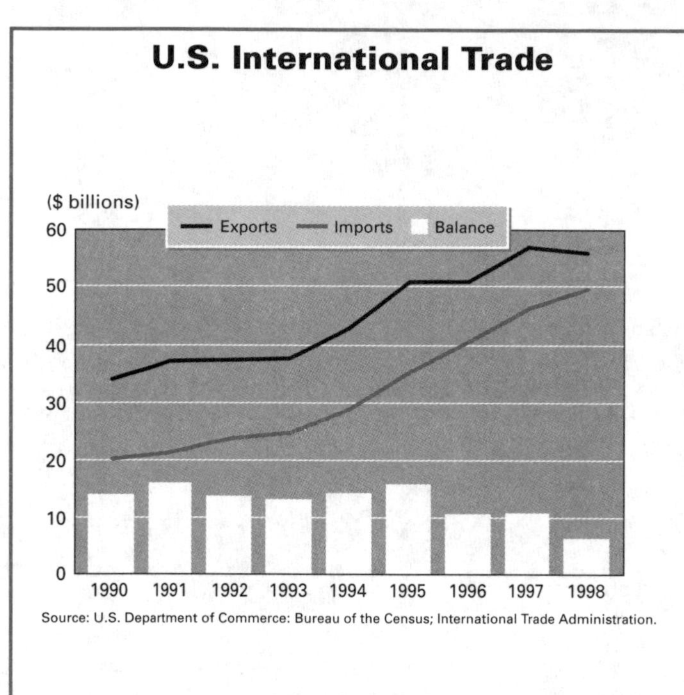

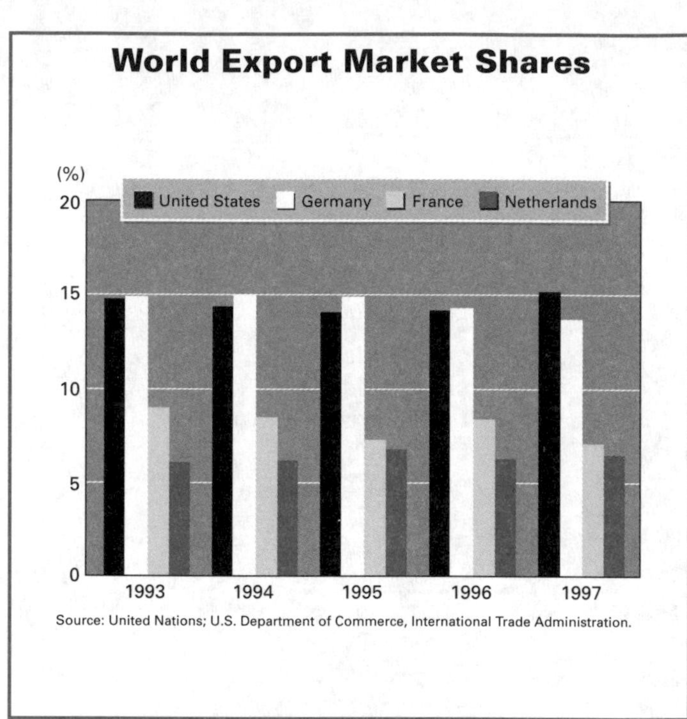

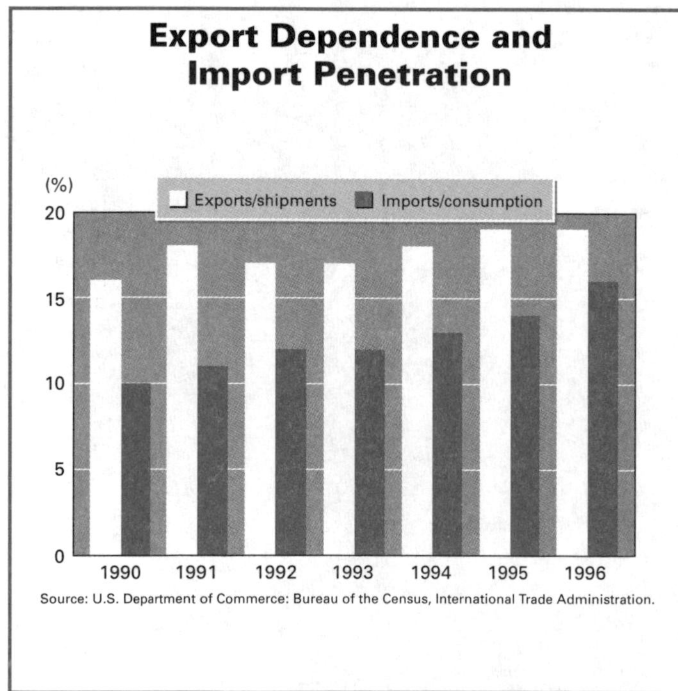

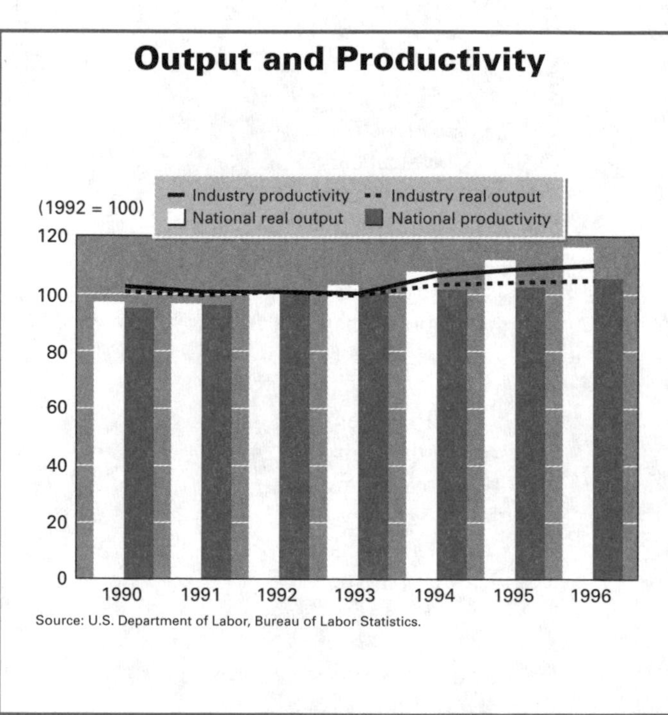

See "Getting the Most Out of *Outlook 2000*" for definitions of terms.

11

Chemicals and Allied Products

INDUSTRY DEFINITION This chapter contains sections on the chemical industry (SIC 28) and the following subsectors: industrial inorganic chemicals (SIC 281), industrial organic chemicals (SIC 286), agricultural chemicals (part of SIC 287), miscellaneous chemical products (SIC 289), plastic materials and resins (SIC 2821), and drugs and pharmaceuticals (SIC 283). Cellulosic and noncellulosic man-made fibers (SIC 2823 and 2824) are covered in Chapter 9, "Textiles."

OVERVIEW

Often referred to as the keystone industry because nearly every other sector of the manufacturing economy uses its products, the U.S. chemical industry ranks among the world's leading industries, with U.S. chemical companies accounting for an estimated one-quarter of total world chemical production. The industry includes hundreds of companies with over 12,000 plants that produce over 70,000 different chemical products, ranging from raw materials for other industries to a wide variety of finished consumer products. Chemical building blocks are used in nearly all nonfood consumer and industrial products.

The U.S. chemical and allied products industry, with about $391 billion in shipments in 1998, is the world's largest supplier of chemicals and accounts for about 25 percent of total world chemical production. Chemicals are one of the nation's largest industries, representing about 11.5 percent of all U.S. manufacturing on a value-added basis and 1.9 percent of gross domestic product (GDP). Chemical companies employ over 1.04 million persons in the United States, equal to 5.5 percent of all the workers employed in manufacturing.

The U.S. chemical industry is also one of the country's largest exporting industries, generating over 10 percent of the nation's total exports and 13 percent of all world exports of chemicals. According to data provided by the Chemical Manufacturers Association (CMA), chemical industry exports in 1998 totaled $68 billion, down 2 percent from 1997, while imports rose 8.5 percent to reach $54.6 billion. The industry's trade surplus narrowed to $10.1 billion, the lowest surplus since 1988. Although the Asian economic crisis was the main factor in the poor trade balance, that decline also reflected reduced demand from the Middle East and central and eastern Europe coupled with increased imports from those regions into the United States. In 1999, exports were expected to decline slightly and imports were expected to rise about 7 percent, and the industry's balance of trade was likely to drop to about $8 billion. Firmer economies in Asia should help lift exports in the year 2000, resulting in an improved trade picture.

In 1998, worldwide chemical shipments of slightly less than $1.6 trillion were up about 0.75 percent from the 1997 level, according to data provided by the CMA. This sluggish growth contrasted with an average annual gain of 4.2 percent in the 1994–1997 period. The softening trend largely reflected the effect of the widespread financial crisis in Asia. Global dollar shipments also were affected by falling prices stemming from oversupply conditions in many principal product categories. Unit shipments to the Asia-Pacific region dropped 2.25 percent in real terms in 1998, including a 4.5 percent decline in Japan. By contrast, most major markets in western Europe grew at rates in excess of the world average, especially in France and Italy. Boosted by new capacity, chemical shipments to Mexico increased 4.25 percent and shipments to Canada rose 3.75 percent. According to the CMA, the Asia-Pacific region accounted for 31 percent of global chemical shipments in 1998, western Europe for 29 percent, North America for 27 percent, Latin America for 6 percent, and other areas for the remaining 7 percent.

World exports of chemicals totaled $510 billion in 1998, according to CMA data. With chemicals now manufactured throughout the world, prices are determined by global supply and demand conditions and the discounting tactics used by leading producers to gain market share. According to Chemical Market Associates, Inc. (CMAI), worldwide capacity in base chemicals (light olefins, aromatics, chlor-alkali, and methanol) will expand from about 250 million tons in 1990 to close to 400 million tons in the year 2000. World chemical consumption of 300 million tons in 1998 was divided as follows, according to CMAI: light olefins (ethylene and propylene), 43 percent; chlor-alkali (chlorine and caustic soda), 30 percent; aromatics (benzene and mixed xylenes), 18 percent; and methanol, 9 percent.

The industry is also capital-intensive, a large user of energy resources, and heavily regulated, factors that provide high entry barriers to new competition. U.S. chemical companies consume about 7 percent of total annual U.S. energy output. Most of the industry's energy consumption involves natural gas and oil, with the balance consisting largely of electricity and coal.

Most of the industry's production consists of commodity chemicals, with demand largely a function of general economic activity in the U.S. market and overseas markets. Industry profitability is determined largely by raw material costs, export demand, pricing trends in world chemical markets, and capacity utilization. Trends in interest rates, inflation, and manufacturing as well as marketing costs also can have a significant impact on profits.

Chemicals are produced from raw materials such as oil, natural gas, metals, minerals, and air, which are further processed into chemical intermediates and industrial and consumer goods. The automobile and housing sectors are key markets, although chemicals find their way into nearly all manufactured products.

Key trends affecting leading U.S.-based chemical companies include specialization, globalization, and consolidation. With an eye toward increasing profits and the return to shareholders, chemical firms are divesting low-margin commodity businesses to concentrate on higher-margin specialty chemical businesses. Other firms are attempting to achieve greater profitability through mergers and acquisitions. The value of all merger and acquisition activity in the worldwide chemical industry was expected to exceed $45 billion in 1999, including the planned $11.3 billion merger of Dow Chemical and Union Carbide. The value of all merger and acquisition activity in 1998 totaled $37.3 billion, according to Young & Partners.

INDUSTRIAL INORGANIC CHEMICALS

This subsector covers developments in the industrial inorganic chemicals industry (SIC 281), which includes four main product groups: alkalies and chlorine (SIC 2812); industrial gases such as nitrogen, oxygen, and carbon dioxide (SIC 2813); inorganic pigments such as titanium dioxide and iron oxide (SIC 2816); and miscellaneous inorganics, including acids, aluminum compounds, potassium and sodium compounds, and catalysts, among many others (SIC 2819). Accounting for the bulk of chemical industry production, inorganic chemicals are derived from earth materials such as minerals and the atmosphere.

Global Industry Trends

With U.S. markets for commodity inorganic chemicals such as the automobile and housing industries considered relatively mature, most future growth for these products is expected to come from developing nations in Asia and Latin America. Exports account for close to 30 percent of total inorganic chemical production, with domestic markets accounting for the remaining 70 percent. Key U.S. export markets include Canada and Mexico, which accounted for 28 percent of inorganic chemical exports in 1998, followed by western Europe at 23 percent, Japan and China at 22 percent, Latin America at 10 percent, the rest of Asia at 11 percent, and other areas at 6 percent (see Table 11-1). With depressed economic conditions, particularly in Asia, continuing to affect this market, exports of inorganic chemicals were expected to decline almost 5 percent in 1999, after a drop of over 8 percent in 1998 (see Table 11-2).

Despite the recent downturn in export volumes, long-term business prospects remain favorable. Some improvement in export volume is anticipated in the year 2000, generated by firming economic trends in Japan and other Asian countries. In addition, key export markets in North America have continued to be resilient. The North American Free Trade Agreement (NAFTA) partners Canada and Mexico, along with Latin America, account for about 38 percent of total U.S. inorganic chemical exports, and growth in those regions is expected to remain respectable.

U.S. Industry Outlook

Key factors affecting domestic demand for inorganic chemicals include the health of end-use markets, environmental regulations, and trends in foreign trade. Inorganic chemicals are used primarily by the construction, paper, packaging, paints and coatings, and fertilizer industries. Those markets are influenced by the overall health of the U.S. economy and by consumer spending trends.

After declining 5.6 percent in 1998, industrial production of inorganic chemicals was sluggish through much of 1999. Demand from export markets remained weak, and many domestic markets slumped. However, this situation is expected to improve somewhat in the year 2000, with growth through 2003 projected to be in the range of 2 percent per year, boosted by cyclical improvement in U.S. industrial production.

The sectors expected to exhibit the best growth are industrial gases and titanium dioxide. Chlorine shipments also should begin to improve over the next few years, helped by better demand from the pulp and paper industry and greater use of polyvinyl chloride (PVC) plastic products. Inorganic chemicals include a large number of items, with the most important being alkalies and chlorine, industrial gases, and inorganic pigments such as titanium dioxide.

TABLE 11-1: U.S. Trade Patterns in Industrial Inorganic Chemicals[1] in 1998
(millions of dollars; percent)

Exports			Imports		
Region[2]	Value[3]	Share, %	Region[2]	Value[3]	Share, %
NAFTA	1,822	28	NAFTA	1,629	27
Latin America	680	10	Latin America	459	8
Western Europe	1,512	23	Western Europe	1,685	28
Japan/Chinese Economic Area	1,408	22	Japan/Chinese Economic Area	747	12
Other Asia	726	11	Other Asia	120	2
Rest of world	389	6	Rest of world	1,375	23
World	6,538	100	World	6,014	100
Top Five Countries	Value	Share, %	Top Five Countries	Value	Share, %
Canada	1,181	18	Canada	1,364	23
Japan	1,057	16	Germany	611	10
Mexico	641	10	Australia	611	10
Belgium	370	6	Russia	459	8
South Korea	331	5	Japan	421	7

[1] SIC 281.
[2] For definitions of regional groupings, see "Getting the Most Out of *Outlook 2000.*"
[3] Values may not sum to total due to rounding.
Source: U.S. Department of Commerce, Bureau of the Census.

Alkalies and Chlorine

The principal products manufactured by the chlor-alkali industry (SIC 2812) include chlorine, caustic soda, soda ash, sodium bicarbonate, and potassium hydroxide. Chlorine and caustic soda dominate the industry, accounting for more over 80 percent of total demand, and soda ash accounts for about 15 percent. Chlorine production totaled 12.8 billion tons in 1998, down from $13.0 billion tons in 1997. Industry shipments were estimated at about $2.8 billion in 1998.

Chlorine and caustic soda (sodium hydroxide) are manufactured by a chemical process called electrolysis. This technique is accomplished by passing electricity through brine (a salt and water solution), triggering a chemical reaction that results in the recombination of salt (sodium chloride) and water (hydrogen and oxygen) to form chlorine and sodium hydroxide. The process yields 1.1 parts of caustic soda to 1 part of chlorine. Because chlorine is difficult to store, production is geared to meet immediate demand. Thus, the availability of caustic soda

TABLE 11-2: Industrial Inorganic Chemicals (SIC 281) Trends and Forecasts
(millions of dollars except as noted)

										Percent Change			
	1992	1993	1994	1995	1996	1997[1]	1998[1]	1999[2]	2000[3]	97–98	98–99	99–00	96–00[4]
Industry data													
Value of shipments[5]	27,332	26,339	25,018	26,667	27,741	28,950	29,600	30,300	31,100	2.2	2.4	2.6	2.9
Value of shipments (1992$)	27,332	26,092	24,358	24,744	25,052	26,100	25,500	25,800	26,200	−2.3	1.2	1.6	1.1
Total employment (thousands)	103	93.7	86.5	81.8	80.2								
Production workers (thousands)	54.9	49.7	46.7	45.4	45.2								
Average hourly earnings ($)	16.59	16.93	17.87	19.00	20.74								
Capital expenditures	1,553	1,179	1,304	1,708	2,002								
Product data													
Value of shipments[5]	22,090	21,845	21,286	23,992	24,920	26,020	26,600	27,240	27,950	2.2	2.4	2.6	2.9
Value of shipments (1992$)	22,090	21,670	20,729	22,064	22,333	23,450	22,900	23,170	23,540	−2.3	1.2	1.6	1.3
Trade data													
Value of imports	4,183	3,998	4,389	5,189	5,882	5,953	6,014	6,100	6,190	1.0	1.4	1.5	1.3
Value of exports	5,324	4,926	5,309	6,145	6,254	7,121	6,538	6,250	6,380	−8.2	−4.4	2.1	0.5

[1] Estimate except imports and exports.
[2] Estimate.
[3] Forecast.
[4] Compound annual rate.
[5] For a definition of industry versus product values, see "Getting the Most Out of *Outlook 2000.*"
Source: U.S. Department of Commerce: Bureau of the Census; International Trade Administration.

is dictated by the level of chlorine production, creating cyclical problems in matching chlorine and caustic supplies with demand. Chlorine is used in the production of both organic and inorganic chemicals, including chlorinated solvents, titanium dioxide, and propylene oxide; as a feedstock in the manufacture of PVC; as a pulp and paper bleach; and as a sanitizing agent in water treatment. Caustic soda is used in soaps and detergents, water treatment, oil drilling, and textiles and fibers.

The chlor-alkali industry experienced a cyclical downturn during 1998 and through the first half of 1999 as prices deteriorated under pressure from increased industry overcapacity coupled with weakness in demand from the pulp and paper industry. On an electrochemical unit (ECU) (a combined price of chlorine and caustic soda) basis, prices of chlor-alkali products during the first half of 1999 were at their lowest level in over 20 years. However, the market showed signs of improvement during the second half of that year, and prices started to firm. The better pricing environment reflected tighter supply and demand conditions as well as improved demand from the pulp and paper and oil refining industries. Prices also benefited from short supplies caused by unplanned outages at several producers, including the effects of a plant explosion at a key producer. Demand from U.S. markets should continue to be healthy over the next few years.

Demand for PVC, which accounts for close to a third of chlorine production, will be a key driver of chlorine demand over the coming years. The second largest volume plastic, PVC, is used primarily by the housing and construction industries. The PVC market has risen in importance for the chlorine industry in recent years as environmental regulations have affected chlor-alkali use in solvents, pesticides, and chlorofluorocarbons (CFCs).

Improving economies in Asia also should bolster this business in the year 2000. Over 40 percent of U.S. vinyl chloride (the raw material for PVC) production is shipped to Asian markets. Boosted by better foreign markets, worldwide chlorine demand is expected to expand 2.5 percent per year through 2002. By comparison, domestic demand is expected to grow only 1.5 percent in that period.

As caustic soda production is linked to chlorine, the 1998–1999 slump in the chlorine market was reflected in caustic soda. Caustic soda prices declined in 1999, largely as a result of reduced demand from the pulp and paper industry, which accounts for about 18 percent of caustic soda production. Pricing also has been under pressure from capacity additions in the United States and abroad. New facilities were expected to boost total U.S. chlor-alkali capacity about 5 percent in 1999. Largely as a result of the new plants, domestic producers were operating at about 91 percent of capacity in 1991, down from 98 percent in 1997. Although operating rates in 2000 are not likely to improve much, increased demand, particularly from emerging markets, should help prices stay firm. Worldwide demand growth over the next 4 years should create a balance between worldwide production and consumption and facilitate an improved pricing environment.

Soda ash (sodium carbonate) is a naturally occurring mineral whose primary use is in glass production, which accounts for nearly half of total demand. It also is used as a sodium source in chemical production, as a detergent builder, in pulp and paper, and in environmental and water treatment products. U.S. soda ash production dropped 9.8 percent to 10.7 million tons in 1998 as the business was affected by the Asian economic slowdown. Exports constitute a vital market for U.S. soda ash producers, accounting for about 35 percent of total domestic production.

With exports to Asia accounting for nearly half of all American soda ash exports, the Asian slump continued to affect this market negatively in 1999, with total production levels not expected to vary appreciably from 1998 levels. A better performance is seen for the year 2000, boosted by economic recovery in Asia and improved demand from the domestic glass market.

Although the overall market for soda ash in the United States is mature, demand from the glass industry has picked up in recent years, with a resurgence of glass usage in many container markets. Accounting for about half of U.S. soda ash consumption, the glass industry has regained market share in certain glass container markets. Although competition from plastic packaging and aluminum beverage cans will limit its growth in soft drink markets, glass remains the preferred bottle material in the wine and beer industries, which are experiencing respectable growth. Demand for soda ash also has increased from the chemical industry, where soda ash has benefited from the increased price of caustic soda, opening up opportunities in swing markets that can use either one as a raw material.

Industrial Gases

Demand for industrial gases in the United States is expected to increase about 5 percent annually through 2004, driven primarily by growth in large-volume gases such as nitrogen, oxygen, and hydrogen. Other important gas products include carbon dioxide, argon, acetylene, and helium. Niche markets exist for krypton, neon, and xenon. Oxygen is used extensively to fire kilns in the steel and building products industries, and liquid oxygen and liquid hydrogen are used in rocket fuel. Nitrogen is used in the brewing industry, rubber tire industry, and other industries, and argon is used in the manufacture of stainless steel and in fluorescent light bulbs.

Production of nitrogen increased 4.2 percent in 1998, but unit volumes of hydrogen dropped 9.1 percent and oxygen production fell 5.1 percent. Demand for industrial gases will continue to be heavily reliant on the chemical, oil refining, and primary metals industries. However, the strongest gains will occur in the electronics industry and in smaller niche markets such as oil recovery and water treatment applications. Hydrogen has been one of the fastest-growing sectors in this market in recent years, boosted by rising demand from the oil refining industry, which uses hydrogen to process crude oil and oil residues.

An important technological development in the industrial gas industry involves the continuing diffusion of noncryogenic air separation technology, particularly membrane systems, pressure swing adsorption (PSA), and vacuum PSA. Although more traditional cryogenic air separation technology will retain the high-volume and high-purity segments of the industrial gas market, noncryogenic methods offer a highly cost-effective alternative for smaller customers for the major atmospheric gases: nitrogen and oxygen. These developments have prompted gas customers to reevaluate their purity requirements and methods of delivery, and most major gas companies now offer customers on-site noncryogenic options in areas where those methods can result in substantial cost savings.

Although the chemical and primary metal industries are mature markets, gas demand from those markets exceeds secular growth in end-market chemicals and metals, reflecting greater usage of industrial gases compared with competing materials. For example, the use of nitrogen for inerting applications in the chemicals industry is growing as a result of the greater availability of less costly noncryogenic materials. Meanwhile, hydrogen is finding greater use in petroleum refineries because of Clean Air Act mandates that necessitate the hydrosulfurization of petroleum products to produce cleaner-burning fuels.

Oxygen is by far the largest-volume gas used in the production of primary metals, where it fuels the basic oxygen furnaces that convert pig iron into steel as well as blast furnaces and open hearth furnaces. Using oxygen instead of air in furnaces enhances combustion, reduces energy consumption, and reduces emissions, particularly of nitrous oxides. These advantages are promoting the use of oxygen in combustion processes in many other industries, such as glass manufacturing. Oxygen and acetylene also provide combustible heat sources in welding operations, while carbon dioxide, argon, and helium are used as shielding gases to protect the welding surface.

The electronics industry will remain a leading outlet for high-purity gases, particularly nitrogen, which is used to create an oxygen-free atmosphere that is conducive to the production of sensitive components such as semiconductors and printed circuit boards. Nitrogen also is being used in new packaging materials that provide longer shelf lives for perishable foods and beverages. However, oil recovery will remain the market's most rapidly expanding sector, boosted by the cost-effectiveness of using gases such as nitrogen and carbon dioxide to improve yields.

Exports in most industrial gases are not significant because of prohibitively high shipping costs. However, foreign trade is important in niche gases such as helium. With its large natural deposits, the United States holds a dominant world position in the supply of helium.

Pigments and Other Inorganic Chemicals

As most of their major markets are relatively mature, growth in demand for inorganic pigments and other inorganic chemicals is not expected to exceed growth in GDP in the foreseeable future. The U.S. market for other inorganic chemicals includes commodity products such as sodium and potassium chemicals, aluminum compounds, and inorganic pigments. Hundreds of chemical compounds can be formed by utilizing sodium and potassium chemicals because of their high reactivity, which allows them to combine with numerous other chemicals. Key end markets include the water treatment, pulp and paper, fertilizer, soap and detergent, food and beverage, metals, textile, and leather processing industries.

Consumption of aluminum compounds such as aluminum oxide, aluminum hydroxide, and aluminum sulfate is expected to roughly track growth in GDP. Aluminum oxide (alumina) should benefit from growing demand for aluminum metal in the packaging, transportation, construction, and electrical equipment and electronics markets. Aluminum hydroxide is increasing its share of the flame retardant products market because of its environmental advantages over competing products, particularly halogenated flame retardants. Demand for aluminum sulfate (alum) will benefit from growing concern about the presence of organic carbon in water supplies. Municipal and industrial water treatment facilities are expected to increase their use of alum to enhance organic carbon removal via coagulation.

Since the United States has virtually no commercially significant deposits of bauxite, the ore from which aluminum metal and chemicals are made, basic bauxite demand will continue to be satisfied by foreign sources, primarily Jamaica and Suriname. However, the United States is largely self-sufficient in downstream aluminum compounds, including alumina, aluminum sulfate, and aluminum hydroxide.

Demand for titanium dioxide, the largest-volume inorganic pigment, is expected to be somewhat stronger than that for most other pigments, stimulated by its unique qualities and increased demand from the pulp and paper industry. Used as the primary white pigment in paper and paperboard, plastics, synthetic rubber, and coatings, titanium dioxide has an extremely high ability to reflect light and add brightness to products. After showing annual compound growth of 3 to 4 percent through 1997, production of titanium dioxide slipped 0.1 percent in 1998, primarily as a result of reduced shipments to Asia, which accounts for about 25 percent of world demand. After another indicated modest decline in 1999, demand should grow in the range of 2 to 3 percent through 2003.

The global titanium dioxide industry has exhibited increased merger and acquisition activity in recent years as companies sought to join forces to compete more effectively during the downturn experienced in 1998 and 1999. Consolidation activity also has been a response to a weaker pricing environment resulting from substantial overcapacity, which has left producers with eroding margins despite robust growth in demand.

INDUSTRIAL ORGANIC CHEMICALS

This subsector covers developments in the industrial organic chemicals industry (SIC 286), which includes organic dyes and pigments, aromatics such as benzene and toluene, gum and wood chemicals, pesticides, alcohols, and various cyclic intermediates, such as cumene, cyclohexane, and styrene, along with many other organic chemicals. All organic chemicals contain carbon and come in liquid and solid forms.

Global Industry Trends

Consisting primarily of petrochemicals, dyes, and pigments, the global organic chemical market is becoming increasingly competitive as new suppliers emerge from developing nations.

Although traditionally dominated by the United States, Germany, and Japan, this sector has had considerable capacity added in recent years from companies in Asia, the Middle East, and Latin America. That trend should continue despite the recent financial crisis in Asia.

The global petrochemical industry had a tough year in 1998 as it was beset by worldwide overcapacity, declining prices, and reduced shipments to Asian markets. Although lingering financial difficulties in Asia continued to affect this business in the first half of 1999, substantial price hikes implemented during that year should help top line comparisons in the year 2000. In 1999, international price increases in major petrochemical products were triggered by increases in raw material (naphtha) prices and increasing demand from some markets. The chemical industry is sensitive to changes in oil and gas prices, as both of those materials represent basic chemical feedstocks and key energy sources that fuel manufacturing processes.

With important derivatives uses in plastics and fibers, ethylene is the largest-selling organic chemical. Reflecting higher oil feedstock costs and better supply and demand conditions, ethylene prices rose materially in 1999. According to estimates by SRI Consulting, ethylene feedstocks should be adequate to meet world demand through 2005 despite projected growth in demand of 4 percent per year and growth of 2 percent in the rate of global production.

U.S. Industry Outlook

Key factors affecting the U.S. organic chemical industry include the prospects for key end-use markets and competition from foreign producers. As a result of the commodity nature of many of these chemicals, currency fluctuations also play an important role in global shipment patterns. Industrial organic chemicals are used primarily in the production of fuels, plastics, fibers, elastomers, fertilizers, and a broad range of other chemical products. Organic chemicals encompass a broad range of products, the majority of which are intermediates in the production of other chemicals.

After rising for many years, production of industrial organic chemicals dropped 5.7 percent in 1998, largely reflecting the downturn in petrochemical production and the reduced export opportunities caused by recession in key Asian economies. Exports of organic chemicals, a good deal of which are shipped to the Far East, dropped almost 9 percent in 1998 (see Table 11-3). Organic chemical production continued to slide in 1999, although the rate of decline subsided somewhat. With recovery in Asian economies, total domestic industrial organic chemicals production was expected to decline modestly in 1999.

However, some improvement is projected for the year 2000, with growth increasing almost 3 percent annually through 2004. That gain should reflect a cyclical upturn in the petrochemical industry and improvement in the overall global economy. The United States is expected to remain a net exporter of organic chemicals but will have a significantly smaller surplus than that which it averaged over the last decade because of strong competition from export-oriented producers in Asia and the Middle East.

The trade balance in industrial organic chemicals has eroded in recent years, with the value of exports exceeding that of imports by only 5 percent in 1998. Important export markets are western Europe, 33 percent; Canada and Mexico, 26 percent; east Asia, 14 percent; Latin America, 13 percent; and other regions, 14 percent (see Table 11-4). About 45 percent of imports came from western Europe, 17 percent from Japan and China, 12 percent from Canada and Mexico, 7 percent from Latin America, and 14 percent from the rest of the world.

TABLE 11-3: Industrial Organic Chemicals (SIC 286) Trends and Forecasts
(millions of dollars except as noted)

										Percent Change			
	1992	1993	1994	1995	1996	1997[1]	1998[1]	1999[2]	2000[3]	97–98	98–99	99–00	96–00[4]
Industry data													
Value of shipments[5]	64,397	64,280	70,096	76,729	75,672	77,100	76,500	78,600	80,900	–0.8	2.7	2.9	1.7
Value of shipments (1992$)	64,397	61,826	65,700	66,020	63,902	66,250	65,500	66,550	67,750	–1.1	1.6	1.8	1.5
Total employment (thousands)	125	123	116	118	126								
Production workers (thousands)	72.3	72.9	68.5	69.7	74.7								
Average hourly earnings ($)	18.55	18.68	19.98	20.31	21.30								
Capital expenditures	4,791	4,061	3,554	4,923	6,269								
Product data													
Value of shipments[5]	59,451	59,912	65,889	73,247	71,478	72,850	72,300	74,300	76,450	–0.8	2.8	2.9	1.7
Value of shipments (1992$)	59,451	57,724	61,955	63,234	60,931	62,600	61,900	62,900	64,700	–1.1	1.6	2.9	1.5
Trade data													
Value of imports	8,179	8,327	9,807	12,276	13,823	15,774	15,364	16,000	16,300	–2.6	4.1	1.9	4.2
Value of exports	11,536	11,839	13,953	17,560	16,158	17,775	16,238	16,800	17,400	–8.6	3.5	3.6	1.9

[1] Estimate except imports and exports.
[2] Estimate.
[3] Forecast.
[4] Compound annual rate.
[5] For a definition of industry versus product values, see "Getting the Most Out of *Outlook 2000.*"
Source: U.S. Department of Commerce: Bureau of the Census; International Trade Administration.

TABLE 11-4: U.S. Trade Patterns in Industrial Organic Chemicals[1] in 1998
(millions of dollars; percent)

Exports			Imports		
Region[2]	Value[3]	Share, %	Region[2]	Value[3]	Share, %
NAFTA	4,233	26	NAFTA	1,810	12
Latin America	2,148	13	Latin America	1,042	7
Western Europe	5,284	33	Western Europe	6,884	45
Japan/Chinese Economic Area	2,299	14	Japan/Chinese Economic Area	2,626	17
Other Asia	1,435	9	Other Asia	794	5
Rest of world	839	5	Rest of world	2,209	14
World	16,238	100	World	15,364	100
Top Five Countries	Value	Share, %	Top Five Countries	Value	Share, %
Canada	2,510	15	Japan	2,073	13
Mexico	1,723	11	Germany	1,491	10
Belgium	1,246	8	Canada	1,325	9
Netherlands	1,137	7	United Kingdom	956	6
Japan	1,088	7	France	908	6

[1] SIC 286.
[2] For definitions of regional groupings, see "Getting the Most Out of *Outlook 2000*."
[3] Values may not sum to total due to rounding.
Source: U.S. Department of Commerce, Bureau of the Census.

Dyes and Organic Pigments

Domestic demand for dyes and organic pigments in the United States is projected to rise about 2 percent annually over the next 5 years, bolstered by growth in key end markets such as packaging and printing inks. Growth in demand for organic dyes also has been stimulated by ongoing shifts from inorganic to organic pigments. However, other important markets, such as plastics and paints and coatings, are expected to continue to be restricted by stringent environmental regulations that have fostered the use of other products. Demand from textile markets also has been muted in recent years.

The U.S. organic pigments business also has been hampered by heightened import competition from low-cost overseas producers of colorants. Competition from developing countries, particularly India, China, and other Asia-Pacific nations, has been especially prevalent in the textiles sector, the largest end use for colorants, because of increased organic pigment production in those countries to support their growing textile markets. U.S. producers also have expanded their operations in the Asia-Pacific region to take advantage of lower labor, environmental compliance, and other costs.

Foreign trade is significant in the organic colorants industry, with the dye sector being affected more significantly than the organic pigments sector. The United States is expected to maintain its position as a net importer of dyes and organic pigments, although exports are expected to increase much more rapidly in the years ahead. Western Europe should remain a dominant supplier to the United States, although less expensive organic colorants (particularly textile dyes) from Asia-Pacific countries should continue to apply downward pressure on most dyestuff prices, squeezing profit margins for U.S. manufacturers. Western Europe, Canada and Mexico, and the Asia-Pacific region are expected to remain the most significant markets for U.S. exports of dyes and organic pigments.

AGRICULTURAL CHEMICALS

Fertilizers

World consumption of fertilizers totaled 136.1 million tons in the 1997–1998 growing season, up 1.3 percent from the comparable 1996–1997 season, according to data provided by the International Fertilizer Industry Association (IFA). Nitrogen fertilizers accounted for 59 percent of world fertilizer consumption, phosphate fertilizers for 24 percent, and potash fertilizers for 17 percent.

The fertilizer industry is a relatively mature business in the United States, reflecting stagnancy or modest growth in the underlying American farm economy. The overall fertilizer business is highly seasonal, with the most sales occurring before the spring and fall plantings. Domestic demand is largely a function of the amount of acreage planted, with farmers' planting decisions importantly influenced by grain prices, federal support programs, and weather conditions. Other important factors affecting this business include carryover inventories from the previous year, production costs, environmental concerns, and soil moisture. A bumper crop in the previous year typically results in lower prices and reduced plantings in the current year. However, when favorable weather causes increased grain and bean yields, additional fertilizer application is needed in the current year to compensate for soil nutrient depletion.

Foreign business is important, representing about one-third of U.S. industry shipments (see Tables 11-5 and 11-6). Thus, changes in economic conditions abroad and fluctuations in currency exchange rates can materially affect the fertilizer business. China accounts for close to 33 percent of U.S. fertilizer exports; other Asia-Pacific markets, 37 percent; Latin America, 25 percent; and all other markets, 5 percent.

After 4 years of increased volume, world fertilizer consumption was expected to decline fractionally in 1999 and remain flat

TABLE 11-5: Agricultural Chemicals Except Fertilizer Mixing (SIC 2873, 2874, 2879) Trends and Forecasts
(millions of dollars except as noted)

	1992	1993	1994	1995	1996	1997[1]	1998[1]	1999[2]	2000[3]	Percent Change 97–98	98–99	99–00	96–00[4]
Industry data													
Value of shipments[5]	16,637	16,669	18,479	19,862	20,963	20,740	21,110	21,450	21,750	1.8	1.6	1.4	0.9
2873 Nitrogenous fertilizers	3,177	3,467	4,246	4,446	4,376	3,960	4,040	4,100	4,140	2.0	1.5	1.0	−1.4
2874 Phosphatic fertilizers	4,318	3,648	4,597	5,337	5,684	5,860	6,030	6,120	6,180	2.9	1.5	1.0	2.1
2879 Agricultural chemicals not elsewhere classified	9,142	9,554	9,636	10,079	10,903	10,920	11,040	11,230	11,430	1.1	1.7	1.8	1.2
Value of shipments (1992$)	16,637	16,637	16,569	16,341	16,825	16,725	16,970	17,250	17,500	1.5	1.6	1.4	1.0
2873 Nitrogenous fertilizers	3,177	3,340	3,617	3,267	3,196	2,890	2,950	3,000	3,030	2.1	1.7	1.0	−1.3
2874 Phosphatic fertilizers	4,318	4,155	4,152	4,083	4,031	4,220	4,300	4,360	4,400	1.9	1.4	0.9	2.2
2879 Agricultural chemicals not elsewhere classified	9,142	9,142	8,800	8,991	9,597	9,615	9,720	9,890	10,070	1.1	1.7	1.8	1.2
Total employment (thousands)	33.3	32.7	31.8	30.7	29.1								
2873 Nitrogenous fertilizers	7.0	7.0	8.0	7.3	7.5								
2874 Phosphatic fertilizers	9.5	9.4	8.5	8.6	7.8								
2879 Agricultural chemicals not elsewhere classified	16.8	16.3	15.3	14.8	13.8								
Production workers (thousands)	21.0	20.5	20.4	20.3	18.7								
2873 Nitrogenous fertilizers	4.7	4.7	5.4	5.1	5.1								
2874 Phosphatic fertilizers	6.7	6.6	6.2	6.5	5.8								
2879 Agricultural chemicals not elsewhere classified	9.6	9.2	8.8	8.7	7.8								
Average hourly earnings ($)	15.00	15.79	17.41	17.89	18.09								
2873 Nitrogenous fertilizers	15.66	16.11	16.69	16.37	16.95								
2874 Phosphatic fertilizers	13.84	14.70	16.69	16.75	17.30								
2879 Agricultural chemicals not elsewhere classified	15.57	16.41	18.40	19.85	19.45								
Capital expenditures	944	692	633	688	967								
2873 Nitrogenous fertilizers	209	186	175	176	305								
2874 Phosphatic fertilizers	307	150	159	194	200								
2879 Agricultural chemicals not elsewhere classified	428	356	299	318	463								
Product data													
Value of shipments[5]	15,743	15,871	17,548	19,368	20,265	20,000	20,370	20,700	20,990	1.9	1.6	1.4	0.9
2873 Nitrogenous fertilizers	3,589	3,737	4,428	4,761	4,864	4,405	4,500	4,570	4,620	2.2	1.6	1.1	−1.3
2874 Phosphatic fertilizers	3,929	3,397	4,272	4,983	5,364	5,535	5,700	5,790	5,850	3.0	1.6	1.0	2.2
2879 Agricultural chemicals not elsewhere classified	8,225	8,737	8,848	9,623	10,038	10,060	10,170	10,340	10,520	1.1	1.7	1.7	1.2
Value of shipments (1992$)	15,743	15,830	15,711	15,896	16,193	16,000	16,240	16,500	16,730	1.5	1.6	1.4	0.8
2873 Nitrogenous fertilizers	3,589	3,600	3,772	3,498	3,553	3,220	3,290	3,340	3,370	2.2	1.5	0.9	−1.3
2874 Phosphatic fertilizers	3,929	3,869	3,859	3,813	3,804	3,930	4,010	4,070	4,110	2.0	1.5	1.0	2.0
2879 Agricultural chemicals not elsewhere classified	8,225	8,361	8,080	8,585	8,837	8.850	8,940	9,090	9,250	1.0	1.7	1.8	1.1
Trade data													
Value of imports	1,521	1,801	2,253	2,536	2,594	2,556	2,632	2,703	2,784	3.0	2.7	3.0	1.8
Value of exports	3,598	3,051	4,039	4,734	4,635	4,874	5,222	5,551	5,928	7.1	6.3	6.8	6.3

[1] Estimate except imports and exports.
[2] Estimate.
[3] Forecast.
[4] Compound annual rate.
[5] For a definition of industry versus product values, see "Getting the Most Out of *Outlook 2000.*"
Source: U.S. Department of Commerce: Bureau of the Census; International Trade Administration.

in the year 2000. The fertilizer business has been hurt by sluggish demand in the United States, economic problems in Asia, and excess global capacity for key products such as ammonia and diammonium phosphate (DAP). Reflecting reduced acreage for corn and certain other crops, DAP consumption dropped an estimated 3 percent in the 1998–1999 growing season.

Domestic dollar fertilizer shipments are expected to post another decline in the year 2000 as continued high grain inventories and depressed grain prices are expected to weaken fertilizer demand in the 1999–2000 growing season. Planted corn and wheat acreage dropped about 2.6 percent in the 1998–1999 season, and a drop of 3.7 percent is expected for 1999–2000.

TABLE 11-6: U.S. Trade Patterns in Agricultural Chemicals[1] in 1998
(millions of dollars; percent)

Exports			Imports		
Region[2]	Value[3]	Share, %	Region[2]	Value[2]	Share, %
NAFTA	1,181	23	NAFTA	1,456	55
Latin America	982	19	Latin America	300	11
Western Europe	444	8	Western Europe	473	18
Japan/Chinese Economic Area	1,391	27	Japan/Chinese Economic Area	62	2
Other Asia	817	16	Other Asia	14	1
Rest of world	407	8	Rest of world	327	12
World	5,222	100	World	2,632	100
Top Five Countries	Value	Share, %	Top Five Countries	Value	Share, %
China	1,093	21	Canada	1,368	52
Canada	923	18	Trinidad and Tobago	245	9
Brazil	415	8	Germany	200	8
Australia	318	6	Russia	112	4
India	309	6	Mexico	88	3

[1] SIC 2873, 2874, 2879.
[2] For definitions of regional groupings, see "Getting the Most Out of *Outlook 2000.*"
[3] Values may not sum to total due to rounding.
Source: U.S. Department of Commerce, Bureau of the Census.

Planted acreage for corn rose fractionally to 80.2 million acres in the 1999 growing season, while plantings for soybeans increased 2.9 percent to 72.0 million acres. Farmers have opted to plant more soybeans in recent years because of attractive prices and new findings of soil benefits from the annual rotation of soybeans with corn.

Nitrogen is the most commonly used fertilizer, with anhydrous ammonia being the principal ingredient in most nitrogen fertilizers. Anhydrous ammonia is produced by combining atmospheric nitrogen with methane. Another related nitrogen fertilizer is urea, a combination of anhydrous ammonia and carbon dioxide. Because nitrogen-based compounds evaporate from the soil, nitrogen fertilizers must be applied each year, resulting in a relatively stable market for this commodity. Phosphate fertilizers are derived from phosphate rock. Phosphate rock is combined with sulfuric acid to yield phosphatic acid, which is further processed into DAP, the most widely used phosphatic fertilizer. Potash is mined primarily from deposits of potassium salts in Canada, Germany, Russia, the United States, and Israel.

World phosphate production rose about 3 percent in 1998, according to IMC Global estimates, with U.S. producers accounting for 41 percent of world concentrated phosphate production. The industry's current phosphoric acid capacity utilization rate is about 77 percent, with utilization expected to remain in that area over the next few years, according to IMC Global. However, by 2005, utilization should reach 85 percent as supply and demand conditions are more closely matched.

The United States exports about 55 percent of its phosphate fertilizer production, with about 30 percent of that volume going to China. About one-fifth of U.S. nitrogen fertilizer production is exported. Despite its leading position, the United States is expected to relinquish its dominant position in phosphate fertilizers to Morocco eventually. With its phosphate deposits estimated at over 50 percent of world rock phosphate reserves, Morocco is currently the largest phosphate rock exporter, with most of its production going to Europe. China, the former Soviet Union, and India are also large phosphate fertilizer producing countries.

World potash production increased about 2 percent in 1998. North America is the leading producer and exporter of potash products. Over 95 percent of world potash output in 1998 consisted of potassium chloride or muriate of potash, with the rest consisting mostly of potassium-based sulfate products. According to IMC Global, world potash consumption is expected to grow 12 percent while capacity is expected to rise only 6 percent, resulting in higher operating rates and firmer prices. Overall potash consumption should track growth rates in the world economy.

Despite prospects for stagnant or declining levels of fertilizer consumption in the United States and western Europe, developing nations in Asia and Latin America represent important growth markets for fertilizers. According to the IFA, Asian countries accounted for 48 percent of fertilizer consumption, North America for 16 percent, western Europe for 16 percent, Latin America for 8 percent, and other areas for 12 percent in 1998–1999.

Strong demographic growth, rising income levels, and efforts to improve diets and general standards of living in developing areas in Asia, Latin America, and Africa should foster greater production of grains and other produce. This should result in increased use of fertilizers to lift production. The total world population is projected to grow from 6 billion in 1999 to over 7 billion in 2010, with most of the growth occurring in emerging or third world countries. Asia currently accounts for about half of world fertilizer consumption.

Pesticides

After several years of declining sales, the $31 billion worldwide pesticide market was expected to increase slightly (less than 1 percent) in 1999, according to data provided by Wood Mackenzie

Consultants, a research firm in Edinburgh, Scotland. Although demand has remained sluggish in the United States and western Europe, shipments have benefited from improved demand conditions in developing countries in Latin America and east Asia. Demand from Asian markets was depressed in 1998 by economic problems and unfavorable weather conditions.

Pesticides are chemical agents that are used to destroy or repel plant or animal pests, with herbicides, insecticides, and fungicides representing the principal product categories. The United States is the leading global manufacturer of chemical pesticides, with Germany and Japan also being important producers. North America is the largest geographic market for pesticides, accounting for 32 percent of 1998 global sales, according to Wood Mackenzie. Other important markets are western Europe (26 percent of 1998 sales), the Far East (18 percent), Latin America (16 percent), and other areas (8 percent). Leading global pesticide producing corporations include Novartis, Monsanto, Astra-Zeneca Corp., Dupont, AgrEvo, Bayer, Rhone-Poulenc, Dow Chemical, BASF, the Cyanamid division of American Homes Products, and FMC Corp.

Global sales of insecticides and herbicides were relatively unchanged in 1998, but demand for fungicides improved as fungus outbreaks increased as a result of wet weather conditions in Europe and Japan. By contrast, weather conditions reduced insect infestation in North America, Europe, and Japan, resulting in a reduced need for insecticides and herbicides in those markets.

Greater use of insect-resistant cotton and herbicide-resistant food crops also has affected the overall pesticide business. Genetically engineered, or transgenic, plants have been developed that have resistance to insects, herbicides, and plant diseases, reducing the need for conventional pesticides. Led by Monsanto, many companies have developed transgenic seeds for corn, cotton, and soybeans. About one-half of all soybean and corn acreage planted in the United States today is used to grow genetically modified seeds. Approximately one-third of that output is exported, primarily to markets in Europe and Japan. Although U.S. producers argue that transgenic seeds provide important quality and cost advantages, there is growing opposition to those products, especially in Europe, because of consumer apprehensions and environmental concerns.

Total domestic sales of U.S.-made and imported pesticides grew 1.1 percent to $8.95 billion in 1998, according to the American Crop Protection Association (ACPA). Exports of U.S.-made pesticides totaling $2.86 billion were essentially unchanged from the level in 1997. With this business affected by price erosion caused by weak markets and increasing use of genetically modified seeds, many companies are exploring ways to divest or merge their agrochemical businesses. Increased consolidation is anticipated in this market in the years ahead.

Corn represents the largest single market for crop protection products, accounting for 26 percent of domestic pesticide sales in 1998. Other important crop markets in that year included soybeans (17 percent), cotton (8 percent), small grains (5 percent), and vegetables (4 percent). The balance (40 percent) was composed largely of fruits, rice, sorghum, peanuts, and potatoes. Revenues from pesticides designed for use in the home, garden, turf, and other noncrop categories totaled $1.64 billion in 1998, representing 14 percent of total domestic pesticide sales.

The pesticide market is a mature business in the United States, with over 90 percent of corn, soybean, and cotton acreage in major producing states being treated each year with pesticides. Changes in yearly sales are largely a function of starting inventory levels, changes in planted acreage, weather, and farm prices.

Representing the largest pesticide category, herbicide sales totaled $6 billion in 1998. Herbicides, which are used to control weeds, brush, and other unwanted vegetation, accounted for 68 percent of total U.S. crop protection sales in 1998, according to the ACPA. About 88 percent of U.S. herbicide sales in 1998 were for crop use, of which corn and soybeans accounted for about two-thirds of total volume. Herbicide sales rose 0.6 percent in 1998.

Used to guard growing or stored crops from insect infestation, insecticides are the industry's second largest product segment and totaled $1.8 billion in sales in 1998, accounting for 20 percent of industry sales. Cotton and corn were the leading end markets for insecticides in 1998, with each one accounting for about 19 percent of total insecticide sales. Corn insecticide sales rebounded 27 percent in 1998, after a comparable drop in 1997. The gain was due entirely to a sharp increase in sales of corn soil insecticides. Total U.S. insecticide sales increased 0.7 percent in 1998, with the gain restricted by the widening market acceptance of insect-resistant plants. Fungicides accounted for 8 percent of total pesticide sales in 1998. While agricultural uses represent the largest end market, fungicides also are used extensively in the lumber, paint, plastics, and pharmaceutical industries. Fungicide sales rose 13 percent in 1998.

MISCELLANEOUS CHEMICAL PRODUCTS

This subsector covers developments in the miscellaneous chemical products industry (SIC 289), which includes five main product groups: adhesives and sealants (SIC 2891), explosives (SIC 2892), printing ink (SIC 2893), carbon black (SIC 2895), and various miscellaneous chemicals, including fatty acids and gelatin.

U.S. Industry Outlook

Shipments of miscellaneous chemicals in current dollars were expected to increase just over 2 percent in 1999, with growth accelerating to 3 percent annually through 2003, essentially in line with expected growth in overall GDP (see Table 11-7). This projection, however, masks many diverse trends that are occurring in individual product markets. The leading importers of these products from the United States are Canada and Japan (see Table 11-8). Included in this category are products ranging from specialty chemicals such as adhesives and sealants and printing inks to commodity chemicals such as carbon black and fatty acids.

Adhesives and Sealants

Domestic demand for adhesives and sealants is projected to grow in the range of 2 to 3 percent annually through 2004, with higher prices expected to raise the annual growth in industry

TABLE 11-7: Miscellaneous Chemical Products (SIC 289) Trends and Forecasts
(millions of dollars except as noted)

	1992	1993	1994	1995	1996	1997[1]	1998[1]	1999[2]	2000[3]	Percent Change 97–98	98–99	99–00	96–00[4]
Industry data													
Value of shipments[5]	20,512	21,851	22,502	23,830	24,508	26,000	26,550	27,050	27,600	2.1	1.9	2.0	3.0
Value of shipments (1992$)	20,512	21,481	21,426	21,662	22,194	23,100	23,150	23,200	23,270	0.2	0.2	0.3	1.2
Total employment (thousands)	83.7	81.8	79.8	81.6	75.9								
Production workers (thousands)	48.2	47.0	46.7	47.7	45.0								
Average hourly earnings ($)	13.63	13.76	14.27	14.42	14.72								
Capital expenditures	751	790	731	807	1,006								
Product data													
Value of shipments[5]	19,440	20,764	20,950	22,215	22,918	24,300	24,800	25,950	26,470	2.1	4.6	2.0	3.7
Value of shipments (1992$)	19,440	20,406	19,954	20,191	20,734	21,570	21,600	22,040	22,480	0.1	2.0	2.0	2.0
Trade data													
Value of imports	1,511	1,702	1,883	2,316	2,625	2,868	2,661			–7.2			
Value of exports	2,881	3,143	3,356	3,863	4,177	4,733	4,533			–4.2			

[1] Estimate except imports and exports.
[2] Estimate.
[3] Forecast.
[4] Compound annual rate.
[5] For a definition of industry versus product values, see "Getting the Most Out of *Outlook 2000.*"
Source: U.S. Department of Commerce: Bureau of the Census; International Trade Administration.

shipments to close to 4 percent in that period. The average price per pound for formulated adhesives and sealants will increase because of continuing shifts in the product mix that favor highly formulated synthetic adhesives.

The global adhesive and sealant market was estimated to be about $22 billion in 1998. Adhesives accounted for about 82 percent of the total global market, with sealants representing 18 percent. North America accounted for 33 percent of the global adhesive and sealant market, followed by Europe with a 30 percent share. The Far East accounted for 19 percent of the world market, with the rest of the world representing 18 percent.

Adhesives are chemicals that are used to attach or bond together materials such as paper, wood, and metal. Also bonding agents, sealants are substances that are used to fill gaps between two materials and prevent the passage of liquids and gases between them. Sealants have the flexibility to adjust to changing conditions, such as the expansion and contraction that occur with heat and cold, without being damaged. Adhesives and sealants are produced from blends of petroleum-derived resins, synthetic rubber elastomers, and related materials.

The largest market for adhesives in 1998 by volume was converting and packaging, with a 34 percent share, according to

TABLE 11-8: U.S. Trade Patterns in Miscellaneous Chemical Products[1] in 1998
(millions of dollars; percent)

Exports			Imports		
Region[2]	Value[3]	Share, %	Region[2]	Value[3]	Share, %
NAFTA	1,284	28	NAFTA	566	21
Latin America	612	13	Latin America	140	5
Western Europe	1,034	23	Western Europe	816	31
Japan/Chinese Economic Area	755	17	Japan/Chinese Economic Area	819	31
Other Asia	493	11	Other Asia	274	10
Rest of world	355	8	Rest of world	46	2
World	4,533	100	World	2,661	100
Top Five Countries	Value	Share, %	Top Five Countries	Value	Share, %
Canada	888	20	Japan	648	24
Japan	493	11	Canada	433	16
Mexico	396	9	Germany	289	11
Singapore	234	5	France	174	7
Brazil	212	5	China	149	6

[1] SIC 289.
[2] For definitions of regional groupings, see "Getting the Most Out of *Outlook 2000.*"
[3] Values may not sum to total due to rounding.
Source: U.S. Department of Commerce, Bureau of the Census.

DPNA International. Other important markets were construction, 17 percent; pressure-sensitive (self-adhesive) materials, 14 percent; woodworking, 9 percent; assembly, 7 percent; and transportation, 2 percent. The balance of shipments (17 percent) went for a wide variety of other uses, including laminates, flexible packaging, disposable products, and consumer do-it-yourself markets. Major applications for adhesives include paperboard, labels and tapes, containers, plywood, laminates, furniture, graphic arts, carpeting, and motor vehicles.

Advances in technology have increased adhesive use in the automotive industry as new adhesives have been developed to allow for lighter and more fuel-efficient cars. Other technological improvements have resulted in the development of adhesives that are less flammable and products with lower solvent content and reduced emissions of volatile organic compounds. The major beneficiaries of these trends include environmentally compatible systems with higher solids contents, such as water-based and hot melt (100 percent solid) adhesives. Because of environmental concerns about their toxic content, the use of solvent adhesives is declining about 2 percent a year.

According to some industry observers, adhesives have the potential to partially replace traditional methods of fastening such as rivets, welding, bolting, and screw joining of materials. However, it is unlikely that adhesives will become the dominant means of fastening materials because of concern about the long-term reliability of adhesive bonds.

Foreign trade does not play a significant role in the adhesive and sealant industry, principally because of prohibitive shipping costs and the fact that most of these products are based on readily available technology. Nonetheless, U.S. producers hold a leadership position in the global market, particularly in higher-margin products such as structural adhesives and sealants used in more advanced applications. Most trade in adhesives and sealants traditionally has been with Canada, although the enactment of NAFTA has increased trade with Mexico in recent years. Asia is another important market, with exports to that region expected to show good growth over the 2000–2004 period, buoyed by alleviation of the financial and economic problems experienced there in 1998 and 1999.

The U.S. adhesive industry is fragmented, with over 500 companies manufacturing adhesive products. By contrast, the sealants industry is highly concentrated, with a small number of firms accounting for the bulk of industry sales. Leading companies in the adhesives and sealants industry include Dow Corning (a joint venture between Dow Chemical and Corning), National Starch & Chemical, Imperial Chemical Industries (United Kingdom), Henkel (Germany), General Electric, Bostick, Solutia, Tremco (a division of RPM Inc.), Dow Chemical, Rohm & Haas, Reichhold Chemical, and Elf Atochem (France).

Consolidation activity in this industry has increased in recent years as companies have joined together to broaden product lines and achieve operating synergies in order to compete more effectively in an increasingly competitive marketplace. The need to reduce costs through mergers and restructuring also has resulted from spiraling costs for regulatory compliance in the United States and abroad. The most recent large merger in this industry was Rohm & Haas's $4.9 billion purchase of Morton Salt in early 1999. Rohm's management said that the merger should enable the company to increase its top line growth from its present range of 4 to 5 percent range to between 6 and 8 percent beginning in 2001 and allow for a reduction of $300 million in annual operating costs.

Explosives

The explosives market is driven by underlying demand conditions in principal global energy, base metal, and construction markets. The coal and metal mining industries account for roughly two-thirds of the total market. While demand from the coal and metal mining industries depends on global economic trends, construction activity varies significantly by geographic region.

Overall demand for explosives, including pyrotechnics and explosive accessories and assemblies, is expected to increase at a rate of slightly over 2 percent annually through 2004. That growth will trail the higher rates experienced during the early and middle 1990s because of a decline in mining activity (partly caused by lower prices for many metals) and decelerating construction expenditures. These markets account for nearly two-thirds of worldwide explosives consumption.

Geographically, the largest explosives market is the North American market, which is dominated by coal and metals mining, quarrying, and construction. Construction represents the principal growth area in western Europe as mining activity continues to decline in that region. Construction also drives most Asian markets, although mining plays a significant role in Australia. Coal and iron ore account for close to one-fifth of Australia's exports. South America is another growing market, boosted by rising open pit coal and metals mining activity in many countries.

Although the United States is the largest consumer of explosives worldwide, the market is becoming increasingly globalized. The greatest opportunities for producers of explosives are in the expanding mining and construction industries of southeast Asia, Latin America (e.g., Argentina, Peru, and Bolivia), and Australia. Many U.S. producers therefore are pursuing growth through exports. Explosives exports are expected to outpace imports significantly in the foreseeable future. Besides direct export business, many U.S. explosives firms are entering international markets through direct investment in local industries, joint manufacturing ventures, and technological licensing agreements.

Currently representing a relatively small part of the overall market, pyrotechnics, or consumer explosives, represent a rapidly growing market. Growth is being driven by increased use of fireworks in holiday celebrations, stage productions, and amusement park displays. Strong demand also is coming from the automotive market, which uses explosive ignitors and propellants in air bag systems. Leading explosives manufacturers include Austin Powder, Dyno Nobel (Sweden), Explosive Technologies International, and LSB Industries.

Printing Inks

Valued at about $12 billion, the global printing ink market is expected to expand at a rate of about 2 percent annually through

2004. Modest growth is projected in the key commercial printing and packaging markets, helped by improved demand for ink-jet inks and other higher-priced formulations. Inks used in commercial printing and packaging, such as newspapers, periodicals, and books, represent the largest segment of the printing ink market, with miscellaneous applications such as business forms and greeting cards accounting for the balance. Ink-jet printing inks are the most rapidly growing ink type, with demand being driven by greater use of personal and commercial digital printing equipment in the desktop printing industry and the development of new substrates and niche markets. Although still a factor to some extent, the switch from solvent-based inks to environmentally attractive alternatives (vegetable oil–based products) in applicable markets has been completed for the most part.

Representing about one-third of the total global market, the U.S. printing ink business is expected to show very little growth over the coming years, reflecting the maturity of its basic markets. However, better gains are projected for emerging overseas markets, especially in many Asian and South American countries, as demand for commercial printing and packaging rises with improving standards of living. The United States should maintain its position as a net exporter of printing inks in the coming years, with the trade surplus widening as U.S.-based suppliers expand their multinational presence.

This industry also has witnessed considerable consolidation in recent years as key players have sought mergers to better deal with stagnant markets and declining ink prices. Two leading companies—Dainippon Ink & Chemical and Flint Ink—have grown through acquisitions of smaller ink companies in recent years.

Carbon Black

Demand for carbon black in the United States is expected to increase about 2.5 percent annually through 2004, essentially tracking growth in rubber tire production, its principal end market. Rubber tires account for more than 90 percent of total demand for carbon black. Carbon black is used as a reinforcement in vulcanized rubber products, since it has the ability to improve an elastomer's tear, abrasion, and flex resistance. A fine powder substance, carbon black is derived from petroleum refining, the distillation of coal tars, and ethylene.

Continued demand growth is forecast in the tire industry, augmented by the increased popularity of performance tires and new formulations of carbon black with properties that reduce tire leaks. Performance tires require higher carbon black loadings in tread compounds compared with all-season radials. Performance tires also have shorter service lives, and so they are replaced more often. In addition, the popularity of sport utility vehicles and full-size pickup trucks has increased demand for larger tires from both original equipment manufacturers (OEM) and replacement markets.

Besides rubber tires, carbon black is used widely in industrial rubber products such as hoses, belts, and mechanical goods. However, demand for carbon black in nontire industrial rubber products will be restricted by the increased use of thermoplastic elastomers, some types of which do not require carbon black while others require much less carbon black than do conventional rubber parts.

Accounting for less than 10 percent of the market, nonrubber applications, called special blacks, are also important, particularly from a value standpoint, since these specialized grades command significantly higher prices than do commodity rubber blacks. In addition to higher margins, a strong position in special blacks offers suppliers greater protection against cyclical swings in the rubber and motor vehicle industries.

The primary nonrubber use for carbon black is as a pigment in plastics, paints and coatings, and printing inks. While growth in the domestic market is expected to remain relatively modest, strong gains are indicated in many foreign regions. The Asia-Pacific region will continue to have the biggest growth markets for carbon black, mainly because of the ongoing development of China's tire industry. Latin America also offers solid opportunities, particularly in Brazil; in eastern Europe, the strongest prospects are in the Czech Republic, Hungary, and Poland.

Herman Saftlas, Standard & Poor's Corporation, (212) 438-9542, November 1999.

DRUGS AND PHARMACEUTICALS

The drugs and pharmaceuticals sector (SIC 283) has four primary components: medicinals and botanicals (SIC 2833), pharmaceutical preparations (SIC 2834), diagnostic substances (SIC 2835), and biological products (SIC 2836). Medicinal and botanical establishments (SIC 2833) are engaged primarily in manufacturing bulk organic and inorganic medicinal chemicals and their derivatives and in processing bulk botanical drugs and herbs. Pharmaceutical preparations (SIC 2834) include those produced by establishments engaged primarily in manufacturing, fabricating, and processing medicinal substances into finished pharmaceuticals for human and veterinary use. Ethical brand-name drugs, generic products, and nonprescription or over-the-counter medications constitute the pharmaceutical preparations subsector. The diagnostic substances subsector (SIC 2835) includes products from companies that make chemical, biological, or radioactive substances for testing blood and other bodily fluids and tissues. These substances may be used for in vitro (test tube) or in vivo (administered in the body) testing. Biologicals establishments (SIC 2836) are engaged primarily in the production of bacterial and viral vaccines, toxoids, and analogous products (such as allergic extracts, serums, plasmas, and other blood derivatives) for human and veterinary use.

Global Industry Trends

The global pharmaceutical market continues its pattern of solid growth, with consistent increases in sales expected over the next 5 years. Growth in the world pharmaceutical market increased from 6.6 percent in 1997 to 7 percent in 1998. Combined worldwide sales of prescription and over-the-counter medications are estimated at over $300 billion. The market is expected to experience annual compound growth of 8 to 10 percent in the next 5 years. Strong growth in North American markets and the recovery in Japan helped drive the global pharmaceutical market upward in 1998. The United States remains the largest pharmaceutical market in the world, followed by Europe and Japan. Global growth in the consumption of pharmaceutical products is likely to be sustained by strong demographic gains with record-setting life expectancies, a rising standard of living in developing countries, and a steady stream of new products and line extensions, including the new frontier of quality-of-life pharmacology.

Demographics are expected to provide a strong market and high demand for pharmaceuticals for the foreseeable future. The World Health Organization (WHO) reports that the global over-65 population is forecast to rise from 380 million in 1997 to more than 690 million by 2025. The elderly are the single largest group of users of prescription drugs. The over-65 population consumes three times as many pharmaceutical medicines as younger patients do. As governments around the world consider various ways to tackle the problems of rising health care costs for the elderly, pharmaceuticals are emerging as an efficient and cost-effective way to address this problem. Pharmaceuticals provide health care savings by shortening hospital stays, reducing nursing home admissions, lessening doctors' visits, and in some cases eliminating the need for surgery. In the last decade, pharmaceutical companies have brought to market more than 150 new medicines for disease of aging. Pharmaceutical company researchers are working on more than 600 new medicines to tackle the major causes of disability among seniors.

Rising standards of living throughout the world are expected to bolster the demand for better health care and increase sales of medical products. Health in developing countries is improving as a result of a rising global economy and the new interaction between science, public health, and business. As issues of trade and health continue to intersect, it is inevitable that the pharmaceutical industry and the WHO are increasing their interaction. The WHO and the pharmaceutical industry continue to search for ways to reduce barriers to the global availability of medicine. Pharmaceuticals are the first line of medical therapy worldwide. The global pharmaceutical industry has the ability to develop products to fight infectious diseases wherever they occur. The challenges are availability, affordability, and effectiveness.

The introduction of new products is expected to accelerate the growth of the global pharmaceutical industry in the years ahead. The leading research-based pharmaceutical companies indicate that there are at least 29 compounds in the global pipeline with "blockbuster" potential. Innovative products have replaced price as the leading factor driving the industry. Higher sales are being achieved through simultaneous multicountry launches of new products, improved sales force productivity, and direct-to-consumer advertising. Advances in biomedical science have given rise to new processes that are expected to assist scientists in developing and discovering new pharmaceutical compounds at even faster rates. Over the next few years, it is expected that pharmaceutical companies will introduce a whole range of new compounds that not only will cure diseases but also will slow the ravages of age. Even with advances in research and development (R&D) and the continued introduction of new pharmaceuticals, there is an urgent need for new and better medicines. According to WHO, there is still no adequate therapy for three-quarters of the 2,500 currently recognized medical conditions.

The global pharmaceutical industry shows no signs of slowing its worldwide consolidation activity. Companies pool resources to compete more effectively and finance the escalating cost of expanded R&D. Mergers are especially prevalent in companies whose principal drugs have lost or are about to lose patent protection. Other likely candidates for mergers are firms whose R&D pipelines are sparse or whose products consist largely of drugs that can be produced by other companies. Foreign drug manufacturers continue to eye U.S. firms as potential candidates for acquisition. In the early 1990s, mergers were driven primarily by a desire to cut costs. In the late 1990s, R&D opportunities appeared to be the driving force. The press is filled with reports of a battle between three leading U.S. research-based pharmaceutical companies to see which two will merge to become the world's largest pharmaceutical company.

U.S. Industry Growth Projections for the Next 1 and 5 Years

The U.S. pharmaceutical industry is divided into three segments: the research-based branded pharmaceutical industry, the generic pharmaceutical industry, and the nonprescription or over-the-counter industry. Research-based pharmaceutical companies invent prescription drugs that can be sold only with a doctor's prescription. Generic forms of prescription drugs are made available once the innovator's patent expires. Generic drugs, like prescription drugs, can be obtained only with a doctor's prescription. Over-the-counter pharmaceuticals are drug products that consumers can obtain and use on their own initiative. All three segments are predicted to have a positive growth rate for the next year, and the momentum is expected to continue over the next 5 years. New drug discoveries, increased interest in health, demographic trends, managed health care, and a more industry-friendly regulatory environment have combined to support the sustained growth of the industry. The nominal value of industry shipments for the U.S. drug sector totaled $107.7 billion in 1998, a 13.1 percent increase over 1997 shipments (see Table 11-9).

The U.S. industry appears to be on the verge of a major new cycle, with a number of potential blockbuster products in the pipeline that should ensure continued industry growth for at least the next 5 years. To satisfy the increased demand for new products, especially among the elderly, U.S. companies have intensified their efforts to create unique, "breakthrough" therapeutic compounds. Examples of new products are more effective cancer drugs, protease inhibitors to treat AIDS patients, oral diabetes therapy, cholesterol reducers, new treatments for arthritis, and impotence treatments. Increased demand for new

TABLE 11-9: Drugs (SIC 283) Trends and Forecasts
(millions of dollars except as noted)

	1992	1993	1994	1995	1996	1997[1]	1998[1]	1999[2]	2000[3]	Percent Change 97–98	98–99	99–00	96–00[4]
Industry data													
Value of shipments[5]	67,792	70,985	75,804	80,907	86,532	95,219	107,692	112,815	121,947	13.1	4.8	8.1	9.0
Value of shipments (1992$)	67,792	68,179	71,142	73,820	76,824	82,952	85,251	86,673	91,488	2.8	1.7	5.6	4.5
Total employment (thousands)	194	200	205	216	213								
Production workers (thousands)	92.7	94.6	102	113	106								
Average hourly earnings ($)	14.78	15.80	16.34	15.99	16.63								
Capital expenditures	3,887	4,047	4,034	4,503	4,301								
Product data													
Value of shipments[5]	60,793	63,970	67,751	71,528	76,293	83,952	94,949	99,466	107,517	13.1	4.8	8.1	9.0
Value of shipments (1992$)	60,793	61,428	63,588	65,285	67,754	73,159	75,186	76,440	80,687	2.8	1.7	5.6	4.5
Trade data													
Value of imports	5,980	6,063	6,905	8,504	11,090	14,110	17,847	23,308	27,969	26.5	30.6	20.0	26.0
Value of exports	6,765	7,214	7,561	7,992	8,884	10,368	11,944	13,616	14,705	15.2	14.0	8.0	13.4

[1] Estimate except imports and exports.
[2] Estimate.
[3] Forecast.
[4] Compound annual rate.
[5] For a definition of industry versus product values, see "Getting the Most Out of *Outlook 2000*."
Source: U.S. Department of Commerce: Bureau of the Census; International Trade Administration.

products has replaced price as the primary force in the U.S. pharmaceutical industry's overall growth.

In the United States, consumer interest in health matters remains at an all-time high. People say they follow health-related stories in the media more than they follow any other subject. The industry is capitalizing on this interest by increasing direct-to-consumer (DTC) advertising. Once considered taboo, DTC advertising is becoming a major marketing force in the U.S. pharmaceutical industry and is likely to be a key driver of the industry's future growth. In 1998, the industry spent $1.33 billion on DTC advertising, a 38 percent increase over the $965 million spent in 1997. Increased DTC advertising is leading to greater consumer recognition of the benefits of pharmaceutical therapies and increasing consumers' confidence in discussing health matters with their doctors and asking for specific medications.

Managed care is lifting pharmaceutical sales in the United States by increasing the use of pharmaceuticals as a viable alternative to other treatment forms, and this trend should continue over the next 5 years. Health maintenance organizations (HMOs), preferred provider organizations, and other managed care firms have grown rapidly in recent years. In the 1980s, managed care's share of the retail pharmaceutical market was less than 30 percent; by the year 2000, that share is expected to be 90 percent. However, the experiment with HMOs has shown that the American people do not like the idea of rationing health care. Complaints have increased that HMOs put financial considerations ahead of patients' needs. In 1999, the U.S. House of Representatives approved a bill to make HMOs subject to lawsuits for liability. Regardless of whether the HMO liability bill becomes law, there is a definite trend toward more people having more of a say in the drugs they are prescribed.

In different ways and degrees, each of the three segments of the U.S. pharmaceutical industry benefits from the growth of managed care. Partly because of the continued trend toward self-care, which increasingly is driven by the managed care industry, retail sales of nonprescription drugs are expected to increase steadily over the next 5 years. Managed care has contributed to the expansion of the markets for generics as well. Generic drugs are forecast to account for nearly two-thirds of all prescriptions written by the end of the decade, a large increase from 42 percent of the market in 1996 and 22 percent in 1985. The generics market is expected to reach $15 billion by the year 2000, up from an estimated $9 billion in 1996. Growth of the generics market also is aided by the fact that over the next 5 years drugs that generated more than $16 billion in 1996 sales are scheduled to lose patent protection. Sales of research-based pharmaceuticals also have been helped by managed care. Managed care providers realize that newly developed branded pharmaceuticals often provide the most effective and cost-efficient means to treat patients. Increasingly, leading-edge branded pharmaceuticals are being used by managed care providers as the preferred form of treatment. To compete with well-established and cheaper generic products and to increase their share of the managed care market, the branded companies have to ensure a full pipeline of new and innovative pharmaceuticals that offer improved effectiveness or unique solutions. To maintain approximately 10 percent annual growth, research-based pharmaceutical companies believe that they must bring two or three new products to market each year.

The U.S. pharmaceutical industry is experiencing a more industry-friendly regulatory environment. Pharmaceutical sales continue to benefit from 1997 legislation that streamlined the U.S. Food and Drug Administration's (FDA) approval process for new prescription drugs and medical devices. FDA's user-fee program has been extended, and the review process for new drugs has been expedited. Under the 1997 law, seriously ill patients have easier access to experiential compounds and new incentives for the development of pediatric medicines are provided. The FDA has cooperated by liberalizing regulatory requirements on DTC ads. The 1997 legislation is expected to continue to aid industry growth over the next 5 years.

International Competitiveness

Highly innovative and technologically advanced, the U.S. pharmaceutical industry has consistently maintained a competitive edge in international markets. In 1997, North America accounted for 34.5 percent of the global pharmaceutical market, Europe, 29.0 percent; Japan, 15.9 percent; Latin America, 7.7 percent; southeast Asia and China, 7.3 percent; and all other regions, 5.6 percent. This geographic breakdown is not expected to change much over the next 5 years.

The introduction of new products is the primary force in the U.S. pharmaceutical industry's overall growth and competitiveness. The United States leads the world in new drug discoveries and R&D expenditures. Research-based pharmaceutical companies invested $18 billion in R&D in 1998 and were expected to invest $24 billion in 1999. Pharmaceutical manufacturers invest a higher percentage of sales revenues in R&D than does any other industry. Innovative pharmaceuticals provide some of the most effective and cost-efficient means to treat patients. U.S. R&D-based pharmaceutical companies have an excellent reputation throughout the world. With the world's rising standard of living and the increasing use of innovative drugs as a way to slow the rise in health care costs, U.S. pharmaceutical exports are expected to continue to do well.

In 1998, the pharmaceutical industry in the United States was expected to export medicines worth more than $11.9 billion (see Table 11-10). Between 1997 and 1998, exports from the United States increased 15.1 percent. U.S. drug makers on average make close to 35 percent of their sales abroad. Some of the leading pharmaceutical customers for the United States are Canada, the Netherlands, Germany, Japan, and United Kingdom.

Although U.S. exports continue to be strong, pharmaceutical imports into the United States are increasing faster than are exports. The United States imported more than $17.8 billion worth of pharmaceuticals in 1998 (see Table 11-10). This was a 25.7 percent increase over the 1997 level. Some of the largest pharmaceutical suppliers to the United States are Germany, Ireland, the United Kingdom, Japan, and Switzerland. There has been a rapidly growing deficit in U.S. pharmaceutical trade since 1997. Possible reasons for the increase in pharmaceutical imports include the number of companies relocating research and manufacturing operations outside the United States, international mergers, and increased sales by European Union (EU) producers in the United States. Two factors also could create the appearance of rapid import growth: a recent change in the methodology used by U.S. firms to set transfer prices from their subsidiaries and an increase in the use of foreign trade zones to manufacture duty-free finished pharmaceutical products from dutiable, imported intermediates and raw materials.

Other concerns threatening the competitiveness of the U.S. pharmaceutical industry in the international arena are inadequate protection for patents, trademarks, trade secrets, and data; price restraints; and barriers to market access. Pharmaceutical intellectual property is threatened in many countries. Protection of pharmaceutical intellectual property provides an incentive to continue R&D investment and is important for the continued international competitiveness of the U.S. industry. The pharmaceutical industry objects to price controls, which it perceives as denying recovery of R&D costs and a fair profit, thus threatening the innovation and viability of U.S. firms. Nontariff barri-

TABLE 11-10: U.S. Trade Patterns in Drugs[1] in 1998
(millions of dollars; percent)

Exports			Imports		
Region[2]	Value[3]	Share, %	Region[2]	Value[3]	Share, %
NAFTA	1,892	16	NAFTA	811	5
Latin America	792	7	Latin America	70	0
Western Europe	6,835	57	Western Europe	14,407	81
Japan/Chinese Economic Area	1,376	12	Japan/Chinese Economic Area	1,766	10
Other Asia	313	3	Other Asia	426	2
Rest of world	735	6	Rest of world	368	2
World	11,944	100	World	17,847	100
Top Five Countries	Value	Share, %	Top Five Countries	Value	Share, %
Canada	1,614	14	Germany	3,548	20
Netherlands	1,292	11	Ireland	3,227	18
Germany	1,121	9	United Kingdom	3,015	17
Japan	1,071	9	Japan	1,445	8
United Kingdom	825	7	Switzerland	1,223	7

[1] SIC 283.
[2] For definitions of regional groupings, see "Getting the Most Out of *Outlook 2000*."
[3] Values may not sum to total due to rounding.
Source: U.S. Department of Commerce, Bureau of the Census.

ers, according to industry estimates, have cost U.S. pharmaceutical companies as much as $9 billion.

Bill Hurt, U.S. Department of Commerce, Chemicals, Pharmaceuticals, and Biotechnology Division, (202) 482-5125, November 1999.

PLASTIC MATERIALS AND RESINS

The plastic materials and resins industry (SIC 2821) includes establishments engaged primarily in manufacturing synthetic resins, plastics materials, and nonvulcanizable elastomers.

Global and Domestic Subsector Outlook

Global Industry Trends. The plastics industry has moved around the world as it has pursued business opportunities in emerging high-growth markets and as suppliers have followed OEMs as those companies have expanded production. The global plastics industry is dominated by large multinational chemical companies that are vertically integrated. Although the industry is expanding globally, it has undergone considerable consolidation and restructuring in recent years as a result of major acquisitions, the formation of joint ventures, and the closing of obsolete facilities. That trend is likely to continue because of the level of competition among producers and the need for cost-cutting measures. Despite this trend toward consolidation, total plastics production remains fragmented because of the number of resins produced and the diversity of the markets served. Production of larger-volume commodity resins such as polyethylene and polypropylene tends to be less concentrated than that of smaller, specialty-type products. In each of the top four resin sectors—polyethylene, polypropylene, PVC, and polystyrene—fewer than five players have significant global positions.

Although the plastics industry is global, the base of production for many commodity resins has shifted to countries such as Saudi Arabia, China, and South Korea. Producers in highly developed markets such as the United States, western Europe, and Japan have responded to these shifts in production by emphasizing the manufacture of specialty and higher-value-added products and by rationalizing their production capacity to improve profitability. Such actions not only capitalize on the comparative advantage of developed countries in highly advanced production technologies and research but also lessen the impact on profitability of swings in levels of resin production capacity and demand.

Key markets for the global plastics industry include the Chinese Economic Area, Japan, North America, South America, southeast Asia, and western Europe. Because of their size and level of economic development, it is no surprise that Japan, North America, and western Europe are the largest regional markets for plastic resin, accounting for some 90 percent of world polymer consumption. Although there is certainly opportunity for expansion in those regions, as epitomized by Canada and Mexico, those markets are in large part established, with a more limited opportunity for growth. Despite the economic difficulties in Asia and South America recently, those regions remain the primary areas of significant growth opportunity in both the short term and the long term.

Research in the plastics industry has focused on the development of new production processes instead of entirely new plastic materials. For example, the development of metallocene catalyst technology was expected to play a key role in the olefin sector through the end of the century. The production of metallocene-catalyzed thermoplastics has been growing rapidly both in the United States and worldwide, yet it accounts for only a minor proportion of total resin production. As technical difficulties are resolved and prices fall, this technology is expected to gain greater importance in the global marketplace. Other research efforts are aimed at expanding applications for plastics and improving the performance properties of existing resins through alloying and blending.

Domestic Industry Trends. Factors affecting growth in the U.S. plastics industry include trends in key end-use markets such as packaging, building and construction, consumer and institutional products, and transportation. Those markets in turn are affected by trends in consumer spending, GDP, and population growth. Other issues that influence the industry's outlook include the cost and availability of raw materials, foreign competition, technological advancements, and intermaterial and alternative material competition.

Noteworthy trends specific to the U.S. plastics industry include consolidation and restructuring of the industry, competition among alternative plastic materials, and the emergence of electronic commerce (E-commerce) as a business tool. Depressed oil and resin prices and overcapacity in resin supply have prompted a number of mergers, acquisitions, and joint ventures, with the most notable in 1999 being the merger announced by the Dow Chemical Company and the Union Carbide Corporation. The same pressures, along with consolidation among OEMs, have played a role in the increased level of intermaterial competition faced by plastics. Such competition is occurring across the spectrum of end-use markets as commodity materials that are enhanced through alloying and blending vie with specialty resins for market share. Last but certainly not least is the advent of E-commerce in the business operations of the U.S. plastics industry. Most U.S. resin producers have a Web site, with some companies offering more comprehensive services such as on-line sales, shipping and inventory information, and technical assistance. The Internet provides these companies with a low-cost, time-sensitive means of communicating product information to current and potential customers. In turn, the ready availability of information on-line has helped reduce the time frame for customer decision making.

Industry and Trade Projections for the Next 1 and 5 Years

Shipment Projections. Constant dollar shipments of plastic materials and resins are forecast to increase only 3 percent in the year 2000 after an unexpectedly strong performance of 7 percent growth in 1999 (see Table 11-11). A variety of factors contributed to the unusual increase in shipments in 1999: the ability of the industry to push through resin price increases, the buildup of inventory after a drawdown in 1998, the anticipation of Y2K problems in sourcing resin, and the strength of sales in virtually all end-use markets. Performance in the year 2000 will be weaker because of expected price and shipment erosion during the first quarter after the inventory buildup of 1999, additional capacity coming on-line without sufficient growth in the domestic economy and the export market to support it, increased competition from imported materials, and a weaker performance in key end-use markets such as building and construction and transportation.

For the near term, 2000–2004, the outlook for plastics will continue to be favorable, with constant dollar shipments growing between 3 and 4 percent. A weaker domestic economy will lead to weakened demand in key end-use markets. However, that trend will be offset somewhat by increased exports as economies in Asia and South America recover and have higher rates of growth.

Export Trade Patterns and Projections. Historically, exports as a percentage of plastic resin shipments have grown at an increasing rate. Large regional export markets in the NAFTA countries and western Europe and double-digit growth in Asia have played a significant role in this trend (see Table 11-12). The economic crisis in Asia and the economic difficulties experienced in Latin America in 1998 saw a reversal of this trend. During most of 1999, U.S. exports of plastics to virtually every region in the world were negative. However, there was sufficient recovery—led by Asia—such that plastic resin exports did end the year with a positive performance, albeit a small one. For the first time since NAFTA's implementation, exports to Mexico fell. U.S. exports to that country were hurt by low oil prices, cuts in spending by the Mexican government, and incremental growth in the domestic economy. Continuing poor economic performance was the largest negative element for exports to Latin America. U.S. exports to western Europe suffered as a result of competition from Asian exports. Bright spots included China, South Korea, Vietnam, Thailand, and Malaysia as the United States expanded trading opportunities in Vietnam and as the Asian economies began to show clear signs of recovery.

In the year 2000, U.S. plastics exports are expected to grow 4.1 percent as the Mexican economy improves its performance and oil prices recover. Exports to Latin America are expected to continue to fall, although not as much as in 1999. Incremental growth is expected in western Europe as competition for market share from Asian resins is not anticipated to be as fierce. Asia will resume its position as the primary growth market for U.S. plastics exports—although growth will have a slower pace—with Vietnam possibly benefiting from a bilateral agreement with the United States. The same factors will contribute to export growth of 4 to 5 percent in the period 2000–2004.

Import Trade Patterns and Projections. Although there was strong demand in the U.S. market, plastic resin imports were negative for most of 1999. Contributing to this scenario were poor domestic economies in Mexico and most of Latin America that prompted those countries to supply resin to their domestic markets as opposed to exporting or importing material. However, U.S. plastic resin imports did ultimately have a positive performance, rising 5.4 percent for the year. The primary reason for the shift in fortunes was a reversal in Canadian imports—from negative to positive—given that they hold

TABLE 11-11: Plastics Materials and Resins (SIC 2821) Trends and Forecasts
(millions of dollars except as noted)

										Percent Change			
	1992	1993	1994	1995	1996	1997	1998[1]	1999[2]	2000[3]	97–98	98–99	99–00	96–00[4]
Industry data													
Value of shipments[5]	31,601	31,546	37,305	43,453	40,097	44,575	47,160	50,980	52,866	5.8	8.1	3.7	7.2
Value of shipments (1992$)	31,601	31,172	35,327	35,156	34,567	37,678	39,486	42,250	43,517	4.8	7.0	3.0	5.9
Total employment (thousands)	61.2	62.2	68.9	70.0	58.6	61.0	60.8	60.5	59.3	–0.3	–0.5	–2.0	0.3
Production workers (thousands)	36.5	36.6	40.4	41.6	36.3	37.5	36.7	36.4	35.8	–2.1	–0.8	–1.6	–0.3
Average hourly earnings ($)	18.61	18.75	19.39	20.04	20.50	21.70	22.62	23.53	24.00	4.2	4.0	2.0	4.0
Capital expenditures	1,712	1,926	2,536	2,324	2,784	2,921	2,727	3,324	3,091	–6.6	21.9	–7.0	2.6
Product data													
Value of shipments[5]	33,299	33,589	38,043	44,017	42,751	45,670	47,862	51,739	53,653	4.8	8.1	3.7	5.8
Value of shipments (1992$)	33,299	33,191	36,025	35,612	36,854	38,623	40,091	42,897	44,184	3.8	7.0	3.0	4.6
Trade data													
Value of imports	2,147	2,606	3,380	4,200	4,311	4,788	4,913	5,178	5,515	2.6	5.4	6.5	6.4
Value of exports	7,091	7,280	8,529	10,461	10,705	11,884	11,282	11,305	11,769	–5.1	.2	4.1	2.4

[1] Estimate except imports and exports.
[2] Estimate.
[3] Forecast.
[4] Compound annual rate.
[5] For a definition of industry versus product values, see "Getting the Most Out of *Outlook 2000*."
Source: U.S. Department of Commerce: Bureau of the Census; International Trade Administration.

TABLE 11-12: U.S. Trade Patterns in Plastics[1] in 1998
(millions of dollars; percent)

Exports			Imports		
Region[2]	Value[3]	Share, %	Region[2]	Value[3]	Share, %
NAFTA	4,720	42	NAFTA	2,344	48
Latin America	1,400	12	Latin America	85	2
Western Europe	2,137	19	Western Europe	1,450	30
Japan/Chinese Economic Area	1,645	15	Japan/Chinese Economic Area	782	16
Other Asia	813	7	Other Asia	175	4
Rest of world	568	5	Rest of world	78	2
World	11,282	100	World	4,913	100
Top Five Countries	Value	Share, %	Top Five Countries	Value	Share, %
Canada	2,816	25	Canada	2,150	44
Mexico	1,904	17	Japan	670	14
Belgium	758	7	Germany	488	10
Japan	590	5	Mexico	194	4
Netherlands	450	4	France	165	3

[1] SIC 2821.
[2] For definitions of regional groupings, see "Getting the Most Out of *Outlook 2000*."
[3] Values may not sum to total due to rounding.
Source: U.S. Department of Commerce, Bureau of the Census.

a 44 percent share of U.S. imports of plastic resin. Although a smaller portion of the market, double-digit imports from Asian economies—predominantly Hong Kong, South Korea, and the Association of Southeast Asian Nations (ASEAN) countries—solidified import growth.

In the year 2000, imports are expected to continue a positive pattern of growth, rising 6.5 percent. Imports from Asia will continue to grow at double-digit levels as the Asian economies continue to recover, but gains will not be as strong, as Asian resin will not be as inexpensive as it was in 1999. This shift in pricing will encourage closer sourcing of material, with the NAFTA countries and western Europe having the most to gain. The same factors will contribute to import growth of 4 to 6 percent in the period 2000–2004.

Kimberly G. Copperthite, Office of Metals, Materials, and Chemicals/International Trade Administration, (202) 482-5124, Kim_Copperthite@ita.doc.gov, November 1999.

REFERENCES

Chemicals

Chemical Marketing Reporter, Schnell Publishing Company, 80 Broad Street, New York, NY 10004. (212) 248-4177.

Chemical Week, McGraw-Hill Publications, 888 Seventh Avenue, New York, NY 10106. (212) 621-4900.

Drugs and Pharmaceuticals

Current Industrial Reports, Manufacturers Shipments, Inventories and Orders (monthly), U.S. Department of Commerce, Bureau of the Census, Washington, DC 20233.

Generic Pharmaceutical Industry Association, 1620 I Street, NW, Suite 800, Washington, DC 20006.

Nonprescription Drug Manufacturers Association, 1150 Connecticut Avenue, NW, Washington, DC 20036.

Pharmaceutical Research and Manufacturers of America, 1100 Fifteenth Street, NW, Washington, DC 20005.

Plastic Materials and Resins

American Plastics Council, 1801 K Street, NW, Washington, DC 20006. (202) 974-5400, plastics.org.

Facts and Figures of the U.S. Plastics Industry, 1998 edition, Society of the Plastics Industry, Inc., 1801 K Street, NW, Washington, DC 20006. (202) 974-5200

Modern Plastics, McGraw-Hill, Two Penn Plaza, New York, NY 10121-2298. (212) 904-6245, modplas.com.

Plastics News, Crain Communications Inc., 740 North Rush Street, Chicago, IL 60611-2590. plasticsnews.com.

Society of the Plastics Industry, Inc., 1801 K Street, NW, Washington, DC 20006. (202) 974-5200, socplas.org.

RELATED CHAPTERS

8: Building Products and Materials
9: Textiles
12: Synthetic Rubber
20: Environmental Technologies and Services
25: Printing and Publishing
35: Processed Food and Beverages
45: Medical and Dental Instruments

SYNTHETIC RUBBER
Economic and Trade Trends

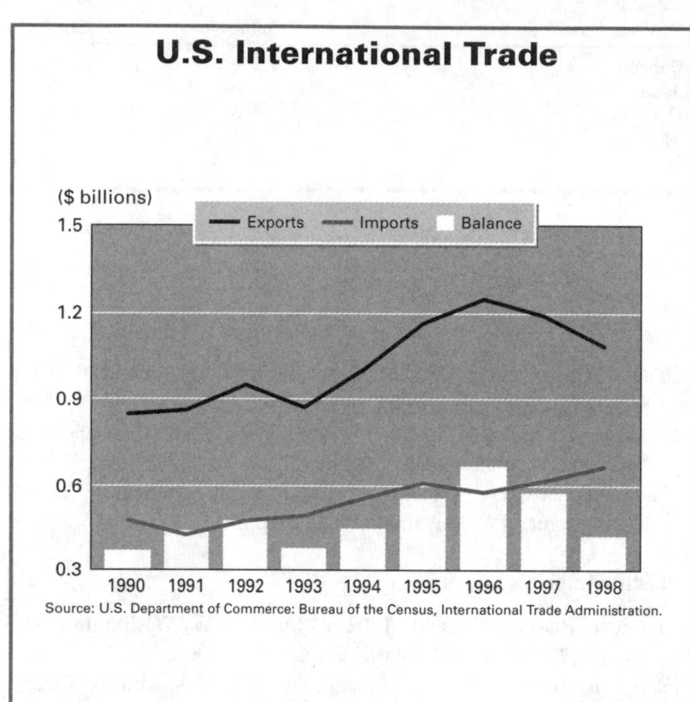

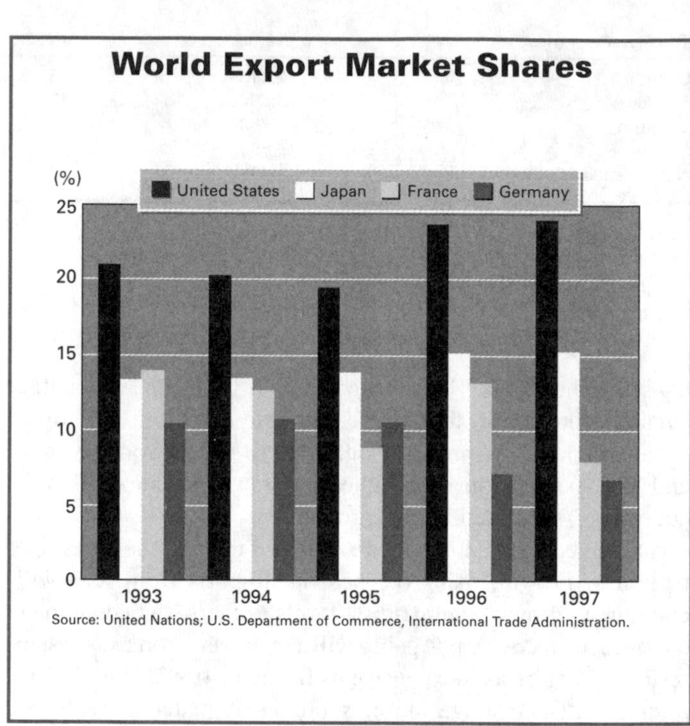

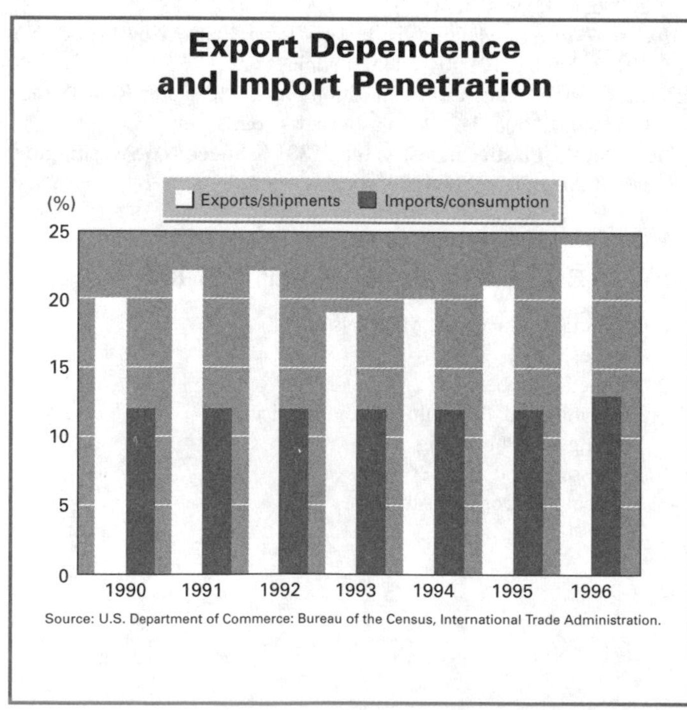

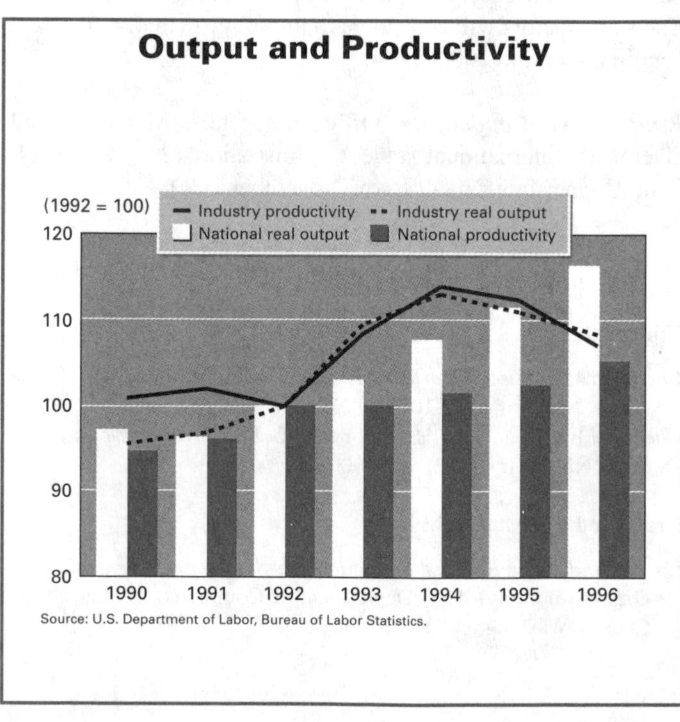

See "Getting the Most Out of *Outlook 2000*" for definitions of terms.

12

Synthetic Rubber

INDUSTRY DEFINITION The synthetic rubber industry (SIC 2822) includes establishments engaged primarily in the manufacture of synthetic rubber (SR), an elastomer, by polymerization or copolymerization. Elastomers are rubberlike materials capable of further processing by vulcanization; they include polymers and copolymers of butadiene and styrene as well as butadiene and acrylonitrile, polybutadienes, chloroprene rubbers, and isobutylene-isoprene copolymers. Butadiene copolymers, however, containing less than 50 percent butadiene are classified under SIC 2821. Similarly, natural chlorinated rubbers and so-called cyclized rubbers are considered semifinished products and are classified under SIC 3069, fabricated rubber products not elsewhere classified. The synthetic materials industry is considered part of the larger U.S. chemical industry. Natural rubber, unlike synthetic, is derived from rubber trees (*Hevea brasiliensis*) and imported largely from southeast Asia. The United States does not produce natural rubber (apart from Gualyule). Production and processing of natural rubber are not included in this industry classification.

OVERVIEW

The U.S. elastomer industry remains the largest, most advanced, and most productive in the world. The United States produced approximately a quarter of world rubber output in 1998 and is also the world's largest consumer of elastomers. In addition, the United States has had a trade surplus in this sector, reaching $421 million in 1998. However, to remain competitive in the twenty-first century, this mature industry must focus on end-product customers while lowering costs, reducing waste, and increasing productivity levels.

GLOBAL INDUSTRY TRENDS

Since its inception in 1906, synthetic rubber has become ubiquitous. People rely on synthetic rubber products for safety in areas ranging from the highway to the doctor's office. As a result of the great resistance to corrosion, poor electrical conductivity, and ability to flex and regain its shape, synthetic rubber uses continue to grow as technology advances. The United States has been and continues to be a leader in the development and production of vulcanizable elastomers.

Two product groups account for the bulk of world production and consumption of synthetic rubber: emulsion styrene-butadiene rubber (SBR) and butadiene rubber (BR). Approximately 87 percent of synthetic rubber capacity is based on the emulsion process (23 to 25 percent styrene and 75 to 77 percent butadiene). The solution process, which has been less popular, produces polymers with a lower molecular weight distribution. The tire industry consumes about 76 percent of dry SBR (15 to 25 percent styrene and 75 to 85 percent butadiene), and much of the tire industry produces SBR exclusively for its own use.

Consumption

Worldwide synthetic rubber consumption reached 10.4 million metric tons in 1998, according to the International Institute for Synthetic Rubber Producers (IISRP). In the aftermath of the Asian financial crisis and as a result of sluggish demand in the automotive sector, world synthetic rubber consumption remained flat at best and by some industry estimates decreased 1.4 percent in 1998 after 3 consecutive years of gains. Western

Europe recorded the greatest growth in 1998, rising 5.4 percent to 2.7 million metric tons. North America showed growth of 3.1 percent thanks to the strong economy, reaching 3.3 million metric tons consumed in 1998. However, Asia continued to experience the aftermath of the economic crisis that hit in 1997. In 1998, Asia decreased synthetic rubber consumption 8.3 percent to 3.2 million metric tons. China experienced a decrease in consumption of 0.8 percent, a substantial drop for a country that has consistently enjoyed growth between 7 and 10 percent. Latin America also suffered from financial turmoil in 1998 and decreased its consumption of synthetic rubber 4 percent to 702 thousand metric tons (kt).

End Use

The bulk of synthetic rubber (SR) is consumed by the automotive industry. Tire applications absorb 62 percent of SR, and automotive mechanical goods account for 8 percent. Nonautomotive mechanical goods account for 6 percent of SR consumption, plastics modification absorbs approximately 8 percent, and 5 percent is consumed by the building and construction industry; other applications account for the remaining 11 percent.

Elastomer Type

With regard to growth by elastomer type in 1998, ethylene propylene rubber [EPR, both ethylene-propylene copolymer (EPM) and ethylene-propylene terpolymer (EPDM)] experienced the largest consumption increases, growing 3.2 percent to reach 814 kt, according to data released by the IISRP. SBR consumption remained stable at 0.8 percent, or 3.3 million metric tons. BR consumption was down 3.4 percent to 1.9 million metric tons, mainly because of significant decreases in Asia and Oceania, China, and Latin America. Acrylonitrile butadiene (NBR) consumption remained relatively flat at –0.2 percent, dropping to 320 kt.

Production

According to data collected by the International Rubber Study Group (IRSG), world synthetic rubber output fell by nearly 2 percent to 9.9 million metric tons in 1998 after 3 consecutive years of growth. During that period, the world experienced a relatively higher increase in the consumption of synthetic rubber, resulting in declining stocks in the second half of 1998.

Synthetic rubber production increased in the United States only slightly, rising .08 percent to 2.6 million metric tons in 1998. Growth was tempered by a strong dollar and weakened Asian and Latin American currencies. Synthetic rubber output fell 11 percent in Canada to 191 kt but increased in Mexico by 8 percent to 167 kt in 1998. In Brazil, synthetic rubber production increased slightly to 340 kt in 1998. However, Argentina experienced a 3 percent decline in production to 54 kt. Certain parts of eastern Europe experienced declines as well: In Romania output fell 24 percent to 22 kt; in Russia, 17 percent to 599 kt; in Bulgaria, 17 percent to 28 kt; and in Poland, 6.5 percent to 94 kt. Neighboring countries experienced moderate growth in synthetic rubber production in 1998, including the Czech Republic (2.5 percent to 82 kt) and Turkey (3.0 percent to 49 kt). In the past, these producers looked eastward for markets, but they recently shifted their focus to western European consumers. Some western European producers experienced growth in output. Output in the Netherlands increased 13 percent to 220 kt; in Germany, 4.5 percent to 580 kt; and in France, 1.2 percent to 606 kt; Finland and Belgium's production remained relatively flat at 39 kt and 120 kt, respectively. Other western European producers experienced declines in output in 1998 mostly as a result of cheaper imports from eastern Europe. The United Kingdom decreased production 14 percent to 252 kt; Spain, 15 percent to 86 kt; and Italy, around 2 percent to 290 kt. Most Asian producers, still suffering from the 1997 financial crisis and overcapacity in that region, experienced declines in production in 1998. China's production declined 2 percent to 589 kt after 8.4 percent growth in 1997–1998. Japan's production declined 4 percent in 1998 to 1.5 million metric tons, Korea's dropped 2 percent to 530 kt, and India's plummeted 12 percent to 66 kt in that period. Only Taiwan weathered the Asian storm with an increase in production, up 5 percent to 428 kt in 1998.

Trade

U.S. exports of synthetic rubber totaled over $1 billion in 1998 (see Table 12-1). Thirty-six percent of those exports were destined for the North American Free Trade Agreement (NAFTA) region, 13 percent for Latin America, 38 percent for western Europe, 7 percent for the Japan/Chinese Economic Area, and 4 percent for Asia. These trade flows reflected the demand of the largest customer, the automotive industry, in particular the huge North American automotive industry and the large auto manufacturers in western Europe.

The synthetic rubber industry had a trade surplus throughout the 1990s; however, that surplus shrank after 1994. In 1998, U.S. imports of synthetic rubber rose 7.8 percent to reach $664 million, whereas, U.S. exports fell by 8.9 percent in that period to $1.1 billion (see Table 12-2). The surge in imports and the dropoff in exports were due to a combination of factors. The Asian economies are still recovering from the 1997 currency crisis. In addition, Asia is experiencing severe overcapacity, with more production coming on-line in 1999 and 2000. Western Europe experienced slow gross domestic product (GDP) growth in 1998, and imports were received from low-cost producers such as the Czech Republic and Turkey rather than from higher-cost producers such as the United States. Economic turmoil and depressed demand in Latin America and Russia also contributed to the decrease in U.S. exports. The strong U.S. economy and the higher value of the dollar hurt U.S. exports but encouraged imports.

Trade estimates for 1999 and 2000 depend on the economic and political situation in troubled regions, such as Asia and Latin America. In addition, they depend on the continued health of the U.S. economy relative to other countries. In 1999, imports are expected to continue to grow at around 7 percent, driven largely by regional NAFTA trade. Overall, imports should continue to grow, but at a more moderate growth rate over time. Exports are expected to remain relatively flat in 1999 due to the recovering

TABLE 12-1: U.S. Trade Patterns in Synthetic Rubber[1] in 1998
(millions of dollars; percent)

Exports			Imports		
Regions[2]	Value[3]	Share, %	Region[2]	Value[3]	Share, %
NAFTA	387	36	NAFTA	256	39
Latin America	143	13	Latin America	22	3
Western Europe	418	38	Western Europe	213	32
Japan/Chinese Economic Area	71	7	Japan/Chinese Economic Area	100	15
Other Asia	44	4	Other Asia	54	8
Rest of world	23	2	Rest of world	19	3
World	1,085	100	World	664	100
Top Five Countries	Value	Share, %	Top Five Countries	Value	Share, %
Canada	288	27	Canada	206	31
Belgium	186	17	Japan	91	14
Mexico	99	9	France	59	9
Brazil	80	7	Germany	56	8
United Kingdom	48	4	Mexico	50	8

[1] SIC 2822.
[2] For definitions of regional groupings, see "Getting the Most Out of *Outlook 2000*."
[3] Values may not sum to total due to rounding.
Source: U.S. Department of Commerce, Bureau of the Census.

state of Asian and Latin American economies, tempered with unexpected pockets of demand in places like Korea and Venezuela. Slower growth for U.S. exports over imports will persist through 2000, particularly if Asian markets fail to grow faster than capacity.

Capacity

World capacity of synthetic rubber remained fairly stable throughout the early 1990s, but as the Asian economies grew rapidly, they began to add capacity in the middle to late 1990s. However, their growth rates went negative in 1998, and Japan's economy slowed during that period; this turn of events caused severe overcapacity in the industry.

In 1998, total world capacity of synthetic rubber is estimated to have reached nearly 13.5 million metric tons. Much of world SR production is located in North America (the United States and Canada), accounting for nearly 28 percent, or 3.8 million metric tons, of the total. However, Europe (including central and eastern Europe and Russia) is the largest source of synthetic rubber capacity, totaling 5.9 million metric tons. However,

TABLE 12-2: Synthetic Rubber (SIC 2822) Trends and Forecasts
(millions of dollars except as noted)

										Percent Change			
	1992	1993	1994	1995	1996	1997	1998[1]	1999[2]	2000[3]	97–98	98–99	99–00	96–00[4]
Industry data													
Value of shipments[5]	4,235	4,739	4,964	5,475	5,291	6,060	6,182	6,244	6,306	2.0	1.0	1.0	4.5
Value of shipments (1992$)	4,235	4,623	4,755	4,543	4,537	5,081	5,130	5,128	5,143	1.0	–0.0	0.3	3.2
Total employment (thousands)	11.9	12.2	11.9	12.0	12.0	12.0							
Production workers (thousands)	7.6	7.7	7.7	8.0	7.9	7.7							
Average hourly earnings ($)	18.73	19.27	19.52	20.61	20.68	21.96							
Capital expenditures	321	256	266	268	279	391	407	411	423	4.1	1.0	2.9	11.0
Product data													
Value of shipments[5]	4,318	4,643	4,983	5,430	5,139	6,160	6,221	6,283	6,345	1.0	1.0	1.0	5.4
Value of shipments (1992$)	4,318	4,530	4,773	4,507	4,407	5,196	5,200	5,190	5,205	0.1	–0.2	0.3	4.2
Trade data													
Value of imports	475	493	554	608	576	616	664	710	745	7.8	7.0	4.9	6.6
Value of exports	950	872	1,003	1,165	1,249	1,191	1,085	1,085	1,095	–8.9	0.0	0.9	–3.2

[1] Estimate except imports and exports.
[2] Estimate.
[3] Forecast.
[4] Compound annual rate.
[5] For a definition of industry versus product values, see "Getting the Most Out of *Outlook 2000*."
Source: U.S. Department of Commerce: Bureau of the Census; International Trade Administration.

these numbers are overstated somewhat because most of Russia's capacity is nonoperational. Asia's capacity has continued to grow, reaching a level of 3.1 million metric tons in 1998. Latin America remains a relatively small player in the synthetic rubber industry, with a reported production capacity of 670 kt in 1998.

FACTORS AFFECTING FUTURE INDUSTRY GROWTH

The synthetic rubber industry is by all accounts mature. Thus, the relatively modest growth rates it has achieved in recent years are quite impressive in light of the mature nature of the industry.

High costs of entry, low profit margins, and the power exerted by established market leaders have resulted in a high level of industry concentration, with huge incentives for further consolidation. Five synthetic rubber producers account for over one-third of total world capacity: Bayer A.G., EniChem SpA, the Goodyear Tire and Rubber Company, Japan Synthetic Rubber Corporation (JSR), and Exxon Chemical. Other major players include DSM, Ameripol Synpol Corporation, DuPont Dow Elastomers, Flexys NV/SA, Nippon Zeon Chemical, Korea Kumbo, Bridgestone Corporation, and Michelin.

In fact, pressure to increase quality and efficiency has motivated many in the industry to pursue mergers and acquisitions. Dow Chemical increased its elastomer reach in June 1999, when it purchased Shell Chemicals' general-purpose rubber business, including its polybutadiene and emulsion SBR businesses. Later in 1999, Dow bid $11.6 billion to acquire Union Carbide Corporation, creating the world's second largest supplier of ethylene-propylene rubber when capacity expansions come on-line. Zeon Chemicals LP acquired DSM Copolymer Inc.'s Nysyn nitrile rubber (NBR) business in March 1999. That deal will give Zeon exclusive purchasing rights for Nysyn NBR produced by DSM at its Baton Rouge, LA, facility. Similar mergers and cooperative arrangements are expected in the year 2000 as synthetic rubber manufacturers look for ways to increase quality and productivity, lower costs, and reach more of the global market.

Overcapacity is a concern in the industry and has affected prices. Asia has been steadily increasing capacity, with much of its output destined for Europe and the United States. Thailand and Indonesia were reported to have several synthetic rubber plants coming on line in 1998 and 1999. Many in the industry believe that capacity in South Korea could be as great as three times domestic demand, with more scheduled to come on-line in 1999. Some industry experts predict that overcapacity in Asia could reach 20 percent by 2002. New entrants into the market, such as Hyundai, which started to export SBR and BR to the United States recently, have pushed prices down. In fact, several South Korean synthetic rubber manufacturers were the subject of investigations during 1999 for dumping product onto the U.S. market (selling below cost). However, these dumping cases were not substantiated by the U.S. International Trade Commission (ITC).

Demand

Globally, the automotive industry accounts for about 70 percent of SR demand, producing tires, gaskets, hoses, belts, sealants, and adhesives. Thus, trends in the automotive sector affect the outlook for the SR industry significantly. Many in the industry have predicted that demand from the automotive sector will decrease over time; however, the popularity of sport utility vehicles (SUVs) has belied that claim, and demand is actually on the rise.

Most trends indicate that vehicle usage is on the rise, with miles driven per year constantly increasing. The Rubber Manufacturers Association (RMA) revised its shipment projections for 1999 upward, including a 5 percent increase in original equipment passenger tire shipments, a 3 percent increase in replacement passenger tires, and a 17 percent increase in the original equipment light truck tire category over 1998 shipments. Also, experts in the automotive industry predict that the next 4 to 6 years will see the scrapping of automobiles originally produced in the period 1984–1989 (a period of record sales), thus boosting new car sales higher than long-range forecasts suggest. These positive forecasts for the automotive industry, including the popularity of SUVs, bode well for the SR industry, as auto and tire manufacturers are always looking for new elastomers that will enhance the functioning and durability of their products.

DOMESTIC TRENDS

The United States continues to be the world's largest consumer of synthetic rubber, absorbing about a quarter of world output. The United States consumed 2.4 million metric tons of SR in 1998, up slightly from 2.3 million metric tons in 1997. Consumption is expected to increase an average of 1 percent per year for the next 5 years.

As a result of relatively strong GDP growth in North America, the use of automotive elastomers rose at an average rate of 3.0 percent in 1998. BR consumption rose 2.7 percent to 280 kt, and SBR solid consumption increased 2.2 percent to 960 kt. EPDM use had a growth rate of 3.7 percent, increasing from 309 kt in 1997 to 321 kt in 1998, while NBR use grew 4.2 percent from 85 kt to 89 kt during that period. Over the next 5 years, according to the IISRP, tire elastomer consumption should climb at a moderate rate of 1.5 percent in North America.

Geography and Industry Statistics

According to industry statistics for 1997, seven states were responsible for over 75 percent of synthetic rubber shipments in the United States: Texas ($1.9 billion), Louisiana ($1.0 billion), Ohio ($757 million), Kentucky ($432 million), New Jersey ($230 million), Indiana ($100 million), and Florida ($96 million). Texas employs the largest number of workers in the synthetic rubber business, with 3,644 employees (2,424 production workers) in 1997. Louisiana employs 1,511 people (1,062 production workers) in the synthetic rubber business, and Ohio employs 1,035 people (594 production workers).

New Capacity

Several domestic producers are set to increase capacity over the next 5 years. Ethylene-propylene (EP) rubber users, who have been caught in a supply-demand price squeeze, may begin to see relief by the end of 1999 and into 2001. Two new sources of supply are coming on stream (Union Carbide in Seadrift, TX, and Dupont Dow Elastomers in Plaquemine, LA), and the industry's largest producer, DSM N.V., is starting expansion projects in the United States and Europe. Global capacity for EP-type elastomers could increase 20 percent over the next 2 to 3 years and reach about 1.1 million tons by 2001. Worldwide demand for EP-type rubber is expected to grow 4 percent annually over that period.

Also moving to increase capacity, Goodyear has begun building a $144 million solution synthetic rubber plant in Beaumont, TX, and has reorganized its chemical division. These developments promise to make the already huge synthetic rubber producer even more aggressive in the commercial synthetic market. Currently, Goodyear uses most of its SR production internally. The new facility will produce 240 million pounds of additional capacity, offering approximately half for commercial sale. In addition, Goodyear plans to build a solution synthetic plant in Europe. Goodyear already ranks as the second largest supplier of tire elastomers in the world, behind Bayer A.G.

Price

Synthetic rubber prices fell in 1998 because of several major factors, including the overall decrease in commodity prices experienced during the period, global overcapacity, and increased import competition from low-cost producers such as South Korea and Malaysia. However, in mid-1999, as commodity prices began to recover, producers had to announce price increases of 2 to 3 cents per pound of SR to absorb the higher costs of raw materials. Prices should continue to rebound in 2000.

PROJECTIONS OF INDUSTRY AND TRADE GROWTH FOR THE NEXT 1 AND 5 YEARS

Worldwide synthetic rubber consumption was forecast by the IISRP to rise 2.0 percent, to 10.7 million metric tons in 1999. Over the next 5-year period, global SR consumption is estimated to average a moderate growth rate of around 3 percent per annum to reach a total of 12 million metric tons by 2004. In real terms, industry shipments in the year 2000 will depend largely on conditions prevailing in the main end-use sectors. Optimistic demand from the tire sector and the health care industry, combined with expected growth in the fabricated rubber products and miscellaneous plastic products sectors, has created a relatively positive outlook for the SR industry in the next 5 years. In addition, rising prices predicted for natural rubber and continued concern about latex allergies will contribute to increased demand for competitively priced, high-performance synthetic elastomers.

Industry experts believe that all geographic regions will show gains in SR use over the coming 5-year period. After a year of negative growth in 1998, China is expected to resume its consumption at pre–Asian crisis levels, rising around 7 percent to nearly 1 million metric tons by 2004. In Asia and Oceania, an annual growth rate of 2 percent is expected through 2004 to 2.2 million metric tons consumed, depending on economic reform and political factors. The situation in the Confederation of Independent States (CIS) remains uncertain. Industry forecasts call for an annual average growth rate of around 2 percent, but that rate will depend on economic stabilization in the region and continued assistance from the International Monetary Fund (IMF). The prospect for growth in central Europe is optimistic, according to many in the industry, averaging near 5 percent per year and rising to 550 kt consumed by 2004. In western Europe, consumption is expected to grow more slowly over the next 5 years. It is forecast to rise at an annual rate of nearly 2 percent to over 3 million metric tons by 2004. In the Middle East and Africa, predictions call for a growth rate of around 2 percent annually to 297 kt by 2004. Latin America should increase its use of SR at a more moderate rate near 2 percent, reaching approximately 758 kt by 2004, depending on growth in recovering economies such as Brazil. North American consumption should rise at an annual rate of around 1 percent, and could reach 3.7 million metric tons by 2004.

Consumption of all elastomer types should grow over the next 5 years, according to the IISRP. Forecasts predict that EPR (EPDM) use will grow around 4 percent per annum to 1 million metric tons by 2004. NBR should show annual average increases of approximately 3 percent to 400 kt. SBR consumption is forecast to grow 3 percent annually as well, reaching nearly 4 million metric tons by 2004, powered by increased demand from the automotive sector. BR consumption is expected to climb an average of 2 percent to reach 2.2 million metric tons by 2004.

The thermoplastic elastomers (TPEs) market is widely viewed as mature, with overcapacity and price competition at the lower end of the market. However, growth is still expected, and companies such as Dupont Dow Elastomers are banking on increased use of TPEs, particularly those of middle to high performance. Worldwide use of TPEs is expected to increase from 1.3 million metric tons in 1998 to 1.8 million metric tons by 2004, an average annual increase of around 5 percent. In North America, TPE use should increase in line with world forecasts, reaching approximately 642 kt by 2004.

GLOBAL MARKET PROSPECTS

Overall, increased global competition in the rubber business is heightening the urgency among producers to lower costs, reduce waste, and utilize plant and labor power more effectively. In short, many rubber suppliers will target productivity improvements in the twenty-first century. This goal implies an increase in cooperative agreements and/or mergers and acquisitions among producers to achieve economies of scale and scope.

In addition, increased cooperation with end-product manufacturers will become more critical to the success of SR producers. In particular, the industry's biggest customer—the tire industry—is actively seeking new, improved varieties of synthetic rubber that will allow it to decrease the weight, and thus the rolling resistance, of tires. Some in the industry suggest that the use of solution polymerization SBR rather than emulsion SBR (the historical favorite) could contribute to a lighter-weight elastomer. The goal for many producers will be to develop lighter elastomers without sacrificing basic performance, safety, and/or durability requirements to meet the needs of an industry that will face growing environmental regulation in the future. In addition, the tire industry continues to search for a synthetic substitute for natural rubber. This search has taken on new intensity as natural rubber prices are forecast to rise sharply over the next 5 years, with supply problems predicted for 2004 and beyond.

The health care industry continues to search for durable, high-performance elastomers that will not pose problems for persons allergic to latex. The best synthetic alternatives to natural latex gloves contain nitrile and neoprene, but those products are significantly more expensive than latex. Synthetic rubber companies are under pressure to develop low-cost, durable elastomers with low latex protein levels.

Overall, the synthetic rubber industry must focus increasingly on end-user demands while working to increase productivity levels and lower costs to ensure its success in the twenty-first century.

Jennifer Yoder, Office of Metals, Materials, and Chemicals, Department of Commerce, International Trade Administration, (202) 482-0131, jennifer_yoder@ita.doc.gov, February 2000.

■ REFERENCES

Primary

Rubber Economic Yearbook 1998, International Rubber Study Group, Heron House, 109/115 Wembley Hill Road, Wembley HA9 8DA, United Kingdom. (44) 181-903-7727; fax: (44) 181-903-2848; www.rubberstudy.com.

Rubber Statistical Bulletin, vol. 53, no. 10, July 1999, International Rubber Study Group, Heron House, 109/115 Wembley Hill Road, Wembley HA9 8DA, United Kingdom. (44) 181-903-7727; fax: (44) 181-903-2848; www.rubberstudy.com.

Worldwide Rubber Statistics 1998, International Institute of Synthetic Rubber Producers, 2077 South Gessner Road., Suite 133, Houston, TX. (713) 783-7253; fax: (713) 783-7253; www.iisrp.com.

Secondary

"Elastomers Overview, January 1995," *Chemical Economics Handbook,* SRI International, Menlo Park, CA 94025. (415) 859-3900.

International Tire and Rubber Association. 3332 Gilmore Industrial Boulevard Louisville, KY 40213-4113. (502) 968-8900 or (800) 426-8835; fax: (502) 964-7859; www.itra.com.

National Tire Dealer and Retreaders Association, 1250 I Street, NW, Suite 400, Washington, DC 20005. (202) 682-3999.

Rubber and Plastics News, Crain Communications, Inc., 1725 Merriman Road, Suite 300, Akron, OH 44313-5251. (330) 836-9180; fax: (330) 836-1005; www.rubbernews.com.

Rubber Manufacturers Association, 1400 K Street, NW, Washington, DC 20005. (202) 682-4800; (202) 682-4809; www.rma.org.

Rubber Products: An Overview of Major Markets and Opportunities for Developing Countries, International Trade Center, UNCTAD/GATT, Geneva, Switzerland, 1995.

■ RELATED CHAPTERS

11: Chemicals and Allied Products
36: Motor Vehicles
37: Automotive Parts
44: Medical and Dental Instruments and Supplies

STEEL MILL PRODUCTS
Economic and Trade Trends

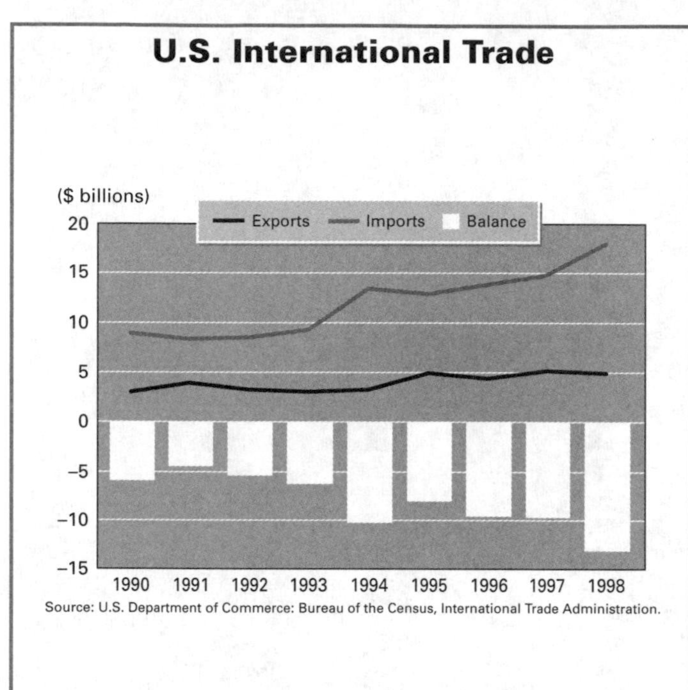

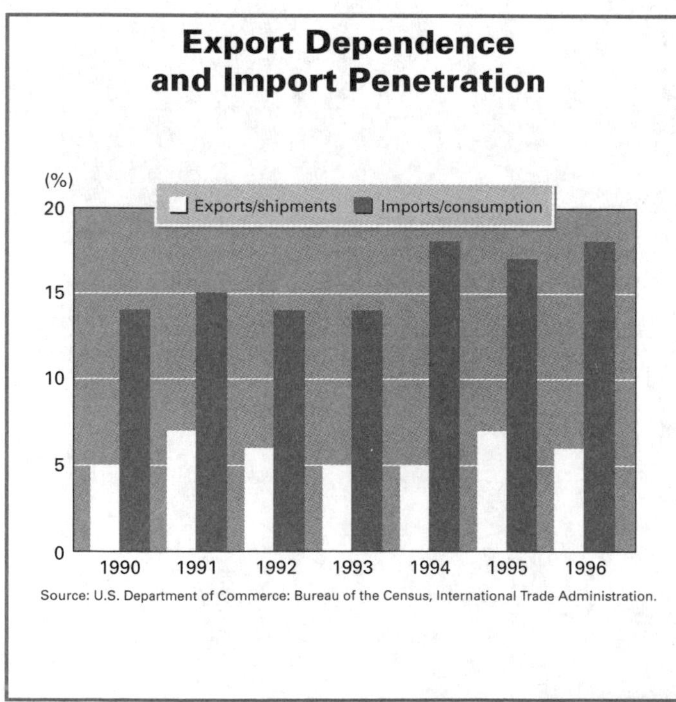

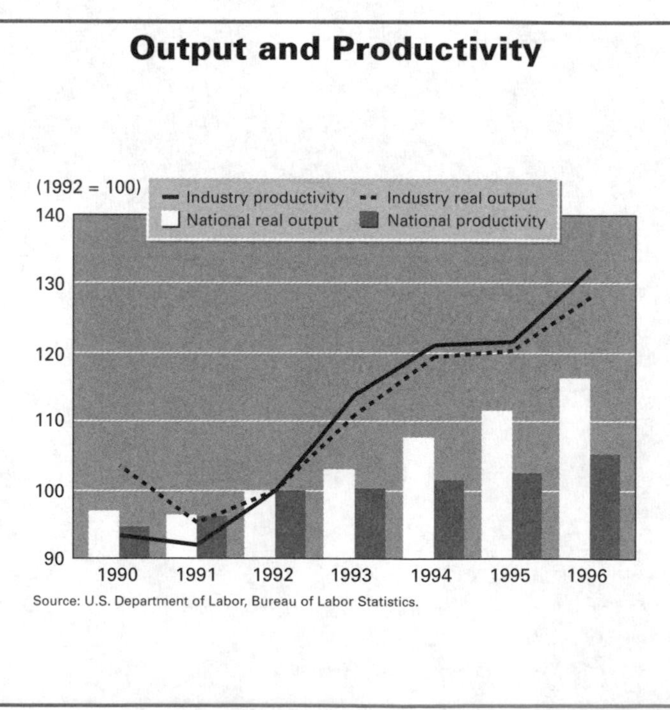

See "Getting the Most Out of *Outlook 2000*" for definitions of terms.

13

Steel Mill Products

INDUSTRY DEFINITION The U.S. steel industry encompasses the products of steel works, blast furnaces, and rolling mills (SIC 3312); steel wiredrawing and steel nails and spikes (SIC 3315); cold-rolled sheet, strip, and bars (3316); and steel pipes and tubes (SIC 3317). The products in SIC 3312 account for the overwhelming share of this sector.

GLOBAL INDUSTRY TRENDS

The severe economic problems that roiled the Asian countries beginning in 1997, together with global overcapacity, precipitated a global "steel crisis" in 1998, with continuing consequences for U.S. steel producers in 1999. The rapidly developing countries in Asia had been major importers of steel. However, as their economies weakened, steel demand fell precipitously. While apparent consumption fell 2 percent (16 million tons) worldwide in 1998, it dropped 37 percent (12 million tons) in the Association of Southeast Asian (ASEAN) countries as well as in South Korea. In Japan, the third largest individual market for steel, the decline was 17 percent (14 million tons).

With limited sales prospects at home, Asian steelmakers shifted to exports to the remaining strong and open markets, principally the United States and the European Union (EU) nations. In addition, countries that had been shipping most of their exports to Asia, notably Japan and Russia, diverted their trade to the United States and EU markets. As a consequence, total U.S. imports jumped 33 percent to a record 37.7 million tons in 1998. Imports from Japan and South Korea soared 163 percent (4 million tons) and 109 percent (1.6 million tons), respectively. Imports from smaller Asian producers such as Indonesia, Taiwan, and Thailand also rose more than 100 percent. Russia, which also experienced falling domestic demand as a result of its own financial crisis, boosted its shipments to the United States by 1.8 million tons (59 percent) to account for 13 percent of total imports. In the European Union, the net trade balance shifted from a surplus of 11.7 million tons to just 0.5 million ton because of a rise in imports and a decline in exports.

Sharply falling prices compounded the difficulties of steelmakers in the United States and elsewhere. The spot composite price for carbon steel product exports worldwide fell 14 percent between 1997 and 1998, dropping to its lowest level since 1993. The price of hot-rolled sheet, the most extensively traded product, dropped more than 19 percent. In the United States, the average unit value of all steel imports fell 9 percent between 1997 and 1998. It continued to fall an additional 10.5 percent between January and June 1999.

Owing to the dramatic shifts in trade and the drop in prices, more than 20 steel-importing countries have taken formal trade action since the start of the crisis, including many of world's biggest importers. In the United States, the U.S. Department of Commerce completed more than 60 antidumping and countervailing duty investigations covering a wide range of products and countries. In most cases, additional duties were imposed after trade agencies determined that there had been dumping and the industry had been injured. As an alternative to prohibitive tariffs, the U.S. Department of Commerce negotiated an agreement that placed quotas and a price floor on imports of certain hot-rolled flat products from Brazil in July 1999. For Russia, which also had been facing very high dumping duties, an agreement was reached to suspend the antidumping investigation on the flat-rolled products and impose a quota and additional minimum prices. The quota volumes increase incrementally over the 5-year life of the agreement. A second agreement was concluded that restricts imports in major product areas not covered by other agreements or investigations. These two agreements and a previous one on plate were designed to reduce 1999 imports of steel from Russia by nearly two-thirds compared with 1998 levels.

During the first 7 months of 1999, U.S. imports decreased 9.5 percent to 18.2 million tons from the level a year earlier, reflecting largely the remedial impact of the trade cases and suspension agreements. Imports of carbon hot-rolled steel fell 65 percent from the November 1998 peak, and those of cold-rolled steel dropped 23 percent; both products were the subject of a number of dumping cases. Still, with U.S. prices remaining well above world prices and many other foreign markets weak, the United States is an attractive market for foreign steel producers. This has encouraged some shifting to other products and countries.

Global overcapacity is cited as the root cause for this surge in "unfair" trading. According to Organization for Economic Cooperation and Development (OECD) Steel Committee estimates, the capacity utilization rate worldwide was only 75 percent in 1998, based on production of 776 million tons and a capacity of 1.04 billion tons. The rate had been 77 percent in 1997; it was forecast to decline to just 71 percent in 1999 owing to an increase in capacity of 30 million tons and a 3 percent decline in production. Other groups have developed somewhat lower and perhaps more realistic capacity estimates that are based on an "effective capacity" measure, but even by those estimates the production surplus is substantial.

Much of the excess capacity is believed to be unjustified economically. For social reasons, governments frequently have supported inefficient mills by maintaining import barriers, providing subsidies, or tolerating cartels. As a matter of industrial policy and national pride, many countries developed state-owned steel sectors, many of which were privatized during the last decade. However, state ownership persists in China and India.

The Newly Independent States of the former Soviet Union and Japan have substantial overcapacity. In Russia, producers have adjusted to the 70 percent decline in domestic demand since 1992 by boosting exports more than 220 percent. Exports now account for more than 69 percent of domestic production. Even with the growth in export markets, however, the industry operated at only 48 percent of capacity in 1998. Very little capacity has been cut because of the critical importance of steel mills to many communities. Japan's steelmakers operated at only 63 percent of capacity in 1998, down from 72 percent in 1997, owing to the previously mentioned contraction in domestic demand (down 17 percent) and in traditional export markets in Asia. In a recent report, the Japanese government warned that overcapacity problems would be chronic and urged the industry to cut capacity and focus on selective product lines. The report concluded that if steps are not taken, the capacity surplus in 10 years will range from 15 million to 32 million tons, or 12 to 24 percent of the total capacity.

Concerned about the difficulties for the steel industry posed by the continuing high levels of unfairly traded imports, the Clinton administration announced a Steel Action Program on August 5, 1999. Key features of the program include a systematic analysis of foreign subsidies and market-distorting trade barriers for steel and steel raw materials, an international conference on unfair trade practices that support economically unjustifiable production capacity, bilateral discussions with key steel exporters (e.g., Japan and South Korea) to ensure that they play by the rules of fair trade and eliminate market-distorting subsidies, and strengthened enforcement of U.S. trade laws.

The difficulties of the steel industry worldwide are one factor in consolidations among major steelmakers as well as scrap processors and steel service centers. Steel firms have viewed mergers as one means of boosting earnings in light of the limited prospect for price increases. Benefits result from combining some mills and shutting others. In mid-1999, British Steel agreed to purchase the Dutch producer Hoogovens, creating the second largest steel company in Europe, with a capacity of more than 24 million tons. This followed the merger in 1998 of Thyssen Krupp, now the third largest European firm, with a capacity of 25 million tons, and a wave of earlier consolidations. The result is that the five largest mills in Europe have an average capacity of more than 20 million tons; Japan's Nippon Steel, the world's largest, has a capacity of 30 million tons. The U.S. industry has undergone some consolidation, but not as much as the steel industry in Europe has; the largest U.S. steelmaker, USX Corporation, has a capacity of 11.5 million tons. In part, this may reflect the entry in recent years of a number of very competitive minimills that are challenging the dominance of the mostly larger integrated mills. Still, AK Steel, once part of Armco, agreed to acquire its former parent during the summer of 1999 to create the country's sixth largest producer, with a capacity of more than 5.3 million tons; as the two firms merged, some mills were to be shut, idled, or sold. Also, three major bar producers USS/Kobe Steel, Republic Engineered Steels, and Bar Technologies—agreed to merge their bar divisions to form the dominant producer of special quality bars, with a capacity of 3.2 million tons. Some bar mills were closed as part of rationalization during the merger.

Some major steel consumers, such as General Motors (GM), are encouraging international consolidation by instituting a global purchasing policy. In early 1999, GM announced agreements to buy 18 million tons of steel over 4 years from 40 global producers. Three-quarters of the steel was to be supplied by U.S.-based producers. Still, this represents GM's first attempt to buy large amounts of steel on a global basis. The length of the contract is also unusual. Typically, contracts are negotiated for much shorter periods owing to price fluctuations.

DOMESTIC TRENDS

Demand for steel mill products has been strong owing to the continuing robust growth of the economy. In 1998, apparent consumption for steel mill products (domestic shipments plus imports minus exports, with no inventory adjustment) rose to a record 125.6 million tons, a 5.8 percent rise over the previous record in 1997 and up nearly 40 percent since 1989.

Many new products and applications, an increase in the steel intensity of the economy [steel consumption per unit of gross domestic product (GDP)], high automobile production, and a favorable shift in the indirect trade of steel (i.e., the net trade in steel-containing products) are factors that have boosted demand since 1989.

However, in the first half of 1999, apparent consumption dropped by 8 percent from the same period in 1998. A partial drawdown of the huge inventory accumulated during the import surge in 1998 is believed to account for a large part of the decline. While estimates of the actual inventory increase during that time are imprecise, industry data suggest that the cumulative inventory buildup between the fourth quarter of 1997 and the third quarter of 1998 may have exceeded 7 million tons.

Even with strong underlying demand, the recent performance of the U.S. steel industry has been dismal by almost any measure, particularly in the second half of 1998 and continuing into first half of 1999. Domestic shipments dropped 3 percent in 1998 from the previous year to 92.9 million tons; in the first half of 1999, they fell an additional 8 percent compared with the same period in 1998. In addition, through September 11, the industry operated at only 80 percent of its raw steelmaking capacity, compared with 90 percent in the same period in 1998. Maintaining high operating rates is important to the bottom line of this capital-intensive industry.

Compounding the steelmakers' difficulties was the sharp drop in prices. According to the Bureau of Labor Statistics (BLS) composite index for steel mill products, prices fell by 7 percent between January 1998 and January 1999. By August 1999, they had fallen an additional 2 percent to only slightly above the December 1984 level. By comparison, the price index for all manufacturing industries rose 29 percent since 1984. Many steelmakers were concerned that they had little price relief in 1999 despite the decline in imports. They attributed the lower prices and shipments to the lingering impact of inventory overhang and drawdown.

Owing to the low prices and low operating rates, profitability has suffered. During the first half of 1999, the industry reported an operating loss of $51 million compared with an operating profit of $537 million during the same months in 1998. Since the steel industry historically is highly cyclical, it has been particularly apprehensive that even at the peak of the economic cycle it is unable to generate the profits that will be necessary to tide it over during a recession. Five companies have declared bankruptcy since the crisis began.

The sharp drop in earnings has made it more difficult to raise capital. With the stock prices of some major steel companies falling by more than half since April 1998, those companies have little prospect of raising new equity on a favorable basis. With some companies encountering difficulties even borrowing money, Congress approved and the President signed legislation in August 1999 authorizing federal loan guarantees up to $1 billion to the steel industry, subject to certain conditions. Individual steel companies will be eligible to borrow up to $250 million at market rates to modernize their plants, and all loans will have to be repaid by 2005. The program will be administered by the U.S. Department of Commerce.

With falling operating rates and mounting pressure to reduce costs, steel companies accelerated reductions in employment. According to BLS data, employment dropped 5 percent between January 1998 and January 1999 to 223,700, the lowest figure then on record. Employment continued to decline during much of 1999, bottoming out at 221,500 in June, a new low. (Data were first collected in 1939, when employment totaled 515,500; the number peaked at 726,100 in 1953.) Over the long term, strong growth in productivity has allowed the industry to boost shipments substantially while decreasing the workforce. Between 1990 and 1998, shipments increased 21 percent while employment dropped more than 16 percent.

Demand from the motor vehicle sector, which alternates with construction as the largest steel-consuming industry, is a major factor in the strong growth in apparent consumption. Between 1991 and 1998, domestic shipments to this sector increased nearly 60 percent as light vehicle production in the United States jumped 5.2 million units. Moreover, with the growing popularity of larger sport utility vehicles and as a result of other factors, such as an emphasis on safety, the average weight per unit rose more than 150 pounds. More than half the increase involved the use of high- and medium-strength steels, many of which have been developed recently. Other products experiencing greater use include tubing made from hot-rolled steel and tailor-welded blanks. Steel's total share of the average vehicle body weight has been fairly steady, rising about 1 percent annually to reach 56 percent between 1991 and 1998.

Steel is facing strong competition from other materials. In 1999, its share of the total weight of a light vehicle edged down very slightly (about 7 pounds) for the first time in several years even as total vehicle weight rose about 13 pounds. While part of the decline may be attributable to increased use of lighter-weight steel in new applications, there appears to be some substitution of lighter-weight materials as automakers try to control the weight of vehicles. Aluminum content, for example, rose 13 pounds in 1999 and 70 pounds since 1991.

The construction industry, particularly the housing sector, is viewed by steelmakers as a major growth market for steel and has contributed to the current strength in market demand. Between 1990 and 1998, shipments to the construction sector rose more than 26 percent to 13.9 million tons, accounting for 15 percent of total shipments. To promote the use of light gauge steel framing in residential construction, in October 1998 the American Iron and Steel Institute established the North American Steel Framing Alliance. Steel's advantages include its strength, steady prices, and recyclability (a typical 2,000-square-foot wood-framed house requires 13,000 board-feet of lumber, the equivalent of the steel recycled from six cars). Its disadvantages are the requirement for rivets and specialized tools, somewhat higher construction costs, and the inexperience of most builders in working with steel. To address this problem, new tools are being developed to facilitate assembly and training for framers is being offered. At present, only a very small percentage of new houses are framed with steel, but the industry aims to boost its share substantially over the next few years. A typical steel-frame house contains about 9 tons of steel.

The growing demand for steel and lower barriers to entry resulting from less capital-intensive steelmaking and rolling technologies have prompted a large increase in steelmaking capacity. During the 1990s, crude steelmaking capacity bottomed out at 98.2 million tons in 1994 and then jumped to 116.2 million tons in 1999. Most of this capacity increase occurred in minimills, which linked the electric furnace to technological developments in thin slab casting and the rolling of flat products. Nearly 15 million net tons of flat rolled capacity has been added. Still, much of the steel that is produced by minimills is not competitive with the high-quality steel manufactured by integrated mills for use in motor vehicles and appliances.

To upgrade their flat products, minimills are adjusting the mix of the raw materials in their furnaces. Scrap is the primary charge in an electric arc furnace (EAF), but it generally cannot be used to produce the highest-quality products. An alternative that is being used is pig iron. However, pig iron, which typically is produced in a blast furnace by an integrated producer, has a price disadvantage except during cyclical downturns. Direct reduced iron (DRI), iron carbide, and hot briquetted iron (HBI) also are being more widely produced by minimills in new plants to meet the higher demand for scrap substitutes. One promising new development is a process that would produce low-cost molten pig iron from iron ore fines and steam coal. If this process, which is in the start-up phase, is successful, the minimill where it is being tried could produce higher-quality flat products owing to the improved properties of its EAF-based crude steel. The process also has lower capital and operating costs (including substantial energy savings) and more favorable economies of scale than the conventional coke oven/blast furnace means of making pig iron. If this project is successful, its use is likely to spread to other minimills.

Steel trading on the Internet is growing rapidly, particularly for the excess prime and secondary steels that reportedly account for about 15 percent of the steel sold in the United States. Two sites have been established that offer buyers and sellers an opportunity to buy and sell steel from a variety of companies. Revenues accrue to the sites through transaction fees and advertising. Sellers at one site include foreign and domestic producers and steel service centers selling steel, plate, and slabs. One major steel company reported that it first offered 90 tons of cold-rolled steel at one of the sites in January 1999 and by July had expanded to 45,000 tons in six products. A major service center created a Website in 1998; 1 year later, Web sales totaled $100 million. E-commerce allows efficient communication between buyers and sellers and seemingly threatens the middlemen companies that historically have played that role.

INDUSTRY AND TRADE PROJECTIONS FOR THE NEXT 1 AND 5 YEARS

With GDP expected to rise at a 2 percent rate in 2000 and inflation prospects modest, underlying steel demand in the United States should continue to be strong. The prospects for major end users appear favorable. The construction market, which accounted for nearly 15 percent of 1998 shipments, is expected to rise about 1 percent, but the steel-intensive highway and private nonresidential building components markets are forecast to rise 8 percent and 2 percent, respectively. Light vehicle production is likely to be relatively flat at the current high level of approximately 12.1 million units. With producers' durable equipment expenditures expected to rise at a solid rate, the capital goods industries important to steel should benefit.

Globally too, demand is expected to rise. The OECD Steel Committee is projecting that apparent consumption worldwide will increase approximately 4 percent, including a nearly 10 percent increase in the ASEAN countries. With growing

TABLE 13-1: Steel Mill Products (SIC 3312, 3315, 3316, 3317) Trends and Forecasts
(millions of dollars except as noted)

										Percent Change			
	1992	1993	1994	1995	1996	1997[1]	1998[1]	1999[2]	2000[3]	97–98	98–99	99–00	96–00[4]
Industry data													
Value of shipments[5]	57,187	61,301	68,753	73,716	73,238	77,600	74,500	72,000	75,000	–4.0	–3.4	4.2	0.6
Value of shipments (1992$)	57,187	60,338	64,732	65,687	67,422	70,700	68,450	69,600	71,000	–3.2	1.7	2.0	1.3
Total employment (thousands)	234	225	222	221	217								
Production workers (thousands)	179	173	172	173	171								
Capital expenditures	2,568	2,166	3,130	3,283	3,402								
Product data													
Value of shipments[5]	56,132	60,199	67,681	72,347	71,293	75,505	72,489	70,056	72,975	–4.0	–3.4	4.2	0.6
Value of shipments (1992$)	56,132	59,266	63,733	64,472	65,609	68,791	66,602	67,721	69,083	–3.2	1.7	2.0	1.3
Trade data													
Value of imports	8,507	9,298	13,442	12,906	13,853	14,814	17,970	14,500	13,900	21.3	–19.3	–4.1	0.1
Value of exports	3,191	2,987	3,204	4,891	4,346	5,116	4,865	4,400	4,800	–4.9	–9.6	9.1	2.5

[1] Estimate except imports and exports.
[2] Estimate.
[3] Forecast.
[4] Compound annual rate.
[5] For a definition of industry versus product values, see "Getting the Most Out of *Outlook 2000.*"
Source: U.S. Department of Commerce: Bureau of the Census; International Trade Administration.

TABLE 13-2: Net Tonnage of Steel Mill Products (SIC 3312, 3315, 3316, 3317), 1988–2000
(millions of net tons except as noted)

	1988	1992	1993	1994	1995	1996	1997	1998	1999[1]	2000[2]	Percent Change 97–98	98–99	1999–2000	Compound Annual Rate of Growth, % 88–98
Raw steel production	99.9	92.9	97.9	100.6	104.9	104.4	108.6	108.8	105.0	107.5	0.2	−3.5	2.4	0.9
Continuous casting (%)	61.3	79.3	85.7	89.5	91.1	93.2	94.7	95.5	96.0	97.0				
Steel mill product shipments	83.8	82.2	89.0	95.0	97.5	100.5	105.9	102.4	104.0	106.0	−3.3	1.6	1.9	2.0
Exports	2.1	4.3	4.0	3.8	7.1	5.0	6.3	5.5	5.0	5.3	−12.7	−9.1	6.0	10.1
Imports	20.9	17.1	19.5	30.1	24.4	29.1	31.2	41.5	34.5	32.0	33.0	−16.9	−7.2	7.1
Apparent domestic consumption	102.7	95.0	104.5	121.3	114.8	124.6	130.8	138.4	133.5	132.7	5.8	−3.5	−0.6	3.0
Exports/shipments ratio	2.5	5.2	4.5	4.0	7.3	5.0	5.9	5.4	4.8	5.0				
Imports as a percent of apparent consumption	20.3	18.0	18.7	24.8	21.3	23.4	23.9	30.0	25.8	24.1				

[1] Estimate.
[2] Forecast.
Source: American Iron and Steel Institute, U.S. Bureau of the Census. Forecasts by the International Trade Association.

TABLE 13-3: Metric Tonnage of Steel Mill Products (SIC 3312, 3315, 3316, 3317), 1988–2000
(millions of metric tons except as noted)

	1988	1992	1993	1994	1995	1996	1997	1998[1]	1999[2]	2000[2]	Percent Change 97–98	98–99	1999–2000	Compound Annual Rate of Growth, % 88–98
Raw steel production	90.6	84.3	88.8	91.3	95.2	94.7	98.5	98.7	95.3	97.5	0.2	−3.5	2.4	0.9
Continuous casting (%)	55.2	79.3	85.7	89.5	91.1	93.2	94.0	95.5	96.0	88.0				
Steel mill product shipments	76.0	74.6	80.7	86.2	88.5	91.2	96.1	92.9	94.3	96.2	−3.3	1.6	1.9	2.0
Exports	1.9	3.9	3.6	3.4	6.4	4.5	5.7	5.0	4.5	4.8	−12.7	−9.1	6.0	10.1
Imports (including semifinished steel)	19.0	15.5	17.7	27.3	22.1	26.4	28.3	37.6	31.3	29.0	33.0	−16.9	−7.2	7.1
Apparent domestic consumption	93.2	86.2	94.8	110.0	104.1	113.0	118.7	125.6	121.1	120.4	5.8	−3.5	−0.6	3.0
Exports/shipments ratio	2.5	5.2	4.5	4.0	7.3	5.0	5.9	5.4	4.8	5.0				
Imports as a percent of apparent consumption	20.3	18.0	18.7	24.8	21.3	23.4	23.9	30.0	25.8	24.1				

[1] Estimate.
[2] Forecast.
Source: American Iron and Steel Institute, U.S. Bureau of the Census. Forecasts by the International Trade Administration.

demand elsewhere, foreign producers will have markets besides the United States to which to ship their steel.

In this environment, domestic steel shipments should grow approximately 2 percent from the 1999 projection of 94 million tons. The excess inventories were expected to be liquidated in 1999 and therefore are unlikely to weigh on the market in 2000. Imports are expected to drop slightly as a result of improving demand elsewhere and the remedial impact of the large and growing number of trade cases.

Through the year 2004, steel shipments should rise at an erratic rate of 1 to 2 percent annually, assuming continued moderate economic growth (see Tables 13-1, 13-2, and 13-3).

GLOBAL MARKET PROSPECTS

Exports historically have accounted for only a small share of total steel shipments. Even in 1995, when they reached a peak of 6.4 million tons, they represented just 7 percent of domestic shipments. Since then, exports have trended downward erratically, falling to 5 million tons in 1998 to account for just 5 percent of shipments. During the first half of 1999, in response to the global steel crisis, they dropped an additional 21 percent compared with the same period in 1998.

Many steelmakers argue that they have little incentive to export, since they do not have the capacity even to supply the domestic market, for which they have demonstrated a marked preference. Also discouraging exports are the current low prices and alleged trade barriers and subsidies in many countries that the Steel Action Program is designed to address.

In 1998, 70 percent of U.S. exports were destined for the North American Free Trade Agreement (NAFTA) partners Canada and Mexico (see Table 13-4). Their large share is a result of proximity, the relative strength of those markets, the presence of the same end users (e.g., automobile companies), and certain market access provisions under NAFTA. Tariffs with Canada have been eliminated, and those with Mexico will disappear completely in 2003. South America and Europe are small (as measured by value) and declining markets for U.S. producers. Asia had developed into a promising market in the mid-

TABLE 13-4: U.S. Trade Patterns in Steel Mill Products[1] in 1998
(millions of dollars; percent)

Exports			Imports		
Region[2]	Value[3]	Share, %	Region[2]	Value[3]	Share, %
NAFTA	3,407	70	NAFTA	3,818	21
Latin America	409	8	Latin America	1,411	8
Western Europe	413	8	Western Europe	4,384	24
Japan/Chinese Economic Area	117	2	Japan/Chinese Economic Area	3,916	22
Other Asia	161	3	Other Asia	1,657	9
Rest of world	358	7	Rest of world	2,785	15
World	4,865	100	World	17,970	100
Top Five Countries	Value	Share, %	Top Five Countries	Value	Share, %
Canada	2,339	48	Japan	3,172	18
Mexico	1,068	22	Canada	2,644	15
United Kingdom	108	2	Russia	1,395	8
Venezuela	77	2	South Korea	1,281	7
Morocco	72	1	Mexico	1,174	7

[1] SIC 3312, 3315, 3316, 3317.
[2] For definitions of regional groupings, see "Getting the Most Out of *Outlook 2000.*"
[3] Values may not sum to total due to rounding.
Source: U.S. Department of Commerce, Bureau of the Census.

1990s, but shipments to that region fell off sharply even before the economic crisis. Exports to Japan totaled just 11,363 tons in 1998.

Some steel companies believe that they can develop export markets for certain niche products where they have a technological edge. For example, manufacturers of light gauge steel framing have indicated that they will be able to develop a market for their product in certain countries in South America. Specialty producers also suggest that their products have export potential in certain markets.

Charles Bell, U.S. Department of Commerce, International Trade Administration, (202) 482-0608, September 1999.

■ REFERENCES

American Iron and Steel Institute, 1101 17th Street, NW, Washington, DC 20036. (202) 452-7100, www.steel.org.

American Metal Market, Capital Cities, Inc. 825 Seventh Avenue, New York, NY 10019. (212) 887-8550.

International Iron and Steel Institute, 120 Rue Colonel Bourg, 1140 Brussels, Belgium. (32)(2)702.89.00; fax: 32-2-702.88.99; www.worldsteel.org; E-mail: steel@iisi.be.

Metal Bulletin, Metal Bulletin, Inc., 220 Fifth Avenue, New York, NY 10001. (212) 213-6202.

Steel Manufacturers Association, 1730 Rhode Island Avenue, NW, Washington, DC 20036-3101. (202) 296-1515, www.steelnet.org.

■ RELATED CHAPTERS

1: Metals and Industrial Minerals Mining
2: Coal Mining
6: Construction
8: Construction Materials
36: Motor Vehicles

NONFERROUS METALS
Economic and Trade Trends

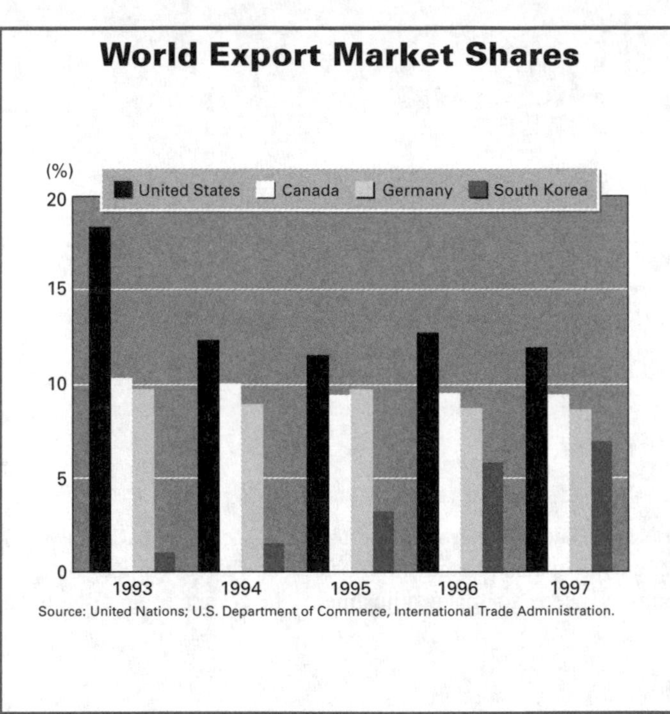

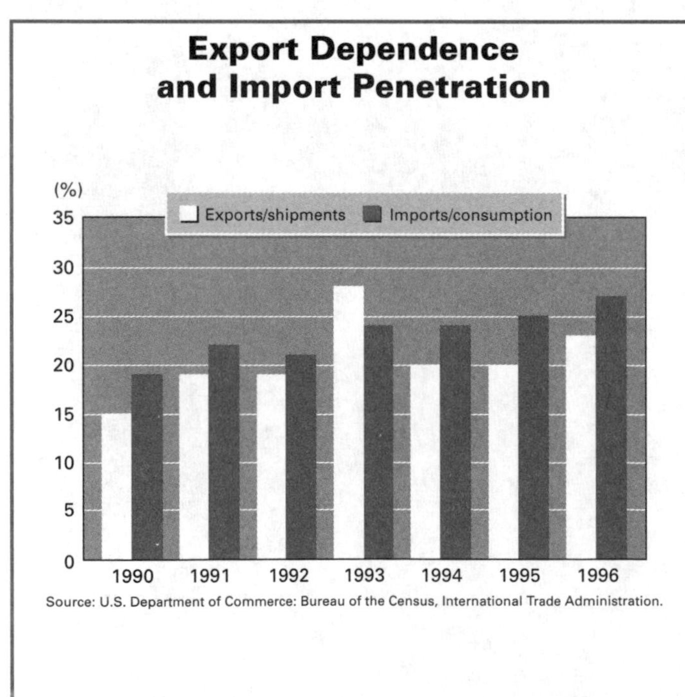

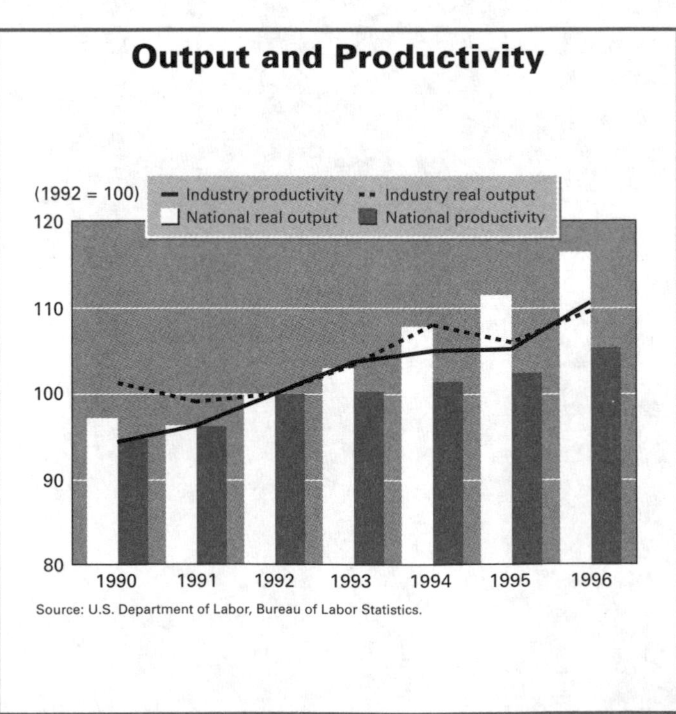

See "Getting the Most Out of *Outlook 2000*" for definitions of terms.

14

Nonferrous Metals

ALUMINUM

The aluminum industry is composed of a primary aluminum sector (SIC 3334), a secondary sector (a portion of SIC 3341), and a semifabricating sector that includes SIC 3353, aluminum sheet, plate, and foil (rolling); SIC 3354, aluminum extruded products; and SIC 3355, aluminum rolling and drawing not elsewhere classified, such as cable, wire, bars, and rods.

Global Industry Trends

The global aluminum industry currently is in the midst of a process of rationalization. This has been spurred in part by worldwide overcapacity, languishing prices, and a recognition that the industry needs to make adjustments to compete against other materials in developing the new end-use markets that will be required for continued growth. Global overcapacity exists despite exceptionally strong demand in the United States and evidence of a return to positive growth rates in the Asian economies, especially South Korea and Taiwan, that were affected by the Asian financial crisis. The economy in Japan also demonstrated hints of a resurgence in demand. However, increases in aluminum production, particularly in Europe and Russia, which the latter country exports in large quantities, have closely matched the increase in demand. As a result, market surpluses are expected to continue, although at increasingly lower levels, for the next couple of years.

Globally, it appears that in 1998, primary aluminum supply exceeded consumption by about 600,000 tons—the combined effect of a 2.5 percent increase in supply and a 1 percent decrease in demand. The fall in primary aluminum consumption in Asia (excluding Japan and China) from 1997 to 1998 was approximately 400,000 tons, or 5.6 percent. Most of the surplus thus can be attributed to the Asian economic crisis. From 1987 to 1998, global primary aluminum consumption increased at a compound annual growth rate of 2.9 percent. In 1998, demand decreased, but a return to recent growth trends was expected in 1999. Demand in the United States was expected to increase 6.6 percent in 1999 (see Table 14-1) and

TABLE 14-1: Aluminum Industry (SIC 3334, 3341, 3353, 3354, 3355) Trends and Forecasts
(thousands of metric tons)

									Percent Change			Compound Annual Growth Rate, %
	1993	1994	1995	1996	1997	1998	1999[1]	2000[2]	97–98	98–99	99–2000	93–98
Total shipments	8,417	9,365	9,565	9,609	10,224	10,518	11,212	11,325	2.88	6.60	1.01	4.56
Primary ingot production	3,695	3,299	3,375	3,577	3,603	3,713	3,800	3,850	3.05	2.34	1.32	0.10
Exports	1,094	1,195	1,310	1,309	1,367	1,265	1,300	1,365	−7.46	2.77	5.00	2.95
Ingot	404	343	373	421	361	277	325	340	−23.27	17.33	4.62	−7.27
Semifabricated products	690	852	937	888	1,006	988	975	1,025	−1.79	−1.32	5.13	7.44
Imports	2,327	3,136	2,702	2,573	2,805	3,264	3,900	3,950	16.36	19.49	1.28	7.00
Ingot	1,850	2,536	1,976	1,940	2,097	2,472	3,050	3,100	17.88	23.38	1.64	5.97
Semifabricated products	477	600	726	633	708	792	850	850	11.86	7.32	0.00	10.67
Primary metal inventories, end of year	4,497	3,733	2,581	2,642	2,258	2,324						
Week Supply	14.7	11.2	8.2	7.6	6.2	6.4						

[1] Estimate: shipments by the Aluminum Association, production by the U.S. Geological Survey.
[2] Forecast.
Source: U.S. Department of Commerce, International Trade Administration (ITA), the Aluminum Association. Estimates and forecasts by ITA; 1997 shipments by the Aluminum Association.

will account for a large portion of the global increase. On the supply side, increases in capacity are expected to average just over 2 percent annually for the next 5 years. However, a further 1.5 million tons of global capacity, 40 percent of which is in the United States, remains idle. Therefore, depending on capacity utilization rates, market surpluses should gradually disappear.

Industry Structure

In 1999, the U.S. industry was dominated by three large integrated, multinational U.S. companies—Alcoa, Reynolds Metals Company, and Kaiser Aluminum and Chemical—as well as the Canadian company Alcan. However, in late summer, Alcoa announced plans to acquire Reynolds for $5.6 billion. At the same time, Alcan announced its plans to merge with Pechiney (France) and Alusuisse (Switzerland). The primary aluminum segment of the industry is composed of 24 smelters operated by 12 companies located principally in the Pacific northwest, while the semifabricating sector is composed of over 200 companies clustered principally in the midwest. Together they account for over 60,000 employees and over $30 billion in shipments.

These mergers would create the world's two largest aluminum companies, both with revenues of approximately $21 billion. As with Alcoa's acquisition of the U.S. aluminum producer Alumax in 1998, the merger will depend on approval by the U.S. Department of Justice. Similar approval must be granted to Alcan by the European Commission. It is expected that these mergers will enable the aluminum industry to compete more effectively against substitute materials.

Domestic Trends

Consumption. In 1998, the U.S. aluminum industry set a record for total shipments, which reached approximately 10.52 million metric tons (mt). Shipments in 1999 were expected to increase 6.6 percent to 11.21 million mt. In descending order, the largest end-use sectors were and probably will remain the transportation sector, the containers and packaging sector, and the building and construction sector. Combined, those sectors represented about two-thirds of all shipments. Over half of all shipments were in the form of rolled products such as plate, sheet, and foil. The transportation sector, which supplanted the containers and packaging sector as the largest end-use sector in 1994, continues to expand its share of overall aluminum shipments. The transportation sector now accounts for approximately one-third of the industry's shipments; just as the aluminum can was the engine for demand growth in the 1970s and 1980s, the transportation sector is expected to provide the impetus for demand growth in the future.

The year 1999 was expected to be another 100-billion year for can shipments, although through the first 6 months, shipments of aluminum beverage cans fell 0.8 percent from the 1998 level. This was due mostly to a decrease in the soft drink sector. It remains to be seen whether a hot summer will boost shipment beyond the 100-billion level. However, June data published by the Aluminum Association on new orders seem to indicate that an upturn beyond that level is unlikely. It seems that the domestic container and packaging sector has reached full maturity and that increases in aluminum sheet shipments will rely solely on increases in beer and soft drink consumption. In fact, it is now the aluminum can that is under substitution pressure, particularly from plastic, rather than, as before, aluminum displacing materials such as glass.

Shipments to the container sector have reached a plateau for a number of reasons. First, the industry continues to improve the technology for producing cans in order to compete with steel and plastic containers. As a result, about 33 cans are made per pound of aluminum compared with 29 in 1992 and 22 in 1972. Second, the market is saturated: Virtually 100 percent of beer and soda cans are aluminum, and the possibility for further substitution in place of glass packaging is minimal. Therefore, increased shipments must rely on increases in soda and beer demand to offset the lightweighting of cans.

Supply. The domestic supply of aluminum can be divided into three components: primary production, secondary production, and imports. Currently, these sectors each supply roughly one-third of the market. This ratio is vastly different from that in 1992, when domestic production accounted for almost half of supply. The change in the ratio is a result of a decrease in primary production and an increase in secondary production and imports.

Primary Aluminum. Primary aluminum production was about 3.7 million mt in 1998. This represents a capacity utilization rate of about 88 percent, compared with 91 percent globally. This is well below the 1987 rate of approximately 97 percent but above the nadir in 1994, when the industry was operating at around 79 percent. U.S. production is expected to increase slowly in the next few years as, depending on global market conditions (the price of aluminum is determined on an international trading exchange), idled capacity is reactivated. The United States is responsible for approximately 40 percent of the idle capacity worldwide, and Alcoa maintains most of that, about 400,000 mt. Primary aluminum production in 1999 was expected to increase slightly to 3.8 million mt.

The production of primary aluminum is an electrolytic process that is energy-intensive. Electricity accounts for approximately one-third of the cost of production, and its cost and availability are the driving forces behind decisions on the location of new or expanded smelter capacity. For example, approximately 40 percent of U.S. smelting capacity is located in the Pacific northwest and utilizes hydropower from the Bonneville Power Administration. Currently, new capacity is planned for locations such as Canada (hydropower) and the Middle East (natural gas). There has not been a new smelter constructed in the United States since 1980.

However, changing economics and, in particular, the impending deregulation of the U.S. power industry have renewed interest in the possibility of smelter expansion in the United States. It is believed that after deregulation, it will be possible for aluminum companies to buy electricity more economically by wheeling power in from areas of the country with excess supply and controlling its cost to the smelter through hedging. As a result, feasibility studies are under way for the possible expansion of smelters in the United States.

Secondary Aluminum. Although its share of total supply has remained constant since 1992 at about one-third, as recently as 10 years ago secondary aluminum production accounted for only one-quarter of supply. Absolute production of secondary aluminum since 1992, though, has increased about 35 percent. In 1997, for the first time, secondary and primary production were approximately equal. However, in 1998 and 1999, primary aluminum production reasserted its supremacy. This probably does not reflect a rejection of aluminum recovery and recycling but instead reflects economic fundamentals. The spread between primary and secondary aluminum prices over that period was very tight, causing primary aluminum to be an attractive alternative to consumers and putting pressure on the profitability of secondary aluminum producers, which subsequently reduced production. Expectations of better prices for primary aluminum and a widening of the price differential in the year 2000 are expected to result in an increase in secondary aluminum production greater than that in primary aluminum production.

In general, a major factor in the increase in secondary production has been the success of the aluminum beverage can and its recyclability. Of the 100 billion aluminum beverage cans produced in 1998, 62.8 percent were recycled. This reflects a slight decrease from 66.5 percent in 1997 and probably is a manifestation of depressed prices for aluminum scrap and secondary material. Over half the content of a new aluminum beverage can comes from recycled aluminum. In 1998, a total of 879 thousand mt of aluminum was recovered from used beverage containers. An additional factor that will have a profound influence on scrap markets and secondary aluminum production is the obsolescence of vehicles containing increasingly larger amounts of aluminum. In the coming years, there will be an increase in aluminum scrap supply as vehicles from the last decade reach the end of their lives.

Another principal factor causing steadily increasing production of secondary aluminum is the energy savings that result. Secondary aluminum production saves 95 percent of the energy required to make aluminum from virgin materials. However, the production of secondary aluminum relies on a loop based on cause and effect. Increased secondary aluminum production is dependent on improved recycling rates and an increasingly larger supply of scrap. A larger supply probably will occur through the obsolescence of a greater number of products and products containing increasing amounts of aluminum, such as autos. These products, however, initially will require an increase in primary metal production. Therefore, as a consequence of this loop and the fact that primary aluminum and secondary aluminum are not perfect substitutes, there is a limit to the potential market share that can be accounted for by secondary aluminum.

Environment. Environmental issues pose economic concerns for the primary aluminum industry, but global climate change and measures that may be implemented to reduce greenhouse gas (GHG) emissions loom as the most threatening factor. Approximately one-half of the electricity consumed by the primary aluminum industry is generated by coal-fired power facilities, which are heavy emitters of GHG. Given the sensitivity of the primary sector to electricity costs, it is quite possible that depending on the structure and timing of GHG reduction measures, a considerable portion of the U.S. industry will become unviable.

Currently, the industry is working with the U.S. Environmental Protection Agency (EPA) to voluntarily reduce some GHG emitted directly by smelters. The EPA and the aluminum industry have developed a joint program, the Voluntary Aluminum Industrial Partnership (VAIP), designed to improve aluminum production efficiency while simultaneously improving the environment through the reduction of emissions of perfluorocarbon (PFC), a potent greenhouse gas. All U.S. producers except one participate in the program, representing 94 percent of U.S. capacity. The industry has committed to reducing PFC emissions 40 percent from 1990 levels by the year 2000. However, these emissions are insignificant in magnitude compared with the problem of indirect emissions from electricity consumption by the industry.

Technology. All segments of the aluminum industry are working to lower costs, improve their environmental performance, and develop new end uses for aluminum. In this regard, in late 1996, the Aluminum Association (U.S.) announced a joint effort with the U.S. Department of Energy to, among other things, develop technology to reduce the consumption of electricity 30 percent in the production of primary metal, increase the use of continuous casting technology in the semifabricating sector, and enhance joining and forming processes for fabricating finished products.

Because of the importance of electricity to the cost structure of the industry, the industry has sought to reduce the number of kilowatt-hours necessary to produce a pound of aluminum. To this end, it has been working to develop modifications to the existing Hall-Heroult electrolytic process for producing aluminum. Two of the most notable techniques under development are a new type of cathode for use in certain prebaked anode cells and a dimensionally stable anode for use in all cells. In addition to improving energy efficiency, this anode would not be consumed during the electrolytic process and would not emit PFC. However, these developments are many years from commercial application.

U.S. Industry Growth Projections for the Next 1 and 5 Years

Total shipments are expected to increase at an average annual rate of 2.5 percent annually from 1999 through 2004, just below the average annual growth rate for the last 10 years. This means that shipments will total 11.33 million mt in 2000 and 12.5 million mt in 2004. Primary aluminum production should increase slowly as idle capacity is reactivated, climbing to 3.85 million mt in 2000 and probably approaching 4.0 million mt in 2004. Despite expected increases in secondary aluminum production, it will be necessary for imports, especially of ingot as a result of domestic capacity constraints, to increase to meet the growing demand.

The transportation sector, light vehicles in particular, should be the driving force behind growth in aluminum demand. Growth in this sector is expected to increase about 4 percent annually through 2004. Although vehicle production will remain fairly constant, the amount of aluminum per vehicle should increase. Aluminum is the fastest-growing major material in light vehicles, outpacing gains made by plastics, glass, and rubber. Aluminum per light vehicle now averages over 250 pounds, compared with 183 pounds in 1992. Currently, the majority of aluminum consumed in this sector is in the form of castings, with engines being the largest end use, followed by transmissions. Although aluminum may be expected to increase its share of these applications, the real growth potential exists in applying sheet aluminum in areas such as body panels.

To further develop what is expected to be the most important growth sector for aluminum in the coming years, the aluminum and automotive industries have established the Auto Aluminum Alliance. The goal of this interindustry alliance is to promote collaboration on research and accelerate the use of new and improved aluminum technologies in light vehicles. This includes, among other things, efforts to reduce the cost of using aluminum sheet in vehicles, developing a process for the cost-effective recovery of aluminum from scrapped autos, and establishing a mechanism to disseminate information about automotive aluminum repair.

The containers and packaging sector will remain a dominant end-use sector for aluminum through the year 2004. However, it will grow at a very lackluster rate, probably only 1 percent annually. Competition from other materials could dampen that already low growth rate. However, a major factor responsible for the widespread acceptance of the aluminum can has been its recyclability. This usually has proved to be a decisive advantage of aluminum over other materials, but as the recycling rates of those materials improve, it will put additional pressure on the aluminum can.

Demand from the building and construction sector should be slightly lower than the overall growth rate for aluminum, particularly as commercial construction begins to slow in the next couple of years. All other sectors should match the overall growth rate for aluminum in general.

Global Market Prospects

In 1999, the global market for aluminum was expected to continue to experience a situation of oversupply. U.S. exports of ingot should remain fairly constant through 2004. Exports of semifabricated products should grow faster than do overall shipments as a result of improved European economic performance and a rebound in growth in Asia. Canada always has been the largest market for U.S. exports, and this will remain the case.

The United States is the largest market for aluminum. Other major markets include Europe and Japan. As an indication of size, per capita consumption of aluminum is 34.2 kilogram (kg) in the United States, 27.8 kg in Japan (which reflects depressed economic conditions in Japan; the rate was 31.8 in 1997), 27.2 kg in Germany, 19.5 kg in France, and 15.0 kg in the United Kingdom. The difference in rates results mainly from the end-use consumption patterns in the different markets. The United States and to an increasing degree Japan are large consumers of aluminum beverage cans; this is not the case in Europe. The transportation sector assumes a much larger role proportionally in aluminum demand in Japan and Europe than it does in the United States.

As was mentioned above, the transportation sector already is a source of considerable aluminum demand. However, consumption in this sector could grow considerably as a result of efforts to reduce the weight of vehicles for the purpose of improving gas mileage, thus conserving energy and reducing GHG emissions. Several programs to develop such vehicles are under way, such as the U.S. government–industry consortium called the Partnership for a New Generation of Vehicles, whose goal is to develop a mass-produced vehicle carrying six people with fuel efficiency of 80 miles per gallon. Such a vehicle is expected to weight about 2,000 pounds, most of which will be aluminum. The University of Wisconsin–Madison aluminum-intensive hybrid electric vehicle has demonstrated that this objective is achievable. In addition, certain regions of the United States have mandated that no-emission vehicles constitute a given percentage of new car sales (see the section on lead). If this situation materializes, it could be a boon for aluminum. For example, the GM EV1 electric vehicle has an aluminum unibody frame that weighs only 295 pounds.

David A. Cammarota, Office of Metals, Materials and Chemicals, (202) 482-5157, david_cammarota@ita.doc.gov, September 1999.

COPPER

The copper sector includes the primary smelting and refining industry (SIC 3331), which produces refined metal from raw materials, and rolling, drawing, and extruding establishments (SIC 3351), which shape refined copper into semifabricated products such as rods, bars, profiles, plates, sheets, strips, tubes, pipes, and wire. The insulating of copper wire is classified under SIC 3357, nonferrous wire drawing and insulating, and copper and alloy foundries are classified under SIC 3366.

Global Industry Trends

World consumption of refined copper reached nearly 13.5 million mt in 1998, 2.9 percent above the 1997 level and a new record. This was the fifth consecutive year of robust growth; world copper consumption rose one-quarter during the 1990s. Western Europe consumed about 3.5 million tons, up about 100,000 tons from 1997. Countries in the east Asia–Pacific Rim region consumed about 4.1 million tons, 30 percent of the world total. This was down from the 1997 level of 4.3 million, as copper demand slackened in many of the struggling economies of this region, such as Indonesia, Japan, and Thailand. China, by contrast, continued to increase its demand for copper, absorbing almost 1.4 million tons, more than 8 percent above 1997 levels and for the first time exceeding the currently depressed Japanese level of 1.25 million.

Production also set new records in 1998. Mine output worldwide reached 12.2 million mt, up more than 5 percent over 1997. Chile remains the world's premier copper miner, increasing its output nearly 9 percent in 1998 to almost 3.7 million mt. Production of refined copper, including metal refined from scrap (secondary metal), rose 3.7 percent to 14 million mt. Although the United States remains the world's largest refining country at 2.46 million mt, Chilean refining continues to expand rapidly, having achieved a level of 2.33 million mt in 1998. This was up 10 percent over 1997 and up 80 percent over the last 4 years.

Earlier in this decade, strong economic growth, particularly in the United States and Asia, led world demand for copper to outpace growth in supply. The resulting period of high copper prices inspired many expansion projects around the world. In 1998, copper mine capacity (facilities that already are operating or whose development is under way) reached 13.4 million mt, an increase of about 2 million tons in 3 years. Chile alone has added more than 1 million mt since 1995, and additional projects there may add a further 800,000 mt by 2001. Worldwide, expansions now under way will boost total mining capacity to as much as 14.7 million mt in 2001. Other announced exploration projects, such as those in Peru, Argentina, and Brazil, could add nearly another million mt to mine capacity between the present time and 2002 if all those proposals are pursued.

With this tide of new output entering the market, production has been growing faster than consumption. The world copper market moved from a deficit of 450,000 mt in 1994 to a surplus of about 530,000 mt in 1998, with stocks held at year end by producers, consumers, merchants, and exchanges rising more than 30 percent during 1998 to approximately 1.35 million mt. Under these circumstances, copper prices have remained depressed, with quotations on the Commodities Exchange (COMEX) in New York averaging about 65 cents per pound over the first 6 months of 1999, less than half the price copper commanded at its 1995 peak. It is believed that many of the world's newer and more efficient properties can continue to operate even at these price levels, but sustained low copper prices have already led to the closing of some higher-cost facilities, delay of expansion plans, and corporate realignment.

Domestic Trends

Total refined output rose 10,000 tons in 1998 to 2.46 million mt (see Table 14-2), while mine production eased 2 percent to 1.86 million tons. Primary refined output grew 2.9 percent to 2.12 million mt, continuing the upward trend of recent years, but secondary refinery production declined more than 12 percent to 336,000 mt, dampened by low prices and tight scrap supplies. Capacity in the secondary refining sector continued to contract with the March 1999 closure of the Warrenton, MO, plant of Philip Services Corp. Including the 1998 closure of Cerro Copper Products' refinery in Illinois, industry capacity has been reduced by more than 85,000 metric tons in the last 2 years. The largest secondary copper refinery in the United States, at Carrollton, GA, remains in operation, but its owner, Southwire Co., is attempting to sell the operation, along with its copper rod mill and an aluminum refinery.

Although some expansion projects are proceeding, such as the 23,000-mt SX-EW facility that Equatorial Mining hopes to

TABLE 14-2: Copper Industry (SIC 3331, 3351, 3357, 3366) Trends and Forecasts
(thousands of metric tons; percent)

	1993	1994	1995	1996	1997	1998[1]	1999[2]	2000[2]	Percent Change 97–98	98–99	99–00	Compound Annual Growth Rate, % 93–97
Refined copper production	2,250	2,230	2,280	2,350	2,450	2,460	2,180	1,820	0.4	−11.4	−16.0	2.2
From primary materials	1,790	1,840	1,930	2,010	2,060	2,120						
From scrap	460	392	352	345	383	336						
Refined copper consumption	2,364	2,680	2,525	2,620	2,790	2,880	2,940	3,000	3.2	2.1	2.0	4.2
By wire rod mills	1,820	2,060	1,950	1,980	2,140	2,170						
By brass mills	503	568	533	588	597	659						
Semifabricate production												
By wire rod mills	1,730	1,910	1,820	1,920	2,080	2,100						
By brass mills	1,320	1,460	1,430	1,550	1,600	1,590						
Exports												
Refined copper and alloys	239	173	232	184	117	105						
Wire mill products	57	67	48	59	63	65						
Brass mill products[3]	87	103	130	144	142	154						
Scrap	262	359	548	393	380	307						
Imports												
Refined copper and alloys	354	486	442	635	669	700						
Wire mill products	32	43	56	72	73	98						
Brass mill products[3]	125	176	196	189	220	255						
Scrap	200	194	222	212	212	166						

[1] Estimate, U.S. Department of Commerce, International Trade Administration (ITA).
[2] Forecast, U.S. Department of Commerce and ITA.
[3] Excluding foil.
Source: U.S. Geological Survey; U.S. Department of Commerce, ITA.

have ready early in the year 2000 at Tonopah, NV, low prices are pressing most primary producers to continue rationalizing their operations. Cutbacks and closures over the last 2 years have claimed around 20 percent of U.S. mine and smelter capacity. In February 1999, Asarco began a planned 3-year shutdown of its 115,000-mt smelter in El Paso, TX; as a result, output of metal from the company's Amarillo refinery is likely to fall as much as 100,000 tons by 2000. Cyprus closed its leaching operations at Tohono, AZ, where mining was already suspended, and curtailed output at the Bagdad and Sierrita mines by 27,000 tons. Phelps Dodge has reduced SX-EW activity by more than 20 percent and concentrate output by one-third at Chino, NM; than closed the 32,000-ton Cobre mine and cut back operations by 68,000 tons at its Morenci mine. Additionally, in June, the company announced temporary closure of its Hidalgo, NM, smelter.

In June 1999, BHP announced that it was closing all its North American copper operations. BHP, which is based in Australia, entered the U.S. copper market with the $1.9 billion acquisition of Magma Copper in January 1996. Company properties include a large smelter and refinery at San Manuel, AZ; the Miami, Pinto Valley, and San Manuel mines in Arizona; and the Robinson mine in Nevada. Some of these are believed to be among the higher-cost facilities in the United States, and the company had been interested in selling off at least some of them for some time. BHP is involved in other metal and mineral activities in other parts of the world, including Latin American copper, and will remain a major factor in the world copper market.

In July, Asarco Inc. and Cyprus Amax Minerals, the second and fifth largest of the five principal U.S. copper companies, respectively, announced plans to merge. The combination would control more than 25 percent of U.S. mine, smelter, and refinery capacity and, including operations abroad, around 8 percent of total western world copper production. With combined revenue estimated at $3.8 billion, it would be surpassed in size only by Chile's Codelco. Industry observers believe that the merger could permit savings as high as $80 million per year.

The Asarco-Cyprus announcement was followed in August by a proposal from Phelps Dodge, the largest U.S. copper producer, to acquire both of the merging firms. With about two-thirds of U.S. primary copper production capacity, such a three-way merger could face a challenge on antitrust grounds. This problem may be mitigated, however, because production of unwrought refined metal, in which U.S. producers concentrate their activities, is the stage of copper production most open to international competition. Thus, although the merged firm would be very large with respect to the remaining domestic producers, it also would be competing with large foreign suppliers such as Chile. Unlike some other metals, the U.S. copper industry does not have a high degree of vertical integration. The primary copper producers are involved in the wire rod sector, but most semifabricated and other "downstream" products are manufactured by other companies.

Such mergers may improve the U.S. industry's international competitive position, permitting the most efficient plants and mines to remain in operation and eliminating substantial duplicative overhead in both domestic and foreign operations, which are concentrated in Peru and Chile. The current depressed price levels also may make the merger seem an attractive alternative to exploration as a means of securing reserves of copper for future production.

Domestic consumption of refined copper set a record again in 1998, reaching 2.88 million mt. This level represents an increase of 3.2 percent over 1997 and nearly a 22 percent increase above the level 5 years earlier. As usual, wire rod mills accounted for about 75 percent of refined metal consumption, with most of the remainder going to brass mills, which also use remelted scrap.

Wire rod mill production edged upward in 1998 to 2.1 million mt (see Table 14-2). Two new wire rod mills opened in the last two years. In June 1998, Encore Wire Corp. began operations at its new mill in McKinney, TX, where it also produces other wire and cable products. United Copper Industries, a division of Mexican conglomerate Industrias Unidas, SA (IUSA), initiated start-up trials of its Denton, TX, rod mill in April 1999. IUSA also has other manufacturing and distribution operations at the Denton site. Each of these mills has an estimated capacity of about 60,000 mt of rod per year.

While output from brass mills was little changed from 1997, easing less than 1 percent from that year's level of 1.6 million mt, the amount of refined cathode used in 1998 increased more than 10 percent, reaching 659,000 mt. Low copper prices have made recovery of scrap less attractive, and tight supply, coupled with the narrowed price spread between cathode and scrap, has encouraged substitution of relatively cheap and available cathode as brass mill feedstock.

International Trade

Although the United States is the world's largest refiner and second largest miner of copper, it is also the world's largest importer of refined metal. Imports of unwrought refined copper and alloys rose 31,000 mt to 700,000 mt in 1998, twice the tonnage of 5 years earlier. The principal category, cathodes, increased about 6 percent in 1998, reaching 613,000 mt. Canada remained the largest source at 238,000 tons, but cathode shipments from Mexico tripled to 178,000 tons and imports from Peru reached 127,000 tons, double their 1996 level. Cathode imports for consumption from Chile slipped nearly 50 percent to only 56,000 mt, but an additional 40,000 tons from that country entered bonded warehouses.

Copper stocks in London Metal Exchange (LME) warehouses in the United States, especially those in California, rose sharply in 1998, reaching 341,000 mt at the end of that year, up from 129,000 tons at the end of 1997. This amounted to more than 80 percent of the worldwide increase in LME copper stocks during that period and left 57 percent of total LME stocks in U.S. warehouses. In September 1998, the LME responded to growing concern about possible market distortions if exchange warehouses became destinations of first resort for copper and announced limits on the California warehouses (at Los Angeles and Long Beach) equal to their stocks on hand effective December 2, 1998. Total LME stocks in the United States continued to grow in the first part of 1999, reaching 424,000 tons at the end of August. Unlike the case in 1998, however, significant stock increases also occurred in Europe, where LME warehouse inventories ballooned from 151,000 mt to 333,000 mt between December 1998 and August 1999.

Imports of all major types of semifabricates increased in 1998. Among brass mill products, plate, sheet, and strip imports rose 14 percent to about 63,000 mt; rods, bars, and profiles amounted to 114,000 tons; and tubes and pipes were up only 4 percent to 78,000 tons. Wire imports grew by one-third to 98,000 mt, triple the volume of 5 years earlier. Canada, Mexico, Germany, and Japan were the principal suppliers in most of these categories; Korea and France were additional major sources of rods, bars, and profiles. Wire exports also increased moderately in 1998 to 65,000 mt, while exports of plate, sheet, and strip were up 36 percent to 66,000 tons, largely on the strength of increased shipments of brass sheet and strip in coils to Canada and Mexico. Rod, bar, and profile exports fell 7 percent to 51,000 mt, and tubes and pipes slipped 4 percent to about 37,000 tons. Canada and Mexico were the most important markets for most of these export items.

Both imports and exports of copper and alloy scrap decreased in 1998 as scrap supplies remained tight in the face of depressed copper prices. Canada received about 107,000 mt of U.S. scrap exports, and China and Hong Kong took 49,000 and 40,000 tons, respectively. The principal sources of imported scrap were Canada (87,000 tons) and Mexico (48,000 tons).

U.S. Industry Growth Projections for the Next 1 and 5 Years

Domestic production was expected to feel the effects of recent closures and cutbacks in 1999, with refined output declining about 11 percent to 2.18 million mt and mine output down 9 percent to 1.7 million tons. This sharp decline in production is expected to continue in the year 2000, with both mine and refinery output off a further 15 percent as industry rationalization proceeds. Recovery in domestic production levels will depend heavily on price developments in the copper market. Many shuttered facilities could reopen if conditions improve sufficiently, but some recent closures are probably permanent, and even a return of strong prices is not likely to boost output levels beyond the range of 2.2 to 2.3 million tons by 2004. Although many U.S. production facilities are as technologically sophisticated as any in the world, the lower grades of ore and inherently higher costs typically encountered in this country make price fluctuations more challenging for domestic operations than they are for lower-cost foreign competitors, particularly the new and planned operations in Latin America.

Domestic copper consumption continues to rise, buoyed by the strong economy. In 1999, consumption was expected to reach about 2.94 million mt, up 2 percent. Construction, whose need for copper in wiring, plumbing, heating, air-conditioning, refrigeration, and power utilities accounts for nearly half of all copper demand, is at record levels, and the value of all new construction put in place was expected to rise another 4 percent in 1999. New housing starts in 1999 may have been down slightly from 1998, but the continuing trend of approximately 2 percent annual growth in the size of the average new unit was expected to offset this, allowing total real spending on new housing to increase 5 percent for the year. Nonresidential building construction other than factories also has been strong, with the office and hotel sectors growing at double-digit rates in 1999. If the economy proceeds, as expected, on a path of moderate 2.5 to 3.0 percent growth, annual increases in copper consumption probably will continue to be in the neighborhood of 2 percent over the next several years, with consumption levels reaching 3 million tons in the year 2000 and exceeding 3.2 million mt in 2004.

Global Market Prospects

Copper use remains on an upward trend throughout the world. The United States and other more developed economies are maintaining or increasing their copper use, but the rapidly industrializing parts of the world have displayed the most impressive growth in copper demand. When the Asian countries whose economies have recently faltered recover, their pattern of growth in copper consumption is likely to resume. China alone now consumes more than 10 percent of all refined copper and appears poised to become the world's second largest consumer, after the United States. Without sufficient economically exploitable copper resources to supply its smelters and refineries, China has become the second largest importer of concentrates (after Japan) and blister and anode (after the United States) as well as the largest importer of scrap (951,000 mt in 1998, accounting for 27 percent of the world total).

Most of the expected increases in world copper production will occur in the major copper mining regions, especially Chile and Peru, and the rapidly industrializing countries. In the long run, these new facilities can be expected to supply most of the coming growth in world copper demand. The major U.S. copper companies are participating in many of these projects, particularly in Latin America, as well as in other metals and minerals.

Robert M. Shaw, U.S. Department of Commerce, Office of Metals, Materials, and Chemicals, (202) 482-0606, robert_shaw@ita.doc.gov, September 1999.

LEAD

The international lead industry consists of primary producers (SIC 3339) that use either lead ores and concentrates or a mixture of lead ores and concentrates and scrap lead as feedstock and secondary producers (SIC 3341) that recycle scrap lead primarily in the form of spent lead-acid batteries (LABs). The most important end use for lead by far is the LAB (SIC 3691), which accounts for an estimated 72 percent of global consumption. Lead is an internationally traded commodity whose value is based on the price set daily by the LME. This price may vary in different countries, depending on local market conditions.

Global Industry Trends

The world's largest producers of lead ores and concentrates are China, accounting for 22.9 percent of total production, followed by Australia with 18.8 percent, the United States with

15.5 percent, Peru with 8.3 percent, and Canada with 6.1 percent. The United States, however, is the world's largest producer of refined lead metal, accounting for 23.8 percent of total production, followed by China with 11.8 percent, the United Kingdom with 6.2 percent, Germany with 5.9 percent, and Japan with 5.1 percent.

In the 1990s, the international lead and lead-acid battery (LAB) industries underwent a process of consolidation and globalization, with a number of major producers expanding their operations to reduce transportation costs and increase market share in foreign markets. U.S. producers have played an important role in this consolidation by purchasing facilities or forming joint ventures in China, Europe, Central and South America, and Saudi Arabia.

The international lead industry continues to experience both increasing opportunities and significant challenges to its markets. The rapid expansion of the economies and automobile fleets in newly industrializing and developing countries, combined with the explosive worldwide growth in telecommunications and the Internet, continues to benefit the lead and LAB industries. At the same time, an increasing number of international environmental negotiations, as well as regional and national regulatory initiatives for the environment, are focusing on lead and some of its end uses. Certain dispersive or readily bioavailable end uses for lead, such as lead in gasoline, as a solder in piping for drinking water and food cans, and in house paints, have been or are being phased out in many countries because of environmental and health concerns. Some of these recently proposed regulations propose banning materials such as lead and cadmium and mandating specific design standards. These bans appear to lack adequate scientific and economic justification and may serve as unnecessary barriers to trade.

Domestic Trends

The domestic lead mining industry includes 17 mines in Alaska, Colorado, Idaho, Missouri, Montana, New York, and Tennessee, with the 9 mines in Alaska and Missouri accounting for about 91 percent of domestic production. Primary lead is produced at Doe Run's Herculaneum and Glover smelter-refineries in Missouri. Asarco's East Helena, MT, smelter produces lead bullion, which it ships to refineries outside the United States. Doe Run is the world's largest primary lead producer as a result of its purchase of Asarco's Glover smelter-refinery in October 1998 and Peru's La Oroya smelter-refinery in September 1997. Secondary lead is produced at 17 recycling facilities in Alabama, California, Florida, Georgia, Indiana, Louisiana, Minnesota, Missouri, New York, Pennsylvania, Tennessee, and Texas. In August 1999, GNB announced that it would close its Columbus, GA, smelter, which has an annual capacity of 80,000 mt, because of the plant's high production costs in relation to current lead prices. Since 1995, Exide Corporation, an integrated LAB producer and recycler, has acquired a number of secondary lead refineries in the United States, France, and Spain as well as battery plants in the United States and across Europe, making it the world's dominant secondary lead and LAB producer. Delphi Automotive Systems was spun off from General Motors to establish greater independence and opened LAB production facilities in China and Saudi Arabia. One of the three largest U.S. automotive LAB producers, JCI, sold its industrial battery division to Charter Power Systems, Incorporated, the second largest domestic producer of industrial LABs. Charter Power Systems also formed a joint venture called Enermex with the Mexican-based IMSA to serve Central America and signed a global agreement with the German-based Varta that has potential for the European and South American LAB markets.

Lead also is sold by the Defense National Stockpile Center (DNSC) as a result of legislation passed in 1992 authorizing the disposal of the entire 555,000 mt in the stockpile over several years. The law, however, requires the task to be completed without undue disruption of commercial lead markets. At the end of August 1999, 268,579 mt of lead remained in the DNSC inventory. The fiscal year (FY) 2000 Annual Materials Plan (AMP) authorizes the disposal of about 54,000 mt of lead between October 1, 1999, and September 30, 2000. Additional authority is being sought by the DNSC to dispose of 54,000 mt of lead for the FY 2001 AMP. However, the AMP represents a limit and not a goal, and typically a smaller amount has been sold annually.

The domestic lead market has experienced robust growth since 1994. Domestic lead mine production, which declined in the early 1990s as a result of low lead, gold, and silver metal prices, grew at an annual rate of 8.3 percent between 1994 and 1998 as several mines expanded or reopened as a result of improved metal prices. Domestic lead mine production rose to 493,000 mt in 1998, slightly below the 497,000 mt produced in 1990. Domestic lead metal production rose at an annual rate of 3.8 percent during that period, climbing to a record high of almost 1.44 million mt in 1998. This increase occurred despite the closure of Asarco's Omaha primary refinery and a number of secondary plants; those closings were more than offset by the opening of a new secondary refinery and an increase in capacity at a number of other secondary refineries. During this time period, secondary lead's share of total metal production increased from 72 percent to 77 percent (see Table 14-3).

Domestically, lead is consumed in about 160 plants that manufacture end-use products such as LABs—the leading end use—ammunition, covering for power and communication cable, building construction materials, and solder for motor vehicles, metal containers, and electrical and electronic components and accessories. The United States accounts for almost 29 percent of global lead consumption and is by far the single largest market worldwide. Domestic lead consumption increased at an average annual rate of 5.7 percent per year between 1991 and 1998, rising from 1,248,000 mt to 1,742,000 mt. While some important lead-consuming countries still have major non-LAB markets for lead, such as lead sheet for roofing and lead chemicals, consumption patterns in the United States have long been shifting to a market dominated by one major end use: the LAB. Increasing domestic LAB demand has more than made up for all the end uses that have significantly declined or been legislated out of existence for environmental and health reasons. The LAB's share of total domestic lead con-

TABLE 14-3: Lead and Lead-Acid Battery Industries (SIC 3339, 3341, 3691) Trends and Forecasts
(thousands of metric tons; percent)

									Percent Change			Compound Annual Growth Rate, %
	1991	1994	1995	1996	1997	1998	1999[1]	2000[2]	97–98	98–99	99–00	91–98
Mine production	477	370	394	436	459	493	499	500	7.4	1.2	0.2	0.5
Metal production	1,195	1,249	1,378	1,372	1,432	1,437	1,434	1,460	0.3	–0.2	1.8	2.7
Primary	346	351	374	326	343	337	348	350	–1.7	3.3	0.6	–0.4
Recycled	849	898	1,004	1,046	1,089	1,100	1,086	1,110	1.0	–1.3	2.2	3.8
Percent recycled production	71.1	71.9	72.9	76.2	76.1	76.6	75.7	76.0				
Apparent metal consumption	1,248	1,514	1,614	1,648	1,664	1,742	1,805	1,795	4.7	3.6	–0.6	4.9
By lead-acid battery industry	1,009	1,286	1,406	1,449	1,435	1,538	1,596	1,594	7.2	3.8	–0.1	6.2
Percent SLI batteries	79.7	79.7	70.7	71.3	68.4	70.6	71.9	70.1				
Percent industrial batteries	20.3	20.3	29.3	28.7	31.6	29.5	28.1	29.9				
Imports for consumption	116	230	264	268	265	267	295	299	0.8	10.5	1.4	12.7
Percent of consumption	9.3	15.2	16.4	16.2	15.9	15.3	16.3	16.7				
Exports	94	48	47	44	37	24	18	18	–35.1	–25.0	–0.0	–17.7

[1] Estimate.
[2] Forecast.
Source: U.S. Department of Commerce, International Trade Administration (ITA); U.S. Department of the Interior, Geological Survey; International Lead and Zinc Study Group; Estimates and Forecasts by ITA.

sumption increased from 80 percent in 1991 to almost 88 percent in 1998. Nonbattery uses of lead, in contrast, declined at an average annual rate of 2.1 percent during that period. Lead used in ammunition, the largest nonbattery end use, remained fairly constant in that period. Other uses, such as cable covering, calking, and solder, have declined significantly. Tetraethyl lead additives for gasoline, which once accounted for 20 percent of domestic consumption, were phased out entirely in 1992.

Environment. Thirty-seven states have enacted legislation to encourage recycling of LABs. The laws adopted by those states, which were proposed by the Battery Council International (BCI), prohibit the disposal of LABs in municipal solid waste streams and require all levels of the collection chain to accept spent LABs. Four other states ban only the landfilling and incineration of LABs. As a result of these bills, which reinforce long-standing industry practices in the collection and recycling of batteries, more batteries are being recycled and fewer batteries are being disposed of improperly. The 1996 annual study released by the BCI reported a domestic LAB recycling rate of 96.5 percent with an average annual LAB recycling rate of 94.5 percent between 1987 (the first year covered) and 1996. The recycling rate should remain near that level in the future.

A number of international, regional, and national environmental negotiations and regulations could have an impact on the domestic and global lead markets. The Basel Convention is an international environmental agreement designed to restrict the transboundry movement of hazardous wastes to protect countries (particularly developing ones) that may not have the capability or technology to manage waste properly. Annex VIII of the convention, which contains a list of materials that Annex VII countries [Organization for Economic Cooperation and Development (OECD) members, the European Union, and Liechtenstein] are prohibited from exporting to non-Annex VII countries after December 31, 1998, includes lead compounds, lead waste and scrap, and scrap LABs. This ban may make it difficult for non-Annex VII countries to obtain feedstock for their secondary lead industries. While some domestic lead waste and scrap is exported to OECD countries, more than half these exports of waste and scrap were destined for non-OECD countries in 1998 (see pages 14-17 to 14-18 for more information on the Basel Convention).

In February 1998, the Convention on Long-Range Transboundary Air Pollution sponsored by the United Nations Economic Commission for Europe (UNECE), which includes all the European countries, Canada, and the United States, concluded a Heavy Metals Protocol that will, among other things, control emissions of lead from stationary sources and restrict the use of leaded gasoline. Strict criteria and procedures were included in this protocol to ensure that additional metals or products containing the metals covered under the protocol are added to the agreement only if, through their use, they contribute significantly to long-range transboundary air emissions of these metals. Currently, only lead, cadmium, and mercury are included in the protocol, which was signed by the United States and other UNECE member countries in June 1998.

The European Commission and a number of countries have recently introduced or are considering initiatives that if enacted would severely restrict the use of lead in various products. The proposed European initiatives could severely affect the international competitiveness of U.S. producers of lead-containing products such as the U.S. automotive, electronics, and telecommunications industries. In most cases, these initiatives focus on nondispersive uses of lead that do not pose unmanageable risks to human health and the environment. The commission's environment director general has proposed a directive on Waste from Electrical and Electronic Equipment (WEEE) that would ban the use of lead in electrical and electronic equipment. The draft WEEE directive is expected to be discussed by the new commission, which was approved by the European Parliament in mid-September 1999. While the United States supports the objectives of this proposal to reduce waste and the environmental impact of discarded products, the manner in which this directive is written raises a number of important trade policy concerns. In addition, the newly elected European Parliament is scheduled to consider a proposed End-of-Life Vehicle (ELV) directive that would, among other things, require all vehicles marketed in the European Union (EU) after January 2003 to be free of most uses of lead and materials such as cadmium and mercury. LABs, lead solder in circuit boards, and a small number of lead-containing components would be exempted from this ban (see page 14-19 for more information on the WEEE and ELV directives).

Denmark has proposed banning the import, sale, and production of most products containing lead compounds and a number of products containing metallic lead. This regulation, which would continue to allow exports of these products, was to go into effect on January 1, 1998. When Denmark submitted this proposal to the European Commission for comments, however, nine EU member states submitted "detailed opinions" opposing it. In addition, the commission informed Denmark that it must first respond to a number of questions and then have its proposal reviewed by a commission scientific review board before the initiative can be enacted. Sweden has drafted legislation that would ban lead in shot for sporting and hunting purposes and the use of lead in polyvinyl chloride (PVC). However, the stated long-term goal of this legislation is to voluntarily discontinue the use of lead in all products, including LABs. In Japan, the Ministry of International Trade and Industry (MITI) has asked domestic automobile producers to voluntarily reduce by almost 70 percent the amount of lead used in automobiles by 2005.

U.S. Industry Growth Projections for the Next 1 and 5 Years

A sharp increase in the production of both automotive replacement and original equipment batteries in 1999, along with continued steady growth in industrial battery demand, is expected to boost domestic lead consumption to a projected average annual increase of 1.5 percent between 1998 and 2000, growing from 1.74 million mt to 1.80 million mt. Colder than normal temperatures nationwide in early 1999 followed by warmer than normal temperatures in the summer of 1999 finished off the large number of replacement batteries produced in 1994 and 1995 that were near the end of their service life. In addition, strong growth in motor vehicle production in 1999 pushed up demand for original equipment (OE) batteries. While production of both replacement and OE batteries is expected to decline in the year 2000, the levels will still exceed those reached in 1998. The domestic industrial battery market is expected to increase at an average annual rate of 11 percent during this time period as a result of continued dynamic growth in the telecommunications and uninterruptible power supply (UPS) markets and solid growth in the motive power sector. Between 2000 and 2004, domestic lead consumption is expected to rise at an average rate of about 1.9 percent per year, reaching 1.93 million mt in 2004, with the LAB's share of total consumption accounting for about 89 percent. The forecast growth rate could be less than anticipated if the EU's WEEE and ELV directives are enacted as currently written.

Lead-Acid Batteries. Both globally and domestically, the LAB is the driving force behind the lead industry. This sector consists of two main markets: starting, lighting, and ignition (SLI) batteries, which currently account for an estimated 72 percent of the market, and industrial batteries, which account for 28 percent. SLI batteries are used in a number of applications, such as passenger cars and light trucks, heavy commercial vehicles, motorcycles, special tractors, marine craft, aircraft, and military vehicles. Demand for replacement SLI batteries, which currently represents 80 percent of the SLI market, is dependent on the size and age of the motor vehicle fleet, extreme temperature fluctuations, and the service life of the battery. Demand for OE SLI batteries is tied to the level of motor vehicle production and sales.

Between 1991 and 1998, SLI battery production increased at an average annual rate of 5 percent, rising from 78.2 million units to 105.6 million units. SLI production is expected to increase to about 108.8 million units in the year 2000. Production should rise at an average annual rate of about 1.2 percent between 2000 and 2004, reflecting both a slight increase in motor vehicle production and a growing automotive fleet. The motor vehicle industry is moving increasingly toward higher-voltage and multielectrical systems. In certain current motor vehicles, a 36-volt battery is used for the high-power requirements in conjunction with a 12-volt battery for common accessories. Other vehicles utilize one high-voltage battery in conjunction with a DC/AC converter to split power requirements. If these systems become widespread, projected growth rates could increase significantly, since either system would increase battery weight and as a result the amount of lead used per battery. Such a change is similar to the industry's switch from 6-volt to 12-volt batteries in the 1950s and 1960s. Extreme temperature fluctuations in large segments of the United States during the forecast period could push this growth rate higher.

The industrial battery market is divided into two sectors: motive power and stationary power. Motive power includes batteries for industrial trucks, mining vehicles, and railroad cars and currently accounts for 40 percent of the industrial battery market, while stationary power includes telecommunications, UPS, miscellaneous standby, security, control and switchgear, emergency lighting, electronics, and medical batteries and represents the remaining 60 percent. This market rose 5.2 percent in 1998 and registered an average annual growth rate of 11.3 percent between 1990 and 1998, with the strongest increase in UPS batteries (24 percent growth) and telecommunications batteries (14 percent growth).

The industrial battery market is forecast to experience continued strong growth between 1998 and 2004, rising at an average rate of about 11 percent per year, as stationary power batteries continue to increase their share of this market to an estimated 66 percent. This growth should be led by telecommunications and UPS batteries, which are tied to the buildup and redefinition of the worldwide telecommunications infrastructure as a result of the advent of new technologies in fiber-optics and broadband communications systems and the explosive growth in Internet and networking servers. Industrial batteries are forecast to account for 32 percent of the lead consumed by the domestic LAB industry in 2004.

Laws passed in California and nine northeastern states mandating the production of electric vehicles (EVs) could influence lead consumption during this period. California and the Coalition of Northeastern Governors (CONEG) require that by 2003, 10 percent of all vehicles sold in these areas be zero-emission EVs and 15 percent be ultra-low-emission vehicles. Since EVs are considerably more expensive than conventional motor vehicles and consumers are not required to purchase EVs, it remains uncertain whether these goals will be achieved (see the section on zinc for a related topic).

Supply. Domestic production of lead is forecast to rise to 1.46 million mt in 2000 and continue increasing to an estimated 1.56 million mt in 2004. While primary production is expected to remain flat during this period, secondary production will continue to rise. Any increase in secondary production, however, is dependent on the availability of scrap LABs. The share of total domestic production accounted for by secondary lead should rise to 78 percent by 2004, reflecting the continued importance of recycling for the lead industry.

Imports of unwrought lead accounted for an estimated 15 percent of consumption in 1998 and are expected to increase to 18 percent by 2004. In 1998, almost all imports came from Canada, China, Mexico, and Peru. Imports of LAB 12-volt automotive batteries increased significantly in 1998, rising from 1.3 million units to 4.8 million units. Mexico's share of these imports jumped from 42 percent to 86 percent, primarily because of the joint venture between JCI and IMSA. Such a large increase in LAB imports could result in lower than anticipated domestic lead consumption. In March and August 1999, imports of industrial LABs from most EU countries declined 35 percent because of a 100 percent tariff being placed on those batteries in retaliation for the EU's discriminatory policy on banana imports. Although the United States exported about 21,000 mt of unwrought lead in 1998, with about 88 percent going to Canada, South Korea, and Taiwan, most exports are in the form of LABs or products containing either LABs or other applications of lead.

Global Market Prospects

Between 1991 and 1998, global consumption of lead rose at an annual rate of 2.1 percent, increasing from 5.23 million mt to 6.01 million mt. LABs accounted for 71 percent of consumption, followed by pigments, 12 percent; rolled extrusions, 7 percent; ammunition, 6 percent; and other uses, 4 percent. Global market conditions for lead are forecast to show continued growth in the near term. Consumption is expected to increase 2 percent to 6.12 million mt, while metal production is projected to rise 3.3 percent, increasing from 5.96 million mt to 6.16 million mt. The United States will maintain its position as the world's largest producer and consumer of lead metal.

Dave Larrabee, Office of Metals, Materials, and Chemicals, (202) 482-0607, dave_larrabee@ita.doc.gov, September 1999.

TITANIUM

Titanium does not have a specific SIC code. Titanium sponge for metal alloy production is included in the basket industry classification code SIC 3339. The secondary recovery of titanium is covered by SIC 3341, while mill product production is covered by SIC 3356, castings by SIC 3369, and forgings by SIC 3463. Titanium is a lightweight metal well known for its corrosion resistance and high strength-to-weight ratio.

There are ample titanium-bearing mineral resources around the world. Australia provides about half the world's titanium raw materials through its production of titanium mineral concentrates; most of the balance consists of concentrates and titanium-bearing slags from the Republic of South Africa, Canada, and Norway. These raw materials are processed primarily by pigment manufacturers and a few integrated titanium metal producers. The bulk of the world's titanium consumption is in the form of titanium dioxide, and its use is dominated by pigments for paints, paper, and plastics. Less than 10 percent of world titanium consumption is in the form of metals. Titanium is an important strategic and critical material that is used in the manufacture of both engines and airframes of high-performance military and civilian aircraft. It also is used in other aerospace and nonaerospace defense, industrial, and consumer applications. This section focuses on metallurgical titanium.

Global Industry Trends

Reduced aerospace and industrial demand, largely as a result of the economic crisis in Asia and Latin America, has resulted in production cutbacks by titanium sponge, the porous basic titanium metal, and ingot producers worldwide. The production of titanium sponge is now limited to eight companies in six countries: the United States, Japan, Russia, Kazakhstan, Ukraine, and China. Sponge consumption for conversion to ingot and slab and the subsequent production of castings and mill products occurs principally in the United States, Japan, Russia, the United Kingdom, France, and Germany.

Another significant global trend is the increased use of titanium products from the former Soviet Union (FSU), especially Russia, in world markets. Substantially reduced demand for titanium in the FSU has resulted in considerable production capacity available for the export market. There has been a net reduction in world sponge capacity of about 30 percent since the early 1990s to an estimated practical capacity of about 106,000 tons per year in 1999. In contrast to this trend, the Zaporozhye Titanium-Magnesium Plant in Ukraine successfully restarted sponge production in the fourth quarter of 1998 with plans to achieve an initial production of about 6,000 mt in 1999. Zaporozhye closed with about 20,000 mt of capacity during the last titanium market downturn in the early 1990s. Owing to higher demand levels between 1994 and 1997 and the lack of sufficient sponge capacity in their home markets, U.S., Japanese, and European titanium producers have entered into long-term supply contracts and other arrangements for sponge from Russia and Kazakhstan. As a result, U.S. imports of sponge from the FSU represented approximately 16 percent of U.S. sponge consumption in 1996 and increased to 29 percent in 1998. The Berenzniki Titanium and Magnesium Works (Avisma) in Russia has a practical capacity of about 26,000 tons of titanium sponge per year, and the Ust-Kamenogorsk Titanium and Magnesium Works in Kazakhstan has a practical capacity of about 22,000 tons of sponge per year. Altogether, the FSU holds about 51 percent of estimated world practical capacity for titanium sponge. Increased purchases of FSU sponge by U.S., Japanese, and European titanium producers underscore the importance of the FSU's sponge production.

Through the mid-1980s, defense applications, led by aerospace, were the leading uses for titanium worldwide, but the end of the cold war and the drive to produce larger and more fuel-efficient aircraft led commercial aircraft manufacturers to design increasing amounts of titanium into their airframes. Commercial aerospace applications for titanium previously had centered on jet engine components. With the growth in titanium usage, the commercial aerospace market has assumed the lead in worldwide titanium consumption. Depending on the engines employed, roughly 14 tons, or 9 percent of the weight, of a delivered Boeing 777 consists of titanium compared with less than 4 percent of the weight of the older and smaller Boeing 737. Approximately 68 tons of titanium mill products are shipped to produce one Boeing 777.

Worldwide demand for titanium declined in 1998 on the back of decreased demand from the aerospace industries of the United States and Europe and continued their decline in 1999. Undelivered commercial jet aircraft orders increased to 3,704 planes at year end 1998, up 951 planes (35 percent) from 1997. Furthermore, pushbacks and extended delivery schedules have led some producers to reduce production rates, especially for the larger, more titanium-intensive, twin-aisle wide-body airplanes. As a result, worldwide titanium demand from the commercial aerospace industry decreased to an estimated 17,300 tons in 1998, down 18 percent, or approximately 35 percent of estimated world titanium demand of 49,500 tons in 1998.

Domestic Trends

Reduced aerospace demand and the buildup of inventory throughout the supply chain have forced U.S. titanium producers to curtail production levels while they continue their planned capacity expansions through the installation of new, more cost-efficient production technology. Owing to reduced commercial aircraft deliveries in 1999 and a projected further reduction in the year 2000, U.S. titanium demand declined 5 percent in 1998 to about 32,300 tons and was projected to fall about 30 percent in 1999 to about 22,000 tons (see Table 14-4). Titanium producers typically do not sell directly to aircraft and jet engine manufacturers but instead sell to companies that fabricate and supply parts and components to the aircraft and jet engine manufacturers. There is generally a lag of about 12 to 18 months between shipments of titanium mill products and the delivery of a finished aircraft.

A significant development for the U.S. titanium industry in 1999 was the awarding of the jet engine contract for Boeing's 777X long-range jet exclusively to the General Electric Company. Trent engines manufactured by Rolls Royce power Boeing's current 777s. The selection of GE should lead to greater domestic titanium consumption for engine manufacture once the 777X goes into production. Boeing hopes eventually to build up to 500 777X's. Rolls Royce will continue to supply Trent engines for the standard Boeing 777.

Actual titanium shipment levels by end-use areas are not known. This estimate is based on an aggregation of producer perceptions derived from their sales and their knowledge of the likely uses of different titanium mill products and castings. However, the International Titanium Association began to collect quarterly shipments data by end use from the association's North American membership in mid-1998 and was expected to begin publishing those data in 1999.

Owing to reduced domestic and world titanium demand, U.S. activity in titanium—production, consumption, and trade in titanium products—generally decreased in 1998, with the exception of scrap consumption and exports. There are three major producers of titanium in the United States: Titanium Metals Corporation (Timet) of Denver, CO; RTI International Metals, Inc., of Niles, OH; and Allegheny Technologies, Inc., of Pittsburgh, PA. Since only Timet and Allegheny Technologies manufacture titanium sponge, U.S. sponge production is withheld to prevent disclosure of company proprietary information. U.S. titanium sponge imports, however, declined one-third in both tonnage and value in 1998 to 10,912 tons valued at $83 million (see Table 14-4). The leading U.S. sponge import sources in 1998 were Russia (68 percent) and Japan (25 percent). The average unit value for imported sponge in 1998 was $3.43 per pound, about the same as it was in 1997.

U.S. sponge consumption decreased 12 percent in 1998 to 28,200 tons (see Table 14-4). The imports' share of U.S. sponge consumption also decreased, falling about 12 percent to a 39 percent share. On average, there is a weight loss of about 10 percent when titanium sponge is converted to ingot, but this ratio is decreasing gradually as the more efficient cold hearth melting, which also allows for greater scrap utilization, is increasingly employed to melt and cast industrial-grade (or commercially pure) single-melt titanium ingot and slab. In contrast, aerospace-grade titanium alloys typically require two or three vacuum arc remelts to meet the technical specifications for aerospace use.

In 1998, U.S. titanium scrap imports declined 8 percent to 9,765 tons valued at about $35 million, down 29 percent. This decline was accompanied by a lower average unit value of $1.61 per pound, down 48 cents per pound. Reported scrap consumption increased 8 percent in 1998 to 28,609 tons, and exports were up 27 percent. Owing to its large aerospace industry, the United States is a major generator of titanium scrap. On average, there is a weight loss of about 30 percent from the conversion of ingot

TABLE 14-4: Titanium Trends and Forecasts
(metric tons except as noted)

	1990	1993	1994	1995	1996	1997	1998	1999[1]	2000[1]	Percent Change 97–98	Percent Change 98–99	Percent Change 99–00	Compound Annual Growth Rate, % 88–98
Sponge metal													
Imports for consumption	1,093	2,160	6,470	7,560	10,110	16,140	10,912	5,000	4,800	(32.4)	(54.2)	(4.0)	23.1
Consumption	23,207	15,100	17,200	21,500	28,400	32,000	28,200	16,000	13,600	(11.9)	(43.3)	(15.0)	3.0
Imports as percent of Consumption	4.7	14.3	37.6	35.2	35.6	50.4	38.7	31.3	35.3				
Industry stocks, Dec. 31	3,267	2,910	5,570	5,270	4,390	7,050	10,600	7,000	6,000				
Price, Dec. 31 ($/lb)	4.50–5.00	3.50–4.00	3.75–4.25	4.25–4.50	4.25–4.50	4.25–4.50	4.25–4.50						
Scrap metal													
Imports	3,037	5,520	5,870	11,100	16,400	10,650	9,765	5,600	6,000	(8.3)	(42.7)	7.1	8.7
Consumption	14,973	15,300	15,700	20,600	26,300	26,400	28,609	20,000	21,700	8.4	(30.1)	8.5	4.7
Exports	5,487	3,890	4,120	3,420	3,410	5,500	7,010	8,700	8,000	27.5	24.1	(8.0)	1.6
Stocks, Dec. 31	8,535	8,130	7,930	9,730	15,900	15,200	13,600	12,000	11,800				
Ingot													
Production	36,809	27,900	29,500	39,800	51,400	58,800	52,500	39,000	35,000	(10.7)	(25.7)	(10.3)	3.1
Imports	*	206	1,463	1,772	2,063	5,189	2,228	1,600	1,400	(57.1)	(28.2)	(12.5)	NA[2]
Consumption	35,320	25,700	24,300	30,600	38,300	45,500	43,000	36,500	32,800	(5.5)	(15.1)	(10.1)	1.9
Exports	513	275	373	483	269	613	528	700	650	(13.9)	32.6	(7.1)	NA
Stocks, Dec. 31	3,725	2,430	3,270	3,560	4,710	4,350	4,050	4,200	4,000				
Mill products and castings													
Net mill product shipments	23,923	16,500	15,600	19,800	25,900	28,200	27,500	18,500	17,000	(2.5)	(32.7)	(8.1)	2.0
Net castings shipments	482	469	540	480	680	1,020	908	700	510	(11.0)	(22.9)	(27.1)	9.0
Imports (including castings)	987	600	802	1,860	6,142	4,592	3,896	2,900	2,600	(15.2)	(25.6)	(10.3)	16.8
Demand, net shipments + imports	25,392	17,569	16,942	22,140	32,722	33,812	32,304	22,100	20,110	(4.5)	(31.6)	(9.0)	3.1
Exports (including castings)	4,526	2,390	3,850	4,580	4,535	5,196	5,798	6,200	5,900	11.6	6.9	(4.8)	8.0

[1] Forecast.
[2] Not available
Source: U.S. Department of Commerce, International Trade Administration (ITA); U.S. Department of the Interior, U.S. Geological Survey; estimates and forecasts by ITA.

to mill products, and most of that loss is recovered as scrap. From mill product to finished aircraft part or component, there is an additional metal weight loss that is recovered as scrap. This fabrication metal weight loss can be quite significant, especially for large forgings for aerospace structural applications, in which as much as two-thirds of the metal weight may be recovered as scrap. U.S. titanium scrap export destinations were led by the United Kingdom with an 84 percent share of total scrap exports. Overall, the average scrap export unit value declined 15 cents per pound to $0.91 per pound.

Reported U.S. titanium ingot production decreased 11 percent to 52,500 tons in 1998, while imports decreased 57 percent in both tonnage and value to 2,228 tons and $37 million, respectively. With 72 percent of the total volume, ingot imports were led by Russia with 1,624 tons valued at about $30 million, each down about 58 percent. Imports from China followed with a 15 percent share, and those from the United Kingdom had a 6 percent share. The average unit value of U.S. ingot imports was $7.56 per pound, down 6 cents per pound. U.S. exports of ingot decreased 14 percent to 528 tons valued at about $9.4 million, down 15 percent, while the average export unit value decreased 5 cents to $7.91 per pound.

The United States is a major producer and exporter of titanium mill products and castings. Reported domestic shipments fell 23 percent in the second half of 1998, yielding an overall decrease in domestic shipments of 3 percent to 28,408 tons. U.S. imports of titanium mill product and castings declined 15 percent in 1998 to 3,896 tons; however, owing to firmer prices, the value increased to about $90 million, up 13 percent. With a 61 percent share of the total import volume, Russia was the leading import source for titanium mill products and castings in 1998. U.S. imports of titanium mill products and castings from Russia totaled 2,363 tons, down 30 percent, valued at about $34 million, down only 6 percent. Meanwhile, U.S. exports of titanium mill products and castings increased 12 percent in 1998 to 5,798 tons valued at about $283 million, up 5 percent (see Table 14-4). If U.S. trade in titanium mill products and castings is included, the United States is a net exporter. U.S. net exports of titanium mill product and castings trade amounted to 1,902 tons and $193 million in 1998, up 214 percent in volume and 2 percent in value from 1997.

U.S. Industry Growth Projections for the Next 1 and 5 Years

The 2000 and 2004 forecast for U.S. and world titanium consumption has changed appreciably from a year ago, as about 65 percent of U.S. and about 40 percent of world titanium consumption is associated with aerospace sales and there has been a significant downturn in the commercial aerospace market for the near term. Worldwide commercial aircraft build rates and planned deliveries have been adjusted downward after the 1999 peak in planned deliveries of about 1,140 aircraft, up 20 percent from 1998. For the year 2000, planned commercial aircraft deliveries will decline about 10 percent to 1,023 units. Planned deliveries of commercial aircraft for 2001 are not available but are expected to be lower than those for 2000. Estimates of the amount of titanium inventories remaining in the supply chain, including aircraft parts subcontractors and titanium mill product, ingot, and sponge producers, vary from about 9 months to 1.5 years. Therefore, no sustained recovery in U.S. or world titanium demand is anticipated until at least the second half of 2000 or perhaps the first half of 2001, as improved build rates draw down titanium inventories.

Worldwide, the defense sector continues to be driven by several aerospace programs and the armor market continues to offer good demand prospects because of its large volume potential. Diminished but stable military aerospace programs are expected to yield fairly flat demand growth of about 6,000 tons per year through 2004. Titanium demand from the nonaerospace industrial and consumer sector could slip to 26,000 tons worldwide in 2000 before growing to about 28,600 tons in 2004. The principal nonaerospace industrial and consumer applications for titanium include chemical processing, pulp and paper equipment, industrial power plants, pollution control equipment, and desalination plants, while emerging applications include end-use areas such as sports equipment, medical implants, automotive, energy extraction and processing, and off-grid power plants.

For 2000, U.S. demand, as measured by domestic shipments of titanium mill products and castings, is projected to decline 9 percent to about 20,100 tons owing to weakness in aerospace demand. The gradual recovery in the economies of Asia and Latin America will lead to improved demand late in the forecast period. As a result, U.S. titanium demand and exports are projected to grow. U.S. titanium demand is projected to grow about 6.3 percent yearly from 22,100 tons in 1999 to about 30,000 tons in 2004, while exports are projected to increase at a rate of about 3 percent per year from 6,200 tons in 1999 to about 7,200 tons in 2004.

Graylin W. Presbury, Office of Metals, Materials, and Chemicals, (202) 482-5158, graylin_presbury@ita.doc.gov, September 1999.

ZINC

The international zinc industry includes primary producers (SIC 3339) that use zinc ores and concentrates as a feedstock and secondary producers (SIC 3341) that recycle scrap zinc and crude zinc calcine obtained from electric arc furnace dust in steel mills. Secondary zinc has become an increasingly important source of metal in recent years. Zinc is consumed primarily by the galvanizing (SIC 3312), zinc-based die-casting alloy (SIC 3369), and brass and bronze (SIC 3364, 3366) markets. Zinc is an internationally traded commodity whose value is based on the price set daily by the LME. This price may vary in different countries, depending on local market conditions.

Global Industry Trends

The structure of the global zinc industry changed significantly in the 1990s. Before the breakup of the Soviet Union, Japan was the world's largest producer of zinc metal, followed by the Soviet Union, Canada, China, and the United States. In 1998, however, China was the dominant producer, accounting for 18.3 percent of the 7.9 million mt produced, followed by Canada, 9.3 percent; Japan, 7.6 percent; South Korea, 4.9 percent; and Spain and the United States, 4.6 percent each. China also has become the world's second largest exporter of zinc metal, with exports rising from 6,000 mt in 1991 to 354,000 mt in 1998. China's increasing production in the early 1990s, combined with declining zinc consumption in Europe, Japan, and other countries in the early 1990s, resulted in a record market surplus in 1993, with the level of excess supply rising from 25,000 mt in 1990 to 619,000 mt in 1993. Improved market conditions after 1993 transformed this surplus into a supply deficit in 1995 and 1996. By 1998, however, a surplus of 152,000 mt had developed as a result of growing Chinese exports and significantly lower demand in Japan.

Domestic Trends

The United States is the world's fifth largest producer of zinc ores and concentrates after China, Canada, Australia, and Peru. Zinc is extracted in 20 domestic zinc mines in seven states. For the eighth consecutive year, Alaska is the leading zinc mining state, followed by Tennessee, New York, and Missouri. In 1998, as was the case in every year since the opening of Cominco's Red Dog mine in Alaska, U.S. mine production greatly exceeded smelter capacity, resulting in significant exports to Canada and Asia. Primary zinc metal is produced at three refineries: Big River Zinc at Sauget, IL; Pasminco USA at Clarksville, TN; and Zinc Corporation of America (ZCA) at Monaca, PA. Secondary zinc metal is produced from waste and scrap materials at 10 plants. The largest secondary producer, ZCA, obtains a substantial part of its feedstock from crude zinc calcine recovered from electric arc furnace dust in steel mills.

Zinc also is sold by the DNSC as a result of legislation passed in 1992 authorizing the disposal of the entire 334,000 mt in the stockpile over several years. The law, however, requires the task to be completed without undue disruption of commercial zinc markets. At the end of August 1999, 183,727 mt of zinc remained in the DNSC inventory. The FY 2000 AMP authorizes the disposal of about 45,000 mt of zinc between October 1, 1999, and September 30, 2000. Additional authority is being sought by the DNSC to dispose of 45,000 mt for the FY 2001 AMP. This AMP, however, is a limit and not a goal, and DNSC has never reached this limit for zinc.

The domestic zinc industry experienced major structural changes in 1998. Asarco sold all its Missouri lead-zinc operations, which consisted of its Sweetwater and West Fork underground mines, to Doe Run. Savage Zinc, which was planning to nearly triple capacity at its 150,000-mt per year Clarksville smelter, was taken over by another Australian producer, Pasminco, and the smelter expansion was put on hold indefinitely. In addition, IMCO Recycling, Incorporated, acquired U.S. Zinc Corporation and its five production facilities with a total of about 100,000 mt, making IMCO the world's largest zinc recycler and second largest supplier of zinc oxide and zinc dust.

Between 1991 and 1998, domestic zinc mine production increased at an average annual rate of 5.4 percent, rising from 547,000 mt to 755,000 mt, primarily reflecting the reopening of Kennecott's Greens Creek mine in Alaska in 1996 and increased production at Cominco's Red Dog mine in Alaska.

Domestic zinc metal production remained relatively flat during that period, falling from 376,000 mt in 1991 to 368,000 mt in 1998 as increased secondary production at a number of facilities, debottlenecking at Pasminco's Clarksville smelter, and increased capacity at Big River Zinc's Sauget smelter offset the 1993 closure of ZCA's Bartlesville, OK, facility. During this period, secondary zinc's share of total metal production increased from 32 percent to about 41 percent (see Table 14-5).

The United States accounts for about 16 percent of global zinc consumption and is the single largest market worldwide. Domestic zinc consumption increased at an average rate of 5.4 percent per year between 1991 and 1998, rising from 931,000 mt to 1,283,000 mt. In 1998, zinc galvanizing accounted for 57 percent of total consumption, followed by zinc-based die-casting alloys at 19 percent and brass and bronze at 13 percent. The remaining 11 percent went to zinc oxides, rolled zinc, and several other zinc uses (see Table 14-5).

Markets. Zinc is found in a large number of manufactured products, but its role is not always obvious because it tends to lose its identity in the product. Almost all zinc consumed domestically and exported and a large share of imported zinc reach the final consumer contained in hundreds of products, such as motor vehicles (galvanized steel body, zinc die castings, and tires containing zinc oxide), appliances (zinc die castings), televisions (zinc sulfide), and animal feed (zinc oxide). Rolled zinc is purchased by the U.S. Mint for the production of pennies.

The largest and fastest-growing segment of the zinc market is galvanized steel, which includes coated steel sheet and strip, structural shapes, fencing, storage tanks, fasteners, nails, and wire rope. Galvanized steel is used in the automotive and construction industries for corrosion protection. Galvanizing in automotive applications increased substantially during the last few years as virtually all domestically produced motor vehicles switched to two-sided galvanized steel. In addition, the sport utility vehicle's increasing share of domestic vehicle production has resulted in an increase in the amount of galvanized steel used per vehicle. Because of its durability, galvanized steel is making inroads into applications such as residential housing and public works, including highways, bridges, and wastewater treatment systems.

As a result of research and extensive marketing, two applications in the construction sector could result in a significant increase in galvanized zinc consumption. The International Lead and Zinc Research Organization has worked extensively to promote the use of galvanized rebar. Corrosion of concrete reinforcement bars is a major infrastructure problem that costs billions of dollars in repairs and replacement of reinforced concrete structures. Currently, less than 1 percent of rebar is galvanized, representing 30,000 mt of zinc worldwide. If this project is successful, zinc consumption for this use could expand to 150,000 mt annually worldwide. Another promising application sponsored jointly by the North American steel and zinc industries is steel framing for residential housing. While steel framing is estimated to cost 3 to 5 percent more than building with lumber, it offers some advantages that could outweigh the increased construction costs. Steel frames often are produced from recy-

TABLE 14-5: Zinc Industry (SIC 3339, 3341) Trends and Forecasts
(thousands of metric tons; percent)

	1991	1994	1995	1996	1997	1998	1999[1]	2000[2]	Percent Change 97–98	Percent Change 98–99	Percent Change 99–00	Compound Annual Growth Rate, % 91–98
Mine production	547	598	644	628	632	755	810	810	19.5	7.3	-0.0	4.7
Metal production	376	356	363	366	367	368	370	380	0.3	0.5	2.7	-0.3
Apparent metal consumption	931	1,182	1,250	1,212	1,244	1,283	1,355	1,365	3.1	5.6	0.7	4.7
Percent galvanizing	49.9	52.8	51.9	53.6	55.9	57.3	58.3	58.2				
Percent zinc alloy	21.5	20.4	20.0	18.9	18.0	19.3	19.2	19.4				
Percent brass and bronze	14.3	14.0	12.6	13.2	13.2	12.9	12.3	12.2				
Percent other uses	14.3	12.8	14.2	14.3	12.9	10.6	10.2	10.0				
Imports for consumption	549	793	856	827	876	879	965	956	0.3	9.8	-0.9	7.0
Percent of consumption	59.0	67.1	68.5	68.3	70.4	68.5	71.2	70.4				
Exports	1	6	3	2	4	2	1	1	-50.0	-50.0	-0.0	10.4

[1] Estimate.
[2] Forecast.
Source: U.S. Department of Commerce, International Trade Administration (ITA); U.S. Department of the Interior, Geological Survey; International Lead and Zinc Study Group. Estimates and forecasts by ITA.

cled steel products and are resistant to fire, natural disasters, and termites. While the participants in this project have a goal of capturing one-quarter of the residential frame market by the year 2002, only 3 to 6 percent of new houses currently are built from steel. If it is successful, this initiative could result in a 7,000-mt increase in galvanizing zinc consumption per year.

Zinc-based die-casting alloys are used to produce die-cast parts, such as handles, grilles, brackets, locks, hinges, gauges, pumps, mounts, and housings, that are used extensively in motor vehicles, heavy machinery, business machinery, appliances, household hardware, and scientific and electronic equipment. Brass and bronze products are used as shell casings in ammunition and in tubes, valves, motors, pipes, refrigeration equipment, heat exchangers, communication units, and electronic devices.

Environment. Laws passed in California and nine northeastern states mandating the production of EVs could influence future zinc consumption. California and CONEG require that by 2003, 10 percent of all vehicles sold in those areas be zero-emission EVs and 15 percent be ultra-low-emission vehicles. One technology that could compete in this market is the zinc-air battery. An Israeli company has developed a prototype zinc-air EV battery system that would allow an EV to perform as well as a gasoline-powered vehicle, with a range of 300 miles or more, a top speed of 80 miles per hour, acceleration from zero to 50 miles per hour in 12 seconds, and refueling (mechanical recharging) in only a few minutes at a recharging station. Annual sales of 100,000 such EVs would translate into 10,000 mt of zinc per year for these batteries.

A proposed European Commission directive on batteries and accumulators would ban the marketing of nickel-cadmium batteries in the EU by 2008. Since cadmium is a by-product of zinc, this proposal, if adopted, would severely affect the price of zinc. This proposed directive is contrary to a joint effort of the OECD and industry to increase the recycling of these batteries. The United States has raised concerns over the apparent lack of adequate scientific and economic justification for such a ban, and industry has proposed a voluntary agreement to collect and recycle these batteries (see page 14-19 for more information on this proposed directive).

U.S. Industry Growth Projections for the Next 1 and 5 Years

Domestic zinc consumption is estimated to increase at an average annual rate of about 3.2 percent between 1998 and 2000 to 1.37 million mt and rise at an average annual rate of 1.5 percent between 2000 and 2004 to 1.45 million mt. The galvanizing segment is forecast to increase from 735,000 mt in 1998 to 795,000 in 2000 and to rise about 1.4 percent annually between 2000 and 2004, reaching 840,000 mt as a result of increases in private nonresidential and public works construction such as highways as well as a slight increase in motor vehicle production. Domestic consumption for the zinc-based alloy segment is expected to increase from 247,000 mt to 265,000 mt between 1998 and 2000 and then rise about 1.5 percent per year between 2000 and 2004, reaching 281,000 mt. This growth reflects the decision by several automobile producers to increase their specifications for zinc die castings in addition to projected growth in the use of zinc die castings in the building hardware market. Consumption in brass and bronze is estimated to grow from 165,000 mt in 1998 to 180,000 mt in 2000. Between 2000 and 2004, the brass and bronze segment is forecast to rise almost 2 percent per year to 180,000 mt as this segment is positively affected by an increase in some of its end-use markets, such as ammunition and plumbing fixtures.

Supply. Domestic production of zinc is forecast to increase to 380,000 mt in 2000 and 405,000 mt by 2004 as a result of increased capacity utilization at Big River Zinc's Sauget smelter, growth in secondary production, and the opening of CalEnergy Minerals LLC's plant for zinc recovery from geothermal brines in Imperial Valley, CA, in mid-2000. This plant, which has been used for power generation, will first pass brine through an ion-exchange plant. Through reverse osmosis, it then will produce a zinc concentrate solution that will go through solvent extraction and electrowinning to produce zinc cathodes for remelting in a casting facility. CalEnergy is expected to produce 25,000 mt of zinc per year.

The United States is by far a net importer of refined zinc, with imports currently accounting for about 69 percent of consumption (see Table 14-5). In 1998, 87 percent of the 879,000 mt imported came from Canada, China, South Korea, Mexico, Peru, and Spain. Imports from Canada, Mexico, and Peru were imported duty-free, while Chinese and Spanish imports were charged a 1.5 percent duty. Zinc alloy imports in 1998 jumped to 5,414 mt from 267 mt in 1997, with Canada, Mexico, and Peru accounting for 99 percent of the total. Despite the large increase in imports, they only account for 6 percent of domestic consumpton of zinc alloys. The tariff for zinc alloy was 19 percent for most countries prior to 1995, but as a result of the Uruguay Round of the General Agreement on Trade and Tariffs (GATT), it decreased to 3 percent in January 1999. Imports of zinc alloy are duty-free from Mexico under NAFTA and from other developing countries eligible for the Generalized System of Preferences (GSP) program. Imports from Canada have been duty-free since January 1998. Pursuant to the Statement of Administrative Action (SAA) accompanying the Uruguay Round implementing legislation, the Department of Commerce will monitor imports of zinc alloy until 2002. The SAA requires monitoring of zinc alloy imports subject to the Uruguay Round tariff reductions, which account for 1 percent of U.S. imports.

Given the domestic zinc industry's reliance on imports, only 2,333 mt of zinc was exported in 1998, with 97 percent going to Canada, India, and South Korea. About 11,000 mt of zinc alloy was exported, with 93 percent going to Canada.

Global Market Prospects

Between 1991 and 1998, global consumption of zinc rose at an annual rate of 2.7 percent, increasing from 6.63 million mt to

7.79 million mt. Galvanizing currently accounts for 47 percent of consumption, followed by brass and bronze, 19 percent; zinc-based alloys, 14 percent; chemicals, 8 percent; zinc semi-manufactures, 8 percent; and other uses, 4 percent. Broken down by end use, 48 percent currently goes into construction, followed by transportation, 23 percent; consumer goods and equipment, 10 percent each; and infrastructure, 9 percent. Global market conditions for zinc are forecast to show continued growth in the near term. Consumption was expected to rise 2 percent in 1999 to 8.1 million mt, while metal production was projected to increase 2.1 percent from 8.03 million mt to 8.20 million mt.

Dave Larrabee, Office of Metals, Materials, and Chemicals, (202) 483-0607, dave_larrabee@ita.doc.gov, September 1999.

INTERNATIONAL ENVIRONMENTAL INITIATIVES AND THE METALS INDUSTRY

Basel Convention

The Basel Convention on the Control of Transboundary Movements of Hazardous Wastes and Their Disposal, which was adopted at a diplomatic conference at Basel, Switzerland, in 1989, was developed under the auspices of the United Nations Environment Program (UNEP) and entered into force in May 1992. As of September 1999, the Basel Convention had 127 contracting parties and one economic integration organization (the EU). The United States has signed but not ratified the agreement.

Basel is the broadest and most significant international treaty on hazardous wastes currently in effect. Its key objectives are to (1) reduce transboundary movements of hazardous wastes and other wastes subject to the convention, (2) minimize their generation and hazardousness, (3) ensure strict control over movements across borders, particularly illegal traffic, through a requirement of written notification and consent, (4) prohibit shipments to countries that lack the capacity to manage and dispose of them in an environmentally sound manner, and (5) assist developing countries and countries in transition with the development of environmentally sound management. The convention affirms the principle that any nation has the sovereign right to ban unilaterally the import of any hazardous waste into its territory.

The Basel Convention lists wastes as either hazardous (Annex VIII) or nonhazardous (Annex IX). The waste lists were formally adopted by the Basel Convention at the Fourth Conference of Parties (COP IV) at Kuching, Malaysia, in 1998. Annex VIII wastes are considered hazardous under Basel so long as the waste or shipment contains a hazardous constituent, listed on Annex I of the Convention, to a degree that causes it to demonstrate a hazardous characteristic, as listed in Annex III. The convention has included introductory language (chapeau) that allows an individual shipment of Annex VIII material to be reclassified if the shipment does not demonstrate an Annex III characteristic. A controversial aspect of the Basel Convention is that it makes few distinctions between the export of a waste for recycling and export of waste for final disposal and classifies wastes on the basis of "intrinsic hazard" as opposed to the risk involved in shipping and storage.

Earlier, in September 1995, at COP III, Decision III/1 (the Ban Amendment) was adopted. That decision immediately prohibited the export of hazardous materials from Annex VII countries (OECD, EU, and Liechtenstein) to non-Annex VII countries for disposal and, after December 31, 1997, for recovery and/or recycling. To come into force, however, this amendment needs to be ratified by three-fourths of the parties. As of September 1999, the ban had been ratified by only 14 nations and the EU. Nevertheless, the EU and Norway already have implemented the ban and have also moved to phase out exports of nonhazardous wastes, such as bulk ferrous and nonferrous scrap, to developing countries that indicated a desire not to receive these products or failed to respond to a European Commission questionnaire (European Council Regulation No. 1420/1999). That move has been construed by many in U.S. industry as veiled protectionism, as it is likely to increase the supply of critical industrial inputs within the EU, thus lowering their price and creating an unfair competitive advantage. The composition of Annex VII, particularly regarding recent (1997) applications by Israel and Monaco to accede to that annex, has been an especially contentious issue in Basel. The United States, joined by the non-EU OECD countries and a number of developing countries, has endorsed a need to develop criteria for accession to and secession to or from Annex VII. However, COP III agreed that Annex VII will remain unchanged until the ban comes into force.

Another important component of the Basel Convention is that it disallows trade in hazardous wastes with nonparties to the convention unless the trade is governed by a bilateral or multilateral agreement with provisions no less stringent than those of Basel. Such agreements are permissible under Article XI. The most important Article XI agreement to the United States, apart from the bilateral agreements with Canada and Mexico, is the OECD agreement Council Decision C(92)39 adopted in 1992 and last amended in 1998. This agreement has governed trade in hazardous wastes destined for recovery operations within the OECD through a control system of notification and consent based on a three-tier system: Green list wastes are nonhazardous and are moved through a system of tacit consent; amber list wastes may be moved but are subject to certain controls, generally written notification and consent; and red list wastes are highly hazardous and not suitable for recovery, and trade in them should be reduced to a minimum.

The OECD agreement differs from Basel in that it was designed to facilitate trade in recyclables, recognizing the economic and environmental benefit of a free market in such products. Its control system is also risk-based as opposed to being based on the intrinsic hazardousness of the waste in question, as in Basel. Recently, the Environmental Policy Committee of the OECD (EPOC) instructed the Working Group on Waste Management Policy (WGWMP) to harmonize the OECD agreement with Basel. Harmonization has the potential to move a number of amber list wastes to Annex VIII, thus increasing the scope of Annex I, even though an amber listing was not an implicit recognition of hazardousness but instead of a potential risk (e.g., flammability). Furthermore, the control procedure and review mechanisms of the Basel Convention are largely untested, and Basel makes few distinctions between a waste export for recycling and a waste export for final disposal. While the OECD is committed in principle to work on this harmonization, largely because of a perceived need for clarity and for budget cutting in the OECD, changes to C(92)39 may occur only by consensus. The status of Article XI agreements in Basel, of which some parties question the validity and tenure (the EU has announced a moratorium on negotiating new Article XI agreements), will ultimately affect what type of OECD agreement will be maintained.

The U.S. Senate has provided notification and consent to the administration to develop implementing legislation for ratification of the Basel Convention. While most issues concerning the annexes have been concluded satisfactorily, U.S. ratification has been on hold largely as a result of the questionable environmental and economic implications of the Ban Amendment (the Senate has not provided notification and consent for the ratification of the ban) and because ratification of Basel will require amending the Solid Waste Disposal Act, the amendment of which is invariably connected to RCRA/Superfund reform, a controversial issue whose resolution has perennially eluded the U.S. Congress.

Climate Change

The United Nations Framework Convention on Climate Change (FCCC), which was signed in Rio de Janeiro in 1992, was ratified as of June 1999 by 179 countries; it entered into force in 1994. The FCCC seeks to address the anthropogenic emissions of the greenhouse gases carbon dioxide (CO_2), methane (CH_4), and nitrous oxide (N_2O) and those of the industrial gases hydrofluorocarbons (HFCs), perfluorocarbons (PFCs), and sulfur hexafluoride (SF_6). These emissions may result directly from metal-processing facilities as well as indirectly from the consumption of raw material inputs such as electricity generated from fossil fuels. Metal-processing industries such as steel and aluminum, despite major reductions in greenhouse emissions, remain significant sources of those emissions, primarily as a result of energy consumption.

At COP III in Kyoto, Japan, in December 1997, the parties agreed to a protocol for reducing greenhouse gas emissions. The Kyoto Protocol calls for industrialized nations to reduce their average national emissions at least 5 percent below 1990 levels by 2008–2012. The United States is required to lower its emissions 7 percent, and the EU has committed to an 8 percent reduction. U.S. negotiators and industry have claimed that such a target is easier for Europe because of the selection of 1990—a period of relative economic slowdown for the United States compared with Europe—as the base year; wider use of nuclear power in Europe; a wholesale conversion from coal-based power to natural gas mandated in Britain by the United Kingdom government; and the inclusion of eastern Germany under the European "umbrella." As of August 1999, the protocol had 84 signatories and 14 ratifications (mostly from small island states). It will come into force when it has been ratified by 55 countries, including developed countries representing at least 55 percent of the total 1990 CO_2 emissions from this group. Important provisions, particularly the means by which to achieve these reductions, will be significant if the protocol is to receive widespread ratification. Most important is the issue of participation by developing countries. Despite being competitive industrial producers, developing countries such as China, India, and Brazil are essentially exempt from the protocol. Other countries, notably Russia and the eastern European countries, it has been argued, are not forced to make a significant reduction in emissions, as the recessions those countries faced after the transition to capitalism resulted in large reductions of output and thus emissions well below 1990 levels, rendering their commitments moot. The ability to extensively use so-called flexible mechanisms such as carbon "sinks" and emissions trading, which the United States strongly supports, is also an important issue currently being debated within the FCCC.

The United States faces strong opposition from the EU and a number of developing countries on most of these issues, although at COP IV in Buenos Aires, Argentina, Kazakhstan and the host country announced that they would set emissions reduction targets, making them the first developing countries to do so. In the meantime, the U.S. administration has begun consultations with industry through the White House Climate Change Taskforce (WHCCTF) to determine the best means of achieving reductions in greenhouse gas emissions on a voluntary basis. The sectors the WHCCTF is focusing on include aluminum, steel, and metal castings. Technological innovation will assume a major role in the ability of industry to further reduce energy consumption and greenhouse gas emissions.

Global Initiatives to Reduce the Impact of Metals on Human Health and the Environment

Because of the risks certain metals may pose to human health and the environment, a number of international and regional initiatives have been or are being considered to reduce those risks. Some of these initiatives are aimed at controlling transboundary emissions of these metals or promoting recovery and recycling, while others focus on product design and the elimination of certain metals from products and product components as a means of managing waste.

Heavy Metals Protocol. The United States is a contracting party to the Convention on Long-Range Transboundary Air Pollution sponsored by the United Nations Economic Commission for Europe. Under this convention, the Heavy Metals Protocol was concluded in February 1998 and signed in June 1998. This protocol, which covers Europe, Canada, and the United States, will control long-range transboundary emissions of cadmium, lead, and mercury. Since the emissions from facilities that produce, recycle, and incinerate these metals or products containing these metals already are covered under the convention as stationary sources, only products containing these metals that directly contribute to such emissions are restricted under the protocol. Currently, this includes only leaded gasoline and most mercury-containing primary batteries. To add other products to the protocol, strict criteria and procedures must be met to ensure that the use of the proposed product significantly contributes to long-range transboundary air emissions of the covered metals and that the risks and benefits of both the proposed product and any possible substitute are examined.

OECD Chemical Classification. Other environment activities of the OECD have the potential to affect the metals industry. One important initiative is the Global Harmonization of Chemical Classification and Labeling Systems (GHS), which is considering a number of metals with which it associates certain criteria, such as persistence, ecotoxicity, and bioaccumulation. Importantly, the GHS has a Mixtures Group that as part of its agenda will consider the classification of alloys. Metal industry representatives have been active in stressing the idea that metals contain properties intrinsically different from those of chemicals (metals are by definition persistent) and that, at the least, alloys are not mixtures (the chemical and physical characteristics of an alloy differ from those of the individual metals in that alloy). Furthermore, the metals in the alloy are not dispersible.

Apart from GHS, the OECD has embarked on work in the areas of waste minimization, closed-loop recycling, sustainable development, and ecolabeling, as have a number of other international forums, including the United Nations, the EU, and Asia-Pacific Economic Cooperation (APEC).

Risk Reduction. In 1990, the OECD began a risk reduction program with pilot projects focused on lead, cadmium, mercury, and two chemicals. As part of the Cadmium Risk Reduction Program, the OECD Working Group on Cadmium Risk Reduction concluded at a 1995 workshop in Sweden that the release of cadmium from incinerators and landfills can be mitigated to insignificant levels through the use of current technologies and proper management practices. The group agreed that it was desirable to increase the collection and recycling of nickel-cadmium batteries, particularly for portable applications. After this workshop, the OECD worked closely with industry to establish a successful collection and recycling chain for these batteries. The October 1997 OECD Workshop on the Effective Collection and Recycling of Nickel-Cadmium Batteries in France concluded that "significant private investment is being made, and will continue to be made, to establish" an environmentally responsible collection and recycling system. The workshop further concluded that "for the continuation of private investment it is important that there be a stable market, a high collection and recycling rate, an adequate return on investment and end product markets for the recovered materials." A recently proposed directive by the European Commission's environment director general, which is discussed further below, could undermine these efforts.

European Commission Waste Directives. The European Commission's environment director general has proposed three waste management directives that could affect the international competitiveness of a number of U.S. industries, such as aviation, automotive, electronics, power tools, and telecommunications, as well as the metals industry. These directives are currently at various stages in the EU legislative process. The environment director general recently completed the third draft of the directives on Batteries and Accumulators and WEEE and submitted those drafts for interservice consultations among the various directorates of the commission. If they are adopted by the commission, those directives will go to the council and parliament in late 1999 or early 2000. While the United States supports the objectives of the drafts to reduce waste and the environmental impact of discarded products, the manner in which these directives are written raises a number of important trade policy concerns. In particular, the draft directives' approach to banning certain materials (such as lead, cadmium, and mercury) and mandating specific design standards appears to lack adequate scientific and economic justification and may serve as an unnecessary barrier to trade. In addition, imposing the sole responsibility for the collection and recycling of used products on the manufacturer is unnecessarily burdensome.

The directive on batteries and accumulators would ban the marketing of nickel-cadmium batteries in the EU by January 1, 2008, while the WEEE directive would ban the use of certain materials in almost all electrical and electronic equipment marketed in the EU by January 1, 2004. In October 1998, industry presented the environment director general with a voluntary industry agreement to collect and recycle those batteries. In this proposed agreement, which is in line with OECD efforts to increase the collection and recycling of these batteries, battery producers, producers and importers of appliances that use nickel-cadmium batteries, and recyclers would make a commitment to increase the quantity of nickel-cadmium batteries recycled each year until the target collection rates stated in the directive are achieved. Effective implementation of such an agreement might achieve the commission's environmental objectives without causing the trade disruption that would result from a ban on nickel-cadmium batteries.

The United States also is concerned about a draft directive on the disposal of end-of-life vehicles (ELVs). As is the case with the other directives, the ELV directive contains substance bans that do not appear to be justified by scientific risk assessment and that would, if implemented, impose onerous burdens on U.S. vehicle producers.

Anthony Renzulli, U.S. Department of Commerce, Office of Metals, Materials and Chemicals, (202) 482-5159, Anthony_Renzulli@ita.doc.gov, September 1999. ***Dave Larrabee,*** U.S. Department of Commerce, Office of Metals, Materials and Chemicals, (202) 482-0607, Dave_Larrabee@ita.doc.gov, September 1999.

TABLE 14-6: U.S. Trade Patterns in Nonferrous Metals[1] in 1998
(millions of dollars; percent)

Exports			Imports		
Region[2]	Value[3]	Share, %	Region[2]	Value[3]	Share, %
NAFTA	5,364	38	NAFTA	9,721	46
Latin America	806	6	Latin America	2,085	10
Western Europe	5,193	37	Western Europe	2,715	13
Japan/Chinese Economic Area	1,312	9	Japan/Chinese Economic Area	1,484	7
Other Asia	587	4	Other Asia	437	2
Rest of world	792	6	Rest of world	4,764	22
World	14,054	100	World	21,205	100
Top Five Countries	Value	Share, %	Top Five Countries	Value	Share, %
Canada	2,943	21	Canada	7,587	36
United Kingdom	2,815	20	Russia	2,351	11
Mexico	2,422	17	Mexico	2,134	10
Switzerland	1,427	10	South Africa	1,263	6
Japan	696	5	China	724	3

[1] SIC 1021, 3331, 3334, 3339, 3341, 3351, 3353, 3354, 3355, 3357.
[2] For definitions of regional groupings, see "Getting the Most Out of *Outlook 2000*."
[3] Values may not sum to total due to rounding.
Source: U.S. Department of Commerce, Bureau of the Census.

Electronic Commerce

Like other industries, the metals industries have recognized the time and cost savings associated with conducting transactions electronically, and industry associations have recognized the capability of the Internet as a means of product promotion. In addition, companies are combining resources to establish Web sites that offer products for sale from a variety of producers. The use of electronic commerce has been very effective in complementing the notion of just-in-time inventory and has been useful for consumers requiring emergency supplies and producers wishing to dispose of excess inventory. In essence, an electronic spot market is being created that is serving to improve the overall functioning of markets through increased transparency.

U.S. trade patterns in nonferrous metals are shown in Table 14-6.

REFERENCES

Aluminum

The Aluminum Association, 900 19 Street, NW, Washington, DC 20006. (202) 862-5100, www.aluminum.org.

American Metal Market, Capital Cities, Inc., 825 Seventh Avenue, New York, NY 10019. (202) 887-8550, www.amm.com.

Metal Bulletin, Metal Bulletin, Inc., 220 Fifth Avenue, New York, NY 10001. (212) 213-6202, www.metalbul.com.

Platts-Metals Week, The McGraw-Hill Companies, 1221 Avenue of the Americas, New York, NY 10020. (212) 512-6126, www.platts.com.

Copper

American Metal Market, 825 Seventh Ave., New York, NY 10019. (212) 887-8550.

Copper Development Association, 260 Madison Avenue, New York, NY 10016. (212) 251-7200, www.amm.com.

International Copper Study Group, Rua Almirante Barroso, No. 38, 6th Floor, 1000 Lisbon, Portugal. 351-1-352-4039, www.icsg.org.

U.S. Department of the Interior, Geological Survey, Office of Minerals Information, 989 National Center, Reston, VA 20192. (703) 648-4978, www.minerals.er.usgs.gov.

Lead

American Metal Market, Capital Cities, Inc., 825 Seventh Avenue, New York, NY 10019. (212) 887-8550, http://amm.com.

Battery Council International, 401 North Michigan Avenue, Chicago, IL 60611-4267. (312) 644-6610, http://www.batterycouncil.org.

The Battery Man/Independent Battery Manufacturers Association, 100 Larchwood Drive, Largo, FL 33770-2811. (727) 586-1408, http://www.thebatteryman.com.

International Lead and Zinc Study Group, 2 King Street, London SW1Y 6QP, United Kingdom. 011-44-171-484-3307, http://www.ilzsg.org.

International Lead Zinc Research Organization, 2525 Meridan Parkway, P.O. Box 12036, Research Triangle Park, NC 27709. (919) 361-4647, http://www.ilzro.org.

Lead Development Association, 42 Weymouth Street, London W1N 3LQ, United Kingdom. 011-44-171-499-8422, http://www.ldaint.org.

Lead Industries Association, 295 Madison Avenue, 19th Floor, New York, NY 10017. (973) 726-5323, http://www.leadinfo.com.

Metal Bulletin, Metal Bulletin, Inc., 220 Fifth Avenue, New York, NY 10001. (212) 213-6202, http://www.metbul.com.

Mineral Commodity Surveys, *Lead Industry Monthly,* U.S. Department of the Interior, U.S. Geological Survey, Reston, VA 20192. (703) 648-77567, http://minerals.usgs.gov/minerals.

Platts-Metals Week, The McGraw-Hill Companies, 1221 Avenue of the Americas, New York, NY 10020. (212) 512-6126, http://www.platts.com.

U.S. Trade Representative, "1999 National Trade Estimate Report on Foreign Trade Barriers—European Union," pp. 114–115, 600 Seventeenth Street, NW, Washington, DC 20506. (202) 395-9624, http://www.ustr.gov.

Titanium

American Metal Market, Capital Cities, Inc., 825 Seventh Avenue, New York, NY 10019. (212) 887-8550, http://www.amm.com.

International Titanium Association, 1871 Folsom Street, Suite 200, Boulder, CO 80302. (303) 443-7515. http://titanium.org.

Metal Bulletin, Metal Bulletin, Inc., 220 Fifth Avenue, New York, NY 10001. (212) 213-6202, http://metalbulletin.com.

Platts-Metals Week, The McGraw-Hill Companies, 1221 Avenue of the Americas, New York, NY 10020. (212) 512-6126, http://www.platts.com.

Titanium Quarterly, Mineral Industry Surveys, U.S. Department of the Interior, U.S. Geological Survey, Reston, VA 20192. (703) 648-7718, http://minerals.usgs.gov/minerals.

Zinc

American Metal Market, Capital Cities, Inc., 825 Seventh Avenue, New York, NY 10019. (212) 887-8550, http://www.amm.com.

American Zinc Association, Suite 240, 1112 Sixteenth Street, NW, Washington DC 20036. (202) 835-0164, http://www.zinc.org.

International Lead and Zinc Study Group, 2 King Street, London SW1Y 6QP, United Kingdom. 011-44-171-839-8550, http://www.ilzsg.org.

International Lead Zinc Research Organization, 2525 Meridan Parkway, P.O. Box 12036, Research Triangle Park, NC 27709. (919) 361-4647, http://www.ilzro.org.

International Zinc Association, 168 avenue de Tervueren, Box 4, B-1150 Brussels, Belgium. 011-32-2-776-00-70, http://www.iza.com.

Metal Bulletin, Metal Bulletin, Inc., 220 Fifth Avenue, New York, NY 10001. (212) 213-6202, http://www.metbul.comhttp://www.platts.com.

U.S. Trade Representative, "1999 National Trade Estimate Report on Foreign Trade Barriers—European Union," pp. 114–115, 600 Seventeenth Street, NW, Washington, DC 20506. (202) 395-9624, http://www.ustr.gov.

International Environmental Initiatives

European Commission, http://europa.eu.int.

Organization for Economic Cooperation and Development (OECD), 2 rue André-Pascal, 75775 Paris Cedex 16, France. http://www.oecd.org.

Secretariat of the Basel Convention (SBC), Geneva Executive Center, 15, Chemin des Anémones, CH-1219 Châtelain, Geneva, Switzerland. (41-22) 979-92-18, http://www.unep.ch/basel.

United Nations Economic Commission for Europe. http://www.unece.org/env/env_eb.htm.

United Nations Environment Program (UNEP), Geneva Executive Center. http://www.unep.ch.

United Nations Framework Convention on Climate Change (UNFCCC), Haus Carstanjen, Martin-Luther-King-Strasse 8, D-53175 Bonn, Germany. (41-228)-815-1000, http://www.unfccc.de.

U.S. Trade Representative, "1999 National Trade Estimate Report on Foreign Trade Barriers—European Union," pp. 114–115, 600 Seventeenth Street, NW, Washington, DC 20506. (202) 395-9624, http://www.ustr.gov.

White House Climate Change Taskforce, 734 Jackson Place, NW, Washington, DC 20503. (202) 395-2310, http://whitehouse.gov/PCSD/tforce/ccft/index.html.

■ RELATED CHAPTERS

1: Metals and Industrial Minerals Mining
6: Construction
21: Aerospace
36: Motor Vehicles

GENERAL COMPONENTS
Economic and Trade Trends

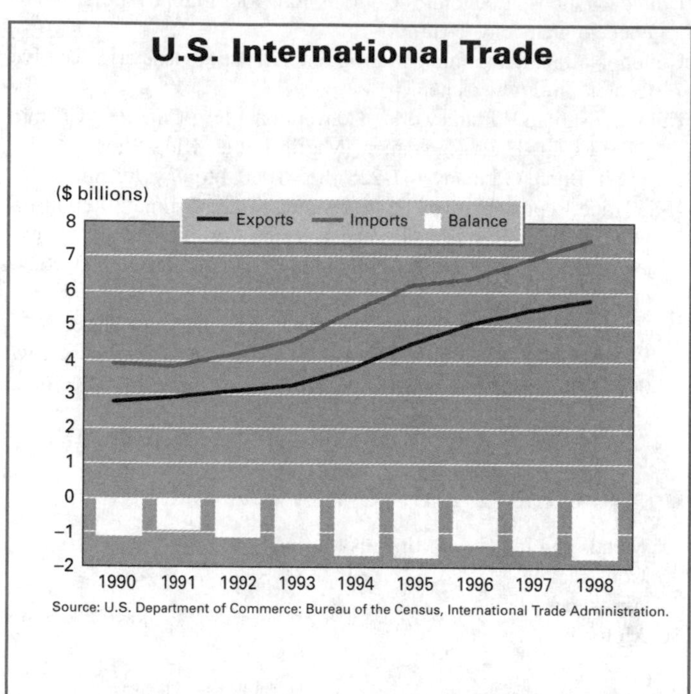

Source: U.S. Department of Commerce: Bureau of the Census, International Trade Administration.

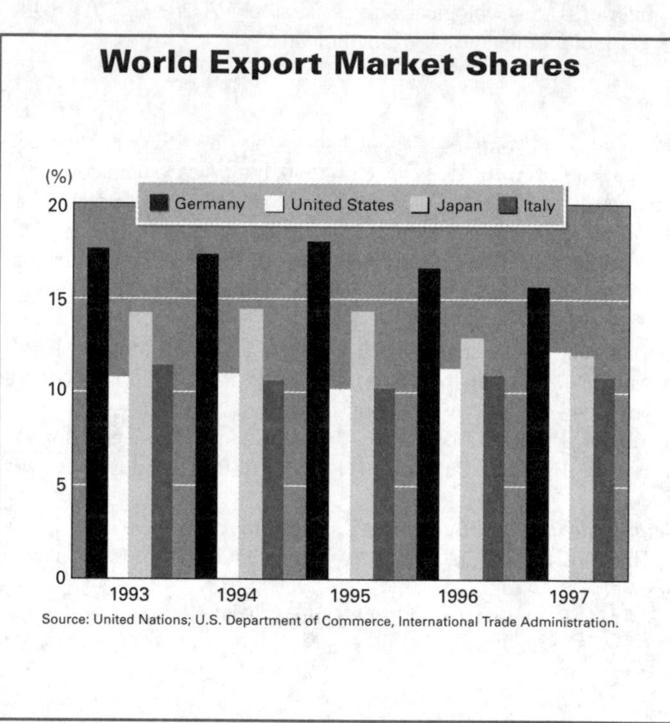

Source: United Nations; U.S. Department of Commerce, International Trade Administration.

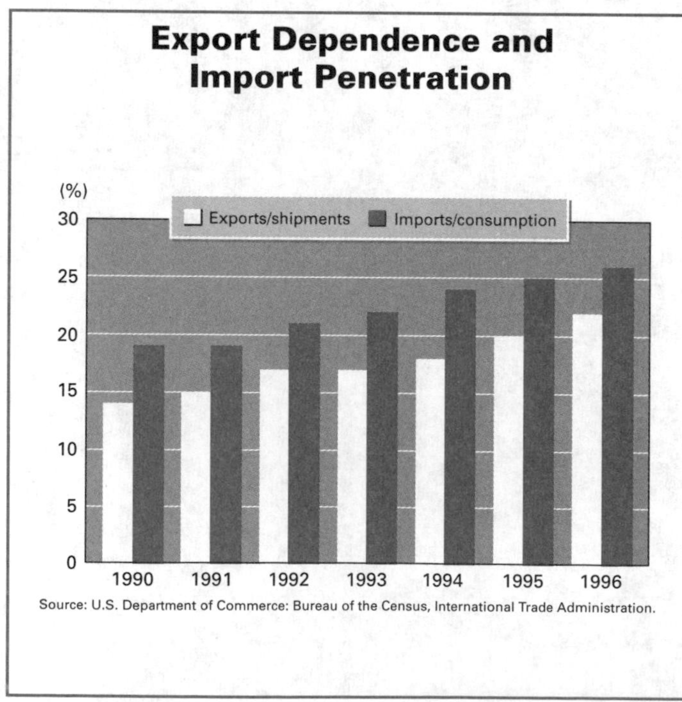

Source: U.S. Department of Commerce: Bureau of the Census, International Trade Administration.

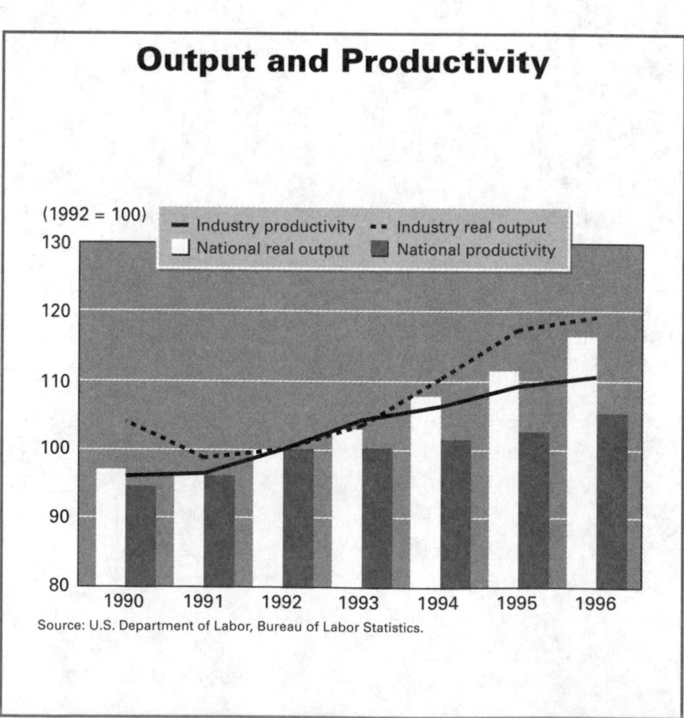

Source: U.S. Department of Labor, Bureau of Labor Statistics.

See "Getting the Most Out of *Outlook 2000*" for definitions of terms.

15

General Components

INDUSTRY DEFINITION The general components sector consists of products used as parts by manufacturers to construct machinery, equipment, buildings, piping systems, and other manufactured goods. This chapter examines screw machine products (SIC 3451), industrial fasteners (SIC 3452), industrial valves (SIC 3491), pipe fittings (SIC 3494), and ball and roller bearings (SIC 352). Among the general components not discussed in this chapter are gaskets, packing, and sealing devices (SIC 3053); fluid power valves and hose fittings (SIC 3492); steel springs (3493); wire springs (3495); speed changers, industrial high-speed drives, and gears (SIC 3566); and mechanical power-transmission equipment not elsewhere classified (SIC 3568).

GLOBAL INDUSTRY TRENDS

General components play a major role in manufacturing worldwide. Most machinery or equipment uses some type of bearings, screw machine products, or industrial fasteners. Valves and pipe fittings are used in most kinds of construction, including industrial plants, power projects, and commercial construction, as well as in pipelines and oil refineries.

General components industries around the world are changing rapidly. Developing countries are establishing their industries, while industrialized countries are using new technology to make new and better products. Competition is getting stronger all the time. End users constantly try to cut costs, and that forces general components manufacturers to try to cut their costs. General components companies are making significant investments in new technology in the form of improved capital equipment and manufacturing processes. There is also a trend toward consolidation. Companies find that the best investment often entails buying up companies or merging rather than building new product lines.

The slump in the world economy precipitated by the financial crises in Asia and South America has had a major impact on the world general components industry. Many general components producers experienced sharp drops in demand for their products from Asian and Latin American manufacturers of machinery and equipment. The competition for customers has been fierce and has precipitated sharp price competition for many general components products. The wholesale prices for some general components sectors actually have declined in the past 2 years.

Technological advances also have facilitated expanded world trade in general components. The general components industries are becoming more globalized. The rapid rate of technology transfers has made it possible for developing countries to become major players in international markets for commodity-type products. Low-tech commodity-type products increasingly are being made in countries with relatively lower costs of production. General components industries that are based in industrialized countries still have a comparative advantage in providing high-quality products and service. Some valve, pipe fitting, and bearing manufacturers in industrialized countries are sourcing components and parts from developing countries.

DOMESTIC TRENDS

U.S. production levels of general components have been strong in recent years. However, profit margins have suffered as a result of pressure to cut costs and prices. A strong domestic manufacturing sector, combined with robust exports, has resulted in healthy sales for the valve, pipe fitting, screw machine product, industrial fastener, and bearings industries. Between 1992 and 1998, combined product shipments for these general components industries in constant dollars increased about 26 percent overall, with a compound annual growth rate of 4 percent.

In 1996, employment in the four components industries covered in this chapter was approximately 212,000 (Table 15-1),

TABLE 15-1: General Components (SIC 345, 3491, 3494, 3562) Trends and Forecasts
(millions of dollars except as noted)

										Percent Change			
	1992	1993	1994	1995	1996	1997[1]	1998[1]	1999[2]	2000[3]	97–98	98–99	99–00	96–00[4]
Industry data													
Value of shipments[5]	22,038	23,202	25,014	27,310	28,648	29,876	31,019	30,474	31,249	3.8	−1.8	2.5	2.2
3451 Screw machine products	3,831	4,170	4,686	5,044	5,278	5,694	6,412	6,476	6,703	12.6	1.0	3.5	6.2
3452 Industrial fasteners	5,195	5,373	5,819	6,385	6,519	6,754	7,065	7,030	7,100	4.6	−0.5	1.0	2.2
349A Valves and pipe fittings[6]	8,723	9,102	9,618	10,600	11,405	11,290	11,177	10,730	11,052	−1.0	−4.0	3.0	−0.8
3562 Ball and roller bearings	4,290	4,557	4,891	5,281	5,446	6,138	6,365	6,238	6,394	3.7	−2.0	2.5	4.1
Value of shipments (1992$)	22,038	22,866	24,174	25,593	26,221	26,884	27,625	26,952	27,507	2.8	−2.4	2.1	1.2
3451 Screw machine products	3,831	4,137	4,599	4,841	4,993	5,362	6,107	6,168	6,383	13.9	1.0	3.5	6.3
3452 Industrial fasteners	5,195	5,320	5,699	6,145	6,209	6,364	6,587	6,587	6,785	3.5	0.0	3.0	2.2
349A Valves and pipe fittings	8,723	8,928	9,174	9,731	10,178	9,852	9,556	8,983	9,073	−3.0	−6.0	1.0	−2.8
3562 Ball and roller bearings	4,290	4,481	4,702	4,876	4,841	5,306	5,375	5,214	5,266	1.3	−3.0	1.0	2.1
Total employment (thousands)	193.5	193.6	195.5	207.1	211.5								
3451 Screw machine products	46.4	47.1	51.9	54.2	57.1								
3452 Industrial fasteners	44.1	43.7	43.4	46.0	46.5								
349A Valves and pipe fittings	68.0	69.0	66.8	71.3	71.9								
3562 Ball and roller bearings	35.0	33.8	33.4	35.6	36.0								
Production workers (thousands)	142.2	144.4	146.8	156.2	159.1								
3451 Screw machine products	36.5	38.5	41.9	44.0	46.0								
3452 Industrial fasteners	31.9	32.0	31.9	34.1	35.1								
349A Valves and pipe fittings	45.6	46.6	45.8	48.9	48.5								
3562 Ball and roller bearings	28.2	27.3	27.2	29.2	29.5								
Average hourly earnings ($)	12.57	12.70	12.90	13.25	13.52								
3451 Screw machine products	11.29	11.36	11.25	11.55	12.26								
3452 Industrial fasteners	12.80	12.74	12.76	13.58	13.36								
349A Valves and pipe fittings	12.39	12.76	12.76	13.17	13.55								
3562 Ball and roller bearings	14.35	14.48	15.97	15.65	15.72								
Capital expenditures	758	778	825	1,194	1,024								
3451 Screw machine products	135	152	226	250	231								
3452 Industrial fasteners	151	163	157	386	190								
349A Valves and pipe fittings	265	257	269	310	331								
3562 Ball and roller bearings	207	206	173	248	273								
Product data													
Value of shipments[5]	20,754	21,930	23,702	25,871	27,030	28,262	29,376	28,698	29,397	3.9	−2.3	2.4	2.1
3451 Screw machine products	3,660	3,986	4,642	5,324	5,608	6,051	6,813	6,881	7,087	12.6	1.0	3.0	6.0
3452 Industrial fasteners	4,854	5,043	5,439	5,916	6,115	6,335	6,626	6,593	6,659	4.6	−0.5	1.0	2.2
349A Valves and pipe fittings	8,100	8,461	8,828	9,501	10,049	9,949	9,850	9,259	9,537	−1.0	−6.0	3.0	−1.3
3562 Ball and roller bearings	4,140	4,440	4,794	5,129	5,258	5,927	6,087	5,965	6,114	2.7	−2.0	2.5	3.8
Value of shipments (1992$)	20,754	21,616	22,913	24,262	24,772	25,473	26,281	25,776	26,289	3.2	−1.9	2.0	1.5
3451 Screw machine products	3,660	3,954	4,555	5,109	5,305	5,698	6,490	6,646	6,845	13.9	2.4	3.0	6.6
3452 Industrial fasteners	4,854	4,993	5,327	5,694	5,824	5,970	6,179	6,179	6,364	3.5	0.0	3.0	2.2
349A Valves and pipe fittings	8,100	8,303	8,422	8,723	8,969	8,682	8,422	7,917	7,996	−3.0	−6.0	1.0	−2.8
3562 Ball and roller bearings	4,140	4,366	4,609	4,736	4,674	5,123	5,190	5,034	5,084	1.3	−3.0	1.0	2.1
Trade data													
Value of imports	4,170	4,574	5,422	6,174	6,372	6,935	7,481	7,184	7,629	7.9	−4.0	6.2	4.6
3451 Screw machine products													
3452 Industrial fasteners	1,231	1,386	1,666	1,894	1,847	1,907	2,020	2,006	2,207	5.9	−0.7	10.0	4.6
349A Valves and pipe fittings	2,048	2,188	2,590	2,907	3,140	3,576	3,923	3,766	3,954	9.7	−4.0	5.0	5.9
3562 Ball and roller bearings	891	1,000	1,166	1,372	1,385	1,452	1,538	1,412	1,468	5.9	−8.2	4.0	1.5
Value of exports	3,093	3,264	3,770	4,475	5,049	5,455	5,738	5,759	6,262	5.2	0.4	8.7	5.5
3451 Screw machine products													
3452 Industrial fasteners	685	710	905	1,061	1,366	1,333	1,470	1,558	1,680	10.3	6.0	7.8	5.3
349A Valves and pipe fittings	1,771	1,917	2,153	2,544	2,794	3,148	3,291	3,258	3,583	4.5	−1.0	10.0	6.4
3562 Ball and roller bearings	638	638	712	870	890	975	976	943	999	0.1	−3.4	5.9	2.9

[1] Estimate except imports and exports.
[2] Estimate.
[3] Forecast.
[4] Compound annual rate.
[5] For a definition of industry versus product values, see "Getting the Most Out of *Outlook 2000.*"
[6] Code 349A represents an aggregation of SICs 3491 and 3494.
Source: U.S. Department of Commerce: Bureau of the Census; International Trade Administration.

with production workers accounting for about 159,000 of those jobs. The industry is faced with a shortage of skilled workers that has been difficult to resolve despite the creation of training programs. The demand for skilled workers continues to grow faster than does the supply. To a limited extent, increased investment in labor-saving machine tools and other production equipment has alleviated the problem.

A major trend facing the U.S. general components industries is consolidation. Most U.S. general components makers were highly fragmented until fairly recently. With increased competition both domestically and internationally, U.S. general components companies are finding it harder to survive. Increased competition has resulted in relatively small profit margins for many companies. Companies are being forced to cut costs in order to survive. Consolidations are one means of cutting costs, allowing companies to take advantage of economies of scale.

The future of the U.S. general components industries is heavily dependent on the growth of the domestic manufacturing base. Despite the growing share of product shipments now being exported, the U.S. general components industry is still heavily dependent on the domestic manufacturing sector; this is especially true for bearings, screw machine products, and industrial fasteners. The automotive industry is the most important end user for all three of these industries. Expanded domestic motor vehicle production is a key to the future of the general components industries.

With the stiff competition they face from imports, it is important for general components companies to remain competitive. Most U.S. general components manufacturers will not be able to compete on a price basis in the commodity products sectors of these industries. U.S. companies need to invest in research and product development and incorporate new production techniques into factory lines. An emphasis on quality and service will be an important competitive factor. U.S. companies need to develop and exploit market segments and niches where they enjoy a comparative advantage.

PROJECTIONS OF INDUSTRY AND TRADE GROWTH

The screw machine product, industrial fastener, industrial valve, pipe fitting, and bearings industries are forecast to register a combined growth rate of about 2 percent in the year 2000. Increases in both machinery and equipment exports and general components exports are major factors in the anticipated rebound in general components shipments in 2000. Strong demand is expected from manufacturers of automobiles, construction machinery, material handling equipment, and light and heavy trucks. The projected expansion of the commercial construction industry is expected to stimulate the valve and pipe fitting industry. Demand from aircraft, machine tool, and farm machinery manufacturers is expected to be soft.

General component exports are expected to expand about 0.4 percent in 1999 and about 9 percent in the year 2000. Canada and Mexico will continue to be the most important foreign markets. The European Union will account for a significant share of exports outside North America (see Table 15-2).

Imports of general components were expected to decline about 4 percent in 1999 and are projected to increase about 6 percent in the year 2000. There could be significant increases in imports from Asian manufacturers because of the high value of the U.S. dollar against most Asian currencies. Strong growth in imports from China is expected to boost the Chinese share of the U.S. general components import market.

TABLE 15-2: U.S. Trade Patterns in General Components[1] in 1998
(millions of dollars; percent)

Exports			Imports		
Region[2]	Value[3]	Share, %	Region[2]	Value[3]	Share, %
NAFTA	3,365	59	NAFTA	1,764	24
Latin America	327	6	Latin America	80	1
Western Europe	967	17	Western Europe	1,981	26
Japan/Chinese Economic Area	391	7	Japan/Chinese Economic Area	3,048	41
Other Asia	380	7	Other Asia	466	6
Rest of world	309	5	Rest of world	142	2
World	5,738	100	World	7,481	100
Top Five Countries	Value	Share, %	Top Five Countries	Value	Share, %
Canada	2,425	42	Japan	1,485	20
Mexico	940	16	Taiwan	1,131	15
United Kingdom	300	5	Canada	904	12
Germany	185	3	Mexico	861	12
Japan	151	3	Germany	596	8

[1] SIC 3451, 3452, 3491, 3494, 3562.
[2] For definitions of regional groupings, see "Getting the Most Out of *Outlook 2000.*"
[3] Values may not sum to total due to rounding.
Source: U.S. Department of Commerce, Bureau of the Census.

In the 5-year period 1999–2003, shipments in the general components industry are expected to increase at an average annual rate of 2 to 3 percent. Exports and imports are both expected to register average annual growth rates between 6 and 12 percent.

SCREW MACHINE PRODUCTS AND INDUSTRIAL FASTENERS

Screw machine products (SIC 3451) are custom-designed products and turned parts that are made on screw machines and other types of turning machinery. With technological advances in the machine tool industry, most products that once were made on screw machines now can be made more efficiently on other types of machines. The trend will continue as companies use more computer numerical control (CNC) machines in their production processes. The industrial fastener industry (SIC 3452) consists of establishments engaged primarily in manufacturing metal bolts, nuts, screws, rivets, washers, formed and threaded wire goods, and special industrial fasteners such as aircraft fasteners.

Global Industry Trends

The "standards" (commodity-type) segment of the industrial fastener industry is global in nature. Countries with relatively low labor costs have an advantage in producing large numbers of standard products at a relatively low price. For a number of years, Taiwan and Japan were the principal suppliers of standards to the world market, but because their labor costs have increased, they now are facing increased pressure from lower-cost producers such as China. Developing countries seeking to build their domestic fastener industries initially are very dependent on exports, as their domestic markets are limited. As a result of the financial crises in many Asian and South American economies, many of the fastener industries in developing countries find it imperative to expand their export markets. Many of the larger fastener companies are pursuing strategies of acquisition and mergers to expand product lines and enter new markets.

Since screw machine products are customized products that cannot be categorized, there is very limited information of the size and growth of world production of those products.

Domestic Industry Trends

The U.S. industrial fastener and screw machine product industries are very competitive in producing custom or specially engineered products. The U.S. competitive advantage lies in providing quality and service. Both industries sell primarily to the North American market. Trade statistics are not available for screw machine products.

The "specials" (custom-designed) segments of the industrial fastener industry and the screw machine products industry are localized in nature. Fastener and screw machine product manufacturers usually are located in close proximity to their major customers. The move toward just-in-time delivery gives an advantage to suppliers that are near major manufacturers. Some industrial fastener companies and, to a limited extent, screw machine product manufacturers follow their major customers overseas. In some cases, they set up manufacturing facilities overseas. For example, many Japanese transplants buy fasteners and screw machine products from their traditional suppliers, some of which have built facilities in the United States. Many U.S. fastener and screw machine product companies have significant exports to the automotive industries in Mexico and Canada. A number of U.S. fastener companies have set up distribution or manufacturing facilities to service Mexico's growing manufacturing base, particularly in the automotive sector.

The U.S. screw machine products (SIC 3451) and industrial fastener (SIC 3452) industries are concentrated in the large manufacturing states in the midwest—Michigan, Ohio, Illinois, Indiana, and Wisconsin—as well as in New York, Pennsylvania, Connecticut, and California. The screw machine product industry consists of about 1,700 establishments that employed 57,100 people in 1996; the industrial fastener industry had 930 establishments with 46,500 workers in that year.

Trends in the U.S. industrial fastener and screw machine product industry are closely related to trends in the major consuming industries. Virtually all machinery and equipment manufacturers use industrial fasteners and screw machine products. An important trend for both industries is the constant pressure to reduce costs. Major industrial fastener and screw machine product end users are facing pressure to reduce costs in order to survive in very competitive markets. End users look to industrial fastener and screw machine products suppliers to reduce the cost of inputs. Economies of scale obtained through mergers are one way to reduce costs. Other companies are trying to reduce costs by improving productivity through worker training, investment in new and improved equipment, and the development of more efficient production methods.

The automotive industry is the major consuming industry for both the industrial fastener and the screw machine product industries. Shipments to the automotive industry account for about 30 to 35 percent of U.S. fastener production and a somewhat smaller percentage for the screw machine products industry. Other major consuming industries are aerospace, defense, construction machinery, mining equipment, machine tools, medical equipment, and computers. Aircraft fasteners represent a special segment of special highly engineered products that are used only by aircraft manufacturers.

The industrial fastener industry continues its trend toward consolidation with more mergers and acquisitions. Despite the consolidations, the industry still can be characterized as fragmented, with many small and medium-size companies that are at a disadvantage in competing in an increasing global marketplace. The small and medium-size manufacturers in this industry have limited resources to invest in improving productivity. The trend toward consolidation is spreading internationally as the largest fastener manufacturers are putting increased emphasis on developing new markets. Consolidations improve the competitiveness of U.S. companies through reduced costs associated with economies of scale and increased financial resources for research and expansion that otherwise would not be available.

Both the industrial fastener and the screw machine product industries are highly competitive. There is a constant need to improve production processes and raise productivity. Major customers are asking suppliers to keep a lid on prices. Many large customers, especially in the automotive sectors, are making few or no provisions for raising prices. It is important for industrial fastener and screw machine product manufacturers to improve efficiency and productivity. Much of that increase in productivity and efficiency is based on utilizing new technology and production processes. Much new or advanced technology is incorporated in new and improved machine tools and other production machinery.

The automotive industry is the major engine behind the industrial fastener industry and, to a lesser degree, the screw machine product industry. When the automotive industry is booming, so is the industrial fastener industry; when the automotive industry is depressed, the fastener industry also slumps. The U.S. fastener and screw machine product industries have prospered in recent years with the strong expansion of the manufacturing sector and high demand from the automotive sector in particular. A rebound in the construction industry also has benefited both industries. New residential construction stimulates the production of appliances, a major consuming industry for screw machine products. Screw machine product shipments in constant dollars registered a modest increase of 2.4 percent in 1999 compared with 1998. Screw machine products had registered a strong increase, estimated at 14 percent, in 1998. Strong demand from the automotive, appliance, and construction sectors largely was offset by weak demand from most major machinery and equipment sectors. Many fastener and screw machine product companies that were dependent on major customers in the heavy equipment and farm machinery sectors registered declines in sales volumes in 1999 compared with 1998.

Industrial fastener shipments were projected to register zero growth in 1999. Strong demand from the automotive sector was offset by weak demand from the farm machinery and heavy equipment sectors. Demand from commercial aircraft manufacturers was soft, but there was increased demand from military aircraft manufacturers.

U.S. industrial fastener exports were expected to reach almost $1.56 billion in 1999 (see Table 15-1), a 6 percent increase from 1998. Fastener exports increased in value every year during the 1990s except 1997. The annual value of fastener exports grew 120 percent between 1993 and 1999. Exports to Canada and Mexico, the two largest U.S. export markets, expanded an estimated 16 and 17 percent, respectively, in 1999 compared with 1998. Combined, Canada and Mexico accounted for 69 percent of U.S. exports of fasteners in 1998 (see Table 15-3). Fastener exports to a number of regions were expected to register strong decreases in 1999. Exports to Asia and the MERCOSUR countries were each expected to decline over 30 percent. Exports to Malaysia, the Philippines, and Thailand were expected to fall over 50 percent. Demand from some Asian countries did improve: Exports to Singapore were expected to increase over 30 percent, making it the fourth largest export market, and exports to South Korea were expected to increase over 60 percent.

The value of U.S. imports of industrial fasteners declined an estimated 0.7 percent in 1999 to about $2 billion. Taiwan remained the largest U.S. supplier in 1998, with a 40 percent share, followed by Japan and Canada with 19 and 14 percent shares, respectively. Fastener imports from Taiwan and Japan both declined an estimated 4 percent, while imports from Canada increased an estimated 4 percent. China replaced Germany as the fourth largest supplier, as imports from China increased about 28 percent.

TABLE 15-3: U.S. Trade Patterns in Bolts, Nuts, Rivets, and Washers[1] in 1998
(millions of dollars; percent)

Exports			Imports		
Region[2]	Value[3]	Share, %	Region[2]	Value[3]	Share, %
NAFTA	1,019	69	NAFTA	302	15
Latin America	44	3	Latin America	7	0
Western Europe	214	15	Western Europe	301	15
Japan/Chinese Economic Area	55	4	Japan/Chinese Economic Area	1,301	64
Other Asia	111	8	Other Asia	97	5
Rest of world	27	2	Rest of world	12	1
World	1,470	100	World	2,020	100
Top Five Countries	Value	Share, %	Top Five Countries	Value	Share, %
Canada	709	48	Taiwan	816	40
Mexico	311	21	Japan	378	19
United Kingdom	113	8	Canada	283	14
Singapore	48	3	China	103	5
Malaysia	32	2	Germany	93	5

[1] SIC 3452.
[2] For definitions of regional groupings, see "Getting the Most Out of *Outlook 2000*."
[3] Values may not sum to total due to rounding.
Source: U.S. Department of Commerce, Bureau of the Census.

Fastener Quality Act

The Fastener Quality Act (FQA), Public Law 101-592, has had a major influence on the U.S. industrial fastener industry. That law addresses the issue of mismarked, substandard, and counterfeit fasteners in the U.S. market. It makes persons who manufacture and sell fasteners responsible for assuring that such fasteners have been manufactured in accordance with the applicable standards and specifications.

The FQA has been amended to make the original legislation, passed in 1990, more focused and less burdensome. The amended FQA was signed by President Clinton on June 8, 1999. The amended law no longer requires the U.S. Department of Commerce's National Institute of Standards and Technology to approve organizations that accredit fastener testing laboratories. Fasteners covered under the FQA are limited to bolts, nuts, screws, and studs (having a nominal diameter of 6 millimeters/0.25 inch or greater) or direct tension-indicating washers that are through-hardened or meet a consensus standard that calls for through-hardening and are manufactured to standards and specifications of consensus standards organizations or government agencies that require a grade mark.

Many fasteners have been exempted from coverage, including those manufactured in accordance with International Organization for Standardization (ISO) 9000, 9001, or 9002 or TS16949; Quality System (QS) 9000; or other fastener quality assurance systems defined by the law or manufactured to a proprietary standard. To encourage the use of quality management systems such as QS 9000, fasteners are exempt from the FQA if they are manufactured in a facility that uses such a system.

To reduce paperwork and record-keeping burdens, companies are allowed to transmit and store electronically all records of fastener quality as long as there are reasonable means to authenticate the source of the document and reasonable protection against alteration. The record required for a covered fastener is the record of conformity that identifies the fastener by description, lot number, and manufacturer and includes other information defined by the law. The text of the amended FQA is available at www.nist.gov/fqa.

Projections of Trade and Industry Growth

Growth in screw machine product shipments is expected to be 3 percent in the year 2000 as demand from the automotive sector remains strong and demand from most major machinery and equipment sectors rebounds from the 1999 level. The expected improvement in machinery and equipment exports to Asia will brighten the outlook for manufacturers of screw machine products in 2000. Sales to appliance manufacturers are expected to remain at a relatively high level because of the health of the residential construction sector. Demand from the telecommunications and computer industries was expected to strengthen in 2000. Only modest growth in shipments to the automotive sector is expected in 2000. Screw machine product shipment are forecast to grow at average annual rate of 3 to 4 percent in the period 2000–04.

Growth in industrial fastener shipments is expected to be 3.0 percent in 2000. Continued strong demand from the automotive sector is expected to be a major fact contributing to expanded fastener shipments. Fastener shipments to the construction machinery and machine tool sectors are expected to increase in the year 2000. Demand from farm machinery manufacturers is expected to remain weak. In the 5-year period 2000–2004, fastener shipments are expected to grow at an average annual rate of 3 to 4 percent in constant dollars. The trend toward consolidation is expected to continue. In order to grow, U.S. companies will need to invest in product development and emphasize quality and service.

Fastener exports are projected to register a moderate increase of just under 8 percent, reaching $1.68 billion in the year 2000. Most of the increased exports will be destined for Mexico and Canada, but exports to South America and Asia are expected to rebound from the sharp declines experienced in 1999. Most exports will be to the automotive sector, with smaller quantities going to the aircraft and heavy equipment sectors.

Fastener imports also are expected to increase in 2000 after declining in 1999. Continued demand from the automotive sector and the construction industry, combined with increased demand from heavy equipment and machinery manufacturers, could see U.S. imports of industrial fasteners grow to $2.2 billion in 2000. The "standards" (mass market products) that represent the majority of fastener imports are very price sensitive, and the availability of low-cost steel could lead to an influx of fastener imports from low-cost producers such as China.

Global Market Prospects

Global demand for industrial fasteners will continue to grow as most industrialized and developing countries expand their manufacturing bases. The world automotive industry will continue to be the most important source of demand for industrial fasteners. The world industrial fastener industry is expected to become even more competitive as developing countries expand their fastener industries and acquire the skilled workers and technology needed to produce higher-quality and more sophisticated fasteners. There will be a global trend toward consolidation as individual companies try to improve their competitiveness.

VALVES AND PIPE FITTINGS

The valve and pipe fitting industry includes industrial valves (SIC 3491) and valves and pipe fittings not elsewhere classified (SIC 3494). It does not include plumbing fixture fittings, which are included under SIC 3432. Industrial valves include a wide range of valve types: gates, globes, angles, water work valves (IBBW, AWWA, and UL), ball, butterfly, plug, nuclear, automatic, and solenoid-operated. Valves and pipe fittings not elsewhere classified include plumbing and heating valves and metal fittings, flanges, and unions for piping systems.

Global Industry Trends

The global valve and pipe fitting industry has been adversely affected by the sluggishness of the world economy resulting from financial crises in many Asian and South American countries. The cutbacks in energy demand resulting from negative economic growth in many important economies have led to lower levels of demand from energy sectors around the world. Increased price competition has been one of the outcomes of lower world demand for valves and pipe fittings. The industrialized countries still constitute the largest market for valves and pipe fittings, but before the financial crises, the developing countries had been the fastest-growing markets. Countries with large oil industries are among the best markets for valves and pipe fittings.

In order to grow, developing countries need to make heavy investments in their manufacturing sectors and infrastructures, all of which use a wide variety of valves. Sectors that purchase a large number of valves are petroleum production and refining, chemical plants, water and sewage, and power generation. Other major valve consuming sectors are pulp and paper and commercial construction.

Developing countries are building their own valve and pipe fitting industries. Initially, production in developing countries far exceeds domestic demand, and so many valves and pipe fittings are exported. Many developing countries have problems competing on a quality basis because their valve industries are still developing and lack the technology and skilled labor of the industries in developed countries.

This industry is very globalized. The developing countries are present in low-tech commodity-type valves, while the industrialized countries dominate in the more high-tech and highly engineered products. There has been a trend toward consolidation in recent years. To expand and compete in a global marketplace, many valve and pipe fitting companies are merging or being acquired by other industrial companies. Merged companies can improve efficiency by achieving economies of scale.

Domestic Trends

The U.S. valve and pipe fitting industries consist of about 648 establishments that employed almost 72,000 workers in 1996. Texas has the largest concentration of plants, with 73 establishments making products covered under SIC 3491 (industrial valves) and 47 companies making products covered under SIC 3494 (valves and pipe fitting not elsewhere classified). Texas-based companies make a wide variety of valves and pipe fittings for the oil and gas sectors. Other states with large concentrations of valve and pipe fitting manufacturers include California, Pennsylvania, Ohio, and Illinois.

The U.S. valve and pipe fitting industry has many different segments. Several large companies make a wide range of valve and pipe fitting products, but most companies in the industry can be characterized as small and medium-size. However, the percentage of small and medium-size companies is shrinking as a result of mergers and acquisitions. The larger companies, with greater financial resources, are better able to compete in international markets.

Small and medium-size valve and pipe fitting manufacturers focus on certain segments or market niches. Some segments of the U.S. industry, such as cast iron valves and fittings, have been contracting, while other segments, such as automated valves, have expanded. To a large extent, the market segments are competing with each other. Many companies are trying to expand their product lines as a means of expanding sales and surviving in the long term. Acquisitions and mergers have been a popular means of expanding product lines. Many smaller valve and pipe fitting companies have limited financial resources as a result of declining profits and have merged or been acquired by larger companies.

Imports will have a major effect on the future of the U.S. industrial valves and pipe fittings industry. Manufacturers of commodity-type valves and pipe fittings have faced stiff competition from the newly industrializing countries and recently from developing countries such as India and China. The depreciations of many Asian currencies as a consequence of financial crises hurt the competitiveness of U.S. valve and pipe fitting products.

In order to survive, U.S. valve and pipe fitting companies need to be diligent in continuously increasing their competitiveness by improving the manufacturing process and expanding product lines to meet the changing needs of their customers. Companies that do not invest in new technology and product development will find their market shares eroding.

Advances in technology are leading to improvements in valve and pipe fitting products. U.S. companies need to work closely with end users to engineer valves for particular applications. World demand for valves and pipe fittings will grow at a faster rate than will U.S. demand. World demand for valves and pipe fittings will continue to grow, but the growth will vary greatly among the different segments. U.S. valve and pipe fitting manufacturers are becoming increasingly dependent on export markets in order to grow. Exports account for about 25 percent of U.S. production. The percentage is higher for valves than it is for pipe fittings and higher for larger companies than it is for smaller manufacturers. Some U.S. valve manufacturers export as much as 50 percent of their production. Small and medium-size companies are coming to realize that to survive in the long term, they need to devote more resources to exporting. Entering into strategic alliances with larger companies is one means by which small and medium-size companies can expand into new export markets. The internet and E-commerce are tools that are allowing valve and pipe fitting manufacturers to develop new export markets.

Safety and environmental concerns will continue to play an important role in the future success of U.S. valve and pipe fitting manufacturers. End users are developing closer working relationships with valve and pipe fitting manufacturers to resolve specific problems associated with piping systems. As valve reliability becomes increasingly important, end users are becoming more knowledgeable about valve technology. Greater emphasis is being placed on training and maintenance. U.S. manufacturers of valves and pipe fittings have a technological advantage over many foreign competitors in providing solutions to safety and environmental problems.

The energy sectors are the major consumers of valves and pipe fittings. Sectors that account for a significant share of total valve and pipe fitting consumption are petroleum production, oil and gas transmission, petroleum refining, gas distribution, and power generation and cogeneration. Together, those sectors account for about 45 percent of total demand for valves and pipe fittings. Other major consuming industries are the chemical industry, the pulp and paper industry, food processing, and commercial construction.

Valve and pipe fitting industry shipments in constant dollars declined an estimated 6 percent in 1999 (Table 15-1), the third consecutive annual decline for the industry. Weak demand from the U.S. industrial construction industry more than offset increased shipments to the commercial and residential construction industries. There has been a dearth of new energy projects, chemical plants, and paper mills in recent years. The sluggish world economy and the resulting low energy prices have the dampened the prospects for energy-related major projects in the United States. Most of the domestic demand for valves and pipe fittings is for maintenance and repair applications. Low capacity operating rates for the chemical and oil refining sectors have resulted in lower demand for replacement valves and pipe fittings.

Exports have been the major growth sector for the U.S. industry, but in 1999, valve and pipe fitting exports declined an estimated 1 percent. It was the first annual decline in exports for the combined valve and pipe fitting industry since 1986. Exports accounted for an estimated 35 percent of U.S. production in 1999. Exports to 10 of the largest U.S. export markets declined in 1999. Exports to Canada, the largest export market, accounting for 38 percent of total exports, declined 2 percent. Increased demand from Mexico resulted in a 10 percent increase in U.S. valve and pipe fitting exports to that country. Mexico's share of total U.S. valve and pipe fitting exports grew to 15 percent in 1998 (Table 15-4). The expansion in exports resulted from increased investment by Mexico in its infrastructure and manufacturing base.

U.S. imports also declined in 1999, contracting by about 4 percent. Imports accounted for approximately 38 percent of valve and pipe fitting consumption in 1999. Mexico remains the largest foreign supplier of valves and pipe fittings to the U.S. market, with a 19 percent share of total imports, but the dollar value of valve and pipe fitting imports from Mexico declined an estimated 11 percent in 1999. The value of imports for 8 of the top 10 suppliers to the U.S. market declined in 1999. Japan, with a 15 percent share, remained the second largest supplier, followed by Canada and Germany with 11 and 10 percent shares, respectively. Imports from Germany increased an estimated 14 percent. In 1999, imports from Taiwan also increased, and that country replaced Italy as the fifth largest supplier with a 7.5 percent share. Imports from a number of smaller European suppliers registered significant increases. Imports from Denmark and Sweden, which were among the top 20 suppliers, increased more than 20 percent. Imports from a number of smaller European suppliers registered increases of more than 100 percent, including Turkey, 300 percent; Portugal, 200 percent; and Hungary, more than 1000 percent.

Projections of Trade and Industry Growth

U.S. industry shipments of valve and pipe fittings are expected to increase 1 percent in constant dollars in the year 2000. Exports will be the major factor in the expected increase as domestic demand is expected to remain relatively soft. Demand from the commercial sectors of the construction industry is expected to increase, but weak demand is expected from the industrial construction sector. Demand from gas and electric utilities is expected to remain weak, and overall demand from the U.S. energy sector is expected to register little or no growth. Strong demand is expected from paper machinery manufacturers as their capacity operating rates continue to improve.

Stronger demand from domestic valve and pipe fitting end-user industries and continued strong overseas demand for U.S.-made valves are expected to lead to a 3 percent expansion in

TABLE 15-4: U.S. Trade Patterns in Valves and Pipe Fittings[1] in 1998
(millions of dollars; percent)

Exports			Imports		
Region[2]	Value[3]	Share, %	Region[2]	Value[3]	Share, %
NAFTA	1,772	54	NAFTA	1,217	31
Latin America	207	6	Latin America	45	1
Western Europe	565	17	Western Europe	1,299	33
Japan/Chinese Economic Area	292	9	Japan/Chinese Economic Area	1,041	27
Other Asia	226	7	Other Asia	239	6
Rest of world	231	7	Rest of world	83	2
World	3,291	100	World	3,923	100
Top Five Countries	Value	Share, %	Top Five Countries	Value	Share, %
Canada	1,265	38	Mexico	795	20
Mexico	507	15	Japan	578	15
United Kingdom	147	4	Canada	422	11
Germany	115	4	Germany	341	9
Japan	89	3	Italy	286	7

[1] SIC 3491, 3494.
[2] For definitions of regional groupings, see "Getting the Most Out of *Outlook 2000.*"
[3] Values may not sum to total due to rounding.
Source: U.S. Department of Commerce, Bureau of the Census.

valve and pipe fitting shipments in 2000. Export growth of 10 percent is forecast for the year 2000, with valve and pipe fitting imports expanding about 5 percent. In the 5-year period 2000–04, industry shipments of valves and pipe fittings are expected to expand at an average annual rate of 3 to 4 percent, with increased overseas demand the major driving force.

The continued growth of the U.S. valve and pipe fitting sector is highly dependent on U.S. valve and pipe fitting companies maintaining their competitiveness. This will require investing in new technology to improve productivity and the development of new product lines. The U.S. edge lies in customizing products to meet the needs of individual customers.

Global Market Prospects

World demand for valves and pipe fittings is expected to outpace U.S. demand during the next 5 years. The expected recoveries of economies in Asia and Europe are expected to stimulate world economic expansion and increased demand for valves and pipe fittings. Increased energy demand precipitated by world economic growth should lead to expanded activity in world oil and gas exploration, energy production, and oil and gas pipelines and result in growing world demand for industrial valves and pipe fittings. As the world economic recovery progresses, large investments in infrastructure projects and manufacturing industries in Asia and the developing countries will foster large increases in demand for valves and pipe fittings.

BALL AND ROLLER BEARINGS

The ball and roller bearing industry (SIC 3562) consists of establishments engaged primarily in manufacturing ball and roller bearings (including ball and roller bearing pillow block, flange, takeup cartridge, and hangar units) and parts. Major product sectors include miniature and precision instrument bearings, integral shaft and integral spindle ball bearings, thrust ball bearings, tapered roller bearings, and cylindrical, spherical, and needle bearings.

Global Industry Trends

A sharp drop in demand for bearings from Asian manufacturers has been an important reason for the significant overcapacity that characterizes the world bearing industry. That overcapacity has precipitated sharp competition among the largest world bearing manufacturers for market share. The competition is particularly stiff in the commodity-type bearing sectors. Estimates put world ball and roller bearing production at about $25 billion. The largest bearing-producing countries continue to be the United States, Germany, and Japan, but those countries face stiff competition from bearing industries in developing countries in Asia and, to a lesser degree, eastern Europe. The largest bearing companies have plants throughout the world to better service individual markets. In recent years, the largest companies have been establishing operations in Asia to better service the emerging automotive manufacturing industries and heavy equipment and machinery operations being developed in the Asian countries.

The largest bearing producers in the United States are also the largest world producers. The large German and Japanese bearing companies have established significant bearing production capacity in the United States through acquisitions and new plant construction. To improve competitiveness, the larger bearing companies have modernized their existing plants. Some older U.S. bearing plants are being closed.

Domestic Trends

The U.S. bearing industry consists of about 183 plants that make a wide variety of ball bearings, roller bearings, mounted bearings, and bearing parts. There are two large U.S.-based bearing companies: the Timken Company and the Torrington Company. Several large foreign-based companies also have large U.S. operations and manufacture a wide range of ball and roller bearing products. The products that they do not manufacture in the United States they import from their other bearing plants, primarily in Europe and Asia. In recent years, a number of acquisitions have contributed to the consolidation of the U.S. bearing industry. There are still a number of small and medium-size bearing companies that make specialty products or have market niches. The recent trend toward building new bearing plants has come to a halt because of overcapacity in the United States. The narrower profit margins resulting from strong price competition also make new bearing plants less attractive. The states with the largest numbers of bearing plants are Connecticut, New York, Pennsylvania, South Carolina, and Ohio. The bearing industry employed about 36,000 workers in 1996.

The U.S. bearing industry is becoming very price competitive. Major bearing consumers, facing the need to reduce production costs to remain competitive, are seeking price savings from bearing manufacturers. The U.S. bearing industry continues to face strong pressure from imports. Because of the intense price competition, dumping has been a problem for U.S. bearing companies. In recent years, U.S. bearing plants have faced growing pressure from imports from China. Increased pressure to reduce the cost of bearing inputs makes imports from China attractive, and as the quality of Chinese bearing products improves, U.S. bearing consumers are expected to buy an increasing number of bearings from that country. After a strong increase in bearing shipments in constant dollars in 1997, the bearing industry registered a slight increase in shipments in 1998, followed by a projected 3.4 percent decline in 1999. In 1999, strong demand from the automotive sector, which accounted for an estimated 30 to 35 percent of bearing consumption, was offset by weak demand from most other industrial sectors. Demand from farm machinery, construction machinery, mining equipment, and machine tool manufacturers was particularly weak. Shipments to the defense sector showed improvement but remained at relatively low levels. After the 30 to 35 percent share consumed by the motor vehicle industry, the other large bearing consuming industries include the aircraft, railroad, construction machinery, mining equipment, machine tool, and farm machinery industries. The aftermarket plays a very important role in bearing sales, accounting for as much as 30 percent of total bearing production. U.S. bearing shipments for the aftermarket registered a significant decline in 1999.

Bearing exports were projected to decline about 3 percent in 1999 but are forecast to grow almost 6 percent in the year 2000. Canada and Mexico, with market shares of 48 and 13 percent, respectively, were the largest U.S. bearing export markets in 1999. The interdependence of the automotive industries in the North American Free Trade Agreement (NAFTA) nations accounts for the large value of bearing exports to those countries, which reached $573 million in 1998 (see Table 15-5). U.S. bearing exports to a number of important markets—the United Kingdom, France, Japan, and Brazil—registered sharp declines in 1999. Exports to Australia, South Korea, Sweden, and Spain registered significant increases in 1999 compared with 1998 levels.

Imports account for about 24 percent of apparent consumption. After increasing almost 6 percent in 1998, U.S. bearing imports declined a projected 8 percent in 1999. The added capacity in their U.S. bearing operations, combined with weaker U.S. demand, led German- and Japanese-based bearing companies to supply a larger percentage of their U.S. bearing demand from domestic plants. Bearing imports from Japan declined 18 percent in 1999, and imports from Germany were an estimated 24 percent lower. China replaced Germany as the third largest bearing supplier to the United States after Japan and Canada. Bearing imports from China increased 5 percent in 1999. Bearing imports from Mexico increased 23 percent as a result of that country's expanding bearing capacity. Imports from Korea, Poland, and Argentina also registered increases of 20 percent or more in 1999.

Projections of Trade and Industry Growth

Bearing shipments are expected to register a slight increase of 1 percent in the year 2000 as demand from a number of major bearing industries improves. Shipments to the construction machinery, machine tool, and farm machinery industries are expected to rebound as overseas markets improve and the U.S. farm industry recovers. Bearing demand from the automotive sector is expected to remain at the relatively high level of 1999, registering little if any growth. Demand from the commercial aircraft industry will remain soft, while demand from military aircraft manufacturers is expected to grow. The rebound of bearing shipments in 2000 will be heavily dependent on the recovery of equipment and machinery exports to the Asian market.

Bearing exports to Canada and Mexico are expected to remain strong in the year 2000, and exports to Europe and Asia are expected to register significant improvements. Bearing exports to South American countries also are expected to rebound as those economies recover from their financial crises. The total value of U.S. bearing exports is forecast to increase almost 6 percent in 2000.

Bearing shipments are expected to expand at an average annual rate of 2 to 3 percent in the next 5 years. Expanding export markets should be a major factor in that growth. The improved competitiveness of the U.S. bearing industry, combined with continued strong demand from the automotive sector and a rebound in demand from major industrial equipment and machinery manufacturers, should lead to healthy growth in bearing shipments. The improved competitiveness of U.S. manufacturing companies should assure a healthy U.S. bearing industry. However, it is important for U.S. bearing companies to remain competitive by investing in research and product development. This will entail developing closer working relationships between bearing companies and end users. As machinery, equipment, and motor vehicles become more sophisticated, bearing end users will demand new and improved bearing products.

TABLE 15-5: U.S. Trade Patterns in Ball and Roller Bearings[1] in 1998
(millions of dollars; percent)

Exports			Imports		
Region[2]	Value[3]	Share, %	Region[2]	Value[3]	Share, %
NAFTA	573	59	NAFTA	245	16
Latin America	76	8	Latin America	28	2
Western Europe	188	19	Western Europe	382	25
Japan/Chinese Economic Area	45	5	Japan/Chinese Economic Area	706	46
Other Asia	43	4	Other Asia	130	8
Rest of world	51	5	Rest of world	47	3
World	976	100	World	1,538	100
Top Five Countries	Value	Share, %	Top Five Countries	Value	Share, %
Canada	452	46	Japan	529	34
Mexico	122	12	Canada	198	13
Germany	48	5	Germany	162	11
United Kingdom	40	4	China	145	9
France	40	4	United Kingdom	61	4

[1] SIC 3562.
[2] For definitions of regional groupings, see "Getting the Most Out of *Outlook 2000.*"
[3] Values may not sum to total due to rounding.
Source: U.S. Department of Commerce, Bureau of the Census.

Global Market Prospects

The rate of growth of bearing exports is expected to exceed growth in domestic bearing demand in the period 1999–2003. Canada and Mexico will remain the most important markets. Outside NAFTA, exports to the European Union will be the major source of expanded exports in the next 5 years. Demand from the developing markets in South America and Asia is expected to rebound when those economies recover. The relative value of the U.S. dollar will be an important factor in the competitiveness of U.S. bearings in international markets.

Industrialized countries' comparative advantage lies in producing high-value bearings of superior quality and in the service those countries provide. In critical applications, reliability often takes precedence over price. The value added by bearing companies will continue to increase as those companies become more integrated into the manufacturing process.

Richard Reise, U.S. Department of Commerce, Office of Energy, Infrastructure, and Machinery, (202) 482-3489, November 1999.

■ REFERENCES

Annual Survey of Manufactures, 1996, M94(AS)-1 and M94(AS)-2, Bureau of the Census, United States Department of Commerce, Washington, DC 20233.

Valves and Pipe Fittings

Census of Manufactures, 1997, EC97M-332911 (EC97M-3329A), Bureau of the Census, U.S. Department of Commerce, Washington, DC 20233

Census of Manufactures, 1997, EC97M-332919 (EC97M-3329D), Bureau of the Census, U.S. Department of Commerce, Washington, DC 20233

Valve Magazine, Valve Manufacturers Association of America, 1050 17 Street, NW, Suite 280, Washington, DC 20036-5503

Screw Machine Products and Industrial Fasteners

American Fastener Journal, published by Mike McGuire, 293 Hopewell Drive, Powell, OH 43065-9350. (614) 848-3232.

Census of Manufactures, 1997, EC97M-332721 (EC97M-3327B), Bureau of the Census, U.S. Department of Commerce, Washington, DC 20233

Fastener Industry News, edited by John Wolz, 2009 NE 16th Avenue, Portland OR 97212-4430. (503) 335-0183.

Fastener Technology International, Initial Publications, Inc., 3869 Darrow Road, Suite 101, Stow, OH 44334. (330) 686-9544.

Ball and Roller Bearings

Antifriction Bearings, 1998, Current Industrial Report, MA332Q(98)-1, Bureau of the Census, U.S. Department of Commerce, Washington, DC 20233

Census of Manufactures, 1997, EC97M-332991 (EC97M-3329E), Bureau of the Census, U.S. Department of Commerce, Washington, DC 20233

■ RELATED CHAPTERS

17: Metalworking Equipment
18: Production Machinery
36: Motor Vehicles
37: Automotive Parts

MICROELECTRONICS
Economic and Trade Trends

Source: U.S. Department of Commerce: Bureau of the Census, International Trade Administration.

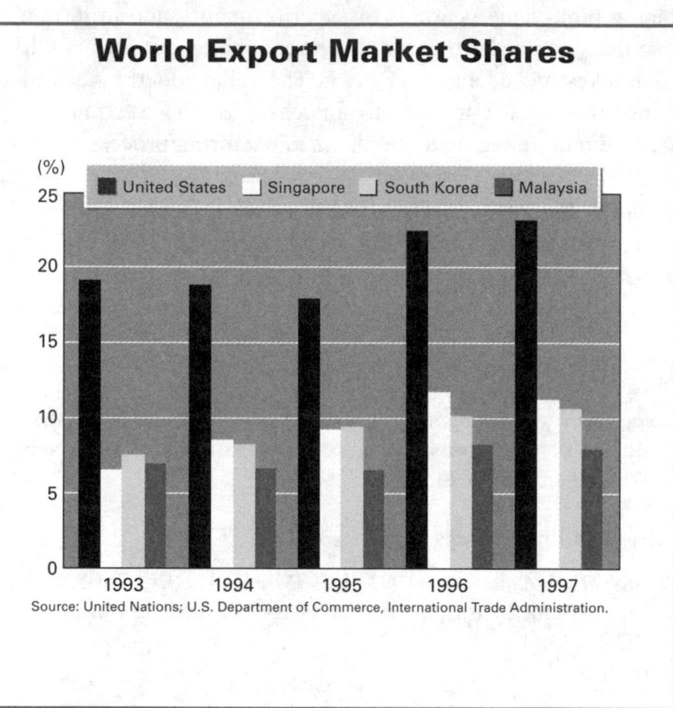

Source: United Nations; U.S. Department of Commerce, International Trade Administration.

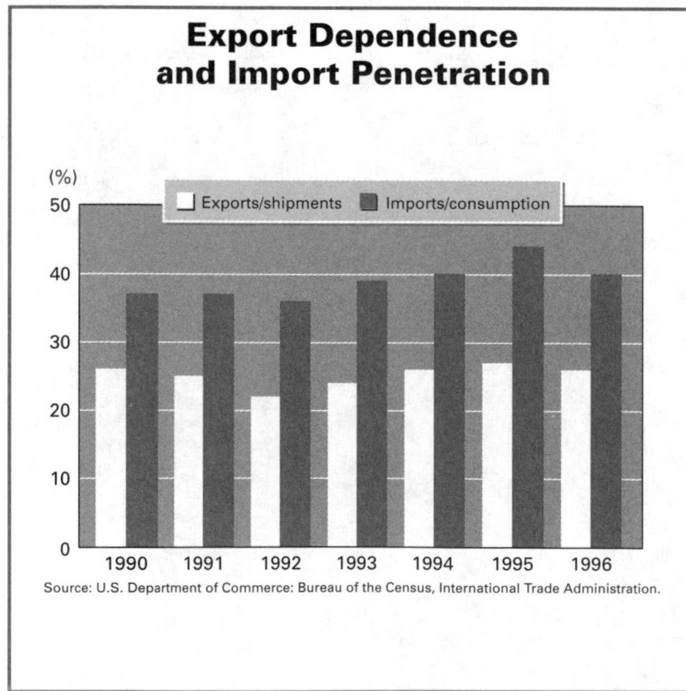

Source: U.S. Department of Commerce: Bureau of the Census, International Trade Administration.

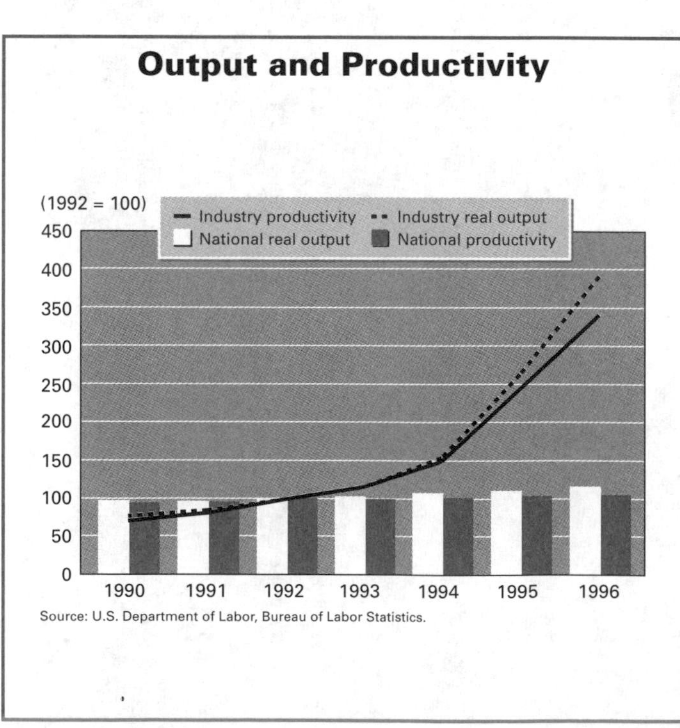

Source: U.S. Department of Labor, Bureau of Labor Statistics.

See "Getting the Most Out of *Outlook 2000*" for definitions of terms.

16

Microelectronics

INDUSTRY DEFINITION This chapter covers electronic components and semiconductor manufacturing equipment (SME). The Standard Industrial Classification (SIC) system includes electronic components and accessories under SIC 367. Electronic components include electron tubes (SIC 3671); printed circuit boards (SIC 3672); semiconductors and related devices (SIC 3764); electronic capacitors (SIC 3675); electronic resistors (SIC 3676); electronic coils, transformers, and other inductors (SIC 3677); electronic connectors (SIC 3678); and electronic components not elsewhere classified (SIC 3679).

GLOBAL AND DOMESTIC INDUSTRY TRENDS

The microelectronics industry manufactures a wide array of products that range from relatively simple electrical connectors that cost a few pennies, to thousand-dollar integrated circuits (ICs) that contain millions of transistors on a single chip, to complex machines for semiconductor manufacturing that cost several millions of dollars per unit. The majority of these products are sold to manufacturing companies in the computer, telecommunications, consumer electronics, automotive, aerospace, medical, and other industrial sectors.

The value of the electronic components contained within individual products is growing. The automotive sector illustrates this trend. Twenty years ago, the value of electronic components in the average automobile was only about 1 percent; today, the figure ranges from 8 to 15 percent, depending on the make and model of car. Auto manufacturers are exploring concepts such as the "network vehicle," the "personal productivity vehicle," and the "auto PC." The addition of communications, navigation, and computing electronics is increasing demand for microprocessors, mass-storage devices, flat-panel displays, and other electronic components. It has been estimated that a minimum of 8 megabytes of dynamic random-access memory (DRAM) will be necessary in a car equipped with an auto PC, while mapping software could require 8 to 12 megabytes and voice recognition would need another 4 megabytes. New packaging, miniaturized connectors, flex circuitry, and additional ruggedization will be required for the new generations of automotive electronics. With these developments, it is possible that the electronics content of the average automobile will reach 25 percent over the next decade.

There is intense pressure for microelectronics manufacturers to be first to market with leading-edge products. By being the first to introduce a new product, a supplier often can gain the high profits necessary to finance research and development for the next generation of product and the purchase of new equipment to manufacture that generation. Efficiency and flexibility in electronic component design and manufacturing are key goals for the industry as it strives to function in a system in which product development and marketing life cycles can average only 18 months in the case of many advanced semiconductor chips.

To meet fierce international competition for worldwide sales, U.S. suppliers of electronic components must sell to all major markets, both domestic and foreign. Profit margins on some "commodity" products, such as DRAM chips, are so slim that only through global sales can a supplier generate sufficient profits to remain in business. Other products, such as semiconductor manufacturing equipment (SME), have higher profit margins but are sold in far fewer and more specialized markets.

Microelectronics companies compete globally for labor as well as sales. U.S. electronic component manufacturers have utilized offshore assembly and test operations in countries such as South Korea, Malaysia, Mexico, and Singapore for many years. The continuing search for skilled labor at a low cost has led some U.S. microelectronics firms to invest in assembly and test operations in locations such as Costa Rica and Thailand.

U.S. companies also have internationalized other stages of electronic component manufacturing, such as circuit design and semiconductor wafer fabrication, to better serve the needs of end users abroad.

While a large proportion of high-skill, high-investment, and high-value-added electronics manufacturing is still done in the United States, American high-tech industry has expressed concern over the difficulty of recruiting adequate numbers of top-quality electrical engineers, software programmers, and other highly specialized workers. Industry pushed Congress to pass legislation, known as the American Competitiveness and Workforce Improvement Act of 1998, that temporarily (through September, 2001) raises existing limits on immigration visas for highly skilled workers. The new, higher limits were quickly surpassed in 1999, however, and new legislation known as the New Workers for Economic Growth Act (S. 1440) was introduced in the 106th Congress that would further raise visa limits for fiscal years 2000 through 2002.

In 1999, the U.S. electronic component industry employed an estimated 605,400 people, of whom roughly 65 percent were production workers. Total employment in the electronic component industry has grown only 1.4 percent a year since 1996 despite increasing industry shipments, indicating the increasing productivity of the industry's workers.

The global microelectronics industry already is benefiting from implementation of the Information Technology Agreement (ITA), which will eliminate import duties on information technology products, including electronic components and SME, by the year 2000. Efforts to expand the number of participants and the scope of goods covered by the ITA are the subject of ongoing multilateral negotiations.

The Asian financial crisis had a significant but not catastrophic effect on U.S. electronic component makers as well as on suppliers of electronics manufacturing equipment. Sales to the Asian region of semiconductors, passive electronic components and connectors, and SME saw little growth in 1998, depressing U.S. export figures. The full effect of the Asian financial crisis on the microelectronics sector has yet to play out. Worldwide sales of electronic equipment recovered fairly well in 1999 as economic growth in many Asian countries strengthened. While economic recovery and industry restructuring seem to be well under way in countries such as South Korea and Thailand, the economies of Japan, Indonesia, and to some extent China are still beset with problems that hinder economic growth and thus demand for electronic components and accessories.

The U.S. printed circuit board industry remains concerned about ripple effects from the Asian financial crisis. Downward pressure on prices continued to affect printed circuit boards and related production equipment in 1999. U.S. board producers are most vulnerable to this in the North American market, which is the primary outlet for their sales. Asia-based semiconductor companies reduced capital spending in 1998 and 1999, and that hurt sales by U.S. suppliers of SMEs. Reduced consumer demand in Asia also contributed to a downturn in the global semiconductor market in 1998, but the market resumed positive growth in 1999.

ELECTRONIC COMMERCE

The worldwide electronic components and assemblies industry has a tremendous and lasting stake in the continued free and open development of the Internet and electronic commerce. As the Internet grows, so grows the electronic components industry, which supplies the capacitors, connectors, printed circuit boards, and semiconductors that make up the computers, modems, and switches that make up the Internet.

CHANGES IN TRADE DATA DUE TO THE TRANSITION TO NAICS

The United States began using the North American Industry Classification System (NAICS) with the release of the 1997 Economic Census statistics. One activity that became a separate industry under the NAICS is printed circuit assembly manufacturing. Under the Standard Industrial Classification (SIC) system this activity was included within SIC 3571, electronic computers; SIC 3679, electronic components, not elsewhere classified; SIC 3661, telephone and telegraph apparatus; and other industries depending upon the intended use of the manufactured product. The NAICS includes all manufacturers of assemblies in the one industry. It is the intent of all U.S. statistical agencies to tabulate and publish statistics according to the NAICS. To facilitate the conversion of trade statistics from SIC-based to NAICS-based groupings, Census reviewed the commodities included in each SIC-based group and adjusted their content, in essence, redefining the SIC-based groupings.

Trade data included in *U.S. Industry and Trade Outlook 2000* are based on the revised Census SIC-based groupings. Prior to this revision, imports and exports of printed circuit board assemblies were included in other SIC-based groups including SIC 3571; they are now included in SIC-based group 3679. Consequently, imports attributed to the passive components reported in Table 16-10 increased dramatically from last year's edition because printed circuit assemblies are now included in SIC 3679. Exports of some commodities previously included with passive components were omitted from the new definitions, reducing the reported value of exports shown in Table 16-10. Trade data for passive components are consolidated into the data for electronic components and accessories (SIC 367), Table 16-1. A larger trade deficit is shown in this summary table than was shown in previous years because of the use of the adjusted Census trade group definitions.

TABLE 16-1: Electronic Components and Accessories (SIC 367) Trends and Forecasts
(millions of dollars except as noted)

	1992	1993	1994	1995	1996	1997[1]	1998[1]	1999[2]	2000[3]	Percent Change 97–98	98–99	99–00	96–00[4]
Industry data													
Value of shipments[5]	73,642	81,236	97,131	120,129	127,996	141,453	150,840	167,575	189,048	6.6	11.1	12.8	10.2
Value of shipments (1992$)	73,642	81,129	97,838	126,734	144,213	169,166	192,669	224,655	263,133	13.9	16.6	17.1	16.2
Total employment (thousands)	530	531	551	584	588	583	589	605	622	1.0	2.7	2.8	1.4
Production workers (thousands)	317	321	340	364	368	385	386	396	408	0.3	2.6	3.0	2.6
Average hourly earnings ($)	10.83	10.98	11.14	11.41	11.70	13.08	13.45	13.88	14.40	2.8	3.2	3.7	5.3
Capital expenditures	4,483	5,521	7,743	11,213	14,345	13,134	14,108	15,125	16,861	7.4	7.2	11.5	4.1
Product data													
Value of shipments[5]	71,372	77,840	92,719	115,202	126,997	139,576	150,482	165,141	184,231	7.8	9.7	11.6	9.7
Value of shipments (1992$)	71,372	77,739	93,343	121,272	142,543	167,384	191,632	218,714	254,278	14.5	14.1	16.3	15.6
Trade data													
Value of imports	31,567	38,767	47,066	66,825	63,033	65,145	65,310	72,511	80,559	0.3	11.0	11.1	6.3
Value of exports	16,216	18,844	24,523	31,095	32,824	39,768	39,871	43,179	47,629	0.3	8.3	10.3	9.8

[1] Estimate except imports and exports.
[2] Estimate.
[3] Forecast.
[4] Compound annual rate.
[5] For a definition of industry versus product values, see "Getting the Most Out of *Outlook 2000.*"
Source: U.S. Department of Commerce: Bureau of the Census; International Trade Administration.

A growing number of electronic component manufacturers and distributors offer a variety of services that range from on-line auctions, to detailed product catalogs, to comparative technical data on their Internet Web sites. While many electronic component manufacturers have deployed Web sites, electronic component distributors may be moving faster toward establishing E-commerce as a standard practice rather than a value-added service. Several distributors noted an increase in Internet business during 1999, with Web site visitors registering for on-line purchasing up by a factor of 10 or more in some cases. Most on-line orders are still small in dollar terms and often come from individuals and smaller customers. The majority of high-value and high-volume electronic component orders are still placed via older, well-established electronic data interchange (EDI) systems.

As in other industry sectors, many electronic component companies are grappling with the best way to define and deploy their E-commerce strategies. For many, the initial approach has been to follow the pack and take "stopgap measures" to counter something the competition has done. The level of investment in electronic commerce has remained relatively low compared with other information technology activities and remains directed primarily at boosting sales. Most electronic component companies see their E-business initiatives as additional channels to serve their customers, while fewer (perhaps half) firms also aim their Web sites at their suppliers. It seems clear that as the Internet evolves from an information-posting opportunity and sales and marketing tool, companies will be more aggressive in using E-business to address supply-chain issues, bringing significant new investment of dollars and resources to the effort.

PROJECTIONS OF INDUSTRY AND TRADE GROWTH FOR THE NEXT 1 AND 5 YEARS

The U.S. electronic component and accessories industry has grown in recent years, though somewhat less than it did during the boom years 1994–1995. Electronic component industry shipments were estimated at over $141 billion in current dollars in 1997, up 10 percent from the 1996 level (see Table 16-1). Industry shipments were estimated at almost $151 billion in 1998 (a gain of 6.6 percent) and over $167.6 billion in 1999, an increase of 11 percent. For the year 2000, industry shipments are forecast to grow another 12.8 percent, reaching $189 billion. The 5-year outlook for electronic components and accessories is favorable, with shipments by U.S. industry expected to grow by 12.5 percent annually through 2004, when their value should exceed $300 billion.

Exports have accounted for approximately 26 percent of total shipments by the U.S. electronic component industry in recent years (see Table 16-2). U.S. exports of electronic components are forecast to grow 10.3 percent in the year 2000, when they should reach a value of $47.6 billion. A significant factor in this growth in exports is the expected economic strengthening of foreign markets hampered by the Asian financial crisis in 1998–1999. Over the long term, exports should grow at a compound annual rate of about 14.4 percent, reaching a value of almost $82 billion in 2004.

U.S. imports of electronic components surpassed $65 billion in 1998, an increase of only 0.3 percent from 1997 (see Table 16-2). The strong U.S. economy absorbed an estimated $72.5 billion worth of electronic component imports in 1999, partly due to reduced prices for Asian components brought on by currency devaluations resulting from the Asian financial crisis. Electronic

TABLE 16-2: U.S. Trade Patterns in Microelectronics[1] in 1998
(millions of dollars; percent)

Exports			Imports		
Region[2]	Value[3]	Share, %	Region[2]	Value[3]	Share, %
NAFTA	11,186	28	NAFTA	10,488	16
Latin America	944	2	Latin America	587	1
Western Europe	5,348	13	Western Europe	5,855	9
Japan/Chinese Economic Area	7,267	18	Japan/Chinese Economic Area	22,200	34
Other Asia	14,603	37	Other Asia	25,569	39
Rest of world	524	1	Rest of world	611	1
World	39,871	100	World	65,310	100
Top Five Countries	Value	Share, %	Top Five Countries	Value	Share, %
Mexico	7,000	18	Japan	10,601	16
Canada	4,186	10	Malaysia	7,715	12
Malaysia	3,719	9	South Korea	6,942	11
Philippines	3,435	9	Taiwan	6,800	10
South Korea	3,302	8	Canada	5,565	9

[1] SIC 367.
[2] For definitions of regional groupings, see "Getting the Most Out of *Outlook 2000*."
[3] Values may not sum to total due to rounding.
Source: U.S. Department of Commerce, Bureau of the Census.

component imports are forecast to increase at a compound annual rate of 12.4 percent through 2004, when they will reach a value of nearly $129 billion.

Robin Roark, U.S. Department of Commerce, Office of Microelectronics, Medical Equipment and Instrumentation, (202) 482-3090, October 1999.

ELECTRON TUBES

Electron tubes (SIC 3671) are active electronic components. SIC 3671 includes receiving tubes, including television picture tubes and computer monitor tubes, and specialty tubes, including vacuum tubes, klystrons, magnetrons, and microwave tubes.

Global and Domestic Industry Trends

There are fewer than 200 manufacturers of electron tubes in the United States, and most are small businesses that employ 1 to 19 people. Cathode-ray tubes (CRTs), a type of receiving tube used in televisions and computer monitors, constitute the largest product segment of SIC 3671. As a result of increased demand around the world for larger-screen televisions and

TABLE 16-3: Electron Tubes (SIC 3671) Trends and Forecasts
(millions of dollars except as noted)

	1992	1993	1994	1995	1996	1997[1]	1998[1]	1999[2]	2000[3]	Percent Change 97–98	98–99	99–00	96–00[4]
Industry data													
Value of shipments[5]	3,145	3,052	3,148	3,500	3,779	3,961	4,079	4,159	4,317	3.0	2.0	3.8	3.4
Value of shipments (1992$)	3,145	3,085	3,126	3,434	3,701	3,895	4,108	4,288	4,396	5.5	4.4	2.5	4.4
Total employment (thousands)	22.2	20.2	20.4	21.6	23.3	21.7	21.4	21.3	22.1	–1.4	–0.5	3.8	–1.3
Production workers (thousands)	16.8	15.3	15.8	16.6	17.9	16.7	16.4	16.4	17.0	–1.8	0.0	3.7	–1.3
Average hourly earnings ($)	13.21	13.73	13.25	13.10	12.95	14.32	14.67	15.08	15.39	2.4	2.8	2.1	4.4
Capital expenditures	62	85	132	142	181	160	157	167	187	–1.9	6.4	12.0	0.8
Product data													
Value of shipments[5]	3,357	3,330	3,561	3,894	4,178	4,349	4,377	4,359	4,496	0.6	–0.4	3.1	1.9
Value of shipments (1992$)	3,357	3,367	3,536	3,822	4,092	4,276	4,408	4,494	4,578	3.1	2.0	1.9	2.8
Trade data													
Value of imports	928	990	1,218	1,390	1,239	1,123	998	942	978	–11.1	–5.6	3.8	–5.7
Value of exports	771	929	1,232	1,541	1,720	2,258	2,471	2,417	2,586	9.4	–2.2	7.0	10.7

[1] Estimate except imports and exports.
[2] Estimate.
[3] Forecast.
[4] Compound annual rate.
[5] For a definition of industry versus product values, see "Getting the Most Out of *Outlook 2000*."
Source: U.S. Department of Commerce: Bureau of the Census; International Trade Administration.

TABLE 16-4: U.S. Trade Patterns in Electron Tubes[1] in 1998
(millions of dollars; percent)

Exports			Imports		
Region[2]	Value[3]	Share, %	Region[2]	Value[3]	Share, %
NAFTA	1,860	75	NAFTA	288	29
Latin America	142	6	Latin America	15	1
Western Europe	163	7	Western Europe	183	18
Japan/Chinese Economic Area	194	8	Japan/Chinese Economic Area	457	46
Other Asia	78	3	Other Asia	49	5
Rest of world	35	1	Rest of world	7	1
World	2,471	100	World	998	100
Top Five Countries	Value	Share, %	Top Five Countries	Value	Share, %
Mexico	1,824	74	Japan	415	42
Brazil	111	4	Mexico	273	27
Japan	85	3	France	63	6
Hong Kong	55	2	Germany	53	5
United Kingdom	52	2	United Kingdom	42	4

[1] SIC 3671.
[2] For definitions of regional groupings, see "Getting the Most Out of *Outlook 2000*."
[3] Values may not sum to total due to rounding.
Source: U.S. Department of Commerce, Bureau of the Census.

larger computer monitors, the fastest-growing segment for CRTs is for those greater than 26 inches in diagonal measurement. CRTs larger than 26 inches account for the bulk of U.S. shipments of electron tubes.

Projections of Industry and Trade Growth for the Next 1 and 5 Years

The European Union countries and South Korea are the leading manufacturers in this sector. U.S. companies will continue to concentrate on high-end, specialty products. Nearly three-quarters of U.S. exports of electron tubes go to Mexico, where there is a substantial television and computer monitor assembly industry, especially in the United States–Mexico border region of "maquiladora" manufacturing. The industry is expected to grow in unit sales but show only slight growth in dollar terms over the next 5 years (see Tables 16-3 and 16-4).

Dorothea Blouin, U.S. Department of Commerce, Office of Microelectronics, Medical Equipment and Instrumentation, (202) 482-1333, October 1999.

PRINTED CIRCUIT BOARDS

The interconnection industry is the backbone of the electronics industry and modern industrial society. Virtually every product that has electronic functions contains interconnected electronic components mounted on printed circuit boards (PCBs). When PCBs have other electronic components assembled on them, they are called printed circuit assemblies or "stuffed boards." Interconnection products have grown in importance with the electronics industry's perpetual emphasis on miniaturization in the packaging of electronic components. The electronic interconnection food chain is composed of PCB manufacturers, suppliers of PCB production equipment and the electronic chemicals and materials used in the PCB fabrication process, and the companies involved in assembling the board products into finished electronic end products. This section, however, focuses primarily on the bare PCB.

Global and Domestic Industry Trends

The production of circuit boards in the United States is performed both by independent PCB firms and electronic system companies known as original equipment manufacturers (OEMs). This relationship also is described as merchant versus captive; the merchant firms are those which sell products into the overall market, and the captive firms are those which produce PCBs for use in their own electronic systems products.

Independent/merchant PCB firms focus almost exclusively on PCB manufacturing and are the dominant contributor to PCB production in the U.S. market. According to the Institute for Interconnecting and Packaging Electronic Circuits (IPC), a leading trade association for the PCB industry, in 1998 there were an estimated 690 independent PCB firms operating in the United States. Approximately 95 percent of the PCBs produced in the United States were made by independent producers in 1998. U.S. PCB makers are primarily small to medium-size companies. According to IPC, only 125 of 690 merchant PCB firms have annual sales of more than $10 million. To put this in perspective, only the top 10 independent PCB companies had sales over $100 million. Those top 10 firms accounted for 44 percent of the U.S. market in 1998.

PCBs fall into either the rigid or the flexible circuit category. Rigid boards dominate U.S. production. Of the $10.6 billion worth of PCBs produced in the United States in 1998, only $874 million worth were flexible circuits. The rigid board category is broken down further into single-sided, double-sided, and multilayer boards. Since 1994, multilayer boards have been the fastest-growing and largest rigid board segment, accounting for approximately 73 percent of the value of the total rigid board market. As electronic end products have become significantly smaller with more electronic functionality, demands for higher electronic packaging densities and higher functionality have driven growth in the multilayer board market.

PCB manufacturers sell their products to firms in the following end markets: automotive, business and retail, consumer electronics and household appliances, computers, industrial machinery, instrumentation, medical equipment, military, and telecommunications. In the United States, the computer industry has traditionally been the major end market for U.S. PCB suppliers. However, as electronics spread to other industries, the computer market declined from a high point in 1980, when it accounted for 52 percent of PCB sales, to 21 percent in 1998. By 1999, the computer industry had fallen to third place, behind communications and contract manufacturing (see Table 16-5).

Newer end-market consumption trends are driven in part by the development of multifunction portable electronic products, such as personal communication assistants, which process voice mail and E-mail messages via the Internet and also function as phones and beepers. Since these devices generally are considered communication products, the communications sector accounted for the largest share (27 percent) of the overall PCB end market.

Another major new end market is the contract electronic manufacturing (CEM) segment, which captured 22 percent of overall PCB production in the United States in 1998. The CEM industry has become increasingly more sophisticated, with some contract manufacturers taking on nearly every aspect of electronic production, including product design and manufacturing, global component sourcing, final assembly and packaging, and electronic systems integration. The term "box building" was coined to describe the new CEM role, meaning that contract manufacturers develop finished products rather than just stuffing printed circuit boards as in the past. In the same way that many OEMs have previously outsourced PCB production, there is a strong trend for OEMs to outsource additional aspects of electronics production and even entire electronic products to contract manufacturers in most major electronic end markets.

TABLE 16-5: Distribution and Volume of Printed Circuit Board (PCB) Sales in 1998
(millions of dollars)

Industry/End Market	PCB Sales	Percent Share
Communication	1,971	27
Contract manufacturing	1,605	22
Computers	1,533	21
Automotive	731	10
Industrial	497	7
Instrumentation	519	7
Consumer	220	3
Government/military	147	2
Business/retail	74	1

Since the mid-1980s, the CEM industry has experienced a 25 percent compound annual growth rate (CAGR). During this dramatic expansion, CEM firms have branched out in overall product design and other manufacturing life-cycle activities. One major area of importance in this regard is the CEM segment's role in component procurement. Contract manufacturers are now major customers for suppliers of electronic components such as PCBs and semiconductors. Contract manufacturing is the fastest-growing end market for PCBs and is expected to surpass communications as the major end market in the next 2 or 3 years. As contract manufacturers continue to expand their involvement in electronic manufacturing and take further control of component sourcing and end-product manufacturing, they will play a powerful role in the overall U.S. and global electronics industry.

Contributions by the interconnection industry to the U.S. economy include the value of bare PCBs produced, the electronic components mounted on PCBs, the service activities involved in the assembly of board products, and overall employment in PCB manufacturing and assembly operations. U.S. interconnection companies have operations in all 50 states. IPC estimates that in 1999, overall U.S. interconnection industry production (PCB plants and assembly operations) was valued at $33 billion and the industry employed more than 330,000 people. Employment specifically in PCB manufacturing (SIC 3672) in 1998 grew by more than 6 percent from 1997 and was estimated at 79,700 jobs (see Table 16-6). A large majority (over 73 percent) of these jobs are for production workers.

Projections of Industry and Trade Growth for the Next 1 and 5 Years

With production at $10.6 billion, 1998 was a somewhat difficult year for many U.S. PCB manufacturers. According to IPC, U.S. production of PCBs was relatively flat in 1998, recording only a 5 percent increase over the 1997 level. This flat market performance was attributed to inventory corrections, reduced equipment exports, global PCB overcapacity, and unfavorable exchange rates. In addition, most market analysts also focus on severe pricing pressures in the U.S. market and abroad caused by the Asian financial crisis.

Shipments of rigid boards rose a scant 3 percent in 1998, and orders and bookings reportedly were down almost 0.5 percent. For flex circuits, shipments in 1998 rose 15.7 percent, with bookings rising about 5 percent. Laminate shipments were up about 10 percent.

U.S. exports of PCBs in 1999 have been estimated at $2.2 billion, roughly equivalent to the previous year's figure. Price competition related to currency devaluations posed serious difficulties for U.S. board exporters in 1999. North America, the largest regional market for U.S. exporters, accounted for nearly 60 percent of total U.S. exports of printed circuit boards. In 1998, Mexico purchased $630 million and Canada bought $613 million worth of U.S.-made PCBs (see Table 16-7).

In 1998, other large export markets (in descending order after Mexico and Canada) included the United Kingdom, Singapore, the Philippines, Ireland, Japan, Malaysia, Germany, and Thailand. Exports to the Philippines were most notable as a hot

TABLE 16-6: Printed Circuit Boards (SIC 3672) Trends and Forecasts
(millions of dollars except as noted)

	1992	1993	1994	1995	1996	1997[1]	1998[1]	1999[2]	2000[3]	Percent Change 97–98	98–99	99–00	96–00[4]
Industry data													
Value of shipments[5]	7,320	7,378	8,416	9,498	10,702	12,200	12,932	13,708	14,941	6.0	6.0	9.0	8.7
Value of shipments (1992$)	7,320	7,551	8,803	9,924	11,067	12,603	13,401	14,324	15,654	6.3	6.9	9.2	9.0
Total employment (thousands)	76.0	73.6	76.9	81.6	88.3	75.1	79.7	84.1	90.7	6.1	5.5	7.8	0.7
Production workers (thousands)	51.0	50.5	54.0	59.6	63.9	56.8	58.6	62.2	67.6	3.2	6.1	8.7	1.4
Average hourly earnings ($)	10.16	10.58	10.49	10.36	10.75	11.92	12.28	12.74	13.37	3.0	3.7	4.9	5.6
Capital expenditures	318	283	381	453	585	691	875	938	1,069	26.6	7.2	14.0	16.3
Product data													
Value of shipments[5]	6,293	6,930	7,555	8,543	8,949	10,112	10,618	11,255	12,268	5.0	6.0	9.0	8.2
Value of shipments (1992$)	6,293	7,093	7,902	8,926	9,254	10,446	11,003	11,761	12,846	5.3	6.9	9.2	8.5
Trade data													
Value of imports	1,243	1,289	1,468	1,840	1,849	2,071	2,045	2,311	2,542	−1.3	13.0	10.0	8.3
Value of exports	1,092	973	1,377	1,651	1,694	2,007	2,178	2,199	2,309	8.5	1.0	5.0	8.1

[1] Estimate except imports and exports.
[2] Estimate.
[3] Forecast.
[4] Compound annual rate.
[5] For a definition of industry versus product values, see "Getting the Most Out of *Outlook 2000.*"
Source: U.S. Department of Commerce: Bureau of the Census; International Trade Administration.

new market prospect, and this trend is expected to continue for the foreseeable future. Growth in U.S. exports to the Philippines and Singapore created an upward surge in U.S. exports to the Asian region as a whole in 1999 as well. It appears that the electronics assembly boom in those countries is fueling dramatic consumption of U.S. PCBs.

U.S. exports to the European Union were expected to grow moderately in 1999. However, U.S. exports may face stronger challenges in Europe and other markets because of the lower costs of Asian board makers. The years 2000 through 2004 are expected to offer strong opportunities for U.S. PCB exports as the global economy recovers and information technology products proliferate.

The world market for PCBs, including both rigid and flexible circuits, was estimated at $34.3 billion in 1998. Industry representatives estimate that the global PCB market will grow to between $36 and $39 billion by the year 2000. According to IPC, total rigid PCB production was estimated at $31.5 billion in 1998.

Japan has emerged as the global market leader for rigid board production. Japan's 1998 PCB production was estimated at $7.96

TABLE 16-7: U.S. Trade Patterns in Printed Circuit Boards[1] in 1998
(millions of dollars; percent)

Exports Region[2]	Value[3]	Share, %	Imports Region[2]	Value[3]	Share, %
NAFTA	1,244	57	NAFTA	410	20
Latin America	53	2	Latin America	6	0
Western Europe	378	17	Western Europe	149	7
Japan/Chinese Economic Area	138	6	Japan/Chinese Economic Area	1,088	53
Other Asia	339	16	Other Asia	371	18
Rest of world	26	1	Rest of world	20	1
World	2,178	100	World	2,045	100
Top Five Countries	**Value**	**Share, %**	**Top Five Countries**	**Value**	**Share, %**
Mexico	630	29	Taiwan	541	26
Canada	613	28	Canada	346	17
United Kingdom	132	6	Japan	297	15
Singapore	131	6	China	168	8
Philippines	116	5	South Korea	133	7

[1] SIC 3672.
[2] For definitions of regional groupings, see "Getting the Most Out of *Outlook 2000.*"
[3] Values may not sum to total due to rounding.
Source: U.S. Department of Commerce, Bureau of the Census.

billion, which accounted for 25.3 percent of total world output, followed by the United States with $7.72 billion, or 24.5 percent of world production. Taiwanese PCB producers experienced the strongest expansion, accounting for 10.5 percent of world production, while China/Hong Kong expanded to 6.6 percent of total output. South Korea surpassed Germany to take the fifth position in world production, accounting for 5.3 percent of the total.

Imports of PCBs from Taiwan have had a dramatic increase over the past 5 years and heavily dominate all board imports into the U.S. market. In fact, the value of PCBs imported from Taiwan was higher than those entering from the North American Free Trade Agreement (NAFTA) countries (Canada and Mexico) and the countries in the European Union. In 1998, board imports from Taiwan accounted for 26 percent of all imports into the U.S. market, followed by Canada (17 percent) and Japan (14 percent).

The Asia-Pacific countries (including Australia), accounted for the largest regional share of the 1998 rigid market with $17 billion, followed by North America, which accounted for nearly $8.5 billion, and Europe with $5.6 billion.

The world market for flexible circuits in 1998 was estimated by IPC to be $2.83 billion. Japan continued to have the largest market, with shipments estimated at $990 million, or 36 percent of the world market, followed by the United States with $874 million (31 percent). From a regional perspective, the Asia-Pacific region contributed $1.5 billion, while North America shipped $902 million and Europe accounted for $385 million.

In 1999, U.S. PCB manufacturers fought hard to regain world market share from their Asian competitors. However, tremendous pricing pressure and exchange rate differentials made this an unattainable goal. To remain competitive globally, U.S. companies must continue to seek ways to reduce costs in PCB manufacturing. However, this challenge has to be met by all global PCB producers and has been a reality since markets became international. In late 1999, the lessons of the Asian financial crisis and subsequent global uncertainty in the electronic markets of Europe and South America reaffirmed the integration of global markets and the vulnerabilities that accompany it. The large volume of board imports into the U.S. market in 1998 underscores this reality for U.S. PCB producers, which not only must compete overseas but also must fight for market share at home to survive.

In their efforts to cut costs, many global PCB makers are expanding their offshore manufacturing in newly developing countries. Japan has been a leader in the use of offshore manufacturing to strengthen its market position. U.S. PCB companies have not embraced offshore manufacturing to the extent that competitors such as the Japanese have. A primary reason for this has been the large and consistent domestic PCB market, since many U.S. PCB firms are running at high capacity just to meet local demand. Instead of investing in offshore production, U.S. firms have tried to develop process improvements that will yield higher volumes and lower-cost boards.

Like Japan, Taiwan, Hong Kong, and South Korea are investing offshore. Although the manufacturing environment there has not become equivalent to that in the United States or Europe, these east Asian producers are contending with higher labor rates and higher prices for industrial development and manufacturing overall. These large east Asian PCB producers have increasingly resorted to moving production to areas with lower manufacturing costs. The general impact of east Asian offshore manufacturing strategies was evident by the mid-1990s and strongly contributed to explosive growth in the PCB markets of southeast Asia and China. Market analysts trace this growth primarily to capital investment from Japan, Hong Kong, and Taiwan. In 1998 and throughout much of 1999, most of these countries also felt the effects of the Asian financial crisis ripple through the PCB markets, and Asian producers have received less new investment in PCB production.

Intensified pricing pressure, particularly from Taiwanese PCB makers, affected most global markets through 1999. Market conditions for individual PCB companies throughout Asia and the world will vary greatly, especially in relation to their level of direct exposure in world markets. The performance of U.S. firms is likely to vary according to their export reliance and sensitivity to imports. Asian firms that export more should perform more strongly than will their domestic counterparts, since they will continue to be paid in U.S. dollars or other strong currencies.

The outlook for the U.S. PCB market in the year 2000 is modestly strong, as world economies are expected to recover fully from the Asian financial crisis and the U.S. economy is projected to remain strong. Moderate growth is expected in the U.S. PCB market in 2000, and many analysts expect the market to grow more rapidly by 2001. Globally, the effect of the Y2K transition is forecast to stimulate computer purchases worldwide and have a positive impact on PCB consumption. Competition from Asian board producers will intensify through the forecast period to 2004. The U.S. PCB market is expected to reach the neighborhood of $9 billion in 1999 and probably will surpass $10 billion by the close of the year 2000.

Growth in PCB bookings is expected to reach 7 to 8 percent in 2000. Shipments by the U.S. PCB industry are estimated to grow by 6 percent in 1999 and 9 percent in the year 2000 (see Table 16-6). Over the next 3 years, most market analysts expect average annual growth in U.S. PCB sales to range between 7 and 10 percent. Possibilities exist in the early part of the twenty-first century for a repeat performance of the banner year of 1998, with shipments growing more than 10 percent. The major drivers of long-term growth should continue to be the increasing level of electronic content in capital goods, expansion of Internet-related products and businesses, and global demand for personal computers and cellular phones.

Barring major unforeseen financial disruptions, the U.S. electronics industry and the U.S. PCB market are expected to maintain their overall strength through 2004. However, U.S. market growth may turn out to be a double-edged sword for domestic PCB firms, as imports increase along with overall market size. However, the United States will not be the only market consuming more PCB imports. Western European electronics firms are expected to rely heavily on imported boards throughout the year 2000, and that should bode well for U.S.

export prospects. Overall, strong long-term growth is expected in PCB-consuming products, and so optimism pervades the U.S. interconnection industry's expectations for growth and expansion through the year 2004.

Judee Mussehl-Aziz, U.S. Department of Commerce, Office of Microelectronics, Medical Equipment and Instrumentation, (202) 482-0429, October 1999.

SEMICONDUCTORS AND RELATED DEVICES

Semiconductors are active electronic components that produce and transfer electricity in electronic circuits. Semiconductor devices covered in this section include discrete semiconductors and integrated circuits classified under SIC 3674. Discrete semiconductors perform a single electronic function—acting as a diode or a transistor, for example—and several discrete semiconductors must be connected to form a working circuit. Integrated circuits (ICs) incorporate thousands or millions of microscopic transistors and other functional components to form complex electronic circuits on the surface of a rigid substrate such as a "chip" of silicon; thus, they sometimes are called computer chips.

Global and Domestic Industry Trends

The U.S. semiconductor industry consists of well over 100 firms that design, manufacture, and sell semiconductors. Most semiconductors are purchased by OEMs for incorporation into electronic products and systems. A small proportion of ICs are purchased by individual end users, mostly for processor and memory chip upgrades in personal computers or electronic hobby applications. Leading U.S. semiconductor companies include Intel, Motorola, Texas Instruments, IBM, AMD, National Semiconductor, Micron Technology, and Lucent Technologies, each of which is active in semiconductor design, manufacture, and marketing. Many small and midsize U.S. semiconductor firms also manufacture chips, and dozens of companies design and/or market semiconductors they do not manufacture themselves.

According to the U.S. Census Bureau, the U.S. semiconductor industry employed roughly 198,000 people in 1997 (see Table 16-8). Approximately 53 percent of total semiconductor industry jobs are in production. Semiconductor industry employment is estimated to have declined about 0.5 percent in 1998, partly as a result of the decline in semiconductor exports to countries hard hit by the Asian financial crisis. However, employment is expected to reach 201,000 workers in 1999 and nearly 206,000 in 2000.

Semiconductors are used in most electronic products and systems, including computers and other data processing equipment; consumer electronics; industrial machinery; telecommunications equipment; automobiles, aircraft, and other transportation systems; medical equipment and analytical instruments; and military electronic systems. According to the World Semiconductor Trade Statistics (WSTS) organization, the computer industry was the largest end user of semiconductors in 1998, when it accounted for 50.4 percent of worldwide sales. Communications products represented 18.8 percent of global semiconductor demand in 1998. The consumer electronic products sector was the third-ranking end use in 1998, taking 14.9 percent of semiconductor sales worldwide. The industrial equipment sector accounted for roughly 8.9 percent

TABLE 16-8: Semiconductors and Related Devices (SIC 3674) Trends and Forecasts
(millions of dollars except as noted)

										Percent Change			
	1992	1993	1994	1995	1996	1997[1]	1998[1]	1999[2]	2000[3]	97–98	98–99	99–00	96–00[4]
Industry data													
Value of shipments[5]	32,191	35,152	47,265	65,922	71,413	78,770	85,307	98,614	115,436	8.3	15.6	17.1	12.8
Value of shipments (1992$)	32,191	35,222	47,790	71,810	85,833	104,608	124,878	152,653	187,701	19.4	22.2	23.0	21.6
Total employment (thousands)	172	163	183	192	190	198	197	201	206	–0.5	2.0	2.5	2.0
Production workers (thousands)	84.8	82.2	92.9	98.1	96.2	106	105	108	110	–0.9	2.9	1.9	3.4
Average hourly earnings ($)	13.55	14.08	14.46	14.89	15.29	16.36	16.97	17.43	17.94	3.7	2.7	2.9	4.1
Capital expenditures	3,121	3,839	5,982	9,182	11,991	10,533	11,206	12,035	13,518	6.4	7.4	12.3	3.0
Product data													
Value of shipments[5]	29,391	33,689	44,064	60,330	67,070	75,367	82,007	95,138	111,229	8.8	16.0	16.9	13.5
Value of shipments (1992$)	29,391	33,757	44,554	65,719	80,613	101,269	120,802	145,627	177,966	19.3	20.6	22.2	21.9
Trade data													
Value of imports	15,275	19,244	25,670	38,618	36,256	36,266	33,157	35,982	39,104	–8.6	8.5	8.7	1.9
Value of exports	11,465	13,744	17,991	23,189	24,001	28,861	29,055	32,114	35,834	0.7	10.5	11.6	10.5

[1] Estimate except imports and exports.
[2] Estimate.
[3] Forecast.
[4] Compound annual rate.
[5] For a definition of industry versus product values, see "Getting the Most Out of *Outlook 2000.*"
Source: U.S. Department of Commerce: Bureau of the Census; International Trade Administration.

of sales in 1998, followed by the automotive industry, with about 5.8 percent of the market. Semiconductor sales to the military market, which declined during the 1990s, represented only 1.1 percent of worldwide demand in 1998, according to WSTS.

Semiconductor manufacturing is a capital- and research-intensive endeavor. The increasing cost of semiconductor manufacturing plants—a state-of-the-art semiconductor wafer fabrication facility cost an average of about $1.5 billion in 1999—has led to growing numbers of mergers, coproduction agreements, and contract manufacturing in the U.S. industry and worldwide. According to the Semiconductor Industry Association (SIA), the U.S. semiconductor industry invested 13 percent of sales revenue in research and development (R&D) in 1997. Total investment in plants, property, and equipment (capital expenditure) by U.S. semiconductor companies was roughly 18 percent of sales in 1997. This combined investment of 31 percent of sales revenue is very high compared with the national average for all manufacturing industries and bodes well for the future growth and health of the semiconductor industry.

The average selling price for many semiconductors continued to fall throughout 1998 and into 1999. Excess production capacity combined with the Asian financial crisis (which dampened demand for semiconductors in the Asian region) to keep semiconductor prices on a downward trend throughout 1998 and much of 1999. DRAM prices in the spot market stabilized and even began to strengthen a bit in the fourth quarter of 1999, as some DRAM producers lowered their production levels. A continuing glut of production capacity is expected to keep downward pressure on semiconductor prices in 2000.

Like the electronic components industry as a whole, U.S. semiconductor manufacturers are concerned about meeting future needs for highly skilled workers and have taken some initiatives to address that problem. In 1998, the SIA released a report titled "Educating Tomorrow's Workforce: A Report on the Semiconductor Industry's Commitment to Youth in K-12," which outlined the industry's best practices in educating and creating interest in young students about mathematics, science, and technology. The report describes the investment of tens of millions of dollars by 16 major U.S. semiconductor makers in developing education programs ranging from hands-on manufacturing training to expanded classroom curricula.

Projections of Industry and Trade Growth for the Next 1 and 5 Years

U.S. semiconductor industry shipments in 1998 increased an estimated 8.3 percent over the previous year, reaching $85.3 billion in current dollars (see Table 16-8). In response to continued growth of the U.S. economy and recovery in Asian markets affected by the Asian financial crisis, U.S. semiconductor industry shipments grew strongly (15.6 percent) in 1999 to reach a value of $98.6 billion. Semiconductor industry shipments are forecast to grow just over 17 percent in 2000 to approximately $115.4 billion. The long-term outlook for industry shipments calls for a CAGR of about 15 percent, with the value of shipments reaching $203.6 billion in 2004.

In 1998, the worldwide semiconductor market contracted to roughly $127.5 billion from the previous year's $140 billion, a drop of 8.9 percent. This decline was due largely to the effects of the Asian financial crisis, as demand for semiconductors dropped sharply in leading Asian markets such as South Korea, Hong Kong, Malaysia, Thailand, Singapore, and Japan. Worldwide semiconductor sales were estimated at $143.3 billion in 1999, an increase of 12.4 percent from 1998. The world semiconductor market is forecast to grow 17 percent in the year 2000, when revenues should reach $167.6 billion. Forecasters expect the global semiconductor market to experience a CAGR of roughly 15 percent per year through 2004.

On a product basis, worldwide demand for memory ICs is expected to rebound strongly in the year 2000, increasing 30 percent over 1999 sales. Demand for memory chips strengthened in 1999 after much slower growth and falling memory prices throughout 1998. The year 2000 should see strong demand for memory chips, as a wide range of new products—from portable phones and hand-held computers to global positioning systems—incorporate increasing amounts of memory, supplementing the worldwide sales of "traditional" memory-rich products such as personal computers (PCs) and computer peripherals. After memory ICs, the next fastest growing semiconductor product in 2000 will be applications-specific integrated circuits (ASICs), up 20 percent over 1999, followed by microcomponents (e.g., digital signal processors, microprocessors, and microcontrollers) and optical semiconductors (each up 12 percent), and discrete semiconductors and analog ICs (each up about 10 percent).

Fast-growing end-use markets for semiconductors over the next 5 years include computers (especially laptops and hand-held computers), communications equipment (especially wireless mobile equipment and wired network and public switching equipment), and digital consumer electronics such as digital video disc (DVD) players, digital televisions and set-top boxes, digital cameras and camcorders, digital videocassette recorders (VCRs), and arcade and home video games.

Global Market Prospects

U.S. semiconductor companies are major players in the global electronics industry, and roughly half of U.S. semiconductor industry revenues are derived from foreign sales. According to the SIA's estimate, the U.S. semiconductor industry's share of the total world market reached 52 percent in 1998, a gain of about 3 percent from the previous year. Foreign sales by U.S. semiconductor companies include direct exports from the United States and sales of chips made in U.S.-owned facilities overseas. In 1998, direct exports of semiconductors from the United States were valued at $29.1 billion, up a modest 0.7 percent from the 1997 figure (see Table 16-9). This relatively flat export performance in 1998 was due largely to the dampening effect of the Asian financial crisis. U.S. exports to six of the eight major country markets in Asia fell, while exports to the Philippines and South Korea showed some growth in 1998. Exports accounted for roughly 39 percent of the $74.5 billion in worldwide semiconductor sales recorded by U.S. companies in 1998.

In 1998, the largest markets for U.S. semiconductor exports were Malaysia, the Philippines, South Korea, Canada, Singapore, Mexico, Japan, Taiwan, Hong Kong, and Thailand. The majority of U.S. semiconductor exports to Malaysia and the Philippines consist of unfinished parts that receive further processing (mostly assembly and testing) and are reexported to the United States and other countries.

On a regional basis, analysts forecast that semiconductor revenue in North America and South America combined will increase 18 percent in 2000. The Asia-Pacific region, excluding Japan, ranks second to the Americas in terms of market size and is expected to grow strongly at 19 percent. The European market, almost equal in size to Japan's, is forecast to grow about 18 percent. The Japanese semiconductor market is expected to grow 13 percent, the lowest rate in the four regions.

Since 1998, Japanese electronic giants have lost billions of dollars in DRAM revenue because of the Asian financial crisis and falling memory prices. These severe losses set the stage for a wave of consolidation, mergers, restructuring, and other cost-cutting moves. Two Japanese firms, Hitachi and NEC, merged their core DRAM businesses in 1999. Other Japanese firms restructured operations, closed plants, streamlined management, combined overseas units, reduced employment, slashed capital spending, forged joint ventures, outsourced production, and focused on nonmemory higher-end computing, consumer electronics, and communications products. These moves will strengthen Japanese semiconductor firms in the long run. The Electronics Industries Association of Japan forecasts that electronic component and device production, including semiconductors, will return to normal levels over the next 2 years.

Taiwan has emerged as an important semiconductor production location in the Asia-Pacific region. According to Taiwan's Ministry of Economic Affairs, the island's production is forecast to reach $35 billion in 2005. Taiwanese firms are among the world's 10 top capital spenders, and the Semiconductor Equipment and Materials International trade association forecasts that Taiwanese capital investment could reach $80 billion over the next 10 years. Taiwanese firms are world leaders in contract or "foundry" manufacturing of semiconductors, a trend that is expected to increase as global firms consolidate, restructure, and focus on new market segments.

South Korea has been a leader in the DRAM segment. Confronting the memory downturn in 1998, Korean semiconductor firms slashed capital spending and curbed DRAM production. In the wake of the Asian financial crisis and economic reforms called for by the International Monetary Fund, the Korean government urged Hyundai Electronic Industries and LG Semicon to merge their vast DRAM operations in 1999. That merger created the world's largest DRAM semiconductor company after Korea's Samsung. In preparation for the mass production of next-generation DRAMs, Samsung's investment in production facilities is expected to reach almost $3 billion. As the memory market returns to good health, Korean firms will increase capital spending and semiconductor-derived revenue should grow strongly.

The European semiconductor industry is well positioned in key growth markets, including the mobile telephone, digital TV and set-top box, chip card, and automotive electronics markets. Only one European manufacturer, Infineon, remains in the DRAM market. Spun off from its parent, Siemens, in 1999, Infineon curbed DRAM output and shifted production to logic and other nonmemory products. As the transition from a personal computer (PC)– to a communications-driven market accelerates, European semiconductor revenue is likely to surge. In terms of sales, three European firms rank among the world's top 10 semiconductor manufacturers.

TABLE 16-9: U.S. Trade Patterns in Semiconductors and Related Devices[1] in 1998
(millions of dollars; percent)

Exports			Imports		
Region[2]	Value[3]	Share, %	Region[2]	Value[3]	Share, %
NAFTA	5,030	17	NAFTA	3,135	9
Latin America	375	1	Latin America	52	0
Western Europe	3,464	12	Western Europe	2,733	8
Japan/Chinese Economic Area	6,199	21	Japan/Chinese Economic Area	10,444	31
Other Asia	13,736	47	Other Asia	16,617	50
Rest of world	250	1	Rest of world	176	1
World	29,055	100	World	33,157	100
Top Five Countries	Value	Share, %	Top Five Countries	Value	Share, %
Malaysia	3,610	12	Japan	5,891	18
Philippines	3,277	11	South Korea	5,223	16
South Korea	3,197	11	Malaysia	4,290	13
Canada	2,644	9	Philippines	3,884	12
Singapore	2,464	8	Taiwan	3,004	9

[1] SIC 3674.
[2] For definitions of regional groupings, see "Getting the Most Out of *Outlook 2000*."
[3] Values may not sum to total due to rounding.
Source: U.S. Department of Commerce, Bureau of the Census.

A NEW MULTILATERAL STATEMENT ON SEMICONDUCTORS

Access to the Japanese market has been an area of concern for the U.S. semiconductor industry since the 1980s. With the help of successive United States–Japan semiconductor arrangements negotiated in 1991 and 1996, the foreign share of the Japanese semiconductor market slowly increased from 16.7 percent in 1992 to 33.3 percent in 1997. Global semiconductor markets will benefit from the new Joint Statement Concerning Semiconductors by the European Commission and the governments of the United States, Japan, and Korea (the Statement), the successor to the 1996 bilateral United States–Japan arrangement. The new Statement, announced on June 10, 1999, ensures barrier-free trade in global semiconductor markets. Taiwan also endorsed the objectives and became a party to the Statement by agreeing to eliminate tariffs on semiconductors promptly.

The Statement supports free and open trade, competition, minimal government intervention, and antidumping measures consistent with General Agreement on Tariffs and Trade (GATT) and WTO principles. The Statement continues the Government Consultative Mechanism (GCM), a forum where government representatives evaluate recommendations on trade and investment liberalization, tariffs and market barriers, regulations, taxation, standardization, the environment, worker health and safety, intellectual property rights, scientific research, and information technology made by the industry-led World Semiconductor Council (WSC).

The new Statement does not specifically address market access in Japan. Since the foreign share of Japan's semiconductor market had exceeded 30 percent for eight consecutive quarters when the new Statement was created, the U.S. semiconductor industry expressed satisfaction with market access in Japan. The foreign market share in Japan was 31.7 percent in 1998, the second consecutive year it was above 30 percent. In the future, the U.S. Department of Commerce and the U.S. Trade Representative will monitor foreign market access, using the GCM as a forum to confront trade and investment barriers in global semiconductor markets.

A new industry-led WSC was established on June 10, 1999, under the Agreement Establishing a New World Semiconductor Council by the members of the Electronic Industries Association of Japan, the European Electronic Component Manufacturers Association, the Korea Semiconductor Industry Association, and the Semiconductor Industry Association. The Taiwan Semiconductor Industry Association became a member of the previous WSC in 1999. The WSC strongly supports free and open markets, intellectual property protection, full transparency of government policies and regulations, nondiscrimination for foreign products, and the ending of investment restrictions that are linked to technology transfer requirements. The WSC also encourages cooperative efforts in global PFC emissions reduction and worker health and safety.

The DRAM market continues to be the focus of trade disputes in the global semiconductor industry. In October 1998, the U.S. DRAM manufacturer Micron filed an antidumping petition involving 11 Taiwanese DRAM manufacturers. Reviews of previous antidumping cases against South Korean DRAM makers continued during 1999 both within the U.S. government and at the WTO. In April 1999, the Taiwanese Semiconductor Industry Association filed an antidumping petition in Taiwan against one U.S. DRAM producer and the U.S. affiliates of two Korean DRAM manufacturers. Taiwan's Ministry of Finance ruled in favor of the petitioner in September 1999. This will be the first imposition of a punitive antidumping duty by Taiwan on a U.S. semiconductor firm if the decision is approved by Taiwan's cabinet, as is expected.

Robert Blankenbaker, (202) 482-3411, ***Robin Roark,*** (202) 482-3090, U.S. Department of Commerce, Office of Microelectronics, Medical Equipment and Instrumentation, October 1999.

PASSIVE COMPONENTS

Passive components cover a wide range of products. The major categories are capacitors (SIC 3675); resistors (SIC 3676); coils, transformers, and other inductors (SIC 3677); electronic connectors (SIC 3678); and other electronic components (SIC 3679), including but not limited to printed circuit assemblies, power supplies, switches, relays, and piezoelectric devices.

Global and Domestic Industry Trends

Passive components are used in computer equipment, telecommunications and navigation equipment, industrial and analytical instruments, medical and dental equipment, consumer electronics, automobiles and other transportation equipment, and other electronic systems. Worldwide, the computer and telecommunications sectors are the largest consumers of passive components and are growing the fastest in terms of demand. The European market is slightly different, with the telecommunications sector being the major consumer of passive components and the automotive sector being a fast-growing market. The worldwide market for passive components was estimated at $66 billion in 1998.

The largest companies and the majority of high-end passive component production are in the United States, Japan, and the European Union. Large passive component manufacturers usually supply more than one type of passive component. Lack of technological know-how is a barrier to entry into the high-end market, although South Korean and Taiwanese firms have gained a substantial share of the market for some high-end passives. A large proportion of low-end, or "commodity," passive components are produced by companies based in Asian countries such as China, Singapore, and Malaysia and in the countries in the Americas, notably Mexico and Brazil.

Price, miniaturization, efficiency, and resistance to cross-noise are important competitive factors for high-end passive components. In commodity passives, price has been the most important factor, though quality has become an issue. Speed of delivery and availability are also important, especially with computer and telecommunications companies outsourcing assembly to subcontractors in many locations. To provide quick delivery and better service, most large passive component manufacturers sell in many overseas markets through a subsidiary or a local distributor. As is true with semiconductors, passive component manufacturers are experiencing price pressure from falling computer prices. As demand for passive components from Asian electronic manufacturers slowed because of the Asian financial crisis, makers of commodity passives tried to compensate by increasing exports from Asia in 1998.

Nearly 40 percent of the capacitors sold are ceramic capacitors. In early 1998, producers of ceramic capacitors, which contain palladium, were affected by shortages and price hikes resulting from a cutoff of palladium exports from Russia, which supplies over 60 percent of the world's palladium. From a low of $129 per troy ounce in 1996, prices skyrocketed to a high of $363 per troy ounce in May 1998 as a result of lower exports from Russia. When shipments resumed in June, prices fell slightly. Prices rose and fell for the rest of the year, depending on the supply and selling price of palladium from Russia.

Resistors are considered a commodity product, but quality is becoming an issue, especially with tiny resistors. The larger U.S. companies have broad product lines, which decreases their vulnerability to price changes for any given type of resistor. The recent recession in Asia caused more Asian producers to export resistors rather than sell them in the home market, forcing prices downward.

Inductor manufacturers are concentrating on miniaturization and current and frequency handling. The driving technology for inductors is telecommunications, especially mobile phones. Unlike the situation for some other electronic components, inductor prices have remained relatively stable.

There are literally hundreds of different designs of electronic connectors. Although the top 50 companies supply more than half the market, many small firms produce electronic connectors. In the United States alone, there were 347 firms producing electronic connectors in 1997. Some of the smaller companies specialize in a certain type of connector or manufacture custom connectors. U.S., Japanese, and European companies, especially French firms, lead in the high end, while China offers the most competitive prices for low-end connectors. Connector manufacturers must meet a difficult set of customer demands: large product line, low prices, volume pricing, just-in-time delivery, high density, no line noise, and durability (especially in consumer electronics).

In 1998, the connector industry experienced falling prices because of decreasing computer prices, flattening computer demand, and a slowing of the Asian market (which caused more exports by Asian connector companies and a greater supply). Because of price competition, especially in the computer market, some end users are beginning to accept a lower standard of quality or connectors made with lower-price materials. This has led to an increase in sales from Chinese and southeast Asian connector companies, putting pressure on U.S. producers.

Printed circuit assemblies are PCBs with electronic components mounted on them. U.S. industry shipments of printed circuit assemblies rose to $23.9 billion in 1997 from $13.7 billion in 1992, an average growth rate of 14.7 percent per year. Of those shipments, 45 percent were computer printed circuit assemblies, 17 percent were for telecommunications equipment, and 20 percent went into instrumentation. Nearly 700 companies in the United States do printed circuit assembly.

The contract manufacturing industry, of which printed circuit assembly is a part, is a $90 billion industry and is expected to nearly double to $178 billion by the year 2001. Because of their greater purchasing power and global presence, large contract manufacturers have a substantial advantage over smaller ones. The contract manufacturing industry is beginning to divide into two different segments—the large international companies and the small niche companies—with the midsize companies being bought out, disappearing, or growing into large companies. Recently, many OEM companies sold their assembly business to contract manufacturing companies, and contract manufacturers are buying one another.

While Asia has long been a center for semiconductor assembly, this is not true for contract electronics manufacturing. Of the top 20 contract electronics manufacturers, 12 are headquartered in the United States, 2 are in Canada, 1 is in France, 1 is in Finland, and only 5 are headquartered in Asia (3 in Singapore, 1 in Japan, and 1 in Taiwan). Most printed circuit assembly plants are located near computer, telecommunications, or other electronics plants. The fastest-growing locations for printed circuit assembly are central and eastern Europe and Brazil. Contract manufacturing in China is expected to grow rapidly. Other countries that are expected to experience an increase in contract manufacturing over the next few years are Australia, India, and Vietnam.

With the increase in outsourcing of computer and other electronics final assembly, printed circuit assembly companies have had to expand their presence into more markets and/or offer improved distribution. Assembly of electronic components onto PCBs is done not only in Asia but also in the United States, Mexico, the European Union (EU) countries, and eastern and central Europe. Mexico is popular because of its closeness to the U.S. market and NAFTA, and eastern and central Europe because of their proximity to the large markets of the EU.

Projections of Industry and Trade Growth for the Next 1 and 5 Years

Shipments by the U.S. passive components industry in 1998 increased an estimated 4.3 percent over the previous year, reaching $48.5 billion in current dollars (see Table 16-10). As the U.S. economy continued to grow and Asian markets recovered from the financial crisis, U.S. passive components shipments grew an estimated 5.3 percent in 1999 to reach a value of $51 billion. Shipments by the passive components industry are forecast to grow 6.4 percent in the year 2000 to approximately $54.4 billion. The long-term outlook for industry shipments calls for a compound annual growth rate of 6.4 percent, with shipments reaching a value of $69.8 billion in 2004.

As is noted in the box titled "Changes in Trade Data Caused by the Transition to NAICS," changes have been made to import and export data for passive components because of the reclassification of certain products in preparation for the use of NAICS to report economic and trade data formerly reported using the Standard Industrial Classification (SIC) system. The value of imports of passive components increased significantly as a result of this change because of the inclusion of imports of printed circuit assemblies in SIC 3679.

Exports of passive components by U.S. suppliers were estimated at $6.5 billion in 1999, up 4.6 percent over the previous year, when U.S. exports fell because of the Asian financial crisis. U.S. passive component exports are forecast to reach $6.9 billion in 2000, an increase of 7 percent. Over the longer term, passive components are forecast to experience a compound growth rate of more than 10 percent, reaching a value of $10.2 billion in 2004. Passive component imports totaled an estimated $33.3 billion in 1999 and are forecast to reach $37.9 billion in 2000, owing in large part to the continued strength of the U.S. economy. The rate of growth of passive component imports is expected to decrease from roughly 14 percent in both 1999 and 2000 to about 11.6 percent from 2000 to 2004, when their value is forecast to reach $58.8 billion.

Global Market Prospects

An upturn in the Asian markets, especially that of Japan, has improved market conditions for passive component manufacturers, especially in the capacitor and connector markets. U.S. exports of capacitors in 1998 were $1 billion and were expected to grow only 1.3 percent in 1999. The top three destinations for U.S. exports were Mexico ($909 million), the EU ($167 million), and Canada ($109 million). U.S. imports of capacitors were $1.4 billion and were expected to grow 7.4 percent in 1999. The top three importers of capacitors into the United States were Japan ($547 million), Mexico ($373 million), and Israel ($103 million).

Ceramic capacitators use palladium, which comes largely from Russia, and shipments were disrupted during the global financial crisis. By November 1999, palladium shipments from Russia were more stable, but prices for palladium rose to $397 per troy ounce, higher than the price of gold, and there were still reports of spot shortages. Palladium prices are expected to remain high because Russia is using palladium to guarantee some of its International Monetary Fund loans. In view of continuing high prices for palladium, U.S. and other ceramic capacitor manufacturers are increasing the nickel content of their products or considering switching to completely nickel-based ceramic capacitors.

In the first half of 1999, capacitor makers posted better quarterly sales and earning figures than analysts expected. Most analysts credit the recovering Asian market for the upturn. Japanese and other Asian capacitor companies are able to concentrate on their domestic customers and are exporting less product. The wireless communications industry is increasing demand for tantalum capacitors, which represent 25 percent of the total capacitor market, and lead times and prices are rising. Tantalum capacitor manufacturers were expected to show double-digit earnings in 1999. Because of their innovations in the use of nickel in their products and improved manufacturing techniques, ceramic capacitor companies were also, with the improvement in the Asian markets, expected to show double-digit earnings growth in 1999.

TABLE 16-10: Passive Components (SIC 3675, 3676, 3677, 3678, 3679) Trends and Forecasts
(millions of dollars except as noted)

	1992	1993	1994	1995	1996	1997[1]	1998[1]	1999[2]	2000[3]	Percent Change 97–98	98–99	99–00	96–00[4]
Industry data													
Value of shipments[5]	30,986	35,656	38,302	41,209	42,102	46,522	48,522	51,094	54,354	4.3	5.3	6.4	6.6
Value of shipments (1992$)	30,986	35,270	38,119	41,565	43,612	48,060	50,282	53,390	55,391	4.6	6.2	3.7	6.2
Total employment (thousands)	260	275	271	290	287	288	291	299	303	1.0	2.7	1.3	1.4
Production workers (thousands)	165	173	177	190	190	206	206	210	214	0.0	1.9	1.9	3.0
Average hourly earnings ($)	9.45	9.48	9.53	9.86	10.16	11.44	11.78	12.11	12.43	3.0	2.8	2.6	5.2
Capital expenditures	983	1,314	1,248	1,436	1,587	1,751	1,870	1,985	2,087	6.8	6.1	5.1	7.1
Product data													
Value of shipments[5]	32,330	33,892	37,540	42,435	46,800	49,748	53,480	54,389	56,238	7.5	1.7	3.4	4.7
Value of shipments (1992$)	32,330	33,523	37,350	42,805	48,584	51,393	55,419	56,832	58,888	7.8	2.5	3.6	4.9
Trade data													
Value of imports	14,122	17,244	18,710	24,977	23,689	25,684	29,109	33,276	37,935	13.3	14.3	14.0	12.5
Value of exports	2,888	3,198	3,924	4,714	5,410	6,642	6,166	6,449	6,900	–7.2	4.6	7.0	6.3

[1] Estimate except imports and exports.
[2] Estimate.
[3] Forecast.
[4] Compound annual rate.
[5] For a definition of industry versus product values, see "Getting the Most Out of *Outlook 2000.*"
Source: U.S. Department of Commerce: Bureau of the Census; International Trade Administration.

U.S. exports of resistors in 1998 were $522 million and were expected to grow 6.3 percent in 1999. The top three destinations for U.S. exports of resistors were Mexico ($185 million), the EU ($92 million), and Japan ($161 million). U.S. imports of resistors totaled $623 million and were expected to fall 5.9 percent in 1999, primarily because of a slowdown in imports from east and southeast Asian countries, especially Japan. The top three sources of U.S. imports of resistors were Japan ($204 million), Mexico ($108 million), and the EU ($92 million). Resistor manufacturers credit the rise in exports and the slowing of imports to the improving Asian market. This improvement has also stabilized resistor prices.

U.S. exports of inductors in 1998 totaled $886 million and were expected to grow only 1.1 percent in 1999. The top three destinations for U.S. exports were Mexico ($373 million), the EU ($162 million), and Canada ($77 million). U.S. imports of inductors totaled $1.2 billion and were expected to grow only 1.5 percent in 1999. The top three importers of inductors into the United States were Mexico ($427 million), China ($181 million), and Japan ($146 million). The U.S. inductor market is expected to continue to be neither a growing nor a shrinking market in the years ahead.

U.S. exports of electronic connectors in 1998 totaled $1,110 million and were expected to grow 9.8 percent in 1999. The top three destinations for U.S. exports were Mexico ($306 million), the EU ($256 million), and Canada ($229 million). U.S. imports of electronic connectors totaled $1,330 million and were expected to grow 4.9 percent in 1999. The top three importers of electronic components into the United States were Mexico ($377 million), Japan ($242 million), and the EU ($215 million). Connector manufacturers are seeing an improvement in their sales in Asia, and sales are continuing to grow in the U.S. market, especially in telecommunications. Consolidation is continuing in this industry, allowing manufacturers to expand their overseas presence.

The top five sources of U.S. imports of printed circuit assemblies (PCAs) are the same countries that are the top five sources for U.S. imports of all passive components. Malaysia is the top supplier of U.S. imports ($3 billion), followed by Canada ($2.5 billion), Taiwan ($2.3 billion), Mexico ($1.9 billion), and Japan ($1.1 billion). With the exception of Japan, PCAs make up more than 50 percent of the total U.S. passive component imports from those countries. U.S. imports of PCAs in 1998 were $18.4 billion, or 63 percent of total passive component imports. U.S. imports are dominated by PCAs for computer use (86 percent of total PCA imports, or $15.8 billion). Imports of PCAs are estimated to have grown by 29 percent from 1998 to 1999 and are expected to see continued growth in the year 2000 (see Table 16-11).

Dorothea Blouin, U.S. Department of Commerce, Office of Microelectronics, Medical Equipment and Instrumentation, (202) 482-1333, October 1999.

SEMICONDUCTOR MANUFACTURING EQUIPMENT

Semiconductor Manufacturing Equipment (SME) includes equipment used to fabricate, assemble, and test semiconductors. The Standard Industrial Classification system does not currently define SME as a separate industry. Its products are classified in such diverse industries as photographic equipment and supplies (SIC 3861); coating, engraving, and allied services (SIC 347); and special industrial equipment (SIC 3559).

TABLE 16-11: U.S. Trade Patterns in Passive Components[1] in 1998
(millions of dollars; percent)

Exports			Imports		
Region[2]	Value[3]	Share, %	Region[2]	Value[3]	Share, %
NAFTA	3,052	49	NAFTA	6,655	23
Latin America	374	6	Latin America	514	2
Western Europe	1,343	22	Western Europe	2,790	10
Japan/Chinese Economic Area	736	12	Japan/Chinese Economic Area	10,211	35
Other Asia	449	7	Other Asia	8,531	29
Rest of world	213	3	Rest of world	408	1
World	6,166	100	World	29,109	100
Top Five Countries	Value	Share, %	Top Five Countries	Value	Share, %
Mexico	2,160	35	Japan	3,997	14
Canada	892	14	Mexico	3,704	13
United Kingdom	362	6	Malaysia	3,356	12
Japan	300	5	Taiwan	3,227	11
Germany	270	4	Canada	2,951	10

[1] SIC 3675, 3676, 3677, 3678, 3679.
[2] For definitions of regional groupings, see "Getting the Most Out of *Outlook 2000*."
[3] Values may not sum to total due to rounding.
Source: U.S. Department of Commerce, Bureau of the Census.

Global and Domestic Industry Trends

The SME industry has grown at a compound rate of nearly 20 percent since 1992. The SME industry is global, capital-intensive, and highly cyclical, subject to boom-bust cycles. These circumstances require SME firms to be highly adaptive. At a time when firms are recovering from a drastic recession in the late 1990s, U.S. firms face increasing R&D, marketing, and customer service costs as products migrate to a new generation and customers become increasingly dispersed geographically.

The health of the SME industry is tied closely to trends in the semiconductor industry. Capital spending decisions of semiconductor producers determine orders to the SME industry. Semiconductor producers buy SME to expand their manufacturing capacity in response to demand for products or to upgrade production capacity for manufacturing more sophisticated products. The semiconductor industry's profitability affects the timing of its capital spending decisions. A collapse in the prices of semiconductor devices generally hurts the profitability of semiconductor manufacturers, which in turn may curtail spending on SME for next-generation semiconductor devices. Conversely, rising prices encourage expansion of semiconductor production capacity for both existing and next-generation devices.

The SME industry is highly cyclical, expanding and contracting in tandem with, but more dramatically than, revenue growth in the semiconductor industry. During the banner expansion of the semiconductor industry in 1995, the global SME industry grew 65 percent, its best performance in nearly two decades. In 1998, at the bottom of semiconductor industry recession of the late 1990s, the SME industry contracted 25 percent.

In recent years, the SME industry has become progressively more global. Today, SME firms in United States, Japan, and Europe—the major suppliers of SME on the world market—earn on average less than half their revenues from their home markets. In recent years, as semiconductor firms have made more offshore investments and entered into more joint ventures, SME firms have had to follow their customers to new markets. In addition, SME suppliers have started serving an emerging market: foreign semiconductor foundries or contract manufacturing plants.

During the last decade, as soaring development costs presented significant barriers to market entry, the SME industry became increasingly concentrated. Equipment prices have increased an average of 15 percent annually as the technology used to make semiconductors has become more sophisticated. According to some analysts, a steadily decreasing number of companies supply the SME market despite its continued growth. The world's 10 largest SME companies supply about 60 percent of the global market; the top 20 firms supply nearly 80 percent. This trend toward concentration probably will continue as large firms benefit from increasing economies of scale and mergers and acquisitions in the SME industry become more common.

The long-term prospects for the SME industry are good. As a result of continued growth in the computer and telecommunications sectors, semiconductor manufacturers will need to add manufacturing capacity to meet growing demand for new generations of the semiconductor devices used by those industries.

Over the next 5 years, the SME industry will begin a major product transition, moving from equipment based on a 200-mm (approximately 8-inch) standard for processing semiconductor wafers to a 300-mm (approximately 12-inch) standard. The 300-mm equipment will be more expensive but will increase productivity in manufacturing semiconductors considerably.

To respond to cyclical market fluctuations while maintaining long-term competitiveness, U.S. SME firms must manage their financial and personnel resources with a high degree of flexibility. In periods of a cyclical downturn, U.S. SME firms often focus on cash flow. Firms on average spend about 15 percent of revenues on R&D. Firms that reduce their absolute level of R&D spending during a downturn can hurt their future competitiveness. During high-growth periods, U.S. firms closely watch their order backlogs to ensure that customers do not defect to rival suppliers that can deliver products more quickly. The availability of qualified engineering and manufacturing personnel became a concern during the last boom cycle in the mid-1990s, when the U.S. SME industry increased production so rapidly that firms had trouble filling design and factory positions.

Projections of Industry and Trade Growth for the Next 1 and 5 Years

The global SME market in 1999 totaled an estimated $23 billion, a 4 percent increase over 1998. The United States is the largest market for SME, accounting for roughly $7.5 billion. Japan's market is valued at $5 billion, Taiwan's at $4 billion, that of the European Union at $3 billion, and Korea's and Singapore's at $1.5 billion each.

In recent years, U.S. SME market growth has closely corresponded to the growth rate of the world market. In the year 2000, analysts forecast growth in the U.S. market of 18 percent to nearly $9 billion, while the worldwide market also will grow 18 percent to $27 billion. Over the next 5 years, analysts forecast a compound growth rate of 15 percent in the United States and worldwide. By 2004, the value of the U.S. SME market will double to $15 billion and the world market will grow to $46 billion.

Historically, the wafer fabrication equipment segment has grown faster than have the assembly and test segments, and this trend probably will continue for the foreseeable future. Wafer fabrication equipment currently accounts for 65 percent of the value of the SME market and should account for 70 percent of that market by 2004. Semiconductor producers are demanding greater functionality from wafer fabrication equipment, and this has spurred strong growth in this segment. The test and assembly equipment segments will experience slightly slower rates of growth, and their shares of the total SME market will decline to an estimated 22 percent and 8 percent, respectively, by 2004.

Global Market Prospects

Japan is the chief competitor of the United States in SME. Currently, U.S. SME firms hold 50 percent of the world market, while Japanese firms have 42 percent. European firms account for the remaining 8 percent. The United States is a net exporter of SME. In 1998, it exported an estimated $3 billion of SME, compared with imports of $1.7 billion. U.S. firms currently supply nearly 70 percent of the U.S. SME market. The major sources of SME imports into the United States, in order of importance, are Japan, the Netherlands, and Germany.

The U.S. SME industry now earns the majority of its revenues from exports, and the export outlook is bright. Analysts expect U.S. SME exports to grow at a compound annual rate of 20 percent through 2004. U.S. exporters are strong in several markets that are expected to experience above-average growth. In 1998, the top five markets for U.S. SME exports, in descending order, were Taiwan, Japan, Korea, Singapore, and Ireland. As the rankings show, Asia is the dominant market for U.S. exporters.

Japan is the second largest SME market after the United States. However, the U.S. share of the Japanese SME market is only 20 percent, and Japan's importance to U.S. exporters has been declining in recent years. Although Japan has historically been the largest export market for U.S. firms, it has been eclipsed by faster-growing markets that are more receptive to U.S. equipment. In 1995, Korea briefly emerged as the top export market, and in 1997, Taiwan assumed that position. Japanese semiconductor firms have been severely affected by that country's financial crisis and declining profit margins from commodity semiconductors such as DRAM. Both factors have resulted in cutbacks and delays in Japanese capital investment. Analysts expect Japanese SME market growth to lag behind the world average during the next 5 years.

Taiwan is now the top market for U.S. exporters and the second largest Asian market for SME after Japan. In 1998, Taiwan bought over $900 million of SME from the United States. Taiwan has over a dozen semiconductor firms, which have ambitious capital expenditure plans. The financial position of Taiwan customers was not hampered by the Asian financial crisis or the collapse in DRAM prices, unlike that of firms in Japan and Korea. Taiwan has become the leading global center of the fast-growing market for semiconductor foundry services, and this will continue to drive capital expansion. Taiwan's chief constraint is the availability of engineering talent. Taiwan is expected to continue to grow considerably faster than the world average during the next 5 years.

Korean semiconductor manufacturers built numerous new plants to make DRAM in the first half of the 1990s, during which time the Korean SME market experienced explosive growth, at a compound annual rate of 50 percent. After peaking in 1996, the Korean SME market collapsed. Korean semiconductor producers faced falling profits from DRAM, a credit crunch, and a sharply devalued currency. In 1998, the value of Korean purchases of SME was one-third the level of the peak year of 1996. Korean semiconductor producers have restructured their industry and resumed purchasing SME, but the Korean market will not grow as fast as will other Asia-Pacific markets.

Other Asian markets will grow faster than the world average. After Taiwan, Singapore has seen the most solid market growth in the Asia-Pacific region and has surpassed many European nations in market size. Malaysia is a major market for assembly and test equipment and still hopes to construct wafer fabrication plants despite current credit difficulties. China is planning to build its competitive wafer fabrication capability during the next 5 years, and this may present opportunities for U.S. exporters.

Analysts expect the EU to experience average growth through 2004. Ireland has emerged as the top European market for U.S. SME exporters. Germany, France, the United Kingdom, Italy, and the Netherlands are other important markets.

Michael Andrews, U.S. Department of Commerce, Office of Microelectronics, Medical Equipment and Instrumentation, (202) 482-2795, October 1999.

■ REFERENCES

Advanced Packaging, IHS Publishing, 17730 West Peterson Road, P.O. Box 159, Libertyville, IL 60048. (847) 362-8711.

American Electronics Association (AEA), 1225 Eye Street, NW, Suite 950, Washington, DC 20005. (202) 682-9110, fax (202) 682-9111, http://www.aeanet.org/.

Bishop and Associates, 1209 Fox Drive, St. Charles, IL 60174. (630) 443-2702, http://bishopinc.com/.

Circuitree, 700 Gal Drive, Suite 200, Campbell, CA 95008-0901. (408) 364-3949.

Circuits Assembly, Miller Freeman Inc., 2000 Powers Ferry Center, Suite 450, Marietta, GA 30067. (404) 952-1303.

CleanRooms, Penn Well Publishing Company, 98 Spit Brook, 4th Floor, Nashua, NH 03062. (603) 891-0123, fax (603) 891-9200, http://www.cleanrooms.com/.

Dataquest, Inc., 251 River Oaks Parkway, San Jose, CA 95134-1913. (408) 468-8000, fax (408) 954-1780, http://www.dataquest.com/.

EDN, Cahners Publishing Company, 275 Washington Street, Newton, MA 02158. (617) 964-3030, fax (617) 558-4470, http://www.ednmag.com/.

EDN Asia, Cahners Asia Limited, 19/F, Eight Commercial Tower, 8 Sun Yip Street, Chaiwan, Hong Kong. (852) 2965-1555, fax (852) 2976-0706.

EDN China, China Electronic News Agency, 23 Shi Jing Shan Road, Beijing 100043, China. (011) 86-10-886-1813, fax (011) 86-10-886-1805.

Electronic Business Asia, Cahners Asia Ltd., 19/F, Eight Commercial Tower, 8 Sun Yip Street, Chaiwan, Hong Kong. (852) 2965-1555, fax (852) 2976-0706, http://www.eb-asia.com/.

Electronic Business Today, Cahners Publishing Company, 275 Washington Street, Newton, MA 02158. (617) 558-4563, fax (617) 558-4470, http://www.ebtmag.com/.

Electronic Buyers' News, CMP Media Inc., 600 Community Drive, Manhasset, NY 11030. (516) 562-5000, fax (516) 562-5123, http://www.ebnews.com/.

Electronic Design, Penton Publishing Inc., 611 Route 46 West, Hasbrouck Heights, NJ 07604. (201) 393-6060, fax (201) 393-0204, http://www.penton.com/ed/.

Electronic Engineering Times, CMP Media Inc., 600 Community Drive, Manhasset, NY 11030. (516) 562-5000, fax (516) 562-5325, http://techweb.cmp.com/eet/.

Electronic Industries Alliance (EIA), 2500 Wilson Boulevard, Arlington, VA 22201. (703) 907-7750, fax (703) 907-7501, http://www.eia.org/.

Electronic Materials Report, Rose Associates, 4 Main Street, Los Altos, CA 94022. (650) 941-1215, http://www.roseassociates.net/.

Electronic News, Electronic News Publishing Corp., 488 Madison Avenue, New York, NY 10022. (212) 909-5916, fax (212) 755-2751, http://www.sumnet.com/enews/.

Electronic Packaging & Production, Cahners Publishing Company, 1350 East Touhy Avenue, Box 5080, Des Plaines, IL 60017. (847) 635-8800, fax (847) 390-2770.

Electronic Products, Hearst Business Publishing Inc., 645 Stewart Avenue, Garden City, NY 11530. (516) 227-1300, fax (516) 227-1901, http://www.electronicproducts.com/.

Electronic Trend Publications, 1975 Hamilton Avenue, Suite 6, San Jose, CA 95125. (408) 369-7000, fax (408) 369-8021, http://www.electronictrendpubs.com/.

European Electronic Component Manufacturers Association (EECA), Avenue Louis 140, Boite 6, B 1050, Brussels, Belgium. (32) 2 646-5695, http://www.eeca.org.

Fabless Semiconductor Association (FSA), 13455 Noel Road, Suite 1000, Dallas, TX 75240. (214) 239-5119, fax (214) 774-4577, http://www.fsa.org/.

Fleck Research, 501 Golden Circle, No. 200, Santa Ana, CA 92705. (714) 953-9000, http://fleckresearch.com/home.htm/.

Freedonia Group, 767 Beta Drive, Cleveland, OH 44143. (440) 684-9600, http://www.freedoniagroup.com/.

Frost and Sullivan, 2525 Charleston Road, Mountain View, CA 94043. (650) 961-9000, http://www.frostandsullivan.com/.

Germany—Electronic Components, Market Research Report, Industry Sector Analysis, U.S. Department of Commerce, Foreign Commercial Service, 1998.

Henderson Ventures, 101 First Street, Suite 144, Los Altos, CA 94022. (415) 961-2900.

HTE Research, Inc., 400 Oyster Point Boulevard, Suite 220, South San Francisco, CA 94080. (415) 871-4377, fax (415) 871-0513, http://www.hte-sibs.com/.

Institute for Interconnecting and Packaging Electronic Circuits (IPC), 2215 Sanders Road, Northbrook, IL 60062. (847) 509-9700, fax (847) 509-9798, http://www.ipc.org/.

Integrated Circuit Engineering Corp., 15022 North 75 Street, Scottsdale, AZ 85260. (602) 998-9780, fax (602) 948-1925, http://www.ice-corp.com/.

Integrated System Design, Verecom Group, Inc., 5150 El Camino Real, Suite D31, Los Altos, CA 94022. (415) 903-0140, fax (415) 903-0151, http://.www.isdmag.com/.

International Microelectronics and Packaging Society (IMAPS), 1850 Centennial Park Drive, Suite 105, Reston, VA 22091. (703) 758-1060, fax (703) 758-1066, http://www.imaps.org/.

International Trade Monitor, Directorate of Intelligence, Central Intelligence Agency, November 1999. http://www.cia.gov/cia/di/.

MA36Q(97) Semiconductors, Printed Circuit Boards, and Other Electronic Components—1997, Current Industrial Reports, U.S. Department of Commerce, Economic Statistics Administration, Bureau of the Census, August 1998.

Manufacturing Market Insider, JBT Communications, P.O. Box 782, Needham Heights, MA 02494. (781) 444-2154, http://www.mfgmkt.com/.

Mexico–Baja California—Electronic Components, Market Research Report, Industry Sector Analysis, U.S. Department of Commerce, Foreign Commercial Service, 1998.

1997 Economic Census: Electron Tube Manufacturing, U.S. Department of Commerce, Census Bureau, Manufacturing and Construction Division, 1999. (301) 457-4673, http://www.census.gov/prod/www/abs/97ecmani.html/.

1997 Economic Census: Electronic Capacitor Manufacturing, U.S. Department of Commerce, Census Bureau, Manufacturing and Construction Division, 1999. (301) 457-4673, http://www.census.gov/prod/www/abs/97ecmani.html/.

1997 Economic Census: Electronic Coil, Transistor, and Other Inductor Manufacturing, U.S. Department of Commerce, Census Bureau, Manufacturing and Construction Division, 1999. (301) 457-4673, http://www.census.gov/prod/www/abs/97ecmani.html/.

1997 Economic Census: Electronic Connector Manufacturing, U.S. Department of Commerce, Census Bureau, Manufacturing and Construction Division, 1999. (301) 457-4673, http://www.census.gov/prod/www/abs/97ecmani.html/.

1997 Economic Census: Electronic Resistor Manufacturing, U.S. Department of Commerce, Census Bureau, Manufacturing and Construction Division, 1999. (301) 457-4673, http://www.census.gov/prod/www/abs/97ecmani.html/.

1997 Economic Census: Other Electronic Component Manufacturing, U.S. Department of Commerce, Census Bureau, Manufacturing and Construction Division, 1999. (301) 457-4673, http://www.census.gov/prod/www/abs/97ecmani.html/.

1997 Economic Census: Printed Circuit Assembly (Electronic Assembly) Manufacturing, U.S. Department of Commerce, Census Bureau, Manufacturing and Construction Division, 1999. (301) 457-4673, http://www.census.gov/prod/www/abs/97ecmani.html/.

N.T. Information LTD., 18 Strawberry Lane, Huntington, NY 11743. (516) 673-8571.

Printed Circuit Directories, P.O. Box 67202, Scotts Valley, CA 95067. (408) 353-4322.

Printed Circuit Fabrication, Miller Freeman Inc., 2000 Powers Ferry Center, Suite 450, Marietta, GA 30067. (404) 952-1303.

Production and Exports/Imports of Electronic Equipment, Electronic Industries Association of Japan (EIAJ), Tokyo Chamber of Commerce and Industry Building, 2-2 Marunouchi 3-chome, Chiyoda-Ku, Tokyo, Japan. (03) 3213-5863, http://www.eiaj.or.jp/english/index.htm/.

Semiconductor Equipment and Materials International (SEMI), 805 East Middlefield Road, Mountain View, CA 94043. (415) 964-5111, http://www.semi.org/.

Semiconductor Industry Association (SIA), 181 Metro Drive, Suite 450, San Jose, CA 95110. (408) 436-6600, fax (408) 436-6646, http://www.semichips.org/.

Semiconductor International, Cahners Publishing Company, 1350 East Touhy Avenue, Des Plaines, IL 60018. (847) 390-2296, fax (847) 390-2770, http://fablink.semiconductor.net/semiconductor/.

Solid State Technology, Penn Well Publishing Company, 98 Spit Brook, 4th Floor, Nashua, NH 03062. (603) 891-0123, fax (603) 891-0597, http://sst.pennwellnet.com/.

Status of Korean Electronics Industry, Electronic Industry Association of Korea, 12th Floor, Electronics Building 648, Yeosam-dong, Kangnam-Ku Seoul, South Korea (135-080). (02) 2646-5695, http://www.eiak.org/.

Surface Mount Technology, IHS Publishing Group, 17730 West Peterson Road, P.O. Box 159, Libertyville, IL 60048. (847) 362-8711, fax (847) 362-3484.

Technology Forecasters, 1420 Harbor Bay Parkway, Suite 295, Alameda, CA 94502. (510) 747-1900, http://www.techforecasters.com/.

VLSI Research, Inc., 1754 Technology Drive, Suite 117, San Jose, CA 95110. (408) 453-8844, fax (408) 437-0608, http://www.vlsir.com/.

RELATED CHAPTERS

23: Industrial and Analytical Instruments
24: Photographic Equipment and Supplies
27: Computer Equipment
29: Space Commerce
30: Telecommunications Services
31: Telecommunications and Navigation Equipment
36: Motor Vehicles
38: Household Consumer Durables
44: Medical and Dental Instruments and Supplies

GLOSSARY

Active component: A nonmechanical circuit component that has gain or switches current flow, such as a diode or transistor.

Analog: Refers to a continuous value that most closely resembles the real world and can be as precise as the measuring technique allows.

Analog circuit: A collection of components used to generate or process analog signals.

Application specific integrated circuit (ASIC): An integrated circuit designed to meet a specific customer requirement.

Assembly: The final stage of semiconductor manufacturing, in which the active device is encased in a plastic, ceramic, or metal package. Also referred to as back-end processing.

Capacitor: An electrical component that builds and stores voltage for release on command.

Chip: An integrated circuit or discrete device. Also called a die.

Circuit board: The generic name for a wide variety of interconnection techniques, which include rigid, flexible, and rigid-flex boards in single-sided, double-sided, multilayer, and discrete wired configurations.

Conductor, electrical: A material capable of carrying (conducting) electricity. Silver is the best electrical conductor. Copper, gold, and aluminum are also popular conductors.

Die: A single square or rectangular piece of semiconductor material into which a specific electrical circuit has been fabricated. The plural is "dice." Also called a chip or device (integrated circuit or discrete).

Digital: Refers to a method of representing information in an electrical circuit by switching the current on or off. Only two output voltages are possible, usually represented by 0 and 1.

Digital circuit: A circuit that operates like a switch and can perform logical functions. Used in computers or similar logic-based equipment.

Digital signal processor (DSP): A primarily digital component used to process either digital or analog signals. In the latter case, the signal may be conditioned and then converted into a digital equivalent by using an analog-to-digital (A/D) converter function. The signal conditioning and A/D functions may be external to the DSP or resident in the device. A typical DSP application is the compression and decompression of video data.

Diode: A two-terminal device that conducts electricity only in one direction; in the other direction, it behaves like an open switch. The term "diode" typically is taken to refer to a semiconductor device, although alternative implementations such as vacuum tubes are available.

Discrete device: A semiconductor containing only one active element, such as a transistor or a diode.

Double-sided: Refers to a printed circuit board with tracks on both sides.

Dry etch: The process that uses radiofrequency energy and gas phase chemicals to remove a specific layer during semiconductor processing.

Dynamic random-access memory (DRAM): A memory device in which each cell is formed from a transistor-capacitor pair. Called dynamic because the capacitor loses its charge over time and each cell must be periodically recharged if it is to retain its data.

Electron tube: An enclosed device consisting of at least two plates that is capable of varying current from one side to the other in response to the characteristics of a signal or under the control of another device. The most basic form of tube having just two plates is called a diode.

Etching: The process of removing material (such as oxides or other thin films) by chemical, electrolytic, or plasma (ion bombardment) means.

Fabless: Refers to a semiconductor company that does not have its own wafer manufacturing facility but subcontracts wafer manufacturing.

Fabrication: In semiconductor manufacturing, usually refers to the front-end process of making devices on semiconductor wafers but usually does not include the package assembly (back-end) stages.

Inductor: A passive component that opposes changes in current flow that result from lagging current changes relative to voltage changes. Inductors acts as antennas and interference suppressors to block out signal interference in television sets, radios, stereos, and telecommunications equipment.

Insulator: A material that is a poor conductor of electricity; used to separate conductors from one another or to protect personnel from electricity.

Integrated circuit (IC): A semiconductor die containing multiple elements that act together to form the complete device circuit.

Interconnect: A conductive connection between two or more circuit elements; the conductors among elements (transistors, resistors, etc.) on an integrated circuit or between components on a printed circuit board.

Leadframe: A stamped or etched metal frame that provides external electrical connections for a packaged electrical device.

Linear circuit: A circuit whose output is an amplified version of its input or whose output is a predetermined variation of its input.

Line width: Usually refers to a dimension on a mask or a feature on an integrated circuit.

Lithography: The transfer of a pattern or image from one medium to another, as from a mask to a wafer. If light is used to effect the transfer, the term "photolithography" applies. Microlithography refers to the process as it is applied to images with features in the submicron range.

Magnetron: An electron tube used to generate microwave radiation for applications that include telephony and radar.

Microcomputer: A microprocessor complete with stored program memory (ROM), random-access memory (RAM), and input/output (I/O) logic. Microcomputers can perform useful work without additional supporting logic. If all functions are on the same chip, it is sometimes called a microcontroller.

Microprocessor: The basic arithmetic logic of a computer; also called a microprocessor unit (MPU).

Monolithic device: A device whose circuitry is completely contained on a single die or chip.

Package: The protective container for an electronic component, with terminals to provide electrical access to the components inside.

Passive component: An electrical component without "gain," or current-switching capability. Commonly used to refer to resistors, capacitors, or inductors.

Printed circuit board (PCB): A substrate on which a predetermined pattern or printed wiring and printed element has been formed. Also called a printed wiring board (PWB).

Perfluorinated hydrocarbons (also called perfluorocarbons) (PFCs): Greenhouse gases emitted as by-products of industrial processes such as semiconductor manufacturing.

Random-access memory (RAM): An element that stores digital information temporarily and can be changed as required. It constitutes the basic (read/write) storage element in a computer.

Read-only memory (ROM): A computer element that permanently stores information that is repeatedly used, such as tables of data and characters of electronic displays. Unlike RAM, it cannot be altered.

Resistor: An electrical component used to modify voltage or current in a circuit by providing resistance.

Semiconductor: A material with the properties of both a conductor and an insulator. Common semiconductors include silicon and germanium.

Silicon (Si): The basic element used in most semiconductor devices, such as diodes, transistors, and integrated circuits.

Substrate: The material on which a microelectronic device is built. Such material may be active, like silicon, or passive, like alumina ceramic.

Transformer: An electrical component used to modify voltage or other characteristics between one circuit and another.

Transistor: An active semiconductor device with three electrodes that may be either an amplifier or a switch.

METALWORKING EQUIPMENT
Economic and Trade Trends

Source: U.S. Department of Commerce: Bureau of the Census, International Trade Administration.

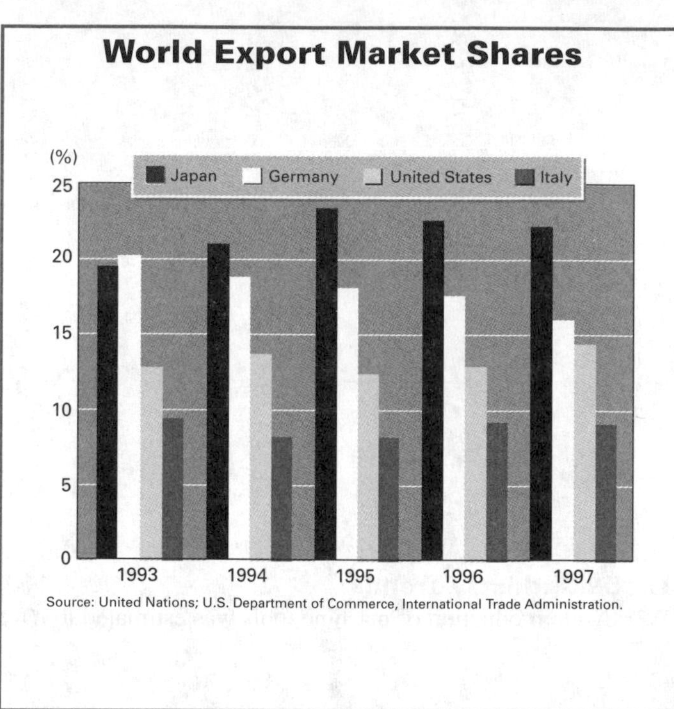

Source: United Nations; U.S. Department of Commerce, International Trade Administration.

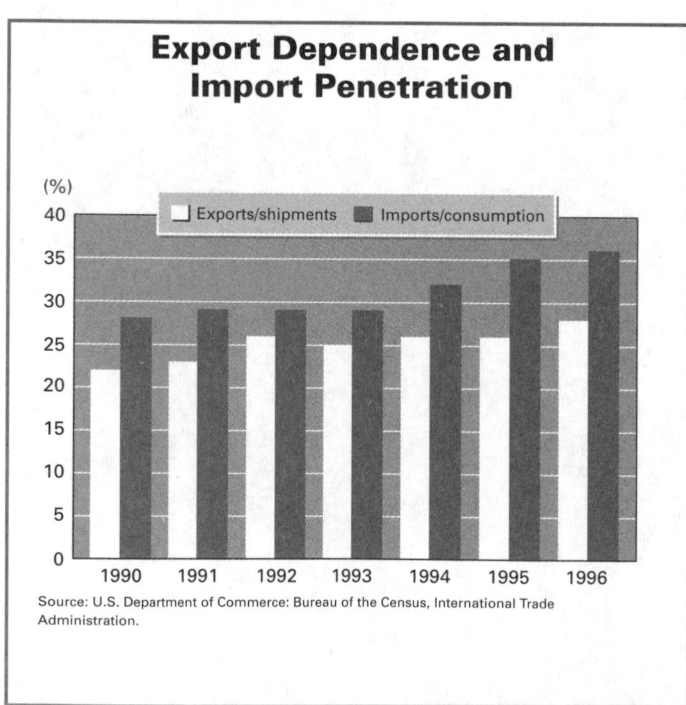

Source: U.S. Department of Commerce: Bureau of the Census, International Trade Administration.

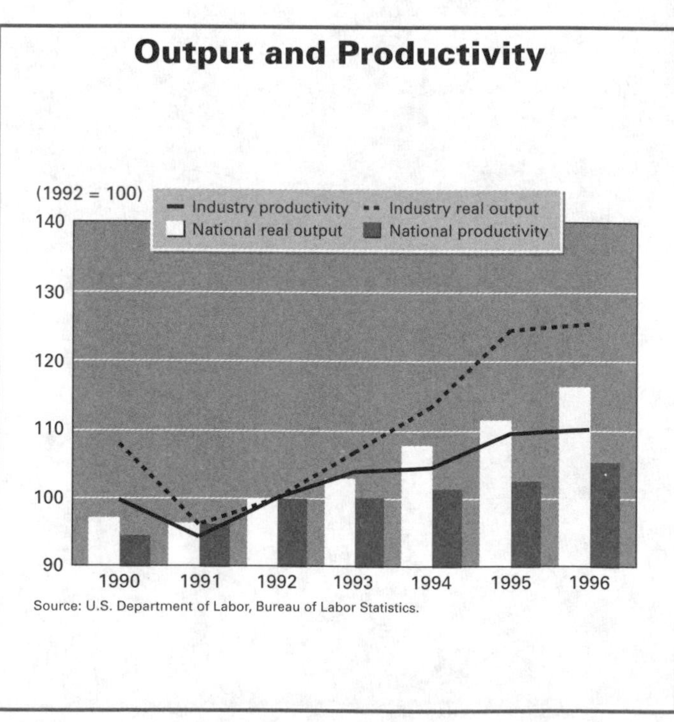

Source: U.S. Department of Labor, Bureau of Labor Statistics.

See "Getting the Most Out of *Outlook 2000*" for definitions of terms.

17

Metalworking Equipment

INDUSTRY DEFINITION Metalworking equipment includes machine tools (SIC 3541, 3542), machine tool accessories (SIC 3545), metal cutting tools (SIC 35415), special dies and tools (SIC 3544), power-driven hand tools (SIC 3546), and welding apparatus (SIC 3548). Trade patterns in 1998 for this industry are presented in Table 17-1.

MACHINE TOOLS

A machine tool is a power-driven, not hand-held machine used to cut, form, or shape metal. The industry consists of about 16 primary product groups under two codes: SIC 3541, metal cutting machines, and SIC 3542, metal forming machines.

Global Industry Trends

Worldwide production of machine tools was estimated to have declined in 1998 and 1999 (see Table 17-2). The major underlying factors were the depressed economies in Asia and South America. Before the financial crises, the countries in those regions had the fastest-growing demand for machine tools. Exports to those countries of products made with machine tools contributed to the robust growth of the global machine tool industry.

In 1998 and 1999, the weakness of the world economy led to significant excess capacity in many manufacturing sectors, negating the need for machine tools for new production lines. The slumping world economy also precipitated lower profits and decreased capital outlays for investments in new capital equipment such as machine tools. Many of the high-technology consuming sectors were still expanding, but at slower rates.

The globalization of many manufacturing industries, which has led to increased price competitiveness, has benefited machine tool manufacturers around the world. As a result of the

TABLE 17-1: U.S. Trade Patterns in Selected Metalworking Machinery[1] in 1998
(millions of dollars; percent)

Exports			Imports		
Region[2]	Value[3]	Share, %	Region[2]	Value[3]	Share, %
NAFTA	2,149	38	NAFTA	785	9
Latin America	449	8	Latin America	70	1
Western Europe	1,558	27	Western Europe	3,462	38
Japan/Chinese Economic Area	746	13	Japan/Chinese Economic Area	4,310	47
Other Asia	425	7	Other Asia	275	3
Rest of world	384	7	Rest of world	290	3
World	5,711	100	World	9,192	100
Top Five Countries	Value	Share, %	Top Five Countries	Value	Share, %
Canada	1,397	24	Japan	3,275	36
Mexico	752	13	Germany	1,387	15
United Kingdom	371	6	Canada	572	6
Germany	371	6	Taiwan	569	6
Japan	296	5	China	427	5

[1] SIC 3541, 3542, 3545, 3546, 3548.
[2] For definitions of regional groupings, see "Getting the Most Out of *Outlook 2000*."
[3] Values may not sum to total due to rounding.
Source: U.S. Department of Commerce, Bureau of the Census.

TABLE 17-2: Machine Tools (SIC 3541, 3542) Trends and Forecasts
(millions of dollars except as noted)

										Percent Change			
	1992	1993	1994	1995	1996	1997[1]	1998[1]	1999[2]	2000[3]	97–98	98–99	99–00	96–00[4]
Industry data													
Value of shipments[5]	5,102	5,231	5,366	6,089	6,357	6,910	6,530	5,812	5,766	–5.5	–11.0	–0.8	–2.4
3541 Metal cutting machines	3,618	3,518	3,672	4,065	4,143								
3542 Metal forming machines	1,484	1,713	1,694	2,024	2,213								
Value of shipments (1992$)	5,102	5,152	5,196	5,695	5,771	6,123	5,633	4,957	4,858	–8.0	–12.0	–2.0	–4.2
3541 Metal cutting machines	3,618	3,476	3,579	3,817	3,770								
3542 Metal forming machines	1,484	1,676	1,617	1,877	2,001								
Total employment (thousands)	39.9	38.0	37.1	40.4	40.4								
3541 Metal cutting machines	27.4	25.3	24.0	27.0	26.9								
3542 Metal forming machines	12.5	12.7	13.1	13.4	13.5								
Production workers (thousands)	23.3	22.3	22.0	24.5	24.7								
3541 Metal cutting machines	15.4	14.5	13.7	16.0	16.2								
3542 Metal forming machines	7.9	7.8	8.3	8.5	8.5								
Average hourly earnings ($)	15.34	15.72	16.16	16.25	16.74								
3541 Metal cutting machines	15.54	15.75	16.31	16.26	16.85								
3542 Metal forming machines	14.93	15.68	15.91	16.24	16.52								
Capital expenditures	124	96	131	190	169								
3541 Metal cutting machines	83	63	106	134	117								
3542 Metal forming machines	41	33	25	56	52								
Product data													
Value of shipments[5]	4,521	4,524	5,098	5,747	6,088	6,618	6,254	5,566	5,521	–5.5	–11.0	–0.8	–2.4
3541 Metal cutting machines	3,093	2,915	3,435	3,906	4,082								
3542 Metal forming machines	1,428	1,609	1,663	1,841	2,006								
Value of shipments (1992$)	4,521	4,455	4,934	5,375	5,528	5,865	5,396	4,748	4,653	–8.0	–12.0	–2.0	–4.2
3541 Metal cutting machines	3,093	2,881	3,347	3,668	3,714								
3542 Metal forming machines	1,428	1,574	1,587	1,707	1,814								
Trade data													
Value of imports	2,350	2,621	3,445	4,456	4,837	5,377	5,782	4,972	5,320	7.5	–14.0	7.0	2.4
3541 Metal cutting machines	1,681	1,882	2,385	3,101	3,415	3,816	4,110			7.7			
3542 Metal forming machines	669	739	1,060	1,354	1,422	1,562	1,673			7.1			
Value of exports	1,902	1,804	2,258	2,412	2,753	2,983	2,944	2,708	2,843	–1.3	–8.0	5.0	0.8
3541 Metal cutting machines	1,017	975	1,353	1,350	1,662	1,768	1,692			–4.3			
3542 Metal forming machines	885	829	905	1,061	1,090	1,215	1,251			3.0			

[1] Estimate except imports and exports.
[2] Estimate.
[3] Forecast.
[4] Compound annual rate.
[5] For a definition of industry versus product values, see "Getting the Most Out of *Outlook 2000.*"
Source: U.S. Department of Commerce: Bureau of the Census; International Trade Administration.

need to cut costs and develop improved and innovative products, many manufacturers must invest in the advanced technology incorporated in machine tools.

Japan remains the largest machine tool producer, followed by Germany and the United States. Other major producing countries include Italy, Switzerland, Taiwan, China, the United Kingdom, France, and South Korea. Japan, the United States, and the European Union (EU) producers dominate the high end of the market but have been overtaken by Taiwan, China, and South Korea in producing commodity-type machine tools. The industrialized countries have an advantage in quality and service but have a hard time competing on a price basis because of their higher costs of production.

Competition among the world's machine tool manufacturers is fierce. To better serve customers in the larger developing countries, many Japanese, European, and American manufacturers are establishing overseas operations in China, Thailand, Indonesia, India, and Brazil. Their operations include service centers, distribution centers, and manufacturing facilities. Many of those operations serve burgeoning automotive industries in those countries.

Overview of the U.S. Machine Tool Industry

Despite the sharp drop in shipments in 1999, the U.S. machine tool industry is relatively healthy. The industry is characterized by sharp swings in demand for machine tools. The decline in 1999 followed a period of relatively high levels of shipments. The number of industry establishments is about 600. There continue to be a number of mergers and acquisitions, but their frequency has fallen off. The U.S. industry has about 40,000 employees, and plants are concentrated in the midwest and northeast. The states with the largest concentrations are Ohio, Michigan, and Illinois.

The industry's customer base continues to follow historical patterns, with the exception of the job shop sector, which has increased in importance in recent years. The automotive sector remains the industry's largest customer group, followed by the job shop and aerospace sectors. The appliance and off-highway and construction machinery industries are also significant markets. The medical equipment industry is one of the fastest-growing customer groups.

The composition of the industry changed during the 1990s as a result of consolidation and foreign investment in U.S. machine tool companies. A spate of buyouts and acquisitions occurred, and a number of privately held companies became publicly owned. A wave of investment in the United States by the European automotive industry precipitated similar investments by European machine tool producers, which established U.S. production facilities to supply their primary customer group. Japanese investment also picked up in the first half of the decade, driven by the strong yen. The newcomers joined a contingent of Japanese machine tool manufacturers that had established U.S. production facilities in the 1980s in response to U.S. import restrictions that later were lifted.

A strong commitment to exporting and the sustained expansion of the U.S. economy are key elements in the machine tool industry's newfound stability. Changes in the automotive sector are also important. The automotive industry is far less cyclical than it was in the past. Automakers are undertaking more frequent and less extensive design changes and are becoming globalized, tailoring their products to individual markets. This has led to ongoing investment programs rather than concentrated purchasing cycles. The increasing globalization of the automotive sector is encouraging a similar trend among machine tool suppliers. U.S. machine tool companies are increasing their worldwide presence, often through joint ventures, cooperative agreements, and strategic alliances. The countries that have attracted the most investment are Mexico, Brazil, India, and China.

Domestic Trends and Factors Affecting U.S. Industry Growth

Advances in technology are effecting major changes in the U.S. machine tool industry. The computerization of the industry is leading to rapid improvements in existing machine tool product lines and the development of new products. Machine tool producers are manufacturing products with vastly expanded capabilities and a significant improvement in precision. The shortage of skilled labor and the relatively high cost of labor are driving the demand for machine tools with greater flexibility that are programmable to replace or reduce the need for more sophisticated operators.

The increased competitiveness of major consuming industries such as the automotive and job shop sectors is driving the demand for more sophisticated machines. End users are investing in machine tools that offer increased performance, flexibility, and productivity.

Rapidly changing consumer tastes and shorter product life cycles are driving the demand for machine tools with greater flexibility. Manufacturers need machine tools that are conducive to short changeover times for small-lot production. End users increasingly are buying machining centers capable of performing a range of functions with minimal setup times. Machining and turning centers are in many cases replacing two to three machines as a result of the more advanced technology available. Machining centers can be more easily integrated into production lines. Traditional transfer line technology often is being replaced by the technology incorporated in these more flexible machines and the use of less expensive manufacturing cells. Some of the greatest growth in demand for machine tools is coming from the job shop sector, which is expanding as a result of outsourcing by large manufacturers.

Demand for high-speed machining technology is coming from a range of user industries. This technology is used increasingly by the aerospace, automotive, and die and mold industries to machine aluminum. Use of the technology is expected to grow steadily as producers across the manufacturing sector face increasing pressure to improve accuracy, efficiency, and productivity. Environmental concerns also are driving investment and research in new technology. Many end users are asking for machines that produce less waste and are less dependent on coolants and other fluids that have environmental and health ramifications.

Machine tool builders are developing new machining techniques to handle the increasing use of alternative materials in place of traditional metal. In addition to the automotive and aerospace sectors, there is an increased use of exotic metals as well as polymers such as cast nylon and plastics by more and more industries. These newer materials also have unique machining requirements not possible on many conventional machine tools.

Some nontraditional cutting methods are gaining ground on traditional methods. There is an increased use of lasers as well as electrical discharge machining (EDM) and waterjet machining. These technologies currently represent niche markets but have the potential for significant growth.

Advances in control technology are contributing to improvements in machining precision, flexibility, and speed. Personal computer (PC)-based controls have the advantage of being easy to upgrade when there are advances in software technology. Another advantage is that more machine functions can be addressed by machine operators, giving operators greater flexibility.

Environmental issues remain a concern for the U.S. machine tool industry. Fluids, mist, and metal scrap are three of the larger environmental issues the industry is dealing with. Dry cutting is a process that is being used to help address fluid and mist problems. To reduce the need for fluids, drill bits and other cutting tools are being treated with heat-resistant coatings such as diamond, cubic boron nitride, and titanium-aluminum-nitride. Dry machining methods and improved cutting tool configurations are resulting in higher metal removal rates and better part geometry.

Global Market Prospects

World demand for U.S. metal cutting and metal forming machine tools declined in 1998 and 1999 as a result of the financial crises in several Asian and South American economies. There was a decline in world exports of machine tools to those markets and sharp drops in exports of machinery and equipment from major machine tool consuming industries. With the globalization of the world's machine tool industries and markets, many machine tool companies have become dependent on exports. U.S. exports currently account for about 40 percent of U.S. production of machine tools. However, many small and medium-size companies with limited resources focus only on a limited number of markets.

Currently there are strong competitive pressures because of the weak world demand for machine tools. The ability of U.S. companies to win orders for their tools depends on a number of factors in addition to the capabilities of their machines. Price is an important factor, and the course of foreign exchange rates will play a major role in the ability of U.S. machine tool companies to increase their exports. The ability to offer competitive financing is a critical factor in competing with foreign competitors, especially in developing countries. European and Japanese machine tool companies often have access to financing that U.S. firms cannot provide.

There are other obstacles that U.S. machine tool producers must overcome in developing foreign markets. U.S. export controls have a significant impact on the ability of U.S. machine tool companies to sell in some foreign markets. The ability to service the machine tools is another critical factor in winning export contracts. U.S. machine tool manufacturers must be able to establish some form of local representation in order to be accepted in foreign markets.

Machine tool exports declined an estimated 8 percent to $2,708 million in 1999 (see Table 17-2). Exports of metal cutting machine tools declined roughly 10 percent, and those of metal forming machine tool declined 5 percent. Mexico replaced Canada as the largest purchaser of U.S. machine tool exports in 1999. Exports to Mexico increased a projected 18 percent, while exports to Canada dropped 18 percent. Machine tool exports to the EU, which accounted for 26 percent of the total, declined about 2 percent in 1999. Asia accounted for 25 percent of total machine tool exports. Exports to Asian markets dropped an estimated 7 percent in 1999 after an 11 percent decline in 1998. The export markets ranked third to tenth were United Kingdom, Germany, Japan, Taiwan, China, France, Brazil, and South Korea. U.S. machine tool exports to France and Brazil increased 17 percent and 42 percent, respectively, while the value of exports to the other six markets registered a decline. Venezuela and Switzerland dropped out of the top 10 markets after declines of approximately 80 percent and 40 percent, respectively.

With the expected recovery of their economies, the newly industrializing countries of Asia and South America are expected to have the fastest-growing demand for machine tools. The trend toward globalization in a wide range of industries, particularly the automotive sector, will ensure continued growth in offshore demand for capital equipment. Global manufacturers are building plants throughout the world to supply markets from local operations.

Mexico. Mexico has been one of the U.S. machine tool industry's most important export markets for many years. With the recovery of Mexico's economy, U.S. exports to that country boomed in 1999. U.S. machine tool exporters have a competitive advantage in Mexico over other major foreign machine tool manufacturers because of the lower tariff rates they face as a result of the North American Free Trade Agreement (NAFTA). Under NAFTA, various U.S.-built machine tool products have received immediate duty-free status, and the remaining duties are being phased out. Tariffs on machine tools from non-NAFTA members range from 10 to 20 percent.

Ambitious investment plans for the Mexican automotive, appliance, and heavy equipment industries bode well for the continued strength of U.S. machine tool exports. New automotive plants are being built to meet expected future growth in automobile demand. Mexico's automotive parts sector also is undergoing a strong expansion.

China. With Asia's ongoing recovery from the financial crisis, prospects for U.S. machine tool exports to China are improving. That country's plans to accelerate domestic manufacturing are still on track. The level of U.S. machine tool exports to China from 1997 to 1999 was significantly below the level reached in 1996, but the agreement China reached with the United States to reduce tariff rates on a wide range of products should stimulate expanded machine tool exports to China.

Brazil. Brazil and the other countries in the Southern Cone region hold significant potential for U.S. machine tool exports. Efforts are under way in Brazil and many other South American countries to revamp domestic industries by lifting import restrictions and lowering tariffs and other barriers to trade. All these actions are favorably affecting demand for machine tool imports. Brazil has a population of over 170 million, and its overall economy is healthy. Its current political stability enhances its potential.

The depressed U.S. demand for machine tools in 1999 had an impact on imports of machine tools, which declined an estimated 14 percent. Despite a 15 percent drop in imports from Japan in 1999, Japan remains the largest foreign supplier to the U.S. market, with a 42 percent share of machine tool imports. Germany remained the second largest supplier with a 16 percent share. The third to tenth largest suppliers were Canada (8 percent), Taiwan (6 percent), Switzerland (5 percent), Italy (5 percent), United Kingdom (3 percent), South Korea (3 percent), China (2 percent), and France (1 percent). Imports from Canada and China increased an estimated 2 percent and 7 percent, respectively, and declines were registered for the other six countries.

U.S. Industry Growth Projections

U.S. machine tool product shipments in constant dollars dropped an estimated 12 percent in 1999. The decline was attributable largely to the financial crises in Asia and South America, which severely weakened the economies of many countries and led to sharp drops in exports of machine tools to those regions. Domestic demand was also weak, particularly from sectors that had been registering large increases in exports to the Asian and South American markets. Demand from the automotive sector, the largest machine tool end user, softened with the leveling off of automotive production. Machine tool shipments to the farm machinery and aerospace industries were particularly weak. Other major consumers include the appliance, construction machinery, and job shop industries. The strength of the construction industry benefited machine tool builders for the appliance and construction machinery sectors. The growth of the job shop industry and its investment in new high-technology equipment to improve quality and precision have led to increased shipments to that sector.

The U.S. machine tool industry is showing signs of rebounding from the drop in product shipments in 1999, but constant dollar shipments are still expected to decline about 2 percent in the year 2000 (see Table 17-2). Weak demand from many foreign markets and relatively low capacity utilization rates in most major machine tool consuming industries are the major reasons for the expected decline. Little growth is expected in demand from the automotive sector as production levels register little if any growth in 2000, and there are few plans for new production lines. A bright spot is the expected continued strong demand from the job shop industry. In their drive to remain competitive, many job shops will continue to upgrade their machining capabilities. The trend toward outsourcing by major manufacturing sectors, particularly the automotive industry, is expected to contribute to an expansion of the job shop industry and lead to increased demand for machine tools. Machine tool demand from farm machinery manufacturers and aerospace companies is expected to remain weak in the year 2000.

U.S. machine tool manufacturers can expect moderate growth in shipments in the period 2000–2004. Projections call for average annual growth of 3 to 4 percent. The rising demand for capital equipment will be driven by manufacturers' need to improve productivity and invest in labor-saving equipment. Price increases will be virtually nonexistent as manufacturers continue to place strong pressure on machine tool suppliers. The metal cutting sector is expected to be somewhat stronger than the metal forming sector.

Prospects for export markets are mixed. Some export markets showed signs of rebounding in 1999, but other markets remain depressed. Exports to Canada are expected to improve and shipments to Mexico are expected to continue to expand, but not at the rate registered in 1999. The forecast is for exports to increase 5 percent in 2000 compared with 1999.

Richard Reise, U.S. Department of Commerce, Office of Energy, Infrastructure and Machinery, (202) 482-3489, November 1999.

MACHINE TOOL ACCESSORIES

The machine tool accessories subsector (SIC 3545) (NAICS 333515) includes establishments engaged primarily in manufacturing cutting tools; machinists' precision measuring tools such as comparators and micrometers; and work and tool holders, including vises, attachments, and accessories for machine tools and other metalworking machinery. The cutting tool subsector (SIC 35451) is the largest subsector in this industry. Metal cutting tools perform the actual cutting operation for a machine tool and require frequent replacement and resharpening. They include drills, taps, reamers, and various forms of indexable inserts. An insert is a form of tool with two or more cutting edges that can be repositioned quickly during the machining process.

Global Trends

The principal markets for machine tool accessories are in the industrialized countries, which account for the large majority of machine tool sales. Most cutting tools are supplied by locally or regionally based manufacturers and distributors. Each leading international market has developed a discrete set of principal suppliers that often are internally based. Consequently, export opportunities for U.S.-based manufacturers of cutting tools have been limited, and most U.S. production has been destined for domestic markets or the NAFTA partners. In an effort to expand sales in foreign markets, U.S. manufacturers have begun to establish more international stocking points and acquire foreign companies that can provide the service and parts needed to maintain an effective presence in a foreign market. The U.S. industry anticipates expanded export opportunities for precision tools.

Domestic Trends

Job shops account for a large share of cutting tool sales in the domestic market. The major end user of these tools is the automotive industry. Other leading customers for cutting tools include manufacturers of industrial machinery, aircraft, off-road vehicles, white goods, tools and dies, and electrical machinery.

The preeminence of small business in this industry is clearly shown in the size and distribution of its establishments. Employing a significant portion of its workforce in small machine shops, the industry reported total 1997 employment of 47,800 employees, of whom 34,700 were production workers (see Table 17-3). In 1997, the industry consisted of 1,816 companies with 1,916 establishments. Only 499 establishments reported having more than 20 employees and only 108 reported having more than 100 in 1997. The production of machine tool accessories is concentrated in the Great Lakes states, with Michigan the leading producer state (349 establishments and 8,582 employees), followed by Illinois (189 establishments and 5,281 employees) and Ohio (179 establishments and 4,837 employees). The rest of the top producer states ranked by total employment are California, Pennsylvania, South Carolina, Wisconsin, Massachusetts, and Connecticut.

Metal cutting tools constitute the largest product class in this industry, averaging 50 to 55 percent of product shipments.

TABLE 17-3: Machine Tool Accessories (SIC 3545) Trends and Forecasts
(millions of dollars except as noted)

										Percent Change			
	1992	1993	1994	1995	1996	1997[1]	1998[1]	1999[2]	2000[3]	97–98	98–99	99–00	96–00[4]
Industry data													
Value of shipments[5]	3,844	4,003	4,698	5,341	5,893	5,336	5,704	6,040	6,310	6.9	5.9	4.5	1.7
Value of shipments (1992$)	3,844	3,940	4,548	5,030	5,416	4,761	4,990	5,175	5,299	4.8	3.7	2.4	–0.5
Total employment (thousands)	43.3	43.3	46.7	51.1	55.6	47.8							
Production workers (thousands)	30.6	30.5	32.7	35.8	39.3	34.7							
Average hourly earnings ($)	12.03	12.79	12.48	12.46	13.06								
Capital expenditures	144	164	188	245	283								
Product data													
Value of shipments[5]	3,606	3,798	4,401	4,864	5,146	4,958	5,316	5,655	5,927	7.2	6.4	4.8	3.6
Value of shipments (1992$)	3,606	3,739	4,260	4,580	4,730	4,276	4,494	4,683	4,819	5.1	4.2	2.9	0.5
Trade data													
Value of imports	535	613	741	908	935	1,001	1,139	1,179	1,226	13.8	3.5	4.0	7.0
Value of exports	427	586	661	771	856	905	919	1,010	1,071	1.5	9.9	6.0	5.8

[1] Estimate except imports and exports.
[2] Estimate.
[3] Forecast.
[4] Compound annual rate.
[5] For a definition of industry versus product values, see "Getting the Most Out of *Outlook 2000.*"
Source: U.S. Department of Commerce: Bureau of the Census; International Trade Administration.

Demand for metal cutting tools is closely linked to production levels for the machine tool industry. Technological advancement in the cutting tool industry also is closely linked to the demands of the machine tool industry for new and improved technology, including competitive pressures to increase productivity.

Metal cutting tools are divided into standards and specials. In 1998, 69 percent of all tooling manufactured was standards and 31 percent was specials, closely approximating the historical 70–30 ratio between the two types. A large percentage of small shops (those with 25 or fewer employees) specialize in producing special tooling. The larger manufacturers (those with over 100 employees) concentrate on standard tooling.

The impact of technology on the value of product shipments has gone in two opposite directions. High-technology products usually carry higher unit prices and tend to increase the value of product shipments; conversely, cutting tools have become more efficient and productive and have a longer life span. In addition, the industry has witnessed advances in casting technology and the greater use of near net shapes, which reduces the need for metal removal and thus for cutting tools. Manufacturing the products without the use of coolants has gained increasing interest in light of environmental concerns.

Mergers and Consolidations

The principal U.S.-based and foreign-based producers of metal cutting tools have engaged in a round of mergers and consolidations in the past 3 years that has reshaped the industry significantly. This activity has taken several different forms. In addition to conventional acquisitions within the industry, some metal cutting tool companies have purchased firms outside the industry and some have been purchased by machine tool manufacturers. The latter mergers have altered the traditional relationship between producers of machine tools and suppliers of metal cutting tools. Such mergers are driven partly by the increasing tendency of cutting tool technology to dictate developments in the machine tool industry rather than vice versa.

Projections of Industry and Trade Growth for the Next 1 and 5 Years

After declining in 1997, both product and industry shipments of machine tool accessories resumed a pattern of modest growth. Product shipments of machine tool accessories were estimated to have risen by 4.2 percent in 1999 to $4.683 billion in constant 1992 dollars. Slower growth in product shipments for machine tool accessories is expected for the year 2000, with a forecast of a 2.9 percent increase to $4.819 billion in constant 1992 dollars. Over the 5 year period 2000–2004, both industry and product shipments should continue to achieve steady growth, rising at an annual average rate of 4 percent (see Table 17-3).

As was noted earlier, international trade remains limited in some segments of this industry, especially the cutting tool segment, in which suppliers traditionally have been located close to their customers. Most exports consist of high-value items (i.e., coordinate measuring machines, comparators) and work and tool holders, although expanding exports of cutting tools are contributing to the growing two-way trade in machine tool accessories.

After a steep 13.8 percent jump to a record $1.139 billion in 1998, U.S. imports of machine tool accessories slowed in the first half of 1999. Estimates are for an increase of 3.5 percent in 1999, which is projected to be followed by a 4 percent rise in the year 2000. U.S. exports of machine tool accessories are estimated to have risen almost 10 percent in 1999, reaching a record level of $1.01 billion, and are forecast to show a further 6 percent increase in current dollars to reach $1.07 billion in 2000 (see Table 17-3).

Global Market Prospects

The metal cutting tool segment of the machine tool accessories industry is largely a domestic industry, with imports amounting to about $100 million per year and exports amounting to an estimated $62.5 million in 1999. Although both export trade and import trade in this segment of the industry rose 4 to 5 percent per annum through the 1990s, future trade growth is expected to be modest. The primary market for metal cutting tools remains small metalworking shops in both foreign and domestic markets. These small shops often prefer to source tooling from local or long-established suppliers that can work within a pattern of occasional orders or "just-in-time" shipments. The volume and frequency of many such individual orders are often below the level at which the product can be exported profitably. The amenability of metal cutting tools to air shipment enhances the prospects for increased exports. The increased use of foreign stocking points should help facilitate export growth.

Exports in the metal cutting tool segment of the industry are focused primarily on NAFTA markets and the Japanese market. In 1999, nearly 43 percent ($42 million) of this segment's exports went to Mexico, and another 23 percent ($23 million) went to Canada. After Japan ($10 million), the remainder of the top 10 markets in this segment together accounted for approximately $20 million in total U.S. exports. On the import side, Japan has long been the leading source for U.S. cutting tool imports, totaling an estimated $56 million in 1999, double the $28 million of second-place China. Other leading U.S. cutting tool import sources were Taiwan ($22 million), Switzerland ($16 million), Germany ($9 million), the United Kingdom ($7 million), South Korea ($4 million), Thailand ($3 million), France ($3 million), and Canada ($3 million.)

Edward D. Abrahams, U.S. Department of Commerce, Office of Energy, Infrastructure, and Machinery, (202) 482-0312, November 1999.

POWER-DRIVEN HAND TOOLS

The power-driven hand tool industry (SIC 3546, NAICS 333991) consists of manufacturers of hand-held and portable electric and nonelectric power tools. These tools include corded and cordless (battery-powered) electric tools, pneumatic and hydraulic tools, powder-actuated tools, and gasoline-powered and electric chain saws. Stationary woodworking tools are classified under SIC 3553. Hand and edge tools are classified under SIC 3423. Gasoline and electric trimmer/brushcutters, hand-held and backpack blowers, and hedge trimmers are classified under SIC 3524. Handsaws and saw blades are classified under SIC 3425.

Global Trends

The power-driven hand tool subsector has evolved into a global industry. Manufacturers are producing tools at locations that yield the greatest efficiencies and largest profit margins while still providing labor sufficiently skilled to manufacture high-quality tools. The industry's products increasingly are being sourced from newly industrializing countries. Distribution channels, which long were confined to national borders, have become global as retail chains in the United States and Europe have established branches outside their domestic markets. Both domestically and abroad, home centers have captured an increased share of the power tool market from hardware stores and industrial distributors. Although the leading brand names have retained their identities and trade dress, mergers in the electric power tool subsector have altered the locus of capital control among the industry leaders. The mergers and joint ventures have involved both foreign capital purchases of U.S.-based entities and U.S. purchases of foreign firms, primarily EU firms. U.S. companies are acquiring the European firms primarily to gain easier entry into the EU. The CE Mark, which is viewed by the industry as a nontariff barrier, has further encouraged the establishment of new U.S.-owned European facilities. Japan-based suppliers have continued to expand their manufacturing capabilities in the United States.

Domestic Trends

The production of nonelectric (hydraulic and pneumatic) power tools is concentrated in New York, Pennsylvania, Ohio, and Illinois. However, the production of electric power tools has settled gradually in a southern crescent running from Maryland through North Carolina, South Carolina, Georgia, Mississippi, Tennessee, Arkansas, and Texas.

The projected increases in power tool shipments in the period 1998–2000 (see Table 17-4) will be driven by several factors. One important factor is the increased availability resulting from the growing number of home center outlets. Other factors include step-up purchasing by do-it-yourselfers seeking higher-quality tools, rising domestic and export sales of cordless tools, and higher levels of exports to previously underexploited markets. Employment in the power-driven hand tool subsector stood at 16,436 employees in 214 establishments in 1997. Approximately three-fourths of those employees, or 12,173, were production workers. Employment remained relatively level in 1998 and 1999, although some U.S.-based facilities closed. Employment at foreign-owned plants appears to have risen over the last 3 years.

Starting with the introduction of the power-driven screwdriver in 1987 and then the arrival of 18- and 24-volt cordless drills, battery-powered electric tools have gained wide acceptability among both do-it-yourselfers and contractors. Battery charging times, which initially were measured in hours, have been compressed to minutes. Cordless tools have proved immensely popular on outdoor job sites and in areas, including many foreign markets, where electric power supplies are unreliable. According to newly released U.S. Census of Manufactures data, product shipments of battery-powered tools rose two-thirds between 1992 and 1997, increasing from $291 million to $489 million in current dollars. Current dollar product shipments of battery-powered tools are estimated to have risen a further 17.5 percent to $575 million in 1999. Manufacturers have broadened the range of tools that use cordless technology.

TABLE 17-4: Power-Driven Hand Tools (SIC 3546) Trends and Forecasts
(millions of dollars except as noted)

	1992	1993	1994	1995	1996	1997	1998[1]	1999[2]	2000[3]	Percent Change 97–98	98–99	99–00	96–00[4]
Industry data													
Value of shipments[5]	2,873	3,480	3,608	3,791	3,744	3,524	3,781	4,031	4,254	7.3	6.6	5.5	3.2
Value of shipments (1992$)	2,873	3,405	3,450	3,566	3,470	3,233	3,408	3,592	3,760	5.4	5.4	4.7	2.0
Total employment (thousands)	16.1	17.0	16.1	17.0	16.3	16.4	15.7	14.7		–4.3	–6.4		
Production workers (thousands)	10.6	11.7	11.2	11.9	11.3	12.2							
Average hourly earnings ($)	11.08	10.98	11.27	12.13	12.17	12.95							
Capital expenditures	72	112	106	118	118	119							
Product data													
Value of shipments[5]	2,415	3,074	3,281	3,368	3,426	3,365	3,551	3,803	4,006	5.5	7.1	5.3	4.0
Value of shipments (1992$)	2,415	3,008	3,137	3,168	3,175	3,093	3,235	3,417	3,579	4.6	5.6	4.7	3.0
Trade data													
Value of imports	742	792	923	1,050	1,175	1,343	1,423	1,570	1,677	6.0	10.3	6.8	9.3
Value of exports	548	580	675	722	701	897	794	754	820	–11.5	–5.0	8.8	4.0

[1] Estimate except imports and exports.
[2] Estimate.
[3] Forecast.
[4] Compound annual rate.
[5] For a definition of industry versus product values, see "Getting the Most Out of *Outlook 2000*."
Source: U.S. Department of Commerce: Bureau of the Census; International Trade Administration.

Shipments of chain saws were reported by industry sources at 2.21 million units in 1998, up approximately 1.5 percent from the 1997 total. Product shipments were projected to increase about 2 percent in 1999 to surpass 2.25 million units. A severe 1999 hurricane season on the east coast helped boost shipments in the second half of 1999, possibly at some expense to new orders in the year 2000. On the regulatory front, the industry has reached an agreement with the California Air Resources Board to implement compliance with its year 2000 Tier II standards for two-cycle engines. In addition to complying with the California standards, the industry must comply with U.S. Environmental Protection Agency Phase I and Phase II exhaust emission standards for two-cycle engines.

Distribution

The distribution channels for electric power-driven hand tools has been altered markedly by the rise of the big box home center. Traditional distribution channels for power tools include hardware stores, home centers, warehouse clubs, lumber dealers, farm stores, industrial distributors, and servicing dealers. The growth of home centers and large warehouse clubs, which often are called big boxes, has forced manufacturers to refocus their methods of distribution. In particular, sales to contractors now frequently occur through home centers, usually at the expense of industrial distributors and hardware cooperatives. Contractors, who often initially resisted buying from home centers, are now the preferred customers, with hours and entrances set to meet their needs. Successful home center chains, warehouse clubs, and hardware stores now feature large tool cribs with offerings from most major manufacturers. Major power tool manufacturers have established divisions to deal directly with home centers and warehouse clubs, especially the market leaders.

The retail environment is undergoing rapid consolidation in a retail market that once was so diverse that no single firm held as much as 10 percent of the market. In particular, the two largest home center chains have gained significant market share as major competitors have consolidated or fallen by the wayside. Other chains have limited expansion to regional bases, notably in the midwest and on the Pacific coast. The expansion of the national chains has produced keen competition for retail sites, especially near interstate highways or at major highway intersections. The availability of such sites in major metropolitan areas is often limited and constricted by zoning regulations or citizens' opposition to the placing of large stores in their communities. The recent failure of a major home center chain set off a scramble for its most desirable sites. Although the number of do-it-yourselfers continues to rise, home centers generally have increased the percentage of their tool sales to contractors and professional do-it-yourselfers as opposed to sales of consumer tools to infrequent users. It is unlikely that any home center chain will continue to succeed without developing a large contractor base. Furthermore, retailers are beginning to develop E-commerce channels for the distribution of high-volume items such as drills and are moving toward full-scale "clicks and mortar" retailing. The leading home center chains now offer information-rich Web sites with detailed instructions on how to execute home projects and suggestions on which tools to use. These sites are designed primarily to educate do-it-yourselfers before customers come to the home center, but they are expected to offer a wider range of products for on-line purchase in the forthcoming years. Expansion and consolidation in the retail environment appear to be offering consumers, both casual users and contractors, a wider variety of tools at a given location. The power tool industry is price-sensitive and highly seasonal, with peak sales in the spring and the holiday season.

Projections of Industry and Trade Growth for the Next 1 and 5 Years

As is indicated in Table 17-4, current dollar product shipments of power-driven hand tools are expected to reach record levels of almost $3.8 billion in 1999 and $4 billion in 2000. In constant 1992 dollars, product shipments of power-driven hand tools are estimated to have risen by 5.6 percent in 1999 and are projected to rise 4.7 percent in 2000. Over the 5-year period 2000–2004, both industry and product shipments are expected to increase at an annual growth rate of 3.5 percent in constant 1992 dollars.

International trade in power-driven hand tools should continue to be robust at the turn of the millennium. U.S. imports of power tools are estimated to have risen by 10.3 percent in 1999 to a record $1.570 billion and are anticipated to register a further increase of 6.8 percent to reach $1.677 billion in the year 2000. The growing U.S. trade deficit in power tools is expected to widen in this period. After peaking at $897 million in 1997, U.S. power-driven hand tool exports fell 11.5 percent to $794 million in 1998 and are anticipated to have fallen by another 5.0 percent to $754 million in 1999. Although a modest 8.8 percent rebound to $820 million is projected for the year 2000, U.S. power tool exports are still expected to be more than 8 percent below the 1997 level. U.S. power-driven hand tool imports are expected to rise at a compound annual growth rate in excess of 5.5 percent per annum between 2000 and 2004. U.S. exports of power-driven hand tools will rebound as the new century begins, rising at an annual rate of 7 percent per annum between 2000 and 2004. Even if, as is noted below, U.S. imports of Japanese power-driven hand tools remain steady or decline over the 2000–2004 period, the projected export increase will barely dent the deficit in the balance of trade stemming from rising imports from China and Taiwan.

Global Trade Prospects

U.S. exports of power-driven hand tools fell sharply in 1998, declining 11.5 percent to $794 million, down from a record $897 million in 1997. The fall in U.S. exports continued in 1999 with an estimated decline of 5 percent to $754 million. Nonelectric power tools, which have a much higher value per unit, accounted for about 60 percent of U.S. exports, and electric power tools constituted approximately 40 percent. Canada held its historical position as the leading U.S. power tool export market in 1999, accounting for $220 million of U.S. power tool exports, or approximately 25 percent of the total. The other NAFTA partner, Mexico, ranked second as a destination for U.S. power tool exports in 1999 with $84 million. The other leading markets for U.S. power-driven hand tools in 1999 were Germany ($75 million), the United Kingdom ($63 million), the Netherlands ($26 million), Australia ($25 million), Japan ($20 million), Brazil ($14 million), China ($14 million), France ($12 million), and Argentina ($12 million). The EU markets received a substantial volume of exports to U.S. subsidiaries, including parts subject to substantive transformation in the manufacturing process.

With estimated U.S. imports of $315 million in 1999, Japan regained its traditional position as the leading import source for power tools. Although still dogged by quality problems, China remained a strong second to Japan as a source of U.S. power tool imports in 1999, accounting for $284 million. Other major import sources for power tools in 1999 included Taiwan ($195 million), Germany ($191 million), Mexico ($175 million), Sweden ($98 million), and the United Kingdom ($75 million). U.S. imports of Mexican power tools have fallen as production has decreased at *maquiladora* (in-bond) plants. The continued shift of Japan-based firms' power tool production to the United States will slow import growth in the years after 2000. However, U.S. production capacity at Japanese-owned plants customarily is dedicated to the production of high-volume, price-sensitive consumer-grade drills and other tools that carry lower price points. Japan will remain a significant import source through this period, although China and Taiwan are likely to achieve further import penetration of the U.S. power tool market. Imports from Italy and Canada also decreased sharply between 1997 and 1999 and are not expected to regain their former prominence.

WELDING APPARATUS

The welding apparatus industry consists of manufacturers of welding power sources, including generators; arc welding equipment; gas welding equipment; resistance welders; plasma, laser, electron beam, and ultrasonic welding equipment; welding robots; welding guns, tips, and torches; soldering equipment; electrodes; and bare and coated welding wire. The industry is formally known as the welding and soldering equipment industry (SIC 3548, NAICS 333992). Manufacturers of shielding gases are classified under SIC 2813 (NAICS 325120). Effective with the NAICS revision, manufacturers of arc welding transformers are classified under NAICS 335311, power distribution and specialty transformer manufacturing.

Global Trends

The United States is the world's largest producer of welding and cutting apparatus, and U.S. welding products maintain a strong competitive position in most industrialized countries, which are the leading markets for these products. The United States remains a leading producer of welding power sources, electrodes, and resistance welding apparatus. Importers have emerged as the primary sources for robotics as well as some types of welding torches and welding power sources. Mergers and consolidation of U.S.-based and foreign-owned firms have placed some traditional competitors under common ownership.

Domestic Trends

Leading markets for welding apparatus include the automotive, automotive repair and aftermarket, nonresidential construction, petrochemical, highway construction and bridge building, and machine and job shop industries. The decline and consolidation of the shipbuilding industry and other traditional welding apparatus markets have forced the industry to seek new applications for welding apparatus. Welding apparatus manufacturers are seeking entry into industries, such as aerospace, from which welding products traditionally were excluded.

Since the welding apparatus industry is a mature industry, technological change tends to be incremental. A prime example can be seen in welding guns and torches. A long secular trend toward lighter and smaller guns and torches has prevailed. The increased use of plastics, silicone rubber, and ceramics has allowed companies to design more compact and versatile guns and torches. Recent improvements have focused on ergonomics designed to allow workers to weld for sustained periods with less fatigue. These improvements include bent or curved gun handles, extended, flexible triggers, and 360-degree swivel.

In 1997, the U.S. welding apparatus subsector employed 22,100 workers, of whom 14,300 were production workers. The industry consists of 217 companies with 249 establishments, of which 47 had at least 100 employees. Welding apparatus plants are widely distributed throughout the United States, with the greatest concentration in the Great Lakes states. Ohio, with 6,162 employees in 20 establishments in 1997, leads in industry employment. Michigan, with its proximity to the automobile industry, dominates in the production of resistance welding equipment. With 4,304 employees in 43 establishments, Michigan ranks second in employment and first in the number of establishments. Third-ranked Wisconsin reported 2,002 employees in 12 establishments. Pennsylvania, Illinois, and Florida each reported between 500 and 1,000 industry employees in 1997. These states constitute the leading producers of welding power sources and equipment for gas-metal and gas-tungsten arc welding. New Hampshire has emerged as a major source of plasma cutting equipment.

Mergers and Consolidations

The welding apparatus industry has experienced a spate of mergers over the last 5 years that have reshaped the industry. This trend toward consolidation is likely to continue. The merger activity has involved both publicly traded and privately held companies. The merger trend has injected a substantial amount of publicly held capital stock into an industry long characterized by closely held firms even among the U.S. industry leaders.

Standards, Workplace Safety, and the Environment

The safety of the welding work environment has been heavily regulated at the federal level by the U.S. Department of Labor's Occupational Safety and Health Administration (OSHA) and by related state agencies. The regulations primarily govern workplace safety and have impelled manufacturers to improve the dust and fume extraction capabilities of machinery and the effectiveness of shielding gases. Safety equipment such as gloves, shields, and eyewear has become a major feature of the industry's trade shows. Environmental concerns also have stimulated greater interest in pulse welding. The industry has long been active in maintaining and revising welding standards through bodies such as the American National Standards Institute and the American Welding Society. These organizations also are working to harmonize international standards. The U.S. industry is concerned that European-influenced or -controlled international standard-setting bodies, including the European Committee for Standardization (CEN) and the International Standards Organization, could create nontariff barriers to the sale of U.S. welding apparatus by establishing standards that are incompatible with U.S. standards.

Welding Education

The welding apparatus industry places great importance on education and training as a central tenet of its efforts to attract more workers to the profession. Education and training also are critical to improving safety in the industry. The education process ranges from the training of apprentice welders to the education of graduate welding engineers. Education and training have centered in a number of venues, including undergraduate and graduate engineering programs at selected colleges and welder education programs at the high school level. These educational programs have begun to attract some state government assistance. The American Welding Society has promoted welding education and launched an "Image of Welding" program that is aimed at middle school students and designed to attract new students to the field.

Projections of Industry and Trade Growth for the Next 1 and 5 Years

Revisions occasioned by the adoption of the North American Industrial Classification System (NAICS) have produced some discontinuities in the product and industry shipment data reported in the 1997 *Census of Manufactures*. Among the major changes is the inclusion of resistance welding apparatus (formerly under SIC 3629) in the welding and soldering equipment industry. That change appears to have raised the value of both industry and product shipments above the level of increase that would have been reported if the statistical definition of the industry had remained unchanged.

As is indicated in Table 17-5, product shipments of welding apparatus are expected to grow an estimated 5 percent in constant 1992 dollars in 1999. Product shipments of welding apparatus are expected to rise 4.7 percent in constant 1992 dollars in the year 2000, as product shipments of welding apparatus are anticipated to maintain an unbroken string of gains through the 1990s and into 2000. Over the 5-year period 2000–2004, both industry and product shipments are estimated to increase at an average rate of 4 percent per annum in constant 1992 dollars.

U.S. exports and imports of welding apparatus should continue to grow modestly between 2000 and 2004. Imports of welding apparatus are expected to rise at an annual average rate of 4 percent in current dollars, while exports are expected to show a slightly smaller increase of approximately 3 percent a year.

Global Market Prospects

The United States remains the world's largest producer of welding apparatus as well as the largest market. A majority of top welding apparatus manufacturers remain U.S.-based. The United States is highly competitive internationally in the pro-

TABLE 17-5: Welding Apparatus (SIC 3548) Trends and Forecasts
(millions of dollars except as noted)

	1992	1993	1994	1995	1996	1997[1]	1998[1]	1999[2]	2000[3]	Percent Change 97–98	98–99	99–00	96–00[4]
Industry data													
Value of shipments[5]	2,738	3,101	3,086	3,303	3,496	4,374	4,702	5,016	5,344	7.5	6.7	6.5	11.2
Value of shipments (1992$)	2,738	2,984	2,871	2,970	3,067	3,800	4,005	4,205	4,403	5.4	5.0	4.7	9.5
Total employment (thousands)	19.6	20.3	18.6	18.9	19.7	22.1							
Production workers (thousands)	11.7	13.1	12.0	12.7	13.0	14.3							
Average hourly earnings ($)	13.87	14.76	15.28	15.92	16.05								
Capital expenditures	65	81	73	89	124								
Product data													
Value of shipments[5]	2,391	2,717	3,043	3,336	3,452	4,062	4,367	4,659	4,958	7.5	6.7	6.4	9.5
Value of shipments (1992$)	2,391	2,615	2,830	3,000	3,028	3,455	3,638	3,820	4,000	5.3	5.0	4.7	7.2
Trade data													
Value of imports	403	559	549	685	778	907	847	847	841	–6.6	0.0	–0.7	2.0
Value of exports	651	682	730	825	894	1,141	1,055	1,050	1,105	–7.5	–0.5	5.2	5.4

[1] Estimate except imports and exports.
[2] Estimate.
[3] Forecast.
[4] Compound annual rate.
[5] For a definition of industry versus product values, see "Getting the Most Out of *Outlook 2000.*"
Source: U.S. Department of Commerce: Bureau of the Census; International Trade Administration.

duction of most types of welding apparatus. However, Japan has established a clear predominance as a supplier of robotic welders used in systems developed by U.S. engineering firms and systems integrators. Germany is also a major supplier of robotic welding systems to the American market. Italy has established a foothold in the U.S. market as a manufacturer of inverters and other welding power sources.

U.S. exports of welding apparatus remained level in 1999 at an estimated $1.05 billion, less than 1 percent below the level of 1998. U.S. exports of welding apparatus are expected to rebound 5.2 percent in the year 2000 to reach $1.105 billion. The industry first reached the billion-dollar export level in 1997 (see Table 17-5). Canada, long the top U.S. export destination for welding apparatus, retained its leading position in 1999 with an estimated $209 million in U.S. exports, down 38 percent from 1998. Mexico followed in second place with an estimated $188 million, a 75 percent increase over the previous year. Rebounding Asian markets keyed an upturn in U.S. exports of welding apparatus to that region. After the NAFTA countries, the leading U.S. markets for welding apparatus in 1999 included Singapore ($61 million), Taiwan ($56 million), Japan ($52 million), South Korea ($51 million), the United Kingdom ($36 million), Germany ($28 million), France ($24 million), China ($22 million), and Hong Kong ($21 million). Despite the Asian financial crisis, U.S. welding apparatus exports to all those markets except South Korea (down 50 percent) held steady or registered small gains in 1999, setting the stage for the 2000 export rebound.

The import penetration rate for the U.S. welding apparatus market rose from 16 percent in 1992 to 24 percent in 1996 as U.S. imports of welding apparatus nearly doubled. After 1996, import penetration fell to an estimated 18 percent in 1999. After reaching a record $907 million in 1997, U.S. welding apparatus imports fell $60 million to $847 million in 1998 and remained flat at an estimated $847 million in 1999 (see Table 17-5). Imports from Japan declined an estimated 53 percent over that 2-year period. This partly reflects the transfer of some Japanese firms' production to other markets. With $201 million in U.S. imports, Japan remains the leading U.S. import source for welding apparatus. Other leading U.S. import sources for welding apparatus in 1999 included Germany ($171 million), Canada ($113 million), Sweden ($40 million), Switzerland ($40 million), Italy ($36 million), Singapore ($34 million), the United Kingdom ($30 million), Austria ($17 million), and France ($14 million). Asian manufacturers of welding apparatus did not increase their export activity significantly in the face of the Asian financial crisis. After Singapore, only Korea ($13.7 million), Taiwan ($10.2 million), and China ($7.5 million) accounted for at least $5 million of U.S. welding apparatus imports in 1999. China ranked sixteenth on the U.S. import source list in 1999, up only two places from 1998. Technical requirements for assembly and the need for a skilled labor force have largely precluded the migration of the industry's manufacturing base to newly industrializing countries.

Edward D. Abrahams, U.S. Department of Commerce, Office of Energy, Infrastructure, and Machinery, (202) 482-0312, November 1999.

■ REFERENCES

Machine Tools

American Machinist, Penton Publishing, Inc., 1100 Superior Avenue, Cleveland, OH 44114-2543. (216) 696-7000; fax: (216) 696-0177; http://www.penton.com/am.

Association for Manufacturing Technology, 7901 Westpark Drive, McLean, VA 22102-4269. (701) 893-2900; fax: (701) 893-1151, http://www.mfgtech.org.

Manufacturing Extension Partnership (MEP), National Institute of Standards and Technology. (800) MEP-4mfg, http://www.mep.nist.gov.

Metalworking Insiders' Report, P.O. Box 107, Larchmont, NY 10538-0107. (914) 834-2300; fax: (914) 834-7035.

Metalworking Machinery, Current Industrial Reports, Series MQ-35W, U.S. Department of Commerce, Bureau of the Census, Industry Division, Washington, DC 20233. (301) 457-4744, http://www.census.gov/econ/www/manumenu.html.

1997 Census of Manufactures, MC92-I-35C, Metalworking Machinery, U.S. Bureau of the Census, Washington, DC 20233.

1999 World Machine Tool Output and Consumption Survey, Gardner Publications, Inc., 6915 Valley Avenue, Cincinnati, OH 45244-3029. Fax: (513) 527-8801, http://www.garnerweb.com.

Machine Tool Accessories

Assembly, Cahners Business Information, 2000 Clearwater Drive, Oak Brook, IL 60523.

Cutting Tool and Machine Tool Accessory Manufacturing, 1997 Economic Census, Manufacturing, Industry Series, EC97-M, 3335E, U.S. Department of Commerce, Economics and Statistics Administration, U.S. Bureau of the Census, Washington, DC 20233.

Cutting Tool Engineering, CTE Publications, Inc., 400 Skokie Blvd., Suite 395, Northbrook, IL 60062-7903.

Job Shop Technology, Edwards Publishing Co., 16 Waterbury Road, Prospect, CT 06712.

Modern Applications News, Nelson Publishing, Inc., 2500 Tamiami Trail North, Nokomis, FL 34275-3482.

Tooling & Production, Adams/Huebcore Publishing, Inc., 6001 Cochran Road, 3rd Floor, Solon, OH 44139.

Power-Driven Hand Tools

Do-It-Yourself Retailing, National Retail Hardware Association, 5822 West 74 Street, Indianapolis, IN 46278.

National Home Center News, Lebhar-Friedman, Inc., 425 Park Avenue, New York, NY 10022.

1997 Census of Manufactures, Power Driven Hand Tool Manufacturing, EC97M-3339H, U.S. Department of Commerce, U.S. Bureau of the Census, Washington, DC 20233.

Power Equipment Trade, Hatton-Brown Publishers, 225 Hanrick Street, Montgomery, AL 36104.

Welding Apparatus

Gases and Welding Distributor, Penton Publishing Company, 1100 Superior Avenue, Cleveland, OH 44114-2543.

Practical Welding Today, The Croydon Group Ltd., 813 Featherstone Drive, Rockford, IL 61107-6302.

Welding and Soldering Equipment Manufacturing, 1997 Economic Census, Manufacturing, Industry Series, EC-97M-3339I, U.S. Department of Commerce, U.S. Census Bureau, Washington, DC 20233.

Welding Design & Fabrication, Penton Publishing Company, 1100 Superior Avenue, Cleveland, OH 44114-2543.

Welding Journal, American Welding Society, 550 NW Le Jeune Road, Miami, FL 33126.

■ RELATED CHAPTERS

1: Metals and Industrial Minerals Mining
6: Construction
8: Building Products and Materials
13: Steel Mill Products
14: Nonferrous Metals
15: General Components
16: Microelectronics
18: Production Machinery
36: Motor Vehicles
37: Automotive Parts

PRODUCTION MACHINERY
Economic and Trade Trends

Source: U.S. Department of Commerce: Bureau of the Census, International Trade Administration.

Source: United Nations; U.S. Department of Commerce, International Trade Administration.

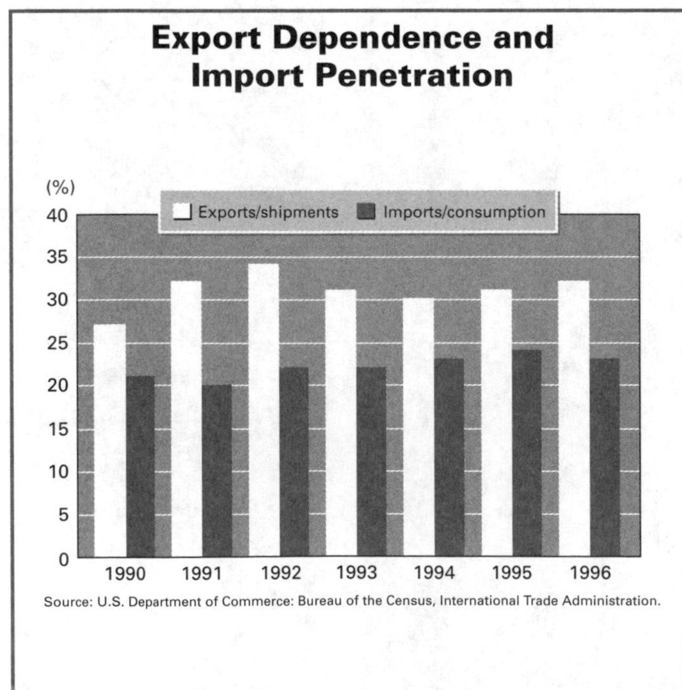

Source: U.S. Department of Commerce: Bureau of the Census, International Trade Administration.

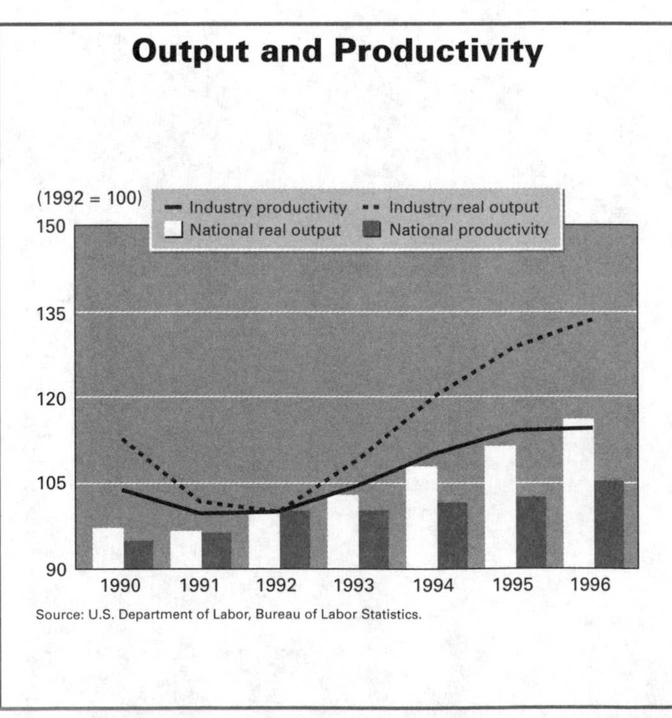

Source: U.S. Department of Labor, Bureau of Labor Statistics.

See "Getting the Most Out of *Outlook 2000*" for definitions of terms.

18

Production Machinery

INDUSTRY DEFINITION This chapter discusses nine production machinery industries: air-conditioning, refrigeration, and heating equipment (SIC 3585); construction machinery (SIC 3531); mining machinery (SIC 3532); oil and gas field machinery (SIC 3533); printing trades machinery (SIC 3555); packaging machinery (SIC 3565); paper industries machinery (SIC 3554); agricultural and farm machinery (SIC 3523); and food products machinery (SIC 3556). Air-conditioning, refrigeration, and heating equipment is the largest subsector, followed by construction machinery and then agricultural and farm machinery. These three subsectors account for 76 percent of 1999 product shipments of the production machinery discussed in this chapter. Trade patterns in 1998 for the nine industries discussed in this chapter are shown in Table 18-1.

CONSTRUCTION MACHINERY

Construction machinery (SIC 3531) consists of earthmoving equipment (bulldozers, shovel loaders, and excavators), off-highway trucks, power cranes, crawlers, draglines, trenchers, compactors, mixers, pavers, graders, and scrapers as well as components, parts, and attachments. This equipment is used for the construction of residential and nonresidential buildings, for new power and manufacturing plants, and for adding to or renovating infrastructures such as sewage and water lines, roads, bridges, and tunnels.

Global and Domestic Outlook

The construction machinery industry is a very cyclical one, with high sales growth during boom years and reductions in output during economic slowdowns and downturns. The industry is affected particularly by factors such as housing starts, consumer confidence, and employment. Since residential and business construction is typically debt-financed, interest rates and the availability of credit are also important factors.

With 1998 being a year of high economic activity, with a 10 percent increase in private housing starts, high consumer confidence, a high level of employment, and low mortgage rates, the construction equipment industry experienced a 10 percent increase in output. Even though the Asian currency crisis that began in 1997 with the devaluation of the Thai bhat did not result in a domestic recession in the United States, it affected the construction equipment industry through a 6 percent decline in exports in 1998. With exports typically constituting over one-quarter of the shipments in the construction machinery industry, severe recessions in many of the large export markets were expected to result in a significant decline in overall product demand in 1999. As a reaction to the cyclical nature of the construction machinery industry, several major firms in the industry are diversifying into other products and services, such as financial services, automobile parts, and engines, to soften the impact of adverse economic conditions on their overall profits.

Companies are diversifying further by expanding globally, although this strategy clearly has risks that were evident during the Ásian crisis. Developing nations with significant infrastructure investment are prime external markets, with exports to countries such as Brazil, South Africa, Russia, Peru, India, and Egypt reaching double-digit annual growth rates from 1992 to 1998. As international trade has become increasingly important to the construction machinery industry, sales have become increasingly vulnerable to currency fluctuations and economic conditions abroad. Because of the sharp rise in the value of the dollar relative to many other currencies since 1997, the construction machinery industry has lost competitiveness with foreign manufacturers, leading to the first trade deficit in this industry in over a decade. The rise in imports and the corresponding fall in exports are not unexpected with economic weakness, with low demand abroad and low prices for imports resulting from the strength of the U.S. dollar.

The continued preference of many customers to rent rather than purchase equipment continues to shape the distribution

TABLE 18-1: U.S. Trade Patterns in Production Machinery[1] in 1998
(millions of dollars; percent)

Exports			Imports		
Region[2]	Value[3]	Share, %	Region[2]	Value[3]	Share, %
NAFTA	7,997	29	NAFTA	4,211	22
Latin America	5,482	20	Latin America	492	3
Western Europe	5,320	19	Western Europe	9,303	49
Japan/Chinese Economic Area	1,574	6	Japan/Chinese Economic Area	3,765	20
Other Asia	2,109	8	Other Asia	851	4
Rest of world	5,053	18	Rest of world	493	3
World	27,534	100	World	19,115	100
Top Five Countries	Value	Share, %	Top Five Countries	Value	Share, %
Canada	5,936	22	Japan	3,402	18
Mexico	2,061	7	Germany	2,789	15
Venezuela	1,288	5	Canada	2,786	15
United Kingdom	1,233	4	United Kingdom	1,787	9
Australia	1,104	4	Italy	1,487	8

[1] SIC 3523, 3531, 3532, 3533, 3554, 3555, 3556, 3565, 3585.
[2] For definitions of regional groupings, see "Getting the Most Out of *Outlook 2000.*"
[3] Values may not sum to total due to rounding.
Source: U.S. Department of Commerce, Bureau of the Census.

channels in this industry. The expansion of renting will continue not only in the United States, where the trend toward consolidation has led to an increase in the size and a reduction in the number of players in the rental market, but also in Europe and Canada as end users demand flexibility, cost reduction, and the latest technology, particularly in specialized equipment.

Revenue in the construction machinery industry is always heavily affected by federal, state, and local government spending, and 1998 was especially favorable to the industry in that regard, as state and local government construction rose in response to the passage in 1998 of the Transportation Equity Act for the 21st Century (TEA-21). That legislation, which was enacted in June 1998, provides for $218 billion in expenditures for highway and other transit systems through 2003, with $175 billion earmarked for highway repair and expansion. This increase of 40 percent over previous spending levels has fueled and will continue to fuel domestic demand for construction equipment, offsetting, at least in part, the reduction in demand caused by international factors.

The Role of Electronic Commerce

Electronic commerce is changing the nature of business-to-business interaction as an ever-increasing number of small and large firms implement electronic business applications using the Internet. The Construction Industry Manufacturers' Association (CIMA), an industry trade group, has organized seminars to assist business leaders in implementing E-commerce solutions designed to reduce costs and provide customers with more information and support. Electronic data interchange (EDI) has proved to be the most useful technology for the industry as product registration and other transactions that were previously paper-based now are conducted electronically, reducing errors and administrative costs for both customers and suppliers.

As firms become more Internet- and technologically savvy, additional applications will be implemented. One-click ordering and E-mail communication with customers regarding the status of orders are used extensively in retail transactions and have the potential to streamline the construction machinery industry further. Sales of parts are expected to lead the rest of the industry in Internet sales as competition is greater and the product is available through a wider range of suppliers. With customer emphasis on specialized construction equipment, customized sales and support applications are another area of potential growth as firms expand into the digital realm. As with companies across the economy, internal transactions and communication, including documentation, reporting, administration, and project management, lend themselves well to electronic solutions.

Industry and Trade Projections

The outlook for the construction machinery industry indicates that the rapid expansion of the mid-1990s will not continue as housing starts level off and exports continue to show weakness in 1999 and 2000. Adjusted for inflation, product shipments are expected to decrease over 5 percent in 1999 and over 4 percent in the year 2000 (see Table 18-2). Continued low mortgage rates and robust government spending on highway maintenance and expansion will not offset sluggish overseas demand and the increased foreign competition brought on by a strong dollar. Over the longer term, however, shipments will pick up again, increasing at an annual rate of nearly 2 percent from 2000 through 2004.

The construction machinery industry is dependent on demand from international customers, with over one-quarter of sales in 1996 consisting of shipments to foreign countries. The Asian economic crisis had a significant impact on the industry's shipments, with exports to Asia dropping 33 percent in 1998

TABLE 18-2: Construction Machinery (SIC 3531) Trends and Forecasts
(millions of dollars except as noted)

	1992	1993	1994	1995	1996	1997[1]	1998[1]	1999[2]	2000[3]	Percent Change 97–98	98–99	99–00	96–00[4]
Industry data													
Value of shipments[5]	13,139	15,444	17,697	19,911	21,627	24,354	27,204	26,687	26,180	11.7	−1.9	−1.9	4.9
Value of shipments (1992$)	13,139	15,097	17,049	18,714	19,860	22,026	24,118	23,371	22,623	9.5	−3.1	−3.2	3.3
Total employment (thousands)	74.6	74.7	77.9	85.4	88.7								
Production workers (thousands)	47.8	49.1	52.9	58.4	61.1								
Average hourly earnings ($)	15.13	15.33	14.84	14.81	14.93								
Capital expenditures	395	346	359	443	450								
Product data													
Value of shipments[5]	12,001	14,122	16,123	18,299	20,259	22,812	25,572	24,600	23,936	12.1	−3.8	−2.7	4.3
Value of shipments (1992$)	12,001	13,804	15,532	17,198	18,604	20,633	22,676	21,519	20,572	9.9	−5.1	−4.4	2.5
Trade data													
Value of imports	2,988	3,900	4,923	5,310	5,284	6,072	7,173	7,263	7,247	18.1	1.3	−0.2	8.2
Value of exports	4,541	4,526	5,425	5,734	6,099	7,061	6,648	6,144	6,746	−5.8	−7.6	9.8	2.6

[1] Estimate except imports and exports.
[2] Estimate.
[3] Forecast.
[4] Compound annual rate.
[5] For a definition of industry versus product values, see "Getting the Most Out of *Outlook 2000.*"
Source: U.S. Department of Commerce: Bureau of the Census; International Trade Administration.

alone. Fortunately, increased sales to North American Free Trade Agreement (NAFTA) countries compensated somewhat for the reduction in shipments to Asian markets. As exports fell in 1998, imports rose, leading to the first trade deficit year the industry had seen in over a decade. Imports were especially strong from manufacturers in Asia, where weak currencies increased their competitiveness. Japan historically had been and continued to be the top supplier of construction machinery to the United States, with a 22 percent share of all imports in the industry in 1998 (see Table 18-3).

Christine Siegwarth Meyer, (315) 637–8831, November 1999.

MINING MACHINERY

The mining machinery industry (SIC 3532) includes excavating, crushing, loader, and haulage equipment used in mining as well as pertinent components of and accessories for extraction equipment. Among the industry's key products are excavating machinery, conveyor systems, LHD (load, haul, and dump) machines, underground trucks, ground support equipment, mine seal equipment, and rock crushers. While the basic machinery standards are fundamental to the industry, technological innovation has automated many of the mechanical processes. New applications of robotic and remote control systems, for instance, stand to replace tradi-

TABLE 18-3: U.S. Trade Patterns in Construction Machinery[1] in 1998
(millions of dollars; percent)

Exports			Imports		
Region[2]	Value[3]	Share, %	Region[2]	Value[3]	Share, %
NAFTA	2,519	38	NAFTA	1,671	23
Latin America	1,224	18	Latin America	205	3
Western Europe	1,260	19	Western Europe	3,232	45
Japan/Chinese Economic Area	223	3	Japan/Chinese Economic Area	1,630	23
Other Asia	394	6	Other Asia	299	4
Rest of world	1,028	15	Rest of world	136	2
World	6,648	100	World	7,173	100
Top Five Countries	Value	Share, %	Top Five Countries	Value	Share, %
Canada	1,991	30	Japan	1,568	22
Mexico	529	8	Canada	1,192	17
Belgium	474	7	United Kingdom	794	11
Australia	360	5	Germany	738	10
Chile	297	4	France	496	7

[1] SIC 3531.
[2] For definitions of regional groupings, see "Getting the Most Out of *Outlook 2000.*"
[3] Values may not sum to total due to rounding.
Source: U.S. Department of Commerce, Bureau of the Census.

tional machinery and yield increased productivity and efficiency in the mining industry.

Global and Domestic Trends

Mine production declined generally in 1998 and 1999 because of low commodity prices worldwide. In the summer of 1999, the price of gold was $258, down from over $400 an ounce in 1996. The price of silver had fallen from over $6 per ounce in 1997 to only $5.25. Copper and other metals showed similar price declines, with much of these declines attributed to falling demand from Asia after its currency crisis and the resulting recessions. The U.S. Geological Survey estimated that total mine production in 1998 fell for metals ($13.1 billion in 1997 to $10.6 billion in 1998) and coal ($19.8 billion in 1997 to $19.6 billion in 1998) and rose for industrial minerals ($28.4 billion in 1997 to $29.5 billion in 1998). The number of coal mines in operation fell from 1,828 in 1997 to 1,750 in 1998, with a reduction in both underground and surface mines. As mine production fell, so did orders for new mining equipment. Firms with low profits are reluctant to purchase new machinery for sectors with such volatile prices. In 1999, purchases of mining machinery fell 6.5 percent in constant dollars from the level in 1998. The uncertainty related to the path of future commodity prices affected capital spending for both domestic and overseas mines, with exports dropping 2.2 percent in 1999. Exports are becoming an increasingly important source of demand for mining machinery as South American and Asian mines are chipping away at the traditional U.S. dominance in the global mining industry.

In June 1998, the U.S. Department of Energy (DOE) and the National Mining Association (NMA) agreed to develop a joint government and industry research and development partnership as part of the DOE's Industries of the Future program. The aims of this partnership are to promote promising research designed to develop environmentally sound, energy-efficient technologies that would not otherwise be developed by companies because of their cost or riskiness. A significant part of the program focuses on the energy efficiency of motors used in the mining industry. Since motors and their related systems utilize over 90 percent of the electricity used in mining, according to the DOE and the NMA, opportunities for energy conservation abound. Practical applications of the Mining Industry Motor Systems Initiative include distributing a software program to assist firms in choosing efficient and economically feasible motor systems, providing NMA members with technical information that can be used in the decision-making process, and funding projects that are in line with the program's goals. The first 10 such projects were announced in 1999 and will address goals such as improving the quality of mine output, reducing the environmental impact of mines, increasing the energy efficiency of mine operations, and cutting costs through increased equipment life, more efficient use of equipment, improved communication throughout a mine, and enhanced productivity.

Industry and Trade Projections

Output in the mining machinery industry was expected to fall 6.4 percent in 1999 as customers took a wait and see approach to evaluating new equipment purchases after the steady level of shipments seen in the early 1990s and the substantial growth seen in 1997 (9.5 percent) and 1998 (12.1 percent) (see Table 8-4). In the longer term, the mining machinery sector will continue to experience flat sales, with shipments forecast to fall 0.8 percent annually between 2000 and 2004.

Internationally, U.S. exports were expected to suffer setbacks in 1999 as they did in 1998, largely as a result of a drop in demand from Asian customers whose revenues slumped because of currency devaluations. Exports to Asian countries were estimated to decline 44 percent in 1998, with the Philippines, South

TABLE 18-4: Mining Machinery (SIC 3532) Trends and Forecasts
(millions of dollars except as noted)

	1992	1993	1994	1995	1996	1997[1]	1998[1]	1999[2]	2000[3]	Percent Change 97–98	98–99	99–00	96–00[4]
Industry data													
Value of shipments[5]	1,548	1,881	1,715	2,181	2,397	2,687	3,020	2,938	3,176	12.4	–2.7	8.1	7.3
Value of shipments (1992$)	1,548	1,844	1,659	2,038	2,193	2,401	2,663	2,578	2,756	10.9	–3.2	6.9	5.9
Total employment (thousands)	12.6	12.6	12.6	13.8	13.7								
Production workers (thousands)	7.4	7.7	8.0	8.9	8.4								
Average hourly earnings ($)	11.92	12.21	13.08	13.30	13.87								
Capital expenditures	33.0	58.9	29.5	29.8	43.8								
Product data													
Value of shipments[5]	1,417	1,745	1,639	2,100	2,202	2,468	2,804	2,632	2,892	13.6	–6.1	9.9	7.1
Value of shipments (1992$)	1,417	1,711	1,585	1,962	2,014	2,205	2,472	2,313	2,507	12.1	–6.4	8.4	5.6
Trade data													
Value of imports	227	256	329	399	439	474	486	495	506	2.5	1.9	2.2	3.6
Value of exports	725	763	894	970	1,089	1,337	1,203	1,177	1,225	–10.0	–2.2	4.1	3.0

[1] Estimate except imports and exports.
[2] Estimate.
[3] Forecast.
[4] Compound annual rate.
[5] For a definition of industry versus product values, see "Getting the Most Out of *Outlook 2000.*"
Source: U.S. Department of Commerce: Bureau of the Census; International Trade Administration.

Korea, and Indonesia all experiencing drop-offs in purchases of over 30 percent. The decline in exports, however, was worldwide, with all the top five markets in 1997 reporting a fall in the value of shipments in 1998. However, U.S. exports still exceeded imports in 1998 (see Table 18-5).

Electronic Commerce

Companies in the mining equipment industry are using E-commerce and the Internet in a variety of ways. As with many firms, electronic internal communications, including human resources, management, and engineering applications, are quite common. Firms also are using the World Wide Web to study their competitors, customers, and suppliers and communicate with component vendors and distributors. However, in light of the specialized and customized nature of the product sold by this industry, large-scale interaction with customers is not as prevalent as it is in retail industries. All the large manufacturers have a Web presence, which emphasizes equipment and product descriptions, dealer locations, and employment opportunities.

Computer modeling is becoming especially important in the design of new equipment models. For example, computer tools and three-dimensional modeling can be used to forecast the impact of various types of stresses on a machine's survivability. This not only increases the reliability of equipment but also allows it to come to market more quickly, since many rounds of simulations can be completed in a short time.

Christine Siegwarth Meyer, (315) 637–8831, November 1999.

OIL AND GAS FIELD MACHINERY

Oil and gas field equipment (SIC 3533) includes machinery, equipment, and components used in oil and gas exploration, well servicing and drilling, and the production and processing of oil and gas in the field. Among the specific kinds of equipment produced are geophysical prospecting machinery, drilling rigs and tools, cementing and well-fracturing units, pumping machinery, dehydrators, separators, treaters, and other field processing machinery.

Global Industry Trends

Procurement for the oil and gas field machinery subsector is a function of international supply and demand for oil and gas. Spurred by the impact of low petroleum prices in 1998, oil and gas field equipment manufacturers continued to focus on diversifying their product lines and reducing costs in 1999. Despite increases in petroleum prices, the oil and gas field machinery industry remained depressed during much of 1999. The majors and most independent producers were recouping lost revenues through conservative spending, so purchases of new machinery were limited. The industry was not hit uniformly by the slump, since oil and gas field equipment used offshore, in subsea services, and in well interdiction services were affected less by the slowdown. Nevertheless, orders were on the rise at the end of 1999, and the industry appeared to be on an upswing.

After the oil price slump of 1998, the emphasis for most producers was on replenishing their balance sheets, so they were cautious with their exploration spending in the early months of 1999. Producers concentrated on capital spending that could add immediately to their revenues or that would provide the best long-run returns. Thus, well interventions and long-term development plans were funding priorities. Many fields in the contiguous United States were put on hold and overall capital spending was cut as producers focused their attention on consolidating mergers and acquisitions and waited to see whether higher petroleum prices would be sustained. Oil and gas field equipment manufacturers also continued to pursue mergers and acquisitions as a means of diversifying their product lines and lowering their costs to weather the cyclical swings of the boom-bust oil and gas industry.

TABLE 18-5: U.S. Trade Patterns in Mining Machinery[1] in 1998
(millions of dollars; percent)

Exports			Imports		
Region[2]	Value[3]	Share, %	Region[2]	Value[3]	Share, %
NAFTA	326	27	NAFTA	96	20
Latin America	349	29	Latin America	7	1
Western Europe	172	14	Western Europe	259	53
Japan/Chinese Economic Area	71	6	Japan/Chinese Economic Area	49	10
Other Asia	84	7	Other Asia	34	7
Rest of world	201	17	Rest of world	43	9
World	1,203	100	World	486	100
Top Five Countries	Value	Share, %	Top Five Countries	Value	Share, %
Canada	219	18	Germany	78	16
Mexico	107	9	Canada	69	14
Colombia	95	8	United Kingdom	50	10
Chile	91	8	Italy	45	9
South Africa	59	5	Japan	32	7

[1] SIC 3532.
[2] For definitions of regional groupings, see "Getting the Most Out of *Outlook 2000.*"
[3] Values may not sum to total due to rounding.
Source: U.S. Department of Commerce, Bureau of the Census.

Baker Hughes, an oil and gas field equipment and services company, provides rig counts that are used commonly in the oil and gas industry as an indicator of sectoral activity. Baker Hughes reported that in the first quarter of 1999, the average number of active rotary drilling rigs totaled 557 compared with a first quarter average of 968 active rigs in 1998. Those figures indicate how significant activity decreased from the first quarter of 1998 to the first quarter of 1999.

The decrease in active rigs was concentrated in land-based drilling, which declined 45 percent from 832 rigs in the first quarter of 1998 to 454 in the first quarter of 1999. The slowdown in offshore activity was comparatively moderate, with a 24 percent decline in that time period. In the second quarter of 1999, the average dropped even further to 521 active rigs, a 42 percent decline from the second quarter of 1998. The decline again was concentrated in the onshore-based drilling arena, where the average fell from 732 rigs in the second quarter of 1998 to 421 in the second quarter of 1999.

The decline in onshore drilling and its impact on the domestic oil and gas field industry were highlighted by an antidumping and countervailing duty petition filed against Iraq, Mexico, Saudi Arabia, and Venezuela on June 29, 1999. The petition was filed by the Committee to Save Domestic Oil, a group composed of independent oil producers and associations of independent oil producers, on behalf of the domestic oil industry. The committee further alleged that there is a regional industry with respect to crude oil that consists of the 48 contiguous states, excluding Arizona, California, Nevada, Oregon, and Washington. In the petition, the committee alleged that crude oil was being sold in the United States at less than its fair market value by the four nations mentioned above. The U.S. Department of Commerce rejected the claim, saying that there was insufficient industry support. However, the action highlights the stress that low petroleum prices placed on the U.S. onshore oil industry. The downturn resulted in significantly lower sales for oil and gas machinery manufacturers that serve this sector of the industry.

Despite their preferable position relative to equipment manufacturers selling to the onshore industry, the price slump of 1998 had a significant impact on U.S. offshore equipment manufacturers. The U.S. Minerals Management Service's (MMS) Central Gulf lease sale number 172 in March 1999 received considerably fewer bids than did the Western Gulf lease sale 169 held in March 1998. According to MMS, the lower number of bids was due to low oil prices and producers being judicious about adding additional leases. There were 1,188 bids received during lease sale number 169 with $810 million in high bids, while lease sale number 172 recorded only 272 bids with high bids totaling $171 million. In bid round number 174 held in August 1999, MMS received 177 bids with $95 million in high bids. Because U.S. offshore activity is located primarily in the Gulf of Mexico, the lower leasing activity should translate into lower near-term U.S. offshore investment levels than otherwise would have been expected.

The difficulties faced by the U.S. onshore industry during this past industry downturn were due to the fact that most contiguous U.S. fields have been exploited extensively. The pockets of oil that remain are in difficult geological formations with high associated costs for exploration, development, and production. Indeed, most U.S. drilling activity is aimed at satisfying the North American gas market, where U.S. production is more competitive. As onshore fields decline in productivity and reservoirs increase in complexity, the economics of their development will hinge increasingly on technological improvements to make their exploitation economically viable. In a similar vein, offshore exploration and development hinge on equipment manufacturers cutting field development costs while allowing producers to work in greater water depths with higher pressures. In both areas, manufacturers are working to fill those needs while producing equipment that meets ever-increasing environmental standards.

Over the last 15 years, U.S. oil and gas field machinery manufacturers have met this challenge while facing increasing product competition. Directional drilling and other oil field technologies are reducing dramatically the number of production wells that must be drilled, particularly in costly offshore operations. Three-dimensional seismic imaging and other advances in seismic technologies are reducing exploration costs per barrel to levels that were unimaginable only 15 years ago. Advances in technology will continue to have a major impact on the industry. Advanced sensor technologies, riserless drilling, composite tubing applications, expanded casing technology, subsea completions, smart wells, and real-time reservoir management systems are expected to have a major impact on the industry in the next 5 years. Smart sensors, downhole refinery, rigless drilling, and laser technologies seem poised to advance the industry in the longer term.

Global Market Prospects

U.S. oil and gas field equipment manufacturers are very competitive in international markets. Indeed, U.S. suppliers are active in virtually all upstream (oil and gas field) petroleum markets, and U.S. technology and quality are considered among the best available in most product categories.

The top five foreign markets for U.S. upstream equipment in 1998 were Venezuela, Singapore, the United Kingdom, Saudi Arabia, and Brazil in that order (see Table 18-6). Those countries remained the top buyers of U.S. equipment in the first 7 months of 1999. However, a strong potential exists for change to this lineup in the year 2000.

In Venezuela, the election of General Hugo Chavez brought about a downward revision of former national petroleum company [Petróleos de Venezuela PDVSA] president Luis Giusti's plan to double Venezuela's oil production capacity by the year 2008. Current plans call for a much slower expansion of petroleum production with more competition and investment in the downstream industries to help diversify that country's petroleum sector. Current plans also call for upstream joint ventures and partnerships, including more small Venezuelan companies. These changes should constrain export opportunities for U.S. upstream equipment manufacturers in Venezuela in the coming years.

The move by Middle Eastern countries such as Kuwait to open participation in their petroleum industries to international competition is likely to shift investment to that region. This change in the flow of investment capital probably will come at

TABLE 18-6: U.S. Trade Patterns in Oil and Gas Field Machinery[1] in 1998
(millions of dollars; percent)

Exports			Imports		
Region[2]	Value[3]	Share, %	Region[2]	Value[3]	Share, %
NAFTA	184	3	NAFTA	121	39
Latin America	2,177	33	Latin America	3	1
Western Europe	973	15	Western Europe	164	53
Japan/Chinese Economic Area	218	3	Japan/Chinese Economic Area	6	2
Other Asia	955	15	Other Asia	15	5
Rest of world	2,025	31	Rest of world	2	1
World	6,533	100	World	311	100
Top Five Countries	Value	Share, %	Top Five Countries	Value	Share, %
Venezuela	862	13	Canada	111	36
Singapore	498	8	United Kingdom	43	14
United Kingdom	467	7	Netherlands	29	9
Saudi Arabia	382	6	France	25	8
Brazil	252	4	Austria	23	7

[1] SIC 3533.
[2] For definitions of regional groupings, see "Getting the Most Out of *Outlook 2000*."
[3] Values may not sum to total due to rounding.
Source: U.S. Department of Commerce, Bureau of the Census.

the expense of locations such as Russia and the Caspian, where oil fields have comparatively higher lifting and transportation costs and many political problems remain.

The south Atlantic holds promise for exceptional offshore oil and gas field exploration and development activity in the coming years. Drilling activity in Brazilian offshore fields is expected to increase dramatically since the Brazilian Ministry of Mines and Energy has a stated policy goal of achieving self-sufficiency in hydrocarbon fuels by the year 2005. As part of those plans, the Brazilian Petroleum Regulatory Agency (ANP) awarded 12 offshore concessions to 10 U.S.- and foreign-owned exploration and production companies in June 1999. Spending on seismic data is believed to have increased 1,000 percent in 1999, and increases are expected in the year 2000 as well.

In Africa, known deepwater reserves are already considerable, and new finds are adding to those totals. Also, a number of African governments, from Cote D'Ivoire to Angola, along Africa's western coast are making changes to attract exploration and production companies to the region. Many African reserves are being developed, and there are plans for substantial increases in investment in the coming years.

Industry and Trade Projections

Figures for the third and fourth quarters of 1999 show increased activity as the impact of higher prices filtered through to the upstream equipment industry. Thus, sustained world market prices for petroleum products are bringing about a recovery in demand for upstream oil and gas products. The U.S. Department of Energy's Energy Information Agency (EIA) predicts that world oil prices will remain high throughout the year 2000 if compliance by the Organization of Oil Exporting Countries (OPEC) remains strong.

The U.S. Bureau of Land Management's lease sale in the Alaskan National Petroleum Reserve in May 1999 should herald increased spending on the North Slope, and other Alaskan leasing rounds such as Cook Island and the Beaufort Sea should bring a resurgence of oil and gas investment in that state. As the first oil and gas lease sale in the National Petroleum Reserve since the mid-1980s, the North Slope bidding in May 1999 was healthy, with 174 bids received, totaling roughly $125 million.

Drilling activity also is expected to increase in the Gulf of Mexico during the year 2000, in part to offset tightening natural gas supplies but also as leaseholders begin to revive investment plans that were put on hold during the oil price downturn. Much of the onshore industry activity in the lower 48 states will be geared toward meeting the needs of the growing U.S. gas market. These expanded domestic activities, combined with international opportunities in the Middle East and the south Atlantic, should herald a welcome comeback for U.S. oil and gas field machinery manufacturers. Exports, which drive industry growth prospects, are expected to increase over 10 percent in 2000. Industry and product shipments should grow by over 9 percent (see Table 18-7). Average annual growth over the period 2000–2005 is forecast to be 3 percent.

Christine Siegwarth Meyer, (315) 637–8831, November 1999.

FARM MACHINERY

The farm machinery subsector (SIC 3523) is defined as consisting of farm field and farmstead machinery used for the production of crops and agricultural livestock. Major product lines for the industry include wheel tractors, planting and fertilizing machinery, tillage equipment (plows, cultivators, and harrows), fertilizer and chemical application equipment, harvesting machinery (e.g., combines, cotton pickers, root/tuber harvesters), haying and mowing machinery (including

TABLE 18-7: Oil and Gas Field Machinery (SIC 3533) Trends and Forecasts
(millions of dollars except as noted)

	1992	1993	1994	1995	1996	1997	1998[1]	1999[2]	2000[3]	Percent Change 97–98	98–99	99–00	96–00[4]
Industry data													
Value of shipments[5]	3,921	3,740	3,758	3,803	4,646	6,240	6,422	4,019	4,430	2.9	–37.4	10.2	–1.2
Value of shipments (1992$)	3,921	3,762	3,677	3,619	4,290	5,586	5,628	3,487	3,806	0.8	–38.0	9.1	–3.0
Total employment (thousands)	26.3	24.5	25.5	24.3	26.4								
Production workers (thousands)	15.4	13.8	14.7	15.0	17.0								
Average hourly earnings ($)	13.63	14.22	15.57	15.05	16.07								
Capital expenditures	105	79.8	77.7	123	157								
Product data													
Value of shipments[5]	2,981	2,939	2,976	3,023	3,814	5,503	6,075	3,813	4,204	10.4	–37.2	10.2	2.5
Value of shipments (1992$)	2,981	2,956	2,912	2,876	3,521	4,927	5,325	3,309	3,612	8.1	–37.9	9.2	0.6
Trade data													
Value of imports	36.2	47.1	67.5	93.2	145	204	311	243	246	52.5	–21.9	1.2	14.1
Value of exports	3,986	3,746	3,546	4,168	5,236	5,907	6,533	4,101	4,520	10.6	–37.2	10.2	–3.6

[1] Estimate except imports and exports.
[2] Estimate.
[3] Forecast.
[4] Compound annual rate.
[5] For a definition of industry versus product values, see "Getting the Most Out of *Outlook 2000*."
Source: U.S. Department of Commerce: Bureau of the Census; International Trade Administration.

balers), milking machines and other farm dairy equipment, poultry equipment (e.g., incubators, brooders, egg collectors), barnyard equipment, sprayers and irrigation equipment, grain driers and blowers, commercial turf and grounds care equipment, and parts for farm machinery. Because of the rugged construction and long service life of many farm machines (e.g., the median age of a farm tractor in the United States is 19 years), replacement parts represent a significant industry segment. While they are not used in farm agriculture, tractor mowers and some irrigation equipment are used as commercial turf and grounds care equipment and are included under SIC 3523.

Global Trends

The farm machinery manufacturing industry is characterized by increased globalization and mergers. Consolidation activity is widespread throughout the agribusiness industry, and there have been numerous mergers of farm cooperatives, grain companies, seed companies, and food processors in the United States and internationally. The largest manufacturers, such as Deere, Case Corporation, Caterpillar, AGCO, and New Holland, are multinational businesses that have manufacturing joint ventures and/or assembly operations on every continent. Many other U.S. farm machinery companies have agents and distribution channels around the world or distribute through export management companies. The products of overseas farm equipment manufacturers such as Kubota and Yanmar of Japan, Claas of Germany, Fiat of Italy, Zetor Tractor of the Czech Republic, Mahindra of India, Baldan of Brazil, and Kvernland of Norway have long been distributed in the United States and throughout the world. Parts and components are shipped globally for use in original equipment manufacturing and as replacement parts. Those parts account for a large share of farm machinery exports and imports (e.g., components exports can constitute as much as half of U.S. exports to European markets). It is difficult to determine accurately the exact local content of machinery produced in the United States and elsewhere because U.S. components are shipped to companies' overseas subsidiaries and U.S. farm machinery can contain parts and components manufactured offshore, particularly in Canada and Europe.

Growth in farm size, along with increased mechanization and the use of larger, higher-production machinery, is a continuing trend in the agricultural industry, especially in sophisticated and mature markets such as the United States, Canada, Europe, Australia, and the larger Latin American markets such as Mexico, Argentina, and Brazil. In the United States, farmers make up only 2 percent of the population, and about 50,000 of the largest farms produce half the crops. The real profits in the industry are realized by the larger agricultural producers. In mature markets, most farm machinery sales are replacement sales, with larger high-efficiency machinery replacing less productive and powerful older models. The growth in average farm acreage has resulted in fewer total farms and fewer units of farm machinery sold. Major food and cereal producers such as Archer Daniels Midland and independent contractors that provide crop services such as planting, nutrient, and pesticide application and harvesting to farms are the major purchasers of farm machinery.

The major categories of farm production machinery correspond to the three fundamental types of farming practiced around the world. Large-scale, highly mechanized agriculture is practiced in North America, Australia, Argentina, Saudi Arabia, Brazil, and South Africa. Russia and Former Soviet Union (FSU) republics such as Ukraine, Uzbekistan, and Turkmenistan, which had large state farms under the Soviet system also continue large-scale operations. Medium-scale but highly sophisticated farming is practiced in most of Europe and some parts of Asia and Latin America, while small-scale farming is the norm in most of Asia, Africa, and the Caribbean.

The farm machinery manufacturing industry is structured on a global basis to produce sizes and models of machinery in economically rational areas where the highest volume of such equipment is used. By exporting tractors, harvesters, and other machinery from consolidated locations to dealers throughout the world, farm equipment producers have been able to offer customers around the globe a wide variety of types and sizes of equipment at the lowest cost possible. The United States and Canada dominate in the manufacturing of powerful high-efficiency, high-horsepower [100 horsepower (HP) and above] equipment. Europe leads in the production of medium-range (40 to 100 HP) equipment, but there is increasing production in Latin America. Japan is the major producer of tractors under 40 HP and other small-scale units.

The world farm machinery industry experienced a major structural decline in the mid-1980s as a result of plant overcapacity and crop surpluses, similar to the conditions that persist at the turn of the century. Many prominent companies, such as International Harvester, Steiger Tractor, and Ford, merged, disappeared, or sold off their farm machinery segments. This resulted in a market dominated by four large producers: Deere & Co., 26 percent; New Holland NV (owned by Fiat of Italy), 17 percent; Case Corporation, 13 percent; and AGCO Corporation, 12 percent. In November 1999, the U.S. Department of Justice approved the $4.6 billion acquisition of the farming and construction equipment manufacturer Case Corporation by New Holland NV. This merger will create a $12 billion company that will rival Deere & Co. as the largest farm machinery manufacturer in the world, and the consolidation will make this company the world's third largest construction machinery manufacturer behind Caterpillar and Kubota of Japan. To obtain Justice Department approval, the companies had to divest ownership in Hay and Forage Industries and the Versatile and Genesis tractor lines that are manufactured in Canada. The worldwide glut of crops and the resultant manufacturing overcapacity were contributing circumstances that led to this merger.

Despite declining sales of large farm machinery in 1999, Caterpillar is moving forward to break ground on a new 350,000-square-foot facility in Nebraska to manufacture the LEXION line of combines in the United States. Full production of combines is expected in 2001, when the plant will be completed; by 2005, the plant is expected to employ 500 workers. Caterpillar and Claas Harvester OHG of Germany formed a joint venture in 1997 to produce the LEXION combines in America. Deere & Co. and the Hattat Group of Turkey agreed to form a joint venture to produce 50- to 90-HP tractors in Turkey and distribute Deere farm machinery throughout that country. Deere also increased its investment in its SLC-John Deere farm machinery company in Brazil. Among other mergers and acquisitions, the Georgia-based AGCO Corporation purchased SPRA-COUPE and Willmar, two leading brands of agricultural sprayers, and completed its joint venture with Deutz AG to produce engines for agricultural equipment in Argentina.

Domestic Trends

Industry shipments of farm machinery in constant dollars grew only 0.8 percent in 1998 (Table 18-8). Strong sales of combines in that year and robust early sales of U.S.-manufactured tractors helped offset the late year slide in tractor sales and the 6.9 percent decline in U.S. exports of farm machinery. Sales of tractors, combines, and other heavy harvesting machinery account for about 65 percent of total farm machinery sales. In 1998, combine sales increased 14.5 percent, but sales of tractors above 100 HP were 3.6 percent lower than the level in 1997. Sales of tractors in the 40- to 100-HP range, many of which are imported, rose 8.9 percent; tractor sales in all horsepower ranges grew 7.6 percent. While combine sales remained high throughout 1998, sales of tractors above 100 HP and other farm machinery began to fall sharply in August; farmers reacted to plummeting crop prices caused by worldwide grain surpluses by reducing equipment purchases. Shortline (specialty) machinery also showed a decline in the second half of 1998. Median shortline equipment sales were down 5 percent in the fourth quarter of 1998, and median orders for new equipment were off 7 percent.

Crop surpluses and the resulting low commodity prices that began in 1998 persisted into 1999. Two primary reasons for the worldwide glut of food products were good weather conditions around the world and the collapse of some Asian economies. Bumper crops in parts of the United States had led to a lack of sufficient storage facilities, forcing farmers to sell crops at prices below production costs. U.S. farmers' income in 1999 is estimated to have been 40 percent lower than it was in 1998, and farmers reflect their general uncertainty by not buying new machinery. Moreover, much of the strength in sales of tractors and combines in the 1990s reflected rollover deals in which farmers would get a new combine almost every year in return for a trade-in and a modest payment. While this benefited machinery manufacturers, it hurt farm equipment dealers. Today, there is an enormous amount of good used equipment available; this also suppresses new equipment sales by giving farmers a good and less costly alternative to purchases of new equipment. In October 1999, unit sales for tractors above 100 HP were down 30.8 percent from the level in October 1998, sales of four-wheel tractors were down 27.6 percent, and self-propelled combine sales were off 45.5 percent from a year earlier. Large tillage equipment shipments were down about 50 percent from 1998, and second quarter median sales of shortline machinery were 9 percent lower than those in 1998. By contrast, in 1997, second quarter shortline equipment sales were 21 percent higher than those in the second quarter of 1996. Currently, shortline equipment manufacturers have no back orders.

U.S. imports of farm machinery rose 6.9 percent in 1998 and totaled $3.6 billion, compared with 1997 imports of $3.4 billion; however, U.S. exports of farm machinery exceeded imports by $505 million. The top suppliers, accounting for 85 percent of U.S. imports, were Japan, Canada, Great Britain, France, Germany, and Italy; those six countries have been the top suppliers to the United States for well over 10 years (see Table 18-9). Japan is the leading supplier of low-horsepower farm machinery, and many of the European imports come from subsidiary operations of major

TABLE 18-8: Farm Machinery and Equipment (SIC 3523) Trends and Forecasts
(millions of dollars except as noted)

	1992	1993	1994	1995	1996	1997[1]	1998[1]	1999[2]	2000[3]	Percent Change 97–98	98–99	99–00	96–00[4]
Industry data													
Value of shipments[5]	9,620	11,190	12,759	13,757	14,469	15,899	16,215	10,586	10,076	2.0	–34.7	–4.8	–8.6
Value of shipments (1992$)	9,620	10,938	12,163	12,773	13,070	14,834	14,952	10,460	9,937	0.8	–30.0	–5.0	–6.6
Total employment (thousands)	61.5	63.5	66.5	65.7	66.6	66.2	64.2	53.0	58.2	–3.0	–17.4	9.8	–3.3
Production workers (thousands)	42.6	45.8	47.7	48.3	48.5	47.8	46.2	38.1	40.5	–3.3	–17.5	6.3	–4.4
Average hourly earnings ($)	13.18	13.18	13.60	14.37	14.24	16.24	16.50	16.40	16.42	1.6	–0.6	0.1	3.6
Capital expenditures	196	229	260	290	294	509							
Product data													
Value of shipments[5]	8,940	10,340	11,911	12,599	13,191	14,966	15,264	9,478	9,023	2.0	–37.9	–4.8	–9.1
Value of shipments (1992$)	8,940	10,108	11,355	11,698	11,916	13,274	13,380	9,366	8,898	0.8	–30.0	–5.0	–7.0
Trade data													
Value of imports	1,935	2,057	2,745	2,837	2,798	3,146	3,352	2,548	2,268	6.5	–24.0	–11.0	–5.1
Value of exports	2,241	2,525	2,723	3,174	3,696	4,510	4,198	3,048	2,682	–6.9	–27.4	–12.0	–7.7

[1] Estimate except imports and exports.
[2] Estimate.
[3] Forecast.
[4] Compound annual rate.
[5] For a definition of industry versus product values, see "Getting the Most Out of *Outlook 2000*."
Source: U.S. Department of Commerce: Bureau of the Census; International Trade Administration.

U.S. manufacturers in those countries. Mexico's 2.5 percent share of U.S. imports of farm machinery reflects the implementation of NAFTA in 1994. The crisis in the farm sector was manifest in 1999 imports, which were down 24 percent through August from the same period a year earlier. While the countries listed above continue to be the leading suppliers, imports are drastically down from Canada (–45 percent), Great Britain (–43 percent), France (–53 percent), and Italy (–19 percent). Over half of U.S. farm machinery imports consist of low- and medium-horsepower tractors and parts and their complementary attachments. The factories of U.S.-based farm machinery firms manufacture field row crop tractors in horsepowers of 100 and above. In 1999, sales increases were realized only for tractors below 40 HP; as a result, imports from Japan increased slightly while imports from most traditional suppliers except Germany fell.

As a result of plant overcapacity and crop surpluses in the mid-1980s, many farmers left the business because of bankruptcy and other factors. The 1998–1999 farm crisis was similar to that of the mid-1980s; however, it was less severe than the earlier crisis in that farmers' ratio of debt to equity was worse in the 1980s. Farmland values are holding up well compared with the 1980s crisis, with fewer farmers facing bankruptcy. However, many midlevel (family) farmers will quit farming because they cannot earn enough money from farming operations. This will continue the trend toward very large farms and sundowners (or hobby) farmers. Even before the current crisis, the continuing trend in American agriculture was toward increased mechanization and growth in farm size. There are approximately 2 million farms today, compared with more than 5.4 million in 1950. Although the number of farms has decreased, acreage under cultivation has not decreased; and agricultural output has increased. American farmers feed twice as many people today as they did 50 years ago while farming about the same amount of land, and about 50,000 of the largest farms produce half the nation's agricultural output.

The U.S. Environmental Protection Agency (EPA) has determined that emissions of off-road engines, including engines used in farm machinery, contribute significantly to air pollution. EPA proposed diesel engine regulations to limit exhaust and smoke emissions from off-road engines and proposed a staggered phase-in period for new engines. Most Tier I requirements have been put into effect, with only engines above 750 HP or below 25 HP to be modified by the year 2000. Tier I requirements were accomplished through relatively moderate design adjustments. However, EPA Tier II (required by 2003) and Tier III (required by 2006) requirements are increasingly stringent. EPA's final rule on Control of Emissions of Air Pollution from Nonroad Diesel Engines was issued on August 27, 1998, to be effective 60 days after its publication in the *Federal Register.* The farm and construction equipment industries challenged many requirements as being unrealistic. Among the specific concerns were that EPA had (1) not considered all classes and categories of off-road vehicles as required by the Clean Air Act, (2) overestimated the industry's ability to transfer highway engine technology to off-road applications and underestimated the costs of the changes, and (3) underestimated the costs of compliance with the proposed rule to the equipment manufacturers. For greater detail on this complex subject, readers can refer to the public policy section on the Equipment Manufacturers Institute (EMI) Web site at www.emi.org.

The EPA estimates that 65 percent of non-point-source water pollution comes from agriculture. The principal pollutants are sediment, animal waste, fertilizers, and pesticides. On August 23, 1999, EPA issued a proposed Clean Water Act (CWA) rule that could significantly revise the guidelines for measuring and reporting total maximum daily loads (TMDLs). TMDLs are measure-

TABLE 18-9: U.S. Trade Patterns in Farm Machinery[1] in 1998
(millions of dollars; percent)

Exports			Imports		
Region[2]	Value[3]	Share, %	Region[2]	Value[3]	Share, %
NAFTA	1,551	37	NAFTA	679	20
Latin America	593	14	Latin America	18	1
Western Europe	1,016	24	Western Europe	1,754	52
Japan/Chinese Economic Area	110	3	Japan/Chinese Economic Area	715	21
Other Asia	56	1	Other Asia	57	2
Rest of world	871	21	Rest of world	129	4
World	4,198	100	World	3,352	100
Top Five Countries	Value	Share, %	Top Five Countries	Value	Share, %
Canada	1,250	30	Japan	668	20
Australia	411	10	Canada	561	17
Mexico	301	7	United Kingdom	501	15
Germany	290	7	Germany	365	11
France	231	5	Italy	356	11

[1] SIC 3523.
[2] For definitions of regional groupings, see "Getting the Most Out of *Outlook 2000*."
[3] Values may not sum to total due to rounding.
Source: U.S. Department of Commerce, Bureau of the Census.

ments of the amount of pollution from a source present in a body of water and are used for waters where effluent technology limitations required by state and local governments are not sufficiently stringent to meet federal water quality standards, as is allowed for under the CWA. This proposed rule would establish a priority ranking system by which state and local governments would have to identify and report bodies of water most impaired by point and non-point-source pollution. It uses the "watershed" approach to water quality management, which allows characteristics of individual watersheds to determine the proper means of quality control. Under the provisions of the CWA, government, agricultural groups, and machinery producers are working to prevent non-point-source water pollution. Precision agricultural equipment, which enables site-specific nutrient, seed, and pesticide inputs, is an example of machinery that reduces pollutants. Additional details on how the CWA affects farm machinery producers can be found in the public policy section of the EMI Web site.

The major manufacturing states for farm machinery are, in rank order, Iowa, Illinois, Wisconsin, Kansas, Nebraska, and Georgia.

Global Market Prospects

Exports account for an average of 25 percent of U.S. farm machinery shipments. In 1998, U.S. exports of farm machinery dropped 6.9 percent after registering a 21 percent increase in 1997. That decrease reflected a global softening of demand for farm machinery caused by crop surpluses and the resulting low commodity prices in most agriculturally productive nations. In 1997, exports had reflected a spike caused by large purchases by the FSU countries of Kazakhstan, Turkmenistan, Ukraine, and Uzbekistan. However, in 1998, Uzbekistan was the only country to show an increase in imports from the United States, largely as a result of the Case Corporation's joint venture in that country. Exports fell dramatically to Ukraine (–20.4 percent), Turkmenistan (–86.5 percent), and Kazakhstan (–93.3 percent). Exports were off more than 8 percent to major markets such as Canada, Australia, and Argentina and were 17 to 20 percent lower in Mexico, the United Kingdom, and South Africa.

The depression in the farm sector deepened in 1999, with exports down about 28 percent through August, and there was little chance for improvement for the remainder of that year. Exports in all the major markets for U.S. farm machinery were in the negative column. The robust sales to Russia and FSU countries of the previous few years continued to drop drastically in 1999. Exports through August were down to Ukraine (–99.3 percent), Russia (–95.3 percent), and Turkmenistan (–98 percent). Increased exports to the few countries that showed some improvement, such as China and Romania, cannot reverse the severe export loss in the major markets.

Projections of Industry and Trade Growth for the Next 1 and 5 Years

In 1998, constant dollar shipments of U.S. farm machinery increased an estimated 0.8 percent, compared with 11 percent growth in 1997. Unit sales of combine harvesters rose a healthy 8 percent, but tractor sales declined steeply starting in August of that year. Unit domestic sales of two-wheel tractors above 100 HP finished the year down 8 percent compared with 1997, while unit sales of four-wheel-drive tractors fell 30 percent. Almost all row crop field tractors manufactured in the United States are two-wheel tractors of over 100 HP or very high horsepower units with four-wheel drive and special rubber crawlers. A limited number of tractors in the 40- to 100-HP range are manufactured in the United States, but most are imported. Unit sales of tractors in the 40- to 100-HP range increased 9 percent in 1998. Export sales declined 10.3 percent in 1998; however, 1997 exports had been unusually high because of shipments for large projects in FSU nations such as Ukraine and Turkmenistan.

While most of the U.S. economy is enjoying almost unparalleled prosperity, the farming sector has been severely depressed. Americans are seeing some of the lowest food price increases in years, but farm income is down approximately 40 percent. The global glut of cash grain crops (wheat, corn, soybeans) that began in 1998 resulted in commodity prices that were the lowest since the agricultural recession of the mid-1980s and had a severe impact on farm machinery sales in 1999. The U.S. Congress passed and the President signed a record $8.7 billion farm aid bill; nonetheless, constant dollar farm machinery sales in 1999 were 30 percent lower than those in 1998. That was the second consecutive year in which U.S. farmers received a substantial bailout package ($5.9 billion in 1998) to help them survive the abrupt income loss caused by price slumps and conditions akin to those during the great depression. Farm machinery factories have been idled or have operated at reduced capacity.

Farm machinery sales in the year 2000 are forecast to continue to fall, but the decline should slow from the steep drop experienced in 1999. Farm machinery sales cannot recover substantially until there is a drawdown of the current huge crop surplus and an increase in crop prices. The crop surplus is not expected to diminish sufficiently in 2000 and possibly not until 2001 or 2002. There has been long-term competition in the wheat market, and there is significant competition from South America in the oilseeds market. With the 1999 harvest almost complete, each new U.S. Department of Agriculture (USDA) crop report predicted higher yields, further suppressing commodity prices. Because of the low commodity prices, farmers may reduce plantings in 2000, further reducing the need for machinery to work the fields. The availability of a large array of good used equipment will inhibit new machinery purchases further in 2000. As a result of these factors, farm machinery sales are projected to fall another 5 percent in 2000.

Increased farm income from rising commodity prices must precede any significant increase in farm machinery purchases. Farmers purchase other farm inputs, such as seed, fuel, nutrients, and fertilizer, before purchasing equipment. Because of the lagged effect of increased farm income on machinery purchases, substantial increases in farm machinery purchases may lag behind a rise in commodity prices by at least a year. In the long run, today's low commodity prices could stimulate future demand as customers increase feed grain purchases at today's low prices and become accustomed to more protein in their diets.

The long-term outlook for agriculture and farm machinery is positive as populations increase globally, with continued demand for dietary improvements. The demand for more protein in the diets of people in developing countries will boost the need for feed grains and the equipment used to produce them. Because water resources are finite, farmers globally are seeking improved farming methods both to conserve water and to achieve water use efficiency. The United States is recognized as the leader in irrigation technology and should benefit from the increased demand for this sophisticated irrigation equipment as well as that for new conservation tillage machinery and other new environmentally sound equipment.

Mary R. Wiening, U.S. Department of Commerce, Office of Energy, Infrastructure and Machinery, (202) 482–4708, November 1999.

PACKAGING MACHINERY

The packaging machinery industry (NAICS 333993, formerly SIC 3565) consists of establishments engaged primarily in manufacturing machinery for uses such as canning, container cleaning, filling, forming, bagging, packing, unpacking, bottling, sealing and lidding, inspection and check weighing, wrapping, shrink film and heat sealing, case forming, labeling and encoding, palletizing and depalletizing, and related uses. More than 100 specialized types of packaging machines are manufactured and are in daily use throughout the world.

The purpose of packaging machinery is to take bulk or finished products—liquid, gaseous, or solid objects—and pack them for final shipment to customers, whether industrial, wholesale, commercial, or retail. The packaging process consists of placing a product into containers made of appropriate materials and of uniform sizes that are designed to protect the product against deterioration or damage and marking and/or labeling them and packing them as required into outer containers ready for shipment.

Global Trends

The packaging machinery industry is steadily becoming more globalized as industrialization and modern agribusiness spread throughout the world, creating new demand and markets for packaging. Although varying by geographic region and industry segment, the outlook for growth of the industry is very favorable.

The United States, the European Union, and Japan are the world's leading manufacturers, distributors, and end users of packaging machinery and technology. Packaging machines of various types and degrees of sophistication also are produced in numerous other countries such as Brazil, Mexico, Taiwan, Hungary, Turkey, and Russia. They often are designed for local or regional use and may be built in factories that are joint ventures or subsidiaries of foreign manufacturers. There are no international standards for packaging machinery; this is a concern among U.S. manufacturers, which are exporting about 20 percent of their production and striving to expand their international market share. U.S. machinery is routinely built to meet Underwriters Laboratory standards, Occupational Safety and Health Administration (OSHA) standards, ISO-9000, and increasingly European Union (EU) seal requirements. When used in sanitary applications such as food processing, pharmaceutical, and cosmetics packaging, the machinery conforms to and is operated in accordance with the Code of Federal Regulations (21CFR, Parts 1–99) of the Food, Drug and Cosmetic Act of 1938 as amended, including the Current Good Manufacturing Practices (CGMP) section. The U.S. industry supports international cooperation in standards development to prevent standards from becoming trade barriers while assuring that uniformly high-quality, safe machinery is delivered to end users throughout the world.

Domestic Trends

The United States is the world's largest market for packaging technology, earning revenues exceeding $100 billion annually and employing more than 200,000 workers. Although this is a huge market, it is still growing, fueled by the highly competitive, industrialized, market-driven U.S. economy. The extensive range of American-made packaging equipment reflects the machinery industry's historical response to the dynamic needs of U.S. and international manufacturers of packaged goods.

A broad base of standard packaging systems is the foundation of an almost infinite number of systems variations that can be customized to meet customers' demands. This requires that machinery suppliers cultivate closer working relationships with their customers to provide them with technical expertise, engineering services, after-sales support, and developmental planning for the future. Eventually, some packaging equipment suppliers may become "full-service" suppliers by building equipment, training operators, and employing packaging system managers in customers' plants.

U.S. industrial consumption of packaging machinery is estimated as follows: The food and beverage industry uses about 55 percent; the pharmaceuticals, cosmetics, and personal care products sectors, about 15 percent; the chemical sector (all types), nearly 10 percent; the consumer durables and nondurables sectors, about 10 percent; and the hardware and automotive sectors and the printing and converting sectors, about 5 percent each.

The U.S. packaging machinery industry includes nearly 690 companies, mainly small and medium-size highly specialized businesses. Most of those companies are privately held. The leading manufacturing states are Illinois, Wisconsin, California, Ohio, and Minnesota, which account for about 40 percent of the industry's employment. With the growing demand for complete packaging lines at home and abroad, specialized machinery builders with limited product lines are collaborating with manufacturers of complementary equipment on projects. Companies are partnering and forming consortia that can undertake very large and diverse projects. There also has been some acquisition activity, both foreign and domestic, as manufacturers attempt to broaden their product lines by acquiring companies in strategic markets. For example, there are European firms that manufacture in the United States to have better access to the U.S. and NAFTA markets and, conversely, American firms that place manufacturing and distribution operations in western Europe to have better access to that and neighboring markets.

Four major factors drive U.S. demand for new machinery. The first is the need to expand production and packaging capabilities, which is spurred by the continuing growth of the U.S. manufacturing base. Packagers are demanding more automated and efficient machinery. Second, despite the legendary long life of U.S. packaging machinery, the replacement of older machinery is often urgently required to improve production and efficiency. With the growing number of business mergers and consolidations, a significant amount of often late-model used machinery is available. This situation has prompted more machinery builders to launch their own programs for upgrading and rebuilding machinery for individual customers and for the used machinery market. Third, the flood of new product introductions, which were estimated to exceed 19,000 in 1999, is causing U.S. packagers to seek machinery that can increase production, reduce changeover time, and handle a wider variety of packaging forms, sizes, and materials. The fourth and most compelling factor is the need for packagers to reduce their production costs in response to intensifying market competition.

Now, more than ever, important technology drivers are supporting demand for new machinery. Those drivers include expanded robotics systems, contributing to cost reductions in general and to worker safety; enhanced vision systems and improved machinery flexibility, permitting quick changeovers without the need for tools and requiring only minimal labor; expanded computer integration; and simpler user-friendly controls. In short, the trends are toward greater efficiency, higher performance, flexibility, automation, cost reduction, and larger profit margins.

Internet Applications

The Internet is rapidly advancing from a passive to an active reference tool for commerce in packaging technology. The majority of machinery builders, industry trade associations, and publications have established their own Web sites. Associations are facilitating access to member companies by putting their membership directories on-line, complete with product locators and contact information, as well as promoting important trade shows and meetings. The trend toward E-commerce is under way as growing numbers of manufacturers are providing technical information and ordering services for selected parts, supplies, and basic machines. Some manufacturers accept complex machinery inquiries by E-mail and respond promptly with conditional equipment recommendations, which are subject to later review, pricing, and final approval by their sales and engineering departments. Long-distance servicing is now possible as a result of the Internet. Manufacturers are using the capabilities of the Internet by incorporating modems into their equipment to permit their customers around the world to log on to their home sites for "real-time" field adjustments and troubleshooting.

Evolution of Packages

A new generation of proprietary, lightweight, and generally reusable shipping containers is replacing the heavy, dedicated, rigid, mass-produced stock containers of the past. The once distinct boundary between rigid and flexible containers has been blurred by ever lighter containers using fewer but stronger materials. Environmental and economic drivers are moving packagers to contain more contents with less packaging material. Packaging designers are responding imaginatively and responsibly to consumer demands such as tamper-resistant packages, child-protective closures, user-friendly packages for the infirm, reusable and reliable resealable packaging, more protection for contents, and, in the case of noxious products, more protection from leakage of contents. However, the market success of this new generation of packages will rely on the ability of machinery manufacturers to engineer, build, install, and service flexible, agile packaging equipment.

Packaging Education

Globalization of packaging is increasing the need for international packaging education at the technical training school, continuing education, and university levels. Education in package design, materials selection, machinery functions, labeling, marketing, and the environmental aspects of good packaging is essential to modern manufacturing, distribution, and trade. Education in the correct specification, installation, maintenance, and operations of packaging machinery lines is equally important. In addition to supporting established academic programs through scholarships and technical assistance, the U.S. machinery industry and its trade and professional associations promote packaging education through the organization of technical seminars and training courses for industry professionals and students. The machinery industry also is publishing technical materials and machinery operations and maintenance manuals.

Projections of Industry and Trade Growth

Aided by high demand and low interest rates, 1997 product shipments of packaging machinery surged 24 percent, registering an all-time high. Market demand was driven upward as packagers, particularly large-volume manufacturers, sought to improve productivity, efficiency, and profitability through the installation of more highly automated packaging lines. Market momentum and technological improvements demanded by new product packaging, combined with moderate growth in the gross domestic product (GDP), produced a 2 percent increase in packaging machinery shipments in 1998 (see Table 18-10). In 1999, product shipments grew 4 percent in nominal terms (2 percent in constant dollars), and that rate is forecast to continue through 2000. In recent years, the U.S. packaging machinery industry has invested heavily in capital equipment, factory modernization, and rationalization programs. The industry should enter the new millennium well equipped, well staffed, and globally competitive.

Global Market Prospects

It is estimated that about one-third of the world market for packaging machinery is located in North America. Owing to the large size of the U.S. market and import competition, American machinery builders must focus a great deal of attention on their home market. However, export business is extremely important to U.S. machinery builders. They have been adept at meeting the special needs of overseas customers and being loyal suppliers in times of difficulty. U.S. packaging machinery has earned a strong position in international markets. The United States exports packaging machinery to about 140 countries annually. In 1998, Canada and Mexico (NAFTA) imported about 36 percent of U.S. exports, western Europe about 28 percent, Latin America 12 percent, the Japan/Chinese Economic Area and Asia about 15 percent, and other nations about 10 percent (see Table 18-11). In 1999, the top 10 U.S. export markets were Canada, Mexico, the United Kingdom, Germany, Japan, the Netherlands, Belgium, Brazil, Australia, and Italy. The downturn in economic conditions in key world markets was reflected by falling exports in 1998 and 1999. With economic recovery under way in Asian and Latin American markets, an upturn in U.S. exports is expected.

As the world's largest market for packaging machinery, the United States has had imports in excess of $1 billion since 1995. It is an outstanding market for international machinery builders that can meet its high production, technical, and competitive price requirements. The U.S. market is open and accessible and offers the greatest variety of machinery applications. Leading supplier nations are Germany, Italy, Canada, Japan, and the United Kingdom, which together supplied 76 percent of

TABLE 18-10: Packaging Machinery (SIC 3565) Trends and Forecasts
(millions of dollars except as noted)

										Percent Change			
	1992	1993	1994	1995	1996	1997	1998[1]	1999[2]	2000[3]	97–98	98–99	99–00	96–00[4]
Industry data													
Value of shipments[5]	3,150	3,418	3,690	4,185	4,056	4,820	4,916	5,113	5,317	2.0	4.0	4.0	7.0
Value of shipments (1992$)	3,150	3,322	3,491	3,864	3,667	4,269	4,267	4,351	4,438	–0.0	2.0	2.0	4.9
Total employment (thousands)	26.4	24.9	24.8	28.0	27.2	31.2							
Production workers (thousands)	15.6	14.2	14.9	16.9	16.3	16.9							
Average hourly earnings ($)	13.86	14.29	14.52	14.69	14.68	15.69							
Capital expenditures	70.6	90.2	98.6	87.0	111	120							
Product data													
Value of shipments[5]	2,861	3,098	3,257	3,658	3,435	4,355	4,442	4,620	4,805	2.0	4.0	4.0	8.8
Value of shipments (1992$)	2,861	3,011	3,081	3,377	3,105	3,857	3,855	3,931	4,010	–0.1	2.0	2.0	6.6
Trade data													
Value of imports	699	719	842	932	1,042	1,104	1,072	1,086	1,097	–2.9	1.3	1.0	1.3
Value of exports	606	672	792	839	841	871	791	746	783	–9.2	–5.7	5.0	–1.8

[1] Estimate except imports and exports.
[2] Estimate.
[3] Forecast.
[4] Compound annual rate.
[5] For a definition of industry versus product values, see "Getting the Most Out of *Outlook 2000*."
Source: U.S. Department of Commerce: Bureau of the Census; International Trade Administration.

TABLE 18-11: U.S. Trade Patterns in Packaging Machinery[1] in 1998
(millions of dollars; percent)

Exports			Imports		
Region[2]	Value[3]	Share, %	Region[2]	Value[3]	Share, %
NAFTA	289	36	NAFTA	159	15
Latin America	92	12	Latin America	3	0
Western Europe	223	28	Western Europe	772	72
Japan/Chinese Economic Area	60	8	Japan/Chinese Economic Area	120	11
Other Asia	52	7	Other Asia	9	1
Rest of world	76	10	Rest of world	10	1
World	791	100	World	1,072	100
Top Five Countries	Value	Share, %	Top Five Countries	Value	Share, %
Canada	168	21	Germany	327	30
Mexico	121	15	Italy	195	18
United Kingdom	50	6	Canada	154	14
Netherlands	36	5	Japan	90	8
Germany	34	4	United Kingdom	65	6

[1] SIC 3565.
[2] For definitions of regional groupings, see "Getting the Most Out of *Outlook 2000*."
[3] Values may not sum to total due to rounding.
Source: U.S. Department of Commerce, Bureau of the Census.

the machinery imported into the United States in 1998, a year in which imports held a 23 percent share of the domestic market. The remaining top 10 import suppliers are Switzerland, the Netherlands, France, Sweden, and Taiwan.

As globalization of the world's economy increases, so will international requirements for packages and containers of every description to protect, promote, and carry the increasing abundance of the world's commerce.

Eugene Shaw, U.S. Department of Commerce, Office of Energy, Infrastructure and Machinery, (202) 482–3494, November 1999.

PAPER INDUSTRIES MACHINERY

The paper industries machinery subsector (SIC 3554, NAICS 333291) consists of firms that manufacture machinery for the production of pulp and paper. The industry produces equipment for the major papermaking stages: woodyard equipment used to prepare wood for pulping, pulping and fiberline equipment used in the manufacture of pulp, paper machines, calendars, on-machine coaters, winders, and machinery and equipment used in converting paper into finished goods. The industry includes machinery for off-machine coating but does not include some machinery and equipment commonly used in paper and allied product mills, such as vacuum pumps, fourdrinier wire, and paper machine clothing.

Global Trends

Despite intense competition from Finland and Germany, the United States remains the largest worldwide manufacturer of paper industries machinery and an effective competitor in international markets. Although paper industries machines are among the largest forms of machinery manufactured for any industry, that machinery is easily exportable in a completely knocked-down form. Consequently, size has not proved to be a barrier to the movement of paper industries machinery in international trade.

The paper industries machinery subsector historically has been subject to the cyclical nature of the paper industry. The long lead times required for paper machinery make industry activity a lagging economic indicator and can mask industry performance. The long lead times cushion the initial impact on the industry of the downturn in its customer base. Conversely, an upturn in the fortunes of the industry's customers may take 1 or 2 years to be reflected in industry shipments. Furthermore, new capital spending by the paper industry is highly cyclical. The cyclicality of those capital expenditures is reinforced by the tendency of mills to cluster new capital spending in periods of greatest profitability.

When a major manufacturer launches a new mill or a major rebuild, competitors often are not far behind. New capital expenditures, especially for rebuilds, often are driven by increased demand for a specific paper grade. New capital expenditures by the U.S. paper industry are constrained by the need to allocate financial resources to meet the EPA's Cluster Rule. Internationally, Asian markets for paper machinery are expected to revive more slowly than those for other types of production machinery.

Domestic Trends

The U.S. paper industry has experienced 7 years of sluggish growth, with increases in product shipments averaging only 1.5 to 2.0 percent annually (see Table 18-12). This slow growth has resulted from a combination of falling prices and overcapacity in paper sectors such as market pulp and key paper grades such as newsprint and tissue. Those factors brought about 3 straight years of declining product shipments from 1996 to 1999 for the U.S. industry. Paper and allied product mills have been reluctant to increase capital spending during the current cycle.

Mergers and acquisitions in the paper and allied products industry have eliminated some existing capacity and consequently have led to reduced demand for both new and rebuilt machinery. Long lead times and a large backlog of orders fueled industry growth before 1997. Now long lead times have hindered the industry's ability to recover from the sluggish performance of its primary customer base. These circumstances have increased the industry's reliance on exports at a time when domestic production capacity has declined and exports to Asian markets such as Indonesia and Malaysia have plummeted.

The industry continues to undergo extensive restructuring through mergers, acquisitions, bankruptcy proceedings, and joint ventures. Manufacturers of pulping equipment and primary paper machinery in particular have been affected by these developments. This activity has increased the industry's concentration, reduced the volume of manufacturing capacity, and increased the proportion of product shipments emanating from the leading U.S., German, and Finnish suppliers. Mergers in the paper and allied products industries also have reduced excess pulp and paper machine capacity. Paper industry mergers have provided new investment capital for greenfield mill projects and paper machine rebuilds. However, these mergers appear to have reduced the number of paper machines in place at U.S. and Canadian mills and also have contributed to the drop in the number of new and rebuilt paper machine projects being announced.

Employment in the paper machine industry continued to fall in 1999 and was estimated at approximately 16,000 at the end of that year, down more than 2,300 from the 18,349 reported in 1997. Industry employment is likely to decline further in the year 2000 in light of announced restructuring plans and the planned closing of some domestic production capacity.

The U.S. industry remains concentrated in its traditional centers of production in smaller, mostly northern communities. The south continues to attract stocking and parts facilities in states such as Alabama, Florida, and Louisiana, which are home to mill operations that use southern yellow pine and other faster-growing wood species. The effect of recent industry layoffs has been particularly severe in several small towns, including Beloit, WI; Dalton, MA; and Watertown, NY. The industry consisted of 331 companies with 365 establishments in 1997. Of those establishments, 42 had 100 or more employees in 1997. Wisconsin, with 48 firms, accounts for approximately one-third of all industry shipments and, despite a decline in its market share, maintains its place as the leading state for paper machinery manufacturing. Massachusetts, Pennsylvania, New Jersey, Ohio, New York, Maryland, and New Hampshire were the next largest leaders in paper machinery industry employment in 1997. Following Wisconsin in the number of establishments were New York (32), Massachusetts (22), Ohio (20), and Pennsylvania (18).

The need to rebuild or replace outdated paper machines in domestic mills may provide the spark needed to revive the depressed U.S. market. An industry-conducted survey reported that in October 1998, more than 36 percent of a large sample of paper machinery operating in domestic mills had been installed before 1986, 31 percent between 1986 and 1990, and 33 percent since 1991. A separate survey in 1999 indicated that under 25 percent of the machines designed to process paper grades such as linerboard and uncoated free sheet are capable of operating at internationally competitive standards. Since approximately 10 percent of operating machines probably will not be rebuilt, a significant volume of machinery awaits upgrading.

Although proposals for greenfield mills in North America are drawn up frequently, only a small proportion are ever built. The

TABLE 18-12: Paper Industries Machinery (SIC 3554) Trends and Forecasts
(millions of dollars except as noted)

										Percent Change			
	1992	1993	1994	1995	1996	1997	1998[1]	1999[2]	2000[3]	97–98	98–99	99–00	96–00[4]
Industry data													
Value of shipments[5]	2,524	2,529	2,828	3,418	3,419	3,396	3,316	3,174	3,124	−2.4	−4.3	−1.6	−2.2
Value of shipments (1992$)	2,524	2,496	2,751	3,283	3,216	3,082	2,944	2,774	2,709	−4.5	−5.8	−2.3	−4.2
Total employment (thousands)	18.2	18.1	17.5	19.3	19.5	18.3							
Production workers (in thousands)	10.2	9.8	9.8	10.9	11.2	10.1							
Average hourly earnings ($)	14.76	15.24	16.11	16.55	17.56	17.60							
Capital expenditures	65.4	55.9	49.7	90.6	75.3								
Product data													
Value of shipments[5]	2,225	2,253	2,479	2,970	3,039	2,971	2,894	2,757	2,704	−2.6	−4.7	−1.9	−2.9
Value of shipments (1992$)	2,225	2,224	2,411	2,853	2,859	2,727	2,604	2,443	2,365	−4.5	−6.2	−3.2	−4.6
Trade data													
Value of imports	637	709	890	970	1,168	1,099	1,029	1,083	1,145	−6.4	5.2	5.7	−0.5
Value of exports	583	652	633	838	836	978	796	704	687	−18.6	−11.6	−2.4	−4.8

[1] Estimate except imports and exports.
[2] Estimate.
[3] Forecast.
[4] Compound annual rate.
[5] For a definition of industry versus product values, see "Getting the Most Out of *Outlook 2000*."
Source: U.S. Department of Commerce: Bureau of the Census; International Trade Administration.

construction of a greenfield mill requires passage through an obstacle course of environmental regulations and planning and zoning processes. This has limited the number of projects completed. Traditionally, rebuilds of machinery in place account for 60 to 70 percent of paper machine orders in North American markets. The rebuilding or replacing of existing machines offers mill operators a less tortuous route to increase production capacity or effect a change of paper grade.

Projections of Industry and Trade Growth

Product shipments of paper industries machinery were expected to drop for the third consecutive year in 1999 as the industry continued to feel the effects of the recession in the North American and Asian paper machinery markets. Product shipments were estimated to have fallen to $2.4 billion in constant 1992 dollars, or 6.2 percent below the already depressed totals in 1998. The decline is expected to continue as product shipments of paper machinery are forecast to register a further 3.2 percent decline in 2000 to a constant 1992 dollar level of under $2.4 billion. Annual U.S. imports of paper machinery exceeded exports throughout the 1990s. However, after approaching parity in 1997, the deficit widened as exports, especially to Asian markets, fell in the next 2 years (see Table 18-13). U.S. paper machinery exports were projected to fall 10.3 percent in 1999 to $704 million, approximately 28 percent below the record level of $978 million reached in 1997. Although imports fell nearly 12 percent between 1996 and 1998, an increase of 5.2 percent to $1.1 billion was projected for 1999. A further widening of the trade deficit is expected in the year 2000 as U.S. imports of paper industries machinery are anticipated to rise 5.7 percent to $1.1 billion in that year. The closing of several U.S. manufacturing facilities and the sharp fall in exports to Asian markets such as Indonesia and Malaysia have contributed to the worsening balance of trade in paper industries machinery. Meanwhile, imports have begun to recover from the long-term sluggishness of the North American paper industry, which had reduced demand for paper machinery products.

Over the 5-year period 2000–2004, product shipments are expected to grow at an annual rate of 4 percent, with stronger growth likely in the later years. With the expected recovery of the paper industries in key Asian markets, U.S. exports of paper machinery are forecast to recover during the 2000–2004 period, with an annual growth rate of 4 to 7 percent. Imports are already rising and are expected to increase at a rate of approximately 5 percent per annum in the 2000–2004 period.

Global Market Prospects

Canada, which accounts for over one-fourth of U.S. paper machinery exports, has long been the leading export market for the U.S. industry. U.S. exports of paper machinery to Canada more than doubled between 1994 and 1997, reaching a record $267 million. By eliminating a 9.5 percent Canadian tariff on paper machinery, NAFTA has encouraged the reorganization of Canadian paper machinery manufacturing facilities and stimulated a sharp rise in U.S. paper machinery exports to Canada. However, U.S. paper machinery exports to Canada retreated in 1998 to approximately the 1996 level of $234 million and were expected to fall another 6 percent to $220 million in 1999. The Canadian pulp and paper industry has been dogged by many of the same difficulties that have depressed shipments to U.S. customers.

U.S. exporters of pulp and paper machinery to Asia were deeply affected by the Asian financial crisis. The inability of a large Indonesian partner to meet its financial obligations to a U.S.-based paper machinery manufacturer directly affected the U.S. parent firm's decision to file for protection under Chapter 11 of the Bankruptcy Act. U.S. paper machinery exports to Brazil and Asian markets fell precipitously in both 1998 and 1999. After

TABLE 18-13: U.S. Trade Patterns in Paper Industries Machinery[1] in 1998
(millions of dollars; percent)

Exports			Imports		
Region[2]	Value[3]	Share, %	Region[2]	Value[3]	Share, %
NAFTA	302	38	NAFTA	160	16
Latin America	99	12	Latin America	11	1
Western Europe	199	25	Western Europe	776	75
Japan/Chinese Economic Area	68	9	Japan/Chinese Economic Area	63	6
Other Asia	65	8	Other Asia	7	1
Rest of world	63	8	Rest of world	13	1
World	796	100	World	1,029	100
Top Five Countries	Value	Share, %	Top Five Countries	Value	Share, %
Canada	218	27	Germany	261	25
Mexico	85	11	Canada	160	16
United Kingdom	52	7	Switzerland	119	12
Germany	39	5	Italy	99	10
Brazil	34	4	Sweden	89	9

[1] SIC 3554.
[2] For definitions of regional groupings, see "Getting the Most Out of *Outlook 2000.*"
[3] Values may not sum to total due to rounding.
Source: U.S. Department of Commerce, Bureau of the Census.

reaching $76.7 million in 1997 to place second among all paper machinery export markets, U.S. exports to Indonesia plunged to $24 million in 1998 and to an estimated $6 million in 1999. However, the revival of other Asian economies is likely to produce a small uptick in U.S. exports in the year 2000 and larger increases in subsequent years. U.S. exports of paper machinery to Brazil dropped from $53.7 million in 1997 to an estimated $16.4 million in 1999. New commodity-grade mills have been constructed in Latin American and Asian markets to manufacture paper grades such as newsprint in exportable quantities. The relative difficulty of siting greenfield mills in Europe and North America as a result of environmental constraints and tight zoning restrictions will continue to make Asia and Latin America attractive locations for the construction of paper mills.

Mexico at an estimated $82 million, Germany ($74 million), the United Kingdom ($65 million), the Netherlands ($27 million), Australia ($25 million), Japan ($20 million), Brazil ($16 million), China ($16 million), and France ($12 million) rounded out the top 10 markets in 1999. Italy, Argentina, Taiwan, Chile, and Indonesia constituted the next five largest markets.

The primary foreign suppliers to the U.S. market in 1999 were Germany ($274 million), Canada ($210 million), Switzerland ($97 million), Sweden ($77 million), the United Kingdom ($74 million), Finland ($52 million), Italy ($50 million), Austria ($40 million), Japan ($31 million), and France ($25 million). Although Finland was the trailblazer in penetrating North American paper machinery markets in the 1960s, its exports of paper machinery to the United States have fallen as its major producers have increased direct manufacturing in the United States and Canada. Imports from some sources, including Canada, Spain, the United Kingdom, and Brazil, include machinery manufactured in U.S.-owned facilities in those countries.

Edward D. Abrahams, U.S. Department of Commerce, Office of Energy, Infrastructure and Machinery, (202) 482-0312.

AIR-CONDITIONING, REFRIGERATION, AND HEATING EQUIPMENT

Air-conditioning, refrigeration, and heating equipment (SIC 3585) includes machinery related to heat transfer and cooling systems. Specific products include air conditioners, humidifiers, dehumidifiers, furnaces, compressors and compressor units, heat pumps, and commercial refrigerators.

Global and Domestic Outlook

The air-conditioning, refrigeration, and heating equipment (HVAC) industry experienced higher growth in 1998 than it did in any year since 1994. In 1998, industry shipments were estimated to be over $30.1 billion, an 8.9 percent increase from 1997 (see Table 18-14). A continuation of favorable economic conditions, including low mortgage interest rates, high consumer confidence, and robust housing starts contributed to that growth. Estimates of 1999 industry growth show a slowdown from the record levels of 1998. However, the industry was expected to sell 3.2 percent more product in real terms in 1999 than it did the previous year. This was due in no small part to the ongoing strength in the housing market, with housing starts estimated to have been in the range of 1.6 million in 1999. Central air-conditioning is fast becoming standard in new house construction. The Air-Conditioning and Refrigeration Institute (ARI) reports that about 83 percent of new homes are currently built with central air conditioning, including 99 percent of those in the south. The housing industry benefited from low mortgage interest rates as well as from the prospect of higher rates in the near future as a result of an expected increase in interest rates by the Federal Reserve. Also favorable was the unemployment rate, which remained at record low levels throughout that year. In addition to providing units for new homes, nearly half the industry's shipments are used to replace outdated systems, both residential and nonresidential.

In addition to economic conditions, weather is an important factor in sales of air-conditioning and heating units. The record heat experienced by much of the country in the summer of 1999 was reflected in a record number of shipments for a single month, with 872,843 central air conditioners and air-source heat pumps shipped in June alone, as reported by the ARI. Scorching weather in July presaged strong shipments in July and August.

One of the major issues for the air-conditioning industry is the replacement or conversion of chlorofluorocarbon (CFC) chillers. Even though a ban on the production of CFCs has been in effect since 1995 because of the ozone-depleting nature of those chemicals, the EPA predicted that by the year 2000, only 44 percent of the CFC chillers that existed in the early 1990s would be replaced or converted. According to a survey conducted by the ARI, at the current pace of replacement, it will take until 2010 to eliminate the use of CFC chillers in the United States. Since so many CFC units are still in service, manufacturers will have steady demand for replacement units for at least another decade. This demand will rely less on economic conditions than it will on the availability and price of CFC refrigerants, which are no longer being produced domestically. While the United States and other developed countries have stopped producing CFCs, developing nations continue to produce CFCs, and some attempt to export them to the United States illegally. For a report on the current status of CFC supply, visit the EPA Internet site at epa.gov/spdpublc/geninfo/sdreport99.pdf.

Since CFCs are no longer in production and their replacements, hydrocholorofluorocarbons (HCFCs), are due to be phased out by 2030, the industry is searching for new, efficient, and environmentally friendly refrigerants. Hydrofluorocarbons (HFCs), which are chlorine-free and thus non-ozone-depleting, are slated to be the next generation of refrigerant, with some possibilities for ammonia and gas applications, particularly for industrial and other large-scale applications.

Electronic Commerce

E-commerce has permeated this industry as it has the entire economy. ARI estimates that the number of manufacturers with Web sites has increased from 0 in 1993 to well over 100 today. Additionally, distributors and contractors also have a Web presence, offering product descriptions and prices, contact information, and

TABLE 18-14: Refrigeration and Heating Equipment (SIC 3585) Trends and Forecasts
(millions of dollars except as noted)

	1992	1993	1994	1995	1996	1997[1]	1998[1]	1999[2]	2000[3]	Percent Change 97–98	98–99	99–00	96–00[4]
Industry data													
Value of shipments[5]	19,739	21,530	24,414	26,217	28,094	27,655	30,123	31,346	31,470	8.9	4.1	0.4	2.9
Value of shipments (1992$)	19,739	21,338	24,029	25,233	26,554	26,120	28,079	28,978	28,833	7.5	3.2	−0.5	2.1
Total employment (thousands)	121	122	131	135	135								
Production workers (thousands)	89.1	90.1	99.1	103	104								
Average hourly earnings ($)	13.26	13.36	13.76	14.16	14.20								
Capital expenditures	557	518	779	672	717								
Product data													
Value of shipments[5]	18,098	19,767	22,441	23,770	25,512	25,113	27,198	28,313	28,483	8.3	4.1	0.6	2.8
Value of shipments (1992$)	18,098	19,591	22,087	22,877	24,114	23,720	25,404	26,192	26,139	7.1	3.1	−0.2	2.0
Trade data													
Value of imports	1,605	1,723	2,128	2,378	2,633	2,557	2,835	3,007	2,923	10.9	6.1	−2.8	2.6
Value of exports	3,310	3,582	3,855	4,373	4,691	5,229	5,140	5,053	5,438	−1.7	−1.7	7.6	3.8

[1] Estimate except imports and exports.
[2] Estimate.
[3] Forecast.
[4] Compound annual rate.
[5] For a definition of industry versus product values, see "Getting the Most Out of *Outlook 2000.*"
Source: U.S. Department of Commerce: Bureau of the Census; International Trade Administration.

on-line newsletters. Perhaps the most significant single commercial Internet entity in the business is hvacmall.com, which provides a directory of services, companies, and products related to the HVAC industry, including residential, commercial, and industrial applications. ARI has an extensive Web site on which members can download industry standards such as purity levels for refrigerants, design specifications, and noise measurement. Additionally, the site has extensive consumer information explaining, for example, how air-conditioning systems work, why the government has banned the production of certain refrigerants, and where to find career opportunities in the industry. On-line business-to-business sales are an emerging area for the HVAC industry. Air-Conditioning & Refrigeration Wholesalers International (ARWI) has launched its HVAC/R Warehouse, where members can list products for sale to other distributors. The extent to which such services are used by wholesalers remains to be seen.

The air-conditioning, refrigeration, and heating industry is composed of firms with worldwide operations. Significant transportation costs and regional product differentiation make it cost-competitive to locate manufacturing plants around the world. E-commerce, particularly in the area of internal communication, is therefore vital to this industry. The sharing of information

TABLE 18-15: U.S. Trade Patterns in Refrigeration and Heating Equipment[1] in 1998
(millions of dollars; percent)

Exports Region[2]	Value[3]	Share, %	Imports Region[2]	Value[3]	Share, %
NAFTA	2,277	44	NAFTA	1,127	40
Latin America	595	12	Latin America	231	8
Western Europe	737	14	Western Europe	341	12
Japan/Chinese Economic Area	541	11	Japan/Chinese Economic Area	695	25
Other Asia	398	8	Other Asia	417	15
Rest of world	593	12	Rest of world	24	1
World	5,140	100	World	2,835	100
Top Five Countries	**Value**	**Share, %**	**Top Five Countries**	**Value**	**Share, %**
Canada	1,654	32	Mexico	769	27
Mexico	623	12	Japan	528	19
Saudi Arabia	215	4	Canada	358	13
Japan	154	3	Brazil	226	8
United Kingdom	153	3	South Korea	206	7

[1] SIC 3585.
[2] For definitions of regional groupings, see "Getting the Most Out of *Outlook 2000.*"
[3] Values may not sum to total due to rounding.
Source: U.S. Department of Commerce, Bureau of the Census.

with engineers around the world in real time allows for a much greater level of efficiency in the design of new processes and products. Technological innovations can be shared instantly without regard for distance.

Industry and Trade Projections

With the U.S. economic expansion in its ninth year in 1999, the Federal Reserve was beginning to worry about early inflationary signs, leading it to raise interest rates. The resulting upward pressure on mortgage rates and the resulting slowdown in housing starts predicted for the year 2000 are forecast to spell an end to the years of consistent growth experienced by the industry. Assuming GDP growth of approximately 2 percent in 2000, constant dollar industry shipments are expected to decrease 0.5 percent in that year.

Exports slowed in 1998 and were expected to continue to do so in 1999, largely because of the Asian economic crisis. Shipments to Asia fell 26 percent in 1998. Despite increases in product demand in Europe, Latin America, and the NAFTA countries, total exports fell 3 percent in 1998 and 2 percent in 1999. Nevertheless, exports exceeded imports in both years (see Table 18-15). The currency devaluations that precipitated the Asian economic downturn also contributed to an 11 percent increase in U.S. imports in 1998, followed by a 6 percent rise in 1999.

Christine Siegwarth Meyer, (315) 637–8831, November 1999.

PRINTING TRADES MACHINERY

Printing trades machinery (SIC 3555) consists of the equipment used in all phases of the printing process, from prepress to bindery. All types of printing presses are included in this category, from conventional offset presses to those incorporating the latest flexographic and digital imaging technologies. This subsector also includes bookbinding machinery and graphic arts accessories used in the prepress stage.

Global and Domestic Trends

In general, the printing trades machinery industry has experienced strong growth in the last decade, with shipments growing at an annual rate of over 6 percent from 1992 through 1997. A healthy U.S. economy with high spending on advertising leading to robust consumer demand, a very literate population, and growing tax revenues and government budgets have all contributed to continued demand for printed products and thus for the machinery that produces them.

The printing trades machinery subsector also has been the beneficiary of healthy investment in new presses by the printing industry as digital technology has infiltrated all aspects of the printing process, according to the Association for Suppliers of Printing and Publishing Technologies (NPES), a U.S. trade association representing companies engaged in manufacturing and importing equipment used in printing and publishing. Digital techniques have been most influential in the preliminary prepress stage of printing. The integration of computers into this stage of the printing process has significantly shortened the time needed to create the print and allowed the increased integration of picture and text processing. Digital production scheduling, steering, and transcription systems have transformed the printing portion of the process as well. As the time needed to program and prepare the machines has decreased with electronic steering techniques, productivity and flexibility have been increased. Digital advances also have made it possible to integrate pre- and postprinting processes into one printing system, whereas they once were handled separately from the printing itself. Continued integration of postpress into the printing process is an area of continued development in the industry. The industry is challenged to continue providing high-quality print through the increased use of color printing, special colors and coatings, and solids and other saturated colors by designers.

Imports have exceeded exports in the printing trades machinery subsector for many years, with the strongest competition coming from Germany and Japan. Germany supplied 37 percent of the imports to the United States in 1998, with Japan accounting for 19 percent (see Table 18-16). U.S. exports are destined mainly for Europe, the NAFTA countries, and Japan. Shipments to Canada exceed those to any other single export destination, with 16 percent of U.S. exports heading north of the border. Exports to Mexico have increased significantly (a threefold increase since 1995) since the enactment of NAFTA and the recovery of the Mexican economy from the peso crisis. The United Kingdom, France, and Japan are traditional markets for U.S. machinery, and demand from those countries continues to be high. Emerging markets such as China and Brazil are beginning to place significant orders for U.S. equipment.

Industry and Trade Projections

As end users of printing press systems continue to make capital investments that will allow them to access the dramatic productivity improvements of the new technologies, the printing trades machinery industry will continue to experience growing sales through 2004. Constant dollar product shipments are forecast to expand 0.7 percent in the year 2000 (see Table 18-17) and nearly 3 percent annually through 2004. Successful firms will recognize that the printing industry is changing in response to new technologies as well. The major growth markets for printing, as reported by NPES, include catalogs, check printing, direct mail, magazines, corporate products, labels, and packaging. Traditional markets such as newspapers, annual reports, greeting cards, and technical literature face strong competition from the Internet and other electronic sources.

Exports of printing trades machinery are expected to increase in the year 2000 after 2 years of decline resulting from weak economies overseas. NPES expects that future export growth will come mainly from Asia and Mexico as those high-growth economies provide expanding markets and as NAFTA and its free trade provisions continue to stimulate trade within North America. China, Hong Kong, Taiwan, and Indonesia are seen as significant potential markets for U.S. printing machinery when their economies recover from their ongoing recessions. Assuming that U.S. firms can capitalize on these large potential markets,

TABLE 18-16: U.S. Trade Patterns in Printing Trades Machinery[1] in 1998
(millions of dollars; percent)

Exports			Imports		
Region[2]	Value[3]	Share, %	Region[2]	Value[3]	Share, %
NAFTA	335	24	NAFTA	144	7
Latin America	183	13	Latin America	3	0
Western Europe	540	38	Western Europe	1,482	67
Japan/Chinese Economic Area	201	14	Japan/Chinese Economic Area	440	20
Other Asia	61	4	Other Asia	10	0
Rest of world	103	7	Rest of world	121	6
World	1,423	100	World	2,199	100
Top Five Countries	Value	Share, %	Top Five Countries	Value	Share, %
Canada	223	16	Germany	810	37
Germany	118	8	Japan	424	19
Mexico	112	8	United Kingdom	183	8
United Kingdom	110	8	Canada	139	6
Japan	103	7	France	118	5

[1] SIC 3555.
[2] For definitions of regional groupings, see "Getting the Most Out of *Outlook 2000.*"
[3] Values may not sum to total due to rounding.
Source: U.S. Department of Commerce, Bureau of the Census.

exports will rise 7.1 percent per year from 2000 through 2004. Despite the expected expansion of exports, the trade deficit in this industry is anticipated to remain in place in the foreseeable future, with strong competition from Germany and Japan leading to a 1.8 percent annual increase in imports through the year 2004.

Electronic Commerce

The major manifestation of E-commerce in this industry is a growing Internet presence among manufacturers, distributors, and sellers of preowned products. Specific applications include product information, download capability for files associated with certain digital processes, press releases, and discussion boards for users of a firm's equipment.

Within the printing firm, electronic communication between the customer and the printing shop has become standard and has resulted in more accurate and flexible as well as quicker conversion of the customer's ideas and needs into final results. Flexible digital printing systems that can handle a quick job-to-job changeover are needed to convert these electronic conversations into tangible flawless output.

Christine Siegwarth Meyer, (315) 637–8831, November 1999.

TABLE 18-17: Printing Trades Machinery (SIC 3555) Trends and Forecasts
(millions of dollars except as noted)

										Percent Change			
	1992	1993	1994	1995	1996	1997[1]	1998[1]	1999[2]	2000[3]	97–98	98–99	99–00	96–00[4]
Industry data													
Value of shipments[5]	2,635	2,727	3,079	3,498	3,654	3,843	3,793	3,854	3,931	−1.3	1.6	2.0	1.8
Value of shipments (1992$)	2,635	2,668	2,972	3,300	3,371	3,496	3,405	3,432	3,466	−2.6	0.8	1.0	0.7
Total employment (thousands)	19.2	18.9	21.4	21.6	21.8								
Production workers (thousands)	10.7	10.3	11.7	12.1	11.0								
Average hourly earnings ($)	13.65	14.59	14.48	14.80	15.90								
Capital expenditures	62.7	52.9	74.0	101	106								
Product data													
Value of shipments[5]	2,342	2,345	2,814	3,213	3,019	3,175	3,112	3,154	3,221	−2.0	1.3	2.1	1.6
Value of shipments (1992$)	2,342	2,294	2,716	3,031	2,785	2,888	2,777	2,795	2,814	−3.8	0.6	0.7	0.3
Trade data													
Value of imports	1,219	1,348	1,555	1,991	1,778	2,022	2,199	2,269	2,296	8.8	3.2	1.2	6.6
Value of exports	1,087	1,102	1,069	1,261	1,385	1,456	1,423	1,419	1,506	−2.3	−0.3	6.1	2.1

[1] Estimate except imports and exports.
[2] Estimate.
[3] Forecast.
[4] Compound annual rate.
[5] For a definition of industry versus product values, see "Getting the Most Out of *Outlook 2000.*"
Source: U.S. Department of Commerce: Bureau of the Census; International Trade Administration.

FOOD PRODUCTS MACHINERY

The food products machinery industry (NAICS 333294, SIC 3556) supplies machinery for all types of operations in the processing of foodstuffs (vegetables, fruits, nuts, meats, poultry, fish, dairy products, grains, cereals, bakery and confectionery products, beverages, and animal foods). Machinery and associated systems for most applications are custom designed and constructed of special materials for highly sanitary operation and ease of thorough cleaning. Depending on their use, machines must conform to one or more of the sanitary standards established by the U.S. Department of Agriculture, the Food and Drug Administration, and the International Association of Milk, Food and Environmental Sanitarians. Food products machinery builders regularly provide machinery to the pharmaceutical, drug, cosmetic, and personal-care-products industries because of their skill in building machines for sanitary applications.

The basic types of food preparation and preservation processes are baking, canning, and thermal preservation; concentration with or without sugar; drying and/or dehydration; fermentation; freezing; frying; radiation; chemicals (sugar, salt, spices, and acids); and others, such as freeze drying, smoking, dehydrofreezing, and refrigeration with or without a controlled atmosphere. These processes are enhanced by the selection and use of appropriate packaging materials and methods. U.S. food machinery, processing plants, and operations must conform to the Code of Federal Regulations (21CFR, Parts 1–199) of the Federal Food, Drug and Cosmetic Act of 1938 as amended, including the CGMP.

Global Trends

Global demand for processed foods and beverages is continuing its upward climb, paving the way for the continued growth of the food products machinery industry. For nearly three decades, the estimated value of world trade in processed foods has increased at an average annual rate exceeding 10 percent. Fully two-thirds of all international trade in agricultural products is in processed foods and beverages. Economic and lifestyle changes caused by industrialization, urbanization, and rising family affluence, coupled with less time for meal preparation, will continue to drive up worldwide demand for processed foods. Moreover, the faster-paced lifestyles and growing personal incomes in highly developed food markets such as North America, western Europe, and Japan are giving rise to consumer demand for a wider selection of new, higher-quality processed foods and beverages. For many of the same reasons, these demands and tastes are being adopted by consumers in developing economies.

To meet this escalating demand and capitalize on new opportunities, the processed foods industry is undergoing sweeping reorganizations and changes. Companies are divesting unprofitable lines, undertaking mergers and acquisitions with companies that have complementary lines and objectives, and making direct capital investments in domestic and foreign markets. Those strategies are leading to increased consolidation and concentration of manufacting and marketing in the hands of fewer, larger, and more powerful multinational companies. The international food and beverage business has developed far beyond its traditional but still very important import and export functions.

Globalization of the processed food industry directly affects food products machinery manufacturers in terms of where, how, and with whom they do business and ultimately determines the types of machinery and equipment that are most salable and appropriate to specific markets. The international market for food products machinery is highly competitive. The leading manufacturers and distributors of food products machinery, especially high-technology equipment and systems, are found in the United States, the EU, and Japan. There also have been significant overseas investments, mergers, and acquisitions by those manufacturers to assure their profitable access to important regional markets. Machines and equipment of various types, operating capacities, and degrees of technology also are produced in other nations, usually for local or regional markets. As with other types of industrial equipment, basic parts and components are often available from international sources at competitive prices.

Capital investment in food processing is extensive because each process requires the use of a range of interdependent machinery and equipment. Every food processing line requires the support and services of equipment such as refrigeration equipment, dry and raw materials handling equipment, storage equipment and facilities, waste treatment systems, clean-in-place (CIP) systems, and packaging machinery lines. Process plants routinely require appropriately equipped laboratories for quality control, hygienic testing, and research and development (R&D) functions. Advances in these technologies are often essential to the development of new food technology and products. With some exceptions, most machinery is custom built by the manufacturer in accordance with government product, safety, and health standards and regulations. Standards such as the 3A standards for dairy equipment, Underwriters Laboratory certification, EU seals, and ISO-9000 are widely recognized and applied. There is no single set of international standards. The U.S. industry supports international cooperation to prevent machinery standards from becoming trade barriers and to assure that uniformly high-quality, safe equipment is delivered to processors throughout the world.

Domestic Trends

U.S. food products machinery manufacturers benefit from the huge domestic market. The processed food industry is the largest manufacturing and distribution sector in the U.S. economy, accounting for more than one-sixth of the nation's industrial activity. In addition, the United States is a major player in the global food industry, manufacturing about one-fourth of the world's processed foods. It is near or at the top in firm size, labor productivity, total production, and international trade. In 1999, U.S. shipments of processed foods and beverages were expected to reach an estimated $486.7 billion. Almost half the world's 50 leading food processing companies are headquartered in the United States. In addition to providing a large and viable home market for U.S. machinery manufacturers and process technologists, the United States is a magnet market for advanced foreign technology machinery suppliers and for direct investment in the food industry. The strategic restructuring by national and multinational food companies to improve their competitiveness, quality control, earnings, and profits is affecting machinery suppliers. Divestitures of low-profit lines, mergers, acquisitions, and particularly consolidation are creating a trend toward fewer and larger food processors with a need for more automated and flexible strategically located processing plants. However, consolidation and expansion demand in-depth analyses of existing, available plant facilities and an assessment of their most cost-effective use as well as their appropriate augmentation with different or new equipment weighed against any advantages of relocation and new construction. Therefore, some lag time in the final decision process is inevitable.

However, once these decisions are made, processors are on tight schedules to bring new products to market, improve their productivity, and make changes efficiently. Therefore, they are demanding expeditious delivery of plant projects whether for renovations, the expansion of existing facilities, or the design and building of new plants. Plant engineers and designers and machinery manufacturers may be called on to work on accelerated schedules to complete projects and equipment. Current construction surveys indicate a record number of food and beverage plant projects under way or in the planning and design stages across a full range of product sectors. Leading regions for new development are the south, the midwest, and the west coast. New plants typically are designed for relatively fast, economical construction and ease of hookup of utilities for machinery installation, cleaning, and maintenance. The most significant trends in plant design and operation are the increased use of computer-integrated process management technology and the use of more automated equipment. The application of information technology systems has gained increased importance in key operations such as in-process technology, sanitation and food safety, and business management. The factors driving this strong trend are market forces, competition, legislation and regulations, quality standards, and optimization of production performance and plant operations to achieve maximum profitability.

Historically, some food processors, particularly larger organizations, have had in-house technical staff to design new production lines and plants and often to manufacture proprietary machinery and production lines for their own use. These capabilities are fading rapidly because of downsizing and outsourcing measures to reduce R&D costs and take advantage of the technology and expertise of dedicated machinery manufacturers, food laboratories, and food plant engineering companies.

The majority of machinery builders are small and medium-size businesses that have developed special market niches and technical expertise. However, processors in the United States and abroad increasingly are demanding complete turnkey production systems that almost preclude single machinery sales except through engineering companies or systems integrators. Therefore, many niche manufacturers are forming working consortia with manufacturers of complementary machines, enabling them to broaden their effective product base in order to offer turnkey systems. Many U.S.-owned and foreign-owned companies are broadening their product lines by acquiring or merging with builders of complementary machinery in order to offer fuller systems capabilities. Machinery manufacturers faced with the added expenses of complying with environmental and occupational safety regulations in polluting or hazardous manufacturing operations such as degreasing, cleaning, metal plating, painting, and waste disposal are farming out those jobs to the growing numbers of small, highly specialized companies that are equipped to perform them on a fee or contract basis. In addition, more machining jobs are being farmed out to job shops, leaving final assembly to the machinery manufacturers.

Other Key Developments

Implementation of Hazard Analysis and Critical Control Point Plans. The use of hazard analysis and critical control point (HACCP) plans is widespread and growing throughout U.S. food processing plants of all types. However, in the greatest single change in its 90-year history, the Food Safety Inspection Service (FSIS) of the U.S. Department of Agriculture has augmented existing food safety regulations by mandating that more than 6,200 slaughtering and meat and poultry processing plants phase in standard operating procedures and HACCP plans for controlling salmonella and *E. coli* bacteria in poultry and meats. FSIS implemented the first stage of the program in January 1998 for more than 300 large plants with 500 or more employees. Smaller plants with 10 to 500 employees were required to implement their plans by January 1999, and very small plants had to implement plans by January 2000. HACCP is a process control system, or operating plan, designed for each specific processing plant to prevent microbial and other hazards from developing in food production. It includes steps to prevent problems before they occur and correct deviations when they are detected. Such preventive control systems with documentation and verification are increasingly recognized by scientific authorities and international organizations as the most effective approach toward producing safe food. The new regulations create the need and opportunity for machinery builders to manufacture HACCP-friendly machinery built of corrosion-resistant materials, featuring the absence of crevices where bacteria can accumulate, that can be disassembled, cleaned, sanitized, inspected, and reassembled easily. Machinery also must be designed for repetitive operation under wet, harsh operating conditions in the presence of strong cleaning chemicals. However, a significant proportion of U.S. machinery already meets or can be adapted to meet HACCP requirements. Opportunities have arisen for the development of HACCP-complementary software programs.

Technologies for Sanitary Food Treatment. Equipment developments that are in the forefront of the movement to assure more consistently sanitary and wholesome food products include pasteurization, ozone treatment methods, and electron beam treatment based on nonnuclear laser beam technology. Irradiation is a proven method of food sanitation that can double the shelf life of foods and substantially increase food safety in regard to microbes. For more than 20 years, irradiation has been an accepted process in many countries. It is used on milk in Europe, cheese and poultry in France, and poultry in Russia, the United Kingdom, the Netherlands, and elsewhere. However, there is a resistance to irradiated foods by consumers in many countries, including the United States, who fear possible radioactivity. Acceptance of the use of irradiation technology may gain in the long run, but not without further public debate.

Home Meal Replacements. The home meal replacement (HMR) sector is the fastest-growing sector in the food industry. HMR arose from the factors of sweeping demographic changes and time. Today, fewer than 20 percent of American homes are traditional households in which a homemaker manages the house and prepares the family's daily meals. There are many more working families and a proportionately higher number of one-person households than there were a generation ago. Today's lifestyles allow less time for meals and food preparation. By 1996, the value of takeout orders exceeded that of restaurant dining for the first time. Takeout is no longer limited to simple sandwiches and snacks. In response to consumers' demands for a variety of interesting, tasty, and wholesome foods, supermarkets and food specialty shops throughout the nation are providing shoppers of all income levels with an increasing variety of international foods, from appetizers and main courses to desserts, that are ready to eat with minimal preparation. By expanding its prepared food lines, the grocery industry has been able to capture a share of the lucrative and growing fast-food market.

Provision of these foods follows one or a combination of three alternatives: in-house preparation, preparation and distribution by central commissaries, and the purchase of packaged HMRs from often distant food processors. These alternatives represent opportunities for a wide range of machinery, equipment, and packaging materials suppliers and the use of sophisticated management and process techniques. In-house preparation may be done by professional chefs using high-quality commercial food service equipment, refrigeration, and appropriate packaging. However, the technologies supporting the processing and delivery of safe refrigerated HMRs require strict sanitary preparations under safe sanitary operating procedures (SSOPs), HACCP, and the application of cold-chain management. Cold-chain management applies from the acquisition of raw materials through processing and packaging in the plant or commissary to transportation and storage of HMRs at sales outlets. Clean room sanitation techniques and the segregation of raw materials from secondary packaging areas are practiced increasingly to prevent cross-contamination of food products. To extend product shelf life, safe food-handling techniques are enhanced by processors that employ high-technology packaging methods such as modified gas atmosphere packaging (MAP) in combination with specially selected packaging materials. HMR production establishes a partnership between skilled R&D food technologists and engineers with food product and packaging machinery manufacturers, packaging materials suppliers, and food distribution experts.

Projections of Industry and Trade Growth

The period 1996–1997 showed a remarkable flattening of industry performance. In time, this may be accounted for by revised statistical information. However, it could be attributed to a number of factors, including delays in domestic projects that have caused postponements of shipments, an abundance of used equipment in the market, a decrease in exports to key markets, and increased imports. The year 1998 saw a 1 percent improvement in product shipments in constant dollars that accelerated to around 3 percent in current dollars in 1999 (see Table 18-18). In the year 2000, shipments of food products machinery are projected to outpace U.S. domestic economic growth by about 1 percent, with an annual growth rate in 1992 dollars of about 4 percent as a result of new construction, reno-

TABLE 18-18: Food Products Machinery (SIC 3556) Trends and Forecasts
(millions of dollars except as noted)

	1992	1993	1994	1995	1996	1997	1998[1]	1999[2]	2000[3]	Percent Change 97–98	98–99	99–00	96–00[4]
Industry data													
Value of shipments[5]	2,417	2,630	2,674	2,819	2,798	2,798	2,882	2,968	3,087	3.0	3.0	4.0	2.5
Value of shipments (1992$)	2,417	2,564	2,520	2,579	2,502	2,437	2,456	2,495	2,595	0.8	1.6	4.0	0.9
Total employment (thousands)	18.9	18.8	19.8	19.9	21.1	18.4							
Production workers (thousands)	11.2	11.3	12.0	12.1	12.1	11.1							
Average hourly earnings ($)	13.08	13.23	13.05	13.46	13.66	15.63							
Capital expenditures	46.8	48.8	48.5	43.0	67.0	77.6							
Product data													
Value of shipments[5]	2,102	2,311	2,266	2,347	2,490	2,513	2,594	2,672	2,778	3.2	3.0	4.0	2.8
Value of shipments (1992$)	2,102	2,252	2,136	2,147	2,227	2,189	2,210	2,246	2,335	1.0	1.6	4.0	1.2
Trade data													
Value of imports	481	445	482	601	558	579	657	643	649	13.5	−2.1	0.9	3.8
Value of exports	682	701	731	785	822	812	803	811	827	−1.1	1.0	2.0	0.2

[1] Estimate except imports and exports.
[2] Estimate.
[3] Forecast.
[4] Compound annual rate.
[5] For a definition of industry versus product values, see "Getting the Most Out of *Outlook 2000*."
Source: U.S. Department of Commerce: Bureau of the Census; International Trade Administration.

vation, and expansion projects in the food and beverage sectors at home and abroad. The introduction of new food products and technology also will have a positive effect on machinery sales.

In 1999, exports resumed modest upward growth in current dollars after small downward adjustments in 1997 and 1998. In the year 2000, U.S. exports are expected to exceed the record level of $821 million reached in 1996. The United States is a net exporter of food products machinery. In 1999, exports accounted for an estimated 30 percent of domestic production. The opportunities in overseas markets are becoming more evident to U.S. manufacturers as the large home market matures and competition intensifies.

The United States is the world's largest food processor, food innovator, and machinery market. Therefore, it is the leading world market for imports, which in 1999 accounted for a 26 percent share of the market. The U.S. market is accessible and competitive, and tariffs are low. Foreign manufacturers of a variety of high-quality state-of-the-art machinery and special niche equipment find a receptive audience among U.S. processors.

Global Market Prospects

Excellent business opportunities for food products machinery lie in the global markets. The outlook for the continued growth of international markets is generally very good but varies regionally and between countries. As in the domestic business, export market opportunities will fluctuate with changes in economic and market conditions. Therefore, it is important for manufacturers to establish a consistent presence in the large and mature markets of western Europe, Japan, North America, and important food processor and distributor nations such as Australia, Brazil, and Argentina and to provide, to the best extent they can, regional coverage in the emerging markets.

In 1998, the United States exported about $803 million of food products machinery to more than 140 countries. Table 18-19 shows the top five export markets. With the gradual improvement of economic conditions in various international markets in 1999, exports rose to about $811 million. Continued steady export growth is forecast through the year 2000. The leading country markets in 1998 were, in order, Canada, Mexico, the United Kingdom, Japan, and Brazil. U.S. machinery has earned an international reputation for its heavy-duty construction designed for continuous operation in hostile environments. It is increasingly noted for its technical quality, excellent electronics, compatibility and ease of integration with other equipment, long service life, serviceability, competitive pricing, and good value.

In 1999, the United States imported an estimated $643 million in food products machinery. Regionally, western Europe, the NAFTA countries, Japan and China, and Latin America were the leading suppliers. The leading supplier countries were, in order, Germany, Italy, the Netherlands, Switzerland, and the United Kingdom.

There is evidence that the financial problems that have dampened the growth of the food industry in important markets such as Brazil and the Pacific Rim are being brought under control, brightening the picture for those markets in the year 2000. Globally, the processed food industry is now well grounded, and progress will continue despite any temporary setbacks.

With notable exceptions, the agricultural and food industries of eastern and central Europe, Russia, and the Newly Independent States are greatly in need of modernization in terms of equipment and technology. The technical level and productivity of the food processing industries in many of those countries are outdated by 10 to 40 years. The need to reduce food waste and improve food quality through better technology is genuine. Even standard western machinery would represent major improvements to many users in those regions. Despite current difficulties in doing business in some of those nations, particularly in terms of financing, their markets offer significant

TABLE 18-19: U.S. Trade Patterns in Food Products Machinery[1] in 1998
(millions of dollars; percent)

Exports			Imports		
Region[2]	Value[3]	Share, %	Region[2]	Value[3]	Share, %
NAFTA	213	27	NAFTA	54	8
Latin America	170	21	Latin America	12	2
Western Europe	201	25	Western Europe	524	80
Japan/Chinese Economic Area	82	10	Japan/Chinese Economic Area	49	7
Other Asia	44	5	Other Asia	4	1
Rest of world	92	12	Rest of world	14	2
World	803	100	World	657	100
Top Five Countries	Value	Share, %	Top Five Countries	Value	Share, %
Canada	136	17	Germany	143	22
Mexico	77	10	Italy	126	19
United Kingdom	54	7	Netherlands	57	9
Japan	33	4	Switzerland	46	7
Brazil	31	4	United Kingdom	43	7

[1] SIC 3556.
[2] For definitions of regional groupings, see "Getting the Most Out of *Outlook 2000.*"
[3] Values may not sum to total due to rounding.
Source: U.S. Department of Commerce, Bureau of the Census.

opportunities to suppliers that will work closely and patiently with potential buyers.

As the world's population grows and industrialization progresses, agribusiness development will continue to spread as a result of the need for increased food production and the reduction of food waste. The increased use of processed and preserved foods is driven by necessity, national government priorities, and foreign direct investment. Those factors are combining to increase international trade in food products and the necessary machinery and technology.

Eugene Shaw, U.S. Department of Commerce, Office of Energy, Infrastructure and Machinery, (202) 482–3494, November 1999.

■ REFERENCES

Construction Machinery

Construction Industry Manufacturers Association, 111 East Wisconsin Avenue, Suite 1000, Milwaukee, WI 53202-4879. www.cimanet.com.

Mining Machinery

National Mining Association, National Mining Association Building, 1130 17 Street, NW, Washington, DC 20036. www.nma.org.

World Mining Equipment, 220 Fifth Avenue, 19th Floor, New York, NY 10001-7781. www.wme.com.

Oil and Gas Field Machinery

Drilling & Production Outlook, October 1999. Spears & Associates, Inc., 5110 South Yale, Suite 410, Tulsa, OK 74135. (918) 496-3434, http://www.spearsresearch.com.

International Energy Outlook 1999, April 1999, DOE/EIA 0484(99). Energy Information Administration, U.S. Department of Energy, Washington, D.C. 20585. http://www.eia.doe.gov.

Issues in Midterm Analysis and Forecasting 1999, August 1999, DOE/EIA 0607(99). Energy Information Administration, U.S. Department of Energy, Washington, DC 20585. http://www.eia.doe.gov.

Lease Information. Gulf of Mexico Outer Continental Shelf (OCS) Region, Minerals Management Service, U.S. Department of the Interior, 1201 Elmwood Park Boulevard, New Orleans, LA 70123-2394. http://www.gomr.mms.gov.

Oil and Gas Field Machinery and Equipment Manufacturing, 1997 Economic Census, Manufacturing Industry Series, October 1999, EC97M-3331E. Bureau of the Census, U.S. Department of Commerce, Washington, DC 20233. http://www.census.gov.

Short-Term Energy Outlook, April 1999, DOE/EIA 0202(99/2Q). Energy Information Administration, U.S. Department of Energy, Washington, D.C. 20585. http://www.eia.doe.gov.

Short-Term Energy Outlook, September 7, 1999. Energy Information Administration, U.S. Department of Energy, Washington, D.C. 20585. http://www.eia.doe.gov/emeu/steo/pub/contents.html.

U.S. Rotary Rig Counts. Baker Hughes, Inc., P.O. Box 4740, Houston, TX 77210-4740. http://www.bakerhughes.com.

Farm Machinery

Ag Industry Watch, Farm Equipment, Johnson Hill Press, Inc., 1233 Janesville Avenue, Fort Atkinson, WI 53538-0460.

Agriculture Online. www.agriculture.com.

Agricultural Outlook, U.S. Department of Agriculture, Economic Research Service, ERS-NASS, 341 Victory Drive, Herndon, VA 22070. www.econ.ag.gov.

Agricultural Resources and Environmental Indicators, Farm Machinery. U.S. Department of Agriculture, Economic Research Service, ERS-NASS, 341 Victory Drive, Herndon, VA 22070. www.usda.gov/nass.

American Feed Industry Association, 1501 Wilson Boulevard, Suite 1100, Arlington, VA 22209. www.afia.org.

American Society of Agricultural Engineers, 2950 Niles Road, St. Joseph, MI 49085-9659. http://asae.org.

Current Industrial Reports: Farm Machinery and Lawn and Garden Equipment. MA-35A (97)-1. U.S. Department of Commerce, Bureau of the Census. Washington, DC 20233. www.census.gov/econ/www/manumenu.html.

Flash Reports, Equipment Manufacturers Institute, Suite 1220, 10 South Riverside Plaza, Chicago, IL 60606. www.emi.org.

Government Information Sharing Project, Oregon State University. http://govinfo.kerr.orst.edu.

Grainnet. www.grainnet.com.

Irrigation, Business & Technology, Irrigation Association, 8260 Willow Oaks Corporate Drive, Suite 120, Fairfax, VA 22031. www.irrigation.org.

1997 Census of Manufacturers: Engines and Turbines and Farm Machinery and Equipment, MC 97-1-35A. U.S. Department of Commerce, Bureau of the Census, Washington, DC 20233. www.census.gov.

Short Liner, Farm Equipment Manufacturers Association, 1000 Executive Parkway, Suite 100, St. Louis, MO 63141. www.farmequip.org.

10-Digit HS U.S. Trade Data. U.S. Department of Commerce, ITA. www.ita.doc.gov/industry/otea/trade-detail.

TVA Rural Studies. www.rural.org.

U.S. International Trade Commission Data Base. http://dataweb.usitc.gov.

World Agricultural Information Center, Food and Agricultural Organization of the United Nations, Vialo delle Terme di Caracalla, 00100, Rome, Italy. www.fao.org.

Packaging Machinery

Institute of Packaging Professionals, 481 Carlisle Street, Herndon, VA 20170. (703) 318-8970, wcp@pkgmatters.com.

Packaging Machinery Manufacturers Institute, 4350 North Fairfax Drive, Suite 600, Arlington, VA 22203. (703) 243-8555, pmmi@pmmi.org.

1997 Economic Census Manufacturing Series, Packaging Machinery Manufacturing, NAICS 333993, EC97M–339, U.S. Department of Commerce, Economics and Statistics Administration, Bureau of the Census, Washington, DC 20233, (301) 457–4100.

1999 U.S. Packaging Machinery Purchasing Plans Study, Packaging Machinery Manufacturers Institute, 4350 North Fairfax Drive, Suite 600, Arlington, VA 22203. (703) 243-8555, pmmi@pmmi.org.

Paper Industries Machinery

Capacity, Paper, Paperboard, and Pulp, 39th Annual Survey: 1997–2001, American Forest & Paper Association, Washington, DC 20036, December 1998.

Converting, Cahners Business Information, 1350 East Touhy Avenue, Des Plaines, IL 60018.

5th Annual Packaging Machinery Shipments and Outlook Study, Packaging Machinery Manufacturers Institute, 4350 North Fairfax Drive, Suite 600, Arlington, VA 22203. (703) 243-8555, pmmi@pmmi.org.

Journal of Pulp & Paper Science, Canadian Pulp & Paper Association, P.O. Box 1144, Lewiston, NY 14092.

1997 Census of Manufactures, Paper Industries Machinery Manufacturing, EC97-M-3332C, U.S. Department of Commerce, Economics and Statistics Administration, U.S. Census Bureau, Washington, DC 20233.

Paper Age, O'Brien Publications, Inc., 51 Mill Street, Suite 5, Hanover, MA 02339-1650.

Paper Industry, Democrat Printing & Lithographing Co., P.O. Box 5613, Montgomery, AL 36103-5675.

PIMA's North American Papermaker, Paper Industry Management Association, 1699 Wall Street, Suite 212, Mt. Prospect, IL 60056-5782.

Pulp & Paper, Miller-Freeman Publishing Co., 525 Harrison Street, Suite 500, San Francisco, CA 94105.

TAPPI Journal, Technical Association of the Pulp & Paper Industry, 15 Technology Parkway, South, Norcross, GA 30092.

Air-Conditioning, Refrigeration, and Heating Equipment

Air-Conditioning & Refrigeration Institute (ARI), 4301 North Fairfax Drive, Suite 425, Arlington, VA 22203. www.ari.org.

Air-Conditioning & Refrigeration Wholesalers International, 1650 South Dixie Highway, 5th Flr, Boca Raton, FL 33432 USA. www.arwi.org.

HVAC&R Research, American Society of Heating, Refrigerating and Air-Conditioning Engineers, 1791 Tullie Circle, NE, Atlanta, GA 30329. www.hvacmall.com.

Printing Trades Machinery

NPES, the Association for Suppliers of Printing, Publishing, and Converting Technologies, 1899 Preston White Drive, Reston, VA 20191-4367. www.npes.org.

Food Products Machinery

AER-742, Globalization of the Processed Foods Market, United States Department of Agriculture, Economic Research Service, Washington, DC 20005. 1-800-999-6779.

The Almanac of the Canning, Freezing, Preserving Industries, Edward E. Judge & Sons, Inc. P.O. Box 866, Timonium, MD 21158. (410) 876-2052, http://www.eejudge.com.

American Meat Institute, 1700 North Moore Street, Arlington, VA 22209. (703) 841-2400, http://www.meatami.org.

Exports and Imports of the United States, U.S. Department of Commerce, Economics and Statistics Administration, Bureau of the Census, Washington, DC 20233. (301) 457-4100, www.census.gov.

Food Engineering, Cahners Business Information, 201 King of Prussia Road, Radnor, PA 19089. (610) 964-4000, foodexplorer.com.

Food Processing Machinery & Supplies Association, 200 Daingerfield Road, Alexandria, VA 22314-2800. (703) 684-1080; E-mail: fpmsa@clark.net; fpmsa.org and iefp.org.

Food Processing, Putnam Publishing Company, 555 West Pierce Road, Suite 301, Itasca, IL 60143. (630) 467-1300.

Food Processors Institute, 1350 Eye Street, NW, Suite 300, Washington, DC 20005. (202) 393-0890, www.fpi-food.org.

Food Production Management, CTI Publications, Inc., 2 Oakway Road, Timonium, MD 21093-4247. (410) 308-2080; E-mail: sales@ctipuns.com; ctipubs.com.

International Association of Food Industry Suppliers, 1451 Dolly Madison Boulevard, McLean, VA 22101. (703) 761-2600, iafis.org.

International Dairy Foods Association, 1250 H Street, Northwest, Suite 900, Washington, DC 20005. (202) 737-4332, idfa.org.

Meat & Poultry, Sosland Companies, Inc., 4800 Main Street, Suite 100, Kansas City, MO 64112. (816) 516-1000; E-mail: meat&poultry@sosland.com; meatpoultry.com.

Meat Marketing & Technology, Marketing & Technology Group, Inc., 1415 North Dayton, Chicago, IL 60622. (312) 266-3311, chicago@meatingplace.com.

1992 Census of Manufactures, Special Industrial Machinery, except Metalworking, SIC 3565, MC92-1-35D. U.S. Department of Commerce, Bureau of the Census, Washington, DC 20233. (301) 457-4100.

1996 Annual Survey of Manufactures, M96(AS)-1 and M96(AS)-2, U.S. Department of Commerce, Bureau of the Census, Washington, DC 20233. (301) 457-4100.

1997 Economic Census Manufacturing Industry Series, Food Product Machinery, NAICS 3332, EC97M-3332. U.S. Department of Commerce, Economics and Statistics Administration, Bureau of the Census, Washington, DC 20233. (301) 457-4100.

Quick Frozen Foods International, E. W. Williams Publications Co., Division of Pioneer Association, 2125 Center Avenue, Fort Lee, NJ 07024. (201) 592-7007, qffimag1@aol.com.

Snack World, Snack Food Association, 1711 King Street, Alexandria, VA 22314. (703) 836-4500, http://www.sfa.org/sfa.

■ RELATED CHAPTERS

1: Metals and Industrial Minerals Mining
2: Coal Mining
3: Crude Petroleum and Natural Gas
6: Construction
9: Textiles
10: Paper and Allied Products
11: Chemicals and Allied Products
12: Synthetic Rubber
15: General Components
25: Printing and Publishing
33: Apparel and Fabricated Textile Products
35: Processed Food and Beverages
38: Household Consumer Durables

ELECTRICAL EQUIPMENT
Economic and Trade Trends

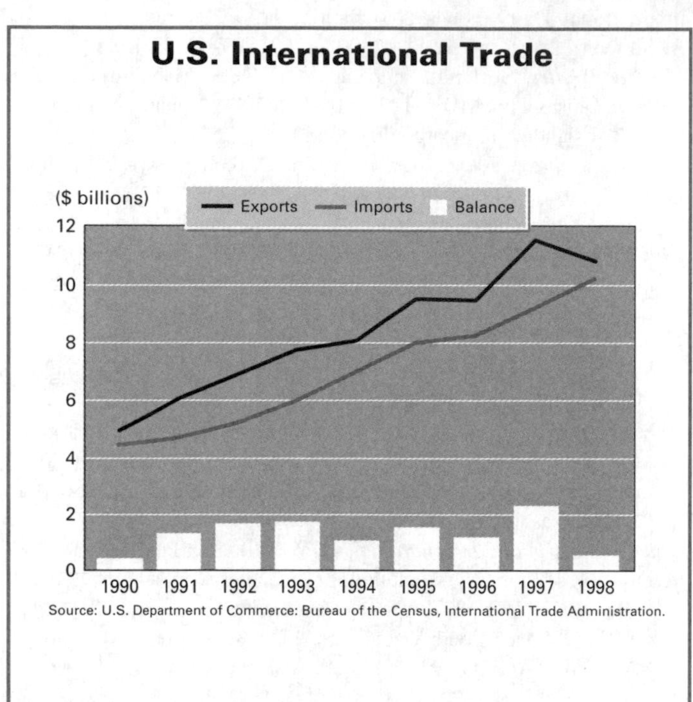

Source: U.S. Department of Commerce: Bureau of the Census, International Trade Administration.

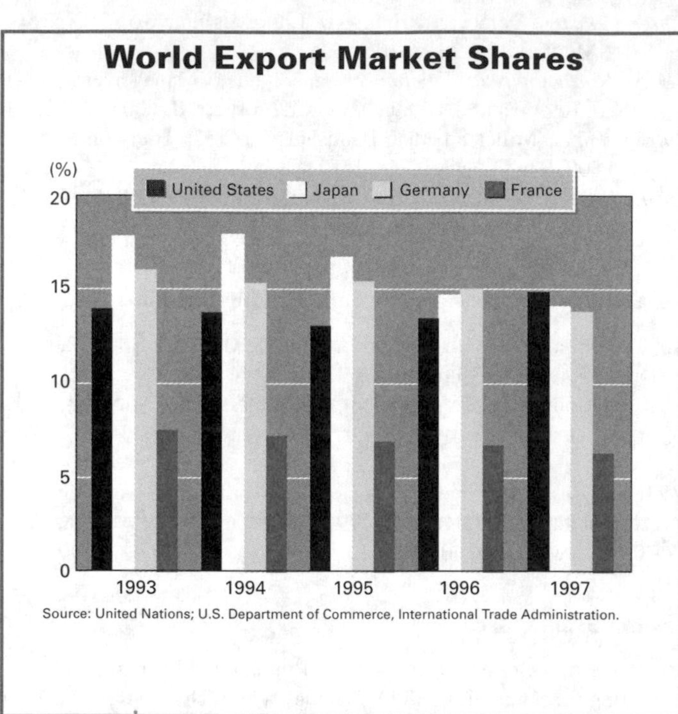

Source: United Nations; U.S. Department of Commerce, International Trade Administration.

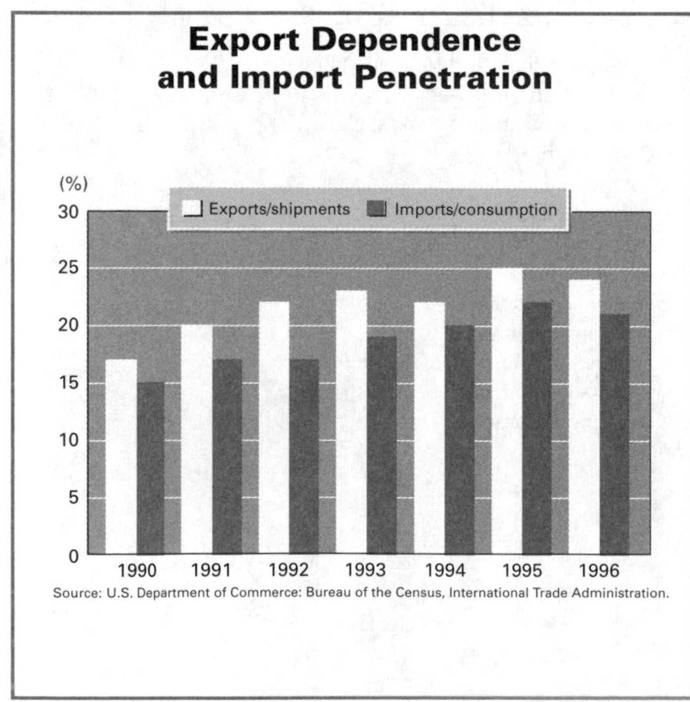

Source: U.S. Department of Commerce: Bureau of the Census, International Trade Administration.

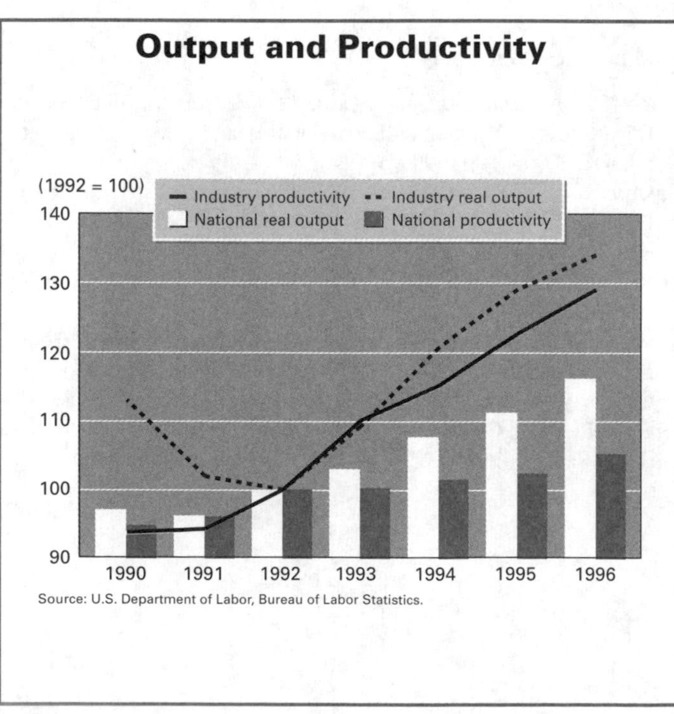

Source: U.S. Department of Labor, Bureau of Labor Statistics.

See "Getting the Most Out of *Outlook 2000*" for definitions of terms.

19

Electrical Equipment

INDUSTRY DEFINITION Electrical equipment includes five subsectors: power, distribution, and specialty transformers (SIC 3612); switchgears (SIC 3613); motors and generators (SIC 3621); industrial controls (SIC 3625); and steam, gas, and hydraulic turbines and turbine generator sets (SIC 3511). For statistical purposes, the last subsector is treated separately from the others.

OVERVIEW

Electrical equipment plays a major role in many of the products used by consumers and many of the machines used by industry to produce those products. Turbines, switchgear products, and transformers are employed by electric utilities to produce power used by households and firms. Motors and generators are incorporated into many consumer products people purchase and use, including refrigerators and other electrical appliances, as well as various modes of transportation. Industrial controls are employed by firms to control the machinery that produces many of the consumer goods used in the economy.

The U.S. electrical equipment industry prospered from the recession of the early 1990s until 1998, with average annual growth of 3.1 percent in real terms since 1992. A strong domestic manufacturing sector driven by ever-increasing consumer confidence that translated into high consumer spending produced robust sales for the turbine, switchgear, transformer, motor and generator, and industrial controls industries. Exports also played a major role in those high sales figures, with shipments to foreign markets increasing 7.9 percent per year in current dollar terms from 1992 through 1998. Competition from foreign manufacturers remains strong, particularly in the transformer and motors and generators subsectors. Imports increased at an annual rate of 11.9 percent during the 6 years before 1998, far outpacing the growth in exports. However, owing in large part to the significant trade surplus in turbines, exports still exceed imports in the electrical equipment industry (see Table 19-1).

TURBINES

This subsector consists of the manufacture of steam turbines, hydraulic turbines, gas turbines except aircraft, and complete steam, gas, and hydraulic turbine generator set units. Also included is the manufacture of wind-powered and solar-powered turbine generators and windmills for generating electric power.

Global and Domestic Trends

The value of shipments for the turbine industry has fluctuated significantly over the past decade as a recession and the subsequent recovery, economic instability abroad, and deregulation of electric utilities have been important determinants of demand for nonaviation turbines. The year 1998 presents a good example of the myriad global economic factors that affect the industry. The rise in shipments of 2.4 percent in constant dollars masks two important trends: a sizable decrease in exports of nearly 13 percent and a phenomenal surge in domestic sales that was reflected in price increases of over 10 percent in that year (see Table 19-2).

The slowdown in exports in 1998 was due in large part to slow economic activity in southeast Asia, with cutbacks in government-financed infrastructure projects, high capital costs brought about by currency devaluations, and sagging demand for electricity. Declines were seen in exports to Japan (down 19 percent), China (down 17 percent), and Korea (down 53 percent). Surprisingly, Thailand continued to buy U.S. turbines in 1998, with increased sales of 13 percent over the previous year, largely as a result of the fulfillment of orders that had been placed before the worst of the economic crisis.

TABLE 19-1: U.S. Trade Patterns in Electrical Equipment[1] in 1998
(millions of dollars; percent)

Exports			Imports		
Region[2]	Value[3]	Share, %	Region[2]	Value[3]	Share, %
NAFTA	4,197	39	NAFTA	4,577	45
Latin America	1,194	11	Latin America	294	3
Western Europe	2,297	21	Western Europe	2,474	24
Japan/Chinese Economic Area	1,162	11	Japan/Chinese Economic Area	2,131	21
Other Asia	940	9	Other Asia	553	5
Rest of world	946	9	Rest of world	124	1
World	10,737	100	World	10,152	100
Top Five Countries	Value	Share, %	Top Five Countries	Value	Share, %
Mexico	2,331	22	Mexico	3,251	32
Canada	1,866	17	Japan	1,365	13
United Kingdom	637	6	Canada	1,326	13
Japan	604	6	Germany	774	8
Germany	314	3	China	566	6

[1] SIC 3511, 361, 3621, 3625.
[2] For definitions of regional groupings, see "Getting the Most Out of *Outlook 2000.*"
[3] Values may not sum to total due to rounding.
Source: U.S. Department of Commerce, Bureau of the Census.

While currently only about 15 percent of the world's electricity is generated by gas turbines, the sales of electrical power gas turbines increased rapidly in the 1990s. The second half of 1998 saw a burst of domestic orders that more than offset the decline in orders from abroad. Nuclear plant shutdowns and poor weather conditions were the major factors influencing this sudden and unexpected investment in new turbine equipment.

New technologies abound in the turbine industry, and some of the most promising developments are not yet in commercial production. Microturbines are an example of a technology that some analysts believe will revolutionize the industry. These small turbines produce between 25 and 100 kilowatts (kW) of power, compared with the largest segment of the gas turbine market, which produces over 50 megawatts (MW) of power. Their uses would be primarily for small retail estab-

TABLE 19-2: Turbines and Turbine Generator Sets (SIC 3511) Trends and Forecasts
(millions of dollars except as noted)

										Percent Change			
	1992	1993	1994	1995	1996	1997[1]	1998[1]	1999[2]	2000[3]	97–98	98–99	99–00	96–00[4]
Industry data													
Value of shipments[5]	5,843	6,234	6,802	6,144	6,268	6,260	7,055	7,656	7,544	12.7	8.5	–1.5	4.7
Value of shipments (1992$)	5,843	6,160	6,565	5,846	6,050	5,979	6,125	6,484	6,294	2.4	5.9	–2.9	1.0
Total employment (thousands)	27.1	26.7	27.1	24.3	21.8								
Production workers (thousands)	15.0	15.0	15.1	14.8	13.2								
Average hourly earnings ($)	18.38	18.62	19.67	19.03	19.44								
Capital expenditures	312	310	247	162	150								
Product data													
Value of shipments[5]	6,003	6,354	6,546	6,134	6,308	6,300	7,138	7,795	7,693	13.3	9.2	–1.3	5.1
Value of shipments (1992$)	6,003	6,278	6,318	5,836	6,089	6,048	6,232	6,647	6,452	3.0	6.7	–2.9	1.5
Trade data													
Value of imports	628	740	803	788	743	797	1,040	1,066	1,090	30.5	2.5	2.3	10.1
Value of exports	2,340	2,967	3,010	3,618	3,253	4,255	3,707	3,623	3,775	–12.9	–2.3	4.2	3.8

[1] Estimate except imports and exports.
[2] Estimate.
[3] Forecast.
[4] Compound annual rate.
[5] For a definition of industry versus product values, see "Getting the Most Out of *Outlook 2000.*"
Source: U.S. Department of Commerce: Bureau of the Census; International Trade Administration.

lishments as well as firms seeking flexible power generation options to capitalize on the increased competition stemming from deregulation.

The U.S. Department of Energy (DOE) believes that wind turbines are another emerging technology that could revolutionize energy markets with their environmentally friendly operations and potential for providing an economical stream of energy. DOE is working with U.S. manufacturers of wind turbines to develop low-cost machines that will be viable in the market. They anticipate that such turbines will enter the market in 2002. It remains to be seen whether such technologies can make inroads into either U.S. or foreign markets.

Industry and Trade Projections

Assuming that U.S. electric utilities continue to view turbines, particularly gas turbines, as a profitable capital investment, domestic demand is forecast to remain strong and was expected to result in a 5.9 percent increase in shipments in 1999. Once this wave of investment is finished and other potential customers wait until the turmoil surrounding deregulation and price competition in the electric utility industry subsides, orders for new turbines will slow down in the year 2000. Modest increases in sales thereafter will bring the volume of sales in constant dollars back to 1999 levels by the year 2004.

Exports were forecast to continue dropping in 1999 as the impact of the Asian economic and financial crisis continued to influence that area's demand for new electrical equipment. Exports of turbines to Thailand were off 68 percent in the first half of 1999 from the same time period in 1998, signaling that the Asian economic hardship had not finished affecting the turbine industry's sales to that region. Shipments to Japan and Korea for the first 6 months of 1999 were also lower than they were during the same months in 1998, which was a year of very low exports to many Asian markets. As demand overseas improves and infrastructure projects are renewed, shipments abroad are expected to rise moderately in the year 2000 and beyond.

The bright spots in U.S. turbine exports continue to be the North American Free Trade Agreement (NAFTA) countries and several emerging countries intent on developing their electrical generating capacity (see Table 19-3). Canada and Mexico both continue to be strong and growing markets for U.S. manufacturers, with shipments to both countries increasing over 40 percent in the first 6 months of 1999 compared with the same period in 1998. Other growing markets include emerging countries such as Saudi Arabia and Brazil, both of which were on track for a record volume of turbine purchases in 1999.

Electronic Commerce

There are several starting points for those interested in E-commerce in the turbine industry. The Power Bank is an on-line database of manufacturers, suppliers, and other groups that are related to the power generation equipment industries, including turbines. The American Society of Manufacturing Engineers (ASME) has developed a Web site that places much of the information from its annual expositions on-line. Included is information from original equipment manufacturers (OEMs) of gas turbines and manufacturers of gas turbine components, drive train equipment, and air, oil and fuel systems, as well as controls, instrumentation, and other ancillary equipment for gas turbines. Firms providing gas turbine education, testing equipment, analytic services, and design processes also are represented.

TABLE 19-3: U.S. Trade Patterns in Turbines and Turbine Generator Sets[1] in 1998
(millions of dollars; percent)

Exports			Imports		
Region[2]	Value[3]	Share, %	Region[2]	Value[3]	Share, %
NAFTA	612	16	NAFTA	311	30
Latin America	492	13	Latin America	4	0
Western Europe	1,055	28	Western Europe	626	60
Japan/Chinese Economic Area	524	14	Japan/Chinese Economic Area	56	5
Other Asia	494	13	Other Asia	25	2
Rest of world	530	14	Rest of world	18	2
World	3,707	100	World	1,040	100
Top Five Countries	Value	Share, %	Top Five Countries	Value	Share, %
Canada	390	11	Canada	259	25
United Kingdom	334	9	Germany	182	17
Japan	333	9	United Kingdom	150	14
Mexico	222	6	Italy	82	8
Italy	173	5	France	73	7

[1] SIC 3511.
[2] For definitions of regional groupings, see "Getting the Most Out of *Outlook 2000*."
[3] Values may not sum to total due to rounding.
Source: U.S. Department of Commerce, Bureau of the Census.

The turbine industry has a significant presence on the World Wide Web that is due, at least in part, to the many new technological innovations being developed. Cogeneration, the simultaneous production of heat and power, has several Web sites listing pertinent links, including manufacturers, consultants, and even legal services related to that technology.

Direct sales of replacement parts are one of the expanding areas of electronic commerce in the turbine industry. Pratt Whitney Canada, for example, allows users to inquire about its inventory of used replacement parts, receive price quotes, and even transmit orders on-line from its Web page.

TRANSFORMERS

This subsector involves economic activity in the manufacture of power, distribution, industrial, and specialty transformers. Transformers play a crucial role in the transmission of electricity as they increase, decrease, and regulate the voltage of electric current efficiently and safely.

Global and Domestic Trends

U.S. transformer manufacturers saw shipments rise 5.1 percent in real terms in 1998, reaching a current dollar value of $5.5 billion (see Table 19-4). The impact of the Asian financial crisis and uncertainty in all the industries that supply electric utilities regarding the effect of deregulation led to reduction in shipments of 0.9 percent in 1999. This drop in shipments occurred despite strong increases in housing starts in 1998 and 1999, which often portend high sales in the industry because the demand for new transformers comes mainly from new construction. Nonresidential construction, however, was weak in 1998, falling 0.1 percent after several years of positive growth. This was a significant factor in the demand for commercial and industrial transformers, while the uncertainty surrounding deregulation moderated capital investments, including those in transformers, by the electric utilities.

The United States continued to sustain a trade deficit in transformers in 1998, with imports rising 8.7 percent and exports falling 14 percent. The leading suppliers of transformers were Mexico, Canada, and China. Mexico was by far the largest supplier, accounting for over 54 percent of total imports. Although Mexico has long been the leading supplier of transformers to the United States, this represents a significant increase in market share for Mexico, which accounted for less than 40 percent of imports in 1992. Among the other countries that have increased substantially in importance in recent years as suppliers of transformers are Canada, China, and Japan. Shipments from China have increased at an annual rate of 52 percent since 1992.

Exports of transformers fell in 1998 after a record value of shipments was recorded in 1997. The leading export markets for transformers were the NAFTA countries of Mexico and Canada, followed by Japan, Ireland, Hong Kong, and the Philippines (see Table 19-5). The Asian currency crisis and the ensuing recessions certainly were a major factor in the export decline, with exports to Hong Kong, the Philippines, Taiwan, and Korea all falling in 1998. However, exports to other major markets, including the NAFTA countries, also fell during that year as competition from low-cost suppliers around the world strengthened.

The U.S. Environmental Protection Agency (EPA) and major manufacturers of transformers expanded the Energy Star program in April 1998 to include commercial and industrial (C&I) transformers in addition to the utility distribution transformers that have been in the program since 1995. The Energy Star program provides a special label for products that meet strict energy conservation standards. The overall program aims to reduce wasted energy in everything from windows, to insulation, to household appliances, with the new C&I transformer program leading to estimated annual savings of up to 20 billion kilowatt-hours (kWh). Since this is a new program for the industry, only 5 percent of all current C&I transformers meet the standards. The EPA is hoping to increase demand for such energy-efficient units through its release of a software program [Commercial and Industrial Transformer Cost Evaluation Model (CITCEM)] that helps building owners and contractors compare the short-term costs with the long-term benefits of the high-efficiency transformers. The ongoing utility distribution transformer program is designed to reduce the annual electricity losses of 61 billion kWh currently experienced by end users of such products.

Industry and Trade Projections

Despite strong housing starts in 1998 and 1999, domestic demand for transformer equipment, which supports the generation of electricity, will remain weak in the year 2000, with a 2 percent reduction in shipments. An increasing amount of the transformer demand coming from the nonresidential sector will be fulfilled by imported units, with total imports rising 9 percent per year from 1996 to 2000. This growing reliance on overseas production will result in a trade deficit that reaches $532 million in the year 2000, a figure that exceeds the value of both exports and imports only 8 years earlier.

Electronic Commerce

The distribution of new, remanufactured, and reconditioned transformers is being taken on-line, with price quotes available via E-mail from several Internet sources. The major benefit of this E-commerce to customers is the speed at which surplus stock can be searched and made available for use. Shipping time can be reduced from several months to a few weeks. Additional uses of technology include taking pictures of the products with a digital camera and then sending those pictures to potential customers for review via E-mail or fax.

More standard E-commerce applications, such as on-line product guides, company information, information request forms, and company newsletters, are widely used by manufacturers and distributors of transformers.

TABLE 19-4: Electrical Equipment (SIC 3612, 3613, 3621, 3625) Trends and Forecasts

(millions of dollars except as noted)

	1992	1993	1994	1995	1996	1997[1]	1998[1]	1999[2]	2000[3]	Percent Change 97–98	98–99	99–00	96–00[4]
Industry data													
Value of shipments[5]	25,706	27,697	29,787	33,429	34,670	35,083	35,763	35,512	35,661	1.9	−0.7	0.4	0.7
3612 Transformers	4,118	3,940	4,708	5,213	5,147	5,332	5,658	5,618	5,556	6.1	−0.7	−1.1	1.9
3613 Switchgear and apparatus	5,679	5,849	6,172	6,866	7,184	7,243	7,440	7,387	7,499	2.7	−0.7	1.5	1.1
3621 Motors and generators	8,168	9,182	9,499	11,163	11,477	11,400	11,457	11,366	11,320	0.5	−0.8	−0.4	−0.3
3625 Relays and controls	7,741	8,727	9,408	10,188	10,862	11,108	11,208	11,141	11,286	0.9	−0.6	1.3	1.0
Value of shipments (1992$)	25,706	27,329	29,082	31,833	32,536	32,660	32,862	32,258	31,972	0.6	−1.8	−0.9	−0.4
3612 Transformers	4,118	4,028	4,819	5,192	5,051	5,241	5,508	5,459	5,349	5.1	−0.9	−2.0	1.4
3613 Switchgear and apparatus	5,679	5,723	5,889	6,363	6,603	6,586	6,614	6,456	6,415	0.4	−2.4	−0.6	−0.7
3621 Motors and generators	8,168	9,064	9,267	10,621	10,787	10,782	10,760	10,642	10,546	−0.2	−1.1	−0.9	−0.6
3625 Relays and controls	7,741	8,514	9,108	9,657	10,095	10,051	9,980	9,701	9,662	−0.7	−2.8	−0.4	−1.1
Total employment (thousands)	199	199	208	215	215								
3612 Transformers	29.0	27.9	30.7	32.3	32.1								
3613 Switchgear and apparatus	39.1	38.5	39.5	41.6	41.5								
3621 Motors and generators	67.9	69.2	73.7	77.1	75.2								
3625 Relays and controls	62.5	63.1	64.3	64.2	66.2								
Production workers (thousands)	136	138	144	151	150								
3612 Transformers	22.0	21.1	21.7	23.0	22.4								
3613 Switchgear and apparatus	26.0	25.7	27.2	29.0	29.0								
3621 Motors and generators	51.9	53.6	58.0	61.7	59.9								
3625 Relays and controls	36.0	37.2	37.3	37.6	38.6								
Average hourly earnings ($)	11.40	11.79	11.80	12.29	12.71								
3612 Transformers	11.62	12.00	11.91	11.93	12.68								
3613 Switchgear and apparatus	12.25	12.89	13.25	13.29	13.61								
3621 Motors and generators	11.22	11.33	10.85	11.90	12.21								
3625 Relays and controls	10.90	11.58	12.18	12.37	12.82								
Capital expenditures	663	664	862	929	938								
3612 Transformers	85.3	77.8	166	132	144								
3613 Switchgear and apparatus	112	120	146	155	164								
3621 Motors and generators	242	249	290	337	349								
3625 Relays and controls	224	217	260	305	280								
Product data													
Value of shipments[5]	25,435	27,123	29,582	31,885	33,379	33,762	34,427	34,169	34,262	2.0	−0.7	0.3	0.7
3612 Transformers	4,066	3,906	4,485	4,632	4,746	4,917	5,273	5,231	5,100	7.2	−0.8	−2.5	1.8
3613 Switchgear and apparatus	5,469	5,718	5,894	6,526	6,816	6,872	7,085	7,092	7,220	3.1	0.1	1.8	1.4
3621 Motors and generators	8,626	9,406	10,255	11,055	11,541	11,464	11,492	11,372	11,327	0.2	−1.0	−0.4	−0.5
3625 Relays and controls	7,274	8,093	8,948	9,671	10,276	10,509	10,577	10,474	10,615	0.6	−1.0	1.3	0.8
Value of shipments (1992$)	25,435	26,770	28,882	30,348	31,319	31,430	31,612	31,093	30,847	0.6	−1.6	−0.8	−0.4
3612 Transformers	4,066	3,994	4,591	4,614	4,657	4,832	5,122	5,074	4,948	6.0	−0.9	−2.5	1.5
3613 Switchgear & apparatus	5,469	5,595	5,624	6,048	6,264	6,248	6,285	6,223	6,229	0.6	−1.0	0.1	−0.1
3621 Motors and generators	8,626	9,285	10,005	10,519	10,847	10,842	10,787	10,648	10,554	−0.5	−1.3	−0.9	−0.7
3625 Relays and controls	7,274	7,896	8,662	9,167	9,550	9,508	9,418	9,148	9,116	−0.9	−2.9	−0.3	−1.2
Trade data													
Value of imports	4,530	5,180	6,116	7,140	7,442	8,343	9,113	9,574	10,151	9.2	5.1	6.0	8.1
3612 Transformers	500	608	574	793	804	949	1,032	1,081	1,136	8.7	4.7	5.1	9.0
3613 Switchgear and apparatus	559	646	748	849	907	1,070	1,212	1,235	1,340	13.3	1.9	8.5	10.2
3621 Motors and generators	2,146	2,365	2,872	3,188	3,233	3,541	4,001	4,270	4,608	13.0	6.7	7.9	9.3
3625 Relays and controls	1,324	1,560	1,922	2,310	2,497	2,782	2,868	2,988	3,067	3.1	4.2	2.6	5.3
Value of exports	4,473	4,693	4,966	5,805	6,127	7,209	7,029	6,937	7,520	−2.5	−1.3	8.4	5.3
3612 Transformers	338	359	384	469	518	659	567	557	604	−14.0	−1.8	8.4	3.9
3613 Switchgear and apparatus	831	826	897	1,005	1,159	1,431	1,425	1,370	1,465	−0.4	−3.9	6.9	6.0
3621 Motors and generators	1,969	2,061	2,129	2,540	2,516	2,974	2,866	2,856	3,087	−3.6	−0.3	8.1	5.2
3625 Relays and controls	1,334	1,447	1,557	1,791	1,934	2,146	2,172	2,154	2,364	1.2	−0.8	9.7	5.1

[1] Estimate except imports and exports.
[2] Estimate.
[3] Forecast.
[4] Compound annual rate.
[5] For a definition of industry versus product values, see "Getting the Most Out of *Outlook 2000.*"
Source: U.S. Department of Commerce: Bureau of the Census; International Trade Administration.

TABLE 19-5: U.S. Trade Patterns in Transformers[1] (Except Electronic) in 1998
(millions of dollars; percent)

Exports			Imports		
Region[2]	Value[3]	Share, %	Region[2]	Value[3]	Share, %
NAFTA	259	46	NAFTA	732	71
Latin America	70	12	Latin America	6	1
Western Europe	77	14	Western Europe	111	11
Japan/Chinese Economic Area	95	17	Japan/Chinese Economic Area	163	16
Other Asia	45	8	Other Asia	18	2
Rest of world	20	4	Rest of world	1	0
World	567	100	World	1,032	100
Top Five Countries	Value	Share, %	Top Five Countries	Value	Share, %
Mexico	173	31	Mexico	573	56
Canada	86	15	Canada	159	15
Japan	50	9	China	122	12
Ireland	34	6	Germany	21	2
Hong Kong	27	5	Netherlands	21	2

[1] SIC 3612
[2] For definitions of regional groupings, see "Getting the Most Out of *Outlook 2000*."
[3] Values may not sum to total due to rounding.
Source: U.S. Department of Commerce, Bureau of the Census.

SWITCHGEARS

Switchgear products include switches, fuses, panel boards, distribution boards, and circuit breakers. They are used primarily in electric generation, transmission, and distribution systems. Switchgears protect electrical systems from problems in voltage, frequency, continuous current, and other operating conditions. They are required for load switching, for short-circuit protection, and in industrial and commercial power systems to protect and control circuit loads.

Global and Domestic Trends

Shipments by the U.S. switchgear industry were expected to decrease approximately 2.4 percent in real terms in 1999 (see Table 19-4). Demand for switchgear equipment is driven by a variety of market forces. Residential and commercial construction requires the expansion of existing electric power distribution systems and thus generates demand for switchgear, circuit breakers, and other products that provide protection for those systems. Weak growth of 1.1 percent in private nonresidential structures along with moderation in residential construction from the phenomenal 10 percent increase in 1998 served to slow demand.

Globally, shipments to Asian markets were expected to fall in 1999, with exports to Japan, Hong Kong, and Singapore off by more than 5 percent for the first half of 1999 compared with the same period in the previous year. The NAFTA countries continue to provide U.S. manufacturers with robust export markets. In 1998, exports to Canada, the leading nondomestic market for U.S. electrical products, accounted for 20 percent of all switchgear exports, while Mexico accounted for 24 percent (see Table 19-6).

Industry and Trade Projections

Housing starts and investment in nonresidential structures, however, are expected to grow slowly until the year 2000, with housing starts actually falling in that year and nonresidential construction increasing only 2 percent per year in 1999 and 2000. The result of these domestic economic trends, together with continued weakness in Asian and Latin American markets, was expected to be flat growth for the industry in 1999. Overall, despite the recessions in countries in the Far East, strong growth in Europe as a result of integration as well as in Canada and Mexico will provide U.S. manufacturers of switchgears and other related products with sufficient demand to see an increase in exports in 2000.

In the longer term, the switchgear industry is well positioned for growth. Constant dollar shipments are forecasted to increase 2 percent annually through 2004, with exports growing 8 percent per year during that period.

Electronic Commerce

Switchgear manufacturers and distributors have a significant Internet presence, with Web sites providing general company information, describing products, and in some cases even providing product literature and specifications electronically. However, because of the specialized and often customized nature of the products these firms produce, selling product directly to the end user on-line has not developed to the extent that it has in other industries.

MOTORS AND GENERATORS

This subsector includes the production of electric motors (other than engine starting motors) and power generators, motor generator sets, railway motors and control equipment, and motors, generators, and control equipment for gasoline, electric, and oil-electric buses and trucks.

TABLE 19-6: U.S. Trade Patterns in Switchgear[1] in 1998
(millions of dollars; percent)

Exports			Imports		
Region[2]	Value[3]	Share, %	Region[2]	Value[3]	Share, %
NAFTA	630	44	NAFTA	553	46
Latin America	241	17	Latin America	82	7
Western Europe	236	17	Western Europe	369	30
Japan/Chinese Economic Area	130	9	Japan/Chinese Economic Area	147	12
Other Asia	90	6	Other Asia	54	4
Rest of world	98	7	Rest of world	7	1
World	1,425	100	World	1,212	100
Top Five Countries	Value	Share, %	Top Five Countries	Value	Share, %
Mexico	339	24	Mexico	413	34
Canada	291	20	Canada	141	12
Dominican Republic	107	8	Japan	105	9
United Kingdom	60	4	Germany	97	8
Japan	56	4	United Kingdom	80	7

[1] SIC 3613.
[2] For definitions of regional groupings, see "Getting the Most Out of *Outlook 2000.*"
[3] Values may not sum to total due to rounding.
Source: U.S. Department of Commerce, Bureau of the Census.

Global and Domestic Trends

Markets for motors and generators include both direct sales to consumers and business-to-business sales to producers of a wide range of end products, including everything from photocopiers to medical equipment, power windows to printing presses, and air conditioners to electric toothbrushes.

Sales of motors and generators have been sluggish since 1996, with constant dollar shipments dropping 0.2 percent in 1998 and 1.1 percent in 1999. Low foreign demand has been the primary factor, with exports falling 3.6 percent in 1998 and forecast to fall 0.3 percent in 1999 (see Table 19-4). The devaluation of the Brazilian currency led exports to that country to fall 32 percent in 1998. The Asian currency crisis further exacerbated the low volume of shipments, with significant percentage reductions in sales to Japan (4 percent), Korea (27 percent), Hong Kong (40 percent), Taiwan (43 percent), and Singapore (54 percent) in 1998. Concurrently, imports rose substantially, with total sales from foreign producers increasing from $559 million in 1992 to $1.2 billion in 1999, representing an annual expansion of 12 percent.

As firms in the motor and generator industry search for cost-reduction strategies, relocation of plants to countries with low-cost labor is becoming an increasingly common approach. This in part accounts for Mexico's large and expanding share of exports to the United States. Shipments of over $1.4 billion from Mexico in 1998 accounted for more than 36 percent of all imports, up from 22 percent in 1992 (see Table 19-7). Japan,

TABLE 19-7: U.S. Trade Patterns in Motors and Generators[1] in 1998
(millions of dollars; percent)

Exports			Imports		
Region[2]	Value[3]	Share, %	Region[2]	Value[3]	Share, %
NAFTA	1,420	50	NAFTA	1,886	47
Latin America	304	11	Latin America	101	3
Western Europe	473	16	Western Europe	806	20
Japan/Chinese Economic Area	246	9	Japan/Chinese Economic Area	917	23
Other Asia	192	7	Other Asia	238	6
Rest of world	232	8	Rest of world	53	1
World	2,866	100	World	4,001	100
Top Five Countries	Value	Share, %	Top Five Countries	Value	Share, %
Mexico	737	26	Mexico	1,471	37
Canada	684	24	Japan	566	14
United Kingdom	104	4	Canada	415	10
Japan	101	4	Germany	278	7
France	76	3	China	262	7

[1] SIC 3621.
[2] For definitions of regional groupings, see "Getting the Most Out of *Outlook 2000.*"
[3] Values may not sum to total due to rounding.
Source: U.S. Department of Commerce, Bureau of the Census.

Canada, Germany, and China followed with significant shares of the import market (14 percent, 10 percent, 7 percent, and 7 percent, respectively). The largest percentage increases in volume since 1992 have come from low-cost producers such as Malaysia (annual growth of 34 percent), China (annual growth of 21 percent), Mexico (annual growth of 20 percent), Thailand (annual growth of 19 percent), and South Korea (annual growth of 16 percent).

Industry and Trade Projections

To combat sluggish demand and the resulting disappointing profits, U.S. motor and generator manufacturers are looking for ways to cut costs as well as engaging in selective acquisitions. For example, in 1999, Emerson Electric Co. acquired Daniel Industries, a manufacturer of oil and gas industry measuring and control instruments, and Kato Engineering, a producer of larger electrical generators, to diversify its target market. In that year, A. O. Smith Corporation, a diversified corporation, acquired the worldwide motor operations of MagneTek, Inc., a manufacturer of motors used in pool and spa pumps, air compressors, and commercial air conditioners. This purchase followed recent acquisitions of two other related businesses by A.O. Smith: the UPPCO subfractional horsepower C-frame motor business in 1997 and General Electric's domestic hermetic motor operation in 1998. These corporate initiatives will begin to bear fruit after the year 2000, with exports projected to increase starting in 2000 and total real shipments expected to rise in the following year. Between 2000 and 2004, output is forecasted to grow 0.4 percent annually despite strong competition from low-cost producers abroad. Imports are expected to increase at an annual rate of 8 percent from 2000 to 2004, continuing to make inroads into the U.S. market.

Electronic Commerce

The motor and generator industry is an area within the electrical products sector where direct Internet sales are feasible and are utilized by the industry. In addition to direct sales, most notably in the area of residential backup power systems, commercial and industrial customers have many on-line options for locating rebuilt and other used motors and generators. Manufacturers of large industrial and commercial motors employ Web sites designed for business-to-business sales, including product descriptions, on-line E-mail forms and information requests, and general corporate information.

INDUSTRIAL CONTROLS

Industrial controls are used primarily for starting, regulating, stopping, and protecting various types of machinery and equipment that incorporate motors and/or other power generating systems. There are two types of industrial controls: advanced industrial controls, which are based on solid-state electronics technology and include programmable logic controllers, computer numerical controls, adjustable speed drives, proximity/positioning systems, and industrial control software, and conventional (electromechanical) industrial controls, such as starters and contractors, limit switches, and resistors.

Global and Domestic Trends

Industrial controls are used in a variety of industries, including but not limited to machine tools, automotive, material handling, pulp and paper, food and beverages and heating, ventilation, and air-conditioning (HVAC). The purchase of such controls for use in new equipment is cyclical, increasing when capital investment and consumer spending are robust and falling when economic activity slows. Constant dollar shipments have not continued to experience the rapid growth seen by the industry between 1992 and 1996, during which time real sales grew nearly 7 percent annually. A moderation in the volume of exports in 1998 and 1999 is partially to blame as exports to the United Kingdom, Germany, Japan, and Hong Kong fell in 1998. At the same time, imports rose, particularly from Mexico, Canada, Germany, and the United Kingdom (see Table 19-8). The largest increases in imports since 1992 have come from the NAFTA countries (with average annual gains of 27 percent) and several key Asian markets, including China, Japan, Malaysia, Taiwan, and Singapore. This has resulted in a trade balance that, while in surplus as recently as 1992, is forecast to have a $703 million deficit by 2000.

Computer technology has influenced industrial controls as it has virtually every sector of manufacturing. Programmable logic controllers (PLCs) are becoming standard in many industrial applications. PLCs are small microprocessor-based units that can control a variety of different functions, including assembly of industrial products, pumps and valves, furnaces and ovens, chemical processing, and even automatic cattle feeders. PLCs are one part of what is known as a process control system, a series of interrelated computers and other equipment customized to perform a specialized task or series of tasks. PLCs are becoming a viable method of process control even for relatively small operations as a result of recent price reductions. PLCs have several advantages over their precursors, relay logic controllers, including their freedom from the need for frequent human involvement, remote reprogramming and visual display capabilities, reliability, and low cost. Although most PLCs are not affected by the Y2K bug because they do not use date-related functions, they may be based on an embedded personal computer (PC), and thus there may be a real-time clock in the system. Because the Y2K bug is not thought to be a major problem for PLCs, no surge in demand for newer models of PLCs or corresponding software is anticipated.

A significant development in the area of PLCs is the development of small units that have many of the features previously found only in much larger machines. Because of advanced programming languages, firms are able to integrate these small machines easily into virtually any manufacturing environment. These small, flexible systems represent an important step toward the integration of computer technology into all aspects of the manufacturing process.

TABLE 19-8: U.S. Trade Patterns in Relays and Industrial Controls[1] in 1998
(millions of dollars; percent)

Exports			Imports		
Region[2]	Value[3]	Share, %	Region[2]	Value[3]	Share, %
NAFTA	1,276	59	NAFTA	1,094	38
Latin America	88	4	Latin America	101	4
Western Europe	457	21	Western Europe	562	20
Japan/Chinese Economic Area	166	8	Japan/Chinese Economic Area	848	30
Other Asia	118	5	Other Asia	218	8
Rest of world	66	3	Rest of world	45	2
World	2,172	100	World	2,868	100
Top Five Countries	Value	Share, %	Top Five Countries	Value	Share, %
Mexico	860	40	Mexico	743	26
Canada	416	19	Japan	628	22
United Kingdom	129	6	Canada	351	12
Germany	87	4	Germany	196	7
Japan	64	3	China	157	5

[1] SIC 3625.
[2] For definitions of regional groupings, see "Getting the Most Out of *Outlook 2000*."
[3] Values may not sum to total due to rounding.
Source: U.S. Department of Commerce, Bureau of the Census.

Industry and Trade Projections

Consistent with forecasts that the economic boom is showing signs of age, constant dollar shipments of relays and controls are expected to decline by 0.4 percent in the year 2000. A moderation in noncomputer business investment and a leveling off of consumer demand would curtail the demand for consumer durables and nondurables as well as industrial machinery and therefore would lead to lower capital investment by the OEMs of these products. However, in the long run, steady demand by maintenance, repairs, and operating (MRO) firms for products to repair and service the original equipment, along with renewed OEM demand, portends robust shipments for the industrial controls industry through 2004, with growth of 2.4 percent annually.

Exports of industrial controls are expected to rise sharply in the year 2000 as Asian and Latin American economies regain their former strength and high-technology U.S. products are in high demand by expanding firms worldwide. As programmable logic controllers and similar computerized relays and controllers, products for which the U.S. is an industry leader, expand into new markets, the growth of U.S. exports (10.7 percent annually) will outpace the growth of imports (4.2 percent annually) from 2000 through 2004. These two favorable conditions will lead to a trade deficit of less than $100 million in industrial controls by 2004.

Christine Siegwarth Meyer, Colgate University, October 1999.

■ REFERENCES

Electricnet. http://www.electricnet.com.

Electric Power Annual, Energy Information Administration, Office of Coal, Nuclear, Electric and Alternate Fuels, U.S. Department of Energy, Washington, DC 20585. http://www.eia.doe.gov/cneaf/electricity/epav1/epav1 sum.html.

Electric Power Supply Association, 1401 H Street, NW, Suite 760, Washington, DC 20005. www.epsa.org.

Turbines

Cogeneration Buyers Guide. http://www.energy.rochester.edu/cogen/chpguide.htm.

International Gas Turbine Institute, ASME International, 5775-B Glenridge Drive, Suite 370, Atlanta, GA 30328-5380. http://www.asme.org/igti.

Turbine Systems International, P.O. Box 333, Piscataway, NJ 08854. http://www.cogeneration.com.

U.S. Department of Energy Wind Energy Program. http://www.eren.doe.gov/wind.

Watts, James H., "Microturbines: A New Class of Gas Turbine Engines," *Global Gas Turbine News* 39(1):1999.

World Co-generation Magazine. http://www.co-generation.com.

■ RELATED CHAPTERS

15: General Components
17: Metalworking Equipment
18: Production Machinery
31: Telecommunications and Navigation Equipment

ENVIRONMENTAL TECHNOLOGIES AND SERVICES
Economic and Trade Trends

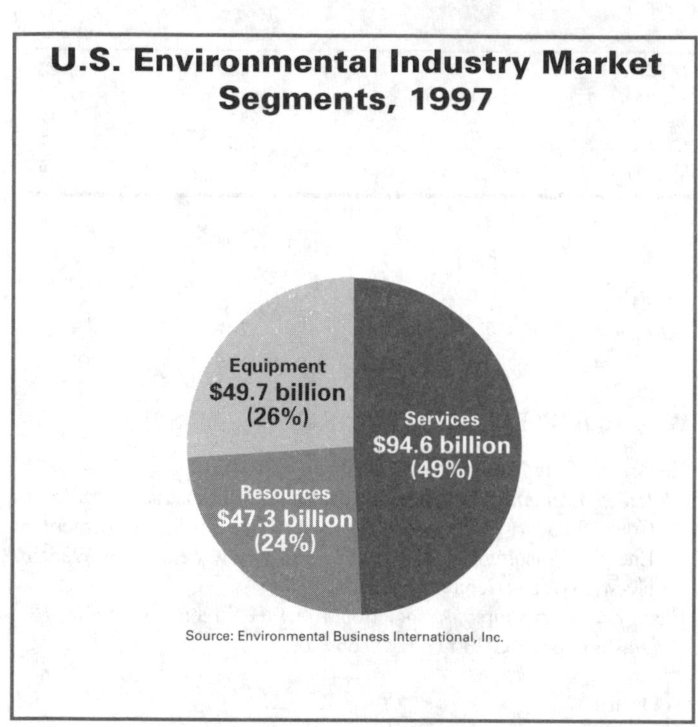

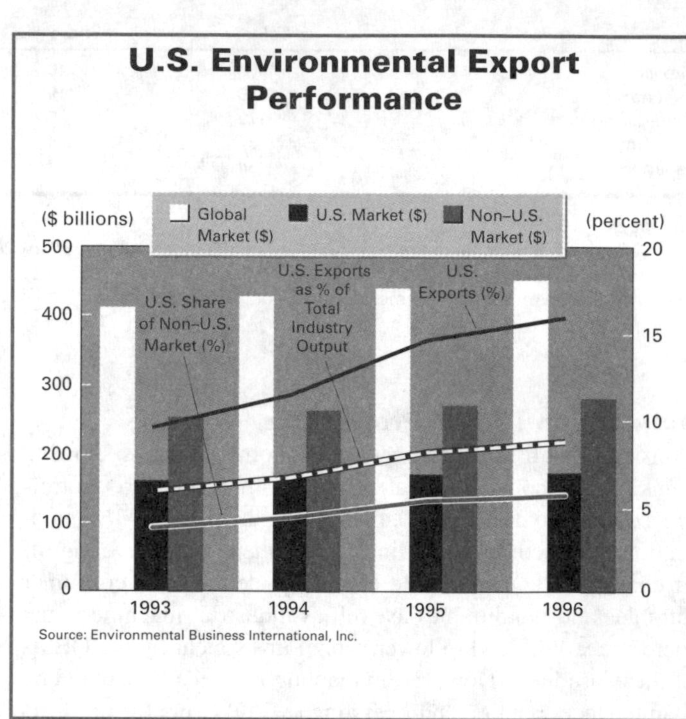

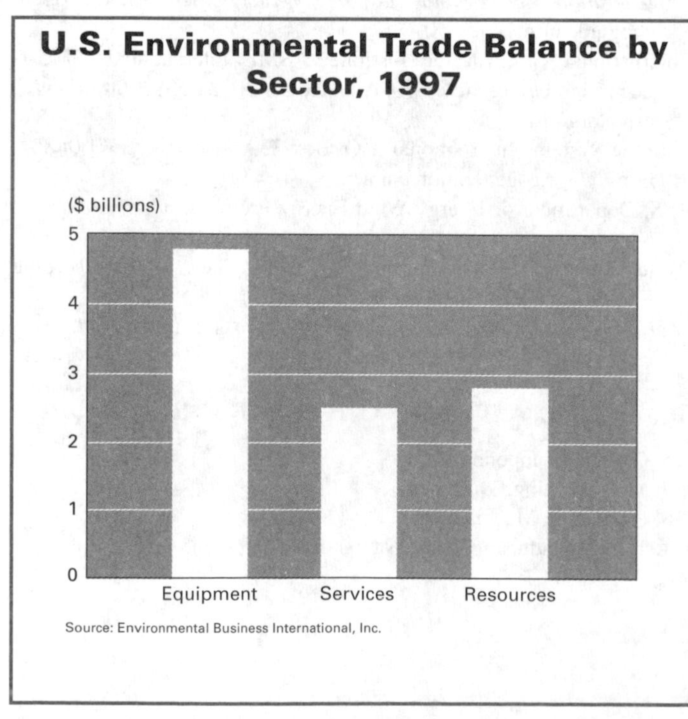

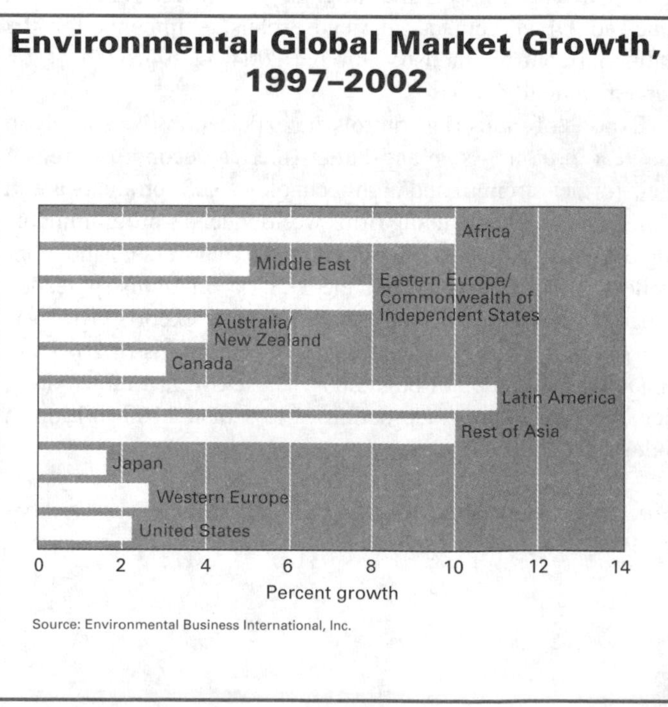

See "Getting the Most Out of *Outlook 2000*" for definitions of terms.

20

Environmental Technologies and Services

INDUSTRY DEFINITION Environmental technologies advance sustainable development by reducing risk, enhancing cost-effectiveness, improving process efficiency, and creating products and processes that are environmentally beneficial or benign. The environmental technology industry includes air, water, and soil pollution control; solid and toxic waste management; site remediation; engineering, design, and consulting services; environmental monitoring; recycling; and industrial and clean process technology. This industry is large and fragmented and has evolved in response to growing concern about the risks and costs of pollution and the enactment of pollution control legislation in the United States and around the world.

OVERVIEW

The highly fragmented U.S. environmental industry is large and complex, consisting of both investor-owned and government entities that provide everything from small-scale consulting services to large-scale water utility operations. According to Environmental Business International (EBI) of San Diego, CA, the industry grew at an annual rate of 2.7 percent in 1997 to produce a total output of $186 billion, up from $181 billion in 1996 (see Table 20-1). The environmental sector's customers range from individual consumers, to local regulated water utility monopolies and partnerships, to major U.S. corporations. Approximately 117,000 U.S. companies are engaged in the business of environmental technologies, with 4,300 of those firms exporting internationally, generating $18.2 billion in export revenues and creating a trade surplus of $9.1 billion in 1997 (see Table 20-2).

The environmental technologies industry encompasses four primary segments: water supply and treatment, solid waste management, air pollution control, and environmental cleanup. Although the four segments have much in common, their operations and demand drivers are somewhat different, as are their trends. An overriding theme for these segments, however, is the challenge of functioning in a mature marketplace with intense competition, slim profit margins, and slow demand drivers. Historically, environmental regulations were the main driving force in the development of environmental technologies in the United States. With growing public concern about the environment and the passage of the Clean Air Act, the environmental sector has expanded to meet new needs. Early technologies stemming from state and federal policies focused on end-of-pipe pollution control and remediation technologies. More recent policy and market shifts toward pollution prevention have stimulated the development of ecoefficient, or green, technologies. Along with these changes, the industry has made major advances in monitoring and assessment techniques to meet industry and government needs.

The new scenario exists in a climate of changing buying patterns among customers that now are motivated by increased resource productivity and technological improvements. In response to this trend, cost reduction for the consumer and the company is fast becoming a key industry driver, leading the public and private sectors to consolidate and diversify to achieve greater distribution of overhead costs. As a result, mergers are redefining big companies as those whose holdings are in the range of $2 billion, twice the figure in 1998. Signs of this movement, especially in the solid waste and environmen-

TABLE 20-1: U.S. Environmental Industry Revenues, Trends, and Forecasts

(billions of dollars; percent)

Industry Segment	1996	1997	1998[1]	1999[2]	2000[2]	2001[2]	2002[2]	97–02[2]
Equipment								
Water equipment and chemicals	17.5	18.2	19.1	20.0	21.2	22.8	24.6	6.2
Instruments and information systems	3.1	3.3	3.4	3.5	3.7	3.8	3.9	3.5
Air pollution control equipment	15.3	15.7	16.2	16.6	17.1	17.5	18.0	2.7
Waste management equipment	9.8	9.8	10.0	10.2	10.5	10.7	10.9	2.2
Process and prevention technology	0.8	0.9	1.0	1.1	1.2	1.3	1.4	7.0
Services								
Analytic services	1.2	1.12	1.13	1.14	1.13	1.12	1.1	0.8
Wastewater treatment works	24.0	24.44	25.30	26.30	27.3	28.3	29.3	3.7
Solid waste management	33.9	34.90	35.90	36.90	37.9	38.9	39.8	2.7
Hazardous waste management	6.0	5.80	5.7	5.50	5.4	5.2	5.0	–2.9
Remediation and industrial services	11.1	11.02	11.4	11.6	11.7	11.7	11.7	0.9
Consulting and engineering	15.2	15.31	15.8	15.9	16.0	16.0	15.8	–0.4
Resources								
Water utilities	26.4	27.60	28.5	29.4	30.3	31.3	32.3	3.2
Resource recovery	14.3	15.30	15.9	16.4	16.9	17.3	17.8	3.1
Environmental energy sources	2.5	2.70	2.9	3.1	3.3	3.5	3.6	6.0
Industry total	181.0	186.0	192.1	197.7	203.5	209.2	215.3	

[1] Estimate.
[2] Forecast.
Source: Environmental Business International, Inc.

TABLE 20-2: U.S. Environmental Trade Balance by Industry Segment, 1997

(billions of dollars; percent)

Industry Segment	U.S. Industry Revenues	U.S. Market	Exports	Imports	Trade Balance	Exports to Industry Revenues, %
Equipment						
Water equipment and chemicals	18.2	15.9	4.55	2.2	2.4	25
Air pollution control	15.7	15.0	2.11	1.4	0.7	13
Instruments and information	3.3	2.3	1.30	0.3	1.0	40
Waste management equipment	9.8	9.2	1.56	1.0	0.6	16
Process and prevention technology	0.9	1.0	0.05	0.1	–0.1	5
Total	47.9	43.4	9.57	5.0	4.8	20
Services						
Solid waste management	34.9	33.8	1.33	0.2	1.1	4
Hazardous waste management	5.8	5.6	0.21	0.0	0.2	4
Consulting and engineering	15.3	13.9	1.67	0.2	1.4	11
Remediation and industrial services	11.2	10.9	0.34	0.0	0.3	3
Analytic services	1.1	1.1	0.03	0.0	0.0	2.9
Wastewater treatment works	24.4	25.9	0.147	1.6	–1.5	1
Total	92.7	91.2	3.73	2.0	2.5	25
Resources						
Water utilities	27.6	28.8	0.14	1.4	–1.3	1
Resource recovery	15.3	12.3	3.29	0.3	3.0	22
Environmental energy	2.7	1.6	1.44	0.3	1.1	53
Total	45.6	42.7	4.87	2.0	2.8	10.7
Industry total	186.2	177.1	18.2	9.0	9.1	.8

Source: Environmental Business International, Inc.

tal services areas, have been going hand in hand with outsourcing activities by industrial companies, which are seeking to free their resources for use in their core functions. Outsourcing has created opportunities for high-quality niche-type services such as conservation planning, natural resource damage assessment, and other investigatory or planning activities at all governmental levels. In addition, the current transfer of defense technologies mandated by the U.S. government at federally supported laboratories, the required implementation of environmentally sound procedures for the cleanup of military bases, and increased U.S. Department of Defense–sponsored research and development (R&D) programs are all encouraging the growth of another niche for the environmental technologies industry.

In another approach to the issue of cost reduction, the environmental sector is turning to more creative financing alternatives, such as public–private sector partnerships and privatization. It is hoped that these new investment strategies will provide solutions for an industry that is wrestling with potential environmental liability and demand uncertainty, dynamic regulatory requirements, and relatively small transaction sizes. In the water supply and wastewater treatment subsector, privatization scenarios are appearing in the form of outright sales of public water utilities to private firms or in some form of a long-term contract for the operation of public water utilities by private firms. Privatization could present enormous opportunities for investor-owned companies driven by the concepts of stewardship and sustainability. Alongside the elements of cost, diversification, and a decreasing focus on regulations, there is an increased emphasis on public health that is shaping the environmental industry's future.

At the policy level, the U.S. government is looking at innovative tools that would complement or substitute for technology-based regulations and direct the environmental industry toward achieving environmental benefits. The use of effluent trading and emission credits, service pricing based on environmental impacts, subsidy reforms that discourage environmental degradation, and increased lobbying by environmental activists and professional organizations are all examples of these tools. Other policy changes have stimulated some activity in emissions trading in sulfer dioxide (SO_2) and the oxides of nitrogen (NO_x). The success of the Acid Rain Emissions Trading Program in bringing down the cost of compliance has encouraged interest in other emissions trading programs, particularly international trading in greenhouse gas emissions (GHGs). However, a viable market is dependent on continued policy development and domestic authority. Industry and government also suggest focusing on information and education campaigns to communicate the financial benefits of key environmental technologies, trade promotion initiatives, and trade liberalization of environmental goods and services (see the box "Trade Liberalization of Environmental Goods and Services") and dispel the notion that such efforts promote "corporate welfare."

TRADE LIBERALIZATION OF ENVIRONMENTAL GOODS AND SERVICES

Environmental goods and services was one of the original eight sectors identified for priority liberalization under the Asia-Pacific Economic Cooperation (APEC) Early Voluntary Sectoral Liberalization (EVSL) initiative. Under this initiative, tariffs would be eliminated on environmental goods and General Agreement on Trade in Services (GATS)–based commitments in environmental services would be expanded.

After several negotiating sessions with APEC member economies, it was agreed that tariffs on environmental goods would be eliminated by 2003, with limited flexibility for extended staging on several items. At the November 1998 APEC ministerial meeting, trade ministers agreed to move the EVSL tariffs package, including environmental goods, to the World Trade Organization (WTO), headquartered in Geneva. APEC members are now seeking WTO support for this initiative.

Trade liberalization of environmental services continues to be negotiated in APEC, where the environmental services portfolio was moved under the umbrella of the Group on Services (GOS). APEC economies agreed on a consolidated list of environmental services, subject to further clarification on a limited number of items. The agreed-on list extends beyond the environmental services indicated in Central Product Classification (CPC) Division 94 to encompass other services vital to this sector, such as environmental engineering, construction, monitoring, and analysis. Inventory work and the definition of environmental services for structuring trade liberalization efforts continue in both APEC and the WTO Services 2000 negotiations.

Work in APEC environmental services will contribute to the WTO 2000 Services negotiations. APEC meetings will continue into the year 2000 in Brunei.

INDUSTRY OUTLOOK

A mature industry such as environmental technologies may be described as a market where more supply is chasing less demand and where customers are experienced in buying its products and services and dictate its prices as well. Under this type of market condition, environmental companies have little to differentiate themselves from each other and thus compete on price, typically bringing down profit margins. According to the Standard & Poor's (S&P) environmental industry survey, remediation, air pollution control, hazardous and nonhazardous solid waste disposal, and treatment services are key environmental subsectors that are approaching or already are in the mature phase of the business life cycle. S&P also identifies the environmental management and information services subsector as being in the development or growth phase of this life cycle. The market research firm says that the outsourcing of service functions such as industrial treatment operation places the subsector between the development and growth stages, where the market is on the verge of exploding and new products and services are easier to introduce. BTI identifies toxic cleanup consulting and third-party industrial water quality contract operations as growth companies as well.

The current condition and forecast for the environmental technologies industry are greatly affected by specific variables or drivers. Gross domestic product (GDP) is a primary driver, for example, in the municipal solid waste (MSW) subsegment, and the Standard and Poor's–based 1998 growth rate of 3.9 percent and mid-April forecast for a 3.7 percent growth rate in 1999 reflect only moderate GDP gains. Many industry observers believe that GDP growth will continue at a similar pace into the next millennium, influencing the MSW subsegment at the same rate. U.S. Bureau of the Census estimates are for an annualized U.S. growth rate of 0.8 percent, from 268 million people in 1997 to 298 million in 2010. The slowing growth of the U.S. population is in turn expected to lead to slow growth in the MSW subsegment. The low-margin $13 billion air pollution control industry continues to suffer from weak markets resulting from the uncertain regulatory environment. The environmental cleanup subsector is suffering for the same reasons and is affected greatly by competition from consolidation and low entry barriers. Along with these and the other slow demand drivers mentioned throughout this chapter, key factors affect the future of the industry. Demand for water is increasing with population growth, and U.S. surface and ground waters increasingly are showing signs of infiltration by nitrates and pesticides, saltwater intrusion, and urban runoff. Hazardous waste management threats continue, with an additional 1,789 sites under consideration for inclusion on the Superfund National Priority List. Climate change and ozone depletion are genuine threats as well.

Major acquisition activity in the environmental marketplace in response to the slowing growth of this mature industry is expected to continue in the near term. The scope of future mergers should diminish, though, as companies focus on integrating the acquired businesses, generating internal growth, and reducing costs. The industry should shift from performing in a manner appropriate to a regulatory-driven milieu to behavior determined by stewardship and sustainability. Sustainable development of renewable energy resources and the protection of those resources should be more heavily supported. Performance-based flexible requirements for compliance as well as higher standards of accountability in fulfilling them are essential to the health of the environmental industry in the next generation.

SOLID WASTE MANAGEMENT

U.S. industry revenues in the solid waste management services and equipment segment were estimated at $45.9 billion in 1998, up 3 percent from $44.7 billion in 1997. The worldwide market was estimated at $138 billion in 1998, up 3 percent from $134.8 billion in 1997. Solid waste management is the largest environmental industry segment and covers collection, transfer, processing, and disposal.

Approximately 240 million tons of municipal solid waste was generated in the United States in 1998, up 14 percent from 210 million tons in 1997. Per capita daily waste generation in 1998 was estimated at 4.5 pounds. Single families generate 51 percent of solid waste, businesses and institutions generate 43 percent, and multifamily residences generate 6 percent.

Collection of waste is the largest revenue producer for the waste treatment system, accounting for 55 percent of all industry revenues. It is also the most expensive and labor-intensive component of the solid waste system to run. Private contractors collect 65 percent of residential solid waste, 80 percent of waste targeted for recycling or landfills, and 95 percent of commercial, industrial, and multifamily waste.

Transferring waste is a growing aspect of solid waste operations; this is due to shifting the concentration of waste treatment to waste diversion. New transfer stations are under construction, and existing ones are being updated and refurbished. Approximately 3,100 transfer stations are in operation today.

Solid waste treatment consists of three types of processes that can be broken down as follows: land filling, accounting for 57 percent of waste treatment and 35 percent of revenues; recycling and composting, accounting for 27 percent of waste treatment and 5 percent of revenues; and incineration, accounting for 16 percent of waste treatment and 5 percent of revenues.

In 1998, approximately 9,349 curbside recycling programs served 139.5 million people, up from the level in 1997, when approximately 8,937 curbside recycling programs served 135.5 million people. Composting yard trimmings facilities in the United States grew from 3,460 in 1997 to 3,807 in 1998. There are 310 materials recovery facilities operating in the United States, 75 percent of which are privately owned.

State regulations stemming from grassroots initiatives for bans on certain wastes and the development of municipal waste diversion goals have been the catalyst for the growing number of curbside recycling and yard trimmings composting programs. However, there is still room for the recycling and composting market to grow as most states are not widely served by those programs. The proportion of communities served by recycling programs is still under 50 percent in over 30 states. In the 1980s, the emphasis was on recycling glass, paper, and metal. Paper is still the primary commodity being recycled, with an average of 70 percent of the revenues and volume of most recycling programs depending on recovered paper. Waste diversion should increase, though, with the evolving knowledge that a significant proportion of organics from yard trimmings, wood, and food wastes enters the waste stream and that the processing of organics into affordable by-products is a reasonable goal.

Primarily because of federal regulations, the number of landfills shrunk by over 4,500 from 1989 to 1995. Since 1995, that number has been steady, and the number of landfills accepting waste dropped slightly from 2,514 in 1997 to 2,314 in 1998. Nationwide capacity has increased, with most sites having more than 10 years of remaining landfill life, as the landfills that have not been closed down by federal regulations are the larger facilities.

The number of landfills owned by the private sector grew from 17 percent in the mid-1980s to 36 percent in 1998. Privately owned landfills accept 56 percent of the solid waste that goes to landfills. The volumes of waste managed by the private sector versus the public sector have followed the same pattern. In the mid-1980s, the ratio of private to public landfill management was 50/50; today, the split is 58/42.

The number of incinerators declined from 131 in 1998 to 114 in 1999. This trend is expected to continue without having a great effect, since the smaller incinerators are the ones shutting down. Nationwide total daily incineration capacity in 1998 was 91,000 tons compared with 94,000 tons in 1999. Incineration is a more costly method of waste treatment and therefore is not as common as landfilling.

While the last decade saw a progression in waste industry consolidations, mergers in the last 2 years have taken industry analysts by surprise. In March 1998, the largest firm, Waste Management Inc., was acquired by the third-ranked USA Waste Service Inc. for $13.5 billion. Retaining the Waste Management name, the new industry giant holds about 25 percent of the market, with 1998 revenues of $11.2 billion. Other 1998 consolidations included Waste Management's takeover of the eighth largest Eastern Environmental Services, the third largest Allied Waste Industries Inc.'s takeover of the ninth largest Rabanco Ltd., and USA Waste's take over of the tenth largest City Management Corp.

In 1999, buyout fever continued with the stunning takeover by Allied of the number two Browning-Ferris Industries, Inc., for $9.1 billion, increasing Allied's revenues to $6.4 billion. Waste Connections Inc. became the fifth largest firm after its purchase of International Environmental Industries Inc., increasing its annual revenues $45 million to $220 million. The third ranked Republic Services Inc. purchased 40 private waste companies with an estimated annual revenue of $74 million. Like the other firms mentioned here, Republic increased its size and ranking not only through purchases but through swaps of properties that facilitated larger market share and consumer density. This consolidation trend decreased the number of U.S. waste firms with an annual income over $100 million from 16 in 1998 to 12 in 1999.

Industry officials predict that the industry will be more aggressive under the new regime. In the process of industry consolidation, larger companies divested themselves of operations in different markets and integrated collection, transfer, recycling, and disposal systems within close geographic proximity. By using their own local operations, they will avoid third-party fees and limit the costs of hauling waste.

Smaller companies are prospering from larger company consolidations. Sales of assets and holdings and market swaps to raise capital and comply with U.S. Department of Justice antitrust rulings opened the door for smaller firms to enter markets previously served by bigger firms. By combining their piecemeal acquisition of assets, these companies are growing rapidly.

Hazardous Waste Management and Remediation/Industrial Services

U.S. Environmental Protection Agency (EPA) data show that in 1997, the hazardous waste market industry was estimated at $5.8 in the United States and $16.8 billion worldwide. This figure includes industrial waste generated by manufacturing industries, medical waste management ($1.1 billion), and nuclear waste management ($1.2 billion) as well as other companies responsible for hazardous waste handling, treatment, storage, recycling, and disposal.

The hazardous waste management market has been flat over the last decade, and no turnaround is expected in the near future as a result of the increased pace of waste minimization and pollution prevention efforts by waste generators. Hazardous waste is burned predominantly in incinerators (commercially operated or captive within a waste generator's plant) or disposed of in special landfills. EPA has special regulations for hazardous waste landfills [Resource Conservation Recovery Act (RCRA) Subtitle C] that are more stringent than those for municipal waste (Resource Conservation Recovery Act Subtitle D). A number of firms offer "fuel blending" services and supply mixed fuel to kilns or other boilers and industrial furnaces. Much of what is termed "recleaning" actually consists of incinerating in cement kilns. Some hazardous waste is disposed of by deep well injection. In its *Treatment Technologies Annual Status Report,* EPA defines soil vapor extraction and thermal desorption as established technologies because of the large number of applications and the availability of cost and performance information.

The global market for remediation and industrial services (RIS) in 1997 was estimated at $27.4 billion, with the U.S. market at $11.2 billion, and no slowdown in that market is expected. Services covered in these figures include only the cleanup portion, not assessments or other work associated with contaminated sites. These firms specifically conduct environmental cleanup or maintenance work at contaminated sites, buildings, and industrial facilities and can be broken down into site remediation, industrial services, and abatement services.

The U.S. government is the RIS sector's biggest client. Superfund and underground storage tank–related work slipped from generating for 40 percent of the work in 1992 to only 22 percent in 1996. In the same time frame, U.S. Department of Defense (DOD) and U.S. Department of Energy (DOE) contracts rose from generating 25 percent of the business in 1992 to generating 46 percent in 1997.

In its latest "Cleaning Up the Nation's Waste Sites: Markets and Technology Trends," EPA reported that in the United States over the next several decades, federal, state, and local governments and private industry will commit billions of dollars annually to cleaning up sites contaminated with hazardous waste. The most recent EPA data show almost half a million sites with potential contamination that have been reported by state or federal authorities; of these sites, over 217,000 in seven market segments will cost about $187 billion in 1996 dollars. Another 300,000 sites were cleaned or found to require no further action. This cleanup commitment has resulted in a continuing demand for site remediation services and technologies; transportation costs account for roughly half the revenues, with the other half coming from disposal or recycling operations.

The hazardous waste management segment has seen rising opportunities in overseas markets, where its total revenue increased to $198 million, 60 percent derived from Canada and a significant portion from Mexico. Because of the localized nature of hazardous waste businesses and the number of U.S. offices in Canada, these percentages are high compared with other segments of solid waste. Much more than half the hazardous waste and RIS market is located in the United States and western Europe with its high concentration of manufacturers. In developing economies, much of the waste volume generated is discharged into waterways or stored with appropriate commercial waste management companies.

Anne Novak, U.S. Department of Commerce, Office of Environmental Technologies Exports, (202) 482-8178, October 1999.

WATER AND WASTEWATER

The value of the water and wastewater utilities market worldwide is estimated at $142 billion; of which $52 billion lies in the

United States. The water industry in the United States is driven and regulated by the Clean Water Act of 1972 and the Safe Drinking Water Act, which was reauthorized in 1996. This legislation facilitated the emergence of a strong high-tech commercial water and wastewater industry in the United States (see Table 20-3). The U.S. domestic water supply consists primarily of publicly owned facilities, a large majority of which are operating beyond their useful lives and need major capital improvements. The American Water Works Association estimates that $325 billion will be needed over the next 20 years to meet water infrastructure needs in the United States. As public pressure mounts to avoid raising taxes or water fees while simultaneously maintaining high water quality standards and improving systems to meet increasingly strict federal regulations, a trend toward more privatization of water treatment facilities probably will result.

The water and wastewater market in the United States can be divided into four subsectors: water supply, wastewater treatment, water equipment and chemicals, and water consulting. The water supply subsector includes government-owned and investor-owned utilities that distribute purified water to consumers. The wastewater treatment subsector consists of government-owned and investor-owned facilities that treat municipal and industrial sewage. The water equipment and chemicals subsector includes companies that make pumps, filters, and chemicals for water purification. The water consulting subsector consists of firms that provide consulting services to water pollution cleanup projects. In terms of spending for water and wastewater treatment, the top U.S. industrial wastewater markets are chemicals, electric utilities, pulp and paper, petroleum refining, food processing, primary metals, and other types of manufacturing. Among these markets, the chemicals sector accounts for 25 percent of spending.

Two major trends that are likely to continue in the water and wastewater industry are the consolidation of major companies through mergers and acquisitions and the trend toward privatization. Privatized systems probably will demand single-source supply companies, possibly resulting in an increased foreign presence in the U.S. market.

Privatization Trends

Historically, the water supply and wastewater treatment business in the United States was largely publicly owned and operated. However, this is changing. One of the most important trends in the water industry in recent years has been the contracting of private companies to operate existing facilities or build and operate new facilities. Public water suppliers have been forced to raise rates to keep up with increased demand for water, tightening environmental regulations, the need to replace an aging infrastructure in every major city in the United States, and decreased federal funding. The pressure to provide more efficient water service at a reasonable price has forced once solely government-owned providers to consider privatizing or issuing concession agreements.

Privatization of a water facility can take many forms, from the outright sale of all assets and facilities to a private sector holder, to a contract for operating or managing the facility while ownership remains in the public domain (this is also called a concession), and everything in between.

Currently, less than 33 percent of U.S. water service companies are privately owned. Privately owned water utilities serve a total of 33 million Americans, 21 million of whom are served by the 330 largest investor-owned companies. These numbers are expected to increase in the near future. In Europe, 70 percent of water and wastewater systems are privately

TABLE 20-3: U.S. Water Industry Growth
(millions of dollars except as noted)

Business Segments	1996	1997	1998[1]	1999[2]	2000[2]	2001[2]	2002[2]
Full-solution companies	1,380	2,900	5,500	4,670	6,800	8,400	10,300
Water equipment and chemicals							
Separation	2,500	2,640	2,300	2,250	2,210	2,170	2,130
Destruction	790	830	870	870	870	870	870
Chemical equipment	370	370	370	370	370	370	370
Delivery equipment	8,100	7,100	6,700	6,630	6,560	6,490	6,430
Biosolids equipment	900	930	900	890	880	870	860
Chemicals	3,410	3,440	3,470	3,500	3,540	3,580	3,620
Total	16,070	15,310	14,610	14,510	14,430	14,350	14,280
Services, consulting and engineering							
Contract operations	1,000	1,180	1,390	1,830	1,920	2,260	2,660
Consulting	1,440	1,500	1,560	1,620	1,680	1,750	1,820
Design engineering	1,630	1,710	1,800	1,890	1,980	2,080	2,180
Maintenance services	1,090	1,160	1,230	1,300	1,380	1,460	1,550
Total	5,160	5,550	5,980	6,440	6,960	7,550	8,210
Instruments	570	600	630	560	690	720	760
Analytic services	410	440	450	460	470	480	490
Wastewater treatment works	24,020	24,440	25,340	26,280	27,250	28,260	29,310
Water utilities	26,360	27,580	28,460	29,370	30,310	31,280	32,280
Total water industry	73,970	76,620	79,970	83,220	86,910	91,040	95,630
Annual growth (%)	4.9	3.9	4.1	4.1	4.4	4.8	5.0

[1] Estimate.
[2] Forecast.
Source: Environmental Business International, Inc.

owned. As U.S. municipalities are evaluating financial opportunities to resolve their funding issues, they are turning to privatization as a resource of revenue. The private sector is more often providing the capital necessary to meet strict federal standards. The European private sector is particularly well poised to take advantage of the privatization of public utilities around the world. In Great Britain, for example, the water and wastewater system was privatized in 1989, creating billion-dollar companies that have built a global presence since that time. In France, $38 billion Vivendi and $33 billion Suez Lyonnaise des Eaux have become the global leaders in water and wastewater systems. U.S. companies have been falling behind both abroad and at home because most of the U.S. water infrastructure remains in the public sector, making it difficult for the United States to win large integrated contracts for major developing cities both domestically and overseas. To date, the best international opportunities for U.S. companies have been in engineering and design, consulting services, and supply of equipment.

Privatization may take on a greater role in the developing world as well. In Malaysia, the largest cities are trying full private management. Mexico, the Philippines, and Argentina all achieved major privatization in the water sector in 1999 alone. China and India have opened some midtier cities to foreign investors.

Consolidation

The major trend toward consolidations and acquisitions by both domestic and foreign companies continued in 1999. Despite these acquisitions, an important role remains for small and medium-size companies. Those firms can offer more customized services and are not subject to the bureaucratic processes inherent in larger organizations.

Some industry experts believe that to survive in the global economy, smaller companies are being pressured into consolidating their operations into large entities that own and operate water and wastewater facilities around the world. As a result of those pressures, many smaller firms are buying equipment manufacturing firms and chemical treatment companies in order to expand a company into a larger conglomerate.

Domestically, Philadelphia Suburban and Consumers Water merged to create the second largest water company in the United States. In 1998, several large U.S.-based companies were acquired by the French. Vivendi (the world's largest water company) bought U.S. Filter, and Suez Lyonnaise (the world's second largest water company) bought Nalco Chemical, United Water Resources, and Calgon Corporation. In addition, the British-based Yorkshire Water merged with the U.S.-based Aquarion. American Water Works, Ionics, Osmonics, and Waterlink are a few of the remaining large, publicly traded companies left in the United States. Industry experts predict that there will be additional acquisitions of U.S.-based companies by French companies.

Enron, which purchased the British water company Wessex Water in 1998, created Azurix to own and operate strategic water and wastewater assets. The company's strategy is to acquire water assets in Latin America and Europe and compete directly against the French giants Vivendi and Suez Lyonnaise.

International Markets

Two important recent trends in the international water business have been privatization and mergers and acquisitions. Privatization of a country's water utilities can create opportunities for U.S. equipment and services providers as well as for private investors. For example, the government of the United Arab Emirates recently decided to privatize its water industry to reduce capital expenditures and federal subsidies, bring in advanced foreign managerial expertise, reduce the price of water services, open job opportunities for local residents, and attract foreign investment.

While the U.S. market is clearly one of the world's most developed and largest, opportunities exist for U.S. firms around the world. Estimates put the market for the rest of the world at three times the revenue volume of the U.S. market. Many modern, developed countries, such as Japan, have a large percentage of the population that is not connected to sewage treatment facilities or does not have access to clean drinking water. In addition, some mature markets may require modernization or replacement of aging water infrastructure.

In Asia, despite the economic downturn, several countries plan to invest in water and wastewater treatment facilities, creating opportunities for U.S. equipment and service companies. For example, the South Korean Ministry of Environment is planning to invest $5.5 billion to build 216 additional wastewater treatment plants throughout that nation by the year 2005. In Indonesia, the market for wastewater pollution equipment reached about $246.3 million in 1996. It has grown at an annual rate of 20 to 25 percent in the last 3 years and is expected to continue to expand no less than 15 to 20 percent over the next 5 years. The other developing countries in Asia will not be far behind in requiring water and wastewater technologies, goods, and services.

Water scarcity continues to be one of the key issues facing China in the next decade. Despite the abundance of raw water resources in China, uneven distribution has created severe shortages in certain areas, especially the northwest region and the North China Plain. If current trends continue, China is expected to incur a water shortage of 20 billion tons per year by the year 2000. According to a recent study entitled "Projection of China's Water Supply Situation and Strategy in the Year 2000," China's agricultural water consumption after 1980 will rise approximately 19 percent to 514 billion tons in 2000. Industrial consumption after 1985 will have increased a projected 47 percent to 100 billion tons in that year. Estimates for municipal consumption will reach 300 percent of the 1985 level, a direct result of rapid population growth in Chinese urban centers. The same study estimates that $700 million in wastewater treatment facilities will be needed each year to meet the projected municipal water demand. In 1997, only 26 percent of municipal and industrial wastewater was treated. The Chinese water supply and treatment subsector has the following features: scarce water resources; numerous competing users along the major rivers, especially the Yellow River; supply problems in the developed lower reach areas; an underdeveloped allocation infrastructure; and inefficient water use by private and public end users. However, water prices remain far too low: They are perhaps two to three times lower than they should be if they are to encourage conservation and generate funds for water supply, treatment, and infrastructure development. Some cities are starting to adjust rates and add wastewater treatment surcharges to their water bills.

Some of the biggest opportunities for U.S. companies may exist in Latin America, especially in the water and wastewater sector. Investment opportunities in that region are estimated to be worth $27.4 billion over the next 5 years. In Mexico, significant growth in these markets is expected because of that country's leadership in regulation development and enforcement. In addition, the Mexican government's Water Resources Sectoral Program for 1995–2000 seeks to extend the population coverage of potable water and sewerage systems to 94 and 82 percent, respectively. Population coverage is currently 85 and 65 percent, respectively.

U.S. companies are also finding success in other Latin American markets. CH2M Hill International, in partnership with a Brazilian engineering firm, recently was awarded a concession to design, construct, own, and operate a wastewater collection and treatment plant in Brazil. This is the first privatized wastewater treatment project in that country. Brazil has one of the largest environmental sectors in Latin America, with trade and investment opportunities worth $1.7 billion in the water and wastewater sector.

For continuing medium- and long-term growth, U.S. water equipment and services suppliers can turn to developing markets in the Middle East and Africa. In the Middle East, 45 million people lack access to safe water and more than 80 million lack access to safe sanitation systems. In southern Africa, the growing need for the provision of new water supply sources for rural and urban areas and for the monitoring of micropollutants provides evidence of an expanding market for U.S. companies.

George Litman and Ellen Zeytoun, U.S. Department of Commerce, Office of Environmental Technologies Exports, (202) 482-5225, October 1999.

AIR POLLUTION CONTROL

The air pollution control (APC) sector includes products and services that remove air pollutants or convert them to an odorless, less polluting form before their release into the atmosphere. This sector includes equipment to control, mitigate, or reduce emissions from both "stationary" (e.g., factories and utilities) and "mobile" (e.g., cars, buses, and mobile power equipment) sources (see Table 20-4). Customers for APC goods and services include electric utilities; incinerators and waste-to-energy processors; various manufacturing sectors, such as pulp and paper, mining, and metal finishing; cement; chemicals; pharmaceuticals; plastic manufacturing; petroleum refining; printing and publishing; electronics; and computers. Vehicle manufacturers buy catalytic converters and related technologies.

The market for stationary source emissions control includes items such as the following:

- Flue-gas desulfurization (FGD) systems ("scrubbers"), which remove sulfur dioxide from the combustion of fossil fuels.
- Electrostatic precipitators (ESPs), which remove small particles [particulate matter (PM)] from the postcombustion process.
- Fabric filters and baghouse equipment used primarily for power plants and other combustion-dependent industries, used in a variety of applications from industrial to home heating and ventilating. Baghouses are like vacuum cleaner bags.
- Oxidation systems including catalytic and thermal types. These systems chemically alter volatile organic compounds (VOCs) that arise from hazardous air pollutants (HAPs), paint and cleaning solvents, and the like, transforming them into nonhazardous substances.
- Selective noncatalytic reduction (SNCR) and selective catalytic reduction (SCR), which are used to control and eliminate NO_x.
- Carbon adsorbers that use activated carbon to collect VOCs and other odors and hold them until they can be used or destroyed.

The principal categories of air pollutants ("criteria pollutants") that EPA controls include SO_2 and nitrogen dioxide (one of the NO_x), which cause breathing problems and acid rain; carbon monoxide (CO), which affects the ability of the blood to carry oxygen to cells; VOC smog formers, some of which are also referred to as HAPs, such as mercury and dioxin; lead (Pb), which causes brain disorders; ground-level ozone or smog (O_3), which reduces lung function and damages trees and plants; and PM, which creates soot and causes lung irritation. These pollutants are created by the burning of fossil fuels (coal, oil, wood, natural gas) and the burning of waste. They also arise from solvents such as paint and glue. Smog is created by a combination of VOCs and NO_x. Coal is the "dirtiest" and natural gas the "clean-

TABLE 20-4: Air Quality Markets in the United States
(billions of dollars)

	1994	1997	2000[1]
Stationary sources market			
Equipment	3.7	3.5	3.7
Consulting and engineering	1.6	1.3	1.4
Instrumentation	0.6	0.5	0.6
Analytic services	0.1	0.1	0.1
Indoor air pollution	0.5	0.5	0.6
Total	6.5	5.9	6.4
Mobile sources market			
Equipment	10.8	12.3	13.5
Consulting and engineering	0.2	0.2	0.2
Instrumentation	0.2	0.3	0.4
Analytic services	0.4	0.6	0.9
Total	11.6	13.4	15
Total air pollution control	18.1	19.3	21.4

[1] Forecast.
Source: Environmental Business International, Inc.

est" among the fossil fuels. According to the EPA's *National Air Quality Trends Report,* emissions of the common criteria pollutants declined 31 percent while the U.S. population increased 31 percent, with GDP up 114 percent.

The clients of APC equipment manufacturers include electric utilities, incinerator operations, and various manufacturing sectors. Electric utilities support a quarter of the APC equipment market in the United States. This proportion is considerably higher in developing countries. Markets for machine production, metal plating, auto painting, and electronics are emerging to control VOCs.

Scope and Size of the Air Pollution Control Market: Industry Revenues

According to EBI, the total U.S. market for APC equipment and related services and stationary and mobile source pollution control technologies and services was $19.3 billion in 1997, somewhat higher than the revenues recorded in 1994 ($18.1 billion). In 1997, mobile source APC technologies, the largest segment in the APC sector, accounted for $13.4 billion in revenues. Revenues in this segment grew from $11.6 billion in 1994. The segment of the industry that provides controls for indoor air pollution showed no change and totaled $0.5 billion in both years (see Table 20-4).

According to EBI, stationary source equipment accounted for $3.5 billion in revenues in 1997, with 13 percent of those sales coming from exports. In that year, the $3.5 billion U.S. market consisted of an estimated 550 firms. Companies that earn under $100 million in APC revenues represent approximately 77 percent of the total market. Large diversified firms dominate the global markets. Mitsubishi in Japan and ABB in Europe are market leaders. The European and Japanese firms are more competitively positioned than are their American counterparts. Their leaders tend to be integrated power systems manufacturers and constructors. Technology has advanced in these countries as a result of more stringent regulatory frameworks.

Research done by H&W Management Science for the Institute of Clean Air Companies (ICAC), which closely tracks the APC equipment market, put total revenues for 1997 at $1.4 billion. These numbers represent normal vendor system scope and are representative of contract values; they differ from EBI numbers because of the different scopes used in creating the database of products and services.

Regulatory Trends and Market Drivers

The APC industry in the United States is driven by government regulations. The first clean air legislation in the United States was enacted in 1955, and the first comprehensive legislation, the Clean Air Act (CAA), was passed in 1963. CAA was reauthorized by Congress in 1970 and amended most recently in 1990 with the Clean Air Act Amendments (CAAA). The CAAA added acid rain and stratospheric ozone depletion to EPA's mandate. Also, revisions were made to mobile source emissions, HAPs, and ambient air quality standards. New industrial sources of pollution also were covered.

Under the CAAA, states and local authorities are required to maintain or "attain" air quality under National Ambient Air Quality Standards, or NAAQs. A final rule issued in July 1997 strengthening NAAQs for ground-level ozone, small particulate matter (PM 2.5) and coarse particulate matter (PM 10) was challenged in court. In May 1999, U.S. court of Appeals for the District of Columbia Circuit remanded the rule to EPA for review and justification. The 8-hour ozone standard within the rule was not vacated, and EPA has suggested that it will require states to submit designations of nonattainment. A state or metropolitan area that is not in conformity with the relevant NAAQs or is not implementing a plan to conform to its NAAQs risks losing federal funding for transportation projects under the Transportation Equity Act for the Twenty-First Century (TEA-21).

While EPA regulations continue to be a major market driver for environmental technologies in the United States and in countries that have strict environmental standards, demand for APC equipment is ultimately driven by popular and consumer demand for cleaner air, even in countries that do not employ a regulatory framework, and especially in rapidly industrializing countries. Another market driver is the recognition that economic and cost efficiencies can be achieved by establishing environmental management systems.

Projected Growth in the Air Pollution Control Market

All analysts agree that there will be some future growth in this market, although different estimates are given. Both EBI and Farkas Berkowitz anticipate moderate (2.5 to 3 percent) growth in the vehicle segment through the end of the decade while admitting that EPA standards could generate increased demand for mobile source APC technologies with strict enforcement. Under new standards, diesel trucks and light-duty vehicles could be affected. Other EPA-proposed standards would affect locomotive engines.

EBI predicts that between 1997 and 2000 the total stationary equipment segment will grow moderately from $3.5 billion to $3.65 billion, with NO_x control technologies experiencing the greatest increase of 35 percent (see Table 20-5). The ICAC and H&W Management study forecasts greater annual increases for the overall sector for 1999, 2000, and 2001: $3.280 billion, $2.470 billion, and $2.620 billion, respectively.

There are three reasons for the increase projected by H&W Management, according to the ICAC's deputy director, Ed Campobenedetto. First, two EPA rules to control ozone, while undergoing court challenges, are forcing utilities and manufacturers to buy NO_x control technologies (SNCR, SCR, and combustion modification). NO_x is a "precursor" of ground-level ozone. In addition to the new NAAQs for ozone cited above, EPA's rule for an Ozone Transport Assessment Region (40 CFR Parts 51, 72, 75, and 96) or "SIP Call," published in September 1998, establishes an annual emissions level for NO. The rule is intended to reduce NO_x during the summer months, when ozone is at its highest levels. EPA found that the eastern U.S. states cannot meet their ozone standards because of pollution that drifts in from the midwest and the south. Even though this rule is under court challenge, the net results of the two rules continue to drive utilities and other producers of NO_x toward

TABLE 20-5: U.S. Air Pollution Control Equipment Market Revenues for Stationary Sources, by Equipment
(millions of dollars)

Equipment Type	1996	1997	1998[1]	1999[1]	2000[2]	2001[2]	2002[2]
Flue-gas desulfurization	793.4	663.0	636.5	611.0	592.7	574.9	557.7
Electrostatic precipitators	684.3	698.8	684.8	671.1	677.8	684.6	691.4
Fabric filters and baghouses	601.3	653.1	863.4	873.7	891.2	909.0	927.2
Oxidation systems	520.2	536.6	563.4	591.6	627.1	664.7	704.6
Carbon absorption	125.2	124.9	121.1	117.5	115.1	112.8	110.6
NO_x control systems	296.2	322.3	354.5	389.9	436.7	489.1	547.8
Delivery systems	48.6	28.7	29.3	29.9	30.8	31.7	32.6
Other equipment	39.7	111.3	114.2	117.2	120.7	124.3	128.0
Materials and supplies	81.2	134.0	141.4	149.1	155.1	161.3	167.7
Total equipment market	3,390	3,473	3,509	3,551	3,647	3,759	3,868

[1] Estimate.
[2] Forecast.
Source: Environmental Business International, Inc.

establishing greater controls. Finally, there is concern in Congress about authority for deregulated entities to meet clean air standards, which could stimulate new legislation.

Campobenedetto also points to the trend toward deregulation of utilities as another positive driver for APC equipment. Deregulation is forcing sales of utility plants and equipment. When a new owner takes over an old asset, the trend is to retrofit it with APC equipment to bring it up to more modern environmental standards. In other words, new plant owners are modernizing their assets as part of their long-term investment in them. Robert McIlvaine of McIlvaine Company agrees. He points out in the January 1999 *EM,* the magazine of the Air and Waste Management Association (AWMA), that "new owners are typically investing more in upgrades and retrofits than they initially paid for the plants themselves" and that strict new ozone standards in combination with deregulation are generating demand in this sector.

McIlvaine also predicts that coal-fired power plant capacity will increase from 1,400,000 megawatts (MW) to more than 2,000,000 MW in the next 15 years. The U.S. power industry, he believes, will be the hottest sector in the world air pollution control market, with China the biggest buyer of electrostatic precipitators, over the next 5 years (*EM,* January 1999, pp. 24–27). Additionally, emissions trading, according to McIlvaine, represents another "positive market factor": "Power plants have justified the installation of redundant SO_2 monitors strictly on the basis of more accurately measuring emissions and ensuring more allowances available for trading than with the single monitor systems." While the price of an SO_2 emissions credit is approximately $200, the price of an NO_x credit is closer to $3,000, requiring careful monitoring.

A study that tracks worldwide growth in demand for vehicle control technologies prepared by Michael P. Walsh forecasts that by the year 2010, the motor vehicle pollution control market will almost double from an estimated 1998 level of $38.6 billion to over $72 billion. This growth is a function of growth in the number of new motor vehicles in Asia and Latin America and an increase in the number of countries using pollution control equipment. According to Walsh, "Continuing air pollution problems from vehicle related pollution have been stimulating innovative pollution control approaches." Walsh further notes that "since 1970 with vehicle miles traveled and U.S. GDP doubling, emissions of almost all pollutants are down significantly" and explains that the rest of the world is following this pattern.

Pollution Prevention: Process and Prevention Technology

In its broadest definition, pollution prevention (P2) or process and prevention technology (PPT) means reducing pollution at its source and refers to equipment or processes designed to achieve waste minimization and resource efficiency rather than end-of-pipe control. PPT can be used in all ET subsectors: water management (treatment, delivery, recycling), waste management, environmental energy sources, strategic environmental management, risk assessment and cost-benefit analysis, brownfields redevelopment, and instruments and information systems. As modern industrial economies shift from a focus on pollution control and mitigation to a focus on prevention and process, from environmental management to resource management, the environmental industry and ultimately other industrial sectors will evolve and change.

PPT can refer to any technology that improves the environmental and economic efficiency of a manufacturing process whether through more efficient use of resources and materials and energy, automation, design, or recycling or through novel uses of chemistry, manufacturing process, or materials that reduce or eliminate waste. P2 technologies may be developed in connection with specific industries (pulp and paper, metal painting, printing).

In general pollution prevention and process strategies include the following:

- Resource recovery and recycling. Waste streams are used and reused as a feedsource in a manufacturing process.
- Material and process substitutions. Existing materials are replaced with less environmentally damaging ones. For example, as a result of the Montreal Protocol, halons and chlorofluorocarbons (CFCs) are being eliminated from the manufacture of plastics and solvents. Biopesticides found in bt-corn and

cotton are used instead of environmentally damaging chemical pesticides, and biodegradable plastics and non-oil-based inks, paints, and detergents are substituted for oil-based products. Contaminants are removed from fuel before combustion, as in coal washing, or fuels are switched and less polluting natural gas is substituted for coal.

- New or "green" chemistry. New catalysts to enhance biological processes to replace toxic products are being developed.
- Process technologies. Engineering changes and process control devices lead to greater material and energy efficiency.
- Energy-efficient products and devices. Lighting systems, compact fluorescent bulbs, appliances, and building materials are being developed.

PPTs are emerging technologies that are dependent on R&D strategies, whose applications can embrace many industries and economic activities. Any new plant or manufacturing system inevitably involves improvement over the last generation. Sometimes efficiencies are sought in the quest for market survival as opposed to pollution prevention. Waste minimization technologies exist in many industries, but many companies have not had enough of an incentive to adopt them, instead deferring the cost of new investment. Only a fraction of metal finishers, generally the larger ones, appear to have taken advantage of some of the promising technologies, such as reverse osmosis, evaporation, and ion exchange. Nevertheless, EBI predicts a 7 percent average annual growth rate for this segment for the period 1998–2002 (see Table 20-1).

While environmental regulation will remain a necessary condition for increased environmental protection, many analysts believe that factors emerging from the economy itself increasingly will become important drivers of the environmental industry, such as cost escalation in raw materials and waste disposal, cleanups based on the economic value of land, economic return for waste minimization, and increased profits and better comparative advantage from increased efficiency. These market factors eventually will overtake regulation as the primary means of achieving higher environmental standards, providing new and expanded markets for environmental technologies and giving rise to a shift from cleanup and control to process and prevention.

Pollution prevention strategies can be promoted under the Clean Water Act and the Resource Conservation and Recovery Act by linking permit approvals to prevention planning and setting stricter discharge standards that may be achievable only through some form of source reduction. The nation's core environmental regulations have thus far stimulated pollution control techniques. Most federal government P2 initiatives are voluntary and educational. The 33/50 program to reduce chemical releases, the Energy Star and Green Lights Program, and numerous R&D and demonstration activities are examples of these programs.

Emissions trading in SO_2 allowances is a hybrid strategy that combines a market mechanism and a regulatory standard. An incentive is provided to the most efficient producer or the one most able to bear the cost of compliance. Efficient producers can buy allowances or permits and use them to expand their productive capacity or sell them. In this way, the cost of compliance is spread out over an entire industry. The success of this strategy in bringing down the cost of compliance for emissions of SO_2 has given rise to an emissions trading market in which brokers (Natsource, BTU Brokers, Cantor Fitzgerald) and traders (Dynegy) are operating. Hagler Bailly Services, Inc., recently prepared a report for the U.S. Department of Commerce titled "Markets for Climate Change Mitigation Technologies and Services in Developing Countries."

Jane Siegel, U.S. Department of Commerce, Office of Environmental Technologies Exports, (202) 482-0617, October 1999.

Recycling

Recycling involves the collection, separation, and recovery of recyclable solid waste. Industry recognizes 35 different business categories within the recycling subsector, identified as part of recycling collection, processing and manufacturing, reuse and remanufacturing, and support businesses. Over the past 25 years, the American public has increasingly made recycling a social priority. It is increasingly appreciated as a waste management tool that reduces the loss of limited natural resources, lessens the amount of waste flowing to landfills and incinerators, and stimulates economic activity.

Economics, along with public sentiment, is a primary driver for recycling activity. Recycling costs appear to be inversely related to recycling quantities, and the recycling industry has been able to implement enough efficiencies of operation as programs have matured to maintain recycling costs over time. In 1997, the U.S. recycling industry was estimated to be a $15.3 billion industry with an 8 percent growth rate. In 1998, the industry was reduced by 11 percent and prices of recyclables dropped to historical lows, mostly as a result of declines in demand and price caused by the Asian economic crisis. Other economic issues affecting recycling are concern over the lack of a sufficient and stable market demand, the extreme price volatility for many recycled materials, shortfalls in the collection of materials such as plastic bottles and aluminum cans (where demand is higher than supply), a recent flattening out of recycling levels related to slowing population growth, and the general cost of recycling in a weaker market.

Government recycling policies also greatly affect the health of this industry. Many local recycling programs are the result of state mandates that were passed during the "rush to legislate" in the early 1990s. Public–private sector partnership programs are increasingly being implemented, using financial grants from a state or a contract between a regional waste authority and a composting firm, for example. Economic policies that account for the true social cost of consuming unsustainable materials will be required if recycling is to reach its full potential as a business.

The United States diverts about 27 percent of all discarded materials for recycling, up from 17 percent in 1990. The largest single category of recyclables is paper of various types, followed by scrap metal and yard trimmings. About 45 percent of all paper used in the United States is recovered, bringing the nation close to the papermaking industry's goal of a 50 percent recovery rate. Recovered paper represents 37 percent of the fiber input in paper production in the United States. The steel industry is also leaner, meaner, and greener than it used to be. Today's U.S. steel mills expend 45 percent less energy than they did 20 years ago, using 70 million tons of recovered materials per year.

Recyclables are collected mostly through the curbside recycling programs sponsored by 80 percent of U.S. municipalities. Multimaterial curbside recycling programs provide service to 140 million Americans in 9,000 communities nationwide. In addition to its focus on the environment and landfills, recycling is about creating new commodities to be used in the manufacture of new products. This subsector of the recycling industry is known as resource recovery (RR) and is defined as the recycling and reuse of materials and the revenues generated from the sale of those materials. RR is discussed further in the solid waste management section of this chapter, above.

Sage Chandler, U.S. Department of Commerce, Office of Environmental Technologies Exports, (202) 482-5225, October 1999.

ENVIRONMENTAL SERVICES

Environmental services refers to a set of activities marketed to reduce, control, and/or monitor environmental pollutants. That set includes consulting, engineering and design, construction, operations and maintenance (facility management), and other services organized around environmental facilities or primarily for environmental benefit. This includes water treatment services, waste and hazardous waste management services, and other elements covered more comprehensively in other sections of this chapter. The global market for environmental services is currently estimated at approximately $247 billion, growing at an estimated average rate of 2 percent.

Overall, this group has been characterized by the marks of a maturing industry. Industry consolidation is the most prominent mark. Strong price competition and the thinning profit margins that result reinforce this trend. Regulatory incentives continue to be the primary driver for the market. However, as a result of the industry integrating regulatory compliance into core operations and remediation and ongoing cleanup activities, the effectiveness of this driver in the domestic market will continue to diminish. A positive trend in domestic regulation is that regulatory agencies are devoting more attention to voluntary programs that encourage industry to look beyond regulatory compliance to find the best comprehensive environmental management solutions. International trade and cooperative agreements as well as the activities of multinational companies are helping to spread this orientation to developing markets.

The strengthening of trade ties is accompanied by the spread of environmental concerns and standards. Multinational manufacturers that are accustomed to operating in more strict regulatory environments than they might find in some developing nations have raised the bar with regard to environmentally responsible operations in many of those nations. This suggests that firms are finding more benefit in the standardization of facilities and practices, environmental risk reduction, and the competitive advantage of sound environmental management than in taking advantage of the lagging regulation and enforcement they may find in developing markets. Also, guidelines such as the ISO 14001 series administered by the International Standards Organization (ISO) and the Kyoto Protocol continue to penetrate international markets through regulatory and industrial channels, helping to drive growth in environmental services.

Stiff domestic competition, industrialization, infrastructure development, and privatization in international markets continue to provide U.S. firms with export opportunities. U.S. exports of environmental services were estimated to be approximately $3.7 billion in 1997. This represents an increase of only about 4 percent over 1996, compared with the estimated 22 percent average annual increase recorded from 1994 through 1996. Continued industry consolidation and uncertainty in international markets are the likely causes for this downturn.

The Asian financial crisis has dampened possibilities in that region, making firms more cautious about investment opportunities there. Latin America remains an attractive region for business expansion, posting the most impressive estimated growth numbers of any global region for the overall environmental technologies market. Many firms are keeping a cautious eye on the Middle East with the hope that the peace process will spur increased industrial investment and create opportunities for environmental services firms. European economic growth and unification activities continue to provide opportunities for U.S. firms in that region. According to industry estimates, over 50 percent of international revenue for U.S. firms resulted from project work in Europe. Research indicates that solid waste management continues to be the largest component of the services group, although growth prospects look strongest in water treatment services. Although U.S. firms continue to have a strong international reputation, they are commonly perceived as second to a strong European environmental services industry, with Germany generally viewed as the world leader.

Although industry consolidation has been the most obvious mark of the maturation of the market, it seems to have spurred activity and creativity in some respects. Some smaller companies have survived by offering more focused client attention in specialized technical or geographic niche markets. Larger firms are solidifying their positions by capitalizing on the contacts and reputations of the smaller firms they integrate. For these firms, mergers, acquisition, and restructuring are often part of a strategy to provide the broader capabilities and deeper technological knowledge needed to respond to more comprehensive environmental management demands from end users.

The long-term future of the industry will depend on the establishment and strengthening of more pure market drivers. There is some evidence that markets are beginning to attach financial value to environmental leadership. One example is the continuing momentum of emissions credit trading and environmental performance bond schemes in domestic and international markets. Industry is starting to seek opportunities to capitalize on these mechanisms. However, since the mechanisms usually are administered by government entities, such vehicles represent only a step in the right direction.

More promising evidence of the strengthening link between financial value and environmental management can be found in the fact that many international financial institutions are asking that borrowers comply with voluntary international environmental management standards, such as the aforementioned ISO 14000 and World Bank environmental guidelines, on large projects. Lenders view compliance as a means of reducing the risk of environmental liabilities later in project life cycles. Also, the continuing popularity of concepts such as environmental cost accounting and design for environment (DFE) illustrates the fact that the world's corporate leaders recognize the value of sound environmental practices and are seeking to quantify that value more accurately. Trends such as these will be important for the long-term future of the market.

Further international education and awareness on the part of both markets and consumers across the board on the cost saving benefits of good environmental management will stimulate future market growth. Also, technological developments in environmental services that make demonstrable contributions to cost reduction as well as environmental compliance can boost growth in the sector.

Marc Lemmond, U.S. Department of Commerce, Office of Environmental Technologies Exports, (202) 482-3889, October 1999.

THE INTERNATIONAL PERSPECTIVE

U.S. environmental exports doubled from $9.4 billion in 1993 to $18.4 billion in 1997, reflecting the U.S. environmental industry's trend toward globalization in recent years. Since 1994, U.S. international revenues have accounted for over one-half of U.S. environmental industry growth. The U.S. share of the international market inched above 6 percent in 1997, with foreign competitors having more success in securing major contracts, particularly in water, wastewater, and solid waste, a segment in which the United States once had a significant advantage (see Table 20-6 and Table 20-7).

The U.S. environmental technologies export industry has considerable competitive advantages in certain U.S. segments and disadvantages in other segments, partly as a result of more progressive environmental policies domestically and more aggressive export promotion activities on the part of competitor nations. According to industry officials, there is a significant volume of European work for U.S. business, but competing for it stateside is extremely difficult. In recent years, the U.S. environmental export market has grown faster than has the domestic market, but U.S. companies have been slow to change their domestic orientation, partly because government assistance has lagged behind that in Japan, Germany, the United Kingdom, Canada, France, and South Korea. There also have been major regional financial crises overseas, leading U.S. firms to be more cautious about expanding globally. The United States nevertheless anticipates foreign growth through projects for overseas facilities of domestic industrial clients and joint ventures, especially in the Pacific Rim. There are also business prospects in China and India, and South Korean companies continue to look for joint ventures with U.S. testing and instrument firms. Thailand has very strong environmental programs, though this market has progressed with caution. In Malaysia, environmental spending is growing and the government is setting up public sector laboratories.

The Asian market on the whole has a lot of promise after a temporary slowdown incurred as a result of the Asian financial crisis. Opportunities exist for U.S. environmental products and services in Indonesia specifically, as the government there is initiating programs for rating domestic manufacturers' adherence to environmental regulations. The government has publicized these ratings and will continue to do so. Its goal is to have at least 750 firms in this rating program by the year 2000. Compliance with these very rigorous laws would require the purchase of environmental goods and services to meet greener standards. Also, the large multinational corporations operating in Indonesia usually adhere to environmental standards and buy U.S. environmental products and services. In addition, new power plants are required to adhere to stricter environmental standards and local manufacturers will be motivated to spend money on pollution control equipment with the implementation of ISO 14000.

TABLE 20-6: U.S. Environmental Industry Trade, 1994–1996
(billions of dollars; percent)

	1994	1995	1996	1997	Percent Change[1] 96–97
U.S. environmental industry revenues[2]	172.1	179.5	181.1	186.2	2.8
U.S. environmental market[2]	165.9	171.6	172.8	176.9	2.3
U.S. environmental exports[2]	11.5	14.5	16.0	18.4	14.8
U.S. environmental imports	5.5	6.6	7.7	9.0	17.4
U.S. industry exports to revenues (%)	6.7	8.1	8.8	9.9	11.7
Trade balance	6.2	7.9	8.3	9.4	13.3

[1] Compounded annual rate change.
[2] U.S. industry is revenues generated by U.S. companies worldwide; U.S. market is revenues generated from U.S. customers. Exports include ownership of overseas companies but do not include repatriated profits.
Source: Environmental Business International, Inc.

TABLE 20-7: U.S. Environmental Export Performance
(billions of dollars except as noted)

	1993	1994	1995	1996	1997
Global market	413	429	441	454	468
U.S. market	160	166	170	173	177
Non-U.S. market	253	263	271	281	291
Exports (% of total industry output)	5.9	6.7	8.2	8.8	9.9
U.S. exports	9.6	11.5	14.7	16	18.4
U.S. share of non-U.S. market (%)	3.8	4.4	5.4	5.7	6.3

Source: Environmental Business International, Inc.

Central America has shown market demand in the environmental instrumentation market, specifically in Guatemala, El Salvador, and Costa Rica. Columbia also is receptive to doing environmental business with the United States, having negotiated cooperative market development initiatives that cover the setting up of an environmental testing capacity.

U.S. environmental industry experts see recycling as a sector with opportunity in foreign markets. Thermo-Retec in Concord, MA, a broad-based environmental technologies company, has been involved in Central America and South America, doing in-process engineering and site conversion for multinational corporations. In Ireland, Thermo-Retec owns a recycling company where the industry drivers are land needs and the specific economies of the site. Also, EPA has partnered with the U.S. Department of Commerce and other agencies to showcase U.S. remediation and field characterization technologies in the Czech Republic and Argentina. EPA's Walt Kovalick, director of the Superfund Technology Innovation Office, sees a marked shift internationally (e.g., Netherlands, the United Kingdom, Germany, and France) toward taking land use into account as well as making site-specific risk assessments.

In the waste management equipment subsector, the transportation costs of the finished equipment are so high that centralized manufacturing is unrealistic. Many companies end up shipping components or finished parts to local partners for final assembly, making U.S. export penetration difficult. Waste Equipment Technology Association surveys indicate that about 15 percent growth of U.S. output in solid waste equipment and vehicles is exported. U.S. exports break out roughly as follows: 40 percent to Canada and Mexico, 30 percent to Asia, 20 percent to Latin America, and 10 percent to Europe. About 70 percent of the Water Equipment Technology Association's membership is involved in exporting, including more than half the firms with revenues of less than $20 million, according to the association's executive vice president.

In Europe, large foreign environmental technologies companies are merging with their counterparts at home and abroad in response to their own needs to improve operations and resolve financial inefficiencies. The water sector is an especially attractive area for acquisition because of its size, global quality, emerging technologies, and primary ownership by the government. U.S. Filter was acquired by the French conglomerate Vivendi for $6.2 billion. By combining Vivendi's strong presence in the municipal water treatment market with U.S. Filter's North American industrial water treatment businesses, the company will provide single-source services to customers in the commercial, industrial, municipal, residential, and agricultural world markets. International industrywide consolidation of larger companies that operate the supply of drinking water appears imminent as well. Enron Corporation, a Houston-based energy company, is targeting the contract service market and is expected to be one of American Water Works's strongest competitors for acquisitions. In October 1998, Enron acquired Britain's Wessex Water plc for $2.2 billion. Leading U.S. environmental consultants are working all over the globe and even acquiring some of their European counterparts. The environmental consulting and engineering company Environ in Arlington, VA, recently purchased the British firm EAG. Such additions have brought in new clients and opportunities, paving the way for U.S. environmental companies to serve transnational clients in the global market (see Table 20-8).

In the municipal sewage treatment industry, several foreign companies are exploiting the trend toward privatization of publicly owned municipal wastewater treatment plants. Vivendi, the French water utility company Suez Lyonnaise des Eaux, and several British water companies have been purchasing large stakes in U.S. water treatment firms. Suez owns a 29 percent stake in United Water Resources, the second largest privately owned water company in the United States. Vivendi owns a 13 percent stake in Philadelphia Suburban Corporation, which recently acquired Consumers Water Company. Suez bought

TABLE 20-8: Estimated Growth in Global Environmental Market
(billions of dollars; percent)

	1996	1997	1998[1]	1999[2]	2000[2]	2001[2]	Percent Change 97–02[3]
United States	171.8	175.5	179.4	183.4	187.4	191.5	2.2
Canada	11.6	11.9	12.2	12.5	12.8	13.1	3
Latin America	8.8	9.8	11.0	12.3	13.8	15.5	11
Western Europe	133.6	137.3	141.2	145.1	149.2	153.4	2.6
Eastern Europe/Confederation of Independent States	7.1	7.7	8.3	9.0	9.7	10.5	8
Japan	87.1	88.8	90.6	92.4	94.3	96.2	1.6
Rest of Asia	20.0	22.0	24.2	26.6	29.3	32.2	10
Australia/New Zealand	6.8	7.1	7.4	7.6	8.0	8.3	4
Middle East	4.3	4.7	5.0	5.4	5.9	6.3	5
Africa	2.2	2.4	2.6	2.9	3.2	3.5	10
Total	453	467	482	497	513	530	

[1] Estimate.
[2] Forecast.
[3] Compound annual rate change.
Source: Environmental Business International, Inc.

Nalco Chemical, a water treatment company based in Chicago, for $4.1 billion in June 1999. Vivendi and Suez have invested more than $10 billion in the United States in the last 5 months, using international financial backing from French equity markets. Both firms show signs of continuing to invest, and Enron also plans to compete with Suez and Vivendi for control of the sewage treatment market.

Asia

The outlook for U.S. environmental goods and services in Asia is very promising. By the year 2015, more than 1 billion Asians will live in cities, putting unfathomable strains on water resources and waste disposal systems. Asia today represents about 20 percent of the global environmental market. Environmental degradation, the demand for clean water, and the inadequacy of waste treatment will only increase as those countries continue to develop. Meeting these needs will provide tremendous opportunities to U.S. firms in the years ahead.

The United States has the largest percentage of market share of imported environmental goods and services in South Korea at 38 percent, followed by Japan at 26 percent and Germany at 16 percent. The South Korean environmental market grew to about $5 billion in 1998. South Korea is a promising market for imports in most environmental technologies in the long term. However, like Japan, it is an extremely difficult market to penetrate because of the dominant role played by that country's chaebols in many aspects of the economy. South Korean companies are typically capable of manufacturing medium- to low-tech components and parts of environmental facilities, but most still lack the core technologies to build large-capacity advanced facilities. Over the years, Japanese and European providers generally have been aggressive in building technology and business linkages with chaebols and thus have had a foothold in meeting technology requirements in most environmental segments.

South Korea's government agencies and chaebols are the primary buyers of environmental goods and services, followed by foreign-based multinational corporations. Domestic environmental firms are the dominant players, while foreign-based suppliers generally shy away from the highly competitive sectors and focus mainly on niche areas.

In recent years, some U.S. firms have been making strides in areas such as water and wastewater and air pollution control, where demand for state-of-the-art technologies and expertise has given determined U.S. players opportunities to participate in otherwise impenetrable markets. Similar requirements in the solid and hazardous waste management sectors will open up further opportunities in the long term.

The national environmental protection system in the Philippines is struggling to catch up with that country's booming economic growth of the last few years. With a fairly comprehensive regulatory framework, the environmental market was estimated at $600 million in 1998. The largest sector is the water and wastewater treatment sector, followed by the solid waste management sector. Imports account for 80 to 90 percent of the total market. The United States has an advantageous position in the import market because of its historical ties with the Philippines as well as price competitiveness and the high quality of U.S.-manufactured equipment.

Taiwan remains one of the strongest environmental markets in Asia but is perhaps one of the toughest to penetrate. Taiwan's biggest environmental challenges are industrial waste disposal, air pollution, and water pollution. The environmental marketplace in Taiwan grew to approximately $5.2 billion in 1998. The disposal of solid waste improved with the construction of 21 new incinerators, of which 9 are now operating. Serious problems still exist with the disposal of industrial waste. Laws are not strictly enforced and need to be modified to include stiffer penalties. Motorcycles and motor scooters are major contributors to air pollution. The majority of imported environmental goods and services come from Japan, Germany, and the United States, in order of market share.

China's environmental problems stem from a deteriorating natural resource base, dense population, heavy reliance on soft coal, outmoded technology, underpriced water and energy, and breakneck industrial growth. The World Bank estimates that air and water pollution cost the Chinese economy up to 8 percent of GDP. In response, the government unleashed a burst of environmental legislation, shut down thousands of small and dirty factories, decreed that all industrial enterprises comply with pollution discharge standards by the end of the year 2000, and elevated the country's environmental protection agency (SEPA) to ministerial status.

Still, local enforcement of environmental laws is spotty, investment in pollution control infrastructure is inadequate, and competition from domestic firms is increasingly strong. Products that enjoy the best sales prospects include low-cost FGD systems, air and water monitoring instruments, drinking water purification products, vehicle emissions control and inspection devices, industrial wastewater treatment equipment, and resource recovery technologies.

In 1998, China spent nearly $10 billion on the environment—about 1 percent of GDP. This figure includes the upkeep of environmental institutes and street sweepers' salaries; the actual market accessible to foreign firms is considerably smaller. Fully achieving the stated environmental objectives of China's current five-year plan (1996–2000) would require an investment of at least $54 billion. The government plans to boost environmental spending to 1.5 percent of GDP early in the twenty-first century and expects actual spending to exceed 1 percent of GDP in 1999. Phase 1 (1996–2000) of SEPA's ambitious Trans-Century Green Plan lists 1,591 priority projects requiring an investment of $23 billion. Finally, the government pledged to boost environmental and other infrastructure investment to stimulate economic growth.

However, the central authorities—whose net tax revenues account for a tiny percentage of GDP—inevitably look to local governments and foreign lenders to provide the lion's share of investment. Determining which projects will ultimately receive funding and necessary approvals is often a daunting task. Most large U.S. environmental firms traditionally looked to World Bank and Asian Development Bank projects for opportunities. The future may be brighter as the affluent coastal cities begin to increase environmental spending dramatically, multinational investors uncork new sources of demand, and municipalities experiment with new project financing models.

China is preparing to revise its clean air act for the second time in 5 years and mandate desulfurization systems on all new power plants and industrial facilities in designated SO_2 and acid rain control zones. China also is embarking on an ambitious campaign to curb vehicle emissions in major cities by phasing out leaded gasoline, issuing new tailpipe standards, developing alternative fuel technologies, and investing in emissions control and inspection equipment.

China and its foreign lenders still spend far more on the water sector than they do on air and waste, especially on the cleanup of priority river basins and lakes, but domestic competition is also stiffest in this market. To meet funding demands, water tariffs are expected to rise, cities are starting to levy wastewater surcharges, and BOT-type concession projects are emerging.

China is slowly beginning to enforce its first comprehensive solid and hazardous waste law, but investment remains low despite a dire need for hazardous waste treatment technologies. Low-cost resource recovery and refuse handling systems enjoy the best prospects.

American firms lag far behind their competitors despite the high regard in China for U.S. technology. Many U.S. companies attribute this lag to the substantial tied aid programs of other countries. Some Chinese end users credit the other countries' aggressive marketing, flexible financing, and ability to provide turnkey solutions as their competitive advantage over U.S. technologies. Some firms find that a successful strategy for lowering manufacturing costs in the face of high import duties and growing local competition is to form joint ventures in China.

Latin America

Latin America purchased approximately $9.4 billion in environmental goods and services in 1997. Unfortunately, the Brazilian financial panic in the fall of 1998 signaled a lack of investor confidence and plunged the countries of South America into a fairly strong recession in 1999. The notable exception to this regionwide recession is Mexico, which has benefited from its strong ties to the robust U.S. economy. This recession in South America has led to a shortfall in government revenues, which will clearly indicate an even greater reliance on Inter-American Development Bank and World Bank funding for environmental projects. In developing economies, the environmental sector is even more dependent on the economic cycle than it is in the United States.

On the positive side in 1999, the privatization of regional water companies in Chile and Argentina continued at a brisk pace. U.S. companies should note that new capital from the private sector will be injected into those water utilities, especially the Buenos Aires provincial water utility OSBA, which is now owned by Enron affiliate Azurix, which paid $438 million to run this 30-year concession.

Still, years of uncontrolled industrial growth, urbanization, and overpopulation have created a society that must face serious environmental issues. The principal market drivers that will be responsible for the approximate 8 percent industry growth rate in the region for the next 2 years are adherence to ISO 14000 standards, especially for multinational corporations (MNCs); stricter enforcement on the part of the government (a common demand by a rising middle class); and tremendous basic unmet needs in water supply and sanitation services.

The Latin American environmental market reflects demand for a broad range of environmental goods and services. These environmental subsectors, from the largest to the smallest, include water utilities, solid waste management, water equipment and chemicals, water treatment works, waste management equipment, air pollution control equipment, consulting and engineering, resource recovery, hazardous waste management, instruments and information systems, analytic services, RIS, and environmental waste-to-energy projects. Among all the environmental submarkets, potable water, municipal sanitation services (sewer systems and wastewater treatment plants), and industrial wastewater treatment offer the best opportunities for U.S. envirotech firms, especially U.S. firms that work with U.S. MNCs.

In addition to the regionwide need for water pollution control and solid waste management, each Latin American country has its own key industry sectors, such as mining (Peru, Chile), petroleum (Venezuela, Mexico), petrochemicals (Brazil), food and beverage processing (Brazil, Argentina), and paper (Chile, Brazil), that offer significant environmental opportunities for U.S. firms.

A new modality for structuring large municipal wastewater projects has emerged under the label of the build-operate-transfer or concession mode. While this mode will be a major trend over the next 5 years, traditional multilateral development bank projects will continue to play the most important role in the region's environmental sector.

David O'Connell, U.S. Department of Commerce, Office of Environmental Technologies Exports, (202) 482-3509, October 1999.

Europe

Europe is the United States' largest export market for environmental technologies, with U.S. exports expected to grow to $158 billion by 2005. U.S. exports to Europe totaled $145.5 billion in 1998, up 3 percent from $148.1 billion in 1997 and up 6 percent from $137.6 billion in 1996.

The European Union

The primary market driver for environmental technologies in Europe is the European Union's (EU) aggressive environmental policies. Since the early 1970s, the European Commission has enacted over 200 environmental directives that mandate and guide member states in enacting national legislation dealing with environmental issues. Since 1992, the European Commission has taken a broader approach to the environment, integrating sustainable development and economic development. Since then EU directives have focused on and encompassed restrictive measures and procedures in the following sectors:

- Water pollution control. The EU has set minimum standards for wastewater treatment and collection; regular monitoring of bathwater; dealing with surface and underground water, both fresh and salt; and the discharge of toxic substances.

- Solid and hazardous waste treatment. The collection, disposal, recycling, and processing of the 2 billion or more tons of waste that the EU produces every year are strictly regulated. Enforced methods include waste diversion by reusing or recycling packaging and packaging waste, stringent rules for the appropriate disposal of batteries and electrical waste, hazardous waste incineration, and the dumping of waste at sea.
- Air pollution control. General measures have been enacted to reduce pollution from large combustion plants, particularly power stations, and reduce motor vehicle emissions. Also, measures have been taken to phase out the production and consumption of CFCs and other substances that contribute to ozone depletion.

In some cases, over 80 percent of EU member states' environmental laws originate from EU directives. However, enforcement of environmental laws, whether EU-mandated or nationally mandated, varies widely from state to state, and thus so does the marketability of environmental technologies. The markets of the Mediterranean countries, where environmental progress has lagged behind that in the northern region, are generally less saturated by domestic and other European suppliers. However, U.S. companies selling to any European country need to incorporate business strategies to compete with European suppliers that enjoy advantages of low or no tariffs, longstanding commercial relationships, and geographic proximity.

The countries profiled in this report represent three of the most promising environmental technologies markets in Europe, though they are each at a different stage in the development of their environmental infrastructures.

Spain. Private sector environmental investments in Spain were estimated at over $14 billion in the period 1995–2000. Public sector environmental investments are creating demand for environmental technologies as well. The Spanish government planned to allocate $14.4 billion through 2005 for the installation of collection, desalination, and purification equipment under the National Plan for Water Cleansing; $1.4 billion through the year 2000 for the National Plan for Hazardous Waste Recycling; $2.6 billion through 2000 to develop a strategy for efficient energy use and renewable energy under the Energy Efficiency and Saving Plan; and $1 billion through the year 2005 to remediate polluted areas under the National Plan for Recovery of Contaminated Land. Spain's environmental technologies market grew from $10.8 billion in 1996 to $12.6 billion in 1998. Total imports from 1996 to 1998 grew from $3.6 billion to $4.37 billion, and the U.S. share grew from $1.1 billion to $1.7 billion.

France. Most spending on environmental technologies in France in the near future will be allocated to the water and wastewater (48 percent) and solid waste (33 percent) sectors. Establishing increased connections to and between existing sewage networks and preserving the quality of groundwater resources are priorities for the French government.

Both industrial and municipal end users employ fully integrated waste processing industry suppliers. Incineration is currently the preferred way of dealing with household wastes; thus, French municipalities are expected to continue to invest in new plants and upgrades of existing incineration plants, and an average of 5 to 10 incineration plants are expected to be brought online each year. This is due to French law, which calls for the closing or upgrading of hundreds of landfills by the year 2002. Municipalities also will invest in solid waste collection and processing technologies to meet the objective of reclaiming 75 percent of all consumer packaging by the year 2002.

The environmental market in France dropped slightly from $23.7 billion in 1996 to $23.2 billion in 1998. Although the market potential is substantial, U.S. companies should be aware that competition is extremely intense from French industry, which not only dominates its own market but has captured markets worldwide through the use of aggressive marketing and operational strategies. Local production of environmental technologies grew from $26.1 billion in 1996 to $26.9 billion in 1998. Within that time frame, imports grew from $4.8 billion to $4.9 billion, and the U.S. share increased slightly from $580 million to $594 million.

Portugal. The Portuguese government budgeted $2.4 billion in the last 5 years for water supply and water treatment infrastructure projects. Plans are under way to provide adequate treatment for about 35 percent of the national urban solid waste generated. Solid waste project expenditures cofunded by the EU and Portugal were expected to total $1.2 billion.

An average annual growth rate of 10 to 15 percent for the Portuguese environmental marketplace is expected during the next 2 years. The best sales prospects for U.S. exporters include filtering and purifying machinery and apparatus, sensors and analyzers, recycling equipment, and heavy metal collecting equipment. The Portuguese environmental market grew from $146 million in 1997 to $185 million in 1999. In that time frame, imports grew from $137 million to $172 million, and the U.S. share grew from $9 million to $12 million.

Central and Eastern Europe

U.S. exports to central and eastern Europe (CEE) were estimated at $8 billion in 1998, up 5 percent from $7.6 billion in 1997 and up 8 percent from $7.4 billion in 1996. Projections put this figure at $18 billion by 2005. The United States has a small (about 5 percent) share of the CEE market.

Since the early 1990s, CEE governments have been enacting legislation to reverse the damage caused by decades of heavy industrialization and to bring their nations into conformity with EU environmental standards. Governments are attempting to reduce air emissions and remediate the polluted water and soil that have threatened public health and the quality of life. However, much of the environmental improvement in CEE can be attributed to the curtailment of industrialization rather than the enforcement of stringent environmental laws.

More developed CEE countries have developed their own domestic environmental industries, supplemented for the most part by western European suppliers. Poland, the Czech Republic, and Hungary, which were among the first tranche of the former communist bloc countries scheduled to accede to the EU, have made the most progress in environmental improvements. Privatization has stimulated the market for environmental technologies in those countries because environmental laws are easier to enforce on privately owned operations. When the industrial sectors were in the governments' hands, they were responsible for policing their own operations and satisfied more immediate needs such as full employment.

The less developed economies are only now beginning to address environmental problems. Still, those countries have well-trained and inexpensive labor forces and potentially good returns on long-term investments because of the absence of serious domestic competition. The commercial challenges are absence of transparency in contract negotiations, government red tape and bureaucracy, corruption, lack of capital markets, and high commercial interest rates.

In all CEE countries, lack of financing is the primary obstacle to more aggressive and rapid progress in the environmental arena. However, U.S. firms have an opportunity to gain a foothold in those markets through U.S. export assistance programs targeted specifically at that region. A program introduced in 1998 is the U.S. Agency for International Development's Ecolinks Program (http://www.Ecolinks.org), which offers grants for businesses or other project leaders interested in partnering with local entities on environmental projects in over 24 countries.

The three countries profiled below represent the most promising markets in CEE because they have the most developed environmental infrastructures that incorporate government authorities that introduce and enforce legislation and have established special environmental funding mechanisms for environmental projects.

Poland. Poland, with a population of 39 million, is the single largest environmental market in CEE. Dealing with air, soil, and water pollution problems is a major priority for the Polish government. After 1990, environmental investments increased from $580 million to reach $2 billion in 1997. The market for pollution control equipment is expected to continue to grow and grow at a faster pace over the next few years. Despite difficult economic conditions, Poland has been very successful in obtaining environmental financing through fees and fines based on the "polluter pays" principle.

The most promising areas are air pollution control, wastewater treatment, waste disposal, and recycling technology. The United States is the fourth largest supplier of environmental technologies to Poland, behind Germany, Switzerland, and Italy.

The Polish environmental technologies market grew from $430 million in 1997 to $514 million in 1999. Within that time frame, imports grew from $319 million to $390 million, and the U.S. share grew from $20 million to $22 million.

The Czech Republic. The Czech Ministry of Environment has announced that in the next 7 years, $15 billion must be invested in environmental improvements to bring the Czech Republic into compliance with EU standards. It is estimated that compliance with EU water protection standards will cost about $3 billion and will be achieved after 2007. This will require 1,500 new wastewater treatment facilities to serve municipalities with fewer than 5,000 inhabitants.

Air protection, water protection, and waste treatment are the government's environmental priorities. The Czech Ministry of Environment estimates that about $6 billion needs to be spent for air protection. The Czech Republic will need to invest in effective technologies for waste separation, environmentally friendly technologies for waste disposal, waste minimization processes, and hazardous waste incinerators. Around $4 billion is targeted for remediation projects.

The Czech Republic's environmental market grew from $668 million in 1996 to $750 million in 1998. In that time frame, imports dropped from $230 million in 1996 to $210 million, and the U.S. share increased from $30 million to $50 million.

Hungary. U.S. environmental technologies have excellent potential to penetrate the market along with new manufacturing technologies. The United States is the largest investor in Hungary, with U.S. environmental consulting companies and technologies having earned a positive reputation from major projects.

Recent government regulations, including the Environmental Act, the Act on Water Management, the new Decree on Hazardous Waste, and the new Clean Air Act, are the primary market drivers. With the privatization of several power, chemical, and pharmaceutical companies, western investors are bringing a higher level of environmental consciousness as well as new technologies to address environmental concerns.

The Hungarian environmental market grew from $65 million in 1997 to $82 million in 1999. In that time frame, imports grew from $55 million to $70 million, and the U.S. share grew from $4.5 million to $5.5 million.

Anne Novak, U.S. Department of Commerce, Office of Environmental Technologies Exports, (202) 482-8178, October 1999.

International Environmental Standards

The growing acceptance by companies of international environmental management standards should lead to increased sales of environmental technologies. The ISO is developing this family of standards, which addresses management systems, including auditing and performance evaluation, and the environmental aspects of products in the areas of life cycle assessment and labeling. These standards have the potential to exert a significant influence on the design, manufacture, and marketing of products. They also are likely to affect the type of environmental data gathered by businesses and the ways in which those data are communicated internally and externally. Although ISO 14000 standards are voluntary, competition could in effect force industrywide conformance, as has been the case with the ISO 9000 series (quality management systems). ISO 14001—the specification for an environmental management system (EMS)—is the only standard in the 14000 series that is applicable to third-party certification. An organization may seek third-party certification of its management system to meet a regulatory requirement or a demand from customers and/or stakeholders for independent verification. Businesses may benefit from implementing ISO 14001 in a facility in any number of ways, such as decreasing waste through efficient energy use, pollution prevention, cost recovery recycling, and decreased liability. EPA recognizes that the implementation of an EMS has the potential to improve an organization's environmental compliance with regulatory requirements; however, at this time, the agency is not basing any regulatory initiatives on the use of EMSs or certification to ISO 14001.

REFERENCES

A Bridge to a Sustainable Future, Office of Science and Technology Policy, Old Executive Office Building, Washington, DC 20500.

Academy of Management Executives, 1998, vol. 12 no. 2, "Proactive Corporate Environmental Management: A New Industrial Revolution," Michael Berry and Dennis Rondinelli.

African Development Bank Report by the Boards of Directors and African Development Fund, January 1–December 31, 1996, 01 B.P. 1387 Abidjan 01, Cote D'Ivoire.

Air Pollution Control Equipment 1995, National Fund for Environmental Protection and Water Management, Warsaw, Poland.

Air Pollution Control Equipment Market Forecasts, Institute of Clean Air Companies, Inc., H&W Management Science Consultants, Washington, DC, January 1996, September 1998. (202) 457-0911.

Air Pollution Management Report, McIllvaine Company, Northbrook, IL, 1996. (847) 272-0010.

Asia Environmental Business Journal, Environmental Business International, Inc., San Diego, CA.

Asia Environment Review, Asia Environment Trading, 55 Exhibition Road, London SW7 2PG, United Kingdom.

Asian Development Bank Annual Report 1996, 6 ADB Avenue, Mardaluyong City, 0401 Metro Manila, Philippines.

BioCycle 11th National Survey, "The State of Garbage," *BioCycle,* April 1999, Emmaus, PA. (610) 967-4135.

China: Environmental Technologies Export Market Plan, Trade Promotion Coordinating Committee, Environmental Trade Working Group, March 1996.

Congressional Research Service, James McCarthy, Environment and Natural Policy Division, Library of Congress. (202) 707-7225.

Demand for Environmental Technologies in Poland, Hungary, the Czech Republic and Slovakia, Regional Environmental Center, September 1997.

Directions in Development Series: Toward Sustainable Management of Water Resources, 1995, The World Bank, Serageldin, Ismail, 1818 H Street, Washington, DC 20433. (202) 477-1234.

EBI Report 510: The U.S. Water & Wastewater Industry, 1996, Environmental Business International, Inc., P.O. Box 371769, San Diego, CA 92137. (619) 295-5743.

EBI Report 2000: The U.S. Environmental Industry & Global Market, August 1996, Environmental Business International, Inc., P.O. Box 371769, San Diego, CA, 92137. (619) 295-5743.

EM: Journal of the Air & Waste Management Association, Pittsburgh, PA, January 1999. (412) 232-3444. From "1999 Air Market Outlook," Robert McIlvaine, McIlvaine Company, Northbrook, IL.

Engineering News-Record, July 5, 1999, "The 'Other' E-Biz Continues to Grow," Andrew Wright, Debra Rubin, Mary Powers, Sherie Winston, William Angelo, Shephen Daniels, and Paul Rosta.

Engineering News-Record, July 6, 1999, "Booming Economy Keeps Green Markets Afloat," Andrew Wright, Debra Rubin, Mary Powers, Sherie Winston, William Angelo, Shephen Daniels, and Paul Rosta.

The Environment Industry and Markets in Selected Central and Eastern European Countries, Organization for Economic Cooperation and Development, 1995, Paris, France.

Environmental Industry of the United States—Meeting the Challenge: U.S. Industry Faces the 21st Century, U.S. Department of Commerce, Office of Technology Policy, Technology Administration, August 1998.

Environmental Industry of the United States—Overview by State and Metropolitan Statistical Area, U.S. Department of Commerce, October 1997.

Environmental Technologies Industry and Exports: A Reference Guide, U.S. Department of Commerce, Washington, DC, June 1999. (202) 482-5225.

Environmental & Waste Management, Industry Surveys, Standard & Poor's, a division of the McGraw-Hill Companies, New York, NY, April 29, 1999.

European Bank for Reconstruction and Development Annual Report 1996, EBRD Procurement Opportunities, Subscription Department, 82–84 Peckham Rye, London SE15 4HB, United Kingdom.

Executive Brief, Environmental Industry Associations, May 1998, 4301 Connecticut Avenue, NW, Suite 300, Washington, DC 20008. (202) 244-4700.

Global Competitiveness of U.S. Environmental Technology Industries: Air Pollution Prevention and Control, International Trade Commission, Publication 2974, June 1996. (202) 205-1806.

Global Competitiveness of U.S. Environmental Technology Industries: Municipal and Industrial Water and Wastewater, March 1995, U.S. International Trade Commission, Publication 2867, Washington, DC 20436.

The Global Environmental Markets and United States Environmental Industry Competitiveness, Environmental Business International, Inc., 1995, San Diego, CA 92137.

Global Water Report, "Weighing the Benefits of Privatization," *Financial Times,* London, United Kingdom, December 17, 1998.

Greener Management International, Autumn 1998, "The Business Case for Sustainable Development," Robert Day and Matthew Arnold.

The Hazardous Waste Consultant, "Commercial Hazardous Waste Management Facilities: 1998 Survey of North America," March/April 1998, vol. 16, issue 2.

India: Environmental Technologies Export Market Plan, Trade Promotion Coordinating Committee, Environmental Trade Working Group, October 1996.

Indonesia: Environmental Technologies Export Market Plan, Trade Promotion Coordinating Committee, Environmental Trade Working Group, August 1996.

Industrial Wastewater, Water Environment Federation, 601 Wythe Street, Alexandria, VA 22314-1994. (703) 684-2400.

Industry, Trade, and Technology Review, U.S. International Trade Commission, June 1999, "Market Trends Affecting the U.S. Environmental Services Sector," Jennifer Baumert.

Infrastructure Finance, "Turning on the Taps," February/March 1996, citing World Bank Statistics.

Inter-American Development Bank Annual Report 1997, 1300 New York Avenue, Washington, DC 20577. (202) 623-1000.

International Environment, The Bureau of National Affairs, Inc., vol. 21, no. 11, May 27, 1998, Washington, DC 20037.

Journal, American Water Works Association, Business—North Carolina, vol. 19, no. 7, Business Dateline, News & Observer Publishing, 6666 West Quincy Avenue, Denver, CO 80235. (303) 794-7711.

Motor Vehicle Pollution Controls: The Growing Global Market, 1996, 1999 update, Michael P. Walsh, 3105 North Dinwiddie Street, Arlington, VA 22207. (703) 241-1297.

The NAWC Privatization Study: A Survey of the Use of Public-Private Partnerships in the Drinking Water Utility Sector, Hudson Institute. Washington, DC, 1999.

National Recycling Coalition, *Building A Strong Foundation for Recycling's Future,* Edgar Miller, October 6, 1999.

Projects & Finance: Lagniappe Monthly on Latin America, vol. 8, no. 6, June 1999.

Public Utilities Topics, Winter 1999, "Public Water Suppliers Look to Privatization," Price Waterhouse Coopers, Philadelphia, PA, 1999.

Puget Sound Business Journal, vol. 18, issue 46, "Asian Market Flat for Enviro Firms—Local Companies Turn Attention Back to Domestic Services."

Solid Waste Disposal Trends; 1999 Update, Environmental Industries Associations, Washington, DC 20008 August, 1999.

South Korea: Environmental Technologies Export Market Plan, Trade Promotion Coordinating Committee, Environmental Trade Working Group, November 1994.

Taiwan: Environmental Technologies Export Market Plan, Trade Promotion Coordinating Committee, Environmental Trade Working Group, July 1995.

Technology for a Sustainable Future, Office of Science and Technology Policy, Old Executive Office Building, Washington, DC 20500.

Tirone Corporation, 44 Main Street, Suite 510, Champaign, IL 61820. (217) 359-5433, mail tirocorp@cu-online.com. Data in Russia/New Independent States section are based on an unpublished study by Tirone Corporation. Data came from an independent national survey of over 500 Russian businesses in 22 cities conducted by Tirone Corporation in 1997.

US-Asia Environmental Partnership (US-AEP), "Country Assessments," 1996.

Waste Age, July 1999, "Consolidation, Rearranging the Pieces," Crain Communications, Detroit, MI.

Waste Age 100, Bethany Barber and John Aquino, September 1997.

Waste News, July 12, 1999, "Hauling and Disposal, Top 100," Intertec Publishing Corp., Atlanta, GA.

Waste News, July 19, 1999, "Republic Acquisitions Top Target," Intertec Publishing Corp., Atlanta, GA.

The Water Business: Understanding the Water Supply and Wastewater Industry, Leonard S. Hyman, Vienna, VA, 1998.

Water & Environment International, International Trade Publications Ltd., Redhill, Surrey, RH1 1QS, United Kingdom. (44) (0)173-776-8611.

Water & Wastewater International, MacDonald Communications, Inc., 3300 South Gessner, Suite 119, Houston, TX 77063. (713) 266-0610.

Water Conditioning & Purification Magazine, Water Quality Association, 4151 Naperville Road, Lisle, IL 60532. (708) 505-0160.

Water Environment & Technology, Water Environment Federation, 601 Wythe Street, Alexandria, VA 22314-1994. (703) 684-2400.

Water Treatment and Supply Concession Projects in China, U.S. and Foreign Commercial Service and U.S. Department of State, July 1999.

WaterWorld, P.O. Box 2847, Tulsa, OK 74101. (918) 835-3161.

World Bank Annual Report 1997, 1818 H Street, NW, Washington, DC 20433. (202) 477-1234.

WorldWater and Environmental Engineering, Faversham House Group Ltd., South Croydon, CR2 8LE Surrey, United Kingdom. (44) (0) 181-651-7100.

■ RELATED CHAPTERS

1: Metals and Industrial Minerals Mining
2: Coal Mining
3: Crude Petroleum and Natural Gas
4: Petroleum Refining
5: Electricity Production and Sales
10: Paper and Allied Products
11: Chemicals and Allied Products
12: Synthetic Rubber
13: Steel Mill Products
14: Nonferrous Metals
23: Industrial and Analytical Instuments

AEROSPACE
Economic and Trade Trends

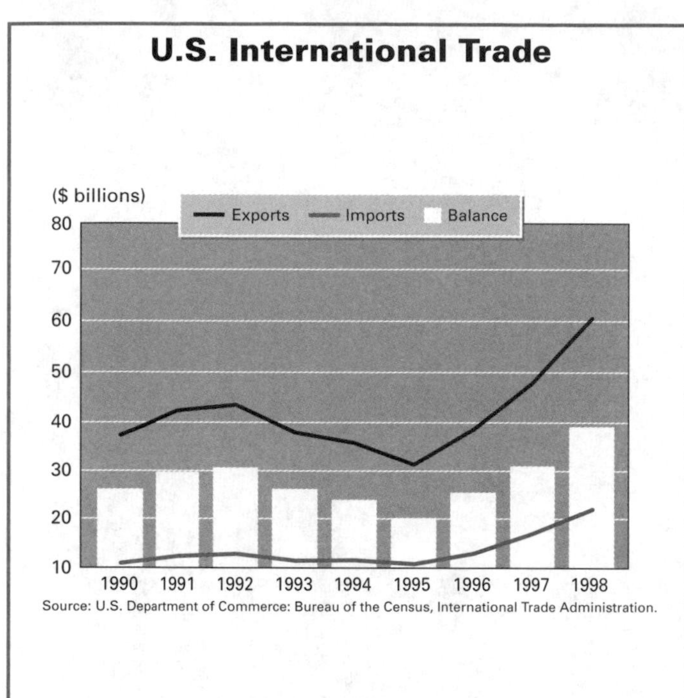

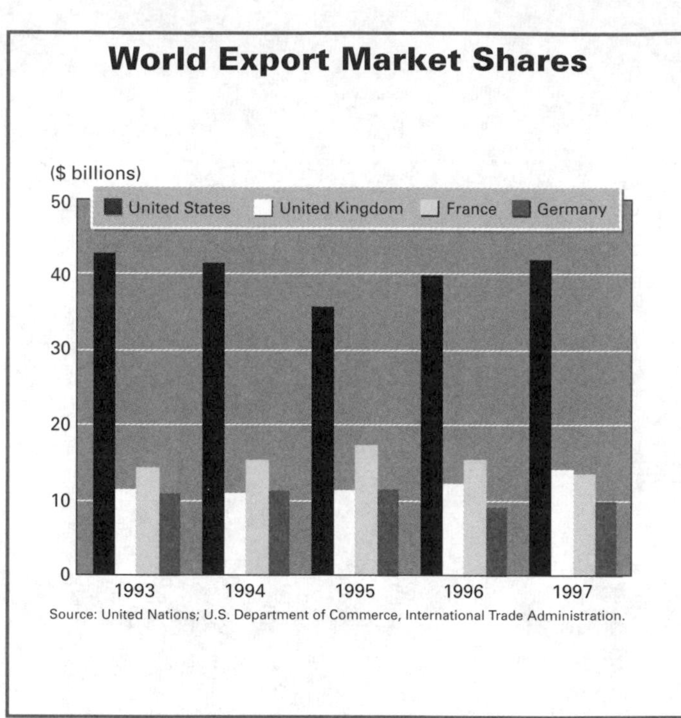

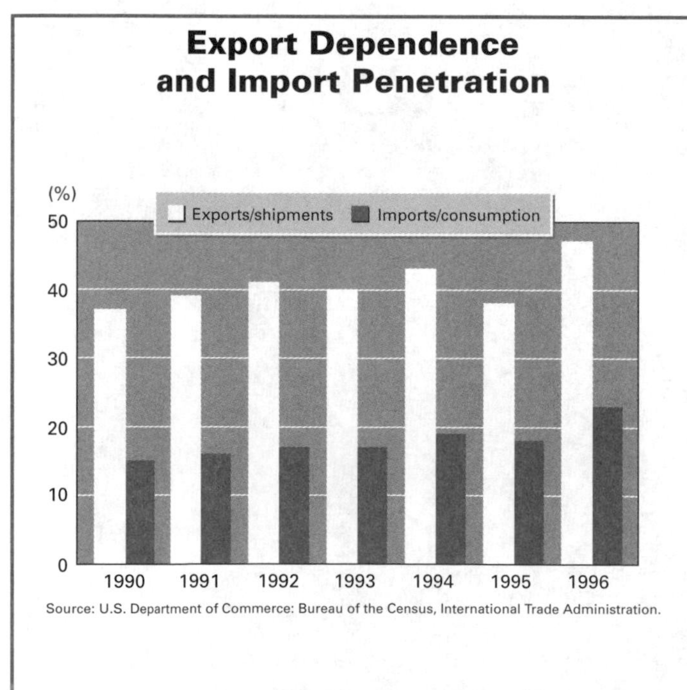

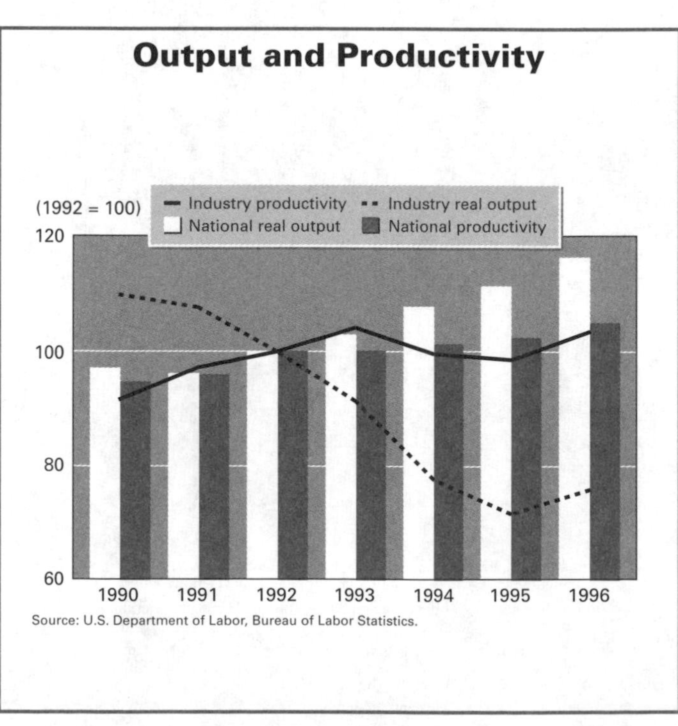

See "Getting the Most Out of *Outlook 2000*" for definitions of terms.

21

Aerospace

INDUSTRY DEFINITION The aerospace industry includes aircraft, aircraft engines and their parts, and aircraft equipment and other parts (SIC 372) and guided missiles and space vehicles, propulsion units and parts, and other parts and auxiliary equipment (SIC 376).

GLOBAL INDUSTRY TRENDS

Global Economy

In October 1999, the International Monetary Fund (IMF) predicted that the world economy would grow about 3 percent in 1999, reflecting a more positive outlook for South Korea, Thailand, and Malaysia than was the case for 1998. This improvement offset the more negative picture for Latin America compared with 1998. The IMF predicts that global gross domestic product (GDP) growth will reach 3.5 percent in the year 2000. Japan was expected to show an economic decline of about 1 percent in 1999 and a 1.5 percent gain in 2000. The IMF report predicted that South Korea's economy would expand 6.5 percent in 1999 and a further 5.5 percent in 2000. As a group, the economies of Indonesia, the Philippines, Malaysia, and Thailand were expected to expand 1.4 percent in 1999 and 3.6 percent in 2000. The IMF believed that the United States and the European Union would continue to experience solid but moderate growth in 1999 and 2000.

Industry experts anticipate that the number of aerospace manufacturers will decline over the next few years through continued consolidation of companies. Key factors that will influence future global growth are rates of productivity, technological innovation, international competition, investment in research and development, improvements in aviation infrastructure, levels of defense spending, and support by governments for their aerospace industries. The high level of world sales and deliveries of aircraft and aerospace products in 1998 and 1999 is expected to decrease to a more normal level in 2000 and remain stable over the period 2001–2004.

Fluctuations in the global economy affect the U.S. aerospace industry because of the importance of the large civil aircraft sector to that industry. (Large civil aircraft account for about a quarter of the total aerospace industry's output.) Changes in passenger travel historically have been proportional to changes in GDP, and demand for large civil aircraft is directly proportional to demand for passenger travel (often with a lag of 3 to 4 years).

The currency crisis in Asia brought about a significant retrenchment by Asian airlines, causing the elimination of many international flights and decisions to delay delivery or cancel high-value orders for large commercial aircraft. Another consequence of the economic crisis and currency devaluation in eastern Asia for the aerospace industry has been the reduced availability of funding for these markets from any source. Japanese banks in part also have less capacity to lend then they did previously. At the end of 1995, Japan had 25 of the largest 100 banks in the world. In the period 1988–1997, Japanese banks provided some 25 percent of the new equipment financing raised by the world's airlines. As of early 1998, however, almost no new funding commitments were made by Japanese banks. Other banks, especially German ones, have become more active in aircraft financing, but they have not filled the gap left by the Japanese, especially in Asia. The potential for bad debt that may materialize in Asia will affect all banks active in that region. In response to the declining availability of financing in traditional capital markets, the Export-Import Bank of the United States (Ex-Im Bank) has dramatically increased its financial support of U.S. aircraft exports worldwide. In 1998, Ex-Im Bank supported $2.6 billion in U.S. aircraft exports, and it expanded those commitments to over $6.6 billion in the first 8 months of 1999.

Industry Consolidation

Consolidation among major aerospace and defense companies has proceeded more rapidly in the United States than it has in other regions of the world, such as Europe. After numerous mergers and acquisitions, three very large companies—The Boeing Company, Lockheed Martin Corporation, and the Raytheon Company—have come to dominate the U.S. aerospace sector. This consolidation has placed enormous pressure on aerospace component suppliers. As those suppliers reposition themselves, they are being forced to improve economies of scale and reduce costs. Recent mergers among major suppliers include Honeywell–AlliedSignal and Hamilton–Sundstrand. Consolidation has been a two-edged sword. On the one hand, it has boosted the U.S. aerospace industry's international competitiveness, better enabling U.S. companies to win contracts overseas. On the other hand, it has increased pressure to eliminate duplicative jobs. Several merged companies have announced layoffs.

Consolidation of the European aerospace industry is accelerating as national governments and aerospace manufacturers acknowledge the need to integrate their defense and commercial aerospace sectors to reduce operating costs and become more competitive with their U.S. counterparts. European aerospace companies are adopting strategies to streamline processes and increase their flexibility in outsourcing aircraft components.

In 1997, the governments of France, Germany, and the United Kingdom agreed that there was an urgent need to restructure Europe's aerospace and defense industries. In 1998, a plan was signed to transform the then four Airbus partners—British Aerospace PLC (BAe), Aerospatiale SA of France, DaimlerChrysler Aerospace AG of Germany (DASA), and Construcciones Aeronauticas SA (CASA) of Spain—into a single corporate entity (SCE) by 1999. This SCE is intended to enhance cycle times, productivity, profitability, and customer support by consolidating authority and responsibility for Airbus under a single corporate management. This transformation, which was set to take place on January 1, 1999, was postponed indefinitely because of the persistent challenges of accommodating the partners' divergent cultural and political concerns, especially the French government's resistance to privatizing Aerospatiale. Transport ministers from the United Kingdom, Germany, Spain, and France have called repeatedly for the four partners in Airbus to accelerate the transformation of the consortium into an SCE, noting that it would be easier for their governments to provide financial support for the development of the "super-jumbo" A3XX aircraft when the consortium is transformed into a single enterprise.

In response, a series of merger announcements were made in 1999. In October 1999, DASA and Aerospatiale-Matra agreed to merge to form European Aeronautic, Defense and Space (EADS). This followed earlier announcements of mergers between BAe and Marconi Electronic Systems from Britain's General Electric Company, Aerospatiale and Matra Hautes Technologies, and DASA and CASA.

These mergers may help facilitate Airbus's transformation into an SCE. With the new makeup of Airbus as a German and French–controlled company as a result of the DASA–Aerospatiale-Matra merger, it is possible that BAe may seek to sever its partnership status in Airbus. Other European companies interested in joining Airbus are Alenia of Italy, Thomson-CSF and Dassault of France, and Saab of Sweden. The precise role of these possible new partners is unclear.

DOMESTIC TRENDS

The industry was expected to have a moderate to strong increase in the value of shipments made in 1999 compared with 1998. The total value of shipments by the U.S. aerospace industry in 1998 was $145 billion, a 2.2 percent increase over 1997. In the first half of 1999, compared with the same period in 1998, shipments increased 1.8 percent and new orders grew 0.8 percent. Deliveries of complete civil aircraft and engines reached $48 billion in 1998, an increase of 34 percent over the 1997 level. U.S. aerospace exports increased 27 percent in 1998 compared with 1997 (see Table 21-1). The top five destinations of U.S. exports in 1998 are shown in Table 21-2. U.S. defense procurement in fiscal year (FY) 1998 (including new buys, modifications, and parts) totaled $14 billion for aircraft and $3.8 billion for missiles and space equipment.

Defense Industry

Reversing 15 years of decline, total procurement from all industry sectors by the U.S. Department of Defense (DOD) in FY 1998 rose slightly to $128.8 billion, in comparison to $128.4 billion in 1997. The total outlay was significantly lower than the peak of $163.7 billion reached in 1985.

The largest prime contractors in the U.S. defense industry—Lockheed Martin and Boeing—were each awarded over $10 billion in prime contracts in FY 1998. The third largest, Raytheon, received $5.7 billion in prime contract awards. Rounding out the list of the top 10 prime contractors in 1998 were General Dynamics, Northrop Grumman, United Technologies, Textron, Litton Industries, Newport News Shipbuilding, and TRW (with $1.3 billion).

The largest military aviation development program is the multirole Joint Strike Fighter (JSF), which will be produced for the U.S. Air Force and Marines and the U.S. and British navies. Three thousand JSFs are planned for manufacture over several years to replace aging F-16s and other aircraft. Competition for the role of primary contractor for the JSF has been narrowed to Boeing and Lockheed Martin as the program enters the prototype and testing stages.

With the United States accounting for 46 percent of the world's inventory of tactical combat aircraft, the export potential of the JSF is envisioned to be high, although it may not be available for exportation before the year 2010. Foreign competition would come largely from the newly developed Eurofighter Typhoon, Dassault's Rafale or Mirage, and Russia's MiG and Sukhoi combat aircraft.

Other aircraft in various stages of development include Lockheed Martin's multi-billion-dollar F-22 Raptor program to replace F-15s, large transports to replace the C-130s, and new bombers, helicopters, and refuelers.

Fearing that a single supplier could emerge in Europe and resisting further domestic consolidation, DOD is encouraging

TABLE 21-1: Aerospace (SIC 372, 376) Trends and Forecasts
(millions of dollars except as noted)

	1992	1993	1994	1995	1996	1997	1998[1]	1999[2]	2000[3]	Percent Change 97–98	98–99	99–00	96–00[4]
Industry data													
Value of shipments[5]	131,367	116,346	103,316	100,062	101,322	118,505	144,833	155,049	136,195	22.2	7.1	−12.2	7.7
Value of shipments (1992$)	131,367	113,815	98,831	94,046	93,799	107,322	131,093	139,355	122,702	22.1	6.3	−12.0	6.9
Total employment (thousands)	694	612	525	471	458	492							
Production workers (thousands)	331	279	241	221	219	252							
Average hourly earnings ($)	18.74	19.05	20.00	20.37	21.33	20.54							
Capital expenditures	3,837	2,725	2,363	2,114	2,513	3,120							
Product data													
Value of shipments[5]	122,800	110,312	97,156	95,311	96,222	112,102	135,010	143,103	126,437	20.0	6.0	−11.6	7.1
Value of shipments (1992$)	122,800	107,905	92,937	89,576	88,974	101,692	121,980	128,232	113,599	19.5	5.1	−11.4	6.3
Trade data													
Value of imports	12,914	11,527	11,642	10,869	13,060	17,205	22,186	22,564	20,835	29.0	1.7	−7.7	12.4
Value of exports	43,562	37,901	35,761	31,304	38,563	48,175	61,375	64,102	62,367	27.4	4.4	−2.7	12.8

[1] Estimate except imports and exports.
[2] Estimate.
[3] Forecast.
[4] Compound annual rate.
[5] For a definition of industry versus product values, see "Getting the Most Out of *Outlook 2000*."
Source: U.S. Department of Commerce: Bureau of the Census; International Trade Administration.

transatlantic partnerships. The Balkan war accelerated the impetus for U.S. partnerships with European industry stemming from concerns about the existing technology gaps and lack of interoperability that hindered NATO's effectiveness.

In 1998, deliveries of new military aircraft to foreign customers rose to $3.6 billion, an increase of 57 percent compared with 1997. U.S. arms exports as measured by agreements signed (actual deliveries can lag several years) totaled $7.1 billion in 1998. While the United States continued to dominate global export markets with almost a third of total military exports worldwide, the market is considerably smaller than the $37 billion in sales reached in 1993.

Developing countries, which can stage the fiercest competition among military suppliers, purchased some $4.6 billion of U.S. arms in 1998, compared with $2.4 billion from France and less than $2 billion each from Germany, the United Kingdom, and Russia. Middle Eastern countries such as Saudi Arabia, Kuwait, the United Arab Emirates, Egypt, and Israel continue to be some of the largest purchasers of arms. In Asia, Malaysia led with $2.1 billion in imports. The top recipients of arms deliver-

TABLE 21-2: U.S. Trade Patterns in Aerospace[1] in 1998
(millions of dollars; percent)

Exports			Imports		
Region[2]	Value[3]	Share, %	Region[2]	Value[3]	Share, %
NAFTA	3,490	6	NAFTA	4,531	20
Latin America	2,996	5	Latin America	892	4
Western Europe	23,176	38	Western Europe	13,589	61
Japan/Chinese Economic Area	12,891	21	Japan/Chinese Economic Area	1,952	9
Other Asia	7,277	12	Other Asia	520	2
Rest of world	11,545	19	Rest of world	701	3
World	61,375	100	World	22,186	100
Top Five Countries	Value	Share, %	Top Five Countries	Value	Share, %
United Kingdom	7,248	12	France	5,539	25
Japan	5,922	10	United Kingdom	4,635	21
Saudi Arabia	4,946	8	Canada	4,445	20
Germany	4,100	7	Germany	1,878	8
France	4,048	7	Japan	1,841	8

[1] SIC 372, 376.
[2] For definitions of regional groupings, see "Getting the Most Out of *Outlook 2000*."
[3] Values may not sum to total due to rounding.
Source: U.S. Department of Commerce, Bureau of the Census.

ies in 1998 were Saudi Arabia, Taiwan, Singapore, and South Korea.

U.S. INDUSTRY GROWTH PROJECTIONS FOR THE NEXT 1 AND 5 YEARS

Shipments of aerospace products were expected to increase in value about 7 percent in 1999 over the 1998 level and decrease about 12 percent in 2000 compared with 1999 (see Table 21-1). Aerospace shipments are estimated to increase about 3 percent per year from 2001 through 2004. U.S. defense procurement in FY 1999 was expected to increase 22 percent for aircraft and 11 percent for missiles and space vehicles from FY 1998 levels. An increase in military procurement in FY 2000 suggests that the decline in defense spending has stopped and that such spending will climb through FY 2004.

AIRCRAFT AND PARTS

The aircraft and parts industry (SIC 372) covers aircraft (SIC 3721), aircraft engines and engine parts (SIC 3724), and aircraft equipment and parts not elsewhere classified (SIC 3728).

DOMESTIC OUTLOOK BY SUBSECTOR

Aircraft

This sector (SIC 3721) consists of large transports, general aviation aircraft, rotorcraft, and unmanned aerial vehicles.

Large Transports. The large civil aircraft sector includes commercial passenger and cargo aircraft with an operating empty weight greater than 15,000 kilograms and two, three, or four engines. Passenger aircraft in this category can accommodate at least 70 passengers. The Boeing Company is the only manufacturer of such aircraft in the United States.

Economic growth is expected to continue to be the main stimulus for aircraft demand. A decline in economic growth that followed the 1997–1998 financial troubles in Asia resulted in a decrease in airline traffic in that region. That decline had a negative impact on the airlines' revenue and overall cash flow, resulting in a decreased demand for aircraft. However, nations such as India and China are expected to experience growth in air travel as they climb the economic development curve.

In mid-1999, there were signs of economic recovery in Asia, especially South Korea, Singapore, and Thailand, as those countries began to emerge from the Asian financial crisis. China, Australia, and New Zealand continued to maintain stable economies, and U.S. and European economies remained strong. Air travel remains brisk, aging domestic fleets are being phased out and replaced with new planes, and overseas travel continues to grow. These factors are expected to spur demand for new aircraft over the next 5 years.

Industry experts foresee an overall production downturn in the year 2000. On the basis of announced manufacturing rates, 1999 was expected to be the peak year in total aircraft production, with the global industry delivering about 920 jets. The outlook for 2000 is estimated to be below 1999 levels, with about 800 jets expected to be delivered. U.S. production of large civilian transports was expected to reach about 620 aircraft in 1999 and about 480 in 2000 (see Table 21-3).

In the early years of the twenty-first century, technology may take a back seat to efficiency. Rather than creating entirely new passenger aircraft that will fly faster, higher, and farther on less fuel, large aircraft manufacturers are more likely to modify existing designs; this will reduce production costs, pollutants, and noise and add more seats. Stiff price competition between Boeing and Airbus will continue.

U.S. government funding for aeronautical research and development decreased significantly with the cancellation in 1999 of the National Aeronautics and Space Administration's (NASA) funding for the High Speed Research and Aviation Subsonic Technology programs.

One of the most significant new influences on twenty-first-century aircraft will be the environment. Next-generation and future aircraft will be required to meet new and increasingly more stringent environmental protection requirements for engine emissions in keeping with the U.S. Clean Air Act and the Kyoto Protocol.

Fair trade principles should stimulate new services in the twenty-first-century air transport market. Improved market access would promote greater freedom for developing commerce, particularly among the three largest trading partners: North America, Europe, and Japan (see Tables 21-4 and 21-5). Air traffic is expected to grow at an average annual rate of 5 percent through 2005.

General Aviation Aircraft. Manufacturers in the general aviation sector produce fixed-wing aircraft for regional airline service, business transportation, recreation, and specialized uses such as ambulance service, agricultural spraying, and pilot training. About 12 companies in the United States manufacture general aviation aircraft. The largest manufacturers, measured by number of aircraft produced, are Cessna, Learjet, Mooney, Piper, and Raytheon.

The General Aviation Manufacturers Association (GAMA) reported that in 1998 its members had their highest billings ever at $5.9 billion, up 26 percent from the level in 1997. This was the third year in a row of record-setting sales and deliveries. Shipments of general aviation aircraft reached 2,213 units, up 42 percent from 1,569 units in 1997. Piston-powered aircraft shipments rose 56 percent, and those of turbine-engine aircraft, including seven Boeing Business Jets, increased 18 percent. Billings in the first half of 1999 reached $3.5 billion, an increase of 45 percent over the same period in 1998; unit shipments increased 13 percent in that period. Units exported in 1998 increased 19 percent compared with 1997 and remained steady in the first half of 1999 compared with the same period in 1998.

TABLE 21-3: Shipments of Complete U.S. Aircraft
(millions of current dollars)

	Aircraft Total		Civil								Military Total	
			Total		Large Transports[1]		General Aviation[2]		Rotorcraft			
Year	Units	Value	Units	Value	Units	Value	Units	Value	Units	Value	Units	Value
1976	17,812	9,299	16,494	4,628	222	3,078	15,451	1,226	821	324	1,318	4,671
1977	19,041	8,968	17,907	4,388	155	2,649	16,904	1,488	848	251	1,134	4,580
1978	19,952	10,136	18,956	6,417	241	4,308	17,811	1,781	904	328	996	3,719
1979	19,280	15,028	18,443	10,598	376	8,030	17,048	2,165	1,019	403	837	4,430
1980	14,677	18,929	13,630	13,037	387	9,895	11,877	2,486	1,366	656	1,047	5,892
1981	11,978	20,093	10,916	13,223	387	9,706	9,457	2,920	1,072	597	1,062	6,870
1982	6,244	18,446	5,085	8,611	232	6,246	4,266	2,000	587	365	1,159	9,835
1983	4,409	21,769	3,356	9,773	262	8,000	2,691	1,470	403	303	1,053	11,996
1984	3,928	21,787	2,992	7,700	185	5,689	2,431	1,681	376	330	936	14,087
1985	3,610	27,269	2,691	10,385	278	8,448	2,029	1,431	384	506	919	16,884
1986	3,262	29,587	2,155	11,859	330	10,309	1,495	1,262	330	288	1,107	17,728
1987	3,010	29,010	1,800	12,148	357	10,507	1,085[3]	1,364[3]	358	277	1,210	16,862
1988	3,323	30,904	2,018	15,860	423	13,603	1,212[3]	1,923[3]	383	334	1,305	15,044
1989	3,709	31,962	2,448	17,129	398	15,074	1,535	1,804	515	251	1,261	14,833
1990	3,321	38,585	2,268	24,476	521	22,215	1,144	2,007	603	254	1,053	14,109
1991	3,092	44,657	2,181	29,035	589	26,856	1,021	1,968	571	211	911	15,622
1992	2,585	47,397	1,832	30,732	567	28,750	941	1,840	324	142	753	16,665
1993	2,585	41,166	1,630	26,390	408	24,133	964	2,144	258	113	955	14,776
1994	2,309	36,568	1,545	20,666	309	18,124	928	2,357	308	185	764	15,902
1995	2,436	33,658	1,625	18,299	256	15,263	1,077	2,842	292	194	811	15,359
1996	2,235	36,247	1,677	20,884	269	17,564	1,130	3,127	278	193	558	15,363
1997	2,777	45,883	2,289	30,715	374	25,810	1,569	4,674	346	231	488	15,168
1998	3,554	55,398	3,112	41,776	559	35,890	2,213	5,646	363	252	419	13,610[4]
1999[4]	3,700	60,140	3,185	45,340	620	39,000	2,220	6,140	345	200	515	14,800
2000[5]	3,574	48,057	3,059	33,057	480	26,600	2,240	6,260	339	197	515	15,000

[1] Includes fixed-wing aircraft over 15,000 kilograms of empty weight, including all jet transports plus the turboprop-powered Lockheed L-100 and the Boeing Business Jet, which is based on the fuselage of the 737-700. To prevent duplication, the Boeing Business Jets are subtracted from the General Aviation Manufacturers Association's shipments.
[2] Excludes off-the-shelf military aircraft.
[3] Revised.
[4] Estimated.
[5] Forecast.
Source: U.S. Department of Commerce; International Trade Administration (ITA); Bureau of the Census; Department of Defense; General Aviation Manufacturers Association (GAMA); Aerospace Industries Association; and company reports. Estimates and forecasts by ITA.

There are several programs to revitalize the U.S. general aviation industry. One is the Advanced General Aviation Transport Experiments (AGATE) program initiated by NASA in 1994. The AGATE Consortium is a cost-sharing industry-university-government partnership—which includes the Federal Aviation Administration (FAA) as well as NASA's Langley Research Center—to develop affordable new technologies, industry standards, and certification methods for airframe, cockpit, flight training systems, and airspace infrastructure for next-generation single-pilot, four- to six-passenger, near-all-weather light airplanes. The latest initiative is called the "highway in the sky," a cockpit display system that includes a computer-drawn highway that the pilot follows to a preprogrammed destination. The displays and other equipment will provide intuitive situational awareness and enough information for a pilot to perform safely, with a reduced workload, in nearly all weather conditions.

Business aviation, one of the most important segments of general aviation, consists of companies and individuals that use aircraft as tools to conduct their business. Business aircraft are used by all types of people and companies, from individuals who fly rented, single-engine, piston-powered airplanes to sales or management teams from the largest multinational corporations, many of which own fleets of multiengine, turbine-powered aircraft and employ their own flight crews, maintenance technicians, and other aviation support personnel. The number of flight departments in U.S. businesses grew nearly 25 percent from 6,747 in 1993 to 8,236 in 1998. Although the overwhelming majority of business aircraft missions are conducted on demand, some companies have scheduled operations, known as corporate shuttles, that essentially are in-house airlines. Most corporations that operate business aircraft use modern multiengine turbine-powered jets, turboprops, or turbine helicopters that are certified to the highest applicable transport-category standards.

Aircraft built specifically for business use vary from four-seat, short-range, piston-powered airplanes to two- and three-engine corporate jets that can carry up to 19 passengers nearly 7,000 miles nonstop. Some companies even use airline-type jets, including the Boeing Business Jet, which uses the fuselage of the 737-700 airliner and the wings and landing gear of the

TABLE 21-4: U.S. Exports of Aerospace Vehicles and Equipment
(millions of current dollars; number of units; metric tons)

	1993		1994		1995		1996		1997[1]		1998	
	Units	Value	Units	Value	Units	Value	Units	Value	Units	Value	Units	Value
Aerospace vehicles and equipment, total		39,334		37,357		33,275		40,272		50,575		63,994
Total Aircraft		21,279		18,810		13,852		18,984		25,560		35,248
Civilian aircraft		19,821		17,718		12,251		15,160		23,164		31,427
Under 4,536 kg unladen weight, new	486	227	436	270	504	296	507	343	492	475	528	345
4,536–15,000 kg unladen weight, new	58	324	66	331	56	306	52	257	83	486	79	486
Over 15,000 kg unladen weight, new	278	18,146	222	15,931	137	10,606	172	13,624	252	21,028	375	29,168
Rotorcraft, new	171	119	159	83	208	170	214	212	259	208	238	148
Used or rebuilt	696	996	640	1,097	614	858	547	715	519	959	506	1,270
Nonpowered aircraft		9		7		15		8		8		10
Military aircraft	629	1,458	436	1,093	520	1,601	428	3,824	416	2,397	364	3,821
New	517	1,403	348	826	462	1,539	316	3,549	360	2,297	269	3,608
Used or rebuilt	112	55	88	266	58	62	112	275	56	99	95	213
Aircraft engines and parts		6,212		6,402		6,144		6,829		8,575		10,537
Piston engines and parts		283		317		360		336		427		409
Complete engines, new and used	7,582	114	6,679	143	7,885	147	7,528	144	17,749	229	10,923	198
Engine parts		169		174		213		192		198		212
Turbine engines and parts		5,929		6,086		5,784		6,493		8,149		10,128
Complete engines, new and used	17,028	2,406	4,950	2,484	7,025	1,802	8,638	2,136	11,028	2,275	12,198	3,365
Engine parts		3,523		3,601		3,982		4,357		5,874		6,763
Propellers, rotors, and parts		307		306	2,584	334	2,974	426	3,360	500	3,157	597
Landing gear and parts		336		313	3,138	386	4,321	527	4,997	559	7,325	970
Aircraft parts and accessories not elsewhere classified		8,316		8,717		9,238		10,374		11,793		13,028
Avionics		646		673		673		778		871		1,022
Flight simulators and parts		197		232	1,714	122	2,056	166	2,044	184	3,738	262
Guided missiles and parts		1,233		1,096		1,467		1,187		1,144		922
Space vehicles and parts		277		240		220		976		1,083		1,126
Missile and space vehicle propulsion units and parts		6		18		42		24		9		10

[1] Revised from previously published data. Revisions to trade data based on U.S. Bureau of the Census, Historical Summary 1989–1993 and 1992–1998.
NOTE: Totals do not correspond to SIC-based trade statistics because of slightly broader coverage. Details may not add to totals due to rounding.
Source: U.S. Department of Commerce: Bureau of the Census; International Trade Administration.

737-800. A rapidly growing alternative to full ownership is fractional ownership, by which companies or individuals own a fraction of an aircraft and receive management and pilot services associated with the aircraft's operation. Growth in this area has been phenomenal. In 1986, there were four owners of fractionally held aircraft; by 1993, there were 89. From 1997 to 1998, the number of companies using fractional ownership grew over 50 percent from 743 to 1,125.

World deliveries of turbine-powered business airplanes were expected to reach about 760 units in 1999 and increase slightly to about 770 units in the year 2000. Deliveries are expected to decrease each year through 2004 until they reach about 680 aircraft a year.

Regional Jets. A number of definitions for regional aircraft exist, from that of the FAA, which defines regional aircraft as aircraft with fewer than 60 seats, to the definition used by U.S. Regional Airline Association (RAA), which defines them as the aircraft used by "the 97 regional airlines in the United States provid[ing] short-haul scheduled passenger and freight service using turboprop and small turbofan powered airplanes connecting small- and medium-sized communities with larger cities and hub airports." The RAA definition is more expansive than that of the FAA because it includes aircraft with up to 100 seats.

Fairchild Aerospace (which acquired Dornier of Germany) and Raytheon Aircraft are the only U.S. manufacturers of regional aircraft. Raytheon's 1900 turboprop aircraft covers the market for regional aircraft with 19 seats. Fairchild Aerospace, based in San Antonio, TX, manufactures a range of aircraft produced both in the United States and in Germany, including the Metro 23 and Dornier 228, turboprops that seat 19 passengers; the Dornier 328, a turboprop that seats 32 passengers; and Fairchild jets seating 32, 44, 55 to 63, 70 to 85, and 85 to 105 passengers, depending on the model and configuration.

Competing against the two U.S. manufacturers are Bombardier of Canada (Regional Jet and the Dash 8-100/200), Embraer of Brazil (EMB-120 and the ERJ145), Aerospatiale of France and Alenia of Italy (ATR72 and ATR42), and BAe of the United Kingdom (BAe146/RJ85, the J31/32, and the J41).

The U.S. market for regional aircraft has changed markedly in the last decade, especially after the introduction of Bombardier's Regional Jet (RJ), which provided regional airlines with an aircraft that offered the opportunity to service longer routes at greater speeds. Pairing turboprops with regional jets has sparked the expansion of regional airlines, as has the strength of the U.S. economy and the reliance of many U.S. airlines on a hub-and-spoke network. The overall outlook for regional aircraft is optimistic, although demand for smaller aircraft in the 15- to 39-seat range is expected to decline over the

TABLE 21-5: U.S. Imports of Aerospace Vehicles and Equipment
(millions of current dollars; number of units; metric tons)

	1993		1994		1995		1996		1997[1]		1998	
	Units	Value	Units	Value	Units	Value	Units	Value	Units	Value	Units	Value
Aerospace vehicles and equipment, total		12,495		12,648		12,050		14,163		18,773		24,172
Total aircraft		3,809		3,722		3,655		3,947		4,562		7,058
Civilian Aircraft		3,798		3,698		3,589		3,920		4,545		7,047
Under 4,536 kg unladen weight, new	143	39	163	25	213	28	278	30	252	22	257	29
4,536–15,000 kg unladen weight, new	130	1,210	152	1,673	157	1,506	209	2,144	206	2,531	271	3,638
Over 15,000 kg unladen weight, new	55	2,078	35	1,137	23	1,050	19	823	23	919	67	2,405
Rotorcraft, new	156	225	215	317	206	300	183	361	241	461	274	536
Powered, used or rebuilt	246	245	313	545	258	703	275	560	298	609	309	436
Nonpowered aircraft		1		1		3		3		2		3
Military aircraft		11		24		66		26		18		11
Powered, new	36	7	54	16	122	64	47	20	58	3	143	3
Powered, used or rebuilt	33	2	42	6	41	1	9	5	22	11	20	5
Nonpowered aircraft		2		2		2		2		3		3
Aircraft engines and parts		5,235		5,254		4,711		5,656		7,714		9,637
Piston engines and parts		76		146		127		168		174		190
Complete engines, new and used	2,511	28	4,480	84	4,781	54	5,735	70	3,458	47	3,359	43
Engine parts		47		62		72		98		127		147
Reaction engines, turbines and parts		5,159		5,108		4,584		5,488		7,540		9,447
Complete engines, new and used	2,423	2,568	2,298	2,672	2,752	1,774	5,964	1,937	4,247	2,949	3,641	4,019
Engine parts		2,590		2,436		2,810		3,551		4,590		5,428
Propellers, rotors, and parts		22		26	162	33	195	51	258	46	435	49
Landing gear and parts		57		64	609	70	923	129	1,226	173	1,608	224
Aircraft parts and accessories not elsewhere classified		2,639		2,661		2,782		3,553		4,979		6,007
Avionics		458		472		567		599		699		646
Flight simulators and parts		75		144	323	56	391	64	550	99	1,123	269
Guided missiles and parts		108		88		96		113		110		97
Space vehicles and parts[2]		138		263		111		81		345		185
Missile and space vehicle propulsion units and parts		1		1		2		17		46		10

[1] Revised from previously published data. Revisions to trade data based on U.S. Bureau of the Census, Historical Summary 1989–1993 and 1991–1997.
[2] Category does not include materials imported by NASA for launching into space.
NOTE: Totals do not correspond to SIC-based trade statistics because of slightly broader coverage. Details may not add to totals due to rounding.
Source: U.S. Department of Commerce: Bureau of the Census; International Trade Administration.

next 20 years. Steady growth is anticipated for turboprop aircraft in the 60- to 99-seat category. Demand for jets in the 40- to 59-seat category is expected to continue the current strong growth. The strongest growth is predicted in the 70-seat jet class as larger regional aircraft capture the medium- and long-haul route segment of the U.S. market.

Rotorcraft. Rotorcraft include helicopters—vertical takeoff and landing aircraft (VTOL)—and tiltrotor or other aircraft that can take off vertically as a helicopter and fly horizontally as an airplane. Some of the special uses of VTOL aircraft are oil rig and pipeline construction, power line construction, logging, transporting crews to offshore oil rigs, law enforcement, fire fighting, search and rescue, emergency medical service (EMS), and electronic news gathering (ENG).

In 1998, U.S. manufacturers shipped 363 civil helicopters—294 piston and 69 turbine—valued at $252 million, up from 346 units worth $231 million in 1997, an increase of 9 percent. The helicopter industry faces a number of problems, including access to heliports, high operating costs, an increasing shortage of realistic access to airspace, the release of surplus military helicopters in the civil marketplace, and the use of helicopters owned by public operators, which compete for services provided by private operators. Despite these handicaps, the helicopter industry is likely to grow because of its outstanding safety record, the variety of missions unique to helicopters, newly improved models, corporate mergers and acquisitions, strong sales of new and used helicopters, and a new focus on controlling maintenance and operation costs.

In February 1999, The Boeing Company sold its light helicopter product lines to MD Helicopters Holding, a subsidiary of RDM Holding of the Netherlands. The Federal Trade Commission had objected to Boeing's previous attempt to sell those programs to Bell Helicopter Textron.

Bell Boeing delivered the first production V-22 Osprey tiltrotor aircraft to the U.S. Marine Corps in May 1999. It was the first of 11 V-22s to be assigned for pilot training; the balance of the 360 Ospreys will be delivered later. After the second aircraft is delivered, production will shift from the facility near Fort Worth, TX, to a new factory near Amarillo, TX. The U.S. Air Force's Special Operations Command has ordered 50 V22s, and the U.S. Navy plans to buy 48. The U.S. Army may be reconsidering its 1987 decision to drop out of the V-22 program. The Osprey is more survivable than, carries twice as many troops as, and is twice as fast as the UH-60 helicopter.

Unlike the V-22, the nine-passenger Bell Agusta BA609 (a U.S.–Italian joint venture) civil tiltrotor is pressurized to travel above the weather. The first delivery is expected in the

2004–2005 time frame. After the first four prototypes are completed, production will shift to the new plant near Amarillo.

Unmanned Aerial Vehicles. A number of unmanned aerial vehicles (UAVs) exist, both domestically and internationally. Their payload capability, accommodations (volume and environment-temperature maintenance, electrical support, and sensors provided), mission profile (altitude, range, and duration), and command, control (how much control is required by operator and how much of its operations can be preprogrammed), and data acquisition capabilities vary significantly. DOD promoted research on UAVs in the late 1980s and well into the 1990s as reconnaissance platforms to prevent the risk of death or capture of a flight crew. Routine civil access to these various UAV assets is at an early stage.

NASA, through its Dryden Flight Research Center, is involved in the Environmental Research Aircraft and Sensor Technology (ERAST) program, which has been developing high-altitude and long-endurance UAVs that will go slower, higher, and longer. The goal of ERAST is to develop aeronautical technologies that will lead to a new family of UAVs that will fly at subsonic speeds—as slow as 24 kilometers per hour—at altitudes as high as 30 kilometers for continuous missions as long as 96 hours. A recent product of this program is a solar-powered UAV with a 75-meter wingspan that is designed to remain in the stratosphere for months at a time.

Growth and Trade Projections for Aircraft

While 10- and 20-year forecasts look good for the world aircraft market, the next 5 years do not hold similar promise. The value of U.S. aircraft shipments was expected to increase 8.8 percent in 1999 over 1998 and then decrease 20 percent in 2000 (see Table 21-6). Shipments are expected to decline about 2 percent a year from 2000 through 2004. In part, this is due to a lack of growth in economies in northeastern Asia, which is a major market for twin-aisle (wide-body) commercial aircraft. Regional jets (those with fewer than 100 seats) are in strong demand for new routes and are replacing single-aisle commercial and turboprop aircraft on current routes. Since U.S. manufacturers represent only a small share of the regional jet market and capacity, they could be affected adversely by Asian airlines' decisions to reduce aircraft size as they purchase new aircraft. U.S. helicopter and general aviation production also seemed to be peaking in 1999.

Aircraft Engines and Engine Parts

Prospects for future sales of U.S.-manufactured aircraft engine "hushkits" and replacement engines suffered a setback with the adoption by the European Union (EU) in April 1999 of legislation aimed at restricting the operation of aircraft modified with that equipment. The regulation is scheduled to take effect in May 2000. It freezes at current levels the number of hushkitted and certain reengined aircraft that may be registered and operated in the EU even though those aircraft are compliant with the most recent and stringent aircraft noise standards established by the International Civil Aviation Organization (ICAO).

No aircraft manufactured in Europe are affected by the regulation. The restrictions fall on U.S. manufacturers and other U.S. companies that produce and install hushkits and replacement engines. The EU legislation also affects U.S. air carriers, whose fleets contain many more hushkitted and reengined aircraft than do European carriers. The restrictions imposed by the regulation reduce the market for noise-modified aircraft and thus the resale value of such aircraft. As of November 1999, the

TABLE 21-6: Aircraft (SIC 3721) Trends and Forecasts
(millions of dollars except as noted)

	1992	1993	1994	1995	1996	1997	1998[1]	1999[2]	2000[3]	Percent Change 97–98	98–99	99–00	96–00[4]
Industry data													
Value of shipments[5]	62,940	55,120	50,970	47,028	47,313	56,843	67,140	73,030	58,250	18.1	8.8	–20.2	5.3
Value of shipments (1992$)	62,940	53,775	48,131	42,909	41,870	49,688	58,638	63,339	50,433	18.0	8.0	–20.4	4.8
Total employment (thousands)	265	241	218	189	188	204							
Production workers (thousands)	122	104	92.9	84.0	84.5	98.6							
Average hourly earnings ($)	20.00	19.90	20.75	22.15	23.12	21.32							
Capital expenditures	1,660	1,154	877	586	622	785							
Product data													
Value of shipments[5]	56,569	51,006	46,814	44,457	44,584	51,026	61,595	67,000	53,440	20.7	8.8	–20.2	4.6
Value of shipments (1992$)	56,569	49,762	44,206	40,563	39,455	44,603	53,795	58,109	46,268	20.6	8.0	–20.4	4.1
Trade data													
Value of imports	3,921	3,738	3,809	3,557	3,948	4,669	6,939	7,000	6,550	48.6	0.9	–6.4	13.5
Value of exports	26,419	21,306	18,831	13,614	18,970	25,509	35,248	36,000	35,000	38.2	2.1	–2.8	16.5

[1] Estimate except imports and exports.
[2] Estimate.
[3] Forecast.
[4] Compound annual rate.
[5] For a definition of industry versus product values, see "Getting the Most Out of *Outlook 2000*."
Source: U.S. Department of Commerce: Bureau of the Census; International Trade Administration.

United States was continuing to seek the EU's withdrawal of its regulation.

One program designed to revitalize the U.S. general aviation industry, the GAP Program, has implications for manufacturers of small aircraft engines. Managed out of NASA's Glenn Research Center, this program is coordinated by the FAA and performed jointly by NASA and Contractor-Led Project Teams formed by industry. The goal of GAP is to develop affordable propulsion systems for general aviation light aircraft and consists of two elements. The goal of the Intermittent Combustion (IC) Engine Element is to reduce engine prices in half while substantially improving reliability, maintainability, ease of use, and passenger comfort. The primary goal of the Turbine Engine Element is to reduce the price of small turbine engines by a factor of 10.

On the military side there is the Integrated High Performance Turbine Engine Technology (IHPTET) Initiative, a joint DOD–NASA–industry effort to provide significant performance and operational improvements for current and future military engines. IHPTET is considered a model program because the technology it is developing is dual-use technology.

Growth and Trade Projections for Aircraft Engines and Parts

The value of shipments in the aircraft engine and parts industry was expected to increase about 10 percent in 1999. Shipments are expected to remain level through 2004 as the market for regional jets replaces that for twin-aisle commercial aircraft. Exports increased about 23 percent in 1998 compared with 1997 and were expected to increase 0.7 percent in 1999 (see Table 21-7) as regional jets are being manufactured outside the United States. Foreign production of regional jets is expected to absorb some of the parts previously consumed by domestic producers.

Aircraft Parts and Equipment

The aircraft parts and equipment subsector (SIC 3728) covers parts and equipment other than engines and their parts. It excludes avionics—navigation and communications equipment for aircraft. Some of the products included are fuselage assemblies, wing assemblies and parts, rudders, landing gear, wheels, brakes, fuel tanks, propellers and rotors, and their parts. Other equipment covered includes dusting and spraying equipment, ejector seat devices, and aircraft arresting device systems. Small individual parts are included in SICs other than 372 and 376 but are not covered elsewhere in this publication.

Electronic commerce has come to U.S. aerospace industry manufacturers and distributors of aircraft parts, including some engine parts. Suppliers to major aerospace contractors increasingly may contact their customers and suppliers on the Internet. Aircraft owners and mechanics may order parts at an increasing number of Web sites.

A central concern of U.S. manufacturers of aircraft parts and equipment is the apparent trend among U.S. airframe producers, both civil and military, to source more components offshore. Parts suppliers and labor unions charge that the increased foreign content of "U.S." aircraft deprives them of contracts and jobs. Manufacturers of airframes and major components (such as engines) justify offshore sourcing as a necessary element in maintaining access to foreign markets for complete aircraft. U.S. airframe manufacturers also cite the substantial number of components U.S. parts producers provide to foreign airframe manufacturers.

TABLE 21-7: Aircraft Engines and Engine Parts (SIC 3724) Trends and Forecasts
(millions of dollars except as noted)

	1992	1993	1994	1995	1996	1997	1998[1]	1999[2]	2000[3]	Percent Change 97–98	98–99	99–00	96–00[4]
Industry data													
Value of shipments[5]	22,408	18,946	16,584	17,519	18,769	22,660	27,700	28,550	26,300	22.2	3.1	−7.9	8.8
Value of shipments (1992$)	22,408	18,538	15,855	16,450	17,315	20,525	24,977	25,582	23,524	21.7	2.4	−8.0	8.0
Total employment (thousands)	120	103	84.2	76.3	75.1	82.9							
Production workers (thousands)	66.5	53.6	45.5	41.9	41.4	48.1							
Average hourly earnings ($)	17.25	17.15	18.79	18.17	19.98	19.60							
Capital expenditures	598	440	435	475	485	669							
Product data													
Value of shipments[5]	20,933	17,995	15,218	15,811	17,017	20,096	25,320	26,080	24,000	26.0	3.0	−8.0	9.0
Value of shipments (1992$)	20,933	17,608	14,549	14,846	15,698	18,203	22,831	23,369	21,467	25.4	2.4	−8.1	8.1
Trade data													
Value of imports	5,745	5,244	5,269	4,699	5,644	7,693	9,605	9,590	8,800	24.9	−0.2	−8.2	11.7
Value of exports	6,639	6,205	6,422	6,101	6,780	8,532	10,476	10,550	10,300	22.8	0.7	−2.4	11.0

[1] Estimate except imports and exports.
[2] Estimate.
[3] Forecast.
[4] Compound annual rate.
[5] For a definition of industry versus product values, see "Getting the Most Out of *Outlook 2000*."
Source: U.S. Department of Commerce: Bureau of the Census; International Trade Administration.

Growth and Trade Projections for Aircraft Parts and Equipment

As with engine and parts manufacturers, U.S. deliveries of aircraft parts and equipment were expected to rise in 1999 compared with 1998 (see Table 21-8) but remain stable for the period 2000–2004. During the latter period, exports should rise about 2 percent per year as foreign regional jet aircraft manufacturers' requirements increase, partially offsetting decreased demand by U.S. aircraft manufacturers.

Air Traffic Control and Navigation

This section covers air traffic control equipment and services, radar, aeronautical instruments, equipment, and navigational services. The air traffic control (ATC) sector encompasses ATC equipment and service providers, airlines, telecommunications companies, satellite service providers and other data-link systems, and airports. The ICAO estimated that more than $10 billion would be spent on global ATC communications, navigation equipment, surveillance, and control center systems in 1999. This was a significant increase over 1998, when aviation telecommunications and satellite service providers and other data-link providers spent just over $5.5 billion on dedicated ATC systems and equipment.

The Air Traffic Control Association (ATCA) has projected that worldwide demand for ATC equipment and services in the period 2000–2010 will reach about $90 billion. This is due in part to efforts by the U.S. government and European governments to modernize their existing infrastructure, especially as they incorporate more satellite-based navigation technology into regional ATC systems.

Total scheduled passenger traffic of the world's airlines is expected to grow around 4 percent in 1999, 5 percent in 2000, and nearly 6 percent in 2001, according to forecasts prepared by ICAO. This increase in air traffic will further stress an already overburdened global ATC system.

ATC demand will vary by geographic region because of specific local or regional factors. The volume of air traffic in the Asia-Pacific region is expected to grow at the highest rate among all regions after a decline in 1998 resulting from unfavorable economic conditions, although at a significantly slower pace than that experienced over the past decade. ATC system operators in Europe and in Latin America and the Caribbean forecast slight operational increases in the year 2000, while ATC operations in the Middle East and Africa are expected to grow at a rate close to the world average. Moderate growth is expected in the mature North American ATC system.

The completion of most east Asian national ATC modernization and the downturn in economies in Latin America are predicted to have little impact on the ATC market. By 2006, U.S. manufacturers and suppliers are likely to have two-thirds of the global ATC equipment market. The best opportunities lie in North America and Europe, followed by the Caribbean.

Several ATC programs that are being implemented around the world are having a positive impact on ATC service and infrastructure. One is the Global Air Navigation Plans for Communications, Navigation, and Surveillance/Air Traffic Management (CNS/ATM) system for the Caribbean. With the help of the United States and ICAO, 23 Caribbean nations are in the process of planning, implementing, and operating a satellite-based ATC system for that region. The improvements in ATC technology being used in this effort are expected to improve the safety, efficiency, and economy of international flights in the Caribbean. Since most of the Caribbean nations' ATC systems are in poor condition, those governments view CNS/ATM as

TABLE 21-8: Aircraft Parts and Equipment Not Elsewhere Classified (SIC 3728) Trends and Forecasts
(millions of dollars except as noted)

	1992	1993	1994	1995	1996	1997[1]	1998[1]	1999[2]	2000[3]	Percent Change 97–98	98–99	99–00	96–00[4]
Industry data													
Value of shipments[5]	19,511	18,264	17,049	16,848	17,312	21,035	25,240	26,000	24,000	20.0	3.0	−7.7	8.5
Value of shipments (1992$)	19,511	17,750	16,206	15,939	16,029	19,210	22,780	23,123	21,314	18.6	1.5	−7.8	7.4
Total employment (thousands)	163	139	122	116	113								
Production workers (thousands)	92.0	78.4	66.1	64.0	64.5								
Average hourly earnings ($)	16.71	18.37	19.20	19.73	19.98								
Capital expenditures	1,112	713	656	673	916								
Product data													
Value of shipments[5]	21,940	18,684	17,710	17,701	18,832	22,882	27,460	28,280	26,300	20.0	3.0	−7.0	8.7
Value of shipments (1992$)	21,940	18,157	16,835	16,747	17,437	20,897	24,783	25,151	23,357	18.6	1.5	−7.1	7.6
Trade data													
Value of imports	3,068	2,390	2,429	2,483	3,288	4,631	5,405	5,670	5,200	16.7	4.9	−8.3	12.1
Value of exports	8,844	8,878	9,257	9,865	11,196	12,677	14,401	16,150	15,700	13.6	12.1	−2.8	8.8

[1] Estimate except imports and exports.
[2] Estimate.
[3] Forecast.
[4] Compound annual rate.
[5] For a definition of industry versus product values, see "Getting the Most Out of *Outlook 2000.*"
Source: U.S. Department of Commerce: Bureau of the Census; International Trade Administration.

the solution to inadequate facilities, at a much lower cost than alternative ground-based ATC equipment.

Europe is addressing its ATC requirements by updating its regional aerospace infrastructure. For example, Eurocontrol, the organization that manages the airspace for 14 European nations, is implementing its new Air Traffic Management (ATM) Strategy for 2000–2015. Despite efforts by many individual European nations to reduce the number of aircraft in flight, regional ATC systems are reaching their operational limits. The Eurocontrol ATM strategy identifies improvements in operational management and ATC infrastructure that are intended to have a unifying effect on the overall European ATC system. There are two key initiatives in the strategy. The first is to enhance the management and use of the airspace of the Eurocontrol states as a gate-to-gate continuum for ATM purposes that is not constrained by national boundaries. The second is to encourage contributions and commitments from member nations to install advanced ATC infrastructure.

Chapter 31, "Telecommunications and Navigation Equipment," contains additional information on air traffic control and navigation markets.

Global Market and Prospects for Aircraft and Parts

Asia. The economic crisis in Asia has caused the postponement or cancellation of commercial and military aircraft orders throughout that region. The crisis has adversely affected U.S. aerospace companies, mainly through canceled or delayed orders from Asian buyers. As a direct result of the economic situation, there have been significant and often drastic changes in the size and structural makeup of the region's aerospace industries and national airlines.

Before the onset of the economic crisis, many Asian airlines anticipated high rates of traffic growth. Responding to the crisis and the resulting depressed demand for air travel, airlines eliminated nearly 200 aircraft from their fleets through cancellations, deferrals, sales, leases, returns, and other methods. Regional air carriers in Indonesia, Malaysia, the Philippines, South Korea, and Thailand have been the most strongly affected.

The region's aerospace industries, which are in various stages of technological development and expertise, were hit especially hard by the Asian economic crisis. The stringent IMF programs for economic recovery in Asia, most notably in Indonesia and South Korea, resulted in a dramatic restructuring and overhaul of those countries' aerospace industries. Among the most important aspects of this overhaul was the implementation of more effective research and development (R&D) programs that required combining R&D centers to reduce costs and eliminate duplicate research. The South Korean government will grant Korea Aerospace Industries, Ltd., exclusive rights for all that government's military and satellite programs.

Possible economic recovery in the region in 2000 or 2001 could cause Asian aircraft orders to rebound in the long run, with orders for wide-body aircraft recovering last. However, the crisis will continue to mean further aircraft delivery delays and cancellations in the short run. The Asian airline industry is expected to recover in 2 or 3 years. By that time, traffic is anticipated to grow approximately 5 percent a year, down from precrisis estimates of 7 to 8 percent a year.

The demand for aerospace products in Asia will continue to be strong, but that demand will be tempered by the lingering economic crisis. Over the next two decades, Asia will continue to be one of the largest aerospace markets in the world. The top emerging aircraft markets for wide- and narrow-body aircraft in the coming decades will include China, India, Indonesia, Singapore, South Korea, and Taiwan.

China. After North America, China is one of the largest single markets for aircraft worldwide. The ongoing Asian financial crisis reduced Chinese airlines' profitability in 1998, with the majority of those airlines ending the year deeply in the red. The General Administration of Civil Aviation of China (CAAC) has led the effort to revitalize the airlines by imposing consolidation, fare restructuring, and other regulatory changes. Those adjustments, combined with an upturn in Asian economies, have allowed forecasts for the Chinese aviation market to remain guardedly optimistic.

Over the next 20 years, aviation experts forecast that demand in China for commercial aircraft will be for up to 1,600 aircraft worth $120 billion. Domestic air travel growth averaged 19 percent annually between 1985 and 1995 and 4 percent annually from 1995 to 1998. In 1998, 57 million passengers flew on China's airlines, and Chinese authorities estimate annual passenger growth rates of 8 percent over the next 10 years. Both The Boeing Company and Airbus Industrie, the European aircraft consortium, seek to fulfill this anticipated demand for transport aircraft.

China's expanding economy has strained its existing transportation infrastructure, limiting its growth. Both airports and ATC systems need modernization to accommodate increasing air travel and trade demand. To address the problems, China is investing significant resources in infrastructure, especially in the areas of passenger and cargo air transport, ATC systems, airports, and highways. More than 40 Chinese airports will be developed, modernized, and upgraded in the next 5 years.

Indonesia. Early in 1998, the government of Indonesia ended all financial support of Industri Pesawat Terbang Nurtanio (IPTN), that country's domestic civil aircraft manufacturer. Operating under these circumstances, the IPTN N250 airliner program (the first indigenously designed and manufactured plane) has not shifted out of the full developmental state. Garuda Indonesia Airlines announced a new business and debt restructuring plan, reducing its fleet of almost 60 large jets to its current fleet of 39 Boeing and Airbus aircraft. That airline has attempted to consolidate its domestic routes to give more service to its marketable routes. In addition, it is seeking more alliances with foreign air carriers as part of its consolidation and rehabilitation program.

Japan. Continuing economic weakness in Japan and the depreciation of the yen have been detrimental to the Asian aviation sector as a whole. Until 1998, Japan was regarded as the catalyst for growth in Asian aviation in terms of revenue and growth. The weak yen has been particularly problematic for Asian air carriers, many of which viewed the yen as the strongest regional currency. Falling passenger traffic and lower yields from a less stable yen have made payment of international debts (often U.S. dollar–denominated) even harder. ANA and Japan Airlines carry heavy debt loads and are prime candidates for restructuring.

South Korea. In the spring of 1999, the government of South Korea took major steps in the restructuring of its aerospace industry. The government's measures consolidated the country's competing aerospace industry manufacturers (Daewoo, Hyundai, and Samsung) into a single entity that will be known as the Korea Aerospace Industries, Ltd. The new company will execute all existing projects from the three companies. This consolidation supports the government's vision that by the year 2015, the South Korean aerospace industry should develop into one of the world's top-ranked aerospace producers. Korean Airlines is financially weak and is trying to sell or lease back aircraft to raise cash.

Thailand. The Thai government has chosen to partially privatize its national carrier, Thai International Airlines. Because the majority of that carrier's passenger traffic is international, the airline has benefited from the drastic decline in the national currency, the baht, enabling it to offer inexpensive seats to non-Thai travelers. The government reduced defense spending nearly 50 percent to about $2 billion in 1999. Purchases during the coming years will consist largely of replacement parts and aging aircraft upgrades.

Europe. Since 1995, global aircraft market growth has had a positive effect on deliveries and orders for Airbus Industrie. With a fivefold increase in the number of its aircraft orders since 1995, Airbus has increased its production dramatically. From 1988 to 1998, the number of Airbus orders increased 46 percent and deliveries of large civil aircraft grew 29 percent. In the past, the European aerospace industry was military-oriented. Today, it has evolved into an increasingly civil-oriented industry. By 1998, the civil share climbed to 63 percent, while the military share declined to 37 percent, according to European aerospace industry statistics. European aerospace companies continued to prosper as Airbus Industrie reported strong sales. DaimlerChrysler Aerospace, BAe, and Aerospatiale-Matra all reported profits rising dramatically and orders swelling to a record number in late 1999.

Despite product line expansion in the period 1992–1999, including the A318, A319, A321-100, A330-300, and A340, to compete with Boeing, Airbus still lacks an entry in the very large aircraft (more than 400 seats) market, which currently is dominated by the Boeing 747. In response, in 1997, the Airbus consortium launched a new family of A340 derivatives. The A340-500 is aimed at the very long range market segment, while the A340-600 is aimed at the large-capacity 747-200 replacement market. Airbus's development of those derivatives will help complete its aircraft product line and help it compete with Boeing 777 and 747 product lines.

The Airbus consortium may launch the "super-jumbo" A3XX to break into the crucial 400- to 600-seat segment, competing with the Boeing 747. Airbus Industrie forecast a demand of 1,300 planes in the A3XX size range over the next 20 years. Other industry analysts do not believe that there is sufficient demand to justify the cost of developing an all-new super-jumbo jet. The estimated development cost is $10 billion to $15 billion.

In the regional transport market, production has ceased for the British Aerospace ATP/J61, the Saab 2000, and the Fokker 50. Among the 50- to 65-seat props, only the ATR 42/72 family remains. Among smaller jets, the BAe Jetstream 41 and Saab 340 have been terminated. Industry experts question whether the market can support the development of all-new regional jets in light of stiff price competition and high production costs. In 1998, Aero International Regional, which was composed of Aerospatiale, Alenia, and British Aerospace, broke up as a result of heavy losses in previous years. Despite the breakup, there are strong indications that the 50- and 30-seat regional jet programs will recover in the years ahead. Industry experts expect that there will be modifications of existing products rather than all-new products.

Russia. Since the breakup of the Soviet Union, the Russian civil aircraft industry has declined dramatically as government subsidies have been cut and procurement of new aircraft has declined. Deliveries of new Russian-made large civil aircraft plummeted from 282 in 1992 to 6 in 1998. Survival of the Russian aircraft sector will depend on the industry and government's ability to adapt to a new market-oriented environment, attract needed capital, establish a new finance and lease system, and consolidate the industry by focusing on a few promising aircraft programs.

In the last 10 years, the Russian civil aircraft industry has been devoting its resources to developing a new generation of large civil aircraft capable of competing in the global market. Its inability to raise capital has been the single largest obstacle facing the Russian aircraft industry. Many U.S. and European parts suppliers saw an opportunity to provide components to "westernize" Russian airframes into internationally marketable aircraft, but progress has been slow in the development of these new hybrids. One new large aircraft model, the Ilyushin IL-96T, which incorporates U.S. engines and avionics, received FAA certification in June 1999. The first production IL-96T model is expected to go into service in early 2000.

The lack of domestic financing and leasing to support sales and leases of Russian aircraft has been a major impediment to the growth of the Russian aircraft industry. Some Russian airlines, mainly Aeroflot and Transaero, have turned to western aircraft to augment their fleets with fuel-efficient, cost-effective aircraft. These transactions have been supported by western leasing and financing institutions. The August 1998 financial crisis, which led to a severe downturn in the economy, stifled near-term aircraft acquisitions by Russian airlines suffering from a major decline in passenger and cargo traffic.

Concerned by the threat of aircraft imports, Russian aircraft manufacturers have sought import relief. In 1994, the Russian Federation imposed a 50 percent tariff on imports of aircraft to protect domestic manufacturers. Over the last few years, the Russian Federation lowered this tariff until it reached the 1999 level of 20 percent. Despite this barrier, U.S. exports of aircraft to Russia rose from $29 million in 1997 to $1.1 billion in 1998, making Russia the fourteenth largest market for U.S. aerospace products in that year. This large jump in exports reflected Aeroflot's purchase of 10 Boeing B737s. Ex-Im Bank provided the financing for this transaction, which marked the first purchase by a Russian airline of western aircraft. All previous transactions had been leases. The Russian Federation facilitated this purchase by providing tariff waivers as set forth in the 1996 Joint U.S.–Russia Memorandum of Understanding on Aircraft Market Access.

Despite its problems, Russia remains a country with a tremendous market demand for aviation services. Huge distances, unsatisfactory railroad services, and a poor highway infrastructure will ensure that the role of air transport will continue to grow. As hundreds of aging Soviet-built aircraft are retired over the next several years and as economic conditions improve, the need for both Russian-built and western-built aircraft will increase.

Latin American and the Caribbean. Latin America is undergoing its deepest economic slump since the debt crisis of the early 1980s. The region is burdened with low commodity prices, soaring public debt, high unemployment, currency destabilization, and a lack of foreign investment capital. The slowdown has raised doubts about whether those governments should continue free-market reforms. The recession is a disappointing cap on a decade in which Latin America and the Caribbean experienced solid economic growth rates fueled mostly by the widespread adoption of free market practices.

The aerospace sector, however, continues to grow despite economic recession. At the end of 1999, Latin American governments were making decisions to upgrade to new tactical fighter aircraft and parts, airlines were acquiring new commercial transport aircraft for their fleets, and governments were continuing to purchase navigational and ATC systems.

Brazil. Empresa Brasileira de Aeronutica S.A. (Embraer) is Brazil's largest aircraft manufacturer and second largest exporter. In June 1999, Embraer announced a record-breaking $4.9 billion purchase order agreement with the Swiss regional carrier Crossair. That contract confirmed the purchase of 40 ERJ-145 50-seat jetliners and 30 firm orders for both the 70-seat ERJ-170 and the 108-seat ERJ-190-200 regional jets. In addition, InterCanadian Airlines placed a firm order for six 50-seat ERJ-145s valued at approximately $230 million.

Embraer may be negatively affected by the 1999 World Trade Organization (WTO) ruling that declared Brazil's "ProEx Program" an illegal export subsidy. (Also cited as an illegal export subsidy by the WTO was Canada's "Technology Partnership Program," which benefits Bombardier.) The WTO ordered both nations to halt their practices.

In 1998, the government of Brazil began reducing its involvement in the airline sector, and that action affected Varig, VASP, TAM, and Transbrasil Airlines. The 1998 aircraft and parts markets were estimated to be $1 billion, with the United States supplying 78 percent of Brazil's import market, followed distantly by Canada (17 percent) and France (5 percent). The demand for aircraft and parts is expected to grow 35 percent in the period 2000–2003.

Middle East. As a result of the short-term reduction in demand for oil by Asian countries, the Middle East experienced a setback in GDP growth that forced those governments to cut spending. Financing difficulties also caused delays in deliveries of new aircraft to Middle Eastern countries such as Saudi Arabia. However, with U.S. banks' willingness to arrange billions of dollars in aircraft loans backed by Ex-Im Bank guarantees, deliveries may be back on track through the year of 2001. According to industry experts, there is a sign of recovery in oil prices that will allow some of the marginally profitable programs in the Middle East to be resuscitated. It is expected that Middle Eastern GDP growth will be approximately 2.2 percent a year for the next 5 years, down from 4.4 percent.

Africa. Africa accounts for 12 percent of the world's population yet accounts for only 2 percent of the world's scheduled airline traffic. In 1998, the United States exported $1.46 billion in aerospace products to African countries, a slight decrease from $1.56 billion in 1997. Ex-Im Bank initiated a recent surge in financing in support of U.S. aircraft to Africa. In the first 6 months of 1999, Ex-Im Bank supported $364 million for Africa and the Mideast, nearly four times the $93 million reported for all of 1998.

Ronald D. Green, U.S. Department of Commerce, Office of Aerospace, (202) 482-3068, ronald_green@ita.doc.gov, October 1999.

MISSILES AND SPACE LAUNCH VEHICLES

The guided missiles and space vehicles and parts industry (SIC 376) covers guided missiles and space vehicles (SIC 3761), guided missile and space vehicle propulsion units and parts (SIC 3764), and guided missile and space vehicle parts and auxiliary equipment not elsewhere classified (SIC 3769). Trends and forecasts in these three categories are shown in Tables 21-9, 21-10, and 21-11, but those definitions differ from the two subsectors that follow, missile systems and launch vehicles.

Missile Systems

Missile systems include guided missiles, guided missile propulsion units and parts, and guided missile parts and auxiliary equipment not elsewhere classified.

Global Industry Trends

The European missile market continued to consolidate in 1999 but experienced budget-related delays. In France, Matra's

TABLE 21-9: Guided Missiles and Space Vehicles (SIC 3761) Trends and Forecasts
(millions of dollars except as noted)

	1992	1993	1994	1995	1996	1997	1998[1]	1999[2]	2000[3]	Percent Change 97–98	98–99	99–00	96–00[4]
Industry data													
Value of shipments[5]	19,423	15,800	13,954	14,315	13,777	14,791	19,656	21,818	21,904	16.0	11.0	0.4	12.3
Value of shipments (1992$)	19,423	15,628	13,899	14,373	14,262	14,674	19,636	21,709	21,752	16.8	10.6	0.2	11.1
Total employment (thousands)	97.7	86.6	68.5	60.8	55.7	52.2							
Production workers (thousands)	30.1	27.6	23.8	20.0	18.6	18.7							
Average hourly earnings ($)	22.58	20.88	21.30	20.65	21.81	22.59							
Capital expenditures	313	308	297	294	367	6.38							
Product data													
Value of shipments[5]	13,972	13,452	10,983	11,756	10,536	12,671	14,406	15,072	16,003	13.0	4.6	6.2	11.0
Value of shipments (1992$)	13,972	13,306	10,939	11,804	10,907	12,571	14,392	14,997	15,892	13.8	4.2	6.0	9.9
Trade data													
Value of imports	4.1	5.2	1.6	2.7	1.1	0.2	2.3	3.4	3.1	1050.0	47.8	–8.8	29.6
Value of exports	599	507	364	718	608	462	537	720	680	16.2	34.1	–5.6	2.8

[1] Estimate except imports and exports.
[2] Estimate.
[3] Forecast.
[4] Compound annual rate.
[5] For a definition of industry versus product values, see "Getting the Most Out of *Outlook 2000.*"
Source: U.S. Department of Commerce: Bureau of the Census; International Trade Administration.

merger with Aerospatiale should increase competitiveness because of its ability to merge or eliminate competing programs. Matra's close relationship with BAe also should move the Europeans into a more competitive position internationally. Programs that overlap will probably be pulled together, such as antiship, air defense, and cruise missiles. As in other aerospace-related areas, Germany is reemerging as a producer of various kinds of missiles and may begin extensive involvement in this sector. Germany is developing the IRIS-T air-to-air infrared guided missile. It also is considering medium-range air-to-air missiles, air defense missiles, standoff missiles, antitank missiles, antiradiation missiles, and air-to-surface missiles. Europe maintains a strong market presence in the low-altitude air defense market, competing against U.S. Stinger missiles. However, Europe has seen a decline in sales of medium-range air defense missiles. Europe is developing standoff aviation missiles, but the U.S. AGM-154 Joint Stand-Off Weapon (JSOW) is further along in development. The development of European

TABLE 21-10: Space Propulsion Units and Parts (SIC 3764) Trends and Forecasts
(millions of dollars except as noted)

	1992	1993	1994	1995	1996	1997	1998[1]	1999[2]	2000[3]	Percent Change 97–98	98–99	99–00	96–00[4]
Industry data													
Value of shipments[5]	5,121	6,201	3,374	2,954	2,715	3,239	3,406	3,743	3,820	12.6	9.9	2.1	8.9
Value of shipments (1992$)	5,121	6,134	3,360	2,968	2,819	3,213	3,392	3,721	3,790	13.0	9.7	1.9	7.7
Total employment (thousands)	32.0	29.2	22.8	19.6	17.2	18.5							
Production workers (thousands)	13.2	8.9	7.8	6.7	5.5	8.3							
Average hourly earnings ($)	23.81	22.03	22.10	19.60	20.61	23.15							
Capital expenditures	121	85.4	68.9	48.8	77.5	65.1							
Product data													
Value of shipments[5]	5,207	5,862	3,705	2,984	2,803	3,127	3,422	3,696	3,712	10.0	8.0	0.4	7.3
Value of shipments (1992$)	5,207	5,799	3,690	2,999	2,911	3,103	3,408	3,674	3,683	10.4	7.8	0.2	6.1
Trade data													
Value of imports	7.6	1.2	0.7	0.9	18.4	46.1	9.9	25.6	22.3	–78.5	158.6	–12.9	4.9
Value of exports	15.5	5.7	2.6	42.3	23.8	9.0	10.1	53.2	45.9	12.2	426.7	–13.7	17.8

[1] Estimate except imports and exports.
[2] Estimate.
[3] Forecast.
[4] Compound annual rate.
[5] For a definition of industry versus product values, see "Getting the Most Out of *Outlook 2000.*"
Source: U.S. Department of Commerce: Bureau of the Census; International Trade Administration.

TABLE 21-11: Space Vehicle Equipment Not Elsewhere Classified (SIC 3769) Trends and Forecasts
(millions of dollars except as noted)

	1992	1993	1994	1995	1996	1997	1998[1]	1999[2]	2000[3]	Percent Change 97–98	98–99	99–00	96–00[4]
Industry data													
Value of shipments[5]	1,964	2,015	1,386	1,398	1,436	899	1,691	1,908	1,921	9.0	12.8	0.7	7.5
Value of shipments (1992$)	1,964	1,991	1,381	1,406	1,504	890	1,669	1,880	1,889	8.7	12.6	0.5	5.9
Total employment (thousands)	16.2	12.3	9.1	8.8	8.1	6.1							
Production workers (thousands)	6.8	5.6	4.7	4.6	4.8	4.2							
Average hourly earnings ($)	18.04	19.95	20.29	21.49	20.98	21.01							
Capital expenditures	33.8	25.3	29.1	37.0	45.0	28.5							
Product data													
Value of shipments[5]	4,179	3,313	2,727	2,602	2,451	2,812	2,807	2,975	2,982	7.0	6.0	0.2	5.0
Value of shipments (1992$)	4,179	3,273	2,718	2,618	2,567	2,784	2,771	2,931	2,932	6.7	5.8	0.0	3.4
Trade data													
Value of imports	169	148	133	127	161	166	225	275	260	35.5	22.2	–5.5	12.7
Value of exports	1,045	1,000	884	963	985	986	703	629	641	–28.7	–10.5	1.9	–10.2

[1] Estimate except imports and exports.
[2] Estimate.
[3] Forecast.
[4] Compound annual rate.
[5] For a definition of industry versus product values, see "Getting the Most Out of *Outlook 2000*."
Source: U.S. Department of Commerce: Bureau of the Census; International Trade Administration.

air-to-air missiles has been focused recently on close-range and medium-range competitions. The British Advanced Short-Range Air-to-Air Missile (ASRAAM) will offer strong competition for the U.S. Aim-9X in the future, along with Rafael's Python-4 and the Russian Vympel R-73. Europe maintains only limited production of lightweight, low-cost infantry antitank missiles (often used against bunkers and other hardened targets) and mostly is purchasing U.S. Hellfire missiles but probably will face increased competition from U.S. programs that are under development. The European Eryx is a strong lightweight option, as are the Israeli NT and Europe's TriGAT-MR.

Russia has not developed any new ballistic missiles and continues to rely on the Topol-M ICBM. It is likely that Russian capabilities will shrink as weapons deteriorate and new ones are not manufactured. Russia's submarine-launched ballistic missiles also are not being upgraded or rebuilt, and new ones are not expected to be ready for several years. However, most of the new activity in ballistic missiles manufacturing has taken place in developing countries, including Pakistan, North Korea, and Iran. Missile tests in emerging markets such as China, Pakistan, and North Korea will continue to keep the industrialized powers working on advanced weapons systems.

Domestic Industry Trends

American manufacturers continue to have the highest sales worldwide and lead the world in the development of all systems. American dominance in the missile market may decrease over the next few years because of increased European competitiveness. Some standard U.S. missiles are getting older and may be replaced by systems with more advanced technology. U.S. government officials are reacting to missile tests held in emerging markets and are placing increased importance on those systems. For improving targeting and guidance, the Global Positioning System (GPS) is being investigated for tracking on several weapons systems since it allows for real-time programming rather than using preprogrammed data.

American firms continue to have a strong lead in the missiles sector. The Advanced Medium-Range Air-to Air Missile (AMRAAM) is dominant in both domestic and foreign markets, with minimal competition. With strong sales of U.S.-manufactured fighter aircraft, sales of AMRAAMs should remain steady. In fact, as a result of program delays, Europe may need to procure AMRAAMs for use on the Eurofighter until a European version can be developed. The U.S. Aim-9X continues to lead the short-range air-to-air market but may face competition from the British ASRAAM in the future. The U.S. Joint Direct Attack Munition (JDAM) has been flight tested and is in production without any competition from the Europeans. Many analysts feel that this GPS-guided bomb could revolutionize the missile business, maintaining the U.S. lead. Europe is developing standoff aviation missiles, but the U.S. AGM-154 JSOW is farther along in development.

Air defense missiles constitute the largest segment of the missiles sector, with the United States focusing on tactical missile defense. The United States finally made progress with the Theater High-Altitude Air Defense (THAAD) missile, posting two successful tests after six failed attempts. The development of new weapons systems in China, North Korea, and Pakistan has reinforced the need to focus on this sector. Israel is the only country other than the United States that is focusing on the development of the Arrow-2 system as an active air defense program against shorter-range threats. Continued development in countries such as India, Pakistan, and North Korea, as well as their continued attempts to acquire technology and/or weapons from other markets, will keep this segment of the U.S. industry strong over the next few years. Surface-to-air missiles (SAMs) are being switched from one-stage to two-stage designs for improved performance and reduced cost. Defense units are switching to only short-range, human-portable SAMs and long-range, high-altitude systems, such as the Patriot despite the high cost of Patriot-type systems. Raytheon has upgraded the Patriot for anti–cruise missile capability, and a Patriot intercepted a target in its first flight test in July 1999.

Manufacturers of air-to-air missiles have focused recently on competition in the close-range and medium-range sectors. The ASRAAM and the AIM-9X are the leaders in this field, with strong competition from the French Rafael Python-4 and the Russian Vympel R-73. Growth in this area has not increased as expected because of the high cost of aircraft-missile integration and delays in procurement. Raytheon's AMRAAM will continue to dominate and may drive some European product lines out of the market. Russia is not expected to provide unique developments in this area in the near future.

The antiship missiles market is stagnant as a result of improvements coming from software upgrades rather than new missile technologies. The Harpoon is the most popular missile, and a replacement is not likely for a decade. Missiles from Russia and China have not had much of an impact on the market.

With the dramatic decline in tank production, shipments of antitank missiles, which often are used against bunkers and other hardened targets, have dropped off sharply. The U.S. Hellfire dominates this market globally, including sales to several European customers. Europe maintains some participation in lightweight, low-cost infantry antitank missiles and may face competition from U.S. programs under development. The European Eryx is a strong lightweight option, and the United States is following with the development of a similar weapon, the Predator/MPIM (Multi-Purpose Individual Munition). Other options include the U.S. Javelin and Europe's TriGAT-MR. The Israeli NT, which uses fiber-optic guidance, is the first missile to do so. Fiber optics probably will be developed in other systems in the United States, Japan, Europe, and Brazil. Funding will be the main issue. Other than the Hellfire, antitank missile production has been stagnant, with almost no foreign competition.

The United States dominates the air-to-surface market with the JDAM, the AGM-154 JSOW, and the Tomahawk Block-3 cruise missile. The JDAM was test launched successfully from an F-15E fighter aircraft in July 1999, marking the first time that aircraft used a JDAM. Europe is incorporating GPS guidance into several systems, such as the Storm Shadow cruise missile and the Taurus standoff missile; this will provide some competition to U.S. GPS-guided missiles.

For ballistic missiles, the U.S. is upgrading the Minuteman fleet with new engines, guidance systems, warheads, and structures and continues to rely on the Trident D-5 submarine-launched ballistic missile. Russia has not developed any new ballistic missiles and continues to rely on the Topol-M ICBM. It is likely that Russian capabilities will shrink as weapons deteriorate and new ones are not manufactured. Russia's submarine-launched ballistic missiles are not being upgraded or rebuilt. The greatest progress in the development of ballistic missiles has been seen in the developing countries of Pakistan, North Korea, and Iran.

DOD acquisition costs for FY 2000 have remained steady on average compared with FY 1999 costs. Only a limited number of programs faced decreases across those 2 years. The Hellfire missile's acquisition cost decreased from $345.1 million to $294.3 million, and the Tomahawk's cost decreased from $201.9 million to $198.1 million. Most other programs increased in acquisition costs. For example, the Trident II program increased from $374.4 million to $537 million, the AMRAAM increased from $187.3 million to $207.3 million, the JASSM increased from $130.9 million to $168.4 million, the JSOW increased from $231.2 million to $275.9 million, and the AIM-9X Sidewinder increased from $117.2 million to $142.3 million.

Industry and Trade Projections for the Next 1 and 5 Years

Depletion of reserves resulting from the conflict in Kosovo was expected to increase production rates in 1999 as inventories were resupplied (see Table 21-9). Most missile-related growth through the next 5 years will continue to be in the air-to-air and air-to-surface sectors, with little to no growth in the antiship, antiradiation, and antitank areas. The use of GPS for targeting has improved accuracy and lowered costs and will be investigated for use in many types of missiles. Europe may see a resurgence as a result of increased competitiveness caused by consolidation.

LAUNCH VEHICLES

This section covers the space vehicles and parts component, space vehicle propulsion units and parts, and space launch vehicle parts and auxiliary equipment.

Global Industry Trends

On a global basis, the international commercial launch services market should thrive over the next 5 years as providers of satellite services have been waiting to get their new satellites into orbit.

Europe. The current world leader is the European consortium Arianespace, which intends to increase its market share of geostationary transfer orbit (GTO) launches while capturing a significant portion of the low earth orbit (LEO) market. To do this, Arianespace intends to reduce production cycle time, invest in upgrades and new facilities, and lower prices. Arianespace probably will maintain its hold on at least 40 percent of launches for the commercial satellite market but will face increasing competition from nonmarket economy providers such as Russia, China, and Ukraine as well as new and/or improved U.S. vehicles such as Sea Launch.

In 1998, Arianespace orbited 14 satellites on 10 Ariane launchers. In 1999, there were 13 or 14 missions scheduled, with 3 of them on the larger Ariane 5. Because of satellite delays, Arianespace had only eight launches through August 1999 but was expected to match the 1998 schedule by holding eight launches from August to December. The Ariane 5 successfully completed its first commercial launch in spring 1999, and a second batch of Ariane 5s has been ordered that cost up to 40 percent less than the first batch. This reduced cost will improve Arianespace's competitiveness against other new-to-market vehicles and allow it to launch a wide range of payload sizes. The Ariane 5 is expected to evolve to carry up to 20 metric tons for LEO launches and eventually will include several new components and technologies. Arianespace plans to grow to eight Ariane 5 launches per year by 2002, with extended use of the Ariane 4 beyond 2002–2003, the original expected retirement date for the Ariane 4. Arianespace is evaluating the development of Ariane 4 Lite, a smaller version that would launch small payloads to geosynchronous earth orbit (GEO) at a lower price. Ariane believes that the market would support six Ariane 4 Lite launches a year. Ariane's backlog is approximately 40 GEO spacecraft and 1 LEO constellation launch, worth a total of nearly $4 billion.

Internationally, Arianespace launches the Russian Soyuz vehicle through its Starsem venture, which was created in 1996. Starsem may launch the Soyuz from the European equatorial launch site in Kourou, French Guyana, as soon as 2001–2002 for added performance (it currently is launched from a Russian launch site in Kazakhstan). Soyuz is one of the world's most reliable vehicles. Some analysts believe that Europe may look to the United States for further alliances, but there are no existing proposals. In addition, Europe is beginning to focus on developing a reusable launch vehicle (RLV). To gain expertise, Europe first will need to develop an "X-vehicle" for testing. Several different proposals exist, but no decision has been made about which will be funded and/or developed.

Italy would like to develop the Vega small launch vehicle, but France postponed its development in the European Space Agency (ESA) ministerial summit held in May 1999 by convincing the ministers to postpone a decision on further development until October 1999. If the project goes forward, Aerospatiale and Fiat Avio will form the Vega Spazio joint venture to build and market the Vega for LEO launches. Vega will be a solid propellant launch vehicle, with launches expected to cost approximately $20 million, and could provide four or five launches per year.

Overall, the ESA ministerial summit reduced budgets and directed the ESA nations to continue reorganization efforts. The ESA approved 90 percent of the requested amount of government financial support for further development of the Ariane 5, Europe's largest launch vehicle, which was an increase from an earlier figure of $479.8 million to $622.5 million through 2001.

Russia. The launch vehicles of the former Soviet Union are being marketed mainly through international joint ventures with western countries. Russia expected to have a busy year of Soyuz (LEO) and Proton (GEO) commercial and military flights, but uncertainties about the Russian space budget left many of the other programs in jeopardy. Eleven of the projected 13 Proton launches in 1999 were to be performed by the International Launch Services (ILS) joint venture with Lockheed Martin. Soyuz had nine LEO missions scheduled for 1999, an increase of one from 1998. Six of those flights will be commercial for Globalstar, with three traveling to the Mir Space Station. With a few launches on other vehicles, the projected number of Russian launches for 1999 was expected to be 25, but it probably will turn out to be lower because of delays and a Proton failure. Russia uses the Plesetsk launch site and the Svobodny space launch center to launch LEO satellites.

Baikonur, in Kazakhstan, remains Russia's predominant GEO launch site. April 1999 marked the first launch of a commercial Russian–Ukrainian Dnepr rocket, based on the RS-20 ICBM, carrying a commercial payload from the Baikonur Cosmodrome. The project serves two purposes in that it increases the supply of launch vehicles for small commercial satellites and removes inventory from Russian ICBM stockpiles. Ukrainian Tsyklon rockets are used by Boeing's Sea Launch consortium to provide commercial launches from a mobile platform in the Pacific Ocean. Russia may convert the SS-19 Strela ballistic missile into a commercial launcher by the end of the year 2000 for the same purposes. Conversion will require numerous tests and adjustments to the Svobodny Far East launch site that are expected to cost $10 million.

China. In 1998–1999, China faced difficulties not from vehicle reliability as in 1996 but from U.S. government concerns about technology transfer, national security, and export licensing. After investigations into whether U.S. companies using the Long March rocket for commercial launches had transferred sensitive technology to China, the U.S. industry thought that the export licensing process became much more difficult, dissuading several firms from selecting a Chinese launch. As a result, China has not sold any new launches since 1996. China did hold a launch for Brazil in October 1999 and several LEO satellites for Iridium. (China has had 14 straight successes since 1996, improving users' confidence.) China has a few commercial launches remaining on its manifest, but most of them are being held up by U.S. export licensing delays.

China is preparing to launch its first manned spacecraft as early as spring 2000 and will perform a test launch of an unmanned capsule before that date. In China's claim for status, it is seeking to build a spaceport in Hainan at a cost of $500 million and develop a full space program, including a space station and reusable spacecraft, to send probes to the moon. China probably will launch a new, larger Long March 2F vehicle from the Jiuquan launch site in its northwest for the manned program.

Japan. Japan remains an up-and-coming participant in the global launch vehicle market. It is planning its first commercial launches of the new H-2A vehicle in July 2001, with the first prototype to launch in spring 2001. Both Loral and Hughes have orders for 10 H-2A commercial launches but will wait until the demonstration launch to select firm launch dates.

Brazil. As a developing space nation, Brazil is hoping to create the first international commercial spaceport at its Alcantara launch site, 3 degrees south of the equator, making it a competitive location for improving the performance of GEO launches. Until now, the Alcantara site has been used only for test flights of sounding rockets and the initial failed flights of Brazil's VLS launch vehicle, but four noncommercial launches are scheduled through 2001. Brazil would like to use this prime location to launch foreign vehicles normally disadvantaged by launch sites in higher latitudes such as Cape Canaveral and Kazakhstan. The Brazilian firm Infraero would like to operate Alcantara in much the same way that it operates Brazil's airports. Several U.S. and foreign firms are interested in using Brazil as a launch site, but current U.S. policy would heavily restrict the ability of firms to transport rockets into Brazil for launch. For this spaceport program to go forward, Brazil will have to meet U.S. concerns about the transfer of sensitive technology. If this can be accomplished, Brazil may become the world's first truly international spaceport.

Israel. Israel Aircraft Industries teamed up with a U.S. firm, Coleman Research Corporation, to market launches for small U.S. government payloads to LEO from Cape Canaveral. NASA selected both this venture and Orbital Sciences to provide small launches for its payloads. The venture will manufacture more than half its components in the United States to comply with U.S. policy.

South Korea. In 1999, the United States and South Korea agreed in principle to lift all existing restrictions on commercial rocket development in South Korea. The agreement will create guidelines under which South Korea will develop vehicles for both commercial and government launches.

India. India launched a commercial payload with its Polar Satellite Launch Vehicle (PSLV) for the first time on May 26, 1999. It carried an oceanographic Indian remote sensing satellite, a South Korean minisatellite, and a German research satellite. The U.S. government has not supported the development of that program in India because of that country's continued attempts to develop nuclear weapons. India is continuing to work on a larger geostationary satellite launch vehicle (GSLV) program, which is expected to have its first experimental launch by early 2000.

Domestic Trends

Strong foreign competition in both large and small launch vehicles has pushed the U.S. industry to examine ways to improve competitiveness vis-à-vis Europe and several emerging competitors. Many vehicles are being improved, new vehicles are being designed, new technologies are being developed, and companies are entering international partnerships and developing unique ways to reduce the cost of access to space through RLVs.

One major program that should improve U.S. competitiveness is the Evolved Expendable Launch Vehicle (EELV). In October 1998, the U.S. Air Force announced that its EELV program would split its procurement between Boeing's Delta IV rocket and Lockheed Martin's Atlas V. Delta was awarded $1.88 billion for 19 launches, and Atlas was awarded $1.15 billion for 9 launches between 2002 and 2006. The program's goal is to reduce the cost of space launch 25 percent, and the U.S. Air Force expects launch cost reductions of $6 billion from 2002 to 2020. This program will provide increased production for these launch vehicles as well as for numerous subcontractors. For example, Aerojet was awarded $500 million to provide solid rocket motors for the Atlas V, and a new launch pad for the Delta IV will be built at a cost of $250 million.

Lockheed Martin is improving its competitiveness through a partnership with Russia's Khrunichev and Energia to provide launches on the Russian Proton and American Atlas launch vehicles, with the Atlas launched from American sites and the Proton launched from the Baikonur site in Kazakhstan. The ILS venture received its first contract in July 1999 for an Atlas 5 launch with Teledesic. The contract calls for three Proton and three Atlas-5 launches, with options for an additional five on each vehicle. These contracts would allow Lockheed Martin to launch a significant portion of the Teledesic satellite communications system. Atlas and Proton have a backlog of at least 34 commercial launches valued at over $3 billion. While making the transition to the Atlas V, Lockheed Martin will use the Atlas 3 rocket, which will be powered by Russian RD-180 rocket engines, the engines that also will be used on the Atlas 5. Based on all forecasts, Lockheed Martin expected 1999 to be its busiest year ever with 11 Atlas and 11 Proton launches; however, a string of launch failures and satellite delays forced a halt to most launches globally.

Continuing the transition toward increased international cooperation in space launch, the Boeing-led Sea Launch venture had its first successful demonstration launch on March 27, 1999. Since that event, Sea Launch has won four additional launch contracts, increasing the manifest to 19 confirmed launches. The venture includes the Boeing Commercial Space Company, Norway's Kvaerner (which is pulling out of the venture as a result of financial problems in the firm), Russia's Energia, and Ukraine's Yuzhnoye. Sea Launch earns a considerable performance gain by launching from a mobile platform on the equator and taking full advantage of the rotational forces of the earth.

In addition to Boeing's international Sea Launch venture, Boeing continues to launch the Delta 2 and 3 rockets, and the Delta 4 will be Boeing's EELV vehicle. The Delta 2 had its most successful year in 1999, launching several payloads in short time frames. However, on May 4, 1999, a Delta III rocket experienced a failure that left the payload in a useless orbit. This failure will delay further development of the program as well as launches on other vehicles (such as the Atlas) that use the same components. Boeing has booked 18 Delta 3 missions through 2002, with Hughes holding 13 and Loral holding the other 5. The Delta 3 is considered a transition vehicle from the Delta II to the EELV/Delta 4 and will be phased out between 2003 and 2005. A new trend in U.S.-manufactured vehicles such as the Delta 3 is the use of numerous major components that are manufactured overseas. On the Delta 3, the propellant tanks for the second stage are built by Mitsubishi in Japan, while the extendable nozzle on the second-stage engine is built by France's SEP.

Subcontractors also are planning improvements. Pratt & Whitney is developing a new cryogenic upper-stage engine that is based on the RL-10 engine but is twice as powerful. The engine is planned to be available in 2003. Boeing is developing the most powerful liquid oxygen–hydrogen engine, the RS-68, the first large U.S. engine since the Space Shuttle Main Engine in the 1970s. It was tested successfully in July 1999 and will be used to power the Delta 4 launch vehicle in 2001.

In addition to large launch vehicles, the United States produces a number of small launch vehicles. Orbital Sciences produces both the Pegasus and Taurus lines of small launch vehicles. The Pegasus is unique in that it is carried to a high altitude on the belly of an L-1011 aircraft and then released and launched from the air. This type of launch gives Orbital the ability to launch from anywhere in the world as long as the political atmosphere allows it. Orbital currently has a backlog of at least 11 launches valued at over $220 million.

Lockheed Martin's Athena rocket program continues to struggle. The program was not picked by NASA to launch the agency's small scientific spacecraft. With this loss, Athena will need to rely heavily on commercial contracts, but this market has not been growing. Athena will need to increase from two to three launches to six launches a year to keep the program alive. Athena also has been stung by failures, including one in April 1999. Out of five missions since the program began launching in 1995, only three have been successful. Athena has three launches on its manifest, including one from a new spaceport in Kodiak Island, AK, in 2000. To prepare, Athena will begin pathfinder exercises from the Kodiak spaceport in the fourth quarter of 1999. However, on April 22, 1999, NASA announced that it had also chosen an Athena I rocket to launch its Vegetation Canopy Lidar (VCL) satellite from Alaska in August 2000.

Another new concept—commercial "spaceports" that would function similarly to airports—may allow launch companies to use additional sites to increase the number of launches. However, many issues need to be worked out before large numbers of launches will occur on those sites. Issues such as who has priority at those sites (commercial entities or the government) and who must pay for common assets are still being determined. Additional issues include who will run the launch ranges and who will provide safety services.

The years 1998 and 1999 were disappointing for the U.S. commercial space launch industry. A large string of failures restricted the launch rate and slowed the development of new vehicles. Both the public and private sectors ordered wide reviews of those failures. The failures included three Titan failures that cost taxpayers over $3 billion, a Delta III failure that grounded Deltas and Atlases because common components were used, and an Athena II small launch vehicle. A Russian Proton rocket also failed in July 1999, delaying launches for several ILS commercial payloads until the failure review could be completed.

With the growth of commercial satellite demand, a number of entrepreneurial ventures have announced plans to manufacture commercial launch vehicles, including a number of private proposals for RLVs. In addition, NASA is cofunding the development of three experimental RLVs: the X-33, X-34, and X-37. The Commercial Space Act of 1998 granted clear licensing authority for RLVs to the U.S. Department of Transportation, the first time commercial RLVs have been approved for launch. This should make it easier for companies to get financing and provide some certainty in the process.

Historically, companies developing new vehicles have had difficulty getting financing, and they will continue to have this problem because of the risky nature of the business. Many investors are adopting "wait and see" strategies as a result of the risks involved in starting new ventures. Many analysts see the ability to raise financing as the biggest hurdle in this development of new technology. All companies are touting their ability to have rapid turnaround times averaging approximately 2 weeks. This would change the face of space launch by providing the ability to launch on demand. In addition, NASA and the Spaceport Florida Authority (SFA) are constructing an $8 million RLV support complex. It will support the Space Shuttle and other RLV and X-vehicles. The facility will include a multipurpose RLV hangar and facilities for ground support equipment and technical support.

NASA's X-33 development will cost NASA $1 billion by the end of the project's 15 test flights, and Lockheed Martin will invest $230 million for the subscale VentureStar test vehicle. That vehicle also will test new technologies, such as the aerospike engine, a hydrogen-cooled engine that will fire its thrusters in a line along 4 feet of copper alloy. The X-33 will launch vertically and land horizontally, similar to the Space Shuttle. VentureStar is examining 15 states for potential launch sites of its reusable vehicle. Sites should be selected in early 2001 for initial flights in 2005. Lockheed Martin expects to roll out the vehicle in January 2000, with the first flight in July 2000.

NASA's X-34 test model, built by Orbital Sciences Corporation, made its first captive-carry test flight with its L-1011 aircraft in June 1999. The X-34 is smaller than the X-33 and is designed to carry small payloads comparable to those carried on Orbital's Taurus launch vehicle, but at a much lower cost. Russian NK-39 engines are being considered to reduce the cost. NASA and Orbital Sciences would like to reduce the turnaround times on the follow-on RLV to 24 hours. The contract is worth $85.7 million to Orbital to design, build, and test fly the vehicle.

In a 50–50 government-industry arrangement, NASA and Boeing are developing an experimental space plane, the X-37 (formerly known as the Future-X Pathfinder), for a contract worth $173 million. The vehicle could be ferried into orbit by the Space Shuttle or launched by an EELV. NASA hopes that the vehicle will be able to do everything from on-orbit satellite repair to becoming a next-generation reusable vehicle. The project will explore new technologies in thermal protection systems, nontoxic liquid propellants, and new aerodynamic features. Plans include the ability to remain in orbit up to 21 days to perform experiments before returning to earth. The first unpowered drop test is planned in fall 2001, with two orbital tests scheduled for 2002.

The private company Kistler Aerospace remains the farthest

along in the development of a reusable vehicle with its K-1 rocket. The K-1 will use Russian NK-33 rocket engines on its first and second stages. Once those stages separate, the first stage will fly back to the launch site on its own and use parachutes and air bags to land. Kistler hopes to have the first stages ready for another use with only 2 weeks between launches. The second stage will continue its ascent to deliver the payload and then return to the launch site to be used again. Kistler also is interested in launching from the Woomera launch range in southern Australia. Currently, Northrop Grumman is under contract to build structures for the K-1 vehicle. Kistler expects to charge approximately $17 million per launch. Kistler has raised approximately $450 million but is still under the amount needed. Taiwan would like to invest $50 million in the future development of the K-1, and Kistler would like to see Taiwan raise up to $200 million for the project.

The Rotary Rocket Company's Roton rocket will launch like a rocket, using kerosene instead of hydrogen fuel to cut costs as much at 90 percent. After deploying the satellite, the Roton will use rocket-tipped helicopter blades to slow the vehicle for landing. The craft will be piloted by a two-person crew and is planned to have a first launch by summer 2000. Roton's demonstrator had its first test flight in July 1999 and proved the flight simulator technology.

Kelly Space & Technology has designed the Eclipse three-stage reusable launch vehicle, which will be towed to 20,000 feet behind a Boeing-B747. At that point, the Astroliner will rise to more than 75 miles and the pilots will release the payload with a small rocket booster attached to deliver the satellite to its proper orbit. The Astroliner returns to the runway just as the Space Shuttle does. If Kelly can get the appropriate financing, the Astroliner is scheduled to provide its first launch in 2002.

Pioneer Rocketplane is specially designing the Pathfinder RLV, which would use conventional jet engines to rendezvous with a tanker between 15,000 and 30,000 feet. It would fill its rocket propellant tanks with liquid oxygen, which would carry the plane to altitudes of up to 120 miles. At that point, it would release a satellite with an expendable upper-stage rocket. Costs would be reduced by fueling in space, which would reduce the weight of the vehicle. Pioneer would like to hold its first launch in 2002.

Other unique ventures include Space Access LLC's development of a multistage reusable launch system that features an aircraftlike first stage powered by ejector ramjets. The firm is in the preliminary design phase but plans to test a full-size vehicle in 2001, with commercial launches beginning in 2002. In addition, Beal Aerospace will launch semireusable three-stage rockets from Sombrero Island in the Caribbean.

Industry and Trade Projections for the Next 1 and 5 Years

The commercial space launch industry is expected to experience steady growth through 2000 and 2001, when delayed launches are rescheduled and new satellite systems are still completing initial launches. After this period, launches should level out for 2 or 3 years, after which time replacement and follow-on systems will increase the number of launches again. The high demand for launches will be addressed by the appearance of several new launch services providers as well as numerous upgrades and improvements in current systems. Small launch vehicles will experience slower but steady growth because of the need for remote sensing satellite systems, scientific experiments, and replacement launches for LEO communications systems (see Tables 21-9, 21-10, and 21-11).

Kim Wells, U.S. Department of Commerce, Office of Aerospace, (202) 482-2232, kim_wells@ita.doc.gov, October 1999.

■ REFERENCES

Aircraft, Engines, and Parts

Aerospace America, American Institute of Aeronautics and Astronautics, 1801 Alexander Bell Drive, Reston, VA 20191. (703) 264-7596, http://www.aiaa.com.

Aerospace Daily, 1156 15 Street, NW, Washington, DC 20005. (202) 822-4600.

Aerospace Facts and Figures, 1997–1998, Aerospace Industries Association, 1250 Eye Street NW, Washington, DC 20005. (202) 371-8400, http://www.aia-aerospace.org.

"Aerospace Industry (Orders, Sales, and Backlog) Current Industrial Report MA37D," Bureau of the Census, U.S. Department of Commerce, Washington, DC 20233. http:/www.census.gov/cir/www.ma37d.html.

Air Transport World, 1350 Connecticut Avenue NW, Washington, DC 20036. (202) 659-8500, http://www.atwonline.com.

Aviation Week & Space Technology, 1221 Avenue of the Americas, New York, NY 10020. (212) 512-2000, http://www.awgnet.com/aviation.

The Boeing Company, P.O. Box 3707, Seattle, WA 98124. http:/www.boeing.com.

Business Aviation Fact Book 1999, National Business Aircraft Association, Inc., 1200 18 Street, NW, Washington, DC 20036. (202) 783-9000, http:/www.nbaa.org.

Business Week, 1221 Avenue of the Americas, 39th Floor, New York, NY 10020. (212) 512-3396, http://www.businessweek.com.

The Changing Structure of the Global Large Civil Aircraft Industry and Market: Implications for the Competitiveness of the U.S. Industry, Investigation No. 332-384, Publication 3143, November 1998, U.S. International Trade Commission, 500 E Street, SW, Washington, D.C. 20436. (202) 205-2000, http://www.usitc.gov.

"Civil Aircraft and Aircraft Engines, Current Industrial Report M37G," Bureau of the Census, U.S. Department of Commerce, Washington, DC 20230. http:/www.census.gov/cir/www.m37g.html.

Defense*LINK,* U.S. Department of Defense, OASD(PA)/DPC, 1400 Defense Pentagon, Room 1E757, Washington, DC 20301-1400. (703) 697-5737, http://www.defenselink.com.

Defense News, 6883 Commercial Drive, Springfield, VA 22159. (703) 658-8400, http://www.defensenews.com.

Empresa Brasileira de Aeronutica S.A. (Embraer), São José dos Campos, Brazil. http://www.embraer.com.

European Association of Aerospace Industries (AECMA), Gulledelle 94-b.5, B-1200 Brussels, Belgium. (32) (2) 775-8110, http://www.aecma.org.

European Commission, Cordis Customer Service, B.P. 2373, L-1023 Luxembourg. (352) (44) 1012-2240, http://www.europa.eu.int/com.

Export-Import Bank of the United States, 811 Vermont Avenue, NW, Washington, DC 20571. (202) 565-3946, http://www.exim.gov.

FAA Aviation Forecasts, Fiscal Years 1999–2010, Office of Aviation Policy and Plans, Federal Aviation Administration, U.S. Department of Transportation, Washington, DC 20591. http://www.api.hq.faa.gov.

Flight International, Quadrant House, The Quadrant, Sutton, Surrey, SM2 5AS, United Kingdom. http://www.reedbusiness.com.

Flug Review. Flug Revue, Ubierstrasse 83, 53173 Bonn, Germany. http://www.flugreview.rotor.com, http://www.flug-revue.rotor.com.

General Aviation 1999 Statistical Databook, General Aviation Manufacturers Association, 1400 K Street, NW, Washington, DC 20005. (202) 393-1500, http://www.generalaviation.org.

"Industrial Production and Capacity Utilization," Board of Governors of the Federal Reserve System, Washington, DC 20551.

Interavia, Swissair Centre, 31 Route de L'Aéroport, P.O. Box 437, CH-1215 Geneva, Switzerland.

International Herald Tribune, 850 Third Avenue, New York, NY 10022. (202) 752-3890. http://www.usadv@iht.com.

Market Research Reports, National Trade Data Bank, U.S. and Foreign Commercial Service, International Trade Administration, U.S. Department of Commerce, Washington, DC 20230. (202) 482-2000, http://www.doc.gov.

National Aeronautics and Space Administration, Dryden Flight Research Center, P.O. Box 273, Edwards, CA 93523. (661) 258-3311, http://www.dfrc.nasa.gov.

National Aeronautics and Space Administration, Goddard Space Flight Center/Wallops Flight Facility, Wallops Island, VA 23337. http://www.wff.nasa.gov.

National Aeronautics and Space Administration, John H. Glenn Research Center, Lewis Field, 21000 Brookpark Road, Cleveland, OH 44135. (216) 433-4000, http:/www.grc.nasa.gov.

National Aeronautics and Space Administration, Langley Research Center, 100 NASA Road, Hampton, VA 23681-2199. http://www.larc.nasa.gov.

Office of Aerospace, International Trade Administration, U.S. Department of Commerce, 1401 Constitution Avenue, NW, Room 2128, Washington, D.C. 20230. (202) 482-1229. http://www.ita.doc.gov/aerospace.

"Procurement Programs (P-1), Department of Defense Budget for Fiscal Year 2000," Office of the Secretary of Defense (Comptroller). http://www.dtic.mil/comtroller.

"Quarterly Financial Report for Manufacturing, Mining, and Trade Corporations," Bureau of the Census, U.S. Department of Commerce, Washington, DC 20233. http://www.census.gov/agfs/www/qfr.html.

Regional Airline Association, 1200 19 Street, NW, Suite 300, Washington, DC 20036-2422. (202) 857-1170, http://www.raa.org.

Rotor & Wing, Phillips Business Information, Inc., P.O. Box 61130, 7811 Montose Road, Potomac, MD 20897-5402. (301) 340-2100.

Transportation Research Board, National Research Council, 2101 Constitution Avenue, NW, Washington, DC 20418. http://www.nas.edu/trb.

The Wall Street Journal, 200 Liberty Street, New York, NY 10281. 1-800-JOURNAL, http://www.interactive.wsj.com.

World Airline News, Phillips Communications and Aerospace Group, 1201 Seven Locks Road, Suite 300, Potomac, MD 20854. (301) 340-2188, http://www.aviationtoday.com.

Missiles and Space Launch Vehicles

Aviation Week & Space Technology, 1221 Avenue of the Americas, New York, NY 10020. (212) 512-2000, http://www.awgnet.com/aviation.

Launchspace, Launchspace Publications, Inc., 7929 Westpark Drive, McLean, VA 22102. http://www.launchspace.com.

Low Earth Orbit Commercial Market Projections, Associate Administrator for Commercial Space Transportation, Federal Aviation Administration, Washington, DC 20590. http://ast.faa.gov.

1999 COMSTAC Mission Model Update, Commercial Space Transportation Advisory Committee, Federal Aviation Administration, Associate Administrator for Commercial Space Transportation, Washington, DC 20590.

Space News, The Times Journal Co., 6883 Commercial Drive, Springfield, VA 22159. (703) 658-8400, http://www.spacenews.com.

Via Satellite, Phillips Publishing Inc., 7811 Montrose Rd., Potomac, MD 20854.

■ RELATED CHAPTERS

16: Microelectronics
29: Space Commerce
30: Telecommunications Services
31: Telecommunications and Navigation Equipment
51: Air Transportation

■ GLOSSARY

Airframe: Assembled structure of an aircraft, together with the system components that form an integral part of the structure and influence strength, integrity, or shape.

Avionics: Aeronautical electronics, including communications and navigation equipment.

Big LEO system: Satellites working together as a system in low earth orbit that will provide all the services of Little LEO systems as well as mobile voice and fax capabilities.

Block buys: A strategy used by satellite manufacturers in which they purchase numerous launches at one time to reserve access to space and receive a price discount based on the volume of launches purchased.

FAA Stage 3 regulations: Requirements that aircraft meet more stringent (lower) noise levels than Stage 2 aircraft as they approach and take off from airports; similar to Chapter 3 of the European Union's regulations.

General aviation aircraft: Fixed-wing aircraft used for regional airline service, business transportation, recreation, specialized uses (such as ambulances and agricultural spraying), and pilot training.

Geostationary earth orbit (GEO): The altitude (22,230 miles) at which a satellite appears to be fixed at a specific spot above the earth.

Global Positioning System (GPS): A system using 24 satellites, all of which report precise time signals, along with location keys. Eight satellites are in each of three 63°-incline-plane circular orbits at 11,000 nautical miles of altitude; the system is used for navigation and to determine positions exactly.

Little LEO system: A system of low earth orbit satellites that will provide mobile data messaging and position determination services on a global level.

Low earth orbit (LEO): For the purposes of this chapter, any orbit lower than geostationary earth orbit.

Payload: The satellite, instrument package, or equipment carried into space by a launch vehicle.

Rotary-wing aircraft or rotorcraft: An aircraft that delivers lift from a system of rotating airfoils; includes helicopters and the tiltrotor aircraft in the vertical mode.

Unmanned aerial vehicle (UAV): An aircraft, whether fixed-wing or rotary-wing, that is directly controlled [remotely piloted vehicle (RPV)] or programmed to do certain operations and return to base.

SHIPBUILDING AND REPAIR
Economic and Trade Trends

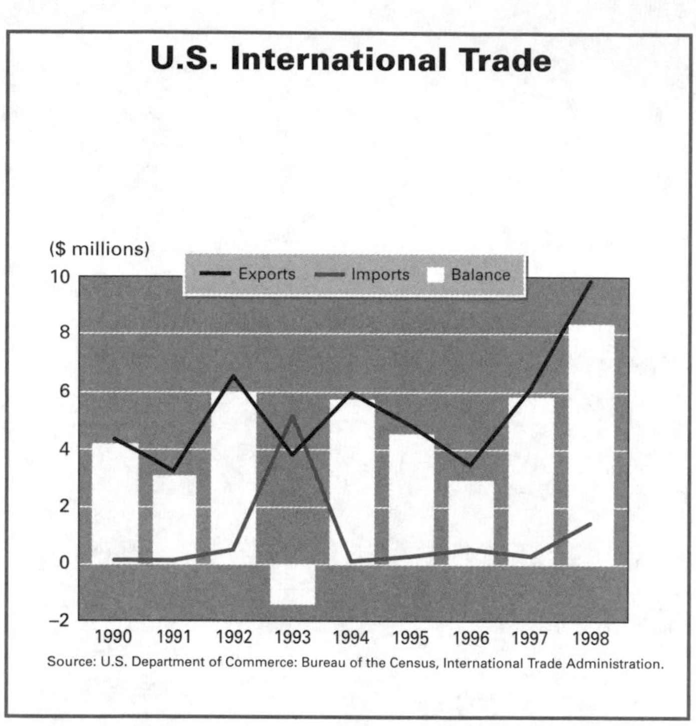

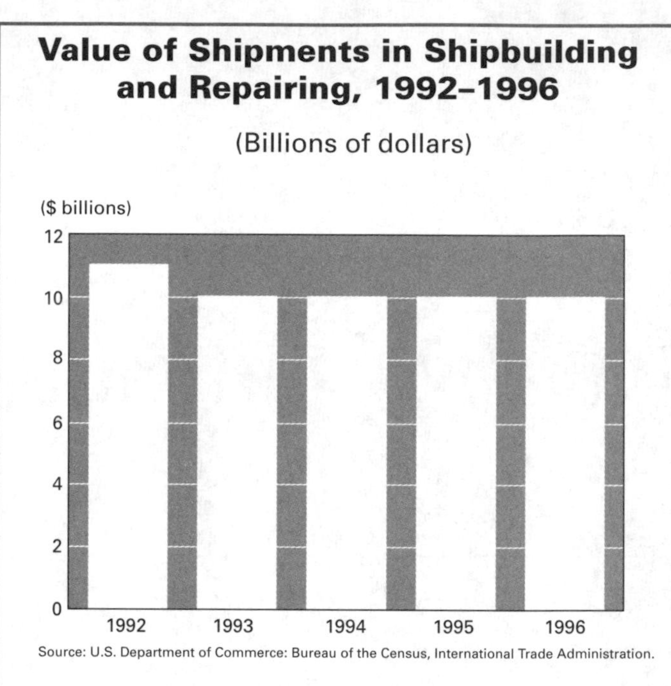

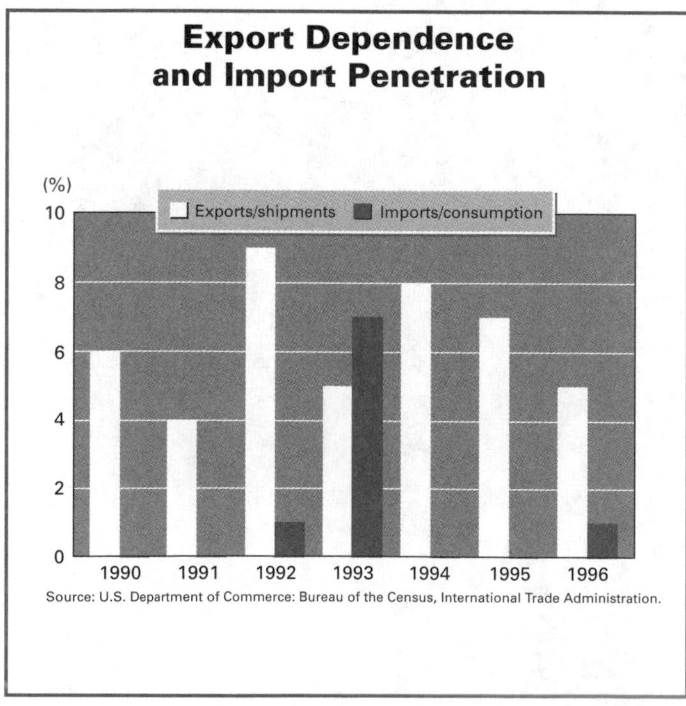

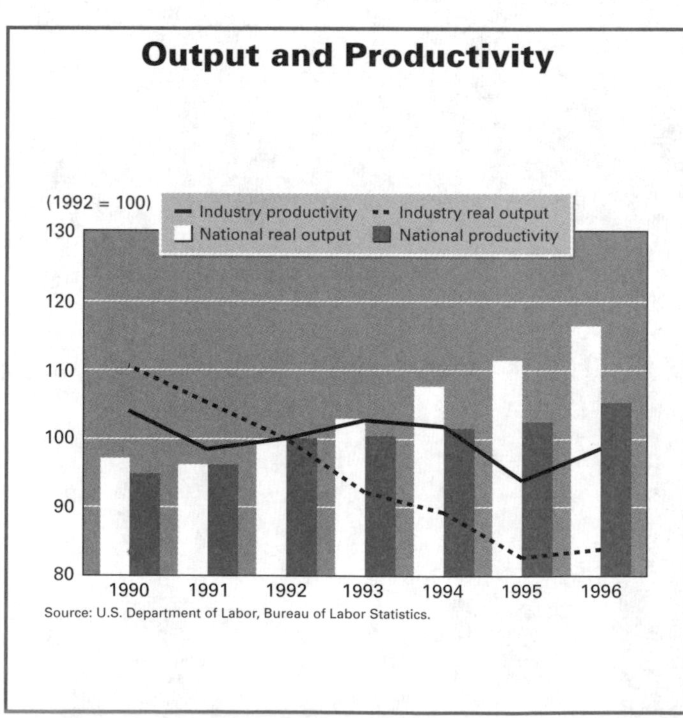

See "Getting the Most Out of *Outlook 2000*" for definitions of terms.

22

Shipbuilding and Repair

INDUSTRY DEFINITION The shipbuilding and repair industry (SIC 3731) includes establishments engaged primarily in building and repairing ships, barges, and lighters, whether self-propelled or towed by other craft. This industry also includes the conversion and alteration of ships and the manufacture of offshore oil- and gas-well drilling and production platforms, whether or not self-propelled. Establishments engaged primarily in fabricating structural assemblies or components for ships and subcontractors engaged in ship painting, joinery, carpentry work, and electrical wiring installation are classified under other industrial codes.

OVERVIEW

The U.S. shipbuilding industry has made progress toward reemerging as an active participant in the commercial shipbuilding markets. The stimulus for this development in the industry and the ability of the industry to enter and compete in these markets aggressively was the National Shipbuilding and Conversion Act of 1993 and the expanded Title XI Federal Ship Financing Guarantee Program.

GLOBAL INDUSTRY TRENDS

According to Lloyd's Register, the world orderbook for new ships, as measured in gross tons, decreased after June 1998. On June 30, 1999, the world orderbook for merchant vessels 100 gross tons (gt) and over consisted of 2,479 vessels totaling 53.8 million gt. This represents a 7 percent decrease from the 2,668 vessels on order at the end of June 1998 and a 3 percent decrease in gross tonnage from 55.6 million gt in June 1998. The average size of merchant ships on order increased 4 percent from 20,829 gt at the end of June 1998 to 21,718 gt at the end of June 1999. South Korea jumped ahead of Japan to regain the dominant position in the world merchant shipbuilding market. South Korea accounted for 35 percent of the gross tonnage of merchant ships on order, followed by Japan with 32 percent and the People's Republic of China with 5 percent of the international commercial shipbuilding orderbook (see Figure 22-1). At the end of June 1999, the United States ranked twelfth among shipbuilding nations with 1.29 percent of world gross tonnage compared with an orderbook of 1.05 percent of the aggregate in June 1998. The U.S. orderbook increased from 582,377 gt to 696,343 gt, an increase of 20 percent in gross tonnage of ships on order.

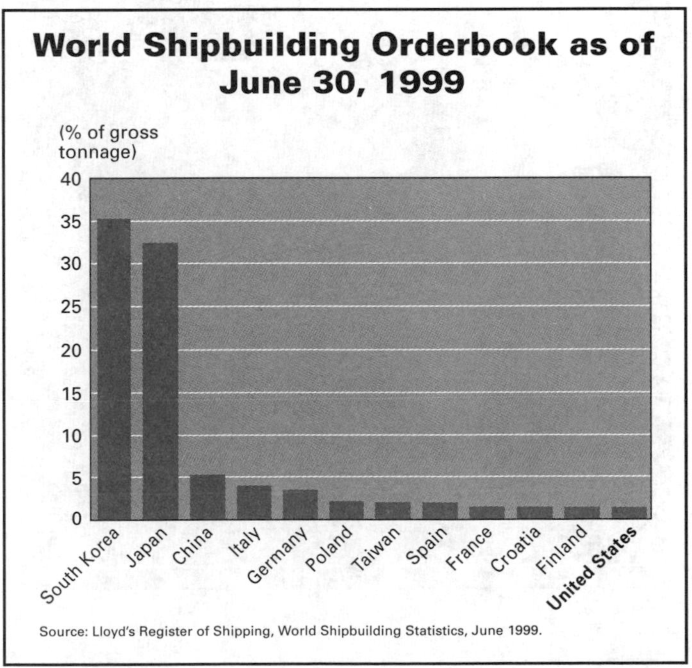

FIGURE 22-1

U.S. SHIPBUILDING TRENDS

The benchmark used for tracking the U.S. shipbuilding industry is the U.S. Major Shipbuilding Base (MSB), which is defined as privately owned shipyards that are open and have at least one shipbuilding position consisting of an inclined way, a launching platform, or a building basin capable of accommodating a vessel 122 meters in length or larger. With few exceptions, these shipbuilding facilities are also major repair facilities with a drydocking capability. On January 1, 1999, there were 19 major shipbuilding facilities in the United States (see Figure 22-2).

According to the U.S. Department of Labor, aggregate employment in the U.S. shipbuilding and repair industry in December 1998 was 100,200, up 500 from the revised December 1997 figure of 99,700. MSB shipyards employ about 60 percent of the total workforce of the shipbuilding and ship repair industry. The remaining 40 percent worked in the 550 additional establishments (with 10 or more employees) classified by the Bureau of Labor Statistics under SIC 3731 (shipbuilding and repairing). Not included in SIC 3731 are the five government-owned shipyards that do not engage in new construction but instead overhaul and repair Navy and Coast Guard ships. In October 1998, total employment in the five government shipyards was 23,116.

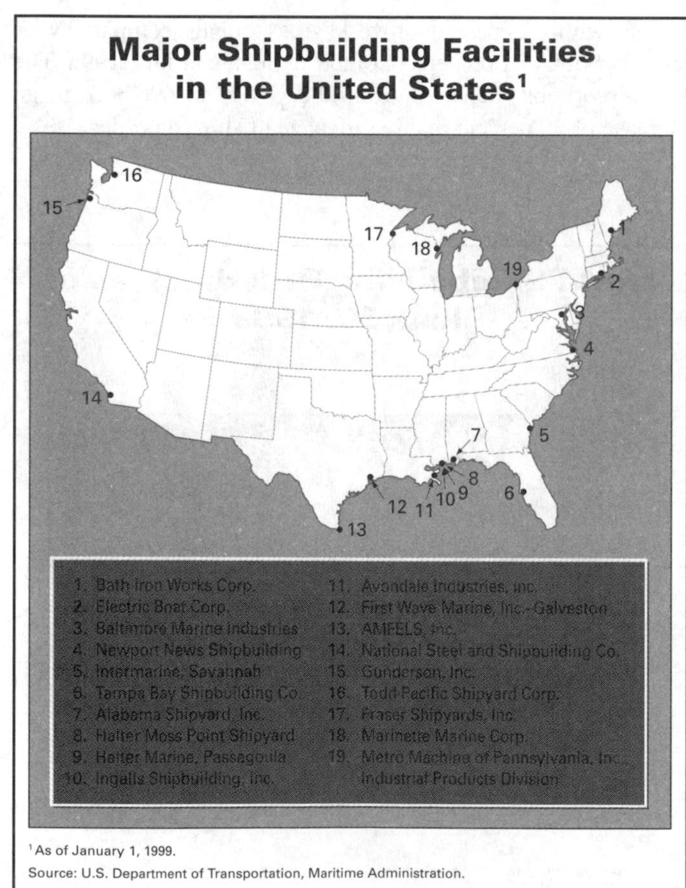

[1] As of January 1, 1999.

Source: U.S. Department of Transportation, Maritime Administration.

FIGURE 22-2

Industry Revitalization Efforts

Recognizing that U.S. shipyards had to be able to compete in the international commercial shipbuilding market to remain viable, the federal government developed a multifaceted program to improve the industry's competitiveness in the international commercial shipbuilding market. In 1993, President Clinton submitted to Congress the report *Strengthening America's Shipyards: A Plan for Competing in the International Market.*

This report formed the basis for the administration's efforts to help the U.S. shipbuilding industry translate its skills from military requirements to a commercial focus in order to compete and obtain orders from international shipowners, substantially increasing the industry's customer base. The President's five-part plan included the following aims:

- Ensuring fair international competition
- Eliminating unnecessary government regulation
- Assisting international marketing
- Financing ship sales through Title XI loan guarantees
- Improving commercial competitiveness through MARITECH

To implement the plan, the President signed into law the National Defense Authorization Act of 1994, which contained the National Shipbuilding and Shipyard Conversion Act of 1993. The latter act expanded the existing Title XI Federal Ship Financing Program by authorizing the secretary of transportation to guarantee obligations issued to finance the construction, reconstruction, or reconditioning of eligible export vessels. It also authorized guarantees for shipyard modernization and improvement projects. The Shipyard Act established a National Shipbuilding Initiative (NSI) program to support the industrial base for national security objectives. Its goal is to reestablish the American shipbuilding industry as an internationally competitive industry.

Federal Assistance Programs

For over 40 years, the Maritime Administration (MARAD) has provided financial assistance to U.S. shipowners through the Federal Ship Financing Guarantee Program (Title XI) and the Capital Construction Fund (CCF). The Title XI program was established by the Merchant Marine Act of 1936, as amended, and provides for a full faith and credit guarantee by the U.S. government for the purpose of promoting the growth and modernization of the U.S. Merchant Marine and U.S. shipyards. The Title XI program provides for federal government guarantees of private sector financing or refinancing. The program may be utilized for the construction or reconstruction of U.S.-flag or export vessels in U.S. shipyards as well as modernization of U.S. shipyards. Vessels eligible for Title XI assistance include but are not limited to commercial vessels such as passenger vessels, bulk carriers, cargo, tankers, tugs, towboats, barges, dredges, oceanographic research vessels, and offshore oil vessels.

U.S. operators are permitted to establish a CCF. They can make qualified withdrawals from the fund of tax-deferred dollars to procure new or reconstructed vessels from U.S. shipyards. In addition, the federal government continues to provide significant direct support to the industry through the procurement of goods and services from a large number of shipyards and related industries to repair government-owned vessels. The principal government contracting agencies include the Naval Sea Systems Command, the Military Sealift Command, the Army Corps of Engineers, the U.S. Coast Guard, the National Oceanic and Atmospheric Administration, the National Science Foundation, and MARAD.

Federal Ship Financing Guarantee Program

Interest and approvals in the Title XI program have reached their highest historical levels as a result of the enactment of the National Shipbuilding and Shipyard Conversion Act of 1993. The act expanded the program to make Title XI financing guarantees available to foreign shipowners and shipyard modernization projects. This resulted in the approval in fiscal year (FY) 1994 through the first quarter of FY 1999 of more than $4.6 billion in Title XI guarantees. MARAD has been asked to consider a variety of projects, including river and power barges, tugs, double-hulled product tankers, and a variety of drilling equipment, including semisubmersible mobile offshore drilling units.

During FY 1998 and the first three-quarters of FY 1999, MARAD approved 20 applications for Title XI financing (see Table 22-1). Included are five export projects and one shipyard modernization project. The total estimated cost of these projects is $2.8 billion, with Title XI guarantees totaling $2.4 billion. The five export projects have a total estimated cost of $652 million, with Title XI guarantees totaling $566 million.

As of June 30, 1999, MARAD had applications for 19 projects pending, including three shipyard modernization projects, at an estimated cost of $1.3 billion, with Title XI guarantees totaling $1.1 billion. The pending Title XI applications included double-hulled product tankers, ferries, various offshore vessels, barges, tug/supply vessels, and dredges.

MARITECH Program

MARITECH was a 5-year federal program that provided matching government funds to encourage the shipbuilding industry to direct and lead in the development and application of advanced technology to improve its competitiveness and preserve its industrial base. The program was industry-led and jointly funded by the government and industry. Administration was provided through the Defense Advanced Research Projects Agency (DARPA) of the U.S. Department of Defense in collaboration with MARAD.

MARITECH had both near-term and long-term objectives. In the near term, it assisted industry in penetrating the international marketplace with competitive ship designs, market strategies, and modern shipbuilding processes and procedures. In the long term, the program encourages advanced ship and shipbuilding technology projects to promote continuous product and process improvement that will maintain and enlarge the U.S. share of the commercial and international market; this will ensure the availability of an experienced industrial base, which is vital to national security in times of crisis.

MARITECH projects awarded during FYs 1994 through 1997 cover a wide range of themes, from the design of various types of

TABLE 22-1: Approved Title XI Applications, Fiscal Years 1998–1999[1]

Company	Reason or Number and Type of Ship	Loan Guarantee Amount, $ millions
Ship Projects		
Noble Drilling Corporation[2]	1 semisubmersible mobile offshore drilling unit	96.8
Tugz International L.L.C.	3 twin Z-drive reserve tractor harbor/escort/towing tugs	41.0
Canal Barge Company, Inc.	30 steel open hopper barges	11.7
	2 260-foot deck barges	
	10 120-foot deck barges	
Attransco, Inc. (refinancing of Title XI debt)	3 tank vessels	48.8
Western Power Co. (Ika Ghana National Petroleum Corp.)[2]	2 power barges	67.0
Marine Cranes (a Washington General partnership)	1 split-hull ABS loadline hopper barge	4.1
Maybank Navation Company, L.L.C.	1 warehouse barge	4.0
Vessel Management Services, Inc.	10 medium-high horsepower tugboats	75.5
Perforadora Central, S.A. de C.V.[2]	1 jack-up mobile offshore drilling unit	70.8
Astro Offshore Corporation[2]	2 platform supply vessels	31.5
Rowan Companies, Inc.	1 self-elevating mobile offshore drilling unit	171.0
Lightship Tankers III-V, L.L.C.	3 46,095-dwt tank vessels	139.0
Empresa Energetica Corinto, Ltd.	1 power barge	50.0
Cashman Equipment Company	5 steel deck barges	7.9
Petrodrill Offshore, Inc.[2]	2 semisubmersible drilling rigs	299.8
Trico Marine International, Inc.	2 230-foot supply vessels	18.8
Torch Deepwater, Inc.	1 300-foot by 75-foot multipurpose DP vessel	45.8
Project America, Inc. (formerly Great Hawaiian)	2 U.S.-flag cruise ships	1,079.5
Ensco Offshore Company	1 semisubmersible drilling rig (EMSCP 7500)	194.7
Shipyard projects		
Bender Shipbuilding & Repair Co., Inc.	Shipyard modernization	14.6

[1] As of July 1, 1999.
[2] Export projects.
Source: U.S. Department of Transportation, Maritime Administration.

small vessels and large oceangoing ships, shipyard technology, and advanced material technology. These projects have been awarded to 24 companies and their subcontractors in 40 states, the District of Columbia, Puerto Rico, and nine foreign countries.

MARAD MARITECH Projects. Since 1994, DARPA and MARAD have jointly selected a total of 65 projects valued at $357 million, of which 40 projects valued at $172 million were assigned to MARAD to administer (Table 22-2). No funding was provided for new projects in FY 1998. Several existing projects, however, were extended with follow-on work phases.

At present, 21 MARITECH projects are ongoing and are being administered by MARAD. Those projects range from innovative design and marketing strategies for high-technology vessels to research in advanced manufacturing technology processes and procedures. Information on MARAD-administered projects is available on the World Wide Web on the National Maritime Resource and Education Center (NMREC) home page (http://www.marad.dot.gov/nmrec/). A MARITECH projects index file lists MARAD-administered projects. From that index, MARITECH project information files are available for review, including information such as project title, project consortium members, project objectives and overview, project status, and government and private sector contacts.

MARITECH Advanced Shipbuilding Enterprise. Funding for MARITECH ended in FY 1998. Recognizing the need to build on MARITECH's success, the industry worked with the Navy, DARPA, the Coast Guard, and MARAD to develop a successor program called MARITECH Advanced Shipbuilding Enterprise (ASE). This program, which received congressional funding in FY 1999, is strategically structured to place the industry in a position to control its own destiny and return U.S. shipbuilders to a position of international strength.

Commercial Ship Construction

New Orders. In 1998 and the first half of 1999, the U.S. shipbuilding industry received orders for the construction of three oceangoing commercial ships. In September 1998, Avondale Industries received a $164 million order from ARCO Marine, Inc., to build an additional 82,545-gt (125,000 deadweight tons or dwt) crude carrier. The tankers built for ARCO are the largest ships ordered from a U.S. shipyard since 1984. In March 1999, Ingalls Shipbuilding received a new order for two 72,000-gt (6,300 dwt) oceangoing passenger cruise ships. These cruise ships are the first oceangoing passenger cruise ships ordered from a U.S. shipyard since the *SS United States* was constructed at Newport News Shipbuilding in 1952.

TABLE 22-2: MARITECH Projects by Fiscal Year
(millions of dollars)

Fiscal Year	Number of Projects	Total Value	Government Funded	Industry Matching Funds
1994	19	92.5	43.3	45.2
1995	26	100.9	46.9	53.6
1996	11	83.8	38.5	45.2
1997	9	79.8	36.6	43.1
Total	65	357.0	165.3	187.1
Projects managed by MARAD	40	172.0	80.0	87.8
Projects managed by DOD	25	185.0	85.3	99.3

Note: Year values do not sum to total due to project administrative costs.
Source: U.S. Department of Transportation, Maritime Administration.

Deliveries. In 1998 and the first half of 1999, U.S. shipyards delivered seven commercial oceangoing ships totaling 262,100 dwt and 174,075 gt.

Newport News delivered the remaining five of six double-hulled product tankers. The 30,415-gt tankers ordered by Hvide Marine were delivered between October 1998 and June 1999. Alabama Shipyard delivered the second of two 11,000-gt chemical carriers, which were ordered in late 1995, to Danneborg Rederi AS of Denmark. Halter Marine delivered a 12,904-gt oceangoing passenger/vehicle ferry in June 1998 to the Alaskan Marine Highway System. In addition, Todd Pacific Shipyard Corp. of Seattle delivered two 4,340-gt non-oceangoing passenger/vehicle ferries for the Washington State Ferry System.

Current Orderbook. As of August 1, 1999, the U.S. orderbook for oceangoing commercial ships consisted of three crude carriers at Avondale and two passenger cruise ships at Ingalls Shipbuilding. The two passenger cruise ships at Ingalls Shipbuilding were made feasible by the assistance of the MARAD's Title XI Federal Ship Financing Program. The crude carriers under construction at Avondale Industries for ARCO Marine, Inc., a subsidiary of Atlantic Richfield Company, are being financed by the parent company and withdrawals from its CCF administered by MARAD. The end-of-year orderbook since 1975, updated to August 1, 1999, is shown in Figure 22-3.

MARAD data indicate that U.S. shipyards had additional orders for approximately 80 commercial self-propelled vessels larger than 100 gt (both oceangoing and non-oceangoing), totaling about 140,000 gt. These orders included tugs, towboats, offshore supply vessels (OSVs), and ferries. Orders for barges and government/military vessels are not included in this count.

As of August 1, 1999, the orderbook for oceangoing commercial vessels totaled five ships with original contract values of approximately $1.73 billion (see Table 22-3). Of those five vessels, two were covered by Title XI with original contract values of $1.23 billion, with MARAD providing $1.08 billion under the Title XI program.

Military Ship Construction

Navy ship construction programs, which have been declining since 1991, are continuing to decline. The Navy's ship acquisition budgets are still well below the level reached in the 1980s, when the Navy commenced its largest peacetime combatant ship construction program, with nearly $100 billion appropriated. Although the Navy's ship construction projects have dominated the workload in U.S. shipyards in recent years, they have done this on a much diminished scale.

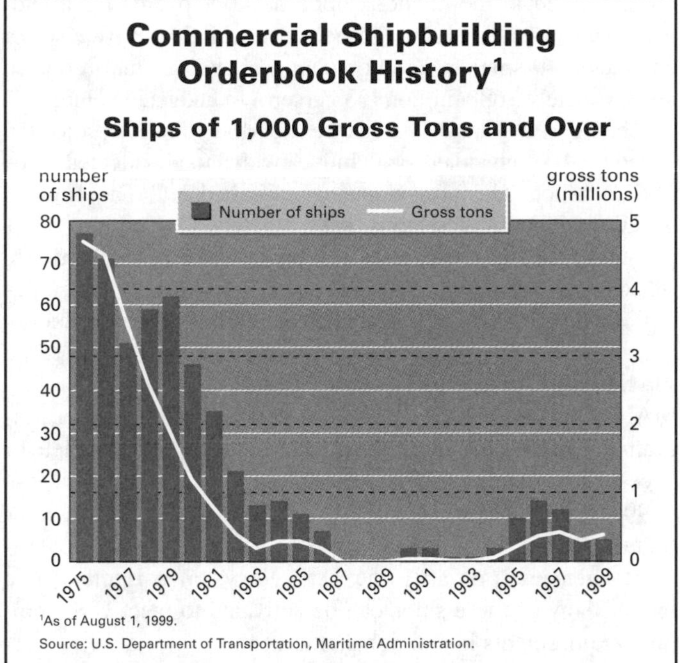

FIGURE 22-3

New Orders. In 1998 and the first half of 1999, the Navy ordered 17 new ships 1,000 light displacement tons (ldt) or larger from U.S. private shipyards, totaling 171,699 ldt with a total original contract value of $6.9 billion. In that period, U.S. private shipyards delivered 15 new Navy vessels and completed two conversions totaling 340,994 ldt with a total original contract value of $6.1 billion. The Navy's shipbuilding orderbook as of July 1, 1999, had declined dramatically in the previous 10 years as a consequence of the austere new construction budget, dropping from 102 vessels in 1989 to 44 in 1999.

Current Orderbook. As of July 1, 1999, the Navy backlog of ships on order or under construction in private shipyards 1,000 ldt or larger consisted of 26 combatants and 18 amphibious ships, auxiliary ships, and T-ships, totaling 44 ships (see Table 22-4). Four Navy vessels were scheduled to be delivered by the end of 1999, 12 before the end of 2000, and 9 by the end of 2001. The naval shipbuilding orderbook encompasses a variety of vessels, from the Seawolf submarine to a Coast Guard icebreaker. The Navy's new construction backlog of 44 ships includes 10 different types of ships, with the orders dispersed among seven private shipyards on the Atlantic (three), Gulf (three), and Pacific (one) coasts.

Most U.S. shipyards do not have the experience, expertise, or infrastructure required to construct sophisticated naval combat vessels. The Navy's T-ship projects, however, have provided some work for private U.S. shipyards that for the last 16 years have relied heavily on military ship construction. These projects involve the building of civilian-manned Navy auxiliary ships that when completed will be placed under the control of the Military Sealift Command (MSC). On July 1, 1999, there were 14 T-ships on order or under construction. Avondale Industries, Inc., of Avondale, LA, received orders for six military sealift ships, and National Steel and Shipbuilding Co. (NASSCO) of San Diego, CA, received orders for five military sealift ships. Halter Moss Point Shipyard of Moss Point, MS, is constructing two ocean survey ships and one ocean surveillance ship.

National Oceanic and Atmospheric Administration

The National Oceanic and Atmospheric Administration (NOAA) currently owns and operates eight fisheries research vessels, four charting and survey ships, and three oceanographic research ships. NOAA is moving forward with plans to replace the aging National Marine Fisheries Service portion of its 15-ship fleet with new acoustically quiet fisheries research vessels (FRVs). Anticipating four new FRV-40 class ships, NOAA has completed the contract definition package and tested the hull and propeller designs to assure their quiet performance, which will significantly enhance survey quality and greatly increase productivity.

The President's budget request for FY 2000 includes funding for the first of these ships and allows annual options for the awarding of an additional three. The detailed design and construction contract is expected in the year 2000. These vessels will replace the existing fleet of aging FRVs and provide expanded capability by using new technology and an improved design. The missions for these new vessels will include stock assessment and life history, physical and biological research, habitat studies, evaluation of fisheries research gear, and atmospheric and sea surface observations and measurement. An extensive suite of state-of-the-art gear and laboratories to support stock assessment

TABLE 22-3: Commercial Shipbuilding Orderbook[1]

Shipyard	Design Type	Vessel Name	Gross Tons	Award Date	Estimated Delivery Date	Approximate Contract Price, $ millions
Avondale Industries	Crude carrier	*Endeavor*	82,545	06/30/1997	8/1/2000	166.0
Avondale Industries	Crude carrier	*Resolution*	82,545	06/30/1997	9/1/2001	166.0
Avondale Industries	Crude carrier	*Discovery*	82,545	09/30/1998	8/1/2002	164.0
Ingalls Shipbuilding	Cruise ship	Unnamed	72,000	03/09/1999	1/24/2003	616.9
Ingalls Shipbuilding	Cruise ship	Unnamed	72,000	03/09/1999	1/23/2004	616.8
Total	5 ships		391,635			1,729.7

[1] Vessels of 1,000 gross tons and over as of August 1, 1999.
Source: U.S. Department of Transportation, Maritime Administration.

TABLE 22-4: Military Ships under Construction[1]

Symbol	Type	Number
New construction		
CVN	Aircraft carrier (nuclear-powered)	1
DDG	Guided missile destroyer	23
LHD	Amphibious assault ship (multipurpose)	1
LPD	Amphibious transport ship	2
SSN-21	Attack submarine (nuclear-powered)	1
SSN-774	Attack submarine (nuclear-powered)	1
T-AKR	Military sealift ship	11
WAGB	Icebreaker	1
T-AGOS-23	Ocean surveillance ship	1
T-AGS-60	Ocean survey ship	2
Total		44

[1] Ships of 1,000 ldt or over as of July 1, 1999.
Source: U.S. Department of the Navy, Naval Sea Systems Command.

and sampling, diving, and oceanography will be required, including state-of-the-art sonar sampling systems, bottom and pelagic trawling equipment, and oceanographic sampling systems. It is anticipated that the ships will have an overall length of 65 meters, be able to carry enough supplies to ensure a self-sustained 40-day mission, and have accommodations for 38 crew members and scientists. The vessels will comply with all U.S. and international rules and standards applicable to oceanographic research vessels. Currently, NOAA is conducting public comment surveys on the technical package and requesting potential sources for design and construction.

A major repair and service life extension also is planned for the NOAA ship *David Starr Jordan,* which currently conducts fisheries research in the Pacific Ocean. Modification of several surplus navy vessels and craft to be used for limited Fisheries and Coastal Ocean Program research also is planned. Normal annual and voyage repairs for the 15 NOAA ships in operation will continue.

Ship Repair and Conversion Work

Activity in the U.S. ship repair industry continues to be robust. Large and small U.S. shipyards continue to compete successfully in domestic and foreign markets for ship repair and conversion work to supplement their diminishing Navy repair work. U.S. shipyards have been successful in using location, timeliness of repairs, and competitive prices to gain an advantage over many foreign repair yards.

U.S. private shipyards perform a variety of ship repair and conversion work on a large array of vessel types. The continued high level of activity in the U.S. offshore oil and gas industry has created a need for additional ship repair and conversion services and has increased maintenance capabilities. There has been a great deal of consolidation activity in Gulf Coast shipbuilding and repair and an expansion of shipyard capabilities achieved through an increase in shipyard property and capital equipment.

The U.S. Navy is another major ship repair market. Each year, the Navy accomplishes maintenance and modernization work on its ships in both public and private shipyards. In FY 1998, the Navy completed 95 availabilities (overhaul/repair work) with a budgeted value of $2.1 billion. Of those availabilities, 46 were accomplished in the public sector's naval shipyards for a budgeted value of $1.4 billion (67 percent), while the private sector completed 49 smaller, less complex availabilities that reflected approximately $688 million (33 percent) in budgeted value.

The FY 1999 Navy Maintenance and Modernization projection called for 100 scheduled availabilities with a total budgeted value of $2.3 billion. The naval shipyards are scheduled to accomplish 36 availabilities representing approximately $1.4 billion, or 61 percent of the budgeted value. The private sector's shipyards are scheduled to accomplish 64 smaller, less complex availabilities representing $875 million, or 39 percent of the budgeted value.

National Defense Reserve Fleet

MARAD's National Defense Reserve Fleet (NDRF) is a program that allows the storage and orderly disposal of obsolete or excess government-owned vessels. At the beginning of FY 1999, the NDRF consisted of 220 ships. There are also an additional 87 vessels held in MARAD's custody for other government agencies, primarily the U.S. Navy, on a reimbursable basis. Many of these ships can be activated to meet U.S. shipping requirements in a national emergency.

A key sealift shipping program that exists as a subset of the NDRF is the Ready Reserve Force (RRF). At the beginning of FY 1999, the RRF was composed of 91 oceangoing cargo ships that are maintained to keep their certificates of inspection current. Vessels in the RRF are owned, managed, and operated by MARAD under authorization found in the Merchant Ship Sales Act of 1946. In peacetime, 93 RRF ships generally are held in various stages of readiness in the United States and are periodically activated in support of U.S. Department of Defense (DOD) peacetime exercises. In 1990, the first mass activation of the RRF took place when 79 RRF ships were activated to support Operation Desert Shield/Desert Storm. By the end of the Gulf War, the RRF had transported 22 percent of all military supplies, including 45 percent of the ammunition, to the Persian Gulf.

The NDRF is funded by DOD through the National Defense Sealift Fund (NDSF). The budget is about $260 million for maintenance and operations. MARAD retains the responsibility for the ownership, custody, maintenance, and operational readiness of the fleet. To reduce the existing surge roll-on/roll-off (RO/RO) shortfall, DOD is pursuing expansion upgrades of selected RRF RO/ROs to obtain an additional 5,980 square meters of lift by the year 2002. A DOD directive calls for the retirement of 19 older breakbulk ships from the RRF to the NDRF by FY 2002 as the Navy's newly constructed and/or converted military sealift ships (T-AKRs), which are large medium-speed RO/ROs, become available.

RRF ship maintenance and repair are conducted primarily in commercial U.S. yards, including the island of Guam, with U.S. marine equipment and service suppliers. The RRF uses commercial ship managers that are authorized to do ship maintenance and repair contracting in accordance with commercial practices. MARAD utilizes a combination of surplus government piers and commercial piers to meet its vessel layberthing needs. A total of 65 RRF ships were outported. Lessons learned from Operation Desert Shield/Desert Storm indicated a need to berth more RRF ships in a higher state of readiness, some with full-time reduced operating status (ROS) crews aboard. MARAD has received 110 no-notice activations from DOD since the 1990–1991 Gulf War, and all but two ships have met or exceeded the assigned level of readiness. Through June 30, 1999, operational RRF ships in prepositioning accumulated over 12,627 operational days while achieving a 99.5 percent full-mission-capable readiness rating. MARAD will continue to rely heavily on the U.S. maritime industrial base for the RRF program, which is now the single largest source of national emergency contingency surge shipping in the world.

Passenger and Cruise Vessels

In March 1999, the U.S. shipbuilding industry reentered the market for the construction of large oceangoing cruise ships. Ingalls Shipbuilding received an order to build two 256-meter-long, 1,900-passenger oceangoing cruise ships for American Classic Voyages Co., with an option for a third vessel. The first vessel is scheduled to be delivered in early 2003, and the second in early 2004. The much heralded "Project America" contract was made possible by the enactment of the 1997 U.S. Flag Cruise Ship Pilot Project statute. These cruise ships are the first oceangoing passenger cruise ships ordered from a U.S. shipyard in over four decades and were made feasible by the assistance of MARAD's Title XI federal ship financing program.

Medium and Small Shipyards

Medium and small shipyards—shipyards that are engaged primarily in supporting inland waterway and coastal operators—constitute an important segment of the U.S. shipbuilding and repair industry. They are active in the construction and repair of smaller vessels such as barges, tugboats and towboats, offshore crew and supply boats, ferries, casino boats, fishing boats, patrol boats, military and nonmilitary craft, and fire and rescue vessels as well as oil rig construction, conversion, and repair.

Dry Cargo Barges

The surge in construction orders for new dry cargo barges experienced in recent years has slowed to a trickle as the operating fleet has moved into a situation of overcapacity. Contributing to the overcapacity situation have been the slower than anticipated pace of barge retirements, their low utilization, and the construction of deeper, larger barges. As retirements have slowed, assets reportedly are being redeployed from grain hauling into the carrying of coal, scrap iron, and other bulk products.

The fleet of covered barges is estimated at about 12,400. Barge operators slowed the new construction pace as the market continued to absorb the influx of the more than 2,500 new dry-cargo bottoms delivered in 1996 and 1997. According to the trade press, many covered barges are having their useful life extended as an alternative to the higher capital investments required for the construction of new bottoms.

Tank Barges

The replacement building boom anticipated as a result of the Oil Pollution Act of 1990 (OPA-90) which will phase out single-skin bottoms by 2015, has not materialized. According to *Workboat Magazine,* only 130 single-skin tank barges were retired from 1995 through 1997. There are about 500 single-skin tank barges operating on the inland waterways that will have to be retired or converted into double-skin tank barges.

The trade press has reported numerous new orders for double-hulled tank barges as well as the delivery of double-hulled tank barges. Conoco, a major integrated energy company, for example, reported that it had completed the conversion of its U.S. barge fleet with the delivery of its fourth new double-hulled tank barge and is now operating a 100 percent, double-hulled fleet of 14 tank barges along the Gulf Coast from Brownsville, TX, to Mobile, AL.

Data available at the Maritime Administration show an assortment of medium and small shipyards with orders for tank barges, with many scheduled to be delivered before the end of 1999.

Offshore Supply Vessels

The decline in oil prices translated into an oversupply situation for the existing fleet of OSVs, and builders of OSVs suffered from a dearth of new orders. It will take a lengthy period of higher oil and gas prices before the level of offshore activity picks up. Some analysts believe that drilling activity is bottoming out and that the outlook for the oil service sector is bullish.

Ferries

U.S. shipyards reportedly account for 30 percent of the world ferry orderbook. A number of U.S. shipyards are currently building ferries: Gladding-Hearn Shipbuilding has been building a variety of aluminum boats, including a second high-speed triple-decked INCAT passenger catamaran for Boston Harbor Cruises; Halter Marine has a contract to build two auto/passenger ferries for North Carolina's Department of Transportation; Derecktor Shipyards built a high-speed 46-meter catamaran passenger ferry capable of operating in excess of 52 knots; and Pequot River Shipworks has built a 35-meter high-speed catamaran and is building two 35-knot, 177-passenger TriCat ferries. Additional ferry projects are under development, and Washington State Ferries reportedly is looking for up to as many as seven new passenger-only ferries. With many cities looking for solutions to high traffic congestion, the passenger waterborne transportation sector may be poised to grow over the next several years.

Export Orders

Medium-size and small shipyards continue to operate in the international market, building a variety of vessels for different clients. Some examples of recent activity for the export market include a high-speed, 45-meter catamaran 300-passenger ferry for the Argentinean company, Buquebus, built by Derecktor Shipyards and a 70-MW power barge for use in Nicaragua built by Todd Pacific Shipyards.

Capital Investment

In FY 1998, the U.S. shipbuilding and repair industry invested more than $292 million in the expansion and upgrading of facilities. Much of this investment was intended to improve efficiency and competitiveness in the commercial shipbuilding arena. Improvements were made to update and convert shipyard facilities to make them more commercially viable. Examples of recent capital investments include new pipe and fabrication shops, drydock extensions, military work enhancement programs, automated steel process buildings, and expanded design programs. Many of these improvements have been made necessary by the increased utilization of U.S. shipyards, particularly those along the Gulf Coast, as a result of the resurgence of the oil patch industry. In 1999, the industry planned to spend about $383 million for the upgrading and expansion of facilities, according to data received by the Maritime Administration. The industry's capital investments since 1970 have totaled approximately $6.5 billion. The actual expenditures between 1985 and 1997, with the exception of 1990, consistently exceeded those planned.

U.S. INDUSTRY OUTLOOK

Only two U.S. shipyards have orders for the construction of oceangoing commercial vessels: Ingalls Shipbuilding has work through early 2004 completing the construction of two passenger cruise ships, and the Avondale Industries, Inc., Shipyards Division has work through the year 2002 for the construction of three tankers for ARCO Marine. The U.S. Navy will continue to be the principal customer for the U.S. shipbuilding and repair industry in the foreseeable future for both conversion and repair work, although the level of activity is expected to be lower than that in the previous decade. Demand for ferries and double-hulled vessels should increase as a result of highway congestion and OPA-90 requirements, respectively. Oil rig demand should remain steady because of the age of the existing fleet.

Major Shipyards

In the 1980s, the Navy's long-term fleet expansion program was begun, with a goal of establishing a modern 600-ship fleet. This fleet expansion program halted with the end of the cold war. Reductions in the Navy ship procurement program, along with the scheduled and early decommissioning of Navy submarines, combatants, and auxiliary vessels, have led to a smaller active U.S. Navy fleet. The Navy's active fleet was reduced by 208 ships between the end of FY 1985 and FY 1998, dropping from 541 to 333 ships. This represents a 38.4 percent decline in the size of the active fleet. The U.S. Navy's shipbuilding plan for FYs 1999 through 2004 includes the construction and conversion of 66 new ships costing about $46.0 billion (see Table 22-5). The 66 Shipbuilding and Conversion, Navy (SCN) ships consist of 45 new construction ships, one nuclear aircraft carrier refueling, eight ship modernizations, and 12 service life extensions (SLEPs). The Navy's shipbuilding program represents a 60.5 percent reduction in the quantity of ships being procured, an average of 7.5 ships per year compared with the average of 19 ships procured annually for Navy programs in the 1980s.

Navy ships require many subcontractors to assist in the construction and installation of a multitude of complex shipboard systems (weapons, radar, etc.). These complex systems dramatically increase the total cost of military ships. The shipyard contract value accounts for only about one-third of the $46 billion budget; the remainder goes for items such as government-furnished equipment placed aboard the vessels and government program costs. The major full-service shipyards, those which constitute the MSB for the foreseeable future, will continue to depend on Navy shipbuilding and repair work as their primary source of employment. Since mid-1992, those shipyards have experienced a sharp decrease in employment as a consequence of deep reductions in new Navy shipbuilding orders, the decline in complex Navy repair activity, and the absence of significant orders for commercial shipbuilding. The Navy's shipbuilding plan for FYs 1999 through 2004 will result in a leveling out of the workforce by the end of 2006. The shipbuilding industry's workload projection (see Figure 22-4) reflects the labor-power requirements for the commercial shipbuilding orderbook as of December 1998 and the proposed Navy FYs 1999 through 2004 shipbuilding plan.

TABLE 22-5: Navy Shipbuilding Plan, 1999–2004[1]

Ship Class	1999	2000	2001	2002	2003	2004	Total
New construction							
CVN			1				1
SSN	1		1	1	1	1	5
DDG-51	3	3	3	3	3		15
DD-21						1	1
LPD	1	2	2	2	2	2	11
T-AGS	1						1
T-AKR (military sealift)	1						1
ADC(X)		1	1	2	2	3	9
JCC(X)						1	1
Subtotal	7	6	8	8	8	8	45
Modernization/ major overhaul							
CVN (refueling)			1				1
LCAC SLEP	1	2	1	2	3	3	12
CG (modernization)				1	3	4	8
Subtotal	1	2	2	3	6	7	21
Total	8	8	10	11	14	15	66

[1] Fiscal years.
Source: U.S. Department of the Navy, Naval Sea Systems Command.

Oil Pollution Act of 1990

OPA-90 established the requirement that all tankers entering U.S. ports by the year 2015 have double hulls. OPA-90 was seen as representing a large step toward reducing the environmental danger from shipping petroleum and petroleum products as well as an opportunity for the U.S. shipbuilding industry to reenter the commercial market through the construction of double-hulled tankers. The U.S. industry has taken numerous steps to improve its ability to capture a comfortable percentage of the demand for replacement tonnage in the world tanker fleet. MARAD data indicate that about 1,500 tankers involved in foreign trade, or about one-third of the world's petroleum tanker fleet, enter U.S. ports. It is difficult to determine the number of tankers that will be rebuilt, scrapped, or constructed as a result of the enactment of OPA-90, but it is known that a

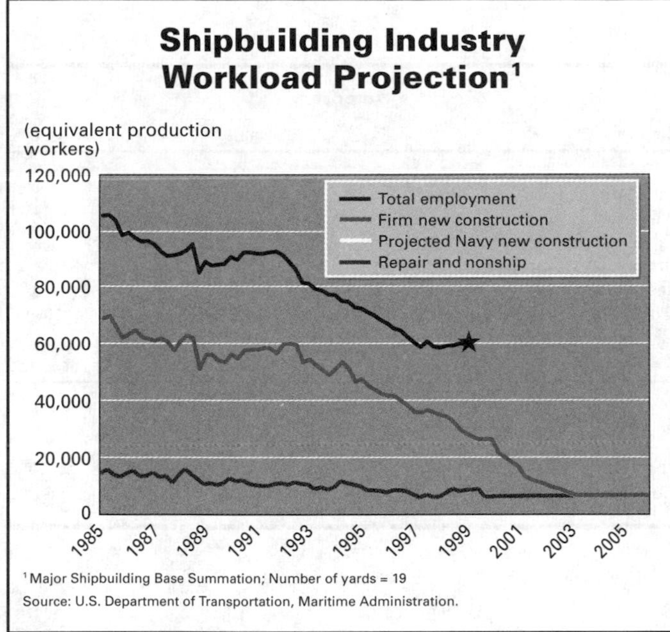

FIGURE 22-4

double hull will be required by the year 2015 for all tankers entering a U.S. port.

World Tanker Fleet

According to *Clarkson's Shipping Review and Outlook* of spring 1999, about one-third of the tankers in the world's operational fleet, measured by number and deadweight tonnage, were built before 1980. While very large crude carriers (VLCCs) represent about 44 percent of the world tanker fleet in terms of deadweight tonnage, about 52 percent of the VLCC fleet, measured by dwt, was more than 20 years old.

Clarkson's reports that it is expected that 9.3 million dwt of VLCC tonnage will be delivered in the year 2000, down very slightly from the 9.6 million tons expected to be delivered in 1999. The large amount of tonnage forecast for delivery is a direct result of the massive amount of orders placed for VLCCs in 1997 and 1998.

Clarkson's reported that the fleet of smaller tankers, Aframax-tankers, those in the range of 80,000 to 120,000 dwt, continued to age. As of March 1999, 21 percent of those tankers were over 20 years old, compared with 17 percent at the end of 1995.

Clarkson's reported that as of March 1999, double-hulled tankers represented about 26 percent of the world's tanker fleet, with 1,325 vessels aggregating to 77.2 million dwt. The double-hulled fleet is fairly young; almost 80 percent of the vessels and 91 percent by tonnage are less than 9 years old.

Much older tanker tonnage remains to be replaced with new tonnage in the twenty-first century so that those vessels will be able to enter U.S. ports. U.S. and foreign shipyards have seen an influx of orders for double-hulled tankers as a result of the requirements of OPA-90. The U.S. shipbuilding industry has benefited from the increased demand for double-hulled tankers generated by OPA-90, receiving orders for 11 new tankers (9 product and 2 chemical tankers) and four major tanker reconstructions. Those orders should be a catalyst for future orders for double-hulled tankers that incorporate design improvements and advanced electronic features. U.S. shipyards continue to make significant capital investments to improve their facilities and increase their productivity in order to participate in the opportunities forecast for the next decade, including Jones Act tanker tonnage resulting from OPA-90. Shipbuilding analysts expect a significant rise in new orders for commercial ships into the twenty-first century. This increase is a result of projections of high growth in the seaborne trade for oil and dry bulk cargoes as well as the continued demand for replacement ships necessitated by the aging of the world fleet. To achieve this level, a significant number of orders will have to be made for tankers and dry bulk carriers.

Organization for Economic Cooperation and Development

In December 1994, the world's key shipbuilding nations (the United States, Japan, Korea, the European Union countries, and Norway) signed an agreement to eliminate shipbuilding subsidies and other trade-distorting practices. The agreement was negotiated under the auspices of the Organization for Economic Cooperation and Development (OECD). This accord eliminates virtually all direct and indirect subsidies, establishes common rules for government-assisted financing, creates an injurious pricing mechanism to prevent ship dumping, and provides a binding mechanism for dispute settlement. The OECD agreement is intended to achieve the goal of ensuring fair international competition for U.S. shipyards. The administration believes that the agreement can help restore the competitiveness of American shipbuilding in the world market, since it requires other countries to give up the much more substantial support they have provided to their yards while requiring relatively modest changes in U.S. programs. Although negotiation of the OECD agreement began as a U.S. initiative, there has been a protracted disagreement within the U.S. shipbuilding industry over its utility. Large military-oriented yards have opposed the agreement, while many commercially oriented small and medium-size yards have supported it. The Clinton administration and congressional supporters of the agreement have sought to address critics' concerns through compromise proposals. Various bills to implement the agreement have been considered, but Congress still must act. All other parties have ratified the agreement, but it will not go into force unless the United States approves it by passing implementing legislation.

If the agreement takes effect, the Title XI program will be modified to meet its terms, which provide for a maximum repayment period of 12 years and a maximum financing coverage of 80 percent. The current Title XI program allows for a maximum 25-year repayment period and maximum financing coverage of 87.5 percent.

Medium-size and Small Shipyards

Medium-size and small shipyards continue to flourish with orders for tugs, ferries, patrol boats, and other shallow-draft vessels. Many yards report that they are continuing to invest in

TABLE 22-6: U.S. Trade Patterns in Shipbuilding[1] in 1998
(millions of dollars; percent)

Exports			Imports		
Region[2]	Value[3]	Share,%	Region[2]	Value[3]	Share,%
NAFTA	49	5	NAFTA	10	7
Latin America	311	32	Latin America	1	1
Western Europe	363	37	Western Europe	123	85
Japan/Chinese Economic Area	3	0	Japan/Chinese Economic Area	3	2
Other Asia	34	4	Other Asia	4	3
Rest of world	222	23	Rest of world	4	3
World	983	100	World	145	100
Top Five Countries	Value	Share,%	Top Five Countries	Value	Share,%
Netherlands Antilles	190	19	Finland	113	77
Netherlands	178	18	Canada	10	7
United Kingdom	162	16	Norway	5	4
Egypt	127	13	Singapore	4	3
Nigeria	42	4	Poland	3	2

[1] SIC 3731.
[2] For definitions of regional groupings, see "Getting the Most Out of *Outlook 2000*."
[3] Values may not sum to total due to rounding.
Source: U.S. Department of Commerce, Bureau of the Census.

their facilities. Some yards acquire other facilities to improve their market positions, gain access to additional workers, and enter new markets. Medium-size and small shipyards saw a growth opportunity in the rig business and moved aggressively into that market. The industry observed that the rig fleet was aging and saw a tremendous opportunity in an expected surge in demand for rig repairs and conversions.

FACTORS AFFECTING FUTURE U.S. INDUSTRY GROWTH

The availability of long-term Title XI guarantees for eligible vessels constructed or reconstructed in U.S. shipyards and for shipyard modernization projects continues to be a major factor in the revitalization of commercial shipbuilding in U.S. shipyards. The U.S. shipbuilding industry has to make significant strides in building efficient ships at lower prices with on-time deliveries for the Jones Act trade to demonstrate to the international market its ability to produce high-quality commercial vessels. (See Table 22-6 for the total value of exports in 1998.) The knowledge and experience gained in the past few years, coupled with a successful domestic building program, should help the U.S. shipbuilding industry secure additional new building tonnage generated by OPA-90, the projected growth in world trade, and the projected demand for replacement tonnage. The U.S. shipbuilding industry has made significant capital investments to enhance its competitive posture by means of productivity improvements. The federal government, suppliers, shipyard managements, and organized labor continue to work together to achieve increased market penetration through the cost-effective production of high-quality ships and products.

The industry sees opportunities in the years ahead, and a sharp focus on product planning, production, and marketing should give it a chance to demonstrate achievement first in the domestic market and then in the more competitive foreign commercial shipbuilding arena.

Daniel Seidman and Elizabeth Gearhart, Office of Ship Construction, Maritime Administration, U.S. Department of Transportation, (202) 366-5841, August 1999.

■ REFERENCES

The Clarkson's Shipping Review and Outlook, Spring 1999, Clarkson Research Studies, 12 Camomile Street, London, EC3A 7BP, United Kingdom. 0171-283-8955.

Marine Log, Simmons-Boardman Publishing Corporation, 345 Hudson Street, New York, NY 10014. (212) 620-7263.

Maritime Reporter and Engineering News, Maritime Activity Reports, Inc., 118 East 25 Street, New York, NY 10010. (212) 477-6700.

1998 Report on Survey of U.S. Shipbuilding and Repair Facilities, Maritime Administration, U.S. Department of Transportation, Office of Ship Construction, 400 Seventh Street, SW, Washington, DC 20590. (202) 366-5841.

Shipyard Chronicle (newsletter), Shipbuilders Council of America, 901 North Washington Street, Alexandria, VA 22314. (703) 548-7447.

Workboat Magazine, Journal Publications, 120 Tillson Avenue, Suite 201, P.O. Box 908, Rockland, ME 04841-0908. (207) 594-6222.

World Shipbuilding Statistics, Lloyd's Register of Shipping, 71 Fenchurch Street, London EC3M4BS, United Kingdom. 071-709-9166.

■ RELATED CHAPTERS

13: Steel Mill Products
17: Metalworking Equipment
31: Telecommunications and Navigation Equipment
52: Water Transportation

INDUSTRIAL AND ANALYTICAL INSTRUMENTS
Economic and Trade Trends

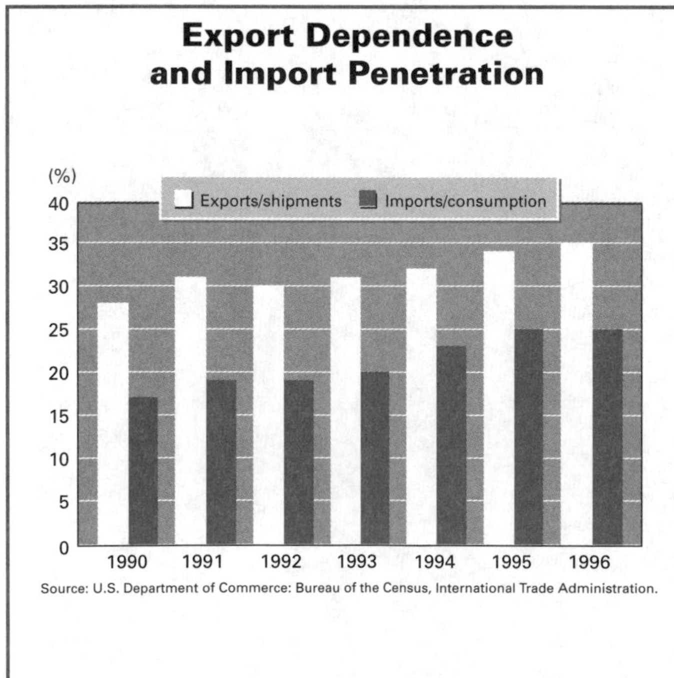

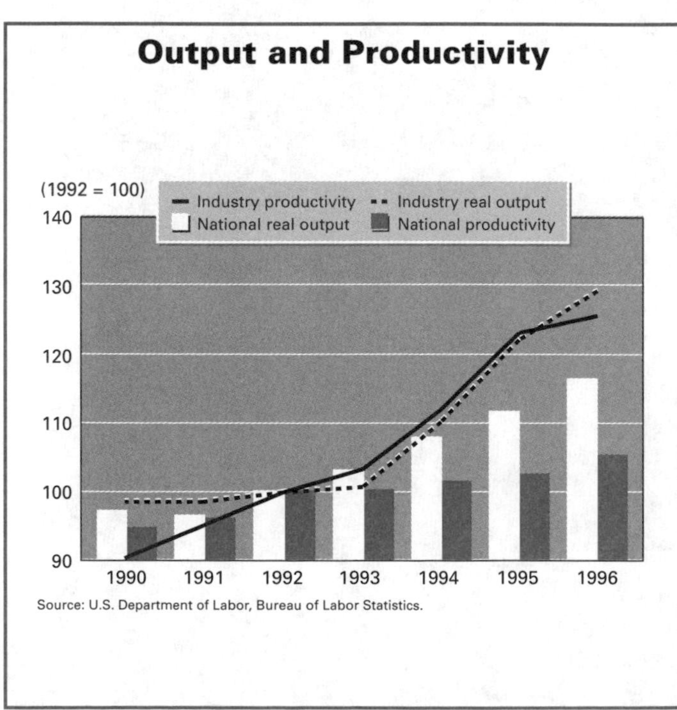

See "Getting the Most Out of *Outlook 2000*" for definitions of terms.

23

Industrial and Analytical Instruments

INDUSTRY DEFINITION The industrial and analytical instruments industry (SIC 382) encompasses three major sectors: laboratory instruments and apparatus (SIC 3821, 3826, 3827), measuring and controlling instruments (SIC 3822, 3823, 3824, 3829), and electrical test and measuring instruments (SIC 3825).

OVERVIEW

Global and Domestic Outlook

The industrial and analytic instruments (I&AI) industry manufactures a diverse range of technically advanced products. Measuring and controlling instruments are used in most manufacturing and processing plants around the world; laboratory instruments and apparatus are crucial to the pharmaceutical industry for drug research and are equally important to the clinical diagnostic market; and electrical test and measuring instruments are used by the semiconductor industry to test semiconductors and loaded circuit boards, the computer industry to test disk drives, and the telecommunications industry to test the rapidly growing voice, data, and video infrastructure.

The I&AI industry is highly competitive, technologically advanced, and globally integrated. The markets in which U.S. companies compete are globalized; therefore, many large U.S. instruments companies have manufacturing operations throughout the world and derive a significant portion of their revenues from international sales. Restructuring, consolidation, and mergers and acquisitions are key elements to growth in today's marketplace. Global competition is constantly driving new standards of quality while reducing manufacturing costs. The keys to success include the selling price, the performance capabilities of an instrument, state-of-the-art technology, technical support, and aftermarket service.

The United States is the largest producer of I&AI in the world. The chief competitors to U.S. companies are based in Japan, Germany, and the United Kingdom.

In 1998 and the first half of 1999, overall business activity for I&AI experienced weak economic conditions, especially in Asia and Latin America and to a lesser degree in Europe. This weakness was partially offset by stronger growth in the domestic market.

The global I&AI industry is benefiting from implementation of the Information Technology Agreement (ITA), which will eliminate import duties on information technology products, including most analytical instruments, by January 1, 2000.

In November 1998, the Asia-Pacific Economic Cooperation (APEC) ministers signed the Early Voluntary Sectoral Liberalization initiative agreeing to lower tariffs and trade barriers in instrumentation and medical devices. This agreement is, however, nonbinding. The APEC ministers also agreed to initiate a process in the World Trade Organization (WTO) for the reduction of tariffs known as Accelerated Tariff Liberalization (ATL) in which the APEC economies have pledged to work constructively to achieve the critical mass in the WTO necessary for concluding agreements in all nine sectors. The lowering of tariffs in all nine sectors, including scientific instruments, has the potential to increase trade on a global basis.

Industry and Trade Projections

Shipments by the U.S. I&AI industry totaled an estimated $46.3 billion in constant dollars (see Table 23-1) in 1998 and were expected to rise slowly to $47.8 billion in 1999. For the year 2000, I&AI shipments are forecast to grow 3 percent to $49.2 billion. During the 5-year period ending in 2004, ship-

TABLE 23-1: Measuring and Controlling Devices (SIC 382) Trends and Forecasts
(millions of dollars except as noted)

	1992	1993	1994	1995	1996	1997[1]	1998[1]	1999[2]	2000[3]	Percent Change 97–98	98–99	99–00	96–00[4]
Industry Data													
Value of shipments[5]	34,730	35,409	38,932	43,730	46,741	49,411	49,909	51,837	54,030	1.0	3.9	4.2	3.7
3825 Electrical measuring devices	8,826	8,746	10,124	12,418	13,371	14,040	13,478	13,950	14,480	–4.0	3.5	3.8	2.0
382A Laboratory instruments[6]	9,823	10,384	11,119	12,254	13,039	13,821	14,235	14,804	15,544	3.0	4.0	5.0	4.5
382B Measuring instruments[7]	16,081	16,279	17,689	19,059	20,331	21,550	22,196	23,083	24,006	3.0	4.0	4.0	4.2
Value of shipments (1992$)	34,730	34,708	37,705	41,659	43,955	45,957	46,279	47,834	49,225	0.7	3.4	2.9	2.9
3825 Electrical measuring devices	8,826	8,608	9,800	11,649	12,543	13,060	12,573	13,001	13,370	–3.7	3.4	2.8	1.6
382A Laboratory instruments	9,823	10,229	10,842	11,761	12,310	13,289	13,583	14,112	14,611	2.2	3.9	3.5	4.4
382B Measuring instruments	16,081	15,871	17,062	18,250	19,102	19,608	20,123	20,721	21,244	2.6	3.0	2.5	2.7
Total employment (thousands)	276	269	266	271	272								
3825 Electrical measuring devices	68.5	64.9	63.0	62.3	63.2								
382A Laboratory instruments	78.2	78.0	76.6	76.8	77.4								
382B Measuring instruments	129	126	126	132	132								
Production workers (thousands)	138	134	139	142	141								
3825 Electrical measuring devices	32.2	30.5	32.0	31.0	33.0								
382A Laboratory instruments	34.3	34.0	35.2	35.1	34.5								
382B Measuring instruments	71.3	69.4	71.3	75.4	73.7								
Average hourly earnings ($)	13.01	13.32	13.52	13.94	14.28								
3825 Electrical measuring devices	14.20	14.56	14.84	15.07	15.53								
382A Laboratory instruments	12.74	13.06	13.47	14.14	14.65								
382B Measuring instruments	12.61	12.91	12.97	13.37	13.54								
Capital expenditures	1,180	1,152	1,156	1,348	1,466								
3825 Electrical measuring devices	324	402	334	398	469								
382A Laboratory instruments	355	330	325	371	401								
382B Measuring instruments	501	420	498	579	596								
Product Data													
Value of shipments[5]	32,914	33,904	36,214	39,747	42,227	44,639	45,099	46,843	48,821	1.0	3.9	4.2	3.7
3825 Electrical measuring devices	7,985	8,180	9,020	10,882	11,964	12,562	12,060	12,482	12,956	–4.0	3.5	3.8	2.0
382A Laboratory instruments	9,481	9,654	10,014	11,062	11,451	12,138	12,502	13,002	13,652	3.0	4.0	5.0	4.5
382B Measuring instruments	15,448	16,071	17,181	17,803	18,812	19,939	20,537	21,359	22,213	3.0	4.0	4.0	4.2
Value of shipments (1992$)	32,914	33,257	35,092	37,910	39,757	41,499	41,788	43,201	44,535	0.7	3.4	3.1	2.9
3825 Electrical measuring devices	7,985	8,051	8,731	10,208	11,224	11,686	11,240	11,633	11,963	–3.8	3.5	2.8	1.6
382A Laboratory instruments	9,481	9,516	9,775	10,626	10,815	11,671	11,929	12,395	12,915	2.2	3.9	4.2	4.5
382B Measuring instruments	15,448	15,690	16,585	17,076	17,718	18,142	18,619	19,173	19,657	2.6	3.0	2.5	2.6
Trade Data													
Value of imports	5,368	5,969	7,293	8,579	9,159	10,269	11,260	11,342	11,731	9.7	0.7	3.4	6.4
3825 Electrical measuring devices	1,184	1,323	1,474	1,834	2,063	2,442	2,487	2,467	2,541	1.8	–0.8	3.0	5.3
382A Laboratory instruments	1,987	2,040	2,303	2,733	3,091	3,526	3,992	4,025	4,075	13.2	0.8	1.2	7.2
382B Measuring instruments	2,197	2,606	3,516	4,011	4,005	4,301	4,781	4,850	5,115	11.2	1.4	5.5	6.3
Value of exports	9,862	10,646	11,724	13,371	14,647	17,165	17,161	17,261	17,957	–0.0	0.6	4.0	5.2
3825 Electrical measuring devices	2,934	3,000	3,228	3,932	4,438	5,151	5,052	4,991	5,191	–1.9	–1.2	4.0	4.0
382A Laboratory instruments	3,011	3,166	3,552	4,131	4,829	5,655	5,763	5,875	6,125	1.9	1.9	4.3	6.1
382B Measuring instruments	3,917	4,479	4,944	5,309	5,380	6,359	6,346	6,395	6,641	–0.2	0.8	3.8	5.4

[1] Estimate except exports and imports.
[2] Estimate.
[3] Forecast.
[4] Compound annual rate.
[5] For a definition of industry versus product values, see "Getting the Most Out of *Outlook 2000*."
[6] The code 382A represents an aggregation of SICs 3821, 3826, and 3827.
[7] The code 382B represents an aggregation of SICs 3822, 3823, 3824, and 3829.
Source: U.S. Department of Commerce: Bureau of the Census; International Trade Administration.

ments are forecast to grow at a compound annual rate of 4 percent to $58.2 billion.

The United States is a net exporter of I&AI. In 1998, the United States exported $17.2 billion (see Table 23-2) of I&AI while importing $11.3 billion. Germany is the largest export market for I&AI in Europe, while Japan is the largest market for exports to Asia. The United States imports the largest amount of I&AI from Japan, followed by Mexico and Germany.

Exports of I&AI were estimated to rise fractionally to $17.3 billion in 1999 and are forecast to rise 4 percent to $18 billion in 2000. Imports of I&AI were estimated to level off at $11.3

TABLE 23-2: U.S. Trade Patterns in Industrial and Analytical Instruments[1] in 1998
(millions of dollars; percent)

Exports			Imports		
Region[2]	Value[3]	Share, %	Region[2]	Value[3]	Share, %
NAFTA	4,114	24	NAFTA	2,982	26
Latin America	932	5	Latin America	99	1
Western Europe	5,359	31	Western Europe	3,913	35
Japan/Chinese Economic Area	3,661	21	Japan/Chinese Economic Area	3,392	30
Other Asia	2,030	12	Other Asia	497	4
Rest of world	1,065	6	Rest of world	377	3
World	17,161	100	World	11,260	100
Top Five Countries	Value	Share, %	Top Five Countries	Value	Share, %
Canada	2,794	16	Japan	2,609	23
Japan	2,208	13	Mexico	1,947	17
Mexico	1,320	8	Germany	1,466	13
Germany	1,212	7	United Kingdom	1,081	10
United Kingdom	1,153	7	Canada	1,035	9

[1] SIC 382.
[2] For definitions of regional groupings, see "Getting the Most Out of *Outlook 2000.*"
[3] Values may not sum to total due to rounding.
Source: U.S. Department of Commerce, Bureau of the Census.

billion in 1999 and are forecast to rise 3 percent to $11.7 billion in the year 2000.

LABORATORY INSTRUMENTS AND APPARATUS

The laboratory instruments industry includes laboratory apparatus and furniture (SIC 3821), analytical instruments (SIC 3826), and optical instruments and lenses (SIC 3827).

Global and Domestic Outlook

The laboratory instruments and apparatus (LI&A) market covers a broad assortment of products that range from large-scale, fully automated robotic laboratory systems to microscopes. The principal products manufactured in the analytical laboratory instruments sector include high-performance liquid chromatographs (HPLC), gas chromatographs, thermal analysis systems, and spectrometers.

The markets for U.S. laboratory instruments and apparatus are highly competitive, globalized, and technologically advanced. Many companies participate in one or more parts of each market segment. Success depends heavily on selling price, the performance capabilities of an instrument, technical support, and aftermarket service. Many larger U.S. companies derive a significant portion of their revenues from international sales and have manufacturing operations throughout the world. Restructuring, consolidation, and mergers and acquisitions are key elements to long-term growth in this increasingly competitive marketplace. Among the major transactions and realignments that took place in 1998 and 1999 were Varian's split into three separate corporations along product lines; EG&G Instruments' purchase of Perkin Elmer's Analytical Instruments Division; the restructuring of Thermo Instrument Systems, the world's largest analytical instruments company; Perkin Elmer's acquisition of PerSeptive Biosystems and its investment in Tecan; Amersham Pharmacia Biotech's purchase of Moleculer Dynamics; Fisher Scientific's purchase of Bioblok; and Roper Industries' acquisition of Varlen's Instruments Division.

The leading U.S. manufacturers of analytical instruments include Thermo Instruments Systems, Hewlett-Packard, Perkin Elmer, Waters Inc., Varian, Sybron, and Beckman Coulter. The chief competitors to U.S. firms are based in Japan, Germany, and the United Kingdom. The largest include Amersham Pharmacia Biotech (United Kingdom), Bruker (Germany), Sartorius (Germany), Kendro (Germany), Shimadzu (Japan), Hitachi (Japan), Horiba (Japan), and JEOL (Japan).

The markets for LI&A products are highly specialized as a result of the differing needs of the industries in which those products are used. LI&A products are used by the pharmaceutical industry for drug research, testing, and quality control; by the clinical diagnostics market, which includes hospital laboratories and physicians' offices; by life science research laboratories, which include corporate, university, and governmental research labs; by the biotechnology industry to study proteins, genomes, peptides, and other biological samples to gain knowledge about diseases and possible treatments and cures; by environmental laboratories for testing air, soil, and water samples for compliance with environmental regulations; by the chemical industry for research and quality control; and by the food and beverage industry for quality control.

The size and growth of the LI&A markets are influenced by a variety of factors, including government funding for basic and disease-related research; spending by biotechnology, pharmaceutical, and chemical companies; the number of new or revised federal, state, local, and foreign environmental regulations; and the level of health care spending.

As a result of the Asian and Latin American economic crises, low commodity prices, and attempts to contain costs among health care providers, industry observers expect short-term growth within the LI&A industry worldwide to be in the low single digits. However, in the long term, industry observers expect an increase in worldwide health care expenditures, a recovery in commodity prices, and increased growth in the economies in Asia and Latin America to stimulate demand for LI&A products, resulting in a 5 percent growth rate by the end of the year 2000. Long-term trends in the life science research industry include the growth in research and development (R&D) funding for new drugs by the pharmaceutical and biotechnology industries and the demand for increased automation and efficiency in the pharmaceutical and biotechnology industries. R&D spending by chemical companies will increase once commodity prices advance significantly.

The field of laboratory automation will continue to be one of the fastest-growing segments, increasing at an annual rate of 15 percent, according to observers, in the industry. Companies that have the ability to automate a wide variety of tests on integrated workstations will have a distinct advantage. The use of advanced software and data output has become an integral part of today's laboratories. Software that can control instruments from different suppliers will be central to the automated laboratories of the future. Microminiaturized analytical devices have the potential to revolutionize chemical and biochemical analysis; some industry representatives refer to these small devices as a lab on a chip.

Standardization of laboratory instruments is a key element to the future of the industry; open architecture and standardization will speed new product development and time to market. This will allow the bigger players to function more as integrators.

Industry and Trade Projections

Shipments by the U.S. laboratory instruments and apparatus industry in 1998 rose an estimated 2 percent over 1997, reaching $13.6 billion in constant dollars (see Table 23-1). The value of U.S. LI&A shipments was estimated to reach $14.1 billion in constant dollars in 1999, an increase of almost 4 percent. In 1998 and the first half of 1999, overall business activity for LI&A companies suffered from weak economic conditions in Asia, Latin America, and Europe. This was offset by stronger growth in the domestic market.

U.S. industry shipments of LI&A are forecast to grow by 4 percent to $14.6 billion in constant dollars in 2000. During the 5-year period ending in 2004, analysts project an annual compound growth rate of 5 percent, with total U.S. industry shipments of LI&A reaching $17.9 billion in constant dollars. However, certain segments—laboratory automation, HPLC and associated software, and thermal analysis equipment—will exhibit double-digit growth through 2004. The need for laboratories to improve efficiency and sample throughput and the need to decrease human error are the driving forces behind the growth of laboratory automation. New sciences, such as genomics and proteinomics are fueling the demand for HPLC, and the search for new and better materials is driving the demand for thermal analysis equipment.

The United States is a net exporter of laboratory instruments and apparatus. In 1998, the United States exported almost $5.8 billion (see Table 23-3) of LI&A, while importing almost $4 billion. Japan is by far the largest export market for U.S. manufacturers. Germany, the United Kingdom, and Canada all received U.S. exports of approximately $500 million each. The United States imported slightly more LI&A from Japan than it exported.

Total U.S. exports of LI&A in 1999 were estimated to rise fractionally to $5.9 billion, while imports were estimated to level off at $4 billion. For the year 2000, exports are forecast to increase at a much faster pace than are imports. The increase

TABLE 23-3: U.S. Trade Patterns in Laboratory Instruments[1] in 1998
(millions of dollars; percent)

Exports			Imports		
Region[2]	Value[3]	Share, %	Region[2]	Value[3]	Share, %
NAFTA	678	12	NAFTA	475	12
Latin America	268	5	Latin America	3	0
Western Europe	2,340	41	Western Europe	1,562	39
Japan/Chinese Economic Area	1,655	29	Japan/Chinese Economic Area	1,565	39
Other Asia	504	9	Other Asia	183	5
Rest of world	317	5	Rest of world	203	5
World	5,763	100	World	3,992	100
Top Five Countries	Value	Share, %	Top Five Countries	Value	Share, %
Japan	1,119	19	Japan	1,194	30
Germany	531	9	Germany	629	16
United Kingdom	486	8	Canada	401	10
Canada	453	8	United Kingdom	315	8
Netherlands	312	5	China	203	5

[1] SIC 3821, 3826, 3827.
[2] For definitions of regional groupings, see "Getting the Most Out of *Outlook 2000.*"
[3] Values may not sum to total due to rounding.
Source: U.S. Department of Commerce, Bureau of the Census.

in exports will be driven by the recovery in Asia and Latin America.

In the first half of 1999, Japan experienced two consecutive quarters of gross domestic product (GDP) growth, a promising sign that the long-awaited recovery had finally begun. Also, Japan must maintain a high level of expenditures for R&D to stay competitive in domestic and overseas markets. The Japanese government has introduced new programs and incentives to encourage and promote basic research. Together with the necessity to stimulate new demand in a weakened economy, these programs and incentives will act as primary drivers to support a comparatively high rate of growth in the market for LI&A. U.S. companies currently command a 60 to 70 percent share of the import market in Japan.

Hong Kong and Taiwan also represent excellent future export opportunities for U.S. companies. Hong Kong has only a few laboratories that provide product safety and international standards certification, and their services generally are considered slow; therefore, manufacturing industry representatives have been urging the Hong Kong government to establish a comprehensive central product testing laboratory. Once built, this laboratory will increase the demand for LI&A. Also, the Hong Kong government is expected to spend more than $1 billion on environmentally related projects in the next 3 years. This huge government expenditure represents outstanding business opportunities for state-of-the-art laboratory instruments. Taiwan has made great efforts to improve its R&D environment. By 2002, more than $14 billion will be devoted to science and technology development. With a number of ongoing and proposed high-tech investment projects, the demand for LI&A will increase.

Germany is the largest export market for U.S.-produced LI&A in Europe. Currently, U.S.-made products command a 40 percent import market share. With Germany's economy expected to grow in the next couple of years, U.S. exports of LI&A will increase. The best sales prospects include laboratory automation technologies, chromatographs, spectrometers, and electrophoresis equipment.

Brazil is the largest export market for LI&A in South America. A strong prospective market for environmental analysis instruments exists because of new Brazilian environmental regulations that should increase the enforcement of environmental regulations and require industry administrators to invest in pollution prevention programs.

Indrek Grabbi, U.S. Department of Commerce, Office of Microelectronics, Medical Equipment and Instrumentation, (202) 482-2846, September 1999.

MEASURING AND CONTROLLING INSTRUMENTS

The measuring and controlling instruments industry includes automatic controls for regulating environments (SIC 3822), process control instruments (SIC 3823), fluid meters and counting devices (SIC 3824), and measuring and controlling devices not elsewhere classified (SIC 3829).

Global and Domestic Outlook

The principal products manufactured by producers of measuring and controlling instruments include process control computers, programmable logic controllers, microprocessor-based distributed control systems, sensors, energy control systems for buildings, flowmeters, level indicators, and pressure gauges. Many of these instruments contain microprocessors that improve the speed, measurement, and process control of these instruments and systems. A recent development is the trend toward integrated products and systems. The enormous impact of personal computers (PCs), computer software, and digital technology is revolutionizing the measuring and controlling industry. The control function is moving rapidly to PC-level systems. The increased use of "intelligent" products is allowing the end user—a manufacturing facility or power plant—to predict problems in advance of costly failures. U.S. companies must continue to invest in key growth technologies such as electronics and software to remain competitive in today's increasingly complex environment.

The keys to growth in today's global marketplace include acceleration of new product introductions and the globalization of the instrument business. Acquisitions, joint ventures, and strategic alliances are critical to American companies that wish to remain competitive in the global marketplace. In 1999, the process control industry saw one of the industry's largest corporate mergers, when Asea Brown Boveri (ABB), a joint venture of companies in Switzerland and Sweden, completed its purchase of the Dutch-based Elsag Bailey, forming ABB/Elsag Baily, one of the world's top suppliers of process control systems, analytical devices, and instrumentation. This trend toward mergers and acquisitions will continue to dominate, with mid-sized players fast disappearing through acquisitions.

The world's leading suppliers of process control and automation technology are the United States, Germany, Japan, and Switzerland. The leading manufacturing companies are ABB/Elsag Bailey (Switzerland), Emerson Electric (United States), Honeywell (United States), Rockwell Automation (United States), Siebe (United Kingdom), Siemens (Germany), Hartmann & Braun (Germany), and Yokogawa (Japan).

Nearly every manufacturing and processing industry around the world requires process control and automation technology. The primary economic driver of this market is industrial capital spending on plant and equipment, particularly in the nondurable goods sector, including chemicals, plastics, pulp and paper, food processing, and petroleum refining. Process control instrumentation also is used heavily by electric and gas utilities and wastewater treatment facilities.

Both globally and domestically, the process control industry has been and continues to be hampered by low commodity prices in the oil, chemical, and pulp and paper industries. As long as commodity prices stay low, these industries will not expand or update their production facilities. Recently, the price of oil started creeping upward, and that bodes well for the petroleum industry. Once commodity prices climb higher, this should stimulate higher capital investment by the nondurable goods industries in plant and equipment, which in turn will result in increased orders and sales for the process control industry.

The market for controls designed for monitoring and controlling residential and commercial environments is driven primarily by the level of construction of commercial buildings and residential housing and secondarily by the refurbishment of existing buildings and houses. The brisk pace of new home and commercial building construction in the United States has been offset by the stagnant residential and commercial market in the European Union countries and the complete stoppage of new home and business construction in Asia. The leading suppliers of commercial and residential controls are Honeywell (United States), Emerson Electric (United States), Johnson Controls (United States), Siemens (Germany), and Siebe (United Kingdom).

Industry and Trade Projections

Shipments by the U.S. measuring and controlling instruments industry in 1998 rose an estimated 3 percent over 1997, reaching $20.1 billion in constant dollars (see Table 23-1). The value of U.S. measuring and controlling industry shipments was estimated to reach $20.7 billion in 1999, an increase of 3 percent. The sluggishness of industry shipments in 1998 and the first half of 1999 is attributed to the Asian and Latin American economic crises. Even though current growth in Asia has been severely dampened by economic weakness, U.S. companies should see long-term shipments to developing countries grow faster than they do in the domestic market. Developing countries still need to modernize their plants to be competitive in world markets. As developing countries become more environmentally conscious, the demand for state-of-the-art process control instrumentation will grow, especially in the areas of wastewater facilities, electric utilities, and nondurable goods manufacturing plants.

U.S. industry shipments of measuring and controlling instruments are forecast to grow 3 percent to $21.2 billion in 2000. During the 5-year period ending in 2004, analysts project an annual compound growth rate of 4 percent, with total U.S. industry shipments of measuring and controlling instruments reaching $24.1 billion.

The United States is a net exporter of measuring and controlling instruments. In 1998, the United States exported over $6.3 billion (see Table 23-4) of measuring and controlling instruments while importing almost $4.8 billion. Canada is by far the largest export destination for measuring and controlling instruments; the United States imports the greatest amount of measuring and controlling instruments from Mexico. In 1998, U.S. exports to Asia were down considerably from 1997 as a result of the stagnation in the major end-use markets, such as chemicals and petroleum. Exports to Japan and the Chinese Economic Area declined 14 percent, while exports to the remaining Asian markets were down 23 percent from 1997. This downward trend in exports to Asia was expected to continue through 1999, with some moderate prospects for growth returning in 2000.

Total U.S. exports of measuring and controlling instruments in 1999 were expected to stabilize at $6.4 billion, while imports were expected to register a small gain to an estimated $4.9 billion. For the year 2000, U.S. exports of measuring and controlling instruments are forecast to show an upward trend (see Table 23-1) to $6.6 billion.

In the short term, Ireland, Spain, and Colombia are growing markets for U.S. exports of measuring and controlling instruments. For U.S. companies with a longer-term strategy, Taiwan, Singapore, and Malaysia offer growth prospects as well, though they will need time to recover from Asia's financial crisis.

The total market size for process control instruments in Ireland was $223 million in 1998. Process control instruments constitute an integral element in Irish manufacturing processes.

TABLE 23-4: U.S. Trade Patterns in Measuring and Controlling Instruments[1] in 1998
(millions of dollars; percent)

Exports			Imports		
Region[2]	Value[3]	Share, %	Region[2]	Value[3]	Share, %
NAFTA	2,667	42	NAFTA	2,179	46
Latin America	383	6	Latin America	90	2
Western Europe	1,588	25	Western Europe	1,224	26
Japan/Chinese Economic Area	694	11	Japan/Chinese Economic Area	983	21
Other Asia	536	8	Other Asia	241	5
Rest of world	477	8	Rest of world	62	1
World	6,346	100	World	4,781	100
Top Five Countries	Value	Share, %	Top Five Countries	Value	Share, %
Canada	1,864	29	Mexico	1,715	36
Mexico	803	13	Japan	667	14
United Kingdom	380	6	Canada	464	10
Germany	360	6	Germany	382	8
Japan	354	6	United Kingdom	374	8

[1] SIC 3822, 3823, 3824, 3829.
[2] For definitions of regional groupings, see "Getting the Most Out of *Outlook 2000*."
[3] Values may not sum to total due to rounding.
Source: U.S. Department of Commerce, Bureau of the Census.

During the last couple of years, the Irish government has provided many benefits to foreign companies that are willing to invest and locate their manufacturing facilities in that country. This has allowed the chemical, pharmaceutical, food processing, and gas and power generation industries to expand substantially. The pharmaceutical sector has 40 international manufacturing subsidiaries. There is an estimated replacement cost of $3.3 billion for capital investment in this sector; this means that when the pharmaceutical plants upgrade their manufacturing facilities, there will be demand for process controls. Sales are expected to be good for programmable logic controllers, control valve systems, pressure gauges, and thermostats.

In Spain, the total market size of process control instruments in 1998 was $1.5 billion. There is a great demand for high-quality process control instruments that is driven by the increasing automation of Spanish industry and the need to upgrade current infrastructures while protecting the environment. Good prospects can be found in the following Spanish industrial sectors: food processing, chemicals, pharmaceuticals, utilities, machine tools, and pollution control.

Colombia's process control instruments market was $78 million in 1998. Intensive oil and gas exploration, expansion and modernization of refineries and other petrochemical facilities, and the increasing use of electric power that calls for the development of several new hydro and thermal projects will spur demand for process control instruments. The most promising products for export include flow and liquid level controls, pressure and temperature instruments, control software, programmable logic controllers, digital displays, and transducers.

Indrek Grabbi, U.S. Department of Commerce, Office of Microelectronics, Medical Equipment and Instrumentation, (202) 482-2846, September 1999.

ELECTRICAL TEST AND MEASURING INSTRUMENTS

The electrical test and measuring (ET&M) (SIC 3825) instruments subsector includes electrical integrating instruments; test equipment for testing electrical, radio, and communications circuits and motors; and instruments to measure electricity.

Global and Domestic Outlook

The electrical test and measuring (ET&M) instruments market covers a broad assortment of products purchased by a diverse range of industries, mostly in the fast-growing information technology area. Products vary from simple analog voltage meters costing a few dollars to sophisticated multimillion-dollar digital diagnostic equipment, with the high-value products representing an increasing share of U.S. shipments in the ET&M subsector. Customers span the computer equipment, automotive, consumer electronics, telecommunications services and equipment, and semiconductor industries. ET&M applications range from R&D, to manufacturing, to field installation and maintenance testing.

The United States is a net exporter of ET&M (see Table 23-5). U.S. ET&M firms are especially competitive in high-end technologies, notably high-speed digital and analog-to-digital ET&M equipment. U.S. ET&M equipment enjoys a well-established reputation for product reliability.

The chief competitors to U.S. ET&M firms are based in Japan, Germany, and the United Kingdom. In recent years, several prominent U.S. ET&M firms have acquired or merged with European firms. Import statistics for Europe include imports from European subsidiaries of U.S. ET&M firms.

The ET&M market is characterized by a high degree of product segmentation. More than 350 U.S. firms manufacture

TABLE 23-5: U.S. Trade Patterns in Instruments to Measure Electricity[1] in 1998
(millions of dollars; percent)

Exports			Imports		
Region[2]	Value[3]	Share, %	Region[2]	Value[3]	Share, %
NAFTA	769	15	NAFTA	327	13
Latin America	281	6	Latin America	6	0
Western Europe	1,430	28	Western Europe	1,127	45
Japan/Chinese Economic Area	1,312	26	Japan/Chinese Economic Area	844	34
Other Asia	989	20	Other Asia	72	3
Rest of world	271	5	Rest of world	111	4
World	5,052	100	World	2,487	100
Top Five Countries	Value	Share, %	Top Five Countries	Value	Share, %
Japan	735	15	Japan	748	30
Canada	477	9	Germany	455	18
Taiwan	338	7	United Kingdom	392	16
Germany	321	6	Canada	170	7
Mexico	291	6	Mexico	157	6

[1] SIC 3825.
[2] For definitions of regional groupings, see "Getting the Most Out of *Outlook 2000.*"
[3] Values may not sum to total due to rounding.
Source: U.S. Department of Commerce, Bureau of the Census.

ET&M instruments. Only three or four of those firms are large enough to sell across product segments. Most firms are small, and many have been successful in exploiting emerging market niches and have developed customized technological solutions, spurring innovation in the industry. At the same time that customer requirements are becoming more specialized, certain underlying ET&M technologies are converging, paralleling the trend toward digital integration in information technology. ET&M firms must deepen their technical expertise and extend it to new product segments.

Industry and Trade Projections

Analysts expect the U.S. ET&M industry to grow a modest 2.9 percent in 2000 (see Table 23-1). During the 5-year period ending in 2004, however, analysts project a more robust compound annual growth rate of 8 percent.

The largest category of ET&M instruments, accounting for roughly half the total of U.S. ET&M shipments, is automatic test equipment (ATE). ATE is utilized to test semiconductors, loaded printed circuit boards, and other electronic component assemblies, such as computer disk drives. Demand for ATE should continue to be strong over the next 5 years.

Communications test equipment, accounting for roughly 12 percent of U.S. ET&M shipments, includes network analyzers, fiber-optic test equipment, and wireless test equipment. Communications test equipment will continue to grow faster than will other ET&M subsectors in response to growth in the Internet, wireless, and other communications markets. The next largest category of ET&M, oscilloscopes and spectrum analyzers, which are used by many electronic industries, should experience average growth in that period. Other ET&M products that will experience continued growth are digital voltage measuring equipment; logic analyzers, microprocessor development systems, and frequency synthesizers; and portable analyzers for internal combustion engines.

Although the United States enjoys a substantial trade surplus in ET&M instruments, in recent years the rate of growth in imports has outpaced the growth rate in exports, and analysts expect this trend to continue over the next 5 years. The strength of the dollar has made U.S. products more expensive in Asian countries suffering from financial crises while offering lower-priced Asian goods in the U.S. market.

Nevertheless, Asia has been the fastest-growing market for U.S. ET&M instruments. The semiconductor industry's demand for ATE in that region is the dominant driver for U.S. exports to Asia. The combination of the semiconductor industry downturn and the Asian financial crisis hurt U.S. ET&M exports in the late 1990s, especially in the major markets of Japan and South Korea. Over the next 5 years, Japan, South Korea, and Taiwan will remain the largest Asian markets, but analysts expect that growth will be fastest in Malaysia and the Philippines, which were less severely affected by the financial crisis.

The product mix of U.S. ET&M exports to Europe is more diversified than that to Asia. Germany will remain the largest European market in the next 5 years, but analysts forecast that the Netherlands will have the fastest rate of growth in Europe.

Michael Andrews, U.S. Department of Commerce, Office of Microelectronics, Medical Equipment and Instrumentation, (202) 482-2795, September 1999.

■ REFERENCES

Analytical Instrument Industry Report, Publisher, Dr. Gordon Wilkinson, P.O. Box 78, East Grinstead, United Kingdom, RH19 2YW. (01342) 835-935.

Analytical Instruments & Life Science Systems Association, 225 Reinekers Lane, Suite 625, Alexandria, VA 22314. (703) 836-1360. Fax: (703) 836-6644.

Automation Research Corporation, 3 Allied Drive, Dedham, MA 02026. (781) 461-9100.

Chemical Engineering, The McGraw Hill Companies, Inc., 1221 Avenue of the Americas, New York, NY 10020. (212) 512-2000.

Chemical Market Reporter, Schnell Publishing Co., 2 Rector Street, New York, NY 10006. (212) 791-4200. Fax: (212) 791-4310.

Control Engineering, Cahners Publishing Co., 8773 South Ridgeline Boulevard, Highlands Ranch, CO 80126. (303) 470-4445.

Control Magazine, Putnam Publishing Company, 55 W. Pierce Road, Suite 301, Itasca, IL 60143. (630) 467-1300. Fax: (630) 467-1124.

Instrument Business Outlook, Strategic Directions International, Inc., 6242 Westchester Parkway, Suite 100, Los Angeles, CA 90045. (310) 641-4982. Fax: (310) 641-8851.

Laboratory Equipment, Cahners Publishing Co., 301 Gibralter Drive, Box 650, Morris Plains, NJ 07950. (973) 292-5100. Fax: (973) 539-3476.

Laboratory Products Association, 225 Reinekers Lane, Suite 625, Alexandria, VA 22314. (703) 836-1360. Fax: (703) 836-6644.

LG-GC, The Magazine of Separation Science, Advanstar Communications Inc., 131 West First Street, Duluth, MN 55802. (218) 723-9477.

McMahon Technology Associates, 135 Fort Lee Road, Leonia, NJ 07605. (201) 585-2050. Fax: (201) 585-1968.

Measurement, Control & Automation Association, P.O. Box 3698, Williamsburg, VA 23187. (757) 258-3100. Fax: (757) 258-9066.

Measurement & Control News, Measurements & Data Corp., 2994 West Liberty Avenue, Pittsburgh, PA 15216. (412) 343-9666. Fax: (412) 343-9685.

Research & Development, Cahners Publishing Co., 2000 Clearwater Drive, Oak Brook, IL 60523. (630) 320-7164. Fax: (630) 320-7160.

Selected Instruments and Related Products, Current Industrial Report (MA)-38B, 1997, Bureau of the Census, U.S. Department of Commerce, Washington DC, 20233. (301) 457-4817.

Test & Measurement World, 275 Washington Street, Newton, MA 02458. (617) 558-4671. www.tm.world.com.

■ RELATED CHAPTERS

6: Construction
16: Microelectronics
18: Production Machinery
19: Electrical Equipment
21: Aerospace
27: Computer Equipment
31: Telecommunications and Navigation Equipment
36: Motor Vehicles
38: Household Consumer Durables
44: Medical and Dental Instruments and Supplies

PHOTOGRAPHIC EQUIPMENT AND SUPPLIES
Economic and Trade Trends

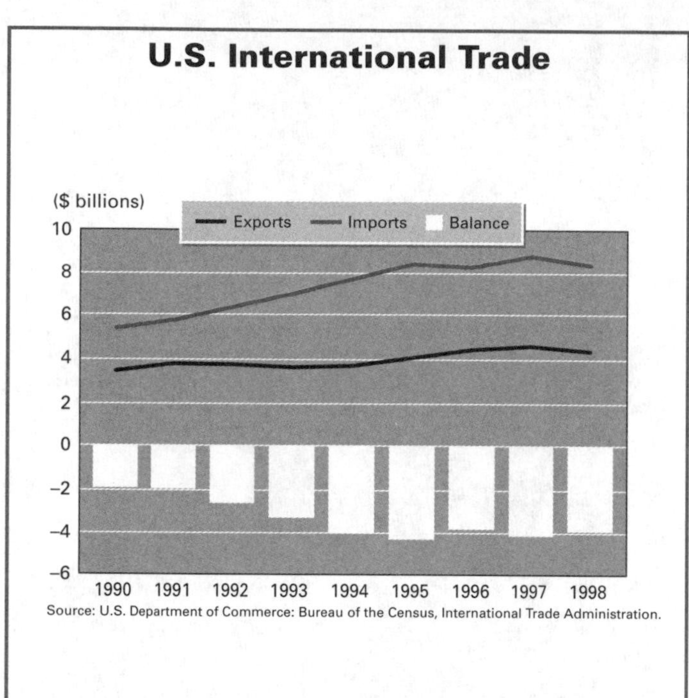

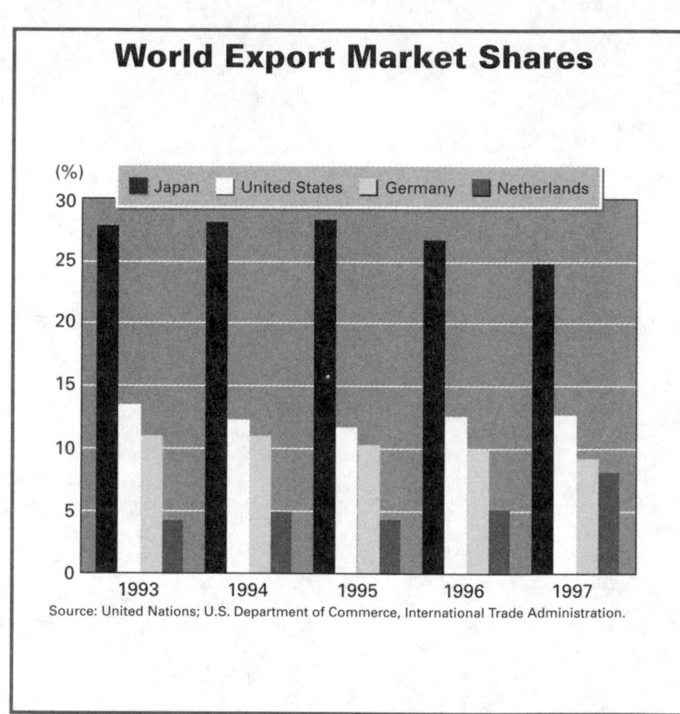

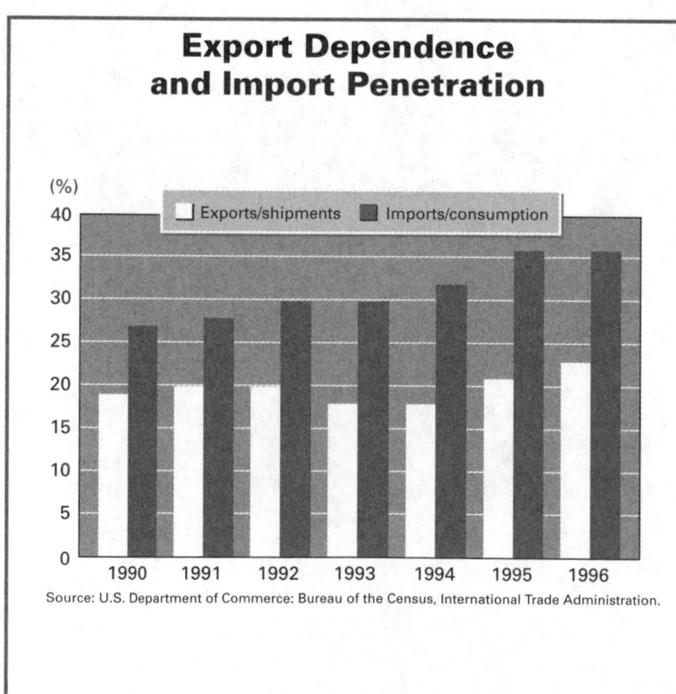

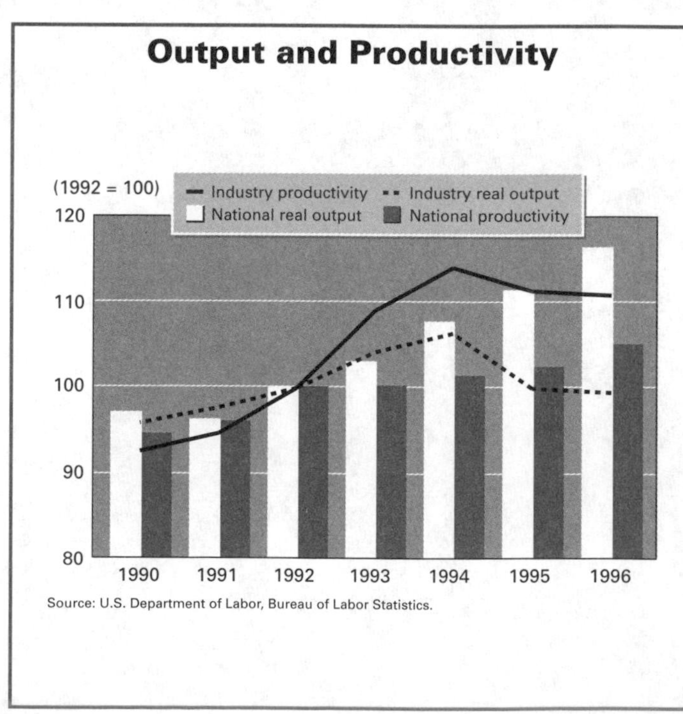

See "Getting the Most Out of *Outlook 2000*" for definitions of terms.

24

Photographic Equipment and Supplies

INDUSTRY DEFINITION The U.S. photographic equipment and supplies industry (SIC 3861) consists of manufacturers of photographic equipment, accessories, and parts such as still and motion picture camera and projection apparatus; photofinishing equipment; photocopy and microfilm equipment; and sensitized film, paper, plates, and prepared photographic chemicals. Establishments engaged primarily in developing film and making photographic prints and enlargements for the trade or the general public are classified under SIC 7384, photofinishing laboratories. Establishments engaged in the manufacture of digital cameras, scanners, and printers are classified under SIC 3577, other computer peripheral equipment.

FACTORS AFFECTING FUTURE INDUSTRY GROWTH

Global Industry Trends

Traditional photographic, digital imaging, and computer technologies have contributed to a change in direction for the photographic equipment and supplies industry. Both silver halide photographic technologies and digital imaging have created a broad array of products that serve a diverse set of end-use markets and customers worldwide. Overseas demand for photographic products remained soft in 1998–1999 because of weak economies and sluggish demand in foreign markets. Consumers delayed spending on leisure goods, and business investment failed to recover. For example, Japan's photographic industry's shipments dropped 9 percent and its consumer photographic market declined 3 percent in 1998. Similarly, the economies of eastern Europe continued to experience weakness. The economies of Latin American and European Union countries fared better and had pockets of growth for certain photographic products. For example, U.S. film exports to Europe were down, but increases were recorded for Latin America. The reverse was true for exports of U.S. still picture equipment, which declined to Latin America but rose modestly to Europe.

The U.S. amateur consumer market gained momentum and benefited from popular products such as the Advanced Photo System (APS) and single-use cameras (SUCs) and the emerging use of on-line storage and access of photographic images. Demand continued to grow for new technologies such as digital cameras and imaging software. In business and professional markets, traditional output in the form of printed documents, photocopying, and faxes is still popular despite the use of electronic means of communications such as E-mail and the Internet. However, to remain competitive, copier suppliers have redefined themselves and expanded their ability to incorporate digital and color technologies. Multifunctional peripheral products (MFPs), for example, made gains in small business markets, where space and budget constraints are significant. MFPs can perform two or more of the following functions: printing, copying, faxing, and scanning.

The recent influx of new digital technology into the photographic marketplace has presented the industry with a unique set of challenges and opportunities. To improve global competitiveness, companies continue to form strategic alliances with firms in the industry, but those companies also are participating in mergers and acquisitions with suppliers in the electronics and imaging sectors. It is common to see alliances formed among firms that range from component manufacturers such as Intel to Internet service providers such as America Online. Because of the global nature of the industry, partnerships are formed with both domestic and foreign firms. For example, consumer choices have expanded with the introduction of digital on-site minilab equipment. As part of its strategy to increase its presence in the on-site minilab market in the United States, Konica of Japan agreed to sell three wholesale photofinishing labs to Qualex, the wholesale photofinishing subsidiary of the Eastman Kodak Company. Mergers such as the one between the Gretag Imaging Group (Switzerland) and Raster Graphics (United States) are allowing companies to redefine and expand their focus on global manufacturing and marketing. Gretag focuses on large format production, digital printing systems, and supplies for the professional laboratory segment. Its investment in Raster Graphics gives Gretag access to new technologies and allows it to expand into related segments such as the graphic arts.

Meanwhile, many industry observers see Asia as a developing photographic market with huge long-term opportunities for growth. CPAC of the United States opened a photographic chemicals manufacturing plant in Thailand to deal with its growing market share in that region. Kodak plans to invest $1 billion in China over the next several years for joint venture manufacturing and to expand distribution and marketing activities for its photographic products. However, offshore manufacturing in developing markets can present risks as well as opportunities. The uncertain and changing economic climates in some developing markets, the need to identify and train source suppliers, and foreign environmental issues can slow a company's investment plans. For example, one U.S. firm had to close an x-ray film plant in China because new wastewater disposal laws made that factory unprofitable.

The use of electronic commerce through Web sites, virtual stores, and on-line catalogs to promote, buy, and sell photographic products and services should continue to expand. For many businesses, experimenting with virtual locations or using stock photo background shots instead of going on location can be a time- and money-saving process. Stock photography was traditionally a trade tool, but now consumers can use stock photos to make brochures, Web sites, newsletters, E-mail greetings, screen savers, and school reports.

The convergence of computer technology with photography also can be seen in the growing popularity of on-line photo services that have expanded opportunities for equipment and film manufacturers, retailers, and photofinishers. For example, on-line photo albums can be used for any event. They allow any number of customers in different locations to view and purchase photographs by using a secure Web-connected computer and a password. Some mail order photofinishing operations have expanded their offerings to include the scanning, posting, and storage of photos on an Internet server. Prints can be purchased, stored on a floppy disk or photo CD, or printed onto products such as T-shirts, calendars, and coffee mugs. Seattle FilmWorks, a leading mail order photofinisher and image management company, recently announced that it is storing more than 30 million personal photographs on-line.

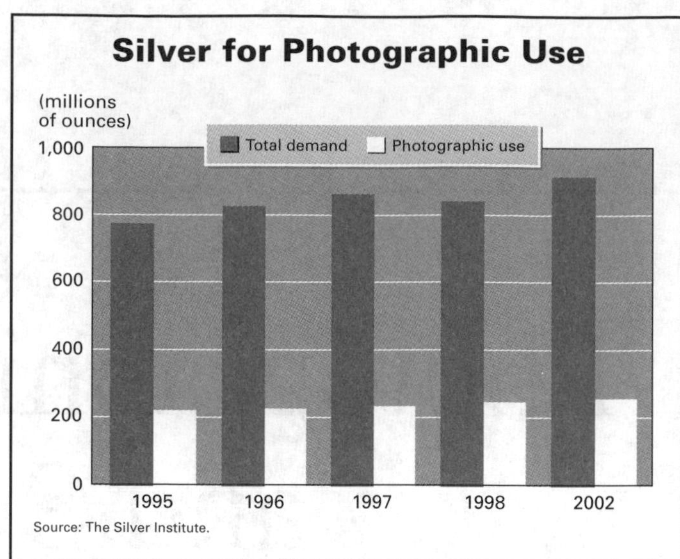

FIGURE 24-1

Silver halide photography continues to be the foundation of the industry, as APS gains momentum among amateur photographers. SUC sales continue at double-digit rates, and color negative film still accounts for about 90 percent of total film sales. These trends support statistics released by the Silver Institute that show that silver use by the photographic industry increased nearly 6 percent to 245 million ounces worldwide in 1998, although total demand for silver fabrication slipped 2 percent. In addition to the consumer segment, increases in silver consumption were noted in other photographic areas, including medical and dental x-ray films, motion picture film, photographic paper, and the graphic arts sector. Photography is one of the top application areas for silver, accounting for 29 percent of total demand in 1998. Other end-use categories include industrial applications, jewelry and silverware, and commemorative coins and medals (see Figure 24-1).

The United States accounted for 36 percent of world demand for silver for photographic use in 1998. U.S. demand has been spurred by the continued expansion of Japanese film and paper production facilities in the United States and the subsequent sourcing of raw materials from domestic suppliers. Japan was the second largest user, with about 25 percent of the world total. In Europe, Belgium was the major user of silver for photographic purposes, with about 11 percent of the world total.

Domestic Trends

Shipments. Despite the industry's diverse array of products and end-use markets that generally help offset periods of weak demand, U.S. photographic industry shipments in constant dollars declined 5 percent to an estimated $24.9 billion in 1999 (see Table 24-1). Although sales increases were recorded in the area of digital imaging, products such as digital cameras and color printers are classified as computer peripheral equipment and thus are not counted in photographic industry shipments. Opportunities for growth in traditional photographic products is dependent

TABLE 24-1: Photographic Equipment and Supplies (SIC 3861) Trends and Forecasts
(millions of dollars except as noted)

	1992	1993	1994	1995	1996	1997[1]	1998[1]	1999[2]	2000[3]	Percent Change 97–98	98–99	99–00	96–00[4]
Industry data													
Value of shipments[5]	22,119	22,368	23,261	21,654	22,297	23,500	23,500	22,000	22,500	0.0	–6.4	2.3	0.2
Value of shipments (1992$)	22,119	23,276	24,825	23,135	23,796	25,850	26,100	24,900	25,400	1.0	–4.6	2.0	1.6
Total employment (thousands)	77.3	75.7	63.9	61.1	60.7	61.3	58.5	54.0	51.0	–4.6	–7.7	–5.6	–4.3
Production workers (thousands)	39.2	38.0	34.7	35.2	35.7	37.0	35.0	32.5	31.0	–5.4	–7.1	–4.6	–3.5
Average hourly earnings ($)	14.65	14.64	15.82	16.41	16.72								
Capital expenditures	805	775	753	746	724								
Product data													
Value of shipments[5]	18,861	19,686	20,227	19,159	19,129	20,450	20,450	19,150	19,125	0.0	–6.4	–0.1	–0.0
Value of shipments (1992$)	18,861	20,485	21,586	20,469	20,415	22,400	22,700	21,600	21,600	1.3	–4.8	0.0	1.4
Trade data													
Value of imports	6,408	7,024	7,711	8,408	8,276	8,784	8,368	7,900	8,000	–4.7	–5.6	1.3	–0.8
Value of exports	3,762	3,637	3,705	4,080	4,460	4,628	4,387	4,200	4,325	–5.2	–4.3	3.0	–0.8

[1] Estimate except imports and exports.
[2] Estimate.
[3] Forecast.
[4] Compound annual rate.
[5] For a definition of industry versus product values, see "Getting the Most Out of *Outlook 2000*."
Source: U.S. Department of Commerce: Bureau of the Census; International Trade Administration.

on the development of new and innovative products, particularly those which combine the best of silver halide and digital technologies. Opportunities also exist in many developing regions where markets are small and penetration is low. The recent economic crisis in developing markets such as Asia and eastern Europe had a negative impact on U.S. photographic industry shipments, since exports to those regions declined 16 percent and 33 percent, respectively, in 1998. Together, those regions accounted for 25 percent of U.S. photographic exports. The downturn in demand for U.S. photographic products in overseas markets also can be seen in the ratio of exports to shipments, which steadily increased between 1994 and 1997 to nearly 23 percent but dipped slightly to about 22 percent in 1999. Growing U.S. demand for new and expensive digital photofinishing equipment has helped boost shipments because a single piece of that equipment can cost about $250,000. Another contributor to U.S.-based shipments is production by foreign firms investing in this country. For example, Fuji Photo Film continues to expand its manufacturing complex in South Carolina.

Employment. After a slight increase in 1997, employment in the U.S. photographic industry resumed its downward course in 1998 and 1999, dropping from its historical peak of 119,300 workers in 1982 to about 54,000 in 1999. Production workers accounted for about 60 percent of total employment, reflecting companies' efforts to downsize management, administrative, and sales personnel. The ratio of production workers to total employment traditionally has been about 50 percent. Recent employment cutbacks have served as a way for U.S. photographic equipment suppliers to reduce costs and improve productivity and operating margins while strengthening their position in the face of strong price competition and intensifying sales competition from computer and consumer electronics firms.

Trade Patterns. U.S. photographic exports were expected to decline for the second consecutive year, dropping 4 percent to about $4.2 billion in 1999 after declining 5 percent in 1998. Despite the overall slowdown in export growth, exports to four of the top five destinations, which accounted for over half the export total, increased in 1998 (see Figure 24-2). However, those gains were offset by steep declines for countries in Asia, eastern Europe, and the European Union as a result of adverse economic conditions. In Asia, for example, photographic exports to Thailand dropped 54 percent, those to South Korea fell 45 percent, and those to Hong Kong were

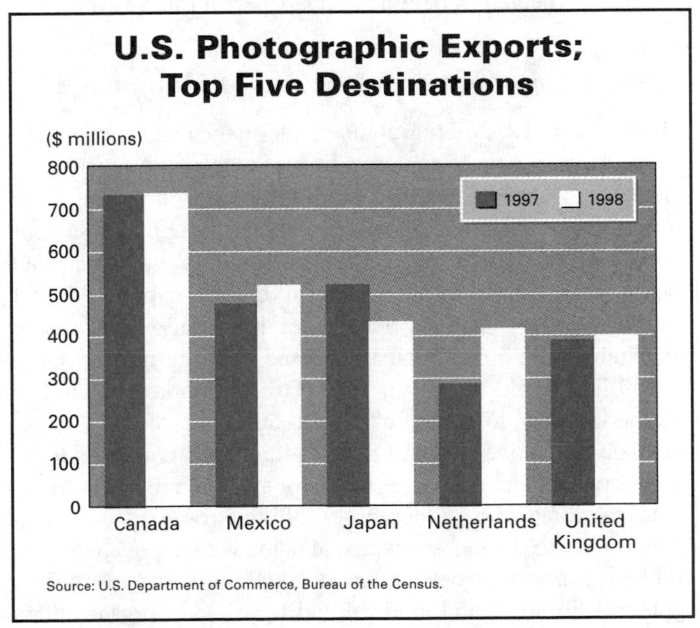

FIGURE 24-2

down 23 percent. The European Union countries received one-third of U.S. photographic exports. Within that region, shipments to Belgium and Italy were down 68 percent and 32 percent, respectively.

Photographic exports in all product groups declined in 1998, with the exception of photocopying and microfilming equipment, which rose 21 percent to $1 billion. Another bright spot was exports of digital cameras, which increased nearly 10 percent to $75 million. The top five destinations, which accounted for 55 percent of digital camera exports, were the United Kingdom, Japan, Canada, Germany, and Mexico.

In terms of its position in global trade, the United States continues to rank as the second largest exporting nation after Japan, with 12 percent of the world export market.

Photographic imports are an important factor in the U.S. market and account for about one-third of domestic consumption. Asia is traditionally the largest supplier and consistently provides about 70 percent of the import total. Japan continues to be the principal source of photographic products, but its share of total imports declined from 61 percent in 1992 to 46 percent in 1998. Meanwhile, a significant increase in imports from other Asian countries has occurred as Japan has continued to move its production of photographic products offshore. Thailand, Taiwan, and Malaysia are among the production sites selected because of lower labor rates, but China has emerged as a principal supplier of U.S. photographic products and now holds the number two position. Between 1992 and 1998, China's share of U.S. photographic imports rose from 1 percent to 14 percent, consisting primarily of still picture equipment and photocopiers. Since the U.S. market experienced a period of contraction with selected areas of growth, total U.S. photographic imports fell nearly 5 percent to $8.4 billion in 1998. Imports were expected to remain soft in 1999, declining another 6 percent to $7.9 billion. As a result, the 1999 U.S. trade deficit in photographic equipment and supplies was expected to decline about 7 percent to $3.7 billion.

Office Equipment and Document Management

Micrographics. Micrographics is an image and storage technology system that is dependent on photographic processing. This technology maintains a prominent position in the document imaging and management market through the sale of existing products. However, it has been paired with electronic document imaging to form hybrid computer-based digital imaging systems. The Association of Information and Image Management estimated that film-based imaging represented a $1.8 billion world market in 1999. Overall market growth has declined slowly in some sectors because microfilm is being used less for active retrieval needs, although it continues to be an effective and inexpensive choice for archival records storage. Concern about the vulnerability of electronic records and changes in hardware, software, and media will keep micrographics as a storage option. Financial institutions, government agencies, libraries, and medical and health care organizations are among the top buyers of micrographics equipment.

Photocopiers. Analog photocopiers have been the mainstay of office copying since their invention and accounted for about 95 percent of U.S. photocopier shipments in 1997. Since this market segment is mature, products and pricing practices are similar among producers and original equipment manufacturing is a typical way to supply the market. However, end users are embracing digital copier technologies at an increasing rate, since those technologies offer many advantages over analog machines and have become less expensive in recent years. Digital copiers scan the original and convert the image into digital data, allowing the user to edit or manipulate, print, copy, store, retrieve, and transmit electronically. As a result, copier manufacturers are incorporating more digital models into their product mix. This transition from analog to digital technology also is promoting the integration of copiers with stand-alone office equipment, such as printers and scanners, to take advantage of electronic imaging and networking capabilities. While the overall copier market is expected to remain relatively flat between 1998 and 2000 at about 1.7 million units, industry sources indicate that the growth rate for digital copier shipments will outpace that for analog shipments and that digital could become the dominant technology by the year 2001 (see Figure 24-3).

Digital copier shipments in the United States were expected to more than double the 1997 level to reach 228,000 units in 1998, according to the International Data Corporation (IDC), a Massachusetts-based research firm. Canon, Ricoh, and Xerox are among the leading producers of this equipment. Digital copiers increasingly will be used to support and enhance the productivity of office environments, since they can serve as network peripherals. This trend supports an industry shift toward multifunctional peripherals from traditional stand-alone copiers and printers.

Color. While prices for color copiers are falling, speeds are increasing. Low-end color copiers can sell for about $500, while high-end models sell for over $100,000. However, most

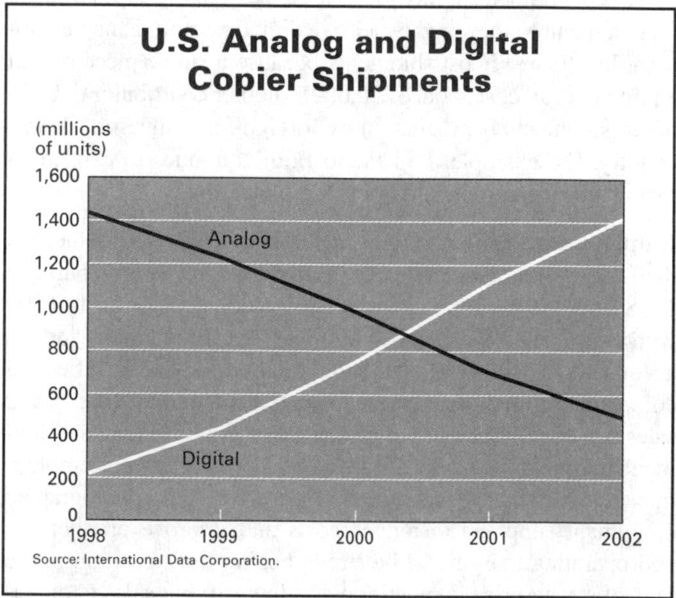

FIGURE 24-3

models sell within the price range of $25,000 to $40,000 and represent a significant price disparity compared with midvolume monochrome copiers that cost less than $10,000. Color laser technology is faster and more costly and offers a higher image quality than does inkjet, but copy resolution on some inkjet models is improving and end-use applications will determine the level of acceptability. In terms of speed, color copiers range between 2 and 40 pages per minute (ppm), with most models operating between 3 and 15 ppm. Another expense that often is overlooked in evaluating color copier prices is the cost for consumable supplies such as toner cartridges and specialty paper. Color output traditionally has been a niche item in offices because of the cost, but the use of color will become more widespread as prices continue to fall and business users reevaluate its benefits. For example, the increased use of color technologies on the desktop (charts, graphs, Web pages) and the preference for color presentations, reports, newsletters, and marketing materials have led to the gradual integration of color into a variety of business documents. CAP Ventures, a Massachusetts-based research firm, estimated that about 2 billion impressions were made by color copiers and printers in 1998 and projects that this number may quintuple by the year 2001. In professional photographic laboratories, digital color laser copiers represent about 80 percent of small-format copiers. Photographic-quality copiers have an almost 20 percent unit share. When it comes to large-format printing, over 40 percent of labs have color copiers and/or printers, according to the Photo Marketing Association International.

Multifunctional Peripherals. Since multifunctional devices can combine copying, printing, scanning, and faxing, many office products are being designed with computer network capabilities to increase productivity for corporate work groups. However, MFPs have a special appeal for small offices and home offices (SOHO) because of their smaller footprint and convenience, competitive prices, and ongoing performance improvements. According to CAP Ventures, the SOHO market is the fastest-growing market segment for office equipment, supplies, and services and will account for 25 percent of some consumable sales, such as inkjet replacement cartridges and cut sheet paper. MFPs used in the SOHO market typically range in price from $400 to $1,000. IDC estimates that MFP shipments to the home office segment totaled about 1 million units in 1998. The total U.S. MFP market increased 51 percent from 1.8 million units in 1997 to 2.6 million units in 1998. Similarly, the value of MFP shipments rose 61 percent from about $3 billion in 1997 to nearly $5 billion in 1998. Increased shipments of digital copiers in multifunction configurations is one factor that is contributing to ongoing growth in the market. Another factor is the change from laser to inkjet printing for low-end multifunctional products, which has resulted in lower prices and thus higher demand. In terms of technology, inkjet MFPs accounted for 58 percent of unit shipments, followed by laser-based units with 28 percent and thermal-transfer-based devices with 14 percent.

The MFP market historically has been a retail-oriented, small office–based market with most equipment sold directly by company sales branches or through photocopier channels of distribution. Retail channels work well for products that are priced under $1,000 and require minimal service and support. However, as they expand their product lines with more expensive, higher-speed models, including those with color capability, manufacturers have taken steps to broaden channels of distribution to include value-added reseller channels and computer superstores that use high-volume sales and large inventories to keep prices low. Also, suppliers have established separate divisions to market digital products and better understand and respond to customers' concerns regarding digital technologies.

Document Management. Document management consists of a broad range of associated technologies that are combined to organize and manage information. This process includes the operations of capture, retrieval, dissemination, printing, archiving, amending, and integration of documents. Since documents today can include text, data, images, and sound, a broad array of products are needed to manage work flow, including scanners, optical character recognition devices, computers and software, micrographics equipment and film, optical and magnetic media, and printers. The Internet is also playing a key role in document storage, retrieval, and dissemination.

Opportunities for sales exist in the area of document management because most corporations continue to store documents on paper despite efforts to move toward the paperless office. According to the IDC, the worldwide document management market was expected to reach $4 billion after rising 36 percent in 1999. A breakdown of the market by category shows that services accounted for about one-half the market revenues and increased at a rate of 39 percent in 1999. In fact, service providers are expected to have an increasingly significant impact on the overall market in administering document management as it becomes more widely accepted and is used increasingly with Web infrastructures. Sales in the software segment increased 29 percent and represented about 20 percent of revenues. Hardware and maintenance revenues together accounted for about 25 percent of total revenues and grew 35 percent and 40 percent, respectively, in 1999. The U.S. market for document management equipment, software, maintenance, and services was expected to increase 33 percent to about $2.7 billion in 1999. The United States is the largest document management market, with about 65 percent of worldwide revenues. Other regional markets are expected to outpace U.S. market development over the next few years as suppliers take advantage of growth opportunities in foreign markets (see Table 24-2).

Consumer Photography

Cameras. Innovative cameras that are convenient, easy to use, and affordable, coupled with a strong U.S. economy, stimulated renewed interest in picture taking in 1998 and 1999. According to the Photo Marketing Association International (PMAI), U.S. traditional still camera sales increased 5 percent to 16.4 million units in 1998 and revenues rose 14 percent to $1.6 billion, reflecting the higher average cost of APS cameras.

TABLE 24-2: Worldwide Electronic Document Management Revenues by Region
(millions of dollars)

Region	1998	1999	2000	2001	2002
North America	1,996	2,658	3,551	4,653	6,070
Latin America	101	146	209	291	392
Europe	677	954	1,309	1,745	2,323
Asia-Pacific	158	231	324	436	583
Rest of world	48	69	104	145	191
Total	2,979	4,057	5,498	7,271	9,560

Source: International Data Corporation.

The APS was introduced nearly 4 years ago with sluggish sales and limited advertising initially but is gaining in popularity and thus has higher demand. APS camera sales increased 29 percent to 3 million units and more than doubled their share of cameras sold to account for 19 percent of total shipments in the United States in 1998. The 24mm silver-based system is designed with drop-in film loading, a choice of three print formats, index prints instead of negatives, and the ability to link to other capabilities, including image scanning, editing, and transmission by computer.

The APS format met resistance at first from the film processing segment because of those cameras' slow sales growth and the need to invest to upgrade photofinishing equipment. That attitude slowed the APS penetration rate because of limited processing outlets, particularly on-site processing. In 1998, about 18 percent of all minilabs were APS-equipped, with the percentage higher for mass merchandisers. With increased consumer awareness and many new models, APS is currently growing at a healthy rate. This trend should continue, with some industry observers forecasting that APS will account for half of all camera sales by the early part of the twenty-first century. Total 35mm camera sales increased 4 percent to 9.9 million sold in 1998 after 2 years of declining sales. This type of camera remains the dominant format, accounting for nearly 60 percent of total camera volume in the United States, according to PMAI. Sales of cartridge cameras have continued to drop, falling to about 1.3 million units as newer camera technologies have displaced them in the marketplace.

The SUC is still a solid performer for U.S. photographic camera sales and continues to experience double-digit growth. Sales reached 88 million units, up 23 percent, in 1997. A 25 percent increase was recorded by PMAI for 1998, which brought total SUC sales to 110 million units. Discount stores have captured the largest percentage of this business, with 32 percent of total sales. The discount segment also relies on private label SUCs as a means of securing profits higher than those generated by leading name brands with lower margins. Many stock their own brands to provide some latitude in price points that appeal to a wide customer base (see the box "International Trade Commission Rules").

After several years of declining sales, instant cameras and film bounced back in 1997. Growth in sales of those cameras increased 17 percent to 2 million units and film sales rose 2 percent to 90 million units, according to PMAI. The introduction of several new products aimed at the preteen, teenage, and young adult markets was a key factor in the rebound. New marketing strategies such as repackaging and new channels of distribution are being used by suppliers in an effort to reach the new generation of instant photographers. Competition from 1-hour photofinishing outlets and low-end digital cameras will continue to put pressure on the instant segment. However, recent competition between manufacturers in some foreign markets has resulted in price cuts for instant products that bring the cost of instant picture taking closer to that of developing and printing film from traditional cameras. Instant camera and film sales in markets outside the United States were mixed in 1998. In Japan, sales gained from the introduction of several new products, including a new instant camera that takes miniature photos. In many emerging markets, such as Russia, sales fell sharply because of weak economic conditions. U.S. instant camera sales declined 5 percent in 1998 to 1.9 billion units (see Figure 24-4).

INTERNATIONAL TRADE COMMISSION RULES IN SECTION 337 INVESTIGATION ON SINGLE-USE CAMERAS

In June 1999, the U.S. International Trade Commission (ITC) issued a permanent general exclusion order that bars the importation into the United States of all one-time-use cameras that infringe on any of Fujifilm's 15 U.S. patents. The ITC exclusion order was the final stage of an action filed in February 1998 by Fuji Photo Film Company, Ltd., of Tokyo. The complaint named 26 respondents and alleged that they either manufacture one-time-use cameras or remanufacture (reload) one-time-use shells manufactured by Fujifilm and others into one-time-use cameras for importation and sale in the United States, in violation of Fuji's patents.

After this favorable ruling, Fuji Photo Film filed complaints against three companies for infringement of one-time-use camera patents. One company appealed and was issued a stay pending the court's decision. The stay prohibits enforcement of the ITC order for that company pending resolution of the appeal.

Film. U.S. film sales revenues totaled about $3 billion and reached 972 million rolls in 1998, according to PMAI. Conventional film accounted for about 90 percent of that total. Growing acceptance of APS and intense price competition helped spur

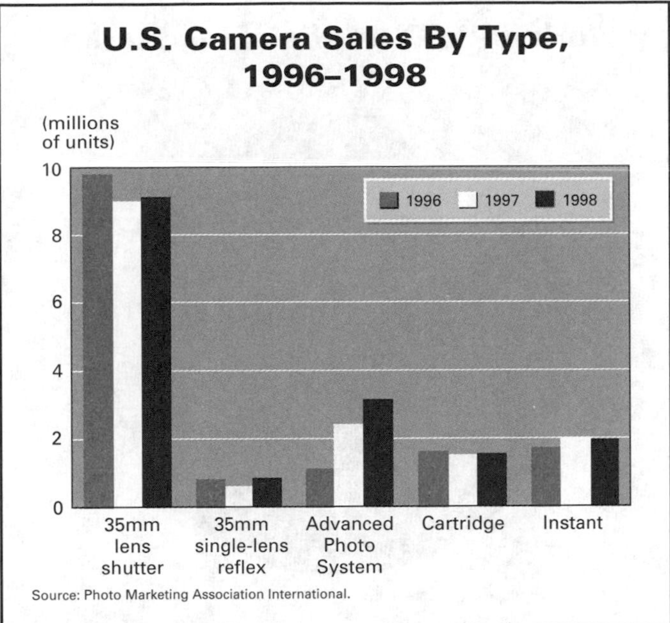

FIGURE 24-4

sales. Brand loyalty and price are driving factors in film sales. Recently, film suppliers have engaged in an aggressive round of price cutting in the U.S. market as a way to gain consumer acceptance and stimulate sales. As a result, companies throughout the film industry have had to adjust their pricing strategies to counter lower prices, maintain sales, and protect market share. Even suppliers of private label film, which generally is priced lower than branded film, have been drawn into the competition as the price gap between branded film and private label film has narrowed. Private label film accounts for about 7 percent of the total market. Multipacks are another contributor to lower film prices. They are sold primarily through discount chains and have a lower price per roll. Companies are using new packaging, advertising and promotions, and improved film technology to generate sales.

In terms of distribution, mass merchants accounted for over 50 percent of film sales, followed by drugstores, about 16 percent; supermarkets, 12 percent; and warehouse clubs, 11 percent. Mail order, camera stores, and minilabs account for the remaining sales. By type and unit volume, 35mm film accounted for close to 80 percent of sales in 1998. APS film sales increased from 3 percent of total volume in 1997 to about 6 percent in 1998, according to industry data.

Digital Cameras. Digital cameras resemble film cameras, but the image is recorded electronically and is available for immediate viewing. Images are stored on memory cards that can be linked to computers for editing or transmission. According to IDC, worldwide shipments of digital cameras reached 3 million units valued at $2.1 billion in 1998. Sales of this product were estimated to grow more than 50 percent to 4.6 million units valued at $2.7 billion in 1999. Falling prices are making digital cameras more affordable to the consumer segment. However, the proportion of digital cameras sold is still relatively small (about 3 percent) compared with that of traditional cameras. Digital image quality and resolution do not match those of silver halide technology but are acceptable for use with many computer applications. Digital resolution moved closer to that of traditional technology with the introduction in 1999 of 2-million-pixel (2-megapixel) digital cameras. Also, lighter weight, smaller sizes, optical zoom lenses, and improved storage devices are being added to digital camera models to improve their attractiveness.

U.S. digital camera shipments, representing 37 percent of the worldwide total, surpassed 1 million units for the first time in 1998 and were expected to increase 54 percent to about 1.7 million units in 1999, according to IDC. There are demographic indicators of those who are likely to buy digital cameras. While average prices have dropped, falling from about $5,000 in 1993 to less than $900, most purchases are made by single men and older consumers in the 55- to 64-year-old age bracket and those with incomes over $40,000, according to PMAI. The peripheral equipment and supplies used with digital cameras, such as batteries, scanners, printers, and specialty papers, increase the overall cost to the consumer. Even with falling prices, penetration into the consumer segment will take time. Demand for digital cameras comes primarily from business and professional users.

Japan is the global leader in digital camera shipments. With an estimated growth rate of 48 percent to 2 million units in 1999, it accounted for about 43 percent of total worldwide sales, according to IDC. Nikkei Market Access, by contrast, projects that the growth rate of the Japanese digital camera market has slowed and that sales were expected to reach 1.8 million units, an increase of only 24 percent from 1998. Most commercial and professional photographers in Japan have shifted to digital technology. Lower prices and the trend toward on-line computer applications should expand sales in the Japanese consumer segment.

Demand for digital cameras lags in Europe compared with the United States and Japan. Shipments are projected to reach around 600,000 in 1999 and represent about 13 percent of the worldwide total. Shipments to the rest of the world accounted for close to 320,000, or 7 percent of the worldwide total (see Figure 24-5).

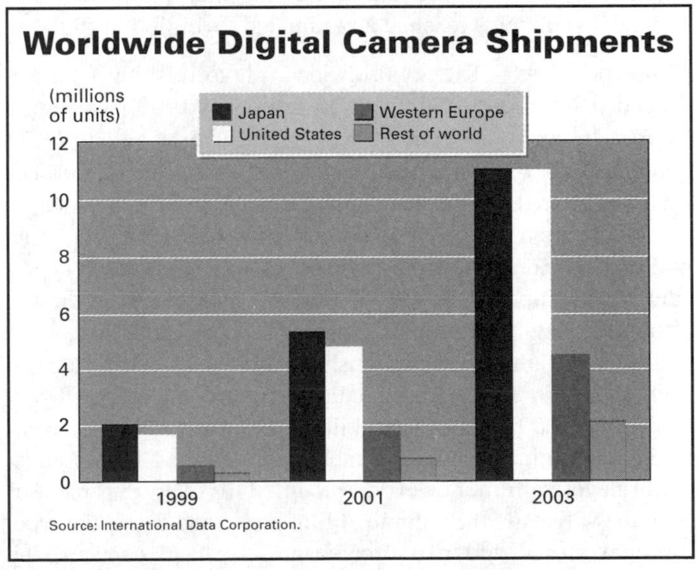

FIGURE 24-5

Worldwide shipments of digital cameras are estimated to reach $8 billion and exceed 28 million units in 2003, according to IDC. Declining prices and improved technology will stimulate sales in the consumer market over the next few years. The average street value of digital cameras is projected to fall under $300 by 2003, partially because 2-megapixel cameras will drive down the prices of older models. The United States and Japan will basically hold their share of the global market, while Europe should increase its share slightly.

Chemicals. Demand for photographic chemicals used to process film and paper is driven by the continued use of 35mm film, which accounts for the majority of the film processed. Supporting chemical demand is double-digit growth in the use of SUCs and the APS, which have gained in their share of film exposures and processing. The shift to larger print sizes and the offer of double prints to consumers also have contributed to the steady demand for photographic processing chemicals. Furthermore, despite advances in digital photography, chemical photography is the primary choice for many medical facilities (x-ray film) and for business use in archival storage of documents.

Environmental concerns have led to a reduction in the amount of photographic chemicals used during photoprocessing. New formulas requiring the use of smaller quantities of chemicals and the employment of chemicals in the form of concentrates, tablets, and cartridges have helped reduce the volume needed for photoprocessing. In addition, recycling efforts have reduced waste and the amounts of chemicals needed to replenish the finishing system.

The nearly $300 million U.S. market for photographic chemicals accounted for about 30 percent of the worldwide total, according to Photofinishing News, Inc., but the greatest growth in sales of photographic chemicals is occurring outside the United States. As developing photographic markets continue to expand, particularly in Asia, so will the need for processing chemicals. Growth rates in developing regions of the world are rising three times faster than they are in the more developed markets of Europe and Japan. The worldwide total for photographic chemical shipments reached an estimated $1 billion in 1998.

Photofinishing. The worldwide photofinishing market dipped 0.2 percent to almost $33 billion in 1998 (see Figure 24-6). The amateur segment accounted for $24 billion, or 73 percent of the total, and the nearly $9 billion professional segment accounted for the remaining 27 percent. Growing acceptance of both APS and digital cameras stimulated the photographic market, and picture taking increased nearly 4 percent worldwide in 1998 to 91.3 billion exposures, according to Photofinishing News, Inc., a Florida-based research firm.

The U.S. amateur photofinishing market rose 7 percent to $6.5 billion in 1998. Total picture exposures increased 8 percent from 24.9 billion to 26.9 billion. Exposures using conventional and digital technology each increased by 1 billion units. Color negative film, however, accounted for over 95 percent of both the value and the volume of film processed. By outlet type, discount stores and mass merchandisers have captured the largest share of amateur photoprocessing volume, with 37 percent of the total rolls processed. Drug stores and supermarkets hold the second and third largest shares, with 24 percent and 18 percent, respectively. By print size, the 4 × 6-inch print continues to gain market share, rising from 36 percent in 1993 to 59 percent of total prints in 1998. Enlargement volume, accounting for about 6 percent of total rolls processed, is expected to increase as digital imaging evolves with new products to manipulate images and restore faded photos.

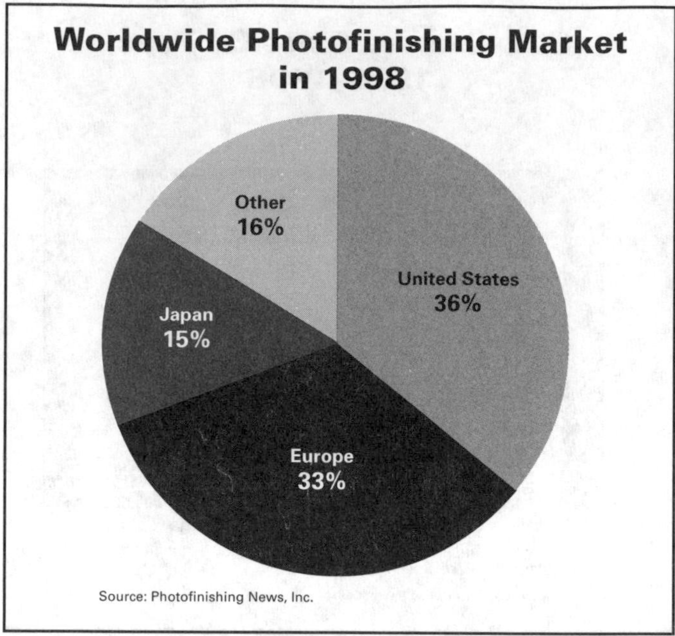

FIGURE 24-6

Restructuring, consolidation, and the formation of company alliances continue in the photofinishing segment of the industry. The introduction of new equipment such as digital minilabs also is changing the face of the industry. Digital lab equipment is capable of performing multiple operations to provide a spectrum of digital and traditional services. Sales of minilabs in 1997 (5,100) more than doubled the 1996 volume (2,800) because of equipment upgrades to accommodate APS, according to Photofinishing News, Inc. In 1998, there were an estimated 34,000 minilabs operating in 28,400 locations in the United States, along with about 2,450 wholesale central labs. Digital equipment increases the opportunity to expand services for all sizes of photofinishing laboratories because it can process and print film and scan the images onto computer CDs or for use online. This trend increases the importance of connectivity between the imaging industry and the information technology industry. In addition, digital imaging kiosks were installed at an unprecedented rate in 1998. By mid-October, there were more than 14,000 of those units in operation throughout the United States.

The professional segment of the U.S. photofinishing market increased nearly 9 percent to $5.3 billion in 1998 after a slight decline in 1997. The portrait and candid segment of the market, with 43 percent of the total, grew for 3 consecutive years, and the number of portrait sittings rose 2 percent in 1998. School-age portrait sittings account for one-fourth of total sittings. Preschool sittings, accounting for 12 percent of the total, declined for the second consecutive year. Other professional services include commercial custom lab work.

Europe's total photofinishing market is second to that of the United States, with 33 percent of the worldwide total. The amateur segment reached $8.6 billion in 1998, accounting for 78 percent of the $11 billion market total. Picture exposures totaled about 17 billion units. Conventional picture taking in Japan declined 5 percent in 1998 to 11.4 billion exposures, but digital camera exposure increases from 1 billion to 2.6 billion were responsible for the nearly 8 percent increase in total exposures to 14.3 billion in 1998. Japan's total photofinishing market declined about 8 percent to $4.8 billion and represented 15 percent of the worldwide total. Growth slowed in photofinishing markets throughout the rest of the world. Together, those markets accounted for about $5.3 billion.

Global Industry Trends

Japan. The Japanese amateur photographic market declined 3 percent to $9.2 billion in 1998, according to Photo Market. By category, photoprocessing accounted for more than half the revenue, with 52 percent of the total, down from 54 percent in 1997. Total film exposures fell 5 percent to 11.7 billion compared with 12.3 billion pictures taken in 1997. Other photo categories included in the market total include film, with 24 percent of the revenues; cameras, 16 percent; and accessories, 7 percent. Demand for APS film and instant cameras showed small gains, but was offset by declines in demand for other photographic equipment and processing services.

Exports helped compensate for weakness in Japan's photographic market. According to the Japan Camera Industry Association, Japanese camera exports showed a modest increase of 0.6 percent to 31.6 million units. APS camera exports increased 12 percent to 4.9 million units and represented 15 percent of the total volume. Exports of SUCs increased 18 percent from 30.8 million units in 1997 to 36.4 million in 1998. This contrasts with Japan's overall shipments of SUCs, which declined 8 percent in 1998, with 35mm models down 13 percent to 64.5 million units, while APS models increased 6 percent to 24.9 million units, according to the Ministry of International Trade and Industry. Japan's camera imports in all product categories declined in 1998. Volume imports of both 35mm and APS cameras declined, but the value of APS cameras increased because of shipments of higher-priced models. A review of the countries of origin indicates that these camera shipments were provided mostly by offshore production sites of Japanese manufacturers (see the box "Monitoring Report on Foreign Access to Japan's Film Market").

China. China has the potential to become a major photographic market, since under 15 percent of Chinese households own cameras. Many U.S. and Japanese photographic companies participate in China's photographic industry through joint venture manufacturing and marketing agreements. According to *Photofinishing News,* 8 million cameras and about 210 million rolls of film were sold in China in 1997. Minilabs continue to proliferate in that country, increasing from 7,000 in 1994 to 20,000 in 1997. Retail kiosks and outlets are another way to make photography accessible to the population. Since 1994, Kodak has opened about three Kodak Express stores a day on the mainland, bringing the total outlets to more than 5,000 nationwide, according to press articles. Fuji has about 2,300 of its Circle shops there.

MONITORING REPORT ON FOREIGN ACCESS TO JAPAN'S FILM MARKET

Access to Japan's photographic film market has been a long-standing problem. After a World Trade Organization's (WTO) panel finding that Japan had not violated its WTO obligations in the photographic film sector, the U.S. Department of Commerce and the U.S. Trade Representative established in 1998 an interagency monitoring committee to review the implementation of formal measures proposed by the government of Japan to the WTO panel.

In its first report, issued in August 1998, the committee revealed that the availability of foreign film doubled over the past 3 years in "nontraditional" outlets, such as supermarkets and convenience stores but declined slightly in traditional photospecialty shops, which account for about half of Japanese film sales by volume. The committee found that to fully live up to its WTO representations, Japan must take significant additional actions to open its photographic materials market and eliminate business practices that unreasonably restrict competition in this sector. The committee urged Japan to abolish measures that favor small and medium-size stores over large stores, eliminate potentially anticompetitive activities, publicize more widely its business practices guidelines, and make a greater effort to ensure compliance with those guidelines by wholesalers and retailers.

The committee's second report, released in June 1999, noted that some marginal improvements were taking place in the photographic film and paper sector but stated that foreign film manufacturers continue to face barriers in the Japanese market. While praising the efforts of the Japan Fair Trade Commission (JFTC) to cease potentially anticompetitive data exchanges, which constituted a potential violation of Japan's antimonopoly law, and improve the transparency of Japanese competition policy, the report highlighted the need for additional Japanese government action to improve market access and stimulate greater competition in this sector. In addition, further actions are required to ensure that JFTC has sufficient resources to investigate complaints, address business practices that restrain trade, open its distribution system to imports, and prohibit practices that discourage the opening of large stores.

INDUSTRY AND TRADE PROJECTIONS FOR THE NEXT 1 AND 5 YEARS

The overall photographic industry is mature, and U.S. demand for traditional photographic products is soft. Industry shipments in constant dollars are projected to rebound, rising a modest 2 percent to $25.4 billion in the year 2000 after declining 5 percent in 1999. Some of the industry's most competitive products, such as SUCs and APS, should continue to increase at a healthy rate, while others, such as analog photocopiers, will experience sluggish growth. Shipment growth also will be fueled by increased demand in overseas markets that are recovering from unfavorable and volatile economic conditions. Photographic trade should recover, with exports expected to rise 3 percent to $4.3 billion in the year 2000. Reflecting the soft demand for certain traditional photographic products in the United States, imports are expected to remain sluggish, growing only 1 percent to $8 billion in the year 2000. Digital products, in contrast, should experience stronger growth rates. Imports of digital cameras, for example, are expected to continue rising at double-digit rates to exceed $700 million. The photographic trade deficit should remain at $3.7 billion in 2000.

Photographic workers should expect to endure another year of employment cutbacks as companies make difficult restructuring decisions to consolidate manufacturing operations and continue to form strategic alliances with companies outside the industry. Total industry employment is expected to drop about 6 percent to 51,000 employees in the year 2000, with production workers accounting for about 60 percent of the total.

The U.S. economy has enjoyed a period of overall healthy growth over the last several years. Discretionary spending and purchases of leisure goods and services have come to include many high-end photographic products, consumer electronics items, and recreational travel. This consumer spending pattern is expected to remain favorable, although indicators suggest that a slowdown in the economy may occur in 2000.

Over the next 5 years, the shift away from traditional photography will continue as manufacturers embrace digital technologies and produce innovative products that reflect this blending. Photographic industry shipments should grow only marginally because of the changing product mix but also because of their dependence on exports to foreign markets to maintain growth. Recovery from financial instability in overseas markets will factor into the growth in shipments and expansion of trade. Industry shipments are forecast to reach $22.8 billion in current dollars by 2004, reflecting a compound average growth rate of less than 1 percent between 2000 and 2004. Silver halide photography will continue to dominate industry shipments, but the estimated $18.2 billion in current dollars in product shipments for 2004 represents a gradual decline in the percentage share of the total. Similar to the pattern for industry shipments, exports and imports will initially expand and then shrink over the 5-year period. Exports should reach about $4.5 billion and imports $8.5 billion, resulting in a $4 billion trade deficit in 2004. China will continue to emerge as a major provider of photographic products since it serves as a base for manufacturing. It also is poised to be a key market for photographic goods because its population is enormous and its market has barely been penetrated.

Manufacturers should continue to incorporate digital products in their product offerings and increase the use of strategic company alliances to participate in the more rapidly growing segments of the market. Digital imaging is a catalyst for long-term industry growth. Digital film finishing and the demand for photos on the Internet will increase. Photofinishers will offer both conventional film and digital finishing services to remain competitive. More film-to-digital conversions and a slowing in sales of film-based micrographic products in favor of digital hybrid imaging systems are expected. The transition from analog to digital photocopiers is projected to take place well before 2004 because of lower prices and the increased functionality of digital products. Color products will become more affordable, with higher speeds and greater resolution stimulating business sales.

Meanwhile, silver halide will continue to play a major role in

TABLE 24-3: U.S. Trade Patterns in Photographic Equipment and Supplies[1] in 1998
(millions of dollars; percent)

Exports			Imports		
Region[2]	Value[3]	Share, %	Region[2]	Value[3]	Share, %
NAFTA	1,257	29	NAFTA	792	9
Latin America	495	11	Latin America	40	0
Western Europe	1,482	34	Western Europe	1,605	19
Japan/Chinese Economic Area	680	16	Japan/Chinese Economic Area	5,336	64
Other Asia	201	5	Other Asia	581	7
Rest of world	272	6	Rest of world	15	0
World	4,387	100	World	8,368	100
Top Five Countries	Value	Share, %	Top Five Countries	Value	Share, %
Canada	736	17	Japan	3,884	46
Mexico	521	12	China	1,134	14
Japan	435	10	Mexico	480	6
Netherlands	418	10	Netherlands	334	4
United Kingdom	401	9	Germany	314	4

[1] SIC 3861.
[2] For definitions of regional groupings, see "Getting the Most Out of *Outlook 2000*."
[3] Values may not sum to total due to rounding.
Source: U.S. Department of Commerce, Bureau of the Census.

the industry and coexist with newer technologies. APS is expected to account for about 50 percent of camera sales and 20 percent of photofinishing sales in by 2004. Because of their convenience and ease of use, SUCs should still be a popular silver-based item. Price competition in the film segment should intensify as the struggle for market share intensifies. The use of niche marketing to address particular customers' needs or interests could help boost sales. The emergence of Internet photo services using images that originated on film for E-mail and the use of photo compact disks with computers will act as a bridge between silver halide digital photography and the newer technologies.

U.S. trade patterns in photographic equipment and supplies in 1998 are shown in Table 24-3.

Joyce Watson, U.S. Department of Commerce, Office of Computers and Business Equipment, (202) 482-0574, joyce_watson @ita.doc.gov, September 1999.

REFERENCES

CAP Ventures, Inc., 600 Cordwainer Drive, Norwell, MA 02061. (781) 871-9000, http://www.capv.com.

International Data Corporation, 5 Speen Street, Framingham, MA 01701. (508) 935-4389, http://www.idcresearch.com.

Manufacturers' Shipments, Inventories and Orders (M3-1), *Current Industrial Reports,* U.S. Bureau of the Census, Washington, DC 20230. (301) 457-4673, http://www.census.gov.

Micrographics and Hybrid Imaging Systems Newsletter, P.O. Box 950, Larchmont, NY 10538. (914) 834-3044, fax (914) 834-3993.

1997–1998 Industry Trends Report, Photo Marketing Association International, 3000 Picture Place, Jackson, MI 49201. (517) 788-8100, http://www.pmai.org.

1997–1998 Digital Imaging Industry Trends, Digital Imaging Marketing Association, 3000 Picture Place, Jackson, MI 49201. (517) 788-8100, http://www.pmai.org.

1998 and 1999 International Photo Imaging Industry Report, Photofinishing News, Inc., 10915 Bonita Beach Road, Suite 1091, Bonita Springs, FL 34135. (941) 992-4421, www.photo-news.com

Photo Electro News, Japan Photographic Enterprises Association, JCII Building, 25 Ichibancho, Chiyoda-ku, Tokyo 102-0082, Japan. 81-3-5226-7900, fax 81-3-5226-7419.

Photo International, World Press, Inc. 807 Chatore Ichigaya, 11-5, Tomishisa-cho, Shinjuku-ku, Tokyo 162, Japan. 81-3-3356-2879.

Photographic Trade News, 445 Broad Hollow Road, Suite 21, Melville, NY 11747. (516) 845-2700, www.ptnonline.com.

The Silver Institute, 1112 16 Street, NW, Suite 240, Washington, DC 20036 (202) 835-0185, http//:www.silverinstitute.org

RELATED CHAPTERS

27: Computer Equipment

38: Household Consumer Durables

GLOSSARY

Advanced Photo System (APS): A 24mm silver-based camera and film system introduced in 1996 that simplifies the picture-taking process and the reprint-ordering process.

Megapixel (million pixels): Refers to the resolution of a graphics device (display, digital camera, etc.). A 2-megapixel digital camera takes a picture that is divided into 2 million pixels, which would be a 1,000 × 1,000 resolution.

Minilab: A retail outlet (freestanding or in-house) that processes photographs (usually within 1 hour), using on-site equipment.

Silver halide photography: A photographic process that uses the interaction of silver compounds coated on a film base and chemicals to make images visible.

Single-use camera (SUC): A camera preloaded with film (the film cannot be removed by the photographer) that must be delivered as a unit to a photofinisher for processing.

Stock photography: Refers to a library of photographic images.

PRINTING AND PUBLISHING
Economic and Trade Trends

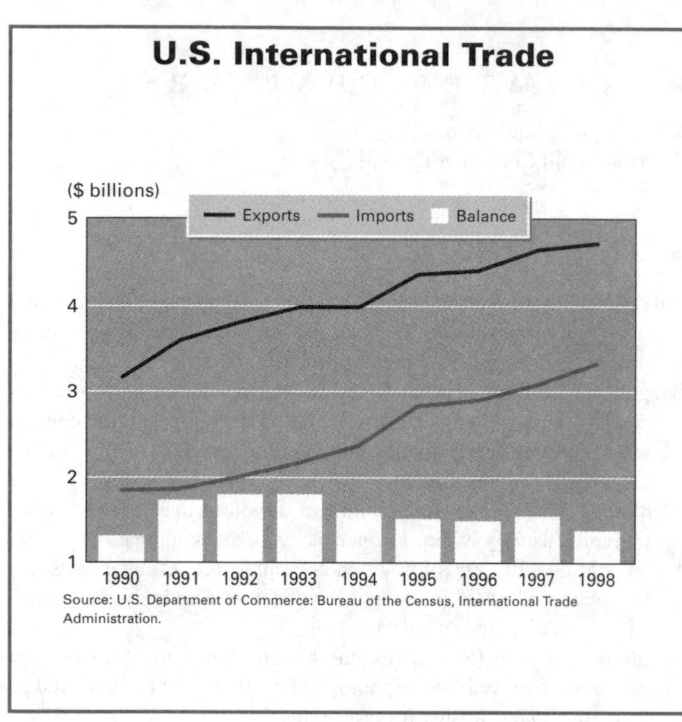

Source: U.S. Department of Commerce: Bureau of the Census, International Trade Administration.

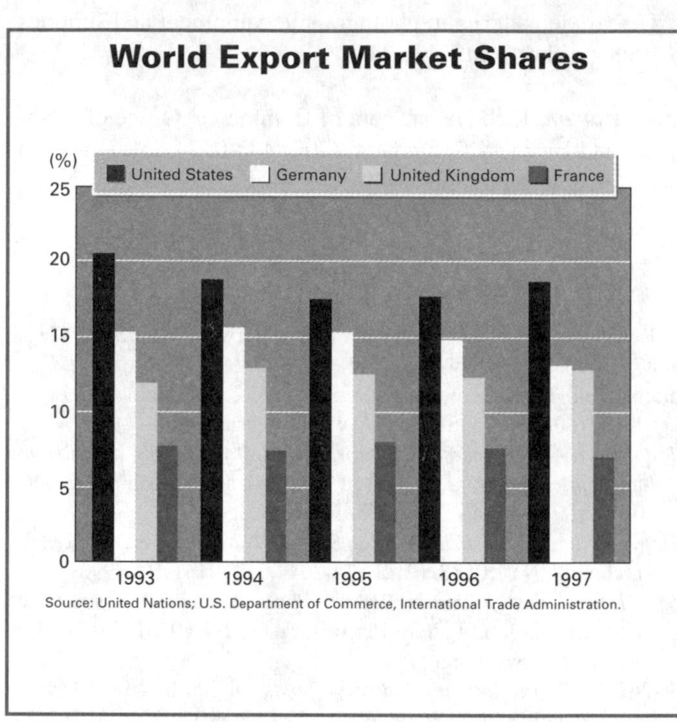

Source: United Nations; U.S. Department of Commerce, International Trade Administration.

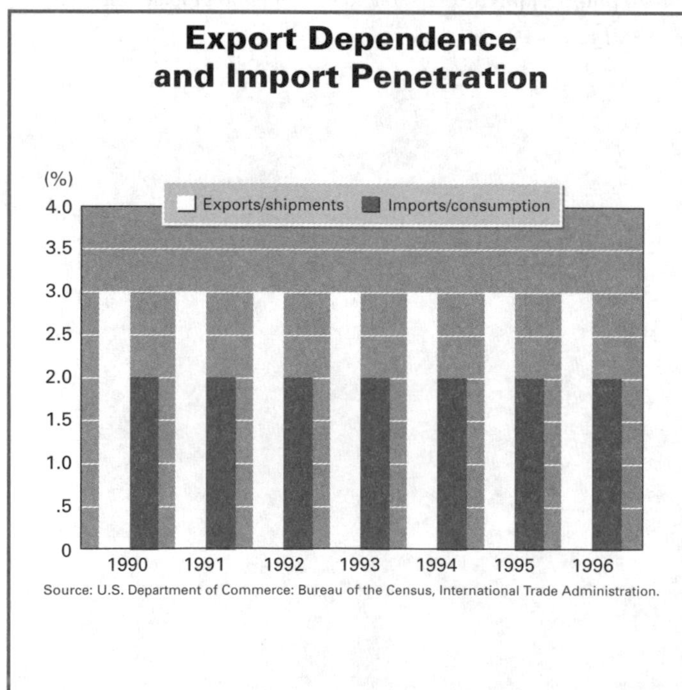

Source: U.S. Department of Commerce: Bureau of the Census, International Trade Administration.

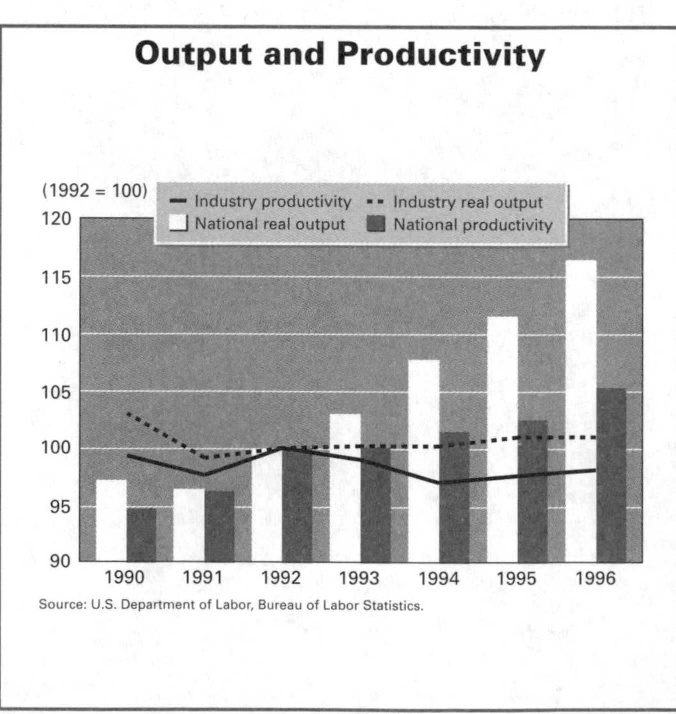

Source: U.S. Department of Labor, Bureau of Labor Statistics.

See "Getting the Most Out of *Outlook 2000* for definitions of terms.

25

Printing and Publishing

INDUSTRY DEFINITION The U.S. printing and publishing industry consists of the following industry sectors: newspapers (SIC 2711); periodicals (SIC 2721); book publishing (SIC 2731); book printing (SIC 2732); miscellaneous publishing (SIC 2741); the commercial printing (SIC 275) industries, which consist of commercial printing, lithographic (SIC 2752), commercial printing, gravure (SIC 2754), and commercial printing not elsewhere classified (SIC 2759); manifold business forms (SIC 2761); greeting cards (SIC 2771); blankbooks and looseleaf binders (SIC 2782); bookbinding and related work (SIC 2789); and printing trade services (SIC 279), which consist of typesetting (SIC 2791) and platemaking services (SIC 2796).

OVERVIEW

As the twentieth century drew to a close, the U.S. printing and publishing industry experienced unparalleled demand for its products. Despite intense competition from the electronic media and people's scarcity of leisure time, the industry's value of shipments from the sale of newspapers, periodicals, books, and trade advertising materials climbed steadily, reaching an estimated $184 billion in 1992 dollars in 1999 (see Table 25-1). Profit margins also advanced, aided by a pattern of low prices in materials costs—especially paper—and gains in worker productivity. Employment in printing and publishing had moderate growth through the decade of the 1990s, exceeding 1.5 million by 1999, but competition and consolidation reduced the number of establishments to an estimated 62,000 in 1999 from 65,000 a decade earlier.

Global Trends

Attending to the informational needs of the huge domestic market is the primary focus of U.S. printers and publishers, but the industry is an active participant in the international economy as well and thus is subject to global forces. These critical forces include changes in technology, new opportunities in global markets, international sourcing of equipment and supplies, and increased cross-border investment.

Technology. The move toward digital (electronic) technology has influenced the world's publishers as well as printers. The previous technology—analog—was based on film, plate, and chemical processes that required intermediary operations before textual input was ready for the printing press. Digital technology removes those intermediary activities and binds the production ties between printers and publishers more closely. The decades ahead will witness a sorting-out process that will determine which parts of the production process will be done at publishers' offices and which tasks will be accomplished at the printing plant.

International Markets. Printers and publishers in the world's major economies face mature domestic markets in which constraints on expansion often encourage a more global view. This is especially true in European countries such as France, Germany, the Netherlands, Spain, and the United Kingdom, where exports of printed products account for 10 to 20 percent of the industry's total revenues. The United States engages in the world's largest trade in printed products (see Table 25-2). Exports of U.S. books, periodicals, and trade advertising materials totaled approximately $4.5 billion in 1999, while imports of printed products reached $3.5 billion. The strongest demand for U.S. printed materials is found in Canada, the United Kingdom, Mexico, Japan, and Australia. Efforts by U.S. printers and publishers to establish larger markets in Latin America and the countries of the Pacific Rim are determined largely by literacy and income levels and the relative strength of regional economies.

Production Requirements. Trends in the acquisition of equipment and supplies find the world's printers and publishers

TABLE 25-1: Printing and Publishing (SIC 27) Trends and Forecasts
(millions of dollars except as noted)

	1992	1993	1994	1995	1996	1997[1]	1998[1]	1999[1]	2000[2]	Percent Change 97–98	98–99	99–00	96–00[3]
Value of shipments[4]	166,153	172,633	176,876	188,133	195,435	205,645	217,200	228,865	240,005	5.6	5.4	4.9	5.3
2711 Newspapers	33,782	34,651	36,091	37,732	39,171	41,200	43,550	46,120	48,655	5.7	5.9	5.5	5.6
2721 Periodicals	22,104	22,653	21,892	23,743	24,930	26,750	28,570	30,570	32,250	6.8	7.0	5.5	6.6
2731 Book publishing	16,698	18,616	19,695	20,484	21,363	21,980	23,385	24,950	26,495	6.4	6.7	6.2	5.5
2732 Book printing	4,681	4,810	4,745	5,392	5,333	5,360	5,525	5,720	5,905	3.1	3.5	3.2	2.6
2741 Miscellaneous publishing	10,908	11,807	11,976	12,025	12,511	13,075	13,600	14,155	14,720	4.0	4.1	4.0	4.1
275 Commercial printing	56,229	58,173	60,411	65,101	67,842	72,930	78,180	82,400	86,520	7.2	5.4	5.0	6.3
2761 Manifold business forms	7,429	7,491	6,958	7,894	7,724	7,440	7,285	7,510	7,770	–2.1	3.1	3.5	0.1
2771 Greeting cards	4,190	4,275	4,546	4,689	5,011	5,185	5,395	5,660	5,900	4.1	4.9	4.2	4.2
2782 Blankbooks and binders	3,758	3,771	4,276	4,544	4,820	5,120	5,260	5,495	5,690	2.7	4.5	3.5	4.2
2789 Bookbinding	1,291	1,258	1,367	1,509	1,608	1,705	1,780	1,865	1,940	4.4	4.8	4.0	4.8
279 Printing trade services	5,085	5,129	4,920	5,020	5,123	4,900	4,670	4,420	4,160	–4.7	–5.4	–5.9	–5.1
Value of shipments (1992$)	166,153	167,352	167,099	168,181	168,517	173,432	177,720	183,946	188,075	2.5	3.5	2.2	2.8
2711 Newspapers	33,782	33,222	33,294	32,782	31,718	31,559	31,527	31,685	32,002	–0.1	0.5	1.0	0.2
2721 Periodicals	22,104	22,014	20,849	21,903	22,379	23,140	23,510	24,474	24,963	1.6	4.1	2.0	2.8
2731 Book publishing	16,698	18,180	18,493	18,257	18,166	18,094	18,727	19,457	19,982	3.5	3.9	2.7	2.4
2732 Book printing	4,681	4,777	4,647	5,043	5,008	4,968	5,018	5,093	5,129	1.0	1.5	0.7	0.6
2741 Miscellaneous publishing	10,908	11,320	11,048	10,604	10,504	10,567	10,609	11,139	11,161	0.4	5.0	0.2	1.5
275 Commercial printing	56,229	56,764	58,252	59,454	60,555	65,097	68,482	72,180	74,923	5.2	5.4	3.8	5.5
2761 Manifold business forms	7,429	7,027	6,240	5,762	5,494	5,208	5,062	5,108	5,185	–2.8	0.9	1.5	–1.4
2771 Greeting cards	4,190	4,040	4,016	3,960	4,064	4,149	4,211	4,232	4,266	1.5	0.5	0.8	1.2
2782 Blankbooks and binders	3,758	3,668	4,049	4,058	4,152	4,347	4,460	4,661	4,778	2.6	4.5	2.5	3.6
2789 Bookbinding	1,291	1,249	1,343	1,431	1,501	1,545	1,584	1,636	1,662	2.5	3.3	1.6	2.6
279 Printing trade services	5,085	5,090	4,867	4,928	4,977	4,758	4,530	4,281	4,024	–4.8	–5.5	–6.0	–5.2

[1] Estimate.
[2] Forecast.
[3] Compound annual rate.
[4] For a definition of industry versus product values, see "Getting the Most Out of *Outlook 2000.*"
Source: U.S. Department of Commerce: Bureau of the Census; International Trade Administration.

TABLE 25-2: U.S. Trade Patterns in Printing and Publishing[1] in 1998
(millions of dollars; percent)

Exports			Imports		
Regions[2]	Value[3]	Share, %	Regions[2]	Value[3]	Share, %
NAFTA	2,369	50	NAFTA	1,130	34
Latin America	286	6	Latin America	42	1
Western Europe	997	21	Western Europe	1,046	31
Japan/Chinese Economic Area	455	10	Japan/Chinese Economic Area	833	25
Other Asia	188	4	Other Asia	221	7
Rest of world	427	9	Rest of world	54	2
World	4,722	100	World	3,325	100
Top Five Countries	Value	Share, %	Top Five Countries	Value	Share, %
Canada	2,018	43	Canada	975	29
United Kingdom	478	10	United Kingdom	474	14
Mexico	351	7	China	376	11
Japan	279	6	Hong Kong	269	8
Australia	221	5	Italy	174	5

[1] SIC 27.
[2] For definitions of regional groupings, see "Getting the Most Out of *Outlook 2000.*"
[3] Values may not sum to total due to rounding.
Source: U.S. Department of Commerce, Bureau of the Census.

fulfilling more of their requirements from international sources. Digital printing presses from Belgium, platesetters from Canada, and text processors and software from the United States point to the globalization of graphic arts equipment. Material inputs also are sourced globally, with ink supplied by the United States, the Netherlands, and Japan and paper obtained from the United States, Canada, and the Scandinavian countries. To a degree, this trend is countered by the large U.S. market for printed products, which encourages foreign suppliers and equipment manufacturers to establish plants in the United States.

Mergers and Acquisitions. The opening of foreign markets to investment opportunities has been seized on by the world's major printing and publishing companies. The leading attraction for foreign investment has been the United States, where up to 50 percent of the largest book and periodical firms are foreign-owned and the second largest printer is headquartered in Canada. U.S. printers have sought market opportunities abroad by merging, acquiring, or establishing printing plants throughout Europe, Asia, and Latin America. The U.S. book and periodical publishing industries are also active internationally through product licensing and joint ventures. This expansion of global publishing is in part the result of greater worldwide protection of intellectual property, a priority of the governments in nations with major publishing economies for the last two decades.

Domestic Trends

The United States is the world's largest market for printed products, and with imports accounting for only 1.5 percent of apparent consumption, its needs are met essentially by the domestic printing and publishing industry. Favorable economic and demographic factors expanded U.S. printed product markets throughout the 1990s, and that trend is expected to continue into the new millennium. Demand for printed products is a function of literacy levels, educational enrollment and attainment, disposable personal income, new business formations, and advertising expenditures. Specific factors influencing U.S. markets for printed products are population growth, expansion of the domestic economy, competition from the electronic media, and the printing and publishing industry's cost structure.

Demographics. U.S. printers and publishers have benefited from growth of the population, an increase in educational enrollment, an expansion in educational attainment, and higher levels of disposable personal income. Since 1980, the U.S. population has grown by 44.7 million, and school enrollments by 10 million. The proportion of U.S. high school and college graduates rose to 83 percent and 25 percent, respectively, in 1999 from 67 percent and 16 percent in 1980. Adjusted for inflation, U.S. disposable personal income per capita rose to over $21,000 in 1999 from $14,867 in 1980.

The Economy. A surging U.S. economy propelled demand for U.S. printed products in the 1990s, a trend that is expected to continue in the decade ahead. Growth of the economy has raised corporate profits and generated an outpouring of expenditures for advertising. Publishers of newspapers and periodicals are strongly dependent on revenues from advertising, and the U.S. printing industry earns over 60 percent of its income from that source. The creation of new businesses boosts demand for insurance, financial, bank, and legal printing, while higher levels of disposable personal income encourage more purchases of newspapers, books, and periodicals. Tax revenues generated by growth of the economy support the purchase of more instructional materials for school rooms and publications for libraries.

Electronic Competition. Printing and publishing is a highly competitive industry, and advances in the electronic media have intensified that factor. Since the 1960s, network television has reduced U.S. markets for evening newspapers; beginning in the 1990s, CD-ROMs have limited demand for encyclopedias. The Internet may become a long-term competitor to the U.S. printing industry as demand increases for newsletters, technical manuals, and reference materials in electronic format rather than printed format. Publishers also may be affected adversely by growth in Internet use as the U.S. population devotes more of its scarce leisure time to the electronic media rather than reading printed newspapers and periodicals.

Structural Factors. The printing and publishing industry's cost structure has benefited since the mid-1990s from low prices for materials, especially paper, and a smooth transition to digital technology. Accounting for up to 20 percent of the industry's total costs, paper prices have plummeted as a result of collapsed demand from economies in the Pacific Rim. Prices of other material and supply inputs have been held in check by import competition and the strong U.S. dollar. The move toward a digitally-based (electronic) technology has involved high capital investment costs, but the result has been greater productivity and a more highly skilled workforce. These new investments by U.S. printers have increased their plant capacity, leading to more competitive pricing in markets for printed products and intensifying the industry's movement toward reductions of and consolidations among printing firms.

Projections of Industry and Trade Growth for the Next 1 and 5 Years

An expanding U.S. economy, coupled with rising levels of advertising expenditures, should lift the value of shipments of the U.S. printing and publishing industry to $188 billion in the year 2000, an increase in constant dollars of 2 percent over 1999. This growth in demand for printed products should be enhanced by two special events: the Sydney, Australia, Olympics and the U.S. presidential election. The U.S. economy's strength is expected to keep both corporate profits and tax revenues at the high levels achieved since the mid-1990s, supporting increases in advertising expenditures and increased funding for schools and libraries. Printers' and publishers' costs are not anticipated to increase significantly in 2000, since global demand for material inputs, especially paper, remains subdued and rises in U.S. workers' wages should not outpace the nation's rate of inflation.

The long-term economic outlook for the U.S. printing and publishing industry is strongly positive. The industry's rate of revenue growth, adjusted for inflation, should average 3 percent annually over the 5-year period through 2004. This growth rate is predicated on a continuation of the favorable U.S. economic trends experienced since the mid-1990s: low levels of inflation and interest rates, steady gains in school enrollment and tax revenues, and high levels of consumer confidence and business employment. Particularly encouraging is a demographic trend favoring expansion of the U.S. population's core reading segment (those in the age group 45 and over), which is expected to expand by 10.1 million through 2004. Less encouraging to U.S. printers is the anticipated expansion of U.S. households' Internet capability, rising to an estimated 40 percent of all households in 2002 from 23 percent in 1998. The transition of some printed materials from paper to electronic format could follow this development, but the Internet's potential long-term threat appears to lie beyond this 5-year projection period. To date, the Internet has aided publishers' sales of books and periodicals and has not had an adverse impact on printers' shipments of catalogs and direct mail materials. U.S. printers and publishers should anticipate greater cost pressures through 2004 as improved global economies lift worldwide demand for paper.

Global Market Prospects

The U.S. printing and publishing industry should have ample international trade and investment opportunities over the next 5 years. Economies in Latin America and along the Pacific Rim are expected to improve, creating increased demand for U.S. printed product exports. Greater enforcement of international copyright protection should take place in Asia, the Middle East, and the newly independent states of the former Soviet Union, offering U.S. book publishers wider markets for their products. Growth in the global economy should expand foreign markets for U.S. consumer goods, providing the global advertising support required by U.S. periodical publishers to establish or license more of their titles overseas.

Exports should remain an important component in the international marketing plans of U.S. printers and publishers. The downturn in U.S. exports of printed products in 1999 was attributed to the strength of the U.S. dollar and softness in foreign demand as a result of stagnant economies. The return of economic growth, especially to countries in Europe and the Far East, should lift U.S. printed product exports to levels well above the 3 percent average annual rate of increase experienced in the 1992–1998 period. Exports of U.S. printed products to the nation's core trading partners—Canada, the United Kingdom, Mexico, Japan, and Australia—usually represent over 70 percent of the export total, but this ratio could decline if the economies in Latin America and the Far East become robust.

The U.S. government has taken a leadership role in supporting the international interests of U.S. printers and publishers. Working through first the General Agreement on Tariffs and Trade (GATT) and then the World Trade Organization (WTO), the United States has reduced significantly foreign trade barriers to exports of printed products. Free trade agreements negotiated with Israel, Canada, and Mexico have increased demand in those countries for U.S. printed products. Largely through U.S. efforts, the World Intellectual Property Organization (WIPO) agreed to strengthen enforcement of international copyright and extend copyright coverage to include materials in the electronic media. Working with the private sector, the U.S. government is determined to help U.S. printers and publishers gain full access to global trade and investment opportunities that stretch into the new millennium.

NEWSPAPERS

The U.S. newspaper publishing industry achieved solid gains in the late 1990s, spurred by a strong domestic economy and a resultant influx of advertising revenues. Competition from both the print and the nonprint media has trimmed the industry's share of total U.S. advertising spending, but publishers' revenues grew as a result of aggressive participation in the expanding U.S. advertising marketplace. The level of U.S. newspaper circulation held steady, but higher prices generated a slight increase in publishers' revenues from subscriptions and newsstand sales. The industry's profit margins expanded because of declines in newsprint prices and a trimming in the number of production workers. Continuing a long-term trend, the total number of U.S. daily newspapers edged downward as competition from the electronic media forced more evening newspapers to consider ceasing operations or converting to morning editions.

Global Industry Trends

The viability of the world's newspapers depends on literacy levels and economic factors, and the United States has long benefited from favorable trends in both areas. The strong U.S. school system fosters high educational attainment levels and enlarges the population of newspaper readers. Steady growth of the U.S. economy is accompanied by gains in demand for advertising, which represents up to 80 percent of U.S. daily newspaper publishers' total revenues. In certain respects, especially in its dependence on advertising, the U.S. newspaper industry is unique among its global colleagues.

The United States is among the world's leaders in newspaper publishing, but its position in regard to other nations invites comparisons and highlights global trends. With the total U.S. newspaper value of shipments having been estimated to reach approximately $32 billion in 1992 dollars in 1999 (see Table 25-3), U.S. publishers rank first among all nations in aggregate revenues and first in total advertising revenues. The U.S. newspaper industry's dependence on advertising for up to 85 percent (daily newspapers) or even close to 100 percent (weekly newspapers) of its total revenues stands in contrast to that of other major publishing countries: Canada, 73 percent; Australia, 69 percent; Germany, 61 percent; United Kingdom, 49 percent; Japan, 41 percent. In many developed economies, the total share of the advertising revenue market held by newspapers is trending downward as a result of competition from other media, principally television.

TABLE 25-3: Newspapers (SIC 2711) Trends and Forecasts
(millions of dollars except as noted)

	1992	1993	1994	1995	1996	1997[1]	1998[1]	1999[2]	2000[3]	Percent Change 97–98	98–99	99–00	96–00[4]
Industry data													
Value of shipments[5]	33,782	34,651	36,091	37,732	39,171	41,200	43,550	46,120	48,655	5.7	5.9	5.5	5.6
Value of shipments (1992$)	33,782	33,222	33,294	32,782	31,718	31,559	31,527	31,685	32,002	–0.1	0.5	1.0	0.2
Total employment (thousands)	414	410	412	415	403								
Production workers (thousands)	134	132	134	135	136								
Average hourly earnings ($)	12.94	12.90	13.39	13.58	13.61								
Capital expenditures	1,665	1,262	1,329	1,229	1,277								
Product data													
Value of shipments[5]	31,933	32,853	34,040	35,577	37,225	39,125	41,315	43,710	46,070	5.6	5.8	5.4	5.5
Value of shipments (1992$)	31,933	31,499	31,402	30,909	30,142	29,961	29,901	30,021	30,291	–0.2	0.4	0.9	0.1
Trade data													
Value of imports	53.4	50.3	9.2	8.7	8.7	9.1	8.7	8.0	9.0	–4.4	–8.0	12.5	0.9
Value of exports	30.1	27.3	34.9	30.8	28.3	33.9	31.2	35.0	38.0	–8.0	12.2	8.6	7.6

[1] Estimate except exports and imports.
[2] Estimate.
[3] Forecast.
[4] Compound annual rate.
[5] For a definition of industry versus product values, see "Getting the Most Out of *Outlook 2000.*"
Source: U.S. Department of Commerce: Bureau of the Census; International Trade Administration.

Although U.S. publishers' revenues from circulation (subscription and newsstand sales, estimated at $9 billion in 1999) are significantly lower than those from advertising, the United States ranks a close second to Japan ($12 billion) and is well ahead of its significant competitors, Germany ($5 billion) and the United Kingdom ($4 billion). Globally, circulation trends are strongest in the rising Asian economies, relatively stable in Europe and North America, and weakest in South America and Africa. Among mature, developed economies, the number of newspaper titles is stable (Germany, Japan, the United Kingdom) or in a slight decline (Canada, the United States). Russia publishes the largest number of newspapers each day (13,000 to 14,000 titles versus 2,500 titles in China and 1,485 in the United States), but Japan's newspapers have a higher aggregate daily circulation (72 million to 73 million versus 57 million in the United States) and a circulation per title (667,000 versus 38,000 in the United States) exceeding that of all other countries.

Aside from levels of literacy and economic growth, the world's newspaper publishers have a commonality of interest regarding costs of materials (newsprint), competition (particularly but not limited to the electronic media), and investment opportunities.

Newsprint. In developed economies, newsprint accounts for approximately 25 percent of a publisher's total costs and has a direct impact on profitability. Newsprint prices are determined by global demand, but production is concentrated in North America (principally Canada) and Scandinavia (principally Finland). Throughout the 1990s, the price of newsprint ranged from $500 to $600 per metric ton, but production shortages coupled with sudden demand from Asian buyers lifted prices to $658 in 1995. Weakness in Asian demand over the period 1997–1999 saw newsprint prices fall below the $500 mark during the first 6 months of 1999. An upturn in the Asian economies and virtually no increases scheduled in newsprint mill capacities are expected to drive newsprint prices back to the range of $500 to $600 in the next 5 years.

Competition. With few exceptions, the share of advertising expenditures held by newspapers is either stable or experiencing a gradual decline in the world's most developed economies. In North America, advertising inroads have been made by television and the direct mail industries, while the deregulation of Europe's television industry has adversely affected the advertising revenues of that region's newspaper publishers. Newspaper publishers in some Asian (Taiwan) and South American (Argentina, Venezuela) countries gained market share of the advertising dollar in the 1990s, but in general the prognosis for continued gains is doubtful. Growth of the electronic media in both developed and developing countries is expected to limit the newspaper industry's share of global demand for advertising.

Foreign Investment. Constrained by a perception of limited market opportunities in mature economies and the prospect of increased competition for advertising, global-minded newspaper publishers seek investment success beyond their national borders. Canadian publishers, for example, have been aggressive purchasers of U.S. newspaper properties for decades. Overseas investment by U.S. publishers has not been significant to date, particularly compared with the foreign ownership activities of newspaper entrepreneurs in Australia, Canada, and the United Kingdom. This focus by U.S. publishers on exclusively domestic markets may change as a result of selective newspaper publishing opportunities in growth regions such as Asia and Latin America.

Domestic Trends

Newspaper publishing is among the largest and most profitable U.S. enterprises. The nation's approximately 1,485 daily newspapers tend to have local market exclusivity, with papers competing directly in only the largest metropolitan areas. Although the total number of daily newspapers has declined 16 percent since 1950, this is not reflective of the industry's economic health. The number of morning newspapers more than doubled to 721 in 1998 from 322 in 1950 and represents over 80 percent of total daily circulation. The number of evening papers plummeted to 781 in 1998 from 1,450 in 1950, the result principally of competition from evening television. Since the United States still has more evening than morning newspapers, declines in the number of evening editions are expected to continue. Weekly newspapers rely almost entirely on revenues from advertising and have benefited from the long-term growth of the economy. While the number of U.S. weekly papers has remained at approximately 8,000 since 1965, average weekly circulation tripled to 75 million in 1999 from 25 million in 1965.

The U.S. newspaper industry's economic climate appeared to undergo a sea change in the late 1990s. A series of critical factors have placed U.S. publishers in a generally positive position for the near term. Circulation levels have stabilized, and advertising revenues are matching or exceeding growth in nominal gross domestic product (GDP). However, cost levels for both plant and materials are on the rise, pressuring the industry's profit margins. In the long term, competition from the electronic media could restrain future growth.

Circulation. The gradual but steady decline in U.S. daily newspaper circulation, to 56.2 million in 1998 from 62.8 million in 1987, may be coming to a close. While 1999 circulation levels were expected to be slightly below those of 1998, U.S. newspapers are expected to achieve stability if not gains in circulation beginning in the year 2000. Despite growth in readership of newspapers on the Internet, an expanding U.S. population continues to prefer to purchase the printed edition rather than viewing the electronic edition. Greater investment in zoned distribution and customer delivery systems is eliminating heretofore unprofitable fringe circulation: readership in geographic areas remote from core or central circulation sectors. Publishers also encouraged circulation growth in 1998 and 1999 by restraining subscription and newsstand price increases in reaction to wide audience disapproval of the significant price hikes levied in 1995–1996 as a result of surging costs of newsprint. According to the Newspaper Association of America, newspaper circulation in 1999 slowed its relative decline in relation to the total U.S. adult population, with weekday readers accounting for 59 percent of the total and weekend and Sunday readers representing 68 percent.

Advertising. After revenue declines in the early 1990s, advertising expenditures in U.S. newspapers have experienced a relative boom since 1994. The industry's gains in advertising revenues tended to match or exceed growth in nominal GDP in each of the last 5 years. These substantial increases in publishers' advertising revenues were predicated on a series of factors. The closings and consolidations of U.S. department stores, whose retail advertising was critical to newspapers, appears to have reached a stage of remission. Department store advertising is on the rise, along with expanded advertising expenditures from other retail establishments, including banks, computer and electronic stores, and home furnishing and appliance stores. Newspaper advertising from national as opposed to locally based sources accounts for just 13 percent of total newspaper advertising, the result of complexity in both newsprint size formats and advertising rate structures. However, publishers recorded rapid revenue gains in the late 1990s as a result of national advertising buying services that simplify the buying of advertising space across a wide spectrum of newspapers. Expenditures on classified advertisements—including employment, automobile, and real estate—surged in response to robust growth of the U.S. economy over the 1994–1999 period.

Material and Plant Costs. The principal factor leading to improved publishers' profit margins in the late 1990s was the substantial decline in the price of newsprint. The 1990–1991 U.S. economic recession led North American newsprint producers to cut back mill capacity. Thus, newsprint was in short supply at the start of the U.S. and Asian economic expansion in 1994–1995, resulting in transaction prices moving to $658 per metric ton in 1995 from $466 in 1994. In response to higher demand, more newsprint production came on line, but the industry was jolted in 1996 as many prominent Asian economies began to falter. Newsprint prices fell to below $500 per ton in 1999 but began to inch upward by that year's end. Although publishers' cost of materials declined in the late 1990s, plant costs rose. Those higher costs resulted from publishers' long-term plans to improve the industry's production facilities. This included printing presses with full-color reproduction capabilities, prepress systems with more efficient film and composition capabilities, and improvements in paper-handling and paper-inserting equipment. Among the largest publishers, plans often specified the transfer of plant facilities from an urban locality's nexus to sites offering greater space as well as more efficient transportation schemes.

Print and Electronic Competition. Until 1996, the U.S. newspaper industry attracted more advertising than did any other medium. Television has displaced newspapers as the leading advertising medium, and the gap between advertising expenditures in direct mail and those in U.S. newspapers is gradually shrinking. Despite these intrusions by competing media, the newspaper industry improved fractionally its share of the U.S. market in 1999. Publishers have been aggressive in defending one of their principal revenue sources: classified advertising. This was accomplished by establishing a series of Web sites on the Internet with the goal of linking electronic advertisements to the industry's newspapers. By offering U.S. advertisers access to both print and electronic media, newspaper publishers are positioning their companies attractively in anticipation of a boom in electronic commerce (E-commerce) activities.

Projections of Industry and Trade Growth for the Next 1 and 5 Years

The value of shipments of the U.S. newspaper industry is expected to exceed $32 billion in the year 2000, an increase in constant dollars of 1 percent over 1999 (see Table 25-3). Increases in newspaper advertising revenues, led by expenditures in retail and classified advertisements, should outpace gains in nominal GDP. Subscription revenues should also increase in 2000 as a result of both price increases and an expanded subscriber base. Publishers' initiatives on the Internet will provide a new revenue stream in 2000, helping to defray the initial Web site investments of the late 1990s. Both plant and material (newsprint) costs should increase in 2000 because of the addition of more color presses and paper-handling equipment and higher newsprint prices brought about by increases in global demand for this commodity.

The U.S. newspaper industry's value of shipments through 2004 is projected to increase 2 percent annually adjusted for inflation. This represents a significant, positive turnaround in the industry's fortunes, especially compared with the period 1985–1995. Revenues from advertising should continue at a high level as a result of a buoyant U.S. economy, an expanding retail sector, and a more appealing newspaper product (a growing subscriber base and the availability of color printing of both photos and advertisements). Publishers expect success in enlarging newspaper circulation through more attractive price offers to subscribers and the visual appeal of color used throughout a newspaper. The industry's production costs also are expected to rise over this 5-year period largely because of higher newsprint prices and greater expenses to improve plant facilities. Although total industry employment is projected to rise, efficiencies in plant production could reduce slightly staffing needs for production workers.

Global Market Prospects

Newspaper publishing has yet to become a global enterprise. Although dozens of the world's most popular newspapers are available each day in many major urban areas, they represent an important but minuscule portion of the world's newspaper readership. In the United States, newspaper publishing's 1,485 daily and 8,200 weekly papers provide content overwhelming geared toward serving the informational interests of local markets. Perhaps as many as six to eight U.S. newspapers achieve their goal of national distribution, and three to four of them reach international markets as a result of contractual production facilities located abroad. As shown in Table 25-4, U.S. trade in newspapers is negligible. However, this review of data belies the international influence of the U.S. newspaper industry. The thoughts and values expressed by U.S. newspapers are projected globally and anticipated and evaluated by small but significant international audiences. Growth of the Internet should provide an even more formidable outlet for the voices of American publishers.

With this almost totally domestic orientation, long-term growth of the U.S. newspaper publishing industry relies on a robust economy and favorable demographics. Through the later half of the 1990s, the U.S. economy provided a series of markers that may prove difficult to emulate in the decade ahead. A pattern of low unemployment and interest rates, stable prices, a federal budget surplus, and healthy growth in GDP resulted in strong consumer confidence and an expansion in advertising expenditures. A continuation of these trends will have a very positive effect on newspaper publishers' receipts. Projected population trends also should contribute to the industry's good

TABLE 25-4: U.S. Trade Patterns in Newspapers[1] in 1998
(millions of dollars; percent)

Exports			Imports		
Regions[2]	Value[3]	Share, %	Regions[2]	Value[3]	Share, %
NAFTA	20	65	NAFTA	2	24
Latin America	1	2	Latin America	0	0
Western Europe	7	22	Western Europe	5	62
Japan/Chinese Economic Area	2	6	Japan/Chinese Economic Area	0	3
Other Asia	0	0	Other Asia	1	10
Rest of world	2	5	Rest of world	0	1
World	31	100	World	9	100
Top Five Countries	Value	Share, %	Top Five Countries	Value	Share, %
Canada	18	59	United Kingdom	4	49
United Kingdom	6	20	Canada	2	19
Mexico	2	6	India	1	10
China	1	5	Spain	1	6
Colombia	0	1	Mexico	0	5

[1] SIC 2711.
[2] For definitions of regional groupings, see "Getting the Most Out of *Outlook 2000.*"
[3] Values may not sum to total due to rounding.
Source: U.S. Department of Commerce, Bureau of the Census.

fortunes. A positive correlation has been shown between age and newspaper readership, and the United States is experiencing an aging of its population. Industry studies indicate that less than half of persons age 18 to 34 read a newspaper each day, compared with 66 percent of persons age 35 and over and 71 percent of those age 55 and over. Through 2004, the U.S. population age 35 and older will increase 6.8 percent (9.4 million persons) and those age 55 and older will increase 11.5 percent (6.6 million persons). In contrast, the U.S. population age 18 to 34 is expected to increase just 1.3 percent (0.8 million persons) over the 1999–2004 time frame.

For most U.S. publishers, a presence on the Internet has become obligatory. Over two-thirds of the industry's daily newspapers now have Web sites whose initial purpose is to provide for the electronic placement of classified advertising. Since classified advertisements account for over 40 percent of the industry's advertising revenues and are becoming increasingly popular on the Internet, it is critical that publishers retain this revenue source by offering advertisers both print and electronic formats. Placement of classified advertisements on a publisher's Web site is provided free or at little charge if the advertisement also appears in the newspaper's printed edition. Beyond offering an electronic format for classified advertising, Web sites reinforce a publisher's brand name and represent electronic portals through which Internet surfers can access information sources or services that often are proprietary to the individual newspaper publisher.

Long-term prospects for the U.S. newspaper industry also are affected by the regulatory environment of the federal government. Since the 1970s the U.S. Federal Communications Commission (FCC) has barred newspapers from owning electronic media (television and radio stations) in the same geographic market. Given the diverse range and expansion of new media in the nation's urban markets, the newspaper industry insists that such cross-ownership regulations are outdated and unfair. Liberalization of cross-ownership rules could strengthen the advertising position of newspapers in local markets and increase publishers' profitability. The U.S. Postal Service (USPS) establishes the structure and level of postal rates (rates are approved by the U.S. Postal Rate Commission and the USPS's board of governors), and publishers perceive the USPS as favorably disposed toward one of the newspaper industry's prime competitors: the domestic direct mail industry. Postal rates are a critical cost variable to direct mailers, and lower rates on third-class mail (direct mail) could translate into a competitive advantage for the direct mail industry.

The focus of the U.S. newspaper industry is not entirely domestic. A principal international concern involves restrictions on U.S. publishers seeking investment opportunities in foreign newspaper properties. Countries that limit foreign ownership of their domestic newspapers include Australia, Brazil, France, India, and Italy. As U.S. publishers become more sophisticated in their Internet operations, they may develop a client base that includes international as well as domestic users. The logical next step for U.S. publishers would involve a global approach to the world's newspaper industry, were current restraints on investment and other barriers to trade removed.

PERIODICALS

The surging U.S. economy, accompanied by rising profit margins in most industries, spurred growth of the U.S. periodical publishing industry in the later part of the 1990s. Higher profits enabled U.S. businesses to increase their advertising budgets, and U.S. magazines became a prime beneficiary of this process. Emboldened by positive trends in advertising revenues, U.S. publishers increased their title output and expanded their presence in both domestic and global markets. Cost controls instituted by publishers in the early 1990s on editorial, marketing, and production operations in response to revenue shortfalls resulting from that period's poor advertising environment paid dividends by the decade's close. Magazine circulation levels improved in the 1996–1999 period, with the industry allocating more funds to its search for new readers. The combination of an expanded revenue base, effective controls on costs, and a substantial cash flow positioned magazine publishing as an industry attractive to investors. As a consequence, an accelerated pace of title acquisitions and new publishing ventures characterized the U.S. magazine industry in the later half of the 1990s.

Global Industry Trends

Despite intense competition from a variety of electronic media, global publishing of periodicals experienced rapid growth in the 1990s. This growth was supported by rising levels of literacy, expanding economies and business profit margins, and the awareness of print media as a powerful means of projecting advertising messages to both mass and special-interest audiences. Astute publishers recognized a series of evolving middle- and upper-class populations whose growth in affluence supported a need for the delivery of printed information and entertainment in a serial format. Global interest in periodical publishing was centered on perceived opportunities in Asia, Latin America, and eastern Europe, but niche markets in North America and western Europe also received attention.

While foreign publishers continued a long-term trend of investments in the U.S. periodical industry, that trend was not totally one-sided. By the decade's close, U.S. publishers had found investment opportunities in Europe, Asia, and Latin America. However, serving international markets was in many cases achieved more efficiently through joint ventures or co-publishing activities rather than through direct exports. To some extent, the expansion of international markets for U.S. periodicals was led by multinational consumer goods and services companies whose need for brand identification and recognition worldwide could be fulfilled by print advertisements delivered to mass and target markets in many countries via periodicals.

With an estimated value of shipments in 1992 dollars exceeding $24 billion in 1999 (see Table 25-5), the U.S. periodical publishing industry is the world's largest, and its huge markets have long attracted the interests of publishers abroad. Foreign investment in U.S. publishing has generally but not exclusively focused on the industry's largest segment: consumer magazines. However, in recent years, foreign publishers have increased their presence in U.S. business, reference, and database publishing. The investment strategy of most foreign firms is essentially to acquire existing U.S. publishing companies. By 1999, 4 of the 10 largest magazine companies operating in the United States were foreign-owned, representing publishers headquartered in Australia, Canada, and Japan and a consortium formed between interests in the Netherlands and the United Kingdom. Publishers in France, Germany, and Italy also have found profitable sectors in the U.S. magazine market.

The vast publishing opportunities afforded by the large and expanding domestic periodical market has precluded many U.S. publishers from seeking sales overseas. As shown in Table 25-5, U.S. exports of periodicals did not grow significantly in the 1990s. Projected exports of U.S. periodicals in the year 2000 ($825 million) are expected to be no higher than the value in 1995. The U.S. focus has always been on the Canadian market, which traditionally garners over 70 percent of U.S. periodical exports (see Table 25-6). To the degree that the U.S. periodical publishing industry seeks profits abroad, the strategy for domestic publishers of consumer magazines is primarily one of linkage through joint ventures or copublishing operations with foreign publishers. However, the international strategy of U.S. publishers of business magazines tends to be more broad-based. Since U.S. business magazines may already have a growing foreign circulation, the initial focus of those publishers is to establish a separate foreign edition to address those audiences more specifically. However, this strategy does not prevent consideration of joint ventures, copublishing, and direct acquisition when those actions are thought to be more appropriate.

The international interests of U.S. periodical publishers are prodded in part by the advertising strategies of global businesses. To establish brand recognition and company identification worldwide, major multinational companies and their advertising agencies are encouraging the largest U.S. publishers to project their well-recognized titles into new regions, especially Asia, Latin America, and eastern Europe. To capitalize on growing markets for consumer goods and services in those regions, global businesses acknowledge the value mass-market periodicals lend to their advertised products and services. Supported by advertising from global sources, some U.S. publishers are finding that the attractiveness of their major periodicals extends beyond national borders.

Domestic Trends

The U.S. periodical publishing industry consists of approximately 4,700 establishments whose 120,000 employees produce just under 18,500 titles annually. The industry's value of shipments in 1992 dollars from subscriptions, newsstand sales, and advertising totaled an estimated $24 billion in 1999. Magazine publishing contains three major segments: consumer magazines (representing 63 percent of total industry revenues), business magazines (28 percent), and all other magazines (farm, comic books, religious, Sunday newspaper comics, and professional journals) (9 percent). The issuance of new titles is strongly correlated with health of the domestic economy. In the 1990s, new title output averaged 788 annually, ranging from 553 new titles in 1991 to 1,067 in 1998. Approximately two-thirds of all new titles fail to survive beyond 4 or 5 years.

TABLE 25-5: Periodicals (SIC 2721) Trends and Forecasts
(millions of dollars except as noted)

	1992	1993	1994	1995	1996	1997[1]	1998[1]	1999[2]	2000[3]	Percent Change 97–98	98–99	99–00	96–00[4]
Industry data													
Value of shipments[5]	22,104	22,653	21,892	23,743	24,930	26,750	28,570	30,570	32,250	6.8	7.0	5.5	6.6
Value of shipments (1992$)	22,104	22,014	20,849	21,903	22,379	23,140	23,510	24,474	24,963	1.6	4.1	2.0	2.8
Total employment (thousands)	115	117	117	122	121								
Production workers (thousands)	20.2	19.7	18.2	17.8	16.4								
Average hourly earnings ($)	13.40	12.51	12.78	13.58	14.85								
Capital expenditures	235	290	308	332	311								
Product data													
Value of shipments[5]	20,942	21,692	21,642	22,951	24,352	26,250	28,165	30,275	32,090	7.3	7.5	6.0	7.1
Value of shipments (1992$)	20,942	21,080	20,611	21,173	21,860	22,603	22,965	23,907	24,385	1.6	4.1	2.0	2.8
Trade data													
Value of imports	134	194	209	222	217	204	217	250	240	6.4	15.2	–4.0	2.6
Value of exports	731	737	788	825	819	864	864	800	825	0.0	–7.4	3.1	0.2

[1] Estimate except exports and imports.
[2] Estimate.
[3] Forecast.
[4] Compound annual rate.
[5] For a definition of industry versus product values, see "Getting the Most Out of *Outlook 2000.*"
Source: U.S. Department of Commerce: Bureau of the Census; International Trade Administration.

TABLE 25-6: U.S. Trade Patterns in Periodicals[1] in 1998
(millions of dollars; percent)

Exports			Imports		
Regions[2]	Value[3]	Share, %	Regions[2]	Value[3]	Share, %
NAFTA	637	74	NAFTA	139	64
Latin America	32	4	Latin America	1	1
Western Europe	148	17	Western Europe	65	30
Japan/Chinese Economic Area	13	2	Japan/Chinese Economic Area	8	4
Other Asia	10	1	Other Asia	1	1
Rest of world	23	3	Rest of world	2	1
World	864	100	World	217	100
Top Five Countries	Value	Share, %	Top Five Countries	Value	Share, %
Canada	617	71	Canada	127	59
United Kingdom	72	8	United Kingdom	42	19
Netherlands	27	3	Mexico	12	6
France	21	2	Japan	6	3
Mexico	20	2	Spain	5	2

[1] SIC 2721.
[2] For definitions of regional groupings, see "Getting the Most Out of *Outlook 2000*."
[3] Values may not sum to total due to rounding.
Source: U.S. Department of Commerce, Bureau of the Census.

Advertising. It is not an understatement to say that while readers are important to a publisher's success, advertisers are crucial. Advertising revenues traditionally account for over 60 percent and 50 percent, respectively, of total revenues for publishers of business magazines and consumer magazines. Growth in business magazine advertising is fueled by corporate profits. The economic dynamism displayed by U.S. businesses in the 1990s led to significant gains in advertising in U.S. business publications, reaching an estimated $8.4 billion by 1999. Four U.S. sectors account for over two-thirds of total business publication advertising: technology, especially computers and telecommunications; health care and pharmaceutical; business and financial; and manufacturing, processing, and industrial. All four sectors recorded annual gains in advertising expenditures in the double-digit range in the period 1996–1999. Publishers of consumer magazines also notched revenue records in U.S. advertising in the 1990s, and their annual gains were only slightly less impressive than those of their business magazine colleagues. In 1999, estimated advertising expenditures in U.S. consumer magazines totaled $10.4 billion. Four U.S. sectors account for over half of total consumer magazine advertising: automotive, accessories, and equipment; toiletries and cosmetics; direct response companies; and computers, office equipment, and stationery.

Circulation. The total number of U.S. magazines circulated annually exceeds 500 million. Consumer magazines represent most of this volume—estimated at 365 million in 1999—and have benefited from the growth of the U.S. population, accompanied by greater disposable personal income. Sales of consumer magazines are generated through two outlets: subscriptions and newsstands (a misnomer, since most single-copy sales occur at supermarkets and drug and convenience stores). Since 1980, circulation levels of consumer magazines from subscriptions have experienced gradual but annual increases except for slight downturns in 1992 and 1996. In contrast, single-copy (newsstand) sales have been in a long-term decline for decades: down to an estimated 66 million in 1999 from 91 million in 1980. The circulation of U.S. business magazines, which totaled an estimated 120 million in 1999, also takes two forms: paid and unpaid (controlled) circulation. Controlled circulation publications, which are sent free of charge to selected individuals engaged in business-specific activities, represent two-thirds of total business magazine circulation and showed a pattern of moderate but continuous growth throughout the 1990s. Business magazines with paid circulation experienced a gradual downturn in circulation levels to 38 million in 1997 from 42 million in 1992.

Operational Costs. Aside from salaries for its workforce, the primary costs facing the U.S. periodical publishing industry involve paper, postage, and distribution. Except for some religious publications, publishers contract out the printing of U.S. magazines to the highly competitive commercial printing industry. Paper represents the principal material cost, and publishers bear this expense directly or indirectly through negotiations with their printers. Paper prices spiked upward in 1994 and 1995 but were relatively steady in the period 1996–1999. Although postal charges did not rise substantially in the 1990s, the price of postage remains a contentious issue for most publishers. The industry argues that the USPS fails to recognize sufficiently the mail-processing costs absorbed by magazine publishers and thus allocates unfairly higher postal charges to the periodical industry. One publishing cost center that has seen a rise in expenses involves the distribution of magazines into single-copy sales channels. In the period 1995–1999, both magazine distributors and many retail establishments required significantly higher payments from publishers for the distribution and display of their newsstand titles.

Shifts in the Magazine Marketplace. The decade of the 1990s had a profound impact on the magazine industry's sources of advertising revenue and the types of magazines that appealed most to U.S. audiences. Combined advertising revenues from the tobacco, liquor, wine, and beer industries declined to less than 5 percent of total consumer magazine advertising in 1999 from approximately 10 percent in 1989. The surge in magazine advertising revenues since 1992 has come from four new sources: direct response companies; computer, office equipment, and stationery firms; business and consumer service operations; and drug and remedy manufacturers. Those four sectors increased their advertising spending in U.S. magazines throughout the 1990s at annual growth rates averaging 15 to 25 percent. By 1999, advertising expenditures in U.S. consumer periodicals by each of those four sectors had reached $1 billion. While the number of U.S. magazines increased in terms of title output by over 40 percent over the past decade (to approximately 30,000 magazine titles in 1999 from 21,344 in 1989), changes in the reading interests of U.S. audiences lifted the fortunes of some publishers while challenging those of others. Among categories experiencing at least a doubling of titles over the past decade are publications classified in antiques and art goods, art and sculpture, collectibles, culture and humanities, museum publications, and lifestyle. Magazine categories showing a loss in title representation have included crossword puzzles, family, genealogy, parapsychology, and poetry and creative writing.

Projections of Industry and Trade Growth for the Next 1 and 5 Years

Publishers' value of shipments is estimated to approach $25 billion in 1992 dollars in the year 2000, an increase, adjusted for inflation, of 2 percent over 1999 (see Table 25-5). Expected gains in advertising receipts should be accompanied by revenue increases in both subscription and single-copy sales of magazines. Continued growth of the U.S. economy and expanding corporate profits are the underpinnings of the U.S. magazine industry's anticipated success in the year 2000. The 10 largest U.S. business sectors, whose annual advertising expenditures in domestic magazines increased at an annual average rate of no less than 8 percent in the period 1996–1999, are expected to match or exceed that rate of growth in 2000. Since the number of periodicals sold by subscription or single copy is anticipated to increase only marginally, the magazine industry's growth in real terms is expected to come almost entirely from gains in advertising revenues. Publishers' profit margins in 2000 should be down slightly from 1999 as a result of higher costs of paper, higher retail display charges, and acquisition efforts to obtain new subscribers.

The U.S. periodical industry should continue a pattern of solid growth in the years immediately ahead. The industry's receipts are projected to expand in constant dollars at an average annual rate of 2 percent through 2004. Certain cost sectors—paper supplies, retail distribution and display activities, and expansion of the subscriber base—should be of increased concern to magazine publishers and will restain growth in profits. Periodical publishing's advertising base should expand over the 2000–2004 period with continued growth of the U.S. economy and rising corporate profit levels. Advertisers in U.S. periodicals should have a wider choice in title selection, since the number of new magazines published each year is expected to maintain its current level of 1,000 new titles annually. The decades-long decline in single-copy sales appeared to have bottomed out in 1999 at 66 million, and that level of newsstand circulation is expected to be maintained through 2004. Magazine circulation through subscriptions should continue its gradual increase, ranging from 0.2 percent to 0.4 percent annually, through 2004.

Global Market Prospects

The U.S. periodical publishing industry is at the genesis of what should become an economic era highly favorable toward its products. Publishers face a confluence of positive factors: increases in segments of the U.S. population critical to magazines, a relative decline in network television as a competitor for advertising, expansion of the public's Internet use that should increase magazine circulation, and new sets of opportunities for the growth of U.S. publishing in international markets. Balanced against these factors are the relative diminishment of leisure time and continued problems in shoring up single-copy sales of U.S. magazines.

The level of U.S. magazine circulation, at least the part generated by subscription sales, should show steady improvement in the immediate future. The U.S. population is increasing, accompanied by greater purchasing power, higher educational attainment levels, and stronger literacy skills. Two population groups are particularly attractive to U.S. magazine publishers: the youth segment (age 24 and under) and the senior segment (age 45 and over). Both segments will increase in numbers in the 1999–2004 period, the youth segment by 3.3 million and the senior segment by 10.1 million. Despite a decline of 3.4 million in the segment of the U.S. population age 25 to 44, magazine publishers and advertisers will compete vigorously for this group's attention. The gradual decline in network television viewership in the 1990s enhanced U.S. magazines as an advertising vehicle: Advertisements placed in a combination of large consumer magazines now have the same level of audience exposure at costs lower than that of television.

The growth of E-commerce is having a profoundly positive effect on the U.S. periodical publishing industry. Virtually all publishers have Web sites, and the popularity of those digital settings is growing rapidly. Publishers use Web sites to deliver information and entertainment, encourage participatory forums, and sell their publications and services. Both business and consumer magazines attribute part of their circulation increases to readers gained as a result of their Web sites. In particular, special-interest magazines are finding their Web sites to be crucial to their circulation strategies. With retail store display space increasingly limited as well as costly, Web sites have become a powerful means to turn viewers into subscribers.

Direct exports of U.S. magazines may be entering a period of gradual decline. The combination of more U.S. publications available internationally through licensing or joint venture operations and Internet access to publishers' Web sites that provide foreign audiences with instant information may have a deleterious effect on U.S. periodical exports. However, the opportunity for direct U.S. exports of periodicals to Canada, by far the largest export market, were strengthened significantly by a 1999 trade agreement negotiated between the United States and that nation in settlement of a WTO dispute. Under this agreement, Canada will permit the importation of U.S. periodicals containing advertising aimed at Canadian audiences as long as those advertisements occupy no more than 18 percent of total advertising space in a publication. Canada will allow Canadian companies to deduct up to 50 percent of their advertising expenses in U.S. periodicals from their corporate income taxes. Canada also agreed to permit foreign investors to achieve 100 percent equity in a periodical publisher in Canada provided that the enterprise is not an existing Canadian-owned enterprise. Removal of these barriers to U.S. periodical exports should enable U.S. periodical publishers to improve their positions in the highly competitive Canadian market.

For many U.S. magazine publishers, adopting a global focus for their publications remains a difficult task. The continuance of trade barriers, both subtle and overt, has thwarted a U.S. export strategy in some countries. India, for example, discourages the domestic printing of foreign periodicals, thus increasing significantly the costs of market penetration. Other countries place restrictions on foreign investment in their publishing enterprises. For the large number of U.S. magazines with small circulations, the rationale for foreign licensing and joint venture arrangements is not compelling. Such arrangements are most viable for mass-market U.S. consumer periodicals already recognized by international audiences.

For most of the nation's periodical publishers, corporate attention centers on the large and expanding domestic market. With both advertising and magazine subscription levels at record levels, the U.S. periodical publishing industry is posed for even greater growth. This optimism is tempered for some by concerns about the costliness and reduced availability of magazine display space at some major retail outlets and a modest decline in the number of hours U.S. audiences spend annually reading magazines, but those issues relate primarily to publishers of mass-market consumer magazines. For the industry as a whole, magazine publishing is filled with opportunities for visionary entrepreneurs.

BOOK PUBLISHING

Growth in disposable personal income coupled with higher levels of educational attainment pushed the receipts of the U.S. book publishing industry to record heights as the millennium closed. Publishers' revenues were spurred by more tax revenues being used to fund schools and libraries and the expansion of technical and professional occupations resulting from growth of the U.S. economy. The dynamics of electronic commerce have created an invaluable marketing and distribution tool for U.S. publishers but also have contributed to a one-third decline in the number of domestic bookstores. The nation's book publishers have increased their product mix, adding audio books, CDs, and Internet-only materials to their traditional reliance on the paper product. A more global perspective is evident at U.S. publishing's managerial levels, with mergers and acquisitions and licensing and marketing opportunities increasingly being determined by international considerations.

Global Industry Trends

Total receipts of the world's book publishing community in 1999 were estimated to reach $120 billion. Publishers in the United States accounted for about 21 percent of this total, or almost $25 billion (see Table 25-7), with approximately 60,000 new titles or editions issued in 1999. The huge American book market has become a magnet for major foreign publishing houses. Imports of books by the United States increased at an average annual rate of 6 percent in the period 1992–1999, and the 1990s saw an influx of foreign firms—primarily British, Dutch, and German—merge with or acquire U.S. book-publishing companies. English-language publications dominate the international trade in books, which has witnessed rapid growth as a result of expanding Internet use.

Factors that influence international demand for books include educational systems, language skills, the pricing and availability of publications, and consumer income levels. The principal trends affecting global book sales are greater protection of copyright, the rise of the Internet, growth in the use of the English language, and the expansion of market opportunities abroad. The U.S. book publishing industry has been both a leader and an active participant in each of those activities.

Protection of Copyright. The protection of intellectual property is the prime determinant of the extent of world trade in books. Although the major European countries had strong copyright protection in place for over a century (the Berne Convention), global enforcement of Berne's provisions was enhanced by U.S. adherence to Berne in the late 1980s and the positive outcome of international trade negotiations involving copyright in the early 1990s under what is now the WTO. For the past two decades, international copyright enforcement has focused on the Far East, a region with enormous market potential and unequal levels of copyright adherence. As copyright protection in the Far East improved, this region became the fastest growing market for imported books in the 1990s. Regions yet to achieve a high degree of adherence to intellectual property rights include the Middle East and the newly independent states of the former Soviet Union.

The Internet. The availability and sale of publications over the Internet has changed international trade in books radically. Foreign buyers using the Internet routinely expect to obtain books faster and at a lower cost with no regard to a book's source of delivery. For publishers, the Internet is a marketing tool without peer. By displaying the availability of titles not simply to regional or national but to global audiences, the Internet encourages publishers to extend the print life of their products in anticipation of future sales. In turn, the Internet places

TABLE 25-7: Book Publishing (SIC 2731) Trends and Forecasts
(millions of dollars except as noted)

	1992	1993	1994	1995	1996	1997[1]	1998[1]	1999[2]	2000[3]	Percent Change 97–98	98–99	99–00	96–00[4]
Industry data													
Value of shipments[5]	16,698	18,616	19,695	20,484	21,363	21,980	23,385	24,950	26,495	6.4	6.7	6.2	5.5
Value of shipments (1992$)	16,698	18,180	18,493	18,257	18,166	18,094	18,727	19,457	19,982	3.5	3.9	2.7	2.4
Total employment (thousands)	79.0	83.2	83.5	83.5	85.4								
Production workers (thousands)	18.2	18.2	18.2	18.5	18.5								
Average hourly earnings ($)	12.51	12.90	13.56	13.61	13.27								
Capital expenditures	327	282	283	345	365								
Product data													
Value of shipments[5]	14,761	16,596	17,229	18,409	19,114	19,340	20,695	22,330	23,580	7.0	7.9	5.6	5.4
Value of shipments (1992$)	14,761	16,207	16,177	16,407	16,254	16,189	16,756	17,409	17,879	3.5	3.9	2.7	2.4
Trade data													
Value of imports	953	966	1,023	1,184	1,240	1,298	1,384	1,425	1,495	6.6	3.0	4.9	4.8
Value of exports	1,637	1,664	1,703	1,779	1,776	1,897	1,842	1,790	1,880	−2.9	−2.8	5.0	1.4

[1] Estimate except exports and imports.
[2] Estimate.
[3] Forecast.
[4] Compound annual rate.
[5] For a definition of industry versus product values, see "Getting the Most Out of *Outlook 2000.*"
Source: U.S. Department of Commerce: Bureau of the Census; International Trade Administration.

the onus for fast delivery on international book distributors, which must consider shipments by plane versus boat and form tighter linkages with in-country package carriers. In one aspect, however, the Internet presents publishers with certain complications. For example, anticipated profits to British publishers from the purchase of licensing rights on U.S. titles can be circumvented by British book buyers who purchase books over the Internet from U.S. rather than British sources.

Growth of the English Language. U.S. publishers benefit significantly from the global popularity of the English language. English is more than the world's second language. Its use is imperative among all educated sectors: business, the professions, and science. International publishers of technical, scientific, and professional books are aware that their publications for export must be in the English language if they are to capitalize fully on global markets. For this reason, more books are translated into English than into any other language. The ubiquitousness of English on the Internet has further enhanced its stature as the critical global language. One estimate indicates that 80 percent of the world's Web sites are displayed in English. Continued growth of U.S. exports of technical, scientific, and professional books has been spurred by the acceptance of English among the world's estimated 50 million to 60 million persons who have professional occupations.

International Markets. Over the past several decades, book publishing has evolved into a global business. Publishers venture where profits, market opportunities, and scale economies are most enhanced. The large U.S. book market has attracted many major companies, accounting for the fact that 5 of the 10 largest publishing firms in the United States are foreign-owned. Publishers' international interests sometimes are served through mergers and acquisitions, but more common routes are direct exports and the licensing of rights to their titles for translation. Revenues to U.S. publishers from exports and rights sales account for approximately 10 percent of the industry's total annual revenues. Major publishing countries in Europe—the United Kingdom, Germany, France, and Spain—find 20 to 40 percent of their industry's revenues coming from international sources. As a result of geographic proximity or historical conditions, certain international markets have established stable relationships with major publishing countries: Canada with the United States, Latin America with Spain, and former colonies in Africa and Asia with France and the United Kingdom. Publishers' interest in other book markets waxes and wanes, depending on copyright enforcement and economic conditions. Book sales to Asia jumped in the late 1980s and early 1990s, only to flag in the mid-1990s in response to that region's weakened financial situation.

Domestic Trends

The U.S. book publishing industry consists of approximately 2,700 firms whose estimated value of shipments of $19 billion adjusted for inflation in 1999 was accomplished through the efforts of 85,000 employees. The nation's largest firms are generally in or near New York City, but publishers can be found in every region and urban area. Most book publishing establishments are small, with well under 20 employees, and few, if any, have their own printing plants.

Domestic markets for U.S. books are determined by the size and growth of the U.S. population, levels of educational attainment, school enrollment, the occupational mix, and disposable personal income. Book markets are both broad and highly segmented, depending on the audience to be reached. The principal product categories are trade books (works of fiction and nonfiction sold primarily through bookstores), educational materials (textbooks and supplementary items), and all other books (religious, university press, reference, book club, mail-order, and technical, scientific, and professional books). The business of publishing is being buffeted by a series of significant trends, including changes in the channels of distribution, funding levels for schools and libraries, shifts in production costs, and fluctuations in demographic characteristics.

Channels of Distribution. A development with important consequences has occurred in the selling of adult and juvenile trade books to U.S. consumers. Beginning in the mid-1980s, chain superstores with upwards of 20,000 square feet of floor space and shelving 50,000 to 100,000 titles began to appear in major urban areas, selling books at both list and discounted prices. In the mid-1990s, selling books over the Internet, especially at discounted prices, began to attract sizable audiences. These sales venues—the Internet and the superstores—had and are continuing to have a deleterious effect on book sales through independent bookstores and small, mall-based chain bookstores. The capacious environments presented by chain superstores have proved attractive to U.S. consumers and, along with the growth of book sales on the Internet, have contributed to a one-third decline in the number of independent domestic bookstores. The economic effect of chain superstores and Internet sales has been less onerous on independent bookstores that have developed an intensely loyal clientele and stores serving a unique segment of the population, such as readers of travel, mystery, or military books.

Funds for Schools and Libraries. The funding of public schools and libraries is a function of tax revenues, which are determined largely by the health of the U.S. economy. In the period 1985–1995, funds for public elementary and secondary schools increased 43 percent while enrollment grew 23 percent. In relative terms, however, funds targeted for instructional materials (textbooks, workbooks, and the like) failed to keep pace with enrollment levels and textbook publishers recorded only modest increases in unit sales. Another adverse factor was the emphasis in some school systems on allocating limited funds to the purchase of computer equipment, further reducing the funds available for textbooks. However, by the mid-1990s, the U.S. economy began to surge and more tax dollars became available for public schools. This growth in educational funding continued through the late 1990s, and sales of textbooks and supplementary materials recorded growth rates higher than those of most book categories. Funding of libraries after 1985 followed a pattern similar to that of the nation's public schools. Funding levels in constant dollars remained relatively stable in the 1985–1995 period, with any increased monies spent for computer-related items. As more tax dollars became available in the mid-1990s, book purchases began to increase, and that favorable situation continued through the balance of the decade.

Book Manufacturing. The production of most U.S. books is contracted out to the highly specialized U.S. book printing industry. Larger publishers apply their economic leverage by purchasing paper directly from paper mills and shipping it to their contracting printers. In recent years, publishers have been blessed with falling paper prices and relatively stagnant printing expenses. Since 1995, publishers have seen paper prices fall 5.6 percent annually as a result of overcapacity at both the domestic level and the international level. Printing costs have increased since 1995, but at an average rate well under 1 percent annually. Neither of these trends in manufacturing costs is likely to continue beyond the year 2000. Although printing costs for books without color illustrations are favorable, a number of U.S. publishers have found that for producing color separations, the craft skill cost compares unfavorably with that of their manufacture abroad. Hence, the use of Asian or European printers for the production of publications containing color remains an attractive option.

Population Characteristics. Favorable demographics have had an extremely positive impact on the U.S. book publishing industry. The U.S. population has grown, increased its level of education, accumulated more disposable personal income, and increased its propensity to buy and read books. Over the past two decades, the population increased 44.7 million, and school enrollment 10.0 million. The percentage of the U.S. population completing 4 or more years of high school rose to an estimated 83 percent—226 million—in 1999 from 67 percent—153 million—in 1980. The percentage of college graduates reached an estimated 25 percent—68 million—of the population in 1999 from 16 percent—36 million—in 1980. Disposable personal income on a per capita basis and adjusted for price increases grew to over $21,000 in 1999 from $14,867 in 1980.

Projections of Industry and Trade Growth for the Next 1 and 5 Years

Growth of the U.S. economy, with resultant increases in disposable personal income and revenues from taxes, should propel the value of shipments of the U.S. book publishing industry to over $23 billion in 2000, an inflation-adjusted gain of 3 percent over 1999 (see Table 25-7). The U.S. market for books should expand as the nation's population increases by an estimated 2.3 million. Gains also should take place in educational enrollments, with an expected addition of 334,000 elementary and secondary school students and 130,000 college students. These enrollment gains should be accompanied by more funds for education as more tax revenues become available for schools and libraries. The year 2000 should witness the scheduling of slightly more state textbook adoptions than took place in 1999, resulting in an expansion of the markets for those products. Exports of U.S. books should approach $1.9 billion in 2000, an improvement over projected exports of just over $1.8 billion in 1999. Aided by improved economies and more book buying over the Internet, major export markets—particularly Canada, Mexico, and countries in the Pacific Rim—are expected to increase their purchases of U.S. books in 2000.

Book publishers' receipts through the year 2004 are projected to increase in constant dollars at a compound average rate of 2 percent. A series of positive demographic and economic factors are expected to support growth of the U.S. book publishing industry over this 5-year period. Continued expansion of the U.S. economy in this time frame, yielding more disposable personal income, should underpin publishers' receipts. The overall domestic market for U.S. books will grow as the U.S. population expands by 11.4 million. Since no growth will take place in the number of U.S. persons under age 45 (growth in the number of persons under age 25 will be negated by a decline in the number of persons in the age group 25 to 44), all this growth will be in the age group of persons 45 or older, a demographic segment with a strong propensity to read. Educational enrollments should increase by 1.8 million at elementary and secondary schools and 0.6 million at the college and university level. Enrollment growth is expected to be accompanied by more tax funds allocated to education. Tax revenues are expected to increase funding levels for U.S. school and public libraries, specifically benefiting publishers of juvenile books. Exports of U.S. books should increase through the year 2004 as a result of strong economies overseas, more familiarity with publications in the English language, greater use of the Internet as a marketing tool, and improved copyright conditions abroad.

Individual U.S. book markets are expected to display significant variations from the 2 percent average annual rate of growth through 2004. Market segments forecast to exceed that average include school and college textbooks, religious books, and technical, scientific, and professional books. Both enrollment levels and funding requirements for U.S. schools and colleges should increase through 2004, expanding unit sales of elementary, high school, and college textbooks. The nation's quest for a spiritual life has been a dominant theme for the past several decades and shows no signs of abating. Publishers of religious books have expanded their title listings to accommodate this increased demand and should experience continued growth in the next 5 years. Markets for U.S. technical, scientific, and professional books should expand significantly through 2004. Employment gains in the United States are becoming concentrated in the service, technical, and professional speciality occupations, requiring informational and educational skills imparted largely through instructional materials.

Demand in some U.S. book categories is not forecast to exceed the 2 percent average growth rate through 2004. These categories include reference books, mass-market paperbound books, and adult trade books. Publishers of reference books are increasingly gravitating toward designing their products for CD and/or on-line formats. The expansion of electronic networks among U.S. libraries could reduce libraries' overall purchasing requirements and place limits on the market for reference books. Sales of mass-market paperbound books declined throughout the 1990s and are not expected to exhibit growth through 2004. The discounting of adult trade hardcover books has been and should continue to be the major factor in reducing demand for paperbacks. Demand for adult trade books in the period 1999–2004 is expected to match but not exceed the book industry's 2 percent average annual rate of growth in that time frame. The rise of book superstores and Internet use has not yet compensated for the one-third decline in the number of independent and small mall-based chain bookstores, thus providing fewer physical outlets for the display and sale of trade books.

Global Market Prospects

The United States is the world's largest book market, and many small and medium-size U.S. publishers focus on it exclusively. With positive demographic characteristics and a robust economy, this emphasis on the U.S. book market is not misplaced, but a more international focus is becoming more evident in the U.S. book publishing industry. This focus is supported by the generally rising level of U.S. book exports, global use of the Internet to purchase books, perceived market opportunities abroad, and recognition of the growth in international copyright protection. However, evidence of a more international orientation on the part of U.S. publishers is often clouded by inadequate data. For example, neither public nor private sources account for U.S. sales of licensing rights to foreign publishers, an activity that brings $200 million to $400 million annually to U.S. publishing houses. Expanding use of the Internet overseas has created a wave of U.S. books destined for foreign buyers, but because U.S. export data exclude shipments valued under $2,500, such electronic-generated traffic in books may not be accounted for adequately in the trade statistics.

The long-range outlook for U.S. book exports is distinctly favorable. English is becoming a dominant language, and products of the U.S. book publishing industry are sought worldwide for their information, knowledge, entertainment, and cultural value. Textbooks, reference books, and technical, scientific, and professional books represent approximately half of all U.S. book exports. Trade books account for most of the rest and represent virtually all the activity in U.S. licensing rights. Data on direct exports of U.S. books show a relatively consistent pattern: Combined purchases from four countries—Canada, the United Kingdom, Australia, and Japan—traditionally account for 70 percent of the export total. Over 40 percent of U.S. book exports are earmarked for Canada, while an additional 13 percent find markets in the United Kingdom (see Table 25-8). Exports of U.S. books are destined for virtually every country in the world, with the purchasing levels of 28 countries exceeding $5 million annually. Viewed regionally, the major market for U.S. books is North America, followed by Europe. Combined book exports to the countries of Latin America and Africa remain well under 10 percent of the trade total.

Markets for U.S. books, both domestic and international, are strongly positive. At the global level, the economies of Canada and the countries of the European Union—traditional markets for U.S. books—are strengthening and should continue to attract large shipments of U.S. books. U.S. publishers view Asia and Latin America as attractive regions for their export efforts but remain skeptical about individual countries' financial situations and the enforcement of international copyright. The fact that copyright is such an overwhelming concern to U.S. publishers is evidenced by the industry's successful legislative efforts in 1998 to have the United States become one of the first

TABLE 25-8: U.S. Trade Patterns in Book Publishing[1] in 1998
(millions of dollars; percent)

Exports			Imports		
Regions[2]	Value[3]	Share, %	Regions[2]	Value[3]	Share, %
NAFTA	866	47	NAFTA	233	17
Latin America	69	4	Latin America	16	1
Western Europe	407	22	Western Europe	604	44
Japan/Chinese Economic Area	195	11	Japan/Chinese Economic Area	370	27
Other Asia	75	4	Other Asia	135	10
Rest of world	228	12	Rest of world	26	2
World	1,842	100	World	1,384	100
Top Five Countries	Value	Share, %	Top Five Countries	Value	Share, %
Canada	808	44	United Kingdom	314	23
United Kingdom	237	13	Canada	216	16
Australia	158	9	Hong Kong	200	14
Japan	133	7	Italy	103	7
Mexico	59	3	China	101	7

[1] SIC 2731.
[2] For definitions of regional groupings, see "Getting the Most Out of *Outlook 2000*."
[3] Values may not sum to total due to rounding.
Source: U.S. Department of Commerce, Bureau of the Census.

countries to provide for the protection of works appearing in electronic format. By endorsing copyright in all its mutations, the United States has demonstrated its commitment to the intellectual property of its citizens. Growth of publishing on a truly global basis will be enhanced when this concept is adopted uniformly at the international level.

COMMERCIAL PRINTING

The explosion of informational materials supplied electronically in the last decade has not dampened U.S. demand for printed products. Catalogs, brochures, direct mail, labels, inserts, and a wide array of other printed items also have witnessed high growth patterns, and their manufacture is accomplished by the U.S. commercial printing industry. Printers reside in every town and county, and their total number—approximately 35,000 establishments with over 600,000 employees—places commercial printing among the largest U.S. manufacturing industries.

The nation's large and growing demand for printed products dictates that U.S. commercial printers focus their efforts almost exclusively on serving domestic markets. The industry contains a sizable number of small firms—over 80 percent of the industry's establishments have fewer than 20 employees—and caters primarily to local markets. In contrast, the industry's biggest firms—250 establishments each with 250 or more employees—meet the needs of national and international clients. The U.S. printing industry's exports, estimated at over $1.3 billion in 1999 (see Table 25-9), represent less than 2 percent of apparent consumption but still place U.S. commercial printers among the world's largest suppliers of printed products.

Global Industry Trends

As one of the world's oldest manufacturing activities, printing has long met the informational needs of a global society. Over the past decade, however, the printing industry has encountered a series of critical challenges that threaten its supremacy in that role. These challenges include responding to technological change, meeting environmental requirements, sourcing equipment and supplies internationally, and positioning for increased competition.

Changes in Technology. The printing industries in virtually every developed economy are moving from the traditional analog-based technology to a digital-based process. This is a change of enormous proportion, requiring large investments of capital, entirely new job skills among employees, and the rapid obsolescence of equipment and supplies. Analog technology is a process that is dependent on photographic film, light-sensitive printing plates, solvent-based inks, and a wide range of chemicals and developers. Digital technology eliminates those articles of manufacture, focusing instead on networks, servers, information technology platforms, and software to process electronically the input received from clients via telecommunication. Digital technology is transforming the printing industry's prepress operations at a significant cost and is beginning to be applied to the printing press itself. The U.S. commercial printing industry is the leading implementor of digital technology, but rapid acceptance of this technology also is occurring in printing plants in Canada, the countries of the European Union (EU), and Japan.

Environmental Regulations. Although moving to digital technology involves high initial costs, the world's printers welcome the digital process for reducing the industry's adverse impact on the environment. By removing the processing of film and light-sensitive printing plates from prepress operations,

TABLE 25-9: Commercial Printing (SIC 275) Trends and Forecasts
(millions of dollars except as noted)

	1992	1993	1994	1995	1996	1997[1]	1998[1]	1999[2]	2000[3]	Percent Change 97–98	98–99	99–00	96–00[4]
Industry data													
Value of shipments[5]	56,229	58,173	60,411	65,101	67,842	72,930	78,180	82,400	86,520	7.2	5.4	5.0	6.3
Value of shipments (1992$)	56,229	56,764	58,252	59,454	60,555	65,097	68,482	72,180	74,923	5.2	5.4	3.8	5.5
Total employment (thousands)	567	572	577	598	604								
Production workers (thousands)	408	415	417	433	437								
Average hourly earnings ($)	11.50	11.69	11.75	11.86	12.31								
Capital expenditures	2,144	2,238	2,708	2,680	2,959								
Product data													
Value of shipments[5]	54,902	56,960	58,902	63,819	66,624	71,685	76,920	81,225	85,445	7.3	5.6	5.2	6.4
Value of shipments (1992$)	54,902	55,577	56,791	58,277	59,466	63,985	67,376	71,149	73,853	5.3	5.6	3.8	5.6
Trade data													
Value of imports	442	505	584	756	748	825	909	965	1,015	10.2	6.2	5.2	7.9
Value of exports	1,056	1,201	1,061	1,197	1,195	1,248	1,393	1,340	1,380	11.6	–3.8	3.0	3.7

[1] Estimate except exports and imports.
[2] Estimate.
[3] Forecast.
[4] Compound annual rate.
[5] For a definition of industry versus product values, see "Getting the Most Out of *Outlook 2000*."
Source: U.S. Department of Commerce: Bureau of the Census; International Trade Administration.

printers eliminate the need for chemicals and developers, a significant source of waste. The industry is reducing the emission of volatile organic compounds (VOCs) from printing inks and printing press cylinder blanket washes by increasing its use of soy-based inks and experimenting with waterless printing techniques. Improvements in printing press automation, along with greater use of lightweight and/or easily recycled materials, are limiting the amount of paper waste. North America, the EU countries, and Japan have the strongest environmental regulations, and the printing industries in those countries are working to comply with ever more stringent requirements. Printers in the EU countries, for example, are striving to meet a target of 52 percent waste recovery by 2001.

Sourcing Equipment and Supplies. The printing industries in the world's developed economies have been forced to become more global-minded. Changes in technology have altered printers' sourcing channels for both equipment and supplies. The United States remains a leader in the supply of equipment for prepress operations, but an increasing quantity of printing and binding equipment, especially digital printing presses, is obtained from abroad. Prices of equipment and supplies often are determined by global market demand, forcing printing plant managers to pay close attention to international economic conditions and currency exchange rates. In general, the U.S. commercial printing industry obtains paper from domestic, Canadian, and Scandinavian sources; inks from the United States, Japan, and the Netherlands; and prepress, printing, and binding equipment from the United States, Israel, Japan, and the countries of the EU.

Foreign Competition. Since printing is a mature industry, the world's major printing companies have long sought market opportunities outside their borders. The size, growth, and vibrancy of U.S. printing markets have attracted increased numbers of foreign competitors. Since the mid-1990s, U.S. imports of printed products have increased at an annual average rate more than twice that of U.S. exports. The second largest printing company in the United States is Canadian-owned, but mergers, acquisitions, and new start-ups have established a U.S. presence for German, French, Dutch, and Japanese printers. Since the early 1990s, several of the largest U.S. printing companies have found market opportunities abroad. A primary focus has been servicing print demand in select countries in Central America and South America, but U.S. printers also have invested in Canada, the countries of the EU, Russia, India, Singapore, China, and Japan.

Domestic Trends

Products of the U.S. commercial printing industry fill the knowledge, informational, and entertainment needs of U.S. business and consumers. Factors influencing domestic demand for those products include the state of the U.S. economy, corporate profits, the level of U.S. advertising expenditures, and demographics. Changes in the U.S. population are particularly significant. Having more senior citizens increases the market for books and newspapers, and having fewer teenagers reduces the market for comics and magazines. School enrollment levels are closely watched, since they influence markets for textbooks, juvenile books, and periodicals. The level of U.S. business formations reflects the status of the economy and determines markets for business forms, binders, directories, newsletters, printed financial and legal products, and an array of trade advertising materials. General growth of the U.S. population, especially of household formations, influences demand for catalogs, magazine and newspaper inserts, and direct mail.

Commercial printers are being challenged by changes in the markets for their products, their industry's structure, and the technology they employ. The principal issues facing the U.S. commercial printing industry concern employment, competition from the electronic media, plant mergers and consolidations, and changes in the advertising environment.

Printing Employment. The printing industry's transition to digital from analog technology has had a profound effect on employment. This transition has increased the industry's substitution of capital for labor and has changed its labor requirements significantly. Printing is shedding much of its craft skill orientation, especially in prepress and printing operations, in favor of persons knowledgeable about digital work flows, but attracting such people into printing careers has not been easy. Such potential employees gravitate more naturally to the information and communications sectors rather than to factory-focused commercial printing plants. The industry's managers are addressing this critical issue in three ways: (1) selecting current staff for exhaustive retraining in digital processing, (2) refocusing the industry's training programs at U.S. schools and colleges toward electronic-based technology, and (3) lifting the industry's stature as a desirable, productive, and profitable employment sector for potential workers.

Electronic Media. Commercial printers are witnessing a gradual erosion in some of their traditional markets as competition from the new electronic media becomes more formidable. The presentation of information in electronic rather than printed format is a continuing process that shows no signs of ebbing. Libraries are replacing printed reference materials such as directories with CD-ROMs. Banks seek greater profitability by encouraging customers to use electronic transactions rather than checkbooks. Households purchase encyclopedias in electronic rather than printed format. Businesses seek information and reference materials from on-line sources rather than from printed technical manuals and paper-based database compilations. Another factor is the gradual increase in the amount of leisure time U.S. households spend on the electronic media (television, videos, CDs, games, and the Internet) and the relative decline of time spent reading. The growth of the Internet is not an encouraging trend for U.S. printers, especially with U.S. household Internet capability projected to rise to 40 percent by 2002 from 23 percent in 1998. Yet these signs of an expanding Internet presence have not adversely affected U.S. demand for printed catalogs, periodicals, books, or direct mail materials, products that account for the bulk of the printing industry's value of shipments.

Industry Structure. The often difficult transition to digital technology coupled with a more competitive market environment has reduced the number of U.S. printing firms, increased merger and acquisition activity, forced more specialization in markets for printing, and induced printers to absorb functions previously done by independent typesetting and platemaking firms. The capital requirements of digitalization, along with market competition, reduced the estimated number of U.S. commercial printers to 35,000 in 1999 from approximately 40,000 a decade earlier. These factors also have led to more mergers and acquisitions, especially among the industry's medium-size and large firms. Such consolidation offers the potential of scale economies in purchasing equipment and supplies, lower administrative overhead, and stronger competitive positions in local and regional markets. The average printer's product mix is becoming more specialized, with equipment purchases geared more to specialized market segments than to offering a range of printed products to all customers. Finally, the demise of analog technology has virtually eliminated the former prepress functions of independently owned typesetters and platemakers, enabling printers to bring in-house and hopefully profit from their new digital prepress operations.

The Advertising Environment. Advertising expenditures in all U.S. media were estimated to exceed $160 billion in 1999, an increase in nominal dollars of 8 percent over 1998. The importance of attracting advertising dollars to the U.S. print media is crucial to the nation's printers: Over 60 percent of the commercial printing industry's total revenues come from advertising. Shifts in advertising expenditures in the various media cause tremors among printers. While the total market for U.S. advertising is expanding, the share of that market held by printed products is slowly contracting. Growth of the electronic media—first radio and television and then cable television and the Internet—is increasing their share of advertising dollars at the print media's expense. Some printed products remain in strong favor among the nation's advertisers: direct mail, catalogs, newspaper and magazine inserts, and coupons. Other print media experienced revenue growth in the later 1990s but have not gained market share, among them newspapers, periodicals, and outdoor and telephone directory advertising.

Projections of Industry and Trade Growth for the Next 1 and 5 Years

The value of shipments of the U.S. commercial printing industry is anticipated to approach $75 million in 2000, a gain in constant dollars of 4 percent over 1999 (see Table 25-9). This bullish demand for U.S. printed products is supported by growth of the U.S. economy, gains in advertising expenditures, rising corporate profits, and population increases. Interest in the year 2000 U.S. election and the Sydney, Australia, Olympics should translate into more advertising revenues and a larger domestic audience for a variety of printed products, including newspapers, periodicals, books, and direct mail. Continued expansion of the U.S. economy and more new business formations should induce greater demand for labels, decals, binders, blankbooks, and financial and legal printing. Growth in U.S. household formations should increase demand for catalogs, direct mail, and newspaper and magazine advertising inserts. Continued pressure from the electronic media, especially the delivery of information on-line, will soften U.S. demand for technical manuals, newsletters, printed directories, and business reference materials in looseleaf formats. Printers' profits, which rose steadily in the later 1990s, are expected to stabilize in the year 2000.

A strong U.S. economy accompanied by favorable demographics and stable prices for material inputs should enable U.S. printers to maintain an average annual rate of growth adjusted for inflation of 4 percent over the next 5 years. This rate of growth is predicated on continued high levels of U.S. corporate profits, steady expansion in U.S. advertising expenditures in the print media, and the formation of more new businesses. Demand for printed products also is determined by demographics, a factor with strongly positive implications for commercial printers. The population of the United States is projected to expand by 11.4 million over the 5-year time frame, including an addition of 5.6 million households. Printed advertising materials—catalogs, flyers, brochures, inserts, coupons, and direct mail—should be in greatest demand, but other printed matter—financial and legal printing, labels, decals, and binders—also is expected to show gains in unit volume. Pricing pressures are not expected to intensify significantly through 2004 even though global demand for paper is projected to rise. Paper mill capacity is underutilized worldwide, and the expected growth of Asia's economies through 2004 should not result in the price spikes on publication and printing paper last encountered in the mid-1990s.

Global Market Prospects

While the near-term fortunes of the U.S. commercial printing industry are relatively positive, the long-term outlook is less sanguine. The printing business is undergoing a period of plant consolidation, the absorption of new technology, and new competitors in the electronic media. Future success in what is now the printing industry may necessitate the evolution of printing firms into communication firms. Under this likely scenario, printers would take on additional tasks, enabling them to supply their customers with informational products in both print and electronic formats. As the U.S. printing industry completes this transition, it must contend with both the reduction in and the consolidation of its plants and seek new markets for its products in domestic and international arenas.

The progressive movement of the global printing industry into digital technology involves the enlargement of some major cost sectors: equipment, retraining, and recruitment. However, once they become skilled in digital communications, printers foresee the forging of closer ties to their customers and envision the supply of new products and services. By acquiring competence in both print and electronic communications, the printing industry can position itself to provide clients with a wide array of value-added options. Those options include the management of customer's databases; the storage of client-supplied materials in an electronic format for later use; the design of Web pages; the development and formatting of customers' materials into printed products, CDs, and applications for the Internet; and the development of training programs to inform customers about the appropriateness and employment of these options. The printing industry recognizes that adherence to a paper-based product mix will not guarantee survival, especially as information in electronic format becomes more popular. Adjusting to and gaining knowledge about digital technology is the printing industry's first step in keeping up with the changing needs of its customers.

The U.S. printing industry's domestic markets are well established, and success in the future depends largely on the continued expansion of advertising revenues in the print media. However, as the U.S. electronic media increase their share of the total market for advertising, printers are developing strategies that include a more global presence. Printers' plans focus less on expanding direct exports of printed products than on merging, acquiring, and establishing new facilities or forming linkages

TABLE 25-10: U.S. Trade Patterns in Commercial Printing[1] in 1998
(millions of dollars; percent)

Exports			Imports		
Regions[2]	Value[3]	Share, %	Regions[2]	Value[3]	Share, %
NAFTA	531	38	NAFTA	529	58
Latin America	145	10	Latin America	10	1
Western Europe	319	23	Western Europe	238	26
Japan/Chinese Economic Area	181	13	Japan/Chinese Economic Area	101	11
Other Asia	75	5	Other Asia	19	2
Rest of world	141	10	Rest of world	12	1
World	1,393	100	World	909	100
Top Five Countries	Value	Share, %	Top Five Countries	Value	Share, %
Canada	343	25	Canada	479	53
Mexico	188	14	United Kingdom	55	6
United Kingdom	118	8	Germany	53	6
Japan	88	6	Mexico	50	6
Germany	61	4	Italy	48	5

[1] SIC 275.
[2] For definitions of regional groupings, see "Getting the Most Out of *Outlook 2000*."
[3] Values may not sum to total due to rounding.
Source: U.S. Department of Commerce, Bureau of the Census.

with their foreign colleagues. Just as large U.S. consumer goods companies have encouraged domestic advertising agencies and periodical publishers to set up global media networks to promote simultaneous advertising campaigns worldwide, U.S. printers are eager to play a role in this consumer goods strategy. Printers envision the same-day production of direct mail, flyers, coupons, and other promotional materials on a global basis, designed to coincide with their multinational clients' advertising campaigns. The largest U.S. commercial printers already are extending their reach into international economies that afford the greatest potential opportunities. The initial strategy is to serve the regional needs of those economies, but this may be expanded in recognition of the global printing needs of multinational businesses.

Although U.S. exports of commercially printed products account for less than 2 percent of the industry's total revenues, the United States is second only to Germany in serving an international clientele. Exports of U.S. printed products totaled an estimated $1.3 billion in 1999 and should continue to trend upward for the indefinite future. The combined markets of Canada, Mexico, the United Kingdom, and Japan account for over 50 percent of the U.S. export total (see Table 25-10). The largest category of U.S. printed product exports is trade advertising materials, but U.S. printers have found strong overseas markets for labels and financial printing. Foreign markets for U.S. printed products are determined by the strength of their economies and their rates of currency exchange, factors that are subject to considerable fluctuation.

As the U.S. commercial printing industry seeks a more global presence, it is supported in those efforts by the federal government. First through GATT and now through the WTO, the government has worked to remove foreign trade barriers to the products and services of U.S. printers. Trade agreements that eliminate tariffs on printed products have been reached with important trading partners such as Canada, Israel, Japan, South Korea, Mexico, and the countries of the EU. These agreements, along with further removal of trade barriers in other countries, should encourage the U.S. commercial printing industry to take a more aggressive approach to opportunities in the international marketplace.

William S. Lofquist, formerly U.S. Department of Commerce, Office of Consumer Goods, (202) 482-0337, August 1999.

REFERENCES

Advertising Age, Crain Communications, Inc., 740 Rush Street, Chicago, IL 60611. (312) 649-5200.

Commercial Printing and Manifold Business Forms, 1992 Census of Manufactures, MC92-I-27B. Bureau of the Census, U.S. Department of Commerce, Washington, DC 20233. (301) 457-4768.

Communications Industry Forecast, Veronis, Suhler & Associates, Inc., 350 Park Avenue, New York, NY 10022. (212) 935-4990.

Employment and Earnings, Bureau of Labor Statistics, U.S. Department of Labor, Washington, DC 20212. (202) 606-6555.

Greeting Card Association Newsletter and Publications, Greeting Card Association, Inc., 1350 New York Avenue, N.W., Suite 615, Washington, DC 20005. (202) 393-1778.

Greeting Cards; Bookbinding; Printing Trade Services, 1992 Census of Manufactures, MC92-I-27C. Bureau of the Census, U.S. Department of Commerce, Washington, DC 20233. (301) 457-4768.

Industrial Production and Capacity Utilization, Industrial Output Section, Mail Stop #2, Division of Research and Statistics, Board of Governors of the Federal Reserve System, Washington, DC 20551. (202) 452-2570.

Newspapers, Periodicals, Books and Miscellaneous Publishing, 1992 Census of Manufactures, MC92-I-27A. Bureau of the Census, U.S. Department of Commerce, Washington, DC 20233. (301) 457-4768.

Producer Price Indexes, Bureau of Labor Statistics, U.S. Department of Labor, Washington, DC 20212. (202) 606-7716.

Statistics for Industry Groups and Industries, 1996 Annual Survey of Manufactures, M96 (AS)-1. Bureau of the Census, U.S. Department of Commerce, Washington, DC 20233. (301) 457-4768.

Value of Product Shipments, 1996 Annual Survey of Manufactures, M96 (AS)-2. Bureau of the Census, U.S. Department of Commerce, Washington, DC 20233. (301) 457-4768.

Newspapers

Editor & Publisher, Editor & Publisher Company, 11 West 19th Street, New York, NY 10011. (212) 675-4380.

Newspaper Newsletter, Morton Research, P.O. Box 40, Spencerville, MD 20868. (301) 879-9806.

Presstime, Newspaper Association of America, Inc., 1921 Gallows Road, Suite 600, Vienna, VA 22182. (703) 902-1600.

Publisher's Auxiliary, National Newspaper Association, 1627 K Street, N.W., Washington, DC 20006. (202) 466-7200.

Periodicals

Business Publication Rates and Data, Standard Rate & Data Service, 3004 Glenview Road, Wilmette, IL 60091. (708) 256-6067.

Consumer Magazine and Agri-Media Rates and Data, Standard Rate & Data Service, 3004 Glenview Road, Wilmette, IL 60091. (708) 256-6067.

Folio: The Magazine of Magazine Management, an Intertec/Primedia publication, P.O. Box 4949, Stamford, CT 06907. (203) 358-9900.

Gale Directory of Publications, Gale Research, Inc., Book Tower Building, Detroit, MI 48226. (313) 961-2242.

Magazine World, International Federation of the Periodical Press, Queens House, 55/57 Lincoln's Inn Fields, London WC2A 3LJ, UK 011-44-171-379-3822.

Newsletter of International Publishing, Magazine Publishers of America, Inc., 919 Third Avenue, New York, NY 10022. (212) 872-3700.

Sumir Husni's Guide to New Magazines, Department of Journalism, University of Mississippi, P.O. Box 2906, University, MS 38677.

Book Publishing

Book Industry Trends, Book Industry Study Group, Inc., 160 Fifth Avenue, New York, NY 10010. (212) 929-1393.

Book Publishing Report, Simba Information, Inc., 11 River Bend Drive South, P.O. Box 4234, Stamford, CT 06907. (203) 358-9900.

Industry Statistics, Association of American Publishers, Inc., 71 Fifth Avenue, New York, NY 10003. (212) 255-0200.

Publishers Weekly, a Cahners/R.R. Bowker publication, 249 West 17th Street, New York, NY 10011. (212) 463-6758.

Publishing Trends, Market Partners International, Inc., 232 Madison Avenue, Suite 1400, New York, NY 10016. (212) 447-0855.

Subtext, Open Book Publishing, Inc., 90 Holmes Avenue, P.O. Box 2228, Darien, CT 06820. (203) 316-8008.

Weekly Bookseller, American Booksellers Association, Inc., 828 South Broadway, Tarrytown, NY 10591. (914) 591-2665.

Commercial Printing

American Printer, an Intertec/Primedia publication, 29 N. Wacker Drive, Chicago, IL 60606. (312) 726-2802.

Graphic Arts Monthly, Cahners Publishing Company, 249 West 17th Street, N.Y. 10011. (212) 463-6828.

Graphic Communications World, Green Sheet Communications, Inc., P.O. Box 727, Hartsdale, NY 10530. (914) 472-3051.

High Volume Printing, Innes Publishing Company, 425 Huehl Road, Building 11, P.O. 368, Northbrook, IL 60062. (312) 563-5940.

Print Business Register, PTN Graphic Arts Network, Inc., 20 E. Jackson Boulevard, Chicago, IL 60604. (312) 922-5402.

Printing Business Report, National Association of Printing Leadership, Inc., 75 West Century Road, Paramus, NJ 07652. (201) 634-9600.

Printing Impressions, North American Publishing Co., 401 N. Broad Street, Philadelphia, PA 19108. (215) 238-5300.

Printing News, PTN Publishing Co., 445 Broad Hollow Road, Melville, NY 11747. (516) 845-2700.

Ratio Studies, Printing Industries of America, Inc., 100 Daingerfield Road, Alexandria, VA 22314. (703) 519-8100.

Technology Forecast, Graphic Arts Technical Foundation, Inc., 200 Deer Run Road, Sewickly, PA 15143. (412) 741-6860.

U.S. & World Printing Industry—1997 & 2002, Clayton/Curtis/Cottrell, 1722 Madison Court, Louisville, CO 80027. (303) 665-2005.

What's News in Graphic Communications, Michael H. Bruno, 228 Orchard Lane, Glen Ellyn, IL 60137. (630) 469-9984.

Worldwide Graphics, Reebius Research Labs, Inc. 3952 N. Southport, Suite 143, Chicago, IL 60613. (773) 935-2135.

■ RELATED CHAPTERS

Chapter 10: Paper and Allied Products
Chapter 18: Production Machinery
Chapter 24: Photographic Equipment and Supplies
Chapter 32: Entertainment and Electronic Media
Chapter 48: Professional Business Services

INFORMATION SERVICES
Economic and Trade Trends

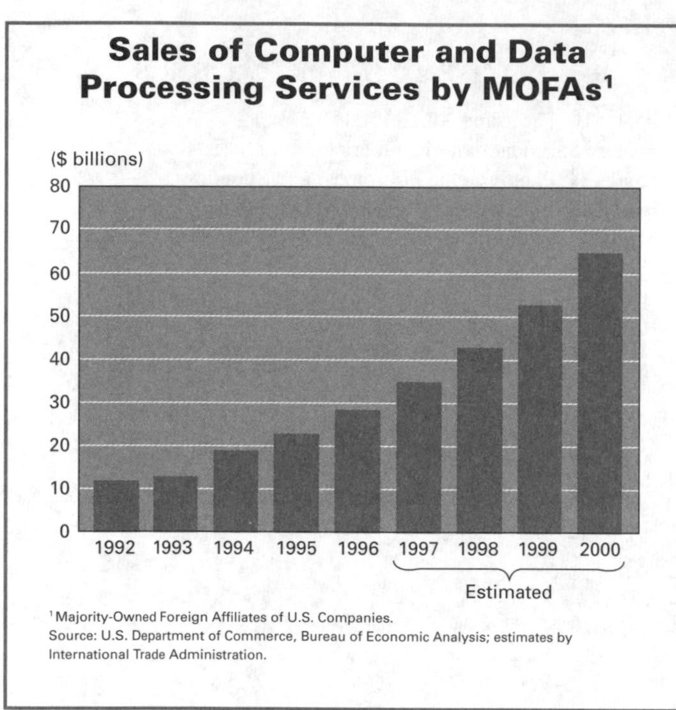

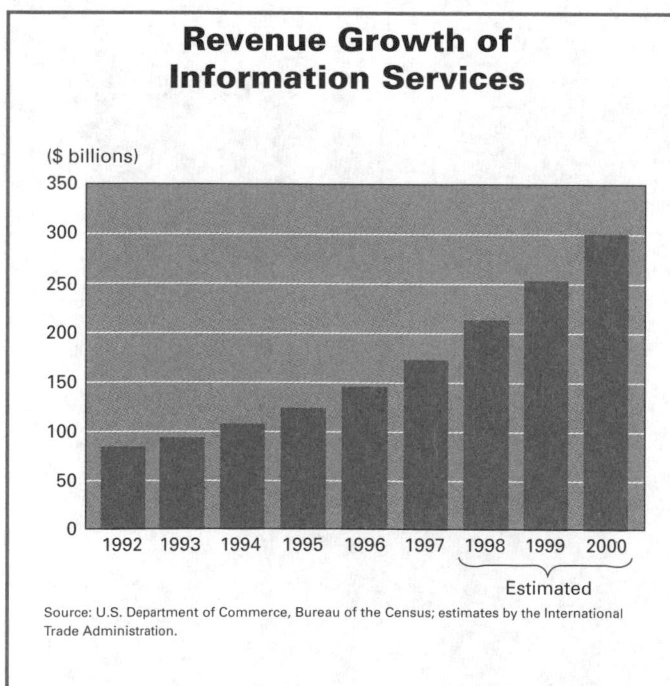

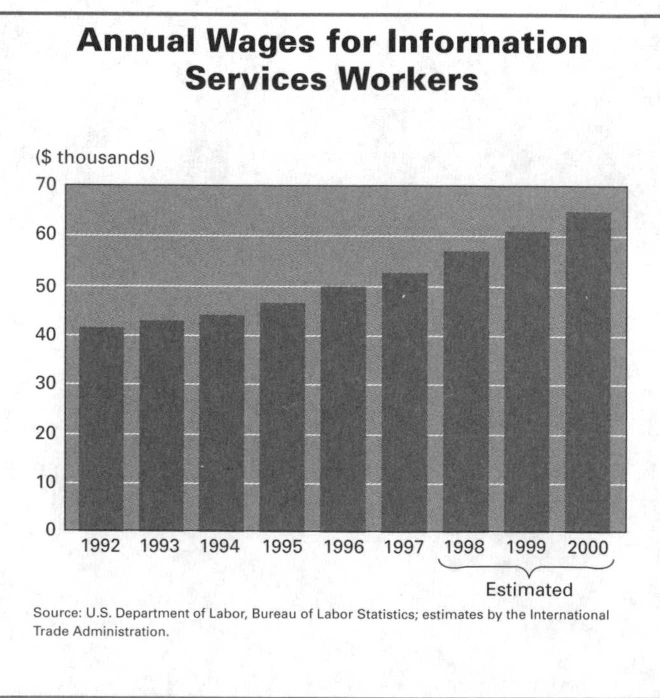

See "Getting the Most Out of *Outlook 2000*" for definitions of terms.

26

Information Services

INDUSTRY DEFINITION Information services have permeated the world economy to such an extent that defining this industry has become difficult. For this chapter's purposes, information services are defined primarily as professional computer services, data processing and network services, and electronic information services. Professional computer services, partially covered by SIC 7371, 7373, 7377, 7378, and 7379, is the largest information services subsector; data processing and network services, partially covered by SIC 7374 and 7376, is the second largest; and electronic information services, under SIC 7375, is third.

OVERVIEW

"Globalization" is a term that perfectly fits the information and communication services industry, which has grown by leaps and bounds during the last two decades through significant technological breakthroughs; this industry has made outstanding contributions to production and productivity levels throughout the world economy. National economies will rapidly become integrated into the global "information economy" in which the information-intensiveness of most goods and services will increase, competition will intensify, and the development of electronic commerce will be a key element.

In the United States, phenomenal growth in the production and consumption of information services and information technology (IT) has been one of the major elements of the record-breaking overall economic growth of the last several years. The importance of information services cannot be overemphasized; they have permeated manufacturing, transportation, utilities, energy, distribution services, financial services, educational institutions, and public administration.

As a result of the changes brought about by IT, new products and services have multiplied and a plethora of markets has emerged to satisfy the seemingly insatiable needs of businesses and consumers. Of course, companies not only have had to reorganize but have often had to revolutionize the way they operate, while governments and regulatory agencies have had to initiate programs and strategies that would have been unimaginable a few years ago.

Two critical issues emanating from the spread of technology are privacy and security. Self-regulation by business has long been accepted in the United States as an integral aspect of a competitive marketplace, while government is responsible for establishing an unimpeded and fair environment. However, as the electronic side of information services spreads worldwide, variance in national laws may become an obstacle that can be surmounted only through the adoption of certain principles, the most important being that market forces in an open and competitive environment should be the instrument that makes available to consumers the array of information services that technology has developed. The second most important principle involves the responsibility of governments to eliminate barriers, coordinate international policies, and build a stable and transparent legal environment.

DOMESTIC AND INTERNATIONAL TRENDS

Information services and computer services are traded primarily through foreign affiliates of U.S. companies in foreign markets, referred to as U.S. majority-owned foreign affiliates (MOFAs). U.S. sales of computer services by MOFAs reached $28.3 billion in 1996, an increase of almost 25 percent over 1995 (see Table 26-1 and Economic and Trade Trends at the beginning of the chapter). Europe is the largest market for the United States, and the Asia-Pacific region is the second largest. In 1996, sales in Europe by MOFAs posted a 21 percent increase over 1995 and sales in the Asia-Pacific region grew 11 percent.

The United States has had a considerable trade surplus in information services for a number of years (See Economic and

TABLE 26-1: Sales of Computer and Data Processing Services by Majority U.S.-Owned Foreign Affiliates
(millions of dollars except as noted)

	1992	1993	1994	1995	1996	1997[1]	1998[1]	1999[1]	2000[2]	2004[2]
Total sales	11,664	12,675	18,777	22,662	28,313	34,824	42,833	52,684	64,801	120,585
Percent change		8.7	48.1	20.7	24.9	23.0	23.0	23.0	23.0	23.0[3]

[1] Estimate.
[2] Forecast.
[3] Compound annual rate.
Source: U.S. Department of Commerce, Bureau of Economic Analysis; estimates by International Trade Administration.

Trade Trends at the beginning of the chapter). Despite strong increases in imports, U.S. information services generated a $2.6 billion surplus in 1997; that surplus is expected to expand well into the next decade as more countries liberalize their telecommunication networks and open their markets to international competition (see Table 26-2).

The largest section of the U.S. information services market, nearly 70 percent of the total in 1997, is the professional computer services subsector, which includes systems integration, computer programming services, consulting, training, facilities management and maintenance, and computer rental and leasing. It has been a fast-growing area, having gone from $79.3 billion in receipts in 1995 to $94.2 billion in 1996 and 116.5 billion in 1997; it is estimated that by 2004 receipts from this subsector will be close to half a trillion dollars (see Table 26-3).

Large U.S. systems integrators and professional computer consultants have found strong demand for their services both domestically and internationally, especially since businesses worldwide are endeavoring to take full advantage of the Internet and its vast potential.

The second largest section of the U.S. information services market, accounting for approximately 25 percent of the total in 1997, is the data processing and network services subsector, which includes data entry, credit card authorization and billing, payroll processing, and a broad range of network services, such as electronic data interchange, electronic mail delivery, file transfer, and electronic funds transfer. Revenues from this subsector grew from $38.5 billion in 1995 to $44.0 billion in 1996 and $46.8 billion in 1997; in 2004, it is estimated that they will top $100 billion (see Table 26-4). The outlook for data processing operations is extremely bright, since the demand for such automated routine functions will parallel the global growth of IT as a whole.

The third section of the U.S. information services market, accounting for around 5 percent of the total in 1997, is the electronic information services subsector, which provides a variety of on-line services with access to the Internet, the World Wide

TABLE 26-2: Information Services Balance of Trade
(millions of dollars except as noted)

	1992	1993	1994	1995	1996	1997	1998[1]	1999[1]	2000[2]	2004[2]
U.S. exports	1,417	1,680	2,332	2,418	2,798	3,047	3,412	3,821	4,280	6,734
U.S. imports	143	211	224	282	287	434	451	469	488	568
Balance of trade	1,274	1,469	2,108	2,136	2,511	2,613	2,961	3,352	3,792	6,166

[1] Estimate.
[2] Forecast.
Source: U.S. Department of Commerce, Bureau of Economic Analysis; estimates by International Trade Administration.

TABLE 26-3: Professional Computer Services (SIC 7371, 7373, 7377, 7378, 7379)[1] Trends and Forecasts
(millions of dollars except as noted)

	1992	1993	1994	1995	1996	1997	1998[2]	1999[2]	2000[3]	2004[3]
Receipts	36,429	62,182	70,326	79,329	94,232	116,535	149,164	178,996	214,795	445,401
Percent change		70.7	13.1	12.8	18.7	23.6	28.0	20.0	20.0	20.0

[1] SIC 7371: computer programming services
SIC 7373: computer integrated systems design
SIC 7377: computer rental and leasing
SIC 7378: computer maintenance and repair
SIC 7379: computer related services
[2] Estimate.
[3] Forecast.
Source: U.S. Department of Commerce, Bureau of the Census; estimates by International Trade Administration.

TABLE 26-4: Data Processing and Network Services (SIC 7374, 7376)[1] Trends and Forecasts
(millions of dollars except as noted)

	1992	1993	1994	1995	1996	1997	1998[2]	1999[2]	2000[3]	2004[3]
Receipts	23,055	26,273	31,829	38,462	43,961	46,761	52,372	58,657	65,696	103,374
Percent change		13.9	21.1	20.8	14.2	6.3	12.0	12.0	12.0	12.0

[1] SIC 7374: computer processing and data preparation and processing services
SIC 7376: computer facilities management services
[2] Estimate.
[3] Forecast.
Source: U.S. Department of Commerce, Bureau of the Census; estimates by International Trade Administration.

TABLE 26-5: Information Retrieval Services (SIC 7375) Trends and Forecasts
(millions of dollars except as noted)

	1992	1993	1994	1995	1996	1997	1998[1]	1999[1]	2000[2]	2004[2]
Receipts	3,931	4,277	4,559	5,343	6,912	9,078	11,801	15,341	19,943	56,958
Percent change		8.8	6.6	17.1	29.3	31.3	30.0	30.0	30.0	30.0

[1] Estimate.
[2] Forecast.
Source: U.S. Department of Commerce, Bureau of the Census; estimates by International Trade Administration.

Web, and global E-mail. This subsector includes proprietary databases and information not only on-line but via CD-ROM, magnetic tape, floppy disk, or audiotext; it also could include bulletin boards, live conferencing, chat rooms, and home shopping. Information provided by this subsector ranges from financial and economic information for business uses to education and entertainment for individual consumers. Revenues for information retrieval services are growing more rapidly than are those for the other two subsectors, having increased from $5.3 billion in 1995 to $6.9 billion in 1996 and $9.1 billion in 1997; in 2004, they are expected to reach approximately $57 billion (see Table 26-5).

EMPLOYMENT AND WAGES

Employment growth in information service industries far outpaces the growth of total private employment (see Table 26-6). Between 1990 and 1997, the average annual growth rate for information services industries was 8.8 percent compared with 1.8 percent for total private employment. As the demand for IT professionals such as computer scientists, engineers, programmers, and systems analysts and managers has risen, so have the annual wages paid to those workers. For instance, the average annual growth in wages for all private industries between 1990 and 1997 was 3.7 percent; for information services workers, it

TABLE 26-6: Information Services Employment, 1990–1997
(thousands except as noted)

Industry	SIC	1990	1991	1992	1993	1994	1995	1996	1997	Change 1990–1997	Average Annual Growth, % 1990–1997
Total private employment		91,098	89,847	89,956	91,872	95,036	97,885	100,189	103,120	12,022	1.8
Computer programming services	7371	150.8	156.9	168.6	188.3	209.9	245.3	276.2	321.7	170.9	10.5
Computer integrated systems design	7373	97.5	98.7	102.5	109.5	116.4	129.9	143.5	162.9	65.4	7.3
Computer processing and data preparation	7374	196.7	198.2	204.4	207.3	209.5	223.1	230.0	248.6	51.9	2.9
Information retrieval systems	7375	47.7	45.2	45.2	46.2	48.0	56.9	70.2	81.3	33.6	8.9
Computer facilities management services, rental and leasing, and computer related services	7376 7377 7379	126.6	131.1	141.2	154.9	172.9	205.3	253.5	309.3	182.7	13.9
Computer maintenance and repair	7378	39.8	42.5	42.8	41.8	44.5	48.6	53.3	57.2	17.4	6.6
Total, information services		659.1	672.6	704.7	748.0	801.2	909.1	1026.7	1181.0	521.9	8.8
Share of total employment (percent)		0.7	0.7	0.8	0.8	0.8	0.9	1.0	1.1		

Source: U.S. Department of Labor, Bureau of Labor Statistics.

TABLE 26-7: Annual Wages for Information Services Workers, 1990–1997
(in dollars except as noted)

Industry	SIC	1990	1991	1992	1993	1994	1995	1996	1997	Change 1990–1997	Average Annual Growth, % 1990–1997
Average for all private industries		23,209	23,952	25,375	25,746	26,248	27,164	28,320	29,787	6,578	3.7
Computer programming services	7371	41,857	43,053	46,222	47,552	50,057	52,731	56,918	60,028	18,171	5.4
Computer integrated systems design	7373	43,795	44,640	48,556	49,689	52,749	54,711	59,352	61,430	17,635	5.1
Computer processing and data preparation	7374	30,452	30,772	34,374	36,131	36,625	39,749	43,341	43,660	13,208	5.4
Information retrieval systems	7375	32,704	35,044	36,704	38,898	38,583	42,197	45,308	49,582	16,878	6.2
Computer facilities management services, rental and leasing, and computer related services	7376 7377 7379	41,185	43,242	45,970	46,830	48,924	51,827	54,647	60,365	19,180	5.7
Computer maintenance and repair	7378	34,296	34,071	36,589	37,488	37,236	37,819	39,546	40,559	6,263	2.5
Average for information services		37,382	38,470	41,403	42,764	44,029	46,506	49,852	52,604	15,222	4.8

Source: U.S. Department of Labor, Bureau of Labor Statistics.

was 4.8 percent (see Table 26-7). In addition, the wage gap between IT workers and other workers continues to widen. In 1990, the average annual wage of all private industry workers was $23,209; it grew to $29,787 in 1997, a 28 percent increase. In contrast, the average annual wage for information service workers rose from $37,382 to $52,604 between 1990 and 1997, a 40 percent increase.

INFORMATION INDUSTRY STATISTICS

In April 1997 the Office of Management and Budget issued a notice in the *Federal Register* publicizing its decision to adopt the North American Industry Classification (NAICS) as the new U.S. economic classification system. The NAICS codes will be used in tabulating federal economic statistical data published for 1997 and later. The former classification system was the Standard Industrial Classification (SIC), which had been used since the 1940s. NAICS was developed in collaboration with Canada and Mexico and will be used by all three countries.

Another initiative launched by the Office of Management and Budget that has special significance for the services sector of the economy is a proposed product-oriented classification system that will improve the identification and classification of service products. This new classification system will be incorporated into the questionnaires for the 2002 Economic Census. Eventually this new system will cover both goods and services, but the focus on services is due to the fact that (1) industries included in the service sectors now account for about 45 percent of private sector gross domestic product (GDP) in the United States and include some of the fastest-growing segments of the economy, such as information services, computer services, communications, management consulting, temporary help services, and health services, and (2) despite the importance of the service sectors in the overall private economy, the United States currently has no product classification system for service industries; in contrast, the government has been collecting product-level data for manufacturing industries for 100 years.

Two reports that are of considerable usefulness and are replete with high-quality economic and statistical data are *Information Technology Outlook* and *Communications Outlook.* They are prepared by the Directorate for Science, Technology and Industry of the Organization for Economic Cooperation and Development (OECD) and are based on data provided by member countries, public telecommunication operators, and the International Telecommunication Union. Both outlooks are biennial, published in alternate years.

Information Technology Outlook provides member governments with internationally comparable data and analyses on trends in the IT sector, specifically, computer hardware, components, software, and services; it generally excludes telecommunications equipment and services, which are covered separately in *Communications Outlook.* In addition to economic and statistical analyses, *Information Technology Outlook* tackles a number of policy issues in detail. One is the standardization process that has become increasingly visible recently, largely as a result of the recognition that success in the deployment of a seamless and open global information infrastructure will depend on the ability to overcome differences in types of equipment, operating systems, and applications so that effective standards can be defined, developed, and implemented.

Another policy issue pertains to protection of intellectual property, protection of personal data and privacy, and security of information systems. The development of complicated and powerful information systems, such as the global information infrastructure (GII), that could be used to transmit to a variety of clients all kinds of data and information—medical, legal, personal, statistical, scientific, educational—makes the need for protection essential. Also essential is that as information crosses national boundaries at an increasing rate, the problems that it may produce be resolved by means of international consultation and cooperation.

Communications Outlook presents the most recent data comparing the performance of the telecommunication sectors in OECD countries and their policy frameworks. As the role of the communications sector in OECD economies expands, the underlying factors in its success seem to be the continuous application of new technologies, the multiplicity of its services, and the contribution it has made to the globalization of economic activity. According to the report, businesses are demanding telecommunication applications support at the international level that is similar to the support they are receiving domestically. Consequently, service providers have shown immense flexibility in a variety of ways: the convergence of telecommunication and information technology, international callback services, cordless and cellular telephones, facsimile machines, television receivers, video services, and other types of user equipment. Information technologies are changing the way networks transmit, receive, and manage information, while with network costs becoming less sensitive to distance, customers are looking for seamless service. Providers are eager to oblige, and whether they own fixed telecommunication networks, mobile telecommunication networks, satellites, cable television networks, or information hardware or software companies, they are trying to enter each other's markets. The challenge to government regulators and policy makers is to ensure a market structure that will enable public telecommunication operators and new entrants to compete in the provision of all telecommunication services on a fair and equitable basis, a situation that should result in price discipline, improved quality, and broader consumer choice.

INTERNATIONAL ACTIVITIES

Policies and issues affecting the information services sector include market access, privacy protection, security and encryption, copyright, and intellectual property protection. National governments and international organizations are working together to harmonize disparate approaches to these issues. The General Agreement on Trade in Service (GATS), the World Intellectual Property Organization (WIPO), the United Nations Commission on International Trade Law (UNCITRAL), the Transatlantic Business Dialogue (TABD), the Asia-Pacific Economic Cooperation (APEC), and the OECD are some of the international forums that work with private sector groups to increase access to information services around the world.

Specifically, the OECD, through its Directorate for Science, Technology and Industry and its various committees, provides a forum in which national policies can be analyzed, discussed, and compared and thus be made more effective; a place for consultations aimed at improved convergence or compatibility of national policies; and a location where analytic work and quantitative indicators are developed.

The OECD also organizes conferences that enhance international cooperation in electronic commerce. A conference entitled "Dismantling the Barriers to Global Electronic Commerce" took place in 1997 in Turku that was hosted by the government of Finland in cooperation with the European Commission. The conference drew together government and private sector policy makers who took stock of the issues and of recent steps to resolve them and discussed the policy principles on which actions may be taken to remove barriers and promote the fruitful development of electronic commerce. At a high-level symposium titled "A Borderless World—Realizing the Potential of Global Electronic Commerce" in October 1998 in Ottawa, Canada, ministers from many countries attempted to achieve a consensus on definitions and principles for the operation and use of global information networks for electronic commerce.

Background reports were prepared by the OECD to provide an analytic basis for these ministerial discussions. They included *The Role of Telecommunications and Information Infrastructures in Advancing Electronic Commerce, The Economic and Social Impacts of Electronic Commerce: Preliminary Findings and Research Agenda, The Year 2000 Problem: Impacts and Actions, Small and Medium-Sized Enterprises and Electronic Commerce, New Developments in Educational Software and Multimedia, Protection of Privacy on Global Networks, Consumer Protection in the Electronic Marketplace, An Inventory of Controls on Cryptography Technologies,* and *An Inventory of Approaches to Authentication and Certification.*

The Ottawa conference adopted three declarations to establish principles and goals and provide guidance for further OECD work:

- *The Declaration on Protection of Privacy on Global Networks* reaffirms the importance of protecting privacy, recognizing that the principles outlined in the 1980 OECD guidelines continue to provide an international foundation for the protection of privacy on any medium and that countries should work together and with the private sector to ensure their effective implementation in an open and global network environment.
- *The Declaration on Consumer Protection in the Context of Electronic Commerce* highlights the need to ensure that consumers who participate in electronic commerce are afforded a transparent and effective level of protection for electronic transactions.
- *The Declaration on Authentication for Electronic Commerce* states the ministers' determination not to discriminate against the authentication approaches taken by other countries and to amend, where appropriate, technology- or media-specific requirements in current laws or policies that might impede electronic commerce.

To maintain the momentum and preserve the coordination that was launched in Ottawa, it was decided to convene a working-level meeting approximately 1 year later to assess the progress made by the OECD, other international organizations, and private sector groups on the issues discussed at the Ottawa conference. The meeting was scheduled to be held in Paris in October 1999, and apart from OECD activities, some time was to be devoted to contributions the OECD can make to the next round of trade negotiations in view of the fact that the World Trade Organization (WTO) ministers were scheduled to convene a few weeks later.

Another major conference that took OECD efforts a step further was organized in May 1999 by the White House's National Economic Council with assistance by the Departments of Commerce, Labor, and Treasury; the National Science Foundation;

the White House's Office of Science and Technology; the Council of Economic Advisers; and the Small Business Administration. Titled "Understanding the Digital Economy," the conference examined not only information services and technology but also digitally delivered services and software; the need for new data, indicators, and tools; and the development of a plan for future research. Specifically, the following six areas were touched on by speakers at the conference:

- *Operational change.* Since IT has the potential to change the structure and performance of organizations and human enterprises, in what ways will it affect relationships within and among firms? To what extent and under what conditions will a digital economy lead to new organizational cultures?
- *Macroeconomic implications.* With IT playing an increasingly important role in growth, capital investment, and other aspects of the economy, what industry-level and economy-wide investments have been made in electronic commerce, including investments in IT equipment and workers? How pervasive is electronic commerce in the relationships among businesses and between businesses and consumers?
- *Market structure and competition.* What are the relationships and interactions between economic characteristics of information technologies, products, and services and the structure and competitiveness of markets? How do producer investment and consumer investment in the Internet and related technologies affect market structure and competition in new and established industries?
- *Access.* Since the growth of information services depends on the ability of businesses and consumers to participate, what barriers impede the diffusions of such services throughout the economy? To what extent does IT increase or decrease opportunities for economic progress for individuals, groups, and geographic areas?
- *Small business.* As much of the innovative activity in IT appears to emanate from small firms, what roles do start-ups and small firms play in different sectors of the economy? How and to what extent do the Internet and electronic commerce benefit or damage small and medium-size companies?
- *Employment and the workforce.* As IT and communications technology transform both the global economy and the size and composition of the labor force, how reliable are current models for projecting the labor market structure, especially in areas where technologies are changing rapidly? Are there any reliable indicators that assess labor market shortages in technologically oriented occupations?

The Impact of Information Services and Information Technology on Selected Service Industries

Virtually every sector of the economy—manufacturing, transportation, finance, retail and wholesale trade, government, and other service sectors—has been feeling the impact of information services and IT. The electronic exchange of information is transforming commercial and household activities and is accelerating faster than expected. It also is affecting the interaction between consumers and suppliers. Professional computers and information services in the marketplace provide new and innovative ways by which businesses can become more closely acquainted and more personal with the client base. This dynamic association provides companies with unbounded capabilities to expand product horizons and satisfy the unending needs and desires of consumers. Following are thumbnail sketches of the effect IT has had on selected service industries.

Direct Marketing. Domestic and international direct marketing have changed dramatically as a result of the influence of IT. The Internet has proved to be a valuable tool in distributing information and promoting goods and services to a mass clientele and potential customers. New technology also allows marketers to test new on-line advertising campaigns and conduct consumer feedback surveys regarding new products and services. The interactive capabilities of the World Wide Web allow companies to immediately assess the effectiveness of these campaigns rather than wait for quarterly reviews and year-end figures. In addition, technological advances in graphics allow consumers to see realistic images from many different angles, nearly allowing the customer to "touch" the product. Banner advertisements and pop-up windows allow companies to increase revenues and cut costs through efficient advertising.

Advances in IT not only have stretched the boundaries of macromarketing, reaching an increasing number of consumers, but also have paved the way for innovations in micromarketing, personalizing companies' relationships with their clients. The Internet has allowed the development of individual client profiles through on-line questionnaires and consumer surveys. These profiles, which are easily accessible through internal databases, allow companies to focus specific advertising campaigns on a narrow group of consumers who have displayed certain purchasing preferences. As a result, the advertising and market access of companies is essentially boundless. A company with well-developed Internet sales can in essence advertise to a customer an item that is very similar to or complements that customer's last purchase. Such a developed knowledge of an extensive customer base helps reduce the cost of advertising media such as flyers, catalogs, and handouts by focusing on a much narrower population of consumers.

Such improvements in the cost and management of electronic business have led to the advent of a multitude of cyberfirms within Internet cyberspace. Priding themselves on low inventory, virtual office space, and discounted goods and services, those companies, by eliminating the middleman, are fast becoming the newest and most profitable followers of progress in the electronic information society.

Education and Training. IT has allowed significant expansion in the fields of education and training. Through IT, services and programs once available only at the provider's place of business are now accessible throughout the world. Distance teaching through faxes and teleconferencing has paved the way for a surge in educational opportunities. Diplomas and certificates can be earned without one leaving the home, and downloadable classes and lessons increase the convenience and compatibility of a student's schedule. This makes it easier for people in their thirties or forties who want to further their education or get executive/management or technical training to deal with an increasingly competitive business world.

Innovative technological tools also are redefining the traditional models associated with training and hiring. Electronic submission of résumés makes the selection process less time-consuming by allowing selection criteria to be more definitive and customized, while expedited enrollment and electronic payment techniques allow more efficient service. The major obstruction to the expansion and worldwide acceptance of such services is the lack of access to Internet services in underdeveloped and developing countries. However, as twenty-first-century technology continues to grow and expand into new markets, this barrier will soon be overcome.

Entertainment. IT has contributed significantly to growth in the entertainment sector, and the Internet in particular is playing a major role in marketing. Record companies as well as retailers have Web sites where consumers can browse titles, listen to sampled music, and purchase titles on-line. Other sites permit customers to select specific titles and create a set for computer download or a customized compact disc. However, as a result of increased Internet traffic and the popularity of data transfer, Internet piracy has become a major problem for the industry, which has taken significant steps against Internet site holders that offer illegal downloads. To curb copyright infringement, retailers have considered charging minimal prices while offering extensive title databases as incentives for on-line music sales.

Financial Services. As IT budgets for banks continue to rise, E-banking and E-commerce, which include payment mechanisms, present the greatest challenge to and opportunity for the commercial banking industry. Engaged in a race to build a bank-centric electronic payments infrastructure, banks are poised to solidify their premier role as a payment processor for the global economy. They also are offering to facilitate interactive banking by allowing customers to monitor account activity, transfer funds, pay bills, and send E-mail to customer service. On the securities side they are gearing up to provide customers with the tools needed to make investment decisions such as trading in stocks, bonds, and mutual funds. Harnessing technology to profitably serve their customers will be the banks' main concern in the future.

Health Care. Telemedicine has been one of the most important applications of IT in the health care services sector. Through technology, health care can be provided even over vast distances. This allows the transmission of basic patient data through computer networks as well as images such as x-rays, ultrasound, and magnetic resonance and makes possible consultations with medical specialists and patient interviews.

Telemedicine's chief benefit is that it eliminates the need for the physician and patient to be in the same geographic region. U.S. hospitals, managed care firms, physician groups, and other providers have recognized the commercial benefits that can be realized by offering such services, especially in rural sections of the United States and developing countries, where they are well suited to providing a cost-effective alternative to the maintenance of expensive medical facilities.

Professional Services. IT has the potential to achieve new levels of productivity, reducing the costs and improving the profitability of professional service providers such as architects, engineers, accountants, and attorneys. It will enhance the way service providers perform their professional responsibilities with clients and the way they communicate with colleagues. Furthermore, it permits providers of services and potential customers to efficiently find each other through Internet search engines and referral services. The Internet also allows increased levels of customer service and customer interaction by creating new opportunities for the customer to communicate directly with the service provider. Internal integration through IT will ensure that all the necessary elements of the organization will receive pertinent information relevant to client service, allowing critical data to be stored digitally in formats that permit instantaneous retrieval and transmission.

Publishing. IT has paved the way for substantial opportunities in the publishing industry. Assuming that copyright protection is obtained for the material, on-line publishing reduces the cost of reproducing manuscripts, documents, and bound works by eliminating the capital associated with printing and binding, advertising and distribution, and inventory costs. It also enables publishers to offer supplementary services to their customers, such as the convenience of making purchases from the home. Another service that has flourished is electronic versions of newspapers. According to the Newspaper Association of America, the number of newspapers providing on-line services has doubled in the last 3 years. One of the most popular and profitable services offered by these newspapers is the publication of on-line classified products.

Retailing. Retailing on the Internet promises to greatly benefit consumers and businesses, since it will allow retailers to reach their customers and suppliers at a relatively low cost. The resulting low prices for goods and services, along with the development of search engines that will be able to find merchandise on the Internet at the lowest quoted price, will benefit the consumer directly. Apart from the price factor, convenience is an important element of the electronic age, allowing consumers to comparison shop without leaving home.

Some catalog retailers, however, are proceeding cautiously in the use of the Internet by advertising their merchandise on the Internet but providing an 800 telephone number for customer orders. Some reasons for this hesitancy include a concern that it might decrease their catalog sales and the perception that going through a catalog is more satisfying to the customer than viewing a Web site. Other retailers are reluctant to devote more resources to the Internet until they feel more confident of consumer interest in the medium. Some international retailers must analyze their pricing and exclusivity arrangements with their affiliates. In response to this hesitancy by businesses and their customers, the private sector and the government are working together to improve the reliability of Internet transactions and tackle issues such as privacy and security and encryption and authentication certification.

Transportation and Travel. On-line services have greatly expanded and transformed the transportation industry. Airlines have developed or become aligned with on-line service providers to allow travelers to plan itineraries and book flights on-line. Through these systems, travelers are also able to rent cars and secure hotel reservations before arriving at their destinations. Corporations that wish to advertise special weekly discounts and travel programs to on-line clients can relay those materials to potential customers through E-mail databases. Since reservations are made directly with airline and rental agencies through Web sites, costs are dramatically reduced through the bypassing of associated advertising and personnel. Cyberspace has helped develop the market of the local and national tourism industries. The Web sites of these industries can provide travelers with train schedules, road maps, and lists of restaurants and even golf courses. This capability allows travelers to develop more complex and accurate itineraries before talking to a travel agent.

Recent advances in IT have allowed expansion in the shipping and air transportation industry. Freight companies such as UPS, DHL, and Federal Express have developed Web sites that serve as important resources for small exporters who rely on expedited and reliable yet cost-effective shipping. Package identification tags enable users to track shipped items, ensuring certifiable delivery of goods. Ocean carriers, railroads, and trucking firms have developed Web sites and use computer-generated documentation. Critical to delivery time is the speed at which goods can pass customs. IT has allowed freight companies to send airway bills, ocean bills of lading, and vessel manifests for customs clearance electronically before a shipment arrives at its destination, saving a significant amount of time.

Wray O. Candilis, U.S. Department of Commerce, Office of Service Industries, (202) 482-0339, September 1999.

■ REFERENCES

Bank Technology News, Faulkner & Grey, 11 Penn Plaza, New York, NY 10001-2006. (800) 535-8403, www.electronicbanker.com

Business America, January 1998, U.S. Department of Commerce, Washington, DC 20230. (202) 482-3809.

Business Software Alliance, 1150 18 Street, NW, Washington, DC 20036. (202) 872-5500, www.bsa.org.

Census of Service Industries, U.S. Department of Commerce, Bureau of the Census, Washington, DC 20230. (301) 457-2689.

Computerworld, International Data Group, Inc., 500 Old Connecticut Path, P.O. Box 9171, Framingham, MA 01701-9171. (508) 879-0700, www.computerworld.com.

Datamation, Cahners Publishing Co., 275 Washington Street, Newton, MA 02158. (617) 558-4281, www.datamation.com.

Electronic Commerce World, 2021 Coolidge Street, Hollywood, FL 33020-2400. (954) 925-5900, www.ecresources.com.

Electronic Industries Association, 2500 Wilson Boulevard, Arlington, VA 22201. (703) 907-7500. www.eia.org.

Electronic Messaging Association, 1655 North Fort Myer Drive, Arlington, VA 22209. (703) 524-5550, www.ema.org.

The Emerging Digital Economy II, U.S. Department of Commerce, Washington, DC 20230. (202) 482-8369, www.ecommerce.gov.

Employment and Earnings, U.S. Department of Labor, Bureau of Labor Statistics, Washington, DC 20212. (202) 606-6373.

European Union News, European Commission Delegation, 2300 M Street, NW, Washington, DC 20037. (202) 862-9500.

Federal Computer Week, FCW Government Technology Group, 3141 Fairview Park Drive, Falls Church, VA 22042-4507. (703) 876-5100.

Government Computer News, 8601 Georgia Avenue, Silver Spring, Maryland 20910. (301) 650-2000, www.gcn.com.

Information Industry Association, 1625 Massachusetts Avenue, NW, Washington, DC 20036. (202) 986-0280, www.infoindustry.org.

Information Technology Association of America, 1616 North Fort Myer Drive, Arlington, VA 22209-3106. (703) 522-5055, www.itaa.org.

Information Today, Information Today, Inc., 143 Old Marlton Pike, Medford, NJ 08055. (609) 654-6266, www.infotoday.com.

Organization for Economic Cooperation and Development, various publications, OECD Washington Center, 2001 L Street, NW, Washington, DC 20036-4922. (202) 785-6323.

Recent Trends in U.S. Services Trade, U.S. International Trade Commission, May 1999. www.usitc.gov.

Service Annual Survey: 1997, U.S. Department of Commerce, Bureau of the Census, Washington, DC 20233. (301) 457-2826.

Software Publishers Association, 1730 M Street, NW, Washington, DC 20036-4510. (202) 452-1600, www.spa.org.

Survey of Current Business, U.S. Department of Commerce, Bureau of Economic Analysis, Washington, DC 20230. (202) 606-9900.

■ RELATED CHAPTERS

24: Photographic Equipment and Supplies
25: Printing and Publishing
27: Computer Equipment
28: Computer Software and Internet
30: Telecommunications Services

Quality and Productivity

COMPUTER EQUIPMENT
Economic and Trade Trends

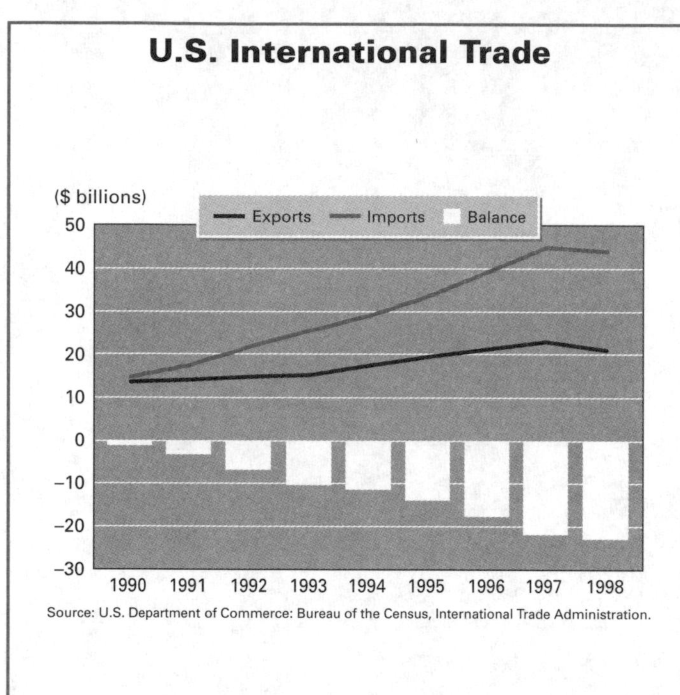

Source: U.S. Department of Commerce: Bureau of the Census, International Trade Administration.

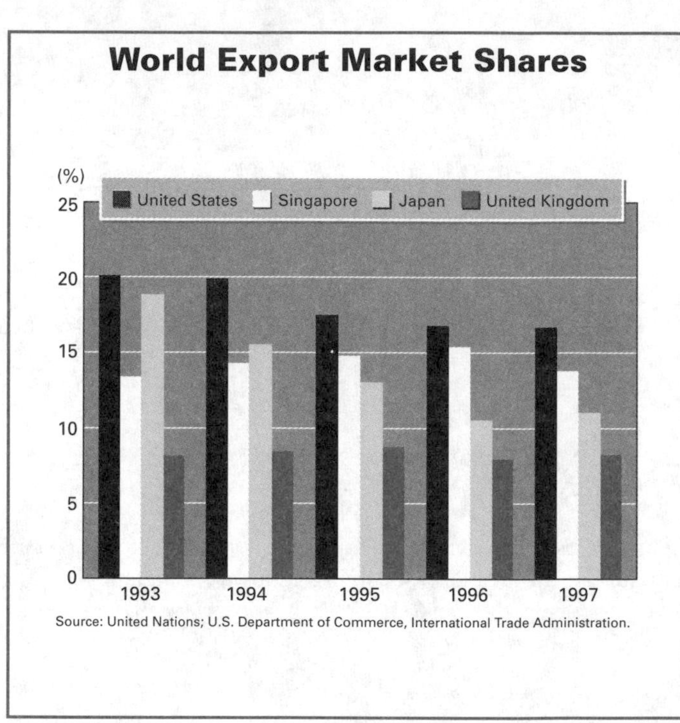

Source: United Nations; U.S. Department of Commerce, International Trade Administration.

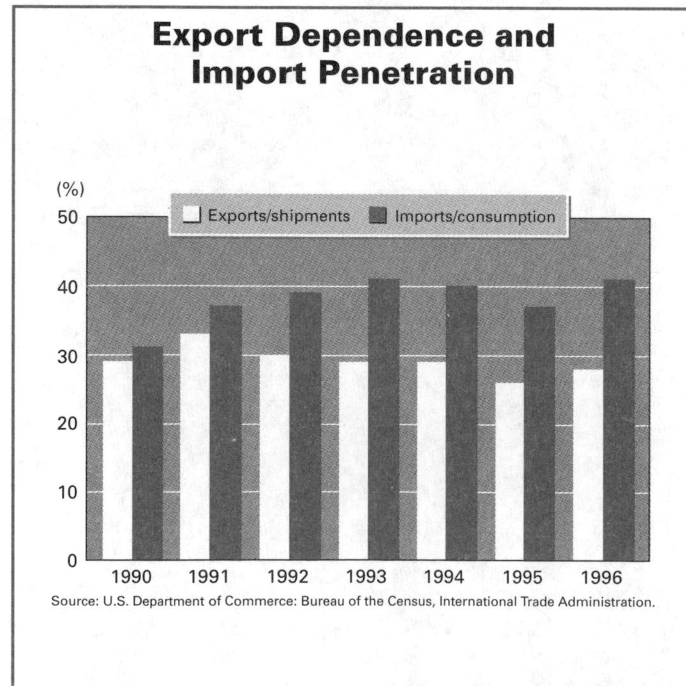

Source: U.S. Department of Commerce: Bureau of the Census, International Trade Administration.

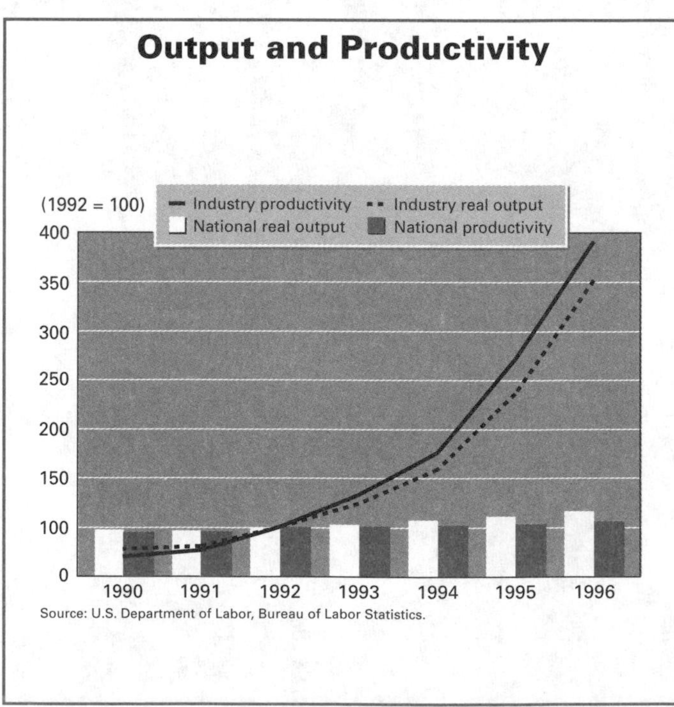

Source: U.S. Department of Labor, Bureau of Labor Statistics.

See "Getting the Most Out of *Outlook 2000*" for definitions of terms.

27

Computer Equipment

INDUSTRY DEFINITION Computer equipment includes computer systems, peripherals, and networking equipment (SIC 3571, 3572, 3575, 3577). Computer parts are not included under product shipments and trade data, and computer modems (SIC 3561) are not included under product shipments.

GLOBAL INDUSTRY TRENDS

The computer equipment industry's entrance into the twenty-first century has been characterized by the continued globalization of the industry and the convergence of information technologies. For computer equipment companies to compete and survive in a quickly evolving industry, maintain market share, and expand their global presence, industry players must rapidly devise and adopt new business strategies to keep up with emerging trends. At the turn of the century, computer equipment firms are facing many challenges, including shortened product life cycles, concern about overhead cost requirements, intense price competition, and the convergence of traditionally distinct markets and technologies as the industry enters a more networked world. If they are strategically leveraged, these challenges can present opportunities to industry players that can ultimately offer more computing alternatives to information technology end users at a lower cost.

Continued Globalization of Production

As the computer equipment industry has become more global, calculating a precise figure for each supplier nation's share of production and exports has become increasingly difficult, since the final products involve many multinational assembly and production operations and alliances. The U.S.-based industry was the leader in worldwide manufacturing of computer equipment in 1998 (the most recent year for which data are available), accounting for 29 percent of global production, followed by Japan and Taiwan. Japan and the United States alone represented half of that production. Computer equipment companies in many principal supplier nations are continuing to increase their offshore production and assembly of key components. For example, in 1998, 89 percent of Taiwan's desktop personal computers (PCs) and 37 percent of its motherboards were produced offshore in China, Malaysia, Thailand, and the Philippines, where production costs are much lower. China has emerged as the sixth largest computer manufacturing country in the world, and some experts expect that nation to account for more than half the PCs manufactured worldwide by 2004.

Globalization of business activity also results from continued investment across geographic boundaries. According to the Bureau of Economic Analysis, the U.S. computer and office equipment industry's overseas investment position fluctuated between 1994 and 1996. The level of U.S. investment activity then began to increase, totaling $17.8 billion by 1998 (the most recent data available), a 7 percent increase over 1997. Europe, Canada, and Mexico together were the recipients of roughly 40 percent of this investment activity in 1998. Although data are not available for all countries and regions, many industry analysts believe that much of the remaining overseas investment occurred in Asia because of that region's lower labor and overhead costs of manufacturing.

In 1998, U.S. direct investment activity abroad in the computer and office equipment industry was over six times greater than foreign direct investment in the U.S.-based industry, which totaled $2.7 billion. The level of foreign investment in the United States actually decreased 25 percent compared with 1997. In 1997, the operations of affiliates of foreign firms in the United States produced $9.6 billion worth of computer and business equipment. Subsidiaries of parents in the European and Asia-Pacific regions accounted for 44 percent and 39 percent of that total, respectively.

Shift to Contract Manufacturing

The traditional supply chain structure of computer equipment manufacturers is changing quickly. In light of the shortened life cycles of today's products compared with the cost of developing and manufacturing new technology, computer equipment companies have balanced their assets carefully to shorten their products' time to market while keeping burdensome overhead and operational costs down. Many traditional original equipment manufacturers (OEMs) and start-up companies in the computer equipment industry have been outsourcing some of their production to contract electronics manufacturers (CEMs) that already have low-cost manufacturing plants in the United States and overseas at key regional hubs. Outsourcing of production has enabled them to devote more time to developing next-generation products and keep up with cutting-edge high-technology trends.

This wide-scale adoption of a new manufacturing strategy has led to an acceleration of CEM production within the OEM supply chain and is exemplified by the record number of OEM divestitures of assembly operations, manufacturing plants, and repair facilities in 1999. As of July 1999, there were at least 13 major OEM divestitures. Industry experts expected this number to exceed 30 by the end of 1999, compared with 24 in 1998 and 13 in 1997. The CEM industry is growing at a rate of almost 25 percent a year, and contractors are accounting for a greater percentage of OEMs' costs of goods sold. Based on International Data Corporation (IDC) estimates, revenues in the worldwide market for outsourcing services covering networking equipment and desktop PCs reached $14.3 billion in 1998, an increase of $2 billion over 1997. By 2003, the outsourcing market is expected to more than double, reaching $30.7 billion.

This trend will continue in the years to come as CEMs are increasingly integrated into the OEM supply chain. According to a Bear Stearns Electronics manufacturing services and supply-chain poll, 90 percent of the leading and emerging OEMs, with costs of goods sold between $10 billion and $50 billion, plan to increase their alliances with CEMs. Some of the OEMs polled stated that they may outsource as much as 50 percent of their final product. Their greater use of outsourcing will put pressure on middle-tier OEMs, those with revenues of $1 billion or less, to do the same thing to stay competitive. CEMs also are diversifying their responsibilities within the OEM supply chain. In addition to their traditional assembly operations, CEMs are increasingly involved in design and support services. By 2002, Dataquest, a market research firm, predicts that the traditional channel assembly method of building PCs will account for no more than 8 percent of total production in the industry.

Fierce Competition and Accelerated Performance

The year 1999 also witnessed the continuation of the long-term trend in technology breakthroughs and price declines across the broad spectrum of computers. The release of Apple's PowerMac G4, containing the equivalent of the first supercomputer on a chip that is capable of operating at up to one gigaflop, signaled convergence between high-performance computing and desktop computing. Price competition was particularly severe in low-end PCs, enabling more people to replace old systems or purchase more than one computer for a household. The pervasive price erosion in this systems area has placed pressure on the U.S. computer equipment industry to balance its pricing strategy with the need to develop new technologies before its competitors do. Although there is increased global demand for PCs because of cheaper prices for these systems, the growth rate for PC unit shipments has greatly surpassed the dollar value of the PCs being shipped. According to IDC, continuing price pressure was expected to slow PC dollar growth to less than 7 percent in 1999, while the growth of shipments was forecast to average 19 percent.

Convergence of Information Technologies

The rapid convergence of computing, telecommunications, information appliances, and the Internet is transforming home- and corporate-based consumer demand for information technology products. Homes, educational institutes, businesses, and the public sector will become more networked through increased use of intranets and extranets, enabling them to increase efficiency and drive costs down. Intranets are computer networks that allow organizations to make internal resources available to their employees by using familiar Internet clients such as Web browsers, while extranets are intranets that businesses open selectively to their suppliers, customers, or strategic partners. More businesses, particularly small to medium-size enterprises, will go on-line to meet their customers' needs through extranets or through the development of electronic commerce strategies. Extranets will enable companies to streamline their business-to-business transactions by speeding delivery times, orders, and payments; extend their services for customers; and allow real-time information sharing along their supply chains.

There is a plethora of new products and services that allow users to become less reliant on the PC. Users are beginning to shift away from desktops and laptops to handhelds, wearable computers, pagers, and cell phones that can perform some of the traditional functions of a desktop model but offer greater convenience. Users increasingly are demanding technologies that can perform the functions of data synchronization, data storage, and scheduling. The advent of higher bandwidth will accelerate the mobile computing age, providing users with more flexibility in the ways they access shared information and synchronize and/or store data.

The Year 2000 Problem

According to IDC, the global costs for fixing the year 2000 (Y2K) problem, including spending on internal and external services and hardware and software purchases and/or upgrades, could reach a cumulative $297 billion by the end of 2001. Most large corporations worldwide addressed the issue in 1998 and 1999. Despite predictions that the Y2K problem would generate skyrocketing revenues for information technology vendors, actual spending on Y2K-related projects was marginal at a global level. Based on IDC reporting, worldwide spending on Y2K peaked in 1998, with Y2K projects accounting for only 6 percent of total worldwide information technology (IT) spending. In that year, purchases and/or upgrades of hardware devices represented 11 percent of the global Y2K spending budget, reaching $10.04 billion. That figure was expected to decrease to $9.44 billion by of the end of 1999 and then decline 56 percent to $4.2 billion by the end of the year 2000. Many small to medium-size enterprises and less developed economies that have been grappling with financial and resource constraints may delay purchasing new equipment until the effects of the Y2K problem are more clearly felt and understood.

Asian Financial Crisis

The financial crisis that plagued many Asian economies and adversely affected the rest of the world in 1997 and 1998 is subsiding, and economies are recovering. Although spending on large-scale systems that require high capital investment may have declined in 1999, growth in the lower-end segments should have offset those budget cutbacks. Rising demand for PCs in the Asia-Pacific region translated into revenue growth compared with the previous year, according to IDC. During the second quarter of 1999, PC sales in that region increased 18 percent over the first quarter, and unit sales grew by 34 percent over the same quarter in 1998. The fastest-growing PC markets in the region were South Korea and Taiwan. Falling PC prices and low PC penetration will drive consumer interest in PCs in the future. IT spending in the Asia-Pacific region is expected to grow 8 percent annually from $145 billion in 1997 to $215 billion by 2002. China, South Korea, India, and Australia are expected to be the fastest-growing IT markets in the region.

Investment in the development of a more sophisticated IT infrastructure has been considered integral to economic recovery and international competitiveness for these countries' industries. For example, Singapore continues to be among the highest IT spenders in the world, allocating 3 percent of its 1999 gross national product to IT investment. The government of Singapore budgeted $205 million for the implementation of IT projects in schools and tertiary institutions in 1998. In Thailand, by 1999 the number of Internet users was expected to grow 50 percent. This increasing demand for the use of Internet services will stimulate demand for networking products. U.S. computer equipment manufacturers are in a good position to take advantage of these investment and business opportunities in light of their strength in the production and marketing of computer hardware and networking equipment.

DOMESTIC TRENDS

Increased Mergers and Acquisitions

The need to stay competitive is the driving force behind the U.S. computer equipment industry's continued trend toward consolidation. To stay ahead of their rivals, companies in many high-tech sectors are continuously seeking cash infusions and cutting-edge product innovations. To meet these competitive challenges, they are turning more and more to mergers and acquisitions as a viable means for growth and development. The acquisition option, no longer the realm of only large public corporations, increasingly has become the preferred liquidity route for many small private enterprises. Leading this trend are U.S. computer manufacturers. According to Broadview, a global investment bank that focuses on high-tech, communications, and media industries, there were 337 mergers and acquisitions in the North American hardware industry in 1998. While this number represented a decline of 14.5 percent from the previous year, the value of those transactions increased 8.2 percent to $52.7 billion. In the first half of 1999, there were 242 transactions totaling $73.7 billion, almost double the value of transactions in the same time period in 1998. Examples of these major transactions include EMC's $952 million acquisition of Data General, IBM's $810 million purchase of Sequent Computer Systems and its $240 million deal for Mylex Corporation, and Cisco Systems' acquisitions of Cerent Corporation and Networks, Inc., for a total of $7.4 billion.

Continued Diversification

Intense competition also has prompted many computer manufacturers to diversify their products and change their business models. For example, several firms have shifted from being exclusively PC manufacturers to being broader-based systems suppliers. Some manufacturers have continued to move beyond hardware production into areas such as computer and information services, software development, and the use of the Internet for electronic commerce, where the profits are larger and the potential for sales growth is greater. For example, IBM has long recognized that hardware sales are no longer its main growth engine. Its services revenues went from $16 billion in 1996 to $23.4 billion in 1998 and now account for 29 percent of total sales and 17 percent of profits. Today, half of IBM's 290,000 employees are involved in this services business. In responding to these market changes, other companies have taken a very broad view of the global IT business. Gateway 2000, for example, recently became an Internet service provider (ISP) as well as a PC vendor, while several of its competitors have linked up with ISPs to sell their products.

Increased Technology and Production Agreements between Rivals

Efforts to cut costs have spawned technology and production agreements between traditional computer industry rivals. These agreements benefit both parties by giving each one access to the strengths of the other. A prime example is Dell Computer's $16 billion agreement with IBM. This pact gives Dell access to IBM's rich storehouse of technological know-how. In return, IBM benefits by having its OEM business supply Dell with storage products, semiconductors, and other parts and gains access to the knowledge behind Dell's coveted build-to-order process.

Shipments Bolstered by Domestic Demand

Strong domestic demand helped product shipments of the U.S. computer equipment industry increase nearly 9 percent to $84.3 billion in 1997 (the most recent data available), according to data from the U.S. Bureau of the Census. Computer systems remained the mainstay of the U.S.-based computer equipment industry, accounting for approximately 65 percent of total product shipment value (see Figure 27-1), and should

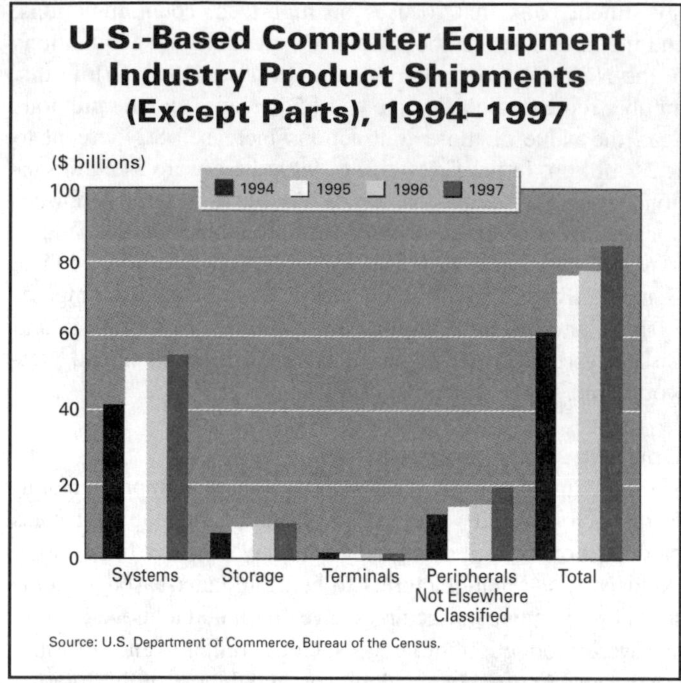

FIGURE 27-1

continue to dominate its output in the future. Severe price competition and lower demand continued to batter shipments of storage devices, which managed only a 2.2 percent increase. After reaching an all-time low in 1996, terminal production rebounded with 15.4 percent growth but still amounted to only around $1.5 billion. Shipments of peripherals not elsewhere classified, of which printers and networking equipment are important products, increased an impressive 30.8 percent between 1996 and 1997.

The U.S. computer equipment market remained vibrant throughout 1998, growing 9 percent from the previous year to an estimated $116 billion. It was expected to increase 6 percent to reach $123 billion by the end of 1999. Business spending to address the Y2K problem continued to drive demand in 1999 but reportedly had less of an effect than it did in the previous year. Other factors that drove demand were increased use of the internet and the building of corporate intranets. Low-priced PCs and easy accessibility to the internet also increased consumer demand. Dell reported exceptionally strong consumer sales and noted that shipments to nonbusiness users in the United States were up 100 percent in midyear 1999 compared with the same period in 1998.

Floundering Trade

Sluggish overseas markets, particularly in Asia, caused U.S. computer equipment industry exports to drop 8.5 percent to $21.2 billion in 1998 (see Table 27-1). This was the first time industry exports actually declined during the 1990s. Computer systems shipments dropped at a much faster rate than did those of peripherals (10 percent versus only 2 percent). On a regional basis, western Europe and the North American Free Trade Agreement (NAFTA) countries remained the principal export markets, accounting for 34.8 and 23.4 percent of the total, respectively (see Table 27-2). With an 18 percent average annual growth rate between 1992 and 1998, Latin America posted the largest increase in demand (see Figure 27-2). Canada, Japan, and the United Kingdom, while remaining the top destinations for exports, experienced declines in computer exports. By contrast, U.S. exports to the Netherlands and Germany increased.

Imports of computer equipment totaled $44 billion in 1998, a 2.1 percent decrease from the level in 1997. Even with that drop,

TABLE 27-1: Computers and Peripherals (SIC 3571, 3572, 3575, 3577) Trends and Forecasts
(millions of dollars except as noted)

	1992	1993	1994	1995	1996	1997[1]	1998[1]	1999[2]	2000[3]	Percent Change 97–98	98–99	99–00	96–00[4]
Industry Data													
Value of shipments[5]	61,969	64,374	73,345	86,078	97,592	105,700	116,300	122,100	131,900	10.0	5.0	8.0	7.8
Total employment (thousands)	221	211	201	210	221	246	251	238	233	2.0	–5.2	–2.1	1.3
Production workers (thousands)	74.2	73.9	75.8	78.9	83.4	101	106	105	103	5.0	–0.9	–1.9	5.4
Average hourly earnings ($)	12.26	12.77	13.67	13.49	14.84	16.02							
Capital expenditures	2,137	2,045	1,907	1,902	2,684	3,288							
Product data													
Value of shipments[5, 6]	49,900	53,254	60,643	76,344	77,503	84,300	92,800	97,400	105,200	10.1	5.0	8.0	7.9
Trade data[6]													
Value of imports	21,783	25,593	29,027	33,618	39,306	44,975	44,015	47,320	50,150	–2.1	7.5	6.0	6.3
Value of exports	14,941	15,367	17,580	19,647	21,439	23,175	21,202	21,290	23,000	–8.5	0.4	8.0	1.8

[1] Estimate except imports and exports.
[2] Estimate.
[3] Forecast.
[4] Compound annual rate.
[5] For a definition of industry versus product values, see "Getting the Most Out of *Outlook 2000.*"
[6] These data are for computers and peripherals, excluding parts.
Source: U.S. Department of Commerce: Bureau of the Census; International Trade Administration.

TABLE 27-2: U.S. Trade Patterns in Computer Equipment[1] in 1998
(millions of dollars; percent)

Exports			Imports		
Region[2]	Value[3]	Share, %	Region[2]	Value[3]	Share, %
NAFTA	4,964	23	NAFTA	4,671	11
Latin America	2,294	11	Latin America	20	0
Western Europe	7,385	35	Western Europe	3,433	8
Japan/Chinese Economic Area	3,616	17	Japan/Chinese Economic Area	16,875	38
Other Asia	1,623	8	Other Asia	18,064	41
Rest of world	1,319	6	Rest of world	952	2
World	21,202	100	World	44,015	100
Top Five Countries	Value	Share, %	Top Five Countries	Value	Share, %
Canada	3,879	18	Japan	9,333	21
Japan	2,059	10	Singapore	9,282	21
United Kingdom	1,948	9	Taiwan	4,677	11
Netherlands	1,528	7	Mexico	3,596	8
Germany	1,421	7	Malaysia	3,007	7

[1] SIC 3571, 3572, 3575, 3577.
[2] For definitions of regional groupings, see "Getting the Most Out of *Outlook 2000*."
[3] Values may not sum to total due to rounding.
Source: U.S. Department of Commerce, Bureau of the Census.

imports in 1998 had doubled since 1992. Asia remained the predominant regional source of these imports, while Japan continued slightly ahead of Singapore as the leading country of origin (see Tables 27-1 and 27-2). Benefiting from its NAFTA ties, Mexico is the only nation among the top five suppliers that increased its shipments to the United States in 1998. At that rate of growth, Mexico was expected to overtake Taiwan and become the third largest supplier of U.S. computer equipment imports by the end of 1999. Contributing to the value of imports is trade between U.S. subsidiary operations overseas and parent companies in the United States. Imports have continued to outpace exports, resulting in a U.S. computer equipment trade deficit that reached $22.8 billion in 1998. This was the first time the deficit total was larger than the export value in the same year.

Concentration in Manufacturing and Changes in Distribution

Computer equipment production in the United States is concentrated primarily in the west and the northeast, according to the 1997 Census of Manufacturing (see Figure 27-3). California

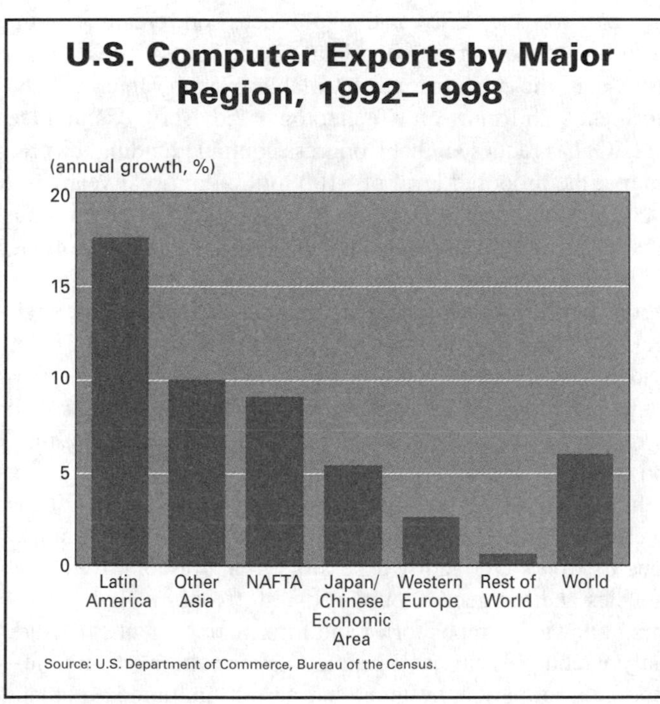

Source: U.S. Department of Commerce, Bureau of the Census.

FIGURE 27-2

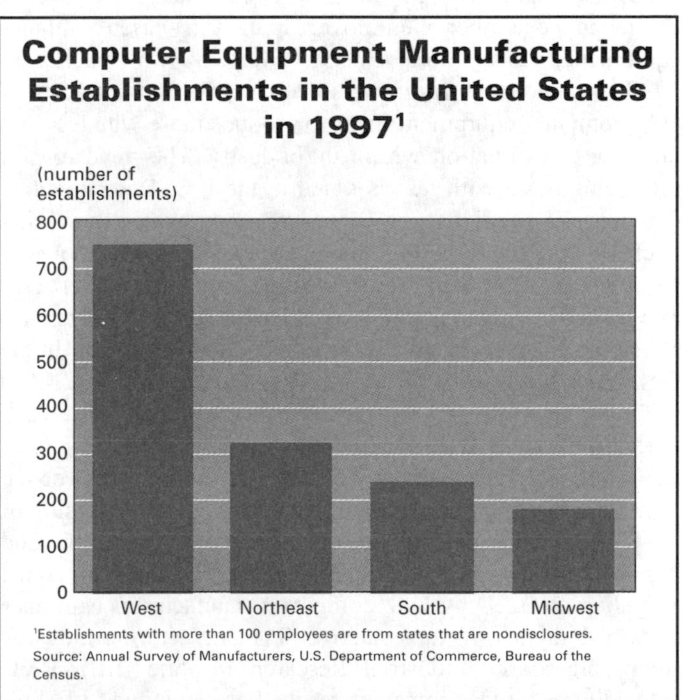

[1]Establishments with more than 100 employees are from states that are nondisclosures.
Source: Annual Survey of Manufacturers, U.S. Department of Commerce, Bureau of the Census.

FIGURE 27-3

accounted for almost 40 percent of these production sites, and Texas was a distant second with 7 percent, followed by New York, Massachusetts, and Pennsylvania.

Build-to-order (BTO) and direct sales over the telephone and the Internet have revolutionized the manner in which U.S. computer equipment manufacturers operate. First pioneered by Dell Computer, these processes are being emulated throughout the computer equipment industry and are rapidly replacing traditional distribution channels. The BTO model owes a large part of its success and widespread adoption to connectivity and the Internet. The use of the Internet as a strategic tool has become a catalyst for change in the computer equipment industry in which inventory control, manufacturing, distribution, and consumption are all part of a continuous process. Companies, such as Dell and Gateway, that recognized this early continue to outperform suppliers that were slower to act. Dell's use of electronic commerce brings in about $6.5 billion annually, or roughly 30 percent of all of its sales.

Reversal of Employment Trend

Total and production worker employment in the U.S.-based computer industry grew for the fourth straight year in 1998. After 1994, an estimated 50,000 new employees were added to the industry's labor force, more than 60 percent of whom were production workers. This growth was tied to the strength of the overall economy and to healthy domestic demand for computer products. The growth of production workers in relation to total employment parallels the industry's increased reliance on the Internet and BTO processes. By using the Internet as a marketing tool and a means to transform production and distribution operations, computer equipment manufacturers have reduced their dependence on nonproduction workers. This trend has contributed and will continue to contribute to the overall decline in the number of employees in the U.S.-based computer equipment industry after a peak of 251,000 was reached in 1998. Also contributing to this decline will be the efforts of U.S. computer equipment firms to produce more with less and ongoing consolidation within the industry. The trend toward producing more with less is noted in the U.S. Department of Commerce's *The Emerging Digital Economy,* which shows that from 1990 to 1997, the U.S.-based computer equipment industry achieved 30 percent growth in value added per worker. This rate is second only to that in the semiconductor industry and far above the 1.4 percent growth in value added per worker in the U.S. economy as a whole.

Research and Development

Research and development (R&D) will continue to be an important factor in maintaining the technological leadership of the U.S. computer industry and determining the capabilities and applications of computer equipment in the years to come. Spending on R&D by U.S. computer manufacturers continues to be the highest in any major U.S. manufacturing industry. According to the Industrial Research Institute (IRI), R&D expenditures by IT companies reached an estimated $12.8 billion in 1998, representing an average of 6.3 percent of its revenues. A sampling from the September 6, 1999, issue of *Infoworld* shows that IBM led the way in 1998 in terms of dollars spent, dedicating over $5 billion to R&D, representing 6 percent of its annual revenue. Compaq spent over $1.3 billion; Sun, more than $1.2 billion; and Hewlett-Packard, over $857 million. Each of those companies dedicated between 4 and 11 percent of annual revenue to R&D efforts. These significant investments should ensure that U.S. manufacturers retain their technological superiority and dominance in the worldwide computer industry for the foreseeable future.

The U.S. industry aggressively pursues R&D that gives it a market advantage in the near term. However, from a business perspective, long-term basic research can be risky and does not necessarily translate to marketable computer products for those companies. In response to the need for long-term basic research, the U.S. government has initiated the broad-based Federal Computing, Information and Communications (CIC) programs to advance the state of the art in supercomputer hardware, software, and networking technologies and to use IT to improve biomedical research, education, emergency response times, manufacturing, national security, public health, and science and engineering. The three largest R&D efforts within the CIC are High End Computing and Computation (HECC), Large Scale Networking (LSN), and Human Centered Systems (HuCS). Other programs include High Confidence Systems (HCS) and Education, Training and Human Resources (ETHR). Among the goals of HECC is the eventual development of computer systems with performance that approaches a million billion floating point operations per second (petaflops), 1,000 times more powerful than the largest massively parallel system today. This program is investigating advanced concepts in quantum, biological, and optical computing.

The Next Generation Internet (NGI) initiative is an important part of the LSN and will focus on creating high-performance networks with data transfer rates 1,000 times faster than the rate currently available over the Internet. The President's Information Technology Advisory Committee (PITAC) has requested that Congress continue funding the program at the proposed level of $100 million in fiscal year (FY) 2000. This initiative is closely associated with the $500 million Internet2 program, an independent cooperative effort involving 122 U.S. universities and firms in the computer and communications industries that will create broadband applications, engineering technologies, and network management tools for academic research and education. It is hoped that both programs will provide the basis for revolutionary applications such as remote medicine, more sophisticated weather forecasting, and distance learning.

In the year 2000, the HuCS program will continue to focus on ensuring that advanced computing systems and communications networks are readily accessible to and usable by federal agencies and the general public. Its efforts will include developing knowledge repositories and information agents that sort, analyze, and present massive amounts of multimedia and multisource information; systems that permit multimodal human-systems interactions such as speech, touch, and gesture recognition and synthesis; and virtual reality environments for scientific research, health care, manufacturing, and training.

Funding levels for these initiatives got a boost in September 1999 when the House Science Committee approved legislation that would authorize a total of $4.8 billion for IT research over the next 5 years. More than half of that funding was directed to the National Science Foundation, which supports and coordinates the federal government's multiagency efforts in the programs mentioned above.

The Research and Experimentation Tax Credit, which was enacted in 1981, is under Section 41 of the Internal Revenue Code. This tax credit provides a research credit equal to 20 percent of the amount by which a company's qualified research expenditures in a taxable year exceed its base amount for that year. The R&D tax credit must be extended repeatedly by Congress and was last extended from June 30, 1998, to June 30, 1999. It has since expired. However, many people in the computer industry are pushing for a 5-year extension or even permanent status for this tax credit. This will be an important issue to continue monitoring through the year 2000, as it will have long-term implications for the continued dominance of the U.S. information technology industry.

PROJECTIONS OF INDUSTRY AND TRADE GROWTH FOR THE NEXT 1 AND 5 YEARS

Product shipments by U.S. computer equipment manufacturers will increase 8 percent in the year 2000 to an estimated $105 billion (see Figure 27-4 and Table 27-1). An anticipated slowdown in U.S. business purchases of computer equipment will carry over from the last quarter of 1999 into the first quarter of the year 2000 as companies assess the effects of the Y2K problem on their operations. After this initial slump, business spending should rebound, stimulated by pent-up demand for equipment upgrades and new systems. Consumer demand will continue to be high because of the increased affordability of PCs resulting from severe price competition. The U.S. government is expected to increase its overall IT budget 4 percent to $34 billion in 2000. Computer equipment purchases should account for a substantial part of this budget. The educational sector also will show brisk demand for computer equipment. IDC estimates that higher education spending on computer equipment will grow 6 percent to reach $1.6 billion in 2000. All these factors will push the U.S. computer equipment market to an estimated $132 billion.

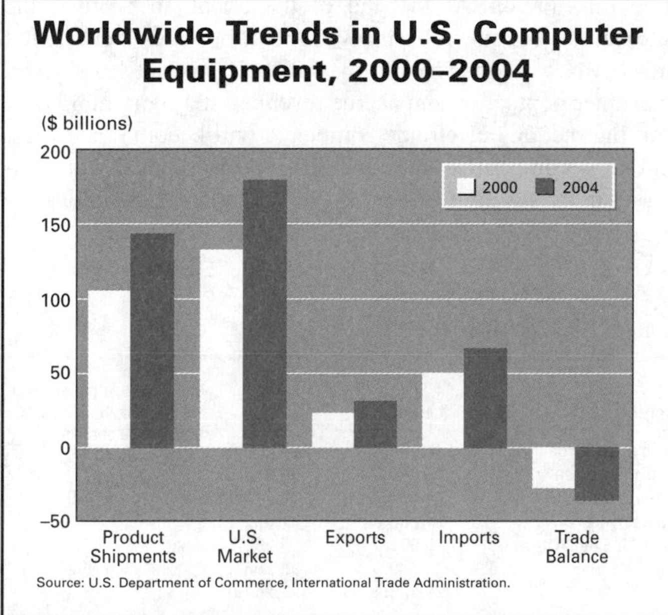

FIGURE 27-4

U.S. computer equipment trade should improve, with exports posting an impressive recovery after minimal growth in 1999 (see Figure 27-4). Exports are expected to rise 8 percent to $23 billion in the year 2000, benefiting from strong economic growth in major trading partners such as Canada, western Europe, and Asia, where the financial crisis of the last few years should no longer be a major hindrance to trade. Corresponding to continued expansion in domestic demand, imports should increase 6 percent to reach $50.2 billion in 2000. If this projection holds, it will be the first time imports have grown more slowly than have exports in the 1990s. However, this lower import growth rate will not be sufficient to arrest the worsening computer trade deficit, which is expected to climb to an estimated $27 billion.

Increased use of the Internet and continued expansion of corporate Intranets will be the principal forces driving demand for computer equipment over the next 5 years. These forces will create an increasing demand for greater computer storage. Computer storage firms will emerge as significant components in the overall U.S.-based computer equipment industry. U.S. firms will continue to develop faster, more powerful computers and networks that will make video telephony and desktop videoconferencing everyday practices. At the same time, PC manufacturers will face a growing challenge from producers of information appliances ranging from smart telephones to television set-top boxes. These new appliances will be linked with computers throughout the home to create a "networked home."

The growing pervasiveness of computers and their declining cost have made the Internet a powerful force for transforming business activity and thinking. In the next few years, the emerging battle between stand-alone computing and thin client computing probably will be settled. Stand-alone computing represents the continuation of the standard that dominates today's computing, while thin client computing would allow users to connect to the Internet or to corporate Intranets through simple terminal-like devices that have minimal operating systems and memory and rely on networked resources for their applications. Many see this approach as benefiting from the economies associated with reduced overhead costs, increased reliability, and superior security. U.S. computer companies are strong in both areas, and so regardless of which camp wins, the industry will be well placed to meet future demand. This future demand should result in U.S.-based computer industry shipments increasing 8 percent each year in current dollars to an estimated $143 billion in 2004 (see Figure 27-4).

Trade

Exports of U.S. computer equipment will remain strong and will continue to sustain the growth of the industry's product shipments. These exports should grow at a healthy 8 percent rate to reach an estimated $31 billion in 2004 (see Figure 27-4). Canada and western Europe will continue to be the principal markets for U.S. computer equipment exports, but as those markets mature, the U.S.-based industry will depend more on demand from Asia and Latin America for future growth. As long as there is economic and financial stability, demand from Asia and Latin America is expected to increase at a faster rate than will demand from any other major trading region. Other markets, such as eastern Europe, Russia, and the Middle East, should offer U.S. computer equipment manufacturers substantial export opportunities.

Imports will continue to play a significant role in the U.S. domestic computer market and should increase 7 percent annually to reach an estimated $66.5 billion in 2004 (see Figure 27-4). Most of those imports will originate from Asia, where U.S. suppliers will continue to source large quantities of computer components. Because of NAFTA, imports from Mexico will grow the fastest as U.S. firms and foreign competitors continue to set up production facilities in that country to serve U.S. demand. In addition to setting up facilities in Mexico, foreign suppliers will continue to establish new production sites in the United States to help meet domestic demand. These affiliates will rely heavily on imports from their parent countries, thus contributing to the growing deficit in computer equipment trade. The U.S. computer equipment trade deficit is expected to climb to a projected $35.5 billion in 2004.

GLOBAL MARKET PROSPECTS

Sources of Future Demand

As major trade barriers to IT products and services continue to fall and worldwide IT spending continues to rise into the twenty-first century, the U.S. computer equipment industry is poised to maintain its leadership position in the world market. According to IDC, worldwide IT spending will grow at a compound annual rate of 9 percent from 1997 to 2002 and exceed $1.1 trillion by the end of that period. By 2002, North America, western Europe, and the Asia-Pacific region will account for 93 percent of worldwide IT spending. The systems markets in those regions represented 44 percent, 26 percent, and 23 percent, respectively, of the worldwide systems market, which totaled $329 billion in 1999. The U.S. market alone represented 45.2 percent of worldwide IT market (excluding telecommunications equipment and services) and 42.2 percent of the world computer systems market in 1999. In 2002, the United States will still be the leading market for these products. Japan and several other Asian nations will continue to be the strongest competitors of the U.S. computer systems industry in that period. Latin America, eastern Europe, and the Middle East/Africa regions are expected to be the fastest-growing markets by 2002 (see Table 27-3). Despite these double-digit growth rates, their combined markets will still be nearly six times smaller than the North American market.

In 2002, lower systems costs resulting from fierce price competition coupled with lower inflation rates, stronger Asian economies, and the growing demand for Internet- and Intranet-based technologies will create a robust environment for the global computer equipment industry.

The expected growth in Internet use is one of the main factors that will fuel demand for computer equipment sales in the future. According to the *Computer Industry Almanac,* there were over 150 million Internet users at the end of 1998 compared with 61 million in 1996. The number of Internet users worldwide is expected to more than double to 320 million by the end of the year 2000 and exceed 720 million in 2005. In 1998, the United States had 76.5 million people connected, or roughly 52 percent of the world total. That figure should grow to more than 207 million by 2005 but account for only a 29 percent share. The PC will remain the primary way for users to access the Internet.

Another significant demand driver will be escalating interest in electronic commerce in the private and public sectors. According to IDC, the number of users that bought and sold goods over the Internet was 142 million in 1998. By the end of 1999, that figure was expected to approach 200 million, and it should surpass 500 million by 2003. In that year, electronic commerce transactions will exceed $1 trillion. Nations are increasingly developing electronic commerce policy frameworks to encourage the growth of E-commerce among businesses. That development will fuel further expansion in corporate demand for computer equipment.

Businesses are moving more of their services on-line, making it easier for their customers and employees to access real-time information. At the end of the twentieth century, the Internet has become a business tool that provides a cheap and quick way for companies to market their products to a broad consumer population and accrue revenues at a more rapid rate. The Internet and electronic commerce will become the fastest and most competitive sales and distribution channels for businesses in the twenty-first century. In the United States alone, 10

TABLE 27-3: Growth in Worldwide Systems Market by Region, 1999–2002
(millions of dollars)

Region	1999	2002	Compund Annual Growth Rate, %
North America	146,000.5	189,089.0	9.0
Latin America	13,059.8	18,082.3	11.4
Western Europe	84,652.7	100,510.9	5.9
Eastern Europe	4,858.6	7,072.1	13.2
Middle East/Africa	5,979.0	9,298.5	15.7
Asia-Pacific	74,642.6	98,205.8	9.6
World	329,193.1	422,267.6	8.7

Source: International Data Corporation.

percent of small businesses were selling products over the Internet in 1998, according to IDC. By the end of 2003, that figure is expected to increase to 46 percent. To compete effectively, all businesses, large and small, will need to maintain a presence on the Internet, and this should spur computer equipment sales.

Effects of International Agreements and Issues

Information Technology Agreement. The Information Technology Agreement (ITA), which was implemented on July 1, 1997, continues to have a positive impact on U.S. computer exports and the computer equipment industry's international competitiveness. Under the terms of the agreement, most of the 48 participating countries eliminated tariffs on covered products by January 1, 2000. When the agreement originally was signed, there were 29 signatories. By July 1999, that figure had grown to 48 signatories, including Australia, Canada, Chinese Taipei, the Czech Republic, Costa Rica, El Salvador, European Union, Estonia, Hong Kong (China), Iceland, India, Indonesia, Israel, Japan, Korea, the Kyrgyz Republic, Latvia, Lithuania, Macao, Malaysia, Mauritius, New Zealand, Norway, Panama, Philippines, Poland, Romania, Singapore, the Slovak Republic, Switzerland (including Liechtenstein), Thailand, Turkey, and the United States. A few developing countries were granted extensions on a limited number of products, but in no case will tariffs be permitted after 2005. Tariff elimination generally took place in four equal steps on July 1, 1997; January 1, 1998; January 1, 1999; and January 1, 2000.

The ITA covers over 93 percent of world trade in IT products. Global trade in products covered by the ITA was expected to exceed $1 trillion by the turn of the century. These products include semiconductors and other electronic components, most semiconductor manufacturing equipment, analytic instruments, computer software, digital photocopiers, most telecommunications equipment, printed circuit boards, and process controls.

Negotiations, initially slated to conclude by June 30, 1998, continued in an effort to expand product coverage, accelerate tariff reductions, and address nontariff measures. This process generally is known as ITA-II. Failure to reach agreement on additional product coverage at those negotiations led to their continuation. Under the terms of the agreement, all signatories must reach consensus on an agreed-on list of product additions. Since no party wanted to close out the negotiation or have a result that could not be accepted by consensus, countries agreed to consult bilaterally and multilaterally with the goal of achieving closure in 1999.

Export Controls. The basic purposes of U.S. export controls in the computer equipment sector are essentially twofold: to protect national security and to further U.S. foreign policy interests. The Bureau of Export Administration at the U.S. Department of Commerce is responsible for the management and enforcement of regulations related to the export of computer equipment from the United States.

To keep pace with the rapid technological advancements in the U.S. computer industry, the administration has revised export parameters on computer equipment three times since 1993. These revisions have taken into account the increased availability and performance of commodity computer products. They also were intended to ease unnecessary regulatory burdens on government and industry while ensuring effective controls on militarily sensitive technology. In its most recent review, the administration determined that widespread commercial availability makes computers with a performance of 6,500 millions of theoretical operation per second (MTOPS) or less uncontrollable.

The revised controls announced by the President in July 1999 maintain the four country groups announced in 1995 but amend the countries in, and control levels for, those groups: Tier I now consists of western Europe, Japan, Canada, Mexico, Australia, New Zealand, Hungary, Poland, the Czech Republic, and Brazil and requires a general license for all computers (no prior government review, but companies must keep records on higher-performance shipments that will be provided to the U.S. government as directed). Tier II now consists of South America, South Korea, the Association of Southeast Asian Nations (ASEAN) countries, Slovenia, and South Africa and requires a general license up to 20,000 MTOPS, with recordkeeping and reporting as directed and an individual license (requiring prior government review) above 20,000 MTOPS. Tier III now consists of India, Pakistan, all Middle East/Maghreb nations, the former Soviet Union, China, Vietnam, and central Europe. General license exports are permitted for civil end users between 2,000 and 12,300 MTOPS, with exporter recordkeeping and reporting required as directed. Tier III requires an individual license for 6,500 MTOPS for military end users and 12,300 MTOPS for civilian end users. The 1998 National Defense Authorization Act (NDAA) imposed a requirement for companies to provide the U.S. Department of Commerce with prior notice of exports of systems above 2,000 MTOPS to all Tier III end users. U.S. export control agencies then have 10 days to inform a company if it must apply for a license. The President's July 1999 decision raised the NDAA notification level from 2,000 MTOPS to 6,500 MTOPS. The President has advised the appropriate congressional committees of his decision to raise the NDAA notification level, and by law, Congress has 6 months to review that decision, after which the change in the NDAA notification level will go into effect in February 2000. Tier IV countries currently include Iraq, Iran, Libya, North Korea, Cuba, Sudan, and Syria. There are no planned changes for Tier IV, and current policies continue to apply (the United States will maintain a virtual embargo on computer exports).

Current export control levels are a moving target, and reviews and revisions undoubtedly will be required on an ongoing basis to make certain that U.S. computer export control policy continues to keep pace with rapidly advancing computer technology. Export control issues will remain a challenge in the coming years as the United States seeks to balance this reality with its national security interests.

Local Area Network Classification Dispute with the European Union. U.S. producers of local area network (LAN) equipment currently are at odds with the European Union (EU) over the classification of that equipment in the Harmonized System (HS). LAN equipment traditionally had been classified in Chapter 84.71 as units of automatic data processing machines (computers). In 1995, the European Commission (EC) began classifying certain LAN products—hubs, routers, bridges, optical converters, and network interface cards (NICs)—as telecommunications equipment within HS Chapter 85.17. As this latter category had a higher tariff than 84.71, the change raised the costs for U.S. LAN equipment producers that export to the EU.

In response, the United States filed a case at the WTO in 1996 accusing the EU of violating its tariff commitments on LAN equipment. The dispute panel decided in favor of the United States. However, without deciding the substantive issue, the appellate body reversed the panel on technical grounds in 1998. In a different venue, the classification issue was brought up at the World Customs Organization (WCO). The WCO twice decided in favor of the U.S. position, but in both cases the EC entered reservations, it is delaying implementation of the WCO decisions. The case was to be addressed in the WCO again in March 2000. The EC argued that under the ITA, EU tariffs on all products in HS Chapters 84.71 and 85.17 would fall to zero on January 1, 2000, and therefore the classification dispute would become irrelevant. However, U.S. firms fear that LAN equipment may be subject to EU telecommunications equipment-related testing and certification requirements, such as those for electromagnetic compatibility, if it is imported under 85.17 and that this would again raise producers' costs and slow their time to market.

Daniel Valverde, Tu-Trang Phan, Richard Dickerson, and Danielle Kriz, U.S. Department of Commerce, Office of Computers and Business Equipment, (202) 482-0571, September 1999.

PERSONAL COMPUTERS

The PC product sector includes a growing variety of devices, among them desktop computers, portable computers (including notebooks, handhelds, and pen-based tablets), thin clients, and, more recently, wearable PCs. Personal computers usually are differentiated from more powerful workstations, which generally are used in financial modeling, graphics design, engineering, and scientific applications. Workstations traditionally have had fast reduced instruction-set computing (RISC) microprocessors, more graphics capabilities, and better display resolution and usually run on a UNIX operating system rather than Windows, OS/2, or the Macintosh OS. However, a new category of PC workstations has emerged as PC-based processors, operating systems, hard drives, and other components have reached higher performance levels. PC servers are covered in the section on high-performance computers. Personal computers fall under SIC 3571, electronic computers.

Market Size and Growth

The United States leads the world in spending on IT and the use of PCs in business as a competitive tool. According to an assessment conducted in 1999 by the European Information Technology Observatory (EITO), in 1998 the United States spent 4.5 percent of its gross domestic product on IT versus 2.6 percent for Japan and 2.3 percent for western Europe. Business use of PCs was also greater. The number of business PCs per 100 white-collar workers reached 105 in the United States, nearly twice the average level in western Europe (55) and four times that in Japan (24).

The U.S. PC market remained fairly healthy in 1998, although unit growth was somewhat below the 1997 rate. Shipments of desktops and portables totaled 35.4 million units, up 15 percent from 1997, according to IDC (see Figure 27-5). Sales revenues, which were severely affected by declining prices, rose a modest 5.5 percent to $69.4 billion after growing 14.2 percent in 1997. These figures cover computers manufactured in the United States by domestic and foreign firms, plus imports. PCs with sixth-generation Pentium-type processors ranging from 200 to 500 megahertz (MHz) in speed represented more than 70 percent of the market. RISC-based PCs using PowerPC, MIPS, and Alpha processors accounted for the remainder of the market. According to the *Computer Industry Almanac,* the U.S. installed base of PCs reached 129 million units in 1998.

Unit demand for PCs in the United States was expected to rise sharply in 1999, benefiting overall from the strong U.S. economy and substantial small business and consumer purchases. Revenue growth again was expected to be restrained by intense price competition. Growing interest in the Internet and the availability of low-cost PCs will continue to be the principal demand drivers. ISPs should have a positive effect on PC sales through their offers of incentives to attract customers, ranging from "free" PCs to hefty discounts from the price of a PC in

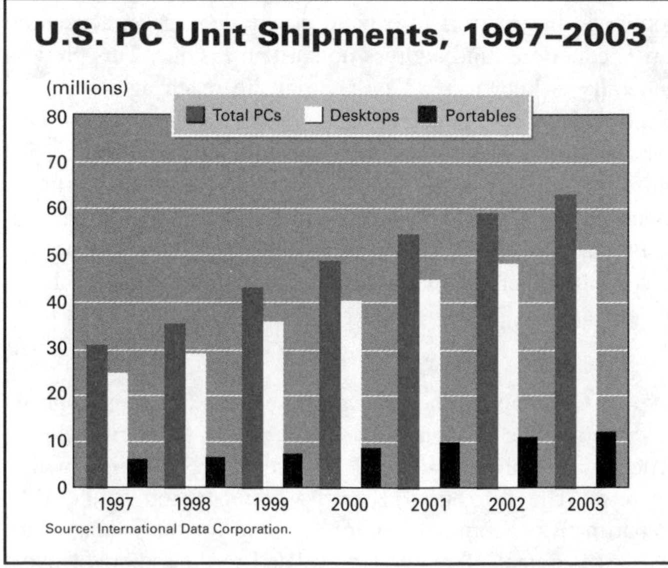

FIGURE 27-5

return for signing a long-term Internet access contract. The price of PCs, which was an obstacle to home and educational PC ownership in the past, should continue to fall, making these systems more affordable for many Americans (see Figure 27-6). As has been the case in the last few years, much of the growth in the market should occur in the sub-$1,000 segment.

First introduced in 1996 to address users' concern about the high cost of ownership of desktop PCs, thin client computers are gaining more interest in the U.S. corporate marketplace. These systems have emerged as a potential competitor to traditional desktops in commercial enterprises and are distinct from them because they focus on access of applications via a network and have a smaller operating system. Two types of thin clients exist. One is the Windows-based terminal (WBT), which relies solely on an NT server to access applications and do its processing. The other is the server-neutral network computer (NC), which can do processing both on the host server and via a Java Virtual Machine (JVM) and keeps all of its applications and data on the server. For example, in an effort to better position itself in this market and to offer an alternative to the WBT, Sun Microsystems unveiled its Sun Ray 1 notebook-sized network appliance in September 1999. This device incorporates a MicroSPARC chip, 8 million bytes (megabytes) of dynamic random access memory (DRAM), and a smart card reader to access applications on a server. Sun Microsystems also acquired Star Division of Fremont, CA, to provide thin client users with a free Web-based suite of spreadsheet and word processing applications that will run on servers that use the Windows, Linux, Solaris, and OS/2 operating systems.

Worldwide shipments of thin clients rose 24 percent to 368,497 units in 1998 and were almost equally divided between NCs and WBTs, according to IDC. However, the value of these shipments dropped 17 percent to $318 million, reflecting the sharp decline in average system price that occurred during that year to make these systems more competitive with sub-$1,000 desktop PCs. The U.S. market remained the predominant consumer of thin client computers, taking 90 percent of the value and unit shipments. The top three vendors—Wyse, IBM, and NCD/Textronix—accounted for about 75 percent of total worldwide unit shipments. Despite the strong position held by a few leading suppliers, many other participants are competing in this market, including smaller firms and new entrants such as Addonics Communications, Athena, Boca Research, Boundless, Cedar Systems, Clientec, Keytronics, NCL Peripherals, and Neoware. Sales of these systems were expected to grow more strongly in both units and value in 1999, benefiting from the emergence of applications service providers (ASPs), the lower cost and improved capabilities of Microsoft's Windows Terminal Server (WTS) software, the availability of greater bandwidth, and the replacing of older terminal and legacy desktop PCs by corporate information systems (IS) managers in response to the Y2K problem.

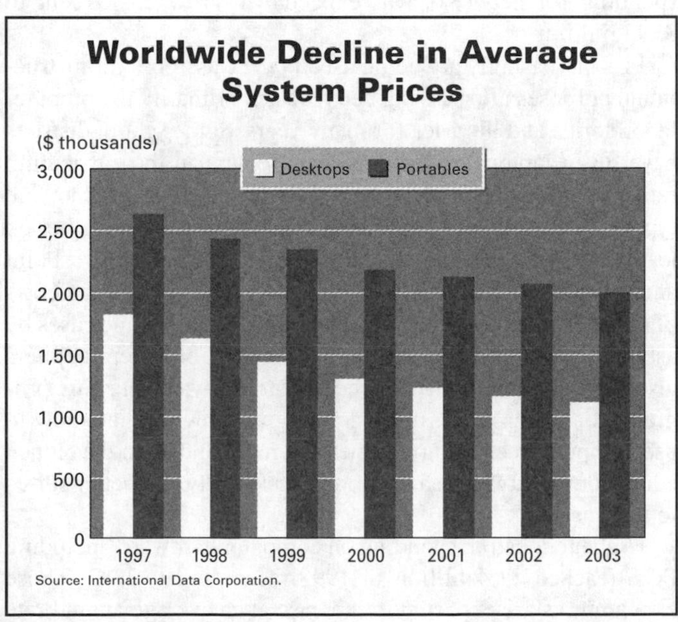

FIGURE 27-6

The U.S. PC market may almost double in regard to the number of systems purchased over the next 5 years, but the unit growth rate is likely to fall into single digits (see Figure 27-5). Revenues will increase very slowly as PC prices continue to decline and stimulate unit demand. More widespread use of the Internet and electronic commerce by businesses for supply-chain management and customer sales and by consumers for personal shopping, airline and hotel reservations, banking services, and on-line purchases of stock, to name only a few uses, will make ownership or access to a PC almost a necessity.

Industry and Market Trends

Manufacturing. U.S. computer firms have begun to move notebook production back to the United States in an attempt to shorten their supply chain, respond more quickly to market changes, and be closer to their customers. They expect that these moves will help cut inventory and delivery times, increasing the slim profit margins on these models. Dell recently announced that it plans to move its assembly of consumer notebooks from Asian contract manufacturers to its plant in Austin, TX. Because product life cycles are longer in the corporate notebook market, Dell will continue to assemble corporate notebooks in several Asian countries. IBM is moving more of its notebook assembly from Asia to Guadalajara, Mexico, and expects to have up to 65 percent of its portables assembled there in the year 2000, up 15 percent from 1999. In contrast to Dell's approach, IBM's strategy is to assemble high-end notebooks in North America and leave low-end assembly in Asia. Compaq, Sanyo, and Sony also are increasing their assembly of notebook and hand-held devices in North America.

As a result of this trend toward North American assembly, some flat panel monitor companies are following their customers back to this region with both assembly and repair facilities, eliminating transportation costs and the time delay necessitated by shipping panels to Asia for repair or alteration. However, on January 1, 2000, the 3 percent tariff levied by the United States on computer imports will be eliminated. The duty-free entry of finished PCs will cut the cost of Asian assembly and may provide a disincentive for further PC assembly investment in the United States.

Technology. Rapid technological advances continue to shorten product life cycles, putting more pressure on companies' bottom lines and making product delivery and inventory control more critical exercises for PC producers. The estimated product life of a PC has decreased from about 22 months in 1988 to less than 6 months today, with R&D and market introduction phases shrinking accordingly. PC product cycles are mainly a function of the introduction of new microprocessors, but the capabilities of these systems also are affected by improvements in other areas, such as semiconductors, storage devices, and software.

There were several important developments in processor technology in 1999. Microprocessor supplies introduced 700-MHz chips for PCs late in that year and are expected to raise this performance to 1 gigahertz (GHz) in the year 2000. Apple Computer also announced a new G4 personal computer (developed by Apple, IBM, and Motorola) that has a sustained speed of over 1 billion floating point operations per second (gigaflop). The Power PC G4 microprocessor that is at the heart of this system is being referred to as a "supercomputer-on-a-chip." The machine's "velocity engine," or AltiVec technology, enables the PC to speed up the data-intensive processing that is needed to run new graphics, video, voice, and other applications. National Semiconductor took a significant step toward further reducing the size and cost of PCs and embedded computers when it placed the MediaPC, or PC-on-a-chip, on the market. This device replaces many of the separate chips typically found in a PC by integrating the central processing unit (CPU) with core logic and input/output (I/O), networking or modem circuitry, graphics, and multimedia functions.

Pricing. A factor that sets computers apart from most other products is their constantly improving price-performance ratios. The prices of desktop PCs now range from below $1,000 to more than $10,000 for the most powerful, fully configured systems. Hard disk capacity in new desktop systems is around 4 gigabytes (4 billion bytes) at the low end and 20 gigabytes at the higher end. CD-ROM (read-only memory) drive access times have increased significantly, ranging from 24X to 40X, and digital video disk (DVD) and recordable CD-ROM drives are now available on many systems. Typical internal memory allocation ranges from 32 megabytes of DRAM at the low end to up to 128 megabytes at the high end. Microprocessor speeds continue to increase, with 400 MHz at the low end and up to 650 MHz on the more high-priced systems. Monitors are now 17 inches and larger. Flat panel displays for notebook computers have expanded to 15 inches, and liquid crystal display (LCD) panels are now available for desktop computers.

Price competition has been unusually intense in PCs compared with other types of computer systems. After 1997, the average system price for a desktop PC globally is estimated to have dropped 21 percent to $1,429 in 1999 while that for portables declined 11 percent to $2,335, according to IDC (see Figure 27-6). These downward price trends should continue over the next 5 years as suppliers benefit from expected declines in the cost of key components such as microprocessors and DRAMs and battle for market share by offering users increasingly less expensive systems with better performance.

Market Subsectors

Small Business. Computer systems suppliers continue to target small businesses (those with fewer than 100 employees), which now are the least penetrated, fastest-growing business sector. IDC estimates that shipments to this sector in the United States should almost double from the 1997 level to reach 13.7 million units in 2002 and represent 25 percent of total U.S. PC shipments. The major factors in this growth include the efforts of PC vendors to address the specific resource and technical needs of those companies and the greater availability of low-cost PCs in retail outlets.

Home Use. PC shipments to the home are expected to increase 11 percent annually to 18.2 million units from 1997 to 2002, representing roughly a third of the U.S. PC market. As was the case in the past, demand should be driven by lower prices for PCs, better and cheaper consumer software, and growing interest in accessing information and services on the Internet. The trend toward working at home, or telecommuting, also should continue to stimulate home sales.

Educational Use. The installed base of computers in U.S. school districts in the 1997–1998 academic year was 6.7 million units, up nearly 5 percent from the previous year's level, and spending on instructional technology reached $2.9 billion in that year, according to IDC. Purchases of computer hardware and networks represented 48 percent and 10 percent of those expenditures, respectively. During the 1998–1999 academic year, U.S. schools were expected to boost their computer hardware spending 22 percent to $1.7 billion, while spending for networks was expected to grow 83 percent to $505 million.

PCs increasingly are being used in the classroom for instructional purposes after having been located primarily in computer laboratories and libraries for many years. Some school districts have given laptops to their students for use in the curriculum rather than just having a room of PCs for teaching Internet and typing skills. Students in lower grades are working together on team projects that involve creating presentations in PowerPoint and similar programs. School districts have defrayed the costs of these PCs through parent volunteer work or in some cases by asking parents to pay a third of their cost. Computer suppliers also have tried to help U.S. school districts by establishing programs that offer professional training to show teachers how to use computer technology in the classroom and have developed educational software that is more user-friendly and better suited to their needs.

Higher education spending on computer hardware, including PCs, reached $1.4 billion in 1998, according to IDC. Those expenditures are expected to increase at an average annual rate of 7 percent to reach nearly $2 billion by 2003. As in elementary and secondary schools, educational use of PCs in universities and colleges has been stimulated by the availability of high-speed Internet access and the growth of on-line educational content for classroom instruction. Mounting interest in providing distance learning to students off campus is becoming another important factor in PC demand.

Government. Federal government spending on PCs jumped 30 percent in 2 years to reach $1.3 billion in fiscal 1998, according to Colmar Inc., a Reston, VA, market research firm that tracks computer purchases by the U.S. government. Its projection for fiscal 1999 was for a 5 percent increase to around $1.4 billion. A factor in this lower growth rate is the current preference of federal agencies for sub-$1,000 systems. Future demand for IT at all levels in the public sector should be spurred by ongoing modernization programs that require government workers to use computers to enhance their productivity.

Future Outlook

The next major phase in the networking era will focus on connecting single and multiple PCs, information and communications devices, entertainment systems, and smart appliances in the home with one another and with the outside world through the use of broadband wired and wireless technologies. A comprehensive survey conducted in mid-1999 by the Yankee Group found that more than 17 million U.S. homes, or about 37 percent of PC households, were interested in home networking for applications such as high-speed Internet access, printer sharing, sharing of video and audio content, and multiuser gaming. Cahners In-Stat Group, a market research firm, predicts that the U.S. home networking market will grow over 600 percent to $1.4 billion by 2003. The increasing availability of cheaper and more powerful PCs will be a principal factor in that growth.

In the not too distant future, computing will become nearly ubiquitous. Computer scientists Marc Weiser and John Seely Brown of Xerox PARC call this paradigm shift third wave computing and characterize it as "deeply imbedding computation in the world" and having "lots of computers sharing each of us." Examples of this new type of computing include devices that are carried in the hand or buried in walls that can find people and perform intuitive tasks for them, clocks that return to the correct time after a power failure, and microwave ovens that download recipes from the Internet. However, further advances in technologies such as speech recognition, graphics, storage, wireless communications, nanocomputers, and biometrics will have to take place before ubiquitous computing becomes a reality. It is likely that both PCs and thin clients will coexist with a wide variety of information appliances in this era.

Global Market Overview

As the domestic PC market matures, U.S. manufacturers are seeking overseas markets with high growth opportunities to survive growing foreign competition, particularly from Asian suppliers. Those markets are becoming even more attractive with the elimination of tariff barriers through bilateral and multilateral agreements such as NAFTA and the ITA. In addition, developing countries will continue to focus on improving their IT infrastructures to expand their economies. Their successful participation in the global economy will require access to the Internet and therefore to computers. To better serve emerging markets, many leading U.S. computer firms have a strong manufacturing presence overseas in key regional hubs and are well positioned to take advantage of sales opportunities in those markets.

Worldwide shipments of PCs (desktops and portables) were expected to increase 19 percent to around 105 million units in 1999, according to IDC (see Figure 27-7). Unit sales should benefit from the recovery in several Asian economies, the continuing strength of the U.S. market, and healthy worldwide consumer demand for low-cost PCs. However, shortages in supplies of LCD panels from Asian sources and major disruptions in shipments of key components, such as motherboards, resulting from the September 1999 earthquake in Taiwan could negatively affect this forecast and industry prospects for the year 2000. Intense price competition was expected to keep growth in the value of worldwide shipments for these computer systems down to 7 percent in 1999, reaching an estimated $166 billion.

The United States and Japan, with a 43 percent share and a 10 percent share of world unit shipments in 1999, respectively, are the largest single-country PC markets. On a regional basis, western Europe receives 26 percent of these shipments, followed by the rest of the world (largely Canada and Latin America) and the Asia-Pacific region with 12 percent each.

IDC forecasts that worldwide unit PC shipments will increase at a slightly lower annual growth rate of 14 percent to about 168 million systems through 2003, while their value will increase 6 percent each year to reach $211 billion. That market research firm believes that the U.S. market will experience more moderate growth that will be counterbalanced by much stronger demand in the Asia-Pacific region, particularly China,

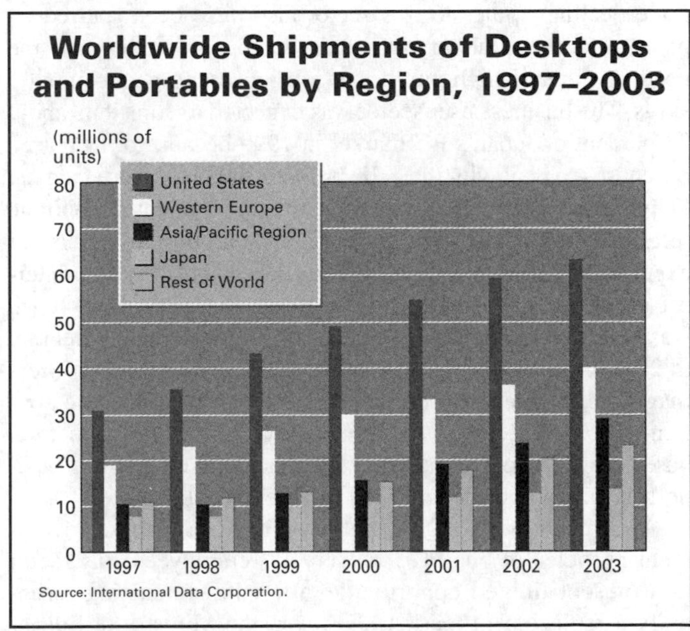

FIGURE 27-7

and in other emerging markets, such as Latin America. Among the major factors fueling worldwide demand will be the small business market, growing interest in electronic commerce, and the rapid spread of the global Internet user base. Average system prices are expected to fall at a faster annual rate for desktops than for portables (down 6.3 percent and 4 percent, respectively) (see Figure 27-6).

Western Europe. Western European countries have relatively developed computer markets that more or less track U.S. trends. Growth will continue to be driven by expanded use of the Internet, increased demand for portable PCs, the growing availability of low-cost PCs, and economic stability. As in the United States, the largest growth in demand will be for sub-$1,000 PCs. According to IDC, the volume of PC shipments was expected to rise 15 percent in 1999, but the annual growth rate should slow to 12 percent through 2003, when it will reach 40 million units (see Figure 27-7). EITO estimates that about 55 percent of the over 102 million PCs already installed in the EU countries are used for business purposes and 45 percent are used at home. U.S. firms remain the dominant PC suppliers in that region.

Japan. After being restrained for a few years by a recession, sales in the Japanese PC market were expected to rebound in 1999 and lead the Asia-Pacific region in growth. IDC estimated that unit demand in Japan would jump 26 percent to 10 million units, while value would grow 29 percent to $20 billion (see Figure 27-7).

According to the *Asia IT Report* published by the Market Intelligence Center (MIC) in Taiwan, continued expansion in the home market, combined with a revival in the business user sector, will be needed to stimulate that growth. Japan's home user market has been particularly vibrant despite that country's economic woes as a result of the release of Windows 98, the popularity of space-saving desktops and slim notebooks, and price declines. Sales to this sector also have been spurred by parental concern about children's computer literacy and the need for Japan's high number of job seekers to gain computer skills. The business user sector was expected to constitute about 33 percent of Japan's PC market in 1999 because of increased purchases to deal with the Y2K problem and assistance from an IT purchase subsidy that is part of the government's economic reform program. PC sales to both home and business users are expected to surge over the next 5 years because of greater interest in the Internet and the use of electronic commerce. Japan was expected to double the number of people using the Internet to 20 million by the end of 1999, according to *Nikkei Business* magazine. To measure Internet use in Japan, the Japanese government is building a National Information Infrastructure, based on fiber-optic networks, that should tie homes, businesses, and government offices together by 2010.

As a result of the high penetration rate in Japanese government agencies of one PC for every 1.3 employees, this sector will present limited opportunities for sales, remaining essentially a replacement market. However, the Ministry of Education's long-term effort to make computer education an essential part of the school curriculum has boosted the demand for PCs. There is currently a shortfall of 276,000 PCs in elementary schools and another 166,000 in junior high schools.

The Japanese market is still difficult to enter because of cultural and commercial factors even though trade barriers to computer imports, such as tariffs and quotas, no longer exist in that country. Japanese sales continue to be dominated by domestic computer manufacturers that control over two-thirds of the domestic PC market, largely through their use of extensive dealer networks. U.S. companies have been able to gain market share in Japan's private sector by selling competitively priced world-class technology. As the popularity of direct sales increases in Japan, U.S. companies that are more experienced in this channel of distribution may be able to strengthen their position in that market. Direct sales in the Japanese PC market were projected to double in 1999 alone to 1.2 million units.

Other Asia-Pacific Countries. Several Asia-Pacific markets are recovering from the economic woes they experienced in 1997 and 1998. As a result of this upturn, IDC forecast regional growth of 24 percent for 1999, with shipments reaching 12.6 million units (see Figure 27-7). The Asia-Pacific region is expected to have some of the fastest-growing economies in the world in the future and contains half the world's population. PC markets should benefit from pent-up demand, higher living standards, and a greater need for IT in this region to support economic development. Regional growth in 1999 was expected to be led by strong PC sales in China, Australia, and India.

According to MIC, China was expected to become the third largest single-country PC market in the world in 1999 if sales increased 32 percent to 6.2 million units as predicted. The 34 percent growth in unit demand in 1998 was stimulated by the home and education markets and significant IT spending by public sector organizations immediately after the reform of state-run enterprises. Market segmentation was as follows: The government user sector accounted for 31 percent of total unit PC sales; business, 26 percent; home use, 25 percent; and educational use, 18 percent.

Government efforts to stop illegal import practices buoyed the PC sales of local firms such as Legend, Founder, Star, and Hisen. As a result, domestic suppliers (including joint ventures with foreign companies) held about 80 percent of the Chinese PC market compared with only 20 percent for foreign imports. Payment problems also remain an issue in China, with limited available capital, fixed exchange rates, and the use of promissory notes making it difficult to conduct business.

Although the Asia-Pacific region is a key area, representing one-quarter of the world's IT market, computer suppliers can encounter many difficulties selling in that region, such as high import taxes, arbitrary customs enforcement, smuggling and gray market activities, investment restrictions, software piracy with inadequate international property rights enforcement, and in some cases skilled labor shortages.

Latin America. According to IDC, regional PC shipments totaled nearly 4.2 million units in 1998, up 14 percent over the previous year's level. Although Latin America represents only 4 percent of the global PC market, it has some of the fastest-growing and least penetrated markets in the world. For example, in Mexico, the installed base of PCs is about 4.6 million units, or approximately 3 per 100 people. Market reforms in Brazil and Mexico, the two largest Latin American PC markets, have facilitated a more competitive market-oriented system in comparison to the protectionist policies of the past. As trade barriers fall with the spread of free trade alliances such as NAFTA and MERCOSUR, commercial relations and confidence in these markets will grow along with their economies. Growth in the region in 1999 was expected to slow as a result of the latest devaluation of the Brazilian real, lower overall gross domestic product (GDP) growth, and higher interest rates. However, demand is expected to rebound, increasing at double-digit levels through 2003.

Robin Gaines and Tim Miles, U.S. Department of Commerce, Computer Systems Division, Office of Computers and Business Equipment, (202) 482-0571, September 1999.

HIGH-PERFORMANCE COMPUTERS AND SERVERS

Supercomputers

The supercomputer segment of the computer equipment industry consists of two main architectural types: parallel vector processing (PVP) and massively parallel processing (MPP). System speeds generally are measured in billions of floating point operations per second (gigaflops). The PVP architecture relies on a relatively small number of very powerful processors using a large shared memory to perform intricate vector calculations. PVPs historically used high-performance emitter-coupled-logic (ECL) technology and a complex liquid coolant system. However, these systems are now based on complementary metal oxide semiconductor (CMOS) technology and are air-cooled. PVPs have dominated the very high end of the supercomputing spectrum because of their reliability, market acceptance, and ability to solve vector-type problems efficiently.

By contrast, the MPP architecture consists of hundreds and sometimes thousands of processing elements strung together in a parallel configuration. This architecture uses distributed memory and CMOS technology. In certain applications, MPPs are challenging PVPs for market share. However, in many cases, MPPs operate at a much lower level of efficiency on vector-type problems.

Some emerging alternative technologies in the supercomputer sector, such as multithreading (executing different parts of a program simultaneously), ultimately could compete for share with the current PVP and MPP architectures. Multithreaded systems are just moving into the marketplace and are intended to address specific application niches in the market, although they face a difficult battle for market share in the near term.

The high-end PVP industry consists of a small number of suppliers, with Cray, the one remaining U.S. company, and three Japanese firms—NEC, Hitachi, and Fujitsu—competing for a relatively small number of global procurements. International Business Machines, SGI/Cray, Hewlett Packard, Sun, Compaq, Fujitsu, and Hitachi all offer MPP systems. Tera, a U.S. company, is offering a machine based on multithreaded architecture.

Formerly consisting of a large number of companies dedicated to developing cutting-edge technologies, the supercomputer sector has undergone considerable reorganization and consolidation in recent years. Several factors have contributed to volatility in the industry, including a shrinking supercomputer market and the inability of smaller suppliers to generate sufficient revenues to fuel R&D efforts. This volatility has brought smaller companies under the umbrella of larger, more diversified organizations that have the resources to pursue R&D and can withstand short-term stagnation in demand. These larger companies have realized the benefits of employing "high-end" technology throughout their product range and have pushed bus and interconnect technologies developed for supercomputers down to the desktop level. Companies without substantial financial resources to commit to R&D may quickly see erosion of their competitive technological advantage. This situation can create a spiraling effect, with decreased revenue from a noncompetitive system providing a decreased revenue base to fuel R&D efforts for future systems.

In August 1999, SGI announced that it would sell Cray, which it had purchased in early 1996. In the following month, SGI stated that it hoped to reach an agreement in the near future with a company that would take a majority stake in the Cray unit. This situation will continue to be an important development to monitor, as Cray is the sole U.S. manufacturer of vector supercomputers.

In light of the fact that vector supercomputers remain vital to U.S. national security and commercial interests, the U.S. Department of Defense and the National Security Agency recently announced that they will provide significant financial support for the development of the next generation of vector supercomputers by Cray, known as SV2. This effort by the U.S. government to support the continuity of this technology can be attributed to the realities of the PVP market outlined below. With the current market dynamics, it remains a challenging business proposition to develop and market vector supercomputers.

Price has become the major determinant in competition for procurements worldwide. In the United States, an antidumping petition was filed against a Japanese supplier in mid-1996 for allegedly offering supercomputer systems below cost to a U.S. government-funded site. While the resulting order has eased the predatory pricing situation in the United States, intense pricing battles continue in the European market. U.S. and Japanese vendors have been facing off in head-to-head competition over procurements at influential research and computer centers throughout Europe.

At the high end of the MPP market, supercomputer suppliers have developed computers that operate at speeds exceeding a trillion floating operations per second (teraflops). The U.S. Department of Energy has awarded contracts to Intel, Cray/SGI, and IBM to build these teraflop systems as part of the

Accelerated Strategic Computing Initiative (ASCI). ASCI is a 10-year, $940 million project to provide a computational alternative to the testing of nuclear weapons. Intel, a former ASCI participant, announced in 1998 that it will no longer manufacture MPP supercomputer systems but instead will provide components and advice to suppliers in the high-performance market. Three of the top six systems on the top 500 list of the world's most powerful supercomputers published in June 1999 were developed for the ASCI program. This list is published twice annually and independently ranks the top 500 supercomputer installations worldwide according to their performance on the LINPACK benchmark for supercomputer performance.

As a snapshot competitive analysis of the supercomputer market, the top 500 list published in June 1999 shows that over 86 percent of the systems surveyed were manufactured by U.S. vendors (36 percent by SGI/Cray, 23 percent by IBM, 19 percent by Sun, and 7 percent by Hewlett-Packard).

The federal High Performance Computing and Communications (HPCC) program is another R&D effort that is important to the future of the U.S. supercomputer industry. It coordinates federal multiagency R&D activities with academia and industry to develop leading-edge applications to support public sector and private sector operations and boost U.S. economic competitiveness. For a more complete discussion of this initiative, see the R&D discussion earlier in this chapter.

Heightened competition through technical innovation and aggressive pricing is expected to continue in the near future. The overall supercomputer market will see limited growth through 2003, with revenue totaling close to $1.2 billion, according to IDC. This represents an annual growth rate of 6.7 percent since 1998. IDC expects the average selling prices of these systems to grow only 2 percent annually through 2003, while unit shipments will increase 4.6 percent.

U.S. supercomputer suppliers face substantial competition in major foreign markets from Japanese suppliers. U.S. and Japanese manufacturers will have to compete against each other for a relatively small number of procurements worldwide and try to win customers by continuing to introduce new, more powerful systems with improved price-performance ratios.

Japan represents the single largest market for supercomputers outside the United States and is expected to maintain that position over the next 5 years. With over 10 percent of the worldwide installed base of supercomputers, this market holds substantial opportunities for both U.S. and Japanese vendors. U.S. suppliers should retain their competitive edge in the Japanese private sector through the turn of the century because of the quality and reliability of their systems.

The U.S.-Japan Supercomputer Agreement, negotiated in 1987, addressed U.S. concerns regarding competition for Japanese public sector procurement. When this agreement failed to increase U.S. access to the Japanese public sector market, the United States and Japan renegotiated the agreement in 1990. The 1990 agreement, which remains in place, contains more detailed procedures for an open, nondiscriminatory public procurement process through which the government of Japan committed to purchase supercomputers on the basis of competitive factors.

During fiscal 1993–94, the U.S. share of the Japanese public sector supercomputer market increased dramatically and approached the 45–50 percent share of the Japanese private sector supercomputer market supplied by U.S. firms. Since then, the U.S. share of the Japanese public sector supercomputer market has not kept pace with the U.S. share of the private sector market. At the annual bilateral meetings to discuss the implementation of the agreement, the United States government expressed concern about Japanese government practices which appear to be inconsistent with the agreement.

Competition for supercomputer procurements in Europe should intensify. Although the number of new sites is expected to increase only slightly, the relatively large installed base of supercomputer users in markets such as Germany, France, and the United Kingdom will continue to stimulate demand for supercomputer system upgrades. Sales of high-performance systems should increase in Asia, Italy, and the Scandinavian countries as their computational needs grow.

Mainframe Computers

Mainframes range from small-scale to large-scale, are based primarily on proprietary processor technology, and provide enormous amounts of throughput by offloading I/O processing to a peripheral channel. Mainframes are capable of supporting hundreds of users and have multiple ports into memory and especially into high-speed caches, which can transfer data 10 times faster than the main memory can. Additionally, the internal bus transfer rates of mainframes are also much higher than those of smaller systems, giving them the ability to process large volumes of data much more efficiently than smaller-scale systems or PCs can.

In spite of predictions that mainframe computers would relinquish the market to networked PCs and workstations, demand for these computer systems continues among users that need significant processing and storage capabilities for a large user base. Typical applications being handled by mainframes include management information systems (MIS), enterprise resource planning (ERP), and on-line transaction processing (OLTP). According to most sources, shipments will continue to decline over the next 5 years as users replace and upgrade their existing systems rather than purchase mainframes for new installations. The ability of these computers to process large amounts of data more efficiently and reliably than existing client/server systems, together with decreased costs resulting from their use of CMOS technology, has kept the replacement market for mainframes viable for the near term. Projections of future revenues for mainframes are included within the data on large-scale servers given below.

Servers

Servers are computer systems in a network that are shared by multiple users and are employed for a wide variety of functions, such as Web servers, application servers, file servers, and network access servers. They support a broad range of applications and range from small PC-based single-processor servers to complex large-scale multiprocessor systems.

Growth of server sales has exploded in recent years, and substantial demand for these systems should continue in the near future. However, according to IDC, large-scale servers will experience a slowdown from $17.2 billion in sales in 1998, falling to around $16.7 billion in 2002. There is no foreseeable development that will reverse this trend, since the price-performance ratios of medium-range to low-range servers continue to improve, making them attractive and viable alternatives to more expensive high-end models. For this reason, PC, low-end, and midrange servers will experience substantial growth. The strongest advances in this systems category will occur in Windows NT–based PC models, which will experience more than 20 percent annual growth in revenue through 2003, according to IDC. Also, sales of midrange servers should rise 10 percent each year during this period. IDC predicts that the server category as a whole will grow about 6.4 percent annually from $68 billion in 1999, reaching nearly $89 billion in 2003.

Larger configurations of processors and improvements in processor speed will allow users to benefit from significant increases in overall system performance in the coming years. Driven by the widespread deployment of corporate and government networks, Intranets, and Internet applications, server sales will continue to represent nearly 20 percent of annual worldwide spending on IT equipment through 2003.

Pricing competition will remain severe in the server market. Although actual unit shipments have increased dramatically in recent years, revenue has not increased proportionately. This trend undoubtedly will continue as manufacturers further refine production processes and sales and distribution channels to maintain profitability in a market based on volume and increasingly thin margins.

The increasing popularity of application servers (computers that are used to handle specific applications) appears to be the next important development in the world computer systems market. These special-purpose servers increasingly are being deployed by application service providers (ASPs), offering access to specific applications via the Internet, and are replacing multipurpose servers in many sites because of their lower cost and their reliability. If current trends continue, these systems can be expected to become an $8 billion business by 2002, according to IDC, with U.S. server manufacturers predicted to be the dominant competitors in this emerging market.

Another interesting development in this sector is the emergence of the nonuniform memory access (NUMA) architecture, which allows multiple operating systems and applications to run on a single multiple-processor server system. As this technology is deployed, both technical and commercial end users in large organizations will have a unique opportunity to perform data processing operations using a variety of computing environments. This will greatly ease system administration for organizations that currently use a variety of platforms and operating systems.

The overall outlook for the U.S. server industry for the next 5 years is bright. Although some consolidation will occur, larger players increasingly will look for innovations and partnering opportunities with firms that can provide incremental performance advantages over their competitors. Based on the current pace of technological development, U.S. server manufacturers will maintain their market leadership for the foreseeable future.

Foreign Markets While the United States remains the dominant consumer of servers, Asian and western European countries will continue to represent the major overseas markets for U.S. vendors. The Middle East and Africa, eastern Europe, and Latin America should present exceptional opportunities for U.S. manufacturers, with IDC and other market researchers projecting substantial and sustained sales growth in those areas through 2003. However, the combined demand of those regions will remain significantly lower than that of Japan or Germany alone. The proliferation of servers in the workplace that has occurred in the United States and other major developed markets around the world will continue to be mirrored elsewhere in the international marketplace as Internet use expands and developing countries exploit the efficiencies afforded by the networking of IT products. As in the domestic market, price competition in overseas markets will remain intense among U.S. and foreign server manufacturers. U.S. vendors that have lowered their production and distribution costs to handle this challenge in the North American market should continue to do well if they apply the same tactics to their overseas marketing efforts.

Workstations

Although the lines between high-end PCs and workstations are blurring because of ever-increasing processor speeds, a workstation is generally defined as a high-performance desktop computer used for technical applications such as computer-assisted design (CAD), digital content creation, mathematical modeling, and programming. Workstations typically have a high-resolution display and powerful graphics processing capabilities. The distinction between PCs and workstations has further blurred with the adoption by both PC and workstation firms of the Peripheral Component Interconnect (PCI) bus. The enhanced graphics capabilities of PCs and faster microprocessors also are significantly diminishing the performance differential between high-end workstations and PCs.

Price and performance enhancements drive global and domestic demand for workstations. Average selling prices are declining steadily as a result of the use of lower-cost components. Constant improvements in DRAM and hard disk drive capacity as well as microprocessor speeds have led to significant increases in workstation performance. According to IDC, worldwide shipments of these computers will grow 16 percent annually through 2003 to reach 4.9 million units. However, revenues from sales of these systems will increase only an estimated 6 percent each year during that period. NT-based workstations have eroded Unix market share, with declines in Unix shipments expected to continue in the near future. IDC predicts that shipments of Unix systems will decline from an estimated 554,185 units in 1999 to 461,955 units in 2003. In addition, revenue from Unix shipments is expected to decline nearly 10 percent annually to $4.6 billion through 2003. NT systems, by contrast, will continue to expand their overall share of the workstation market. IDC predicts significant volume growth of over 20 percent each year to 4.4 million units through 2003. Revenue from these systems will increase steadily at an annual rate of 16 percent to reach $14.9 billion during this time frame but will not keep pace with the growth in unit shipments because of continued price declines.

U.S. firms remain the leading suppliers, with five companies accounting for 88 percent of the worldwide installed base of traditional workstations in 1998, according to IDC. Systems are currently on the market with clock speeds exceeding 600 MHz and the ability to handle more than one instruction per clock cycle. Leading vendors include Sun Microsystems, Hewlett-Packard, SGI, IBM, and Compaq.

As was stated above, Intel-based windows NT workstations that use Pentium III microprocessors are continuing to challenge Unix vendors for market share. Unix offers superior scalability and high systems resource availability, but Windows NT has a superior price-performance ratio. Both offer the ability to run on a multitude of microprocessor platforms, a sophisticated graphical user interface, high-performance networking capabilities, and cutting-edge Intranet and Internet functionality.

The availability of new computing applications such as image processing, videoconferencing, speech recognition, transaction and database processing, and data warehousing, coupled with constantly falling prices, should stimulate steady, consistent growth for Windows NT workstations over the next 5 years. Unix-based systems, while continuing to meet the needs of highly technical users, should experience a continuing decline in unit shipments during this period. Linux, the shareware operating system that is emerging as a possible contender to Windows NT, will be an important factor to monitor in the near future (for a detailed discussion of Windows NT, Unix, and Linux, see Chapter 28). Regardless of which operating system ultimately wins the competition, U.S. equipment suppliers will continue to control this market. Further improvements in the price-performance ratios of these systems will enable users to obtain very powerful workstations with more sophisticated graphics capabilities at a fraction of today's costs in the near future.

As a result of the technical sophistication and computational needs of their user bases, steady demand in Asia and Europe for workstations should continue over the next 5 years. Outside the United States, Japan, Germany, the United Kingdom, France, and Canada will remain the top five country markets for U.S. workstation manufacturers. IDC predicts that sales in Japan, the leading overseas market, will increase 5 percent annually from $2.6 billion in 1998 to more than $3.3 billion in 2003. This is in contrast to many other developed markets, where demand is expected to remain relatively flat or increase only slightly.

The developing markets that show significant promise for U.S. manufacturers are Venezuela and Saudi Arabia. Although their current size is relatively small compared with other markets, both of these markets are expected to experience substantial double-digit increases in annual demand through 2003, according to IDC.

Richard Dickerson, U.S. Department of Commerce, Computer Systems Division, Office of Computers and Business Equipment, (202) 482-1987, September 1999.

NETWORKING EQUIPMENT

The networking equipment covered in this section includes various switches, routers, hubs, bridges, NICs, and remote access products such as modems. Other products related to networks, such as servers and network operating systems, are covered elsewhere in this chapter and in Chapter 28, respectively. Networking equipment does not fall under a single SIC category. Shipments data for networking equipment are not included in this chapter.

Computer networking is one of the fastest-growing and most dynamic segments of the IT industry. Although PC networks began to be used widely in the 1980s with the rise of client/server computing, a number of recent trends have greatly accelerated their adoption and expansion. As firms try to enhance efficiency and worker productivity to remain competitive, they are increasing their use of Intranets for shared applications and internal files, Extranets to connect to external suppliers and customers, and the Internet, particularly for E-commerce. In addition, the growing number of network users and the increasing average size of electronic files sent through them require networks with greater speed and bandwidth, driving users to upgrade or expand their networking technologies.

Networks are essentially the connection of computers, including PCs, servers, and workstations, and peripherals for sharing files and services such as databases, E-mail, and printing. Networks typically run over a common medium such as copper wire or optical fiber and until recently were used solely to transmit packets of data. Conventionally, the term *computer network* is used to refer to LANs, which accommodate relatively small groups of users, usually at the office or building level. Whereas LANs technologically can cover only relatively short distances, wide area networks (WANs) connect users and LANs over longer distances, encompassing a city, a country, or, in the case of the Internet, the world. Although WAN users generally lease lines from public networks, some WANs are privately owned. LANs and WANs traditionally have used different equipment and transport technologies, and purchasers of LAN and WAN equipment also have been distinct. Enterprises, such as private firms and governments, more often buy LANs, and telecommunications carriers and ISPs typically purchase the WANs. For the most part, this analysis focuses on the LAN equipment industry. However, as the use of both LANs and WANs increases, there is a growing interrelationship between LAN and WAN technologies and trends. WAN-related issues are discussed where appropriate.

The main LAN products are NICs, hubs, bridges, routers, switches, and remote access products such as modems. NICs, also known as adapter cards, are printed circuit boards that provide the interface and connectivity between a computer and the

LAN. Hubs are simple devices that transmit data among groups of LAN users at the work group level. Bridges are used to join and extend the physical reach of LANs by passing traffic from one LAN segment to another. Switches are intelligent hubs that can determine the destination of a data packet and forward it only to the intended recipients. Routers are one step smarter, as they can determine the most efficient path on the network for packets to follow. In addition, unlike hubs, routers can link networks with different transport protocols, such as Ethernet and Token Ring (these and other technologies are discussed in detail in a later section of this chapter) and can interface LANs and WANs. Modems connect networks to telephone lines, allowing users to access LANs from external sites.

Global Industry Trends

Network use is most prevalent in the United States with its high level of PC penetration and Internet use. Major end users include the public sector, the banking and finance sectors, and multinational corporations in a variety of industries. Other developed countries also are adopting networks at an increasing rate. Dataquest reported that in 1998, nearly three-quarters of the European enterprises surveyed had over 90 percent of their PCs connected to a LAN. Although developing countries lag behind the United States and Europe in both PC penetration and Internet use, interest in networking technologies is high in many regions, especially in countries that have pinpointed IT investment as the key to future economic growth. The market research firm Datamonitor predicts that the United States will continue to lead in overall investment in networks, although its market share will drop as investments in other regions increase.

Companies that compete in the networking equipment industry typically are very large firms with a variety of products or smaller players competing in niche markets. U.S. firms are global leaders in the networking equipment industry, largely as a result of the extensive use of networks in the United States. Until recently, the U.S. industry was dominated by four main firms: Cisco Systems, 3Com, Cabletron, and Bay Networks. However, Cisco has drawn ahead and is now the industry leader in almost every technology segment. *Business Week* reported that Cisco's revenues increased from $1.3 billion to $12.2 billion in the 1994–1999 period. Cisco's success has come in part from a broad line of networking products that it has acquired by acquiring smaller software and hardware firms. According to *Business Week,* it has paid nearly $20 billion to acquire 40 start-up firms since 1993.

Cisco's acquisition strategy reflects trends in the networking equipment industry as a whole. Driven by customers' growing desire to procure end-to-end solutions from one supplier and the need to offer the latest technologies, large vendors are investing in or acquiring other companies to broaden their product portfolios, resulting in rapid consolidation in the industry. 3Com, a leader in NIC cards, acquired U.S. Robotics in 1997, achieving market leadership in modems, and Cabletron recently bought Digital Equipment's networking unit to increase its own equipment sales. These mergers and acquisitions are likely to continue, rendering it increasingly challenging for smaller networking companies to compete in the industry. Nonetheless, industry analysts predict that the number of competitors providing niche products for transporting data, video, and voice traffic will increase.

A new trend in merger and acquisition activities is the growing participation by large telecommunications equipment producers that are aiming to compete in the networking equipment industry by investing in or acquiring networking equipment suppliers, particularly ones that focus on leading-edge technologies. Two major recent acquisitions that shook up the industry were Lucent's 1999 acquisition of Ascend Communications and Nortel's 1998 acquisition of Bay Networks (and the subsequent name change to Nortel Networks). IDC analysts observe that purchasing Ascend, a leader in WAN switching, has not strengthened Lucent's position in the LAN market. However, its announced acquisition of Xedia Corporation, a maker of LAN routers, should help fill that gap. The Bay Networks purchase has strengthened Nortel's competitiveness in LAN routers as well as its presence in the enterprise market, as it now has access to Bay Networks' distribution channels. This trend is being countered as Cisco and some other traditional networking equipment suppliers are attempting to enter the market for telecommunications equipment by purchasing start-up telecommunications firms. Industry observers believe that competing with Lucent and Nortel Networks will be difficult, as both companies have supplied these markets for years and have solid reputations with telecommunications carriers, the principal customers for such equipment.

Traditional computer hardware firms such as IBM, Compaq, and Hewlett-Packard (HP) also produce some networking products, such as switches, hubs, and NICs, although they are not major players. IBM announced in August 1999 that it was for the most part leaving the networking equipment industry by selling its portfolio of router and switch patents to Cisco. IBM will supply Cisco with network components and consulting services and resell Cisco's networking equipment to its own customers. This deal is expected to augment Cisco's market share.

Globally, the U.S. networking equipment industry faces limited competition from suppliers in Japan and Europe. Fujitsu, Hitachi, and Siemens are competitive in networking, although mostly in servers. Similar to U.S. firms, foreign telecommunications equipment vendors are purchasing smaller networking equipment firms in an attempt to compete in that market. European firms in particular are beginning to enter the U.S. market. Siemens's recent purchase of the U.S.-based Redstone Communications will allow it to compete in router technologies. France's Alcatel recently purchased the U.S.-based Xylan, a LAN equipment vendor, and Sweden's Ericsson purchased Torrent Network Technologies to acquire carrier-class routing switches.

Domestic Industry Trends

Very few trends in the networking industry are strictly domestic. However, most of the technological trends and industry issues can be discussed from a domestic angle, largely because U.S. firms are at the leading edge of the networking equipment industry.

Technology Trends. The rapid pace of technological change is a key driver in the networking equipment industry. As networks proliferate, networking equipment must handle the torrent of data resulting from an increasing number of users and larger applications that in many cases now incorporate multimedia—voice and video—in addition to data. As a result, as is the case in many other IT industry segments, firms must invest continuously in R&D to improve their product performance and invent their own next-generation technologies to avoid being left behind. Standard and Poor's estimates that networking companies spend approximately 10 percent or more of their sales on R&D.

The basic thrust of technological developments has been increased network bandwidth and transmission speed to alleviate congestion. The most prominent developments include new transmission technologies, switched LANs, wireless LANs, converged networks, and next-generation networks. Many new technologies do not gain widespread acceptance. Even when they do, they may take years to gain acceptance, in part because of the high cost of installing new equipment and training people to run it. Firms also find it difficult to justify discarding the huge investments they have made in what were considered the best technologies at the time.

Transmission Technologies. Major changes and battles are occurring in the area of LAN transmission protocols, or the rules and coding specifications for sending packets. As protocols evolve, they become more scalable and enable network sizes to grow, and so emphasis has been placed on increasing transmission speeds. Currently, the most widely used LAN transmission technology is Ethernet. IDC estimates that currently approximately 80 percent of networks use some form of Ethernet technology. The most basic Ethernet is a 10 megabits per second (Mbps) technology dating from the 1970s. However, it is too slow for many current network needs, and vendors have been investing in R&D to increase its speed and abilities.

Fast Ethernet, which runs at 100 Mbps, has been adopted by many enterprises, although 1,000 Mbps (gigabit) Ethernet has gained widespread attention. Gigabit Ethernet's deployment had been delayed pending the release of approved international standards by the Institute of Electrical and Electronics Engineers (IEEE), which sets standards for networking equipment. IEEE approved a standard for running gigabit Ethernet over fiber-optic cable in 1998, increasing its acceptance. A standard for running it over copper wire was finally approved in June 1999. The widespread use of copper wire in Ethernet LANs has caused many industry analysts to predict rapid deployment of gigabit Ethernet. Gigabit Ethernet's acceptance is likely to be enhanced because new Ethernet technologies are compatible with existing Ethernets and users can upgrade to them without changing existing wiring or applications. This compatibility gives both fast Ethernet and gigabit Ethernet an advantage over other networking protocols such as Token Ring and Asynchronous Transfer Mode (ATM) because of Ethernet's existing large installed base. In addition, upgrading on a continuous Ethernet path saves time and money in network training and management tools.

Notwithstanding the publicity, gigabit Ethernet's deployment in LANs is not yet widespread. Many PCs and workstations do not have the power to handle 1,000 Mbps of bandwidth, and so networks cannot take full advantage of gigabit Ethernet's capacity. As a result, according to a survey by *Government Computer News,* most firms are not adopting gigabit Ethernet but are upgrading to fast Ethernet or staying with their current transmission technologies. However, gigabit Ethernet does have a market in enterprise backbones, where its speed can be optimized. It is used for communication between high-performance servers, where its high speed is ideal for transferring large databases, backing up applications, or making connections for Web site traffic. Nonetheless, the prices of gigabit Ethernet products are dropping rapidly, and that should drive further deployment of that technology.

Despite its slow start in the LAN market, gigabit Ethernet increasingly is being used in WANs. One reason for this trend is its high bandwidth. Another reason is the fact that network managers seek easy connectivity between Ethernet-based LANs and WANs. As a result, some analysts view gigabit Ethernet as having the potential to become a single unifying transmission technology for LANs and WANs in the future; that is what ATM, as described below, was supposed to be. There is even talk of 10-gigabit Ethernet, although standards work on it remains in the embryonic stage. Nonetheless, *Network World* reports that MCIWorldcom and other service providers are considering 10-gigabit Ethernet's possibilities for WANs.

Token Ring LAN technology, which was introduced by IBM in the 1980s, continues to be deployed in most non-Ethernet LANs. Its use is declining as some enterprises are replacing Token Ring backbones with Ethernet and, to a lesser extent, ATM. *PC Week* predicted that worldwide Token Ring hub and switch revenues would be slightly less than $800 million in 1999, decreasing from nearly $1.2 billion in 1996. In 1997, vendors were investing heavily in high-speed Token Ring, with transmission speeds of 100 Mbps, and discussing gigabit Token Ring, hoping to give users an upgrade path similar to that of Ethernet users. However, competition from newer Ethernet technologies and Token Ring's high cost and complexity of deployment have reduced its popularity. Only two high-speed Token Ring vendors remain: IBM and Madge Networks. Token Ring will continue to serve a niche market in environments where users value performance over cost. Because Token Ring is reliable and redundant and allows no data collision, it remains the protocol of choice in businesses where networks are time-sensitive or need careful control, such as assembly, process control, and hospital environments.

A few years ago, ATM, a transmission technology widely deployed by carriers to transmit voice, data, and other traffic across WANs, was regarded by many analysts as the dominant future technology for LANs. It was seen as a technology that if deployed through both LANs and WANs could offer seamless transmission among networks. ATM has virtually unlimited bandwidth, a key feature for transmitting multimedia, and can send data, voice, and video simultaneously. ATM routers and switches also have quality of service (QOS), or the ability to prioritize the transmission of packets, such as video and voice, that cannot be delayed if they are to function properly.

Despite the initial excitement, ATM has not gained widespread acceptance in LANs. It is expensive, and not all users need its voice and video integration abilities. It also has proved relatively complex to implement on the enterprise side. Further, when it was introduced, ATM's 155 Mbps of bandwidth was 50 percent faster than fast Ethernet. It now faces competition in LANs from gigabit Ethernet, which is 10 times faster than fast Ethernet.

Internet Protocol (IP), the protocol for data transmission over the Internet, also has been deployed to a limited extent in LANs. Although IP is not widely used in LANs, it sometimes is used to ensure data integrity. Industry analysts note that as other transport technologies come to dominate LANs, IP may remain marginalized.

Switched LANs. The migration from shared media to switched LANs is another important development in LAN technologies. In shared media LANs, routers play a prominent role. However, routers are expensive and can slow networks as they must stop each packet to read its destination and determine its most efficient route. As a result, vendors have been developing higher-speed switches designed to be as intelligent as but faster than routers. Layer 3 switches are one such switch. Faster and less expensive than routers, Layer 3 switches separate each data packet and read only what is needed to make a forwarding decision. With both routing and switching functions in one device, Layer 3 switches are easier to maintain and manage.

As a result of this migration to switched LANs, switches are one of the fastest-growing network equipment market segments, causing a related decline in router demand. A recent survey by Infonetics Research Inc. found that 80 percent of the companies surveyed planned to adopt Layer 3 switches by the year 2000, especially as switch prices drop. However, Layer 3 switches cannot handle as many transport protocols as routers can, ensuring routers a place in the market. Some vendors recently introduced even faster and more intelligent Layer 4 gigabit Ethernet switches. However, as was discussed above, gigabit Ethernet technologies are gaining slow acceptance in LANs. For the most part, Layer 4 switches are being deployed at the edge of LANs for access to WANs and are owned by telecommunications service providers.

Wireless LANs. Much attention has been paid to the idea of wireless LANs. Wireless LANs consist of radio receivers and transmitters attached to computers and points along a conventional LAN. They are most commonly used in situations where wiring is impossible, inconvenient, or costly or where the mobility of users is important, as in the case of employees entering warehouse inventory data into a hand-held computer.

Although wireless LANs were long considered a niche technology because few customers were interested in them as a result of their high cost, their use is increasing. According to IDC, worldwide wireless LAN equipment shipments were valued at approximately $700 million in 1999 and are likely to grow continuously to reach $1.6 billion in 2003. Various trends are driving increased wireless LAN use. The IEEE ratified standards for wireless LANs in 1997, giving vendors a greater incentive to produce the equipment. Notably, major network equipment vendors such as Cabletron, Lucent, and Nortel Networks have begun to manufacture wireless LAN products, and this has made enterprises more comfortable investing in these technologies. Also, computer vendors have introduced an increasing number of portable computing devices necessary for wireless LANs, such as Palm Pilots and Microsoft CE devices. Finally, recent advances in radio frequency (RF) technologies allowing larger bandwidth have increased wireless LAN speeds.

Wireless LANs must overcome several hurdles before they are more widely used. One is a perception issue, as many users are more comfortable with cable-based networks. Wireless LAN equipment is still expensive, and despite new standards, many products are not interoperable. Wireless LANs also have relatively low speeds and distance limitations. As is the case with other leading-edge networking technologies, the future widespread acceptance of wireless LANs is uncertain.

Convergence. The convergence of voice, data, and video traffic over a single network is another trend that has gotten off to a slower start than was anticipated. Many industry experts agree that convergence will occur eventually but are not sure when and how. Analysts at Forrester Research predict that it may take 10 years for converged networks to become a reality and expect that voice and data networks will continue to exist side by side until then.

Voice over Internet Protocol (VOIP) is the first convergence service to have gained momentum and early demand. VOIP products transmit digitized voice signals across IP-based packet-switched networks, whereas traditional telephone service uses analog signals that are transmitted over circuit-switched networks. Although it has received much press coverage, recent studies suggest that most enterprises will not adopt VOIP in the near future. Forrester Research's poll of 50 of the largest U.S. firms found that two-thirds have no plans to use it. Vendors such as 3Com, Nortel Networks, and Cisco are offering VOIP products to enterprise customers. Currently, the biggest sales of VOIP products are for WANs and are made to carriers such as AT&T, MCIWorldcom, and Sprint.

Progress in integrating video is even further behind, largely because of the bandwidth constraints of current networks. Other obstacles hindering the use of converged networks include a lack of QOS. While slight delays do not affect the performance of traditional LAN traffic, such as file transfers and database queries, delays in voice or video result in unnatural-sounding voices and stilted images. Achieving QOS will require expensive upgrades of entire networks, since switches must be smarter to regulate voice and video traffic effectively.

Next-Generation Networks. A new area of LAN technologies that is receiving press coverage is the concept of next-generation networks (NGNs). Compared to traditional "dumb" networks, which administrators must control, smarter networks can adapt to the needs of an enterprise without an administrator's intervention. NGNs are expected to have distributed intelligence, using directory services to identify on-line users and act accordingly by assigning particular files or services only to certain users. Vendors are promoting this networking concept in response to rising user demand for reliability as networks become increasingly critical to firms' day-to-day operations and competitiveness and as essential services begin to cut across LANs and WANs. Layer 4 gigabit Ethernet switches are expected to be central to NGNs. However, NGNs are in the embryonic stage since gigabit Ethernet is only slowly being adopted in LANs. Even though vendors tout NGNs' faster network access and simpler network administration, they are expected to be more complex to administer at first, slowing their adoption.

Other Trends

Remote Access. Users increasingly are accessing networks remotely, a trend driven by the growing number of telecommuting employees, sales and service personnel, and business travelers who must access LANs from outside the office. IDC reports that over 85 percent of U.S. and western European companies own remote access products or lease remote access services and that laptop use is rising (24 percent of the PCs purchased by U.S. businesses with more than 100 employees are laptops). In-Stat forecasts that the number of ports in the United States for remote access products will grow 24 percent over the 1999 level to reach 3.4 million in the year 2000.

Analog modems, which convert digital computer signals to analog for transmission over circuit-switched telephone lines, are the most commonly used remote access products. The fastest analog modems run at 56 kilobits per second (Kbps) and were developed by U.S. Robotics, which is now owned by 3Com. Their widespread use was delayed by two factors: lack of a common standard and a dearth of ISPs offering the 56 Kbps transmission speed that allows consumers to use them. However, a standard was agreed to in 1998, and most ISPs have upgraded to 56 Kbps technologies. Standard and Poor's predicts that these events will spur demand for analog modems.

Cable modems, a newer remote access product, allow users to access the Internet through existing cables used for cable television. They are extremely fast and maintain a constant connection to the Internet, in contrast to analog modems, which require users to dial in for each Internet connection. However, cable modems are not yet widely used. Users must share the connection with multiple users on a neighborhood's cable system. This means that access can become slower as subscribership increases. In addition, few U.S. network users have access to upgraded cable systems that are compatible with cable modems.

Pricing. Prices in the networking equipment industry are declining because of intense competition among vendors. As a result, many producers' margins are slim. The most rapid price declines typically occur in older shared media or commodity products such as hubs, routers, NICs, and slower-speed analog modems, which are particularly sensitive to price competition. Prices for products based on older transmission technologies also are falling. For example, IDC reports that prices for Token Ring switches have been dropping in recent years.

Prices for even newer products such as fast Ethernet and gigabit Ethernet switches also are declining because of fierce competition among vendors. IDC reports that prices for fast Ethernet switches will fall from $450 per port in 1999 to $232 per port in 2002. Prices for gigabit Ethernet switches will fall by more than half from $1,300 to $520 per port. However, functionality and performance gains are expected to increase as vendors upgrade their products. The trend of continuously falling prices in the networking equipment industry is expected to continue.

Issues and Challenges. Two of the most significant issues currently facing the networking industry are the increasing need for network security and the possibility of network disruptions resulting from the Y2K computer problem. As network use grows and networks become critical to enterprises' day-to-day functioning and competitiveness and as remote access becomes more common, security for information on the networks and infrastructure is becoming critical.

Enterprises use a variety of methods to increase security. Many enterprises have physically separated their Intranets and Extranets. Enterprises also are purchasing from software firms products such as firewalls to keep out intruders and authentication applications to verify users' identities. Several networking equipment vendors have acquired security companies or have developed their own security features for their products. However, setting up firewalls and comprehensive security packages can be expensive, and although almost all large and most medium-size companies implement them, only slightly more than half of smaller firms do, according to Cahers In-Stat Group. The need for security products and services will multiply as network use grows and fear of intrusion or a network attack increases. At the same time, firms will increase their use of Extranets as security issues are addressed.

The Y2K issue is not expected to have a major impact on the networking equipment industry. Some network applications that rely on time stamping and other scheduled processes may be disrupted if devices cannot read the correct date. However, many experts say that most network products will not malfunction since they deal with shorter time spans, usually within the same minute, hour, or day. *Network World* posits that Y2K could pose a security risk if devices that cannot read the correct date allow unwanted packets into the network. Equipment vendors have been working to ensure that their products are Y2K-compliant, but most major vendors are not fixing Y2K bugs in equipment made before 1997.

Markets

IDC reports that the worldwide market for LAN equipment was $43.3 billion in 1998, of which the U.S. market accounted for 43.8 percent, or just under $19 billion. Although much smaller, Japan had the second largest market, valued at almost $3.8 billion, or 8.7 percent of the global market. The next largest markets were those of the United Kingdom, Germany, France, China, and Brazil (see Table 27-4).

IDC predicts that the global LAN equipment market will grow at an average annual rate of 8.4 percent to reach $59.7 billion in 2002 as enterprises in developed countries install,

TABLE 27-4: Networking Equipment: Global Market Shares by Country, 1998 and 2002

Country	1998 Market, $ millions	Global Share, %	Estimated 2002 Market, $ millions	Estimated Global Share, %	Compound Annual Growth Rate, % 98–02
United States	18,972.3	43.8	25,419.4	42.5	7.6
Japan	3,752.0	8.7	4,674.3	7.8	5.6
United Kingdom	2,607.3	6.0	3,024.8	5.1	3.8
Germany	2,398.2	5.5	3,186.2	5.3	7.4
France	1,122.3	2.6	1,545.4	2.6	8.3
China	1,269.1	2.9	2,614.1	4.4	19.8
Brazil	1,111.8	2.6	1,792.3	3.0	12.7
Other	12,069.5	27.9	17,484.8	29.3	9.7
Total	43,302.2	100.0	59,741.3	100.0	8.4

Note: IDC figures include remote access servers.
Source: International Data Corporation.

upgrade, and replace networks to remain competitive and as increasing PC penetration and greater Internet use spur network use in developing markets (see Table 27-4). The developed countries' share of the global market is expected to fall as those markets mature and demand for networking equipment accelerates in other regions. For example, the U.S. market is expected to grow quickly in absolute terms, at an average annual rate of 7.6 percent to reach $25.4 billion in 2002, but its share of the global market will fall to 42.5 percent. The Japanese market, which is expected to grow 5.6 percent annually to reach almost $4.7 billion in 2002, will fall to 7.8 percent of the world market. Other developed markets, such as those in western Europe, also will represent a slightly smaller share of the global market.

The fastest-growing regional markets for LAN equipment will be in Asia and Latin America. According to IDC, the Asian financial crisis dampened many Asian economies' overall investments in IT in 1998, except for China and Taiwan. U.S. networking equipment producers such as Cisco have reported that Japan's recession and the lingering effects of the Asian financial crisis have slowed the growth of their sales in Asia. Nonetheless, recovery in the networking equipment industry is expected in the future, as networking budgets are becoming less discretionary for Asian firms, many of which aim to be globally competitive. IDC predicts that the networking equipment market in Asia will grow from $9.3 billion to $13.4 billion in the period 1998–2002, registering an average annual growth rate of 9.6 percent. During that period, the Latin American market is expected to grow at an average annual rate of 14.4 percent, increasing from $2.1 billion to $3.6 billion. These regions' growth will be led by China and Brazil, whose markets are projected to be $2.6 billion and almost $1.8 billion, respectively, in 2002 and, combined, will account for 7.4 percent of the world market at that time (see Table 27-4).

U.S. firms supply most of the U.S. and foreign networking equipment markets. In fact, Cisco and 3Com obtain 50 percent of their sales from foreign markets. U.S. exports of LAN equipment are estimated to have been approximately $4.8 billion in 1998, with Europe and Japan the leading export markets. U.S. imports of networking equipment were valued at approximately $4 billion in 1998 and came principally from Singapore, Ireland, and Taiwan. Most U.S. exports consist of higher-end products such as switches and routers, while imports are dominated by commodity items, including NICS and hubs, many of which are made in countries where labor costs and other costs are lower. Some of these foreign manufacturers are U.S. subsidiaries. For example, 3Com has manufacturing facilities in Ireland and Singapore. In other cases, imports come from contract manufacturers that manufacture networking equipment in lower-cost regions for firms such as Cisco, Nortel Networks, and 3Com.

In developed countries and regions, where LAN adoption is high and markets are relatively mature, the most dynamic markets are those for products based on leading-edge technologies. Fast Ethernet and gigabit Ethernet switches are among the fastest-growing market segments in those regions, reflecting the conversion of many enterprises to switched LANs. The market for fast Ethernet NICs also is growing quickly; Standard and Poor's attributes this in large part to increased demand for PCs that allow Internet access. The market shares for older networking transmission technologies, such as products based on Token Ring, are falling, although vendors continue to sell to the installed base. In addition to switches, remote access products are another fast-growing LAN market segment. Demand for modems is increasingly rapidly as more networks are accessed remotely. Sales of all products also are driven by falling prices.

The movement to switched LANs has resulted in an overall decline in sales of older shared media products such as bridges, routers, and hubs. Nonetheless, according to Standard and Poor's, routers continue to command the largest share of the market even though their sales are slowing. Upgrading networks is expensive, and not all enterprises can afford to replace their current networks with those based on Layer 3 switches. Routers and other more mature products also continue to serve certain markets in developed countries. Standard and Poor's notes that while larger companies buy the bulk of their networking equipment in the United States, small and medium-size firms as well as home offices represent the fastest-growing networking equipment markets. Those firms, which cannot afford to invest as much as larger enterprises do in leading-edge technologies, are driving demand for less expensive products such as low-end hubs and routers. Home networks also are expected to grow as residential users link multiple systems together within the home and increase their access to the Internet. The market for network equipment in the home, currently valued at $250 million, could increase to $4 billion in 2002, according to *Business Week.* LAN equipment purchases for the home probably will consist of lower-end products.

Danielle Kriz, U.S. Department of Commerce, Software Division, Office of Computers and Business Equipment, (202) 482-0568, September 1999.

REFERENCES

Articles

"Alternatives: Co-Location, Contract Manufacturing and BTO—Channel Assembly Loses Its Momentum," Pedro Pereira, *Computer Reseller News,* May 10, 1999. www.crn.com.

"Big Blue At Your Service," Ira Sager, *Business Week,* June 21, 1999, New York, NY. (800) 635-1200, www.businessweek.com.

"Cisco Sees the Light in Twin Deals," John Rendleman, *PC Week,* August 30, 1999, 10 Presidents Landing, Medford, MA 02155. (781) 393-3690, www.zdnet.com/pcweek.

"The Coming Age of Calm Technology," Mark Weiser and John Seely Brown, October 5, 1996, Xerox PARC, Palo Alto, CA. www.ubiq.com.

"Compaq Shows Alpha-Based Servers, Workstations," Margaret Quan, *EE Times Online,* July 19, 1999. www.eet.com.

"Computing After Silicon," David Rotman, *Technology Review,* July–August 1999, MIT Technology Review, 201 Vassar Street, W59-200, Cambridge, MA 02139. (617) 253-8250, www.techreview.com.

"Convergence: The Future of Networking," Brian Robinson, *Federal Computer Week,* July 19, 1999, PO Box 3023, Northbrook, IL 60065. (847) 291-5214, www.fcw.com.

"Deal Gives IBM Access to Dell's Build-to-Order Process," Anne Knowles, *PC Week News Online,* March 12, 1999. www.zdnet.com/pcweek.

"Ethernet beyond the LAN," Jeff Caruso, *Network World Fusion,* July 30, 1999. www.nwfusion.com.

"Federal Budgets for IT Are Expected to Climb," Peter Behr, *Washington Post,* May 6, 1999. www.washingtonpost.com.

"The Ferrari of Throughput," Mark Kellner, *Government Computer News,* November 1998, Silver Spring, MD. (301) 650-2111, www.gcn.com.

"Firewalls for the Rest of Us," *Network Magazine,* September 1999, 600 Harrison Street, San Francisco, CA, 94107. (415) 905-2200, www.networkmagazine.com.

"Frame Relay Rolls On . . . ," Steve Taylor and Joanie Wexler, *Network World Fusion,* April 26, 1999. www.nwfusion.com.

"Gigabit Ethernet Adoption Expected to Soar," *Network World Fusion,* July 15, 1999. www.nwfusion.com.

"Giving Research the Business," Ted Smalley Bowen, *Infoworld,* September 6, 1999, 155 Bovet Road, Suite 800, San Mateo, CA 94402. (415) 572-7341, www.infoworld.com.

"Guru Ponders Problems with the Post-PC Era," Rick Boyd-Merritt, *Electronic Engineering Times,* April 19, 1999, CMP Media, Inc., 600 Community Drive, Manhasset, NY 11030. (516) 562-7405, www.techweb.cmp.com/eet.

"How Far Can Gigabit Ethernet Go?" Jeff Caruso, *Network World Fusion,* May 10, 1999. www.nwfusion.com.

"IBM Has All but Thrown in the Towel on Its Networking Hardware Division," Marc Songini, *Network World Fusion,* August 31, 1999. www.nwfusion.com.

"IBM Plans Flexible Next-Generation Server Architecture," *Infoworld,* February 15, 1999, 155 Bovet Road, Suite 800, San Mateo, CA 94402. (415) 572-7341, www.infoworld.com.

"In the New Age of Data, EMC Rules," David Kirkpatrick, *Fortune,* August 16, 1999. www.fortune.com.

"Industry Outlook Upbeat," Heidi Elliot, *Electronic News,* June 21, 1999, 2105 Landings Drive, Mountain View, CA 94043. (415) 691-1690, www.electronicnews.com.

"Information Technology Will Change Everything," Paul M. Horn, *Research-Technology Magazine,* January–February 1999, Industrial Research Institute, 1550 M Street, NW, Washington, DC 20005. (202) 776-0759, www.irinc.org.

"Into the Big Blue Yonder," Robert Buderi, *Technology Review,* July–August 1999, MIT Technology Review, 201 Vassar Street, W59-200, Cambridge, MA 02139. (617) 253-8250, www.techreview.com.

"Is This Token Ring's Last Gasp?" *PC Week,* February 16, 1998, 10 Presidents Landing, Medford, MA 02155. (781) 393-3690, www.zdnet.com/pcweek.

"IT's Upcoming Shift," Paul A. Strassmann, *Computerworld,* August 2, 1999. www.computerworld.com.

"A Labs Special Report: Next-Generation Networks," *PC Week Online,* May 5, 1998. www.zdnet.com/pcweek.

"LAN Hardware and Y2K," Jeff Caruso, *Network World Fusion,* August 16, 1999. www.nwfusion.com.

"Large Vendors' Sales Rise," John S. McCright, *PC Week,* August 25, 1999, 10 Presidents Landing, Medford, MA 02155. (781) 393-3690, www.zdnet.com/pcweek.

"Lucent Snaps up Excel for $1.7 Billion," *PCWeek Online,* August 18, 1999. www.zdnet.com/pcweek.

"Lucent to Buy Xedia for about $246 million in Stock," *Infobeat,* August 13, 1999. www.infobeat.com.

"Meet Mr. Internet," *Business Week,* September 13, 1999, New York, NY. (800) 635-1200, www.businessweek.com.

"Networking Deals Continue," John Rendelman, *PC Week,* April 26, 1999, 10 Presidents Landing, Medford, MA 02155. (781) 393-3690, www.zdnet.com/pcweek.

"Networking Essentials: Basic Components of Networks," Cisco Systems. www.cisco.com.

"No Longer Just Board Stuffers, CEMs Will Enter the New Century as a Proven Industry," Darrell Dunn, *Electronic Buyers' News,* June 7, 1999, CMP Publishing, 600 Community Drive, Manhasset, NY 11030. (516) 562-5899, www.ebnonline.com.

"North America Gaining Rep as PC Assembly Site," Jack Robertson, *Electronic Buyers' News,* August 9, 1999, CMP Publishing, 600 Community Drive, Manhasset, NY 11030. (516) 562-5899, www.ebnonline.com.

"OEMs Planning for Larger Role for EMS," Thomas Hopkins, *Electronic Buyers' News,* July 1, 1999, CMP Publishing, 600 Community Drive, Manhasset, NY 11030. (516) 562-5899, www.ebnonline.com.

"Old Switches, Routers Pose Y2K Threat," Jim Duffy, *Network World Fusion,* April 26, 1999. www.nwfusion.com.

"Quality-of-Service Options for Real-Time Traffic," Anita Karve, *Network Magazine,* February 1999. www.networkmagazine.com.

"Recovery Boosts Asia-Pacific PC Sales to 3 million," David Legard, *Computerworld Hong Kong,* August 19, 1999, www.cw.com/hk.

"Research Gets Multi-Billion Boost," Juliana Gruenwald, *Technology Daily,* September 9, 1999.

"Server to Open New Doors for Intel," Henry Baltazar, *PC Week Online,* August 16, 1999, 10 Presidents Landing, Medford, MA 02155. (781) 393-3690, www.zdnet.com/pcweek.

"Soul of a New Company," Arik Hesseldahl, *Electronic News,* August 16, 1999, 2105 Landings Drive, Mountain View, CA 94043. (415) 691-1690, www.electronicnews.com.

"Special Report: Gigabit Ethernet," *Network World Magazine,* September 1998, 600 Harrison Street, San Francisco, CA, 94107. (415) 905-2200, www.networkmagazine.com.

"Technology in the Coming Century," Arno A. Penzias, *Research-Technology Magazine,* January–February 1999, Industrial Research Institute, 1550 M Street, NW, Washington, DC 20005. (202) 776-0759, www.irinc.org.

"10G Ethernet WANS?" Jeff Caruso, *Network World Fusion,* August 16, 1999, www.nwfusion.com.

"These Growth Figures Won't Set Off Any Alarms at the End," James C. Cooper and Kathleen Madigan, *Business Week,* August 2, 1999, New York, NY. (800) 635-1200, www.businessweek.com.

"Token Ring Shakeup," Jeff Caruso, *Network World Fusion,* September 14, 1999, www.nwfusion.com.

"The Top of the Heap," Gina Fraone and Stanley H. Brown, *Electronic Business,* July 1999, 275 Washington Street, Newton, MA 02158. (617) 964-3030, www.eb-mag.com.

"To Wire or Not to Wire," Jeff Caruso, *Network World Fusion,* May 31, 1999. www.nwfusion.com.

"US Drives Progress in the Internet Age," *Financial Times,* March 3, 1999. www.ft.com.

"Voice on the Network," *Network Magazine,* January 1999. www.networkmagazine.com.

"Will IP Networks Suffer from Too Much Complexity?" Steve Taylor and Joanie Wexler, *Network World Fusion,* August 20, 1999, www.nwfusion.com.

"Wireless LANs Going Mainstream," Stephen Lawson, *Infoworld,* February 15, 1999, 155 Bovet Road, Suite 800, San Mateo, CA 94402. (415) 572-7341, www.infoworld.com.

"Wires Not Included," Peter Ruber, *Network Magazine,* June 1999. www.networkmagazine.com.

Books and Reports

Asia Commercial Overview, National Trade Data Bank, January 8, 1999, and March 5, 1999, U.S. Department of Commerce, Washington, DC 20230. www.stat-usa.gov.

Asia IT Report, Market Intelligence Center, March 1999, Taiwan. http://mic.iii.org.tw/english/asiait.

Basic Facts, European Information Technology Observatory Task Force, January 1, 1999. www.ispo.cec.be/esis/Basic

Communications Systems and Networks: Voice, Data, and Broadband Technologies, Ray Horak, M&T Books, IDG Books Worldwide, Inc., 1997, 919 East Hillsdale Boulevard, Suite 400, Foster City, CA 94404.

Computer Industry Almanac, 8th Edition, Karen Petska (Juliussen) and Egil Juliussen, Computer Industry Almanac Inc., 1013 South Belmont Avenue, Arlington Heights IL 60005.

Computers: Networking, Standard & Poor's Industry Surveys, August 6, 1998, 55 Water Street New York, NY 10041. (212) 438-2000, www.standardpoor.com.

E-Commerce: Implications for Firm Strategy and Industry Configuration, Martin Kenney and James Curry, University of California E-conomy Project, July 1999.

Export Administration Act, Issue Brief, American Electronics Association, August 1999. www.aeanet.org/aeanet/.

Foreign Direct Investment in the United States: Detail for Historical-Cost Position and Related Capital and Income Flows, 1998, Jeffrey H. Lowe, Survey of Current Business, September 1999, Bureau of Economic Analysis, U.S. Department of Commerce, Washington, DC 20230. www.bea.doc.gov.

Foreign Direct Investment in the United States: Preliminary Results From the 1997 Benchmark Survey, William J. Zeile, Survey of Current Business, August 1999, Bureau of Economic Analysis, U.S. Department of Commerce, Washington, DC 20230. www.bea.doc.gov.

The Global Market Forecast for Internet Usage and Commerce: Based on Internet Commerce Market Model, Version 5, Carol Glasheen and John Gantz, International Data Corporation, June 1999, 5 Speen Street, Framingham, MA 01701. (800) 343-4952, www.idcresearch.com.

High-Performance Technical Computer Census, Review, and Forecast, 1999–2003, Christopher Willard, PhD, and Debra Goldfarb, International Data Corporation, September 1999, 5 Speen Street, Framingham, MA 01701. (508) 872-8200. www.idcresearch.com.

IDC Analyzes Lucent's Acquisition of Ascend, International Data Corporation, January 25, 1999, 5 Speen Street, Framingham, MA 01701. (800) 343-4952, www.idcresearch.com.

IDC Intranet Fact Book: First Half 1999, International Data Corporation, 5 Speen Street, Framingham, MA 01701. (800) 343-4952, www.idcresearch.com.

IDC Worldwide Black Book, International Data Corporation, December 1998, 5 Speen Street, Framingham, MA 01701. (800) 343-4952, www.idcresearch.com.

Information Technology Frontiers for a New Millennium, High Performance Computing and Communications, National Science and Technology Council, Committee on Technology, Subcommittee on Computing, Information, and Communications R&D, Supplement to the President's FY2000 Budget, April 1999.

IT Spending Forecast for Higher Education Institutions, 1998–2003, Ray Boggs and Sau Lau, International Data Corporation, June 1999, 5 Speen Street, Framingham, MA 01701. (800) 343-4952, www.idcresearch.com.

1997 Annual Survey of Manufacturers and *Current Industrial Report,* Bureau of the Census, U.S. Department of Commerce, Washington, DC 20230. (301) 457-4673. www.census.gov.

1998 High-Performance Computer Market Review and Outlook, International Data Corporation, January 1999, 5 Speen Street, Framingham, MA 01701. (508) 872-8200, www.idcresearch.com.

1999 NIC Market Share Overview, International Data Corporation, June 1999, 5 Speen Street, Framingham, MA 01701. (800) 343-4952, www.idcresearch.com.

Policy-Based Networking: Creating the Business-Driven Network (White Paper), Lucent Technologies, 1999.

Presidents' Information Technology Advisory Committee Report to the President, Information Technology Research Investing in Our Future, National Coordination Office of Computing, Information and Communications, February 1999, 4201 Wilson Boulevard Suite 690, Arlington, VA 22230.

Quarterly Networking Market Watch—Routers, LAN Switches, and Shared Media Hubs: Second Quarter 1998, Dataquest, September 14, 1998, 1290 Ridder Park Drive, San Jose, CA 95131. (408) 437-8000, www.dataquest.com.

Research and Development (R&D) Tax Credit, Issue Brief, American Electronics Association, August 1999. http://www.aeanet.org/aeanet.

Sequent and IBM, International Data Corporation, August 1999, 5 Speen Street, Framingham, MA 01701. (508) 872-8200, www.idcresearch.com.

Server Market Review and Forecast, 1995–2003, International Data Corporation, August 1999, 5 Speen Street, Framingham, MA 01701. (508) 872-8200, www.idcresearch.com.

The State of Technology Usage in K–12 Education, 1999, Ray Boggs and Sau Lau, International Data Corporation, May 1999, 5 Speen Street, Framingham, MA 01701. (508) 872-8200, www.idcresearch.com.

Technology M&A Report: First Half 1999, Broadview, July 1999, 1 Bridge Plaza, Fort Lee, NJ 07024. (201) 346-9000, www.broadview.com.

Top 500 Supercomputer Sites, University of Mannheim, Germany, June 1999. www.top500.org.

U.S. Direct Investment Position Abroad on a Historical-Cost Basis: Industry Detail for Selected Countries, 1998, Bureau of Economic Analysis, U.S. Department of Commerce, Washington, DC 20230. www.bea.doc.gov.

The U.S. Segment of the 1999 Global IT Survey, Carol Glasheen, International Data Corporation, April 1999, 5 Speen Street, Framingham, MA 01701. (508) 872-8200, www.idcresearch.com.

Wireless LANs: Worldwide Market Review and Forecast, 1997–2003, International Data Corporation, June 1998, 5 Speen Street, Framingham, MA 01701. (800) 343-4952, www.idcresearch.com.

Worldwide Application Service Provider Review and Forecast, 1998–2003, International Data Corporation, March 1999, 5 Speen Street, Framingham, MA 01701. (508) 872-8200, www.idcresearch.com.

The Worldwide Financial Impact of the Y2K Problem for Vendors, Thomas D. Oleson, International Data Corporation, September 1998, 5 Speen Street, Framingham, MA. (800) 343-4952, www.idcresearch.com.

Worldwide Local Area Networks Market Share and Forecast, 1998, Dataquest, September 28, 1998, 1290 Ridder Park Drive, San Jose, CA 95131. (408) 437-8000, www.dataquest.com.

Worldwide PC Forecast Update, 1999–2003, Schelly Olhava et al., International Data Corporation, August 1999, 5 Speen Street, Framingham, MA 01701. (508) 872-8200, www.idcresearch.com.

Worldwide Workstation Review and Forecast, 1998–2003, International Data Corporation, May 1999, 5 Speen Street, Framingham, MA 01701. (508) 872-8200, www.idcresearch.com.

Yearbook of World Electronics Data 1999/2000, Volume 4: *East Europe and World Summary,* Reed Electronics Research, Quadrant House, the Quadrant, Sutton, Surrey SM2 5AS, United Kingdom.

Trade Associations

American Electronics Association, 1225 Eye Street, NW, Suite 950, Washington, DC 20005. (202) 682-9110.

Information Technology Association of America, 1616 North Fort Meyer Drive, Suite 1300, Arlington, VA 22209. (703) 522-5055, www.itaa.org.

Information Technology Industry Council, 1250 Eye Street, NW, Suite 200, Washington, DC 20005. (202) 626-5736.

Institute for Information Industry, 11F, No. 106, Sec. 2, Ho-Ping E. Road., Taipei, 106, Taiwan, Republic of China.

Interactive Multimedia Association, 48 Maryland Avenue, Suite 202, Annapolis, MD 21401-8011. (410) 626-1380.

Internet Society, 12020 Sunrise Valley Drive, Suite 270, Reston, VA 22091-3429. (703) 648-9888.

RELATED CHAPTERS

Chapter 16: Microelectronics
Chapter 26: Information Services
Chapter 28: Software and Internet Technologies
Chapter 30: Telecommunications Services
Chapter 31: Telecommunications and Navigation Equipment

SOFTWARE AND INTERNET TECHNOLOGIES
Economic and Trade Trends

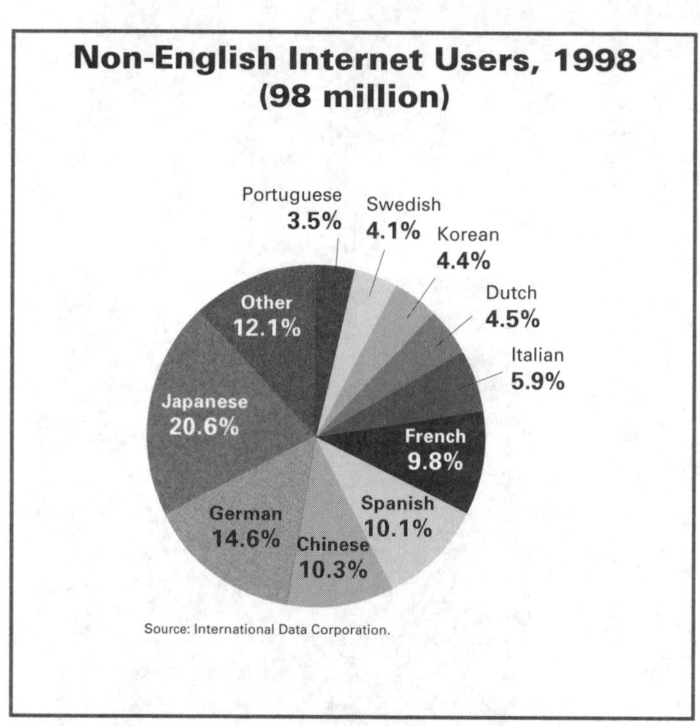

Source: International Data Corporation.

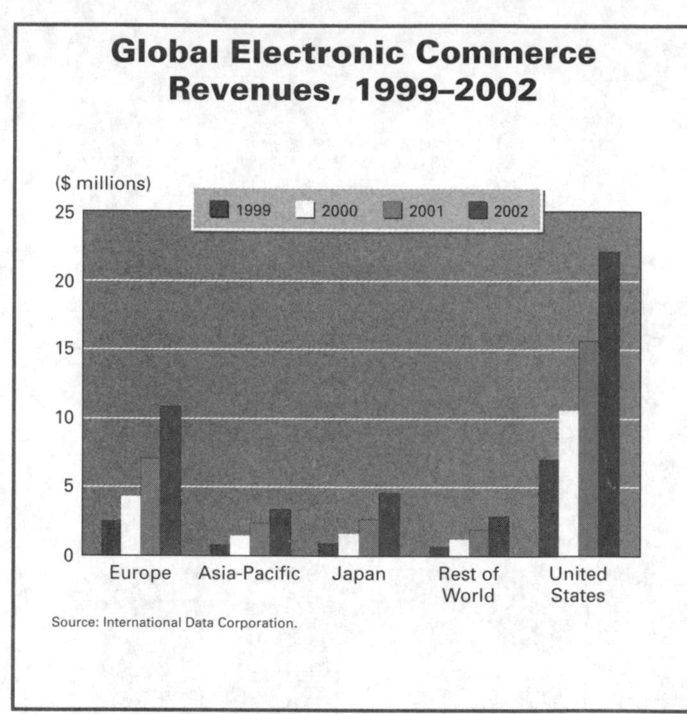

Source: International Data Corporation.

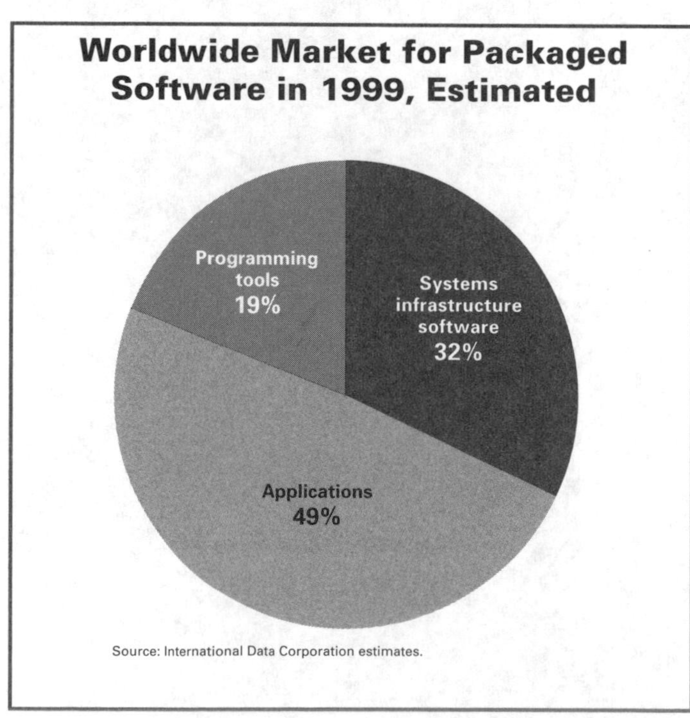

Source: International Data Corporation estimates.

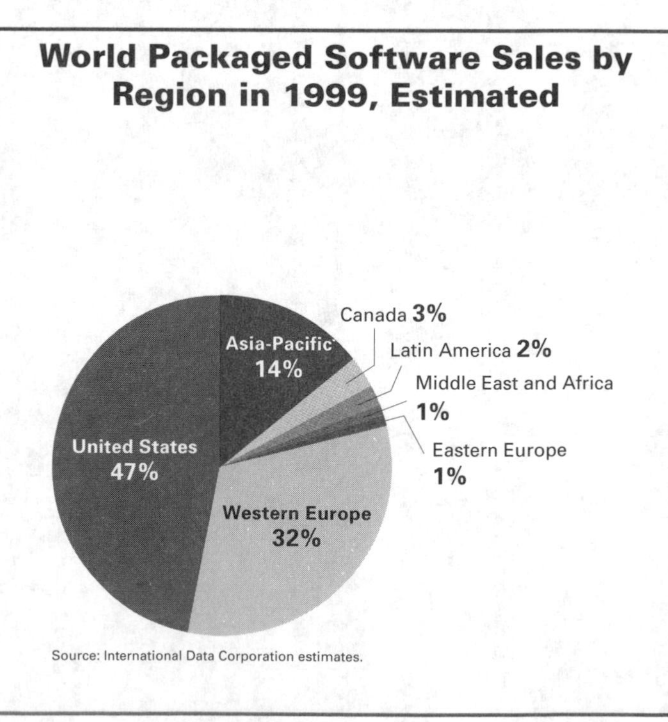

Source: International Data Corporation estimates.

See "Getting the Most Out of *Outlook 2000*" for definitions of terms.

28

Software and Internet Technologies

INDUSTRY DEFINITION The computer software industry consists of three parts: companies that design and publish packaged software programs for commercial sale or lease; companies that develop internet and electronic commerce technologies and provide on-line information and services, such as Web page designers and internet portals; and companies that provide traditional computer services, such as systems integration design, custom computer programming, consulting, and software installation and training. This chapter covers the first two groups; computer services are discussed in Chapter 26, Information Systems. Packaged software is subdivided into systems infrastructure software (operating systems, utilities, systems management programs, etc.), applications packages (solutions for businesses, consumers, government, and organizations), and software development tools (programming languages, application development programs, etc.). The software covered in this chapter operates on all computer hardware platforms: personal computers (PCs), network servers, and mainframes.

As a key component of information technology (IT), software increasingly pervades all areas of society. It has become one of the fastest-growing and innovative economic sectors as businesses and governments around the world expand software expenditures to increase their operational efficiencies. Software solutions allow organizations to better manage internal operations, automate external relationships with clients and suppliers, and improve worker productivity. It is an integral part of the global economy as more international business is conducted electronically, stock markets are automated, and money is transmitted across the globe in seconds.

As a key contributor to the economy, software is one of the fastest-growing industries in the United States. According to the trade association the Business Software Alliance (BSA), sales of software products and services rose 18 percent to reach $140.9 billion in 1998. The industry has grown three times as fast as U.S. gross domestic product, created jobs at five times the rate of the private sector, and paid wages twice the national average over the last 5 years. Employment has grown at an annual rate of 10 percent over the last 10 years and 13 percent over the last 4 years. Because of its dominant position worldwide, the industry accounts for an important share of U.S. exports. BSA estimates that packaged software firms had a trade surplus of $13 billion in 1997 and forecasts that the surplus will exceed $20 billion in the year 2000 as U.S. firms increase their overseas sales.

INDUSTRY STRUCTURE AND DYNAMICS

The scope and variety of the software industry have expanded exponentially over the past several decades as a result of improvements in hardware performance and software programming techniques and changes in market needs and expectations. What was once a relatively small industry with a limited number of programs has exploded into one with a rapidly expanding volume and variety of products that are performing increasingly sophisticated tasks and serving new and unanticipated markets.

Programs have increased in size, complexity, and diversity to meet the demands of growing computer networks and exploit the escalating power of computers. As firms cut costs by automating and integrating management and production functions, the enterprise resource planning (ERP) software segment has grown. Computer-aided design (CAD) software, which once was used solely on workstations by engineers and scientists, is now employed widely on personal computers (PCs) by nontraditional users such as landscape architects. Software developed for home use (education, home finance, and entertainment) is becoming more widespread as home PC penetration increases. The rapid growth in computer networks from local area networks (LAN) to internet-based computing and E-commerce has driven the development of network management and internet-related software. The development of software for use in remote access, wireless, and portable computer applications is pushed by the insatiable demand for instant and ubiquitous communications.

The U.S. software industry is composed of thousands of establishments of all sizes, including some large firms with annual software sales above $1 billion that dominate major market segments, a good number of midsize companies, and many small firms that work in niche technologies and markets. Like other literary works, computer software has been created over the years by many types of organizations and individuals for self-use or sale. However, most commercial software is developed either by computer systems manufacturers that produce both hardware and software, such as IBM, Sun Microsystems, and Hewlett-Packard, or by independent software vendors (ISVs) that focus exclusively on software, such as Oracle and PeopleSoft. Recently, to maintain revenue flow and take advantage of new markets and technologies, some traditional software firms have begun to move into the on-line information services arena. For example, Microsoft has introduced Microsoft Network, an internet portal offering Web site hosting, E-mail, and internet access, and IBM provides "E-business" services that give customers electronic commerce strategies.

Like other IT sectors, the software industry is characterized by growing consolidation as firms merge with and acquire other software producers to augment their products' capabilities, participate in leading-edge technologies, and expand their marketing reach. According to *Software Magazine*'s ranking of the 500 leading software companies around the world, the top 10 vendors accounted for $50.7 billion, or 55 percent of total revenues, in 1998 and employed two-thirds of the workforce. Mergers and acquisitions in the North American software industry rose 21 percent from 1997 to 1998, according to Broadview International, LLC. *Software Magazine* reports that 32 percent of the top 500 software firms merged with or acquired another company in 1998. Examples include America Online's purchase of Netscape Communications to acquire Netscape's strength in Web browsers and Microsoft's acquisition of Spyglass, which also is an internet vendor.

With the limited exception of several large foreign companies, U.S. firms dominate almost all software sectors in the United States and abroad and account for over 90 percent of worldwide packaged software revenues. Eight of the top 10 firms on *Software Magazine*'s top 500 list are headquartered in the United States. Germany's SAP AG, a leader in ERP software, and Japan's Hitachi are the exceptions (see Table 28-1).

TABLE 28-1: Worldwide Software Revenues and R&D Expenditures of the Top 20 Software Companies in 1998
(millions of dollars; percent)

	Software Revenue	Revenue Spent on R&D, %
Microsoft	16,660	16
IBM Corp.	11,863	6
Oracle Corp.	5,317	9
Computer Associates, Inc.	4,854	8
Hitachi, Ltd.	4,184	n/a
SAP AG	3,154	12
Hewlett-Packard	1,412	7
Sun Microsystems	1,367	11
Compaq Computer Corp.	1,174	4
PeopleSoft, Inc.	1,042	16
Parametric Technology Corp.	1,009	10
Network Associates, Inc.	990	n/a
BMC Software, Inc.	975	13
Candence Design Systems	960	n/a
Compuware Corp.	929	8
Adobe Systems, Inc.	895	23
Sybase, Inc.	868	17
SAS Institute, Inc.	846	31
The Learning Company, Inc.	839	12
Andersen Consulting LLP	830	n/a

Source: *Software Magazine,* June 1999.

A major event with major implications for the software industry is the ongoing antitrust case against Microsoft. The case was filed in May 1998 by the U.S. Department of Justice and twenty state attorneys general, after a lengthy period of government investigation and court actions by both sides. The trial began in October of that year, during which Justice Department lawyers challenged a variety of Microsoft's practices designed to protect the company's alleged monopoly position in the PC operating systems market and to dominate the internet browser market. The complaint alleged that among other things, Microsoft illegally bundled its internet browser with its Windows operating system, attempted to divide markets with its competitors, and imposed exclusionary terms and conditions with various customers and vendors in violation of the Sherman Antitrust Act.

In November 1999, U.S. District judge Thomas Penfield Jackson issued his Findings of Fact, which according to the Justice Department, found that Microsoft is a monopolist engaged in anticompetitive activity harming innovation and limiting consumer choice. The judge also appointed a mediator to spur an out-of-court settlement between the parties. Justice Department lawyers are exploring options to limit Microsoft's market power if they win the case, such as breaking up the company into separate firms along product lines, such as operating systems, applications, programming tools, and internet products; or restricting Microsoft's future marketing and software development activities. Whatever the outcome of this landmark case, the industry will be deeply affected.

Workforce Issues

Job creation in the U.S. software industry is increasing rapidly. According to the Bureau of Labor Statistics, employment grew an estimated 11 percent in 1999 to exceed 915,000 workers. Jobs in packaged software firms, which employ about one-third of the industry's workforce, grew faster at 16 percent. BSA reports that in 1998, total wages for the industry reached $55.6 billion, having increased at an average annual rate of 8 percent since 1994 to reach an annual average of $68,900 per employee. Although most programmers work for software development firms, a variety of firms and organizations employ software professionals to develop and maintain in-house computer systems.

The industry requires a large number of highly skilled software engineers to develop and maintain software code; however, companies are facing acute shortages in the United States, causing the delaying or abandonment of projects, computer system failures, and wage inflation. This shortage has encouraged firms to establish software development facilities overseas, import trained engineers, and contract work to overseas programmers, principally in India, Ireland, and Israel, which have a large pool of English-speaking, highly skilled workers.

Immigration has become a contentious issue as U.S. software companies argue that to remain competitive internationally and avoid moving jobs overseas, they must be able to bring in foreign workers. Partly to address this need for technical labor, the H-1B visa program allows foreigners to reside temporarily in the United States while working in high-tech positions. Since 1990, the annual cap on H-1B visas has been 65,000. However, this limit was met before the end of the year in both 1997 and 1998. In response to industry pressure, in 1998 Congress enacted legislation to raise temporarily the number of H-1B visas issued annually. The cap on visas will rise to 115,000 in fiscal year (FY) 2000, increase to 107,500 in FY 2001, and then revert again to 65,000 in FY 2002.

Capital Investment

The software industry is characterized by perpetual change and innovation resulting from rapid technological advances in the IT sector and the consequent short product life cycles. Success for any company in this highly competitive arena depends on creating new product generations and markets in very short periods, a process that requires a continuing supply of research and development (R&D) investment. Five of the top 10 U.S. firms in terms of R&D expenditures were in the IT and software sector in 1997, according to *Inside R&D.*

In 1998, the packaged software industry spent $4.1 billion on research, placing it eighth among industry sectors in total dollars spent, behind automobiles and chemicals but ahead of photographic equipment and semiconductors. However, according to the Industrial Research Institute, the industry ranks third behind medical chemicals and biological products in terms of research intensity, or the ratio of R&D expenditures to total revenue. While average R&D expenditures for all U.S. industries amount to 7 percent of revenues, the software industry averages nearly 11 percent (see Table 28-1).

Because of the importance of R&D, the software industry, along with other industries, is seeking a permanent R&D tax credit. The Research and Experimentation Tax Credit under Section 41 of the Internal Revenue Code provides for a tax credit equal to 20 percent of any company's qualified research expenditures during a taxable year. Originally enacted in 1981, the credit is temporary and can be extended only through the legislative process. Since its inception, the R&D tax credit has been extended nine times, most recently in 1998, when Congress approved a 1-year extension through June 30, 1999. In 1999, a 5-year extension to the credit was proposed as part of a broader tax bill but was not adopted. While the software industry has lobbied for a permanent extension, Congress and different administrations have been unable to agree on this issue.

The software industry is characterized by a large number of small start-up companies, which are a major source of rapid innovation. These firms possess intellectual capital and new technologies but lack operational and product development funds. To provide funding, a venture capital industry has emerged that provides money to young, rapidly growing companies that have viable business plans and good market prospects. Although most start-up companies do not receive venture capital, it is an essential source of equity for many and is important to the competitive strength of the entire industry. In the IT sector, the majority of venture capital is directed toward computer software and services companies, especially internet-related ventures. Funding totaled nearly $5 billion in the first half of 1999, double that of the first half of 1998 (see Tables 28-2 and 28-3).

Other countries do not have a U.S.-style venture capital system, and that lack limits access to capital for their new companies and impedes industry growth, innovation, and risk taking. In response to the successful U.S. experience, venture capital firms have emerged in countries such as the United Kingdom. However, in some cases, those firms do not specialize in IT as they do in the United States and may not emphasize high-tech investing. In addition, as a result of the rapid pace of technological change, U.S. venture capitalists do not necessarily penalize company founders who fail and will give them access to future funding if their new proposals warrant it. This is not always the case abroad, where more conservative lending policies may prevent the creators of failed projects from receiving funding for their new ideas.

TABLE 28-2: Venture Capital Investments by Industry
(millions of dollars)

	1999, first half	1998, first half	Percent Change
Computer software and services	4,916	2,326	111
Communications	2,588	1,133	128
Medical and health	986	1,175	–16
Semiconductors and other electronics	598	320	87
Biotechnology	520	492	6
Computer hardware	310	270	15

Source: National Venture Capital Association.

TABLE 28-3: Internet-Related Venture Capital Investments in the First and Second Quarters in 1999

	Second Quarter		First Quarter	
Internet Category	No. Companies	Investment, $millions	No. Companies	Investment, $millions
E-commerce and content	179	1,688	117	957
Internet software and tools	91	769	64	339
Internet services	61	731	39	286
Other Internet-related	27	304	19	273
Communications and infrastructure	23	273	14	252
Internet hardware	12	100	11	93
Total	393	3,865	264	2,200

Source: National Venture Capital Association.

Markets and Growth

Markets for computer software are growing rapidly in all countries, although economic slowdowns and currency devaluations in Asia, Russia, and parts of Latin America have dampened demand in those regions. Software is still growing faster than are the computer hardware and services sectors, although it represents less than one-fifth of the total IT market. International Data Corporation (IDC), a research firm, estimates that worldwide revenues for packaged software were $155.3 billion in 1999. The industry is divided into systems infrastructure software (23 percent), applications (51 percent), and programming tools (26 percent). The market is forecast to grow at an average annual rate of 14.5 percent to exceed $268 billion by 2003.

The United States is the largest software market, accounting for about 47 percent of global software sales, and should grow over 15 percent annually in the next several years. The next largest market is western Europe with 34 percent of world sales, followed by the Asia-Pacific region, 12 percent; Canada, 3 percent; Latin America, 2 percent; Middle East and Africa, 1 percent; and eastern Europe, 1 percent. Table 28-4 shows the percentage of the world market and near-term growth rates for selected countries.

TABLE 28-4: Share of Worldwide Packaged Software Market and Growth Rates for Selected Countries in 1998

Country	Share, %	Compound Annual Growth Rate 98–03, %
Japan	7.6	13
Germany	8.6	13
Italy	2.4	8
Norway	0.5	13
Korea	0.3	18
Brazil	0.4	12
South Africa	0.6	20
China	0.6	48
Israel	0.4	8
Mexico	0.3	12
Poland	0.2	12
India	0.1	39

Source: International Data Corporation.

MARKETING AND TECHNOLOGY TRENDS

The rapid growth of the internet and the parallel emergence of E-commerce are having a profound effect on the industry by changing how software is developed, marketed, and distributed. Changes in the quality and sophistication of electronic communications, such as high-speed connections and multisite databases, have led firms increasingly to globalize software development, with programmers in different locations collaborating and sharing code electronically. Globalized development is increasing as firms seek specialized talent or try to reduce development costs, particularly when using lower-wage programmers in countries such as India, China, and Russia. Firms also engage in collaborative development to reduce time to market, gain customer proximity, and create a global presence.

Software products increasingly are marketed and sold on-line, and those sales are expected to approach $900 million in the year 2000, according to BSA. The internet has introduced a unique distribution channel that is able to provide consumers with on-line sales and downloads as well as much broader product selections than they can find at retail stores. The internet provides publishers and channel partners with swifter ways to introduce their software products and services to global markets compared with previous methods. Today, most internet sales consist of consumers paying by credit card on-line for software that then is shipped by regular mail. However, software increasingly will be downloaded by users from the internet via electronic software distribution (ESD). Currently, ESD is hampered by limits on the amount of data that can be effectively downloaded (bandwidth) and relatively slow transmission times. As software programs continue to expand in size, it will be impractical for many consumers to download entire programs until bandwidth is increased.

Increasing business use of the internet has enabled a new sales model for software: the renting or leasing of Web-based software applications. This option is attractive to smaller firms that cannot afford to pay for software licenses or maintain software internally. Application rental is especially prevalent in the ERP and E-commerce industry segments and is discussed in more detail in "Internet Technologies," below.

The internet is driving the creation of new products such as Web page design and influencing the development of existing products. For example, many products are being redesigned to have Web functionality. The proliferation of intranets, extranets, and E-commerce also has increased the demand for software security products that can insulate networks and protect data and for back-end payment systems and credit/fraud management software. However, other technologies also are propelling the industry, such as three-dimensional (3-D) techniques, virtual reality, and voice recognition. Increasing computer memory and processor speeds are allowing the development of software technologies that depict more lifelike situations.

3-D technology creates an illusion of depth by using perspective, colors, shadows, shading, and texture. These characteristics are "rendered," or applied to the specific scene, through the use of modeling tools. These techniques have become a well-known software solution in many industries, including medical imaging, chemistry, home design, and games. In the health care industry, 3-D software has been integrated into diagnostic equipment in medical visualization for digital x-rays, magnetic resonance imaging, and nuclear medicine. In scientific simulation software, 3-D capability allows a computer to design models for simulations to help scientists decide which chemical compounds to make and how to make them. Builders can design and visualize a structure before breaking ground, including landscaping and decor within the structure. Video game developers use 3-D technologies to create increasingly sophisticated games to meet the demands of players, who want game experiences to be as lifelike as possible.

Virtual reality (VR) technology refers to systems that simulate real-world environments in which users can move and interact. The technology began with elaborate flight simulators built for pilot training during World War II and today is widely found in game arcades and amusement parks, using a combination of movie screens and movable platforms to create virtual experiences. It is a technology that is being incorporated into a small but growing number of products in many areas. Fire investigators use VR to simulate walking into a fire scene. Heavy equipment in a VR factory can be moved with the touch of a finger on a computer mouse, allowing designers to identify safety problems before building new plants. VR is used in schools to enhance students' understanding of science and history.

Virtual reality applications require a computer, a head-mounted display helmet, and data gloves, which allow the user to interact within fabricated surroundings. The helmet creates a 3-D world by limiting visual and audio contact to a small screen mounted inside that surrounds the user with high-fidelity sights and sounds. Sensors in the glove measure the movements of the fingers and hand and translate them into coordinates, which are fed into the computer; the virtual world is changed as a user points or grips and pushes objects. Feeling a virtual object requires a specialized system that transmits forces back to the user's hand in a way that mimics the sensation of touch. This allows users to feel objects created by the computer in the way that a graphic display lets users see computer-generated objects.

Voice or speech recognition technology is a computer-user interface that enables computers to recognize the natural human voice, interpret it, and carry out a spoken command. Through voice recognition, users can operate applications by speaking words or short phrases instead of inputting commands with a mouse or keyboard. Spoken words are converted into a sequence of numbers and matched against coded vocabulary dictionaries that identify the words or recognize speech algorithms. The words then are stored in the computer and matched with future words, along with speech patterns on the hard drive, that are loaded into memory when the program is run. The vocabulary size and word matching speed of a voice recognition program vocabulary are directly related to the computer's memory and processing speed. Dragon Systems and IBM, with its OS/2 operating system supporting voice recognition, are the leaders in this field.

Voice recognition technology allows computer users to be more productive and work at a faster rate. One of the most common uses of this technology has been in dictation, where the computer interprets and translates human speech into text and displays it in a document on a screen. Voice recognition software can handle the dictation of 30 to 70 words per minute (wpm) compared with the average typing speed of 5 to 25 wpm on a keyboard. Voice recognition technology has become commonplace in telephones with voice dialing and answering. In the medical and legal professions, where a significant amount of time is spent recording and documenting, voice recognition systems will be used to boost productivity. Voice recognition software also is used by the disabled in working and communicating with others and will become a standard feature of word processing programs. In the future, voice recognition technology will be available in automobiles, cellular phones, televisions, and temperature control systems and will have many other uses.

The year 2000 (Y2K) transition problem was a major concern of the software industry over the past several years. This problem resulted from the fact that software programs traditionally used a two-digit format to represent a particular year; this is not an adequate system and will provide incorrect dates when the century changes. The Y2K problem created new markets for products that could remediate noncompliant computers and software and for companies that had the expertise to troubleshoot computer code in old legacy systems. However, software developers also incurred costs not only to repair their own in-house systems but to establish Web sites to inform customers about the Y2K compliance of their products and provide free downloadable software fixes. The Y2K problem both hampered and helped software sales. Y2K concerns prompted some users to delay new software purchases as they shifted their IT budgets to Y2K remediation, while others made purchases to implement new solutions instead of repairing existing systems. Pent-up demand for delayed procurements will spur software sales in the year 2000.

TRADE POLICY ISSUES

Maintaining open markets around the world for software and IT products is important to the strength of the global economy and the competitive strength of the U.S. software industry. Computer software provides modern productivity tools to struggling economies and makes the trading system, which is highly IT-dependent, more efficient. The industry's hefty positive trade balance, resulting from its strong global position, is important to the U.S. economy. Some U.S. companies earn over half their revenue from overseas sales, and as the U.S. market becomes saturated, firms will rely more on foreign sales. Although U.S. software exports face few restraints around the world, partly because of the lack of competitive national software industries, there are government policies and practices that stifle trade. Among the most consequential are the lack of intellectual property rights (IPR) protection, market access issues, industrial policy regimes, and export control regulations.

Intellectual Property Rights Protection

Software, like a book or movie, is a creative product with a high information content, but its electronic digital format is more easily copied and distributed. Therefore, software firms depend on strong and enforceable IPR regimes to discourage the unauthorized copying of their products. Some countries lack essential copyright and trademark laws, and others fail to enforce the laws that have been adopted; this has resulted in the proliferation of software theft. Piracy also is facilitated by the ease of copying software sold on CD-ROM disks, which can be replicated on inexpensive equipment, and the growing practice of downloading programs from the internet. BSA reports that thousands of sites providing illegal software can be found on the World Wide Web.

The lack of adequate copyright protection results in monetary losses, inhibits technological innovation and R&D investment, and leads some exporters to avoid certain markets. The U.S. software trade associations the Software and Information Industry Association (SIIA) and BSA estimated that in 1998, 38 percent of all packaged business software used around the world was pirated; this resulted in losses of $11 billion for software producers. This was a slight improvement over 1997 piracy estimates of 40 percent and $11.4 billion.

The principal international organizations that address IPR issues are the World Intellectual Property Organization (WIPO), which is part of the United Nations and has 171 member states, and the 135-member World Trade Organization (WTO), which adopted the Agreement on Trade-Related Aspects of Intellectual Property Rights (TRIPS) in 1994. WIPO develops international norms for IPR protection and helps developing countries comply with those conventions. The agency recently extended basic copyright protection into the electronic environment and now protects copyrighted works that are on-line, including software. TRIPS obligates WTO members to establish and enforce a base level of IPR protection and provides dispute settlement procedures. The agreement calls on countries to recognize software as a literary work with 50 years of protection that is eligible for full legal protection against copying or other improper use. The more developed economies in the WTO have been required to comply with TRIPS provisions since January 1, 1996, while developing countries have been directed to comply by January 1, 2000. Many developing countries are still deficient in establishing TRIPS-mandated IPR protection and enforcement mechanisms.

The U.S. government and various trade associations work with foreign governments to establish adequate IPR protection legal regimes. The United States also attempts to address the IPR violations of its trading partners through the use of its trade laws, specifically the "Special 301" process. Under Special 301, the United States identifies and, if appropriate, can impose sanctions against countries that fail to provide adequate protection for U.S. products. In April 1999, the U.S. Trade Representative (USTR) announced the results of its tenth annual Special 301 review of IPR protection and IPR-related market access practices of U.S. trading partners. As a result, 16 countries were placed on the "priority watch list" and 37 were placed on the "watch list," which identify countries with IPR deficiencies. The USTR also will continue to monitor Paraguay and China under Section 306 of the Trade Act of 1974 to ensure that those countries comply with IPR commitments made under bilateral agreements with the United States.

Market Access Restrictions

There are three ways to export software overseas: physically shipping or mailing it to the end user, sending master disks of the software to the end user or reseller with a license to make a prescribed number of additional copies for use in that country or for further export, and transmitting the software electronically over the internet or other networks. In some cases, the programs are localized (translated into the local language and culture) in the recipient country. Today, most software is exported by using the first two methods, but electronic distribution will increase as bandwidth limitations are overcome and E-commerce applications become more generally accepted.

Although software is subject to certain foreign packaging and labeling requirements and to content censorship as programs increasingly contain information components other than computer code, the principal impediment to trade is import tariffs. Countries vary in their valuation of and assessment of duties on software imports. According to a 1984 General Agreement on Tariffs and Trade (GATT) ruling, the valuation of software should be based on the value of the underlying medium (the cost of the unrecorded magnetic and optical disks) rather than on that of the information residing on that medium. Since the value of a software program is significantly greater than the cost of a blank disk, tariffs assessed only on the media are much lower. The United States and the other major software markets apply software duties in this manner. However, application of the GATT ruling is not mandatory, and customs entities in some countries still assess duties on the total price of the software, which can be significant for expensive programs. Further, the language of the GATT ruling explicitly excludes audio and video recordings, and this raises issues of its applicability to modern software that incorporates sound and image. Royalties from foreign software sales also are subject to withholding, value-added, and other types of taxes, which generally are assessed on the full value of a product, although certain taxes can be waived if the United States has a tax treaty with the recipient country.

The Information Technology Agreement (ITA) that was concluded in 1997 eliminates some tariffs for software exporters. The 52 participating countries agreed to a staged elimination of tariffs on a variety of IT products, including software, in most cases by January 1, 2000. Duty-free treatment significantly reduces import duties on software, which had been as high as 60 percent in some countries. This will effectively eliminate the issue of whether duties should be assessed on the value of the media or the content in the signatory countries. However, growing markets, such as China, Brazil, Mexico, and Chile, have not signed the agreement. With the fast pace of technological change, there is also a problem regarding how software is defined, which could affect how products are covered under this agreement. This could create implementation issues at customs' agencies and require further modifications of the ITA. For example, there is a question whether programs that include recorded music or video clips fall under the definition of computer software of the ITA. In addition, game software written for television consoles, such as those produced by Nintendo and Sega, is not covered under the ITA.

Industrial Policy Regimes

Establishing a software industry and attracting software companies are one of the primary economic development goals of many countries as well as a key strategy of many communities in the United States. Software firms have high potential earnings, employ highly trained workers, and are considered "environmentally clean." However, those companies require a highly developed technical infrastructure within a country and thus tend to congregate in "technology parks." Factors that helped the U.S. software industry flourish included a skilled workforce, distinguished universities, highly developed communications and transportation systems, a large affluent domestic market, readily available investment funding, and an entrepreneurial spirit. The U.S. industry also was helped because computers and software were first commercially developed in the United States, and the early widespread adoption of PCs created a growing demand for software products that thousands of new companies emerged to satisfy. The birth of the software industry in the United States resulted in English-language programming code becoming the industry standard, giving U.S. software companies, with their access to a large English-speaking population, an advantage over foreign competitors.

Notwithstanding global competitors such as Germany's SAP AG and the Netherlands' Baan, most foreign software firms are not competitive globally. Many foreign firms tend to target their own markets, selling products in the local language and focusing on niche markets. However, in recent years a number of governments have attempted to develop indigenous software industries. The British and German governments have established regional economic development agencies that provide business advice and development services to software developers. Those entities help software firms secure funding, assist with business plans and in locating potential partners, and aid market expansion. Software incubators are becoming more widespread in those countries, where start-ups are given offices, access to communications, and business counseling at subsidized rates.

Developing countries also are trying to establish software industries. India provides a great deal of custom programming services for U.S. companies and subsidiaries, and the number of Indian-owned software firms with successful export businesses is growing. Since this industry is a major foreign exchange earner, the Indian government provides incentives to promote its growth, including reduced import duties on hardware and software, incentives for export sales, and accommodations in software technology parks. With demand for software programmers outpacing supply, the Indian government has established several software engineering programs in conjunction with private computer educational institutes. One reason for India's international success is that its programmers have strong English-language skills. The Philippine government also offers overseas investors incentives to establish computer software businesses, particularly for export, and those companies also benefit from a large English-speaking population. The Chinese government has invested in many software start-up firms and has built a number of software production facilities in technology parks. However, much of the software developed by those firms is written in Chinese for an exploding domestic market. While China has a large number of programmers, it has not been successful in competing overseas because of a lack of English-language proficiency.

Export Controls

Since the beginning of the cold war, exports of encryption technologies, including software, that encode, scramble, and recover data sent over electronic networks have been subject to government control in the United States. Those controls have engendered intense debate between industry advocates, who complain of lost sales as a result of license denials and license approval delays, and government agencies concerned with law enforcement and national security demands. Recently, the pervasiveness and commercial use of the internet have increased the demand for encryption products, and privacy advocates argue that export controls deprive internet users of the most advanced technologies to protect the confidential nature of personal data and business dealings. As the speed, efficiency, and cost-saving benefits of internet and electronic commerce technologies increase, the demand for highly secured transmissions of confidential data will grow. In recognition of the realities of the emerging digital economy and to support its development, the U.S. government relaxed controls on the export of encryption software in January 2000. The new regulations give U.S. companies more liberalized access to all global markets (see "Internet Technologies," below).

R. Clay Woods, Danielle M. Kriz, Duaine A. Priestley and Patricia A. Johnson, Office of Computers and Business Equipment, (202) 482-0572, October 1999.

SYSTEMS INFRASTRUCTURE SOFTWARE

Systems infrastructure software, such as operating systems, is used to manage and control individual computer systems as well as networks of computers. This sector includes all programs that oversee and direct the internal operations of a computer system and enhance basic system functionality. The sector is divided into four areas: system-level software, system and network management products, middleware, and security software. The sector is robust, and all of its segments will continue to grow rapidly as a result of explosive growth in E-commerce and internet applications and corporate enterprise computing. Microsoft has a leading position in this market. However, other technologies, such as the Linux operating system and thin-client computing networks, are gaining support.

The systems infrastructure software industry experienced strong worldwide growth of 12 percent in 1999, reaching $46 billion. Annual growth should average 15 percent through 2003, with sales reaching almost $80 billion (see Table 28-5). U.S.-based vendors lead in this market. The top four suppliers—IBM, Microsoft, Computer Associates, and Hewlett-Packard—held a 48 percent market share in 1998, followed by Hitachi and Fujitsu in Japan with shares of 2.5 and 2.4 percent, respectively. Microsoft's rapidly rising sales growth was expected to place it in the number one spot in 1999, as Intel microprocessor–based machines running with Windows operating systems increased their performance levels to compete in areas previously dominated by Unix and RISC-based workstations. Nevertheless, the accelerating expansion of the internet, electronic commerce, and enterprise database sectors will increase demand for all software platforms, including mainframe systems software.

System-level software is the largest segment of the systems infrastructure industry and consists of operating systems (OS), utilities, and networking software. Operating systems are master programs that perform basic computer functions as well as act as underlying platforms for application programs. OS software is required for all computer platforms. The most common are Windows, Unix, and Macintosh. Utilities are programs that enhance a computer's capabilities or perform support functions such as file management and file compression. Norton Utilities, for example, provides system diagnostic and monitoring capabilities. Network operating systems such as Novell's Netware and Windows NT contain the interconnecting communications software that links autonomous computers and peripherals. Network operating systems manage network resources and provide file/print and directory functions, along with other services.

Worldwide revenues for system-level software increased 7 percent in 1999 to reach $23.5 billion. Sales of operating systems are expected to grow at an 11 percent compound annual growth rate (CAGR) to reach $28.6 billion in 2003. Utilities software should grow 7 percent to register sales of $2 billion in 2003. The total systems level segment is expected to reach $33.8 billion by 2003 (see Table 28-5).

The best-selling operating system continues to be 32-bit Windows 95, 98, and NT, which had over $6.2 billion in sales, or 37 percent of the world OS market, in 1998. Mainframe OS software such as IBM's OS/390 was second with 27 percent of the market, followed by Unix products, 19 percent; NetWare, 4 percent; and Apple's Mac OS, 1 percent. Operating systems for portable devices, such as Windows CE and Palm OS, had only $16 million in sales in 1998, but IDC states that this market could grow to $132 million by 2003.

The OS market is concentrated in a few vendors mainly because users want well-supported and stable operating systems that have a wide range of applications. Microsoft, IBM, Hewlett-Packard, Sun Microsystems, and Novell accounted for over two-thirds of revenues in 1999; Microsoft accounted for over one-third of those sales. Nearly 90 percent of all businesses use a 32-bit Windows operating system, and 75 percent of all PCs worldwide use some version of Windows. NetWare and Unix are resident on 49 and 45 percent of corporate systems, respectively.

Several factors account for the continued success of Windows at both the client level and the server level. First, the move to networked and distributed computing has suppressed the growth of mainframe and proprietary minicomputer software and increased the demand for desktop and network operating system products. Another factor is Microsoft's successful high-volume, low-price strategy, which is tied to the dominance and growth of Intel processor-based, or "Wintel," PCs. Although a strategy initially devised for the desktop market, it is proving effective for servers, particularly on the low end. Despite the fact that Windows NT servers are sold at lower prices than are typical Unix packages, the higher volume of Microsoft's sales results in comparable revenues for NT. Many IT managers are expressing a preference for the cost savings of NT servers versus Unix/RISC-based products and are moving to standardize all their systems

TABLE 28-5: Trends and Forecasts in Worldwide System Infrastructure Software Revenues
(billions of dollars)

Market Segment	1998	1999	2000	2001	2002	2003	Compound Annual Growth Rates 00–03, %
System-level	22.0	23.5	25.3	27.8	30.7	33.8	10
Middleware	4.0	5.1	6.7	9.0	12.2	16.6	35
System management	12.6	13.1	14.7	16.4	18.4	21.2	13
Security	3.2	4.4	5.6	6.6	7.5	8.3	14
Total	41.7	46.0	52.3	59.8	68.8	79.9	15

Source: International Data Corporation.

on NT. Microsoft also is "bundling" more functionality into its OS software, such as Web browsers and other internet applications. Shipments of Windows NT totaled 1.8 million units in 1998, an increase of 24 percent from the 1997 level, and IDC projects that revenue for 32-bit Windows (including NT) will have a CAGR of 18.9 percent from 1998 to 2003.

Despite the success of Windows, the surging growth of the internet, enterprise databases, and Web-based applications will continue to drive the demand for high-end scalable application server software built on Unix and other platforms. For example, most internet service providers and other companies prefer to use Unix for their Web server environments. Unix sales also will continue to be boosted by increased demand for work group application support, work group databases, and the need to provide file-and-print services for more users. Unix is a highly flexible operating system with greater compatibility with a wide variety of networking standards than Windows NT Server has. Unix is the dominant operating system for hosting relational database management systems on midrange servers. Applications running on NT Server, Novell NetWare, or IBM's OS/2 often receive data from Unix-run databases. The leading midrange server systems, such as Sun's Solaris, Hewlett-Packard's HP-UX, and IBM's AIX, are all Unix operating environments. However, Unix will face tough competition from Windows NT Server on entry-level server hardware priced at less than $100,000. According to IDC, the Unix operating environment will experience a 1998–2003 CAGR of 11.4 percent, maintaining an OS market share of 18.5 percent.

NetWare 5 from Novell, with support for multiple networking protocols and advanced remote management features, will remain a major player in this sector. NetWare has the largest installed base of any server operating environment, with 4 million units worldwide and an estimated 80 million end users. IDC projections indicate that NetWare will have a robust CAGR of 9.4 percent from 1998 to 2003. However, NetWare's share of the worldwide OS market is forecast to decline from 4.2 percent to 3.9 percent. Sales of other network operating systems, such as Banyan Vines, LANtastic, and other LAN-centric OS products, have declined dramatically. Banyan has terminated its OS business and is focusing on internet technologies; it has sold Microsoft an equity position of roughly 10 percent as well as access to Banyan's installed base. Therefore, it is likely that many of the sites currently running Vines will migrate to Microsoft's Windows NT Server.

Unix, NetWare, and OS/2 will continue to be major products in this sector because of installed bases numbering in the millions and brand loyalty among users that have invested heavily in these products. Although Windows NT Server is having great success in the large enterprise market, many users are purchasing Unix in addition to NT Server and then matching each system with the appropriate workload and applications. Corporate sites with large installed bases of NetWare and OS/2 are continuing to buy those operating environments. Even mainframe OS products such as IBM's OS/390 will experience some growth, as many internet applications require the level of robustness that only large-scale systems can provide. IDC projects that mainframe operating systems will have a CAGR of 3.5 percent from 1998 through 2003.

Middleware is defined as software that allows shared use, or interoperability, of resources across interconnected, heterogeneous computer systems. These products usually operate on top of host OS software environments. Subsegments include legacyware (software used to access legacy applications) and Web server products such as Netscape's FastTrack Server and Microsoft's Internet Information Server, which enable external Web browsers to communicate with other programs, such as database applications. Other major vendors include IBM, BEA Systems, and TIBCO. Worldwide revenues for middleware software were expected to grow 27.1 percent from $4.0 billion in 1998 to $5.1 billion in 1999. IDC forecasts that sales of middleware will reach $16.6 billion by 2003, representing a CAGR of 35 percent from 1999 (see Table 28-5). Much of this growth will be driven by programs that integrate software applications.

The market will be driven by the need to integrate new systems with "legacy" applications and data, which represent significant IT investments for corporations, and the desire to manage distributed or networked computer systems. There is also demand, particularly in vertical industry sectors such as health care and telecommunications, for software that will integrate disparate applications, which is known as enterprise application integration (EAI). E-commerce applications will push growth in Web server middleware products.

System management software governs computing resources. Examples include tools to manage data storage, job scheduling, and output, such as printer spoolers and fax servers. Network management software controls the components of the computing infrastructure, addressing network performance, configuration, and fault management. The U.S. firms Computer Associates, IBM, and Hewlett-Packard are global leaders in this industry segment. Major foreign vendors include Fujitsu, Hitachi, and Bull, a French company. The worldwide market for system management software was expected to increase 4.3 percent from $12.6 billion in 1998 to $13.1 billion in 1999. Growth will be strong into the next century, with IDC predicting that the market will expand to $18.1 billion by 2003, a 13 percent annual increase from 1998 (see Table 28-5).

The security software industry segment encompasses firewall, encryption, and antivirus software. Firewall software restricts unauthorized users from entering an internal network. Encryption programs secure information and data by encoding them through the use of cryptographic algorithms. Antivirus software protects systems against attack by computer viruses through prevention or remediation. This segment also includes authentication, authorization, and administration (3A) products, which cover diverse applications such as intrusion detection, single sign-on software, and security management products.

Sales of security software worldwide were expected to increase 37.2 percent from $3.2 billion in 1998 to $4.4 billion in 1999. Much of this growth was driven by the firewall and 3A areas, which benefited from internet-related demand. Firewall software was expected to grow 50 percent to reach $662 million in 1999, and 3A products, the largest of these subsectors, expanded 34.4 percent to $2.2 billion. Encryption, the smallest sector, had 1999 worldwide sales of $119 million. According to IDC, the security software market will reach $8.26 billion by 2003 (see Table 28-5). With continued growth of distributed systems, E-commerce, and the internet, concern about protection from unauthorized network intrusion, viruses, and illicit data access will accelerate the growth of the data security market. Sales of applications that incorporate or use encryption technologies, for example, have risen dramatically in recent years as the need for secure transactions, particularly on the internet, has grown.

Market Trends

Although Microsoft clearly holds the leading position in the systems infrastructure software industry through its Windows family of products, other vendors are attempting to challenge the company by pushing changes in the way software is engineered and distributed. Some of these changes include the growth of the open-source software development model and thin-client, or servercentric, computing. These trends are gaining adherents to varying degrees, but so far the effect of open-source software or other technologies on Microsoft's revenues has been negligible. A recent survey of 1,300 IT professionals by *Survey.com* found that over 80 percent intended to begin deploying Windows 2000 by fourth quarter of 2000.

The open-source software movement represented by Linux could reshape the market landscape dramatically. This type of software is free, although a third-party distribution of Linux that includes proprietary add-ons and support can be obtained for a fee. The source code is open to all, and development is done in a collaborative manner involving a myriad of programmers worldwide. Linux, which is a Unix-like operating system created by the Finnish computer scientist Linus Torvalds, is an open-source product that has been gaining grassroots acceptance rapidly in the IT community. Because of its stability, Linux is finding success particularly among internet service providers (ISPs) as the operating system of choice for hosting Web servers. From 1997 to 1998, shipments of Linux grew over 181 percent, making it the fastest-growing server operating system that year in terms of unit and volume growth. Actual usage growth could be higher, however, because Linux can be downloaded free from the internet.

On the client side, Linux was installed on 2 percent of the 89 million PCs that were shipped in 1998, representing 11 percent growth over the 1997 level. IDC projections show that Linux could become the fourth most popular client operating system by 2003 after Windows 95/98, Windows NT/2000, and Mac OS. An August 1999 IDC survey of business users showed that 13 percent are now using Linux, up from little more than zero in 1997. Uncertainties in the near term about switching to Windows 2000 also may be helping Linux. Not only are companies wary of the possible effects of the Y2K problem and initial reliability concerns, there may be a high cost involved in switching desktops to Windows 2000. A September 1999 Gartner Group study concluded that it will cost corporations between $1,250 and $3,100 per PC to migrate to Windows 2000 from earlier versions. Hence, some companies may find Linux a cost-effective alternative in the 12- to 18-month time frame.

Linux's gain also is due to a rapid increase in support from major IT companies. Many third-party software vendors have announced Linux ports of their applications, and major hardware makers have started to provide Linux on their client and server systems. Those vendors include some of the biggest names in IT: IBM/Lotus, Oracle, Informix, Sybase, SCO, Corel, Sun, Netscape, and Novell. Dell, Compaq, Hewlett-Packard, Micron, and others have announced that they will begin to offer Linux-based PC systems. In August, Silicon Graphics revealed that it will spin off its Cray and NT workstation businesses and instead focus on internet servers built on Linux. SCO has formed a "Linux and Open Source Professional Services Team" that will offer enterprise consulting services to customers interested in open-source software. IBM's Lotus recently came out with a Linux version of Domino. Netscape's Navigator is available on Linux.

Although revenues from Linux are currently minuscule compared with those of Windows, various factors could continue to drive its growth and open new profit avenues. There are potentially large revenue opportunities in providing service and support for associated products. As an open-source product, Linux is not backed by a single company's technical support and assistance. This opens the door to third-party support providers. Several firms, such as Red Hat and Caldera Software, offer support along with their distribution of Linux. The Linux OS also requires fewer system resources. While older hardware such as 386 and 486 PCs cannot run resource-intensive operating systems such as Windows 98 and NT Workstation, Linux has relatively lower hardware requirements and can easily operate on those platforms. Finally, there are generally no licensing requirements for Linux. Linux and its source are free. Hardware vendors that sell Linux-based machines do not pay a third party for each system they sell.

Another potential challenger to the hegemony of the Windows system is thin-client, or servercentric, computing. This is a computing architecture in which most of the data, the applications software, and even a great deal of the user interface are stored on the server. In this model, the client supports only the graphic-user interface (GUI) and a limited number of other input and output functions. This is an architecture that harkens back to "timesharing," or host-based processing, during the mainframe era of the 1960s and 1970s. Instead of loading software on client systems, all applications can be loaded once on the server, making maintenance and support easier. This computing model traditionally has been supported by Unix, OpenVMS, OS/390, OS400, and recently the Linux OS. Many midrange and mainframe systems have been using the servercentric approach for years. Clients in the thin-client model include everything from automated teller machines (ATMs), to X-Windows terminals, to Wintel personal computers. Servercentric computing is efficient and offers lower staffing costs compared with a highly distributed computing environment. A May 1999 study by Datapro found that thin-client enterprise deployments reduced support staff costs by at least 80 percent compared with "fat-client" PCs.

Five times as many personnel were required to support a fat-client environment than a thin-client environment.

Microsoft's Windows NT did not initially support the server-centric approach, and that opened the door to third-party software vendors. Citrix, Prologue, New Moon, and others developed virtual user interface (VUI) software that was loaded on top of Windows NT and offered thin-client functionality. These VUI products would take a Windows application's input and output, virtualize it, and transmit it on the network. Client software received that information and displayed it locally. This approach gave even non-Windows clients the ability to use VUI software to work with Windows applications. Eventually, the success of those thin-client solutions spurred Microsoft to release a thin-client version of NT, Windows NT Server 4 Terminal Server Edition (TSE), in 1998. Although TSE's pricing model makes it relatively more expensive than comparable Unix-based solutions, current trends show that most new thin-client deployments are to TSE and Citrix Systems' MetaFrame software.

While thin clients will represent only 5 to 10 percent of all client deployments over the next several years, the development and increasing acceptance of Java- and Web-based applications and Java-capable Web browsers could spur increased growth in the long term. Furthermore, growing use of Java-based applications could promote the use of network computers instead of Windows-based terminals. In fact, Datapro predicts that full-function PCs will not be needed at all as the servercentric computing model becomes more prevalent. Another development that is likely to promote the use of thin-client computing is the emergence of application service providers (ASPs), which may greatly change the way softwarc programs are distributed, sold, and used (see "Application Hosting," below).

Raymond H. Cho, Office of Computers and Business Equipment, (202) 482-0551, October 1999.

APPLICATIONS SOFTWARE

Applications software encompasses computer programs that allow users to perform specific jobs or activities, such as word processing, product design, and accounting, in contrast to system infrastructure software, which works in the background as an intermediary between the software application and the computer hardware components. The three major application areas covered in the following sections are enterprise resource planning software, CAD/CAM, and consumer software.

This large and varied segment of the software industry is divided into applications for businesses and organizations and those for consumer and home use, such as entertainment, education, and personal productivity programs. This business segment is subdivided into cross-industry and vertical industry products. Cross-industry products apply across many different types of corporate environments and are not targeted at a single industry sector such as payroll or customer support software. Vertical industry applications are designed to address the particular needs of a single industry sector, such as automobile manufacturing, retail establishments, and banking.

According to IDC, the overall applications software sector was expected to grow 14.7 percent in 1999 to reach over $62 billion worldwide (see Table 28-6). Growth through 2003 is estimated at a compound annual rate of 15.1 percent to reach $125.5 billion by 2003. In 1999, business applications were expected to grow 14.7 percent and consumer applications 12 percent. Most applications sales were divided equally between the Unix and 32-bit Windows platforms at $20.7 billion and $23.9 billion, respectively; however, it is anticipated that demand for Windows applications will grow faster and may exceed $60 billion by 2003, while sales of Unix systems will approach $35 billion.

Cross-industry sales reached $33.1 billion in 1999 and represented half the business market. The three largest firms—Microsoft, SAP, and IBM—accounted for about one-fourth of this market. This area includes Microsoft's popular office suite products, which include word processing, spreadsheet, database, personal calendar, and E-mail components. IDC projects that this sector will grow at a CAGR of 18.5 percent to reach $66 billion in 2003. The top three vendors in the vertical industry software area are Cadence Design Systems [CAD/computer-aided manufacturing (CAM)], Parametric Technology Corp. (CAD/CAM), and McKesson HBOC (health care). Sales of vertical industry software were expected to total $32.3 billion in 1999 with a growth rate of 12.5 percent and are projected to grow 50.2 percent to reach $50.2 billion by 2003.

Consumer applications will continue to experience steady growth in the future. However, this segment's rate of growth is heavily dependent on the speed at which PCs penetrate the 50 percent of U.S. households that do not own a computer. Increas-

TABLE 28-6: Trends and Forecasts in Worldwide Applications Software Revenues
(billions of dollars)

Market Segment	1998	1999	2000	2001	2002	2003	Compound Annual Growth Rate 00–03, %
Cross-industry business	28.3	33.1	39.1	46.3	55.1	66.0	19
Vertical industry business	28.8	32.3	36.1	40.1	44.8	50.2	12
Consumer and home	5.0	5.6	6.4	7.3	8.2	9.2	13
Total	62.1	71.0	81.6	93.6	108.1	125.4	15

Source: International Data Corporation.

ing consumer interest in accessing the internet may transfer demand toward on-line services and away from traditional shrink-wrapped software products, and this trend will force vendors to incorporate internet technologies into their product offerings. This sector was expected to grow 12 percent in 1999 to reach $5.6 billion and is projected to reach $9.2 billion by 2003. Major firms include The Learning Company, Microsoft, and Knowledge Adventure, which is owned by Havas of France.

The United States accounted for about half the applications market in 1998, followed by western Europe with one-third of sales and the Asia-Pacific region and the rest of the world with almost 10 percent each. The top four vendors—Microsoft, IBM, SAP, and PeopleSoft—had a combined market share of 16 percent. Other major U.S. suppliers included BMC and Oracle. U.S.-based vendors accounted for about 68 percent of industry revenues in 1998, while foreign firms accounted for 32 percent, or roughly $20 billion. Major non-U.S. firms include Baan (Netherlands), Misys (United Kingdom), and Fujitsu (Japan).

Market Trends

Strong growth is predicted for business applications over the next several years. Corporate demand is high for ERP products as companies seek stable, highly integrated software systems to handle general administrative functions such as payroll, procurement, and human resources management and to automate supply-chain operations more effectively. As computer systems become larger and more complex, corporations will tend to purchase third-party packaged software rather than develop their own in-house solutions. This will mean greater demand for vertical industry applications that have some cross-industry functionality, such as products equipped to handle both manufacturing and retail sector elements. Deregulation in certain sectors also will help fuel growth for vertical industry applications as new competitive pressures arise. For example, the repeal of the Glass-Steagall Act, which separated investment banks from savings and loans institutions, has had a major impact on the banking and financial services sector.

The internet is pushing corporations to look for new ways to stay competitive in the rapidly evolving and increasingly competitive information economy. Many enterprises are reassessing their operations and adjusting to the internet economy in both their external customer relationships and their internal process management. Firms want applications that easily interface with the internet and are equipped to handle on-line business transactions in order to open new revenue streams. Thus, enterprisewide software systems with built-in E-commerce functionality are becoming more common in response to growing market demand. Zona Research predicts that sales of business-to-business E-commerce applications will grow nearly 80 percent to reach $93.2 billion in the year 2000.

The distribution and rental of programs through ASPs is another emerging trend (see "Application Hosting," below).

Raymond H. Cho, Office of Computers and Business Equipment, (202) 482-0551, October 1999.

ENTERPRISE RESOURCE PLANNING SOFTWARE

ERP software consists of cross-industry applications that automate firms' business processes. Common applications include human resources (personnel administration, recruitment, and career planning), manufacturing (supply-chain planning, plant operations, and production planning), and financial management (general ledger, asset management, and accounts payable).

ERP software traditionally has been implemented in the "back office" by specially trained employees and has not been accessible to most employees. ERP systems are used mostly in large enterprises, especially multinationals, where managers need to control a variety of locations and entities efficiently. Demand for ERP solutions is growing quickly as businesses become more decentralized and face the need to integrate their back-office functions. The use of ERP is extending into supply-chain and customer relationship management with the rise of intranets and extranets.

As the use of intranets grows, opportunities for ERP vendors will increase. IDC predicts that worldwide revenues for the four main ERP segments—accounting, human resources, manufacturing, and materials management—will reach $20.5 billion in 1999 and grow to $33.6 billion in 2002 (see Table 28-7). A recent survey of U.S. corporate sites found that 45 percent had implemented ERP systems.

TABLE 28-7: Trends and Forecasts in Worldwide Enterprise Application Software License and Maintenance Revenues
(billions of dollars)

Market Segment	1997	1998	1999	2000	2001	2002	Compound Annual Growth Rate 00–02, %
Accounting	5.3	6.1	7.1	8.1	9.3	10.5	14.8
Human resources	1.9	2.4	2.9	3.5	4.1	4.8	19.7
Manufacturing	4.8	5.6	6.4	7.3	8.3	9.4	14.2
Materials management	2.4	3.1	4.1	5.4	7.0	8.9	30.3
Total	14.4	17.2	20.5	24.3	28.6	33.6	18.4

Source: International Data Corporation.

Until recently, the majority of licenses of U.S.-based firms, such as Peoplesoft, was sold in the United States and Canada, with most international sales made to overseas affiliates of their U.S. customers. However, these firms have stepped up their efforts to sell overseas. Peoplesoft recently took aggressive steps to enter the European market. However, the U.S. and western European large enterprise markets for ERP software are maturing. Thus, vendors not only are targeting smaller customers in the United States and Europe but also are looking at opportunities outside those regions.

Market Trends

ERP software applications consist of a number of individual modules that automate separate tasks. For example, a financial management application may have general ledger, assets, and accounts payable modules. Customers can purchase only the modules of the application they need, and modules can be expanded or added on to as a company grows. Many ERP vendors, such as SAP, Peoplesoft, and Oracle, also sell applications development tools to allow end users to modify or customize their ERP modules. ERP applications are designed to work with relational database management systems (RDBMS), which are produced by vendors that include Oracle, IBM, and Informix. ERP software runs on a variety of operating systems, including Windows, NT, Unix, and AS400, as well as a variety of hardware platforms such as mainframes and client/server systems.

The ERP software segment is led by four large firms that traditionally have sold to large multinational customers. European firms are particularly strong in this area; this is due in large part to their early strategies of partnering with large U.S.-based consulting firms that helped implement their software for customers in the United States. The German-based SAP AG is the leading ERP vendor, commanding nearly one-third of the market. Its flagship product, R/3, is used by many of the world's largest manufacturing, petrochemicals, and pharmaceuticals companies as well as in an increasing number of IT companies. The Netherlands-based Baan and the U.S.-based Oracle and Peoplesoft are the other major ERP firms. J.D. Edwards, a U.S. vendor, recently began to compete with the big four firms as they have tried to sell more of their products to medium-size enterprises, which have been J.D. Edwards's main market.

A growing number of smaller vendors, such as Geac Computer Corporation and Systems Software Associates, are competing in the ERP sector but mostly focus on market niches, such as human resources and financial management, and sell to small- and midsize businesses. In the past year, a number of Web-enabled competitors emerged, gaining market share since the larger firms have been slow to implement E-commerce and Web-based applications and strategies (see below).

Growth in the ERP industry has been strong. *Software Magazine* reports that average revenue growth was 17.4 percent in 1998 and that Peoplesoft and J.D. Edwards have been the fastest-growing ERP vendors. However, the large ERP vendors are facing slowing sales partly because ERP sales were affected by Y2K concerns, which led many customers to shift their IT budgets to Y2K remediation at the expense of new software procurement. Although this became less of a problem after January 2000, other long-term issues are depressing larger suppliers' sales. Vendors have been slow to address growing customer demands resulting from the increased use of intranets and extranets and the need for Web-based business integration systems, particularly those involving E-commerce. As a result, larger vendors have seen their sales taken over by smaller ERP vendors that have more quickly adopted internet-based strategies. In addition, the larger vendors' major market—large enterprises—is approaching saturation. In response to these changing market conditions, large ERP vendors have undertaken a variety of strategies to stem slowing sales, most of which involve implementing Web strategies and making efforts to enter the rapidly expanding ERP market in small and medium-size firms.

A major factor precluding smaller customers from purchasing ERP software from large vendors has been their products' long-standing reputation for being costly and complex to implement. Average implementation periods for full ERP systems can run from 18 to 36 months and in many cases involve a complete overhaul of a customer's existing business systems. Implementation usually requires the assistance of third-party consultants and systems integration firms such as Anderson Consulting, PriceWaterhouseCoopers, and Deloitte and Touche, and this also raises costs for customers. ERP vendors have taken a number of steps to address the cost concerns of smaller firms. Peoplesoft, Oracle, SAP, and Baan all have shortened their product implementation cycles. For example, SAP reports that depending on the vertical market and customer, it now can take just a month to implement one of its financial packages. Vendors also are working to make their products more interoperable with those of their competitors, allowing customers to choose modules from different vendors and allowing increased integration in supply chains and customer relations. Efforts include building application programming interfaces (APIs), which allow third-party products to hook onto their packages, and partnering with other vendors. These integration steps are still nascent, and some experts wonder whether ERP vendors truly want to allow easy integration of their applications with those of their competitors.

ERP vendors are implementing applications hosting strategies in an attempt to increase sales to small and medium-size customers. Hosting strategies allow users to lease ERP applications through the Web on a per-person, per-use basis. SAP, Oracle, and Peoplesoft have unveiled plans to host applications such as SAP's mySAP.com, a Web-hosted ERP package it introduced in July 1999. MySAP.com, with a simplified interface, also addresses the growing demand by ERP customers for less complex "front-office" applications that automate functions, such as sales and marketing, performed by a large number of employees, as opposed to traditional back-office applications used by specially trained workers. Front-office applications are becoming more integral as extranets grow and supply chains become automated and as more workers need access to these automated systems. Baan entered the front-office market by acquiring the sales and marketing vendors Aurum and Beologic, and J.D. Edwards is attempting to expand its front-office presence through a recent agreement with Siebel Systems, a leader in front-office sales and service automation software. In fact, as in the software industry as a whole, the ERP segment is characterized by a growing number of mergers and acquisitions as firms attempt to round out their product lines.

Expanding into E-commerce has become a key priority for ERP vendors, all of which have launched E-commerce strategies that go beyond simple applications hosting. Vendors are interested in creating or partnering with other firms to build vertical, industry-specific business-to-business E-commerce platforms such as Web sites that are intended to bring together buyers and sellers from specific vertical industries and tools that allow collaboration among partners. Larger ERP vendors are collaborating with smaller ERP firms as well as smaller software firms that have Web-enabling technologies. Oracle's Oracle Exchange supports a business-to-business on-line marketplace, as does mySAP.com. The E-commerce strategies of these large suppliers are fairly new, and most have only been announced or demonstrated, not implemented on a large scale. IDC does not expect these E-commerce strategies to be a major factor in those firms' sales until the year 2000 or later.

In fact, although ERP traditionally has been designed for cross-industry uses, the movement to develop products for vertical markets is another prominent trend in ERP as vendors try to increase sales. SAP, Baan, and Oracle, which traditionally have had a manufacturing-specific focus, have begun to offer products in other areas. SAP recently shipped a version of R/3 for retail and has announced programs or products for other nonmanufacturing industries, including health care, banking, insurance, and government. Oracle also plans to offer retail-specific software. Peoplesoft, which has focused primarily on human resource management and financial management packages, has added manufacturing, communications, health care, and retail suites to its offerings. However, it will be difficult for those vendors to compete with software firms that have a strong reputation in the vertical industries.

As a result of these market forces and firm strategies, the future of competition in the ERP industry segment is unclear. Despite larger ERP vendors' recent efforts to penetrate the small and medium-size market segment and remodel their products for the Web, their slow start in doing so has cost them customers as smaller competitors have taken advantage of the delays. However, industry analysts note that the large companies will continue to sell to their large enterprise customer base.

Danielle M. Kriz, Office of Computers and Business Equipment, (202) 482-0568, October 1999.

CAD/CAM AND CAE

The computer-aided design, computer-aided manufacturing, and computer-aided engineering (CAD, CAM, and CAE) sector has four major segments: mechanical computer-aided design and engineering (MCAD/MCAE); electronic design automation (EDA); architectural, engineering, and construction (AEC); and geographic information systems (GIS)/mapping. CAD systems use high-speed workstations or desktop computers that enable engineers and architects to design and manufacture products.

MCAD and MCAE include tools used to design, analyze, document, and manufacture single-function parts, components, and assemblies for products ranging from chairs, to cars, to aircraft. EDA encompasses tools that automate the design process for a variety of electronic products, such as designing circuits on a chip and simulating their performance. EDA includes electronic computer-aided engineering (ECAE), integrated circuit (IC) layout, and printed circuit board (PCB)/multichip module (MCM)/hybrids.

AEC refers to software tools used by architects, contractors, and plant and civil engineers to aid in the design and management of buildings, industrial plants, and ships and the construction of roads and bridges. GIS/mapping software enables users to capture, edit, display, and analyze various geographic data, such as topographic maps, property lot lines, and city planning maps.

Factors Affecting Future U.S. Industry Growth

The CAD, CAM, and CAE industry is projected to grow steadily over the next 5 years as many CAD companies continue to form alliances and partnerships and make acquisitions to remain competitive in the development of new products. Some of the dynamics driving the growth of the industry are the need to develop new ways to design highly complex ICs, making it possible to integrate more functions onto a single chip. These new tools will allow engineers to integrate complex subsystems such as television, audio, and video onto a single chip. In automotive design, the integration of new CAD tools with digital styling tools will help car designers meet the changing demands of consumers.

Previously, high-end CAD software was costly and was available only to elite designers, but the increased performance of the PC has given CAD software developers a platform on which to offer powerful software to nontraditional users in emerging markets such as landscape design and crime scene reenactment. The PC has spurred the growth of CAD software market as engineers have begun to move from higher-priced Unix-based systems to lower-priced NT-based CAD systems. The PC has evolved to challenge the power of the Unix-based systems and is becoming the platform of choice for CAD users. Windows NT is in competition with Unix to become the standard operating system of choice for workstations used by CAD designers and engineers. Today, CAD users, particularly those in the EDA market, are leaning toward NT, although NT is seen as being less robust in its file system and reliability. Currently, many new workstation models offer a choice of NT or Unix.

Additionally, in the CAD industry, to spur growth, several CAD software vendors have formed strategic alliances to offer CAD/CAM/CAE products to civilian agencies in the U.S. government. As a result, federal civilian agencies now have access to the product development technology and technical expertise on which military and large corporate clients depend.

Innovative technologies have fueled the growth of the EDA industry and continue to be a driving force. For example, to gain an advantage in time to market, design teams need verification models for system-on-a-chip (SOC) design. SOC technology and application-specific standard products (ASSPs) for products such as digital cameras and cell phones will contribute to fast growth in the logic design market.

From the CAD user to the financial manager, from the GIS professional to the structural engineer, from the facility manager to the process plant designer, and from the architect to the office manager, AEC technology offers many exciting new features as it continues to lead the industry to new growth. Three-dimensional CAD technology will promote growth when it is used to construct roads, buildings, bridges, power plants, and airports. This new growth is expected as users move from two-dimensional (2-D) to 3-D technical drawings. According to Dataquest, a market research firm based in San Jose, CA, both replacement sales at the high end of the market and the movement from 2-D to 3-D at the lower end of the market will generate revenue growth over the next 2 years. There also will be growth in peripheral CAD markets: products such as visualization software and product data management. This is software that is not focused directly on design but uses and manages CAD data.

Mechanical CAD/CAM and CAE

According to Daratech Inc., a market research and technology assessment firm in Cambridge, MA, worldwide users are expected to spend more on mechanical CAE (computer-aided analysis and simulation) software. Driving that growth will be strong manufacturing economies in North America and Europe, together with new products from leading CAE software suppliers. Growth in the mechanical CAE market remains impressive, but is slightly lower than that in the mechanical CAD/CAM and CAE market as a whole. The traditional market for CAE tools, which includes specialty analysts and some advanced mechanical engineers, is smaller than the broad-based market of mechanical engineers, designers, and drafters who use CAD systems. New software licenses for mechanical CAD/CAM and CAE, license renewals, recurring licenses, maintenance, updates, and hot line support are expected to promote market growth. Engineering and manufacturing companies are expanding their capital investments in product process reengineering and globalization to compress schedules, shorten time to market, improve quality, and strengthen their global competitiveness.

Several suppliers have introduced improved mechanical CAD software solutions for design, modeling, and drafting. SolidWorks 99 is a 3-D CAD software package used in designing custom walk-in vans, parcel delivery vans, and truck bodies for various industries, including laundry, baking, utility, package delivery, and other commercial-type applications. Unigraphics Solutions offers Solid Edge, a mechanical CAD software package used in developing products for the mobile equipment industry, including mining, construction, and agriculture. Autodesk markets AutoCAD Mechanical 2000 and Mechanical Desktop 4, a 3-D modeling package. Structural Dynamics Research Corp. (SDRC) offers I-DEAS, a software package used to engineer new product development.

New CAE software solutions have been released, such as Prescient Technologies' GeometryQA, an engineering software package used in the aerospace, automotive, electronics industries and other industries with complex design, manufacturing, and assembly processes. IBM's CATIA V5 Grant program is being used to bring advanced CAD technology to colleges and universities by offering software, hardware training, and technical support.

Electronic Design Automation

The EDA industry has become a multi-billion-dollar industry with double-digit growth worldwide. This growth is attributed to the need for electronic designers to shorten the time to market for their products. This market is expected to have steady growth between 2000 and 2004. Major breakthroughs in technology are needed to promote continued growth in the EDA industry. The industry faces the tough challenge of developing tools to design semiconductors with interconnect line widths so tiny that the laws of physics will be tested. In the so-called deep submicron range, chip makers will be looking to the EDA industry to help them design more powerful chips to drive everything from dental equipment to palm-sized cell phones. Continuing dialogue between chip makers and tool makers in solving the deep submicron design problem will help increase design productivity.

With the incorporation of greater amounts of semiconductor intellectual property (IP) content and the need to verify and correct designs, new methodologies and tools are needed to meet time-to-market goals. Design data interoperability has to be improved to promote design reuse. To gain a time-to-market advantage, design teams need verification models for the most popular processor, memory, and peripheral devices used in SOC designs. At one time, the use of point tools was the most important technology in the EDA industry. Then logic simulation became the key, followed by design languages and then synthesis. Each new technology has contributed to the automation of the design function.

It is expected that by the year 2002, designers will have the capability of integrating 100 million transistors on a chip. To succeed, chip makers may have to build their own design tools to gain a competitive advantage, because such tools may not be available from the EDA industry by that time. To address this issue, companies in the EDA industry may decide to work cooperatively with semiconductor manufacturers in R&D partnerships to help speed the development of these tools.

Architectural, Engineering, and Construction

The AEC/CAD software market is expected to show steady growth between 2000 and 2004 as designers move to the new generation of 3-D CAD technology. The need for architects to visualize their designs and evaluate a design has been a problem for the many users. With the new generation of 3-D design software, users can design and view all their plans, sections, elevations, colors renderings, and walk-through animations. Three-dimensional CAD software is changing the way designers produce conventional drawings. With the addition of 3-D views, designers have moved from drafting lines to being masters of virtual reality. In addition to developing and viewing a design at a faster speed, designers have the ability to compare the different options for architectural designs side by side. Powerful new software makes it easier for designers to deal with drastic changes to a design and see how those changes affect the overall design. Three-dimensional CAD software permits several architects to collaborate simultaneously on a very large project and allows interactive redlining by many people across the internet.

Architectural CAD software specifically addresses the needs of the construction industry (architects, interior designers, builders, building engineers, etc.), which has to easily place walls, windows, doors, roofs, stairs, and other architectural elements as components into a 3-D model. There are two primary implementations of architectural CAD. One is used when a second program adds architectural features to and modifies a core generic drawing program (such as ArchT or AutoArchitect on top of AutoCAD). The other is used to design buildings from the beginning (such as ArchiCAD and AllPlan). Architectural CAD software allows a designer to easily create proper floor plans and show complete and comprehensive plans.

Geographic Information Systems/Mapping

The GIS software market is expected to grow steadily between 2000 and 2004. Several factors have contributed to growth in the use of GIS technology in federal and state governments. Most states and large cities have dedicated GIS organizations to maintain standard base maps and central data clearinghouses and provide metadata, Web distribution, and technical support for client services. Innovations in computer technology have made it possible for sophisticated GIS operations to be performed on the desktop. Faster and cheaper computers, network processing, electronic data publishing, and improved and easier to use GIS technology are fueling rapid growth in the desktop area. Private businesses are adopting GIS as a decision support tool and have access to mapping applications on the Web.

Increased use of GIS by the federal government and state governments continues to promote growth in this segment. With the coming of the millennium, GIS will be used in the U.S. Bureau of the Census's 2000 census to give federal, state, and local governments the means to establish demographic data based on street addresses. Locations of homes and businesses, coupled with statistics on health, human services, education, income, and crime, will make demographic information the most effective planning and operational resource of government. GIS/mapping will provide the ability to link census data to spatial data, providing a demographic information system that is expected to be unprecedented in quality and usefulness.

U.S. Market Leaders

According to *Software Magazine,* the top CAD/CAM/CAE software leaders are IBM, Parametric Technology, Cadence, Synopsys, Autodesk, Intergraph, Mentor Graphics, and Environmental Systems Research Institute (ESRI). The top three CAD software leaders are Autodesk, Intergraph, and Bentley Systems, Inc. Parametric Technology Corp. (PTC) is a leading supplier of CAD/CAM/CAE mechanical product development and information management tools used in all areas of mechanical design, production, simulation, styling, and surfacing. Autodesk is the world's leading supplier of PC-based design software used to visualize and manage architectural design, mechanical design, spatial data management, and mapping applications. The top leaders in CAE software tools are Cadence, Synopsys, Mentor Graphics, and Bentley Systems. Cadence has evolved as the world's leading supplier of EDA software and services to help improve time to market, quality, and productivity. ESRI is the world's leading supplier of GIS/mapping software used for managing geographic information.

U.S. Industry Growth Projections for the Next 1 and 5 Years

In 1998, the U.S. CAD/CAM/CAE software market was estimated to have grown 10 percent, with revenues reaching over $2.9 billion (see Table 28-8). The growth in revenues for EDA and GIS/mapping exceeded growth for mechanical CAD/CAE and AEC applications.

In 1999, the U.S. CAD/CAM/CAE software market was forecast to increase 11 percent over its level in 1998, with revenues over $3.2 billion. Mechanical CAD/CAE was expected to continue to dominate the market with revenues of almost $1.4 billion (42 percent), followed by EDA with revenues over $1

TABLE 28-8: Trends and Forecasts in the U.S. CAD/CAM/CAE Software Market
(millions of dollars; percent)

Application	1998[1]	1999[1]	2000[2]	2001[2]	2002[2]	2003[2]	2004[2]	Compound Annual Growth Rate 00–04, %
Mechanical	1,243	1,373	1,530	1,720	1,944	2,206	2,526	13
Electronic design automation	908	1,026	1,165	1,335	1,541	1,796	2,110	16
Architectural, engineering, and construction	419	442	473	508	552	605	669	9
Geographic information systems/mapping	353	395	445	505	579	668	778	15
Total	2,923	3,237	3,613	4,068	4,616	5,275	6,084	14

[1] Estimate.
[2] Forecast.
Source: U.S. Department of Commerce, International Trade Administration (ITA).

TABLE 28-9: Trends and Forecasts in the Worldwide CAD/CAM/CAE Software Markets
(millions of dollars; percent)

Region	1998[1]	1999[1]	2000[2]	2001[2]	2002[2]	2003[2]	2004[2]	Compound Annual Growth Rate 00–04, %
North America	3,452	3,787	4,222	4,733	5,353	6,113	7,055	14
Europe	2,634	2,861	3,158	3,505	3,940	4,452	5,093	13
Japan	1,623	1,727	1,853	2,009	2,185	2,410	2,685	10
Asia-Pacific	457	479	509	547	591	644	712	9
Rest of world	136	142	149	158	169	182	200	8
Total	8,302	8,999	9,892	10,952	12,238	13,803	15,745	12

[1] Estimate.
[2] Forecast.
Source: U.S. Department of Commerce, International Trade Administration (ITA).

billion (32 percent), AEC with revenues of $442 million (14 percent), and GIS/mapping with revenues of $395 million (12 percent). In 1999, the fastest-growing segments were expected to continue to be EDA and GIS at 13 percent and 12 percent, respectively.

In the year 2000, the U.S. CAD/CAM/CAE software market should increase 12 percent over the 1999 level, reaching an estimated $3.6 billion. The 5-year (2000–2004) growth projections show that the U.S. CAD/CAM/CAE software market should increase to almost $6.1 billion at a CAGR of 14 percent. The EDA and GIS/mapping segments will continue to be the fastest growing markets in the period 2000–2004.

Global Market Prospects

In 1998, the worldwide CAD/CAM/CAE software market reached an estimated $8.3 billion in revenues, growing 7 percent over 1997. North America was the largest region, with revenues of almost $3.5 billion (42 percent), followed by Europe with revenues of over $2.6 million (32 percent), Japan with over $1.6 billion (20 percent), the Asia-Pacific region with $457 million (6 percent), and the rest of world with $136 million (2 percent) (see Table 28-9). The world market leaders were IBM, Parametric Technology, Dassault, Autodesk, SDRC, Cadence, Synopsys, Intergraph, Mentor Graphics, and ESRI.

In 1999, the worldwide CAD/CAM/CAE software markets were projected to increase 8 percent over 1998, with revenues of almost $9.0 billion. North America was again the largest region, accounting for 42 percent of the total. Europe followed with revenues of almost $2.9 billion (32 percent), and Japan was next with over $1.7 billion (19 percent). The Asia-Pacific region stood at $479 million (5 percent), and the rest of the world accounted for $142 million (2 percent). European growth nearly reached that of North America, registering a rate of 9 percent. In the year 2000, the worldwide CAD/CAM/CAE software market is expected to increase 10 percent, reaching an estimated $9.9 billion. For the 5-year period 2000–2004, the worldwide CAD/CAM/CAE software market is expected to grow at a steady CAGR of 12 percent, exceeding $15.7 billion by 2004.

In 1998, mechanical CAD/CAE accounted for the largest share of the market with 42 percent, followed by EDA with 39 percent, AEC with 13 percent, and GIS/mapping with 6 percent. In the period 2000–2004, EDA will grow to have the largest market share, followed by mechanical CAD/CAE. The fastest-growing segments are expected to be EDA and GIS/mapping (see Table 28-10).

The Asia-Pacific Region and Japan. In 1998, the CAD/CAM software market in the Asia-Pacific region reached $457 million. In 1999, the Taiwanese IC industry was expected to be the largest in Asia, excluding Japan. To meet the demand for deep submicron design capability, Taiwanese chip makers and foundries are leading the way in capacity expansion, followed by those in Malaysia and Singapore, in spite of the Asian economic crisis. Asian electronics makers are trying to recover from the regional financial crisis that began in 1997. After 2 years of economic crisis, Japan is slowly restructuring its econ-

TABLE 28-10: Trends and Forecasts in the Worldwide CAD/CAM/CAE Software Market
(millions of dollars; percent)

Application	1998[1]	1999[1]	2000[2]	2001[2]	2002[2]	2003[2]	2004[2]	Compound Annual Growth Rate 00–04, %
Mechanical	3,506	3,737	4,055	4,440	4,907	5,471	6,166	11
Electronic design automation	3,260	3,602	4,038	4,543	5,156	5,904	6,837	14
Architectural, engineering, and construction	1,069	1,140	1,228	1,333	1,459	1,613	1,803	10
Geographic information systems/mapping	467	516	570	636	715	815	939	13
Total	8,302	8,995	9,891	10,952	12,237	13,803	15,745	12

[1] Estimate
[2] Forecast
Source: U.S. Department of Commerce, International Trade Administration (ITA).

omy, and that should help boost the global economy. The Thai electronics industry is made up largely of foreign-owned subassembly builders and semiconductor test and assembly operations. Components are brought in, and products are assembled and then reexported.

Chinese enterprises are expected to take advantage of the latest EDA tools and services. The Chinese EDA market surged in the early 1990s, when many research institutes, universities, and state-run enterprises set up CAD centers using government research funds. Nevertheless, the growth rate for EDA slowed after the government began to evaluate productivity and investment. The result was a decline in the Chinese EDA tool market, which grew at a relatively sluggish 10 percent annual rate between 1995 and 1998. The market is beginning to rebound again. Research funding from the government's ninth 5-year plan is expected to boost growth.

Europe. The European CAD/CAM/CAE software market is projected to grow at a CAGR of 13 percent between 2000 and 2004. The markets with highest expected growth are Germany, the United Kingdom, and France. European electronics sales should continue to benefit from a strong economy. The Organization for Economic Cooperation and Development forecasts that the European Union economy will grow 2.4 percent in 1999 and 2.9 percent in 2000. There is a prospect for future growth in CAD software in the design of plastic products and molds.

Export Market Size

In 1999, the total worldwide CAD/CAM/CAE market for software, hardware, and services was estimated to increase 11 percent from its level in 1998, with revenues reaching an estimated $25 billion. CAD/CAM/CAE software accounted for about 37 percent of the market, with hardware accounting for 40 percent and services at 23 percent.

The total worldwide CAD/CAM/CAE market is expected to continue to experience double-digit growth in all segments. In the 5-year period 2000–2004, the market is forecast to grow at a 13 percent CAGR, reaching $46.3 billion. Software is forecast to represent the largest share with 39 percent, followed by hardware with 36 percent and services with 25 percent. The top market leaders are forecast to be IBM, Parametric Technology, Cadence, Synopsys, and Autodesk.

U.S. and Foreign Competition

In 1998, U.S. vendors continued to be the major suppliers in the worldwide CAD/CAM/CAE software market with a 35 percent market share, followed by vendors from Europe with 32 percent. Japan and other suppliers in the Asia-Pacific region accounted for 25 percent, and suppliers from the rest of the world accounted for 2 percent. The top foreign competitors include Dassault, Fujitsu, Zuken-Redac, Siemens Nixdorf, and Hitachi. The leading foreign competitors in Asia are Japan's Fujitsu and NEC. In Europe, the leaders are the French firm Dassault and the German firm Siemens. Foreign suppliers of CAD/CAM/CAE products have had limited success in penetrating the U.S. market. U.S. market leaders continue to dominate, although there have been some business alliances and partnerships with foreign companies, such as Advanced Enterprise Solution (AES), Dassault, and IBM.

Prospects for the Year 2000

In the year 2000, the total worldwide CAD/CAM/CAE market is forecast to increase 12 percent over 1999, with revenues reaching an estimated $25 billion. CAD/CAM/CAE software will account for 38 percent of the market with revenues of $10.5 billion. North America will continue to lead with the largest market share at 43 percent, followed by Europe with a 32 percent market share.

Vera A. Swann, Office of Computers and Business Equipment, (202) 482-0396, October 1999.

CONSUMER SOFTWARE

Although business remains the dominant software market, software increasingly is bought for home use to satisfy a variety of needs and interests. Demand is fueled by increasing sales of PCs to households as computer prices drop and internet use expands and by online mass marketing strategies. Consumer programs increasingly are sold over the internet and through traditional consumer channels such as department stores, bookshops, and video/music CD outlets. According to IDC, 48 million households, or almost half of all U.S. households, owned PCs in 1998, and almost one-third of them owned more than one. Most retail PCs sold today come with CD-ROM drives as standard equipment and include a variety of bundled consumer software on compact disks, which hold considerably more information than do magnetic diskettes. CD-ROM also permits the development of larger, faster, and more complex programs; this is particularly important to game publishers.

Consumer software is divided into three segments: education/edutainment, home productivity, and games/entertainment (see the boxed note "Customer Software Market Segments"). About two-thirds of households with PCs use some type of educational software. These products allow self-paced learning in the privacy of the home, can track the user's progress and target specific areas of difficulty, and may feature Web site interactivity. Educational software includes products sold for specific instructional purposes, such as teaching reading, writing, and arithmetic, in addition to study aids and reference materials. Test-taking software, which allows students to take practice tests, review background materials on specific areas, and learn score improvement strategies, has widespread use. Programs tied to specific curricula for exclusive sale to schools are not considered part of consumer software.

Edutainment software is designed to educate the user in a particular subject, but in a game-oriented or entertaining manner devised to hold the user's interest. Edutainment software creatively exploits the use of graphics, audio, video, and interactivity. Examples include Microsoft's *Flight Simulator;* the *Where in the World is Carmen Sandiego?* series by Broderbund, which

CONSUMER SOFTWARE MARKET SEGMENTS

The worldwide consumer software market is made up of three areas:

Education and Edutainment	
Edutainment products.	**Software products that are designed to simultaneously educate and entertain, such as *Carmen Sandiego* series, *Math Blaster,* home and auto repair, and CD-ROM encyclopedias and typing programs.**
Home education products.	**Products sold to homes for specific educational purposes to teach a process or subject, such as preschool storybooks and study aids. Includes reference works but not courseware designed for structured learning within schools.**
Home Productivity	
Personal creativity.	**Help, how-to, home graphics, and lifestyle software, including diet, cookbook, and creative music software.**
Personal productivity.	**Software used in the home for nonbusiness purposes, such as word processing, banking and personal finance, tax preparation, home design, and personal newsletters. Software intended for commercial use, such as Lotus 1-2-3 and Microsoft Word, is excluded.**
Games and Entertainment	**Software primarily differentiated by the presence of a scoring function; a win/lose scenario for entertainment purposes; as arcadelike games, simulation, or strategy. Proprietary platform game systems as Nintendo, Sega, and Sony Playstation are excluded.**

Source: International Data Corporation, 1998.

teaches geography within a crime-scenario adventure; and the various editions of *Math Blaster* by Knowledge Adventure, which teach math through learning adventures, games, and puzzles. CD-ROM encyclopedias are also popular edutainment applications. The publishers of the *Encyclopedia Britannica* and other publishers produce comprehensive references that include thousands of articles, advanced multimedia technology, interactive animation, internet search engines, and on-line updates.

Home productivity software is divided into programs that deal with home and family management activities and programs oriented toward hobbies and recreation. The first category, which is the largest, includes applications such as money management, tax preparation, genealogy, and résumé writing. Intuit's *Quicken* and *Microsoft Money* are examples of personal finance applications that allow users to monitor investments and pay bills. Some versions interface with the user's bank. Home creativity and recreation software covers a wide variety of how-to topics (canning, cooking, scuba diving, etc.) as well as graphics and music creation programs.

Games and entertainment, the most popular consumer software sector, continue to sustain tremendous sales growth. First introduced in the 1970s, computer and video games have progressed from simple graphics and animation to games of virtual reality in which the player becomes a character in the game. Games are designed both for PCs and for proprietary console devices that attach to the user's television, such as those sold by Sega, Sony, and Nintendo. These proprietary consoles are becoming more like PCs as they increase in performance and functionality. To take advantage of both markets, some developers design their games for both hardware platforms.

The games industry is extremely competitive and is characterized by constant change. Developers must design games that players will want to use repeatedly and that satisfy consumers' desires for better, faster, and more realistic experiences. As competition increases, marketing becomes more important as game vendors forge comarketing arrangements with mass market concerns such as food chains and retail stores and spend more money on celebrity endorsements. For example, in 1999, Nintendo partnered with the Kentucky Fried Chicken food chain to promote the Pokemon game, which resulted in in-store promotions and cobranding efforts worth an additional $16 million. On-line or head-to-head gaming is also a growing trend in which participants can download software that enables them to play games with other players on the internet. With players demanding faster download and response times, the technological limits are being challenged.

Although U.S. firms are leaders in the games industry, there are major competitors in Japan and the United Kingdom, and some foreign companies locate product development in the United States because of the large U.S. market, the global popularity of U.S. games, and the availability of talented developers and technical support. The Japan-based Nintendo, Sega, and Sony have long been leading drivers of industry growth and have made gains in key technologies through acquisitions. These firms produce both game software and proprietary hardware on which to play games. This gives them a competitive advantage in game development, although third-party developers may license the right to write software for these platforms. Since the appeal of these games depends on the capabilities of the corresponding hardware, these firms must continuously upgrade the processing speed and graphics ability of their consoles. Sega's new Dreamcast machine features a 200-MHz microprocessor, a 128-bit graphics engine with more graphics processing power than a Pentium II computer, a built-in 56K modem, and access to the internet for head-to-head gaming. Nintendo has developed a 256-bit console, code-named Dolphin, that relies on two processors: a customized PowerPC chip

TABLE 28-11: Consumer Software Revenues in 1999
(billions of dollars)

	Entertainment and Games	Education and Edutainment	Home Productivity	Total
United States	1.6	1.2	1.1	3.9
World	2.3	1.7	1.5	5.6

Source: International Data Corporation estimates.

and a graphics chip for translating 3-D graphics. Sony's 128-bit Playstation II features powerful 3-D graphics, internet links, and a DVD-ROM drive for playing music and videos.

As is the case in other sectors, the consumer software industry has been marked by consolidation, as 6 of the top 10 companies engaged in some type of acquisition in 1998 that directly contributed to broadening their technology portfolios and product offerings. According to IDC, the top 10 consumer software vendors accounted for 59 percent of worldwide revenue of $5 billion in 1998. This figure does not include sales of proprietary game systems by Sega, Nintendo, and Sony or business software such as Microsoft's suite of word processing, spreadsheet, and database programs. The top 10 vendors in 1998 were The Learning Company, Microsoft, Cendant/Havas Software, Intuit, Electronic Arts, Activision, GT Interactive, InterPlay Productions, Mattel, and Infogames. Some of these firms serve an individual niche, while others have wider coverage in the industry. The Learning Company was the leading supplier of educational software, followed by Microsoft and Cendant/Havas Software. Microsoft led in the home productivity area, followed by Intuit and The Learning Company. Electronic Arts leads in games and entertainment applications, followed by Microsoft and Activision, Inc.

As with video movies, some vendors are experimenting with consumer software rentals through retail stores. In this model, customers pay a relatively low price to try a game or entertainment title for a set period, such as 3 days. After renting a title, the customer connects to a specific authorizing Web site, which verifies the software rental through information encoded on the CD and submits an access code to initiate play. At the end of the rental period, the user may purchase additional days at a discounted price or purchase the title outright. The CD becomes disabled after the set period expires, and so the disk does not have to be returned.

According to IDC, the worldwide consumer software market totaled $5.0 billion in 1998 and was estimated to reach $5.6 billion in 1999. It is forecast to increase nearly 13 percent annually through 2003. The U.S. market accounted for about 71 percent of the world market, followed by Western Europe, 25 percent; the Asia-Pacific region, 2 percent; and the rest of the world, 2 percent. The games and entertainment segment dominated the world market with 42 percent of sales, followed by education/edutainment with 31 percent and productivity applications with 27 percent (see Table 28-11). Entertainment software is growing at a slightly faster rate than the other two segments. With the exploitation of new distribution channels, principally the internet and mass market retailers, prices should decline despite vendor's attempts to maintain premium price points. The U.S. market totaled $3.6 billion in 1998 and is forecasted to grow at an average annual rate of 12 percent through 2003. Growth in markets outside the United States will be slightly higher over the next several years but will remain in the range of 11 to 15 percent.

Patricia A. Johnson, Office of Computers and Business Equipment, (202) 482-2053, October 1999.

SOFTWARE DEVELOPMENT TOOLS

Software development tools help computer programmers design, develop, and implement software programs. This industry segment has four components: database management system tools; components, objects, and development environments (CODE); development life-cycle management (DLM); and internet tools, a small but rapidly growing area.

The industry will experience continued growth driven by the demand for E-commerce and internet applications and services, such as the need to create Web-accessible databases and retrofit existing systems with newer Web-based technologies. The focus on the internet also will increase the demand for platform-independent processes and tools such as object-oriented programming (OOP). Another market driver will be the demand for new tools to create software for emerging products, such as portable and remote access devices, and equipment with embedded microchips. According to IDC, the industry will grow at an average annual rate of 14.0 percent from 1998 to 2003, resulting in a $64.7 billion market by 2003, up from $35.4 billion in 1999. Growth will be highest in the emerging internet tools segments of the industry (see Table 28-12).

Most current programming tools are unique to a specific software platform. Sales of tools engineered for the Windows operating environment totaled $6.8 billion in 1998 and accounted for 28 percent of the total market. As the Windows NT and Windows 98 operating systems continue to penetrate more areas of the IT industry, the tools for writing software applications for these systems are increasingly in demand. Sales of tools for writing software for Unix operating systems, which are used mostly for workstations and internet servers, and for mainframe systems are growing more slowly. Unix tools constituted 30 percent of the market in 1998 ($7.4 billion), and mainframe tools 29 percent ($7.2 billion). The Y2K remediation of legacy mainframe computer systems, along with the need to retrofit those systems for the internet age, has significantly benefited the market for mainframe programming tools. Areas of future growth include platform-independent tools such as Java.

The United States is the largest market for programming tools, accounting for 48 percent of worldwide sales in 1999. The second largest market is western Europe with a 32 percent market share, followed by the Asia-Pacific region with 13 percent and the rest of the world with 7 percent. U.S.-based companies are responsible for over 87 percent of global sales. The top five American vendors—Oracle, IBM, Microsoft, Computer Associates, and Compuware—receive about 45 percent of world rev-

TABLE 28-12: Trends and Forecasts in Worldwide Software Development Tool Revenues
(billions of dollars)

Market Segment	1998	1999	2000	2001	2002	2003	Compound Annual Growth Rate 00–03, %
Database management systems	12.4	13.6	14.7	16.6	18.9	21.1	13
Components, objects, and development environments	7.2	8.1	9.3	10.7	12.7	15.3	18
Development life cycle management	4.5	4.9	5.5	6.2	7.0	7.9	13
Internet tools	0.3	0.5	0.7	0.9	1.1	1.3	23
Total	24.5	27.1	30.1	34.4	39.6	45.7	15

Source: International Data Corporation.

enues. The leading foreign vendors are the Japanese companies Fujitsu, NEC, and Hitachi and the British company MERANT plc. Those firms account for 4.8 percent of the world market.

Database management systems (DBMS) tools, representing over 50 percent of this industry in 1998, are used to manipulate information in a database, providing retrieval, storage, and organizational capabilities. They are especially important in maintaining the large multiuser databases employed by large organizations and corporations and ensuring seamless connectivity with other systems and software. Revenues for this segment grew 9.7 percent in 1999 to reach $13.6 billion and should grow at an average annual rate of 11 percent over the next several years. DBMS tools will experience strong demand as the popularity of conducting business-to-business transactions over the internet increases demand for the provision of Web access for enterprise applications and data warehousing. Embedded chip environments that employ database engines represent another area that will spur demand. Personal digital assistants (PDAs) such as the Palm hand-held computer, cell phones, smart cards, and set-top boxes incorporate embedded database technology. IBM's DB2 Everywhere DBMS, which was released in May 1999, is a product for accessing data from these types of devices. After virtually no sales in 1998, IDC predicts that revenue for these products will grow over 80 percent annually over the next several years to exceed $750 million by 2003.

CODE products include programming languages that are used to write code for software programs. This includes traditional high-level languages such as COBOL, Basic, C, and Pascal and object-oriented programming tools such as C++ and Java, which employ reusable, self-contained program modules that perform a specific task such as opening a window on screen. C is a general-purpose procedural language that is used by most major software publishers, while Visual Basic is a Windows-based programming process that is used by many shareware developers. The demand for Java, a hardware-platform-independent programming language, will be driven by the internet's reliance on OOP techniques. Sales of CODE products were expected to grow 11.9 percent to reach $8.1 billion in 1999 and to have a 30 percent share of the total programming tools market. Growth through 2003 is forecast by IDC to be in the range of 17 percent.

DLM packages support the software development process, managing all stages from conceptual design to deployment, including software quality maintenance and configuration management. Revenues for DLM software grew 9.4 percent in 1999 to reach $4.9 billion and will increase at a 12.8 percent annual rate over the next several years. This area has an 18 percent share of the tools market. Demand for DLM solutions is driven by the increasing necessity to manage the costs of software development. Demand also is pushed by the decisions of large organizations to prolong the life of older computer systems by integrating them with newer technologies. As E-commerce applications continue to expand, companies will seek ways to Web-enable legacy systems. This will benefit the DLM market segment, which includes software reengineering and transformation products that are used to interpret and convert data from legacy systems.

The market for internet tools grew over 40 percent to reach $470 million in 1999, but sales accounted for less than 2 percent of the overall software tools market. This area will continue to show rapid growth as enterprises seek new and more effective ways to implement E-commerce solutions. This segment should grow around 30 percent per year through 2003.

Internet-Based Applications Development

The major factor driving the development tools market is the popularity and growth of the internet. The explosion in business transactions over the internet has created a demand for "Web-enabled" applications tools that make it easier to build E-commerce Web sites and services. The Java programming language created by Sun Microsystems is playing an increasingly important role in the development of server-side internet applications for the enterprise. While Hypertext Markup Language (HTML) is a document display format for the Web, Java is a complete programming language that is used to create sophisticated Web and intranet applications.

The use of object-oriented tools will result in future applications development centered less on an operating system environment and more on next-generation Web development portals. These common Web sites will be development platforms to make available object-style components and dynamic data links that can be used to fashion Web sites and other on-line services. For example, a developer might use a portal to combine Microsoft's Passport single sign-on Web service with an Oracle database, and Java would be used to provide interoperability. Major vendors such as Microsoft and IBM have begun to provide portal-related products and services.

Microsoft has reworked its programmer development tools offerings to accommodate industry trends. The company announced in September 1999 that it will release new development tools and revise Windows 2000 to make it easier for programmers to create Web-enabled software. These products, collectively known as Windows Distributed interNet Architecture (DNA) 2000, are a response to the growing popularity of Java, which is gaining wide acceptance among Web developers. A Forrester Research report indicates that large enterprises currently prefer Sun Microsystems' Java and the Common Object Request Broker Architecture (CORBA) to Microsoft's Component Object Model (COM) for object-oriented development of large-scale applications.

Microsoft also enables Web developers to download objects from its Microsoft Network (MSN) Web site, which contains software snippets, such as its Hotmail service and MSN Instant Messenger. In addition, the company will XML-enable all its operating system and applications software. XML, or eXtensible Markup Language, is a method that allows data, components, and applications to work together over the internet. IBM, Hewlett-Packard (HP), and Oracle also have announced major moves into the Web development area. In August 1999, HP and Oracle agreed to collaborate closely to produce an integrated platform for E-commerce programmer tools. HP will combine its E-speak developer product with the Oracle8i database and other Oracle internet platform software. IBM has unveiled tools that offer strong Java and XML support, in line with that company's overall E-business strategy.

Raymond H. Cho, Office of Computers and Business Equipment, (202) 482-0551, October 1999.

INTERNET TECHNOLOGIES

The internet is a global network of interconnected networks that transmits information (text, graphics, voice, and data) in digital format. Its unstructured approach allows extra networks to be added at any point. According to *Network Wizards,* the internet has grown exponentially since it was commercialized. The number of computers connected to the internet increased from 1.3 million in 1993 to 29.7 million in 1998. By July 1999, it had reached 56.2 million. While the rate of increase will slow, the number of users will increase to the hundreds of millions in the near future, since every second, seven people log on to the internet for the first time. According to IDC, the number of people who used the internet reached an estimated 100 million in 1998, 40 percent of whom lived outside the United States. IDC forecasts that the number of internet users will reach a half a billion by 2003.

The use of the internet has evolved to include what is termed electronic commerce, or the electronic conducting of business functions such as marketing, price quotes, and sales. Electronic commerce has the potential to fundamentally change the way companies conduct their business by reducing costs, reaching new customers, and finding new markets. While 1997 witnessed the emergence of the internet and electronic commerce as the beginning of the digital economy, 1998 may be remembered as the year in which corporate America embraced the internet as a core business function.

Internet Service Providers

Commercial ISPs provide fee-based access to internet applications and resources for individuals and companies. ISPs range from very large telecommunications companies (telcos) to very small local service providers. Approximately 5,000 ISPs are operating in the United States today. Local ISPs currently control 31 percent of dial-up accounts in the United States, while telcos and national ISPs control the remaining 69 percent. Competition among ISPs is fierce and probably will become even more so in the near term. There are three categories of ISPs.

Long-distance carriers/cable/on-line companies include long-distance telecommunications companies such as AT&T and Sprint, Regional Bell Operating Companies (RBOCs), such as Ameritech and Bell Atlantic, cable television operators, such as Time Warner and TCI, and on-line service providers, such as America Online (AOL). Consolidations are taking place among the largest players, as was evidenced by AT&T's acquisition of TCI in 1999. AOL is by far the largest ISP, with more than 17 million subscribers, accounting for 13 percent of the market.

Regional/national independents are for-profit companies that offer internet connectivity services either domestically or internationally. They are generally well positioned in the ISP marketplace but do not have subscriber rates similar to those in the first category. PSINet, UUNET, Mindspring, Concentric, and Rocky Mountain internet are examples of this category. Several ISPs in this category, such as UUNET and PSINet, are expanding aggressively into international markets, focusing on the business community. Recent consolidations in this group include that of Mindspring and EarthLink.

Local service providers sometimes are referred to as "mom and pop shops." These ISPs typically cater to a very small number of users, operate in one physical location, and offer services to businesses and individuals in a single metropolitan area or rural town. Increasingly, they target small- and medium-size companies that do not have networked PCs but want internet access.

All three segments of the ISP market will have continued subscriber growth, but competition will remain very intense as firms focus on customer satisfaction, marketing strategies, and profitability. Thus far, local ISPs have been profitable because they run streamlined operations and generate more revenue per customer. Larger ISPs continue to struggle to develop a successful business model, and only a small percentage of them are profitable. Given the immense competition that characterizes the industry, the domestic ISP industry probably will experience considerable consolidation in the next few years. Increased competition has emerged in several areas, all of which will apply pressure to ISP profitability. The first area is competition from ISPs that offer free internet access versus those which continue to charge dial-up fees. This marketing strategy has caused smaller ISPs to offer bundled services such as free PCs included with a 2- or 3-year service contract. Whether this business model will prove to be sustainable is unclear. There are also questions of the benefits to the consumer. Smaller ISPs also are focusing on sales of on-line advertising, Web hosting, and electronic commerce applications as ways to maintain a competitive edge. Competition also is coming from the availability of increases in bandwidth resulting from new technologies such as Digital Subscribe Line (DSL) services and cable modems. Consumers are unlikely to keep their current ISPs at rates of $20 a month for 56-Kbps dial-up service if they are offered high-speed access for a slightly higher fee of $25 to $30 a month.

The large ISPs will continue to dominate the corporate market and attract a majority of individual users by integrating their existing internet services such as Web hosting and multiple E-mail addresses with broadband services such as videoconferencing and movies on demand (see Table 28-13). The smaller ISPs will be most strongly affected by broadband technologies because they lack the technical capabilities to keep up with new developments or do not have access to "last mile" cable access to the home. In addition to the competitive pressures outlined above, small ISPs will seek distribution alliances with value-added resellers (VARs), competitive local exchange carriers (CLECs), incumbent local exchange carriers (ILECs), and traditional distributors to find new customers in the small business sector.

Web Hosting

For a variety of reasons, companies choose to outsource Web site design and maintenance to third-party companies. This is especially true of small and medium-sized firms that lack the funding or personnel to build a Web site. However, outsourcing a Web site is not limited to small companies. Many of the largest companies that run complicated and elaborate Web sites use third-party service providers, including Yahoo! The most commonly cited factors for this decision include lack of internal resources, cost, network connectivity, security, and business integration. Moreover, the cost of building and maintaining an electronic commerce Web site averages between $500,000 and $2.5 million, and many companies have decided that such activities are outside their core competencies. Web hosting is offered by both ISPs and third-party service providers, and growth in this subsector is expected to accelerate in the next several years. Web hosting services vary according to customers' needs and range in cost from tens of dollars to tens of thousands of dollars, depending on the complexity of a site.

According to IDC industry forecasts, the market for Web hosting services will continue to experience strong growth well into the next century as companies further integrate the internet into their core business functions and existing back-end systems, such as inventory control and procurement (see Table 28-14). In addition, broadband access, increased use of intranets and extranets, and implementation of virtual private networks (VPNs) by businesses will fuel the Web hosting market. Small to midsize companies probably will use Web hosting service providers, since those providers offer a myriad of services tailored to a company's financial resources.

For small companies eager to participate in electronic commerce, Web hosting offers a viable and affordable route to on-line commerce. It gives them the opportunity to access suppliers, distributors, and customers, especially as larger corporations employ total electronic commerce solutions through extranets and VPNs.

Application Hosting

Many ISPs are beginning to act as ASPs. This emerging business model offers remote access to mission-critical applications ranging from low-end productivity programs such as E-mail and word processing to complex ERP modules on a subscription basis. These network-based application services allow a company to access as needed one or more software applications that are resident on an ISP's server or at a third-party's data center through the internet. The inherent advantages to the company of this model are the pricing flexibility based on use and the reduced support costs.

This type of outsourcing is a fast-growing trend that has been made possible by three developments: the internet, which serves as a standard platform for product delivery; the Web browser, which has standardized the user interface; and technologies such as XML, which has simplified integration with legacy systems.

There are three types of ASPs, each of which offers slightly different services:

TABLE 28-13: Top 10 ISPs and Web Hosts by Revenue in 1998
(millions of dollars)

Rank and Host	Revenue
1. America Online	3,300
2. PSINet	390
3. EarthLink	245
4. MindSpring	215
5. Verio	188
6. Prodigy	142
7. Concentric	110
8. Exodus	108
9. Excite@Home	86
10. OneMain	74

TABLE 28-14: Worldwide Web Hosting Revenues, 1998–2002

	1998	1999	2000	2001	2002
Revenues ($millions)	770	1,479	3,018	6,095	11,825
Growth (%)	86	92	104	102	94

Source: International Data Corporation.

Application outsourcing. These are ISPs/ASPs that offer top-tier enterprise applications on a pay-as-you-go basis. An example of this type of ASP is Usinternetworking.

Application hosting. These are software applications that are offered by an ISP from an interactive Web site that augments and is integrated with a company's existing in-house systems.

Web sourcing. These are value-added services that are offered on a monthly subscription fee basis that give the user access to a variety of applications. E*Trade and Intuit are examples of Web sourcing companies. ASPs can specialize in specific professional or business activities such as customer relationship management and human resources or in vertical markets such as finance and banking.

Common applications hosted by ASPs include E-mail and certain types of ERP products. This situation may change as many major IT corporations, as well as start-up operations have rushed into the ASP arena. Product and service differentiation among ASPs is occurring quickly and mirroring the growth of the industry. Industry segmentation is occurring primarily along lines of service breadth, specialization, and vendor type. Whereas the initial ASP model included only the hosting of applications, some ASPs are beginning to offer a broad array of integrated solutions, such as end-to-end support of E-commerce services. This category includes Intira and the bandwidth provider Qwest Communications.

Large firms that have declared themselves ASPs or have begun to offer ASP-like services include Oracle, Sun Microsystems, IBM, Intel, Hewlett-Packard, the telecommunications carriers AT&T and Qwest, the consultancy KPMG, and the financial services firm Merrill Lynch. Newer, start-up ASP companies include Verio, AristaSoft, and Intira.

Other ASPs, such as AristaSoft, are targeting vertical industry segments. AristaSoft is offering suites, anchored by ERP products from J.D. Edwards, of 10 to 30 hosted applications for specific vertical markets. Major software vendors also are unveiling ASP-like offerings of their own applications. Oracle, for example, has eschewed licensing its products to independent ASPs and is instead promoting its own hosting service, Business Online. Its rival, Microsoft, is planning to invest over $67 million in a partnership with the internet systems integrator USWeb/CKS to develop a framework for delivering and managing its applications over the Web.

While ASPs initially appealed to small and medium-size businesses that lacked the internal expertise and finances to develop or host applications on their own, larger firms are beginning to move many of their data and applications to ASPs. For instance, General Motors (GM) is moving its expense management functions to the Web, using applications from Captura Software hosted by the telecommunications firm Qwest Communications. This system will allow GM employees to file and process various expenses, such as travel and phone charges, on-line. When fully installed, the system will be able to handle as many as 100,000 users. Other companies, such as Delta Airlines and ToySmart.com, have undertaken or are planning similar ventures.

Various factors have driven the growth of the ASP industry: the IT labor shortage; the speed of industry change, particularly in E-commerce; and the high costs of purchasing and maintaining applications. For software vendors, the ASP model may help eliminate the fraudulent distribution and use of software, allow automatic software upgrades, and provide a potential long-term revenue stream through licensing arrangements. Growth in this market is expected to be extremely strong. The ASP market for 1999 was $2.7 billion (Gartner Group), and growth forecasts have ranged from $4.5 billion (IDC) to $22.7 billion (Gartner Group) by 2003 (see Table 28-15).

Outlook for Other Sources of Revenue

While Web hosting is an established and successful business model, ASP is still in its infancy. Its inherent technical challenges mean that an effective business model still has to be developed. However, ISPs can continue to rely on a number of other applications outsourced by users to remain competitive. E-mail will continue to be the leading application, followed by videoconferencing and audioconferencing, which consume significant network resources. Other outsourcing opportunities include scheduling/calendaring/groupware applications, knowledge management, human resource applications, and accounting.

Electronic Commerce

While most of the attention paid to the internet is focused on the consumer side of electronic commerce, such as buying books on-line, and on the wealth generated by many of the initial public offerings (IPOs) of internet companies, the real revolution that is taking place is in business-to-business (B2B) E-commerce. This type of E-commerce is having a profound effect on the way companies operate by reducing the cost of doing business along the entire value chain, from supplier to customer. In some cases, it is transforming entire industries, such as the travel and leisure industry. More and more companies, both large and small, are embracing electronic commerce solutions that will restructure their business processes, the way they define themselves, and their relations with their customers and partners. According to a University of Texas study, the internet generated nearly $301 billion in revenue in the United States in 1998, rivaling the U.S. automobile industry in revenues and making it as large as the economy of Switzerland.

TABLE 28-15: Spending in ASP Market by Region
(millions of dollars except as noted)

Region	1999	2003	Compound Annual Growth Rate 99–03, %
North America	135.9	1,415.0	80
Western Europe	9.1	390.1	156
Asia-Pacific	1.8	34.2	108
Japan	2.5	110.4	157
Rest of world	1.1	50.4	161
Total	150.4	2,000.0	91

Source: International Data Corporation.

Business-to-business electronic commerce comes in many forms. Electronic data interchange (EDI), which allows the electronic exchange of documents between two parties, is a form of B2B that has been used for decades. The internet, however, has expanded EDI's capabilities greatly. Documents can be exchanged in real time, legally recognized signatures can be authenticated, browsers are used to access customers' and partners' systems through extranets and VPNs, and transactions can be completed. More important, internet-based solutions are more affordable for small and medium-size companies, thus integrating a new level of business partners into the supply chain. Increasingly, companies are using internet-enabled solutions to integrate their purchasing and selling systems with the rest of their business processes. While many Fortune 1000 companies keep their electronic commerce applications in-house for security reasons, small businesses are apt to exploit the capabilities of ISPs that offer a range of electronic commerce solutions.

There are three business models in today's B2B environment. Each model has its individual advantages, but the net result is an increase in competition.

1. *Seller-controlled Web sites.* These sites usually are set up by a single company seeking many buyers and increased cost reductions through greater process efficiencies. An example of a seller-controlled Web site is Cisco Systems, the company that manufacturers most of the internet's routers. Cisco Systems' Web site allows buyers to configure their routers according to their specifications and check prices and order and shipping status. It also allows buyers to speak with technical specialists about their orders. Cisco Systems indicated that its Web site generates $3 billion in sales a year, approximately 40 percent of the company's total. Cost reductions are realized through reduced printing expenses and customer management services, including technical support. Cisco estimates cost savings of $270 million a year from its Web site.
2. *Buyer-controlled Web sites.* These sites typically are established to increase a buyer's purchasing power in the marketplace through lower prices. Buyer-controlled sites allow a single company to post procurement notices on the internet for bidding by suppliers. Often, buyer-controlled Web sites include an intermediary that acts as an agent or aggregator of information in finding the best price for the buyer's specifications. Perhaps the best example of this is TPN Register, a joint venture between General Electric (GE) and Thomas Publishing. Increased process efficiencies reduced order processing times from a week to a day for GE Lighting and resulted in cost reductions of 10 to 25 percent. The initiative spread to all of GE's operating units and led its chief executive officer, Jack Welsh, to call on all GE's businesses to integrate the power of the internet.
3. *Intermediaries.* One of the greatest myths about the internet is that it will lead to the extinction of the middleman or broker. Entirely new concepts have been created, such as "disintermediation" to describe the demise of the middleman as power shifts to the consumer. However, the opposite has occurred, with B2B intermediaries growing. One reason for this is the sheer mass of information that is available to both buyers and sellers. Intermediaries act as collectors, aggregators, and synthesizers of volumes of information, especially information about buying patterns for a range of products, which can be sold to sellers. They also bring the advantage of scale in transaction processing by making a Web site more efficient by spreading the cost across many product lines. A Web site that carries one product from a supplier may not be sufficient to support the expense of that site. An intermediary that can accommodate a number of products and sellers has sufficient scale to keep costs down for buyers and sellers. Intermediaries also can function in the areas of order fulfillment/logistics, payment processing, and customer data analysis. Photodisc.com is an example of a successful intermediary. That company allows its customers to search and browse its databases of images, purchase or license images on-line, and download a selected image.

TABLE 28-16: Total Corporate Web Purchases, 1999–2003
(billions of dollars except as noted)

Category	1999	2003	Percent of Total Sales
Services	22.10	220.00	7.80
Goods	109.30	1,330.80	9.40
Total	131.40	1,550.80	

Source: International Data Corporation.

Corporate investment in internet-enabled technologies is expected to grow in the United States and abroad, further fueling B2B E-commerce. IDC estimated that domestic spending on Web-enabled technology would reach $174 billion, or 57 percent of the global total, by the end of 1999. By 2003, IDC estimates that total Web purchases will reach $1.5 trillion (see Table 28-16). Computing equipment and electronic equipment will be the largest categories of goods traded on-line between companies, followed by automobiles and petrochemicals. Business services, particularly financial and professional services, will probably experience significant gains as well.

Small businesses will invest heavily in internet-enabled technologies. While they account for 98 percent of all the businesses in the United States, they generate only 34 percent of all sales. By 2002, small businesses are expected to more than double the $39 billion they spent on IT in 1998. B2B E-commerce will benefit small businesses that incorporate their business functions into the supply chains of their larger customers. In addition, it will give them another channel to seek buyers, particularly if they work through an intermediary's Web site (see Tables 28-17 and 28-18).

These new business models illustrate how efficiently businesses can adopt new, cost-effective technology and underscore how electronic commerce has become a business strategy. The biggest challenge facing companies that buy and sell on the

TABLE 28-17: Spending on Information Technology by Small Businesses, 1998 and 2002

Area of Spending	Percent of Total 1998	Percent of Total 2002
Hardware	36	18
Software	23	21
Network	10	17
Telecommunications	11	14
Personnel	14	19
Consulting	6	11
Total IT spending	$39 billion	$87 billion

Source: International Data Corporation.

internet will be the relationships they form with customers who now have access to nearly perfect market information.

Factors Affecting Future U.S. Industry Growth

Although the number of internet users in the United States will slow because of saturation, the outlook for growth internationally is excellent. One of the qualities that make the internet unique—its unstructured approach—is proving to be one of its greatest challenges, particularly for ISPs that host Web sites or data centers. If, as many experts project, the internet grows to billions of users, its infrastructure will need to be improved dramatically to make it more scalable and secure. Providing increased reliability for a system in constant use will be the biggest challenge. While many ISPs are building excess capacity into their infrastructure to allow for increased use in the future, this may not be sufficient to handle the dramatic projected increase in network traffic. Industry representatives suggest that a number of advanced technologies will be introduced in the next 5 years to mitigate potential problems. Among the new technologies that are expected to debut are the following:

Internet Protocol version 6 (IPv6). This is a new version of the Internet Protocol (IP) that will allow virtually unlimited numbers of IP addresses and contain increased security (the current version—IPv4—is limited to 4 billion addresses).

Dense Wavelength Division Multiplexing (DWDM). This technology will allow telecommunications companies to combine data from different sources on an optical fiber. Each signal will carry its own separate light wavelength. Using DWDM, up to 80 separate wavelengths or channels of data can be multiplexed into a light stream transmitted on a single optical fiber. In a system where each channel carries 2.5 billion bits per second, up to 200 billion bits can be delivered a second by the optical fiber.

TABLE 28-18: Small Business Internet Access, 1996–2001

	1996	1997	1998	1999	2000	2001
Total small businesses (millions)	7.1	7.2	7.4	7.5	7.7	7.8
PC penetration (%)	74	78	80	81	83	84
Internet access (%)	20	39	44	48	51	54

Source: International Data Corporation.

Security. For electronic commerce Web sites, security will be paramount. The industry's development of strong encryption technologies will continue. An example is the development of an encryption technology to replace the current 64-bit Digital Encryption Standard (DES) with the 128-bit Advanced Encryption Standard (AES).

Caching servers. This internet-based server stores copies of the user's most frequently accessed content near the user, with the practical result of faster response times and an easing of performance spikes across the internet.

Standards. RosettaNet, a consortium of major IT companies around the world, is working to define standards for B2B transactions in the IT industry. The standards will define the many aspects of supply-chain processes so that manufacturers, distributors, retailers, and purchasers can track each product as it moves through the supply chain. In establishing these standards, RosettaNet is intended to provide significant cost saving and efficiencies throughout the supply chain. The goal is to establish standards by February 2000.

Three technologies that are making their way to market are DSL, cable modems, and wireless internet. Digital Subscriber Line is the next generation of internet access technology for bringing high-bandwidth information into homes and small businesses over ordinary copper telephone wires. DSL will increase the speed at which a consumer can download information. For a typical DSL connection, the speed will vary between 1.5 and 6.1 megabits (millions of bits, or Mbps) per second when receiving data and 128 kilobits (thousands of bits, or Kbps) per second when sending data. Ordinary modems currently are limited to 56 Kbps. A DSL line can carry both voice and data signals, with a constant data connection. The deployment of DSL began in late 1998, and demand is expected to increase as more ISPs and RBOCs offer the service. There are several limitations to DSL, however. The price of DSL services is high compared with that of most dial-up services, ranging from $40 to $100 a month, depending on the level of service (speed). As more subscribers are added, that price will fall. Dataquest, a market research firm, estimated that 5.8 million lines would be installed by the end of 1999. Another problem for DSL is proximity. The subscriber must be within 18,000 feet (about 3.5 miles) of a telephone switching station or ISP. Moreover, for other types of DSL, the higher the bandwidth is, the closer the user must be to the switch.

Cable modems are another technological advancement that will increase internet access speed. Cable modems are devices that allow high-speed data access via the existing cable television network. The ubiquitous nature of cable television makes cable modems an attractive business model. On-line access through cable modems will allow internet access at speeds nearly 100 times faster than that of a typical 56-Kbps computer modem. In addition, cable modem lines are always open, which means that dial-ups are unnecessary. They allow for multiple users in a household, do not tie up telephone lines, and provide users with true multimedia capability. The growth potential for cable modems is enormous. Pioneer Consulting estimates that 1.5 million subscribers worldwide currently use cable modems for internet access, with more than half in the United States. That firm expects global cable modem use to exceed 45 million internet connections by 2007, with the U.S. share approximately one-quarter of that total.

Wireless communications offer another promising technology for internet access via either a standard wireless digital cell phone or PDAs such as the Palm Pilot. The emergence of digital networks with increased infrastructure capability, coupled with software technology that allows wireless devices to connect to the internet, will foster increased growth in the internet. More than 220 million people are estimated to be wireless subscribers today, and about 150 million people have internet access. Some market research firms estimate that within 5 years, those numbers will be 1 billion and 2 billion people, respectively. In the short term, however, wireless internet access will be limited to text-based messages. Satellite technology is another alternative for providing internet access, especially for broadband-intensive industries such as entertainment and multimedia. However, its viability remains to be seen in light of the slow adoption of current satellite technologies as a result of the expense.

Policy Trends

The emergence of the internet as an engine of global business growth is challenging government policy makers across a spectrum of issues. Work is under way in many countries to develop policies that will foster the growth of the internet and electronic commerce. In the United States, both the administration and Congress have not enacted legislation that could undermine the potential of the industry.

Domain Name System. Domain names are familiar and easy-to-remember names such as www.mydomain.com. The names correspond to unique numbers for each computer connected to the internet, for example, 98.37.241.30, which serve as routing addresses on the internet. The internet domain name system (DNS) is very hierarchical and requires only 13 "root servers" to link all points on the internet. The DNS was developed in the 1980s as a mechanism to simplify addressing for a growing number of computers. In 1992, when commercial traffic was first permitted on the network, the internet rapidly became a global medium for commerce, education, and communications. With the commercialization of the internet, the DNS became a lucrative market. Projections show that the DNS will be worth more than $2 billion annually, based on a 20-fold increase in the demand for domain names by the year 2003 (see Table 28-19).

In 1997, the U.S. government decided to privatize the DNS in a manner that would increase competition and facilitate global participation in its management. After releasing a series of papers, the government invited the global community of private sector internet stakeholders to work together to form a new private sector, not-for-profit corporation to manage DNS technical functions currently performed by or on behalf of the U.S. government. In response, the global internet community created the Internet Corporation for Assigned Names and Numbers (ICANN), a private sector, not-for-profit corporation with a board of directors from around the world. After extensive consultations with the private sector and other governments, the U.S. government entered into a memorandum of understanding with ICANN to design, develop, and test a plan under which the private sector will manage DNS functions.

TABLE 28-19: Internet Population Forecast

	1998		2003	
	Millions of Users	Percent of Total	Millions of Users	Percent of Total
United States	62.8	43	177	35
Canada	10	7	23.9	5
Western Europe	40.9	28	168.5	34
Japan	8	6	32	6
Asia-Pacific (excluding Japan)	10.2	7	47.7	9
Latin America	4.8	3	19.1	3
Rest of world	8.5	6	38.9	8
Total	145.2	100	507.1	100

Source: International Data Corporation.

In October 1998, the U.S. government secured a commitment to permit the development of global competition in domain name registration in the .com, .net, and .org domains. ICANN is currently responsible for accrediting companies that want to register names in .com, .net, and .org through uniform, fair, and transparent processes. Five companies—AOL, the Council of Registrars, France Telecom, Melbourne IT, and Register.com—were named to participate in the initial testing phase of the new competitive domain name registration system. After the completion of the test phase, the registration system will be open to all registrars accredited by ICANN. Approximately 37 entities from around the world have been accredited to participate in the posttesting phase. The U.S. government intends to move the management of DNS functions completely to the private sector as soon as possible but no later than September 2000.

Data Privacy. The free flow of information across the internet is one of its most important benefits, but it is posing new challenges, particularly to individual privacy. The widespread availability of vast amounts of data and rapidly developing technologies now enable organizations to integrate data from several sources to create an information-rich packet about individuals and their preferences. Such capabilities increasingly will allow businesses to customize offerings and information to specific consumer demands but could lead to an unprecedented erosion of individual privacy. Numerous polls and surveys show that the protection of personal data on the internet is a key concern among current and potential users. In fact, privacy concerns often are cited as one of the main reasons why users do not make a purchase on the internet and nonusers do not surf the internet. The potential economic effect is significant. An August 1999 report by Jupiter Communications found that privacy concerns among on-line shoppers could cut $18 billion from a projected $40 billion in total E-commerce revenues by 2002. In an effort to address privacy concerns on the internet, a number of private organizations in the United States have strengthened on-line privacy protection through self-regulation. For example, the

Online Privacy Alliance (www.privacyalliance.org) is helping define privacy policies for the internet and encouraging companies to adopt and post effective privacy policies. Also, the Better Business Bureau (www.bbbonline.org), TRUSTe (www.truste.org), and Web Trust (www.webtrust.org) have developed independent third-party enforcement regimes that award a "seal" or trust mark to notify consumers that an organization follows fair information practices on-line. New technologies are giving consumers greater control over their personal information on the internet.

Some companies have addressed the privacy challenge through specific corporate actions. For example, in early 1999, IBM, one of the biggest Web advertisers, announced that it would not advertise on Web sites that do not post privacy policies. Several other major Web advertisers, including Microsoft, Disney, Intel, and Proctor & Gamble, announced similar policies. Those actions raise awareness and put pressure on commercial Web sites to institute effective privacy policies.

Although privacy concerns most directly affect the growth of business-to-consumer electronic commerce, they also can affect business-to-business operations and cross-border trade. For example, the European Commission's Directive on Data Protection, which went into force in October 1998, gives the European Commission the authority to cut off transfers of personal data to countries whose data protection practices are deemed inadequate. Since many U.S. companies receive countless data transfers from their European offices, partners, and other sources, the directive has the potential to disrupt business operations and trade between Europe and the United States. Because of this, the European Commission and the U.S. Department of Commerce have sought to create a "safe harbor" that would facilitate compliance by U.S. organizations with the European directive. Under the proposal, which was under discussion in late 1999, U.S. organizations that adhere to certain data protection principles would be presumed to be in compliance by the European Commission and data transfers would continue uninterrupted to those firms (see www.ita.doc.gov/ecom for up-to-date information on this proposal).

Taxation. When Congress passed the internet Tax Freedom Act in 1998, it set a 3-year moratorium on internet sales and use taxes. What happens when the moratorium expires has not been determined and is the subject of intense debate in the Advisory Commission on Electronic Commerce. The commission was established by Congress to examine a number of issues related to electronic commerce, including taxation, and includes state and local elected officials and representatives from the internet industry. Many analysts suggest that imposing taxes on internet sales will stymie growth and be especially burdensome for small and medium-size companies. For state and local governments, sales taxes are the single largest source of revenue, totaling nearly $147 billion in 1997. If, as some market research firms suggest, internet sales reach $100 billion by 2003, an estimated $4 billion in sales taxes will go uncollected. One of the biggest problems policy makers will have to address is how an internet sales tax, if it is implemented, will be levied and who will collect it. A recent study by Ernst & Young LLP's Economic Consulting and Quantitative Analysis Group suggests that companies that collect sales taxes from multiple jurisdictions spend nearly as much on collecting taxes as they receive. Moreover, internet taxes are unpopular in Congress, and recent polls indicate that American consumers want electronic commerce to remain tax-free.

Internationally, in May 1998, the WTO agreed to a 2-year standstill on the imposition of duties on goods and services that are delivered electronically. The standstill does not apply to transactions in which goods and services are ordered electronically and are delivered by normal mechanisms. The United States supports the extension of the moratorium and hopes to make it permanent.

Jurisdiction and Consumer Protection. One of the most vexing problems related to the internet and electronic commerce is the issue of jurisdiction. The internet has no geographic borders and challenges the generally accepted notion of jurisdiction, since no single government or entity controls it. This is especially troublesome in regard to traditional consumer protection laws. Clearly, existing concepts of jurisdiction do not fit today's electronic environment, especially when buyers and sellers live in different countries and complete transactions directly on-line. The prevailing legal precedent that appears to work best in the absence of a specific contract that clearly designates the applicable law and forum or a new body of jurisprudence is the notion of "country of origin," which states that the applicable law applies to the country in which the party fulfilling the contract resides. In the on-line environment, that would mean the seller.

A draft regulation by the European Commission to amend the Brussels Convention, which covers civil and commercial matters, including consumer protection rules, would allow the buyer to seek redress in the buyer's country of residence in cases of disputes involving international contracts that were transacted on-line. The implications of this draft regulation are enormous for electronic commerce and Web-based merchants. Critics charge that it would treat all Web sites as cross-border advertising and a form of active solicitation. They claim that it would require businesses that sell on-line to be familiar with the consumer protection laws of all 18 European Union countries, as well as the myriad state and local regulations. Opponents state that the regulation could stifle practical and nonregulatory solutions that provide consumers with more protection.

The use of robust encryption technology is vital to the future of electronic commerce. In recognition of the realities of the emerging digital economy and in support of its development, the U.S. government made significant changes in its export control policies in January 2000 by relaxing government controls on the exportation of data encryption technology. The new regulations give U.S. companies the opportunity to sell their products to most end users in global markets. Under the new policy, any encryption commodity or software, (including retail products) of any key length may be exported under license exception, that is, without a licence, after a one time technical review. Commodities can be exported to individuals, commercial firms, and other nongovernment end users in any country except Iran, Iraq, Libya, Syria, Sudan, North Korea, and Cuba. Streamlined post-export reporting of any product above 64 bits will provide the U.S. government with an understanding of where encryption is exported and reflect the types of industry business models and distribution channels used. These policy changes have the practical effect of opening U.S. encryption products to the global marketplace. Exports previously allowed only for a company's internal use now can be used for communication with other firms, supply chains, and customers. Moreover, ISPs can use any encryption commodity or software to provide services to commercial firms and nongovernment end users. Exports to governments still must be approved for a license.

The distribution of broadband networks will bring new opportunities to businesses and consumers and enable consumers to have "always-on" connection to the internet at speeds 100 times faster than those of dial-up modems. The ubiquity of cable television makes it an excellent mechanism for broadband internet access. However, mergers between long-distance telephone operators (which operate as ISPs) and cable companies will challenge many small ISPs that operate in niche marketplaces. At issue is whether cable operators should be compelled to offer high-speed internet access through their cable networks, which they consider proprietary, to competitors, that is, ISPs. Few markets in the United States have more than one company providing broadband internet access, and so consumers are limited in their selection of high-speed ISPs that offer DSL. By contrast, dial-up internet access markets have many competitors, even in small markets. In June 1999, the City of Portland, OR, ruled that AT&T must open access to competing ISPs. The city's decision was upheld by a federal court, and an appeal is pending. The key issue is whether cable access should be determined by local officials or federal regulators. The Federal Communications Commission (FCC), which has jurisdiction over national telecommunications policy, has not resolved how to determine internet access via cable modems.

Global Market Trends

While the United States clearly has had the lead in the adoption of internet and electronic commerce, that position will erode. Through 1999, the United States was responsible for three-quarters of the total electronic commerce revenues generated in the world, and it still has a significant lead in the development of internet and electronic commerce applications. A confluence of government policies and agreements and commercial developments will cause western Europe and the Asia-Pacific region to experience strong growth in internet use and electronic commerce over the next 5 years. Latin America and central and eastern Europe will trail because of low per capita incomes, inadequate infrastructure, and low internet and PC penetration rates (see Tables 28-20 and 28-21).

Western Europe. Europe has a population of more than 320 million and a single market that generates $7 trillion in gross domestic product (GDP), second only to the United States. Europe has the potential to be the next big market for internet commerce because of its advanced economies and infrastructure. In addition, with the implementation of a common currency, the Euro, businesses should find it more efficient to operate in Europe. The IDC estimates that at the end of 1998, there were approximately 41 million internet users in western Europe. That number is expected to increase to nearly 170 million by 2003. IDC estimates that western Europe's internet commerce will grow from $5.6 billion in 1998 to more than $430 billion by 2003, a CAGR of 138 percent.

TABLE 28-20: Worldwide Revenue from Internet Commerce
(billions of dollars except as noted)

Region	1998	2003	Compound Annual Growth Rate 98–03, %
United States	37.25	707.92	80
Western Europe	5.61	430.37	138
Japan	1.98	44.94	87
Asia-Pacific (excluding Japan)	0.72	32.59	109
Rest of world	1.41	53.02	107

Source: International Data Corporation.

Although the use of intranets and extranets is on the rise and a significant number of PCs have been sold in Europe, the wholesale adoption of electronic commerce by European consumers and businesses is still 1 to 2 years behind that in the United States. For a variety of reasons, the internet and electronic commerce will grow unevenly and in clusters in Europe. With the highest internet penetration rate in the world, the Nordic countries were the first to develop an on-line market through their early adoption of internet services via mobile phones. However, their small population base will hinder their market growth. The area that promises the greatest growth rate and contains the biggest markets will be the United Kingdom, Germany, and the Benelux nations. Another factor pushing the development of the internet and electronic commerce is free internet access. A number of companies, including AOL UK, recently adopted a new business model that provides subscription-free internet access to increase the number of users. A factor influencing the growth of internet commerce in Germany and the United Kingdom is the increase in mergers and acquisitions (M&A) such as the one between Daimler-Benz and the Chrysler Corporation. U.S. companies gen-

TABLE 28-21: Top 10 Countries for Worldwide Internet Traffic in 1998

Rank	Country	Share, %
1	United States	59.4
2	Japan	12.5
3	Germany	4.2
4	United Kingdom	2.6
5	Australia	1.9
6	Canada	1.9
7	Italy	1.6
8	France	1.5
9	Netherlands	1.3
10	Sweden	1.0
	Rest of world	11.4

Source: StatMarket (www.statmarket.com).

erally are farther along in the adoption of internet technologies than European companies are. To fully integrate their business lines, European companies will need to adapt their business processes to reflect their U.S. counterpart's lead. Low internet and PC penetration rates will keep the southern European countries such as France, Italy, and Greece behind (see Table 28-22). One area of significant growth potential for internet and electronic commerce applications in western Europe is wireless connectivity. Europe has a very high rate of wireless phone use. Technological advances in mobile telecommunications are facilitating the migration of internet and electronic commerce applications to the wireless phone.

The internet and electronic commerce face a number of challenges in western Europe. A factor that will affect the internet's growth potential is the slow pace of telecommunications deregulation in some countries, which can translate to technical issues such as bandwidth shortages. For example, despite the fact that the European Union (EU) is a signatory to the WTO Basic Telecommunications Agreement and a European Commission (EC) Directive on Telecommunications was implemented in 1996, deregulation has been slow in many countries. High internet access charges can slow the rate of consumer use of the internet. Some European ISPs have addressed this issue by offering free internet access to increase their customer base. They generate revenue by sharing local call charges with the telecom carrier and through advertising. FreeServe, the largest ISP in the United Kingdom, recently announced a service that will enable users to accumulate up to 10 hours of free internet access a month, depending on the amount of national and international phone calls they make. AOL UK introduced flat-rate pricing of 1.65 cents per minute for its 600,000 subscribers by connecting them to a toll-free number. Subscribers still pay a fee of approximately $16.45 a month.

Asia-Pacific Region. With over half the world's population, the Asia-Pacific region has enormous growth potential for the internet and electronic commerce. Some observers argue that the recent financial crisis necessitated a new approach to conducting business, including the use of the internet. Businesses in that region are beginning to realize significant benefits from operating cost reductions and returns on investments resulting from the use of the internet and electronic commerce technologies. Fueled in part by falling PC prices, internet use in the Asia-Pacific region (excluding Japan) is expected to grow from approximately 10 million users in 1998 to some 48 million in 2003. The electronic commerce market will grow from $700 million in 1998 to more than $32 billion in 2003. Two other factors that are influencing the projected growth of the internet in this region are telecommunications liberalization as a result of the WTO Basic Telecommunications Agreement and the Information Technology Agreement reducing duties to zero on IT equipment imports, of which most Asia-Pacific countries are signatories.

Australia, China, and Japan are projected to experience the greatest growth in internet and electronic commerce opportunities, although in different ways. Japan has the biggest economy in the region, second only to that of the United States worldwide. However, it is just starting to show signs of sustained economic growth after a prolonged recession. With per capita income rates similar to those in the United States, a high PC penetration rate, and an internet population expected to grow from 10.2 million in 1998 to 47 million in 2003, Japan probably will lead the region's growth. IDC estimates that Japanese internet users will generate nearly $45 billion in electronic commerce revenues by the year 2003. However, high internet access charges, lack of access to broadband technologies, and the lack of a standardized payments system will hinder growth beyond those estimates. Although recent developments suggest that the government of Japan and the Ministry of Posts and Telecommunications may introduce flat-rate internet access, charges for unlimited internet access would still be more than three times higher than the U.S. rate. Nippon Telegraph and Telephone (NTT), the leading national telecommunications firm, continues to strongly support ISDN, although technologies such as DSL offer better performance. Because of NTT's decision to encourage the use of competing technologies such as ISDN, DSL probably will not be available in the near term. Internet access through cable modems is a weak option because of the low penetration of cable television in that country.

It is impossible to look at the Asia-Pacific region without thinking about the Chinese market. With nearly one-quarter of the world's population and a sizable but underdeveloped economy, China is an attractive market. China has several large metropolitan populations and a technically competent workforce, and the number of PCs and Web users is growing daily. However, China still must resolve several issues to foster the growth of electronic commerce. For example, foreign ownership of Chinese ISPs remains illegal, and the status of foreign investment in companies that provide internet content and services remains an open question. The other major challenge electronic commerce faces is that China remains a cash-oriented society, with few people using credit cards.

By almost any measure, Australia leads the Asia-Pacific region in adapting to the emerging digital economy. Nearly one-third of Australia's 18 million people (5.1 million) are internet

TABLE 28-22: Western European Internet Usage in 1998

Country	Percent of Population
Finland	31.0
Sweden	28.0
Norway	23.0
Denmark	22.6
Netherlands	19.6
United Kingdom	15.1
Switzerland	14.4
Germany	12.4
Ireland	8.6
Belgium	7.7
France	6.9
Italy	5.4
Spain	5.1
Portugal	4.7
Greece	2.6

Source: International Data Corporation.

users, and even more impressive is the number of Australian businesses that use the internet. From 1998 to 1999, the number of business Web sites that were hosted by ISPs doubled to 48,000, and more than 50,000 Australian companies have their Web sites in-house. Moreover, Australia has a very competitive ISP market, with more than 640 ISPs in business. The two largest ISPs, OzEmail and Telstra, control almost half the market. Australian consumers are gravitating to the internet as well. According to one study, nearly 66 percent of Australian internet users shop on-line, and they spent over $88.2 million on-line in 1998. The Australian government recognized the potential of electronic commerce by drafting an electronic commerce bill that would, among other things, recognize the validity of electronic commerce communications and on-line transactions and ensure that electronic communications comport with existing off-line requirements such as the requirement for signatures. The bill also will validate electronic contracts and provide specific rules to govern electronic communications.

Singapore is positioning itself as the internet and electronic commerce gateway for southeast Asia. In addition to its having perhaps the best infrastructure and telecommunications system in southeast Asia, over the past year, Singapore's government made several significant policy changes in an effort to capitalize on the potential of electronic commerce. The government identified the internet as a priority and implemented a plan to provide the entire nation with high-speed access. It also overturned a ban on home offices so that Singaporeans can now work out of their homes and relaxed a number of restrictive censorship laws, including some that affect ISPs. The impact of these policies is being realized. Electronic commerce transactions were expected to increase 25 percent by the end of 1999 to reach nearly $750 million, of which 99 percent were B2B transactions.

India is another country whose government has recognized the enormous potential of the internet and electronic commerce. India has the largest number of English-speaking citizens outside the United States and a highly educated and technically competent, growing middle class. Through a number of policy initiatives and international agreements, successive Indian governments have appeared to be committed to opening the IT sector to foreign imports and investment. The emergence of the internet as a medium to conduct business is also a factor in these policy initiatives. IT investment grew 26 percent in 1998. Furthermore, according to IDC, India's IT investment will continue to increase well into the next century, especially in regard to PCs. IDC expects PCs to experience a compound growth rate of 33.6 percent through 2003. Price reductions are fueling much of this growth. In addition, foreign investment in the ISP sector has been liberalized, although foreign ownership is limited to 49 percent. The biggest challenge facing the internet sector is telecommunications liberalization. Although India is a member of the 1998 WTO Agreement on Basic Telecommunications, the government did not accept the procompetitive regulatory principles in total and agreed to only a 25 percent share of foreign ownership despite the fact that existing basic and cellular joint ventures are allowed at 49 percent.

One area that cannot be overlooked in the Asia-Pacific region is television. There are more than 110 million cable television subscribers in Asia, and countries such as Singapore and Hong Kong are increasingly focusing on cable television networks to provide internet services.

Duaine A. Priestley, Office of Computers and Business Equipment, (202) 482-0397, October 1999.

■ REFERENCES

Business Software Alliance, 1150 18 Street, NW, Washington, D.C. (202) 872-5500, http://www.bsa.org.

Business Week, 1221 Avenue of the Americas, 39th Floor, New York, NY 10020. http://www.businessweek.com.

Business Wire. http://www.businesswire.com.

Cahners Publishing, 1350 East Touhy Avenue, Des Plaines, IL 60018. http://www.cahners.com.

CMP Media, Incorporated, 600 Community Drive, Manhasset, NY 11030. http://www.cmp.com.

CommerceNet & Nielson Media Research. http://www.commerce.net.

Computer-Aided Engineering, 270 Madison Avenue, New York, NY 10016. http://www.penton.com/cae.

Computerworld, 375 Cochitutate Road, Framingham, MA 01701-9171. http://www.computerworld.com.

Datapro, 600 Delran Parkway, Delran, NJ. 08075. http://datapro@gartner.com. Tel. 800 328-2776.

Dataquest, Inc., 1290 Ridder Park Drive, San Jose, CA 95131. http://www.dataquest.com.

Daratech, Inc., 255 Bent Street, Cambridge, MA 02141-2001. 617-354-2339. http://www.daratech.com/index.htm.

Electronic Engineering Times, 600 Community Drive, Manhasset, NY 11030. http://pubs.cmpnet.com/eet.

Electronic News, 475 Park Avenue South, 2d Floor, New York, NY 10016. http://www.electronicnews.com.

eMarketer. http://www.emarketer.com.

Financial Times, The Financial Times Limited, 14 East 60 Street, New York, NY 10022. http://www.ft.com.

Forrester Research, Inc., 400 Technology Square, Cambridge, MA 02139. http://www.forrester.com.

Foster's Research. (617) 497-7090.

Government Computer News, Cahners Publishing Co., 8601 Georgia Avenue, Suite 300, Silver Spring, MD 20910. http://www.cahners.com.

Government Executive, "GIS Puts Information on the Map," October 1997. http://www.governmentexecutive.com.

IDG Company, One Exeter Plaza, 15th Floor, Boston, MA 02116. http://www.idg.net.

Infoworld, InfoWorld Publishing Co. and IDG Co., 155 Bovet Road, Suite 800, San Mateo, CA 94402. http://www.infoworld.com.

Inside R&D, John Wiley & Sons, 605 Third Avenue, New York, NY 10158. (212) 850-6000, http://www.wiley.com.

The Interactive Services. http://www.cyberatlas.com.

International Data Corporation, 5 Speen Street, Framingham, MA 01701. (508) 872-8200. http://idcresearch.com.

Internet World, Mecklermedia, 20 Ketchum Street, Westport, CT 06880.

Jupiter Communications, 627 Broadway, New York, NY 10012. (212) 780-6060. http://www.jup.com.

National Venture Capital Association, 1655 North Fort Myer Drive, Suite 850, Arlington, VA 22209. (703) 524-2549.

Network Wizards. http://www.nw.com. *Network Wizards* information also is found at www.cyberatlas.com.

Pioneer Consulting, 125 Cambridge Park Drive, Cambridge, MA 02140. (617) 441-3900.

Software & Information Industry Association, 1730 M Street, NW, Suite 700, Washington, DC 20036. (202) 452-1600.

Software Magazine, 257 Turnpike Road, Suite 100, Southboro, MA 01772. (508) 366-2031. http://www.softwaremag.com.

Survey.com, 5021 Almaden Expressway, San Jose, CA 95118. (408) 979-8230, http://www.survey.com.

U.S. Department of Labor, Bureau of Labor Statistics, 2 Massachusetts Avenue, NE, Washington, DC 20212. http://stats.bls.gov/blshome.html.

U.S. Trade Representative, 600 17 Street, NW, Washington, DC 20006. http://www.ustr.gov.

Wired Magazine, 520 Third Street, 3d Floor, San Francisco, CA 94107.

The Yankee Group. http://www.emarketer.com.

ZDNet, Suite 4000, 650 Townsend Street, San Francisco, CA 94103. http://www.zdnet.com.

Zona Research, Inc., 900 Veterans Boulevard, Suite 500, Redwood City, CA 94063. (650) 298-4000.

■ RELATED CHAPTERS

26: Information Services

27: Computer Equipment and Networking

30: Telecommunications Services

31: Telecommunications and Navigation Equipment

SPACE COMMERCE
Economic and Trade Trends

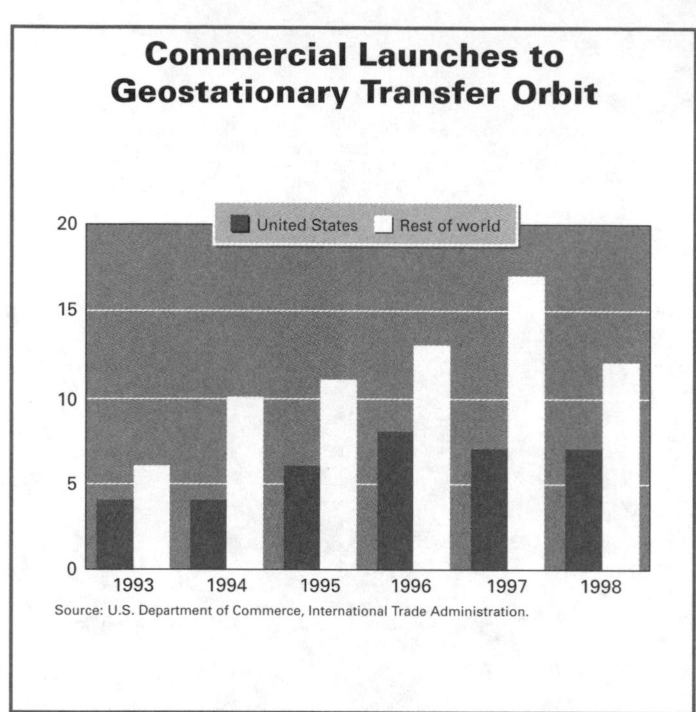

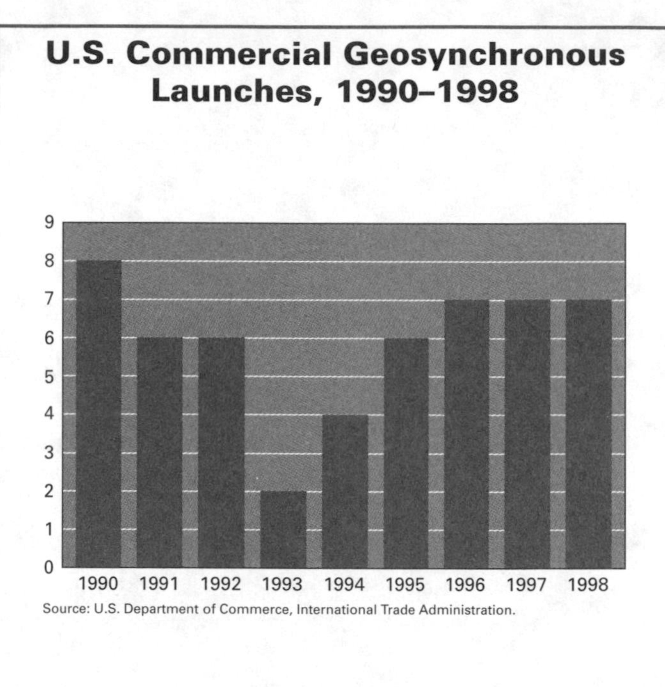

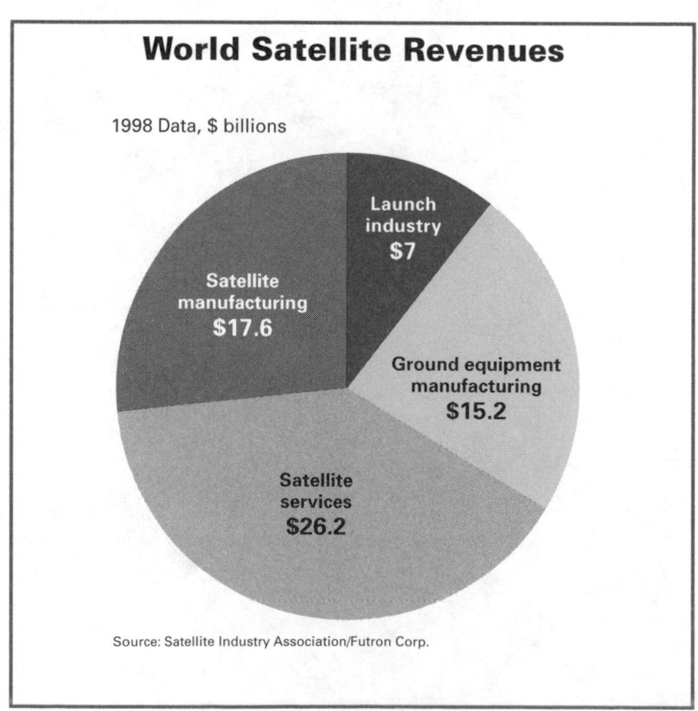

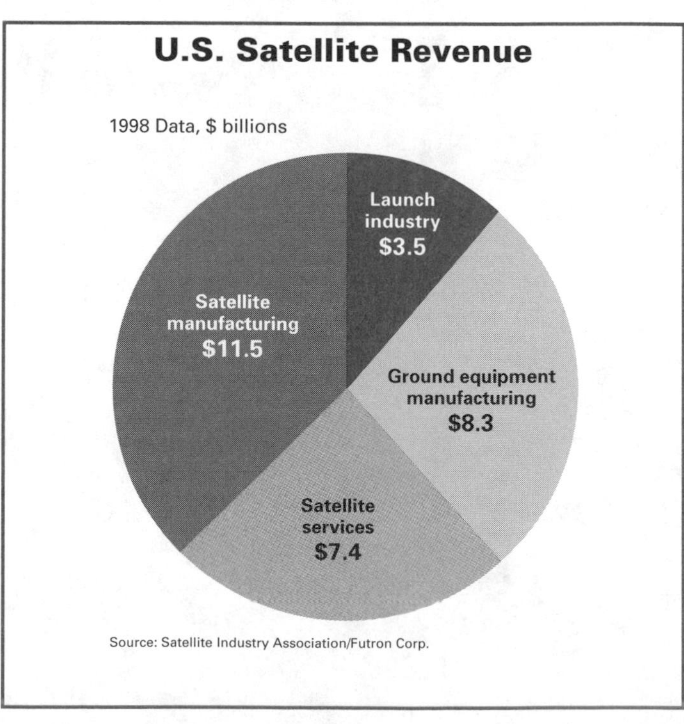

See "Getting the Most Out of *Outlook 2000*" for definitions of terms.

29

Space Commerce

INDUSTRY DEFINITION Space commerce consists of a number of major areas, six of which are covered in this chapter: commercial space launch vehicles and launch services, satellite communications systems, satellite communications services, satellite remote sensing services, space insurance, and noncommercial activities that relate to future commercial prospects. Included in the noncommercial activities category are emerging applications such as microgravity research and manufacturing, solar power activities, waste removal, space infrastructure, and less developed sectors such as space tourism.

Satellite communications systems can be divided into two categories: the space and ground segments. The space segment includes satellite and satellite subsystems that are placed in orbit around the earth; the ground segment includes equipment used to receive and/or transmit signals to satellites in orbit and consists of everything from large earth stations to small dishes used to receive satellite-delivered television. Satellite communications services include one- and two-way delivery of voice, video, and data via satellite, including international phone calls, broadcasting, and enhanced data services, to discrete geographic locations. Fixed satellite services (FSS) refer to broadcasting, data transmission, and telephony using fixed earth stations, while mobile satellite services (MSS) utilize mobile receivers, such as cellular-size phones, that can receive and transmit satellite signals.

GLOBAL TRENDS

The leading competitors in the commercial space market are generally countries that have had a strong historical interest in space: the United States, France and other European nations, Russia and Ukraine, China, and more recently Japan and Canada. These countries have developed the ability to manufacture, operate, and launch communications satellites and, in most cases, remote sensing satellites.

There were approximately 200 commercial communications satellites in geosynchronous earth orbit (GEO) in April 1999, with another 56 GEO satellites on order. The number of GEO contracts signed annually has declined from a peak of 36 in 1996. In 1998, 31 commercial satellites were ordered, although it remains to be seen how many of those satellites actually will be produced. However, 1998 proved to be a difficult year for satellite manufacturers. There were a number of in-orbit satellite anomalies or failures that led manufacturers to delay satellite production schedules and place more of an emphasis on quality control in the production process.

Euroconsult predicts that 108.7 million earth stations will be sold in 2006, with revenues of $46 billion. The growth in this market can be attributed to several factors, including technological improvements that have led to smaller, less expensive, and more sophisticated equipment; global deregulation; and new satellite applications that have translated into higher demand for equipment to utilize satellite technology. Ground equipment sales will continue to be driven by strong growth in very small aperture terminal (VSAT) and direct broadcast satellite (DBS) services in developed regions, while demand for large earth stations for telecommunications services will continue to grow in developing areas. While the space segment will continue to receive most of the attention, the earth station market is critical to the success of the overall industry.

The landscape of the international satellite services sector continues to change as two of the major international treaty satellite services organizations—INMARSAT and INTELSAT—undertake privatization efforts. INMARSAT was privatized in April 1999, and INTELSAT plans to privatize fully in 2001. It is thought that these newly privatized entities will be better suited to compete with the other private sector international satellite companies that have emerged in the last 10 years. The regulatory environment for satellite services continues to improve as 47 countries implement commitments made under the World Trade Organization (WTO) Agreement on Basic Telecommunications. The United States also has signed a number of bilateral satellite services agreements with countries such as Mexico and Argentina to ensure access to those markets. Direct broadcast satellite services continue to thrive in Europe, Latin America, and the Asia-Pacific region. In some cases, U.S. companies have made significant inroads in foreign countries, such as Hughes's DIRECTV Japan and Galaxy Latin America. New satellite-delivered telephony services were expected to grow as Iridium restructured and Globalstar prepared to launch service in October 1999.

These new low earth orbit (LEO) communications systems will encourage growing demand for commercial launches in the next several years, with only a slight dip in demand around 2001 before the launch of two major LEO systems, Skybridge and Teledesic. European and U.S. providers are operating at or near capacity and are sold out until 2001. The current trend is to launch groups of satellites, or at least two satellites at a time, to lower costs. For LEO systems, the main requirement is to get all the system's satellites in orbit as fast as possible. Many countries and companies are examining reusable concepts to meet this demand, but these developments will not be available in the near term. In the long run, new reusable vehicles will require additional personnel, infrastructure, and legal guidance. Other creative attempts to address this market through lower-cost vehicles will continue in both the public and private sectors. However, financing is not readily available for this type of high-risk project, and so the future of these reusable vehicles is undetermined. Until reusables are fully developed, upgraded versions of existing launch vehicles and continued cooperation and globalization between western and former Soviet countries will have to meet the demand.

In 1998, there was a global decline of about 11 percent from 1997 in commercial launch revenues because of increased difficulty obtaining export licenses for U.S. satellites launched from foreign countries, political uncertainty, the Asian financial crisis, and postponed launches caused by satellite manufacturing delays. Several of these problems occurred in 1999 as well, including the aftereffects of the Asian financial crisis, as canceled programs have not yet been restarted. In addition, a string of failures in 1998–1999 and satellite manufacturing delays have reduced the overall number of launches but will encourage greater reliability and quality checks at least in the short term. This should start a trend toward increased reliability. As a result of the size and functions of satellites, large, heavy payloads will grow larger while LEO payloads will get smaller, creating growth at both ends of the launch market. Smaller LEO satellites will be launched several at a time, encouraging growth in the middle to heavy end of the launch market.

Europe has invested around $10 billion to develop the Ariane 5, and the United States has developed the Evolved Expendable Launch Vehicle (EELV). In the future, the industry will need to consolidate further domestically and work jointly with international partners to provide funding for major projects, improve performance, reduce costs, and pursue global markets for projects such as large launch vehicles, reusable launchers, and satellite communications systems.

A main source of interest, especially at the United Nations's UNISPACE 3 conference in July 1999, has been the challenge of bringing the benefits of space to developing countries around the world. Through programs such as telecommunications and remote sensing, it is believed that developing countries can improve their quality of life. Many nations have made a commitment to achieving this goal, but no specific programs have been created to address it.

DOMESTIC TRENDS

The United States dominates the world satellite manufacturing industry in large satellites and is also very competitive in the manufacture of new smaller satellites that will provide a variety of new satellite services. Hughes Space and Communications, Lockheed Martin Telecommunications, and Space Systems/Loral are currently the top three manufacturers of traditional commercial communications satellites. U.S. manufacturers are facing serious competition from newly consolidated satellite companies in Europe and up-and-coming manufacturers in Japan and are subject to government export controls. U.S. companies also are active in the manufacture of smaller satellites, including Motorola, Boeing, Orbital Sciences, Spectrum Astro, and TRW. These relatively new, smaller satellites are being used to provide satellite messaging and satellite telephony services.

U.S. companies such as Hughes Network Systems and Scientific Atlanta are strong in the market for large earth stations and VSAT equipment, while companies in Asia and Europe tend to excel in the manufacture of consumer electronics products such as small satellite television dish receivers and receivers for satellite telephony. In 1998, there was a tremendous amount of merger and consolidation activity in the earth station industry. These mergers reflect a trend toward product integration and efforts to enter overseas markets.

Growth in the satellite services sector has been driven by satellite television, mobile satellite data, VSAT, and Global Positioning System (GPS) services. Revenues from mobile satellite services did not increase as rapidly as anticipated as Iridium initiated service later than expected and had difficulty attracting subscribers. U.S. domestic providers of fixed satellite services (FSS) include COMSAT, PanAmSat, Loral Skynet, GE American Communications, and Columbia Communications Corporation. Although FSS traditionally have accounted for the majority of satellite service revenues, new mobile services are expected to generate a significant portion of future earnings.

The United States saw a decline in launch revenues of about 3 percent from 1997 to 1998. Launch revenues were $6.9 billion in

1996, with the U.S. share equal to 46.4 percent; in 1997, the figure was $7.9 billion, with the U.S. share equal to 45.6 percent; and in 1998, it was $7 billion, with the U.S. share equal to 50 percent. While most basic rocket technology is approximately 20 to 30 years old, the U.S. industry is searching for ways to improve performance, reduce the time between launches, and reduce costs. In an attempt to meet commercial demand, substantial investments have been made to improve the performance of existing commercial vehicles and develop less expensive reusable vehicles. In addition, U.S. firms continue to explore international ventures, especially with Russia and Ukraine. Because of the growing demand for commercial launches, there is also a need to upgrade launch range infrastructure. Most commercial launch providers have been operating at or near capacity for several years, and launches are sold out into 2001. Additional discoveries about the usefulness of microgravity for scientific research and the development of pharmaceuticals, semiconductors, and new materials are driving the demand for the commercialization of space assets. Growing applications for remotely sensed images are pushing software manufacturers to design new and better programs that can quickly provide customers with value-added, easily understood images.

INDUSTRY AND TRADE PROJECTIONS FOR THE NEXT 1 AND 5 YEARS

The United States will continue to dominate the market for large GEO satellites in 2000, although further consolidation in Europe may create increased competition in the longer term. Orders for GEO satellites will remain at an average of about 30 per year, while contracts for new and next-generation small satellites may not meet previous expectations as initial difficulties in the mobile satellites services sector have weakened the prospects for future systems. In the next 5 years, an increase in the manufacture of smaller satellites for use in both voice and data systems most likely will balance out any potential downturns in the growth of the GEO satellite manufacturing market.

While growth in the satellite ground equipment market is solid, competition is intensifying among manufacturers of this equipment. This intense competition is driving manufacturers to lower prices while improving features and performance, differentiate and continually redevelop products, and tolerate low profit margins. In the early 1990s, U.S. manufacturers retained a large share of the world market for most satellite ground segments, but that share has decreased as competition from Japan and Europe has become more intense. As the industry has grown, so has the number of competitors. The ground segment will retain its current growth rate or grow slightly in 2000, and is expected to remain steady over the next 5 years.

The satellite services market will continue to be one of the fastest-growing segments in the industry, driven by growth in satellite television, satellite messaging, VSAT, and GPS services. Although Iridium's service did not meet expectations in 1999, Globalstar may prove that there is a market for satellite-delivered mobile telephone services. Satellite messaging services are likely to see substantial growth as ORBCOMM expands its customer base and other providers come on-line in 2001. Most observers expect that satellite radio and satellite broadband will add substantial growth to the satellite services market when those services are launched in the 2001–2002 period. In terms of revenues, satellite services grew substantially from 1997 to 1998, and that rapid rate of growth should continue in the year 2000. Over the next 5 years, the satellite services sector will continue to demonstrate significant growth as new services are launched.

U.S. industry reports that export controls will continue to cause delays in the year 2000 in shipping satellites to other nations for launch. This will maintain the delay in satellite launches that began in 1998. In addition to inhibiting U.S. satellite customers from choosing foreign launches, they may steer foreign customers away from U.S. satellite manufacturers in an attempt to avoid the cumbersome export licensing process. These problems will continue until the U.S. State Department is better staffed to handle the large number of export license applications and/or export licensing application processes are improved.

The launch market is expected to remain robust because the launch manifests will remain fully booked. GEO launches are expected to remain steady, with LEO launches adding to the market, as they have for the last 2 or 3 years. With new vehicles being developed, a chance of oversupply in the launch market exists in a few years. Many of these vehicles are being developed on the basis of encouraging market projections that show that launches could increase to 40 per year in the next decade, up from 34 in 1998. In addition, with higher-capacity vehicles being built, the number of multiple satellite launches will increase. If new vehicles enter the market, the costs of launching could decline, but because of the need to recover high development costs, it is unlikely that this will happen.

As Figures 29-1 and 29-2 demonstrate, the United States maintains a higher percentage of market share for launches than for actual payloads launched. This is due to the ability of Arianespace to launch more than one payload at a time to GEO. In addition, Table 29-1 shows that while the United States has made a steady number of launches to GEO over the past few years, the overall market has increased, causing the GEO market share of the United States to decline.

Revenues from sales of remote sensing imagery will increase as more systems are launched, making more images commercially available. Segments of this market will compete directly with the aerial photography market, which probably will lose revenue. Space insurance providers are facing a difficult year and are likely to raise their premiums to cover the losses paid for in 1998 and 1999. Because of those losses, fewer insurers are covering this market; this increases the risk to insurers and forces them to raise premium prices again.

Prices for launch services are expected to remain approximately the same but may shrink over time as new competitors enter the market. Recouping development costs will limit that reduction. Prices for remote sensing imagery will shrink as more systems are launched, more applications for the data are found, and greater amounts of data are purchased. Value-added services for interpreting imagery also will vary by application.

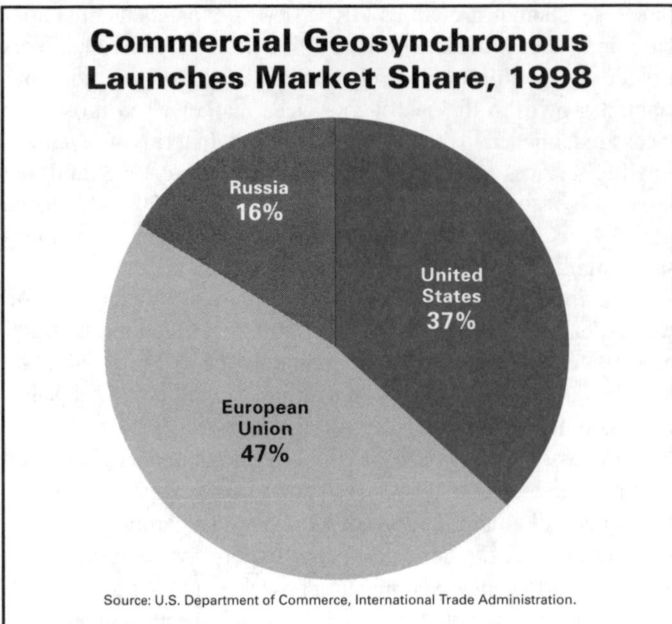

FIGURE 29-1

TABLE 29-1: Commercial Launches to Geostationary Transfer Orbit

	1993	1994	1995	1996	1997	1998
United States	4	4	6	8	7	7
Rest of world	6	10	11	13	17	12
Total	10	14	17	21	24	19

Source: U.S. Department of Commerce, International Trade Administration.

Space insurance premiums may rise over the next 2 years as a result of the number of recent launch failures, satellite in-orbit failures, and manufacturing delays that postpone the initial date of system operation and thus revenues.

The remote sensing imagery market remains in its early stages but is blossoming with the appearance of 1-meter resolution images on the commercial market. Several high-resolution systems are planned for launch in the next 5 years. The number of satellites developed will depend on the demand for value-added data images. The demand for those images will be directly related to the number of applications that find a use for these data and whether the data will be available at a reasonable price. Several foreign providers have footholds in this industry, including Russia, India, and Canada, but U.S. systems coming on-line should offer stiff competition.

Export of U.S. launch services will increase as additional foreign customers demand launches of their telecommunications systems. The sale of remote sensing systems and data from those systems also may increase U.S. exports. However, this positive effect on the trade balance may be offset by increased U.S. purchases of foreign remote sensing data.

Employment in the commercial space sector will remain steady or increase as new systems begin to provide commercial services. Entrepreneurial launch ventures will increase employment in the launch sector. Employment in remote sensing will be centered on the value-added computer software and data processing industries, but a slight increase will occur as turnkey remote sensing systems are sold internationally. Employment related to programs such as the Space Shuttle will decrease as the ongoing programs become more efficient and cost-effective. In the near term, employment in microgravity experiments and space research will be concentrated largely in the public and academic sectors.

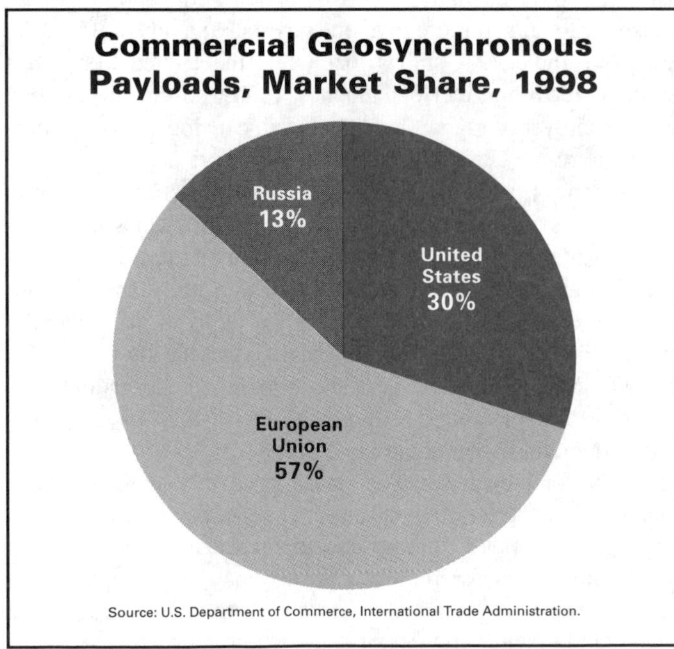

FIGURE 29-2

LAUNCH VEHICLES

Launch vehicles are included in SIC 376, guided missiles and space vehicles and parts. This section covers the space vehicles and parts component (SIC 3761), space vehicle propulsion units and parts (SIC 3764), and space launch vehicle parts and auxiliary equipment. Guided missile parts, propulsion units, and auxiliary equipment also are included in these SIC codes and are addressed in Chapter 21, Aerospace.

Global Trends

The current world leader in this sector is the European consortium Arianespace, which has set a goal of increasing its geostationary transfer orbit (GTO) market while capturing a significant portion of the LEO market. Arianespace is owned by 49 European aerospace and financial companies and the French Space Agency, Centre National d'Etudes Spatiales (CNES), which is the largest owner. In 1998, Arianespace orbited 14 satellites on 10 Ariane launchers. Like U.S. launch providers, the producers of the Ariane 4 and 5 are trying to reduce the production cycle time to 12 months for the Ariane 4 and 25 to 30 months for the Ariane 5 to match the production cycle of satellite manufacturers. To do this, huge investments will be required even though upgrades in rockets and launch facilities have already cost billions of dollars. Arianespace is slashing costs to maintain its 50 to 60 percent market share while new vehicles such as Sea Launch and the Delta 4 begin service. Ariane has ordered a second batch of Ariane 5's, which are expected to cost up to 40 percent less than the first batch. This reduced cost will improve Arianespace's competitiveness against other new-to-market vehicles. The Ariane 5 is expected to evolve to carry up to 20 metric tons for LEO launches and eventually will include an updated cryogenic stage, increased propellant capacity, and a lighter-weight stage structure. The new upper stage will give customers increased flexibility because of the reignitable engine. Arianespace is planning to build for an average of eight Ariane 5 launches per year by 2002 and probably will extend the use of the Ariane 4 beyond 2002–2003, as was originally expected. Arianespace also is evaluating the development of Ariane 4 Lite, a smaller version of the Ariane 44LP that would launch small payloads to GEO, but for a much lower price. Ariane believes that the market would support six Ariane 4 Lite launches a year. Ariane's backlog is approximately 40 GEO spacecraft and one LEO constellation launch worth nearly $4 billion.

The year 1999 started with 13 to 14 missions scheduled, with 3 of those missions on the larger Ariane 5. The Ariane 5 successfully completed its first commercial launch in spring 1999. Owing to satellite delays, Arianespace only had eight launches through August. As a result, Arianespace expected to match the 1998 schedule by holding eight launches from August to December 1999.

Internationally, Arianespace launches the Russian Soyuz vehicle through its Starsem venture, which was created in 1996. Starsem, which also includes the French satellite manufacturer Aerospatiale, the Russian Space Agency, and two Russian firms, is considering launching the Soyuz from the European equatorial launch site in Kourou, French Guiana, as early as 2001–2002 for added performance. The Soyuz currently is launched from the Russian launch site in Kazakhstan and is one of the world's most reliable vehicles.

Talk of a consolidated European space company continues with rumors about alliances between DaimlerChrysler Aerospace (DASA) and Alenia of Italy after DASA finalizes its merger with Construcciones Aeronauticas SA (CASA) of Spain. Some observers believe that these companies also may be looking to the United States for further alliances, but there are no existing proposals.

Europe, especially Arianespace and CNES, is beginning to focus on developing a reusable launch vehicle to maintain its position in the commercial launch market. To master reusable launch vehicle (RLV) technology on a system level, Europe will have to develop an "X-vehicle" for testing. Several different proposals exist, but no decision has been made about which one will be funded and/or developed.

Italy would like to develop the Vega small launch vehicle, but France blocked its development in the European Space Agency (ESA) Ministerial Summit held in May 1999 by getting the ministers to postpone a decision on further development until October 1999. If that program goes forward, Aerospatiale and Fiat Avio will form the Vega Spazio joint venture to build and market the Vega for LEO. Vega will be a solid-propellant launch vehicle with launches expected to cost approximately $20 million. The companies expect to provide four or five launches a year.

Overall, the ESA Ministerial Summit reduced budgets and directed the ESA nations to continue their reorganizational efforts. ESA approved 90 percent of the requested amount for further development of the Ariane 5, Europe's largest launch vehicle. A total of $708.6 million was allocated for the Living Planet remote sensing program, and $359.1 million was allocated for the International Space Station for the period 2000–2001. Ariane 5 was awarded an increase from $479.8 million to $622.5 million through 2001.

While Russia expected to have a busy year of Soyuz and Proton commercial and military flights, uncertainty about that country's space budget left many of its other programs in jeopardy. Eleven of the projected 13 Proton launches in 1999 were to be performed by the International Launch Services (ILS) joint venture with Lockheed Martin. Soyuz had nine missions scheduled for 1999, an increase of one from 1998. Six of those flights would be commercial for Globalstar, with three traveling to the Mir Space Station. With a few launches on other vehicles, the projected number for 1999 was expected to be 25, but the actual number was likely to be lower.

Russia uses the Plesetsk launch site and the Svobodniy space launch center to launch LEO satellites, but Baikonur in Kazakhstan remains the predominant Russian launch site, especially for GEO launches. In April 1999, the first launch of a commercial Russian–Ukrainian Dnepr rocket based on the RS-20 ICBM launched a commercial payload from the Baikonur Cosmodrome. The project serves two purposes in that it increases the supply of launch vehicles for small commercial satellites and takes inventory out of Russian ICBM stockpiles pursuant to U.S.–Russian arms reduction negotiations. Russia claims to be converting the SS-19 Strela ballistic missile into a commercial launcher by the end of 2000 for the same purposes. Conversion will require numerous tests and adjustments to the Svobodny Far East launch site that are expected to cost $10 million. As was mentioned above, Russia also has commercialized the Soyuz rocket, which launched two Globalstar communications satellites in 1999 through the Starsem venture.

In 1998–1999, China faced difficulties not from vehicle reliability but from U.S. government concern over technology transfer, national security, and export licensing. After investigations into whether U.S. companies that used the Chinese Long March rocket for commercial launches transferred sensitive technology to China, the export licensing process became much more difficult, dissuading several firms from selecting a Chinese launch. As a result, China has only one new launch. However, it held a launch for Brazil in October 1999, launched several LEO satellites for Iridium, and is proposing to build a spaceport in Hainan, China's second largest island. The site would cost $500 million to build and would include the launch site, a tourist center, and an industrial park. China also improved the performance of its Long March 4B rocket. China has had 15 straight successes since a string of failures in 1996, improving users' confidence. China has a few commercial launches remaining on its manifest, but most of them are being held up by U.S. export licensing delays.

China is preparing to launch its first manned spacecraft as early as spring 2000 and performed a test launch of an unmanned capsule in November 1999. In a claim for status, it seeks to build a full space program, including a space station, reusable spacecraft, and lunar probes. China probably will launch a new, larger Long March 2F vehicle from the Jiuquan launch site in northwest China for the manned program.

Japan remains an up-and-coming participant as its Rocket System Corporation is planning its first commercial launches on the new H-2A vehicle in July 2001, with the first prototype scheduled to launch in spring 2001. Both Loral and Hughes have orders for 10 H-2A commercial launches but will wait until the demonstration launch to select firm dates.

As one of the leading developing space nations, Brazil is hoping to create the first international commercial spaceport at its Alcantara launch site. The launch site is 3 degrees south of the equator, making it a competitive location for improving the performance of launch vehicles placing satellites into GEO orbit. Until now, the Alcantara site has been used only for test flights of sounding rockets and two failed flights of Brazil's VLS launch vehicle, but four noncommercial launches are scheduled through 2001. Brazil would like to use this prime location to launch foreign vehicles that otherwise would be launched from sites at higher latitudes, such as Cape Canaveral and Kazakhstan. The Brazilian firm Infraero would like to operate Alcantara in much the same way that it operates Brazil's airports. Several U.S. and foreign firms are interested in using Brazil as a launch site, but current U.S. policy would heavily restrict the ability of firms to transport rockets into Brazil for launch. For example, Italy's Fiat Avio would like to use Alcantara to launch the Tsyklon 4 Ukrainian rocket, an improved rocket being developed jointly by Fiat Avio and Ukraine's NPO Yuzhnoe. Boeing, Lockheed Martin, and Orbital Sciences Corporation also have considered launching from Brazil. For this spaceport program to go forward, Brazil would have to meet American concerns about sensitive technology transfer. If that can be accomplished, Brazil might have the world's first truly international spaceport.

Israel Aircraft Industries teamed up with the U.S. firm Coleman Research Corporation to market launches for U.S. government payloads. The partnership takes advantage of a loophole in U.S. government policy forbidding U.S. payloads to be launched on foreign rockets by ensuring that the vehicles used have just enough U.S. content to meet its requirements. The National Aeronautics and Space Administration (NASA) selected this venture and Orbital Sciences to provide small launches for its payloads. The venture will attempt to manufacture more than half its components in the United States to comply with the policy. The Israeli/Coleman Shavit launch vehicle will launch payloads of less than 2,000 pounds into LEO, most likely from Cape Canaveral, Florida.

The United States and South Korea have agreed in principle to lift all existing restrictions on commercial rocket development in that nation. The agreement will create guidelines under which South Korea will develop launch vehicles for both commercial and government launches.

India launched its Polar Satellite Launch Vehicle (PSLV) for the first time on May 26, 1999, carrying a commercial payload. It carried an oceanographic Indian Remote Sensing (IRS) satellite, a South Korean minisatellite, and a German research satellite. The U.S. government has not supported the development of such a program in India because of that country's continued attempts to develop nuclear weapons. India is continuing to work on a larger Geostationary Satellite Launch Vehicle (GSLV) program, which is expected to have its first experimental launch in early 2000.

Bilateral Commercial Space Launch Agreements

In the period 1993–1996, the United States signed bilateral trade agreements with Russia, China, and Ukraine to give U.S. satellites increased opportunities for space launch. The agreements allowed those countries to enter the international commercial space launch services market, which previously had been restricted for national security reasons. With the growing satellite market and increasing demand for space launch services, the U.S. government developed those agreements to provide for a gradual entry of these nonmarket economies into the commercial market, increasing supply and competition while avoiding undue market disruption. The agreements allow each of those countries to provide up to 20 launches to GEO through the years 2000 (Russia) and 2001 (China and Ukraine). In addition, the agreements contain pricing provisions that state that those foreign providers must price launches on a par (within 15 percent) with the prices of western commercial providers. While these agreements are scheduled to remain in place for another 1 or 2 years, the booming commercial launch industry and the changing international partnerships have driven the US. aerospace industry to request that the quantitative restrictions be removed from the agreements. The U.S. government is considering several options related to that request. Any action taken will be aimed at further encouraging free and fair trade in the commercial launch industry.

Domestic Trends

Because of the projected growth in the commercial launch industry, the United States has been examining several ways to improve competitiveness vis-à-vis Europe and several emerging competitors. Many existing vehicles are being improved, and new vehicles are being designed. Companies are entering international partnerships and developing unique ways to reduce the cost of access to space through the development of reusable launch vehicles. Unfortunately, the U.S. industry has been hit by a number of failures as well as satellite manufacturing delays that have caused the growth of this market to slow in the short term. Because backlogs continue to grow, the market will remain strong in the future.

To move toward commercial procurement for military launches, in October 1998, the U.S. Air Force announced that its EELV program would split its procurement between Boeing's Delta IV rocket and Lockheed Martin's Atlas V. Delta was awarded $1.88 billion for 19 launches, and Atlas was awarded $1.15 billion for 9 launches. The launches will be performed between 2002 and 2006. The goal of the program is to reduce the cost of military space launches by 25 percent. EELV is expected to reduce U.S. Air Force launch costs by $6 billion from 2002 to 2020. This program provides increased production not only for these launch vehicles but also for numerous subcontractors. For example, Aerojet was awarded $500 million to provide solid rocket motors for the Atlas V, and a new launch pad for the Delta IV will be built at a cost of $250 million.

Lockheed Martin participates in a partnership with Russia's Khrunichev and Energia firms to provide launches on the Russian Proton and American Atlas launch vehicles. ILS launches the Atlas from American launch sites and the Proton from Baikonur, Kazakhstan. The ILS venture received its first contract in July 1999 for an Atlas 5 launch with Teledesic. The contract calls for three Proton and three Atlas-5 launches, with options for an additional five with each one. These contracts would allow Lockheed Martin to launch a significant portion of the Teledesic satellite communications system. Atlas and Proton have a backlog of at least 34 commercial launches valued at over $3 billion. While transitioning to the Atlas V, Lockheed Martin will use the Atlas 3 rocket, which will be powered by Russian RD-180 rocket engines, the engines that will be used on the Atlas 5. All forecasts indicated that Lockheed Martin expected 1999 to be its busiest year ever. However, a string of launch failures and satellite delays forced a halt to most launches globally. Atlas had planned to launch 11 rockets and 11 Protons in 1999.

Continuing the transition toward increased international cooperation in space launching, the Boeing-led Sea Launch venture had its first successful demonstration launch on March 27, 1999. Since that demonstration, Sea Launch has won four additional contracts, increasing the manifest to 19 confirmed launches. The venture includes the Boeing Commercial Space Company, Norway's Kvaerner (which pulled out of the venture as a result of financial problems in the firm), Russia's Energia, and Ukraine's Yuzhnoye. Sea Launch achieves a considerable performance gain by launching from a mobile platform on the equator and taking full advantage of the rotational forces of the earth.

In addition to its international Sea Launch venture, Boeing continues to launch the Delta 2 and 3 rockets, and the Delta 4 will be Boeing's EELV vehicle. The Delta 2 had its most successful year in 1999 by launching several payloads in short time frames. However, on May 4, 1999, a Delta III rocket experienced a premature shutdown of its second-stage engine, which left the payload in a useless orbit. That failure will delay further development of the program as well as launches on other vehicles (such as the Atlas) that use the same upper-stage engine. Boeing has booked 18 Delta 3 missions through 2002, with Hughes holding 13 of those reservations; Loral holds the other 5. The Delta 3 is considered a transition vehicle from the Delta 2 to the EELV/Delta 4 and will be phased out between 2003 and 2005. A new trend in U.S. manufactured vehicles such as the Delta 3 is the use of numerous major components that are manufactured overseas. On the Delta 3, the propellant tanks for the second stage are built by Mitsubishi in Japan, while the extendable nozzle on the second-stage engine is built by France's SEP.

Subcontractors also are planning improvements. Pratt & Whitney is developing a new cryogenic upper-stage engine that is based on the RL-10 engine but is twice as powerful. The engine is planned to be available in 2003. Boeing is developing the most powerful liquid oxygen/hydrogen engine, the RS-68, which was tested successfully in July 1999 and will be used to power the Delta 4 launch vehicle in 2001. This is the first large liquid-fueled rocket engine developed in the United States since the Space Shuttle Main Engine in the 1970s.

In addition to large launch vehicles, the United States produces a number of small launch vehicles. Orbital Sciences produces both the Pegasus and Taurus lines of small launch vehicles. The Pegasus is unique in that it is carried to a high altitude on the belly of an L-1011 aircraft and then released and launched from the air. This gives Orbital the ability to launch from anywhere in the world as long as the political situation allows it. Orbital currently has a backlog of at least 11 launches valued at over $220 million.

Lockheed Martin's Athena rocket program continues to struggle. The program was not picked by NASA to launch the agency's small scientific spacecraft. Because of that loss, Athena will need to rely heavily on commercial contracts, but that market has not been growing. Athena will have to increase from two or three to six launches a year to keep the program alive. Athena also has been stung by failures, including one in April 1999. Of five missions since the program began launching in 1995, only three have been successful. Athena has three launches on its manifest, including one from a new spaceport in Kodiak Island, Alaska, in 2000. To prepare, Athena will begin pathfinder exercises from the Kodiak spaceport in the fourth quarter of 1999. However, on April 22, 1999, NASA announced that it had also chosen an Athena I rocket to launch its Vegetation Canopy Lidar (VCL) satellite from Alaska in August 2000.

Another new concept—commercial "spaceports" that would function similarly to airports—may give launch companies additional sites for increasing the number of launches. However, many issues need to be worked out before large numbers of launches will occur on those sites. Issues such as who has priority at those sites (commercial entities or the government) and who must pay for common assets are still being determined. Other issues include who will run the launch ranges and who will provide safety services.

String of Failures

The year 1999 was disappointing for the U.S. commercial space launch industry. A string of failures involving both government and commercial payloads restricted the launch rate and slowed the development of new vehicles. Both Lockheed Martin and Boeing, as well as the U.S. Air Force and the U.S. government's executive branch, ordered wide reviews of those failures, which could be damaging to both companies' desire to build their launch businesses. The three Titan failures alone cost taxpayers $3 billion. The failures in 1998 and 1999 included the following:

- A Titan exploded on August 12, 1998, destroying a $344 million Titan 4 and a top-secret payload worth $700 million.

It cost the military $1 billion because of the high cost of the national security payload that was lost and the expense of the largest American rocket. The failure was blamed on a damaged electrical wiring harness that cut power to the rocket's guidance system. On April 9, 1999, a Titan 4 that carried a $250 million missile warning satellite failed. On April 30, a third Titan 4 failed to place an $800 million *Milstar* military communications satellite into the correct orbit, causing a $1.2 billion loss for the Air Force. The failure was caused by incorrect information placed in the Titan software.

- On May 4, 1999, a Delta III rocket experienced a premature shutdown of its second-stage engine, which left the payload in a useless orbit. The combustion chamber probably ruptured as a result of a new manufacturing process, something that will affect all vehicles that use the Centaur upper stage. The upper stage also is used on the Atlas launch vehicles and caused that program to be grounded while the precise cause was determined.
- On April 27, 1999, a Lockheed Martin Athena II small launch vehicle's payload fairing did not separate properly, and the *Ikonos-1* remote sensing satellite was not placed into orbit.
- On July 5, 1999, a Russian Proton rocket with a military *Raduga* payload fell to earth because of a failure and explosion of the Proton's second stage. While this was not a U.S. launch, the same vehicle is used by ILS for commercial Proton launches, and delays were incurred. Kazakhstan at first banned all future launches from the Baikonur Cosmodrome but then allowed them to proceed when Russia agreed to pay its back rent, which had been owed for several years.

Reusable Launch Vehicles

With the growth of commercial satellite demand, a number of entrepreneurial ventures have announced plans to manufacture commercial launch vehicles, including a number of private proposals for RLVs. In addition, NASA is cofunding the development of three experimental RLVs: the X-33, X-34, and X-37. The Commercial Space Act of 1998 granted clear licensing authority for RLVs to the U.S. Department of Transportation, the first time commercial RLVs have been approved for launch. This should make it easier for companies to get financing and provide some certainty in the process.

Historically, companies developing new vehicles have had difficulty getting financing, and they will continue to have that problem because of the risky nature of the business. Many investors are adopting wait-and-see strategies because of the high risks involved in starting new ventures. Many see the ability to raise financing as the biggest hurdle in the development of new technology. All these companies are touting their ability to have rapid turnaround times of approximately 2 weeks. This would change the face of space launch by providing the ability to launch on demand. In addition, NASA and the Spaceport Florida Authority (SFA) are constructing an $8 million RLV support complex that will support the Space Shuttle and other RLV and X-vehicles. The facility will include a multipurpose RLV hangar and facilities for ground support equipment and technical support.

NASA's X-33 development will cost $1 billion by the end of the project's 15 test flights, and Lockheed Martin will invest $230 million for the subscale VentureStar test vehicle. That vehicle also will test new technologies, such as the aerospike engine, a hydrogen-cooled engine that will fire its thrusters in a line along 4 feet of copper alloy. The X-33 will be similar to the Space Shuttle in launching vertically and landing horizontally. VentureStar is examining 15 states for potential launch sites for its reusable vehicle. Sites should be selected in early 2001 for initial flights in 2005. Lockheed Martin expects to roll out the vehicle in early 2000, with the first flight in late 2000.

NASA's X-34 test model, built by Orbital Sciences Corporation, made its first captive-carry test flight with its L-1011 aircraft in June 1999. The X-34 is smaller than the X-33 and is designed to carry small payloads comparable to those carried on Orbital's Taurus launch vehicle, but at a much lower cost. Russian NK-39 engines are being considered to reduce the cost. NASA and Orbital Sciences would like to reduce the turnaround times on the follow-on RLV to 24 hours. The contract is worth $85.7 million to Orbital to design, build, and test fly the vehicle.

In a 50-50 government-industry deal, NASA and Boeing are developing an experimental space plane, the X-37 (formerly known as the Future-X Pathfinder), for a contract worth $173 million. The vehicle could be ferried into orbit by the Space Shuttle or launched by an EELV. NASA hopes that the vehicle will be able to do everything from in-orbit satellite repair to becoming a next-generation reusable vehicle. The project will explore new technologies in thermal protection systems, nontoxic liquid propellants, and new aerodynamic features. Plans include the ability to remain in orbit up to 21 days to perform experiments before returning to earth. The first unpowered drop test is planned for fall 2001, with two orbital tests scheduled for 2002.

The private company Kistler Aerospace remains the farthest along in the development of a reusable vehicle with its K-1 rocket. The K-1 will use Russian NK-33 rocket engines in its first and second stages. Once those stages separate, the first stage will fly back to the launch site on its own and use parachutes and air bags to land. Kistler hopes to have the first stages ready for another use after only 2 weeks. The second stage will continue its ascent to deliver the payload and then return to the launch site to be used again. Kistler also is interested in launching from the Woomera launch range in southern Australia. Currently, Northrop Grumman is under contract to build structures for the K-1 vehicle. Kistler expects to charge approximately $17 million per launch. Kistler has raised approximately $450 million but is still shy of the amount needed. Taiwan would like to invest $50 million in future development of the K-1, and Kistler would like to see Taiwan raise up to $200 million for the project.

The Rotary Rocket Company's Roton rocket will launch like a rocket with kerosene instead of hydrogen fuel to cut costs by as much at 90 percent. After deploying the satellite, the Roton will use rocket-tipped helicopter blades to slow the vehicle for landing. The craft will be piloted by a two-person crew and is planned to have a first launch by summer 2000. Roton's demonstrator had its first test flight in July 1999 and proved the flight simulator technology.

Kelly Space & Technology has designed the Eclipse three-stage reusable launch vehicle, which will be towed to 20,000 feet behind a Boeing B747. At that point, the Astroliner, the third stage, will rise to more than 75 miles and the pilots will release the payload with a small rocket booster attached to deliver the satellite to its orbit. The Astroliner will return to the runway, just as the Space Shuttle does. If Kelly is able to get financing, the Astroliner is scheduled for its first launch in 2002.

Pioneer Rocketplane is specially designing the Pathfinder RLV, which would use conventional jet engines to rendezvous with a tanker between 15,000 and 30,000 feet. It would fill its rocket propellant tanks with liquid oxygen that would carry the plane to altitudes up to 120 miles. At that point, it would release a satellite with an expendable upper-stage rocket. Costs would be reduced by fueling in space, which would reduce the weight of the vehicle. Pioneer would like to hold its first launch in 2002.

Other unique ventures include Space Access LLC's development of a multistage reusable launch system that features aircraftlike first-stage power supplied by ejector ramjets. The firm is in the preliminary design phase but plans to test a full-size vehicle in 2001, with commercial launches beginning in 2002. Beal Aerospace hopes to launch semireusable three-stage rockets from Sombrero Island in the Caribbean.

Industry and Trade Projections for the Next 1 and 5 Years

As a result of the many delays in 1998 and 1999, launch manifests are booked, and so launch providers will operate at maximum capacity for at least the next 2 years. Continued demand for satellite services will allow this strong performance to continue through the next 5 years as new satellite communications constellations are readied for launch. Demand may level off slightly in 2001–2002 as some satellite systems require only maintenance of their systems rather than the launching of new satellites. Small launch vehicles will see steady performance because of the market for launching scientific and remote sensing satellites as well as replacement LEO launches. The small launch vehicle/satellite market has continued to develop more slowly than expected. This is causing damage to small launcher programs, such as Athena, which cannot rely solely on government contracts to maintain thriving programs.

In 1997, for the first time, commercial launches outnumbered government ones, and this trend will accelerate in the next decade. The growing commercial satellite market is spurring investment in new launch vehicles and increased capability. It is hoped that this investment will decrease launch costs over the long run. Most observers believe that the high cost of launch is inhibiting many scientific programs and that if costs were lowered, more programs would be more viable. As LEO satellites grow smaller and GEO satellites grow larger, launch providers will have to address both ends of this spectrum to meet the market's demands.

SATELLITE COMMUNICATIONS SYSTEMS

Satellite communications systems can be divided into two categories: the space and ground segments. The space segment includes satellite and satellite subsystems that are placed in orbit around the earth. The satellite itself consists of several major components, including transponders or channels, a power system (battery modules and solar panels), an antenna system, a command and control system, and satellite housing. The ground segment includes equipment used to receive and/or transmit signals to satellites in orbit and everything from large earth stations used for tracking, telemetry, and control of the satellite to dishes as small as 18 to 24 inches that are used by consumers to receive direct broadcast satellite services.

Global Industry Trends: Space Segment

GEO Satellites. In many ways, the 46-year cold war between the United States and the Soviet Union (1945–1991) was responsible for the development of satellite technology. As early as 1950, the U.S. government began secret research to develop a series of spy satellites. Although satellites were traditionally the purview of governments attempting to develop advanced reconnaissance satellites, the technology soon was developed to use satellites for a variety of telecommunications services. The launch of the world's first commercial satellite, INTELSAT 1 (also known as "Early Bird"), in April 1965 marked the advent of a new age in telecommunications. To this day, many countries enter the satellite manufacturing business for the sole purpose of developing satellite reconnaissance capabilities. Governments worldwide still play a role in spurring advances in this technology by encouraging private companies, either directly or indirectly, to improve satellite information-gathering capabilities.

There were approximately 200 commercial communications satellites in GEO, carrying some 4,500 transponders, in April 1999. The geostationary orbit is the orbit 22,237 miles above the earth at which a satellite appears to move at the same rotational speed as the surface of the earth, therefore appearing to stay "fixed" over a specific place. Since the launch of the first satellite in 1957, satellites traditionally have been placed in this orbit to provide the most efficient global service. A transponder is an electronic component of a satellite that shifts the frequency of an uplink signal and amplifies it for retransmission to the earth in a downlink. *Via Satellite* reports that there are 56 more GEO satellites on order, and this will make 1,800 additional transponders available in the near future. The number of GEO contracts signed annually has been declining from a peak of 36 in 1995 (there were 25 contracts in 1996 and 21 in 1997). Thirty-one commercial satellites were ordered in 1998, although it remains to be seen how many actually will be produced.

Despite these strong numbers, 1998 was a difficult year for satellite manufacturers. *Via Satellite* reports that there were 24 in-orbit satellite anomalies or failures, resulting in approximately $1.4 billion in insurance claims. In the United States, the most notable failure occurred in May 1998, when a Hughes Galaxy 4 satellite experienced difficulties and the outage affected almost

90 percent of U.S. paging companies. Satellite manufacturing companies, which are increasingly concerned about in-orbit performance, are taking longer periods to produce satellites and delaying scheduled launches. In the United States, new export licensing procedures are making it more difficult for companies to establish firm satellite production and delivery targets.

Despite these short-term difficulties, advances in technology and new applications for satellites ensure that the market for GEO satellites will not diminish greatly in the near term and that overall growth in the global satellite manufacturing industry will continue to expand. Satellites traditionally have been used to provide voice and telecommunications services, but new applications such as DBS services, mobile telephone services, Internet access, and data broadcasting will expand their use significantly. According to analysts at J.P. Morgan, capacity saturation in the west coupled with economic challenges in the east will lead to a reduction in satellite manufacturing in the next 2 to 3 years. By 2002, however, a new growth cycle is expected to begin as replacement satellites are ordered, further telecommunications deregulation occurs, and strong economic recoveries take hold in Latin America and the Far East.

According to a market survey completed by Euroconsult in March 1998, the world's satellite operators will order approximately 300 GEO satellites over the next 10 years (approximately 30 orders per year). These satellites are valued at an estimated $30 billion to $38 billion. Euroconsult notes that nearly 500 non-GEO satellites were under contract as of February 1998, but it is unclear how many of those satellites will be launched. Over the last few years, a wide variety of systems have been proposed to offer many similar satellite-based services. As a result of regulatory hurdles, increased competition, and financing needs, many of these systems may not be implemented.

Although the United States dominates the world market for large GEO satellites and is among the leaders in the market for the new smaller satellites that will be used in LEO and medium earth orbit (MEO) systems, U.S. manufacturers face challenges from the consolidation of satellite competitors in Europe, up-and-coming manufacturers in Japan that are increasingly taking on the responsibility of being a prime contractor, and U.S. government export controls that provide incentives for global customers to purchase satellites from non-U.S. companies.

U.S. industry perceives that U.S. government export controls continue to affect the ability of U.S. companies to enter into joint venture projects overseas. On March 15, 1999, licensing authority for commercial communications satellites was officially transferred from the U.S. Commerce Department's Bureau of Export Administration to the U.S. State Department's Office of Defense Trade Controls, as mandated by the National Defense Authorization Act. This shift in authority has resulted in a much more stringent export control regime and has had a significant effect on the ability of U.S. companies to compete for major international projects. As many countries attempt to develop their own satellite manufacturing capabilities, export controls and technology transfer issues are having a significant impact on the ability of U.S. companies to enter into joint ventures with government and private entities in countries such as Russia and China.

The strongest competition for U.S. manufacturers for GEO commercial communications satellite contracts comes from European manufacturers. Tremendous consolidation in the European satellite industry has created formidable competition for U.S. companies such as Hughes Electronics, Lockheed Martin, and Space Systems/Loral. In mid-1998, the Paris-based Aerospatiale merged with Matra Marconi Space (also based in France), forming Aerospatiale-Matra. It is expected that Aerospatiale-Matra eventually will acquire the space divisions of DaimlerChrysler Aerospace (Germany) and Alenia Aerospazio (Italy). The new French-German-British-Italian entity is expected to be named Astrium. While plans for these mergers have been announced, all the relevant regulatory approvals must be obtained before the new entity is completely integrated. It also will take considerable effort to consolidate operations, employees, and business plans. The other major player in Europe will be Alcatel Space, which purchased Aerospatiale's spacecraft business in July 1998. Alcatel Space reported 1998 revenue of $1.85 billion and is ranked among the largest satellite manufacturers in the world. Alcatel is set to build satellites or satellite payloads for SkyBridge, WorldSpace, and XM Satellite Radio. U.S. companies have been in direct competition with these companies in numerous tenders for satellites in Europe and the Middle East.

Countries such as Japan, Russia, Canada, India, China, and Israel are active in the manufacture of communications satellites for domestic use. They also export parts, components, and subassemblies to U.S. satellite manufacturers.

Japan. Japan continues to pose a serious competitive challenge to U.S. manufacturers of advanced components and parts. In Japan, Mitsubishi Electric Corp., NEC, and Toshiba produce internationally competitive satellite components but have not yet served as primary contractors for complete satellites. The government of Japan has funded a satellite called the Unmanned Space Experiment Recovery System (USERS), which will give Mitsubishi significant experience in integrating satellite components. The satellite is scheduled to be launched in 2002. Mitsubishi is also coordinating the construction of the Optus C1 satellite for Australia's Cable & Wireless Optus. It hopes to obtain work on other commercial satellite projects that will allow it to grow into the role of a prime contractor. Japan's Ministry of International Trade recently announced that it is accepting bids for another experimental satellite, the Space Environment Reliability Verification Integrated System (SERVIS), to reduce that country's satellite production costs and delivery schedules, making Japanese companies more competitive in the commercial satellite business. Many analysts believe that these companies will have the ability to manufacture GEO commercial communications satellites in the next 5 years. In February 1999, the Japan Forum on Satellite Communications was initiated to ensure better collaboration in Japan's satellite industry. The forum includes Mitsubishi Electric Corp., NEC Corp., Toshiba Corp., Fujitsu Corp., NTT Satellite Communications, Japan Satellite Systems, and Space Communications. One of its goals is to collaborate in an effort to compete better in international markets.

Russia. Russia has a significant domestic satellite manufacturing capacity, although its satellite industry has suffered enormously as that country makes the transition to a market economy. Employment in the industry has fallen to record lows, and a lack of financial resources has led to deteriorating manufacturing facilities. Russia has built many satellites for domestic use, although it has not been as successful in selling its satellites to overseas customers. Nauchno-Proivzvodstvenoe Obiedinenie Prikladnoi Mekhaniki (NPO-PM) is the leading designer of Russian satellites, and RSC Energiya, NPO Lovachkin, and JSC Gascom also are involved in satellite manufacturing. Russia is eager to upgrade its satellite manufacturing technology and capabilities and has encouraged partnerships with foreign companies to accomplish that goal. RSC Energiya is planning to construct four satellites using the Yamal design, with some components from NEC of Japan and Space Systems/Loral. NPO-PM is said to be working with Alcatel Space and Aerospatiale of France to build two additional satellites. In 1999, Russia was said to be in talks with Korea regarding a proposal to jointly develop and manufacture telecommunications and remote sensing satellites.

Canada. In 1998, Spar of Canada retreated from the satellite manufacturing business, selling off most of its satellite-related businesses. In that year, Spar sold Comstream, Astro Aerospace, and its satellite products division. It has been reported that Spar decided to get out of the satellite business because of tough competition from the United States and Europe as well changing Canadian government dynamics. MacDonald Dettweiler of British Columbia is a wholly owned subsidiary of Orbital Sciences of Virginia.

India. According to a Euroconsult survey entitled "Government Space Programs," the Indian government has increased its space budget more than 50 percent since 1996. India is developing its own rocket series and is building third-generation communications satellites (Insat 3). The first Insat 3 was expected to be launched in late 1999. Government investment in satellite manufacturing eventually will lead to a strong commercial satellite business in India. In June 1999, the Indian Space Research Organization (ISRO) bid on a contract to build a new communications satellite for Iran. ISRO is competing with satellite manufacturers from France, Russia, and China for that $500 million project.

China, Taiwan, Israel, and South Africa. The Chinese Academy of Space Technology (CAST), established in 1968, reports that it has developed and launched 40 satellites, including communications, meteorology, earth exploration, and experimental scientific satellites. CAST reportedly is marketing its platform for commercial use and anticipates greater commercial sales in the next millennium. Israeli Aircraft Industries (IAI) was designated by the Israel Space Agency as the prime contractor for that country's space programs and will continue to develop lightweight GEO satellites, LEO surveillance satellites, and earth remote sensing observation satellites. IAI developed and manufactured the *AMOS-1* communications satellite in cooperation with DASA of Germany and Alcatel Space of France. IAI is also an investor in the Ellipso mobile satellite project, which is scheduled to launch service in 2002. Taiwan is hoping to become more involved in satellite manufacturing through the Republic of China (*Rocsat*) program. Although TRW was heavily involved in the manufacture of *Rocsat 1,* Taiwan's National Space Program Office plans to take on a larger role in *Rocsat 2* and *Rocsat 3.* In February 1999, the first South African–designed and –produced satellite (*Sunsat*) was launched by NASA from Vandenberg Air Force Base in California. *Sunsat* will be used for environmental research purposes.

Although contracts from international treaty organizations such as the International Telecommunications Satellite Organization (INTELSAT) and the International Mobile Satellite Organization (INMARSAT) and from U.S. and foreign government entities continued to represent a significant portion of the satellite market in 1998, contracts from privately owned customers are on the rise. This increase can be attributed to some extent to the trend toward privatization of telecommunications institutions in many areas of the world. A new private entity, New Skies Satellites, was created in 1998 from a spin-off of five of INTELSAT's satellites. The complete privatization of INTELSAT has been a topic of much debate in the U.S. Congress and among INTELSAT members. It is expected that INTELSAT will be fully privatized at some point in the 2001–2002 period. INMARSAT completed its privatization on April 15, 1999.

According to information from *Via Satellite,* of the 200 commercial communications satellites in GEO orbit, 24 percent serve the Asia-Pacific region, 23 percent serve Europe, 20 percent serve North America, 5 percent serve Latin America, and 6 percent serve the Middle East and north Africa. The remaining 22 percent serve the transatlantic, trans–Indian Ocean, and transpacific regions. WorldSpace launched its Afristar satellite in October 1998 to provide digital audio broadcasting services to the African region. It is one of the first satellites to be dedicated solely to Africa, and service was initiated in October 1999. The Regional Satellite Communications Organization (RASCOM) is reportedly in talks with Alcatel regarding a satellite that would provide communications, television and radio services to Africa. South Africa is said to be studying a plan to purchase its own satellite. Although the Asia-Pacific region leads the world in the number of satellites, the financial crisis and the impact of export control issues has had a dampening effect. Many observers view the impact as temporary, stating that the demand for rural telephony and telecommunications services is so great that satellites will certainly play a role in the region. The temporary economic downturn in the Asia-Pacific region has generated renewed interest in Latin America. Developments such as the rapid growth of direct-to-home (DTH) services in the region and the trend toward deregulation ensure that Latin America will offer significant opportunities in the long term.

Non-GEO Satellites. With advances in satellite technology, the number of manufacturers of small satellites has increased. These satellites orbit the earth at much lower altitudes (500 to 1,000 miles, as opposed to 4,000 to 7,000 miles for MEO and 22,237 miles for GEO). As satellites have become much more powerful and orbit much closer to earth, the reception device does not need to be as powerful and is therefore much more compact. Instead of the larger earth stations that are necessary to receive signals directly from a GEO satellite, hand-held cellularlike phones can easily receive signals from a LEO or MEO satellite. U.S. manufacturers of these smaller satellites include Boeing, Motorola, Orbital Sciences, Spectrum Astro, and TRW. As companies rush to offer services using LEO and MEO satellites, the market for these smaller satellites will grow tremendously. For example, the Teledesic system, which promises to offer broadband services including Internet, two-way videoconferencing, and telemedicine services in 2004, plans to build 176 satellites over the next 5 years to operate its service (see the section on satellite services for an in-depth discussion of these systems). The small satellite market forecast will be influenced by the future of systems such as Teledesic. Teledesic has continually scaled back the number of satellites for its system. Originally, Teledesic planned 840 satellites, then 288, then 176, and further reductions have been predicted.

A clear trend toward truly global ventures has emerged in the market for smaller satellites for use in LEO and MEO systems. As providers try to find the best technology, the lowest prices, and guaranteed access to markets all over the world, U.S. and foreign companies have formed numerous partnerships. Globalstar, for example, has established strategic partnerships with DACOM/Hyundai (Korea), France Telecom/Alcatel, Daimler-Benz (Germany), and Alenia Spazio (Italy). Major components of the Globalstar satellites were built at Loral's facilities in northern California, but final assembly and testing of the satellites was done in Italy by Alenia Spazio. As an increasing number of international ventures are created, it is becoming more difficult to identify precisely the U.S. contribution to many of these ventures. However, the United States is still considered the world leader in the advanced technologies that are critical to the success of these projects.

Satellite manufacturing and sales were tremendously strong in the 1990s. Although many observers predicted that satellites would lose out to fiber optics in the late 1980s and early 1990s, satellites have been resilient because of the inherently global "instant" infrastructure they provide. In fact, according to *Via Satellite,* more GEO satellites were launched in the 1990s than in the past three decades combined. Numerous research reports indicate the strength of the worldwide commercial satellite industry, but it is important to consider several factors before forecasting growth in this sector over the next 5 years: continued competition from both wireline and other wireless technologies, more advanced satellites with longer lifetimes that will not need to be replaced as often, large up-front investment requirements, the significant risks inherent in launching highly sophisticated equipment into space, and the need to surmount the domestic and international regulatory hurdles operators face in trying to offer global service. As the number of commercial satellites in orbit increases, the allocation of valuable orbital slots and parts of the radiofrequency spectrum becomes more challenging. The International Telecommunication Union (ITU), which is part of the United Nations, provides an international forum for the coordination of slots and parts of the spectrum. It has become increasingly difficult to ensure that adequate frequencies are available for the large number of satellite services that companies are promising to provide.

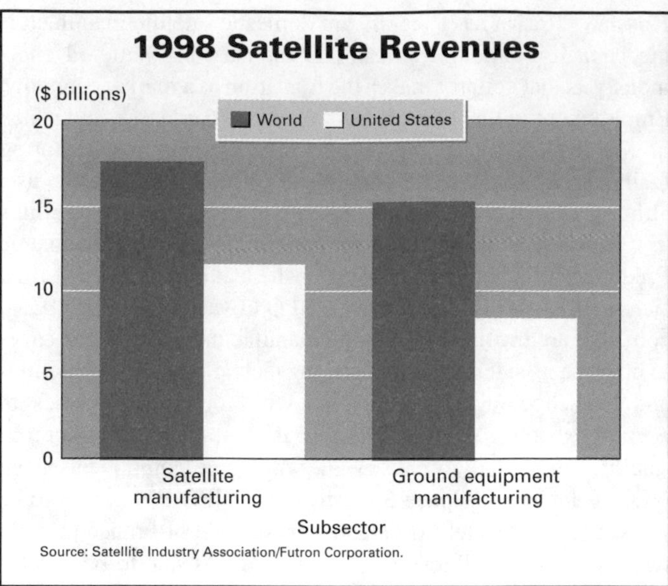

FIGURE 29-3

Domestic Trends: Space Segment

Despite recent in-orbit satellite malfunctions and the impact of changes in U.S. export control regulations, the United States continues to lead the world in satellite manufacturing. Hughes Space and Communications (Hughes), Lockheed Martin Telecommunications (Lockheed Martin), and Space Systems/Loral (SS/L) are the top three manufacturers of traditional commercial communications satellites built for operation in geostationary orbit. While Hughes, Lockheed Martin, and SS/L remain the key U.S. players in the manufacture of large communications satellites, Boeing, Motorola, Orbital Sciences, Spectrum Astro, and TRW are gaining increased recognition for the manufacture of smaller satellites that will be used for a variety of emerging satellite services. A Satellite Industry Association (SIA)/Futron Corporation report estimates that in 1998, the United States had approximately 65.3 percent of the global satellite manufacturing market ($11.5 billion of $17.6 billion, including payments to subcontractors) (Figure 29-3). The report also notes that satellite manufacturing supported approximately 64,100 jobs in the United States in 1998.

According to *Via Satellite*'s "1998 Global Satellite Survey," Hughes has built more than one-third of the GEO satellites in orbit and has contracted to build more than a quarter of those under construction. With regard to satellites in orbit, Hughes has 37 percent, Lockheed Martin has 17 percent, and SS/L has 12 percent (foreign manufacturers account for the remaining 34 percent). With regard to satellites under construction, Hughes has 25 percent, Lockheed Martin has 20 percent, and SS/L has 25 percent. Lockheed Martin and SS/L are strong competitors and will continue to challenge Hughes's leadership in this area.

The manufacturing of GEO satellites is highly capital-intensive, and the process does not lend itself easily to new competitors. Lockheed Martin, Hughes, and SS/L have upgraded their satellite manufacturing facilities over the past few years to implement more efficient "modular" manufacturing practices. This involves reducing complexity by lowering the number of parts and part types, simplifying design and testing procedures, moving toward assemblylike products, using common buses, and tailoring user payloads. Implementation of these procedures has resulted in lower costs as well as reductions in the length of time it takes to manufacture a large GEO satellite from more than 30 months to 18 to 24 months. The pressure to reduce production times has in some cases led to quality control problems that many analysts argue were the cause of several in-orbit satellite failures in the last year. As a result of the high-profile failures that have tarnished the industry's reputation, many manufacturers have recommitted to a focus on quality and reliability. It will be interesting to see how companies balance the need to deliver larger, more complex, longer-lasting satellites in short time frames with the need to ensure quality and dependability.

As a result of customs tracking procedures, U.S. government statistics for exports of communications satellites (HS 8802.60 .3000) are representative only of the countries where satellites are launched. Since only certain countries have commercial communications satellite launch facilities, the statistics are not meaningful in tracking the number of satellites that are sold to entities in foreign countries. According to Figure 29-4, U.S. "exports" (i.e., foreign sales) of GEO commercial communications satellites (based on estimated ranges of contract values for foreign customers) was between $690 million and $805 million in 1998.

Satellite Parts and Components

U.S. manufacturers contribute technology to many of the commercial communications satellites made today. U.S. government trade statistics indicate a continued positive trade balance for U.S.-made parts for communications satellites (HS

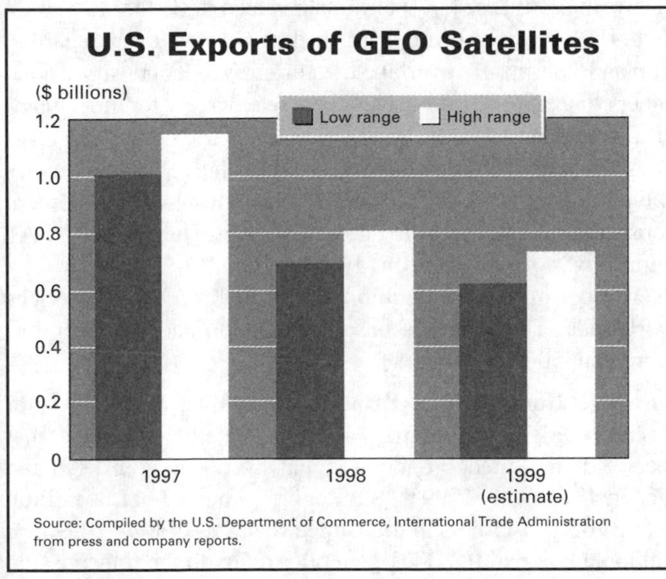

FIGURE 29-4

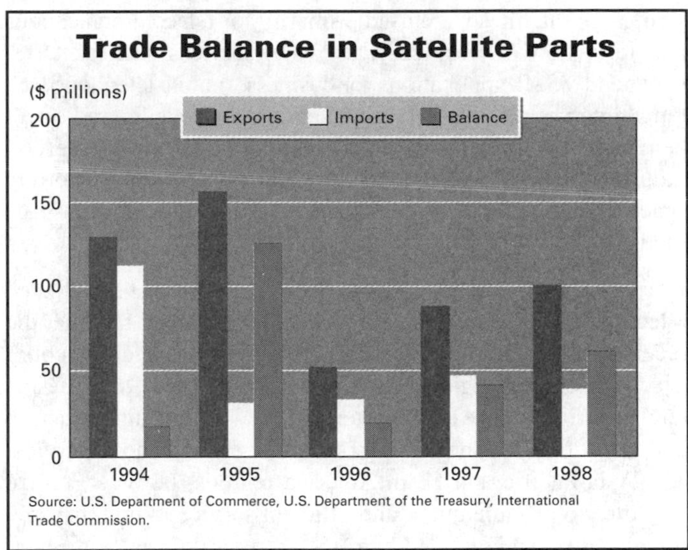

FIGURE 29-5

8803.90.3000) from 1994 to 1998. U.S. exports of satellite parts totaled $100 million in 1998, up from $88 million in 1997. Nonetheless, U.S. exports have fallen dramatically from a peak of $156 million in 1995. This drop in exports of satellite parts can be attributed to several factors, including an increase in the technological capabilities of manufacturers in other countries (see Figure 29-5). In addition, U.S. industry perceives that stricter enforcement of U.S. export controls may affect the ability of U.S. manufacturers to sell to foreign customers. It is expected that U.S. exports of satellite parts may decline sharply in 1999 but should see some recovery in 2000 as export licensing issues are addressed more effectively.

GROUND SEGMENT

The satellite ground equipment industry includes manufacturers of large fixed earth stations; complex telemetry, tracking, and control (TT&C) equipment; very small aperture terminals (VSATs), direct broadcast satellite (DBS) dishes; and smaller mobile receivers. An earth station is a piece of equipment that can send or receive a satellite signal and consists of an antenna, a low-noise amplifier, a down-converter, and receiver electronics. The high end is represented by large earth stations that cost between $1 million and $10 million, and the low end by DBS receivers priced as low as $199. In the middle, VSATs are priced between $3,000 and $15,000.

Global Trends: Ground Segment

Euroconsult estimates that 21.4 million earth stations were sold worldwide in 1996, accounting for about $18 billion in total annual sales. Euroconsult predicts that 108.7 million earth stations will be sold in 2006, with revenues of over $46 billion (see Table 29-2). The growth in this market can be attributed to several factors: technological improvements that have led to smaller, less expensive, and more sophisticated equipment; global deregulation; and new satellite applications that have translated into higher demand for equipment to utilize satellite technology. Ten years ago, satellites were used primarily for telecommunications and television delivery services. New services such as DBS, expanded VSAT applications for business, mobile telephone systems, Internet protocol (IP) applications, and satellite radio will help boost the ground equipment market to new heights. Several industry analysts note that the ground segment for supporting space systems is one of the largest single markets in the space industry and is typically the most underestimated.

Large Earth Stations. Large earth stations used for "fixed" telecommunications services ("fixed" refers to the fact that the receiver is not mobile) are still in demand in developing countries. Developed regions such as North America and Europe tend to utilize the extensive terrestrial wireline infrastructure and do not rely as heavily on satellites for telephone service. The Asia-Pacific and Latin America regions, however, utilize satellites to provide quick and efficient service to both densely populated urban areas and hard-to-reach rural areas. Some analysts predict that satellite-delivered telephone services will decrease in popularity as the terrestrial infrastructure develops in those areas. Although many regions are still in dire need of telecommunications services (including India, China, and Africa), satellites do not always provide the lowest-cost solution. Euroconsult predicts that 759,635 fixed telecommunications earth stations, or 62 percent of the world total, will be sold in regions other than North America and Europe by 2006.

Some of the largest gateway manufacturers include Hughes Network Systems, NEC, IDB Systems Corporation, Scientific Atlanta, and Stanford Telecommunications. In 1998, there was a tremendous amount of merger and consolidation activity in the earth station industry. Although Hughes Network Systems (HNS) remains one of the largest players, several companies are gearing up to take on that company. Recent activity includes Gilat's purchase of GE Spacenet; L-3's purchase of STS (a division of California Microwave), Essco, Storm, Microdyne, and Aydin; the merger of Trexcom and LNR; the merger of Radyne and ComStream; the merger of RSI and Prodelin to form Tripoint Global Communications; and the purchase of Matra Marconi's civil ground segment by Globecomm. These mergers and acquisitions reflect a trend toward product integration and efforts to enter overseas markets.

The advent of mobile satellite services spurred the market for large earth stations in 1998 as companies such as Iridium and Globalstar constructed large earth stations to connect signals from satellites to terrestrial networks. Scientific Atlanta constructed 57 global gateways for Iridium, and Qualcomm is the prime contractor for the construction of the 38 gateways for Globalstar. As of August 1999, Globalstar had 8 gateways in operation, with 16 additional gateways to be activated by the end of 1999 and all 38 to be on-line by mid-2000. As Iridium struggles to restructure its business and the mobile satellite services industry undergoes a degree of consolidation, demand for these types of gateways may decrease in the short term.

TABLE 29-2: World Satellite Communications Ground Equipment Market in 1986, 1996, and 2006

Year	1986	1996	2006
Annual sales (units)*	510,000	21.4 million	108.7 million
Annual sales ($)*	$2.48 billion	$18.13 billion	$46.28 billion
Average price ($)	$4,860	$850	$425

* On average.
Source: Euroconsult, May 1997.

Telemetry, tracking, and control (TT&C) systems are used to monitor the operations of a satellite. Telemetry involves reporting the status of satellite systems, such as voltage, current, temperature, and transponder configuration. Tracking equipment is used to enable controllers to locate a satellite's exact position and track the direction of the antennas. Control equipment entails sending commands to a satellite to operate systems, configure transponders and antennas, and perform orbital maneuvers such as adjusting the position of a satellite in orbit.

Very Small Aperture Terminals. A VSAT is a small earth station, usually a satellite dish between 1.2 and 2.4 meters in diameter, that is used to provide one-way or two-way narrowcast transmission of video, voice, and data to a satellite. VSATs are most commonly used for business applications. Growth in this segment can be attributed to several factors, including the development of new VSAT applications such as credit authorization, electronic payment systems, transmission of sales and pricing information between retail outlets and headquarters sites, travel- and financial-related services, hotel and motel management, automatic tellers, and real-time inventory control. Other factors that will contribute positively to the growth of the industry include price reductions, technological advancements, and the demand for greater bandwidth. The world's largest VSAT equipment manufacturers include HNS, Scientific Atlanta, NEC, Fujitsu, Bosch Telecom, and Gilat Satellite Networks. C.E. Unterberg, Towbin, a Wall Street investment analysis firm, notes that HNS and Gilat Satellite Networks account for more than 80 percent of VSAT business. In 1999, those two companies publicly battled for a large contract to provide VSATs to BP Amoco that was said to be involve more than 24,000 terminals valued at $1,000 to $3,000 each. HNS emerged triumphant, dealing Gilat a blow in regard to its plan to ultimately overtake the current VSAT industry leader. Other companies in the business compete fiercely for the remaining 20 percent.

According to C.E. Unterberg, Towbin, the VSAT market was valued at over $1 billion in 1999 and will have a 22 percent compound annual growth rate until 2003. The Global VSAT Forum was established in 1998 to combat regulatory and license constraints that inhibit the growth of VSAT services worldwide. The forum is based in London and currently has more than 50 members.

Direct to Home, Direct Broadcast Satellite, and Television Receive-Only Equipment. Sales of satellite antennas that receive digital direct broadcast signals were strong in 1998 and the first half of 1999. "SkyReport" counted 11.6 million DTH/DBS subscribers in the United States as of May 1999 (1.8 million are C-band). (DTH generally refers to the transmission of television signals directly to satellite dishes placed outside viewers' homes. DBS is considered a subset of the DTH industry and refers to service delivered by a high-power satellite that requires smaller satellite dishes. Many people use the two terms interchangeably.) C.E. Unterberg, Towbin predicts that DTH households in the United States will number 21 million in 2005 and approach 24 million in 2007. Worldwide subscribers of DTH totaled 39.6 million in 1998, according to "SkyReport," and many analysts expect tremendous growth in Asia and Latin America. DTH services include transmission of signals to both large C-band dishes and smaller 18- to 24-inch dishes. Although these DBS services face stiff competition from the cable industry and in the future from digital cable, many observers predict that this segment of the industry, and thus the equipment necessary to utilize these services, will continue to grow.

U.S. government statistics show that the United States had a negative trade balance in television receive-only (TVRO) equipment, the only category in the ground equipment sector for which data are available, from 1994 to 1998. The trade deficit in TVRO deteriorated to $336 million in 1998 from $127 million in 1997. The negative trade balance in this area can be attributed in large part to the competitive strength of Asian manufacturers of these products (see Figure 29-6). Although sales of DBS equipment will continue to be strong, the main producers of these products reside outside the United States.

U.S. manufacturers of DTH equipment include Thomson Consumer Electronics, HNS, and Channel Master. General Instrument Corp. no longer produces DBS hardware for consumers in North America after losing a contract with its major customer, PrimeStar. DirecTV announced plans to acquire PrimeStar in January 1999. Japanese manufacturers include Hitachi, Mitsubishi, Toshiba, Sony, and JVC. Philips Electronics, which is owned by Royal Philips Electronics of the Netherlands, is also a major player in the DTH equipment market. The DTH equipment sector has seen a steep drop in equipment prices since the introduction of these services in 1994. Originally totaling $699 a set, prices have dropped to as low as $199.

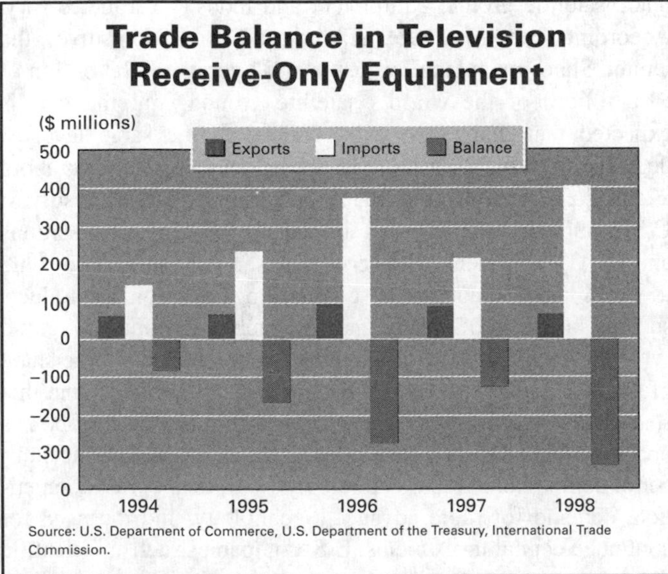

Source: U.S. Department of Commerce, U.S. Department of the Treasury, International Trade Commission.

FIGURE 29-6

Two primary components are necessary for satellite television: the 18- to 24-inch dish placed outside the home and the set-top box (or integrated receiver-decoder) that sits on top of the television set. The manufacture of these components is highly competitive, and service providers frequently subsidize the equipment to gain subscribers and earn monthly service fees. Prices for this type of equipment have been driven down by competition in the service market, as service providers have forced equipment prices to fall below actual costs. There is, however, high potential for growth in the satellite television industry, ensuring a large future market for this equipment.

Mobile Services Equipment. With the advent of several new services, prices for commercial mobile satellite services and handsets have decreased substantially. Recent figures put unit sales of INMARSAT's mini-M laptop-sized mobile satellite phones at about 50,000 since they were introduced in July 1997. These telephones cost approximately $3,000, with charges starting at about $2.70 per minute. Manufacturers of the mini-M phones include KVH (United States), NEC (Japan), NERA (Norway), and Thrane (Denmark). INMARSAT's mini-M is facing competition from Iridium and Globalstar which offer mobile telephone services with hand-held phones.

Sales of mobile handsets should increase as companies such as Globalstar, ICO, and several regional systems roll out their services over the next 2 to 4 years. These services will allow customers to use hand-held cellularlike phones to make and receive telephone calls anywhere on earth. Iridium launched service in November 1998 with somewhat disappointing results. As of May 1999, Iridium reportedly had sold fewer than 11,000 phones, far below the 100,000 it had estimated it would sell by the end of 1998. Manufacturers of Iridium handsets include Motorola and Kyocera (Japan). Globalstar was expected to launch partial service in October 1999 and estimated that 35,000 handsets would be available by fall 1999 and a total of 100,000 by the end of that year. Globalstar's handsets are being made by Ericsson, Qualcomm, and Telital. ICO is expected to launch service in 2000, and its handsets will be produced by HNS, Matsushita, Mitsubishi, NEC, Samsung, and NERA. Frost & Sullivan predicts that spending on mobile satellite earth stations (including hand-held phones and computer receivers) will grow to $6.4 billion in 2001, with sales of over 3 million mobile stations.

Under the auspices of the ITU, there has been an attempt to facilitate common procedures among countries for licensing, marking, customs, and type approval of handsets and terminals for mobile satellite systems. This effort has been formalized in the Global Mobile Personal Communications by Satellite (GMPCS) Memorandum of Understanding (MoU). Currently, 129 entities (including governments, operators, service providers, and manufacturers) are signatories to the MoU. It is hoped that this agreement will increase mobile satellite phone use by ensuring that customers can bring their handsets across borders freely.

Mobile services for paging, messaging, tracking, and data (referred to as Little LEOs) are expected to be offered by a number of companies, such as ORBCOMM, LEO One USA, E-Sat, and Final Analysis, in the next several years. ORBCOMM was the first to offer two-way data and messaging services, initiating service in 1998. C.E. Unterberg, Towbin estimated that ORBCOMM would ship almost 200,000 terminals by the end of 1999, at a cost of approximately $400 each. Pagers and other equipment necessary for the rollout of these services will increase over the next several years. A surge in sales of satellite telephones and pagers is expected as companies seek unconventional ways of maintaining communications links during the Y2K transition period.

Global Positioning System. Sales of receivers using the U.S. GPS constellation of radio-emitting satellites for location, tracking, and timing services are expected to continue to grow rapidly in the next 5 years. U.S. companies involved in the GPS equipment market include Garmin, Honeywell, Magellan (a unit of Orbital Sciences), Motorola, Rockwell, Trimble Navigation, and the NOMOS Corporation. GPS is used for a variety of different industrial and consumer applications. Although industrial market GPS applications such as surveying and aircraft navigation have been growing steadily, the consumer market for GPS has shown dramatic growth. Consumer applications such as car navigation and hand-held GPS receivers used for fishing, camping, hunting, and other outdoor sports have taken off as prices have decreased. Hand-held GPS receivers sell for as little as $100.

The recent decision by the U.S. Federal Communications Commission to require cellular and personal communications services (PCS) networks to incorporate enhanced 911 (E-911) features such as caller location by the year 2001 will ensure that GPS consumer applications will increase. Cellular and PCS handset manufacturers are already incorporating GPS into their equipment in anticipation of E-911 implementation.

Car navigation systems such as OnStar, PathMaster, and Guidestar cost from $1,000 to $2,500 and are one of the fastest-growing segments of the GPS market. GPS car navigation systems are now installed in many luxury and rental car vehicles, but it is expected that they will soon become standard in many midpriced vehicles. Some analysts predict that car navigation systems will be a standard option for most U.S. vehicles and trucks in the next 3 years. Japan already has a large market for car navigation equipment, and it continues to grow.

A recent report by Allied Business Intelligence (ABI) predicts that the commercial market for GPS will be worth $14 billion by 2005. ABI notes that although the United States currently retains 65 percent of the GPS hardware and software market, foreign firms will capture 50 percent of the total market by 2005.

Digital Audio Radio Satellite and Digital Audio Broadcasting Services. Digital audio radio satellite (DARS) services from companies such as CD Radio and XM Satellite Radio (formerly American Mobile Radio Corporation) are expected to increase demand for satellite receiver radios in the United States over the next few years. CD Radio is expected to launch its service in late 2000, with radios manufactured by Panasonic (a division of Matsushita) and Alpine. XM Satellite Radio will initiate service in 2001, and its radios will be manufactured by Pioneer, Sharp, and Alpine. C.E. Unterberg, Towbin estimates that there will be 1.84 million U.S. DARS subscribers in 2001 and 21.5 million in 2005.

WorldSpace planned to offer digital audio broadcasting services (DABS) primarily to developing markets around the world beginning in late 1999. The system will include satellites serving Africa, the Caribbean, Central America and South America, and north, southeast, and west Asia. WorldSpace launched its first satellite, *Afristar,* in October 1998. *Afristar* was slated to begin providing service to customers in South Africa, Kenya, and the Middle East by October 1999. Current estimates place the cost of a WorldSpace radio at about $300. WorldSpace has signed contracts with several Japanese companies for the manufacture of this equipment, including Hitachi, JVC, Sanyo, and Matsushita (Panasonic). WorldSpace anticipates that it will sign up 500,000 subscribers in the first year of service. C.E. Unterberg, Towbin predicts 930,000 international satellite radio subscribers in 2000 and 8.4 million in 2003. Japan's Nihon Mobile (a joint venture involving Toshiba, Toyota Motors, and Fujitsu) is planning to offer satellite radio services to customers throughout Japan beginning in 2001. The company forecasts 2 million subscribers by 2003 and 10 million by 2010. The radios are expected to cost between $1,150 and $1,500.

Many satellite radio manufacturers are outside the United States; thus, growth in this market will benefit foreign consumer electronics companies more than U.S. firms.

While growth in the satellite ground equipment market is solid at this time, competition is intensifying among manufacturers of this equipment. This intense competition is driving manufacturers to lower prices, improve features and performance, differentiate and continually redevelop products, as well as tolerate low profit margins.

Domestic Trends: Ground Segment

There are no official production or revenue statistics for U.S.-made satellite ground equipment, and industry estimates vary. According to the May 1999 SIA/Futron Corporation survey, the United States manufactures just over 54 percent ($8.3 billion of $15 billion) of the world's satellite ground equipment. It is expected that that share will continue at the same level or decrease slightly. The ground equipment industry supports about 22,500 jobs in the United States, according to the same survey. U.S. companies are strong in the market for large earth stations and VSAT equipment, while companies in Asia and Europe tend to excel in the manufacture of consumer electronics products such as smaller DBS dishes and new mobile terminals.

In the early 1990s, U.S. manufacturers retained a large share of the world market for most satellite ground segments, but that share has decreased as competition from Japan and Europe has become more intense. As the industry has grown, so has the number of competitors. Manufacturers face significant price competition, demand for more advanced technology, and the need for continued capital investments. U.S. companies such as Scientific Atlanta and STM Wireless face fierce competition from NEC, Alcatel, and Gilat.

With regard to large earth stations, U.S. companies have benefited from the launch of new mobile satellite systems such as Iridium and Globalstar, although competition from Japanese and European manufacturers is growing for other large projects. While the VSAT market is expected to grow overall, the U.S. share of that market may slip as companies such as NEC, Fujitsu, and Gilat Satellite Networks make inroads in world markets. Although many analysts predict that DBS subscriptions will grow significantly over the next 5 years, manufacturers from Asia have gained a large portion of this equipment market. The United States continues to import more TVRO than it exports, and the imbalance has increased significantly since 1997. The market for mobile handsets and pagers will see significant growth in the next few years as new services for voice, paging, and messaging are introduced. The United States should retain a fair share of this market. Many U.S. companies excel in the production of the higher-technology GPS receivers used for location, tracking, and timing services, although Japanese companies are also strong in this area. The market for satellite receiver radios should increase, although much of that business may go to European and Japanese companies.

Industry and Trade Projections for the Next 1 and 5 Years

The U.S. commercial satellite communications systems industry (both the space and ground segments) generated revenues of $19.8 billion in 1998, according to the SIA/Futron Corporation survey report published in May 1999. The U.S. share represents about 60 percent of world revenue, although future revenues may be affected by new export licensing procedures that make it difficult for U.S. companies to market and sell to overseas customers. Although U.S. satellite component manufacturers strengthened their hold on the market in 1998, the size of the surplus may slip as a result of export licensing issues and technological advances by manufacturers in other countries. The ground segment will retain its current growth level or grow slightly, although there is strong competition in this segment.

The United States will certainly dominate the market for large GEO satellites in 2000, although the consolidation of several companies in Europe may create increased competition in the longer term. Orders for GEO satellites will remain at an average of about 30 per year, while contracts for new and next-generation LEO satellites may not meet previous expectations as initial difficulties in the mobile satellite services sector have weakened the prospects for future systems. In terms of the outlook for the overall commercial satellite manufacturing industry over the next 5 years, an increase in the manufacture of smaller satellites for use in both voice and data systems most likely will balance any potential downturns in the growth of the GEO satellite manufacturing market.

Ground equipment sales will continue to be driven by strong growth in VSATs and DBS in developed regions, while demand for large earth stations for telecommunications services will continue to grow in developing areas. The areas of high growth most likely will continue to be VSATs, DBS, and mobile terminals (including GPS). While the space segment will continue to receive most of the attention, the earth station market is critical to the success of the overall industry. Without equipment to effectively receive signals from satellites, no satellite system can be commercially viable.

Continued international demand, coupled with new applications such as mobile telephony, DBS, satellite radio, satellite messaging, and data services, will sustain U.S. satellite equipment industry revenues through the early part of the next century. Many analysts predict some consolidation as the industry grows, but the United States should continue to have a strong presence in both the space and ground segments.

The U.S. satellite manufacturing industry will continue to dominate the GEO satellite market for the short term, and companies such as Boeing, Motorola, Orbital Sciences, Spectrum Astro, and TRW will continue to represent the United States in the manufacture of smaller, non-GEO satellites. The ground equipment industry will continue to see strong growth as these new applications are rolled out. Although the U.S. industry will see more pronounced competition from overseas competitors and more stringent implementation of export control regulations, U.S. companies should be able to maintain their lead in the space segment and remain competitive in certain segments of the ground equipment market, such as large earth stations, VSAT systems, and GPS receivers.

The future of the industry will rely to some extent on three main factors: deregulation that will allow companies to offer global services, rising demand for telephony and data services, and continued technological developments. Many analysts believe that the ability of companies to overcome regulatory hurdles, coordinate spectrum and orbital slot allocations at the ITU, and work with foreign governments will be key factors in the future success of the industry.

SATELLITE COMMUNICATIONS SERVICES

Satellite telecommunications services include one- and two-way delivery of voice, video, and data via satellite, including international telephone calls, broadcasting, and enhanced data services, to discrete geographic locations. Fixed satellite services (FSS) refer to broadcasting, data transmission, and telephony using fixed earth stations, while mobile satellite services (MSS) utilize mobile receivers, such as cellular-size phones, that can receive and transmit satellite signals. FSS traditionally have accounted for the majority of satellite service revenues, but new mobile services are expected to generate a significant percentage of future earnings.

Global Trends

There are no official U.S. government data on satellite service revenues. According to SIA/Futron Corporation, revenues from global satellite services (both fixed and mobile) amounted to $26.2 billion in 1998, up from the 1997 adjusted figure of $21.2 billion. The United States accounted for $7.4 billion, or 28 percent, of that total (see Figure 29-7). Dramatic growth in DBS and other subscription services was largely responsible for the increase in satellite services revenues from 1997 to 1998. The rapid growth that had been expected in revenues from the mobile satellite services sector (such as those offered by Iridium) did not materialize in 1998 as service was initiated later than expected and suffered from a number of technical glitches during the first several months. SIA/Futron breaks down satellite service revenues into two primary categories: transponder leasing and subscription/retail services. Satellite operators derive revenues by leasing out a specific number of transponders (transmit-receive devices) that are physically part of a communications satellite. Subscription/retail services receive the revenues generated through direct broadcast satellite, mobile satellite telephone, mobile satellite data, VSAT, and value-added remote sensing services. SIA/Futron reported $20.1 billion in revenues from subscription/retail services and $6.0 billion in revenue from transponder leasing in 1998.

INTELSAT, an international treaty organization founded in 1964, was the first organization to provide global satellite coverage. It continues to provide voice, data, video, and Internet services to more than 200 countries. In March 1998, INTELSAT's 143 member nations agreed to partially privatize and form a new company, New Skies Satellites, N.V. Six of INTELSAT's 24 satellites (5 operational and 1 to be launched in 1999) were transferred to New Skies in November 1998. Building on the momentum of the partial privatization, INTELSAT's members endorsed full privatization of the entity in April 1999. This privatization is still subject to final approval by the members but is expected to take place in 2001. The global telecommunications marketplace has changed dramatically since INTELSAT was created. It is thought that the "New INTELSAT" will be better suited to compete with other private sector international satellite and cable companies and respond more rapidly to changes in the marketplace.

INTELSAT's activities in the United States are carried out through COMSAT Corporation. In September 1998, Lockheed Martin Global Telecommunications Inc. announced plans to purchase COMSAT. The purchase is contingent on the resolution of several regulatory issues involving the U.S. Federal

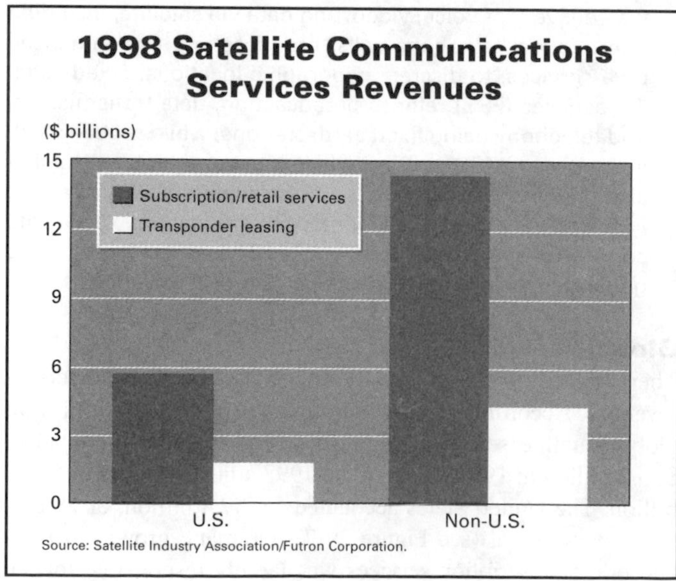

FIGURE 29-7

Communication Commission, the U.S. Department of Justice, and Congress (legislation needs to be passed that would repeal a 10 percent ownership limit in COMSAT). Many observers are optimistic that these hurdles will be overcome in the year 2000. Lockheed has said that its purchase offer requires all legislative issues to be resolved by September 2000.

While INTELSAT concentrates on fixed satellite services (FSS), INMARSAT provides mobile satellite services (MSS) worldwide. Established in 1979 as an intergovernmental treaty organization, INMARSAT has 86 member countries and provides global mobile satellite communications for air, sea, and land applications. In April 1999, INMARSAT became the first intergovernmental treaty organization to fully make the transition to a private company. Headquartered in London, the newly privatized company is governed by a 14-member board of directors. In the next several years, INMARSAT is planning to launch a four-GEO satellite system to provide broadband, high-speed, mobile multimedia services that is called Project Horizons. It anticipates that the first Horizons satellite will be operational in 2002.

The PanAmSat Corporation, which merged with Hughes in 1997, was the world's first private international satellite service provider. It maintains a fleet of 19 satellites and was preparing for the launch of 7 additional or replacement satellites from November 1999 to the end of 2001. PanAmSat reported earnings (before interest, taxes, depreciation, and amortization) of $553.3 million in 1998.

Other global satellite service providers include GE Americom Communications, Loral Space and Communications (which purchased Orion Network Systems in 1997), and Columbia Communications Corp. In many areas of the world, the number of private satellite operators has begun to increase significantly. The result has been heightened competition, lower prices, and better technology.

Another factor that will influence the future of the global satellite service industry is the increasing use of digital compression technology. Digital compression, or the ability to include multiple digital feeds into the space formerly occupied by a single analog channel, allows more efficient use of satellite technology and lower transponder costs. The primary markets for digital compression are expected to be DTH, business television, and satellite news gathering. Irwin Communications estimates that almost 1,000 transponders were carrying some form of digital traffic in 1998, up from 400 in 1997. Although many firms are hesitant to switch from analog to digital because of the short-term costs associated with the transition and a general lack of familiarity with the new technology, long-term price advantages are expected to persuade the majority of businesses to make the switch as early as 2001.

Regulatory Developments

In February 1997, the United States and 47 other countries made binding commitments to open satellite markets to competition in the WTO Agreement on Basic Telecommunications Services. To ensure implementation of the WTO agreement, the U.S. Federal Communications Commission issued orders in November 1997 that effectively liberalized market access for foreign telecommunications providers in the United States and provided for enhanced competition in the U.S. satellite services market. The objective of these regulations is to ensure that foreign and U.S. carriers will have new opportunities to compete in previously inaccessible markets.

In addition to the WTO agreement commitments on satellite services, the United States has negotiated several bilateral agreements pertaining to the provision of satellite services (see Table 29-3). In December 1998, the United States and Mexico signed an agreement regarding the provision of mobile satellite services. Previously, in October 1997, those two countries signed a bilateral agreement on FSS that allows U.S. and Mexican satellites to provide these types of services in both countries. A separate agreement on the provision of DTH satellite services was signed in November 1996. The United States and Argentina signed a similar agreement in June 1998 that will allow U.S. and Argentine companies to provide FSS (including DTH) in both countries. These agreements should ensure that U.S. operators are poised to take advantage of opportunities to serve Latin America, which is a very promising market for DBS services.

Domestic Trends

Fixed Satellite Services. FSS provides point-to-point or point-to-multipoint telecommunications between fixed locations. Applications include telephony, video broadcasting, data transmission, and teleconferencing. Users of these services were previously limited to INTELSAT and several regional and national systems, many of which were owned by governments or quasi-governmental agencies.

According to *Via Satellite,* the number of GEO satellite operators doubled, from about 25 operators in the 1980s to about 50 in 1996. It is estimated that there will be up to 60 operators by the year 2000. U.S. domestic FSS operators include but are not limited to Columbia Communications Corporation, COMSAT, GE American Communications (GE Americom), Loral Skynet, and PanAmSat. Satellite manufacturers such as Loral have increasingly become involved in the services side of the business, integrating vertically to manufacture the satellites while also offering services to consumers. Although the number of operators is expected to continue to increase, industry consolidation, increased competition from new mobile systems, and systems that most likely will be phased out over time will mitigate the increase in the number of new operators over the next 10 years.

The 1990s saw an increase in the number of agreements between satellite manufacturers in search of valuable orbital slots and service providers with orbital slots that lacked access to the most sophisticated satellites. Two examples of this trend include the Lockheed Martin Intersputnik (LMI) venture formed in 1997 and a Loral/SatMex venture announced in 1998.

With regard to LMI, Intersputnik is contributing valuable orbital slots and satellite coordinating services for the venture, while Lockheed Martin will provide launch services and the latest-generation A2100 satellites for the system. LMI currently is using two Intersputnik Gorizont satellites to provide service in Russia and Asia, but these older satellites are expected to be replaced in the next several years. LMI planned to launch an A2100 satellite, the LMI-1, in the third quarter of 1999. Despite cutbacks in its London office and a restructuring effort, LMI was hoping to sign additional customers and provide specialized regional service in 1999. In October 1997, Loral (United States) and Telefonica Autrey (Mexico) won a 75 percent interest in SatMex, which owns orbital slots above North America. These slots will allow the new company to provide television and data services throughout the Western Hemisphere.

Transponders may be leased on a full-time or occasional-use basis. Full-time applications typically include radio and television network broadcasting, cable television, private satellite

TABLE 29-3: Recent International Market-Opening Agreements on Satellite Services

Title of Agreement	Countries Covered	Date Signed
U.S.–Mexico Framework Agreement on Satellite Services	United States and Mexico	April 1996
U.S.–Mexico Agreement on Direct-to-Home Satellite Services	United States and Mexico	November 1996
World Trade Organization Agreement on Basic Telecommunications Services—Market Access for Satellite Service Suppliers	Argentina, Australia, Austria, Belgium, Bolivia, Brunei, Bulgaria, Canada, Chile, Colombia, Czech Republic, Denmark, Dominican Republic, El Salvador, Finland, France, Germany, Greece, Grenada, Guatemala, Hungary, Iceland, Indonesia, Ireland, Israel, Italy, Jamaica, Japan, Korea, Luxembourg, Malaysia, Mexico, Netherlands, New Zealand, Norway, Peru, Poland, Portugal, Romania, Singapore, Slovak Republic, Senegal, Spain, Sri Lanka, Sweden, Switzerland, Thailand, Trinidad and Tobago, Turkey, United Kingdom, United States, Venezuela Limited market access: Brazil, Cote d'Ivoire, Ghana, Hong Kong, Mauritius, South Africa.	February 1997
U.S.–Mexico Agreement on Fixed Satellite Services	United States and Mexico	October 1997
U.S.–Argentina Agreement on Fixed Satellite Services (including DTH, BSS)	United States and Argentina	June 1998
U.S.–Mexico Agreement on Mobile Satellite Services	United States and Mexico	December 1998

Source: U.S. Department of Commerce, International Trade Administration.

networks, and the restoration of terrestrial cables. Occasional-use transponders typically are employed for sports and news events such as the Olympics, network feeds, and satellite news gathering. The cost of leasing transponders varies significantly, depending on time of day, frequency of use, power, level of protection, length of lease contract, orbital position, and type of satellite. Satellites are utilized by the major television networks to distribute regular programming to affiliates across the country and transmit special-events programming. In addition, cable television may be transmitted via satellite to cable headends for terrestrial distribution to approximately 66 million households in the United States. Cable television may also be distributed directly to households through DTH satellite services.

Direct Broadcast Satellite Services. DBS is one of the fastest-growing FSS. [DBS services are formally defined by the FCC as radiocommunication services in which signals transmitted or retransmitted by space stations are intended for direct reception by the general public, including both individual reception and community reception. The FCC does not have a formal definition for Direct-to-Home fixed satellite services (DTH-FSS), but it does note that there are differences between DBS and DTH-FSS in terms of frequencies, allocation of orbital positions, and interference coordination. Many people use the two terms interchangeably.] DBS services involve the delivery of audio and video signals directly to a household via a receiver dish placed outside the home. DBS subscribers receive from 150 to 200 channels by paying approximately $200 for equipment and about $40 in monthly programming fees (this varies with the service provider and the programming package selected). The U.S. DBS industry underwent a dramatic consolidation in 1998 when Hughes DIRECTV purchased both its former rival, Primestar, and its former premium programming partner, United States Satellite Broadcasting (USSB). As of early 1999, only two U.S. DBS providers remained: DIRECTV and EchoStar's DISH network. In June 1999, there were 11.8 million DBS subscribers in the United States, according to the Satellite Broadcasting and Communications Association (SBCA) (see Figure 29-8).

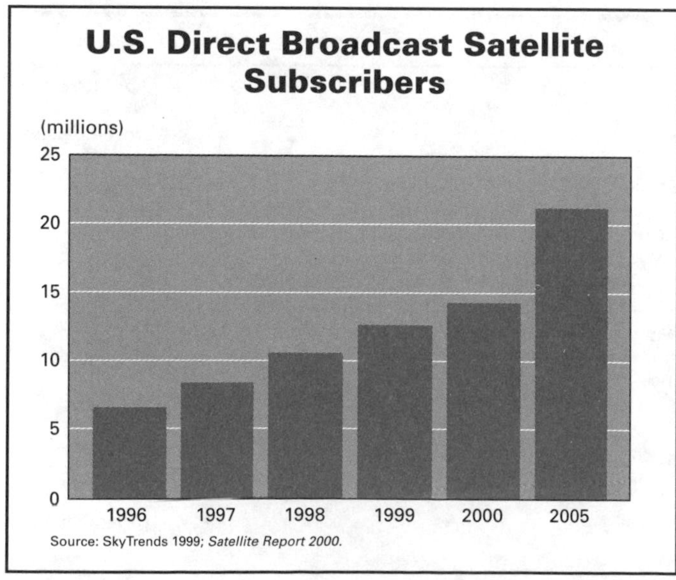

Source: SkyTrends 1999; *Satellite Report 2000.*

FIGURE 29-8

DIRECTV, a business unit of Hughes Electronics, is the largest single player in the market. DIRECTV also has made inroads overseas through its PanAmSat/Galaxy partnership in Latin America and its DIRECTV Japan partnership in Japan. DIRECTV increased its subscriber base 35 percent in 1998, adding 1.2 million subscribers. DIRECTV had a total of 4.46 million subscribers at the end of 1998.

EchoStar's DISH network has been growing steadily and hopes to draw new customers by offering several local stations via satellite, a service that is not currently available from the other providers. EchoStar ended 1998 with a total of 1.9 million subscribers. Both EchoStar and DIRECTV are competing for former PrimeStar subscribers (totaling 2.3 million at the end of 1998). Despite the fact that DIRECTV purchased PrimeStar, it did not necessarily acquire all of PrimeStar's subscribers. Aside from DIRECTV, EchoStar, and PrimeStar, about 1.9 million people in the United States still subscribe to C-band services. C-band services typically are delivered via large satellite dishes (5 to 12 feet) placed in a subscriber's backyard. This is considered an "open" satellite system in that the dishes are designed to receive all signals transmitted in the C-band. Subscribers are free to use the dish to receive programming from multiple providers. Research from the Yankee Group indicates that although the C-band market has shown very little growth, only 1 percent of C-band subscribers state that they will convert to DIRECTV or EchoStar's DISH service using the smaller satellite dishes.

Although it has been claimed that DIRECTV's Digital Satellite System has been the fastest-selling consumer product in history, selling more quickly than the video cassette recorder (VCR), the DBS industry faces many challenges from the established cable industry, which has 67 million subscribers in the United States, as opposed to 11.8 million DBS subscribers. There are a number of hurdles the industry must overcome in order to thrive, including competition from digital cable, regulations pertaining to the carriage of local channels, higher copyright fees for DBS companies compared with those paid by cable operators, regulations inhibiting the growth of DBS in multiple-dwelling units (MDUs), increasing "churn" (subscriber turnover rates), and infighting among U.S. DBS companies. Although only 20 percent of cable households currently have access to digital cable, a report from Morgan Stanley Dean Witter predicts that 16 million households will have digital cable by 2003.

Cable continues to rule the urban markets, while DBS has made strong inroads in rural areas where cable is not as readily available or offers low channel capacity. DBS has great potential in MDUs such as high-rise apartments and condominiums in urban areas but thus far has been limited by regulatory and technological challenges. A final decision on a 1998 FCC ruling concerning the ability of apartment residents to install dishes and antennas on rental properties without the consent of the property owner will affect the ability of DBS companies to increase subscriber numbers in urban areas. DBS companies also are rolling out new products that will give them the ability to better penetrate MDUs. Other trends that will have a positive impact on the DBS industry in the next few years include DBS alliances with Internet service providers and interactive television services (such as DIRECTV's deals with AOL and Wink), continued increases in the number of channels and programming packages (such as EchoStar's announcement that it will soon offer 500 channels), and resolution of regulatory issues that will allow DBS companies to offer local programming. Analysts predict that there will be 17 million DBS subscribers in the United States by 2005.

International Direct Broadcasting Satellite Services

The global DBS market has been very strong, and most analysts predict continued growth despite competition from cable and a number of governmental regulations banning the service because of concerns about foreign programming content. According to SIA/Futron, there were approximately 30 million subscribers worldwide (excluding the United States), generating programming revenues of approximately $9 billion, in 1997. In 1998, subscribers reached an estimated 39 million, with programming revenues of $12.2 billion (see Figure 29-9). The United States is the largest market for DBS based on revenue, but other regions appear to have high growth potential, including western Europe, Latin America, the Asia-Pacific region, and the Middle East and Africa.

Europe. According to C.E. Unterberg, Towbin, 35 million Europeans receive television by satellite. However, many of those subscribers receive the signal via Satellite Master Antenna Television (SMATV). SMATV usually is used to provide satellite television to residents of MDUs. The signal is received by the master antenna and then transmitted to individual units by cable. Regardless of how the signal is received, Europe is one of the largest markets for satellite television. Factors that may inhibit growth in the coming years include the growth of digital terrestrial broadcasting, complexities stemming from the presence of different regulations in each country, and the need to provide programming in over 24 different languages. Euroconsult research shows that 510 channels in over 24 languages were available in western Europe in 1997.

Société Européenne des Satellites (SES), based in Luxembourg, operates the Astra satellite system. The Astra system currently consists of nine satellites, but four more are under construction or procurement. SES was the pioneer of DBS in Europe, and many providers now use its system to reach customers throughout that continent. Other providers in the region include the United Kingdom's British Sky Broadcasting (with over 1 million subscribers), France's Canal Satellite (also with more than 1 million subscribers), Germany's DF1, and Spain's Via Digital.

DBS services are poised for growth in eastern Europe, although low per capita incomes in that region and a lack of appealing local programming may hinder their rapid expansion. Russia, Poland, and Slovakia already have significant DBS penetration, which is expected to grow substantially because of the lack of cable infrastructure in those countries.

Latin America. The Strategis Group predicts that cable and satellite subscribers will increase from 13 million in 1997 to 57 million in 2007, with revenues growing from $4.2 billion to $26.9 billion. Hughes's Galaxy Latin America and Sky Latin America (backed by TCI International and News Corp.) compete fiercely for subscribers in that region. Galaxy reported 570,000 subscribers in May 1999, while Sky Latin America reported 750,000 in the second quarter of 1999. The Strategis Group notes that the top five markets for cable and satellite are Brazil, Mexico, Argentina, Colombia, and the Caribbean. Further privatization, regulatory liberalization, and continued economic growth all send positive messages about the growth of DBS services in that region. Factors that may hinder growth include a lack of local programming, local content restrictions on foreign programming, and a large consumer base that may not be prepared to pay fees for television.

Asia-Pacific Region. The Asia-Pacific region is thought to be one of the areas with the greatest future growth potential. Paul Budde Communication of Australia predicts up to 67 million subscribers to DBS services in Asia by 2005. In countries where populations are spread out over large areas, such as Indonesia, satellite-delivered services are much more efficient than most wireline technologies. In Japan, DirectTV Japan (backed by Hughes and Japanese companies such as Matsushita Electric, Space Communications Corp., and Mitsubishi Electric) is waging a fierce battle for subscribers against SkyPerfecTV (formed by a merger of PerfecTV Corporation and Japan Sky Broadcasting in May 1998). SkyPerfecTV reported 1.2 million subscribers in August 1999, while DirecTV Japan had acquired only 299,300 customers. DirecTV continues its efforts to attract subscribers through new channel and package offerings, new interactive services, and strengthened relationships with retail distributors. In January 1999, Hughes increased its ownership of DirecTV Japan to 42 percent to become the largest shareholder.

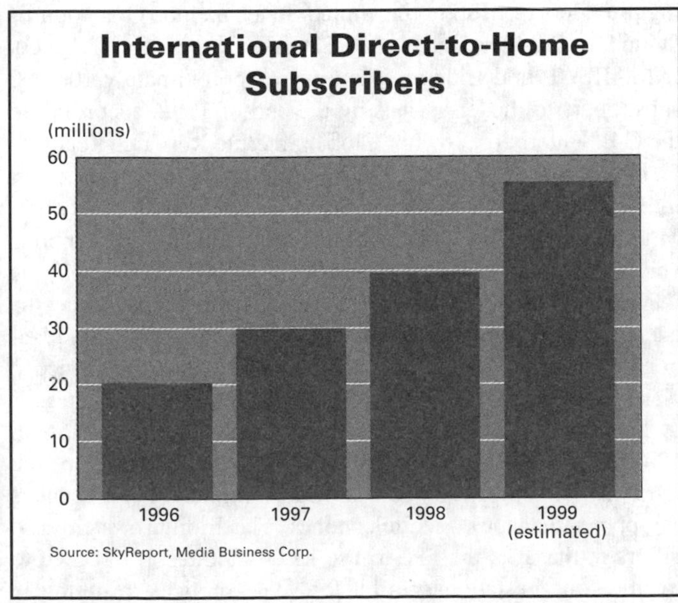

FIGURE 29-9

China banned the use of satellite television dishes by consumers in 1993, although hotels and some organizations are allowed to obtain DBS services. Although there is an official ban, it has not always been enforced strictly by the government. Hong Kong-based Star TV (backed by Phoenix Satellite Television, an affiliate of Rupert Murdoch's News Corp.) apparently is received illegally by many consumers in China. Although the government can ban the equipment, it cannot prevent Star TV from beaming its satellite signals into the country. There was a crackdown on illegal dishes in June 1999 during the tenth anniversary of Tiananmen Square, but history has demonstrated that such crackdowns usually are forgotten after a few months. In the meantime, Star TV has attracted a number of big-name advertisers and appears to be thriving against competition from Chinese state television. In August 1999, it was reported that DiviCom Inc. had been selected by the China Broadcasting Film Television Co. Ltd. to implement the first DBS service in China. It will be interesting to see how this legitimate and domestic DBS system will compete against the already entrenched but illegal Star TV.

DBS has been a source of great speculation in India. Many analysts believe that the large number of television households and the current lack of channel variety offered by cable operators make India an ideal growth market for DBS. Unfortunately, political and regulatory uncertainty have hampered the efforts of DBS companies to break into this market. The Indian parliament had been considering the passage of a sweeping Broadcast Bill in 1998–1999, but the government dissolved before a decision was made and no action on the bill is expected until early 2000. The Broadcast Bill reportedly will create an entity called the Broadcast Authority of India, which will have responsibility for licensing cable and satellite operators. In July 1997, the government decided to ban ku-band DTH broadcasting until the Broadcast Bill was finalized. In the two years that have passed since DBS was banned in India, those with hopes of providing DBS have begun to retreat from the country. News Corp.–backed Star TV significantly reduced its operations in India from about 1,000 employees in 1996 to only 150 in 1999. It has been rumored that Doordarshan (DD), the Indian government broadcaster, has been lobbying the government for an exclusive 5-year DTH license that would allow it to develop its DBS business while keeping foreign competitors out of the market. No decisions on this license or the Broadcast Bill are expected until late 1999 or 2000. Even after the DBS licensing issue has been resolved, local content restrictions will present a hurdle.

Africa and the Middle East. Despite government bans on satellite dishes because of concerns about content, challenging economic conditions, and a relatively low number of television households, several companies are succeeding in providing DBS services to consumers in certain countries. In the Middle East, ORBIT Radio and Television Network and ART, both based in Saudi Arabia, are the two primary DBS providers. In February 1999, Israel awarded a DBS license to a consortium that includes Bezeq and Gilat. In Africa, MultiChoice Africa of South Africa provides DBS services in South Africa, Namibia, Zimbabwe, Swaziland, Lesotho, Mozambique, and Botswana. South Africa and Nigeria have great potential for DBS, as subscribers in those countries are most likely to have enough disposable income to pay for the equipment and services.

Canada. There are currently two Canadian companies providing DBS service in Canada: StarChoice and Expressvu. StarChoice is owned by Canada's Shaw Communications (a large cable company) and Canadian Satellite Communications (CanCom). As of August 1999, StarChoice had 225,000 subscribers. Bell Expressvu uses EchoStar's (United States) DISH Network trademark to sell its service and is controlled by Canada's largest telephone company, Bell Canada. Bell Expressvu had 230,000 subscribers at the end of August 1999. According to the Canadian Association of Broadcasters, StarChoice and Expressvu should attract 1.9 million subscribers by 2007. Telesat Canada's *Nimiq* satellite was launched successfully in May 1999. *Nimiq* is a high-powered DBS satellite that will allow Canadian DBS providers to offer small dish services, like those offered in the United States.

Despite the fact that there are now two Canadian DBS providers, there is still a relatively large "gray" market of Canadian customers receiving U.S. programming not approved for distribution in Canada. In 1997, it was estimated that 300,000 to 800,000 Canadians received illegal DBS service from the United States. The Royal Canadian Mounted Police continue to raid stores that sell illegal DBS equipment, with the most recent raid occurring in April 1999. With the enhancement of service offerings by StarChoice and Expressvu and the launch of Canada's first DBS satellite, many observers expect that the size of the gray market will begin to decrease. Several U.S. companies have expressed an interest in offering legitimate DBS services in Canada, but their efforts have been hindered by strict content and license requirements.

Mobile Satellite Services

Mobile satellite services transmit voice and data by satellite to mobile receivers such as pagers and cellular-size phones. Existing providers of MSS in the United States include Qualcomm's OmniTRACs, American Mobile Satellite Corporation (AMSC), INMARSAT, and Iridium. There were approximately 100,000 subscribers to those services by the end of 1998, according to the C.E. Unterberg, Towbin Global Satellite Research Team.

In January 1997, INMARSAT introduced the world's first truly portable global satellite phone service. INMARSAT's mini-M terminal is a laptop-size mobile satellite phone that supports voice, fax, and data communications. COMSAT markets the INMARSAT mini-M phone service in the United States under the name Planet 1. At this time, Planet 1 is subject to FCC authorization in the United States, meaning that one may use the service to place calls to the United States but not from the United States.

Iridium made history when it launched its global MSS in November 1998. Iridium's service is different from the INMARSAT mini-M in that subscribers use hand-held receivers as opposed to laptop-size telephones. The Iridium system also differs in that it is the first to use LEO satellites as opposed to satellites in geostationary orbit for voice services, resulting in significantly less delay in transmitting voice signals (the signal travels only 500 miles from the earth, as opposed to 22,237 miles using the INMARSAT system). Iridium was also the first system to market its global satellite telephone service aggressively to businesses, governments, and consumers worldwide.

Iridium experienced several financial, legal, marketing, distribution, and personnel challenges in 1999. Although Iridium had anticipated 100,000 subscribers by December 1998, it had only 10,294 customers by March 1999, and the situation did not improve significantly in the subsequent months. While some analysts blame the firm's difficulties on marketing and management missteps, others say that the price for its service was too high. With handsets initially priced in the range of $3,000, monthly service charges of about $60, and rates of $2 to $7 a minute, Iridium proved that the international businessperson seeking telephone access anywhere, anytime was not necessarily willing to pay those kinds of prices for global connectivity. On August 13, 1999, the company filed for Chapter 11 bankruptcy. Despite the bankruptcy, Iridium service will continue and the company hopes to restructure and remain in the satellite telephone business it largely pioneered.

In addition to Iridium, two mobile satellite services are in the process of being deployed and constructed: Globalstar and ICO Global Communications. Two more companies—Ellipso and Constellation Communications—are still in the development stages but are hoping to enter the market in 2002. While many observers believe that Globalstar may be able to distinguish itself from Iridium with lower prices and better marketing and distribution, the Iridium saga has had a tangible impact on the ability of ICO to raise the financing for its system and will affect investors' assessments of systems such as Ellipso and Constellation.

If all five services survive, Iridium, Globalstar, ICO Global Communications, Ellipso, and Constellation are expected to compete fiercely for subscribers (see Table 29-4 for information on investors, charges, and system characteristics). [These systems are also referred to as Big LEOs, a term that generally refers to LEO satellite systems used for voice and paging, while Little LEO generally refers to LEO systems used for nonvoice (E-mail, paging, and messaging) services.] These systems are not expected to compete directly with existing cellular services of PCS but instead to serve the geographical areas that cellular and other wireless services do not cover, such as rural areas with poor telephone coverage. All the MSS target slightly different market niches or will take different approaches to interacting with terrestrial telephone service providers. Although there is some concern about the demand for all these services, it is important to note that the systems differ both in structure and in target markets.

Iridium's 66-satellite system is the only one that uses intersatellite links to transfer a call from satellite to satellite until the call reaches one gateway of 13 that is closest to the end user. This system architecture allows the calls to bypass long-distance networks. Although Iridium initially targeted the international business traveler, it has significantly revised its marketing and pricing strategy to build up its fledgling customer base and is now focusing on vertical markets such as the oil and gas industry. Iridium announced a new pricing strategy in June 1999, lowering prices on both handsets and phone charges and simplifying its pricing plans. On July 1, 1999, handset prices were cut to about $1,500, and service charges were also reduced substantially.

Globalstar's 48-satellite "bent-pipe" network relies to a larger extent on earth stations on the ground. The satellite is used to provide the final link in a particular call, but the call is beamed down to the local terrestrial network as soon as possible. Globalstar has partnered with service providers all over the world, which will set the final charges. Globalstar's architecture is expected to allow for lower costs, with the handset selling for $750 and per minute charges to the retailer set at 35 to 55 cents. Globalstar is targeting international businesses but also is advertising its ability to provide rural telephony solutions. By August 1999, Globalstar had launched 36 satellites, and it planned to launch an additional 16 satellites by the end of 1999 (a total of 52 satellites total, including 48 active and 4 spares). Globalstar launched its service to coincide with ITU Telecom 99 in Geneva in October 1999.

ICO is a London-based private subsidiary of INMARSAT that was set to offer service in 2000, using 12 MEO satellites. ICO experienced several financing problems in 1999, culminating in a bankruptcy filing in August 1999. In addition, it has been reported that Hughes (ICO's satellite supplier) was behind schedule in manufacturing the 12 satellites that were to be used for the system because of quality control problems with certain parts and components. ICO could emerge from bankruptcy with a restructuring, but its future currently appears uncertain. Ellipso has a patented satellite orbit that will allow the satellite to serve the most populated areas during daylight hours and rotate to less populated areas during the evening hours, when traffic is not as heavy. In May 1998, Boeing became the project's primary contractor and took an equity stake in the system. Constellation will focus on providing coverage in equatorial countries, such as Brazil and Indonesia, with remote villages and low-density populations spread throughout vast geographic regions. In May 1998, Orbital Sciences invested in the Constellation system and ended its relationship with Ellipso.

Although it appears that there is a need for these types of services, especially in developing regions, the main determinants appear to be cost and whether customers are willing to pay higher prices for satellite-delivered telephone services. As the Iridium experience demonstrates, these complex satellite systems must overcome many hurdles, both technological and regulatory, to ensure that customers are able to use the services effectively. Iridium's challenges in gaining subscribers hindered ICO's ability to get financing, and it remains to be seen whether the market can support additional systems such as Constellation and Ellipso. Globalstar appears to have the best chance of success, but it will still have to win customers with low prices, conveniently sized handsets, and truly global service. With all these satellite-delivered telephone services, there remain potential launch problems, in-orbit satellite difficulties, a need to obtain the necessary interconnection and regulatory approvals from governments all over the world, and the problem of ensuring that customers have easy access to the handsets and services. C.E.

TABLE 29-4: Mobile Satellite Systems for Telephony

Name of System/ Applications	Major Investors	Number of Satellites/ Orbit	Estimated Cost of Project/ Service[1]	Operational in
Iridium Hand-held dual-mode phones, paging, low-speed data transmission	Motorola, Raytheon, Lockheed Martin, Sprint, Khrunichev State Research (total of 20 strategic investors)	66/low earth orbit	$5 billion *Handset:* Originally $3,000, reduced to $1,500 as of July 1999 *Charges:* $3–$5/minute (retail) *Access fee:* Varies by country	November 1998 Declared bankruptcy in August 1999, though service will continue
Globalstar Hand-held dual-mode phones, fixed ordinary phones, paging, low-speed data transmission	Loral Space & Communications, Qualcomm Inc., AirTouch Communications, and others	48/low earth orbit	$2.6 billion *Handset:* $750 *Charges:* 35–55 cents/ minute (wholesale) *Access fee:* Service providers will set fees	Fourth quarter of 1999 Globalstar had launched 36 of 48 satellites as of August 1999
ICO Global Communications[2] Hand-held dual-mode mobile phones, phones for cars, ships, aircraft, fixed phones in developing areas	ICO is a London-based private offshoot of INMARSAT. 59 investors, including TRW and Hughes. Declared bankruptcy in August 1999, though it is expected to reemerge through restructuring	12/medium earth orbit	$4.7 billion *Handset:* $1,000 *Charges:* $1.00–$3.50/minute (retail) *Access fee:* Varies by country	2000 ICO had been expected to launch its first satellites in late 1999. Now in restructuring.
MCHI/Ellipso Hand-held phones for mobile and fixed uses Will use smaller satellites in highly inclined and equatorial orbits to provide low-cost service	Mobile Holdings Communications Inc. (Boeing, Lockheed Martin, Israel Aircraft Industries, Vula Communications, and Harris Corp.)	17/ medium-earth orbit	$1.1 billion *Handset:* $1,000 *Charges:* 35 cents/minute *Access fee:* $35/month	2001 (partial) 2002 (full)
Constellation Hand-held phones for mobile and fixed uses Focus on providing telecommunications coverage in equatorial countries, such as Indonesia and Brazil, with remote villages and low-density populations spread throughout vast geographic areas	Constellations Communications (Orbital Sciences, Bell Atlantic, Raytheon, Space Vest)	12 in initial phase/low earth orbit	$1.2 billion *Handset:* $750–$1,000 *Charges:* 60–90 cents/minute *Access fee:* $20–$40/month	2002

[1] Service charges are estimated and are subject to change.
[2] Odyssey announced in December 1997 that it had relinquished its license and invested in ICO.
Source: Company materials compiled by the U.S. Department of Commerce, International Trade Administration.

Unterberg, Towbin predicts that mobile satellite telephony systems will serve over 10.3 million subscribers by 2005.

These Big LEOs will face competition from several regional systems that will provide mobile satellite services in the next 3 years. There are several primary regional systems, including (1) Asian Cellular Systems (ACeS), which is expected to serve Indonesia and Asia in 2000, (2) ASC/Agrani, which will serve India and Asia in 2001, (3) Thuraya, which will serve the Middle East, central Asia, India, and eastern Europe in 2000, and (4) Euro-African Satellite Telecommunications (EAST), which will serve Africa, the Middle East, and parts of Europe in 2002. The future of another regional system, Asia Pacific Mobile Telecommunications (APMT), that was to have provided service in eastern Asia in 2000 has been called into question since Hughes was denied an export license by the U.S. government to sell one of its satellites to APMT in April 1999. Most of these systems utilize satellites in geostationary orbit, meaning that there may be significant delays in voice transmission. Although these regional systems are disadvantaged by voice delays, they have an advantage in terms of tailoring the service specifically to the local market as well as the ability to offer lower prices. Many of these regional systems have suffered significant delays caused by financing problems.

Little LEO services offer store-and-forward communications such as E-mail, two-way paging, and messaging. These services are different from the Big LEO systems in that they provide data-only services (no voice) and use less bandwidth. This means that both the satellites and the user equipment are less expensive, reducing the cost of service to the consumer. Subscriber costs are anticipated to be 25 cents per message, with terminals costing from $100 to $400. Little LEO services are particularly well-suited for a number of monitoring and tracking applications in the transportation, shipping, utilities, security, agriculture, and environmental industries.

ORBCOMM, owned by Orbital Sciences Corporation and Teleglobe of Canada, entered the market in November 1998, becoming the first commercial provider of satellite messaging services. ORBCOMM was expected to ship almost 200,000 satellite messaging units by the end of 1999. Leo One (owned by dbX Corporation) is expected to be the second player to market, with service commencing in late 2001 or early 2002. Other possible competitors include FAISat (Final Analysis), and E-Sat (a joint venture between DBS Industries and EchoStar). Both FAISat and E-Sat plan service in 2001.

Broadband Systems

VSATs already provide a very effective means of delivering "narrowband" data for business applications. The VSAT market has grown significantly in the last few years, and it is predicted that this growth will continue in 2000–2001 (see the discussion of VSATs in the equipment section for additional information). Two companies are currently offering two-way data services: Hughes's DirecPC and Gilat's SkySurfer. These two services have not experienced significant growth in consumer and commercial markets because of their relatively high prices. New services are being developed that will focus on delivering two-way data-intensive (broadband) transmissions to businesses and consumers at lower prices.

In addition, several satellite systems have been proposed to offer high-speed, two-way data communications such as Internet, corporate Intranet, and videoconferencing. Some of the players in this market are Loral's CyberStar, Alcatel's SkyBridge, Lockheed Martin's Astrolink, Hughes Spaceway, and Teledesic (backed by Bill Gates, Craig McCaw, Motorola, Boeing, and Saudi Arabia's Prince Alwaleed Bin Talal).

In October 1998, CyberStar launched service in the United States by using an already operational Loral satellite (*Telstar*). Loral has said that if there is enough demand for this partial service, it will move forward with plans to build three GEO satellites at a cost of $1.6 billion. Service utilizing the three GEO broadband-only satellites is slated to commence in 2003. Loral also is involved in the SkyBridge project (also backed by Alcatel, Toshiba, and Aerospatiale), which will use 80 LEO satellites for broadband services and is scheduled to commence service in 2002.

Lockheed Martin's Astrolink (also backed by TRW and Telecom Italia) plans to initiate service in 2003 by using four GEO satellites and expanding to nine as demand grows. Hughes Spaceway plans to use a combination of GEO and MEO satellites to provide a range of broadband and multimedia applications. In March 1999, Hughes announced a $1.4 billion investment in the system, which is scheduled to begin partial operation in North America in 2002. Eight GEO satellites are planned for the first phase, with as many as 20 MEO satellites to be added as the business matures.

Teledesic's $9 billion "Internet in the Sky" project has been scaled back significantly over the last year, and the service commencement date has moved to 2004. In July 1999, Teledesic signed Motorola as prime contractor on the project and awarded Lockheed Martin a contract for several launches. Although originally planned as an 840-LEO-satellite system, it has been reconfigured with 176 satellites.

With the large number of companies proposing broadband satellite services (13 of which have been licensed by the FCC), it is certain that consolidation, lack of financing, and demand factors will limit the number of systems that are implemented. The trend toward consolidation was exemplified by the May 1998 announcement that Teledesic would join forces with Motorola's Celestri project. In June 1997, Motorola had proposed its own $12.9 billion, 64-satellite system, called Celestri, to offer high-speed data services in 2002. Celestri and Teledesic were characterized as fierce competitors that would have to fight each other for financing and customers. For many reasons, Motorola decided to abandon its own project and become the primary contractor for the Teledesic project. Many analysts believe that the move significantly strengthens Teledesic's position by bringing Motorola's experience in mass-producing LEO satellites (it already has built approximately 70 of them for the Iridium system) and ensuring that the project will be able to attract the necessary financing.

These systems must overcome an array of challenges, including the ability to produce a large number of technologically sophisticated satellites at very low cost; ensuring a way to launch a large number of satellites by the planned service dates, surmounting domestic and international regulatory hurdles; and combating a problem known as "rain fade," or ensuring the transmission of high-frequency signals through rain. In addition, these broadband services face competition from fiber-optic cable, which has proved to be an effective and economical mode of transmitting large amounts of data. Satellites offer a more appropriate solution when there is a need to deliver data to multiple locations, however.

One project that may compete with the proposed broadband satellite systems is Sky Station International. Sky Station will provide Internet connectivity and other interactive communications services via approximately 250 high-powered balloons 13 miles above the earth beginning in 2002. Although the technology behind the project is unproven, Sky Station maintains that it can compete with satellite-based systems in price and quality.

It claims that it will be able to offer high-quality broadband services for only a few cents a minute.

C.E. Unterberg, Towbin estimates that satellite broadband providers will capture 10 percent of the entire broadband market by 2007, with 131 million broadband subscribers in that period. The majority of this growth will occur between 2002 and 2004, when many of these dedicated broadband satellite systems will initiate service. As none of these services has been launched (with the exception of the partial operation of Cyberstar), it is difficult to estimate future revenues.

Electronic Commerce

The explosive growth of the Internet offers many growth opportunities for satellite service companies. Many of the proposed broadband operators listed in the previous section are counting on continued growth in Internet and electronic commerce applications to fuel demand for these services. Compared with terrestrial modes of Internet delivery, satellites offer several advantages. First, satellite transmissions are distance-insensitive in that the price of delivery does not depend on the distance traveled. Second, satellites provide the most effective means of point-to-multipoint transmission. Information may be delivered effectively from one headquarters to hundreds of distribution points simultaneously. Third, installing a satellite dish to receive signals is much more efficient in terms of both time and money than deploying a fiber-optic network. However, fiber has a much greater capacity for delivering large amounts of data more efficiently and in a shorter period. For countries that have a developed terrestrial infrastructure, fiber thus will be the mode of choice. In developing countries, however, satellites are the only means of gaining access to the Internet.

According to Pioneer Consulting, Internet access is the main demand factor driving the growth of broadband satellite services. Electronic commerce is one of the components that is fueling the worldwide push for Internet access. Dynamic Web pages (those capable of processing electronic commerce transactions) are projected to be the second leading element in bandwidth demand (after multimedia applications) in the period 1999–2008. Thus, electronic commerce is one of the primary factors driving the growth of broadband satellite services.

By 2002, 400 million people are expected to be using the Internet, generating billions of dollars in annual revenue. Broadband satellite operators are certain to gain a significant share of the revenue from the boom in electronic commerce.

Digital Audio Radio Services

Several companies plan to offer satellite-delivered radio directly to consumers. These systems will allow the delivery of up to 100 channels of digital radio to vast geographic areas. In the United States, CD Radio (backed by Loral Space and Communications of the United States and Arianespace of France) and XM Satellite Radio (formerly American Mobile Radio Corporation, backed by American Mobile Satellite Corporation) are the key players. A third consortium that was planning to compete in the U.S. DARS market, WCS Radio, withdrew its FCC license application in June 1999, citing unanticipated obstacles.

CD Radio will offer a subscription-based satellite radio system to deliver 100 channels of news and music to vehicles across the United States. Subscribers should be able to insert a radio card into a car's radio cassette or compact disc slot and place a battery-powered satellite dish the size of a silver dollar on the car's rear window. The cost of both the radio card and the satellite dish is expected to be about $200 to $250, with monthly subscription fees of about $10. Space Systems/Loral is building four satellites for the CD Radio system. The first satellite launch is expected in January 2000, with service commencing later that year. CD Radio has contracts with Alpine, Panasonic, Delphi Delco, and Recoton for the satellite receivers and has an alliance with Ford Motor Company to install the satellite radios in all Ford cars.

XM Satellite Radio will offer a similar service beginning in early 2001, charging about $400 for an AM/FM/XM satellite radio, with monthly fees of about $10. Hughes Space and Communications and Alcatel are building the satellites for XM and plan to launch the first in 2000. In 1999, XM signed agreements with Alpine, Pioneer, Sharp, and Delphi Delco to manufacture the satellite radios. XM also is teaming with General Motors (GM) to offer XM service in GM vehicles.

The two companies will compete to attract the consumers who purchase 12 million new cars and trucks annually, the 5 million people who install upgraded car stereo systems each year, and the 174 million vehicles already equipped with radios and CD players. The critical determinant in the success of satellite-delivered radio services is whether consumers will pay fees to receive radio programming anywhere in the United States. Estimates for DARS subscriber growth in the United States vary greatly, with analysts from C.E. Unterberg, Towbin predicting 1.84 million subscribers in 2001 and 21.5 million in 2005.

WorldSpace (Alcatel Space of France, Matra Marconi of the United Kingdom, and others) plans to offer its portable digital direct audio broadcasting services to Africa, the Middle East, Asia, Latin America, and the Caribbean via three satellites (*AfriStar, AsiaStar,* and *AmeriStar*). Over 100 radio stations providing news, music, sports, talk, and drama will be delivered via portable or hand-held radios to consumers in homes, offices, cars, parks, shops, and restaurants. *AfriStar* was launched in October 1998 and was expected to commence service in 1999. *AsiaStar* and *AmeriStar* were also slated for launch in 1999, but manufacturing glitches may have delayed this schedule. A WorldSpace receiver is expected to cost about $300 initially, but it is assumed that the price will decrease over time. In addition to the first-generation portable model, future generations will be incorporated into automobiles, laptop computers, and multifunction home stereo systems. WorldSpace's satellite radio service will be free for listeners. WorldSpace plans to get revenues from advertising, royalty fees, receiver sales, and the leasing of satellite capacity to programmers. The WorldSpace Foundation, a charitable and educational organization, plans to distribute radio receivers to poor families and remote villages. Many analysts question the ability of consumers in those developing regions to pay up to $300 for a radio, but the idea of delivering news, information, and educational programming to people in vast geographic areas certainly has potential. C.E. Unterberg, Towbin predicts 930,000 international satellite radio subscribers by 2000, growing to 8.4 million by 2003.

Nihon Mobile Broadcasting Corp. of Japan also is planning to enter the satellite radio market in 2001, but will focus its service solely on Japan.

Global Positioning System

The Global Positioning System is a constellation of 24 radio-transmitting satellites operated by the U.S. Department of Defense and used for both military and nonmilitary applications to determine the precise position of a radio receiver on the ground. By determining the time it takes a radio signal to arrive from each satellite's known position in space to a GPS receiver on the ground, the receiver calculates its own position with a high degree of accuracy. The signals derived from these satellites are used to produce precise timing, location, and velocity information.

Commercial applications of the U.S. government's GPS are expected to expand significantly in the next 5 years. Approximately 300 companies provided some form of GPS equipment or services in 1997. GPS is used in a variety of applications, including aviation, communications, environmental protection, forestry and agriculture, ground transportation, health care, law enforcement and safety, maritime, mining and construction, recreation, infrastructure development, and public safety. In 1995, the number of users in the United States alone surpassed 500,000. This is expected to increase to more than 2.5 million users by the year 2000. A September 1998 study by the U.S. Department of Commerce estimates that worldwide sales of GPS products will reach $8 billion by 2000 and could exceed $16 billion by 2003. Allied Business Intelligence predicts that the commercial GPS market will be worth $14 billion by 2005.

Industry and Trade Projections for the Next 1 and 5 Years

The satellite services market will continue to be one of the fastest-growing segments in the industry, driven by growth in satellite television, satellite messaging, and VSAT and GPS services. Although Iridium's service fell far short of expectations in 1999, Globalstar may prove that a market exists for MSS by learning from Iridium's missteps. If Globalstar's service is successful, revenues from satellite telephony could rise substantially in the year 2000. ICO's bankruptcy filing makes it difficult to believe that there is room in the MSS market for future systems such as Constellation and Ellipso. Satellite messaging services are likely to see substantial growth as ORBCOMM expands its customer base and other providers come on-line in 2001. Most analysts expect that satellite radio and satellite broadband will add substantial fuel to the satellite services market when those services come on-line in the 2001–2002 period.

SIA/Futron noted that worldwide revenue from satellite services grew from $21.2 billion in 1997 to $26.2 billion in 1998, an increase of 23 percent. Although the services industry has experienced setbacks in terms of financing, marketing, and postponement of expected launch dates, there is nothing in the 2000–2003 time frame that should substantially hinder growth. Despite the fact that some service offerings are not meeting expectations, satellite television, satellite messaging, VSAT, and GPS should continue to drive growth.

The Pioneer Consulting Group estimates that the global satellite services market will exceed $131 billion by 2007, with fixed data representing 18 percent of the market and DBS/DTH and mobile voice and data representing 35 and 40 percent, respectively. These estimates are quite optimistic, and untested technology, unknown demand, consolidation, regulatory issues, and other factors may mitigate some of the explosive growth rates that have been predicted. Although these growth rates may be overstated, it is clear that the satellite services industry will enjoy healthy growth rates over the next 1 and 5 years.

REMOTE SENSING SATELLITES

Remote sensing satellites collect images of the earth by using various methods, including electro-optical sensors and radar. Electro-optical sensors may collect images by using one light frequency (panchromatic) or several frequencies (multispectral) or may collect images contiguously over a broad range of frequencies (hyperspectral). Radar satellites bounce radar signals off the earth's surface and record the energy that is returned. Radar imagery can be used to "see" through clouds and collect images in the daytime or at night. The sharpness and detail of photographs can be related to a satellite sensor's resolution, which usually is measured in meters.

Global Trends

Over the last several years, a number of commercial firms have contracted with foreign government agencies that sell data from remote sensing satellites in the international marketplace. Simultaneously, a number of U.S. firms have begun to develop commercial private systems that would distribute their own data to the commercial market. This has initiated a fierce competition between satellite operators-owners and data distributors that should drive down the price of imagery.

The Asia-Pacific region is a prime market for European and North American satellite imagery to tackle problems related to increasing populations and dwindling resources. In that area, India and Japan support global data-gathering efforts, South Korea is working with TRW on a joint project for a land-ocean imaging satellite, Australia is developing a new satellite, and Thailand, China, Indonesia, and Taiwan are increasing their use of imagery. Mapmaking is more important in this region than in developed areas because of a lack of infrastructure. Maps may be used for forestry mapping, watershed mapping, road construction, infrastructure improvements, and industrial investment. Digital three-dimensional maps also may be used to create car navigation systems, building on the two-dimensional navigation systems already used in millions of Japanese cars.

The SPOT satellite Earth Observation System was designed by CNES of France and developed with the participation of Sweden and Belgium. As the current global leader in remotely sensed images, SpotImage had revenues of approximately $43 million in 1998, up from $37 million in 1997. The *Spot 4* satellite, provides 10-meter resolution panchromatic images, 20-meter resolution multispectral images, and infrared images used mainly to monitor vegetation. The satellite also is used to improve cartography, wetlands studies, and geological studies. *Spot 5* is currently being built and will be launched in 2001; it will provide 5-meter resolution panchromatic and 10-meter multispectral images.

The ESA operates the *ERS-1* satellite, which provides synthetic aperture radar (SAR) imagery with a resolution of 30 meters. Its imagery is sold in the United States by Space Imaging.

The Indian Remote Sensing Program was begun as a federal-state partnership and is now a leader in commercial remote sensing imagery. The program was intended to address issues such as overcrowding, inadequate transportation, water conservation, crop planning, and disaster relief. Space Imaging is now its commercial marketer and distributor. The *IRS-1C/1D* satellite has 5.8-meter panchromatic resolution and 23.5-meter resolution in three visible and near-infrared bands and 71-meter resolution in a short-wave infrared band. India also was planning the *Cartosat-1* satellite to provide 1-meter resolution imagery starting in 1999.

The Canadian Space Agency provides 8-meter resolution radar images from the *Radarsat-1* satellite. SAR is a powerful instrument that can transmit and receive signals that "see" through clouds, haze, smoke, and darkness and obtain high-quality images of the earth in all types of weather, 24 hours a day. *Radarsat-2* will be launched in 2001 and is worth $200 million; it will be operated by MacDonald Dettwiler rather than the Canadian Space Agency. *Radarsat-2* will have 3-meter SAR resolution.

The Australian Resource Information and Environment Satellite (*Aries-1*) is intended to investigate land surface biophysical properties and geologic composition for commercial customers using 10-meter panchromatic imagery and 30-meter resolution hyperspectral imagery that images the earth's surface in the visible, near-infrared, and short-wave infrared spectra. The satellite is being developed by a consortium that includes Australia's Commonwealth Scientific and Industrial Research Organization (CSIRO), the Australian Centre for Remote Sensing (ACRES), and Auspace Limited (a subsidiary of Matra Marconi). *Aries* is slated for launch in early 2002.

Besides the shutdown of the *JERS* satellite, Japan's National Space Development Agency (NASDA) lost the $1 billion Advanced Earth Observing Satellite (*Adeos-1*). The satellite quit operating, possibly because of a solar array failure. A replacement, *Adeos-2,* is scheduled for launch in late 2000 and will feature a mix of Japanese and foreign components. Japan is scheduling a launch in September 2002 of an Advanced Land Observing Satellite (*ALOS*) to complement the Adeos system. *ALOS* will image with both optical and SAR instruments to determine land elevations and the heights of ground objects for land classification studies.

In early 1998, Russia launched the *Spin-2* photo reconnaissance satellite, which took pictures at 2-meter resolution for commercial customers. The satellite's path allowed it to image most of North America, and the images are kept in a database to be sold by a joint venture of the Russian firm Sovinformsputnik Interbranch Association and three U.S. firms: Aerial Images, Lambda Tech International, and Central Trading Systems. The venture has developed detailed maps for farmers, agriculturalists, rescue services, and many other users. Russia also sells raw remote sensing data from Russian government satellites and historical archives on the Internet.

Brazil is cooperating with China on the Chinese-Brazil Earth Resources Satellites (*CBERS*), which was slated to be launched on a Chinese Long March rocket in 1999. The second satellite is scheduled in 2000. The program will provide high-resolution imagery through a widefield camera and will collect data in the visible and infrared bands. As a result of its large size and vast unpopulated areas, Brazil has used remote sensing data for studies of the environment (especially forest and jungle monitoring), weather prediction, drug enforcement, and urban planning.

Israel is developing the EROS series of high-resolution satellites. These satellites will produce panchromatic images with a resolution of 1 meter. Launch was expected in 1999.

The *Korean Multi-Purpose Satellite* (*KOMPSAT*), which was launched in 1999, was built, tested, and operated by teams of personnel from TRW and the Korea Aerospace Research Institute (KARI). *KOMPSAT* will house instruments to map Korea and monitor earth resources. The satellite will provide 10-meter resolution panchromatic and 20-meter multispectral images.

Alenia Aerospazio of Italy is developing plans for the Skymed/COSMO constellation of earth observation satellites, which will consist of seven satellites: four radar and three optical. The radar satellites will have X-band SAR instruments capable of 3-meter imagery. The optical satellites will include a high-resolution (2.5-meter) panchromatic camera, a coarse-resolution multispectral imager, and a medium-resolution infrared camera. The launch of the first satellite is planned for 2001.

Domestic Trends

After the launch failure of the *Ikonos-1* satellite in April 1999, the United States has had to wait longer than expected for the first 1-meter commercial remote sensing satellite to begin operation. Historically, the *Landsat* satellite system has been the primary source of remote sensing data in the United States. In 1984, *Landsat* was commercialized through the Land Remote Sensing Commercialization Act, which allowed the Earth Observation Satellite Company (EOSAT) to operate the satellite and market the raw data.

Under the U.S. policy allowing high-resolution satellites to market data commercially, the U.S. industry is leading the world in the development of these high-resolution remote sensing satellites. Three U.S. companies are developing high-resolution (less than 1-meter) satellites that should be in operation by the end of the decade. These satellites will compete directly with aerial photography for the high-resolution imagery market. Satellites offering pictures of the earth that have the same clarity as aerial photographs will compete in terms of price and the timeliness of the images.

While no other commercial providers have developed 1-meter resolution systems, the market demand that evolves will determine how many systems with that level of detail are needed in the marketplace and whether the data can be made available at a reasonable cost. Many experts argue that only moderate resolution (10 to 20 meters) is necessary for most purposes and that a wider field of view (usually available on lower-resolution systems) is acceptable for many applications. However, SpotImage is concerned that Earthwatch's 5-meter imagery (obtained through joint ventures with India's IRS spacecraft and data from the U.S. *Landsat* system and Canada's *Radarsat*) may take market share from the *Spot 1, 2,* and *4* satellites' 10-meter images.

Space Imaging/Eosat markets not only U.S. *Landsat* data but also imagery from India's *IRS-1C/1D* and Japan's Earth Resources Satellite, which was shut down in 1998. The company has ground stations around the world (Australia, Japan, Thailand, and China) and archives in India and Japan. Space Imaging suffered a huge setback when its *Ikonos-1* satellite with 1-meter resolution was destroyed during launch. However, the company launched *Ikonos-2,* an exact duplicate, in 1999.

Earthwatch's *QuickBird* satellites will take 1-meter panchromatic images and 4-meter multispectral images. *QuickBird-1* will launch in late 1999 or early 2000 on a Russian Cosmos launch vehicle. *Quickbird-2* probably will be launched in 2001. Earthwatch originally hoped to be the first commercial firm to provide high-resolution images through its *Earlybird* satellite, but communication with the satellite was lost soon after its 1997 launch.

Through its subsidiary Orbimage, Orbital Sciences will launch its *OrbView-3* satellite in 2000 and will provide 1-meter resolution panchromatic and 4-meter resolution multispectral imagery in real time. *Orbview-4* is planned for a 2000 launch and will be the first commercial hyperspectral imager in addition to offering the same products as *OrbView-3.* Data from the hyperspectral sensor will be used for mineral exploration, agricultural management, environmental monitoring, and security purposes.

Research & Development Laboratories (RDL) is licensed to build and operate an SAR satellite, *Radar-1,* with 1-meter resolution. RDL will launch in 2001, and its satellite will circle the planet 14 times daily.

In coordination with the government of Israel, West Indian Space (WIS) planned to provide high-resolution imaging services for 8 years, starting in 1999. WIS is a joint venture between Israel Aircraft Industries, two other Israeli companies, and Core Software Technology of the United States. The company will launch eight Earth Remote Observation Satellites (EROS) between 1999 and 2003 and will provide global real-time high-resolution images commercially.

Industry and Trade Projections for the Next 1 and 5 Years

The remote sensing market should grow quickly as new high-resolution, 1-meter images become available. This includes U.S. and foreign government customers of the 1-meter images, including an initiative by the U.S. Department of Defense, the Central Intelligence Agency, and the National Reconnaissance Office to increase the amount of data purchased and the investment made in commercial imagery satellites, with half of the $1 billion budget being placed between 2001 and 2005. In this way, the government would allow commercial firms to provide basic images while the government maintained advanced technology systems. Satellite images should take over markets now served by aerial images. Many analysts believe that satellites will control more than half the imagery marketplace by 2005, though their share was only 10 percent in 1998. Satellites will take market share because they can cover an increased area in a shorter time and for a lower cost per image.

Foreign providers of remote sensing imagery will offer strong competition to the U.S. industry by providing a large assortment of services. The U.S. industry will need to develop applications for value-added products, offer lower-cost services, and provide timely images to remain competitive. Growth in remote sensing imagery for the next 1 and 5 years will occur in both the space-based sector, which includes the manufacture and sale of satellites, ground stations, and hardware, and the value-added sector, which converts raw data for specific uses. Growth in the value-added sector will be stronger. Growth in the hardware area will result from the sale of satellite systems internationally and the sale of ground stations for receiving and interpreting data. Growth in the value-added sector will come from end-user demand driven by the ability to adapt the data to specific purposes in a timely, low-cost manner.

Revenues for raw data and value-added images should reach over $1 billion in the year 2000, with approximately 90 percent of the revenues coming from the value-added sector. Reportedly, satellite imaging revenues reached $165 million in 1998 and could reach $2.7 billion by 2007. With higher-resolution images and the ability of computer software companies to convert satellite data into useful end products, the remote sensing industry will begin to cut into the aerial photography market. Therefore, competition will occur not only among satellite remote sensing providers but also between the satellite industry and the aerial photography industry. The amount of competition will be determined by the public's demand for images in the resolution range provided by aerial photography and the development of new applications for remote sensing data. It also will depend on the speed and cost at which satellite data can be converted to support such applications. New applications include forestry, urban planning, telecommunications system planning, search and rescue operations, fleet management, product tracking, zoning, and fishing. Of course, each market segment will require specific information relative to its function. It will be the responsibility of value-added providers to meet the needs of this market. If that happens, the market will grow consistently.

The remote sensing industry will earn commercial profits from the development of several purely commercial systems and the presence of worldwide data distributors that use many countries' satellites to compile image libraries for future use. In addition, the demand for different types of images, such as radar and hyperspectral imagery, will increase the demand for remotely sensed images of the earth. Most satellite imagers are planning to distribute images via the Internet, which should increase the customer base.

SPACE INSURANCE

Space insurance is a growing subsector of the insurance industry that provides coverage for all aspects of commercial space. Included are a satellite's preparation, assembly, and transportation; its mating with the launch vehicle; the launch and delivery of a satellite into the proper orbit; and the testing and operation of a satellite for a specified period. Satellites often are insured against delays in the launch schedule, during which time a company could lose revenue.

Global Trends

Space insurance providers lost approximately $1.7 billion to $2 billion in 1998 for a 200 percent insurance loss ratio for 1998. An unusually high number of launch failures in the first half of 1999 has continued to hurt the industry. An increase in insurance rates was not immediately apparent in 1999 because of overcapacity in the insurance market but was expected to follow as the market shrinks. Under the new export licensing restrictions, launch providers and satellite manufacturers may not be able to provide as much technical information to the insurance community as they had under the former export guidelines. With less information to analyze potential risk, insurers may increase rates to counter the risk. Because of the high risk, capacity in the reinsurance market has shrunk from a high of nearly $1 billion and could force major changes in the industry. On a positive note for insurers, the recent Titan launches were not insured and will have no impact on the launch insurance market.

Many firms entered the market after the successful launch markets of the 1995–1997 period. In-orbit insurance rates tend to be higher, which means that capacity continues to be lower, reaching a high in 1997–1998 at approximately $750 million. This will continue and probably worsen as a result of the string of in-orbit satellite failures that occurred in 1999. Premium rates currently range from 15 to 20 percent for GEO launches and 12 to 20 percent for LEO launches. Most rates cover the launch and an initial operating period, with insurance only for launch ranging around 6 to 12 percent. The majority of the insurance market is located in the United Kingdom, France, Germany, and the United States. Insurance companies are becoming increasingly conservative as new launch vehicles enter the market without demonstrable track records. A string of failures has reminded insurers that with new ventures comes high risk. The total global space insurance capacity for the year is only about $1.3 billion. Any more failures will seriously injure commercial insurance providers. Insurers are hopeful that the increased attention being paid to launch failures will increase reliability.

Domestic Trends

As a result of the recent string of failures, it is not expected that many U.S. insurance providers will enter this risky market in the near future. As with global providers, U.S. providers may raise premiums to cover the costs of failures in 1998 and 1999. It is possible that investigations into many vehicles' manufacturing and assembly processes following failures may increase the success rates of future launches. This could draw more insurance companies back into the space insurance market.

Industry and Trade Projections for the Next 1 and 5 Years

The space insurance market will struggle in the year 2000, and its success will be dependent on the occurrence of additional failures. The market should stabilize within 5 years, and vehicles should return to a more reliable condition after launch failure investigations. In the long run, as new vehicles prove their reliability, the space insurance market will expand, premiums will drop, and volume and capacity will increase.

OTHER NONCOMMERCIAL SPACE VENTURES

This section deals with projects that are on the verge of becoming commercial but remain in the government realm and have not begun to be exploited. It includes the commercialization of human space flight, the commercialization of the International Space Station, and projects such as microgravity experiments, manufacturing in space, space-based solar power, and space tourism.

Global Trends

The drive to commercialize space has gained momentum as government space budgets have been cut, pushing this market toward the commercial sector. Driving this commercialization are government agencies such as NASA, which is trying to shed its operational functions and focus its limited resources on core research and development missions such as space exploration. NASA is working with commercial space firms to explore ways in which LEO space projects can be financed with private funds so that it can focus on the exploration of Mars and other planets. Both the public sector and the private sector recognize that the development of commercial space will rely on public-private partnerships and hope that those relationships will spread the risk of these projects enough that more projects will materialize.

Historically, the commercialization of space was restricted by high risk and the high cost of developing and launching space assets. For investments in commercial space to be worthwhile, end markets have to be developed that will drive demand for these products. The government has tended to fund all space science activities, but new companies are beginning to establish entrepreneurial ventures to capitalize on the resources of space.

Domestic Trends

Although it often goes unrecognized, NASA research has already provided the world with creations such as vehicle controllers for the handicapped, weather forecasting, firefighter breathing systems, water recycling technologies, scratch-resistant glass, advanced turboprops, anticorrosion paint, laser heart surgery, and new flame-resistant materials. Continuation of the development of commercial products based on space-related research is a priority for the U.S. government.

The Commercial Space Act of 1998 makes commercializing the International Space Station (ISS) a priority. SPACEHAB is the first company to commercially develop, own, and operate habitable modules that provide laboratory facilities and logistics resupply aboard NASA's Space Shuttles. For the ISS, SPACEHAB signed its first customer, the Colorado School of Mines' Center for Commercial Applications of Combustion in Space (CCACS), which will use the SPACEHAB-funded furnace called Space DRUMS to process exotic glass and ceramic materials, using a unique combustion technique in the microgravity environment aboard the ISS. Space-DRUMS is a partnership between SPACEHAB and Guigne Technologies Ltd. of Canada and uses acoustic levitation, or sound waves, to hold fluid or solid material samples in place in microgravity while they are being processed aboard the Shuttle or ISS. This eliminates physical defects and opportunities for contamination. The unique glass and ceramics eventually could be used for bone replacement, industrial filters, and fiber-optic telecommunications cable. This will be the first commercial research facility on the ISS when it is delivered in 2000.

NASA believes that commercial activities could account for up to approximately one-third of the ISS's space for scientific experiments in its first 10 years of operation. The ISS is currently projected to cost approximately $21 billion, but many aerospace experts believe that the cost could go up, perhaps by another $3 billion, and many also assume that further delays will increase the price farther. The ISS is being developed mainly by the United States, Russia, Japan, and Europe, with 180 companies working on the space laboratory. Efforts are under way to turn over the facility completely to private industry at the end of its 10-year government occupancy.

Of great concern to the operators of the ISS is orbital debris, which has been accumulating in space since the beginning of the space program. Approximately 9,000 objects are regularly tracked, but the real amount of space debris is much greater. Orbital debris is a concern to the ISS because impact could damage the orbiting station. Several proposals have been made for reducing the amount of orbital debris, but none of them has been developed.

Emerging Markets

Even though the use of satellites for telecommunications has become standard, several other sectors of this industry have just begun to enter the commercial market, while others are poised to enter in the next few years. In addition to remote sensing and GPS, emerging markets such as asset tracking, data processing, logistics, fleet management, and remote management and control will increase their dependence on space assets. One application is the use of a microgravity atmosphere for the development of tissues, proteins, crystals, and semiconductors in space. Manufacturing such materials in a microgravity environment produces much larger and purer specimens than can be produced on the ground. NASA has performed several experiments on the Space Shuttle and the Russian Mir Space Station. NASA and several pharmaceutical firms are interested in the use of microgravity to speed biomedical research toward cures for diseases such as AIDS and cancer. While not all microgravity experiments are performed on the Space Shuttle or the ISS, approximately 20 companies perform experiments related to physical properties in the absence of gravity. Companies interested in the manufacture of thin semiconductor films and crystal development believe that profits are still a few years away. Limited short-term access to the microgravity atmosphere is available through parabolic aircraft flights, and long-term access is available through the European "Eureka" platform and SPACEHAB. The ISS and reusable launch vehicles will greatly increase this segment's ability to perform microgravity experiments.

A number of new U.S. companies have developed proposals for commercial space ventures. For example, Lunar Exploration Inc. plans to return rock samples from the moon to the earth for analysis that would expand the work started by the Apollo program. The commercial ventures would sell the samples to NASA and other space agencies and would like to begin missions in 2002. In addition, SpaceDev, the world's first commercial space exploration and development company, is providing the Near Earth Asteroid Prospector (NEAP), which is slated to launch in 2001. The mission is intended to be the first in a series of profitable commercial deep space missions. SpaceDev will sell the data gathered from its instruments to scientists, researchers, universities, and other purchasers.

Two companies are offering trips to space a few years hence: Adventure Tours Inc., a partnership between Omega Travel and Quark Tours, and Zegrahm Space Voyages, a partnership between Zegrahm Expeditions and Vela Technology Development Inc. Independent market surveys indicate that there is a huge potential for public space travel and tourism, and many of those polled say they are willing to pay a significant price for the experience.

A number of other applications have not been tapped. Examples of other ideas for commercializing space include solar power satellites, lunar power stations, the exploitation of lunar or asteroid materials for sale on earth, dedicated space theme parks associated with suborbital and orbital flights, orbiting resort hotels, the collection of orbital debris, and eventually lunar cruises and visits.

Industry and Trade Projections for the Next 1 and 5 Years

Space commercialization, research and manufacturing in space, and more established sectors such as GPS and remote sensing will continue to experience growth, but several of these sectors will not enter the commercial realm for a few years. Scientific research in space for the most part will remain in the domain of governments in the near term. With the development of the ISS, the commercial use of space for scientific (especially pharmaceutical) research will move this market toward profitability.

Kim Wells, U.S. Department of Commerce, Office of Aerospace, (202) 482-2232, kim_wells@ita.doc.gov; ***Krysten Jenci,*** Office of Telecommunications, (202) 482-4466, krysten_jenci@ita.doc.gov, August 1999.

REFERENCES

Aviation Week & Space Technology, McGraw-Hill, Inc., 1221 Avenue of the Americas, New York, NY 10020.

GPS 2005, Allied Business Intelligence (ABI), 202 Townsend Square, Oyster Bay, NY 11771. (516) 624-3113, www.alliedworld.com.

Low Earth Orbit Commercial Market Projections, Federal Aviation Administration, Associate Administrator for Commercial Space Transportation, Washington, DC 20590.

1999 COMSTAC Mission Model Update, Commercial Space Transportation Advisory Committee, Federal Aviation Administration, Associate Administrator for Commercial Space Transportation, Washington, DC 20590.

Satellite Communications Ground Stations Market Survey—Worldwide Prospects, 1997–2006, Euroconsult, 71,79 boulevard Richard Lenoir, 75011 Paris, France. 33-1-49-23-75-30, www.euroconsult-ec.com.

Satellite Communications Industry Overview—Third Quarter 1999, Banc of America Securities. (212) 583-8011.

Satellite Industry Indicators Fact Sheet, Satellite Industry Association/Futron Corporation. (703) 549-8697, www.sia.org.

Satellite International, Baskerville Communications Corp., 15165 Ventura Blvd., Suite 310 Sherman Oaks, CA 91403. (310) 978-6073, www.baskerville.co.uk.

Satellite Markets, Spring and Summer 1999, Media Business Corp., Futron Corporation, Satellite Industry Association, 807 Arapahoe Street, Golden, CO 80401. (303) 271-9960, www.skyreport.com.

Satellite Report 2000, William Kidd, satellite analyst, C.E. Unterberg, Towbin, 10 East 50th Street, New York, NY 10022. (212) 572-8000, www.unterberg.com/satcom.

SkyTrends Annual Report 1999, Media Business Corp., 807 Arapahoe Street, Golden, CO 80401. (303) 271-9960, www.skyreport.com.

Space News, Army Times Publishing Co., 6883 Commercial Drive, Springfield, VA 22159. (703) 750-8696, www.spacenews.com.

State of the Space Industry—1999 Outlook, International Space Business Council, 2055 North Fifteenth Street, Suite 300, Arlington, VA 22201. (703) 524-2766, www.spacebusiness.com.

Via Satellite, 1998 Global Satellite Survey, Phillips Business Information Inc., 1201 Seven Locks Road, Suite 300, Potomac, MD 20854. (301) 340-7788, www.satellitetoday.com/viaonline.

World Satellite Ground Segment Equipment Markets, Frost & Sullivan, 2525 Charleston Road, Mountain View, CA 94043. (415) 961-9000, www.frost.com.

World Transmission Equipment Markets, 1997 Edition, Northern Business Information/Dataquest, 251 River Oaks Parkway, San Jose, CA 95134. (408) 468-8000, gartner11.gartnerweb.com/dq/.

RELATED CHAPTERS

21: Aerospace
30: Telecommunications Services
31: Telecommunications and Navigation Equipment
32: Entertainment

GLOSSARY

Big LEO system: A system of satellites working together as a system in low earth orbit that will provide all the services of Little LEO systems as well as mobile voice and fax capabilities.

Block buys: A strategy, used by satellite manufacturers, of purchasing numerous launches at one time to reserve access to space and receive a price discount based on the volume of launches purchased.

Broadband LEO system: A satellite system in low earth orbit that will provide wireless video, voice, and broadband high-speed data services to small satellite dishes.

Digital elevation mapping/model: The process of using computer software to develop a three-dimensional image from remote sensing data to depict elevations.

Direct-to-Home (DTH): A term that is used to refer to the satellite television and broadcasting industries. An example is DirecTV.

Evolved Expendable Launch Vehicle (EELV): A U.S. Air Force program that incorporates existing launch vehicles into the development of a family of more capable, less expensive launch vehicles.

Geostationary earth orbit (GEO): The altitude (22,230 miles) at which a satellite appears to be fixed at a specific spot above the earth.

Geostationary transfer orbit (GTO): An orbit to which GEO satellites often are launched before their final orbital maneuvers.

Little LEO system: A system of low earth orbit satellites that will provide mobile data messaging and position determination services on a global level.

Low earth orbit (LEO): For the purposes of this publication, any orbit lower than geostationary earth orbit.

Payload: The satellite, instrument package, or equipment carried into space by a launch vehicle.

Remote sensing: The process of imaging the earth from space.

Seamless imaging: The process of incorporating a number of remotely sensed images to make a large image.

TELECOMMUNICATIONS SERVICES
Economic and Trade Trends

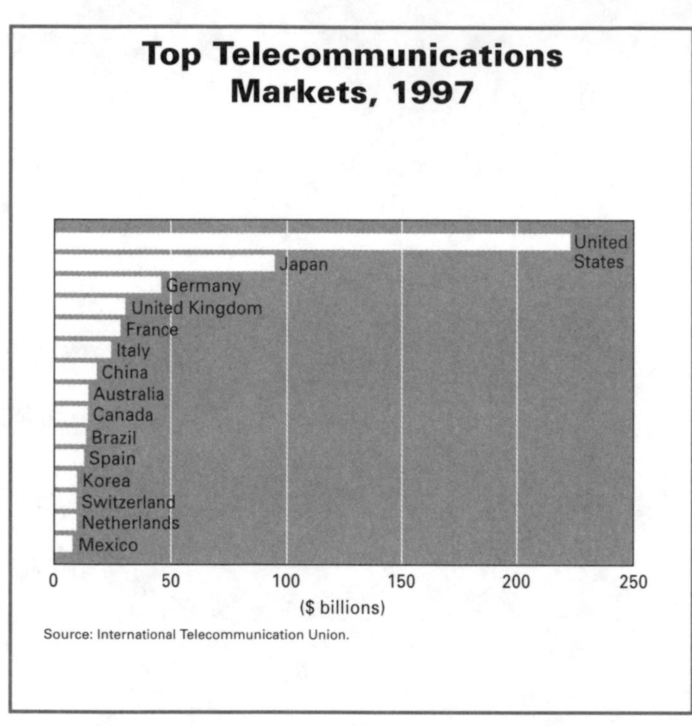

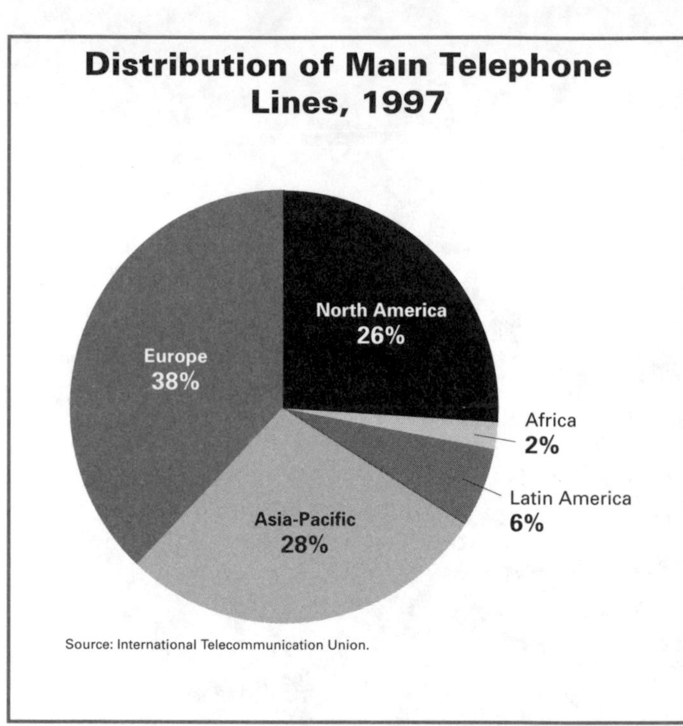

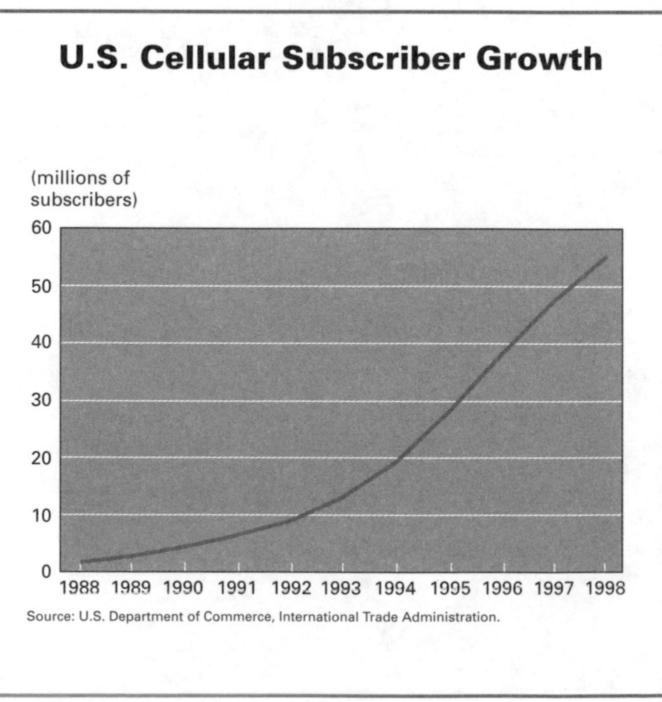

See "Getting the Most Out of *Outlook 2000*" for definitions of terms.

30

Telecommunications Services

INDUSTRY DEFINITION The telecommunications services industry (SIC 4812, 4813, 4822) is broadly divided into providers serving the communications markets for basic voice and data services. These services include local exchange, cellular telephony and paging, long-distance (toll), and international services, whether provided by wire (coaxial or fiber cable) or wireless (terrestrial radio systems or satellite) technologies. This chapter focuses on telecommunications firms, both regulated and unregulated, offering basic services that transmit information of the user's choosing without change in the form or content of the information as it is sent and received.

OVERVIEW

Traditional telephone services include local, long-distance, and international voice telephony and data transmission services. The "wireline" services industry (SIC 4813 and 4822) uses terrestrial cable and fiber-optic technology to provide voice and data communications. Some wireline services are now provided through the use of wireless technologies or a combination of wireline and wireless facilities. Radiotelephone communications (SIC 4812), including cellular, paging, and personal communication services (PCS), are discussed in the wireless communications services section of this chapter. The satellite services sector, which includes fixed and mobile services (voice, data, and video) provided through communications satellites, is discussed in Chapter 29.

The Telecommunications Act of 1996 removed the last domestic barriers to competition in telecommunications services. However, competition in local markets still is generally restricted to large urban business markets, and some former Bell companies are just beginning to secure authorization to offer long-distance services within their own service areas. The opening of many international markets to competition, which was formalized by the entry into force of the World Trade Organization's (WTO) Agreement on Basic Telecommunications Services in 1998, was a major milestone in the industry. Major American and foreign telecommunications firms already are competing in large segments of the estimated $900 billion worldwide market for telecommunications services.

GLOBAL INDUSTRY TRENDS

Historically, telecommunications companies in virtually all countries were state-owned enterprises (generically known as PTTs for the postal, telegraph, and telephone services they offered). PTTs had exclusive rights to provide telephone services both domestically and internationally. Privatizing some or all of its monopoly carrier has become one many governments take as they get out of the telephone business and allow greater participation by the private sector. Governments do this for several reasons: to raise capital to invest in telecommunications infrastructure; to bring "market discipline" to an often inefficient, poorly managed bureaucratic enterprise so that it can develop into a competitive business operation; and to help set the stage for competition by separating the government regulator from the provider of telecommunications services. In the United States, however, the government never owned or controlled a telephone company, and so it had no financial interest in perpetuating the AT&T monopoly. British Telecom was the first PTT to go private, with a 51 percent public offering that raised $5.2 billion in 1984. Since that time, governments in countries such as Mexico, Brazil, Denmark, Pakistan, and Singapore have sold stakes in their telecommunications operators.

Mergers and business alliances continue to take place in the U.S. and foreign telecommunications markets. These strategic alliances provide ways for companies to enter new markets and strengthen their competitive positions in the markets they already serve. U.S. companies with long experience in the telecommunications sector are potentially desirable partners for foreign firms eager to gain access to the U.S. market. As competition increases within and beyond the United States, companies are looking for new business partners that can provide capital, customers, and/or the marketing and technological expertise needed to develop and sell new services.

Continued market liberalization, accompanied by growing competition, is a third global trend. Some governments have introduced competition by allowing private sector participation in building and operating networks for cellular communications and paging services. Since PTTs have never provided these services, they do not view the new carriers as competitive threats. A more significant step in market liberalization is the opening of all sectors of telephony to competition without limiting the number of firms authorized to provide service, sharply limiting the types of services they can offer, or restricting the degree of foreign participation (investment) in the market. Under legislation passed by the European Union (EU), 10 of its member states fully opened their markets to competition on January 1, 1998. All the EU member states except Greece and Portugal have liberalized the provision of telecommunications services. There are now 78 WTO members with post-Uruguay Round commitments in basic telecom services.

FACTORS AFFECTING FUTURE U.S. INDUSTRY GROWTH

New laws, together with judicial and regulatory decisions, have played a critical role in introducing and promoting competition in telecommunications services in the United States. After a 20-year effort, Congress passed the Telecommunication Act of 1996, which promised far-reaching changes in the industry. However, widespread dissatisfaction remains, because local competition has not developed in the residential market to a significant degree. Future legal decisions and modifications of regulatory policy will continue to have an impact on the pace of competition in local telephony.

The fundamental role telecommunications now plays in the operations of all businesses and its importance in promoting economic growth and increasing trade assure its future growth. The United States is the world's largest telecommunications services market, accounting for about 30 percent of world market revenues. Hence, gaining access to the U.S. market is a key strategic objective of many foreign firms.

U.S. companies are world leaders in the development and marketing of telecommunications services and, unlike most foreign telecommunications operators, already have considerable experience functioning in a competitive marketplace. U.S. firms have demonstrated expertise in utilizing new technologies to lower the costs and improve the quality of their services. Many new features and applications in telecommunications are based on sophisticated software programs, such as billing systems that provide valuable information to the customer and the carrier alike.

Growth in the U.S. telecommunications industry also will be fueled by expanding opportunities in foreign markets. U.S. companies, often in partnership with a firm in the host country, have won scores of bids to build and operate cellular networks abroad. As more countries have adopted policies that allow the construction of new networks to provide basic telephony, U.S. firms are in an excellent position to compete in the bidding process. Expanding opportunities abroad for U.S. service firms also will stimulate the domestic market for network equipment, since many of the countries where new telecommunications networks will be built do not manufacture the advanced equipment that will be needed.

U.S. firms also participate in foreign markets by investing in privatized national operators and/or new private sector telecommunications firms. In Mexico, for example, SBC Communications is part of a consortium of companies investing in Telmex. MCI WorldCom is a 45 percent co-owner of the competitive Mexican long-distance carrier Avantel. U.S. firms also have invested in the former PTT carriers in Belgium, Ireland, and Italy and in European consortia, one of whose partners owns a telecommunications network that competes against the former PTT. AT&T is an investor in Arcor, a German private network operator formed by an alliance of Mannesmann, Unisource, and DBKom, which owned the telecommunications facilities of the German railway system. Bell Atlantic has a 20 percent interest in BayanTel, a telecommunications operator that serves metropolitan Manila and southern Luzon. Among the major foreign telecommunications services markets, only China remains closed to any type of foreign investment in or operation of its networks.

Although the United States continues to register a large net deficit in international telecommunications services, this is more a reflection of the inadequacies of foreign market conditions (service monopolies, high prices, less extensive and lower-quality telecommunications networks) and artificially high accounting rates than of the competitiveness of the U.S. industry. (An accounting rate is a negotiated rate between carriers for the handling of international traffic.) Net settlement payments ("imports") that amounted to $4.7 billion in 1998 (down from $5.2 billion in 1997) should continue to decline as the forces of competition lower accounting rates closer to the costs of service (see Figure 30-1). Real progress has been made in reducing accounting rates in the last 2 years. Carriers in 35 countries are at or below the relevant Federal Communications Commission (FCC) benchmark rate, and carriers in 17 other countries have agreed to reach that rate on schedule. The countries involved account for two-thirds of total U.S. settlement minutes, and those minutes make up about half of U.S. settlement payments. The net result has been good for the consumer.

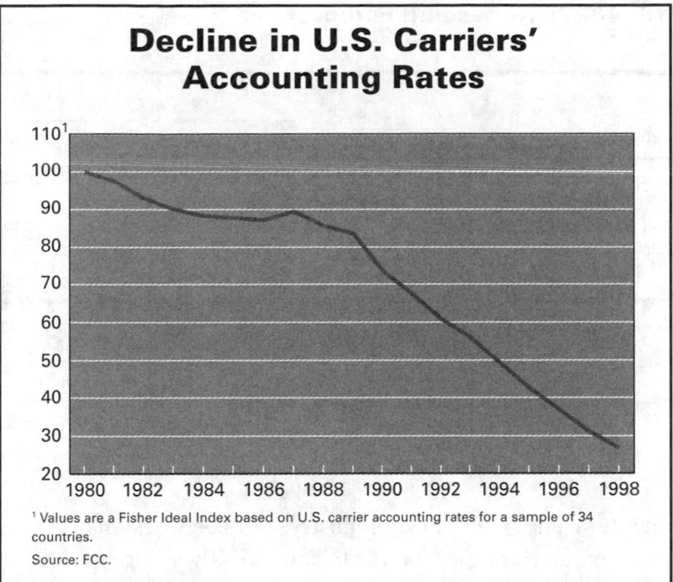

FIGURE 30-1

The average global rate from the United States was 63 cents a minute in 1997; by September 1999, that rate was down to 43 cents a minute.

U.S. INDUSTRY GROWTH PROJECTIONS FOR NEXT 1 AND 5 YEARS

It is a challenging exercise to forecast U.S. local, long-distance, and international telephone revenues. Increased competition continues to affect prices, traffic volumes, and revenue growth, and the trend toward convergence (e.g., offering telephone services on cable television networks) and the development of Internet Protocol (IP) networks make the timing and extent of competition in important submarkets uncertain. AT&T is gearing up to provide local telephony in many markets, but how quickly those services will be made available and how many subscribers will sign up are unanswered questions.

In the long-distance sector, the drama is still entitled *Waiting for Godot.* The former Bell companies have been waiting several years to obtain authorization to provide long-distance and international services to customers in their respective service areas. In return, they have been required to open their networks to potential competitors, as specified in a 14-point checklist. In 1998, experts predicted at least one Bell firm would be in the long-distance business by mid-1999. With that date having been missed, the new predictions cluster around the first quarter of 2000. Other unanswered questions include the following: Will the entry of large incumbent local exchange carriers (ILECs) result in price wars? Will IP telephony services stimulate overall demand or reduce aggregate long-distance revenues or have only marginal effects in the year 2000? Will large foreign firms try to buy a large U.S. telecommunications carrier in 2000? At this point, the answers are unknown.

What can be said with confidence is that telecommunications services remain a dynamic and growing industry. Although the fortunes of individual firms and subsectors may ebb and flow, consumer demand for telecommunications services and business needs for new and improved applications will continue to flourish. The demand for all telecommunications services will remain strong, and revenues will increase, although at different rates, in the three primary basic services market segments. Local service revenues should increase about 5 percent in 2000 and 5 to 6 percent in the following 4 years to reach about $156 billion in 2004. Growth in interstate long-distance domestic minutes was 9 percent in 1998, maintaining an annual growth rate of about 10 percent. Revenue growth for all toll services was under 4 percent in 1998 and should be close to 3 percent in the next few years, and so total toll revenues could reach $118 billion in 2004.

Fairly dramatic changes in international revenues and traffic first occurred in 1998, and those trends are expected to continue. Those reductions were due to both falling prices and the routing of more traffic over private line networks and the Internet, for which traffic and revenue figures are unavailable. Carriers report figures only for traffic carried by public circuit-switched telephone networks. Thus, current reports do not capture all international traffic. Those reports indicate that international outbound U.S. minutes of traffic grew at only a 4 percent rate in 1998 and should grow at an annual rate of 4 percent or less from 2000 to 2004. Inbound minutes to the United States grew less than 1 percent in 1998, with no or at best minimal growth expected during the next 5 years. End-user billed revenues for international calls dropped 11 percent annually in 1998 and may amount to about $15 billion in 1999, probably remaining at about that level through 2004.

Total U.S. revenues for basic voice and data services are expected to increase about 7 percent in 2000 to reach just over $282 billion (see Table 30-1). Annual revenue growth is expected to continue at that level, bringing industry telecommunications service revenues to $370 billion in 2004.

The number of jobs in the telecommunications services industry increased 3 percent in 1998, but from 1994 to 1998, jobs in the industry increased 13 percent. Most of the growth occurred in the wireless sector, where jobs increased 97 percent during that period. This sector, however, has only about one of every five industry jobs. The forecasts for continued substantial growth rates in wireless subscribers and revenues and the continued entry by foreign competitors into the open U.S. telecommunications market suggest that overall the telecommunications services industry will continue to create new jobs.

GLOBAL MARKET PROSPECTS

Prospects are good for overall 6 to 7 percent annual growth in the global telecommunications services market. Continued expansion of foreign networks (leading to improvements in service quality and increases in the number of subscribers on the network) and lower prices resulting from competition

TABLE 30-1: Telecommunications Services (SIC 4812, 4813, 4822) Trends and Forecasts
(millions of dollars except as noted)

	1993	1994	1995	1996	1997	1998	1999[1]	2000[2]	Percent Change 95–96	96–97	97–98	93–99
Operating revenues	165,342	174,890	190,076	211,782	231,168	246,392	263,640	282,094	11.42	9.15	6.59	59.45
Operating revenues (1992$)	160,995	165,820	175,817	197,135	215,823	229,348			12.13	9.48		
Total employment (thousands)	886	901	908.2	919.8	984.2	1,013.3			1.28	7.00		
Production workers (thousands)[3]	668.4	668.7	678.8	703.2	736.7	710.1			3.59	4.76		
Average hourly earnings ($)[3]	15.61	15.92	16.22	16.63	17.51	17.61			2.53	5.29		

[1] Estimate.
[2] Forecast.
[3] Production or nonsupervisory workers only.
Source: U.S. Department of Commerce: International Trade Administration (ITA), Bureau of the Census; U.S. Department of Labor, Bureau of Labor Statistics; Federal Communications Commission. Estimates and forecasts by ITA.

and/or the use of newer, cost-effective technologies will fuel demand.

There are two significant aspects of future global demand for telecommunications services. One is the demand for "traded" telecommunications services: U.S.-originated and -terminated international voice traffic. Outbound call volume should continue to increase, although a higher percentage of traffic will go over private leased circuits. Large manufacturing and service companies in the United States are and will continue to be heavy users of telecommunications services. Strong U.S. industries such as financial services, travel and tourism, software development, and some manufacturing sectors maintain close overseas business connections with subsidiaries, customers, and suppliers and depend heavily on private telecommunications networks and services to carry out their business operations. In addition, the presence of large immigrant populations in the United States and the prospect of lower international calling rates will encourage residential use of international voice services. The value of U.S. telecommunications services "exports" (traffic received from foreign destinations) dropped to $2.4 billion in 1998 and is expected to fall to about $2.0 billion in 2000, providing further evidence of the effects that lower settlement rates and alternative networks (private leased lines and the Internet) are having on international telephony.

A second aspect of global market prospects involves the new business opportunities that have emerged for U.S. firms as the large telecommunications service markets in Europe and many in the Far East and Latin America have opened to U.S. service suppliers. In pursuing commercial opportunities of these sorts, U.S. telecommunications firms often establish a commercial presence in the foreign country either directly or through joint venture arrangements. Although the future revenues and exports those ventures generate can become a source of profit to a company, the revenues earned do not show up in U.S. market figures.

There are tremendous unmet demands throughout the global telcommunications services marketplace. Many nations have ambitious plans to invest huge sums in their infrastructures and make telecommunications services more widely available to their citizens. Under China's Ninth Five Year Plan, the communications and information industry has been designated as a strategic area for development. The objective is to establish a national information infrastructure based on the broadband integrated service digital technologies by 2010. In 1999, China aimed for an annual capital investment of $12 billion with a network that would reach every village. India's government hopes to see $41 billion invested in that country's telecommunications sector over the next 15 years. Public telecommunications investment in EU member states has increased as a result of market liberalization during the last few years and may total $55 billion in the year 2000.

In developing countries, where typically less than 10 percent and often under 5 percent of the population has ready access to a telephone, the priority is to expand "universal service." In the United States, Japan, and western Europe, where 85 percent to 95 percent of households have telephone service, the emphasis is on upgrading existing networks (popularly referred to as information superhighways or national information infrastructures) to accommodate advanced multimedia (combining voice, data, and video applications) and other information technology services.

TELEPHONE SERVICES

Telecommunications Service Providers

Although well over 90 percent of wireline service revenues are controlled by a few large companies (the former regional Bell firms and the three largest long-distance companies), the introduction of new services based on new or improved technologies provides ample scope for niche market players in telecommunications services. There are 2,000 companies and subsidiaries providing local telephone services in the United States. About 150 firms offer long-distance services over network facilities of which they own at least a part. Another 350 companies provide toll services by reselling the long-distance services of the large carriers that have built their own nationwide networks (e.g., AT&T, MCI WorldCom, and Sprint). About 300 competitive local exchange carriers (CLECs) have built fiber networks in urban business districts that connect with the networks of long-distance carriers. Some of the carriers mentioned above are discussed in more detail below.

Approximately 60 firms own part (e.g., a switch) of the facilities they use to provide international telecommunications services, and at least 350 firms offer international services on a resale basis. Other companies that report toll revenues include operator service providers and pay telephone operators. On the wireless side, about 900 firms provide cellular, paging, and other mobile services. Although the precise number of firms providing telecommunications services in the United States is unknown, since many are unregulated, small, privately held enterprises, the total probably is around 4,100.

Of the approximately 350 firms that provide some form of international voice and data services, the three biggest players account for about 80 percent of international revenues. Each of those three companies has established business relationships with leading foreign telecommunications companies. The benefits of those alliances include instant access to the large foreign markets already served by the partners, the ability to provide domestic customers with a greater range of seamless global services carried over the partners' network, a stronger competitive position against traditional rivals, and the ability to expand into domestic markets by obtaining funds to invest in building new network facilities and developing new services.

Mergers and Business Alliances

Mergers continued to occur at all levels of the telecommunications industry in 1998 and 1999, and that trend is expected to continue in the absence of sharp antitrust or regulatory opposition in the year 2000 and beyond. Seven of the top 10 mergers in the telecommunications industry have occurred or been proposed within the last 2 years. Eight of those mergers have been between U.S. companies (see Table 30-2). Some believe that before these activities end, the structure of the telecommunications industry in the United States will be altered fundamentally. They predict that ultimately only three of the original seven Bell regional companies may remain, each allied or merged with one of the two or three big U.S. long-distance carriers (AT&T, MCI WorldCom, and Sprint) or with a foreign carrier or at least will have investments in or exclusive business relationships with large international (European or Asian) telecommunications firms. Industry leaders claim that in a few years there may only be a handful of truly global telecommunications carriers and that recent mergers are only a reflection of the financial and marketing alliances necessary for a company to be a global competitor. The fundamental unanswered question is whether the creation of such national and ultimately global behemoths will increase competitive choices for consumers or whether a telecommunications oligarchy will be created whose firms all offer essentially similar services at similar prices.

Clearly, one can make a case that "market forces" are largely responsible for this wave of mergers, but others argue that misguided or vague legislation, combined with regulatory micromanagement and a strategy of some firms to remove potential competitors by taking them over, is also part of the explanation. It was anticipated that the 1996 Telecommunications Act would lead to vigorous competition in the last segment of the telecommunications market dominated by monopolies: local telephone services. The theory was that allowing cable television companies to offer local telephony and long-distance carriers to serve local markets while allowing the former Bell companies to enter the domestic long-distance and international markets would spur innovation and competition that would benefit consumers.

There has been widespread criticism because competition in the "local loop" has not developed or at least does not yet benefit residential customers. Some want to revisit sections of the Telecommunications Act, while others allege that the act tried to please all sides and established contradictory objectives of promoting universal service by maintaining billions of dollars of industry subsidies for local telephone service while encouraging competition in the same market, where the costs of service have been skewed in favor of rural and residential users. In areas where prices have been subsidized historically, competition can result in an increase, not a decrease, in prices as they rise toward the true costs.

Similarly, all the former Bell companies are not yet allowed to offer in-region long-distance and international services. Some observers believe that consolidation among local exchange carriers has become a key strategic goal because those companies have not been granted the authority to expand into long distance or because they and other large telecommu-

TABLE 30-2: Top 10 Telecommunications Mergers

Date Announced	Buyer	Target	Value of Deal, $ billions
10/05/99	MCI WorldCom	Sprint	129.0
05/11/98	SBC Communications	Ameritech	72.4
07/28/98	Bell Atlantic	GTE	71.3
01/18/99	Vodafone Group Communications	AirTouch Communications	65.9
05/06/99	AT&T	MediaOne	58.0
06/14/99	Qwest Communications	US West	48.5
10/01/97	WorldCom	MCI Communications	43.4
02/20/99	Ing.C. Olivetti	Telecom Italia	34.8
04/22/96	Bell Atlantic	Nynex	30.8
04/01/96	SBC Communications	Pacific Telesis Group	22.4

Source: Adapted from Thomson Financial Securities Data.

nications firms see little to gain from a fierce struggle to compete in new markets that could result in greater costs, loss of market share, and lower profits.

Local telecommunications companies have a different explanation for their desire to grow through mergers. Merging is the best way for a telecommunications company to gain a presence internationally and strengthen its position in the U.S. market. Merging increases the financial and marketing resources at the company's disposal and lets it invest the large sums necessary to compete in local markets outside its own service territory. With a greater geographic coverage in the United States and telecommunications alliances abroad, those companies are better able to offer more customers end-to-end connectivity and seamless services among global locations. Do mergers essentially eliminate the possibility of future competition among rival firms or enhance the prospect of such competition, although among a reduced number of firms?

Several factors account for this trend toward creating larger companies in the telecommunications market. Traditional telecommunications companies (providing basic voice and data services) are becoming information and communications companies (offering integrated voice, enhanced data, video, and multimedia services) and are looking for partners that can increase the ability of the combined firms to compete in the global marketplace. Telecommunications firms may look for partners that can help them maintain market share in already competitive markets and achieve revenue growth by entering newly opened markets. Telecommunications companies are likely to seek out partners that offer different types of services in adjacent markets or that have developed expertise in new technologies. Voice, data, and video communications markets are merging, and different technologies (Internet, digital wireless, broadband networks, and low-orbiting satellite systems) have been developed to transmit digital signals. A company that wants to provide its customers with one-stop shopping for all their communications needs (domestic and international voice, cellular, paging, cable television, Internet, on-line and information services, etc.) is unlikely to have the necessary resources and expertise in-house and will need to buy or form a joint venture with niche market companies.

Local Exchange Firms

The Bell Atlantic–GTE "merger of equals" that was announced in July 1998 has continued to receive approval from state and federal regulators. The companies agree that the merger will enhance the strength of GTE's Internet backbone and data services, add a fourth national facilities-based carrier to the long-distance market, and create a provider of global communications services. The new company would serve more than 60 million U.S. access lines and about 13 million wireless subscribers. It also would have a major international presence with investments or operations in more than 30 foreign countries.

The SBC–Ameritech merger also appears to be close to completion, as the FCC and the companies have proposed 28 merger conditions in an effort to boost local competition in home markets and accelerate SBC's entry into new markets. Among the proposals, SBC would agree to enter and compete in 30 markets outside the firms' combined 13-state territory, using its own facilities within 30 months after the merger is approved, or pay a $40 million penalty for each market missed. Within its service territory, SBC would provide promotional discounts to local competitors of up to 32 percent for resold service and 25 percent for leasing unbundled local loops, the copper wires that connect a customer's home with the telephone company's local switching center. The objective is to increase competition in the local residential market, where few customers have a choice of local telephone service providers. The new SBC company would serve 57 million access lines in three separate geographic regions of the country.

US West, another former Bell company, was acquired by Quest in July 1999 in a $48 billion merger. With this acquisition, Quest becomes one of the few communications supercarriers expected to offer all types of communications services and connect its customers directly or through joint partnership arrangements to all major markets around the world by the end of the next decade. The merger combined US West's local networks with Quest's long-distance backbone. Quest, which went public only in 1997, was the nation's fourth largest long-distance telephone company and operated an 8,500-mile fiber-optic network linking 150 U.S. cities. The company has expanded into Mexico, where it is constructing a 1,400-mile network and has formed a partnership with a Dutch telecommunications company to build and operate a fiber network that will span 9,000 miles in Mexico by 2001. Quest also owns undersea cable connections to Europe. With this acquisition, Quest gained direct access to US West's 25 million customers across 14 midwestern and western states. The firm plans to offer a full menu of data services and Internet connections to businesses, particularly targeting midsize firms in 25 major cities not served by US West.

The long-distance market, where prices of 5 to 10 cents a minute now apply to domestic and many foreign locations, is not attractive as a distinct market to local exchange carriers, but those carriers need to be able to offer those services to their local customers in the future as part of a one-stop-shopping package. Only one former Bell company has met the 1996 Telecommunications Act's conditions for entry into long distance, and observers think that no more than 15 states will see the introduction of such competition by the end of the year 2000. Carriers believe that they need to combine ("bundle") as many services as possible to market an appealing product to customers: a single bill and a single contact for customer service. Bundled services can be packaged in ways that provide special discounts or value-added features to distinguish them from standard telephone services. Many telecommunications companies would like to achieve one-stop shopping by which they could offer their customers a variety of voice, data, and Internet-related services, providing a solution to all of a customer's communications needs.

Global Crossing, a Bermuda-based company founded in 1997, made an initial bid to acquire US West in May 1999 but ended up acquiring Frontier Communications for $12.5 billion.

Global Crossing has an undersea fiber-optic cable connecting the United States to Europe and plans cable routes to connect the United States to Asia and Latin American locations. It has been a "pipe provider," a transmission path for services offered by other telecommunications firms. Frontier had telephone operating companies in 14 states serving more than 1 million access lines as well as two international firms in Canada and the United Kingdom. Global Crossing acquired Frontier's U.S. fiber network along with its Internet and other value-added IP service capabilities. The company has announced plans to build an 11,000-mile land-and-undersea cable network over which high-speed services can be provided to Japan, China, Singapore, Hong Kong, the Philippines, and South Korea. The new firm's next step may be to acquire U.S. and European CLECs in major financial centers.

Competitive Local Exchange Carriers

CLECs are companies whose facilities bypass the bottleneck in the last mile of today's communications networks. Many began as competitive access providers (CAPs) and provided local loop bypass services to long-distance carriers. They include firms that have installed local fiber-optic rings around a metropolitan area as well as wireless cable operators. These companies operate in an increasingly competitive environment against entrenched incumbents (local telephone companies) that have much greater financial resources. Many CLECs are unprofitable, and future technological breakthroughs could undermine the viability of their current systems. However, some CLECs may be attractive acquisition targets, and others may be long-term players and become significant providers of broadband access. The 20 largest U.S. CLECs provide service to more than 4.3 million business lines, accounting for nearly 8 percent of the total market. Total market revenue of all CLECs reached $3.35 billion in 1998. CLECs also are attempting to position themselves as full-service providers, combining voice (including long-distance and international), data [frame relay, integrated series digital network (ISDN), and private lines], and Internet services into a single package.

MCI WorldCom (MCIW) has local city networks operating in more than 100 U.S. cities that connect 30,000 buildings. AT&T bought a CLEC, TCG, in 1998 as a way to enter the local business market. Sprint has spent about $1 billion acquiring CLECs, including small wireless cable providers, giving it access to nearly 25 million homes. Sprint is expected to use this spectrum to deliver broadband connectivity to households and small and medium-size businesses. So-called midtier CLECs tend to focus on a particular region of the country but are expanding the number and types of services they offer. Some of these CLECs will expand further by merging with fellow CLECs or become the acquisition targets of larger fiber-based carriers such as Quest. A growing number of start-up CLECs compete with a local telephone company in a small geographic area. Power and water utilities are using this method as a way to break into the telecommunications industry. Even large telecommunications companies such as SBC are planning to establish CLECs in some of the out-of-region urban markets in which they hope to compete.

Long-Distance Telecommunications Providers

Competition continued apace in the U.S. long-distance market, driving down prices in the process. Consumer price plans of 10 cents a minute have been replaced by offers of 7 cents and 5 cents a minute depending on the time of day. The calling plans carry a monthly service fee as well. AT&T probably has more than 60 percent of the nation's long-distance subscribers but only about 42 percent of switched toll revenues. MCIW has about 25 percent of those toll revenues, while Sprint's share is about 10 percent. The remaining competitors, facilities-based carriers, resellers, and firms offering IP telephony services (see below) claimed 23 percent of those revenues. FCC-mandated reductions in the access charges long-distance carriers pay to local telephone companies for access to their networks are one element helping to reduce the charges consumers pay.

AT&T

One of the most significant telecommunications mergers of 1999 was AT&T's $60 billion acquisition of MediaOne, which was the country's fourth-largest cable company. Earlier in that year, AT&T closed its $48 billion purchase of another cable firm, Tele-Communications. The two deals made AT&T the country's largest cable provider, giving it access to nearly 60 million households. In the future, such cable connections could carry telephone calls, E-mail, faxes, movies, and entertainment and provide access to the Internet. As AT&T upgrades its cable systems, it will be able to offer high-speed Internet service. AT&T also has announced agreements with Microsoft to work together on the deployment of next-generation broadband and Internet services.

An important policy issue that has not been resolved is whether AT&T should be required to let its cable customers use Internet providers other than Excite@Home, which AT&T partially owns, at no extra charge. AT&T does not want the obligation to serve as a carrier for other Internet providers. Some consumer groups worry about customer choice if one communications company gets control over the facility a customer uses to access all types of voice, data, and video services. Other observers point out that the local telephony company wire, as well as future wireless (including satellite) technologies, can provide competition for a telecommunications and cable company. As a condition for AT&T's acquiring the cable company in Portland, OR, that city required AT&T to open its Portland cable lines to any Internet company on the same terms as those for Excite@Home. This case is now in the courts. What is clear is that telecommunications companies believe that an important key to their future success is the ability to provide high-speed Internet access.

A breakdown of AT&T's estimated 1999 revenues shows how important new growth businesses such as wireless services and high-speed Internet access will be to the firm's future revenue growth. The revenue mix of services included business (42 percent), consumer (35 percent), wireless (11 percent), and broadband and Internet (7 percent).

During 1999, AT&T made several moves to strengthen its position in the international communications marketplace. To capture and retain the multinational corporate customers a telecommunications carrier has to increase the scope of its current services, develop innovative new services, devise communications solutions on a global basis, and make competitive bids on global outsourcing contracts. In May 1999, AT&T and Japan's NTT agreed to work together in business ventures to provide value-added networking solutions for global businesses and industries. AT&T acquired the IBM Global Network backbone that was deployed in 59 countries to utilize in meeting business demands for networking solutions across national boundaries. AT&T and NTT will cooperate in developing and marketing services that use that backbone network in the Asia-Pacific region.

AT&T and British Telecommunications (BT) agreed to acquire jointly a 30 percent stake in Japan Telecommunications for nearly $2 billion. Japan Telecommunications, a growing carrier that offers domestic and international telephone and data and mobile communications services, will distribute IP-based network services provided by the AT&T–BT joint venture. These joint ventures with two Japanese telecommunications firms illustrate a common feature of many current telecommunications alliances in which participants that cooperate with each other in certain market segments or geographic regions may compete in others.

AT&T's agreement to acquire Netstream, a Brazilian IP-network-based carrier that serves local business customers (a $9 billion market) over urban fiber-optic networks, was another example of AT&T's strategy of extending its network to local business markets in other countries where there is growing demand for advanced communications and Internet services.

MCI WorldCom–Sprint

Like AT&T, MCIW took steps to enhance its position as a global competitor in 1999. In October, it announced that it would acquire Sprint, the nation's third largest long-distance carrier, in what would amount to the largest corporate takeover in history. The new company, to be known as WorldCom, would have revenues of nearly $50 billion. To secure regulatory approval, MCIW is likely to divest itself of Sprint's Internet backbone facilities. The merger would give MCIW, which lacks an extensive wireless infrastructure, control of Sprint's wireless operations, which reach nearly all parts of the country. This would allow the new firm to expand the scope of its integrated wireless, wireline, and data services. The equity for a deal of such magnitude is not cash but an exchange of MCIW stock. The new company would become the biggest telecommunications firm in the world, not in terms of annual revenues but with a stock market value of more than $200 billion.

MCIW became the first foreign-owned company in Japan to offer local and international voice and data services to Japanese customers over its fiber-optic network in the business districts of Tokyo and Osaka. MCIW also received a license to build a fixed wireless access network in Japan to give customers access to the company's global infrastructure without relying on the incumbent's local loop. MCIW is building a metropolitan fiber network in Sydney and Melbourne, Australia, and is offering value-added and international simple resale services in Hong Kong. It also is offering value-added services in Singapore. MCIW has been attempting to secure licenses to construct its own facilities in both Hong Kong and Singapore. In addition, MCIW offers comprehensive Internet services to businesses in the Asia-Pacific region through its Internet services division, UUNET.

In Belgium, MCIW began to offer services over its first facilities-based national network in Europe in January 1999. The company has built and operates local networks in Paris, Frankfurt, London, Amsterdam, Rotterdam, Stockholm, and Zurich and plans to build a pan-European long-distance network to connect those city networks. MCIW also is a founding investor in a submarine cable system that will link South Africa with Europe and Asia and plans to begin offering commercial services in 2001. Once the cable is completed, African countries such as Senegal, Ghana, Nigeria, and Angola will have access to broadband services and new technologies that will spur the development of their telecommunications markets.

Viatel

Viatel is a newer U.S. carrier that has changed its service offerings and business strategies drastically to keep up with the rapidly changing telecommunications marketplace and position itself to be a player in global communications in the next decade. Founded in 1991, with its first public stock offering only in 1996, Viatel offered primarily international callback telephone and value-added services from foreign destinations to the United States.

In 1998, with the liberalization of telecommunications in EU member states and the coming into effect of the WTO Agreement on Basic Telecommunications Services, Viatel obtained licenses to construct a pan-European network to offer a full range of voice and data services. This five-ring fiber-optic network, in which Viatel is investing more than $1 billion, is projected to be 8,700 kilometers long upon completion in June 2000. Two of the fiber rings are already in operation, carrying traffic in the United Kingdom, the Netherlands, Belgium, France, and Germany. The remaining rings, when completed, will extend the network to Switzerland and link more than 40 major European cities. In addition, Viatel has received licenses to own and operate network infrastructure in Ireland, Italy, and Spain.

Internet Protocol Telephony

Originally, the concept of Internet telephony referred to making telephone calls over the Internet by using computers at both ends. First introduced in 1995 with the release of software allowing for computer-to-computer phone calls, what is commonly referred to as IP telephony now has a broader and more dynamic meaning. Still including computer-to-computer calls on the Internet, IP telephony now can refer to any calls (computer, telephone, or any combination of the two) that originate and/or terminate on the public switched telephone network (PSTN) but are carried using IP packets on a data network in the middle.

One often sees other terms used in referring to IP telephony, including *Internet telephony* and *Voice Over Internet Protocol*

(*VOIP*). Internet telephony is just that: voice traveling over the public Internet. VOIP, like IP telephony, describes any voice transmission using IP regardless of whether it travels on the public Internet, a corporate Intranet, private lines, or a virtual private network (VPN).

IP telephony is made possible by gateways, equipment introduced in 1996 that formed the basis for the development of the IP telephony industry. The primary function of a gateway is to convert a voice signal to IP packets to be transmitted over a data network. The packets are reassembled and converted back into voice signals at the receiving end by another gateway, which then puts the call back on the PSTN. Data traffic over packet-switched networks is growing rapidly, but the role VOIP will play in that growth is debated. Bellcore has estimated that data will account for approximately 90 percent of the traffic (but not revenue) on the U.S. public network sometime in the next 5 to 10 years. Some analysts have estimated that the current U.S. data market is approximately $20 billion annually and that it will double or triple in the next 10 years. Estimates of the IP telephony market vary, generally ranging from $3 billion to $5 billion annually in the United States over the next 5 years and $4 billion to $8 billion worldwide.

Regardless of the exact share of the data market IP telephony will generate, its impact on the telecommunications sector will be important for a variety of reasons. Some of the drivers behind IP telephony and VOIP are the following:

- IP lowers prices for suppliers and service providers. First and foremost, IP telephony, whether delivered over the public Internet, Intranets, or VPNs, can reduce prices for service providers and consumers. IP telephony allows users to make calls at a lower price per minute than that for calls through the PSTN. In addition, IP-router networks are much cheaper to build than are traditional circuit-switched networks of comparable size. Internationally, toll bypass could be one of the largest drivers of IP telephony, particularly in areas where Internet or packet-based data services are not regulated as heavily as are basic voice services.
- IP may serve as the platform for future multimedia applications. Some companies, both domestic and international, look beyond the use of IP telephony as a cheaper means of making phone calls and faxes. For those companies, IP is viewed as a platform from which the next generation of multimedia services will be built. Voice over IP will be one piece of a package of services that will include video, data, fax, and a host of other services marketed to the end user.
- IP can help facilitate electronic commerce. IP telephony allows operators to receive calls directly from Web pages. This allows customers and companies to exchange information more easily.
- IP allows more efficient utilization of corporate networks. In addition to the inherent efficiency of packet-switched versus circuit-switched networks, corporations may be able to make telephone calls more cheaply on their Intranets by using IP telephony. Also, the use of a single network for a wide-area network (WAN) or local-area network (LAN) may simplify administration by running voice and data over one network rather than two.
- IP telephony will benefit from the growing popularity of the Internet. As the Internet grows, IP telephony equipment can be integrated easily into existing networks. In addition, Internet service providers (ISPs) can offer IP telephony as a value-added service that will attract new subscribers.

A number of issues may impede or delay the widespread application of IP telephony. First and foremost, quality of service is problematic for any company using the public Internet for voice services. The Internet may drop packets or suffer from congestion problems, leading to unacceptable delays and transmission quality. This problem may be solved, at least in part, by moving traffic onto private networks. However, one may face quality of service issues on private networks as well. Some analysts have argued that the technology and equipment surrounding VOIP are evolving so quickly that quality of service issues will be resolved in the near future.

For those providing international IP telephony simply as a cost-saving device over traditional telephony, falling per-minute costs for traditional telephony throughout the world may have a long-term negative impact on demand in this sector. Increased competition and decreasing accounting rates are making international telephony cheaper for consumers. This may not be as large an issue for those who view IP as a long-term platform for multiple applications in which IP telephony will play a role rather than simply being a mechanism for toll bypass.

Another major issue involves the lack of standardization among equipment manufacturers for IP telephony equipment, particularly manufacturers of gateways. Service providers face the challenge of integrating voice, video, and data in an IP-based platform that provides seamless service to the customer. (See Chapter 31 for further discussion of the standardization problem.)

Several types of companies are currently involved in IP telephony services. Discount telephony companies market international telephone calls below standard rates. Prepaid telephone calling card companies capitalize on inexpensive transmission costs made possible by voice over the Internet or over private lines. Internet telephony exchange carriers (ITXCs) sell wholesale minutes on their backbone networks and offer global termination to other Internet telephony service providers, such as the discount telephony companies mentioned above. Terminating companies use their own gateways to terminate traffic originating elsewhere through agreements with Internet telephony exchange carriers. They receive IP packets from one side of the gateway and send out local PSTN calls to the other side. Some traditional telephony companies, including present and former monopoly foreign carriers, are investigating the potential of IP telephony. Long-distance voice carriers are evaluating how IP packets could transport voice more cheaply than does circuit-switched telephony. Some companies are taking this a step further and looking at IP as a platform for future multimedia offerings to compete with new firms loosely referred to as "next-generation telecom companies" that hope to offer Internet-related advanced services, Internet access, and local and long-distance telephony on one bill.

Regulatory Environment for IP Telephony

The FCC set forth its policy toward ISPs and IP telephony in a 1998 report to the U.S. Congress. The FCC noted that Internet access providers offer enhanced information services, not telecommunications services, and thus are unregulated. The FCC concluded that computer-to-computer IP telephony is not a telecommunications service and therefore is not subject to regulation. The FCC stated that phone-to-phone IP telephony may have characteristics similar to those of basic telecommunications. However, the FCC noted that it would need to compile a more complete record focused on phone-to-phone Internet telephony service offerings before reaching any conclusions. In April 1999, US West filed a petition with the FCC in which it argued that ISPs that provide Internet telephony are acting as long-distance carriers and therefore should pay access charges. The FCC is studying this issue.

In 1998, the European Commission (EC) issued a notice addressing the status of voice communications on the Internet under European Community law and in particular under the directive on competition in the markets for telecommunications services. A major issue the notice posed was the extent to which the elements of the regulatory framework applicable to the provision of voice telephony services should be applied to voice services provided over the Internet. The EC observed that voice communications over the Internet could be considered voice telephony only if each of four specific criteria was met. The EC notice concluded that current Internet voice services could not be considered "voice telephony" but said that it would review the situation in light of technological and market developments by the end of 1999.

In many other countries, there is regulatory uncertainty, in part because no systematic investigation or analysis of IP telephony has been conducted and no clear policy has been enunciated. Licenses may be issued to ISPs, and data communications service providers, some of which may offer a type of IP telephony, receive licenses in some countries, but there is ambiguity about whether such an IP telephony service has been authorized. Some countries have explicitly prohibited some forms of IP telephony. However, it is not clear just which existing or future services such a ban applies to. The objective appears to be to prevent IP telephony services from eroding the very lucrative profits being earned by the monopoly state-owned carriers in long-distance and international voice services. Critics are skeptical that such a ban could be legally or technologically enforceable. The current impact of IP telephony on voice revenues is minimal in any case, since the number of IP telephony service firms and subscribers is still insignificant.

The future of Internet telephony will be affected greatly by whether regulators define it as a form of ordinary voice telephone service or, by virtue of its use of Internet protocols, as a distinct information service. If Internet-related telephony became subject to access charges and universal service obligations, the prices charged to consumers would have to be increased substantially, making the service less attractive and perhaps undermining the growing utilization of the Internet

Packetized voice traffic also can flow over private networks, and private corporate Intranets represent a significant potential market. International fax traffic currently may account for as much as 40 percent of the total international telecommunications services market. Faxing over the Internet may become a major application because of the cost savings that can be realized. One consulting group envisions one-third of the long distance telephone calls being carried on packet networks by 2005. During the next few years, it is not expected that Internet telephony will have a large impact on the established long-distance services. Internet telephony revenues will remain modest in absolute terms, and the growth of all types of Internet services should help stimulate, not reduce, continued growth in toll volumes.

Electronic Commerce

Telecommunications networks provide the critical enabling infrastructure for electronic commerce in other industries. However, most telecommunications companies are not yet involved in E-commerce, such as on-line retailing, and the industry may not be adaptable for widespread E-commerce applications. An Arthur D. Little executive has noted the great difference between an Internet provider with its specific service applications and a conventional telecommunications firm that focuses on expanding its network facilities. The large telecommunications companies need to make up-front investments in switches and network facilities, which are depreciated over a decade or so. The business model for E-commerce is based on windows of commercial opportunities that last 3 to 6 months, after which new models must be designed and invested in. To date, Web-based E-commerce has been driven more by the software industry than by the telecommunications industry.

One example of telecommunications capacity and services being sold in an E-commerce environment can be mentioned here. Although millions of minutes on established international networks go unused every day, new telecommunications start-ups, especially ISPs, may have trouble finding capacity. There now is an on-line electronic market for buying and selling bandwidth. Telephone resellers can post bids for international phone minutes offered by companies with international network facilities. Currently, it may take some time to conclude deals because of the technical and commercial arrangements that must be sorted out between the two parties. The goal is to create a true commodities spot market in which traders can agree on amounts, quality, and price at the same time for prompt exchange.

U.S. Industry Growth Projections for the Next 1 and 5 Years

The number of telephone access lines in the United States is expected to exceed 180 million in the year 2000. A healthy overall 4 percent annual growth rate can be anticipated as a result of continued increases in the number of households with demand for second or third lines. Those lines will be used to support home-based businesses and heavy use of on-line/

Internet services and to give family members individual personal communications links in addition to pagers and cellular and portable phones. The number of business access lines has been growing 7 percent annually.

Wireline telecommunications services generated 85 percent of telecommunications services revenue in 1998, while the share of wireless could increase from the current 15 percent to 20 percent of total revenues in 2004. Wireless revenues should grow at an annual rate of 15 percent as price competition cuts into earlier annual growth rates of 20 percent and more. Local exchange service revenues are expected to increase at an annual rate of 10 percent to reach $71 billion in 2000 and about $105 billion in 2004. New entrants (cable television companies and long-distance firms) will incur expenses in building their own facilities to offer services and are unlikely to offer local telephony at a significant discount. Access charges, which totaled $18.5 billion in 1998, will continue to decline. Their amounts in 2004 will depend on developments in FCC access charge policy.

Growth in total long-distance use should continue to increase at a 10 percent annual rate, but prices may decline somewhat, particularly when the former Bell companies enter the market. Total toll service revenues (switched and private line) are projected to increase 5 percent in the year 2000 to reach about $115 billion. Entry by the Bell local exchange carriers into the interexchange toll market should reduce the 75 percent-plus market share now held by the three large carriers: AT&T, MCIW, and Sprint. In future years, toll revenue growth should increase at a 3 percent annual rate, bringing toll revenues to $130 billion by 2004.

U.S. internationally billed revenues for telecommunications services amounted to $14.5 billion in 1998. International minutes of use (sent over the public switched network) are expected to increase only 5 percent annually over the next 5 years. Demand should remain strong during this period, with price reductions resulting from increased competition from the former regional Bell companies and new foreign competitors. Continuing reductions in accounting rates will bring lower rates for callers and stimulate international call volume. High volumes of fax traffic that are recorded by networks as international voice calls are also likely to continue. On some U.S.–Asian routes, where time and language differences are obstacles to voice communications, 40 to 50 percent of international calls may be fax transmissions.

Telecommunications Liberalization in Foreign Markets

With one exception, the largest international carriers are based in open or soon to be open telecommunications markets. The entry into force of the WTO Basic Telecommunications Services Agreement on February 5, 1998, provided formal recognition of the increasing degree of telecommunications service liberalization in the world's major markets. The agreement codifies existing policies in some countries and challenges other nations to ensure that their new regulatory structures operate effectively to promote real marketplace competition. The words *privatization, liberalization, competition,* and *deregulation* sometimes are used interchangeably to refer to this general trend, but it is useful to make distinctions among those terms. Privatization may refer to the sale of state-owned telecommunications operators to private investors or to allowing private sector firms to participate in a market formerly reserved for government-owned companies. Privatization may be a first step toward liberalization and competition, but in other cases, a government-owned PTT may not be privatized until years after other firms enter the market. Most experts would agree that continued state ownership of dominant carriers makes it harder for a country to deal successfully with operational and policy decisions to promote fair competition. The WTO agreement did not address the question of privatization directly, and some countries maintain investment limitations in their government-owned carriers.

Liberalization refers to improved or unrestricted market access to provide telecommunications services. It also has a more theoretical connotation, suggesting the absence of legal and nontariff barriers in this market. The term *competition,* by contrast, refers to marketplace realities. If the market has been liberalized (old laws and regulations have been changed) but no new players have appeared to offer services, there still is no competition. However, some competition may exist even though the market has not been liberalized, as is the case in China.

The word *deregulation* often is used interchangeably with *competition,* but in fact, introducing competition into a formerly monopolistic industry may call for new regulations, at least for a transitional period. Once the market has become truly competitive, there is less need for regulations and the industry may be deregulated. Because of the current structure of many national telecommunications regimes and the dominant roles of large firms in the industry, deregulation may not be advisable for some time.

Liberalization has not proceeded at the same pace in all countries or even within all sectors or submarkets of telecommunications. The equipment market usually has been the first to be liberalized, followed by value-added or enhanced services and then by basic (voice) services. In the United States, liberalization in voice telephony proceeded over a number of years, driven by the development of new technologies and equipment and supported by regulatory policy and court decisions. Now basic voice telephony is regarded as a service that can (although many countries choose not to do so) be liberalized all at once whatever its geographic reach or technology base.

Five of the six heaviest U.S. international traffic routes are to fully liberalized markets, and Hong Kong, also liberalized, accounts for nearly two-thirds of U.S. traffic with China (see Figure 30-2). However, traffic volumes are increasing the fastest in many countries whose telecommunications markets are not yet fully open to competition. For example, 7 of the 10 markets with the highest growth rates for U.S. telecommunications services trade during the 1992–1997 period have yet to liberalize their international services markets. (see Figure 30-3).

Asia. Asia encompasses a large number of telecommunications markets with strikingly different telecommunications ser-

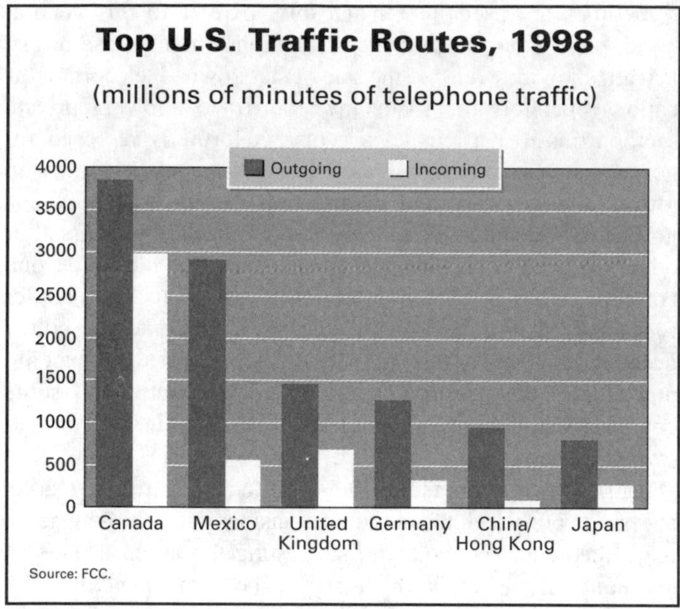

FIGURE 30-2

vices regimes. Some—such as Australia, New Zealand, and Japan—are fully liberalized, while others—the Philippines, India, and Singapore—have taken significant steps toward liberalization but still limit foreign investment or have other restrictions on the supply of telecommunications services. Countries such as China, Indonesia, and Vietnam have introduced multiple suppliers of some services but have taken few steps to truly liberalize their markets.

The aggregate value of the telecommunications services market in Association of Southeast Asian Nations (ASEAN) countries is about $15.5 billion. Wireline revenues probably account for more than 90 percent of the total. Singapore and Malaysia are striving to become regional telecommunications and information technology hubs but have not liberalized their markets fully. Malaysia is upgrading its telecommunications infrastructure rapidly to provide electronic commerce, multimedia, and value-added services.

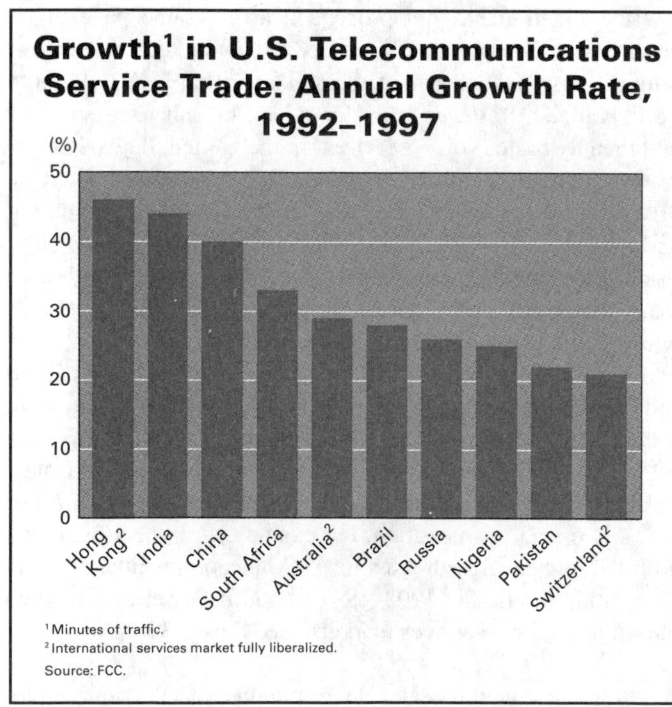

FIGURE 30-3

ASEAN telecommunications markets that are on the rise include Thailand and the Philippines. Telecommunications services are still a legal state monopoly in Thailand, but the government appears to be committed to liberalization, although at a slow pace. The current tariff structure does not produce the returns needed to encourage further private sector investment, but changes to the system are expected once the new National Telecommunications Committee is established. In the Philippines, almost 90 percent of telecommunications-related projects are private sector–driven and directed under Philippine government deregulation policies. Although the telecommunications market in general has performed well in spite of the Asian financial crisis, the demand for telecommunications services has decreased in recent years.

Southern Asia. Southern Asia has a total population that matches China's. Private industry participates in the telecommunications service sectors of the four largest markets: Bangladesh, India, Pakistan, and Sri Lanka. Partial privatization of state-owned carriers has occurred in Pakistan and Sri Lanka. Teledensity (the ratio of main lines per 100 inhabitants) has yet to reach 2.0 in this region, and so there is an enormous potential for infrastructure growth. The annual value of the telecommunications services market is more than $6 billion.

India is the region's largest market, but progress in opening up its telecommunications services market to privatization and competition has been agonizingly slow. In 1994, the government adopted a policy that aimed to introduce two new cellular carriers in each of 20 regions around the country and one wireline carrier in each region to compete with the incumbent state-owned telephone company. As a result of many factors, including mismanagement of the tendering process, corruption, and delays in setting up an independent regulator, implementation of the policy was only a partial success. A new telecommunications policy was announced in March 1999, but many details regarding the timing and extent of its implementation remained unclear. For example, the new policy promised to open India's domestic long-distance market to competition on January 1, 2000, but in late 1999 some observers feared that restrictions and the imposition of burdensome requirements on new entrants would largely defeat the purpose of the policy. India did allow private firms to offer Internet services to the public on a local, regional, or national basis in late 1998, and more than 115 firms have been issued ISP licenses.

China. China's telecommunications services market, which was valued at about $27.5 billion in 1999, is essentially closed to foreign investors. Chinese law currently prohibits foreign entities from owning, operating, or managing telecommunications networks in that country. The government is adding 15 million to 20 million lines to its wireline network every year, and wireless expansion is averaging 1 million lines per month.

A number of foreign companies have tried to circumvent the Chinese restriction on foreign investment by establishing joint ventures that would be considered Chinese entities under Chinese law. Those joint ventures then would invest in telecommunications services operations, generally cellular systems. Approximately 50 of these so-called China-China-Foreign (CCF) joint ventures were established, with foreign investments estimated at $1.4 billion, before the Chinese government decided in 1998 that they were illegal. Currently, many foreign investors are in limbo, waiting to see what the government ultimately decides to do with their investments. Discussions between China and the United States on terms for China's accession to the WTO have been held on and off for several years. China is expected to offer some degree of liberalization in its telecommunications services sector in return for U.S. approval of its accession, but the degree and timing of its steps toward liberalization are unknown.

Africa. In the last several years, several African countries have taken important steps to liberalize, privatize, and establish independent regulatory regimes to oversee and encourage growth in the telecommunications sector. As an important indicator of this change, six Sub-Saharan African nations—Côte D'Ivoire, Ghana, Mauritius, Senegal, South Africa, and Uganda—have signed on to the WTO Basic Telecommunications Agreement. Privatization of state-owned telecommunications companies is well under way. It is expected that roughly a dozen additional countries will privatize their operators over the next few years. In addition, many African nations, including Ghana and Tanzania, have opened their cellular and value-added services markets to foreign operators.

According to the International Telecommunication Union (ITU), Botswana, Gambia, Cape Verde, and Mauritius experienced the highest rates of growth in main lines in the 1990s and are considered telecommunications role models for sub-Saharan Africa. Ghana has begun one of the most liberal telecommunications restructuring plans in Africa. Certain sectors are open to competition and there are no foreign investment limitations for telecommunications service providers, 30 percent of the national operator—Ghana Telecommunications—was sold in early 1997, and an independent regulator was established recently, although it has yet to enact regulations. Cote d'Ivoire recently sold off 51 percent of its national operator—Côte d'Ivoire Telecommunications—to France Telecommunications and has opened several subsectors to competition.

Since the passage of the Telecommunications Act of 1996, South Africa has privatized 30 percent of Telkom, S.A., the national operator, and created the South Africa Telecommunications Regulatory Authority (SATRA) as an independent regulator. As a result of the liberalization program, large-scale basic telecommunications infrastructure building plans are under way and certain sectors have been opened to competition, including cellular services. The privatization of Nigeria's national operator, NITEL, has been promised since 1997, but this has not occurred. There are, however, private service providers that work alongside, though not in direct competition with, NITEL. Ten firms have been licensed by the Nigerian Communications Commission (NCC) to be interconnected to NITEL to provide various telecommunications services.

Latin America. Recent and upcoming basic services liberalization continues to drive telecommunications growth and convergence in Latin America. Service revenues in the region exceeded $50 billion in 1998 and are growing at about 20 percent annually. Many countries in the region completed privatization of their national operators in the 1990s, and six countries are planning privatization of their network operators.

Despite dramatic market liberalization throughout Latin America over recent years, there is a lack of uniformity in regulatory environments. The telecommunications market in Chile is the most liberalized in the region, while Uruguay's is one of the least liberalized. Investments in the Chilean telecommunications sector, whose long-distance sector is the most competitive in Latin America, are projected to run about $700 million annually, with the market expanding 20 to 25 percent a year. The market has entered a consolidation phase after several years of cutthroat competition. Two dominant operators are emerging—CTC and ENTEL—the original state monopoly long-distance providers.

The government of Argentina has begun to license competitors to the two national operators, including six personal communications services (PCS) license awards in 1999 that generated over $1.2 billion, and the market will be opened to full competition in November 2000. The regulatory situation remains problematic, however, as the legal framework is vague and the regulatory authority (CNC) has yet to establish itself as a strong institution. Virtually all its major decisions are appealed in the courts.

The biggest recent event in Latin America telecommunications was the privatization of Telebras and the licensing and sale of "mirror" companies in Brazil, and the market is an active one as companies build out their networks in preparation for full competition in 2002. The market for domestic long-distance services was opened in 1999, and ANATEL took further steps to open the data communications market. In addition, analysts project that demand for Internet access in Latin America will quadruple over the next 5 years and that Brazil, with at least 50 percent of the region's Internet users, will lead the way.

Many other changes in recent years have opened up opportunities for U.S. companies. Mexico, following the lead of Argentina, Chile, and Peru, has completed wireless local loop and PCS auctions. In Colombia, the national operator now competes with private local, long-distance, and cellular providers, and auctions for nationwide PCS licenses were planned for late 1999 or 2000. Telefonica del Peru's monopoly was terminated a year ahead of schedule, and both cellular and long-distance competitors are entering the market. In Venezuela, the telecommunications sector has been absorbing investments of approximately $1 billion a year as the government has made plans to sell off a third national cellular license before the end of 1999, and the monopoly on basic telephone services is set to end in November 2000. The Central American states continue to push toward introducing modern liberalizing telecommunications legislation and privatizing state-owned telecommunications companies, and some Caribbean governments are trying to move toward liberalization by ending the U.K.-based Cable & Wireless monopolies.

Central and Eastern Europe. The telecommunications sector in central and eastern Europe remained strong in 1999 despite the financial crises that affected markets in many developing economies. Currently, a number of wireless licenses have been tendered or are under discussion in the region, and there is strong competition among providers of value-added services. The telecommunications services market for this region is estimated to total $7.5 billion, of which probably 85 percent or more is held by wireline carriers. Some countries in this section of Europe—the Czech Republic, Hungary, and Romania—have begun the process of privatizing their national telecommunications operators. In addition, nearly all the countries in central Europe have signed the WTO Agreement on Basic Telecommunications Services and have made a legal commitment to liberalize their markets within the next 2 to 5 years.

While most countries in central and eastern Europe are continuing to progress toward privatization and market liberalization, Poland has undertaken changes in its telecommunications sector over the past 3 years that have put it at the forefront of the eastern European market for telecommunications services. In November 1998, the government sold a 15 percent share of the Polish national operator, Telekomunikacja Polska (TPSA). The government of Poland announced a tender for an additional 25 to 35 percent stake in the company in August 1999.

Poland also has undergone extensive market liberalization. Two additional cellular licenses were granted in 1999, and tenders for 65 licenses to provide local service competition with TPSA have been completed. Tenders for two long-distance licenses have been issued, and so the monopoly on long-distance voice services will end in 2000; the intention is to open international public services to competition in 2003. The Polish parliament is considering a new telecommunications law that promises significant changes in that market. When enacted, the law will provide for an independent regulatory body, create a level playing field for all competitors, and terminate TPSA's authority to operate without a license.

Western Europe. Five EU member states (Denmark, Finland, the Netherlands, Sweden, and the United Kingdom) liberalized voice telephony by 1997 and are the farthest along in establishing a competitive market for telecommunications services. Five more EU member states (Austria, Belgium, France, Germany, and Italy) liberalized their markets on January 1, 1998, but still are grappling with key issues (prices and terms of interconnection, regulating the former monopoly carriers, establishing nondiscriminatory policies) that must be settled before competition can flourish. Spain liberalized its telecommunications market on December 1, 1998, and Ireland followed suit on January 1, 1999. The German government already has licensed more than 80 operators, although it has not resolved important competitive issues regarding interconnection and pricing. As the largest telecommunications market in Europe, Germany is a bellwether and is critical for the ultimate success of telecommunications liberalization throughout Europe.

In 1998, the EU market for telecommunications services was valued at $162 billion, 81 percent of which was for voice telephony and network services, and the remainder mobile communications. However, mobile communications are growing at an annual rate of 21 percent in the EU, considerably faster than are network services, which are growing 14 percent annually.

One indication of the benefits competition has brought to the EU market is the increase in the number of operators authorized to offer public network services. By September 1998, 526 local operators had been licensed, while 189 national and 256 international operators had been authorized to offer services. It is too early to measure any decrease in the market power of incumbents in the fixed, wireline market. The best available indication is that Deutsche Telekom, the incumbent in Germany, has lost some 30 percent of the long-distance market to private competitors but only 2 percent of the market for local services. Another indication of the impact of competition is a decline in prices for telecommunications services, especially for long-distance services, which have fallen as much as 70 percent in many EU countries, such as Germany, which accounts for 25 percent of the total EU telecommunications market.

A wave of privatization and corporate alliances has been sweeping through western Europe since 1997. While most governments in the EU retain a majority stake in their former monopoly carriers, many have plans to sell off most of their holdings and get government out of the business of managing a telecommunications service provider. In April 1999, reports surfaced that Deutsche Telekom, in which the German government still owns a majority share, was ready to merge with Telecommunications Italia (TI) in an $80 billion deal that would have created the second largest telecommunications service provider in the world, with $65 billion in revenues. The firms noted that their intent was to form a company that could respond to the expanding presence of American companies in Europe. Some analysts were not convinced that this "merger of monopoly dinosaurs" made sense. Would combining two such companies, both in need of restructuring and with similar corporate cultures, really create a competitive superpower? The issue became moot when the deal fell through, and a private Italian firm, Olivetti, then made a successful bid to acquire control of TI. In the end, a private company that had led the most successful challenge to TI in cellular communications was viewed as a better match for TI, which was facing a nascent competitive market for telecommunications services in Italy.

Implementation of the WTO Agreement on Basic Telecommunications

Sixty-nine countries, accounting for more than 90 percent of the world's telecommunications revenues, reached a telecommunications services agreement on February 15, 1997, under the auspices of the WTO in Geneva. The agreement entered into force on February 5, 1998. Since that time, several of those countries have adopted policies that go beyond the degree of liberalization they made a commitment to under the WTO, and four more countries have joined the agreement. Three countries have failed to ratify the agreement: Brazil, Papua New Guinea, and the Philippines. All WTO members are bound to apply the most-favored-nation (MFN) principle in the telecommunications sector as a result of the agreement, which is fully enforceable under WTO dispute settlement procedures.

The Agreement on Basic Telecommunications has three parts: market access, national treatment, and procompetitive regulatory principles. With regard to market access, U.S. companies are given varying degrees of market access in other markets, based on individual country commitments, for local, long-distance, and international services. Services can be provided through any network technology, either on a facilities basis or through the resale of existing network capacity. As a result of the national treatment obligation, U.S. companies can acquire, establish, or hold a significant stake in telecommunications companies around the world, with the exact percentage of ownership dependent on individual countries' commitments. Sixty-four countries adopted procompetitive regulatory principles based on the landmark 1996 U.S. Telecommunications Act.

Implementation of the agreement has made it apparent that some countries face greater challenges in conforming their institutions and policies to their commitments to liberalize than do others. During the annual "Section 1377" congressionally mandated review of telecommunications trade agreements entered into by the United States, U.S. companies filed complaints against Mexico, Japan, the EU, and Germany regarding implementation of their WTO obligations.

For more than a year, U.S. carriers have raised questions about international service and domestic regulatory issues in Mexico. Six competitors of Telmex, the dominant former monopoly supplier of wireline voice telephony services, requested permission to provide international simple resale (ISR) services on Mexico's international routes in late 1998, which the regulator denied. U.S.-affiliated carriers also have concerns about competition-neutral universal service policies and the implementation of dominant carrier regulation vis-à-vis Telmex. In June 1999, the U.S. Trade Representative (USTR) announced the extension of an out-of-cycle review of Mexico's compliance with the WTO Basic Telecommunications Agreement while noting that Mexico's ongoing consultative policy review provided a credible basis for expecting improved implementation of its WTO commitments. The situation deteriorated in August as Telmex refused to provide new local circuits for the interconnection of its long-distance customers to new and growing customer access points. AT&T and MCIW are considering whether to press immediately for the initiation of a WTO dispute case.

AT&T and Telmex earlier announced agreement on a 19-cents-per-minute international accounting rate (down from 39.5 cents), a reduction that should reduce retail prices for telephone calls between the United States and Mexico. This action should reduce considerably the $800 million per year settlement payments (U.S. trade deficit) that U.S. carriers make to Mexico under international accounting rates. Implementation of ISR could lower retail prices for calls to Mexico to 10 cents a minute or less and further reduce uneconomical price distortions brought about by the accounting rate regime.

U.S. carriers that have invested in networks in Japan have asserted that NTT's interconnection regime has effectively prevented them from competing against NTT in the provision of local service. They have pointed to evidence that NTT has been pricing elements of interconnection significantly above its costs and engaging in anticompetitive behavior, including anticompetitive cross-subsidization. Japan also prohibited facilities-based carriers from using leased lines to provide long-distance services. This adversely affected international carriers by not allowing them to carry their traffic inland via leased circuits (thus reducing their costs) and closer to the end customers.

The commitments made by Japan under the May 1999 bilateral "Enhanced Initiative on Deregulation and Competition Policy" include making procompetitive reforms that would address many of the issues raised by U.S. carriers. Specifically, Japan agreed to take action to ensure that interconnection rates did not impair local competition and to permit carriers to combine owned and leased facilities to provide services. NTT began work on a proposal to revise its interconnection tariff that is expected to reflect substantial reductions in interconnection rates for all types of phone calls and provide discounts from retail rates that will ensure that vigorous competition is possible. If NTT's new tariff does not achieve this, the USTR has indicated that it will begin preparing for a possible WTO dispute settlement case.

In Germany, U.S. telecommunications companies complained that the German regulatory authority was not requiring Deutsche Telekom (DT) to provide interconnection on a nondiscriminatory, cost-based, and timely basis. DT, the dominant German carrier, has advocated policies that, if adopted, would severely hamper the ability of U.S. firms to compete in the German market. While the German regulatory authority made two decisions in May 1999 that denied DT's demands for more burdensome interconnection terms and conditions, the regulator also announced its willingness to consider DT's proposals for the interconnection regime that it plans to announce for the year 2000 and beyond. At the same time, DT reportedly is negotiating potentially precedent-setting interconnection contracts with one or more competitors.

U.S. carriers have insisted that DT not be allowed to continue delaying the supply of interconnection facilities to its competitors and that it inform its competitors when and where such facilities will be most promptly available. The USTR announced in August 1999 that it would continue an out-of-cycle Section 1377 review of the German regulatory framework to assure that upcoming decisions on the interconnection regime receive prompt scrutiny for consistency with Germany's WTO commitments.

Daniel W. Edwards, U.S. Department of Commerce, Office of Telecommunications, (202) 482-4331, October 1999.

WIRELESS SERVICES

Cellular and PCS service providers continued to thrive in the United States in 1999, and the potential for growth remains strong as the industry enters the new millennium. A significant number of new networks have come into service globally over the last few years, increasing competition and driving prices down. Those factors combined with strong demand and advances in technology to make 1999 a banner year for wireless.

While voice communications continued to account for the bulk of wireless traffic in 1999 and are expected to continue to do so, that year also was marked by the rollout and continued expansion of new wireless applications, including advanced messaging, data and video transmission, location technology, and remote monitoring. In addition, that year heralded the trend toward the convergence of wireline and wireless services—termed fixed/mobile convergence (FMC)—and the transitioning of networks to IP, which allows service providers to make more efficient use of existing network capacity and offer a greater range of services to wireless users. Many remaining obstacles to wireless Internet access have been overcome, prompting the *Wall Street Journal* to dub 1999 the year "the Internet cut the cord." As a result of those developments, an increasing percentage of consumers are using wireless handsets as a primary, as opposed to secondary, means of communication.

Commercial networks for mobile voice communications services in the United States generally are divided into two categories: cellular and PCS. Those systems are distinguished mainly by the frequency used: Cellular in the United States uses the 800-megahertz (MHz) band range, while PCS uses the 1,900-MHz range (see Table 30-3). In addition, PCS systems are digital, while most cellular networks in the United States are still analog. In 1999, cellular operators continued to convert their networks from analog to digital and position themselves to be all but indistinguishable from PCS operators. In fact, several PCS carriers offer both cellular and PCS capabilities with dual-band, dual-mode handsets. Competition between PCS carriers and existing cellular carriers continued in 1998 as PCS service providers sought sufficient market share to recover their development costs and established cellular carriers fought to maintain their market share. Few analysts predict that PCS will eclipse cellular in the United States in the near term; however, the gap is expected to close gradually over the next 5 years as PCS takes the majority of net additions.

TABLE 30-3: Spectrum Summary

Service	Spectrum Allocation
Cellular	825–850 MHz, 865–890 MHz
PCS	A: 1,850–1,865 MHz, 1,930–1,945 MHz
	B: 1,870–1,885 MHz, 1,950–1,965 MHz
	C: 1,895–1,910 MHz, 1,975–1,990 MHz
	D: 1,865–1,870 MHz, 1,945–1,950 MHz
	E: 1,885–1,890 MHz, 1,965–1,970 MHz
	F: 1,890–1,895 MHz, 1,970–1,975 MHz

Source: FCC.

Industry Growth

The number of new cellular subscribers in the United States increased markedly from 1992 to 1997, and this dramatic growth has continued. For the third year in a row (1996–1998), the annual increase in new subscribers exceeded 10 million, with a record 13.9 million net new subscribers in 1998, reaching more than 69 million wireless subscribers at the end of that year. The number of net new subscribers in the United States was expected to top 10 million in 1999, exceeding 80 million total subscribers by the turn of the century. Although projections differ, the number of cellular and PCS subscribers in the United States from 1997 to 2002 generally is expected to have a compound annual growth rate (CAGR) of 12 percent. Most of this growth is expected to occur by 2001, when there may be a slowdown before the advent of third-generation (3G) wireless.

The cellular and PCS industries continued to attract more nonbusiness than business users in 1998 and 1999, largely as a result of a decline in the cost of handsets and bundled services packages that are attractive to consumers. Wireless service providers continued to make inroads into a broad cross section of demographic groups. One analytic firm believes that more than 80 percent of U.S. adults from households with an income greater than $35,000 per year (approximately 90 million people) will be subscribers by 2002. A 1999 study by the Yankee Group showed that the use of wireless phone services among consumers with an annual income below $20,000 nearly doubled from about 9 percent in 1997 to 17.4 percent in 1998. Research by Peter Hart Associates claims that the heaviest users of wireless services—those who use wireless 3 hours or more per week—constituted 16 percent of the market and were disproportionally young and upper income. The Yankee Group study also found that household penetration of wireless phones among 50- to 59-year-old users increased from 29.5 percent in 1997 to 46.4 percent in 1998.

According to an annual survey conducted by the Cellular Telecommunications Industry Association (CTIA), the average wireless customer's local service bill dropped about 7.8 percent to $39.43 per month at the end of 1998, down from $42.78 at the end of 1997. Overall revenues for cellular and PCS operators exceeded $33.1 billion in 1998, up 20 percent from $27.5 billion in 1997. Roaming revenues in 1998 grew 17.9 percent from $2.97 billion to $3.5 billion, accounting for about 10 percent of total revenues. Industry revenues should continue to increase over the next few years as higher-capacity digital networks are expanded and new service providers increase competition. Cumulative capital investment grew 31.5 percent in 1998, increasing from $46 billion at the end of 1997 to $60.5 billion. Wireless operators added nearly 135,000 additional jobs in 1998 and accounted for more than 1.3 million jobs in the U.S. economy at the beginning of 1999.

Although cellular services still dominate the wireless sector in the United States, PCS is poised for tremendous growth in the period 2000–2001. Before the introduction of PCS, there were only two cellular operators in a market with accompanying duopoly pricing. With the introduction of PCS, however, there can now be up to nine competitors in each market, including six PCS carriers and one specialized mobile radio (SMR) provider. PCS networks normally are located in urban areas because rural areas generally have a higher buildout cost per subscriber. PCS networks also require a greater number of towers to cover the same area.

Although PCS is only a few years old, the number of subscribers in the United States nearly tripled in 1998 to 6.2 million from 2.2 million in 1997 (see Table 30-4). Although predictions vary widely, on average it is projected that PCS subscribers will account for about 40 percent of wireless subscribers and about half of total service revenues by the end of 2001. PCS users reportedly tend to use their phones more than cellular users do, with an average of 300 minutes per month for PCS users as opposed to about 140 minutes for cellular users.

As was noted above, incumbent cellular service providers face competition from both PCS carriers and SMR providers with designs on their customers. The last few years have seen industry giants such as Sprint, AT&T Wireless, and other operators aggressively rolling out their PCS networks, and although PCS licensees continue to carry heavy debt burdens, declining prices eventually will lead many consumers to consider PCS as their primary wireless carrier. Increasing competition from PCS is affecting decisions made by incumbent cellular service providers in a variety of ways, including decisions about how to structure prices, what services to offer in the future, and what alliances will be most beneficial.

Large, established U.S. telecommunications services organizations such as AT&T Wireless and the Regional Bell Operating Companies (RBOCs) continue to dominate wireless services. Many analysts predict that four or five national service providers of cellular/PCS will remain preeminent over the next 5 years. Dataquest notes the following criteria for successful operators: financial viability, marketing acumen, wireless expertise (i.e., a well-crafted business plan), an adequate subscriber base, and the ability to construct a network properly and the human resources to sustain it.

Wireless communications sectors of telecommunications companies have contributed greatly to overall revenues. In 1999, Bell Atlantic reported that wireless services generated $1.12 billion during the first quarter, an 18.6 percent increase compared with the second quarter of 1998; its digital data revenues rose 26.3 percent to reach $691 million. BellSouth reported that wireless revenues grew over 18 percent to $796 million, while revenues from digital and data services jumped 32 percent to $615 million.

TABLE 30-4: The PCS Service Market in the United States

Year	Subscribers, millions	Average Local Monthly Spending, $	Annual Spending, $Millions
1997	2.2	56.88	1,502
1998	6.2	50.00	3,720
1999	12.2	46.00	6,734
2002	34.6	40.00	16,608

Source: Multimedia Telecommunications Association.

Market Trends

Analysts point to a number of factors that caused rapid growth in the wireless services industry and subscriber gains over the last 3 years, including increased competition from new market entrants, the introduction of digital technology, wider area coverage at lower rates, declining service costs, the increasing availability of advanced services, and modest reductions in handset prices. The principal reason for the growth of wireless services, however, remains the fact that consumers want an affordable, untethered alternative to wireline networks. These trends are expected to continue into the next decade.

Fixed/Mobile Convergence. In 1999, a notable trend in wireless services was growing "convergence." In its broadest sense, convergence in the communications industry entails combining various services—voice and data transmission (including Internet access), video, cable television, and/or other multimedia broadband applications—into a single package. FMC, which is part of this larger integration movement, involves the offering of fixed and wireless in the same service package. FMC allows operators to have only one core network to manage and one set of services common to both mobile and fixed users and allows customers to have a single access device independent of the network. At present, demand for voice services is driving the integration of fixed and mobile services; however, as mobile data evolves it will play a greater role in the movement toward convergence. FMC will present many opportunities for telecommunication services, but it also will present dilemmas, most notably whether to become an integrated content provider or stay with basic services.

As convergence proceeds, most analysts agree that wireless will continue to draw significant amounts of voice telephony traffic from wireline, especially in highly penetrated markets. According to one consulting group, by 2005, around 16 percent of call minutes will be made on mobile phones, compared with just 5 percent in 1999, as mobile operators use innovative pricing to encourage people to use mobile phones as a substitute for fixed phones.

Consumer awareness is cited as a major reason why FMC is not yet ubiquitous. Unaware of progress in this area, most users have not objected to receiving wireless or wireline services from different operators so long as those operators provide low prices and high-quality services. Analysts believe that operators need to educate subscribers about the advantages of FMC. Some operators plan to market the service as a convenience, touting the "one-number, one-point-of-contact" approach in marketing FMC services. Perhaps the most common approach, however, especially to the price-conscious consumer market, is selling FMC as a packaged service that can decrease the price of the combined total bill.

Intelligent Networks and Internet Access. To achieve convergence and as part of a long-term strategy for achieving advanced intelligent networks (AINs), many existing service providers are converting to IP-based networks and many new operators are building networks based entirely on the IP. Intelligent networks allow seamless switching of wireless calls from data-ready, hand-held devices seeking access to the Internet by assigning those wireless transmissions a specific IP address. Intelligent networks recognize these signals as a wireless call and process the call accordingly. While convergence of fixed and mobile networks does not necessarily involve IP, IP holds the promise of more efficient use of network capacity and a greater range of services, thus increasing revenue and reducing operating costs. Billing is simplified, fixed and mobile networks can merge their marketing and sales efforts, and services can be integrated.

As operators convert to IP-based networks, increasing the use of server-run as opposed to conventional switches, fixed and mobile networks will become harder to distinguish. Mobile transmission towers and fixed local exchanges will become devices on a single network, with both transmitting IP packets to their destinations. The perceived benefit of mobile intelligent networks lies in how they shape the use of mobile wireless by designing an entirely personal mobile service package to suit the customer's personal needs.

For the future, AIN services are considered vital to the continued growth of an operator's revenue and subscriber base. AIN platforms are equally vital for the number portability needed to encourage competition. AIN also will help service providers achieve further and better segmentation of their customer bases and customization of their service offerings. Other advantages include greater economies of scale, increased interoperability, and the facilitation of mergers and alliances. At present, there are only a few intelligent networks in existence, and those which are operational are leasing bandwidth from other providers.

Pricing. The declining price of wireless services has been a key driver of the wireless market. According to a number of studies, most wireless consumers base their choice of a service largely on price, even when the operator does not offer cutting-edge services. In a 1998 study by the Yankee Group, 42 percent of the respondents reported basing their purchase decisions on the lowest price for services. When nonusers were polled about incentives to subscribe, affordable service rates and free handsets were cited the most frequently. Among all the pricing incentives presented in a study by Strategy Analytics, nonusers were most receptive to the rate of 10 cents a minute. Many operators are using price-oriented service plans termed "buckets of minutes" to attract customers. Some analytic groups have noted that significant price reductions may be required to sustain the surge in usage seen to date and to penetrate the next socioeconomic layer of customers.

Although average PCS and cellular airtime prices have continued to decline over the last few years, the rate of decline has slowed somewhat. Some analysts predict that service prices will fall significantly over the next 5 years, perhaps as much as 40 percent. According to the Strategis Group, the average price of wireless phone usage will fall from 33 cents per minute in 1998 to 20 cents per minute in the year 2000 as mobile voice telephony evolves toward commodity-based competition.

Recently mandated demands on carriers, however, may slow the trend toward reduced prices. In 1998, for example, wireless carriers were ordered to provide police with the locations and telephone numbers of 911 callers. In addition, in 1999, local number portability (LNP), which allows consumers to keep the same telephone number when they switch carriers, will be required for highly populated service areas that request it. Such requirements will add to the cost of providing wireless services and undoubtedly will create upward price pressures.

Even though mobile data is still in its early stages, the growth of intelligent networks already is forcing telecommunications service providers to reconsider their pricing structures. If mobile users are to remain connected to the Internet for extended periods, price structures must be modified to avoid discouraging them from going on-line when they are mobile.

One of the main areas where cost is often an issue is interconnection fees, since wireless operators are charged a fee to access the wired network. These fees, particularly those charged for access to the local loop, can be very high. Some wireless operators have cautioned that the recent rapid growth in the wireless services market may lead to overly complex pricing schemes that could confuse customers and hurt the industry. Also of concern, according to some officials, are potentially overinflated promises about users' ability to access the Internet through new mobile phones.

As prices decline throughout the industry, service providers will have to differentiate themselves by a variety of other methods, including voice quality, customer service, and features such as caller identification and voice-activated dialing.

Beyond Voice: The Movement toward Multimedia and Internet Access. As was noted above, voice services will continue to drive the cellular and PCS market. However, the shift in fixed network traffic from voice to data is expected to permeate wireless communications over the next 5 to 10 years, since users want to access high-speed data and multimedia applications. The use of short messaging service (SMS), a form of E-mail between wireless phones, is already available, and in the future, enhanced services (Internet access and E-mail) increasingly will become the norm as enabling technologies lead to the development of more sophisticated equipment. The eventual goal of service providers is to deliver ubiquitous, affordable wireless services to small, lightweight handsets that can handle voice, data, and video.

Although wireless data services are expected to continue to have a low rate of growth for another year because of relatively slow transmission speeds on existing networks and relatively high costs, data transmission is expected to constitute an ever-increasing portion of the future wireless services market. Predictions are that the wireless data market will grow rapidly as access devices become more prevalent and affordable. Wireless applications to query databases and access E-mail through cellular modems and phones, while not ubiquitous, are available. Some industry observers predict that within the next 5 years, data transmission will account for up to 70 percent of wireless traffic (see Figure 30-4). Others note that wireless access to the

Internet will force the extinction of analog systems except in areas with modest traffic. To meet this shift in demand, existing operators are making plans to evolve their networks toward 3G services with progressively faster data speeds.

A notable event in 1999 was Microsoft Corp.'s introduction of MSN Mobile, which provides consumers with a variety of wireless information services on interactive pagers and cellular phones. MSN Mobile offers wireless information services such as news, sports, weather, stock quotes, horoscopes, and personal alerts. In conjunction with the launch of MSN Mobile, Microsoft acquired OmniBrowse Inc., a wireless data services company that specializes in applications for wireless hand-held devices. Also in 1999, the SABRE Group, the airline reservation provider, along with IBM and Nokia, developed an interactive wireless service that allows travelers to adjust their itineraries and access flight schedules.

Much of the technological development in telemetry has focused on automatic meter reading and tracking vehicles, and there will be continued growth in this mobile data application. The Yankee Group expects wireless telemetry revenues to grow to more than $6.6 billion by 2004. Growth will be driven by the convergence of wireless, computing, and Internet technologies and the need for wireless service providers to diversify their revenue streams. LoJack, the stolen vehicle recovery provider, says that its wireless technology has enabled law enforcement entities to recover 30,000 vehicles since its inception.

Instant messaging, sometimes referred to as on-line "buddy lists," is used by more than 50 million PC-based users and is becoming available to users of hand-held computers and mobile phones. One analysis firm claims that in 5 years, the interface to most cell phones and wireless personal digital assistants (PDAs) will include a buddy list that will transform the way people communicate by replacing the number of routine real-time two-way phone calls.

Following is a brief description of other recent issues and trends of note in the wireless services industry:

- *Alternative distribution channels.* Wireless services are distributed through a number of different marketing channels. In the past, this was done mainly through direct marketing by service providers. Many carriers have opened retail specialty stores to sell branded equipment and services. Carriers also distribute through alternative channels, such as electronics stores and general retailers as well as through resellers, agents, and third-party telemarketers. Wireless carriers are expected to increase the use of alternative distribution channels. In 1998, carriers' sales through indirect channels totaled 43 percent, according to Cahners In-Stat, and sales are expected to increase to 48 percent in the year 2000. Cahners cited alternative distribution channels such as catalog showrooms, home office stores, warehouse clubs, and on-line Internet Web sites.
- *Churn.* Generally speaking, consumers' satisfaction with wireless services remains high, but increased competition in the industry is leading consumers to comparison shop and switch carriers more frequently. In addition, as wireless carriers continue to develop their networks and convert to digital, it is inevitable that some customers will grow disenchanted with spotty coverage or surprisingly high phone bills and that some will discontinue use or change operators. (Price was reportedly the primary reason customers switched service providers.) Cahners In-Stat Group reports that while more than 13 million new subscribers signed on for wireless services in 1998, more than 16 million customers either discon-

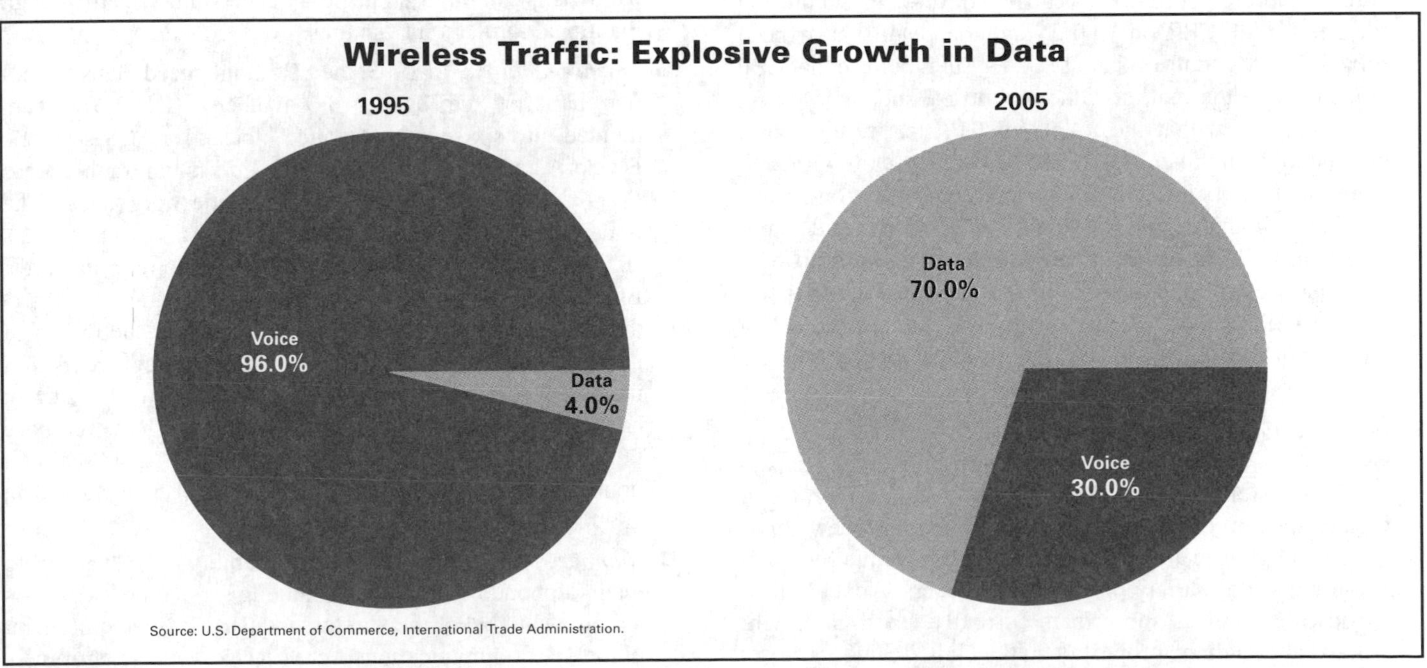

FIGURE 30-4

tinued service or changed service providers. Total annual churn in the cellular and PCS market may reach nearly 40 million subscribers by 2002. Analysts generally agree that the future success of many carriers could be determined by their level of churn. As challengers to incumbent cellular operators, PCS operators are expected to benefit from high churn rates. To combat churn, service providers are applying longer-term customer-focused strategies. Operators are using network information and relating it back to the services they deliver to subscribers, for example, compensating some customers for dropped calls. Call assessments include analysis of voice quality, handoff failures, dropped call rates, call connectivity, and blocked service.

- *Coverage.* While the goal of many service providers is to expand coverage of their networks—in the case of larger operators, the goal is national coverage—some analysts claim that a nationwide footprint is not necessarily a prerequisite for success. According to Allied Business Intelligence (ABI), the inability of a wireless carrier to offer a "one-price" coast-to-coast wireless plan that includes free roaming and long-distance calls does not mean that that carrier cannot be competitive. Users who work and live locally and do not travel often still constitute the bulk of the untapped wireless market. Bell Atlantic Mobile, for example, whose parent still is trying to establish a national footprint, estimates that 70 percent of its customers never roam. In fact, just over 10 percent of cellular revenues are generated by roaming. Nationwide PCS carriers are offering airtime packages with no roaming charges within their networks.

- *Calling party pays (CPP).* In the United States, calling charges for wireless phone calls mainly have been billed to the recipient of a call. In Europe and other parts of the world, the reverse is the case: It is the calling party that pays for calls to mobile phones. U.S. carriers have been monitoring the impact of CPP on traffic, and the results have been mixed. Many countries that use this system believe that CPP helps expand the market. Other countries, such as Mexico, have discovered that the rollout of CPP has resulted in a decline in the number of wireline-to-wireless calls, although some analysts believe that high interconnection rates may play a role in that result. In 1999, the FCC adopted a declaratory ruling and a notice of proposed rule making to help facilitate the introduction of CPP as an optional wireless service to U.S. consumers. Comments were sought regarding the role of the states and the FCC in developing a uniform notification requirement.

- *Digitalization.* While analog systems remain the most pervasive systems in the United States, many are reaching capacity. Conversion to digital technologies holds the promise of greater spectral efficiencies as well as a range of new applications. Digital features translate to more revenue for carriers and a wider variety of services for users. About half of worldwide wireless subscribers currently use digital technology, although the proportion in the United States is closer to one-quarter. The number of U.S. subscribers using digital technologies is expected to overtake the number of analog subscribers around 2002.

- *Fraud prevention.* The war against fraud remains a notable phenomenon in cellular services. One analysis group claims that U.S. wireless carriers are losing as much as half a million dollars a day, although others question that estimate because the growing numbers of digital networks are arguably more secure against fraud than are analog cellular services. In addition, cloning has been reduced through the use of sophisticated antifraud software. Nevertheless, internal fraud remains a problem, and carriers continue to look for innovative ways to reduce it.

- *Industry consolidation.* As is the case in the wireline industry—with the mergers of AT&T and TCI, SBC Communications and Ameritech, and Bell Atlantic and GTE—consolidation is occurring rapidly in the cellular services industry as major players ally. Market share growth and the need to combine to become more efficient and generate funds for the tremendous capital costs required are two primary reasons. Mergers and joint ventures are often the fastest way to expand into new markets and cut costs by eliminating overlapping operations. Some new market entrants are simultaneously building their own networks and buying other companies to gain immediate access to customers. Perhaps the most notable merger in 1999 was the Vodafone Group's $77 billion purchase of AirTouch Communications. That merger created the world's largest wireless company, with more than 29 million customers in 23 countries. Vodafone/AirTouch and Bell Atlantic reportedly plan to craft a coast-to-coast U.S. wireless network. Other examples include the merger of US West Wireless and Touch America and MCIW's acquisition of Wireless One. This trend also is occurring globally, but in the future wireless carriers probably will establish partnerships through strategic alliances rather than through traditional formal joint ventures.

- *License auctions.* In 1993, the FCC announced plans to auction parts of the 1.8- to 1.9-gigahertz (GHz) spectrum divided into six segments, called blocks, for PCS services. Blocks A and B were designed for the 51 major trading areas (MTAs), which included multiple cities or states. The remaining blocks were allocated to the basic trading areas (BTAs), each of which included only one metropolitan area. Blocks A through C were allocated 30 MHz, and blocks D through F were allocated 10 MHz each. The auctioning of new licenses by the FCC over the last few years has increased competition and helped bring about the current boom in wireless services. Some participants, however, have fallen by the wayside. Of the 493 C-Block licenses auctioned, more than half were returned to be reauctioned in 1999.

- *Number portability.* Number portability—the ability to retain a phone number after changing service providers—is a prominent goal of the wireless industry. It is a requirement of the Telecommunications Act of 1996 to enable customers to keep their existing phone numbers after switching from one local telephone company to another. Number portability is seen as essential by wireless carriers if they are to achieve convergence or compete head to head with wireline carriers for local exchange customers.

- *Prepaid services.* Prepaid wireless services are services that are purchased in advance of their use and do not require a service contract with a wireless provider. Prepaid services are being mass-marketed by most service providers, with notable success. Prepaid appeals to segments of the market that otherwise are not eligible for or do not want an open-ended or monthly contract and are willing to pay substantially higher rates per minute of airtime for the freedom of not being tied down. Prepaid service offerings also cut down on fraud and bad debt and relieve the operator of the need to do expensive credit checks. U.S. carriers, observing the successful experience of other countries with prepaid, no doubt noted that in less than 2 years prepaid showed 170 percent growth worldwide and represented one-third of all cellular subscriptions in western Europe. Foreign network operators found that not only were costs of acquisition and operational costs low with prepaid, there was no billing or debt collection to worry about, and prepaid users generally made twice as many calls. Prepaid also opened up entirely new market segments and lines of distribution. Prepaid is less widely used in the United States, but the Yankee Group predicts that the number of prepaid users in the United States will grow from 3.5 percent of all wireless subscribers in 1998 to 22 percent in 2003.

Global Market Trends

The international wireless communications sector took on an added dimension in 1999 as manufacturers and operators began to position themselves for the evolution to the next-generation, or 3G, wireless systems beginning in 2001. The industry has continued to experience extraordinary growth globally, surpassing 300 million subscribers at the end of 1998 and approaching 350 million by mid-1999. Incumbent players are investing in their networks to add high-speed data capabilities and improve quality, coverage, and capacity. In addition, new 3G licenses contemplated over the next several years will act as a market catalyst.

The ITU, a treaty organization of the United Nations, is coordinating the worldwide process to establish global 3G wireless standards though a project dubbed International Mobile Telecommunications–2000 (IMT-2000). The ITU's goal is to establish new standards that will allow global roaming (use outside the user's home service area), high-speed data and Internet access, full-motion video, and other sophisticated multimedia services. The ITU was scheduled to complete its final recommendation on a set of standards by December 1999.

Although it appeared that the 3G process might be delayed because of disputes over standards and intellectual property, in February 1999, the TransAtlantic Business Dialogue (TABD) broke the lengthy impasse on 3G standards by fashioning a multiple standards compromise that subsequently was used by the ITU as the basis for its 3G standard. The resolution of outstanding intellectual property disputes further set the stage for the resolution of the issue to everyone's (manufacturers and operators) satisfaction. A group including European, North American, Asia-Pacific region, and other operators, whose current share of the global wireless telecommunications services market is near 90 percent, then developed an Operators' Harmonization Group (OHG) agreement in June 1999. That agreement established the technical framework for interoperability between the various air interfaces and the two wireless core networks in use today and subsequently was accepted by the ITU. Consequently, the forthcoming ITU standards will provide the technical capability for extensive roaming arrangements between new 3G and existing second-generation (2G) operators.

In December 1998, the European Council of Ministers and the European Parliament adopted a Common Position and Decision that mandated that licensing processes move forward immediately for 3G services. It specified that "E.C. Member States shall adopt an authorization system for UMTS by January 1, 2000 and allow the introduction of UMTS services by 1/1/2002" (with the possibility of a 1-year extension). Finland, the sole EU member state (and any country in any region) to have licensed 3G systems as of September 1999, selected four 3G service licensees in March 1999. Japan and several EU member states planned to begin issuing licenses to operators late in 1999, although the systems will not be deployed commercially until 2001–2002. Some 50 3G licenses are expected to be auctioned between 1999 and 2000.

In the 1990s, the benefits of cellular telephony—mobility, usability, and, more recently, affordability—made cellular attractive to consumers in developed countries and an urgent requirement in many developing countries. The degree to which wireless has developed in different regions of the world depends largely on factors such as level of economic development, income distribution, cost of entry, affordability, free market orientation, and effectiveness of distribution systems. Wireless coverage is approaching ubiquity in developed countries, with most nations having an array of as many as nine competing networks. In developing countries, wireless technology is increasingly a substitute for wireline networks as developers have come to recognize that wireless networks are often less expensive to construct and operate than are traditional landline networks and can be brought to market in one-third the time. The auctioning of licenses has become increasingly prevalent as digital technologies have provided foreign governments and regulators with an opportunity to create competition in line with the prevailing political trend toward a more open environment in telecommunications services. This in turn provides a better deal for users and attracts potential foreign investors to the country.

The year 1998 ended with some 308 million cellular subscribers worldwide, an increase of nearly 100 million, bringing worldwide penetration to 5.8 percent, up from 3.9 percent at the end of 1997 (see Figure 30-5). Strong growth of about 68 percent enabled western Europe to surpass Asia (excluding Japan) and North America as the largest regional market, with about 31 percent of the world's subscribers. The number of subscribers in the Asia-Pacific region continued to grow rapidly, up about

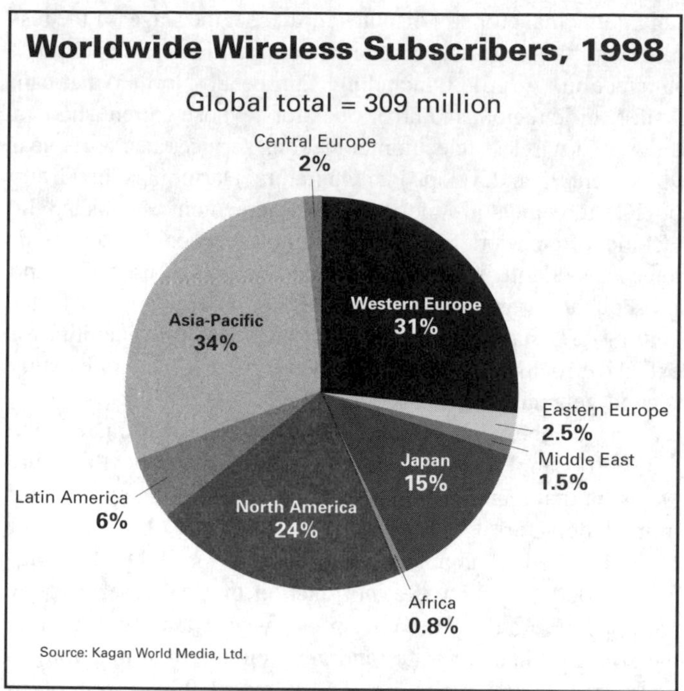

FIGURE 30-5

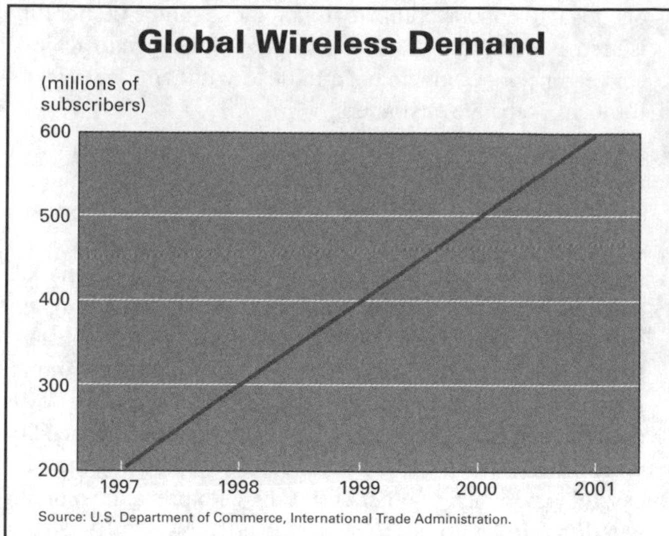

FIGURE 30-6

31 million to more than 106 million, ending that year with 34 percent of the world total. North American subscribers were up about 25 percent to nearly 75 million and accounted for about 24 percent of the world total. Though starting from a much smaller basis, Latin America experienced strong growth of 73 percent in 1998, accounting for about 6 percent of the world total. Africa and the Middle East had a combined total of about 6.7 million, or about 2.3 percent of the world's subscribers (see Table 30-5). Many forecasters expect the number of wireless subscribers to exceed 500 million in the year 2000, and some believe that there will be 1 billion subscribers by 2003 or 2004 (see Figure 30-6).

Of the more than 300 million wireless handsets in service worldwide at the beginning of 1999, about 50 percent of users subscribed to analog services (mainly AMPS), and the remainder were digital (or dual-mode) users. The majority (74 percent) of digital subscribers are Global System for Mobile (GSM) handset users. However, the share of analog is expected to decline markedly to about 20 percent worldwide by 2002.

TABLE 30-5: Cellular Subscribers by World Region

Region	1997[1]	1998[1]	Percent Change	Percent of Total
Western Europe	56.77	95.64	68.5	30.9
Eastern Europe	3.88	7.69	98.2	2.5
Middle East	3.30	4.38	32.7	1.5
Africa	1.85	2.35	27.0	0.8
North America	59.36	74.46	25.4	24.1
Latin America	10.27	17.79	73.2	5.7
Asia-Pacific region	74.40	106.62	43.3	34.5
Total	209.83	308.93	47.2	

[1] Millions of subscribers at end of year.
Source: Kagan World Media, Ltd.

The global value of the wireless services market in 1998 was estimated at more than $125 billion, and some analysts project that it will reach $275 billion by 2001. According to Analysys, mobile communications revenues will reach $420 billion in 2005 and grow a further 47 percent to nearly $620 billion by 2010.

The vast majority of wireless subscribers are cellular users, although PCS has continued to experience remarkable growth levels, with the number of global subscribers increasing 80 percent from 14 million at the end of 1997 to more than 25 million at the end of 1998. PCS subscribership is projected to reach 150 million worldwide by 2001.

The year 1998 ushered in new advances in hemispheric roaming. BellSouth International's roaming and clearinghouse operation, International Wireless Services, for example, began offering telecommunications carriers in the Americas hemispheric roaming, connecting wireless carriers in South America and Central America to one another and to carriers in North America. France Telecom and Deutsche Telekom plan to offer wireless roaming between Europe and North America. Those companies plan to open the service to all GSM operators. While dual-band handsets have been in service for some time, new triband handsets allow users to access or roam on up to three different frequencies. The first "world phone" affording access to GSM 900/1800/1900 appeared on the market in 1999.

Latin America. According to the Strategis Group, cellular and PCS markets throughout Latin America will achieve impressive growth over the next 5 years despite uncertainty in Latin American economies. Privatization and liberalization programs are boosting wireless growth in Central America and South America. Other market drivers include the low cost of development relative to wireline and the introduction of CPP and prepaid services. The Latin American cellular market is forecast to grow at a compound annual growth rate (CAGR) of 40 to 45 percent in the 2000–2002 period, outperforming growth in the wired network. Various assessments predict that wireless subscribership in Latin America will grow from around 18 million in 1998 to as many as 55 million in 2002. A study by Baskerville Communications in 1999 estimated that more than 71 million mobile lines will be in service in Latin America by 2007, when revenues will reach more than $81 billion. A number of principal U.S. wireless companies participate actively in the Latin American market.

Brazil is clearly the premier market in the region. The wireless market in Brazil exploded in 1998, as was evidenced by the more than 1 million cellular customers added in less than 8 months in that year, with even stronger growth predicted for 1999. In the cellular market alone, the government expected 2.9 million new lines to be contracted for installation in 1999, drawing foreign suppliers to manufacture in-country.

Mexico also is considered one of the region's most promising markets. Over the last 2 years, Mexico's new regulatory authority has moved aggressively to auction spectrum, introduce competition in new sectors, and license new technologies. The auctioning of PCS licenses in nine regions of Mexico was completed in May 1998. The number of cellular//PCS subscribers in that country is expected to increase about 42 percent by the year 2000.

Venezuela and Chile also posted above-average growth in 1998. In March 1998, Chile became one of the first Latin American countries to launch PCS services, and after a number of delays, Argentina auctioned PCS licenses in mid-1999. Some smaller Latin American markets—notably, El Salvador, Panama, Paraguay, and Bolivia—performed remarkably well.

As was noted above, prepaid systems, deregulation, and, in some areas, CPP have accelerated growth in much of Latin America. Only 3 years after its introduction, prepaid cellular/PCS was generating more than 25 percent of new Latin American subscribers, and the Strategis Group forecasts that by 2005, two-thirds of all new cellular/PCS subscribers in that region will sign up through prepaid plans. Wireless prices are dropping in the Latin American market, and by lowering the effective cost of cellular and providing for usage and spending flexibility, prepaid service in most markets is expanding the addressable market.

Time Division Multiple Access (TDMA) digital technology has benefited the most from the upgrading of analog AMPS networks and buildout of new systems throughout the region. Code Division Multiple Access (CDMA) 1900 subscribership grew 120 percent to reach 124,000 at the end of 1998. The Global Mobile Suppliers Association predicts that there will be at least one GSM operator in every country in Latin America within 2 years. The Strategis Group projects that 60 percent of the subscriber base in Latin America will use GSM or TDMA and that most of the remainder will use CDMA.

Asia-Pacific Region. Subscriber levels in the Asia-Pacific region grew from 75 million at the end of 1997 to 106 million at the end of 1998. That region (including Japan) accounted for more than one-third of the world's 1998 subscriber base. Emerging markets in the Pacific Rim have abundant populations and low telephone densities, making them highly attractive markets for wireless services. Some analysts have forecast that that region may have more than 200 million subscribers by 2002, for a regional penetration rate of about 6.5 percent, although this will vary significantly by country. Cellular service revenues for the Asia-Pacific region exceeded $60 billion in 1998 and are projected to exceed $100 billion by 2001.

The Asia-Pacific region, however, is far from monolithic. While China's market has been burgeoning and seemed relatively unscathed by the regional economic downturn in 1998, currency woes have caused southeast Asian nations such as Thailand to reevaluate their wireless network development plans. Wireless licensing procedures have run the gamut from no public tendering to spectrum auctions. Ownership stipulations on operating entities also differ throughout the region, ranging from complete state ownership to total foreign control, with varying degrees in between. Japan and China account for 63 percent of the regional market and are expected to remain the largest markets in the region, with China poised to overtake Japan's lead in terms of total subscribers.

The most spectacular growth in the region occurred in Japan, where cellular subscriber totals rose 133 percent to nearly 50 million in mid-1999, in large part reflecting falling service prices and enhanced services such as SMS and E-mail. The vast majority of subscribers—nearly 90 percent—are cellular users, and the remainder are users of Personal Handyphone System (PHS), an affordable but less functional service whose popularity has waned for the last 2 years. Japan's last remaining operator accepting applications for analog cellular service ceased issuing new analog accounts in August 1999. The Japanese market is set for spectacular growth as 3G comes to the fore. The Japanese carrier NTT DoCoMo will initiate nationwide IMT-2000 service with high-speed data and video capabilities in Tokyo, Osaka, and Nagoya by 2001, with nationwide service scheduled for 2003.

Growth in China's wireless market is expected to remain strong. China grew from 14.4 million subscribers to 24.9 million in 1998, and a number of analysts claim that that country will have 45 million subscribers by 2001. In anticipation of future growth, China's Ministry of Information Industry added an extra digit to mobile numbers to increase the cellular numbering system capacity to 500 million numbers. Chinese officials have made a commitment to open that country's wireless markets to nearly 50 percent foreign ownership. This move was taken in part to pave the way for membership in the WTO. There is speculation that China's existing operators—China Telecom and China Unicom—may have additional competition in the near future when new wireless licenses are issued in the year 2000.

In India, the cellular industry all but ran aground in 1998, running up losses of over $600 million. This was due mainly to license fees charged by India's Department of Telecommunication (DoT) that were way out of proportion to revenues. Cellular operators also pay DoT retail access charges for mobile–to–fixed line calls, and for some operators this amounts to half the amount invoiced to mobile subscribers.

All countries in the Asia-Pacific region with the exception of a handful of smaller nations have at least three licensed wireless operators. Uncertainties in regard to continued growth include the residual economic impact of the Asian monetary crisis. South Korea, which scaled back its development plans sharply in 1997, began to increase expenditures in 1998, and the number of subscribers doubled from 6.6 million to 13.9 million. Taiwan was the fastest-growing market (133 percent) in 1998, with 3.5 million users as opposed to 1.5 million in 1997.

Europe. The remarkable growth of the wireless market in western Europe is expected to continue, with some studies claiming that sales and penetration levels will grow an average of 10 percent a year over the next 5 years. Subscribership in the region grew more than 68 percent, rising from about 56 million at the end of 1997 to about 95 million at the end of 1998, resulting in an average penetration level of more than 21 percent. Total subscribers in western Europe are projected by *Global Mobile* to reach 108 million by 2000 and 158 million by 2004. Other analysts predict that overall wireless penetration in western Europe will exceed 27 percent by 2001, with some projecting over 40 percent by 2006. New wireless licenses, declines in service prices in some countries resulting from increased competition, and the increased availability of dual-band (GSM 900 and DCS 1800) handsets will continue to propel the market. The growing migration of voice traffic from fixed networks to cellular/PCS networks and the increased revenues generated by wireless data and value-added services are also among the reasons cited for the increase. Prepaid services also have had a significant impact on the market, with more than 40 percent of all subscribers on a prepaid basis at the end of 1998.

The western European cellular services market was estimated to be worth about $42 billion at the end of 1998 and is forecast to grow at a CAGR of more than 10 percent over the next 5 years, reaching about $150 billion in revenues by 2004. As new licenses have been awarded throughout the region, increased competition has increased pressure on incumbent operators. Third and fourth mobile licenses were awarded by the end of 1998 in most European countries, with many new entrants launching services in the last quarter of 1998 and the first quarter of 1999. Prices are expected to decrease markedly, dropping up to 10 percent per year on average in most countries, because of increased competition. It is assumed that 3G wireless will not have a significant impact until at least 2002 and even later in some countries. Nonetheless, many incumbent operators already are contracting with vendors for technology to give them high-speed data capability.

The four largest markets in the region—Italy, Germany, France, and the United Kingdom—accounted for about two-thirds of total regional growth. Italy had the highest growth rate in western Europe, adding more than 8 million new subscribers in 1998 for a total of more than 20 million users, and was projected to reach 27 million subscribers by the end of 1999. Italy launched a third operator in 1998 and planned to award a fourth operating license in 1999. Italy's wireless growth is attributed in large part to attractive pricing. Italy reportedly offers the least expensive wireless service; at less than $0.16 per minute, this is 54 percent below the average for Europe. Germany increased its subscriber levels from 8.3 million to 13.8 million, and the United Kingdom effectively used prepaid to expand its market 53 percent to over 13 million. Other countries also showed notable growth. Greece, for example, more than doubled subscribership in 1998, as did the Netherlands, Portugal, and Turkey. For some time, Finland has been a vanguard country for wireless penetration; however, analysts generally agree that the boom in dual-band mobile phone sales could slow markedly in the year 2000 because about 60 percent of that country's population now owns at least one mobile phone. Faster networks and the emergence of the wireless Internet could help fuel the market in the future.

Despite efforts by the European Commission, rates of fixed to mobile calls throughout the region vary markedly. Many network operators in Europe had a good revenue year in 1998. Total revenue in western Europe was estimated at $33.2 billion in 1998, and some analysts project that that market will be worth $84 billion in 2003. A report from the Strategis Group finds that while European wireless operators earn reasonably high revenues per customer and have low churn, they also incur high operating expenses per customer, resulting in lower operating margins in Europe than in the United States. The Strategis Group estimates that wireless margins in Europe are less than 40 percent, while in the United States, margins were about 42 percent in 1998. According to *Global Mobile,* the average European mobile user generated about $41 per month in revenue in 1998, ranging from $69 per month in the Netherlands to about $20 per month in Luxembourg.

International Data Corporation (IDC) predicts that average revenue per user (ARPU) in western Europe will decrease at an annual rate of 5.6 percent over the next 5 years; however, price declines soon will be mitigated by increasing revenue from wireless data and value-added services in that period. IDC expects the total number of mobile data subscribers to grow from around 2 percent of the total GSM subscriber base to 12 percent at the end of the 5-year period. The main growth is expected to start toward the end of 2001, fueled by the launch of General Packet Radio Service (GPRS) toward the end of the year 2000 in the most developed GSM markets.

Some industry observers believe that the future use of wireless throughout the world can be predicted by looking at what is happening in Europe today. Subscribers there are using their phones to pay bills, conduct banking, and schedule travel. By early in the next decade, one in four Europeans is expected to own a mobile phone. The British company Strategy Analytics claims that 47 percent of European households already have more than one cell phone, while 12 percent have three or more.

The wireless services market in central and eastern Europe (CEE) grew markedly in 1998—many CEE markets experienced triple-digit growth rates in that year—as competition and digital networks expanded. The number of cellular subscribers in the 15 largest CEE countries more than doubled to 7.5 million, reaching 2.3 percent of that region's population. CEE's wireless market entered an era of fierce competition propelled by the new digital standards (GSM 900 and DCS 1800).

In recent years, the region's largest growth markets were Poland, Hungary, and the Czech Republic, while Romania, Bulgaria, and Yugoslavia recorded the fastest rates of growth, but from a lower base. Russia's marked cellular slowdown must be viewed in light of the economic slowdown there in the second half of 1998. Kagan World Media anticipates that the CEE cellular market will explode within the next 10 years, with an estimated 75.2 million mobile phone users by 2008, representing 10-fold growth.

Average monthly revenue per subscriber in CEE markets ranges from $66 a month in Slovakia to $290 a month in Russia. Russia continues to report the highest monthly revenue per subscriber, although the economic problems caused the ARPU to drop in 1998.

Africa and the Middle East. The use of wireless telephony is extremely popular in Africa; in fact, cellular service has become so popular in some African countries that it sometimes is difficult to make or receive cellular calls because of network congestion. Africa was estimated to have about 2.4 million cellular users at the end of 1998. African nations realize the need for communications capabilities to expand their economies. There is a movement toward liberalization in various countries as well as increasing private sector participation, and most countries in Africa now have multiple operators. In countries where they are offered, prepaid packages have been effective in driving market growth. While Africa has many analog networks, digitalization is taking hold and digital networks are growing in number. GSM has become the dominant mobile technology.

Companies pursuing wireless opportunities in Africa have had to face a number of disappointments. Economic stagnation, political unrest, and corrupt bureaucracies have hampered progress, and in many countries there is an unstable or confusing regulatory climate. With the exception of South Africa, handsets usually are not subsidized as they are elsewhere, and the cost of a basic handset can run as high as $1,000 or more in many African countries. In addition, getting equipment through customs can be difficult, and power sources are not always reliable.

The Middle East, which added more than 1 million subscribers in 1998, had about 4.3 million users at the end of that year. That region has had selected successes in wireless. Just as South Africa dominates the African continent, Israel dominates wireless subscribership in the Middle East. With 57 percent of the regions subscribers, Israel was projected to have spent an estimated $1 billion to set up its third mobile phone network in 1998. The New Territories of Palestine are also planning to establish a wireless network.

The Arabian Gulf states have invested enormous sums in developing their telecommunications infrastructures over the last decade, and mobile communications has played a leading role in this investment program. The average level of monthly traffic per subscriber is significantly higher—almost three times larger—than the average for western Europe. The largest single market in the Gulf states is Saudi Arabia, which has nearly half a million subscribers.

Although a monopoly operator is still the regional norm, this is changing gradually, and there are likely to be major steps toward a more competitive environment over the next 2 or 3 years. For example, Saudi Arabia's national telephone operator, STC, was privatized in May 1998, although the government still retains all the shares.

Linda Astor and Richard Paddock, U.S. Department of Commerce, Office of Telecommunications, (202) 482-4466, September 1999.

■ REFERENCES

America's Network, 201 Sandpointe Avenue, Suite 600, Santa Ana, CA 92707. (714) 573-8400; fax: (714) 573-8634.

APEC Telecom Working Group. www.apec-wg.com/.

Cellular Telecommunications Industry Association. www.wow-com.com/.

Communications Week International, P.O. Box 550, Bromley BR2 9TA, United Kingdom. (44) 181-956-3017; www.commweek.com.

CTIA Semi-Annual Data Survey, Cellular Telecommunications Industry Association, 1250 Connecticut Avenue, NW, Suite 200, Washington, DC 20036. (202) 785-0081; fax: (202) 785-0721.

European Messaging/Paging Markets: 1998, Inside Paging, The State of the U.S. Paging Industry: 1997, the Strategis Group, 1130 Connecticut Avenue, NW, Suite 325, Washington, DC 20036-3915. (202) 530-7500; fax: (202) 530-7550.

FAA Office of Commercial Space Transportation. www.dot.gov/faa/cst/.

Global Wireless, Crain Communications Inc., 777 East Speer Boulevard, Denver, CO, 80203-4214. (303) 733-2500; fax: (303) 733-9941; www.globalwirelessnews.com.

Industry Analysis Reports from the FCC's Common Carrier Division. www.fcc.gov/ccb/stats.

International Cellular, Kagan World Media, Ltd., 126 Clock Tower Place, Carmel, CA 93923-8734. (408) 624-1536; fax: (408) 625-3225.

International Telecommunication Union. www.itu.ch.

Long Distance Market Shares, Federal Communications Commission, 1919 M Street, NW, Room 533, Washington, DC 20254. (202) 418-0940.

Lynx Global Telecom Database, Lynx Technologies, 710 Route 46 East, Fairfield, NJ 07004. (973) 256-7200; fax: (973) 882-3583.

Market Demand Forecast for Terrestrial Third Generation (IMT-2000) Services, Personal Communications Industry Association, 500 Montgomery Street, Suite 700, Alexandria, VA 22314-1561. (703) 739-0300; fax: (703) 836-1608; www.pcia.com.

Mobile Communications International, MCI Subscriptions, Central House, 27 Park Street, Croydon CRO 1YD, United Kingdom. (011) 44-081-686-5654 or (011) 44-071-383-5757; fax: (011) 44-071-383-3181.

Mobile Phone News, PCS Week, Wireless Business & Finance, Phillips Business Information, Inc., 1201 Seven Locks Road, Potomac, MD 20854. (301) 340-1520; fax: (301) 424-2058; www.phillips.com.

New International Carriers Online Database, Telegeography, 1730 Rhode Island Avenue, NW, Suite 400, Washington, DC 20036. (202) 467-0017; fax: (202) 467-0851.

1998 PCIA Wireless Market Portfolio, Compiled by the Personal Communications Industry Association, 500 Montgomery Street, Suite 700, Alexandria, VA 22314-1561. (703) 739-0300; fax: (703) 836-1608.

1999 Multimedia Telecommunications Market Review and Forecast, MMTA/TIA, 2500 Wilson Boulevard, Arlington, VA 22201. (703) 907-7470.

Office of Telecommunications of the International Trade Administration, U.S. Department of Commerce, http://.infoserv2.ita.doc.gov/ot/home.nsf.

Personal Communications Industry Association. www.pcia.com/.

RCR Radio Communications Report, RCR Publications Inc., 777 East Speer Boulevard, Denver, CO 80203. (800) 678-9595; www.rcrnews.com.

Reference Book of Rates, Price Indices, and Household Expenditures for Telephone Service, Federal Communications Commission, 1919 M Street, NW, Room 533, Washington, DC 20036. (202) 418-0940.

Statistics of Communications Common Carriers, Federal Communications Commission, 1997/1998, 1919 M Street, NW, Room 533, Washington, DC 20036. (202) 418-0940.

Telecommunications Industry Revenue: TRS Fund Worksheet Data, Federal Communications Commission, 1919 M Street, NW, Room 539, Washington, DC 20254. (202) 418-0940.

Telecommunications Reports, Business Research Publications, Inc., 1333 H Street, NW, 11th Floor-West, Washington, DC 20005. (202) 842-3006.

Telegeography 1999, Telegeography, Inc., 1730 Rhode Island Avenue, NW, Suite 400, Washington, DC 20036. (202) 467-0017; fax: (202) 467-0851.

Telephony, Telephony Publishing Corp., P.O. Box 12976, Overland Park, KS 66282-2976.

3G Mobile, Global Mobile, Baskerville Communications Corp., 15165 Ventura Boulevard, Suite 310, Sherman Oaks, CA 91403. (818) 461-9660; fax: (818) 461-9661.

Trends in the International Telecommunications Industry, Federal Communications Commission, 1919 M Street, NW, Room 539, Washington, DC 20254. (202) 467-0017.

U.S. Long Distance Markets; Local Exchange Carrier Markets: 1995 Edition, Northern Business Information, DataPro Information Services Group, 1221 Avenue of the Americas, New York, NY 10020-1095. (212) 512-2900.

WirelessNow (daily wireless update). www.commnow.com.

WirelessNOW (on-line service), CommunicationsNOW, Inc., the Strategis Group, 1130 Connecticut Avenue, NW, Suite 325, Washington, DC 20036-3915. (202) 530-7500; fax: (202) 530-7550.

Wireless Week, Chilton Publications, 600 South Cherry Street, Suite 400, Denver, CO 80222. (303) 393-7449; fax: (303) 399-2034.

World Telecommunications Development Report 1998/99, International Telecommunication Union, Geneva, Switzerland, available from Telegeography, Inc., Suite 1000, 1150 Connecticut Avenue, NW, Washington, DC 20036. (202) 467-0017.

■ RELATED CHAPTERS

26: Information Services
27: Computer Equipment
28: Software and Internet Technologies
29: Space Commerce
31: Telecommunications and Navigation Equipment

TELECOMMUNICATIONS AND NAVIGATION EQUIPMENT
Economic and Trade Trends

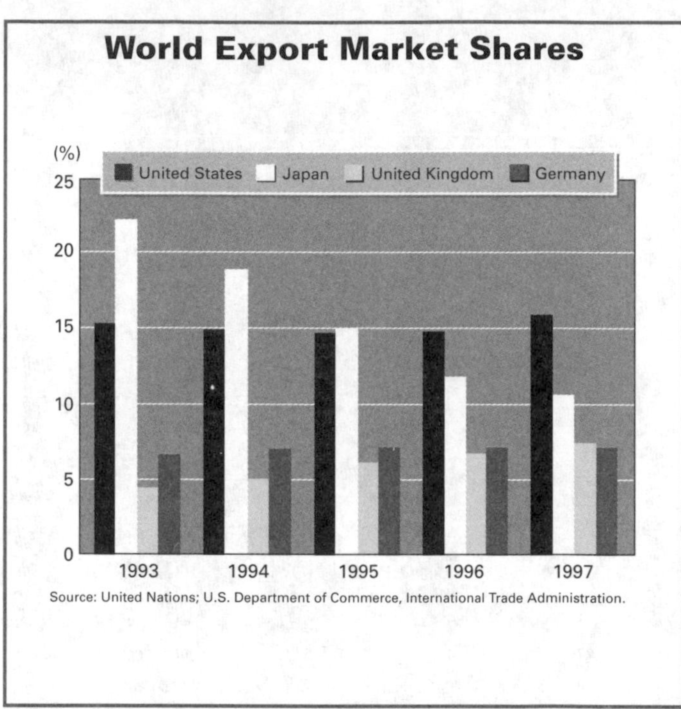

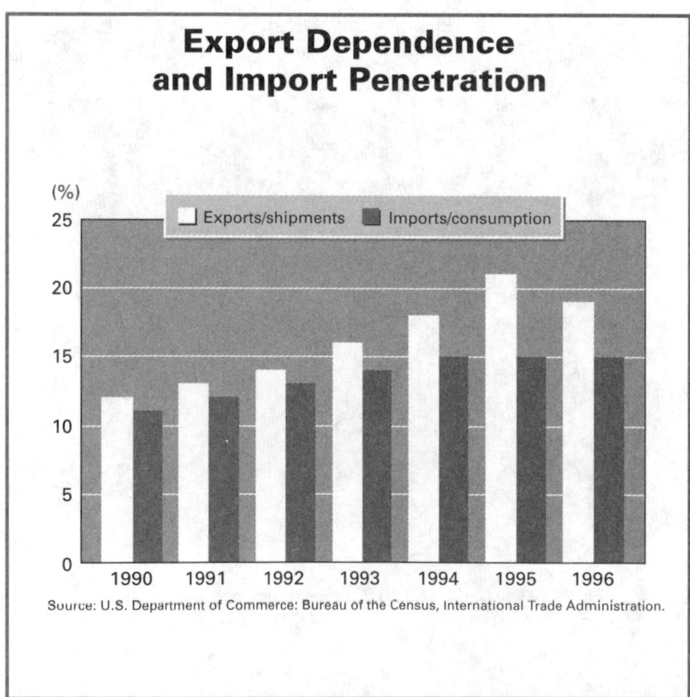

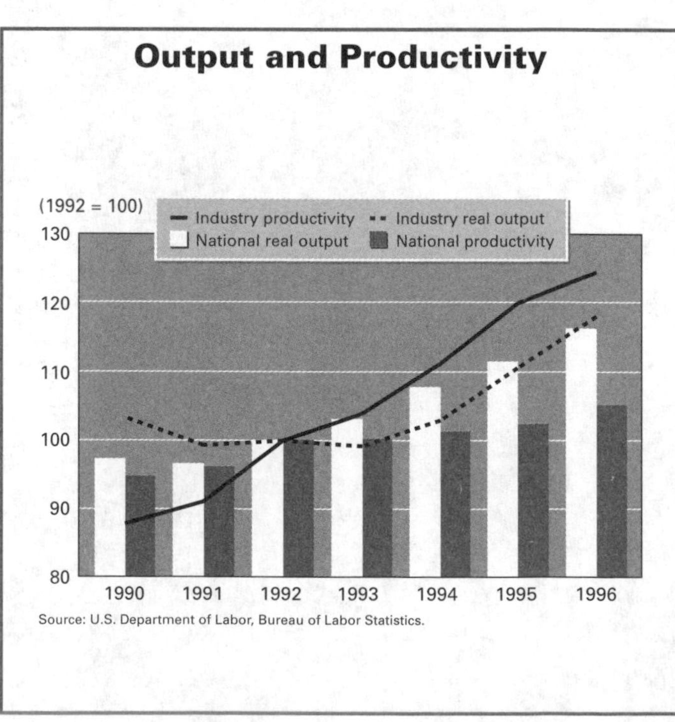

See "Getting the Most Out of *Outlook 2000*" for definitions of terms.

31

Telecommunications and Navigation Equipment

INDUSTRY DEFINITION This chapter covers network equipment, which includes switching and transmission equipment; customer premises equipment that can be attached to a telephone network, such as telephones, answering machines, and fax machines; fiber optics, including optical fiber and fiber-optic cable; wireless communications equipment, including cellular, paging, and personal communications systems; and satellite communications systems, including communications satellites and related ground equipment. Search and navigation equipment, which covers radar and sonar systems, and surveillance equipment also are included. The chapter omits radio and television broadcasting equipment [closed-circuit and cable television transmission equipment and studio (audio and video) equipment] and terrestrial microwave communications equipment.

GLOBAL INDUSTRY TRENDS

Driven by vibrant demand for Internet access and mobile telephony, the global market for telecommunications equipment was expected to surpass $325 billion in 1999 and is projected to grow at an average annual rate of 15 percent to reach over $400 billion in 2001. The wireless sector generally is regarded as the fastest-growing component of the telecommunications equipment industry. Research by the DMG Technology Group (DMG) estimated that wireless infrastructure equipment will increase from 16 percent of overall telecommunications equipment spending in 1999 to 21 percent in 2001. Just as the fixed telephony market is shifting from a circuit-switched to a packet-based architecture to meet the increasing demand for data, wireless operators worldwide are seeking solutions that will enable them to offer their customers high-speed wireless Internet access as well as access to a wide range of new data applications.

Growing demand for telecommunications equipment is being driven by the confluence of a number of factors: the continued expansion of wireless networks and preparations for meeting expected demand for high-speed wireless data; continued liberalization and deregulation of telecommunications services, in many cases stemming from commitments made in the World Trade Organization (WTO) Agreement on Basic Telecommunications Services; and significant unmet demand for basic telecommunications services in developing countries as well as additional lines for Internet access in developed markets.

Growth is robust across all continents. Europe was expected to surpass North America as the largest regional equipment market. The majority of European countries have authorized competition in basic telecommunications services and the related infrastructure. In addition to hundreds of new network operators that have been licensed to offer public telecommunications services in individual countries as well as businesses that are establishing corporate networks, incumbent European operators are investing in their networks to help maintain their share of domestic wireline markets. Many are expanding into new markets or new lines of business such as wireless communications and the Internet. Asia, one of the fastest-growing markets in the world, is continuing to rebound from the financial crisis that dampened demand in many countries. The Latin American market, though considerably smaller, also is growing at a rapid pace. Many governments have introduced competition by allowing private sector participation in the delivery of wireless services.

In a capital-intensive business requiring high outlays for research and development, a handful of suppliers command the majority of the world telecommunications market, and most have a substantial manufacturing presence on every continent. Trade accounts for a substantial portion of U.S. production and consumption, with nearly 23 percent of U.S. product shipments being exported and imports accounting for 20 percent of apparent consumption in 1998. For SIC 3661, 20 percent of U.S. product shipments were exported and imports accounted for 20 percent of apparent consumption in 1998. For SIC 3663, 26 percent of U.S. product shipments were exported and imports accounted for 20 percent of apparent consumption in 1998.

DOMESTIC TRENDS

Shipments by the U.S. telecommunications equipment industry were estimated to have increased over 10 percent in 1999, reaching $91.5 billion, up from $82.9 billion in 1998, and were equally divided between telephone and telegraph apparatus (SIC 3661) and radio and television broadcasting and communications equipment (SIC 3663). Industry shipments of telephone and telegraph apparatus approached $46.0 billion in 1999, up over 11 percent from $41.4 billion in 1998. Industry shipments of radio and television broadcasting and communications equipment were estimated to have risen almost 10 percent to $45.5 billion in 1999, up from $41.6 billion in 1998 (see Table 31-1).

TABLE 31-1: Telecommunications Equipment (SIC 3661, 3663) Trends and Forecasts
(millions of dollars except as noted)

										Percent Change			
	1992	1993	1994	1995	1996	1997[1]	1998[1]	1999[2]	2000[3]	97–98	98–99	99–00	96–00[4]
Industry data													
Value of shipments[5]	40,031	42,190	49,371	54,915	63,807	73,251	82,944	91,527	—	13.2	10.3		
3661 Telephone apparatus	20,510	21,540	23,243	26,183	31,727	36,867	41,383	45,987	51,600	12.2	11.1	12.2	12.9
3663 Radio/TV communications equipment	19,521	20,650	26,128	28,733	32,080	36,384	41,561	45,540	—	14.2	9.6		
Value of shipments (1992$)	40,031	41,736	48,498	54,166	62,619	71,451	81,249	90,154	100,225	13.7	11.0	11.2	12.5
3661 Telephone apparatus	20,510	21,411	23,081	26,052	31,412	36,500	41,055	45,941	51,591	12.5	11.9	12.3	13.2
3663 Radio/TV communications equipment	19,521	20,325	25,416	28,114	31,206	34,951	40,194	44,213	48,634	15.0	10.0	10.0	11.7
Total employment (thousands)	216	208	220	216	234	238	243	240	—	2.1	−1.2		
3661 Telephone apparatus	91.1	84.9	86.5	89.3	93.6	98.1	103	100	—	5.0	−2.9		
3663 Radio/TV communications equipment	125	123	133	127	140	140	140	140	—	0.0	0.0		
Production workers (thousands)	103	94.5	100	103	107	107	106	102	—	−0.9	−3.8		
3661 Telephone apparatus	44.8	38.5	41.3	40.8	38.1	38.9	38.0	37.9	—	−2.3	−0.3		
3663 Radio/TV communications equipment	58.6	56.0	59.0	61.7	68.9	68.2	67.5	64.2	—	−1.0	−4.9		
Average hourly earnings ($)	14.28	14.35	14.25	15.69	16.33	17.65	17.80	17.78	—	0.8	−0.1		
3661 Telephone apparatus	14.90	15.34	15.35	16.65	16.57	17.50	17.29	17.05	—	−1.2	−1.4		
3663 Radio/TV communications equipment	13.82	13.66	13.51	15.08	16.18	17.80	18.30	18.50	—	2.8	1.1		
Capital expenditures	1,317	1,445	1,518	1,899	2,088								
3661 Telephone apparatus	615	595	662	742	731								
3663 Radio/TV communications equipment	702	851	856	1,157	1,357								
Product data													
Value of shipments[5]	36,106	38,151	45,495	52,481	60,706	69,640	78,913	87,389		13.3	10.7		
3661 Telephone apparatus	18,328	19,589	21,661	24,816	30,516	35,399	39,801	44,532	49,587	12.4	11.9	11.4	12.9
3663 Radio/TV communications equipment	17,778	18,562	23,834	27,665	30,190	34,241	39,112	42,857		14.2	9.6		
Value of shipments (1992$)	36,106	37,742	44,695	51,762	59,582	68,002	77,272	85,788	95,307	13.6	11.0	11.1	12.5
3661 Telephone apparatus	18,328	19,472	21,510	24,692	30,214	35,110	39,446	44,179	49,537	12.3	12.0	12.1	13.2
3663 Radio/TV communications equipment	17,778	18,269	23,185	27,069	29,368	32,892	37,826	41,609	45,770	15.0	10.0	10.0	11.7
Trade data													
Value of imports	7,923	8,802	10,047	10,537	11,283	12,730	15,118			18.8			
3661 Telephone apparatus	5,172	5,633	5,942	5,898	6,277	7,169	7,824			9.1			
3663 Radio/TV communications equipment	2,752	3,169	4,106	4,639	5,006	5,561	7,294			31.2			
Value of exports	7,364	9,185	11,559	14,681	14,971	18,562	17,976			−3.2			
3661 Telephone apparatus	3,278	4,010	4,799	5,783	6,576	7,326	7,883			7.6			
3663 Radio/TV communications equipment	4,086	5,174	6,760	8,898	8,395	11,236	10,093			−10.2			

[1] Estimate except imports and exports.
[2] Estimate.
[3] Forecast.
[4] Compound annual rate.
[5] For a definition of industry versus product values, see "Getting the Most Out of *Outlook 2000*."
Source: U.S. Department of Commerce: Bureau of the Census; International Trade Administration.

Employment in the telecommunications equipment industry declined slightly to about 240,000 in 1999, reflecting continued pressure to reduce costs and improve productivity in a highly competitive market environment. In addition, mergers and consolidations among manufacturers probably contributed to the lack of employment growth in that year. Many telecommunications companies are finding it essential to join forces with networking companies to remain competitive as the demand for data traffic continues to rise.

Regulatory Developments

As was noted in Chapter 30, the opening of many international markets to competition, formalized by the entry into force of the WTO Agreement on Basic Telecommunications Services in February 1998, was a major milestone in the telecommunications industry. Under this accord, 73 countries have liberalized, in whole or in part, their telecommunications markets on a multilateral basis and many other countries are liberalizing more services and conditions of foreign investment on a phased-in basis. As an increasing number of countries adopt policies that allow the construction of new networks to provide basic telephony, U.S. firms are well positioned to compete for opportunities abroad, since many of the countries where new telecommunications networks will be built do not manufacture the advanced equipment that will be needed.

In the United States, Congress passed the Telecommunication Act of 1996, which promised far-reaching changes in the industry. However, local competition has not materialized to a significant extent in the residential market. Future legal decisions and modifications of regulatory policy will continue to have an impact on the pace of competition in local telephony. Many new competitors use installed networks on a resale basis rather than building their own independent networks. Moreover, the well-publicized mergers and business alliances that are taking place both within the U.S. market and in foreign markets are enabling carriers to combine their resources and thus reduce their capital outlays.

PROJECTIONS OF INDUSTRY GROWTH FOR THE NEXT 1 AND 5 YEARS

Shipments by the telecommunications equipment industry are projected to increase over 11 percent in the year 2000, exceeding $100 billion in constant dollars. Shipments of telephone and telegraph apparatus (SIC 3661) should increase over 12 percent, while shipments of radio and television broadcasting and communications equipment (SIC 3663) are expected to rise about 10 percent in 2000. The product areas leading this growth are wireless communications equipment and network equipment, including that for wireless networks. Although the outlook for telecommunications equipment shipments through 2004 continues to be positive, the rate of growth is expected to decline to an average of 5 percent per year as new wired and wireless networks are more fully built out.

New market entrants and the emergence of enhanced services will continue to drive demand for equipment both in the United States and abroad. New technologies will generate growth in many sectors of the telecommunications equipment industry. For example, the trend toward the deployment of fiber-optic cable in the local loop will spark growth in both fiber-optic equipment and new network equipment such as optical switching and transmission equipment. The continuing conversion of wireless networks to fully digital networks that can support high-speed data rates over the next few years will continue to fuel demand for radio base stations and antennas as well as a variety of new wireless end-user devices. In the longer term, as users increasingly seek E-mail and Internet access on demand, networks will become largely software-driven.

U.S. Trade Performance

The trade data in Table 31-1 are based on a concordance between SICs 3661 and 3663 and the harmonized tariff schedule. Although this concordance corresponds closely with most commonly accepted definitions of telecommunications equipment, there are some notable exceptions. First, a number of products classified in SIC 3663—CB radios, walkie-talkies, and infant nursery monitors—are included in Table 31-1 even though they typically are not considered telecommunications equipment. This largely affects imports. Second, television cameras used in broadcasting are included in Table 31-1 even though they similarly are not regarded as telecommunications equipment. Third, optical fiber, fiber-optic cable, and coaxial cable, which all are widely used in telecommunications systems, technically reside in other SIC codes and therefore are not included in Table 31-1. The United States registers a sizable surplus ($800 million) in these products. As a result, the following discussion of U.S. trade performance and global market prospects is based on an adjusted SIC-based trade concordance that was modified as noted above to correspond as closely as possible to generally accepted perceptions of telecommunications equipment.

The United States registered a surplus in telecommunications equipment trade in 1998 for the sixth consecutive year. However, the surplus dropped 75 percent from that registered in 1997 ($5.1 billion in 1997 and $1.3 billion in 1998). That change resulted from an increase in imported telecommunications equipment, which rose 20 percent from $14.7 billion in 1997 to $17.6 billion in 1998. U.S. exports of telecommunications equipment fell 5 percent, dropping from $19.8 billion in 1997 to $18.9 billion in 1998. Although export growth resumed in 1999, up 8.5 percent over 1998, imports surged about 35 percent, and a deficit was likely for the first time since 1992.

Canada remained the largest telecommunications export market in 1998, with U.S. telecommunications equipment exports to that market rising 9 percent ($231 million) to slightly over $2.9 billion, a record high (see Table 31-2). Canada accounted for 15 percent of total U.S. telecommunications equipment exports. Exports to Mexico grew 35 percent in 1998, placing Mexico as the second largest export market and pushing

TABLE 31-2: U.S. Trade Patterns in Telecommunications Equipment[1] in 1998
(millions of dollars; percent)

Exports			Imports		
Region[2]	Value[3]	Share, %	Region[2]	Value[3]	Share, %
NAFTA	4,533	25	NAFTA	5,229	35
Latin America	2,983	17	Latin America	170	1
Western Europe	3,852	21	Western Europe	1,232	8
Japan/Chinese Economic Area	3,576	20	Japan/Chinese Economic Area	5,230	35
Other Asia	1,149	6	Other Asia	2,670	18
Rest of world	1,883	10	Rest of world	587	4
World	17,976	100	World	15,118	100
Top Five Countries	Value	Share, %	Top Five Countries	Value	Share, %
Canada	2,640	15	Canada	2,638	17
Mexico	1,893	11	Mexico	2,591	17
Japan	1,777	10	Japan	2,011	13
United Kingdom	1,273	7	China	1,788	12
Brazil	939	5	Taiwan	1,316	9

[1] SIC 3661, 3663.
[2] For definitions of regional groupings, see "Getting the Most Out of *Outlook 2000.*"
[3] Values may not sum to total due to rounding.
Source: U.S. Department of Commerce, Bureau of the Census.

Japan to the third position. Exports to Mexico were $1.95 billion, accounting for 10 percent of the total in 1998, up from $1.4 billion and 7 percent of the total in 1997. Exports to Japan fell $137 million, or almost 7 percent, to $1.9 billion in 1998. This placed Japan as the third largest U.S. export market, although it retained 10 percent of total U.S. telecommunications equipment exports (the same as in 1997).

Exports to the European Union (EU) increased in 1998 by $509 million (16 percent) to reach $3.7 billion. The EU share of total U.S. telecommunications exports, after declining slightly in 1997 and 1996, moved up to 19 percent of the total in 1998. The United Kingdom, the Netherlands, and Germany led.

Telecommunications equipment exports to Asia declined 26 percent in 1998, yet on a regional basis, Asia remained the largest market for export sales at over $5.1 billion. The top export markets in Asia for U.S. telecommunications equipment were Japan, China, Hong Kong, Taiwan, and South Korea.

Telecommunications equipment exports to Latin America were flat compared to 1997, growing less than 1 percent to $5 billion. The top three export markets in that region were Mexico, Brazil, and Argentina. Exports to the Middle East and North Africa increased 8 percent to $879 million.

Canada was again the largest source of U.S. telecommunications equipment imports in 1998. Imports from Canada grew by $503 million, or 18 percent, to reach $2.9 billion. Imports from Mexico grew 39 percent (to $2.9 billion) in comparison to 16 percent growth (to $2.7 billion) in imports from Japan, which placed Mexico as the second largest source of imported telecommunications equipment and pushed Japan down to third. Asia continued to be a dominant supplier of telecommunications equipment imports, representing 50 percent of U.S. telecommunications imports, or $8.9 billion. Telecommunications equipment imports from the EU rose 18 percent in 1998, a smaller rate of growth than in 1997, when those imports rose 24 percent.

In keeping with past history, the United States again tallied a substantial deficit of $3.5 billion in customer premises equipment. This was a sizable increase from 1997 and was larger, in fact, than the deficit registered in 1996 in relatively low-end, commodity-type customer premises equipment, much of which is no longer manufactured domestically. This was more than offset by the surplus in network/transmission equipment, which increased 4 percent in 1998 to $3.96 billion. The United States also tallied a surplus of $1.1 billion in "other" telecommunications equipment (largely wireless communications equipment, radio and television broadcasting equipment, and basket categories of telephone equipment that cannot be allocated to either network equipment or customer premises equipment).

Parts continue to represent a substantial percentage of U.S. telecommunications equipment trade. In 1998, parts exports of $5.6 billion accounted for 30 percent of total telecommunications exports, about the same percentage as in 1997. Parts for radio equipment accounted for about half of U.S. telecommunications parts exports, with telephonic apparatus accounting for most of the rest. Parts imports of $4.2 billion accounted for 25 percent of total telecommunications equipment imports, down slightly from 26 percent in 1997. Definitive comparisons to parts import and export activity in 1997 are complicated by new categories that were created in mid-1997.

Trade Agreements

Three kinds of trade agreements applying to the telecommunications sector have gone into force since 1997: the WTO Agreement on Basic Telecommunications Services, the WTO Information Technology Agreement (ITA), and the U.S.–EU Mutual Recognition Agreement (MRA). The most important of these agreements is the WTO Basic Telecommunications Agreement, which committed over 70 countries to liberalize their regulatory regimes for basic telecommunications services (implementation of this agreement is described in Chapter 30). This agreement will serve as an important stimulus for equipment purchases by numerous new service providers in these countries for years to come.

The Information Technology Agreement (ITA) commits 49 countries, including the entire EU, to eliminate tariffs on most telecommunications products by January 1, 2000. A few developing country signatories have been granted extensions for a limited number of information technology products, but in no case beyond the year 2005. The 49 ITA signatories account for 95 percent of world trade in information technology products. Negotiations for a second agreement that will be known as ITA-II have been under way since 1998 to expand the product coverage of the ITA and add coverage of related nontariff measures. The United States had hoped to complete the ITA-II negotiations by November 1999.

An MRA with the EU entered into force on December 1, 1998. An MRA provides for recognition by the importing party of the conformity assessment bodies (e.g., Underwriters' Laboratories) in the exporting country as well as acceptance of the testing results and equipment certification procedures undertaken by those bodies in evaluating the conformity of equipment to the importing party's technical regulations. Three of the six annexes to the U.S.–EU MRA apply to equipment for attachment to public telecommunications networks: the annexes on telecommunications terminal equipment, electromagnetic compatibility (EMC), and electrical safety. Implementation of the first two annexes is proceeding as planned, but implementation of the Electrical Safety Annex has been delayed by a disagreement that has not been resolved concerning on-site inspections of test laboratories in the EU. The telecommunications and EMC annexes are currently in a 2-year transition period, during which they authorize mutual recognition of product testing by recognized conformity assessment bodies to each other's regulatory requirements. After the completion of the transition period, these two annexes provide for mutual recognition of product approvals to each other's requirements. The United States and the EU are preparing to proceed to full implementation of the telecommunications and EMC annexes ahead of schedule, possibly by the middle of the year 2000.

An MRA for conformity assessment of telecommunications equipment was endorsed by the Asia-Pacific Economic Cooperation (APEC) Telecommunications Ministerial Meeting in June 1998. Like the U.S.–EU MRA, the APEC MRA should facilitate trade in telecommunications equipment by reducing the time and cost of testing and certifying equipment. The MRA establishes a process that will allow APEC members to test and/or certify equipment to other members' standards. Since 1998, APEC member economies have been negotiating bilateral agreements to implement the APEC framework arrangement. It is expected that such bilateral agreements will go into force within a year or two of ratification to allow for changes in national laws and regulations. Negotiations are also under way in the Organization of American States' Inter-American Telecommunications Commission (CITEL) to establish a framework MRA similar to that of APEC.

GLOBAL MARKET PROSPECTS

The priority being given to infrastructure development in most nations means that enormous sums are being invested in telecommunications networks. Worldwide demand for basic dial tone in emerging markets and for additional lines for Internet and E-mail applications in developed markets, the continued robust demand for wireless services, and public policies that promote deregulation and competition are all fueling equipment demand. The International Telecommunication Union (ITU), based on a historically constant growth trend, estimates that the number of main telephones will increase from an estimated 800 million in 1997 to nearly 1 billion by the year 2000. The number of wireless subscribers is expected to more than double from 308 million at the end of 1998 to 1 billion by 2004. The following sections address regional market prospects.

Western Europe

Expenditures on telecommunications equipment in western Europe are expected to continue to grow at the current annual rate of 13 percent, increasing the estimated value of that market from $68 billion in 1998 to $112 billion in 2002. This boom is being driven primarily by increasing competition in telecommunications and multimedia services as well as new technologies for offering those services. Since the beginning of 1999, all but three west European countries (Greece, Luxembourg, and Portugal) have authorized unlimited competition in basic telecommunications services and related infrastructure. Although they are allowed to postpone liberalization until 2003, those three countries are likely to follow the examples of Spain and Ireland, which chose complete liberalization of basic telecommunications services by December 1998 and January 1999, respectively, ahead of the deadlines set by the European Commission. The most rapidly growing telecommunications sector in western Europe continues to be cellular communications, which was opened to competition in 1996. A large majority of the 92 million cellular subscribers in that region use digital technology. In Finland and Italy, the penetration rate of mobile communications is already higher than it is for wireline communications, and west European countries use wireless communications for E-mail at a much higher rate than in the United States.

U.S. exports of telecommunications equipment to the EU, which accounts for virtually all of western Europe, increased 16 percent in 1998 to reach $3.7 billion. The best opportunity for U.S. suppliers to maintain or increase their share of the western European market lies in selling to the hundreds of network operators that have recently been licensed to offer public telecommunications services in individual countries and to businesses establishing corporate networks. The trend is for new operators to build pan-European networks or merge with other companies so that they can offer both long-distance and international services over their own transnational networks. In addition, European regulators are pressing telecommunications operators such as Deutsche Telekom to divest themselves of cable television networks so that their competitors will develop capacity for broadband applications and be able to offer not only voice and data communications but also multimedia services. The convergence of voice, data, and multimedia technologies is allowing networks to respond rapidly to the growing demand for high-speed data and mobile communications, frequently over the same network. To that end, the EU planned to complete licensing arrangements for third generation (3G) wireless systems by January 1, 2000 and to begin the licensing process in the first half of the year 2000. Even the former national monopoly carriers in western Europe welcome U.S. equipment if it helps them offset their shrinking share of domestic wireline markets by expanding into new markets or new lines of business, such as wireless communications and the Internet.

Central and Eastern Europe and the Newly Independent States

As the countries in central and eastern Europe (CEE) enter the twenty-first century, virtually all have recognized that efficient, reliable, and cost-effective telecommunications will be essential for economic growth and development. Regional authorities clearly recognize the shortcomings of existing networks and are working diligently to expand and improve their communications systems. Since 1990, increased investment has occurred in almost every segment of telecommunications: satellite, mobile telephony, paging, fiber optics, switching, transmission systems, and other network equipment. Many countries have laid out ambitious modernization plans, moved toward international norms for regulation and competition, revised their legal climates to establish a transparent regulatory environment, begun privatization, and introduced competition in some sectors. Accordingly, heavy investment in telecommunications will continue for the foreseeable future, and there is great potential for U.S. companies interested in selling equipment or providing services in that region. Estimates for the combined services and equipment markets in that region range from $13 billion to $19 billion in 2000, and $15 billion to $21 billion in 2004.

The Newly Independent States (NIS) also are struggling to remove obstacles to economic growth and development, including aging communications systems. Governments in that region must contend with insufficient capacity, low telephone penetration rates, highly variable call completion rates, and antiquated equipment. This, combined with vast distances, high demand for basic telecommunications infrastructure, and the lack of modern network services, makes the NIS a potentially lucrative market for U.S. telecommunications companies. Governments in that region have made great strides in expanding and modernizing their networks and services, and a number of U.S. companies already are active in the region. However, telecommunications companies interested in doing business in the NIS have to contend with a number of difficulties, including unclear regulatory and legal structures, inconsistent enforcement of laws, standards issues, cumbersome equipment certification and approval procedures, and confusing and multilayered authorities and licensing procedures. Despite these challenges, the NIS represents a large potential market for U.S. telecommunications companies. Reliable figures regarding the size of the equipment and services markets in the NIS have always been difficult to find, and since the early 1990s estimates have varied widely. Since the economic crisis began in the second half of 1998, it has become even more difficult to procure credible statistics on the size of the equipment and services markets in the NIS.

The Asia-Pacific Region

The Japanese telecommunications market, which was estimated at $27 billion in 1999, is the largest market in the Asia-Pacific region and the second largest in the world after the United States. Japan ranked as the third largest U.S. telecommunications equipment export market in 1998, with exports totaling $1.9 billion, down from $2.1 billion in 1997. The fastest-growing segment of the telecommunications market is the wireless sector. Japanese regulatory changes, some stemming from commitments under the WTO Basic Telecommunications Agreement, have resulted in a number of new opportunities for foreign suppliers. However, the pace of change continues to be slow, and it is unclear how quickly such changes will translate into meaningful increases in market share for competitors in light of the market power of the two incumbent carriers, NTT and KDD.

China presents a potentially vast but extremely challenging market for U.S. telecommunications equipment suppliers. China's telecommunications equipment market was estimated at $20 billion in 1999. China has been expanding its network at a rapid rate, and about 20 million new fixed lines and about 12 million mobile lines were added in 1999. Chinese government policies are designed to develop an indigenous telecommunications manufacturing capability rather than rely on imported products. Foreign companies that want to sell in that country must deal with pressure to form joint ventures with Chinese partners as well as domestic content and technology transfer requirements, standards issues, and other policies designed to discourage direct imports and promote the development of the domestic industry. U.S. telecommunications equipment exports to China amounted to $780 million in 1998.

Hong Kong represents an important market for U.S. telecommunications equipment exports both in its own right and as a gateway to China. Hong Kong gradually has been opening its telecommunications services market to competition and new entrants, creating new opportunities for telecommunications equipment providers. U.S. telecommunications equipment exports to Hong Kong amounted to $791 million in 1998.

Taiwan, like Hong Kong, has been liberalizing its telecommunications services sector, first in the mobile sector and now in the fixed line sector. U.S. telecommunications equipment exports to Taiwan amounted to $528 million in 1998.

As South Korea recovers from the effects of the Asian financial crisis, it promises to offer increased export opportunities to U.S. suppliers. Although U.S. telecommunications equipment exports to South Korea declined significantly as a result of the crisis, the economic reforms initiated as a result of that crisis should create a more open and competitive telecommunications market and increased demand for new services and equipment. U.S. telecommunications equipment has always had a good reputation in South Korea and a strong position in the market. U.S. exports of telecommunications equipment to South Korea amounted to $449 million in 1998.

The telecommunications market in southeast Asia will continue to be important for U.S. equipment manufacturers, particularly as those countries continue to recover from the Asian economic crisis. Telecommunications services are opening up in key southeast Asian markets under the auspices of the WTO Agreement on Basic Telecommunications Services. In addition, a number of those countries are striving to become regional high-technology hubs by building intelligent cities and industry parks and offering business incentives to foreign companies. In particular, the telecommunications markets in Indonesia, Malaysia, the Philippines, Singapore, and Thailand are showing improved or continued strength and opportunities. Each of these countries has signed the WTO Basic Telecommunications Agreement.

Indonesia has demonstrated a strong commitment to the development of its telecommunications infrastructure. In 1997, the United States was the largest supplier of telecommunications equipment to Indonesia, capturing 39 percent of imports into that country. The 1999 total market size was estimated to be $2.1 billion and should grow at least 2 percent in the year 2000. U.S. telecommunications equipment exports to Indonesia reached $56 million in 1998.

Malaysia is working to establish itself as a regional high-technology hub. Toward that goal, the government created the Multimedia Super Corridor (MSC), which consists of 300 square miles of land outside the capital, Kuala Lumpur. The MSC contains state-of-the-art telecommunications facilities that will create numerous opportunities for the telecommunications industry, especially in fiber optics, asynchronous transfer mode (ATM), and assymetric digital subscriber line (ADSL). The MSC project will cover a period of 10 years and will provide opportunities not only for laying new infrastructure but also for upgrading the telecommunications network over the designated period. Cyberjaya, the newly opened "intelligent city," serves as the centerpiece of the MSC. As of July 1999, 285 companies had applied for MSC status, and 21 have already moved into Cyberjaya. The country is looking for and purchasing state-of-the-art equipment and technology, and unlike the situation in many countries in that region, the telecommunications sector has been privatized, making it a highly competitive market. In 1998, U.S. manufacturers exported $100 million of telecommunications equipment to Malaysia.

In the Philippines, the Asian economic crisis has led to consolidation in the telecommunications industry, exemplified by the takeover of the telecommunications giant Philippines Long-Distance Telephone (PLDT) by the Hong Kong–based First Pacific. Despite economic setbacks, the Philippines is looking toward new technologies and trends such as computer telephony integration (CTI) and Internet Protocol (IP) telephony. Those technologies, combined with the Philippine government's interest in promoting them, will determine where future opportunities lie. In 1999, the total market size was estimated to be $2 billion. U.S. telecommunications equipment exporters performed well in the Philippines in 1998, achieving $124.6 million in sales.

Singapore has made no secret of the fact that it wants to be a regional high-technology hub. With its advanced network, openness to foreign companies, and high penetration rates, it provides excellent opportunities for U.S. companies. The government of Singapore is building an information superhighway infrastructure to link every home, office, and government agency through a nationwide network called Singapore ONE. By the year 2000, all of Singapore will be linked by 300,000 kilometers of fiber. Singapore's efforts to liberalize services will give U.S. operators greater opportunities in that sector. Promising subsectors for equipment manufacturers include switching and transmission equipment, fiber optics, and wireless transmission equipment. In 1998, U.S. telecommunications equipment exports to Singapore totaled $295.7 million.

The telecommunications market in Thailand shrank in recent years but is on the rise. The market was estimated to be $2.6 billion in 1999, a 4 percent increase from the 1998 level. As in other southeast Asian countries, Thailand has been moving toward privatization. In 1997, the government reorganized the regulatory structure and created a plan for turning its state-owned enterprises into stock companies before privatization and liberalization of its services sector. In the equipment sector, switching equipment, fiber-optic cable, mobile telephone equipment, and private branch exchanges (PBXs) are in highest demand. In 1998, U.S. manufacturers exported $79 million worth of telecommunications equipment to Thailand.

Latin America

U.S. exports of telecommunications equipment to Latin America remained strong despite a regional economic downturn driven by the economic crisis in Brazil in early 1999. U.S. exports of telecommunications equipment to Latin America in 1998 totaled over $5 billion, about the same level as in 1997. The top three export markets in that region were Mexico, Brazil, and Argentina. Exports to Mexico increased 35 percent to $1.95 billion, while exports to Brazil fell 22 percent to $957 million and those to Argentina fell 16 percent to $386 million. Despite those declines, both countries still imported from the United States significantly more telecommunications equipment in 1998 than they did in 1996. Exports to Chile were up considerably (59 percent), reaching a total of $189 million.

The devaluation of the Brazilian real in early 1999 affected the region greatly, and the Argentinian economy was hit especially hard because of its close ties with Brazil. In particular, the devaluation caused problems for companies with U.S. dollar–denominated obligations. The region's economies were expected to recover from recession in late 1999 and pull into positive economic growth in 2000. The privatization of major national operators and continued market liberalization, as well as new license awards for personal communications services (PCS), wireless local loop, cable television, and cellular telephony, will continue to spur considerable network expansion and the offering of new services throughout the region.

The wireless segment continued its strong rate of growth as underdeveloped telecommunications markets in the region took advantage of more advanced wireless technologies such as cellular and wireless local loop to increase teledensity and improve the quality of service. The growing demand for access to the Internet is another powerful driver of growth. Analysts expect that there will be approximately 27 million Internet users in the region by 2003, and the Brazilian market especially is expected to see surging demand for Internet access in the near future. According to a recent Business Communication study, the Latin American telecommunications equipment market was worth $22.8 billion in 1998, accounting for about 8.5 percent of the worldwide total, and should reach almost $31 billion by 2002.

Many changes in this region in recent years have opened up export and investment opportunities for the United States. Chile continues to be the most open and competitive market in the region. Mexico, following the lead of Argentina, Chile, and Peru, has completed wireless PCS auctions. The Brazilian market is experiencing a tremendous amount of activity; nine cellular Band-B licenses were sold in 1998, Telebras was privatized, the domestic long-distance sector was opened to competition, and telecommunications companies have been gearing up for full market competition in 2001. The government of Argentina has begun to license competitors for Telefonica and Telecom Argentina, the two dominant telecommunications operators. In Colombia, the national operator began competing with private long-distance providers in late 1998, and auctions for nationwide PCS licenses were planned for late 1999 or 2000. Telefonica del Peru's monopoly was terminated a year ahead of schedule, and both cellular and long-distance competitors are entering the market. In Venezuela, the telecommunications sector was absorbing investments of approximately $1 billion a year as the government planned to sell off a third national cellular license before the end of 1999, and the monopoly on basic telephone services is set to end in November 2000.

The Central American states continue to push toward introducing modern, liberalizing telecommunications legislation and privatizing state-owned telecommunications companies. Some Caribbean governments are making a strong move to break the United Kingdom–based Cable & Wireless monopolies and open their markets to competition.

There are an estimated 60 million main telephone lines in Latin America for a teledensity rate of approximately 12 percent, according to Baskerville Communications. By 2003, it is estimated that the number of main lines will surpass 80 million and teledensity will reach 16 lines per 100 inhabitants. Equipment demand will remain high for the next several years as the region's economies pull out of recession and markets rapidly expand to meet unmet demand for telecommunications services.

Africa

U.S. exports of telecommunications equipment to sub-Saharan Africa totaled $206 million in 1998, an increase of 39 percent over the level in 1997. Exports to South Africa accounted for nearly two-thirds of the total. Thus, Africa represents only 1 percent of the market for U.S. telecommunications equipment exports. Teledensity in this region of over 700 million people is approaching 2 telephones per 100 inhabitants, and Africa has only 2 percent of the world's telephone lines. Cellular services have been introduced in many countries, with over 5 million subscribers reported at the end of 1998.

Although there is a vast potential market for telecommunications equipment in Africa, it is not clear whether the necessary financial and technical resources can be harnessed to expand that region's telecommunications infrastructure significantly in the near future. Most African countries have adopted policies that allow some private sector participation in telecommunications, and some have been seeking to privatize parts of their national telephone companies. Nearly 20 countries have established independent regulatory authorities to lay the groundwork for competition. Although six countries have committed to some degree of liberalization under the WTO Agreement on Basic Telecommunications Services, efforts to promote competition throughout all sectors of the African telecommunications industry are just beginning.

One large project promises to link countries in Africa to one another and to growing global broadband telecommunications networks. Africa ONE is an independent fiber-optic cable system scheduled to be completed in 2002 that will extend nearly 40,000 kilometers at a cost of $1.6 billion. Thirty African countries have formally indicated their interest in participating in the project. Many countries are hopeful that new Internet service providers and global as well as regional satellite systems will help meet the growing telecommunications needs of the region. The remainder of this chapter consists of analyses of specific segments of the telecommunications industry, followed by a discussion of the search and navigation equipment industry.

Linda Gossack Astor, U.S. Department of Commerce, Office of Telecommunications, (202) 482-4466, October 1999.

NETWORK EQUIPMENT

Network equipment includes transmission and switching equipment purchased by public or private network operators. Switches complete connections between calls and route information from one network user to another. Transmission systems include the multiplexing equipment, repeaters, and line conditioning equipment used to transmit information. Network equipment is classified under SIC 3661.

Global Industry Trends

The worldwide market for wireline network equipment is estimated to reach $54.5 billion in the year 2000, up 0.5 percent from $54.0 billion in 1999. [That figure does not include fiber-optic transmission systems (FOTS), satellite transmission systems, or microwave communications systems.] Within this category, switching equipment will decrease slightly from approximately $34.2 billion in 1999 to $34.1 billion in 2000 after peaking at $36.2 billion in 1996.

U.S. exports of network equipment have increased steadily since the early 1990s. In 1998, U.S. exports reached nearly

$10.5 billion, up 7.9 percent from $9.7 billion in 1997. The top markets for U.S. exports of network equipment in 1998, beginning with the largest, were Canada, Mexico, Japan, the United Kingdom, and Hong Kong.

Although aggregate exports have grown, differing trends in the exportation of network equipment from the United States can be discerned at the regional level. After the Asian economic crisis of 1997, exports of network equipment to that region declined, and the same was true in eastern Europe and the former Soviet states after the devaluation of the ruble in 1998. At the same time, exports to the EU, Latin America, sub-Saharan Africa, and within North America (Mexico and Canada) increased.

World demand for network equipment is driven by a variety of market forces. In less developed regions of the world, network expansion and investment can be attributed to meeting the vast infrastructural needs of relatively new market-based economies; a desire to modernize aging and technologically obsolete communications infrastructures; the need to provide telephony to a larger number of residents, especially in rural areas; the need to provide greater overall reliability and better service in both telephony and data transmission; and a desire to be connected to and reap the benefits of access to the Internet. In more developed regions, new equipment is being deployed to provide advanced new services. Technological advances in network equipment allow network operators not only to offer the new services that customers demand but also to realize cost savings from improvements in network operating efficiencies.

Worldwide, liberalization and competition in the telecommunications services sector attract new entrants that need to build new networks, while existing operators are forced to upgrade their networks to remain competitive. The Agreement on Basic Telecommunications Services under the WTO will reinforce this trend over the next few years as signatories of the agreement, accounting for over 90 percent of the world's telecommunications services market, introduce competition into their markets. Also, the growth of the Internet and new technologies and services that rely on packet-based switching will continue to spur demand for new and expanded networks.

Software is becoming increasingly important in the public switching market as manufacturers continue to produce switches that can be upgraded by using software rather than requiring the installation of new equipment. Northern Business Information (Gartner Group) predicts that in some developed markets, software revenues may account for as much as 50 percent of total revenues by 2001. In addition, for most switch-producing companies, software upgrades to installed switches will be the largest source of revenues over the next decade, and reliability and maintenance of software will be essential for revenue and market share.

Programmable switches, in conjunction with larger preexisting switches or standing alone, probably will make further inroads into the equipment market. Although programmable, scalable packet-based switches do not currently have the call-processing power of a traditional central office switch, they allow carriers to modify services quickly and expand capacity rapidly, features that are particularly attractive to start-up companies. Similar to the personal computing model, these switches give the user choices regarding both software and hardware, allowing the user to customize the switch and network to his or her needs. Also, as voice, data, and integrated services come together, the ability to react quickly to changing switching needs will become increasingly important.

Despite this flexibility, programmable switches will not immediately push traditional switches aside. Network operators have invested enormous amounts of money in traditional equipment that is still functioning well, and carriers want to get the maximum return on investment before moving wholesale to new technologies. Additionally, traditional equipment offers tremendous capability and a wide variety of features in one switch. Smaller programmable switches will experience healthy growth and pull the market in their direction, but the need for large-scale switches will not disappear.

Another notable trend is that companies that provide central office switches are moving closer to the local area network (LAN). As the line between voice and data blurs, so does the line between what services and equipment are at the customer's premises or enterprise level versus what exists at the central office. Telecommunications vendors will have to serve all their customers' needs, looking beyond their immediate customers at the enterprise level to the needs of the final consumer, the end user. For example, it has been predicted that virtual private networks (VPNs) will displace many of the private networks in existence today. Also, equipment vendors will have to integrate their equipment seamlessly into a variety of networks domestically and abroad, possibly managing those networks as well.

Factors Affecting U.S. Industry Growth

The future of the network equipment industry in the United States will be determined to a large extent by changes in the U.S. telecommunications services industry resulting from the Telecommunications Act of 1996. That complex piece of legislation promises to restructure the telecommunications, computer, and cable television industries fundamentally by removing many of the barriers to market entry and cross-ownership that previously existed.

For example, local service companies and long-distance service providers will be permitted to compete in each other's markets, while the previous ban on the provision of video programming by telephone companies within their service areas has been eliminated. Cable television companies also will be permitted to offer local telephone service in their franchise areas, an activity that previously was prohibited. However, implementation of the act is not moving forward as quickly as originally envisioned, so its full impact has not been felt yet by network equipment suppliers hoping to reap the benefits of greater competition in telecommunications services.

Nevertheless, the new law has shaken up the telecommunications industry as players try to reposition themselves to gain the maximum advantage. Despite the fact that protracted legal and regulatory battles are slowing implementation of the law, it is widely expected that the legislation will promote increased demand for network equipment as new companies are created and existing service providers develop new service offerings. U.S. equipment companies are considered to be in the best position to take advantage of these new opportunities.

Another major factor driving the network sector is the increasing amount of data traffic and the convergence of voice and data networks. This convergence is fueled largely by the expanding presence of the Internet and related applications. Bellcore has estimated that data will account for approximately 90 percent of the traffic (but not revenue) on the U.S. public network in the next 5 to 10 years. Some analysts have estimated that the U.S. data market is worth approximately $20 billion (annual voice traffic is worth about $200 billion) and will double or even triple in the next 10 years. Dataquest estimated that in the United States, data traffic is growing 4 to 5 times faster than is voice traffic, approximately 30 percent per year versus 6 to 7 percent per year.

As demand for Internet access grows, new breeds of companies emerge, existing companies move business to the Web, and service providers demand more bandwidth, there will be continued demand for upgraded and new equipment. Companies such as Level3, Qwest, DeltaThree, and Net2Phone are investing heavily in fiber, gateways, and other Internet-related equipment. While increasing data traffic is not a new phenomenon, a variety of IP-based services that have been recently introduced or are just around the corner promise an even greater focus on packet-switched networks in the United States. The expanding suite of applications based on IP technology serves as an example of how the Internet and an increased emphasis on data may change the network sector.

Most industry analysts believe that IP-based networks and services will exert a noticeable influence on the network. Some believe that IP technology such as voice over Internet (VOIP), fax over Internet (FOIP), and E-commerce applications will change the face of telecommunications dramatically and rapidly. Others believe that IP technologies will have a more gradual impact. Still others believe that IP may become a ubiquitous platform for multimedia services but that specific technologies such as VOIP will develop as only one element of value-added telecommunications services offered to business and residential customers.

All these cases present opportunities for vendors of network equipment, whether using IP or any other platform. The underlying trend is the continued shift toward increased data traffic on the network, with the line between voice and data transmission beginning to blur. The specifics of how data will move on the network are still being decided.

What is certain, however, is that the network sector is changing and that new and incumbent service providers will need equipment with which to build the networks of the future. For example, some industry executives envision the public switched telephone network (PSTN) of 2005 centering on converged voice and data and circuit-switched to packet/IP carriers. Also part of this vision is an emphasis on multiservice switching at the edge of the network, where the interaction between networks with differing technologies and speeds must occur. These switches, which are open and programmable like those mentioned above, will push the network to become more decentralized, as in the computing world. They also will provide opportunities for savvy manufacturers to profit from the changing network.

Another example of convergence giving birth to new types of equipment is the development of the gateway. IP telephony is made possible by gateways that form the basis for the development of the budding IP telephony industry. The primary function of a gateway is to convert a voice signal to IP packets for transmission over a data network. The packets are reassembled and converted back into voice signals at the receiving end by another gateway, which then transfers the call to the PSTN.

The use of gateways in the network has exploded since they were introduced in 1996. Gateway sales grew at a rate of 906 percent in 1997 (total revenues of $47.3 million) and 417 percent in 1998 (revenues of $244.8 million) and are predicted to fall to a still impressive growth rate of 27 percent in 2002 (totaling $3.16 billion in revenues). This represents a compound annual growth rate of 132 percent between 1996 and 2002. While the rate of growth is likely to continue to decline gradually through 2004, gateways—a direct result of converging networks—will have moved from under $5 million in revenue in 1996 to well over $3 billion in 2002, according to Frost and Sullivan.

Convergence also has made the network equipment market more dynamic, with a frenzy of mergers and partnerships among players both large and small in recent years. Nortel's (now Nortel Networks) purchase of Bay Networks combined Nortel's core competency of central office equipment with Bay's reputation in the data world, reflecting the importance Nortel is placing on data in the future. Similarly, Lucent's purchase of another data networking leader, Ascend Communications, and the Internet equipment–focused Nexabit was a way to quickly gain access to greater data communications and Internet capabilities. Similar moves have been made by foreign switching giants, including Siemens of Germany and Newbridge Networks of Canada.

There is a potential for rapid growth in today's network equipment market. Cisco Systems, a leader in Internet technologies, has emerged in recent years as one of the largest companies in the Internet industry. After shipping its first product in 1986, the company now holds the number one or number two market share in virtually every market segment in which it participates. After Cisco became a public company in 1990, its annual revenues increased from $69 million to $8.46 billion in fiscal year 1998.

Not only large companies have benefited from the explosion of new technologies and the convergence of voice and data. Since 1993, Cisco alone has purchased nearly 30 smaller companies that will add strength to various aspects of its networking capabilities. The same is true of almost every other major equipment vendor in the telecommunications equipment sector. Those which are not purchasing companies (and many that are) also are announcing strategic partnerships that will allow them to remain nimble in an era of rapidly developing services and investment in networks.

The demand drivers outlined above will be offset partially by the maturation of the U.S. market. In the year 2000, central office switches in the United States will be over 91 percent digitized, a figure that is expected to rise to well over 95 percent by 2004. Vendors in the United States and other mature markets will derive much of their revenue, as was mentioned above in regard to the global switching market, from upgrading features on the installed base of switches rather than from selling new equipment.

Internationally, the continuing worldwide trend toward privatization, liberalization, and competition in telecommunications services markets not only will sustain the demand for equipment but will help erode market access barriers and allow U.S. equipment suppliers to compete for business in markets that formerly were closed to them. This trend will be bolstered by the WTO Agreement on Basic Telecommunications Services and the ITA.

While worldwide demand for network equipment will remain strong, U.S. suppliers will continue to face strong competition from long-established suppliers in Europe and Japan as well as from newer manufacturers in countries such as South Korea and Taiwan. Industry experts generally agree that there is surplus production capacity in certain sectors, such as central office switching equipment, and predict that some sort of consolidation is inevitable.

Projections of U.S. Industry Growth for the Next 1 and 5 Years

U.S. shipments of network equipment are expected to reach \$13.3 billion in the year 2000, increasing to approximately \$14.7 billion in 2004, with an average annual growth rate of 2.5 percent (these figures do not include FOTS, satellite transmission systems, or microwave systems).

Global Market Prospects

The world market for network equipment is expected to remain strong for the foreseeable future as developing countries continue to build out their telecommunications infrastructures and developed countries invest in new technologies. Worldwide demand for network equipment is expected to grow to \$58.9 billion in 2004, although the value of the worldwide switch market will continue to decline gradually to \$33.0 billion.

Again, convergence and the rise of data traffic on the PSTN are the primary drivers of change in this sector. Dataquest asserts that while voice market revenue is growing an estimated 10 percent per year, the data market is growing about 65 to 70 percent per year. A news organization in the United Kingdom cited statistics indicating 1,000 percent per year growth for IP traffic worldwide, compared with public switched telephone network traffic growth of under 10 percent.

In November 1998, British Telecommunications was the first of the major European telecommunications carriers to announce that data traffic had overtaken voice traffic on its domestic network. This is due largely to increased Internet usage, E-mail transmission, and E-commerce applications. Other major carriers are sure to follow with similar announcements. This level of growth demands significant investment in network infrastructure.

Nevertheless, the high growth rates seen in worldwide demand for network equipment in past years are expected to gradually taper off over the next 5 years, although this will vary regionally with the level of economic development. Strong growth is expected to continue in the developing world, where infrastructure is generally weak and telephone penetration rates are still very low. However, this growth will be offset by stagnation and decline in mature markets, where the demand will be primarily for product replacement and new software offerings.

The strongest growth is expected to occur in central and eastern Europe, where digital local lines will grow approximately 18 percent per year between 2000 and 2004. That region will be followed by Latin America with 17.8 percent and Africa and the Middle East with 17.0 percent. The Asia-Pacific region is predicted to have an annual growth rate of only 0.9 percent, reflecting a slowing of demand in mature markets that growth in developing markets will not offset. The growth rates for the mature markets of North America and western Europe will decline 0.9 percent and 1.4 percent, respectively.

Asia's low growth rate in switching does not imply that it is not an important market. In fact, the opposite is true. Asia will continue to be the world's largest market for switching equipment, with approximately 30 percent of world main lines in service. China is the largest market in Asia and the world. Asia has surpassed North America and western Europe in the size of its installed base of main lines.

Competition in the network equipment market will continue to intensify worldwide, with large telecommunications equipment vendors such as Lucent, Alcatel, Siemens, NEC, Nortel Networks, and Fujitsu emphasizing their ability to provide total network solutions while firms serving niche markets offer expertise in specialized equipment subsectors. This intense competition has led to significant downward pricing pressures, a trend that will continue. Fueled by privatization, liberalization, and new technologies, price declines have resulted in declining margins for manufacturers. This too, in conjunction with the convergence of voice and data, has contributed to the trend toward industry mergers and consolidation.

Jason Leuck, U.S. Department of Commerce, Office of Telecommunications, (202) 482-4202, September 1999.

CUSTOMER PREMISES EQUIPMENT

Customer premises equipment (CPE), or terminal equipment, consists of a wide range of privately owned telecommunications equipment that attaches to the public network. CPE shipments are classified under SIC 3661. The largest CPE product sectors are modems, private branch exchanges (PBXs), voice processing equipment, video communications equipment, telephones, key telephone systems (KTSs), and facsimile machines.

Global Industry Trends

The customer premises industry encompasses a wide variety of products that range from simple telephone handsets that cost a few dollars to complex PBX systems that can cost millions of dollars. Most are mature markets characterized by intense competition and declining unit prices. The majority of low-end products (e.g., telephone handsets and answering machines) are commodity products that are manufactured in countries with low labor (production) costs. In the United States, most of these low-end products are imported, primarily from manufacturing facilities in Asia. Domestic manufacturing tends to be centered on the more technically sophisticated products, such as videoconferencing and voice processing equipment, which have high value-added content and in which U.S. manufacturers are the technological leaders.

Domestic Trends

Manufacturers of high-end customer premises equipment increasingly are influenced by trends in the computer industry. This movement toward convergence between voice and data is commonly known as computer telephony integration (CTI). The influence of CTI is particularly noticeable in the customer premises equipment industry, where vendors of everything from PBXs to voice processing equipment are working to integrate voice, data, and video communications for desktop users.

CTI is most prevalent in the call center arena, where the ability to converge the traditional inbound/outbound call accounting software with the Internet and the agent's telephone line allows these centers to provide enhanced customer service. Its potential uses include Web-enabled call centers, unified messaging, and videoconferencing. CTI products are expected to become more widespread as prices drop, new applications are developed, business customers learn about the benefits of CTI features, and the technology moves beyond the traditional call center environment.

In the PBX and key telephone system (KTS) markets, manufacturers have turned their attention to developing advanced features that provide additional value to their customers. PBXs and KTSs have changed from being stand-alone equipment to being part of a company's communications network. PBX/KTS manufacturers have moved from proprietary to open systems to meet the needs of customers who want to integrate their premise switching equipment with the rest of the enterprise network. CTI and call centers have brought increased complexity to the task of integrating the different components of the enterprise network. PBX vendors consequently have become increasingly software-focused. In fact, most PBX and KTS manufacturers have formed alliances with computer software and hardware companies for application development.

As in the PBX/KTS industry, manufacturers of voice processing equipment are becoming more software-intensive in their development as they move to open, personal computer (PC)-based architectures. Manufacturers also are intensifying their focus on developing enhanced applications for the business and home markets, such as voice-activated dialing.

Wireless capabilities are another promising feature offered by some PBX and KTS vendors. Although the technology has been around for some time, it has taken off only recently. Wireless applications within buildings have considerable potential since they allow corporate users mobility without losing contact within the office setting. The proliferation of wireless phones in the consumer market also is helping to popularize this feature in the office, as users have come to expect added mobility there as well. Some wireless PBXs promise interoperability with public personal communications services or cellular phone system allowing consumers to use the same handset in the office that they use on the road. However, most wireless PBXs are limited to 1,000 feet or less. The market for this equipment should grow significantly once prices drop below $1,000 per station.

Increased interest in on-line technologies and sales of PCs bundled with modems have spurred dramatic growth in the modem market while blurring the line between telecommunications and computer equipment. Despite this growth, the modem sector has experienced a decline in recent years that is primarily attributable to a strong reduction in shipments of low-speed modems and the drop in demand for external modems now that most new PCs have internal modems that satisfy new users' needs. Most sales in this sector come from replacements of and upgrades to existing equipment.

The U.S. market for consumer customer premises equipment (CPE) products is well established. Falling prices have contributed to growth in sales of consumer products such as modems, answering machines, and cordless telephones. The Consumer Electronics Manufacturers Association reports that in 1997, 66 percent of U.S. households had a cordless phone, 65 percent had an answering machine, 34 percent had a cellular phone, 19 percent had a modem, 18 percent had caller ID equipment, and 9 percent had a facsimile machine. Most of this equipment is imported.

Projections of Industry Growth for the Next 1 and 5 Years

The value of domestic CPE shipments is estimated to grow about 8 percent to just over $7 billion in the year 2000. Growth in U.S. shipments will occur principally in the high-end and technically sophisticated product segments. The value of overall CPE shipments is forecast to grow annually at around 8 percent, reaching an estimated $10.3 billion by 2004. Performance of individual CPE product sectors will vary as a result of trends mentioned above.

The PBX market is very mature, so replacements and upgrades account for the majority of shipments. PBX shipments are expected to experience solid growth over the next 5 years. Growth will come primarily from manufacturers providing value-added features such as CTI and wireless applications. U.S. shipments of PBX equipment will grow about 5 percent yearly through 2004.

Growth in the KTS market will be fueled by small start-up companies looking for low-cost voice processing solutions and advancements in KTS functionality. However, growth in this sector is expected to be slower over the next few years compared to previous years. As companies grow and start to demand more from their voice processing systems, they probably will migrate to PBXs.

According to various sources, the worldwide modem market should decline in 2000 but regain its momentum in 2001 and experience steady, although slower, growth through 2004. Shipments of high-speed modems are expected to continue to increase 10 percent per year over the next few years, driven primarily by consumer demand for faster Internet access for their existing PCs. While shipments of conventional modems should continue to grow through 2004, integrated services digital network (ISDN) terminals, digital subscriber lines, and cable modems will occupy a significant portion of the overall market as demand for broadband applications increases.

In 1998, some industry analysts predicted that year-on-year growth of videoconferencing systems may reach up to 40 percent by the year 2000. While that may prove overly optimistic, videoconferencing equipment should experience increased growth as compression technologies improve, standards issues are resolved, and broadband transmission facilities become more readily available.

Global Market Prospects

The global market for CPE should continue to be characterized by intense competition, and in many markets U.S. companies will continue to face stiff competition from European and Asian manufacturers. While the United States runs a consistent trade deficit in CPE, primarily because of imports of commodity-type products (e.g., telephones, answering machines, and fax machines), there are significant opportunities in the international market for U.S. exports, especially in product sectors that incorporate advanced and convergent technologies.

During the forecast period, the developing economies in Latin America and the Asia-Pacific region should offer the most promising growth markets for the CPE industry, as growth in the mature markets of North America and western Europe is expected to slow.

Most analysts predict that the top growth markets for PBX and KTS equipment will be in the Pacific Rim economies, eastern Europe, and Latin America. The market for voice processing products outside North America is expected to grow at a healthy rate as foreign companies recognize the cost and productivity benefits of voice processing products. U.S. manufacturers should stand to gain from this trend, as U.S.-based multinationals have been some of the first global companies to implement worldwide voice processing systems. In order to maintain compatibility, these companies tend to favor manufacturers with a large U.S. presence.

In the short term, the most promising international markets for modems will be in western Europe and Japan, where there is the highest penetration of PCs outside the United States. The developing markets in Asia and Latin America should present additional opportunities as the penetration of PCs increases in those regions.

Over the next few years, the worldwide market for videoconferencing equipment is expected to experience its strongest growth outside North America, in Europe and the Pacific Rim.

Paulette Blanscet, U.S. Department of Commerce, Office of Telecommunications, (202) 482-0399, October 1999.

TERRESTRIAL BROADCASTING AND CABLE TELEVISION EQUIPMENT

The broadcast and pay television equipment subsector consists of equipment utilized by traditional over-the-air broadcasters and by cable system operators to transmit the same information and programming to many recipients, either through wireless technology or over fiber-optic and/or coaxial cable. This equipment is classified under SIC 3663. Products under this classification include amplifiers; AM, FM, and television transmitters; broadcasting transmitting antennas; cable television headend equipment, including modulators/demodulators and control units; subscriber converters and decoders; and broadcast and studio equipment.

Television and radio broadcasters transmit audio and video content over terrestrial antennas to multiple receivers. The United States is the largest and one of the most technologically advanced broadcasting markets in the world. There are over 1,200 commercial television stations on the air in the United States. BIA Research reports that the top 10 television groups own 304 stations. There are over 10,000 commercial radio stations in the United States. The cable television industry originated in the United States in the late 1940s as a means of transmitting over-the-air broadcast signals to communities out of the reach of then existing broadcast transmitters. Individual homes were wired with cable from a central antenna through which mostly local area broadcast signals were transmitted. These systems gradually evolved to transmitting distant signals, and cable operators began to compete against terrestrial broadcasters for viewers. The primary revenue source for cable system operators is subscription fees, with advertising revenue a secondary source.

By number of subscribers, the U.S. cable television market is the second largest in the world, and cable penetration is high at approximately 68 percent of television households. According to Nielsen Media Research, there were 67.6 million wired cable subscribers and 10,844 cable headends in the United States in 1998. The cable industry's share of multichannel video households has been declining slightly as a result of competition from other providers, especially direct broadcast satellites (DBS). The top 20 multiple system operators (MSOs) serve approximately 90 percent of cable subscribers in the United States, indicating a high level of consolidation in the domestic cable industry. This allows operators to address declining levels of public funding and the challenges brought by newer competitors. In addition, operators can leverage the advantages of fiber optics, digital terrestrial compression, and transmission technologies to tap new consumer demands. In August 1999, the top five MSOs were AT&T, Time Warner Cable, Comcast, MediaOne, and TWE-Advance/Newhouse, as reported by *Cablevision* magazine. Other major MSOs include Cox Communications, Charter Communications, Adelphia Communications, Cablevision Systems, and Century Communications. Revenues for the cable industry were approximately $32 billion in 1998 and are expected to grow about 9 to 10 percent annually in the coming years, driving demand for investment in cable television networks.

Major producers of television cable and broadcasting equipment include Panasonic, Sony, Scientific Atlanta, General Instrument, Harris, Andrew Corporation, Lucent Technologies, Motorola, NEC, Phillips, Thomcast, Thomson, and Zenith. U.S. government statistics indicate that U.S. manufacturers shipped $3.35 billion in broadcast, studio, and related electronic equipment in 1997, the most recent data available. U.S. manufacturers exported $1.15 billion in broadcasting equipment in 1998, down 26 percent from 1997 levels. The total amount exported in 1997 represented the peak in a long-term trend of growth in exports of broadcasting equipment, after which recessions in Asia and Latin America dampened demand somewhat. The total for 1998 exports of broadcasting equipment was only slightly less than the total for 1996, and except in Asia, exports were showing growth trends again in 1999. The top markets for exports of U.S. broadcasting equipment in 1998 were Canada, the United Kingdom (UK), Hong Kong, Brazil, Mexico, China, France, Japan, Taiwan, and Germany. Baskerville Communications lists the largest foreign markets for television broadcasting equipment, based on the number of television households, as China, India, Russia, Japan, Brazil, Germany, Indonesia, the UK, France, and Italy. The largest markets in the world for cable television equipment, based on the number of cable television subscribers, are China, India, Germany, Canada, Japan, the Netherlands, Argentina, Taiwan, and Brazil, according to Baskerville Communications.

Domestic Trends

The cable industry in the United States appeared moribund through much of the 1980s but turned around in the 1990s. The turning point in the industry's fortunes was Microsoft's $1 billion investment in Comcast, after which the idea of cable infrastructure as the most logical broadband route into U.S. households and onto the Internet gained life. The industry entered a period, still ongoing, of rapid and extensive system buildouts, overbuilds, and upgrades. The two most significant factors currently affecting the broadcasting and cable television equipment sector in the United States are the transition to digital transmission technologies and the changing competitive landscape created by the 1996 Telecommunications Act.

Investments in the cable sector in recent years to implement digital compression technology and upgrade infrastructure have placed cable networks at the core of developing voice, data, and video networks. These improvements also have placed operators in a strong competitive position as they prepare for competition from telephone companies, DBS, and the Internet. Digital compression and fiber-optic technologies allow operators to build capacity, attract more subscribers, increase revenue per subscriber, and therefore better compete against alternative providers (primarily DBS, which recently has slowed the cable industry's subscriber growth). For instance, cable operators currently rely largely on coaxial cable to carry services to subscribers. Hybrid fiber-coaxial cable is utilized increasingly in system upgrades and network expansions to provide greater capacity, speed, and quality of signal transmission; greater reliability; reduced expenses; and two-way transmission, allowing additional revenue-producing service offerings to subscribers. The Federal Communications Commission (FCC) calculated that capital expenditures for upgrading facilities were up 21 percent from 1996 to 1998. Approximately half of all cable plant in the United States was expected to be two-way-capable by the end of 1999. Some of the major operators will have spent upward of $1 million each in 1999 on capital expenditures and will have 100 percent of their systems two-way-capable by the end of the year 2000. Time Warner, MediaOne, Comcast, Cox, and Cablevision Systems are the leaders in offering two-way services to their subscribers. Analysts report that in 1998 the U.S. cable industry spent approximately $8 billion for infrastructure construction and upgrades, an increase of $1 billion from 1997.

The 1996 Telecommunications Act has mobilized competitive pressures and opportunities similar to those experienced in other liberalizing telecommunications markets. The cable industry is utilizing consolidation and clustering as two tactics to face competition and more effectively enter the telephony local loop. The last few years have been marked by mergers and acquisitions on a truly grand scale. Some of the larger deals were U.S. West's purchase of Continental Cablevision, Charter Communications' acquisition of Falcon Cable and Fanch Communications, AT&T's purchase of TCI, and AT&T's proposed acquisition of MediaOne. The trend toward consolidation has meant not only acquisition but also system clustering. Several major MSOs have traded system ownership in efforts to obtain economies of scale in certain geographic markets and subdue developing competition. TCI, Adelphia, Comcast, and Jones in particular have been active in system trades in recent years.

Terrestrial radio and television broadcasters also are experiencing consolidation, mostly as a result of relaxed ownership limits implemented by Congress and the FCC in recent years. The FCC eased television ownership rules in August 1999 to reflect growth in competing services, such as cable and DBS, and allow broadcasters to leverage their resources to operate more efficiently and strengthen their ability to compete. The proposed Viacom acquisition of the CBS network, the largest media deal in U.S. history, worth approximately $37 billion, is the beginning of what is expected to be a rush of consolidation activity. This deal also exhibits how both broadcast networks and cable operators are evolving into components of larger integrated multimedia and telecommunications companies such as Disney (which purchased ABC), Time Warner (which merged with Turner Broadcasting), and News Corporation (which owns Fox).

In addition to other changes in the industry wrought by the 1996 Telecommunications Act, the act specified the terms under which U.S. broadcasters would make the transition to digital terrestrial transmission. Digital telecommunications transmission technologies are a means by which problems in the nation's analog terrestrial broadcasting system, such as ghosting, interference, limited picture resolution, and limited presentation of color, can be addressed. The FCC developed a plan for switching to digital broadcasting, including the allocation of a second frequency channel to each station for simultaneous digital transmissions, and a time schedule. The transition officially commenced in the fall of 1998, when stations in the top 10 markets across the country began transmitting digital television (DTV). The FCC schedule calls for a staged transition in which all commercial stations must be on the air with a digital signal by May 1, 2002. Analog broadcasts are scheduled to be terminated in 2006, at which point the broadcasters will return to the government one of their two spectrum channels. The schedule will be reviewed periodically by the FCC and can be extended if certain conditions relating to the number of consumers receiving DTV signals are not being met.

Work originally commenced on developing a standard for advanced television services over a decade ago. A struggle between competing factions, including equipment manufacturers, broadcasters, and the computer industry, resulted in recommendations to the FCC that included 18 distinct formats under one umbrella standard. The range of formats reflects a dispute between the computer and the consumer electronics industries that is based on the capabilities of two methods of scanning, interlaced and progressive. The standard includes five technical subsystems covering scanning, video compression, audio compression, packetized data transport, and frequency transmission.

The FCC approved a standard within a range of allowable formats to give broadcasters flexibility and allow innovation to respond better to market forces. The Advanced Television Systems Committee (ATSC) standard, referring to the industry group that worked with the Advisory Committee on Advanced Television Service in developing the standard, allows for both high-definition television (HDTV) broadcasting and standard-definition television (SDTV) broadcasting. HDTV offers a more dramatic improvement in picture resolution than does SDTV and uses less of the broadcast spectrum. The 18 allowable formats include six HDTV formats (three with progressive scanning and three with interlaced scanning), eight formats that are SDTV, and four formats that are of lower quality than the current analog National Television Standards Committee (NTSC) standard. The "Big Three" networks have announced their decisions regarding HDTV format: ABC chose 720p (720 lines using progressive scanning), and CBS and NBC selected 1080i (1080 lines using interlaced scanning). Fox has not yet announced a decision.

Neither the 1996 Telecommunications Act nor the FCC mandated that broadcasters use their spectrum allotments for HDTV broadcasting, allowing broadcasters to decide whether to use the spectrum for HDTV broadcasts, multiple SDTV broadcasts ("multicast"), or SDTV broadcasts that use the extra frequency for auxiliary services such as data transmission ("datacast"). Beyond the question of the appropriate model for service delivery, several questions remain regarding a successful transition to digital. The lack of digital programming, the level of consumer demand, questions about revenue models, and technical issues still must be resolved.

Depending on station size, television stations are spending $8 million to $10 million on average to make the transition to digital, according to the National Association of Broadcasters. Small stations spend approximately $5 million to $6 million, and large stations may spend up to $20 million. Equipment needs include antennas, transmitters, transmission lines, switching equipment, converters, and exciters. Specific costs and equipment needs vary widely, depending on whether a station is simply passing through network signals or is originating digital programming.

Digital Audio. Work continues on establishing a U.S. standard for digital audio radio (DAR), also called digital audio broadcasting (DAB), which promises to offer compact disc–quality audio, greater channel capacity, reduced interference, and some types of information and subscription services. Lucent Digital Radios, USA Digital Radio, and Digital Radio Express were conducting field tests in 1999, and an industry standards panel was expected to make a decision by the end of 1999. Digital radio service should begin in late 2000. Each radio station should spend considerably less on the transition to digital than are television stations, with estimates running about $70,000 to $100,000 per radio station. New equipment may include exciters, amplifiers, transmitters, and antennas.

Global Industry Trends

The broadcasting and cable television industry worldwide is marked by interlinked trends toward increased competition, industry consolidation and ownership clustering, and the transition to digital compression and digital transmission technologies. As markets liberalize their telecommunications regulatory structures, cable systems are becoming a valuable alternative infrastructure for the provision of not only audio and video programming but also telephony and data transmission. In fact, some analysts believe that cable is the only provider in position today to offer multiple advanced digital services. These trends are especially advanced in the mature markets of North America and Europe. Other foreign markets are just beginning to enter a high-growth phase as the cable infrastructure is expanded and higher-technology equipment is utilized to tap pent-up demand for telephony and data and video services for which the existing traditional voice infrastructure is ill suited. Subscription revenues in several markets grew over 20 percent over the last 2 years. Some analysts estimate that multichannel revenues in Latin America alone will more than quintuple over the next decade. Although Asia offers incredible potential in terms of market size and potential demand, there is a wide range of regulatory environments, and the industry has been struggling as a result of the regional economic crisis.

In most mature markets, market liberalization and increased

competition have spurred a trend toward consolidation through mergers and acquisitions. Europe's second largest cable operator, United Pan-European Communications, went on a buying spree in recent years, acquiring pay television and cable operators in Poland, France, and Sweden and bidding on the Deutsche Telekom cable systems. Also in Europe, the cable sector in the UK is consolidating to compete with BSkyB, the country's digital satellite programming provider. NTL recently moved to become that country's largest cable operator after acquiring Comtel, Diamond Cable, and most of the Comcast systems in the UK and purchasing the residential cable operations of Cable & Wireless. Industry observers predict that NTL soon may acquire the country's one remaining large MSO, Telewest. In less mature markets, where broader economic pressures are of primary concern, system consolidation can provide operators with the means to weather turbulent economic conditions. For instance, pay television operators in the Philippines and in Thailand consolidated operations in 1998 to ease competitive pressures.

As in the U.S. domestic market, increased bandwidth and the capabilities of digital compression and digital terrestrial broadcasting are the major factor in the broadcasting and cable industry's promising future. The satellite industry began implementing digital transmission technologies for video programming earlier than cable operators and terrestrial broadcasters did, although in most countries cable operators are following closely behind. Relatively little of the cable plant in other countries has been upgraded to two-way capability, but that is changing rapidly as demand for cable telephony, cable modems, and data over cable soars.

Several countries are moving into commercial digital terrestrial broadcasting, most notably the United States, the UK, and other European countries. The first commercial terrestrial digital broadcast service in the world, ONdigital, was launched in the UK in November 1998. ONdigital was available at launch to 65 percent of the population and eventually will reach 85 percent. The company has been battling the satellite digital broadcasting service, BSkyB's Sky Digital, for subscribers ever since. The company's offer of free digital set-top boxes have spurred growth in the number of subscribers and greatly increased equipment needs. Datamonitor Europe predicts that there will be 600,000 terrestrial digital viewers in the UK in 2002.

Digital terrestrial service also has commenced in Sweden. Several other countries have published plans for the implementation of digital terrestrial television broadcasting services, including Australia, Canada, Finland, France, Germany, Italy, Japan, South Korea, the Netherlands, Singapore, Spain, and Taiwan. Other countries are just beginning to consider alternative standards for terrestrial digital broadcasting, namely, the ATSC standard or Europe's digital video broadcasting (DVB) standard, including China, Hong Kong, Brazil, Mexico, Venezuela, Paraguay, Ecuador, and Uruguay. The DVB standard has been selected by the European countries as well as Australia and Singapore. The ATSC standard has been adopted by the United States, Canada, South Korea, Taiwan, and Argentina. In addition, Japan has developed the Integrated Services Digital Broadcasting–Terrestrial (ISDB-T) standard for digital terrestrial broadcasting, based on the European standard.

Advances in the technology utilized in the cable and broadcasting sector to maximize revenue streams from each subscriber have highlighted certain areas of special interest: set-top boxes, Internet access over cable, interactivity, and telephony over cable. The increased capabilities of upgraded cable infrastructure and digital terrestrial transmissions have caused not only growth in the market for digital transmission and digital studio production equipment but also explosive growth in demand for digital set-top boxes that can deliver the full range of advanced services. A set-top box that incorporates proprietary technology is familiar to many cable subscribers as the device that decodes signals from the cable headend for viewing on a consumer's television set.

Compelled by provisions in the 1996 Telecommunications Act calling for standardized set-top boxes to be available in the retail market by July 2000, cable operators and equipment manufacturers have joined forces to develop interoperability standards under CableLabs' OpenCable effort. Beyond decoding and security functions, the newer generations of digital set-top boxes will allow telephony, digital radio, data services, electronic mail and Internet access (utilizing a cable modem), interactive electronic program guides, electronic gaming, video on demand (VOD), and electronic commerce. Consumers will require an advanced digital set-top box to access these services through the cable operator, surf the Internet on the television set by using telephone lines, or receive digital terrestrial broadcasting transmissions on an analog television set. OpenCable standards will allow the use of hardware and software from different vendors without limits on interoperability from proprietary technology and allow the consumer to purchase a box directly on the retail market. The standards will stimulate greater competition among equipment vendors, resulting in lower costs to operators and consumers.

Cable operators have begun purchasing large quantities of advanced digital set-top boxes that incorporate proprietary technology and in most cases leasing those boxes to their subscribers. High consumer response to free digital set-top box offers from SkyDigital satellite service and ONdigital's terrestrial digital service in the UK has pushed some manufacturers to increase production quickly to meet demand. Major MSOs in the United States that are implementing two-way services are also placing huge orders. The U.S. market for digital set-top boxes with advanced capabilities is the largest in the world, and worldwide demand for those set-top boxes will remain strong for the next several years. In future years, demand for digital set-tops will grow in foreign markets where the telephony infrastructure is poor, computers have not achieved high penetration, and the television set would be a more affordable means to access the Internet. However, the market eventually will shift toward digital televisions that incorporate a set-top box's functions. International Data Corporation predicts that 5 million units will be shipped in the year 2000, increasing to 11 million units in 2002. General Instruments is the largest supplier of set-top boxes in the United States, with 60 percent of the domestic market. By late 1999, the company had shipped 2 million digital set-tops, with commitments from operators to purchase 15 million over the next 3 to 5 years. Other major U.S. manufacturers include Scientific Atlanta, Hewlett Packard, and Zenith. Primary foreign manufacturers include Toshiba, Pace, Phillips, Panasonic, and Matsushita.

Just as consumer demand for Internet access and interactive services is pushing demand for set-top boxes, it also is driving demand for cable modems. Cable operators generated $432 million in Internet access fees from 1.2 million cable modem users in 1999, according to Veronis, Suhler & Associates. Access to the Internet through cable infrastructure soon will receive stiff competition from the digital subscriber line (DSL) technology being rolled out by local telephone operators. The Multimedia Telecommunications Association reports that it currently costs less to upgrade a subscriber to cable modem service than to DSL, an average of $1,000 per subscriber versus an average of $1,500, although consumers' preference remains unclear. Allied Business Intelligence predicts that the total market for broadband subscribers in the United States will be 21 million by the end of 2004 (up from 4.2 million in 1999) and that cable modems will have a 26 percent share of that market, less than that of asymmetric digital subscriber line's (ADSL) projected 36 percent share.

Although cable operators usually lease cable modems to individual subscribers, cable modems with proprietary technology have been on the retail market for some time. A CableLabs industry coalition has developed a common standard, Data Over Cable Service Interface Specification (DOCSIS), to facilitate the widespread deployment of cable modems. The DOCSIS standard has been approved by the ITU as an international standard, although there is a rival European standard from the European Cable Communications Association based on DVB and Digital Audio Video Council (DAVIC) technology. Major producers of DOCSIS cable modems include Motorola, Nortel, Scientific Atlanta, Lucent, LAN City, Zenith, Com21, and Terayon. More than 20 manufacturers in total are manufacturing to the DOCSIS standard. Motorola is the largest cable modem manufacturer in the United States, with about 40 percent of the domestic market, followed by Toshiba and Thomson. The common standard has brought down the final price for cable modems in some cases to less than $300. Very few of the cable systems in the United States are DOCSIS-enabled, though, and DOCSIS cable modems are not expected on the retail market for many more months. Both computer and set-top box manufacturers soon will begin incorporating DOCSIS modems into their products.

In the United States, operators are well along in upgrading the cable infrastructure to allow two-way communications, and several major MSOs have rolled out cable modems to their subscribers. Analysts estimate that approximately one-quarter of U.S. households currently have access to cable systems that offer high-speed residential cable Internet access services. The major operators in Canada have achieved a higher penetration rate in their systems for cable modems. By mid-1999, approximately 1.2 million households in the United States and Canada subscribed to high-speed cable modem services. Time Warner leads with the most high-speed data subscribers, followed by AT&T, MediaOne, Shaw, Cox, Rogers, Comcast, CableVision, Charter, and others. Gecko Research estimates that 35 million homes worldwide are passed by cable modem services, with 20 million of those homes in the United States and Canada.

Although the cable infrastructure in western Europe is generally less developed, operators have been active in upgrading infrastructure, conducting cable modem trials, and beginning to offer Internet access. The penetration rate for cable modems in the Netherlands is high. The demand for high-speed Internet access is also high in Germany, although the installed infrastructure is poor. Spain, Sweden, and Italy also offer good opportunities for high-speed cable Internet access. International Data Corporation projects that revenues from cable modem shipments in western Europe will increase from $33 million in 1998 to almost $550 million in 2003. Although operators in Latin America have much less digital infrastructure in place, they are moving ahead on implementing Internet access over an analog infrastructure. The Strategis Group projects that the cable modem market in Latin America will grow from 54,000 in 1999 to over 1.2 million in 2003.

Other major potential markets include China, Japan, and South Korea. The Japanese government announced in mid-1999 that the number of subscribers to residential high-speed Internet access over cable had grown well over 300 percent over the previous 8 months and that there were over 70 providers of the service in Japan. China already has more cable subscribers than does the United States, yet the penetration rate for multichannel video remains comparatively low, indicating a large growth potential. Cable operators have begun to offer some advanced services, signs of industry consolidation are appearing, and there is a shift toward more commercially based operations. The Chinese government's plans to construct a nationwide fiber backbone would further support the development of high-speed cable access.

Consumer demand for interactive services is driving much of the market for digital set-top boxes and cable modems. There is little to no industry consensus on the exact definition of interactive services, although interactivity may encompass services that include electronic programming guides, VOD, surfing the Internet, electronic gaming, filtered data services such as weather and sports, auxiliary datacasts, viewer-defined television ("personal television"), applications downloads, and electronic commerce applications such as shopping and banking.

"Interactive services" delivered over cable have been predicted for several years, and Time Warner conducted ultimately unsuccessful trials of its "Full Service Network" in Florida from 1994 to 1997. The level of technology and equipment prices have evolved since then, and consumer acceptance is growing. Requirements for implementing interactive services include set-top boxes, the 750-megahertz (MHz) cable infrastructure in nodes of 100 or fewer subscriber homes, security and authentication capability, network control and signaling systems, end-to-end IP capability, a scalable reverse path from the subscriber back to the cable headend, file servers at the headend, and an operating system. VOD in particular is viewed as the "killer application," offering a high revenue stream for operators. The Yankee Group predicts that revenues from VOD alone will reach $1 billion in the year 2000. Several operators have been preparing plans for aggressive rollouts of interactive services in 2000, including Time Warner's plan to begin trials of VOD in late 1999. CableLabs is building on its OpenCable and DOCSIS efforts through its PacketCable project, through which the industry group will build IP-based standards to facilitate the development of interoperable equipment for interactive applications. Vendors and manufacturers involved in interactive television include DIVA, Intertainer, TVN Entertainment, NCube, Wink, TiVO, ICTV, ACTV, WebTV, MyWeb, WorldGate, NetChannel, HBO, Showtime, and Viewer's Choice. Forrester Research estimates that interactive applications will generate $63 billion in revenues in 2004.

Another area worthy of mention is the provision of telephony over cable infrastructure. Although the 1996 Telecommunications Act allowed local exchange carriers (LECs) to enter into video delivery, there has been relatively little activity by LECs in this arena. Interest is growing, and in some areas, LECs are becoming more competitive in video delivery. For example, Ameritech, Bell South, and RCN are entering the video market. Cable operators, in contrast, have been very proactive in taking advantage of the 1996 act to enter the local loop. Cox and MediaOne have led the way, rolling out telephony services to several domestic markets, and AT&T and TimeWarner also offer local telephony services. By mid-1999, Cox claimed almost 60,000 telephony customers and MediaOne claimed about 26,000. The Strategis Group predicts that cable telephony subscriptions will rise to over 7 million in 2004.

While cable operators are just beginning to enter the local loop in the United States, telephony has been bundled with video service by operators in the UK since the early 1990s and currently is offered in other European markets as well. Telecommunications regulatory liberalization is opening opportunities for cable operators and equipment providers around the world. The Strategis Group predicts that cable telephony equipment and service revenues in 2003 will surpass $2 billion in the UK, almost $1.5 billion in the United States, $230 million in China, and almost $200 million in the Netherlands.

Global Market Prospects

The technology to upgrade cable infrastructure and offer advanced services over cable has in many cases been available for several years. The United States is the most advanced country in terms of cable infrastructure and advanced service offerings, with many major world markets anticipating strong growth in the near future. The mature cable markets in Europe, including the UK, the Netherlands, Switzerland, Belgium, Denmark, and Germany, are experiencing many of the same trends seen in the Canadian and U.S. markets. Germany in particular offers opportunities in that it represents a large percentage of the continent's cable subscribers. The cable infrastructure, although well established, uses older technology and needs upgrading before advanced services can be distributed reliably and widely. Italy also has potential, with over 20 million television households and an extremely low cable penetration rate.

Cable operators and broadcasters in Asia have been struggling with the impact of the regional economic crisis, although that region represents a large potential market for broadcasting and cable television equipment. The region covers well over 500 million television sets. A few countries are planning to implement digital terrestrial broadcasting within the next 5 years, cable penetration remains low but is growing, and demand for the Internet and a wider range of entertainment options is growing rapidly. Some markets, such as Japan, are relatively well advanced technologically with high cable penetration, and others, especially China but also Thailand, Malaysia, and Indonesia, present opportunities simply because of their size and unmet demand.

Despite the economic downturn throughout Latin America, there is demand for access to the Internet, competition in the local loop, and a wider range of entertainment options. Again, plans to implement digital terrestrial broadcasting offer additional opportunities for equipment manufacturers. Some markets in Latin America are already very competitive, and several of the cable markets in that region are experiencing rapid growth in subscribership, which will lead to greater equipment needs to service subscribers and offer more advanced services to an increasingly sophisticated consumer market. Brazil is a large potential market with over 35 million television households and substantial unmet demand for video, telephony, and data services. In addition, the Brazilian government recently awarded new cable and multichannel multipoint distribution services (MMDS) concessions that offer opportunities for equipment providers. While DBS is gaining subscribers in the region rapidly, it remains an option primarily for the wealthy. The cable infrastructure in markets with a poor telephony infrastructure provides strong opportunities as a competitive alternative to voice and high-speed data services.

Projections of Industry Growth

The primary factors mobilizing strong growth in the market are regulatory changes, the speedup in infrastructure upgrades, rapidly growing demand for high-speed access to the Internet, new technology rollouts, digital terrestrial broadcasting, and cable telephony. The end result is that broadcasting and cable television equipment manufacturers are anticipating strong growth in demand worldwide over the next several years. While foreign demand will remain level for the next year because of lingering suppressed demand from economic recessions in Latin America and Asia, demand for access to the Internet both domestically and worldwide will push the deployment of cable infrastructure and equipment. Equipment manufacturers should see demand begin to rise at a strong and increasing rate of growth. The rollout of digital terrestrial broadcasting in foreign markets will further support a healthy rate of growth over the latter part of the forecast period.

Elizabeth Farrand, U.S. Department of Commerce, Office of Telecommunications, (202) 482-2953, October 1999.

WIRELESS COMMUNICATIONS EQUIPMENT

Wireless communications equipment consists of complete radio-based communications systems, including mobile switching, transmission, and subscriber equipment for the provision of cellular, paging, and personal communications services (PCS). Switches complete connections between mobile users or between mobile users and the public switched telephone network. Transmission equipment includes radio transmitters, receivers, and transceivers as well as other base station equipment, such as antennas and amplifiers. Subscriber equipment includes mobile and portable handsets. Wireless communications equipment is classified under SIC 3663.

The wireless communications industry in the United States has few rivals in terms of its rate of growth. In the span of about 15 years, wireless telephony in the United States has attracted more than 70 million subscribers, bringing the penetration rate to close to 30 percent. A 1999 study predicted that 77 percent of U.S. workers eventually will use a wireless phone for business purposes, and a number of industry experts believe that wireless may become the dominant voice network for households in the United States by the middle of the next decade. No other communications medium, including telephone, radio, and television, can claim the same dramatic rate of penetration into the population. Globally, growth also has been spectacular: In 1998, more wireless phones were sold worldwide than automobiles and PCs combined.

For the purposes of this report, the wireless communications equipment industry consists of suppliers of handsets and related infrastructure equipment for analog and digital cellular as well as PCS. Wireless telephony uses the radio spectrum rather than fixed wires to provide communications services. Signals are transmitted between wireless handsets and a network of base stations that consist of radio transmitters and receivers. Each base station operates within a set geographic region called a cell. As users travel from one cell to another, calls are handed off from one base station to the next, allowing for mobility. Base stations are connected to a mobile switching center by microwave or fiber links.

Although most cellular operators are digitizing their networks, cellular equipment can be either analog or digital, while PCS equipment is only digital. The difference between PCS and digital cellular lies mainly in the spectrum allocation. In the United States, PCS operates at 1.8 to 1.9 gigahertz (GHz), a higher band than the 800-MHz frequencies used for digital cellular (see Table 31-3). PCS and digital cellular both use code division or time division multiplexing technology to maximize the use of assigned frequencies. Signals cannot travel as far at the higher frequencies used by PCS; therefore, PCS requires more transmitting towers, and its geographic cells are smaller than cellular cells. PCS base stations are smaller and generally cheaper to operate. While this affords PCS an operating cost advantage over cellular, overall infrastructure costs tend to be higher for PCS, and PCS technology imposes limits on the economics of wide-area coverage. As a result, PCS networks are centered largely in urban areas and are often unavailable in rural areas.

TABLE 31-3: U.S. Cellular/PCS Spectrum Summary

Service	Spectrum Allocation
Cellular	825–850 MHz, 865–890 MHz
PCS	A: 1,850–1,865 MHz, 1,930–1,945 MHz
	B: 1,870–1,885 MHz, 1,950–1,965 MHz
	C: 1,895–1,910 MHz, 1,975–1,990 MHz
	D: 1,865–1,870 MHz, 1,945–1,950 MHz
	E: 1,885–1,890 MHz, 1,965–1,970 MHz
	F: 1,890–1,895 MHz, 1,970–1,975 MHz

Source: FCC.

While demand for wireless equipment fluctuates in response to the licensing of new operators and technological innovations, demand for wireless equipment in the United States is expected to remain strong. Factors that will affect growth include the increased adoption of wireless technology by businesses and growing telecommunications budgets, the reallocation of funds from telecommunications budgets to wireless, and wider acceptance of wireless by diverse demographic groups.

Domestic Trends

According to the *1999 Multimedia Telecommunications Market Review and Forecast* published jointly by the Telecommunications Industry Association (TIA) and the Multimedia Telecommunications Association (MMTA), aggregate U.S. spending on wireless communications equipment rose about 4 percent from about $11.5 billion in 1997 to about $12.0 billion in 1998. Aggregate spending was projected to increase another 4 percent to about $12.4 billion in 1999. TIA predicts that overall U.S. wireless equipment expenditures will decline to $10.9 billion by 2002 (see Table 31-4). The factors discussed below, however, may mitigate this decline.

Spending for wireless infrastructure equipment, including switches, base stations, and peripherals, declined about 17 percent in 1998 from $5.63 billion to $4.67 billion and was projected to decline modestly in 1999 to $4.38 billion. TIA and MMTA predict that overall spending on wireless infrastructure equipment will decrease over the 1998–2002 period, with the compound annual growth rate (CAGR) for 1998–2002 for infrastructure expenditures projected to be –10 percent. Cellular operations reportedly still represent the bulk of infrastruc-

TABLE 31-4: Wireless Communications Spending
(millions of dollars)

Year	Services	Handsets	Infrastructure	Total
1997	32,479	5,867	5,630	43,976
1998	38,245	7,336	4,667	50,248
1999	45,479	8,032	4,383	57,894
2002	70,838	7,950	3,010	81,798

Source: The Strategis Group; CTIA; InfoTrack for In-Building Wireless (Phillips InfoTeck); Electronics Industry Association; Donaldson, Lufkin & Jenrette; Paul Kagan Associates; MMTA.

ture spending as a result of the digitization of networks, with about 56 percent versus 43 percent for PCS. The 1998–2002 CAGR for cellular infrastructure is projected to be –15 percent versus –2.3 percent for PCS.

From 1997 to 1998, handset spending increased about 25 percent, rising from $5.9 billion to $7.3 billion. The number of handsets sold in the United States rose to 18.9 million units in 1998, up 3.3 percent from 18.3 million units in 1997. Original projections for 1999 showed a modest increase of about 2 percent in 1999 and then a leveling off and slight decline in the year 2000. However, mobile handset sales exceeded the 10-million-per-quarter mark for the first time in 1999, according to a report from Dataquest that put second-quarter sales of handsets at 10.3 million. Dataquest also reported that about 78 percent of sales consisted of digital handsets, indicating, as expected, an accelerating decline of analog handset sales. Code Division Multiple Access (CDMA) handset sales also are increasing more rapidly in the United States than are Global System for Mobile communications (GSM) handset sales.

The Yankee Group reported that in 1999, 65 percent of wireless subscribers in the United States used analog networks, while 19 percent used digital cellular and 16 percent used PCS. In the future, however, digital handset sales increasingly will outpace analog handset sales. By 2003, as many as 95 percent of the handsets sold in the United States will be digital, and with the continuing decline of analog, many analysts are focusing their predictions exclusively on the digital handset market. This trend is even more pronounced globally: Analog phones accounted for only about 15 percent of the world handset market in 1998, as most new wireless licenses have been for GSM or PCS networks. Operators prefer digital handsets because they provide the ability to offer more sophisticated and diversified (and revenue-generating) service offerings.

U.S. wireless subscriber forecasts vary markedly, as do the percentages of cellular and PCS subscribers. Phillips Group Info Tech, for example, predicts 80.6 million cellular subscribers and 47.5 million PCS subscribers in the United States by 2004, for a combined total of 128.1 million, while Paul Kagan Associates predicts that there will be a total of 185 million subscribers by 2004, with 99.4 million cellular subscribers and 74.9 million PCS subscribers.

According to TIA and MMTA, the average retail price of a cellular handset, about $175 in 1997 rose to about $210 in 1998 and was projected to drop to $185 in 1999. The average price is predicted to continue to decline, falling to $150 by 2002. The average price of a PCS handset, estimated at $325 in 1997, declined to $275 in 1998 and was projected to decline further in 1999 to $225. The average price of all handsets is projected to have a 1998–2002 CAGR of about –8 percent.

In considering these average prices, it should be noted that the operative word is *average,* and although they may reflect the retail cost, these figures do not give a complete picture of the market. Average prices have been skewed by a number of factors, including the recent introduction of new models with more sophisticated componentry designed for future applications such as E-mail and Internet access. In addition, consumers can easily find handsets on the market that satisfy their basic voice communications requirement for under $100. Handset prices often are kept artificially low by service providers that bundle handsets with service packages. Price declines would be much greater if it were not for the shift to digital equipment in general as well as the increased use of multimode phones to increase coverage in areas where compatibility issues are prevalent.

As was noted earlier, spending on cellular infrastructure equipment trended downward in 1998, mainly because networks for the first wave of PCS operators (A-Block and B-Block licensees) approached completion. Although cellular networks in the United States are largely built out, cellular carriers are continuing to invest in infrastructure equipment to convert their networks to digital in response to competition from PCS.

The bulk of spending will continue to be on digital technologies. Although digital equipment is more expensive than comparable analog equipment, it can support a substantially higher number of subscribers. On a per-subscriber basis, therefore, digital infrastructure costs are approximately 30 percent lower than those for analog.

Accordingly, infrastructure spending changed markedly between 1997 and 1998. In 1997, analog infrastructure spending accounted for about two-thirds of total spending; however, by 1998, analog infrastructure spending fell to only $442 million, representing less than 15 percent of total infrastructure spending. The percentage of digital infrastructure spending went up even more dramatically in 1998–1999. Spending on Time Division Multiple Access (TDMA) infrastructure doubled in 1998, rising from just over $1 billion to almost $2.1 billion, while spending on CDMA infrastructure more than quadrupled, rising from $131 million to $634 million. Over the 1999–2002 period, $3.7 billion is expected to be spent on TDMA infrastructure and $1.5 billion on analog infrastructure, for a total of $8.2 billion. According to TIA, spending on cellular infrastructure totaled over $3.1 billion in 1998 (see Table 31-5).

Although a number of analysts predict that infrastructure equipment purchases will continue to trend downward through 2003, others note that the market may accelerate beyond projections in 2000 as a result of the increasing digitization and expanded coverage of cellular and as wireless data services become more popular. The national coverage of cellular networks will help it remain competitive, and the number of cellular subscribers is projected to continue to grow, although at a somewhat slower rate. As the number of new cellular sub-

TABLE 31-5: Cellular Infrastructure Spending
(millions of dollars)

Year	Analog	TDMA	CDMA	Total
1997	2,379	1,026	131	3,536
1998	442	2,054	634	3,130
1999	425	1,274	798	2,497
2000	393	1,202	786	2,381
2001	367	610	733	1,710
2002	321	632	657	1,610

Source: TIA, MMTA, Donaldson, Lufkin & Jenrette.

scribers decreases over time, however, average spending per subscriber is expected to rise.

Total spending for PCS networks has not caught up to investments in cellular networks. PCS networks are more limited in scope; as was noted above, PCS is centered largely in urban areas because rural areas have a higher build-out cost per subscriber. Nevertheless, PCS has been the fastest-growing component of the wireless market, and PCS subscribership should continue its rapid expansion. While PCS infrastructure spending is expected to slow in the longer term, expenditures for PCS handsets are expected to increase from $2.9 billion in 1999 to $3.2 billion in 2002.

The telecommunications industry is outpacing most other industries in terms of innovation, and the wireless sector is a significant contributor to this trend. Wireless services, which are managed by advanced software platforms, are changing the nature of the industry, and the Internet is expected to play a significant role in the growth of the next generation of wireless networks.

Most analysts are predicting that the next 5 years will see the long-anticipated commercialization of wireless data. While wireless Internet currently has only a small foothold, future Internet access clearly will have a significant wireless element, and the wireless sector will benefit from the Internet and data movement that has taken hold in the wireline sector. The Yankee Group estimated that there were about 3.4 million mobile data subscribers in the United States in 1999 and predicts that that number will exceed 20 million by 2004. The first wave of "smart phones" and personal data assistants (PDAs) with wireless Internet access came to market in 1999. Subsequent generations of wireless access devices will have far greater capabilities because the bandwidth will be much larger and users will be able to access data more rapidly at much higher speeds.

Although the arrival of wireless data has been touted for a number of years, industry experts cite the lack of existing networks that can support data as the biggest obstacle to the marketing of data-ready handsets. As was reported in *Wireless Review* in mid-1999, in the United States, "the cars are ready, but the highway is still under construction . . . the networks [that can handle high-speed data] aren't ready and the applications are not complete." Delays reportedly stem from the fact that existing IP standards were not designed for wireless access: Handset screens generally cannot display much of the Web's hyper-text markup language (HTML) content efficiently.

To solve this problem, a veritable alphabet soup of protocols is evolving, designed to facilitate wireless data and increase transmission speeds, leading the way toward the third-generation (3G) wireless discussed at the end of this section. Some industry analysts predict that in the year 2000, the World Wide Web will begin to deal routinely with wireless markup language (WML). At that point, sales of data-ready wireless devices should begin to take off, and some company officials believe that by 2001 there will be as many as 10 million wireless phones globally accessing the Internet. Remarkably, by 2005, more handsets than PCs are projected to be connected to the Internet.

Wireless Application Protocol (WAP), a set of protocols that allow greater compression of data and maximize low to medium bandwidths, became available in late 1999. WAP was developed by the founders of the WAP Forum formed in June 1997—Unwired Planet (now Phone.com), Nokia, Ericsson, and Motorola—in recognition of the fact that wireless Internet needed its own dedicated access standard. WAP handsets began to appear on the market in 1999. Motorola and Nokia, for example, began shipping WAP handsets priced at about $575 in the last quarter of 1999. According to *Global Mobile,* however, WAP will not have a significant presence until 2001 and will reach critical mass only in 2002. *Global Mobile* predicts that only 5 percent of cellular phones in circulation will be WAP-enabled by the end of 2000; however, that figure will rise to 15 percent in 2001 and 65 percent in 2004.

Several wireless protocols are likely to coexist for a number of years. The development of WAP will facilitate the rollout of General Packet Radio Service (GPRS), which is under development, to increase bit rates even further and allow users to remain connected to the network while being billed only for time in use. GPRS systems reportedly will enable operators to offer wireless Internet and other IP-based applications at speeds 10 times as fast as those of current mobile networks. Motorola and Ericsson delivered GPRS systems to operators in the Americas, the Asia-Pacific region, and Europe for GPRS field trials in the fourth quarter of 1999. GPRS is projected to appear commercially in 2000, followed by Enhanced Data for Global Evolution (EDGE), a standard designed to boost bit rates further on GSM and TDMA networks up to 384 kilobytes per second (kbps). Additionally, High Speed Circuit Switched Data (HSCSD), currently available for GSM networks, boosts wireless data access speeds from 9.6 kbps up to 57.6 kbps, discussed at the end of this section.

Handsets. The current handset market is a good harbinger of where the wireless industry is going. In its report on the global handset market, Morgan Stanley Dean Witter (MSDW) declared 1998 a "transition year" for the global handset market, mainly because of the growing level of electronic components dedicated to data. This increasing level of sophisticated circuitry has had the effect of accelerating the product cycle for digital handsets from about 2 years to 1 year.

Innovative handset features will become an increasingly important marketing tool, and many analysts believe that success in the wireless handset market will depend on having the right product in place at the right time as wireless data unfolds. For example, some manufacturers are reportedly considering a "handset" that would consist of an earpiece, a small microphone, and a transmission device that would eliminate the keypad and be operated by voice-activated dialing.

Handsets that can access the Internet, such as Motorola's i1000, Nokia's 7100 Communicator, Neopoint's 1600 smart phone, and the Palm VII PDA, have been on the market for some time. The Motorola i1000, for example, combines the capabilities of a digital cellular phone and two-way radio with text messaging and data capabilities and allows users to hold an instant conference call at the push of a button. In 1999, Nokia introduced a dual-band, high-speed data terminal that operates on both GSM 900 and GSM 1800 networks. The Nokia Card Phone 2.0. is a PC card with a built-in GSM phone that supports HSCSD and enables data transmission of up to 43.2 kbps without data compression.

Manufacturers that have developed smart phones believe that data-ready networks will emerge early in the next decade. Once data services in North America are rolled out, growth in digital handset sales is expected to take off again, driven by demand for E-mail, Internet access, and information management. Some analysts believe that carriers initially will offer a package with E-mail and customized Internet access (e.g., news, sports, weather, movies) to build a customer base. Others note that to attract business clients, carriers will have to demonstrate that users can access personal data wherever they go. New software that allows subscribers to synchronize data between their wireless devices and their PCs addresses this need.

Wireless video also has arrived, although on a limited basis. In 1999, Kyocera Corp. of Japan introduced a new VP-210 mobile telephone with a built-in video camera, claiming it as the first commercial handset that makes videoconferencing possible in a mobile environment. The handset has a 2-inch color liquid crystal display (LCD), and Kyocera built a hands-free function into the handset. In 1999, Nokia developed a prototype handset called the MediaScreen that it claims is a combination wireless phone, television, and Internet access system.

Speech recognition technology has not made a significant mark on the industry, however. At the end of 1998, only about 1.5 million U.S. subscribers were using voice-activated services. In the near future, however, voice activation is expected to come to the fore. Developments in voice recognition software—termed interactive voice recognition (IVR), the simplest example of which is voice-activated dialing—have some analysts predicting that keypads will become a thing of the past. A number of leading handset manufacturers, including Motorola, Nokia, Ericsson, and Neopoint, have introduced voice dialing features into their product lines in recent years. Some of these handsets have limited capabilities, including voice dialing directories. However, newer voice-responsive models that combine phones and PDAs are expected to be on the market in the year 2000. Industry observers forecast that the global market for these wireless products was $200 million in 1999 and will reach $675 million in 2000 and $2.4 billion in 2001.

In addition to the development of sophisticated applications in handsets, a number of manufacturers are using cosmetic changes to handsets to capture the attention of prospective buyers. Nokia, for example, has introduced handset faceplates in a wide variety of designer colors. An Ericsson handset introduced in 1999, a dual-mode GSM 900 and GSM 1800 phone, comes in "juicy blue, mustang yellow, shocking pink, funky purple and crispy turquoise." NEC's NEX series, Nokia's 8810, and Sony's CMZ-200 all offered a brushed silver or chrome-finish faceplate in the 1999 models.

In addition to adjustments in color and finish, handset designers are searching for the right combination of shape, size, weight, display size, keypad size and placement, and conformity to the hand. Some manufacturers, including Qualcomm and Nokia, have introduced small, ultrathin handsets. Qualcomm's Thin Phone weighs about 4 ounces and fits into a shirt pocket, and Nokia's 8810 weighs just under 4 ounces and is about 0.7 inch thick. Ericsson also designed a water-, dust-, and shock-resistant phone, the R250 Pro, that operates on GSM 900 and GSM 1800 networks.

While consumer surveys suggest that the market wants smaller phones with new data capabilities, manufacturers face the dilemma of how to cram the electronics needed for advanced applications into ever-smaller phones. Research and development resources required by the increasing number of data components in handsets also may make it difficult for all but the largest manufacturers to set their handsets apart in terms of innovation.

Nokia, Ericsson, and Motorola are widely viewed as the Big Three in the wireless handset market, with a combined share of 57 percent of the world cellular handset market (68 percent of the total market excluding Japan) in 1998. The Big Three have nearly 70 percent of the world's GSM market: Nokia, 27 percent; Ericsson, 22 percent; and Motorola, 19 percent. MSDW predicts that Nokia will show some of the strongest growth in the handset market through the growing replacement market in GSM and TDMA phones and market share gains in the evolution to 3G. MSDW also predicts a gradual loss of market share for Ericsson because of its late arrival in the narrowband CDMA market. The analog market has been dominated by Motorola, with 57 percent of the world market in 1998, followed by Nokia with 25 percent. Ericsson has only a 3 percent share of the U.S. analog market.

Nokia reached the number one position globally in mid-1998 largely by jettisoning other product lines and focusing on innovations in wireless handsets and infrastructure equipment. With $70 billion in sales in 1998, Nokia had a 34 percent market share in the United States. By the third quarter of 1999, Nokia increased its U.S. share to 40 percent, most likely because of its ties to AT&T's Digital One Rate plan introduced earlier that year. Motorola also experienced a near doubling of its market share, from 6.3 percent in 1998 to 11.5 percent in 1999, while Ericsson and Qualcomm both lost market share in 1999. Notably, Qualcomm, after selling its infrastructure manufacturing division to Ericsson, subsequently announced that it also would abandon its handset business.

Ericsson has been losing share in the digital handset market in recent years. In the first half of 1999, administrative costs reportedly grew 30 percent while sales increased only 12 percent, prompting a restructuring program that included significant employee layoffs. Ericsson believes it can regain market share in 2001 or 2002 and introduced a number of new phones in 1999 toward that end. Ericsson's professed goal for the year 2000 is to achieve 20 percent sales growth.

Motorola had been losing ground in the handset market largely as a result of its slow start in the digital market. Motorola had 13 percent of the digital handset market and 57 percent of the analog market in the United States in 1998. A successful CDMA product line placed Motorola in the number two position in the overall U.S. mobile handset market in 1999, spurred by a contract with Bell Atlantic to supply about 1 million CDMA phones. Motorola claims that it is poised to assume the number one position in 2000.

Alcatel has made inroads into GSM handset sales, more than doubling its share of the market since 1996. Alcatel reportedly is gaining market share and may rival Motorola in the near future. Alcatel's market share in western Europe was 12 percent compared with Motorola's 15 percent. Excluding Japan, Alcatel was number four in the world in 1998, with 6.3 percent of the market. Panasonic is fourth when Japan is included, with about 8 percent, followed by Alcatel with 4 percent.

There is cooperation as well as competition among the Big Three. In 1998, Nokia, Ericsson, Motorola, and the British handset manufacturer Psion formed an alliance called Symbian, a private consortium for the advancement of 3G wireless. The objectives of the Symbian alliance include accelerating the development of higher-speed networks and making wireless access to the Internet ubiquitous.

Other suppliers also are involved in cooperative ventures. AT&T Wireless reportedly has been negotiating with Ericsson and Nokia to market a "world phone" that can roam across the GSM networks that are common overseas and, by mid-2000, across TDMA networks in the United States and the western hemisphere. A partnership of Mitsubishi Wireless Communications and AT&T says that its MobileAccess T250 is the first and only wireless voice/data communicator to work on both digital voice and packet data networks. The "Quad-Mode" phone handles cellular digital packet data (CDPD), 800-MHz and 1,900-MHz TDMA systems, and analog networks for voice services.

As competition has increased, some manufacturers have abandoned certain markets or withdrawn from the handset market altogether. For example, in 1999 Sony made the decision to leave the North American handset market and disbanded its engineering, sales, and marketing offices, leaving only a research and development (R&D) center working on CDMA 2000 technology. That decision was reached despite the fact that the region accounted for 40 percent of the company's mobile handset business. Sony cited lost market share in the region over the past few years and reports that future operations will be focused on the Asian and European markets. Qualcomm and Philips Consumer Communications (PCC), perhaps the most conspicuous companies to depart the handset market recently, have not been alone. Over the past 3 years, Nortel, Oki, and Mitsubishi have all pulled out of handset manufacturing markets. One of the major challenges facing new entrants to the American handset market, particularly the second wave of CDMA vendors, is that the three industry giants are so entrenched that new entrants are forced to compete on the less desirable basis of price.

Standards. According to Dataquest, in 1999, CDMA pulled ahead of TDMA in the U.S. wireless handset market. Dataquest reports that 3.2 million CDMA handsets were sold in the first quarter of 1999, more than TDMA's 2.8 million. One Dataquest analyst warns that wireless handset manufacturers that do not have CDMA products should be concerned. That research firm predicts that CDMA will continue its upward momentum, increasing the distance between itself and rival standards in the next few years. That firm also said that as CDMA becomes stronger in the United States, the technology's prospects in other parts of the world, such as Latin America and the Pacific Rim, will improve.

The cellular market has entered a mature phase in its growth cycle. Major near-term developments in that market are the migration of analog customers to digital services and the attempt by cellular carriers to maintain their customer base in the face of competition from PCS. 3G technologies (discussed below) will allow carriers to offer high-bandwidth services. Implementation of 3G will require renewed infrastructure spending. These developments, however, probably will not play a material role until the next decade.

Global Industry Trends

The international wireless communications sector took on an added dimension in 1999 as manufacturers and operators began to position themselves actively for the evolution to the next-generation, or 3G, wireless systems beginning in 2001. The industry has continued to experience extraordinary growth globally, surpassing 300 million subscribers at the end of 1998 and approaching 500 million toward the end of 1999. Incumbent players worldwide are investing in their networks to add high-speed data capabilities and improve quality, coverage, and capacity. In addition, new 3G licenses contemplated over the next several years will act as a market catalyst for infrastructure equipment and handset sales.

In the 1990s, the benefits of cellular telephony—mobility, usability, and, more recently, affordability—made cellular attractive to consumers in developed countries and an urgent requirement in many developing countries. The degree to which wireless has developed in different regions of the world depends largely on factors such as level of economic development, income distribution, cost of entry, affordability, free market orientation, and effectiveness of distribution systems. Wireless coverage is approaching ubiquity in developed countries, with most nations having as many as nine competing networks. In developing countries, wireless technology is increasingly a substitute for wireline networks as developers have come to recognize that wireless networks are often less expensive to construct and operate than are traditional landline networks and can be brought to market in one-third of the time. The auctioning of licenses has become increasingly prevalent as wireless services have provided foreign governments and regulators with an opportunity to create competition in line with the prevailing political trend toward a more open environment in telecommunications services. This provides a better deal for users and attracts potential foreign investors to a country.

The year 1998 ended with some 308 million wireless subscribers worldwide, an increase of nearly 100 million, bringing worldwide penetration to 5.8 percent, up from 3.9 percent at the end of 1997. Strong growth of about 68 percent enabled western Europe to surpass Asia (excluding Japan) and North America as the largest regional market, with about 31 percent of the world's subscribers. The number of subscribers in the Asia-Pacific region continued to grow rapidly, up about 31 million to more than 106 million, ending that year with 34 percent of the world total. North American subscribers were up about 25 percent to nearly 75 million and accounted for about 24 percent of the world total. Although starting from a much smaller base, Latin America experienced strong growth of 73 percent in 1998, accounting for about 5.7 percent of the world total. Africa and the Middle East had a combined total of about 6.7 million, or about 2.3 percent of the world's subscribers. Many forecasters expect the number of wireless subscribers to reach 500 million in the year 2000, and most believe that there will be 1 billion subscribers by 2004 (see Figure 31-1).

According to a study from the Strategis Group, wireless handset sales were expected to reach worldwide volumes of 205 million in 1999 and grow to approximately 303 million in 2004, when annual handset revenues will reach $47 billion. Allied Business Intelligence (ABI) estimated that there were about 1.43 million base stations deployed throughout the world in 1999, up more than 40 percent from about 822,000 in 1998. ABI estimates a 21 percent compound annual average growth (CAAG) rate through 2003, when there will be 2.5 million base stations deployed globally.

Among the more than 300 million wireless users worldwide at the beginning of 1999, about one-third used analog devices, mainly advanced mobile phone system (AMPS), and the remainder used digital (or dual-mode) devices. The share of analog is expected to continue its marked decline to about 10 percent worldwide by 2002. The majority of digital subscribers—about three-quarters—use GSM handsets. The remaining digital subscribers use TDMA, 6 percent; CDMA, 7 percent; Pacific Digital Cellular (PDC), 11 percent; and Personal Handyphone Service (PHS), 2 percent (see Figure 31-2).

The vast majority of wireless subscribers are cellular users, although PCS has continued to experience remarkable growth levels, with the number of global subscribers increasing 80 percent from 14 million at the end of 1997 to more than 25 million at the end of 1998. PCS subscribership is projected to reach 150 million worldwide by 2001. Several operators, primarily in Europe, provide dual-band services.

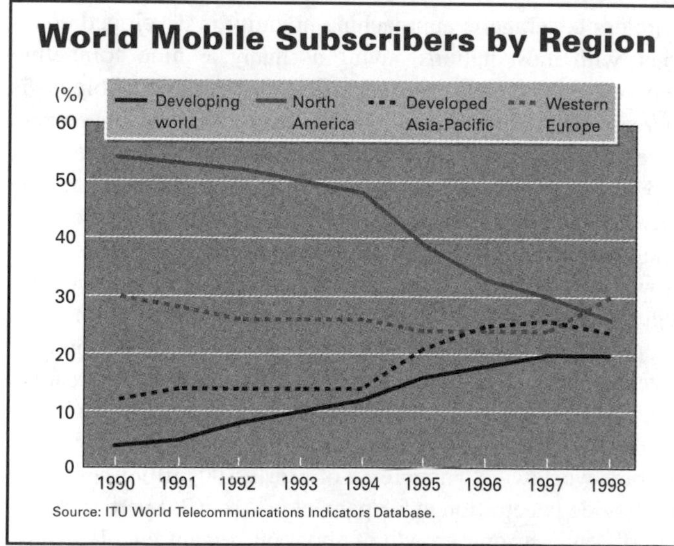

FIGURE 31-1

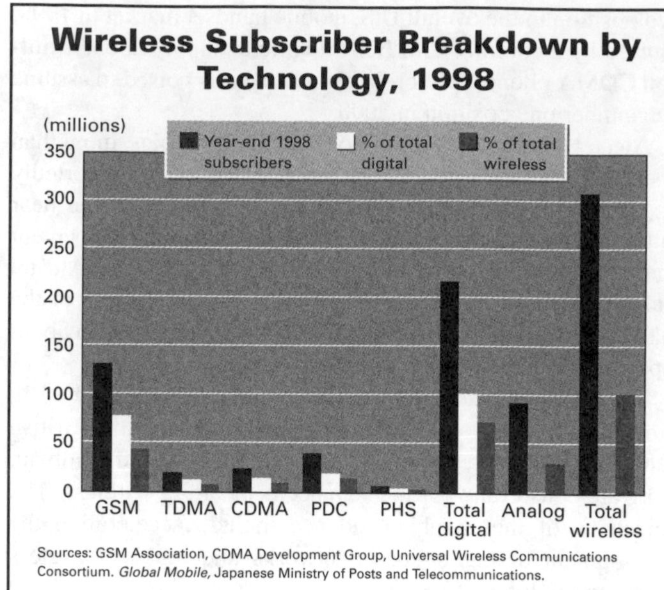

FIGURE 31-2

According to the Strategis Group, global cellular/PCS handset shipments reached approximately 68 million units in the second quarter of 1999, increasing 14 percent compared with the previous quarter. Western Europe showed the highest growth in GSM handset sales, accounting for 61 percent of sales in the second quarter of 1999, followed by the Asia-Pacific region with 18 percent. Total second quarter cellular/PCS handset sale revenues reached $12.4 billion, of which about $7 billion came from GSM handset sales. Growth of GSM was most prevalent in China, Italy, and the United Kingdom, while significant increases in CDMA occurred in Japan and the United States.

New advances in equipment that allow greater hemispheric roaming began to take hold in 1998. While dual-band handsets have been in service for some time, new triband handsets allow users to access or roam on up to three different frequencies. The first "world phone" affording access to GSM 900/1800/1900 appeared on the market in 1999.

Asia-Pacific Region. Subscriber levels in the Asia-Pacific region grew from 75 million at the end of 1997 to 106 million at the end of 1998. When Japan is included, the Asia-Pacific region accounted for more than one-third of the world's 1998 subscriber base. Emerging markets in the Pacific Rim have abundant populations and low telephone densities, making them highly attractive markets for wireless services. Some analysts have forecast that that region may have more than 200 million subscribers by 2002, for a regional penetration rate of about 6.5 percent, although this will vary significantly by country. According to the

Strategis Group, the number of handsets sold in the Asia-Pacific region is expected to increase from about 35 million in 1997 to 54.2 million in 2001. Handset sales revenues (reflecting a notable decline in price per unit) for the entire region are expected to grow from about $18 billion in 1997 to $19.7 billion in 2001, with analog handsets garnering only about 17 percent of the total in 2001. By 2004, the Asia-Pacific region is forecast to lead the world in sales of mobile computing devices.

The Asia-Pacific region has adopted virtually every global wireless standard as well as a few that are unique to the region. Japan's PDC standard, which has remained limited to Japan, has one of the largest installed subscriber bases in the region, with 46.3 million subscribers as of September 1999. Another digital wireless market segment in Japan is PHS, which has certain limitations. For example, the system does not lend itself to either vehicular use or conventional roaming. Although 45 percent of the traffic on PHS networks is data traffic and a 384-kbps upgrade is available, Japan's cellular carriers are now offering competitive high-speed data services. As a result, the number of PHS subscribers has been declining since mid-1997 and stood at 5.65 million in September 1999.

GSM is the most widely used local standard at present, with GSM carriers in the Asia-Pacific region reportedly serving more than 53 million subscribers. The region's GSM infrastructure equipment market, which was robust in 1999, is expected to exceed those in all other regions by 2001. CDMA and TDMA are in use in a growing number of countries in the region. Australia, for example, is in the middle of a significant buildout of CDMA networks, with the goal of 50 percent coverage by 2001. Telecom New Zealand is continuing its migration from AMPS to TDMA. CDMA service was expected to be available in Hong Kong later in 1999.

Japan and China accounted for 63 percent of the Asia-Pacific market in 1999 and are expected to remain the largest markets in that region, with China poised to overtake Japan in terms of total subscribers. The most spectacular growth in the region in 1998 occurred in Japan, where cellular subscriber totals rose 133 percent to nearly 50 million in mid-1999, in large part reflecting falling service prices and enhanced services such as wireless Internet. NTT DoCoMo had over 3 million subscribers to its iMode wireless Internet service. Japan's last remaining operator accepting applications for analog cellular service ceased issuing new analog accounts in August 1999. The Japanese equipment market is set for even more spectacular growth as 3G comes to the fore.

Growth in China's wireless market is expected to remain strong. China grew from 14.4 million subscribers in 1997 to 24.9 million in 1998, and a number of analysts claim that that country will have 45 million subscribers by 2001 and as many as 100 million by 2004. While China's telecommunications equipment manufacturing industry slowed in the first half of 1999, the wireless sector surged. Demand from the country's rapidly expanding cellular industry saw the production of mobile telephone handsets rise 45.3 percent to 10.7 million sets. In anticipation of future growth, China's Ministry of Information Industry added an extra digit to mobile numbers to increase the cellular numbering system capacity to 500 million numbers.

In India, the cellular industry all but ran aground in 1998, running up losses of over $600 million. This was due mainly to license fees charged by India's Department of Telecommunication (DoT), which were way out of proportion to revenues. Cellular operators also pay DoT retail access charges for mobile–to–fixed line calls, and for some operators this amounts to half the amount invoiced to mobile subscribers.

All countries in the Asia-Pacific region with the exception of a handful of smaller nations have at least three licensed wireless operators. Factors that may limit growth include the residual economic impact of the Asian monetary crisis. South Korea, which scaled back its development plans sharply in 1997, began to increase expenditures in 1998, and the number of subscribers doubled from 6.6 million to 13.9 million. Three major Korean manufacturers of CDMA handsets reportedly account for 57 percent of CDMA handset sales worldwide. Taiwan was the fastest-growing market (123 percent) in 1998, with 3.5 million in 1998 compared with 1.5 million in 1997. Despite its economic difficulties, Indonesia's Association of Cellular Telephone Dealers reported that between 30,000 and 50,000 units were sold in each of the first 6 months of 1999, compared with just 15,000 per month in 1998. Thailand was hit the hardest by the currency turmoil, and its recovery was still under way in 1999.

Europe. The remarkable growth of the wireless market in western Europe is expected to continue, with some studies claiming that sales and penetration levels will grow an average of 10 percent a year over the next 5 years. Subscribership in that region grew more than 67 percent, rising from 56 million at the end of 1997 to 95 million at the end of 1998, and resulting in an average penetration level of more than 21 percent. Total subscribers in western Europe are projected by *Global Mobile* to reach 108 million by 2000 and 158 million by 2004. Other analysts predict that overall wireless penetration in western Europe will exceed 37 percent by 2001, with some projecting over 50 percent by 2006. New wireless licenses, declines in services prices in some countries resulting from increased competition, and the increased availability of dual-band (GSM 900 and GSM 1800) handsets will continue to propel the market. The growing migration of voice traffic from fixed networks to cellular/PCS networks and the increased revenues generated by wireless data and value-added services are also among the reasons cited for the increase in wireless infrastructure buildout. Prepaid services also have had a significant impact on the market, with more than 40 percent of all subscribers on a prepaid basis at the end of 1998.

The four largest markets in the region—Italy, Germany, France, and the UK—accounted for about two-thirds of total regional growth. Italy had the highest growth rate in western Europe, adding more than 8 million new subscribers in 1998 for a total of more than 20 million users, and was projected to reach 27 million subscribers by the end of 1999. Italy launched a third operator in 1998 and planned to award a fourth operating license in 1999. Germany increased its subscriber levels from 8.3 million in 1997 to 13.8 million in 1998, and the UK effectively used prepaid to expand its market 53 percent to over 13 million. Other countries also showed notable growth. Greece, for example, more than doubled subscribership in 1998, as did the Netherlands, Portugal, and Turkey. For some time, Finland has been a vanguard country for wireless penetration; however, analysts generally agree that the boom in mobile phone sales could slow markedly in the year 2000 because over 60 percent of that country's population now owns at least one mobile phone. Faster networks and the emergence of the wireless Internet could help fuel the market in the future.

Across Europe, as many as 1 billion short messages are transmitted every month. Since today's mobile phones have slow transmission rates (9.6 kbps), small screen displays, and awkward keyboards, the enormous popularity of short messaging is surprising and bodes well for the future of wireless text. Although short messaging service (SMS) is very popular in Europe, only 2 percent of GSM subscribers used wireless data services in 1999. International Data Corporation (IDC) expects the total number of mobile data subscribers to grow to 12 percent at the end of the 5-year period. The increase in growth is expected to start toward the end of 2001, fueled by the launch of GPRS (discussed below) in the second half of 2000 in the most developed GSM markets.

Some industry observers believe that the future use of wireless throughout the world can be predicted by looking at what is happening in Europe today. Subscribers there are using their phones to pay bills, conduct banking, and schedule travel. By early in the next decade, one in three Europeans is expected to own a mobile phone. The UK company Strategy Analytics claims that 47 percent of European households already have more than one cellular phone, while 12 percent have three or more.

The wireless services market in central/eastern Europe (CEE) grew markedly in 1998—many CEE markets experienced triple-digit growth rates in that year—as competition and digital networks expanded. The number of cellular subscribers in the 15 largest CEE countries more than doubled to 7.5 million, reaching 2.3 percent of that region's population. CEE's wireless market entered an era of fierce competition propelled by the introduction of digital standards (GSM 900 and GSM 1800).

The region's largest growth markets were Poland, Hungary, and the Czech Republic, while Romania, Bulgaria, and Yugoslavia recorded the fastest rates of growth, but from a lower base. Russia's marked cellular slowdown must be viewed in light of the economic slowdown there in the second half of 1998. Kagan World Media anticipates that the CEE cellular market will explode within the next 10 years, with an estimated 75.2 million mobile phone users by 2008, representing a 10-fold increase.

Latin America. According to the Strategis Group, cellular and PCS markets throughout Latin America will achieve impressive growth over the next 5 years despite uncertainty in several Latin American economies. Privatization and liberalization programs are boosting wireless growth in Central America and South America. Other market drivers include the low cost of wireless development relative to wireline and the introduction of calling party pays and prepaid services. The Latin American cellular market is forecast to grow at a CAGR of 40 to 45 percent in the 2000–2002 period, outperforming growth in the wired network. Various assessments predict that wireless subscribership in Latin America will grow from 18 million in 1998 to as many as 55 million in 2002. A study by Baskerville Communications in 1999 estimated that more than 71 million mobile lines will be in service in Latin America by 2007, when revenues will reach more than $81 billion. Most of the principal U.S. wireless equipment companies participate actively in the Latin American market.

Dataquest reported that wireless networks in Latin America were exceeding traditional wireline buildouts, and handset sales in that region were projected to reach 24.5 million by the end of 1999. In the first half of 1999, handset sales in Latin America exceeded 9.8 million units, with Nokia, Ericsson, and Motorola accounting for 78 percent of all sales. Analog handsets had 54 percent of overall sales in the region in 1998, but that number reportedly dropped to about 30 percent in 1999.

Brazil is clearly the premier market in the region. The wireless market in Brazil exploded in 1998, as was evidenced by the more than 1 million cellular customers added in less than 8 months, with even stronger growth predicted for 1999. In the cellular market alone, the government expected 2.9 million new lines to be contracted for installation in 1999, drawing foreign suppliers to manufacture in-country.

Mexico also is considered one of the region's most promising markets. Over the last 2 years, Mexico's new regulatory authority has moved aggressively to auction spectrum, introduce competition in new sectors, and license new technologies. Networks were constructed for the PCS licenses auctioned in nine regions of Mexico in 1998. The number of cellular/PCS subscribers in that country is expected to increase over 40 percent by the year 2000.

Venezuela and Chile also posted above-average growth in 1998. In March 1998, Chile became one of the first Latin American countries to launch PCS services, and after a number of delays, Argentina auctioned PCS licenses in mid-1999. Some smaller Latin American markets—notably El Salvador, Panama, Paraguay, and Bolivia—also performed remarkably well.

Several new CDMA 1900, TDMA 1900, and GSM 1900 systems were inaugurated in 1998 in the region, positioning 1999 as a potentially significant year in the battle of wireless technologies. TDMA digital technology benefited most from the upgrading of analog AMPS networks and the buildout of new systems throughout the region. CDMA 1900 subscribership grew 120 percent to reach 124,000 at the end of 1998. The Global Mobile Suppliers Association predicts that there will be at least one GSM operator in every country in Latin America within 2 years. The Strategis Group projects that 60 percent of the subscriber base in Latin America eventually will use GSM or TDMA and that most of the remainder will use CDMA.

Africa and the Middle East. African nations realize the need for communications capabilities to expand their economies. There is a movement toward liberalization in various countries as well as increasing private sector participation, and most countries in Africa now have multiple operators. In countries where they are offered, prepaid packages have been effective in driving market growth. While Africa has many analog networks, digitalization is taking hold and digital networks are growing in number. GSM has become the dominant digital technology. According to the GSM Association, GSM has seen almost a 75 percent increase in subscribers, growing from 2.9 million subscribers to around 5 million toward the end of 1999. The popularity of prepaid services and the continued investment in and deployment of new GSM networks across several countries are some of the factors that have leveraged this rapid growth.

Companies pursuing wireless opportunities in Africa have to face a number of challenges, including economic stagnation, political unrest, and corrupt bureaucracies. In addition, many countries still have an unstable or confusing regulatory climate. With the exception of South Africa, handsets usually are not subsidized as they are elsewhere, and the cost of a basic handset can run as high as $1,000 or more in many African countries. In addition, getting equipment through customs can be difficult, and power sources are not always reliable.

The Middle East, which added more than 1 million subscribers in 1998, had about 4.3 million users at the end of that year. The region has had selected successes in wireless. Just as South Africa dominates the African continent, Israel dominates wireless subscribership in the Middle East. With 57 percent of the region's subscribers, Israel was projected to have spent an estimated $1 billion to set up its third mobile phone network in 1998. The New Territories of Palestine also are planning to establish a wireless network.

The Arabian Gulf states have invested enormous sums in developing their telecommunications infrastructures over the last decade, and mobile communications has played a leading role in this investment program. The average level of monthly traffic per subscriber is significantly higher—almost three times larger—than the average for western Europe. The largest single market in the Gulf states is Saudi Arabia, which had nearly half a million subscribers at the end of 1998.

Although a monopoly operator is still the regional norm, this is changing gradually, and there are likely to be major steps toward a more competitive environment over the next 2 or 3 years. For example, Saudi Arabia's national telephone operator, STC, was privatized in May 1998, although the government still retains all the shares.

Evolution to the Third Generation

As the new millennium begins, standards for 3G wireless communications systems are nearing completion. (Analog cellular is considered the first generation, and digital cellular/PCS the second generation). The much-anticipated standardization of 3G wireless systems on which the ITU began work in 1985 to establish the basic vision and spectrum requirements for 3G services has been the major focus of wireless standards organizations around the world for the last several years. International Mobile Telecommunications–2000, (IMT-2000), the name given to the 3G project by the ITU, was chosen to represent deployment around the year 2000, using 2,000-MHz spectrum bands and offering data rates up to 2,000 kbps. The ITU is coordinating this worldwide process to establish global recommendations for 3G systems that will allow automatic global roaming (use outside the user's home service area), high-speed data and Internet access, full-motion video, and other sophisticated multimedia services from mobile devices. The minimum performance capabilities established by the ITU for data transmission were 144 kbps at vehicular speeds, 384 kbps at pedestrian speeds, and 2 million bytes per second (Mbps) in fixed applications, far higher data transmission rates than those available with current wireless communications networks. The ITU completed its evaluation of candidate technical proposals for 3G wireless systems in September 1998 and is scheduled to finalize its recommendations in May 2000.

In December 1998, the European Council of Ministers and the European Parliament adopted a Common Position and Decision on the coordinated introduction of Universal Mobile Telecommunications Systems (UMTS) in the European Community (EC). The decision requires that (1) UMTS be provided only using a common radio technology that has been standardized by the European Telecommunications Standards Institute (ETUI) and (2) EU member states adopt an authorization system for UMTS by January 1, 2000, and allow the introduction of UMTS services by January 1, 2002, with the possibility of a 1-year extension. The Common Position and Decision made no provision for the deployment of 3G services other than UMTS on any specific time scale. [In January 1998, ETSI approved the single European-proposed standard—UMTS Terrestrial Radio Access (UTRA). The Commission has since stated that only one 3G license has to be for UMTS.]

Finland, the sole EC member state to have licensed 3G systems, selected four 3G service licensees in March 1999. Finland did not stipulate use of a specific standard as a license condition, although all four licensees are known to favor UMTS. Japan and several EC member states planned to begin issuing licenses to operators in the first half of 2000, although the systems will not be deployed commercially until 2001–2002. In September 1999, the Japanese Ministry of Posts and Telecommunications announced the approval of two standards for 3G (both CDMA).

At the end of 1998, prospects appeared dim for the successful resolution of the contentious issues that threatened to derail the IMT-2000 standardization process within the time frame that had been established by the ITU. Then, in a breakthrough agreement demonstrating an unprecedented level of global cooperation, the global wireless industry came together to resolve virtually all the outstanding issues concerning the direction of 3G standards. The first agreement, announced in February 1999 by a working group of the TransAtlantic Business Dialogue (TABD), created a practical solution to the market needs for backward compatibility with existing systems, global roaming, smooth evolution to 3G, and the timely introduction of 3G services. That agreement also affirmed the strong desire of wireless operators to have the opportunity to choose which technologies and standards they use in their networks to meet their customer and business needs. The TABD agreement was submitted to the ITU in March 1999, where it was incorporated into the IMT-2000 recommendations. Thus, although the ITU initially sought a single 3G air interface standard, it has accepted a "Family of 3G Systems" concept that envisions the evolution of 3G networks from the existing base of second-generation (2G) networks. This will provide mobile users, through five ITU-specified interfaces, with the potential for seamless support of 3G services across different families of networks.

Another major obstacle to IMT-2000 standardization was removed in March 1999, when Qualcomm and Ericsson announced the successful conclusion of negotiations that resolved their ongoing confrontation over intellectual property rights related to CDMA technology. With the resolution of this legal dispute, the ITU received the assurances it required that IMT-2000 standards utilizing CDMA technologies would be licensed in accordance with the ITU's established intellectual property rights (IPR) policies.

Wireless standards activities have been under way to define the air interfaces, core networks, interfaces, and services for 3G networks. The 3G standardization activities within the ITU and related SDOs have been complemented by the global 3G Partnership Projects—3GPP and 3GPP2—which are essentially consortia of SDOs. The ITU will adopt those specifications upon their completion. The focus of the technical specifications work in the 3GPPs is on intrasystem evolution from 2G to 3G, complementing the ITU's work on the standardization of IMT-2000.

An important positive development assisting the focusing and completion of all IMT-2000 proposals was the engagement of the global operator community through the efforts of groups such as the Operators' Harmonization Group (OHG) for aligning various CDMA-based proposals, and the collaboration of the GSM Association and Universal Wireless Communications Consortium (UWCC) operators regarding the convergence of TDMA-based systems. The coordinated input of these operator organizations has greatly assisted the work of the individual SDOs, the 3GPP groups, and the ITU.

In June 1999, the OHG, which included the major operators and equipment suppliers of 13 North American, European, and Asia-Pacific nations, reached agreement on a technical framework that would combine the various 3G CDMA proposals into a single, "three-mode" Global 3G (G3G) CDMA standard. The three modes are Multi-Carrier (MC), formerly CDMA2000, which is most likely to be used by existing CDMA operators that want to overlay 3G services on top of their existing 2G operations; Direct Spread (DS), formerly W-CDMA, which is most likely to be used when an operator has a clear spectrum; and Time Division Duplex (TDD), which is to be used for unpaired spectrum. This framework called for modifications to a variety of technical parameters as well as provisions for all CDMA modes to operate with both of the existing major wireless network infrastructures (ANSI-41, which is used by current CDMA and TDMA systems, and GSM MAP, which is used in GSM systems). The details to implement this framework are being worked out by the industry. The ITU, also in June 1999, endorsed this approach.

Separately from the OHG, the UWCC has been working in tandem with the GSM Association to codevelop specifications for high-speed data applications. Some observers have speculated that TDMA could well become the "standard" 3G technology in the medium term by using some of these jointly developed specifications, particularly with mergers, such as that between AT&T and British Telecom, that create a ready-made market.

As it has become clear that operators want to be able to evolve their installed infrastructure to provide their customers with high-speed data applications, equipment vendors have developed a number of "2.5G" technologies that will be commercially available beginning in mid-2000 at a fraction of the cost of constructing new 3G networks. All major wireless vendors are competing for these interim upgrades to better position themselves for subsequent 3G contracts. One such upgrade for use with TDMA-based networks is General Packet Radio Service (GPRS). GPRS is designed to support efficient, cost-effective access to Internet-based data communications services, including E-mail, Web access, and mobile banking, over GSM networks at speeds up to 172 kbps. GPRS overlays a packet-based air interface over a circuit-switched architecture. It allows GSM operators to tailor packet-switching capacity in line with the predicted data traffic increases over GSM networks and to engage the radio channels only when actually sending or receiving data. Rather than having a radio channel dedicated to a mobile data user for a fixed period, the available radio channel can be shared concurrently among several users. This efficient use of scarce radio resources means that large numbers of GPRS users potentially can share the same bandwidth and be served from a single cell. Eventually, all GSM operators are expected to implement GPRS, and an estimated 60 percent of handsets will be GPRS-enabled by 2004. For manufacturers, GPRS is viewed as the first stage in the transformation of the GSM business from delivering basic voice services to delivering wireless data and eventually wireless multimedia. Thus, although GPRS contracts are not particularly lucrative, they represent an entry point to a massive new wave of network investment. According to Baskerville Communications, as of November 1999, vendors had received 43 GPRS contracts, and as many as 200 new contract awards are expected by the end of 2000. If GPRS services are commercially successful, base station orders are likely to skyrocket in 2001. EDGE will enable operators of 2G GSM and TDMA networks to offer Internet-based services at speeds of up to 384 kbps on their existing networks and further improve spectrum efficiency.

CDMA carriers will be implementing the first phase of 3G CDMA, which is known as 1XRTT in technical circles. The 1XRTT standard lays the foundation for a wide array of high-speed wireless information services and has the added advantage of a twofold increase in voice capacity as well as extended battery life. It provides 144-kbps packet data in mobile applications and significantly higher speeds in a fixed environment. CDMA carriers in the United States, Japan, Canada, South Korea, and Australia already have announced their intention to implement the 1XRTT upgrade.

All these 2G upgrades allow operators with existing spectrum to take advantage of 3G capabilities without having to acquire new spectrum. In addition, Baskerville Communications reported that the comparative costs of 2.5G base stations such as GPRS to be one-fourth the cost of UMTS base stations.

Costs for GPRS are relatively minimal, involving primarily a software upgrade. Thus, in western Europe's four largest cellular markets—Germany, France, Italy, and the UK—operators should be able to provide national GPRS coverage for $100 million to $120 million, according to the Yankee Group. Western European operators alone are expected to spend a combined $2 billion on upgrading to 2.5G capabilities.

Looking toward the future, the ITU has forecast that 160 MHz of additional spectrum will be needed by 2010 for the terrestrial component of IMT-2000. The ITU's 1992 World Administrative Radiocommunication Conference (WARC-92) identified 230 MHz (1,885 to 2,025 MHz and 2,110 to 2,200 MHz) for use on a worldwide basis by administrations wishing to implement IMT-2000 systems, which then were termed Future Public Land Mobile Telecommunications Services (FPLMTS). The next ITU World Radiocommunication Conference (WRC-2000), scheduled for May 2000, will include a review of spectrum and regulatory issues related to IMT-2000 services, including additional terrestrial spectrum needs. The industry is strongly advocating for globally harmonized spectrum. The outcome of this process has important implications for both manufacturers and service providers.

Japan probably will be the first country to deploy 3G networks commercially; this is planned for the second half of 2001. In September 1999, Japan announced its decision to approve two 3G standards, with licensing expected to take place in the spring of 2000. Earlier in 1999, NTT DoCoMo, the world's largest wireless carrier, and its competitors, DDI and IDO, introduced high-speed data and wireless Internet services on their respective 2G networks, and the market response was very enthusiastic. NTT DoCoMo and Japan Telecom both anticipate being awarded 3G licenses in the year 2000. NTT DoCoMo's network is scheduled for completion in early 2001. Japan Telecom says that it will spend at least $6.7 billion during the next 2 years to build a rival service, aiming for a late 2001 kickoff.

In Europe, some 80 3G licenses are expected to be offered, beginning in the spring of 2000. As member states were still finalizing their 3G licensing procedures and timetables at the end of 1999, it is unclear how many new networks actually will be built out as well as the pace at which the buildout will occur.

In the United States, domestic operators already have the flexibility in their operating licenses to deploy 3G services in their existing spectrum allocations, and several U.S. carriers conducted trials of 3G technologies and services in 1999. Most operators are expected to upgrade their networks to meet the demand for high-speed data applications. In addition, the FCC will be proposing additional spectrum that could be used in the future for 3G operations in the United States.

According to Baskerville Communications, 3G-enabled handset demand is expected to reach 210 million in 2008 and account for over 30 percent of all wireless handsets. Most of those handsets will be multimode, that is, incorporating two or more digital technologies. The majority of 3G subscribers will be located in Asia and Europe (see Table 31-6). Ericsson has forecast that there will be 120 million 3G users by the end of 2004, based on current interest on the part of network operators in the evolution of mobile communications technology to wideband, multimedia-capable mobile services across all digital standards. Ericsson claims that operators are making aggressive investments in new packet-data equipment and showing tremendous interest in 3G licenses and the timely rollout of new services. In 1999, sales of GPRS packet-data equipment that gives operators the ability to offer new and more content-rich applications to their subscribers were accelerating. Others, such as the UK telecommunications consultancy Ovum, do not believe that rapid 3G subscriber growth will occur until 2007. Although Ovum predicts that 3G subscribers will reach 1 billion and account for nearly two-thirds of the world's wireless subscribers by 2010, it believes that most of the traffic on 3G networks will be for voice or low-speed data applications (see Table 31-6).

The implementation of packet-based upgrades to existing wireless networks over the next several years represents one of the most significant changes in the ability of mobile networks to deliver new services to date. The ability of operators to market

TABLE 31-6: 3G Regional and Global Subscriber Forecasts

	2002	2003	2004	2005	2006	2007	2008	2009	2010
3G subscriptions (thousands)									
Africa and Middle East				252	1,342	2,632	4,131	5,845	7,781
Asia-Pacific region	11,156	18,786	34,245	54,572	104,197	141,499	162,275	169,587	172,118
Europe	10,088	27,322	46,392	69,252	105,552	140,437	160,904	173,837	177,035
Latin America	0	0	0	979	2,850	4,963	7,298	9,670	16,584
North America	3,588	8,166	18,775	31,063	59,939	75,814	93,214	112,083	132,336
World	24,832	54,274	99,412	156,118	273,880	365,345	427,822	471,022	505,854
3G subscriptions as a percent of total subscriptions									
Africa and Middle East				0.50	2.60	4.70	6.80	8.90	11.00
Asia-Pacific region	4.40	6.70	11.40	17.20	31.50	41.40	46.30	47.50	47.50
Europe	4.00	9.70	15.30	21.50	31.30	40.20	44.80	47.30	47.30
Latin America	0.00	0.00	0.00	0.90	2.60	4.20	5.80	7.30	12.00
North America	2.20	4.50	9.50	14.50	26.00	30.70	35.50	40.30	45.00
World	3.20	6.30	10.60	15.60	25.80	32.90	36.90	39.20	40.80

Source: Baskerville Communications Corporation.

these services effectively will determine the need for 3G networks over the forecast period.

Linda Gossack Astor and Richard H. Paddock, U.S. Department of Commerce, Office of Telecommunications, (202) 482-4466, October 1999.

SEARCH AND NAVIGATION EQUIPMENT

Search and navigation equipment (SIC 3812) consists of search, detection, navigation, guidance, aeronautical, and nautical systems, instruments, and equipment. It includes radar and sonar systems, light reconnaissance and surveillance equipment, and electronic warfare equipment.

Domestic and Global Industry Trends

This industry consists of establishments engaged primarily in manufacturing search, detection, navigation, guidance, aeronautical, and nautical systems and instruments. Products fall under SIC 3812. Important products of this industry are radar systems and equipment; sonar systems and equipment; navigation systems and equipment; flight and navigation sensors, transmitters, and displays; gyroscopes; airframe equipment and instruments; and speed, pitch, and roll navigational instruments and systems.

Search and detection, ground navigation, and guidance systems and equipment account for approximately 92 percent of shipments in this industry. Aeronautical, nautical, and navigation equipment accounts for the other 8 percent.

U.S. shipments of search, detection, navigation, guidance, aeronautical, and nautical systems instruments, and equipment continued their downward trend in 1999 (see Table 31-7). Industry shipments totaled just over $25 billion in constant dollars, representing a 3.7 percent decrease from 1998. Since 1992, shipments have been decreasing at an average annual rate of 4 percent. Defense spending directly affects demand in the search and navigation industry as military aircraft, ships, guided missiles, early warning radar systems, and weapons systems all incorporate products from this industry. Defense spending has been in decline since the end of the cold war era, and this decline has adversely affected demand for products from this industry. Continued cutbacks in defense spending were reflected in the fiscal year 1999 defense budget. Many defense programs were not funded or were funded at diminished levels, and defense opportunities have continued to shrink.

Consolidation in the industry—marked by mergers and acquisitions—coupled with the recession of the early 1990s prompted numerous layoffs. The latest census data indicate that the total number of U.S. companies that produced search, detection, navigation, guidance, aeronautical, and nautical systems dropped from 315 in 1996 to 295 in 1997. After 1992, total employment in this industry declined at an average annual rate of approximately 4 percent, decreasing from a high of 253,000 in 1992 to an estimated 177,000 in 1999. Production workers, or workers engaged in the actual production of search and navigation equipment, have experienced similar declines. The number of production workers declined sharply from 103,000 in 1992 to an estimated 63,000 in 1999.

Many defense-dependent manufacturers of search and navigation equipment have been diversifying their operations to take advantage of the emerging commercial applications of radar technology. After the early 1990s, defense contractors began to place more emphasis on defense conversion and dual-use programs that incorporate leading-edge military technologies into civilian markets. A number of government technology investment programs have been funded to aid companies in developing products and services for commercial use. One DOD program

TABLE 31-7: Search and Navigation Equipment (SIC 3812) Trends and Forecasts
(millions of dollars except as noted)

										Percent Change			
	1992	1993	1994	1995	1996	1997[1]	1998[1]	1999[2]	2000[3]	97–98	98–99	99–00	96–00[4]
Industry data													
Value of shipments[5]	35,039	33,546	30,110	32,000	30,371	29,459	28,575	27,718	26,886	−3.0	−3.0	−3.0	−3.0
Value of shipments (1992$)	35,039	32,856	29,204	30,506	28,925	27,661	26,312	25,336	24,353	−4.9	−3.7	−3.9	−4.2
Total employment (thousands)	253	225	199	200	186	185	184	177	170	−0.5	−3.8	−4.0	−2.2
Production workers (thousands)	103	88.5	80.3	71.6	67.8	64.0	63.0	63.0	63.0	−1.6	0.0	0.0	−1.8
Average hourly earnings ($)	17.28	18.79	18.84	19.95	20.31								
Capital expenditures	849	706	688	730	1,223								
Product data													
Value of shipments[5]	34,171	31,203	29,160	27,755	26,653	25,053	23,550	22,137	20,809	−6.0	−6.0	−6.0	−6.0
Value of shipments (1992$)	34,171	30,561	28,283	26,458	25,383	23,525	21,685	20,384	18,849	−7.8	−6.0	−7.5	−7.2
Trade data													
Value of imports	965	862	828	959	1,013	1,225	1,271	1,319	1,450	3.8	3.8	9.9	9.4
Value of exports	2,133	2,105	2,031	1,978	2,046	2,515	2,613	2,699	2,872	3.9	3.3	6.4	8.8

[1] Estimate except imports and exports.
[2] Estimate.
[3] Forecast.
[4] Compound annual rate.
[5] For a definition of industry versus product values, see "Getting the Most Out of *Outlook 2000.*"
Source: U.S. Department of Commerce: Bureau of the Census; International Trade Administration.

responsible for assisting firms in this conversion process is the Defense Advanced Research Project Agency program. Under this program, Lockheed Martin developed the antenna for the Multi-Purpose Airport Radar, which was conceived to fulfill requirements for next-generation terminal area surveillance systems.

Under the Federal Radio Navigation Plan, a joint document by DOD and the U.S. Department of Transportation, the Global Positioning System (GPS) is being phased in as the primary radio navigation system. This satellite-based navigation system will be the future technology for aviation internationally. The International Civil Aviation Organization (ICAO) already has endorsed the use of a global navigation satellite system (GNSS) to serve as the important element of an international system for communications, navigation, and surveillance (CNS) and air traffic management (ATM). CNS/ATM is expected to be implemented between 2000 and 2002 and will be the backbone of the concept of "free flight," which will free pilots from navigating along a predetermined route. The Federal Aviation Administration (FAA), which has the responsibility for developing and implementing U.S. radio navigation systems to ensure safe and efficient air navigation, is well on its way to implementing phases of this transition to GPS.

One of the phases being implemented in conjunction with GPS is the Wide Area Augmentation System (WAAS), which will provide navigation services for all phases of flight through Category I precision approach landings by providing a signal in space. This system will augment GPS by monitoring flights from the ground. FAA's prime contractor, Raytheon, conducted flight trials in 1999, and the WAAS performed solidly. The WAAS is expected to reach its full operational capability in 2001. The implementation of WAAS in conjunction with the introduction of CNS/ATM should provide U.S. producers of search and navigation equipment with sales opportunities as the aviation community makes the transition to WAAS avionics. The WAAS also is expected to be used extensively for numerous other civil applications in which improved accuracy, integrity, and availability are needed.

Global Market Prospects

Exports of search and navigation equipment totaled over $2.6 billion in 1998, which represented an increase of almost 4 percent from 1997. Imports totaled almost $1.3 billion in 1998, up 3.8 percent from the 1997 level. Because of their ability to provide technologically advanced equipment, U.S. suppliers were able to maintain a strong trade surplus in this industry. Increased foreign competition will result in further import growth, but the United States will continue to maintain its trade surplus.

In 1998, Canada remained the largest export market for U.S.-manufactured search and detection equipment, accounting for 16 percent of total exports. The other major export markets were Japan (12 percent), the United Kingdom (11 percent), France (8 percent), and Germany (5 percent). Those five countries accounted for approximately 51 percent of all U.S. exports (see Table 31-8).

Radar apparatus and parts for radar apparatus were the major products in this category exported from the United States. Combined, those products accounted for 31 percent of all U.S. exports. Exports of radar apparatus totaled approximately $491 million in 1998, representing an 8 percent increase from the 1997 total of $456 million. Parts for radar apparatus, which always had been the top item exported in this industry, were second in 1998, with approximately $317 million in exports. Export sales of radar apparatus were spurred by purchases from Saudi Arabia and Romania, which together constituted 25 percent of all purchases of radar apparatus. Accounting for 38 percent of the export total, Japan was the major purchaser of parts for radar apparatus.

On the import side, Canada and the UK supplied almost 37 percent of all U.S. imports for this industry. The leading prod-

TABLE 31-8: U.S. Trade Patterns in Search and Navigation Equipment[1] in 1998
(millions of dollars; percent)

Exports			Imports		
Region[2]	Value[3]	Share, %	Region[2]	Value[3]	Share, %
NAFTA	446	17	NAFTA	376	30
Latin America	118	5	Latin America	1	0
Western Europe	989	38	Western Europe	429	34
Japan/Chinese Economic Area	423	16	Japan/Chinese Economic Area	288	23
Other Asia	282	11	Other Asia	111	9
Rest of world	354	14	Rest of world	66	5
World	2,613	100	World	1,271	100
Top Five Countries	Value	Share, %	Top Five Countries	Value	Share, %
Canada	376	14	Canada	259	20
Japan	308	12	United Kingdom	204	16
United Kingdom	272	10	Japan	135	11
France	210	8	Taiwan	134	11
Germany	142	5	Mexico	117	9

[1] SIC 3812.
[2] For definitions of regional groupings, see "Getting the Most Out of *Outlook 2000*."
[3] Values may not sum to total due to rounding.
Source: U.S. Department of Commerce, Bureau of the Census.

ucts imported were radio remote control apparatus ($198 million) and radio navigational aid apparatus, reception only ($166 million). Imports have been growing at an annual average rate of 9 percent over the last 5 years.

U.S. search and navigation equipment manufacturers should be able to capture sales opportunities in domestic and foreign airport construction projects. Procurement of air traffic control (ATC) equipment would include ground-based navigational aids such as instrument landing systems (ILS), distance measuring equipment (DME), VHF omnidirectional radio ranges (VOR), radar equipment, terminal control centers, microwave landing systems, voice switching systems, secondary surveillance radars, remote control equipment, radio navigation devices, antennas, and compasses. Japan plans to build three major new airports within the next decade and has already started procuring GPS systems. German investment in navigation equipment is expected to grow rapidly as ground support equipment is needed to increase the capacity of 46 existing airports in that country. The UK also is expected to be one of the fastest-growing markets as a result of its plans to procure guidance and detection equipment. Russia, China, and some Latin American countries offer excellent sales opportunities for U.S. companies as they upgrade their existing air traffic control systems.

Procurement of radar, search, detection, and navigation equipment under NATO's Security Investment Program (NSIP) continues to provide export opportunities for U.S. manufacturers. NATO funds the construction of military facilities such as airfields and radar installations in member countries for dual-use purposes. Procurement of three-dimensional radar for Greece and Turkey was among the projects solicited in 1999. The Czech Republic, Poland, and Hungary will offer additional sales opportunities for U.S. manufacturers as those countries modernize their air defense systems to meet NATO standards. According to the General Accounting Office, Hungary and the Czech Republic plan to invest nearly $1 billion a year in their military forces by 2001 and maintain that level for several years. Poland has budgeted nearly $2.5 billion, almost a $1 billion increase, between 1999 and 2003.

Projections of Industry Growth for the Next 1 and 5 Years

Shipments of search and navigation equipment declined an estimated 3 percent in 1999, with the same rate of decline anticipated for 2000. The U.S. search and navigation industry will continue to be the world's technological leader in producing leading-edge products and should begin to experience positive growth over the next 5 years (2000–2005).

U.S. manufacturers can expect many procurement opportunities from military end users of their products. President Clinton's proposed budget authorization for fiscal years 2000–2005 calls for increasing DOD funding by an additional $112 billion. The defense appropriations bill authorized $267.8 billion, reflecting $12.6 billion in additional funding. A procurement budget of $53 billion has been allocated for fiscal year (FY) 2000, with increases projected to reach approximately $75 billion by FY 2005. A large portion of DOD procurement spending will go to modernize navigation aids. The proposed FY 2000 budget continues the implementation of DOD's comprehensive Quadrennial Defense Review (QDR), out of which initiatives to modernize and upgrade aging weapons systems often emerge. If enacted, the $112 billion in added funding over the FY 2000–2005 period will go to augment DOD's previous modernization plans. The FY 2000 budget proposed to allocate $53 billion for defense procurement, with a goal of $75.1 billion in FY 2005. This additional funding would enable the DOD to add eight ships to the U.S. Navy's shipbuilding plan and procure additional aircraft.

Modernization efforts by DOD will involve major avionics upgrades to the C-5 transport and all KC-135 tankers, replacing Navy F/A-18C aircraft and Air Force F-16 aircraft with the new Joint Strike Fighter (JSF). The National Missile Defense (NMD) program will continue to receive high priority as the United States moves to deploy a nationwide missile defense system. One of the key programs under the NMD is the Theater High Altitude Area Defense (THAAD) system. THAAD will provide a theaterwide area defense consisting of four integrated subsystems, including a radar system, a command and control station, a launcher, and missiles.

The Ballistic Missile Defense Organization (BMDO) is the technology-developing organization for the Pentagon that is responsible for technology development related to missile defense efforts. Radar development is a vital part of that effort. Research into radar technologies is expected to be one of BMDO's top priorities under its Advanced Radar Technology (ART) program. This program is the first stand-alone radar development effort in BMDO in over 5 years. Among the systems that are expected to benefit from ART are the Patriot's C-band radar, THAAD's X-band radar, NMD's Ground-Based Radar, and the ship-based Aegis radar used for both the Navy Area Wide and Navy Theater Wide programs.

Civilian applications of search and navigation equipment also will provide the impetus for future growth. As the global ATM system evolves, the market for search, detection, and navigation equipment will continue to grow. The use of GPS signals for navigation is the backbone of the new ATM system. Radio navigation equipment is also vital to the development of intelligent transportation systems (ITS). Although fleet management, in-vehicle navigation, and vehicle location services are some of the applications already in use, ITS is an emerging market that will create many opportunities for manufacturers of search and navigation equipment.

Alexis Kemper, U.S. Department of Commerce, Office of Telecommunications, (202) 482-1512, October 1999.

■ REFERENCES

General Reports and Studies

Datapro (titles listed under each section), McGraw-Hill Building, 37th Floor, 1221 Avenue of the Americas, New York, NY 10020-1095. (212) 512-2900.

Dataquest (titles listed under each section), 251 River Oaks Parkway, San Jose, CA 95134-1913. (408) 954-1780; fax: (408) 954-1780.

1999 Multimedia Telecommunications Market Review & Forecast, Multimedia Telecommunications Association & Telecommunications Industry Association, Arlington VA.

Telecom Market Report: China, India & Pacific Rim, Telecom Market Report: Latin America & the Caribbean, Wireless Local Loop: Prospects for Profits, International Technology Consultants, 4340 East-West Highway, Suite 1020, Bethesda, MD 20814-4411. (301) 907-0060; fax: (301) 907-6555; www.intl-tech.com.

Trends in the International Telecommunications Industry, Federal Communications Commission, 1919 M Street, NW, Room 539, Washington, DC 20254. (202) 467-0017.

World Telecommunications Development Report 1998, International Telecommunication Union, Geneva, Switzerland, available from Telegeography, Inc., Suite 1000, 1150 Connecticut Avenue, NW, Washington, DC 20036. (202) 467-0017.

General Publications

Communications Week International, CMP Publications, Inc., 600 Community Drive, Manhasset, NY 11030. (516) 562-5000, www.commweek.com.

Global Telephony, Telephony, Telephony Publishing Corporation, 55 East Jackson, Chicago, IL 60604. (312) 922-2435.

Telecommunications Reports, Business Research Publications, Inc., 1333 H Street, NW, 11th Floor-West, Washington, DC 20005. (202) 842-3006.

Web Sites

Allied Business Intelligence. www.alliedworld.com.

APEC Telecom Working Group. www.apec-wg.com.

Analog2Digital (Tektronix Inc.). www.analog2digital.com.

Bureau of the Census, U.S. Department of Commerce. www.census.gov/ftp/pub/industry/ma36p97.txt.

Cable Datacom News (Kinetic Strategies). CableDatacomNews.com.

CableLabs. www.cablelabs.com.

Cable Today (Phillips International). www.cabletoday.com.

Cablevision magazine. www.cvmag.com.

CATV CyberLab (Gecko Publishing). www.catv.org.

Cellular Telecommunications Industry Association. www.wow-com.com.

Communications Week. www.commweek.com.

Consumer Equipment Manufacturers' Association. www.cemacity.org.

Datapro. www.datapro.com/datapro1.html.

Dataquest. www.dataquest.com.

DigitalBroadcasting.Com. www.digitalbroadcasting.com.

DTV Online (Broadcasting & Cable). www.dtvonline.com.

Federal Communications Commission. www.fcc.gov.

Frost & Sullivan. www.frost.com.

International Cable Protection Committee (ICPC). http://elaine.teleport.com/~ptc/iscw/iscw.shtml.

International Data Corporation (IDC). www.idc.com.

International Telecommunication Union. www.itu.int.

Kagan & Associates. www.kagan.com.

National Association of Broadcasters. www.nab.org.

National Cable Television Association. www.ncta.com.

Office of Telecommunications of the International Trade Administration, U.S. Department of Commerce. www.infoserv2.ita.doc.gov/ot.

Personal Communications Industry Association. www.pcia.com.

Strategis Group. www.strategisgroup.com.

Telecom Insider. www.clnewsnet.com/telecom.html.

Telecommunications Industry Association. www.industry.net/tia.

Total Telecom. www.totaltele.com.

Veronis, Suhler & Associates, Inc. www.veronissuhler.com.

Wireless Communications Association International (WCAI). www.wcai.com.

WirelessNow (Daily Wireless Update). www.commnow.com.

Yankee Group. www.yankeegroup.com.

Network Equipment

America's Network, Advanstar Communications Inc., 131 West First Street, Duluth, MN 55802.

Central Office–North America, Dataquest, 251 River Oaks Parkway, San Jose, CA 95134-1913. (408) 468-8000.

Financial Times On Line. www.ft.com.

The Shift to Data by Two Major U.S. Suppliers, Dataquest, 251 River Oaks Parkway, San Jose, CA 95134-1913. (408) 468-8000.

Telecommunications Equipment: U.S. Performance in Selected Major Markets, December 1998, U.S. International Trade Commission, Washington, DC 20436.

Telephony, Intertec Publishing Corp., 9800 Metcalf, Overland Park, KS 66212-2215.

Total Telecom. www.totaltele.com.

World Markets for IP Telephony, Frost & Sullivan, 90 West Street, Suite 1301, New York, NY 10006.

World Public Switching Markets: 1997 Edition and Database, Northern Business Information (Dataquest) (see above).

World Transmission Equipment Markets: 1997 Edition and Database, Northern Business Information (Dataquest) (see above).

Customer Premises Equipment

1995 North American Modem Market; Modems North American Market Share and Forecast, August, 1996, Dataquest (see above).

Voice Networking Systems Strategic Analysis, July 1996; *World PBX and KTS Markets, Telefacts,* December, 1996; Datapro Information Services Group.

World PBX and KTS Markets: 1995 Edition, *U.S. PBX, KTS, and Related Markets* 1995 Edition, *U.S. Voice Processing Equipment Market:* 1994 Edition, Northern Business Information.

Broadcasting and Cable Equipment

Annual Assessment of the Status of Competition in Markets for the Delivery of Video Programming, Federal Communications Commission, 1919 M Street, NW, Room 539, Washington, DC 20254. (202) 467-0017.

Broadcasting & Cable Magazine, Cahners Business Information, 245 West 17 Street, New York, NY 10011. (212) 645-0067.

Cable Trends, International High-Speed Internet Access: The Residential Marketplace, World Two-Way Cable Modem Manufacturers, Operators, and Shipments, World Cable and Satellite Markets, The Strategis Group, 1130 Connecticut Avenue, NW, Suite 325, Washington, DC 20036-3915. (202) 530-7500; fax: (202) 530-7550.

Charting the Digital Broadcasting Future, Advisory Committee on Public Interest Obligations of Digital Television Broadcasters, The Benton Foundation, 1800 K Street NW, Second Floor, Washington DC 20006. (202) 638-5770.

Digital Broadcast 99: Worldwide Market for Digital Broadcast Systems and Equipment, CATV Infrastructure 1999, Allied Business

Intelligence, 202 Townsend Square, Oyster Bay, NY 11771. (516) 624-3113.

Industry Survey: Broadcasting & Cable, Standard & Poor's, 2 Broadway, New York, NY 10004.

International Cable, Phillips Business Information Inc., 1201 Seven Locks Road, Potomac, MD 20854.

Multichannel News, Multichannel News International Cahners Business Information, 245 West 17 Street, New York, NY 10011. (212) 645-0067.

TV International, TV International Sourcebook, Latin American Television, Asia Pacific Television, European Television, Japan: Cable and Satellite Strategy, U.S. Interactive Entertainment Forecast, DTV Market Overview and Forecasts, European Cable Telephony, TV Sourcebook, Baskerville Communications Corp., 15165 Ventura Boulevard, Suite 310, Sherman Oaks, CA 91403. (818) 461-9660; fax: (818) 461-9661.

World Television 2000, Financial Times, FT Business, Maple House, 149 Tottenham Court Road, London W1P 9LL. 44 (0) 171-896-2748.

Wireless Communications Equipment

Cellular Infrastructure Worldwide, 1992–2001 Market Trends (PERS-WW-MT-9703), December 31, 1997, Dataquest (see above).

CTIA Semi-Annual Data Survey, Cellular Telecommunications Industry Association, 1250 Connecticut Avenue, NW, Suite 200, Washington, DC 20036. (202) 785-0081; fax: (202) 785-0721.

International Cellular, Kagan World Media, Ltd., 126 Clock Tower Place, Carmel, CA 93923-8734. (408) 624-1536; fax: (408) 625-3225.

Mobile Communications International, MCI Subscriptions, Central House, 27 Park Street, Croydon CRO 1YD, United Kingdom (011) 44-081-686-5654 or (011) 44-071-383-5757; fax: 011-44-071-383-3181.

Mobile Phone News, PCS Week, Wireless Business & Finance, Phillips Business Information, Inc., 1201 Seven Locks Road, Potomac, MD 20854. (301) 340-1520; fax: (301) 424-2058; www.phillips.com.

1999 PCIA Wireless Market Portfolio, Compiled by Personal Communications Industry Association, 500 Montgomery Street, Suite 700, Alexandria, VA 22314-1561. (703) 739-0300; fax: (703) 836-1608.

Personal Communications North America (PERS-NA-MT-9701), December 15, 1997, Dataquest (see above).

RCR Radio Communications Report, RCR Publications Inc., 777 East Speer Boulevard, Denver, CO 80203. 1-800-678-9595.

3G Mobile, Global Mobile, Baskerville Communications Corp., 15165 Ventura Boulevard, Suite 310, Sherman Oaks, CA 91403. (818) 461-9660; fax: (818) 461-9661.

WirelessNOW (daily wireless update), The Strategis Group, 1130 Connecticut Avenue, NW, Suite 325, Washington, DC 20036-3915. (202) 530-7500; fax: (202) 530-7550.

Wireless Systems Outlook: 1998 The Evolving Landscape, Allied Business Intelligence, Inc., P.O. Box 452, 202 Townsend Square, Oyster Bay, NY 11771. (516) 624-3113; fax: (516) 624-3115.

Wireless Telecom Equipment, Deutsche Morgan Grenfell (DMG) Technology Group, 31 West 52 Street, New York, NY 10019. (212) 469-5000; fax: (212) 469-5381.

Wireless Week, Chilton Publications, 600 South Cherry Street, Suite 400, Denver, CO 80222. (303) 393-7449; fax: (303) 399-2034.

Search and Navigation Equipment

ATC Market Reports, 4001 North 19 Street, Suite 904, Arlington, VA 22203. (703) 524-1630.

Aviation Week & Space Technology, McGraw-Hill, 1200 G Street, NW, Suite 922, Washington, DC 20005. (202) 383-2403.

Avionics News, Aircraft Industries Association, 13700 East 42 Terrace, Suite 102, Independence, MO 64055. (816) 373-6565.

Federal Radio Navigation Plan, U.S. Department of Transportation (OST/P), Washington, DC, and U.S. Department of Defense (USD/A&T), Washington, DC 20301.

ICAO Journal, magazine of the International Civil Aviation Organization, Suite 1205, University Street, Montreal, Quebec, Canada, H3C5H7. (416) 259-9631; fax: (416) 259-9634.

Journal of Electronic Defense, Horizon House Publications, Inc., for the Association of Old Crows, The AOC Building, 1000 North Payne Street, Alexandria, VA 22314-1696.

Signal, Armed Forces Communications and Electronics Association, 4400 Fair Lakes Court, Fairfax, VA 22033-3899. (703) 631-6100.

State of the Space Industry, 1997 Outlook, KPMG Peat Marwick, 2001 M Street, NW, Washington, DC 20036. (202) 467-3083; fax: (202) 239-5437.

RELATED CHAPTERS

27: Computer Equipment
28: Software and Internet Technologies
29: Space Commerce
30: Telecommunications Services

ENTERTAINMENT AND ELECTRONIC MEDIA
Economic and Trade Trends

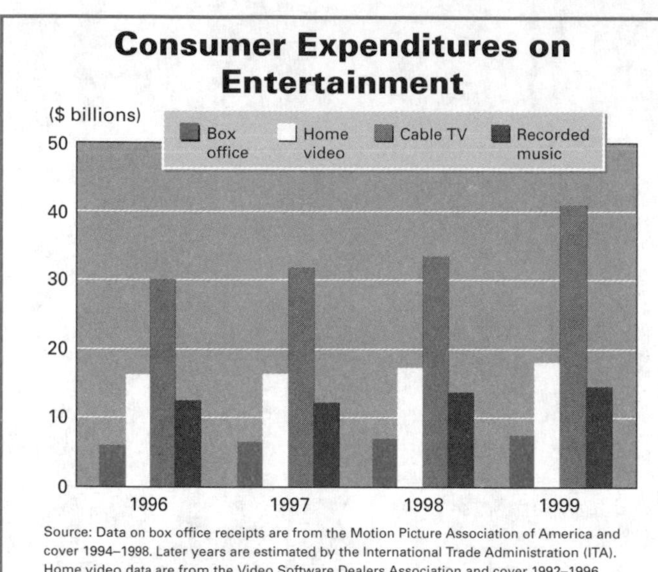

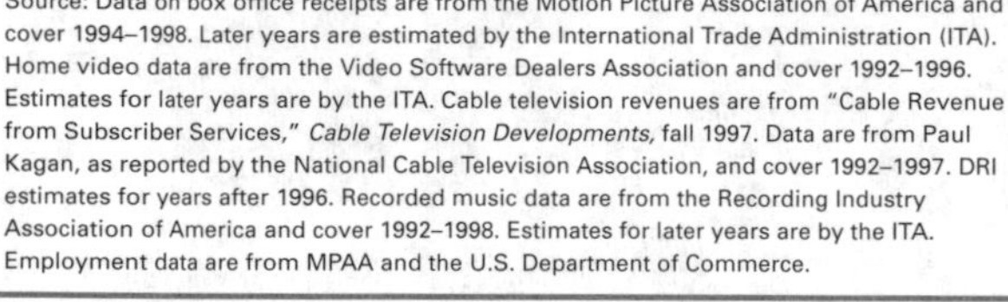

Source: Data on box office receipts are from the Motion Picture Association of America and cover 1994–1998. Later years are estimated by the International Trade Administration (ITA). Home video data are from the Video Software Dealers Association and cover 1992–1996. Estimates for later years are by the ITA. Cable television revenues are from "Cable Revenue from Subscriber Services," *Cable Television Developments*, fall 1997. Data are from Paul Kagan, as reported by the National Cable Television Association, and cover 1992–1997. DRI estimates for years after 1996. Recorded music data are from the Recording Industry Association of America and cover 1992–1998. Estimates for later years are by the ITA. Employment data are from MPAA and the U.S. Department of Commerce.

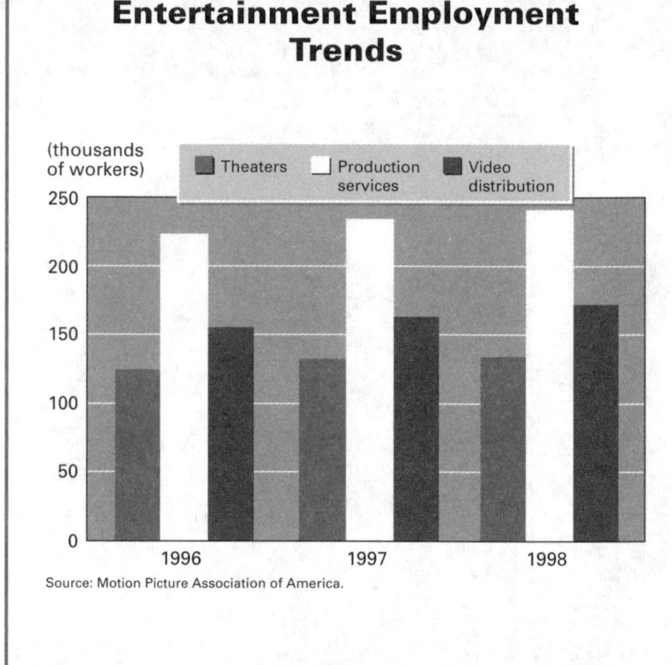

Source: Motion Picture Association of America.

Source: Data are from the BEA survey published in the *Survey of Current Business* every September. Data are available through 1997 for cross-border sales and through 1996 for sales by subsidiaries. All other figures are estimates by the International Trade Administration; U.S. payments under "Sales by foreign subsidiaries" includes sales in the United States by film companies that are subsidiaries of foreign companies.

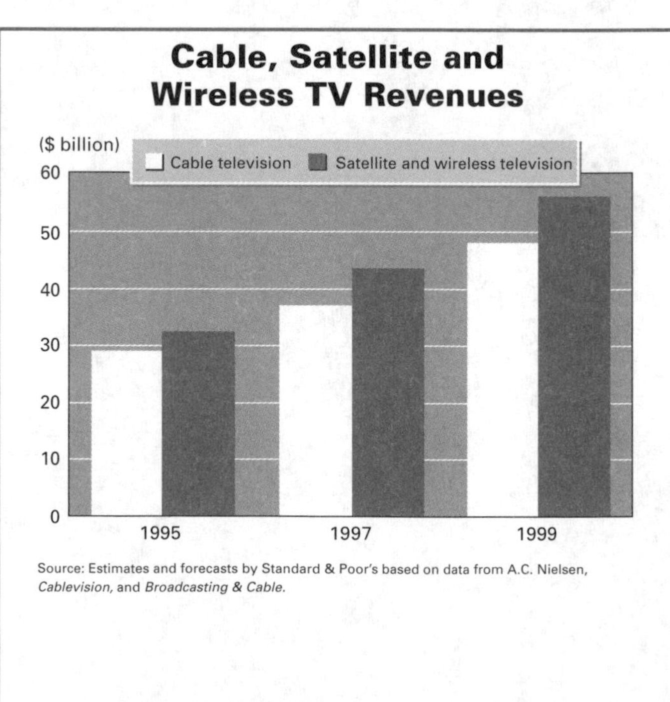

Source: Estimates and forecasts by Standard & Poor's based on data from A.C. Nielsen, *Cablevision*, and *Broadcasting & Cable*.

See "Getting the Most Out of *Outlook 2000*" for definitions of terms.

32

Entertainment and Electronic Media

INDUSTRY DEFINITION Entertainment covers recorded music and filmed entertainment, which includes movies and series television programming, whether shown on movie screens, broadcast on network or cable television, or viewed on videocassettes. The industries are motion picture and videotape production (SIC 7812), motion picture and videotape distribution (SIC 7822), motion picture theaters (SIC 783), phonograph records and prerecorded audiotapes and disks (SIC 3652), record and prerecorded tape stores, retail (SIC 5735), videotape rental (SIC 7841), radio broadcasting stations (SIC4832), television broadcasting stations (SIC 4833), and cable and other pay-television services (SIC 4841).

OVERVIEW

Global Industry Trends

The U.S. entertainment industry continues to lead the world in terms of size and revenues, and international markets are crucial to its continued success. For at least the last 5 years, those markets have accounted for about 40 percent of the revenues of the major U.S. film companies, up from 34 percent in 1988. New technology continues to offer opportunities and challenges to the entertainment industry. At the same time that growth in the videocassette and cable television markets has slowed, the digital versatile disk (DVD) and the Internet are beginning to offer new possibilities as delivery systems for entertainment programming. New technologies no doubt will continue to contribute to the worldwide success and even dominance of the U.S. entertainment industry. However, those technologies have brought new problems, primarily video piracy and the need for protection of copyrights. Adequate protection is urgent for DVD and the Internet, where recorded music is now available through MP3 technology and filmed entertainment soon will be available.

Audiovisual services, one of many service sectors covered by the General Agreement on Trade in Services (GATS), will be the subject of renewed negotiations beginning in the year 2000. The United States is one of 19 countries that have made commitments regarding audiovisual services—13 countries during the Uruguay Round and 6 countries that have acceded since 1994. These commitments can cover one or more subsectors, including principally motion picture and videotape production and distribution services, motion picture projection services, radio and television services, and sound recording. The GATS, an agreement under the World Trade Organization (WTO), is the first multilateral, legally enforceable agreement covering trade and investment in services. It includes basic trade-liberalizing rules such as most-favored-nation treatment, national treatment, market access, transparency, and the free flow of payments and transfers. In the negotiations that will begin in the year 2000, U.S. goals include increasing the number of country commitments in audiovisual trade and encouraging broader, more liberalizing commitments. Some major trading partners, such as the European Union, have not made a commitment involving audiovisual services.

Important Factors Affecting Future Growth of the U.S. Industry

Worldwide demand for U.S. entertainment remains strong and is likely to grow in the long run. Sales of U.S. entertainment both domestically and abroad will depend in part, as they always have, on general economic conditions. In addition, sales will depend on how new technologies are used to deliver entertainment and the barriers, such as weak intellectual property rights (IPR) protection, that U.S. entertainment encounters in foreign markets. New technologies include the Internet; satellite delivery systems for programming, especially Direct Broadcast Satellite (DBS); DVD; and telephone company entry into the markets for video programming and music. These technologies are expected to play an increasingly large role in the delivery of filmed entertainment and recorded music. Many industry observers believe that within a decade, the Internet will become a crucial method for delivering filmed entertainment and recorded music to homes. The rapid growth of DBS appears likely to continue through 2003.

Electronic Commerce

Internet distribution of entertainment products has grown significantly, a trend that surely will continue, but unresolved problems, principally IPR protection, may delay its full utilization. For example, increased use of the Internet will depend on meeting the needs of entertainment companies for IPR protection of programming and recorded music and nondiscriminatory access to the network for all users. The recording industry already is facing unauthorized distribution of recordings through the use of MP3 files. Aside from the Internet, trade barriers limiting market access for U.S. entertainment, coupled with a lack of IPR protection, can impede the growth of U.S. sales abroad. These trade barriers can include quotas on importing and exhibiting foreign films, import monopolies, and film censorship. Despite these problems, the outlook for U.S. entertainment abroad is good, with steady growth a likely prospect.

U.S. Industry Growth Projections for the Next 5 Years

Consumer expenditures in the United States on movies, home video, and recorded music will continue to grow through 2004. Spending by consumers totaled about $35 billion in 1997 and is expected to climb to more than $41 billion in 2000, and $49 billion in 2004 in current dollars. Between 1998 and 2000, the industry overall should grow 12.3 percent; from 2000 to 2004, growth is estimated at 19 percent. In 1998, all these subsectors of the entertainment industry improved on their 1997 results (see Table 32-1). In the case of home video, the improvement was substantial after a lackluster year in 1997. One question is whether these subsectors will continue to have such successful results through 2004. Another is whether growth projections for industry revenues will translate into high profitability. For example, the film industry continues to struggle with controlling costs, and the home video industry may face significant competition from other means of delivering entertainment (see Table 32-1).

Global Market Prospects

The Bureau of Economic Analysis (BEA) of the U.S. Department of Commerce collects official data on U.S. trade in film. Those data include recordings of film and television programming as well as home video. After 1987, total sales of filmed entertainment to foreign buyers increased from $3.73 billion to about $17 billion in 1997, with some ups and downs along the way. For at least the next 5 years, similar growth probably will continue, with neither sharp increases nor large declines.

According to the BEA, U.S. revenues from exports of film and television tape rentals totaled roughly $5 billion in 1996 and

TABLE 32-1: Trends and Forecasts in Selected Entertainment Industries
(billions of dollars except as noted)

	1992	1993	1994	1995	1996	1997	1998[1]	1999[2]	2000[2]	Percent Change 97–98	98–99	99–00	96–00[3]
Box office receipts[4]	4.9	5.2	5.4	5.5	5.9	6.4	6.9	7.4	7.8	7.8	7.2	5.4	7.2
Home video rental revenues[5]	11.8	12.8	14.2	15.0	16.2	16.3	17.2	18.0	18.7	5.5	4.7	4.4	3.7
Recorded music sales[6]	9.0	10.0	12.1	12.3	12.5	12.2	13.7	14.6	15.4	0.1	1.6	10.7	4.4
Employment (thousands)													
Theaters	110.2	110.6	113.4	118.7	123.9	131.8	133.5			1.3			
Production services	148.8	152.7	169.6	200.7	222.5	233.4	240.2			2.9			
Videotape rental	127.1	132.4	138.8	146.1	155.1	162.9	171.9			5.5			

[1] Estimate.
[2] Forecast.
[3] Compound annual growth rate.
[4] SIC 783, motion picture theaters.
[5] SIC 7841, video rental stores.
[6] SIC 3651, phonograph records and prerecorded audiotapes and disks.
Source: Data on box office receipts are from the Motion Picture Association of America and cover 1994–1998. Later years are estimated by the International Trade Administration (ITA). Home video data are from the Video Software Dealers Association and cover 1992–1996. Estimates for later years are by the ITA. Recorded music data are from the Recording Industry Association of America and cover 1992–1998. Estimates for later years are by the ITA. Employment data are from MPAA and the U.S. Department of Commerce.

TABLE 32-2: Trends & Forecasts for International Receipts and Payments (Trade) in Film and Tape Rentals: Sales by Foreign Subsidiaries of Motion Picture Companies, Including Television, Tape, and Film
(billions of dollars; percent)

	1992	1993	1994	1995	1996	1997[1]	1998[1]	1999[2]	2000[2]	Percent Change 97–98	98–99	99–00	96–00[3]
Cross-border sales													
U.S. receipts	2.6	3.3	4.4	4.8	5.0	6.2	6.9	7.6	8.2	11.3	10.1	7.9	13.2
U.S. payments	0.1	0.1	.23	.23	.25	.25	.25	.27	.29	0.0	8.0	7.4	3.8
Sales by foreign subsidiaries													
U.S. receipts	5.5	5.9	6.6	7.5	9.6	10.6	11.6	12.6	13.6	9.4	8.6	7.3	9.1
U.S. payments	7.3	6.9	7.7	8.5	9.0[4]	9.5	9.9	10.2	10.6	4.2	3.0	3.9	4.2

[1] Estimate.
[2] Forecast.
[3] Compound annual growth rate.
[4] Estimated by ITA.
Source: Data are from the BEA survey published in the *Survey of Current Business* every September. Data are available through 1997 for cross-border sales and through 1996 for sales by subsidiaries. All other figures are estimates by the International Trade Administration; U.S. payments under "Sales by foreign subsidiaries" includes sales in the United States by film companies that are subsidiaries of foreign companies.

$6.2 billion in 1997. That figure is expected to rise to $8.2 billion by the year 2000 and $10.6 billion by 2004. Foreign affiliates of the major U.S. film companies play a crucial role in distributing American films abroad. BEA data show that in 1996, foreign affiliates of U.S. companies sold $9.6 billion worth of rights to motion pictures, including television, tape, and film. Those sales are expected to rise to $13.6 billion in 2000 and $17.5 billion in 2003. BEA data include revenues from home video but do not identify them separately (see Table 32-2).

MOTION PICTURES

The motion picture subsector includes motion picture and videotape production (SIC 7812), motion picture and videocassette tape distribution (SIC 7822), and motion picture theaters (SIC 783).

Although the film industry continued to realize substantial revenues in 1998, costs continued to grow and put pressure on profits. Thus, for several months the industry emphasized reducing costs at all levels of production and distribution. The results of those cost reduction efforts may be starting to improve profitability. Thus, according to the Motion Picture Association of America (MPAA), the average cost to its members of producing a motion picture declined 1.4 percent from $53.4 million in 1997 to $52.7 million in 1998, the first decline since 1991. However, that decline followed an increase of 34 percent from 1996 to 1997, the highest year-to-year increase since 1980 (the earliest year for which data are available). The number of new film releases by MPAA member companies remained stable at 221 in 1998 compared with 219 in 1997. This minor year-to-year change may indicate growing caution in approving large new filmmaking projects, in part to reduce costs. However, releases by all U.S. companies, including independent film companies, rose from 461 in 1997 to 490 in 1998, an increase of 6.3 percent. Thus, the usually smaller independent film companies, which rely less on well-known and highly paid stars, may be affected less by these trends, although they face many problems from the major studios' marketing muscle.

The cost of distributing films, which often is handled by film production companies or their subsidiaries, has been one of the more difficult expenses to reduce. Thus, for MPAA members, the average costs of printing (making prints of films) and advertising for new releases have risen every year since 1986. According to the MPAA, the combined average costs per film of printing and advertising for its member companies in 1998 were $25.3 million, up 13.5 percent from $22.3 million in 1997; even the 13.5 percent increase was higher than the 12.2 percent increase from 1996 to 1997. Advertising costs have increased faster than have printing costs.

Theatrical exhibition of films remains the principal method for introducing new movies to the public. For the last 3 years, box office receipts have shown sizable growth, while the growth in admissions has been somewhat lower. Specifically, box office receipts increased 9.1 percent in 1998 to $6.9 billion and are expected to reach $7.4 billion in 1999 and $9.4 billion in 2004. Admissions increased from 1.39 billion in 1997 to 1.48 billion in 1998, a growth rate of 6.7 percent. After 1992, admissions increased in every year except 1995. However, the earnings of film companies from theatrical exhibition as a percentage of total revenues probably will continue their slow decline. Total revenues consist of box office, videocassette, and television revenues (see Table 32-2).

The steady increase in the number of U.S. movie screens is a sign that the exhibition industry has been profitable for both film companies and exhibitors. According to the MPAA, the total number of screens (indoor and outdoor) was 34,186 in 1998, up 8 percent from 1997. This percentage increase was slower than it had been in preceding years but maintained the trend of slight annual increases every year since 1990. Smaller increases are likely over the next few years. As a result of growth in multiplex theaters, the number of screens is five to six times the number of sites. Generally, owners of film rights and exhibitors divide box office receipts roughly in half, with the owners' share referred to as film rentals.

The need to reduce the costs of film production and distribution may be contributing to another trend that affects much of the U.S. film industry: the movement of film and TV production from the United States to foreign countries, especially Canada. Both the favorable Canadian exchange rate and provincial government incentives for film production have contributed to this trend. California in particular has been considering legislation intended to bring production back.

International

U.S. movies continue to dominate international trade in motion pictures, including film rentals (a percentage of box office receipts), videocassette rentals and sales, and sales of television rights (including pay television).

In many country markets, theatrical exhibition appears to have stabilized after declining for a number of years. As in the United States, other methods of exhibition, such as videocassettes and cable, have grown. In many regions, year-to-year results do not fit easily into long-term trends. Recently, however, some foreign markets have shown increases in film production, box office receipts, or admissions. For example, *Variety* reported that in 1998 France had a record 170 million theater admissions but French films fell to an all time low of 30 percent of box office receipts. In Latin America, box office receipts rose about 20 percent, reaching close to $800 million, thanks to new multiplex theaters and several blockbuster films. *Titanic* was a major blockbuster in many countries, contributing 5 or 10 percent of total box office receipts. It has long been true that as U.S. films acquire a share of foreign box office receipts equal to or higher than that of domestic films, protectionist sentiment is likely to grow.

Official data from the BEA for film rentals from theatrical exhibition are unavailable. The American Film Marketing Association (AFMA) publishes figures on behalf of its 140 members. The AFMA reported that its members earned $705 million from foreign film rentals in 1998, up 25 percent from $565 million in 1997. Theatrical earnings in 1998 accounted for about 31 percent of AFMA members' total foreign revenues of $2.3 billion. The MPAA has concluded that in 1997 total revenues of U.S. film companies from foreign theatrical exhibition of U.S. films were about $3 billion.

MUSIC

The music subsector includes manufacturers of phonograph records and prerecorded audiotapes and disks (SIC 3652).

Sales of prerecorded music in all formats—CDs, cassettes, vinyl records, singles, and music videos—were $13.7 billion in 1998, according to the Recording Industry Association of America (RIAA). That figure represents an increase of 12.1 percent over sales of $12.2 billion in 1997. This increase in manufacturers' dollar value—manufacturers' recommended list price for recordings—was welcome news for the industry after it had registered a 2.4 percent decline from 1996 to 1997. In addition, unit sales of 1.1 billion in 1998 also showed an increase of 5.7 percent from 1997 (see Table 32-2).

Sales growth in 1998 represented the first instance of a healthy year-to-year increase in record sales since 1994, when revenues surpassed $12 billion for the first time. The RIAA offers several reasons for the improvement in record sales in 1998: the "continued diversity of recordings, hit product releases spread throughout the year, a hot fourth quarter, and increased consumer demand for full-length CDs." The industry also noted that retailers have become more effective in managing inventories. Indeed, 1998 retail sales, referred to as total retail value by the RIAA, increased to $12.2 billion from $10.8 billion in 1997. The percentage increase in total retail value of 12.8 percent exceeded the growth rate of the industry as a whole.

Electronic Commerce

The Internet is playing an increasingly important role in making recorded music available to consumers. Sales of recorded music over the Internet are expected to grow very fast, increasing from about $200 million in 1998 to about $2.5 billion in 2003. These sales take two forms. The first is sales of CDs or cassettes ordered over the Internet. Record companies as well as retailers and other distributors have Web sites where the public can order and pay for CDs and other recorded music. The second is the downloading of music over the Internet to files on a buyer's computer. This method permits a customer to select music and create a customized CD or receive music in a digital format on a computer disk. There is a trend for record companies to position themselves, in part through acquisitions, to compete for Internet sales. Independent, or smaller, music companies tend to see the Internet as a means to improve their ability to compete with the major record companies in marketing recordings.

The recording industry views Internet piracy as a serious threat. The primary threat is from MP3 technology, which permits the posting of computer files of music, known as MP3 files, at Web sites; other Web users then can access and download those files onto their computers at no cost. The MP3 files can be played on the computer or other audio devices designed to play them. Under current conditions, these steps can be accomplished without the payment of copyright royalties. It is noteworthy that "MP3" is among the most common search terms used on Internet search engines. The RIAA views the potential harm to copyright owners from infringement on the Internet as "exponentially greater" than that from traditional piracy. To cope with the situation, the RIAA and several technology companies announced the "Secure Digital Music Initiative" (SDMI), which will attempt to develop a secure music format that would include an open architecture to provide access to recorded music, ensure interoperability among digital products and services, and provide copyright protection. In June 1999, over 100 companies agreed to specifications for a portable device for digital music, the first step in the SDMI process.

In 1998, CDs accounted for approximately $11.4 billion, or 83 percent, of all recorded music sales, a figure that has increased steadily over the last 10 years. However, the dominant position of CDs looks less secure than it did in recent years because of the rapid growth in the use of the Internet to distribute music through downloadable files, as was described above. Some industry observers believe that high-speed Internet connections for downloading music will largely replace the CD.

For the second consecutive year, the RIAA reported a continuing trend toward increased recorded music purchases by older consumers. Thus, in 1998, consumers 35 years old and older accounted for 39 percent of purchases. Purchases by young consumers, long crucial to the industry's success, accounted for a lower percentage of total purchases in 1998 (28 percent) than they did in the two preceding years (32.2 percent in 1996).

International

Two important international trends in recorded music are the increasing globalization of recorded music and the growing role of the Internet in the distribution and consumption of music. U.S. music has long been successful internationally. A recent trend is that the music of other countries has been successful in international markets. Thus, large record companies have been willing to promote pop artists from southern Asia and elsewhere, some of whom have scored major successes in the United States.

By empowering the consumer to download music into MP3 files onto a computer and make CDs, the Internet is likely to contribute to the globalization of the industry. The new technology will permit a consumer abroad to access U.S. music, download the desired music, and bypass local record stores. In many cases the price of the downloaded music compared with that of the locally sold CD may determine the consumer's decision. Industry's receptivity to Internet marketing, however, will depend on IPR protection for recordings.

Another recent trend is the increasing success of recordings of local music in competing with foreign, primarily U.S., music. Local groups may benefit from two phenomena: Current styles that are popular in the United States have not gained wide acceptance abroad, and local groups have attracted increased consumer attention in their own countries.

Despite these trends and concerns, the volume of worldwide sales of recorded music increased 3 percent in 1998 to reach $38.7 billion, according to the International Federation of the Phonographic Industry (IFPI), an international trade association based in London. World sales in 1997 were $38.1 billion. Sales growth over several years remains impressive, with 1998 sales representing an increase of 46.6 percent from 1991 sales of $26.4 billion. The United States remains the world's largest country market, with 24.1 percent of the world market in 1998.

Determining U.S. sales of music overseas is difficult, in part because, according to the RIAA and the IFPI, most major record companies use licensing agreements with foreign manufacturers to serve foreign markets. With this type of agreement, very little, if any, merchandise crosses a border, as opposed to recorded music shipped in merchandise trade. Sales of music downloaded over the Internet will further complicate the determination of foreign sales.

The U.S. government reports trade in recorded music under "records, tapes, and other recorded media for sound or other similarly recorded phenomena." Despite the more detailed product descriptions used since 1996 and further refinements in 1998 that allow better identification of exports of recorded music, uncertainty remains in regard to the volume of U.S. exports of recorded music. In any case, U.S. government data indicate that total exports of recorded music were $314 million in 1998, a decline of 15 percent from $369.3 million in 1997. The 1998 data also indicate a U.S. trade deficit of about $111.1 million, whereas the data for 1997 show a surplus of $85.4 million.

These numbers give an incomplete picture of U.S. trade in recorded music, primarily because they do not include U.S. receipts from licensing agreements with foreign record companies. U.S. licensing receipts from recorded music are certain to be large because many U.S. record companies sell to foreign markets by entering into license agreements with local companies, which then produce recorded music to meet demand in the local market. An additional problem is the valuation of recorded music shipments according to their wholesale value rather than retail value. Most industry observers believe that the percentage of total foreign recorded music revenues from licensing agreements is high, although the exact figure is unknown. Based on U.S. domestic sales in 1998 of about $13.7 billion, total sales of music worldwide of $38.7 billion, and the assumption that U.S. music accounts for about 50 percent of all sales worldwide, foreign sales of U.S. music amounted to approximately $5.7 billion.

VIDEOCASSETTES

The videocassette subsector includes videocassette rental (SIC 7841) and recorded and prerecorded tape stores (SIC 5735). Establishments that sell videotapes are more diverse than those which rent tapes and therefore fall under the SIC of the establishment's primary business, such as department stores, variety stores, grocery stores, and the like.

The retail videocassette industry consists of both the rental and the sale of videocassette tapes, and the revenue of the U.S. videocassette market includes both rental and retail sales figures. Results for the retail home video industry over the last 3 years indicate that the industry has considerable resilience but is nonetheless a mature industry that is unlikely to return to double-digit growth in the future. However, the DVD offers the retail home video industry an opportunity for diversification and renewal. After earning revenues of about $16.3 billion in 1997, a modest increase over the 1996 results, the home video industry recovered in 1998 with a 5.5 percent increase in sales and rentals to reach $17.2 billion. The largest increase was in the sell-through market (sales of videos), where sales, including those of videocassettes and DVDs, increased 9.7 percent, growing from $7.4 billion in 1997 to $8.1 billion in 1998. Over the last 2 years, the size of the sell-through market has equaled that of the rental market. Among industry commentators, it is commonplace to assert that the video business is hit-driven, and the popularity of the blockbuster hit *Titanic* contributed to the growth in sell-through business. For 1999 and 2000, the International Trade Administration (ITA) estimates that home video revenues will reach $18.7 billion and $19.4 billion, respectively.

Flat 1997 revenues at retail video outlets may have resulted in part from insufficient rental copies of hit videos on store shelves or, in industry parlance, lack of "copy depth." To remedy this problem while limiting costs, video retailers conceived a plan for "revenue sharing." Under this plan, which first was employed by independent retailers to increase the availability of titles to consumers, the video retailer pays the video supplier up front much less than the full purchase price and then pays the rest of the price from rental revenues. This system is profitable for both the retailer and the studio. On the one hand, the retailer at first pays much less than full price for a "to be rented" video, diminishing the costs and problems associated with box office failure and copy depth. On the other hand, the studios benefit as they receive a prorated payback that is based on the success of rental videos. Major players in the videocassette industry have begun to embrace revenue sharing to expand the availability of videocassettes in the rental industry and efficiency in the sell-through video market. This program, which was employed in the past primarily by independent and specialty retailers, has been undertaken by Blockbuster Video/Viacom, Inc. It also has led to tension between the independents and the large video retailers because of the independents' conviction that the large retailers have gained concessions from video suppliers that the smaller retailers cannot get.

Although sales of home videos and VCRs rose in 1998, several problems remain that are inhibiting the growth of the retail videocassette industry. The first is competition from DBS, which employs small satellite systems to deliver multichannel digital broadcasting directly to subscribing customers. DBS provides access to more movies and broadcasts than standard cable does. Given the shorter time periods (called windows) between the date of a movie's release on video and that on pay per view, DBS (and cable) has begun to make inroads in the market for videocassette rentals. DBS subscription rates through program suppliers such as DirectTV and EchoStar reached about 10 million in 1998. *DBS Digest* indicates that those sales represented strong consumer interest in the industry and that subscriptions would continue to rise in 1999.

Another issue facing the retail videocassette industry is DVD. This industry poses a threat to videocassettes, since DVDs provide better picture and sound quality and versatility, often for a lower price than that of a standard videocassette. According to *DVD Wire,* DVD player sales were expected to increase over 265 percent from 1998 to 1999, reaching more than 1 million players. In response, over 10 million DVD movies have been sold in the United States, with sales continuing to rise. However, this concept appears not to be a significant threat to retail video stores, since those stores could shift to rental and sales of the new format.

Digital Video Express (DIVX) is a service closely related to the DVD home video product. The DIVX technology was developed for the purpose of competing with retail video stores. The consumer rents a DIVX disc from a retailer and then, through a modem connection on the DIVX player, receives 48 hours of unlimited viewing of the movie. After that period is over, the consumer has the option to purchase the right to view the movie for a new period or simply dispose of the disk. The consumer can also pay, via modem, to receive unlimited viewing of the recorded materials. These pay-per-view DVD discs were slow to gain popularity with consumers, and production and sales were halted in late 1999.

Despite the maturity of the rental home video industry and competition from DBS, DVD, and cable television, the industry seems to be holding its own, with profitability assured for many years to come. Whereas rentals of prerecorded home videos were flat in 1997, sales of tapes increased, and sales of VCRs have continued to rise over the past 2 years. VCR penetration into U.S. households remains on the rise, increasing from 80.1 percent of television households in 1997 to an all-time high of 84.1 percent in 1998. This increase in sales seems to be closely related to eroding prices of VCRs and the increased availability of lower-priced VCRs.

International

The continued popularity of U.S. filmed entertainment in foreign markets appears to indicate that home videos of U.S. filmed entertainment also will be popular. Thus, revenues of U.S. film companies from foreign countries should continue to be a strong contributor to the total foreign revenues of those companies. The MPAA estimated that in 1997 foreign home video revenues of all U.S. film companies were $4.4 billion, or about 36 percent of total foreign revenues of about $12.3 billion. That percentage is almost the same as the percentage of film companies' home video revenues in the U.S. market. In addition, the AFMA, which publishes the foreign revenues of its 140 independent film company members, reports that in 1998, AFMA members earned foreign revenues of $643 million from home video in foreign countries, or 28 percent of their total foreign revenues. Finally, *Variety* reports that the VHS format has not yet faced competition from the new DVD technology.

John Siegmund, U.S. Department of Commerce, Office of Service Industries, (202) 482-4781, August 1999.

CABLE TELECOMMUNICATIONS

The cable telecommunications subsector (SIC 48) includes cable system operators that transmit programming over their systems to cable subscribers.

Cable television is a delivery system that provides from 30 to several hundred channels of video programming to subscribers through a coaxial cable or optical fiber network connected to the subscriber's television set. For a monthly fee, subscribers receive basic cable service and have the option to subscribe to additional channels of video programming, audio, and other services for extra monthly fees.

Unlike broadcast television stations, cable system operators derive most of their revenues from monthly subscriber fees. In addition to recurring subscriber programming revenues, cablers get revenues from installation charges, sales of pay-per-view movies and events, set-top converter rentals, remote control sales and rentals, advertising, and carriage fees from home shopping channels and other, including advertorial and infomercial, presenters.

In recent years, the industry has upgraded the technological capabilities of its broadband network so that in addition to the services outlined above, cablers offer new services such as digital video, high-speed Internet access, local and long-distance telephone service, and commercial competitive local exchange carrier operations. High-definition television, video on demand, and E-commerce are among the newest offerings.

Total revenues for U.S. cable system operators, including subscription fees, advertising, new services, and other fees and charges, are expected to increase nearly 15 percent in the year 2000 after an estimated 14 percent rise in 1999. The average annual rate of gain through 2004 is projected at over 15.4 percent (see Table 32-3). Those gains reflect several positive factors, including explosive growth in new broadband services; an increase in the number of subscribers; price inflation; growth in demand for higher-priced programming packages, including digital services; and strong advertising revenues.

Although cable television is a relatively mature industry, it continues to experience moderate growth in the number of subscribers, largely because of gains in household formation but also as a result of gains in household penetration. The number of U.S. cable subscribers should grow roughly 2.2 percent in the year 2000, followed by increases in the narrow range of 1.9 percent to 2.9 percent in each year through 2004. The average annual rate of growth in the 5 years through 2004 should be roughly 2.2 percent.

These gains continue in spite of explosive growth in DBS service. The inroads of DBS into cable's market thus far have been relatively minor. DBS systems provide sharper, clearer pictures than does cable and also provide more programming choices. Both factors are becoming less advantageous with the cable industry's current roll-out of digital broadband capabilities. Beginning in 1998, cable began to make a significant start in upgrading to digital system delivery, which provides exceptional picture quality and superior channel capacity. DBS has several shortcomings relative to cable, including cost. Although prices continue to drop, the customer bears the cost of the DBS dish and its installation and maintenance. With cable, equipment costs and maintenance are borne by the cable system operator. In most markets, DBS subscribers cannot receive locally originated over-the-air broadcast signals but must put up a rabbit-ear antenna or subscribe to cable to receive the local channels. That explains why roughly one-fourth of DBS subscribers also subscribe to cable. DBS reception is limited to one television set per household unless there is a special hookup for a second set. More than two television sets require additional DBS dishes. Furthermore, without another special hookup, all the sets in a DBS household must be tuned to the same program. Cable systems do not have those limitations. In addition, DBS reception can be lost or disturbed in bad weather. In November 1999, the House passed a satellite television bill that will allow customers to receive local channels. The measure, which probably will gain senatorial and presidential approval eventually, is aimed at putting DBS on a more equal footing with cable. It is doubtful whether the eased restrictions will have much of an impact on cable subscriber growth, largely because DBS operators plan to tack another $5 to $6 or more on to subscribers' monthly bills. DBS will still have drawbacks relative to cable.

In addition to sustained subscriber growth, cable is benefiting from rising rates charged for service. Passed in 1992, the Cable Television Consumer Protection and Competition Act reimposed rate regulation on the industry and forced some operators to lower their rates for basic service packages such as equipment rental and installation. Then the Telecommunications Act of 1996 put in place a regulatory framework in which cablers have been allowed to raise rates for various services, depending on a number of factors. Because of the politically sensitive nature of cable charges, few operators have taken full advantage of the increases allowed by the Federal Communications Commission (FCC). Nevertheless, rate hikes have been generous in comparison to inflation, averaging an estimated 6.5 percent in each of the 4 years through 1990. (Those rates actually declined in 1994, reflecting the impact of the 1992 act.) Average price hikes of 6 to 7 percent through 2004 are expected in spite of the phasing out of the regulatory guidelines and ceilings.

Although cablers are spending heavily to upgrade their systems and program offerings, escalating programming costs are also a major driver of the rising rates to subscribers. Not only are cablers

TABLE 32-3: Cable Television Trends and Forecasts
(billions of dollars except as noted)

	1995	1996	1997	1998	1999	2000	2001	2002	2003	2004
Cable Subscribers (millions)	61.5	63.1	65.0	67.0	68.4	69.9	71.1	72.7	74.8	76.2
Basic subscription revenues	15.2	17.0	18.4	20.3	22.5	24.7	27.8	30.5	34.1	37.4
Advertising revenues	5.1	6.4	7.5	9.1	11.8	15.0	18.0	21.6	25.5	32.1
Other revenues	9.1	9.9	11.1	12.6	14.2	16.7	19.4	22.7	26.8	31.2
Total cable revenues	29.4	33.3	37	42	48.5	56.4	65.2	74.8	86.4	100.7

Source: S&P estimates and forecasts based on data from A.C. Nielsen, *CableVision,* and *Broadcasting & Cable.*

adding channels each year, cable program suppliers are hiking their fees substantially. Many of the programming cost increases are justified by higher spending to acquire sports, news, original and first-run movies, and other programming. Cable's enhanced program offerings draw new subscribers and draw existing subscribers to the more expensive programming packages.

Cablers' advertising revenues continue to grow rapidly, outpacing the growth rate of both television and radio. U.S. cable advertising revenues are expected to advance roughly 22 percent on average each year through 2004 (see Table 32-3) and 27 percent in 2000. (Roughly one-third of advertising revenues on cable accrues directly to cable system operators from sources such as infomercials and advertisements sold on some syndicated programs; roughly two-thirds of the advertising revenue goes into the coffers of cable networks such as American Movie Classics and Nickelodeon for advertisements sold on their programs.) Special marketing and promotions related to the new millennium have boosted advertising in 1999 and 2000. The Summer Olympics in 2000 and 2004 and the Winter Olympics in 2002 also will provide a boost to cable advertising in those years.

William H. Donald, Standard & Poor's, (212) 208-8153, November 1999.

SATELLITE AND WIRELESS TECHNOLOGY

The sky appears to be the limit for satellite and wireless technology in the new millennium. DBS companies are gaining strength by bypassing ground-based lines and beaming their signals directly into consumers' homes. Direct-to-home (DTH) companies currently employ DBS, DISH, SMATV, and MMDS technologies.

Ever since the first 18-inch satellite dish was placed on a house roof in early 1995, the primary industry participants have consistently lowered the price and stepped up their marketing efforts. At the forefront of this effort have been the industry leaders GM Hughes (with its DIRECTV service) and EchoStar Communications (with the DISH Network). Dish prices have plunged from their initial $1,000-plus price tag to become quite reasonable (generally priced from $149 to $239) with some pre-paid programming. Installation initially was a big issue but has become an add-in, with personal installation kits included with systems (professional installation usually costs between $49 and $99). With the price of the hardware becoming less of an issue, operators have been focusing on adding channels (some systems offer more than 200 channels) and leveraging digital audio and video capabilities. These companies are poised to offer one-way Internet access, with two-way service being at least a couple of years away.

DBS operators are projected to produce annual subscriber growth of 17 percent in the 6 years through 2005 (Table 32-4). Projected subscriber additions of about 36 percent in 1999 will be tempered by about 7.5 percent growth in 2005. Industry revenues during that time period should expand about 15 percent on average. Companies initially lost money on the cost of acquiring customers but are recouping much of this loss through the additional premium packages offered. The industry has risen from a subscriber base of 8.7 million and revenues of over $7 billion in 1998 to an expected 23 million subscribers and $19 billion of revenues by 2005.

The rapid growth of and impact on the cable market by DBS can no longer be ignored. The growth rate for cable subscriptions has declined to a 2 percent per year pace, with this sector's market share and growth prospects viewed as possibly passing the mature phase and heading for the decline stage. DBS systems, with their digitally enhanced clear picture and sound, have become not only a viable complement to cable but also its potential replacement. With AT&T entering the cable market in recent months, this slide will be slowed somewhat by the

TABLE 32-4: Satellite and Wireless TV Trends and Forecasts
(billions of dollars except as noted)

	1995	1996	1997	1998	1999	2000	2001	2002	2003
Direct broadcast satellite									
Subscribers (millions)	2.3	4.4	6.2	8.2	11.2	14.5	18.9	24.0	30.0
Revenues	1.5	3.3	4.8	6.8	8.0	11.2	14.0	17.3	20.9
Wireless (MMDS)									
Subscribers (millions)	0.8	1.2	1	1	0.9	0.9	0.9	0.9	0.9
Revenues	0.4	0.6	0.5	0.5	0.5	0.5	0.5	0.6	0.6
Satellite master antenna (SMATV)									
Subscribers (millions)	0.9	0.8	1	1.1	1.1	1.1	1.2	1.2	1.3
Revenues	0.4	0.3	0.5	0.6	0.6	0.7	0.8	0.9	1
Satellite dish (C-band/Ku band)									
Subscribers (millions)	1.8	1.7	1.6	1.4	1.2	1.2	1.1	1	1
Revenues	0.7	0.7	0.7	0.7	0.8	0.8	0.8	0.8	0.8
Total revenues for all segments	32.4	38.2	43.5	49.8	56.1	63.5	71.5	80.1	92.1

Source: Standard & Poor's; A.C. Nielsen; Cablevision; Broadcasting & Cable; Multichannel News Online; DBS Dish.com!; skyreport.com. Forecasts by Standard & Poor's.

upgrading of cable wires to broadcast a digital signal. However, the gap between DBS and cable continues to narrow as price becomes less of an issue. DBS also has broken the local logjam, and its systems now carry locally originated over-the-air broadcast signals. DBS is projected to become a competitor to cable and eventually an important complement to consumer communications systems that utilize telephony. The industry must devise hardware that can convert a signal into reception on all the television sets in a household. The extra cost of purchasing a second dish, or converter, seems to be pushing consumers who are on the fence over to cable.

The outlook for other DTH technologies is not as rosy as that for DBS or even its slower-growing counterpart, cable. With roughly 1 million subscribers, a level that has remained stable for a number of years, wireless (or MMDS) has been limited by poor visibility, weak signal quality, and limited channel capability. This system, which is based on microwave broadcasts to huge rooftop or backyard antennas, has all but been replaced by the smaller, more capable DBS systems. The C-band (backyard satellite dish) market also has declined and should have worsening prospects over the next 5 years. These systems will continue to be nonentities in the industry, clearing the way for the battle between cable and DBS. As cable wires are updated, it will become a more difficult fight for DBS operators looking to compete on the basis of quality. The battle essentially will be won through price and breadth of service offered. To this point, cable has the stability and price and DBS has a huge channel offering. The race has just begun, and a clear winner may not emerge for a number of years.

Phil Wohl, Standard & Poor's, (212) 438-9511, November 1999.

RADIO AND TELEVISION BROADCASTING

Radio broadcasting refers to the transmission of sound. Television signals—technically another form of radio—involve the transmission of both visual and aural content. With federal deregulation, the number of U.S. radio stations expanded from roughly 10,500 in 1985 to 12,582 on July 31, 1999. In the United States, commercial television broadcasting is conducted on 68 channels. The U.S. television market is the largest in the world, served by 1,229 commercial television stations—668 UHF stations and 561 VHF stations—as of July 31, 1999.

Radio and television stations derive the bulk of their revenues from advertising. In each market, stations use program formats and on-air talent to attract specific demographic audiences. A station's program ratings (audience size measures), the time of day the advertising runs, and the demographic qualities—mainly age and sex—of each program's typical listener or viewer determine the advertising rates station owners charge and the attractiveness of a station or program to advertisers.

Factors Affecting U.S. Industry Growth

Size and clout are becoming more important for broadcasters. The radio and television industries consist of tens of thousands of individual companies, most of which are small business operations. Within each segment, however, the biggest players claim a disproportionately large share of business, and the industries are becoming more top-heavy each year.

Audience size and demographic range are sought so that broadcasters can woo large national advertisers. At the same time, broadcasters are narrowing their focus, usually on a station-by-station or program-by-program basis, to attract narrowly defined audiences with distinct consumer profiles that appeal to particular advertisers. The challenge of reaching these niche groups is magnified by their growing elusiveness. Expanded choices for consumers and media users essentially splinter audiences, making them hard to target and making it even harder to reach them with an advertising pitch.

The Big Three television networks—ABC, CBS, and NBC—generally take in more than 40 percent of the broadcast television industry's annual advertising revenues and as much as 47 percent or more in winter or summer olympics years. The top 25 owners of television stations together controlled 36 percent of the more than 1,200 U.S. commercial television stations as of January 1999, up from 33 percent in 1997 and 25 percent in 1996.

In general, the Big Three networks' (their combined affiliates number roughly 650 television stations) share of the prime-time television audience has declined over the last few decades. That share has been whittled away in recent years by the growing popularity and availability of cable television (see Table 32-3), the success of the 12-year-old Fox network, and, since January 1995, the growth of two new networks: United Paramount Network (UPN) and Warner Brothers Television Network (WB).

The 10 largest radio broadcasters, which own about 14 percent of all U.S. stations, accounted for nearly 41 percent of radio industry advertising revenues in 1998. In 1996, the 15 largest owners of radio stations controlled 6 percent of the stations and accounted for 34 percent of advertising revenues.

Facilitating this trend toward consolidation, and thus the reshaping of radio and television, are the Telecommunications Act of 1996, rules changes by the FCC, and other recent federal legislation.

Most recently, in August 1999 the FCC revised its local market television ownership rules—the "TV duopoly" rule and the radio-television cross-ownership (or "one-to-a-market") rule—to reflect dynamic changes in the U.S. media marketplace. These changes include rapid growth in the number and variety of media outlets in local markets, including cable, the Internet, and DBS.

The changes in the duopoly rule permit common ownership of two television stations within the same Nielsen Designated Market Area (DMA) if eight full-power independent television stations (commercial and noncommercial) remain after the merger and one of the stations is not among the top four stations in the market on the basis of audience share.

Cross-ownership rule changes permit a party to own a television station and a second television station if that is permited under the new duopoly rules, plus any of the following radio station combinations in the same market:

- Up to six radio stations (any combination of AM or FM stations) in any market where at least 20 independent voices remain after a merger
- Up to four radio stations (any combination of AM or FM stations) in any market where at least 10 independent voices remain after a merger
- One radio station (AM or FM) notwithstanding the number of independent voices in the market

The FCC let stand its rule prohibiting television broadcasters from owning stations reaching more than 35 percent of the nation's television households. The loosened rules have been a particular boon for television stations, since radio already had received a powerful boost to its fortunes from the FCC's relaxation of ownership rules when it passed the landmark Telecommunications Act of 1996. With the passage of that act, one owner was given the right to own up to 20 FM and 20 AM radio stations in any market. Now the largest companies own hundreds of radio stations. Consolidation and station trading should remain robust for the foreseeable future.

Consolidation allows the centralization of back-office functions such as advertising sales, billing, and marketing. In some instances, combining certain operations in the news rooms also has saved owners money. Cost savings are being redeployed successfully into programming and advertising sales efforts as well as other areas, such as facilities upgrades. The concentration of ownership across local markets and regions appeals to advertisers and advertising agencies as well. Marketers can reach larger markets and wider audiences with fewer ad buys. This one-stop-shopping concept boosts the attractiveness of radio as an advertising medium whether the advertiser is a local merchant, a regional advertiser, or a national marketer. The recent loosening of television ownership rules should provide that industry group with some of the same benefits radio has been enjoying.

Radio and television broadcasters will benefit from several unusual events in the near future. Both will receive additional mileage from advertising and marketing programs related to the new millennium in both 1999 and 2000. Although the old millennium technically closes on December 31, 2000, the event was celebrated at the end of 1999 as well. Although the leisure and entertainment industries will be at the forefront of this marketing opportunity, all marketers can be expected to take advantage of this once-in-a-lifetime occurrence. There will be untold opportunities to market consumer products in "collector's editions," "limited editions," "boxed gift sets," and so forth. One can expect to see greater marketing of items and services such as cars, toys, magazines, books, mementos, alcoholic beverages, hotels, restaurants, airlines, and vacation packages.

With 2000 and 2004 being presidential election years, advertising spending will be boosted by advertising related to the national elections. Those 2 years will also contain the Summer Olympics, whose impact on television is substantial: The Olympics could add to revenues over $800 million in 2000 and over $1.1 billion in 2004. In addition, the year 2002 will include the Winter Olympics, which also boosts spending on television advertising.

Dire predictions that the Internet would spell death for traditional media advertising—that the new medium would supplant advertising in newspapers and magazines, on television and radio, and in outdoor media—have not come true. On the contrary, the outlook for traditional media advertising is as bright as ever. Ironically, radio and television, along with other traditional media, are seeing a surge in advertising from the very businesses that are supposed to be putting them out of business. Some of the largest gains in advertising in traditional media have come from the new media.

Companies that are promoting new media enterprises are savvy enough to know that they must quickly establish their service as a "name brand" or be drowned out by others trying to make a name for themselves. The contestants span the spectrum, ranging from AT&T Corp., America Online Inc., and Microsoft Corp., which are promoting new services in the areas of telecommunications, broadband/digital, on-line, and software, to relative newcomers such as Yahoo Inc., eBay Inc., Ameritrade Holding Corp., Amazon.com Inc., and theglobe.com. These companies must reach large audiences quickly not only to establish their brands but also to drum up business.

Although penetration is rising rapidly, only about 37 million homes (37 percent of U.S. households) have Internet access. By comparison, some 98 percent of American households have televisions; more than 123 million people read newspapers on a daily basis; 99 percent of U.S. households have radio, with an average of 5.6 radios per household; billboards are ubiquitous; and in any given month, 367 million magazines are purchased at newsstands or by subscription in the United States. Thus, while advertising in cyberspace is exploding (it nearly doubled to almost $2 billion in 1998), traditional media also are benefiting. No change in these ratios is foreseen any time in the near future.

U.S. Industry Growth Projections for the Next 1 and 5 Years

The outlook for radio and broadcast television advertising is good both on a relative basis (compared with the growth of total U.S. advertising) and on an absolute dollar basis. In addition to the factors cited above, advertising demand will be bolstered over the next 5 years by a fairly healthy U.S. economy, although one that is likely to grow only at a moderate pace. Viewed as a whole, the radio and broadcast television industries should increase their share of the total U.S. advertising market over the next 5 years. Broadcast television garnered nearly 20 percent of total U.S. advertising in 1998, up from 17 percent in 1993, while radio accounted for close to 8 percent of total advertising spending in all media (compared with nearly 7 percent in 1993). By 2004, the share of broadcast television should be nearly 21 percent, while radio's share should be over 9 percent.

Combined advertising spending in broadcast television and radio is expected to rise to $67.5 billion in 2000, up 13 percent from the $59.7 billion estimated for 1999 (see Table 32-5). Combined gains should average 9.1 percent in each of the 5 years through 2004.

Radio was expected to exhibit the stronger growth of the two media, advancing 12 percent in the year 2000 after registering a

TABLE 32-5: Radio and Television Advertising Revenues, Trends and Forecasts
(millions of dollars)

	1995	1996	1997	1998	1999	2000	2001	2002	2003	2004
Broadcast television	27,919	31,270	36,890	39,170	42,250	48,000	50,500	54,600	57,700	63,639
Radio	11,470	12,410	13,490	15,410	17,445	19,520	21,710	23,880	26,300	28,670
Total	39,389	43,680	50,380	54,580	59,695	67,520	72,210	78,480	84,000	92,309

Source: Television Bureau of Advertising; Radio Advertising Bureau. Forecasts by Standard & Poor's.

more than 13 percent gain in 1999. Radio's average annual growth in the 5 years through 2004 should be 10.4 percent.

Radio and television advertising will benefit from the factors enumerated above, including ownership deregulation; an explosion in new media, technologies, and services; and one-time events. In addition, advertising is benefiting from a healthy economy, buoyant consumer confidence, and a continuing shift from trade promotions to consumer advertising and business-to-business advertising. As the business environment changes in response to deregulation in telecommunications and advances in technology, advertisers in various segments should continue to intensify their marketing programs to keep up with the competition. As was noted above, brand building among the newer media also is fueling growth.

William H. Donald, Standard & Poor's, (212) 208-8153, November 1999.

REFERENCES

Call the Bureau of the Census at (301) 457-2820 for information on ordering Census documents.

Government Publications

Annual Survey of Communication Services: 1997, U.S. Department of Commerce, Bureau of the Census, Washington, DC 20230. (301) 457-2766. The report covers telephone communications services, broadcasting services, and cable and other pay television services. www.census.gov/svsd/www/ascs/html.

Census of Service Industries, U.S. Department of Commerce, Bureau of the Census, Washington, DC 20233. (301) 457-2668, www.census.gov/econ/waa/servmenu.htm#services.

U.S. International Sales and Purchases of Services, Survey of Current Business, Bureau of Economic Analysis, U.S. Department of Commerce, Washington, D.C. 20230, October 1998. (202) 606-9573, www.bea.doc.gov/bea/ai1.htm.

Industry Associations

American Film Marketing Association, Suite 600, 10850 Wilshire Boulevard, 9th Floor, Los Angeles, CA 90024. (310) 446-1000, www.afma.com.

Motion Picture Association of America, Inc., 1600 Eye Street, NW, Washington, DC 20006. (202) 293-1966, www.mpaa.org.

National Association of Theater Owners, 4605 Lankershim Boulevard, Suite 340, North Hollywood, CA 91602. (818) 506-1778.

National Cable Television Association, 1724 Massachusetts Avenue, NW, Washington, DC 20036. (202) 775-3680, www.cable-online.com/ncta.htm.

Recording Industry Association of America, Suite 300, 1330 Connecticut Avenue, NW, Washington, DC 20036. (202) 775-0101, www.riaa.com.

Video Software Dealers Association (VSDA), 16530 Ventura Boulevard, Encino, CA 91436. (818) 385-1500, www.vsda.com.

Publications

Billboard, Billboard Publications, Inc., 1515 Broadway, New York, NY 10036. (202) 764-7300, www.billboard-online.com.

Boxoffice, RLD Communications, Inc., 1800 North Highland Avenue, Hollywood, CA 90028. (213) 465-1186.

Broadcasting and Cable, Broadcasting Publications, Inc., 1735 DeSales Street, NW, Washington, DC 20036. (202) 659-2340, www.broadcastingcable.com.

Movie & Home Entertainment, Standard and Poor's, October 2, 1997, 25 Broadway, New York, NY 10004.

Variety, Variety, Inc., 154 West 46 St., New York, NY 10036. (212) 779-1100, www.variety.com.

Consulting Companies

Alexander & Associates, 38 East 29 Street, 10th Floor, New York, NY 10016. (212) 684-0291.

Cambridge Associates, Inc., 157 Breezy Hill Road, Stamford, CT 06903. (203) 322-6600.

Paul Kagan Associates, Inc., 126 Clock Tower Place, Carmel, CA 93923. (408) 624-1536.

Veronis, Suhler & Associates, 350 Park Avenue, New York, NY 10022. (212) 935-4990.

Radio and Television Broadcasting and Cable

Advertising Age, Crain Communications, 220 East 42 Street, New York, NY 10017. (800) 992-9970, http://www.adage.com.

American Demographics, Cowles Business Media, 108 North Cayuga Street, Ithaca, NY 14850. (800) 828-1133, http://www.demographics.com.

Broadcasting & Cable, Cahners Publishing Co., 245 West 17 Street, New York, NY 10011. (212) 645-0067, World Wide Web: http://www.broadcastingcable.com.

Cable Television Advertising Bureau (CAB), 757 Third Avenue, New York, NY 10017. (212) 751-7770, http://www.cableTVadbureau.com.

CableVision, Chilton Publications, 245 West 17 Street, New York, NY 10011. (212) 645-0067, http://www.cablevisionmag.com.

DBS Dish.com, http://www.dbsdish.com.

Federal Communications Commission (FCC), 1919 M Street, NW, Washington, DC 20554. (202) 632-7260, http://www.fcc.gov.

Multichannel News Online, Cahners Business Information, http://www.multichannel.com.

National Association of Broadcasters (NAB), 1771 N Street, NW, Washington, DC 20036. (202) 429-5366, http://www.nab.org.

National Cable Television Association (NCTA), 1724 Massachusetts Avenue, NW, Washington, DC 20036. (202) 775-3550, http://www.cableonline.com/ncta.htm.

Radio Advertising Bureau (RAB), 261 Madison Avenue, New York, NY 10016. (212) 681-7200, http://www.rab.com.

Radio Business Report and *Radio Business Source Guide,* Radio Business Report, 6208-B Old Franconia Road, Alexandria, VA 22310. (703) 719-9500.

Television Bureau of Advertising (TVB), 850 Third Avenue, New York, NY 10022. (212) 486-1111.

TVB News, Television Bureau of Advertising, 850 Third Avenue, New York, NY 10022. (212) 486-1111.

Variety, Variety Publications, 475 Park Avenue South, New York, NY 10016. (212) 779-1100, http://www.variety.com.

Veronis, Suhler & Associates, 350 Park Avenue, New York, NY 10022. (212) 935-4990, http://www.vsacomm.com.

RELATED CHAPTERS

29: Space Commerce

APPAREL AND FABRICATED TEXTILE PRODUCTS
Economic and Trade Trends

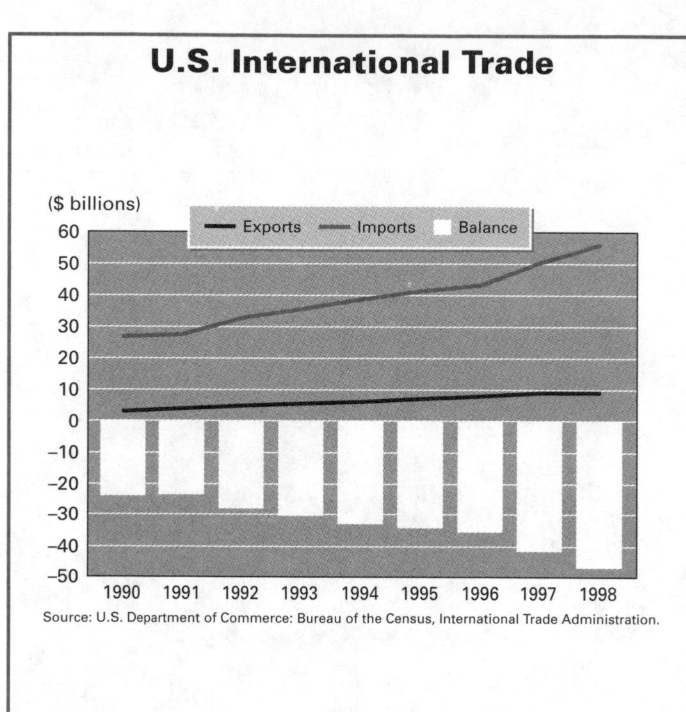

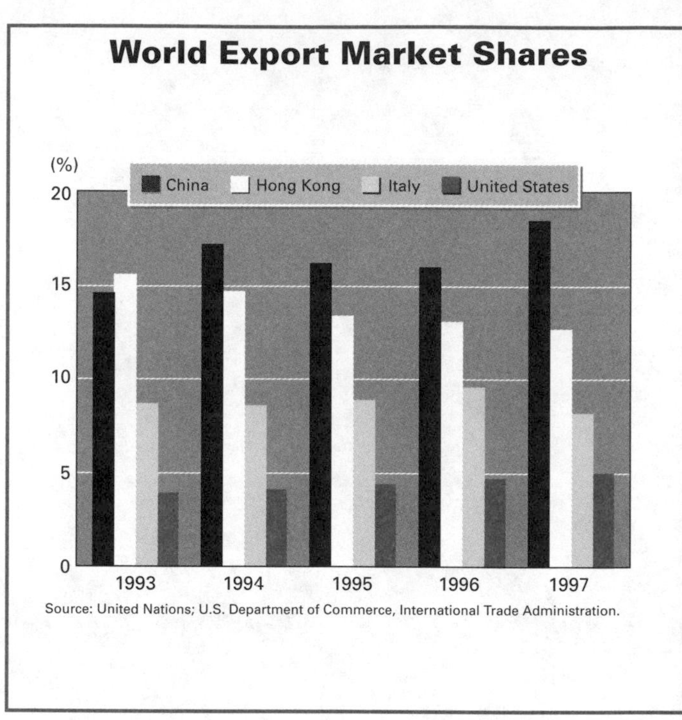

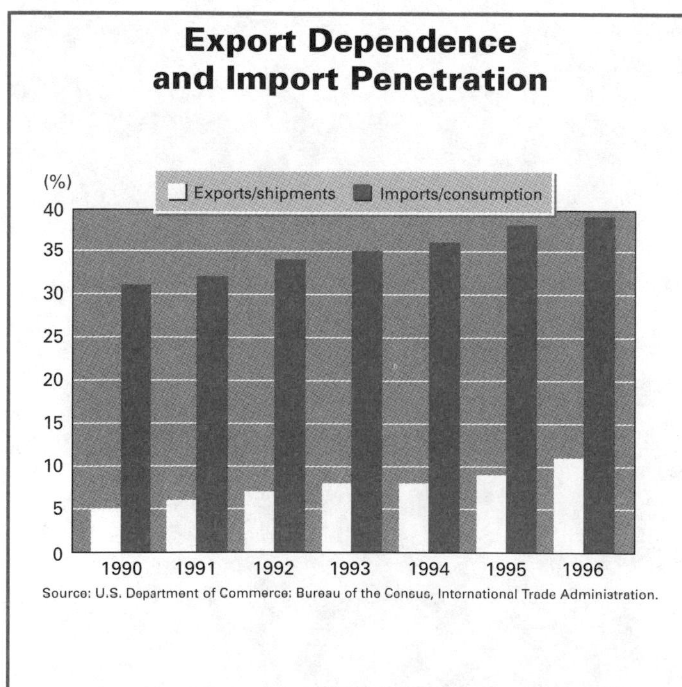

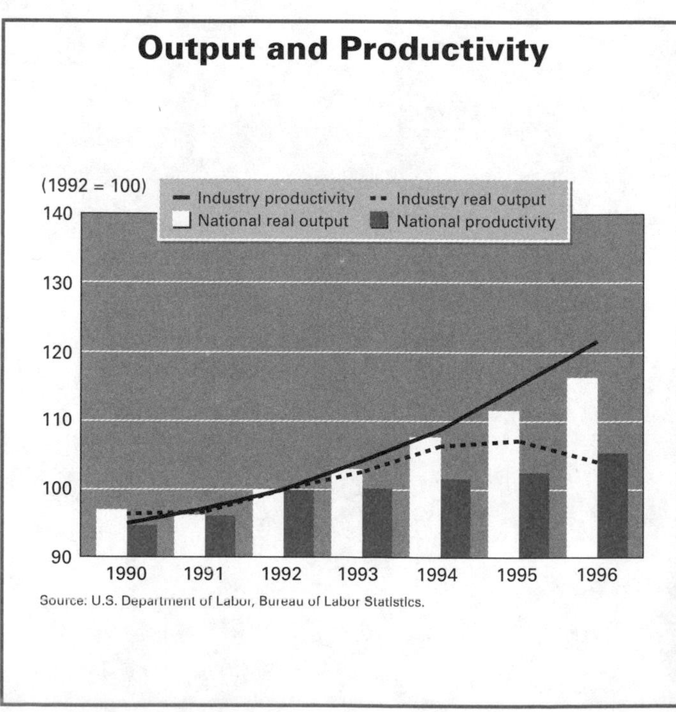

See "Getting the Most Out of *Outlook 2000*" for definitions of terms.

33

Apparel and Fabricated Textile Products

INDUSTRY DEFINITION SIC 23 covers 31 distinct four-digit industries. Those industries fall into the following nine groupings, as defined by the third SIC digit: men's and boys' suits, coats, and overcoats (231); men's and boys' furnishings, work clothing, and allied garments (232); women's, misses', and juniors' outerwear (233); women's, misses', children's, and infants' undergarments (234); hats, caps, and millinery (235); girls', children's, and infants' outerwear (236); fur goods (237); miscellaneous apparel and accessories (238); and miscellaneous fabricated textile products (239). The fabricated textile products industry consists of eight four-digit industry SIC groups: curtains and draperies (2391), home furnishings (2392), textile bags (2393), canvas and related products (2394), pleating and stitching (2395), automotive and apparel trimmings (2396), schiffli machine embroideries (2397), and fabricated textile products not elsewhere classified (2399). Products in the last group include miscellaneous items such as banners and flags, sleeping bags, nondisposable diapers, fishing nets, parachutes, and seat belts.

OVERVIEW

The products covered in this chapter are a diverse group, ranging from suits to fishing nets and from neckwear to draperies. They are all products of a mature industry that continues to face intense competition from growing levels of imports. As in other industries, globalization, technological advances, and changing business practices are changing the way companies do business and where they do business. The industry is trying to become more efficient and productive by restructuring and reorganizing, but many times these moves have led to employment declines and plant closings or relocation to offshore production.

The apparel and fabricated textile products industry consists primarily of firms that produce and coordinate the production of wearing apparel, both cut and sewn and knit to shape, for all population groups. Apparel accounted for 70 percent of total SIC 23 shipments in 1998, while fabricated textile products, which include home furnishings, canvas products, and automotive trimmings, accounted for 30 percent. Those shares are unchanged from the previous 2 years.

FACTORS AFFECTING FUTURE INDUSTRY GROWTH

The growth of the U.S. apparel and fabricated textile products industry has been slow (see Table 33-1). The industry's future growth depends on several factors, including the health of the U.S. economy, changing demographics, industry price trends, ability to meet the challenge of increasing imports, growth in exports, and the effects of new and expiring trade agreements.

The gross domestic product (GDP) is growing steadily, inflation remains lower than it has been in the past 40 years, interest rates have risen slightly but are still low, employment growth remains strong, joblessness is at its lowest level in three decades, consumer confidence is high, and expectations are that the econ-

TABLE 33-1: Apparel and Fabricated Textile Products (SIC 23) Trends and Forecasts
(millions of dollars except as noted)

	1992	1993	1994	1995	1996	1997[1]	1998[1]	1999[2]	2000[3]	Percent Change 97–98	98–99	99–00	96–00[4]
Industry data													
Value of shipments[5]	71,658	74,010	76,979	78,103	77,628	79,025	76,496	76,879	77,602	–3.2	0.5	0.9	–0.0
Value of shipments ($1992)	71,658	73,339	76,063	76,601	74,976	75,645	72,403	72,503	72,612	–4.3	0.1	0.1	–0.8
Total employment (thousands)	985	980	954	947	865								
Production workers (thousands)	824	825	799	792	726								
Average hourly earnings ($)	7.12	7.34	7.44	7.56	7.67								
Product data													
Value of shipments[5]	68,844	70,986	73,258	73,780	73,319	74,639	72,250	72,612	73,294	–3.2	0.5	0.9	–0.0
Value of shipments ($1992)	68,844	70,345	72,382	72,370	70,843	71,446	68,384	68,479	68,581	–4.3	0.1	0.1	–0.8
Trade data													
Value of imports	32,658	35,485	38,571	41,219	43,087	50,203	55,864	59,551	65,441	11.3	6.6	9.9	11.0
Value of exports	4,767	5,505	6,099	7,061	7,905	8,988	9,032	8,806	9,186	0.5	–2.5	4.3	3.8

[1] Estimate except imports and exports.
[2] Estimate.
[3] Forecast.
[4] Compound annual rate.
[5] For a definition of industry versus product values, see "Getting the Most Out of *Outlook 2000*."
Source: U.S. Department of Commerce: Bureau of the Census; International Trade Administration.

omy will continue to grow. Growth in consumer spending has contributed a significant portion of overall economic growth.

Consumer expenditures for clothing did not keep up with overall consumer spending in the earlier part of the decade. Between 1990 and 1997, total consumer spending grew at a faster rate than did spending for clothing. In 1998–1999, however, that trend reversed and apparel expenditures outpaced overall spending. Between 1997 and midyear 1999, overall consumer expenditures rose an average of 5.4 percent per year while expenditures for clothing rose 6.3 percent per year.

Apparel demand is influenced by a variety of factors, including demographic trends. Growth in the number of households headed by baby boomers (born between 1946 and 1964), who are in their prime earning years, accounts for a large portion of apparel sales. The members of the "echo boom" (also known as generation Y), the children of baby boomers, are becoming significant consumers in their own right. Teens have more available income than ever before and have an impact on apparel spending as they prefer to buy trendy and brand name clothes, while older echo boomers are establishing their own households. Significant growth in the population of older Americans also bodes well for apparel spending. Those consumers are less concerned about fashion and concentrate more on comfort and function, spurring demand for casual clothing.

A trend that is accelerating spending on casual clothing is the movement toward dressing down in the workplace. "Casual Fridays" are being adopted at more companies each year. The practice is accepted at major firms as well as smaller companies. In addition, casual Fridays have led some companies to soften dress codes or adopt a more casual dress code on other days. Other companies have relaxed dress codes for the summer months. The trend toward dressing down in the workplace has led to sharply higher sales of casual dress. Indeed, more articles of casual attire can be purchased with the same funds that would be spent on tailored clothing, because casual clothing is less expensive. While dressing down for work has been a boon to apparel companies that have taken advantage of the trend, it has led to significant production and employment declines for companies that specialize in tailored clothing.

As with other consumer items, the focus in apparel spending is on value. Consumers are demanding higher-quality apparel at lower prices. This demand is being met largely through low-priced imports that exert downward pressure on the prices of domestically produced apparel. As a result of these import and pricing pressures, U.S. apparel producers are not benefiting significantly from greater personal consumption expenditures on apparel.

GLOBAL INDUSTRY TRENDS

U.S. producers of apparel and fabricated textile products continue to face intense global competition from more sources than ever before. Low-cost imports from traditional Asian suppliers coupled with imports from new suppliers continue to put pressure on domestic manufacturers to cut costs in order to remain competitive in the domestic market (see Table 33-2). Apparel production sharing arrangements under the North American Free Trade Agreement (NAFTA) and the Caribbean Basin Initiative (CBI) have helped domestic manufacturers compete with imports from the Far East.

Under production sharing arrangements in the CBI countries and Mexico, U.S. firms export apparel components to those countries for assembly and return to the United States so that they can qualify for quota preferences and, in the case of Mexico, tariff preferences. Offshore operations enable domestic manufacturers to take advantage of lower wages for labor-intensive assembly operations in the CBI nations and Mexico

TABLE 33-2: U.S. Trade Patterns in Apparel and Fabricated Textile Products[1] in 1998
(millions of dollars; percent)

Exports			Imports		
Region[2]	Value[3]	Share, %	Region[2]	Value[3]	Share, %
NAFTA	3,687	41	NAFTA	9,399	17
Latin America	3,952	44	Latin America	8,914	16
Western Europe	512	6	Western Europe	3,834	7
Japan/Chinese Economic Area	583	6	Japan/Chinese Economic Area	14,753	26
Other Asia	66	1	Other Asia	16,062	29
Rest of world	231	3	Rest of world	2,902	5
World	9,032	100	World	55,864	100
Top Five Countries	Value	Share, %	Top Five Countries	Value	Share, %
Mexico	2,715	30	China	7,795	14
Dominican Republic	1,100	12	Mexico	7,692	14
Honduras	1,001	11	Hong Kong	4,497	8
Canada	972	11	Taiwan	2,373	4
Japan	500	6	Dominican Republic	2,336	4

[1] SIC 23.
[2] For definitions of regional groupings, see "Getting the Most Out of *Outlook 2000*."
[3] Values may not sum to total due to rounding.
Source: U.S. Department of Commerce, Bureau of the Census.

while retaining in the United States capital- and knowledge-intensive operations such as product design, marketing, and distribution. Until recently, most products sent offshore for assembly required simple assembly operations, standardized runs, and few changes. In an effort to reduce their costs further, U.S. apparel producers are expanding their production sharing operations to assemble garments requiring higher levels of sewing skills. Some large apparel manufacturing companies are cutting costs and providing better service to consumers by consolidating or divesting company-owned manufacturing facilities in favor of forming new partnership-oriented sourcing strategies in which buyers and sellers are encouraged to form long-term relationships based on mutual dependencies.

Much of the growth in U.S. apparel imports can be attributed to Mexico, as U.S. apparel firms continue to seek an advantage from the duty and quota provisions offered by NAFTA. More than two-thirds of U.S. imports from Mexico are made up of U.S. components, in contrast to Asian imports, which use virtually no U.S. components. Mexico caught up with China as the largest supplier of U.S. apparel in 1998 with a 13 percent share of the total, up from 11 percent a year earlier. China's share of total apparel imports declined from 15 percent in 1997 to 13 percent in 1998 (see Table 33-3). Imports from the CBI countries, which had been posting significant increases during the previous few years, increased 8 percent in 1998. CBI countries continued to lose share of the assembly market to Mexico

TABLE 33-3: U.S. Trade Patterns in Selected Apparel[1] in 1998
(millions of dollars; percent)

Exports			Imports		
Region[2]	Value[3]	Share, %	Region[2]	Value[3]	Share, %
NAFTA	2,637	40	NAFTA	7,962	16
Latin America	2,883	44	Latin America	8,782	17
Western Europe	377	6	Western Europe	3,251	6
Japan/Chinese Economic Area	471	7	Japan/Chinese Economic Area	13,215	26
Other Asia	32	0	Other Asia	14,951	29
Rest of world	132	2	Rest of world	2,734	5
World	6,532	100	World	50,895	100
Top Five Countries	Value	Share, %	Top Five Countries	Value	Share, %
Mexico	2,095	32	China	6,606	13
Dominican Republic	842	13	Mexico	6,581	13
Honduras	658	10	Hong Kong	4,466	9
Canada	542	8	Dominican Republic	2,318	5
Japan	419	6	Taiwan	2,087	4

[1] SIC 231, 232, 233, 234, 235, 236, 238.
[2] For definitions of regional groupings, see "Getting the Most Out of *Outlook 2000*."
[3] Values may not sum to total due to rounding.
Source: U.S. Department of Commerce, Bureau of the Census.

because of Mexico's preferential access to the United States. Imports from the traditional big four suppliers (China, Hong Kong, Taiwan, and South Korea) continued to lose share of the U.S. market to imports from Mexico and the CBI countries. However, other Asian countries, particularly those which experienced serious economic crisis, aided by inexpensive inputs and devalued currencies, increased their share of total imports to the United States.

As global competition intensifies in the coming years, imports probably will continue to increase. Mexico probably will continue to expand its share of U.S. imports as U.S. apparel producers and suppliers of apparel fabric relocate their operations to that country. CBI countries, in the absence of NAFTA-equivalent duty and quota treatment, will continue to lose share to Mexico. Various proposals for "Caribbean Basin Trade Enhancement" have been introduced by the administration and Congress in recent years. Those proposals differ in specifics, but in general they would provide CBI beneficiary countries with access to the U.S. apparel market similar to that accorded to Mexico under the terms of NAFTA, particularly for products made from U.S. components.

Of particular relevance to U.S. manufacturers is the elimination of apparel quotas on imports as mandated by the World Trade Organization (WTO) Agreement on Textiles and Clothing. On December 31, 2004, the phaseout of quotas will be complete for current members of WTO. This undoubtedly will intensify competition from low-cost suppliers in Asia and heighten the importance of preferential arrangements that offer benefits for products made from U.S. components.

DOMESTIC TRENDS

The U.S. apparel and fabricated textile products industry is highly fragmented and quite labor-intensive. Of the approximately 24,000 establishments producing apparel and fabricated textile products, nearly two-fifths are establishments with four or fewer employees. More than half these establishments have fewer than 100 but more than 4 employees. The remaining establishments are mainly large-scale operations. In some industry segments, such as underwear and jeans, a few companies command very large market shares.

Employment trends in the industry have been downward. Just over 670,000 workers were employed in the apparel and fabricated textile products industry in mid-1999, less than half the number employed during the peak years of the early 1970s. Employment declines occurred across all industry segments except fabricated textile products, where employment has held steady for several years. To remain competitive, many U.S. companies have downsized or restructured. Other, financially weaker firms have gone out of business or have been acquired by other companies. Several companies, both large and small, announced significant layoffs in the last few years. Production jobs account for more than 80 percent of total employment, compared with 69 percent for all U.S. manufacturing. Industry productivity has increased sharply. Output per hour in the industry increased 29 percent between 1990 and 1996, the latest year for which data are available.

Industry wages are typically lower than those in other manufacturing industries because apparel production jobs tend to require fewer skills. Average hourly earnings increased an average of 1.9 percent per year from 1992 to 1996 and are estimated to have grown at a rate of 3.8 percent through midyear 1999. The sharpest increases from 1992 to 1996 occurred in men's neckwear and work clothing (see Table 33-4). Average hourly earnings in several categories declined, including men's and boys' underwear (see Table 33-5), some women's undergarments (see Table 33-6), and women's blouses (see Table 33-7). Some companies are having trouble finding enough workers to operate their businesses because of the availability of higher-wage jobs in other industries. The main industry union, the Union of Needletrades, Industrial and Textile Employees (UNITE), organized several more assembly plants in the last year.

While wages have increased, prices for apparel and fabricated textile products have stagnated, continuing the trend of the last few years. Wholesale prices for industry products grew only 2 percent between 1996 and mid-1999. During that period, consumer prices for apparel declined by more than 3 percent. Consumer prices for all items, including apparel, increased more than 6 percent during that period. Retail prices for men's and boys' apparel showed little change over the period, but retail prices for women's and girls' clothing declined sharply. These price trends reflected the intense competition and anti-inflationary pressures in the overall market and also, in the retail price data, the impact of increased imports of lower-priced apparel from other countries.

Retail sales of apparel and accessory stores picked up in 1998 and 1999, as did sales of apparel through catalogs and the Internet, as consumers increased spending on apparel. As consumers searched for value, however, they shifted more of their purchases from traditional apparel sales sources to discount stores, which accounted for nearly one-half of all apparel sales in 1998. One way stores are fighting to remain competitive is by merging. In 1998, six department store chains accounted for 90 percent of all department store apparel sales. The concentration of retail sales among a decreasing number of large retailers has emboldened those companies to demand price and other concessions from suppliers. As consumers spend less time shopping in stores, price, quality, variety, and value have become more important in the effort to capture retail dollars. Retailers' determination to hold or reduce price levels and, until the last year, increases in the prices of raw materials have led to a profit squeeze on U.S. apparel producers.

Structural Changes

Restructuring trends in the apparel and fabricated textile products industry continue unabated. Restructuring has taken two forms: (1) mergers and (2) reorganization of companies to include more overseas sourcing at the expense of domestic manufacturing, with a concentration on design and marketing.

TABLE 33-4: Selected Men's and Boys' Apparel (SIC 231, 2321, 2323, 2325, 2326) Trends and Forecasts

(millions of dollars except as noted)

	1992	1993	1994	1995	1996	1997[1]	1998[1]	1999[2]	2000[3]	Percent Change 97–98	98–99	99–00	96–00[4]
Industry data													
Value of shipments[5]	16,991	16,819	17,088	17,426	17,208	17,440	16,906	16,992	17,130	−3.1	0.5	0.8	−0.1
231 Men's/boys' suits/coats	2,430	2,463	2,362	2,078	1,968	1,988	1,933	1,936	1,947	−2.8	0.1	0.6	−0.3
2321 Men's/boys' shirts	5,921	5,012	5,082	5,186	4,939	5,045	4,852	4,874	4,903	−3.8	0.4	0.6	−0.2
2323 Men's/boys' neckwear	618	619	705	792	652	597	641	640	647	7.3	−0.0	1.1	−0.2
2325 Men's/boys' trousers	6,519	7,055	7,226	7,506	7,658	7,785	7,523	7,569	7,641	−3.4	0.6	1.0	−0.1
2326 Men's/boys' work clothing	1,503	1,670	1,714	1,863	1,991	2,025	1,956	1,973	1,991	−3.4	0.9	0.9	0.0
Value of shipments ($1992)	16,991	16,538	16,669	16,837	16,437	16,635	15,991	15,982	15,937	−3.9	−0.1	−0.3	−0.8
231 Men's/boys' suits/coats	2,430	2,471	2,338	2,044	1,915	1,909	1,783	1,756	1,754	−6.6	−1.6	−0.1	−2.2
2321 Men's/boys' shirts	5,921	4,938	5,017	5,104	4,880	5,021	4,948	5,025	5,040	−1.4	1.6	0.3	0.8
2323 Men's/boys' neckwear	618	611	695	772	628	569	606	602	603	6.6	−0.8	0.2	−1.0
2325 Men's/boys' trousers	6,519	6,889	6,975	7,169	7,190	7,293	6,888	6,831	6,794	−5.6	−0.8	−0.5	−1.4
2326 Men's/boys' work clothing	1,503	1,629	1,644	1,748	1,823	1,843	1,766	1,768	1,746	−4.2	0.1	−1.2	−1.1
Total employment (thousands)	245	229	225	216	185								
231 Men's/boys' suits/coats	44.0	41.2	34.0	31.1	27.1								
2321 Men's/boys' shirts	84.4	72.7	73.8	71.0	59.1								
2323 Men's/boys' neckwear	7.5	6.3	6.2	5.6	4.7	4.9							
2325 Men's/boys' trousers	78.9	78.5	82.2	79.4	70.9								
2326 Men's/boys' work clothing	30.4	30.0	28.5	28.6	23.4								
Production workers (thousands)	214	199	197	190	163								
231 Men's/boys' suits/coats	37.4	34.7	28.7	26.3	22.2								
2321 Men's/boys' shirts	74.2	64.1	67.0	64.4	53.1								
2323 Men's/boys' neckwear	5.8	4.8	4.6	4.0	3.5	3.8							
2325 Men's/boys' trousers	69.8	68.4	71.9	70.4	64.3								
2326 Men's/boys' work clothing	26.4	26.5	24.4	24.8	19.6								
Average hourly earnings ($)	6.94	7.21	7.18	7.45	7.67								
231 Men's/boys' suits/coats	7.96	8.32	8.35	8.13	8.40								
2321 Men's/boys' shirts	6.85	6.90	6.96	7.20	7.38								
2323 Men's/boys' neckwear	7.39	8.43	9.21	9.82	10.16								
2325 Men's/boys' trousers	6.81	7.15	7.03	7.40	7.69								
2326 Men's/boys' work clothing	6.06	6.47	6.49	7.19	7.17								
Product data													
Value of shipments[5]	15,810	15,405	16,129	16,096	15,441	15,660	15,170	15,247	15,370	−3.1	0.5	0.8	−0.1
231 Men's/boys' suits/coats	2,387	2,257	2,417	2,020	1,913	1,933	1,879	1,882	1,893	−2.8	0.1	0.6	−0.3
2321 Men's/boys' shirts	5,318	4,632	4,709	4,792	4,303	4,395	4,227	4,246	4,271	−3.8	0.4	0.6	−0.2
2323 Men's/boys' neckwear	544	529	594	618	574	537	564	564	570	5.0	−0.0	1.1	−0.2
2325 Men's/boys' trousers	6,065	6,338	6,636	6,771	6,757	6,869	6,638	6,679	6,742	−3.4	0.6	1.0	−0.1
2326 Men's/boys' work clothing	1,495	1,650	1,773	1,895	1,894	1,926	1,861	1,877	1,894	−3.4	0.9	0.9	0.0
Value of shipments ($1992)	15,810	15,147	15,733	15,550	14,744	14,930	14,335	14,324	14,282	−4.0	−0.1	−0.3	−0.8
231 Men's/boys' suits/coats	2,387	2,263	2,393	1,986	1,861	1,856	1,733	1,706	1,705	−6.6	−1.6	−0.1	−2.2
2321 Men's/boys' shirts	5,318	4,563	4,649	4,717	4,252	4,374	4,311	4,378	4,391	−1.4	1.6	0.3	0.8
2323 Men's/boys' neckwear	544	521	586	602	553	512	534	530	530	4.3	−0.8	0.2	−1.0
2325 Men's/boys' trousers	6,065	6,190	6,405	6,467	6,344	6,435	6,077	6,028	5,995	−5.6	−0.8	−0.5	−1.4
2326 Men's/boys' work clothing	1,495	1,609	1,700	1,777	1,734	1,753	1,680	1,682	1,661	−4.2	0.1	−1.2	−1.1
Trade data													
Value of imports	6,792	7,500	8,376	9,845	10,372	12,075	13,909	15,228	16,971	15.2	9.5	11.4	13.1
231 Men's/boys' suits/coats	768	829	999	1,036	1,110	1,242	1,385	1,424	1,561	11.5	2.8	9.6	8.9
2321 Men's/boys' shirts	4,020	4,511	4,908	5,865	6,001	6,806	7,793	8,237	9,105	14.5	5.7	10.5	11.0
2323 Men's/boys' neckwear	151	158	156	167	174	184	186	199	206	1.4	6.9	3.6	4.4
2325 Men's/boys' trousers	1,853	2,002	2,313	2,777	3,087	3,843	4,545	5,368	6,098	18.3	18.1	13.6	18.6
2326 Men's/boys' work clothing	0	0	0	0	0	0	0	0	0				
Value of exports	1,310	1,578	1,765	1,854	2,068	2,388	2,253	2,429	2,536	−5.7	7.8	4.4	5.2
231 Men's/boys' suits/coats	121	133	170	157	143	136	95	79	75	−30.1	−17.0	−5.1	−14.9
2321 Men's/boys' shirts	467	612	734	854	953	1,147	1,098	1,270	1,349	−4.3	15.7	6.2	9.1
2323 Men's/boys' neckwear	15.5	21.1	17.9	18.4	21.1	20.6	17.6	10.8	9.7	−14.6	−38.4	−10.7	−17.7
2325 Men's/boys' trousers	707	813	844	825	952	1,084	1,042	1,069	1,102	−3.9	2.6	3.1	3.7
2326 Men's/boys' work clothing	0	0	0	0	0	0	0	0	0				

[1] Estimate except imports and exports.
[2] Estimate.
[3] Forecast.
[4] Compound annual rate.
[5] For a definition of industry versus product values, see "Getting the Most Out of *Outlook 2000*."
Source: U.S. Department of Commerce: Bureau of the Census; International Trade Administration.

TABLE 33-5: Men's and Boys' Underwear and Nightwear (SIC 2322) Trends and Forecasts

(millions of dollars except as noted)

	1992	1993	1994	1995	1996	1997[1]	1998[1]	1999[2]	2000[3]	Percent Change 97–98	98–99	99–00	96–00[4]
Industry data													
Value of shipments[5]	820	581	664	592	590	595	602	608	614	1.1	1.0	1.0	1.0
Value of shipments ($1992)	820	578	660	586	578	576	580	589	592	0.6	1.6	0.5	0.6
Total employment (thousands)	14.2	11.3	10.5	7.8	6.9								
Production workers (thousands)	13.1	10.5	10.1	7.5	6.5								
Average hourly earnings ($)	6.67	6.48	7.03	7.10	6.46								
Product data													
Value of shipments[5]	808	689	743	674	578	583	590	596	601	1.1	1.0	1.0	1.0
Value of shipments ($1992)	808	685	738	667	567	565	568	577	580	0.6	1.6	0.5	0.6
Trade data													
Value of imports	396	529	652	963	1,229	1,662	1,892	2,096	2,417	13.8	10.8	15.3	18.4
Value of exports	237	343	361	470	566	715	695	887	972	−2.8	27.6	9.6	14.5

[1] Estimate except imports and exports.
[2] Estimate.
[3] Forecast.
[4] Compound annual rate.
[5] For a definition of industry versus product values, see "Getting the Most Out of *Outlook 2000.*"
Source: U.S. Department of Commerce: Bureau of the Census; International Trade Administration.

TABLE 33-6: Women's and Children's Undergarments (SIC 234) Trends and Forecasts

(millions of dollars except as noted)

	1992	1993	1994	1995	1996	1997[1]	1998[1]	1999[2]	2000[3]	Percent Change 97–98	98–99	99–00	96–00[4]
Industry data													
Value of shipments[5]	3,943	3,943	4,245	4,577	4,244	4,301	4,182	4,191	4,243	−2.8	0.2	1.2	−0.0
2341 Women's/child underwear	2,368	2,155	2,438	2,494	2,330	2,356	2,296	2,298	2,322	−2.5	0.1	1.0	−0.1
2342 Bras and allied garments	1,575	1,789	1,807	2,083	1,914	1,946	1,886	1,892	1,921	−3.1	0.3	1.5	0.1
Value of shipments ($1992)	3,943	3,884	4,129	4,418	4,071	4,096	3,953	3,926	3,934	−3.5	−0.7	0.2	−0.9
2341 Women's/child underwear	2,368	2,135	2,390	2,431	2,264	2,280	2,215	2,208	2,214	−2.9	−0.3	0.3	−0.6
2342 Bras and allied garments	1,575	1,748	1,739	1,988	1,807	1,816	1,739	1,719	1,720	−4.3	−1.1	0.1	−1.2
Total employment (thousands)	53.7	52.1	47.1	45.9	38.1								
2341 Women's/child underwear	41.6	38.0	33.5	30.2	25.5								
2342 Bras and allied garments	12.1	14.1	13.6	15.7	12.6								
Production workers (thousands)	45.4	43.7	39.4	38.0	32.0								
2341 Women's/child underwear	35.8	33.0	29.0	26.3	22.6								
2342 Bras and allied garments	9.6	10.7	10.4	11.7	9.4								
Average hourly earnings ($)	6.74	6.89	6.70	7.01	7.31								
2341 Women's/child underwear	6.46	6.54	6.51	6.96	7.21								
2342 Bras and allied garments	7.80	7.93	7.22	7.09	7.53								
Product data													
Value of shipments[5]	3,821	3,587	3,917	4,180	3,922	3,975	3,864	3,872	3,921	−2.8	0.2	1.3	−0.0
2341 Women's/child underwear	2,237	1,928	2,128	2,135	1,980	2,002	1,951	1,953	1,973	−2.5	0.1	1.0	−0.1
2342 Bras and allied garments	1,584	1,659	1,789	2,045	1,941	1,973	1,913	1,919	1,948	−3.1	0.3	1.5	0.1
Value of shipments ($1992)	3,821	3,532	3,808	4,032	3,758	3,779	3,645	3,619	3,626	−3.5	−0.7	0.2	−0.9
2341 Women's/child underwear	2,237	1,911	2,086	2,081	1,924	1,937	1,882	1,876	1,881	−2.9	−0.3	0.3	−0.6
2342 Bras and allied garments	1,584	1,621	1,722	1,951	1,833	1,842	1,763	1,743	1,744	−4.3	−1.1	0.1	−1.2
Trade data													
Value of imports	1,519	1,787	2,067	2,442	2,492	2,885	3,285	3,849	4,355	13.9	17.2	13.1	15.0
2341 Women's/child underwear	985	1,168	1,342	1,540	1,646	1,938	2,200	2,462	2,799	13.5	11.9	13.7	14.2
2342 Bras and allied garments	534	619	725	902	845	946	1,085	1,388	1,556	14.7	27.9	12.2	16.5
Value of exports	407	466	521	654	650	816	771	839	921	−5.5	8.8	9.8	9.1
2341 Women's/child underwear	155	186	222	267	273	347	306	301	327	−11.8	−1.7	8.5	4.6
2342 Bras and allied garments	252	280	299	387	376	468	465	538	595	−0.8	15.8	10.5	12.1

[1] Estimate except imports and exports.
[2] Estimate.
[3] Forecast.
[4] Compound annual rate.
[5] For a definition of industry versus product values, see "Getting the Most Out of *Outlook 2000.*"
Source: U.S. Department of Commerce: Bureau of the Census; International Trade Administration.

TABLE 33-7: Selected Women's Outerwear (SIC 2331, 2335, 2337) Trends and Forecasts
(millions of dollars except as noted)

	1992	1993	1994	1995	1996	1997[1]	1998[1]	1999[2]	2000[3]	Percent Change 97–98	98–99	99–00	96–00[4]
Industry data													
Value of shipments[5]	13,733	14,123	14,598	14,413	13,851	14,117	13,775	13,879	14,001	−2.4	0.8	0.9	0.3
2331 Women's/misses blouses	3,970	4,012	4,147	3,797	3,649	3,700	3,623	3,634	3,669	−2.1	0.3	0.9	0.1
2335 Women's/misses dresses	5,366	5,602	6,396	6,928	6,606	6,730	6,571	6,632	6,696	−2.4	0.9	1.0	0.3
2337 Women's suits and coats	4,397	4,509	4,055	3,688	3,596	3,687	3,581	3,612	3,636	−2.9	0.9	0.7	0.3
Value of shipments ($1992)	13,733	14,063	14,644	14,604	14,248	14,567	14,068	14,150	14,369	−3.4	0.6	1.5	0.2
2331 Women's/misses blouses	3,970	3,976	4,053	3,686	3,563	3,651	3,543	3,544	3,556	−2.9	0.0	0.4	−0.0
2335 Women's/misses dresses	5,366	5,597	6,507	7,128	6,896	6,992	6,773	6,847	6,983	−3.1	1.1	2.0	0.3
2337 Women's suits and coats	4,397	4,491	4,084	3,790	3,789	3,924	3,752	3,758	3,830	−4.4	0.2	1.9	0.3
Total employment (thousands)	188	190	182	186	169								
2331 Women's/misses blouses	56.1	52.9	51.8	47.8	42.9								
2335 Women's/misses dresses	83.2	87.1	87.5	99.3	93.3								
2337 Women's suits and coats	48.3	49.6	43.1	38.8	33.0								
Production workers (thousands)	156	159	151	156	143								
2331 Women's/misses blouses	47.1	44.7	42.2	39.3	35.6								
2335 Women's/misses dresses	71.0	74.5	74.8	85.1	80.5								
2337 Women's suits and coats	37.8	40.0	34.1	31.1	26.8								
Average hourly earnings ($)	6.88	7.02	7.09	6.99	6.92								
2331 Women's/misses blouses	6.44	6.96	6.61	6.55	6.35								
2335 Women's/misses dresses	6.82	6.71	7.10	6.93	6.87								
2337 Women's suits and coats	7.56	7.64	7.68	7.75	7.95								
Product data													
Value of shipments[5]	13,581	14,275	14,400	14,083	13,734	13,997	13,658	13,760	13,881	−2.4	0.7	0.9	0.3
2331 Women's/misses blouses	4,195	4,580	4,425	4,012	3,752	3,804	3,726	3,737	3,772	−2.1	0.3	0.9	0.1
2335 Women's/misses dresses	5,278	5,431	6,042	6,397	6,336	6,455	6,302	6,361	6,422	−2.4	0.9	1.0	0.3
2337 Women's suits and coats	4,108	4,264	3,933	3,674	3,646	3,738	3,630	3,662	3,686	−2.9	0.9	0.7	0.3
Value of shipments ($1992)	13,581	14,211	14,433	14,253	14,119	14,439	13,944	14,022	14,237	−3.4	0.6	1.5	0.2
2331 Women's/misses blouses	4,195	4,539	4,325	3,896	3,664	3,754	3,643	3,644	3,657	−2.9	0.0	0.4	−0.0
2335 Women's/misses dresses	5,278	5,426	6,146	6,582	6,614	6,706	6,496	6,567	6,697	−3.1	1.1	2.0	0.3
2337 Women's suits and coats	4,108	4,247	3,961	3,775	3,842	3,978	3,805	3,811	3,883	−4.4	0.2	1.9	0.3
Trade data													
Value of imports	7,469	8,149	8,645	9,283	9,910	10,846	11,952	12,534	13,808	10.2	4.9	10.2	8.6
2331 Women's/misses blouses	4,224	4,538	4,743	4,805	4,959	5,887	6,759	7,489	8,430	14.8	10.8	12.6	14.2
2335 Women's/misses dresses	1,054	1,130	1,339	1,688	1,871	1,930	1,992	2,183	2,365	3.2	9.6	8.3	6.0
2337 Women's suits and coats	2,191	2,480	2,563	2,790	3,080	3,029	3,201	2,862	3,013	5.7	−10.6	5.3	−0.6
Value of exports	514	602	603	737	788	880	848	761	781	−3.6	−10.2	2.5	−0.2
2331 Women's/misses blouses	189	242	267	377	421	452	428	429	440	−5.3	0.3	2.4	1.1
2335 Women's/misses dresses	98.3	105	103	112	115	148	124	100	104	−16.2	−19.7	4.0	−2.6
2337 Women's suits and coats	227	255	233	247	253	280	296	232	237	5.7	−21.5	2.1	−1.6

[1] Estimate except imports and exports.
[2] Estimate.
[3] Forecast.
[4] Compound annual rate.
[5] For a definition of industry versus product values, see "Getting the Most Out of *Outlook 2000.*"
Source: U.S. Department of Commerce: Bureau of the Census; International Trade Administration.

The apparel industry is still highly fragmented, with many companies experiencing slow growth and depressed stock prices, and so mergers are seen as a way to cut expenses by eliminating duplicate functions and streamlining business. As is the case among retailers, mergers among apparel companies are a way to enhance bargaining power in the marketplace. Mergers also are used by companies to expand their brand names into new product categories or to broaden their range of offerings. Although most recent mergers have involved small and medium-size companies, several larger manufacturers have conducted high-profile mergers recently.

Many apparel and fabricated textile products companies that have reorganized have in the process also changed focus from manufacturing to become consumer marketing companies. These companies have shifted at least part of their production overseas or have outsourced to contractors. Many participate in production-sharing programs in Mexico and the CBI countries to reduce costs and provide a quick turnaround. This allows them to offer competitively priced merchandise and respond quickly to changes in consumer demand. Many of these companies provide packaging services that stores now request. The U.S. International Trade Commission estimates that 55 percent of the apparel sold in the United States in 1998 was imported.

The trend toward retailers becoming apparel manufacturers and apparel manufacturers becoming retailers continues. Some retailers have established private label lines that allow them to deal directly with contractors. Some retailers use private labels to differentiate themselves from other retailers and fill in gaps in their product lines. Consumers increasingly associate national brands with consistency in quality and size, and this has allowed rapid growth in private label brands. Some U.S. apparel companies have established their own merchandise stores. Combining retailing and apparel manufacturing allows companies to create efficiencies by eliminating middlemen.

Some textile companies are becoming apparel manufacturers. A few large U.S. textile companies have established sewing operations as well as spinning, knitting, and weaving mills in Mexico and are able to produce garments with their own fabric and take advantage of the NAFTA apparel trade provisions. Combining mill operations with sewing leads to cost reduction and greater efficiencies and also is intended by some companies to increase export sales to third countries.

Technology improvements have enabled apparel and fabricated textile products manufacturers to enhance the quick response programs that have become essential to compete in today's rapidly changing markets. "Supply-chain management" is a broader term that includes timely product development and quick response to market demand. Sophisticated programs start with data from a cash register sale and automatically transmit the information needed to replenish stock quickly. Supply-chain management ties together design, inventory, suppliers, cutters, sewers, and delivery systems to eliminate inefficiencies and reduce inventory and delays in responding to customer demand. Aided by technology, some large U.S. apparel firms have formed "strategic alliances" with their retail customers that involve developing plans regarding production, inventory management, and automatic replenishment.

Other technological improvements are leading to increased efficiency and increases in productivity in manufacturing processes, such as computer-aided design (CAD) systems for cutting and embroidery layouts. Many companies are using technology to establish programs to improve quality control.

Electronic Commerce

Among all the structural changes affecting the apparel and fabricated textile products industry, however, the Internet is proving to be one of the largest and most promising. The Internet is factoring into all facets of the industry, from direct sales to consumers, to ordering from suppliers, to speeding designs to distant cutters and assembly plants.

The Internet has become a quick way to shop for busy families that want to reduce the amount of time spent in stores, and apparel is one of the items most frequently purchased on-line. Internet shopping for apparel is not yet as large as the other method of nonstore retailing: catalogs. Catalogs have been around for many years, are portable, offer generally good pictures and descriptions of merchandise, and provide telephone ordering and assistance. However, Internet sales are growing at a much faster rate than are catalog sales. It is estimated that 140 million Americans have Internet access, with over 40 percent of adults going on-line every month.

Apparel manufacturers, catalog companies, and retailers all use the Internet to promote sales. On-line apparel sales were estimated to exceed $300 million in 1998. Approximately 21 percent of households that made on-line purchases in 1998 bought apparel. Manufacturers often offer more complete or different merchandise lines and sizes on the Internet than can be found in many retail stores, and they can vary the selection quickly if necessary, for example, in response to unexpected weather patterns. Other Internet sites have store locators for consumers who want to to purchase at retail. Innovative companies have added features such as the ability to mix and match separates, view coordinating articles, and custom design outerwear to their Web sites. One catalog company invites users to enter their personal measurements and characteristics and then builds a model to interactively display different apparel choices and make recommendations.

The Internet has begun to redefine the relationship between manufacturers and retailers, and the transition has not always proceeded smoothly as retailers see themselves threatened with becoming increasingly less essential to sales of apparel and fabricated textile products. Retailers are deciding how large a presence they want on the Internet and whether to regard on-line retailing as an extension of their store networks or as competition for them. Nearly two-thirds of on-line revenues in 1998 went to retail or catalog companies whose businesses predated their Internet sites.

The Internet is becoming a more significant factor in export sales, reaching consumers who otherwise might not have access to U.S. products, although on-line shopping has not spread as quickly in the rest of the world as it has in the United States. It is estimated the United States accounted for 80 percent of global on-line sales in 1998. In seven foreign countries, at least 10 percent of the population is able to access the Internet. Connecting to the World Wide Web is generally much more expensive abroad, and in some countries Internet availability is not widespread. Language barriers, import taxes, and restrictions also may hinder the spread of Internet retailing to other countries.

As the Internet has made shopping more efficient for millions of consumers and reduced costs for manufacturers and retailers, it has streamlined the apparel business and made it more efficient. Manufacturers use the Internet and a range of information technologies such as Intranet and electronic data interchange (EDI) to cut costs and increase efficiency. Apparel companies use the Internet to hold fashion shows for retail buyers, beam new designs and specifications to manufacturing facilities around the world, order from suppliers, and integrate manufacturing and distribution processes with accounting and payroll via sophisticated supply-chain management systems. This technology increases sales by allowing more of the right product to be in stock when the consumer is ready to buy.

Labor Standards

More and more apparel and fabricated textile product companies are taking initiatives to guarantee that they and their contractors do not participate in sweatshop operations in the United States and abroad. For example, the Apparel Industry Partnership (AIP), initiated by President Clinton in 1996, is a group of industry, labor, nongovernmental, and consumer groups that have agreed to a code of conduct and independent monitoring systems that will help assure that the clothing and shoes available in the marketplace are made under decent and humane working conditions. The strong workplace code of conduct, which companies voluntarily adopt and require their contractors to adopt, includes prohibitions against child labor, worker abuse or harassment, and discrimination; recognition of workers' right to freedom of association and collective bargaining; a minimum or prevailing industry wage; a cap on mandatory overtime to 12 hours per week; and a safe and healthy working environment. There are 18 participants in the partnership. In November 1998, the partnership released its agreement on a global monitoring plan. Under the plan, an independent body called the Fair Labor Association (FLA) was established that will oversee the monitoring of the working conditions of the member companies.

In late 1998, the American Apparel Manufacturers Association launched a separate effort called the Worldwide Responsible Apparel Production (WRAP) certification program. The WRAP program is an international plant certification plan based on a set of 12 minimum standards for production facilities that are designed to eliminate workplace abuses.

The AIP's FLA and WRAP have many elements in common, differing mainly in their approach to monitoring. The FLA approach requires companies to ensure that their factories and those of their suppliers are in compliance with the AIP code of conduct. Outside monitors randomly audit a company's compliance. The WRAP program takes a factory-based approach in which plants may be certified for compliance with WRAP principles through inspection by an outside monitor.

Consumers have become increasingly aware of the sweatshop issue, and some have become activists. Initiatives have been introduced on several college campuses to require that bookstore merchandise not be produced by sweatshop or child labor. Over 120 colleges and universities have joined the FLA. In addition, five of those schools participate in a program to help manufacturers and subcontractors comply with new fair labor codes at factory sites. Those codes cover payment of a just wage and the identification of factories that manufacture school goods.

PROJECTIONS OF INDUSTRY AND TRADE GROWTH

Prospects for the apparel and fabricated textile products industry include slight growth in industry shipments, but imports are expected to continue to claim a growing share of the market. Consumer confidence is expected to remain high, economic conditions should stay good, and the number of "affluent" households is increasing. Those households account for a significant share of apparel spending.

The twin problems of import competition and stagnant pricing remain formidable for the industry. With the phaseout of import quotas in 2005 under the WTO Agreement on Textiles and Clothing, these problems will continue to grow. Large apparel companies are expected to expand as they implement globalization strategies and continue to consolidate. Smaller companies that cannot afford the latest technology to streamline operations and shorten delivery times will increasingly rely on niche markets. The development of new fabrics by the textile industry, such as smart fabrics that automatically adjust to changes in temperature and high-performance fabrics, gives apparel companies opportunities to produce new products.

Time-pressed consumers increasingly will turn to catalogs and on-line shopping as an alternative to traditional retail formats. Less time will be spent in fewer stores. Apparel companies will spend more on information technology even as they source more manufacturing abroad to reduce costs and improve their ability to respond quickly to consumer demand.

Many apparel companies that manufacture upscale goods are working to improve the fit of clothing. Answering a chronic complaint of consumers, new technology using body scans and lasers is under development by several companies. The resulting three-dimensional models allow customers to "try on" clothes that match their measurements or order custom-made apparel. These projects, some of which include worldwide body measurement surveys, are expected to improve sizing standards in the industry.

Government agencies are helping the industry develop and apply new technologies. The American Textile Partnership (AMTEX), a joint venture of the industry and the U.S. Department of Energy, is working to link textile mills, apparel manufacturers, wholesalers, and retailers in a business-to-business electronic commerce network that allows all industry segments to respond more quickly and efficiently to changing consumer spending patterns. The National Textile Center (NTC), a research consortium of six universities, and the Textile/Clothing Technology Corp. (TC^2), both of which receive funds through the U.S. Department of Commerce, are working with industry to develop technology to automate product design, production, and distribution.

GLOBAL MARKET PROSPECTS

Exports of apparel and fabricated textile products accounted for 12.5 percent of product shipments in 1998, up from 6.9 percent in 1992. In the 1993–1998 period, exports of those products achieved a compound annual gain of 10 percent, but they were nearly flat from 1997 to 1998.

Exports of apparel declined 4 percent from 1997 to 1998, when they totaled $6.5 billion. Apparel export data include cut parts exported for assembly in other countries and returned to the United States as imports under HTSUS 9802. Exports to the NAFTA member Mexico and the CBI beneficiary countries, which are the main partners in such production sharing arrangements, have advanced dramatically in recent years and accounted for about 75 percent of total apparel exports in 1998.

Canada, Japan, and the European Union (EU) countries are the major destinations for finished apparel exports. Exports to those countries are concentrated in men's and boys' apparel, with trousers and knit shirts being among the strongest categories. Although apparel exports to Canada increased in 1998, exports to Japan and the EU countries declined. The ongoing integration of the North American economy driven by NAFTA, coupled with a solid Canadian economy, resulted in a 7 percent increase in apparel exports to Canada. Japan, suffering from a weak economy, sharply curtailed its imports of U.S. apparel in 1997 and 1998. The level of apparel exports to Japan in 1998 stood at less than half the level in 1996 as spending for discretionary consumer products plummeted. While exports to Japan continued to decrease in the first half of 1999, the rate of decline was only 10 percent, and a possible rebound in the Japanese economy is cause for optimism about U.S. apparel sales. Apparel exports to the EU nations declined 19 percent from 1997 to 1998 as those economies lost momentum during the course of 1998. Data for the first half of 1999 show further erosion of exports to the EU. Among smaller markets for U.S. apparel exports, South America also experienced economic difficulties in 1998, particularly Brazil, where U.S. apparel exports were cut in half from the previous year's level.

While the performance of U.S. apparel exports is driven in large part by economic conditions in their major markets, the migration of U.S. apparel producers to low-cost countries is another significant factor. As U.S. companies are becoming more global, they increasingly are serving foreign markets from their low-cost production sources. Thus, while exports from the United States have not been robust in recent years, this does not necessarily indicate weakness in the appeal of U.S. apparel brands around the world.

Exports of fabricated textile products expanded in 1998, exceeding $2.4 billion, 14 percent higher than the previous year (see Table 33-8). NAFTA partners Canada and Mexico are by far the largest markets for these products. Exports of fabricated textile products to the EU countries were stable in 1998, but those to the Far East declined.

The U.S. Department of Commerce's Office of Textiles and Apparel (OTEXA) provides assistance to firms that sell in foreign countries, including an export database, Export Advantage, which includes information on country markets and listings of overseas buyers and U.S. exporters. OTEXA also facilitates participation in trade fairs in many parts of the world and assists firms in overcoming foreign countries' restrictions on their exports.

INDUSTRY SUBSECTORS

Many of the industry trends discussed so far cut across all segments of the sewn products industry. The following sections provide information on the three major sectors of that industry. To provide an indication of the relative importance of the apparel sectors, personal consumption expenditure data show that women's and girls' apparel accounted for 56 percent of consumer apparel expenditures in 1998, men's and boy's apparel 36 percent, and infants' apparel 8 percent.

Men's and Boys' Apparel

Shipments of men's and boys' apparel remained fairly stable over the last several years, but shifts within some segments were marked. Shipments of suits, coats, and shirts declined sig-

TABLE 33-8: U.S. Trade Patterns in Fabricated Textile Products[1] in 1998
(millions of dollars; percent)

Exports			Imports		
Region[2]	Value[3]	Share,%	Region[2]	Value[3]	Share,%
NAFTA	1,043	43	NAFTA	1,372	29
Latin America	1,047	43	Latin America	126	3
Western Europe	128	5	Western Europe	555	12
Japan/Chinese Economic Area	96	4	Japan/Chinese Economic Area	1,484	31
Other Asia	34	1	Other Asia	1,109	23
Rest of world	96	4	Rest of world	162	3
World	2,444	100	World	4,806	100
Top Five Countries	Value	Share,%	Top Five Countries	Value	Share,%
Mexico	618	25	China	1,142	24
Canada	425	17	Mexico	1,109	23
Honduras	343	14	Pakistan	362	8
Dominican Republic	257	11	India	340	7
El Salvador	183	7	Taiwan	286	6

[1] SIC 239.
[2] For definitions of regional groupings, see "Getting the Most Out of *Outlook 2000.*"
[3] Values may not sum to total due to rounding.
Source: U.S. Department of Commerce, Bureau of the Census.

nificantly, while those of trousers, underwear, and work clothing increased (see Tables 33-4 and 33-5).

The trend toward casual dressing remained a significant influence in the men's and boys' wear markets, displacing sales of tailored clothing. Many tailored clothing manufacturers have followed the trend, cutting back on their tailored lines and concentrating on casual clothing. Some new products gave dressy clothing a boost. One involves the use of stretch fabric in dress slacks; another is dress slacks with finished bottoms. Khaki clothing continues to make inroads in casual dressing in all age groups, while newer types of denim are gaining acceptance in the jeans market. As sales of sports logo apparel and sweats have fallen off, sales of branded apparel have grown sharply, especially with younger consumers.

Employment in men's and boys' clothing categories declined across the board between 1992 and 1996, and those declines accelerated in the following years. Wages rose in all men's and boys' apparel segments except underwear, with neckwear showing the largest wage gains in the 1992–1996 period.

Women's, Girls', and Children's Apparel

Women's, girls', and children's apparel shipments (see Tables 33-6, 33-7, and 33-9) showed very little growth in the last several years as import penetration in the American market continued to increase. As is the case in men's wear, tailored women's clothing has been negatively affected by the trend toward casual dressing. Sales of sportswear and sports apparel were highlights in this segment. Along with value, consumers are looking increasingly for comfort when they select apparel, leading to the popularity of stretch fabrics. Ease of care also is of growing importance to customers. The children's market is expanding as more children are born to older, more affluent parents. Many adult apparel manufacturers are expanding into the lucrative children's market.

TABLE 33-9: Girls' and Children's Outerwear (SIC 236) Trends and Forecasts
(millions of dollars except as noted)

										Percent Change			
	1992	1993	1994	1995	1996	1997[1]	1998[1]	1999[2]	2000[3]	97–98	98–99	99–00	96–00[4]
Industry data													
Value of shipments[5]	3,145	3,221	3,926	3,605	3,874	3,935	3,818	3,835	3,870	−3.0	0.5	0.9	−0.0
2361 Child's dresses/blouses	1,619	1,567	1,716	1,631	1,636	1,663	1,612	1,620	1,636	−3.0	0.5	1.0	0.0
2369 Children's outerwear nec	1,525	1,655	2,210	1,973	2,238	2,272	2,205	2,215	2,233	−2.9	0.4	0.8	−0.1
Value of shipments ($1992)	3,143	3,203	3,932	3,594	3,832	3,917	3,800	3,837	3,861	−3.0	1.0	0.6	0.2
2361 Child's dresses/blouses	1,619	1,570	1,728	1,572	1,567	1,603	1,568	1,567	1,566	−2.2	−0.0	−0.1	−0.0
2369 Children's outerwear nec	1,525	1,633	2,203	2,022	2,265	2,314	2,232	2,269	2,295	−3.5	1.7	1.1	0.3
Total employment (thousands)	53.3	49.2	48.0	42.7	33.5								
2361 Child's dresses/blouses	23.9	23.1	19.5	17.3	11.6								
2369 Children's outerwear nec	29.4	26.1	28.5	25.4	21.9								
Production workers (thousands)	43.6	39.8	38.4	34.1	27.4								
2361 Child's dresses/blouses	19.1	18.6	15.2	13.1	8.8								
2369 Children's outerwear nec	24.5	21.2	23.2	21.0	18.6								
Average hourly earnings ($)	6.36	6.63	6.78	6.54	7.01								
2361 Child's dresses/blouses	6.49	6.24	6.53	6.33	7.36								
2369 Children's outerwear nec	6.26	6.97	6.96	6.65	6.87								
Product data													
Value of shipments[5]	3,503	3,452	3,636	3,565	3,585	3,642	3,533	3,549	3,581	−3.0	0.5	0.9	−0.0
2361 Child's dresses/blouses	1,719	1,626	1,680	1,616	1,590	1,616	1,567	1,575	1,590	−3.0	0.5	1.0	0.0
2369 Children's outerwear nec	1,784	1,826	1,957	1,949	1,995	2,026	1,966	1,975	1,991	−2.9	0.4	0.8	−0.1
Value of shipments ($1992)	3,503	3,432	3,642	3,554	3,542	3,621	3,514	3,546	3,568	−3.0	0.9	0.6	0.2
2361 Child's dresses/blouses	1,719	1,629	1,692	1,557	1,523	1,558	1,524	1,523	1,522	−2.2	−0.0	−0.1	−0.0
2369 Children's outerwear nec	1,784	1,803	1,951	1,997	2,019	2,063	1,990	2,023	2,046	−3.5	1.7	1.1	0.3
Trade data													
Value of imports													
236 Girls' and children's outerwear	7,748	7,899	8,407	8,211	8,425	10,475	11,705	12,677	14,027	11.7	8.3	10.7	13.6
Value of exports													
236 Girls' and children's outerwear	453	484	594	698	829	914	1,031	847	953	12.8	−17.8	12.5	3.6

[1] Estimate except imports and exports.
[2] Estimate.
[3] Forecast.
[4] Compound annual rate.
[5] For a definition of industry versus product values, see "Getting the Most Out of *Outlook 2000.*"
Source: U.S. Department of Commerce: Bureau of the Census; International Trade Administration.

TABLE 33-10: Miscellaneous Fabricated Textile Products (SIC 239)
(millions of dollars except as noted)

	1992	1993	1994	1995	1996	1997[1]	1998[1]	1999[2]	2000[3]	Percent Change 97–98	98–99	99–00	96–00[4]
Industry data													
Value of shipments[5]	19,118	20,264	21,738	22,488	22,934	23,588	22,983	23,136	23,380	−2.6	0.7	1.1	0.5
239A Home furnishings[6]	6,886	7,154	7,411	7,616	7,517	7,698	7,510	7,567	7,649	−2.4	0.8	1.1	0.4
239B Miscellaneous textile products[6]	12,232	13,110	14,327	14,872	15,418	15,890	15,472	15,569	15,731	−2.6	0.6	1.0	0.5
Value of shipments ($1992)	19,118	20,034	21,318	21,740	21,236	21,463	20,373	20,572	20,525	−5.1	1.0	−0.2	−0.8
239A Home furnishings	6,886	7,022	7,217	7,305	7,002	7,109	6,856	6,860	6,866	−3.5	0.1	0.1	−0.5
239B Miscellaneous textile products	12,232	13,012	14,101	14,436	14,234	14,354	13,517	13,711	13,659	−5.8	1.4	−0.4	−1.0
Total employment (thousands)	211	212	222	228	224								
239A Home furnishings	73.7	72.1	71.3	74.4	68.6								
239B Miscellaneous textile products	137	140	151	154	155								
Production workers (thousands)	168	171	179	182	179								
239A Home furnishings	61.0	59.5	59.0	60.0	55.8								
239B Miscellaneous textile products	107	112	120	122	123								
Average hourly earnings ($)	8.34	8.61	8.78	8.90	9.02								
239A Home furnishings	7.24	7.79	7.90	7.98	8.20								
239B Miscellaneous textile products	8.98	9.06	9.21	9.33	9.39								
Product data													
Value of shipments[5]	18,220	19,555	20,738	21,240	21,866	22,490	21,912	21,644	21,644	−2.6	−1.2	0.0	−0.3
239A Home furnishings	6,540	6,980	7,230	7,096	7,071	7,241	7,065	7,425	7,425	−2.4	5.1	0.0	1.2
239B Miscellaneous textile products	11,681	12,575	13,508	14,143	14,795	15,248	14,847	14,219	14,219	−2.6	−4.2	0.0	−1.0
Value of shipments ($1992)	18,220	19,331	20,339	20,534	20,243	20,461	19,420	19,254	19,011	−5.1	−0.9	−1.3	−1.6
239A Home furnishings	6,540	6,851	7,043	6,808	6,587	6,687	6,450	6,732	6,665	−3.5	4.4	−1.0	0.3
239B Miscellaneous textile products	11,681	12,480	13,296	13,726	13,657	13,774	12,971	12,522	12,346	−5.8	−3.5	−1.4	−2.5
Trade data													
Value of imports	2,720	3,135	3,446	3,577	3,637	4,221	4,806	5,474	6,022	13.9	13.9	10.0	13.4
239A Home furnishings	1,160	1,318	1,538	1,718	1,709	2,054	2,546	2,930	3,228	24.0	15.1	10.1	17.2
239B Miscellaneous textile products	1,559	1,817	1,909	1,859	1,928	2,168	2,261	2,544	2,794	4.3	12.5	9.8	9.7
Value of exports	1,081	1,221	1,286	1,519	1,878	2,139	2,444	2,535	2,662	14.3	3.7	5.0	9.1
239A Home furnishings	338	349	362	350	371	439	469	445	457	6.8	−5.1	2.6	5.3
239B Miscellaneous textile products	742	872	924	1,169	1,507	1,700	1,975	2,090	2,205	16.2	5.8	5.5	10.0

[1] Estimate except imports and exports.
[2] Estimate.
[3] Forecast.
[4] Compound annual rate.
[5] For a definition of industry versus product values, see "Getting the Most Out of *Outlook 2000.*"
[6] 239A includes SIC 2391 and SIC 2392; 239B represents all other components of SIC 239.
Source: U.S. Department of Commerce: Bureau of the Census; International Trade Administration.

Employment in the women's, girls', and children's apparel segments declined sharply from 1992 to 1996 across all segments except dresses, although in the following years significant declines continued, including in the dress segment.

Fabricated Textile Products

Home furnishings (see Table 33-10) is one of the brighter areas in the apparel and fabricated textile products industry. This market is growing because of the boom in construction and home sales prompted by low interest rates and the trend toward consumers spending more time at home and dressing up the home to make it as comfortable as possible. Unlike apparel, the home furnishings market is dominated by a few U.S. (mainly textile) companies and traditionally was unaffected by imports because most items are significantly less labor-intensive than apparel and because shipping charges are relatively high for bulkier and heavier home textiles. Imports are making inroads in this market, however, and in 1998 accounted for over 25 percent of the market.

Many of the large textile companies that dominate this market have reduced or eliminated their apparel fabric manufacturing and diversified their home furnishings offerings and expanded product lines to take advantage of the expanding home market. Some designers have established their own home furnishings product lines.

Employment in home textiles declined in the 1992–1996 period as productivity improved, and it continued to fall in the following years, although at a slower rate than in the remainder of the apparel and fabricated textile products industry. Wages for fabricated textile product workers are among the highest in the industry.

Joanne Tucker, Office of Textiles and Apparel, U.S. Department of Commerce, (202) 482-4058, September 1999.

■ REFERENCES

Apparel Industry Magazine, Shore Communications, 180 Allen Road, Suite 300-N, Atlanta, GA 30328. (404) 252-8831, http://www.aimagazine.com.

Apparel Manufacturing Strategies, American Apparel Manufacturers Association, 2500 Wilson Boulevard, Arlington, VA 22201. (703) 524-1864, http://www.americanapparel.org.

Bobbin, Bobbin International, Inc., 1110 Shop Road, P.O. Box 1986, Columbia, SC 29202. (803) 771-7500.

Current Industrial Reports, SIC 23, U.S. Department of Commerce, Bureau of the Census, Industry Division, Washington, DC 20233. (301) 457-4100, http://www.census.gov.

Daily News Record, Fairchild Publications, 7 West 34 St., New York, NY 10001. (212) 630-4000.

Focus: Economic Profile of the Apparel Industry, American Apparel Manufacturers Association, 2500 Wilson Boulevard, Arlington, VA 22201. (703) 524-1864, http://www.americanapparel.org.

Home Textiles Today, 245 W. 17 St., New York, NY 10011. (212) 337-6900, http://www.hometextilestoday.com.

Industry & Trade Summary, Apparel, USITC Publication 3169, March 1999, U.S. International Trade Commission, Office of Industries, Washington, DC 20436. (202) 205-3486.

Monthly Labor Review, U.S. Department of Labor, Bureau of Labor Statistics, Washington, DC 20211. (202) 606-5900.

OTEXA, Export Advantage, U.S. Department of Commerce, International Trade Administration, Office of Textiles and Apparel, Washington, DC 20230. (202) 482-3400, http://otexa.ita.doc.gov.

Seidman News Bulletin, 51 Pine Mountain Road, West Redding, CT 06896. (203) 544-8249.

Women's Wear Daily, Fairchild Publications, 7 West 34 St., New York, NY 10001. (212) 630-4000.

■ RELATED CHAPTERS

9: Textiles
18: Production Machinery
42: Retailing

FOOTWEAR, LEATHER, AND LEATHER PRODUCTS
Economic and Trade Trends

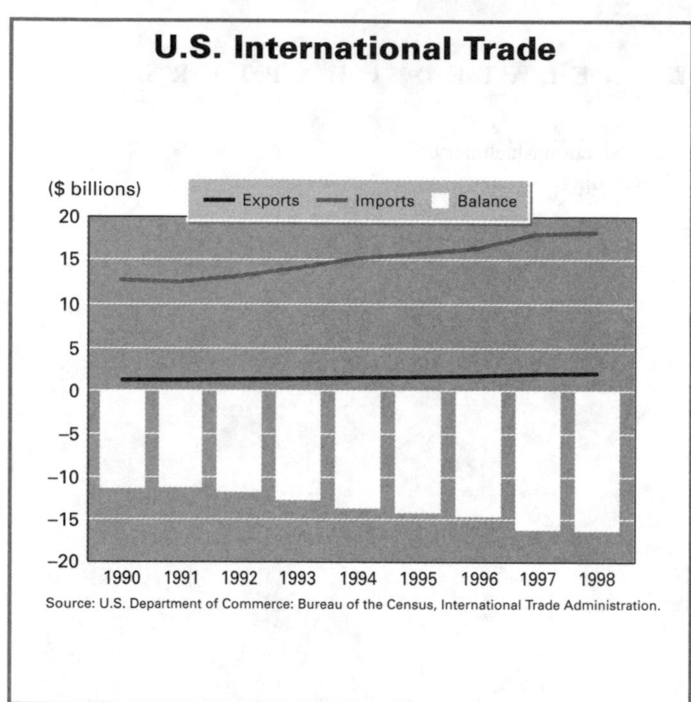

Source: U.S. Department of Commerce: Bureau of the Census, International Trade Administration.

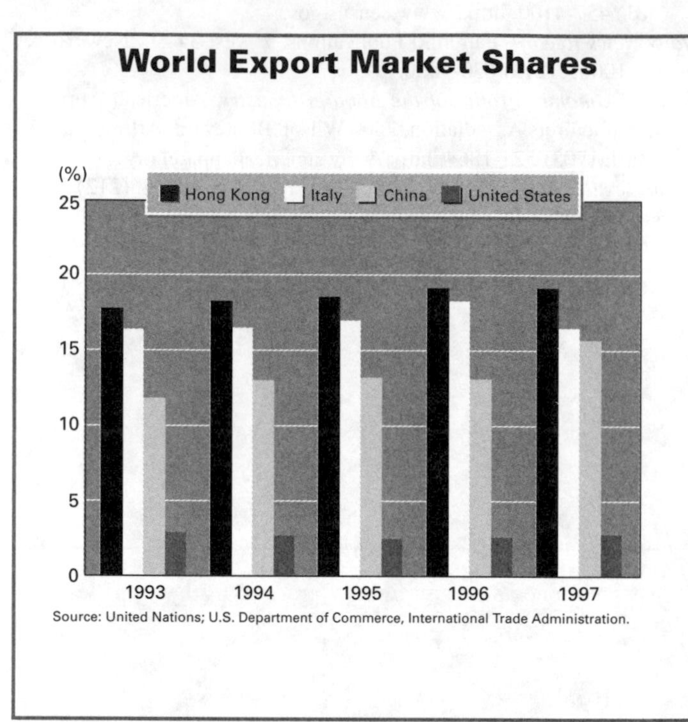

Source: United Nations; U.S. Department of Commerce, International Trade Administration.

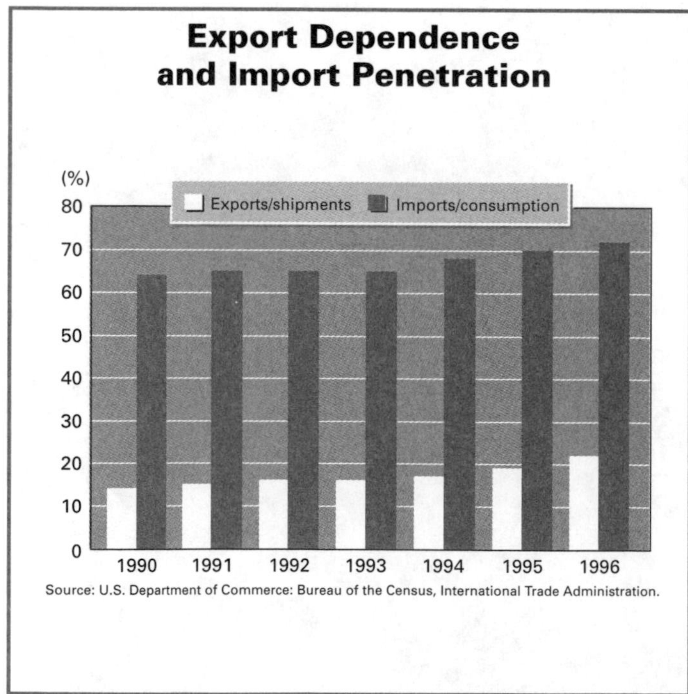

Source: U.S. Department of Commerce: Bureau of the Census, International Trade Administration.

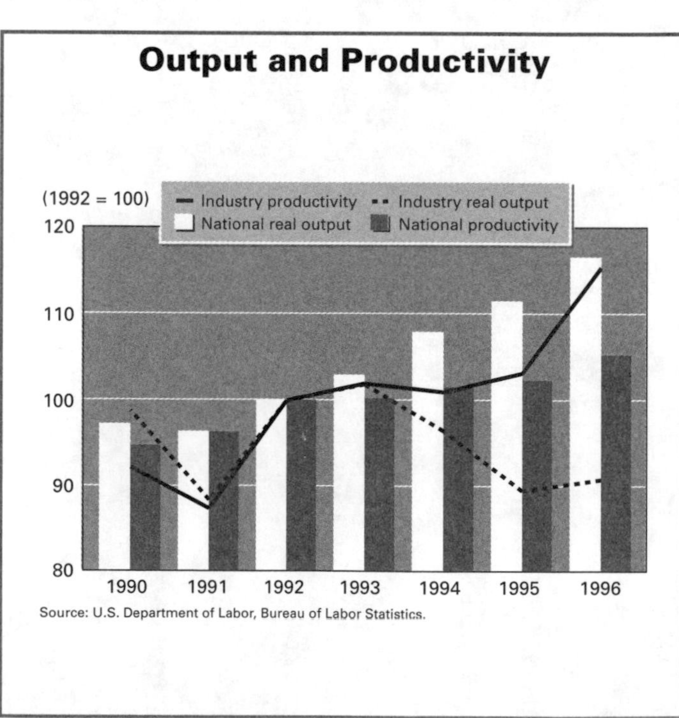

Source: U.S. Department of Labor, Bureau of Labor Statistics.

See "Getting the Most Out of *Outlook 2000*" for definitions of terms.

34

Footwear, Leather, and Leather Products

INDUSTRY DEFINITION The footwear, leather, and leather products group consists of seven industries: nonrubber footwear (SIC 314), leather tanning and finishing (SIC 3111), leather gloves and mittens (SIC 3151), luggage (SIC 3161), handbags (SIC 3171), small personal leather goods (SIC 3172), and leather wearing apparel (SIC 2386)

OVERVIEW

Industry shipments of nonrubber footwear, leather, and leather products declined about 7 percent in 1999 to an estimated $7.65 billion. In constant dollars, the value of shipments declined about 6 percent in 1999 as strong competition from imports and lower domestic demand limited production in all industry segments except leather tanning and leather wearing apparel. Tables 34-1 and 34-2 show the distribution and change in industry shipments in current dollars and constant dollars.

GLOBAL INDUSTRY TRENDS

U.S. imports of nonrubber footwear, leather, and leather products increased about 1.5 percent to $18 billion in 1999. China was the largest supplier by far, accounting for 51 percent of total U.S. imports of those products (see Table 34-3). All these industries, with the exception of leather tanning and finishing, are extremely labor-intensive. In comparison with U.S. producers, manufacturers in China and developing countries have a substantial cost advantage as a result of their lower labor compensation rates.

In 1999, U.S. exports of nonrubber footwear, leather, and leather products totaled about $1.8 billion, down about 8 percent from 1998. Thus, in 1999 imports of these products exceeded exports by about $16.2 billion, a decrease in the sector trade deficit of less than 1 percent from the 1998 level. Nonrubber footwear accounted for $11 billion of that deficit. By value, imports accounted for 76 percent of apparent consumption (product shipments plus imports minus exports) for the nonrubber footwear, leather, and leather products group in 1999. The handbag industry had the highest ratio of imports to apparent consumption at 88 percent, followed by 86 percent for leather apparel, 82 percent each for nonrubber footwear and luggage, 73 percent for gloves, and 62 percent for personal leather goods. Leather tanning had the lowest ratio at 44 percent.

LEATHER TANNING AND FINISHING

The leather tanning and finishing industry (SIC 3111) includes establishments engaged primarily in tanning, currying, and finishing hides and skins into leather. It also includes leather converters, which buy hides and skins and then have them processed into leather on a contract basis, and finishers, which color and finish crust leather under contract for others, including leather importers.

Global Trends

The most recent estimated data published by the Food and Agriculture Organization (FAO) of the United Nations show that in 1998 the United States ranked fourth in world bovine (cattle, calf, and buffalo) population with 99.5 million head, behind India (301.3 million), Brazil (162.7 million), and China (147 million). The world bovine population totaled 1,495 million head; the sheep and lamb population, 1,062 million head; and the goat and kid population, 707 million head. Data on the hog population were not included in the FAO report. Goatskin production is con-

TABLE 34-1: Distribution of Industry Shipments of Footwear, Leather, and Leather Products in 1999
(millions of dollars; percent)

SIC and Industry	Shipments[1]	Percent of Total
3111 Leather tanning and finishing	3,296	43.1
314 Nonrubber footwear	2,702	35.3
3161 Luggage	928	12.1
2386 Leather wearing apparel	243	3.2
3172 Small personal leather goods	229	3.0
3171 Handbags	153	2.0
3151 Leather gloves and mittens	96	1.3
Total	7,647	100.0

[1] Estimate.
Source: U.S. Department of Commerce, International Trade Administration.

TABLE 34-2: Industry Shipments of Footwear, Leather, and Leather Products, 1999–2000
(millions of 1992 dollars)

SIC and Industry	1999[1]	2000[2]	98–99	99–2000
3111 Leather tanning and finishing	3,063	3,065	5.1	0.1
3142 House slippers	125	121	−13.1	−3.2
3143 Men's footwear except athletic	1,665	1,682	−13.5	1.0
3144 Women's footwear except athletic	447	434	−13.2	−2.9
3149 Footwear except rubber nec[3]	221	230	−17.5	4.1
3151 Leather gloves and mittens	80	73	−25.2	−8.8
3161 Luggage	894	848	−10.9	−5.1
3171 Handbags	157	136	−13.3	−13.4
3172 Small personal leather goods	216	193	−9.2	−10.6
2386 Leather and sheepskin-lined clothing	251	256	5.5	2.0
Total	7,119	7,038	−5.5	−1.1

[1] Estimate.
[2] Forecast.
[3] nec = not elsewhere classified.
Source: U.S. Department of Commerce, International Trade Administration.

centrated in developing countries, primarily those in Africa and Asia. China was the largest producer of sheepskins and goatskins. The U.S. livestock population consists mainly of cattle.

Developing countries have about 77 percent of the world bovine herd but produce only 49 percent of the world supply of bovine hides and skins. The United States produced about 37 million cattlehides and calfskins in 1998, making it the largest producer in the world. The European Union group of 15 countries ranked second, followed by the group of countries in the former Soviet Union, China, and India. Extensive U.S. feedlot operations permit cattle to be grown in a relatively short period of time to an average in excess of 1,000 pounds before being slaughtered. As a result, the average weight per hide recovered from slaughter in the United States is far higher than that for most other countries. Total world production of hides was estimated at 286.1 million in 1998 and increased at an annual rate of only 0.7 percent between 1996 and 1998. The FAO report noted that China had become one of the five largest hide-producing countries and was expected to remain the leading producer among the developing countries.

The United States and the European Union have the highest takeoff, or recovery, rates (38 percent) for hides among all countries. By contrast, recovery rates in the developing countries average about 15 percent. However, some countries, such as China, improved their rates considerably during the 1990s, and if major producers such as Brazil, China, and India increase their levels to those of the United States and the European Union, the available world supply of hides will increase about 5 percent.

Hides and skins are by-products of the much larger meat and wool industries. The quantity of raw material produced depends in most cases on the animal population, which is affected by the demand for meat, dairy products, and wool. The quality and yield of the raw material produced in a country depend largely on animal husbandry, feeding, slaughtering, preservation, and transportation practices. Leather tanners constitute the only market for these raw materials, and the entire takeoff is utilized by the tanning industry and converted into leather.

Domestic Trends

The current dollar value of leather tanning and finishing shipments increased almost 3 percent in 1999, reaching an estimated $3.3 billion (see Table 34-5 later in this chapter). That increase resulted from a rise of about 5 percent in the quantity and a decline of 2 percent in the price of leather shipped. In 1999, product shipments also increased by about 3 percent to $3.3 billion. The quantity of leather shipped by U.S. tanners rose about 5 percent to an estimated 21.3 million equivalent cattlehide units from 20.3 million units in 1998. Included in those totals are leather produced from the hides and skins of cattle, calves, goats, sheep, lambs, cabretta, pigs, horses, and other animals and reptiles. Shipments of cattlehide leather accounted for 20.7 million units, or 97 percent of the total (see Table 34-4).

The shoe industry consumes about 35 percent of all domestic leather shipments. In 1998, about 60 percent of domestic and 53 percent of imported nonrubber footwear was produced with leather uppers. Leather use for outsoles is now limited mostly to high-priced men's and women's footwear of welt or cement construction with uppers of calfskin, hand-sewn moccasins, and more expensive styles of western boots. Synthetic outsoles are favored over leather because new equipment and technology have reduced labor costs in shoe bottoming operations.

The fastest-growing and potentially largest markets for leather in the United States are those for automotive and furniture upholstery. The industry estimates that upholstery leather accounted for about 50 percent of all leather shipped in 1998. Leather is used to upholster about 20 percent of all furniture and over 10 percent of all automotive vehicles sold in the United States. Leather is an option in most medium-priced cars and sport utility vehicles and trucks; it is standard in higher-priced foreign and domestic models. The United States exports automotive upholstery leather to a number of countries, primarily Mexico, Canada, and Japan.

In 1999, the quantity of cattlehides derived from total commercial slaughter increased less than 1 percent from the 1998 level to an estimated 35.7 million head, down substantially

TABLE 34-3: U.S. Trade Patterns in Footwear, Leather, and Leather Products[1] in 1998
(millions of dollars; percent)

Exports			Imports		
Region[2]	Value[3]	Share, %	Region[2]	Value[3]	Share, %
NAFTA	697	35	NAFTA	1,141	6
Latin America	203	10	Latin America	1,597	9
Western Europe	279	14	Western Europe	2,963	16
Japan/Chinese Economic Area	608	30	Japan/Chinese Economic Area	9,820	54
Other Asia	146	7	Other Asia	2,494	14
Rest of world	66	3	Rest of world	213	1
World	2,000	100	World	18,228	100
Top Five Countries	Value	Share, %	Top Five Countries	Value	Share, %
Mexico	456	23	China	9,383	51
Japan	353	18	Italy	1,658	9
Canada	242	12	Brazil	1,071	6
Hong Kong	154	8	Mexico	998	5
South Korea	67	3	Indonesia	726	4

[1] SIC 2386, 3111, 314, 3151, 3161, 317.
[2] For definitions of regional groupings, see "Getting the Most Out of *Outlook 2000.*"
[3] Values may not sum to total due to rounding.
Source: U.S. Department of Commerce, Bureau of the Census.

from the record high of 43 million in 1976 but up from the more recent low of 32.7 million in 1991.

Cattlehides are a by-product of the meatpacking industry, and supply depends solely on the demand for meat, not on the demand for leather. A long-term decline in the demand for red meat, accompanied by increased consumption of poultry, has discouraged rebuilding of cattle herds to the levels of the 1950s to 1970s even though feed grains have been favorably priced since the mid-1980s.

Cattle population in January 1999 dropped 1.5 percent from that in January 1998 to 97.9 million head, far lower than the record high of 131.8 million recorded in 1975. Large numbers of cattle, including breeding stock, were moved to feedlots in 1999 as herd liquidation continued. Beef herds were not expected to increase until 2001 at the earliest as competition from pork and chicken held down prices, forcing many growers to leave the business entirely. As a result, slaughter is expected to drop almost 6 percent in the year 2000 to 33.6 million head and not turn higher until 2002 or later.

In 1999, the U.S. Bureau of Labor Statistics (BLS) wholesale price index for cattlehides dropped an estimated 9 percent from 1998. This decline followed one of 22 percent in 1998. The BLS producer price index for leather declined about 5 percent in 1999.

TABLE 34-4: U.S. Trade Patterns in Leather Tanning and Finishing[1] in 1998
(millions of dollars; percent)

Exports			Imports		
Region[2]	Value[3]	Share, %	Region[2]	Value[3]	Share, %
NAFTA	529	41	NAFTA	651	41
Latin America	80	6	Latin America	396	25
Western Europe	109	8	Western Europe	434	28
Japan/Chinese Economic Area	430	33	Japan/Chinese Economic Area	15	1
Other Asia	125	10	Other Asia	39	3
Rest of world	17	1	Rest of world	36	2
World	1,290	100	World	1,571	100
Top Five Countries	Value	Share, %	Top Five Countries	Value	Share, %
Mexico	404	31	Mexico	614	39
Japan	199	15	Argentina	261	17
Hong Kong	137	11	Italy	221	14
Canada	125	10	United Kingdom	66	4
South Korea	60	5	Brazil	61	4

[1] SIC 3111.
[2] For definitions of regional groupings, see "Getting the Most Out of *Outlook 2000.*"
[3] Values may not sum to total due to rounding.
Source: U.S. Department of Commerce, Bureau of the Census.

Raw cattlehide exports declined about 9 percent in 1999 to 16.1 million hides. This quantity represented about 45 percent of the total commercial slaughter, the lowest ratio since 1971. In 1972, Argentina, also a major producer of cattlehides, imposed an embargo on hide exports, diverting worldwide demand to the U.S. hide market and pushing up hide prices to historically high levels. Argentina has maintained export restrictions ever since. The United States exported a record 27.3 million cattlehides, or 70 percent of domestic supply, in 1986. Both U.S. hide exports and the ratio to domestic supply have declined gradually since that time.

Trends in Technology

The U.S. Environmental Protection Agency (EPA) promulgates and administers environmental regulations affecting the tanning industry. The EPA has established standards to control pretreatment of wastes that tanners discharge indirectly into publicly owned waste treatment facilities. These standards do not require biological treatment to reduce oxygen demand of the effluent, but they do require the control of sulfides, chromium, and acidity. Most tanners meet the federal standards, although local restrictions and more stringent standards in some states have forced some tanners to cease production or confine it to the further processing of wet-blue or crust leathers, which produce fewer pollutants.

The EPA requires that tanneries that discharge wastes directly into waterways and all new plants must control conventional pollutants such as solids and biological oxygen demand in addition to sulfides, chromium, and acidity. Furthermore, these tanners must operate with EPA-approved permits. Control of these wastes requires both primary and secondary (biological) treatment. In the future, even tertiary treatment may be required if the EPA further tightens standards and broadens them to include other pollutants, such as ammonia, biocides, chlorides, and surfactants. These waste products, however, probably can be controlled through less costly process modifications.

The EPA has excluded from hazardous waste regulations waste scrap leather, wet-blue trimmings and shavings, and tannery sludges that contain chromium, the principal tanning agent. No studies have proved that nontoxic trivalent chromium in these products is oxidized in landfill disposal to the toxic hexavalent form. Therefore, the majority of chrome-containing solid wastes may not be classified as hazardous and do not require treatment before land disposal. The industry has developed and is adopting new tanning systems that will use other nontoxic metal salts to replace some or all of the chromium currently used. Vegetable, synthetic resin, and other organic tanning materials also can be substituted for some of the chromium. Tanning systems that recycle chromium are used extensively throughout the industry to reduce chromium concentrations in the effluent. Additionally, the industry has successfully curbed emissions of volatile organic compounds by adopting low-solvent or solvent-free finishing and coating technologies.

The recycling of materials, the introduction of new processes that reduce the quantities of chemicals used, and the installation of new equipment have reduced the industry's impact on the environment and at the same time have lowered material and labor costs, making U.S. leather even more price-competitive in world markets.

Trade

In 1999, U.S. leather imports declined over 3 percent to an estimated $1.52 billion from $1.57 billion in 1998 (see Table 34-5). The decline was due primarily to a 7 percent decline in the quantity of leather imported. In January–June 1999, the United States imported leather from 72 countries. In that period, the largest supplier was Mexico, which provided 43 percent of total U.S. leather imports. Argentina and Italy each had a 16 percent share, followed by Brazil with 4 percent and Germany and Uruguay with 3 percent each. Cattlehide upholstery leather, including both uncut and cut-to-pattern seat parts, accounted for 70 percent of total leather imports. Mexico was the largest supplier of upholstery leather, capturing 53 percent of upholstery leather imports. Argentina ranked second at 20 percent.

Leather exports also declined in 1999, dropping 13 percent to an estimated $1.1 billion from $1.3 billion in 1998, mainly in response to lower demand from footwear and leather products manufacturers in the Far East and for automotive leather in Mexico (see Table 34-5). By mid-1999, the United States had exported leather to 61 countries, of which Mexico was the largest recipient with more than 28 percent of the total. China, including Hong Kong, ranked second with a 16 percent share, followed by Japan with 11 percent, Canada with 10 percent, and South Korea with 7 percent.

In 1999, cattlehide upholstery leather, including both uncut and cut-to-pattern seat parts, accounted for an estimated 43 percent of total leather exports, down from 49 percent in 1998. Mexico received the largest share: 52 percent of total U.S. upholstery leather exports. Over 17 percent of U.S. exports are wet-blue leathers, or leathers that have been tanned but not processed or finished further. South Korea and Italy were the largest markets for wet-blue leathers. International trade in wet-blue leathers has increased because of lower shipping costs, quality advantages, and the environmental benefits of these products compared with raw cattlehides. The largest meatpacker in the United States produces an estimated 4 million wet-blue hides annually, and one large independent tanner produces more than 3 million annually. Much of the production of these two companies is exported. An increasing share of U.S. leather exports goes to China and the beneficiary developing countries, or those countries which are accorded special tariff treatment under U.S. trade laws. Increasing demand for leather from those countries reflects the steady movement to low-wage countries of labor-intensive footwear and leather products production.

Trade Actions

Australia. In June 1999, a World Trade Organization (WTO) dispute settlement panel ruled that the government of Australia had provided an illegal subsidy of about $18 million to a large Australian tanner of automotive upholstery leather. As a result, Australia was required to withdraw the subsidy by September

TABLE 34-5: Leather Tanning and Finishing (SIC 3111) Trends and Forecasts
(millions of dollars except as noted)

	1992	1993	1994	1995	1996	1997[1]	1998[1]	1999[2]	2000[3]	Percent Change 97–98	98–99	99–00	96–00[4]
Industry data													
Value of shipments[5]	2,905	3,198	3,041	3,119	3,134	3,353	3,212	3,296		−4.2	2.6		
Value of shipments (1992$)	2,905	3,096	2,808	2,717	2,821	2,949	2,915	3,063	3,065	−1.2	5.1	0.1	2.1
Total employment	16.6	16.9	15.9	15.3	14.8	14.7	14.0	14.7	14.0	−4.8	5.0	−4.8	−1.4
Production workers (thousands)	13.3	13.8	13.4	12.5	12.4	12.3	11.7	12.3	11.7	−4.9	5.1	−4.9	−1.4
Average hourly earnings ($)	10.56	10.65	10.62	10.54	10.98	11.14	11.31	11.54		1.5	2.0		
Capital expenditures	48.5	52.2	45.5	57.6	51.9								
Product data													
Value of shipments[5]	2,952	3,218	3,064	3,138	3,184	3,407	3,264	3,349		−4.2	2.6		
Value of shipments (1992$)	2,952	3,115	2,829	2,733	2,866	2,996	2,962	3,112	3,115	−1.1	5.1	0.1	2.1
Trade data													
Value of imports	631	736	960	1,089	1,139	1,376	1,571	1,520	1,680	14.2	−3.2	10.5	10.2
Value of exports	705	764	812	870	951	1,146	1,290	1,120	1,198	12.6	−13.2	7.0	5.9

[1] Estimate except imports and exports.
[2] Estimate.
[3] Forecast.
[4] Compound annual rate.
[5] For a definition of industry versus product values, see "Getting the Most Out of *Outlook 2000.*"
Source: U.S. Department of Commerce: Bureau of the Census; International Trade Administration.

1999. Several U.S. upholstery leather tanners alleged that the subsidy allowed the Australian tanner to underbid them on leather contracts awarded by auto seat manufacturers in the U.S. and Mexico and thereby capture a large share of the automotive upholstery leather market. In January 2000, the WTO dispute settlement panel further determined that measures taken by Australia in September 1999 were insufficient to comply with the previous ruling requiring Australia to withdraw the prohibited subsidies within 90 days. At the time of this writing, the Australian government had not announced what actions would be taken in response to the latest WTO finding.

U.S. Industry Growth Projection for 2000

Leather shipments are expected to remain unchanged at 21.9 million equivalent cattlehide units in the year 2000 as a result of the industry's tanning a large proportion of the smaller available cattlehide supply in that year.

Long-Term Prospects

The longer-term outlook for the leather tanning and finishing industry continues to be unsettled. The U.S. hide supply will remain tight at least until 2002, and so U.S. tanners and packers must be able to convert a larger proportion of that supply to wet-blue and finished leather without pushing leather prices up to levels where other materials are substituted for leather. Wet-blue leather's share of total U.S. production should continue to increase, although new joint production ventures overseas involving U.S. tanners and other tanners may have an adverse effect on domestic finished leather production by reducing the supply of wet-blue leather available for further domestic processing and pushing up hide prices. New waste treatment technology and equipment, which often are incorporated in new wet-blue plants, should help tanners control waste discharges. Some of these newer plants may add capacity and equipment to further process wet-blue hides into crust or finished leather. Improved opportunities to expand exports are essential for U.S. tanners to achieve at least some growth over the long term. In this regard, the U.S. leather industry perceives that access to raw materials and foreign market barriers remain key obstacles.

NONRUBBER FOOTWEAR

The nonrubber footwear industry (SIC 314) produces all types of footwear, including house slippers (SIC 3142), men's footwear except athletic (SIC 3142), women's footwear except athletic (SIC 3144), and footwear except rubber not elsewhere classified (SIC 3149). Nonrubber footwear does not include rubber-fabric and rubber-protective footwear, both of which are classified under SIC 3021.

Global Trends

The footwear manufacturing process is highly labor-intensive, requiring a large number of cutting, sewing, and stitching operations. For that reason, manufacturing activities have been transferred to countries that can provide cheap labor. Wholesalers, distributors, and retailers of branded, unbranded, and private label footwear continuously search for countries with lower-cost manufacturers. Because production machinery and equipment for making most types of footwear do not require large investments, manufacturing operations can be moved readily from one country to another with little difficulty.

For these reasons, Asia, including China, has become the largest shoe manufacturing area, and according to the industry publication *World Footwear Markets, 1999,* that area produced almost 71 percent of all footwear manufactured in the world in 1997. That publication also estimated world production of all types of footwear at 11 billion pairs, up about 5 percent from 1996. After Asia, the largest production areas were western Europe with 9.9 percent of total world footwear output and South America with 6.9 percent. In Asia, production has moved away form Taiwan and South Korea, the leading producers and exporters in the 1970s and 1980s, to low-labor-cost labor countries such as China, Indonesia, Thailand, India, and, more recently, Vietnam. In 1997, China's footwear production totaled 5.2 billion pairs, 47.5 percent of the world total of 11 billion pairs. Between 1993 and 1997, China's footwear production grew at a rate of 8.5 percent annually. In 1997, India produced 680 million pairs, or 6.2 percent of total world production. Indonesia and Brazil had 4.7 percent each, and Italy had 4.2 percent. Thailand, Turkey, Mexico, Spain, and Vietnam, in that order, filled out the top 10. For the first time, the United States was not ranked among the top 10 producers in 1997.

In 1997, the United States was by far the world's largest footwear importer, receiving 1.5 billion pairs, or 22 percent of total world imports of 6.5 billion pairs. European Union imports totaled about 4.2 billion pairs in 1997. That represented 65 percent of total world exports. China's share far exceeded that of the second largest exporter, Italy, which shipped 414 million pairs, or 6.3 percent of total world footwear exports. Indonesia (3.5 percent), Vietnam (2.7 percent), and Thailand (2.4 percent) had the next largest shares. The shares for Taiwan and South Korea each fell below 1 percent of total world exports in 1997.

Total world footwear consumption in 1997 was estimated at 11.051 billion pairs. U.S. consumption was 1.622 billion pairs, or 14.7 percent of the world total. China's share was 21 percent, but U.S. per capita consumption of 6.2 pairs for 1997 far exceeded China's 1.8 pairs and that of most other countries. Per capita consumption worldwide was 1.91 pairs.

World Footwear Markets, 1999, also estimates that shoes with leather uppers accounted for almost 46 percent of total world footwear production in 1997. This amounted to about 5 billion pairs of shoes that used 11.8 billion square feet of leather, or 2.3 square feet per pair. The equivalent quantity of leather-making raw material consumed approximated 296 million equivalent cattlehide units.

The publication estimates world sports footwear production at 1.9 billion pairs, or 18 percent of total footwear produced. Eighty percent of sports footwear is produced in Asia, and most international sports companies source their shoes from that region. The majority of people buy sports footwear for leisure purposes rather than for active sports participation. World production of safety footwear was estimated at 125 million pairs in 1997, slightly more than 1 percent of total world production.

In 1997, wage rates in U.S. dollars per month for footwear manufacturing were $85 per month for China compared with $1,263 per month for the United States, a rate 15 times larger. Vietnam, at $50 monthly, was the only major producing country with a lower rate than China.

Domestic Trends

Shipments of nonrubber footwear declined about 14 percent in 1999 to about 106 million pairs. Shipments of footwear not elsewhere classified (nec) declined about 18 percent, and those for the other three types declined 13 percent each. Over the long term, nonrubber footwear shipments dropped from 642 million pairs in 1968 to the 1999 level, a compound annual rate of decline of 5.6 percent. Production was relatively stable only during the 4-year period of the Orderly Marketing Agreements with South Korea and Taiwan from 1977 to 1981 and the 3 years from 1986 through 1988.

Domestic production of nonrubber footwear declined about 14 percent in 1999 to an estimated 105.9 million pairs. In 1999, the value of industry shipments declined almost 15 percent to an estimated $2.7 billion. The decline affected all segments of the industry. Unit shipments of house slippers declined 13 percent in 1999 to 37.6 million pairs, shipments of men's footwear except athletic dropped 13 percent to 29.3 million pairs, shipments of women's footwear except athletic declined 13 percent to 32.2 million pairs, and shipments of footwear except rubber nec declined 18 percent to 6.8 million pairs. Imports increased more than domestic production declined, and apparent consumption of nonrubber footwear increased in 1999 to 1.372 billion pairs from 1.335 billion pairs in 1998. About 93.5 percent by quantity of apparent consumption in 1999 was supplied by imports. In 1999, per capita consumption of nonrubber footwear was about 4.7 pairs, up from 4.5 pairs in 1998 but down significantly from the historically high levels recorded during the 1980s, when consumption consistently exceeded 5 pairs per capita. These higher levels resulted from soaring demand for athletic-type footwear. Before 1980, annual per capita consumption of nonrubber footwear seldom reached four pairs.

Personal consumption expenditures (PCEs) on all types of footwear reached an annual rate of $41.5 billion in the second quarter of 1999, about even with the second quarter in 1998. The price deflator index for all footwear PCEs in 1999 was lower than that in 1992. In January–July 1999, the consumer price index (CPI) for nonrubber footwear was down about 1 percent from the same period in 1998. From 1992 to 1998, the CPI increased at a compound annual rate of only 0.4 percent, reflecting the substantial impact of low-priced imports on pricing at the retail level. The BLS's international price index for imported footwear has not increased since 1990.

The Census of Manufacturers for 1992 listed 318 companies operating 391 establishments in the nonrubber footwear industry. In 1968, more than 1,000 plants were operating. Published reports indicate that 11 plants were closed in 1997 and 5 were closed in 1998. More than 10 plant closures were expected for 1999. In 1999, total employment and production employment dropped about 13 percent each to 25,600 and 21,600, respectively.

Trends in Technology

The widespread use of computers has shortened production time, reduced costs, improved quality, and allowed manufacturers to respond rapidly to customers' orders. To maintain competitiveness, manufacturers must respond to trends in fashion within days or even hours rather than weeks. Computer-aided design (CAD) and computer-aided manufacturing (CAM) shoemaking systems help manufacturers improve competitiveness through better quality and by greatly expanding design capability, shortening delivery time, and lowering inventory and production costs. Three-dimensional CAD systems are used for developing styles, visualizing three-dimensional shoe designs, engineering patterns, doing three-dimensional designing of unit soles, producing lasts, and determining material requirements.

Programmable machines are now available for virtually every operation in the shoe manufacturing process, including cutting, sewing, folding, lasting, making, and bottoming. Continuous cutting machines can be used for leather and synthetic materials, producing material savings above 10 percent in some cases. The latest developments in automatic stitching use some of the most advanced techniques in vision and computer technologies to improve quality and vastly increase productivity in the high-cost labor operations where Far Eastern manufacturers have a substantial advantage.

Robots reduce labor and material costs and increase quality. As a result, they are being used increasingly in shoemaking to perform some of the tedious repetitive tasks that used to be done manually. Currently, robots are being used for direct injection molding operations, but they also can be used for roughing, cement application, spraying, trimming, last pulling, and general handling on production lines.

Much of this new technology has been developed and used in Europe and, depending on the availability of capital, can be transferred readily to Far Eastern producers. However, the benefits of such labor-saving technology would not be as great for producers with low labor costs. The net effect of such technology would be to reduce the cost, increase the quality, and shorten response times for U.S. production relative to Far Eastern production, although the Far East would continue to maintain a competitive though more narrow cost advantage for most footwear.

BLS labor productivity indexes for nonrubber footwear increased at a compound annual rate of 6 percent from 1991 to 1996 after a long period of stable or declining productivity. The increase was 7 percent for men's footwear. Further productivity increases could lead to increased investment in the domestic industry, improve its competitiveness, and return the production of some types of footwear to the United States.

Trade

Imports of nonrubber footwear in 1999 increased about 4.5 percent over 1998 to 1.3 billion pairs. The customs value declined about 1 percent to an estimated $11.4 billion. The unit value of imports in 1999 was $8.86, down about 5 percent from 1998 and almost 62 percent below the unit value of domestic production. In 1999, the unit value of imports from China was $6.84, about 6 percent below the $7.39 recorded in 1998 and the lowest unit value of all the major foreign suppliers. This unit value was only 30 percent of that for U.S. production at an estimated $22.60.

In 1999, the five largest suppliers by quantity of nonrubber footwear to the United States were China (74 percent of the total), Brazil (11 percent), Indonesia (5 percent), Italy (4 percent), and Spain (1.5 percent). Those five countries accounted for over 91 percent of all U.S. nonrubber footwear imports in that year. Although the United States imported nonrubber footwear from over 90 countries in 1999, only 3 other countries—Mexico, Thailand, and Taiwan—accounted for more than a 1 percent share of U.S. nonrubber footwear imports.

In 1999, imports of nonrubber footwear from China increased 9.5 percent and reached a record high of 980 million pairs valued at an estimated $6.78 billion. Taiwan and South Korea, which had been the two major U.S. suppliers until the mid-1980s, are no longer major producers or exporters because of their higher labor costs. Furthermore, Taiwan in particular is now supplying China's expanding footwear manufacturing operations with a large measure of technological and financial support.

In 1999, China was the leading supplier in all 19 major gender and upper material subcategories of nonrubber footwear imports. Italy ranked second for men's leather footwear; Brazil and Italy second and third, respectively, for women's leather footwear; and Indonesia second for athletic footwear. U.S. leather footwear imports accounted for about 52 percent of total nonrubber footwear imports in 1999. By comparison, leather footwear's share of domestic production was about 60 percent. Leather footwear imports averaged an estimated $13.04 per pair in 1999, down 4 percent from 1998, primarily because of a decline in worldwide leather prices in 1999. Leather footwear imports from China were $10.91 per pair, down almost 6 percent from 1998.

U.S. manufacturers export large quantities of cut footwear parts and other component materials to many developing countries, where they are reexported to the United States as partly finished or finished footwear. Under the U.S. Tariff Schedule (Heading No. 9802), import duties are assessed only on the value-added content. Moreover, imports of such footwear from Caribbean Basin countries, by statute, are accorded duty-free treatment if they are produced in those countries with 100 percent U.S. components. U.S. duties on unlasted nonrubber footwear are less than 5 percent, compared with 8.5 percent or more for completed footwear. Frequently, final manufacturing operations that require less labor, such as lasting, bottoming, finishing, and packing, are performed in the United States. In 1999, the value of imports of such unlasted footwear uppers was $295 million, down about 8 percent from 1998.

In 1999, U.S. exports of nonrubber footwear increased about 1 percent to an estimated 19.2 million pairs valued at $331 million. About 18 percent of U.S. production of nonrubber footwear was exported. The weaker U.S. dollar encouraged export growth to high-cost developed country markets, particularly the United Kingdom, France, and Italy. In 1999, Canada was the largest export market, receiving 18 percent by quantity of total U.S. nonrubber footwear exports, followed by Japan with 14 percent, Mexico with 13 percent, and the United Kingdom with 10 percent. The average unit price for the year was $17.31, down slightly from the price in 1998. Table 34-6 shows U.S. trade patterns by value in 1998.

TABLE 34-6: U.S. Trade Patterns in Footwear Except Rubber[1] in 1998
(millions of dollars; percent)

Exports			Imports		
Region[2]	Value[3]	Share, %	Region[2]	Value[3]	Share, %
NAFTA	69	21	NAFTA	264	2
Latin America	67	20	Latin America	1,096	10
Western Europe	73	22	Western Europe	2,024	18
Japan/Chinese Economic Area	81	24	Japan/Chinese Economic Area	6,773	59
Other Asia	7	2	Other Asia	1,187	10
Rest of world	34	10	Rest of world	142	1
World	332	100	World	11,486	100
Top Five Countries	Value	Share, %	Top Five Countries	Value	Share, %
Japan	72	22	China	6,611	58
Canada	54	16	Italy	1,138	10
Netherlands	24	7	Brazil	1,009	9
Mexico	15	5	Indonesia	575	5
Venezuela	11	3	Spain	379	3

[1] SIC 314.
[2] For definitions of regional groupings, see "Getting the Most Out of *Outlook 2000.*"
[3] Values may not sum to total due to rounding.
Source: U.S. Department of Commerce, Bureau of the Census.

In 1999, U.S. exports of nonrubber footwear to Japan declined about 6 percent, indicating the continuing difficulty U.S. producers have had in overcoming Japan's restrictive global tariff rate quotas on imported leather nonathletic footwear. These quotas, combined with the import licensing procedures required to administer them, discourage U.S. manufacturers from engaging distributors and expanding exports in Japan. The Japanese market for leather footwear is estimated at more than 200 million pairs, but Japan's quotas, which are legal under WTO trade rules, restrict leather footwear imports to less than 15 million pairs, or 7 percent of the Japanese market for those types.

Trade Actions

In 1995, the government of Argentina increased tariffs on certain textile, apparel, and footwear imports to levels substantially above their WTO-bound rates, which for footwear was 35 percent. Subsequently, a WTO dispute settlement panel found the duty increase on textiles to be illegal, but the Argentinian government was able to avoid such a determination on footwear by reimposing the higher duties under the WTO-legal safeguard rules. This action has stymied the efforts of several major U.S. exporters of branded athletic footwear to increase exports to Argentina, and it is unlikely that the safeguards will be removed until after the year 2000.

House Slippers

Shipments of house slippers (SIC 3142) declined about 13 percent in 1999 to an estimated 37.6 million pairs. Their product value dropped to about $121 million in constant dollars. Slippers accounted for 36 percent of the quantity but only 5 percent of the value of total nonrubber footwear product shipments in 1996, primarily because most slippers are of simple construction and are produced from lower-cost vinyls and textiles rather than leather. In 1999, the ratio of imports to apparent consumption for slippers was an estimated 61 percent by quantity, the lowest among the four sectors (see Table 34-7).

Men's Footwear Except Athletic

Shipments of men's footwear, which includes dress, casual, and work shoes and boots, totaled an estimated 29.3 million pairs in 1999, down about 13 percent from 1998. Their value declined about 15 percent from that in 1998. Leather is by far the most widely used upper material for men's footwear. By quantity, the ratio of imports to domestic consumption for men's footwear was an estimated 87 percent in 1999. Work shoe production accounted for about 50 percent of total men's footwear production.

Women's Footwear Except Athletic

Shipments of women's footwear declined about 13 percent in 1999 to an estimated 32.2 million pairs, and their value declined about the same percentage to an estimated $639 million. Women's footwear accounted for about 28 percent by quantity and 27 percent by value of all nonrubber footwear product shipments in 1999. By quantity, import penetration for this sector exceeded 94 percent, the highest among the four sectors.

Footwear Except Rubber Not Elsewhere Classified

Shipments of youths' and boys', misses', children's, infants' and babies', and athletic and other miscellaneous types of footwear declined about 18 percent in 1999 to an estimated 6.8 million pairs. Their value dropped about 16 percent to $167 million. Shipments of footwear in this group accounted for 6 percent by quantity and 7 percent by value of all product shipments of nonrubber footwear in 1999.

About 99 percent of all nonrubber athletic footwear is imported. In 1999, consumption of athletic footwear declined for the sixth consecutive year as high worldwide inventories were gradually reduced. Athletic footwear's share of the total

TABLE 34-7: Footwear Except Rubber (SIC 314) Trends and Forecasts
(millions of dollars except as noted)

	1992	1993	1994	1995	1996	1997[1]	1998[1]	1999[2]	2000[3]	Percent Change 97–98	98–99	99–00	96–00[4]
Industry data													
Value of shipments[5]	3,898	3,974	3,923	3,688	3,605	3,575	3,164	2,702		–11.5	–14.6		
3142 House slippers	285	302	204	113	128	138	154	133		11.6	–13.6		
3143 Men's footwear	2,210	2,351	2,461	2,420	2,413	2,522	2,169	1,846		–14.0	–14.9		
3144 Women's footwear	1,095	1,010	950	758	555	478	555	482		16.1	–13.2		
3149 Footwear nec	309	310	309	397	509	437	286	241		–34.6	–15.7		
Value of shipments (1992$)	3,898	3,907	3,816	3,477	3,345	3,250	2,852	2,458	2,467	–12.2	–13.8	0.4	–7.3
3142 House slippers	285	310	205	109	122	130	144	125	121	10.8	–13.2	–3.2	–0.2
3143 Men's footwear	2,210	2,305	2,382	2,257	2,218	2,260	1,925	1,665	1,682	–14.8	–13.5	1.0	–6.7
3144 Women's footwear	1,095	987	927	730	522	448	515	447	434	15.0	–13.2	–2.9	–4.5
3149 Footwear nec	309	305	302	381	483	412	268	221	230	–35.0	–17.5	4.1	–16.9
Total employment (thousands)	48.8	48.5	46.8	44.4	36.7	33.7	29.6	25.6	25.0	–12.2	–13.5	–2.3	–9.2
Production workers (thousands)	41.4	41.3	40.3	37.7	31.1	28.5	24.9	21.6	21.0	–12.6	–13.3	–2.8	–9.4
Average hourly earnings ($)	7.33	7.43	7.44	7.85	8.32	8.78	9.26	9.77		5.5	5.5		
Capital expenditures	51.2	40.3	58.8	34.1	34.5								
3142 House slippers	2.1	2.5	4.8	1.5	1.2								
3143 Men's footwear	32.8	26.1	43.3	23.6	25.8								
3144 Women's footwear	10.5	6.8	7.6	4.3	2.4								
3149 Footwear nec	5.8	4.9	3.1	4.7	5.1								
Product data													
Value of shipments[5]	3,608	3,707	3,739	3,402	3,128	3,074	2,804	2,398		–8.8	–14.5		
3142 House slippers	259	256	208	122	116	125	140	121		12.0	–13.6		
3143 Men's footwear	1,807	1,970	2,040	1,926	1,924	2,011	1,729	1,471		–14.0	–14.9		
3144 Women's footwear	1,229	1,188	1,190	959	735	634	736	639		16.1	–13.2		
3149 Footwear nec	314	293	301	394	354	304	199	167		–34.5	–16.1		
Value of shipments (1992$)	3,608	3,643	3,639	3,217	2,906	2,801	2,534	2,185	2,183	–9.5	–13.8	–0.1	–6.9
3142 House slippers	259	263	209	118	110	118	131	113	110	11.0	–13.7	–2.7	0.0
3143 Men's footwear	1,807	1,931	1,975	1,797	1,768	1,802	1,534	1,326	1,339	–14.9	–13.6	1.0	–6.7
3144 Women's footwear	1,229	1,160	1,161	924	692	594	683	593	575	15.0	–13.2	–3.0	–4.5
3149 Footwear nec	314	289	294	378	336	287	186	153	159	–35.2	–17.7	3.9	–17.1
Trade data													
Value of imports	8,616	9,290	9,698	9,984	10,478	11,544	11,486	11,370	11,711	–0.5	–1.0	3.0	2.8
Value of exports	343	332	382	370	385	378	332	331	325	–12.2	–0.3	–1.8	–4.1

[1] Estimate except imports and exports.
[2] Estimate.
[3] Forecast.
[4] Compound annual rate.
[5] For a definition of industry versus product values, see "Getting the Most Out of *Outlook 2000*."
Source: U.S. Department of Commerce: Bureau of the Census; International Trade Administration.

footwear market dropped to 529 million pairs, or 31 percent of combined nonrubber and rubber footwear consumption, totaling about 1.716 million pairs in 1999.

U.S. Industry Growth Projections for the Next Year

Shipments of nonrubber footwear are expected to remain relatively unchanged in the year 2000. Shipments by quantity of slippers and women's footwear will decline about 3 percent each. Men's footwear and footwear nec will increase 1 percent and 4 percent, respectively.

Long-Term Prospects

The production of footwear has become a truly global business. The U.S. market is dominated completely by imports, and large domestic manufacturers, importers, wholesalers, and retailers all continue to transfer product sourcing to countries with abundant low-cost labor, particularly those in Asia, such as China, Indonesia, Thailand, India, and Vietnam. Per capita consumption of footwear will increase slightly, but the gains will be recorded in casual and other types rather than in athletic footwear as the average age of the population increases. This shift in demand will result in the production of fewer pairs of higher quality, more comfortable footwear that wears longer than do most of the current styles.

The industry has demonstrated an ability to respond quickly and effectively to changes in the market. However, large producers in the Far East, particularly in China, have adopted some of the new technology and could become even more price-competitive than they are today. A stronger U.S. dollar could enlarge their price advantage over U.S. producers. Consequently, lower-cost foreign production could continue to provide stiff competition for domestic producers and limit their opportunity to increase their share of the U.S. footwear market. Only if a branded manufacturer were to build a plant in the United States incorporating all the latest technology would it be possible to demonstrate whether U.S. production could sufficiently narrow the cost gap to make the industry competitive again.

LUGGAGE AND PERSONAL LEATHER GOODS

The luggage and personal leather goods industries produce a wide variety of consumer goods, including leather gloves and mittens (SIC 3151), luggage (SIC 3161), women's handbags and purses (SIC 3171), personal leather goods (SIC 3172), and leather and sheepskin-lined clothing (SIC 2386).

The total value of industry shipments for all five of these industries declined about 10 percent in current dollars in 1999 to an estimated $1.65 billion. The value of product shipments fell about 9.5 percent to approximately $1.47 billion. When measured in constant (1992) dollars, both industry and product shipments declined about 9.5 percent from 1998. In 1999, total employment in these industries dropped almost 11 percent to 14,200 and production employment declined almost 14 percent to 10,100.

Global Industry Trends

The luggage and leather goods industries continue to encounter severe competition from low-cost imports, especially from China and developing countries, since labor costs represent a large proportion of total production costs. In 1999, the value of imports of luggage and personal leather goods totaled about $5.1 billion, which represented 83 percent of domestic consumption. In 1999, the value of exports for the group was an estimated $381 million, unchanged from 1998.

Leather Gloves and Mittens

The U.S. leather glove industry includes manufacturers of both dress and work gloves but excludes sports gloves. Work gloves account for more than 90 percent of domestic production. These products are made from leather or from combinations of leather and cotton, wool, or synthetic fibers.

The value of product shipments of these products declined about 25 percent in 1999 to $84 million. In constant dollars the decline was also about 25 percent (see Table 34-8). Total employment dropped about 24 percent to 1,480, and production employment fell about 25 percent to 1,290. In 1999, apparent consumption of gloves and mittens declined to $319 million from $388 million in 1998.

Imports declined about 14 percent to an estimated $284 million. However, the quantity of imports declined only about 6 percent because of lower leather prices and the substitution of lower-cost imported leather-fabric types for imports of leather gloves. Imports represented about 76 percent of apparent consumption. China captured 73 percent by value but 87 percent by quantity of total imports of leather gloves in 1999. The Philippines was the next largest supplier with a 5 percent share by value. In 1999, exports of leather gloves and mittens increased about 20 percent to an estimated $8.6 million. Canada was the largest customer for these exports, but China, Mexico, and Hong Kong received significant quantities of cut glove parts that were assembled in those countries and then reentered the United States under Section 9802 of the Harmonized Tariff Schedule of the United States. That section subjects such items to U.S. duties only on the value-added content.

Luggage

The luggage industry produces a wide variety of products, including suitcases, briefcases, attaché cases, hand luggage, tote bags, backpacks, occupational cases, computer cases, and musical instrument cases. The materials used include leather, plastics, textiles, metals, and various combinations. Leather use is highest in attaché cases and briefcases. Construction methods include sewing, molding, and laminating. A growing proportion of luggage is made of fabric and incorporates wheels, which allow the traveler to pack more clothes with very little increase in weight compared with earlier styles of luggage.

In 1999, the product value of shipments of these products declined about 11 percent from the 1998 level to a real $691 million. Measured in constant dollars, product shipments fell almost 11 percent. Total employment dropped about 16 percent to 4,400, and production employment declined 11 percent to 3,200. Apparent consumption by value of luggage dropped to $2.9 billion in 1999 from $3 billion in 1998.

The value of imports remained unchanged in 1999 at $2.45 billion, but the quantity of imports rose about 11 percent, primarily because a strong U.S. dollar during most of 1999 allowed major suppliers such as China to reduce export prices. By value, imports were 84 percent of apparent consumption. The principal sources of luggage imports were China with 39 percent of the total, Thailand with 12 percent, the Philippines with 9 percent, and South Korea and Taiwan with 6 percent each. The top 10 suppliers captured 90 percent of total luggage imports. In 1999, U.S. luggage exports increased 2 percent to an estimated $233 million. The largest export markets were Canada, Japan, Germany, and Mexico.

Handbags

The U.S. handbag industry produces women's handbags and purses made of leather and other materials except precious metal. About 64 percent of handbag shipments in 1992 were made wholly or partially of leather. In 1999, the value of handbag product shipments declined about 13 percent to an estimated $161 million in current dollars from $185 million in 1998 (see Table 34-8). Product shipments in constant dollars also dropped about 13 percent. Total employment was 2,200, and production employment was 1,100. In 1999, apparent consumption of handbags dropped about 2 percent to $1.16 billion. Imports of handbags totaled $1.02 billion, or 89 percent of apparent consumption. Although the value of imports was vir-

TABLE 34-8: Luggage and Personal Leather Goods (SIC 2386, 3151, 3161, 3171, 3172) Trends and Forecasts
(millions of dollars except as noted)

	1992	1993	1994	1995	1996	1997[1]	1998[1]	1999[2]	2000[3]	Percent Change 97–98	98–99	99–00	96–00[4]
Industry data													
Value of shipments[5]	2,207	2,106	2,070	1,891	2,030	1,993	1,828	1,649		−8.3	−9.8		
2386 Leather and sheepskin-lined clothing	209	224	237	206	190	216	230	243		6.5	5.7		
3151 Leather gloves and mittens	140	169	145	114	145	146	128	96		−12.3	−25.0		
3161 Luggage	968	930	991	946	1,115	1,136	1,044	928		−8.1	−11.1		
3171 Women's handbags and purses	463	387	304	305	286	229	176	153		−23.1	−13.1		
3172 Personal goods nec	428	395	393	321	294	266	250	229		−6.0	−8.4		
Value of shipments (1992$)	2,207	2,090	2,064	1,888	2,007	1,944	1,767	1,598	1,506	−9.1	−9.6	−5.8	−6.9
2386 Leather and sheepskin-lined clothing	209	225	247	218	201	225	238	251	256	5.8	5.5	2.0	6.2
3151 Leather gloves and mittens	140	168	137	103	125	124	107	80	73	−13.7	−25.2	−8.8	−12.6
3161 Luggage	968	922	979	942	1,102	1,104	1,003	894	848	−9.1	−10.9	−5.1	−6.3
3171 Women's handbags and purses	463	385	313	307	291	236	181	157	136	−23.3	−13.3	−13.4	−17.3
3172 Personal goods nec	428	389	388	317	289	255	238	216	193	−6.7	−9.2	−10.6	−9.6
Total employment (thousands)	26.4	24.3	22.1	18.5	18.1	17.0	15.9	14.2		−6.5	−10.7		
Production workers (thousands)	21.1	19.0	17.7	14.8	14.4	13.2	11.7	10.1		−11.4	−13.7		
Average hourly earnings ($)	7.43	7.41	7.55	7.85	8.13								
Capital expenditures	27.9	28.2	26.8	30.9	36.7								
2386 Leather and sheepskin-lined clothing	1.3	1.6	0.1	0.6	0.2								
3151 Leather gloves and mittens	0.5	0.3	12.2	18.4	12.3								
3161 Luggage	15.9	16.4	9.5	6.1	17.8								
3171 Women's handbags and purses	3.4	4.2	3.1	3.7	3.6								
3172 Personal goods nec	6.8	5.7	1.9	2.1	2.8								
Product data													
Value of shipments[5]	2,109	2,013	2,050	1,818	1,822	1,769	1,621	1,468		−8.4	−9.4		
2386 Leather and sheepskin-lined clothing	199	216	222	194	183	208	221	233		6.3	5.4		
3151 Leather gloves and mittens	114	115	115	93	125	126	111	84		−11.9	−24.3		
3161 Luggage	864	814	880	778	830	846	777	691		−8.2	−11.1		
3171 Women's handbags and purses	411	366	328	315	301	241	185	161		−23.2	−13.0		
3172 Personal goods nec	522	503	505	438	384	348	327	299		−6.0	−8.6		
Value of shipments (1992$)	2,109	1,997	2,045	1,816	1,804	1,728	1,570	1,424	1,336	−9.1	−9.3	−6.2	−7.2
2386 Leather and sheepskin-lined clothing	199	217	231	205	193	217	229	240	245	5.5	4.8	2.1	6.1
3151 Leather gloves and mittens	114	114	109	85	108	107	93	70	64	−13.1	−24.7	−8.6	−12.3
3161 Luggage	864	807	869	775	820	822	746	666	631	−9.2	−10.7	−5.3	−6.3
3171 Women's handbags and purses	411	364	338	318	305	248	191	166	144	−23.0	−13.1	−13.3	−17.1
3172 Personal goods nec	522	495	498	433	378	334	311	282	252	−6.9	−9.3	−10.6	−9.6
Trade data													
Value of imports	3,882	4,068	4,560	4,670	4,771	5,103	5,171	5,108		1.3	−1.2		
2386 Leather and sheepskin-lined clothing	1,229	1,221	1,238	989	910	974	931	894		−4.4	−4.0		
3151 Leather gloves and mittens	171	214	261	291	295	309	284	244		−8.1	−14.1		
3161 Luggage	1,273	1,403	1,700	1,965	2,042	2,312	2,453	2,448		6.1	−0.2		
3171 Women's handbags and purses	890	910	959	972	1,055	1,051	1,018	1,016		−3.1	−0.2		
3172 Personal goods nec	319	321	401	454	470	457	485	506		6.1	4.3		
Value of exports	270	283	311	355	384	408	379	381		−7.1	0.5		
2386 Leather and sheepskin-lined clothing	65	69	65	89	68	71	67	51		−4.9	−24.1		
3151 Leather gloves and mittens	12	14	14	13	10	7	7	9		9.1	19.4		
3161 Luggage	135	138	166	176	231	250	228	233		−8.8	2.2		
3171 Women's handbags and purses	35	41	42	50	46	46	41	37		−10.8	−11.6		
3172 Personal goods nec	23	20	24	27	29	34	35	51		3.9	46.9		

[1] Estimate except imports and exports.
[2] Estimate.
[3] Forecast.
[4] Compound annual rate.
[5] For a definition of industry versus product values, see "Getting the Most Out of *Outlook 2000*."
Source: U.S. Department of Commerce: Bureau of the Census; International Trade Administration.

tually unchanged from 1998, their quantity increased about 6 percent as the price per unit dropped. Most manufacturers, distributors, and retailers of well-established and higher-priced brands are sourcing a large proportion of their handbag requirements from overseas manufacturers. In 1999, China was the largest supplier of handbags to the U.S. market with a 62 percent share of total U.S. imports; Italy had a 17 percent share. In 1999, exports of handbags were down 12 percent to $36.7 million. Japan, Mexico, and Canada were the leading export markets, although a large proportion of U.S. handbag exports to

Mexico consisted of cut handbag parts that were assembled there and reexported to the United States.

Personal Leather Goods

Manufacturers in this industry sector produce small articles carried on the person or in a handbag, such as billfolds, wallets, key cases, French purses, credit card cases, and cases for eyeglasses and cigarettes. These products often are referred to as flat goods. They are made mostly of leather or leather combined with textiles or plastics.

In 1999, product shipments of flat goods declined 8.5 percent to $299 million in current dollars from $327 million in 1998. Product shipments in constant dollars declined 9 percent from 1998. In 1999, total employment dropped 6 percent to 4,000 and production employment declined 9 percent to 2,700.

Apparent consumption of flat goods fell about 3 percent to $754 million from $777 million in 1998. Imports rose 4.5 percent to an estimated $506 million and accounted for 67 percent of apparent consumption, the lowest percentage for all the industries in the luggage and leather goods group. The largest suppliers were China with a 55 percent share of total imports and India and Italy with 9 percent each. In 1999, U.S. exports of personal leather goods were up 47 percent to about $51 million and went primarily to Japan and Canada.

Leather and Sheepskin-Lined Clothing

Manufacturers of leather wearing apparel produce leather coats, jackets, and other garments for men, women, and children. Shipments include leather pants, vests, dresses, skirts, suits, caps, and other clothing. Demand for these products is highly seasonal, with most retail sales concentrated in the fall and winter, and is directly related to trends in fashion. Therefore, consumer spending on leather wearing apparel is largely discretionary, and consumption patterns can vary widely from year to year because of fluctuations in the price of leather, weather conditions, and styles.

In 1999, product shipments of leather wearing apparel increased almost 6 percent to $233 million in current dollars from $221 million in 1998. Measured in constant dollars, product shipments increased over 5 percent. Total employment rose 8 percent to 2,100, and production employment increased 5 percent to 1,900. In 1999, apparent consumption of leather wearing apparel declined slightly to $1.08 billion.

In 1999, imports of leather apparel declined 4 percent to an estimated $894 million from $931 million in 1998. Import penetration in 1999 was 83 percent, down from 86 percent in 1998 and a high of 90 percent in 1994. China was by far the largest supplier in 1999, with 59 percent of total leather wearing apparel imports. Italy and Pakistan had 8 percent and 7 percent shares, respectively. U.S. exports of leather wearing apparel in 1999 were down about 24 percent to $51 million, and Canada was the largest market.

U.S. Industry Growth Projections for the Next 1 and 5 Years

In the year 2000, consumption of luggage and leather products is expected to increase 1 percent to an estimated $6.26 billion. Imports are expected to rise about 3 percent and reach 84 percent of consumption. As a result, product shipments in constant dollars are expected to drop 6 percent. The rate of decline varied among categories: luggage, –5 percent; leather gloves and mittens, –8.5 percent; personal leather goods, –11 percent; and handbags, –13 percent. Shipments of leather wearing apparel will increase about 2 percent.

Consumer demand for luggage and leather products is expected to strengthen over the next 5 years. Increased employment in the white-collar segment of the services and high-tech industries should lead to increased purchases of leather office products. Leather work glove consumption directly correlates with changes in manufacturing output and should increase. Larger numbers of professional women should lead to higher sales of business cases, computer cases, and luggage. Large numbers of senior citizens and retirees with higher disposable income should stimulate more travel and corresponding increases in luggage sales.

However, relentless competition from abroad will continue, and U.S. manufacturers are unlikely to regain much, if any, of the domestic market share lost to imports over the last two decades. Nevertheless, with the help of a favorably valued dollar, innovative and aggressive producers can expect to expand exports and at least share in the future expansion of domestic consumption of luggage and leather products.

Over the next 5 years, the constant dollar value of luggage and leather product shipments is expected to decrease at a compound annual rate of about 3.5 percent. Four sectors are expected to decline: luggage and leather gloves and mittens, 1 percent each; handbags, 7 percent; and personal leather goods, 8 percent. Leather wearing apparel will increase 2 percent.

James E. Byron, U.S. Department of Commerce, Office of Consumer Goods, (202) 482-4034, September 1999.

REFERENCES

American Shoemaking (monthly), *World Footwear* (monthly), and *American Shoemaking Directory,* 1999, Shoe Trades Publishing Co., Inc., 61 Massachusetts Avenue, Arlington, MA 02474-0023. (781) 648-8160, info@shoetrades.com.

Footwear: Current Industrial Report (quarterly, with annual summary), MQ31A, U.S. Department of Commerce, Bureau of the Census, Industry Division, Washington, DC 20233. (301) 457-4673 or 1-800-STAT-USA, www.stat-usa.gov or www.census.gov.

Footwear Manual and *World Footwear Markets* (*SATRA*), Footwear Industries of America, Inc., 1420 K Street, NW, Washington, DC 20005. (202) 789-1420.

Footwear News (weekly), Fairchild Publications Inc., 7 West 34 Street, New York, NY 10001-8191. (800) 360-1700, plotkina@fairchildpub.com.

Journal of the American Leather Chemists Association, Leather Industries of America Research Laboratory, Campus Station, Cincinnati, OH 45221.

Leather Gloves, Luggage and Miscellaneous Leather Goods, SIC 3151, 3161, 3171, 3172; 1992 and 1997 Census of Manufacturers, U.S. Department of Commerce, Bureau of the Census, Washington, DC 20233.

Leather International Journal of the Industry (monthly), and *International Leather Guide, 1999,* Miller Freeman UK Ltd., Sovereign Way, Tonbridge, Kent TN91RW, United Kingdom. (44)(0)1732364422, andrew.lee@unmf.com.

Membership Bulletin Leather Industry Statistics, 1999 Edition, Leather Industries of America, Inc., 1000 Thomas Jefferson Street, NW, Suite 515, Washington, DC 20007. (202) 342-8086.

Miscellaneous Apparel and Accessories, SIC 2371, 2385, 2386, 2387, 2389; 1992 and 1997 Census of Manufacturers, U.S. Department of Commerce, Bureau of the Census, Washington, DC 20233.

Nonrubber Footwear Quarterly Statistical Reports, U.S. International Trade Commission, Washington, DC 20436.

Travelware, Business Journals, Inc., 50 Day Street, Norwalk, CT 06854.

World Footwear Markets, 1999, Shoe and Allied Trades Research Association (SATRA), Kettering, Northants NN169JH, United Kingdom. (44)1-536-410000.

World Statistical Compendium for Raw Hides and Skins, Leather and Leather Footwear, 1976–1995, Seventh Edition, Food and Agriculture Organization of the United Nations, United Nations Publications.

RELATED CHAPTERS

12: Synthetic Rubber

33: Apparel and Fabricated Textile Products

42: Retailing

PROCESSED FOODS AND BEVERAGES
Economic and Trade Trends

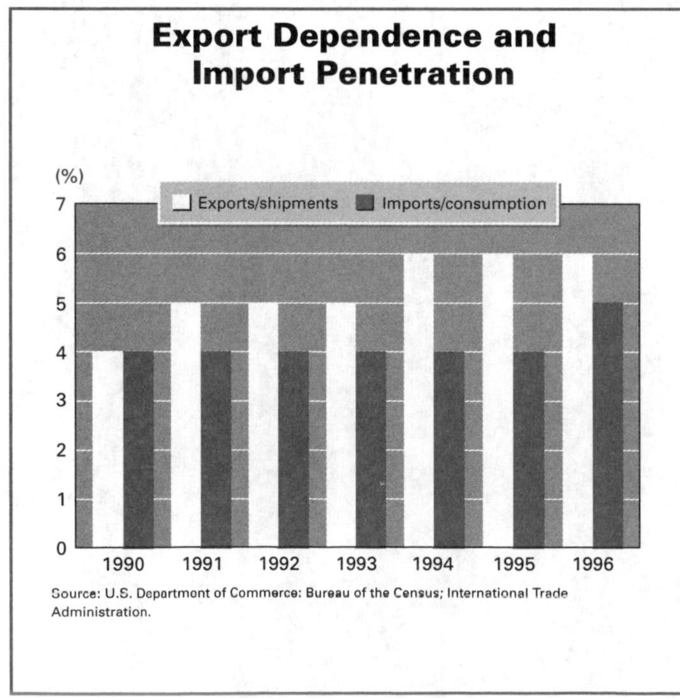

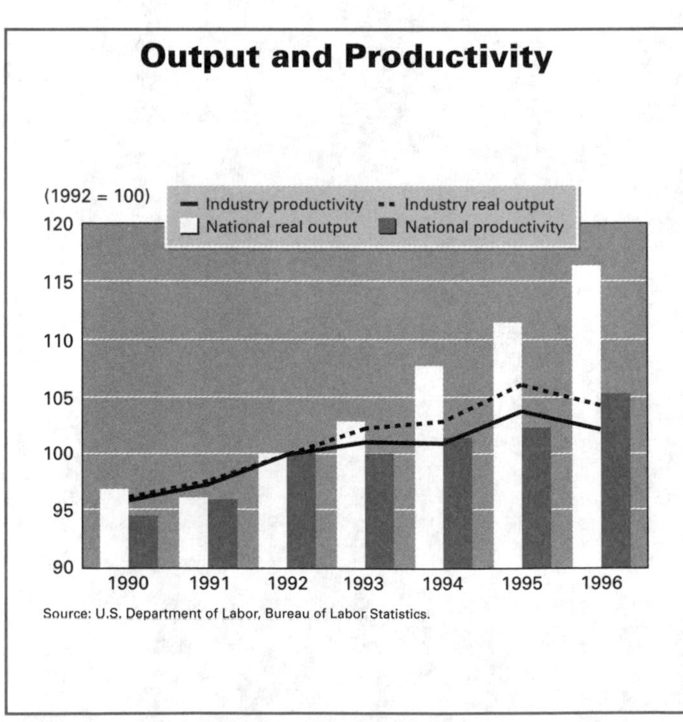

See "Getting the Most Out of *Outlook 2000*" for definitions of terms.

35

Processed Foods and Beverages

INDUSTRY DEFINITION This industry includes establishments that manufacture or process foods and beverages for human consumption and related products such as manufactured ice, chewing gum, vegetable and animal fats and oils, and prepared feeds for animals and fowl. Subsectors in this chapter include red meats and poultry (SIC 2011, 2013, 2015), snack foods (SIC 2068, 2096) and other assorted items related to snack foods, and alcoholic beverages such as malt beverages (SIC 2082), wines and brandy (SIC 2084), and distilled spirits (SIC 2085).

OVERVIEW

Globalization in the processed food and beverage markets is increasing at a tremendous rate as most developed countries face mature domestic markets. Food and beverage companies are becoming more aware of the excellent opportunities resulting from exporting or making foreign direct investment. The U.S. processed food and beverage industry is a major participant in this global economy. Almost half the world's top 50 food processing firms are headquartered in the United States.

The processed food and beverage industry (SIC 20) is one of the United States' largest manufacturing sectors, accounting for about one-sixth of industrial activity. In 1999, the value of food and beverage shipments was expected to reach an estimated $486.7 billion. In constant dollars, shipments were expected to rise 2.4 percent. In the year 2000, the U.S. food and beverage industry is projected to grow 1.8 percent in constant dollars (see Table 35-1).

The world economic situation and the strength of the U.S. dollar have taken a toll on U.S. exports of processed food and beverages. In 1999, for the first time in more than two decades, the United States was expected to import more processed foods and beverages than it exported: $25.4 billion versus $24.8 billion. U.S. exports fell 6 percent, while imports grew 7.5 percent from 1998 levels (see Table 35-2). U.S. exports of more price-sensitive items were affected (e.g., nonbranded commodity-type items such as fats and oils, meats, and wet corning milling).

In 1999, U.S. exports of these low-valued-added items fell more than 13 percent while consumer branded food items (beverages, candy, snacks, canned foods) showed a modest increase of about 0.2 percent. This indicates that even though the strength of the U.S. dollar puts U.S. exports at a price disadvantage, U.S. consumer-ready food items still are popular around the world.

The price sensitivity of low-value-added exports is a phenomenon not just in the United States but in other developed nations as well. A possible indicator of this is the composition of U.S. processed food and beverage imports. Most of the growth in U.S. imports came from imports of consumer branded-type imports rather than lower-value-added items (10 percent versus 1 percent).

Consolidation is continuing in the processed food and beverage industry as less efficient plants close or merge with more efficient ones. In 1998, mergers and acquisitions in this industry increased more than 20 percent. In the next 5 years, constant dollar shipments are expected to grow 1.4 to 2.6 percent annually.

Electronic Commerce

The U.S. on-line population is poised to explode. According to a report by the International Data Corporation, the number of people on-line totals 90 million and is expected to double by 2003.

TABLE 35-1: Food and Kindred Products (SIC 20) Trends and Forecasts
(millions of dollars except as noted)

										Percent Change			
	1992	1993	1994	1995	1996	1997[1]	1998[1]	1999[2]	2000[3]	97–98	98–99	99–00	96–00[4]
Industry data													
Value of shipments[5]	406,963	422,220	430,963	446,869	461,324	469,944	476,565	486,686		1.4	2.1		
Value of shipments (1992$)	406,963	415,099	419,135	430,949	422,920	428,143	439,660	450,202	458,115	2.7	2.4	1.8	2.0
Total employment (thousands)	1,503	1,520	1,511	1,520	1,517	1,518	1,525	1,528	1,527	0.5	0.2	–0.1	0.2
Production workers (thousands)	1,100	1,118	1,112	1,120	1,113	1,112	1,120	1,126	1,125	0.7	0.5	–0.1	0.3
Average hourly earnings ($)	10.41	10.58	10.74	10.96	11.17	11.45	11.77	12.08		2.8	2.6		
Capital expenditures	9,898	9,389	10,093	11,812	11,717								
Product data													
Value of shipments[5]	382,889	397,633	405,490	421,507	435,009	442,730	448,720	458,470		1.4	2.2		
Value of shipments (1992$)	382,889	391,076	394,419	406,235	398,663	403,214	413,832	423,866	431,522	2.6	2.4	1.8	2.0
Trade data													
Value of imports	15,967	15,779	17,106	18,109	20,637	22,421	23,565	25,440		5.1	8.0		
Value of exports	19,134	19,954	22,419	25,143	26,015	27,625	26,457	24,832		–4.2	–6.1		

[1] Estimate except imports and exports.
[2] Estimate.
[3] Forecast.
[4] Compound annual rate.
[5] For a definition of industry versus product values, see "Getting the Most Out of *Outlook 2000.*"
Source: U.S. Department of Commerce: Bureau of the Census; International Trade Administration.

The number of transactions could reach 2.1 billion by that year. According to a study by Forrester Research, the large volume of small parcels that needs to be delivered will spark logistics suppliers to develop new solutions that will get small orders from low-volume vendors to private individuals in a cost-effective manner.

Also according to Forrester Research, in 1998 approximately $40 billion to $50 billion in commerce was conducted over the Internet. Of that amount, about one-eighth was consumer retail and the rest consisted of business-to-business transactions. The total figure could exceed $400 billion by 2003. The U.S. Bureau of the Census estimates the retail figure in 1998 to be between $3 billion and $18 billion, depending on the definition of on-line sales.

The convenience factor is expected to fuel the growth in on-line grocery shopping. According to Forrester Research, over the next 5 years consumers are projected to spend 45 times the

TABLE 35-2: U.S. Trade Patterns in Food and Kindred Products[1] in 1998
(millions of dollars; percent)

Exports			Imports		
Region[2]	Value[3]	Share, %	Region[2]	Value[3]	Share, %
NAFTA	7,459	28	NAFTA	7,508	32
Latin America	2,783	11	Latin America	2,404	10
Western Europe	3,933	15	Western Europe	7,813	33
Japan/Chinese Economic Area	7,200	27	Japan/Chinese Economic Area	886	4
Other Asia	1,899	7	Other Asia	2,618	11
Rest of world	3,183	12	Rest of world	2,336	10
World	26,457	100	World	23,565	100
Top Five Countries	**Value**	**Share, %**	**Top Five Countries**	**Value**	**Share, %**
Japan	4,737	18	Canada	5,608	24
Canada	4,671	18	Mexico	1,900	8
Mexico	2,788	11	France	1,710	7
Hong Kong	1,022	4	Italy	1,366	6
South Korea	854	3	United Kingdom	968	4

[1] SIC 20.
[2] For definitions of regional groupings, see "Getting the Most Out of *Outlook 2000.*"
[3] Values may not sum to total due to rounding.
Source: U.S. Department of Commerce, Bureau of the Census.

$235 million spent on on-line groceries in 1998, generating an estimated $11 billion in E-commerce grocery sales by 2003. Of those sales, about 60 percent will be spent on specialty items such as kosher products, upscale chocolate, and gift baskets, with the remaining 40 percent spent on full-line groceries.

In an effort to reach consumers, food processors are using the Internet through electronic couponing. While coupons on-line account for only 0.004 percent of the 259 billion coupons offered through the print media, the redemption rate is 7.5 percent compared with a rate of 1.5 to 2 percent for coupons offered through newspapers and mailings.

Internet sales of alcoholic beverages face obstacles that food and nonalcoholic beverages do not face. While states cannot prohibit interstate commerce in food and nonalcoholic beverages, they can do so for alcoholic beverages. Because of the Twenty-First Amendment to the U.S. Constitution, it is unlawful to transport liquor into any state that prohibits such transactions. It is the only item in the Constitution that allows state rights to supersede federal regulation of interstate commerce. This has been upheld in the courts (*Utah v. Beer Across America*). As a result of the three-tiered system (producers can sell only to wholesalers that can sell to retailers or other end users) that many small producers feel stifles growth, these small producers of wine or microbeers have fully embraced the Internet. For example, a small winery in California now can sell directly to individuals in Connecticut, who otherwise may not be able to purchase the item in Connecticut unless a Connecticut wholesaler stocks the item.

With the increased use of the Internet for buying alcoholic beverages, state and federal agencies are studying the issue for three major reasons: (1) revenue lost by the state, (2) variation in the legal drinking age from state to state, and (3) whether the state prohibits such transactions (Who is going to keep tabs on shippers to make sure the "little brown package" does not contain an alcoholic beverage?).

ALCOHOLIC BEVERAGES

The alcoholic beverage industry consists of establishments engaged primarily in manufacturing malt beverages (SIC 2082), wines, brandies, and brandy spirits (SIC 2084) and establishments engaged primarily in manufacturing alcoholic liquors by distillation and manufacturing alcoholic cocktails through blending processes or by mixing liquors and other ingredients (SIC 2085).

Global Industry Trends

The alcoholic beverage industry has three major sectors: beer, wine, and distilled spirits. Except in a handful of situations, producers do not venture out of their respective sectors. Per capita consumption in many major developed countries has leveled off. As a result, most producers have had to find niche markets for their products overseas to continue to grow. Malt beverage and distilled spirit companies have had to establish licensing agreements and joint ventures in addition to exporting to continue to satisfy their owners' desire to increase profits.

Beer. According to a *Euromonitor* study, world beer output grew in volume more than 7 percent between 1993 and 1997 and is expected to grow almost 10 percent through 2002. Average world per capita consumption is 5.6 gallons. Among the 56 major beer markets, the Czech Republic leads in per capita consumption with 45.3 gallons. Other markets include Germany with just over 34 gallons; Australia, New Zealand, and the United States with 20 to 22 gallons; South Africa with just over 12 gallons; Brazil with 9 gallons; Russia with just over 3 gallons; China with almost 3 gallons; and India with only 0.1 gallon. The regions experiencing the greatest consumption growth rates have been Asia, the Middle East, eastern Europe, and Latin America.

Despite the economic crisis in Asia, beer consumption in that region as a whole has been stable. The differences have occurred among individual countries. While Indonesia suffered a 40 percent drop in consumption between 1997 and 1998, consumption continued to increase in Thailand and Vietnam and, to a lesser extent, in Singapore. Between 1997 and 2003, beer output in Asia is expected to increase over 75 percent.

The beer market in Latin America will continue to develop positively, according to the Latin American beverage expert José J. Yordan. The main reason for this optimistic outlook is that (1) the population grows faster than it does in industrialized countries, (2) the average age is lower, and as a consequence, the beer-drinking age group will increase more rapidly than will the total population, (3) per capita consumption is still comparatively low, a factor that characterizes emerging beer markets, and (4) the tropical climate is favorable to beer consumption. Per capita beer consumption in the region is highest in Venezuela at 16.5 gallons, followed by Colombia at 12.4 gallons, Brazil at 9 gallons, Chile at 7.5 gallons, and Argentina at 6.5 gallons. Overall, beer output in all of Latin America has increased over 36 percent since 1990 to 2.76 billion gallons (12.55 billion liters).

Wine. Internationally, although the wine industry in each country still relies heavily on exports to increase sales, many countries are realizing that countries should work together to find ways to reduce barriers to the wine trade. The international wine industry is evolving into a global, market-oriented industry. Marketing strategies have shifted. In the past, western Europe (old world regional wines) set the standard in the wine trade, but that situation is changing. Wines from the new world (branded varietals), although accounting for only about one-seventh of world production and 5 to 7 percent of world exports, have been gaining a more prominent active role in international trade. In 1998, the first of several meetings was held among the new world wine producers (NWWPs) to discuss actions needed to reduce trade barriers for wine. Two more meetings were held in 1999. Members of this organization include Argentina, Australia, Canada, Chile, New Zealand, South Africa, Uruguay, and the United States.

Distilled Spirits. The international distilled spirits industry has faced hard times because of economic crises in the fastest-growing markets for their products. As a result, according to *Impact,* a major alcoholic beverage trade publication, major multinationals have moved inexorably toward the creation of powerful core premium brand groups that are responsible for growth in the global marketplace, while their other brands are tapped on a more narrow strategic basis, usually according to regional or local strengths. Globally, white spirits account for about 42 percent of the branded distilled spirits markets, followed by local spirits with 28 percent and whiskey with 18 percent.

Domestic Trends

Between 1990 and 1997, total U.S. production of alcoholic beverages declined 2 percent to 6.7 million gallons; however, between 1996 and 1997, it registered a modest 0.6 percent increase. There continued to be modest growth between 1997 and 1999. Per capita consumption has remained relatively stable in recent years as consumers have shifted to higher-priced

TABLE 35-3: Alcoholic Beverages (SIC 2082, 2084, 2085) Trends and Forecasts
(millions of dollars except as noted)

										Percent Change			
	1992	1993	1994	1995	1996	1997[1]	1998[1]	1999[2]	2000[3]	97–98	98–99	99–00	96–00[4]
Industry data													
Value of shipments[5]	25,035	24,739	24,983	25,652	27,441	28,277	28,770	29,651		1.7	3.1		
2082 Malt beverages	17,340	16,656	16,795	17,151	18,220	18,408	18,638	19,404		1.2	4.1		
2084 Wines and brandy	4,301	4,514	4,301	4,798	5,548	6,087	6,304	6,492		3.6	3.0		
2085 Distilled liquor	3,394	3,569	3,888	3,703	3,673	3,782	3,828	3,755		1.2	–1.9		
Value of shipments (1992$)	25,035	24,802	25,333	25,251	26,160	26,499	26,870	27,245	27,635	1.4	1.4	1.4	1.4
2082 Malt beverages	17,340	16,859	17,332	17,100	17,655	17,700	17,870	18,135	18,335	1.0	1.5	1.1	0.9
2084 Wines and brandy	4,301	4,465	4,267	4,723	5,175	5,435	5,600	5,710	5,855	3.0	2.0	2.5	3.1
2085 Distilled liquor	3,394	3,478	3,734	3,429	3,330	3,365	3,400	3,400	3,445	1.0	0.0	1.3	0.9
Total employment (thousands)	55.6	56.4	53.8	55.6	57.6	56.0	55.6	55.7	56.0	–0.7	0.2	0.5	–0.7
2082 Malt beverages	34.5	35.3	33.5	32.6	34.0	32.3	31.7	31.7	31.8	–1.9	0.0	0.3	–1.7
2084 Wines and brandy	14.0	14.1	13.7	16.3	17.0	17.0	17.4	17.5	17.6	2.4	0.6	0.6	0.9
2085 Distilled liquor	7.1	7.0	6.6	6.7	6.6	6.7	6.5	6.5	6.6	–3.0	0.0	1.5	0.0
Production workers (thousands)	36.7	37.0	34.9	35.9	36.8	35.7	35.2	35.2	35.5	–1.4	0.0	0.9	–0.9
2082 Malt beverages	25.1	25.3	23.6	23.6	24.6	23.4	22.9	22.9	23.0	–2.1	0.0	0.4	–1.7
2084 Wines and brandy	6.5	6.6	6.6	7.5	7.5	7.5	7.7	7.7	7.8	2.7	0.0	1.3	1.0
2085 Distilled liquor	5.1	5.1	4.7	4.8	4.7	4.8	4.6	4.6	4.7	–4.2	0.0	2.2	0.0
Average hourly earnings ($)	19.83	19.81	20.15	20.37	20.22	20.75	20.81	20.95		0.3	0.7		
2082 Malt beverages	22.89	22.71	23.01	23.92	23.39	23.86	24.00	24.16		0.6	0.7		
2084 Wines and brandy	12.68	12.80	13.53	13.05	13.56	13.83	13.90	13.99		0.5	0.6		
2085 Distilled liquor	15.05	15.49	15.43	15.38	16.07	16.39	16.47	16.58		0.5	0.7		
Capital expenditures	736	668	754	1,138	1,200								
2082 Malt beverages	565	479	564	861	877								
2084 Wines and brandy	115	146	151	209	269								
2085 Distilled liquor	56	42	40	67	54								
Product data													
Value of shipments[5]	24,607	24,324	24,370	25,155	26,794	27,596	28,080	28,975		1.8	3.2		
2082 Malt beverages	17,302	16,629	16,714	17,108	18,196	18,380	18,610	19,380		1.3	4.1		
2084 Wines and brandy	4,050	4,355	4,196	4,675	5,411	5,936	6,150	6,335		3.6	3.0		
2085 Distilled liquor	3,255	3,340	3,460	3,372	3,188	3,280	3,320	3,260		1.2	–1.8		
Value of shipments (1992$)	24,607	24,394	24,735	24,780	25,568	25,894	26,254	26,630	27,010	1.4	1.4	1.4	1.4
2082 Malt beverages	17,302	16,831	17,249	17,057	17,631	17,674	17,844	18,110	18,310	1.0	1.5	1.1	0.9
2084 Wines and brandy	4,050	4,308	4,163	4,601	5,047	5,300	5,460	5,570	5,710	3.0	2.0	2.5	3.1
2085 Distilled liquor	3,255	3,255	3,324	3,122	2,890	2,920	2,950	2,950	2,990	1.0	0.0	1.4	0.9
Trade data													
Value of imports	3,527	3,386	3,668	3,979	4,618	5,194	5,695	6,460	6,781	9.6	13.4	5.0	10.1
2082 Malt beverages	881	961	1,072	1,192	1,341	1,514	1,732	1,920	2,016	14.4	10.9	5.0	10.7
2084 Wines and brandy	1,347	1,152	1,268	1,402	1,724	2,031	2,239	2,600	2,730	10.2	16.1	5.0	12.2
2085 Distilled liquor	1,299	1,274	1,327	1,386	1,553	1,649	1,723	1,940	2,035	4.5	12.6	4.9	6.9
Value of exports	742	766	973	1,242	1,342	1,409	1,367	1,279	1,337	–3.0	–6.4	4.5	–0.1
2082 Malt beverages	221	234	391	526	453	418	338	290	300	–19.1	–14.2	3.4	–9.8
2084 Wines and brandy	182	184	201	246	330	423	543	549	577	28.4	1.1	5.1	19.0
2085 Distilled liquor	339	349	380	470	559	568	486	440	460	–14.4	–9.5	4.5	–4.8

[1] Estimate except imports and exports.
[2] Estimate.
[3] Forecast.
[4] Compound annual rate.
[5] For a definition of industry versus product values, see "Getting the Most Out of *Outlook 2000*."
Source: U.S. Department of Commerce: Bureau of the Census; International Trade Administration.

alcoholic beverages. In a number of instances, imports have competed successfully for the consumer's dollar. Total constant dollar shipments of alcoholic beverages rose 1.4 percent in 1999. While industry shipments remained flat for distilled spirits, wine and brandy shipments rose 2 percent and malt beverages rose about 1.5 percent (see Table 35-3).

Beer. The fourth largest U.S. brewery, Stroh Brewing Company, left the business in 1999 after 149 years in the beer industry. Stroh sold its assets to Miller Brewing and Pabst Brewing. Also in 1999, it appeared that imports earned the microbrewer's crown and now reign as the hottest segment in the U.S. beer market. Microbreweries had registered double-digit growth yearly throughout the 1990s until 1998, but are now experiencing a "shakeout." Many that expanded too fast are seeing declines, while those which emphasized regional sales are doing better. Despite mergers, brand acquisitions, and closings, new brew pubs and microbreweries continue to open across the country, and many of those companies are registering single- or double-digit growth.

Wine. While there was little growth in volume in 1998, it was another successful year as upscale premium varietal wines and exports grew dramatically even though there was a drop in shipments of popular-priced jug and generic wines. In 1999, because of a hot summer, grape crushings for wine rose, but the quality of crushings increased. In 1999, the United States and the European Union commenced bilateral negotiations in an effort to reduce trade impediments. Those negotiations are scheduled to be concluded in the year 2000 with an agreement signed by 2001. A successful deal will result in greater U.S. access to the European wine market.

Distilled Spirits. Although the volume of total spirits rose a modest 1 percent in 1998, premium/superpremium brands outperformed the total market. The top 25 premium/superpremium spirits, which account for 28 percent of the total spirits market, rose at an aggregate rate of almost 4 percent, while the remaining sector grew only 0.2 percent.

U.S. Industry Growth Projections for the Next 1 and 5 Years

Even though domestic consumption of alcoholic beverages will remain relatively stable, constant dollar industry shipments will increase 1.4 percent in the year 2000 and 1.3 to 1.8 percent over the next 5 years as U.S. consumers continue to consume higher-priced alcoholic beverages. Exports, after a 6.4 percent drop in 1999, will rebound in 2000, increasing 4.5 percent (see Table 35-3). As the Asian economies rebound and other markets continue to open, U.S. exports of alcoholic beverages are expected to increase 3 to 7 percent annually in the next 5 years.

Global Market Prospects

In 1999, U.S. total exports of alcoholic beverages dropped 6.4 percent from 1998 levels (see Table 35-4). The only sector that experienced any increase was the wine and brandy sector, which grew 1.1 percent after a 28 percent increase in 1998. As the domestic alcoholic beverage market has been stable, exports have played a bigger role in the growth of the industry. Total U.S. alcoholic beverage exports since 1992 grew at a compound annual rate of 8.1 percent.

Malt Beverages. In 1998, three-quarters of U.S. exports in this category consisted of beer, followed by brewing dregs and waste with 21 percent, which other countries import as a feed input. In 1998, the top five country markets for U.S. beer were Japan (20 percent), Canada (14 percent), Taiwan (11 percent), Hong Kong (9 percent), and the United Kingdom (8 percent) (see Table 35-5). In the top five markets, only U.S. exports to Canada increased in 1999, rising an estimated 10 to 15 percent. As was mentioned earlier, imports have gained a greater role in

TABLE 35-4: U.S. Trade Patterns in Alcoholic Beverages[1] in 1998
(millions of dollars; percent)

Exports			Imports		
Region[2]	Value[3]	Share, %	Region[2]	Value[3]	Share, %
NAFTA	208	15	NAFTA	1,239	22
Latin America	85	6	Latin America	190	3
Western Europe	575	42	Western Europe	3,955	69
Japan/Chinese Economic Area	335	24	Japan/Chinese Economic Area	37	1
Other Asia	26	2	Other Asia	11	0
Rest of world	140	10	Rest of world	263	5
World	1,367	100	World	5,695	100
Top Five Countries	Value	Share, %	Top Five Countries	Value	Share, %
Japan	258	19	France	1,318	23
United Kingdom	207	15	Mexico	713	13
Canada	170	12	United Kingdom	670	12
Germany	74	5	Netherlands	598	11
Netherlands	73	5	Italy	559	10

[1] SIC 2082, 2084, 2085.
[2] For definitions of regional groupings, see "Getting the Most Out of *Outlook 2000.*"
[3] Values may not sum to total due to rounding.
Source: U.S. Department of Commerce, Bureau of the Census.

TABLE 35-5: U.S. Trade Patterns in Malt Beverages[1] in 1998
(millions of dollars; percent)

Exports			Imports		
Region[2]	Value[3]	Share, %	Region[2]	Value[3]	Share, %
NAFTA	59	18	NAFTA	742	43
Latin America	38	11	Latin America	30	2
Western Europe	108	32	Western Europe	912	53
Japan/Chinese Economic Area	105	31	Japan/Chinese Economic Area	25	1
Other Asia	5	2	Other Asia	7	0
Rest of world	22	7	Rest of world	17	1
World	338	100	World	1,732	100
Top Five Countries	Value	Share, %	Top Five Countries	Value	Share, %
Japan	52	15	Netherlands	570	33
Canada	39	12	Mexico	551	32
United Kingdom	32	10	Canada	190	11
Taiwan	28	8	Germany	137	8
Ireland	26	8	United Kingdom	101	6

[1] SIC 2082.
[2] For definitions of regional groupings, see "Getting the Most Out of *Outlook 2000*."
[3] Values may not sum to total due to rounding.
Source: U.S. Department of Commerce, Bureau of the Census.

the U.S. market. U.S. companies seizing on this trend have negotiated agreements to become U.S. distributors. Imports as a share of the U.S. market increased from 6.7 percent in 1995 to an estimated 9.1 percent in 1999.

In 1998, beer imports from the top five countries accounted for almost 90 percent of the total. In value, the Netherlands was the largest supplier with 33 percent, followed closely by Mexico with 32 percent. The other three countries were Canada (11 percent), Germany (8 percent), and the United Kingdom (6 percent). Based on quantity, Mexico was the largest supplier. In 1999, Mexico was the largest supplier of imports to the United States in both value and quantity. On the basis of value, Mexico accounted for almost 35 percent of the total, followed by the Netherlands with 33 percent, Canada with 9 percent, Germany with 7 percent, and the United Kingdom with 6 percent.

Wine. Wine industry exports include grape wine, sparkling wines, brandy, and fermented beverages (i.e., other fruit wines, wine coolers) (see Table 35-6). In 1998, grape wine accounted for about seven-eighths of wine industry exports, followed by sparkling wines (5 percent), fermented beverages (4 percent), and brandy (2 percent). The top five countries accounted for three-quarters of U.S. grape wine exports. The United Kingdom was the largest export market for grape wine with 29 percent, followed by Canada (17 percent), Japan (15 percent), the Netherlands (9 percent), and Switzerland (5 percent). Japan is

TABLE 35-6: U.S. Trade Patterns in Wines and Brandy[1] in 1998
(millions of dollars; percent)

Exports			Imports		
Region[2]	Value[3]	Share, %	Region[2]	Value[3]	Share, %
NAFTA	94	17	NAFTA	13	1
Latin America	25	5	Latin America	142	6
Western Europe	295	54	Western Europe	1,899	85
Japan/Chinese Economic Area	117	22	Japan/Chinese Economic Area	10	0
Other Asia	8	1	Other Asia	1	0
Rest of world	5	1	Rest of world	175	8
World	543	100	World	2,239	100
Top Five Countries	Value	Share, %	Top Five Countries	Value	Share, %
United Kingdom	144	26	France	1,190	53
Japan	99	18	Italy	494	22
Canada	90	17	Australia	150	7
Netherlands	47	9	Chile	116	5
Switzerland	23	4	Spain	102	5

[1] SIC 2084.
[2] For definitions of regional groupings, see "Getting the Most Out of *Outlook 2000*."
[3] Values may not sum to total due to rounding.
Source: U.S. Department of Commerce, Bureau of the Census.

the largest export market for U.S. sparkling wine (45 percent of total exports) and brandy (60 percent of total exports).

By 2004, U.S. wine exports could almost double if there is (1) a substantial agreement among the NWWP group on avenues to reduce or influence wine duties and on other reductions in nontariff impediments through bilateral negotiations or the next World Trade Organization (WTO) round and (2) a successful wine agreement signed by the United States and the European Union by 2001.

Distilled Spirits. In 1998, almost 71 percent of U.S. distilled spirit exports consisted of branded items such as whiskey (59 percent), rum (7 percent), liqueurs and cordials (3 percent), vodka (1.3 percent), and gin (0.4 percent). Japan was the largest export market for U.S. whiskey, accounting for 23 percent of the total, followed by Germany (16.5 percent), Australia (14 percent), the United Kingdom (9 percent), and France (5 percent). Japan, Germany, and Australia were the top three export markets for all distilled spirits (see Table 35-7).

In 1999, the estimated 9.5 percent decline in total U.S. distilled spirit exports could be attributed to a decline in grain spirit exports or in those of other distilled spirits products used in the production of vodka and possibly gin. As the demand for grained spirits as inputs for vodka has declined, U.S. exports of branded distilled spirits have garnered a greater share of total U.S. exports of distilled spirits. In 1999, branded spirits accounted for 80 percent of total distilled spirits exports, up from 71 percent in 1998. Between 1998 and 1999, U.S. exports of branded spirits grew about 10 percent while exports of nonbranded spirits fell almost 50 percent. In the year 2000, U.S. exports of distilled spirits are expected to increase over 4 percent, with branded spirits accounting for most of the increase. Over the next five years, exports of U.S. branded spirits should increase as countries that were in violation of WTO policy, which prohibits countries from discriminating against imports, adhere to WTO rulings. The United States was successful in its cases against Japan (1998–1999) and Korea (1999–2000). Also in December 1999, the WTO Appellate Body upheld the WTO panel decision finding the Chilean tax regime inconsistent with its WTO obligations.

SALTED SNACKS AND SNACK FOODS

The salted snack industry consists of establishments engaged primarily in manufacturing potato chips, corn chips, and similar snacks (SIC 2096) and establishments engaged primarily in manufacturing salted, roasted, dried, cooked, and canned nuts or processing grains or seeds in a similar manner for snack purposes (SIC 2068). Salted snacks are part of snack foods, a broader category that also includes consumer-ready packaged cookies and crackers, snack nuts, popcorn (microwavable or unpopped), meat snacks, and other types of foods that are ready to eat in casual, between-meals settings. Although much of this section focuses on salted snacks (the only part of snack foods for which industry-level census value of shipments data are available), data and information on other snack foods are presented whenever they are available.

Global Industry Trends

Since 1992, the world snack food market has grown over 25 percent, and it is projected to reach almost $55 billion by the year 2000. The United States continues to be the largest market, accounting for about a third of the world total; Japan and the United Kingdom together account for another quarter of the world total.

The spread of western eating habits to other parts of the world continues as lifestyles in those parts of the world become busier and traditional family mealtimes become a thing of the past. As

TABLE 35-7: U.S. Trade Patterns in Distilled Spirits[1] in 1998
(millions of dollars; percent)

Exports			Imports		
Region[2]	Value[3]	Share, %	Region[2]	Value[3]	Share, %
NAFTA	55	11	NAFTA	484	28
Latin America	22	5	Latin America	19	1
Western Europe	172	35	Western Europe	1,144	66
Japan/Chinese Economic Area	113	23	Japan/Chinese Economic Area	3	0
Other Asia	13	3	Other Asia	2	0
Rest of world	112	23	Rest of world	71	4
World	486	100	World	1,723	100
Top Five Countries	Value	Share, %	Top Five Countries	Value	Share, %
Japan	108	22	United Kingdom	558	32
Germany	51	10	Canada	332	19
Australia	43	9	Sweden	164	10
Canada	40	8	Mexico	152	9
United Kingdom	30	6	Ireland	132	8

[1] SIC 2085.
[2] For definitions of regional groupings, see "Getting the Most Out of *Outlook 2000*."
[3] Values may not sum to total due to rounding.
Source: U.S. Department of Commerce, Bureau of the Census.

a result, the demand for snack foods continues to increase, especially for healthier types that are lower in fat. Many manufacturers around the world are responding to this trend.

Domestic Trends

While sales of snack foods sold through traditional-type supermarkets have had only modest gains, most of the growth has taken place in mass merchandising stores. For the salted snacks segment, constant dollar shipments of salted snacks increased an estimated 2.2 percent in 1998 and were expected to increase another 6.8 percent in 1999 (see Table 35-8).

Although the nationally known manufacturer Frito-Lay continues to dominate the U.S. snack food industry, regional manufacturers have prospered by finding niche markets that accommodate changes in consumers' preferences. While a couple of national brands of snack products using the fat-free Olestra ingredient were introduced in 1998 (Frito-Lay's WoW and Procter & Gamble's Fat Free Pringles), two regional brands have introduced contenders into the arena (Utz's Yes and Herr's Rave). According to industry sources, Olestra-containing snacks will capture 4 to 12 percent of the snack food market. The sustained growth of the snack food industry also will be dependent on its ability to tap overseas markets where western eating habits are having an influence.

U.S. demographics continue to affect the growth of this industry. Three major population sectors have had a balancing effect on the growth of this industry. According to the latest U.S. Bureau of Labor *Consumer Expenditures Survey* and U.S. Bureau of the Census population estimates, the age group (35 to 44 years) that consumes more snack food annually than the

TABLE 35-8: Snack Foods (SIC 2068, 2096) Trends and Forecasts
(millions of dollars except as noted)

										Percent Change			
	1992	1993	1994	1995	1996	1997[1]	1998[1]	1999[2]	2000[3]	97–98	98–99	99–00	96–00[4]
Industry data													
Value of shipments[5]	10,146	10,779	11,266	11,997	12,523	13,036	13,372	14,333		2.6	7.2		
2068 Snack nuts and seeds	2,837	3,044	3,098	3,248	3,390	3,636	3,807	4,183		4.7	9.9		
2096 Potato chips and snacks	7,309	7,735	8,167	8,749	9,133	9,400	9,565	10,150		1.8	6.1		
Value of shipments (1992$)	10,146	10,479	10,712	11,182	11,445	11,785	12,050	12,870	13,500	2.2	6.8	4.9	4.2
2068 Snack nuts and seeds	2,837	2,955	2,934	2,905	2,973	3,104	3,200	3,470	3,640	3.1	8.4	4.9	5.2
2096 Potato chips and snacks	7,309	7,524	7,778	8,277	8,472	8,681	8,850	9,400	9,860	1.9	6.2	4.9	3.9
Total employment (thousands)	45.3	45.1	44.1	45.4	45.4	46.2	46.4	47.1	49.4	0.4	1.5	4.9	2.1
2068 Snack nuts and seeds	10.5	10.0	9.8	10.5	9.4	9.3	9.3	9.0	9.4	0.0	−3.2	4.4	0.0
2096 Potato chips and snacks	34.8	35.1	34.3	34.9	36.0	36.9	37.1	38.1	40.0	0.5	2.7	5.0	2.7
Production workers (thousands)	32.1	32.0	31.1	33.0	32.6	33.1	33.3	33.8	35.4	0.6	1.5	4.7	2.1
2068 Snack nuts and seeds	8.1	7.7	7.9	8.4	7.1	7.0	7.0	6.8	7.1	0.0	−2.9	4.4	0.0
2096 Potato chips and snacks	24.0	24.3	23.2	24.6	25.5	26.1	26.3	27.0	28.3	0.8	2.7	4.8	2.6
Average hourly earnings ($)	9.94	10.17	10.55	11.55	12.42	12.66	13.13	14.30		3.7	8.9		
2068 Snack nuts and seeds	8.79	9.07	9.35	9.27	10.06	10.50	10.75	11.20		2.4	4.2		
2096 Potato chips and snacks	10.35	10.56	11.00	12.44	13.16	13.26	13.80	14.25		4.1	3.3		
Capital expenditures	304	321	349	400	611								
2068 Snack nuts and seeds	45	70	75	72	195								
2096 Potato chips and snacks	259	250	273	328	415								
Product data													
Value of shipments[5]	10,199	10,739	11,016	11,466	11,718	12,170	12,465	13,340		2.4	7.0		
2068 Snack nuts and seeds	2,671	2,820	2,854	2,860	2,514	2,700	2,820	3,100		4.4	9.9		
2096 Potato chips and snacks	7,527	7,919	8,163	8,607	9,204	9,470	9,645	10,240		1.8	6.2		
Value of shipments (1992$)	10,199	10,441	10,476	10,700	10,743	11,051	11,300	12,055	12,640	2.3	6.7	4.9	4.1
2068 Snack nuts and seeds	2,671	2,738	2,702	2,558	2,205	2,302	2,375	2,575	2,700	3.2	8.4	4.9	5.2
2096 Potato chips and snacks	7,527	7,703	7,774	8,142	8,538	8,749	8,925	9,480	9,940	2.0	6.2	4.9	3.9
Trade data													
Value of imports	35.4	35.5	37.7	37.2	40.6	53.1	72.8	79.6	82.2	37.1	9.3	3.3	19.3
2068 Snack nuts and seeds	12.6	12.6	12.5	12.8	10.8	20.4	30.8	34.6	36.3	51.0	12.3	4.9	35.4
2096 Potato chips and snacks	22.9	22.9	25.2	24.4	29.8	32.6	42.0	45.0	45.9	28.8	7.1	2.0	11.4
Value of exports	437	508	572	366	451	416	467	488	507	12.3	4.5	3.9	3.0
2068 Snack nuts and seeds	301	333	321	140	229	191	164	165	167	−14.1	0.6	1.2	−7.6
2096 Potato chips and snacks	137	176	252	226	222	225	303	323	340	34.7	6.6	5.3	11.3

[1] Estimate except imports and exports.
[2] Estimate.
[3] Forecast.
[4] Compound annual rate.
[5] For a definition of industry versus product values, see "Getting the Most Out of *Outlook 2000.*"
Source: U.S. Department of Commerce: Bureau of the Census; International Trade Administration.

TABLE 35-9: U.S. Exports of Snack Food Products by Product Category
(millions of dollars)

Product Category	1989	1992	1995	1996	1997	1998	Percent of 1998 Total
Salted snacks							
Potato chips	20.7	94.6	168.4	158.8	161.7	247.2	29.6
Corn chips and pretzels	14.9	42.2	57.7	63.2	63.1	56.0	6.7
Snack nuts	137.7	300.6	140.2	229.1	190.8	163.8	19.6
Subtotal	173.3	437.4	366.2	451.1	415.7	467.0	56.0
Other snacks							
Cookies and crackers	64.9	152.6	184.8	190.4	208.7	211.7	25.4
Meat snacks	15.8	41.1	71.8	69.9	67.1	65.9	7.9
Popcorn	49.5	84.9	87.1	98.1	100.5	89.4	10.7
Subtotal	130.2	278.7	343.7	358.4	376.3	366.9	44.0
Total	303.5	716.1	710.0	809.6	792.0	833.9	100.0

Source: Compiled from Official Statistics of the U.S. Department of Commerce.

national average ($112.75 compared with $84.53) grew 10 percent between 1992 and 1997 and accounts for 16 percent of the population. This growth is offset by the 25- to 34-year-old and 65-and-over age groups. Although the numbers in those two age groups declined about 1 percent after 1992, the two groups account for 28 percent of the population and consume almost 20 percent less than the national average.

The U.S. industry not only has been innovative in successfully marketing Olestra-type products to win back snack food consumers but also has introduced innovative flavored snack foods as a means to entice new consumers or produce a high-value-added product to increase the profit margins of snack food companies. Chesapeake crab and cheeseburger-flavored potato chips, hot cheese curls and tortilla chips, and butter-flavored pretzels as well as soynuts and mixed vegetable chips are examples of such innovative snack foods.

U.S. Industry Growth Projections for the Next 1 and 5 Years

Because U.S. demographics and consumption patterns will remain similar to those previously mentioned, constant dollar shipments of salted snacks probably will increase no more than an estimated 5 percent in the year 2000. While U.S. exports to Asia will continue to decline in 2000, U.S. salted snack exports to the rest of the world, especially to Western Hemisphere neighbors, will be strong. Exports are expected to increase 4 percent in the year 2000.

Demographic projections continue to indicate less than substantial growth in the salted snack food sector. Even though the 35- to 44-year-old age category consumes approximately a third more than the national average, this category will experience a population decline of about 1 percent annually through 2004. Also, the 65-and-over age group, which consumes about 30 percent less than the national average, will continue to grow annually at about 1 percent. These factors, coupled with expectations of growing exports, indicate that the salted snack food industry should grow 2 to 3 percent annually over the next 5 years.

Global Market Prospects

The discussion in this section is based on trade data for salted snacks (potato chips and similar snacks and snack nuts) and other consumer-ready snacks, including packaged cookies and crackers, popcorn, and meat snacks. In 1998, U.S. exports of those snack foods increased 5.3 percent. Except for a minor increase in U.S. exports of cookies and crackers (1.45 percent), that 5.3 percent increase can be attributed to an increase in potato chip exports, since all other categories experienced a decline. In 1998, exports of potato chips rose 52.8 percent and became the largest export category. In past years, potato chips were either the second or the third largest category. In 1998, potato chip exports accounted for almost 30 percent of total U.S. snack food exports, followed by cookies and crackers (25.4 percent), snack nuts (19.6 percent), popcorn (10.7 percent), meat snacks (7.9 percent), and corn chips and pretzels (6.7 percent) (see Table 35-9 and Figure 35-1 for details).

The North American Free Trade Agreement (NAFTA) countries continue to be the largest U.S. export market for these snack food items, accounting for more than 39 percent in 1998, followed

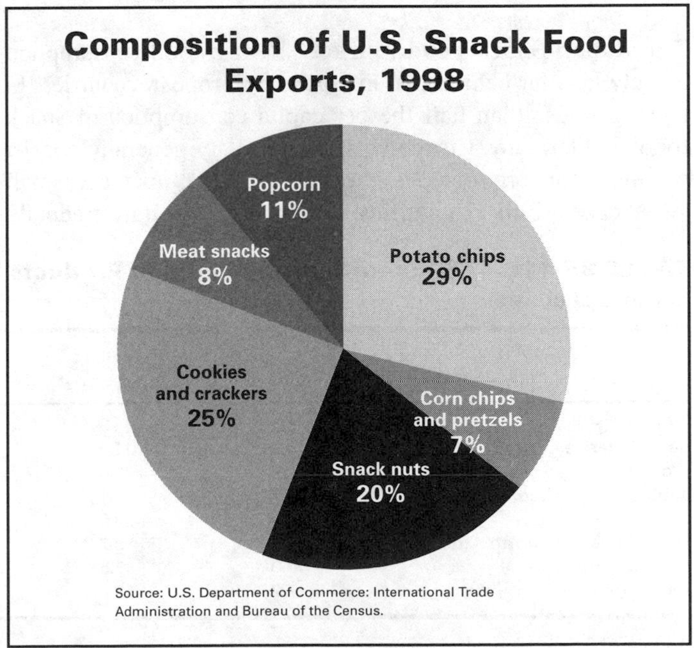

FIGURE 35-1

TABLE 35-10: U.S. Exports of Snack Food Products[1] in 1998
(millions of dollars)

Region	Value	Share, %
NAFTA	327.3	39.2
Latin America	89.4	10.7
Western Europe	155.0	18.6
Japan/Chinese Economic Area	128.4	15.4
Other Asia	40.1	4.8
Middle East and north Africa	27.2	3.3
Rest of world	66.5	8.0
World	833.9	100.0
Top Five Countries	**Value**	**Share, %**
Canada	244.6	29.3
Mexico	82.7	9.9
Japan	69	8.3
Hong Kong	41.3	5.0
United Kingdom	36.6	4.4

[1] Includes potato chips, corn chips, pretzels, cookies and crackers, snack nuts, popcorn, and meat snacks.
Source: Compiled from Official Statistics of the U.S. Department of Commerce.

by western Europe with more than 18 percent, the Japan/Chinese Economic Area (Japan, Hong Kong, China, and Taiwan) with just over 15 percent, and Latin America (except Mexico) with almost 11 percent. While U.S. snack food exports to Asia as a whole fell approximately 21 percent, U.S. exports to the Western Hemisphere (Canada, Mexico, and Latin America) grew almost 17 percent (see Tables 35-10, 35-11, and 35-12 for details).

The following discussions of selected country markets are based on reports prepared for the U.S. Department of Agriculture. For the complete reports contact the U.S. Department of Agriculture Web page at http://www.fas.usda.gov/scriptsw/AttacheRep/default.htm (Italy: AGR Number 8734, New Zealand: AGR Number 9028, and Saudi Arabia: AGR Number 8030).

The Italian Snack Food Market. Snack food consumption in Italy lags far behind that in northern European countries. In fact, it is less than half the per capita consumption of snack foods in Germany. Currently, snacks in Italy generally consist of chips, popcorn, cookies, pretzels, crackers, nuts, and small sweet cakes similar to muffins. Eating snacks in Italy gradually is becoming a more common practice. Traditionally, fruits were used as snack foods, and sweet cakes often are served to school-age children in the afternoon when they return home from school. While the traditional lunch for students and northern Italian office workers is a sandwich, it seldom is accompanied by a side item such as potato chips or French fries except at McDonald's.

The Italian snack market has expanded more than 6 percent a year since 1992. Imports account for nearly 40 percent of the market supply. Imported products establish general snack food prices. This sector provides high profits for domestic Italian products. High profit margins are expected to remain an important factor in this sector.

The changing lifestyle of Italian consumers has boosted snack consumption. The major factors causing this change in consumption patterns are more active lifestyles combined with more flexible eating habits and fewer home-prepared meals.

According to Italian sources, snack food prices are relatively inelastic. Italian snack food prices are generally 25 to 50 percent higher than those in the United States. Consumers often purchase snack food without comparing the prices with those of other items available to them. In fact, many Italian bars and other snack food outlets do not display prices, leading consumers to base their purchase decisions on packaging or experience.

Most snack food production is done by large companies that combine their own production with imported products or ingredients. Many of those companies belong to multinational groups and may import technologies or final products only from their foreign units. Most snack food production is located in industrial northern Italy, which is also the area with the highest disposable income.

The main snack food competitors are other European Union (EU) member countries that have a distinct transportation and tariff advantage over U.S. products. Competition among major domestic companies and brands is stiff, especially in cookies, crackers, and sweet cakes. Competition is based on expensive publicity campaigns based on television commercials and newspaper and magazine advertisements. This represents a steep barrier for market newcomers. Competition is so fierce that few imported cookies, crackers, or sweet cakes are available in supermarkets. Also, there is little to no advertisement for chips, popcorn, nuts, and other salty snacks.

TABLE 35-11: U.S. Exports of Snack Food Products by Region and Product Category in 1998
(millions of dollars)

Region	Potato Chips	Corn Chips and Pretzels	Snack Nuts	Cookies and Crackers	Meat Snacks	Popcorn	Total
NAFTA	69.1	14.3	27.0	141.9	47.0	27.9	327.3
Latin America	30.0	11.2	7.9	26.3	3.1	10.9	89.4
Western Europe	22.2	7.0	76.6	23.3	1.8	24.1	155.0
Japan/Chinese Economic Area	61.7	7.1	35.7	8.0	5.1	10.8	128.4
Other Asia	15.6	5.6	6.9	3.3	2.0	6.6	40.1
Middle East and north Africa	8.6	3.2	3.2	4.6	1.2	6.5	27.2
Rest of world	40.0	7.5	6.5	4.3	5.8	2.5	66.5
World Total	247.2	56.0	163.8	211.7	65.9	89.4	833.9

Source: U.S. Department of Commerce.

TABLE 35-12: U.S. Trade Patterns in Snacks[1] in 1998
(millions of dollars; percent)

Exports			Imports		
Region[2]	Value[3]	Share, %	Region[2]	Value[3]	Share, %
NAFTA	83	28	NAFTA	37	87
Latin America	41	14	Latin America	1	2
Western Europe	29	10	Western Europe	1	2
Japan/Chinese Economic Area	69	23	Japan/Chinese Economic Area	1	3
Other Asia	21	7	Other Asia	2	4
Rest of world	59	20	Rest of world	1	3
World	303	100	World	42	100
Top Five Countries	Value	Share, %	Top Five Countries	Value	Share, %
Canada	52	17	Mexico	22	52
Japan	38	13	Canada	15	35
Mexico	31	10	South Korea	1	2
Russia	27	9	Israel	1	2
Belgium	18	6	Japan	1	2

[1] SIC 2096.
[2] For definitions of regional groupings, see "Getting the Most Out of *Outlook 2000*."
[3] Values may not sum to total due to rounding.
Source: U.S. Department of Commerce, Bureau of the Census.

The distribution channel in Italy is interesting and complex. Large supermarket chains usually have their own distribution channels. "Cash and carry" wholesale outlets are available to small retailers. There are also small companies that distribute products to bars, institutional cafeterias, and other snack food outlets. Most domestic snack food producers use agents to distribute their products. Some have distribution and storage units spread all over Italy. Only a few producers sell directly to the supermarkets or cash and carry chains.

Discount stores and supermarkets account for roughly half of snack food sales. Italian retailers and wholesalers are actively adopting just-in-time distribution patterns. Consequently, stocks are small and distributors supply stores two to three times per week, ensuring freshness and high product quality.

Adolescents account for one-third of snack food purchasing decisions. Italian youth make up the largest portion of the snack food market, as they are willing to try new products. They are strongly influenced by MTV-type programs and advertisements. Typically, Italian consumers are influenced by packaging, novelty items, and the implied concept that a product brings happiness, encourages friendships, and is good for parties or school vacations. Young Italian consumers often prefer sweet snacks to salty ones. In general, Italians perceive traditional sweet cakes as being healthier than chips or other salty snack foods because the sweet cakes could have been prepared at home.

The New Zealand Snack Food Market. New Zealanders are eating more and more snack foods, but that category, worth around $100 million, is by no means mature. The top five snack food product categories in New Zealand are potato chips, lunch box snacks, extruded cereal snacks, corn chips, and nuts.

At $39 million, potato chips have the largest share of the snack market. The five top selling potato chip flavors—salted, salt'n'vinegar, chicken, sour cream & chives, and cheese & onion—account for an estimated 75 percent of sales, but new variants such as BBQ, Cajun, and spicy chicken are quickly gaining market share.

At $27 million, lunch box snacks is a rapidly emerging category. This category includes dried fruits, fruit roll-ups, snack logs, individually wrapped biscuits and muesli bars, tear-tab biscuits and cheese, small chips, jellies, and fruit fingers. This category is expanding swiftly, and consumers are prepared to pay a premium for unique products that provide novelty and excitement. The move toward more wholesome lunch box fillers has resulted in the introduction of more fruit-filled bars, but taste, ease of eating, and fun are key factors for children. Single-serve dried fruit snacks are rising in popularity with shoppers, with raisins and prunes at the top.

The $14 million extruded cereal snack market is a more traditional segment in which most of the brands are well established. Cereal snack promotions generally target children 5 to 13 years old. Consumption usually peaks at Christmas and Easter, but those seasonal skews are small. Cereal snack sales also are experiencing a growing trend toward multipacks.

Although currently representing only $8 million in sales, corn chips offer the greatest opportunity for growth in terms of volume and sales. In the last couple of years, most of the growth came from the large bag segment of the market. Rather than reducing the box segment, bagged corn chips are filling a separate niche. The top-selling flavors of bagged corn chips, in order, are cheese, salsa, BBQ, jalapeno, and natural. The boxed segment accounts for around 70 percent of total sales, but this is declining because of the impact of bag sales. Corn chips now compete with potato chips but often appeal to consumers as a more substantial, lower-fat alternative to potato chips.

The packaged nut category is very quiet compared with the other snack food categories. Sales through supermarkets in the year ended January 1999 were $4.8 million.

The Saudi Arabian Savory Snacks and Popcorn Market. The Saudi market for popcorn and savory snacks (potato chips, corn chips, and the like) is substantial, valued at $80 million to $90 million retail. Consumption is estimated at 18,000 metric tons (mt). There is no production of popcorn in that country. Annual popcorn consumption is estimated at 1,500 mt. Over the last decade, domestic production of savory snacks increased significantly. Ten years ago, imports accounted for the major share of total consumption of savory snacks; today, imports represent about one-third. Potato chips account for about 50 percent of the market, followed by corn chips and the like at 28 percent.

More than 60 different brands of savory snacks are sold in Saudi retail outlets. Local brands account for two-thirds of the total, with two brands, Tasali and Lays, commanding a leading market share. Several U.S.-origin brands are found on the Saudi market, including Nalley, Planters, Pringles, Dragon, El Rio, S&W, Super Snack, Wise Borden, Fairco, and Panthers. Leading U.S. popcorn brands sold in Saudi supermarkets include Jolly Time, Pop's Rite, ShopRite, and Orville Redenbacher.

About 60 percent of chips and other savory snacks are sold in retail outlets such as supermarkets and corner stores. The balance is sold in the hotel and restaurant, catering, and food service sectors. Popcorn is sold primarily at retail outlets. According to a survey taken in Jeddah, Saudi Arabia has about 25 producers of snacks. About 50 percent of those companies are located in Jeddah, with the balance in the Eastern Province and Riyadh. In addition to the leading brands Tasli and Lays, other major producers are Ghandor, Naghi, Al Gosaibi, SADAFCO, El Essayi, and Basamh. There are more than 55 local brands on the market.

The United States is the only supplier of popcorn to Saudi Arabia and has a 20 to 25 percent share of the savory snack market. The largest savory snack supplier, as a group, is the Gulf Cooperation Council (GCC) countries, accounting for 47 percent of Saudi imports in terms of weight (based on 1996 Saudi import statistics). However, a significant percentage of these imports consists of transshipments from other sites of origin, such as the United States. Other suppliers are Malaysia, Singapore, the United Kingdom, and the Philippines. According to Saudi Arabian trade statistics, Saudi Arabia increased imports of popcorn, chips, and similar salted snacks from $6.7 million in 1992 to an estimated $12.5 million in 1997.

With the emergence of several large-scale modern supermarkets, consumers have become accustomed to a wide variety and choice of food products from all corners of the world. In 1999 alone, 3 new Tamimi supermarkets were scheduled to be completed in Riyadh, bringing the total number of Tamimi markets in the kingdom to 10. The major share of Tamimi products is produced and processed in the United States. Saudi Arabia has about 260 large-scale modern western-style supermarkets.

Saudis consider U.S. food products as being of high quality. Based on the high population growth rate (3.75 percent annually) and changing lifestyles, the demand for U.S. popcorn and savory snacks should continue to be strong over the next few years.

RED MEAT AND POULTRY

Red meat production includes establishments engaged primarily in slaughtering, for their own account or on a contract basis for the trade, cattle, hogs, sheep, lamb, and calves for meat to be sold or to be used on the same premises in canning, cooking, curing, and freezing and in making sausages, lard, and other products (SIC 2011), and establishments engaged primarily in manufacturing sausages, cured meats, smoked meats, canned meats, frozen meats, and other prepared meats and meat specialties from purchased carcasses and other materials (SIC 2013). Poultry production includes establishments engaged primarily in slaughtering, dressing, packing, freezing, and canning poultry, rabbits, and other small game or in manufacturing products from such meats for their own account or on a contract basis for the trade. This industry also includes the drying, freezing, and breaking of eggs (SIC 2015).

Global Industry Trends

According to the U.S. Department of Agriculture (USDA), global production by most producing and trading countries of red meat (beef and pork) and poultry after 1994 increased approximately 2.4 percent annually to about 179 million metric tons. Worldwide production gains have been led by increased poultry production and, to a lesser extent, pork production. Since 1994, poultry meat production has expanded approximately 5 percent annually, followed by 2 percent annual growth in pork production and less than 0.5 percent annual growth in beef production. Global poultry meat production surpassed beef production in 1996, and the gap has continued to widen as beef production has remained stagnant. Pork is the most widely produced meat, accounting for 43 percent, followed by poultry with 30 percent and beef with 27 percent. China accounts for almost half the world's total production of pork.

Domestic Trends

The red meat industry, the largest sector in the processed food and beverage industry, was expected to experience a modest 1 percent increase in constant dollar product shipments in 1999 (see Table 35-13). The U.S. red meat industry continues to be dependent on the forces of nature and demand for red meats at home and abroad. According to USDA, total red meat production was up less than 1 percent in 1999. Pork production increased only 1.4 percent in 1999 to 19.25 billion pounds, compared with a 12 percent increase between 1997 and 1998. Although beef production increased only 2.1 percent between 1996 and 1999, it reached its highest level in more than two decades. While U.S. cattle inventories will continue to decline and beef cow liquidation has largely ended, heifer slaughter remains strong, and that will push beef production to record highs. Heifer retention for herd rebuilding rather than placement in feedlots remains the key to reduced beef supplies.

While the U.S. beef industry has been slowly gaining back the share of the hotel and restaurant market that it had before chicken's tremendous inroads in the 1980s, this has occurred somewhat at the expense of the retail market trade, where more

TABLE 35-13: Red Meat (SIC 2011, 2013) Trends and Forecasts

(millions of dollars except as noted)

	1992	1993	1994	1995	1996	1997[1]	1998[1]	1999[2]	2000[3]	Percent Change 97–98	98–99	99–00	96–00[4]
Industry data													
Value of shipments[5]	70,107	73,941	70,701	72,025	71,943	73,844	76,437	77,200		3.5	1.0		
Value of shipments (1992$)	70,107	71,389	71,609	74,312	71,003	71,150	73,881	74,650	74,650	3.8	1.0	0.0	1.3
Total employment (thousands)	207	209	204	214	218	219	222	223	220	1.4	0.5	−1.3	0.2
Production workers (thousands)	171	173	169	178	180	180	184	185	182	2.2	0.5	−1.6	0.3
Average hourly earnings ($)	8.99	9.06	9.43	9.81	9.64	9.86	10.15	10.53		2.9	3.7		
Capital expenditures	719	703	699	862	1,135								
Product data													
Value of shipments[5]	64,351	68,216	64,839	65,878	65,839	67,600	69,900	70,600		3.4	1.0		
Value of shipments (1992$)	64,351	65,856	65,679	67,977	64,988	65,120	67,600	68,300	68,300	3.8	1.0	0.0	1.3
Trade data													
Value of imports	2,899	3,041	2,946	2,649	2,605	2,968	3,139	3,485	3,570	5.8	11.0	2.4	8.2
Value of exports	4,704	4,606	5,187	6,230	6,145	6,126	5,563	5,585	5,565	−9.2	0.4	−0.4	−2.5

[1] Estimate except imports and exports.
[2] Estimate.
[3] Forecast.
[4] Compound annual rate.
[5] For a definition of industry versus product values, see "Getting the Most Out of *Outlook 2000*."
Source: U.S. Department of Commerce: Bureau of the Census; International Trade Administration.

lower-quality meats are being offered. The trend of offering lower-quality meat with great variability in eating quality on the retail market could make it more difficult to recapture the consumer acceptance maintained under the old choice grades. This difficulty could result in increased prices for beef at retail. Both white meat chicken and pork loin are increasingly able to compete strongly against beef, and both provide a consistency and size of cut very acceptable to consumers, particularly at lower relative prices. In this effort to regain market share, the beef industry has started a $25 million marketing campaign featuring the slogan "Beef. It's what's for dinner."

Constant dollar product shipments of the poultry and poultry products industry were expected to grow 5 percent in 1999 (see Table 35-14). The health of the domestic poultry industry in the last decade has been affected not only by what happens domestically but also by what happens internationally. U.S. production continues to increase. In 1999, domestic production of poultry reached almost 35.1 billion pounds, a 5.2 percent

TABLE 35-14: Poultry Slaughtering and Processing (SIC 2015) Trends and Forecasts

(millions of dollars except as noted)

	1992	1993	1994	1995	1996	1997[1]	1998[1]	1999[2]	2000[3]	Percent Change 97–98	98–99	99–00	96–00[4]
Industry data													
Value of shipments[5]	23,965	25,501	27,415	28,929	30,160	31,075	31,500	31,595		1.4	0.3		
Value of shipments (1992$)	23,965	24,783	25,937	27,525	27,122	28,000	28,330	29,750	31,270	1.2	5.0	5.1	3.6
Total employment (thousands)	194	205	216	214	215	218	221	225	226	1.4	1.8	0.4	1.3
Production workers (thousands)	173	184	193	192	190	192	194	198	199	1.0	2.1	0.5	1.2
Average hourly earnings ($)	7.39	7.40	7.49	8.09	8.27	8.49	8.80	9.02		3.7	2.5		
Capital expenditures	469	555	594	726	697								
Product data													
Value of shipments[5]	23,592	24,983	27,027	28,708	29,981	30,820	31,240	31,330		1.4	0.3		
Value of shipments (1992$)	23,592	24,279	25,570	27,315	26,961	27,770	28,100	29,500	31,000	1.2	5.0	5.1	3.6
Trade data													
Value of imports	25.8	29.9	25.3	30.5	44.7	45.7	53.5	66.9	69.0	17.1	25.0	3.1	11.5
Value of exports	990	1,157	1,633	2,097	2,585	2,537	2,261	1,900	1,900	−10.9	−16.0	0.0	−7.4

[1] Estimate except imports and exports.
[2] Estimate.
[3] Forecast.
[4] Compound annual rate.
[5] For a definition of industry versus product values, see "Getting the Most Out of *Outlook 2000*."
Source: U.S. Department of Commerce: Bureau of the Census; International Trade Administration.

increase over 1998. Net returns for producers, which were fairly high in 1998 (more than 14 cents per pound), although down in 1999, still were expected to register double-digit levels as lower feed costs offset the lower prices producers received for their product. Major U.S. poultry producers are continuing to develop joint ventures around the world (Russia, China) instead of relying solely on U.S. poultry exports for international opportunities.

U.S. Industry Growth Projections for the Next 1 and 5 Years

For the first time in recent history, total red meat and poultry production and exports will be down in the year 2000. Production will decline about 1.4 percent to 80.1 billion pounds, and exports will experience an estimated 2.5 percent decline to 8.9 billion pounds. Three factors are contributing to the slowdown of U.S. exports: the collapse of the Russian economy (affecting poultry and pork), the downturn in and slow recovery of Asian economies, and currency devaluations among both importers and competitors.

Constant dollar product shipments of red meat are expected to be flat in the year 2000, and the current value of exports is expected to drop about 2 percent. Total red meat production will decline about 5 percent to 43.3 billion pounds (beef down 6.2 percent to 24.4 billion pounds and pork down 3.2 percent to 18.6 billion pounds). U.S. cattle inventories are set to decline through the year 2000, with beef production probably declining through 2001. Given the lackluster return scenario for hog producers, the mid-2000 pig crop is expected to be about 3 percent below that of 1999. Record-setting pork production in 1999 forced prices down, encouraging producers to reduce their herds. This is expected to lead to a reduction in pork production in 2000.

Although U.S. poultry exports will be flat in 2000, U.S. poultry production will increase about 4 percent to 36.6 billion pounds. In 2000, constant dollar product shipments of poultry and poultry products are forecast to rise approximately 3 percent, while the current value of exports will be flat.

Per capita consumption of poultry has increased steadily from 90 pounds in 1996, to an estimated 96 pounds in 1999, to a forecast 100 pounds in the year 2000. In contrast, per capita beef consumption was flat at 67 to 68 pounds between 1996 and 1999 and is forecast to drop to 63 pounds in 2000. Per capita consumption of pork, after declining from 52 pounds in 1995 to 49 pounds in 1997, rebounded to 53 pounds in 1998 and 1999 and is forecast to decline to 50 pounds in 2000.

Over the next 5 years, the red meat industry should experience a compound annual growth rate of 1 to 1.5 percent. The industry will still face sluggish domestic demand and less than optimum export markets, especially in Asia. Also, domestic red meat supplies will be tight until after the new millennium. Once the economic crisis in Asia plays itself out, export markets will again play a greater role in the profitability of the U.S. red meat industry.

Although per capita poultry consumption will increase over the next 5 years, it will not grow as fast as it did during the past decade. As other countries become more proficient in poultry production, U.S. poultry exports will not see major increases. As a result, a compound annual growth rate of 2 to 3 percent over the next 5 years is expected for the U.S. poultry industry.

Global Market Prospects

In 1999, U.S. red meat imports reached an estimated $3.6 billion, an increase of 11 percent over 1998. On the other hand, U.S. exports registered a slight increase of 0.4 percent to almost $5.6 billion. Although there was a 90 percent drop in U.S. red meat exports to Russia (once the sixth biggest U.S. export market and now in thirtieth place), U.S. exports to Asia have rebounded as those countries have started to recover from their economic problems. U.S. red meat exports to South Korea and Taiwan rose 49 and 23 percent, respectively.

The EU remains one important export market to which U.S. industry does not have full access. Even though the WTO ruled against the EU ban on imports of U.S. beef treated with growth hormones, the EU has continued the ban. This ban affects over $122 million in U.S. beef exports to the EU (based on 1998 trade data). As a result, the United States exercised its WTO-sanctioned right to apply a 100 percent ad valorem duty to 34 products from the EU. Some of the major imported products affected by that duty are an assortment of pork products, Roquefort cheese, some canned tomato products, soups, chocolate, rusks, cherry and berry juices, and yarn.

The top five export markets in 1999 for U.S. red meat products accounted for more than 85 percent of total exports. Japan was the largest market with 43 percent of the total, followed by Mexico with 16 percent, South Korea with 12 percent, Canada with 9 percent, and Taiwan with 5 percent. Trade patterns for 1998 are shown in Table 35-15.

In 1999, the top five export markets for beef accounted for almost 93 percent of total exports. Japan was the largest U.S. export market for beef, accounting for 52 percent, followed by Mexico with 17 percent, South Korea with about 12 percent, Canada with 10 percent, and Taiwan with 2 percent. U.S. beef exports to Korea were expected to more than double in 1999, as that country appeared to have started to rebound from its financial crisis.

The top five U.S. export markets for hides and skins accounted for about 80 percent of the total in 1999. Korea was the largest U.S. export market, accounting for about 31 percent of the total, followed by Taiwan with 17 percent, Mexico with 16 percent, China with 9 percent, and Japan with 8 percent.

The top five export markets for U.S. pork accounted for 89 percent of the total. As with beef, Japan is by far the largest market with 58 percent, followed by Canada with 15 percent, Mexico with 10 percent, Taiwan with 4 percent, and Korea with 3 percent.

While U.S. poultry imports rose over an estimated 25 percent in 1999, they still represented only 0.2 percent of domestic supply. U.S. exports of poultry fell about 16 percent as the Russian market for U.S. poultry collapsed. Russia was the largest U.S. export market for poultry, accounting for about 30 percent of U.S. poultry exports between 1995 and 1998 (see Table 35-16). In 1999, Russia was the sixth largest export market

TABLE 35-15: U.S. Trade Patterns in Red Meat[1] in 1998
(millions of dollars; percent)

Exports			Imports		
Region[2]	Value[3]	Share, %	Region[2]	Value[3]	Share, %
NAFTA	1,404	25	NAFTA	1,363	43
Latin America	167	3	Latin America	363	12
Western Europe	311	6	Western Europe	298	9
Japan/Chinese Economic Area	2,885	52	Japan/Chinese Economic Area	52	2
Other Asia	520	9	Other Asia	24	1
Rest of world	276	5	Rest of world	1,039	33
World	5,563	100	World	3,139	100
Top Five Countries	Value	Share, %	Top Five Countries	Value	Share, %
Japan	2,362	42	Canada	1,322	42
Mexico	877	16	Australia	581	18
Canada	527	9	New Zealand	420	13
South Korea	472	8	Denmark	189	6
Taiwan	226	4	Brazil	146	5

[1] SIC 2011, 2013.
[2] For definitions of regional groupings, see "Getting the Most Out of *Outlook 2000.*"
[3] Values may not sum to total due to rounding.
Source: U.S. Department of Commerce, Bureau of the Census.

(5 percent of total U.S. poultry exports) as U.S. exports to that country fell almost 90 percent. Even with the decline in total U.S. poultry exports, these exports still represent about 6 percent of domestic production.

The top five U.S. export markets for poultry account for about 62 percent of total exports. Now Hong Kong is the largest U.S. export market with 22 percent of the total, followed by Canada with 13 percent, Mexico with about 10 percent, Japan with 9 percent, and Latvia with almost 8 percent.

For the first time in a decade, U.S. chicken exports are expected to decline 1 percent to 4.6 billion pounds in the year 2000. Exports to the Baltic States are expected to decline from their exceptional growth in 1999. A number of these countries, as well as Mexico, have expanded their own domestic poultry production to meet domestic demand.

U.S. turkey exports are estimated to reach 400 million pounds in 2000, about the same as in 1999. Gains in sales to Mexico and some Asian countries, chiefly South Korea, are expected to offset reduced shipments to Russia and other eastern European markets. Because Mexico is the leading buyer of U.S. turkey (more than 50 percent in 1999), its economy will largely determine the level of U.S. turkey exports. Mexico's gross domestic product is forecast to grow a relatively healthy 2 to 3 percent in both 1999 and 2000. U.S. exports to South Korea, which was a major market for U.S. turkey before economic adversity struck in 1998, could

TABLE 35-16: U.S. Trade Patterns in Poultry[1] in 1998
(millions of dollars; percent)

Exports			Imports		
Region[2]	Value[3]	Share, %	Region[2]	Value[3]	Share, %
NAFTA	485	21	NAFTA	28	53
Latin America	193	9	Latin America	0	0
Western Europe	59	3	Western Europe	2	3
Japan/Chinese Economic Area	591	26	Japan/Chinese Economic Area	6	11
Other Asia	36	2	Other Asia	5	10
Rest of world	898	40	Rest of world	12	23
World	2,261	100	World	53	100
Top Five Countries	Value	Share, %	Top Five Countries	Value	Share, %
Russia	535	24	Canada	28	53
Hong Kong	371	16	New Zealand	10	19
Mexico	243	11	Taiwan	4	7
Canada	242	11	Vietnam	3	5
Japan	172	8	Indonesia	2	4

[1] SIC 2015.
[2] For definitions of regional groupings, see "Getting the Most Out of *Outlook 2000.*"
[3] Values may not sum to total due to rounding.
Source: U.S. Department of Commerce, Bureau of the Census.

rebound sharply if the Korean economy continues to improve in 2000. Export prospects to South Korea are better for turkey than they are for pork since domestic turkey production is limited.

U.S. beef exports are forecast to drop 6 percent to 2.3 billion pounds in 2000. The expected drop in U.S. beef production in 2000 will be greater than the decline in domestic consumption, leaving less beef available for export. At the same time, demand for high-quality hotel and restaurant beef is likely to increase in Asia, Mexico, and some other foreign markets. The gap between increased demand in these markets and reduced U.S. supply is likely to be filled by pulling beef out of the retail market and increasing U.S. imports from Canada and Argentina. Only recently has the United States imported fresh, chilled, or frozen beef from Argentina, after those products were declared free of foot-and-mouth disease by the USDA. Argentina is building up its fed-beef sector to compete with the United States in Asian markets. Australia is also a major beef producer, but it has a small fed-beef sector whose size is limited by feed grain availability.

As with U.S. turkey exports, healthy economic growth will increase demand for U.S. beef in Mexico in the year 2000, continuing a rebound from the lows in the mid-1990s, when the devaluation of the peso depressed sales. Mexico's domestic beef production is limited by declining cattle inventories caused by drought conditions in 1998 and 1999. Also limiting Mexican beef production are high interest rates, the indebtedness of Mexican producers, and the weak peso, which makes imported breeding cattle more expensive and increases the export value of domestic cattle.

U.S. pork exports probably will total 1.2 billion pounds in 2000, down slightly from the 1998 level and the 1999 estimate. The core U.S. markets—Japan, Canada, and Mexico—are each expected to register smaller gains in 2000. Secondary markets such as Korea, Taiwan, and Hong Kong, which saw a small gain in 1999, probably will remain steady in 2000 as U.S. pork prices rise. Export prospects have dampened from the rapid gains of recent years, because Japanese demand for U.S. pork appears to have leveled off and Russia has largely dropped out of the commercial market.

Donald A. Hodgen, U.S. Department of Commerce, Office of Consumer Goods, (202) 482-3346, November 1999.

REFERENCES

Call the U.S. Bureau of the Census at (301) 457-4100 for information about ordering Census documents.

General Information

Agra Europe, Agra Europe (London) Ltd., 25 Frant Road, Tunbridge Wells TN2 5JT, United Kingdom. (011) 0-1892-533813; fax: 011-0-1892-544895/524593.

Agricultural Outlook, Economic Research Service, U.S. Department of Agriculture, 1800 M Street, NW, Washington, DC 20036. (800) 999-6779 or (202) 694-5050.

Consumer and Producer Price Indexes, U.S. Department of Labor, Bureau of Labor Statistics, Washington, DC 20211. (202) 606-6950 and (202) 606-7700.

Consumer Expenditure Survey, U.S. Department of Labor, Bureau of Labor Statistics, Washington, DC 20211. (202) 606-6900.

Euromonitor, 60-61 Britton St., London EC1M 5NA, United Kingdom. (011) 44-171-251-8024; fax: (011) 44-171-608-3149.

Food Engineering, Cahners Business Information, 201 King of Prussia Road, Radnor, PA 19089. (610) 964-4000; fax: (610) 964-2915.

Food Engineering International, Chilton Company, Chilton Way, Radnor PA 19089. (610) 964-4000; fax: (610) 964-4273.

Food Institute Report, American Institute of Food Distribution, 28-12 Broadway, Fairlawn, NJ 07410. (201) 791-5570; fax: (201) 791-5222.

Food Marketing Institute, 800 Connecticut Avenue, NW, Washington, DC 20006-2701. (202) 452-8444; fax: (202) 429-8272.

1992 Census of Manufacturers, Meat Products, Dairy Products, Canned, Frozen and Preserved Fruits, Vegetables, and Specialty Foods, Grain Mill Products, Bakery Products, Sugar and Confectionery Products, Fats and Oils, Beverages, and Miscellaneous Food Preparations, U.S. Department of Commerce, Bureau of the Census, Washington, DC 20233.

Population Projections of the United States by Age, Sex, Race and Hispanic Origin: 1995 to 2050, Series P-25, No. 1130, U.S. Department of Commerce, Bureau of the Census, Washington, DC 20233.

Prepared Foods, Cahners Publishing Company, 1350 East Touhy Avenue, Des Plaines, IL 60018-3358. (847) 635-8800; fax (847) 390-2445.

Statistics for Industry Groups and Industries, 1996 Annual Survey of Manufacturers, M96(AS)-1, U.S. Department of Commerce, Bureau of the Census, Washington, DC 20233.

Supermarket News, Fairchild Publications, P.O. Box 10600, Riverton, NJ 08076. (609) 786-0963; fax: (609) 786-4415.

Thomas Food Industry Register, 5 Penn Plaza, New York, NY 10001. (212) 290-7262; fax: (212) 290-7373.

Value of Product Shipments, 1996 Annual Survey of Manufacturers, M96(AS)-2, U.S. Department of Commerce, Bureau of the Census, Washington, DC 20233.

Alcoholic Beverages

Alcoholic Beverage Executives' Newsletter, Alcoholic Beverage Executives' Newsletter Inc, P.O. Box 3188, Omaha, NE 68103. (402) 397-5514; fax: (402) 397-3843.

Beverage Aisle, Strategic Business Communications, 226 West 26 St., Tenth Floor, New York, NY 10001. (212) 822-5930; fax (212) 822-5931.

Brauwelt, Fachverlag Hans Carl GmbH & Co. KG, P.O.B. 99 01 53, D-90268 Nurnberg, Germany. (011) 49-911-952850; fax: (011) 49-911-9528548.

Brewing and Beverage Industry-International, Verlag W. Sachon GMBH+CO, D-87714 Mindelheim, Germany. (011) 49-08261-966-0; fax: (011) 49-08261-999-132.

Drinks International, Wilmington Publishing Ltd., 5-8 Underwood Street, London N1 7JQ, United Kingdom. (011) 44-181-841-3970; fax: 011-44-181-845-7696.

Food & Drink Weekly, Sparks Publishing, 6708 Whittier Avenue, McLean, VA 22101. 703-734-8787; fax: (703) 556-7865.

Impact International, M Shanken Corporation, 387 Park Avenue South, New York, NY 10016. (800) 848-7113; fax: (212) 481-0722.

International Wine Industry Report, Wine Institute and JBC International, 1620 I Street, NW, Suite 615, Washington, DC 20006. (202) 463-8493; fax: (202) 463-8497.

Liquor Handbook, Adams/Jobson Publishing Inc., 1180 Avenue of the Americas, New York, NY 10036. (800) 827-4700; fax: (847) 427-2006.

Monthly Statistical Release, Beer, Wine and Distilled Spirits, Marketing Compliance Division, Department of the Treasury, Bureau of Alcohol, Tobacco and Firearms, Washington, DC 20226. (202) 927-8130.

1996 Statistical Information for the U.S. Distilled Spirits Industry, Distilled Spirits Council of the United States, Inc., 1250 Eye Street, NW, Suite 900, Washington, DC 20005. (202) 628-3544.

1998 Brewers Almanac, Beer Institute, 122 C Street, NW, Suite 750, Washington, DC 20001. (202) 737-2377; fax: (202) 737-7004.

Wine Business Monthly, New World Wine Communication, 867 West Napa Street, Sonoma, CA 95476. (707) 939-0833; fax: (707) 939-0833.

The Wine Institute, 914 Post Street, San Francisco, CA 90505, (415) 512-0151; fax (914) 442-0742.

World Drink Trends, NTC Publications Ltd., Farm Road, Henley-on-Thames, Oxfordshire RG9 1EJ, United Kingdom. (011) 44-1491-411000; fax: (011) 44-1491-571188.

Salted Snacks and Snack Foods

Milling and Baking News, Sosland Publishing Company, 4800 Main Street, Suite 100, Kansas City, MO 68112. (816) 756-1000; (816) 756-0494.

Snack Food & Wholesale Bakery, Stagnito Publishing, 1935 Sherner Road, Suite 100, Northbrook, IL 60062. (847) 205-5660; fax: (847) 205-5688.

State of the Snack Food Industry Report and Snack World, Snack Food Association, 1711 King Street, Suite 1, Alexandria, VA 22314. (703) 836-4500; fax: (703) 836-8262.

Red Meat and Poultry Products

American Meat Institute, P.S. Box 3556, Washington, DC 20007. (703) 841-2400; fax: (703) 527-0938.

Livestock and Poultry: World Markets and Trade, U.S. Department of Agriculture, Foreign Agricultural Service, AG Box 1044, South Agriculture Building, Washington, DC 20250. (202) 720-8252.

Meat: Marketing & Technology, Marketing and Technology Group, 1415 North Dayton, Chicago, IL 60622. (312) 266-3111; fax: (312) 266-3363.

National Broiler Council, 1155 15 Street, NW, Suite 614, Washington, DC 20005. (202) 296-2622; fax: (202) 293-4005.

Poultry: Marketing & Technology, Marketing and Technology Group, 1415 North Dayton, Chicago, IL 60622. (312) 266-3111; fax: (312) 266-3363.

Render, National Renderers Association and Sierra Publishing, 2820 Birch Avenue, Camino, CA 95709. (530) 644-8428; fax: (530) 644-8429.

MOTOR VEHICLES
Economic and Trade Trends

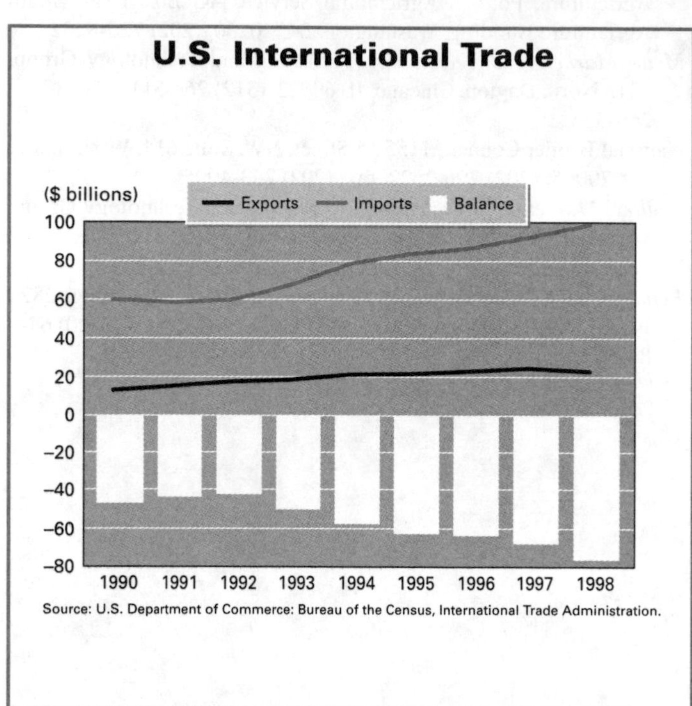

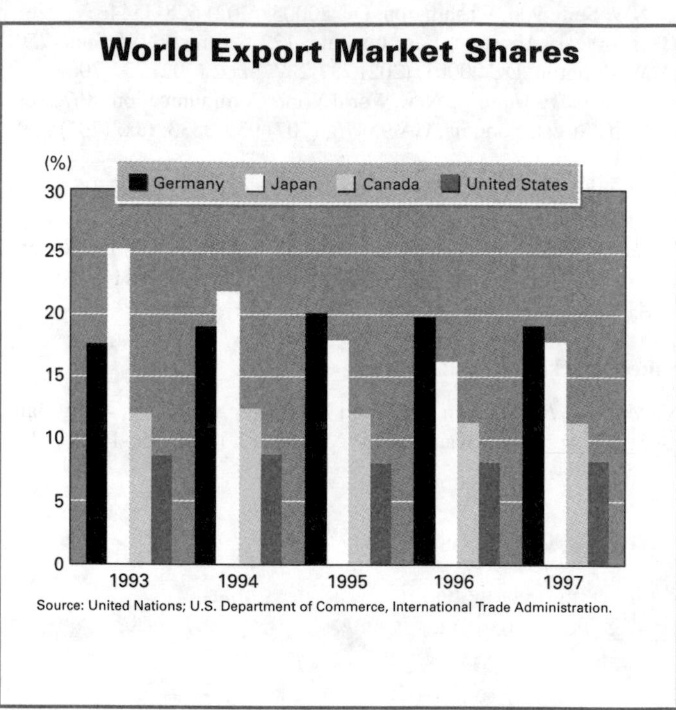

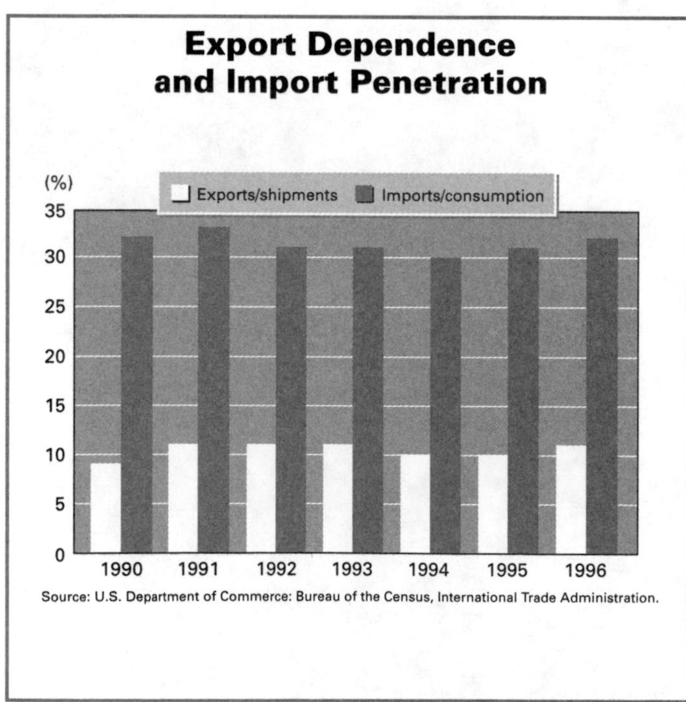

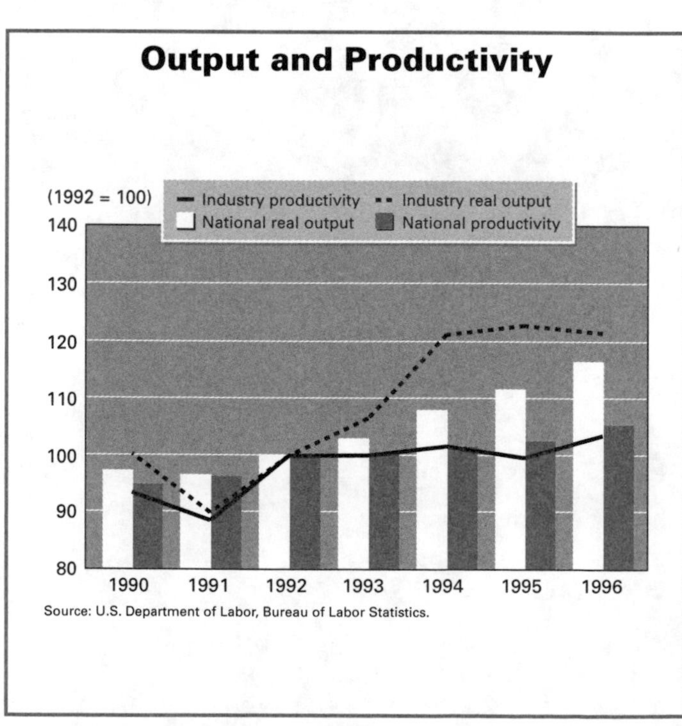

See "Getting the Most Out of *Outlook 2000*" for definitions of terms.

36

Motor Vehicles

INDUSTRY DEFINITION The motor vehicle industry includes new on-road, volume-produced completed vehicles that carry cargo or passengers (SIC 3711, 3713). The automotive parts and accessories industry is covered in Chapter 37.

OVERVIEW

The United States is a major player in the world automobile industry. There are a relatively small number of automobile and truck manufacturers in the world. The largest two, General Motors (GM) and Ford, are U.S.-based but have global operations. Most major foreign manufacturers manufacture or sell vehicles in the large and important U.S. market.

The most important trends in the automotive industry generally pertain to two related developments: intensifying competition and increasing globalization. Increased domestic competition pressures manufacturers to leverage their brands and engineering, development, and production costs by entering and competing in foreign markets. As more producers enter new markets around the globe, competition escalates worldwide.

GLOBAL INDUSTRY TRENDS

The Internet, faster communication, lower trade barriers, and rising incomes in many parts of the world have changed the face of the international automotive market. Competition, which once came primarily from local sources, can now come from or go to virtually anywhere on the planet. The resulting globalization of the auto industry has led to improved product quality and lower costs and has spurred companies to reposition themselves through mergers.

Industry Consolidation

As automakers move toward producing a reduced number of parts, the industry is trending toward a reduced number of manufacturers and component suppliers. That does not imply an impending wave of business shutdowns but instead a consolidation of smaller companies into larger ones. For example, in 1999, Ford, which already effectively controls Mazda and owns the British makes Jaguar and Aston Martin, acquired Volvo's car operations. GM has interests in Isuzu and Suzuki and is expected to purchase the 50 percent of the Swedish automaker Saab that it does not already own. Renault recently invested $5.4 billion for a 37 percent stake in debt-laden Nissan, which owns part of Subaru. Since the 1998 announcement of the merger of Daimler-Benz AG and the Chrysler Corp. that created DaimlerChrysler, German rival Volkswagen AG has made several acquisitions, including the premium brands Rolls Royce Cars of Britain; Automobili Lamborghini SpA, the Italian luxury sports car maker; and Bugatti Automibili, the bankrupt Italian sports-car manufacturer. In addition, Hyundai Motor Co. of South Korea purchased the bankrupt Kia Motors Corp. and Asia Motors Corp. at auction.

These recent acquisitions, following on the heels of the 1998 merger of Germany's Daimler-Benz AG and Chrysler Corp., may represent a peak in automaker merger activity. Additional deals may take place, but the most attractive participants have been sold or are busy digesting their recent acquisitions.

At this point, joint ventures and alliances rather than outright sales may be viewed as the preferred intercompany linkup. They allow companies to both maintain their independence and benefit from the synergies and cost savings of combining certain operations and activities.

Potential buyers include cash-rich global producers such as GM, Ford, DaimlerChrysler, Volkswagen, Toyota Motor Corp., and Honda Motor Co. The list of potential targets includes Samsung Motors Inc., Daewoo Motor Co., Mitsubishi Motor Corp., Fiat Auto SpA, and PSA Peugeot-Citroen. These firms may suffer from a lack of cash, a heavy debt load, a limited international presence, a weak product line, and/or poor manufacturing productivity and quality.

Not everyone, however, feels the urge to merge. Fiat, for example, wishes to remain independent, although it probably will continue to develop joint ventures such as its agreement to combine foundry operations for metal casting with Renault. That venture, which establishes the world's largest auto foundry business, will allow Fiat and Renault to increase revenue while reducing costs.

The trend toward consolidation is not new. Foreign and U.S. auto manufacturers have been following a path of consolidation for some time. Before it became part of DaimlerChrysler, Chrysler grew out of Maxwell and Dodge Brothers and previously had purchased AMC/Jeep. AMC was in turn the sum of a number of companies, including Kaiser's Jeep (formerly Willys-Overland), Nash, and Hudson.

Consolidation activity also has been occurring on the supplier side. Merged suppliers benefit from economies of scale and the ability to shift from doing component and parts production to being module and system manufacturers and suppliers. For example, rather than supplying only seats for a given model, a system supplier may produce the complete interior.

Joint Ventures

Historically, the former Big Three and foreign-based manufacturers formed joint ventures and alliances as a way for the foreign-based producers to gain access to the North American marketplace and for the Big Three producers to fill gaps in their vehicle lineups. Although several transplant manufacturers simply set up shop in North America, others, such as Toyota, decided to test the waters first. The resulting alliance with GM, the New United Motors Manufacturing, Inc. (NUMMI)—the first of its kind in North America—is located in Fremont, CA.

Ford and Mazda's alliance (joint ventures in Thailand and the United States, plus Ford's 38 percent share of Mazda) is interesting because the line between the two companies has started to fade. In fact, as Mazda has continued to struggle with falling market share, its dependence on Ford has been increasing.

World Commonality

The combined trends of globalization and greater competitive pressures have made the construction of a "world car" a priority for automakers. A world car can be defined as a vehicle based on a single platform that a manufacturer intends to produce and sell in multiple regions of the world.

In theory, the goal of building a world car is to leverage costs. By maximizing sales of a single platform that is distributed in a variety of markets, a company leverages its engineering, development, and marketing costs. It also allows for the sharing of best practices as well as economies of scale. While the rationale for building a world car is straightforward, the ability to do so successfully is not. For example, local tastes, infrastructure, government regulations, and other factors may make it difficult for a manufacturer to keep variations to a minimum.

In 1981, Ford introduced its first attempt at a world car, the Escort. That vehicle was not a financial success—it lost money, as do most small cars in the United States. Also, Ford admits that the Escort was not a real world car; it used two platforms (one in Europe and one in the United States) and did not share a sufficient number of components.

In the 1990s, Ford made a second attempt at a world car: the Mondeo/Contour/Mystique. The models shared 70 percent of their components, making them more of a world car than the Escort. However, the effort was ultimately unsuccessful, as Ford still lost money.

Ford's latest entry in the world car category is the Focus sedan. Although built on one platform, the Focus targets a variety of consumer segments. In the United States, in a planned fall 1999 launch, Focus was to replace the Escort as Ford's entry-level vehicle. In Europe, the Focus already serves as a trade-up from the Ford Fiesta. In poorer countries, the Focus would be considered a luxury model.

The Focus will differ from its world car predecessors. Ford has cut engineering and development costs by allowing outside suppliers to manufacture 15 major subassemblies, such as seats and suspensions. While the Focus will be cheaper to produce than were its predecessors, it probably will not be profitable in the United States, although foreign profitability is possible. Still, the Focus will help reduce companywide average vehicle emissions levels.

If Ford can show improved profitability through its world car, other manufacturers will be more likely to follow suit.

Roaming the Globe

To lower costs and meet projected demand from emerging markets, and to avoid existing trade and investment restrictions, vehicle manufacturers have increased production in developing countries, including Mexico, Brazil, and some nations in eastern Europe. Despite recent economic retrenchment, developing markets are expected to provide growth to automakers in the long term. In addition, these markets generally have lower cost structures than do traditional markets.

Mexico, for example, is an attractive production locale for automakers worldwide because of its low labor costs and proximity to the U.S. border. The North American Free Trade Agreement (NAFTA) has eliminated most tariffs on trade between Mexico and the United States.

Brazil, with South America's largest economy, is an important market for U.S.-based manufacturers. Until the recent currency turmoil slowed its economic expansion, Brazil had been a source of sales and profit growth for car makers. The country's austerity measures should create a short-term drag on its economy but could help hasten a rebound.

Since the fall of the former Soviet Union, several manufacturers have built production facilities in eastern Europe. Producers anticipate growth in those markets, where per-capita auto ownership is low. However, this process may take longer than expected.

As automakers have expanded around the globe, parts suppliers have been forced to follow. It is no longer enough to supply parts for GM, Ford, and Toyota in their respective home markets. To be successful, suppliers must be able to produce parts wherever their automaker customers are located. The most successful become automakers' primary vendors and are designated as Tier One suppliers.

DOMESTIC TRENDS

Improving Quality

Beginning in the 1970s, Japanese automakers were able to capture significant U.S. market share largely as a result of their quality advantage over the Big Three. Domestic producers were forced to improve quality in order to compete. Although a gap still remains, this fierce competition has raised the minimum quality level required for participation in the automotive manufacturing industry.

In fact, because of the significant improvement in quality, along with greater consumer knowledge, J.D. Power and Associates redesigned its initial quality study in 1998. With better manufacturing, cars today are more sophisticated and longer-lasting than their predecessors. Consumers are not afraid to use older vehicles as those cars are more reliable than they were in the past.

Factory Transplants

Currency fluctuations have encouraged the production of foreign models in North America and reduced the flow of imports. In particular, the long-term appreciation of the Japanese yen versus the dollar (a trend that until 1999 had been reversed after a mid-1995 peak) made many Japanese automakers step up their North American transplant manufacturing capacity to maintain competitive prices on their core products.

At present, most moderately priced Japanese vehicles sold in the United States are made here. The transfer process is in the early stages for luxury cars, but eventually almost everything Japanese automakers sell in the United States may be built in North America.

European automakers are also increasing their U.S. production capacity. The German-based Bayerische Motoren Werke AG (BMW) has announced plans to expand its U.S. facility. Its compatriot Daimler-Benz is seeking to minimize the effects of currency fluctuations and improve the cost-competitiveness of its Mercedes-Benz line through production at its Alabama facility, its first U.S. plant. Daimler-Benz's 1998 merger with Chrysler could be considered the ultimate currency hedge for producing in the U.S. market. Foreign automakers will continue their efforts to soften the impact of currency fluctuations. This will require them to produce more in foreign markets and source parts and components locally in those markets. Some 3 million units of transplant production capacity are already in place in the United States and Canada. This transplant capacity should grow as foreign companies expand in the U.S. truck market.

Product Cycles and Design

Years ago, car body styles seemed to change almost yearly with the addition of at least some new sheet metal. In the 1960s, body styles began to last longer, with minor trim changes being the only indication of a new model year. Some models today have cycles as long as 8 or 10 years. These longer product cycles most often are associated with the Big Three, as the Asian nameplates generally have cycles of 4 to 5 years.

Freshness of product was one of the key factors that cost American companies market share. When most Asian nameplate production took place overseas, the loss of shares resulted in increased vehicle imports and cuts in U.S. car production. In recent years, with more import nameplate transplant production in North America, the negative effect of longer cycles on U.S. and North American companies has been mitigated somewhat. In addition, the increased popularity of light trucks has helped the production picture because the Big Three dominate the U.S. light truck market. Thus, the trend toward light trucks should result in an increase in U.S. and North American production, all else being equal. Interestingly, trucks tend to have longer product cycles than do cars because consumers do not seem to demand freshly styled trucks as often as they do cars; this also works to the Big Three's advantage.

Price

After years in which price increases outstripped income growth, several developments in recent years—including competition, consumer demand for affordability, currency fluctuations, and cost cutting by manufacturers—have kept a lid on automotive prices.

According to the U.S. Bureau of the Census, in 1973, the average American needed 17.5 weeks of family earnings to buy a car; by 1994, that figure had risen to 25.0 weeks. However, costs then declined sequentially through 1998 to 23.6 weeks. A further decline in 1999 was considered possible as a result of the highly competitive nature of the domestic sedan market.

Even more surprising is the fact that some manufacturers have reduced prices on certain new vehicle models. Increased manufacturing efficiencies and other successful cost-cutting efforts allowed car makers to price certain 1999 model-year vehicles below the comparable 1998 editions even after adding new standard features. For example, Chrysler sold the redesigned and better-equipped 1999 Jeep Grand Cherokee for $25,695, compared with $25,945 for the 1998 model.

Heated competition has contributed to the weak automotive pricing environment. With overall improved quality among most manufacturers, buyers feel more free to use price to differentiate similar offerings. When one manufacturer offers incentives such as rebates or discounted financing, the others generally follow suit or risk losing market share.

Additionally, consumers are increasingly better informed about a vehicle's actual cost and less likely to accept large annual price increases. In an era of low inflation, customers armed with dealer cost information from consumer publications and the Internet have learned to drive a hard bargain when negotiating the purchase of a vehicle.

Dealer Consolidation

The number of franchised auto dealers in the United States has declined since the end of World War II. In 1949, 49,000 dealers were operating in the United States; in January 1998 (the latest available figures), there were about 22,367, according to *Automotive News*. The total is expected to fall below 20,000 early in the next decade.

Large, well-financed entrepreneurs increasingly dominate the dealership base. These modern multifranchise dealerships aim for high unit volume and often are willing to take a smaller profit per vehicle sold. They advertise extensively and often cluster different franchises on one large property to allow customers to shop several nameplates at one time and increase the likelihood of securing a sale.

Impact of Technology and the Internet

The Internet is a growing force in the buying and selling of a wide variety of products, including automobiles. According to International Data Corp., a leading provider of information technology data, aggregate U.S. Internet commerce across all industries was estimated to have been $37 billion in 1998 and is projected to soar to $708 billion in 2003. Use of the Internet to aid new and used car and truck purchasing also should surge dramatically in the coming years. In addition, according to J.D. Power and Associates, 25 percent of new vehicle purchasers used the Internet to assist them with their purchases in 1998—for researching new cars, shopping for used cars, and conducting sales transactions—and this number will increase to approximately 65 percent by 2000.

The primary reason consumers are turning to the Internet to purchase a car is convenience. The Internet provides a relatively easy way to gather information and shop for the best deals in terms of both price and needed attributes.

Through Web sites, consumers can more easily read a variety of vehicle reviews to compare models and ascertain which ones meet their needs. They can view, search, and screen for prices, features, and other important information, such as invoice prices for new cars and published values for used cars. In addition, many Web sites allow consumers to choose insurance, financing, leasing, and warranty options. Once they decide what to purchase, consumers can be referred to one of the dealers affiliated with a Web site or begin negotiations with a dealer. After they receive a Web site referral, dealers are expected to promptly offer a competitive price for the selected vehicle.

Dealers like the Internet too. Not only can dealers increase volume through Internet leads that are converted to sales, they also can decrease incremental marketing, advertising, and personnel costs per sale. Referrals via affiliation with retail Web sites can help dealers improve profits. In fact, dealers eventually can be expected to take the next step and enhance their brands by creating and using their own corporate Web sites.

Web sites are already beginning to provide more than just product and dealer information. In March 1999, GM began offering a $500 discount coupon—its first electronic coupons for automobiles—on its Buick Regal sedans to buyers who fill out a questionnaire on the company's Web site.

Also growing in popularity are Internet auto-buying services such as Autobytel.com, Autoweb.com, and Microsoft Corp.'s Carpoint. Yet Standard & Poor's is cautious about such sites' longer-term prospects in that it expects more competition from dealers' and manufacturers' own Web sites.

As Internet commerce is in its infancy, further evolution is expected in the way buyers and sellers use the medium.

The use of the Internet and supercomputers has allowed automobile designers to create engines, interiors, and even an entire vehicle in record time. Many automakers have expressed interest in shortening the time to market to 24 months or less. This includes designing, testing, and producing a vehicle once corporate decision makers have given the final approval. That allows the production of state-of the art designs and prevents the situation in which designs are dated by the time they reach the market. The Internet allows engineering teams in different parts of the globe to work and view three-dimensional designs simultaneously over computer networks. It also allows for 24-hour-a-day development as tasks are handed off from shift to shift across different continents, countries, and time zones.

The use of computer-aided design ultimately should lead to more uniform product cycles because key design questions can be answered in days rather than months. Similarly, a part can be modeled and prototyped in an hour instead of days. These technological innovations save time and also reduce development costs. In addition, the design and production aspects of the U.S., North American, and world industries may become so integrated that once a part design is complete, computer-driven production equipment will be able to instantly configure the tooling needed to make the part so that actual part production can begin immediately after completion of the design.

Regulatory and Environmental Issues

Automakers often are caught between conflicting regulatory requirements and consumer demands, especially in relation to the design and engineering of vehicles. Automakers must comply with government regulations regarding safety, fuel consumption, and pollution control, but doing so typically has repercussions in other areas. For instance, the most effective way to improve a vehicle's fuel economy is to lighten its weight, yet this leaves the car more vulnerable in a crash and makes the job of designing a safe vehicle more challenging. Also, pollution regulations, which are tightened periodically, require emissions equipment that hurts fuel economy.

Compliance with government rules also can fly in the face of consumer demand. For much of the past decade, consumers have clamored for sport utility vehicles and for larger and more powerful engines. Those desires have been in direct conflict with the government's goal of reducing fuel consumption, because large-engine cars and sport utility vehicles consume more fuel than do smaller vehicles.

Air Quality Standards. The Clean Air Act Amendments of 1990 (CAAA) mandated that automakers reduce emissions from their manufacturing plants and contained several new vehicle regulations. First phased in with 1994 models, CAAA tailpipe standards required that nitrogen oxide and hydrocarbon emissions be cut 60 percent and 40 percent, respectively, by

1996. A second round of cuts may be required in 2003, depending on the nation's air quality at that time.

That legislation raised the required warranty period for catalytic converters and electronic diagnostic equipment to 8 years or 80,000 miles; for all other pollution gear, it was reduced to 2 years or 24,000 miles. Additionally, automobiles sold in the United States must be equipped with fuel-vapor recovery canisters to prevent gasoline fumes from being released when the tank is filled. Gas stations in 39 smoggy metropolitan areas were required to install vapor recovery equipment by 1994.

Alternative Fuels. In those 39 metropolitan areas, the CAAA also required the use of cleaner-burning fuels, including reformulated gasoline. Beginning with 1998 models, centrally fueled fleets of more than 10 vehicles in the 39 areas were required to cut hydrocarbon and toxic chemical emissions 75 percent, which probably portends the use of alternative fuels.

All domestic and most foreign automakers are conducting research on how to use alternative fuels. They also are marketing limited numbers of modified vehicles that can run on either gasoline or alternative fuels such as ethanol, methanol, propane, and natural gas or electricity derived from batteries or solar power.

Technological obstacles notwithstanding, the single greatest barrier to the commercial success of alternative fuel vehicles is the higher cost of operating them compared with conventional gasoline-powered vehicles as long as fuel in the United States remains cheap.

LIGHT TRUCKS

When a nation first has sufficient per capita income to make vehicle ownership feasible on a large scale, the first vehicles purchased are usually trucks, such as compact pickups. Businesses typically make such purchases because they need trucks to get goods to markets. As the market matures, personal-use vehicles, beginning with small cars, begin to take a share of the market, causing light truck sales to dwindle. The U.S. market has shown an uncharacteristic rebound in light truck sales.

Domestic Trends

Over the past decade, the U.S. automobile industry has witnessed a dramatic change in truck offerings and a resulting jump in the demand for and market share of light trucks. The U.S. market provides a sound illustration of the evolution of the light truck from a primarily business and commercial product to a consumer-oriented product. Despite the maturity of the U.S. market, the light truck share in the United States is on the way up and is approaching parity with the car share. However, today's U.S. truck purchases are different from those of an emerging market in that they are not primarily business-related. The models are larger and more luxurious, designed for personal transportation. Part of the U.S. demand for trucks can be attributed to more open space and lower gasoline prices in the United States compared with western Europe and Japan, where the light truck share remains low.

Passenger car sales have slowed to recessionary levels. Car volume has declined each year since 1994 as consumers have shown a preference for sport utility vehicles and minivans, which are classified as light trucks.

Meanwhile, the growth of the truck market has contributed to the profit gains achieved by U.S. automakers. Given their dominance in this segment, the Big Three's profit margins will continue to benefit as the truck market—largely consisting of light trucks—outpaces the slower-growing car market.

Sport utility van (SUV) models include GM's Chevrolet Blazer and Tahoe, Ford's Explorer and Expedition, and DaimlerChrysler's Jeep Cherokee, Grand Cherokee, and Dodge Durango. In the minivan category are DaimlerChrysler's Dodge Caravan and Plymouth Voyager, Ford's Aerostar and Windstar, and GM's Chevrolet Venture and Pontiac Trans Sport.

Foreign companies are increasing their penetration of the light truck, minivan, and SUV market. About 8.9 percent of the light-duty trucks sold in the United States in 1998 were imported from countries other than Canada. Although down from a peak of 16 percent in 1990, this figure is up from 8.5 percent in 1997 and 7.7 percent in 1998 as non-U.S. companies target this bastion of Big Three profits. With new product lines, non–Big Three firms can be expected to continue to take market share.

Toyota, Nissan, Mazda Motor Corp., and Isuzu Motors Ltd. are pursuing strategies to manufacture light trucks in the United States. Nissan and Mazda already have arrangements with Ford, which manufactures vehicles to their specifications. Meanwhile, Toyota has shifted production of its midsize pickup truck to this country. Recent market gains by these foreign companies reflect weaker currencies and attractive products, such as Toyota's Sienna minivan and Nissan's XTerra.

Faced with the potential for greater competition in this segment, GM, Ford, and Chrysler are renewing their truck lines. Some of their new and/or redesigned models, such as GM's Silverado full-size pickup and Ford's Super Duty truck, are already on the market.

Global Trends

Although overseas markets are relatively small, light trucks are starting to increase in popularity as personal use vehicles in western Europe and Japan. Minivans are gaining ground in Europe as most of the major manufacturers have begun to offer models, and Japanese purchases of compact sport utilities and smaller minvanlike offerings are on the rise.

North American light vehicle capacity also is growing. A majority of the gains in plant space have resulted from an expansion by the transplant manufacturers. However, domestic manufacturers in North America are planning to convert plant output from cars to trucks in response to market demand.

Globally, total capacity and production will continue to be affected by the Asian economic crisis. South Korea, which was the most overcapacitized country, was strongly affected by the crisis, and expansion plans probably will be put on hold, perhaps reducing some of the worldwide underutilization problems. Although the crisis has not affected U.S. sales or production, it is likely to affect emerging economies that have significantly higher income elasticity for car demand and from which most of the world's net new growth in demand has been expected to come.

Long-Term Prospects

Sales growth of light vehicles domestically should reflect the maturing age of the U.S. driving population. Unlike previous periods, there is no untapped portion of the population that is about to enter the market. For example, when women entered the workforce en masse, a part of the population with low demand for light vehicles began to purchase them. Similarly, when the baby boomers were old enough to afford new vehicles, sales surged. Over the forecast period, most of the growth in the population will be in the 40- to 60-year-old age bracket. As these buyers are already in the buying pool, growth in this age bracket will not affect the total number of new vehicles sold, although it is likely to affect the types of vehicles purchased.

In general, trucks worldwide probably will offer more car-like amenities such as heated seats, power windows, and traction control. These added features should broaden the range of consumers who choose a light truck over a car. In addition, partly in the interest of reducing unique platforms (and costs) and partly to further soften ride characteristics, many of the latest small truck models are actually based on cars (e.g., many minivans). As many cars are beginning to follow truck styling cues, the world market most likely will offer hybrid models that have the styling and visibility of light trucks and the comfort and features traditionally offered by cars.

GLOBAL MARKET PROSPECTS

The motor vehicle industry in the United States is a large, mature market, and most of the cars and light trucks produced here are geared to the unique U.S. market. For example, many vehicles are large, have powerful engines, and are well equipped compared with products in the rest of the world. This is the case even in comparison with other mature markets, such as those in Japan and western Europe, both of which demand much smaller models than those sold in the United States, in part because of the high price of fuel overseas.

Canada is the market that is most accepting of U.S.-made vehicles. However, because of lower incomes, higher taxes and vehicle prices, and a weak Canadian dollar, the best-selling models in Canada tend to be smaller and less expensive than the U.S. best-sellers. As the Mexican market continues to expand, automakers will increase the number of models tailored for that market. DaimlerChrysler is expected to introduce a model below the Neon in both price and size for the 2000 model, and the forthcoming Fiesta should boost Ford sales. Unfortunately, the Canadian light vehicle market in total is expected to reach only 1.5 million units by 2002, with the Mexican market reaching 700,000 to 800,000 units. In other words, the two export markets with the greatest potential for U.S.-made products have limited growth potential and are far smaller than the U.S. market.

Japanese automakers with plants in the United States have begun exporting vehicles from the United States to Japan. Honda, for example, is exporting Accords made in Ohio to Japan and Europe, and Toyota is exporting Camry coupes and wagons to Japan. European automakers are following suit. Although the volumes of these vehicles will be fairly minimal compared with those of some of the high-volume products made in the United States, their unit value will be higher.

Unfortunately for the U.S. industry, most of the growth in the world's markets will take place in the developing auto markets, such as those in China, India, Latin America, and eastern Europe. The typical product made in the United States has a very limited sales potential in these growing markets because it is overequipped and prohibitively expensive. Even without local production requirements, the low vehicle prices needed to be successful in evolving markets are incompatible with the product costs associated with U.S. manufacturing efforts.

Effects of NAFTA

Five years after its implementation, NAFTA has been boosting automotive trade across borders, NAFTA has enabled vehicle producers to rationalize their production in the United States, Canada, and Mexico (the three member countries), improving their productivity and profitability. Additional volume for the United States is being sourced from Mexico, and U.S. vehicle shipments to Mexico have grown substantially. In 1994, the year the agreement was implemented, exports of all road motor vehicles to Mexico jumped from $167 million to $656 million, according to data assembled by the U.S. Department of Commerce's Office of Automotive Affairs. In 1995, a severe slump in the Mexican economy resulted in a drop in U.S. vehicle exports to $383 million; that figure was still twice the 1993 level. With a rebound in the Mexican economy, U.S. exports to Mexico increased 16 percent compared to 1997, reaching $2.3 billion in 1998. At the same time, imports from Mexico increased nearly 8 percent to $13.2 billion, allowing it to edge out Germany as the third largest source of imports into the United States. Canada accounts for the majority of U.S. exports and imports. Most bilateral trade is generated from intracompany shipments by GM, Ford, and DaimlerChrysler. Total exports to Canada declined 7 percent in 1998 to $13.2 billion. At the same time, imports from Canada rose 4 percent, reflecting strong demand in the U.S. market. Thus, Canada represented 58 percent of the total value of U.S. exports in 1998 and 38 percent of total U.S. imports (see Table 36-1).

Before NAFTA was in place, duty-free treatment existed on virtually all automotive trade between the United States and Canada. As a result, the implementation of NAFTA did not have as dramatic an effect as it did on trade with Mexico.

TABLE 36-1: U.S. Trade Patterns in Motor Vehicles[1] in 1998
(millions of dollars; percent)

Exports			Imports		
Region[2]	Value[3]	Share,%	Regions[2]	Value[3]	Share, %
NAFTA	15,418	68	NAFTA	50,531	51
Latin America	1,154	5	Latin America	3	0
Western Europe	2,768	12	Western Europe	18,164	18
Japan/Chinese Economic Area	1,400	6	Japan/Chinese Economic Area	28,865	29
Other Asia	104	0	Other Asia	1,692	2
Rest of world	1,694	8	Rest of world	168	0
World	22,538	100	World	99,424	100
Top Five Countries	Value	Share, %	Top Five Countries	Value	Share,%
Canada	13,160	58	Canada	37,324	38
Mexico	2,258	10	Japan	28,864	29
Germany	1,157	5	Mexico	13,207	13
Japan	1,113	5	Germany	12,439	13
Saudi Arabia	653	3	Sweden	2,011	2

[1] SIC 371, 3713.
[2] For definitions of regional groupings, see "Getting the Most Out of *Outlook 2000*."
[3] Values may not sum to total due to rounding.
Source: U.S. Department of Commerce, Bureau of the Census.

U.S. INDUSTRY PROJECTIONS FOR THE NEXT 1 AND 5 YEARS

Although the U.S. market is expected to grow only a little over the forecast period, domestic production increased faster than did sales during the 1990s. This reflects the import share of U.S. sales falling significantly as major Japanese and German manufacturers moved vehicle production to North America. Also related to import penetration is the increasing popularity of light trucks, which have far lower import penetration than do passenger cars.

Over time, the former Big Three may have greater production percentage increases in Canada and Mexico than they do in the United States. Offsetting this effect will be continued efforts by the import nameplates to make inroads into U.S. markets. Toyota, Honda, Nissan, Mazda, Mitsubishi, Subaru, Isuzu, BMW, and Mercedes all produce vehicles in the United States. The import nameplates also are expected to continue to increase production elsewhere in North America, in particular, Honda and Toyota in Canada and Nissan and Volkswagen in Mexico.

From 1990 to 2002, the United States may lose some of its light vehicle production predominance in NAFTA as its share of total North American light vehicle output is expected to fall. On a percentage point basis, Mexico will gain the most from this loss by the United States. However, despite a loss in the North American share, U.S. production is expected to remain at approximately 12 million units.

Comparisons of capacity with production indicate that North American factory utilization hit 91 percent in 1997. This represents a slight imbalance between plant space and actual output, but it offers manufacturers room to breathe in years with stronger demand. While some automakers are struggling to make use of their plant floor space, others are finding themselves in need of extra space to keep up with demand. For example, Nissan is working hard to rearrange its production in North America to take advantage of its greatly underutilized Mexican plants. Honda, in contrast, is expanding its North American production capabilities. As these adjustments are made over the next few years, North American automakers should achieve capacity utilization above 90 percent.

According to the 1999 edition of *Ward's Automotive Yearbook*, in 1998, the United States produced 23 percent of world vehicle output. The U.S. share of worldwide production is forecast to rise through 2003 to 27 percent of total output. Although U.S. output will expand at a low single-digit rate over this period, other regions, such as eastern Europe and Latin America, are expected to grow at a much faster rate. One reason for this is that U.S. light vehicle demand is expected to be relatively flat for the next several years. After an expected near-term peak in 1999, production should decline slightly in the year 2000 before slowly rebounding. At the same time, other regions are expected to increase production more rapidly.

In the long term, the markets with the greatest potential for growth include India, China, Latin America, and eastern Europe. Unfortunately, average income levels in those countries are far below those in the mature markets and cannot bear the cost of U.S.-made products. Also, in the short term those developing areas will have to deal with the effects of the economic conditions in Asia and may experience short-lived dips in production. Moreover, the size and relative fuel inefficiency of U.S.-made vehicles would make most of them incompatible with market conditions in those countries. Finally, many of those countries have trade barriers in the form of tariffs or domestic content requirements. For U.S. car companies to be

TABLE 36-2: Motor Vehicles and Bodies (SIC 3711, 3713) Trends and Forecasts
(millions of dollars except as noted)

	1992	1993	1994	1995	1996	1997[1]	1998[1]	1999[2]	2000[3]	Percent Change 97–98	98–99	99–00	96–00[4]
Industry data													
Value of shipments[5]	156,309	173,702	204,373	209,035	209,184	218,596	219,254	228,706	225,400	0.3	4.3	−1.4	1.9
Value of shipments (1992$)	156,309	167,951	190,691	192,975	190,849	195,689	198,115	204,700	201,250	1.2	3.3	−1.7	1.3
Total employment (thousands)	263	259	271	278	263								
Production workers (thousands)	219	217	230	239	225								
Average hourly earnings ($)	20.64	21.28	22.03	22.93	23.04								
Capital expenditures	3,059	4,113	4,419	4,681	4,503								
Product data													
Value of shipments[5]	151,629	168,682	201,307	205,644	205,930	215,359	216,017	225,315	222,163	0.3	4.3	−1.4	1.9
Value of shipments (1992$)	151,629	163,091	187,816	189,846	187,892	192,801	195,190	201,714	198,360	1.2	3.3	−1.7	1.4
Trade data													
Value of imports	59,758	67,753	78,744	83,958	86,898	92,756	99,424	107,378	109,525	7.2	8.0	2.0	6.0
Value of exports	17,124	18,166	20,904	21,267	22,653	24,224	22,538	21,727	22,161	−7.0	−3.6	2.0	−0.5

[1] Estimate except imports and exports.
[2] Estimate.
[3] Forecast.
[4] Compound annual rate.
[5] For a definition of industry versus product values, see "Getting the Most Out of *Outlook 2000.*"
Source: U.S. Department of Commerce: Bureau of the Census; International Trade Administration.

competitive in many large untapped markets, they need to manufacture there, further limiting the likelihood that cars and light trucks made in the United States will be sold in quantity in the emerging markets.

Altogether, U.S. industry shipments were expected to grow 4 percent in 1999, reaching $229 billion in current dollars in that year and $244 billion by 2004 (a further 7 percent gain) (see Table 36-2). Gains are expected to come from a variety of sources, including increased exports to the recovering Mexican market, increased import penetration of North American–made products in Asia and Europe, and increased output from transplant manufacturers.

The movement by the import nameplates over the past decade has allowed both U.S. and North American production to increase faster than have U.S. sales for the first time in recent memory. From 1996 to 2004, however, the outlook is not likely to be as bright for North American producers overall. Like U.S. sales, U.S. production levels are expected to change little from today's levels. In contrast, light vehicle production in North America overall is expected to continue to grow. The strongest growth is expected in Mexico as a result of the use of that country as a base for export production to other Latin American countries and the United States as well as to Europe and the rebound of the Mexican economy, which will boost sales and production for the local market.

Efraim Levy, Standard & Poor's Equity Group, (212) 438-9531, October, 1999.

REFERENCES

Automotive News, Detroit, MI 48202. (313) 875-2090, www.ai-online.com.

International Data Corp., Framingham, MA. www.idcresearch.com.

J.D. Power and Associates, 1999 New Autoshopper.com study. Agoura Hills, CA 91301. (818) 889-6330, www.jdpower.com.

Standard & Poor's, the McGraw-Hill Companies, New York, NY 10041. www.standardandpoors.com.

U.S. Department of Commerce, Bureau of the Census.

U.S. Department of Commerce, Office of Automotive Affairs, International Trade Administration.

Ward's Automotive Yearbook, 1999, a division of Primedia Inc., Southfield, MI 48075. (248) 357-0800, www.wardsauto.com.

RELATED CHAPTERS

13: Steel Mill Products
16: Microelectronics
37: Automotive Parts

AUTOMOTIVE PARTS
Economic and Trade Trends

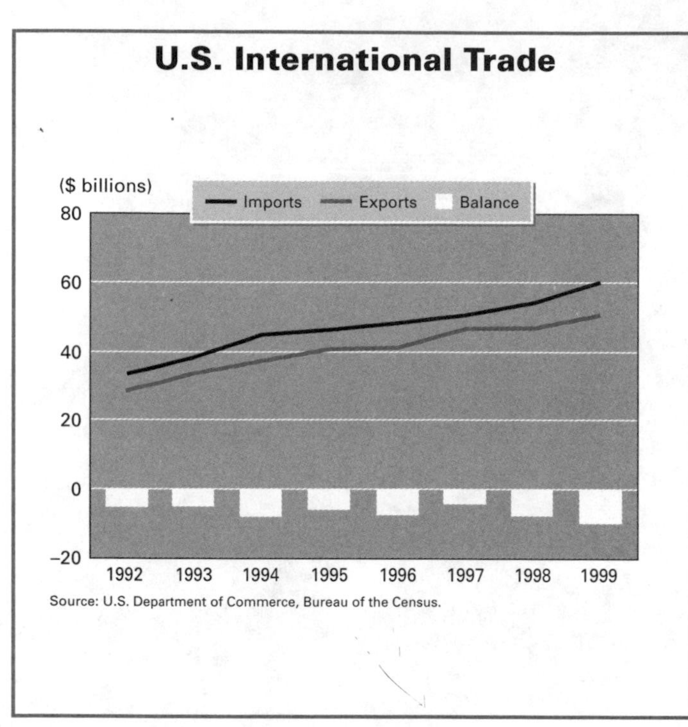

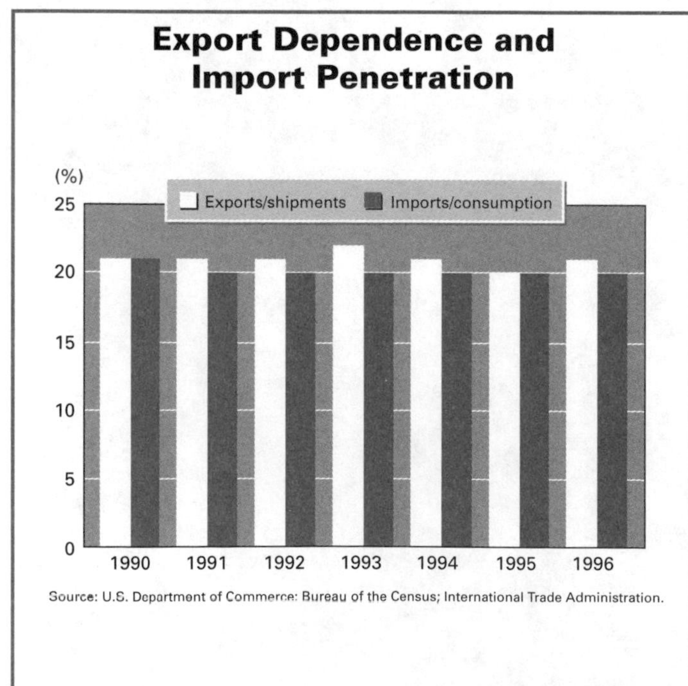

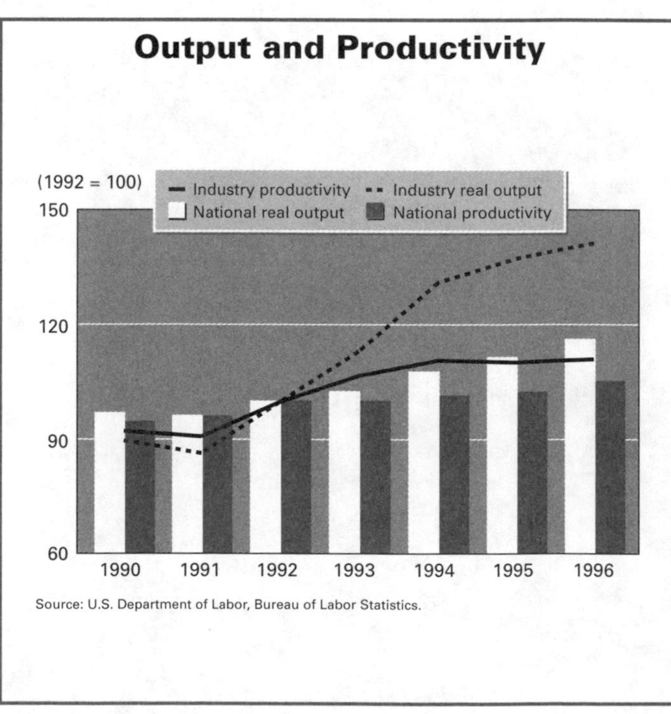

See "Getting the Most Out of *Outlook 2000*" for definitions of terms.

37

Automotive Parts

INDUSTRY DEFINITION The U.S. automotive parts industry includes manufacturers of automotive stampings; carburetors, pistons, piston rings, and valves; vehicular lighting; storage batteries; engine electrical equipment; and other motor vehicle parts (SIC 3465, 3592, 3647, 3691, 3694, and 3714, respectively).

Two different sets of trade data are used in this chapter: a narrow set based solely on the six automotive parts SIC codes and a broad set based on more detailed Harmonized System (HS) codes that include parts from the six SIC codes and other parts, such as tires and tubes and glass, which are included under other nonautomotive SIC codes. Another important difference between the two sets is that the narrow set is based on "imports for consumption" and the broad set is based on "general imports." Imports for consumption include products coming out of U.S. Foreign Trade Zones, some of which have undergone a transformation. General imports measure all imports into the country in the condition in which they arrived. The trade data in the chart titled "Export Dependence and Import Penetration" on the facing page are based on the narrow set. The broad data are used in the chart titled "U.S. International Trade" on the facing page, in Table 37-3, and in the text. The U.S. government uses the broad definition for trade policy purposes.

OVERVIEW

The automotive parts industry supplies two markets: the original equipment (OE) market for parts used directly in the manufacture of vehicles and the replacement (repair) and add-on accessories market, or aftermarket. The U.S. industry consists of approximately 5,000 firms, including about 500 affiliates of Japanese, European, and Canadian manufacturers. The industry is dominated by 100 large manufacturers that supply both the OE market and the aftermarket and account for the vast majority of sales. The industry and trade data cited in this chapter are not collected or reported in a way that allows a distinction to be made between the OE market and the aftermarket.

The OE automotive parts industry is divided into three tiers. Manufacturers of Tier One automotive parts supply finished parts and components to automakers for use in vehicle production, Tier Two suppliers produce subcomponents for Tier One manufacturers, and Tier Three manufacturers supply raw materials used in the production of components. Increasingly, Tier One manufacturers are producing complete major subassemblies and modular components that are installed into a vehicle as a unit.

FACTORS AFFECTING FUTURE INDUSTRY GROWTH

Global Industry Trends

The automotive parts industry naturally is affected by the state of the motor vehicle industry: Increased production of vehicles results in increased demand for automotive parts. U.S. vehicle sales reached a new all-time high, surpassing the record sales of 16 million cars and light trucks set in 1986. World automotive production has been driven by a strong U.S. economy with attendant high consumer confidence, low unemployment, low inflation, and low savings (a high ratio of personal spending to debt). Manufacturers, anticipating a flat 1999 market after an unprecedented 4 consecutive years of sales above 15 million units annually, were pleasantly surprised that U.S. sales in 1999 were around 16.9 million units, up 9 percent from 1998's 15.5 million units and significantly higher than 1986's record 16.1 million units. The demand for light trucks played a substantial part in those unprecedented sales. In 1986, the last all-time peak in total U.S. light vehicle sales, trucks accounted for 29.1 percent of the market. Their share has risen every year since and accounted for 48.4 percent of the total U.S. market in 1999. Not surprisingly, then, demand in the light truck accessories aftermarket has increased as consumers have decided to customize and personalize their trucks.

According to *Ward's Automotive Reports,* in response to record sales, DaimlerChrysler and Ford expanded capacity so that North American (including Mexican) annual capacity probably reached around 18.4 million units in 1999. The success of the U.S. automotive market and the impact of the Asian financial crisis also led to a significant increase in automotive imports to the United States and in the U.S. automotive trade deficit.

The world's major motor vehicle manufacturers continue to restructure their manufacturing operations in the important markets of North America, Europe, Asia, and Latin America, with each one striving to create its own "global car." Industry analysts report that in 1999, 1-million unit platforms were expected to account for 14 percent of total global production, and by 2004, it is expected that about 33 percent of the vehicles produced will come from such platforms. Leading automotive parts manufacturers are responding to this form of globalization by revamping their operations to manufacture products and supply their customers in markets worldwide. This trend has resulted in a sharper focus by parts manufacturers on core competencies as they become systems integrators and assume more of the research and development responsibilities that once were the province of motor vehicle manufacturers. These major trends are changing the face of the global automotive parts industry, which has been undergoing strategic mergers and making crucial acquisitions to pool resources and gain a competitive advantage as a global supplier. Increasing globalization of the industry offers automotive suppliers an opportunity to reduce the impact of regional downturns. Manufacturers that are unable to adapt to these trends are disappearing from the market.

According to industry studies, the value of mergers and acquisitions in the automotive aftermarket (SIC 3714 only) soared to a record $21.8 billion in 1998. The increase in the value of those acquisitions was the result of several large deals, including Johnson Control's acquisition of Becker, Dana Corporation's merger with Echlin, and FederalMogul's acquisitions of T & N, Fel-Pro, and Cooper Automotive (see Table 37-1). The average transaction value of acquisitions in the industry increased to more than $450 million from just over $100 million in 1995. This trend toward large acquisitions carried over into 1999 with Lear Corporation's acquisition of UT Automotive and TRW's acquisition of LucasVarity. Additional high-value deals are expected over the next 5 years.

Some industry experts predict that the merger and acquisition wave among automotive suppliers may recede in the near future because of low return on key profit indicators, heavy debt incursion by large acquisitions, and easy acquisition targets disappearing. To pare debts from acquisitions, some companies have turned to selling off parts of their purchases or more drastic measures. For example, Federal-Mogul reported that it will sell part of its Cooper Automotive acquisition; TRW is selling parts of its Lucas-Varity acquisition; and Breed Technologies has filed for Chapter 11 bankruptcy protection, blaming its purchase of AlliedSignal for much of its financial problems.

The independence of Delphi Automotive Systems was also a result in part of the trend toward a sharper focus on core competencies. Delphi, the number one global manufacturer of automotive parts, was officially spun off from General Motors in 1999. Delphi became the world's largest independent automotive supplier, with sales of $31.4 billion and $1.2 billion in pretax profits in 1997. Industry speculation regarding Ford's auto parts manufacturing division, Visteon, includes a possible spin-off similar to Delphi's.

As motor vehicle manufacturers increasingly seek to supply overseas markets with vehicles produced in those markets, Tier One suppliers follow their customers into those markets by establishing new production facilities or entering into joint ventures with local manufacturers. Global sales by the world's top 10 automotive parts manufacturers rose to $120 billion in 1998, up 5 percent from their level in 1997 (see Table 37-2). In 1999, the world's number one supplier, Delphi Automotive Systems, attempted to augment its overseas sales by purchasing several auto parts businesses from the Korean Daewoo Group and buying a stake in the Tokyo-based Akebono Brake Industry Co. Ltd., the number one supplier of wheel brakes to Japanese automakers.

Globalization, however, is not limited to the largest automotive parts firms: Smaller suppliers also are looking for partners in foreign markets to expand and maintain their current customer base. In some cases, to defend themselves in a time of consolidation, smaller companies have joined the acquisition drive, while some large conglomerates, such as UT Automotive, Cooper Industries, and Tenneco, have left the competitive automotive parts business. The impact of the Asian financial crisis on Asian auto parts suppliers opened opportunities for investment in those markets. In response, some Asian automakers tightened control over their auto parts suppliers to prevent foreign intrusion and acquisition.

In the past decade, motor vehicle manufacturers began requiring their Tier One parts manufacturers to become systems integrators: suppliers of modular or preassembled units that can be installed in a vehicle as a single system such as an entire fuel supply system. In Brazil, Volkswagen (VW), Daimler-Benz, General Motors (GM), and Ford are experimenting with new vehicle assembly facilities that locate some suppliers within a vehicle assembly plant. In late 1996, VW pioneered this practice with the production of a commercial truck: Eight of VW's Tier One suppliers provide modular components and essentially assemble the vehicle. This practice probably will become more prevalent as motor vehicle manufacturers begin a worldwide consolidation of platforms that will be common to several vehicle models.

While these new production processes have enabled vehicle manufacturers to save time and money in product development, they have forced multinational automotive parts manufacturers to

TABLE 37-1: Selected Mergers and Acquisitions in the Automotive Parts Industry, 1998 and 1999

Date	Merger or Acquisition	Value
January 1998	Dana acquired Eaton Corp.'s Axle and Brake	$287 million
February 1998	Magna International acquired majority of Steyr-Daimler-Puch	$275 million
February 1998	Lear acquired Delphi Seating	$250 million
March 1998	Federal-Mogul acquired T&N PLC	$2.4 billion
March 1998	Federal-Mogul acquired Fel-Pro Inc.	$720 million
April 1998	Dura Automotive Systems Inc. acquired Trident Automotive	$87.5 million
June 1998	Dana Corp. merged with Echlin Corp	$4.2 billion
July 1998	Johnson Controls Inc. acquired Becker Group	$548 million
July 1998	Valeo SA of France acquired ITT Electrical Systems	$1.7 billion
August 1998	Continental AG of Germany acquired ITT Brake and Chassis	$1.9 billion
August 1998	Federal-Mogul acquired Cooper Automotive	$1.9 billion
May 1999	Lear acquired UT Automotive	$2.3 billion
May 1999	TRW acquired LucasVarity	$6.5 billion
May 1999	Delphi became independent of GM	
August 1999	Delphi was to acquire several auto parts businesses from Daewoo Group	$396 million
November 1999	Delphi purchases Lucas Diesel Systems from TRW, Inc.	$871 million
	Potential Deals	
	Tenneco plans to sell its automotive parts unit for $4 billion	
	TRW plans to sell four auto businesses	
	Dana plans to sell three subsidiaries	

Source: Compiled by the U.S. Department of Commerce from news reports.

revamp their operations to focus on core competencies. In preparation for the production of global vehicles, leading Tier One suppliers are shedding diverse divisions or snapping up firms with complementary product lines. For example, megasuppliers in the seating and interiors sector emerged when the U.S. seat maker Johnson Controls Inc. acquired the French seat supplier Roth Freres SA and the Canadian giant Magna International purchased the seat manufacturer Douglas and Lomason Co. The braking system giant Lucas-Varity plc was established through a $4.8 billion merger between the U.S.-based Varity Corp. and Lucas Automotive of the United Kingdom. In 1999 Lucas-Varity was purchased by TRW Inc. for $6.5 billion; this was the largest supplier acquisition in history. After its purchase, TRW reorganized into two main business units: TRW Automotive, which included LucasVarity automotive, and TRW Aerospace and Information Systems, which included Lucas Aerospace. TRW also reported that it would sell four units—LucasDiesel Systems Unit, TRW Engine Components, TRW Nelson Stud Welding, and LucasVarity Wiring—to pare debt from its purchase. The world's largest supplier of safety systems was formed when the merger between Sweden's Autoliv AB and Morton International Inc.'s Automotive Safety Products operations led to the establishment of Autoliv Inc. Another company, Tenneco Inc., announced plans to split its automotive and packaging businesses into two independent companies, allowing each of the two to focus on core competencies.

TABLE 37-2: Sales of Top 10 Global Automotive Parts Suppliers in 1998
(millions of dollars)

Rank	Company	Sales
1	Delphi Automotive Systems	26,421
2	Robert Bosch GmbH	18,200
3	Visteon Automotive Systems	17,800
4	Denso Corp.	11,805
5	Lear Corp.	9,100
6	Johnson Controls Inc.	8,600
7	TRW Inc.	7,200
8	Dana Corp.	7,105
9	Aisin Seiki Co. Ltd.	7,076
10	Valeo SA	6,696
	Total	120,003

Source: *CRA/Automotive News,* June 21, 1999, copyright Crain Communications, Inc. All rights reserved.

Today the supplier's role does not end at parts production but has expanded into areas once controlled solely by motor vehicle manufacturers. For example, Ford announced in fall 1998 that it was essentially turning its transmission plant in Batavia, OH, over to ZF, the German transmission company. Automakers are focusing on their primary concern—assembling cars—and leaving the production of components to suppliers that will commit resources and capital to their core competencies. In addition to producing parts for vehicle manufacturers, Tier One suppliers increasingly have been required to take on engineering, managerial, and financial responsibilities. Vehicle manufacturers increasingly are relying on their suppliers for design, research and development expertise, and new product ideas. This trend has resulted in significantly shorter product development cycles for supplier-engineered parts. Some automaker engineers are worried about losing quality control over components and technological capabilities or sharing among outside suppliers, and unions are concerned that such moves will affect job numbers and security. As vehicle manufacturers cull the pool of suppliers with which they deal directly, the surviving Tier One megasuppliers have formed their own strategic partnerships with lower-tier suppliers, managing the sourcing of parts from Tier Two and Tier Three suppliers. Finally, Tier One suppliers now are required to finance those engineering and managerial duties while complying with vehicle manufacturers' requirements for lower-priced parts.

As the evolution of the automotive parts industry into a community of world suppliers continues into the twenty-first century, the ability of Tier One suppliers to adapt to these major trends will determine their fate. The reduced ranks of Tier One suppliers will shrink further. Many will go out of business, be acquired, or channel their resources into other business ventures. The survivors will be divided into three categories: very large, diversified multinational Tier One parts manufacturers with major financial resources; smaller, specialty Tier One firms with partners in strategic global markets; and lower-tier suppliers.

Domestic Trends

In the 1990s, the U.S. automotive parts industry restructured itself in an effort to maintain its competitive position relative to its main rival, Japan. The ability to maintain its standing as a worldwide leader as it enters the twenty-first century will depend not only on its ability to comply with the specific requirements of its current customers—an increased foreign presence, finely honed core competencies, and the assumption of traditional functions normally handled by vehicle manufacturers—but also on its ability to deal successfully with larger domestic and international factors.

Electronic Commerce. The automotive parts industry is not immune to the increasing role of E-commerce in the market. According to industry analysts, an annual transaction level of $9.8 billion was expected in 1999. This figure includes sales over the Automotive Network Exchange (ANX). Auto parts suppliers are offering consumers aftermarket replacement and accessory parts directly through the Internet. The Internet represents novel methods for growth in the global marketing and distribution of products. It has the potential to reach an international audience of consumers that suppliers might never reach through traditional methods. The automotive industry is a leader in just-in-time delivery. E-commerce has increased just-in-time performance by allowing better and faster communications between automakers and consumers and between automakers and suppliers.

A private network, ANX, linking suppliers and automakers, was launched in 1998. ANX is administered by the original equipment coalition, the Automotive Industry Action Group, and is becoming an industry standard as E-commerce takes on an increasingly significant role in automotive parts sales. In early 1999, General Motors, Ford, and DaimlerChrysler encouraged suppliers to join ANX. By late 1999, GM and Ford announced they would be introducing their own supplier sites. ANX is designed to improve communications between assemblers and suppliers, speed order-to-delivery time, and reduce inventories. Many smaller suppliers cannot afford to join the network, potentially leaving them out of the loop.

After an initial attempt to establish an E-commerce supplier network in 1997, Ford Motor Company retooled its on-line network in mid-1999. Ford is hoping to inspire suppliers to use E-commerce for nearly all purchasing communications. Ford already has 1,600 suppliers and about 16,000 individuals who have subscribed to its user group and expects the number of users to increase to 100,000 or even 200,000. GM also plans to expedite car manufacturing and reduce costs through E-commerce. In August 1999, GM formed a new Internet business unit, e-GM. The new unit could link consumers, dealers, suppliers, and factories in such a way that the automaker could deliver customized cars in less than 10 days. GM speculated that the unit, which requires little capital investment, could bring in about $5 billion in revenue over the next 5 years.

In November 1999, General Motors Corporation and Ford Motor Company announced they would launch new business-to-business e-commerce portals for their respective suppliers in 2000. GM plans to move much of its $87 billion component and materials purchases and more than 30,000 suppliers to its portal, TradeXchange. Likewise, Ford plans to conduct much of its $80 billion purchases from more than 30,000 suppliers over its portal, AutoXchange. Because of the significance of the automakers in the U.S. economy and the scale of the operations, the announcements of the new portals mark a coming of age of e-commerce.

GM teamed up with Commerce One to create TradeXchange. GM executives estimate that the site could be handling sales of as much as $500 billion within a few years, and they expect GM to do 100 percent of its purchasing around the world through TradeXchange by 2001. GM's aggressive push to develop its new Internet site for suppliers is expected to do $50 billion in business through the portal by the end of 2000. GM has been encouraging other auto makers with which it has close relations, including Isuzu Motor Co., Suzuki Motor Co., Fuji Heavy Industries, and Honda Motor Co., to join the network and increase trading volume on the system. GM has also invited Toyota to join TradeXchange.

Ford joined with Oracle to create a joint venture to develop AutoXchange. The new portal is expected to result in significant savings on procurement and inventory and a shortening of the product cycles. Ford estimates that the savings as a result of the new site could be about 20 percent. Ford and Oracle hope that other automakers will join in AutoXchange and have suggested that AutoXchange may go public. The site is expected to collect fees of $1 billion in the first 18 months and $5 billion within 5 years.

Visteon Automotive Systems has started selling aftermarket electronics equipment directly to on-line consumers and is buying parts from suppliers on-line. Visteon planned to expand its on-line sales of aftermarket video systems, navigation devices, and CD changers in 1999 and may expand to sell parts made by other companies. One of the goals of the new Internet plan is to double Visteon's aftermarket sales by 2002. The electronic commerce plan, eVisteon, is also being developed to handle on-line auctions of supply contracts. In a trial attempt, 17 suppliers, 6 of which had no previous business with Visteon and many of which were new to the automotive industry, bid on $150 million in supply contracts for printed circuit boards.

Despite the potential benefits of on-line services, smaller suppliers (those with less than $25 million in annual sales) are expressing a reluctance to enter E-commerce because of the costs of joining networks and concerns about investing in technology that may become obsolete as the process develops and automakers move on to the next innovative industry application of information technology. To attract smaller suppliers, networks, including ANX, are designing lower-cost options. Many suppliers cannot or do not want to commit limited time and manpower for such initiatives but instead plan to take a wait-and-see attitude toward such new business techniques.

E-commerce can assist suppliers by improving communications with their customers, whether those customers are automakers, repair shops, or do-it-yourselfers. It reduces the paperwork needed for requisitions, helps suppliers control inventories better by offering more precise production forecasts, and provides electronic payment options. It is fast becoming a critical factor that will determine the eventual success or failure of the firms competing in this industry.

Competitive Pricing. A chief domestic factor affecting the growth of the U.S. parts industry has been U.S. motor vehicle manufacturers' continued demand for improved quality and lower costs. This issue continues to be a long-term concern for U.S. suppliers. In the mid-1980s, the Big Three motor vehicle manufacturers, faced with competition in their own market from state-of-the-art Japanese vehicle manufacturers, were forced to revamp their operations to remain competitive and demanded lower-price, higher-quality parts from their suppliers. As a result, supplying high-quality, continuously improved parts with falling price tags has become an industry norm. Since 1993, productivity has increased slightly more than 2 percent annually and product quality has improved measurably. Despite the parts industry's past successes, vehicle assemblers continue to demand significant cost cuts from their suppliers. Ford sought cost cuts averaging 5 percent annually through 1999, and DaimlerChrysler required its Tier One suppliers to propose money-saving ideas equal to 5 percent of their sales to that company. In 1999, Visteon sought to cut costs by $400 million because it had had to cut prices more than 10 percent in each of the previous 2 years. To accomplish its goal, Visteon requested its suppliers to reduce prices 10 percent in addition to other price reductions already agreed on. Although bigger and more efficient suppliers with low unit costs, such as TRW and Dana, have been able to increase their profit margins despite lower prices, many smaller suppliers have encountered diminishing returns as each additional improvement has become more costly and technologically more difficult to achieve, resulting in lower growth in profits.

Consolidation. The consolidation and strategic partnerships that improved the competitive stance of many U.S. suppliers during the industry's restructuring promise to play a key role in the future growth of the industry. As a result of restructuring, each of the U.S. domestic motor vehicle manufacturers reduced its pool of Tier One suppliers, preferring to source entire systems from a single supplier. To meet those demands, suppliers consolidated their operations, becoming systems integrators by forming strategic partnerships with other firms or by shedding unwanted product lines.

The independent supplier community has continued to undergo mergers, acquisitions, and bankruptcies. Between 1993 and 1996, the industry giant Dana completed 24 purchases or joint ventures. In May 1999, Lear Corp. acquired United Technologies Automotive and TRW Inc. acquired LucasVarity. In 1998, Dana announced its acquisition of Echlin and Johnson Controls acquired Becker Group, while Delco Electronics Corp. was absorbed by Delphi Automotive Systems. Even U.S. domestic assemblers' in-house parts operations underwent change: GM ended its ownership of Delphi in May 1999, creating the largest independent parts supplier. Delphi spent 1998 in preparations for its spin-off from GM by selling 14 different business units worth about $6 billion a year in revenues while making 38 acquisitions, a pace Delphi intends to continue. Industry speculation continues over what Ford will do with Visteon, now the number three global supplier after having been overtaken by Robert Bosch GmbH. A spin-off similar to that involving Delphi has not been ruled out. The actions of the U.S. domestic make vehicle assemblers regarding their parts divisions will sharpen competition in an already highly competitive supplier community. Delphi and Visteon will have to compete with independent suppliers for contracts with their respective former parent companies and hope to increase component sales to other customers.

Technology. Future growth for U.S. automotive parts firms will continue to be technology-driven as a result of increasingly stringent safety, fuel efficiency, and environmental regulations as well as increasing demand for enhanced passenger comfort systems. The Clean Air Act of 1990 has been the major catalyst for this change, prompting U.S. suppliers to develop new technologies to produce lightweight body materials and weight-saving mechanical components. In recent years, U.S. suppliers have developed composite materials—a mix of plastics with glass and carbon fibers or another substrate—to substitute for metal in vehicles, while new heat-resistant technologies have enabled the automotive industry to use more plastic in engine blocks, significantly lowering an engine's weight.

In-car electronics, which have risen to 15 percent of total content from nominal levels in the 1950s, are expected to rise to 20 percent by 2010. Electronic systems will continue to control more functions in vehicles, which thus will require more computer-based technology. As a result, computer software and hardware companies will be more involved in vehicle production, becoming major suppliers to the industry. A difficulty is that the computer technology development cycle is measured in months, while vehicle development and production take years. It takes 2 years to develop a new car or truck; the vehicle is in production for about 5 years and is designed to last 10 years. Suppliers have to develop technology that reconciles computer technology development time with the time needed for automotive development and usage.

The development of new technology is also a key factor in the Clinton administration's Partnership for a New Generation of Vehicles (PNGV). The long-term goal of PNGV is to develop technologies for a new generation of affordable midsize passenger cars that will get 80 miles per gallon. Currently, more than 300 U.S. suppliers are involved in this historic industry-government partnership, which includes the development of new power plant, drive train, and chassis technologies. With safety, noise absorption, exhaust-cleaning, and passenger ergonomic systems adding about 440 pounds of indispensable weight to a vehicle, continued improvement of the technology in those areas will become an even more critical factor in vehicle weight reduction as traditional options dwindle. Steelmakers have been developing the ultralight steel auto body, or body-in-white, which weighs about 25 percent less than traditional bodies and costs less to make than do bodies made from traditional materials and composites. They hope that this development will allow them to become more involved in the PNGV program.

Several automakers revealed vehicles utilizing fuel-cell technology in 1999 and announced release dates within the next decade. In 2004, California's zero-emission vehicle law will take effect, calling for 10 percent of an automaker's vehicles sold in that state to be zero-emission vehicles. Automakers hope that fuel-cell-powered vehicles will satisfy this new requirement and increasing worldwide environmental demands, but many technological and cost hurdles must be overcome before they are feasible alternatives to combustion engine vehicles. Industry analysts predict that automotive fuel-cell use will advance rapidly after 2005 and that fuel-cell annual volumes will hit the million-unit level by around 2010. This new technology will open several opportunities for suppliers. Since fuel cells add a lot of weight, there will be increased demand for lightweight materials. Fuel-cell technology will replace or eliminate many internal combustion components.

Because the development of fuel-cell vehicles is still not cost-effective, the technology is in its infancy, and the infrastructure is not in place, many vehicle manufacturers have been developing alternative fuel vehicles and hybrid vehicles, which combine a gasoline combustion engine with an electric-battery motor. For example, GM offered the first all-electric vehicle, the EV-1, in 1997. As for hybrid vehicles, Honda announced that it would release the Insight to U.S., European, and Japanese markets in fall 1999. Toyota's mass-produced hybrid vehicle Prius, of which Toyota has already sold 28,000 units in Japan, will be sold in America beginning in June 2000. Ford, GM, and DaimlerChrysler expect to deliver hybrid vehicles to the U.S. government as part of contracts approved before the creation of PNGV. U.S. domestic make assemblers are trailing Japanese makers in bringing hybrid vehicles to the U.S. market. GM hopes to have one ready by 2001, and Ford is shooting for 2003.

Production Issues. The domestic make vehicle assemblers' contracts with the United Auto Workers (UAW) Union expired on September 14, 1999. In addition to traditional demands concerning wages and safety, the UAW was concerned about job security and union membership. The tendency of vehicle assemblers to outsource component work and the spin-off of internal parts units concern the union. Workers' protests against the outsourcing of work formerly done in-house resulted in a strike in March 1996 at GM's Delphi brake plants in Dayton, OH. UAW leaders opposed the separation of Delphi from GM and oppose separating Visteon from Ford because of concerns about workers' job security. This situation has caused difficulties in the negotiations between UAW and automakers. GM spun off Delphi early in 1999, but Ford still retains ownership of Visteon. The UAW and GM and Delphi reached an agreement late September 1999. As part of the agreement, Delphi will give union members the same wages and benefits received by GM employees covered by the GM agreement, and if there are layoffs at Delphi, employees will be eligible to return to GM as jobs become available. In the case of Ford, the situation was more difficult because of Ford's plans for Visteon.

One of the points of contention between the UAW and automotive assemblers is the development of a modular assembly, where preassembled modules are constructed at suppliers' facilities and combined into a vehicle by automakers. This process allows automakers to cut costs and increase profits. The UAW is concerned that this is an attempt to outsource work and cut union jobs. Vehicle assemblers setting up shop in Brazil are experimenting with modular assembly and are having suppliers locate near, if not inside, the automotive plant.

Foreign Competition. Foreign competition in the U.S. market will continue to challenge American automotive parts producers as they attempt to comply with the worldwide sourcing strategies of vehicle manufacturers. Foreign, mainly Japanese, competition in the U.S. market was a major catalyst for the industry's restructuring, and U.S. suppliers increasingly have been challenged by imports and U.S.-based foreign-affiliated automotive parts manufacturers. Since 1992, U.S. imports of automotive parts have grown an average of 8.7 percent annually, resulting in import penetration levels just above 19 percent. Parts imports from Japan, which have increased to supply the growing number of U.S.-produced Japanese vehicles, have accounted for the largest percentage of the U.S. deficit in automotive parts trade since the mid-1980s. In response, the United States and Japan negotiated a U.S.–Japan Framework Agreement in 1995, which is set to expire in December 2000. As a result of the agreement, imports from Japan fell 19 percent and U.S. exports to Japan rose 26 percent between 1995 and 1998, resulting in a 25 percent decrease in the parts deficit with Japan for that period. However, annualized data for 1999 reveal that these trends appear to be reversing as a result of a good U.S. economy and the Japanese financial crisis. U.S. automotive parts imports from Japan were up 7.0 percent and U.S. exports to Japan were down 18.8 percent, resulting in a 11.6 percent increase in the deficit for the January–October 1999 period compared with the same period in 1998 (see Figure 37-1).

The share of U.S. production held by foreign-affiliated, U.S.-based parts producers continues to increase. Leading Japanese suppliers, facing demands for drastic price cuts from Japanese vehicle manufacturers intent on lowering production costs, are breaking away from their *keiretsu* relations with vehicle companies and turning to foreign vehicle manufacturers, including the traditional U.S. domestic make vehicle assemblers, for business. While the vast majority of foreign investment in U.S. parts producers is Japanese, European firms also have increased their investments as they have followed BMW and Mercedes-Benz into the U.S. market. High domestic manufacturing and labor costs forced many German automotive parts manufacturers to

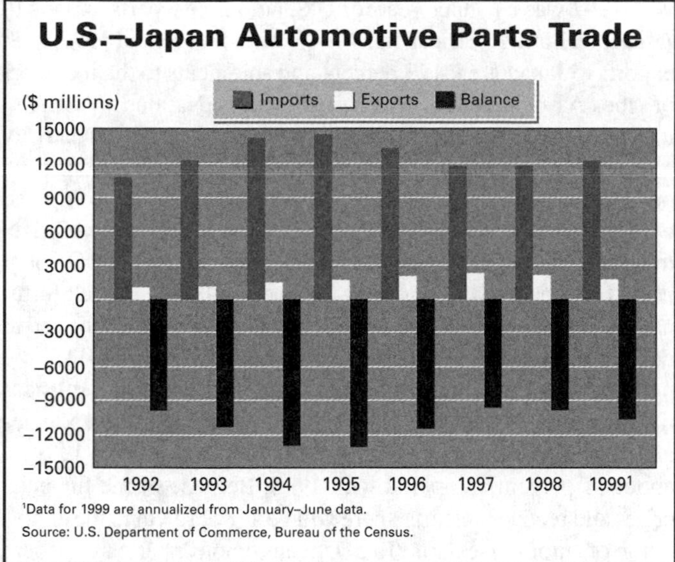

FIGURE 37-1

invest in plants outside Germany. However, east European markets, including Poland and the Czech Republic, are proving to be dicey as manufacturing costs there have increased considerably, driving German manufacturers out of eastern Europe and toward the United States. The trend among German manufacturers is toward expansion, cooperation, or a buyout in the United States rather than investing in new facilities.

Finally, intense foreign competition will pose challenges to U.S. automotive parts manufacturers that are attempting to capitalize on growth opportunities in key emerging markets. The Japanese automotive industry is firmly entrenched in Asian markets, while the European industry is eyeing key east European countries. The U.S. industry can expect to see the Japanese and Europeans work hard to win more of the Mexican market, while recent Japanese and European plans for investment in the Brazilian automotive industry should heat up competition in Latin America.

PROJECTIONS OF INDUSTRY TRADE GROWTH FOR THE NEXT 1 AND 5 YEARS

The U.S. automotive parts industry historically has played a vital role in the U.S. economy. In 1996, industry shipments accounted for almost 4.1 percent of total U.S. manufacturing shipments and the 691,000 jobs provided by the industry accounted for 3.7 percent of total manufacturing employment. Among the top 50 global automotive parts suppliers, 22 are headquartered in the United States. Those 22 U.S. companies accounted for 39 percent of the top 50 companies' worldwide sales in 1998. In addition, this industry is one of the largest U.S. export industries, accounting for 6.9 percent of total U.S. merchandise exports in 1998 and 7.5 percent of total U.S. merchandise exports in the January–June 1999 period.

In 1998, industry shipments totaled an estimated record $188 billion in current dollars, an 8.7 percent increase over 1997 (see Table 37-3). North American sales by the top 50 U.S. automotive parts suppliers totaled $116 billion, down 1 percent from 1997 (see Table 37-4). Although sales by the top 50 may have dipped slightly in 1998 industry shipments increased to an estimated $204 billion in 1999 and are expected to grow to $214 billion in the year 2000 (see Table 37-3). Dramatic growth in U.S. vehicle sales in 1999 resulted in growth in production. U.S. light vehicle production in 1999 exceeded 12.6 million units for the first time, up 9 percent over the 1998 level of 11.6 million units. Despite the inevitable eventual slowing of the U.S. econ-

TABLE 37-3: Automotive Parts and Accessories (SIC 3465, 3592, 3647, 3691, 3694, 3714) Trends and Forecasts
(millions of dollars except as noted)

										Percent Change			
	1992	1993	1994	1995	1996	1997[1]	1998[1]	1999[2]	2000[3]	97–98	98–99	99–00	96–00[4]
Industry data													
Value of shipments[5]	105,841	119,678	138,982	147,773	152,134	173,100	188,100	203,800	214,200	8.7	8.3	5.1	8.9
Value of shipments (1992$)	105,841	119,264	137,842	145,124	148,775	170,800	185,600	200,700	210,900	8.7	8.1	5.1	9.1
Total employment (thousands)	609	633	679	706	691								
Production workers (thousands)	482	506	548	566	558								
Average hourly earnings ($)	15.84	16.22	16.57	17.05	17.05								
Capital expenditures	4,585	5,308	6,010	7,824	7,572								
Product data													
Value of shipments[5]	104,109	118,293	134,462	143,859	148,201	167,600	181,700	196,600	206,400	8.4	8.2	5.0	8.6
Value of shipments (1992$)	104,109	117,882	133,371	141,294	144,954	163,200	176,300	190,000	199,100	8.0	7.8	4.8	8.3
Trade data													
Value of imports	20,407	22,657	26,465	27,948	29,892	32,044	34,486	37,700	39,500	7.6	9.3	4.8	7.2
Value of exports	22,262	25,889	27,725	29,471	30,411	35,214	35,363	36,700	38,700	0.4	3.8	5.4	6.2

[1] Estimate except imports and exports.
[2] Estimate.
[3] Forecast.
[4] Compound annual rate.
[5] For a definition of industry versus product values, see "Getting the Most Out of *Outlook 2000.*"
Source: U.S. Department of Commerce: Bureau of the Census; International Trade Administration.

TABLE 37-4: North American Original Equipment Sales of Top 50 Suppliers in 1998
(millions of dollars)

Rank	Company	Sales
1	Delphi Automotive Systems	20,635
2	Visteon Automotive Systems	14,489
3	Johnson Controls, Inc.	5,590
4	Dana Corp.	5,542
5	Lear Corp.	5,369
6	Magna International Inc.	3,780
7	TRW Inc.	3,528
8	Robert Bosch Corp.	3,458
9	Denso International America Inc.	3,000
10	Eaton Corp	2,380
11	Cummins Engine Co.	2,344
12	Yazaki North America Inc.	2,216
13	Meritor Automotive Inc.	2,149
14	American Axle and Manufacturing Inc.	2,002
15	UT Automotive Inc.	1,939
16	Budd Co.	1,920
17	Textron Automotive Co.	1,827
18	Tower Automotive Inc.	1,752
19	LucasVarity Automotive	1,739
20	New Venture Gear Inc.	1,485
21–50	Other	28,733

Source: Extracted from *CRA/Automotive News '99 Market Data Book,* May 1999, copyright Crain Communications, Inc. All rights reserved.

omy, vehicle production capacity continues to increase and is expected to be about 13.5 million units in 2000, according to *Ward's Automotive Reports.* This production increase resulted in increased OE market and aftermarket demand, especially in the growing light truck share of the market. A 2 to 3 percent annual growth rate in sales of aftermarket parts should sustain the domestic supplier industry over the next few years.

During the industry's restructuring in the late 1980s and early 1990s, foreign trade became an important issue for U.S. automotive parts suppliers. Not only was the influx of imports a catalyst in the industry's restructuring, exports accounted for about 20 percent of total product shipments in 1998 (see Table 37-3). Even with continued growth in exports, the United States has posted a deficit in automotive parts since the early 1980s. While attempts have been made to reduce the deficit, the Asian and South American financial crises in 1998 and 1999 resulted in a substantial increase in the automotive parts trade deficit. The $7.5 billion deficit in 1998 was up 85 percent from the 1997 figure of $4.1 billion. A 56.2 percent increase over the 1998 deficit rate was predicted for 1999. Based on January–October data, much of this deficit was a result of dramatically increased imports, up nearly 13 percent from 1998, and a smaller increase in exports, up only 7 percent from 1998.

In 1998, U.S. exports of automotive parts totaled nearly $47 billion, an increase of only 0.4 percent from 1997 (see Table 37-5). The majority of those exports were shipped to traditional U.S. automotive markets, with over 74 percent going to the North American Free Trade Agreement (NAFTA) partners Canada and Mexico. The European Union (EU) accounted for 9.5 percent, and Japan for under 5 percent. The U.S. automotive parts industry continued to penetrate key Asian and Latin American markets. The year 1997 was a banner year for U.S. automotive parts exports to Asian and Latin American markets. Between 1992 and 1997, U.S. exports to Japan grew 123 percent and shipments to the members of the Association of Southeast Asian Nations (ASEAN) increased 145 percent. The Asian financial crisis negatively affected U.S. exports to that region in 1998, which declined 7.5 percent to Japan and 42 percent to ASEAN countries compared with 1997. This decline was showing signs of reversal in ASEAN trade for 1999, which was up 18 percent in the January–October period compared with January–October 1998 exports. Unfortunately, this was not the case for sales to Japan, which continued to decline, down 14 percent compared with the January–October period in 1998. U.S. exports to Brazil also experienced a substantial increase after 1992, up 536 percent by 1998. Brazilian policies and a financial crisis there threatened to reduce exports in 1999 by about 51 percent compared with 1998. Because of the financial crises and recovery efforts, there will be slow growth in the exportation of automotive parts. Total U.S. automotive parts exports are expected to reach $50 billion in 1999 and $53 billion in 2000. By 2004, exports should be near $59 billion. Much of this growth will occur because of accelerating European light vehicle production and sustained growth in vehicle output in rapidly developing countries such as Mexico, China, and Brazil. Demand for aftermarket parts should rise because of the increasing popularity of light vehicles in the rapidly growing markets in Asia and Latin America.

U.S. imports of automotive parts totaled $54.4 billion in 1998, up 7.2 percent from 1997 (see Table 37-5). The NAFTA countries were the source of the majority (53.7 percent) of those imports, with Mexico experiencing a 133 percent increase in exports to the United States after 1992. Shipments from Japan accounted for almost 22 percent of U.S. automotive parts imports. Other foreign suppliers have had increased penetration of the U.S. market since 1992, with imports from ASEAN countries and Brazil up 82 percent and 121 percent, respectively. U.S. imports of automotive parts should continue to grow slowly, reaching an estimated $61 billion in 1999 and $63 billion in the year 2000. In 2004, imports are expected to reach $74 billion.

GLOBAL MARKET PROSPECTS

The emerging markets in Asia and Latin America were depressed by financial crises, while Japan faced its own financial crisis. Forecasts of flat vehicle sales in western Europe, like those in the United States, failed to materialize in 1998. Instead, vehicle sales in western Europe increased 6.8 percent and those in eastern Europe stayed on course despite financial and political problems in Russia. Despite some reluctance to invest in uncertain markets, U.S. automotive parts suppliers continue to explore and invest in opportunities in other parts of the world, especially in key Latin American and Asian countries. Financial problems have driven many Asian companies to foreign companies for assistance, creating opportunities for joint ventures, mergers, and acquisitions. Some Asian vehicle manufacturers and governments concerned

TABLE 37-5: U.S. Trade Patterns in Automotive Parts and Accessories
(millions of dollars)

Region	Exports[1] 1998	1997	Share of 1998 Total, %	Region	Imports[2] 1998	1997	Share of 1998 Total, %
World	46,807	46,643	100	**World**	54,354	50,720	100
Asia and the Pacific				**Asia and the Pacific**			
Select ASEAN[3]	360	623	0.77	Select ASEAN[3]	1,260	1,251	2.32
Total Chinese Economic Area	535	882	1.14	Total Chinese Economic Area	2,023	1,691	3.72
Select Other Asia and the Pacific				Select Other Asia and the Pacific			
Australia	590	652	1.26	Australia	179	149	0.33
India	42	44	0.09	India	162	134	0.30
Japan	2,139	2,312	4.57	Japan	11,876	11,830	21.85
South Korea	364	661	0.78	South Korea	762	657	1.40
Europe				**Europe**			
Total European Union[4]	4,434	4,121	9.47	Total European Union[4]	6,737	5,877	12.39
Select eastern Europe				Select eastern Europe			
Hungary	53	54	0.11	Hungary	120	111	0.22
Poland	20	12	0.04	Poland	19	14	0.03
Russia	28	66	0.06	Russia	4	6	0.01
Western Hemisphere				**Western Hemisphere**			
Total Andean Community[5]	778	970	1.66	Total Andean Community[5]	194	168	0.36
Total MERCOSUR[6]	1,472	1,059	3.14	Total MERCOSUR[6]	1,338	1,283	2.46
Total Central America[7]	191	173	0.41	Total Central America[7]	28	25	0.05
Total NAFTA	34,799	33,969	74.35	Total NAFTA	29,192	27,139	53.71
All others	969	998	2.07	All others	422	355	0.78
Top Five Countries				Top Five Countries			
Canada	25,298	24,387	54.05	Canada	14,712	13,825	27.07
Mexico	9,502	9,582	20.30	Mexico	14,480	13,314	26.64
Japan	2,139	2,312	4.57	Japan	11,876	11,830	21.85
Austria	1,086	757	2.32	Germany	3,109	2,616	5.72
Germany	1,019	1,006	2.18	Brazil	1,240	1,223	2.28

[1] Total exports, f.a.s.
[2] General imports, customs value.
[3] The selected ASEAN countries include Brunei, Indonesia, Malaysia, Philippines, Singapore, Thailand, and Vietnam.
[4] The European Union includes Austria, Belgium, Denmark, Finland, France, Germany, Greece, Ireland, Italy, Luxembourg, the Netherlands, Portugal, Spain, Sweden, and the United Kingdom.
[5] The Andean Community includes Bolivia, Colombia, Ecuador, Peru, and Venezuela.
[6] The MERCOSUR countries are Argentina, Brazil, Paraguay, and Uruguay.
[7] Central America includes Costa Rica, El Salvador, Guatemala, Honduras, and Panama.
Source: U.S. Department of Commerce, Bureau of the Census.

about foreign acquisitions tightened control over key parts makers. Although short-term growth has been affected severely, most analysts agree that Asia will continue to be one of the world's fastest-growing markets over the next decade. Already there are indications of a turnaround in several Asian countries, and U.S. automotive parts exports to ASEAN countries, China, and South Korea rose in 1999.

U.S. suppliers' export efforts have been supplemented by recent trade agreements and other U.S. government initiatives. NAFTA, the Uruguay Round of the General Agreement on Tariffs and Trade, and the U.S.–Japan Automotive Framework Agreement were negotiated in the early and middle 1990s to facilitate trade and investment with and access to these major and emerging markets. New initiatives, including the Global Automotive Standards Agreement under the auspices of the Transatlantic Business Dialogue and the Asia-Pacific Economic Cooperation (APEC) Early Voluntary Sector Liberalization discussions in the automotive sector, may offer further opportunities for increased trade and investment.

Asia

Many Asian markets have favorable long-term potential, especially the nine members of ASEAN (Brunei or Oarussalam, Indonesia, Malaysia, Philippines, Singapore, Thailand, Laos, Cambodia, Myanmar, and Vietnam), China, and South Korea. Despite the Asian financial crisis, which negatively affected short-term prospects for that region's automotive markets, the ASEAN region remains the most promising for U.S. automotive parts firms over the next decade. In the early 1990s, the Big Three vehicle manufacturers began assembling in that region, as did several leading U.S. suppliers, including Dana Corp., Lear Corp., and Delphi. Between 1992 and 1997, exports of U.S. automotive parts to ASEAN members more than doubled. However, in 1998, exports were reduced nearly to 1993 rates. Early data for January–October 1999 reveal an increase of 18 percent compared with the previous year, indicating a potential recovery.

U.S. automotive parts manufacturers' investment in and exports to the region are expected to expand as those companies try to take advantage of the potential of the ASEAN members to become the hub of Asian automotive manufacturing. This speculation is based on industry forecasts that Thai and Indonesian vehicle production capacity will reach 1 million and 600,000 units, respectively, by the year 2000. Those forecasts have been pushed out to between 2002 and 2004 for Thailand and even later for Indonesia. Thailand, referred to as "Motown East" because of its large and mature automotive industry, peaked at 589,126 units in 1996. After that year, most vehicle and parts manufacturers slashed production in Thailand. The ASEAN region will continue to be the Asian base for manufacturers that plan to export components and finished vehicles in significant quantities to the rest of Asia and other markets. Long-term opportunities, however, will not be realized easily, largely because ASEAN markets are proving difficult to penetrate as a result of Japan's virtual monopoly in the automotive sector, prohibitively high tariffs, stringent investment restrictions, and low annual per capita income. Foreign market penetration is especially difficult in Indonesia and Malaysia, which have automotive programs that discriminate against foreign vehicles and parts. However, Indonesia's national car program was abolished as a result of the International Monetary Fund (IMF) bailout package. As a result, U.S. automotive producers' interest in Indonesia may be revitalized. Much will depend on Indonesia's adherence to its agreements with the IMF and the time it takes that country's economy to recover. The ethnic violence in Timor also threatened to stall the country's economic recovery and scare away potential investors. The APEC Early Voluntary Sector Liberalization automotive dialogue, of which ASEAN members are a part, may lead to further liberalization in access to those markets.

China, while somewhat insulated by a currency that is not fully convertible, was not immune to the effects of the Asian financial crisis and took the opportunity to reform its banking system, restructure loss-making state enterprises, and streamline bureaucracy. The Chinese market combines a high rate of economic growth with one of the lowest vehicle density rates, a meager nine vehicles per 1,000 people. With plans to expand its vehicle product capacity to 3 million vehicles by 2000, China has the potential to become one of the world's largest vehicle markets. U.S. exports of automotive parts have been limited by 20 to 30 percent tariff rates and restrictive local content requirements. The U.S. acceptance of China's accession into the World Trade Organization in 1999 shows promise of opening a window of opportunity for the automotive industry, especially auto parts suppliers. China agreed to reduce tariffs on automobile parts to an average of 10 percent and tariffs on automobiles to 25 percent by 2006. China also agreed to phase out quotas on automobile imports and to eliminate local content requirements. In 1997, U.S. exports to China increased 139 percent over the 1996 level to reach $311 million but fell nearly to the 1996 level with $132 million in 1998. The first 10 months of 1999 showed promise with an increase of 77 percent over the same period in 1998, reaching $191 million. GM's $1.57 billion joint venture with Shanghai Automotive Industry Corporation began full production in 1999 and should generate an estimated $1 billion in U.S. exports over the next 5 years.

After 17 years of nonstop growth, South Korea's automotive industry slumped with the bankruptcy of its third largest vehicle producer, Kia, and the financial problems of its largest automotive parts maker, Mando Machinery. Kia was saved from bankruptcy by the government and sold to Hyundai. Mando Machinery was mostly taken over by foreign automotive parts manufacturing corporations. Additionally, Daewoo, South Korea's second largest automaker, took over Ssangyog Motor, that country's fourth largest vehicle manufacturer, in 1998. Many of South Korea's automotive sector companies began talks with foreign companies. For example, in 1999, Daewoo began discussions to sell off its automotive parts units to Delphi and may auction off Daewoo Motor Co. Ltd. to GM or Ford, which would give either GM or Ford a base to expand sales in Asia. U.S. parts exports to South Korea began to decline in 1997 rather than 1998. In 1996, the United States exported $942 million worth of automotive parts to South Korea and imported $606 million, resulting in a $336 million surplus. However, U.S. automotive parts exports declined 30 percent to $661 million in 1997 and 45 percent to $364 million in 1998, while imports from South Korea increased to $657 million in 1997 and $762 million in 1998, resulting in a meager $4 million surplus in 1997 and a $398 million deficit in 1998.

The United States and the Republic of Korea agreed to a memorandum of understanding in October 1998 that could improve market access to South Korea's historically closed automotive market. South Korea will cut taxes, streamline standards and certification procedures, and introduce a financing system for the purchase of motor vehicles, enabling that country's consumers to finance purchases of U.S. vehicles.

Mexico

Mexico, Brazil, and other Latin American markets may have the greatest potential for U.S. automotive parts manufacturers in the near term. Mexico has been one of the U.S. automotive industry's most significant foreign markets since the early 1980s. In their efforts to rationalize North American production, U.S. motor vehicle manufacturers and suppliers regard the Mexican market as part of their North American operations.

U.S. domestic make assemblers and most leading U.S. automotive parts suppliers manufacture in Mexico, which has become the second most important U.S. export market after Canada. Implementation of NAFTA in January 1994 enhanced the importance of Mexico, providing U.S. suppliers with increased access to the growing Mexican market and an opportunity to structure their overall North American manufacturing operations to achieve economies of scale and maximize quality and international cost competitiveness. With an influx of U.S., Canadian, European, and Asian suppliers, locally owned firms must become more productive to remain competitive.

Mexico is on the road to full recovery from the December 1994 devaluation of the peso and the subsequent economic crisis that severely affected its automotive industry. The parts industry's performance in Mexico was assisted by the increased availability of "cheaper" credit, interest-free factory financing, lower down payments, and extended payment terms, which made vehicles more affordable. Industry analysts report that Mexican vehicle production increased 7.7 percent to 1.4 million units in 1998 compared with 1.3 million in 1997 and is expected to reach 1.6 million by 2001. It also was reported that vehicle sales in Mexico in 1998 hit 643,300 units, up 16 percent from 1997 levels. Mexican vehicle sales were the second highest ever in Mexico in 1998, after the 670,799 units in 1992. Despite production and sales increases, U.S. parts exports were down slightly in 1998, when $9.5 billion was exported, a 0.8 percent decrease from 1997. On January 1, 1998, the 5-year staging for duty elimination on light trucks and many automotive parts was completed. As the Mexican economy improves and Mexico phases out and eliminates all automotive tariffs by 2003, U.S. automotive parts exports should experience a resurgence of growth in Mexico. In the coming years, U.S. producers of replacement parts should benefit from supplying the Mexican market for the increasing number of U.S.-made models now being sold in Mexico.

Mexico also promises to be a springboard for supplying other Latin American countries. The Mexican government has negotiated preferential trade agreements with Costa Rica, Columbia, Venezuela, and Chile and is negotiating similar agreements with other countries, including Ecuador and Peru and the Southern Common Market (MERCOSUR) nations. Negotiations with the EU may result in an agreement by the year 2000. As Mexico's preferential trade arrangements are fully implemented, cost advantages for producers in Mexico exporting to these countries will range from 10 to 35 percent in terms of duties saved.

Brazil

As a result of Brazil's fiscal plan of November 1997, currency devaluation, and political turmoil, vehicle production and economic growth slowed. After a record 2.1 million units produced in 1997, Brazilian vehicle production declined 24 percent to only 1.6 million units in 1998, dropping that country from the world's number eight automobile producer to number nine. Brazil's domestic motor sales picked up as a result of government tax incentives in early 1999, and analysts believe that Brazil has turned the corner economically; however, its stagnant market led manufacturers to scale back production forecasts for 1999. Every vehicle manufacturer in Brazil has cut schedules and laid off workers because of the recession. Brazil might have reached the number four global ranking if proposed new automotive investment expected to surpass $19 billion, which would have increased production capacity to 995,000 units, had been made. However, GM and Ford Motor Company have experienced difficulty getting promised tax relief and incentives for infrastructure investment. As a result, GM decided to delay the start-up of the Blue Macaw assembly plant. Ford may decide to leave the Rio Grande do Sul region, having advised its major suppliers against investing in that region. Brazil has become a testing ground for automakers as they experiment with alternative production methods, including modular assembly. The lessons learned in Brazil may be put into practice in other plants around the world.

U.S. automotive parts exports to Brazil jumped 536 percent between 1992 and 1998 as a result of growth in the market in that period. U.S. investment in the Brazilian supplier industry also has increased. Ford, for example, brought 20 of its U.S. suppliers, including Budd Co., ITT Industries, Inc., and Johnson Controls, to Brazil to supply its Fiesta. TI Group Inc., a subsidiary of Bundy Corp., which built a plant in Brazil to supply Fiat's Palio world car, hopes to land similar contracts with Fiat as Palio production spreads to Argentina and other Latin American countries. Under the March 1998 Memorandum of Understanding Concerning Trade in the Automotive Sector between the U.S. government and the Brazilian government, vehicle assembly companies had until June 30, 1998, and parts manufacturers had until December 31, 1998, to apply for benefits that included lower tariffs and export credits for imports into Brazil or purchases of new capital equipment.

MERCOSUR was formed in 1991. Its members include Brazil, Argentina, Paraguay, and Uruguay. After the NAFTA area, the European market, and Japan, MERCOSUR is the fourth largest integrated market in the world. This is not a full free trade agreement but does allow free movement of most goods and services and imposes a common external tariff on "exempted" products. The automotive aspect of MERCOSUR was one of the most controversial and frequently negotiated issues in the pact, especially between Brazil and Argentina, regarding regional and local content and a common external tariff. A common MERCOSUR automotive policy is planned to be implemented in early 2000, but details of this policy have not been finalized. However, it is expected that most trade barriers among the four member countries will be removed and a common external tariff will be implemented.

Trade Agreements

The 1994 passage of the Uruguay Round of the General Agreement on Tariffs and Trade (GATT) greatly improved the exportation and foreign investment prospects of the U.S. supplier industry in most of the world's major and emerging automotive markets. The Uruguay Round agreement, which established the World Trade Organization (WTO), included a 58 percent reduction in automotive parts tariffs in major markets and put a ceiling on tariffs in many developing countries. In agreeing to these provisions, major automotive markets made a commitment to keep import duties on their automotive parts below certain "bound" rates. The Uruguay Round provisions on trade-related investment measures (TRIMs) and dispute settlement procedures should help eliminate nontariff trade barriers that have long plagued U.S. automotive parts firms in foreign markets. This agreement requires the elimination of performance requirements such as local content and foreign exchange balancing requirements. The dispute settlement procedures will improve the enforcement of these WTO agreements.

In 1996, the U.S. government examined the legality of the automotive regimes of several foreign countries under the WTO. The United States held several rounds of consultations with

Brazil, in which the EU and Japan also participated, on that country's automotive regime and with Indonesia on its national car program, completing the preliminary steps needed to request the formation of WTO Dispute Settlement Panels in both cases. As a result of bilateral consultations between the United States and Brazil, the WTO case was dropped, and early in 1998 the two countries entered into a memorandum of understanding concerning the Brazilian regime. On January 15, 1998, as part of its agreement to receive $43 billion in financing from the IMF, Indonesia agreed to end support for its WTO-violating national car program. The United States also filed a case against India's automotive regime for TRIM violations in 1999 and will continue to pursue any violations that impede the conduct of U.S. automotive business. In addition, as key emerging countries such as China and the newly independent states in Europe join the WTO, the reduction of trade barriers should help U.S. auto parts manufacturers gain a stronger foothold in those markets.

The U.S.–Japan Automotive Framework Agreement signed in 1995 improved opportunities for U.S. automotive parts suppliers with the Japanese industry both in Japan and in the United States. U.S. parts companies that were unsuccessful in penetrating the Japanese market before the agreement reported significant new contracts and sales opportunities during the first 2 years after the agreement. The Japanese Ministry of Transport completed deregulatory actions that should provide new opportunities for U.S. firms in Japan's lucrative aftermarket. However, the current economic crisis in Japan has significantly decreased opportunities for U.S. parts suppliers.

In response to the Asian financial crisis, the Japanese government enacted a variety of macroeconomic measures and financial sector reforms but was reluctant to actively deregulate and fully open the economy, especially in the automotive sector. These policies and the protracted recession have had a negative effect on automotive parts companies. Japanese automotive unit production fell to a 20-year low in 1998, and the value of U.S. parts exports to Japan fell 7.4 percent in 1998 compared with 1997, dropping to $2.1 billion. This was the first decline in U.S. automotive parts exports to Japan since the agreement was signed. The U.S.–Japanese Automotive Framework Agreement is due to expire in December 2000. Whether the agreement should be allowed to lapse, be renewed, or be renegotiated was scheduled to be discussed at the annual Framework Agreement consultations in Vancouver in October 1999.

As the automotive industry becomes more global, differing safety and environmental standards have become major impediments to automotive trade. What began under the auspices of the Transatlantic Business Dialogue, initiated in late 1995, evolved into a proposal for a Global Automotive Standards Agreement. Under the Transatlantic Business Dialogue, U.S. and European industries and governments began discussions on international automotive regulatory harmonization. Those discussions included the intergovernmental regulatory process necessary to achieve such harmonization and the coordination of vehicle safety and environmental research. In March 1998, the United States, the EU, and Japan approved the text of an Agreement on Global Technical Regulations to supplement the revised 1958 United Nations/Economic Commission for Europe Working Party on the Construction of Vehicles (known as Working Party 29) to provide for the development of global technical regulations for motor vehicles and motor vehicle equipment (automotive parts). The text of the agreement is still subject to a final round of comments from the interested governments. The establishment of harmonized or functionally equivalent standards should increase the U.S. industry's export potential to European and other markets and reduce the costs of regulatory compliance for the industry, give consumers more choices and lower prices, uphold and improve safety and environmental standards, and improve the competitiveness of producers.

The APEC automotive dialogue was held in Bali in July 1999. The dialogue produced agreement on actions to seek ways to support the supplier industry during the Asian financial crisis, support step-by-step liberalization of automotive trade in APEC countries, and prepare a joint report on impediments to growth in the APEC automotive sector by April 2000 that will be authored by industry representatives. The Japanese, who have the largest presence in the region, resisted attempts to make concrete progress on trade liberalization in the APEC region.

OUTLOOK FOR U.S. AFTERMARKET SUPPLIERS

The size of the U.S. aftermarket in 1998 was estimated to be $152 billion to $159 billion and probably increased another 5 percent in 1999, according to industry associations. Traditionally, growth in U.S. aftermarket sales has been directly related to the size and age of the vehicle fleet as well as the number of miles driven. According to industry resources, in 1998, there were 205 million vehicles on U.S. roads, up from 176 million in 1989. The median age of cars in operation was 8.3 years in 1998, compared with 6.5 years in 1989. Vehicle ownership increased in the 1990s, and there is no indication of reduced levels any time soon. This is a positive indication of continued growth in the automotive parts industry. The Motor and Equipment Manufacturers Association (MEMA) reported that the "degree of vehicle usage is at the root of most aftermarket demand, and long-term trends in miles driven indicate continued growth in the automotive aftermarket." MEMA estimated that vehicle utilization will increase about 1.1 percent annually from the 2.5 trillion miles driven in 1996. Thus, by 2004, total miles driven will be over 2.7 trillion miles per year. There has been dramatic improvement in the quality and durability of OE parts, with vehicle manufacturers' specifications for a part's life rising from 50,000 miles to 100,000 miles in certain product lines. These improvements have held average annual U.S. automotive parts sales growth at around 2 to 3 percent, an annual growth rate that probably will continue into the twenty-first century.

Light trucks represent a steadily increasing percentage of new vehicle sales, accounting for 48.4 percent in 1999, up from 29.1 percent in 1986. Industry analysts predict that the light truck share of vehicle sales will easily exceed 50 percent in the near future. As a result, light truck aftermarket and specialty equipment products account for an increasing share of the auto parts industry. The Specialty Equipment Market Association (SEMA) reported that light truck product sales accounted for 29 percent of the overall specialty equipment market in 1998. Industry analysts report that the 1998 light truck accessories aftermarket was $1.6 billion in 1998, up 9.6 percent over 1997.

Consolidation and competition will remain major issues for U.S. aftermarket suppliers in the long term. In recent years, U.S. aftermarket manufacturers, like OE suppliers, have been undergoing dramatic restructuring. The Automotive Parts and Accessories Association (APAA) reported that the value of mergers and acquisitions among U.S. aftermarket manufacturers (SIC 3714 only) totaled $21.8 billion in 1998, up 339 percent from the previous year despite the fact that the actual number of mergers and acquisitions went down, indicating that the value of mergers and acquisitions has risen dramatically. Similar consolidations are expected to continue into the next decade as firms regroup to reduce costs and debt and enhance their competitive positions at home and abroad. Competition in the aftermarket increased dramatically in the 1990s. OE suppliers, squeezed by automakers' restructuring plans, are vying for a greater share of the replacement parts market.

Many U.S. aftermarket parts manufacturers found it difficult to supply the increasing number of Japanese imports in the U.S. fleet, since replacement parts for Japanese imports historically were manufactured by Japanese OE suppliers. The 1995 signing of the U.S.–Japan Automotive Framework Agreement aided U.S. aftermarket manufacturers in their efforts to supply parts for Japanese vehicles in the United States, Japan, and other markets where Japanese vehicles are sold. The agreement encourages Japanese automakers to purchase more U.S. parts for use in their U.S.-based operations, some of which will be used to supply the aftermarket for transplant and imported Japanese vehicles, and makes it easier for Japanese consumers to modify their vehicles with independent aftermarket parts and accessories. As of August 1996, the Japanese Ministry of Transport (MOT) released eight parts—shock absorbers, struts, trailer hitches, power steering systems, torque rods, stabilizers, torsion bar springs, and clutches for motorcycles—from the requirement to use government-approved mechanics and garages to remove or replace certain critical or safety-related parts. MOT also liberalized its regulations regarding the number of government-qualified mechanics required for approved garages as well as the requirements for government-approved garages. This includes the creation of specialized certified garages that need only facilities appropriate for the repair of any one or more of the seven, rather than all seven, critical parts systems. In August 1999, MOT established a new classification of chassis certified mechanics, further deregulating certified mechanics requirements and thus establishing conditions more favorable for increased competition and enhanced opportunities for U.S.-made automotive parts. These regulatory changes should increase the opportunities for U.S. suppliers to break into the $60 billion Japanese aftermarket as they allow smaller, independent garages and automotive parts stores that tend to use a larger percentage of imported parts to perform work they formerly could not do. These changes also create an incentive for more garages to carry competitive foreign parts. Because of the recent financial crisis, U.S. automotive parts exports declined in 1998 and 1999, and the Japanese government has expressed reluctance toward further trade liberalization in the region during the crisis. The U.S. and Japanese governments continue to monitor progress under the agreement.

One of the best growth markets for U.S. aftermarket parts manufacturers is Mexico, as a result of NAFTA. Between 1998 and 2004, the Mexican aftermarket is expected to more than double to $11.4 billion as the Mexican fleet of 13 million vehicles grows and ages. U.S. parts currently account for about 23 percent of the replacement parts market, as the Mexican fleet contains a high level of U.S.-origin parts. As the Mexican automotive industry recovers from the peso devaluation and subsequent market collapse and Mexican duties on automotive parts are phased out under NAFTA, U.S. exports of replacement parts are expected to exceed pre-1995 growth levels. In addition, the increasing use of Mexico as an automotive export platform to other Latin American markets should pave the way for increased sales of U.S. parts in those markets.

Forrest Nielsen, U.S. Department of Commerce, Automotive Parts and Suppliers Division, (202) 482-1418, December 1999.

■ REFERENCES

Automotive Industries, Cahners Business Information, 8773 South Ridgeline Boulevard, Highlands Ranch, CO 80126-2329. (303) 470-4445.

Automotive Industry Status Report 1998, Motor and Equipment Manufacturers Association, P.O. Box 13966, Research Triangle Park, NC 27709-3966. (919) 549-4800.

Automotive News, Crain Communications Inc., 965 East Jefferson, Detroit, MI 48207-3185. (800) 678-9595.

The Autoparts Report, International Trade Services, P.O. Box 5950, Bethesda, MD 20824-5950. (301) 857-8454.

Impact of the North American Free Trade Agreement on U.S. Automotive Exports to Mexico: Fourth Annual Report to Congress, U.S. Department of Commerce, International Trade Administration. (202) 482-1418, http://www.ita.doc.gov/auto.

Motor Vehicles Facts and Figures, 1997 (annual), American Automobile Manufacturers Association, Suite 900, 1401 H Street, NW, Washington, DC 20005. (202) 326-5500.

1998 APAA Aftermarket Factbook, Automotive Parts and Accessories Association, 4600 East-West Highway, Third Floor, Bethesda, MD 20814. (301) 654-6664.

1998 SEMA Market Study, Specialty Equipment Market Association.

Report to President William Jefferson Clinton by the Interagency Enforcement Team Regarding the U.S.–Japan Agreement on Autos and Auto Parts, June 3, 1999, U.S. Department of Commerce, International Trade Administration. (202) 482-0554. http://www.ita.doc.gov/auto.

The Shape and Size of the USA Motor Vehicle Aftermarket: A Profile, 1998 Edition, Automotive Service Industry Association, 25 Northwest Point Boulevard, Suite 425, Elk Grove Village, IL 60007-1035. (847) 228-1310.

U.S. Department of Commerce, Office of Automotive Affairs, http://www.ita.doc.gov/auto.

U.S.–Japan Automotive Agreement and Supporting Documents, August 23, 1995, U.S. Department of Commerce, International Trade Administration. (202) 482-0554, http://www.ita.doc.gov/auto.

Ward's Automotive Reports (weekly), *Ward's Automotive International* (bimonthly), and *Ward's Automotive Yearbook,* Ward's Communications, Suite 2750, 3000 Town Center, Southfield, MI 48075. (313) 962-4433.

WEFA, Inc., 111 Broadway, Eighth Floor, New York, NY 10006-1091. (212) 406-2095, www.wefa.com.

World Motor Vehicle Data 1996 (annual), American Automotive Manufacturers Association, Suite 900, 1401 H Street, NW, Washington, DC 20005. (202) 326-5500.

RELATED CHAPTERS

12: Synthetic Rubber
13: Steel Mill Products
14: Nonferrous Metals
36: Motor Vehicles

HOUSEHOLD CONSUMER DURABLES
Economic and Trade Trends

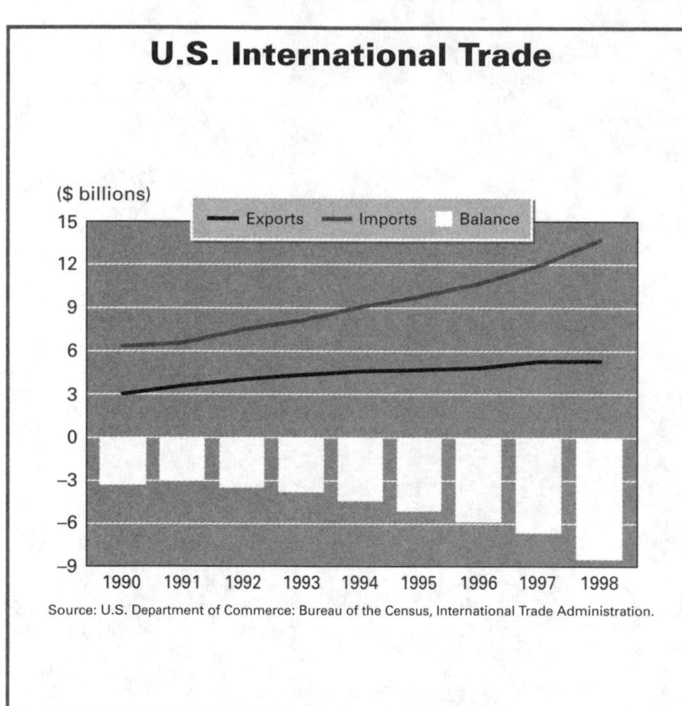

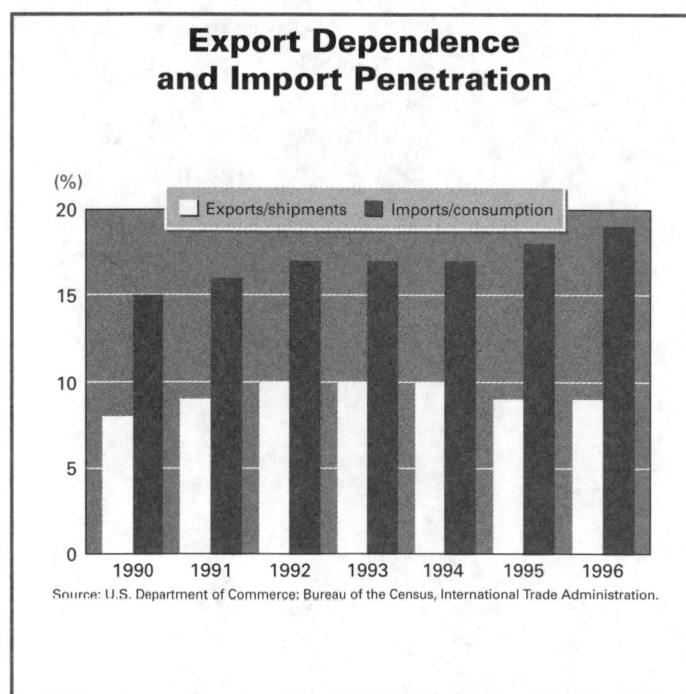

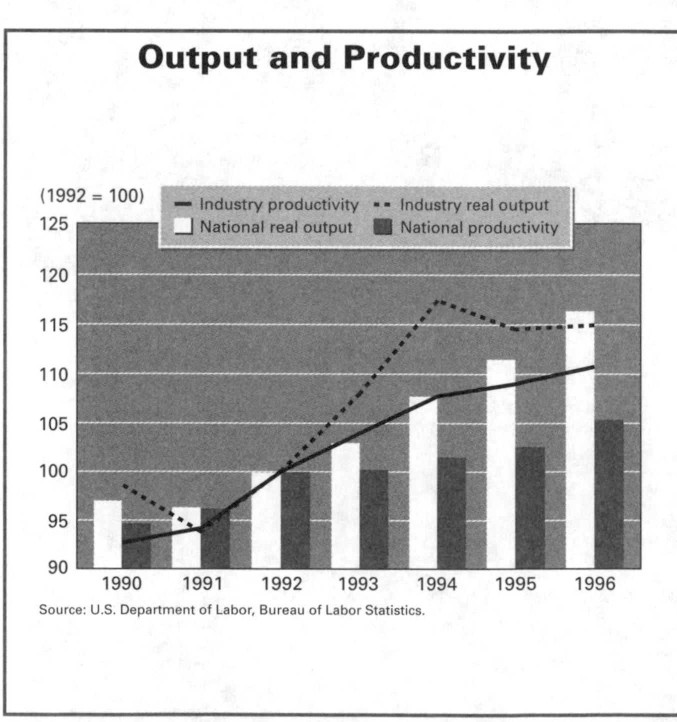

See "Getting the Most Out of *Outlook 2000*" for definitions of terms.

38

Household Consumer Durables

INDUSTRY DEFINITION The household consumer durables sector includes household furniture (SIC 251), household appliances (SIC 363), and lawn and garden equipment (SIC 3524).

OVERVIEW

Factors Affecting Future Industry Growth

Purchases of household durable goods are highly discretionary, and these industries therefore are cyclical, reflecting general trends in the consumer economy, especially housing activity. The lawn and garden equipment industry is heavily dependent on weather, and its shipments are highly seasonal. The U.S. economy continued its remarkable expansion in 1999, with real gross domestic product (GDP) growth expected in the range of 3.5 to 4.0 percent. The lowest unemployment rate in nearly three decades—it remained at 4.2 to 4.3 percent for most of 1999—spurred growth in real disposable personal income (DPI), which averaged 3.4 percent in the first two quarters of 1999. The Blue Chip Economic Indicators consensus estimate was for 3.4 percent real DPI growth for the year. If achieved, that would be the largest full-year gain since 4.1 percent in 1988 (see Figure 38-1). This strong growth was reflected in record median household income of $38,885 in 1998, which exceeded the previous inflation-adjusted high set in 1989, the year before the last U.S. recession.

The powerful performance of the stock market, which has roughly doubled over the last 5 years, is another factor contributing to strong consumer spending. During this period, stock ownership has broadened considerably, mainly through ownership of mutual funds and retirement accounts. Some economists are questioning whether this wealth effect is having a greater impact on consumer spending than it did in the past. They point to the negative savings rate (which is based on income rather than wealth; see Figure 38-2), as evidence that consumers are relying more on wealth (based on stock market appreciation) than on current income to finance consumption. This may be particularly true for big-ticket household consumer durable goods. With unexpectedly large gains in stock prices, consumers may consider gains above some "normal" level as a bonus and thus spendable. Furthermore, with the strong labor market, consumer uncertainty about future earnings may decrease, leading to a greater willingness to spend from current wealth. Traditional macroeconometric models estimate that a dollar's worth of increase in stock market wealth boosts consumer spending 3 to 7 cents per year, with modern estimates putting it closer to 3 percent. Whether this effect has

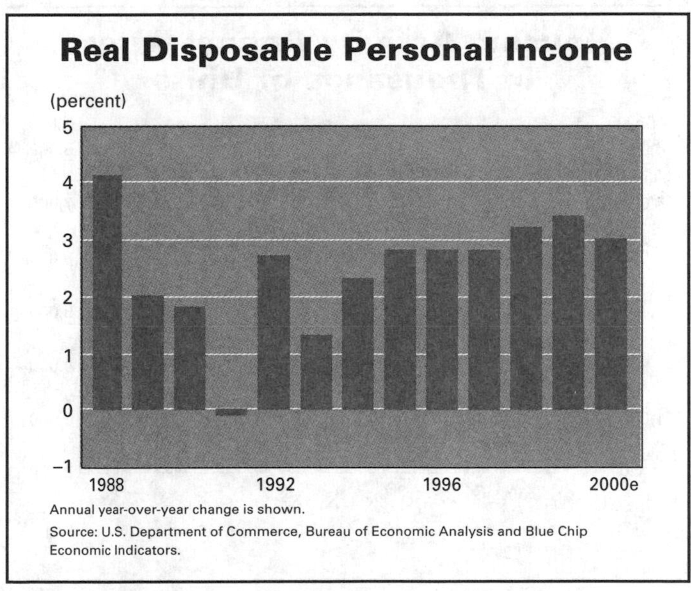

Annual year-over-year change is shown.
Source: U.S. Department of Commerce, Bureau of Economic Analysis and Blue Chip Economic Indicators.

FIGURE 38-1

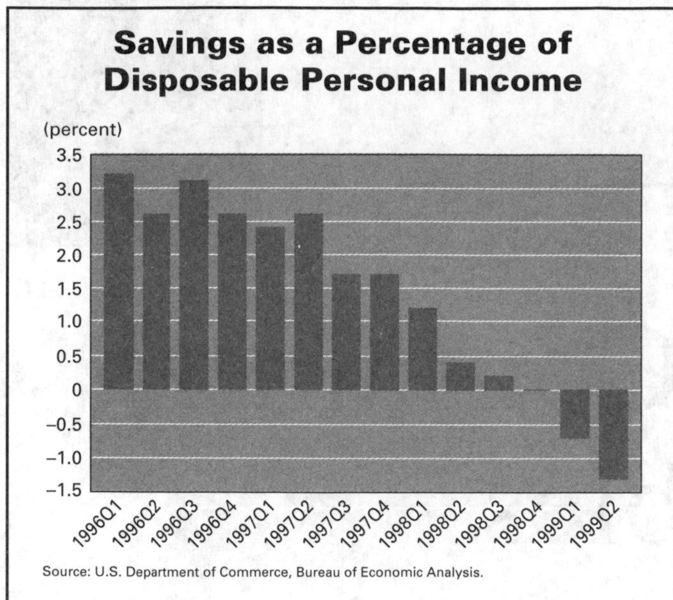

FIGURE 38-2

increased is being debated. Even if consumers still spend the same portion of each new dollar of wealth, with stock market wealth double what it was in 1994, that means that that proportion will have twice the impact on spending.

Spending on household durables is closely associated with housing activity. The housing market had another stellar year in 1999. Housing starts, which are a leading indicator of spending on furniture, appliances, and lawn and garden equipment, had another strong year, totaling an estimated 1.6 million units, with single-family units continuing to be the primary source of strength. Despite repeated predictions that housing sales would decline from their record levels, they continued to set new records in 1999 (see Figure 38-3).

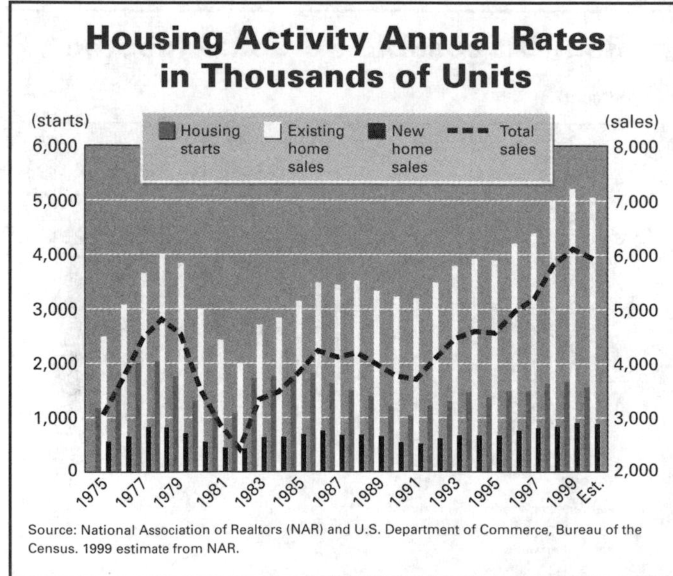

FIGURE 38-3

Along with these positive indicators, there are some cautionary signs for the year 2000. The higher interest rates of 1999 are likely to have an impact on the housing market; there were signs of slowing activity in the third quarter of 1999. In addition, high levels of consumer debt mean that consumers, already with negative savings, are not in a strong position to maintain high levels of spending indefinitely. As consumer spending continued to outpace income in most of 1999, consumer borrowing made up for some of the difference. Still, the strong income gains in 1999 actually resulted in a slight decline in the ratio of consumer debt to personal income (see Figure 38-4), indicating that consumers still have some ability to keep spending. At some point, however, consumers will use their income gains to build savings or pay off debt.

There is also speculation about a U.S. financial markets "bubble." That is, the stock market is overvalued, and when it returns to more "normal" levels, the U.S. economy will be significantly affected. Under such a scenario, the wealth effect will be negative, possibly resulting in a contraction in demand. These concerns were reflected somewhat in consumer confidence, which declined 3 months in a row in the third quarter of 1999. Despite the decline, confidence was still high: The September consumer confidence index remained just 4.8 points off its all-time high of 139.0 in June and well above the recent dip to 119.3 in October 1998 that was caused by concern at that time about stock market volatility and the financial crisis abroad (see Figure 38-5).

Global Trends

A strong U.S. economy and a strong dollar have spurred a surge in U.S. imports and dampened U.S. exports. The main drag on growth for furniture and appliances in 1999 was the high value of the dollar (the highest in 8 years versus the yen in 1998) combined with weaker economies abroad, which boosted imports to the U.S. market and lowered exports. U.S. imports of furniture jumped 20 percent in 1999 to an estimated $8.4 billion, and

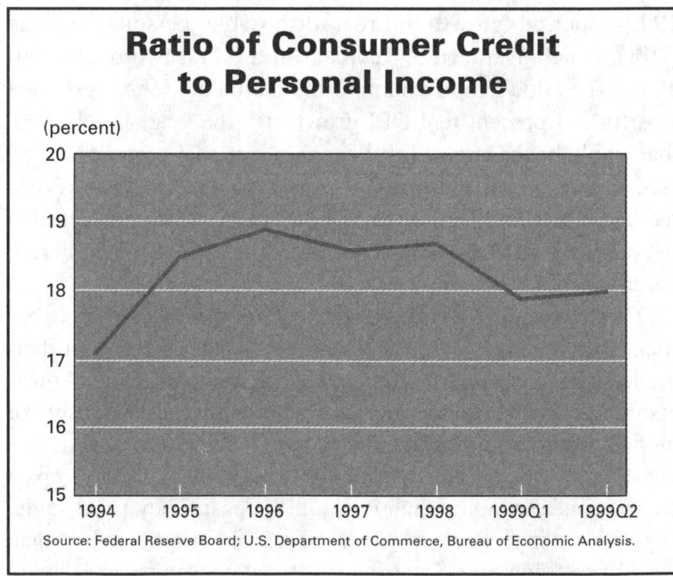

FIGURE 38-4

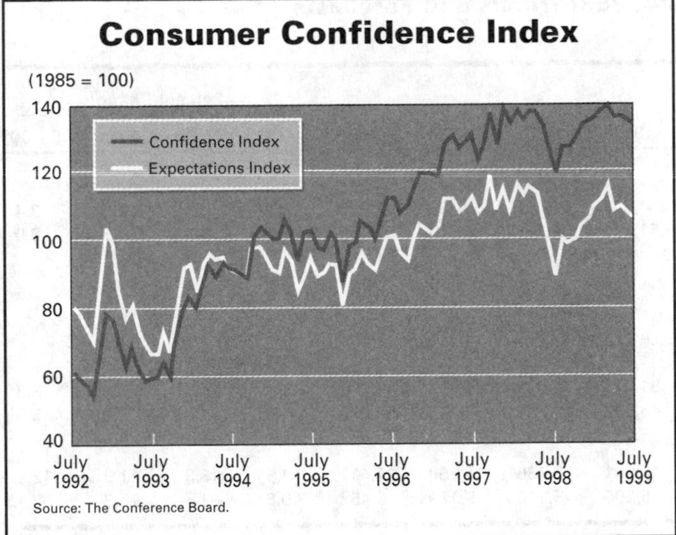

FIGURE 38-5

appliance imports rose 7 percent to an estimated $6.9 billion. Although the dollar declined significantly against the yen in 1999, it remained relatively strong against most currencies. The lagged effect of exchange rates on trade resulted in significant declines in exports in 1999; U.S. exports of furniture and appliances declined 3 percent and 6 percent, respectively.

The lawn and garden industry was an exception to this pattern. While 1999 U.S. trade in furniture and appliances had estimated imbalances of $6.8 and $4.1 billion, respectively, the lawn and garden sector had a positive balance of $0.6 billion after experiencing an estimated growth of 10 percent in exports.

Domestic Trends

There is a continuing trend toward consolidation in the household durable industries at the manufacturing level to leverage brands, manufacturing, and distribution in order to remain competitive in a marketplace that is more exposed to the proliferation of niches and product lines, international competition, and pressure from large retailers. The major appliance industry is already largely consolidated, with five companies dominating sales. The trend toward acquisitions and mergers in the furniture industry continued in 1999 with the announcement that the third largest manufacturer, La-Z-Boy, and the seventh largest, LADD Furniture, would merge in the year 2000 to create the largest U.S. furniture company, with over $2 billion in annual sales.

Electronic Commerce

Most manufacturers of household consumer goods have established some kind of presence on the World Wide Web. These have tended to be sites that provide information and direct consumers to traditional retail outlets. Manufacturers are concerned about competing directly with their dealers or, in the case of more integrated companies, their own retail outlets. There is some question whether large, big-ticket items such as washing machines, armoires, and garden tractors lend themselves to distribution on the Web the way that music and books do. It seems plausible that niche products and products that are easy to ship, such as ready-to-assemble or knock-down furniture, small appliances, and replacement parts for lawn and garden products, are more suitable for distribution and will find a market on the Internet.

The greater benefits from the Internet for these manufacturers may lie in establishing brand awareness and creating a direct link to consumers and in business-to-business transactions. Many companies have done an excellent job of providing extensive product information, customer service, and information about the location of dealers of their products. In the future, it will become increasingly important to have detailed information about consumer segments to anticipate and quickly respond to consumers' needs. The use of the Internet in linking to suppliers and customers—managing inventories (e.g., automated stock replenishment), tracking orders, electronic payment, and after-sales service—could result in the emergence of logistics as a key competitive factor for these industries. Forrester Research estimated that business-to-business Internet transactions for the consumer goods sector will surge from $1.4 billion in 1998 to $51.9 billion in 2003.

Projections of Industry and Trade Growth for the Next 1 and 5 Years

With the length of the current expansion entering record territory in the year 2000, the consensus is still for continued growth in 2000, although at a slower pace. Real GDP was projected to grow 2.0 to 2.5 percent in 2000, although many economists revised their estimates upward late in 1999. Combined U.S. shipments of the appliances, furniture, and lawn and garden industries totaled an estimated $60 billion in 1999 (see Table 38-1). Inflation-adjusted growth of these industries' shipments is expected to slow to 1.9 percent in 2000, down from estimated real growth of 4.4 percent in 1999. Notable for its absence has been any price inflation during this expansion. Growth in the weighted deflator for these combined industries was estimated at a negligible 0.3 percent annually between 1996 and 2000. This was down from an already low compound annual rate of 1.5 percent between 1992 and 1996. Combined U.S. exports are expected to rebound, increasing 5.3 percent in 2000 after a decline of 2.5 percent in 1999. U.S. imports of household durables will continue to rise, up 11.9 percent in 2000, as imports will account for a record one out of every four dollars of apparent consumption.

Over the long term, household demographics play a major role in shaping demand. The baby boom generation continues to have a major effect and over the next 5 years will continue to be a positive factor. Households headed by 45- to 54-year-olds will grow rapidly, and by 2005 people in that age range will become the largest age category, totaling 23.9 million households, according to Census Bureau projections. Meanwhile, the 35 to 44 years old age group will be declining as the tail end of the baby boom moves into the 45-plus cohort. However, this will still be the second largest age group, totaling 22.6 million households. These age groups tend to spend more on expensive, luxury products with extra features. In addition, the trend toward bigger homes means more space to furnish and larger

TABLE 38-1: Household Consumer Durables (SIC 251, 3524, 363) Trends and Forecasts
(millions of dollars except as noted)

	1992	1993	1994	1995	1996	1997[1]	1998[1]	1999[2]	2000[3]	Percent Change 97–98	98–99	99–00	96–00[4]
Industry data													
Value of shipments[5]	44,305	48,169	53,268	53,206	54,406	54,899	57,705	60,490	62,089	5.1	4.8	2.6	3.4
Value of shipments (1992$)	44,305	47,339	51,557	50,783	51,206	51,835	54,200	56,561	57,632	4.6	4.4	1.9	3.0
Total employment (thousands)	381	385	405	409	408								
Production workers (thousands)	316	322	342	341	341								
Average hourly earnings ($)	9.29	9.70	9.72	9.84	10.25								
Capital expenditures	1,027	967	1,083	1,284	1,322								
Product data													
Value of shipments[5]	40,650	43,736	48,261	49,686	51,059	51,518	54,072	56,671	58,204	5.0	4.8	2.7	3.3
Value of shipments (1992$)	40,650	42,970	46,667	47,418	48,041	48,598	50,785	53,045	54,085	4.5	4.5	2.0	3.0
Trade data													
Value of imports	7,497	8,148	9,085	9,793	10,717	11,951	13,730	15,560	17,411	14.9	13.3	11.9	12.9
Value of exports	4,026	4,342	4,606	4,697	4,833	5,280	5,310	5,179	5,452	0.6	–2.5	5.3	3.1

[1] Estimate except imports and exports.
[2] Estimate.
[3] Forecast.
[4] Compound annual rate.
[5] For a definition of industry versus product values, see "Getting the Most Out of *Outlook 2000.*"
Source: U.S. Department of Commerce: Bureau of the Census; International Trade Administration.

kitchens with larger appliances. The average new U.S. home is 40 percent larger than it was in 1980.

Global Market Prospects

Total U.S. imports in 1998 of $13.7 billion were 2.5 times higher than total U.S. exports of $5.3 billion for household consumer durables. The largest market for U.S. household consumer durables consists of the North American Free Trade Agreement (NAFTA) countries, which accounted for 49 percent of total exports in 1998 (see Table 38-2). Canada was the largest single market, with exports totaling over $1.9 billion, accounting for 36 percent of total exports. Mexico was the second largest single market with $682 million, nearly 13 percent, of total U.S. exports. Canada and Mexico accounted for 55 percent of all U.S. exports of household furniture and over half of exports of household appliances. Canada continues to be on top in lawn and garden equipment, totaling $194 million in 1998. The western European region was the second largest market for U.S. household durables, with almost 20 percent of total exports, valued at almost $1.1 billion in 1998. The United Kingdom was the third largest single-country market with $240 million; France was the fourth largest with $211 million of total household durables

TABLE 38-2: U.S. Trade Patterns in Household Consumer Durables[1] in 1998
(millions of dollars; percent)

Exports: Regions[2]	Value[3]	Share, %	Imports: Regions[2]	Value[3]	Share, %
NAFTA	2,603	49.0	NAFTA	3,999	29.1
Latin America	691	13.0	Latin America	253	1.8
Western Europe	1,055	19.9	Western Europe	2,314	16.9
Japan/Chinese Economic Area	302	5.7	Japan/Chinese Economic Area	4,884	35.6
Other Asia	112	2.1	Other Asia	2,124	15.5
Rest of world	549	10.3	Rest of world	158	1.2
World	5,310	100.0	World	13,730	100.0
Top Five Countries	**Value**	**Share, %**	**Top Five Countries**	**Value**	**Share, %**
Canada	1,920	36.2	China	3,425	25.0
Mexico	682	12.9	Mexico	2,035	14.8
United Kingdom	240	4.5	Canada	1,964	14.3
France	211	4.0	Taiwan	1,134	8.3
Taiwan	177	3.3	Italy	881	6.4

[1] SIC 251, 363, 3524.
[2] For definitions of regional groupings, see "Getting the Most Out of *Outlook 2000.*"
[3] Values may not sum total due to rounding.
Source: U.S. Department of Commerce, Bureau of the Census.

exports. The Japan/Chinese Economic Area was the smallest market of the economic regions with less than 6 percent of total exports, but it was the largest supplier for U.S. household consumer durables imports, accounting for almost 36 percent in 1998.

The largest single foreign supplier of household durables imports was China, totaling over $3.4 billion, accounting for 25 percent of U.S. imports. With its low labor rates, China probably will continue to increase its market share for labor-intensive products in the household appliances and furniture industries. In 1998, China became the number one source of foreign furniture in the United States, accounting for 22 percent of imports. The NAFTA region was the second largest source of household durables, with 29 percent of U.S. imports in 1998. Mexico and Canada benefit from low costs as a result of their geographic location near the U.S. market. The Latin American region had $253 million in total U.S. imports in 1998, only a 2 percent share of the U.S. import market; this was due to the economic troubles in several Latin American countries (see Figure 38-6).

The household furniture and appliances industries accounted for most of the trade in the household consumer durables sector, registering 51 percent and 47 percent, respectively, of total imports in 1998. The lawn and garden industry accounted for 2 percent of total imports of household consumer durables. The same goes for total U.S. exports in 1998, with household furniture and appliances industries dominating household consumer durables with 34 percent and 59 percent of total exports, respectively; lawn and garden equipment accounted for 7 percent of those exports.

Kevin M. Ellis, (202) 482-1176, Kevin_M_Ellis@ita.doc.gov, and ***Anhthu D. Tran,*** U.S. Department of Commerce, Office of Consumer Goods, http://www.ita.doc.gov/ocg., October 1999.

HOUSEHOLD FURNITURE

The household furniture industry (SIC 251) consists of firms that produce furniture in six industry sectors; wood household furniture (SIC 2511); wood upholstered furniture (SIC 2512); metal furniture (SIC 2514); mattresses, foundations, and convertible beds (SIC 2515); wood television, radio, phonograph and sewing machine cabinets (SIC 2517); and household furniture not elsewhere classified (SIC 2519), which includes furniture made from rattan, bamboo, rubber, and similar materials. Office furniture, although sometimes used in the home, is included under SIC 252 and will not be discussed in this analysis.

Global Industry Trends

U.S. imports of houschold furniture totaled $7 billion in 1998. From 1992 to 1998, imports grew at an annualized rate of 15 percent. A portion of that increase can be attributed to the labor-intensive furniture parts imported by U.S. manufacturers to enhance product lines, but the increase also signifies the growing importance of the U.S. furniture market to foreign firms. While some U.S. manufacturers operate showrooms, galleries, and retail outlets in foreign markets, few sell internationally on a large scale. In 1998, U.S. furniture exports totaled $1.6 billion, accounting for only 6 percent of all U.S. product shipments.

The success of the new breed of furniture retailers such as IKEA and Pier One indicates that there is potential for the sourcing and marketing of furniture on a global scale. The Swedish franchise IKEA sources products from around the world for sale in 29 different countries and was ranked 1999's eleventh top U.S. furniture store by the industry trade publication *Furniture/Today.* The success of these stores indicates that trade barriers and tariffs are low enough for furniture manufacturers to look beyond domestic markets and build international brands.

Domestic Trends

U.S. Furniture Industry. U.S. manufacturers produce furniture in four broad categories: traditional, which reflects styles

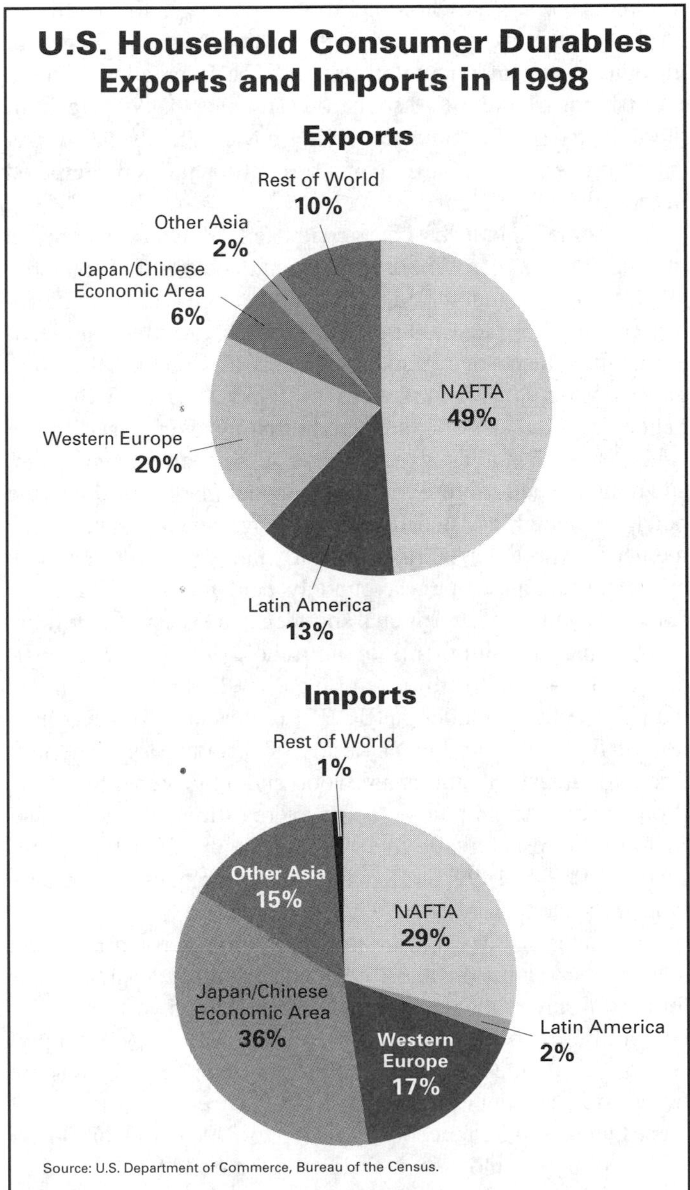

FIGURE 38-6

popular in past centuries; transitional, which is influenced by traditional lines but is blended with newer designs; contemporary, which is reflective of current design trends; and modern, which is completely original in design and form. Despite the range of furniture styles, consumer demand is not uniform across the country. Regional tastes and differences influence the design of the furniture sought in many markets. For example, white finishes are more popular in Florida and Arizona than they are in northern states and modern designs have stronger demand on the west coast than they do on the east coast. Some companies even create furniture lines that appeal to the taste of a specific region, such as Lexington's Southern Living Collection.

North Carolina is the furniture industry hub of the United States. Many of the top manufacturers are located in that state, but even those which produce in other parts of the country have a North Carolinian presence. The state has hosted the Market, a biannual furniture trade show, in High Point since 1913. The Market is the largest wholesale furniture show in the world and a very popular event for manufacturers, which use the forum to introduce new lines to retail buyers. The International Home Furnishings Marketing Association estimates that 90 percent of the industry's U.S. domestic buying power attends the Market and that over 74,500 participants from 106 nations participated in the April 1999 event.

The domestic industry changed in late 1999 with the proposed merger of two major U.S. furniture manufacturers. In September 1999, La-Z-Boy announced that it would purchase LADD Furniture Inc. for close to $300 million. The two companies are leaders in their respective market segments and produce furniture under a variety of brand names (see Table 38-3). La-Z-Boy is a major U.S. producer of upholstered furniture and recliners, while LADD manufacturers a wide range of bedroom, dining room, and upholstered furniture for the residential market as well as the hotel and motel, assisted living, and government markets. The merger is expected to be finalized early in the year 2000 and will create the country's largest publicly held residential furniture company, with expected annual shipments in excess of $2 billion.

U.S. product shipments of household furniture were estimated to reach $29 billion in 1999 (see Table 38-4). The six industry sectors included in SIC 251 represent a diverse collection of firms that produce a variety of furniture for home use. The two largest categories are wood and upholstered furniture. Product shipments in those sectors were estimated at $11.7 and $10 billion, respectively, in 1999. See Figure 38-7 for a comparison of 1998, 1999, and 2000 product shipment estimates by industry sector.

Low interest rates and a strong economy created a vibrant housing market in 1998 and 1999 that translated into strong gains for most furniture manufacturers. Over the last 25 years, new single-family American homes have grown in size. In 1998, 33 percent of new homes were built with four or more bedrooms, up from just 21 percent in 1975. Similarly, the average square feet of homes increased 33 percent from 1975 to 1998 (see Table 38-5).

The domestic industry is following the trend toward foreign production by sourcing labor-intensive hand-carved and painted furniture pieces from low-wage economies around the globe. In addition, many manufacturers are buying furniture abroad and offering it in specialized import collections. In 1998, the household wood furniture, metal furniture, and upholstered furniture industry sectors accounted for 61, 20, and 10 percent, respectively, of all U.S. imports (see Figure 38-8).

TABLE 38-3: Top 10 U.S. Furniture Manufacturers
(millions of dollars; excludes nonfurniture sales)

Manufacturer	Brands	1998 Shipments	Percent Change from 1997
Furniture Brands International	Thomasville, Lane, Broyhill	1,960.3	8.4
Lifestyle Furnishings	Beacon Hill Showrooms, Benchcraft, Berkline, Drexel Heritage, Henredon, La Barge, Lexington, LifeStyle Contract Furnishings, Maitland-Smith, Robert Allen/Ametex, Sunbury, Universal	1,744.7	3.0
La-Z-Boy, Inc.	Centurion, England/Corsair, Hammary, Kincaid, La-Z-Boy Canada, Sam Moore Furniture	1,244.0	15.8
Klaussner	Klaussner of California, Klaussner International, Stylecraft, Paoli, Realistic	725.0	8.5
Ashley Furniture	Ashley, Millennium	651.0	22.8
Ethan Allen Interiors	Ethan Allen, Knob Creek	610.8	17.3
LADD Furniture	American Drew, American of Martinsville, Barclay, Clayton Marcus, Lea Industries, Pennsylvania House, Pilliod	571.1	8.7
Sauder		530.0	11.6
Bassett Furniture Industries, Inc	Bassett, E.B. Malone	397.6	−11.0
Bush Furniture		384.3	27.1

Source: *Furniture/Today,* May 10, 1999.

Internationally, the most competitive U.S. industry sectors are the wood furniture, furniture made of other materials, and upholstered furniture categories, which accounted for 88 percent of the $1.6 billion in exports in 1998. See Figure 38-9 for a breakdown of exports by industry sector.

Trends in Manufacturing. The furniture industry is undergoing a significant change in the way manufacturers market their brands. Traditionally, it was not the manufacturer's name that brought customers to stores but the reputation of the retailer that sold furniture on the basis of price points and style. This resulted in poor brand awareness at a time when name recognition for other high-ticket items, such as cars, computers, and home appliances, was high. To increase brand awareness and attract a devoted customer base, manufacturers increasingly are establishing their own dedicated retail outlets. For example, in the summer of 1999 Furniture Brands International opened its fifth Thomasville store and in May 1999 Baker opened a flag-

TABLE 38-4: Household Furniture (SIC 251) Trends and Forecasts
(millions of dollars except as noted)

	1992	1993	1994	1995	1996	1997[1]	1998[1]	1999[2]	2000[3]	Percent Change 97–98	98–99	99–00	96–00[4]
Industry data													
Value of shipments[5]	20,507	21,906	23,603	24,458	25,426	26,702	28,528	30,495	31,424	6.8	6.9	3.0	5.4
Value of shipments (1992$)	20,507	21,373	22,363	22,563	23,010	23,863	25,126	26,560	27,017	5.3	5.7	1.7	4.1
Total employment (thousands)	253	255	267	271	273								
Production workers (thousands)	213	217	229	231	232								
Average hourly earnings ($)	8.36	8.77	8.83	8.89	9.21								
Capital expenditures	346	393	436	528	481								
Product data													
Value of shipments[5]	19,517	20,825	22,690	23,530	24,571	25,607	27,328	29,191	30,078	6.7	6.8	3.0	5.2
Value of shipments (1992$)	19,517	20,328	21,508	21,739	22,270	22,884	24,069	25,423	25,860	5.2	5.6	1.7	3.8
Trade data													
Value of imports	2,995	3,397	3,965	4,448	4,988	5,882	7,009	8,408	9,837	19.2	20.0	17.0	18.5
Value of exports	1,113	1,183	1,307	1,320	1,326	1,530	1,641	1,594	1,651	7.3	−2.9	3.6	5.6

[1] Estimate except imports and exports.
[2] Estimate.
[3] Forecast.
[4] Compound annual rate.
[5] For a definition of industry versus product values, see "Getting the Most Out of *Outlook 2000*."
Source: U.S. Department of Commerce: Bureau of the Census; International Trade Administration.

ship store in the Georgetown area of Washington, DC, and plans to open 25 additional brand-dedicated stores by 2004. Manufacturers also are using famous names such as the Thomasville Ernest Hemingway Collection and the Thomas Kinkade Collection from La-Z-Boy and sporting events such as Century's British Open Collection and Drexel Heritage's Pinehearst Collection to attract new customers.

Furniture increasingly is being designed with attention to function. A prime example of this trend is the new Oasis recliner by La-Z-Boy. At first glance, the chair appears to be a common recliner; however, it comes equipped with heated massage, a telephone with caller ID and a remote control under one armrest, and a cooler and cup holder hidden under the other armrest. Similar functional yet attractive products are sold by countless other manufacturers. It is not uncommon to find sofas with built-in recliners, coffee tables with hidden drawers for quick cleaning of the living room, and bedroom dressers with concealed openings for jewelry and personal items. Youth furniture has been especially influenced by this trend, as can be seen in space-saving creative units that combine bunk beds, lofts, computer desks, and hidden drawers.

The use of leather in upholstered furniture lines has increased over the last 6 years, and the trend shows no sign of abating. Currently, leather accounts for approximately 19 percent of all upholstery sales, but that figure is expected to increase to 30 percent over the next few years, according to the

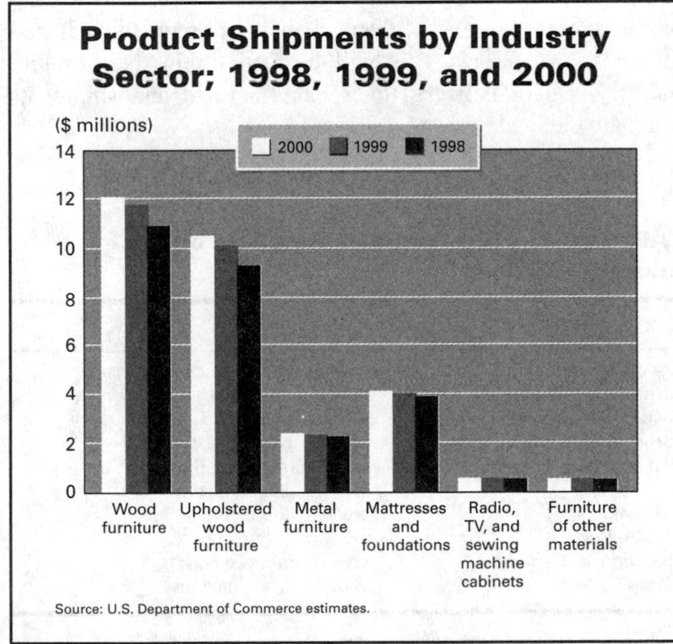

FIGURE 38-7

TABLE 38-5: New Single-Family Homes
(thousands of houses except as noted)

Year	New Homes Completed	Four or More Bedrooms[1]	Two or More Stories[1]	2,400 Square Feet or More[1]	Average Square Feet
1975	875	21	23	11	1,645
1980	957	20	31	15	1,740
1985	1,073	18	42	17	1,785
1990	966	29	46	29	2,080
1995	1,065	30	48	28	2,095
1996	1,129	31	47	30	2,120
1997	1,116	31	49	31	2,150
1998	1,160	33	NA[2]	NA[2]	2,190

[1] Percentage of total homes.
[2] NA = figures not available.
Source: U.S. Bureau of the Census and National Association of Home Builders, http://www.nahb.com/facts/forecast/sf.html.

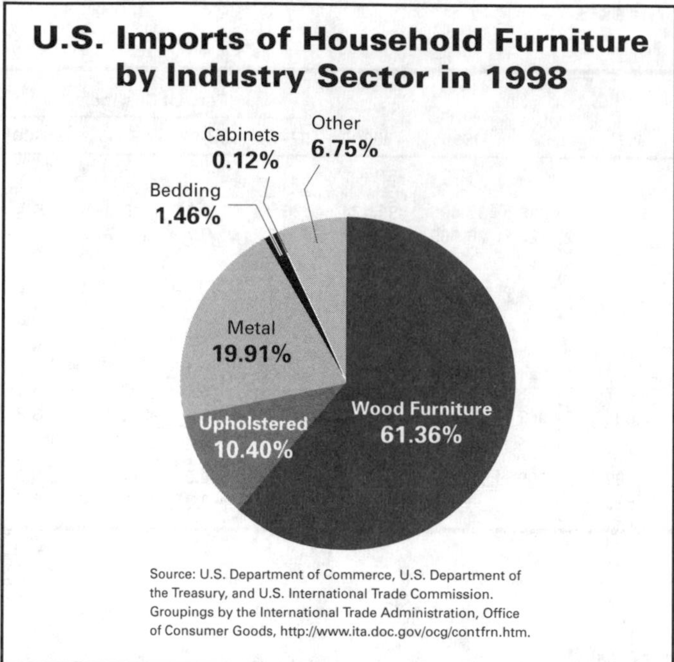

FIGURE 38-8

industry publication *Furniture/Today.* The increased use of leather is attributed to changing customer tastes, an increase in its quality, and a decrease in its price. Industry experts expect the trend toward leather to continue as consumers increasingly view that material as an affordable luxury.

Electronic Commerce. Every major U.S. manufacturer has a Web site, although most are used for marketing and brand building rather than for the sale of furniture. In June 1999, Furniture Brands International, which includes the Broyhill, Lane, and Thomasville brands, announced that it had no intention of allowing direct sales to consumers via Web sites and would not allow Internet furniture pricing or sales even by authorized mortar and brick dealers without prior approval. However, the company did state its support of dealers that use the Internet to advertise and provide product information. In the fall of 1999, La-Z-Boy and Ethan Allen announced that they would begin selling on-line in mid-2000 but stressed that Internet-only retailers would not be allowed to sell their products and that Internet sales would occur only through arrangements with local dealers who would receive a percentage of sales that occurred in their regions as well as compensation for filling on-line orders.

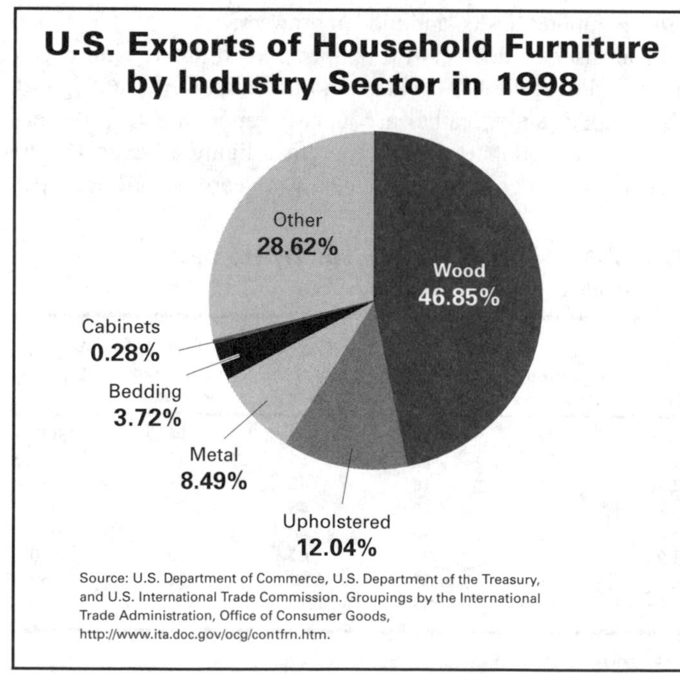

FIGURE 38-9

For smaller, less well-known furniture manufacturers, the Internet provides an opportunity for large-scale visibility that was impossible in traditional mortar and brick stores where expensive floor space was limited to major brands. There are numerous virtual furniture stores on the Web, but there is no clear industry leader. The Internet research firm Gomez.com ranks the most visible furniture retailing sites by ease of use, customer confidence, on-site resources, and personalized service on a quarterly basis (see Table 38-6).

The Internet's future impact on the industry is unclear. On-line retailing is successful when consumers can compare prices and delivery is prompt and efficient. However, most major furniture manufacturers have indicated their unwillingness to sell directly to the public or in any forum that does not involve their established mortar and brick retailers. If major brands use the Internet only to drive consumers to traditional stores, it is unlikely that furniture consumers will realize the price benefits that shopping on-line has created in other industries. Furthermore, for consumers who turn to the Internet for instant gratification purchases, on-line furniture retailers will need to ship within days, not weeks, of the placement of orders to meet customers' expectations. This will be difficult in the furniture industry, where delivery times can fluctuate and shipments often are delayed.

TABLE 38-6: Top Furniture Retailers on the Internet, Winter 1999

Internet Retailer	Web Address
GoodHome.com	www.goodhome.com
Furniture.com	www.furniture.com
Living.com	www.living.com
FurnitureFind.com	www.furniturefind.com
HomePoint.com	www.homepoint.com
Eddie Bauer	www.eddiebauer.com
BeHome	www.behome.com
RTA Online	www.rtaonline.com
The Bombay Company	www.bombayco.com
Puerta Bella	www.puertabella.com

Source: http://www.gomezadvisors.com/scorecards/index.cfm?topcat_id=41.

Industry and Trade Outlook for the Next 1 and 5 Years

The U.S. economy is expected to slow from its record 9-year expansion and grow at a rate of 2 to 2.5 percent in the year 2000. Signs of a possible slowdown were evident in the second half of 1999 as the U.S. Federal Reserve raised interest rates on two separate occasions, signaling the possible threat of inflation in the economy. The increase in interest rates translated into higher mortgage rates that threatened to slow the housing market. In August 1999, the average mortgage rate crossed the 8 percent threshold, a level that had not been seen since mid-1997. However, because of the strength of the U.S. stock market and rising wages, the housing market remained strong as people across the country continued to buy homes, often paying more than the asking price in the hope of securing a mortgage before another rate increase. U.S. product shipments of furniture grew 5.6 percent in constant dollars from 1998 to 1999 (see Table 38-4).

The furniture industry is not expected to see similar gains in 2000. A further rise in interest rates could cause Americans to defer home buying to future periods in hopes of attaining lower financing rates. A decline in home sales would result in decreased demand for furniture products, although it would not translate into an immediate decline for the industry. The strong home sales of late 1998 and 1999 are likely to propel the industry to modest growth in 2000 as consumers gradually purchase furniture for new homes. Therefore, it is estimated that U.S. product shipments will increase 1.7 percent in constant dollars in 2000 (see Table 38-4).

Over the next 5 years, U.S. furniture shipments are expected to slow from their recent highs and attain only modest growth. From 1992 to 1998, the furniture industry was exceptionally strong. Product shipments grew at an annualized rate of 3.6 percent after adjusting for inflation, and it is unlikely that the industry can sustain similar growth in future periods. If the Federal Reserve increases interest rates in 2000, it is likely that the furniture industry will experience a decline in U.S. consumer demand for household furniture. Furthermore, U.S. producers are expected to benefit from a gradual decline in the value of the U.S. dollar, which would make American furniture products more competitive internationally, and the resulting increase in exports could offset declines in the domestic market.

Population demographics have an impact on the furniture industry over the long term. It is estimated that those between ages 34 and 44 spend the most on furniture purchases per year. However, by age 34, most consumers have had some experience buying furniture. In an effort to attract and retain consumers at earlier ages, some furniture manufacturers are targeting generation X with the hope that their attention to this traditionally underserved segment of the market will translate into long-term furniture buying relationships as that generation ages. A prime example of this trend can be seen in a recent collection by Broyhill entitled "GX by Broyhill: A Collection So Hot, It's Cool." In 1999, those between ages 35 and 44 were estimated to make up the largest percentage of U.S. households. However, the population of this age group is expected to decline gradually, and by 2005, those between ages 45 and 54 are expected to hold the largest share of U.S. households (see Figure 38-10).

The Internet's long-term effects on the industry are uncertain. If manufacturers allow top branded furniture to be sold over the Internet, the price competition that is occurring in other industries could result in increased total consumer expenditures on furniture products despite the anticipated slowdown in the industry.

Global Market Prospects

U.S. manufacturers have not focused on international markets because the strong domestic economy has reduced the need for producers to look to foreign markets to meet sales expectations. However, if domestic demand for household furniture declines as a result of changes in the U.S. economy, manufacturers will need to reconsider foreign markets for future growth.

The NAFTA partners Canada and Mexico accounted for 55 percent of all U.S. exports of household furniture in 1998, up from 48 percent in 1997 (see Table 38-7). Total U.S. exports are estimated to have reached \$1.6 billion in 1999, a slight decline from 1998, partly as a result of the strength of the U.S. dollar, which raised the prices of American products for most international consumers.

U.S. exports are expected to grow 3.6 percent in 2000 because of the increasing strength of many of the economies previously devastated by the Asian financial crisis. The economies of Mexico and Brazil, the second and sixth largest U.S. furniture export markets, are expected to see positive growth as their currencies strengthen relative to the U.S. dollar, making American furniture more affordable to their consumers.

U.S. furniture tariffs were reduced beginning in 1995 and eliminated completely by 1999 as part of the General Agreement on Tariffs and Trade (GATT) Uruguay Round "zero-for-zero" agreements. Other signatories to the agreement, including the European Union, followed phased-in tariff reduction sched-

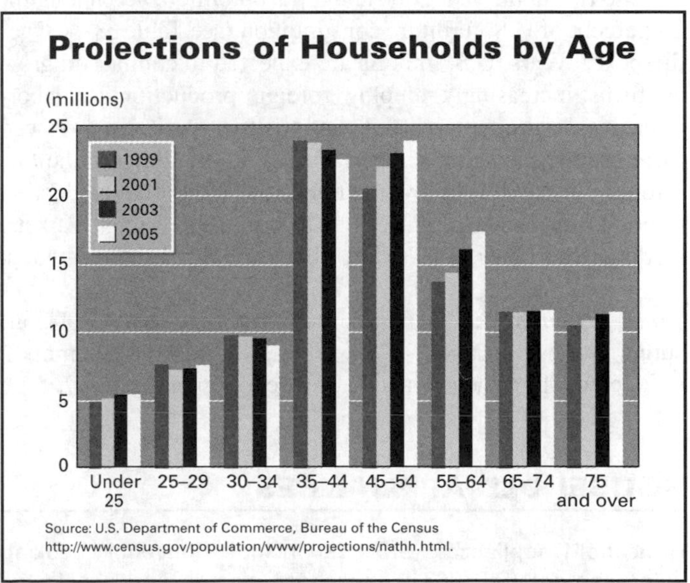

FIGURE 38-10

TABLE 38-7: U.S. Trade Patterns in Household Furniture[1] in 1998
(millions of dollars; percent)

Exports			Imports		
Regions[2]	Value[3]	Share, %	Regions[2]	Value[3]	Share, %
NAFTA	896	55	NAFTA	1,942	28
Latin America	210	13	Latin America	175	2
Western Europe	199	12	Western Europe	1,314	19
Japan/Chinese Economic Area	124	8	Japan/Chinese Economic Area	2,299	33
Other Asia	31	2	Other Asia	1,147	16
Rest of world	180	11	Rest of world	133	2
World	1,641	100	World	7,009	100
Top Five Countries	Value	Share, %	Top Five Countries	Value	Share, %
Canada	721	44	China	1,551	22
Mexico	175	11	Canada	1,301	19
Japan	91	6	Italy	760	11
United Kingdom	68	4	Taiwan	687	10
Saudi Arabia	68	4	Mexico	641	9

[1] SIC 251.
[2] For definitions of regional groupings, see "Getting the Most Out of *Outlook 2000.*"
[3] Values may not sum to total due to rounding.
Source: U.S. Department of Commerce, Bureau of the Census.

ules. Trade in most furniture products between Canada, Mexico, and the United States is duty-free under NAFTA. China's accession to the WTO could result in increased U.S. furniture exports. In 1998, China accounted for only 0.17 percent of U.S. furniture exports. However, during that year, China became the number one source of foreign furniture to the United States, accounting for 22 percent of imports. Liberalization of tariff and nontariff barriers that have prohibited U.S. manufacturers from reaching their full potential probably would result in increased exports to China.

U.S. imports of household furniture were estimated at $8.4 billion in 1999 and accounted for 23 percent of American consumption of household furniture. Imports are expected to continue to rise in the year 2000 and top $9.8 billion, accounting for 25 percent of U.S. furniture consumption (see Table 38-4). Over the next 5 years, U.S. imports are expected to continue to grow as firms increasingly employ foreign production for labor-intensive furniture pieces and continue to buy foreign-produced furniture for specialized import lines. It is possible that the furniture industry will follow the trend toward foreign production of goods that can be produced at a lower cost in foreign markets, leading to a further increase in U.S. household furniture imports.

Jamie J. Lemm, U.S. Department of Commerce, Office of Consumer Goods, (202)-482-5783, fax: (202) 482-3981, LemmJ@ita.doc.gov, http://www.ita.doc.gov/ocg, September 1999.

HOUSEHOLD APPLIANCES

Household appliances (SIC 363) include household cooking equipment (SIC 3631: household electric and nonelectric cooking equipment such as stoves, ranges, and ovens, including microwave and convection ovens); household refrigerators and home and farm freezers (SIC 3632); household laundry equipment (SIC 3633: laundry equipment such as washing machines, dryers, and ironers for household use, including coin-operated); electric housewares and fans (SIC 3634: electric housewares for heating, cooking, and other purposes and electric household fans except attic fans); household vacuum cleaners (SIC 3635); and household appliances not elsewhere classified (SIC 3639: household appliances such as water heaters, dishwashers, food waste disposal units, and household sewing machines).

Factors Affecting Future Industry Growth

The household appliance industry recorded another growth year in 1999 as product shipments expanded to $21.9 billion. This was an increase of 5.4 percent in constant dollars over 1998 (see Table 38-8). The industry benefited from a robust economy in its ninth year of expansion. GDP increased about 4 percent during that year. Real disposable income rose briskly, up an estimated 3.5 percent, aided by strong growth in employment and wages. However, growth in consumer spending increased even more, as the personal saving rate declined from 0.5 percent to a negative 0.5 percent during that year. Rather than being a danger signal, the negative savings rate was attributed by many to a sharp rise in household net worth as a result of the rising stock market in recent years. This enabled consumers to spend more than their incomes normally would allow.

The economy also benefited from relatively low interest rates, which declined in late 1998. Housing starts, which are an important factor in the underlying demand for appliances, totaled an estimated 1,630,000 in 1999. While this was an increase of only about 1 percent from 1998, it was the highest rate of housing starts since 1986. Housing starts remained strong despite two federal funds interest rate increases of 0.25

TABLE 38-8: Household Appliances (SIC 363) Trends and Forecasts
(millions of dollars except as noted)

										Percent Change			
	1992	1993	1994	1995	1996	1997[1]	1998[1]	1999[2]	2000[3]	97–98	98–99	99–00	96–00[4]
Industry data													
Value of shipments[5]	18,633	20,435	22,829	21,776	22,157	21,203	22,014	23,103	23,829	3.8	4.9	3.1	1.8
3631 Household cooking equipment	2,950	3,010	3,849	3,918	3,565	3,540	3,625	3,886	4,041	2.4	7.2	4.0	3.2
3632 Household refrigerators	4,232	4,463	5,149	5,200	5,605	4,826	5,110	5,275	5,433	5.9	3.2	3.0	–0.8
3633 Household laundry equipment	3,329	3,871	4,612	4,133	4,233	3,723	3,865	4,140	4,306	3.8	7.1	4.0	0.4
3634 Electric housewares and fans	2,897	3,106	3,053	3,298	3,032	3,435	3,574	3,678	3,715	4.0	2.9	1.0	5.2
3635 Household vacuums	1,905	2,096	1,933	2,045	2,425	2,398	2,473	2,642	2,748	3.1	6.8	4.0	3.2
3639 Home appliances nec	3,320	3,889	4,233	3,183	3,297	3,281	3,367	3,482	3,586	2.6	3.4	3.0	2.1
Value of shipments (1992$)	18,633	20,179	22,512	21,498	21,717	21,330	22,213	23,380	24,114	4.1	5.3	3.1	2.7
3631 Household cooking equipment	2,950	2,911	3,755	3,856	3,481	3,484	3,658	3,878	4,033	5.0	6.0	4.0	3.7
3632 Household refrigerators	4,232	4,436	5,068	5,154	5,538	4,980	5,180	5,490	5,655	4.0	6.0	3.0	0.5
3633 Household laundry equipment	3,329	3,887	4,668	4,191	4,258	3,878	4,072	4,337	4,510	5.0	6.5	4.0	1.4
3634 Electric housewares and fans	2,897	3,087	3,065	3,328	3,066	3,572	3,679	3,753	3,790	3.0	2.0	1.0	5.4
3635 Household vacuums	1,905	2,037	1,843	1,941	2,303	2,341	2,458	2,630	2,735	5.0	7.0	4.0	4.4
3639 Home appliances nec	3,320	3,820	4,114	3,028	3,070	3,075	3,166	3,292	3,391	3.0	4.0	3.0	2.5
Total employment (thousands)	103	105	111	110	108	98.0	99.0	100		1.0	1.0		
Production workers (thousands)	83.2	85.0	90.6	87.7	87.0	79.9	82.0	85.1		2.6	3.8		
Average hourly earnings ($)	11.34	11.72	11.74	12.23	12.81	13.65	13.95	14.50		2.2	3.9		
Capital expenditures	556	481	517	630	721								
Product data													
Value of shipments[5]	16,789	18,027	19,841	20,095	20,581	19,855	20,542	21,512	22,207	3.5	4.7	3.2	1.9
3631 Household cooking equipment	3,007	3,162	3,821	3,904	3,766	3,607	3,693	3,959	4,117	2.4	7.2	4.0	2.3
3632 Household refrigerators	4,048	4,309	4,995	5,121	5,356	4,775	4,949	5,109	5,262	3.6	3.2	3.0	–0.4
3633 Household laundry equipment	2,995	3,299	3,671	3,541	3,699	3,587	3,724	3,989	4,149	3.8	7.1	4.0	2.9
3634 Electric housewares and fans	2,653	2,710	2,651	2,875	2,501	2,638	2,778	2,790	2,818	5.3	0.4	1.0	3.0
3635 Household vacuums	1,809	2,015	1,788	1,907	2,341	2,334	2,407	2,571	2,674	3.1	6.8	4.0	3.4
3639 Home appliances nec	2,279	2,531	2,916	2,748	2,919	2,914	2,991	3,094	3,187	2.6	3.4	3.0	2.2
Value of shipments (1992$)	16,789	17,792	19,559	19,834	20,160	19,963	20,775	21,889	22,595	4.1	5.4	3.2	2.9
3631 Household cooking equipment	3,007	3,058	3,727	3,842	3,677	3,549	3,726	3,950	4,108	5.0	6.0	4.0	2.8
3632 Household refrigerators	4,048	4,283	4,916	5,075	5,292	4,927	5,124	5,431	5,594	4.0	6.0	3.0	1.4
3633 Household laundry equipment	2,995	3,312	3,715	3,592	3,721	3,736	3,923	4,178	4,345	5.0	6.5	4.0	4.0
3634 Electric housewares and fans	2,653	2,694	2,662	2,902	2,529	2,742	2,797	2,846	2,874	2.0	1.8	1.0	3.2
3635 Household vacuums	1,809	1,958	1,705	1,809	2,223	2,279	2,393	2,560	2,662	5.0	7.0	4.0	4.6
3639 Home appliances nec	2,279	2,486	2,834	2,614	2,717	2,730	2,812	2,924	3,012	3.0	4.0	3.0	2.6
Trade data													
Value of imports	4,368	4,588	4,945	5,172	5,504	5,805	6,461	6,885	7,300	11.3	6.6	6.0	7.3
Value of exports	2,315	2,488	2,574	2,628	2,802	2,979	2,912	2,750	2,925	–2.2	–5.6	6.4	1.1

[1] Estimate except imports and exports.
[2] Estimate.
[3] Forecast.
[4] Compound annual rate.
[5] For a definition of industry versus product values, see "Getting the Most Out of *Outlook 2000*."
Source: U.S. Department of Commerce: Bureau of the Census; International Trade Administration.

percent each by the Federal Reserve during the summer of 1999. Those rate increases caused mortgage interest rates to increase from approximately 7 percent in the spring to 8 percent by mid-September. However, housing starts remained strong into the fall because of the strength of home sales. Nevertheless, higher mortgage interest rates are likely to dampen the housing market in 2000.

Other factors influencing consumer demand for appliances were the low unemployment rate and the high consumer confidence level. In the first 8 months of 1999, the unemployment rate fluctuated at a 4.2 to 4.3 percent level, the cyclical bottom to that point. Most consumers were well aware of this pleasant situation since news articles about employment generally concerned difficulties finding workers, not finding employment. Consumer confidence reflected those rosy conditions. As measured by the Conference Board, consumer confidence hit a cyclical peak of 139.0 (1985 = 100) in June before dipping in August to 135.8, still an extremely high level. Consumer confidence is important for relatively large purchases such as appliances (see Figure 38-5).

Global Industry Trends

The U.S. appliance industry is a relatively mature industry, with five companies producing a full line of major household appliances—cooking, refrigeration, and laundry—and many more companies specializing in more narrow lines of product categories. There are also many companies that produce small household appliances. Since many appliances have changed only slightly over recent decades, there is little to differentiate one manufacturer's products from another's. The result has been intense price competition as appliances have tended to be considered more and more like commodities by consumers.

About 10 years ago, the industry began a globalization process that started when Electrolux of Sweden acquired White Consolidated Inc. of the United States with the Frigidaire, Kelvinator, and White Westinghouse brands. This was followed by Whirlpool's acquisition of Phillips's European appliance business. Since that time, there have been several international acquisitions, consolidations, and restructurings. Along the way there have been a few missteps and retreats. Today, the two global market leaders are Electrolux and Whirlpool, with a strong presence in most of the important markets around the world. In addition, there are several other manufacturers with a strong market position in one or more local markets.

Many of the manufacturers moving into foreign markets found the competition much more intense and unremitting than they expected. Maytag, which had acquired Hoover with plants in the United Kingdom and Australia in addition to the United States, sold off the foreign operations because of fierce competition. Whirlpool, which entered into several joint ventures in China and India to produce refrigerators and laundry equipment, experienced large losses in China as a result of falling prices caused by industry overcapacity. Another problem in recent years has been currency devaluations and economic difficulties in several countries in Asia and South America as well as Russia, which slowed appliance sales drastically. In addition, the economies of several countries in Europe have been far from robust in recent years, with high rates of unemployment.

In spite of these difficulties, the trend toward globalization will continue. The introduction of the Euro at the beginning of 1999 is having a major impact in the European markets by facilitating price comparisons between goods such as appliances produced in different European countries. This will encourage increased trade among the European countries. Further industry consolidation probably will result as weaker companies are forced out of the industry.

Electronic Commerce

The larger appliance manufacturers have all established corporate Web sites in recent years that generally contain basic information about a company and its products. Many do an excellent job of product promotion by providing extensive product information, such as on-line catalogs, warranty and financing information, and a list of local retail dealers. Some companies also supply additional information such as recent press releases, news articles, executives' speeches, and financial statements. Other information sometimes provided includes recipes, owner's manuals, and tips on using appliances. At present, appliance manufacturers generally do not sell products other than parts and accessories directly to the public from these sites. However, there is substantial interest by manufacturers in the sales potential of the Internet. Some manufacturers have plans for some form of Internet sales. General Electric (GE) plans to sell directly to builders via the Internet, and Whirlpool has a joint venture that will sell several product categories, including appliances, on the Internet.

Some national retail chains, such as Sears and Circuit City, are already selling appliances on the Internet. In addition, appliances are being sold on several Internet shopping sites by companies that sell only through the Internet and do not have brick and mortar stores. Most of these sites sell appliances from several manufacturers. Deliveries of major appliances sold on the Internet by the major retail chains can be arranged easily through the chains' local outlets. Other Internet sellers are using special carriers, since most major appliances exceed the weight limits of national shippers such as United Parcel Service (UPS). Smaller appliances can be sent readily without these delivery problems.

Energy Efficiency

The U.S. Department of Energy (DOE), pursuant to the National Appliance Energy Conservation Act of 1987, sets national energy efficiency standards for several categories of major household appliances, including refrigerators and freezers, water heaters, dishwashers, clothes washers and dryers, and kitchen ranges and ovens. After setting the original standards, DOE has since tightened the standards for several of the product categories at various dates.

One major revision consists of the energy efficiency standards for refrigerators and freezers that will take effect in July 2001. Appliances meeting the new standards will be 23 to 30 percent more efficient than those manufactured in 1997, when the final revised standards were published by DOE. Manufacturers will meet the revised standards through changes such as improved insulation, more efficient motors and compressors, and defrost control sensors.

In September 1998, DOE decided not to set standards for electric ranges, ovens, and microwave ovens, since the design options being considered were not economically justified. However, DOE is expected to publish final rules for gas ranges and ovens in early 2000. The revised standards in the rules would ban the use of gas pilot lights for all ranges and ovens. Currently, pilot lights are banned only for gas ranges and ovens that also have an electric cord, which often is used to power electric clocks and timers. The revised standards would save substantial amounts of natural gas since the pilot lights in these appliances use approximately the same amount of gas that is used in the actual cooking.

Revised standards for water heaters are expected to be published in the fall of 2000. These new standards are expected to result in the use of improved heat traps, flue baffles, flue dampers, insulation, heat exchangers, and electronic ignition.

Revised standards for clothes washers are also expected to be published in fall 2000. Since 90 to 95 percent of the energy used by clothes washers is used to heat the water, reducing the amount of water is an obvious way to save energy. Of the two types of clothes washers, horizontal-axis (front load) washers use one-third the amount of water as vertical-axis (top load) washers use. DOE has decided to treat both types of washers as being in the same category, with the same applicable energy efficiency standard, rather than in two categories. While some improvements can be made in vertical-axis washers, such as the use of sprayers for washing and rinsing, they will never be as efficient as horizontal-axis machines. However, more than 95 percent of the washers sold in the United States are vertical-axis washers. In addition, basic horizontal-axis washers currently cost about double what a basic vertical-axis washer costs.

In addition to energy standards, DOE and the U.S. Environmental Protection Agency have created the Energy Star label, which is used to identify the more energy-efficient products on the market. Appliances have been eligible to carry the label since 1996. The appliance categories in SIC 363 that are eligible for the label are refrigerators, clothes washers, and dishwashers. The program may be extended soon to cover water heaters. Energy Star–labeled appliances significantly exceed existing DOE energy standards: dishwashers by 13 percent, refrigerators by 20 percent, and clothes washers by 100 percent. Consumers can be assured that an Energy Star–labeled appliance is a high-performance product that will have a substantially reduced operating cost over its lifetime.

The voluntary Energy Star label is in addition to the Energy Guide label that is required by the U.S. Federal Trade Commission. That label, which has been required since 1980, shows the estimated kilowatt-hours of electricity consumed per year on a horizontal graph, with the end points showing the highest and lowest amounts consumed by models of similar size. The estimated annual operating cost also is provided. These Energy Guide labels are required for refrigerators, refrigerator-freezers, freezers, dishwashers, clothes washers, and water heaters.

Premium Appliances

One bright spot for the appliance industry in the past few years has been the rising demand for premium, high-priced appliances. In recent decades, appliances increasingly have been viewed as commodities. Since there were relatively few product advancements, manufacturers often competed on price. However, fueled by rising income and consumer confidence caused by the strong stock market and an especially long economic expansion, consumers increasingly are opting for high-end appliances as opposed to the basic models. Also contributing to the demand for such appliances is the fact that the baby boom generation has entered its high-income years. The result has been booming sales of premium appliances, while sales of cheaper appliances have been relatively flat.

There are several examples of manufacturers trying to meet the needs of this swelling consumer demand. In 1997, Maytag introduced its new top-of-the-line washer, the Neptune. This horizontal-axis product generated a lot of interest because of its energy- and water-saving ability. It was successfully priced at $1,000, substantially more expensive than any of its competitors' products. Maytag's success with the Neptune spurred other manufacturers' planned introductions of appliances with new features for the high end of the market. In 1998, Whirlpool introduced a high-efficiency vertical-axis washing machine with a spray rinse system and water temperature sensor that reduced water and energy consumption substantially compared with regular fill and rinse washers.

GE introduced the Triton dishwasher in August 1999. This washer has a third wash arm above the top rack that cuts the need for prerinsing. It features a speed cycle that cuts the washing time for lightly soiled or prerinsed dishes from the usual 90 minutes to 60 minutes. It is also especially quiet because of its improved motor and insulation. Maytag's new Intellisense dishwasher senses how dirty dishes are and adjusts the water temperature and cycle time accordingly. It adds washing time if the consumer doesn't use enough detergent.

Several manufacturers' top-end side-by-side refrigerators now feature water filtration. Sub-Zero has a refrigerator model with multiple temperature zones that allows consumers to program specific temperatures for specific foods. It also has an alarm in case the door is left open.

Several appliance manufacturers have also introduced faster-cooking appliances using differing technologies, often combined with microwaves. GE's Advantium oven uses halogen light waves and microwaves to cook the outside of food much as conventional radiant heat does but also to penetrate the surface so that the inside is cooked at the same time. Frigidaire has a new convection oven with a fan system controlled by the cook, while Maytag is introducing a household oven with jet air impingement cooking that shoots hot air from the top of the oven around the food and out the bottom, to be filtered and recirculated. That system is already used in commercial cooking.

Industry Growth for the Next 1 and 5 Years

Appliance product shipments are expected to increase 3.1 percent in 2000 in constant dollars from the record levels of 1999. The economy is expected to grow at a slower rate in the year 2000, with GDP falling from the 4 percent rate of growth of 1999 to an estimated 2 percent growth rate in 2000 (see Table 38-8). Over the next 5 years, U.S. shipments of household appliances are expected to increase at an estimated compound annual rate of 2 percent.

Real disposable income is expected to rise about 3 percent in 2000, while the increase in total consumption is expected to be slightly more than 2 percent as the consumer savings rate rises out of negative territory. The interest rate increases by the Federal Reserve in 1999 should slow the housing market somewhat in 2000 for both new housing starts and housing resales. Housing starts are expected to decline to about 1.5 million starts from slightly over 1.6 million in 1999. In addition, rising interest rates on installment purchases' such as major appliances will discourage appliance sales.

In the United States, most of the demand for household appliances is due to housing construction, kitchen remodeling, and replacements, since for basic appliances such as ranges, refrigerators, and laundry equipment, the market is virtually saturated. However, there appears to be a trend for more households to have a second of some types of appliances. For example, nearly 20 percent of homes are estimated to have two refrigerators. Many dens or family rooms with wet bars now have a small under-the-counter refrigerator. There are even outdoor refrigerators for use with backyard barbecues. There is often a second microwave oven in the home. Aiding this trend is the increasing size of the houses currently being built, providing the needed space for these extra appliances (see Table 38-5).

Population growth and the number of household formations are key underlying determinants of new housing and appliance demand. The outlook for demand in this regard is favorable, since current expectations are that the U.S. population will increase about 0.8 percent annually over the next 5 years and the number of households will increase 1.0 percent annually.

As was mentioned before, the baby boom generation has been an important factor in the increased demand for high-end appliances. This cohort, now 34 to 53 years of age, will continue to be an important source of consumer appliance spending for several more years as its members pass through their high-income years. Consumers in this age range have the highest average annual expenditures for major appliances and tend to replace an old appliance with an improved model with more advanced features.

Global Market Prospects

In 1999, appliance imports increased approximately 7 percent to an estimated $6.9 billion (see Table 38-8). The leading suppliers were China, Mexico, Canada, South Korea, and Taiwan. China continued to increase its market share as its imports increased about 16 percent during that year. It now accounts for about 30 percent of total appliance imports. It is a particularly important source of small electrical appliances, accounting for about 45 percent of total imports of that category in 1999. As a result of China's low labor compensation rates, it is likely that that country will continue to increase its market share for those labor-intensive products. Mexico is a particularly important source of refrigerators, accounting for about 42 percent of imports. Canada is important for laundry products and vacuum cleaners, accounting for nearly 40 percent of imports in both categories. For trade in the larger appliances, both Mexico and Canada benefit from relatively low transportation costs resulting from their proximity to the U.S. market. In addition, leading U.S. appliance companies have interests in appliance production in both countries for distribution in the United States. As a result of Mexico's low wage rates and proximity, additional shifts in the production of large appliances such as refrigerators, stoves, and laundry equipment are likely to occur between the United States and Mexico (see Table 38-9).

U.S. exports of appliances totaled an estimated $2.7 billion in 1999, a decrease of approximately 6 percent. U.S. exports were adversely affected by the strong U.S. dollar as well as economic troubles in several Latin American countries. Exports decreased in all appliance categories except vacuum cleaners, where they increased only marginally. The leading U.S. export markets in 1999 were Canada, Mexico, the United Kingdom, Japan, and Germany. Canada and Mexico accounted for over half of U.S. exports: 35 percent and 18 percent, respectively. However, a portion of the exports to Canada and Mexico were parts for use in appliance production. Many of the appliances produced with those parts were shipped back to this country.

The most recent U.S. tariff reductions for appliances occurred over the 5 years beginning in 1995 as a result of the Uruguay Round of tariff negotiations. The final tariff cut for appliances became effective in 1999. These reductions resulted in the complete elimination of U.S. tariffs on many larger appliances, including refrigerators and freezers, stoves, water heaters, vacuum cleaners, and disposers. The remaining tariffs on large appliances, such as those on laundry equipment and

TABLE 38-9: U.S. Trade Patterns in Household Appliances[1] in 1998
(millions of dollars; percent)

Exports			Imports		
Regions[2]	Value[3]	Share, %	Regions[2]	Value[3]	Share, %
NAFTA	1,504	52	NAFTA	1,908	30
Latin America	444	15	Latin America	78	1
Western Europe	452	16	Western Europe	969	15
Japan/Chinese Economic Area	156	5	Japan/Chinese Economic Area	2,506	39
Other Asia	76	3	Other Asia	976	15
Rest of world	281	10	Rest of world	25	0
World	2,912	100	World	6,461	100
Top Five Countries	Value	Share, %	Top Five Countries	Value	Share, %
Canada	1,005	35	China	1,865	29
Mexico	499	17	Mexico	1,334	21
United Kingdom	105	4	Canada	574	9
Venezuela	90	3	South Korea	521	8
France	74	3	Taiwan	439	7

[1] SIC 363.
[2] For definitions of regional groupings, see "Getting the Most Out of *Outlook 2000*."
[3] Values may not sum to total due to rounding.
Source: U.S. Department of Commerce, Bureau of the Census.

dishwashers, are now relatively low, ranging from 1.4 to 3.4 percent. While tariffs on some small appliances, such as travel irons, also were eliminated completely, the overall tariffs on small electrical appliances were not reduced as much as they were for larger appliances. In fact, for several small appliances, tariffs were not reduced at all. The current tariffs for small electrical appliances generally range from 2 to 5.3 percent.

Some special programs permit duty-free entry of appliances into the United States. Mexico and Canada benefit from NAFTA and the U.S.–Canadian Free Trade Agreement. For developing countries, the most important program is the Generalized System of Preferences (GSP), which permits certain products to enter duty-free from eligible developing countries. All appliances are eligible for GSP treatment. However, all the major suppliers of appliances to the United States, including China, South Korea, Taiwan, and Hong Kong, are not eligible for GSP treatment. Thailand is the only country among the 15 largest suppliers of appliances to the United States that is eligible for GSP treatment. It appears that tariffs on appliances are now so low that duty-free treatment is not enough to offset the low labor rates in China or the advantages the more developed countries gain by producing high-quality appliances for their own home markets that are similar to those used in this country.

John M. Harris, Office of Consumer Goods, U.S. Department of Commerce, (202) 482-1178, john_harris@ita.doc.gov, September 1999.

LAWN AND GARDEN EQUIPMENT

Lawn and garden equipment (SIC 3524) consists of a variety of non-hand-held consumer outdoor power equipment. This group includes riding lawn mowers, walk-behind lawn mowers, walk-behind rotary tillers, electric lawn mowers, leaf and snow blowers, and similar equipment. Not included in SIC 3524 are commercial mowing and turf equipment and grounds care equipment, which are included under SIC 3523. Hand-held lawn and garden shears and pruners are included under SIC 3421, and other garden hand tools are included under SIC 3423.

Global Industry Trends

U.S. exports of lawn and garden equipment amounted to nearly three times the value of imports in 1998. This positive trade balance, which is typical for the lawn and garden equipment industry, is expected to continue. The markets for U.S. lawn and garden exports tend to be the major western industrialized nations, and exports thus are tied to the overall strength of those economies. U.S. domestic exports dropped 1.8 percent from 1997 to 1998 for all lawn and garden equipment, largely as a result of a 5 percent decline in exports to Germany. The German market has been weaker than that in the rest of Europe because of its dependence on manufacturers and exports. As the rest of Europe and Asia recover, the German economy is expected to benefit. The first 6 months of 1999 showed an increase in U.S. exports to the Netherlands over the same period in 1998, with unexpectedly strong growth in the first half of 1999. Notably, imports from China increased substantially from 1992 to 1998. In those 6 years, China moved from the sixteenth largest U.S. import source for lawn and garden equipment to the fifth.

The lawn and garden equipment industry is influenced by several factors. Although it is a fairly steady industry, it is very dependent on weather conditions, and its sales thus can be difficult to predict. There is also currently a shift away from smaller retail lawn and garden equipment dealers toward large home distribution centers. Environmental issues and changes in engine emission standards are creating new regulations for manufacturers to comply with. Lawn and garden equipment tends to track small engine sales, and industry sources indicate a positive outlook for engines.

Domestic Trends

The industry realized a very strong 1998 model year. Total product shipments rose about 15 percent from 1997. According to an Outdoor Power Equipment Institute (OPEI) study, unit shipments of walk-behind powered mowers, all riding units, and tillers rose approximately 9 percent from 1997 to 1998. Both exports and imports were up during the 1998 model year as well. While the 1999 and 2000 model years are expected to be down from 1998, no overall serious drop in the industry is forecast for the next 5 years.

Recent lifestyle trends in American households are having a substantial effect on the lawn and garden industry. According to *Yard & Garden* magazine, the rapidly growing commercial lawn and landscape contractor sector will be the primary factor in changes in the industry. As dual-income American families are making more money on average, they also find themselves with less personal time. This is one key reason why landscape and lawn services are becoming increasingly popular. According to a study conducted by the Associated Landscape Contractors of America (ALCA), American households spent an estimated $16.8 billion on landscape, lawn care, and tree services in 1998, a $2.2 billion increase over 1997. This mirrors strong market growth as well as peer pressure to keep a well-maintained yard. Consumers consider this an investment, as a well-maintained lawn can increase real estate value 15 percent, according to the ALCA. *Lawn & Garden* magazine expects that unless lawn and garden equipment dealers incorporate these rising landscaping demands, the projected dealer population will drop from approximately 25,000 dealer locations in 1995 to 16,000 in 2005.

A report from the U.S. Bureau of Labor Statistics shows that the number of weekend work hours for professionals and managers has increased for both men and women since 1982. The study also found that the average number of workweek hours for both men and women has increased since 1976. This leaves less time for individuals to spend maintaining their lawns, and they are therefore more inclined to hire others to provide this service. Women have increased their presence in the U.S. workforce, and their jobs are professional and managerial, according to the U.S. Bureau of Labor Statistics.

A large segment of lawn and garden equipment sold in North America comes from large retailers, discount retailers, and discount home improvement warehouses. These outlets include stores such as Sears, Wal-Mart, Home Depot, and Costco. Consumers who choose this approach place a greater emphasis on price, convenience, and availability. While most of these stores do not service the equipment after purchase, some are beginning to establish their own service departments.

Environmental and Safety Issues

Several studies indicate that American consumers are increasingly insistent on lawn and garden equipment that is environmentally sound and safe. They also are looking to purchase more durable high-quality products. The white paper *Catalyst for Change* published by *Yard & Garden* magazine states that as consumers become increasingly concerned about environmental issues, they support equipment that has been proved to be environmentally friendly. This is a key advantage for manufacturers in producing products to minimize emissions.

The lawn and garden equipment industry has made significant advances in terms of environmental and safety concerns and ease of operation. Recent safety features on lawn and garden tractors include an operator presence control (OPC) that automatically shuts down the engine and attachments when the operator vacates the seat. Independent suspension was introduced on riding mowers, allowing better stability and rider comfort. Today's engines are typically 70 percent cleaner than those sold in 1990. The Ferris ProCut Z, created by Ferris Industries, Inc., was the first riding lawn mower with independent suspension. This traction feature allows all the wheels to remain on the ground for better mower stability. Toro, a leading name brand manufacturer, introduced new models of cordless electric mowers that are quiet, require little maintenance, and allow a significant amount of mowing time after just one battery charge.

One of the most significant changes affecting the lawn and garden equipment industry has been more stringent engine emissions standards. In March 1999, the U.S. Environmental Protection Agency (EPA) published a regulatory announcement detailing Phase 2 emissions standards for small spark-ignition (SI) non-hand-held engines. The Phase 2 emissions standards apply to Class I (under 225 cc) and Class II (over 225 cc) engines for non-hand-held engines, such as lawn mowers and lawn tractors. This follows the July 1995 Phase 1 regulations, which took effect in 1997. Phase 2 standards are scheduled to be implemented between 2001 and 2007. According to the EPA, these strict Phase 2 standards are expected to reduce hydrocarbons (HC) and oxides of nitrogen (HC and NO_x) 59 percent beyond existing Phase 1 standards.

The emissions standards have been established to aid compliance with the National Ambient Air Quality Standards (NAAQS) under the Clean Air Act. According to the EPA, small SI engines account for about one-tenth of U.S. mobile source HC emissions, which play a role in forming ozone. Phase 2 standards require engine manufacturers to build cleaner and more durable engines in addition to ensuring that they continue to meet these standards throughout the life of the engine. EPA estimates that the new standards will reduce fuel consumption 15 percent. Taking into account the cutback on fuel consumption generated by the new emissions standards, an EPA study found that the projected costs of the new engine requirements are quite low.

The transition schedule between Phase 1 and Phase 2, to be implemented from 2001 to 2007, is designed to alleviate the compliance burdens that engine manufacturers could potentially encounter. Overall, the EPA is expecting a smooth transition, considering the technological changes already being used on Class I engines to attain these standards.

The EPA had originally planned on publishing Phase 2 SI engine emissions standards for hand-held equipment around the same time as those for non-hand-held equipment. These standards have been postponed because of information on recent technologies that could require more rigid standards than those initially proposed. A final decision is expected in March 2000.

To reduce emissions in California, the California Air Resources Board (CARB) implemented Tier I emission standards in June 1995 and extended the implementation of Tier II standards until January 2000. These standards are meant to control emissions from small off-road engines found in lawn and garden equipment as well as other types of maintenance utility equipment. In terms of lawn and garden equipment, CARB Tier II standards will require all rotary mowers to have overhead valve technology in California. Since their implementation, Tier I standards have succeeded in reducing emissions 30 to 70 percent. Tier II regulations pertaining to non-hand-held equipment, primarily lawn mowers, require a 67 percent emission reduction by 2010. While California's standards are more stringent than EPA regulations, the EPA stated that for the most part its new Phase 2 standards coincide with California emissions standards.

Electronic Commerce

As the popularity of the Internet grows, lawn and garden equipment manufacturers and dealers are attempting to keep up with this trend. Realizing the increasing need to utilize electronic commerce measures in the lawn and garden equipment industry, many companies have created Web sites. Those sites are designed to help promote lawn and garden equipment, answer questions about product maintenance and design, and encourage safe practices. A few companies are beginning to offer online ordering of lawn and garden equipment directly through their Web sites.

Internally, many lawn and garden equipment manufacturers are implementing in-house network systems that increase information flow and communication with dealers. This in turn improves customer relations. This technology allows dealers to check the availability of parts, place equipment orders, and verify the status of orders on the Internet. OPEI developed a standards-based electronic data interchange (EDI). These guidelines are meant to facilitate consistent transactions between manufacturers, dealers, and distributors. A report put out by OPEI in March 1999 stated that this EDI format is the only universal model for the outdoor power industry that ensures the use of one standard of communication between all industry players. The goal is to improve efficiency, which would help reduce overall the cost of doing business and lead to better customer service. EDI is used in industry warranty claims, product registrations, claims, purchase orders, and invoices.

Projections of Industry and Trade Growth for the Next 1 and 5 Years

Factors affecting demand for lawn and garden equipment include weather conditions, consumer confidence, housing starts, and employment.

Industry statistics show that overall, constant dollar shipments of lawn and garden equipment have grown since 1990. The weather is a major factor in determining sales of lawn and garden equipment. The full effect of the 1999 drought that hit most of the United States on the industry has not been determined. Most lawn and garden equipment is purchased in the spring. Combined with an April 1999 industry prediction of slower 1999 domestic sales compared with those in 1998, the drought most likely will reinforce this outlook. The OPEI stated that 1999 model year shipments of snow throwers declined 53 percent from the level in 1998. This drop is attributed to mild winter weather conditions in certain parts of the United States. The drought is expected to have the same effect on equipment used mainly in the summer. This includes gas-powered riding and walk-behind mowers, walk-behind rotary tillers, and electric lawn mowers.

According to recent statistics on U.S. housing starts, total single-unit structures have been increasing steadily for the most part over the last several years. Single-unit housing is the most appropriate indicator in terms of housing starts, which affect the lawn and garden equipment industry. Generally, when people purchase a single-unit house, they also purchase some type of lawn and garden equipment. The number was expected to increase for 1999, but the forecast for the next 5 years shows total housing starts as well as single-unit structures decreasing.

Overall, consumer confidence was strong in the first 6 months of 1999. According to the Conference Board Consumer Research Center, the Consumer Confidence Index dipped for the first time in July 1999 after 8 months of gains. This does not necessarily indicate that consumer confidence will continue to drop considerably over the long term. While consumer confidence is always considered in determining the outlook for lawn and garden equipment, it is not expected that a slight drop in consumer confidence will have an extensive negative effect on the industry.

A combination of these industry indicators of forecast industry shipments of lawn and garden equipment, weather conditions, housing starts, consumer confidence, and labor statistics are used in determining a forecast for lawn and garden equipment. This industry typically realizes steady overall growth. Inflation for lawn and garden equipment has averaged approximately 1 percent annually and is expected to continue at that rate. Constant dollar shipments of lawn and garden equipment are expected to decline approximately 0.8 percent in the year 2000. This follows an estimated 3.8 percent drop in 1999 after a strong 1998 model year (see Table 38-10). After these 2 years

TABLE 38-10: Lawn and Garden Equipment (SIC 3524) Trends and Forecasts
(millions of dollars except as noted)

	1992	1993	1994	1995	1996	1997[1]	1998[1]	1999[2]	2000[3]	Percent Change 97–98	98–99	99–00	96–00[4]
Industry data													
Value of shipments[5]	5,164	5,828	6,836	6,971	6,823	6,994	7,163	6,892	6,836	2.4	–3.8	–0.8	0.0
Value of shipments (1992$)	5,164	5,788	6,682	6,723	6,480	6,642	6,861	6,621	6,501	3.3	–3.5	–1.8	0.1
Total employment (thousands)	24.9	25.7	28.0	27.7	27.0	29.1	27.7	27.0		–4.8	–2.5		
Production workers (thousands)	19.9	20.5	22.4	22.3	21.5	23.3	21.8	21.5		–6.4	–1.4		
Average hourly earnings ($)	10.73	10.88	10.56	10.26	11.05	11.35	11.97	11.62		5.5	–2.9		
Capital expenditures	125	92.0	129	126	120								
Product data													
Value of shipments[5]	4,344	4,884	5,730	6,061	5,908	6,056	6,202	5,968	5,919	2.4	–3.8	–0.8	0.0
Value of shipments (1992$)	4,344	4,850	5,601	5,845	5,611	5,751	5,941	5,733	5,630	3.3	–3.5	–1.8	0.1
Trade data													
Value of imports	134	162	175	172	225	264	260	267	274	–1.5	2.7	2.6	5.0
Value of exports	599	671	725	749	705	771	757	835	876	–1.8	10.3	4.9	5.6

[1] Estimate except imports and exports.
[2] Estimate.
[3] Forecast.
[4] Compound annual rate.
[5] For a definition of industry versus product values, see "Getting the Most Out of *Outlook 2000.*"
Source: U.S. Department of Commerce: Bureau of the Census; International Trade Administration.

TABLE 38-11: U.S. Trade Patterns in Lawn and Garden Equipment[1] in 1998
(millions of dollars; percent)

Exports			Imports		
Regions[2]	Value[3]	Share, %	Regions[2]	Value[3]	Share, %
NAFTA	203	27	NAFTA	149	57
Latin America	37	5	Latin America	0	0
Western Europe	404	53	Western Europe	31	12
Japan/Chinese Economic Area	22	3	Japan/Chinese Economic Area	79	30
Other Asia	5	1	Other Asia	1	0
Rest of world	88	12	Rest of world	0	0
World	757	100	World	260	100
Top Five Countries	Value	Share, %	Top Five Countries	Value	Share, %
Canada	194	26	Canada	88	34
France	124	16	Mexico	61	23
United Kingdom	67	9	Japan	59	23
Australia	56	7	Sweden	14	5
Germany	48	6	China	9	4

[1] SIC 3524.
[2] For definitions of regional groupings, see "Getting the Most Out of *Outlook 2000.*"
[3] Values may not sum to total due to rounding.
Source: U.S. Department of Commerce, Bureau of the Census.

of a slight downturn, the industry most likely will continue to grow about 1 percent annually until 2004.

The strong U.S. export market most likely will continue to show average annual growth for the next 5 years of approximately 5 percent. Imports can be expected to remain steady and continue to grow about 2 percent annually during this period.

Global Market Prospects

Total U.S. exports and imports of lawn and garden equipment have realized steady growth. U.S. exports of lawn and garden equipment totaled $757 million in 1998. Canada continues to be the top export destination for lawn and garden equipment. U.S. domestic exports to Canada totaled $194 million in 1998, compared with $183 million in 1997. Trade data for the first 6 months of 1999 indicated a similar trend. Following behind Canada for U.S. exports in 1998 were France, the United Kingdom, Australia, and Germany (see Table 38-11). Japan was the tenth largest U.S. export market for this industry in 1998, totaling $15 million. U.S. exports of all riding mowers accounted for 35 percent ($218 million) of total exports for lawn and garden equipment in 1998. This number increased from 1997, with riding mowers accounting for $210 million of total U.S. exports. Exports of electric lawn mowers were considerably lower than they had been in previous years. Total electric lawn mower exports for 1998 were $8 million, compared with $84 million in 1995.

Lawn and garden equipment imports totaled $260 million in 1998. The top five U.S. import sources in 1998 were Canada with $88 million, Mexico, Japan, Sweden, and China (see Table 38-11). While Canada still retains the top position for lawn and garden equipment imports to the United States, the first 6 months of 1999 showed a sharp percentage decrease compared with 1998 figures. Interestingly, imports from Mexico in the first 6 months of 1999 exceeded the 1998 total. Total U.S. imports of riding mowers in 1998 were $29 million. Canada accounted for $28 million of this total, followed by Japan with less than $1 million. Canada was also the top U.S. import source for electric mowers, with $17 million.

Linda Burlingame, U.S. Department of Commerce, Office of Consumer Goods, (202) 482-0380, Linda_Burlingame@ita.doc.gov, September 1999.

REFERENCES

U.S. Government

To order U.S. Bureau of the Census documents, call (301) 457-4100. A growing number of Census documents and services, including shipment and demographic data, are available via the Internet. The Census Home Page is http://www.census.gov.

Civilian Labor Force by Sex, Age, Race, and Hispanic Origin, 1986, 1996, and Projected 2006, Bureau of Labor Statistics, U.S. Department of Labor, Washington, DC 20212. (202) 606-5711, http://stats.bls.gov/emphome.htm.

Consumer Expenditure Survey, Bureau of Labor Statistics, U.S. Department of Labor, Washington, DC 20212. (202) 606-6900, http://stats.bls.gov/csxhome.htm.

Employment and Earnings, Bureau of Labor Statistics, U.S. Department of Labor, Washington, DC 20212. (202) 606-7705, http://stats.bls.gov/ceshome.htm.

1992 Census of Manufactures, Bureau of the Census, U.S. Department of Commerce, Washington, DC 20233. http://www.census.gov/prod/www/abs/msmfg02a.html.

1996 Annual Survey of Manufactures, Bureau of the Census, U.S. Department of Commerce, Washington, DC 20233. http://www.census.gov/prod/www/abs/m96as1.html.

Personal Consumption Expenditures, Bureau of Economic Analysis, U.S. Department of Commerce, Washington, DC 20230. (202) 606-9375.

Population Estimates and Projections, Bureau of the Census, U.S. Department of Commerce, Washington, DC 20233. (301) 457-2422, http://www.census.gov/population/www.

Producer Price Indexes, Bureau of Labor Statistics, U.S. Department of Labor, Washington, DC 20212. (202) 606-7705, http://stats.bls.gov/ppihome.htm.

Survey of Current Business, Bureau of Economic Analysis, U.S. Department of Commerce, Washington, DC 20230. (202) 606-9900, http://www.bea.doc.gov/bea/pubs.htm.

Trade Associations

National Association of Home Builders (NAHB), 1201 15 Street, Washington, DC 20005. (800) 368-5242 or (202) 822-0555; fax: (202) 822-0377; http://www.nahb.com.

National Association of Realtors (NAR), 700 11 Street, NW, Washington, DC 20001. (202) 383-1225; fax: (202) 383-7563; http://nar.realtor.com/databank/home.htm.

Household Furniture

American Furniture Manufacturers Association, P.O. Box HP-7 High Point, NC 27261. (336) 884-5000; fax: (336) 884-5303; http://www.afmahp.org.

Bed Times: The Business Journal for the Sleep Products Industry, International Sleep Products Association, 501 Wythe Street, Alexandria, VA 22314. (703) 683-8371; fax: (703) 683-4503; http://www.sleepproducts.org.

The Board of Govenors of the Federal Reserve System, http://www.bog.frb.fed.us/rnd.htm.

Furniture/Today: The Weekly Business Newspaper of the Furniture Industry, Cahners Business Information. 7025 Albert Pick Road, Greensboro, NC 27409. (800) 395-2329; fax: (336)-605-1143; http://www.furnituretoday.com.

Gomez.com: The eCommerce Authority. http://www.gomezadvisors.com

HFN: The Weekly Newspaper of Home Products Retailing, Fairchild Publications, Inc., P.O. Box 10521, Riverton NJ 08076-0521. (800) 424-8698; fax: (212) 630-4201; http://www.hfnmag.com.

International Home Furnishings Marketing Association, Inc., 300 South Main Street, P.O. Box 5687, High Point, NC 27262. (336) 889-0203; fax: (336) 889-7460; http://www.ihfc.com.

1996 Annual Survey of Manufacturers: Product of Value Shipments, U.S. Census Bureau. http://tier2.census.gov/asm/asm3_25.htm.

1997 Economic Census: Manufacturing Industry Series: Household Furniture (Except Wood and Metal) Manufacturing, U.S. Census Bureau, http://www.census.gov/prod/www/abs/97ecmani.html.

1997 Economic Census: Manufacturing Industry Series: Mattress Manufacturing, U.S. Census Bureau. http://www.census.gov/prod/www/abs/97ecmani.html.

1997 Economic Census: Manufacturing Industry Series: Metal Household Furniture Manufacturing, U.S. Census Bureau. http://www.census.gov/prod/www/abs/97ecmani.html.

1997 Economic Census: Manufacturing Industry Series: Wood Television, Radio, and Sewing Machine Cabinet Manufacturing, U.S. Census Bureau. http://www.census.gov/prod/www/abs/97ecmani.html.

Household Appliances

Call the U.S. Bureau of the Census at (301) 763-4100 for information about how to order Census documents.

Appliance, Dana Chase Publications, Inc., 1110 Jorie Boulevard, Oak Brook, IL 60522. (630) 990-3484.

Appliance Manufacturer, Business News Publishing Co., 5900 Harper Road, Suite 105, Solon, OH 44139. (216) 349-3060.

Dealerscope Consumer Electronics Marketplace, North American Publishing Co., 401 North Broad Street, Philadelphia, PA 19108. (215) 238-5300.

Electric Housewares and Fans, Current Industrial Reports, MA-36E, Bureau of the Census, U.S. Department of Commerce, Washington, DC 20233. (301) 457-1604.

HFN Home Furnishing News, Fairchild Publications, 7 West 34 St., New York, NY 10001. (212) 630-4000.

Household Appliances, 1992 Census of Manufactures, MC92-1-36B, Bureau of the Census, U.S. Department of Commerce, Washington, DC 20233.

Household Cooking Appliance Manufacturing, 1997 Economic Census, EC97M-335221, EC97M-3352C, Bureau of the Census, U.S. Department of Commerce, Washington, DC 20233.

Household Laundry Equipment Manufacturing, 1997 Economic Census, EC97M-335224, EC97M-3352E, Bureau of the Census, U.S. Department of Commerce, Washington, DC 20233.

Household Refrigerator and Home Freezer Manufacturing, 1997 Economic Census, EC97M-335222, EC97M-3352D, Bureau of the Census, U.S. Department of Commerce, Washington, DC 20233.

Household Vacuum Cleaner Manufacturing, 1997 Economic Census, EC97M-335212, EC97M-3352B, Bureau of the Census, U.S. Department of Commerce, Washington, DC 20233.

Major Household Appliances, Current Industrial Reports, MA-36F, Bureau of the Census, U.S. Department of Commerce, Washington, DC 20233. (301) 457-1604.

1996 Annual Survey of Manufactures, Bureau of the Census, U.S. Department of Commerce, Washington, DC 20233.

Lawn and Garden Equipment

Associated Landscape Contractors of America, 1250 I Street, NW, Suite 500, Washington DC 20005-3922. (202) 789-2900; fax: (202) 789-1893.

California Air Resources Board (CARB), Mobile Sources Lab, 9420 Telstar Avenue, El Monte, CA 91731. www.arb.ca.gov.

Catalyst for Change, Outdoor Power Equipment, "White Paper," *Yard & Garden* magazine, Johnson Hill Press, Inc., P.O. Box 803, Fort Atkinson, WI 53538-0803. (920) 563-6388; fax: (920) 564-1699.

Conference Board Reports, Consumer Confidence Index, 845 Third Avenue, New York, NY 10022-6679. (212) 759-0900; fax: (212) 980-7014.

Engines and Turbines and Farm Machinery and Equipment, 1992 Census of Manufacturers, SIC 3524, Bureau of the Census, U.S. Department of Commerce, Washington DC 20233.

Farm Machinery and Lawn and Garden Equipment 1997, 1997 Current Industrial Reports, Series MA35A (97)-1, Bureau of the Census, U.S. Department of Commerce, Washington DC 20233.

Monthly Labor Review, U.S. Bureau of Labor Statistics, Division of Labor Force Statistics, 2 Massachusetts Avenue, NE, room 4675, Washington DC 20212. Fax: (202) 606-6426.

National Drought Summary, National Oceanic and Atmospheric Administration, U.S. Department of Commerce, Camp Springs, MD 20746.

Outdoor Power Equipment Institute (OPEI), 341 South Patrick Street, Old Town Alexandria, VA 22314. (703) 549-7600; fax: 703-549-7604; www.opei.mow.org.

U.S. Consumer Product Safety Commission, Office of Information and Public Affairs, Washington, DC 20207.

U.S. Environmental Protection Agency, Office of Mobile Sources, National Vehicle and Fuel Emissions Laboratory, 2000 Traverwood Drive, Ann Arbor, MI 48105.

Weekly Weather and Crop Bulletin, NOAA/USDA Joint Agriculture Weather Facility, U.S. Department of Agriculture, South Building, Washington DC 20250. (202) 720-1444.

■ RELATED CHAPTERS

6: Construction
42: Retailing

RECREATIONAL EQUIPMENT
Economic and Trade Trends

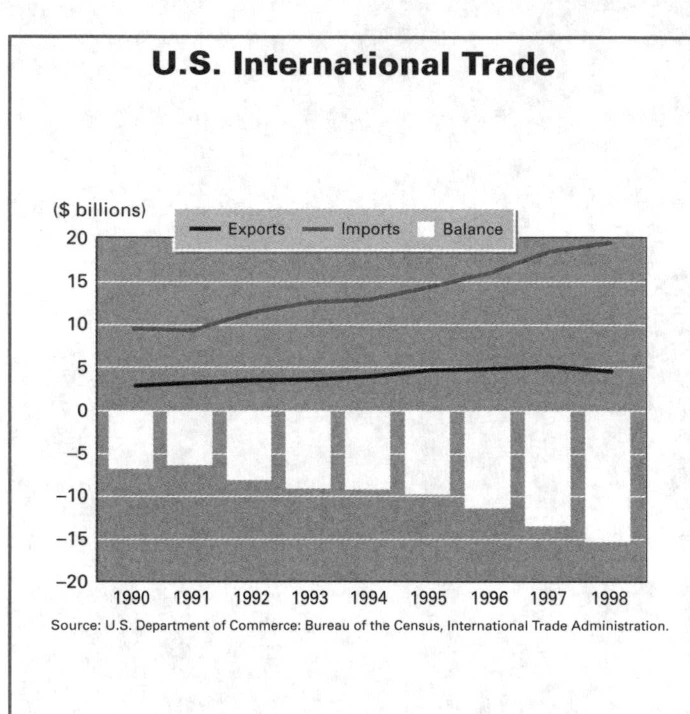

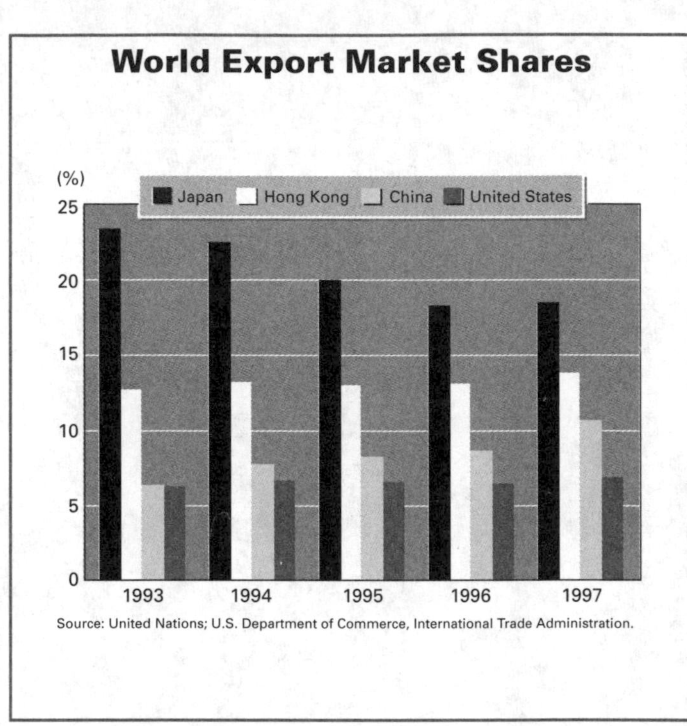

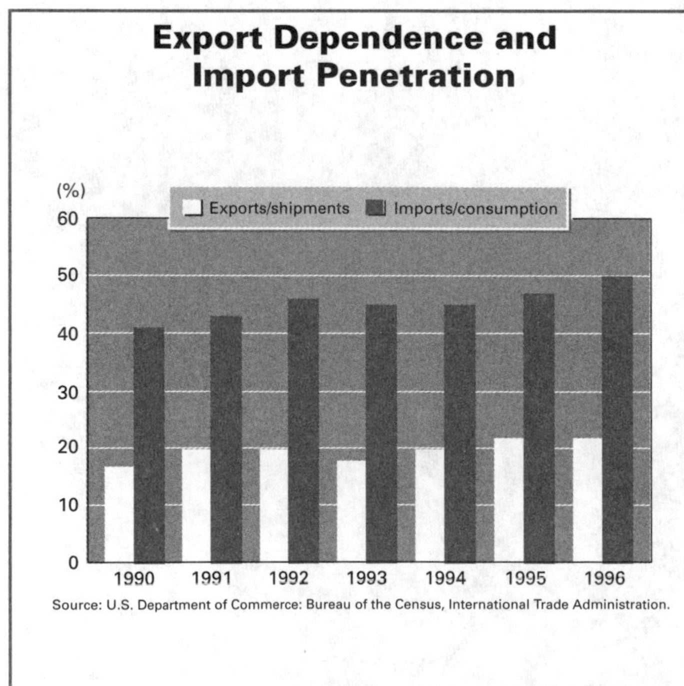

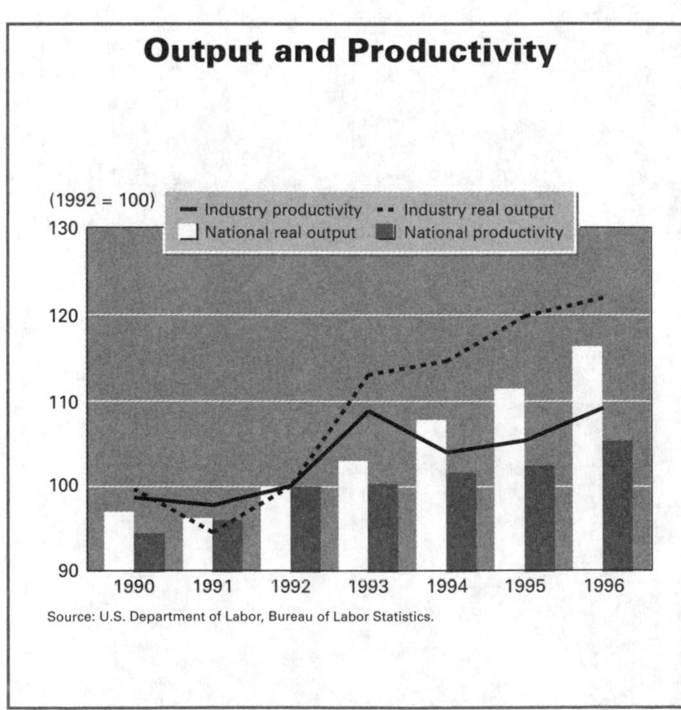

See "Getting the Most Out of *Outlook 2000*" for definitions of terms.

39

Recreational Equipment

INDUSTRY DEFINITION This chapter includes analyses of SIC 3949, sporting and athletic equipment; SIC 3942 and 3944, dolls, toys, and games; SIC 37511, bicycles and parts; SIC 37512, motorcycles and parts; and SIC 3732, boat building and repairing. Among the products not included in this chapter are camping equipment, sports apparel and footwear, coin-operated games, large ships and vessels, and recreational motor homes and camping trailers. More specific industry definitions appear with certain individual industry descriptions.

GLOBAL INDUSTRY TRENDS

International trade is an important aspect of the recreational equipment industry because many of these companies import lower-quality branded products, use overseas parts, or face stiff competition from importers. Labor is an important input in the production of many recreational products, particularly entry-level products. The less developed countries have wage rates that are significantly lower than those in the United States. Many firms import their products with U.S. brand names; this practice is prevalent in the dolls, toys, games, sporting goods, and bicycle industries. The motorcycle industry relies on imported parts from both developed and developing countries; many of those parts are no longer manufactured in the United States. Another major factor in the competitiveness of imports has been the strength of the U.S. dollar relative to foreign currencies. As a result of these trends for both completed products and parts, the ratio of imports to apparent consumption in the recreational equipment industry is high: 52 percent in 1998. The exception to this trend is the U.S. boating industry, where that ratio was only 14 percent in 1998.

A trend that spans virtually all industries in the recreational equipment sector is the increasing demand for "made-in-the-USA" products. U.S. products such as golf clubs, Harley-Davidson motorcycles, inboard-outdrive boats, and high-quality toy trains have high demand overseas. Despite this desire for U.S. products, exports of the recreational equipment industries declined almost 11 percent in 1998. The Asian financial crisis and the high value of the dollar against other currencies have affected the foreign demand for and price competitiveness of U.S. products. The U.S. industry manufactures primarily high-quality recreational equipment products and is viewed by overseas consumers as a leader in product development. As a result, U.S. name brands are recognized and sought throughout the world. However, consumers in Asia were wary of that economy and were not looking to buy expensive U.S. equipment. Other overseas consumers probably were concerned about the loss of the price competitiveness of U.S. recreational equipment. There are several competitive high-quality manufacturers from Europe and Asia from whom overseas consumers can choose.

Innovations such as mountain bikes, in-line roller skates, and snowboards were developed in this country by small entrepreneurs and firms, many of which now are large, profitable companies. Servicing the world's largest market for recreational equipment in the United States, large American firms are aware of consumers' tastes and preferences for recreational products. Many U.S. firms realize their advantages in overseas markets. Export sales are an important factor in U.S. manufacturers' business plans. The ratio of exports to domestic shipments was almost 20 percent for the entire recreational equipment sector in 1998.

Electronic Commerce

E-mail and the Internet have had a major impact on the recreational equipment segment. Product marketing, distribution, retail sales, and production costs of recreational equipment companies have all been affected by the expanding Internet. Manufacturers, both large and small, can promote and advertise their products easily with little expense. The Internet has opened up new overseas opportunities as overseas consumers "surf the Web" to get information about all types of recreational products. In addition, many distributors and retailers have popped up on the Internet, selling toys, sporting goods, and bicycles. It probably will not be long before boats and motorcycles are sold on the Web. Finally, business-to-business E-commerce has increased dramatically, allowing more rapid responses and better inventory control.

IMPORTANT FACTORS AFFECTING THE FUTURE GROWTH OF U.S. INDUSTRY

Current dollar product shipments of recreational equipment totaled an estimated $22.6 billion in 1998, declining nearly 1 percent in real terms (see Table 39-1). Shipments were expected to reach $22.9 billion in 1999, up 0.7 percent in real terms. The shifting of production from the United States to overseas sourcing, particularly for the toys, dolls, games, and bicycle industries, weakened domestic manufacturers' growth. Constant dollar product shipments of bicycles and parts fell an estimated 12 percent and 19 percent, respectively, in 1998 and 1999; constant dollar product shipments of dolls, toys, and games fell just under 1 percent annually in 1998 and 1999. U.S. exports of recreational equipment totaled just under $4.5 billion, decreasing 11 percent, in 1998 and were expected to fall to $4 billion, down 10 percent, in 1999 (see Tables 39-1 and 39-2). U.S. imports of recreational equipment totaled $20.4 billion in 1999, growing 3.5 percent after 7 percent growth in 1998. These increases are related to the shifting of the production of bicycles and toys and to the Asian financial crises. U.S. imports of bicycles and toys increased 15 percent and 5 percent annually, respectively, from 1997 to 1999. In addition, most Asian currencies fell against the dollar, making the price of products imported from Asia significantly lower. However, U.S. imports of sports equipment declined 3 percent. Demand in the U.S. market grew, partly in response to cheaper imported products. As real gross domestic product (GDP) and disposable income increased 4 and 3 percent, respectively, in 1998, apparent consumption climbed 5 percent in real terms to total $37.8 billion in current dollars. In 1999, GDP was expected to grow between 3.5 and 4.0 percent while apparent consumption for the recreational equipment sector was expected to total $39.3 billion, increasing 3 percent in real terms. Consumer confidence, as measured by the Conference Board, remained high at over 130 throughout most of 1998 and the first half of 1999.

TABLE 39-1: Recreational Equipment (SIC 3732, 3751, 3942, 3944, 3949) Trends and Forecasts
(millions of dollars except as noted)

											Percent Change			
	1992	1993	1994	1995	1996	1997[1]	1998[1]	1999[2]	2000[3]	2004[3]	97–98	98–99	99–00	99–04[4]
Product Data														
Value of shipments[5]	17,461	19,385	19,891	21,023	21,411	22,462	22,557	22,878	23,342	27,622	0.4	1.4	2.0	3.8
Value of shipments (1992$)	17,461	19,181	19,410	20,055	20,061	20,692	20,533	20,680	20,958	23,266	−0.8	0.7	1.3	2.4
Apparent consumption	25,491	28,496	28,949	30,798	32,681	35,965	37,837	39,279	40,011	45,166	5.2	3.8	1.9	2.9
Real apparent consumption	25,491	28,245	28,340	29,502	30,863	33,609	35,122	36,320	36,864	39,980	4.5	3.4	1.5	1.9
Trade data														
Value of imports	11,423	12,582	12,901	14,370	16,007	18,491	19,745	20,428	20,861	21,965	6.8	3.5	2.1	1.5
Imports to apparent consumption (%)	44.8	44.2	44.6	46.7	49.0	51.4	52.2	52.0	52.1	48.6	1.5	−0.3	0.3	−1.3
Value of exports	3,394	3,471	3,844	4,595	4,738	4,988	4,465	4,027	4,192	4,421	−10.5	−9.8	4.1	1.9
Exports to shipments (%)	19.4	17.9	19.3	21.9	22.1	22.2	19.8	17.6	18.0	16.0	−10.9	−11.1	2.0	−1.9
Industry data														
Value of shipments[5]	18,649	20,968	21,459	23,065	23,543	24,555	24,812	25,140	25,467	30,200	1.0	1.3	1.3	3.7
Value of shipments (1992$)	18,649	20,754	20,941	22,007	22,065	22,621	22,588	22,729	22,880	25,453	−0.1	0.6	0.7	2.3
Total employment (thousands)	154	165	167	170	171									
Production workers (thousands)	115	123	127	130	130									
Average hourly earnings ($)	9.12	9.44	9.61	10.12	10.29									
Capital expenditures	433	494	523	567	636									

[1] Estimate except imports and exports.
[2] Estimate.
[3] Forecast.
[4] Compound annual rate.
[5] For a definition of industry versus product values, see "Getting the Most Out of *Outlook 2000*."
Source: U.S. Department of Commerce: Bureau of the Census; International Trade Administration.

TABLE 39-2: U.S. Trade Patterns in Recreational Equipment[1] in 1998
(millions of dollars; percent)

Exports			Imports		
Region[2]	Value[3]	Share,%	Region[2]	Value[3]	Share,%
NAFTA	1,341	30	NAFTA	1,787	9
Latin America	389	9	Latin America	56	0
Western Europe	1,401	31	Western Europe	1,442	7
Japan/Chinese Economic Area	869	19	Japan/Chinese Economic Area	15,266	77
Other Asia	115	3	Other Asia	1,084	5
Rest of world	349	8	Rest of world	110	1
World	4,464	100	World	19,745	100
Top Five Countries	Value	Share,%	Top Five Countries	Value	Share,%
Canada	994	22	China	9,983	51
Japan	639	14	Japan	3,695	19
United Kingdom	402	9	Taiwan	1,294	7
Mexico	346	8	Mexico	910	5
Germany	266	6	Canada	877	4

[1] SIC 3732, 3751, 3942, 3944, 3949.
[2] For definitions of regional groupings, see "Getting the Most Out of *Outlook 2000.*"
[3] Values may not sum to total due to rounding.
Source: U.S. Department of Commerce, Bureau of the Census.

U.S. INDUSTRY GROWTH PROJECTIONS FOR THE NEXT 1 AND 5 YEARS

Current dollar product shipments are forecast to exceed $23.3 billion in the year 2000, up 1.3 percent in constant dollars. Constant dollar product shipments for the sports equipment, boat, and motorcycle industries are forecast to increase, while shipments for the bicycle and dolls, toys, and games industries are expected to be down, a continuation of the trend toward imports displacing domestic production. Apparent consumption will grow to a forecast $40 billion, up 1.5 percent in real terms. Imports are the primary beneficiaries of increased U.S. demand as U.S. imports of recreational equipment are forecast to increase over 2 percent to total $20.9 billion in the year 2000. The ratio of imports to apparent consumption will remain at 52 percent in 2000. U.S. exports of recreational equipment will increase 4 percent in 2000 as the weighted sum of the top 20 overall export markets is forecast to grow 3 percent. The ratio of exports to shipments will remain at 18 percent in 2000. Highlighting the expected growth of exports are the 13 percent and 5 percent projected increases in U.S. exports of motorcycles and sports equipment, respectively.

Over the next 5 years, 1999–2004, current dollar product shipments are forecast to reach $27.6 billion, increasing only about 2 percent annually in real terms. Trade will continue to be one of the important factors affecting shipments: U.S. exports are expected to grow 2 percent annually. Meanwhile, imports will continue to increase 1.5 percent annually. The ratio of imports to apparent consumption probably will remain at 52 percent through 2000, depending on fluctuations in exchange rates.

Demographic trends will be a key factor for these industries. The baby boom generation has helped these industries over the last three decades. The boomers' parents bought them toys and bicycles in the 1960s, and they themselves bought sports equipment and motorcycles in the 1970s and boats in the 1980s. In the early 1990s, they upgraded to high-quality recreational products of all kinds. Over the next 5 years, this generation will be entering the 45- to 64-year-old age group. The older part of the group, the 55- to 64-year-old age group, will be the fastest-growing age group over the next 5 years. Getting these soon to be senior citizens to continue to participate in recreational activities will be a growing concern as this period progresses. However, early indications are that they will continue to enjoy recreational activities, especially less strenuous activities such as exercising with equipment, golfing, and motorcycle touring. The age group 45 to 54 also will be growing and will be much larger in total than the age group 55 to 64, totaling about 41 million and 28 million, respectively. Individuals in the 45- to 54-year-old age group are reaching their peak earning potential and typically have more discretionary income. This group may constitute a big factor in the growth trend of the industry, helping to boost industry shipments an estimated 2 percent from 1999 to 2004.

GLOBAL MARKET PROSPECTS

Overseas markets for recreational equipment are growing faster than is the domestic market as leisure time is increasing more rapidly in most overseas markets, particularly in the newly industrialized nations and the big emerging market economies. Western Europe currently is the largest foreign market for U.S. recreational equipment, accounting for 31 percent of U.S. exports in 1998. The next largest markets are the North American Free Trade Agreement (NAFTA) countries (Canada and Mexico); U.S. exports of recreational equipment to this region accounted for 30 percent of total recreational equipment exports (see Table 39-2). The Japan/Chinese Economic Area accounted for 19 percent of exports. In 1998, U.S. exports of recreational equipment to western Europe grew 0.4 percent and those to the NAFTA countries increased 1 percent. However, because of the Asian financial crisis, U.S. exports of recreational equipment to the Japan/Chinese Economic Area fell 23 percent.

The largest single-country market for U.S. recreational equipment exports in 1998 was Canada, totaling $994 million. U.S. exports of sports equipment and dolls, toys, and games to Canada reached $664 million, accounting for 67 percent of U.S. recreational equipment exports to that country. U.S. exports to Japan, the next largest export market, totaled $639 million. U.S. exports of sports equipment to Japan totaled $393 million, accounting for 62 percent of U.S. recreational equipment exports; Japanese consumers have increased leisure time and a passion for many sports activities, especially golf. The United Kingdom was the third largest market, as U.S. exports to the that country totaled $402 million, up 9 percent, in 1998. Mexico and Germany were the fourth and fifth largest markets, as U.S. exports to those nations totaled $346 million and $266 million, respectively, in 1998.

The balance of trade for the recreational equipment sector was negative, as U.S. imports of recreational equipment surpassed U.S. exports by $15.3 billion. Among the recreational equipment sectors, only the golf industry had a favorable balance of trade in 1998.

China was the largest foreign supplier of recreational products, as U.S. imports from that country totaled almost $10 billion, or 51 percent of total U.S. recreational equipment imports, up 11 percent in 1998. China is the world's largest exporter of several recreational products, such as dolls, toys, and bicycles. U.S. imports from Japan, the second largest foreign supplier of recreational equipment, totaled almost $3.7 billion in 1998. Imports of motorcycles and parts accounted for a significant share, 27 percent, of total U.S. imports of recreational products from Japan. U.S. imports from Taiwan, the third largest foreign supplier, totaled just under $1.3 billion. Taiwan has become a major supplier of medium-price and medium-quality recreational products, especially bicycles and sports equipment. The fourth largest foreign supplier in 1998 was Mexico, from which U.S. imports of recreational equipment totaled $0.9 billion. Mexico was a major supplier of dolls, toys, and games, which accounted for 61 percent of all recreational equipment imports from Mexico.

It is likely that imports will continue to grow over the next 5 years, although at a slower rate. With disposable income rising and with many consumers reaching an age at which they have the highest level of discretionary income, consumers may be more apt to purchase higher-quality domestic products.

SPORTING AND ATHLETIC GOODS

The sporting and athletic equipment industry (SIC 3949) produces equipment for golf, fishing, tennis, physical fitness, gymnastics, archery, bowling, billiards, winter sports, and team sports. This industry does not include camping equipment, athletic apparel and footwear, hunting equipment, or most leisure-related vehicles, such as boats, bicycles, motorcycles, and snowmobiles.

Global Industry Trends

With the dollar relatively strong against other major currencies, U.S. exports of recreational equipment declined in 1998 and 1999. However, U.S. brand names are well respected for quality and service throughout the world. Many overseas consumers have become familiar with U.S. athletes and sports leagues from the media and seek to emulate them, using equipment "made in the USA." In addition, many industrialized countries have discovered the benefits of exercising, and increased leisure time has led to greater participation in sports activities. U.S. manufacturers have capitalized on these export opportunities; the ratio of exports to shipments was consistently over 18 percent in the 1990s, peaking at 25 percent in 1996. However, while U.S. manufacturers produce high-quality products, the overseas retail price is an important factor in sales. As a result of the high dollar and higher labor costs, U.S.-produced equipment costs more to produce than does equipment manufactured in Asia or Latin America. Many U.S. manufacturers have production capacity in Asia or Latin America to take advantage of lower wage rates, producing cheaper, lower-quality items. When exchange rates are not favorable for U.S.-produced equipment, U.S. companies try to sell more overseas-produced sports equipment to foreign markets, maximizing their price competitiveness. An additional problem for U.S. exports resulted from an oversupply of certain sports equipment in foreign markets. Overseas dealers and distributors of U.S. products could not sell all of their current inventories and therefore did not demand new products from the United States.

Domestic Trends

The U.S. sporting goods market performed well in the 1990s as real apparent consumption grew 4 percent annually from 1989 to 1999. In the first half of the decade, the sporting goods industry grew faster than did the national economy. From 1989 to 1994, real apparent consumption for the sporting goods industry grew 6 percent annually while real GDP grew only 2 percent. However, in the second half of the decade, the sporting goods industry was outperformed by the national economy. From 1994 through 1999, real apparent consumption of sports equipment grew only an estimated 1.5 percent while real GDP grew 3.0 percent.

The causes of that slow growth can be traced to changes in demographics and consumer preferences. The baby boom generation has traditionally been a consuming generation. For the last 30 years, the effect has been positive on sports equipment sales as the baby boomers participated in sports and stayed fit. In the 1970s, baby boomers engaged in and purchased equipment for strenuous activities such as running, football, and tennis. In the 1980s, that generation mellowed a bit as its members swelled the ranks of the "thirty-somethings," pushing activities such as weight training, baseball, and softball to peak participation rates. In the first half of the 1990s, with baby boomers reaching middle age, fitness activities became one of the most popular forms of sports recreation. However, now that generation is reaching the fifties and lacks the energy it once had but still has high levels of discretionary income and leisure time. Walking, stretching, golfing, camping, and fishing are the top activities among the over-55 age group, according to a survey conducted by American Sports Data Inc. (ASD). The first two activities are not equipment-intensive, and their popularity may be contributing to slower growth for sports equipment. Golf and fishing, which are equipment-intensive activities, are discussed later in this chapter. Camping products are included under several different SIC categories, making it difficult to quantify the camping industry.

Other demographic issues affecting sporting goods sales involve female spending power, growing ethnic populations, and youth activity. Women control an estimated 60 percent of U.S. wealth and make more than 80 percent of sports apparel purchasing decisions, according to the Sporting Goods Manufacturers Association's Sports Apparel Market Index. (Data on purchasing decisions for sports equipment are not available.) The sporting goods industry has tried to cater to this group, offering products designed and promoted specifically for women. According to the ASD survey, in 1998, 37 million women participated frequently in some sort of sport, a 16 percent increase from 1987. The most popular sports activities among women were exercising with equipment, walking, and in-line roller skating. Since the passage of Title IX, federal legislation that prohibits sex discrimination in educational programs that receive federal funds, more women have had opportunities to participate in athletics. The percentage of girls participating in high school activities increased from 1 in 27 girls in 1972 to 1 in 3 girls in 1997, according to the Women's Sports Foundation. Much of the growth in female participation occurred in the 1990s. The number of female competitors in college athletics increased 38 percent from 1990 to 1997, while the number of male competitors increased only 9 percent. These increases in women's participation have meant that more equipment has been purchased for or by women. An additional opportunity will come from the growth of key ethnic groups. The percentage of the U.S. population that is of Asian or Hispanic descent is expected to grow significantly. Individuals of Hispanic and Asian descent are projected to constitute 17 percent of the total population by 2005, compared with 12 percent in 1990. According to a study by the New American Group, the average annual spending of Hispanics increased from $18,800 to $21,700 between 1995 and 1997. Asian-American spending power increased from $26,600 in 1995 to $31,100 in 1997. The Hispanic and Asian populations constitute an important market for many sporting goods activities, such as soccer and baseball. As these populations increase their spending power, sporting goods manufacturers will have more opportunities to sell equipment to them.

Additional opportunities exist among today's teenage generation. However, the members of this generation has many more diversions than did their parents, the baby boom generation. Keeping this group interested in sports activities will not be easy; video games, computers, and the Internet have grown in popularity, taking up the leisure time of today's youth. The ASD study revealed that the 12- to 17-year-old age group was the only one to lose ground in overall sports participation. The Center for Disease Control and Prevention (CDC) reported that 12 percent of all teenagers are overweight, compared with 6 percent 30 years ago. The sporting goods industry faces the challenge of getting children off the sofa and away from the Internet and persuading them to participate in sports activities.

Electronic Commerce

While the industry would prefer that youths spend less time on the Internet and more time participating in sports, the Internet has become an important factor in the distribution of sports products. Most sporting goods companies have Web sites to promote and provide information about their product offerings. In June 1999, nearly 100 million people in the United States had access to the Internet (37 percent of the population), according to Nua, an Internet strategy firm. Both small and large companies are now able to reach a bigger audience. An increasing number of individuals are surfing the Web to find out about products they intend to buy. In addition, more consumers are making purchases over the Web through on-line distributors, from traditional dealers with Internet Web sites, and in some cases directly from manufacturers. This distribution outlet will have a significant impact on the traditional dealer network in terms of competition and aftermarket support of products such as exercise machines. Business-to-business E-commerce is also an important trend in the sports equipment business. Forrester Research estimated that business-to-business E-commerce will total $17.3 billion versus $5 billion for consumer Internet sales in 2001. Administrative costs and processes, such as mailing, can be improved significantly by business-to-business E-commerce, which benefits both manufacturers and dealers.

While dealers certainly are affected by the Internet, there are other significant trends involving traditional retail outlets. Large chains of stores have increased their market share through consolidation and attrition of smaller dealers. These large chains not only affect their competitors but also wield substantial power over manufacturers in regard to price and product offerings. Many manufacturers find themselves in a partnership with retailers in order to lower costs to consumers and maximize profits for the retailer and the manufacturer. U.S. retailers also have instituted better programs to acquire point-of-sale information, which gives companies more control over inventory. As a result, U.S. retailers have asked for a more responsive supply of products. The move to just-in-time inventory and supply probably will give U.S. manufacturers a competitive advantage over imports from the Far East, which can take up to a couple of months to be shipped.

Important Factors Affecting the Future Growth of U.S. Industry

Factors affecting the growth of U.S. sports equipment consumption and U.S. manufacturers' shipments include macroeconomic trends such as disposable income and changes in consumers' preferences. With the U.S. economy continuing to grow, the U.S. sports equipment market has benefited. As disposable personal income (DPI) has grown, so have consumers' expenditures for sporting goods. In 1998, real DPI grew 3 percent while real personal consumption expenditures for sporting goods increased 9 percent. In the first half of 1999, real DPI grew 4 percent from the same period in 1998 while real personal consumption expenditures for sporting goods jumped 11 percent. Personal consumption expenditures for sporting goods are not directly comparable to apparent consumption of sports equipment, as expenditures probably include sports apparel and camping equipment, both of which are growing rapidly, according to industry experts.

Positive factors such as rising personal income have been offset by changes in consumer preferences. In at least two major product segments of the sporting goods industry, U.S. manufacturers and retailers have been hurt by changing consumer preferences that have left dealers and manufacturers with an oversupply of unwanted products. Both golf and in-line skating experienced continued growth in the 1990s. However, both industries misjudged consumer tastes and were left with product they could not sell. The glut of in-line skates resulted from misjudging the growth of the in-line skate market. In addition, in-line skate manufacturers were trying to respond to dealers' complaints about the lack of just-in-time supply. While the demand for skates continues to increase, that growth is in the low single digits, not at the two- and three-digit growth rates that manufacturers and some retailers had hoped for. Golf club manufacturers have experienced the same problem of oversupply. Until recently, golf club makers successfully promoted and sold bigger-headed clubs made with expensive lightweight components. Golf club manufacturers were making drivers with bigger heads with lighter and more expensive materials, mainly titanium. However, several manufacturers went away from bigger is better and toward new designs that moved the balance of weight lower in the club head and used a combination of metals. These manufacturers captured consumers' interest, and sales began switching to those types of clubs. Several manufacturers of big head clubs were left with an excess supply of expensive large club heads. Both in-line skate and golf club manufacturers were trying to sell off these products as best they could from late 1997 through 1999.

Constant dollar product shipments of sporting and athletic goods were expected to grow 1 to 2 percent in 1999 after declining an estimated 3 percent in 1998. A 17.5 percent drop in exports was the primary reason for the decline in shipments in 1998. U.S. imports also declined, falling 0.4 percent in 1998 and an estimated 5 percent in 1999. However, U.S. shipments to the domestic market increased an estimated 3 percent and 5 percent in 1998 and 1999, respectively. As a result, apparent consumption in real terms was up an estimated 2 percent in 1998 and 1999 (see Table 39-3).

Low inflation in the sporting goods industry also helped fuel the demand for sports equipment. The industry's producer price index rose only 1.2 percent in 1998 and was expected to remain virtually the same in 1999. In fact, annual inflation has not topped 3 percent since 1990 and averaged an estimated 2 percent from 1989 to 1999. Over that period, the overall consumer price index had only 3 years with inflation under 3 percent and

TABLE 39-3: Sporting and Athletic Goods nec (SIC 3949) Trends and Forecasts
(millions of dollars except as noted)

											Percent Change			
	1992	1993	1994	1995	1996	1997[1]	1998[1]	1999[2]	2000[3]	2004[3]	97–98	98–99	99–00	99–04[4]
Product data														
Value of shipments[5]	6,994	7,865	8,285	8,802	9,203	9,510	9,350	9,510	9,850	12,450	−1.7	1.7	3.6	5.5
Value of shipments (1992$)	6,994	7,810	8,091	8,440	8,698	8,838	8,586	8,717	8,938	10,596	−2.9	1.5	2.5	4.0
Apparent consumption	8,223	8,918	9,656	10,023	10,362	10,675	10,913	11,092	11,279	14,400	2.2	1.6	1.7	5.4
Real apparent consumption	8,223	8,856	9,430	9,610	9,794	9,921	10,021	10,167	10,235	12,255	−1.0	1.5	0.7	3.8
Trade data														
Value of imports	2,518	2,543	3,129	3,392	3,472	3,531	3,516	3,340	3,275	4,450	−0.4	−5.0	−1.9	5.9
Imports to apparent consumption (%)	30.6	28.5	32.4	33.8	33.5	33.1	32.2	30.1	29.0	30.9	−2.6	−6.5	−3.6	0.5
Value of exports	1,289	1,490	1,758	2,171	2,313	2,366	1,953	1,758	1,846	2,500	−17.5	−10.0	5.0	7.3
Exports to shipments (%)	18.4	18.9	21.2	24.7	25.1	24.9	20.9	18.5	18.7	20.1	−16.0	−11.5	1.4	1.7
Industry data														
Value of shipments[5]	7,581	8,459	8,943	9,543	9,882	10,225	10,200	10,375	10,700	13,500	−0.2	1.7	3.1	5.4
Value of shipments (1992$)	7,581	8,400	8,733	9,150	9,340	9,503	9,366	9,510	9,710	11,489	−1.4	1.5	2.1	3.9
Total employment (thousands)	62.0	64.4	68.2	67.7	66.1									
Production workers (thousands)	44.2	46.8	49.7	48.8	47.6									
Average hourly earnings ($)	8.52	8.74	8.67	9.26	9.51									
Capital expenditures	178	218	192	222	254									

[1] Estimate except imports and exports.
[2] Estimate.
[3] Forecast.
[4] Compound annual rate.
[5] For a definition of industry versus product values, see "Getting the Most Out of *Outlook 2000.*"
Source: U.S. Department of Commerce: Bureau of the Census; International Trade Administration.

grew 3 percent between 1989 and 1999. Manufacturers became much more efficient, cutting their largest input cost—employment—3 percent from 1994 to 1996 while increasing real product shipments 7 percent over that period. The retailer pressures mentioned earlier and pressures for low-cost imports have also been factors in low inflation rates for the sports industry.

Golf Equipment

The golf industry experienced strong growth through most of the 1990s. Apparent consumption of golf equipment increased 6 percent annually in real terms from 1992 to 1999 (see Table 39-4). As was noted earlier in this chapter, participation rates in golfing have increased over the last 10 years. According to a study by the National Sporting Goods Association, the number of individuals participating in golf increased 2 percent annually from 1988 to 1998. From 1996 to 1998, the increase in participation was 9 percent annually. However, actual sales and market shares have fluctuated recently. Apparent consumption in real terms increased an estimated 2 percent and declined an estimated 3 percent in 1998 and 1999, respectively. U.S. imports of

TABLE 39-4: Major Sports Industry Segments Trends and Forecasts
(millions of dollars except as noted)

	1992	1993	1994	1995	1996	1997	1998[1]	1999[2]	Compound Rate 92–97	Percent Change 96–97	97–98	98–99
Golf equipment (SIC 39492)												
Product data												
Value of shipments[3]	1,782	1,926	1,976	2,370	2,648	2,941	2,941	2,941	10.5	11.0	0.0	0.0
Value of shipments (1992$)	1,782	1,903	1,930	2,272	2,503	2,733	2,700	2,695	8.9	9.2	–1.2	–0.2
Trade data												
Value of imports	461	492	541	579	639	784	788	589	11.2	22.7	0.5	–25.2
Imports to apparent consumption (%)	25.4	25.5	27.4	25.6	25.3	26.8	26.2	20.2	1.1	5.9	–2.5	–22.9
Value of exports	428	491	542	690	766	804	718	610	13.5	5.0	–10.7	–15.0
Exports to shipments (%)	24.0	25.5	27.4	29.1	28.9	27.3	24.4	20.7	2.6	–5.5	–10.7	–15.0
Market data												
Apparent consumption	1,816	1,927	1,976	2,260	2,521	2,921	3,011	2,920	10.0	15.8	3.1	–3.0
Real apparent consumption	1,816	1,913	1,929	2,167	2,383	2,714	2,765	2,676	8.4	13.9	1.8	–3.2
Fishing equipment (SIC 39491)												
Product Data												
Value of shipments[3]	493	629	657	756	814	682	682	800	6.7	–16.1	0.0	17.2
Value of shipments (1992$)	493	621	642	725	769	634	627	733	5.2	–17.5	–1.2	17.0
Trade data												
Value of imports	321	289	309	388	358	349	387	357	1.7	–2.5	10.9	–7.8
Imports to apparent consumption (%)	43.4	34.7	35.7	38.1	35.2	39.5	41.0	34.0	–1.9	12.2	3.7	–16.9
Value of exports	76	85	102	126	155	148	124	108	14.4	–4.5	–16.1	–13.0
Exports to shipments (%)	15.3	13.5	15.5	16.7	19.1	21.7	18.2	13.5	7.2	13.8	–16.1	–25.8
Market data												
Apparent consumption	738	833	864	1,017	1,017	883	945	1,049	3.7	–13.1	7.0	10.9
Real apparent consumption	738	827	844	975	961	821	868	962	2.1	–14.5	5.8	10.7
Exercise and gymnastic equipment (SIC 39494)												
Product data												
Value of shipments[3]	1,376	1,407	1,370	1,343	1,360	1,236	1,236	1,236	–2.1	–9.1	0.0	0.0
Value of shipments (1992$)	1,376	1,397	1,338	1,287	1,285	1,149	1,135	1,133	–3.5	–10.6	–1.2	–0.2
Trade data												
Value of imports	382	384	513	517	751	638	569	535	10.8	–15.0	–10.8	–5.9
Imports to apparent consumption (%)	24.3	24.0	31.4	33.0	42.1	42.0	38.6	36.4	11.6	–0.1	–8.1	–5.7
Value of exports	183	191	249	290	325	355	331	301	14.2	9.1	–6.9	–8.9
Exports to shipments (%)	13.3	13.6	18.2	21.6	23.9	28.7	26.7	24.4	16.7	20.0	–6.9	–9.0
Market data												
Apparent consumption	1,575	1,600	1,633	1,570	1,785	1,519	1,474	1,470	–0.7	–14.9	–2.9	–0.3
Real apparent consumption	1,575	1,589	1,595	1,505	1,688	1,412	1,354	1,347	–1.9	–16.3	–4.1	–0.5

[1] Estimate except imports and exports.
[2] Estimate
[3] Value of products classified in the sporting and athletic goods, nec industry produced by all industries.
calculations based on more detailed statistics

golf equipment increased 0.5 percent in 1998 before falling an estimated 25 percent in 1999. Meanwhile, in real terms, U.S. shipments of golf equipment declined 1 percent in 1998 before leveling off in 1999. Exports certainly contributed to the decline in 1998, as U.S. exports of golf equipment dropped almost 11 percent in that year. However, U.S. exports of golf equipment continued to decline, falling an estimated 15 percent in 1999. As was mentioned previously, the industry has had to deal with excess supply. In 1999, that problem abated somewhat as domestic manufacturers were able to sell off much of the excess through nontraditional distribution channels such as wholesale club retailers and other discount brokers on the Internet and in outlet stores. However, finding such channels overseas to sell excess supply has not been as successful. In addition, technologies such as low-center-of-gravity clubs have not been as accepted in foreign markets as they have in the United States.

Demographic factors in the United States have played a large role in the growth of consumption. The baby boom generation has high levels of disposable income in a period when their leisure time is high. Golf is an equipment-intensive activity with participants eager to have the proper tools to maximize their talent. Golfers want the latest clubs, balls, shoes (spikeless), gloves, and even apparel that will make them play or look better. Now this generation has the income to purchase the best equipment. As a result, there are many new manufacturers with new products they hope will become the next big trend, such as low-center-of-gravity clubs.

To market new ideas, many companies have used infomercials and the Internet to promote and advertise their products. New entrants need to increase marketing to make their companies stand out. Several new companies, such as Olimar, Alien, and Pure Spin, have been very successful in using this approach to promote and sell their products. Promotion of products over the Internet is meeting with some success.

Fishing Tackle and Equipment

In 1998, apparent consumption of fishing equipment was estimated at $945 million, up 6 percent in real terms from 1997. U.S. imports of fishing equipment led that growth, increasing almost 11 percent and totaling $387 million, while U.S. exports of fishing equipment fell over 16 percent, totaling $124 million in 1998. Such exports drove down domestic shipments, which declined an estimated 1.2 percent in real terms. In 1999, domestic shipments of fishing equipment rebounded, increasing an estimated 17 percent and totaling $800 million in current dollars. However, U.S. imports of fishing equipment fell an estimated 8 percent and U.S. exports of fishing equipment declined an estimated 13 percent. With domestic shipments growing and imports falling, U.S. apparent consumption of fishing equipment increased 11 percent.

U.S. real apparent consumption of fishing equipment grew 2 percent annually from 1989 to 1999. Imports, domestic shipments, and exports have had their ups and downs as the fishing equipment market has seen fluctuations in exchange rates and frequent changes in consumer preferences play an important role in the composition of apparent consumption. The U.S. dollar fluctuated over the last decade. When the dollar has been relatively high against other currencies, U.S. imports of fishing gear have increased while U.S. domestic shipments and exports of fishing equipment have declined. In addition, both domestic and foreign suppliers have introduced new products to take advantage of changes in consumers' buying habits, and those products have changed the disposition of apparent consumption.

While it was expected that demographic trends would lead to strong growth in the fishing sector in the latter half of the 1990s and the first few years of the next decade, strong growth has not yet materialized. Fishing typically has been popular with individuals in the 55- to 64-year-old age group, which is expected to be the fastest-growing age group from 1995 to 2005. In a 1997 survey of average annual consumer expenditures conducted by the Bureau of Labor Statistics, the age group 55 to 64 spent the highest amount on hunting and fishing equipment. However, participation in fishing has actually declined since 1992, when the National Sporting Goods Association (NSGA) survey reported 47.6 million participants. In 1998, only 43.6 million participated in fishing. One cause of the lack of strong growth might be decreasing opportunities to fish. Developers continue to build resort housing and other projects along waterways, lakes, seas, and oceans. The increase in population typically drives fish and fishermen away. Development can mean polluted water and other negative factors that force the fish away. In addition, fishermen typically desire quiet isolation and have difficulty finding such conditions. In addition, it is likely that other activities, such as golfing, have garnered more leisure time and disposable income.

Exercise and Gymnastic Equipment

Real apparent consumption of exercise and gymnastic equipment declined an estimated 0.5 percent in 1999, remaining at $1.6 billion in current dollars. Imports declined an estimated 6 percent, totaling $535 million in 1999, while U.S. exports of exercise equipment decreased 9 percent to $301 million. Current dollar shipments remained at an estimated $1.2 billion in 1999. Manufacturers have reported that there has been a strong increase in the demand for equipment for exercise clubs and gyms. This type of equipment typically consists of sophisticated high-quality machines, many of which are manufactured in the United States.

Participation in exercising with equipment increased 5 percent annually from 1988 to 1998, according to the NSGA study. Increasingly, baby boomers and women have been using fitness equipment to get into shape or improve strength. Fitness club memberships for individuals in the 45- to 54-year-old age group and the 55-and-over age group increased significantly from 1987 to 1997 at 125 percent and 102 percent, respectively. In several fitness activities, women's participation is greater than men's, such as training with hand weights and using abdominal trainers. In addition, according to the ASD study, the number of women using free weights nearly tripled from 6.8 million to 18.6 million from 1987 to 1998.

Stimulating this increase has been the industry's development of new products and new routines that make exercising fun. The industry continued to develop new products in the 1990s, such as stair climbers, abdominal trainers, cross-country ski machines, and elliptical motion machines. In addition, the industry has developed new training methods that can involve the use of equipment, such as step aerobics, slide boards, and martial arts fitness. These products and methods not only make participation fun, they increase manufacturers' shipments.

Playground Equipment and Other Sporting and Athletic Goods

This category includes all other sporting goods products, including skiing, water sports, swing sets, and team sports equipment. Major segments that have experienced growing participation rates include snowboarding, windsurfing, and baseball. Snowboarding participation increased nearly 29 percent from 1997 to 1998, according to the NSGA survey. The inclusion of snowboarding in the 1998 Nagano Olympics helped fuel the growth of that sport, which already had seen participation double since 1988. However, much of snowboarding's popularity has come at the expense of Alpine skiing. From 1988 to 1998, Alpine skiing lost 4.7 million participants.

Baseball has seen participation drop over the last decade. However, in 1998, participation increased 12 percent, according to the NSGA study. Many analysts believe that excitement over events in major league baseball inspired youths to participate in the sport. Events such as the home run chase, rookie Kerry Wood's strikeout record, and the Yankee's 118-win season were well publicized. The home run chase of Mark McGwire and Sammy Sosa in particular captured the attention of the nation. It is likely that youths participated in baseball in an effort to mimic the exploits of home run hitters. A key to industry growth may be maintaining and building on this increased participation.

U.S. Industry Growth Projections for the Next 1 and 5 Years

Real apparent consumption in the sports equipment industry will grow an estimated 1 percent in the year 2000, mirroring the growth of the national economy. U.S. product shipments are expected to reach $9.9 billion, growing 2 to 3 percent in real terms. U.S. imports of sports equipment will decline an estimated 2 percent. Meanwhile, U.S. exports are forecast to increase 5 percent. Strong growth in overseas markets combined with slowing growth in the U.S. economy will lead to increased exports for U.S. manufacturers. If, in addition, the exchange rates between the U.S. dollar and other major currencies become more favorable, exported U.S. products will be more price competitive. Products imported into the United States will lose some price competitiveness, which has helped them hitherto, thus contributing to the decline in U.S. imports of sports equipment.

The economy is expected to continue to experience modest annual growth. Restraining that growth may be the low level of savings and the high level of debt. Savings as a percentage of disposable income was actually –1 percent in the first half of 1999, meaning that consumers were dipping into their savings in order to continue spending. In addition, the ratio of consumer debt to personal income was high at 18 percent in the first half of 1999. One scenario as the year continued would have consumers becoming apprehensive, seeking less credit, paying more on their debts, and building up their savings again. However, if personal income continued to increase at the end of 1999, consumers were expected to work to improve some of those ratios while continuing to increase their spending slightly, including that on sports equipment.

Constant dollar product shipments of sports equipment are expected to grow 4 percent annually over the next 5 years. The long-term outlook for the U.S. sporting goods industry will be affected by two major factors: demographic trends and the growth of foreign economies. More aging baby boomers probably will participate less in many sports activities. The effects on shipments, however, will not be that significant because the baby boomers who continue to participate probably will engage in equipment-intensive activities such as golf and exercising with equipment. The real challenge will be to entice the next generation, usually called generation X, to participate in and spend on sports activities. These individuals have shown some interest in such activities but have not sustained their level of participation. Individuals in this generation typically are entertained by many different activities besides sports, such as computers, the Internet, and media entertainment (television and motion pictures).

Female participation in sports activities is at an all-time high. Some of the activities in which women have strong participation rates are fitness activities and sports such as softball, in-line skating, and soccer. The success of the women's soccer team at the 1999 World Cup and the continuation of Title IX legislation that was discussed above will boost women's participation even more.

Another positive demographic factor to which it appears the industry can look forward is the echo baby boomers, the offspring of the baby boomers. Although not as large a group as their parents, this age group appears to have many of the same propensities toward sustained sports participation. The echo boomers will be entering the 10- to 19-year-old age group over the next 5 years. The members of this group also appear to have significant purchasing power, perhaps because their parents are at their maximum income levels. Many sports equipment manufacturers are already directing advertising toward this group. Popular sports activities among 10- to 19-year-old individuals include snowboarding, in-line skating, and mountain biking.

If the major industrialized economies continue to expand as expected, U.S. exports of sports equipment will continue to support the growth of domestic manufacturers. Many industrialized countries are experiencing a boom in sports participation that is similar to what happened in the United States in the 1970s and 1980s. However, consumers in those markets are not as committed to leisure spending and typically cut back purchases of sports equipment at the first sign of economic hardship. GDP in major sports equipment markets such as Canada, the United Kingdom, and Germany is expected to grow an estimated 3.5 percent in the year 2000. U.S. brand names are well respected for quality and service in those countries. Opportunities for U.S. exports of sports equipment also will be opening

TABLE 39-5: U.S. Trade Patterns in Sporting and Athletic Goods nec[1] in 1998
(millions of dollars; percent)

Exports			Imports		
Region[2]	Value[3]	Share,%	Region[2]	Value[3]	Share,%
NAFTA	534	27	NAFTA	636	18
Latin America	88	5	Latin America	35	1
Western Europe	578	30	Western Europe	414	12
Japan/Chinese Economic Area	529	27	Japan/Chinese Economic Area	1,892	54
Other Asia	78	4	Other Asia	504	14
Rest of world	146	7	Rest of world	34	1
World	1,953	100	World	3,516	100
Top Five Countries	Value	Share,%	Top Five Countries	Value	Share,%
Japan	393	20	China	1,260	36
Canada	361	18	Taiwan	480	14
United Kingdom	245	13	Canada	341	10
Mexico	173	9	Mexico	295	8
Germany	93	5	South Korea	125	4

[1] SIC 3949.
[2] For definitions of regional groupings, see "Getting the Most Out of *Outlook 2000*."
[3] Values may not sum to total due to rounding.
Source: U.S. Department of Commerce, Bureau of the Census.

up in the big emerging markets, particularly in Latin America and the rebounding Asian economies.

Global Market Prospects

The U.S. sports equipment industry is focused on global competitiveness, especially in terms of the manufacturing process. The production process of sports equipment is diverse in that varying amounts of labor and capital are needed to manufacture the different types of sports products. Sports balls are a good example of the varying cost of production inputs. Inflatable and stitched balls such as basketballs and baseballs require a high labor input, while solid and noninflatable hollow balls such as golf balls and tennis balls rely more on capital and machinery. As a result, the U.S. industry manufactures and competitively exports many capital-intensive products, such as golf and exercise equipment. Labor-intensive products such as team sports equipment tend to be manufactured overseas through licensing contracts or joint ventures, since labor costs are generally lower in many less developed countries, and then imported into the United States. U.S. manufacturers rely on imported products to complete their product lines; the ratio of imports to apparent consumption was 32 percent in 1998.

In 1998, China was the largest foreign supplier and sold almost $1.3 billion of sporting goods to the United States, an increase of 8 percent from 1997. U.S. imports from Taiwan were down 17 percent in 1998, yet Taiwan remained the second largest foreign supplier at $480 million. China and Taiwan combined accounted for 50 percent of U.S. imports. Many sporting goods firms are changing their source for imports from Taiwan to China to take advantage of lower labor costs in China. U.S. sports equipment imports from Canada, the third largest foreign supplier, totaled $341 million in 1998, up 10 percent, and accounted for 10 percent of total imports. Sports equipment imports from Mexico, the fourth largest foreign supplier, totaled $295 million, down 2 percent. This decrease probably was due to the decline in popularity of the big titanium golf club heads that at least one major manufacture imported from Mexico. U.S. imports from South Korea were down 20 percent, totaling $125 million in 1998 (see Table 39-5).

Many products that have a capital-intensive production process and that are made in the United States are price-competitive worldwide. The ratio of exports to shipments for the U.S. sports equipment industry was 21 percent in 1998, down from a modern-day high of 25 percent in 1996. However, U.S. exports fell 18 percent to total just under $2.0 billion in 1998 (see Table 39-5).

Exports to Japan accounted for the largest share of total U.S. sports equipment exports at 20 percent, totaling an estimated $393 million, down 24 percent in 1998. The financial crisis weakened the Japanese market for most U.S. exports, most notably golf equipment. U.S. exports of golf equipment to Japan decreased 17 percent in 1998, when the Japanese became apprehensive about purchasing high-cost golf equipment from the United States. Exports to Canada, the second largest foreign market for U.S. sports equipment, totaling $361 million, were virtually unchanged from a year earlier. Canada is the largest foreign market for exercise equipment, as U.S. exports of exercise equipment totaled $86 million, down 20 percent from 1997. The United Kingdom moved up to become the third largest market, with U.S. exports increasing 21 percent to $245 million. Mexico was the fourth largest market for U.S. sports equipment exports, as exports to that country fell 21 percent to $173 million. U.S. exports of sporting goods to Germany, the fifth largest market, fell 8 percent in 1998 (see Table 39-5).

John A. Vanderwolf, U.S. Department of Commerce, Office of Consumer Goods, (202) 482-0348, John_Vanderwolf@ita.doc.gov, September 1999.

DOLLS, TOYS, GAMES, AND CHILDREN'S VEHICLES

The toys, games, and dolls industry consists of firms that produce a wide variety of children's products under two U.S. Standard Industry Classifications. SIC 3942 includes establishments that produce dolls and stuffed toys. SIC 3944 includes companies that produce toys, games, and children's vehicles. Computer CD-ROM games and related computer software are not considered toys by the current U.S. classification system and are included under SIC 7372.

Global Industry Trends

Today, the toy industry is global in both the production and the sale of products. Worldwide toy sales totaled $53.5 billion in 1998; see Figure 39-1 for a breakdown of sales by region. The two major U.S. producers are Mattel, which markets Barbie, Cabbage Patch Kids, Matchbox Cars, Hot Wheels, and Fisher Price toys, among others, and Hasbro, whose brands include Star Wars, Furby, Teletubbies, Pokeman, Milton Bradley, Parker Brothers, and Playschool. Mattel and Hasbro are publicly held and reported 1998 revenues of $4.8 billion and $3.3 billion, respectively. Major international companies include Nintendo of Japan and LEGO of Denmark, which reported 1998 revenues of $4.7 billion and $1.1 billion, respectively.

The leading international toy companies have strong brand awareness across cultures and localize their products to meet the tastes and demands of consumers in more than 100 nations. Their size and scope allow them to enter markets with ease, and they rarely form joint ventures to gain access to new markets. However, in spring 1999, Mattel joined forces with the Japanese company Bandai Co. Ltd in a unique global marketing alliance. Under the partnership, the companies agreed to market each other's products in their home territories. This arrangement is expected to enable those companies to capitalize on each other's diverse product lines, marketing expertise, and strong regional distribution networks. The major U.S. toy retail outlets, Wal-Mart and Toys "R" Us, operate international retail outlets and play a role in the global distribution of the most popular children's products. However, regional and national stores play a more important role in international distribution.

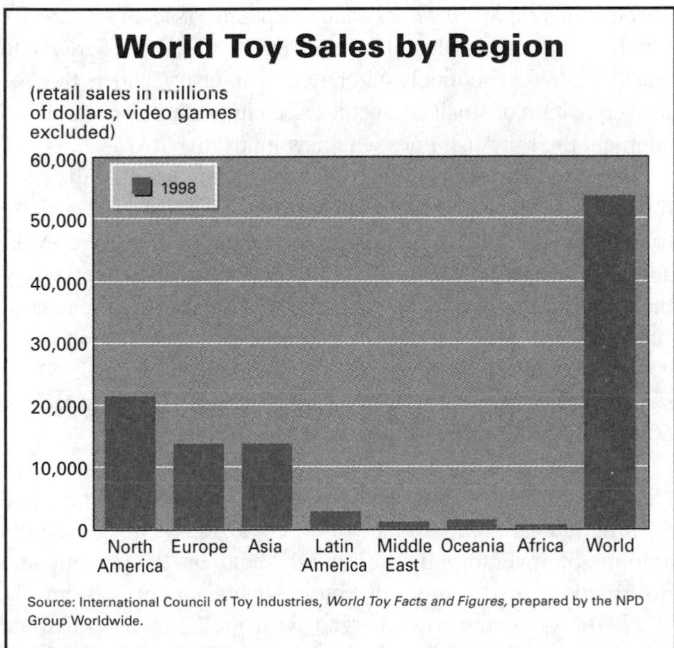

Source: International Council of Toy Industries, *World Toy Facts and Figures*, prepared by the NPD Group Worldwide.

FIGURE 39-1

To achieve profitable economies of scale, toy manufacturers have shifted production away from domestic markets to licensed or wholly owned production facilities in low-wage economies, primarily in Asia. To augment their product lines, they also purchase components, accessories, and finished products from international sources. Evidence of this trend is seen in the U.S. market, where imports of toys have increased steadily to meet the demand not satisfied by U.S.-based producers.

Domestic Trends

As the industry enters the twenty-first century, many of the most popular toys are merchandise based on movies. *Star Wars* episode I toys and action figures drove demand for toys in 1999 and attracted middle-aged fans of the original series as well as a new younger audience. Lucas Films will release *Star Wars* episodes II and III over the next 5 years, both of which are expected to continue to drive sales of a variety of children's merchandise. Similarly, *Toy Story 2* and a movie based on the Japanese toy Pokémon were released late in 1999 and are expected to boost sales into the year 2000. Pokemon became a national obsession among grade-school children in 1999 and led to phenomenal sales of trading cards, figures, and video games. Popular nonmovie toys include yo-yos, Furbies, and Magic the Gathering card game. In the fall of 1999, the producer of Beanie Babies, Ty Inc., announced the retirement of all Beanies on December 31, 1999. However, based on public reaction, Ty later reversed its decision.

The majority of toys sold in the United States are no longer produced domestically. In 1998, imports accounted for 80 percent of U.S. apparent consumption, up from 69 percent in 1992. Large-scale production of toys in the United States has decreased over the last decade as companies have shifted from domestic to international production. Total U.S. employment in SIC 3942 and SIC 3944 in 1997, the latest year for which official Census data are available, indicate that total employment and production workers decreased 11 percent and 15.5 percent, respectively, from the previous year. A closer look at the two industry classifications reveals that the employment changes were not uniform between sectors. Companies that produce dolls and stuffed toys reported a decline of 3 percent, while those which produce toys, games, and children's vehicles reported a decline of almost 17 percent. Additionally, from 1992 through 1997, 92 companies employing fewer than 20 people left the industry. Of the total, 42 entered the doll and stuffed toy sector and 134 left the toys, games, and children's vehicles sector.

The decline in employment does not indicate a loss of competitiveness by the industry, as shipments of U.S. products did not decline by a similar amount during that period. According to the U.S. Bureau of the Census, the industry reported a decrease in industry shipments of 0.6 percent in 1997, while product shipments grew 2.6 percent. Toys, games, and children's vehicles companies saw a decline of 1.7 percent, while dolls and stuffed toys companies reported an increase of 18.5 percent. The production of dolls and stuffed toys is significantly smaller than that of toys, games, and children's vehicles. Therefore, that increase in production did not have a significant effect on the industry as a whole. The downward trend in employment and shipments may indicate that U.S. companies have lost their competitive advantage. However, their performance suggests that the declines are more accurately attributed to technological and productivity advances and increased reliance on foreign labor. Company financial data support this interpretation. During that period of production and employment declines, the major toy companies reported an average 6 percent increase in total revenue.

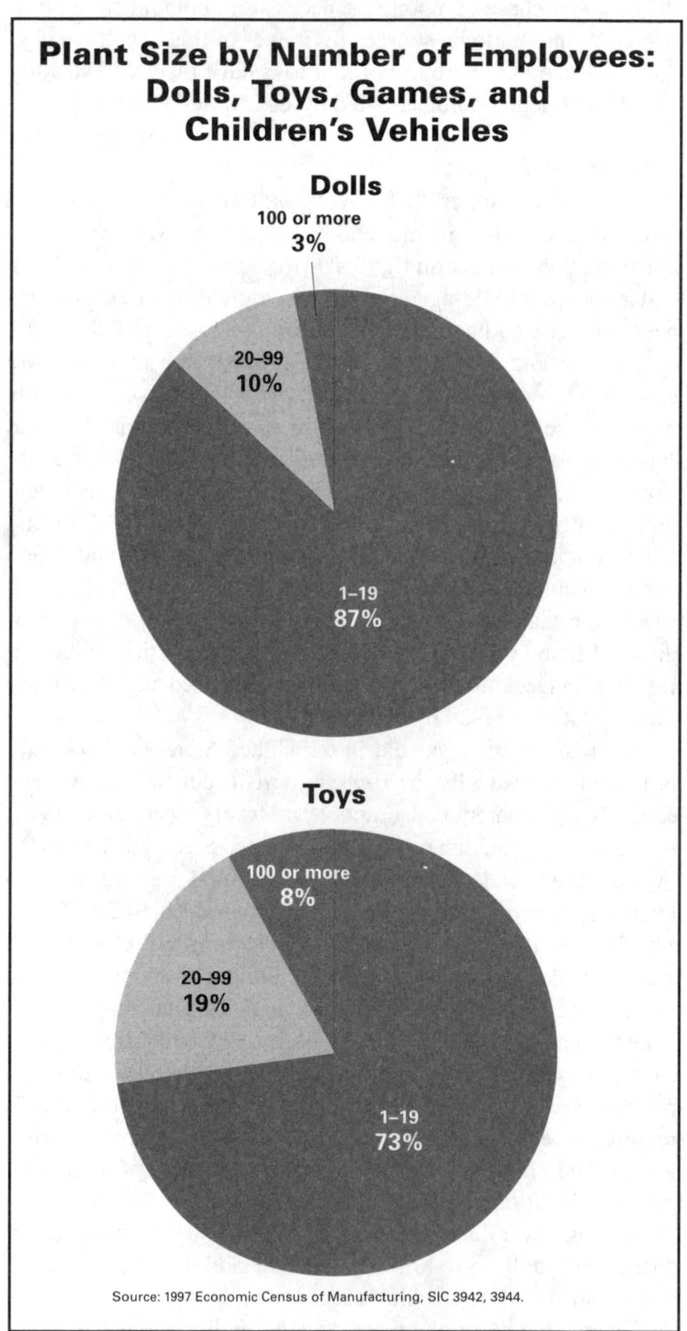

FIGURE 39-2

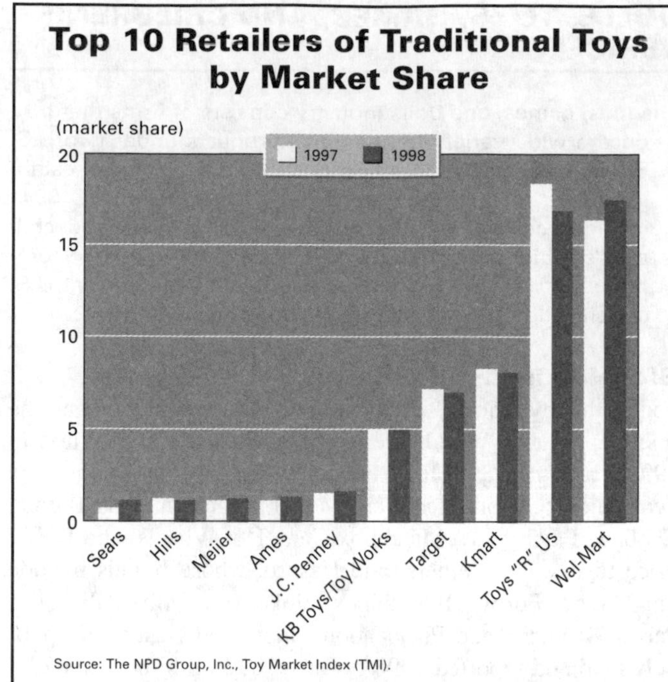

FIGURE 39-3

The U.S. industry is characterized by a few large manufactures and many small producers. Of the 240 establishments that produced dolls in 1997, 87 percent employed fewer than 20 people. Similarly, of the 781 establishments that produced toys in 1997, 73 percent employed fewer than 20 people (see Figure 39-2). Small toy companies do not have the ability to meet U.S. demand and are therefore routinely purchased by industry leaders that see the acquisition of small companies as an important opportunity to augment their product lines with new innovative toys.

The domestic retail industry has changed substantially over the last few years as dedicated toy stores have lost market share to nontraditional retail outlets. In the spring of 1999, Wal-Mart surpassed Toys "R" Us as the number one toy store, reflecting the growing importance of supercenter stores to American consumers. The top 20 retailers of traditional toys, excluding video games, accounted for 67 percent of the retail values of U.S. toy sales in 1998. Among those retailers, the top 10 accounted for 60 percent of all retail sales of toys (see Figure 39-3).

Wal-Mart took the lead in toy retailing at a time when Toys "R" Us was undergoing changes in its business structure and fighting a legal battle. In late 1998, Toys "R" Us decreased the amount of inventory it traditionally held by 24 percent and instituted a just-in-time inventory management system. In 1997, the company was charged with violating federal trade laws by colluding with manufacturers to keep prices for some of the industry's most popular toys artificially high. A tentative settlement of the case was issued in July 1999 and called for Toys "R" Us, Mattel, and Little Tikes to donate over $50 million in cash and toys to charities for needy children.

Technology

The universal mantra of the industry going into the twenty-first century is "Kids are getting older younger." In other words, children are graduating from traditional toys at earlier ages than did their predecessors. Recognizing this trend, Mattel recently teamed up with Patriot Computers to create software designed to emulate the characteristics of its Barbie and Hot Wheels brands. Toy manufacturers also are integrating technology into the production of toys, games, and dolls in ways that were unimaginable just a few years ago. One need look no further than 1998's electronic Christmas hit Furby, Talking Teletubbies, or Microsoft's Actimates, for which the manufacturer prefers the term "learning system" rather than toy, for examples. Further evidence of the trend toward high-tech toys was seen in the Toy Manufacturers of America's announcement that special exhibit space will be dedicated to electronic "smart toys" at the nation's largest toy trade show, Toy Fair, in the year 2000.

New technology gives manufacturers the ability to customize toys to meet specific market demands, and in some cases it even allows the consumer to create the final product. A prime example of this trend is Mattel's "Barbie: My Design" Web site, which allows consumers to create a Barbie fashion doll by choosing the doll's eye and hair color, hairstyle, and other characteristics. Mattel's Web site represents an innovative attempt to increase sales that declined 14 percent in 1998 and fell another 2 percent in the first half of 1999 by making each doll a collectible. It also gives the company the power to produce on demand rather than manufacturing and holding inventory of a product for which demand is uncertain.

Internet technology allows manufacturers to create a central advertising space where all the products relating to a specific brand can be clustered by using a series of connected pages within a Web site, an impossible task in traditional mortar and brick toy stores, where space is limited. Manufacturers are using Web sites to target their most loyal customers and solicit real-time feedback on new product offerings through chat rooms and interactive games. The Internet is expected to drive sales of toys, games, and dolls in the twenty-first century for both manufacturers and retailers. Mattel expects 1999 revenues from its E-commerce business to exceed $60 million. The Internet's effects on toy retailing will be discussed in the following section.

The drive to acquire Internet intelligence and computer technology led to consolidations in the industry in late 1998 and early 1999. Mattel purchased the computer software entertainment business The Learning Company and the girl's entertainment company Purple Moon. With those companies, Mattel expects to operate over 80 Internet sites centered on its most powerful brands. Similarly, Hasbro acquired Tiger Electronics, the maker of Furby, as well as Galoob Toys and Wizards of the Coast, giving that company increased competencies in the production of electronic toys. Technology mergers also occurred in the retailing side of the industry as KB Toys bought the specialized Internet company Brainplay.com. Meanwhile, Toys "R" Us merged with Benchmark Capital to gain Internet retailing competencies. However, soon after their agreement, the two companies split over disagreements about the ownership of ToysRUs.com.

Electronic Commerce

It is anticipated that toys, games, and dolls will lend themselves to on-line purchasing for the same reasons that many firms have turned to the Internet for books and music. Consumers shopping for toys usually know what they will buy before they reach a toy store because children are brand-loyal and only reluctantly accept substitutes for the hot toy of the season. Therefore, for those seeking a specific toy, the Internet promises a convenient and efficient alternative to the long lines and poor selection found at many toy retailers. However, the convenience of shopping on-line will come at the cost of paying full retail prices at the on-line divisions of established mortar and brick stores. Most toy manufacturers have refused to offer the discounts made popular by eToys.com and Amazon.com to avoid undercutting their retail shops.

Established in October 1997, eToys.com is the current leader in Internet toy market, with reported sales in excess of $30 million in the 1998 fiscal year. The retailer clusters a wide selection of children's products into six stores: traditional toys, books, software, videos, music, and video games. Visitors to the site also can browse toys under a variety of categories, including eToys recommendations, and favorites by age, brands, and categories. Although still the leader, eToys.com is no longer the only Internet retailing toy site. Every major toy manufacturer and retailer has a Web site with attributes similar to those of eToys.com. However, there is significant variation in the selection and the degree to which manufacturers are selling directly to the public.

In spring 1999, Amazon.com, the undisputed leader in on-line sales of books, music, and videos, added toys to its portfolio. Amazon.com is expected to be a strong competitor in this area because of its reputation for customer service and extensive national and international distribution systems. In the second quarter of 1999, Amazon.com reported that 70 percent of its orders came from existing customers but did not disclose what percentage of its sales was accounted for by toys.

Projections of Industry and Trade Growth for the Next 1 and 5 Years

The U.S. economy is expected to slow from its record 9-year expansion and grow at a rate of 2 to 2.5 percent in the year 2000. Signs of a possible slowdown were evident in the first half of 1999 as the U.S. Federal Reserve raised interest rates on two occasions, signaling the threat of inflation in the economy. A further rise in interest rates could lead to a decline in the U.S. stock market and result in decreased consumer spending that could slow production and sales in the domestic industry. Therefore, U.S. product shipments of toys, games, and dolls are expected to decline in 2000 at the rate of 0.5 percent in constant dollars (see Table 39-6). Similarly, employment is expected to continue its gradual decline, following the industry trend toward foreign production. The Internet is expected to drive

TABLE 39-6: Dolls, Toys, and Games (SIC 3942, 3944) Trends and Forecasts
(millions of dollars except as noted)

	1992	1993	1994	1995	1996	1997[1]	1998[1]	1999[2]	2000[3]	Percent Change 97–98	98–99	99–00	96–00[4]
Industry data													
Value of shipments[5]	4,542	4,968	4,550	5,092	4,867	4,835	4,787	4,745	4,705	–1.0	–0.9	–0.8	–0.8
Value of shipments (1992$)	4,542	4,954	4,510	4,967	4,708	4,662	4,627	4,599	4,574	–0.8	–0.6	–0.5	–0.7
Total employment (thousands)	35.5	39.0	35.3	38.7	36.8								
Production workers (thousands)	26.8	28.8	27.5	30.0	28.5								
Average hourly earnings ($)	8.43	9.03	9.31	9.58	9.59								
Capital expenditures	146	142	140	138	142								
Product data													
Value of shipments[5]	3,983	4,248	4,170	4,495	4,154	4,261	4,218	4,181	4,146	–1.0	–0.9	–0.8	–0.0
Value of shipments (1992$)	3,983	4,235	4,132	4,384	4,019	4,109	4,077	4,053	4,031	–0.8	–0.6	–0.5	0.1
Trade data													
Value of imports	7,111	7,897	7,445	8,041	9,523	12,063	12,970	13,348	13,686	7.5	2.9	2.5	9.5
Value of exports	719	743	867	915	898	973	930	814	806	–4.4	–12.5	–1.0	–2.7

[1] Estimate except imports and exports.
[2] Estimate.
[3] Forecast.
[4] Compound annual rate.
[5] For a definition of industry versus product values, see "Getting the Most Out of *Outlook 2000*."
Source: U.S. Department of Commerce: Bureau of the Census; International Trade Administration.

demand for toys, dolls, and games, but it is uncertain what overall affect on-line purchasing will have on the industry. In the short term, on-line sales may come at the cost of traditional retail sales.

The next 5 years will be an interesting and challenging period for the industry. Growth in the demand for toys, games, and dolls is correlated with growth in the population of children. Between 1999 and 2003, the population of children up to age 14 is expected to grow at an annual rate of only 0.9 percent. This, coupled with the trend in play habits away from traditional toys and toward interactive computerized toys, could further slow shipments and employment in the industry. However, on-line retailing may help sustain demand for toys in the long term because Internet retailers have the potential to reach significantly more customers, with a much broader product selection, than traditional toy stores can reach. An increased selection and the price competition that is already occurring between Internet toy sites such as Amazon.com and eToys.com could result in an increase in total consumer expenditures on toys in the future.

Global Market Prospects

The United States and Canada consumed approximately 40 percent of total world sales of toys, games, and dolls in 1998, according to the International Council of Toy Industries. However, these markets contain only a fraction of the world's children. With the possibility of a slowdown in the U.S. economy on the horizon and the very slow increase in the population of children expected over the next 5 years, U.S. toy companies will have to look to foreign markets to sustain their profitability.

U.S. exports of toys declined 4.4 percent in 1998 (see Table 39-7). However, while exports declined overall, several key markets increased their consumption of U.S. toys. Canada, the number one export destination across all toy categories, increased consumption 14 percent. Growth of exports for U.S. toys also was seen in Ecuador, 63 percent; China, 41 percent; Russia, 37 percent; Italy, 27 percent; and Germany, 23 percent. However, those increases were not enough to offset declines in other markets. The strength of the U.S. dollar and the lingering effects of the global financial crisis priced U.S. toy products out of the reach of most international consumers. The largest percentage declines occurred in the following countries: South Korea, 74 percent; Chile, 46 percent; Argentina, 40 percent; Paraguay, 33 percent; and Brazil, 29 percent. However, the decrease in U.S. exports did not occur across all toy categories: Exports of dolls and stuffed toys increased 30 percent, while exports of toys, games, and children's vehicles declined 7 percent.

A portion of the decline in exports to Brazil and Argentina resulted from two provisional safeguard measures placed on toys originating outside the MERCOSUR trading bloc. Brazil originally imposed an increase in customs duties on toys ranging from 20 to 70 percent for a period of 200 days in 1997, but the safeguard measure has now been extended until 2004. In January 1999, Argentina imposed an import duty of $3.80 per kilo on toys produced outside MERCOSUR, which resulted in an effective ad valorem rate of 40 to 60 percent, depending on the weight of a toy. Argentina anticipates that the duty increase will be in effect until March 1, 2000. These actions, coupled with the strength of the U.S. dollar, made American toys too expensive for consumers and contributed to the decline in U.S. exports to that region.

U.S. exports were estimated to reach just $814 million in 1999, a decline of 12 percent from 1998 (see Table 39-7). The declines were due in large part to the continued financial difficulties in many international markets. Future U.S. export growth depends on the relative strength of the U.S. dollar. If the decline in the value of the U.S. dollar continues, U.S. exports of

TABLE 39-7: U.S. Trade Patterns in Dolls, Toys, and Games[1] in 1998
(millions of dollars; percent)

Exports			Imports		
Region[2]	Value[3]	Share,%	Region[2]	Value[3]	Share,%
NAFTA	432	46	NAFTA	735	6
Latin America	160	17	Latin America	8	0
Western Europe	147	16	Western Europe	445	3
Japan/Chinese Economic Area	114	12	Japan/Chinese Economic Area	11,241	87
Other Asia	19	2	Other Asia	523	4
Rest of world	57	6	Rest of world	19	0
World	930	100	World	12,970	100
Top Five Countries	Value	Share,%	Top Five Countries	Value	Share,%
Canada	303	33	China	8,308	64
Mexico	129	14	Japan	2,464	19
Japan	74	8	Mexico	558	4
United Kingdom	59	6	Hong Kong	246	2
Hong Kong	28	3	Taiwan	223	2

[1] SIC 3942, 3944.
[2] For definitions of regional groupings, see "Getting the Most Out of *Outlook 2000.*"
[3] Values may not sum to total due to rounding.
Source: U.S. Department of Commerce, Bureau of the Census.

toys and related children's products could pick up in the year 2000, but they are not expected to exceed the 1999 level. U.S. exports of toys are expected to reach $806 million in 2000, down 1 percent from 1999.

Over the next 5 years, U.S. exports are expected to increase gradually, aided by the recovery of the economies weakened by the 1997 Asian financial crisis. In addition, tariff barriers that have hindered the ability of U.S. toys to compete abroad may be reduced.

U.S. toy tariffs were reduced beginning in 1995 and eliminated by 1999 as part of the General Agreement on Tariffs and Trade (GATT) Uruguay Round "zero-for zero" negotiations. Other signatories to the agreement, including the European Union, Japan, and South Korea, followed phased-in tariff reduction schedules. Toy trade between Canada, Mexico, and the United States is duty-free under NAFTA. China's possible accession to the WTO is promising for the industry because it would open more markets for U.S. manufacturers.

U.S. imports totaled almost $13 billion in 1998, a record 14 times total U.S. exports. Sixty-four percent of toy imports originated in China, and 19 percent were Japanese-made (see Table 39-7). The NAFTA partners Canada and Mexico increased their shipments of toys to the United States 8 percent and 14 percent, respectively. A closer look at the two industry sectors shows that while imports have increased overall, they have increased more dramatically in the dolls and stuffed toys sector. Imports of dolls and stuffed toys increased 21 percent in 1998, while those of toys, games, and children's vehicles increased only 1.6 percent.

U.S. imports of toys are expected to increase into the year 2000 at a rate of 2.5 percent. Over the next 5 years, imports are expected to continue to grow at a steady rate as long as manufacturers continue to produce toys for domestic consumption in foreign countries.

International trade in toys between all countries is expected to increase over the next 5 years as tariff and nontariff trade barriers are eliminated. A significant step toward the harmonization of toy safety standards was made in mid-1999 and is expected to facilitate international trade in toys. In that year, the International Organization for Standardization (ISO) drafted the first international safety standard for the production of toys. The standard is based on existing standards in the United States and Europe and specifically addresses the mechanical, physical, chemical, and flammable properties of toys. The ISO standard, No. 8124, must be ratified at the national level by all ISO member countries before it becomes a universal standard. Toy Manufacturers of America and its European counterparts are working to develop seminars to help countries understand and implement the standard in their production facilities. Once it is endorsed, the ISO standard will facilitate international trade in toys by harmonizing standards, improving productivity, and fostering competition among producers.

Jamie J. Lemm, U.S. Department of Commerce, Office of Consumer Goods, (202) 482-5783, LemmJ@ita.doc.gov, September 1999.

BICYCLES AND PARTS

Global Industry Trends

The sources of supply of bicycles have been undergoing major changes over the last few years as imports have risen while U.S. shipments have dropped. As late as 1994, U.S.-manufactured bicycles accounted for 52 percent of U.S. consumption. However, foreign suppliers, mainly China, Taiwan, and Mexico, have captured more of domestic consumption. In 1998, domestically manufactured products accounted for only 34 percent of consumption. After the writing of this chapter, the two largest domestic producers, Huffy and Brunswick, announced independent plans to close domestic manufacturing operations and source bicycles from overseas suppliers. While some layoffs and production declines were expected before these announcements, the estimates and figures may not fully reflect the closing of these major U.S. producers.

Labor compensation typically accounts for most of the total costs of producing a bicycle; therefore, foreign suppliers in countries with lower labor costs have an advantage over U.S. manufacturers. In the past, U.S. manufacturers were able to improve production efficiency and quality through capital investments while maintaining low bicycle costs. However, recently U.S. manufacturers have been unable to match the average unit cost of bicycles produced in several countries, most notably China. The high value of the dollar against other foreign currencies has compounded the impact on U.S. firms' competitiveness, further lowering the average unit cost of foreign-made bicycles. Beginning in 1998, U.S. companies began closing some domestic plants and started sourcing bicycles from Mexico and China. Imports of bicycles from those markets increased 77 percent and 21 percent annually, respectively, over the last 4 years.

The effects of increasing imports have been felt particularly in the mass-merchandiser markets. One large U.S. manufacturer serving that market has stopped offering bicycles to U.S. consumers and has shifted its production resources to other products. Currently, only two U.S. manufacturers supply bicycles to the mass-merchandiser market. The Brunswick Corporation, which recently acquired several bike companies, including Roadmaster and Mongoose, is now the largest supplier of bikes, selling primarily under the Mongoose brand name. Huffy Corporation is the other U.S. manufacturer of mass-merchandiser bikes. Both manufacturers gradually have been moving production away from the United States to foreign countries.

The other segment of the market, the independent bicycle dealer (IBD) market, is supplied primarily by imported products. U.S.-produced products for this market consist of high-quality bikes and bike components. U.S. manufacturers commonly use high-tech materials such as graphite and titanium and have developed innovative component technologies. U.S. manufacturers of mass-merchandiser markets are trying to supply products to this market segment as well. The Mongoose brand was primarily a dealer brand that Brunswick has tried to maintain. These companies hope to build brand loyalty that will transcend distribution channels. However, independent dealers often try to distance and differentiate themselves from the mass merchandisers since they cannot compete with them on price.

Domestic Trends

The bicycle industry is a mature industry that has not had any major new product developments over the last 5 years. As a result, growth in the industry has mirrored the growth of the domestic economy. Apparent consumption totaled over $1.7 billion in 1999, growing an estimated 2.1 percent in 1998 and 2.6 percent in 1999 in real terms. Real personal consumption expenditures for bicycles increased 3 percent in the first 5 months of 1999. The strong economy was the primary reason for the growth of apparent consumption. The U.S. economy remained strong the last 2 years as real disposable personal income grew 3 percent in 1998 and 4 percent in the first half of 1999.

Hybrid bikes and children's bikes, particularly BMX-style bikes, have experienced the strongest demand, leading the growth in consumption. Hybrid bikes combine some of the lightweight features of racing bikes with some of the comfort aspects of mountain bikes. BMX bikes are children's bikes for racing on dirt.

With U.S. manufacturers closing several plants and not particularly strong demand for biking products, U.S. shipments were expected to be weak in 1999. Constant dollar product shipments of bicycles and parts decreased an estimated 12 percent in 1998 and 19 percent in 1999. Current dollar product shipments totaled an estimated $700 million in 1999, down from peak shipments of $1.1 billion in 1994. In addition, export growth has been weak the last several years because of the strength of dollar against other major currencies and weak growth in overseas markets. U.S. exports of bicycles and parts decreased almost 6 percent in 1998 and an estimated 7.6 percent in 1999, adding to U.S. manufacturers' woes. Meanwhile, imports have taken advantage of the high dollar, increasing 14 percent in 1998 and an estimated 17 percent in 1999 (see Table 39-8).

Electronic Commerce

Since quality and product knowledge are key elements in the sale of medium- and high-quality bicycles, most manufacturers have established Web sites to promote and occasionally to sell their products. In addition, several new companies plan to sell most of the major bicycles brands directly on the Internet. These sites have not yet recorded any sales; however, the owner of one site, www.bike.com, believes that his firm could eventually capture 2 percent of total bike market. Although figures of bicycle sales on the Internet are not yet available, the U.S. Department of Commerce estimates that retail E-commerce totaled $7 billion to $15 billion in 1998. The potential of E-commerce is great, as old optimistic estimates of the size of the digital economy typically are far exceeded by new revised estimates. In addition, future sales opportunities should expand as more overseas consumers and businesses get access to the Internet. However, increasing sales over the Internet may strain current manufacturer-distributor relationships as dealers may be asked to increase service on products purchased through E-commerce channels.

Important Factors Affecting the Future Growth of U.S. Industry

While E-commerce probably will have a significant impact on the distribution of bicycles, total sales probably will be influenced by the popularity of bikes. Bicycles have long been an important part of childhood. However, past experience may not induce younger generations to participate in bicycling. Participation in bike riding declined 21 percent from 1990 to 1999, according to a survey by the NSGA. That survey also showed

TABLE 39-8: Bicycles and Bicycle Parts (SIC 37511) Trends and Forecasts
(millions of dollars except as noted)

	1992	1993	1994	1995	1996	1997[1]	1998[1]	1999[2]	2000[3]	Percent Change 92–97[4]	97–98	98–99	99–00
Product data													
Value of shipments[5]	1,023	1,083	1,103	1,048	996	975	860	700	630	−1.0	−11.8	−18.6	−10.0
Value of shipments (1992$)	1,023	1,092	1,112	1.039	981	987	869	704	631	−0.7	−12.0	−19.0	−10.4
Apparent consumption	1,583	1,727	1,729	1,760	1,606	1,644	1,683	1,735	1,765	0.8	2.4	3.1	1.7
Real apparent consumption	1,583	1,741	1,743	1,744	1,582	1,664	1,700	1,744	1,767	1.0	2.1	2.6	1.3
Shipments to domestic market	849	886	903	791	728	665	568	430	365	−4.8	−14.6	−24.3	−15.1
Trade data													
Imports	734	841	825	968	878	979	1,115	1,305	1,400	5.9	13.9	17.0	7.3
Imports to apparent consumption (%)	46	49	48	55	55	60	66	75	79	5.1	11.3	13.5	5.5
Value of exports	175	197	200	257	268	310	292	270	265	12.2	−5.7	−7.6	−1.9
Exports to shipments (%)	17	18	18	25	27	32	34	39	42	13.3	6.9	13.5	9.1

[1] Estimate except imports and exports.
[2] Estimate.
[3] Forecast.
[4] Compound annual rate.
[5] For a definition of industry versus product values, see "Getting the Most Out of *Outlook 2000.*"
Source: U.S. Department of Commerce: Bureau of the Census; International Trade Administration.

that participation among youth declined over that period, dropping 15 percent for children between 7 and 11 years and 13 percent for children between 12 and 17. Greater access to other activities, such as skating, video games, and basketball, is probably the major factor in that decline.

U.S. manufacturers will try to increase interest in the sport over the next several years. Aiding their quest is a recently passed Transportation Bill, TEA-21, which designates an estimated $3 billion over the next several years for the expansion of nonmotorized transportation. Several bicycle organizations and manufacturers have hired advocacy specialists to help steer that money toward projects such as bicycle paths. Increasing access to bicycling through friendly roads, paths, and parks may bring more people into the sport. This commitment also seems to indicate a "maturing" of bicycling from a childhood activity to a mode of adult transportation and recreation as the baby boomer generation has aged.

U.S. Industry Growth Projections for the Next 1 and 5 Years

Imports of bicycles probably will increase over 7 percent in 2000, slowing from the double-digit growth of the last several years. U.S. manufacturers probably will continue to move production to overseas factories in Mexico and China. Constant dollar product shipments of bicycles and parts are forecast to fall over 10 percent in the year 2000. U.S. exports will continue to decrease, but at a lower rate, an estimated 2 percent in 2000, totaling $265 million (Table 39-8). Slightly stronger GDP growth in the top 20 trade-weighted foreign markets of about 3 percent in 2000 compared with an estimated 1.8 percent in 1999 should help export performance. Meanwhile, U.S. apparent consumption adjusted for inflation is forecast to increase an estimated 1.3 percent. With growth of real disposable income expected to grow in the year 2000, the domestic bicycle market should be able to sustain limited growth.

An increase in sales of parts may be a key reason for the growth of apparent consumption. Several manufacturers have developed new seats to respond to medical concerns about impotency and injury. Many bicyclists have purchased and will continue to purchase new seats to avoid potential medical complications and increase comfort. In addition, hard-core mountain bicycling has increased the demand for parts to upgrade to new technologies or replace broken parts. Mountain bike racing, with the pounding of downhill areas and the muddy terrain, can be very hard on parts, causing more frequent replacements. Parts such as fork suspensions, brake pads, chains, and tires are the most likely to be replaced.

Five-year growth in the market probably will be modest at a forecast 1 percent annually. Demographics will play a key role in the modest growth. According to the U.S. Bureau of the Census, the increase in the number of children in the 5- to 14-year-old age group is expected to be lower than population growth of the nation from 1999 to 2004. Historically, U.S. shipments have tended to be correlated with growth in this age group. However, real domestic product shipments probably will decline by a forecast 5 percent compound annual rate, with imports increasing 7 percent over that period. Exports will improve slightly, growing 1 percent annually, as the manufacturers remaining in the United States will have competitive advantages that should give them opportunities overseas. Many of these firms manufacture high-quality products in which price may not be the most important factor in deciding on a purchase.

Global Market Prospects

U.S. imports of bicycles and parts totaled $1.1 billion in 1998, increasing 13.9 percent over 1997 (see Table 39-9). Imports

TABLE 39-9: U.S. Trade Patterns in Bicycles and Parts[1] in 1998
(millions of dollars)

Exports				Imports			
Region[2]	Value[3]	Share, %	Percent Change 97–98	Region[1]	Value[3]	Share, %	Percent Change 97–98
NAFTA	53	18.3	–10.9	NAFTA	52	4.7	150.0
Latin America	22	7.7	–25.3	Latin America	0	0.0	0.0
Western Europe	120	41.0	-9.3	Western Europe	54	4.8	0.0
Japan/Chinese Economic Area	71	24.2	6.6	Japan/Chinese Economic Area	984	88.2	10.3
Other Asia	6	2.1	26.7	Other Asia	23	2.1	8.6
Rest of world	20	6.7	17.5	Rest of world	2	0.2	0.0
World	292	100.0	-5.7	World	1,115	100.0	13.9
Top Five Countries	Value	Share, %	Percent Change 97–98	Top Five Countries	Value	Share, %	Percent Change 97–98
Taiwan	44	15.0	14.9	Taiwan	475	42.6	13.5
Netherlands	37	12.7	-3.7	China	406	36.4	25.7
Canada	31	10.8	-8.3	Japan	99	8.9	–11.4
Mexico	22	7.5	–14.4	Mexico	46	4.1	93.4
Japan	21	7.0	–16.1	Italy	24	2.2	1.2

[1] SIC 37511.
[2] For definitions of regional groupings, see "Getting the Most Out of *Outlook 2000*."
[3] Values may not sum to total due to rounding.
Source: U.S. Department of Commerce, Bureau of the Census.

accounted for 66 percent of apparent consumption. Taiwan, China, Japan, and Mexico are the largest foreign suppliers of bicycles and parts, accounting for a combined 92 percent of U.S. imports. Taiwan remains the largest supplier of bicycles and parts to the United States, supplying $475 million, or 43 percent of total U.S. imports, in 1998; U.S. imports from Taiwan grew 14 percent in that year. While Taiwan remains the largest supplier, bikes from Chinese manufacturers are primarily responsible for the loss of U.S. manufacturers' shares as unit prices for Chinese bicycles produced for the mass-merchandiser market were significantly lower than those for U.S. products. As a result, U.S. imports of bicycles from China increased considerably, growing 26 percent in 1998, to total $406 million, or 36 percent of total U.S. imports. U.S. imports from Japan in 1998 fell 11 percent, totaling $99 million and accounting for 9 percent of total U.S. bicycle imports.

Mexico has been the fastest-growing foreign supplier over the last several years, growing 91 percent annually from 1994 to 1998. U.S. imports from Mexico totaled $46 million in 1998, accounting for 4.1 percent of total U.S. bike imports. U.S. manufacturers have sought to move as much production to Mexico as possible. However, growth has been limited by the time needed to expand facilities and difficulties in acquiring parts. Currently, there are not many Mexican parts manufacturers, and so Mexican plants must import virtually all their parts from the United States or Taiwan. Further hampering production efforts are Mexican tariff rates, which are 18 percent for imported parts from Taiwan. U.S. firms are hoping that Taiwanese parts manufacturers will open plants in Mexico over the next several years to supply the needed parts. An additional concern is that the finished products remain eligible for duty-free treatment under NAFTA by maintaining a certain level of content produced in North America. The U.S. tariff rates for non-NAFTA countries (most favored nations) are 5.5 percent or 11 percent for most imported bicycles.

Taiwan is the world's largest exporter of bicycles in value but second in terms of units. Labor is a significant input into the cost of producing a bicycle. As Taiwan's wage rates have risen, the price competitiveness of its products for the mass-merchandiser market has declined. However, the quality of the products of Taiwanese manufacturers has improved greatly, and those manufacturers supply many of the world's high-quality bicycles, which are sold through bicycle dealers rather than mass merchandisers. Wage rates in China have remained much lower, making that country's products much more competitive. China has maintained its position as the world's largest producer of bicycles by servicing its domestic population of more than 1 billion people. However, with the improved quality of its bikes, China has become a major exporter. China could have become the largest exporter of bicycles if Chinese manufacturers had not had to face high tariffs as a result of safeguard or antidumping actions enacted in several major markets, including the European Union, Canada, Mexico, and South Korea.

In 1998, U.S. exports of bicycles and parts decreased 6 percent from the 1997 level, totaling $292 million. U.S. exports of bicycles and parts accounted for an estimated 34 percent of domestic production in 1998. Several manufacturers have been able to sell products overseas by producing unique and high-quality products. High-quality mountain and BMX bikes and accessories have been particularly in demand. U.S.-made and -branded mountain bikes and parts have a favorable product image in many industrialized nations. However, the high value of the dollar against other major currencies has dampened overseas opportunities.

Taiwan was the largest market for U.S. exports of bicycles and parts in 1998, with U.S. exports totaling $44 million, an increase of 15 percent. Virtually all (97 percent) U.S. exports to Taiwan were bicycle parts in 1998. The Asian financial crisis has not had a great effect on Taiwan. Sales opportunities for U.S. part manufacturers remain strong and have not been affected by the strength of the U.S.

dollar against Asian currencies. Only slightly behind Taiwan in the amount of U.S. exports was the Netherlands. U.S. exports to that country fell almost 4 percent in 1998, totaling $37 million. U.S. exports of bicycles and parts to Canada, the third largest market for U.S. bicycles, totaled $31 million, down over 8 percent. Mexico was the fourth largest market for U.S. exports of bicycles and parts in 1998, with those exports totaling $22 million, a decline of over 14 percent. U.S. bicycles and parts exports to Japan, the fifth largest market for U.S. bicycles, totaled $21 million, down 16 percent.

MOTORCYCLES AND PARTS

Global Industry Trends

Foreign motorcycle and parts markets are very different from U.S. markets. One of the main differences is the greater popularity of motorcycling in most foreign markets. Per capita levels of motorcycle usage are estimated to be higher in many European and Asian markets. However, the motorcycle markets in Asia are dominated by smaller motorcycles, unlike the United States, in which large motorcycles predominate. Some of the Asian markets' preference for smaller motorcycles is due to the fact that larger motorcycles traditionally were not allowed on the market, but many of those restrictions have been lifted. However, Asian consumers have not had the resources to purchase larger motorcycles, and this factor has been compounded by the recent financial crisis in that region. European markets have a much more even distribution between small and large motorcycles. Income and spending power are similar to those in the U.S. market, yet consumers in those markets do not seem as enamored with the cruiser-style motorcycle that is so popular in the United States.

Domestic Trends

The U.S. motorcycle industry experienced positive growth throughout the 1990s. From 1990 to 1999, apparent consumption grew an estimated 11 percent annually in real terms, reaching an estimated $2.4 billion in 1999 (see Table 39-10). Over that period, U.S. real product shipments increased 8 percent annually, totaling an estimated $2 billion in 1999. U.S. imports of motorcycles and parts more than tripled from $450 million in 1990 to an estimated $1.5 billion in 1999. U.S. exports of motorcycles and parts increased from $306 million to an estimated $530 million in 1999, an estimated annual growth rate of 6 percent over the 1990–1999 period. U.S. exports of motorcycles and parts peaked at $666 million in 1997.

This occurred in spite of the fact that the number of motorcycle riders did not increase in the 1990s. Registration figures compiled by the Motorcycle Industry Council (MIC) show that registrations were virtually the same in 1997 as they were in 1990: In 1990, there were 4.088 million motorcycles registered in the United States, compared with 4.011 million in 1997. However, several aspects of these market segments have changed. Sales of large motorcycles (with engines over 750 cc) increased dramatically in the 1990s. The MIC estimates that population for on-highway or street motorcycles over 750 cc grew an estimated 9 percent annually from 1990 to 1997. These motorcycles have a high unit value, boosting U.S. apparent consumption and manufacturing. U.S. producers made primarily large motorcycles, and their shipments thus mirrored the growth of the large motorcycle population. U.S. product shipments of motorcycles increased an estimated 8 percent annually from 1990 to 1997.

In an effort to capture some of the growth of large motorcycle market, there have been several new entrants in the market. Polaris, Excelsior/Henderson, and Indian all have begun to produce large cruising motorcycles. Currently, annual output from these manufacturers is at modest levels. However, Polaris manufactures several small engine products and probably has the capacity to increase production substantially if demand increases. The Indian was a popular U.S. brand name in the

TABLE 39-10: Motorcycles and Parts (SIC 37512) Trends and Forecasts
(millions of dollars except as noted)

	1992	1993	1994	1995	1996	1997[1]	1998[1]	1999[2]	2000[3]	Percent Change 97–98	98–99	99–00	92–97[4]
Product data													
Value of shipments[5]	968	1,277	1,228	1,387	1,585	1,636	1,795	1,975	2,125	9.7	10.0	7.6	11.1
Value of shipments (1992$)	968	1,225	1,143	1,215	1,309	1,375	1,486	1,611	1,707	8.1	8.4	6.0	7.3
Apparent consumption	1,274	1,648	1,654	1,952	2,018	2,074	2,462	2,945	3,075	18.7	19.6	4.4	10.2
Real apparent consumption	1,274	1,581	1,539	1,714	1,740	1,743	2,038	2,402	2,470	17.0	17.9	2.8	6.5
Shipments to domestic market	472	772	717	791	881	970	1,169	1,445	1,525	20.6	23.6	5.5	15.5
Trade data													
Imports	803	877	937	1,162	1,137	1,104	1,293	1,500	1,550	17.1	16.0	3.3	6.6
Imports to apparent consumption (%)	63	53	57	60	56	53	53	51	50	–1.4	–3.0	–1.0	–3.3
Value of exports	497	506	511	593	638	666	626	530	600	–6.1	–15.3	13.2	6.1
Exports to shipments (%)	51	40	42	43	42	41	35	27	28	–14.4	–23.1	5.2	–4.5

[1] Estimate except imports and exports.
[2] Estimate.
[3] Forecast.
[4] Compound annual rate.
[5] For a definition of industry versus product values, see "Getting the Most Out of *Outlook 2000.*"
Source: U.S. Department of Commerce: Bureau of the Census; International Trade Administration.

past. The company name has been bought and sold frequently. The current owner of the name believes that it can return the brand name to popularity.

The growth of sales of large motorcycles can be traced to several factors, including the rebound of the popular motorcycle maker Harley-Davidson and the spending power of motorcyclists in the baby boom generation. Harley-Davidson is a company rich in tradition. It was founded in 1903 and through the years has been a symbol of the American lifestyle. In the mid-1980s, the firm reorganized and worked to transform its products into high-quality machines with nostalgia appeal and the styling of the past, thus increasing demand for its products. The second reason for the growth in popularity of large motorcycles was the increased spending power of the baby boom generation. As baby boomers matured and as their average age and income increased, motorcycle owners traded up for newer, bigger, more comfortable, and more expensive motorcycles. Large touring, racing, and custom-styled motorcycles have been the most popular motorcycles among the baby boom generation.

In off-highway, or off-road, category, the estimated population of these motorcycles increased an estimated 9 percent annually from 1990 to 1997. The popularity of off-road motorcycles can be traced back to the first-time riders and young adults experimenting with motorcycling. Typically, off-road motorcycling has attracted younger consumers who enjoy the thrill and excitement of riding. Generally, these younger consumers have less disposable income and therefore tend to purchase small off-road motorcycles, which are less expensive. Despite the decline in suitable land for dirt bike riding, the number of these motorcycles continues to grow. In addition, as young dirt bike enthusiasts have matured, they have stayed involved in the off-road sport, progressing to medium-size and large off-road motorcycles. Sales of these larger bikes grew 9 percent annually from 1990 to 1997, maintaining the percentage share of the dirt bike market that they had in 1990 and 1997.

If large highway and off-highway motorcycles were the best-selling bikes, street bikes under 750 cc performed the worst. The population of street motorcycles under 750 cc declined an estimated 3 percent annually from 1990 to 1997. Sales of smaller on-highway motorcycles have been affected by the lack of a significant crossover from off-highway to on-highway bikes, the decline in popularity of scooters, and the lack of products that capture young consumers' attention as the large cruiser bike has captured the older age group's. Typically, there has been some crossover from dirt bikes to on-highway bikes. This may be happening, but not in the small motorcycle market. This is illustrated by the decline in sales of dual-purpose motorcycles, which fell an estimated 2 percent annually from 1990 to 1997. The decline in scooter sales also has depressed small motorcycle sales. The decreasing popularity of scooters may be the result of increased congestion on most major roads, making the use of smaller motorcycles such as scooters a more dangerous choice for riding enthusiasts. A final reason for the decline of smaller on-highway motorcycles could be the fact that manufacturers have been unable to offer products that appeal to consumers as the chrome-laden large cruisers do.

Important Factors Affecting the Future Growth of U.S. Industry

Current dollar product shipments for motorcycles and parts totaled an estimated $1.8 billion and $2 billion in 1998 and 1999, respectively (see Table 39-10). Constant dollar product shipments increased over 8 percent in both 1998 and 1999. Sales of heavyweight motorcycles (those with engines over 750 cc) accounted for an estimated 23 percent of the domestic market by units in 1990 versus 43 percent in 1997. Moderate to slow growth in the other motorcycle segments, such as entry-level

TABLE 39-11: U.S. Trade Patterns in Motorcycles and Parts[1] in 1998
(millions of dollars; percent)

Exports				Imports			
Region[2]	Value[3]	Share, %	Percent Change 97–98	Region[2]	Value[3]	Share, %	Percent Change 97–98
NAFTA	100	16.0	−0.1	NAFTA	18	1.4	3.0
Latin America	35	5.6	−24.4	Latin America	3	0.2	6.3
Western Europe	301	48.2	−3.8	Western Europe	204	15.8	22.5
Japan/Chinese Economic Area	111	17.8	1.0	Japan/Chinese Economic Area	1,042	80.6	16.9
Other Asia	6	0.9	−55.1	Other Asia	7	0.5	0.2
Rest of world	72	11.5	−13.3	Rest of world	19	1.5	−0.9
World	626	100.0	−6.1	World	1,293	100.0	17.1
Top Five Countries	**Value**	**Share, %**	**Percent Change 97–98**	**Top Five Countries**	**Value**	**Share**	**Percent Change 97–98**
Japan	109	17.5	3.5	Japan	993	76.8	17.0
Canada	95	15.2	1.6	Italy	70	5.4	37.1
Germany	93	14.8	12.5	Germany	65	5.0	12.0
Netherlands	49	7.9	−0.6	Taiwan	45	3.5	13.6
United Kingdom	44	7.0	28.2	United Kingdom	37	2.9	13.4

[1] SIC 37512
[2] For definitions of regional groupings, see "Getting the Most Out of *Outlook 2000.*"
[3] Values may not sum to total due to rounding.
Source: U.S. Department of Commerce, Bureau of the Census.

motorcycles, has negated some of the positive benefits of the heavyweight markets. U.S. imports of motorcycles and parts totaled an estimated $1.3 billion, increasing over 17 percent in 1998 (see Table 39-11), and reached an estimated $1.5 billion in 1999, a 16 percent increase. The Asian financial crisis gave Japanese manufacturers favorable exchange rates and lower prices to offer to U.S. consumers, particularly in 1998. Meanwhile, U.S. exports of motorcycles and parts decreased 6 percent in 1998 and an estimated 15 percent in 1999. The demand for U.S.-manufactured motorcycles overseas was hurt by the high value of the dollar against other major currencies and slow overall economic growth in many top motorcycle markets. In 1998 and 1999, apparent consumption totaled $2 billion and $2.4 billion, increasing 17 percent and 18 percent in real terms, respectively.

A major restraint on foreign and domestic sales has been the lack of supply of Harley-Davidson motorcycles. Although the company has increased production significantly over the last several years, it has not been able to keep up with demand. Dealers typically have domestic waiting lists of a year or more for buyers wishing to purchase a Harley. Overseas, the expected wait is longer and there are high prices on the used market. However, the company opened a new facility in 1998 and improved production capacity at existing facilities; this will increase production substantially by 2003, the firm's centennial anniversary. With the increased capacity, the company believes that it will be able to meet the growing worldwide demand for its products.

U.S. Industry Growth Projections for the Next 1 and 5 Years

Constant dollar product shipments of motorcycles and parts are forecast to increase 6 percent in the year 2000. Apparent consumption will continue to grow an estimated 3 percent in real terms. Slower growth in personal disposable income probably will slow the growth of personal consumption expenditures on motorcycles. Exports will rebound and increase an estimated 13 percent in 2000. This increase is due largely to an increasing supply of Harley-Davidson motorcycles and a forecast improvement in Asian and European markets in 2000. Real GDP in the top 20 markets for U.S. total exports is expected to grow 3 percent on average in 2000. U.S. imports are expected to rise over 3 percent, again based on slowing of consumer spending among U.S. consumers.

Real domestic product shipments are expected to grow at an annual rate of 2 percent between 1999 and 2004, benefiting from growth in the export sector and domestic demand for touring and custom-style motorcycles. Domestic and foreign demand for large motorcycles should remain strong, particularly in the early years of this time period.

Demographics have played a key role in the growth that will continue over this time period. Motorcyclists of the baby boom generation are primarily in the 45- to 54-year-old age group. This is a time when individuals have their highest levels of discretionary income. The 55- to 64-year-old age group will be the fastest growing, and the age group 45 to 54 the second fastest growing age group, increasing at annual rates of 4 percent and 3 percent, respectively, from 1999 to 2004.

An additional factor affecting future growth will be the expansion of the Internet and E-commerce. More individuals are getting on the Internet and learning about products such as motorcycles and parts. It is likely that more sales of parts will occur over the Internet. Business-to-business transactions will lower administrative costs and streamline paperwork and documentation. An informed consumer with more outlets to purchase equipment that might cost less as a result of lower production expenses is certainly a positive development associated with increased Internet activity.

Global Market Prospects

In 1998, U.S. imports of motorcycles approached $1.3 billion and accounted for 53 percent of apparent consumption. Japan was the largest foreign supplier of motorcycles, accounting for almost 77 percent of total U.S. imports, or $993 million. Imports from the four major manufacturers of motorcycles in Japan—Honda, Kawasaki, Suzuki, and Yamaha—account for an estimated 40 percent of U.S. consumption. Italy and Germany were the other major suppliers of motorcycles to the United States, supplying a total of $70 million and $65 million, respectively; each accounted for roughly 5 percent of U.S. imports of motorcycles in 1998, with many of those imports coming from Ducati in Italy and BMW in Germany.

U.S. exports have become a more important factor in domestic production. The ratio of exports to shipments was 35 percent in 1998 (see Table 39-10). Harley-Davidson continues to have difficulty meeting foreign demand, providing most foreign markets with an allocated percentage of available supply. As was stated earlier, demand exceeds supply in many foreign markets. As a result, many entrepreneurs have stepped in and begun exporting used or new Harleys, inflating the ratio to some degree. In addition, the U.S. manufacturer has faced unfavorable exchange rates, making its product appear even more expensive.

The European Union (EU) was the largest foreign market for U.S. motorcycle exports, totaling $283 million in 1998, or 45 percent of these exports. However, the European markets are primarily performance markets where manufacturers such as BMW, Honda, Kawasaki, and Ducati dominate the overall market. In addition, the EU has the strictest noise emission standards in the world. Owners of larger motorcycles, including cruisers such as Harley-Davidson motorcycles, often modify the exhaust system to produce more power and noise. Finally, U.S. manufacturers are pushing the EU to lower motorcycle tariffs, which are currently 9 percent, during the next round of WTO negotiations.

U.S. motorcycle manufacturers exported $109 million to Japan, which was the largest single-country export market for U.S. motorcycles in 1998. Those exports grew 3.5 percent in 1998. U.S. exports to Japan benefited from new regulations that make it easier for consumers to obtain an operator's license for large motorcycles (those with engines over 400 cc). These changes came about after several years of efforts by Harley-Davidson and the U.S. government to persuade Japanese officials to change rigorous and cumbersome test procedures for the potential operators of large motorcycles. Export sales to the Japanese market are still hampered by the prohibition of tandem riding and a lower speed limit on expressways. Many potential Japanese owners of heavyweight motorcycles pass up the opportunity to own a Harley-Davidson because riding with a passenger is prohibited on Japanese expressways and because other roads are slow and potentially dangerous.

Canada was the second largest market for U.S. exports of motorcycles and parts; those exports increased 1.6 percent in 1998 to total $95 million. U.S. exports of motorcycles and parts to Germany and the Netherlands, the third and fourth largest markets in 1998, totaled $93 million and $49 million, up 12.5 percent and down 0.6 percent, respectively.

Increasing motorcycle sales to Asian markets will be an important factor in the future outlook of the industry. As was stated earlier, Asian markets have a strong proclivity toward using motorcycles but have not yet used large motorcycles. U.S. manufacturers are expecting that personal income levels in those markets will rise so that consumers will be able to purchase larger U.S.-made motorcycles. U.S. motorcycle officials believe that the Asian consumers desire these large bikes and that U.S. exports of motorcycles will increase rapidly over the next decade.

BOAT BUILDING AND REPAIRING

The boat building and repairing industry (SIC 3732) consists of manufacturers that produce primarily pleasure boats, including motorboats, sailboats, rowboats, and canoes. The industry does not include ship building and repairing, inflatable boats, or marine engines. Although this industry also includes small commercial and military craft, this discussion will center on trends in leisure craft.

Domestic Trends

The U.S. pleasure boat industry has had several years of growth, with real domestic shipments growing 3 percent annually from 1992 to 1998 (see Table 39-12). Over that period, real apparent consumption also rose, growing 5 percent annually, thanks mostly to an annual growth rate of 22 percent in U.S. imports of pleasure boats. The boating industry has kept pace with the national economy, which grew 3 percent annually from 1992 to 1998 as measured by real GDP. Growth in personal income and consumer spending have been the highlights of GDP growth, and those factors are key indicators of growth for the boating industry. Real disposable personal income grew 2 percent annually from 1992 to 1998, while total real personal consumption expenditures grew 3 percent annually over that period. Real personal consumption expenditures on boats increased 15 percent annually over that period.

However, in 1999, the boating industry saw growth slow down while the national economy continued to have strong growth. In the first 6 months of 1999, GDP and disposable personal income each increased 4 percent compared with the first 6 months of 1998, while personal consumption expenditures increased 5 percent in real terms after double-digit annual growth from 1992 through 1998. In 1999, real domestic shipments increased an estimated 1 percent, totaling $6.2 billion in current dollars. Fueled by an estimated 10 percent growth in U.S. boat imports, apparent consumption increased 2.3 percent

TABLE 39-12: Boat Building and Repairing (SIC 3732) Trends and Forecasts
(millions of dollars except as noted)

											Percent Change			
	1992	1993	1994	1995	1996	1997[1]	1998[1]	1999[2]	2000[3]	2004[3]	97–98	98–99	99–00	99–04[4]
Product data														
Value of shipments[5]	4,331	4,632	4,887	5,072	5,214	5,750	6,000	6,175	6,250	7,400	4.3	2.9	1.2	3.7
Value of shipments (1992$)	4,331	4,550	4,722	4,762	4,731	5,044	5,150	5,198	5,230	5,649	2.1	0.9	0.6	1.7
Apparent consumption	3,874	4,523	4,945	5,221	5,591	5,891	6,188	6,455	6,525	7,725	5.0	4.3	1.1	3.7
Real apparent consumption	3,874	4,443	4,777	4,903	5,073	5,167	5,311	5,434	5,460	5,897	2.8	2.3	0.5	1.7
Trade data														
Value of imports	257	425	564	807	997	814	851	935	950	1,175	4.6	9.9	1.6	4.7
Imports to apparent consumption (%)	6.6	9.4	11.4	15.5	17.8	13.8	13.8	14.5	14.6	15.2	–0.4	5.3	0.5	1.0
Value of exports	714.4	534.2	507	658	621	673	663	655	675	850	–1.4	–1.3	3.1	5.4
Exports to shipments (%)	16.5	11.5	10.4	13.0	11.9	11.7	11.1	10.6	10.8	11.5	–5.5	–4.1	1.8	1.6
Industry data														
Value of shipments[5]	4,648	4,975	5,334	5,597	5,823	6,420	6,700	6,870	6,825	8,200	4.4	2.5	–0.7	3.6
Value of shipments (1992$)	4,648	4,887	5,154	5,255	5,284	5,632	5,751	5,783	5,711	6,260	2.1	0.6	–1.2	1.6
Total employment (thousands)	44.5	47.0	47.6	47.9	49.2									
Production workers (thousands)	34.4	36.8	38.4	38.9	40.1									
Average hourly earnings ($)	9.58	9.57	9.70	10.49	10.57									
Capital expenditures	63.6	83.2	98.9	89.0	109.0									

[1] Estimate except imports and exports.
[2] Estimate.
[3] Forecast.
[4] Compound annual rate.
[5] For a definition of industry versus product values, see "Getting the Most Out of *Outlook 2000.*"
Source: U.S. Department of Commerce: Bureau of the Census; International Trade Administration.

in real terms. Several indicators for the boat industry began to slow or decline. While consumers continued to spend, they began to dip into savings in 1999. Savings as a percentage of disposable income averaged −1 percent in the first half of 1999. The ratio of consumer debt to personal income also remained high, above 18 percent, for the fifth consecutive year. In addition, interest rates increased modestly throughout the first half of the year. These indicators made consumers more concerned about taking on the significant additional debt associated with the purchase of a boat. This consumer wariness can be measured to a degree by consumer expectations surveys. According to a University of Michigan survey, consumers' expectations dipped in the first half of 1999, down 3.8 percent from 1998. Indicators such as consumer expectations were at or near record highs. It is likely that the negative growth may only slow growth in the industry rather than signaling a decline. In addition, some manufacturers are reporting a shift of consumer preferences toward larger, more expensive boats, offsetting any negative growth trends in the industry. Industry shipments were expected to increase almost 1 percent in 1999 in 1992 dollars.

A further concern of the boating industry in regard to today's consumers is whether they continue to enjoy boating. Participation in boating and boating activities declined over the last 10 years. According to an NSGA survey, 25.7 million people participated in power and motor boating in 1998, down from 32.5 million in 1988. Participation in sailing decreased from 6.7 million to 3.6 million individuals from 1988 to 1998. Several activities associated with boating also declined, such as water skiing and fishing. Over that period, participation in water skiing dropped from 12.8 million to 7.2 million individuals. Fishing lost 2.1 million individuals from 1988 to 1998, when it had 43.6 million participants. Overdevelopment of water locations, higher participation costs versus those for other recreational activities, and a lack of a concerted effort to promote the activity are the reasons most commonly cited for the decline in participation.

Electronic Commerce

The Internet could give the boating industry many additional sales opportunities. For many consumers, the process of buying a boat does not involve a lot of choices. Typically, many communities have one or two dealers with only a few product lines. Because of the cost of floor space, those dealers cannot display a full product line. However, with much greater information exchange over the Internet, consumers probably will learn about many more products and have more choices. Currently, few, if any, manufacturers sell complete boats on the Internet. In the future, that may change as manufacturers will be able to reach more consumers and add custom features that can be expensive to purchase through the current limited dealer network. One segment of the boating industry that is already using the Internet extensively to sell products is the boat accessory and parts market. There are several on-line parts and accessory distributors that provide consumers with greater choices in products, typically at a lower price. Manufacturers also have benefited from business-to-business sales, improving the manufacturing process by speeding the order and efficiency of purchasing parts and allowing manufacturers to shrink their inventory of parts.

However, the development of E-commerce could provide problems for manufacturers and distributors in terms of its effects on service for sold products. Where will consumers go for after-sales questions and service? Companies will have to be formed that will service and repair boats for on-line dealers or the expansion of E-commerce in the boating industry will be short-lived. Much like a car, a boat needs continuing care, and currently that usually is done by boat dealers or small service shops at marinas. Dealers may be apprehensive about working on boats that they did not offer or sell, while small service shops will not have the capacity to satisfy the additional demand for repairs and service. This problem can be overcome if on-line dealers, manufacturers, and service companies work together to address these concerns before expanding.

E-commerce also will provide U.S. manufacturers with additional opportunities. More foreign consumers will learn about the quality and price of U.S. boating products through the Internet. Since Web pages can be accessed worldwide, smaller manufacturers will be able to reach a larger audience to show the merits of their products. If manufacturers are savvy about regulations and tariffs in foreign markets, overseas E-commerce may represent their best opportunity to increase sales by reaching untapped markets. Again, as manufacturers start to make sales on the Internet, they will have to be able to provide aftermarket service for their products or foreign consumers will choose products already available to them locally.

Global Industry Trends

Despite the potential of international E-commerce, foreign market demand has been weak over the last several years. U.S. exports of pleasure boats fell 1 percent annually from 1992 through 1998. In 1999, U.S. exports were estimated to lose over 1 percent. Overall economic conditions in many overseas markets have not been as strong as those in the U.S. market. Real GDP growth in the top 20 overseas markets, as weighted by U.S. total manufacturing exports, increased only 2 percent in 1998 and an estimated 1.8 percent in 1999 compared with 3.9 percent and an estimated 3.5 percent for the U.S. market in 1998 and 1999, respectively. As was the case more recently in the United States, this probably meant that consumer confidence and disposable income growth were lower, making consumers slightly more apprehensive about buying a boat. In addition, it is likely that less was spent on capital investments, particularly marina development. Furthermore, overseas pleasure boat markets are smaller and therefore typically have fewer dealers and distributors that are willing to take risks when the economy is weak or unstable.

The U.S. pleasure boat market is the largest in the world. U.S. consumption of pleasure boats and marine accessories accounts for an estimated 60 percent of the worldwide market for such products. Typically, U.S. manufacturers hope for a strong U.S. market to bolster sales and profits. A strong U.S. market also helps exports to a degree, as economies of scale are an important factor in the production of boats. If U.S. manufacturers are able to produce a large number of boats for the U.S. market, prices will decline for domestic and international buyers, making the U.S. firms more price-competitive overseas.

An additional concern for the boat industry is the increased cost associated with new legislation regulating and taxing the boating industry. The U.S. Environmental Protection Agency (EPA) and the industry have begun implementing stricter emissions standards that will be gradually phased in over the next 6 years and probably will add noise standards over the next several years. These stricter emissions standards require a large capital investment by marine engine companies such as Brunswick and OMC. Similar outboard engine emissions standards are being drafted in the EU. The engine industry has been negotiating with the Europeans for a phase-in period similar to the EPA phase-in. If emissions regulations have no phase-in, they will cause a severe disruption in the supply of outboards to the EU. Other regulations being considered, including operator licensing, upgraded standards for boat components, marine wildlife protection laws, and various user fees and taxes, also may have a significant impact on the boating industry.

Important Factors Affecting the Future Growth of U.S. Industry

Consumer spending has been the key to the growing U.S. economy. However, most economic experts believe that consumer spending will slow in the year 2000. One of the first items households typically would cut back on would be a boat, as consumers typically are not willing to take on additional debt that can be avoided. U.S. shipments of boats often have fallen before a slow or declining year in the general economy. From 1989 to 1991, annual real GDP growth slowed, reaching 2.5 percent in 1989, 1.2 percent in 1990, and –0.6 percent in 1991; meanwhile, real industry shipments declined annually over that period, falling 9 percent in 1989, 16 percent in 1990, and 30 percent in 1991.

U.S. Industry Growth Projections for the Next 1 and 5 Years

U.S. apparent consumption is expected to increase 0.5 percent in real terms, totaling $6.5 billion in current dollars in the year 2000. U.S. imports are expected to total $950 million, up 1.6 percent. U.S. product shipments of boats will grow to a forecast $6.2 billion, increasing 0.6 percent in real terms in 2000. Meanwhile, U.S. exports of boats are expected to grow a modest 3.1 percent for the first time since 1997 to reach $675 million (see Table 39-12). The top 20 trade-weighted economies, based on U.S. exports of total manufacturing products, are expected to grow faster, recording an estimated rate of 3 percent. The overall U.S. economy as measured by GDP and total consumption is expected to grow 2 to 2.5 percent in 2000. This slowdown in growth will prompt the decline of the U.S. boating market as real industry shipments for boats will decline an estimated 1 percent. Consumers probably will start reducing their debt burden before seeking additional credit to purchase a boat. Also important in regard to the forecast will be consumer confidence. Greater declines in industry shipments will be avoided if consumer confidence does not fall dramatically. For consumers who lose confidence in the economy, a highly discretionary purchase such as a boat probably will be deferred.

Five-year growth in the market will be dependent on demographic trends and the continuation of favorable economic trends. More and more baby boomers are preparing for retirement. With retirement comes additional leisure time to participate in boating. However, this group is passing its peak wage-earning years and may be wary of taking on the additional debt burden of a boat. From 1999 through 2004, the 55- to 64-year-old age group will be the fastest-growing population segment. This age group, according to the 1997 Consumer Expenditures Survey of the Bureau of Labor Statistics, spends 56 percent less than does the age group 45 to 54 on boats with a motor. However, the latter age group also will be growing and is much larger, about 10 million, than the age group 55 to 64. According to the survey, consumers between the ages of 45 and 54 are the most likely to purchase a boat with a motor.

With some mixed demographic trends, boat sales also will be dependent on factors such as the growth of real personal disposable income, interest rates, consumer confidence, and the consumer debt ratio. If these indicators remain positive as forecast, constant dollar industry shipments are expected to grow 1.7 percent from 1999 to 2004. Imports and exports probably will grow about 5 percent each annually over that period. As a result, real apparent consumption will grow at an estimated 1.7 percent annual rate from 1999 to 2004.

Global Market Prospects

Despite the fact that U.S. exports of boats are declining, export opportunities are still important factors in U.S. manufacturing trends. Foreign consumers are discovering the pleasure of boating. Their governments and land developers are trying to respond to that desire by building the proper infrastructure. The ratio of exports to shipments for boat building and repairing was an estimated 11 percent in 1998. The U.S. boat building industry is the world's largest supplier of recreational craft. Supplying the sizable U.S. market gives U.S. manufacturers many advantages in overseas markets, including economies of scale and product innovation insights. Many consumers in overseas markets look for the "made in the USA" label because they believe that U.S. manufacturers provide the highest-quality products. U.S. manufacturers are competitive overseas and produce high-quality products. Overseas markets are typically volatile from year to year, as managing the proper amount of supply can be tricky, particularly for many small dealers and suppliers.

In 1998, Canada was the largest market for U.S. exports of boats, with those exports totaling $203 million, a 15 percent increase over the previous year. Canada's proximity to the United States and its numerous navigable lakes and rivers provide many opportunities for U.S. manufacturers. U.S. exports of boats to Canada account for 31 percent of all U.S. boat exports (see Table 39-13). The Netherlands was the next largest market for U.S. boat exports, with exports totaling $51 million, growing 24 percent in 1998 and accounting for 8 percent of all U.S. boat exports. The Netherlands also has many navigable canals and

TABLE 39-13: U.S. Trade Patterns in Boat Building and Repairing[1] in 1998
(millions of dollars; percent)

Exports			Imports		
Region[2]	Value[3]	Share,%	Region[2]	Value[3]	Share,%
NAFTA	221	33	NAFTA	346	41
Latin America	83	13	Latin America	10	1
Western Europe	252	38	Western Europe	324	38
Japan/Chinese Economic Area	44	7	Japan/Chinese Economic Area	107	13
Other Asia	5	1	Other Asia	27	3
Rest of world	58	9	Rest of world	38	4
World	663	100	World	851	100
Top Five Countries	Value	Share,%	Top Five Countries	Value	Share,%
Canada	203	31	Canada	345	41
Netherlands	51	8	United Kingdom	91	11
Japan	42	6	Italy	80	9
United Kingdom	39	6	Taiwan	72	8
Germany	34	5	Germany	56	7

[1] SIC 3732.
[2] For definitions of regional groupings, see "Getting the Most Out of *Outlook 2000.*"
[3] Values may not sum to total due to rounding.
Source: U.S. Department of Commerce, Bureau of the Census.

rivers and the North Sea, which can be used for recreational purposes. In 1998, Japan was the third largest market for U.S. boat exports, with exports totaling $42 million. U.S. exports of boats to Japan fell 28 percent as declining real GDP growth (–2.8 percent) affected the boating market. Japan has numerous inlets and coastlines that could be used for recreational boats. However, currently there is a lack of adequate marina facilities as expected development projects have been delayed by the weak growth of the Japanese economy. The United Kingdom was the fourth largest market for U.S. exports of boats, with those exports totaling $39 million and increasing 12 percent. The fifth largest market for exports of boats was Germany, where U.S. exports decreased 6 percent to $34 million in 1998.

U.S. imports of pleasure boats grew 5 percent in 1998, thanks in large part to the high value of the dollar against other major currencies. The ratio of imports to apparent consumption was almost 14 percent in 1998. The largest foreign supplier of pleasure boats to the United States was Canada. U.S. imports from Canada totaled $345 million in 1998, a decrease of 23 percent. Weak demand for personal watercraft probably was the major cause of this decline, as one of the major suppliers of these boats produces in Canada. The United Kingdom was the second largest foreign supplier in 1998, with U.S. imports from that country climbing 32 percent to reach $91 million. U.S. imports from the United Kingdom experienced double-digit growth from 1992 to 1998. Italy was the third largest foreign supplier to the U.S. market; U.S. imports from that country totaled $80 million, up 10 percent in 1998. Italian manufacturers produce primarily large yachts and sailboats. Taiwan and Germany were the fourth and fifth largest foreign suppliers, with imports from those countries totaling $72 million and $56 million, respectively, in 1998. U.S. imports from Germany increased exponentially in 1998, possibly as a result of a temporary surge in the sale of large yachts, possibly previously owned craft. U.S. imports from Germany were down 93 percent during the first half of 1999 compared with the same period in 1998.

John A. Vanderwolf, U.S. Department of Commerce, Office of Consumer Goods, (202) 482-0348, John Vanderwolf@ita.doc.gov, September 1999.

REFERENCES

Call the Bureau of the Census at (301) 457-4100 for information about how to order Census documents.

Bicycle Business Journal, 1904 Wenneca Street, Fort Worth, TX 76102. (817) 870-0341.

Bicycling Magazine, 33 East Minor Street, Emmaus, PA 18049. (215) 967-5171.

Boat and Motor Dealer, 3949 Oakton, Skokie, IL 60076. (312) 982-1810.

Boating, Diamandis Communications, Inc., 1633 Broadway, New York, NY 10019. (800) 525-0643.

Boating Industry, 850 Third Ave., New York, NY 10022. (212) 715-2600.

Boating 1998, National Marine Manufacturers Association, 200 East Randolph Drive, Suite 5100, Chicago, IL 60601. (312) 946-6200.

Dealernews, Edgell Communications, Inc., P.O. Box 19531, Irvine, CA 92714. (800) 346-0085.

Marine Business Journal, 1766 Bay Road, Miami Beach, FL 33139. (305) 538-0700.

Motorcycle Product News, P.O. Box 2338, 6633 Odessa Avenue, Van Nuys, CA 91406. (818) 997-0644.

1992 Census of Retail Trade, SIC 5941, Sporting Goods Stores and Bicycle Shops, Retail, Series RC92-A-52 (quinquennial), Bureau of the Census, U.S. Department of Commerce, Washington, DC 20233. (301) 457-2687.

1997 Economic Census: Manufacturing Industry Series: (EC97M-EC97M-3366B) Boat Building, U.S. Bureau of the Census. http://www.census.gov/prod/www/abs/97ecmani.html.

1997 Economic Census: Manufacturing Industry Series: (EC97M-EC97M-3399F) Doll and Stuffed Toy Manufacturing. U.S. Bureau of the Census. http://www.census.gov/prod/www/abs/97ecmani.html.

1997 Economic Census: Manufacturing Industry Series: (EC97M-EC97M-3399G) Game, Toy, and Children's Vehicle Manufacturing. U.S. Bureau of the Census. http://www.census.gov/prod/www/abs/97ecmani.html.

1997 Economic Census: Manufacturing Industry Series: (EC97M-EC97M-3369A) Motorcycles, Bicycles, and Parts, U.S. Bureau of the Census. http://www.census.gov/prod/www/abs/97ecmani.html.

1997 Economic Census: Manufacturing Industry Series: (EC97M-EC97M-3399E) Sporting and Athletic Goods, U.S. Bureau of the Census. http://www.census.gov/prod/www/abs/97ecmani.html.

The 1998 Motorcycle Statistical Annual, Motorcycle Industry Council, 2 Jenner Street, Suite 150, Irvine, CA 92718. (714) 727-4211.

Playthings, Cahners Business Information, 51 Madison Avenue, New York, NY 10010. (212) 689-5302; fax: (212) 683-7929.

Personal Consumption Expenditures, Bureau of Economic Analysis, U.S. Department of Commerce, Washington, DC 20230. (202) 606-5302.

Ship and Boat Building, Railroad and Miscellaneous Transportation Equipment, SIC 3732 and 3751, 1992 Census of Manufactures, Series MC92-I-37C (quinquennial). Bureau of the Census, U.S. Department of Commerce, Washington, DC 20233. (301) 763-7304.

Soundings Trade-Only, Pratt Street, Essex, CT 06426. (203) 767-3200.

Sporting and Athletic Goods, SIC 3949, 1992 Census of Manufactures, Series MC92-I-39B, Bureau of Census, U.S. Department of Commerce, Washington, DC 20233. (301) 457-7304.

Sporting Goods Business, Gralla Publications, 1515 Broadway, New York, NY 10036. (212) 869-1300.

Sporting Goods Dealer, Sporting News Publishing Co., 1212 North Lindbergh Boulevard, St. Louis, MO 63132. (314) 997-7111.

The Sporting Goods Market in 1998, National Sporting Goods Association, Mt. Prospect, IL 60056. (847) 439-4000.

Sports Participation in 1998, National Sporting Goods Association, Mt. Prospect, IL 60056. (847) 439-4000.

Sport Style, Fairchild Publications, 7 East 12 Street, New York, NY 10003. (212) 741-5971.

Sports Trend, Shore Communications Inc., Suite 300, N Building, 180 Allen Road, NE, Atlanta, GA 30328. (404) 252-8831.

Toy Book, Adventyre Publishing Group, Inc., 1501 Broadway, Suite 500, New York, NY 10036. (212) 575-4510; fax: (212) 575-4521.

Toy Manufacturers of America, 1115 Broadway, New York NY 10010. (212) 675-1141; fax: (212) 633-1429; http://www.tma-toy.com.

Wall Street Journal, 200 Liberty Street, New York, NY 10281. http://wsj.com.

■ RELATED CHAPTERS

16: Microelectronics
22: Shipbuilding and Repair
36: Motor Vehicles
37: Automotive Parts
42: Retailing

OTHER CONSUMER DURABLES
Economic and Trade Trends

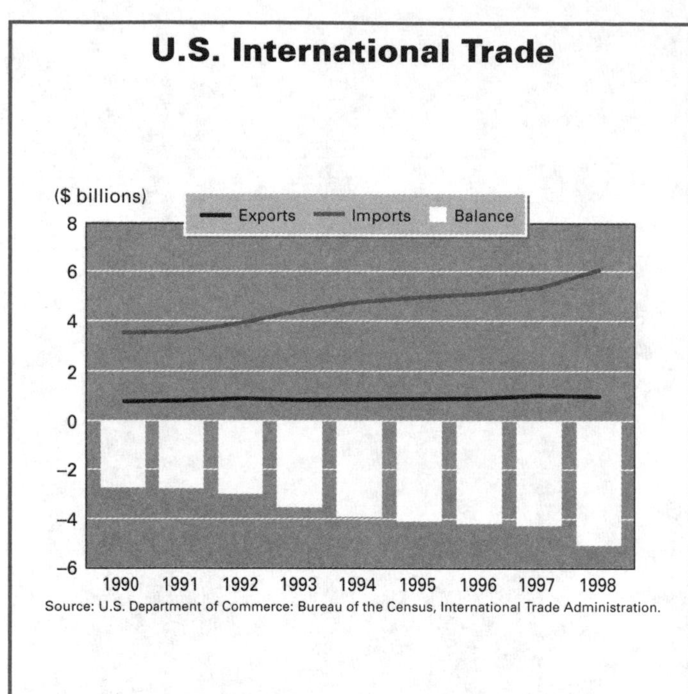

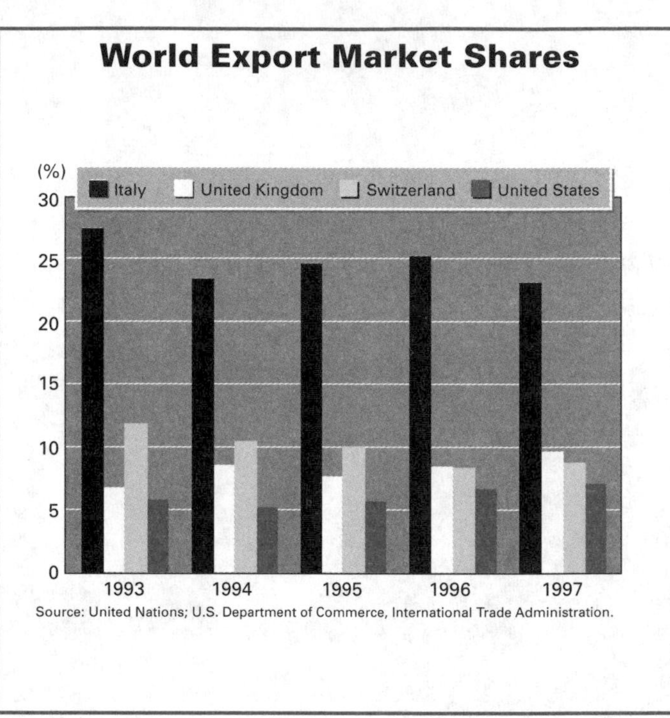

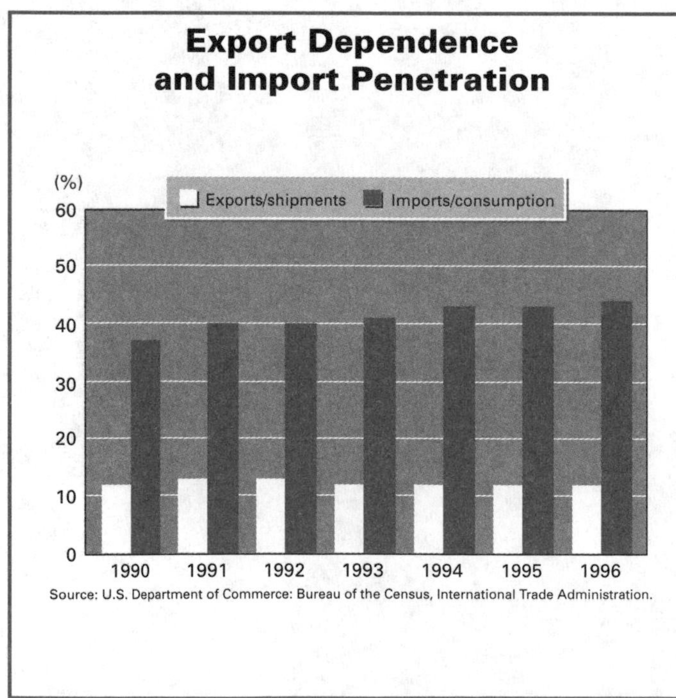

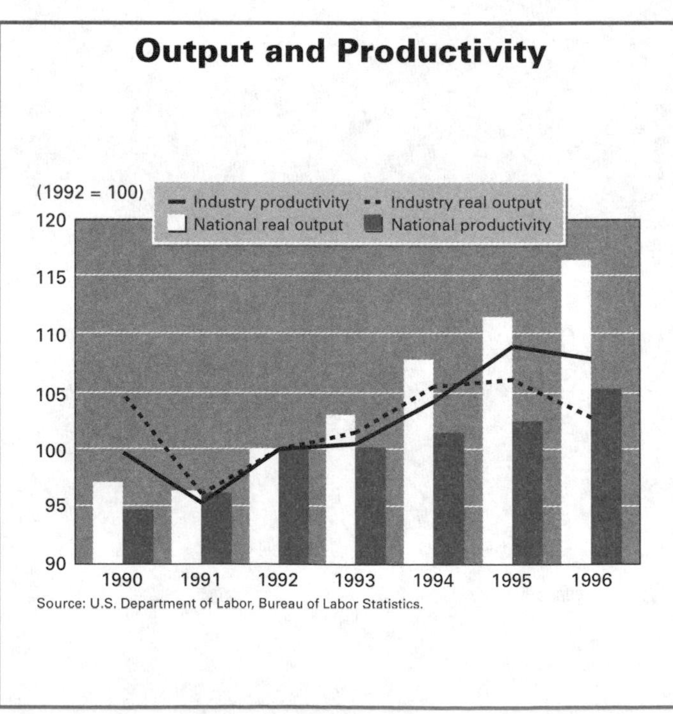

See "Getting the Most Out of *Outlook 2000*" for definitions of terms.

40

Other Consumer Durables

INDUSTRY DEFINITION The other consumer durables group includes jewelry (SIC 3911 and 3961) and musical instruments (SIC 3931)

JEWELRY

Precious metal jewelry (SIC 3911) includes jewelry and other articles worn on or carried about the person, made of precious metals (including base metals clad or rolled with precious metals), with or without stones. Costume jewelry and costume novelties (SIC 3961) includes costume jewelry, costume novelties, and ornaments made of all materials except precious metal, precious or semiprecious stones, and rolled goldplate and gold-filled materials.

Global Industry Trends

Since the early 1990s, the U.S. economy has been expanding steadily, resulting in increased sales of all categories of consumer goods. However, the conditions in many foreign countries have not been nearly as favorable. Demand for luxury items such as jewelry was severely affected by the Asian economic crisis that began in mid-1997 when Thailand devalued the baht. That devaluation was followed by devaluations in several other countries in Asia and South America throughout 1998. After Brazil's devaluation in January 1999, a period of economic recovery began in most of the afflicted regions. Consumers in those countries once again are making nonessential purchases. This bodes well for the jewelry industry, one of the most cyclical industries.

Also benefiting the industry in 1999 was the relatively low price of gold, an important raw material for jewelry. At the beginning of 1999, gold was priced at about $287 a troy ounce. By midsummer, the price had dropped to $253 a troy ounce, a 20-year low, after Great Britain began a series of auctions of more than half its reserves. This was the latest in a series of high-profile central bank sales that have come as gold has lost its luster in favor of better-returning investments.

Gold, traditionally a safe haven in times of turmoil, peaked at $875 per troy ounce in 1980, when the U.S. inflation rate was in double digits and prices for real estate, commodities, and collectibles were rising rapidly as investors sought hedges against inflation. Now, with inflation seemingly tamed, interest in that metal has fallen even among many diehard doomsday investors. While gold still plays a large role in industry and art, many nations are less interested in holding it for their reserves. They believe they can maintain economic confidence by making other investments that appreciate and cost less to hold. Downward pressure on gold prices is expected for some time to come since, in addition to the United Kingdom, Switzerland and the International Monetary Fund are considering gold sales.

Domestic Trends

The U.S. jewelry industry consists of a large number of relatively small companies that produce precious metal jewelry and costume jewelry. There are approximately 2,200 precious metal jewelry manufacturers and 900 costume jewelry manufacturers. In 1999, they employed 35,400 and 12,200 workers, respectively. Several thousand more work in supporting industries. The industry is concentrated in the northeastern United States. New York and Rhode Island account for nearly half of precious metal jewelry shipments and two-thirds of costume jewelry shipments. In recent years, the industry has faced many challenges, including consolidation among retailers through the growth of retail chains, catalog showrooms, and TV home shopping networks; a decline in the number of wholesalers; reduced tariffs; increased imports; expanding jewelry industries in developing countries; and increased competition in third-country markets.

Over the past few decades, import penetration increased from 14 to 54 percent of domestic consumption of precious metal jewelry while import penetration for costume jewelry increased from 14 to 37 percent.

The jewelry companies most threatened by imports are those producing low-end, labor-intensive products whose production often cannot be economically automated or otherwise improved. It is likely that some of these companies will switch to producing high-end categories of jewelry with better materi-

TABLE 40-1: Jewelry, Precious Metal (SIC 3911) Trends and Forecasts
(millions of dollars except as noted)

	1992	1993	1994	1995	1996	1997[1]	1998[1]	1999[2]	2000[3]	Percent Change 97–98	98–99	99–00	96–00[4]
Industry Data													
Value of shipments[5]	4,190	4,278	4,459	4,444	4,443	5,409	5,420	5,494	5,604	0.2	1.4	2.0	6.0
Value of shipments (1992$)	4,190	4,215	4,350	4,297	4,243	5,203	5,254	5,305	5,358	1.0	1.0	1.0	6.0
Total employment (thousands)	32.5	34.0	31.1	30.1	29.4	34.6	35.3	35.4		2.0	0.3		
Production workers (thousands)	22.5	23.6	20.1	20.3	20.1	24.3	24.7	24.3		1.6	−1.6		
Average hourly earnings ($)	9.41	9.53	9.78	9.61	10.06	11.09	11.44	11.71		3.2	2.4		
Capital expenditures	36.8	45.3	49.2	58.0	91.4	60.8							
Product Data													
Value of shipments[5]	3,739	4,006	4,063	4,034	4,016	4,724	4,735	4,763	4,859	0.2	0.6	2.0	4.9
Value of shipments (1992$)	3,739	3,947	3,964	3,902	3,836	4,508	4,553	4,598	4,644	1.0	1.0	1.0	4.9
Trade Data													
Value of imports	2,711	3,142	3,438	3,573	3,766	3,959	4,505	4,840	5,080	13.8	7.4	5.0	7.8
Value of exports	476	388	366	375	392	471	494	700	725	4.9	41.7	3.6	16.6

[1] Estimate except exports and imports.
[2] Estimate.
[3] Forecast.
[4] Compound annual rate.
[5] For a definition of industry versus product values, see "Getting the Most Out of *Outlook 2000.*"
Source: U.S. Department of Commerce: Bureau of the Census; International Trade Administration.

als or styling. Others will shift more production overseas while keeping styling and marketing jobs in the United States or will leave the industry.

U.S. product shipments of precious metal jewelry totaled an estimated $4.6 billion in 1999, an increase of 1 percent in constant dollars. Costume jewelry shipments were an estimated $1.2 billion, down 2 percent in constant dollars. Costume jewelry manufacturers continue to be under particularly heavy import pressure from Asian manufacturers (see Tables 40-1 and 40-2).

Electronic Commerce

Today, in addition to traditional retail jewelry stores, jewelry can be purchased through department stores, mail order, catalog stores, discount stores, TV shopping, and now the internet. Internet or on-line vending has developed over the past few years.

In 1999, the internet was in the news as many companies involved with it in any way became hot issues on the stock market regardless of their profitability. Companies rushed to set up Web sites as vendors or auctioneers, hoping to capture a sizable

TABLE 40-2: Costume Jewelry (SIC 3961) Trends and Forecasts
(millions of dollars except as noted)

	1992	1993	1994	1995	1996	1997[1]	1998[1]	1999[2]	2000[3]	Percent Change 97–98	98–99	99–00	96–00[4]
Industry Data													
Value of shipments[5]	1,444	1,429	1,627	1,660	1,525	1,223	1,194	1,174	1,162	−2.4	−1.7	−1.0	−6.6
Value of shipments (1992$)	1,444	1,417	1,603	1,624	1,472	1,153	1,129	1,106	1,084	−2.1	−2.0	−2.0	−7.4
Total employment (thousands)	17.4	17.1	18.8	16.1	16.2	14.0	13	12.2		−7.2	−6.2		
Production workers (thousands)	12.5	12.0	14.3	12.4	12.5	10.1	9.7	8.9		−4.0	−8.2		
Average hourly earnings ($)	7.25	7.50	8.06	7.77	8.41	9.10	9.65	9.75		6.0	1.0		
Capital expenditures	12.8	9.7	13.6	11.8	10.1								
Product Data													
Value of shipments[5]	1,532	1,556	1,679	1,770	1,666	1,229	1,202	1,182	1,170	−2.2	−1.7	−1.0	−8.5
Value of shipments (1992$)	1,532	1,542	1,654	1,732	1,608	1,160	1,138	1,115	1,093	−1.9	−2.0	−2.0	−9.2
Trade Data													
Value of imports	550	561	586	513	484	486	516	560	600	6.2	8.5	7.1	5.5
Value of exports	121	135	148	140	128	163	140	155	165	−14.1	10.7	6.5	6.6

[1] Estimate except exports and imports.
[2] Estimate.
[3] Forecast.
[4] Compound annual rate.
[5] For a definition of industry versus product values, see "Getting the Most Out of *Outlook 2000.*"
Source: U.S. Department of Commerce: Bureau of the Census; International Trade Administration.

market share. Many of those sites attempted to sell jewelry, which is considered to have a relatively high markup. Soon there were thousands of Web sites offering jewelry for sale, ranging from well-known long-established retailers to inexperienced entrepreneurs. Many of those whose Web sites were tied to frequently visited Web links or had easily recognizable names have had reasonable sales. Others, without such advantages, are as easy to find by potential buyers as a needle in a haystack.

Nevertheless, it is likely that a substantial amount of retail jewelry will be sold over the internet in future years, just as TV shopping has become an important channel of distribution for the jewelry industry. One major retailer expects that its on-line sales eventually will reach 5 percent of its total sales. It also has been estimated that internet sales will account for 6 percent of total U.S. consumer retail spending by 2003. One advantage for on-line shoppers is that they can easily comparison shop for a particular type of jewelry from several suppliers rather than passively looking at what is offered as with TV shopping or being restricted to shopping in stores in the immediate vicinity. Shopping on-line with a vendor across the country is as easy as shopping with one in the same town. Since the costs of an on-line vendor are substantially less than those for a fixed-site vendor, major price discounts are often available. Already, some vendors are selling gold and silver jewelry by the ounce, as is common in parts of Asia. Price comparison shopping is thus facilitated. Some types of jewelry, such as chains, as well as graded diamonds seem especially well suited for such comparison shopping. It remains to be seen how well established jewelers with traditional retail stores will be able to compete on the internet without substantially undercutting their store prices.

The internet offers jewelry manufacturers similar opportunities to increase sales. Many industry trade associations now offer Web sites for their members. Those sites are often searchable by type of product. Access to those Web sites often is restricted to the trade. Many manufacturers have taken advantage of these easy-to-find sites by providing useful product information. Some manufacturers report sizable increases in business from the internet. Many more companies will learn to use the internet productively to promote their products.

It appears that many internet jewelry vendors are not providing purchasers with all the required information about their products. In January 1999, the Federal Trade Commission (FTC) reported that a review of 100 internet Web sites that advertise and sell jewelry had shown that many sites were not providing consumers with information required under the FTC's Jewelry Guides. The Jewelry Guides describe the types of jewelry marketing claims the FTC considers false or misleading and provide examples of nondeceptive claims.

The Web sites reviewed included those of major jewelry chains, small retailers, and on-line auction firms. Less than 30 percent of the sites disclosed whether the pearls used in their jewelry were cultured or imitation, as is required by the Guides. Disclosure for diamonds was better, with two-thirds advertising stone weights correctly. However, among the sites selling gemstone jewelry, only 5 percent correctly disclosed gem treatments, while 37 percent of auction site sellers correctly disclosed treatments.

Industry Growth for the Next 1 and 5 Years

Assuming that the U.S. economy continues its current expansion through the end of the year 2000, constant dollar product shipments of precious metal jewelry are forecast to increase 1 percent that year, while costume jewelry shipments are forecast to decrease 2 percent. Overall consumer spending for jewelry is expected to be more favorable, but imports are expected to capture a larger share of the domestic market.

Several long-term factors affecting the U.S. industry over the next 5 years are favorable. The total population is expected to increase about 0.8 percent per year. The age group that purchases the most jewelry per person is the 45- to 54-year-old group, which spends about $209 per person on jewelry annually. This group is expected to increase about 2.4 percent annually over the next 5 years. The proportion of women participating in the labor force is expected to increase nearly 1 percent during this period. This is meaningful, since women are purchasing more jewelry for themselves every year. In addition, real disposable income is expected to increase over 2 percent per year because of improved labor productivity.

Offsetting these favorable conditions will be the continued threat of higher levels of imports. If U.S. tariffs are reduced to 5 percent for jewelry per the World Trade Organization (WTO) negotiations discussed below, there will be little adverse effect on precious metal jewelry producers since tariffs will drop only from 6 percent to 5 percent. However, costume jewelry producers would be more adversely affected, since most U.S. tariffs for such jewelry are now 11 percent. Therefore, shipments of precious metal jewelry are expected to grow at an average annual rate of 1 percent in real terms through 2004, while costume jewelry shipments are expected to decrease 2 percent annually.

Global Market Prospects

A notable feature in foreign trade in jewelry in 1999 was the sharp increase in U.S. exports of precious metal jewelry, which jumped over 40 percent to an estimated $700 million. In spite of this increase, exports still constitute only a small fraction compared to U.S. imports of precious metal jewelry, which increased 7 percent to $4.8 billion in 1999. Exports of costume jewelry increased nearly 11 percent to $155 million as imports increased 8.5 percent to $560 million. The 1999 economic recovery in several countries in Asia, Latin America, and Europe was a key factor in the increase in U.S. precious metal jewelry exports.

The leading U.S. export markets for precious metal jewelry in 1999 were Switzerland, Mexico, the Netherlands Antilles, Japan, and Canada. Export shipments were up sharply to all these markets but Canada during the year. Together, these five markets account for nearly 60 percent of U.S. exports of precious metal jewelry (see Tables 40-3 and 40-4).

The leading U.S. export markets for costume jewelry in 1999 were Japan, Canada, South Korea, the United Kingdom, and Switzerland. Exports to those five markets accounted for

TABLE 40-3: U.S. Trade Patterns in Fine Jewelry[1] in 1998
(millions of dollars; percent)

Exports			Imports		
Regions[2]	Value[3]	Share, %	Regions[2]	Value[3]	Share, %
NAFTA	133	27	NAFTA	318	7
Latin America	123	25	Latin America	438	10
Western Europe	122	25	Western Europe	1,908	42
Japan/Chinese Economic Area	79	16	Japan/Chinese Economic Area	540	12
Other Asia	13	3	Other Asia	951	21
Rest of world	24	5	Rest of world	349	8
World	494	100	World	4,505	100
Top Five Countries	Value	Share, %	Top Five Countries	Value	Share, %
Canada	80	16	Italy	1,455	32
Switzerland	58	12	India	443	10
Netherlands Antilles	54	11	Hong Kong	405	9
Mexico	53	11	Thailand	377	8
Japan	51	10	Israel	232	5

[1] SIC 3911.
[2] For definitions of regional groupings, see "Getting the Most Out of *Outlook 2000.*"
[3] Values may not sum to total due to rounding.
Source: U.S. Department of Commerce, Bureau of the Census.

nearly 60 percent of U.S. exports of costume jewelry during that year.

The leading foreign suppliers of precious metal jewelry to the United States are Italy, India, Hong Kong, Thailand, and Israel, while the leading suppliers of costume jewelry are China, South Korea, Taiwan, Hong Kong, and Thailand. Italy, which in the early 1990s accounted for about 40 percent of U.S. imports of precious metal jewelry, has seen its share whittled to about 30 percent. During that period, several developing countries substantially increased their shipments of precious metal jewelry to the United States. Those countries include India, Turkey, China, and Oman. Those countries all benefit from low labor costs. Imports of costume jewelry from China have increased sharply over the decade. China's share of U.S. imports more than doubled from 18 percent in 1992 to nearly 40 percent in 1999. This increase came primarily at the expense of Taiwan, whose share of imports dropped from 26 percent to 5 percent in that period.

Gems and jewelry tend to be widely traded global products because of their ease of transportation. However, since they generally are considered luxuries, many countries traditionally have restricted their importation. The developing countries generally have substantially higher tariffs on gems and jewelry than

TABLE 40-4: U.S. Trade Patterns in Costume Jewelry[1] in 1998
(millions of dollars; percent)

Exports			Imports		
Regions[2]	Value[3]	Share, %	Regions[2]	Value[3]	Share, %
NAFTA	31	22	NAFTA	27	5
Latin America	14	10	Latin America	9	2
Western Europe	43	31	Western Europe	42	8
Japan/Chinese Economic Area	34	24	Japan/Chinese Economic Area	257	50
Other Asia	13	9	Other Asia	174	34
Rest of world	5	4	Rest of world	7	1
World	140	100	World	516	100
Top Five Countries	Value	Share, %	Top Five Countries	Value	Share, %
Japan	28	20	China	190	37
Canada	25	18	South Korea	130	25
South Korea	11	8	Taiwan	35	7
United Kingdom	10	7	Hong Kong	26	5
Switzerland	9	6	Thailand	22	4

[1] SIC 3961.
[2] For definitions of regional groupings, see "Getting the Most Out of *Outlook 2000.*"
[3] Values may not sum to total due to rounding.
Source: U.S. Department of Commerce, Bureau of the Census.

do the developed countries. However, several recent events, such as the Uruguay Round of General Agreement on Tariffs and Trade (GATT) negotiations and unilateral tariff reductions by several developing countries, are removing many tariff and nontariff barriers to international trade in gems and jewelry.

Currently, most of the gem categories enter the United States free of tariffs. There are tariffs on some semimanufactured stones and metals, generally under 5 percent. U.S. tariffs generally are about 6 percent for precious metal jewelry and 11 percent for costume jewelry. All these categories are eligible for duty-free treatment under the Generalized System of Preferences (GSP) and the North American Free Trade Agreement (NAFTA).

Since 1976, GSP has permitted several categories of goods, including gems and jewelry, to enter duty-free from most developing countries. China, South Korea, Taiwan, and Hong Kong are not eligible for GSP treatment. In 1998, imports from GSP countries accounted for 36.1 percent of total precious metal jewelry imports and 10.6 percent of total costume jewelry imports.

In November 1997, the Asia-Pacific Economic Cooperation (APEC) forum selected gems and jewelry as a sector for early liberalization of tariff and nontariff measures as part of the Early Voluntary Sectoral Liberalization initiative. In June 1998, APEC agreed to a target tariff rate of 0 to 5 percent by the year 2005 in this sector, and in November 1998 APEC decided to seek broader participation in this initiative in the WTO.

If the WTO initiative is successful, reduction of tariffs to 5 percent or less would continue the trend toward lower barriers to trade. Manufacturers would benefit from increased foreign markets and lower production costs from economies of scale. Consumers would benefit from lower prices as a result of lower taxes and increased competition as well as a greater choice of products. As tariffs dropped, all manufacturers would be competing on a more even basis. Local manufacturers would have less of an advantage from tariff protection, while more manufacturers from different countries would face the same or nearly the same tariff in entering a third country. Tariff preferences under various schemes would have less of an effect on trade as the maximum tariff declined. Although the jewelry industries in many countries, including the United States, are under growing pressure from imports, primarily from China with its low labor costs, they are interested in better foreign market access in developing countries through lower tariffs.

Discussions with several non-APEC countries in the WTO indicate substantial interest in reducing trade barriers in the gems and jewelry sector.

The European Jewellers Associations' Group, representing jewelry trade associations in several European countries, has a stated objective of total eliminating tariffs on a reciprocal basis. Owing to the high interest in this sector by many countries, it is likely that some sort of agreement for tariff reduction will be reached for gems and jewelry.

John M. Harris, Office of Consumer Goods, U.S. Department of Commerce, (202) 482-1178. E-mail: john_harris@ita.doc.gov, August 1999.

MUSICAL INSTRUMENTS

Musical instruments (SIC 3931) includes pianos with or without player attachments, organs, other musical instruments, and parts and accessories for musical instruments.

Global Industry Trends

After a period of sharply restricted demand for consumer goods such as musical instruments in several Asian and South American countries in recent years, the trend in demand for such goods is becoming more favorable. Several Asian countries that were hard hit economically after currency devaluations in 1997, such as South Korea and Thailand, had strong rebounds in their stock markets followed by expanding economies and increased consumer spending in 1999. Economic activity also is showing some improvement in South America as well as Europe.

Domestic Trends

The value of U.S. product shipments of musical instruments was $1.3 billion in 1999, an increase of 1 percent in constant dollars from 1998. This trend reflected the continued economic expansion in the United States during that year. The year 1999 represented the ninth year of growth in this economic cycle. While this economic cycle has continued for a record length of time, consumer confidence, employment, and the stock market were all strong during that year. These were factors in consumers' continued willingness to spend (see Table 40-5).

Major categories of musical instruments included in SIC 3931 and their 1997 product shipments as a percentage of total product shipments are as follows: pianos, 14.7 percent; organs, 7.0 percent; electronic musical instruments and synthesizers, 8.7 percent; others, such as woodwind, brass wind, string instruments, and percussion, 39.1 percent; and accessories and parts, 16.2 percent.

ITC Study of Piano Industry

In May 1999, the U.S. International Trade Commission (ITC) released a study of the U.S. piano industry. The study, titled *Pianos: Economic and Competitive Conditions Affecting the U.S. Industry,* was instituted at the request of the House Ways and Means Committee. It investigated the current conditions affecting the domestic piano industry and included an overview of the global market; a profile of the U.S. piano industry; profiles of leading manufacturers in Japan, South Korea, China, and Indonesia; and a comparison of the competitive strengths and weaknesses of U.S. and foreign producers.

The study found that of the approximately 400,000 vertical pianos and 60,000 grand pianos that were sold globally in 1997, South Korea, China, the United States, and Japan were the major markets for vertical pianos while the United States and Japan were the major markets for grand pianos. Imports, by quantity, supplied 46 percent of U.S. consumption of vertical pianos in the first 9 months of 1998, up from a 35 percent market share in the same period in 1997. Imports accounted for

TABLE 40-5: Musical Instruments (SIC 3931) Trends and Forecasts
(millions of dollars except as noted)

	1992	1993	1994	1995	1996	1997[1]	1998[1]	1999[2]	2000[3]	Percent Change 97–98	98–99	99–00	96–00[4]
Industry Data													
Value of shipments[5]	982	1,037	1,062	1,144	1,173	1,220	1,288	1,325	1,365	5.6	2.9	3.0	3.9
Value of shipments (1992$)	982	990	976	998	986	995	1,025	1,035	1,045	3.0	1.0	1.0	1.5
Total employment (thousands)	12.2	12.5	12.3	12.8	12.9	13.1	13.5	13.5		3.1	0.0		
Production workers (thousands)	9.4	9.7	9.8	10.4	10.3	10.4	10.7	10.8		2.9	0.9		
Average hourly earnings ($)	9.87	10.14	9.63	10.61	10.59	10.70	11.05	11.82		3.3	7.0		
Capital expenditures	13.8	17.1	11.4	23.7	15.3								
Product Data													
Value of shipments[5]	902	965	977	1,167	1,182	1,230	1,298	1,335	1,375	5.5	2.9	3.0	3.9
Value of shipments (1992$)	902	922	898	1,018	993	1,003	1,033	1,043	1,053	3.0	1.0	1.0	1.5
Trade Data													
Value of Imports	666	711	751	880	855	905	1,052	1,030	1,100	16.2	–2.1	6.8	6.5
Value of exports	327	340	370	397	413	411	377	340	390	–8.3	–9.8	14.7	–1.4

[1] Estimate except exports and imports.
[2] Estimate.
[3] Forecast.
[4] Compound annual rate.
[5] For a definition of industry versus product values, see "Getting the Most Out of *Outlook 2000.*"
Source: U.S. Department of Commerce: Bureau of the Census; International Trade Administration.

most of the market for grand pianos in 1998. Imports of vertical and grand pianos from Japan, South Korea, China, and Indonesia accounted for 93 percent, by quantity, of total U.S. imports of pianos in 1998. U.S. producers are major importers, buying foreign-produced pianos to complement their product lines.

Growth of Chinese production and exports in the 1990s was notable from both independent Chinese producers and operations established in China by other Asian producers. In the first 9 months of 1998, the quantity of U.S. vertical pianos imported from China more than tripled compared with the same period in 1997, increasing China's share of U.S. consumption from 6 percent to 16 percent.

U.S. piano producers faced numerous competitive disadvantages in the period 1994–1998: Japanese and Korean producers' operations in Asia were more automated than operations in the United States; Asian producers, with the exception of Japan, have considerably lower labor costs than do U.S. producers; the east Asian financial crisis drastically curtailed piano sales in the home and regional markets of principal Asian piano manufacturers, and it appeared that pianos were redirected from these markets to the U.S. market; and the currencies of three of the four principal Asian competitors depreciated significantly in real terms against the dollar during that period. U.S. producers, however, have the following advantages: close proximity to wood resources, a more experienced labor force in making furniture-style pianos, and lower transportation costs when selling in the U.S. market.

Electronic Commerce

Several of the major manufacturers of musical instruments have established corporate Web sites on the internet to promote their products. As might be expected, their sites vary widely in content. They generally all have some basic information about their products and dealers. Many provide additional information, such as corporate history, production processes, clinics and product demonstrations at dealers, music festivals, promotions such as contests, and posters. Others include corporate press releases, newsletters, detailed product literature, product specifications, and warranty information. Some have details about employment opportunities and even the sounds of various instruments. While manufacturers generally do not sell their instruments directly to consumers on the internet, to protect their dealer networks, some have promotional items for sale, such as clothing, mugs, and key chains with corporate logos. Some craftsworkers, retailers, importers, and mail order houses have begun to use the internet for direct sales of musical instruments, both new and used. Many of those Web sites list prices for several instrument brands. For some brands, purchasers must contact the vendor for a price quote.

When properly utilized, the internet provides the public with substantial information about a manufacturer's or other vendor's products at a relatively low cost. Smaller manufacturers with limited promotion budgets may find the results of a well-designed internet site particularly rewarding. Increased use of the internet to sell certain musical instruments directly to the public probably will place increased price pressure on traditional fixed-site retailers of those types of instruments. Comparison shopping will be encouraged by the internet because of the ease of obtaining price information. Smaller manufacturers and importers without extensive dealer networks to protect may increasingly try to use the internet to market their products directly to consumers.

Industry Growth for the Next 1 and 5 Years

U.S. shipments of musical instruments are expected to increase at a 1 percent growth rate in the year 2000 in constant dollars; this

TABLE 40-6: U.S. Trade Patterns in Musical Instruments[1] in 1998
(millions of dollars; percent)

Exports			Imports		
Regions[2]	Value[3]	Share, %	Regions[2]	Value[3]	Share, %
NAFTA	59	16	NAFTA	79	8
Latin America	33	9	Latin America	2	0
Western Europe	148	39	Western Europe	153	15
Japan/Chinese Economic Area	105	28	Japan/Chinese Economic Area	552	52
Other Asia	12	3	Other Asia	244	23
Rest of world	22	6	Rest of world	23	2
World	377	100	World	1,052	100
Top Five Countries	Value	Share, %	Top Five Countries	Value	Share, %
Japan	90	24	Japan	349	33
United Kingdom	44	12	South Korea	153	15
Canada	41	11	Taiwan	101	10
Germany	35	9	China	101	10
Mexico	18	5	Germany	58	6

[1] SIC 3931.
[2] For definitions of regional groupings, see "Getting the Most Out of *Outlook 2000.*"
[3] Values may not sum to total due to rounding.
Source: U.S. Department of Commerce, Bureau of the Census.

is the same as the estimated rate of growth for 1999. Both imports and exports are also expected to increase in the year 2000, reversing their declines in 1999. Imports are expected to increase 7 percent, while exports are expected to increase 15 percent.

During the 5-year period 2000 to 2004, constant dollar shipments of musical instruments are expected to increase 1 percent annually. After the sustained economic growth of the 1990s, a period of slow growth is more likely than a period of robust growth over the next few years. As the economy continued its expansion in 1999, many economic measures, such as consumer confidence, consumer debt, employment, and the stock market, reached relatively high levels. It is becoming increasingly more difficult for the economy to continue its growth indefinitely from this high point.

Changing demographics will have only a slightly positive effect on sales of musical instruments during this period. The total number of children age 5 to 17 is expected to increase only 2 percent during those 5 years. The number of younger children, age 5 to 13, is expected to decline 5 percent. This is the age group most favorable for piano sales. This group's decline will be more than offset by the 14- to 17-year age group, which is expected to increase 7.5 percent, although data are not available to allow extrapolation on the effect on musical instrument sales.

Global Market Prospects

U.S. exports of musical instruments, which peaked in 1996, fell an estimated 10 percent to $340 million in 1999. The industry was adversely affected by the strong dollar and weak economies in several of its key foreign markets in 1999. For example, the economies of several Asian countries were still depressed to varying degrees after the Asian currency devaluations of 1997. Similarly, the economies of several South American countries were adversely affected by the devaluation of the Brazilian peso early in 1999. Demand for consumer goods such as musical instruments declined in Brazil and its neighbors during that year. In addition, Brazilian manufacturers became more competitive and captured greater market share in South American markets as their export prices declined after the devaluation. In Europe, the value of the Euro also declined after its introduction at the beginning of 1999, making U.S. manufacturers less competitive in that market.

Japan is the largest foreign market for U.S. goods, accounting for approximately 25 percent of U.S. exports of musical instruments in 1999. Japan's share of U.S. exports has remained steady over the past 5 years as demand for musical instruments has continued to be strong in spite of its economy being stagnant during those years. Other major export markets are the United Kingdom, Canada, Germany, and Mexico. Those five countries accounted for approximately 60 percent of U.S. exports of musical instruments in 1999. (see Table 40-6).

U.S. imports of musical instruments declined about 2 percent to $1 billion in 1999. The major suppliers were Japan, South Korea, Taiwan, China, and Germany, which together accounted for about 72 percent of imports. Japan accounted for a third of total imports in 1999. In the early 1990s, it had accounted for nearly half of total imports. China and Indonesia are among the countries substantially increasing their market shares in recent years. Both gained market share in 1999 as their shipments to the United States increased by an estimated 35 percent and 15 percent, respectively. Both countries continue to gain market share owing in large measure to their low labor costs. Pianos, guitars, and electric keyboard instruments are important categories for both Chinese and Indonesian exporters.

John M. Harris, Office of Consumer Goods, U.S. Department of Commerce, (202) 482-1178, john_harris@ita.doc.gov, August 1999.

■ REFERENCES

Call the Bureau of the Census at (301) 763-4100 for information about how to order Census documents.

Jewelry

American Jewelry Manufacturer, Manufacturing Jewelers and Suppliers of America, Inc., 1 State Street, Providence, RI 02908-5035. (401) 274-3840, http://mjsa.polygon.net/ajm.

Costume Jewelry and Novelty Manufacturing, 1997 Economic Census, EC97M-339914 EC97M-3399D. Bureau of the Census, U.S. Department of Commerce, Washington, DC 20233.

Jeweler's Circular-Keystone, Cahners Business Information, 201 King of Prussia, Radnor, PA 19089. (610) 964-4486. http://www.jck.group.net.

Jewelry (Except Costume) Manufacturing, 1997 Economic Census, EC97M-339911 EC97M-3399A. Bureau of the Census, U.S. Department of Commerce, Washington, DC 20233.

Jewelry, Silverware, and Plated Ware, 1992 Census of Manufactures, MC92-1-39A, Bureau of the Census, U.S. Department of Commerce, Washington, DC 20233.

Modern Jewelers National, Cygnus Publishing Inc., Broad Hollow Road, Suite 21, Melville, NY 11747. (516) 845-2700.

National Jeweler, Miller Freeman, Inc., 1 Penn Plaza, New York, NY 10119. (212) 279-1300. http://www.national-jeweler.com.

1996 Annual Survey of Manufactures, Bureau of the Census, U.S. Department of Commerce, Washington, DC 20233.

Office Suppliers, Costume Jewelry and Notions, 1992 Census of Manufactures, MC92-I-39C, Bureau of the Census, U.S. Department of Commerce, Washington, DC 20233.

Musical Instruments

Call the Bureau of the Census at (301) 763-4100 for information about how to order Census documents.

Musical Instrument Manufacturing, 1997 Economic Census, EC97M-339992, EC97M-3399N, Bureau of the Census, U.S. Department of Commerce, Washington, DC 20233.

Musical Instruments and Parts, 1992 Census of Manufactures, MC92-1-39B, Bureau of the Census, U.S. Department of Commerce, Washington, DC 20233.

Music, Inc., Maher Publications, Inc., 102 North Haven Road, Elmhurst, IL 60126. (630) 941-2030. E-mail: musicincupbeat @worldnet.att.net.

The Music Trades, The Music Trades Corporation, 80 West Street, P.O. Box 432, Englewood, NJ 07631. (201) 871-1965. E-mail: MUSIC@MUSICTRADES.com.

Music USA 1999, National Association of Music Merchants, 5790 Armada Drive, Carlsbad, CA 92008. (760) 438-8001. http://www.namm.com/namm. E-mail: namm@namm.com.

1996 Annual Survey of Manufactures, Bureau of the Census, U.S. Department of Commerce, Washington, DC 20233.

Pianos: Economic and Competitive Conditions Affecting the U.S. Industry, May 1999, Investigation No. 332-401, Publication 3196, U.S. International Trade Commission, Washington, DC 20436.

■ RELATED CHAPTERS

7: Wood Products
16: Microelectronics
42: Retailing

WHOLESALE DISTRIBUTION
Economic and Trade Trends

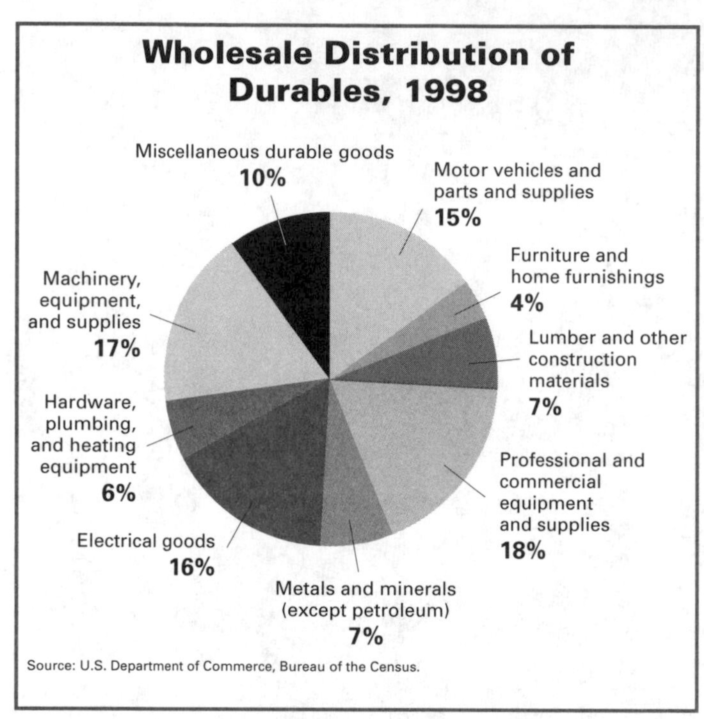

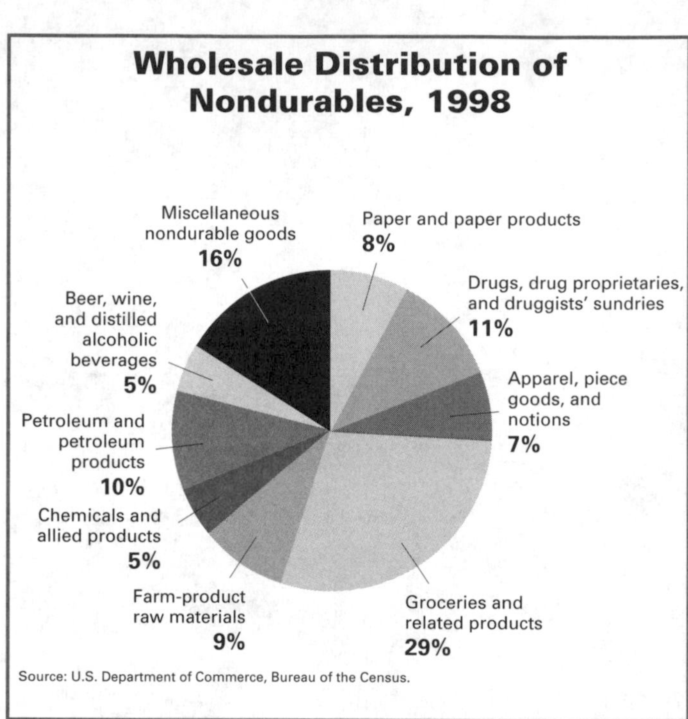

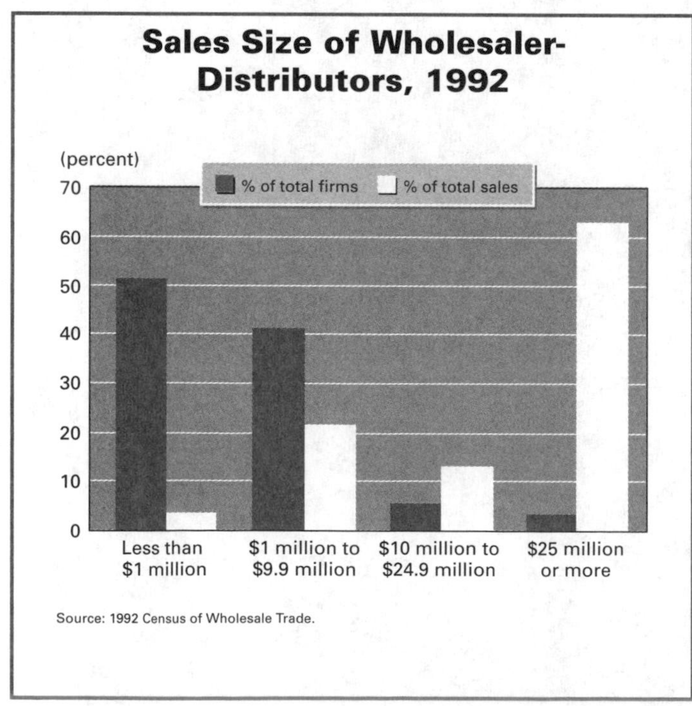

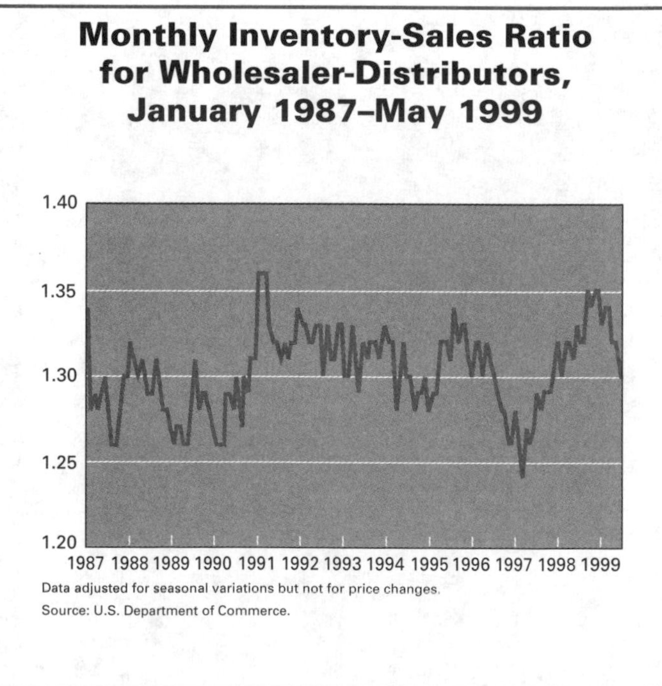

See "Getting the Most Out of *Outlook 2000*" for definitions of terms.

41

Wholesale Distribution

INDUSTRY DEFINITION The wholesale trade industry includes establishments (places of business) that sell products to retailers, merchants, contractors, and/or industrial, institutional, and commercial users but do not sell in significant amounts to ultimate household consumers. The industry includes companies that distribute both durable goods (SIC 50) and nondurable goods (SIC 51). Durable goods are principally items that can be used repeatedly because they are not consumed (or are consumed very slowly) as they are used. Examples include furniture (SIC 5021), office equipment (SIC 5044), plumbing and heating equipment and supplies (SIC 5074), and industrial supplies (SIC 5085). Nondurable goods are principally items that are consumed as they are used, such as printing and writing paper (SIC 5111), groceries (SIC 5141), chemicals (SIC 5169), and books and periodicals (SIC 5192). The implementation of the North American Industry Classification System (NAICS) will replace SIC 50 and 51 with NAICS 421 and 422, respectively.

OVERVIEW

Three types of operations can perform the functions of wholesale trade: wholesaler-distributors, manufacturers' sales branches and offices, and agents, brokers, and commission agents. Wholesaler-distributors are independently owned and operated firms that buy and sell products to which they have taken ownership. Generally, wholesaler-distributors operate one or more warehouses in which they receive and inventory goods for later reshipping. Manufacturers' sales branches and offices are captive wholesaling operations that are owned and operated by manufacturers. Agents, brokers, and commission agents buy or sell products for a commission or fee but do not take ownership of those products. Certain customers, particularly larger multiestablishment retail firms, can and sometimes do perform the functions of wholesale distribution. However, limited comparative data exist about the overall magnitude or importance of those activities.

This chapter uses the general term "wholesaler-distributor." The U.S. Census Bureau refers to wholesaler-distributors as "merchant wholesalers," a term that does not reflect the true range of companies represented in its data. Typically, the term "wholesaler" refers to a company that resells products to another intermediary, while the term "distributor" refers to a company that resells a product to the customer that will use that product. Thus, a pharmaceutical wholesaler resells prescription drugs to a retail pharmacy, which then resells the product to a household consumer. An industrial maintenance, repair, and operations (MRO) distributor sells products such as cutting tools to an industrial customer that may use the tools in its manufacturing facilities. However, terminology varies from industry to industry. For example, distributors of printing paper are called "merchants" and distributors of automotive aftermarket products are called "jobbers."

Total wholesale trade sales in 1998 were approximately $4.3 trillion, of which $2.5 trillion was booked by wholesaler-distributors. As a result, wholesaler-distributors are the largest and most important of the three groups in wholesale trade. Wholesaler-distributors' sales have been growing faster than has the overall economy during the recent economic expansion. According to preliminary data from the 1997 Economic Census, wholesaler-distributors accounted for 59 percent of wholesale sales volume versus 57 percent in 1992. Wholesaler-distributors' share of wholesale trade has been increasing steadily from 48 percent in 1958.

There were 341,376 wholesale distribution firms operating 414,836 establishments at some point in 1992. Only 301,167 of those firms were operating during the entire Economic Census year. In 1997, preliminary estimates indicate 440,211 establishments, an increase of 29 percent. Note that the 1997 Census data show 375,155 wholesale establishments under the new North American Industry Classification System (NAICS), or 65,000 fewer than the 1997 figures based on the SIC classification. Although detailed data have not been released, this apparent decline probably reflects both establishment rationalization and consolidation by individual companies and reclassification of establishments from wholesale to retail in certain industries, such as office supplies and computer equipment.

The majority of wholesaler-distributors are very small companies that operate in a single location (establishment). Ninety-two percent of wholesaler-distributors had annual sales of less than $10 million in 1992, the most recent year for which complete data are available. These companies represented 25 percent of total wholesaler-distributor sales. In contrast, the largest group of wholesaler-distributors (companies with sales greater than $250 million) represented 0.2 percent of total firms but 37 percent of sales (see Table 41-1). It has been estimated that those large firms accounted for 40 percent of sales in 1998.

The size difference between the smallest and largest firms has been growing over time. In 1982, wholesaler-distributors with sales less than $10 million represented a slightly higher proportion of total wholesale distribution firms (94 percent) but a much greater percentage of sales (31 percent). Another important disparity between large and small firms involves their geographic scope of operation. In 1992, wholesaler-distributors with sales less than $10 million operated in one or two locations, while the largest wholesaler-distributors (those with sales of $250 million or more) operated at an average of 29 locations. The disparity in establishment size is even greater. Wholesaler-distributors with total firm sales above $250 million operated establishments that averaged $38.5 million in sales, roughly 10 times as large as the establishments operated by firms with sales below $10 million. More current data are not available (see Table 41-1).

Despite these trends toward consolidation, traditional measures of industry concentration are low relative to most manufacturing sectors. The average four-firm concentration ratio among wholesaler-distributors was 17 percent at the four-digit SIC level in 1992. (The four-firm concentration ratio is the percentage of total industry sales accounted for by the four largest companies.) To some extent, the low level of concentration reflects the fact that competition among wholesaler-distributors traditionally occurs in geographically distinct markets. A wholesaler-distributor can dominate one region of the country yet account for a very small proportion of national sales. Thus, the apparent fragmentation of wholesale distribution may not accurately reflect the nature of concentration in any single region.

The Value of Wholesale Distribution

Wholesale trade contributed 5.8 percent of U.S. national income in 1997. Furthermore, the wholesale distribution industry has consistently accounted for roughly 1 in every 20 jobs in the United States throughout the last century. The wholesale distribution industry is represented by the National Association of Wholesaler-Distributors (NAW), a federation of 112 national wholesale distribution line of trade associations and 45 state, local, and regional associations. NAW collectively represents more than 40,000 individual companies.

Wholesaler-distributors add value in the economy by performing multiple activities in the sales and marketing of products. In other words, wholesaler-distributors are "paid" for taking on specific tasks and functions in the channel on behalf of customers and/or manufacturers. Even if wholesale distribution were eliminated, those functions would still exist and would have to be performed. It has often been said: "You can eliminate the middleman, but you can't eliminate the functions he performs."

At the most basic level, customers want to purchase small quantities of many different products, while manufacturers produce large quantities of a few products. Wholesaler-distributors simplify product, payment, and information flows between the principals to a transaction—a customer and a supplier—by bridging the gap between the assortments of goods and services available from individual producers and the assortments demanded by industrial, retail, institutional, and commercial customers.

Another key function is "breaking lots." This function provides solutions to the quantity discrepancies mentioned above. In this case, the wholesaler-distributor takes in a large quantity of product—a "lot"—and supplies it to customers in smaller

TABLE 41-1: Sales Size Distribution of Wholesaler-Distributors, 1992

Sales Size of Firm	No. Firms	No. Establishments	Total Sales, $ millions	Average Number of Locations per Firm	Average Firm Size, $ thousands	Average Location Size, $ thousands
Less than $1 million	153,657	155,072	61.6	1.0	401	397
$1 million to $9.9 million	123,689	143,252	389.7	1.2	3,151	2,721
$10 million to $24.9 million	15,256	27,797	232.2	1.8	15,222	8,354
$25 million to 49.9 million	4,819	13,001	165.5	2.7	34,344	12,730
$50 million to $99.9 million	2,145	9,331	146.2	4.4	68,163	15,669
$100 million to 249.9 million	984	8,134	147.1	8.3	149.540	18,090
$250 million or more	617	17,619	679.1	28.6	1,100,676	38,545
Total	301,167	374,206	1,821.6	1.2	6,048	4,868

Source: 1992 Census of Wholesale Trade, Table 6. Includes firms that operated during the entire year only.

quantities, or lots. The size of the wholesaler-distributor's purchase satisfies the manufacturer's need for the efficiency and economies that are available when it manufactures and ships in sufficiently large quantities. Access by customers to smaller lots of the same product satisfies their need to receive quantities that more closely match their rate of consumption, reduces the need for inventory storage space, and reduces inventory investment.

Some manufacturers require long lead times to process orders and manufacture product. Wholesaler-distributors keep goods on hand that customers need and have them accessible instantly. That availability very often makes the wholesaler-distributor a backup for and an extension of the customer's own inventory system. In breakdown emergencies and when there are unplanned repairs or maintenance, distributors are an invaluable resource for supplying products that minimize downtime.

Wholesaler-distributors also perform additional sales and marketing functions for manufacturers, such as sales contact, order processing, customer support, and market research information. Functions performed for customers include product availability, credit and finance, customer service, sales advice, and technical support. One reason wholesaler-distributors have increased their share of total wholesale sales is that they can perform these functions more effectively and efficiently than can either manufacturers or customers.

GLOBAL INDUSTRY TRENDS

In 1992, 7.8 percent of wholesaler-distributor sales were for export, a sharp increase from 6.1 percent in 1987. This growth represents a dollar increase in export sales by wholesaler-distributors of $53.9 billion. The following industries had the highest proportion of wholesaler-distributor sales for export in 1992: grain and field beans (SIC 5153), 41%; coal and other minerals and ores (SIC 5052), 37%; farm-product raw materials (SIC 5159), 35%; and transportation equipment and supplies excluding motor vehicles (SIC 5088), 31%. Collectively, those four industries represented 6.5 percent of total wholesaler-distributor sales.

The reality of globally sourced products appears to have arrived for domestic wholesaler-distributors. According to the 1998 *Facing the Forces of Change* report, wholesaler-distributor panelists indicated that 20 percent of their sales come from products manufactured outside North America. Wholesaler-distributor panelists report that their sales of foreign-sourced goods will grow even further to 29 percent over the next five years. Most wholesaler-distributors also expect that their suppliers will increase their offshore production.

At the same time, domestic wholesaler-distributors are expanding internationally, often by acquiring foreign wholesaler-distributors. According to the *Mergers & Acquisitions Journal*'s annual compilation of publicly announced transactions, there were 86 acquisitions of foreign wholesaler-distributors by domestic companies in 1998, up from 9 such cross-border acquisitions in 1981. These figures probably understate the magnitude of the internationalization trend because *Mergers & Acquisitions Journal* tracks only relatively well publicized transactions.

For example, Avnet, Inc., one of the world's largest distributors of electronic components and computer products, recently announced the acquisition of Eurotronics, a division of SEI, a distributor of electronic components that is owned by Sonepar, a global electrical distributor. Eurotronics distributes electronic components in 10 European countries. Avnet also recently acquired Marshall Industries, the fifth largest electronics distributor in North America and the owner of 16 percent of Eurotronics.

International expansion by wholesaler-distributors meets the needs of both customers and suppliers. Global manufacturers and customers are asking that their distribution partners have a presence in all major markets. The reduced costs of cross-border shipping and falling trade barriers also are encouraging expansion. For the same reasons, foreign wholesaler-distributors are making inroads into the domestic market. There were 57 acquisitions of U.S.-based wholesaler-distributors by foreign companies in 1998, mirroring the overseas expansion of US companies. For example, Sonepar, which sold Eurotronics to Avnet, is simultaneously an active acquirer of electrical distributors in the United States. Another prominent cross-border transaction was the acquisition of Rental Service Corporation, an equipment distributor and rental company, by Atlas Copco, a Swedish-based industrial group.

DOMESTIC TRENDS

Industry Consolidation

Today, industry consolidation in wholesale distribution is being led by distributor consolidators that use sequential buy-and-build acquisition strategies to replace a multitude of small "mom and pop" companies with a national, professionally managed, publicly traded corporation. Well-known consolidators include Arrow Electronics (electronic components), Airgas (industrial, medical, and specialty gases), Bergen Brunswig (pharmaceuticals), US Office Products (contract stationers), MSC Industrial (industrial products), and Hughes Supply (construction supplies).

Consolidation in Wholesale Distribution: Understanding Industry Change, a report published by the Distribution Research & Education Foundation (DREF) of NAW, found significant consolidation between 1985 and 1995 in 42 of the 54 wholesale distribution industries included in the study. In 14 of those 42 industries, the number of wholesaler-distributors declined more than 40 percent. According to *Merger & Acquisition Journal*'s annual survey, wholesale distribution is now the second most active industry in the United States for merger and acquisition activity. (Note that Census data have not documented a pronounced decline in the number of wholesaler-distributors. This discrepancy exists partly because SIC codes aggregate firms more than conventional industry definitions do and partly because industry participants underestimate the number of very small wholesaler-distributors.)

The strategy used by consolidators involves building a national network, leveraging buying power with suppliers, and reinvesting profits to meet the emerging requirements of larger customers and suppliers. With their size comes the financial clout to make operating decisions about product assortment and geographic territories independently of their suppliers, the manufacturers. For instance, geographic expansion by distributors has forced many manufacturers to change territory exclusivity agreements and has reduced manufacturers' ability to enforce limits on carrying competing product lines.

Consolidation among downstream customers has been an important trigger for consolidation in the distribution channel. Customer consolidation can occur in a number of ways: through the emergence of a few dominant customers, through the exit of small companies that form the traditional distribution customer base, and when customer organizations band together into cooperative purchasing groups. This creates the necessary conditions for distributor consolidation by providing incentives to grow geographically and exploit the benefits of operating in multiple regions.

Large national manufacturers, multiunit retailers, and national purchasing groups often welcome the mix of broad geographic coverage and wide brand availability, finding it more efficient to deal with distributors that can provide access to multiple manufacturers across multiple geographic regions. Similarly, industrial purchasers that operate multiple regional manufacturing facilities but use local or regional distributors in each area can present an opportunity for a national distributor. Customer consolidation limits the business prospects of distributors that cannot provide the geographic reach or level of service required by large customers.

Consolidators embark on growth-by-acquisition strategies to react quickly to these changes in customers' purchasing patterns. For example, changes in customers' buying practices were the primary driver of rapid and intense consolidation among periodical and magazine wholesalers. Retailers put their contracts up for competitive bidding, encouraging wholesalers to cross previously exclusive geographic boundaries. Contract-winning companies rapidly acquired former competitors in an effort to cover larger territories and service larger accounts. Smaller, regional wholesalers that did not or could not react were forced to sell out or dissolve. As a result, the number of periodical and magazine wholesalers dropped from nearly 182 companies in 1990 to fewer than 40 in 1999. The largest three wholesalers now control an estimated 65 percent of the national market. Similar changes in the customer base have driven consolidation in industries as diverse as drug wholesaling, electronic components distribution, and food distribution. Many industrial product distributors now face similar pressures.

Private equity buyout funds are spurring consolidation activity by investing in buy-and-build and roll-up strategies. Examples of consolidators and their financial backers include Industrial Distribution Partners (Windpoint Capital), American Sanitary (GTCR), and QDS Partners (Aurora Capital). There have been a number of initial public offering (IPO) roll-ups ("poof companies") that have simultaneously consolidated and gone public. US Office Products is probably the best known example of this strategy. Many IPO roll-ups have been unsuccessful at integrating the acquired companies and there is great disenchantment with the "poof company" business model. This disenchantment has slowed consolidation activities in some wholesale distribution industries.

Nonetheless, smaller wholesaler-distributors are banding together into alliances. Members can bid for national or multiregional contracts, offering the same geographic reach that a larger, multiestablishment company offers. The groups also can take advantage of volume purchasing opportunities from suppliers. At the same time, the alliance members retain operational autonomy, enabling them to maintain high levels of service for their local customers. According to *Modern Distribution Management,* two of the largest alliances are Affiliated Distributors, which has 280 members, and iPower Distribution Group, which has 220 members. Both alliances have combined aggregate sales of more than $10 billion.

Despite pressure for consolidation, the total number of wholesaler-distributors is not likely to decline sharply. The disparity between large and small firms shown in Table 41-1 will continue. In many lines of business, there will be a top tier of very large national distributors that coexist with much smaller local firms. The continued success of these groups may provide a way for smaller companies to survive as independent companies.

On-Line Consumer Retailing

Electronic commerce—the process of buying and selling using the Internet—is fundamentally changing the role of wholesaler-distributors. Contrary to conventional wisdom, wholesaler-distributors appear to be benefiting from these changes in consumer retail channels.

Currently, Internet retailing is thriving in areas where wholesale distribution is highly consolidated, such as books, music, videos, and pharmaceuticals. On-line retail intermediaries are creating electronic interfaces with end consumers in place of a physical location. Prominent examples include Amazon.com (books), CD Now (compact discs), and PlanetRx (pharmaceuticals) (see Chapter 42). On-line retailing is leading to growth at the larger consolidated distributors because those Internet companies have a "virtual," drop-ship model. They rely on large wholesaler-distributors for fulfillment, returns, and service. In the examples cited above, this includes Ingram Books for Amazon, Valley Media for CDNow, and McKesson for PlanetRx.

Wholesaler-distributors also represent a small part of many traditional (physical) retail channels under the influence of "power retailers." The 1995 DREF report *Competing for Customers: How Wholesaler-Distributors Can Meet the Competitive Challenge* describes two different types of power retailers: (1) general merchandise power retailers that sell a broad variety of product lines, either discount department stores such as Wal-Mart and Kmart or membership warehouse clubs such as Price/Costco and Sam's Club, and (2) category-dominant power retailers that concentrate on one or more closely related merchandise lines. Examples include Toys R Us (toys), Petco (pet supplies), Staples (office supplies), and Home Depot (home improvement). Since direct purchases by retailers are not included in the Census of Wholesale Trade, the aggregate sales impact of these power retailers is hard to determine.

Power retailers typically buy in large quantities in select product categories, giving them a very prominent position in the channel. This purchase volume has caused many power retailers to adopt a "buy direct" approach. Retailers such as Wal-Mart have squeezed costs out of the channel by creating in-house distribution systems in which wholesaler-distributors play a small role. Manufacturers have been forced to respond to the demands of dominant buyers, often at the expense of wholesaler-distributors. In addition, power retailers have triggered industry consolidation among the small and medium-size retailers that were traditional wholesale distribution customers.

This reduction or elimination of the role of wholesaler-distributors in retail channels during the last 20 years has left fewer but larger wholesaler-distributors among the survivors. As a result, there are few wholesaler-distributors for the Internet to affect. At the same time, the hyperefficient retail distribution systems used by power retailers are ill suited for the "unit of one" shipping required for on-line buying and shipping to a consumer's home. Currently, many power retailers are partnering with wholesaler-distributors or third-party fulfillment companies such as Fingerhut.

Wholesaler-distributors face a potential future threat in regard to products that can be shipped by small-package carriers and delivered overnight almost anyplace in the world. For those products, large public warehouses or third-party shipping organizations could perform the logistics roles, eliminating the need for specialized wholesaler-distributors.

Wholesaler-distributors are also highly vulnerable in industries in which the product can be digitized and transmitted over the Internet, eliminating the need for physical intermediation. For example, Valley Media, a wholesaler-distributor of music products, claims to be the largest reseller of compact audio discs on the Internet as a result of its relationships with companies such as CDNow and Amazon.com. However, music now can be distributed "virtually" over the Internet by using new technologies such as the MP3 file format. Wholesaler-distributors of products such as magazines and software also face this threat.

Business-to-Business E-Commerce

It is likely that the Internet's impact will be greatest in business-to-business marketing channels because wholesaler-distributors by definition do not sell in significant amounts to ultimate household consumers.

Electronic commerce offers the opportunity for customers to compare prices and product availability quickly and efficiently to a degree that was not possible previously. This reduction in customer procurement cost has the potential to reduce a wholesaler-distributor's control over prices and delivery conditions. In theory, logistics and manufacturing firms that specialize in the delivery of small-package orders could eliminate wholesale distribution in many industries. So far, wholesaler-distributors have not been replaced by electronic commerce solutions because it is extremely complex to replace all the valuable functions performed by wholesale distribution intermediaries.

Currently, business-to-business electronic commerce Web sites take three common forms.

Auction Sites. Auction sites most often are operated by a neutral "third-party" company that takes neither possession nor ownership of the product. The site operates a bulletin board arrangement by which sellers, and on some sites buyers, can post lots for sale by a number of technical specifications. Buyers and sellers can negotiate via the site or off-line by traditional means. These sites are increasingly common in industries with highly commoditized products, such as metals (MetalSite, eSTEEL) and printing papers (PaperExchange.com, The Paper Site).

To date, it appears that auction sites are benefiting wholesaler-distributors. In the metals industry, wholesaler-distributors are called "service centers" because they provide a variety of value-added, customer-specific processing functions. Since metals are highly freight- and time-to-receipt-sensitive products, many contracts arranged on auction Web sites are being fulfilled by service centers. In addition, distributors are using auction sites as a way to produce larger, more efficient lots for "make-to-order" product runs and market the excess product on an on-line site. They can identify lower-cost supply sources to meet unique customer requirements or locate emergency supplies when there are customer inventory shortages.

Catalogers of Catalogs. These sites host (or link to) multiple manufacturer or wholesaler-distributor on-line catalogs. A buyer can search the catalogs by a number of criteria and order directly on-line. The Web site operator then forwards the order to the supplier, which arranges shipment. Examples include laboratory supplies (Chemdex, SciQuest) and industrial MRO supplies (OrderZone.com). These sites pose a potential threat because manufacturers can use the Internet to gain direct access to customers, taking on important marketing functions currently being performed by wholesaler-distributors.

Cataloger of catalog sites are expected to pose a minimal threat to the overall wholesale distribution industry, however, because many wholesaler-distributors are actively innovating to remain relevant in the distribution channel. For example, OrderZone.com was developed by W.W. Grainger, a large industrial distributor. Grainger has linked with large distributors from complementary product categories such as office supplies and laboratory products to offer a broad range of products.

VWR Scientific Products, a large distributor of laboratory supplies, recently entered into a strategic relationship agreement with Chemdex, an on-line cataloger of catalogs. The agreement gives Chemdex the right to offer approximately 350,000 VWR-distributed products to its customers. In exchange, Chemdex receives no fee for orders of VWR core products from VWR's 40 largest customers and receives a minimal fee for orders of those core products forwarded to VWR. The two companies expect VWR's existing customers to use Chemdex to package together their VWR and non-VWR orders, thus benefiting both companies. In addition,

VWR and Chemdex are jointly developing a hosted, cobranded Internet procurement solution for VWR's existing and future customers that will provide access to an even wider range of products.

Distributor Web Sites. Many wholesaler-distributors are seeking to build their own E-commerce hubs aimed at corporate purchasers. These Web sites are essentially on-line storefronts for an established company. For instance, Grainger.com allows W.W. Grainger customers to access their standard accounts and price discounts and the company catalog on-line.

It is thought that these sites will allow individual distributors to reach much larger, potentially global marketplaces that were previously unavailable because of advertising and servicing costs. Niche market distributors and distributors with specialized processing skills may be able to expand a previously limited customer base significantly. Larger wholesaler-distributors may be able to channel significant portions of their overall customer base through an in-house Web site, lowering the costs of customer ordering and gaining greater control in the customer relationship.

Integrated Supply

Integrated supply, a more sophisticated type of customer-distributor relationship, is changing wholesale distribution in industrial markets. In an integrated supply arrangement, a customer gives a single wholesaler-distributor or a selected group of wholesaler-distributors all of its business in a product category or categories. In exchange, the distributor agrees to provide a high level of service on the entire product mix at set prices. Alternatively, the distributor may agree to cost-plus product pricing in combination with a service management fee.

Unlike supply-chain solutions that are imposed from above, such as the Efficient Consumer Response movement in the grocery industry, these new arrangements have sprung up organically among channel partners acting in their own best interests. Large customers face enormous organizational costs for purchasing the lowest-cost, most frequently used items. These customers are essentially looking for a complete outsourcing of the procurement function to the merchant wholesale distribution channel. Larger customers are attempting to minimize their total acquisition costs by reducing the supplier base, shrinking internal purchasing staffs, and applying supply chain management technologies such as electronic data interchange (EDI) to reduce inventory.

The wholesaler-distributor's role in an integrated supply relationship varies widely, ranging from simple warehouse storeroom management at the low end to becoming the outsourced procurement department for a customer. In the latter role, the integrator is hired to transform an entire procurement process by managing MRO buying at individual sites (inventory, delivery, and the transaction process) while providing the information technology (IT) infrastructure to optimize the purchasing process across multiple locations. As a result, the integrated supply customer forfeits significant management responsibility for indirect materials purchasing.

Wholesaler-distributors have been successful in offering this new type of service to customers. Some wholesaler-distributors with leading positions are Fairmont Supply and Cameron & Barkley. There are also two "pure integrators": Bruckner Supply and ISA. These companies focus their entire business on integrated supply contracting. They do not have a traditional branch-based distribution business. In contrast, wholesaler-distributors that provide integrated supply use their existing operations to service customers.

U.S. INDUSTRY GROWTH PROJECTIONS FOR THE NEXT 1 AND 5 YEARS

In 1998, sales of wholesaler-distributors reached $2.5 trillion, a 2.2 percent increase from 1997 (see Table 41-2). Sales growth for wholesaler-distributors has been very strong in recent years, exceeding overall economic growth. The compound annual growth rate (CAGR) for durable good wholesale distribution from 1993 to 1998 was 6.6 percent. The CAGR for nondurable wholesale distribution during that period was 4.5 percent (see Table 41-3.) These strong aggregate growth rates indicate clearly that wholesaler-distributors have been an attractive channel for manufacturers and customers during the ongoing economic expansion.

Unfortunately, it is very difficult to interpret growth rates for the subsectors of wholesale distribution. Total sales growth for wholesale distribution can be broken down into the following four underlying components: (1) changes in the volume of product handled, (2) changes in the prices of products, (3) changes in revenues from value-added services, and (4) changes in the proportion of channel volume going through wholesaler-distributors. These four elements cannot be disaggregated in a meaningful and consistent manner across lines of trade.

Sales by wholesaler-distributors are forecast to match or exceed the growth rate of the overall U.S. economy. Growth has been forecast to be steady through 1999, with a slight weakening by the end of 2000. There is some indication that 1999 sales could have been artificially inflated by inventory buildups as a result of concerns about the year 2000 computer problem. By 2001, sales by wholesaler-distributors are expected to approach $2.7 trillion (see Table 41-3). According to the U.S. Department of Commerce, gross profit margins have been remarkably steady for wholesaler-distributors at approximately 21 percent of sales in each of the last 10 years. Gross margins as a percentage of sales are forecast to remain at approximately the same level during the next 3 years.

Many of the domestic trends discussed earlier in this chapter support favorable prospects for wholesale distribution.

In on-line retailing aimed at consumers, electronic commerce is a growth driver because of the efficiency and sophistication of consolidated wholesaler-distributors. As was noted

TABLE 41-2: Wholesaler-Distributor Sales by Category, 1987–1998
(billions of dollars)

	SIC	1987	1988	1989	1990	1991	1992	1993	1994	1995	1996	1997	1998
Durable Goods													
Motor vehicles and parts and supplies	501	156	167	167	174	167	171	175	188	189	193	195	203
Furniture and home furnishings	502	27	30	32	34	32	33	35	37	41	43	46	48
Lumber and other construction materls	503	58	61	63	64	58	64	72	79	79	86	90	92
Professional and commercial equipment and supplies	504	85	94	110	114	124	140	161	171	203	224	240	256
Metals and minerals (except petroleum)	505	68	79	80	78	76	77	79	89	95	94	100	96
Electrical goods	506	94	102	113	116	113	115	138	164	193	195	205	212
Hardware, plumbing, and heating equipment	507	41	45	49	53	50	53	55	63	67	70	74	77
Machinery, equipment, and supplies	508	118	138	149	157	146	149	163	175	191	206	223	241
Miscellaneous durable goods	509	84	86	89	91	93	107	112	125	138	135	139	135
Total	50	731	802	852	881	860	909	990	1,091	1,196	1,246	1,312	1,360
Nondurable goods													
Paper and paper products	511	41	47	51	52	52	55	59	66	80	80	84	90
Drugs, drug proprietaries, and druggists' sundries	512	34	40	45	52	60	67	69	76	84	94	107	124
Apparel, piece goods, and notions	513	47	53	61	65	64	68	70	72	70	75	85	86
Groceries and related products	514	223	236	259	273	277	279	288	293	312	320	332	347
Farm-product raw materials	515	102	124	120	108	105	106	98	99	120	138	125	108
Chemicals and allied products	516	26	34	33	36	37	39	40	43	50	53	55	55
Petroleum and petroleum products	517	125	122	136	149	140	143	132	130	131	149	145	121
Beer, wine, and distilled alcoholic beverages	518	42	43	45	49	52	50	51	52	53	56	58	62
Miscellaneous nondurable goods	519	105	113	123	131	133	133	138	143	160	173	175	183
Total	51	745	812	874	913	920	941	944	975	1,058	1,138	1,168	1,175
Grand total		1,476	1,614	1,725	1,794	1,780	1,850	1,935	2,067	2,255	2,384	2,480	2,535

Source: U.S. Department of Commerce, Bureau of the Census.

above, consolidation has transformed fragmented wholesale distribution industries with many small local companies into channels with larger, professionally managed corporations that focus on return on investment and shareholder value. Thus, wholesale distribution channels provide an infrastructure for "virtual" companies. In a very real sense, wholesaler-distributors are "making the Web happen." Although power retailers pose an ongoing competitive threat to wholesaler-distributors, there are few consumer products for which implementation of the power retailer concept has not already been attempted. Power retailers now face a competitive threat from on-line intermediaries.

In contrast, on-line intermediaries are expected to dramatically alter the specific channel functions performed by wholesaler-distributors in business-to-business channels. However, the Internet will revolutionize business procurement only to the extent that it can eliminate the time wasters and costs of procurement, not simply by reverting to a price-driven mentality. Business customers still value suppliers that can lower a customer's total cost of acquiring products. In many (but not all) industries, wholesaler-distributors have excelled at lowering their customers' total cost of procurement and delivery through consolidation and the application of IT. In contrast, many on-line auction sites focus on the lowest price instead of the lowest total procurement cost. For example, large industrial buyers have begun to experiment with dynamically priced open sourcing over the Internet, using companies such as FreeMarkets Inc., a Pittsburgh-based company that manages Internet-based auctions for clients such as Caterpillar, United Technologies, and General Motors.

TABLE 41-3: Wholesale Distribution (SIC 50, 51) Trends and Forecasts
(billions of dollars)

	1993	1994	1995	1996	1997	1998	1999[1]	2000[2]	2001[2]	Percent Change 98–99	99–00	00–01	93–98[3]
Industry sales													
Durable goods	990	1,091	1,196	1,246	1,312	1,360	1,416	1,447	1,513	4.1	2.2	4.6	6.6
Nondurable goods	944	975	1,058	1,138	1,168	1,175	1,206	1,221	1,255	2.6	1.3	2.8	4.5
Total	1,935	2,067	2,255	2,384	2,480	2,535	2,621	2,668	2,769	3.4	1.8	3.8	5.6

[1] Estimate.
[2] Forecast.
[3] Compound annual growth rate.
Source: U.S. Department of Commerce, Bureau of the Census; author's analysis.

Continued consolidation of the purchasing function by industrial customers will fuel a need for integrated supply contracts. Frank Lynn & Associates, an international consulting firm, estimates that the integrated supply market will exceed $11 billion by the year 2000 versus a $700 million market in 1994. During the next 5 years, wholesaler-distributors' strategies to service integrated supply contracts will lead to a blurring of traditional industry definitions. A few very large multicategory wholesaler-distributors will emerge to service the needs of larger customers. The integrated supply trend also will increase the proportion of wholesale sales that are made through wholesaler-distributors because manufacturers will be unable to fully service the multicategory needs of industrial customers.

The inventory-sales ratio measures the monthly turnover of inventories at current sales rates. From 1991 through 1995, the ratio averaged 1.31, indicating that wholesaler-distributors held inventory that would be used up in roughly 6 weeks if inventories were not replenished. The ratio began trending downward in late 1995, reaching a low of 1.22 in February 1997. However, the inventory-sales ratio then increased to its previous level, standing at 1.30 in May 1999. The ratio for wholesaler-distributors is forecast to decline slightly throughout 2000, driven by increased supply chain efficiencies among larger wholesaler-distributors, the use of electronic commerce by all participants in the supply chain, and the drawdown of year 2000 stockpiles. These figures represent a mix of durable and nondurable goods. The inventory-sales ratio for nondurable wholesale distribution was to 0.99 at the end of 1998, while the ratio for durable goods was 1.64.

GLOBAL MARKET PROSPECTS

The importance of wholesaler-distributors in international trade will grow substantially in the next 5 years. In certain industries, wholesale distribution is globalizing, creating a top tier of wholesaler-distributors that compete across multiple countries. Export activity is expected to continue to expand, and the nondomestic operations of wholesaler-distributors will grow in importance. By 2002, more than 10 percent of wholesaler-distributor sales will be for export.

Large, sophisticated, and well-funded wholesaler-distributors will continue to expand internationally. As suppliers move overseas to take advantage of advantageous labor rates, they cannot always find reliable distribution and logistics support. Wholesaler-distributors have the opportunity to follow their suppliers into global markets. Furthermore, globalizing manufacturers are beginning to require that their original equipment manufacturer (OEM) suppliers have a presence in all major markets. In the most recent *Facing the Forces of Change* study, wholesaler-distributors indicated that about half their suppliers have ventured beyond the borders of North America to sell product overseas and anticipate that that number will increase to about two-thirds by the year 2003.

There are also substantial international growth opportunities in countries with unsophisticated distribution infrastructures. During the next 10 years, domestic wholesaler-distributors are expected to leverage their superior operating procedures, access to capital, and information technology systems to become market leaders in those countries.

Despite these growth trends, the vast majority of domestic wholesaler-distributors will consider international expansion as being rightfully outside the scope of their current business strategies. As Table 41-1 demonstrates, the vast majority of wholesaler-distributors operate at a single geographic location today. For these companies, growth within the United States still represents a first step before venturing abroad. While products or brands often can be standardized across countries (Disney, Coca-Cola, and Microsoft), distribution channels are substantially more complex. This makes it very difficult for suppliers, customers, and wholesaler-distributors to pursue a truly global supply-chain strategy. The few successful examples come from industries in which almost all the participants in the channel are global, such as the electronic components and computer industries.

Adam J. Fein, President, Pembroke Consulting, Inc., Philadelphia, PA, 215-523-5700, http://www.PembrokeConsulting.com; research assistant: James Solodar, January 2000.

REFERENCES

Arthur Andersen, *Facing the Forces of Change: Four Trends Reshaping Wholesale Distribution,* Washington, DC, Distribution Research and Education Foundation, 1998, http://www.nawpubs.org.

Fein, A. J., *Consolidation in Wholesale Distribution: Understanding Industry Change,* Washington, DC, Distribution Research and Education Foundation, (1997, http://www.nawpubs.org).

Fein, A. J., "The Future of Distributor Alliances," *Modern Distribution Management,* September 1998, http://www.PembrokeConsulting.com.

Fein, A. J., "Macroshock: How Wholesale Distribution Industries Are Being Revolutionized," Lehman Brothers, Equity Research Report, 1999, http://www.PembrokeConsulting.com.

Fein, A. J., and S. Jap, "Managing Consolidation in Your Channel," *Sloan Management Journal,* 1999.

Lusch, R. F., and D. Zizzo, *Competing for Customers: How Wholesaler-Distributors Can Meet the Power Retailer Challenge,* Washington, DC, Distribution Research and Education Foundation, 1995, http://www.nawpubs.org.

Lusch, R. L., and D. Zizzo, *Foundations of Wholesaling: A Strategic and Financial Chart Book,* Washington, DC, Distribution Research and Education Foundation, 1996, http://www.nawpubs.org.

Lynn, F., and J. Baden, *Integrated Supply 2: Shaping the Future of the Industrial Marketplace,* Chicago, IL: Frank Lynn & Associates, 1998, http://www.franklynn.com.

Merrifield, B., and S. Epner, *Electronic Commerce for Distributors,* Washington, DC, Distribution Research and Education Foundation, 1997, http://www.nawpubs.org.

Purchasing magazine, *How Industry Buys MRO,* 1992, Cahners Publishing, Newton, MA, (617) 964-3030, ext. 4348.

Rosenbloom, B., *Marketing Functions and the Wholesaler-Distributor: Achieving Excellence in Distribution,* Washington, DC, Distribution Research and Education Foundation, 1987, (202) 872-0885.

Skinner, M., and A. J. Fein, "Build a Value-Creating Integrated Supply Strategy," *Modern Distribution Management,* July 1999, http://www.PembrokeConsulting.com.

Stern, L. W., and A. El-Ansary, *Marketing Channels,* 4th ed., Prentice-Hall, Englewood Cliffs, NJ, 1992.

Wade, W., and C. Vollman, *HD Distribution & The Power of One,* Itasca, IL, QDS Partners, 1999.

Vurva, R., "The Allied Invasion," *Progressive MRO Distributor,* January/February 1998.

RELATED CHAPTERS

6: Construction
7: Wood Products
26: Information Services
38: Household Consumer Durables
42: Retailing

RETAILING
Economic and Trade Trends

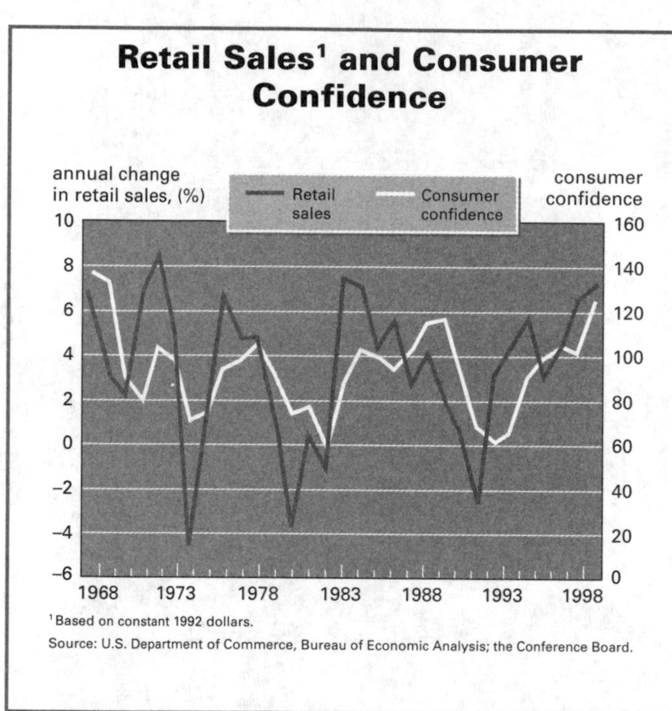

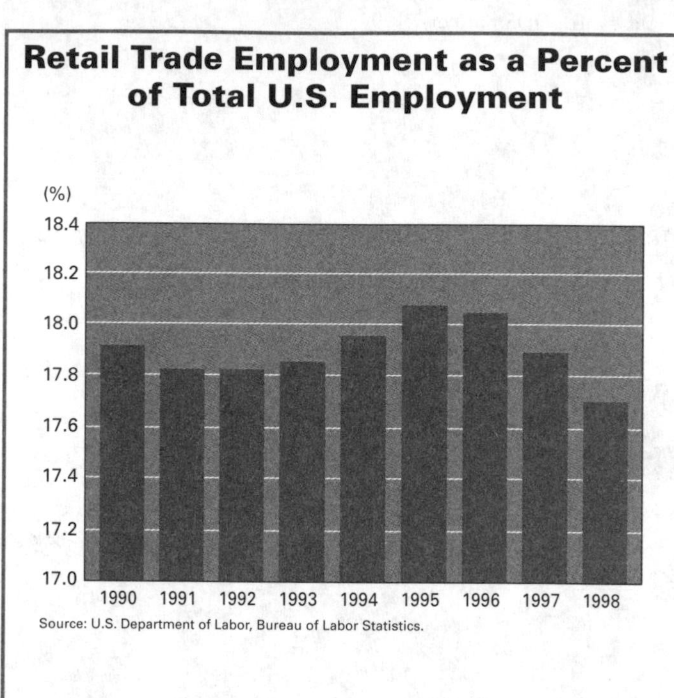

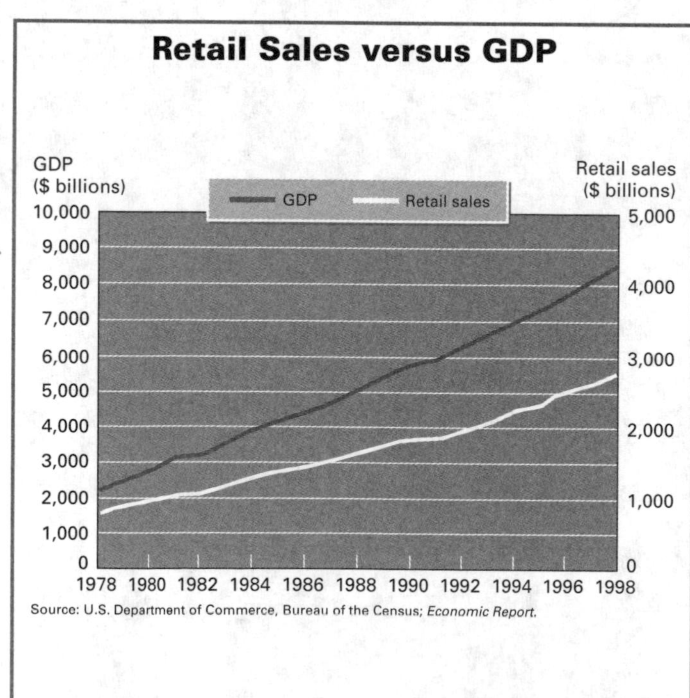

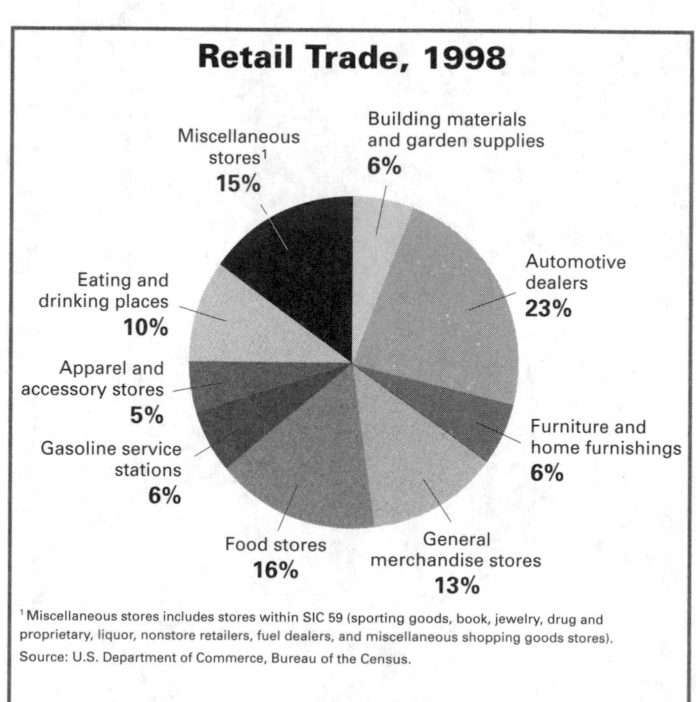

See "Getting the Most Out of *Outlook 2000*" for definitions of terms.

42

Retailing

INDUSTRY DEFINITION Retailers generally sell merchandise primarily for personal or household consumption. In some instances, retailers may further process goods before sale, but such processing is relatively minor. Building materials and garden supply stores (SIC 52), automobile dealers (SIC 55), and home furnishings and equipment stores (SIC 57) primarily sell durable goods, which are expected to last at least 3 years. General merchandise stores (SIC 53), food stores (SIC 54), gasoline service stations (SIC 55), apparel and accessory stores (SIC 56), and eating and drinking places (SIC 58) largely sell nondurables. Miscellaneous retailers (SIC 59), which include book, jewelry, drug, liquor, and toy stores and catalog and mail-order houses, among others, sell a mix of durable and nondurable goods.

DOMESTIC RETAIL TRADE PROSPECTS

Growth in retail sales is expected to be moderate between 1999 and 2000, increasing approximately 4.5 percent annually in nominal terms (see Table 42-1). This growth is slightly less than the 5.9 percent average annual growth rate between 1992 and 1998. Retail sales are expected to increase 6.0 percent in 1999, slow to 4.5 percent in 2000, and register average annual increases from 1999 to 2004 of 4.3 percent, primarily as a result of a slowdown in spending on new homes and related durable and nondurable home furnishings and building and garden supplies. Because consumer spending accounts for two-thirds of the gross domestic product (GDP) and because about 42 percent of consumer spending takes place at retail establishments, it is expected that as GDP changes, so will retail sales.

Changes in several indicators offer guidance in determining trends in consumer spending and, consequently, retail sales over the near term. These indicators include consumer confidence, unemployment, and housing sales. The Conference Board's Consumer Confidence Survey measures the level of confidence individual households have in the performance of the economy over the next 6 months. At 131.7, the consumer confidence index stood at its highest level in 1998, having increased steadily over the 1992–1998 period. Much of the recent optimism is due to the rising value of the stock market, which has added considerably to the wealth of numerous households. Many people have cashed in some of their stock gains to purchase houses, cars, boats, and other large items that have bolstered retail sales in recent years. Consumer confidence is expected to drop gradually between 1999 and 2004, dampening consumers' enthusiasm for spending on "big ticket" durables.

Unemployment has been unusually low, helping to fuel increases in consumer confidence. The unemployment rate has been dropping fairly steadily since 1992, and at 4.9 percent in 1998 it was the lowest it had been in 30 years. The unemployment rate is expected to decline still further in 1999 and 2000 but then rise through 2004, helping to dampen consumer confidence and, consequently, retail sales. As long as consumers are not concerned about their employment prospects, they are more willing to spend current and future income (by increasing debt) on items sold by retailers, but when those employment prospects are less certain, they put off spending on major retail items.

Low interest rates and potential down payments drawn from stock market gains can be expected, at least in the short term, to continue to spur sales of homes, both new and existing, as well as home improvement projects, which in turn will support retail sales growth for home furnishing stores and building and garden supply stores. Mortgage rates are expected to remain stable in 1999 and 2000, and housing starts to continue to increase modestly in 1999 but decline slightly from 2000 to 2004. As spending on new homes declines, retail spending can be expected to shift back somewhat to purchases of nondurables such as apparel.

TABLE 42-1: Retail Trade (SIC 52–59) Trends and Forecasts
(millions of dollars unless otherwise noted)

										Percent Change				
	1992	1993	1994	1995	1996	1997	1998	1999[1]	2000[1]	96–97	97–98	98–99	99–00	96–00
Total retail sales	1,951,589	2,072,788	2,227,325	2,324,038	2,506,141	2,615,669	2,746,011	2,912,061	3,044,422	4.4	5.0	6.0	4.5	5.0
Total, durable goods	703,604	776,126	873,408	925,017	1,020,861	1,066,087	1,138,286	1,207,117	1,261,984	4.4	6.8	6.0	4.5	5.4
Building materials and garden supplies	100,838	109,444	122,342	125,831	141,935	150,482	165,331	185,557	192,051	6.0	9.9	12.2	3.5	7.9
Automotive dealers	406,935	456,332	518,492	551,330	608,781	632,885	668,658	732,047	752,269	4.0	5.7	9.5	2.8	5.5
Furniture and home furnishings	96,947	105,399	118,649	127,270	135,149	140,776	152,044	163,598	168,839	4.2	8.0	7.6	3.2	5.7
Total, nondurable goods	1,247,985	1,296,662	1,353,917	1,399,021	1,485,280	1,549,582	1,607,725	1,704,944	1,782,439	4.3	3.8	6.0	4.5	4.7
General merchandise stores	246,420	264,613	283,203	299,169	313,342	330,216	351,436	381,510	389,742	5.4	6.4	8.6	2.2	5.6
Food stores	377,099	384,978	398,845	409,617	415,390	425,170	438,212	460,277	485,236	2.4	3.1	5.0	5.4	4.0
Gasoline service stations	136,950	138,172	141,671	146,080	168,320	171,527	162,095	167,932	172,970	1.9	–5.5	3.6	3.0	0.8
Apparel and accessory stores	104,212	107,176	109,862	110,429	116,101	120,575	126,939	135,787	140,513	3.9	5.3	7.0	3.5	4.9
Eating and drinking places	200,164	213,461	223,485	232,060	238,474	253,551	266,544	285,263	295,234	6.3	5.1	7.0	3.5	5.5
GAF, total[2]	519,230	552,967	593,788	622,940	656,527	685,577	729,178	784,073	806,062	4.4	6.4	7.5	2.8	5.3
Employment (thousands)	19,356	19,773	20,507	21,187	21,597	21,966	22,296	22,483	22,582	1.7	1.5	0.8	0.4	1.1
Percent of total nonfarm employment	17.8	17.9	18.0	18.1	18.1	18.0	17.7							

[1] Forecast.
[2] GAF represents stores that specialize in department store types of merchandise (general merchandise, apparel, furniture, miscellaneous shopping goods).
Source: U.S. Department of Commerce, Bureau of the Census; Department of Labor, Bureau of Labor Statistics, September 1999.

More broadly, some real changes not only in demographics but also in retailing itself will affect the direction of retail sales and the structure of the industry over the next 5 years. Those changes include the aging of the "baby boom" generation, a shift to casual clothing in the workplace, and the increasing time pressure most consumers feel. As one of the largest segments of the population ages, the baby boom generation (individuals born between 1946 and 1964) is facing new spending priorities. Many consumers in this generation are now focused on sending children to college, caring for elderly parents, and planning for retirement. Instead of spending the disposable income that is left after paying for daily living expenses on purchases of career clothing, for example, these consumers are redirecting their spending to home improvement items, including appliances, personal computers, and automobiles—durable goods sold by specialty retailers and frequently by mass retailers. In addition, mass retailers are benefiting from the penchant of these consumers to buy basic apparel items such as underwear, T-shirts, and jeans at mass retailers such as Wal-Mart and Kmart rather than at the traditional department stores where they used to purchase those items. This demographic-driven shift in buying patterns is expected to continue in the near term, particularly as the increasingly casual dress code expands its presence in workplaces. Retail sales probably will stay strongest at building and garden supply stores, home furnishings stores, discount department stores, and other similar stores.

A third major factor affecting retailing is time: Consumers have less and less of it. Consequently, they care increasingly about convenience. Convenience today is defined as how long it takes a customer to complete the shopping experience from the time he or she leaves home until the time the purchased goods are stored. Convenience thus entails more than a nearby store location; it also entails customer familiarity with a store's layout, how fast the checkout process is, and whether the store can be reliably expected to have the brands sought by the customer. This has fueled and will continue to fuel growth in Internet retailing, sales of brands, and greater efforts of retailers to locate outlets as near as possible to busy customers. Electronic commerce (E-commerce), although still in its infancy, caters to customers who crave convenience. They need not shop only when the store is open and use valuable time and energy to drive to the outlet only to discover that the store is out of stock of the items they seek. Internet retailers ship the product to the doorstep. This trend will grow significantly in the future and is described in more detail below. More consumers are being drawn to purchases of brand items such as Gap jeans, Land's End polo shirts, Dell computers, and Black and Decker hand tools because they know what they are getting. They do not have to worry that they will waste time having to return an item because it does not fit or does not perform to their expectations. Retailers that offer brand merchandise will continue to draw sales from those which do not offer strong national brands. Finally, convenience also demands that retailers have store outlets as close as possible to their customers. A customer with no time will not travel far to pick up toothpaste or milk; the store needs to be on the customer's way to work, home, or school and easily accessible. Thus, for example, in a phenomenon known as backfilling, some cities have outlets of the same retail chain—Starbucks or CVS pharmacy, for example—seemingly on every other downtown corner.

American retailing is a highly competitive industry. Despite the moderate growth in retail sales projected for the future, consolidation in the industry is expected to continue. However, such consolidation has not tempered the intense competition that is characteristic of this industry. No matter how large they are, retailers generally are unable to raise prices to increase margins, in large part because customers can still resist such price increases because they continue to have many retailing options including the Internet. Retail industry analysts continue to point out that the industry is "overstored" and "overcataloged"; despite bankruptcies and closures, multiple retail options continue to fuel competition.

To win this competition, retailers are looking for new ways to build customer loyalty. An increasingly popular method is focused, individual-customer-driven marketing initiatives. By using information collected about their customers at the cash register or through sign-in forms on their Web sites, for example, retailers are targeting their messages, promotions, and loyalty programs to individual customers. According to the International Mass Retail Association, approximately 46 percent of the U.S. population belongs to a customer loyalty program through which retailers are able to collect reams of valuable customer information. These programs, which are particularly strong at supermarkets, increase retail profits by reducing operating expenses.

Electronic Commerce

The Internet is helping retailers collect the information they need to target their marketing efforts more directly at time-starved consumers who are armed with information about the prices and qualities of the products offered by different retailers. The advent of the Internet and E-commerce is revolutionizing the way retailers market their products and interact with their consumers and suppliers. Retailers have flocked to the Internet in hopes of capturing a share of the emerging on-line sales. The products available through the Internet have expanded swiftly from books, CDs, and computer software to almost everything imaginable, including automobiles, groceries, flowers, sporting goods, and apparel.

Although on-line retail sales represented a small share of total retail sales in 1998, that share is growing rapidly each year. In fact, on-line retail sales are growing so rapidly that estimates of those sales vary widely. For example, data derived from a Shop.org study conducted by the Boston Consulting Group predicts total on-line retail sales of $34.2 billion in 1999, while Forrester Research estimates on-line sales of $20 billion in that year.

On-line retailers can be divided into two categories: on-line-only and multichannel. On-line-only retailers sell their products exclusively on the Internet, while multichannel retailers use the Internet in addition to traditional means such as "brick and mortar" stores, catalogs, and call centers. On-line-only retailers may have pioneered E-commerce but do not dominate the on-line sales market. According to the Shop.org survey, multichannel retailers earned 62 percent of total on-line retail revenues in 1998, while on-line-only retailers accounted for only 38 percent.

As both types of on-line retailers continue to develop their on-line business, they will face different sets of challenges and obstacles. On-line-only retailers must invest sizable amounts of capital to acquire and retain customers. Unlike multichannel retailers, on-line-only retailers are not easily recognized by consumers and generally lack brand name recognition. The Shop.org survey revealed that on-line-only retailers must spend an average of $42 to acquire a customer, while multichannel retailers spend only $22 per customer. In addition to marketing expenses, on-line-only retailers will continue to make significant investments in cutting-edge technology. The high cost of marketing and expenditures on technology will continue to inhibit the profitability of on-line-only retailers. As category leaders emerge in the on-line retail industry, many smaller on-line retailers will be unable to compete and will be consolidated into larger companies.

Unlike on-line-only retailers, multichannel retailers already have a customer service, distribution, and marketing infrastructure in place. The challenge for multichannel retailers is to integrate their existing business with E-commerce. Given the complex organizational structures of multichannel retailers, responding rapidly to changing technologies and consumer demands is key if they hope to compete against the easily adaptable structure of on-line-only retailers.

One of the most significant ways in which E-commerce is altering retailing is through the exchange of information between retailers and their customers. The true value of E-commerce to retailers lies in the ability to track and monitor consumers' spending habits. Retailers that hope to win customer loyalty can tailor products and services directly to a particular individual and anticipate customer preferences. In addition, multichannel retailers can apply information obtained on-line to modify the marketing strategies employed in existing brick and mortar stores and catalogs.

E-commerce has the added benefit of empowering consumers to make educated and informed purchasing decisions. Because consumers can scour the Internet to ensure that they are receiving the lowest price possible for a product, it is imperative that retailers provide additional benefits to their customers beyond competitive prices. As on-line shopping continues to grow, retailers will strive to make the on-line experience as convenient and easy to use as possible.

Retailers are incorporating new Internet technologies to enhance the on-line shopping experience. For example, Eddie Bauer has introduced a "virtual dressing room" on its Web site to allow customers to simulate the brick and mortar shopping experience. Land's End's "Shop with a Friend" technology allows two people in different parts of the country to share the same Web page and communicate by phone or text-based chat as they browse merchandise. eWish allows shoppers to create a "wish list" of desired products from all the affiliated eWish merchants, which friends and family members then can access when shopping for birthdays, holidays, or graduation. In addition, many on-line retailers offer 24-hour-a day real-time customer service on-line.

E-commerce also is transforming the relationships between retailers and their suppliers. Manufacturers also have the ability to sell their products on-line directly to consumers, thus bypassing retailers. On-line retail ventures by manufacturers could place them in direct competition with the retailers they supply. In some instances, the supplier may value the relationship with a particular retailer enough to limit its on-line sales to keep that retailer from looking for another supplier with which it is not competing on-line. Other suppliers could realize greater benefits from direct on-line sales and risk competing directly against retailers on-line.

The ability of anyone in the world to access a U.S. retailer's Web site is one of the major advantages of E-commerce. Although E-commerce has had the greatest impact in the United States, the rest of the world, particularly Europe, is catching up. A study by Andersen Consulting predicts that the on-line marketplace in Europe will total $430 billion by 2003 and that the number of European Internet users will reach 170 million, with a similar number projected for the United States.

The expansion of E-commerce in Asia continues to be sluggish because of limited use of credit cards, a lack of personal computers, and Internet security concerns. Beyond technological concerns, Asian culture tends to be wary of sharing information, which could impede the rapid spread of on-line retail sales in that region. With the majority of on-line retail sites in English only, many Asians face an on-line language barrier as well.

INTERNATIONAL RETAILING

Despite the financial troubles experienced by half the world's economies in the late 1990s, U.S. retailers continue to expand sales and increase market share by moving into international markets. Although U.S. retailers generally have been slow to expand overseas, the liberalization of trade and investment through the World Trade Organization and the North American Free Trade Agreement has made it easier for them to do so.

As a result of the high saturation of stores and intense competition in the domestic market, several U.S. retailers have turned to international markets to boost growth. Not only does international retailing offer the possibility of higher sales, it can offset the impact of poor economic conditions in a retailer's home market. Through international expansion, U.S. retailers may provide specialized products or target a unique market niche that is not being served by local retailers. Given the global spread of U.S. popular culture, many U.S. retailers and their products are already well known in foreign countries. In many cases, this gives those retailers an advantage over other competitors in the market.

Despite the considerable opportunities for U.S. retailers in international markets, a number of obstacles must be overcome to succeed in international retailing. Adapting store format, products, and marketing to new cultures requires comprehensive research and planning. Legal restrictions on foreign investment, workers' rights, operating hours, and store location must be evaluated carefully in each country in which retailers operate. U.S. retailers must deal with supply and distribution systems that may differ dramatically from those in their domestic operations.

The trend toward consolidation that is affecting the U.S. retailing industry also applies to international retailing. Recent examples of international retail consolidation include Wal-Mart's acquisition of the British retailer ASDA and the merger of the French retailers Carrefour and Promodes, which created the world's second largest retailer after Wal-Mart. This international concentration of retailers is not expected to dampen the intense competition characteristic of this industry. In addition, large international retailers increasingly are urging their suppliers to mirror their organizational structure to increase efficiency and provide consistent international pricing.

The opportunities in international retailing differ with the market. Mature markets in industrialized countries contain discriminating consumers with large amounts of disposable income. In these markets, U.S. retailers generally face high levels of competition from local retailers as well as other international retailers. Mature markets also have a lack of prime retail space, making acquisitions and joint ventures a popular entry strategy for U.S. retailers. In Europe, governmental restrictions on greenfield developments are driving consolidation.

The prospects for the European Union's economies are strong, with GDP growth expected to increase from 2.2 in 1999 to 3.0 percent in the year 2000. The introduction of a common European currency, the Euro, will be one of the most important factors affecting retailers in the region. The Euro is expected to increase consumer demand as interest rates decline and competition between retailers increases. Improvements in transportation and distribution resulting from the Euro also should benefit retailers in Europe.

The main challenge the Euro presents for retailers relates to pricing. Although Euro notes and coins will not be introduced until 2002, retailers must prepare for a 6-month transition period, January 1 to June 30, during which products will be required to be priced in both Euros and the national currency. This will limit the price flexibility of retailers and cause difficulties in handling transactions. For example, everything from cash registers to accounting systems will have to be adapted to handle different prices and currencies. In addition, retailers must undertake efforts to educate consumers about the new pricing system. Despite these short-term conversion costs, U.S. retailers with operations in Europe, including Staples, Costco, Gap, Toys "R" Us, TJX Companies, Wal-Mart, and Woolworth, are expected to benefit from the efficiencies created by the Euro.

Japan, another mature retail market, was mired in a recession throughout the 1990s. Japanese GDP is expected to decline 1.0 percent in 1999 but reverse the downward trend and rise 0.3 percent in 2000. Even though Japan is recovering slowly, substantial investment opportunities exist there for U.S. retailers. The Japanese retail market is highly developed, and consumers expect high-quality, affordable products. One advantage for U.S. retailers is that Japanese consumers have large personal incomes and are highly conscious of trends and new high-tech products from the United States. U.S. retailers that operate stores in Japan include Toys "R" Us, Gap, and OfficeMax.

Japan is undergoing substantial reforms in the banking and financial sector that should favor retailers in the future. A liberalization of the economy is expected to open the Japanese market further to U.S. retailers. Japan's Large-Scale Retail Store Law, which controls the locations and operations of stores, is scheduled to be revised again in 2001. The law was created in 1973 to protect smaller local retailers but has been progressively weakened. Retailers should expect a further liberalization of this restrictive law in 2001.

The challenges retailers encounter in emerging markets differ from those in the mature markets discussed above. The retail sector in emerging markets is often small and cannot fully meet consumer demand. Many emerging markets also may not have well-developed, stable legal and financial systems, a situation that can harm U.S. retailers.

With one-fifth of the world's population, China is a valuable emerging market for international retailers. China's GDP grew nearly 10 percent annually during the 1990s. As consumer incomes rise and the Chinese government opens more segments of the retail market to foreign investors, rapid growth of retail sales is expected. The Chinese government is placing special emphasis on opening foreign investment in supermarkets and convenience stores, two sectors that are struggling to meet consumer demand. In addition, the government plans to eventually give foreign retailers access to more cities and regions beyond the current six coastal cities and five special economic zones. Wal-Mart and a number of food franchises have opened outlets in China.

In South America, the fallout from the Asian financial crisis continues to batter the Brazilian economy. The high level of government debt has forced the Brazilian government to implement a strict austerity program that is hampering employment growth and income gains. Brazilian GDP is expected to decline 4.0 percent in 1999 but then recover in 2000, increasing 3.3 percent. The fear of unemployment and high interest rates have caused many Brazilian consumers to avoid high-priced purchases; however, consumer spending on low-priced goods remains steady.

As the most populous country and the largest economy in South America, Brazil should not be ignored by U.S. retailers. Wal-Mart and Sherwin-Williams are two U.S. retailers that have already opened stores in Brazil. The Brazilian food store sector was estimated to be worth over $104 billion in 1998 and continues to grow rapidly. Convenience stores in Brazil are growing as a result of strong consumer demand.

When investing in retail operations abroad, retailers need to take a long-term approach, particularly in emerging markets. Retailers must be prepared to commit the necessary resources and time to develop a presence in a foreign retail market. International retailing involves great risks, but its potential for rewards is so great that U.S. retailers must not miss these opportunities.

Because the allure of some retailers is their American image, U.S. retailers with stores abroad often operate as exporters of American-made goods. However, more significant to retailers is the need to import. According to the NRF Foundation, while retailers generally source most of the goods they sell from U.S. producers, some products must be imported, and some retail formats (such as that of Pier 1 Imports) revolve around selling imports. Thus, special U.S. trade programs provide retailers with valuable ways to import the goods they need at prices that enable them to compete successfully in a U.S. market that is notoriously resistant to price increases. Key among these programs is the U.S. Generalized System of Preferences (GSP) program, which provides duty-free treatment to selected imports from certain developing countries. Consumer hard goods are the primary products imported by retailers under the GSP program, including consumer electronics, jewelry, basketry, and brassware.

BUILDING AND GARDEN SUPPLY STORES

The boom in the housing market continues throughout the country. Many homeowners who are not in the market for a different home are undertaking renovation projects that range from the modest—room makeovers—to the ambitious—new stories and other additions. Each project seems to require a trip to the increasingly local building and garden supply store for paint, tools, drywall, landscaping materials, lighting, and even kitchen supplies. Not surprisingly, sales of building and garden supply stores have been booming, having increased at a rate from 1997 to 1998—9.9 percent—that is almost double the retail average.

This strong growth picture is expected to continue as long as interest rates on home mortgages and home equity loans remain relatively low, the stock market remains strong, and consumers feel secure in their employment prospects. Mortgage rates have started to inch up since the Federal Reserve began to increase short-term rates in 1999; however, the increases have not been great enough to stifle enthusiasm in the housing market. Consequently, building and garden supply stores' sales were projected to be 12.2 percent higher in 1999 than in 1998. Helping to maintain the momentum is a strong stock market, which is padding consumers' bank accounts and providing the money needed for down payments and do-it-yourself home improvement projects. Although mortgage rates are expected to remain steady through the year 2000, the unemployment rate is expected to inch up slightly, but more significantly, new housing starts are expected to decline. Consequently, retail sales growth for this segment is projected to drop to 3.5 percent in 2000 from the very strong levels in 1999.

At least three factors are key to success in this sector: customer service, good prices, and in-stock merchandise. Failure to meet two of these factors—service and adequate supplies of merchandise—forced one major regional building and garden supply store, Hechinger/HQ/Builders Square, out of business in 1999 as customers increasingly shifted their purchases to The Home Depot and Lowes, which more effectively provided them with service and reliable sources of merchandise.

Several important building and garden supply stores are undertaking new initiatives designed to keep customers interested. In 1999, Home Depot, the largest retailer in this segment (it also sells significant volumes of goods typically classified in the furniture and home furnishings retail segment), began efforts to cater to customers seeking upscale designer fixtures with its Expo Design outlets; meet the need for a local, easy-in, easy-out hardware outlet with a "neighborhood" store format called Villagers Hardware; and expand its specialty lighting offerings through its acquisition of Georgia Lighting, which operates the largest consumer-oriented store devoted to lighting. It also has begun two mail-order businesses, National Blinds and Maintenance Warehouse (which provides products sought by property maintenance firms). The Home Depot's Web site (www.homedepot.com) offers on-line ordering as well as a "how to" feature for customers to find information about how to undertake a particular do-it-yourself project and what materials will be needed.

The next largest retailer in this category, Lowe's, is adding more housewares and other nonhardware merchandise in its stock of building and garden supplies. It acquired Eagle Hardware & Garden to give it a stronger presence in the west. Lowe's also offers detailed "how to" advice on its Web site (www.lowes.com), which caters not only to "do it yourself" customers but also to commercial builders.

MOTOR VEHICLE RETAILERS

The outlook for motor vehicle retailers was strong through 1999 but is expected to slow somewhat in 2000. Spending on motor vehicles in 1998 continued to benefit from consumers' confidence about their employment prospects, a financial condition made stronger by the stock market, home appreciation, and a large number of mortgage refinancings. Strength in these parameters continued to outweigh any negative fallout that would otherwise result from rising interest rates in 1999, which may increase the costs of financing a motor vehicle purchase, pushing up the value of motor vehicle retail sales by 5.7 percent in 1998 with a projected increase of 9.5 percent in 1999. Projections for a slower U.S. economy generally underlie expectations for a slight decline in the volume of new motor vehicle sales in 2000, although value increases resulting from options as well as general price increases are expected to push total category sales up 2.8 percent in that year.

The strong economy has helped increase the contribution of new car sales to dealership profits, which, according to the National Automobile Dealers Association (NADA), averaged just 1.7 percent in 1998. Typically, these profits are earned primarily on sales of used cars and service and parts. In 1998, NADA reported that new vehicles contributed almost 30 percent to total profit for the average dealership, a sharp turnaround from the typical break-even contribution of new-car sales.

Strong sales and profitability aside, the motor vehicle dealership segment of retailing has been undergoing a series of consolidations. Mergers and acquisitions and motor vehicle producers' efforts to reduce the number of franchises have continued to cause the number of dealerships to drop, declining from 6,725 in 1989 to 4,256 in 1999, according to NADA.

FOOD STORES

There has been much turmoil in the food store sector recently. Sales increased just 3.1 percent in 1998, just above the 6-year average annual growth rate of 2.5 percent. Sales at food stores are expected to increase about 5.0 percent in 1999 and 5.4 percent in 2000.

Supermarkets, which account for the bulk of sales in this category, have been undergoing a series of consolidations and mergers over the last few years. For example, a pending merger of Kroger, the largest supermarket chain, with Fred Meyer, a grocery and general merchandise store that acquired a number of food stores recently, will result in a food retail operation that probably will account for almost 10 percent of the food retail segment's total sales. Safeway and Albertson's have each bought other grocery chains, and Dutch Royal Ahold bought Washington, DC's, Giant Food in 1998, followed by New Jersey's Pathmark grocery chain. Other Ahold holdings include Stop & Shop, Tops Markets, and BI-LO. SuperValue is buying Richfood Holdings, which owns the Shoppers Food Warehouse, Farm Fresh, and Metro market chains.

Part of the problem for these stores is growing competition from nontraditional food retailers, including Wal-Mart, Costco, and Kmart, which are increasingly stocking food items they are able to sell at prices lower than those in most standard supermarkets. Customers with little time prefer to combine their shopping trips as much as possible, and if they can purchase socks at the same store that sells peanut butter and bread, many will choose the retailer that offers them time savings as well as lower prices.

The time crunch also has been decreasing consumers' interest in raw ingredients for at-home cooking in favor of prepared hot foods. Food stores have had to respond with expanded sections of prepared hot foods that customers can easily pick up on the way home from work. In addition, retailers that specialize in prepared foods, such as EatZi's from Dallas, have begun to open new outlets in markets in the northeast that have large numbers of high-income, time-strapped customers.

In addition to large and more varied prepared foods displays, supermarkets have been responding to the intense competition from discounters with customer loyalty programs. Safeway, Inc., introduced a "Safeway Club" card that gives customers discounts from the prices of different products each month. In exchange for the discounts, Safeway is able to use the information it receives from card use to know which customers are purchasing what items and to tailor special discounts on related products, given out at the cash register, that Safeway believes the customer may want to purchase on the next visit.

EATING AND DRINKING PLACES

The booming economy of the late 1990s has been a mixed blessing for eating and drinking places. Sales have been increasing strongly. Two of every five dollars spent by households on food is spent on meals prepared away from home. Sales at eating and drinking places increased 5.1 percent in 1998 and were projected to grow 7.0 percent in 1999. Sales were strong in part because households with spendable income and no time to cook increasingly took their meals in restaurants. However, a drop in sales growth to 3.5 percent is expected for 2000 as a result of the expected slowdown in the economy overall, a slight increase in the unemployment rate, the beginnings of a decline in real disposable personal income, and a decline in consumer confidence. When consumers decide it is time to cut back on spending, dinners out are among the first expenses to be cut.

Low unemployment means that a shortage of qualified labor continues to put upward pressure on retail costs in this segment. The labor pool has shrunk not only because it was so much easier in 1998 to get a higher-paying job in another sector but also because the usual pool of labor for restaurants—employees age 16 to 24—is much smaller than it was in the past because of the sharp decline in births in the 1960s and 1970s. Consequently, the National Restaurant Association reports that restaurants and other eating and drinking establishments are increasingly offering incentives to retain employees or draw new employees, including pay raises, bonuses, profit sharing, health insurance, employee recognition programs, and scholarships.

GENERAL MERCHANDISE STORES

The general merchandise retail category includes department stores (discount, chain, and conventional), variety stores (another type of discount store), and other retailers (typically small) of a mixture of hard and soft lines (such as might be sold in a dry goods country store). This category, however, increasingly is dominated by discount stores. Largely as a result of their success, general merchandise store sales have been growing at faster rates than the retail average: up 6.4 percent in 1998 and projected to increase 8.6 percent in 1999. However, a slight increase in the unemployment rate, coupled with a projected decline in consumer confidence, is expected to slow sales in this category to a growth rate of 2.2 percent from 1999 to 2000.

Consumers' search for convenience and value, coupled with a demographic-induced shift in the products at the top of the customer's shopping list, has enabled discount retailers to increase sales at the expense of department stores, general merchandise chains, and food stores. While discount department stores' market share increased 28 percent from 1992 to 1998, the shares of conventional department and chain stores declined 21 percent and that of food stores (including supermarkets) declined 17 percent in that period. While food stores are fighting back, over the short term this trend can be expected to continue.

The strong showing of discounters aside, some individual general merchandise stores continue to draw customers. Acquisitions as well as consolidations are helping these stores provide customers with quality products at better prices, while they cut costs by, for example, consolidating logistics, focusing more on store brands (called private labels), and employing more productive point-of-sale technology. Conventional department stores are fighting the discounters by emphasizing greater fashion selection, quality, service, and ambience.

APPAREL AND ACCESSORY STORES

Retail sales of apparel and accessory stores have been showing increasing strength, although that strength is expected to moderate in the near future. Sales grew 5.3 percent in 1998 and, based on increases in the first half of 1999, were expected to rise 7.0 percent in that year. However, the general slowdown in the economy expected for the year 2000 will moderate sales growth in this category to an expected 3.5 percent.

Apparel and accessory stores are highly vulnerable to a number of ever-changing factors: demographics, fashion, and competition from a variety of fronts. As was noted above, the baby boom generation is spending less on apparel in favor of other retail items and nonretail spending. When it purchases basic apparel items, many of those purchases have shifted to discount retailers. Apparel and accessory stores find themselves increasingly focusing on much younger consumers: teens and customers in their twenties and early thirties. These customers are highly fashion-conscious, with "fashion" frequently defined by what friends are wearing rather than by the runways in Paris. Trends, fads, and fashions change seemingly monthly, and it is very difficult for many apparel and accessory stores to stay ahead of the curve.

The successful stores have been those which have managed to turn store brands into fashion. Most notable are Gap, Inc., and Limited. Increasingly, these stores and their related divisions (including, for example, Banana Republic, Old Navy, BabyGap, and GapKids for Gap and Victoria's Secret, Express, Structure, and The Limited for Limited) tend to dominate shopping malls around the country. These retailers are also well aware that their primary customer is highly Internet-savvy, and many have on-line shopping sites.

Laura Baughman (baughman@tradepartnership.com) and ***Alan Mauldin*** (mauldin@tradepartnership.com), The Trade Partnership, (202) 347-1041, October 1999.

■ REFERENCES

Annual Benchmark Report for Retail Trade, August 1999, U.S. Bureau of the Census, Economics and Statistics Administration, U.S. Department of Commerce, Washington, DC 20230. (301) 457-2706.

Asia Commercial Overview, U.S. and Foreign Commercial Service, May 21, 1999, National Trade Database.

"Asia's Culture Hampers Net Commerce," Julie Schmidt, *USA Today,* February 16, 1999, www.usatoday.com.

Brazil—Supermarkets—an Overview, Market Research Reports: International Market Insights, Judith Henderson, U.S. and Foreign

Commercial Service and U.S. Department of State, May 12, 1999, National Trade Database.

China—Chain Stores and Retail Sector, Industry Sector Analysis, Mary Cao and Diane Shen, U.S. and Foreign Commercial Service and U.S. Department of State, December 4, 1998, National Trade Database.

Consumer Confidence, the Conference Board, 845 Third Avenue, New York, NY 10022. (212) 759-0900, www.conference-board.org.

Consumer Expenditure Survey, 1997, Office of Prices and Living Conditions, Bureau of Labor Statistics, U.S. Department of Labor, 2 Massachusetts Avenue, NE, Washington, DC 20212. (202) 606-6900, http://stats.bls.gov.

eEurope Take Off, Andersen Consulting, September 9, 1999, 100 Wacker Drive, Suite 1059, Chicago, IL 60606. (312) 693-0161, www.ac.com.

"E-Tailing: Forecasts Keep Swelling," Dick Silverman, September 21, 1999, *Women's Wear Daily,* 7 West 34 Street, New York, NY 10001. (212) 630-4000, www.wwd.com.

"Gift Giving Online Gets Easier," *Business Wire,* September 15, 1999, www.businesswire.com.

"Global Powers of Retailing," Deloitte Touche Tomatsu, *Stores,* February 1999, National Retail Federation, 325 Seventh Street, NW, Suite 1100, Washington, DC 20006. (202) 783-7971, www.nrf.com, www.stores.org.

Industry Analysis and Outlook, National Automobile Dealers Association, 8400 Westpark Drive, McLean, VA 22102. (703) 821-7088, www.nada.org.

Insights on European Retailing 2010, PricewaterhouseCoopers, April 1999, 130 Avenue of the Americas, New York, NY 10019. (212) 596-7000, www.pwcglobal.com.

International Retailing, Brenda Sternquist, 1998, Fairchild Publications, 7 West 34 Street, New York, NY 10001. (212) 630-4000.

"Land's End Sets Gold Standard for Customer Service Online with Two New Collaborative Shopping Aids," *Reuters,* September 15, 1999. www.reuters.com.

"NADA Data," *Automotive Executive,* August 1999, National Automobile Dealers Association, 8400 Westpark Drive, McLean, VA 22102. (703) 821-7088, www.nada.org.

National Restaurant Association, 1200 17 Street, NW, Washington, DC 20036. (202) 331-5900, www.restaurant.org.

"1999 Top 100 Retailers," David P. Schulz, *Stores,* July 1999, National Retail Federation, 325 Seventh Street, NW, Suite 1100, Washington, DC 20006. (202) 783-7971, www.nrf.com and www.stores.org.

"1999 Top Specialty Stores," David P. Schulz, *Stores,* August 1999, National Retail Federation, 325 Seventh Street, NW, Suite 1100, Washington, DC 20006. (202) 783-7971, www.nrf.com and www.stores.org.

1to1 Marketing . . . A Foundation for Building Customer Loyalty, International Mass Retail Association, 1700 North Moore Street, Suite 2250, Arlington, VA 22209, 1998. (703) 841-2300, www.imra.org.

Post-Web Retail, Seema Williams, September 1999, Forrester Research, 400 Technology Square, Cambridge, MA 02109. (617) 497-7090, www.forrester.com.

Prospects for Exporting Textiles and Clothing to the United States over the Next Decade, Laura M. Baughman, March 1997, for the International Textiles and Clothing Bureau, 15 Route des Morillons, 1218 Grand Saconnex, Switzerland. 41-22-929-1616.

Retail News, Ernst & Young, Winter 1999, 787 Seventh Avenue, New York, NY 10019. (212) 773-3000, www.ey.com.

The State of Online Retailing 2.0, the Boston Consulting Group, July 1999, Shop.org, 8403 Colesville Road, Suite 865, Silver Spring, MD 20910. (301) 650-2321, www.shop.org.

Understanding Your Customer, Part II: Consumer Logistics, International Mass Retail Association, 1700 North Moore Street, Suite 2250, Arlington, VA 22209, 1998. (703) 841-2300, www.imra.org.

■ RELATED CHAPTERS

6: Construction
7: Wood Products
8: Building Products and Materials
33: Apparel and Fabricated Textile Products
34: Footwear, Leather, and Leather Products
35: Processed Food and Beverages
36: Motor Vehicles
37: Automotive Parts
38: Household Consumer Durables
39: Recreational Equipment
40: Other Consumer Durables

HEALTH AND MEDICAL SERVICES
Economic and Trade Trends

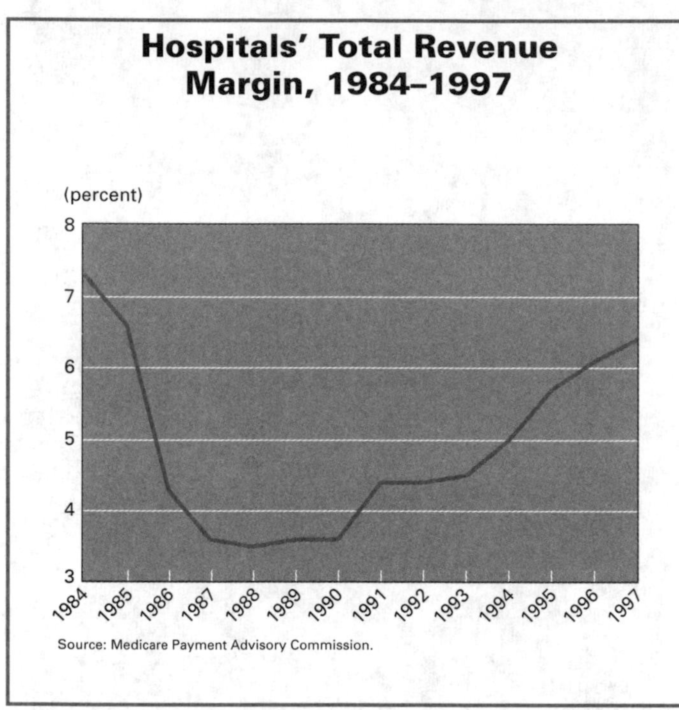

Source: Medicare Payment Advisory Commission.

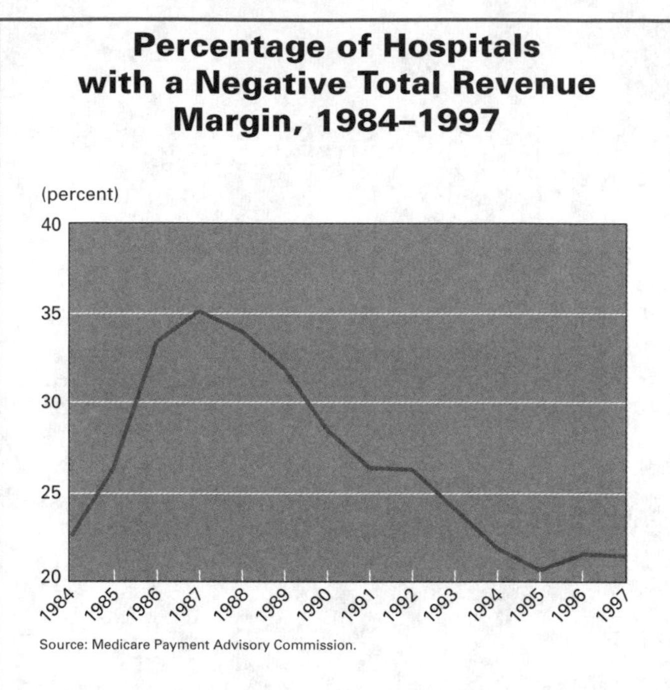

Source: Medicare Payment Advisory Commission.

World's 12 Largest Dedicated Health Care Service Firms

Company	Type of Service	1998 Sales ($billion)
Columbia/HCA Healthcare	Hospital services, home care	18.4
UnitedHealth Group	Managed care	17.8
Aetna/US Healthcare	Managed care	16.0
Tenet Healthcare	Hospital services	10.5
Humana	Managed care	9.7
Pacificare Health Systems	Hospital services	9.6
Foundation Health Systems	Managed care	8.9
Wellpoint Health Networks	Managed care	6.5
Oxford Health Plans	Managed care	4.6
HealthSouth	Rehabilitation, surgery centers	4.1
Medpartners	Home and clinical care	2.8
Beverly Enterprises	Long-term health care, nursing	2.8

Source: The Economist Intelligence Unit, *Healthcare International,* second quarter, 1999.
Note: All firms are based in the United States.

See "Getting the Most Out of *Outlook 2000*" for definitions of terms.

43

Health and Medical Services

INDUSTRY DEFINITION The health care industry (SIC 80) consists of public, private, and nonprofit institutions. Those institutions include hospitals, offices and clinics of medical doctors, nursing homes, and home health care facilities; other specialized health care facilities; and managed care organizations consisting of prepaid plans such as health maintenance organizations (HMOs), preferred provider organizations (PPOs), and independent practice associations (IPAs). The health care industry includes thousands of independent medical practices and partnerships as well as public and nonprofit institutions and major private corporations that have assets of billions of dollars and are major employers in the U.S. economy.

GLOBAL INDUSTRY TRENDS

With the exception of the poorest nations, the rising costs of health care show few signs of abating as a worldwide phenomenon, even if certain countries have achieved greater success in cost containment than others have. Recent economic downturns in Asia and Brazil, for example, have intensified the necessity for reform and new sources of capital for the health care sector, and the volatility of markets has led to some retrenchment in investment. As populations increasingly demand high-quality care across a broad spectrum of services that require access to sophisticated, expensive technology and pharmaceutical treatment, governments have been hard pressed to square those demands with the realities of medical price inflation.

Although the movement toward managed care in the United States represents one of the most noted responses to cost pressures, other countries have adopted varied and more hybrid strategies. Examples are the imposition of price caps on physician and hospital services, ceilings on national health care budgets, and a higher level of copayments. Equally apparent is the trend toward rationalization of hospital care in the face of increasingly expensive inpatient care. The result has been a substantial reduction in the number of hospital beds in western Europe, together with the growth of more cost-effective alternatives such as outpatient surgery centers and home health care. The global expansion in the cost of providing medical services also has encouraged health care decision makers and the medical community to focus on preventive, as opposed to curative, approaches to assuring the health of populations. This type of strategy typically puts more emphasis on health care education and altering harmful behaviors (e.g., smoking, drinking, deficient nutrition) as well as regular medical checkups.

In areas where people have begun to distrust public health care systems because of perceived inadequate care or where budgetary constraints have mounted, governments in regions such as Latin America have taken steps to allow a more significant role for private health care delivery and insurance. However, the ultimate success of such undertakings is more than ever a function of the ability to secure local venture capital and reliable data on populations' health and risk factors.

American managed care's attainment of some degree of success in reducing the rate of growth in health care expenditures has raised the question of the suitability of this form of care for other countries. Although a degree of emulation has taken place in Latin America, local conditions strongly influence its feasibility. The paucity of medical specialists in numerous countries tends to discourage the selective contracting that is an integral component of managed care operations in the United States. Moreover, an absence of reliable health care data on populations and financing severely hinders the management decisions needed for this type of delivery.

The World Bank estimates that investment in medical services worldwide was approximately $1.5 trillion in 1998, a figure that could rise to $4 trillion in 2010. One-quarter of this total will be accounted for by emerging markets.

The health care service subsector in which commercial expectations have arguably been the highest in recent years is telemedicine, or the diagnosis and treatment of distant patients by means of telecommunications systems. Rural and poor communities in particular are considered the most logical beneficiaries of this form of treatment because of their lack of physical proximity to medical centers. However, challenges to the technology's utilization are significant, including physicians' concerns about the maintenance of medical standards as well as questions of liability, confidentiality of data, and payment.

DOMESTIC TRENDS

According to the Health Care Financing Administration (HCFA), the cost of health care in the United States grew about 4.8 percent in 1998, reaching an estimated $1.15 trillion, or about $4,000 per capita. Total health care expenditures amounted to 13.5 percent of U.S. gross domestic product (GDP) in 1998. Managed care, which dominates the industry, provides health care services to over 85 percent of employed Americans. For the past 6 years, managed care has effectively stabilized health care costs, which had been rising at an unprecedented rate over the three decades since the Medicare and Medicaid programs were introduced. From 1993 to 1998, the rate of growth for health care expenditures fluctuated from 4.8 to 7.4 percent per year, compared with 11.0 to 12.9 percent per year from 1970 to 1990. As a proportion of GDP, health care expenditures remained at about 13.6 percent from 1993 to 1998, whereas they grew from 12.2 percent in 1990 to 13.6 percent in 1993. In addition to managed care, the reduction in traditional fee-for-service care, as well as the Balanced Budget Act (BBA) of 1997 that reformed Medicare and Medicaid payments to health care providers, assisted in keeping growth rates low.

Increases in health insurance premiums in the next 3 years are expected to compensate investors for losses incurred in the managed care market. Managed care is reacting to market forces, and the major health care plans increased their premiums in the range of 6 to 9 percent in 1999.

Competition and for-profit activity are fundamentally restructuring the health care services industry. These pressures have resulted in mergers, consolidations, and concentration for managed care investors, for-profit hospitals, nursing home care, and home care, as well as some pressures for physicians' unionization. *Health Affairs* reports that during the period 1987–1997, there were 2,753 mergers and acquisitions involving health services companies and 162 involving health maintenance organizations (HMOs). Merger and acquisition activity for health services and HMO companies peaked in 1996, when there were 483 completed mergers and acquisitions of health care service companies valued at $27 billion and 33 of HMOs worth $13.3 billion.

The number of health care services institutions operating at a profit as well as nonprofit HMOs now operating for profit is increasing. Between 1981 and 1997, for-profit HMOs increased from 18 percent to 75 percent of total HMO plans. Similarly, the number of for-profit community hospitals grew from 13 percent to 15 percent of the total of community hospitals during the period 1981–1996.

At the same time that these structural changes are occurring in the industry, the number of individuals without health insurance has reached an all-time high of about 43 million. Some consumers are dissatisfied with the quality of care as well as access to health care services. These issues have raised policy considerations of how best to allocate the government budget surplus to provide cost-effective health care to the uninsured and underinsured.

Fraud and abuse are major issues in the industry and are estimated to account for about 10 percent of total health care spending. The Office of the Inspector General will continue to investigate fraudulent practices in the industry. The media have been reporting instances in which managed care plans control and limit care to recipients. Patients want to receive high-quality care, but deficiencies exist in the system for managed care organizations as well as for indemnity plans. To establish a national consensus on this vital issue, the Clinton administration created the Advisory Commission on Consumer Protection and Quality in the Healthcare Industry to evaluate the state of information and protection available to consumers, measure the quality of health care, and make recommendations for improvements.

The commission produced the Consumer Bill of Rights and Responsibilities for the benefit of patients and the public (see Table 43-1). The eight general categories identify consumers' rights and responsibilities in the health care system and propose ways to deal with them. Although the Consumer Bill of Rights has not been incorporated into law, it is likely that any future health care reform will encompass elements of it.

DOMESTIC PROJECTIONS

Outlays for the U.S. health care industry (SIC 80) are estimated to be over $1.3 trillion in 2000, a 7.1 percent increase over $1.2 trillion in 1999 (see Table 43-2). In the next 5 years, increases in expenditures are expected to fluctuate in the range of 6.5 to 7.5 percent per year. Hospitals' share of total expenditures is expected to decline from 34.6 percent in 1996 to about 32 percent by the year 2001, a faster rate of decline than has occurred in recent years. Medicare spending for inpatient hospital services is expected to grow at its lowest rate in the program's history, having declined from an average annual high of 8.2 percent in 1993–1996 to 3 percent annually in the period

TABLE 43-1: Consumer Rights and Responsibilities Recommended by the President's Advisory Commission on Consumer Protection and Quality in the Health Care Industry, November 1997

Statement of Right/Responsibility	Summary of Included Protections
Information. Consumers have the right to receive accurate, easily understood information, and some require assistance in making informed health care decisions about their health plans, professionals, and facilities and have the right to receive it.	Consumers have the right to receive information about Covered benefits and cost sharing Licensure, certification, and accreditation status for plans, professionals, and facilities Measures of quality and consumer satisfaction Provider network composition Rules relating to access to specialists and emergency services Care management information, including preauthorization rules and utilization review procedures
Participation in treatment decisions. Consumers have the right and responsibility to participate fully in all decisions related to their health care. Consumers who are unable to participate fully in treatment decisions have the right to be represented by parents, guardians, family members, or advance directives, both living wills and durable powers of attorney for health care.	Patients have the right to receive easily understood information and to decide among treatment options consistent with the informed consent process. They and their designated family members have the right to know about the use of other conservators. Patients have the right to know about factors such as methods of compensation, ownership of or interest in health care facilities, and matters of conscience that could influence medical advice or treatment decisions. They have the right to be treated by health care providers who are not subject to "gag clauses" or other contractual mechanisms that restrict providers' ability to communicate with and advise patients about medically necessary treatment options.
Access/choice. Consumers have the right to a choice of health care providers that is sufficient to ensure access to appropriate high-quality health care.	Consumers have the right to Have access to sufficient numbers of providers without unreasonable delay Choose a qualified provider for the provision of routine and preventive women's health care services Have direct access to specialists for persons with complex or serious medical conditions who require frequent specialty care Have continued access to a nonparticipating specialty provider if they have a chronic or disabling condition and are involuntarily required to change plans or providers.
Emergency services. Consumers have the right to access emergency health care services when and where the need arises. Health plans should provide payment when a consumer presents to an emergency department with acute symptoms of sufficient severity, including severe pain, such that a "prudent layperson" could reasonably expect the absence of medical attention to result in placing that consumer's health in serious jeopardy, serious impairment to bodily functions, or serious dysfunction of any bodily organ or part.	Emergency services should be available 24 hours a day, 7 days a week. Health plans should educate their members about the availability, location, and appropriate use of emergency and other medical services and cost-sharing provisions for emergency services. Health plans should cover emergency services both in network and out of network without prior authorization consistent with the prudent layperson standard.
Nondiscrimination. Consumers have the right to nondiscriminatory treatment in the marketing, enrollment, and delivery of health care services.	Consumers have the right to considerate, respectful care from all members of the health care system at all times and under all circumstances. An environment of mutual respect is essential to maintain a quality health care system. Consumers must not be discriminated against in the delivery of health care services consistent with the benefits covered in their policies or as required by law based on race, ethnicity, national origin, religion, sex, age, mental or physical disability, sexual orientation, genetic information, or source of payment. Consumers who are eligible for coverage under the terms and conditions of a health plan or program or as required by law must not be discriminated against in marketing and enrollment practices based on race, ethnicity, national origin, religion, sex, age, mental or physical disability, sexual orientation, genetic information, or source of payment.
Dispute resolution. All consumers have the right to a fair and efficient process for resolving differences with their health plans, health care providers, and the institutions that serve them, including a rigorous system of internal review and an independent system of external review.	Internal appeals systems should include Timely written notification of coverage decisions and decisions to reduce or terminate services or deny payment, including an explanation of the underlying reasons and appeals mechanisms Timely resolution of all appeals with expedited consideration for decisions involving emergency or urgent care Claims review processes conducted by health care professionals who are appropriately credentialed with respect to the treatment involved and who were not involved in the initial decision
Confidentiality. Consumers have the right to communicate with health care providers in confidence and to have the confidentiality of their individually identifiable health care information protected. Consumers also have	With few exceptions, individually identifiable health care information should be disclosed only for health purposes, including the provision of health care, payment for services, peer review, health promotion, disease management, and quality assurance.

TABLE 43-1: Consumer Rights and Responsibilities Recommended by the President's Advisory Commission on Consumer Protection and Quality in the Health Care Industry, November 1997 *(Continued)*

Statement of Right/Responsibility	Summary of Included Protections
the right to review and copy their own medical records and request amendments to their records.	Disclosure of individually identifiable health care information without written consent should be permitted in very limited circumstances where there is a clear legal basis for doing so, including medical or health care research for which an institutional review board has determined that anonymous records will not suffice, investigation of health care fraud, and public health reporting.
Consumer responsibilities. In a health care system that protects consumers' rights, it is reasonable to expect and encourage consumers to assume reasonable responsibilities to help increase the likelihood of achieving the best outcomes and support a quality improvement, cost-conscious environment.	Recommended responsibilities include the following: Take responsibility for maximizing healthy habits Become involved in specific health care decisions Disclose relevant information and clearly communicate wants and needs Work collaboratively with providers in developing and carrying out treatment plans Use the plan's internal complaint and appeal processes to address concerns that may arise Avoid knowingly spreading disease Recognize the risks and limits of the science of medical care and the human fallibility of health care professionals Be aware of a health care provider's obligation to be reasonably efficient and equitable in providing care to other patients and the community Become knowledgeable about the health plan's coverage and plan options Show respect for other patients and health workers

Source: Adapted from Advisory Commission on Consumer Protection and Quality in the Health Care Industry, Consumer Bill of Rights and Responsibilities: Report to the President of the United States, November 1997.

1998–2000. Growth in expenditures for outpatient services also is expected to decelerate from its historically rapid pace. Medicare's scheduled switch to a prospective payment system for outpatient services in 1999 is expected to contribute to this slowdown.

However, growth in expenditures for physician services is expected to climb from an annual rate of 3.3 percent in 1996 to 7.1 percent by the year 2000 as Medicare beneficiaries enroll in managed care plans and physician services are substituted for hospital care. Spending for other professional services such as specialist clinics and independent practitioners is projected to rise from a 7.3 percent annual growth rate in 1996 to 7.8 percent by 2001.

Since 1993, health care spending as a percentage of GDP has remained relatively stable at about 13.6 percent, except in 1997, when it fell to 13.5 percent. By 2007, health care spending as a percentage of GDP will have risen to a projected 16.2 percent.

Managed care will continue to dominate the health care industry, with a share of about 93 percent of patients by 2005. HMOs can be expected to modify their operational practices to accommodate patients' complaints and increase access and quality care. Managed care premiums probably will increase about 7 to 9 percent per year in the period 2000–2002 and thus help enhance profits for investors and providers. Mergers and acquisitions will continue to occur among health care organizations such as for-profit hospitals, HMOs, and home care, but at a much slower rate than in the late 1990s. Small and inefficient hospitals, HMOs and preferred provider organizations (PPOs) will be closed or bought by larger ones.

The nursing homes and home health care providers that went out of business because of the impact of the BBA of 1997 will soon be replaced by new entrepreneurs to accommodate the growing elderly population that needs such care. The rate of growth of health care spending in the next 5 years will provide a clearer indication of the effects of managed care in containing medical inflation.

TRADE TRENDS

It is probable that a significant amount of medical services is hidden in other international trade transactions, such as royalties, fees, and licensing costs for medical consulting projects. Services such as health care training and equipment repair often are "bundled" into contracts for purchases of medical equipment. Moreover, it is likely that official figures underestimate the scale of medical service transactions between Mexico and the U.S. border states; much of that care is purchased out of pocket and performed by individual physicians' offices and small providers.

The bulk of U.S. medical service exports (see Table 43-3) is still accounted for by foreign citizens travelling to the United States for treatment. U.S. medical service exports rose to a value of $888 million in 1997, a 1.8 percent increase over 1996. These exports have experienced a marked slowdown since the mid-1990s, when annual growth averaged about 6 percent. Revenues from U.S. management of foreign health care facilities remain considerably more modest, although the $33 million registered in 1997 represented almost a doubling from 1996.

Official statistics for U.S. imports of medical services are unavailable. Foreign revenues from the management of U.S. health care facilities in 1997, however, expanded significantly

TABLE 43-2: Health and Medical Services Trends and Forecasts
(billions of dollars; percent)

	1992	1993	1994	1995	1996	1997[1]	1998[2]	1999[3]	2000[3]	Percent Change 97–98	98–99	99–00	96–00[4]
National health expenditures	836.5	898.5	947.7	993.7	1,042.5	1,092.4	1,151.7	1,228.5	1,316.2	5.43	6.67	7.14	6.00
Health services and supplies	809.0	869.5	917.2	963.1	1010.6	1,057.5	1,114.7	1,189.7	1,275.5	5.41	6.73	7.21	5.99
Personal health care	740.7	790.5	834.0	879.3	924.0	969.0	1,018.0	1,078.3	1,150.9	5.06	5.92	6.73	5.64
Hospital care	305.3	323.0	335.7	347.2	360.8	371.1	382.7	401.3	424.0	3.13	4.86	5.66	4.12
Physicians' services	175.9	185.9	193.0	201.9	208.5	217.6	228.0	241.5	258.7	4.78	5.92	7.12	5.54
Dental services	37.0	39.5	42.4	45.0	47.5	50.6	53.5	56.6	60.2	5.73	5.79	6.36	6.10
Other professional services	42.1	46.1	49.6	53.6	57.5	61.9	66.8	72.1	77.9	7.92	7.93	8.04	7.89
Home health care	19.6	23.0	26.2	29.1	31.2	32.3	32.3	33.8	36.0	0.00	4.64	6.51	3.64
Drugs and other medical nondurables	71.2	76.2	81.6	88.9	98.3	108.9	120.9	132.6	145.5	11.02	9.68	9.73	10.30
Prescription	46.6	50.6	55.2	61.1	69.1	78.9	90.0	100.6	112.1	14.07	11.78	11.43	12.86
Other nondurable medical Products	24.6	25.6	26.4	27.9	29.2	30.0	30.9	32.0	33.4	3.00	3.56	4.38	3.42
Vision products and other medical durables	11.9	12.3	12.5	13.1	13.4	13.9	13.8	14.3	15.0	−0.72	3.62	4.90	2.86
Nursing home care	62.3	66.4	71.1	75.5	79.4	82.8	87.0	90.1	94.1	5.07	3.56	4.44	4.34
Other personal health care	15.4	18.0	21.9	25.1	27.4	29.9	33.0	36.0	39.5	10.37	9.09	9.72	9.58
Program administration and net cost of private health insurance	44.9	53.7	55.1	53.3	52.5	50.0	54.5	65.1	74.5	9.00	19.45	14.44	9.14
Government public health activities	23.4	25.3	28.2	30.4	34.0	38.5	42.3	46.2	50.2	9.87	9.22	8.66	10.23
Research and construction	27.5	29.0	30.5	30.6	32.0	34.9	37.0	38.8	40.7	6.02	4.86	4.90	6.20
Research[5]	14.2	14.5	15.9	16.7	17.2	18.0	18.8	19.7	20.6	4.44	4.79	4.57	4.61
Construction	13.4	14.5	14.6	13.9	14.8	16.9	18.2	19.2	20.1	7.69	5.49	4.69	7.95

[1] Preliminary.
[2] Estimate.
[3] Forecast.
[4] Compound annual growth rate.
[5] Research and development expenditures of drug companies and other providers and suppliers of medical equipment are excluded from research expenditures but are included in the expenditure class in which a product falls.
Source: U.S. Department of Health and Human Services, Health Care Financing Administration, Office of the Actuary.

from their modest base. Foreign companies received $43 million for those services, a rise of 87 percent over 1996.

Health care service companies receive significant revenues from owning or operating affiliates abroad. Foreign providers' success in the United States, notably that of providers active in hospital services and cancer treatment, has increased in recent years. In the most recent year for which data are available (1996), foreign health care service firms received $3.45 billion in revenues from their U.S. affiliates, a 126 percent increase over 1995. Canadian and German companies have traditionally turned in strong performances in this sphere, accounting for 98 percent of these revenues in 1995.

TABLE 43-3: U.S. International Trade in Medical Services, 1992–1998
(millions of dollars)

	1992	1993	1994	1995	1996	1997[1]	1998[2]
Medical Services							
Exports	708	750	794	841	872	888	915
Imports	Not available						
Sales to Foreigners by U.S. Nonbank Affiliates							
	367	381	476	677	360	470	520
Sales to Americans by Foreign Nonbank Affiliates							
	[3]	1,514	1,630	1,526	3,451	3,100	3,500

[1] Estimate except exports.
[2] Estimate.
[3] Suppressed to avoid disclosure of individual companies.
Source: U.S. Department of Commerce, Bureau of the Census. Estimates by the International Trade Administration.

U.S. sales to foreigners through foreign affiliates, in contrast, fell to only $360 million in 1996, an almost 47 percent drop from the previous year. The wider permissible range for commercial health care operations in the United States accounts for part of the U.S. deficit in sales through foreign affiliates. Moreover, recent years have witnessed the sale of foreign holdings of the largest U.S. investor-owned hospitals. Except for New York, no ban on for-profit hospitals in the United States or ceilings on hospital and physician charges through central budgets.

U.S. exports of medical services are expected to climb 3.7 percent to about $970 million in the year 2000. Assuming a gradual recovery from the recent economic downturn in Asia and to some degree in Latin America, these exports should experience annual growth of approximately 4.5 to 5.0 percent in the period 2000–2004.

Sales to foreigners by U.S. health care service affiliates abroad should rebound from their nadir in 1996 and rise 11 percent to approximately $640 million in the year 2000. A modest annual growth of just over 3 percent is likely in the 2000–2004 period. Similarly, it appears unlikely that health care service sales to Americans by foreign affiliates can match their growth of over 200 percent in 1996. These purchases should nonetheless increase by about 5 percent in the year 2000, with annual growth of around 4 percent in the period 2000–2004. It is expected that foreign profit margins here will remain in a fairly narrow range in the presence of a continued emphasis on cost control in the U.S. health care sector.

GLOBAL MARKET PROSPECTS

The imperative of health care cost containment follows from the recognition that governments everywhere face profound challenges in financing the level of medical care now available to their populations. Central government expenditures for health care continue to be trimmed as the costs of procuring new technologies and treating aging populations expand. Moreover, in regions such as east Asia and Latin America, overall economic growth has declined or remained stagnant, posing the question of how future medical delivery will be funded.

Health care systems are thus in a state of flux globally, a condition that features increasingly hybrid forms of national health care with varying degrees of state supervision and private commercial activity. Among the most common are national health systems, in which treatment facilities are owned by governments and/or medical practitioners are state employees, and government-subsidized compulsory health insurance systems. The latter form of medical care generally entails coverage of a country's entire population: Citizens are by law required to purchase health insurance. Under this approach, which is employed in Germany, France, Malaysia, South Africa, and a number of other countries, health insurers are governmental or government-designated agencies. Although China has also established a variant of this model, health authorities are moving to modify its structure in the direction of one that relies on medical savings accounts. The latter method, which is in place in Singapore, requires that employers provide money for employees and encourages the recipients to save for their own medical treatment.

A third popular form of national health care that is especially prevalent in Latin America combines contributions from the government, employers, and employees into social insurance funds that cover health care costs. Although the neediest members of the population are covered through taxes, patients under the social funds are often subject to copayments for their own care.

Along with identifying means to finance medical treatment, countries are compelled to discover ways to slow rising costs in a finite budgetary environment. A survey of global cost containment efforts in health care reveals a wide array of tools used by foreign governments toward this end. The most frequently employed practices are copayments for pharmaceutical products and the setting of ceilings for the prices of supplies. Countries such as France, Italy, and Denmark impose national budgets for hospitals and physicians and have moved to expand competition between providers, while Chile, the Netherlands, and Malaysia have done the same thing among payers. Several countries, including China, Canada, Switzerland, and South Africa, have passed measures that limit coverage of basic medical services. Moreover, the "gatekeeping" common among American HMOs, in which access to specialists is determined on a case-by-case basis by a central gatekeeper, has been introduced by managed care providers entering Asia and Latin America. However, this cost-cutting instrument has aroused some opposition among those countries' populations and health care professionals.

Prospective providers of health care services abroad should harbor no illusions about the level of commitment needed to acquire and sustain a successful operation. With few exceptions, such undertakings are associated with a lengthy time horizon: Ventures in which a health care firm operates at a loss for the first 3 to 5 years of operation are not uncommon. An entrepreneur begins by accumulating all the relevant information about the targeted subsectors of a country's health care system, investment requirements, and cultural attitudes toward health care that will have a bearing on success. Often a reliable local partner is necessary for both the initial informational needs and the later day-to-day activities associated with the enterprise. Because of the human welfare dimension of medical treatment, successful firms invariably benefit from stressing their contribution to improving the well-being of the subject population.

Internationally active medical service firms have long focused on Asia because of the high per capita income in a number of Asian countries and the propensity for a large proportion of out-of-pocket payments for health care. Nearly every government in that region is under pressure to at least trim expenditures on health care. As in other industries, the medical service industry is not neglecting the potential for business in China, whose vigorous expansion of GDP, growing middle class, and rising per capita income, notably in its larger cities, are spurring interest. The probability of a broader role for private activity in the medical sphere has been confirmed by the Chinese government's admission that it can no longer maintain cradle-to-grave health care coverage. Recent cuts in state subsidies for health care ensure that a growing number of Chinese citizens will have to assume a larger proportion of medical payments themselves.

In the next 3 to 5 years, Chinese authorities will inaugurate a unified health care system in that nation's cities that will be predicated on payroll taxes, personal responsibility, and trimming waste. The government-administered program will be financed by obligatory contributions from employers and employees. The government thus seeks to extend medical insurance to urban workers but also aims at providing incentives for expanded commercial health insurance.

Despite this official recognition of the need for significant reform of health care, strict conditions are attached to foreign participation in Chinese health care service arrangements. Central government regulations established in 1997 forbid majority foreign control of health care enterprises, although majority stakes have been granted to a few foreign investors in Beijing and Shanghai hospitals and clinics. Chinese authorities as a rule permit the establishment of hospital joint ventures for the teaching and training of Chinese medical personnel but require Chinese employment and subject such undertakings to a needs test.

For the immediate future, foreign hospital undertakings in China will serve a relatively small segment of wealthier citizens, foreigners, and tourists who demand high-quality care. In addition to the Beijing United Family Hospital, which opened in 1998 with 90 percent U.S. investment, a Canadian-Chinese joint venture was inaugurated in the capital in 1999. Some foreign providers of membership-based emergency services were notably successful in the establishment of joint ventures earlier in the 1990s. Those firms provided both inpatient and outpatient services to members, primarily in Beijing. China also is experiencing the introduction of higher quality, western-style treatment centers in regions such as Guangzhou, Shanghai, and Dalian.

Singapore's success in avoiding the most damaging effects of the Asian economic downturn qualifies it as one of the most promising health care service markets. A large middle class and a compulsory medical savings scheme that accounts for almost two-thirds of all private medical spending have attracted the interest of foreign providers. Although expenditures for health care accounted for only 3.1 percent of GDP in 1998, projections are for those costs to grow to 7 percent or more in the future. Both a gradually aging population and the prevalence of unnecessary laboratory tests for patients have inflated demand. Employers, who provide medical plans for their employees, are becoming more interested in adopting managed care techniques to constrain costs.

With a middle class exceeding 200 million inhabitants, India remains an area of interest to the health care service industry. That country's health care delivery is provided by a sizable and growing private sector, together with a smaller, poorly financed web of public hospitals and clinics. Approximately four-fifths of Indian health care is accounted for by out-of-pocket payments to private providers, a sector that is largely unregulated. In addition to the expected expansion of the private insurance market as a result of modified regulations, further opportunities should emerge in telemedicine and managed care plans that feature affordable services.

Elsewhere in Asia, the lasting effects of recession have resulted in more modest overall prospects for health care providers despite the fact that countries such as Thailand and Malaysia in previous years introduced steps to shift health care treatment toward the private sector. A number of Thai hospitals went into bankruptcy after the Asian currency crisis, while Indonesia experienced an almost complete inability to purchase medicine. In Malaysia, inhabitants have significantly less money for purchasing private medical treatment, a development that has shifted a larger number of patients into the state health system, straining its resources.

In only a few regions is the medical service industry changing as rapidly as it is in Latin America. In particular, that region's customary overreliance on hospitals even for routine procedures is giving way to a demand for more economical forms of treatment. Both an expansion in the numbers of those who can pay for services and a growing market for managed care are driving this trend. In this environment, the decentralization of hospital care has spurred those facilities to establish their own rate structures and receive reimbursement commensurate with actual performance.

The World Bank estimates that approximately one-quarter of all Latin American hospital stays take place outside the public sector. This divergence from traditional practice has opened up significant opportunities in a number of health care service subsectors, including hospitals specializing in tertiary care, extended care centers, ambulatory surgery centers, and home health care. Health care providers also see the region as promising for ventures in community hospitals, physician practice management groups, senior living centers, rehabilitation centers, and stand-alone diagnostic facilities. The favorable prospects for home health care and senior living centers are largely a function of the available supply of specialists: Countries such as Argentina, Brazil, and Colombia do not have a shortage of physicians but do not have enough nurses.

It is expected that the market for HMOs and health insurance in Latin America's six largest countries will be near $40 billion by the year 2000. The Brazilian market, at $20 billion, will account for more than half this total, while it is estimated that the market in Argentina will rise to about $13 billion, a 30 percent increase over 1997. It is anticipated that the combined market volume for Chile, Colombia, Mexico, and Venezuela will reach $6.62 billion, with a quadrupling of the Mexican market in just 3 years. Coverage of the population is greatest in Colombia, which, after its 1996 health care reform, raised the percentage of those covered from 16 percent to 50 percent in only 2 years. By contrast, approximately one-quarter of Brazil's populace is covered, compared with 33 percent in Argentina, 27 percent in Chile, and only 2 to 5 percent in Mexico.

Partnerships between U.S. and Latin American hospitals are a common and important feature in the transformation of the region's delivery systems. While Mexico has thus far proved to be the single most attractive magnet for foreign investors, interest in the construction of hospitals and clinics also has risen in Chile, Argentina, Peru, and Colombia. Clinics treating patients in low- to medium-income groups as well as fertility treatment facilities and travelers' health centers are among the most common undertakings in these countries. Also, indigenous insurance companies and managed care providers are purchasing and constructing hospitals to establish health care networks.

Brazil, along with Mexico and Venezuela, offers the most promising market for medical service companies in the region as a whole. By 1998, more than 45 million of Brazil's citizens had joined private health plans, a fourfold increase over 1988. Others received treatment in private hospitals under contracts with the public health system. The best health care service opportunities are in Brazil's hospital, managed care, home health care, and diagnostic subsectors. The U.S. insurers CIGNA, AIG, and Aetna, along with some Spanish and Asian health care companies, have concluded joint ventures in managed care or hospital care with Brazilian entities. Issues relating to the regulation of managed care facilities as well as to quality, however, remain unresolved.

Mexico offers commercial possibilities across a broad range of specialties, including managed care, border clinics, and regional hospitals. It is expected that there will be a significant expansion of cross-border health plans, outpatient clinics, and diagnostic treatment.

Prospects for outpatient clinics, managed care, and diagnostic treatment in Venezuela are favorable. Broad dissatisfaction with the public health care system and what is viewed as exorbitant, arbitrary fees by private physicians and hospitals has fueled the search for alternatives. Recent legislation has broadened the Venezuelan population's latitude in choosing among numerous public and private providers.

In Argentina, Chile, and Colombia, reasonable prospects for the growth of health care services exist in some specialized areas. Argentinian diagnostic treatment, managed care, and medical clinics are drawing the attention of foreign providers. At least 16 arrangements between foreign, primarily U.S., firms and Argentinian health entities have been concluded in the health care services area.

Chile, a forerunner in Latin American health care privatization, offers opportunities in assisted living and care of the elderly as well as outpatient clinics and diagnostic treatment. Moreover, the market for "low-end" managed care has been largely untapped in that country. Over a quarter of the Chilean populace is currently enrolled in private health plans. A considerable number of private and a smaller number of public hospitals have decided to expand their facilities and are planning the construction of additional ones. Private hospitals are particularly well financed to upgrade existing services.

While foreign entry into the Colombian market has been relatively modest, hospital services, outpatient clinics, and diagnostic care represent areas of opportunity. Reforms introduced in 1996 were followed by an expansion of health plan enrollment from 16 percent to 50 percent in only 2 years.

More than ever, health care service opportunities in Canada are a function of providers' success in offering affordable services. Since 1995, both federal and provincial health care authorities have effected substantial cuts in spending in the publicly run, comprehensive health care system, resulting in the closing of hospitals and greater restrictions on the services provided. Recent years also have witnessed a marked emigration of Canadian physicians to the United States. Long-term private spending on health care has continued to rise, increasing from 25 percent of total health care spending in 1984 to 31 percent, or roughly $52 billion, in 1998.

With waiting time for operations lengthening, patients are in some cases looking to the United States for surgery such as heart bypass operations and eye care. In larger cities such as Calgary and Toronto, health centers have been established that receive private payment for specialties such as dental, orthopedic, and diagnostic services. Canada's aging population should present commercial opportunities in assisted living centers and home health care, particularly for firms that can offer a cost-effective alternative to that country's expensive pharmaceuticals. Consulting expertise is another promising area in Canada's cost-cutting environment.

Both governmental regulation and a widespread preference for setting strict limits to the range of permissible commercial health care activities have prevented the emergence of opportunities in western Europe that are commensurate with that region's income level. Both France and Italy, for example, have a large segment of private hospitals, but this condition has not led to a high level of activity there by U.S. hospital firms. Low overall Italian expenditures on health care, which accounted for only 4.9 percent of that country's GDP in 1996, as well as a sizable surplus of physicians and inefficiencies in pricing and information systems have discouraged foreign medical service firms' interest.

The region has for some time engaged the interest of health care providers because of its affluent middle classes; U.S. health care consultants in particular look for opportunities in fields such as hospital management and administration. Germany is viewed as a prospective consumer of home health care services owing to its rapidly aging population. This optimism has been tempered, however, by the current stagnation in demand resulting from a growing emphasis on cost cutting that is expected to persist through the year 2000. Germany's passage of health care reform legislation has intensified cost containment objectives in the medical services sector.

Health care service companies continue to explore business ventures in the Middle East, especially the Gulf states. Current health care service export opportunities in Saudi Arabia and the United Arab Emirates (UAE) are dominated by the reality of substantially less oil revenue, which has led to a trimming of health care expenditures and in a number of cases a decline in the scale and quality of medical treatment.

Saudi Arabia currently spends less than 4 percent of GDP on health care for its citizens, a proportion that is low by the standards of the Organization for Economic Cooperation and Development (OECD) and most Latin American countries. With the long-term drop in oil prices, the kingdom has scaled back the ambitious spending plans of the 1980s. Recent oil price increases may alleviate these constraints, however. At present, the country has a total of 285 general and specialized hospitals, and almost 42,000 beds are now in use; 74 hospitals are privately operated. There are about 1,800 polyclinics and primary health care facilities.

In the last decade, some U.S. health care providers have obtained business in Saudi Arabia in specialties such as cardiac care and hospital management. With respect to the UAE, the Mayo Clinic in 1998 established a Dubai office to assist indigenous patients who seek the clinic's medical treatment in the United States. In addition, Johns Hopkins was awarded a $107 million contract for the management and operation of the Khalifa Medical Hospital. In the UAE, the best prospects for U.S. providers are in the specialties of pediatric care and infectious diseases, for which authorities are constructing hospitals. MOH also seeks expertise in the field of geriatric, handicapped, and rehabilitation services as well as cardiac disease and surgery.

In an attempt to take up the slack left by falling government financing of health care, Saudi Arabia is witnessing a rise in the number of private hospitals and clinics and an upgrading of some existing medical facilities, which could offer possibilities for U.S. firms. MOH is currently undertaking the conversion of polyclinics into 30- to 50-bed general hospitals in an attempt to replace the mobile clinics that are now operating. The challenge for U.S. hospital service firms is to provide high-quality treatment at affordable prices to serve a broader segment of the Saudi Arabian populace.

Saudi Arabia also offers opportunities for U.S. health insurers that can provide standard policies for small to medium-size companies or families through a local partner or agent. As a result of the relatively immature state of the insurance market, however, U.S. firms could best benefit from efforts to educate patients about the advantages of medical insurance by employing vehicles such as handouts and seminars.

The UAE has made attempts to privatize some health care services. In 1998, Abu Dhabi passed legislation to establish an autonomous corporation for the development of health care. That corporation will act as the responsible authority for approving the participation of foreign hospitals in management operations. In addition, the Ministry of Health (MOH) asked for an allocation of $27 million for 1999 to meet the operational costs of public hospitals and other medical facilities as well as medical equipment and supplies. The public health care system is "free" for the nation's 2.6 million citizens but is of variable quality, something that has motivated health authorities to participate in joint economic programs with U.S. academic institutions such as Johns Hopkins University and the Cleveland Clinic Foundation.

GLOBAL BARRIERS TO TRADE IN HEALTH CARE SERVICES

Barriers to the provision of health care vary widely from country to country. In Japan, for-profit activity by hospitals is virtually prohibited. As was noted earlier, China ordinarily requires that hospital joint ventures be geared toward teaching Chinese health specialists and makes a needs test mandatory. Other barriers stem from the internal structure of the health care delivery system, as in the case of the tight collaboration among Japanese physicians, hospitals, and insurers that tends to discourage foreign competition.

In much of the developing world, particularly Africa, the desperate need to combat disease and provide treatment has resulted in minimal barriers to foreign entry. Elsewhere, domestic providers' fear of foreign competition is typically the driving force behind such protective measures.

During the General Agreement on Trade in Services (GATS) negotiations on services trade concluded in 1994, only about a third (33 nations) of the participating countries offered commitments in health care services. A commitment by a country in a sector such as health care assures that the market in that country is open to firms from other World Trade Organization (WTO) member states. However, those commitments frequently include a listing of existing restrictions on the extent of their application. Significant U.S. trading partners such as Argentina, Chile, Hong Kong, Korea, and Indonesia made no commitments in this sector and thus are not bound to any degree of liberalization. A number of countries made relatively narrow commitments, with Canada, for example, stipulating only that "measures related to the supply of services" in health "may result in differential treatment in terms of price." Although the European Union submitted commitments, the provision and sale of health care services are left to the individual national governments.

In those negotiations, it was relatively rare for a member offering commitments in the health care service sector to restrict its citizens' right to travel abroad to receive medical treatment. However, U.S. trading partners generally reserved the right to independently regulate the licensing and qualifications of physicians and medical personnel as well as maintain residency and citizenship requirements for the practice of medicine. However, these requirements generally are applied on a most favored nation (MFN) basis.

In a similar fashion, equity investment proved to be a category that was almost always subject to special national conditions. Many countries applied ceilings for the share of foreign equity in a health care service venture (e.g., 50 percent in Mexico, 49 percent in Brazil, 30 percent in Malaysia) as well as needs tests, in which a foreign provider must show that there is demand for its service beyond the level currently being provided. Medical services such as telemedicine and remote diagnostics, which recently have emerged as cost-effective alternatives to the maintenance of expensive facilities, were areas where countries reserved the right to impose unilateral restrictions.

GOVERNMENT PROGRAMS

The U.S. Department of Health and Human Services (HHS) is the federal government's lead agency for health programs. The mission of HHS is to enhance the health and well-being of Americans by providing for effective health and human services and fostering strong, sustained advances in the services underlying medicine, public health, and social services. The department also helps expand health care coverage to veterans, uniformed military personnel, native Americans, and indigenous Alaskans. The federal government provides health grants to help sponsor biomedical research. Besides providing billions of dollars for Medicare and Medicaid programs and medical research through the National Institutes of Health, federal tax laws assist in financing health insurance for employers and employees.

Medicare

Medicare is a federal program that reimburses hospitals, physicians, and other medical providers for serving patients 65 years of age and older, certain disabled people, and most persons with end-stage renal disease. Medicare has an enrollment of about 39 million elderly and disabled people. There are two basic programs under Medicare: Hospital Insurance (HI), which pays for inpatient hospital care, and Supplementary Medical Insurance (SMI), which pays for physicians' services, outpatient hospital services, and some other services.

Medicare will spend about $230 billion in 1999 on benefit and administrative services. Medicare has increased access to the quality of care for the elderly and disabled. Access and high-quality care have risen from 60 percent in 1966 to almost 100 percent today. Net Medicare outlays are expected to rise about 30 percent from 1998 to 2003, increasing from $194.2 billion to $252 billion in that period. Those amounts include federal spending on Medicare benefits but do not include spending financed from beneficiaries' premium payments and administrative costs. Medicare Part A expenditures will increase from $130.3 billion to $160 billion, a 4.2 percent average annual increase, from 1998 to 2003, while Medicare Part B will grow from $63.8 billion to $92 billion, an average annual rate of 7.6 percent.

Although Medicare is a public program financed by the federal government, most of the services rendered by the program are provided by private and/or nonprofit organizations. Hospital inpatient and outpatient facilities, physicians' offices, and nursing home care and home health agencies receive revenues from the program.

In 1996, hospitals received over $115 billion and 787,513 physicians were paid $41.7 billion for their services under Medicare (see Table 43-4).

The BBA of 1997 (PL105-33) legislated changes that affect almost every aspect of the Medicare program. Those changes are designed to produce significant savings, expand beneficiaries' choices among a wider selection of health plan options, and strengthen the traditional Medicare program.

In the BBA, Congress mandated major reforms in Medicare's role. The law created a new managed care program called Medicare + Choice that expands options for beneficiaries by allowing many private health plans to offer coverage to Medicare enrollees. This created competition among health plans such as HMOs, PPOs, and provider-sponsored organizations (PSOs). Beneficiaries may enroll in a private fee-for-service plan or a high-deductible plan with a medical savings account (MSA). The BBA also reduces future payment increases for some providers and requires the HCFA of HHS to develop and implement prospective payment systems for a variety of providers that previously were reimbursed on a cost basis. These providers include skilled nursing homes, hospital outpatient facilities, inpatient rehabilitation facilities, home health agencies, and Medicare physician services.

Even with these reforms, the aging of the population and the continuing development of new medical technologies and treatments will increase the costs of Medicare programs in the future.

The President has proposed reserving 15 percent of the projected federal budget surpluses over the next 15 years for the Medicare Trust Fund to prolong the program's solvency from 2008 to 2020.

Medicare is consuming a growing share of the federal budget. In 1980, federal spending for Medicare benefits accounted for only 5.2 percent of all federal outlays. This proportion rose from 10 percent in 1995 to 12 percent in 1998, and a high of 16 percent is envisaged for 2008. Medicare enrollment is expected to grow slowly until 2010 and then explode when the baby boom generation begins to reach age 65. From 1995 to 2010, enrollment is estimated to grow at an average annual rate of 1.5 percent, from 37.6 million to 46.9 million enrollees. Enrollment will rise to 61.3 million by 2020.

Medicaid

This jointly funded federal-state health care program provides medical care to low-income people, including children and pregnant women, the elderly, the blind, and the disabled. Total Medicaid enrollment decreased from 33.2 million in 1996 to 32.1 million in 1997. That decline may have been due to a reduction of welfare assistance and Medicaid benefits under the Personal Responsibilities and Work Opportunity Reconstruction Act of 1996 and the replacement of traditional Aid to Families with Dependent Children (AFDC) welfare payments with Temporary Assistance to Needy Families (TANF) that severed

TABLE 43-4: Medicare Payments, Providers, and Beneficiary Use by Fee-for-Service Sector

Provider/ Service Type	Total 1996 Outlays ($ billions)	Percent of Total 1984 Outlays	Percent of Total 1996 Outlays	Number of Providers	Number of Beneficiaries Who Used Services (thousands)	Percent of All Beneficiaries	Average Medicare Payment per User in 1996	Beneficiary Cost Sharing as Percent of Total Payment
Hospital inpatient	98.6	65	49	5,075	6,964	19	11,336	9
Skilled nursing facility	11.7	1	6	15,553	1,233	3	6,325	n.a.
Home health agency	18.3	3	9	9,886	3,468	9	9,240	0
Hospice	2.0	—	1	2,135	309	1	6,058	n.a.
Physician	41.7	24	21	787,513	29,539	79	1,409	20[2]
Outpatient[1]	16.6	6	8	n.a.	19,709	53	778	40
Other	11.6	4	6	n.a.	n.a.	n.a.	n.a.	n.a.

[1] Includes payments for outpatient services provided by hospitals, freestanding dialysis facilities, skilled nursing facilities, comprehensive outpatient rehabilitation facilities, rural health clinics, and other providers of covered services.

[2] Excludes balance bills, which are limited to 15 percent of Medicare's approved payment.

Source: Medicare Payment Advisory Commission compilation of data from the Health Care Financing Administration. n.a. indicates that estimates are not currently available.

the link between the receipt of welfare benefits and automatic Medicaid enrollment.

The program's total spending rose from $159.9 billion in 1997 to $182.0 billion in 1999. Total spending increased only 3.8 percent in 1997, rising to $159.9 billion, the slowest growth since Medicaid's inception nearly 30 years ago. Preliminary data suggest that the slowdown can be attributed to decreases in enrollment in 1995, 1996, and 1997 as well as reductions in the rate of spending growth per enrollee. The Congressional Budget Office estimated that Medicaid provides care for 20 percent of the nation's children and is the largest single purchaser of maternity care, nursing home services, and other long-term care services. The program covers about two-thirds of nursing home residents. Although the elderly and disabled make up less than one-third of Medicaid beneficiaries, they consume almost two-thirds of the spending on benefits. Medicaid serves at least half of all adults with AIDS and about 90 percent of children with AIDS. The BBA has allowed states to mandate managed care enrollment for the Medicaid population without getting federal approval. States are encouraging enrollees to join managed care plans. The number of managed care enrollees in Medicaid programs increased from 4.8 million in 1993 to over 15 million in 1997 (see Table 43-5).

The proportion of the Medicaid population in managed care increased from 9.5 percent in 1991 to 47.8 percent in 1997. In 1997, the BBA made important changes to Medicaid to reduce spending, mainly by reducing the Disproportionate Share of Hospital Program and giving states more flexibility. The BBA gave states the option of requiring most beneficiaries to enroll in managed care plans without seeking a federal waiver and also made it easier to set hospital and nursing home reimbursement rates. States now have the option of guaranteeing Medicaid eligibility to children for 12 months regardless of changes in a child's family's income and restore Medicaid benefits for certain groups of immigrants who would otherwise lose them under the 1996 welfare law. About 10 million American children lack health insurance; the BBA established the state Children Health Insurance Program (CHIP), which provides $24 billion over the next 5 years for states to expand health insurance to low-income uninsured children.

TABLE 43-5: Managed Care as a Percentage of Total Medicaid Enrollment, 1991–1997

Year	Total Medicaid Population	Managed Care Enrollees	Percent Managed Care Enrollment
1991	28,280,000	2,696,397	9.5
1992	30,926,390	3,634,516	11.8
1993	33,430,051	4,808,951	14.4
1994	33,634,000	7,794,250	23.2
1995	33,373,000	9,800,000	29.4
1996	33,241,147	13,330,119	40.1
1997	32,092,380	15,345,502	47.8

Source: U.S. Department of Health and Human Services, Health Care Financing Administration.

Domestic Subsectors

Managed care has transformed the health care services delivery system in the United States. Hospital and physician services continue to be the largest subsectors of the health care delivery system, but their share of total spending is diminishing. These subsectors, which accounted for 57.6 percent of total national health spending in 1990, accounted for only 52.4 percent in 1999. The drop of 5.2 percentage points in spending was shifted to home health care agencies, nursing home care, prescription drugs, other professional services, and other alternative delivery services.

There are over 5,244 community hospitals in the nation, with about 15 percent of them privately owned and the rest being nonprofit institutions. Major private hospital corporations such as Columbia/HCA and Tenet Healthcare have become giant corporations through mergers and acquisitions. The 10 largest for-profit multihospital systems have maintained their share of the total market of for-profit hospitals with 16 percent of the total beds in the nation in 1996 compared with 15 percent in 1986. There is an overcapacity of hospital beds in the nation, as reflected by the rate of occupany. Efforts to reduce that surplus have not been successful. The average occupancy rate for community hospitals increased from 58.7 percent in 1996 to 59.6 percent in 1997.

Between 1983 and 1996, Medicare payment for hospital outpatient services rose more then 13 percent per year on average. The contributing factors were (1) an increase in the number of Medicare beneficiaries, (2) payment policies that encourage a shift from inpatient to outpatient settings, and (3) advances in medical technologies that have increased the supply of and demand for hospital outpatient services. In the 1983–1996 period, hospitals were operating with stable profit margins and increased their revenues by engaging in the business of post-acute home health care and providing nursing home services. Hospital expenditures grew from $360.8 billion in 1996 to $371.1 billion in 1997, a 2.9 percent increase (see Table 43-2). The BBA has developed a new payment system for hospitals, and in this competitive environment hospitals will have to become more creative in cutting costs while attracting patients.

Expenditures for physicians' services rose to an estimated $241.5 billion in 1999, a 5.9 percent increase over 1998. Spending on physicians' services have grown at a low rate since 1990 because of the expanding role of managed care contracts and changes in physician practices. Outlays for nursing home care amounted to $90.1 billion in 1999. Annual spending growth for nursing home care fell from a high of 23.4 percent in 1992, to 5.2 percent in 1996, to 3.6 percent in 1999. As a result of BBA determination to implement corrective actions in that sector, the number of home health care agencies fell from 10,027 in 1996 to about 9,886 in 1998. This was due partly to the detection of fraud and abuse in the industry. As a result, there is a moratorium on the licensing and certification of new Medicare-participating home health agencies.

Home Health Care

Home-delivered health and medical services have become an integral part of the U.S. health care system. The high cost of hospital and nursing home care has intensified the need for alternative, less expensive ways of delivering care to elderly, sick, and disabled people who in many cases require continuous skilled nursing care. One of the most effective ways of containing health care costs is by providing care in a patient's home.

The home care industry consists of home health agencies, home care aid organizations, and hospices. Currently, there are over 20,000 home care organizations in the United States that deliver home care services to 8 million individuals with an acute illness, a long-term medical condition, a permanent disability, or a terminal illness.

Medicare payments for home care accelerated the industry's growth. From 1967 to 1985, the number of agencies certified to participate in the Medicare program rose from 1,753 to 5,983. However, the number of agencies certified decreased from 1985 to 1990 because of the huge increase in Medicare paperwork and unreliable payment policies. This resulted in a lawsuit with an outcome in favor of the National Association for Home Care. The conclusion of this conflict provided the association with the opportunity to participate in rewriting Medicare's payment policies for home health care. The number of Medicare-certified home health agencies increased from 5,793 in 1990 to a high of 9,886 in 1996, a 73.1 percent increase.

Medicare and Medicaid programs are the largest sources of funding for home health care. For instance, in 1996, Medicare and Medicaid paid 38.7 and 27.2 percent, respectively, of total home health care costs. Out-of-pocket expenses accounted for 20.5 percent, and private insurance accounted for only 12.2 percent; the remaining 1.4 percent went to nonprofit organizations.

During the period 1992–1996, Medicare payments for home health services rose from $8 billion to $18 billion while the number of visits more than doubled, rising from 132 million to 284 million. Annual visits per user increased nearly 50 percent from 53 to 79. Payments per user rose 12 percent annually during that period (see Table 43-6).

Poorly defined standards for home health care have given home health agencies leeway to interpret Medicare rules to their advantage. The HHS investigative unit has suggested that abusive and fraudulent activities exist within the home health industry and may account for an important share of Medicare home health expenditures. This information assisted BBA advocates in restricting Medicare reimbursement payments for home health care.

The BBA stipulated strict coverage and administrative guidelines, such as normative standards for home health claims denial and the inclusion of physician identification numbers on home health agency bills, which should help reduce inappropriate billing practices. The BBA also mandated the implementation of a prospective payment system for home care by fiscal year 2000. This payment system must account for number, types, and duration of visits; differences in the mix of services to beneficiaries; and variation in the cost of providing those services.

The number of Medicare-certified home health agencies declined to 9,886 in 1996 and decreased further to 9,655 in 1998. The home health care sector is labor-intensive. Employment in the home care industry rose from 510,000 in 1993 to over 700,000 in 1997 but fell 7.2 percent in 1998 as a result of the reforms instituted by the BBA.

TABLE 43-6: Medicare Home Health Use, 1988–1996

Year	Number of Beneficiaries Receiving Home Health Services (thousands)	Number of Visits (thousands)	Visits per User	Payments per User
1988	1,582	37,130	23	1,287
1989	1,685	46,297	27	1,500
1990	1,940	69,389	36	1,986
1991	2,226	98,650	44	2,487
1992	2,523	132,494	53	3,061
1993	2,868	168,029	59	3,556
1994	3,175	220,495	69	4,179
1995	3,457	266,261	77	4,621
1996	3,583	283,939	79	4,819

Source: Health Care Financing Administration, Office of the Actuary.

Hospital Margins

The financial performance of hospitals was better in 1997 than it had been since 1986. Despite declining occupancy, hospital closures, Medicare program regulations, the BBA, and competition from managed care, the hospital industry has remained financially sound.

In a report to Congress, the Medicare Payment Advisory Commission (MedPAC) indicated that trends in hospital revenues and expenses have tended to move in the same direction. In the 1980s and early 1990s, both revenues and expenses per adjusted admission in hospitals rose at an annual rate of about 9 percent. In 1993, however, there was a sharp decrease in revenues and expenses per adjusted admission. This lower rate of growth in both areas has continued in recent years, but hospitals' aggregate total revenue margin increased from 3.6 percent in 1990 to 6.1 percent in 1996, the last year for which full data are available, a gain of 2.5 percentage points (see Economic and Trade Trends at the beginning of the chapter). MedPAC indicated that these margins compare favorably with data as far back as the early 1970s, when Medicare payment was based on reimbursement of costs.

Preliminary data show that total margins continued to increase in 1997, and more current data show that hospitals succeeded in controlling the growth in their expenses through mid-1998. However, 21.6 percent of hospitals had a negative total revenue margin in 1996; that was less favorable than the 20.7 percent recorded in 1995, which was the lowest percent since the Prospective Payment System was introduced in 1987. This percentage was as high as 35.1 percent in 1987 (see Economic and Trade Trends at the beginning of the chapter).

Health Insurance in the United States

About 70 percent of the U.S. population is covered by health insurance obtained from the private or public sector. Those with private health insurance obtain coverage through direct purchase from an insurance company or through the workplace, either from their own employment or indirectly from that of a family member. More than 1,000 private U.S. insurance companies write individual and group health policies. In addition to commercial insurance companies, there are private insurers such as Blue Cross and Blue Shield and numerous managed care organizations. A growing number of health insurance plans are self-insured, in which case an employer or union assumes all or part of the responsibility for paying claims. Also, health care benefits are available through various government programs, including Medicare for persons 65 and older and those with certain disabilities and Medicaid for a portion of the indigent population and certain categories of the medically needy.

Despite the expansion of government programs and the reduction in the rate of increase in health care costs, the number of uninsured persons is increasing rapidly. In 1997, there were about 43 million persons in the United States without health insurance coverage. There are numerous reasons for the high number of uninsured persons including but are not limited to (1) the erosion of Medicaid coverage for the poor, (2) an increase in part-time workers, (3) the growing number of workers employed by small establishments that are less likely to offer group health insurance, and (4) demographic shifts involving certain subgroups of the population, such as young workers, low-wage workers, and workers who do not understand the English language.

For many years, the media as well as many health analysts have reported that insurers are raising premiums to restore their profit margins and that underlying health care insurance costs will cause health care prices to escalate. Some analysts also claim that managed care is a one-time savings device and will not hold down health costs. However, a look at premium increases for the period 1997–1998 does not substantiate these views. An industry study of medium-size and large companies in the United States indicated that the average increase in health premiums in that period was only 3.5 percent. Single and family coverage premiums rose 2.9 and 4.3 percent, respectively, while the consumer price index rose 1.7 percent in that period. The percentage increases per employee for single coverage fee-for-service premiums and HMO premiums were almost the same at 1.1 percent and 1.2 percent, respectively, while per family the increases were 4.2 percent and 3.1 percent, respectively. However, PPOs' and point of service plans' premiums for employee and family coverage rose an average of 6.3 percent and 4.6 percent, respectively, during that period.

Medical cost trends for managed care and fee-for-service plans typically follow 3-year cycles, and there is a lag before premium increases become effective. Other variables, such as Medicare and Medicaid cost containment policies, demographic factors, future macroeconomic conditions, and health sector developments, also affect health care prices. Some analysts predicted a substantial increase in medical costs for 1997, 1998, and 1999. The rate of increase in medical costs, however, actually decreased to 5.5 percent in 1995, 4.9 percent in 1996 and 1997, and 4.8 percent in 1998, the lowest percentage increases in the more than three decades since the Medicare and Medicaid programs were introduced.

Employment in the Health Care Services

Growth in employment in health care services, which increased significantly in the 1980s and early 1990s, has begun to slow; however, the health industry continues to be a major source of job creation in cities and states. In 1998, the private health care industry employed over 9.9 million people, a 1.9 percent increase over 1997; however, hospitals, the largest subsector in the industry, employed more than 3.9 million people, a 2.2 percent rise over 1997 (see Table 43-7). It is noteworthy that in the period 1987–1992, hospital job growth was 608,000, whereas in 1992–1997 it fell to 119,000, reflecting the competitive forces of managed care in the industry. This period witnessed a growing shift of jobs from hospital inpatient services to outpatient services.

There appears to be a correlation between health care spending, employment, and earnings in this industry. As health care workers experienced smaller gains in employment and earnings in the late 1990s compared with the 1980s, the rate of growth in health care costs decreased. Health services have been accounting for a growing proportion of the private economy in the United States. Private health services employment rosc at an average rate of 4.6 percent from 1987 to 1992 compared with 3.8 percent for services as a whole during that period. For 1992 to

TABLE 43-7: Annual Average Growth in Employment, Total Services, and Health Care Services, 1987–1998

		1987–1992		1992–1997		
Industry	1998 Total Employment (thousands)	Job Growth (thousands)	Annual Average Percent Change	Job Growth (thousands)	Annual Percent Change	1997–1998 Percent Change
Services	37,525	4,942	3.8	6,988	4.4	4.1
Health services	9,904	1,385	4.6	1,230	2.7	1.9
Offices of medical doctors	1,817	324	5.1	280	3.6	4.3
Offices of other health practitioners	464	129	10.5	112	6.1	5.6
Nursing and personal care	1,757	250	3.6	222	2.7	.1
Hospitals	3,953	608	3.6	119	.6	2.2
Home health services	680	182	16.5	315	12.4	4.5

Data series available beginning in 1988; therefore, the average shown is a 4-year average for the 1987–1992 period.
Source: Bureau of Labor Statistics.

1997, however, the rate of growth of health services decelerated to 2.7 percent annually, while the annual rate of growth of total services increased to 4.4 percent. The rate of growth further deteriorated from 1997 to 1998, reaching a low of 1.9 percent. Cost reductions, federal government reimbursement policies, competition from managed care, and mergers and acquisitions have been major contributing factors to the reduction in health services employment. The Bureau of Labor Statistics reported that most of the increases in health care jobs over the 1987–1992 period came from hospitals and the offices and clinics of medical doctors. Home health care employment surpassed all other components in every year of the last decade except 1998. Medicare expenses for home health services grew at an annual rate of 28.6 percent between 1990 and 1996 but were estimated to grow only 0.2 percent annually in the 1996–1998 period. This was due to federal reimbursement policies for home health care and nursing homes that were in place during the late 1990s, when millions of Medicare and Medicaid enrollees shifted from fee-for-service plans to managed care plans.

In addition to affecting employment, cost containment dampened wage growth in health care sectors. In 1998, the rate of growth in average hourly earnings for nonsupervisory workers in health services was only half of the 1987–1992 rate. Wage growth in health services had been higher than that for all services in the 1987–1992 period but dropped to the same rate in 1992–1997 and fell considerably below the rate of increase for all services in 1998. While wage growth declined, average hourly earnings for health service workers were 83 cents more than those of workers elsewhere in the services industry in 1998.

Despite the decline in the rate of growth in health care industry employment, the Bureau of Labor Statistics identified 6 health care occupations among the 10 occupations with the fastest projected employment growth from 1996 to 2006: personal and home care aides, physicians and corrective therapy assistants and aides, home health aides, medical assistants, physical therapists, and occupational therapy assistants and aides. In terms of employment growth, health services are projected to be the second fastest growing industry, surpassed only by computer and data processing services, in the period 1996–2006.

Twenty-First-Century Health Care Reform

The Clinton administration and Congress are eager to reform the health care industry or at least the Medicare and Medicaid programs. However, differences in approach between the parties have been so at variance that reform efforts have been hindered.

The aging population and the millions of uninsured persons will require more and better care and will demand attention and create political issues that must be addressed. Any health care reform in the first decade of the twenty-first century will have to address the following issues:

- Access to health services, including specialists such as obstetricians, gynecologists, and pediatricians, without referrals
- Guaranteed emergency care
- Banning gag rules and provider incentives to physicians to deny care
- Securing privacy of medical records and medical information on patients
- Allowing tax credits to individuals and small businesses for long-term care expenditures
- Using the federal budget surplus to keep the Medicare program solvent
- Providing prescription drug benefits to Medicare recipients
- Allowing injured patients to seek redress in the courts
- Allowing choices and continuity of care
- Holding health care plans accountable to individual patients and the marketplace
- Using a plan similar to the Federal Employee Health Benefit Plan to replace the Medicare program.

Medicare's Payment Policies for Graduate Medical Education and Teaching Hospitals

The BBA of 1997 requires that MedPAC examine and recommend to Congress federal policies that affect payments to graduate medical education (GME) and teaching hospitals as well as federal workforce issues. In general, MedPAC is authorized under Section 1805 of the Social Security Act to develop recommendations on GME and teaching hospitals' payment policies.

In carrying out its work, MedPAC recognizes that Medicare was enacted to improve access and provide high-quality health care to the elderly and certain disabled people. Another purpose of Medicare is to alleviate the financial burden to beneficiaries seeking medical care in an appropriate setting. Consequently, MedPAC has concluded that Medicare's payment system should induce providers to supply care efficiently, account for differences in the intensity and complexity of care provided, recognize the value of enhanced patient care provided in teaching hospitals and other settings where residents and other health professionals are trained, and not intentionally distort the supply of physicians and other health professionals.

Considering these goals, MedPAC has formulated and sent the following six recommendations to Congress.

1. Medicare should pay more for patient care in teaching settings when the enhanced value of that care justifies its higher costs.
2. Congress and the secretary of HHS should change the diagnosis related groups to reflect more accurately the relationship between illness severity and the cost of inpatient care, making Medicare payments more consistent with efficient providers' costs.
3. Congress should revise Medicare's payments to recognize the higher value of patient care services provided in teaching hospitals through an enhanced patient care adjustment.
4. Congress should phase in the payment adjustment for enhanced patient care and any related policies that substantially change payments to individual providers.

5. Congress and the secretary of HHS should develop payment adjustments for enhanced patient care in all settings where residents and other health care professionals train when the added value of patient care justifies higher costs.
6. Federal policies intended to affect the number, specialty mix, and geographic distribution of health care professionals should be implemented through specific targeted programs rather than through Medicare.

GLOBAL SUBSECTORS

Because of the dominance of managed care in the U.S. health care system, the question of its attractiveness for export to other nations is much debated. American HMOs, as was noted earlier, have made significant inroads in a number of foreign markets, notably Latin American countries such as Mexico, Brazil, Argentina, and Venezuela. The success of such undertakings elsewhere in the world will continue to be influenced strongly by peculiarities of local health care systems such as their structure, financing, and costs.

Countries with substantially lower levels of proportionate expenditures on health care lack the cost-cutting urgency for retooling the cycle of delivery that exists in the United States. Moreover, much of the momentum behind the expansion of managed care in the United States was driven by cost-conscious employers, an impulse less striking in Europe, where the employer-based component of health care is considerably smaller. Other conditions in the United States tend to favor the growth of managed care. The large number of U.S. physician specialists allows for the selective contracting that is one of the hallmarks of managed care; in many other countries, by contrast, physician specialists are in short supply. In addition, U.S. superiority in data systems permits the more effective quality management vital to managed care. Data management in other countries is often less sophisticated.

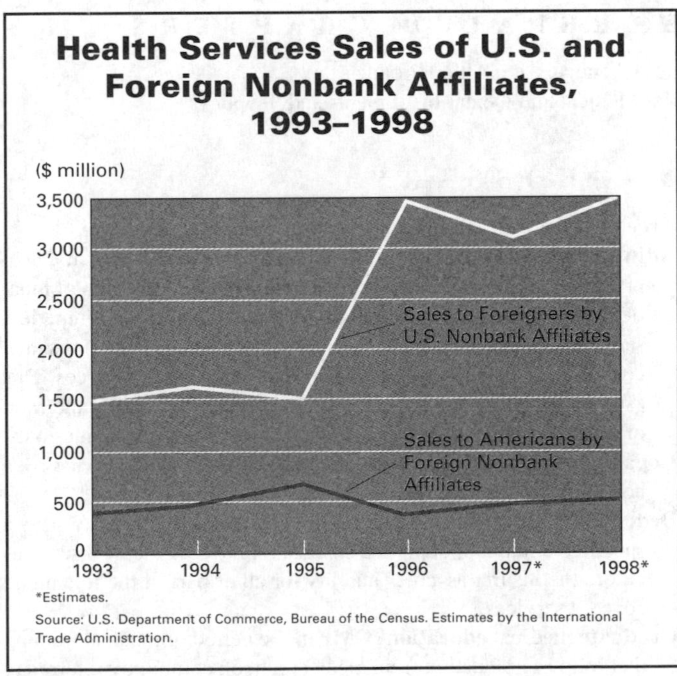

*Estimates.
Source: U.S. Department of Commerce, Bureau of the Census. Estimates by the International Trade Administration.

FIGURE 43-1

It is nonetheless true that concern for rising costs has led governments in nations such as Canada, France, and Germany to impose curbs on spending in areas such as physicians' fees and pharmaceutical purchases and to seek additional vehicles for a reduction in overall spending. Each member state of the European Union now confronts the problem of escalating health care costs. Moreover, since 1994, the U.S. managed care firm United Health Global Consulting has worked with the leading German "sickness fund" to contain escalating costs in that fund's Berlin hospitals.

However, the uniqueness of local conditions makes it unlikely that wholesale adoption of American HMO models will take place abroad. A more piecemeal adoption of U.S. managed care cost-cutting practices is probable. In the case of the German venture mentioned above, for example, the establishment of new channels of communication between physicians, hospital administrators, chiefs of nursing, and medical directors resulted in a reduction in the duration of hospital stays. Managed care practices that can be shown to affect the cost and quality of health care favorably thus can enjoy a positive foreign response.

As was noted earlier, industry analysts view telemedicine as an increasingly important means of medical treatment in the future despite the surfacing of technical and commercial challenges to the use of this form of care. Although initially more often practiced in urban areas, telecommunications technology for long-distance transmission of x-ray imagery and other patient information is being applied in remote, rural sections of developing countries that therefore can forgo the maintenance of expensive medical facilities. In India, China, and some countries in the Middle East, telemedicine ventures with foreign providers are becoming a familiar part of the landscape.

The expanded international resort to telemedicine has not been a uniform process but has taken place in a piecemeal fashion. Teleradiology, in which transmitted images are digitized, was the earliest instance and was characterized by transmission to a central urban hospital unit, a process that reduced the total number of radiologists required. Excess radiological capacity in the United States is leading some providers to look more seriously at foreign markets.

Although much of the growth in telemedicine so far has occurred in university research centers, it is anticipated that future activity will be more concentrated in the private sector, fueled in part by enhanced Internet applications. In addition to the cost-effective advantages this activity offers to developing countries that were cited above, other practical benefits can be discerned. By removing the necessity for patient travel, telemedicine treatment can eliminate the associated risk to patients as well as delays in treatment. The probability of a mistaken diagnosis is reduced through the second opinion provided, and telemedical care also cuts the length of hospital waiting lists and permits a more effective allocation of a facility's resources.

Since hospitals and private physicians can access specialists by means of telecommunications links, the necessity for referrals is eliminated. This form of treatment also introduces the option of home monitoring of patients who do not require hospital care, such as asthmatics and diabetics. Equally significant is the possibility for the continuation of physicians' medical education through telecommunications, entailing medical technicians' contact with senior colleagues and courses.

Despite these clear benefits of telemedical treatment, fuller international exploitation of this method awaits the resolution of a number of issues. The telecommunications and computer equipment required can be expensive even if digital networks are increasingly minimizing transmission costs. However, the weightiest barriers are more closely related to concerns such as licensing, liability, and the confidentiality of data. In addition to the fact that some physicians have practical and ethical concerns about remote treatment, issues of reimbursement remain unclear. Moreover, there is no recognized global standard with respect to the authority of a physician to provide treatment in a foreign country. The same is true in regard to the confidentiality of data, an area in which different governments' positions on matters such as passwords and encryption are in the process of being established. An additional problem is that of incompatible data formats and standards both among organizations and among countries for medical information transmitted from one location to another.

With the aging of populations in key markets such as Germany, Japan, and Brazil, the potential for sales of home health care, assisted living, and retirement home services will be considerable in the next several decades. The extent to which health care service companies can capitalize on these demographic trends, however, will be a function partly of the development of nondiscriminatory regulation regarding equity ownership as well as cultural preferences. In Latin America, for example, care of the elderly is still regarded as a family responsibility even though that attitude appears to be changing in more urban areas. Companies may succeed in bypassing equity restrictions by obtaining consultancy contracts for retirement homes, home care, or other services for the elderly.

With regard to the health care service subsector for which import-export figures are available—management of health care facilities—it is unlikely that either U.S. or foreign firms will experience constant, linear growth. Instead, revenue earned in this subsector will fluctuate more with governmental budgetary developments than with countries' overall growth rates. In the year 2000, the earnings of U.S. providers should increase approximately 3 percent to $41 million. Revenue in this category should rise 6 to 7 percent in the 2000–2004 period. For foreign firms managing U.S. facilities, revenue is expected to increase 8 percent in 2000 and level off at about 5 percent annual growth from 2000 through 2004.

Simon Francis, (202) 482-2697, and ***Ernest Plock,*** (202) 482-4783, U.S. Department of Commerce, Office of Service Industries, September 1999.

■ REFERENCES

Budget of the United States Government, Fiscal Year 1999, U.S. Government Printing Office, Washington, DC 20402.

The Economic and Budget Outlook; Fiscal Years 1999–2008; A Report to the Senate and House Committees on the Budget, January 1998, U.S. Government Printing Office, Washington, DC 20402.

Economist Intelligence Unit, *Healthcare International,* 111 West 57 Street, New York, NY 10019.

Engel, Cynthia, *Health Services Industry: Still a Job Machine? Monthly Labor Review,* March 1999. Bureau of Labor Statistics, Washington, DC. 20212.

Health Affairs, Project Hope, 7500 Old Georgetown Road, Suite 600, Bethesda, MD 20814.

Healthcare Trends Report, 4405 East-West Highway, Suite 406, Bethesda, MD 20814.

Hospitals and Health Networks, American Hospital Publishing, Inc., 737 North Michigan Avenue, Chicago, IL 60611.

Hospital Outlook, Federation of America Health Systems, 1111 19th Street, NW, Suite 402, Washington, DC 20036.

Latin American Healthcare Reform (Sept. 1998), Latin American Information Services, Inc., 159 West 53 Street, New York, NY 10019-6050.

National Trade Data Bank, U.S. Department of Commerce, Washington, DC 20230.

Report to the Congress, Medicare Payment Policy, Medicare Payment Advisory Commission, 1730 K Street, NW, Suite 800, Washington, DC 20006.

Report to the Congress, Rethinking Medicare's Payment Policies for Graduate Medical Education and Teaching Hospitals, MedPAC, Suite 800, Washington, DC 20006.

Report to the Congress, Selected Medicare Issues, Medicare Payment Advisory Commission, 1730 K Street, NW, Suite 800, Washington, DC 20006.

Survey of Current Business, U.S. Department of Commerce, Bureau of Economic Analysis, Washington, DC 20230.

■ RELATED CHAPTERS

11: Chemicals and Allied Products
44: Medical and Dental Instruments and Supplies

■ GLOSSARY

Access: The ability to obtain needed health care services.

Adjusted admissions: A measure of all patient care activity in a hospital, including both inpatient and outpatient care. The sum of inpatient admissions and an estimate of the volume of outpatient services, expressed as the number of inpatient admissions that could have been produced with the same amount of resources. This estimate is calculated by multiplying outpatient visits by the ratio of outpatient charges per visit to inpatient charges per admission.

Copayment: A fixed dollar amount paid for a covered service by a health insurance enrollee.

Deductible: A type of cost sharing in which the insured party pays a specified amount of approved charges for covered medical services before the insurer assumes liability for all or part of the remaining covered services.

Graduate medical education (GME): The period of medical training that follows graduation from medical school; commonly referred to as internship, residency, and fellowship training.

Health maintenance organization (HMO): A type of managed care plan that acts as both the insurer and the provider of a comprehensive set of health care services to an enrolled population. Benefits typically are financed through capitation with limited copayments, and services are furnished through a system of affiliated providers.

Hospital Insurance (HI): The part of the Medicare program that covers the cost of hospital and related posthospital services. Eligibility normally is based on prior payment of payroll taxes. Beneficiaries are responsible for an initial deductible per spell of illness and copayments for some services. Also called Part A coverage or benefits.

Managed care: Any system of health service payment or delivery arrangement in which a health plan attempts to control or coordinate the use of health services by its enrolled members to contain health expenditures, improve quality, or both. Arrangements often involve a defined delivery system of providers with some form of contractual arrangement with the plan. See *health maintenance organization* and *preferred provider organization.*

Medicare: A health insurance program for people over age 65, those eligible for Social Security disability payments, and those who need kidney dialysis or transplants. See *Hospital Insurance* and *Supplementary Medical Insurance.*

Medicare + Choice: A program created by the Balanced Budget Act of 1997 to replace the existing system of Medicare risk and cost contracts. Beneficiaries will have the choice during an open season each year to enroll in a Medicare + Choice plan or remain in traditional Medicare. Medicare + Choice plans may include coordinated care plans (HMOs, PPOs, and plans offered by provider-sponsored organizations), private fee-for-service plans, or high-deductible plans with medical savings accounts.

Point-of-service (POS) plan: A managed care plan that combines features of both prepaid and fee-for-service insurance. Health plan enrollees decide whether to use network or nonnetwork providers at the time care is needed and usually are charged sizable copayments for selecting the latter. See *health maintenance organization* and *preferred provider organization.*

Preferred provider organization (PPO): A managed care plan that contracts with networks or panels of providers to furnish services and be paid on a negotiated fee schedule. Enrollees are offered a financial incentive to use providers on the preferred list but may use nonnetwork providers as well. See *managed care.*

Premium: An amount paid periodically to purchase health insurance benefits.

Prospective payment: A method of paying health care providers in which rates are established in advance. Providers are paid those rates regardless of the costs they actually incur.

Supplementary Medical Insurance (SMI): The part of the Medicare program that covers the costs of physicians' services, outpatient laboratory and x-ray tests, durable medical equipment, outpatient hospital care, and certain other services. This voluntary program requires the payment of a monthly premium, which covers 25 percent of program costs, with the rest covered by general revenues. Beneficiaries are responsible for a deductible and coinsurance payments for most covered services. Also called Part B coverage or benefits.

Total margin: A measure that compares total hospital revenues with expenses for inpatient, outpatient, and nonpatient care activities. The total margin is calculated by subtracting total expenses from total revenues and dividing by total revenues.

MEDICAL AND DENTAL INSTRUMENTS
Economic and Trade Trends

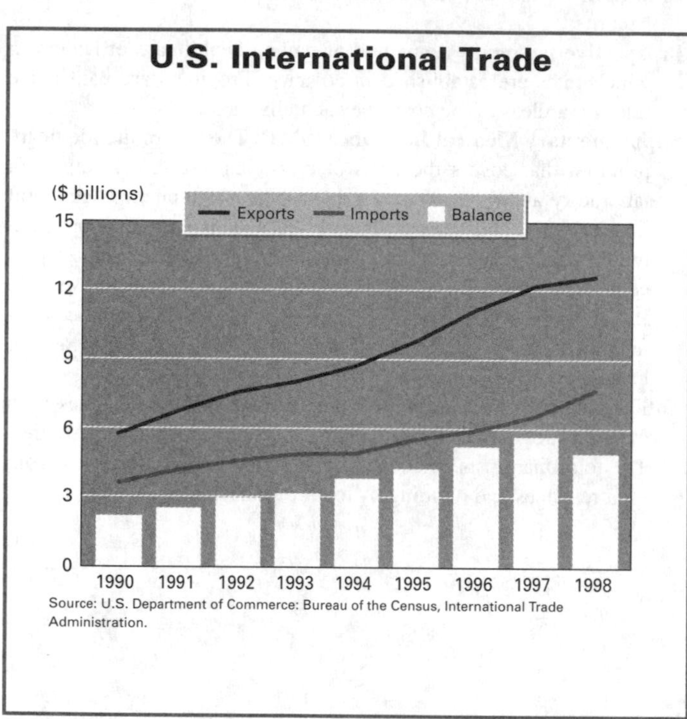

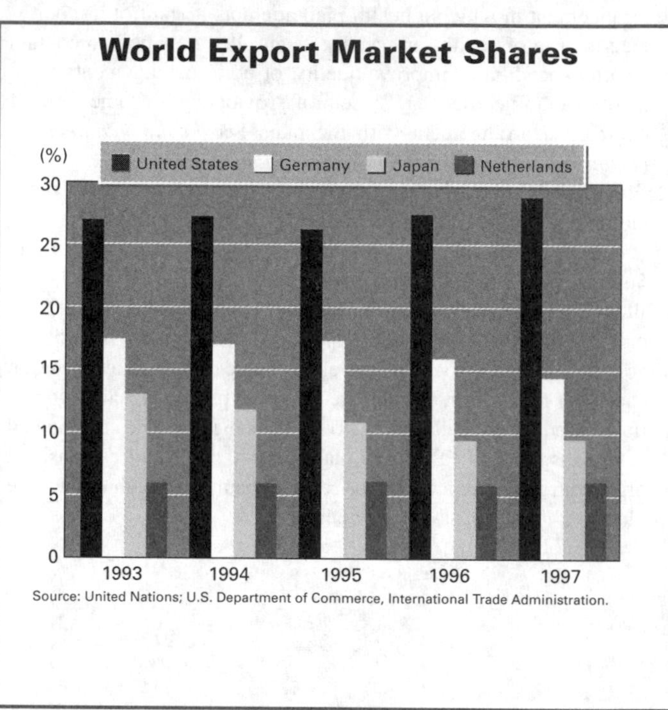

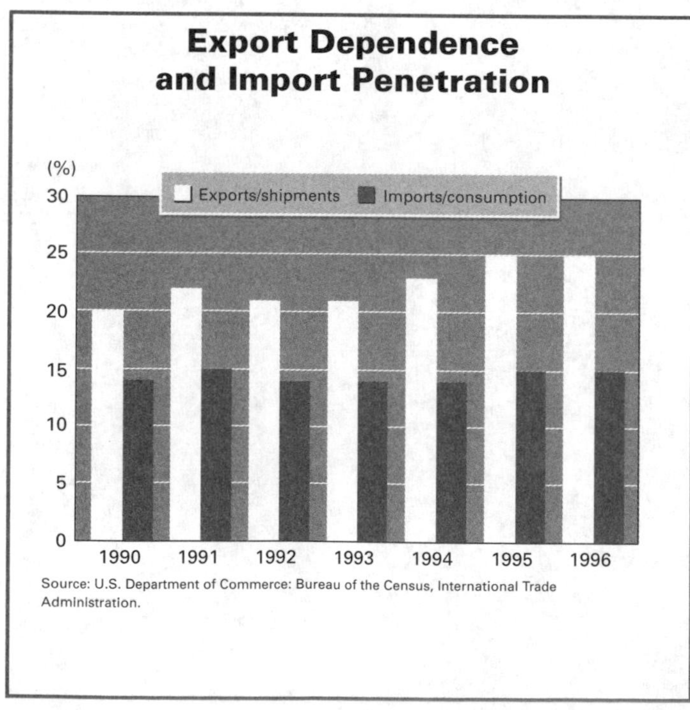

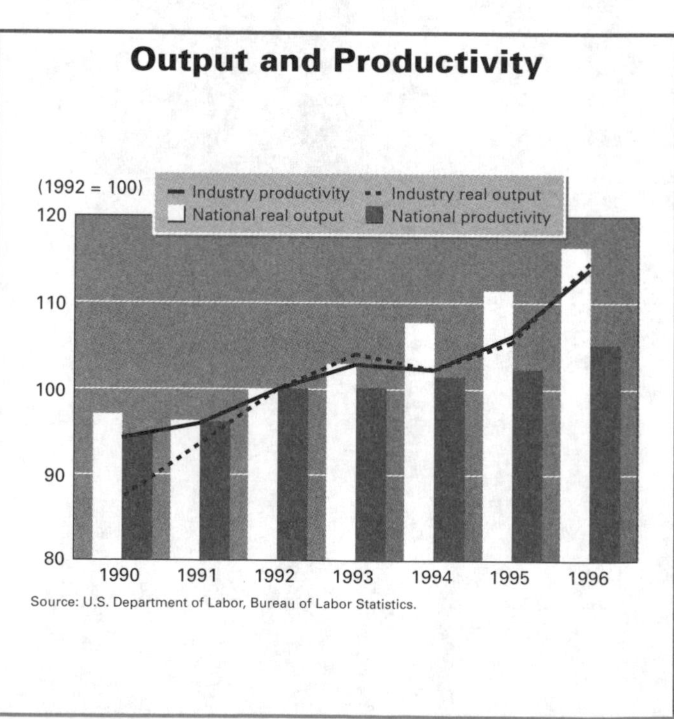

See "Getting the Most Out of *Outlook 2000*" for definitions of terms.

44

Medical and Dental Instruments and Supplies

INDUSTRY DEFINITION This chapter covers surgical, medical, and dental instruments and supplies (SIC 384). This includes surgical and medical instruments and apparatus (SIC 3841); orthopedic, prosthetic, and surgical appliances and supplies (SIC 3842); dental equipment and supplies (SIC 3843); x-ray apparatus and tubes and related irradiation apparatus (SIC 3844); and electromedical and electrotherapy apparatus (SIC 3845).

OVERVIEW

The medical and dental equipment and supplies industry is one of the most exciting, dynamic, and innovative industries in the world. It takes advances from a number of different industries, such as microelectronics, telecommunications, advanced materials, biotechnology, pharmaceuticals, and health care services, and often harnesses its own technologies to the technologies of those industries, so that each one powerfully affects the direction of and innovation in medical devices. It is also an industry that saves lives. Medical technology helps increase productivity in all other industries by reducing the number of sick days. More nations around the world are experiencing growth in gross domestic product (GDP), allowing them to increase spending on health care by building hospitals and clinics, establishing public health insurance, and focusing more attention on the health of their citizens. This is increasing demand for medical and dental equipment and supplies at double-digit growth rates in much of the world. The largest markets for medical equipment are the United States, the European Union (EU), Japan, and Canada. While the United States, EU, Japan, and Canada are extremely large and lucrative markets for medical devices, they are maturing. To facilitate expansion, medical device firms must look increasingly at developing economies for future growth. For this reason, the medical equipment industry is now and will always be a globalized industry.

FACTORS AFFECTING FUTURE GROWTH OF THE GLOBAL INDUSTRY

The U.S. medical and dental equipment and supplies industry is the global leader in a $138 billion world market (this figure does not include the $15 billion in vitro diagnostics market, which is covered in Chapter 11). The United States shipped over $52 billion in medical equipment in 1998. Industry shipments were expected to grow to more than $55 billion in 1999, supplying 40 percent of world demand (see Table 44-1). The United States is also the largest consumer, with a market valued at $51 billion, consuming approximately 37 percent of all the medical equipment produced in the world.

Even though total U.S. industry shipments are still growing, the rate of growth is slowing slightly. The estimated growth for 1999 was steady at 6 percent, and although that is just below the 1998 rate of expansion, it reflects the slowest growth since 1995. Exports continued to show positive growth in 1999. The United States exported $12.6 billion in medical equipment in 1998. Exports in 1999 grew an estimated 6 percent, up from just over 3 percent in 1998, to almost $13.4 billion, earning the U.S. industry a hefty $5 billion trade surplus. Exports have accounted for an increasing proportion of total industry shipments since 1993, when they represented 21 percent, rising to 25 percent in 1995, 27 percent in 1998, and an estimated 28 percent in 1999. This pattern reflects the maturation of the U.S. market, and the trend of U.S. device firms

TABLE 44-1: Medical Instruments and Supplies (SIC 384) Trends and Forecasts
(millions of dollars except as noted)

										Percent Change			
	1992	1993	1994	1995	1996	1997[1]	1998[1]	1999[2]	2000[3]	97–98	98–99	99–00	96–00[4]
Industry data													
Value of shipments[5]	39,535	42,237	42,309	43,413	47,406	49,674	52,253	55,383	57,780	5.2	6.0	4.3	5.1
Value of shipments (1992$)	39,535	41,386	41,057	41,960	45,629	47,005	48,965	51,088	52,605	4.2	4.3	3.0	3.6
Total employment (thousands)	264	271	264	265	268	270							
Production workers (thousands)	154	157	152	154	157	159							
Average hourly earnings ($)	11.22	11.48	11.68	12.00	12.23	13.20							
Capital expenditures	1,560	1,627	1,433	1,477	1,648								
Product data													
Value of shipments[5]	36,001	38,733	38,715	39,963	44,130	46,574	49,035	52,014	54,351	5.3	6.1	4.5	5.3
Value of shipments (1992$)	36,001	37,949	37,568	38,657	42,549	44,242	46,291	48,448	50,051	4.6	4.7	3.3	4.1
Trade data													
Value of imports	4,584	4,869	4,909	5,530	5,932	6,546	7,670	8,953	10,265	17.2	16.7	14.7	14.7
Value of exports	7,574	8,041	8,734	9,802	11,167	12,213	12,606	13,398	14,301	3.2	6.3	6.7	6.4

[1] Estimate except imports and exports.
[2] Estimate.
[3] Forecast.
[4] Compound annual rate.
[5] For a definition of industry versus product values, see "Getting the Most Out of *Outlook 2000*."
Source: U.S. Department of Commerce: Bureau of the Census; International Trade Administration.

turning increasingly to global markets for continued sales growth.

The largest regional market for U.S. exports is the EU, where 47 percent of all U.S. medical equipment exports were shipped in 1998 (see Table 44-2). U.S. export sales to the EU grew 3 percent to $6 billion in 1999. The second largest region is the Japan/Chinese Economic Area, which accounted for 20 percent of all U.S. exports of medical devices. The United States sells more medical equipment to Japan than to any other single country. Exports to Japan in 1998 totaled $1.9 billion, or 16 percent of total exports. In 1999, Japan was expected to increase its purchases almost 7 percent to $2.1 billion. Canada moved ahead of Germany and the Netherlands into the number two spot in 1998, growing from 8.8 percent of the export market to 10 percent. Exports to Canada were expected to rise almost 16 percent in 1999, the largest growth rate of any of the top markets for U.S. medical equipment.

The strong dollar has made U.S. equipment more expensive overseas and has had a dampening effect overall on the level of exports. Conversely, the strong dollar has made purchasing foreign equipment cheaper, and imports experienced double-digit growth for the last several years. In 1998, imports grew over 17 percent to $7.7 billion. In 1999, imports were expected to con-

TABLE 44-2: U.S. Trade Patterns in Medical Instruments and Supplies[1] in 1998
(millions of dollars; percent)

Exports			Imports		
Region[2]	Value[3]	Share, %	Region[2]	Value[3]	Share, %
NAFTA	1,742	14	NAFTA	1,253	16
Latin America	985	8	Latin America	405	5
Western Europe	5,906	47	Western Europe	3,274	43
Japan/Chinese Economic Area	2,472	20	Japan/Chinese Economic Area	1,717	22
Other Asia	441	3	Other Asia	523	7
Rest of world	1,060	8	Rest of world	498	6
World	12,606	100	World	7,670	100
Top Five Countries	Value	Share, %	Top Five Countries	Value	Share, %
Japan	1,980	16	Germany	1,266	17
Canada	1,220	10	Japan	1,218	16
Germany	1,165	9	Mexico	982	13
Netherlands	1,026	8	Israel	381	5
France	882	7	China	371	5

[1] SIC 384.
[2] For definitions of regional groupings, see "Getting the Most Out of *Outlook 2000*."
[3] Values may not sum to total due to rounding.
Source: U.S. Department of Commerce, Bureau of the Census.

tinue to register just under 17 percent growth to an estimated total of $9 billion. The EU was the largest foreign supplier of medical equipment to the United States in 1998, providing 43 percent of the total import market. The Japan/Chinese Economic Area was second with 22 percent of the import market. In that year, Germany took the lead over Japan as the number one foreign supplier of medical equipment to the United States, capturing 17 percent of the U.S. import market, giving the United States a $101 million trade deficit in medical equipment with Germany. Estimates for 1999 show that German medical device suppliers would continue to perform extremely well, with sales to the United States growing almost 19 percent to $1.5 billion. Japan is battling it out with Germany for dominance in the U.S. import market; in 1999, Japan was expected to again fall behind Germany, growing only 8 percent to $1.3 billion. In 1998, a new supplier came on the scene with an extremely vigorous performance. Israel sold $381 million in medical devices to the United States that year, earning 5 percent of the import market share and becoming the fourth largest exporter of medical equipment to the United States. Growth was expected to continue to be very strong for Israel in 1999, and that country may increase its market share considerably by the year 2000.

The medical device industry is globalized, with an increasing number of multinational firms that have pursued the global market aggressively by focusing on international sales and revenue, joint ventures, and mergers and acquisitions. As the increasing import numbers and decreasing export numbers demonstrate, the U.S. industry is facing increased competition from all corners. Certain U.S. export markets have experienced severe financial instability that has had major implications for the industry. Devalued currencies in Brazil and Colombia have severely affected U.S. sales to those markets, which have dropped 15 and 54 percent, respectively. Ever since Russia's financial crisis in August 1998, U.S. sales have plummeted, and in 1999 they plunged 43 percent from the already paltry levels of 1998. Developing economies in central Europe that looked promising instead appeared to be disappointing in 1999. Exports to Poland dropped 35 percent, exports to the Czech Republic dropped 25 percent, and exports to Hungary declined 10 percent. The entire region dropped an average of 25 percent. By contrast, Asia is on the upswing, and growth in 1999 was expected to be positive.

Because the medical device industry is so highly regulated, the regulatory environments at home and abroad also have serious implications for industry performance. Fortunately, the regulatory environment is much less restrictive now than it was in the past. In late 1998, the United States and the EU entered into a Mutual Recognition Agreement (MRA), which includes a 3-year confidence-building period. The MRA allows U.S. device firms to use U.S-based third parties called Conformity Assessment Bodies (CABs) to test some products to EU Medical Device Directive (MDD) requirements for sale in the EU market and allows EU firms to use EU-based third parties also called CABs to test some products to U.S. Food and Drug Administration (FDA) requirements for sale in the U.S. market. Use of the MRA is limited to a selected list of Class II (medium risk) medical devices and also calls for firm audits with no product classification limitations. The MRA is expected to be ready shortly for firms to use during the 3-year confidence-building period. This represents an important easing of regulations between the two largest trading partners in the world and should foster continued globalization of the industry. In addition, at home, the Food and Drug Administration Modernization Act of 1997 (FDAMA) has made important improvements to the system that have eased the way for domestically produced and imported medical devices to enter the U.S. market by exempting low-risk devices from filing requirements, eliminating excessive regulations, providing firms with an option for third-party reviews for certain Class II devices, and lessening restrictions on "off-label" or unapproved uses of approved devices.

At the same time, global regulations have had a negative impact on the U.S. industry. Many countries around the world are facing the same skyrocketing costs of health care seen in the United States and are trying to trim costs by cutting back on reimbursement rates—the rates at which medical devices are reimbursed to hospitals or other purchasers under health insurance or national health-care systems—by making it more difficult to have a product approved for reimbursement at all or by establishing price caps. Germany, France, and Japan are markets where the reimbursement rate has been set lower than what U.S. firms deem appropriate in light of the level of technology and quality of production. In addition, some countries have devised reimbursement formulas that take into consideration all costs for a particular diagnostic related group (DRG). Those formulas establish the maximum amount that will be reimbursed for treating a particular condition. A hospital thus has the incentive to purchase the least expensive equipment needed in order to save money or increase profits. This has a strong negative impact on U.S. medical equipment sales in those markets, because U.S. equipment tends to be of the highest quality, makes the best use of advanced technology, and therefore is often the most expensive. In addition, global reimbursement strategies work against U.S. equipment when they do not take into consideration incremental improvements made to existing technologies and refuse to put those improved device alternatives on the reimbursement list. U.S. firms lead the global industry in research and development and are known for providing continuous improvements and upgrades to existing medical devices.

An increasingly common practice among developing economies is the establishment of their own national regulatory requirements apart from international standards. Device firms are devoting tremendous amounts of time and money to determining what is required to sell a device in a foreign market, conducting extra clinical trials, and paying for the necessary certifications. These national requirements may become trade barriers that protect the domestic industry, earn hard currency for the government, or both. Many developed countries are moving toward global harmonization of regulatory standards. The Global Harmonization Task Force (GHTF) is a voluntary organization of regulators and regulated industries from the United States, the EU, Canada, Japan, Australia, and New Zealand whose work involves the harmonization of global requirements for medical devices. The U.S. industry would like a standard that would guarantee "tested once, accepted everywhere." Many developing countries have been invited to participate in these meetings, and regional working parties are part of the proceedings. In 1999, the Latin American Working Party met for the first time, an important addition to the GHTF, and the Asian Working Party met for the third time.

FACTORS AFFECTING FUTURE GROWTH OF THE DOMESTIC INDUSTRY

The U.S. medical and dental instruments and supplies industry is one of the most robust and innovative industries in the country, and it continues to grow every year. Industry shipments rose 6 percent to $55 billion in 1999, and by the year 2000, shipments should grow another 5 percent to $58 billion measured in constant dollars. Employment held steady from 1996 to 1997, increasing less than 1 percent to 270 thousand people, while wage rates increased 2 percent during that period. Consumption of medical and dental instruments and supplies also increased. The U.S. market in 1998 was $49 billion in constant dollars, and it is expected to increase 6 percent in 2000 to $52 billion.

There are approximately 8,000 medical device firms, mostly small and medium-size. Those firms are spread across the country but tend to be concentrated in certain regions with other high-technology industries, such as microelectronics and biotechnology. Orange County, CA, has the highest concentration of medical device firms in the world. In addition to California, states that have significant medical device manufacturing are Massachusetts, Pennsylvania, Minnesota, New York, Texas, and Florida.

The U.S. industry is characterized by the production of high-quality equipment and the use of advanced technology. The U.S. industry leads the world in medical device innovation as a result of its commitment to investing heavily in research and development and close association with medical research and microelectronics. Despite fluctuations over the years in the domestic and world economies, the U.S. medical device industry remains a vibrant and progressive industry, a situation that is not likely to change. One of the reasons for this is that the industry is self-sustaining. New medical discoveries sustain demand for new innovations to serve those new advances. As medicine improves and lives are prolonged, more people have more years in which they need medical treatment, especially those age 65 and over, among whom the average person's medical requirements increase dramatically. Innovation plays an important role as a sustaining force on its own: As the population grows and health care costs rise, the world seeks easier, cheaper, and more effective ways to satisfy medical needs. The medical device industry is going nowhere but up, and the United States is strategically positioned to remain a dominant player in the world market.

However, the U.S. domestic medical device industry is undergoing radical change in direct response to the factors that affect it. The trends that will affect and change the device industry the most in the next 5 years are cost containment, consolidation, demographics, innovation, the regulatory environment, and global financial instability. Cost containment already has had a serious impact on device firms. Many firms have changed the way they do business as a result of the pinch, yet this factor has only begun to affect the industry, and many more changes are on the horizon.

Health Care Cost Containment

According to the Congressional Budget Office (CBO), the United States will spend $1.3 trillion on health care in 2000. By 2007, that number will explode to a projected $2 trillion, thanks in large part to the growing number of elderly who will be eligible for Medicare. Currently, private health insurance pays a slightly higher percentage of the overall health care costs, but by 2007, that ratio will invert, and the U.S. government will account for more than half the total outlay. The U.S. Bureau of the Census reports that in 1995, 13 percent of the population was age 65 or over; by 2050, the projection is 20 percent. Costs will skyrocket. Employers and workers cannot keep up the pace in premium increases expected for the private sector, and taxpayers will not be able to shoulder the growing burden of Medicare spending.

The Balanced Budget Act of 1997 (BBA) addressed these issues in an effort to keep spending under control. Although it put a damper on the growth rate, spending is expected to increase approximately 4 percent a year.

These attempts at cost containment have had a direct impact on the U.S. medical device industry. Specifically, they directly affect which kinds of products are produced. As Medicare attempts to lower costs by encouraging the use of less costly sites for health care, new technology is introduced to accommodate that shift. The setting and its changed needs help determine the devices that are produced and encourage the introduction of new innovations, including fiber-optics and sophisticated diagnostic and treatment technologies.

While alternative care settings may help encourage innovation in some ways, cost-containment pressures also have a dampening effect on innovation. To justify paying for medical devices, insurance companies are demanding that firms offer "proof" that the new technology provides clear outcome-based benefits before they agree to accept a new device as a reimbursable product. Since small firms are usually the innovators in this industry, many cannot afford to bear the burden in time and expense these proofs require. These conditions have led to another major trend in the domestic industry: consolidation through mergers and acquisitions.

Mergers and Acquisitions

The middle to late 1990s was a time of tremendous numbers of mergers and acquisitions, and this is a trend that will continue in the twenty-first century. The long-term effects are not fully known, but the consolidation of the medical device industry is already changing the structure of firms and the delivery of medical technology to patients. As small firms are finding it too expensive to devote significant resources to providing proof data about their new innovations, they are teaming up with larger firms that have the financial resources to provide such data. Large firms receive the benefit of the new technology and therefore maintain market share; small firms can afford to continue to produce and get the benefit of a large firm devoting resources to the continued incremental improvements that are crucial to the industry.

Large firms have many reasons for pursuing lucrative mergers and acquisitions. They purchase the competition, as occurred when Johnson & Johnson bought DePuy. They purchase the "pipeline" of new technology in their segment, as occurred when Medtronic bought Arterial Vascular Control (AVE). Finally, they attempt to control a vast range of products and become a one-stop shop. The one-stop shop is a direct response to another consolidation trend: purchasers are merging too.

Large buyers have an advantage in the medical device market. In recent years, many hospitals, insurance providers, and other medical equipment purchasers have organized themselves into group purchasing organizations (GPOs), leveraged their purchasing power, and commanded lower prices. The GPO phenomenon has device companies strategizing to retain profits in this new purchasing environment. Siemens recently signed a 5-year contract with a GPO based in Atlanta that purchases for every hospital in the southeast. Firms are merging to take advantage of economies of scale in production, sales, and distribution in the new age of the GPO. Some small firms find that they cannot compete with large firms for GPO business and feel pressured to merge. Some in the industry are concerned about the disappearance of the small firms that made the industry dynamic and innovative and the dominance of a few megafirms. Johnson & Johnson, Baxter, GE Medical Systems, Abbott Labs, Tyco, and Medtronic are the leading U.S. firms. Of the 10 largest firms, 6 are U.S. companies. Consolidated device firms and GPOs are changing the landscape of purchasers, and so will two other groups of purchasers in the next several years: the elderly and women.

Demographics

The elderly will influence the direction of the medical device industry through their particular health needs and how and where they will be treated. As the U.S. population ages and the pressure to contain cost increases, expensive hospital stays will be discouraged and health care increasingly will be delivered in alternative settings such as nursing homes, hospices, and especially the patient's own home. Home health care products are one of the fastest-growing segments of the industry and are branching out into new areas. What used to be limited to only the lowest-technology products now encompasses critical care equipment and a whole new area: high-technology medical devices that are intended to be used by unskilled health care workers or even by the patient.

The elderly population is increasing in numbers and living longer, requiring more years of care. This will benefit to some degree almost all segments of the medical device industry but especially those segments used by the elderly, such as respiratory therapy, disposables such as incontinence products, and devices to treat sleep disorders. By 2005, an estimated 2.5 million people will require some level of respiratory oxygen therapy, and increasingly this will take place in the home, requiring more portable and less complex devices. In 1998, the sleep disorder diagnostic and therapeutic device market earned $298 million, with the obstructive sleep apnea (OSA) sector earning the most revenue. Because the patient population typically requiring OSA devices will increase tremendously, the OSA market is expected to grow 80 percent or more by 2005.

Because of the increasing costs of health care, the shift to home health care and alternative setting care has been astounding, but home health care has not been immune to the belt-tightening that has affected each segment of the industry. When Medicare directed more of its spending into home health care and alternative settings for health care and away from inpatient hospital care, spending on home health care and alternative site care increased sharply. Medicare slashed reimbursement rates on many home health care products. However, over the long run increased spending on home health care is always cheaper than inpatient hospital care. Funding will increase, and this will continue to be the direction of the future.

The shift toward providing health care in the home and other alternative settings will affect certain medical device markets more than others, although almost every market segment will be affected. In vitro diagnostics will see continued rapid growth and innovation in response to advances in biotechnology and change in the setting for health care. Increasingly, diagnostic tests will be easier to use so that patients will test and monitor themselves, negating the need to send samples to a laboratory for analysis. New diagnostic tests will become available as more is learned about the human gene structure.

Other segments expected to benefit from this trend are cardiology, in an increased move toward catheter laboratories, and the needle and syringe market. As more people will be treating themselves, research will be aimed toward producing safer needles and syringes and, even more important, needleless devices. This will affect the huge diabetic population in the United States as well as any patient needing intravenous (IV) drug therapy.

Women will have a greater impact on the medical device industry in the next several years because women outnumber and outlive men. They often require more gender-specific health care and are the ones who tend to make the health care purchasing decisions for the family. The U.S. Bureau of the Census estimates that by 2005 there will be 14 million more women than men age 18 years and older. Women make up the majority of the elderly population as well. The Census Bureau also reports that in 2005, 84 percent of the rapidly growing 100-year-old and older category will be women. Medical device firms will respond to the statistical facts about the role of female consumers of medical devices. For example, demand is rising for technology devoted to early diagnosis, treatment, and follow-up care for breast cancer. Women are the primary purchasers of cosmetic surgery; with increased disposable income and the larger number of women electing to have this surgery, medical lasers will be a major growth area for electromedical products. Some analysts estimate that the medical laser market is already worth more than $1 billion and will grow rapidly.

Innovations and Technological Advances

The U.S. medical device industry funnels a tremendous amount of money into research and development to fund innovation, which will affect some markets especially. Wound care is an important example. In a traditionally low-tech industry valued at $10 billion worldwide, high-technology products are being introduced into the wound care market that will create enormous market growth. Artificial skin is replacing traditional bandages and sutures. As more cardiac catheterization takes place, high-tech incision sealants become necessary. Owing to advances in surgery, wound care will keep pace by providing closures and repair to brain membranes, heart valves, and knees beyond what is typically thought of in this sector. Care of diabetic foot ulcers is an important market in wound care and will keep pace with the increased incidence of this disease in the U.S. population. In 1998, the FDA approved the first fibrin sealant for the U.S. market. Fibrin sealant is a human blood product that aids in clotting and is used to control bleeding during surgery. Fibrin sealants are expected to revolutionize the wound care industry and increase the value of the U.S. market significantly by 2005.

Another area that will see tremendous interest is drug delivery. As new pharmaceuticals are developed to treat illness, the medical device industry will be called on to deliver those pharmaceuticals into the patient's body. This can be done by an IV infusion, a conventional hypodermic needle, an asthma inhaler, an oxygen tent, and so on, but the future of drug delivery will be needleless technologies, which will greatly affect the millions of diabetics in the United States. Many diabetics face painful daily injections of insulin. The method of delivery is a disincentive to take the insulin, and so the competition is fierce among firms that are racing to develop insulin inhalers and other methods of delivery. Microprocessing and advanced materials companies are joining forces with the device industry as firms are also experimenting with loading drugs onto tiny microchips and implanting them in a person's body to achieve accurately timed and automatic delivery of drugs. Particularly for patients who must take numerous doses or juggle numerous different medications, each with a different dose and timing requirement, as in the treatment of AIDS or tuberculosis, human error and the lack of desire to take the medicines are requiring otherwise unnecessary hospitalizations, costly services of social and health care workers to ensure that the patient takes the medicines, and premature deaths. Better drug delivery methods are an exploding growth area for the medical device industry.

Regulatory Improvements

FDAMA has greatly improved the regulatory environment. According to the FDA's Center for Devices and Radiological Health's (CDRH) 1998 annual report, approval time for premarket authorizations (PMAs) was reduced 25 percent, average total time for 510(k) clearance was cut 12 percent, and for 2 years in a row there were no 510(k)s, PMAs, or PMA supplements overdue at the close of the year. This improved performance is an enormous financial asset to U.S. medical device firms, which can bring their products to market faster and easier. Third-party reviews of medical devices will provide for even more efficient review times. However, the same cannot be said for the global environment, an important consideration to a U.S. industry that must become globalized to compete over the long term. What happens in other countries will affect the U.S. industry.

Electronic Commerce

The introduction of E-commerce is having a significant effect on the medical device industry that is likely to continue over the next decade. Most noticeable to consumers is the proliferation of on-line sites featuring product and purchasing information. Institutional purchasers of medical equipment in the United States and overseas are integrating on-line procurement into supply-chain management programs to save time and money. Patients are gathering treatment and product information on the Internet and having more input in decisions affecting their health care.

In addition to manufacturers' Web pages used for direct marketing and sales, there has been a proliferation of third-party Web sites that connect manufacturers with purchasers. On those Web pages, manufacturers may display product information at no cost in a forum where consumers may receive brief overviews of many companies' products at once. Small and large manufacturers benefit equally from this emerging practice because all sizes of producers receive equal space and time on those Web pages. Buyers also may share feedback with one another concerning the quality of products and their recommendations to other possible purchasers of the same merchandise. This new type of connection between manufacturers and consumers probably will yield greater product knowledge on the part of consumers as well as more opportunities for small businesses to enter the manufacturing market.

E-commerce is changing the medical device trade in the regulatory arena as well. In 1997, the FDA implemented the Electronic Records and Signatures Regulation. This rule (21 CFR 11) establishes the criteria under which the FDA will deem electronic records and electronic signatures equivalent to paper records and traditional handwritten signatures. While electronic filing should lighten the burden on manufacturers, there are significant differences between electronic records and signatures and traditional paper systems that necessitate additional controls. Issues relating to confidentiality, permanency, and the integrity of electronic signatures have challenged both the FDA and industry. However, as systems are established and evaluated, electronic submissions probably will become standard.

U.S. INDUSTRY GROWTH PROJECTIONS FOR THE NEXT 1 AND 5 YEARS

From 1993 to 1995, the industry experienced a sharp decline in growth as a result of cost-cutting measures in the health care sector. However, between 1996 and 1999, the industry grew at an average annual rate of 7.4 percent, although every year since 1996 the growth rate was slightly lower than it had been the year before. The pattern will continue in the year 2000, with strong growth yet at the same time an incremental slowdown from the previous year's rate of growth. Industry shipments will grow just under 6 percent to a projected value of $58 billion.

From 1996 through 2000, industry shipments will experience a compound annual growth rate of 5 percent. The next 5 years look very positive for the industry as it takes advantage of a more liberal regulatory environment, an aging population, shifts to home health care and alternative sites, and more efficient manufacturing and distribution. Industry shipments should grow 5 to 8 percent annually through 2004. Fueling this growth in particular will be orthopedics, in vitro diagnostics, cardiology-related technologies, and drug delivery equipment.

The global financial environment is improving for U.S. exports. Economic recovery is taking place in Asia. Developing economies are continuing to place increased emphasis on health care for their countries, and many nations are experiencing the aging of their populations. The United States–EU MRA will be functioning, and the industry will be taking advantage of the established relationships with the CABs established for the MRA to make entering the EU market easier. The industry continues to seek improved reimbursement formulas and will succeed in improving the system or adapt to the new environment.

The United States continues to invest a significant amount of profits into research and development (R&D). Particularly in the diagnostics segment, approximately 50 percent of firms invest up to 50 percent of their profits in research for in vivo and in vitro diagnostic products. Since this industry is fueled by innovation and the ongoing quest for better ways of treating or diagnosing medical problems, the future of the U.S. industry looks very bright. The industry is not adversely affected by lower labor costs in developing countries. Instead, it relies heavily on the new advances that the dynamic U.S. industry continues to create.

In addition, the United States holds a competitive advantage in the complementary industries on which the medical device industry relies, including microelectronics, telecommunications, biotechnology, and software development. The new technologies that will continue to come from these sectors will fuel growth in U.S. shipments and exports. By the year 2000, the decline in the growth of exports seen in the late 1990s will end, and the value of exports is expected to increase almost 7 percent to $14 billion, representing a compound annual growth rate of 6.4 percent between 1996 and 2000. Exports will grow at a projected average annual rate of 8 percent through 2004.

The growth of imports and the shrinking trade surplus have been matters of concern to some industry analysts. In 2000, the growth rate of imports will begin to decline, although it will remain in the double digits. By 2000, the value of imports is expected to reach $10 billion, growing 15 percent, but the rate of growth will slow by 1.5 percent over 1999 levels. As a result of the expected strengthening of the yen and the slight weakening of the dollar, imports will not grow as fast after 2000 as they did in the late 1990s. One can expect imports to remain at higher levels than in the early 1990s as a result of the globalization of the industry and increased manufacturing capacities in Asia and relative newcomers such as Israel. Growth should slow slightly but remain robust at an average annual rate of 8 to 10 percent through 2004.

Valerie Barth, U.S. Department of Commerce, Office of Microelectronics, Medical Equipment and Instrumentation, (202) 482-3360, Valerie_Barth@ita.doc.gov, September 1999.

SELECTED GLOBAL MARKET PROSPECTS

Western Europe

The EU has historically been the largest export market for U.S. medical devices and is expected to continue to receive exports of American-made high-tech products. Steady economic growth, low unemployment, and political and currency stability make that region an attractive market, accounting for 26 percent of the medical device global market. The largest individual European markets, in descending order, are Germany, France, Italy, the United Kingdom, and Spain. In terms of per capita spending, Switzerland, Denmark, Norway, Germany, and Austria are among the markets with the highest rates in the world.

Sales of U.S. medical and dental equipment and supplies to Europe consistently have expanded over the decade and are expected to increase for the foreseeable future. The aging populations of developed economies typical of Europe account for a heavy demand for medical and dental appliances and supplies. Furthermore, economies of scale have contained the price of higher-technology goods that are more efficient in keeping health care expenditures in check. The United States leads in the production of these higher-technology goods. Soaring general health care costs and the trends toward restraining related overall expenses make U.S. merchandise more attractive in cost-cutting European economies. Funds used for medical purposes therefore are increasingly more effective in maintaining community health.

The EU maintains a uniquely open and transparent regulatory system for medical devices that is based on international standards and is a single system for all the member countries. Medical devices sold within the EU must meet the health and safety requirements of the EU Medical Device Directive (93/42/EEC). This directive consolidates regulatory requirements in EU member countries under one system, meaning that if a device can be sold in one country, it is approved for sale in all EU countries.

In this system, a product approval is based on evaluations of the safety and effectiveness of a device. If a product satisfies the requirements of the directive, the manufacturer may affix the "CE mark" to the product, indicating that the device may legally enter the commerce of any EU member country. Some products may fall under the jurisdiction of more than one EU directive and therefore must meet the requirements of all the applicable directives to receive the CE mark. Electrical medical devices must meet the requirements of both the MDD as well as Directive 84/539/EEC relating to electromedical equipment.

U.S. medical and dental instrument and supplies exporters shipped $5.5 billion worth of product to the EU in 1998, representing 44 percent of their medical device exports. Exports from the United States to the EU came close to breaking the $6 billion mark in 1999. Sales of x-ray equipment, which had dropped in the mid-1990s, increased in 1998 and then leveled off at roughly $580 million. Sales of electromedical equipment increased in 1998 and tapered off in 1999, with an expected shipment rate approximating $1.75 billion.

Surgical and medical instruments, surgical and medical supplies, and dental equipment and supplies are the best-sellers in the EU market. All three categories saw steady increases in the latter half of the decade up to and including 1999 and continue to look promising.

Since its inception in December 1998, the United States and the EU have made strides in the confidence-building period of the United States–European Union medical device annex of the medical device MRA. That MRA is a bilateral agreement between the United States and the EU that establishes procedures to facilitate transatlantic trade in medical devices. The medical device MRA recognizes that certain CABs in the United States can conduct type testing (for certain devices only) and quality evaluations according to the EU MDD. Similarly, it recognizes that certain CABs in Europe can conduct, in accordance with U.S. regulatory requirements, product approval–type testing (certain devices only) and quality system evaluations (all devices) in a fashion equivalent to those conducted by the FDA.

The purpose of the medical device MRA is not for FDA-approved products to be accepted in the EU or for EU-approved (CE-marked) products to be accepted in the United States. The United States and the EU still maintain their own unique requirements within their respective borders. Under the medical device MRA, to sell a device in the EU, a U.S. device manufacturer submits an application to a CAB in the United States for review based on the EU MDD. After conducting its review, the CAB recommends approval, if appropriate, to an EU notified body. Once the product is approved by the EU notified body, it can be sold in the EU market. Similarly, a European manufacturer that wants to sell in the United States is required to submit a premarket notification [510(k)] application to a CAB in the EU for review based on FDA requirements. If appropriate, the CAB recommends approval to the FDA. Although the FDA will confirm recommendations by EU CABs, U.S. law prohibits it from delegating its responsibility to grant formal approval. Once the EU CAB recommendation is accepted by the FDA, the product can be sold in the U.S. market.

Only those products (97 product categories), generally lower-risk Class I and Class II devices, listed in the medical device MRA are eligible for this procedure. This list probably will expand over time.

U.S. manufacturing facilities will be inspected by U.S. CABs according to the EU's MDD and quality system requirements. Similarly, manufacturing facilities in the EU will be inspected by EU CABs according to U.S. quality systems good manufacturing practices (GMPs). Although product approvals and EU type testing requirements are limited to specific devices identified in the medical device annex of the MRA, plant inspections apply to all U.S. and EU medical device manufacturing facilities.

During the 3-year confidence-building period that began on December 7, 1998, the United States and the EU will develop an understanding of the procedures used by each party to designate and evaluate CABs. The National Institute of Standards and Technology (NIST), an entity within the U.S. Department of Commerce, has completed screening and reviewing documentation for 10 U.S. CABs, and the FDA has nominated those organizations, along with supporting information, to the European Commission for approval. Similarly, the EU nominated 15 EU CABs that were submitted to the FDA along with supporting information. Each nominated CAB has the ability to perform both product reviews and quality system inspections. The FDA and the EU have agreed that the nominated CABs will participate in the medical device MRA during the 3-year confidence building period.

Over the next 3 years, each party will review technical documentation on CABs and provide annual progress reports regarding confidence-building activities. During this period, the performance of the CABs with regard to product reviews and plant inspections under the medical device MRA will be assessed. By the end of the confidence-building period, the CABs will have been evaluated and the United States and the EU will have exchanged quality-system evaluation reports and product evaluation reports generated by those assessment bodies. After this 3-year confidence-building period, the CABs that meet performance requirements are expected to be authorized to continue to operate within the medical device MRA process.

The goal of the medical device MRA is to establish a model agreement between the EU and the United States under which each party will normally endorse the reports of listed CABs for certain medical device product approvals and plant inspections, thus simplifying and improving two-way trade. The medical device MRA probably will be continued and product coverage will be expanded after the 3-year confidence-building period.

Medical device manufacturers in the United States may be able to save resources by relying on evaluations of manufacturing processes and products conducted domestically under the requirements of the EU's MDD. EU manufacturers would enjoy similar benefit in gaining approval for products sold in the United States.

The success of the United States–European Union medical device MRA will be an important step toward global harmonization of medical device regulatory requirements currently being addressed by the GHTF. The United States does not support or seek multiple MRAs with other countries because it is utilizing its limited resources to ensure the success of this MRA with the EU.

N. Gerard Zapiain, U.S. Department of Commerce, Office of Microelectronics, Medical Equipment and Instrumentation, (202) 482-2410, Gerry_Zapiain@ita.doc.gov, September 1999.

Asia

In the latter half of the 1990s, nearly all the Asian markets were hurt by the Asian financial crisis. While this affected U.S. exports of medical devices to some markets, demand continued to grow in countries that did not have currency devaluations. In 1999, the region began to recover, with U.S. medical device exports totaling $3.24 billion, only 2 percent short of their high in 1997. Those relatively strong export figures suggest that the governments and citizens of Asian nations greatly value health care and are willing to make sacrifices in other areas to preserve it. U.S.-manufactured medical devices, although more expensive than comparable equipment manufactured in Japan or the EU, enjoy a reputation for quality and innovation throughout Asia. Asian economies should continue their recovery with projected regional growth of 3.5 to 4.5 percent in the year 2000, and the outlook for the medical device market in Asia beyond 2000 appears healthy.

For U.S.-manufactured medical devices, the Japanese market is second only to the EU, totaling $2.1 billion in U.S. exports in 1999, accounting for two-thirds of U.S. exports to Asia. Although Japan's economy was in recession in the latter half of the decade, U.S. exports dipped only 2.7 percent in 1998 and more than made up for that decrease in 1999 by rising 7.4 percent. The main forces driving Japan's demand for medical devices are its rapidly aging population and the escalation of health care costs. Thus far, U.S.-manufactured devices have resisted government cost-cutting measures by appealing to the Japanese preference for high quality and innovation, particularly in areas such as computed tomography (CT) systems, pacemakers, laser surgery equipment, and magnetic resonance imaging (MRI) systems. In addition, the Health Industry Manufacturers Association, working in conjunction with the U.S. Trade Representative and the U.S. Department of Commerce, has aggressively advanced the economic benefits of innovative products and lobbied against price control policies. As a result of the bilateral Medical Equipment and Pharmaceuticals Market-Oriented, Sector-Selective (MOSS) negotiations in 1999, local governments in Japan are authorized to base medical device purchases on the best overall value for performance and specification requirements, not simply on the initial cost of devices. With increasing demands for health care, the continuing recovery of the Japanese economy, and more liberal reimbursement practices, U.S. medical device exports to Japan will increase 5 to 10 percent annually for the next 5 years.

China, including the Special Administrative Region of Hong Kong, is the second largest market for U.S. medical device exports in Asia. From 1996 to 1999, U.S. exports to China and Hong Kong increased 20 percent. This reflected increasing government emphasis on health care spurred by an aging and more affluent population's demand for better medical services. In addition, the Chinese government's 1998 prohibition against secondhand medical equipment will continue to benefit exporters of new equipment in this price-sensitive market. Most of the large, well-known U.S. manufacturers have representative offices and sales networks in China's coastal cities. However, lack of funding and distribution difficulties have kept foreign-manufactured equipment out of the vast interior. In the year 2000, the Chinese government will have in place a national health insurance scheme and will introduce private health insurance. These developments will increase rural health care institutions' access to medical technology and improve the market for U.S. exports. The Chinese domestic medical device industry is growing quickly but is unlikely to affect the growing market for technologically advanced U.S. medical devices over the next 5 years. Assuming economic stability in China and a continuation of the Chinese policy of avoiding currency devaluation, the market for U.S. medical devices should increase 5 to 10 percent over the next 5 years.

India is one of the fastest-growing markets in Asia for U.S. medical equipment, rising 44 percent between 1996 and 1999 to $89 million. Although export sales are currently lower than those for Japan, China, Taiwan, South Korea, and Singapore, the industry is enthusiastic about India's potential. A number of factors have made India appealing: immunity from the Asian financial crisis, rapid population growth, the potential introduction of private health insurance, and the lack of a device regulatory system. Serving the growing middle class and relieving the public services burden, India's private health care services sector has been expanding rapidly and fueling the demand for medical equipment. Legislation introducing Indian and foreign health insurance programs to the market should be passed in early 2000 and should increase health care access and the demand for more and better medical devices. Large U.S. manufacturers such as GE Medical Systems and Agilent (HP) already have manufacturing operations in India and have plans for expansion. Because medical devices are exempt from current sanctions, U.S. sales to India are forecast to increase 15 percent annually over the next 5 years.

In South Korea and the southeast Asian countries that devaluated their currencies during the Asian financial crisis, governments are making efforts to maintain public confidence in the health care systems while instituting difficult economic reforms. However, exports of medical devices to these markets were greatly affected by the economic turmoil in 1997 and 1998. While these markets are showing signs of recovery, they are unlikely to reach previous levels until after 2001. Assuming future economic stability, these markets should grow 5 to 10 percent annually over the next 5 years.

Lauren Saadat, U.S. Department of Commerce, Office of Microelectronics, Medical Equipment and Instrumentation, (202) 482-4431, Lauren_Saadat@ita.doc.gov, September 1999.

Latin America

In 1998, Latin American markets were lucrative for U.S. medical device manufacturers, with sales approaching $1 billion. However, in early 1999, Brazil's currency suffered a 30 percent devaluation that sent uncertainty throughout the region. The currency devaluation resulted in no real growth for Brazil in 1999, and other countries such as Argentina and Chile had sharp recessions. Several countries instituted fiscal austerity plans, resulting in less money being spent on health care budgets. As a result, medical device market growth for the entire region declined 8 percent in 1999.

Despite the problems associated with Brazil's downturn, Latin America continues to be a promising market for U.S. medical device manufacturers and, as one of the regions most highly dependent on imported medical products, provides opportunities for U.S. exporters. Several positive trends have emerged in the Latin American health care sector. For example, many countries in that region embarked on health care reform programs as early as the mid-1990s, and results are slowly emerging. Mexico's National Development Program, created in 1995, has seen results in the form of an increase in health care spending, an expansion of coverage under the government's social security program, and a decentralization of management. Chile's 1994–2000 Health Sector Reform Project has doubled the health budget since 1990 and increased the construction of therapeutic diagnostic centers and hospitals to enhance primary care and improve emergency and ambulatory care services.

Another beneficial change in the region is governments' emphasis on comprehensive health insurance coverage. Health ministries are reforming insurance plans to provide comprehensive coverage, private and public, with efforts to reach marginal populations. As nations have attempted to form their own regulatory systems for medical devices, the GHTF formed in 1999 a Latin American Working Party, which bodes well for this region in terms of working toward harmonized regulatory requirements. U.S. industry strongly supports the Latin American Working Party.

Although many countries are implementing positive reforms, several obstacles still exist for U.S. medical device exporters in Latin America. For example, U.S. firms must deal with high registration fees, lengthy review times, and burdensome requirements to enter the Brazilian market. Reimbursement policies need to be updated to add new medical devices to social security coverage and to ensure payment. Despite efforts by the Southern Cone Common Market (MERCOSUR), countries still lack harmonized regulatory systems.

Overall, the Latin American markets continue to provide good prospects for medical device suppliers. U.S. medical equipment is seen as a best prospect not only in the larger economies but also in smaller economies such as the Dominican Republic, Costa Rica, Honduras, and Panama. High quality, reliability, durability, favorable prices, good maintenance service, and timely delivery are the main factors in increasing sales in the medical sector. In Central America, the aftermath of Hurricane Mitch brought reconstruction funds for rebuilding the infrastructure of those nations, and emphasis is being placed on the health of the citizens. New hospitals and health clinics are being built that provide numerous opportunities for U.S. firms to supply the region with medical devices. The Andean region has been a promising but often overlooked area. Colombia and Ecuador in particular have been focusing attention on health care infrastructure, building hospitals and refurbishing others at a fantastic rate. However, beginning in early 1999, the region has become mired in financial and political instability, and that has had a dampening effect on U.S. exports.

Mexico remains the top market for U.S. medical equipment exports in Latin America and continues to appear promising. Total U.S. exports of medical devices and supplies grew 48 percent from 1996 to 1999. Representing over a third of the total U.S. medical device exports to Latin America in 1999, Mexico remains favorable for the industry. Over 50 percent of the medical device import market in Mexico belongs to U.S. firms. Many of the imports are used in the "maquiladora" area as inputs of U.S. medical device companies and then exported to the U.S. market. Under the North American Free Trade Agreement (NAFTA), tariffs have been eliminated on almost all medical devices, providing added interest in the market. The final elimination of tariffs on remaining medical devices will be complete by 2003. In addition, registration fees remain comparatively low and the sale of used equipment is allowed, although only for private health facilities.

Even though the currency devaluation in Brazil triggered a 5.5 percent decrease in overall U.S. exports of medical equipment in 1999, Brazil remains the second leading importer of U.S.-manufactured medical devices in Latin America. From 1995 to 1998, U.S. exports to Brazil increased 25 percent. By 1998, Brazil's imports of medical equipment had grown to $308 million. With the financial crisis, the government made significant cuts in social security and health care budgets. However, despite those cuts, Brazil's GDP continues to be larger than the combined economies of Mexico, Argentina, and Chile, making it an attractive market. Brazil's economic slowdown affected government investment plans for public hospitals. To combat the increased cost of imported equipment and supplies, the government lowered import duties on 42 products in March 1999.

The Brazilian Ministry of Health announced plans to concentrate investments in basic health services through clinics, particularly for the poorer population, and by remodeling 2,138 existing public hospitals. The government also plans to invest $900 million in hospital infrastructure in the next 2 years, using mostly World Bank and Inter-American Development Bank loans.

In late 1998, the government created a new regulatory agency known as Agencia Nacional de Vigilancia Sanitaria (ANVS) to inspect and register medical devices. Fees increased significantly in 1999 to allow the ANVS to be self-supporting, and many U.S. firms are trying to learn the new regulations that Brazil is introducing on a regular basis. Although disruption is to be expected with the creation of a new agency, U.S. medical device manufacturers would benefit from efforts by Brazil to harmonize regulations. U.S. exports can be expected to grow in 2000 rather than decline as they did in 1999. One can expect modest but positive growth of less than 3 percent in 2000. The best prospects for U.S. exports include anesthetics, cardiac catheters, automated blood cell counters and analyzers, autoscanners, diagnostic systems, automatic positioning beds, blood equipment, cardiac pacemakers, dental restoration materials, electrosurgical and electrotherapy apparatus, endoscopic devices, enzyme immunoassay systems, high-performance liquid chromotography (HPLC) imaging equipment, laser equipment for dentistry, magnetic resonance tomography, x-ray equipment and parts, ophthalmic instruments, surgical instruments, ultrasonic scanning devices, visible and ultraviolet (UV) lights, spectofluorometers, and orthopedics products.

From 1996 to 1998, Argentina saw 52 percent growth in its medical equipment market, and that nation continues to have growth in U.S. imports of medical devices in Latin America while other countries' imports have declined. Several hospitals formerly run by the Argentine federal government have been transferred to the provinces and municipalities. Even though the federal government has not increased its budget for hospital equipment, the facilities that were transferred have been upgrading their equipment. While an important market, Argentina has not been immune to the financial instability, and in 1999 every subsector declined sharply except electromedical equipment, which grew 35 percent. The electromedical performance boosted overall growth to 2 percent in 1999. The outlook for 2000 may be about the same. The World Bank is providing project financing and loans to upgrade the Argentinian public health system. However, because of an overall decrease in economic activity and presidential elections in October 1999, decisions to reform investment in the health care sector have been delayed.

Trade barriers are few in the Argentinian medical equipment market, but financing is crucial in selecting foreign suppliers. Competition from local manufacturers is low, particularly in the high-technology end of the market. The best sales prospects for new medical equipment are in prosthetics, imaging systems, dental chairs, and lasers.

Chile has one of the most developed and open economies in Latin America. In 1999, Chile spent 7 percent of its GDP on health care, representing $2 billion of the fiscal budget, making health care one of the largest government expenditures. Although the Chilean government has assigned priority to the improvement of the national public health care sector, the recent financial crises in Asia and Brazil have forced the government to cut back funding by approximately 1 percent. The budget cut delayed new 1999–2000 infrastructure projects; however, all other health care purchases remained untouched. Although the market has suffered slightly, it is dynamic and healthy. Several programs for large-scale purchases of modern equipment as part of an effort to upgrade the public and private health sectors have received government approval.

U.S. medical device manufacturers do not face significant trade barriers in the Chilean market. Chile has launched a tariff reduction program that aims for a 6 percent tariff by 2003, with 1 percent reductions annually. As a result of the openness of its trade practices and overall economic system, Chile remains among the best-rated emerging economies. The United States has been Chile's most important supplier of medical equipment for years. U.S. exports to Chile grew 36 percent from 1997 to 1999.

With reforms under way in the larger economies of the region and an emphasis on new infrastructure in terms of hospitals and health clinics in Central America and the Andean countries, projected regional growth in the industry in the year 2000 should be positive at about 3 percent, marking an improvement over the 8 percent decline in 1999.

Valerie Barth, U.S. Department of Commerce, Office of Microelectronics, Medical Equipment and Instrumentation, (202) 482-3360, Valerie_Barth@ita.doc.gov, and Marnie Morrione, U.S. Department of Commerce, Trade Information Center, September 1999.

SURGICAL AND MEDICAL INSTRUMENTS AND SUPPLIES

Surgical and medical instruments and supplies (SIC 3841) constitute the largest sector of the U.S. medical device industry, accounting for approximately 36 percent of total industry shipments and employing 38 percent of its workers. This category covers a broad spectrum of products, including anesthesia apparatus, biopsy instruments, blood pressure apparatus, blood transfusion equipment, bronchoscopes except electromedical, cannulas, catheters, surgical clamps, physicians' diagnostic apparatus, hemodialysis apparatus, hypodermic needles and syringes, IV transfusion apparatus, inhalation therapy equipment, operating tables, oxygen tents, surgical probes, retractors, suction therapy apparatus, trocars, and, since 1999, bone drills, plates, and screws.

Domestic shipments of surgical and medical instruments have grown steadily since 1994. Over the period 1996–2000, industry shipments of surgical and medical instruments will grow at an estimated compound annual rate of over 6 percent. Shipments valued in constant dollars will total $20 billion in 2000, an increase of $3.4 billion since 1997. The industry employed 17 thousand people in 1997, an increase of 0.5 percent over 1996 levels (see Table 44-3). As in other sectors of the medical device industry, employment has stayed relatively constant while production has expanded, resulting in a productivity increase. These productivity gains have made the industry more competitive in the world market.

Global and Domestic Outlook

U.S. manufacturers exported 23 percent of their surgical instrument shipments in 1999. Despite the strong dollar and unstable global financial markets, exports rose almost 5 percent in 1999 to over $4.7 billion and are expected to increase 7 percent in 2000 to over $5 billion (see Table 44-3). The largest export category is bougies, catheters, drains, and sondes, representing 25 percent of all U.S. exports of surgical instruments and growing 15 percent in 1999 to $1.3 billion. Numerous other categories also showed double-digit export growth, including bone plates, screws, nails, and other internal fixation devices or appliances, which grew 17 percent to $340 million. This market was classified as SIC 3842 until 1999.

Japan was the largest single export market in 1998, with a 16 percent share of the export market, although it has experienced a downward trend since 1997 (see Table 44-4). Export sales dropped 17 percent in 1999 to $677 million. The EU is the largest regional market, purchasing 46 percent of U.S. surgical instrument exports in 1998. In 1999, exports to the EU increased 8 percent to an estimated $2 billion. The Netherlands is the number one market in Europe, growing 8 percent in 1999 to $472 million. The Japan/Chinese Economic Area follows the EU with a 20 percent share of U.S. exports. In the Americas, exports to Canada in 1999 soared 24 percent to $581 million, making that nation the second largest single export market, as U.S. exporters turned increasingly to Canada in 1999 in response to the economic troubles in Mexico and the rest of the Americas.

The outlook for exports to the EU in 2000 is for steady growth, with an expected increase of 6 to 8 percent. As Japan begins a slow recovery in 2000, it will face an aging population and soaring health care costs. Growth for this sector may be hindered by a cost-conscious Japan seeking cheaper and lower-technology products from other countries. Improvements in Japan's reimbursement policies and a strong demand for high-

TABLE 44-3: Surgical and Medical Instruments (SIC 3841) Trends and Forecasts
(millions of dollars except as noted)

	1992	1993	1994	1995	1996	1997[1]	1998[1]	1999[2]	2000[3]	Percent Change 97–98	98–99	99–00	96–00[4]
Industry data													
Value of shipments[5]	13,396	15,113	14,809	15,681	17,042	18,018	19,560	20,815	22,063	8.6	6.4	6.0	6.7
Value of shipments (1992$)	13,396	14,860	14,448	15,136	16,262	16,807	18,195	19,238	20,168	8.3	5.7	4.8	5.5
Total employment (thousands)	98.2	103	99.7	101	104	104	107			2.9			
Production workers (thousands)	58.5	61.4	59.6	60.4	61.8	62.4							
Average hourly earnings ($)	10.88	11.32	11.53	11.83	12.16	12.73							
Capital expenditures	689	809	619	619	673	697							
Product data													
Value of shipments[5]	13,276	14,759	14,264	14,936	16,192	17,278	18,660	19,779	20,767	8.0	6.0	5.0	6.4
Value of shipments (1992$)	13,276	14,512	13,916	14,417	15,450	16,117	17,358	18,280	18,983	7.7	5.3	3.8	5.3
Trade data													
Value of imports	1,224	1,429	1,511	1,714	1,897	2,048	2,421	3,123	3,748	18.2	29.0	20.0	18.6
Value of exports	2,596	2,694	2,658	2,991	3,622	4,223	4,504	4,715	5,045	6.7	4.7	7.0	8.6

[1] Estimate except imports and exports.
[2] Estimate.
[3] Forecast.
[4] Compound annual rate.
[5] For a definition of industry versus product values, see "Getting the Most Out of *Outlook 2000.*"
Source: U.S. Department of Commerce: Bureau of the Census; International Trade Administration.

tech products such as coronary catheters may support export growth of 2 to 5 percent in 2000. U.S. exports to China grew sharply in 1999 at 62 percent, and demand should remain high in 2000 as that nation continues to make health care improvements for its citizens. Latin America faces economic uncertainty in 2000, with the Andean region in recession, and slow growth for Mexico and Brazil. U.S. exports of surgical instruments may grow 2 percent in 2000, an improvement over a decrease of 5 percent in 1999.

While exports of surgical instruments continued to grow overall, the real story in 1999 was the 29 percent growth rate of imports. The United States bought $3.1 billion in surgical instruments and supplies from foreign sources in 1999. One of the factors behind this dramatic increase was devalued currency in certain key foreign markets that made U.S. equipment more expensive and a strong dollar that made purchasing foreign equipment cost-effective. This sector includes numerous price-sensitive lower-technology devices, making the substitution of imported products easier than it is in higher-technology sectors. Another important factor was the sudden increase in U.S. imports of cannulae, up 155 percent, and bougies, drains, and sondes, up 60 percent in 1999. These numbers were strongly

TABLE 44-4: U.S. Trade Patterns in Surgical and Medical Instruments[1] in 1998
(millions of dollars; percent)

Exports			Imports		
Region[2]	Value[3]	Share, %	Region[2]	Value[3]	Share, %
NAFTA	779	17	NAFTA	440	18
Latin America	304	7	Latin America	392	16
Western Europe	2,060	46	Western Europe	765	32
Japan/Chinese Economic Area	852	19	Japan/Chinese Economic Area	493	20
Other Asia	150	3	Other Asia	176	7
Rest of world	358	8	Rest of world	155	6
World	4,504	100	World	2,421	100
Top Five Countries	Value	Share, %	Top Five Countries	Value	Share, %
Japan	731	16	Mexico	385	16
Canada	469	10	Dominican Republic	320	13
Netherlands	437	10	Germany	281	12
France	394	9	Japan	230	9
Mexico	311	7	China	221	9

[1] SIC 3841.
[2] For definitions of regional groupings, see "Getting the Most Out of *Outlook 2000.*"
[3] Values may not sum to total due to rounding.
Source: U.S. Department of Commerce, Bureau of the Census.

influenced by Israel and Ireland, which affected the overall import statistics with their staggering quadruple-digit export growth of cannulae and, to a lesser extent, bougies, drains, and sondes and nonhypodermic syringes. A portion of this growth can be attributed to the fact that Ireland assembles some syringes and surgical instruments from U.S. components for reexportation to the United States; however, the numbers are small in comparison. Ireland has invested heavily in its medical equipment manufacturing industry and has concentrated on one of the growth and volume leaders in this sector: catheter-related technology. At the same time, U.S. exports to Ireland of surgical instruments dropped 30 percent in 1999. The Dominican Republic's 13 percent share of the U.S. import market can be explained by the significant amount of U.S. components shipped there for assembly and then reexported back to the United States. Instruments and appliances used in medical, surgical, dental, and veterinary sciences are the second largest import item from the Dominican Republic of products assembled from U.S. parts or components. Despite some of these high import growth rates, the United States had a $2 billion trade surplus in surgical instruments in 1999.

Two areas of this sector lead the way for the U.S. industry currently and will provide the best opportunity for continued market dominance: advances in catheters and minimally invasive surgery (MIS). These areas are also extremely competitive, and this has encouraged continued incremental improvements as U.S. firms battle for market share.

The catheter market is the single largest export segment, and it continues to grow. The United States dominates the market with approximately 75 percent of world market share. The catheter market is one of the most dynamic markets in this sector as advances in technology are changing use, design, and demand worldwide. The largest segment of the catheter market consists of dialysis and urinary catheters, which are used routinely in health care and are benefiting from increasing demand in emerging markets. Production and demand for vascular interventions such as stents and other catheters used in cardiac-related procedures, while representing a much smaller segment, are growing at double-digit rates. As the need for cardiac care increases and as competition heats up in this sector, the United States will continue to dominate and demand will continue to rise steadily for the next several years.

Minimally invasive endoscopic surgery (MIES) is another rising star in the surgical instruments sector and a technology that has benefited from cost-cutting pressures. Increasingly, certain surgical procedures are conducted by inserting either a rigid or a flexible endoscope into a small incision in the body. MIES technology slashes health care costs, as most of these procedures are performed on an outpatient basis, eliminating the need for expensive hospital stays. It also eliminates much of the pain and complications associated with traditional surgical procedures, and these factors have made it very appealing to managed care providers. The use of minimally invasive procedures is clearly the trend now and for the future. While MIES is in its infancy, it should grow enormously as surgeons become more comfortable using it. Simpler surgeries, such as gallbladder removal, are performed using minimally invasive laparoscopy so often that the cost savings, ease of procedure, and concern for the comfort of the patient have caused a sharp increase in the incidence of gallbladder removal; that, say managed care providers, is a cost increase, not a decrease. As the industry and the technology progress over the next few years, minimally invasive techniques will be used in cardiovascular surgeries, quite possibly making "open heart surgery" a thing of the past. The MIES market is expected to grow 5 percent annually through the year 2003. Another high-growth area of MIS is minimally invasive cardiothoracic surgery (MICS), which should experience double-digit growth for the next 4 years.

One of the reasons MIS is such a dynamic field of technology is its ability to be linked with other advanced technologies, such as robotics. Two California firms have created surgical robotic systems: the Zeus Robotic Surgical System designed by Computer Motions Inc. and the da Vinci Surgical System designed by Intuitive Surgical, Inc. In 1999, those two systems broke new ground by successfully performing heart bypass surgery through only three small holes rather than with the patient's chest cracked open. The Zeus system used three-dimensional (3-D) imaging and voice-activated technology to guide robotic arms and a camera through three holes in the patient's chest. Da Vinci uses similar 3-D imaging and robotic arms, yet the surgeon moves his or her hands on "virtual" pencil-sized instruments resting below a monitor that transfers the surgeon's movements to the robotic surgical instruments. Neither system has received FDA approval, but both have the CE mark. This method of heart surgery may not be quickly adopted by surgeons, but it demonstrates the direction of the industry. It also demonstrates how integral the fields of computing, software, micromanufacturing, and telecommunications are to modern medical technology; as advances in those fields continue, sales of new medical devices will increase.

Other factors will play an important role in the surgical instruments market in the next several years. The movement to home health care will increase demand for and spur innovation in traditional lower-tech technologies such as IV drug infusion equipment, blood pressure equipment, and medical furniture by making them more compact, lighter, and easier to use by the patient. The needle and syringe markets will be greatly affected by home health care and the need to protect health workers from accidental needlesticks. Already U.S. firms are responding to the proposed Health Care Worker Needlestick Reduction Act by improving the safety of needles with retraction, blunting, and other mechanisms. As blood-borne pathogens such as the human immunodeficiency virus (HIV) and the hepatitis virus remain at epidemic levels worldwide, health care workers and public health policy makers will demand safer technologies for treating patients, and sales and innovation will increase. U.S. instruments will be preferred as they will lead the way in this innovative technology to improved safety.

Valerie Barth, U.S. Department of Commerce, Office of Microelectronics, Medical Equipment and Instrumentation, (202) 482-3360, Valerie_Barth@ita.doc.gov, September 1999.

SURGICAL APPLIANCES AND SUPPLIES

In 1999, the value of U.S. shipments of surgical appliances and supplies (SIC 3842) increased 6.5 percent to $18 billion and is expected to continue a steady climb to almost $19 billion by the year 2000 (see Table 44-5). This industry segment produces a broad array of products, ranging from sutures and bandages to wheelchairs, prosthetics, and implantable devices.

Total employment increased 2.1 percent in 1999 over 1998. Sixty-three percent of those workers were production workers.

Global and Domestic Outlook

U.S. exports of surgical appliances and supplies increased 8.9 percent in 1999 to reach 2.7 billion. Assuming similar growth in 2000, exports should exceed $2.9 billion. The largest markets for this type of medical devices are in western Europe, where almost half of U.S. exports are destined. The United States has enjoyed a healthy trade surplus with this region: In 1998, exports were almost double imports. The single largest country market for surgical appliances and supplies is Canada, which purchased equipment valued at $350 million. Again, the United States has had a sizable trade surplus with this trading partner: Exports to Canada were over three times imports from that country. U.S. manufacturers enjoy a zero-for-zero tariff structure with Canada under the provisions of NAFTA (see Table 44-6).

Despite recent economic uncertainty in Japan, that country has maintained its status as a principal purchaser of U.S. surgical appliances and supplies. No longer the largest single country market for this merchandise, Japan nevertheless imported $307 million of U.S.-made appliances in 1998. Japan's aging population is the element that makes that country a stable market for most health care devices. Significant need for health care in Japan, despite economic downturns, accounts for a relatively inelastic demand curve.

In the year 2000, the value of U.S. industry shipments is expected to increase 4 percent to $18.8 billion. Innovative cost-cutting measures are a driving factor in expanding sales of these products. Growing reliance on outpatient rather than inpatient procedures fuels sales of items in this category, especially those intended to reduce labor expenses, curtail hospital stays, and permit patient care in less expensive settings. A burgeoning trend toward limiting reimbursement rates has placed emphasis on lowering overall costs in this product category. For example, patient infection control in any setting is essential to the maintenance of community health and prevents further health care expenditures. As newer-technology products are developed, overall health care costs diminish. Occupational Safety and Health Administration (OSHA) regulations specify sterilization and other procedures to prevent the spread of infection in health care settings. Sterilization equipment has enjoyed constant demand as a result. Technological advances and the desire to improve the safety of the workplace for health care providers will guarantee continued prosperity for the industry.

Industry experts predict that the surgical appliances and supplies industry will continue to expand in 1999 and 2000. The aging populations of developed economies, including the United States, western Europe, and Japan, create a heavy demand for appliances and supplies. Furthermore, economies of scale have contained the price of higher-technology goods, where the United States leads in production. Decreasing unit costs make this merchandise more attractive to developing economies. Funds used for medical purposes are therefore increasingly more effective in maintaining community health. Increasing expenditures on health care in general, including the construction of clinics and improved access to health care, are becoming more prevalent in developing

TABLE 44-5: Surgical Appliances and Supplies (SIC 3842) Trends and Forecasts
(millions of dollars except as noted)

	1992	1993	1994	1995	1996	1997[1]	1998[1]	1999[2]	2000[3]	Percent Change 97–98	98–99	99–00	96–00[4]
Industry data													
Value of shipments[5]	13,801	14,553	14,423	14,759	15,874	16,447	17,041	18,150	18,880	3.6	6.5	4.0	4.4
Value of shipments (1992$)	13,801	14,034	13,479	13,794	14,630	14,854	15,082	15,500	15,765	1.5	2.8	1.7	1.9
Total employment (thousands)	96.4	98.0	95.4	92.4	93.1	94.0							
Production workers (thousands)	61.6	61.9	58.9	58.2	59.7	60.0							
Average hourly earnings ($)	10.84	10.93	11.14	11.51	11.58	11.77							
Capital expenditures	504	433	372	396	519	531							
Product data													
Value of shipments[5]	12,438	13,285	13,145	13,317	14,304	14,822	15,358	16,350	17,008	3.6	6.5	4.0	4.4
Value of shipments (1992$)	12,438	12,811	12,285	12,446	13,184	13,386	13,591	13,975	14,215	1.5	2.8	1.7	1.9
Trade data													
Value of imports	765	766	830	1,020	1,116	1,334	1,631	1,845	2,097	22.3	13.1	13.7	17.1
Value of exports	1,493	1,630	1,777	1,988	2,173	2,436	2,479	2,699	2,938	1.8	8.9	8.9	7.8

[1] Estimate except imports and exports.
[2] Estimate.
[3] Forecast.
[4] Compound annual rate.
[5] For a definition of industry versus product values, see "Getting the Most Out of *Outlook 2000.*"
Source: U.S. Department of Commerce: Bureau of the Census; International Trade Administration.

TABLE 44-6: U.S. Trade Patterns in Surgical Appliances and Supplies[1] in 1998
(millions of dollars; percent)

Exports			Imports		
Region[2]	Value[3]	Share, %	Region[2]	Value[3]	Share, %
NAFTA	437	18	NAFTA	489	30
Latin America	252	10	Latin America	3	0
Western Europe	1,119	45	Western Europe	617	38
Japan/Chinese Economic Area	375	15	Japan/Chinese Economic Area	204	13
Other Asia	86	3	Other Asia	126	8
Rest of world	210	8	Rest of world	192	12
World	2,479	100	World	1,631	100
Top Five Countries	Value	Share, %	Top Five Countries	Value	Share, %
Canada	350	14	Mexico	385	24
Japan	307	12	Israel	106	7
United Kingdom	215	9	Canada	103	6
Netherlands	184	7	United Kingdom	99	6
Germany	173	7	Denmark	93	6

[1] SIC 3842.
[2] For definitions of regional groupings, see "Getting the Most Out of *Outlook 2000.*"
[3] Values may not sum to total due to rounding.
Source: U.S. Department of Commerce, Bureau of the Census.

economies, allowing for an improving community health care picture worldwide.

The importance of infection control in any health care setting has always been paramount to ensure community health and forestall complications. During the 1999–2000 period, many developing economies will focus on improving the health care environment by decreasing the spread of infection in hospitals and clinics. These nations also will purchase more disposables and equipment to protect health care workers. Adding importance to infection control is concern for improved safety of health care workers. Sterilization equipment as well as disposable and reusable barrier equipment (goggles, masks, gloves) will be of growing relevance in established as well as new medical facilities worldwide.

N. Gerard Zapiain, U.S. Department of Commerce, Office of Microelectronics, Medical Equipment and Instrumentation, (202) 482-2410, Gerry_Zapiain@ita.doc.gov, September 1999.

DENTAL EQUIPMENT AND SUPPLIES

The U.S. dental equipment and supplies industry (SIC 3843) covers U.S. manufacturers of equipment, instruments, and supplies used by dentists, dental hygienists, laboratories, and colleges. Specific products include dental hand instruments, plaster, drills, amalgams, cements, sterilizers, and dental chairs.

Global and Domestic Outlook

In the United States, the widening availability of fluoridated water and improved in-home dental products from toothpaste to bleaching processes since the mid-1980s has improved dental health. Despite the proliferation of home products, the number of dentists has increased as Americans have become more aware of dental health.

In the year 2000, the value of shipments of U.S. dental equipment and supplies is expected to increase 5.1 percent over 1999, reaching $3.1 billion (see Table 44-7). The driving force behind growth in the domestic market is a fundamental redefinition of the dental industry. Demand for dental equipment will continue to rise as Americans change their attitude toward dentistry. No longer is a visit to the dentist a painful but necessary experience to prevent losing teeth. Dental appointments are now frequently part of a self-improvement program, similar to exercise and a proper diet. Americans are returning to the dentist more often to improve the appearance of the teeth as well as to maintain health.

Besides advances in technology, in which the United States has historically led the way, an increase in disposable income has allowed more individuals to opt for more elective dental procedures, especially cosmetic and restorative procedures. An amalgam filling, functional or not, can be replaced with a color-matched composite, and gold crowns can be deposed by white porcelain.

Pain management has assumed an important role in dentistry as practitioners have learned that many individuals avoid visits to the dentist for fear of discomfort or to avoid an unpleasant experience. For this reason, dentists are employing creative means to make patients feel as comfortable as possible and make the visit almost enjoyable. Recently, the FDA approved the use of lasers to remove tooth decay. Unlike even the highest-speed drill, lasers produce no vibration, are noiseless, and cause less trauma to healthy tissue.

Another innovation that has become more prevalent in recent years is the intraoral camera, a device that allows the patient to use a screen to monitor work as it progresses. With the intraoral camera, uncertainty is replaced by a vivid image. The intraoral camera also helps the dentist explain to the patient the nature and importance of procedures. Practitioners are thus able to demon-

TABLE 44-7: Dental Equipment and Supplies (SIC 3843) Trends and Forecasts
(millions of dollars except as noted)

	1992	1993	1994	1995	1996	1997[1]	1998[1]	1999[2]	2000[3]	Percent Change 97–98	98–99	99–00	96–00[4]
Industry data													
Value of shipments[5]	1,914	2,012	2,191	2,237	2,366	2,525	2,715	2,950	3,100	7.5	8.7	5.1	7.0
Value of shipments (1992$)	1,914	1,946	2,087	2,100	2,196	2,325	2,480	2,660	2,780	6.7	7.3	4.5	6.1
Total employment (thousands)	15.1	15.4	15.2	16.5	16.4	16.8							
Production workers (thousands)	8.9	9.2	9.7	10.5	11.2	11.9							
Average hourly earnings ($)	11.50	11.89	11.49	11.66	11.46	11.45							
Capital expenditures	48.6	58.5	51.7	75.6	45.8	48.2							
Product data													
Value of shipments[5]	1,621	1,664	1,917	2,027	2,172	2,350	2,555	2,800	3,029	8.7	9.6	8.2	8.7
Value of shipments (1992$)	1,621	1,609	1,826	1,903	2,017	2,159	2,325	2,525	2,705	7.7	8.6	7.1	7.6
Trade data													
Value of imports	230	226	221	262	274	312	348	374	402	11.5	7.5	7.5	10.1
Value of exports	448	498	512	574	632	637	633	671	712	–0.6	6.0	6.1	3.0

[1] Estimate except imports and exports.
[2] Estimate.
[3] Forecast.
[4] Compound annual rate.
[5] For a definition of industry versus product values, see "Getting the Most Out of *Outlook 2000*."
Source: U.S. Department of Commerce: Bureau of the Census; International Trade Administration.

strate to patients the need for preventive treatments without taking more drastic measures later, such as root canals and tooth extractions, practices that are becoming less prevalent.

The intraoral camera, coupled with other video devices, has enabled practitioners to show patients how they can improve the appearance of their dentition. Sales of image-improving products and services that until recently were scarcely used or unavailable have soared.

The United States has historically accounted for approximately 50 percent of the global market for dental equipment and supplies. U.S. manufacturers of dental equipment and supplies have proved to be competitive in recent years. Total exports of these products in 1998 totaled $633 million, representing a trade surplus of $285 million.

The largest markets for U.S. dental equipment continue to be in western Europe, particularly France and Germany. Sales of U.S.-made dental equipment and supplies totaled $277 million in 1998, representing 44 percent of total exports of subject merchandise that year (see Table 44-8). The single largest country market for U.S. dental equipment and supplies is Canada, which purchased $105 million in 1998, creating a trade surplus of $77 million with that country. Total sales of dental equipment and supplies to Canada alone in 1998 represented an increase of over 20 percent since 1996. Furthermore, U.S. dental manufac-

TABLE 44-8: U.S. Trade Patterns in Dental Equipment and Supplies[1] in 1998
(millions of dollars; percent)

Exports			Imports		
Region[2]	Value[3]	Share, %	Region[2]	Value[3]	Share, %
NAFTA	135	21	NAFTA	47	13
Latin America	43	7	Latin America	5	1
Western Europe	277	44	Western Europe	219	63
Japan/Chinese Economic Area	80	13	Japan/Chinese Economic Area	64	18
Other Asia	22	3	Other Asia	7	2
Rest of world	76	12	Rest of world	6	2
World	633	100	World	348	100
Top Five Countries	Value	Share, %	Top Five Countries	Value	Share, %
Canada	105	17	Germany	114	33
Germany	73	11	Japan	53	15
Japan	52	8	Switzerland	37	11
France	47	7	Canada	28	8
Australia	34	5	Mexico	19	5

[1] SIC 3843.
[2] For definitions of regional groupings, see "Getting the Most Out of *Outlook 2000*."
[3] Values may not sum to total due to rounding.
Source: U.S. Department of Commerce, Bureau of the Census.

turers enjoy a zero-for-zero tariff preference with Canada under the provisions of NAFTA.

The industry has also seen an upsurge in sales to the Japan/Chinese Economic Area. Sales of $28 million to that area represent an increase of 40 percent since 1996. As is the case in many countries, the Japan/Chinese Economic Area's increase in demand for U.S. dental products is spurred by economic growth, higher income levels, increased access to dental clinics, and greater awareness of dental hygiene.

The European Union is still the most promising export market for the foreseeable future. As in the United States, elective procedures there constitute an ever-increasing source of revenue for the industry.

During the 1999–2004 period, the market for dental equipment should continue to expand. In the United States as well as in other developed markets, consumers will be willing to spend increasing amounts of disposable income on new technologies intended to improve their dental health and refine their dental appearance. Dental practitioners have worked hard to change the image of their industry from a last-resort means of preventing tooth loss to a first-line means of promoting overall health and appearance. As GDP expands, more emphasis is put on dentistry. The Chinese Economic Area (CEA) is a good example of this trend. Although the CEA is not the largest market for dental equipment and supplies, increases in purchases in that region have followed the expanding economy. Manufacturers, given the nature of current dental procedures, would do best to target markets whose economies have increasing disposable income.

N. Gerard Zapiain, U.S. Department of Commerce, Office of Microelectronics, Medical Equipment and Instrumentation, (202) 482-2410, Gerry_Zapiain@ita.doc.gov, September 1999.

X-RAY AND ELECTROMEDICAL EQUIPMENT

Electromedical equipment (SIC 3845) manufacturers produce a variety of powered devices, including pacemakers and patient-monitoring systems, as well as diagnostic imaging equipment, including informatics equipment, ultrasonic scanning devices, and MRI machines. X-ray apparatus (SIC 3844), which includes computed tomography equipment, is also imaging equipment. Because of the significant trends common to all types of imaging equipment, this section will discuss both industry segments.

Global and Domestic Outlook

In the latter half of the 1990s, domestic shipments of electromedical and x-ray equipment experienced minimal growth. Measured in constant dollars between 1996 and 2000, shipments of electromedical devices are expected to grow 13 percent to almost $10.3 billion, while x-ray apparatus and tubes will grow only 1 percent to just under $4 billion. The most recent employment figures for both segments of the industry at the time of publication, 1992–1996, also indicate slight growth, increasing only 1 to 2 percent yearly. However, for the same period, total employment for x-ray apparatus and tubes alone decreased yearly by 1 to 2 percent (see Tables 44-9 and 44-10).

The minimal growth in electromedical and x-ray shipments is partially linked to the Y2K problem, which has the potential to affect many electromedical and x-ray devices. While manufacturers are responsible for compliance, health care institutions have expended capital and personnel resources on Y2K that otherwise might have been spent on new purchases. Additionally, cost containment has been a powerful domestic trend affecting sales of diagnostic electromedical and x-ray equip-

TABLE 44-9: Electromedical Equipment (SIC 3845) Trends and Forecasts
(millions of dollars except as noted)

	1992	1993	1994	1995	1996	1997[1]	1998[1]	1999[2]	2000[3]	Percent Change 97–98	98–99	99–00	96–00[4]
Industry data													
Value of shipments[5]	7,189	7,186	7,512	7,116	8,491	8,915	9,093	9,548	9,739	2.0	5.0	2.0	3.5
Value of shipments (1992$)	7,189	7,193	7,713	7,382	9,013	9,463	9,652	10,134	10,336	2.0	5.0	2.0	3.5
Total employment (thousands)	40.1	39.9	39.2	41.1	42.0	42.4	43.0	43.4	43.8	1.4	0.9	0.9	1.1
Production workers (thousands)	18.1	17.6	17.6	17.8	18.0	18.2	18.6	18.8	19.0	2.2	1.1	1.1	1.4
Average hourly earnings ($)	11.94	12.12	12.60	12.88	13.43	13.70	14.00	14.25	14.54	2.2	1.8	2.0	2.0
Capital expenditures	255	241	306	290	350								
Product data													
Value of shipments[5]	6,306	6,515	6,895	6,988	8,502	8,927	9,105	9,560	9,846	2.0	5.0	3.0	3.7
Value of shipments (1992$)	6,306	6,521	7,079	7,249	9,025	9,476	9,665	10,148	10,452	2.0	5.0	3.0	3.7
Trade data													
Value of imports	1,263	1,281	1,285	1,396	1,475	1,691	1,995	2,274	2,615	18.0	14.0	15.0	15.4
Value of exports	2,255	2,396	2,820	3,092	3,559	3,630	3,684	3,942	4,139	1.5	7.0	5.0	3.8

[1] Estimate except imports and exports.
[2] Estimate.
[3] Forecast.
[4] Compound annual rate.
[5] For a definition of industry versus product values, see "Getting the Most Out of *Outlook 2000.*"
Source: U.S. Department of Commerce: Bureau of the Census; International Trade Administration.

TABLE 44-10: X-Ray Apparatus and Tubes (SIC 3844) Trends and Forecasts
(millions of dollars except as noted)

	1992	1993	1994	1995	1996	1997[1]	1998[1]	1999[2]	2000[3]	Percent Change 97–98	98–99	99–00	96–00[4]
Industry data													
Value of shipments[5]	3,235	3,372	3,373	3,620	3,634	3,769	3,844	3,920	3,998	2.0	2.0	2.0	2.4
Value of shipments (1992$)	3,235	3,352	3,330	3,549	3,528	3,556	3,556	3,556	3,556	0.0	0.0	0.0	0.2
Total employment (thousands)	14.3	14.2	14.0	13.9	13.4	13.2	13.0	12.8	12.2	–1.5	–1.5	–4.7	–2.3
Production workers (thousands)	7.1	6.9	6.6	6.6	6.3	6.1	6.1	6.0	6.0	0.0	–1.6	0.0	–1.2
Average hourly earnings ($)	14.79	15.44	15.28	15.35	16.05	16.37	16.70	17.03	17.37	2.0	2.0	2.0	2.0
Capital expenditures	63.6	85.6	84.8	95.9	60.0								
Product data													
Value of shipments[5]	2,360	2,510	2,494	2,695	2,960	3,197	3,357	3,525	3,701	5.0	5.0	5.0	5.7
Value of shipments (1992$)	2,360	2,495	2,462	2,642	2,874	3,104	3,352	3,520	3,696	8.0	5.0	5.0	6.5
Trade data													
Value of imports	1,102	1,167	1,062	1,139	1,170	1,161	1,274	1,337	1,403	9.7	4.9	4.9	4.6
Value of exports	782	824	966	1,158	1,182	1,286	1,306	1,371	1,467	1.6	5.0	7.0	5.5

[1] Estimate except imports and exports.
[2] Estimate.
[3] Forecast.
[4] Compound annual rate.
[5] For a definition of industry versus product values, see "Getting the Most Out of *Outlook 2000.*"
Source: U.S. Department of Commerce: Bureau of the Census; International Trade Administration.

ment and will continue to be significant for the foreseeable future. Radiology tests have been identified as a significant source of expenditure, and this has led to the adoption of utilization management programs. These programs attempt to reduce the number of tests ordered by physicians and ensure the maximum use of each piece of equipment. These factors have combined to reduce demand for ultrasound, MRI, CT, and other diagnostic imaging devices.

The integration of radiology with information systems is the most significant trend affecting diagnostic imaging and will profoundly influence product development and purchasing decisions over the next 5 years and beyond. The initial indication of this trend is the growing popularity of picture archiving and communications systems (PACS). PACS replace traditional film with digital technology that may be stored with a patient's medical history. Doctors have remote access to this information, reducing reviewing time and allowing for an increased caseload per doctor. PACS also eliminate the need for film, developing chemicals, and processing labor, leading to considerable savings. According to *Medical Imaging,* U.S. health care systems spend up to $7 billion a year on film alone. Upcoming innovations include the integration of digital diagnostic imaging with the Internet and other clinical and business information systems. GE, Agilent (formerly HP Medical), and other imaging equipment manufacturers are partnering with information technology companies to ensure that their products are Web-compatible and become part of other networks used by health care institutions.

Demographics and technological advances will continue to increase demand for pacemakers and defibrillators well into the twenty-first century. While under significant price pressure from group purchasing and heavy competition, leading manufacturers such as Medtronic and Guidant report yearly double-digit growth in cardiac rhythm management products. Demand for automatic external defibrillators (AEDs) is growing rapidly as a result of technological advances and published studies indicating that faster access to AEDs increases survival rates among victims of sudden cardiac arrest. Businesses that serve large numbers of people at one time, such as airlines, as well as private citizens are purchasing AEDs in record numbers. AEDs, once used exclusively by hospitals and paramedics, are being produced in portable, easy-to-use models at increasingly affordable prices. As the population ages and more people learn about AEDs, sales are likely to increase.

In the global arena, the United States is maintaining a trade surplus in the electromedical equipment and x-ray apparatus sectors, but the gap is narrowing. An increase in imports suggests that U.S.-manufactured electromedical and x-ray equipment is facing stronger competition from overseas. Imports of electromedical equipment jumped 77 percent from $1.48 billion in 1996 to an estimated $2.6 billion in 2000. More than half those imports were from the EU, led by Germany, and Japan. Most of the remaining imports were from Singapore and Israel. Similarly, imports of x-ray equipment increased 20 percent from $1.17 billion in 1996 to an estimated $1.4 billion in 2000. More than half those imports were from Germany and Japan. The bulk of the remainder was sourced from other EU countries.

Exports have also increased, but at a slower rate than have imports. Exports of electromedical equipment are expected to increase an average of 16 percent to over $4.1 billion between 1996 and 2000. Exports of x-ray apparatus and tubes should increase 24 percent to $1.4 billion during this period.

Overseas demand for U.S.-manufactured pacemakers and cardiac defibrillators doubled from 1993 to 1998, reaching a total of $273 million. The top three countries receiving U.S. exports—Germany, Japan, and Canada—represent 51 percent of the exported pacemaker and defibrillator market. Three of the top 10 largest markets for U.S.-manufactured pacemakers and defibrillators—Japan, Korea, and Brazil—contracted between 1997 and 2000 because of the economic recession in those countries. Demand in those markets will increase as the recovery in their economies strengthens.

In terms of regions, the EU has the highest demand and also the highest rate of growth, averaging 45 percent per year from 1996 through 1999. As the European population ages, the need for pacemakers and cardiac defibrillators will increase. While the European market for implantable pacemakers and defibrillators matures, price and public health reimbursement policies are likely to be the biggest factors affecting future growth. Demographic factors indicate that for external defibrillators, the greatest demand will be from Europe, which will follow the high-sales trend for compact, user-friendly models that are popular in the United States. The emerging economies of Latin America and Asia also hold great potential as markets for implantable pacemakers and defibrillators. In preparation, all the leading manufacturers have established direct sales forces in those regions. One U.S. company, Medtronic, has begun manufacturing in China for sale in China and exportation to other emerging markets.

The largest export markets for U.S.-manufactured imaging equipment are Japan and the EU countries, led by Germany. These markets are reaching maturity and are under severe cost-cutting pressure, making innovation and reimbursement policies the key to future market growth for U.S. exports. Throughout the EU, shifts from institutional care toward outpatient care and a move from curative care toward preventive care suggest an increase in demand for diagnostic imaging equipment. However, growing health costs will require an increased effort on the part of manufacturers to provide a cost-benefit justification for purchases. In Japan, U.S. exporters will see benefits from similar shifts to outpatient and preventive care as well as deregulation measures negotiated between the U.S. and Japanese governments. As a result of the U.S. Department of Commerce–led MOSS talks in 1999, local governments in Japan were authorized to base medical device purchases on the best overall value for performance and specification requirements, not simply on the initial cost of the devices. However, as the Japanese government searches for solutions to rapidly inflating health care costs, exporters may experience additional reimbursement obstacles.

In the developing economies of Asia and Latin America, growing populations, increases in per capita income, and popular demand for improved health care suggest strong markets for exports of imaging equipment; however, the future of imaging equipment exports is largely dependent on overall economic stability. Since 1996, widely fluctuating regional export figures have reflected regional economic turmoil.

Among the developing countries in Asia, China has the greatest demand for U.S.-manufactured imaging equipment. Figures from the 1996–1999 period indicate fluctuation in the demand for most types of imaging equipment. However, x-ray apparatus and tubes for radiography and radiotherapy and scintigraphic apparatus, which are used in the practice of nuclear medicine, have sustained strong growth rates. While most U.S. manufacturers of imaging equipment have a significant presence in China, India's new policy on trade liberalization and its growing middle class have recently drawn the attention of those manufacturers. In addition to the potential of India's market, which increased demand for U.S. imaging equipment exports by an annual average of 15 percent from 1996 through 1999, manufacturers see India as a manufacturing base for exports to other south Asian countries. In 1999, GE Medical Systems decided to set up its fifth production unit in India to manufacture accessories for x-ray machines. GE Medical Systems eventually will export ultrasound equipment and x-ray system components.

TABLE 44-11: U.S. Trade Patterns in Electromedical Equipment[1] in 1998
(millions of dollars; percent)

Exports			Imports		
Region[2]	Value[3]	Share, %	Region[2]	Value[3]	Share, %
NAFTA	274	7	NAFTA	256	13
Latin America	280	8	Latin America	1	0
Western Europe	1,842	50	Western Europe	697	35
Japan/Chinese Economic Area	851	23	Japan/Chinese Economic Area	706	35
Other Asia	124	3	Other Asia	208	10
Rest of world	313	9	Rest of world	127	6
World	3,684	100	World	1,995	100
Top Five Countries	Value	Share, %	Top Five Countries	Value	Share, %
Japan	668	18	Japan	633	32
Germany	479	13	Germany	354	18
Netherlands	332	9	Mexico	193	10
Canada	203	6	Singapore	141	7
France	194	5	Israel	119	6

[1] SIC 3845.
[2] For definitions of regional groupings, see "Getting the Most Out of *Outlook 2000*."
[3] Values may not sum to total due to rounding.
Source: U.S. Department of Commerce, Bureau of the Census.

TABLE 44-12: U.S. Trade Patterns in X-Ray Apparatus and Tubes[1] in 1998
(millions of dollars; percent)

Exports			Imports		
Region[2]	Value[3]	Share, %	Region[2]	Value[3]	Share, %
NAFTA	117	9	NAFTA	21	2
Latin America	106	8	Latin America	3	0
Western Europe	608	47	Western Europe	975	77
Japan/Chinese Economic Area	313	24	Japan/Chinese Economic Area	249	20
Other Asia	59	5	Other Asia	6	1
Rest of world	103	8	Rest of world	19	1
World	1,306	100	World	1,274	100
Top Five Countries	Value	Share, %	Top Five Countries	Value	Share, %
Japan	222	17	Germany	435	34
Germany	153	12	Japan	246	19
France	121	9	Netherlands	172	14
Canada	94	7	France	144	11
Belgium	93	7	United Kingdom	75	6

[1] SIC 3844.
[2] For definitions of regional groupings, see "Getting the Most Out of *Outlook 2000*."
[3] Values may not sum to total due to rounding.
Source: U.S. Department of Commerce, Bureau of the Census.

In Latin America, Brazil has the greatest demand for U.S. imaging equipment exports, accounting for 44 percent of the entire Latin American market in 1998. Demographics, the responsiveness of the Ministry of Health to public demand for improved access to health care, and growth of the private health sector indicate that this market should continue to grow. However, economic instability and escalating registration fees may prevent continued increases in exports to this market. Expansion of regional trade agreements such as MERCOSUR and NAFTA will benefit U.S. exports of imaging equipment to other Latin American countries.

Imaging equipment exports to the Middle East and eastern Europe have grown rapidly in recent years as a result of aid from international organizations such as the World Bank and the World Health Organization. While the need for equipment in those regions is great, resources are limited. U.S. manufacturers enjoy name recognition and a reputation for high quality; however, exports to those regions probably will continue to depend on foreign aid (see Tables 44-11 and 44-12).

Lauren Saadat, U.S. Department of Commerce, Office of Microelectronics, Medical Equipment and Instrumentation, (202) 482-4431, Lauren_Saadat@ita.doc.gov, September 1999.

PREOWNED MEDICAL EQUIPMENT

Since the mid-1980s, the market for preowned equipment (ranging from "as is" to remanufactured) has been stimulated by a variety of factors on both the supply and demand sides, especially in the United States. On the supply side, the widespread U.S. practice of leasing rather than purchasing medical device capital equipment generates a steady stream of used equipment. While depreciated, such capital equipment still has a useful life. In addition, noncapital medical equipment often is replaced by health care providers eager to adopt updated technologies. Much of this equipment also has remaining useful life. On the demand side, the effort to trim health care costs and shift care to nonhospital settings has created a demand for preowned equipment. In addition to lowering equipment costs, the purchase of preowned equipment can enable health care providers to obtain low-cost backup equipment and simplify training by replacing equipment with similar refurbished equipment. Preowned medical equipment is exported to foreign countries seeking lower-cost equipment.

Because leasing arrangements are less common in Europe and Japan, the United States has been the dominant source of capital medical equipment in the secondary market. According to industry observers, approximately 80 percent of preowned capital equipment came from U.S. sources in 1998, compared with just 10 percent from Europe, 5 percent from Japan, 4 percent from Canada, and 1 percent from Australia. In 1999, however, industry observers reported that an increased percentage of used medical devices was coming from Europe and Japan, with the percentage from the United States correspondingly declining. This trend was expected to continue in the year 2000, but the United States remains far and away the largest source of preowned capital medical devices. Although no similar data exist for noncapital preowned medical equipment, the United States is believed to be the dominant global supplier to this market as well.

The United States is also the largest market for preowned medical devices. U.S. trade statistics, however, do not differentiate between new and preowned equipment. In the absence of such data, industry estimates of the market for preowned medical equipment vary widely. For 1998, for example, one industry source estimated the U.S. market at $200 million to $300 million while placing the combined market of Europe, the Middle East, and Africa at $90 million to $120 million, Latin America at $30 million to $50 million, the republics of the former Soviet Union (i.e., the Commonwealth of Independent States) at $20 million to $30 million, and India and Pakistan together at $30 million to $50 million. Combined, the market for preowned medical equipment in those regions added up to $370 million to $550 million. Because such estimates of market size typically are based on a sampling of vendors, some industry observers view these estimates as suspect.

A key market not included in these estimates was China, which had been projected by industry observers to import between $130 million and $550 million of preowned medical equipment in 1998. Effective January 1, 1998, however, China barred all importation of used machinery and electric products, including medical devices, except for special needs with the approval of the State Machinery and Electric Products Import and Export Office. In addition to the direct loss of sales, the closure of the China market has depressed prices worldwide for preowned medical equipment.

China is not alone in banning or restricting the importation of preowned equipment. Kuwait, South Korea, and Thailand also ban the importation of such equipment, and at least seven other countries—Argentina, Brazil, Colombia, India, Indonesia, Pakistan, and Turkey—impose restrictions of various severity. Those restrictions range from the imposition of prohibitive taxes on equipment over 5 years old to requirements that the equipment have been refurbished by the original manufacturer. In practice, such restrictions may be tantamount to a prohibition, especially for certain types of preowned equipment. The impact of these restrictions imposed by these 11 markets—all of which are low- or middle-income countries where buyers might be attracted to the lower cost of preowned devices—is significant, since the combined population of these 11 markets represents 52.9 percent of the total population of the U.S. export market. Because the United States does not export to itself, the population of the U.S. export market is equal to world population minus U.S. population.

Countries that permit the importation of preowned equipment, however, are not necessarily good markets. In countries with the economic means to buy the latest equipment and technology, such as Germany and France, there may be a strong disposition against preowned equipment. In other cases, such as Mexico, government procurement policy forbids the purchase of used or refurbished equipment by government-funded hospital and clinics. Although no definitive data exist on the number of firms active in the secondary medical equipment market, the International Association of Medical Equipment Remarketers and Servicers (IAMERS) estimates that as many as 3,400 businesses in the United States, most very small, dealt in or refurbished medical equipment for resale in 1998. Those companies include leasing companies that refurbish equipment coming off lease, brokers that buy equipment and refurbish it for resale, independent service organizations, and original equipment manufacturers who take trade-ins for new equipment and refurbish them for resale. The closing of the China market may have led to a shake-out in the industry, however, since IAMERS estimated that about 18 percent of these U.S. firms focused on supplying the China market.

The U.S. preowned equipment industry has several ongoing activities that may improve the market for U.S. exports by addressing concerns about quality and the need for warranties, postsales maintenance, and parts. IAMERS has developed a code of ethics with which its members have agreed to comply. IAMERS publishes a directory of its members and responds to complaints against them. On several occasions, IAMERS has removed member firms for failure to comply with its ethics code.

A joint effort of IAMERS, the FDA, the American Association of Medical Instrumentation (AAMI), and several new-product industry associations—the Health Industry Manufacturers Associations (HIMA), the National Electrical Manufacturers Associations (NEMA), and the Medical Device Manufacturers Association (MDMA)—has led to a draft agreement for self-regulation of the preowned medical device industry. The proposed self-regulation includes voluntary labeling that tracks the preowned equipment, registration of medical device resellers, and mandatory FDA review of medical devices when the original specifications are modified in any way. The draft agreement also foresees a system for distributing recall and hazard notices. Pending approval of the draft agreement by the FDA, self-regulation of the U.S. preowned medical device industry should be implemented in the next several years.

Under this proposed voluntary system of self-regulation, the participating organizations would label the used equipment they service or remarket with the following information:

- The name of the servicing or remarketing organization;
- a toll-free telephone number or other contact information for the organization;
- service documentation describing the work performed using standardized terminology (see below);
- the date the work was performed and/or the date the transaction was completed; and
- the appropriate device condition code (see below).

The proposed voluntary regulations include definitions for 12 key terms relating to activities that could be undertaken as part of the equipment refurbishing process. The defined terms are *calibration, cleaning, cosmetic restoration, decontamination, installation, performance verification, preventive maintenance, remarketing, repair, safety testing, scheduled (planned) maintenance,* and *service*. The service documentation included on the label would have to use this terminology to describe work done on the device.

Two device condition codes were defined for use on the label:

DC 1—Device may have received cosmetic restoration but otherwise is in as is/unknown condition. Prior to use, device must be checked for proper performance and safety.

DC 2—Device is performing properly and safely and is ready for clinical use. If installation is required, the device must be checked again after installation.

For devices labeled DC 2, the required service documentation provides information on the service(s) performed.

Another key element of the voluntary regulations includes the establishment of a registry operated by a third party to make hazard, recall, and safety related service notices available to all participants. Remarketers would also be obliged to make information on FDA and manufacturer hazard, recall, and safety related service notices available to their customers.

Steven Harper, U.S. Department of Commerce, Office of Microelectronics, Medical Equipment and Instrumentation, (202) 482-2991, Steven_Harper@ita.doc.gov, October 1999.

REFERENCES

"Advances in Less-Invasive Endoscopic & Minimally Invasive Surgical Procedures," *Biomedical Market Newsletter* 800-875-8181, January 31, 1999, pp. 8–11.

Annual Survey of Manufacturers, 1996 Statistics for Industry Groups and Industries, U.S. Census Bureau, http://www.census.gov/econ/www/manumenu.html.

Arnot, Bob, "Pain-Free Dentistry? Lasers Promise Less Grief," MSNBC Online, September 13, 1999.

"Big Companies Targeting New Woundcare for Growth," *Clinica* No. 872, August 23, 1999, pp. 12–13.

Bronson, Judith Gunn, "New Directions for MRI," *Decisions in Imaging Economics,* March/April 1999.

Cannavo, Michael, "Debunking Financial Myths," *Decisions in Imaging Economics,* March/April 1999.

Chadha, Olivia, "Infusion Therapy: Safety Is the New Frontier," *HomeCare Magazine.*

Cicione, Maryellen, "Providing Solutions: The Evolution of Healthcare Consulting," *Medical Imaging,* March 1999.

"21 CFR Part 11: Electronic Records; Electronic Signatures," http://www.fda.gov/cder/esig/part11.html.

Dental Equipment and Supplies Manufacturing, 1997 Economic Census; U.S. Census Bureau, July 1999, http://www.census.gov/prod/www/abs/97ecmani.html.

"Dentists Finding Ways to Make Their Work Painless," CNN Interactive, January 10, 1997.

Electromedical and Irradiation Equipment (MA38R) 1997, Current Industrial Report, U.S. Census Bureau, June 1998, http://www.census.gov/econ/www/manumenu.html.

"European Cardiac Rhythm Market Expected to Reach $1.2 Billion," *Medical Design Online,* July 6, 1999.

Everett Ellin, J.D., "The High Road to Filmless Radiography: A Swift Surer Route to Radiology's All-Digital Domain," *Medical Imaging,* March 1999.

Farnsworth, Leslie, "Crisis Down Under," *Decisions in Imaging Economics,* March/April 1999.

"FDA Approves Laser Treatment for Tooth Decay," CNN Interactive, May 7, 1997.

Flaherty, Megan, "Taking the Measure of the Women's Market," *HomeCare Magazine.*

Hedges, Martin, "Feeding Frenzy as U.S. Firms Go on the Acquisition Trail," *Clinica.*

Hejlik, Karl J., "The Difference Between U.S. & E.U. Laser Standards," *Medical Device & Diagnostic Industry,* August 1998.

"Imagyn Finishes Trials on Site Select Biopsy System," *Medical Imaging,* March 1999, (Anonymous).

Katz, Jon, "Prescription for the Future: Drug-Delivery Product Embodies Development Trends," *Medical Device & Diagnostic Industry Magazine,* July 1999.

Kelly, Donna, "New Device Takes Bite out of Dental X-rays," CNN Interactive, June 12, 1996.

Medistat World Medical Market Analysis, ESPICOM Business Intelligence, Lincoln House, City Fields Business Park, West Sussex, United Kingdom, August 1998.

"New Growth Predicted for U.S. Wound Closure Products Markets," *Medical Design Online,* June 23, 1999.

Plotz, David, "Defining Decay Down: Why Dentists Still Exist," *Slate Magazine Online,* August 17, 1999.

Proval, Cheryl, "Considering the Big Boom Effect," *Decisions in Imaging Economics,* March/April 1999.

Ogle, Peter, "X-Ray Vision: Y2K But a Glitch in the Integration of Images and Health," *Diagnostic Imaging,* April 1999.

Ridley, Erik, "Radiology Entangled in the Web of the Web," *Diagnostic Imaging,* May 1999.

Smith, Rich, "Baystate Health System: Building Unity," *Decisions in Imaging Economics,* March/April 1999.

Stern, Sheldon, "Ultrasound Resonants," *Decisions in Imaging Economics,* March/April 1999.

Surgical and Medical Instrument Manufacturing, 1997 Economic Census; U.S. Census Bureau, August 1999, http://www.census.gov/prod/www/abs/97ecmani.html.

Surgical Appliance and Supplies Manufacturing, 1997 Economic Census; U.S. Census Bureau, August 1999, http://www.census.gov/prod/www/abs/97ecmani.html.

"The Medical Device Industry: A Market Perspective," L.E.K. Consulting, (617) 951-9500, May 1999.

Tierney, Mary C, "Take it to Heart," *Medical Imaging,* March 1999.

"TMG Survey Predicts Healthy PACS Market," http://www.dimag.com/db_area/archives/1998/9801nc5.html.

Trends in Health Care Spending by the Private Sector, Congressional Budget Office, U.S. Congress, April 1997.

Tuchman, Gary, "America Sinks its Teeth Into Digital Future," CNN Interactive, February 4, 1997.

U.S. Markets for Cardiovascular and Cardiothoracic Surgery Devices, Medical Data International (MDI), 800-826-5759, July 1999.

U.S. Medical Device Industry Outlook, Frost & Sullivan, March 1999, (650) 961-9000, http://www.frost.com.

U.S. Wound Closure Products Markets, Frost & Sullivan, (650) 961-9000, www.frost.com.

Worldwide Markets for Medical and Dental Lasers, Medical Data International (MDI), 1998.

RELATED CHAPTERS

16: Microelectronics
27: Computer Equipment
31: Telecommunications and Navigation Equipment
43: Health and Medical Services

FINANCIAL INSTITUTIONS
Economic and Trade Trends

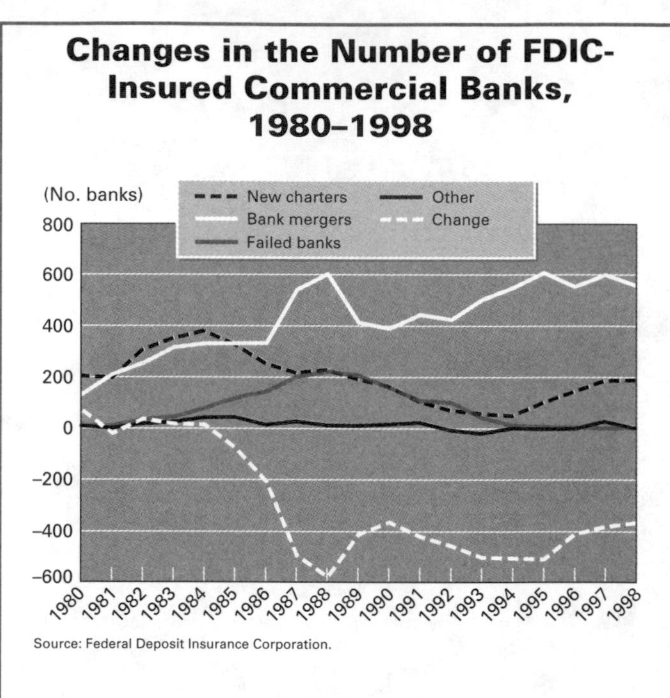

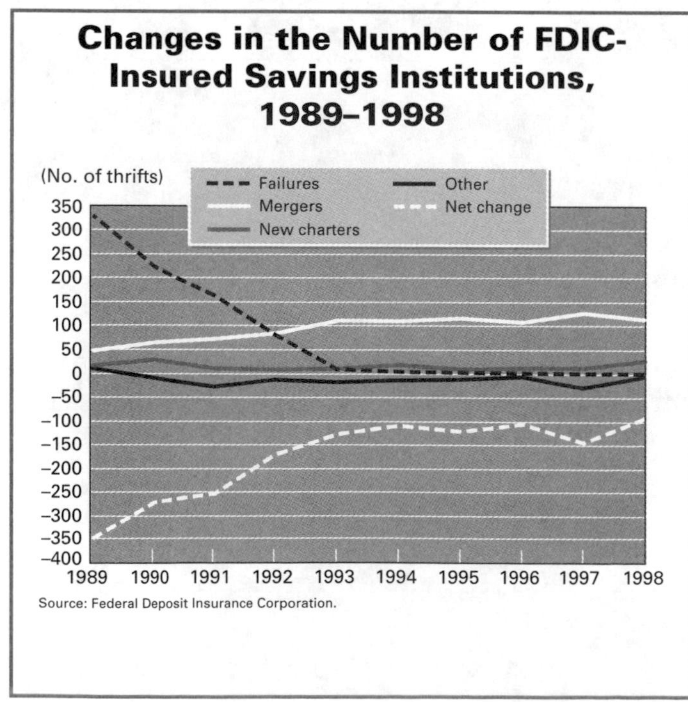

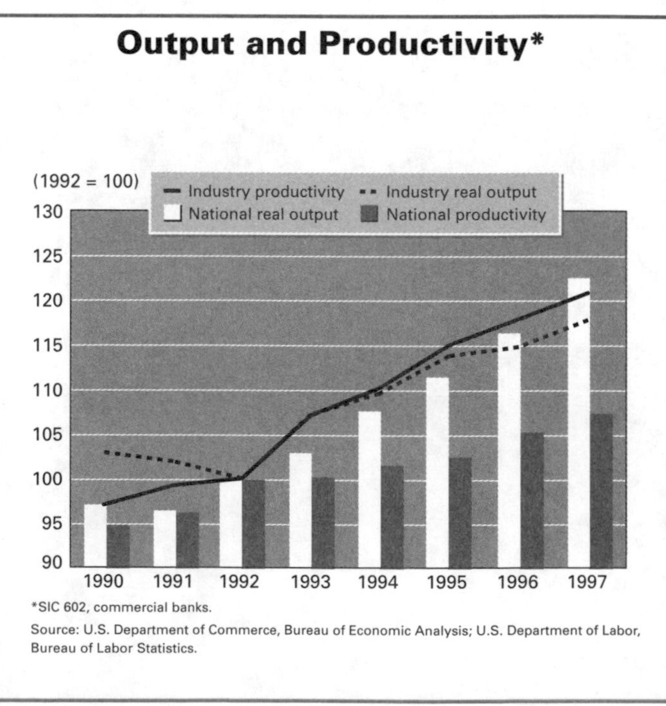

See "Getting the Most Out of *Outlook 2000*" for definitions of terms.

45

Financial Institutions

INDUSTRY DEFINITION Financial institutions include commercial banks (SIC 602) and savings institutions (SIC 6035, 6036), which accept deposits and conduct other related banking functions.

COMMERCIAL BANKING

The year 1998 was challenging for many of the smallest U.S. commercial banks as well as some of the largest institutions. The smaller banks' dependence on traditional lending and deposit taking combined with heightened competitive pressures to erode profitability. For larger banks, economic disruptions in Asia and Russia caused declines in overseas earnings, and expenses related to a number of mergers of large banks further limited profitability. Nevertheless, domestic operations remained robust. Overall profitability was only slightly lower than its all-time high set in 1997, and the industry could look ahead to the prospect of a rebound in profitability in 1999.

Insured commercial banks posted a seventh consecutive year of record earnings in 1998. Net income for the 8,774 commercial banks insured by the Federal Deposit Insurance Corporation (FDIC) rose to $61.8 billion, an increase of $2.7 billion (4.5 percent) over 1997. That increase in earnings reflected strong growth in noninterest revenues and interest-earning assets and a relatively benign credit-quality environment. The industry's return on assets (ROA) declined to 1.19 percent from the record high of 1.23 percent registered in 1997. Almost two of every three commercial banks (63.2 percent) reported an ROA of 1 percent or higher in 1998 (see Figure 45-1).

Domestic economic conditions remained highly favorable for bank performance in 1998. A growing economy, coupled with low and declining interest rates, supported strong demand for loans and fee-based services. Net interest income was $8.3 billion (4.7 percent) higher than it had been in 1997, and noninterest income increased by $19.2 billion (18.4 percent). The growth in net interest income was attributable to an 8.4 percent increase in banks' interest-bearing assets; the industry's net interest margin—the difference between the average yield on interest-bearing assets and the average cost of funding those assets—declined for the sixth consecutive year, falling to 4.07 percent from 4.21 percent in 1997. Margins were at their lowest level since 1990.

The increase in noninterest revenues occurred despite a decline in revenues from trading activities. Heightened volatility in global financial markets in the second half of 1998 caused trading income (proceeds from trading cash instruments and off-balance-sheet derivative contracts) to decline at a number of banks. Overall trading income totaled $7.7 billion, a decline of $318 million (4 percent) from 1997. Weakness in trading income was outweighed by continued strength in fees and other noninterest income. Noninterest income provided 40.4 percent of commercial banks' net operating revenue (net interest income plus noninterest income) in 1998, up from 37.5 percent in 1997 (see Figure 45-2).

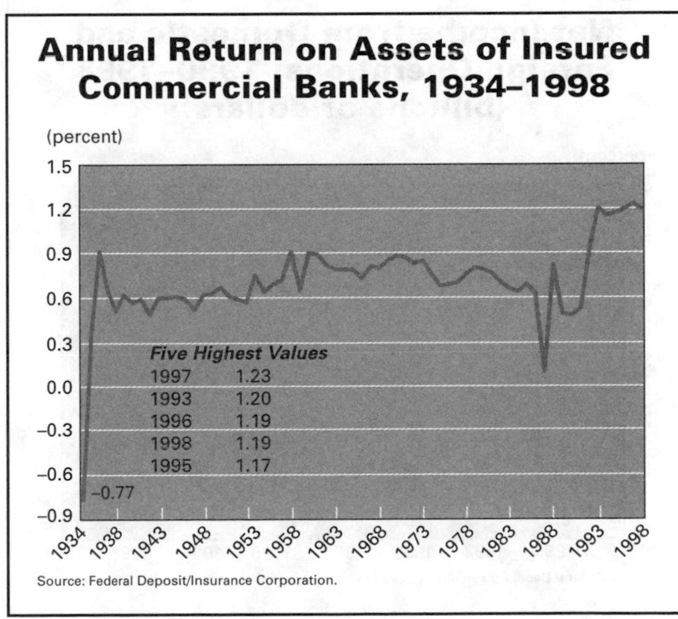

FIGURE 45-1

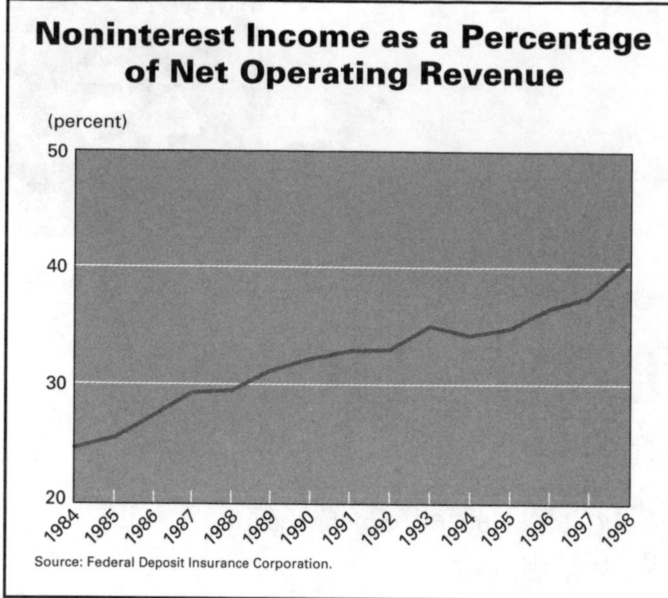

FIGURE 45-2

Earnings from overseas operations declined for the second consecutive year (see Figure 45-3). Commercial banks earned $5.2 billion on their international operations in 1998, $860 million (14.1 percent) less than they did in 1997 and $1.1 billion (17.5 percent) less than they did in 1996. The share of total commercial bank profits accounted for by international operations fell to 8.4 percent in 1998 from 10.3 percent in 1997 and 12.02 percent in 1996. That decline in overseas earnings resulted from lower noninterest revenues, which were $832 million (5.4 percent) lower than in 1997, and higher expenses for loan-loss provisions, which were $739 million (45.4 percent) higher than in 1997. The 1998 loss provision for international operations, at $2.4 billion, was more than 2.5 times the level of 1996.

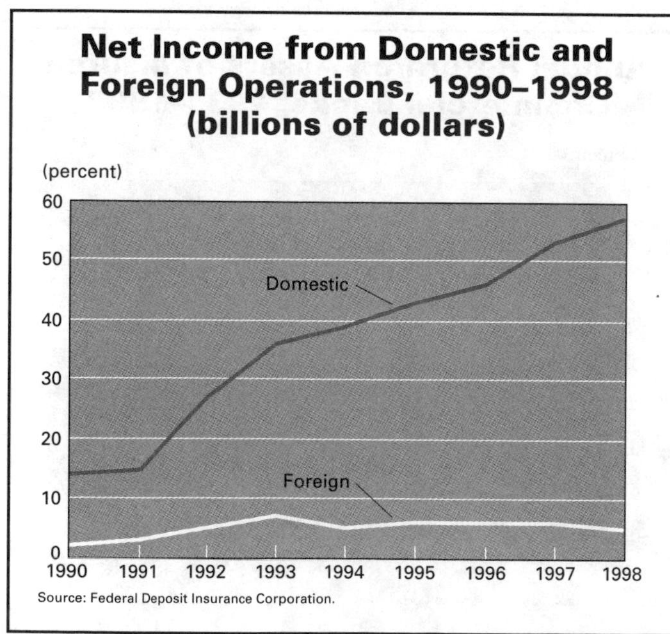

FIGURE 45-3

In contrast, banks' domestic earnings remained strong. Net income from domestic operations was $3.6 billion (6.81 percent) above the level in 1997. The improvement would have been greater except for the sharp increase in merger-related expenses. The industry's net operating revenues from domestic operations were $27.1 billion (10.8 percent) higher than in 1997.

The low level of interest rates, especially in the second half of 1998, supported strong growth in home mortgage lending both for refinancing existing loans and to fund new home purchases. The increased mortgage lending was evidenced by growth in banks' home mortgage portfolios, their holdings of mortgage-backed securities, and their mortgage-servicing assets. With interest rates at cyclically low levels, borrowers with adjustable-rate mortgages try to convert to fixed-rate loans and lock in low rates. Lenders are reluctant to retain too many long-term, fixed-rate loans in their loan portfolios, and so institutions frequently securitize and sell many of the mortgages they originate. Real estate loans secured by one- to four-family residential properties increased $48.1 billion (7.7 percent), while banks' mortgage-backed securities rose $85.9 billion (22.4 percent). Mortgage-servicing assets, which provide an indication of securitization activity, increased $2.9 billion (29 percent).

Loans to commercial and industrial borrowers remained the fastest-growing lending category, increasing by $103.7 billion (13 percent); however, growth in loans to non-U.S. commercial borrowers slowed in 1998, reflecting weakness in overseas economies. Commercial and industrial loans to non-U.S. addressees increased by only $8.4 billion (6.2 percent) compared with an increase of $19.1 billion (16.4 percent) in 1997.

Even though a fourth quarter surge lifted the growth rate for bank deposits to a 12-year high in 1998, the share of commercial bank asset funding provided by deposits declined for the seventh consecutive year. As recently as 1993, deposits funded more than three-quarters of all commercial bank assets; at the end of 1998, deposits funded slightly more than two-thirds of those banks' assets. Total deposits increased 7.6 percent ($260 billion) in 1998, the highest annual growth rate since 1986, but that growth failed to keep pace with the 8.5 percent expansion of commercial bank assets. Domestic savings deposits grew by a record $177 billion (15.1 percent) in 1998, while domestic time deposits were up $40 billion (3.6 percent) and domestic demand deposits declined by $3.5 billion (0.6 percent). Deposits in foreign offices increased $45.8 billion (8.7 percent). Nondeposit borrowings grew $75.4 billion (22.8 percent), and equity capital rose by $44.4 billion (10.6 percent).

Asset quality deteriorated slightly in 1998 as loan losses and noncurrent loans increased. Commercial banks charged off (removed from their books because of uncollectability) $20.7 billion in bad loans in 1998, a $2.4 billion (13.1 percent) increase over 1997. Despite the increased pace of charge-off activity, noncurrent loans—loans 90 days or more past due or in nonaccrual status—registered their first full-year increase since 1990, rising $2.7 billion (9.5 percent). Much of the deterioration occurred in commercial and industrial loans. Commercial and industrial loan charge-offs increased $1.4 billion (65.3 percent), and noncurrent commercial and industrial loans increased $2.1 billion (30.5 percent). As has been the case since 1995, credit card loans accounted for more than half of all commercial banks' loan charge-offs in 1998 (55.4 percent) even though credit card charge-offs were $243 million lower than they had been in 1997.

Despite the problems in commercial and industrial loans, commercial bank asset quality remained good by recent historical standards. The net charge-off rate in 1998 was 0.67 percent of average total loans, compared with 0.64 percent in 1997. This was still well below the recent cyclical high of 1.59 percent in 1991. The industry's noncurrent loan rate was 0.96 percent at the end of 1998, unchanged from a year earlier and only slightly above the lowest level reached in the 16 years during which banks have reported noncurrent loan data.

The pace of industry consolidation slowed for the third consecutive year as the number of insured commercial banks declined by 368. Merger activity eased slightly in 1998 but remained at a historically high level. In 1998, 557 commercial banks were absorbed by mergers, down from 598 in 1997. In contrast to 1997, when almost half (47.1 percent) of all bank mergers involved consolidations within banks' existing holding companies, in 1998 almost two-thirds (63.3 percent) of merged banks were acquired by previously unrelated organizations. This shift reflects the completion of restructuring changes by bank holding companies with subsidiary banks in several different states as they consolidate into fewer separate institutions after the removal of restrictions on interstate branching. Interstate mergers, in which banks are absorbed by banks headquartered in other states, accounted for almost one-third of all mergers for the second consecutive year. The number of new commercial banks beginning operation rose to 190 in 1998 from 187 in 1997. Three insured commercial banks failed in 1998.

As a result of megamergers and strong profits, U.S. banking companies took three of the top five places in an *American Banker* world ranking of market valuations as of June 30, 1999. U.S. companies also accounted for 36 of the top 100 in market capitalization, whereas only 16 U.S. institutions appeared among the top 100 in assets as of year end 1998.

The use of the Internet as a vehicle for delivering financial services is very much in its infancy. At the end of 1998, there were only a few "cyberbanks," offering a limited range of products and services. However, it is estimated that approximately 3,000 insured commercial banks and thrifts now have Web sites, and more than 600 institutions offer some degree of Internet transaction capability.

Outlook

The prospects for commercial banks in 1999 were generally favorable. To the extent that overseas economies in Asia rebounded from their 1998 problems, the profitability of banks' international operations could be expected to improve as well. A lower level of volatility in foreign exchange and interest rate markets should continue to contribute to a recovery in trading revenues. Modest increases in domestic interest rates may have a positive near-term impact on banks' net interest margins. Much of the increased spending by banks for Y2K compliance has already occurred, and the large merger-related charges that inflated the industry's overhead expenses during 1998 were not expected to recur in 1999. The main qualifier of an otherwise favorable outlook is whether recent increases in nonperforming commercial loans continue. Late in 1999, public apprehensions about the impact of the Y2K date change might have prompted larger than usual deposit withdrawals by access-oriented retail depositors. However, such outflows could have been offset by inflows of investment-oriented deposits seeking safe havens, including increased deposits at overseas branches of U.S. banks.

However, some analysts predict that U.S. dominance, especially in market capitalization, will be challenged in the coming years as economies in Europe and Japan improve and banks

TABLE 45-1: Commercial Banking Trends and Forecasts
(billions of dollars exceptions noted)

												Percent Change				Annual Average
	1990	1991	1992	1993	1994	1995	1996	1997	1998	1999[1]	2000[2]	96–97	97–98	98–99	99–2000	93–97
Consumer debt, excluding mortgages	789	777	780	839	961	1096	1182	1234	1300	1382	1472	4.4	5.4	6.3	6.5	10.1
Commercial and industrial loans at all commercial banks	642	624	600	589	643	717	778	846	947	989	1046	8.8	11.9	4.5	5.7	9.5
Real estate loans at commercial banks	819	874	894	916	966	1053	1107	1190	1280	1423	1527	7.5	7.5	11.2	7.3	6.8
Deposits at commercial banks	2298	2428	2489	2513	2527	2605	2756	2998	3233	3446	3606	8.8	7.9	6.6	4.6	4.5
Commercial bank prime rate (%)	10.0	8.5	6.3	6.0	7.1	8.8	8.3	8.4	8.4	8.0	8.5					
Conventional 30-year mortgage rate—all lenders (%)	10.1	9.3	8.4	7.3	8.4	8.0	7.8	7.6	6.9	7.5	7.7					
11th District cost of funds at insured S&Ls—San Francisco (%)	8.2	7.1	5.1	4.1	3.9	5.1	4.9	4.9	4.9	4.6	5.1					

[1] Estimate.
[2] Forecast.
Source: Federal Reserve Board; Freddie Mac; 11th District Federal Home Loan Bank; estimates and forecasts by Standard & Poor's DRI.

there become more bottom-line-oriented. The same analysts argue that after years of pruning their operations, U.S. banks are limited in their ability to sustain substantial earnings growth. Challenging the rise of European and Japanese banks' prospects, other analysts foresee difficulty for them in becoming more efficient because local laws prohibit massive layoffs or make them prohibitively expensive.

Table 45-1 shows trends and forecasts in the banking industry provided by Standard and Poor's DRI. Any discrepancies between these figures and other data in this chapter are due to the use of disparate source materials.

Ross Waldrop, Federal Deposit Insurance Corporation, Division of Research and Statistics, (202) 898-3951, September 1999.

SAVINGS INSTITUTIONS

At the end of 1998, the FDIC was insuring the deposits of 1,687 savings institutions with $1.09 trillion in assets. The thrift industry had lost almost 2,000 institutions since the beginning of 1988, when there were 3,622 institutions. Mergers and failures accounted for most of the decline. While failures have been absent in recent years, merger activity continues the trend of industry consolidation. The number of savings institutions absorbed by mergers in 1998 was 114. The pace of consolidation was slightly slower that year than it had been in 1997, when 127 savings institutions were merged into other institutions. In each of the past 5 years, more than 100 institutions have been merged into other thrifts or banks. There were no failures in 1998, the second year in a row that no insured savings institution had failed.

In 1998, 28 new institutions were chartered, the most since 1986, and 7 uninsured institutions acquired FDIC insurance, the most since 1988. Many firms outside the banking and thrift industries found a thrift charter an attractive addition to their product lines. Several brokerage firms, insurance firms, and trust operations established new institutions, usually through a unitary thrift holding company. Unlike a bank holding company, a unitary thrift holding company can have virtually any type of owner, and that freedom makes a thrift charter attractive to firms that want to align their products with deposit services. A federal thrift charter also allows an institution to branch across state lines with ease even compared with the branching powers that commercial banks have had since the passage of the Riegle-Neal Interstate Banking and Branching Efficiency Act of 1994.

Several Internet-based institutions also have thrift charters. The thrift charter was particularly suitable for on-line activities, since a thrift holding company could affiliate with other Internet providers with fewer restrictions than could commercial bank holding companies. The Gramm-Leach-Bliley Act of 1999 prohibits acquisitions of a unitary thrift holding company by a commercial firm, but previous affiliations are grandfathered until the thrift is sold. This act prevents an Internet-based commercial firm from obtaining a thrift charter.

Profitability

In 1998, the savings institution industry reported over $10 billion in earnings for the first time. Aggregate ROA, at 1.01 percent, was the highest since 1946 (see Figure 45-4). The aggregate return on equity (ROE) in 1998 did not set a record (see Figure 45-5). The ROE of 11.36 percent remained below the level reached in 1985, when savings institutions registered an ROE of 13.91 percent, because capital levels were far higher at the end of 1998. In 1985, an ROA of 0.46 percent provided a large return on capital, since capital was just 3.52 percent of assets. At the end of 1998, capital was 8.68 percent of assets, only slightly below the recent high of 8.71 percent at the end of 1997. Capital levels have been above 8 percent for 4 years in a row, something that had not happened since the early 1950s (see Figure 45-6). At year end 1998, 98 percent of savings institutions were considered well capitalized under regulatory risk-based capital rules.

Net Interest Margins

Net interest margins remain the industry's primary source of profitability. Margins rose above the 3 percent level in 1992 and have exceeded this level every year since then. Margins declined somewhat in 1998 to 3.1 percent from 3.23 percent in 1997, and yield curves remained flat and therefore damaging to small thrifts. Persistently flat yield curves made it difficult for savings institutions to borrow at lower, short-term, rates and make loans at higher, longer-term, rates. The yield on earning assets declined 25 basis points (a basis point is one one-hundredth of 1 percent) in 1998 to 7.55 percent from 7.8 percent in 1997. The cost of funding earning assets also declined, but by a smaller amount (12 basis points). Noninterest income and expenses have both increased recently, but the net effect on earnings has been fairly consistent for several years, with a net expense of about 1.5 percent. Gains on the

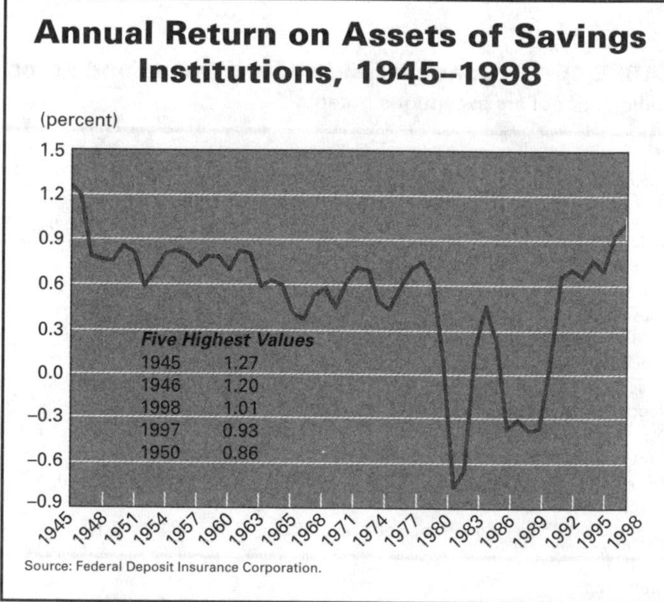

FIGURE 45-4

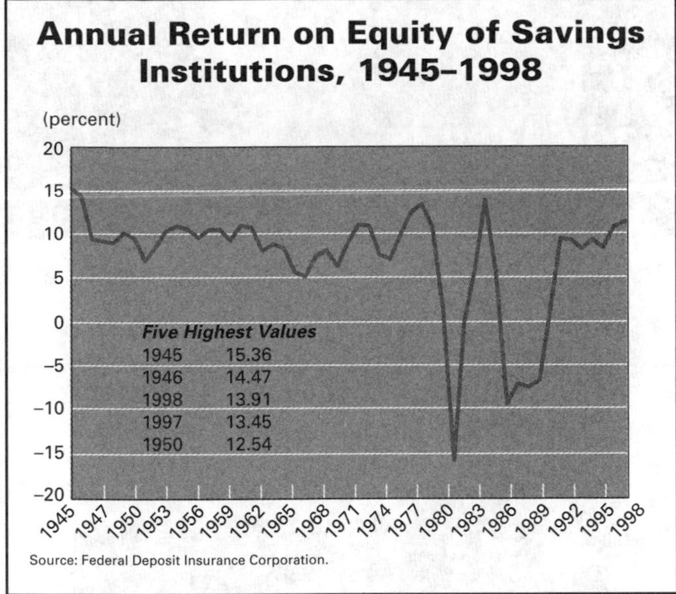

FIGURE 45-5

sales of securities contributed $2.5 billion to earnings, nearly twice as much as they did in 1997, when those gains amounted to $1.3 billion.

Disparity in Performance between Large and Small Thrifts

Small thrifts, with less than $100 million in assets, did not keep pace with the rest of the industry. Those institutions reported an ROA of 0.77 percent in 1998, up only slightly from 0.75 percent in 1997. Asset yields at smaller thrifts fell almost three times as much (20 basis points) as the cost of funding earning assets (7 basis points) in 1998, resulting in a decline of 13 basis points in net interest margins. Smaller thrifts tend to rely heavily on net interest margins for profitability, since they have lower levels of fee income and higher average overhead expenses. Noninterest expense as a percentage of earning assets at small thrifts was 3.14 percent in 1998, down slightly from 3.17 percent in 1997, while the industry average was 2.50 percent. Just 43 percent of small thrifts reported higher earnings in 1998 than in 1997, while over half the larger thrifts in the industry reported earnings gains.

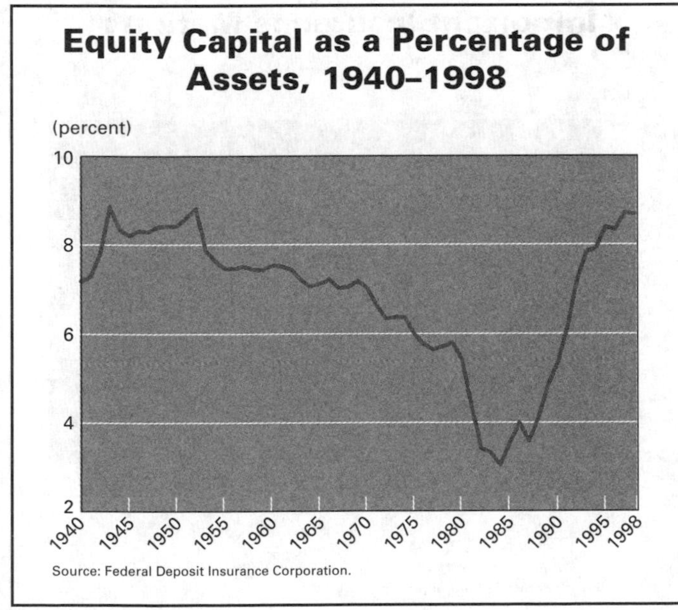

FIGURE 45-6

Asset Quality

Noncurrent loans (loans that are 90 days or more past due and loans in nonaccrual status) continued to improve, declining to the best levels—in percentage of total loans and in dollar amounts—in the 8 years in which all institutions have been reporting consistent measures of noncurrent loans. Only 0.86 percent of total loans were noncurrent at the end of 1998, down from 1.09 percent at the beginning of that year. All loan categories showed improvement.

With the improvement in asset quality, loan losses declined and reserves for loan losses improved relative to noncurrent loans. Total loan charge-offs fell to a record low of 0.22 percent of total loans in 1998, down from 0.25 percent in 1997. Reserves for loan losses fell to 0.96 percent of total loans. This was the first time in a decade that a year ended with reserves below 1 percent of total loans. However, savings institutions held $1.11 in reserves for every dollar of noncurrent loans at the end of 1998, the third straight year in which this ratio showed improvement.

Outlook

In 1998, savings institutions reported record earnings and the federal thrift charter attracted increased interest from outside the industry. Net interest margins are likely to remain under pressure if the yield curve remains flat, and this would mean continued pressure on small thrifts. There are no signs of deteriorating asset quality, and the economy remains strong. In the near future, industry profitability should remain strong, especially at larger institutions.

Tim Critchfield, Federal Deposit Insurance Corporation, Division of Research and Statistics, (202) 898-8557, September 1999.

RELATED CHAPTERS

43: Health and Medical Services
47: Securities and Commodity Futures Trading
48: Professional Business Services

INSURANCE
Economic and Trade Trends

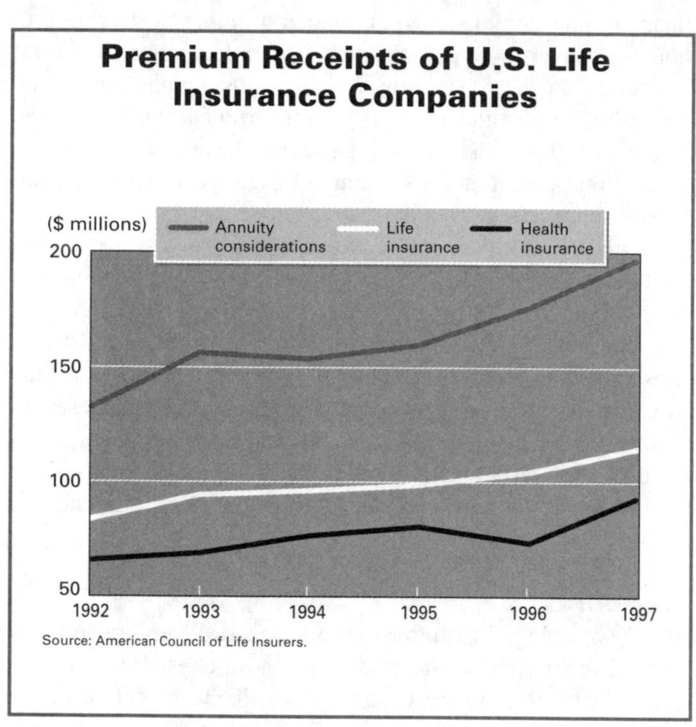

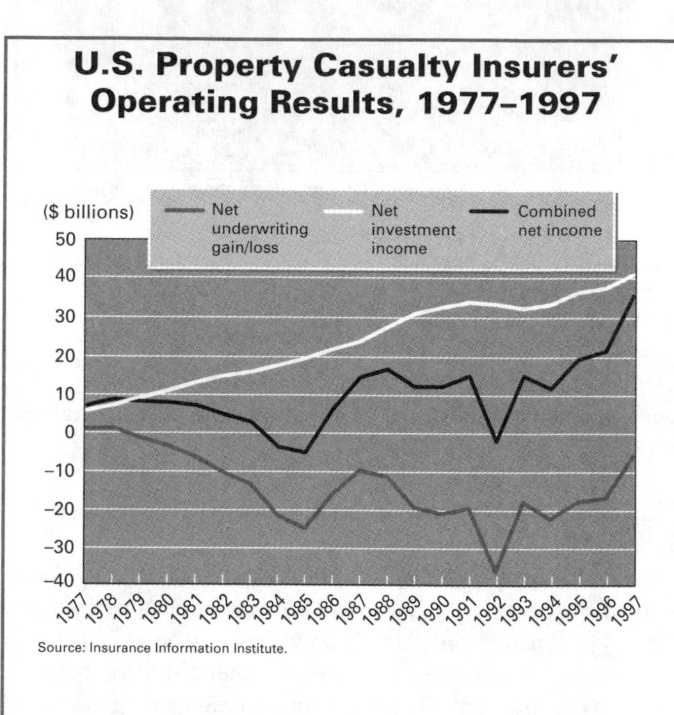

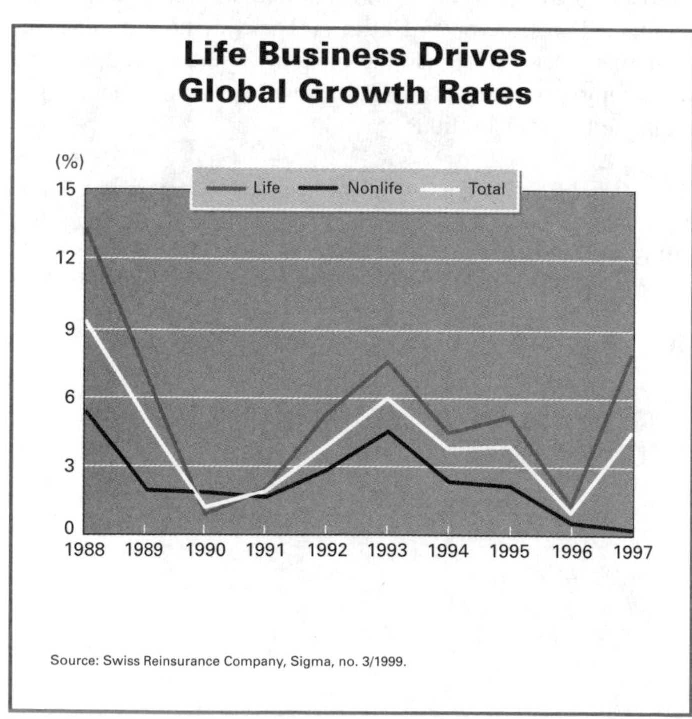

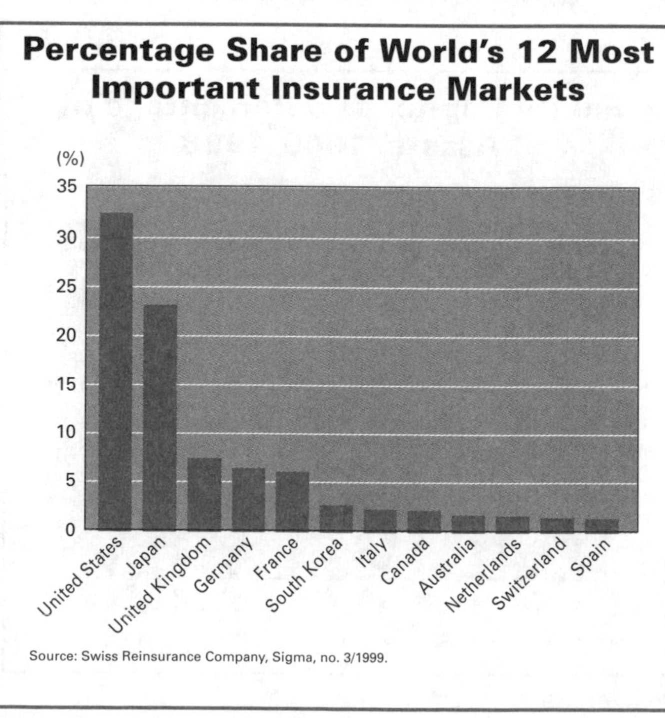

See "Getting the Most Out of *Outlook 2000*" for definitions of terms.

46

Insurance

INDUSTRY DEFINITION Insurance provides financial protection for individuals, commercial businesses, and others against illness, death, loss of property, or losses by a third party for which the insured is liable. Insurance companies are classified mainly under life insurance (SIC 631), accident and health (SIC 632), and property/casualty (i.e., fire, marine, and casualty insurance) (SIC 633).

OVERVIEW

Insurance in the United States can be divided into two broad categories: life and health insurance and property and casualty (p/c) insurance. Approximately 7,900 domestic insurance companies are based in the United States. Together, the life and p/c markets provide 2.3 million jobs and accounted for assets totaling $3.4 trillion at the end of 1997.

The insurance market is a vital component of the U.S. economy, providing individuals and businesses with financial security and generating huge amounts of capital for investment. Insurance companies account for a significant proportion of financial assets in the U.S. economy. Additionally, life insurers maintain about one-quarter of the assets of privately administered pension plans in the United States, valued at $1 trillion in 1997.

Individuals and their families rely on life, retirement income, health, automobile, and homeowner insurance for protection against financial loss. Businesses count on insurance products to protect factories against fire losses, provide worker's compensation in the event of a workplace injury, pay for product liability losses, and provide health and retirement benefits to workers and their families.

The U.S. insurance market is the largest in the world with more than $688.5 billion in premiums in 1997, according to the Swiss Reinsurance Company, followed by Japan, the United Kingdom, Germany, and France. It is arguably the most competitive market in the world. Many analysts consider the U.S. market to be essentially saturated; therefore, future growth of premiums in the United States will be limited. The U.S. insurance industry as a whole is financially healthy, although the threat of environmental liabilities and catastrophic losses could affect the well-being of the p/c industry.

Increased competition in the U.S. market, by far the dominant trend in the industry, will come from banks and other financial institutions, alternative risk mechanisms such as captives and increased self-insurance, and foreign providers as the market becomes more global. These competitive pressures will continue to force insurance providers to reduce costs through new information technology, product specialization, and consolidation. Reducing the costs of distribution, particularly through agency systems, should remain especially important in an increasingly competitive environment.

Growth in the U.S. insurance industry will come primarily from markets outside the United States. U.S. companies continue to invest overseas, where markets are growing faster and are becoming more profitable than the U.S. market. Global trends toward open markets and deregulation are giving U.S. insurers opportunities for growth that cannot be found in the mature U.S. market. Trade agreements directly affecting insurance, including bilateral agreements and multilateral pacts such as the World Trade Organization (WTO) financial services agreement concluded in December 1997, have strengthened these trends. In response to these global trends, foreign insurers from Europe and elsewhere are entering the U.S. market, mainly through acquisitions, to compete with U.S. insurers on a global basis.

Life Insurance

At the end of 1997, the U.S. life insurance industry consisted of nearly 1,620 companies engaged in underwriting life insurance and annuities, a decline of 3.5 percent from 1996. Life insurance companies also underwrite accident and health insurance and manage pension and trust funds. These companies are classified mostly under life insurance (SIC 631) and accident and

TABLE 46-1: Insurance Trends and Forecasts
(millions of dollars except as noted)

	1990	1994	1995	1996	1997	2000	2004	Percent Change 95–96	96–97	90–97
Life insurance										
Premium receipts	264,010	338,151	351,193	378,197	405,305	469,190	538,190	7.7	7.2	53.5
Investment income	111,853	125,999	143,967	152,700	170,713	225,134	292,243	6.1	11.8	52.6
Profit/loss	290,347	366,629	384,087	408,387	439,933	499,618	566,825	6.4	7.7	51.5
Total income	402,200	492,628	528,054	561,087	610,646	724,752	859,068	6.2	8.8	51.8
Assets	1,408,208	1,942,273	2,143,544	2,327,924	2,579,078	2,976,599	3,726,420	8.6	10.8	83.1
Nonlife insurance										
Premium receipts	217,825	250,634	259,803	268,553	276,128	289,436	309,712	3.4	2.8	26.8
Investment income	32,901	33,687	36,834	37,962	41,499	47,513	55,075	3.1	9.3	26.1
Profit/loss	−19,448	−22,191	−17,793	−16,722	−5,827	−8,143	−6,239	5.8	65.1	70.0
Total income	13,453	11,496	19,140	21,239	35,671	39,370	44,457	10.9	67.9	165.1
Assets	556,313	704,600	765,230	801,081	870,056	968,796	1,091,237	4.7	8.6	56.4

Source: American Council of Life Insurance; Insurance Information Institute; A.M. Best; *National Underwriter;* forecasts by U.S. Department of Commerce.

health insurance (SIC 632). The majority of life insurance firms are stock companies (owned by shareholders), while most of the rest are mutual companies (owned by policyholders). Together, stock and mutual life insurers provide 98.2 percent of all the life insurance underwritten by U.S. companies.

Life insurance companies receive funds from two main sources: premiums paid by policyholders and earnings on their investments. Overall, premium growth for life insurance companies increased steadily from 1990 to 1997 to bring premiums to a total of $405.3 billion (see Table 46-1).

Life insurance companies get premium income from three major product areas: life insurance, annuities, and health insurance. The growth of annuity income and the relative decline of premiums from life policies have become an industry trend. In 1997, life policies accounted for 29 percent of premium income, or $115 billion, while annuities accounted for nearly half at $197.5 billion. This is in stark contrast to the 1970s, when life premiums accounted for nearly half of all income and annuities accounted for only 22 percent. Income from health insurance rebounded from a slight decline in 1996, increasing in 1997 to $92.7 billion, or 23 percent of total premium income (see Figure 46-1).

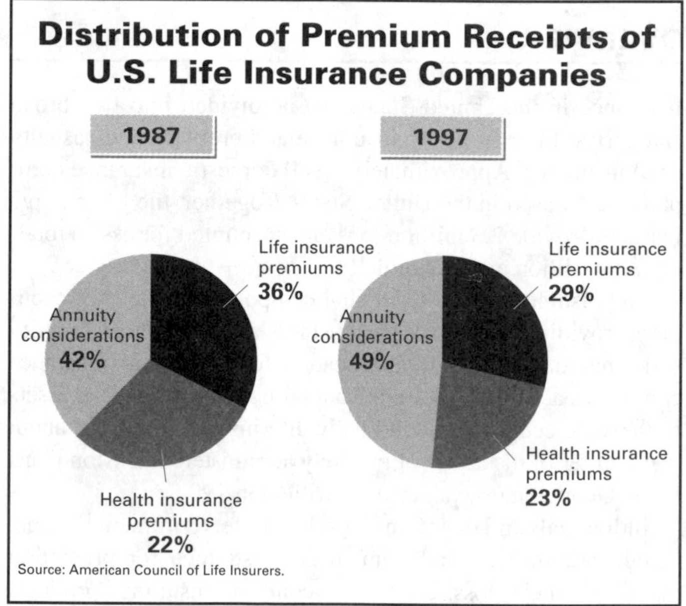

FIGURE 46-1

Increases in 401(k) plans accounted for an 11 percent rate of growth in group annuities to $107.4 billion in 1997, while individual annuities were up 10 percent to reach $90.2 billion. First-year annuity considerations also increased, up 15 percent from 1996. Renewal income also was up, reaching $15.3 billion, a 10 percent increase. In 1997, 3.4 percent of disposable personal income was placed in annuity products. The growth in annuities is attributed largely to increases in group annuities related to tax-favored 401(k) pension plans. This shift from traditional life insurance products to annuity and retirement products—or from managing mortality risks to managing investment risks—has brought life insurers into direct competition with banks, securities firms, and mutual funds. Figure 46-2 shows the distribution of private pension plan reserves in 1997. The slowing of growth in health care costs and the move to managed care have constrained the growth of premiums for health insurance.

Assets of life insurance companies have increased steadily over the last few years, totaling $2.6 trillion in 1997, an increase of 11 percent from 1996, compared with a growth rate of 9 percent in the previous year. Life insurance ranks third among institutional sources of funds, providing $199 billion, or 14 percent of all funds going into U.S. capital markets; commercial

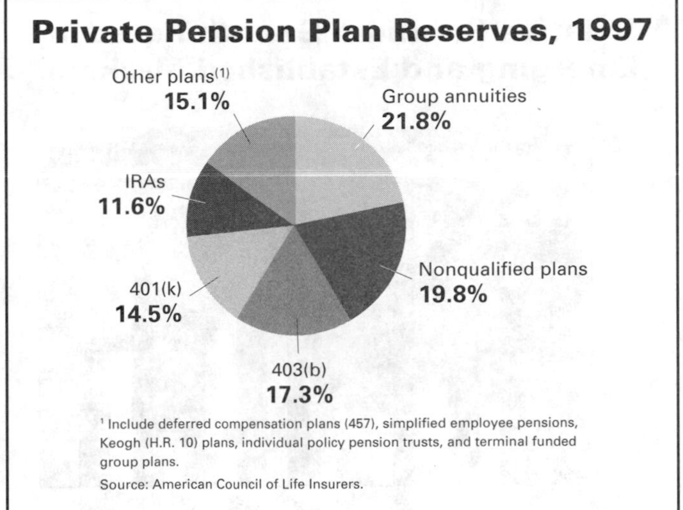

FIGURE 46-2

banks ranked first with $457 billion, followed by mutual funds with $421 billion. Assets of life insurers are placed into four major investment areas: bonds (government and corporate), stocks, mortgages and real estate holdings, and policy loans. The mix of assets in life insurers' portfolios changed significantly from 1986 to 1997 (see Figure 46-3). Holdings of mortgage and real estate declined in 1997 to 8 percent and 1.8 percent of total assets, respectively, while stock holdings rose to 23 percent of total assets. Bond holdings also have increased, rising from 46 percent of total assets in 1986 to 56 percent in 1997. Although bond holdings continue to constitute a majority of assets for life insurers—prompted in part by solvency concerns in the early 1990s and the adoption of risk-based capital standards by state regulators—changes in investment yields contributed to the growth in stock assets. Life insurers shifted

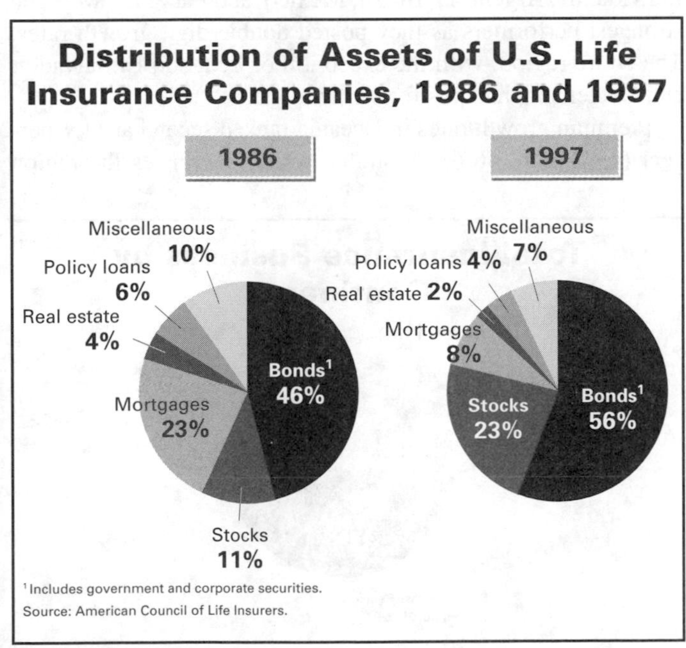

FIGURE 46-3

much of their reliance on mortgages during the 1980s to other sources.

Employment by companies selling mainly life insurance increased to 561,900 in 1997, up from 521,600 in 1996 but representing a slight decline since 1987. Employment by insurers that sell primarily health insurance increased to 347,400 in 1997, up from 322,100 in 1996. The latter increases are attributed mainly to growth in the operation of health maintenance organizations and other managed care entities by insurance companies.

Property/Casualty Insurance

The property/casualty insurance industry (referred to globally as nonlife) provides financial protection for individuals, commercial businesses, and others against losses of property or losses by third parties for which the insured is liable. These insurance companies are classified under fire, marine, and casualty insurance (SIC 633). More than 3,300 companies sell some form of p/c and related lines of insurance, including marine coverage and security and fidelity bonds. Most p/c insurers are organized as stock companies, with some organized as mutual companies.

Property/casualty products include individual and commercial automobile, homeowners, commercial property (e.g., fire, multiple peril), general liability, medical malpractice, and marine insurance. These insurers also write accident and health insurance policies.

Net premiums for p/c insurers totaled $276.1 billion in 1997, up 3 percent from the previous year's level of 268.6 billion. The increase was led by automobile (5 percent), homeowners (6 percent), and farmowner (9 percent) premiums. The highest growth rate in net premiums occurred in the area of financial guaranty, which grew 15 percent from 1996 to 1997 but accounted for only $3.1 billion worth of total premiums in 1997 (see Figures 46-4 and 46-5).

Net underwriting losses improved 65.2 percent in 1997 from their 1996 levels, while income investment grew 9.3 percent.

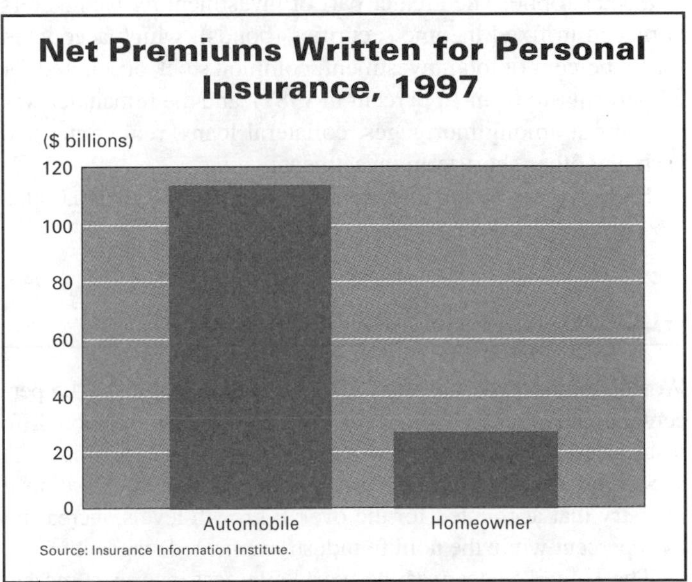

FIGURE 46-4

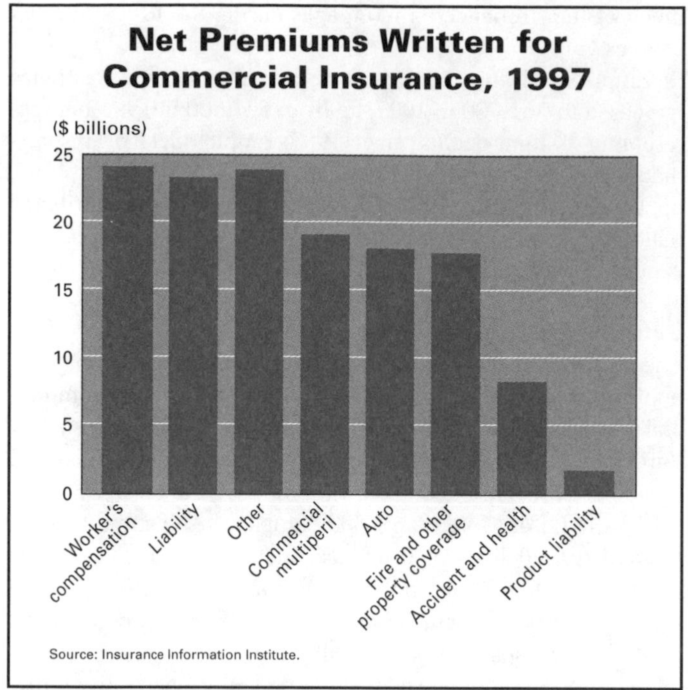

FIGURE 46-5

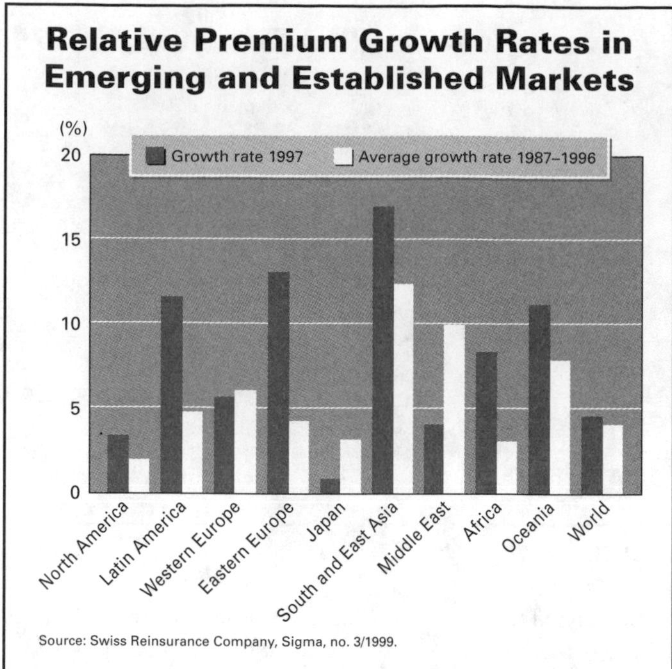

FIGURE 46-6

Profits and losses for p/c insurers are subject to large fluctuations, largely as a result of unforeseen risks such as natural catastrophes. However, investment of capital and surplus accounts and money set aside as loss reserves and unearned premium reserves have allowed p/c insurers to generate enough income to continue their operations despite underwriting deficits.

Property/casualty companies' investments totaled $766.1 billion in 1997, representing 88 percent of total assets, which stood at $870.1 billion. Funds used for investment by p/c insurers tend to be invested in vehicles, such as stocks and bonds, that can provide a solid rate of return in a short time, since p/c insurers need to have ready access to cash to pay claims in case of a catastrophe. The greater part of investment by p/c insurers is placed in fixed income securities (bonds), which accounted for 67 percent of total investment; common stock accounted for 23 percent (up from 15 percent in 1987), and the remainder was spread out among mortgages, collateral loans, real estate, and cash and other short-term investments.

Employment by p/c insurers increased in 1997 to 610,000, a 1.5 percent gain over 1996.

GLOBAL MARKET PERFORMANCE

World premium volume stood at $2.13 trillion in 1997, a 4.5 percent increase over the 1996 level when adjusted for inflation. Life insurance accounted for 58 percent of the volume; nonlife (p/c) accounted for 42 percent. However, it was the life insurance industry that accounted for the overall growth levels, increasing by 8 percent while the nonlife industry remained stagnant.

The United States was the world's largest insurance market in 1997, with 32 percent of worldwide premiums, amounting to $688.5 billion. Japan ranked second with $490.6 billion, or 23 percent of world premiums. The United Kingdom, Germany, and France were the next largest markets, accounting for 7.4 percent, 6.4 percent, and 6.1 percent of worldwide premiums, respectively.

Growth rates varied considerably from region to region (see Figures 46-6 and 46-7). Latin America's growth rate was the highest at 11 percent. The six largest markets (Brazil, Argentina, Mexico, Chile, Colombia, and Venezuela) accounted for nearly 90 percent of the total volume of premiums. Individually, Argentina, Brazil, Mexico, and Paraguay were the strongest performers as they posted double-digit growth rates. The entire region, with the exception of Ecuador, El Salvador, and Guatemala, had positive growth rates.

Premium growth rates in Oceania ranked second at 11.1 percent (see Figure 46-6). Australia, which dominates the region

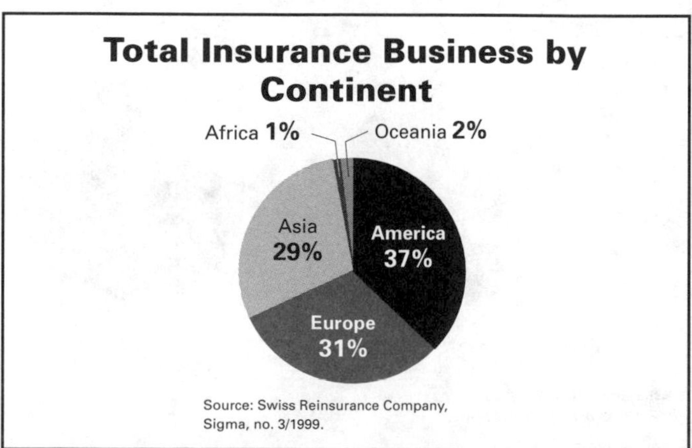

FIGURE 46-7

with 90 percent of premiums, saw its market grow nearly 12 percent, while New Zealand's market increased over 5 percent.

Europe was third, with an overall growth rate of 6 percent. Although western Europe remained stagnant at –0.1 percent overall, central and eastern Europe saw business boom, with nonlife insurance increasing 15 percent and life insurance up 9 percent. Growth rates varied widely across Europe: Latvia (44 percent), Luxembourg (49 percent), Poland (28 percent), Ireland (22 percent), Turkey (20 percent), Italy (18 percent), Slovakia (16 percent), and Ukraine (11 percent, estimated) posted double-digit growth rates. Five countries had negative premium growth: Austria (–8 percent), Sweden (–7 percent), Iceland (–3 percent), Romania (–1 percent), and Bulgaria (–35 percent).

Behind Europe was Asia, which saw its premium level increase 4 percent. The highest growth rates in the region were in China (35 percent), Singapore (20 percent), South Korea (20 percent), Taiwan (14 percent), Syria (13 percent), and Indonesia (12 percent). Premium levels fell in Thailand (–7 percent), the United Arab Emirates (–5 percent), and Pakistan (–7 percent). The Japanese market remained stagnant. Not counting Japan, overall nonlife insurance premiums increased by 7 percent, while life insurance premiums grew 25 percent.

North America had the lowest growth rate in the world at 3.3 percent. The market is dominated by the United States, which holds 94 percent of the region's premiums. The U.S. market grew 2.6 percent, while the Canadian market grew 7 percent.

FACTORS AFFECTING FUTURE U.S. INDUSTRY GROWTH

Financial Market Integration

With the freeing up of interest rates and reform in capital markets, the traditional regulatory distinctions among banks, securities brokers, and insurance companies that existed in the United States since the 1930s are being eroded by the realities of the marketplace and the actions of regulators, courts, and legislatures. As was stated above, life insurers have shifted their focus from traditional life insurance products to annuities and other investment-type products. Banks have changed their emphasis by seeking to deliver a broader array of financial products to their customers, including investment products such as annuities and asset management services. Life insurers and banks therefore are competing head to head with securities firms, including mutual funds, to manage personal and institutional savings and investments. Furthermore, banks are seeking additional fee income through the sale of insurance company products. An expansion of this sales outlet will continue to put pressure on the high-cost agency systems most insurers now have in place.

This trend has been supported by recent Supreme Court decisions that have held that annuities are investment products, not insurance products, and that national banks in towns with 5,000 persons or less can sell insurance. The comptroller of the currency, who regulates national banks, has been actively approving the right of banks to engage in insurance activities. The 106th Congress recently reached an agreement with the White House on the Financial Services Competition Act (H.R. 10). This legislation will alter the landscape of U.S. financial services by repealing many of the aspects of the Glass-Steagal Act and addressing issues of functional regulation and affiliations among financial institutions. This adds up to more competition for insurance companies in the future.

Globalization

As with the economy in general, insurance and financial markets are becoming increasingly global. The rise in personal income and savings in many areas around the world, combined with the need to protect that wealth, provides significant opportunities for life insurers. The growth of multinational companies and international trade and investment has prompted the growth of international nonlife insurance companies and insurance brokers to serve the local and global needs of companies for protection from all types of risk. Therefore, insurers from Asia, Europe, Latin America, and the United States have expanded internationally. In addition to providing insurance products, insurance companies create jobs, provide for capital formation, and transfer services and technologies such as claims adjusting, risk management, actuarial and investment services, and information technologies in foreign markets.

Because of globalization, most countries around the world are moving toward more liberal insurance markets. The pressure of the global economy, the lack of local insurance capacity, and the demand for trade liberalization have pushed many countries to accelerate insurance market reforms, privatize government-owned insurers, and invite more foreign participation. Private insurance markets have proved to be a very effective means to deal with some of the larger economic and social issues all governments face, including providing pension and retirement income, financing and delivering health care, and encouraging sound worker safety and environmental practices.

With multilateral and bilateral trade actions such as the General Agreement on Trade in Services and the financial services pact reached in December 1997, barriers to insurance that limit foreign participation and opportunities in domestic markets are falling. In adjusting to globalization, governments, insurance regulators, and insurance companies are working to strengthen the regulatory and supervisory capacities in those countries to reduce regulatory barriers and improve the market environment. Their efforts are being aided by the attempt by the International Association of Insurance Supervisors (IAIS) to set common standards, guard against problem companies, and prevent fraud and abuse.

However, barriers persist. Some markets, such as India and China, are completely closed to foreign competition or maintain a high degree of government control over the licensing process, denying equal opportunities to foreign insurers. Other countries place restrictions on foreign ownership. Local companies often receive preferential treatment, such as exclusive government procurement or tax benefits. Brokers are not recognized as brokers in many countries, and the lack of transparency of government regulations in many markets remains a major barrier.

Consolidation

Over the last few years, the new global competitive environment and the search for cost efficiencies have spurred mergers and acquisitions in the financial services arena on a global basis. The resulting merger and acquisition boom is expected to continue. Foreign firms are moving to increase their presence in the United States, having committed $29.6 billion to buy U.S. financial companies in the first half of 1999 alone. That volume was 50 percent higher than that in all of 1998 and six times higher than that in the first 6 months of 1998. Part of this reflects a buy-in to the globalization argument: Companies that do not create a global presence are at a competitive disadvantage in regard to those which do.

Many high-profile deals have involved acquisitions by U.S. banks, but many other deals have been made by insurers. There are cross-border deals pending between Aegon NV of the Netherlands in its proposed $10.8 billion purchase of TransAmerica Corp. and Ace Ltd. of Bermuda's $3.4 billion deal for Cigna Corp.'s p/c division. According to analysts, foreign insurers are interested in the U.S. market in large part because it is the world's largest and most efficient.

However, the trend moves both ways, and U.S. companies continue to pursue overseas opportunities. U.S. financial services companies invested $12 billion in international corporate acquisitions in the first half of 1999. U.S. insurers were involved in 14 of the 52 deals in which U.S. financial services firms agreed to buy foreign companies.

Technology

Advances in information and communications technology are changing the nature of the insurance and financial markets rapidly. The insurance industry has invested heavily in information technology equipment, and there is evidence that this investment has resulted in lower operating costs. Competition in the industry, especially among personal lines, suggests that these cost savings are passed on to customers in the form of lower prices and better service. State insurance regulators also are exploring ways to use information technology to reduce regulatory costs and burdens on the industry. An example is the Insurance Regulatory Information Network, in which standard information on agents and brokers will be kept to allow more efficient multistate licensing.

Information technology should continue to have a profound long-term effect on the structure and operation of the industry. Technology will allow niche players to compete locally and financial conglomerates to compete globally and vice versa. Much of the consolidation under way is being driven by a desire to capture information cost efficiencies. Technology will allow the development of new products and new businesses as insurance and financial risks are unbundled. Certainly, advances in information technology are establishing a basis for the integration of financial services.

Electronic Commerce and the Internet

Increased use of the Internet by insurance companies is seen as a way to reduce marketing and selling costs. Such use will grow as the Internet gains acceptance as a tool for obtaining information and conducting business. One study found that 60 percent of insurance companies will offer on-line purchasing services within the next 4 years. Already, companies have developed Web sites and offer on-line quotes, and some sell products over the Internet.

Interestingly, the growth of the Internet also increases the liability for businesses that use it to distribute information, products, and services. Insurance companies have identified this new potential for business by modifying existing products or developing new products to cover the risks involved in E-commerce.

U.S. INDUSTRY GROWTH PROJECTIONS

In general, the insurance industry should grow at the same rate as the economy but probably will be restricted by the forces that have determined its performance over the past few years. The maturity of the U.S. market and the high degree of competition in the industry will keep prices down, profit margins thin, and consolidation the norm. The market should favor insurance consumers. Insurers will look to offer new financial services and enter foreign markets, although cautiously, to achieve their revenue and profit goals. While the balance sheet of the industry should remain strong, results for the first 6 months of 1999 hinted at a slowdown in surplus growth for life insurance companies. For nonlife insurers, which have faced higher than expected large-scale losses, any potential downturn in the market resulting in lower than expected investment gains may place a greater focus on the industry's underwriting losses.

Premium receipts for life insurers were expected to grow in 1999, but at one of the lowest rates in recent years at around 3 percent. Premium receipts for p/c insurers were expected to grow even more slowly than life premiums at 1 to 2 percent. Total income for both life and nonlife insurers will continue to increase, in part because of investment income, but an increase in underwriting losses for nonlife insurers (although not as severe as in the early to middle 1990s) will counter gains from investment. These basic trends are expected to continue at least through the year 2000. The long-term view through 2004 looks somewhat stronger, with both life and nonlife insurers increasing premium receipts and posting stronger results from their investments. By 2004, life premiums should total over $538 billion, while nonlife premiums will reach over 300 billion (see Table 46-1).

Income growth, wealth accumulation, population and workforce changes, and home ownership will determine the demand for the products of life insurers over the long term. The aging of the baby boom generation is placing a demand for products to provide for retirement income and health care financing. The concern with health care costs, however, should maintain the trend toward managed care insurance.

Competition in insurance markets should increase. With the passage and implementation of H.R. 10, banks will be authorized to sell insurance and securities and insurers will be able to enter banking and securities markets. In any event, banks, mutual funds, and other financial institutions will be offering investment and savings products that compete directly with insurance and annuity products. Banks also should increase their sales of automobile and homeowner insurance. Foreign insurers should continue to expand into the largely unrestricted U.S. market, and U.S. insurers probably will expand abroad to capture faster-growing and more profitable foreign markets.

Insurers will be seeking new information and communications technology to increase their efficiency in underwriting, distributing, investment, claims, and administrative activities. There also will be pressure on the distribution system to reduce costs. Insurers will continue to look for cost-efficient alternatives, including the Internet and E-commerce.

Consolidation in the industry should proceed as larger, better capitalized companies take a bigger share of the market from less efficient insurers, but smaller niche players should be strong in selected markets, especially in reinsurance. Reinsurers will compete with capital market products as insurers look for ways to better use their capital to underwrite larger and more volatile risks such as catastrophes and environmental liabilities.

GLOBAL INDUSTRY TRENDS

Regulatory, market, and trade developments around the world continue to create opportunities for U.S. insurance companies.

Europe

In some ways, European Union (EU) countries have a more liberal market than does the United States. Insurers established in the EU are able to structure and price their products freely throughout the EU with only one license. There also is long experience in Europe with bank and insurance affiliations, including the sale and underwriting of insurance products and ownership affiliations; this provides inherent marketing and distribution advantages for domestic European insurers that compete with U.S. or other foreign companies.

Although the western European market remains stagnant and the expected impact of the Euro in improving market conditions has not materialized in regard to increased insurance transactions, a few countries in central and eastern Europe, most notably Poland, have led the charge in the region's market growth. The economies of central and eastern Europe are striving to develop quickly as those countries look to join the EU. Countries such as Poland have taken significant steps toward developing their insurance, pension, and health care markets, and other central and eastern European countries are following suit. Many of these economies are small but are developing strong insurance markets, such as Slovenia and the Baltic republics of Lithuania, Latvia, and Estonia. Other countries, both large and small, remain underdeveloped and mired in macroeconomic and social problems, especially Russia. However, the region has strong long-range prospects despite the fact that many countries continue to struggle with the establishment of basic market and regulatory institutions.

Latin America

The economies of Latin America continue to grow, although recent reports have spoken of recession. Many Latin American countries are liberalizing their insurance markets by privatizing government-owned insurers, allowing foreign investment, and deregulating their markets to make them more competitive. Chile privatized its pension system in 1980 with individually controlled pension accounts, and U.S. insurers are major providers of pension services in that country. The success of the Chilean system has sparked similar changes in Argentina, Colombia, Mexico, and Peru; Brazil also has taken steps in that direction. Other insurance reforms have led and are leading to opportunities in private life and health insurance, commercial insurance, and worker's compensation. Insurance technology firms are finding new markets with Latin American insurance firms that are looking to become more competitive.

Asia

Even larger opportunities are available in the economies of Asia. That region appears to have turned the corner toward economic recovery from its financial crisis. Taiwan's market potential will improve with its accession to the WTO, South Korea's nonlife market had a very strong year in 1998, and Indonesia's life market continues to grow despite that country's political problems. China remains a top priority market for U.S. insurers and is poised to enact significant market access reforms in the context of its accession to the WTO. India is another top priority market and was expected to pass long awaited and much anticipated legislation at the end of 1999 or early in 2000 to open its insurance market to private competition, including foreign participation. Despite stagnant economic and insurance sector growth figures, Japan is progressing with major regulatory reform in financial services and insurance that should create more commercial opportunities for U.S. insurers and brokers over the next few years, including in the private pension area.

Multilateral Trade Agreements

Long-term opportunities for U.S. insurers in foreign markets will depend in part on the effectiveness of the rules and principles negotiated by the United States in the WTO's General Agreement on Trade in Services (GATS). GATS establishes a multilateral framework of principles and rules for trade in services. Among other things, GATS promotes transparency in laws and regulations and treats service providers from all countries on an equal basis (the most-favored-nation principle). Perhaps most important, GATS sets up a strong, binding dispute settlement system to enforce adherence to its members' commitments. A country found in violation of GATS could face WTO-sanctioned retaliatory actions such as punitive tariffs or license denials by injured parties to compensate for the economic harm done to the trade of the injured parties.

A major component of GATS is its annex covering financial services, which was completed in December 1997. The financial services pact covers 95 percent of the global financial services market measured by revenue. Under the agreement's insurance component, 45 countries will permit full foreign ownership of subsidiaries and entry through branches and another 9 countries will permit majority control. In total, those countries account for over 93 percent of insurance premiums worldwide.

The ability of U.S. financial services companies to own and establish companies overseas was greatly improved in 1997. However, impediments remain in certain countries that negatively affect the ability of U.S. insurance companies to establish and operate in a fully competitive market. The United States will address this issue in the next round of talks scheduled to begin in 2000. The United States will focus on the following objectives:

- Getting the 10 countries that as of October 1999 had not ratified their 1997 financial services commitments to do so
- Urging those countries to bind in the WTO current levels of market access, which in some cases are better than what they bound into their 1997 commitments
- Spurring countries that did not make specific commitments on insurance to do so
- Pushing for deeper commitments that allow U.S. insurance companies to operate under a majority or 100 percent equity stake

Changes in the global financial services market such as financial convergence and the advent of new technology are redefining the traditional laws of competition. Banks, securities firms, and insurance companies in Latin America and Europe can cross-sell products. Insurance companies and other financial services firms are able to market, sell, and distribute their products over the Internet. Country commitments in the next round of financial services negotiations must reflect these changes in the industry so that U.S. companies can compete on a level playing field with competitors from other markets.

However, it is important for countries to realize that market access alone does not guarantee fair competition. There is a need to address issues, such as lack of transparency and unequal regulatory requirements, that act as burdens on and barriers to the open participation of foreign insurance companies.

For the next round of financial services negotiations, U.S. industry has been advocating the inclusion of regulatory discussions in addition to further meaningful commitments to market access liberalization. This is not an argument for eliminating appropriate regulation of financial services. In fact, EU and U.S. insurance industries strongly support effective and competitive regulation. Regulations should focus in part on assuring consumers that companies are solvent and are providing accurate information on their financial and business operations. Moreover, transparency and effective enforcement are critical to a regulatory system that will provide for fair and equal competition among foreign and local firms. The benefits of liberalization will come only with true and fair competition.

The U.S. government will be paying close attention to these issues, which, in addition to market access issues, include promoting transparency and fairness of domestic regulatory regimes with appropriate regard for the prudential clause and a review of whether existing definitions of insurance include all important commercial activities. The U.S. government intends to pursue these issues vigorously and through the use of all possible negotiating approaches in the upcoming round of services negotiations.

Tim Fisher, U.S. Department of Commerce, Office of Finance, International Trade Administration, (202) 482-0346, October 1999.

REFERENCES

A. M. Best Company, Ambest Road, Oldwick, NJ 08858. (908) 439-2200.

American Banker, various.

American Council of Life Insurers, 1001 Pennsylvania Avenue, NW, Washington, DC 20004.

Business Insurance, various.

Insurance Information Institute, 110 William Street, New York, NY 10038. (800) 331-9146.

Journal of Commerce, various.

National Underwriter, various.

Swiss Reinsurance Company, 50/60 Mythenquai, P.O. Box 8022, Zurich, Switzerland. 0041-1-285-21-21.

RELATED CHAPTERS

43: Health and Medical Services

45: Financial Institutions

47: Securities, Mutual Funds, and Commodity Futures Trading

SECURITIES, MUTUAL FUNDS, AND COMMODITY FUTURES TRADING
Economic and Trade Trends

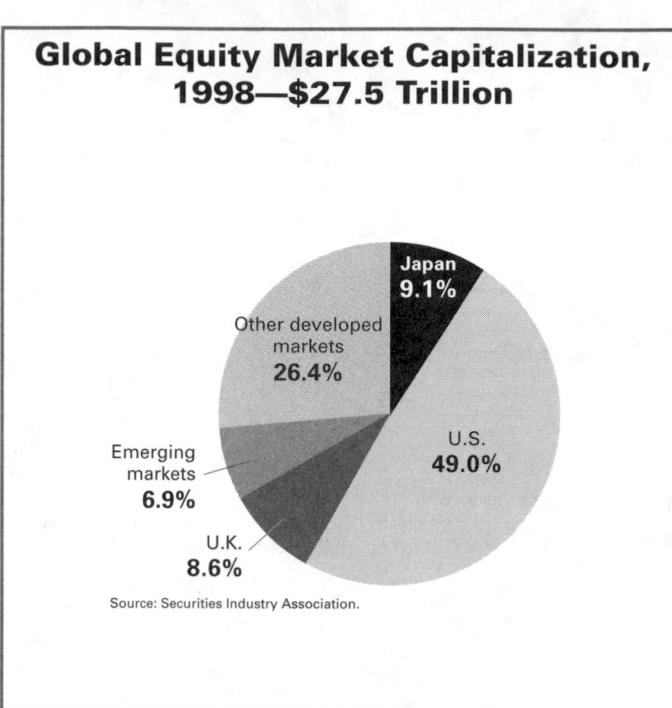

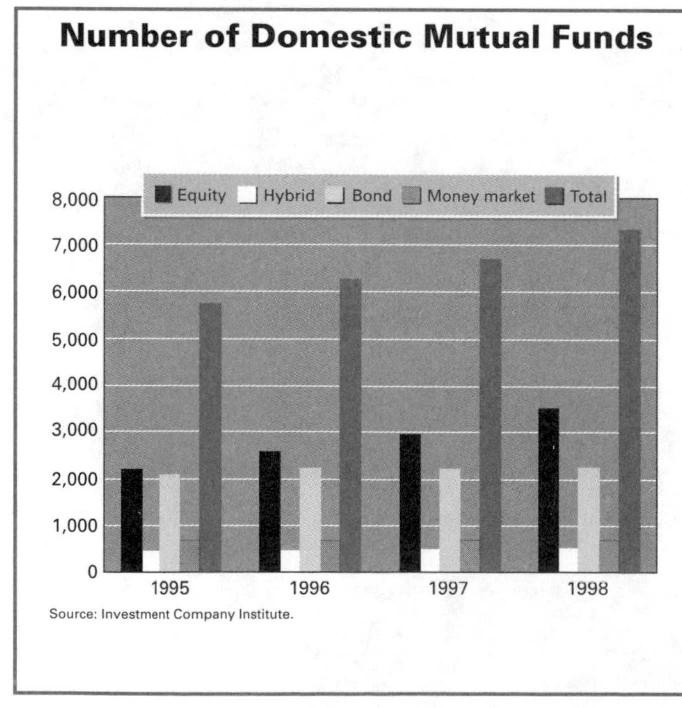

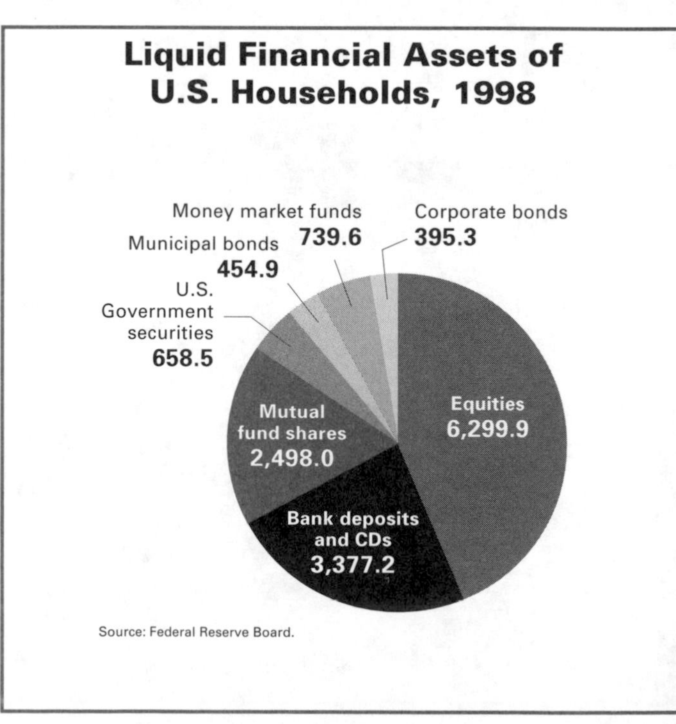

See "Getting the Most Out of *Outlook 2000*" for definitions of terms.

47

Securities, Mutual Funds, and Commodity Futures Trading

INDUSTRY DEFINITION This chapter describes the industries defined in SIC 62 (security and commodity brokers, dealers, exchanges, and services) and SIC 672 (investment offices). The companies involved trade and underwrite stocks, bonds, options, futures, and other financial instruments and provide investment services, including mutual fund management.

SECURITIES

The securities industry (SIC 6211), which serves as an intermediary between investors and issuers of securities, includes firms and individuals engaged in the underwriting, purchase, sale, and brokerage of securities for their own accounts or the accounts of others.

Global Industry Trends

Individual global equity markets had a mixed year in 1998, although overall equity market capitalization continued to increase. At the end of 1998, global equity market capitalization was at a record level of $27.5 trillion, up from $23.5 trillion a year earlier (see Table 47-1), as a 20 percent rise in the value of developed markets outweighed a 13 percent decline in the value of emerging markets. Meanwhile, the value of shares traded on global exchanges increased 17 percent to reach $22.9 trillion.

Global economic turmoil in the 1997–1998 period centered on the way in which emerging markets in Asia, Russia, and to a lesser extent Latin America negatively affected domestic desire for international equity ownership, with U.S. investors selling a net $8 billion of foreign securities in 1998. However, the development and implementation of the European Monetary Union (EMU) on January 1, 1999, as well as economic recovery in many international markets was expected to have a positive impact on U.S. ownership of foreign securities in 1999 and beyond.

Designed partly to eliminate the uncertainty created by currency fluctuations and individual countries' interest rate policies, the EMU was made possible by the formation of the European Central Bank, which sets the direction of monetary policy for all participating EMU countries. With economic stability as the goal, EMU founding country members needed to meet several criteria, including government deficits and debts of no more than 3 percent and 60 percent, respectively, of gross domestic prod-

TABLE 47-1: Capitalization of Global Equity Markets

(billions of dollars)

	1998	1997	1996	1995
United States	13,451	11,309	8,484	6,858
Japan	2,496	2,217	3,089	3,667
United Kingdom	2,374	1,996	1,740	1,408
Germany	1,094	825	671	577
France	991	674	591	522
Other	7,056	6,498	5,837	4,756
Total	27,462	23,519	20,412	17,788

Source: International Finance Corp.

uct. Also included was a fiscal stability pact that guaranteed that member countries would adhere to healthy fiscal policies after the EMU's creation. Accordingly, easing concerns about currencies, interest rates, and general economic risk should give U.S. investors more confidence in owning foreign securities.

The EMU and the establishment of the Euro have sparked a merger and acquisition explosion throughout Europe. Recent high-profile mergers include Olivetti's hostile run on Telecom Italia and the transaction between Banque Nationale de Paris, Societe Generale, and Paribas. Interestingly, global investment banks could have ignored Europe 5 or 10 years ago and still be top-ranked in merger and acquisition activity, but today that is not the case. In fact, booming European merger and acquisition activity bodes well for the future profitability of U.S.-based global investment banks, since European industry is well behind the massive corporate consolidation and downsizing wave American industry has witnessed in the last decade.

In the United States, which alone accounted for 49 percent of global equity market capitalization at the end of 1998 (see Table 47-1), records or near records were set for capital raising, merger and acquisition activity, corporate underwritings, and trading volume. Despite a midyear disruption in the financial markets caused by fallouts in Asia and Russia, both the S&P 500 (up 27 percent for 1998) and the Nasdaq Composite (up 40 percent) indexes witnessed an unprecedented fourth year of annual returns better than 20 percent. The Dow Jones Industrial Average climbed 16 percent, ending its 20 percent growth string at 3 years.

International markets had a spotty year in 1998. Among the major indexes, gains for the year were recorded in France's CAC 40 (up 31 percent), Germany's DAX (up 18 percent), and the United Kingdom's FT-SE 100 (up 15 percent), while declines were seen in Japan's TOPIX (down 7.5 percent), Hong Kong's Heng Seng (down 6.3 percent), and Canada's TSE 300 (down 4.0 percent).

Equity valuations are largely a function of corporate profitability, which has been helped by an environment characterized by low interest rates and inflation, technological and other efficiency improvements, and strong demand for products in a growing global economy. Global consolidations and restructurings also have played a role in making corporations more efficient and competitive and have led to improvements in profitability.

Domestic Trends

Trends in the domestic securities industry were particularly positive in 1998. Capital raised for U.S. businesses and government totaled $3.2 trillion, up from $2.6 trillion in 1997, while $2.0 trillion of merger and acquisition deals were announced, in contrast to $1.2 trillion in 1997. Average daily volume on the New York Stock Exchange (NYSE) was a record 674 million in 1998. Industry pretax profits, however, at $9.8 billion, fell short of the 1997 record of $12.2 billion, hurt by losses in the third quarter of 1998 related to international turmoil. Industry employment reached a record 664,600 at the end of 1998. NYSE firms recorded a record of almost $171 trillion in income in 1998 (see Table 47-2).

As was noted earlier, a low interest rate and inflation environment and technological and other efficiency improvements have led to rapid profit expansion for U.S. businesses in recent years and necessitated reinvestment in core businesses, a process that has spurred greater capital raising efforts. In the meantime, fierce competition domestically and abroad has forced corporations to operate as efficiently as possible, and this has been at least partly responsible for increased merger and acquisition activity. The average daily volume gain is partly a function of the meteoric rise in Internet trading and a continuing decline in the average price per trade resulting from technological improvements and competition.

In addition to following the normal supply-demand equation, in which the volume of trading is expected to rise as commissions decline, less expensive trading lowers the break-even point per trade and encourages higher trading volume. The number of on-line equity trades per day is estimated to have increased from under 100,000 in early 1997 to over 500,000 in early 1999. During that period, on-line trades increased from 7 percent to 16 percent of all equity trades.

The Internet also is credited with making information about specific equities and the equity markets in general much more

TABLE 47-2: New York Stock Exchange Firms' Income Statement Trends and Forecasts
(millions of dollars)

									Percent Change			
	1993	1994	1995	1996	1997	1998	1999[1]	2000[1]	96–97	97–98	98–99	99–00
Commissions	13,707	13,504	15,998	18,400	21,331	24,188	27,800	32,100	15.9	13.4	14.9	15.5
Trading and investment gains	18,473	13,338	18,902	20,134	23,029	21,251	24,300	26,500	14.4	–7.7	14.3	9.1
Underwriting profits	10,061	5,856	7,799	11,165	12,496	14,651	16,800	18,300	11.9	17.2	14.7	8.9
Margin interest	3,130	4,525	6,239	7,120	10,078	12,119	13,500	14,600	41.5	20.3	11.4	8.1
Mutual fund sales	3,541	3,192	3,406	4,472	5,412	6,213	6,950	7,700	21.0	14.8	11.9	10.8
Other	24,270	30,940	43,959	58,958	72,658	92,383	102,600	112,100	23.2	27.1	11.1	9.3
Total	73,182	71,355	96,303	120,249	145,004	170,805	191,950	211,300	20.6	17.8	12.4	10.1

[1] Forecast.
Source: Securities Industry Databank.

readily available. Accordingly, individual investors have been able to overcome some of the information advantages that historically worked to the benefit of professional money managers. This has encouraged individual investors to feel more confident about trading for themselves without the use of a broker. In addition, the nearly 8-year bull run in stock prices has created a "can't lose" psychology among the investing public, drawing even more investors into the fray. The Securities and Exchange Commission, in view of the rampant growth of on-line trading, has been critical of on-line brokers, stressing the need for ensuring service capabilities, adequate client disclosure, and responsible advertising. Highly publicized crashes of on-line systems during which customers were unable to execute trades or check account information were partly responsible for the more watchful eye of regulators.

Consolidation also has made its way into the securities industry. As of 1998, the number of registered broker-dealers had declined to 7,408, down from a peak of 9,515 in 1987, as a result of both mergers and liquidations. As a result, the securities industry has become even more highly concentrated, with the 25 largest NYSE firms accounting for some 79 percent of the industry's total capital and 75 percent of its revenues.

The industry's pretax return on equity (ROE) declined to 17.9 percent in 1998 from 27.9 percent in 1997; this was attributable to the continued entrance of bank securities subsidiaries and their larger than average equity balances. Interestingly, discount brokers had the highest ROE, at 29.7 percent, reflecting their lower relative equity base resulting from limited capital raising needs.

Industry Projections for the Next 1 and 5 Years

The outlook for the securities industry remains positive, although expectations for a continuation of the growth rates seen over the last 3 years are unrealistic. Securities industry profitability should benefit from continued healthy economic conditions and a greater level of investor participation in the markets, which reflects demographics, as an aging population saves for retirement, and technological improvements, which have made access to information more convenient and the cost of individual trades less expensive. Table 47-3 shows the distribution of U.S. household liquid financial assets.

U.S. macroeconomic trends are not expected to change dramatically in the near future. In 1999, growth in the economy was expected to be 3.5 to 4.0 percent, declining modestly to 2.0 to 2.5 percent in the year 2000. Unemployment was expected to be 4.2 to 4.5 percent in 1999, rising only slightly to 4.3 to 4.7 percent in 2000. These are important considerations, since the continuation of a healthy economy assumes a strong rise in corporate profitability and a related increase in equity market valuations and trading volumes, which in turn drive securities industry profitability.

The heights to which the equity markets have climbed in the past 5 years create inherent risks. First, the recent records in traditional price-earnings valuations in the market dictate that investors have a substantial amount of confidence that the nearly perfect environment for equities will continue. Any upset to that environment could erode confidence and stock prices. Second, higher valuations require increasing investment inflows. Simply put, a 30 percent rise in stock values means that it takes $1,300 to buy the same number of shares that $1,000 purchased before the rise.

Meanwhile, individual investors have been participating more actively in the equity markets on both a direct and an indirect basis through mutual funds and increased 401(k) and other methods of retirement savings. With a majority of Americans desiring to retire by age 65 and demographics showing that there will be a substantial burden on public retirement plans, individuals have been realizing the necessity for additional savings.

The investment process has become easier, for example, through employer 401(k) plans. In fact, the automatically deducted money that often is invested regularly in the equity markets through payroll deductions has resulted in greater participation by retail investors. This trend is favorably compounded by employers offering matched contributions.

The concentration of household liquid financial assets at the end of 1998 was 77 percent equities (23 percent bank deposits), in contrast to 49 percent (51 percent bank deposits) at the end of 1995. Accordingly, a greater proportion of the population has a strong desire to see rising equity market valuations, encouraging increased participation in the investment process by individuals. As more equity market information has become available, individual investors have begun to trade equities for themselves. According to Forrester Research, the number of online investing accounts is expected to increase from under 4 million at the end of 1998 to over 20 million by 2003.

TABLE 47-3: Household Liquid Financial Assets
(billions of dollars)

	Equities	Bank Deposits and CDs	Mutual Fund Shares	U.S. Government Securities	Municipal Bonds	Money Market Funds	Corporate Bonds	Total
1994	2,990.4	2,787.2	1,052.1	937.3	502.2	351.3	370.4	8,990.8
1995	3,994.8	2,892.9	1,265.0	854.4	459.0	449.2	457.0	10,372.4
1996	4,524.6	2,998.8	1,586.0	917.7	435.5	505.3	469.6	11,437.4
1997	5,319.1	3,163.4	2,057.6	759.6	423.6	589.9	457.2	12,770.3
1998	6,299.9	3,377.2	2,498.0	658.5	454.9	739.6	395.3	14,423.4

Source: Federal Reserve Board.

The volatile nature of the securities markets makes forecasting profits particularly difficult, but several trends remain in place. Corporate earnings continue to grow at a reasonable pace. This trend, coupled with a 30-year-bond yield below 7.0 percent, should continue to encourage long-term investors to favor equities. Healthy demand from retail investors, who increasingly are turning to the securities markets to meet the financial needs they expect to face at retirement, should continue to spur strong cash inflows into equities; this in turn will have a favorable effect on equity prices. Higher valuations for equities will continue to entice companies in need of capital to offer securities to the public, thus driving securities industry profits.

The securities industry is, however, facing major challenges. One of its principal desires is to reduce the inherent cyclicality of its earnings stream. Many securities firms have succeeded in this regard by using variable compensation plans, which tie employment costs to profits, and moving into less cyclical business lines such as asset management. Separately, the industry is confronting margin pressure in many key businesses through competition both within the industry as securities firms consolidate and from the outside as commercial banks encroach on the basic underwriting and merger and acquisition advisory businesses.

In the absence of a sudden sharp rise in interest rates or a significant market correction, pretax profits for NYSE firms were expected to be $14.2 billion in 1999, with a rise to $15.6 billion in the year 2000. The major drivers will continue to be commission revenues, which should benefit from the secular trend of higher trading volumes while offsetting the declining cost per trade; strong asset management fees aided by a resilient stock market and retirement investment savings; and robust underwriting fees in a low-interest-rate environment.

MUTUAL FUNDS

The mutual fund industry (SIC 672) creates and manages pools of securities, such as stocks, bonds, and money market instruments, on behalf of others. Open-end mutual funds (SIC 6722), which issue and redeem shares on demand, account for the great majority of the economic activity in this industry. Closed-end funds and unit trusts maintain a fixed number of shares, and investors who wish to buy or sell after an initial public offering do so in the securities markets.

TABLE 47-4: Worldwide Assets of Open-End Investment Companies
(millions of dollars)

	1998	1997	1996	1995
Brazil	113,441	108,606	103,786	63,637
Canada	189,210	197,984	154,529	107,812
France	604,381	499,881	534,145	519,376
Germany	175,375	146,889	137,860	134,543
Italy	394,486	209,410	129,755	79,878
Japan	310,810	311,335	420,103	469,980
Spain	223,507	177,192	144,134	99,923
United Kingdom	249,030	235,683	201,304	154,452
Other Non-U.S.	501,498	901,998	990,045	944,844
U.S.	4,889,880	4,468,201	3,526,270	2,811,537
Total	7,651,618	7,257,179	6,341,931	5,385,982

Source: Investment Company Institute.

TABLE 47-5: Domestic Mutual Fund Assets
(billions of dollars)

	Equity	Hybrid	Bond	Money Market	Total
1990	245.6	37.2	284.3	498.3	1,065.5
1991	411.2	54.2	385.4	542.5	1,393.2
1992	522.1	78.8	495.4	546.2	1,642.6
1993	748.1	142.6	614.4	565.3	2,070.1
1994	865.1	156.9	522.4	611.0	2,155.4
1995	1,266.8	204.8	587.0	753.0	2,811.5
1996	1,726.1	252.9	645.4	901.8	3,526.3
1997	2,368.0	317.1	724.2	1,058.9	4,468.2
1998	2,978.2	364.7	830.6	1,351.7	5,525.2

Source: Investment Company Institute.

Global Industry Trends

Worldwide assets in mutual funds continued to increase in 1998, although the growth rate was substantially lower than it had been in the previous 2 years. As of the end of 1998, worldwide mutual fund assets totaled almost $7.7 trillion (see Table 47-4), up 5.4 percent from 1997's $7.3 trillion, in contrast to 18 percent and 14 percent growth in 1996 and 1997, respectively. The United States accounted for all of the growth in 1998, with aggregated non-U.S. mutual fund assets declining fractionally as the economic turmoil centered on emerging markets in Asia, Russia, and to a lesser extent Latin America in both 1997 and 1998 clearly affected overseas markets. The overseas environment for the better part of 1999, however, greatly improved, with many foreign markets improving dramatically.

U.S. mutual fund companies continued to enjoy an efficiency advantage over their European counterparts in 1998, partly explaining their ability to register better growth. Although compensation for fund managers tends to be higher in the United States, the ability to hold down administrative costs, economies of scale, the generally larger size of U.S. funds, and the popularity of low-cost index funds help explain the higher efficiency levels.

The worldwide mutual fund industry has benefited in recent years from the globalization of capital markets, a desire among investors to go outside their own markets for diversification purposes, and the opening of their markets to international investments by less developed countries.

While 1998 witnessed a slowdown in international investing by U.S. investors as a result of international economic turmoil, the early 1999 implementation of the Euro, which is intended to provide economic stability to participating countries, should ease U.S. investors' concerns about interest rates and foreign currency risk and result in greater U.S. investment abroad. With most U.S. investors lacking the knowledge needed to invest in specific foreign markets as well as the resources required to have an adequately diversified portfolio, global mutual funds will continue to remain the preferred method of investing internationally.

Domestic Trends

By any measure, the domestic mutual industry had a spectacular year in 1998. Mutual fund assets increased to over $5.5 trillion at the end of that year, up 24 percent from 1997 and the fourth consecutive year of better than 20 percent growth (see Table 47-5). The rise in assets was almost evenly divided between investment performance (53 percent) and net new cash flow or the creation of new funds (47 percent). While net new cash flow into mutual funds hit a record $477 billion, the mix of new investments changed. In the 1992–1997 period, equity mutual funds took in the majority of new fund flows. However, in 1998, money market funds handily outpaced the new fund flows category, most likely because of investors' concern about market volatility. This was particularly evident in August 1998, when a substantial market correction led to the first net monthly outflow of equity funds since 1990. This trend also is seen in the fact that mutual funds that invest in large capitalization companies, which tend to provide greater liquidity during market disruptions, have recently attracted the majority of new fund flows, seemingly at the expense of funds that invest in small capitalization issues.

Meanwhile, the total number of U.S. funds continues to increase rapidly to satisfy investors' appetite for new investment vehicles. At the end of 1998, investors could choose from 7,314 mutual funds, of which 48 percent were equity funds, 31 percent were bond funds, 14 percent were money market funds, and 7 percent were hybrid funds. Equity funds, benefiting from performance advantages, accounted for nearly all of the increase in the number of funds (see Table 47-6).

The mutual fund industry remains extremely competitive, although a few large players have emerged, including Fidelity Investments, whose popular Magellan Fund reached a milestone $100 billion in assets in July 1999, and Vanguard Group. The largest mutual fund companies have certain advantages of scale, especially with respect to advertising, where bragging about a fund's performance relative to a benchmark, the most practical of which is the S&P 500, is commonplace. Past performance is clearly on the minds of investors contemplating new or additional investments in mutual funds. Interestingly, some 80 percent of mutual funds do not beat the investment return of the S&P 500 on an annualized basis. This has led to a substantial rise in the amount of assets held in Vanguard's 500 Index Fund, which attempts to mimic the performance of the S&P 500 and is now the second largest individual mutual fund in the United States, with over $90 billion in assets. Mutual fund companies tend to compete on investment performance and shareholder fees and operating expenses. Over the last decade, mutual fund shareholders overall have benefited from a lower cost of mutual fund ownership. According to an Investment Company Institute study, the average cost of investing in equity funds declined to 1.49 percent of each dollar invested in 1997 from 2.25 percent in 1980. This is attributable to investors increasing their purchases of funds with relatively lower costs, declining distribution expense, and the economies of scale of the largest fund portfolios.

TABLE 47-6: Number of Domestic Mutual Funds

	Equity	Hybrid	Bond	Money Market	Total
1990	1,116	203	1,024	508	3,086
1991	1,207	226	1,154	554	3,408
1992	1,346	257	1,362	586	3,830
1993	1,604	309	1,704	628	4,537
1994	1,930	387	2,049	644	5,329
1995	2,193	460	2,079	672	5,729
1996	2,572	470	2,224	666	6,254
1997	2,951	501	2,219	682	6,684
1998	3,513	525	2,250	685	7,314

Source: Investment Company Institute.

Mutual fund size also can be a disadvantage. Funds tend to put a cap, often 10 percent, on the percentage they own of any one company. For a very large fund, this may limit the fund manager's choices to larger capitalization issues. The fund then approximates the market at large, and this makes it difficult to outperform its benchmark and smaller funds, whose investment choices are broader. Realizing this, Fidelity's Magellan Fund was closed to most new investors in late 1997.

The mutual fund industry has benefited from an expansion in the available outlets for purchasing funds. In addition to mutual fund companies, intermediaries such as banks and brokerage firms now offer a wide variety of both proprietary and third-party mutual funds to their customers. Separately, employers have made it increasingly simple to invest in mutual funds through 401(k) investment plans and direct payroll deductions, which serve as an automatic source of new funds.

Industry Projections for the Next 1 and 5 Years

Growth in the mutual fund industry is tied to investment performance and net new fund inflows. Investment performance was better than 20 percent in the 4 consecutive years ending in 1998, but it is unrealistic to assume that this trend will continue. Nonetheless, corporate profitability, which ultimately drives stock price performance, is expected to remain strong thanks to the low interest rate and inflation environment, rapid growth in the desire for new technology products, and strong consumer spending. More likely, investment performance will return to the historical range of 10 to 12 percent in the 1999–2000 period.

Meanwhile, favorable population trends should continue to generate a high level of mutual fund inflows. Demographics probably remains the greatest single factor that will favorably affect new inflows. The 77 million baby boomers born between 1948 and 1955 have entered their peak earning years and most aggressive savings period. Because of medical advancements, this group is expected to live longer than prior generations did and thus will require greater retirement savings. In addition, baby boomers tend to be better educated and therefore have higher earnings potential, as well as growing skepticism about the ability of Social Security to support them in their retirement years.

Mutual funds will remain a favorite avenue for those without the time or resources to invest directly. The equity markets, for instance, continue to become more volatile, leaving little room for error in investing in individual stocks. Although the Internet has displaced some of the information advantage professionals enjoyed historically, direct investing requires a solid hands-on approach. In addition, the diversification that investing in mutual funds brings cannot be duplicated effectively by individual investors, who tend to lack the resources to purchase a large number of stocks.

Investors also have turned to mutual funds because of dissatisfaction with the low yields on historically popular investments such as passbook savings and certificates of deposit. Equity mutual fund investors have realized that the returns between 3 and 6 percent offered by such investments will not provide adequately for retirement. The industry also should benefit from the increasing number of funds, which are able to suit practically any investment objective and time horizon.

In the longer term, baby boomers are expected to begin reaching the earliest retirement age of 55 in the year 2003, at which time withdrawls from mutual fund assets can be expected. However, mutual fund assets may only shift from aggressive growth funds to more stable money market and bond funds as pending retirees begin to preserve capital.

Equity market setbacks probably will continue to result in a slowdown in net cash inflows. However, historical data suggest that such setbacks do not result in significant outflows and that the pause in inflows tends to be short-lived. Equity mutual fund investors, at least, appear willing to ride out short-term market fluctuations in favor of long-term investment performance. In addition, since taxes are incurred on gains, current tax laws favor holding mutual fund assets.

COMMODITY FUTURES

Commodity futures trading is covered largely under SIC 6221, commodity contracts brokers and dealers. Firms in this industry trade contracts on behalf of others as members of national commodity exchanges or trade for their own accounts. The exchanges themselves are combined with securities exchanges in SIC 6231.

TABLE 47-7: Futures and Options Volume
(millions of contracts; percent)

	1997	1998	Percent Change
Futures			
U.S. volume	444	503	13.3
Non-U.S. volume	757	798	5.4
Total	1,201	1,301	8.3
Options			
U.S. volume	462	530	14.7
Non-U.S. volume	269	345	28.3
Total	731	875	19.7
World Future and Options			
U.S. volume	906	1,033	14.0
Non-U.S. volume	1,026	1,143	11.4
Total world volume	1,932	2,176	12.6

Source: Futures Industry Association.

Global Industry Trends

According to the Futures Industry Association, world trading in futures and options increased 13 percent to reach 2,175,798,209 contracts in 1998. The breakdown of trading by futures and options on U.S. and international exchanges is shown in Table 47-7. Futures and options volume on non-U.S. exchanges was 1,142,648,478 for January–December 1998, an 11.4 percent gain over 1997. Total U.S. futures and options volume grew to 1,033,149,791, a 14 percent increase over the previous year's figures. This performance was notable in an environment in which the U.S. share of the world market had been declining, at least on the basis of these measures. U.S. volume represents less than half the world futures and options volume. Moreover, the top 10 international contracts accounted for just 26.3 percent of the total 1998 world futures and options contract volume (see Table 47-8). This demonstrates the growing number and wide proliferation of the types of derivatives traded on those exchanges worldwide. Some background, however, is required to understand what the numbers mean.

Futures originally evolved from forward contracts, in which farmers and other commodity producers entered into agreements with the owners of grain elevators or with other consumers or intermediaries to deliver specified quantities of commodities to a particular location on a certain date in exchange for a specified price. This allowed the producers to protect themselves from falling prices and allowed consumers to protect themselves from rising prices that were influenced by demand and uncontrollable factors such as weather. Whereas a forward contract was typically an individual arrangement between two parties, futures contracts developed around recognized commodity exchanges in major trading centers. They differed from forward contracts in that their specifications (date, place, quantity, grade, etc.) were standard and in that while they could be settled by the physical exchange of a product, they did not have to be.

Options on futures became major trading vehicles in the mid-1980s. Although futures buyers do not necessarily have to deliver or accept 10,000 pork bellies, they are exposed to significant financial risk because futures are so highly leveraged. That is, traders commit only a small fraction of the contract value in cash but are liable for the value of the entire contract. Options give traders a way to participate in futures ownership while limiting their potential loss to the amount they invest. Futures contracts originally involved commodities such as grain, precious metals, and silver, but financial instruments have long dominated commodity trading (Table 47-8). Futures on Treasury bonds were the most actively traded contracts in 1998, with 112,224,081 contracts changing hands. The 3-month Eurodollar followed closely with 109,472,507 contracts traded. Earning the number three spot with the second largest percentage gain was the German government bund (EUREX/Frankfurt), which traded 89,877,840 contracts, representing a 187 percent increase over the previous year. KOSPI 200 stock index options (Korea Stock Exchange) edged into the ninth slot. As world financial markets have

TABLE 47-8: Top 10 International Contracts
(millions of contracts; percent)

Contract	Exchange		Jan.–Dec. 1997	Jan.–Dec. 1998	Percent Change
1. U.S. T-bonds	CBOT	United States	99.8	112.2	12.4
2. 3-Month Eurodollar	CME	United States	99.8	109.5	9.7
3. German Bund	DTB/Eurex	Germany	31.3	89.9	186.8
4. 3-Month Euromark	LIFFE	United Kingdom	43.3	54.6	25.9
5. U.S. T-bond options	CBOT	United States	30.8	39.9	29.7
6. Interest rate	BM&F	Brazil	36.5	35.2	–3.6
7. S&P 100 Index Options	CBOE	United States	36.6	33.4	–8.7
8. 3-Month Eurodollar options	CME	United States	29.6	33.1	12.0
9. KOSPI 200 options	KSE	Korea	4.5	32.3	613.5
10. BOBL	DTB/Eurex	United Kingdom	24.3	31.7	30.4
Total			436.6	571.8	
Percent of World Futures and Options Contract Volume			22.6	26.3	

Source: Futures Industry Association.

become increasingly sophisticated, the type and volume of exchange-traded derivatives and over-the-counter (OTC) derivatives have exploded. Electronic trading systems are replacing open outcry floor trading at exchanges around the world, and instantaneous international communication and transactional capabilities are creating truly global markets. Consequently, domestic exchanges and industry professionals are eager to offer their products to U.S. customers. While futures exchanges are grappling with these technological developments, the number and type of derivative products offered over the counter continue to mushroom even as the volume of transactions in that market increases exponentially. In 1999, the OTC derivatives market was estimated by the Bank of International Settlements to have a $70 trillion notional value. Table 47-9 shows the top 10 international exchanges and the percentages of futures and options trading.

As the market has grown in diversity with the development of a multitude of new products and increased interest in new market mechanisms, the Commodity Futures Trading Commission (CFTC) has been put under review. The CFTC oversees exchange rule enforcement and conducts its own surveillance of trading in futures and related cash markets as part of its mission to prevent market abuse and enhance the operations of the market. The responsibility of the CFTC might best be summarized by saying that its purpose is to ensure fair practices and honest dealing in futures trading in order to permit accurate price discovery and opportunity for efficient hedging through competitive, manipulation-free markets. In September 1998, when a large hedge fund, Long-Term Capital Management LP (LTCM), nearly defaulted on $1.25 trillion in the notional value of exchange traded and OTC derivatives, the long-running assurances made by Wall Street that it could control the increasingly complex world of derivatives and global trading without more regulation were questioned.

In any case, there is fierce competition among exchanges to establish new products and attract trading. This is forcing alliances both overseas and within the United States to cut costs and improve service. In September 1997, the three largest European exchanges—Germany's Deutsche Borse, the French Matif, and the Swiss Schweizer Borse—agreed to standardize their contracts and develop a common trading system called EUREX. In March 1998, the Chicago Board of Trade (CBOT) and the Chicago Mercantile Exchange (CME) agreed to consolidate their clearing functions and the New York Cotton Exchange and the Coffee, Sugar, and Cocoa Exchange agreed to merge to form the New York Board of Trade. CBOT and EUREX also entered into an alliance that allowed their members to trade on each other's floors. In late 1999, the CME and the London Interbank Financial Futures and Options Exchange (LIFFE) reached a cross-margining plan that will net the positions of two of the world's most popular interest rate contracts, the Eurodollar and the Euribor, as well as the Eurodollar/Euribor spread contract. Also included in the agreement was the ability for the members of each exchange to have electronic access to products listed on the other exchange, including stock indexes (LIFFE members will be able to trade CME products). This enhanced liquidity comes at a time when international

TABLE 47-9: Top 10 International Exchanges
(millions of contracts; percent)

	Jan.–Dec. 1997	Jan.–Dec. 1998	Percent Change
1. CBOT	242.7	281.2	15.9
2. Eurex[1]	152.3	248.2	63.0
3. CME	200.7	226.6	12.9
4. CBOE	187.2	206.9	10.5
5. LIFFE	209.4	194.4	–7.2
6. Amex	88.1	97.6	10.8
7. NYMEX	83.9	95.0	13.3
8. BM&F	122.2	87.0	–28.8
9. Amsterdam	48.7	64.8	33.1
10. Pacific Stock Exchange	43.4	59.0	36.0
Total	1,378.5	1,560.7	
Total futures and options (%)	71.4	71.7	
[1] Eurex Frankfurt (formerly DTB)	112.2	209.6	86.8
Eurex Zurich (formerly SOFFEX)	40.1	38.7	–3.6

Source: Futures Industry Association.

TABLE 47-10: U.S. Commodities Futures Trading
(millions of contracts; percent)

Exchange	Fiscal Year 1997	Fiscal Year 1998	Percent Change
Chicago Board of Trade (CBT)	179.293	218.205	21.7
Kansas City Board of Trade (KCBT)	2.119	2.156	1.7
Minneapolis Grain Exchange (MGE)	1.075	1.058	−1.6
MidAmerica Commodity Exchange (MCE)	3.321	3.358	1.1
Chicago Mercantile Exchange (CME) and International Monetary Market (IMM)	147.875	181.052	22.4
New York Mercantile Exchange (NYMEX) and Commodity Exchange, Inc. (COMEX)	68.213	78.374	14.9
New York Cotton Exchange & Associates (NYCE) and New York Futures Exchange (NYFE)	5.805	6.540	12.7
Coffee, Sugar, and Cocoa Exchange (CSCE)	9.603	9.813	2.2
Philadelphia Board of Trade (PBOT)	0.036	0.006	−82.4
Total	417.342	500.563	19.9

Source: Commodity Futures Trading Commission.

commodity trading is high and global demand is increasing on the heels of the information technology revolution.

Domestic Trends

Table 47-10 shows the volume of futures trading on U.S. exchanges. Since the time period (fiscal year versus calendar year) is different from that of Table 48-7, the data do not match, but similar growth trends are evident. As in stock trading, aggregate volumes and volumes associated with individual contracts vary widely with both macroeconomic and microeconomic factors. The most significant macro driver in 1997 was the Asian financial upheaval, which started as a currency crisis (translating immediately into high volatility and volume in currency-related futures) and then spread to other commodities, such as copper. Otherwise, 1997 was a down year in commodities, with that trend continuing into 1998.

A brief overview of the types of contracts traded on the U.S. exchanges is seen in Table 47-11. Financial contracts with interest rate futures posted a rise of 14 percent in 1998, with equity indexes soaring over 64 percent and futures contracts and options on futures contracts gaining over 20 percent. (see Table 47-12) The increase in equity indexes is a direct result of the introduction of several products late in 1997 based on popular stock indexes. On September 9, 1997, the CME introduced the "F-mini" contract based on the Standard & Poor's (S&P) 500 stock index, which,

TABLE 47-11: Number of Futures Contracts Traded on U.S. Exchanges
(millions of contracts; percent)

	1997	1998	Percent Change
Interest rate	244.6	279.2	14.1
Agricultural commodities	74.9	73.3	−2.1
Energy products	52.9	63.8	20.6
Foreign currency	26.6	27.0	1.5
Equity indexes	25.8	42.4	64.3
Precious metals	15.4	13.8	−10.4
Nonprecious metals	2.4	2.5	4.2
Other	1.1	1.2	9.1
Total	443.7	503.2	13.4

Source: Commodity Futures Trading Commission.

compared with the existing S&P 500 contract, required a margin (or down payment) of only $2,100 that was based on the index price then in effect: one-tenth of the existing S&P 500 future. Then, just 1 month later, on October 6, the rival CBOT started trading a contract based on the Dow Jones Industrial Average (DJIA). Despite substantial pressure, the Dow Jones had never before licensed anyone to list derivatives on its key index. Also unveiled in October was the first-ever stock index based on the DJIA on the Chicago Board Options Exchange.

Also traded electronically and over the Internet, these contracts are intended to appeal to retail investors. In the future, the big story may not be the introduction of additional stock index products but the ability to trade them electronically (see Table 47-13)

Industry Projections for the Next 1 and 5 Years

As all financial and product markets continue their trend toward globalization, investors need to find new ways to hedge risk, and derivatives creators are responding to that need with ever-increasing sophistication. As electronic trading takes the industry by storm, many issues are being raised about how business will be conducted in the futures industry in the coming years. While electronic trading has been around since the late 1980s, the last few years have seen dramatic changes in the available technology, the demands of the intermediaries and their customers, and the shift from the trading floor to the computer screen.

The major risk, or potential catalyst, for change that may affect the futures industry is the reauthorization of the CFTC on September 30, 2000. Since its inception, there has been debate about what the CFTC's role should be. The question is whether the current definition of a commodity is too broad. Specifically, should financial derivatives be regulated differently from physical commodity derivatives or regulated at all? Should OTC derivatives be regulated in the same manner as exchange-traded instruments? As Brooksley Born steps down as chairperson of the CFTC, among the critical issues to be discussed are OTC derivatives regulation; regulatory reform for exchange-traded derivatives; the ability of futures exchanges to list and trade equity-based products, including

TABLE 47-12: Commodity Trading Industry (SIC 6221, 6231, 628) Trends and Forecasts
(millions of contracts; percent)

	Fiscal Year								Percent Change			
	1993	1994	1995	1996	1997	1998	1999[1]	2000[1]	96–97	97–98	98–99	99–00
Futures contracts	325.5	411.1	409.4	394.2	417.3	500.5	555.6	616.7	5.9	19.9	11.0	11.0
Options on futures	76.9	99.2	95.4	100.3	105.1	124.1	137.8	152.9	4.8	18.1	11.0	11.0

[1] Forecast.
Source: Commodity Futures Trading Commission; forecast by Standard & Poor's.

futures on individual equities; and whether foreign terminals can be placed in the United States, enabling U.S. customers to place orders (and perhaps effect trades) by electronic access. In view of rapid improvements in trading technology, the globalization of markets, and increasingly open avenues of international trade, is there a need for more regulation or regulation of a different kind? How much is enough? Those opposed to stricter regulation believe that care must be taken to assure that domestic regulation is not too strict because that would chase the business offshore.

In October 1999, LIFFE announced that trading in its most popular futures contracts would be done only on computer screens beginning in November 1999. This will mark the end of the open outcry trading pits that only a few years ago were filled with more than 1,000 traders using hand signals and shouts to trade everything from government bond futures to British 3-month money contracts. The end comes as no surprise, as trading in its number one European rival, the Swiss-German EUREX, is already all electronic.

This event provides evidence of the drastic changes that technology is bringing about in the entire financial services industry. From the replacement of floor trading with screen-based trading to the presence of foreign terminals on U.S. desktops, the technological changes are numerous. With the increasing flow of information and in the face of continuing technological enhancements allowing better liquidity, the outlook for commodities trading is for continued growth. In the absence of significant regulatory reform that could transform the industry, the estimated growth in futures and options volume for both 1999 and 2000 is 10 to 12 percent, although with a small decrease in early 2000 with an adjustment to the new millennium clock.

TABLE 47-13: Number of Options Contracts Traded on U.S. Exchanges
(millions of contracts; percent)

	1997	1998	Percent Change
Equity	269.6	325.8	20.8
Stock index	78.2	74.8	–4.3
Foreign currency	2.6	1.8	–30.8
Interest rate	0.1	0.1	0.0
Futures	111.1	127.5	14.8
Total	461.6	530.0	14.8

Source: Commodity Futures Trading Commission.

Stephen Biggar, Standard & Poor's DRI, (212) 438-9504, November 1999.

REFERENCES

Commodity Futures Trading Commission, *Annual Reports,* 1155 21 Street, NW, Washington, DC 20581. (202) 418-5000, http://www.cftc.gov.

Federal Reserve System, Board of Governors, 20 Street and C Street, NW, Washington, DC 20551. (202) 452-3215, http://www.bog.frb.fed.us.

Futures Industry Association, *Futures Industry Magazine,* 2001 Pennsylvania Avenue, NW, Washington, DC 20006. (202) 466-5460, http://www.fiafii.org.

Investment Company Institute, *Mutual Fund Fact Book,* 1401 H Street, NW, Suite 1200, Washington, DC 20005. (202) 326-5800, http://www.ici.org.

Securities Industry Association, 120 Broadway, New York, NY 10271. (212) 608-1500, http://www.sia.com.

U.S. Securities and Exchange Commission, 450 Fifth Street, NW, Washington, DC 20549. (202) 942-8088, http://www.sec.gov.

The Wall Street Journal, 200 Liberty Street, New York, NY 10281. http://www.wsj.com.

RELATED CHAPTERS

45: Financial Institutions
46: Insurance
48: Professional Business Services

GLOSSARY

Broker: A person or firm acting as an intermediary between the buyers and sellers of securities.

Commodity future: A contract tied to a particular commodity's price movement; determined on the floor of a commodity exchange.

Derivative: A contract whose value is based on the price of an underlying financial asset, index, or other investment.

Exchanges: Locations where securities or futures trading take place, such as the New York Stock Exchange.

Mutual fund: A pool of money raised from individual shareholders and managed by an investment company that invests in stocks, bonds, options, futures, and money market and other securities.

Option: A contract that gives the holder the right, but not the obligation, to buy or sell a certain security at a predetermined price, typically until an agreed upon date.

Security: A financial instrument that represents ownership interest in a corporation, a creditor relationship with a company or government, or another underlying right.

PROFESSIONAL BUSINESS SERVICES
Economic and Trade Trends

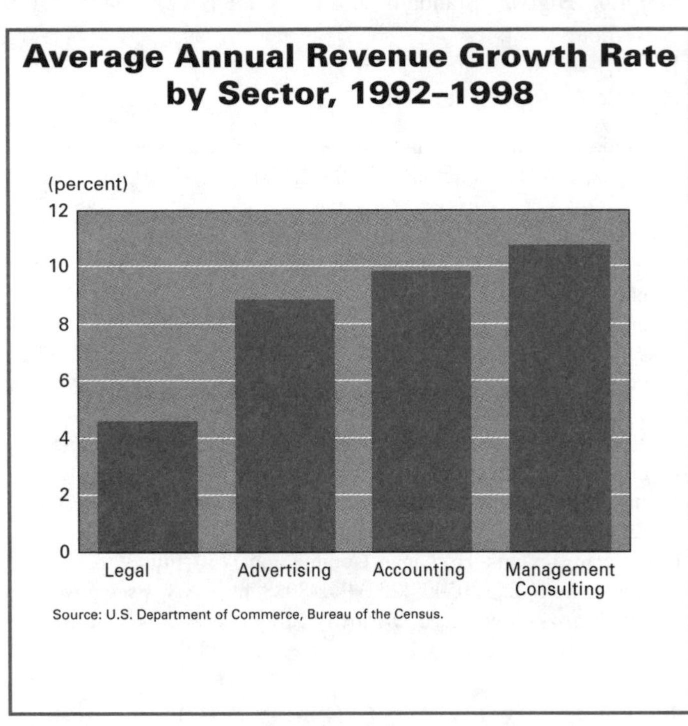

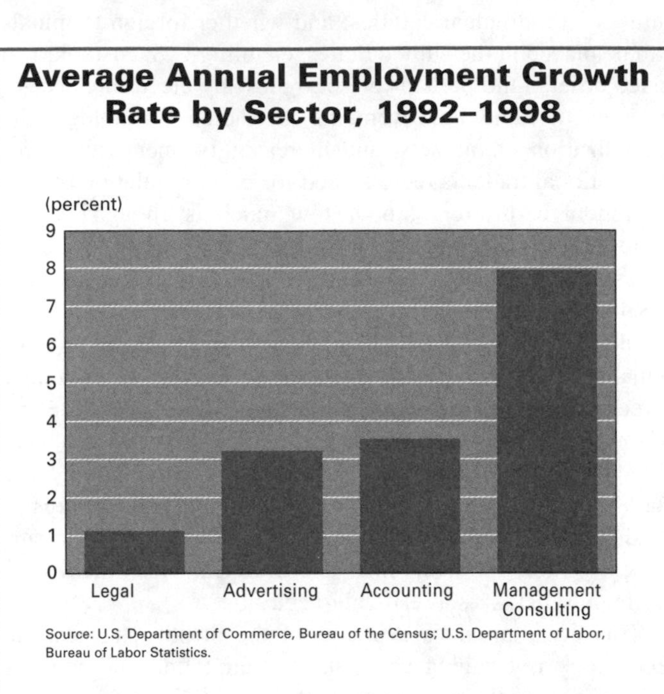

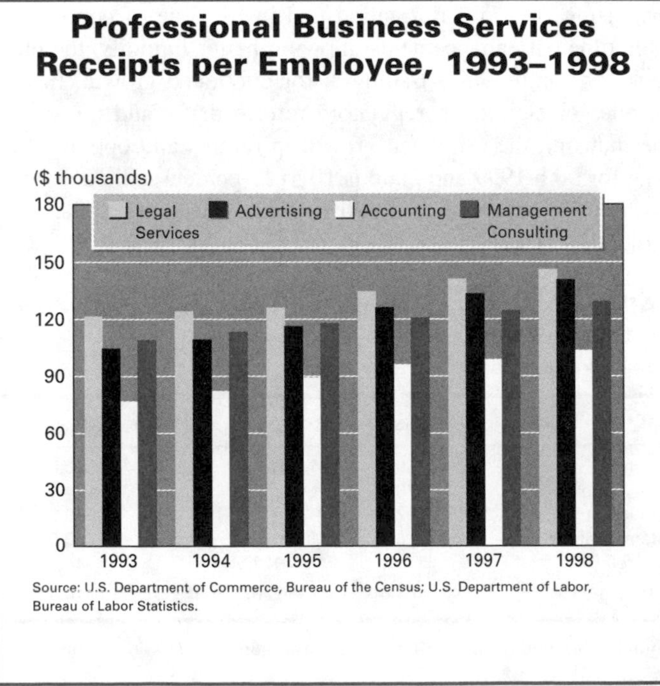

See "Getting the Most Out of *Outlook 2000*" for definitions of terms.

48

Professional Business Services

INDUSTRY DEFINITION The professional business services industry includes accounting, auditing, and bookkeeping services (SIC 8721); advertising services (SIC 731); legal services (SIC 81); and management consulting and public relations services (SIC 874).

OVERVIEW

The professional service industries are undergoing enormous changes and experiencing a powerful surge in business around the world. Record revenue growth rates were reported for many U.S. professional services firms in 1998. The health of the U.S. economy, a return to relative stability in Asian and Latin American markets, and a boom in the globalization of businesses around the world have created significant opportunities for professionals whose expertise is required in international business transactions, such as mergers and acquisitions and corporate finance.

U.S.-based corporations, especially the Big Five accounting firms and the top law firms, are world leaders in the professional services industry. Revenue per employee has risen steadily in each of these professions since the early 1990s, and all the sectors have contributed to the healthy surplus in trade with the rest of the world. The biggest purchasers abroad of U.S. professional services have been from the United Kingdom, Canada, Japan, Germany, France, and Australia.

Consolidation is on the rise among professional service firms, a trend that is reducing the number of companies in the field and combining the revenues of already huge multinational firms. The Big Five accounting industry leaders are now also the top suppliers of management consulting services around the world as well as some of the largest employers of attorneys. The recent attempt to allow multidisciplinary partnerships (MDPs) in the United States could change the structure of the professional service industries irreversibly.

The use of the Internet is catching on rapidly among professional services firms. Companies are using the World Wide Web to market their services, enhance communication with clients and between branch offices, and deliver services electronically.

The World Trade Organization (WTO) launched a new round of trade negotiations focusing on services in January 2000. More than 130 WTO member countries were to participate in the round, known as GATS 2000 (General Agreement on Trade in Services), which will take several years to complete. To further liberalize world trade in professional services, the negotiators will attempt to reduce restrictions on professionals providing services across national borders and encourage regulatory authorities around the world to recognize the educational and professional qualifications of service providers from other nations.

The U.S. government and industry representatives, in cooperation with Canada and Mexico, have begun to develop a new system to classify services, that is known as the North American Industry Classification System (NAICS). The revised classifications will recognize new services and industries that have emerged since the Standard Industrial Classification (SIC) system was devised and will allow the collection of more detailed and accurate data on North American service industries, including professional business services. For more detailed information, see "Getting the Most Out of *Outlook 2000*."

ACCOUNTING, AUDITING, AND BOOKKEEPING

Domestic Trends and Performance

The scope of services offered by accounting firms is expanding rapidly. Advances in technology, coupled with changes in

TABLE 48-1: Worldwide Revenues of the Top Eight U.S. Accounting Firms in Fiscal Year 1998

	Revenues, millions of dollars	Percent Change 97–98
Andersen Worldwide	13,900	23
PricewaterhouseCoopers	15,312	19.8
Ernst & Young	10,900	19.8
Deloitte & Touche	9,000	21.6
KPMG	9,259	15.5
Grant Thornton	1,506	7.3
McGladrey & Pullen	1,179	11.2
BDO Seidman	1,601	10.4
Total[1]	62,657	19.3

Source: *Public Accounting Report,* February 1999, Strafford Publications, Inc., Atlanta, GA. (404) 881-1141.

clients' demands, are enabling and encouraging increasing numbers of accounting firms to offer a wide array of services in addition to traditional accounting, auditing, attest, bookkeeping, and tax services.

The Big Five accounting firms (Andersen Worldwide, PricewaterhouseCoopers, Ernst & Young, Deloitte & Touche, and KPMG) dominated the global market in 1998 with combined global revenue exceeding $58 billion, well over half the industry's total revenue. In terms of revenue growth, 1998 was a record-breaking year for the Big Five, attributable primarily to the boom in consulting services. Andersen Worldwide led the pack with net revenues of $13.9 billion, a 23 percent increase over 1997 (see Table 48-1). On average, fees from management consulting services accounted for nearly half of all the revenue earned by the top eight accounting firms in fiscal year (FY) 1998, surpassing the revenue generated by accounting, auditing, attest, and tax services combined. The July 1998 merger of Price Waterhouse and Coopers & Lybrand to form PricewaterhouseCoopers created the largest accounting network in the world, whose FY 1998 net global revenue exceeded $15.3 billion.

All the Big Five firms reported double-digit growth rates in 1998. However, some of the most spectacular growth was achieved by firms outside the top 10, some of which registered increases of nearly 60 percent over 1997 revenues. Ninety of the top 100 firms had revenue increases, and 58 of them achieved double-digit gains.

Accounting firms and certified public accountants (CPAs) nationwide have begun offering a wide array of services in addition to traditional accounting, auditing, and bookkeeping services. This trend is partially a response to clients' demand for "one-stop shopping" for all their professional services needs. Another cause is the relatively flat growth in demand for traditional accounting and auditing services over the past 10 years and the desire of CPAs to develop more value-added services. The addition of management consulting, legal, and other professional services to the practice mix of large national accounting networks is transforming the industry and has engendered the new category of MDPs.

Many firms are beginning to offer technology consulting because of growing client demand for Internet and electronic commerce services. *Accounting Today*'s 1999 survey of CPA clients indicates that keeping up with technology is the strategic issue of greatest concern to clients, followed by recruiting and retaining staff, competing with larger companies, planning for executive succession, and maximizing productivity.

CPA firms will continue to develop their capabilities and/or alliances to meet clients' demands. Some other areas of expansion among accounting firms are administrative services, financial and investment planning services, general management services, government administration, human resources, international operations, information technology and computer systems consulting, litigation support, manufacturing administration, marketing, and research and development.

A trend toward consolidation is under way in the accounting industry. Many small and medium-size independent firms are merging or forming alliances with large service companies such as American Express Company, H&R Block Incorporated, and Century Business Services. Consolidation is causing a decline in the number of independent accounting firms that offer only tax and accounting services. The New York State Society of CPAs estimates that there is a strong possibility that up to 50 of the largest accounting firms in the United States will dissolve or merge with other entities by the end of the year 2000. The incredibly large increase in revenue among the top 100 accounting firms between 1997 and 1998 may be partially attributable to this trend toward consolidation.

Several factors are fueling the drive toward consolidation. Consolidators want access to the large volume of business currently being done by independent CPAs. The trust that small businesses and individuals have in their CPAs is considered very valuable, and consolidators want to maximize its potential in expanding their own businesses.

From CPA firms' perspective, to compete effectively in today's market requires high levels of expertise in a growing

TABLE 48-2: U.S. Accounting, Auditing, and Bookkeeping Services (SIC 8721) Trends and Forecasts
(millions of dollars, except as noted)

	1992	1993	1994	1995	1996	1997	1998	1999[1]	2000[2]	2004[2]
Receipts	37,191	39,807	42,633	48,769	54,401	58,855	65,414	73,264	82,056	115,829
Employment (thousands)	513	508	519	546	566	596	632	670	703	855

[1] Estimate.
[2] Forecast.
Source: U.S. Department of Commerce: International Trade Administration (ITA), Bureau of Census; U.S. Department of Labor: Bureau of Labor Statistics. Estimates and forecasts by ITA.

array of services, plus strict quality control capabilities. This is increasingly difficult for smaller independent firms to achieve. To add new services to their offerings, firms must hire experts in new fields, outsource for those services, join strategic alliances to enable them to meet clients' demands, or merge with large firms that have more resources. The need for capital will continue to increase as firms attempt to expand their service offerings, and merging with larger firms is often the best way to acquire the necessary capital. Frequently the home office of the consolidation partner will provide firms with centralized advertising and marketing materials. As consolidations continue, brand name recognition is likely to benefit firms acquired by "big-name" consolidators, and this may make it more difficult for independent CPA firms to compete.

The U.S. Securities and Exchange Commission (SEC) is investigating consolidation activities to determine whether they could result in violations of the rules that guarantee the independence of accountants and auditors. One concern is that accounting firms that, as part of their financial services practice recommend to clients the investment products of their new partners could develop a bias in audits done on those public companies. Under current rules, auditors are not allowed to accept commissions for recommending investment products or services to their audit clients. Thus, the terms of consolidation deals are important: Partners in accounting firms that are purchased by large financial services companies become employees of a large company, but they also may choose to retain ownership in the firm that does audits. This type of arrangement could create a conflict.

Growing demand for diverse services is leading traditional accounting firms down new paths. Many firms are expanding their business by developing specialties to respond to specific clients' needs and developing their personnel, operations, and software accordingly. Some examples of industry specialization areas are construction, real estate, auto dealerships, hotels, nonprofit organizations, and international businesses. CPAs are increasingly finding that specialization is the key to remaining competitive, since knowledge of a particular industry is an important criterion for clients in selecting a service provider.

CPAs are now expected to know more about many different subjects than they did in the past. This trend has forced many accountants to make decisions about whether they will become generalists or specialists and in which areas they will specialize.

There is a growing trend for smaller, independent accounting firms to create strategic alliances with other firms with complementary areas of expertise. Formal and informal networks of alliances may come about in a number of ways. A CPA firm may seek out a specialist to fulfill a specific client's need, and the specialist will bill the client directly. Alternatively, the firm may hire a consultant on a short-term basis to assist with some part of the ongoing work being done for a client. Another possibility is that the CPA may go to the alliance in search of expertise on a particular client issue, pay for the service directly, and pass the expertise on to the client. In any case, strategic alliances benefit all concerned and are an effective means for small firms to retain their clients, small-firm character, and independence.

Many accounting firms are responding to the growing demand among corporate clients for business process outsourcing. A recent survey conducted by PricewaterhouseCoopers indicated that more than half of Fortune 500 companies had outsourced at least one business function, such as accounting, treasury, tax compliance, and other "back office" functions, to professional service providers. Among the benefits of outsourcing are that it frees corporate management to focus on developing new business, which improves shareholder value, reduces costs, and increases efficiency. This high-growth area has led to lucrative opportunities for accounting and professional services firms, including some of the Big Five. The energy, financial services, technology, entertainment, media, communications, and consumer and industrial products industries are leaders in the trend toward outsourcing business services.

Perhaps more than any other invention of the twentieth century, computers have changed the way companies do business. They allow professionals to accomplish more in a given time frame and do things more creatively than before. Instantaneous access to virtually limitless information, combined with communication advances, has transformed the accounting industry and the entire economy.

CPAs are rapidly adopting new technologies to help them compete in the global marketplace and provide expanded services to meet their clients' ever-growing demands. Many firms are developing plans to maximize the value of their technology purchases and ensure their positive impact on productivity, efficiency, and profitability. E-mail, voice mail, laptops, remote access, Internet, cellular phones, scanners, and software choices all affect a firm's ability to deliver services to its clients, and the options are increasing at a dizzying pace. A recent study estimated the annual cost to own a computer for a typical company at $10,000 per employee and perhaps even more for accounting firms, which use more mission-critical software applications than do most other businesses. With such a large investment, it is not surprising that many accounting firms are opting to outsource their technology planning to experts in the field.

Software for the accounting industry has developed rapidly in recent years and continues to improve as more companies attempt to write better programs that are easier to learn and use. Financial and estate planning programs for CPAs are abundant, as are reviews of the strengths and weaknesses of the many programs available. Critical questions for accounting firms to answer before purchasing software are as follows: What client needs will be served? How much time will be required to train staff in the use of the software? What return can be expected from employing the new programs?

Tax software has become extremely popular with CPAs and taxpayers. Nearly every tax preparer in the country now uses a personal computer to prepare client returns, according to the National Association of Computerized Tax Processors. The Internal Revenue Service (IRS) states that more than 21 percent of U.S. tax returns were filed electronically in 1998, and the IRS wants at least 80 percent of returns to be filed electronically by the year 2007.

Practice management software is becoming essential to help with tasks such as timekeeping, time and billing, project tracking, accounting systems, and client write-up. Another popular software option is the personal information manager to keep track of client data, appointment schedules, and the like.

The Internet also has changed the way many CPAs do business. It has enabled firms to access more data more quickly than ever before and inexpensively market their services to a wide audience on the Web. It enables them to offer convenient training and development opportunities for staff at much lower cost than traditional training venues, and it allows them to efficiently and inexpensively communicate and share information with clients and affiliate offices. In short, it has allowed CPAs to provide more services more quickly than in the past and hence has created new profit opportunities.

Many CPA firms now have Web sites. In a recent survey of CPAs who use the Web, the most popular reasons cited for creating home pages were to help firms keep up with technology, improve services to clients, and maintain a firm's reputation as an information expert. Other uses of Web sites are to recruit new employees and reduce postage and printing costs.

In 1998, the American Institute of CPAs (AICPA) and the Canadian Institute of Chartered Accountants developed the CPA WebTrust program to meet the needs of the expanding on-line marketplace. Its purpose is to develop customer confidence and trust in buying on-line. Studies have shown that most people avoid purchasing on-line because of fears regarding the security of their credit cards and personal financial information on the Internet. According to the AICPA, CPAs are uniquely qualified to provide independent assurance to consumers who want to do business on-line.

Electronic commerce businesses that apply to participate in the CPA WebTrust program are examined by a licensed CPA in the following areas: on-line business practices and disclosures, such as the way in which orders are taken and fulfilled, how back orders are processed, and so on; transaction integrity, including the ability of an on-line business to deliver what was ordered at the agreed-on price and time frame; and information protection and privacy, or the ability of the company to ensure that personal information will be transmitted securely and confidential information will be kept private. A consumer complaint resolution mechanism is built into the assurance service.

Once it is approved by a CPA, the on-line company is issued a CPA WebTrust seal to display on its Web site. Consumers visiting the site can click on the seal and access the CPA's report of the results of the examination of the on-line business, the CPA WebTrust principles and criteria, and links to other sites that have been granted the seal.

Approximately 20 companies currently participate in the program, including E-Trade, a Web site for on-line investors; Bell Canada, the largest Canadian telecommunications company; and Competitor Communications, Inc., the E-commerce site of Toronto Blue Jays pitcher Roger Clemens. The service is now available to on-line businesses through licensed accountants in the United States, Canada, Puerto Rico, the United Kingdom, and Ireland.

International Activities

The WTO Council for Trade in Services established a Working Party on Professional Services (WPPS) in the early 1990s whose mandate is to examine worldwide domestic regulation issues that may affect international trade in professional services and make recommendations for improvements. So far, WPPS has focused on the accountancy sector.

One of the concrete achievements of the WPPS was to create guidelines that regulators could use to determine cross-border recognition of qualifications in the accountancy sector. The guidelines should make it easier for national governments and regulators to negotiate agreements with other countries on the mutual recognition of professional qualifications.

The WPPS also has developed a set of disciplines on domestic regulation in accountancy that applies to all WTO member countries that made commitments related to accounting during the previous round of services trade negotiations, which ended in 1994. The disciplines are intended to facilitate trade in accounting services by ensuring that regulations related to professional licensing requirements and procedures, technical standards, and qualification requirements and procedures in WTO member countries do not constitute unnecessary barriers to trade.

Differences in national accounting rules have been the focus of worldwide attention for several years, and pressure is growing around the globe to formulate a harmonized set of international accounting rules that corporations anywhere could use to list on any stock market in any country. Considerable progress was made on this issue in 1999. The United Kingdom–based International Accounting Standards Committee (IASC) has nearly completed its work on a core set of accounting standards, which are now under review by the International Organisation of Securities Commissions (IOSCO) and securities regulatory bodies around the world, including the SEC. The review will determine whether regulators will allow foreign companies to use the common set of international rules on their home country stock markets.

Proponents believe that uniform accounting standards can reduce the costs associated with preparing financial statements, make it easier to compare financial information about companies in different countries, and generally create a smoother flow of capital around the world. They also could accelerate global mergers, since companies would not have to spend time and resources converting their books to satisfy the rules of other nations before mergers could be completed.

The SEC and the Financial Accounting Standards Board (FASB) have reservations about the proposed core set of international accounting rules. Their view is that the proposed standards are not of the same high quality as the U.S. Generally Accepted Accounting Principles (GAAP) and do not require the same level of detail in financial reporting as do current U.S. rules and therefore would be subject to wider interpretation;

TABLE 48-3: Balance of Trade in Accounting, Auditing, and Bookkeeping Services
(millions of dollars)

	1993	1994	1995	1996	1997	1998
U.S. exports	164	132	181	222	331	344
U.S. imports	103	130	170	218	280	329
Balance	61	2	11	4	51	15

Source: U.S. Department of Commerce, Bureau of Economic Analysis.

that could mean that they would not adequately protect investors. The SEC is conducting a careful technical review and soliciting public comment on the IASC standards.

Another important area of consideration is the type of organization that ultimately will oversee international accountancy standards issues in the future. The IASC is a likely candidate, but many changes would have to take place before the United States and other nations would give the IASC the authority to set global standards. Intense debate is under way on the subject, and models for the future structure and role of IASC are being discussed. It will be difficult to achieve the delicate balance of power required to satisfy the many organizations that have an important stake in any future global standard setting and enforcement activity.

The balance of trade in accounting, auditing, and bookkeeping services is shown in Table 48-3.

Karen Holderman, U.S. Department of Commerce, Office of Service Industries, (202) 482-0345, September 1999.

ADVERTISING

The U.S. advertising industry consists of advertisers, the media, and advertising agencies. Advertisers are manufacturers of consumer products and service providers; media services include broadcast television, cable television, magazines, newspapers, and radio; and advertising agencies create advertising campaigns and place advertisements in the media.

In 1998, 7 of the top 10 advertising agencies in the world in terms of gross income were in the United States (see Table 48-4). The U.S. advertising industry accounts for almost 50 percent of all advertising expenditures worldwide. Total spending by national advertisers in the United States is approximately $120 billion, compared with the second largest market, Japan, with about $36 billion, and the third largest, the United Kingdom, with about $21 billion.

Advertisers will continue to make significant changes in the way they do business during the next few years. Recent and pending court decisions and proposed government regulations will affect what products can be advertised (e.g., advertising restrictions on tobacco products and sweepstakes offers) and could restrict how marketers obtain personal information. Although there will be significant limits on tobacco marketing and advertising, advertisers will gain revenues from antismoking products and campaigns. Discussions on privacy matters in bilateral and multilateral governmental settings could result in limits on information flow from one national market to another if government authorities determine that proper control over personal data is not being exercised. Advertising opportunities should increase in the year 2000, driven by several factors: the year 2000 political elections, the Olympics, and the continued advertising of "millennium" activities until 2001.

Domestic Trends and Performance

U.S. advertising expenditures continued to be strong throughout 1998, outpacing the economy for the fifth consecutive year. Industry analysts predict that expenditures by all advertisers in 1999 will be about $212 billion, a gain of almost 6 percent over 1998. According to *Advertising Age,* General Motors Corporation was the top U.S. advertiser, spending about over $2 billion, followed by Proctor & Gamble with almost $2 billion. DaimlerChrysler, Philip Morris, and Ford Motor Company rounded out the top five spenders in 1998 for advertising expenditures. The top advertising categories are automotive, retail, telecommunications, food, and restaurants.

In response to a class action suit filed in almost every state against two major sweepstakes companies, Congress passed a sweepstakes bill in 1999 that will restrict certain advertising promotions. The lawsuits allege that sweepstakes companies use fraudulent marketing practices. This bill could have large repercussions, since publishing companies generally rely on sweepstakes mailings to generate about one-third of their total subscriptions. Some titles get as much as 50 percent of their business from sweepstakes. The bill becomes law April 13, 2000, and requires companies to state that no purchase is necessary to enter and to offer toll-free numbers for individuals to call to be removed from sweepstakes lists.

Total U.S. advertising media spending grew 6.9 percent to $16.3 billion in 1998. Television advertising spending is expected to get an added boost from a U.S. Federal Communi-

TABLE 48-4: Worldwide Gross Income of the Top 10 Advertising Firms in Fiscal Year 1998
(millions of dollars; percent)

Firm	Income	Percent Change 97–98
Omnicom Group (New York)	4,812	12
Interpublic Group of Companies (New York)	4,305	13
WPP Group (London)	4,157	15
Dentsu (Tokyo)	1,786	–10
Young & Rubicam (New York)	1,660	11
Havas Advertising (Paris)	1,298	10
True North Communications (Chicago)	1,242	3
Grey Advertising (New York)	1,240	9
Leo Burnett (Chicago)	950	8
Publicis (New York)	930	29
Total/Average	22,380	10

Source: *Advertising Age,* 1999.

cation Commission's action that will permit a company to own more than one television station in a local market. One of the new media approaches some of the major marketers use in scheduling television advertising is recency planning. Rather than continuous scheduling and focusing on the frequency of advertisements, recency planning focuses on the timing of advertisements and influences consumers in regard to the brands being purchased.

One recent focus of television advertising is prescription drugs. Prescription drug marketers have significantly increased their television advertising spending since 1994 as a result of the loosened U.S. Food and Drug Administration guidelines on product-specific commercials. In 1998, prescription drug marketers spent about $664 million on television ads, compared with $310 million in 1997 and $36 million in 1994.

Spot television advertising grew 6.6 percent to $15.5 billion in 1998. Prices in television's spot market for 1999 are expected to rise about 5 percent over the 1998 level, with large increases from automobile marketers.

Syndication television may double or triple its total advertising dollars with an increase of $200 million to $300 million to reach $2.3 billion in 1999–2000. However, some purchasers believe that prices for some of the top shows are too high. The top advertiser on syndicated television for 1998 was Proctor & Gamble, followed by MCI WorldCom and General Motors Corporation.

National cable television advertising continues to surge, up 15.4 percent to $6.6 billion in 1998, and analysts predicted that expenditures in this sector would be approximately $8.6 billion in 1999, a gain of $2 billion from 1998. U.S. household delivery of basic cable reached 2.7 million homes in 1999, an increase of 12.8 percent from 1998. A new study shows that viewers who watch cable television programming pay more attention to commercials than do viewers who watch broadcast television programming. Top cable advertisement categories include long-distance telephone service, national restaurants, and motion pictures.

Advertising on spot cable television totaled an estimated $280 million in 1998. This is expected to increase through the use of advanced technology, which should reduce purchaser's buying steps and increase electronic data interchange. In August 1999, this industry began posting availabilities on the Internet, creating the first end-to-end electronic sales tool for buying local cable spots. As a result, agencies will be able to process local cable television programming electronically, from perusing what is available on the Internet to receiving affidavits and invoices by electronic transmission.

U.S. advertising spending for magazines was up 8.5 percent to $13.7 billion in 1998, but the first half of 1999 was difficult for 8 of the 10 largest-circulation magazines, with total circulation being flat or down. There is no clear evidence that widespread subscription losses were due to depressed response rates to direct-mail packages and sweepstakes offers. For the moment, these magazines have been able to offset lower subscription rates because paper prices are favorable and advertising has continued to be strong, but many magazines may be forced to reduce their rate bases. Another result of the decline in circulation may be the Ford Motor Company's decision to drop several magazine publishing houses from its list of media buys. Magazine companies are concerned that print will suffer as each of the top 50 advertisers begins to spend more money on the Internet, and they are looking for ways to adapt to the new medium.

According to the Newspaper Association of America, newspaper advertising expenditures totaled almost $44 billion in 1998, an increase of 6.3 percent over 1997. National advertising expenditures reached $5.7 billion, retail ads $20.3 billion, and classified ads $17.8 billion. Nationally, more than 56 million newspapers are sold daily and 60 million are sold on Sunday. However, daily newspaper circulation fell about 0.5 percent, according to the latest Audit Bureau of Circulation report. The top-ranked daily newspaper, the *Wall Street Journal,* was down 1.5 percent to about 1.79 million subscribers, while the second-ranked newspaper, *USA Today,* was up 1.4 percent to 1.73 million subscribers. Circulation managers are concerned about stagnant circulation and readership and are looking for solutions. Advertisers consider newspapers the most commonly used source by consumers for purchasing groceries, cars, and homes; they also view most newspapers as regional.

The newspaper is the top source for recruitment advertisements and the primary advertising source for new and used vehicles. According to the Newspaper Association of America, overall print classified revenue increased to a record $17.8 billion in 1998, up almost 7 percent from 1997. By comparison, on-line newspaper classifieds generated about $92 million in revenue in 1998. Newspaper sites offer a ready-made local audience, a trusted brand name, and a variety of classified advertising resources. They also offer on-line auctions similar to eBay, a leading Internet site for on-line auctions. Both on-line classified revenue and on-line auction market sizes are expected to grow in the next few years. Jupiter Communications predicts that total on-line classified advertising will expand to almost $2 billion in 2002 from about $500 million in 1999.

Outdoor advertising revenues were up 7.5 percent to $503.5 million in the first quarter in 1999 compared with the same period in 1998. New companies from the Internet sector and public utility area have begun purchasing advertisements, while some investment companies have returned to purchasing outdoor ads. Times Square in New York has become a center for outdoor media. Several new technologies have made it easier for advertisers to run very good creative images while maintaining a consistent brand image.

Vinyl and vinyl mesh technologies enable advertisers to create large images for placement on billboards and buses (the vinyl covering bus windows is semitransparent). Mapping technologies allow marketers to pinpoint the particular neighborhood or city district where sales occur so that they can focus future campaigns on those buyers. Geodemographic technology allows marketers to determine the specific features of an audience (age, buying patterns, gender) on a street-level or dwelling-by-dwelling basis.

Advertising on the Internet has tremendous potential but is still in the embryonic phase. Although the Internet has experienced unprecedented growth in the number of users and hours of usage, marketers are evaluating the effectiveness of marketing expenditures and looking for additional improvements in technology before they increase their advertising expenditures. Worldwide expenditures for on-line marketing reached $6.2 billion in 1998, up 81 percent from $3.4 billion in 1997. Forecasters predict that expenditures will surpass $30 billion in 2002. Currently, only 1 to 2 percent of U.S. marketing expenditures are directed to the Internet. Most of the largest advertising and marketing spenders allocate less than 0.5 percent of expenditures for on-line spending, while leading technology companies spend considerably more. The top advertisers on the Web are TrustE, Microsoft Corp, Amazon.com, Cdnow, Yahoo! and AmericaOnline.

Internet advertising expenditures should follow patterns similar to those seen in the beginnings of broadcast and cable television advertising, which began slowly, increased over time, and in the case of national advertising eventually commanded very high prices. Besides being a mass medium, however, the Internet offers advertisers the opportunity to target individual consumers' interests. The Internet also allows advertisers to fine-tune their campaigns to focus on which site or interstitial (an advertisement that flashes pages for several seconds before a selected site fully loads) produces the most revenue. A shift is taking place in many business organizations, making the marketing department responsible for the Web site, which used to be the responsibility of the information technology department. Another factor marketers are considering in regard to the Internet is customers' demographic characteristics. Generally, online users are an upscale group and tend to be big spenders. Also, on-line households tend to have more children than the average household. This generation of children, the biggest since the baby boom, could make on-line marketing the medium of choice for many years to come.

Consumer attention will continue to migrate to the Internet as performance improves through increased bandwidth, speed, and quality of access. Digital subscriber line and cable modems are recent improvements in network infrastructure that address those needs. Some companies are not waiting. They are luring consumers to the Web by giving them computers in exchange for personal information, an agreement to use the computer for a set number of hours per month, and receipt of constant advertisements on their screens. Advertisers also are developing more powerful methods of reaching consumers. Banner advertisements, which are the boxes that usually appear at the top of a Web page, accounted for the majority of on-line spending in 1998, while interstitials are increasing in use.

The Internet also has other challenges for marketers to resolve. Current measurement systems do not offer precise gauges of Internet traffic. One of the biggest difficulties is accurately measuring the on-line behavior of people at work, since the workplace is an essential sector of Internet traffic, with more users visiting more pages per day and spending more time on-line than do home users.

International Activity

More and more multinational marketers are consolidating power over global advertising decisions at corporate headquarters and consolidating their large advertising budgets for use by only a few agencies worldwide. Many marketers are opting for one or two networks. While more advertising decisions are controlled by headquarters, marketers are using local input to plan and develop product launches and build brand awareness. Worldwide advertising expenditures increased approximately 5 percent in 1999 to reach about $435 billion. Advertising expenditures are generally down in Asia. They are slightly down in Japan and significantly down in Indonesia, Malaysia, and the Philippines. However, they are up significantly in China.

U.S. advertising agencies are suffering declines internationally as a result of economic recessions and lower consumer spending in many markets. A significant drop in consumer demand caused major decreases in advertising rates and revenues in Asia, Brazil, and Russia. Market disruptions in Hong Kong, Indonesia, Malaysia, the Philippines, South Korea, and Thailand have pushed U.S.-based multinationals to focus on Europe and the thriving home market. The key market for U.S. marketers has been Europe, followed by Latin America and then Asia. Many multinationals consider China the most promising emerging market, followed by Brazil, Mexico, eastern Europe, and India.

Many analysts predict that economic problems will continue for another year in some Asian markets, although some of those markets may have started to show signs of recovery for advertisers. In particular, consumer spending and advertising are on the rebound from the 2-year recession in South Korea, but some foreign firms are still experiencing difficulties with monopoly control over the allocation of television and radio advertising time. Although air time supply exceeded demand during the recent economic downturn, foreign firms reported that the government-affiliated Korean Broadcast Advertising Corporation was demonstrating considerable versatility in offering air time in lengths other than the Korean standard of 15 seconds but that the pricing for the nonstandard time lengths was financially unattractive. Also, the laws and regulations on advertising censorship procedures are nontransparent and add considerable risk and costs to the development of new advertising campaigns and the introduction of new products in South Korea. Although China's advertising expenditures have been increasing, there is uncertainty in that market too. NATO's accidental bombing of the Chinese embassy in Belgrade caused Beijing to shut down cable and satellite systems that pick up overseas channels, creating tremendous uncertainty for those channels and their advertisers.

On a positive note, Canada will open its magazine market to U.S. publishers of split-run editions as part of a deal by U.S. and Canadian officials to resolve a long-running trade dispute. Non-Canadian publishers will be able to sell up to 18 percent of advertising space to Canadian advertisers in "split-run" editions, which reprint existing content for the Canadian market and then sell advertising space to local companies. The percentage will be phased in over 3 years. Magazines interested in selling more Canadian advertising space would be required to carry majority Canadian editorial content. Canadian advertisers will be able to deduct 50 percent of their

TABLE 48-5: Advertising Services (SIC 731) Trends and Forecasts
(millions of dollars except as noted)

	1993	1994	1995	1996	1997	1998	1999[1]	2000[2]	2004[2]
Receipts	23,416	24,212	27,068	30,634	33,832	37,641	37,980	40,050	49,999
Employment (thousands)	223.7	222.5	232.9	242.8	254.5	268.2	283	299	373

[1] Estimate.
[2] Forecast.
Source: U.S. Department of Commerce: International Trade Administration (ITA), Bureau of Census; U.S. Department of Labor: Bureau of Labor Statistics. Estimates and forecasts by ITA.

advertising costs if they place ads in foreign magazines with up to 79 percent non-Canadian content, or they will be able to deduct the full costs of advertising in foreign magazines with more than 80 percent non-Canadian content. Prior to this agreement, there was no such deduction.

The Internet offers huge global marketing opportunities. In a survey by the Direct Marketing Association, almost half the respondents said that they were making money from marketing on the Internet and received many inquiries from overseas. However, U.S. marketers generally have been slow to react to overseas markets, in part because the American market is so profitable, with more Internet users in the United States than in the rest of the world combined. Growth of E-commerce overseas has been stymied by high tariffs on products, government regulations, poor infrastructure (quality is poor and transmission rates are slow, and so visual content has to be slimmed down), and high phone costs. Marketers also have to contend with numerous differences in value added tax rates, pricing, culture, currency exchanges, and languages.

Projections

Spending for all advertising in the United States was expected to reach $212 billion in 1999, up 5.5 percent over 1998. U.S. ad spending has increased every year since 1980 except for 1991. Advertising agency receipts were expected to grow 5.5 percent in 1999 to $38 billion (see Table 48-5). (Agency receipts are only a small portion of total advertising spending.)

Trade in U.S. advertising services, which includes both cross-border trade and affiliate transactions, should continue to reflect a deficit in this service sector through 2002 (see Table 48-6). Sales by foreign advertising affiliates of U.S. firms should continue to grow steadily and are likely to contribute to U.S. parent firms' advertising revenue growth. Affiliate transactions are the dominant mode of trade, since firms with a local presence and understanding of the local media environment generally develop a competitive advantage over agencies that primarily export advertising services from home offices. In 1997, sales by U.S.-owned advertising affiliates abroad totaled more than $6.5 billion, compared with $581 million earned through cross-border exports of advertising services. The top U.S. markets for advertising services in 1997 were Canada, the United Kingdom, Japan, Germany, and Hong Kong. U.S. imports of advertising services were highest from Japan, the United Kingdom, Germany, Canada, and France.

TABLE 48-6: Balance of Trade in Advertising Services
(millions of dollars)

	1993	1994	1995	1996	1997	1998
U.S. exports	338	487	425	543	624	575
U.S. imports	646	728	833	971	859	1,046
Balance	–308	–241	–408	–428	–235	–471

Source: U.S. Department of Commerce, Bureau of Economic Analysis.

Worldwide forecasts for advertising spending for 1999 showed about a 5 percent increase over 1998 to $435 billion. Since advertising expenditures tend to fluctuate with changes in the economic climate, the financial crises in Asia and Brazil will continue to cause some decline in advertising spending in those markets.

The year 2000 should be strong for the advertising industry as it reflects continued consumer confidence in the economy. The categories of telecommunications, health care and medical, and retailing should continue to lead the increases. The Internet will continue to grow in use as a medium for advertisers.

Bruce Harsh, U.S. Department of Commerce, Office of Service Industries, (202) 482-4582, September 1999.

LEGAL SERVICES

Domestic Trends and Performance

The legal services industry is in the middle of a boom, riding the strong U.S. economy and the huge demand for legal services in several lucrative practice areas, including corporate deal making, financing for business start-ups in emerging technologies, intellectual property practices, and litigation. Revenue growth in the legal services sector has increased significantly since the slump in 1995, when receipts increased only 1.2 percent over 1994 (see Table 48-7). Specifically, the revenue growth rate between 1995 and 1996 was 7.5 percent, and from 1996 to 1997 it was 6.5 percent. Combined revenues for the top 100 law firms reached $23 billion in 1998, according to *American Lawyer* magazine, exceeding those in the previous year by nearly 15 percent; industry analysts expected 1999 to be even more profitable.

One of the difficulties faced by firms in 1998 and 1999 was recruiting enough law school graduates and associate lawyers from other firms to keep up with growing demand. That growth spurt has led to increases in associate-level salaries at many firms: starting salaries paid by some of the leading New York firms increased to $108,000 per year for new law school graduates, and some firms are paying as much as $120,000 per year.

A trend toward consolidation has created larger, more profitable firms that are better able to compete. Many firms feel the need to make large capital investments in order to keep up with the competition, and consolidation is a popular path, especially for larger firms. Midsize firms especially are feeling the squeeze, with a record number of disappearances in 1998.

Firms' profits are enhanced by the use of computers, software, and the Internet. Those technologies allow faster delivery of services, involvement of fewer people to complete case work, greater efficiency and cost savings, and more client satisfaction.

Revenue growth is expected to remain strong over the next few years. However, if the American Bar Association (ABA) decides to change its code of professional conduct and state bar associations begin to permit multidisciplinary partnerships (MDPs) in their jurisdictions, accounting and other professional services firms eventually may represent serious competition for law firms.

Rapid globalization of business has spurred increased demand for partnerships that can satisfy all of a client's professional service needs under one roof. As nearly all business and financial activity involves some amount of legal work, many accountancy firms want to add legal services to their offerings to provide a more seamless full range of services to their clients.

Accounting firms are currently the largest employers of lawyers around the world. To date, three of the Big Five accounting firms have purchased or forged affiliations with law firms in many countries, enabling them to offer legal services to their clients. Ernst & Young employs more than 2,400 attorneys worldwide, more than does any single law firm. Arthur Andersen has a network of law firms in more than 30 countries and has become one of the fastest-growing law firms in the United Kingdom by purchasing many small regional solicitors.

CPA ownership of law firms is not permitted in the United States, although it is a widely accepted practice in many countries in Europe, Latin America, and elsewhere. Most Canadian provinces also do not allow partnering or fee splitting among lawyers and nonlawyers. Those who are pushing for MDPs to be permitted in the United States argue that professional services firms should be able to provide a seamless range of multidisciplinary services to their clients to achieve greater efficiency, cost-effectiveness, and client satisfaction. They believe that to remain competitive, professional services firms must include legal services in their practice mix.

The trend toward MDPs is cause for concern to people in the legal profession who believe that lawyers need exclusive partnerships to protect the core values of the profession, such as independence of judgment, confidentiality, and loyalty to clients. Opponents of MDPs believe that clients generally do not desire seamless, one-stop shopping for all their professional services needs and that the disadvantages of marrying legal and accounting services, especially the threat to independent advice, outweigh the advantages. There is also concern over increased competition to the legal profession from MDPs that provide legal services.

Two events in 1998 served to further the case for allowing MDPs in the United States. The IRS Restructuring and Reform Act of 1998 granted (for noncriminal proceedings) privileged status to communications between taxpayers and any individual authorized to practice before the IRS, similar to the client confidentiality privilege shared by lawyers and their clients although not as broad. Also in 1998, in a highly publicized case, the state bar in Texas did not rule against Arthur Andersen for alleged unauthorized practice of law.

The U.S. legal profession is actively involved in this contentious issue, which could drastically change the practice of law in this country. In May 1999, after months of organized debate and feedback from lawyers around the country, the ABA Commission on Multidisciplinary Practice agreed on a set of recommendations that would allow lawyers to share fees and practice under the same roof with other professionals, such as accountants, financial planners, stockbrokers, and management consultants. The commission believed that the recommendations would place enough restrictions on the practice of law in MDPs to avoid endangering the core values of the legal profession or the interests they protect. The recommendations, which, if accepted, would eventually be implemented through amendments to the ABA Model Rules of Professional Conduct, were presented to the ABA House of Delegates at the August 1999 annual meeting. However, two-thirds of the delegates voted to delay any rule change to allow MDPs at least until studies can be completed that show that a rule change would not hurt the public or sacrifice lawyers' independence or loyalty to their clients.

Legal Services and the Internet

Many law firms and legal service organizations are using the Internet to help clients and make referrals. Entrepreneurs inter-

TABLE 48-7: Legal Services (SIC 81) Trends and Forecasts
(millions of dollars except as noted)

	1993	1994	1995	1996	1997	1998	1999[1]	2000[2]	2004[2]
Receipts	112,145	114,603	116,000	124,659	133,015	141,827	150,337	158,605	192,785
Employment (thousands)	924	924	921	927	944	972	1,001	1,021	1,105

[1] Estimate.
[2] Forecast.
Source: U.S. Department of Commerce: International Trade Administration (ITA), Bureau of Census; U.S. Department of Labor: Bureau of Labor Statistics. Estimates and forecasts by ITA.

ested in starting a business can do some of the necessary work without hiring an attorney by downloading forms and instructions from the Web sites of organizations such as the U.S. Small Business Administration (www.sba.gov) and the National Federation of Independent Business (www.nfibonline.com). Legal documents are also available at www.teneron.com and www.nolopress.com.

The Nolo self-help law center (www.nolo.com) site offers a legal encyclopedia on the Web that covers a wide range of topics, including small business, wills, estate planning, employment, Social Security, patents, copyrights, debt, credit, landlord-tenant issues, and marriage law. The purpose of the site is to help ordinary citizens handle their routine legal issues without hiring a lawyer.

Another Internet service is Lawyers.Com (www.lawyers.com), which includes a database of more than 420,000 lawyers around the world who offer basic legal information targeted mainly to small business owners. Businesspeople can E-mail legal questions to the company via the Web site. Questions with broad application are selected, and lawyers' answers are published on the Web site to benefit as large an audience as possible. The ABA's Lawyer Referral Program is available on the Web at www.abanet.org/referral.

Legal negotiating also has gone high-tech. A site called cyber$ettle.com was established in 1998 to help settle cases, mostly personal injury claims, through a blind-bidding system over the Internet. Parties in a dispute never meet face to face. Instead, bids are entered electronically by using encrypted software and confidential passwords. The computer compares the bids and settles the case automatically if the bids from both sides are within $5,000 or 30 percent of one another. Lawyers and companies have settled hundreds of cases on-line that might have taken years if they had gone to court.

Mediation via electronic mail is another use of the Internet that is gaining in popularity. The Web site of eBay Inc. gives customers a chance to mediate disputes with companies on the Web over things such as goods that were damaged during shipment.

The courts also have begun to make use of the Internet. Using modern videoconferencing technology, digital courtrooms have been set up to enable virtual meetings of judges, juries, expert witnesses, prison inmates, court stenographers, and others. This has the potential to reduce courthouse expenses significantly by eliminating the need to transport prisoners and make it possible for trials to be broadcast on the Internet.

Law firms increasingly rely on the Internet to market their services to clients, do case research, and communicate with colleagues, clients, and bar associations. A recent survey by *The Internet Lawyer* indicates that 71 percent of the legal profession is on-line in some capacity and that 33 percent of legal firms have Web sites.

Many lawyers are benefiting from the improved efficiency and cost savings afforded by the use of computers and software designed for the legal profession. Scanners allow loads of casework documents to be digitized and thus easily accessed on the desktop or in the courtroom. Software programs enable attorneys in different locations of the same firm to work simultaneously on the same documents. Intranets allow multiple-location firms to access password-protected on-line libraries, case files, and so on. Many firms now rely on encrypted E-mail to transport documents. E-mail transmission speed can be important to law practices, since knowing something sooner than an opponent does can be advantageous in certain cases.

These tools are especially vital in today's global economy, where more and more cases involve players in different countries. The use of technology enables those in the legal profession to do their jobs more efficiently and deliver services to clients much faster than before and ultimately leads to increased profits. This trend is leading those in the profession to examine the way clients are billed for work that, depending on the method used, can be done very quickly and efficiently electronically rather than in the traditional way.

Because of technological advances, laypeople also have access to an ever-widening array of tools to enable them to complete work on their own for which they traditionally would have had to hire a lawyer. New software packages have been introduced that nonlawyers can use to generate wills and living trusts, conduct estate and financial planning, and keep real estate and medical records. Most of these packages contain templates that make the preparation of legal documents possible on a home computer. Even if a lawyer is necessary to make documents official, laypeople can complete much of the basic document preparation work themselves before going to a lawyer and thus save money on routine legal tasks.

Acquiring a legal education is now possible on-line. Students can receive instruction over the Internet, download videotaped lectures, take interactive tests, and join chat rooms with professors. Law school programs that are entirely on-line (no physical campus) cannot be accredited under ABA rules, since they are considered correspondence schools, but more accredited institutions are using the Internet as part of their teaching tool kits to supplement coursework, and the ABA is examining the issue of allowing schools to give credit for distance learning.

Another trend that has increased in popularity over the last year is the use of prepaid legal service insurance plans. For a relatively low monthly fee, business owners and others can purchase plans that ensure access to basic legal services when they are needed without the need to pay high retainer fees. Such plans are increasing access to legal services by middle-class citizens and small businesses that in the past would have forgone those services because of the fees. Services covered in these plans might include will preparation, home sale or purchase documents, telephone consultations, and traffic court issues but generally do not include major legal work, such as representation in lawsuits. The ABA supports the concept and lists prepaid legal insurance providers on its Internet site (www.abanet.org).

International Activities

Globalization of capital markets and increased cross-border business activity are rapidly expanding the need for international legal services. International business clients see great advantages in having one legal service provider handle all their transactions around the world, and this is the major impetus for law firms to go global. This need has prompted much merger and acquisition activity among law firms worldwide, a trend that is likely to pick up speed in the years ahead. Another major impetus for law firms to internationalize is to keep up with the competition and capture new business abroad.

Differences among national legal systems have long been one of the difficulties faced by international businesses. Local legal expertise and qualifications combined with international business experience are essential to providing high-quality services to clients. The most popular ways in which law firms go global are to establish offices in foreign jurisdictions; arrange associations with local firms; establish network relationships with local law firms in foreign countries, using client referrals and information exchange; and hire foreign lawyers to obtain expertise that is lacking internally. Some firms opt to grow steadily by hiring lawyers to form practices in each country; this is known as the "grow-your-own" strategy and is usually a slow process. Others have poached teams of lawyers from their competitors in targeted countries. A full merger is generally the most difficult and expensive method of globalization.

Difficulties law firms face when expanding overseas are hiring local lawyers who are capable of meeting their high standards of service; economic and political turbulence in foreign markets; corruption, cultural differences, and regulatory hurdles; and government roadblocks. It can take several years for a new establishment abroad to become profitable. Other difficulties include large differences in partner pay scales between corporations and a lack of suitable partners with which to merge in targeted countries.

The International Lawyers Network is a U.S.-based association that was established to help law firms meet the international needs of their clients without opening offices overseas, merging, or hiring foreign lawyers. The network, which includes more than 60 firms, mostly medium-size, enables its members to confidently recommend to their clients the legal services of other network providers in nearly 60 countries. Another such network in the United States is Lex Mundi, which has approximately 145 member firms. These networks rely increasingly on Internet technology to communicate and exchange information worldwide.

Despite the difficulties involved, a merger and acquisition boom is under way in the legal services industry, as it is in the accounting and management consulting industries, especially in the United States and Europe. Law firms on the European continent are striving to keep up with the competition from consolidated practices in the United Kingdom and the United States by merging and forming alliances with other firms, especially in the profitable areas of commercial finance, corporate mergers and acquisitions, property, and litigation. Cameron McKenna, a British firm, is working to create an alliance with five continental European firms that would result in the largest European legal service group, with combined revenue of $265 million and more than 1,400 lawyers.

Most U.S. law firms have declined to join their corporate clients and set up offices in foreign markets. Many partners believe that establishing a branch network internationally is not necessary for participation in big global deals. Chicago's Baker & McKenzie, which ranked number two on the 1998 AmLaw list, has more lawyers (2,400) and more operations overseas (34 countries) than any other U.S. firm.

TABLE 48-8: Balance of Trade in Legal Services
(millions of dollars)

	1993	1994	1995	1996	1997	1998
U.S. exports	1,442	1,617	1,667	1,943	2,152	2,451
U.S. imports	321	383	469	615	560	688
Balance	1,121	1,234	1,198	1,328	1,592	1,763

Source: U.S. Department of Commerce, Bureau of Economic Analysis.

The most highly publicized merger activity in 1999 was the decision by the New York–based Rogers & Wells and London's Clifford Chance to join forces to create the world's largest law firm in terms of both revenue and number of lawyers. A third firm, Germany's Punder, Volhard, Weber & Axster, will join the joint venture. Partners cited the needs of their multinational corporate clients as the driving force behind the merger. The three-way combination will be official on January 1, 2000, and will be known as Clifford Chance Rogers & Wells in the United States and as Clifford Chance elsewhere. The firm will have 2,700 lawyers in 30 offices around the world and was expected to earn more than $1 billion in fees in 1999.

U.S. law firms are world leaders in exported services. Exports of legal services approached $2.5 billion in 1998, a 14 percent rise over the 1997 level (see Table 48-8). This figure does not include sales of services by majority-owned foreign affiliates (MOFAs) of U.S. law firms, which in 1997 totaled $265 million. The largest markets abroad for U.S. legal services in 1997 were Japan, the United Kingdom, France, Germany, and Canada.

Karen Holderman, U.S. Department of Commerce, Office of Service Industries, (202) 482-0345, September 1999.

MANAGEMENT CONSULTING AND PUBLIC RELATIONS

Domestic Trends and Performance

The management consulting industry has grown and specialized to meet the needs of today's global businesses. The practice of consulting continues to change rapidly as new technology develops and as competition within the sector requires that firms innovate and improve their service offerings. To compete effectively, firms are investing in advertising campaigns, employee training programs, and overseas expansion through mergers and acquisitions. The Big Five accounting firms, which are now also five of the world's six largest management consulting firms, will continue to dominate the professional services global marketplace as the twenty-first century begins (see Tables 48-1 and 48-9).

In the past few years, management consulting firms have experienced unprecedented levels of expansion. According to

TABLE 48-9: Revenues of the Top Six U.S. Management Consulting Firms in 1998
(millions of dollars)

Firm	Global Consulting	U.S. Consulting	Percent Change 97–98
Andersen Consulting	7,129	3,578	25
PricewaterhouseCoopers	6,000	2,700	40
Ernst & Young	3,870	2,400	35
Deloitte Consulting	3,240	1,480	40
CSC	3,000	1,900	17
KPMG	3,000	1,516	30

Source: Quoted with permission from *Consultants News,* Kennedy Information LLC, Fitzwilliam NH. (800)531-0007, www.kennedyinfo.com. Copyright 1999.

Consultants News, combined revenues of the 50 largest firms experienced a 27 percent increase in 1998.

In the last fiscal year all consulting sectors enjoyed revenue increases. Information technology practices reported the highest aggregate growth, followed by operations management, human resources, and management strategy practices. Most forecasters predict that this upward trend will continue as a result of innovation in electronic commerce, heightened competition, and increasing globalization of business.

Some analysts have predicted that growth rates in the management consulting industry will decline and eventually stagnate. However, predictions of slowing growth made in previous years have not been realized, and there are few signs of a slowdown. Instead, expansion of the global economy and new technological advances continue to fuel the consulting industry. Firms are under pressure to hire more consultants, and demand for specialized services is on the rise as customers' needs diversify. As a result of the rapid development of electronic commerce, information technology consulting is expected to rise faster than are all the other specializations. The consolidation trend is likely to continue and ultimately could lead to vast alterations in the regulation and structure of the professional service sectors if MDPs are permitted.

Recruitment, training, and attrition issues continue to pose challenges for consulting firms, but, as a whole, the industry is booming and rapid expansion is likely to lead to an overall increase in the workforce (see Table 48-10). Forecasters predict that firms will continue to engage in recruitment wars and salaries will escalate as firms fight for the top talent among MBA graduates.

As a result of the increasing demand for consultants, training and retraining have become important in retaining employees and fostering company loyalty. According to a recent Kennedy Information Research Group survey, firms with 500 or more employees spend an average of 5.3 percent of annual revenue on training, whereas firms with 50 to 99 employees spend 2.5 percent of annual revenue. In the future, computer-aided training using the Internet probably will be used to help reduce the high costs of employee training programs. Firms will continue to invest in training employees in critical areas such as computer use and public speaking.

Public relations continues to be a vital component of the marketing strategies of the leading consulting firms, especially the Big Five. Expensive advertising campaigns are being launched to reestablish those companies as "professional service firms." For instance, the 1998 merger of Price Waterhouse and Coopers & Lybrand into PricewaterhouseCoopers provided the impetus for the new company's current multi-million-dollar worldwide advertising campaign. Increased competition and globalization in the consulting industry are likely to continue to necessitate strong brand recognition campaigns. Each of the Big Five firms has already spent tens of millions of dollars on public relations fees and will continue to do so in the coming years. The added publicity enables firms to distinguish themselves and raise their visibility to attract clients.

Technological advances in the Internet and electronic commerce are changing business operations within consulting firms. A survey of 525 chief executive officers and executives conducted by Booz-Allen & Hamilton indicated that 9 of 10 executives believe that their organizations and cultures will change radically as a result of the Internet by the year 2001. More and more firms are launching innovative Web sites and investing in electronic commerce services. Trends indicate that consulting firms will expand their services through the formation of market and business alliances with software and technological companies. For instance, in April 1999, Ernst & Young formed an alliance with Microsoft Corporation. Such strategic alliances will enable consulting firms to provide electronic commerce services and information technology solutions to customers and perform time-intensive tasks such as customized E-mail messages with greater facility.

Virtual consulting is emerging rapidly as a new service. Instead of paying consultants for their advice by the hour, customers now can pay a flat rate for on-line consulting. This type of service is being offered by small groups of speciality firms

TABLE 48-10: Management Consulting and Public Relations Services (SIC 874) Trends and Forecasts
(millions of dollars except as noted)

	1992	1993	1994	1995	1996	1997	1998	1999[1]	2000[2]	2004[2]
Receipts	72,490	75,026	81,439	94,787	104,831	116,712	133,398	152,474	170,771	268,711
Employment (thousands)	655	688	719	805	869	939	1,023	1,105	1,171	1,478

[1] Estimate.
[2] Forecast.
Source: U.S. Department of Commerce: International Trade Administration (ITA); Bureau of the Census; U.S. Department of Labor: Bureau of Labor Statistics. Estimates and forecasts by ITA.

that band together and by some of the larger consulting firms. The flat fee allows business clients to E-mail questions and receive prompt responses from live consultants. Customer queries are sorted and routed to the consultants who can best answer them. Currently, Ernst & Young and Arthur Andersen are pioneering on-line products and have already developed computer software to replace some types of face-to-face consulting. Dataquest, a high-tech market research firm, predicts that virtual consulting could produce $100 million of revenue over the next 5 years. However, some analysts believe that effective consulting service requires teamwork and face-to-face contact between consultants and clients.

International Activities

The international consulting market is in the middle of a rapid expansion. The Big Five companies are actively pursuing new business and consolidation in many overseas markets, including central and eastern Europe, China, and India. The Asia-Pacific region is likely to afford significant opportunities for new business as well; now that the worst of the financial crisis is over, there is a high demand for professional services among Asian companies that need help rebuilding.

The European market for consulting services is expected to expand in the coming years. Demand for electronic commerce services and information technology consulting in Europe is likely to increase because of the adoption of the euro and year 2000–related work. According to *Consultants News,* the market for management consultancy in Europe in 1999 exceeded $16 billion and is expected to increase 13 percent annually over the next few years. Italy is demonstrating prospects for an especially strong market for consultancy as a result of changing business attitudes and a developing financial market.

Many U.S. firms have gained access to international consulting markets by integrating with national firms in other countries. More and more, local firms are under pressure to merge with global competitors, and as this globalization continues in many business sectors, customers around the world expect consulting firms to have an international presence.

Mergers and acquisitions continue to play an important role in the professional services industry. Aggressive growth strategies among the largest consulting firms have reduced what were once known as the Big Eight to the current Big Five firms. PricewaterhouseCoopers (PwC) led the industry's expansion and acquisitions in 1999, placing it second in size behind Andersen Consulting. As part of its worldwide expansion agenda, PwC acquired an entire KPMG consulting practice in Belgium plus two other independent firms in Italy and France; the Belgian arm of KPMG subsequently sued PwC for $23.6 million for damages caused by that activity. In April 1999, KPMG's Canadian practice successfully avoided a buyout by Arthur Andersen. Although forecasters predict that the Big Five will remain as such for the next couple of years, trends indicate that consolidation and poaching by rivals probably will increase because of the need for specialization of services and an increased capacity for investment among the world's largest firms.

TABLE 48-11: Balance of Trade in Management Consulting and Public Relations Services
(millions of dollars)

	1992	1993	1994	1995	1996	1997	1998
U.S. exports	728	826	1,134	1,489	1,460	1,596	1,657
U.S. imports	243	287	321	465	497	731	914
Balance	485	539	813	1,024	963	865	743

Source: U.S. Department of Commerce, Bureau of Economic Analysis, *Survey of Current Business,* October 1998.

The balance of trade in management consulting and public relations services is shown in Table 48-11.

Karen Holderman and ***Anbinh Phan,*** U.S. Department of Commerce, Office of Service Industries, (202) 482-0345, September 1999.

■ REFERENCES

ABA Journal, American Bar Association, 750 North Lake Shore Drive, Chicago, IL 60611. (312) 988-6018; E-mail: abajournal@abanet.org; internet: www.abanet.org/journal/home.html.

Accountant, Lafferty Publications, Ltd., 6 King Street Cloisters, Clifton Walk, London W6 0GY, United Kingdom. (44) (181) 741-8266, www.lafferty.co.uk.

Accounting Today, Faulkner & Gray, Inc., 11 Penn Plaza, New York, NY 10117-0373. (212) 967-7000; E-mail: AcToday@aol.com; internet: www.electronicaccountant.com.

Advertising Age, Crain Communications, Inc., 740 Rush Street, Chicago, IL 60611. (312) 649-5200, www.adage.com.

American Association of Advertising Agencies, 666 Third Avenue, New York, NY 10017. (212) 682-2500, www.aaaa.org.

American Bar Association, 750 North Lake Shore Drive, Chicago, IL 60611. (312) 988-5000; E-mail: info@abanet.org; internet: www.abanet.org.

American Lawyer, American Lawyer Media, 345 Park Avenue South, New York, NY 10010. (212) 779-9200, info@amlaw.com.

Business Week, McGraw-Hill Companies, Inc., 1221 Avenue of the Americas, 39th Floor, New York, NY 10020. (212) 512-2511, www.businessweek.com.

Business Wire, Business Wire, 40 East 52 St., Nineteenth Floor, New York, NY 10022. (212) 752-9600, www.businesswire.com.

CA Magazine, Canadian Institute of Chartered Accountants, 277 Wellington Street West, Toronto, Ontario M5V 3H2, Canada. (416) 977-3222, www.cica.ca.

Census of Service Industries, U.S. Department of Commerce, Bureau of the Census, Washington, DC 20233. (301) 457-2689, www.census.gov.

Consultants News, Kennedy Information, LLC, 1 Kennedy Place, Route 12 South, Fitzwilliam, NH 03447. (603) 585-3101; E-mail: editor@kennedyinfo.com; internet: www.kennedyinfo.com.

CPA Journal, New York State Society of CPAs, 530 Fifth Avenue, Fifth Floor, New York, NY 10036. (212) 719-8300, www.nysscpa.org.

Crain's Chicago Business, Crain Communications, Inc., 740 Rush Street, Chicago, IL 60611. (888) 909-9111, www.crainschicagobusiness.com.

Crain's New York Business, Crain Communications, Inc., 220 East 42 Street, New York, NY 10017. (888) 909-9111, www.crainsny.com.

Direct, 11 River Bend Drive South, P.O. Box 4949, Stamford, CT 06907. (203) 358-9900, www.directnewsline.com.

Direct Marketing Association, 11120 Avenue of the Americas, New York, NY 10036. (212) 768-7277, www.the-dma.org.

DM News, 100 Avenue of the Americas, New York, NY 10013. (212) 925-7300, www.dmnews.com.

Economist, The Economist Newspaper Ltd., 25 St. James's Street, London SW1A 1HG, United Kingdom. (44) (171) 830-7000, www.economist.com.

Electronic Accountant, Faulkner & Gray. www.electronicaccountant.com.

Employment and Earnings, U.S. Department of Labor, Bureau of Labor Statistics, 2 Massachusetts Avenue, NE, Washington, DC 20212-0001. (202) 606-6569; E-mail: oesinfo@bls.gov; internet: http://stats.bls.gov.

Financial Post, The Financial Post Company, 33 King Street East, Toronto, Ontario M5A 4NZ, Canada. (800) 661-7678; E-mail: fpdg@fpdata.finpost.com; internet: www.fpmarkets.com.

Financial Times, Financial Times Ltd., 1330 Avenue of the Americas, New York, NY 10019. (800) 628-8088, www.ft.com.

Forbes, Forbes, Inc., 85 Fifth Avenue, Second Floor, New York, NY 10003. (212) 620-2200, www.forbes.com.

Global IT Consulting Report, Kennedy Information, LLC, 1 Kennedy Place, Route 12 South, Fitzwilliam, NH 03447. (800) 531-0007; E-mail: editor@kennedyinfo.com.

Independent, Independent Newspapers (UK) Ltd., 1 Canada Square, Canary Wharf, London E14 5DL, United Kingdom. (44) (171) 293-2802; E-mail: newseditor@independent.co.uk; internet: www.Independent.co.uk.

Industry Week, Penton Publishing, Inc., 1100 Superior Avenue, Cleveland, OH 44114. (216) 696-7000, www.industryweek.com.

Insider's Report by Robert Coen Presentation on Advertising Expenditures, McCann-Erikson, 750 Third Avenue, New York, NY 10017. (212) 697-6000, www.mccann.com.

Journal of Accountancy, American Institute of Certified Public Accountants (AICPA), 1211 Avenue of the Americas, New York, NY 10036-8775. (212) 596-6200; E-mail: joaed@aicpa.org; internet: www.aicpa.org.

Journal of Commerce, 2 World Trade Center, 27th Floor, New York, NY 10048. (800) 223-0243; E-mail: editor@mail.joc.com; internet: www.joc.com.

Knight Ridder/Tribune Business News, The Dialog Corp., 11000 Regency Parkway, Suite 400, Cary, NC 27511. (919) 462-8600, www.profound.co.uk.

Management Consultant International, Lafferty Publications Ltd, IDA Tower, Pearse Street, Dublin 2, Republic of Ireland. (212) 557-6726, www.lafferty.co.uk.

Management Review, American Management Association, 1601 Broadway, New York, NY 10019-7420. (800) 262-9699, www.amanet.org.

Newspaper Association of America, 1160 Sunrise Valley Drive, Reston, VA 22091. (703) 648-1100, www.naa.org.

New York Times, The New York Times Company, 229 West 43 St., New York, NY 10036. (800) NYTIMES, www.nytimes.com.

PR Newswire, PR Newswire Association, Inc., 890 Seventh Avenue, 32d Floor, New York, NY 10019. (800) 832-5522, www.prnewswire.com.

Practical Accountant, Faulkner & Gray, Inc., 11 Penn Plaza, New York, NY 10001. (800) 535-8403, www.faulknergray.com.

Services Annual Survey, December 1998, U.S. Department of Commerce, Bureau of the Census, Washington, DC 20233. (301) 457-2826, www.census.gov.

Survey of Current Business, October 1998, U.S. Department of Commerce, Bureau of Economic Analysis, Washington, DC 20230. (202) 482-1000, www.doc.gov.

Target, 401 Broad street, Philadelphia, PA 19108. (215) 238-5300, www.targetonline.com.

Tax Notes, Tax Analysts, 6830 North Fairfax Drive, Arlington, VA, 22213. (703) 533-4400; E-mail: webmaster@tax.org; internet: www.tax.org.

Wall Street Journal, Dow Jones & Company, Inc., World Financial Center, 200 Liberty Street, New York, NY 10281. (800) 568-7625, http://interactive.wsj.com.

■ RELATED CHAPTERS

25: Printing and Publishing
26: Information Services
28: Computer Software and Internet
32: Entertainment

EDUCATION AND TRAINING
Economic and Trade Trends

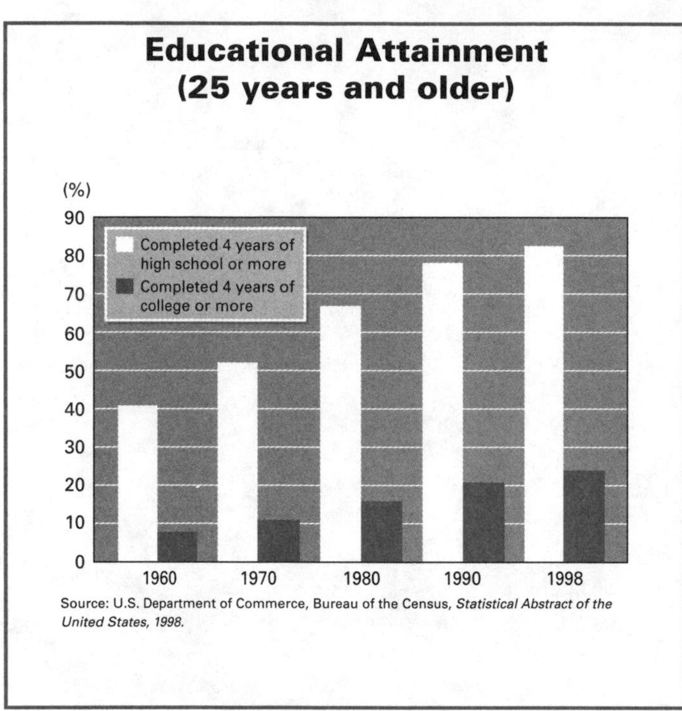

Source: U.S. Department of Commerce, Bureau of the Census, *Statistical Abstract of the United States, 1998.*

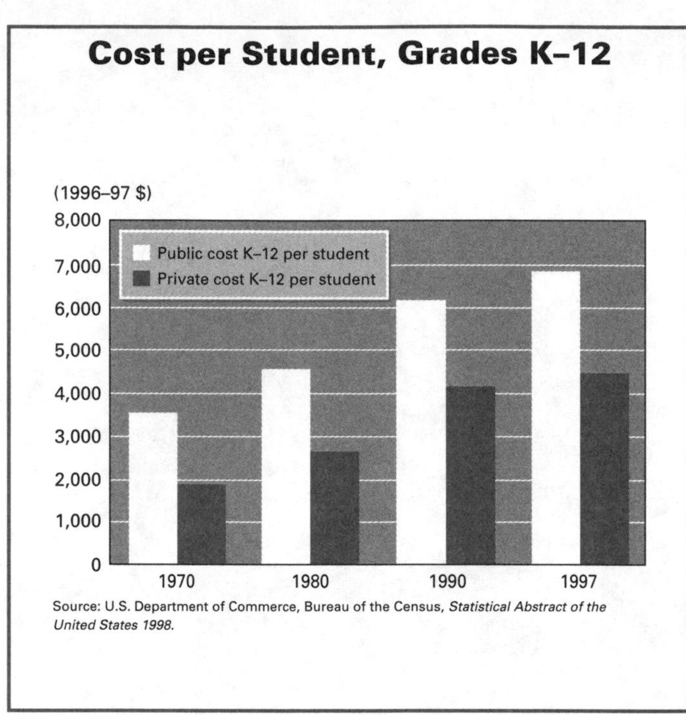

Source: U.S. Department of Commerce, Bureau of the Census, *Statistical Abstract of the United States 1998.*

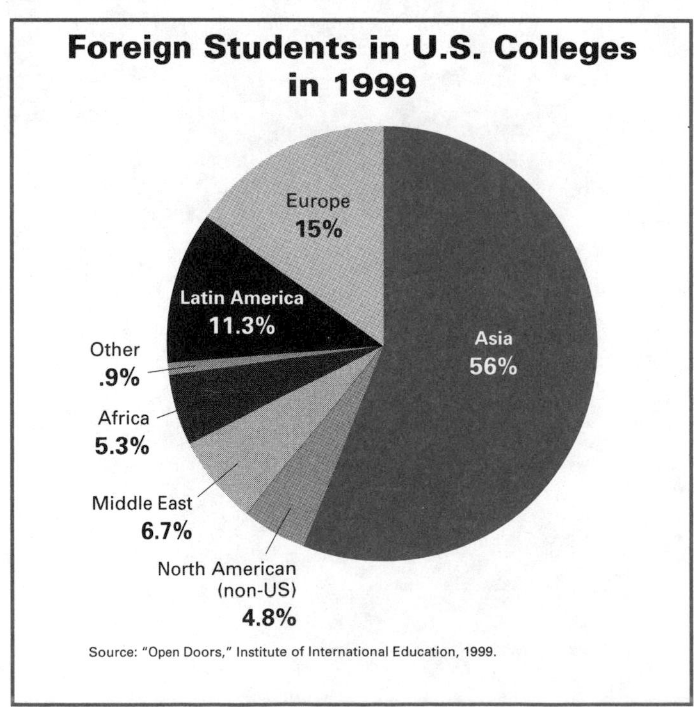

Source: "Open Doors," Institute of International Education, 1999.

Source: U.S. Department of Commerce, Bureau of Economic Analysis.

See "Getting the Most Out of *Outlook 2000*" for definitions of terms.

49

Education and Training

INDUSTRY DEFINITION The education and training industry consists of all public and private institutions engaged in educational activities, including public and private schools for kindergarten through twelfth grade (SIC 821), 2-year community colleges, public and private colleges and universities, vocational schools, and other certificate-granting institutes (SIC 822). Private providers of training and education, particularly formal training programs in public entities and private corporations, whether employer-provided or contracted out (SIC 833), also are discussed.

OVERVIEW

At 7.3 percent of gross domestic product (GDP), the $583.8 billion spent for all public and private educational institutions in 1997–1998 and the additional $60.7 billion spent on workplace training, the education sector remains a robust part of the economy. In 1998, the education industry employed an estimated 8 million teachers, university faculty members, administrators, and support staff. In that year, about 67.3 million children and adults, more than 25 percent of the total U.S. population, attended school for part of the year (see the box "U.S. Education Sector Statistics"). Even if the economy moderates slightly as is expected in 2000–2001, education-related services will retain their strong position relative to overall GDP through the first decade of the new millennium.

According to the National Center for Education Statistics (NCES), enrollment at all educational institutes will continue to grow 1 to 2 percent annually between 1989 and 2009 in what Secretary of Education Richard W. Riley calls "a long, slow, rising wave." Over that period, elementary school enrollment will rise 4.7 million, secondary enrollment 3.6 million, and college enrollment 2.8 million. In the 1999–2000 school year alone, total private and public school enrollment was predicted to rise for the fourth year in a row, this time by about 350,000 pupils, to reach a record 53.5 million students. Total enrollment for higher education was projected to increase from 14.3 million in 1995 to 14.6 million in 1999 to 16.4 million by the year 2009. Unlike the post–World War II baby boom, which saw birthrates plummet to 3.1 million in the early 1970s, the current "baby boom echo" shows no sign of abating in the new century.

U.S. EDUCATION SECTOR STATISTICS

According to *The Digest of Education Statistics 1998* and the U.S. Bureau of the Census, in 1997

The United States had 14,891 school districts and 61,165 public elementary schools with 1,582,000 elementary teachers.

There were 75.4 million people in the education industry as teachers, students at all levels, university faculty, support staff, and special education teachers.

There were 20,997 public secondary schools with 1,084,000 teachers and 27,686 private schools with 387,000 teachers at all levels

There were 2,167 special education and vocational schools with over 32,000 teachers.

There were 9,962 postsecondary institutions, of which 2,189 were public schools, 2,877 were private nonprofit schools, and 4,551 were proprietary schools.

There were 2,244 4-year colleges with 935,000 higher education teaching faculty; among those 4-year institutions, 608 were public colleges or universities with 657,000 teachers, 1,509 were private nonprofits with 278,000 staff members and 117 were proprietary schools. University-level teaching staff is projected to reach over 971,000 by the 2000–2001 academic year.

Source: U.S. Department of Education, National Center for Education Statistics, Common Core of Data and Private School surveys, Higher Education General Information Survey.

TABLE 49-1: School Enrollment
(millions of students)

	1992	1993	1994	1995[1]	1996[1]	1997[2]	1998[2]	1999[2]	2000[2]	2001[2]	Percentage Change 97–98	98–99	99–00	Annual Average 93–97	97–01
Public elementary and secondary	42.82	43.46	44.11	44.84	45.63	45.31	46.79	47.14	47.44	47.70	3.3	0.7	0.6	1.0	1.3
Private elementary and secondary	5.38	5.47	5.60	5.69	5.78	5.87	5.93	5.97	6.01	6.04	1.0	0.7	0.6	1.8	0.7
Total K–12	48.20	48.94	49.70	50.53	51.41	51.18	52.72	53.11	53.45	53.74	3.0	0.7	0.6	1.1	1.2
Public, postsecondary	11.39	11.19	11.13	11.09	11.09	11.21	11.40	11.53	11.63	11.70	1.7	1.1	0.9	0.0	1.1
Private, postsecondary	3.10	3.12	3.15	3.17	3.21	3.14	3.19	3.23	3.26	3.29	1.6	1.2	0.9	0.2	1.2
Total postsecondary	14.49	14.30	14.28	14.26	14.30	14.35	14.59	14.76	14.89	14.99	1.7	1.2	0.9	0.1	1.1
Total	62.69	63.24	63.98	64.79	65.71	65.53	67.31	67.87	68.34	68.73	2.7	0.8	0.7	0.9	1.2

[1] Estimate.
[2] Forecast.
Source: U.S. Department of Commerce, Bureau of the Census, *Statistical Abstract of the United States 1999.*

Indeed, births will rise slowly over the next 10 years and beyond, according to long-range projections by the U.S. Bureau of the Census. In 2009, births are expected to be 4.2 million, growing to 4.8 million by 2028 (see Table 49-1).

This enrollment picture is accelerating the demand for well-trained teachers. To meet the increased number of students, many school districts are hiring uncredentialed teachers or allowing staff members to teach academic subjects outside their undergraduate major or minor fields of study. Some states that are facing critical teacher shortages are offering incentive packages to lure new teachers to their districts. These bonuses range from the $1,000 signing incentive offered by Howard County, Maryland, to $3,000 for anyone with a background in special education, to the $20,000 bonus Massachusetts is offering certified teachers. These incentives in September 1999 came on top of a $3,700 average increase in starting salaries and underline the urgent need for certified, qualified teaching professionals.

Total elementary and secondary school expenditures (kindergarten through twelfth grade) for the school year 1997–1998 were estimated to have been $351.3 billion; expenditures for colleges and other higher learning centers were about $232.5 billion in that period. The group of students forming the so-called baby boom echo will drive expenditures for secondary and elementary schools upward for a net increase of about 25 percent between the 1995–1996 and the 2008–2009 academic years, according to the middle scenario in the NCES's "Projections of Education Statistics to 2009." This may seem to be a large jump, but public elementary and secondary education expenditures are estimated to have increased from $234 billion in 1987 to $316 billion in 1997 (using constant 1997–1998 dollars deflated by the Consumer Price Index), an increase of 35 percent. This continued rise in education expenditures over the next decade assumes that the economy will remain steady, the annual rate of inflation will remain between 2.8 percent and 4 percent, the fertility rate will remain around 2.1 births per woman, mortality will continue to decline, and immigration will stay at about 821,000 annually.

Education expenditures will continue their upward trajectory not only because of the baby boom echo but also because of the need to build new schools. Los Angeles Unified School District has to build 50 new schools in 1999–2002 to absorb the influx of new students. The National Clearinghouse for Educational Facilities estimates that $19.5 billion was spent in 1999 to modernize rapidly deteriorating schools or build new ones. The average public school building in the United States is 42 years old, and many are in dire need of repairs. In fact, the American Society of Civil Engineers gave school modernization and construction the lowest grade, an F, in its "1998 Report Card for America's Infrastructure."

Adding to this bleak picture of a national school system in disrepair are increased parental and community pressures on schools to offer more prekindergarten programs. The proportion of parents who put their 3- to 5-year-olds in a preschool program rose from 37 percent in 1970 to 61 percent in 1996, according to the 1998 *Statistical Abstract of the United States.* Other trends influencing expenditures include moves by school districts to lengthen the school year through longer hours, double sessions, or round-the-year school; efforts to increase school choice by offering charter public schools or, more controversial, voucher programs; and the need to renovate one-third of the nation's schools and build thousands of new ones. Demographic trends will compel the hiring of 2.2 million new teachers by 2009 as teachers from the early 1970s begin to retire. Federal and state funds to implement Standards 2000 (a U.S. Department of Education initiative to improve curriculum and performance from kindergarten through twelfth grade) also will push education costs up.

Total domestic expenditures for education are up from 1993–1994, when public and private education in the United States accounted for 4.2 percent of GDP for the primary and

TABLE 49-2: Cost of Education
(billions of constant 1997–98 dollars)

	1992	1993	1994	1995[1]	1996[1]	1997[1]	1998[2]	1999[2]	2000[2]	Percentage Change 96–97	97–98	98–99	Annual Average 92–96	96–00
Public education	409.3	417.7	425.7	437.2	446.3	458.2	469.8	475.9	482.1	2.7	2.5	1.3	2.2	1.9
Elementary and secondary	282.1	287.0	293.5	300	307.4	315.7	324.3	327.3	330.3	2.7	2.7	0.9	2.2	1.8
Postsecondary	127.2	130.7	132.3	137.2	139.0	142.5	145.5	148.6	151.8	2.5	2.1	2.1	2.2	2.2
Private education	97.4	99.8	102.2	104.7	108.0	111.2	114.0	116.3	118.8	3.0	2.5	2.1	2.6	2.4
Elementary and secondary	23.6	24.3	24.6	25.2	25.8	26.3	27.0	27.3	27.6	2.0	2.8	1.0	2.2	1.7
Postsecondary	73.8	75.5	77.6	79.5	82.3	85.0	87.0	89.1	91.2	3.3	2.4	2.4	2.8	2.6
Total public and private	506.7	517.6	527.9	541.9	554.4	569.5	583.8	592.2	600.8	2.7	2.5	1.4	2.3	2.0

[1] Estimate.
[2] Forecast.
Source: U.S. Department of Commerce, Bureau of the Census, *Statistical Abstract of the United States 1999.*

secondary levels, 2.5 percent for higher education, and 6.8 percent overall. In 1996, combined education expenditures—without factoring in workplace training—accounted for 7.3 percent of GDP. That percentage is expected to hold steady for most of the next decade, as current-fund expenditures for public and private education are expected to increase annually by roughly 5 percent, or 25 percent between 1995 and 2009 (see Tables 49-2 and 49-3).

Trends in Higher Education

Between 1985 and 1995, combined fees for college tuition and room and board at 4-year universities rose from an average of $4,146 to an average of $7,448, an increase of 44 percent over that 10-year period. This increase was due in part to an expanding economy, a rise in enrollments, and an attempt to offset a dip in government funding for postsecondary education in roughly the same period. The rate of growth in higher education expenditures that marked the early 1990s is projected to continue, with total current fund expenditures projected to increase 36 percent from 1995–1996 to 2008–2009 in constant dollars, provided that the economy grows at its current rate and inflation is held in check. Current-fund expenditures per student are projected to increase 19 percent in that period. Even public 2-year institutions will see a rise in per-student expenditures. By 2009, spending for 2-year postsecondary schools is projected to reach $29 billion, with per-student expenditures topping $8,397 in that year. Higher college enrollments have pushed up tuition rates and will continue to do so for most of the next decade, although not as rapidly as they did in the late 1980s and early 1990s.

Women played a major role in the enrollment picture between 1984 and 1997, according to "Projections of Education Statistics to 2009." The number of women going on to college jumped from 6.4 million in 1984 to an estimated 8.1 million in 1997, an increase of 27 percent for the 13-year period, or a yearly increase of 1.8 percent. Women made up 52 percent of all college students enrolled in 1997, and their total share is expected to rise to 58 percent by 2009. In contrast, men increased their numbers in college from 5.9 million in 1984 to 6.5 million in 1992 before dropping to about 6.3 million in

TABLE 49-3: Per-Student Cost
(1997–98 constant dollars)

	1992	1993	1994	1995[1]	1996[1]	1997[1]	1998[2]	1999[2]	2000[2]	Percentage Change 96–97	97–98	98–99	Annual Average 92–96	96–00
Public elementary and secondary	6,588	6,604	6,653	6,691	6,742	6,871	6,931	6,943	6,963	1.9	0.9	0.2	0.6	0.8
Private elementary and secondary	4,398	4,439	4,388	4,418	4,453	4,476	4,555	4,569	4,587	0.5	1.8	0.3	0.3	0.7
Public, postsecondary	11,170	11,681	11,880	12,370	12,532	12,714	12,769	12,894	13,054	1.5	0.4	1.0	2.9	1.0
Private, postsecondary	23,785	24,245	24,675	25,087	25,633	27,041	27,239	27,552	27,950	5.5	0.7	1.2	1.9	2.2

[1] Estimate.
[2] Forecast.
Source: U.S. Department of Commerce, Bureau of the Census, *Statistical Abstract of the United States 1999.*

1997. By 2009, men will increase their numbers in college to 6.9 million, a 10 percent jump from 1997.

Students age 18 to 24 increased their numbers on college campuses from 7.8 million in 1989 to 7.9 million in 1997, an increase of 2 percent. That number, however, is projected to increase to 9.8 million by 2009, a 24 percent increase. As a result, the proportion of university students 18 to 24 years old, which fell from 57 percent in 1989 to 55 percent in 1997, is projected to be 60 percent by 2009. Students age 25 and older will account for about 6.3 million of the university student population in 2009, about the same percentage as in 1997.

Community colleges will continue to see their numbers grow. Since the 1970s, the number of educational institutions offering associate degrees has nearly doubled, from about 900 to about 1,742. Community colleges now teach at least 39 percent of all students in postsecondary institutions, with total full-time and part-time enrollments expected to exceed 5.5 million for the 1997–1998 school year when final tallies are done.

Graduate school enrollment rose from 1.3 million in 1984 to an estimated 1.7 million in 1997, an average annual increase of 2 percent and a 30 percent jump for the entire 13-year period. Using the middle scenario, graduate enrollment is expected to continue to climb, reaching 1.8 million by 2009. According to the *Chronicle of Higher Education,* 490,933 of all postsecondary students in 1998–1999 were foreign students, compared with 218,700 in 1976. The Asian financial crisis put only a modest dent in the number of foreign students who took advantage of the U.S. educational system in 1998. The top five countries sending students to the United States in 1997–1998 were Japan (47,073 students), China (46,958), Korea (42,890), India (33,818), and Taiwan (30,855). The Republic of Korea had the biggest 1-year increase (15.5 percent) in the number of citizens studying in the United States. China and India were a close second and third, posting 10.5 percent and 10.4 percent gains, respectively, over 1996–1997 enrollments. Only Hong Kong showed a drop (11.7 percent) in that period (see Economic and Trade Trends at the beginning of the chapter).

According to the *Statistical Abstract of the United States,* foreign students accounted for nearly 26 percent of the 44,645 doctorates awarded in 1996, a 50 percent increase since 1981, when they earned 12.8 percent of all doctoral degrees. The high representation of foreign students is especially striking in graduate computer science, information technology, and medical and engineering programs. In fact, more than half of engineering doctorates went to foreign students in 1997, according to the National Academy of Sciences (NAS). NAS states that increasing the number of American students in science and engineering will require a significant improvement in the number and caliber of precollege courses. It urges professional scientists and engineers to continue to work with state committees to improve K–12 standards and promote "best practices" in the teaching of courses that expand science and technological literacy.

HOW MUCH IS YOUR DEGREE WORTH?

In a tight labor market, a high level of educational attainment translates into an almost instant asset for job seekers and is a good predictor of high future earnings. In an increasingly high-tech, skills-based marketplace, it is no longer possible to support a family with only a high school diploma. In 1997, a 4-year college degree was worth nearly 55 percent more in wages than was a high school diploma. In manufacturing, workers with less than a high school education made less in constant dollars in 1996 than they did in 1959, while college graduates in manufacturing earned nearly one-third more (about $67,000). Across all jobs, men 25 and older with only a high school diploma earned an average of $27,642 a year in 1997, according to the U.S. Census Bureau; women in the same age and education bracket fared far worse, netting an average of $22,067. In stark contrast, male and female college graduates age 25 and older in 1997 made about $48,616 and $35,379, respectively.

Ironically, despite the long-term economic advantages of staying in school, the high school dropout rate has stagnated at about 15 percent in the last two decades. African-American and Hispanic teenagers are about six times as likely to drop out of high school before graduation than are white students. According to the Educational Testing Service (ETS), the robust economy and tight labor market are at least partly responsible for this dismal statistic. Low-skill jobs in fast-food restaurants, gas stations, and the custodial services help lure teenagers away from school with the illusion of a high-paying job. However, the same ETS study found that within a decade, people who earned a high school diploma surpassed the low wages of their peers who dropped out.

To track the relationship between education and earning power, the U.S. Census Bureau's education branch has created a popular link on its Web site called "How Much is Your Degree Worth?" To visit, go to www.census.gov and click on E for "education." You will find current population and educational attainment figures along with information on top-earning careers.

Source: U.S. Department of Commerce, Bureau of the Census, *Outcomes of Education, Current Population Reports,* Series P-60.

Educational Attainment

Americans are entering the new millenium better educated than ever before, but the U.S. literacy rate is still well below that of industrialized nations such as Germany, Sweden, and Japan. Between 1999 and 2009, the number of U.S. high school graduates will increase 16 percent. According to the U.S. Bureau of the Census's *Current Population Survey,* 82 percent of all people over age 25 in the United States were high school graduates in 1997 and 24 percent had completed 4 years of college (see Economic & Trade Trends at the beginning of the chapter). This represents a healthy increase since 1980, when 67 percent finished high school and only 16 percent had graduated from a 4-year college or university. Professional degrees were up in 1997, with 5.3 percent of those over age 25 earning a master's degree. In that year, just 1.4 percent held a professional degree

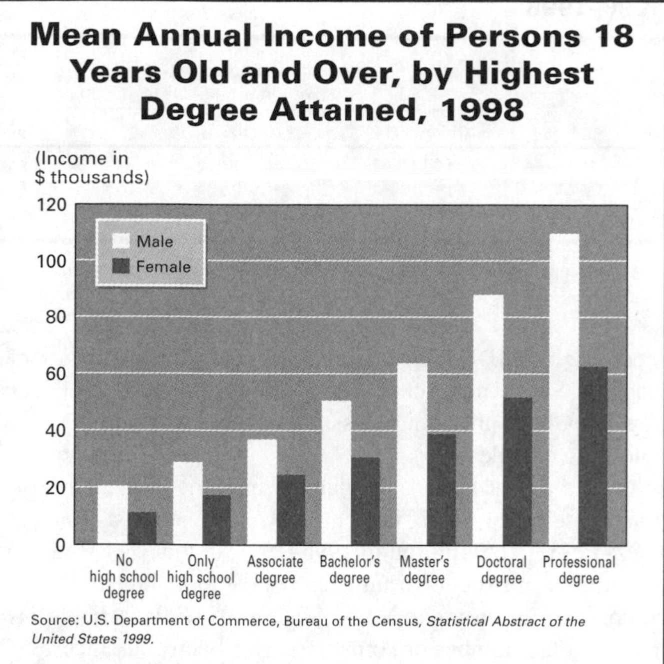

FIGURE 49-1

in medicine or law and 1 percent earned a doctorate in any field (see the boxed note "How Much Is Your Degree Worth?" and Figure 49-1). Men edged out women in the number of doctoral degrees conferred in 1997, earning 26,836 doctorates in 1997 while women earned 17,809.

High schools continue to struggle to meet or beat the standardized test score levels on the Scholastic Achievement Test (SAT) (formerly called the Scholastic Aptitude Test) set in 1970–1971, although students have posted modest gains in mathematics in recent years. In 1987, for example, all students scored an average of 501 on the mathematical portion of the SAT; by 1997, that score had inched up to 511, a 10 percent improvement over the decade. The number of Hispanics and African-Americans taking the SAT continued to climb, but minority students continue to score below the average (423 for African-Americans in 1997) on the mathematics portion. Asian-Americans continued to outpace all other minority groups in mathematics (460 in 1997). Average SAT scores in mathematics for college-bound high school seniors were 492 in 1980; in 1997, they were 511.

In 1996, the most recent year in which the test was given, the National Assessment of Educational Programs (NAEP) found that 97 percent of all 17-year-olds in public high schools performed at or above selected mathematical proficiency levels when asked to do basic numerical operations (balancing a checkbook, adding a column of numbers) and problem solving. However, when NAEP measured the same students' proficiency at problems using moderately complex procedures and reasoning, only 59 percent were found to be proficient. Algebraic equations involving multistep procedures posed an even greater challenge, with only 7 percent of students reaching NAEP's proficiency target levels. Students attending private schools did considerably better at the moderately complex problems (72 percent reached the target score) but only marginally better at the most advanced level, with 10 percent mastering multistep algebra problems. Tests measuring knowledge in history and geography were similarly discouraging, although students' scores improved across all categories the higher their parents' level of education was.

In 1996, President Clinton reacted to educators' concern about the inability of U.S. workers to adjust to a rapidly changing marketplace by calling for a new initiative, Standards 2000, to increase school performance. Standards 2000 calls on states to enact programs to meet uniform national academic goals. In some states, businesses are actively collaborating with high schools in learning partnerships, helping students translate their career goals into business plans or tutoring the college-bound in the skills needed to succeed at the university level.

Overcrowded schools and poor scores in reading, math, science, and critical thinking tests have parents clamoring for more rigorous instruction and smaller classes. In response, nearly a dozen states are offering politically controversial school voucher programs that allow residents of certain districts to opt out of public education altogether. Most of the voucher programs, including one in Cleveland, are facing court challenges because they may violate the constitutional separation of church and state. Public concern about the quality of US public schools helped President Clinton get a $1.2 billion education allocation in 1998 from Congress to fund the hiring of 100,000 new teachers in 1999–2000, a move designed to reduce class sizes and encourage more one-on-one interaction between pupils and teachers. The President also suggested allocating $65 million in additional funding for public charter schools.

EDUCATIONAL INNOVATIONS AT SCHOOL AND WORK

The classroom technology revolution advanced by leaps and bounds in 1998–1999 as computers continued to transform the learning environment. Fueling spending on computer technology in education is President Clinton's 1996 Technology Literacy Challenge, which pledged to provide all eighth-graders with access to the Internet by the year 2000, a goal that has been largely accomplished. According to Market Data Retrieval (MDR), a private marketing company that surveyed 86,600 public schools in 1998, the number of public elementary and secondary schools with Internet access increased from 35 percent in 1994 to 65 percent in 1996. Between 1996 and the 1998–1999 school year, the number of computers in classrooms increased 30 percent (8.2 million computers), and today 90 percent of all schools have at least some computers wired to the World Wide Web. Administrators also are more dependent on computers for tasks that include daily attendance, counseling, grading, scheduling, and payroll. Many school-based computers now use dedicated T-1 lines rather than telephone lines with the slower dial-up technology. A significant number of schools now have computers in computer laboratories/media centers,

TABLE 49-4: Public Schools with Access to the Internet, 1996–1998

	Percent of Schools with Internet Access			Percent of Instructional Rooms with Internet Access		
	1996	1997	1998	1996	1997	1998
Total schools	65	78	89	14	27	51
Elementary	61	75	88	13	24	51
Secondary	77	89	94	16	32	52

Source: U.S. National Center for Education Statistics, "Internet Access in Public Schools and Classrooms: 1994–98," from U.S. Department of Commerce, Bureau of the Census, *Statistical Abstract of the United States, 1999.*

libraries, and individual classrooms; satellite dishes, cable, local area networks (LANs), CD-ROMs, modems, and other hallmarks of the information age are becoming much more common, especially in affluent school districts (see Table 49-4).

Classroom Technology Explosion

The physical plant of new schools today is changing to accommodate the expanding role of computer technology in education. This often means a larger construction footprint to incorporate separate media centers, libraries, and/or computer research and learning laboratories into the floor plans of elementary, middle, and high schools (see Chapter 6 for a discussion of school construction). While significant progress has been made in outfitting schools to hook up to the Internet, the wiring of classrooms for the Internet still lags. According to a 1998 report by the American Society of Civil Engineers, "46 percent of all classrooms lack basic wiring to support computer systems."

The ratio of computers to pupils has risen significantly since the computer age took root in the classroom in the early 1980s. In the 1984–1985 school year, there were 62.7 students for each computer in all schools. By 1998–1999, the national average was projected to drop to 5.9 students per computer. Some states, such as Wyoming, posted even more impressive gains with 3.5 students per machine. California—the nation's most populous state—had the least favorable ratio at 8.5 students per computer, according to MDR. The national average is 6.3 students per machine. Senior high schools do slightly better than do elementary schools at providing classroom access to computer technology (see Table 49-5).

TABLE 49-5: Students per Computer in Elementary and Secondary Schools, 1985 and 1997

Students per computer	1984–1985	1997–1998	1998–1999
U.S. total	**62.7**	**6.4**	**5.9**
Public schools, total	63.5	6.3	5.7
Elementary	79.3	6.9	6.3
Middle/junior high	61.2	5.6	5.8
Senior high	51.5	5	5.1
Catholic schools, total	73.5	8.5	7.6
Elementary	85.1	8.8	7.7
Secondary	57.8	7.8	7.3
Other private schools, total	40.5	7.6	6.9
Elementary	42.7	8.2	7.2
Secondary	40.1	5.3	4.7

Source: Market Data Retrieval, Shelton, CT, unpublished data (copyright), from U.S. Department of Commerce, Bureau of the Census, *Satistical Abstract of the United States, 1999.*

Over a 5-year period, the number of computers for instructional use grew 105 percent from 3.6 million units in 1992–1993, to 6.3 million in 1996–1997, to today's 8.2 million (7.5 million instructional units and 600,000 administrative-use computers), according to MDR. Since 1995–1996, schools have increased the number of computers by 30 percent; since 1997, the number of school-based computers has jumped 10 percent.

According to MDR, nearly 80 percent of all schools use a LAN to communicate electronically within the school. In a new trend, 60 percent of the nation's largest schools use wide area networks (WANs) and half use satellite dishes and videodiscs. Some elementary schools are still being built without telephone hookups in the classrooms to support computer modems, but many others are installing fiber-optics as an alternative way to deliver technology to school learning centers.

Although MDR reports a big jump in the number of teachers who use computers each day in the classroom, it also reports a continuing need to increase technology training for educators. Some studies show that between 25 and 38 percent of elementary and secondary teachers are just beginning to learn basic computing or are totally computer-illiterate. *Education Week* reports that while 50 percent of all full-time teachers participated in a professional development activity in 1994 to learn technology applications, only 15 percent of teachers had at least 9 hours of training in computer use. The Office of Technology Assessment (OTS) estimates that it takes 5 years to effectively introduce technology into a school's curriculum. OTS said that support and ongoing professional development are crucial during that period. Unfortunately, although many school districts invest in computer hardware, they fail to encourage or require staff members to upgrade their skills on a regular basis or budget enough money for ongoing technology education of staff.

Not all students or school districts have equal access to these cutting-edge educational technologies. MDR's data show that equity is still an issue at schools with high percentages of minority students, high poverty levels, or both. Schools that are more than 50 percent African-American or Hispanic have 7.1 students per computer, which is above the national average. The discrepancy is largest when it comes to Internet hookups. In districts where 30 percent or more of the students are impoverished, only

78 percent of schools have access to the Internet. In contrast, in districts with poverty rates under 6 percent, 90 percent of all schools have Internet access. Conversely, school districts with the most poverty-level students are much more likely to use a satellite dish to enhance their ability to access resources outside the school's walls than are their more affluent counterparts.

At the university level, MDR predicted that total spending for computer hardware and software would reach $2.5 billion for the 1998–1999 school year, a decrease of 11 percent over the $2.8 billion spent in the previous school year. MDR states that this drop reflects a shift in spending away from hardware and into software. Spending on hardware will be $1.7 billion, a decline of 17 percent; spending on software will increase by 9 percent to $814 million. Administrative programs will account for about $422 million of that sum, while $392 million will go toward instructional software. Many more libraries are upgrading their electronic catalogs and interactive database search services for students at remote dormitory locations; administrative departments are linking most university computers in enhanced systemwide networks. Colleges with enrollments over 10,000 are spending the most on computer hardware and software upgrades. Most university professors now routinely use computer communications technology to deepen academic discussions between formal class sessions by making on-line debates of written work a required part of classroom participation.

Business and School Partnerships

The Bureau of Labor Statistics' (BLS) Office of Employment Statistics predicted that job openings for systems analysts, computer engineers, and computer scientists will increase 108 percent from the 1996 figure of 933,000 jobs to 1.9 million high-tech jobs in 2006. Educators fear that many of those positions will go unfilled or go to better-educated foreign students unless the skills taught in U.S. secondary and postsecondary schools improve dramatically. This means creating curriculum that teaches both critical thinking skills and expertise in computer programming and repair. Employees need skills that can travel from job to job. This entails training workers who are committed to precision craftsmanship, high manufacturing and repair standards, and quality control.

To that end, in June 1999, the U.S. Congress directed the National Research Coucil (NRC) of the NAS to launch a 15-month study of various industries in the information technology field and profile their workforce needs. Government and industry are concerned about the availability of a well-trained labor force, and the study will try to pinpoint the needed skill mix for future high-tech workers. It also will look at meeting labor needs from foreign immigration, examine the best business-school partnerships, and evaluate the effectiveness of various employer training programs. Controversial issues such as age discrimination and worker displacement by immigrants will be studied as well.

The National Science Foundation's (NSF) advanced technology education program is promoting partnerships between potential employers and community colleges in an effort to target curriculum to fit the hundreds of thousands of high-technology jobs the economy is expected to create over the next 5 years. About 200 NSF-sponsored partnership programs began in 1998, and employers and educators are analyzing the preliminary results. Other collaborative learning programs are being developed by the Institute for Policy Studies at Johns Hopkins University in Baltimore. This work is part of the follow-up to the 1991 report "What Work Requires of School: A SCANS Report for America 2000." Some pilot programs involve building basic skills at the high school level, collaborative efforts between local employers and secondary schools, and training college students in how to make a business plan. To learn more, one can visit the Johns Hopkins Web site at www.scans.jhu.edu.

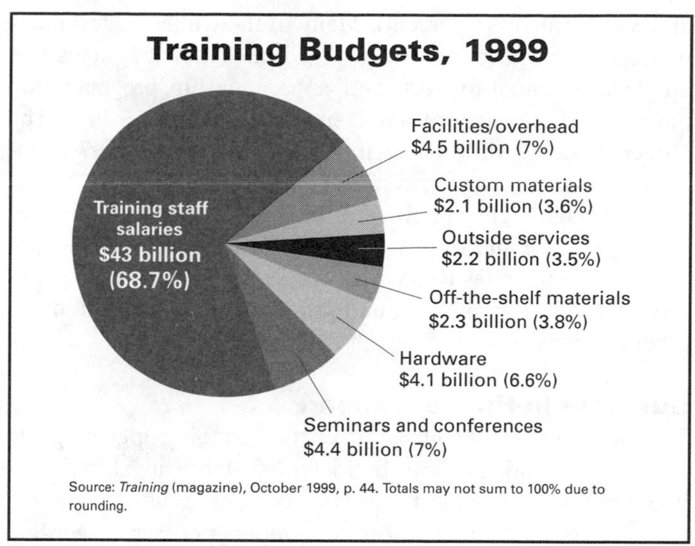

Source: *Training* (magazine), October 1999, p. 44. Totals may not sum to 100% due to rounding.

FIGURE 49-2

On-the-Job-Training

According to *Training* magazine's annual Industry Report (October 1998), U.S. companies with 100 or more employees spent an estimated $60.7 billion on formal workplace training in 1998, a 3.6 percent increase over 1997 and a 26 percent rise since 1993. According to Dun and Bradstreet, 138,850 U.S. businesses employed 100 or more people in 1998. The $60.7 billion figure for formal training expenditures does not include informal, on-the-job training or account for training given at thousands of companies with fewer than 100 workers (see Figure 49-2).

While the trend is for U.S. employers to invest an increasing percentage of their overall budget for honing workplace skills, the United States is being outspent by its global competitors in the G-7 countries in all categories that measure on-the-job training. According to the Organization for Economic Cooperation and Development (OECD), 34 percent of all workers between the ages of 25 and 64 in the United States took part in a job-related program to acquire new skills in 1998, either self-financed or employer-sponsored. The OECD found that more workers took part in similar programs in Australia (38 percent), Finland (45 percent), France (40 percent), Sweden (42 percent), and Switzerland (35 percent). Many of the United States' international rivals have more formalized educational systems that emphasize school-to-work and apprenticeship programs and have a longer history of university-business partnerships. The United States—while outperformed by students in G-7 countries on tests measuring complex problem solving and verbal skills through high school—is still generally perceived to have better graduate and professional school training, and the U.S. workplace continues to produce workers who are perceived as more flexible, competitive, and productive than those in many other countries.

Business In-House Training

The most successful companies say that ongoing upgrading and retooling of workers' skills build a more stable, loyal, and flexible workplace. The most profitable companies usually guarantee workers a set number of training hours per year. According to the American Society for Training and Development (ASTD), the best companies use innovative practices such as self-directed teams that emphasize access to business information, profit sharing, group-based pay, or team-productivity bonuses. Some companies hire individual mentors to coach teams of workers. For example, in the transportation and public utilities sector, which makes up about 8.2 percent of the economy and includes power, water, and gas utilities and the trucking, airline, and railroad industries, companies spend the most on job-specific training to improve delivery mechanisms, including computerized simulator programs.

The people most likely to get workplace training are production workers (16.9 million), professionals (10 million), customer-service personnel (7.2 million), administrative employees (5.2 million), salespeople of all backgrounds and first-line supervisors (4.2 million each), middle managers (3.6 million), senior managers (1.7 million), and executives (1.3 million). According to the BLS, about 70 percent of workers at the 1,000 businesses polled had received some kind of training in the year before the most recent survey (1997). White men in midcareer jobs were more likely to get training than were women and minorities or people younger than 24 and older than 55. College graduates get more opportunities to improve their workplace skills than do those with only a high school education, another clear sign that a high level of educational attainment is a predictor of future workplace success and high earnings. According to the ASTD and BLS, those who receive regular workplace training earn up to 16 percent more than did their similarly educated nontrained peers.

Business Outsourcing of Training

Companies on the leading edge of the economy in the United States are devoting about one-third of their overall training budgets to hiring outside consultants to upgrade workers' computer, technical, interpersonal, managerial, and team-based skills. However, outsourcing has not created a management stampede to hire outside specialists to conduct training workshops. Surveys show that despite predictions that the use of outside experts would skyrocket, the percentage of training that is outsourced (provided by contract employees outside the firm) has not changed in the last 2 years. *Training* magazine says that 69 percent of all formal training is provided by internal staff, compared with 31 percent delivered by outside sources. According to *Training*'s survey, at least 54.5 million workers got some form of formal training in 1997, and 70 percent of them were taught by a live teacher in a classroom.

ASTD reported that of the 500-plus companies it polled, leading-edge firms—those which met several benchmark standards—spent the most on worker training. Most of those leading-edge firms spent $150 to $300 more per employee on job skills training in 1998 than they did in 1997. ASTD said that most of those firms delivered 11.8 percent of their training by using learning technologies such as CD-ROMs, Intranets, LANs, and the Internet. Training expenditures for these so-called benchmark companies fell into the following categories: tuition reimbursements for workers, 13.3 percent; wages for the training staff, 41.4 percent; outsourcing training payments, 27 percent; and other expeditures, 18.3 percent.

INTERNATIONAL EDUCATION COMPARISONS

In general, the greater a country's wealth, the higher the percentage of GDP it spends on education. This is still true for the United States, but other global competitors are quickly catching up. In 1997, France and Canada spent a larger percentage of GDP on primary and secondary education than did the United States, but only Canada spent more on higher education and on all education levels combined. The ratio of U.S. expenditures on education to GDP to the percentage of per capita GDP is also fairly healthy, but not as high as it is in some of our global competitors.

High teacher attrition and dropout rates, especially in the first 3 years of teaching, continue to stymie education policy makers seeking to attract and hold quality educators in a tight labor market. Lack of job status is also a problem in the United States. Many educators complain that young teachers do not get support from their school colleagues or from the larger school community for the tough job they do. In September 1999, with the opening of school looming, districts across the United States scrambled to fill thousands of teaching slots. To recruit candidates, many districts increased base starting salaries and/or offered signing bonuses to new hires. Starting salaries for U.S. teachers are competitive with those of other similarly educated professionals, but career salary maximums lag well behind those of teachers in other industrial, G-7, and Pacific Rim countries. Between 1990 and 1996, average teacher salaries in public elementary and secondary schools increased 24 percent from $20,292 to $25,167. Even with that increase, when salaries are adjusted for inflation, average beginning teacher salaries are relatively low compared with salaries in other fields college graduates can enter. In 1995, salaries for career teachers with 10 years or more in the classroom averaged

$38,456 compared with $45,773 for other professionals over 25 with a bachelor's degree, using 1996 constant dollars.

CHALLENGES FOR THE NEW MILLENNIUM

One of the main challenges in the first decades of the twenty-first century will be to increase opportunities in poorer, high-minority school districts. This means not only making concerted efforts to ease overcrowding but also taking measures to ensure that schools are secure, nonviolent refuges where learning can take place. Educators need to find ways to increase the number of minority students who successfully complete high-level math and sciences courses and go on to college. By 2015, some 19 states will have school enrollments that are at least 30 percent nonwhite. Studies show that schools with high percentages of nonwhite students tend to be less well funded and lag in the acquisition of cutting-edge instructional materials, computers, and educational technologies. In the Los Angeles Unified School District, the Manual Arts High School has doubled its enrollment to over 4,000 students. Many are housed in portable classrooms or in rooms where the pupil-to-teacher ratio far exceeds the national average. They are not alone. From Florida to Illinois, from New York to Washington, DC, students are being crammed into spaces that are not conducive to learning. Perhaps student opportunities can be enlarged through Title I and the new Technology Literacy Challenge Fund, among other programs. Without such an effort, the high school graduates now entering community colleges and vocational schools in record numbers will continue to arrive without the minimal computer and problem-solving skills needed to succeed in tomorrow's workforce. An inadequate education will continue to act as a potential social and economic destabilizing agent unless opportunities are expanded for all.

Joan McQueeney Mitric, Washington, DC, (301) 933-3042, jmitric1@aol.com, December 1999.

■ REFERENCES

Contact the U.S. Bureau of the Census at (301) 457-4701 for information on ordering Census documents, call the Census Education Branch at (301) 457-2464, or contact Steve Turkin at 202-457-3791. Visit www.census.gov for the latest population interim data.

"The Baby Boom Echo: No End in Sight," a Back to School Special Report, U.S. Secretary of Education Richard W. Riley, August 19, 1999.

Beyond the School Doors: The Literacy Needs of Job Seekers Served by the U.S. Department of Labor, September 1992, Educational Testing Service, ISBN 0-88685-136-X.

"Community Colleges: A Vision Deferred," by Anthony P. Carnevale, Donna M. Desrochers, and Stephen J. Rose.

The Condition of Education 1998. National Center for Education Statistics (NCES 98-388), U.S. Department of Education, National Library of Education, 555 New Jersey Avenue, NW, Washington, DC, 800-424-1616 or 202-205-4956. See numerous databases at www.ed.gov, www.fedstats.gov, or www.access.gpo.gov/usbudget/.

"Declining Job Security," by Robert G. Valletta, November 1997, Economic Research Department, Federal Reserve Bank of San Francisco.

Digest of Education Statistics 1998, NCES 98-015 (see address above).

Education and Training for America's Future, by Anthony P. Carnevale, 1998 Growth Papers for the Manufacturing Institute, Suite 600, 1331 Pennsylvania Avenue, NW, Washington, D.C. 20004-1790.

Educational: Mailing Lists & Customized Services 1995–1996. Contact Maureen Hands or Kathleen Brantley at Market Data Retrieval, 1 Forest Parkway, Shelton, CT 06484-9913, (203) 926-4800 or 1-800-333-8802. Or visit www.schooldata.com.

Education at a Glance: OECD Indicators 1997, Centre for Educational Research and Innovation, Organization for Economic Cooperation and Development. Or contact the U.S. office at 2001 L Street, Washington, DC 20036-4922, (202) 785-6323. For economic assumptions underlying this document and other data, visit the OECD Web site at www.oecd.org/els/stats/els_stat.htm.

Education Market News Data Points, various 1998 reports by Market Data Retrieval and the Dun & Bradstreet Corporation, including "Technology Explosion: Key Trends in Public Schools (July 1998), "School Construction in the U.S." (March 1998) and "MDR Unveils Initial Higher Education Technology Survey Findings" (December 1998).

"Employer Training: The High Road, the Low Road and the Muddy Middle Path," by Anthony P. Carnevale and Donna M. Desrochers of the Educational Testing Service. Prepared for the Conference on Restoring Broadly Shared Prosperity at the University of Texas–Austin and sponsored by the Economic Policy Institute and the Lyndon B. Johnson School of Public Affairs, May 1997.

"The Great Outsourcing Stampede That Never Happened," by Jack Gordon in *Training* magazine, February 1998. Or E-mail jgordon@trainingmag.com.

"Harnessing Science and Technology for America's Economic Future: National and Regional Priorities," from the National Academy Press for $29, (202) 334-3313 or 800-624-6242.

Involving Employers in Training: Literature Review (97-K), U.S. Department of Labor, Employment and Training Administration 1997. To obtain a copy, call (202) 219-7664.

"Learning Ecologies," by David Stamps, in *Training* magazine January 1998. See above or E-mail dstamps@trainingmag.com.

Literacy, Economy, and Society, results of the first International Adult Literacy Survey, OECD 1995. See above.

Los Angeles Times, "Baby Boom Echo Putting a Strain on Schools, Study Finds," by John Balz, August 20, 1999.

The National Education Goals Report Summary 1997, National Goals Panel, 1255 22 Street, NW, Suite 502, Washington, DC 20037, (202) 724-0015, visit www.negp.gov, or E-mail NEGP@goalline.org.

The National Research Council, *1999 Study of Information Technology and Work-Force Needs.* To obtain more information about the study, contact the NRC at (202) 334-2138 or visit www.cstb.org.

New York Times, "Other Countries Catching Up to U.S. in Education, Study Finds," by Ethan Bronner, November 24, 1998. Visit NYTimes.com.

New York Times, "Despite Low Prestige and Pay, More Answer the Call to Teach," by Mary B.W. Tabor, July 11, 1999.

New York Times, "Putting Private Education to the Test," by Anemona Hartocollis, July 11, 1999.

New York Times, "As Students Return, Schools Cope with Severe Shortage of Teachers," by Jacques Steinberg, August 31, 1999.

The 1999 ASTD State of the Industry Report, by Laurie J. Bassie and Mark E. Van Buren (mvanburen@astd.org), January 1999. Results of the American Society for Training and Development Human Performance Practices Survey on employer-provided formal training done with the U.S. Department of Labor and Employment and Training Administration, (202) 219-6871. To get a copy, call ASTD at (703) 683-8100 or visit www.astd.org.

Occupational Outlook Quarterly Winter 1997–98 (OOQ), U.S. Department of Labor, Bureau of Labor Statistics, 800 North Capitol Street, Washington, DC 20211, (202) 606-5902 or visit stats.bls.gov.

One-Stop Career Centers and Learning Lab for state-by-state information on vocational education and retraining grants, the Job-Training Partnership Act, adult and veterans education opportunities, www.ttrc.doleta.gov/sites.htm.

Pennsylvania State University international study on correlation between class size and achievement in mathematics. Contact education professors David Post at (814) 863-3786 or dmp10@psu.edu or Suet-ling Pong at (814) 863-3770 or E-mail sxp21@psu.edu.

Pennsylvania State University study surveying 6,994 students at 371 public schools on possible negative consequences of restructuring schools in low-socioeconomic neighborhoods. Contact Professor Roger C. Shouse at (814) 863-3773 or E-mail rcs8@psu.edu.

"The Problem of Out-of-Field Teaching," R. Ingersoll for the U.S. Department of Education, 1996. Visit www.pdkintl.org/kappan/king9806.htm.

Projections of Education Statistics to 2009, National Center for Education Statistics (NCES 98-382), September 1999. See address above.

Statistical Abstract of the United States 1997. U.S. Department of Commerce, Bureau of the Census, Washington, DC.

Technology in Education 1998, Market Data Retrieval. See address above.

Training (magazine), October 1998, "Industry Report," annual report on employer-provided training in the United States, Lakewood Publications, 50 South Ninth St., Minneapolis, MN. Call managing editor Chris Lee at (800) 328-4329 or (612) 333-0471 or E-mail www.lakewoodpub.com.

Washington Post editorial, "Classrooms and Class" and "Science," www.washingtonpost.com.

Washington Post, "Teachers' Choice: Shortage Forces Area School Systems to Compete for Education Graduates," Christina A. Samuels, June 28, 1999.

Washington Post, "Not Just More Teachers—Better Ones Too," by George Miller, August 8, 1999.

What Work Requires of Schools: A SCANS Report for America 2000. U.S. Department of Labor, June 1991. The follow-up of the SCANS report is being done at the Institute for Policy Studies at Johns Hopkins University. Contact Arnold Packer at (410) 516-7160 or Melissa Siberts, education programs coordinator, at (410) 516-5196 or visit www.scans.jhu.edu.

RELATED CHAPTERS

6: Construction
27: Computer Equipment
28: Computer Software and Networking

TRAVEL AND TOURISM
Economic and Trade Trends

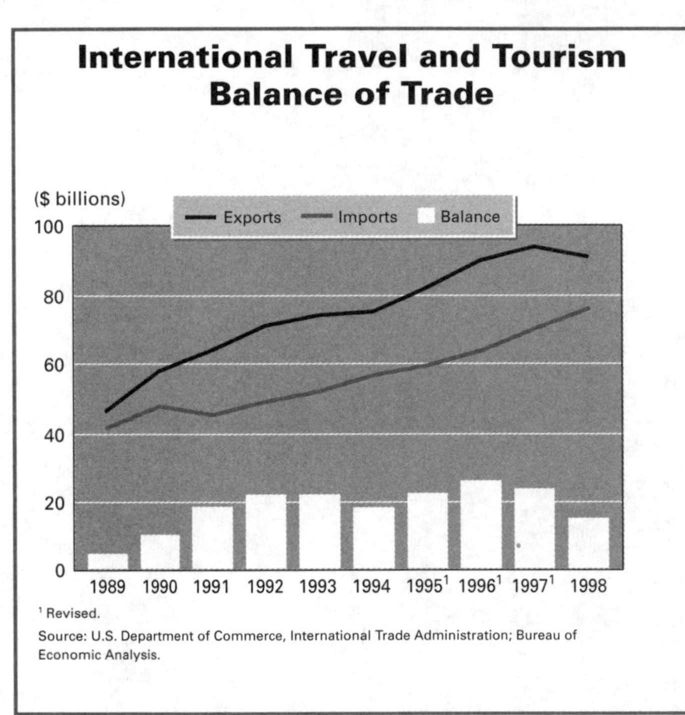

[1] Revised.

Source: U.S. Department of Commerce, International Trade Administration; Bureau of Economic Analysis.

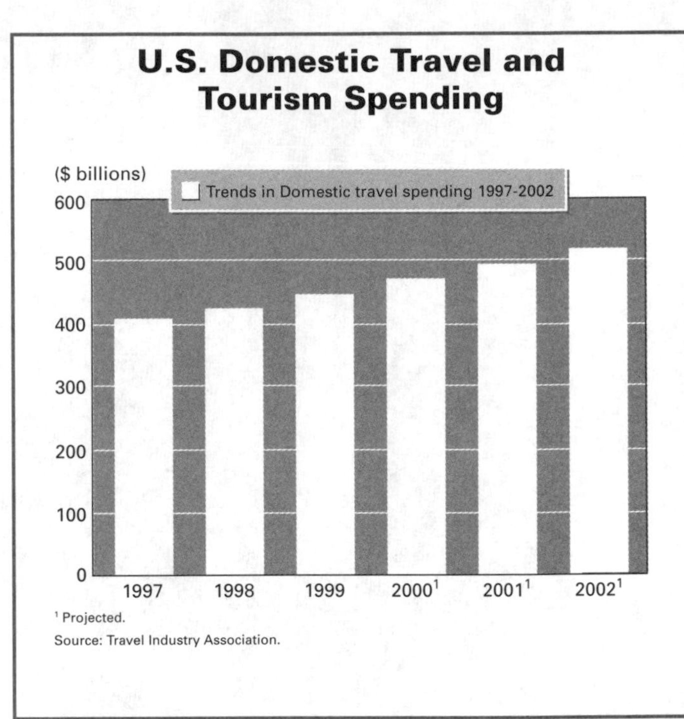

[1] Projected.

Source: Travel Industry Association.

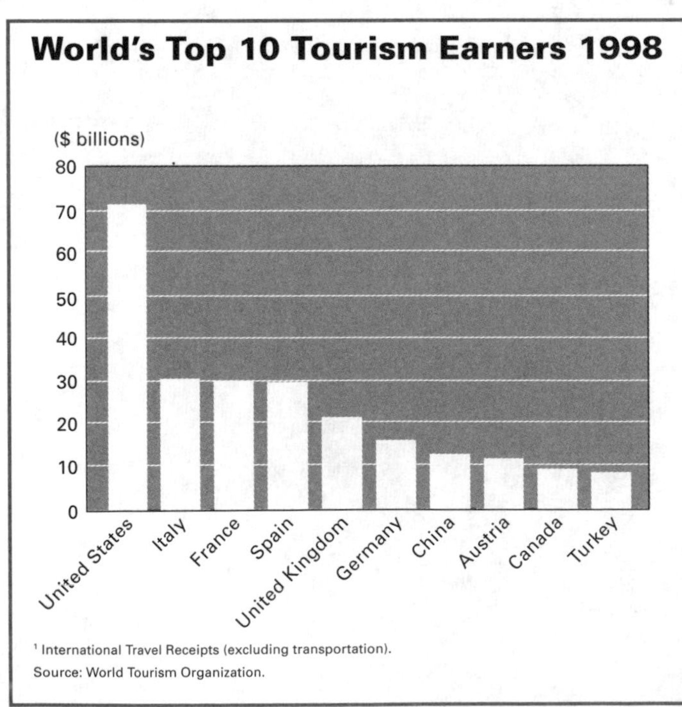

[1] International Travel Receipts (excluding transportation).

Source: World Tourism Organization.

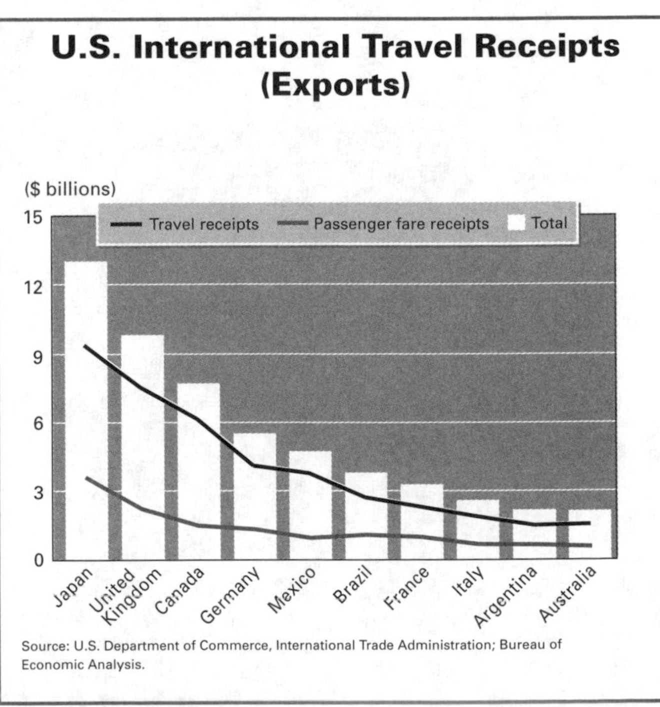

Source: U.S. Department of Commerce, International Trade Administration; Bureau of Economic Analysis.

See "Getting the Most Out of *Outlook 2000*" for definitions of terms.

50

Travel and Tourism

INDUSTRY DEFINITION Tourism includes the activities of persons traveling to and staying in places outside their usual environment for not more than one continuous year for leisure, business, or other purposes.

OVERVIEW

The travel and tourism industry in the United States consists of many industries. It is the second largest U.S. service export and fourth largest overall export category, one of the largest employers, and the third largest U.S. retail sales industry. Total 1998 expenditures for domestic travelers and international visitors were over $515 billion, up from $502 billion in 1997 (see Table 50-1). Over 7 million jobs are directly supported by tourism spending, including 684,000 executive-level positions, and the industry generates $71 billion in federal, state, and local tax revenue annually. The outlook for spending by travelers to and within the United States is excellent. Total travel spending is forecast to grow 4.2 percent annually, increasing from $502 billion in 1997 to $630 billion in 2002. Domestic travel spending is forecast to grow 5 percent to reach $518 billion in 2002. Spending by international visitors is expected to reach $119 billion in 2003, growing 5.5 percent annually between 1998 and 2003.

GLOBAL TOURISM

According to the United Nations' World Tourism Organization, international arrivals worldwide numbered 635 million in 1998, up 2 percent from the 1997 level despite the Asian economic crisis, which depressed travel and tourism throughout the Pacific Rim countries, as well as economic problems in Brazil and parts of Europe. From 1988 to 1998, international arrivals worldwide increased from 395 million to 635 million, a 61 percent increase (see Table 50-2). Spending by international travelers worldwide

TABLE 50-1: Travel and Tourism in the United States Trends and Forecasts
(billions of dollars except as noted)

	1997	1998	1999[1]	2000[2]	2001[2]	2002[2]	2003[2]	Percent Change			
								97–98	98–99	99–00	98–03[3]
Expenditures											
Domestic spending	408	424	446	471	494	518		3.9	5.2	5.5	
International spending	94	91	94	99	105	112	119	–3.2	3.3	5.3	6.9
Total travel and tourism spending	502	515	540	570	599	630		2.6	4.9	5.6	
Number of travelers (millions)											
Domestic travelers	1,026.6	1,035.6	1,061.2	1,081.9	1,095.5	1,107.4		0.9	2.5	1.9	
International visitors to the United States	47.8	46.4	47.0	48.5	50.4	52.4	54.6	–2.9	1.3	3.2	4.2
Rate of inflation in travel services, %	3.4	2.0	3.3	3.6	3.6	3.6					

[1] Estimate.
[2] Forecast.
[3] Compound rate.
Source: Travel Industry Association of America; U.S. Travel Data Center; U.S. Department of Commerce: Bureau of Economic Analysis, International Trade Administration.

TABLE 50-2: Worldwide and U.S. International Visitor Arrivals and Receipts[1]

	Arrivals, millions		U.S. Share of World Arrivals, %	Receipts, billions		U.S. Share of World Receipts, %
	World	United States		World	United States	
1984	316.4	26.9	8.5	112.7	17.2	15.2
1985	327.2	25.4	7.8	118.1	17.8	15.0
1986	338.9	26.0	7.7	143.5	20.4	14.2
1987	363.8	27.8	7.6	176.8	23.6	13.3
1988	394.8	33.9	8.6	204.3	29.4	14.4
1989	426.5	36.4	8.5	221.2	36.2	16.4
1990	458.2	39.4	8.6	267.8	43.0	16.1
1991	464.0	42.7	9.2	277.6	48.4	17.4
1992	502.8	47.3	9.4	313.6	54.7	17.5
1993	518.3	45.8	8.8	323.1	57.9	17.9
1994	553.3	44.8	8.1	352.6	58.4	16.6
1995	568.5	43.3	7.6	403.0	63.4	15.7
1996	599.6	46.5	7.8	437.6	69.8	15.9
1997	619.6	47.8	7.7	438.2	73.3	16.7
1998	635.1	46.4	7.3	439.4	71.3	16.2

[1] All figures are revised estimates except 1998 data, which are original estimates.
Source: U.S. Department of Commerce, International Trade Administration; World Tourism Organization.

totaled $439 billion in 1998, a $1 billion increase from the 1997 level. This spending was equivalent to nearly 13 percent of world goods exports. An estimated 230 million people are directly employed in the travel and tourism industries, accounting for over 9 percent of the world's labor force. Global international spending on travel more than doubled in a decade, going from just over $204 billion in 1988 to over $439 billion in 1998.

The U.S. share of world travel and tourism receipts in 1998 was over 16 percent, down from a peak of just under 18 percent in 1993. The United States has seen international arrivals decline in 4 of the last 6 years, though receipts declined only once in that period. The United States remains the world's top tourism earner, according to the World Tourism Organization (see "Economic and Trade Trends" at the beginning of this chapter). In 1998, the United States' $71.3 billion in travel receipts was more than twice as large as that of the number two earner, Italy ($30.4 billion).

DOMESTIC, INBOUND, AND OUTBOUND TRAVEL AND TOURISM TRENDS

Domestic Tourism

An improved economy and greater consumer confidence have improved travel and tourism industry revenues in the United States. Unemployment has been falling, interest rates and inflation have remained low, and the growth of gross domestic product has been strong. Relatively steady growth of disposable income has benefited the industry because travel and tourism consistently ranks as one of the most common ways Americans choose to spend their free time.

According to the Travel Industry Association of America (TIA), total domestic travel revenues reached $424 billion in 1998, up 4 percent from the 1997 level. American travelers took 898 million pleasure trips and 272 million business trips. Those trips lasted an average of 3.6 days, and more than 80 percent were by automobile. Minivacations of less than 4 days seem to dominate travel and tourism in the United States, perhaps because Americans are becoming less likely to spend significant time away from their jobs. Over one-third of trips in the United States continue to be visits to friends and relatives.

Shopping is the most popular activity on trips by domestic travelers that last a week or more. Outdoor activity is second, followed by visits to historical sites and museums (see Table 50-3).

Over the years, visits to theme parks and national parks have been one of the measures of travel and tourism industry activity. The amusement and theme parks industry in the United States includes approximately 750 parks and has grown an average 2 to 5 percent annually for the past two decades in terms of attendance and revenues. Similar growth is expected to continue over the next several years. According to the International Association of Amusement Parks and Attractions, attendance figures in 1998 were about the same as those in 1997 at 300 million. Revenues were estimated at $8.7 billion in 1998, up from $8.4 billion in 1997. In comparison, national parks had 287 million visitors, up 4 percent from 1997 levels, reversing declines in 1993, 1994, and 1996. The National Park Service forecast no growth in recreational visits to park sites in 1999 and less than 2 percent growth in the year 2000.

Adventure travel (e.g., whitewater rafting, mountain climbing, and photographic safaris) has spawned a number of new tour companies. The TIA reports that half the U.S. adult population has taken at least one such trip. Educational travel (to culinary institutes for cooking classes or tours centered on museums and art galleries) is booming. Another growing area is tour programs that focus on literature and the arts and feature opera and theater performances.

Because family travel accounts for much of summer travel and tourism, an increasing number of programs are being designed to accommodate families. According to the TIA, half

TABLE 50-3: Top 10 Activities of Inbound Overseas Travelers to the United States and Domestic Travelers in 1998

	Inbound Overseas Travelers		Domestic Travelers	
Rank	Activity	Percent Participating in	Activity	Percent Participating in
1	Shopping	89	Shopping	33
2	Dining in restaurants	83	Outdoor activities	17
3	Sight-seeing in cities	45	Historical places and museums	15
4	Amusement and theme parks	33	Beaches	11
5	Visiting historical places	33	Cultural events and festivals	10
6	Visiting small towns and villages	30	National and state parks	9
7	Water sports and sunbathing	26	Theme and amusement parks	8
8	Touring the countryside	24	Nightlife and dancing	8
9	Visiting national parks	21	Gambling	7
10	Visiting art galleries and museums	20	Sports events	6

Source: U.S. Department of Commerce, International Trade Administration; Travel Industry Association.

of all summer travelers are likely to participate in programs aimed at children, such as family discounts, children's menus, and children's activities at hotel and resorts. Hotels increasingly are creating travel packages that appeal to retirees and offering accommodations for travelers with pets.

The Effect of International Travel and Tourism on Trade

International travel and tourism to the United States is an export for the country. Technically, it is classified as a service export in the same manner as freight, insurance, telecommunications, royalties, and education. Although exports typically entail sending and selling U.S. goods abroad, when an international traveler visits the United States and spends money on lodging, food, or any other item or service during the visit, those expenditures are counted as exports.

International travel is a significant export category for the United States despite occasional small declines. In 1998, receipts amounted to $91.2 billion (46.4 million visitors spent $71.2 billion for travel within the United States and paid $20 billion in fares to U.S. carriers), making international travel and tourism the fourth largest U.S. export category, accounting for 34 percent of all service exports and 10 percent of total exports in that year. Travel receipts in 1998 were down 3 percent from those in the previous year but were expected to rise again in 1999 (see Table 50-1). International travel receipts supported over 1 million U.S. jobs in 1998 and generated $9.1 billion in federal, state, and local taxes. The United States regularly has a trade surplus in international travel and tourism, with the largest surplus to date occurring in 1996 ($26.3 billion).

International Arrivals in the United States

The United States hosted almost 46.4 million international visitors in 1998, almost a 3 percent decline from the level in 1997. Economic difficulties in Asia and Canada, economic volatility in South America, and a sluggish economy in Europe contributed significantly to that decline (see Table 50-4).

Canadian arrivals declined over 11 percent in 1998 as a result of that country's weak economy and a poor currency exchange rate, bringing visitation from Canada to its lowest level since 1987. Despite the decline, Canada remains the largest single market for the United States, accounting for more than 13 million visitors in 1998.

Mexican visitation continued to have positive growth in 1998, up 10 percent, and accounted for over 9 million visits to the United States. Mexican visitors traveling to the United States by air increased only 9 percent and totaled 1.4 million in 1998, making Mexican air arrivals the fifth largest market for the United States.

Overseas arrivals in the United States (excluding Mexicans and Canadians) totaled 23.7 million in 1998, a 2 percent decline from the record set in 1997. The Asian economic crisis was a

TABLE 50-4: Top International Travel Markets to the United States (Inbound)
(thousands of arrivals except as noted)

	1997	1998	2003[1]	Percent Change 97–98	Percent Change 1998–03[2]
North America					
Canada	15,127	13,422	15,035	–11.3	2.3
Mexico	8,433	9,276	10,648	10.0	2.8
Overseas					
Japan	5,368	4,885	5,188	–9.0	1.2
United Kingdom	3,721	3,975	5,056	6.8	4.9
Germany	1,994	1,902	2,345	–4.6	4.3
France	978	1,013	1,167	3.6	2.9
Brazil	941	909	891	–3.4	–0.4
Italy	580	611	700	5.3	2.8
Venezuela	488	541	748	10.9	6.7
Argentina	503	524	657	4.2	4.6
Netherlands	473	490	576	3.6	3.3
Australia	501	461	510	–8.0	2.0
Total arrivals	47,754	46,395	54,607	–2.8	3.3

[1] Estimate.
[2] Forecast.
Source: U.S. Department of Commerce, International Trade Administration.

major factor in that decline, with arrivals from that region down more than 13 percent, nearly twice as large a decline as was expected. Growth in select markets in Europe and South America helped moderate the drop in total overseas arrivals.

Travel and tourism from Asia was affected significantly by a severe contraction in the number of Japanese arrivals to the United States, which fell more than 9 percent, a reflection of the Japanese economic crisis in fall of 1997. The bright spot in Asia was India, which accounted for over 210,000 visitors to the United States, up 22 percent from 1997 arrivals. Mainland China and Hong Kong experienced smaller declines than expected, with nearly a half a million visitors between them (209,000 and 213,000, respectively) in 1998.

Conversely, western European visitation in 1998 continued to grow (up 3 percent), although at a slower rate than it did in 1997 (up 7 percent). Despite Germany's economic downturn in 1998, five of the top six western European markets set an all-time record for arrivals in 1998. The United Kingdom continued to grow (up nearly 7 percent) and almost reached a milestone of 4 million visitor arrivals in 1998, gaining ground on Japan, which holds the number one overseas visitation slot. Germany's economic ties with southeast Asia and a cutback in the world's need for machinery and equipment (a major portion of Germany's exports) contributed to the 4.6 percent decline in the number of German arrivals in the United States in 1998. Arrivals from France exceeded expectations by increasing nearly 4 percent and topping the 1 million visitor mark for the first time. Another record in 1998 was the over 5 percent gain in Italian visitors (611,000 arrivals). Arrivals from both the Netherlands and Sweden had positive growth (up nearly 4 percent and 3 percent, respectively) and also set a new record.

Eastern European visitation sustained positive growth for most of 1998, up nearly 5 percent for the year, despite a 1 percent downturn in the fourth quarter. Overall, eastern European arrivals reached a record level with over 400,000 visitors in 1998.

Visitation from South America at nearly 3 million (a 4 percent increase) was better than had been projected in nearly all markets despite Brazil's economic downturn and weakened exchange rate. In 1998, over 900,000 Brazilians visited the United States. Arrivals from Brazil were forecast to be down as much as 8 percent, yet the year-end results showed a contraction of only 3 percent from 1997. Two of the major markets in South America had much higher than expected growth. Colombia was up nearly 16 percent in 1998 over 1997. Venezuela's visitation level displayed double-digit growth, up 11 percent for the year, and at 541,000 surpassed the record level set in 1982 (532,000). Countering the effects of the Brazilian downturn, Argentina showed a 4 percent growth in arrivals in 1998.

Central America accounted for nearly 700,000 visitor arrivals to the United States in 1998 with solid double-digit growth for that region, up 24 percent. Three countries led that growth: Guatemala, up 22 percent; Costa Rica, up 19 percent; and El Salvador, up nearly 46 percent.

Oceania, particularly Australia and New Zealand, was affected by the Asian economic crisis, and visits from those countries were down 8 percent and 3 percent, respectively. Other factors, such as the drop in the Australian dollar against the U.S. dollar (down nearly 17 percent since 1997), cheap packages to Asia, and extremely low air fares to Europe, contributed to nearly an 8 percent decline in Australian visitation to the United States in 1998.

Arrivals from the Caribbean decreased 2 percent in 1998 but still accounted for nearly 1.2 million arrivals in the United States. African arrivals registered double-digit growth in 1998, up more than 10 percent to 258,000. The Middle East performed well in terms of growth, up nearly 7 percent to 587,000 arrivals.

Spending by Country

Although arrivals in a country are a useful measure of the international travel and tourism market, the real impact of travelers results from the export dollars they generate. Although one might expect Canada and Mexico, which send the most tourists, to generate the highest travel receipts, Table 50-5 shows a different picture. Japan has been the top generator of travel receipts (over $13 billion in 1998). Japanese travelers spent $2,817 per trip compared to $568 for Canadian visitors. Similarly, a comparison of the expenditures of domestic and international travelers shows that international travelers on average spent more than five times as much as domestic travelers did ($1,967 per trip versus $412 per trip) in 1998. Therefore, while international travelers are a small-volume market, they have a large dollar impact. Spending figures need to be watched over time because changes in the global economy can have a dramatic effect on spending by international visitors.

Purposes of International Travel and Tourism

International visitors to the United States come for many reasons. The top three purposes for Canadian visitors in 1998 were vacation (78 percent), visiting friends and relatives (25 percent), and business (22 percent). Overseas travelers in 1998 had

TABLE 50-5: U.S. International Travel Receipts (Exports)
(millions of dollars)

	1997	1998	Percent Change 97–98
All countries	94,090	91,246	–3.0
Japan	16,510	13,040	–21.0
United Kingdom	9,266	9,798	5.7
Canada	8,156	7,683	–5.8
Germany	5,502	5,469	–0.6
Mexico	4,297	4,752	10.6
Brazil	3,862	3,823	–1.0
France	3,412	3,309	–3.0
Italy	2,188	2,558	16.9
Argentina	2,460	2,146	–12.8
Australia	2,260	2,110	–6.6

Source: U.S. Department of Commerce: International Trade Administration, Bureau of Economic Analysis.

a similar pattern: vacation (64 percent), visiting friends and relatives (32 percent), and business (30 percent).

Destinations within the United States

Travel and tourism exports are unique in that the buyer travels to the United States to purchase the product, and unlike other merchandise and service exports, the destination is one of the products purchased. In 1998, there were some very interesting shifts in the visitation patterns of overseas travelers to the United States.

Florida became the top state visited by overseas travelers (6.1 million), surpassing California (almost 6.0 million visitors). (Florida and California have traded places over the years as the top destination.) The other top states visited in 1998 were New York (5.3 million), Hawaii (2.8 million), Nevada (1.9 million), Illinois (1.3 million), Massachusetts (1.2 million), and Texas (1.1 million). Guam received 1.0 million overseas visitors, and Arizona and New Jersey were tied for the tenth spot at 853,000. Of the top 11 states, 7 saw declines in 1998.

In 1998, the top destinations (city or island) for overseas travelers were New York City (5.0 million), Los Angeles (3.6 million), Miami (3.3 million), Orlando (2.9 million), San Francisco (2.6 million), Honolulu (2.2 million), Las Vegas (1.8 million), Washington, DC (1.4 million), Chicago (1.2 million), and Boston (1.0 million). New York City and Los Angeles have held the number one and two position for many years. The third through fifth most popular destinations have switched over time, but Miami has held the third spot since 1993. Honolulu has held the sixth position since 1991, Las Vegas has held the seventh spot and, Washington, DC, has been ranked eighth since 1993.

Impact on Transportation and Lodging

Overseas travelers tend to move around the country during their visits. The average number of destinations visited is over two, and 10 percent of those visitors spend time in five or more destinations. The transportation sectors that benefit from international visitors are rental cars (used by 36 percent of visitors in 1998) and taxis (41 percent). Almost 28 percent of those visitors took another domestic flight during their visit, and 27 percent had access to company or private automobiles. Overseas visitors also use public transportation, with almost 20 percent using the subway, tram, or bus systems of their destination cities. Another 11 percent opt to see the country by bus, and Amtrak had 1.8 million overseas travelers (7.5 percent) take to the rails to see the country.

Canadian visitors have very different transportation patterns. Because of their proximity, the main mode of transportation is automobiles (85 percent). Another 39 percent take a flight to or within the United States, and 7 percent use bus transportation.

International travelers have a considerable impact on the hotel industry. In 1998, 19.8 million overseas travelers stayed in a hotel or motel. Their average length of stay in a hotel was 7.7 nights with an average of 1.7 people in a travel party. Although almost 84 percent of overseas visitors stayed in a hotel or motel during their trips to the United States, only 66 percent of Canadian travelers used that option. Twenty-one percent of Canadian visitors spend time with friends and relatives, and another 12 percent go camping.

Top Activities

Since international travelers come to see America, their time is packed with activities. Shopping, dining in restaurants, sightseeing in cities, spending time in amusement and theme parks, and visiting historical places are the top five activities of overseas travelers (see Table 50-3). International visitors are almost twice as active as domestic travelers in general and are four times as likely to visit amusement or theme parks. One reason they appear to do so much on each trip is the length of stay. Overseas travelers' visits last 15.4 nights on average, versus 4 nights for domestic travelers.

The top five activities for Canadian visitors to the United States in 1998 were shopping (68 percent), sight-seeing (52 percent), visiting friends and relatives (43 percent), outdoor and sport activities (43 percent), and dining in restaurants (36 percent). Canadian visitation to the United States was down in 1998, and the length of stay declined slightly as well. Of the 19 activities of Canadian travelers to the United States tracked in 1998, only 2 saw increases: attending sport events and cross-country skiing.

International Travel and Tourism from the United States

When U.S. residents visit another country, their expenditures are an import for the United States. Although the number of U.S. citizens traveling internationally is growing, it still constitutes a small percentage of the population, and the volume of international travel and tourism is small compared with U.S. domestic travel and tourism. In 1998, U.S. domestic travel and tourism was an industry with 1.3 billion person-trips. U.S. outbound travel and tourism grew 6.3 percent in 1998. In the last 10 years, U.S. outbound travel has declined only once. This occurred in 1991, when the Gulf War and a slower U.S. economy kept people at home. International travel and tourism by U.S. residents grew from 41.1 million trips in 1989 to 56.3 million in 1998 and was projected to grow to 59.8 million in 1999. The top destination for U.S. outbound travelers has been Mexico since 1987. In 1998, U.S. visits to Mexico reached 18.3 million, up 2.4 percent over the level in 1997. Canada is the second most popular destination for U.S. international travelers. In 1998, 14.9 million travelers visited that country for 1 night or longer. This was an 11 percent increase over 1997, and it was due primarily to the low exchange rate for Canadian dollar and aggressive marketing by Canadians to lure travelers from the United States to visit their country. Over the past 10 years, U.S. outbound travel to Canada has seen its ups and downs. Declines were registered in 1989, 1991, 1992, and 1996. U.S. travel northward grew from 12.2 million in 1989 to 14.9 million in 1998. The forecast for 1999 was a slight increase over the 1998 total. The top overseas destinations visited in 1998 were the United Kingdom, France, Germany, Italy, and Jamaica.

Spending by U.S. international travelers reached a record $72.6 billion in 1998, including $53.7 billion in travel and

$18.9 billion in passenger fares, according to the Bureau of Economic Analysis. U.S. outbound travel still accounts for almost 40 percent of all service imports for the country. Spending by U.S. travelers over the last 10 years declined only in 1991. Total travel spending by U.S. travelers grew from $41.7 billion in 1989 to $72.6 billion in 1998. TIA forecasts that travel spending by U.S. outbound travelers would reach $80.4 billion by 1999 as outbound travel set yet another new record.

INDUSTRY SUBSECTORS

Transportation

The primary transportation sectors in the travel and tourism industry are airlines, rental cars, Amtrak, intercity buses, cruise lines, and airports. A short synopsis of each industry follows.

Airlines. According to the Air Transport Association, 1998 was the fourth successive year of profitability for the U.S. airline industry. Passenger revenues for U.S. scheduled airlines were $81 billion, and total revenues reached a record $113 billion. Competition in the industry remained intense as 85 percent of passengers had a choice of two or more airlines. Fuel prices declined dramatically, offsetting cost increases in other areas and allowing carriers to lower their prices. As a result, 1998 profits for the airlines declined to $4.9 billion from the record $5.2 billion in 1997. Total departures increased to over 8.3 million flights, and passenger enplanements rose to a record 614 million. Airline capacity has more than doubled in the 20 years since deregulation, reaching 874 billion available seat miles in 1998. The Federal Aviation Administration forecasts that in response to customer demand, U.S. airlines will continue to increase capacity 4.5 percent per year through 2010.

Rental Cars. The car rental industry has grown steadily in both fleet size and revenue over the past 15 years, reaching 1.6 million vehicles and total revenue of $17.2 billion in 1998. The top three companies control about 60 percent of the daily rental market. Fierce competition, high operating costs, and slim profit margins have forced those companies to control internal costs stringently. Many companies have slashed frequent-flier awards drastically, greatly reducing their payments to the airlines; maximized their use of yield-management systems; and reduced fleet sizes in certain areas to avoid having idle cars on their lots.

Industry revenues increased at rates of 3 to 5 percent across the board in 1998, although by the end of the second quarter of 1999, rates had dropped again. Rates continue to be almost flat, a scenario the industry has struggled with over at least the last 10 years.

Ownership of the major companies continues to change hands. HFS (now Cendant) bought Avis in 1996, and the car rental company went public in 1997. Republic Industries (now AutoNation) bought Alamo in 1995 and National in 1997. AutoNation announced in August 1999 that it will sell (or perhaps spin off) both companies. Budget was purchased by a former Budget licensee and then went public in 1997. Thrifty and Dollar had been owned by Chrysler, but also went public under the umbrella corporation Dollar Thrifty Automotive Group in 1997. Ford now owns 80 percent of Hertz.

The bull market and low interest rates have buttressed the industry and allowed it to grow steadily. Increased business and leisure travel and tourism also have contributed to the health of the industry. The prediction is for increased use of yield management systems to keep internal cost down; tight management of fleets, causing some shortages at peak demand times in some areas; continuing proliferation of taxes and fees on rentals, registration, and other components of the business; and small increases in rates to keep pace with rising costs.

Amtrak. Congress created Amtrak in 1971 to take over the intercity passenger rail operations of the nation's railroads. In 1998, Amtrak operated as many as 265 trains daily in its 22,000-mile national passenger rail system. Today, the passenger rail network serves more than 500 destinations in 45 states, excluding Alaska, Hawaii, Maine, South Dakota, and Wyoming. In 1998, Amtrak ridership rose to more than 21 million customers, an increase of 4.5 percent over the level in 1997 and the highest in a decade. Passenger revenues surpassed $1 billion (a record), and total revenues reached $1.7 billion. On-time performance improved to 79 percent, its highest level in 13 years.

In 1998, Amtrak reduced federal support of $359 million for its day-to-day operations, down from $407 million in 1997. It is slated to operate without federal support by 2002. Amtrak's business plan projects that revenues will grow to $2.5 billion in 2002. Chief among the revenue generators will be the Acela high-speed service between Boston, New York, and Washington, DC, which is projected to add $180 million in revenues when it is fully operational in 2001.

Intercity Buses. According to the U.S. Department of Transportation, the top 17 bus carriers in the United States served 33.7 million revenue-generating passengers in 1996. Overall operating revenue for those carriers was $835.8 million in 1996. The direct economic impact of the group tour business in North America was more than $11.6 billion, a 12 percent increase over 1995. North American motor coach charter and tour departures reached 624,000 in 1996, and the passenger count was 25 million, both increases over the levels in 1995, accordng to the National Tour Association and the International Association of Convention and Visitor Bureaus. In 1996, the number of places in the United States served by intercity bus service was over 4,250, a reach far wider than that of airplane or rail service. Various government statistics indicate that approximately 4,000 private motor coach companies operate in the United States. According to the American Bus Association, there are 35,000 to 40,000 commercial buses in use for charters, tours, regular route service, and special operations in North America. Carriers involved in the regular-route industry operate approximately 9,000 intercity coaches.

Cruise Lines. In 1998, more than 5.4 million North American travelers took a cruise, an 8 percent increase over the previous year, according to the Cruise Lines International Association (CLIA). The growth in cruises in 1998 was aided by a booming economy, a fleet of new ships, and aggressive promotions by individual lines and the industry. The growth in cruises over the years has been impressive. In 1980, the first year in which official numbers were recorded, the cruise industry entertained fewer than 1.5 million passengers. By 1989, the number of passengers had doubled to 3.2 million. For 1999, CLIA predicted an 8 percent increase to around 6 million passengers. The growth in 1999 is attributed to more new ships with new and more sophisticated features and consumers' increased awareness of the availability and value of cruise vacations. The top destinations for cruisers are the Caribbean and Bahamas area (42 percent), Europe (20 percent), Alaska (9 percent), and the Panama Canal and transcanal cruises (7 percent).

According to CLIA, cruise lines have committed over $10 billion to building and launching more than 35 new ships, including the world's largest passenger vessel ever, by the end of 2002. CLIA expects that nearly 7 million travelers will take a cruise vacation in the year 2000.

Airports. The United States has the world's most extensive airport system with more than 18,000 airports, of which 413 are classified by the Federal Aviation Administration as primary commercial service airports. As described in an economic impact report issued by the Airports Council International–North America (ACI-NA), over 3.2 million passengers rely on U.S. airports for business and leisure travel and over 38,000 tons of cargo go through U.S. airports each day. The U.S. airport industry plays a major role in the economy, generating $380 billion a year in total economic activity and 5.8 million jobs at airports and in the local community that translate into $155 billion in earnings. Because of the importance of air service in linking their communities to the global economy, most U.S. airports are very active in seeking domestic and international air service.

Worldwide, four of the top five airports with respect to total (domestic and international) passenger traffic over the last 5 years have been U.S. airports. According to statistics released by ACI-NA, U.S. airports handled 1.3 billion total passengers in 1998, an increase of 2.3 percent over 1997. The top five U.S. airports in terms of total passengers in 1998 were Hartsfield–Atlanta (73.5 million), Chicago O'Hare (72.5 million), Los Angeles International (61.2 million), Dallas–Fort Worth International (60.5 million), and San Francisco International (40.1 million). However, being a busy domestic airport does not always translate into having the most international traffic, and so the rankings for the top five U.S. airports for international passengers are somewhat different: New York JFK, Miami International, Los Angeles International, Chicago O'Hare, and San Francisco International, in descending order.

To meet the projected continued growth in aircraft operations, air passenger travel, and air cargo, there is an urgent need for investment in airports. ACI-NA surveys have established that U.S. airports require at least $10 billion annually over the next 6 years to meet the need for capital development projects, including runways, taxiways, noise mitigation, safety, and security as well as terminals and access roads.

Other Travel and Tourism Industry Subsectors

Hotels and Motels. According to Smith Travel Research, 1998 surpassed 1997 as the most profitable year in the history of the U.S. lodging industry. Total revenues reached an estimated $93 billion. Pretax profits were estimated at $20.9 billion, up from $17 billion in 1997. This was the sixth straight year of record profits for the hotel industry. There were 1.16 million people directly employed by the industry full-time and part-time. Total wages paid were $18.9 billion in 1998. Room occupancy peaked in 1995 at 65 percent and then declined slightly to 64 percent in 1997 and 1998. Room rates continued to climb, reaching an average of $78.62 in 1998, up from $75.31 in 1997. In 1998, there were 51,000 properties in the United States, with 3.9 million rooms.

The outlook for the industry is optimistic to bullish on the long term. Demand growth is forecast to be consistent. As the U.S. economy continues to shift from a manufacturing-based economy to a service-oriented economy, this will prove beneficial to the travel and tourism industry because this new economy creates jobs whose occupants have a higher propensity to travel and stay in hotels. The hotel industry overall is starting to shift from its developmental cycle to an operational cycle, although the supply of hotel rooms was forecast to grow 3.5 percent in 1999 while demand growth was expected to slow to only 2.6 percent. This means that the industry will face increasing problems with occupancy rates, which were projected to fall around 1 percent to 63 percent in 1999. With the shifting focus to operations in the next couple of years, the efficiency of hotels should continue to increase, keeping revenue growth strong and profits high. Room rates were expected to continue to rise, but at a slower rate, in 1999. In this scenario, the forecast for the hotel industry in 1999 was for profits of around $22 billion.

Restaurants. In 1999, according to the National Restaurant Association (NRA), restaurant sales were expected to reach $354 billion, a 4.6 percent increase over 1998. With an increase in sales in 1999, that will mark the eighth consecutive year of real sales growth for the restaurant industry. Menu prices were projected to increase 2.8 percent in 1999, somewhat higher than the 2.5 percent increase in 1998. Restaurant industry sales have grown at an average annual rate of 7.6 percent since 1970, when total sales were around $43 billion. NRA estimates that there are approximately 815,000 food service establishments and that 44 percent of every dollar Americans spend on food goes for dining out. This industry is extremely labor-intensive. More than 10.2 million people are employed in the restaurant industry, making it the number one retail employer. The industry provides work for around 8 percent of those employed in the United States, and it is estimated that one-third of all American adults have worked in the restaurant industry at some time. While restaurants cater to the local population, they also obtain business from the travel and tourism industry, as 83 percent of all international travelers dine in restaurants while visiting the country. While no similar figure is available for domestic travelers, according to the Tableservice Operator Survey by the

NRA, in 1997, travelers and visitors accounted for 20 to 25 percent of sales in restaurants.

The biggest challenge for the restaurant industry is the shortage of qualified and motivated workers. To ease labor challenges, many restaurateurs are investing in upgrading technology, stepping up efforts to improve productivity, and providing training and rewards tied to performance. Restaurant sales were projected to increase around 2 percent in real terms in 1999. The NRA forecasts that restaurant industry employment will reach 12 million by 2006.

Travel Agencies. Retail travel agencies sell 80 percent of all airline tickets, book 90 percent of all cruises, and make 25 percent of all hotel reservations, according to the American Society of Travel Agents (ASTA). For this service, travel agencies generally are paid a standard commission that averages around 10 percent by the airline, hotel, cruise line, or wholesaler. The Airlines Reporting Corporation (ARC) states that in 1998, there were 45,542 accredited agency locations. Retail locations accounted for 32,694 of the sites (down 2 percent), and satellite ticket printer (STP) delivery locations were the second largest vendor, offering 12,848 locations (down 6 percent compared with 1997). The remaining locations are airlines and railroads. STPs, which became available in 1991, allow a traveler to purchase a ticket from a travel agency and pick it up in another location. Total sales by travel agencies in 1998 were over $73.4 billion, up 4 percent over 1997. Of the total sales volume in 1998, $67.3 billion was from domestic and international air fares. Domestic fares sales accounted for 68 percent of total sales, and commissions on domestic flights averaged around 7 percent. The average commission for international flights in 1998 was just over 14 percent.

A 1999 ASTA survey indicates that the travel agent industry is still going strong. Despite the decline in airline commissions and the rise in on-line booking options, consumers are still turning to travel agents for assistance and expertise. Even though 13 percent of the agents surveyed acknowledged losing customers to the Internet, nearly half the respondents stated that their client base has grown. Agents are looking to cruise lines and package vacations to increase revenues in the future.

LONG-TERM PROJECTIONS

Global Tourism

The World Tourism Organization projects continued record arrivals for the world, with 5 percent average annual growth between 1998 and 2000. By 2010, the number of world travelers will double to more than 1 billion. Global revenues from travel and tourism are projected to exceed $1.5 trillion in 2010.

International Travel and Tourism to the United States

With healthy growth projected for international travel and consistent growth expected for domestic travel, total spending for travel and tourism in the United States will grow at least 5 percent annually, reaching a record $630 billion in 2002 (see Table 50-1). Growth in travel and tourism will start slowly, but expected recoveries in Europe and Asia will spur the United States into a record-breaking international visitation level in 2003, when international arrivals will reach nearly 55 million visitors. Receipts are projected to surpass $119 billion, also a record. Over the next 4 years, arrivals from each world region are projected to increase (see Table 50-6). By 2003, however, Mexico and Canada will account for just over 47 percent of total arrivals and the share of overseas visitors will increase.

Mexico and Canada

The peso devaluation of April 1999 dampened Mexican travel to the United States an estimated 1.5 percent in 1999 after 10 percent growth in 1998. However, arrivals should grow steadily by over 3 percent a year through 2003, assuming sustained growth in Mexico's North American Free Trade Agreement (NAFTA) partners, which will help support Mexico's upward gross domestic product (GDP) trend and the stabilizing effect of the $24 billion financial agreement reached with the International Monetary Fund, the World Bank, and the Inter-American Development Bank.

A key factor in Canadian visitation is the exchange rate. The Canadian dollar fell from about 73 cents per U.S. dollar early in 1997 to about 66 cents in March 1999. The impact of this consistent decline is visible in the arrivals trend; arrivals declined marginally (–1 percent) in 1997 and dramatically (–11 percent) in 1998. The Canadian dollar is expected to appreciate slowly through 2003. In addition, the recent strength of Canada's GDP and that country's strong job creation over the last couple of years have helped reverse the decline in travel to the United

TABLE 50-6: International Travel to the United States
(thousands of arrivals)

Country of Origin	1998[1]	2003[2]	Percent Change 98–03[3]
Mexico	9,276	10,648	2.9
Canada	13,421	15,035	2.3
Overseas	23,697	28,923	4.1
Europe	10,675	13,041	4.0
Asia	6,724	8,147	3.9
Middle East	587	984	10.9
South America	2,957	3,563	4.4
Central America	697	874	5.2
Oceania	639	728	3.1
Africa	258	341	8.4
Caribbean	1,161	1,244	1.4
Total	46,395	54,607	3.3

[1] Estimate.
[2] Forecast.
[3] Compound annual rate.
Source: U.S. Department of Commerce, International Trade Administration.

States. In 1999, arrivals were estimated to increase nearly 1 percent, a major change from the 11 percent decline in 1998. For the rest of the forecast period, annual increases should track GDP growth, averaging over 2.5 percent a year.

Overseas Visitation

Arrivals from overseas will increase an average of over 4 percent annually between 1998 and 2003, reaching almost 29 million (see Table 50-6). Europe, Asia, and South America will lead that growth in terms of volume. Oil price increases in the global market will buoy the Middle East to surge almost 11 percent to become the sixth largest region for arrivals to the United States by 2003. In addition, improved economic conditions, airline route expansions, and promotional efforts in Central America will help sustain a strong increase in arrivals from that region (874,000 by 2003). Africa is expected to grow by a third to reach 341,000 visitors, while slow growth is forecast for Caribbean arrivals because of slow capital flow and strong domestic (regional) promotion.

Tourism growth from Japan, the top U.S. dollar market, continues to be depressed (see Table 50-4). Japan's economy reached the nadir of its recession in 1998, but its recovery has been slow. Despite some improvement, positive increases have been hampered by the weak yen, making it expensive to travel to the United States. All this contributed to the 4 percent decrease estimated for Japanese arrivals in the United States in 1999. Assuming a strong stock market recovery, which would boost consumer confidence, and exchange rate growth of 2 percent in 2000 and 3 percent in 2001, an increase in arrivals to nearly 5.2 million by 2003 can be expected.

Consumer spending in the United Kingdom has been increasing steadily as a result of the British government's relaxed monetary policies. In addition, declining unemployment has helped boost consumer confidence, encouraging spending. Real GDP was expected to grow about 1.5 percent in 1999 (fueled mainly by the consumer sector) and 2.4 percent in 2000. Travel to the United States should grow an average of 5 percent annually through 2003, reaching 5.1 million arrivals.

Germany, the third largest U.S. tourism market, should post consistent real growth through 2003 as international conditions improve and gains from the Euro are realized. Consumer spending continues to rise at a record-setting pace, and business confidence remains high. German arrivals were expected to grow nearly 4 percent in 1999 and average over 4 percent annual growth through 2003, reaching 2.3 million visitors.

Brazilian arrivals to the United States decreased an estimated 17 percent in 1999. Nevertheless, sound government reforms should help stabilize the current economic conditions, and an increase of 2 percent in travel to the United States is projected for the year 2000.

Despite slow economic growth in Italy in 1998 and 1999, Italian consumers' discretionary income may increase as a result of large increases in service sector employment and labor negotiations for wage increases. As a result, Italian arrivals to the United States should average steady 3 percent growth through 2003, keeping Italy in the top tier for visitors to the United States.

After a 5.8 percent decline in real GDP in 1998, South Korea posted an estimated 7 percent growth in 1999, indicating that the worst may be over for its economy. Inflation remains under control, and the national currency has appreciated against the dollar, spurring an estimated 29 percent increase in travel to the United States in 1999. Fiscal measures by the South Korean government also point to continued recovery. As a result, South Korean arrivals to the United States are projected to double in volume, from 364,000 in 1998 to 839,000 by 2003, and South Korea will regain its standing as one of the top 10 countries of origin for overseas visitors to the United States.

Domestic Tourism

Over the next 5 years, domestic travel in the United States is projected to grow relatively slowly compared with international travel to the United States. According to the TIA, by the end of 1999, a healthy growth of 2.5 percent was expected to occur, bringing domestic travel to a height of 1.08 billion person trips. Considerably slower growth is projected for each of the remaining years to 2002, leading to 1.1 billion person-visits by 2002. Expenditures are expected to be measurably stronger, however, amounting to $518 billion by 2002, an 18 percent jump since 1998.

Electronic Commerce

The travel and tourism industry is a leader in E-commerce. Web sites proliferate, including those of airlines; national, state, and local tourism offices; convention and visitor bureaus; and all the other sectors listed in this chapter. In addition, numerous sites indirectly support the travel and tourism industry. Many people now check weather sites before traveling to their destinations and use Internet map sites to find directions and obtain information about a particular airport, attraction, restaurant, or hotel. International travelers check exchange rates on the Web and use an automated teller machine to obtain money.

Dozens of sites provide alternatives to traditional ways of booking trips. According to the TIA, 70 million travelers used the Internet for a travel-related or other purpose in 1998, up from only 29 million in 1996. The number of travelers who used the Internet for travel planning in 1998 reached 11.7 million, up from 3.1 million in 1996. Furthermore, 6.7 million American adults (9 percent of Internet users) have used the Internet to make travel reservations in the last year.

According to Forrester Research, the travel and tourism industry will account for 32 percent of all business-to-consumer on-line sales in 2002. On-line sales of travel surged 200 percent in the last year, increasing from $3.1 billion to $7.8 billion. The travel and tourism industry is expected to generate almost three times as much as originally was predicted, surging to $20.7 billion in 2001. Forrester predicts that on-line travel and tourism will become the largest business-to-consumer product on-line in terms of dollar volume, accounting for 12 percent of the overall travel market by 2003.

REFERENCES

Abstract of International Travel to and from the United States, U.S. Department of Commerce, Tourism Industries, Washington, DC.

Agency Budgeting and Profitability Survey, 1999, American Society of Travel Agents, 1101 King Street, Suite 200, Alexandria, VA 22314.

Airline Reporting Corporation, 1530 Wilson Boulevard, Suite 800, Arlington, VA 22209-2448. arccorp.com.

Airport Council International, 1775 K Street, NW, Suite 500, Washington, DC 20006. aci-na.org.

Air Transport Association, 1301 Pennsylvania Avenue, NW, Suite 1100, Washington, DC 20004-1707. air-transport.org.

Air Transport 1999 Report: Windows of Opportunity, Air Transport Association of America, Washington, DC.

American Bus Association, 1100 New York Avenue, NW, Suite 1050, Washington, DC 20005-3934. buses.org/frameset.cfm.

American Car Rental Association, 1225 Eye Street, NW, Washington, DC 20006.

American Hotel and Motel Association, 1201 New York Avenue, NW, Suite 600, Washington, DC 20005-3186. ahma.com/ahmahome.htm.

American Society of Travel Agents, 1101 King Street, Suite 200, Alexandria, VA 22314. astanet.com.

Amtrak, 60 Massachusetts Avenue, NE, Washington, DC 20002. amtrak.com.

Cruise Lines International Association, 500 Fifth Avenue, Suite 1407, New York, NY 10110. cruising.org/index2.htm.

Forecast for International Travel to and from the United States, U.S. Department of Commerce, Tourism Industries, Washington, DC., May 1999.

Forrester Research, 1033 Massachusetts Avenue, Cambridge, MA 02138. forrester.com.

International Association of Amusement Parks and Attractions, 1448 Duke Street, Alexandria, VA 22314. iaapa.org.

International Association of Convention and Visitor Bureaus, 2000 L Street, NW, Suite 702, Washington, DC 20036. iacvb.org.

National Park Service, 18 & C Street, NW, Room 3122, Washington, DC 20240. nps.gov.

National Restaurant Association, 1200 17 Street, NW, Washington, DC 20036-3097. restaurant.org.

National Tour Association, 546 East Main Street, Lexington, KY 40508.

1998 In-Flight Survey Report on Overseas Travelers to the United States, U.S. Department of Commerce, Tourism Industries, Washington, DC, June 1999.

1998 In-Flight Survey Report on U.S. Travelers to Overseas Destinations, U.S. Department of Commerce, Tourism Industries, Washington, DC, September 1999.

1998 Lodging Profile, American Hotel and Motel Association, Washington, DC.

"1998 Outlook for Domestic Tourism," Dr. Suzanne Cook, National Outlook Forum, October 1998.

1998 Report on Canadian Travel to the United States, U.S. Department of Commerce, Tourism Industries, Washington, DC, September 1999.

Recommendations on Tourism Statistics, World Tourism Organization, Madrid Spain.

Smith Travel Research, 105 Music Village Boulevard, Hendersonville, TN 37075. str-online.com.

Summary of International Travel to the United States, 1998. U.S. Department of Commerce, Tourism Industries, Washington, DC, April 1999.

"Tourism Works for America," Travel Industry Association of America, 1100 New York Avenue, NW, Suite 450, Washington, DC 20005.

Travel Industry Association of America, 1100 New York Avenue, NW, Suite 450, Washington, DC 20005-3934. tia.org.

U.S. Department of Commerce, International Trade Administration, Trade Development, Tourism Industries, 14th & Constitution Avenue, NW, Room 1860, Washington, DC 20230. tinet.ita.doc.gov.

U.S. Department of Commerce, Economic Statistics Administration, Bureau of Economic Analysis, 1441 L Street, NW, Washington, DC 20230. bea.doc.gov.

U.S. Department of Transportation. 400 Seventh Street, SW, Washington, DC 20590. doc.gov.

U.S. International Air Travel Statistics Report, 1998, U.S. Department of Commerce, Tourism Industries, Washington, DC, July 1999.

U.S. Travel Receipts and Payments Analysis, 1998, U.S. Department of Commerce, Tourism Industries, Washington, DC, September 1999.

World Tourism Organization, Capitan Haya 42, Madrid 20 Spain. world-tourism.org.

RELATED CHAPTERS

36: Motor Vehicles
42: Retailing
51: Air Transportation
52: Water Transportation
53: Railroads

GLOSSARY

Domestic traveler: Any person residing in a given country who travels to a place within that country outside his or her usual environment for a period not exceeding 12 months.

Inbound travelers: All passengers traveling to a country other than their country of origin.

International tourism: Inbound travel and outbound travel.

International traveler: Any person who travels to a country other than that in which he or she has his or her usual residence for a period not exceeding 12 months.

International travel receipts: The expenditures of international inbound visitors, including their payments to national carriers for international transportation and other prepayments made for goods and services received in the destination country.

Outbound travelers: All passengers traveling away from their country of origin to other countries.

Overseas travelers: International travelers to or from the United States from all countries except Canada and Mexico.

Passenger fares: The total amount individual passengers pay for individual tickets to carriers that provide passenger services by land, water, and air.

Person trip: One person taking one trip of 100 or more miles, one-way, away from home.

Revenue passengers enplaned: The revenue generated by domestic airline carriers from embarking domestic and international travelers.

Travel and tourism related SICs: The following SICs have travel and tourism segments: public transportation, which includes air transport (SIC 45), taxicab companies (SIC 412), and intercity highway passenger transportation (SIC 413); auto transportation, which includes gasoline service stations (SIC 55) and automobile rental and leasing without drivers (SIC 751); lodging, which includes hotels, motels, and motor hotels (SIC 701) as well as camps and trailer parks (SIC 703); food service, which includes eating and drinking places (SIC 58); entertainment and recreation, which includes amusement and recreation services (SIC 79); and general retail trade, which includes general merchandise group stores (SIC 53) and miscellaneous retail stores (SIC 59).

Travel expenditure: The total consumption expenditure made by a visitor or on behalf of a visitor for and during his or her trip and stay at the destination.

Travel exports: Goods and services purchased by international travelers while visiting a country other than that of their usual residence.

Visitation: The period any person spends outside his or her usual environment for a duration not exceeding 12 months.

AIR TRANSPORTATION
Economic and Trade Trends

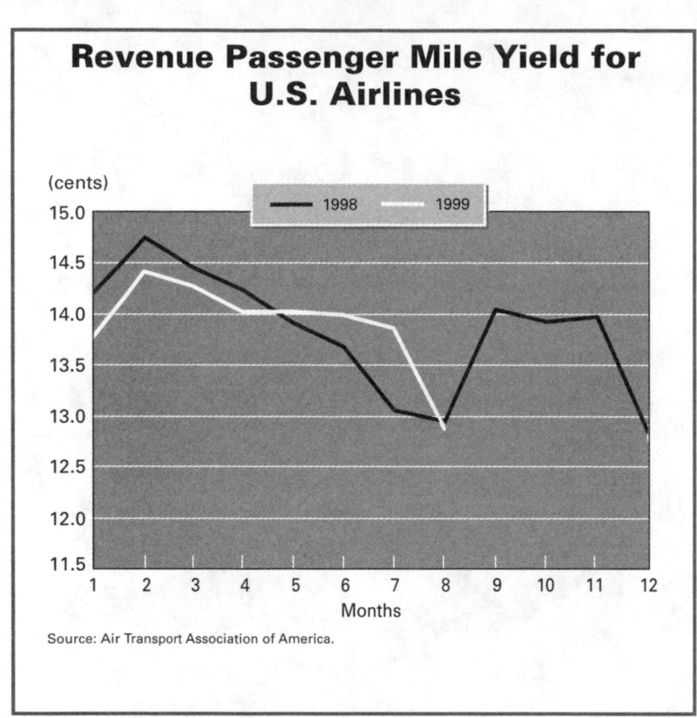

Source: Air Transport Association of America.

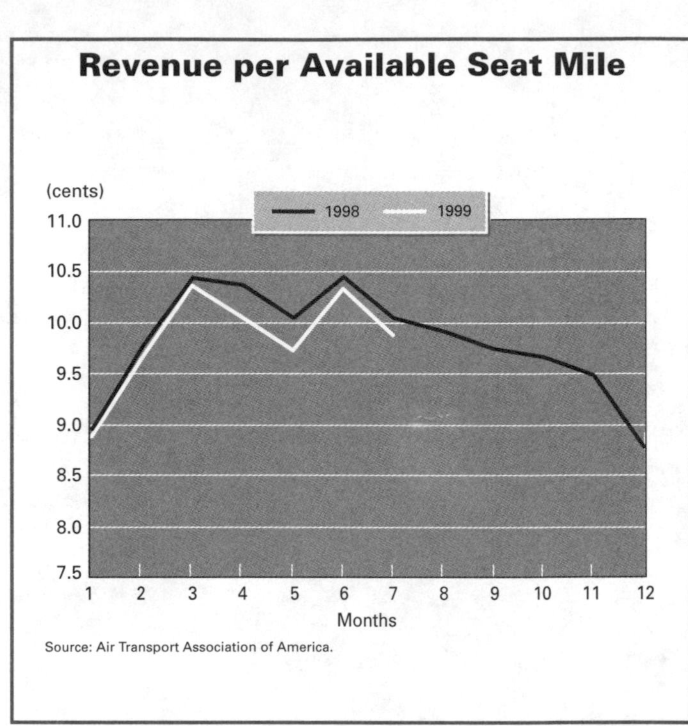

Source: Air Transport Association of America.

Source: U.S. Department of Commerce, Bureau of Economic Analysis.

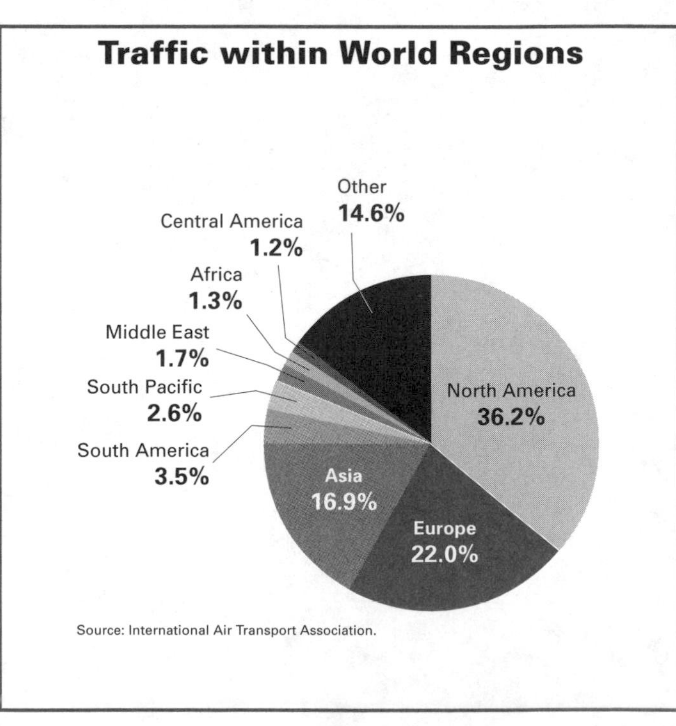

Source: International Air Transport Association.

See "Getting the Most Out of *Outlook 2000*" for definitions of terms.

51

Air Transportation

INDUSTRY DEFINITION Airlines (SIC 4512, 4513, 4522) provide regularly scheduled and nonscheduled air transportation of passengers, cargo, and mail. Integrated air express operators constitute a sector of this industry whose operations are limited to the delivery of letters, parcels, and packages.

AIRLINES

Air Transport Services

The world's airlines have produced operating profits in each of the last 6 years, dating to 1993. In 1998, the airlines generated nearly $300 billion in operating revenues and produced operating profits of $16.5 billion, reflecting a generally healthy world economy (see Table 51-1). In 1998, the airlines carried 1.5 billion passengers and moved more than 25 million metric tons (27.5 million tons) of cargo in total worldwide revenue services. The airlines' operating margin was an acceptable 5.5 percent. A windfall came in the form of comparatively low fuel prices in 1998 and through the first quarter of 1999. In that period, the airlines kept capacity (seats offered) in check, resulting in strong earnings in spite of flat traffic.

The Montreal-based International Civil Aviation Organization (ICAO), the United Nations affiliate that sets standards for aviation, has forecast that scheduled passenger traffic on all airlines will grow 4 percent in 1999, 5 percent in 2000, and 6 percent in 2001 (see Table 51-2). The 1999–2003 forecast of the International Air Transport Association (IATA), the airline industry group cobased in Montreal and Geneva, issued in October 1999 reflects a new caution for the period through 2003. That organization predicted that the annual average growth rate for scheduled international traffic will be 5.02 percent, down 0.5 percentage point from the average level in the organization's 1998–2002 forecast and 1.5 percentage points below the 1997–2001 forecast. Both the ICAO and the IATA forecasts indicate that improving economies in the Asia-Pacific region will restore traffic growth there. However, the IATA forecast is less optimistic about South America, as is reflected in its more cautious predictions. The IATA forecast is based on a 1999 annual survey of the world's major airlines, airports, and civil aviation authorities.

U.S. airlines have been benefiting from a healthy economy and will share in the positive general growth pattern. Passenger traffic on U.S. airlines is not growing, however, at the pace of the U.S. economy, dividing experts on the reasons why. At the same time, U.S. airlines are contending with a sharp rise in fuel costs that is affecting all carriers, rising costs resulting from contracts favorable to labor, and a jump in capacity as a result of new aircraft entering the U.S. fleet. These influences are putting strong economic pressures on carriers.

The airlines begin the year 2000 with a history of positive earnings extending back to 1993–1994. In recent years, the airlines have posted record profits in spite of comparatively sluggish traffic demand. In 1998, U.S. scheduled airlines that are members of the Air Transport Association of America (ATA)

TABLE 51-1: Trends and Forecasts in Traffic, Capacity, and Load Factor for U.S. Commercial Carriers

	Historical Data				Forecast						
	1995	1996	1997	1998	1999	2000	2001	2002	2003	2004	2005
Revenue passenger miles (billions)	537	570	599	614	638	657	679	699	727	756	786
Available seat miles (billions)	804	828	854	867	903	939	977	1,006	1,046	1,083	1,126
Load factor (percent)	66	68	70	70	70	70	69	69	70	70	70

Source: FAA and author's estimates.

TABLE 51-2: Forecast for Scheduled Passenger Traffic
(billions of passenger kilometers)

				Average Annual Growth Rate, %	
	1995	2005[1]	2005[2]	1995–2005[1]	1995–2005[2]
Asia Pacific	550	1,260	1,081	8.5	7.0
World	2,228	3,807	3,629	5.5	5.0

[1] 1997 forecast.
[2] Revised forecast, October 1998.
Source: International Civil Aviation Organization.

enplaned 614.2 million passengers and produced total revenues of $113.3 billion. Operating profits reached an all-time record of $9.3 billion, representing the sixth consecutive year of earnings gains. The operating profit margin was 8.2 percent. The outlook for the airlines continues to be favorable largely because of the health of the U.S. economy and an expected moderate rise in average prices. While traffic growth through 1999 was uneven, the improving economy should boost traffic to the 3 to 4 percent range in the year 2000. The world air transport system has been undergoing vast changes under the influence of the trend toward globalization. Restricted by national laws from merging, international airlines are forming alliances and developing flight networks that serve many of the world's regions. Four huge alliances have taken shape that may form the basis of the future world air transportation system. The U.S. government has supported this trend and granted antitrust immunity to alliances whose airline members represent nations that have accepted free trade open skies agreements with the United States. European governments have tolerated alliances and adopted a more critical view of their impact on competition.

Global alliances are the latest outgrowth of the trend toward government deregulation of the airlines, which began in the United States in 1978. As the government withdrew its authority to limit airlines to specific routes and set prices, competition displaced regulation as the driving force in the marketplace. Deregulation, or liberalization, as it is referred to in Europe, has spread across the world. Many national flag carriers have been privatized under its influence, being transformed from public utilities to profit-seeking companies. In the drive to extend their flight networks through cooperative efforts, nearly all of the top 25 international airlines in the world are members of the four alliances. The lowest form of an alliance is a partnership under which two airlines share their two-letter designator codes used in computer reservations systems, allowing agents for one airline to sell seats on the partner's carriers. The four major alliances are more structured and attempt to link individual airline flight schedules into a global flight network. The rush to form alliances will continue as the aligned carriers add new members from among second-tier markets in the world.

The U.S. government has been a leader in negotiating open skies aviation agreements. The United States and the Netherlands signed the first open skies agreement on September 4, 1992, and the U.S. Department of Transportation exempted Northwest Airlines and KLM Royal Dutch Airlines from U.S. antitrust laws. The exemption allows officials of the two airlines to discuss fares and joint flight schedules. The United States–Netherlands agreement and the Northwest-KLM partnership have become models for other international agreements among nations and for airline alliances and code-sharing relationships, including Star (United and Lufthansa are principals), Oneworld (American and British Airways), and the as yet unnamed alliance involving Delta Airlines, Air France, and AeroMexico.

Even as these new airline-to-airline business relationships have developed, nations around the world have continued to negotiate bilateral air service agreements under a system adopted in Chicago in 1944. Today, more than 3,000 bilateral nation-to-nation agreements exist, setting forth requirements for airline services. Alliances and code-sharing arrangements between airlines have largely superseded the bilateral system, which is regarded as too restrictive. The U.S. government is attempting to persuade other governments to establish a new system that would accommodate the changed environment of world aviation. As of December 1999, the United States had negotiated open skies agreements with 40 nations. The United States has also reached liberalization agreements with key aviation partners, including Canada, France, and Japan. The world of aviation is evolving slowly, however, toward free trade.

On a world basis, the introduction of new technologies and growth in demand have combined to improve airline productivity for the scheduled airline industry. A review of data by the Forecast Branch of the ICAO indicates an average annual improvement in airline productivity of 3.5 percent per year in the 1987–1998 period. New fuel- and labor-efficient aircraft have contributed significantly to improved productivity. Other benefits have come from increased aircraft utilization rates and an increase in the load factor, or the percentage of seats occupied in an aircraft.

U.S. Industry Trends

Laboring against rising costs and comparatively weak demand in 1999, U.S. passenger carriers performed better than the majority of Wall Street airline analysts had forecast. In the second quarter, the airlines posted operating earnings of $3 billion, some $300 million less than the record-breaking earnings in the second quarter of 1998 but much better than expected. Anticipating a run-up of costs for fuel and labor and increased flying, the airlines raised fares several times early in 1999. Weak demand deprived the airlines of the full effect of those increases in fares, however, and only by heavy discounting did carriers fill seats and lift passenger traffic numbers. In the first 7 months of 1999, passenger enplanements increased 6.3 million over the same period of 1998, reaching 329.3 million. The average yield (the average ticket price paid) had begun a slide in August 1998 that continued through much of 1999 despite fare increases. While U.S. airlines in the aggregate have produced profits, earnings began a slow downward slide in the third quarter of 1998 and remained in decline through 1999 compared with the record-breaking financial performance of 1998.

A midyear fare increase in 1999 was related solely to the rise in fuel prices. The higher fuel costs will increase the airlines' 1999 fuel bill by $1 billion over the bill in 1998, according to the ATA. Analysts at Standard & Poor's/Pratts attribute the cost rise to the increased jet fuel demand created by the air invasion of Yugoslavia during the Kosovo crisis by the armed forces of the North Atlantic Treaty Organization nations. Demand for jet fuel continued to be strong during the summer travel season, further strengthening prices. Fuel prices are expected to remain at these higher levels in the short term.

Wages and benefits represent 35 percent of U.S. airlines' operating costs. These costs are growing as the U.S. airline labor force continues to expand and average compensation rises. At the end of 1998, airline members of the ATA reported a 5 percent increase in the workforce, an additional 34,500 employees, increasing the total workforce to 621,058. In 1998, the average compensation per employee was $63,797, including benefits, a minimal increase from $63,265 in 1997, but the financial impact from a spate of labor contracts began taking full effect in 1999. The number of passengers handled per employee fell from 1,021 in 1998 to 989 in 1999, and that trend is expected to continue.

U.S. airlines have been in an expanding mode, and expansion is costly. Each aircraft requires five cockpit crews on average. Pilots and other cockpit personnel for ATA airlines now number more than 75,000. Productivity was expected to improve as U.S. carriers added 84 mostly new aircraft to the U.S. commercial fleet in 1998. ATA airlines were scheduled to receive 350 new transports in 1999, including 125 Boeing 737's, 73 Airbus Industrie A320's, 36 Boeing 757's, 34 Boeing 777's, and 24 MD-80's. U.S. airlines are scheduled to receive 236 new aircraft in 2000 and 205 in 2001. Another 456 aircraft are already on order for the year 2002 and beyond.

The 85 U.S. commercial airlines doing business in the United States operate approximately 7,400 aircraft that are over 75,000 pounds. The total was revised downward slightly at the end of 1999, when the Airport Noise and Capacity Act of 1999 was to take full effect and ban the operation of all aircraft that do not comply with Stage 3 noise requirements. In 1998, 479 Stage 2 aircraft were removed from service and 745 Stage 3-compliant aircraft entered service (this includes reengined and new aircraft and those whose engines have been modified by hush kits). The Federal Aviation Administration (FAA) projects that the U.S. commercial fleet will increase on average by 260 aircraft each year, a 4 percent capacity increase through to 2010, adding to concerns over congestion (see Table 51-3).

Passenger rage and passenger rights dominated the airlines' agenda in 1999. Incidents of unruly passenger behavior have been increasing for years and have become a matter of growing concern to flight attendants, unions, and management. Industrywide statistics are not maintained, and so a full grasp of the extent of the problem is not possible. In 1998 congressional testimony by the ATA, officials offered data from a case study of an unidentified airline and its encounters with unruly passengers. The airline reported the following incidents of passengers' interference with a cabin attendant or flight crew member: 882 incidents in 1995, 836 in 1996, 921 in 1997, and 258 in the first 3 months of 1998. Airlines have instituted training programs for employees to defuse potential incidents. After an incident in Newark in summer 1999 in which a Continental Airlines employee was injured, Continental's chairman, Gordon Bethune, called on Congress to pass a law that would permit an airline to ban violent passengers from using an airline's services.

TABLE 51-3: U.S. Commercial Air Carriers in Fiscal Years 1999–2010

Fiscal Year	Passengers, millions	Revenue Passenger Miles, billions	Jet Aircraft	Domestic Departures, millions
1999	623.9	638.4	5,433	7.2
2000	639.8	661.8	5,610	7.4
2001	656.9	687.7	5,822	7.6
2002	682.9	721.3	6,052	7.8
2003	710.2	756.8	6,320	8.0
2004	738.2	792.7	6,572	8.3
2005	767.4	830.3	6,903	8.6
2006	798.0	869.3	7,170	8.8
2007	830.0	910.0	7,448	9.1
2008	862.4	951.9	7,737	9.4
2009	896.1	995.9	8,040	9.6
2010	931.1	1,041.6	8,360	9.9

Source: Federal Aviation Administration.

In 1999, Congress considered several bills that outlined airline passengers' rights, but none got out of committee. The trigger for the push for passenger rights was a snowstorm in early January that struck hard at midwestern U.S. airports. Hundreds of passengers aboard Northwest Airlines airplanes were stranded in a parking area for 8 hours or more at Detroit Metropolitan International Airport. Some passengers have taken legal action against Northwest. In June 1999, the ATA announced a new customer service plan, Customer First, designed to improve the delivery of air fare and schedule delay information along with other steps to improve relations.

Factors Affecting U.S. Industry Growth

Under deregulation influences, U.S. airlines have developed a series of domestic transportation hubs at airports across the nation. Those hubs have grown rapidly in terms of passenger traffic as the carriers provide frequent daily services to and from key domestic and international destinations, offering improved service but also contributing to congestion and delays. A report of the National Civil Aviation Review Commission, chaired by former Representative Norman Mineta of California, called for sweeping changes in management and funding of the FAA, which provides air traffic services and federal resources directed to airports. The commission, which reported in December 1997, said that unless the stakeholders, including Congress, the executive branch, the FAA, and the aviation community, take action to bring about changes both "internal and external to the FAA," the nation's air transportation system will succumb to gridlock. The commission recommended that FAA services related to the air traffic control system be placed in a performance-based organization managed by a chief operating officer and a board of public interest directors. Progress toward a new management system has been hindered by the failure of the FAA to determine its costs for providing air traffic services. FAA's administrator, Jane Garvey, has placed a high priority on establishing a credible cost accounting system.

The FAA is implementing improvements to air traffic control capability, including new radar and other equipment for the 21 en-route centers across the nation. Raytheon's Standard Terminal Area Replacement System (STARS), the computer and display system that will replace current equipment in major air traffic control terminal facilities, has been accepted conditionally by the FAA and is undergoing operational testing and evaluation. STARS equipment is scheduled for installation in 172 FAA facilities and 199 U.S. Department of Defense air traffic control facilities.

Increases in scheduling delays in 1999 placed new urgency on the Mineta commission's call for change at the FAA. Delays per 1,000 aircraft operations in the first 5 months of 1999 were up 267 percent at Detroit Wayne County Metropolitan Airport, a Northwest Airlines hub; 142 percent at Cincinnati/Northern Kentucky International Airport, a hub for Delta Air Lines and Comair; 131 percent at Dallas/Fort Worth International Airport, a hub for American Airlines and Delta; 105 percent at Cleveland Hopkins International airport, a Continental Airlines hub, and 98 percent at O'Hare International Airport, Chicago, a hub for United Airlines and American.

Experts are divided about why passenger traffic has not grown as fast as the U.S. economy has. Edmund S. Greenslet, president of ESG Aviation Services of Ponte Vedra Beach, FL, believes that the airline industry has matured and will not grow at the same pace as the economy. He further believes that low fuel prices in 1998, a windfall for the carriers, masked the mature state of the domestic portion of the business. David A. Swierenga, chief economist with the ATA, provides a second reasonable explanation, stating that international currency crises in 1998 and 1999 may have contributed to caution in the business sector and left management inclined to cut travel costs. In the United States, international traffic tapered off in 1999 from its high levels in 1998. Domestic traffic took up the slack and outpaced international gains for the first time in years. Sam Buttrick, an airline analyst with Paine Webber, found evidence of softness in the high-yield portion of business flier traffic and noted a greater tendency of business fliers to seek discount fares. In the first 4 months of 1999, discounted miles flown by the U.S. major airlines, except Southwest Airlines, reached 93 percent of the total miles flown, leaving only a small minority of travelers paying the full fare.

Those paying full fares are largely business fliers whose schedules deny them access to the many discounts available to more flexible leisure passengers. Between February 1996 and June 1999, published business fares increased 51 percent, whereas the average business fare actually paid in that period increased 30 percent, according to Bob Harrell of Harrell Associates, an air fare consultant to American Express Travel. In June, the actual average round-trip business fare was $600, compared with the published fare of $970. The gap between the two types of fares has been widening. Harrell interprets the data as providing evidence that companies are taking aggressive actions to find low fares, negotiating directly with airlines for greater discounts, and tightening company travel policies.

U.S. Major Airlines

The 10 largest U.S. airlines, those carriers which produce revenues of $1 billion or more a year, have survived a difficult decade by restructuring and adjusting to the demands of the dynamic world marketplace. Two majors—Pan American World Airways and Eastern Airlines—ceased operations at the beginning of the decade, when an economic recession and international tensions from the Persian Gulf War combined to wound the industry. Three majors—Continental, Trans World, and America West—reorganized in 1991 after filing bankruptcy petitions. Industry net losses totaled more than $10 billion in the 3-year period 1990–1993 (a total of $7.67 billion in operating losses for the major carriers alone in that period).

With the cooperation of labor, the major airlines adopted a series of survival tactics such as cutting costs, rolling back the delivery of some aircraft, and negotiating concessionary contracts with unions. By 1995, the majors had restructured and a new breed of executive, not necessarily with airline experience, began to take control. Concentrating on their airport hub-and-spoke operations, the major carriers have developed traffic feed systems through connections with regional airline partners and have grown internationally, frequently in alliances with foreign airlines.

Alliance fever has also affected the domestic operations of major airlines. Northwest and Continental have signed a 10-year agreement to unite their flight networks. Additionally, Northwest has a code-sharing relationship with Alaska, another major carrier, and with Horizon and a handful of regional carriers. Code sharing between domestic airlines has been permitted in the United States since the 1970s. The Allegheny Commuter System shared codes with a predecessor of the present-day US Airways. More domestic alliance activity can be expected.

To combat the rise of low-fare airlines in recent years, several majors, including United, Delta, and US Airways, have inaugurated services that offer low-fare alternatives: the Shuttle by United, Delta Express, and Metro Express by US Airways. The fastest expanding major airline has been Southwest Airlines, the Dallas-based point-to-point operator, which offers low fares and a no-frills style of cabin service that has won wide acceptance, ranking it fourth in terms of passengers carried. The current top 10 airlines in terms of passengers carried in scheduled airline service in 1998 are Delta, 105.2 million; United, 86.7 million; American, 81.4 million; Southwest, 59 million; US Airways, 57.9 million; Northwest, 50.4 million; Continental, 41.6 million; Trans World, 23.8 million; America West, 17.7 million; and Alaska, 13 million.

Over the last 5 years, in the interest of operational efficiency, major airlines and their partner regional carriers have developed fleets of turbofan-powered regional jet aircraft, ranging in seating capacity from 35 to 70 or more, that serve destinations as long as 2 hours' flight time from hubs. Turbofan-powered regional jets have revolutionized air services to and from medium-sized communities in the United States and have the potential to increase congestion problems. The trend toward regional jets replacing turboprop equipment will increase. The FAA forecasts that regional jets under 60 seats, which numbered 206 aircraft in 1998, will increase to 1,100 aircraft in the regional-commuter fleet by 2010.

National and Regional Airlines

Some 28 U.S. airlines providing scheduled and charter passenger service are classified as national airlines, producing annual revenues of $100 million to $1 billion. In 1999, the Regional Airline Association counted 102 air carriers as regional airlines, with annual revenues of under $100 million. Airlines in these categories have witnessed great changes in the postderegulation period. These airlines are the survivors among the hundreds of airlines that started up since the deregulation act in 1978, though a minority, such as World Airways and American Trans Air, existed before deregulation.

National carriers also include operators such as Midwest Express of Milwaukee, a full-service airline that developed from a corporate aviation department of Kimberly Clark Corp.; Aloha and Hawaiian Airlines; Sun Country, a charter operator that has grown into scheduled operations at Minneapolis/St. Paul International Airport; and Frontier Airlines, the Denver-based successor to a local service airline dating to the period before airline deregulation. Some well-known regional carriers, such as Comair, a Delta Connection partner based in Cincinnati, qualify as national carriers by virtue of their annual revenues. Comair may become the first regional-national carrier to attain status as a major airline if its revenues keep climbing at the fast pace of recent years.

The regional airline industry has experienced the greatest change, beginning with the early 1980s trend toward code sharing and alliances with major U.S. airlines. Majors then acquired or took equity investments in regional carriers and turned over many short-haul markets to them. In this process, the number of regionals declined. In 1988, 163 airlines of this type were operating. In 1999, according to the Regional Airline Association, the number dropped to 97. The introduction of regional jets represents the latest trend revolutionizing the regional industry. The range and seating capacity of these aircraft permit the carriers to serve markets 2 hours' flying time or more from airport hubs. They have become an essential part of the traffic flows required to make a hub-and-spoke operation work. While the regional airlines typically associate with majors in a common effort, the capability of regional jets has placed these airlines in line for eventual competition with major airlines.

Growth of the regionals will continue to outpace that of the major carriers. The FAA forecasts that airline enplanements for regional aircraft with 60 seats or under will increase 7.4 percent to 71 million in 1999. The Regional Airline Association has different figures because its database includes aircraft with more than 60 seats. Basing its projections on a forecast that the U.S. economy will slow, the FAA has said that enplanements will increase through 2002 at an annual average increase of 5.5 percent and then increase at an average annual increase of 5.4 percent until 2010, when enplanements will reach 123.8 million.

Growth rates of national carriers are not predicted separately. Midwest Express grew at double-digit rates through the 1990s and is a carrier with strong local ties to its base in Milwaukee. Other operators, such as Sun Country and American Trans Air, offer trips to vacation destinations at comparatively low charterlike prices. The national carriers generally occupy niches in the U.S. marketplace, as opposed to the regionals, which usually work as local traffic feeders to major airline partners. Growth rates can be expected to be higher than those of the majors but lower than those in the regional field.

Air Cargo

In 1998, some 25 million metric tons (27.5 million tons) of cargo was moved by air. Cargo shipments include freight, mail, and express. Forecasts for cargo shipments (especially air express) are positive after a slowdown in 1998 resulting largely from the Asian economic crisis. Signs of recovery in Asia in 1999 improved the outlook for that region. Boeing has predicted 8.2 percent annual growth for the intra-Asian freight market through 2017. For the world, the Boeing Co. predicts an average annual growth rate of 6.4 percent in that period. MergeGlobal, Inc., of Arlington, VA, forecasts a similar growth pattern: an average of 6.6 percent annual growth in air freight weight.

Air express has become a driving force in the world cargo market just as it has revolutionized the cargo industry in the United States. Express now represents 60 percent of the U.S. market, providing overnight and time-definite delivery of packages and cargo. Express services are performed by providers, known as integrators, that include FedEx and UPS, which have expanded their ground modes of transportation. Integrators also have moved into the field of logistics, acting as third-party distributors of warehoused goods as a service to a variety of companies. Express air shipments in the United States showed a slight decline in 1999 as a result of a shift to second-day and third-day shipments and the expanding use of trucks for deliveries to regional destinations. Express is now making an impact on the international marketplace. Currently at 6 percent of that market, express services are expected to approach 40 percent by 2017.

Along with the scheduled passenger airlines, cargo operators are battling declines in yield. Since 1970, the average yield has declined approximately 2.8 percent per year. This trend is due largely to increased competition. Operators have combated the decline with more efficient aircraft, including dedicated large-capacity wide-body transports. Boeing expects wide-body freighters to represent 54 percent of the world fleet in 2017, up from 27 percent today. MergeGlobal predicts a need for 619 replacement freighters by 2008.

Corporate Strategies

The U.S. airline industry is increasingly dividing into full-service airlines and niche operators. The full-service carriers are engaged in their own brand of consolidation through alliances and partnerships with other carriers. They are aligning with foreign airlines to develop international networks and with regional-commuter airline affiliates for their ability to serve local markets and provide traffic feed. Niche operators are thriving in several forms. The classic form is patterned after Southwest Airlines, the low-cost, low-fare aerial bus service that serves point-to-point markets. Dallas-based Southwest moved nearly 60 million passengers in 1998, ranking it fourth in the United States in terms of passengers enplaned. Detroit's Pro Air has established a local market niche and is expanding the concept, serving principally two corporations: General Motors (GM) and the Chrysler Corp. Pro Air provides Boeing 737 service to eight cities for GM and Chrysler employees under a 1998 agreement. In 1999, Pro Air, in a new partnership with GM, was scheduled to operate three Saab 2000 turboprop aircraft serving other cities. Such unique operations will increase in the United States, especially if congestion and hubbing difficulties overwhelm the major airlines and passenger service becomes a greater issue.

Alliances are having a profound effect on U.S. airlines. Close ties between Northwest and Continental, a partnership that also extends to their regional airline affiliates, has created a domestic network that rivals the size of the domestic operations of the Big Three: American Airlines, Delta Air Lines, and United Airlines. "This is a business, whether we like it or not, where scale and scope matter," said Douglas C. Birdsall, senior vice president for alliances at Northwest. "Passengers tend to want to find a product that can pretty much do for them most everything they want to do." Because of the alliance, Northwest and Continental have become more viable competitors of the Big Three. Partnerships with regional airlines provide local feed to the flight networks. The dynamics of the traffic flow may be seen at airport hubs, such as Cincinnati/Northern Kentucky International and Cleveland Hopkins, where regional carrier terminals have developed in recent years. The regional airline terminals are in close proximity to gates where wide-body transports await passengers for trips to U.S. and foreign destinations. The system by which airlines set fares in the United States, an unwieldy many-tiered system, is a product of the competitive marketplace. Fares are adjusted by each airline for all local markets in a continuing process daily in the computerized electronic marketplace operated by the Airline Tariff Publishing Company, the airlines-owned unit based at Washington's Dulles International Airport. In the past, airlines were unable to agree on how to simplify the system or whether to change it. In 1992, American Airlines attempted to inject order in the system by offering a four-tier fares structure called Value Pricing. The principal effect would have been to reduce fares for business fliers and increase fares slightly for leisure passengers. Unable to agree on the plan, the airlines instead initiated a series of fare wars. Part of the problem in that period was excess capacity (too many seats offered to meet the demand), a condition that usually results in intense fare competition.

Airlines face a dilemma over how to increase revenues to meet rising labor and fuel costs and fill seats while capacity (seats offered) is rising. In 1999, the airlines increased fares several times. Traffic demand has been sluggish, however, and heavy discounting has been the chief means of attracting traffic to growth levels since 1998. If the U.S. economy enters a slow period, the squeeze on the airlines will grow tighter. Discounting is reflected by pressures on revenue passenger mile yield (the price paid) and on the revenue per available seat mile.

Passengers who have been paying full fares, usually business fliers, have been vocal over dissatisfaction with high fares and coach seating. Leisure passengers whose personal schedules meet the stringent requirements for buying advanced-purchase coach tickets (usually requiring a Saturday night stay at the destination) sit in the same seats as business fliers, but at deeply discounted rates. To many business fliers, paying high fares to sit in coach represents a galling inequity.

In August, United Airlines announced an Economy Plus program to improve the flying experience of full-fare-paying and frequent-flier passengers. The Chicago-based carrier began to install improved seating in the first 6 to 11 rows of the coach cabin in 450 aircraft to accommodate "premier" passengers. The seat pitch, typically 31 inches, is being increased to between 35 and 36 inches at a cost of $30 million. Frequent fliers and full-fare passengers will be assigned to Economy Plus seats on a first-come, first-served basis. Other airlines have begun to improve business class amenities. In another effort to enhance value, the airlines amended frequent flier programs to extend the redeemability of frequent flier mileage points acquired by passengers. Under the new rules, which may vary, passengers are required to earn additional miles only once in a 3-year period.

U.S. Industry Growth Projections for the Next 1 and 5 Years

The growth of U.S. airlines will depend, as always, on the health of the national economy. The domestic portion of the airline business may be showing signs of maturity, however. Passenger traffic has been growing, but not at the pace, as in decades past, a waxing economy has engendered. International service offers U.S. airlines the greatest potential for growth, as it has for more than a decade.

Marketplace circumstances are forcing U.S. carriers to conduct a balancing act in terms of ticket prices charged and discounts offered. Airline costs are rising, partly as a result of increasing labor and fuel prices. The carriers raised fares on several occasions in 1999 yet continued to offer a wide range of discounts. The average revenue passenger mile yield (the actual price paid) scarcely changed in this seesaw practice. In the first quarter, the yield was slightly lower than it had been in the same period in 1998; in the second quarter, it was slightly higher.

To keep abreast of rising costs, airlines will continue to raise fares. The ATA expects the revenue passenger mile yield to rise

1 percent in 1999 and 1.5 percent in 2000. On the basis of its analysis, the association expects traffic to grow 4.8 percent in 1999 and as much as 3.5 percent in 2000. Capacity increases should match the growth rates. Don Carty, chairman of AMR Corp. and chief executive officer of American Airlines, has called for world airlines to maintain a close check on growth in the coming years to avoid capacity overload, a condition that usually results in fare wars. American is planning to speed the retirement of its Boeing 727's and DC-10's and will cap capacity gains at 3 percent in 2000 while maintaining its transatlantic flying at the 1999 level.

The growth of E-commerce on the Internet is beginning to have an impact on airline ticket distribution. The dominant airline information technology company, AMR Corp's SABRE, Inc., was forecast to generate more than $1 billion in gross sales from E-commerce in 1999, four times the level in 1998. As E-commerce sales rise, cost-conscious airlines are reducing their dependence on third-party travel agents for ticket distribution. In recent years, many airlines have reduced travel agents' commissions from 10 percent to 8 percent of the value of a transaction. In October 1999, the air carriers joined in reducing these commission rates to 5 percent.

The possibility of a cyclical recession in the U.S. economy looms during the 5-year forecast period. If this does occur, traffic probably will grow at a slower rate, reflecting the economic downturn. International traffic will tend to show a greater traffic reduction compared with domestic.

Global Industry Trends

Over the decade ending in 1998, international scheduled passenger services grew at a faster rate than did domestic services, reflecting the trend toward globalization and the growth of world trade and tourism. Approximately one-third of the 1.6 billion passengers in 1998 crossed national borders. International passengers increased 3 percent in 1998 and 6 percent, on an average annual basis, over the 10-year period. The more than 1 billion passengers on domestic flights in 1998 reflected a 1 percent decline from 1997 and an average 2 percent gain annually over the decade.

North America continues to represent the largest share of world aviation traffic. Scheduled passenger traffic in North America accounted for 36.2 percent of total traffic. Europe ranked second with 22 percent. Other regions and their contribution to traffic were Asia, 16.9 percent; South America, 3.5 percent; southwest Pacific, 2.6 percent; the Middle East, 1.7 percent; Africa, 1.3 percent; and Central America, 1.2 percent. Traffic flow between Europe and North America was the highest between regions at 3.7 percent of the total; between Europe and Asia, it was 1.8 percent; and there were lower percentages between other regions of the world.

The fortunes of the airline industry are particularly vulnerable to economic cycles. The world economy has endured through several cycles in the last two decades. Between 1983 and 1989, the world economy averaged a growth rate of 3.7 percent a year. In 1990, the United States, the United Kingdom, and Canada entered a recession that was followed by an economic slowdown that spread around the world. While the U.S. recovery started as early as 1992, the recession lingered elsewhere. Financial and economic problems worsened in the Asia-Pacific region in 1997 and 1998, resulting in a devaluation of currencies. Asia-Pacific traffic declined 1.5 percent in 1998. The outlook for that region has improved along with that for the rest of the world.

Forecasts for Scheduled Services for the Period 1999–2001 by Region

Asia-Pacific. This region showed signs of a recovery in 1999. Passenger kilometers performed grew an estimated 4.3 percent to 657.2 billion. Traffic is forecast to grow 5.9 percent in 2000 and 6 percent in 2001.

Europe. Passenger kilometers performed in Europe grew an estimated 4.4 percent to 721.9 billion. Traffic is forecast to increase 5.7 percent in 2000 and 6 percent in 2001.

Middle East. This region recorded an estimated 3.6 percent growth in 1999 to 80.5 billion passenger kilometers performed. Traffic is forecast to grow 4.8 percent in 2000 and 5.8 percent in 2001.

North America. Traffic grew at a 3.9 percent rate to 1082.8 billion passenger kilometers performed. It is forecast to grow 3.8 percent in 2000 and 4.6 percent in 2001.

Latin America and the Caribbean. Traffic rose 4.1 percent to 139.3 billion passenger kilometers performed. It is forecast to rise 5.7 percent in 2000 and 6.5 percent in 2001.

These regional forecasts were provided by the Forecast Branch of the ICAO.

James Ott, *Aviation Week,* The McGraw-Hill Companies, (606) 341-8484, December 1999.

REFERENCES

Air Cargo Revolutions in Logistics: Opportunities for the 21st Century, Chris Raymond and Ron Henderson, presented to the Council of Logistics Management's 1997 Conference, Chicago, October 5–8, 1997.

The Airline Monitor, August 1999, ESG Aviation Services, PO Box 1781, Ponte Vedra Beach, FL.

Annual Report, 1999, the Air Transport Association of America, 1301 Pennsylvania Avenue, Washington, DC 20004-1707.

Annual Report, 1999, the Regional Airline Association, 1200 19 Street, Washington, DC 20036-2422.

Aviation Week & Space Technology, 2 Penn Plaza, New York, NY 10121.

Boeing Current Market Outlook, State of the Industry, http://www.boeing.com.

Global Aviation Forecast, 1999–2018, Airbus Industrie, 31707 Blagnac Cedex, France.

FAA Aerospace Forecasts, fiscal years 1999–2010, Office of Aviation Policy and Plans, Washington, DC 20591.

Report to Congress on funding of the nation's civil aviation programs by the National Review Commission, Norman Y. Mineta, Chairman, December 1997, http://www.faa.gov.

Special Report 255: Entry and Competition in the U.S. Airline Industry, Issues and Opportunities, Transportation Research Board, National Research Council, 2101 Constitution Avenue, NW, Washington, DC 20418.

World Air Cargo Forecast 1998/1999, The Boeing Company, Seattle, Washington.

World Air Transport Statistics, No. 43, WATS 6/99, International Air Transport Association, Montreal, Quebec, and Geneva, Switzerland.

World Outlook to 2001, Forecast Branch, International Civil Aviation Organization, 999 University Street, Montreal, Quebec, Canada H3C 5H7.

Interviews

David Bowes, Ph.D., Center for Economic Education, Economics Research Group, the University of Cincinnati, who has developed a linear, multivariate regression model in conjunction with the author to aid in the forecast of U.S. revenue passenger miles and available seat miles.

Sam Buttrick, airline analyst with PaineWebber Inc., New York.

Brian Clancy, Principal, MergeGlobal, Arlington, VA.

Edmund S. Greenslet, president, ESG Aviation Services, Ponte Vedra Beach, FL.

Bob Harrell, president of Harrell Associates of New York, a consultant to American Express.

David Pierce, regional director, marketing-cargo, the Boeing Co., Seattle.

David A. Swierenga, chief economist, Air Transport Association of America, Washington, DC.

U.K. Wickrama, Forecast Branch, International Civil Aviation Organization, Montreal.

■ RELATED CHAPTERS

21: Aerospace
26: Information Services
29: Space Commerce
42: Retailing

■ GLOSSARY

Available seat mile (ASM): One seat flown 1 mile. A transport configured with 100 seats flying 100 miles flies 10,000 available seat miles.

Code sharing: A growing practice in which airlines share the same two-letter designator code (NW for Northwest, for example) on certain flights as they are presented in the computer reservations systems used by airlines and travel agents. Sharing of codes permits a travel agent to sell a ticket that includes routings on both airlines.

Revenue passenger mile (RPM): The principal measure of the airline passenger business. It represents one paying passenger flown 1 mile.

Yield: Basically, the price paid for transportation. It is a measure of airline revenue and may be derived by dividing passenger revenue by passenger miles. It usually is expressed in cents per mile.

WATER TRANSPORTATION
Economic and Trade Trends

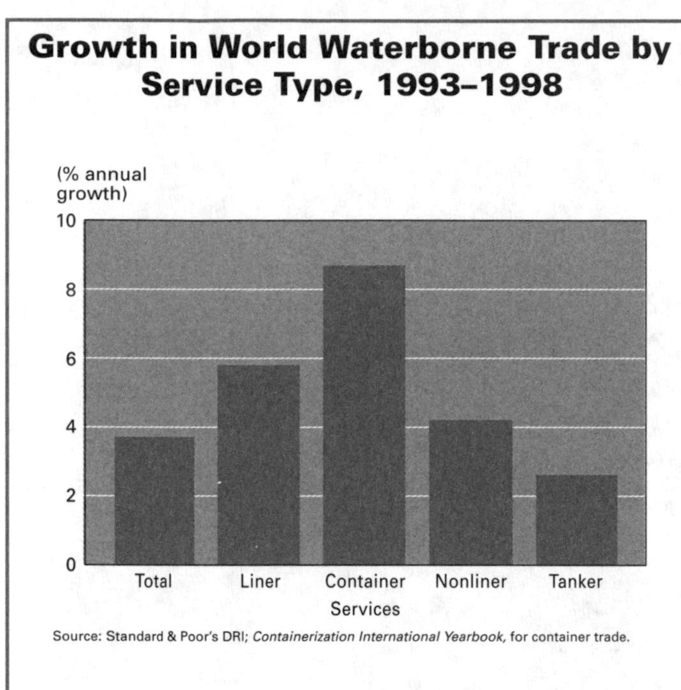

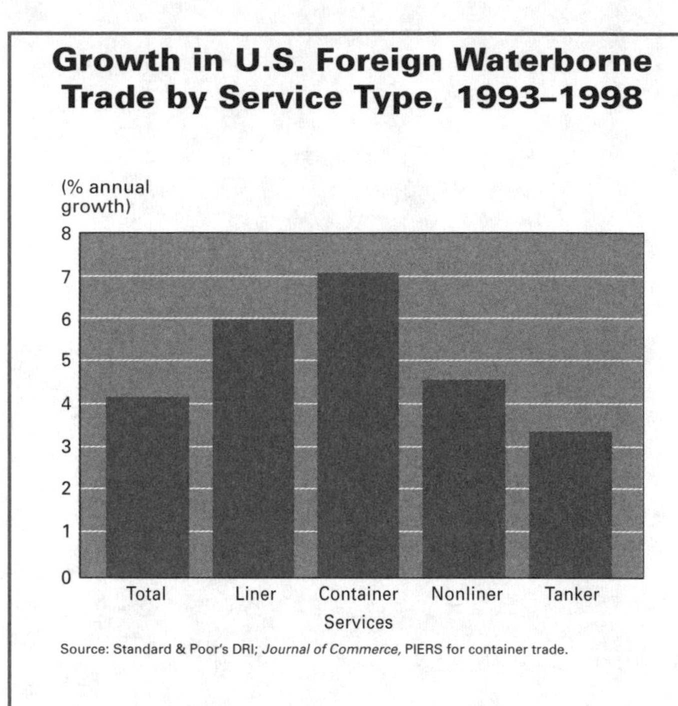

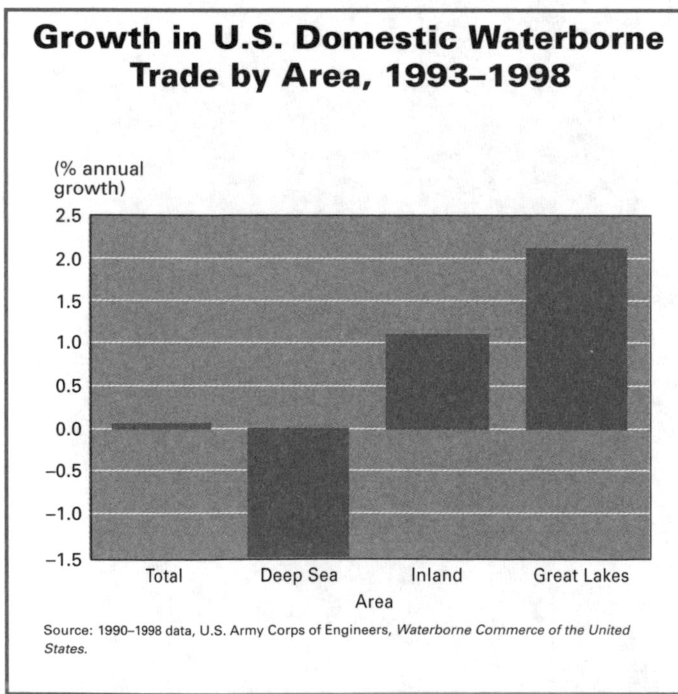

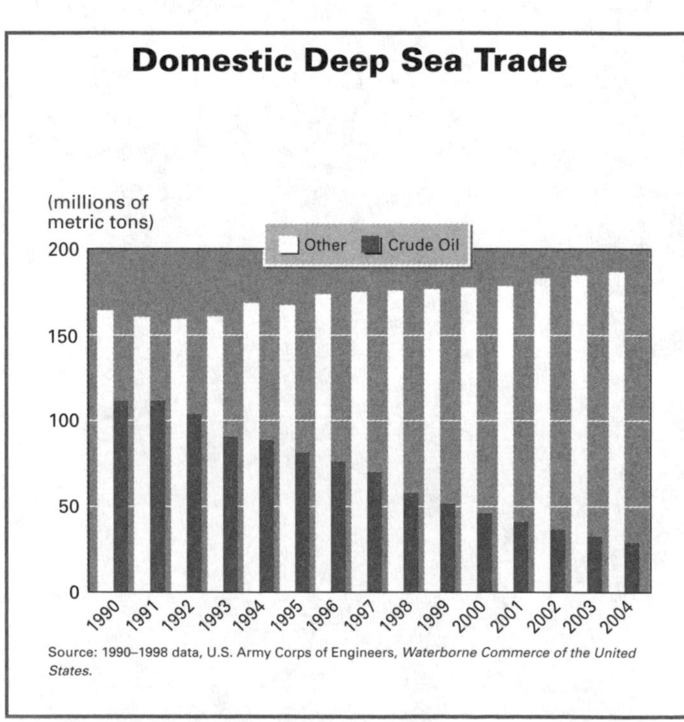

See "Getting the Most Out of *Outlook 2000*" for definitions of terms.

52

Water Transportation

INDUSTRY DEFINITION The U.S. water transportation industry (SIC 44) consists of companies that carry freight or passengers on the open seas or inland waterways and companies that offer lighterage and towing services, operate canals and terminals, charter vessels, and handle cargo. The major segments of the industry are deep-sea foreign transportation of freight (SIC 441), deep-sea domestic transportation of freight (SIC 442), Great Lakes and St. Lawrence Seaway transportation of freight (SIC 443), inland waterways transportation of freight (SIC 444), passenger transportation (SIC 448), and port and cargo-handling services (SIC 449).

GLOBAL INDUSTRY TRENDS

Three types of vessels operate in the deep-sea trade: liners, which offer scheduled service; nonliners, which carry dry cargo on demand; and tankers, which carry liquid cargo on demand. In the period 1993–1998, global waterborne trade increased 3.7 percent per year. In that period, the world liner trade increased 5.8 percent per year, the nonliner (bulk) trade increased 4.2 percent per year, and the tanker trade increased 2.6 percent per year (see Table 52-1). Container trade, a major segment of the liner trade, increased 8.7 percent per year from 1993 to 1998.

Global waterborne trade declined 0.8 percent from 1997 to 1998, largely as a result of the Asian economic crisis (waterborne imports to the Far East fell 7 percent, while waterborne imports to the rest of the world increased 5 percent). Over that period, liner trade fell 0.4 percent, nonliner trade fell 0.7 percent, and tanker trade fell 0.9 percent.

Despite the decline in waterborne trade and vessel earnings, world fleet capacity continued to grow from 1997 to 1998, although at a rate about half that of the previous four years. Over this period 32 million dwt of new capacity was added to the fleet while 22 million dwt of old capacity was removed from the fleet. (See Figure 52-1.)

Several factors are driving new construction in the world merchant fleet, including the age of the existing fleet. New vessels are being built to replace old and obsolete ones and, in the case of tankers, to comply with the double-hull regulations imposed by the United States and the International Maritime Organization (IMO). Product tankers also are being built to accommodate the expansion of refinery capacity in the Middle East and southeast Asia. New construction in the liner segment of the fleet has been driven by the deployment of large [4,000-plus 20-foot equivalent units (TEUs)], shared containerships in the mainstream (transatlantic, transpacific, Europe–Far East) liner trades, and containerization of intraregional trade.

A major trend for containership operators has been the increasing use of vessel-sharing agreements. These agreements

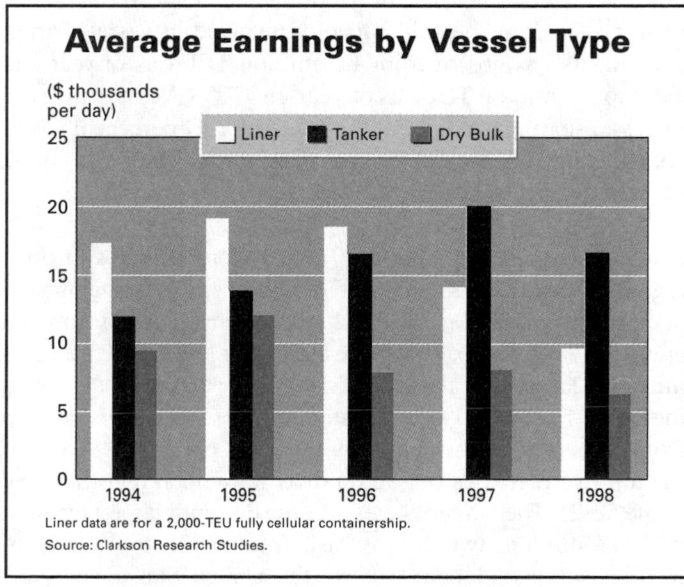

FIGURE 52-1

TABLE 52-1: Water Transportation (SIC 44) Trends and Forecasts

	1993	1994	1995	1996	1997	1998[1]	1999[2]	2004[3]	Percent Change 98–99	93–98	99–04[3]
Industry data											
Employment (thousands)	163	167	167	166	171	171	172	176	0.5	1.0	0.5
Real GDP ($ billion 1992)	10.5	10.8	11.0	10.7	11.0	11.2	11.3	11.9	1.0	1.2	1.0
GDP ($ billion)	10.1	10.9	10.9	11.7	12.8	13.0	13.5	16.5	4.0	5.2	4.0
Net capital stock ($ billion)	45.6	44.7	44.8	45.3	45.5	46.9	48.3	56.0	3.0	0.6	3.0
Waterborne trade data (million metric tons unless otherwise specified)											
World Trade (imports)	3,571	3,769	4,126	4,127	4,310	4,276	4,323	5,322	1.1	3.7	4.2
Liner	354	398	446	433	472	470	478	671	1.7	5.8	7.0
Nonliner	1,572	1,684	1,842	1,852	1,947	1,933	1,961	2,526	1.4	4.2	5.2
Tanker	1,645	1,688	1,838	1,842	1,891	1,873	1,885	2,125	0.6	2.6	2.4
Crude	1,138	1,144	1,283	1,271	1,294	1,306	1,316	1,422	0.8	2.8	1.6
Products	317	333	328	343	353	335	333	359	–0.6	1.1	1.5
Other	190	211	227	228	244	232	236	344	1.7	4.1	7.8
Container lifts (million TEUs)	112	128	136	151	164	170	182	254	7.0	8.7	7.0
U.S. foreign trade	894	939	982	1,020	1,068	1,097	1,123	1,244	2.4	4.2	2.1
Imports	539	599	571	626	678	724	744	855	2.8	6.1	2.8
Liner	55	57	62	64	74	82	85	113	3.7	8.3	5.9
Container (million TEUs)	6.0	6.6	6.8	6.9	7.8	8.9	9.5	13.4	7.0	8.2	7.0
Nonliner	106	134	131	137	150	164	166	192	1.2	9.1	3.0
Tanker	378	408	377	425	455	478	493	550	3.1	4.8	2.2
Crude	275	301	294	323	342	366	378	416	3.3	5.9	1.9
Products	84	85	63	81	89	87	90	99	3.4	0.7	1.9
Other	19	22	20	21	24	25	25	35	0.0	5.6	7.0
Exports	355	340	411	393	390	373	379	422	1.6	1.0	2.2
Liner	60	66	80	73	77	72	74	93	2.8	3.7	4.7
Container (million TEUs)	5.0	5.7	6.4	6.5	7.0	6.6	6.9	8.8	5.0	5.7	5.0
Nonliner	229	228	284	273	266	255	259	278	1.6	2.2	1.4
Tanker	66	46	48	47	46	46	46	51	0.0	–7.0	2.1
Crude	1	1	0	2	3	1	1	1	0.0	0.0	0.0
Products	48	28	27	27	26	27	27	28	0.0	–10.9	0.7
Other	17	17	21	18	17	18	18	22	0.0	1.1	4.1
North American cruise passengers (millions)	4.5	4.4	4.3	4.7	5.0	5.4	5.8	8.5	7.4	3.7	7.9
U.S. domestic trade	969	997	991	998	1,009	997	1,000	1,016	0.3	0.6	0.3
Domestic deep sea	251	257	248	249	244	233	230	213	–1.5	–1.5	–1.5
Inland waterways	618	636	638	645	654	653	660	692	1.0	1.1	1.0
Great Lakes	100	104	105	104	111	111	111	111	0.0	2.1	0.0
Passengers (millions)	139	141	142	143	148	153	155	168	1.5	1.9	1.5

(alliances) enhance vessel utilization, and reduce average shipment costs. Containership capacity involved in vessel-sharing agreements has grown from 1.3 million TEUs as of year-end 1993 to 3.0 million TEUs as of year-end 1998. Vessels involved in vessel sharing agreements accounted for 73 percent of world containership capacity (TEUs) as of year-end 1998, up from 61 percent five years earlier.

Another cost-reducing trend in the 1990s was flagging out, that is, switching national-flag registrations of ships to open registries (see the glossary for definitions). By flagging out, operators typically avoid the higher labor costs of national crews, pay less in taxes, and are subject to less restrictive manning regulations. At the end of 1998, 60 percent of the world merchant fleet (dwt) was registered under open registries, up from 50 percent at the end of 1993. At the end of 1998, four of the top five registries (based on dwt) were open registries (see Table 52-2). The United States was the eleventh largest registry, with 17 million dwt. In contrast, four of the top five shipowning nations—Japan, Greece, the United States, and Norway—were non-open-registry countries.

GLOBAL INDUSTRY PROSPECTS

The growth of world deep-sea trade, which is projected at 4.2 percent per year over the next 5 years, generally will exceed fleet growth (2.0 percent per year) in that period, improving earnings for water carriers.

The rate at which tankers and bulk carriers are scrapped (broken up) is expected to accelerate as vessels built during the boom in the years 1974–1977 reach 25-plus years in service (see Figure 52-2). The age of the fleet is only one factor in the replacement of tankers. Also at work are U.S. and IMO safety and environmental regulations. The Oil Pollution Act of 1990 (OPA-90) mandates that single-hull tankers serving U.S. ports be phased out in stages, based on age and size, beginning in 1995. IMO regulations for tankers serving foreign ports require that new tankers delivered after July 6, 1996, have double hulls and that 25-year-old single-hull tankers be retrofitted with double hulls beginning in 1995. At the end of 1998, Clarkson's Tanker Register (a comprehensive registry of seagoing tankers) reported that only 26 percent of the world's tankers were equipped with double hulls.

TABLE 52-1: Water Transportation (SIC 44) Trends and Forecasts (*Continued*)

	1993	1994	1995	1996	1997	1998[1]	1999[2]	2004[3]	Percent Change		
									98–99	93–98	99–04[3]
Fleet Data (million metric dwt unless otherwise specified)											
World oceangoing fleet	678	687	697	719	744	755	770	851	2.0	2.2	2.0
Container	35	39	43	48	55	61	65	92	7.0	11.8	7.0
Bulk	250	251	261	271	281	277	280	294	1.0	2.1	1.0
Tanker	298	298	294	300	308	317	320	336	1.0	1.2	1.0
Other	95	99	99	100	100	99	99	99	0.0	0.8	0.0
North American cruise capacity (million passengers)	5.3	5.2	5.3	5.7	5.8	6.5	7.2	9.9	10.8	4.2	6.6
Domestic fleet											
Dry cargo ships	2.7	2.7	2.5	2.7	2.7	2.8	2.7	2.5	−1.3	0.7	−1.3
Deep sea	0.7	0.7	0.6	0.8	0.8	0.9	0.9	0.8	−2.0	5.2	−2.0
Great Lakes	2.0	2.0	1.9	1.9	1.9	1.9	1.8	1.8	−1.0	−1.0	−1.0
Tankers	9.1	8.2	7.6	7.7	7.1	7.2	6.7	4.6	−7.0	−4.7	−7.0
Deep sea	9.1	8.1	7.5	7.6	7.1	7.1	6.6	4.6	−7.0	−4.7	−7.0
Great Lakes	0.0	0.1	0.1	0.1	0.0	0.0	0.0	0.0	0.0	0.0	0.0
Dry cargo barges	35.1	35.0	36.2	38.7	39.6	40.0	40.4	42.4	1.0	2.6	1.0
Coastal	4.3	4.4	4.4	4.5	4.6	4.7	4.7	5.0	1.0	1.7	1.0
Great Lakes	0.4	0.3	0.3	0.4	0.3	0.3	0.3	0.3	0.0	−5.6	0.0
Inland	30.5	30.4	31.7	34.0	34.9	35.2	35.6	37.4	1.0	2.9	1.0
Tank barges	9.7	10.0	10.2	10.3	10.2	10.1	10.0	9.5	−1.0	0.8	−1.0
Coastal	3.4	3.5	3.4	3.4	3.5	3.5	3.6	3.7	1.0	0.7	1.0
Great Lakes	0.0	0.0	0.1	0.1	0.1	0.1	0.1	0.1	0.0	0.0	0.0
Inland	6.3	6.5	6.7	6.8	6.7	6.8	6.6	6.0	−2.0	1.4	−2.0
Tugs/towboats (number)	5,985	5,790	5,656	5,558	5,509	5,403	5,295	4,786	−2.0	−2.0	−2.0
Coastal	2,079	1,982	1,941	1,876	1,846	1,785	1,749	1,581	−2.0	−3.0	−2.0
Great Lakes	231	223	220	218	215	209	205	185	−2.0	−2.0	−2.0
Inland	3,675	3,585	3,495	3,464	3,448	3,409	3,341	3,020	−2.0	−1.5	−2.0
Passenger/ferries (thousands of passengers)	328	349	348	353	353	360	364	382	1.0	1.9	1.0

[1] Estimate.
[2] Forecast.
[3] Compound annual rate.
Source: Industry data: U.S. Bureau of Economic Analysis; world trade: Standard & Poor's DRI; cruise: *Cruise Industry News;* world container lifts: Clarkson Research Studies; U.S. container trade: *Journal of Commerce,* PIERS; domestic (fleets and trades): U.S. Army Corps of Engineers; world fleet: Lloyd's Maritime Information Services.

In terms of safety, the IMO Safety of Life at Sea (SOLAS) convention requires that all ships of at least 500 gross registered tons meet International Safety Management (ISM)-mandated safe-management standards. Passenger ships, tankers, bulk carriers, and high-speed cargo ships had to be ISM-certified by July 1, 1998. Other cargo ships must be ISM-certified by July 1, 2002. Vessels that do not have ISM certification will be denied access to U.S. ports. So far, ISM certification has not restricted the shipping capacity available for the deep-sea trade.

For passenger vessels, the SOLAS convention requires significant changes to shipboard infrastructures. By 1997, ships were required to have low-level lighting, smoke detection, alarm systems, and sprinkler systems. By the year 2000, ships are required to have steel frames in stairways, ventilation ducts equipped with fire dampers, and fire-extinguishing systems for certain machinery. For many shipowners, the steel-frame stairway requirement in the year 2000 represents a significant expense and probably will accelerate the removal of older vessels from service.

Reflecting the fact that the expansion of global refinery capacity has been concentrated in crude oil producing areas (the Middle East and Asia), it is expected that the growth of the product tanker fleet will be faster than that of the crude oil tanker fleet and that the average size of product tankers will grow in response to long-haul shipping requirements.

The containership fleet is expected to grow at a significantly higher rate than will other vessel types as larger, shared containerships are introduced into the mainstream east-west trade and containerships continue to replace traditional breakbulk ships in the world liner trade. The containerization of fleets will be most rapid in the intraregional trade.

FACTORS AFFECTING FUTURE U.S. INDUSTRY GROWTH

U.S. waterborne trade, both foreign and domestic, drives the growth of the U.S. water transportation industry. From 1993 to 1998, U.S. foreign waterborne trade grew 4.2 percent per year, while domestic waterborne trade increased only 0.6 percent per year. The Jones Act (Section 27 of the Merchant Marine Act of 1920) precludes foreign-owned, foreign-built, and foreign-flagged vessels from participating in the U.S. domestic trade. Thus, U.S.-based companies receive all payments for domestic water transportation, including payments for port and cargo-handling services. However, foreign com-

TABLE 52-2: World Merchant Fleet: Top Five Registries and Ship-Owning Countries, 1998

Registries	Millions of Deadweight Tons	Ship-Owning Countries	Millions of Deadweight Tons
Panama	146	Japan	92
Liberia	97	Greece	72
Greece	44	United States	44
Bahamas	41	Norway	41
Malta	39	**Singapore**	36
Top Five	367		285
World Total	755		755

Open registry countries are in boldface.
Source: *Lloyd's Register of Ships,* January 1, 1999.

TABLE 52-3: U.S. Balance of Payments in Water Transportation: Passengers and Freight
(millions of dollars)

	1993	1994	1995	1996	1997	1998
Receipts						
Passenger fares	237	287	285	329	329	329
Export freight	4,056	4,506	5,282	4,703	4,571	3,786
Total	4,293	4,793	5,567	5,032	4,900	4,115
Payments						
Passenger fares	341	353	353	453	453	453
Import freight	10,462	11,369	11,514	11,259	11,908	13,652
Total	10,803	11,722	11,867	11,712	12,361	14,105
Balance, passenger	−104	−66	−68	−124	−124	−124
Balance, freight	−6,406	−6,863	−6,232	−6,556	−7,337	−9,866
Balance	−6,510	−6,929	−6,300	−6,680	−7,461	−9,990

Source: U.S. Department of Commerce, Bureau of Economic Analysis.

panies receive significant water transportation payments from U.S. foreign trade (see the discussion of the balance of payments, below).

In the 1990s, growth of real gross domestic product (GDP) from water transportation was below that for other transportation services (excluding trucking), reflecting the heavy involvement of water carriers in primary product trades such as grains, crude oil, coal, and ores, which tend to grow at lower rates than do manufactured trades. Also, real GDP from water transportation accounted for only 5 to 6 percent of real GDP from all transportation services in the 1990s. This low percentage can be attributed to the following factors:

- Freight rates per ton-mile for water transportation tend to be substantially lower than those for shipments by other modes. For example, the Bureau of Transportation Statistics (BTS) estimates that the average freight per ton-mile for rail transportation is about four times that for water transportation.
- The United States has a persistent balance of payments deficit in the ocean freight account. For example, in 1998, U.S. carriers received $3.8 billion for carrying U.S. exports to foreign ports, while foreign carriers received $13.7 billion for transporting foreign goods to U.S. ports, resulting in a net $9.9 billion drain on U.S. GDP (current dollars) from water transportation (see Table 52-3).

Similarly, the growth in capital stock for water transportation (vessels) did not keep pace with that of other transportation modes in the 1990s because of the following factors:

- A surge in new vessel construction in the late 1970s and early 1980s depressed freights in the 1980s and 1990s, limiting financial resources for new vessel construction and dampening expected returns on investment in water transportation.
- Large, unexpected year-to-year fluctuations in traffic and freight rates in primary product trades in the 1990s generated uncertainty about expected returns on investment in water transportation.

Nevertheless, a substantial part of the U.S. commercial fleet will have to be upgraded and/or replaced as existing vessels reach 25-plus years in service over the next 5 years.

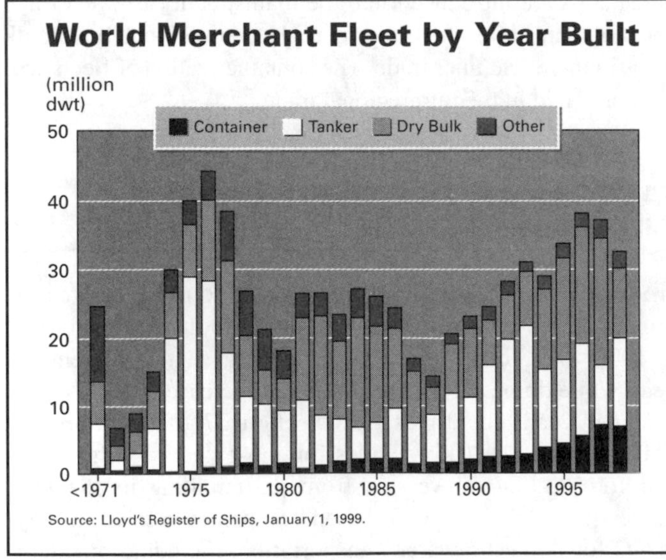

FIGURE 52-2

U.S. INDUSTRY GROWTH PROJECTIONS FOR THE NEXT 5 YEARS

The contribution to the nation's real GDP from water transportation is expected to increase about 1.0 percent per year from 1999 to 2004. This is significantly lower than the projected growth in the international waterborne trade but above the projected growth for the domestic trade. The primary drag on the industry will be the decline in Alaska North Slope production of crude oil, which will reduce domestic deep-sea crude oil movements. Employment in water transportation is expected to increase at a rate of about 0.5 percent per year from 1998 to 2004. For water transportation, employment growth historically has not kept pace with real GDP growth—a sign that productivity is going up—and this relationship is expected to continue.

The capital stock for water transportation is expected to increase about 3 percent per year over the next 5 years as a significant part of the domestic fleet is replaced with new vessels.

Freight Transportation

Four of the major segments of the U.S. water transportation industry carry freight: deep-sea foreign transportation, deep-sea domestic transportation, inland waterways transportation, and Great Lakes and St. Lawrence Seaway transportation.

Deep-Sea Foreign Transportation. This segment of the water transportation industry carries imports and exports on the deep seas between the United States and foreign ports. Servicing this segment are liners, nonliners, and tankers. Between 1993 and 1998, the U.S. liner trade increased 6.0 percent per year, the U.S. nonliner trade increased 4.6 percent per year, and the U.S. tanker trade increased 3.4 percent per year. The U.S. container trade increased 7.1 percent in that period, reflecting the continuing containerization of the U.S. liner trade.

In 1998, liner service accounted for 14 percent of U.S. waterborne trade on a metric ton basis but 61 percent on a value basis. Of the 155 million metric tons of U.S. liner cargoes in 1998, manufactured and semimanufactured products accounted for 88 percent, with crude materials and petroleum products accounting for the remainder.

Liner vessels, largely containerships with some breakbulk and roll-on/roll-off ships, operate between advertised ports of loading and discharge on a regular basis.

Containerships generally move faster and spend much less time in port than do traditional breakbulk ships. Liners carry a variety of manufactured and semimanufactured products. With containerization, different commodities are handled in the same way, facilitating cargo transfers. As a result, highly specialized line-haul/feeder services, connecting carrier services, vessel-sharing agreements, and intermodal services have been developed, increasing carrier productivity in the liner trade.

At the end of 1998, approximately 39 percent of the containership capacity (dwt) deployed in the U.S. liner trade was deployed in round-the-world (RTW)/tricontinental services, up from 31 percent 5 years earlier. The average age of the containership fleet deployed in those services was 5 years, compared with 8 years for vessels deployed in other services. The average container capacity of vessels in those services was 3,600 TEUs, compared with 2,300 for vessels deployed in other services.

The growth in RTW/tricontinental services reflects the fact that major shippers prefer shipping lines that operate on a worldwide scale. Shipping lines want to be able to offer a global service package, with operations on all the major routes (transatlantic, transpacific, and Europe–Far East) supplemented by operations or operating agreements covering the north-south trades.

In contrast to liner vessels, nonliner dry cargo vessels do not operate on fixed schedules or itineraries; instead, they are hired for specific jobs. Of the 419 million metric tons of U.S. nonliner cargoes in 1998, coal and coke accounted for 22 percent, grains accounted for 21 percent, limestone and cement accounted for 17 percent, and ores and scrap accounted for 12 percent. These trades are affected by general economic conditions as well as external shocks such as midwest floods (grains in 1993–1994), United Mine Workers' strikes (coal in 1994), and the expansion of trade with China (grains in 1995).

Tankers carry liquid cargoes in bulk: crude oil, petroleum products, liquid chemicals, liquified gases, vegetable oils, water, and wine. Of the 524 million metric tons that moved in U.S. tanker trades in 1998, crude oil accounted for 70 percent, petroleum products accounted for 22 percent, and liquid chemicals accounted for 5 percent. In 1998, a sharp decline in crude oil prices and an increase in refinery margins encouraged U.S. importers to switch to crude oil at the expense of petroleum products.

In the period 1999–2004, U.S. liner trade (imports and exports) is expected to grow 5.3 percent per year, compared with 2.0 percent per year for the nonliner trade and 2.2 percent per year for the tanker trade. The comparatively high growth for liner trade is attributable to the fact that reductions in trade barriers, privatization, and technological advances in transportation, distribution, and communications have a more immediate positive impact on the supply of and demand for manufactured products, which are shipped in liner service, than they do on the supply of and demand for primary commodities.

U.S. petroleum product imports are expected to recover from 1998 to 1999 and increase steadily over the next 5 years, contributing to a recovery in product tanker earnings. U.S. crude oil imports will continue to grow from 1999 to 2004 (at lower rates than in the previous 5 years) as domestic (Alaska) production declines.

Overall, U.S. foreign deep-sea trade is expected to grow 2.1 percent per year in the period 1999–2004, down from 4.2 percent in the period 1993–1998. The slowdown can be attributed to the following factors:

- Growth in the 1993–1998 period encompassed the 1994–1995 recovery in U.S. coal and grain exports.
- The expected recovery in crude oil prices will dampen growth in U.S. crude oil imports.
- U.S. economic growth is expected to slow from 3 to 4 percent per year from 1993 to 1998 to 2 to 3 percent per year from 1999 to 2004, contributing to a slowdown in the growth of U.S. waterborne imports as a whole.

Deep-Sea Domestic Transportation. This segment of the market includes carriers that transport freight on the deep seas between U.S. ports, including noncontiguous U.S. territories.

Of the 233 million metric tons moved in domestic deep sea trade in 1998, petroleum products accounted for 47 percent, crude petroleum accounted for 25 percent, crude materials accounted for 7 percent, chemicals accounted for 6 percent, coal accounted for 6 percent, manufactured products accounted for 6 percent, and food products accounted for the remainder (see Table 52-4). Manufactured products, the traditional liner cargoes, move primarily in the noncontiguous trades (U.S. mainland to Alaska, Hawaii, Puerto Rico, and Guam) on both self-propelled vessels and deck barges.

Total cargo moving in the domestic deep-sea trade declined steadily in the 1990s, reflecting the decline in Alaska North Slope crude oil shipments (see Figure 52-3). Domestic deep-sea trade declined about 1.5 percent per year from 1993 to 1998. In

TABLE 52-4: Major Commodities Shipped in the U.S. Domestic Deep Sea Trade in 1998

Commodity	Millions of Metric Tons	Billions of Metric Ton-Miles	Average Miles
Coal and coke	13.9	9.2	659
Petroleum	167.2	210.0	1,256
Crude	57.8	107.3	1,777
Product	109.4	102.7	981
Chemicals	13.9	28.5	2,042
Crude materials	17.1	10.5	617
Primary manufactures	6.7	4.5	680
Farm products	6.3	10.8	1,694
Manufactures	7.9	12.8	1,632
Total	233.1	286.4	1,229

Source: U.S. Army Corps of Engineers, *Waterborne Commerce of the United States.*

that period, crude oil shipments declined 8.6 percent per year and other shipments increased 1.8 percent per year. Furthermore, the decline in long-haul crude oil shipments contributed to a 25 percent decline in average haul (miles) in the domestic deep sea trade from 1993 to 1998.

Starting in 1995, the Clean Air Act Amendments of 1990 required that reformulated (oxygenated) gasoline be used year-round in high–carbon monoxide areas, principally on the Atlantic and Pacific coasts. According to the U.S. Department of Energy, methyl tertiary butyl ether (MTBE) production capacity is concentrated at U.S. Gulf refineries. MTBE-gasoline blends cannot be shipped through pipelines from U.S. Gulf refineries to the U.S. west coast. Consequently, long-haul (5,000 to 6,500 nautical miles) product tanker shipments of reformulated gasoline from the U.S. Gulf to the U.S. west coast doubled from 1993 to 1998.

While the U.S. Gulf–west coast petroleum product trade is a significant source of demand for product tanker services, it represents only 1 percent of domestic ocean shipments in terms of metric tons and therefore has had little impact on the overall domestic deep-sea traffic volume discussed above.

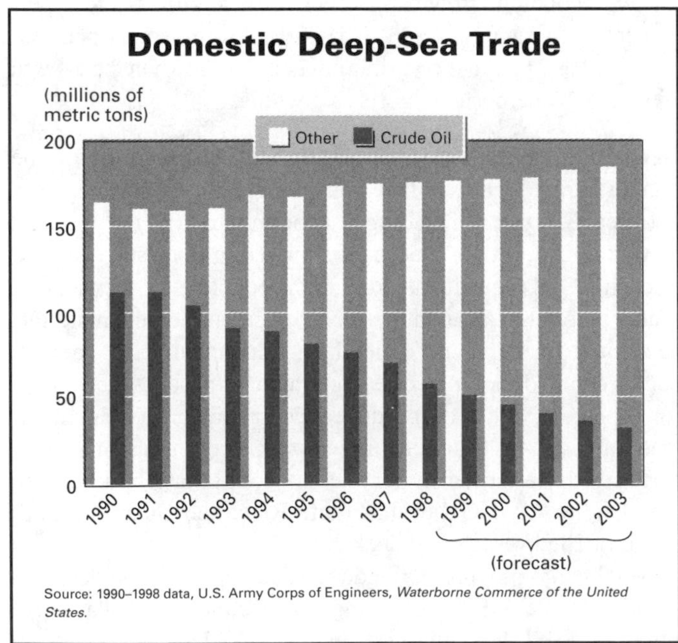

Source: 1990–1998 data, U.S. Army Corps of Engineers, *Waterborne Commerce of the United States.*

FIGURE 52-3

For the period 1999–2004, total domestic deep-sea shipments are expected to decline about 1.5 percent per year. Most of that decline will be in shipments of crude oil, which are expected to fall about 11 percent per year. Shipments of other commodities are expected to increase about 1 percent per year. For other commodities, the expected growth rate is below the 1994–1998 growth rate, primarily as a result of an expected recovery in petroleum product imports (see "Deep-Sea Foreign Transportation," above).

At the end of 1998, the fleets serving the U.S. domestic deep-sea trade included 41 dry cargo vessels (0.9 million dwt), 102 tankers (7.3 million dwt), 3,337 dry cargo barges (4.7 million dwt), and 664 tank barges (3.5 million dwt).

Self-propelled vessels generally are preferred in long-haul, time-sensitive trades because they are faster than barges (15 to 20 knots versus 8 to 12 knots) and are not as likely to be weatherbound. In 1998, barges carried approximately 85 percent of the metric tons in domestic deep-sea trade involving less than 500 miles; self-propelled vessels carried approximately 89 percent of the metric tons moved in domestic deep-sea trade over 1,500 miles (see Table 52-5).

The capacity of the dry cargo vessel fleet is expected to decline about 2 percent per year over the next 4 years as containerships over 25 years old are removed from service. While some limited construction of tankers is under way for the domestic trade (two 125,000-dwt crude oil tankers), the capacity of the tanker fleet is expected to decline about 7 percent per year from 1999 to 2004. At the end of 1998, approximately 64 percent (4.7 million dwt) of the tanker fleet was at least 20 years old (see Figure 52-4). A significant part of this fleet probably will be scrapped or removed from service from 1999 to 2004 as domestic crude oil trades continue to decline and those ships approach their next special survey and/or OPA-90 phase-out dates.

The capacities of the dry cargo and tank barge fleets are expected to increase at about 1 percent per year from 1999 to 2004. The projected growth in tank barge capacity reflects increasing demand for barges in the intracoastal and short-haul intercoastal petroleum products trades. The projected growth of the dry cargo barge fleet reflects an increase in demand for deck

TABLE 52-5: Domestic Deep-Sea Trade, by Length of Haul, 1998
(millions of metric tons; percent)

Miles	Barge	Self-Propelled Vessel	Total	Percent Barge
<500	54.4	9.6	64.0	85.0
500–1,000	33.4	12.4	45.8	72.9
1,001–1,500	12.5	39.6	52.1	24.0
>1,500	7.6	63.5	71.1	10.7
Total	108.0	125.0	233.1	46.3

Source: U.S. Army Corps of Engineers, *Waterborne Commerce of the United States.*

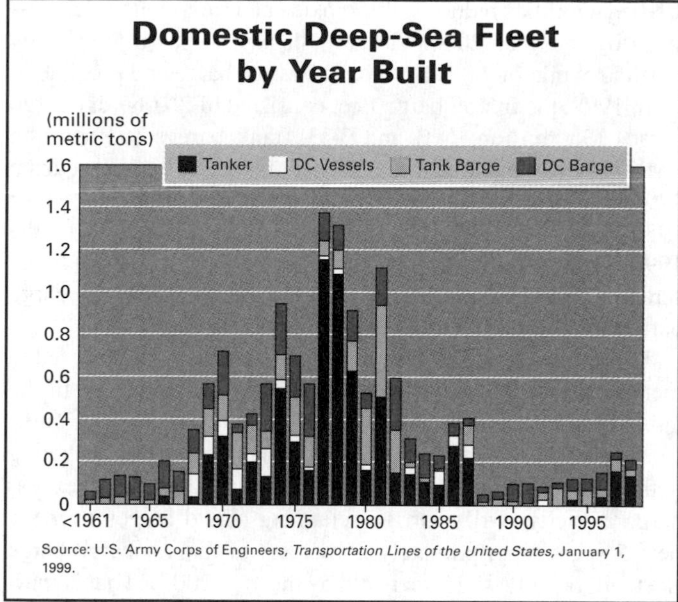

FIGURE 52-4

barges in short-haul container/trailer trades (e.g., Florida–Puerto Rico), penetration of overland (truck and rail) container trades, and expansion of offshore oil field construction projects (installation and removal of offshore oil platforms, pipelines, and associated subsea structures) in the U.S. Gulf.

In recent years, there has been a clear preference for large-capacity barges in deep-sea domestic trade. While only 29 percent of the tank barge fleet was 5,000 dwt or greater at the end of 1998, 62 percent of the tank barges built in the period 1993–1998 were 5,000 dwt or greater. For dry cargo barges, only 20 percent of the year-end 1998 fleet was 1,500 dwt or greater, but 66 percent of the dry cargo barges built in the period 1993–1998 were 1,500 dwt or greater.

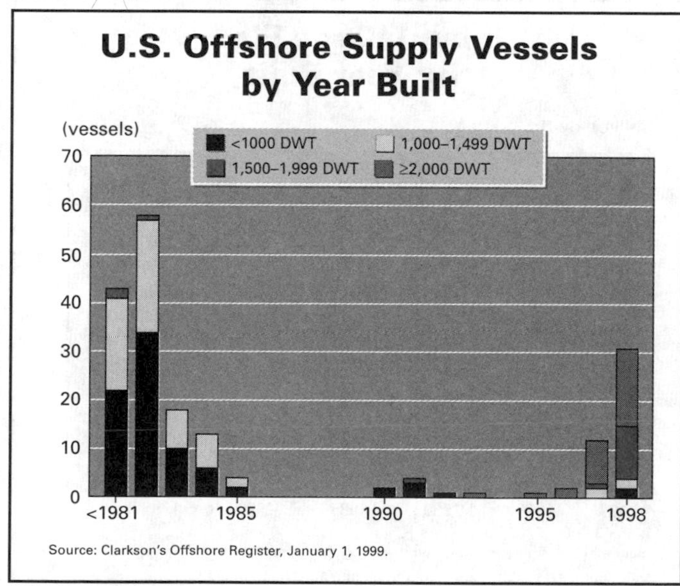

FIGURE 52-5

Offshore Supply Vessels. Offshore supply vessels (OSVs) are used primarily for the transportation of drillwater, potable water, fuel, cement, barite, casings, drillpipe, personnel, and provisions to offshore drill rigs and/or production platforms. At the end of 1998, the U.S. (flag) OSV fleet, which operates primarily in the U.S. Gulf, amounted to 356 vessels. Forty-six of them were large (1,500 or more dwt) OSVs. Forty of the 46 large OSVs were built from 1995 to 1998 (see Figure 52-5).

In the middle to late 1990s, drilling contractors ventured farther offshore into deeper waters, generating demand for large OSV services. The growth in deepwater drilling has been due primarily to the following factors:

- Technological advances such as dynamic (anchorless) positioning systems for drill rigs and three-dimensional seismic geological surveys have reduced the cost of finding and developing large deepwater oil reservoirs. According to Nationsbanc/Montgomery Securities, finding and development costs for deepwater reservoirs fell from $3.60 per barrel in the early 1990s to $2.60 per barrel in 1998.
- The Deepwater Royalty Relief Act of 1995 significantly reduced the royalties payable on production from deepwater (water depths greater than 200 meters) leases in the U.S. Gulf.

Recent lease sales suggest continued growth in deepwater drilling. Deepwater leases accounted for 73 percent (2,210 tracts) of the tracts bid on in the U.S. Gulf in 1997–1998, up sharply from 52 percent (1,251 tracts) in 1995–1996

Large OSVs will continue to replace smaller OSVs in servicing deepwater exploration and development projects. Approximately 37 percent of the year-end 1998 fleet, or 131 OSVs, were built before 1980 (all are less than 1,500 dwt), and a significant number of those OSVs will be removed from service over the next 5 years.

Inland Waterways. In 1998, 653 million metric tons moved on the inland waterways (including the intracoastal waterways on the Atlantic and Gulf coasts). Most of it (96 percent) moved by barge. The primary commodities were coal (27 percent), petroleum (27 percent), crude materials (19 percent), and farm products (12 percent) (see Table 52-6).

However, in terms of ton-miles (demand for transport services), farm products accounted for 28 percent of inland waterway traffic in 1998. The average haul for inland shipments of farm products was 978 miles, compared with 337 miles for all other inland shipments. The temporary surge in shipments of farm products (grain exports) in 1995 had a significant positive impact on the demand for inland dry cargo barge services and freight rates (see Figure 52-6).

The projected growth rate for inland waterways trades (dry and liquid cargoes) is 1.0 percent per year, slightly below actual growth for the period 1993–1998 (1.1 percent per year).

Dry cargo trades are expected to increase at about 1.2 percent per year, largely as a result of a projected increase in domestic consumption of eastern coal. In the 1990s, many coal-burning utilities complied with the emissions requirements of

TABLE 52-6: Major Commodities Shipped in the U.S. Domestic Inland Waterway Trade in 1998

Commodity	Millions of Metric Tons	Billions of Metric Ton-Miles	Average Miles
Coal and coke	174.3	63.2	363
Petroleum	177.8	35.6	200
Crude	35.8	4.2	118
Product	141.9	31.4	221
Chemicals	56.0	27.4	489
Crude materials	125.9	43.8	348
Primary manufactures	27.5	22.9	832
Farm products	76.0	74.3	978
Manufactures	11.0	1.0	93
Other	4.8	0.3	68
Total, excluding farm products	577.3	194.4	337
Total	653.3	268.7	411

Source: U.S. Army Corps of Engineers, *Waterborne Commerce of the United States.*

the Clean Air Act of 1990 (CAA) by substituting low-sulfur western coal carried primarily by rail for high-sulfur eastern coal carried primarily by barge. To satisfy the CAA's more stringent year 2000 emissions requirements, coal-burning utilities will have to install emissions-reducing equipment. As this equipment is put into use, demand for eastern coal and related dry cargo barge services will increase.

However, inland tank barge traffic is expected to decline about 0.5 percent per year as utilities substitute natural gas for fuel oil. At the end of 1998, approximately 28 percent of U.S. fossil-fuel electric utility capacity was capable of burning either fuel oil or natural gas. According to the Energy Information Agency, the substitution of natural gas for fuel oil by electric utilities will be spurred by a significant expansion of the natural gas pipeline system and requirements under the Clean Air Act Amendments of 1990 that utilities reduce sulfur dioxide and carbon dioxide emissions by the year 2000. Virtually all natural gas is moved by pipeline, while fuel oils are moved by both barge and pipeline.

In 1998, the inland barge fleet consisted of 26,069 dry cargo barges (35 million dwt) and 3,332 tank barges (6.8 million dwt). Total inland barge capacity increased 6.2 percent from 1995 to 1996, the largest annual increase in capacity since 1980–1981. The 1996 increase was largely a function of the 1995 surge in barge freight rates that limited dry cargo barge scrapping and led to a sharp increase in orders of new dry cargo barges for delivery in 1996 and 1997 (see Figure 52-7).

Dry cargo barge capacity on inland waterways is expected to increase about 0.5 percent per year from 1999 to 2004. In the late 1990s, the growth of dry cargo barge capacity was significantly above the growth of dry cargo barge traffic, contributing to the decline in freight rates. The decline in freight rates (excess barge capacity) will spur the scrapping of old barges over the next 5 years (approximately 35 percent of the dry cargo barge fleet will be at least 25 years old by the year 2003). That is, new barges generally will replace old barges over the next 5 years.

Inland tank barge capacity is expected to decline about 2 percent per year over the next 5 years. The decline reflects the following factors:

- A decline in inland tank barge traffic.
- Tank barge replacements are largely tied to affreightment contracts (traffic levels).
- Fleet productivity increases; that is, new tank barges require less maintenance and drydocking time than do those they replace.

Great Lakes. Ships in this segment of the water transportation industry move freight on the Great Lakes and the St Lawrence Seaway, either between U.S. ports or between U.S. ports and Canadian ports.

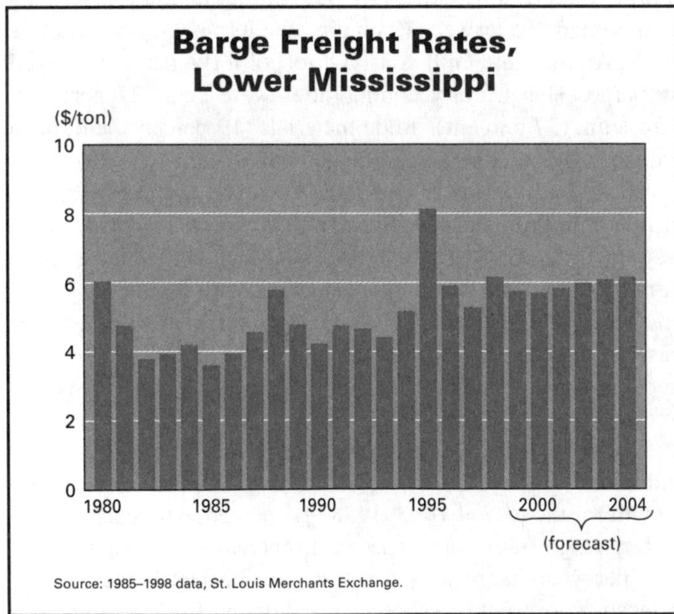

FIGURE 52-6

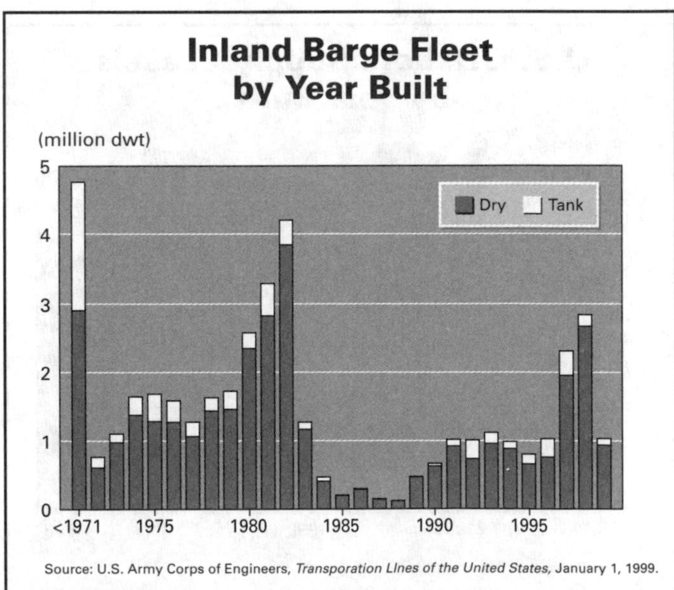

FIGURE 52-7

In 1998, 111 million metric tons of cargo moved in the Great Lakes domestic trade. The major commodities moved were iron ores (48 percent), limestone (24 percent), and coal (18 percent) (see Table 52-7). Iron ores, limestone, and coal are used in steel production. Coal also is used in electric utilities.

In the 1990s, U.S. Great Lakes trade generally was in the range of 104 to 105 million metric tons. However, in 1997 and 1998, trade surged to 111 million metric tons, largely because of abnormally mild weather, which extended shipping seasons.

Shipments (imports plus exports) between U.S. and Canadian ports on the Great Lakes amounted to 46 million metric tons in 1998, and are included in U.S. foreign trade. The major commodities moved were coal (35 percent); cement, lime, and stone (31 percent); and iron ore (27 percent).

At the end of 1998, the U.S. Great Lakes fleet consisted of 101 dry cargo vessels (1.9 million dwt), 4 tankers (0.02 million dwt), 249 dry cargo barges (0.3 million dwt), and 49 tank barges (0.1 million dwt). In 1998, 89 percent of Great Lakes domestic trade was moved in dry cargo vessels. Great Lakes vessels tend to have significantly longer economic lives than do deep-sea vessels: At the end of 1998, the average age of Great Lakes vessels was 33 years compared with 24 years for domestic deep-sea vessels. In the period 1993–1998, the average age of vessels removed from the Great Lakes fleet was 40 years.

From 1993 to 1998, U.S. Great Lakes fleet capacity (mainly self-propelled vessels) declined about 1 percent per year. The decline of the fleet, coupled with nondeclining traffic levels, suggests increased fleet utilization and/or productivity in the 1990s. These trends are expected to continue over the next 5 years.

Tugs and Towboats. The tug and towboat fleet consists of coastal tugs and inland towboats (pushboats). Coastal tugs are used in ship assisting, tanker escorting, barge towing, and salvage. Some recently built coastal tugs have oil spill skimming equipment, contributing to their usefulness in the U.S. tanker and tank barge trades. In contrast, inland towboats are used primarily for pushing barges.

The number of tugs and towboats declined steadily from 5,985 in 1993 to 5,403 in 1998. This decline can be attributed to the fact that newer tugs have greater horsepower and are more productive than those they replace. The average horsepower for tugs built from 1993 to 1998 was 2,424, compared with 1,757 for the rest of the fleet. These trends are expected to continue over the next 5 years.

TABLE 52-7: Major Commodities Shipped in the U.S. Domestic Great Lakes Trade in 1998

Commodity	Millions of Metric Tons	Billions of Metric Ton-Miles	Average Miles
Coal and coke	19.8	10.4	525
Petroleum	1.9	0.6	304
Chemicals	0.2	0.05	324
Crude materials	85.4	43.7	511
Iron ore	53.7	34.0	633
Limestone	27.9	8.4	301
Primary manufactures	3.1	0.9	295
Farm products	0.3	0.3	930
Total	110.8	55.9	504

Source: U.S. Army Corps of Engineers, *Waterborne Commerce of the United States.*

Water Transportation of Passengers: Cruise Ships and Ferries

Cruise ships are floating resorts that tend to offer round trips of 3 days or more. In contrast, passenger/ferry vessels tend to convey passengers on daily one-way trips between two or more points.

Cruise Ships. After a 2-year decline in passengers in the mid-1990s, North American cruise passenger growth was 7.9 percent per year from 1995 to 1998 (the long-term average rate of growth for 1980–1998 was 8 percent per year).

The recovery in passenger growth is due primarily to two factors. The first was the introduction of new ships. The market traditionally has been driven by the introduction of new ships that attract new and repeat passengers. New ships offer new technologies and a rich mix of cabins and amenities. Forty-one of the 122 cruise ships serving U.S. ports in 1998 were introduced as newbuilds after 1994. An additional 47 newbuilds will be introduced from 1999 through 2004.

The second factor is consolidation. At the end of 1998, the top four North American cruise lines—Carnival, Royal Caribbean, Princess, and Norwegian—controlled 82 percent of North American cruise capacity, up from 62 percent at the end of 1994. In fact, these companies control an even larger share of the market because their vessels are newer and tend to sail fuller than do those of smaller lines. Consolidation has provided the top companies with more financial strength and marketing muscle to promote their ships and control costs, contributing to the stability of the industry in the late 1990s.

Passenger/Ferry Vessels. As of year end 1998, there were 1,242 passenger/ferry vessels serving U.S. waterways, 181 of which were fast ferries capable of attaining speeds of at least 25 knots. In terms of passenger capacity, 33 percent of the overall fleet was built before 1975, and a substantial proportion of these vessels will be replaced over the next 5 years. In contrast, only 12 percent of fast ferry passenger capacity was built before 1975 (see Figure 52-8).

Fast ferries have replaced other ferries on existing routes and have allowed new longer-haul ferry routes to open up. In 1998, fast ferries accounted for 9 percent of total ferry traffic, up from 5 percent in 1993. In the period 1993–1998, fast ferry traffic (passengers) increased 12.4 percent per year, while other passenger/ferry traffic increased only 2.6 percent per year. These trends are expected to continue over the next 5 years.

Because existing databases do not include speed for U.S. passenger/ferry vessels, the fast ferry segment of the fleet was estimated from other vessel characteristics: horsepower (1,500 or greater), net registered tons (1,500 or less), and overall length (165 feet or less). These ranges were derived from data on non-U.S. fast ferries.

Section 1207 of the Transportation Equity Act for the 21st Century (TEA-21) calls for the secretary of transportation to

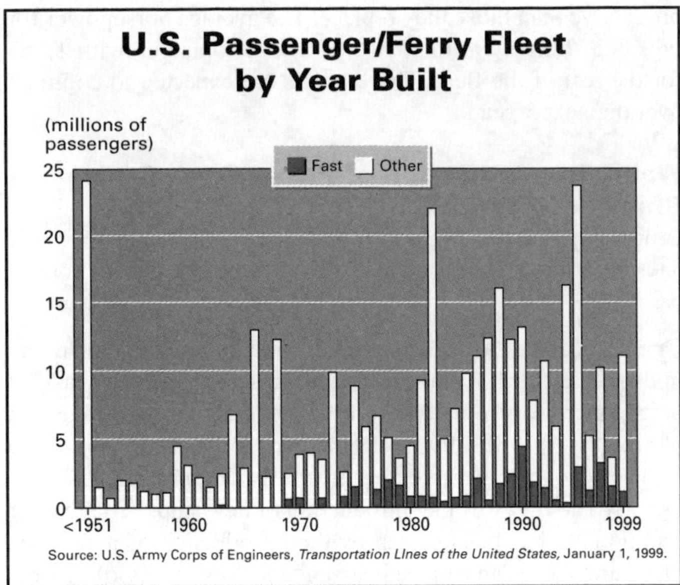

FIGURE 52-8

conduct a study of ferry transportation in the United States and its possessions. As part of the study, the Volpe Center will develop a comprehensive U.S. ferry database that will include speed as one of the data elements.

Port and Cargo-Handling Services

This segment of the water transportation industry handles foreign and domestic marine cargo from the time cargo (for or from a vessel) arrives at a dock, pier, terminal, staging area, or in-transit area until the cargo is loaded or unloaded. This segment also involves the operation and maintenance of piers, docks, and associated buildings and facilities.

In 1997, a total of 350 U.S. ports handled foreign and/or domestic waterborne trade. By tonnage, the top 10 coastal and inland ports handled only 29 percent of waterborne trade that year (see Table 52-8). Seven of the top 10 ports are in the U.S. Gulf, reflecting the heavy involvement of Gulf ports in the tanker and dry bulk trades.

TABLE 52-8: U.S. Waterborne Trade, Top 10 U.S. Ports
(millions of metric tons except as noted)

Port	1993	1994	1995	1996	1997
Port of South Louisiana	176	168	186	172	167
Houston	128	130	123	134	150
New York	106	114	108	119	123
New Orleans	61	66	70	76	81
Corpus Christi	54	71	64	73	79
Baton Rouge	77	78	76	73	76
Valdez	78	77	73	70	67
Plaquemines	48	59	66	61	58
Long Beach	49	51	49	53	52
Texas City	49	40	46	51	51
Total, top 10 ports	826	854	861	882	904
Total, all ports	2,832	2,933	2,964	3,016	3,086
Top 10 ports, percent of total	29.2	29.1	29.0	29.2	29.3

Source: U.S. Army Corps of Engineers, *Waterborne Commerce of the United States.*

TABLE 52-9: Top 10 U.S. Container Ports
(thousands of TEUs except as noted)

Port	1993	1994	1995	1996	1997	1998
Long Beach	1,543	1,939	2,137	2,357	2,673	2,852
Los Angeles	1,627	1,786	1,849	1,873	2,085	2,293
New York	1,306	1,404	1,537	1,533	1,738	1,884
Charleston	579	655	758	801	955	1,035
Seattle	781	967	993	939	953	976
Oakland	772	879	919	803	843	902
Norfolk	519	570	647	681	770	793
Houston	392	419	489	538	609	657
Miami	469	497	497	505	624	602
Savannah	406	418	445	456	529	558
Total, top 10 ports	8,394	9,534	10,271	10,486	11,779	12,552
Total, all ports	10,972	12,238	13,173	13,328	14,794	15,556
Top 10 ports, percent of total	76.5	77.9	78.0	78.7	79.6	80.7

Source: *Journal of Commerce,* Port Import/Export Reporting Service.

In contrast, international container trade through U.S. ports is highly concentrated. In 1997 and 1998, the top 10 container ports accounted for about 80 percent of container traffic, measured in TEUs, moving in U.S. foreign trade (see Table 52-9). Of the top 10 container ports, 5 were on the east coast and 4 were on the west coast. Long Beach had by far the largest absolute growth in container traffic between 1994 and 1998, but Houston and Charleston showed the highest rates of growth over the period, reflecting high growth in the U.S.–Latin America container trade.

■ REFERENCES

Clarkson Research Studies, *Shipping Review and Outlook,* Clarkson Research Studies, London, Spring 1999.

Drewry Shipping Consultants, *Fast Ferries: Shaping the Ferry Market for the 21st Century,* Drewry Shipping Consultants, London, October 1997.

Drewry Shipping Consultants, *Product Tankers,* Drewry Shipping Consultants, London, August 1997.

Drewry Shipping Consultants, *Short Sea Container Markets,* Drewry Shipping Consultants, London, September 1997.

Energy Information Administration, *Annual Energy Outlook 1999* Washington, DC, U.S. Government Printing Office, December 1998.

Energy Information Administration, *Natural Gas, 1998: Issues and Trends,* Washington, DC, U.S. Government Printing Office, June 1999.

Energy Information Administration, "Oxygenate Distribution," *Petroleum Supply Monthly,* December 1994.

Energy Information Administration, *Petroleum Supply Annual 1998,* Washington, DC, U.S. Government Printing Office, June 1999.

Fearnley, Astrup, ed., *Fearnleys Review, 1998,* Fearnresearch, Oslo, Norway, February 1999.

Fox, Douglas, ed., *Survey of Current Business,* Washington, DC, Bureau of Economic Analysis, June 1999.

Holland, D. J. *Future IMO Legislation, to Enter into Force between 1993 and 2010,* Lloyd's Register, London, 1993.

International Maritime Organization, MARPOL 73/78, 1992, Amendments to Annex I, IMO, London, 1992.

International Maritime Organization, Safety of Life at Sea (SOLAS) Convention, Amendments to Ch. II-1, IMO, London, 1992.

Journal of Commerce, PIERS, Port Import/Export Reporting Service, computer files, New York, February issues.

Lambert, Mark, ed., *Containerization International Yearbook, 1999,* Emap Business Communications, London, 1998.

Lamotte, Michael, *The Deepwater Opportunity,* NationsBanc Montgomery Securities, San Francisco, July 1998.

Latta, Cynthia, ed., *Container Watch, 1999/1,* Standard and Poor's DRI, Lexington, Mass., Summer 1999.

Latta, Cynthia, ed., *Maritime Watch, 1999/1,* Standard and Poor's DRI, Lexington, Mass., Spring 1999.

Lloyd's Maritime Information Services, 1994, 1998. Ship Particulars Extract, computer file. Lloyd's of London Press, London, January issues.

Mathisen, Oivind, ed., *Cruise Industry News, 1999 Annual,* Cruise Industry News, New York, 1999.

MDS Transmodal, Containership Databank on Diskette, computer file. Chester, United Kingdom, February issues.

Melancon, M., and R. Baud, Gulf of Mexico Outer Continental Shelf Daily Oil and Gas Production Rate Projections from 1999 through 2003, Minerals Management Service, New Orleans, February 1999.

Ocean Shipping Consultants, *Fast Ferries: Fleet and Market Prospects to 2010,* Ocean Shipping Consultants, Surrey, United Kingdom, 1999.

Public Law 105-178, Transportation Equity Act for the 21st Century, June 9, 1998.

Public Law 101-380, Oil Pollution Act of 1990, August 18, 1990.

Sullivan, Eric, *The Marine Encyclopaedic Dictionary,* Lloyd's of London Press, London, 1996.

Waterborne Commerce Statistics Center, *Transportation Lines of the United States, 1997,* U.S. Army Corps of Engineers, New Orleans, Louisiana, 1997.

Waterborne Commerce Statistics Center, *Waterborne Commerce of the United States, 1997,* Part 5, U.S. Army Corps of Engineers, New Orleans, Louisiana, 1997.

■ RELATED CHAPTERS

22: Shipbuilding and Repair
50: Travel and Tourism

■ GLOSSARY

Barge: A nonmotorized water vessel, usually flat-bottomed, that is towed or pushed by a tug or towboat.

Breakbulk vessel: A cargo ship that carries a variety of products of nonuniform sizes, often bound on pallets to facilitate loading and unloading.

Bulk carrier: A vessel designed to carry dry-bulk cargo such as grain, coal, and ore.

Container lifts: Containers loaded/unloaded from ships.

Containerization: The act of stowing cargo in large rectangular containers that usually are made of corrugated steel to avoid rough handling from ship to shore and back.

Containership: A ship constructed so that it can easily stack containers near and on top of each other. It has cell guides into which containers are slotted for safe stowage.

Deadweight ton (dwt): A measure of vessel carrying capacity. The total cargo, bunkers, and stores that a ship can carry up to its watermarks, measured in metric tons.

Deck barge: A non-self-propelled vessel, usually flat-bottomed and rectangular in structure, that has an intact deck for the carriage of bulk materials, containers, or trailers.

Dry cargo barge (other than deck barge): A non-self-propelled vessel, usually flat-bottomed and rectangulatr in structure, with cargo space below the deck.

Flag (registry): The nation to which a ship is registered and which holds legal jurisdiction over the operation of the ship.

Intermodal: Refers to the transportation of unit loads using a combination of two or more land, sea, or air systems.

International Maritime Organization (IMO): A permanent body established by the 1948 United Nations Maritime Conference convened to address safety at sea. IMO's purpose is to determine acceptable standards and develop treaties (conventions) related to shipping, monitor their implementation by governments, and keep them up to date with advances in technology.

Knot: A measure of speed in navigation; the rate of nautical miles per hour. One nautical mile is equal to 6,083 feet.

Laker: A long, narrow dry-bulk vessel that trades on the Great Lakes.

Open registry: Generally refers to the flag of registry of a ship owned by foreign nationals or corporations that derive financial benefits from the registry. Open registries include Antigua and Barbuda, Bahamas, Belize, Bermuda, Cayman Islands, Costa Rica, Cyprus, Danish International, Gibraltar, Honduras, Hong Kong, Isle of Man, Kerguelen Islands, Liberia, Luxembourg, Madeira, Malta, Marshall Islands, Mauritius, Netherlands Antilles, Norwegian International, Palau, Panama, São Tome and Principe, Singapore, Sri Lanka, St. Vincent, Turks and Caicos, and Vanuatu.

RTW/tricontinental service: Service that includes port calls on three continents.

Tank barge: A non-self-propelled vessel with the hulls subdivided to serve as tanks for the transportation of one or more liquid products.

Tanker: A self-propelled vessel with the hulls subdivided to serve as tanks for the transportation of one or more liquid products.

Tug: A small, powerful, and highly maneuverable vessel designed for towage or salvage operations. Also called a towboat.

Twenty-foot equivalent unit (TEU): A measure of containership cargo-carrying capacity determined by totaling the length of all containers a vessel can carry measured in feet and dividing the total by 20.

Vessel sharing agreement: An agreement between ocean common carriers by which a carrier or carriers agree to provide vessel capacity for use by another carrier in exchange for compensation or services.

RAILROADS
Economic and Trade Trends

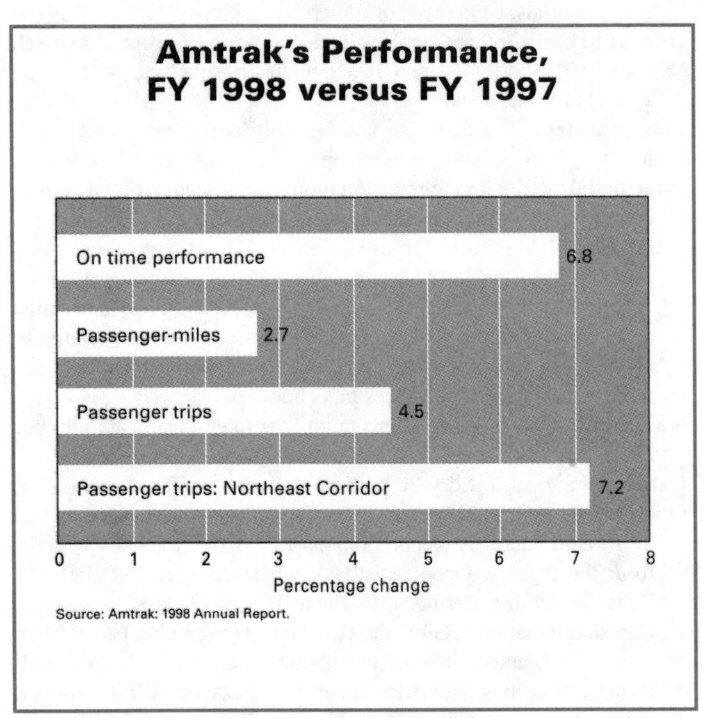

Source: Amtrak: 1998 Annual Report.

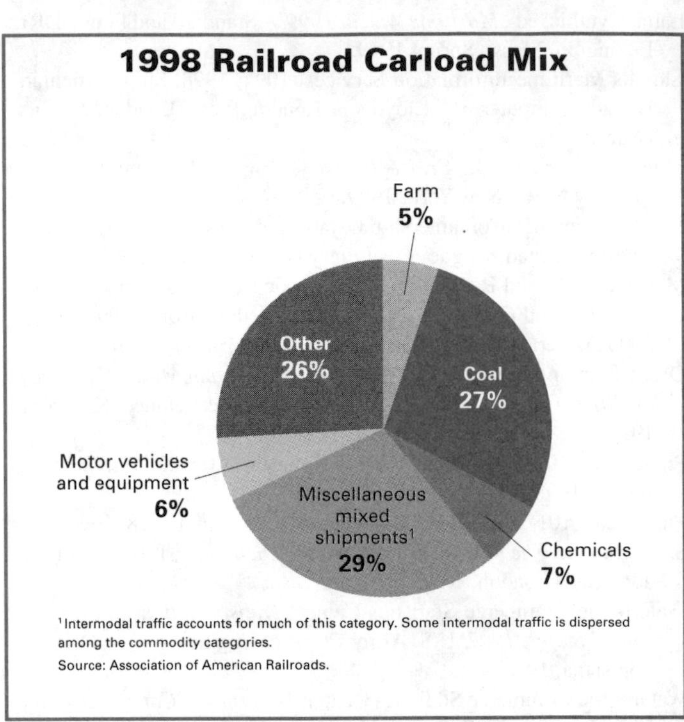

[1] Intermodal traffic accounts for much of this category. Some intermodal traffic is dispersed among the commodity categories.

Source: Association of American Railroads.

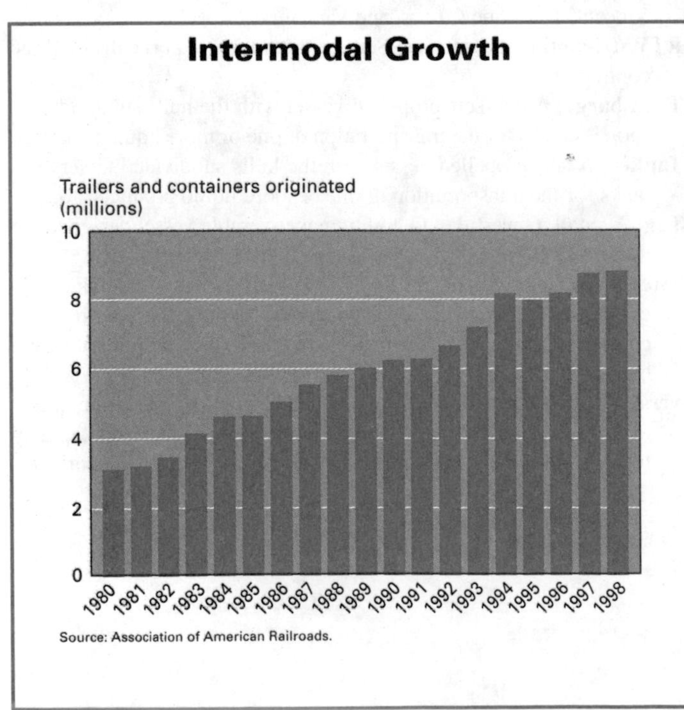

Source: Association of American Railroads.

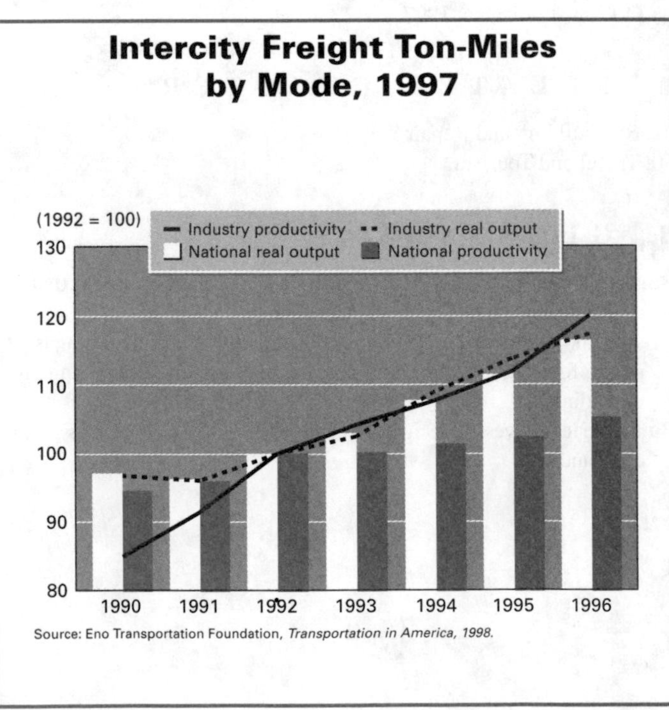

Source: Eno Transportation Foundation, *Transportation in America, 1998.*

See "Getting the Most Out of *Outlook 2000*" for definitions of terms.

53

Railroads

INDUSTRY DEFINITION Railroads (SIC 4011) are establishments engaged primarily in intercity (line-haul) railroad passenger and freight operations.

OVERVIEW

In 1998, the railroad freight industry generated an estimated $35 billion in revenue. Nine major railroad systems accounted for roughly 90 percent of that total. In its fiscal year 1998 (October 1997 through September 1998), Amtrak, the quasi-governmental railroad passenger corporation serving 45 states and Washington, DC, had estimated revenues of $2.3 billion.

Freight Service

In 1998, the railroad industry set a new high for freight traffic of 1.38 trillion revenue ton-miles (a unit of measurement that incorporates both weight and distance), up 2 percent from 1997 (see Table 53-1).

Structure. In 1998, there were nine Class I freight railroad systems—systems with an annual operating revenue of approximately $255 million or more—operating in the United States. Those systems employed 178,222 people, up slightly from 177,981 in 1997, representing the first increase since 1984 but down sharply from 235,880 employees in 1988. In 1997, there were 34 regional railroads (line-haul railroads operating at least 350 miles of road and/or earning revenue between $40 million and the Class I threshold) that employed 10,995 workers, down from 12,092 in 1988. Approximately 500 local railroads (line-haul railroads smaller than regional railroads) employed 11,741 people compared with 13,686 in 1988. Between 1988 and 1997, 219 regional and local railroads were created, while the number of Class I systems dropped from 16 to 9, primarily because of mergers.

Mergers continued to restructure the industry in the late 1990s, as they had since the mid-1980s. The Union Pacific acquired the Chicago and North Western in 1995 and the Southern Pacific in 1996, and the Burlington Northern merged with the Atchison, Topeka and Santa Fe in 1995. In June 1998, the Surface Transportation Board (STB), formerly the Interstate Commerce Commission (ICC), approved the acquisition of Conrail by Norfolk Southern (NS) and CSX. The two railroads split Conrail and began operations over their respective shares of Conrail property on June 1, 1999. CSX and NS created shared asset areas in northern New Jersey, southern New Jersey (including the Philadelphia area), and Detroit, where each railroad can compete for all the traffic previously served only by Conrail. After the splitting of Conrail, rail yards became congested, the inventory of cars on each carrier's system grew, the average system train speed fell, and rail customers complained of service breakdowns. The most significant operating problems occurred in information technology, where computer software caused the misrouting of cars. Although service problems persist, the situation is improving despite seasonal increases in traffic.

In March 1999, the STB approved the Canadian National Railway's (CN) acquisition of the Illinois Central Railroad (IC), allowing the CN (which operates from Vancouver to Halifax, Canada) to serve the rapidly growing north-south trade corridor between Detroit, Chicago, St. Louis, Memphis, Jackson, New Orleans, and Mobile. CN/IC started integrated operations on July 1, 1999, and will invest in automotive, intermodal, and transload facilities in Memphis, Dallas, Kansas City, and Chicago. The STB also approved an access agreement between CN/IC and the Kansas City Southern Railway (KCS) that allows KCS to serve former IC customers in Geismer, LA. These shippers planned to construct a new rail line to reach the KCS line and thus receive service from a second railroad. The STB extended KCS service along this line to additional shippers who claimed during the proceeding that service to customers provided through the access agreement would undermine the economics of the KCS construction project and their future option of obtaining service from a second railroad. In response to concerns voiced by the U.S. Department of

TABLE 53-1: Railroads (SIC 4011) Trends and Forecasts

	1992	1993	1994	1995	1996	1997	1998	1999[1]	2000[2]	Percent Change 97–98	98–99	99–00	96–00[3]
Carloads (thousands)	21,206	21,683	23,179	23,726	24,159	25,016	25,705	25,855	26,100	2.8	0.6	0.9	2.0
Tons (millions)	1,399	1,397	1,470	1,550	1,611	1,585	1,649	1,655	1,665	4.0	0.4	0.6	0.8
Ton-miles (billions)	1,067	1,109	1,201	1,306	1,356	1,349	1,377	1,390	1,405	2.1	0.9	1.1	0.9

[1] Estimate.
[2] Forecast.
[3] Compound annual growth rate.
Source: *Railroad Facts, 1998,* and *Analysis of Class I Railroads 1998,* Association of American Railroads; estimates and forecasts by the author.

Transportation regarding competition between these railroads in the area of overlapping operations between Baton Rouge and New Orleans, the STB instituted a 5-year oversight period to monitor competition in this corridor.

In April 1998, separate from the merger proceeding, the now CN/IC and KCS signed a 15-year marketing alliance with the goal of coordinating sales and marketing, operations, use of equipment, and application of information systems. This agreement provides the customers of these two systems with a single-transaction movement and new competitive options in key north-south continental freight markets. The agreement does not cover shippers with competitive service from both railroads.

In December 1999, the Burlington Northern Santa Fe Corp. and Canadian National Railway Company announced that they had reached agreement to merge the two systems. The proposed system would extend from Los Angeles to Halifax, Nova Scotia, and from the Gulf of Mexico to Vancouver, British Columbia. They expect to file their application with the STB in late March or early April 2000.

Commodities. In 1998, the major rail-carried commodities (in terms of total carloads) included intermodal traffic (trailers and containers on flat cars), 29 percent; coal, 27 percent; chemical products, 7 percent; motor vehicles and equipment, 6 percent; and farm products (predominantly grain and soybeans), 5 percent. The fastest-growing segment of rail traffic has been intermodal traffic, with the number of trailers and containers increasing substantially from an average of 3.4 million loadings in the early 1980s, when doublestack container trains were introduced, to 8.7 million in 1997. The busiest traffic corridor for intermodal traffic is between California and Illinois, reflecting the land portion of container shipments between the United States and Asia's Pacific Rim. With the opening of the Powder River Basin in Wyoming in the late 1970s, coal shipments grew dramatically from 4.8 million carloads to 6.7 million carloads in 1997 as the railroads delivered low-sulfur coal to help electric utilities achieve Clean Air Standards. The largest rail coal movements are from the Powder River Basin to electric generating plants in Illinois, Texas, and Missouri.

Rates. Freight rates adjusted for inflation declined an average of 1.3 percent a year between 1994 and 1998 and an average of 1.4 percent a year since the passage of the Staggers Rail Act of 1980, compared with an average increase of 2.9 percent per year in the 5 years before 1980. Between 1994 and 1998, Class I freight railroads averaged a 7.5 percent return on their net investment, up from a 2 percent average in the 1970s.

The Staggers Rail Act gave the ICC the authority to regulate rates only for traffic where competition is not effective in protecting shippers. In 1995, the ICC estimated that only 16 percent of the revenue earned by freight railroads came from traffic that is subject to maximum-rate regulation. Rates are not regulated when competition keeps them at levels below the statutory threshold for STB authority, in areas where a shipper has effective transportation alternatives, or in areas where traffic moves under contract. The STB/ICC also has exempted certain types of traffic when experience has indicated that regulation is not needed. In the early 1980s, all traffic moving in boxcars or in trailers or containers on flatcars was exempted, but rates are still regulated for specific commodities, including grain, coal, ores, certain food products, certain pulp and paper products, and certain oversized heavy machinery. By legalizing railroad-shipper contracts, the Staggers Rail Act has had a significant impact on the industry's ability to market its services. Today, roughly 70 percent of all freight shipped by rail moves under contract.

Productivity. The railroads are responsible for maintaining their track, rights-of-way, and fleet of railcars and locomotives. Over the years, through mergers and rationalization of their plant, numerous low-density or redundant lines have been abandoned or sold to smaller railroads. Since 1980, Class I railroads have increased their traffic (ton-miles) by 50 percent, while their network (miles of road owned) declined 39 percent. This has increased traffic density by concentrating traffic over a smaller network. Because of this increased density, the railroads have expanded capacity in their highest-density corridors by double-tracking track, as CSX has done in Ohio (or even triple- or quadruple-tracking in some cases) in the last few years.

Between 1980, the year the Staggers Rail Act partially deregulated rail rates and services, and 1998, the railroads have spent $290 billion on capital and maintenance of track and equipment. Capital expenditures grew 70 percent from $3.7 billion in 1988 to $6.3 billion in 1997, more than double the 33 percent increase in the price level of railroad purchases of inputs. Capital expenditures on roadway and structures increased 52 percent from $2.7 billion in 1988 to $4.1 billion in

1997 as railroads increased the percentage of rail weighing 130 pounds per yard or more from 45 percent of mileage in 1988 to 61 percent of mileage in 1997 to accommodate heavier loadings, such as increased coal shipments.

Capital expenditures for equipment more than doubled from $1.0 billion to $2.1 billion between 1988 and 1997. In terms of the capacity of railroad equipment, the total horsepower of the locomotive fleet, which is predominantly railroad-owned, increased 15 percent during this period, enabling the railroads to haul heavier trains, particularly trains moving coal out of the Powder River Basin, and high-speed long-distance intermodal trains. Total freight car capacity, however, has increased only 6 percent, with nonrailroads, such as large shippers and leasing companies, increasing their fleets' capacity by 50 percent while the capacity of the railroad-owned fleet has declined 17 percent.

Between 1988 and 1997, freight railroads made major strides in improving productivity. In that period, the railroads nearly doubled their productivity from 4.2 million to 7.6 million revenue ton-miles per employee as traffic increased and employment dropped. Less labor is needed because of smaller crew sizes and the need for fewer interchanges between railroads as a result of mergers. More traffic, as measured by revenue ton-miles, has resulted from more frequent and heavier traffic moving longer distances. For example, increased coal shipments from Wyoming are moving farther east to electric utility plants.

Freight railroads also are making more efficient use of fuel. Between 1988 and 1997, ton-miles per gallon of fuel consumed rose from 315 to 377. To make their operations more fuel-efficient, railroads have been moving longer distances between interchanges, rebuilding equipment and buying more fuel-efficient locomotives, using innovative equipment (for example, aluminum freight cars and double-stack cars), and reducing locomotive idling time.

To maintain or increase their share of intercity traffic, the railroads must continue to market their services aggressively to existing and potential customers. To satisfy shippers' needs for reliable service, the railroads need to continually adopt cost-effective technological improvements; operate their plant, equipment, and labor force safely and efficiently; and expand their trackage where necessary.

Future Growth. The railroads' major commodities—coal, chemicals, intermodal traffic, and farm products—account for roughly two-thirds of railroad traffic measured in carloads, tons, and ton-miles. Each of these measures is forecast to increase over the next several years for each commodity.

Coal traffic is expected to continue to grow modestly as the demand for coal by electric utilities increases, but at a slower rate than in the past. Coal-burning electric utilities that have not installed scrubber equipment or used emissions credits to satisfy the emissions standards under the Clean Air Act will continue to increase the use of low-sulfur coal mined in the western part of the country. The expansion of demand for western coal will occur partially at the expense of the demand for coal mined in the east. As a result, western coal is expected to continue its increased penetration of more distant eastern utility markets.

Chemical traffic should continue to grow moderately as plastics continue to be substituted for wood, paper, metal, glass, and rubber in the economy. Another application favoring plastic is the development and use of plastic beer bottles. The demand by plastics producers such as makers of plastic packaging will continue to increase the demand for the resins used in making plastics and the raw materials used in making resins. Additional growth in the international demand for resins made by U.S. manufacturers could result if delays are experienced in the growth of foreign resin-making capacity. To a lesser extent, the demand for whitening agents by textile and paper mills also is expected to grow.

Intermodal traffic is expected to grow strongly over the next several years as rail intermodal service continues to compete actively with truck traffic for longer-distance shipments. While Japan is expected to continue to be the largest overseas exporter of containers to the United States, the number two overseas exporter, China, is expected to continue to grow more rapidly. In addition, rail traffic crossing the Canadian and Mexican borders in both directions will continue to increase.

Grain traffic is expected to increase modestly based on U.S. Department of Agriculture (USDA) forecasts of strong growth in U.S. exports of wheat and corn, while the growth in U.S. soybean exports is expected to be hampered by competition from Brazilian and Argentinian exporters. The demand for U.S. exports to north Africa, the Middle East, and southeast Asia is expected to grow as those areas increase their imports of grain to feed livestock.

Passenger Service

Amtrak. The National Railroad Passenger Corporation (Amtrak) operates more than 200 intercity trains a day over a 22,200-mile route system, serving more than 500 communities in 45 states and the District of Columbia. In fiscal year (FY) 1998 (October 1, 1997, to September 30, 1998), Amtrak carried 75.1 million passengers (21.1 million on its intercity trains and 54.0 million metropolitan commuters), generating a total of 5.3 billion passenger miles (up about 3 percent from 5.2 billion in FY 1997).

Amtrak continues to face financial and operational challenges, although the company has been able to show improvement in recent years. Several years ago, inadequate capital investment, stagnant traffic and passenger revenues levels, outdated equipment in need of modernization, and declining federal subsidies worsened Amtrak's performance. In FY 1994, the company incurred a cash operating loss of $578 million and an operating loss of $834 million, the worst in its history.

In FY 1995, under new management, the corporation implemented a reorganization that divided the company into several strategic business units and set in motion a strategic business plan that called for revenue enhancement initiatives and programs to reduce overhead expenses and improve productivity, including major service improvements. The plan was also designed to pursue major initiatives such as high-speed rail along the Northeast Corridor (NEC) and the company's new mail and express operation as well as a program to recapitalize the company's assets, make the company more efficient, and transform its passenger business into a more profitable operation. Since that time, Amtrak has demonstrated improvement, and by the end of FY 1998 its cash operating loss had fallen to $525 million, a reduction of 9 percent from FY 1994.

Despite this improvement, Amtrak still spends almost $2 for every dollar it earns in revenues from its intercity passenger service. In fact, only 1 of its 40 intercity routes, the Metroliner service between Washington, DC, and New York City, was profitable in FY 1998. Controlling expenses and increasing operating efficiencies, on the one hand, and increasing revenues, on the other, particularly in its intercity passenger operation, remain difficult obstacles.

Lower federal operating subsidies have exacerbated Amtrak's financial problems in recent years. Since FY 1995, Congress has lowered Amtrak's operating subsidies and plans to eliminate them altogether by FY 2002, except for excess railroad retirement payments. In FY 1998, the corporation received a federal subsidy of $426 million, including $82 million for equipment and overhaul support, and an additional $250 million to continue electrification along the line between New Haven, CT, and Boston as part of the Northeast Corridor Improvement Project. In constant dollars, Amtrak's FY 1998 subsidy was more than 60 percent lower than its FY 1991 subsidy.

In response to its financial challenges, Amtrak has undertaken an aggressive capital improvement program, primarily to replace outdated equipment and improve service. Over the past several years, Amtrak has ordered and taken delivery of nearly 200 bilevel Superliners designed to replace the aging Heritage equipment and 50 Viewliners, scheduled for service in the midwest and the East Coast. The Viewliner equipment represents the first single-level sleeping cars manufactured in the United States in 40 years.

More recently, Amtrak purchased close to 150 locomotives from General Electric and General Motors to replace aging F-40 locomotives. Furthermore, an international consortium led by Bombardier, Inc., of Canada and GEC Alsthom of France is completing the building of 20 high-speed all-electric train sets. This contract is a vital component of Amtrak's plan to introduce high-speed passenger service along the Washington–Boston Northeast Corridor in spring 2000. The new trains are equipped with tilt technology (designed to improve ride quality through curves), reach speeds of 150 mph, and offer the latest in communications technology to the traveling public. The first of these trainsets arrived at the Transportation Technology Center (TTC) in Pueblo, CO, for functional and performance testing in March 1999. A second trainset began testing along the NEC in June. The first of these trains are scheduled to enter revenue service in spring 2000. The $750 million contract also includes 15 additional high-powered locomotives and three trainset maintenance facilities. The locomotives are being tested at Pueblo, CO, and along the NEC, and all three maintenance facilities are complete. Finally, Amtrak signed a $100 million contract with GEC Alsthom for the acquisition of eight trainsets to be used in Amtrak's San Diegans service from San Diego to Los Angeles, Santa Barbara, and San Luis Obispo, CA.

Other developments in performance have also improved the long-term outlook. First, Amtrak's ridership has shown healthy gains, increasing 4.5 percent in FY 1998 over FY 1997 levels, while ridership during the first half of FY 1999 grew close to 4 percent over the prior year's levels. Strong ridership growth in both the west and the NEC was made possible by improved marketing and a relatively mild winter despite some weather-related service disruptions in the west. The company also surpassed $1 billion in passenger revenues in FY 1998 for the first time. Second, Amtrak's mail and express business improved, earning $83 million in FY 1998, roughly 20 percent higher than revenue in the previous year. Third, Amtrak's customer satisfaction index, which measures responses from riders to 12 indicators of service quality, improved from 81 in FY 1995 to 84 in FY 1998. Gains also were evident in on-time performance, which improved from 71 percent in FY 1997 to 79 percent in FY 1998.

Finally, the passage of two Amtrak-related statutes is likely to have an important effect on Amtrak's future. The Taxpayers Relief Act of 1997 (TRA) and the 1997 Amtrak Reform and Accountability Act (ARAA) provided Amtrak with sufficient capital and needed reform to improve the company's chances for survival and operating self-sufficiency by the year 2002. These laws provided $2.2 billion toward capital investment in Amtrak through two direct payments from the U.S. Treasury, authorized future appropriations and allowed Amtrak to operate more like a private business, replaced Amtrak's existing board of directors with a new seven-member Reform Board, and increased flexibility in the negotiation of future labor contracts.

SAFETY AND TECHNOLOGY

Safety and Regulatory Initiatives

Safety Enforcement Innovations. The Federal Railroad Administration (FRA) has initiated several innovative programs to supplement its regulatory approach to ensuring safety on the nation's railroads. In 1995, FRA developed the Safety Assurance and Compliance Program (SACP), a new approach to safety inspection and compliance that focuses on systemic problems facing the railroads. Through the creation of partnerships with railroads, shippers, and their employees, the parties responsible for implementing a solution are directly involved in identifying and incorporating the corrective actions in the SACP plan. FRA monitors the implementation of the action plans to ensure that commitments are fulfilled, focusing on results, as measured by the level of compliance with safety laws and the frequency of accidents and injuries.

FRA has used this method to improve safety on many large railroads and has begun applying it to smaller railroads and hazardous-materials shippers. In the 6 years since SACP was introduced, railroad-related fatality rates and injury rates are down and the train accident rate has been reduced.

During FY 1998, FRA began conducting SACP safety audits at a number of smaller regional and local railroads. On the Norfolk Southern, the Manpower, Staffing and Crew Utilization SACP Team developed a mentoring and training program for employees who participate in accelerated conductor training, and the Train and Engine Safety Analysis SACP Team developed a training and compliance program to reduce the number of employee accidents. Union Pacific SACP teams have concentrated on fatigue management; crew utilization/crew management systems; dispatcher workload; inspection and testing requirements for signals, maintenance of way, locomotives, and cars; electronic record keeping; and alternatives to employee discipline.

Another new program, the Railroad Safety Advisory Committee (RSAC), chartered on March 25, 1996, provides FRA with a continuing forum for advice and recommendations on the development of the railroad safety regulatory program. This collaborative rule-making approach involves all segments of the railroad community to accommodate rapidly evolving changes in the rail transportation industry.

RSAC task force members have participated in developing final rules for revision of the Track Safety Standards and Rules on Railroad Communications. In addition, RSAC groups are engaged in other regulatory topics, including requirements for locomotive event recorders, standards for locomotive crashworthiness, improvement of cab working conditions, safety enhancements to on-track roadway equipment, performance standards for processor-based signal and train control systems, and the future of positive train control systems.

New Regulations. Among the railroad safety and efficiency issues FRA has addressed through regulation since 1998 are railroad communications, passenger equipment safety standards, track safety standards, passenger train emergency preparedness, power brake end-of-train devices–passenger train operations, and technical amendments to alcohol and drug control rules. Additionally, final rules on credit assistance for surface transportation projects, part II, and adjustment of monetary threshold for reporting rail equipment accidents/incidents were published during that time period.

Technology Initiatives

The U.S. rail industry, in cooperation with FRA, continues to develop new technology to make the rails safer and more efficient. The Magnetic Levitation Transportation Technology Deployment Program is a public-private partnership for the installation of a 35-mile-long maglev transportation system in the United States. The first stage will be the award of federal preconstruction planning grants to several states to assess the feasibility of their proposals. FRA expects to select one of these projects for deployment by FY 2001.

Another technology initiative, the Next Generation High Speed Rail (NGHSR) Program, will demonstrate the feasibility of incrementally upgraded high-speed rail (HSR) passenger service, at speeds of over 110 mph, that can be operated on upgraded existing rights-of-way as a viable alternative to increased investment in intercity highway and airport capacity. Further technology development and demonstration are needed to provide cost-effective high-quality service in applications in the United States.

FRA has identified four program areas in which development and demonstration activities have a potential return on investment when high-speed rail upgrade programs are implemented. They are advanced train control systems that will maximize the capacity of railroads to carry a mix of high-speed passenger, commuter, and freight trains with minimal risk of collision and lower cost than conventional methods of upgrading railroad signal and control systems to support high-speed operations; nonelectric locomotives, which can achieve the speed and acceleration capability of electric trains without the expensive infrastructure of railroad electrification; grade crossing hazard mitigation, including barrier systems and innovative warning devices and methods that provide security similar to that of grade separations but at lower cost; and enhanced track and structures to increase route capacity or improve performance of the infrastructure on existing corridors to permit shared heavy freight and high-speed passenger use.

Role of E-Commerce

The Association of American Railroads (AAR), the trade association of the Class I railroads, through its affiliate, RAILINC, coordinates electronic data interchange (EDI) standard-setting activities for the railroads, the shipping community, and the third-party network that translates business data into EDI transactions. The railroad industry has adopted the widely used Accredited Standards Committee X12 format of EDI for these transactions. Through the use of EDI, railroads and their participating customers, suppliers, and U.S. government agencies such as U.S. Customs are able to exchange information covering all facets of railroad operations.

HIGH-SPEED RAIL

High-speed ground transportation (HSGT), a family of technologies ranging from upgraded existing railroads to magnetically levitated vehicles, is a passenger transportation option that can best link cities lying about 100 to 500 miles apart. Common in Europe and Japan, HSGT in the United States already exists in the NEC between New York and Washington, DC, and will soon serve travelers between New York and Boston.

Major high-speed passenger corridor initiatives include the following.

California Corridor. A very high speed (186 mph, grade-separated) service from Los Angeles to San Francisco will be proposed in addition to a high-speed feeder network operating at 100 mph to serve San Diego, Sacramento, and other system routes. Under FRA's Maglev Deployment Program, a maglev system is being developed between Los Angeles International Airport and Union Station, with an easterly extension.

Pacific Northwest Corridor. Washington State's Department of Transportation and Amtrak have purchased four high-speed trainsets operating in this corridor, which extends from Eugene, OR, to Vancouver, British Columbia.

Chicago Hub Network. Nine midwestern states, known as the Midwest Regional Rail Initiative, are seeking funding to operate at speeds of up to 110 mph by upgrading tracks and signals on routes now in place and purchasing equipment.

Detroit–Chicago Segment. The State of Michigan, FRA, Amtrak, and localities have invested to incrementally upgrade the federally designated route to high-speed rail standards.

St. Louis–Chicago Segment. The use of nonelectric locomotive technology is being evaluated under an award from FRA. The midwestern states and Amtrak are expected to provide additional funding for continuation of the Midwest Regional Rail Initiative Study.

Twin Cities–Chicago Segment. FRA and state funds are supporting phase II of the Twin Cities–Milwaukee–Chicago high-speed rail feasibility study, which is exploring technologies for 110, 150, and 185 mph.

Cincinnati–Indianapolis–Chicago Segment. This segment was added to the Chicago Hub corridor in January 1999, making it eligible for grade crossing hazard elimination funds.

Southeast Corridor. This corridor extends from Washington, DC, to Jacksonville, FL. Among the corridor's developments, the North Carolina Department of Transportation has instituted the Sealed Corridor Initiative to improve or close every highway/rail crossing along the North Carolina portion of the corridor to ensure safe high-speed operation along the line. Solutions include four-quadrant gates, longer gate arms, inexpensive median barriers, and video enforcement.

Florida Corridor. Florida is supporting a project to build a short maglev facility at the Titusville Executive Airport, with possible extensions to Port Canaveral and Orlando. FRA's Maglev Deployment Program selected this project as one of seven eligible for planning funds. Another proposal, privately funded, would use maglev technology to build a system from Orlando Airport west to International Drive and east to Port Canaveral, utilizing the Bee Line Expressway right-of-way.

Gulf Coast Corridor. In May 1999, the Greater New Orleans Expressway Commission, along with six other states and authorities, received a grant under the Maglev Technology Deployment Program for preconstruction planning for magnetic levitation high-speed ground transportation for a system linking the northern suburbs of New Orleans to the airport and downtown across Lake Ponchartrain.

Keystone Corridor. The Port Authority of Allegheny County has applied for and been designated to receive planning funds for a 45-mile maglev system linking Pittsburgh International Airport, Pittsburgh, and Greensburg.

Empire Corridor. In late 1998, Amtrak officials and New York's governor announced a 5-year $185 million plan to upgrade the New York City–Albany–Buffalo line and rebuild trains used on the route. A second track would be built between Albany and Schenectady. In addition, Amtrak and the state are splitting the cost of rebuilding five Turboliner trains.

NAFTA IMPLEMENTATION

The U.S. railroad industry interfaces with the railroad systems of its North American Free Trade Agreement (NAFTA) partners, Mexico and Canada. Changes in the operating environments of those rail systems affect U.S. rail operations. FRA continues to work with its counterparts in Canada and Mexico to ensure continued safe and efficient international rail movements.

In 1998, U.S. railroads carried $52 billion worth of goods between the United States and Canada (excluding transshipments, i.e., traffic moving through Canada to or from a third country). U.S. railroads carried $18 billion worth of goods between the United States and Mexico in 1998, excluding transshipments. Excluding transshipments, motor vehicles and motor-vehicle parts hauled by railroads in 1998 accounted for 34 percent of the rail-delivered U.S. exports to Mexico and 78 percent of the U.S. imports shipped by rail from Mexico. This commodity group accounts for 54 percent of rail-delivered U.S. exports to Canada and 49 percent of rail-delivered imports from Canada. For example, a number of automobile assembly plants have opened on the Mexican side of the border in the last several years. U.S. companies ship motor vehicle parts to those plants for assembly, and the assembled vehicles are shipped back to the United States. Other major shipments include over $5 billion worth of imports of wood and paper and allied products from Canada.

Mexican Railroad Privatization

The 16,415-mile Mexican rail system, Ferrocarriles Nacionales de Mexico (FNM), which consists of three main lines—the Northeast Railroad, the Pacific-North Railway, and the Southeast Railway—several short lines, and the Mexico City terminal railroad, has been privatized.

In December 1996, the consortium of KCS and Transportacion Maritima Mexicana, Mexico's largest ocean freight company, acquired the first concession, Mexico's 2,661-mile Northeast Railroad. Transportacion Ferroviaria Mexicana (TFM) started operations in June 1997, linking Mexico City, Monterrey, and Guadalajara to the Mexican border cities of Nuevo Laredo and Matamoros and the U.S. cities of Laredo and Brownsville, TX.

In July 1997, Grupo Mexico, Ingenieros Civiles Asociados, and the Union Pacific Railroad acquired the concession for the 3,885-mile Pacific-North Railway. Grupo Ferroviario Mexicano (FerroMex) started operations in February 1998 from Mexico City to its interchanges with the Union Pacific at Eagle Pass and El Paso, TX; Nogales, AZ; and Calexico, CA. In 1997, the Burlington Northern Santa Fe Railway gained trackage rights to interchange traffic with FerroMex at Eagle Pass.

In October 1997, the steelmaker Grupo Acerero del Norte and the mining company Grupo Industrias Penoles won a 30-year concession to operate the 604-mile Coahuila–Durango short line. Genessee & Wyoming Inc., the operator, initiated service in April 1998 and provides technical support.

In July 1998, Grupo Tribasa acquired the 1,360-mile Southeast Railway connecting the Gulf of Mexico ports of Coatzacoalcos and Veracruz to the Mexico City Terminal. FerroSur plans new locomotive purchases and infrastructure upgrades on the line.

Canadian Rail Operations

The Surface Transportation Board's July 1, 1999, approval of the Canadian National–Illinois Central merger creates the possibility of through train operations linking Canada, the United States, and Mexico. The FRA Safety Integration Plan developed for the end-to-end merger enables FRA to oversee safety as the systems are integrated over the next 5 years and report to the board on its progress.

Additionally, FRA continues to work with Transport Canada through a Technical Review Working Group to identify regulatory and operating issues that may affect the movement of railroad freight and passenger traffic across the U.S.–Canadian border. FRA and Transport Canada have conducted joint cross-border inspections to ensure good working relationships between the countries and increase understanding of each country's regulatory regimes and compliance policies.

EXPORTING U.S. TECHNOLOGY AND KNOW-HOW

In 1998–1999, the pace of commercialization, privatization, and/or concessioning of government-owned and -operated railways around the world continued. Many of the world's railroads are making these changes to one degree or another. The most common model used is the Swedish model, in which the government retains ownership and maintenance of the infrastructure while operations are spun off and commercialized or privatized. Information about the world's railroads can be found on the Internet. A good starting point is the international rail association's Web site, http://www.uic.assoc.fr.

The U.S. privately owned and operated rail system remains the model for other countries to emulate. Its highly efficient and effective rail-related products and services have clearly proved to have materially and positively affected the profit margin of U.S. railroads, and this has not gone unnoticed by foreign governments.

Concessioning has emerged as the most promising avenue for debt-ridden railways to regain profitability. When a railway is allowed to operate in a free market enterprise environment, financial stabilization and even profitability most often result. To date, the great success story remains the privatization/concessioning of the Argentinian railway system, a story that has prompted countries as far away as Africa's Ivory Coast to venture into this arena by restructuring and concessioning national railways.

Commercialization, privatization, and concessioning and therefore export opportunities in the new millenium continue to appear most likely in sub-Saharan Africa, southeastern and central Europe, central Asia, and China. Although recent economic recessions have affected economies to one degree or another, major rail project planning has not suffered as a result. Furthermore, a number of large projects and/or initiatives remain in various planning stages, including the Trans-Asia Rail Project (Malaysia, Thailand, Cambodia, Vietnam, and points north), the rail system in southeastern Europe (Bulgaria, Romania, Hungary) and Turkey; and continued rapid expansion of the rail system in China, where only 65 to 70 percent of demand currently is being met.

Rolling stock, signaling and train control, safety, management systems, management expertise, and financing all provide opportunities for U.S. rail-related manufacturers, suppliers, and service providers to contribute to the process.

Joel Palley, U.S. Department of Transportation, Federal Railroad Administration, (202) 493-6409, October 1999.

REFERENCES

Amtrak Annual Report, National Railroad Passenger Corporation (Amtrak), 400 North Capitol Street, Washington, DC 20001. (202) 906-3939.

Analysis of Class I Railroads (annual), Policy, Legislation and Economics Department, Association of American Railroads, 50 F Street, NW, Washington, DC 20001. (202) 639-2211.

Commodity Compass (formerly *Transportation Review: Rail Traffic Focus*) (annual), Standard & Poor's DRI, 24 Hartwell Avenue, Lexington, MA 02173. (800) 933-3374.

Directory of Transportation Data Sources (annual), Bureau of Transportation Statistics, U.S. Department of Transportation, 400 Seventh Street, SW, Washington, DC 20590. (202) 366-DATA.

Employment and Earnings (monthly), Bureau of Labor Statistics, U.S. Department of Labor, Washington, DC 20212. (202) 606-6555 or (202) 606-6373.

Freight Commodity Statistics (annual), Policy, Legislation and Economics Department, Association of American Railroads, 50 F Street, NW, Washington, DC 20001. (202) 639-2211.

National Transportation Statistics (annual), Bureau of Transportation Statistics, U.S. Department of Transportation, 400 Seventh Street, SW, Washington, DC 20590. (202) 366-DATA.

1993 Commodity Flow Survey: State Summaries, September 1996, Bureau of Transportation Statistics, U.S. Department of Transportation, 400 Seventh Street, SW, Washington, DC 20590. (202) 366-DATA.

1993 Commodity Flow Survey: United States, October 1996, U.S. Department of Commerce, Economics and Statistics Administration, Bureau of the Census, Commodity Flow Survey Branch, Services Division, Washington, DC 20233. (301) 457-2788 or (301) 457-2114.

1997 Economic Census: Transportation—1997, Commodity Flow Survey: United States (Preliminary) (December 1998), U.S. Department of Commerce, Economics and Statistics Administration, Bureau of the Census, Commodity Flow Survey Branch, Services Division, Washington, DC 20233. (301) 457-2788 or (301) 457-2114.

PPI [Producer Price Index] Detailed Report (monthly), Bureau of Labor Statistics, U.S. Department of Labor, Washington, DC 20212. (202) 606-7705.

Privatization of Intercity Rail Passenger Service in the United States, Federal Railroad Administration, U.S. Department of Transportation, 400 Seventh Street, SW, Washington, DC 20590. (202) 493-6379.

Profiles of U.S. Railroads (annual), Policy, Legislation and Economics Department, Association of American Railroads, 50 F Street, NW, Washington, DC 20001. (202) 639-2211.

Rail Rates Continue Multi-Year Decline, February 1998, Office of Economics, Environmental Analysis and Administration, Surface Transportation Board, 1925 K Street, NW, Washington, DC 20423. (202) 565-1596.

Railroad Facts (annual), Policy, Legislation and Economics Department, Association of American Railroads, 50 F Street, NW, Washington, DC 20001. (202) 639-2211.

Railroad Regulation: Changes in Railroad Rates and Service Quality since 1990 (GAO/RCED-99-93), April 1999, General Accounting Office, P.O. Box 37050, Washington, DC 20013. (202) 512-6000.

Railroad Regulation: Current Issues Associated with the Rate Relief Process (GAO/RCED-99-46), February 1999, General Accounting Office, P.O. Box 37050, Washington, DC 20013. (202) 512-6000.

Railroad Safety Statistics: Annual Report (annual), includes the *Accident/Incident Bulletin,* the *Highway-Rail Crossing Accident/Incident and Inventory Bulletin,* and the *Trespasser Bulletin,* Office of Safety, Federal Railroad Administration, U.S. Department of Transportation, 400 Seventh Street, SW, Washington, DC 20590. (202) 493-6293. Also available at http://safetydata.fra.dot.gov/officeofsafety/.

Railroads and States—1997, January 1999, (annual), Policy, Legislation and Economics Department, Association of American Railroads, 50 F Street, NW, Washington, DC 20001. (202) 639-2211.

Railroad Ten-Year Trends (annual), Policy, Legislation and Economics Department, Association of American Railroads, 50 F Street, NW, Washington, DC 20001. (202) 639-2211.

Railway Age (monthly), Editorial and Executive Offices, 345 Hudson Street, New York, NY 10014. (212) 620-7233. Circulation: (800) 895-4389.

Road and Rail (formerly *Transportation Monitor*) (quarterly), Standard & Poor's DRI, 24 Hartwell Avenue, Lexington, MA 02173. (800) 933-3374.

Short-Term Energy Outlook Quarterly Projections, Energy Information Administration, U.S. Department of Energy, Washington, DC 20585. (202) 586-8800.

Sources of Financial Improvement in the U.S. Rail Industry, 1966–1995, Carl D. Martland, Massachusetts Institute of Technology, *Transportation Research Forum Proceedings, 39th Annual Meeting, 1997,* vol. 1, pp. 58–86.

Traffic World (weekly), Editorial Office, 741 National Press Building, Washington, DC 20045. (202) 383-6140. Circulation: (800) 245-8723.

Transportation Expressions 1996, Bureau of Transportation Statistics, U.S. Department of Transportation, 400 Seventh Street, SW, Washington, DC 20590. (202) 366-DATA.

Transportation in America (annual), Eno Transportation Foundation, Inc., 44211 Slatestone Court, Lansdowne, Va 22075. (703) 729-7200.

Transportation Statistics Annual Report (annual), Bureau of Transportation Statistics, U.S. Department of Transportation, 400 Seventh Street, SW, Washington, DC 20590. (202) 366-DATA.

The Ultimate ICCTA [Interstate Commerce Commission Termination Act] Outline, Mark J. Andrews and Richard H. Streeter, *The Transportation Lawyer,* vol. 5, no. 1, July 1996, pp. 38–52.

USDA Agricultural Baseline Projections to 2008 (annual), World Agricultural Outlook Board, U.S. Department of Agriculture, www.econ.ag.gov/briefing/baseline, (202) 694-5275.

World Agricultural Supply and Demand Estimates (monthly), U.S. Department of Agriculture, Agricultural Marketing Service, Economic Research Service, www.usda.gov/oce/waob/wasde/wasde.htm, (202) 694-5275.

Selected Web Sites

Association of American Railroads (AAR), http://www.aar.org for the Web sites of the Class I railroads and AAR speeches, press releases, data, catalog of publications and services.

Bureau of Transportation Statistics (BTS), U.S. Department of Transportation, http://www.bts.gov for national transportation library; geographic information systems; BTS programs, products, and services; and searchable databases.

Federal Railroad Administration, U.S. Department of Transportation, http://www.fra.dot.gov for news releases, public education campaigns and programs, safety data, FRA's High speed ground transportation (HSGT) Web site: http://www.fra.dot.gov/hsgt/ for information on high-speed rail passenger transportation.

U.S. Department of Transportation (DOT), http://www.dot.gov for news and press releases, DOT Web search, browse DOT modal administrations, what's new, transportation, and government Internet sites.

Additional DOT Sources

DOT's Bureau of Transportation Services provides statistical information line at (800) 853-1351, fax-on-demand at (800) 671-8012, technical assistance for customers experiencing difficulties in accessing or using BTS electronic products at (800) 366-6664.

TRUCKING
Economic and Trade Trends

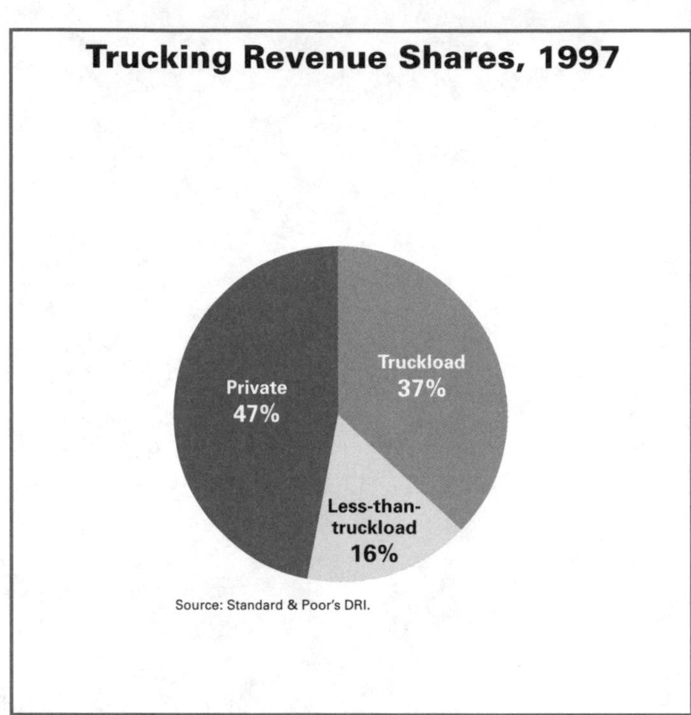

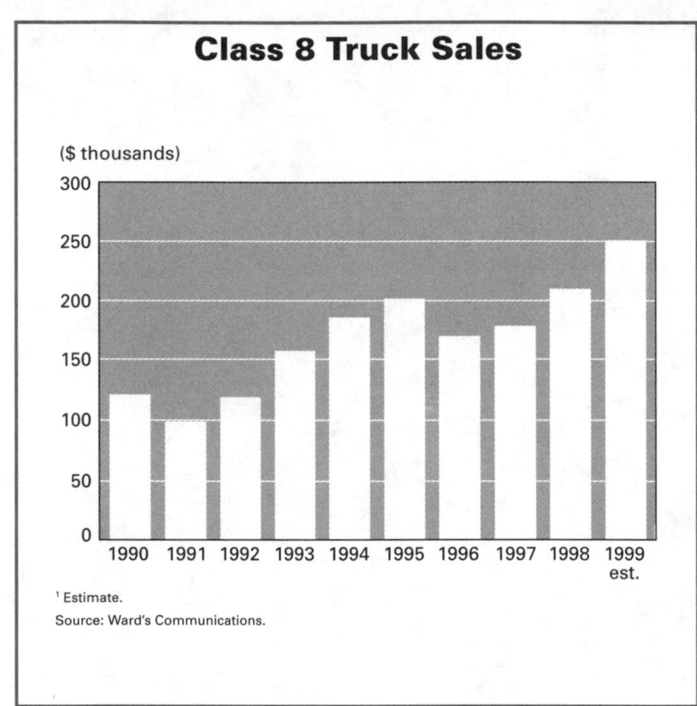

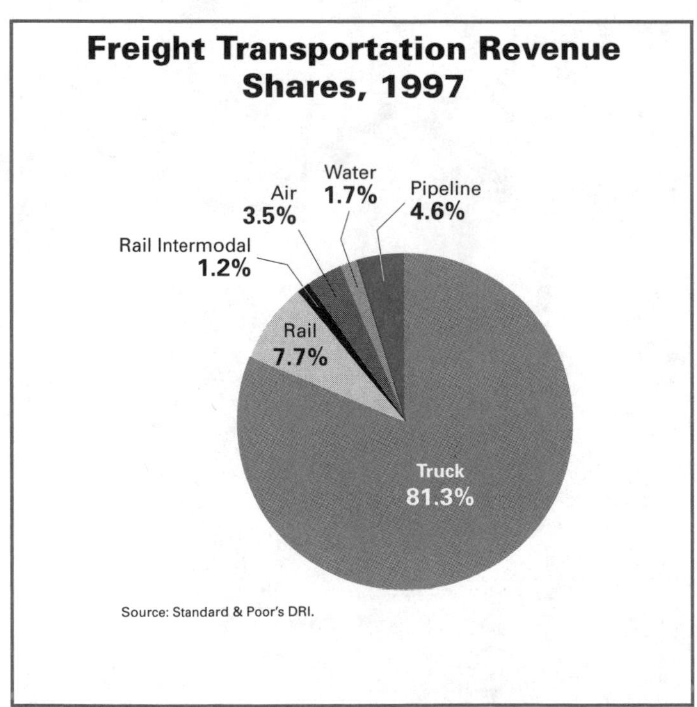

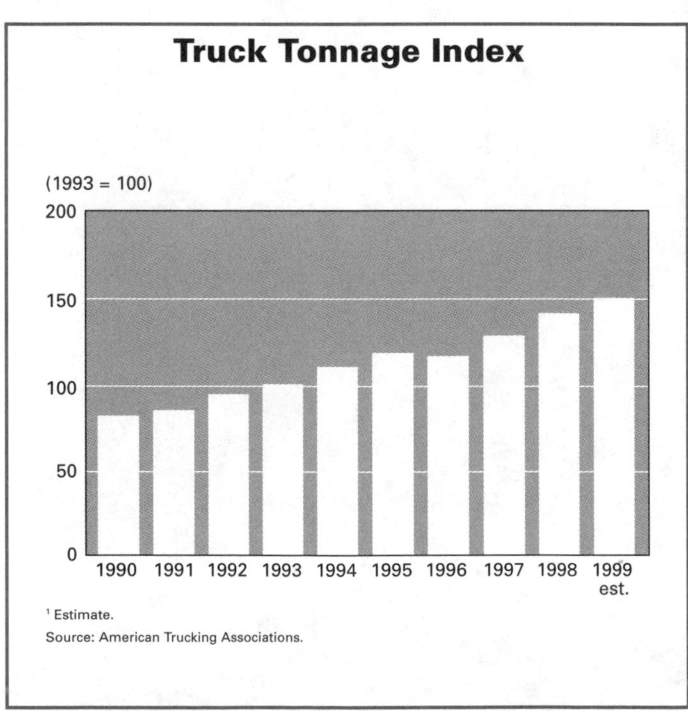

See "Getting the Most Out of *Outlook 2000*" for definitions of terms.

54

Trucking

INDUSTRY DEFINITION Trucking companies (motor carriers) provide ground-based transportation of raw materials, including dry bulk and liquid commodities, as well as semifinished and finished manufactured products. Freight is transported by dry van, refrigerated truck, flatbed, bulk, tank, or auto trailers. Local carriers (SIC 4212) are those which handle shipments exceeding 100 pounds within a single municipality, between contiguous municipalities, or between a municipality and its suburbs. Trucking, except local (SIC 4213), provides highway transport of commercial and household items. Package, parcel, and courier services (SIC 4215) transport items generally weighing less than 100 pounds and may move locally or over long distances.

DOMESTIC TRENDS

Although there were no trucks at the beginning of the twentieth century, the trucking industry has become a linchpin in the supply chain as the U.S. economy starts the twenty-first century. According to a study by Standard & Poor's DRI conducted for the American Trucking Associations (ATA), the trucking industry is a $372 billion industry that accounts for 81 percent of all freight revenues. It hauls 60 percent of all of tonnage, or 6.7 billion tons annually.

For much of the current period of economic expansion, the trucking industry has been a major beneficiary. By hauling freight in all sectors of the supply chain from suppliers, to manufacturers, to wholesalers, to retailers, to home delivery, trucking grows as the general economy improves. Some of the most important drivers of growth for motor carriers are industrial production, retail sales, personal consumption, construction, imports, and exports. Domestic production is more important to trucking activity than are imported goods, as a product completely produced in the United States has several more freight movements during the production process than does an import; nevertheless, imports often are transported three or four times before reaching their final destination. In addition, trucking prospers as other modes of freight transportation grow. Airplanes, ships, and, most often, trains cannot pull up to manufacturing plants, distribution centers, or retail outlets, and so trucking is the link in intermodalism. This ensures growth for the industry as the freight transportation pie expands.

Motor carriers have experienced significant growth over the last few decades. For instance, in 1960, trucking accounted for 68 percent of freight revenues and was a $30 billion industry. In revenue terms, trucking has grown 12-fold since that year. The number of truck-tractors on the highways also has surged during this time frame, increasing from 618,000 to nearly 1.5 million today (this is the active population; there are many more truck-tractors, but they are used very little). The number of miles traveled by large trucks has increased 29 percent since 1990 and now stands at more than 124 billion annually.

Deregulation

A major event in trucking history was the Motor Carrier Act of 1980, which allowed for interstate competition in the for-hire trucking industry. A second key change stemmed from the Trucking Industry Regulatory Reform Act of 1995, which prohibited state governments from regulating carriers' rates, routes, and services. There are still regulations in the areas of safety, vehicle sizes and weights, and hazardous materials movements, but carriers now can compete in the open market for both interstate and intrastate hauls.

Deregulation of the industry has had a significant structural effect, completely changing the way carriers run their business. Most important, the government no longer sets rates. Before 1980, growth in rates, as broadly measured by revenue per mile, nearly matched that of general inflation [the consumer price index (CPI)]. Since then, however, revenue per mile has only grown by 11 percent compared with a 95 percent increase in the

CPI. This has been beneficial for the overall economy, since up to 10 percent of the final price of a good consists of transportation costs. However, this fierce competition drove many participants out of the market and continues to do so. Before deregulation, there were roughly 200 carrier failures a year on average. Since then, according to Dun & Bradstreet, the number has surged to nearly 1,500 per year. In real dollars, total revenue per mile from 1979 to 1997 fell an astounding 44 percent. As a result, carriers have had to become much more efficient to survive. In fact, during that 19-year period, real expenses per mile also fell 44 percent.

Deregulation of trucking created a very fragmented industry. There are now fairly low barriers to entry. Equipment is relatively easy to obtain, and if a driver with a commercial driver's license adheres to insurance and safety rules and regulations, he or she is in business. Today, according to the Office of Motor Carriers, over 450,000 interstate motor carriers are operating in the United States, not including the thousands of intrastate carriers. This is one reason why freight rates remain relatively low. Since June 1992, the producer price index (PPI) for truckload freight has increased only 5.7 percent. Industry fragmentation also has suppressed profit margins. In 1997, the average profit margin for all types of carriers, excluding household goods carriers, was only 1.95 percent.

Another factor that has increased competition in trucking is low barriers to exit. If a driver decides to start his or her own business and fails, that person can fairly easily sell the truck and return to being a company driver or leave the industry entirely. Low barriers to entry and exit are due partly to trucking being a high-variable-cost, low-fixed-cost industry. One industry analyst estimates that over 90 percent of all trucking costs vary with the level of activity.

The ATA has estimated that the percentage of total industry revenue accounted for by the top 50 for-hire carriers increased from 11 percent in 1990 to 13 percent in 1997 (see Table 54-1). Consolidation is likely in a turbulent industry that faces a driver shortage, high operating expenses, and extreme competition. Nevertheless, it is unlikely that consolidation will ever reduce the fragmentation caused by the highly competitive nature of the industry.

TABLE 54-1: Leading Trucking Companies in 1998
(billions of dollars)

Company	Revenue
United Parcel Service	24.79
FDX Corp.	15.87
CNF Transportation	4.94
Yellow Corp	2.90
Schneider National	2.71
Roadway Express	2.65
Consolidated Freightways Corp.	2.24
J. B. Hunt Transport Services	1.84
USFreightways Corp.	1.83
UniGroup Inc.	1.81

Source: *Transport Topics,* August 9, 1999.

Just-in-Time Inventory Management

The use of just-in-time (JIT) inventory management throughout the supply chain has increased the use of trucks. In the early 1990s, customers of the trucking industry, whether manufacturers, distributors, or retailers, began to demand quicker and more reliable and flexible freight transportation as they initiated the use of the JIT process. An estimate by the government showed that JIT was used 45 percent of the time in the production process in 1995. The ratio of inventory to sales also provides evidence of the increasing use of JIT; that ratio has fallen dramatically in recent years.

Thus, the trucking industry has witnessed a substantial increase in scheduled freight. Scheduled freight has a definite time of delivery, not just a day but a specific window. Arriving an hour early often is just as bad as arriving an hour late. While JIT is a process and the motor carrier industry is an invaluable tool in that process, it is clearly a work in progress. Specifically, the trucking industry is plagued with a problem termed "hurry up to wait." This means that many shippers and receivers try to implement JIT but are not ready for the freight when it arrives. One study produced by the industry reported that drivers of refrigerated freight wait nearly 43 hours a week to drop off and pick up freight. Dry van freight drivers wait over 33 hours, according to a similar study. If the waiting times were reduced by just 10 percent, then 6 percent of the trucks dedicated to that activity could be taken off the highways altogether.

Operating Expenses

In 1997, on average, it cost $1.92 to operate a truck for 1 mile (the average revenue per mile was $1.94) (see Table 54-2). For all types of trucking companies, labor is typically the largest component of total operating expenses. However, category shares of expenses vary with the type of operation. For instance, labor is a larger factor for less-than-truckload (LTL) carriers compared with truckload (TL) carriers. Conversely, TL carriers spend a larger percentage of total operating expenses on fuel than do LTL carriers.

TABLE 54-2: Cost Per Mile, 1997

	Cents per Mile
Drivers' wages	36.7
Nondrivers' wages	34.4
Vehicle rentals with or without a driver	24.1
Miscellaneous operating expenses	19.7
Fringe benefits	19.1
Purchased transportation	16.3
Fuel	12.5
Depreciation	9.7
Tax and license fees	6.6
Insurance	5.8
Outside maintenance	5.4
Tires	2.0
Total	$1.92

Source: American Trucking Associations.

Diesel Fuel. As was noted above, trucking is a high-variable-cost industry, with one of the largest expenses being a commodity: diesel fuel. Consequently, carriers can have a difficult time managing costs. The industry as a whole consumes more than 30 billion gallons of diesel fuel a year. Therefore, fluctuations in the price of diesel fuel have a profound impact on the industry. Class 8 trucks (those weighing over 33,000 pounds and typically part of tractor-trailer combinations) average about 6 miles per gallon.

In 1999, carriers witnessed a significant jump in the price of diesel fuel. After bottoming out at 95 cents per gallon (national average) in February, diesel fuel surged to $1.23 per gallon in mid-October, an increase of 29 percent. That rapid rise was due to several factors, of which the most important was a reduction in oil output by the Organization of Petroleum Exporting Countries (OPEC) that propelled the price of West Texas Intermediate Oil upward from $12 per barrel in February to $25 in October. Another factor pushing the price of oil was a rebound in demand, primarily from the Asian countries.

As the price of diesel fuel surged, trucking companies found themselves in a precarious situation. On average, carriers have very slim profit margins. As the price of diesel fuel began to rise through the spring and into the summer, most carriers attempted to pass on those higher costs to shippers, often through fuel surcharges. There are no set industry standards for fuel surcharges, and they usually are set on a contract-by-contract basis between a carrier and its shippers. As thresholds were attained for many surcharges, numerous carriers began billing their customers; however, often the shippers refused to pay, usually for two reasons. First, they claimed that they were unable to pass along those costs to their customers because of intense price competition in an environment of very low inflation. Second, they knew that trucking is a highly competitive industry and that other carriers would be willing to haul the freight. By the end of the summer, with no break in fuel prices, most carriers finally were able to implement fuel surcharges. Without that change, many carriers, particularly small ones, would have faced closure.

There are management techniques that carriers can utilize to minimize large swings in fuel prices. The first technique is to buy in mass quantities, which is easier for carriers that operate in a defined region or utilize terminals. Carriers also can employ fuel management software that indicates which truck stops across the country offer the cheapest prices. They then can inform their drivers at which truck stops they should purchase fuel. Finally, some carriers, usually the largest ones, employ fuel hedging practices. This typically is limited to larger operations that have a staff dedicated to purchasing fuel.

Drivers' Wages. Carriers' largest expense is labor, specifically drivers' wages. According to the U.S. Department of Labor, there are over 3 million truck drivers in the United States, among whom 6 percent are women and 25 percent are members of minority groups. In recent years, it has become increasingly difficult for carriers to find qualified drivers. In fact, the Federal Reserve frequently mentioned the driver shortage in its Beige Book reports in 1999.

This shortage of qualified drivers has put upward pressure on drivers' wages, which have been fairly constant in real terms over the last decade. On average, a driver today makes $36,000 and often is paid on a per-mile basis. However, specialized drivers who operate unique equipment can make upward of $100,000 per year. Owner-operators also make significantly more than $36,000, but they have to pay for their own insurance, fuel, and maintenance. Several large truckload carriers, such as J.B. Hunt and Schneider National, have increased wages significantly in recent years.

Two major problems for carriers are the shortage of and the extremely high turnover among long-haul drivers. A study by ATA and the Gallup Organization states that the industry will have to hire 82,000 new drivers each year until 2005: 48,000 to replace drivers lost to attrition and 34,000 to meet the needs of industry growth. The unemployment rate is so low that this shortage will only get worse, and some larger TL companies are acquiring other carriers simply to increase their driver pools. Truck manufacturers also are building class 8 trucks with automatic transmissions, thinking that this will attract new drivers by making trucks easier to operate.

Arguably an even larger problem is industry turnover (or churning), particularly in the TL sector, a problem that got worse in 1999, according to ATA research. In the second quarter of 1999, ATA data showed that TL annualized turnover was over 90 percent, escalating from a low of 77 percent in the fourth quarter of 1997. The total cost incurred in hiring a new driver is around $9,000. This puts the total annual cost of turnover to the industry in the hundreds of millions of dollars.

The longer a driver stays with a particular carrier, the more his or her turnover rate drops. Therefore, carriers are using both monetary and nonmonetary incentives to retain drivers. This often includes bonuses, new trucks, going home more often, and phone cards. Since drivers are paid by the mile, companies are attempting to assist them in getting more miles (within hours of service rules) by reducing waiting times. To accomplish this, some carriers that do large amounts of consistent business with certain shippers are implementing a drop-and-hook routine. This means that instead of waiting for a trailer to be filled or emptied, the driver drops off an empty trailer with the shipper and picks up a filled one that is waiting for him or her.

Drivers sometimes are asked to load and unload trailers themselves because shippers and/or receivers do not always have freight handlers. While this often is difficult to achieve, some carriers are taking only "no touch" freight when acquiring new business, and so the driver does not have to load or unload at all.

Highway User Fees and Taxes. The trucking industry pays approximately $25 billion a year in federal and state highway user fees such as fuel taxes, motor vehicle excise taxes, and registration fees. Highway user fees go toward the maintenance of the existing highway system and capacity expansion to meet the continuing growth in freight transportation demand. The 1997

Federal Cost Allocation Study found that trucks pay over 36 percent of total highway user fees even though they travel less than 8 percent of the total mileage.

Truck Sales

Truck sales have been on the rise over the last few years, with new records set in 1998 and 1999. Over 250,000 new class 8 units were expected to be sold in the United States in 1999, up from 209,500 in 1998. There are two important reasons why carriers have been purchasing a record number of new trucks. The first is the high level of demand for trucking services. As freight grows and maximum weight limits are maintained, more and more trucks are needed to haul the added freight. Since 1990, trucking tonnage has grown 45 percent.

A second reason for the surge in truck sales is the lower power unit cycle times employed by carriers. Despite the fact that new trucks are being built to last longer than ever (some have warranties up to 1 million miles), major TL companies have reduced cycle times from more than 5 years to around 3, about the time it takes a long-haul driver to put 300,000 miles on a truck (a typical mileage level for a trade-in). This is often done for driver retention. Conversely, LTL carriers have not necessarily reduced cycle times. These carriers usually buy a truck and first use it for line-haul activities. The trucks then are used for regional hauls and finally for local pickup and delivery.

With a boom in truck sales and lower cycle times, there has been a glut in the secondhand market, driving down the prices of used trucks. This has helped smaller carriers add capacity. Used truck dealers are finding new markets in Central and South America as they acquire more trucks.

Trailer sales also have been on the rise, with 344,000 units sold in 1998 and even more sales expected in 1999. When carriers add trailers, they typically add capacity. The ratio of trailers to tractors was 3.7 in 1997, up from 2.6 in 1990. This ratio has been on the increase in part because of the use of drop-and-hook practices.

The Shrinking Share of Private Trucking

Over the last couple of decades, especially since deregulation, there has been a conversion of private fleets to for-hire carriers. In other words, manufacturers, retailers, and private carriers have been getting out of the trucking business and contracting out their freight transportation to for-hire carriers. It is primarily line-haul movements that are being converted, as opposed to local and even regional pickup and delivery. In 1997, private carriage's market share was 47 percent in terms of revenue, but it is expected to shrink to 42 percent by 2007. With trucking rates so reasonable, many private carriers are finding it unnecessary to maintain their own fleets. Many private fleets are used only in regional or local hauls. The average length of haul for private carriers is in the range of 50 to 100 miles, compared with 375 to 425 miles for for-hire carriers.

One reason why there has been a conversion from private to for-hire is the use of dedicated fleets by for-hire carriers for some customers, especially shippers that used to operate their own trucks. This practice of providing a specific number of trucks only for a specific customer provides a sense of security for shippers, since they will have the trucks when they need them. While still fairly limited, the use of dedicated fleets is expected to increase in the future. Nevertheless, there will always be private trucking because some manufacturers and distributors believe they gain competitive advantage by offering delivery services that are directly under their control.

Economies of Scale and Scope

Another change in the industry is the trend toward shippers reducing the number of carriers they utilize to a core few. This allows better coordination and logistics while assuring a high level of service. Carriers are no longer being judged simply on price but also on the level of service. Economies of scale and scope therefore have become very important. If a carrier is large enough to take advantage of economies of scale, it can provide a premium service at a reasonable price. The premium service is related to economies of scope.

Many carriers are not just transportation companies but also logistics and information companies. Large carriers have started logistics divisions or subsidiaries to advise their customers how best to manage their shipping. This often supplies added freight to the transportation division as well. Therefore, as in many industries across the United States, in trucking it is important to be either large enough to take advantage of economies of scale and scope or small enough to be able to target a particular niche.

Third-Party Logistics

In addition to motor carriers offering logistics services, there has been an expansion of non-asset-based logistics companies. These companies act as consultants and/or intermediaries between manufacturers or distributors and transportation companies. Often asset-based, third-party logistics companies (3PL) have an advantage because in a time of capacity constraints they give priority to their own customers. However, asset-based 3PLs must realize that their own fleets are not always the most efficient and price-competitive method to move freight and give transportation business to their competitors.

Electronic Commerce

According to one estimate, 6 percent of retail sales will be made over the Internet in 2003. This certainly will have an impact on the trucking industry. The potential winners will be package and parcel carriers such as United Parcel Service (UPS); FDX, the parent company of Federal Express; and the U.S. Postal Service, since many Web-based sales are business-to-home sales. Other probable beneficiaries from this boom in E-commerce include LTL carriers, which specialize in smaller consolidated freight. However, LTL carriers will have to decide whether they want to get into the home delivery market to compete with UPS and FedEx. Most are fairly reluctant to do this because of the complexities and the addition of costly equipment such as delivery vans. E-commerce winners will also include fleets that have economies of scope in the warehousing business, as more regional distribution centers will emerge. Finally, typical line-haul movements are not expected to be negatively affected by E-commerce and should increase.

Some carriers are starting their own Web pages to take advantage of the surge in Web sales. Carriers move more than just freight; they also move data. On the Web pages of several large carriers, especially in the LTL segment, shippers can get rates, schedule pickups, trace shipments, pull invoices, and make payments on-line. Consequently, the industry's use of E-commerce is expected to increase in the near future.

Regulatory Issues

The trucking industry is largely free of regulation in the area of rates and entry into the industry; however, it is still subject to governmental rules in respect to safety and the environment. These regulations can affect operating expenses and capital spending significantly.

National Motor Carrier Administration. In what some analysts are calling the most significant change in federal oversight of trucking since deregulation, in 1999 Congress established a separate motor carrier safety administration within the U.S. Department of Transportation (DOT). The industry has been lobbying for this move for over a decade. DOT has separate agencies for railroads, aviation, and maritime, but trucking has always been a part of the Federal Highway Administration (FHWA). Proponents of the new motor carrier agency say that the FHWA can no longer promote highway transportation and enforce federal motor carrier safety rules simultaneously.

Environmental Regulation. The U.S. government's policies concerning air quality are shaping the trucking industry's cost structure and capital investment patterns. A July 1, 1999, court-approved settlement between diesel engine manufacturers and the U.S. Environmental Protection Agency (EPA) will require all existing engines to be rebuilt to cleaner standards as a means of rectifying manufacturers' alleged violations of the Clean Air Act that first were identified in 1998. This change may reduce the fuel efficiency of these engines by up to 3 percent. In addition to regulations on new engines, existing engines are being targeted for roadside smoke emission checks in 13 states, and fines can go as high as $1,000 per violation for vehicles with high levels of smoke emissions.

New lower diesel engine emissions rules already on the books for 2004 will further reduce the levels of allowed emissions of smog-precursor nitrogen oxides by 50 percent from current levels. In the year 2000, EPA is expected to finalize a rule that will lower diesel engine emissions in 2007 by as much as 70 to 90 percent of 2004 levels. Meeting those stringent levels is expected to require, for the first-time, the widespread use of particulate traps and catalytic converters. These devices require cleaner-burning, lower-sulfur diesel fuel that will drive up fuel costs an estimated 4 to 7 cents per gallon.

Truck fleets also face costly environmental regulations governing water quality at their maintenance facilities and terminals. Storm water permit requirements affect nearly every company and often require the monitoring of discharge and limitations on activities such as truck washing. These permits typically range in cost from $1,500 to $5,000 per facility. New federal rules expected in early 2000 probably will ban the discharge of water from vehicle maintenance facilities into septic tanks and other wells, affecting thousands of trucking facilities in areas without public utility access.

Highways and Tolls. Highway congestion is increasing across the nation, delaying shipments, adding to expenses, and contributing to air pollution. To alleviate this congestion, states and metropolitan planning organizations are implementing a series of measures to mitigate congestion that focus on providing transportation alternatives to commuters. Projects such as mass transit developments, HOV lanes, and pedestrian access are attracting an ever-growing share of highway user fees. The industry believes that none of these alternatives significantly helps trucking.

There is growing concern in the industry that even as the need for goods movement grows and as more businesses demand JIT delivery to streamline their organizations, few of the transportation improvements made will benefit truckers. Highway capacity expansion in urban areas is increasingly held up by the expense, local residents' concerns, and environmental effects. Trucks depend on the upkeep of a good highway and local street system to deliver their goods but also require transportation improvements to keep pace with demand.

The introduction of new highway tolls is opposed by the trucking industry, which already pays 36 percent of highway user fees. Tolls add to operating costs, traffic delays, and air pollution. Under the Transportation Efficiency Act for the 21st Century (TEA-21), the federal government has made available funding for pilot toll programs for interstate variable pricing and infrastructure rehabilitation. To date, none of these pilot projects has been undertaken, partly because of the industry's continued opposition. With the interstate system already paid for, congestion pricing is viewed as increasing extra taxes, while funding infrastructure projects through tolls when highway user fees already are being spent on many nonhighway projects is seen as inequitable.

Longer Combination Vehicles. Longer combination vehicles (LCVs) offer the trucking industry one possibility for improving productivity in the face of driver shortages and increasing demand for goods movement. The use of triple trailers or other combinations, which is allowed in many western states, reduces the need for vehicles and drivers in moving goods. Proposals have been presented for a federal pilot program to allow harmonization of the limits of those states and permit the operation of LCVs along designated corridors. This would require federal legislation to amend the LCV freeze enacted by the Intermodal Surface Transportation Efficiency Act (ISTEA) and extended by its successor, TEA-21. Opponents of the proposal state that the bigger LCV trucks are more dangerous; however, a 1996 FHWA study found that LCVs, whose use is tightly controlled and monitored by the authorizing states, have lower accident rates than does the general trucking population.

Hours of Service. With qualified drivers in very short supply, particularly in the long-haul segment of the industry, the trucking industry wants to ensure that upcoming revisions in the 60-year-old hours of service regulations are designed to promote both safety and productivity. Since late 1996, as a result of a congressional mandate, the DOT's Office of Motor Carrier Safety (OMCS) has been working to revise its current set of one-size-fits-all regulations. Implementation of the new rules is anticipated by the end of the year 2000.

Although driver fatigue has not been identified as a primary cause of crashes involving heavy trucks, the trucking industry believes that highway safety can be improved if reasonable, flexible, science-based hours of service regulations are implemented. Under the current rules, workers can drive 10 hours, followed by an 8-hour off-duty rest break, and cannot drive after having been on duty for 70 hours in an 8-day period. These rules, which apply across all industry segments, generally are considered to be less than ideal since they are inflexible and promote 18-hour work-rest schedules that are not aligned with a person's natural body clock and cause a shift in sleep patterns. Truckers believe that the current system can lead to fatigue since drivers' sleep patterns are constantly shifting.

The trucking industry believes that new regulations should provide additional off-duty time for drivers each day and promote 24-hour work-rest schedules. To achieve that objective, the industry is promoting a maximum of 14 hours of on-duty time followed by a minimum of 10 consecutive hours of off-duty time. Under this system, a driver would be more likely to perform a driving shift at the same time each day and rest or sleep at the same time each day, leading to more alert drivers overall.

Advocacy groups critical of the trucking industry also are advocating changes in the current rules and are looking for OMCS to reduce the number of hours drivers may drive significantly. These groups also are pressuring OMCS to force truck fleets to install onboard computers (black boxes) on their trucks to ensure compliance with current and future hours-of-service rules. While many larger trucking companies already have devices that perform this function, the vast majority of companies in the industry operate fewer than 20 trucks and do not have the financial resources to implement this technology. According to the industry, the installation of black boxes, coupled with reduced work hours, would place a significant burden on both motor carriers and the economy.

INTERNATIONAL TRENDS

The North American Free Trade Agreement (NAFTA) is a rules-based covenant among the United States, Canada, and Mexico that went into effect on January 1, 1994. In December 1995, NAFTA was supposed to allow free entrance and exit of both U.S. and Mexican trucks across the border. Such trucks could deliver goods to border states in both countries. The U.S. government has delayed the process of border opening, citing safety concerns. The rescheduled date for border opening was January 2000, but the current administration has announced that the border situation will not change for now. That border opening would have allowed Mexican and U.S. trucks to go to any state in either country, as opposed to just the bordering states. Currently, trade is transacted through "commercial zones" at the border, where trailers are transferred from Mexican to American truckers and vice versa (depending on the origin of freight). This process usually takes up to three truck movements.

Between 1994 and 1998, truck-transported trade with Mexico expanded 70.5 percent based on the value of shipments. Canadian truck trade advanced only 32.7 percent during that period. Despite the delays in NAFTA rules implementation, trucks still manage to haul most of the goods that cross the southern border, having carried 83 percent of Mexico–United States surface trade in 1998. Trucks also transport the majority of trade with Canada, with a 74 percent share. By far, Texas and California have the largest proportion of the trade with Mexico; combined, they accounted for 56.2 percent of the total truck trade in 1998. Trade with Canada is more diversified across U.S. states, with Michigan, Ohio, and New York capturing the largest single-state shares of truck commerce with that country.

OUTLOOK

On the cusp of a positive overall economic outlook, freight transportation as a whole is expected to grow nearly 28 percent in terms of revenue by 2007. Trucking will account for the bulk of this growth but will increase slightly more slowly at 26 percent. Tonnage for trucking will increase 1.3 billion tons during that time period, 55 percent of total tonnage growth for all modes of freight transportation.

The near-term outlook for trucking is good. As the manufacturing sector rebounds and consumers continue to spend record amounts of money, trucking activity will keep attaining historical highs. Profits, while still very low compared with those in the prederegulation period, have rebounded over the last couple of years. However, recent spikes in fuel prices could put a short-term strain on profits for the entire industry despite the surge in activity.

In 1997, the LTL market accounted for roughly 16 percent of trucking general freight revenue but only 3 percent of the industry's tonnage (see Table 54-3). The LTL market is expected to flourish over the next decade, growing much faster than both the TL and private sectors. Specifically, LTL tonnage and rev-

TABLE 54-3: General Freight Truck Shipments in 1997

	Tonnage Share, %
Truckload	45.3
Less than truckload	3.1
Private	51.6

Source: American Trucking Associations.

enue are each forecast to increase 45 percent. This also indicates, however, that average revenue per ton will be stagnant. This segment of the industry has benefited from three major closings in the LTL market. For the year 2000, this has created a tighter capacity environment, which should help rates, at least in the short run.

The truckload segment accounts for about 45 percent of the general freight trucking market in terms of tonnage. That market share is anticipated to increase moderately, primarily at the expense of private carriers. On the revenue end of general freight truck shipments, TL carriers are expected to witness growth of 35 percent over the next 10 years, slower than the 45 percent expected for LTL carriers. Nevertheless, TL carriers will not lose market share to LTL carriers, as both will gain shares while private carriers will lose it. The challenge to TL carriers will consist of attracting new drivers, which has been a constraint on growth over the last several years. If they can somehow increase the number of drivers at a faster pace than is expected, TL activity will grow significantly faster than has been forecast.

Bob Costello, American Trucking Associations, (703) 838-1799, October 1999.

REFERENCES

American Trucking Trends, 1999, American Trucking Associations, 2200 Mill Road, Alexandria, VA 22314-4677. (703) 838-1966.

Empty Seats and Musical Chairs, 1997, American Trucking Associations Foundation, 2200 Mill Road, Alexandria, VA 22314-4677. (703) 838-1966.

Engel, Cynthia, "Competition Drives the Trucking Industry," *Monthly Labor Review,* U.S. Department of Labor, Bureau of Labor Statistics, Washington, DC 20212, April 1998.

Financial & Operating Statistics, 1997 Motor Carrier Annual Report, American Trucking Associations, 2200 Mill Road, Alexandria, VA 22314-4677. (703) 838-1799.

Hays, Thomas, *Successful Trucking after Deregulation,* Pacific Standard, 1995.

Highway Statistics, 1997, U.S. Department of Transportation, Federal Highway Administration, Washington, DC 20590.

Hof, Robert D., et al., "A New Era of Bright Hopes and Terrible Fears," *Business Week,* October 4, 1999, McGraw-Hill Companies, 1221 Avenue of the Americas, New York, NY 10020. (212) 512-2000.

National Refrigerated Drivers Survey, 1998, Truckload Carriers Association, 2200 Mill Road, Alexandria, VA 22314-4677. (703) 838-1950.

1999 Dry Van Drivers Survey, Truckload Carriers Association, 2200 Mill Road, Alexandria, VA 22314-4677. (703) 838-1950.

Transportation Expressions, 1996, U.S. Department of Transportation, Bureau of Transportation Statistics, 400 Seventh Street, SW, Room 3430, Washington, DC 20590. (202) 366-3282.

Transportation in America, 1998, Eno Transportation Foundation, Inc., One Farragut Square South, Suite 500, Washington, DC 20006-4003. (202) 879-4700.

Trucking Activity Report, 1999, American Trucking Associations, 2200 Mill Road, Alexandria, VA 22314-4677. (703) 838-1799.

U.S. Freight Transportation Forecast, 2007, 1999, American Trucking Associations, 2200 Mill Road, Alexandria, VA 22314-4677. (703) 838-1799.

RELATED CHAPTERS

4: Petroleum Refining
36: Motor Vehicles
41: Wholesale Distribution
42: Retailing

GLOSSARY

Less-than-truckload (LTL) Freight: Refers to a quantity of freight less than that required for the application of a truckload rate; usually less than 10,000 pounds and generally involves the use of terminal facilities to break and sort shipments.

Truckload (TL): Refers to the quantity of freight required to fill a trailer. When used in connection with freight rates, the quantity of freight necessary to qualify a shipment for a truckload rate typically exceeds 10,000 pounds.

Private motor carrier: A company whose primary business activity is not transportation and whose transportation activities are conducted only to supplement and advance its primary activities.

For-hire motor carrier: A company engaged in the transportation of the goods of others for compensation; can be both TL and LTL.

Index

A

B

C

D

E

F

G

H

I

L

M

N

O

P

Q

R

S

T

U

X

Y

Z

Permissions

Advertising Age
Crain Communications, Inc.
740 Rush Street
Chicago, IL 60611
(312) 649-5200

Aerospace Industries Association
1250 I Street, N.W., Suite 1200
Washington, D.C. 20005-3924
(202) 371-8563

Air Transport Association of America
1301 Pennsylvania Avenue, N.W.
Suite 1100
Washington, D.C. 20004-1707
(202) 626-4178

Allied Business Intelligence, Inc.
Post Office Box 452
2500 Townsend Square
Oyster Bay, NY 11771
(516) 624-3113

American Council of Life Insurance
1001 Pennsylvania Avenue, N.W.
Washington, D.C. 20004
(202) 624-2319

American Iron and Steel Institute
1101 17th Street, N.W.
Washington, DC 20036
(202) 452-7100
www.steel.org

Association of American Railroads
50 F Street, N.W.
Washington, D.C. 20001
(202) 639-2309

Automotive News
Crain Communication, Inc.
965 E. Jefferson
Detroit, MI 48207-3185
(800) 678-9595

Baskerville Communications Corp.
15165 Ventura Blvd., Suite 310
Sherman Oaks, CA 91403
(818) 461-9660, ext. 279

Broadview International LLC
One Bridge Plaza
Fort Lee, NJ 07024
(201) 346-9000

C.E. Unterberg, Towbin
10 East 50th Street
New York, NY 10022
(212) 572-8184

Clarkson Research Studies
12 Camomile Street
London EC31 7BP, England
44-(0)-171-3343134

The Conference Board
845 Third Avenue
New York, NY 10022
(212) 759-0900

Consultants News
Kennedy Information, LLC
One Kennedy Place
Route 12 South
Fitzwilliam, NH 03447
(603) 585-3101
www.kennedyinfo.com

Cruise Industry News
Nissen-Lie Communications, Inc.
441 Lexington Avenue, Suite 1209
New York, NY 10017
(212) 986-1025

Dataquest
251 River Oaks Parkway
San Jose, CA 91534
(408) 468-8076

Economist Intelligence Unit
Healthcare International
111 West 57th St.
New York, NY 10019

Eno Transportation Foundation
One Farragut Square South
Washington, D.C. 20006
(202) 879-4700

Environmental Business International, Inc.
P.O. Box 371769
San Diego, CA 92137
(619) 295-5743

Euroconsult
71-79, Boulevard Richard-Lenoir
Paris, France 75011
33-01-4338-06-00

Furniture Today
P.O. Box 2754
High Point, NC 27261
(336) 605-0121

General Aviation Manufacturers Association
1400 K Street, N.W., Suite 801
Washington, D.C. 20005-2485
(202) 637-1377

Gomez Advisors, Inc.
55 Old Bedford Road
Lincoln, MA 01773
(781) 257-2010

Insurance Information Institute
110 William Street
New York, NY 10038
(800) 331-9146

International Air Transport Association
800 Place Victoria
P.O. Box 113
Montreal, Quebec H4Z IMI
Canada
(514) 874-0202

International Civil Aviation Organization
999 University Street
Montreal, Quebec H3C 5H7
Canada

International Data Corporation
Five Speen Street
Framington, MA 01701
(508) 872-8200

International Telecommunications Union
Sales and Marketing Service
Place des Nations
CH-1211 Geneva 20, Switzerland
41-22-730-61-41

Investment Company Institute
Mutual *Fund Fact Book*
1401 H St., N.W., Suite 1200
Washington, D.C. 20005
(202) 326-5800
http://www.ici.org

J.D. Power and Associates
Agoura Hills, CA 91301
(818) 889-6330

Kagan World Media, Ltd.
126 Clocktower Place
Carmel, CA 93923-8746
(831) 624-1536

Lloyd's Register of Shipping
100 Leadenhall Street
London RC3A 3BP, England
011-44-171-709-9166

Market Data Retrieval
Shelton, CT
(203) 926-0734

Media Business Corporation
807 Araphoe Street
Golden, CO 80401
(303) 271-9960

Motion Picture Association of America
1600 I Street, N.W.
Washington, D.C. 20006

Multimedia Telecommunications Association
2500 Wilson Blvd.
Arlington, VA 22201
(703) 907-7470

National Association of Realtors
700 11th Street, N.W.
Washington, D.C. 20001
(202) 383-1215

National Petroleum News
Adams Business Media
2101 S. Arlington Heights Road
Suite 150
Arlington, IL 60005
(847) 427-9512

National Venture Capital Association
1655 N. Fort Meyer Drive
Arlington, VA 22209
(703) 524-2549

National Railroad Passenger Corporation (Amtrak)
400 North Capitol Street, N.W.
Washington, D.C. 20001
(202) 906-3939

Panel Publishers
Division of Aspen Publishers, Inc.
P.O. Box 1454
Alexandria, VA 22313
(703) 739-6524

Photo Marketing Association International
3000 Picture Place
Jackson, MI 49201
(517) 788-8100

Photofinishing News
10915 Bonita Beach Road, Suite 1091
Bonita Springs, FL 34135
(941) 992-4421

Public Accounting Report
Strafford Publications, Inc.
590 Dutch Valley Road, N.E.
Postal Drawer 13729
Atlanta, GA 30324
(404) 881-1141

Satellite Industry Association
225 Reinekers Lane, Suite 600
Alexandria, VA 22314
(703) 549-9188

Securities Industry Association
120 Broadway
New York, NY 10271
(212) 608-1500
http://www.sia.com

Sigma Securities
The Silver Institute
1112 16th Street, N.W., Suite 240
Washington, D.C. 20036
(202) 835-0185

StatMarket Division
Web Side Story, Inc.
10182 Telesis Court
San Diego, CA 92121
(858) 546-0040
www.statmarket.com

The Strategis Group, Inc.
1130 Connecticut Avenue
Washington, D.C. 20036
(202) 530-7500

Toy Manufacturers of America
1115 Broadway, Suite 400
New York, NY 10010

Training Magazine
Lakewood Publications
50 S. 9th Street, Suite 400
Minneapolis, MN 55402-3165

Video Software Dealers Association
16530 Ventura Boulevard, Suite 400
Encino, CA 91436